STATISTICAL REFERENCE INDEX 1985 ANNUAL

A selective guide to American statistical publications from private organizations and state government sources

Abstracts

CIS

Congressional Information Service

Staff

Editorial Director
Susan I. Jover

Director of Statistical Services
Darlene J. Montgomery

Managing Editor
Lynn K. Marble

Assistant Managing Editor, Abstracts
Joseph H. McNally

*Assistant Managing Editor
Collection Development*
Jeanne Long

Assistant Managing Editor Index
Jeffrey E. Strandberg

Review Editor
Thomas A. Stock

*Abstracting and
Indexing Staff*
Deborah Marlatt Kitchin
Lisette B. Lawson

Jane L. Lean
William S. Nelson
Mary R. Nolan
Pamela Patchin
David Platt
James Shields
Polly Todd
Edie Wett

Accuracy Editors
Donna M. Shea
Katharina C. Wendel

Editorial Assistant
Elizabeth J. Holliday

Acquisitions Editors
Kevin G. Kendrick
Edward Kianka

Diane L. Kinney
Cheryl M. Waldman

Acquisitions Assistant
Gregory Crisostomo

Documents Control
Sally L. MacArthur

Production Coordinator
Dorothy W. Rogers

*Production Services
Supervisor*
Esther R. Aikens

Production Staff
Helene E. Gaffney
Elizabeth Naccarato
Debra Turnell

Congressional Information Service, Inc.

President
Paul P. Massa

*Vice President
and Editorial Director*
Susan I. Jover

Vice President, Marketing
James F. Connolly

*Vice President,
Planning, Research
and Development*
Michael P. Stern

Vice President, Research
Donald G. Tacheron

*Sr. Vice President,
Finance, Manufacturing
& EDP*
Peter M. Bjonerud

*Vice President,
EDP & Technology*
Ralph James

*Manager, Applications
Programming*
William DeRoche

Software Engineers
Mojtaba Anvari
Andrew Ross

Systems Programmer
Robert Better

Programmer/Analyst
Yvonne Malcom

Computer Operators
Susanna Ferro
Mel Turner

Controller
Max Venegas

Accounting Staff
Stuart Abramowitz
Barry Blacka
Gina Bramante
Susan Fasano

Karen Hendren
Sheila Moore
Rita Skolnik
Emmy Wong

*Manager, Administrative
Services*
Lee Mayer

Personnel Director
Susie G. Schwarz

Assistant Personnel Director
Anne F. Starbird

Personnel Assistant
Karen W. Lucas

Director, Manufacturing
William C. Smith

Plant Operations Manager
William Idol

*Micropublishing
Production Staff*
Susan Anderson
Lukman Bazarah
Tobi Barnhill
Rita Berry
Patty Bettencourt
Margarett Boyle
Soon Chea
Desmond Davis
Frank Day
Brezeetha Dhanireddy
Donna Edwards
Sharon Foster
Kathleen Frazzetta
Sharon Garey
Christine Gass
Jean Ann Gibson
Kimberly Goba
Christopher Gorczyca
Norma Herbert
Claire Keister
Jeffrey Kessler
Rhonda Libert
Joyce Lowery
Betty Lyles
Kathleen Lyons
Diana Machen
Brian McCary
Jane Miers
Jeff Miller

Luke Murdock
Tai Nguyen
Edgar O'Bannon
Jennifer Offenbacher
Vatsaladevi Panneerselvam
Patricia Poppen
Juanita Prather
Margaret Reid
Winnie Robertson
Jean Shields
Leonilza Silva
Michelle Slaviero
Victor Smith
Poonam Srivastava
Doris K. Stevens
Mark Steo
Nancy Taylor
Betty Trinquero
Terri Van Houten
Rosario Vargas
Lucy Villagra
Mary Kay Williams
Kim Wilson
Bruce Woodhams
Shaun Woolcock
Jeffrey Zahn

Assistant Director of Research
Mark Vonderhaar

Research Staff
Marilynn Bynum
George Codrea
Jay Fletcher
Cindy Friel
Lois Gearhart
Debra Green
Mary Haygood
Sandra Friedman
Sarah Heron
Angela Hitti
Betty Leonard
Eric Massant
Vandana Mathur
David Molenda
Mary Phillips
William Reilly
Nina Schuster
Jeffrey Showell
Kate Talev

Director of Market Research
Alexander D. McRae

Documents on Demand
Sharon L. Schmedicke

National Sales Manager
John P. Beil

Sales Representatives
Thomas Ball
John Cox
Donald Crowley
Paul Davidson
Charles De Grasse
Jane Edwards
E. Donald Fitch
Paul A. Hennrikus
James Tucker

Marketing Services Coordinator
Laima Rivers

Marketing Services Assistants
Ellie Kasten
Bethann Prather

Director, Communications
Richard K. Johnson

*Advertising, Publicity,
and Promotion Staff*
Barbara Busby
Jack Carey
Shanon Huestis
Marcia Taylor
Leslie Wilson

Secretary to the President
Karen L. Grossnickle

*Secretary to VP Planning,
Research and Development*
Helene Grant

*Secretary to Sr. VP,
Finance, Manufacturing & EDP*
Susan Savage

Staff Assistants
Bonnie Balzer
Marian Fowler
Charles Luther
Delwin Martin
Teresa McVeigh
John Nazarian

International Book Number
  For the Set: 0-88692-082-5
  For Index Volume: 0-88692-083-3
  For Abstract Volume: 0-88692-084-1

Congressional Information Service, Inc.
4520 East-West Highway
Bethesda, Md. 20814
(301) 654-1550

This issue of the Statistical Reference Index has been compiled and
composed with the aid of SAMANTHA™, an electronic data processing
technique developed by Information and Publishing Systems, Inc. of
Bethesda, Md.

SRI 1985 ANNUAL CONTENTS

The Statistical Reference Index 1985 Annual
is published in two volumes, the
contents of which are summarized below.

Abstracts

Index

NOTE: For comprehensive access to U.S. Government statistical publications, consult the American Statistics Index. ASI is published by Congressional Information Service, Inc. and is available in many major libraries. Coverage begins with the early 1960s and is updated monthly.

Detailed Table of Contents: Abstracts Volume

Issuing Sources and SRI Accession Numbers

BUSINESS ORGANIZATIONS

COMMERCIAL PUBLISHERS

INDEPENDENT RESEARCH ORGANIZATIONS

STATE GOVERNMENTS

ALABAMA

ALASKA

ARIZONA

ARKANSAS

CALIFORNIA

UNIVERSITY RESEARCH CENTERS

USER GUIDE

INTRODUCTION TO SRI

Basic Objectives and Coverage

Each year, thousands of U.S. private organizations and State government agencies prepare and issue countless publications and articles, many of which contain important statistics on business, industry and finance, general economic conditions, government programs and politics, and social trends. These data are typically authoritative, timely, and well-researched, and often present results of original surveys and research. In many cases, they complement or fill important gaps in data prepared and issued by the Federal Government, and also frequently are more current than Federal data.

The *Statistical Reference Index* (SRI) service, which includes printed abstracts and indexes and a companion microfiche collection of source data, is designed to provide a reliable, centralized means of access to this large and significant body of business, financial, and social statistical data, much of which has previously been difficult to locate or obtain for research use.

Specifically, SRI has as its purpose the following functions:

- **Survey and review** current statistical publications issued by major U.S. associations and institutes, business organizations, commercial publishers, independent research centers, State government agencies, and universities.

- **Identify** current publications containing substantial statistical material of general research value.

- **Catalog** the publications in which the data appear, providing full bibliographic data and availability information for each publication.

- **Describe** the contents of these publications fully.

- **Index** this information in full detail for access by subject, category, issuing source, and title.

- **Micropublish** the entire content or the statistical portions of the publications covered. (During 1985, SRI obtained microfilming rights for over 90% of the publications abstracted and indexed.)

SRI data selection criteria, more fully detailed below, have been established with the objectives of covering a wide array of data publishing organizations and subject matter. Criteria also emphasize prompt coverage of currently published sources of statistics and focus on continuing time series data wherever possible. Priority is also given to maintaining coverage of basic social, governmental, economic, and demographic data for each of the 50 States and the District of Columbia.

This 1985 SRI Annual contains abstracts and indexing for more than 1,900 titles, including approximately 1,320 annual or other recurring reports, 200 monographs, 375 periodicals with regularly appearing statistical features, and over 2,000 individual statistical articles. Included are reports from all 50 States and the District of Columbia, and statistical compendia from 32 States.

During 1986, SRI will maintain current coverage of all periodicals, annuals, and other recurring reports covered since its inception in 1980, and will continue to expand that coverage with additional current titles.

Issuing Sources Covered

SRI staff have conducted comprehensive surveys of current sources of data in order to establish a well-rounded sphere of coverage for SRI. Identification and selection of issuing sources currently covered are based on:

- Review of secondary sources, including *Directory of Business and Financial Services, Business Information Sources, Guide to Special Issues and Indexes of Periodicals, Statistical Abstract of the U.S.,* and numerous other bibliographies.

- Review of the Harvard University Baker Library industry statistics file.

- Canvass of national associations with annual budgets over $1 million.

- Canvass of business-oriented periodicals ranked in order of sales in *Folio 400.*

- Canvass of 2,000 State government agencies to identify offices publishing the most comprehensive reports on State administered programs.

- Consultations with librarians who are specialists in information fields such as banking and finance, State documents, and others.

- Follow-up on references cited in current periodicals and other news media.

SRI acquisitions staff are continually reviewing additional publications and canvassing additional sources in an effort to maintain and extend SRI coverage. Within this 1985 Annual, over 1,000 issuing source organizations are represented in the following categories:

- **Trade, professional, and other nonprofit associations and institutes,** including those representing manufacturing and nonmanufacturing industries, and academic, occupational, recreational, public interest, and religious groups.

- **Business organizations,** including banks, accounting firms, stock and commodity exchanges, public opinion survey and research firms, and other private companies and corporations.

- **Commercial publishers** of business, trade association, and industry periodical and annual publications, including such major publishers as R. R. Bowker, Chilton Co., Crain Communications, Dun and Bradstreet, Forbes, Lebhar-Friedman, McGraw-Hill, and PennWell Publishing.

- **Independent research organizations,** including public policy, education, demographic, and economic research organizations.

- **State government agencies,** including those with primary responsibility in such areas as State education, employment, health and vital statistics reporting, public assistance, elections, crime and correctional institutions, the judicial system, agriculture, and regulated industries.

- **Universities and affiliated research centers,** including those focusing on demographic research, and research in the fields of business and industry, agriculture, and economic forecasting.

Criteria for Publication Selection

In selecting publications for coverage, SRI seeks to include:

- Publications presenting business, industrial, financial, and social statistics of general research value, and having national, regional, or statewide breadth of coverage. Where there is redundancy of content among groups or related series of publications, emphasis is placed upon selecting those publications presenting time series or regularly updated statistics, and those with the most comprehensive, detailed coverage.

- Publications containing statistics in subject areas or in geographic detail not well covered by Federal data, and statistics useful for comparison with Federal data.

- Publications presenting data that, while in some respects limited in scope, geographically or otherwise, are the best or most authoritative found for a given subject, or present a unique analysis or statistical base.

SRI coverage excludes:

- Ephemeral or highly localized data of very limited interest.

- Scientific or highly technical data, and instructional handbooks and manuals.

- Publications with very limited or exclusive distribution for which microfiche reproduction rights cannot be obtained, that are thus unlikely to be available to libraries in any form.

- Publications which simply republish Federal data from a single source without analysis or without additional data collected from other sources (comprehensive coverage of Federal data can be found in *American Statistics Index,* published by Congressional Information Service, Bethesda, Md.).

- Publications of municipal and county governments (coverage of this material can be found in the *Index to Current Urban Documents,* published by Greenwood Press, Westport, Conn.).

In addition, SRI excludes coverage of published current securities quotations or price data intended primarily for investment or purchasing reference purposes, as well as coverage of widely publicized and commercially distributed monographs that are already well known and easily accessible.

Selection criteria for inclusion and exclusion are reviewed and refined on a continuing basis. We welcome comments and suggestions from SRI users that will help us in shaping future coverage policies and improving abstracting and indexing procedures.

Types of Statistics Covered

Publications covered by SRI provide users access to the following types of data:

- **National Data** — Production, costs, and earnings in major industries and business sectors; operating and market characteristics of business and commerce; rankings of products and corporations; data related to key areas of social or public interest; professional worker supply and demand; public opinion and salary surveys; demographic data; and national economic trends.

- **Statewide Data** — State statistical compendia, and 10-15 additional periodicals or annual basic reports for each of the 50 States, presenting data on such areas as vital statistics, crime, health, agriculture, business conditions and economic indicators, employment, education, taxation, State government finances, insurance, banking, public utilities, the judicial system, corrections, elections, libraries, population, and motor vehicle accidents; and State reports presenting data from the 1980 Census of Population and Housing.

- **Data on Foreign Countries** — World economic and demographic trends; international finance, investment, and trade data; and foreign country social and economic indicators, frequently organized to permit comparison with data for the United States.

- **Local or Otherwise Narrowly Focused Data** — Detail by county and municipality is provided in most State reports selected for inclusion. In addition, selected local or narrowly focused studies or articles, from any source, may be included if the subject matter is judged to have research value beyond the limited area of coverage.

Coverage of SRI Monthly and Annual Editions

SRI indexes and abstracts are issued on a monthly basis except for the combined January/February issue, and are cumulated in an annual edition, published in the spring of the following year.

SRI 1985 Annual. This sixth SRI Annual cumulates the abstracts and indexes originally published in SRI monthly issues January through December 1985, generally covering publications issued October 1984 through September 1985. A selected number of earlier publications are also included, if they retain their value as current research sources. For publications abstracted and indexed prior to 1985, see SRI 1980, 1981, 1982, 1983, and 1984 Annuals.

The 1985 Annual provides full descriptions and index- ing for all publications covered by SRI during 1985, in- cluding "base" descriptions for all periodicals. The SRI 1985 Annual replaces and fully supersedes all 1985 SRI monthly issues.

SRI 1986 Monthly Issues. In general, SRI monthly issues cover periodicals, annuals and other serials, and monographs acquired 8–12 weeks previously. Thus, the SRI monthly issue dated April and shipped in April, for the most part will cover publications acquired during February, the issue dated May will cover March publica- tions, and so forth.

All SRI indexes cumulate monthly during each quarter; that is, the SRI May Index contains all indexing

appearing in the April and May issues. Each quarterly issue (March, June, September, December) cumulates all indexing for the quarter. Thus, users need only search the Annuals, the latest monthly SRI index volume, and any previously published quarterly index volumes, in order to search the entire current file. All indexing for the year will be cumulated in the SRI 1986 Annual cloth- bound issue.

During 1986, in addition to covering new titles, SRI will maintain full current coverage for all new editions of recurring publications, and all new issues of periodicals covered in previous years. Full or "base" abstracts and indexing will be published for all periodicals in the first 1986 SRI monthly issue in which they are covered.

HOW TO USE THE SRI 1985 ANNUAL

ORGANIZATION OF SRI INDEXES

SRI provides access to statistical data through compan- ion volumes of indexes and abstracts. Ordinarily, research will begin with the Index volume. The Index volume contains four basic indexes to lead the user to the information he seeks from a variety of starting points:

- **Index by Subjects and Names**
- **Index by Categories**
- **Index by Issuing Sources**
- **Index by Titles**

Index by Subjects and Names

This index section contains references to specific sub- jects, places, personal authors, and data source organizations other than issuing sources. Each index entry under a subject term contains a "notation of con- tent," which consists of a brief description of the prin- cipal subject matter of the publication as it relates to that term, the date of data coverage or publication, ma- jor data breakdowns, and the publication periodicity. These are followed by the SRI accession number identi- fying the individual document as described in the abstract volume.

Notation of content entries for data of general, na- tional, or international scope are listed first, followed by those for publications limited to individual States and local areas. The initial or key word of these notations of content is selected to provide an added level of specifici- ty under each subject term, and serves, in a general way, to group together entries for similar data under that term.

It should be noted that the notations of content in the *State and local* section of a term (see example below), taken together constitute a unique and useful compila- tion of the major sources of State data on that subject. (Data in publications not focusing on a particular State, but showing breakdowns *by State*, are most easily ac- cessible through the Index by Categories, under the heading, "By State," as detailed below.)

This index also contains *see* cross references to guide the user to the relevant term formats used in SRI; and *see also* cross references to guide the user to addi- tional material to be found under the related or narrower terms cited.

Subject index terms are assigned for each publication abstracted to represent all subject matter and data that are covered in sufficient depth to have research value. Unusual items or items of special interest that occur in the body of a report or article, or in individual tables or groups of tables, are indexed regardless of whether they are related to the primary focus of the publication at hand.

Subject terms and cross references in the Index of Subjects and Names are based on a controlled hierar- chical vocabulary. When indexing a publication to which a hierarchy of vocabulary terms might apply, SRI uses the most specific, generally applicable term or terms, and generally does not also index to broader or narrower terms that, while relevant, do not reflect so well the focus of the publication. In some cases, where the focus of the document is equally upon the more general and the more particular subject term, index references have been placed under both terms.

In general, individual cities and counties, occupa- tions, or other commonly appearing subject breakdowns of data *within* tables are indexed in the Index by Categories and *not* also in the Index by Subjects and Names. Users are urged to review indexed category breakdowns (see section below) and to keep in mind the added depth of coverage provided. A sample search us- ing the Subject Index is illustrated on p. xxx.

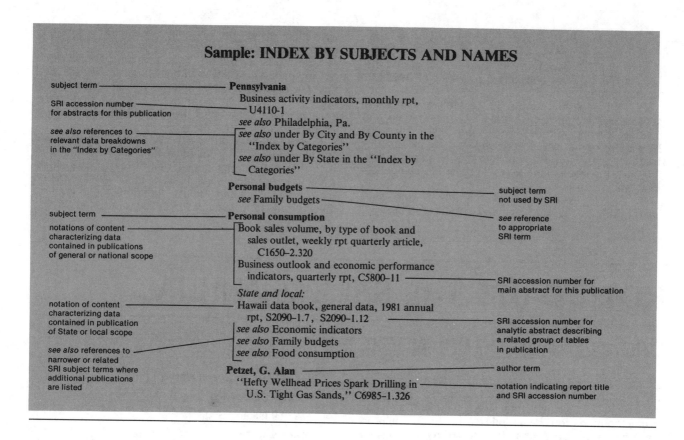

Sample: INDEX BY SUBJECTS AND NAMES

subject term ——————————— **Pennsylvania**
Business activity indicators, monthly rpt,
SRI accession number ———————— U4110-1
for abstracts for this publication
see also Philadelphia, Pa.
see also references to ————————— *see also* under By City and By County in the
relevant data breakdowns   "Index by Categories"
in the "Index by Categories"   *see also* under By State in the "Index by
Categories"

Personal budgets ———————————————————— subject term
see Family budgets ———————————— not used by SRI

subject term ———————————— **Personal consumption** —————————————— *see* reference
notations of content ————————— Book sales volume, by type of book and   to appropriate
characterizing data   sales outlet, weekly rpt quarterly article,   SRI term
contained in publications   C1650–2.320
of general or national scope   Business outlook and economic performance
indicators, quarterly rpt, C5800–11 ————————— SRI accession number for
main abstract for this publication

State and local:
notation of content ————————— Hawaii data book, general data, 1981 annual
characterizing data   rpt, S2090–1.7, S2090–1.12 ——————————— SRI accession number for
contained in publication   *see also* Economic indicators   analytic abstract describing
of State or local scope   *see also* Family budgets   a related group of tables
see also Food consumption   in publication
see also references to —————
narrower or related
SRI subject terms where   **Petzet, G. Alan** ———————————————————— author term
additional publications   "Hefty Wellhead Prices Spark Drilling in ——————— notation indicating report title
are listed   U.S. Tight Gas Sands," C6985–1.326   and SRI accession number

Index by Categories

This index provides special access to detailed statistical data found in tabular breakdowns and cross classifications. This index includes references to all publications that contain comparative tabular data broken down in any one or more of the following twenty standard categories:

GEOGRAPHIC BREAKDOWNS

By Census Division	By Region
By City	By SMSA or MSA
By County	By State
By Foreign Country or World Area	By Urban-Rural and Metro-Nonmetro

ECONOMIC BREAKDOWNS

By Commodity	By Individual
By Government Agency	Company
By Income	or Institution
By Industry	By Occupation

DEMOGRAPHIC BREAKDOWNS

By Age	By Marital Status
By Disease	By Race
By Educational Attainment	By Sex

For subject searches relating to any of the above breakdowns (e.g., a search for data for a specific city or county, for data on women or income, or on a particular commodity or industry), the Index by Categories is an important access tool. For all categories, this index will generally provide an added depth of coverage beyond that available through the Index by Subjects and Names.

For example, data on individual cities and counties found in detailed breakdowns in State reports will be indexed only in the Index by Categories. In addition, for searches where comparative data are desired (e.g., comparative data for different countries, different companies, different age groups or occupations), the Index by Categories is the most logical starting point.

Within each category in the index, entries are grouped according to subject matter, under one of the following 21 subject headings:

Agriculture and Food
Banking, Finance, and Insurance
Communications
Education
Energy Resources and Demand
Geography and Climate
Government and Defense
Health and Vital Statistics
Housing and Construction
Income
Industry and Commerce
Labor and Employment
Law Enforcement
Natural Resources, Environment, and Pollution
Population
Prices and Cost of Living
Public Welfare and Social Security
Recreation and Leisure
Science and Technology
Transportation and Travel
Veterans Affairs

Definitions and conventions used in assigning these headings are summarized in an introductory section preceding the Index by Categories.

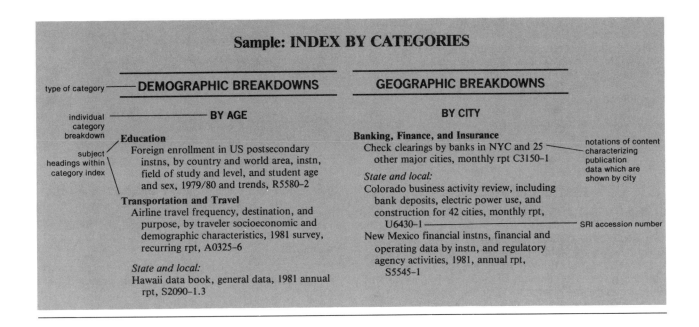

Sample: INDEX BY CATEGORIES

type of category

DEMOGRAPHIC BREAKDOWNS

GEOGRAPHIC BREAKDOWNS

individual category breakdown

BY AGE

BY CITY

subject headings within category index

Education
Foreign enrollment in US postsecondary instns, by country and world area, instn, field of study and level, and student age and sex, 1979/80 and trends, R5580–2

Transportation and Travel
Airline travel frequency, destination, and purpose, by traveler socioeconomic and demographic characteristics, 1981 survey, recurring rpt, A0325–6

State and local:
Hawaii data book, general data, 1981 annual rpt, S2090–1.3

Banking, Finance, and Insurance
Check clearings by banks in NYC and 25 other major cities, monthly rpt C3150–1

State and local:
Colorado business activity review, including bank deposits, electric power use, and construction for 42 cities, monthly rpt, U6430–1
New Mexico financial instns, financial and operating data by instn, and regulatory agency activities, 1981, annual rpt, S5545–1

notations of content characterizing publication data which are shown by city

SRI accession number

Index by Issuing Sources

This index contains references showing issuing source and publication title for all associations, business organizations, commercial publishers, independent research organizations, State agencies, and university departments or research centers whose publications have been abstracted and indexed by SRI. Periodicity and SRI microfiche status are also shown for each publication title.

Names of issuing sources generally appear in natural word order, with report titles listed below. Where issuing source names have been inverted for purposes of alphabetization by surname (e.g., Best, A.M., Co.), a cross reference from natural word order is provided. University research centers are listed first by university, and secondly by specific center or department issuing the report. In general, titles of State reports are listed under State issuing sources at the Department or highest organizational level, with cross references provided, as necessary, from names of responsible State subagencies. (See example, below.)

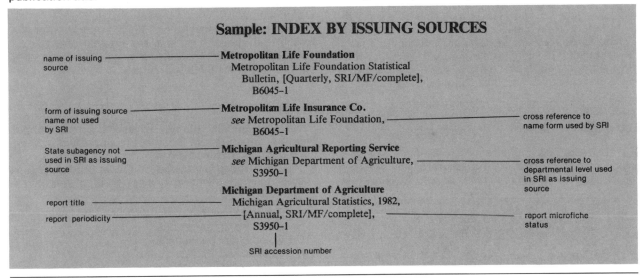

Sample: INDEX BY ISSUING SOURCES

name of issuing source

Metropolitan Life Foundation
Metropolitan Life Foundation Statistical Bulletin, [Quarterly, SRI/MF/complete], B6045–1

form of issuing source name not used by SRI

Metropolitan Life Insurance Co.
see Metropolitan Life Foundation, B6045–1

cross reference to name form used by SRI

State subagency not used in SRI as issuing source

Michigan Agricultural Reporting Service
see Michigan Department of Agriculture, S3950–1

cross reference to departmental level used in SRI as issuing source

report title

Michigan Department of Agriculture
Michigan Agricultural Statistics, 1982,

report periodicity

[Annual, SRI/MF/complete], S3950–1

report microfiche status

SRI accession number

Index by Titles

This index lists titles of all publications, including individual reports within a publication series. Titles are listed alphabetically in natural word order, without initial articles (a, an, the), as they appear in the abstracts.

Titles beginning with arabic numerals appear at the end of the index (e.g., 1982 Commodity Year Book), as well as alphabetically under the first key word (e.g., Commodity Year Book, 1982).

Titles of individual articles within a given publication are not generally included in the Title Index, unless the title itself is considered to be sufficiently well known to be a useful searching tool. However, articles or publications that carry an author's name on the title page or otherwise prominently acknowledged, are listed by author in the Index by Subjects and Names.

Each title listed in the Title Index is followed by an SRI accession number, directing the user to the abstract of the publication.

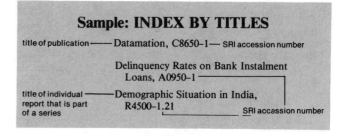

Sample: INDEX BY TITLES

title of publication —— Datamation, C8650–1 — SRI accession number

Delinquency Rates on Bank Instalment Loans, A0950–1

title of individual report that is part of a series —— Demographic Situation in India, R4500–1.21 —— SRI accession number

Lists of Selected Standard Classifications

Statistical data breakdowns indexed in the Index by Categories are frequently presented in accordance with several standard classification systems, and SRI abstracts generally make note of their use. To provide an easily accessible reference for the user, we have printed a number of major classification systems or lists in the "List of Selected Standard Classifications." It includes the following lists:

- Census regions and divisions; outlying areas of the U.S.; Federal Reserve Districts.
- Metropolitan Statistical Areas (MSAs); Consolidated Metropolitan Statistical Areas (CMSAs); cities with population over 100,000; and Consumer Price Index cities.
- Standard Industrial Classification (SIC), providing 1-to 4-digit codes for industry divisions through individual industries.
- Standard Occupational Classification, providing 1- to 4-digit codes for major and minor occupational groups.
- Standard International Trade Classification, a system of 3-digit codes for commodities in world trade, developed by the United Nations, used for foreign trade data, and consistent with the 7-digit codes used for U.S. import-export data.
- List of Part I (Index) and Part II (non-Index) crimes used in Uniform Crime Reporting Systems of the States.

ORGANIZATION OF SRI ABSTRACTS

SRI abstracts are based upon examination of the entire document. Abstracts differ substantially in degree of detail, depending on the type of publication and the kind of data being described. However, all abstracts are written to fulfill certain basic objectives.

These objectives are to describe a publication fully enough to allow the user to determine if it is likely to contain the specific statistical data he seeks; to tell the user how the contents of the publication are organized; to provide basic bibliographic data, availability address, price, and other ordering information; and to identify those publications for which SRI provides microfiche reproductions.

This section explains how SRI abstracts are organized in the abstract volume, the internal structure of abstracts, and the special way in which SRI handles periodicals each month.

Accession Numbers

SRI abstracts are organized by accession numbers assigned to each document abstracted and indexed. This accession number identifies not only the individual

Sample: SRI ACCESSION NUMBER ELEMENTS

issuing agency is an association

SRI serial number for the publication

A 1600–2.2 —— 2nd analytic abstract for the publication

particular issuing source is American Federation of Teachers

publication, but also the type of issuing source and the individual organization. It contains four basic elements, illustrated and outlined below.

- **Type of Issuing Source:** The initial letter of an accession number identifies type of issuing source, as follows:

  A – Associations
  B – Business organizations
  C – Commercial publishers
  R – Independent research centers
  S – State agency or subagency
  U – Universities, and affiliated research organizations.

- **Individual Issuing Source:** The four digits following the initial letter, up to the hyphen, identify the individual issuing source within the issuing source type.

  (Numbers have been assigned in such a way that individual sources are listed in alphabetical order within a source type.)

- **Sequential SRI Serial Number:** The digits after the hyphen form a unique serial number, sequentially assigned, basically in order of SRI acquisition, so that every publication has its own unique number which can be easily found in the abstracts volume of SRI.
- **Analytic Number:** In many cases, SRI describes publications by using a main abstract in coordination with subordinate or "analytic" abstracts. These analytic abstracts are identified by a decimal number (.1, .2, .3, etc.; or .601, .602, .603, etc.) at the end of the accession number. The analytic abstracts have the following purposes:

  (1) To describe and individually index distinct parts of a large publication, or to identify separate publications in a series. [These analytic abstracts are assigned single digit decimal numbers (A1600-1.1, A1600-1.2, etc.), followed by a heading or title.]

  (2) To describe individual issues of, or specific articles in, current issues of periodicals regularly covered by SRI. [These analytic abstracts are identified by 3-digit decimal numbers (U2735-1.301, U2735-1.302, etc.), followed by cover date of the periodical. A further explanation of periodical abstracts may be found in the section on how SRI handles periodicals, below.]

Generally, once SRI has assigned an accession number to a publication, all successive issues or updates of that publication will receive the same accession number. If the number is changed, cross-references between the old and new numbers are included in the abstracts. This will happen if, for example, the issuing agency of the publication changes.

To use SRI indexes and abstracts effectively, it is not necessary to know how SRI codes and assigns accession numbers, but familiarity with components of the accession number can speed interpretation of entries in the indexes.

Internal Organization of Abstracts

SRI abstracts provide the following information for each publication:

- Title, periodicity, publication date, collation (except for periodicals with inconsistent collation), report number (if assigned by the issuing agency), ISSN or ISBN number and Library of Congress card number (if available), and SRI microfiche coverage information.

- Overview of the publication, including principal subject and purpose, major data topics and breakdowns, geographic areas and time periods covered by data, and data sources.

- Contents summary, with page ranges, covering organization and format of the publication and the number of charts and tables presented.

- Description of statistical content. SRI abstracts present either a summary description of all tables, brief paragraphs describing groups of tables, or a complete listing of individual tables, depending on the level of detail necessary to give a clear picture of the publication's statistical content.

- Complete availability information, including issuing source address for ordering, price, and SRI microfiche coverage.

- For periodicals, cover dates of publications reviewed by SRI, and identification of cover date as either a publication date (P), or as the date of the statistical data presented (D).

Please refer to sample abstracts (p. xxvii-xxix) for illustrations of the above.

Special Handling of Periodicals

SRI observes a few special conventions in describing periodicals. Since most statistical periodicals retain at least some features and tables that are of constant format from issue to issue, it would be redundant to provide full abstracts for each issue. Therefore, a "base" abstract is written for each periodical, to indicate the features common to all issues and to describe tables that appear in each issue or at regular intervals.

For many periodicals, this "base" abstract suffices to describe statistical contents for all issuances during the year, since statistical contents are totally constant in format from issue to issue. However, many periodicals also contain nonrecurring feature articles and special tables, or present recurring tables at irregular intervals. These articles and tables are individually described in analytic abstracts under the heading "Statistical Features."

The "Statistical Features" analytic abstracts use 3-digit analytic numbers and are identified by the cover date of the relevant periodical issue (e.g., A1250-1.601, Nov. 5, 1984 (Vol. 62, No. 45)). For illustration of a typical "Statistical Features" abstract, see sample abstracts, p. xxviii

In composing base abstracts for periodicals, we do not give specific time coverage of the data stated as a specific month or year, but describe it in a general way that will apply to all issues. Similarly, the base abstracts do not include page ranges, which may change from issue to issue.

1986 Monthly Issues

During 1986, SRI will continue covering current issues of periodical titles covered in previous years. The combined January/February issue of SRI contains the initial or "base" abstract for all such periodicals for which issues were received in preceding November or December. For periodicals such as quarterlies which were not received for the 2-month issue, the "base" abstract will be published in the first issue for which they are reviewed in 1986. And, as additional periodicals are included during the year, the initial or base abstract will be provided in the SRI issue in which coverage of that periodical begins.

Throughout the year, whether or not "Statistical Features" abstracts are required to describe particular statistics, each SRI monthly issue will contain both a summary abstract and full indexing of statistical contents for each periodical for which one or more current issues were received during the period of coverage. The monthly summary abstracts will indicate all issues reviewed to date for a periodical, and either present a description of statistics appearing in and indexed for current issues, or refer the user to the SRI issue with the "base" periodical abstract that describes the indexed statistics.

HOW TO ACQUIRE SOURCE PUBLICATIONS

Acquiring Publications from a Library

Many of the publications abstracted in SRI are available in library collections. Ask your librarian for assistance in determining availability of specific titles.

Libraries that subscribe to the SRI Microfiche Library will have source material reproduced on microfiche as indicated in individual abstracts. (See explanation of SRI Microfiche Program, below.)

Requesting or Purchasing Publications from the Issuing Source

Information for requesting or purchasing copies of publications from the issuing source is provided in an Availability section in the SRI abstract for each publication. This information is as current and complete as possible as of SRI date of publication. See sample abstracts (p. xxvii-xxix) and symbols list (p. xxxii) for examples of information provided, and explanation of symbols employed.

The SRI Microfiche Program

Over 90% of the publications covered in SRI are included in the SRI Microfiche Library, available on a subscription basis and included in the collections of many major libraries. An entry in the bibliographic data section of each abstract will describe the microfiche status of that publication in one of the following ways:

- **SRI/MF/complete:** the entire publication is available in the SRI Microfiche Library. (In some series designated SRI/MF/complete, only reports with statistics are abstracted and filmed. Such exceptions are noted in the base description of the series.)

- **SRI/MF/excerpts:** only statistical portions have been filmed and are available on SRI microfiche.

  Many periodicals covered in SRI are less than 50% statistical or have only one or two statistical issues per year, yet each issue averages more than 100 pages collation. Rather than inflate the size and price of SRI Microfiche Library with nonstatistical materials, only the cover, title page, table of contents, statistical content, and any accompanying narrative analysis of the statistical content will be filmed. Issues containing no statistics will not be filmed. A few large directories and calendar handbooks with limited statistical sections will also be filmed in excerpted form for similar reasons. Excerpted portions will be specified in the abstract availability information section.

- **SRI/MF/not filmed:** the publication is copyrighted, and SRI has been unable to obtain permission from the issuing agency to micropublish it.

  SRI will make a continuing effort to obtain reproduction rights to provide as inclusive a microfiche library as possible.

  Publications that have very limited distribution and cannot be micropublished by SRI will not be covered in SRI.

- **SRI/MF/complete, delayed; SRI/MF/excerpts, delayed:** the issuing agency has stipulated that SRI must wait to distribute the microfiche of the publication for a specified period of time as a condition of granting reproduction rights. The delay period will always be stated in the abstract availability section. Every effort will be made to keep instances of delayed shipment to a minimum.

Microfiche generally are shipped monthly and correspond to abstracts appearing in SRI monthly issues, except for selected periodicals (averaging less than 60 filmed pages) that are shipped on a quarterly basis to minimize waste space in the microfiche collection. Periodicals with quarterly microfiche shipment schedules are identified in the abstract bibliographic information following SRI/MF (e.g., SRI/MF/complete, shipped quarterly; or SRI/MF/excerpts, shipped quarterly).

SRI microfiche are sheets of film that measure 105 × 148 mm (approximately 4″ × 6″), and contain up to 98 document pages. Each has an eye-readable "title header" that identifies the accession number, series title (if any), the document title, issuing organization, and dates of periodical issues, of each publication filmed. Items are filmed separately, and they are plainly sequenced for file integrity and quick retrieval according to SRI accession number.

Automatically updated collections of SRI current publications are available on a subscription basis. Retrospective collections, shipped in their entirety and ready for use, may also be purchased. Collections may be ordered to contain the entire range of SRI publications; or subsets may be ordered to cover only publications issued by State governments or to cover only publications issued by private organizations and universities.

RELATED CIS SERVICES

American Statistics Index and Index to International Statistics

Since 1973, Congressional Information Service has published the American Statistics Index, a comprehensive monthly abstract and index publication with annual cumulations, covering the thousands of statistical reports and publications prepared and issued by the U.S. Federal Government each year.

Beginning in January 1983, Congressional Information Service initiated publication of the Index to International Statistics, a comprehensive monthly index and abstracting service, covering the statistical publications of international intergovernmental organizations, including UN, OECD, EC, OAS, and approximately 80 other important intergovernmental organizations.

SRI abstracts and indexes are similar to ASI and IIS in many respects, and researchers generally can use SRI,

ASI, and IIS without significantly changing their search methods. However, several differences exist among the abstracts and indexes of the three services that should be noted. Major differences are:

- **Accession Number Periodicity Element**—SRI accession numbers do not indicate periodicity. IIS accession numbers include an indication of periodicity in the first letter after the hyphen, as do ASI accession numbers in the last digit before the hyphen.

- **Issuing Sources Indexing**—SRI and IIS issuing sources are indexed in a separate Index by Issuing Sources. ASI issuing agencies for publications are indexed in the ASI Index of Subjects and Names.

- **Periodicals Indexing in Monthly Issues**—SRI and IIS monthly abstracts and indexing cover all statistical contents of all periodicals received during each month. ASI monthly abstracts and indexing for periodicals cover only articles appearing in current issues, and changes from the "base" description for a periodical in the ASI Annual.

- **Periodical Currency Information in Monthly Issues**—ASI lists current issues of periodicals in a monthly "Periodicals Received and Reviewed" section. SRI and IIS incorporate this information in monthly abstracts for current periodicals.

- **Cumulation Patterns**—IIS indexes and abstracts are cumulated quarterly in the 3rd, 6th, 9th, and 12th issues each year. For ASI and SRI, only indexes are cumulated. ASI indexes are cumulated quarterly on the same schedule as IIS. SRI indexes are cumulated quarterly, but also cumulate throughout the quarter, so that the 2nd issue of a quarter includes indexing from the 1st issue, replacing the earlier monthly index.

All of the documents covered in ASI are included in the ASI Microfiche Library, available on a subscription basis, or through an individual Document on Demand service. The IIS Microfiche Library provides full text availability of over 95% of the publications indexed.

Other CIS Services

Since 1970, Congressional Information Service has published the CIS/Index, a monthly abstract and index publication with annual cumulations, which covers all publications of the U.S. Congress. The CIS/Microfiche Library and CIS/Documents-on-Demand services provide full-text availability of CIS/Index publications.

Through cooperative arrangements with on-line computer services, direct on-line interactive searching of the abstracts and indexing contained in the American Statistics Index and CIS/Index databases is available to the public.

Full details on CIS publications and microform collections are available upon request from the CIS Marketing Department.

ACKNOWLEDGEMENTS

In the development of the Statistical Reference Index, we have had the help and support of so many people that it would be impossible to acknowledge them all individually.

We do wish to thank the hundreds of business organizations, publishers, associations, State government agencies, and research centers that have cooperated in providing us the information to be indexed. We appreciate the many editors, company executives, program and research directors, and State government officials and staff who have shared their expertise and often directed us to other useful sources.

Librarians and information specialists especially have offered useful advice and encouragement as we have discussed with them various aspects of SRI over the years. Our special thanks go to the many State librarians and others who have assisted with the development of selection criteria for the publications to be covered.

The original concept of an SRI data base was developed from suggestions from Jack Leister, Head Librarian at Institute of Governmental Studies, University of California, Berkeley; and Judy Myers, Documents Division of University of Houston Library. Important suggestions in expanding and developing the concept were contributed by Morris Ullman and Ruth Fine.

Sample Abstract—Individual Publication

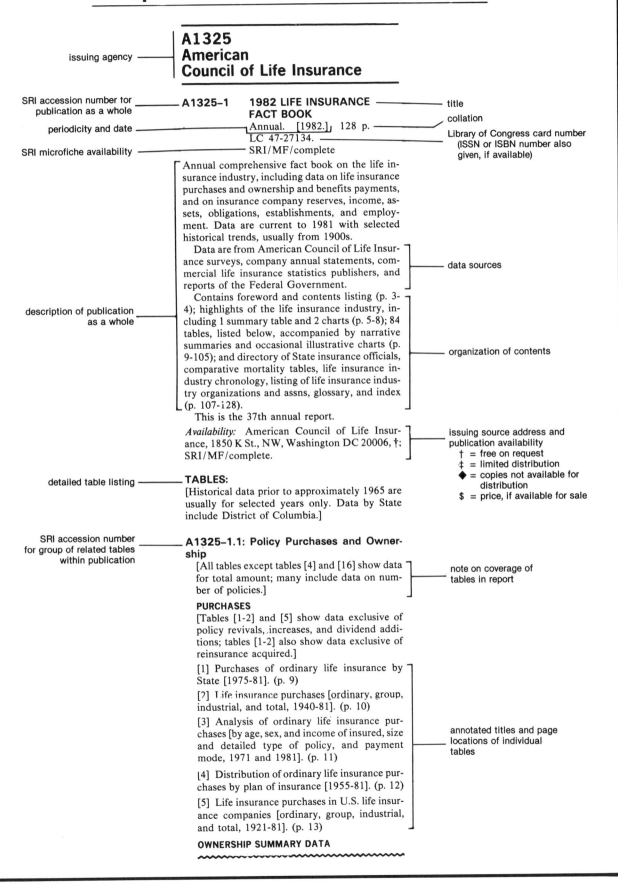

issuing agency ——

**A1325
American
Council of Life Insurance**

SRI accession number for
publication as a whole ——— **A1325-1**   **1982 LIFE INSURANCE** ——— title
FACT BOOK

collation

periodicity and date ——— Annual. [1982.] 128 p. ———

LC 47-27134. ——— Library of Congress card number
(ISSN or ISBN number also
given, if available)

SRI microfiche availability ——— SRI/MF/complete

Annual comprehensive fact book on the life insurance industry, including data on life insurance
purchases and ownership and benefits payments,
and on insurance company reserves, income, assets, obligations, establishments, and employment. Data are current to 1981 with selected
historical trends, usually from 1900s.

Data are from American Council of Life Insurance surveys, company annual statements, commercial life insurance statistics publishers, and
reports of the Federal Government. ——— data sources

description of publication
as a whole

Contains foreword and contents listing (p. 3-
4); highlights of the life insurance industry, including 1 summary table and 2 charts (p. 5-8); 84
tables, listed below, accompanied by narrative
summaries and occasional illustrative charts (p.
9-105); and directory of State insurance officials, ——— organization of contents
comparative mortality tables, life insurance in-
dustry chronology, listing of life insurance industry organizations and assns, glossary, and index
(p. 107-128).

This is the 37th annual report.

Availability: American Council of Life Insur-
ance, 1850 K St., NW, Washington DC 20006, †; ——— issuing source address and
publication availability
SRI/MF/complete.
† = free on request
‡ = limited distribution
◆ = copies not available for
distribution
$ = price, if available for sale

detailed table listing ——— **TABLES:**
[Historical data prior to approximately 1965 are
usually for selected years only. Data by State
include District of Columbia.]

SRI accession number
for group of related tables ——— **A1325-1.1: Policy Purchases and Owner-**
within publication **ship**
[All tables except tables [4] and [16] show data ——— note on coverage of
for total amount; many include data on num- tables in report
ber of policies.]

PURCHASES
[Tables [1-2] and [5] show data exclusive of
policy revivals, increases, and dividend additions; tables [1-2] also show data exclusive of
reinsurance acquired.]

[1] Purchases of ordinary life insurance by
State [1975-81]. (p. 9)

[2] Life insurance purchases [ordinary, group,
industrial, and total, 1940-81]. (p. 10)

[3] Analysis of ordinary life insurance pur-
chases [by age, sex, and income of insured, size ——— annotated titles and page
and detailed type of policy, and payment locations of individual
mode, 1971 and 1981]. (p. 11) tables

[4] Distribution of ordinary life insurance purchases by plan of insurance [1955-81]. (p. 12)

[5] Life insurance purchases in U.S. life insurance companies [ordinary, group, industrial,
and total, 1921-81]. (p. 13)

OWNERSHIP SUMMARY DATA

Sample Abstract—Periodical Publication

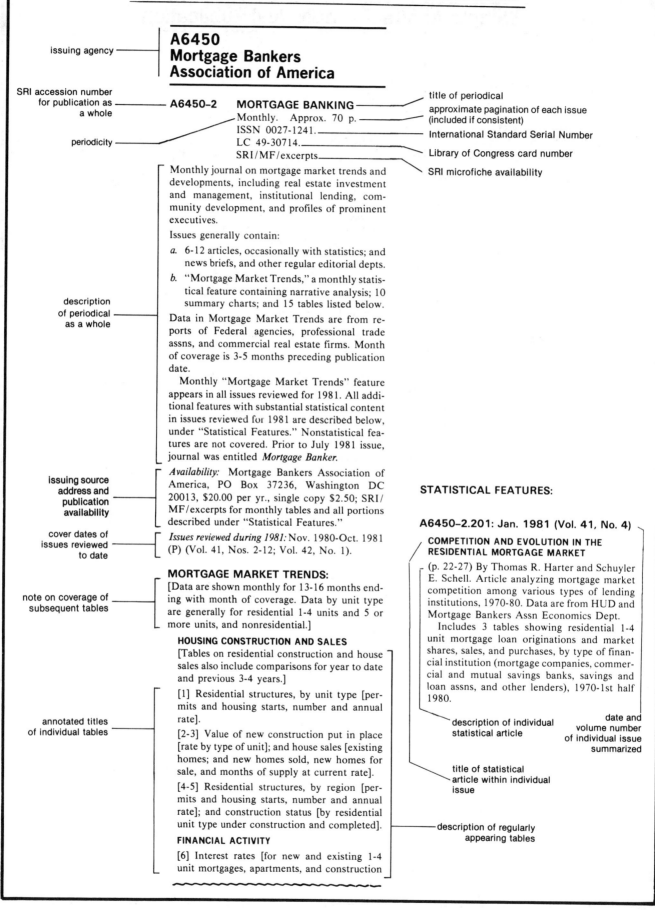

issuing agency

A6450
Mortgage Bankers Association of America

SRI accession number for publication as a whole

A6450–2 MORTGAGE BANKING

title of periodical

Monthly. Approx. 70 p.

approximate pagination of each issue (included if consistent)

ISSN 0027-1241.

International Standard Serial Number

periodicity

LC 49-30714.

Library of Congress card number

SRI/MF/excerpts

SRI microfiche availability

description of periodical as a whole

Monthly journal on mortgage market trends and developments, including real estate investment and management, institutional lending, community development, and profiles of prominent executives.

Issues generally contain:

a. 6-12 articles, occasionally with statistics; and news briefs, and other regular editorial depts.

b. "Mortgage Market Trends," a monthly statistical feature containing narrative analysis; 10 summary charts; and 15 tables listed below.

Data in Mortgage Market Trends are from reports of Federal agencies, professional trade assns, and commercial real estate firms. Month of coverage is 3-5 months preceding publication date.

Monthly "Mortgage Market Trends" feature appears in all issues reviewed for 1981. All additional features with substantial statistical content in issues reviewed for 1981 are described below, under "Statistical Features." Nonstatistical features are not covered. Prior to July 1981 issue, journal was entitled *Mortgage Banker.*

issuing source address and publication availability

Availability: Mortgage Bankers Association of America, PO Box 37236, Washington DC 20013, $20.00 per yr., single copy $2.50; SRI/MF/excerpts for monthly tables and all portions described under "Statistical Features."

cover dates of issues reviewed to date

Issues reviewed during 1981: Nov. 1980-Oct. 1981 (P) (Vol. 41, Nos. 2-12; Vol. 42, No. 1).

MORTGAGE MARKET TRENDS:

note on coverage of subsequent tables

[Data are shown monthly for 13-16 months ending with month of coverage. Data by unit type are generally for residential 1-4 units and 5 or more units, and nonresidential.]

HOUSING CONSTRUCTION AND SALES

[Tables on residential construction and house sales also include comparisons for year to date and previous 3-4 years.]

annotated titles of individual tables

[1] Residential structures, by unit type [permits and housing starts, number and annual rate].

[2-3] Value of new construction put in place [rate by type of unit]; and house sales [existing homes; and new homes sold, new homes for sale, and months of supply at current rate].

[4-5] Residential structures, by region [permits and housing starts, number and annual rate]; and construction status [by residential unit type under construction and completed].

FINANCIAL ACTIVITY

[6] Interest rates [for new and existing 1-4 unit mortgages, apartments, and construction

STATISTICAL FEATURES:

A6450–2.201: Jan. 1981 (Vol. 41, No. 4)

COMPETITION AND EVOLUTION IN THE RESIDENTIAL MORTGAGE MARKET

(p. 22-27) By Thomas R. Harter and Schuyler E. Schell. Article analyzing mortgage market competition among various types of lending institutions, 1970-80. Data are from HUD and Mortgage Bankers Assn Economics Dept.

Includes 3 tables showing residential 1-4 unit mortgage loan originations and market shares, sales, and purchases, by type of financial institution (mortgage companies, commercial and mutual savings banks, savings and loan assns, and other lenders), 1970-1st half 1980.

description of individual statistical article

date and volume number of individual issue summarized

title of statistical article within individual issue

description of regularly appearing tables

Sample Abstract—Publications in Series

U4370
Purdue University:
Credit Research Center

SRI accession number
for series as a whole

U4370–1 CREDIT RESEARCH CENTER ——— title of series
WORKING PAPERS
Series. For individual
publication data, see below.
SRI/MF/complete

description of
series as a whole

Continuing series of preliminary drafts of research study reports examining consumer and
mortgage credit trends and practices, and their
impact on the credit industry, consumers, and
government.

Reports generally contain narrative analyses
with interspersed tables and charts presenting
data from government and private published
sources, or from original surveys and/or survey
analyses.

Recently issued report is described below.

Availability: Purdue University: Credit Research Center, Krannert Graduate School of
Management, West Lafayette IN 47907, $1.50
each; SRI/MF/complete.

availability information for
all reports in series

SRI accession number
for individual report
in series

U4370–1.17: Second Mortgage Survey, ——— title of individual report
1981

bibliographic data for
individual report

[Annual. 1982. iii+33 p. Working Paper
No. 43. SRI/MF/complete.]

Annual report, by Richard L. Peterson et al.,
on a survey of the volume, profitability, and
operating policies of the second mortgage
lending market, 1980. Data are based on responses of 69 National Second Mortgage Assn
members to a 1981 survey.

description of report
subject matter

Includes narrative analysis, with 1 table
showing survey responses, by institution type;
and 10 tables generally showing low, high, average, and/or median, for the following in
1980:

contents summary

description of statistical
content and page
locations of tables

a. Characteristics of second mortgage loans,
including number, value, and average size
of loans outstanding, extensions, and loan
purchases and sales, with selected comparisons to 1979; average size of household and
business extensions; ratio of new money to
loan extensions; liquidation rates; and loan
maturity and equity ratio requirements.
Tables 2-5. (p. 6-12)

b. Operating ratios, including revenues from
interest and other sources, pretax rate of
return on equity and average receivables,
and ratios of borrowing to receivables, and
interest paid to borrowings. Table 6. (p. 14)

c. Delinquency rates by time past due; and
chargeoff, foreclosure, and loss allowance
ratios. Tables 7-10. (p. 16-20)

d. Comparative data, by lender type, including growth in loans and extensions, selected loan characteristics, operating ratios,
delinquency rates, and foreclosures. Table
11. (p. 22)

Sample SRI Search

" How many stores in each of the big convenience grocery store chains sell gasoline? "

Step 1

Check the SRI Index volume

Start with a "subject" approach, where extensive cross-references will lead to the proper index reference from almost any likely point of entry.

Index by Subjects and Names

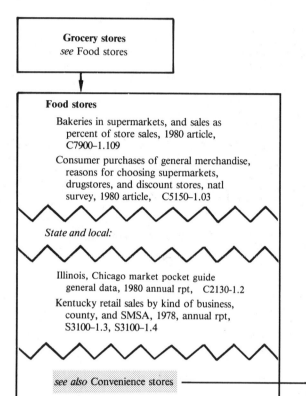

Grocery stores
see Food stores

Food stores

Bakeries in supermarkets, and sales as percent of store sales, 1980 article, C7900–1.109

Consumer purchases of general merchandise, reasons for choosing supermarkets, drugstores, and discount stores, natl survey, 1980 article, C5150–1.03

State and local:

Illinois, Chicago market pocket guide general data, 1980 annual rpt, C2130-1.2

Kentucky retail sales by kind of business, county, and SMSA, 1978, annual rpt, S3100–1.3, S3100–1.4

see also Convenience stores

Convenience stores

Fast food product mix and sales potential, convenience stores, 1979 article, C5800–1.106

Financial and operating data, including gasoline sales, for top 13 convenience store companies, 1971–79, annual rpt. C8115–1

Sales by commodity, and earnings of top 12 companies, 1977–79, annual rpt, C7900–1.105

Gasoline

Agricultural energy use by type of fuel, crop, and farm operation, 1965-80, annual rpt, S2205–1

Consumer expenditures, percent for gasoline by age and household income, monthly rpt special chart, A7475–1.107

Convenience food store chain establishments, profits, total and gasoline sales, stock performance, and operating data for top 13 companies, 1971-79, annual rpt, C8115–1

An alternate approach is through the "Index by Categories." Since you are looking for information about particular firms, you can find it under "By Individual Company or Institution."

Index by Categories

BY INDIVIDUAL COMPANY OR INSTITUTION

Energy Resources and Demand

Auto mileage for 1980 model cars, EPA estimates by size group and model, annual data book, C2700–1.118

Canadian natural gas amounts approved for export to US, by exporting company, 1980-87, article, C7100–1.112

Convenience food store chain establishments, profits, total and gasoline sales, stock performance, and operating data for top 13 companies, 1971-79, annual rpt, C8115–1

Step 2

Go from the index to the data description in the Abstracts Volume

The SRI accession number in the index will lead you to a publication entry that fully describes the document and pin-points the tables containing the statistics you need.

C8115
Roscoe, John F.

C8115–1   NINTH ANNUAL DOLLARS PER DAY SURVEY
Annual. 1979. 107 p.
SRI/MF/complete

Annual report, for 1979, on financial conditions and operations of the 13 largest publicly held convenience store chains in the small food store industry, presented on a dollars per day (DPD) per store basis. Includes profit trends by individual companies, 1971-79; store and gasoline sales, and individual company profiles.

Report is based on the 9th annual survey of company annual reports, proxy statements, or 10-K reports filed with SEC.

Contents:

a. Brief introduction (1-3); and store annual report and DPD analyses, with 36 interspersed tables, listed below (p. 3-26).

b. Historical summaries, 13 companies, each with 1 table showing number of stores, sales per day, DPD sales growth, pre- and after-tax profit DPD, closures, gasoline units, and DPD ranking, 1st-9th surveys, 1971-79. (p. 27-40)

Availability: John F. Roscoe, Dollars Per Day Survey, 391 Castle Crest Rd., Walnut Creek CA 94595, $50.00 1st copy, $5.00 each additional copy; SRI/MF/complete.

TABLES:
[Tables show data for 1979, unless otherwise noted.]

C8115–1.1: Annual Report and DPD Analyses

PROFIT AND SALES

[1-2] Pretax dollars of profit per store per day ranking; and small store industry ranked by profit per store per day [including sales, by company]. (p. 3-5)

[3-5] An aggregate [13 surveyed chains], an annual [average store surveyed]; and average store by day profit and loss statements. (p. 6)

GASOLINE SALES

[21] Number and percentage of stores with gasoline units [by company]. (p. 16)

[22] Gasoline [number of stores, stores with gas units, gas units added, and percent of stores with gas, 1974-79 surveys]. (p. 16)

Step 3

Retrieve the publication

The abstract contains the bibliographic information you need to locate the publication in a library's hardcopy collection or to obtain it from the issuing source, if copies are available.

Alternatively, if you have access to an SRI/Microfiche Library collection, the SRI accession number will lead you directly to the correct microfiche.

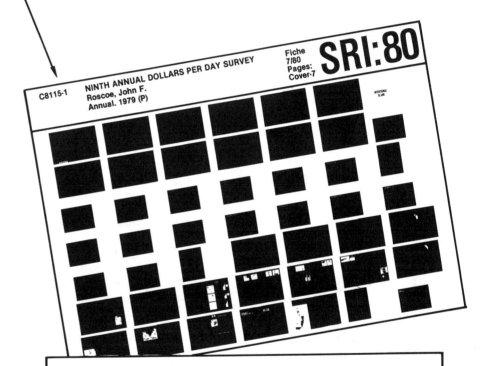

Fiche 7/80
Pages: Cover-7
SRI:80

C8115-1   NINTH ANNUAL DOLLARS PER DAY SURVEY
Roscoe, John F.
Annual. 1979 (P)

Number and Percentage of Stores with Gasoline Units

$DPD Ranking Company	# of Stores	# of Gasoline Units	% of Stores With Gasoline	# of Gasoline Units Added During Year	# of Stores Added During Year
1. Circle K	1,158	681	59%	39	53
2. Shop & Go	379	225	59	--	8
3. Dillon	305	186	61	20	21
4. Southland	6,599	1,857	28	284	242
5. Lil' Champ	130	31	24	6	8
6. National Convenience	806	418	52	[1] 91	81
7. Convenient	316	218	69	[2] 45	31
8. Hop-In	132	108	82	19	20
9. Sunshine Jr.	316	230	73	39	28
10. Li'l General	515	165	32	- 5	- 26
11. UtoteM	934	511	55	21	6
12. Mini Mart	119	11	9	- 2	- 9
13. Munford	1,211	512	42	12	- 140
Totals	12,920	5,153	39.88%	569	323

[1] Purchased 85 when Texas Super Duper Markets were acquired May 1, 1979.
[2] Purchased 15 when gasoline retailing corporation in North Carolina was acquired.

16

ACRONYMS, SELECTED ABBREVIATIONS, AND SYMBOLS

The following acronyms, abbreviations, and symbols may be used without further identification.

Admin	Administration	GSA	General Services Administration	PPI	Producer Price Index
AFDC	Aid to Families with Dependent Children	GSP	Gross State Product	PRC	People's Republic of China
		HHS	Department of Health and Human Services	Pub.	Publication
AFL-CIO	American Federation of Labor-Congress of Industrial Organizations			Qtr	Quarter
		HMO	Health Maintenance Organization	R&D	Research and Development
		HUD	Department of Housing and Urban Development	Res	Research
AMEX	American Exchange			ROTC	Reserve Officers Training Corps
Amtrak	National Railroad Passenger Corp.	Hwy	Highway	Rpt.	Report
Assn	Association	ICC	Interstate Commerce Commission	SALT	Strategic Arms Limitation Talks
Bibl	Bibliography	ILO	International Labor Organization	SBA	Small Business Administration
BLS	Bureau of Labor Statistics	IMF	International Monetary Fund	SEC	Securities and Exchange Commission
Btu(h)	British thermal units	Info	Information		
Bull.	Bulletin	Inst	Institute	SIC	Standard Industrial Classification
Bur	Bureau	Instn	Institution	SITC	Standard International Trade Classification
CAB	Civil Aeronautics Board	Intl	International		
CETA	Comprehensive Employment and Training Act	IRS	Internal Revenue Service	SMSA	Standard Metropolitan Statistical Area
		kWh	Kilowatt hours		
CIA	Central Intelligence Agency	Metro	Metropolitan	SSA	Social Security Administration
CPI	Consumer Price Index	Mgmt	Management	SSI	Supplemental Security Income
DEA	Drug Enforcement Administration	MSA	Metropolitan Statistical Area	TSUSA	Tariff Schedules of the U.S. Annotated
Dept	Department	NASA	National Aeronautics and Space Administration		
Dev	Development			TTPI	Trust Territory of the Pacific Islands
Div	Division	NASDAQ	National Assn of Securities Dealers Automated Quotations		
DOD	Department of Defense (not DON or DOA)			TV	Television
		Natl	National	TVA	Tennessee Valley Authority
DOE	Department of Energy	NATO	North Atlantic Treaty Organization	UK	United Kingdom
DOT	Department of Transportation	NCES	National Center for Educational Statistics	UN	United Nations
EC	European Community			UNESCO	United Nations Educational, Scientific and Cultural Organization
EPA	Environmental Protection Agency	NCHS	National Center for Health Statistics		
FAA	Federal Aviation Administration	NIH	National Institutes of Health		
FBI	Federal Bureau of Investigation	NIMH	National Institute of Mental Health	UNICEF	United Nations International Children's Emergency Fund
FCC	Federal Communications Commission	NLRB	National Labor Relations Board		
		Nonmetro	Nonmetropolitan	USDA	Department of Agriculture
FDA	Food and Drug Administration	NRC	Nuclear Regulatory Commission	USITC	U.S. International Trade Commission
FDIC	Federal Deposit Insurance Corp.	NSA	National Security Agency		
Fdn	Foundation	NSC	National Security Council	USMC	Marine Corps
Fedn	Federation	NSF	National Science Foundation	USPS	U.S. Postal Service
FERC	Federal Energy Regulatory Commission	NYC	New York City	USSR	Union of Soviet Socialist Republics
		NYSE	New York Stock Exchange	VA	Veterans Administration
FHA	Federal Housing Administration	OAS	Organization of American States	WPI	Wholesale Price Index
FHLBB	Federal Home Loan Bank Board	OASDHI	Old-Age, Survivors, Disability, and Health Insurance		
FmHA	Farmers Home Administration				
FNMA	Federal National Mortgage Association	OECD	Organization for Economic Cooperation and Development		
FSLIC	Federal Savings and Loan Insurance Corp.	OMB	Office of Management and Budget		
		OPEC	Organization of Petroleum Exporting Countries		
FTC	Federal Trade Commission				
FTE	Full time equivalent	OSHA	Occupational Safety and Health Administration		
FY	Fiscal Year				
GDP	Gross Domestic Product	PAD	Petroleum Administration for Defense (abolished in 1954 but acronym is still used)		
GNMA	Government National Mortgage Association				
GNP	Gross National Product	PHS	Public Health Service		
Govt	Government	P.L.	Public Law		
Govtl	Governmental				

Document Availability Symbols

† - copies are generally available free of charge from issuing source, while supplies last; inquire of issuing source

‡ - copies are distributed by issuing source on a limited basis; inquire of issuing source

◆ - copies are not available from issuing source; do not inquire of issuing source

SRI/MF/ - notation indicating publication availability in SRI Microfiche Library; see full explanation on p. xxiv

Abstracts of Statistical Publications

A0175
Administrative Management Society

A0175-1 AMS 39th ANNUAL OFFICE SALARIES DIRECTORY: Salary and Benefit Information for Office Employees in the U.S. and Canada
Annual. 1985. 41 p.
ISSN 0731-4434.
LC 82-640803.
SRI/MF/complete

Annual survey report on salaries and benefits for clerical and word processing employees in U.S. and Canada, as of Jan. 1985. Presents median, average, and 1st and 3rd quartile weekly salaries, by position, shown for total U.S. and Canada, for U.S. by region and employer category, and for 100 U.S. and 6 Canadian cities and MSAs.

Employer categories are manufacturing/processing, banking/insurance/financial, retail/wholesale sales/distribution, government agencies, and all others.

Also includes employee benefit and salary administration policies, for U.S. (by region) and Canada; U.S. salary comparison to 1983, by position; and U.S. employees by salary range, by position.

Data are primarily from an AMS survey of 4,732 member and nonmember companies employing 331,548 clerical and word processing personnel in 106 cities.

Contains introduction, map, contents listing, and user guide (p. 3-9); personnel policy summary and highlights, with 2 tables (p. 10-12); statistical section with 5 tables (p. 13-40); and conversion chart (p. 41).

Availability: Administrative Management Society, 2360 Maryland Rd., Willow Grove PA 19090, members $60.00, nonmembers $100.00; SRI/MF/complete.

A0175-2 THIRTEENTH ANNUAL GUIDE TO MANAGEMENT COMPENSATION, 1985
Annual. 1985. 44 p.
ISSN 0278-1506.
LC 81-643450.
SRI/MF/complete

Annual report on a survey of salaries paid by U.S. and Canadian companies for 20 middle management staff positions, as of Sept. 17, 1984. Includes median, average, and quartile salaries; and number of companies and employees represented; shown for Canada, U.S. by region and type of business, and 101 U.S. and 11 Canadian cities or metro areas, all by position.

Also includes summary comparison to 1983; and data on employee benefit policies, including insurance by type, physical examinations, prepaid legal coverage, and pension plans.

Types of business are manufacturing/processing, banking/insurance/financial, retail/wholesale sales/distribution, utilities, and all others.

Data are from a survey of 2,813 companies representing 40,494 employees.

Contains introduction, map, contents listing, methodology, and job titles and descriptions (p. 3-9); personnel policies and survey highlights, with 4 tables (p. 10-14); statistical section, with 4 extended tables (p. 15-43); and salary conversion chart (p. 44).

Availability: Administrative Management Society, 2360 Maryland Rd., Willow Grove PA 19090, members $60.00, nonmembers $100.00; SRI/MF/complete.

A0175-3 THIRD ANNUAL DATA PROCESSING SALARIES REPORT, 1985
Annual. 1985. 44 p.
SRI/MF/complete

Annual report on a survey of salaries paid by U.S. and Canadian companies for 20 electronic data processing (EDP) positions, as of Sept. 17, 1984. Includes median, average, and quartile salaries; and number of companies and employees represented; shown for Canada, U.S. by region and type of business, and 103 U.S. and 11 Canadian cities or metro areas, all by position.

Types of business are manufacturing/processing, banking/insurance/financial, retail/wholesale sales/distribution, utilities, data processing service bureaus, and all others.

Also includes summary comparison to 1983; and data on sample characteristics, including distribution of companies by sales and EDP expenditure ranges.

Data are from a survey of 2,360 companies representing 57,479 EDP employees.

Contains introduction, map, contents listing, methodology, job titles and descriptions, personnel policies and training programs, survey highlights, and 3 summary tables (p. 3-14); statistical section, with 4 extended tables (p. 15-43); and salary conversion chart (p. 44).

Availability: Administrative Management Society, 2360 Maryland Rd., Willow Grove PA 19090, members $60.00, nonmembers $100.00; SRI/MF/complete.

A0175-4 1985 AMS OFFICE TURNOVER SURVEY for the U.S. and Canada
Biennial. 1985.
5 p. no paging.
SRI/MF/complete

Biennial report, by Edward G. Thomas, on office employee turnover in the U.S. and Canada, 1984, with selected comparisons to 1982 and/or 1980. Covers employment, terminations, and turnover rate, by U.S. region and for major U.S. and Canadian metro areas; and U.S./Canadian turnover rates, by type of business, office size, and employee type (exempt and nonexempt). Also includes distribution of employee terminations, by reason and length of service.

Data are from a survey of 1,760 firms in 74 metro areas, conducted by Administrative Management Society.

Contains narrative report and 7 tables.

Previous report, for 1982, is described in SRI 1984 Annual, under this number.

Availability: Administrative Management Society, 2360 Maryland Rd., Willow Grove PA 19090, $20.00; SRI/MF/complete.

A0250
Aerospace Industries Association of America

A0250-1 AEROSPACE
Quarterly. Approx. 15 p.
ISSN 0091-9321.
LC 67-5475.
SRI/MF/complete

Quarterly aerospace industry journal, including aerospace economic indicators, and articles on industry sales, employment, R&D, aviation history, commercial and military aircraft design, and space technology and applications. Journal also includes an annual industry review and forecast feature. Indicator data are from the Aerospace Industries Assn.

Issues contain articles, sometimes including statistics; and a recurring aerospace economic indicators table (inside front or back cover) showing the following:

a. Aerospace shipments, new orders, unfilled order backlog, and capacity utilization.

b. DOD obligations and outlays for aircraft and missiles; and NASA R&D obligations and expenditures.

c. Value of exports and imports (total and civil), and exports of new commercial transports.

d. Employment for aircraft and missiles/space.

e. Profit as percent of sales, for aerospace and all manufacturing; plant/equipment expenditures; and GNP deflator index.

Indicator data are shown for quarter 2-3 quarters prior to cover date, preceding quarter, same period of preceding year, and average 1966-75.

Indicator data on shipments, orders, capacity utilization, imports, and plant/equipment expenditures begin with Spring 1985 issue. Prior to Spring 1985 issue, table also included data on aerospace sales, prime contract awards, and production worker earnings; and backlog orders were shown separately for Government and other customers.

Recurring table appears on a space-available basis. All additional features with substantial statistical content are described, as they appear, under "Statistical Features;" page location and latest period of coverage for recurring table are also noted. Nonstatistical contents are not covered.

Availability: Aerospace Industries Association of America, 1725 De Sales St., NW, Washington DC 20036, †; SRI/MF/complete.

Issues reviewed during 1985: Winter 1984-Summer 1985 (P) (Vol. 22, No. 4; Vol. 23, Nos. 1-3) [Vol. 22, Nos. 1 and 4 are both designated "Winter 1984"].

STATISTICAL FEATURES:

A0250–1.601: Winter 1985 (Vol. 23, No. 1)

AEROSPACE REVIEW AND FORECAST, 1984/85, ANNUAL FEATURE

(p. 12-17) Annual article presenting summary trends and forecasts for aerospace industry operations, with 6 charts, and 1 table showing civil aircraft shipments and value by type (commercial transport, general aviation, and helicopters), 1968-85. Data are from company reports and industry assns.

A0250–1.602: Spring 1985 (Vol. 23, No. 2)

RECURRING TABLE

Aerospace economic indicators, 4th quarter 1984. (inside back cover)

For data description, see A0250-1 above.

A0250–2   AEROSPACE FACTS AND FIGURES, 1984/85

Annual. Sept. 1984. 176 p.
LC 46-25007.
SRI/MF/complete

Annual report on civil and military aerospace industry production, R&D, foreign trade, employment, and financial condition, 1983 and trends. Includes data on aircraft and helicopter transportation, and missile and space programs, with selected worldwide comparisons.

Data are compiled from Federal Government reports, AIA, and other industry sources by the Economic Data Service of the Aerospace Research Center.

Contains contents listing and foreword (p. 5-7); 10 chapters with narrative analyses, 8 summary charts, and 124 tables described below (p. 8-161); and glossary, index, and list of AIA manufacturing members (p. 162-176).

This is the 32nd edition of the report.

Previous report, for 1983/84, is described in SRI 1983 Annual under this number.

Availability: Aviation Week and Space Technology, 1221 Ave. of the Americas, New York NY 10020, $10.95; SRI/MF/complete.

TABLES:

[Data are for U.S., unless otherwise noted, and are generally shown for 1983 with trends from as early as 1955. Budget and Federal outlay estimates are generally shown through FY85.]

A0250–2.1: Aerospace Summary and Aircraft Production

AEROSPACE SUMMARY

a. Aerospace industry: sales and backlog, in current and constant dollars, by product group and customer (U.S. Government and other), with sales comparisons to durable goods and all manufacturing industries and GNP. 5 tables. (p. 13-19)

b. Defense budget vs. all Federal outlays and GNP; Federal outlays for DOD and NASA aerospace products/services and total budgets, with detail for DOD aerospace and military outlays by function; and Federal price deflators for GNP, defense expenditures, PPI, CPI, and aerospace industry. 7 tables. (p. 20-27)

AIRCRAFT PRODUCTION

c. Aircraft/parts and engines/parts sales (in current and constant dollars), new orders, and backlog, for U.S. Government and others; and domestic and export shipments of civil and military aircraft by type. 3 tables. (p. 30-32)

d. Civil aircraft: shipment volume and value, by type; civil transport aircraft domestic and foreign orders and value, shipments, and specifications; and commercial helicopter and general aviation aircraft shipments and value; with detail by company and model. 7 tables. (p. 33-39)

e. Military aircraft: number accepted by all U.S. military agencies and value, by type; DOD aircraft procurement and outlays, by type and model, for each branch of service; and active military aircraft in continental U.S., FY75-85. 8 tables. (p. 40-46)

A0250–2.2: Missile and Space Programs

MISSILE PROGRAMS

a. DOD missile program procurement and outlays, and major missile projects status and major contractors, most by branch of service and missile type and model; outlays for missile R&D/test/evaluation (RDT&E); and sales (in current and constant dollars), new orders, and backlog of missile systems/parts and of military and nonmilitary missile/space vehicle engines/propulsion units. 6 tables. (p. 50-57)

SPACE PROGRAMS

b. Spacecraft attaining earth orbit or beyond, for U.S. (also showing failures), and by foreign country; and U.S. major launch record, space launch vehicles, and manned space flight dates, crew members, and mission highlights. 5 tables. (p. 60-66)

c. Space activity outlays and budget authority for NASA, DOD, DOE, Commerce Dept, and other agencies, with detail for NASA and DOD by function and program; and sales, new orders, and backlog of military and nonmilitary space vehicle systems; generally in current and constant dollars. 12 tables. (p. 68-79)

A0250–2.3: Air and Helicopter Transportation

AIR TRANSPORTATION

a. Airline operations: U.S. and world airline detailed operating revenues and expenses; world airline scheduled passenger and cargo traffic, and fleet composition by model with totals by world region and for U.S. aircraft; and U.S. airline jet fuel cost and consumption, assets and equipment value, load factor, revenue ton- and passenger-miles, and average flight length and seat capacity, with detail for domestic and international operations. 13 tables. (p. 82-96)

b. Civil/joint-use aircraft facilities (public, paved, and lighted), by State and selected U.S. territory; air carrier and general aviation active civil aircraft, by type and use, with detail for general aviation hours flown; and active airman certificates by type. 6 tables. (p. 97-103)

HELICOPTER TRANSPORTATION

c. Civil helicopters and operators, by user type (commercial, corporate/executive, and civil government agencies), by State, and for Mexico, Canada, and Puerto Rico; and heliports/helistops and hospital heliports, by census division and for Canada and Puerto Rico. 4 tables. (p. 106-109)

A0250–2.4: R&D and Foreign Trade

RESEARCH AND DEVELOPMENT

a. R&D Federal and company funds (total and as percent of net sales), for all industries vs. aerospace industries, with detail by manufacturing industry group, and for aerospace applied R&D vs. basic research and energy R&D; and Federal aeronautics R&D budget authority and/or outlays, for NASA, DOD, DOT, DOE, and other programs; most in current and constant dollars. 7 tables. (p. 112-117)

b. RDT&E: DOD appropriations, outlays, prime contract awards, and military aircraft and missile program costs, variously shown by branch of service, research or contractor type, function, missile or aircraft type and model, and census division. 6 tables. (p. 118-123)

FOREIGN TRADE

c. Total and aerospace balance of trade; aerospace foreign trade volume and/or value, by product category and use, including aircraft, gliders, balloons/airships, helicopters, and engines. 6 tables. (p. 127-132)

d. Import and/or export volume and value for civil helicopters, general aviation aircraft, and heavy commercial transport aircraft, by world region or country of origin or destination, and for military aircraft and aircraft engines, by product category and use; and Export-Import Bank authorizations of loans and guarantees. 11 tables. (p. 133-139)

A0250–2.5: Employment and Finance

EMPLOYMENT

a. Employment and payroll for aerospace vs. durable goods and/or all manufacturing industries, with detail for aircraft/parts industry employment; production worker earnings and hours, including overtime; and occupational illness/injury rates for aerospace vs. all manufacturing; most by product group. 8 tables. (p. 142-149)

b. Employment of R&D scientists/engineers and average cost, for all industries vs. aerospace; work stoppages in aerospace industry, workers involved, and worker-days idle; and number of NASA vs. contractor employees in NASA programs. 3 tables. (p. 150-151)

FINANCE

c. Net profit as percent of sales, assets, and equity, for all manufacturing and/or nondurable and durable goods, and for aerospace industry; combined aerospace companies' income statement, and balance sheet; and new plant/equipment expenditures for manufacturing, durable goods, aerospace, and all industries. 4 tables. (p. 155-158)

d. Top 30 NASA and DOD contractors ranked by value of prime contract awards; and total value of DOD prime contract awards of $25,000 or more, for aircraft, missiles/space systems, and electronics/communications equipment, by census division. 3 tables. (p. 159-161)

A0300
Air Conditioning and Refrigeration Institute

A0300–1 **NEWS RELEASE FROM THE AIR-CONDITIONING AND REFRIGERATION INSTITUTE**
Semimonthly, with annual summaries. Approx. 2 p.
LC 31-35153.
SRI/MF/complete, shipped quarterly

Semimonthly press release, with annual summaries, on unitary air conditioner/heat pump domestic shipments, by Btu(h) size. Covers equipment used in most residential central installations, plus some commercial and industrial installations using packaged equipment.

Data are from Institute records. Release is issued approximately 2 months after month of coverage.

The 1st issue of each month contains narrative summary with text data on shipment trends, and 1 table showing total shipments by Btu(h) size and type of condenser. The 2nd issue repeats the narrative summary of shipments and also includes text data on shipments, factory stocks, distributor shipments and inventories, and bookings. All data are shown for month of coverage. Revised data for previous issues are also occasionally included.

In addition to the semimonthly release, 3 annual summaries are issued, reporting on number and value of residential and commercial installations, and installed value of field-engineered equipment. Annual summaries are described as they are published.

Prior to issues presenting data for Mar. 1985, news release was published monthly, without the 2nd issue text data. No 2nd issues were received for June, July, and Aug. 1985; the text data described above for 2nd issues appeared in the single June and Aug. issues received but not in the July issue.

Availability: Air Conditioning and Refrigeration Institute, 1501 Wilson Blvd., Suite 600, Arlington VA 22209, †; SRI/MF/complete, shipped quarterly.

Issues reviewed during 1985: Sept. 1984-Aug. 1985 (D).

ANNUAL SUMMARIES:

A0300–1.1: Unitary Air-Conditioning Equipment: Estimated Installed Value Jumps 25.8% in 1984
[Annual. June 5, 1985 2 p. SRI/MF/complete.]

Annual press release on installed value of residential and commercial unitary air conditioning equipment, 1956-84. Includes 1 table.

A0300–1.2: Field-Engineered Equipment: Estimated Installed Value Climbs 9.7% in 1984
[Annual. June 5, 1985 2 p. SRI/MF/complete.]

Annual press release on installed value of field-engineered air conditioning equipment, 1969-84. Includes 1 table.

A0300–1.3: Unitary Equipment Shipments: Commercial Paces 1984 Surge
[Annual. June 5, 1985 6 p. SRI/MF/complete.]

Annual press release on shipments of unitary air conditioners, for U.S. residential and commercial installation 1953-84, and for export 1960-84. Includes 1 table.

Table column title incorrectly reads "value" instead of "units."

A0325
Air Transport Association of America

A0325–1 **PRELIMINARY PASSENGER TRAFFIC STATISTICS: U.S. Scheduled Airline Industry**
Monthly. 2 p.
SRI/MF/complete, shipped quarterly

Monthly press release on scheduled airline passenger traffic on domestic and international flights. Data are from reports of approximately 25 commercial carriers, and are issued 3-4 weeks after month of coverage.

Contains narrative summary; and 1 table showing revenue passenger miles, available seat miles, and load factor, for domestic and international flights, for month of coverage, year to date, and same periods of previous year.

Availability: Air Transport Association of America, 1709 New York Ave., NW, Washington DC 20006, †; SRI/MF/complete, shipped quarterly.

Issues reviewed during 1985: Oct. 1984-Sept. 1985 (D).

A0325–2 **CARGO FLOWN IN SCHEDULED DOMESTIC AND INTERNATIONAL SERVICE: U.S. Airline Industry**
Monthly. 2 p.
SRI/MF/complete, shipped quarterly

Monthly press release on scheduled airline freight and mail revenue ton-miles on domestic and international flights. Data are from reports of approximately 25 commercial carriers, and are issued 4-5 weeks after month of coverage.

Contains narrative summary; and 1 table showing freight and mail revenue ton-miles, for domestic and international flights, for month of coverage, year to date, and same periods of previous year.

Availability: Air Transport Association of America, 1709 New York Ave., NW, Washington DC 20006, †; SRI/MF/complete, shipped quarterly.

Issues reviewed during 1985: Sept. 1984-Aug. 1985 (D).

A0325–5 **AIR TRANSPORT, 1985**
Annual. June 1985. 17 p.
LC 70-613485.
SRI/MF/complete

Annual report presenting summary statistics on finances and operations of scheduled air carriers, 1984 and trends. Includes selected data by individual carrier and for top airports.

Data are from ATA, Airport Operators Council International, Transport Policy Associates, and other sources.

Contains summary table (inside front cover); 8 charts and 16 tables listed below (p. 2-14); and list of airlines, glossary, and ATA directories (p. 15-17).

Availability: Air Transport Association of America, 1709 New York Ave., NW, Washington DC 20006, †; SRI/MF/complete.

CHARTS AND TABLES:
[Data are shown for 1974 and 1983-84, unless otherwise noted.]

A0325–5.1: Operations, Aircraft, and Finances

[1] 1974-84 highlights, U.S. scheduled airlines [including passengers and average trip length; freight ton-miles; operating revenues, expenses, and profits; investment return rate; and employees]. (p. 2)

[2-5] Passengers, cargo, revenues, and net profit/loss [1982-84]. [charts] (p. 3)

[6] Safety, U.S. air carriers, scheduled service [departures, fatal accidents, and fatalities], 1975-84. (p. 4)

[7] Leading U.S. airports [in passenger and freight traffic], 1984. (p. 4)

[8] Intercity passenger travel in the U.S. [miles traveled by transport mode]. (p. 5)

[9] Employment, U.S. scheduled airlines [flight and ground personnel, by position]. (p. 5)

[10-11] Passenger and freight/express yields [for domestic and international flights]. (p. 5)

[12] ATA airline statistics [aircraft, employees, passengers, departures, revenue passenger miles, passenger and freight revenues, total operating revenues, and operating and net profit/loss, by carrier], 1984. (p. 7)

[13] Aircraft on order [options, and firm orders by delivery date, by aircraft model, aggregated for] ATA airlines, as of Dec. 31, 1984. (p. 8)

[14] Air carrier and general aviation fleets [by aircraft type]. (p. 8)

[15] Operating fleet [by aircraft model, for individual] ATA airlines [no date]. (p. 9)

[16] Top 30 airlines [ranked by passengers, revenue passenger and freight ton-miles, and operating revenues] in 1984. (p. 10-11)

[17-20] Express package traffic (domestic operations) [shipments and revenues]; fares vs. [CPI]; discount traffic (majors, domestic operations); and travel agent sales [and commissions, and number of agency locations; mostly 1982-84]. [charts] (p. 12)

[21-24] Traffic [passenger and cargo] and service, operating revenues and expenses, income statement, and balance sheet [aggregate for U.S. scheduled airlines, 1983-84]. (p. 13-14)

A0325–6   1984 AIR TRAVEL SURVEY
Annual. 1984. 23 p.
SRI/MF/complete

Annual report on commercial airline travel frequency, destination, and purpose, 1984, with selected trends from 1962. Includes data on adults who have ever flown and who have flown in the past year, with number of recent trips; air travel within the U.S. and to Canada, Mexico/Caribbean, and other international points; and number of recent trips taken for business and pleasure/personal reasons.

Selected data are shown by traveler sociodemographic characteristics, including sex, race, age, occupation, community size and region, and family income. Most data are shown as distributions.

Data are based on interviews with 4,571 adults, conducted June 29-July 22, 1984 by Gallup Organization, Inc., and on previous surveys.

Contains introduction (p. 1-4); 14 tables, with accompanying narrative (p. 5-18); 1 historical trend table (p. 19); and sample composition and design, with 1 table (p. 20-23).

Prior to the 1984 survey, report was titled *Frequency of Flying Among the General Public.*

Availability: Air Transport Association of America, 1709 New York Ave., NW, Washington DC 20006, $25.00; SRI/MF/complete.

A0400
Aluminum Association

A0400–1   ALUMINUM SITUATION
Monthly. 4 p. no paging.
SRI/MF/complete, shipped
quarterly

Monthly report on estimated aluminum production, shipments, orders, inventories, and foreign trade. Data are compiled by the Aluminum Assn, primarily from member reports and Dept of Commerce sources. Month of coverage is 1-2 months prior to publication date.

Contains brief narrative interspersed with 3 summary charts, 1 summary table showing shipments for year to date, and 4 monthly tables listed below. Report also occasionally includes data revisions for previous issues.

Availability: Aluminum Association, Publications Department, 818 Connecticut Ave., NW, Washington DC 20006, †; SRI/MF/complete, shipped quarterly.

Issues reviewed during 1985: Nov. 1984-Oct. 1985 (P).

MONTHLY TABLES:
[Data are shown for month of coverage and year to date, for current and previous year, unless otherwise noted.]

[1] Net shipments [including mill products by type, ingot, mill product net imports, and total exports].

[2-3] Order receipts [domestic, for mill products by type, ingot, and total exports]; and month-end aluminum inventories, by type of producer [integrated, smelter, and nonintegrated, and for ingot and scrap, for current year to date and selected previous periods].

[4] Imports and exports [of mill products, ingot, and scrap].

**A0400–2   ALUMINUM STATISTICAL
REVIEW for 1984**
Annual. [1985.] 64 p.
LC 72-131.
SRI/MF/complete

Annual report on U.S. aluminum ingot and mill product supply, demand, and foreign trade, 1984, with trends from as early as the 1940s. Includes data by end-use market, company, and trading partner. Also includes data on scrap recovery and aluminum plants; and world aluminum supply and demand, by country.

Data are compiled by the Aluminum Assn Statistical and Marketing Research Committee from Commerce Dept, Bureau of Mines, National Assn of Aluminum Distributors, and other sources.

Contains contents listing, and introduction with 1 summary table (p. 1-3); 5 sections, with brief narrative, 5 maps, 8 charts, and 22 tables listed below (p. 4-61); and glossary and list of Aluminum Assn publications (p. 62-64).

This is the 17th annual report.

Availability: Aluminum Association, Publications Department, 818 Connecticut Ave., NW, Washington DC 20006, members $12.50, nonmembers $25.00; SRI/MF/complete.

TABLES:
[Data are for 1974-84, unless otherwise noted.]

**A0400–2.1: U.S. Shipments, Markets, and
Supply**

SHIPMENTS

[1] Total industry shipments [ingots, U.S.-produced and imported mill products, and total domestic and exports]. (p. 5)

[2] Mill products imports [total, and to consumers and aluminum producers, for 3 product categories]. (p. 5)

[3] Net shipments of ingot and mill products (excludes mill product imports to consumers) [by product category], 1952-84. (p. 6-7)

[4] General line distributor shipments [and total U.S. shipments excluding direct mill uses, by mill product category]. (p. 8)

[5] Shipments of castings [by type], 1963-84. (p. 9)

MARKETS
[Major markets are building/construction, transportation, consumer durables, electrical, machinery/equipment, containers/packaging, and other.]

[6] Shipments by major market [and exports, 1983-84]. (p. 12)

[7] Product net shipments [for ingot and 14 mill products], by major market [and exports]. (p. 13-17)

[8] Trends in selected markets [shipments of ingot and mill products, by end use]. (p. 18-20)

SUPPLY

[9] Total supply [includes domestic primary production, primary and mill product imports, and secondary recovery from domestic and imported scrap], 1942-84. (p. 23)

[10-11] Suppliers' inventories; and total supply adjusted for [Federal] stockpile. (p. 24)

[12-13] Production of primary aluminum; and primary aluminum capacity [by producer]. (p. 25-26)

[14] Number of plants [by type of aluminum product, 1967, 1977, amd 1982]. (p. 27)

SCRAP

[15-16] Aluminum can reclamation data [weight, number, and percent of cans collected]; and scrap consumption [by secondary smelters, primary producers, and others], and recovery [from new and old scrap], 1946-84. (p. 30-31)

**A0400–2.2: U.S. Foreign Trade, and World
Production and Consumption**

U.S. FOREIGN TRADE

[1] Imports and exports [of ingot, semifabricated products by type, scrap, and dross/skimmings (imports only)]. (p. 36-37)

[2-3] Imports and exports, by product and country [arranged by world area], 1984. (p. 38-41)

WORLD PRODUCTION AND CONSUMPTION

[4] World primary aluminum production [by country and world area]. (p. 45)

[5-6] Per capita aluminum consumption of selected countries [total, and components used in calculation including primary production, imports, secondary recovery, exports, total consumption, inventory change, and population; by country]. (p. 47-61)

A0600
American Apparel
Manufacturers Association

**A0600–1   FOCUS: Economic Profile of
the Apparel Industry**
Annual. 1985. 36 p.
LC 79-109885.
SRI/MF/not filmed

Annual report on apparel industry trends and developments, including production, employment, finances, and demand, 1950s-84. Data are primarily from Census Bureau, BLS, and other Federal agency reports.

Contains contents and table listing (p. 2); introduction and overview, with 4 summary charts (p. 3-7); and statistical section, with 1 chart, and 28 tables described below (p. 8-36).

Report was previously published biennially; for description of previous report, with data through 1981, see SRI 1982 Annual, under this number.

Availability: American Apparel Manufacturers Association, 1611 N. Kent St., Suite 800, Arlington VA 22209, members $15.00, nonmembers $40.00; SRI/MF/not filmed.

TABLES:
[Data generally pertain to the apparel and/or textile industries and are shown for various years 1950-84, with selected comparisons to other industries and monthly detail for 1983-84.]

a. Economic trends and employment, including payroll, materials cost, shipment value, establishments, total and women's employment, and production worker hours and earnings, by SIC 2- to 4-digit industry; employment by State; black and Hispanic employment shares; unemployment rates; and fiber consumption by type and end use. Tables 1-15. (p. 8-21)

b. Production, prices, and investment, including PPI and CPI; apparel production by garment type; capital expenditures, by SIC 2- to 4-digit industry; and business failures and liabilities. Tables 16-20. (p. 22-27)

c. Demand, including retail sales by type of outlet; personal consumption expenditures by general category and for clothing/accessories; value of imports and exports; imports, by fiber and garment type, and exporting country; and import/production ratios. Tables 21-28. (p. 28-36)

A0610
American Association for Public Opinion Research

A0610–1   PUBLIC OPINION QUARTERLY

Quarterly.   Approx. 150 p.
cumulative pagination
throughout year.
Pub. No. 449380.
ISSN 0033-362X.
LC 32-5920r85.
SRI/MF/excerpts

Quarterly journal presenting results of scholarly research on problems of communication and public opinion measurement. Includes articles on polling methodology and on implications of public opinion survey results. Publication is editorially sponsored by the Advisory Committee on Communication, Columbia University.

Issues generally contain original articles, frequently including statistics; "The Polls" feature, usually reporting on trends in public opinion on a single topic as measured by several major research organizations; and book reviews and reader comments.

Features with substantial statistical content are described, as they appear, under "Statistical Features." Nonstatistical features are not covered.

Availability: Elsevier Science Publishing Co., Inc., Journals Fulfillment Department, 52 Vanderbilt Ave., New York NY 10017, institutions $42.50 per yr., individuals $22.00 per yr., single copy price on request; SRI/MF/excerpts for all portions described under "Statistical Features."

Issues reviewed during 1985: Winter 1984-Fall 1985 (P) (Vol. 48, No. 4; Vol. 49, Nos. 1-3).

STATISTICAL FEATURES:

A0610–1.601: Winter 1984 (Vol. 48, No. 4)

PUBLIC'S USE AND PERCEPTION OF NEWSPAPERS

(p. 709-719) By Leo Bogart. Article on public opinion and use of newspapers and other news media. Data are based on a May 1982 survey of 1,979 adults conducted by Audits and Surveys, Inc.

Includes 5 tables showing survey responses concerning use of newspapers and TV as news source; societal institutions with greatest effect on people's lives; personal identification with newspaper, TV channel, or radio station used most; and strengths and qualities of newspaper read most often; 1982, with selected comparisons to similar 1961 and 1971 surveys.

PUBLIC OPINION DU JOUR: AN EXAMINATION OF THE SPIRAL OF SILENCE

(p. 731-740) By Carroll J. Glynn and Jack M. McLeod. Article analyzing the relationship between perceived public support for 1980 presidential candidates and willingness to discuss political opinions and candidate preferences. Data are based on telephone interviews with approximately 400 Wisconsin voters, conducted Sept.-Nov. 1980. Includes 3 tables.

CONSTITUENCY, PARTY, AND REPRESENTATION IN CONGRESS

(p. 741-756) By Benjamin I. Page et al. Article examining correlation between public opinion in congressional districts and the voting records of the districts' representatives, and including analysis of the effects of political party and personal background on voting records. Data are primarily based on responses of residents in 108 districts participating in the 1978 National Election Study, and on voting records of the 1977/78 Congress. Includes 3 tables.

ALTERNATE QUESTION FORMS FOR ATTITUDE SCALE QUESTIONS IN TELEPHONE INTERVIEWS

(p. 766-778) By Peter V. Miller. Article discussing telephone survey responses as affected by 2 survey techniques requiring respondents to rank their opinions on a numerical scale. Most data are based on 4,300 responses to a survey taken in conjunction with a larger study on the feasibility of telephone interviewing conducted by Survey Research Center for the National Health Interview Survey. Includes 4 tables.

COMPARISON OF METHODS OF INCREASING PARENTAL CONSENT RATES IN SOCIAL RESEARCH

(p. 779-787) By Teresa L. Thompson. Article discussing methods of increasing the number of parental consent forms received for surveys involving children. Data are from a 1979-82 study of elementary school children in a selected school district of an unspecified Mid-Atlantic State.

Includes 2 tables showing parental responses to consent requests (granted, denied, and no reply), by race by method used for request (follow-up letter, incentive to child and parent, and additional communication with child and parent).

CONTENT OF SURVEY INTRODUCTIONS AND THE PROVISION OF INFORMED CONSENT

(p. 788-793) By Jeffery Sobal. Article, with 1 table showing number of survey introductions disclosing selected types of information about the researcher and the survey. Data are based on a study of 78 recent survey introductions written by members of the American Assn of Public Opinion Research.

INCENTIVES FOR INCREASING RETURN RATES: MAGNITUDE LEVELS, RESPONSE BIAS, AND FORMAT

(p. 794-800) By J. Scott Mizes et al. Article discussing mail survey response rates and response bias when monetary incentives of $1 and $5 are used, and when the survey response form appears on the reverse side of the incentive check. Data are from a Mar.-June 1982 survey of 200 physicians. Includes 1 table.

BIAS IN A DIRECTORY SAMPLE FOR A MAIL SURVEY OF RURAL HOUSEHOLDS

(p. 801-806) By Frederick J. Kviz. Article, with 1 table comparing rates of response, cooperation, completion, post office return, and eligibility, for mail surveys using the telephone directory or a private listing to obtain a sample of rural area households. Data are based on a 1978 survey of households in Illinois counties considered at least 50% rural in the 1970 census.

COMMENTS AND LETTERS

(p. 809-814) Includes corrected tables for article on religious preference and social tolerance.

For article description, see SRI 1984 Annual under A0610-1.502.

THE POLLS: BRITAIN AT THE POLLS 1945-83

(p. 824-833) By Robert M. Worcester. Article on trends in UK elections, including poll results and characteristics of voters. Data are from various surveys conducted by Market and Opinion Research International, Ltd. and other major UK survey organizations.

Includes 6 tables showing election results, distribution of voters, and voting intentions, variously by political party, and voter characteristics, including sex, age, socioeconomic status, trade union membership, and region; and election poll prediction accuracy; various years 1945-83.

A0610–1.602: Spring 1985 (Vol. 49, No. 1)

UNCOVERING RAPE: THE WATCHDOG PRESS AND THE LIMITS OF AGENDA SETTING

(p. 19-37) By David L. Protess et al. Article examining impact of a Chicago newspaper investigative series about rape on crime-related concerns of the general public and of policy makers, and on the newspaper's subsequent coverage of rape. Most data are from telephone interviews conducted with Chicago residents and policy makers before and after the publication of a 1982 Chicago *Sun-Times* series. Includes 3 tables.

TV NEWS, REAL-WORLD CUES, AND CHANGES IN THE PUBLIC AGENDA

(p. 38-57) By Roy L. Behr and Shanto Iyengar. Article examining interrelationships among actual events and conditions, TV news coverage, and public concerns, with regard to the issues of inflation, energy, and unemployment. Data are based primarily on public opinion surveys conducted by Gallup, Yankelovich, and University of Michigan, and on a study of CBS national news programs, for 1974-80 period. Includes 3 tables.

CRITICAL ANALYSIS OF AUSTRALIAN TV COVERAGE OF ELECTION OPINION POLLS

(p. 58-79) By Ted J. Smith III and Derek O. Verrall. Article analyzing TV coverage of election polls during the 1980 Australia Federal election. Data are from a study of news programs broadcast in the State of Victoria Sept. 30-Oct. 15, 1980.

Includes 4 tables showing content of poll coverage; and errors in poll interpretation, and reasons for rejection or acceptance of poll results, by source of report.

FAILURE OF LIBERAL/CONSERVATIVE IDEOLOGY AS A COGNITIVE STRUCTURE

(p. 80-93) By Norman R. Luttbeg and Michael M. Gant. Article analyzing public's ability to define liberal and conservative political ideologies, with comparison to voting patterns. Data are based on responses to a 1980 Center for Political Studies survey.

Includes 6 tables showing accuracy of ideological definitions, with detail by educational attainment; and correlation between accuracy of definitions and choice of candidate most representative of own views concerning major issues.

DOES TIME OF VOTING AFFECT EXIT POLL RESULTS?

(p. 94-104) By Ronald J. Busch and Joel A. Lieske. Article examining effects of exit poll timing on the accuracy of poll results, based on interviews with 547 Cleveland residents voting on a 1981 tax referendum. Includes 3 tables comparing demographic characteristics, party affiliation, and reported vote, for voters polled at various times of day.

IMPORTANCE OF REPLICATING A FAILURE TO REPLICATE: ORDER EFFECTS ON ABORTION ITEMS

(p. 105-114) By George F. Bishop et al. Article examining effect of question sequence and context on survey responses concerning a woman's right to choose abortion. Data are based on 2 telephone surveys of Cincinnati residents, conducted 1981-82. Includes 2 tables.

THE POLLS: THE EUROPEAN PEACE MOVEMENT AND DEPLOYMENT OF NUCLEAR MISSILES

(p. 119-132) By Connie de Boer. Compilation of survey results on Western European public opinion concerning NATO deployment of U.S. nuclear missiles and related issues. Surveys were conducted by 20 research organizations, in various countries (mostly European), various periods 1981-84.

Includes distribution of responses to 42 questions concerning use and deployment of nuclear weapons, and demonstrations against deployment, with selected detail by country and by respondent sex and age.

A0610–1.603: Summer 1985 (Vol. 49, No. 2)

WOMEN'S GENDER CONSCIOUSNESS

(p. 143-163) By Patricia Gurin. Article discussing women's awareness of their gender as a unified social group. Data are from national election surveys conducted by Institute for Social Research in 1972, 1976, and 1983.

Includes 1 chart and 2 tables showing women's responses to questions concerning identification with their gender, collective social action, legitimacy of status disparities between men and women, and discontent with womens' social power, with selected comparisons to responses of men and racial groups, and detail by education, age, and labor force and marital status.

MYTH AND REALITY: THE ERA AND THE GENDER GAP IN THE 1980 ELECTION

(p. 164-178) By Jane J. Mansbridge. Article analyzing effect of Equal Rights Amendment (ERA) on 1980 presidential voting. Data are from a Nov. 4, 1980 survey of 15,201 voters conducted by CBS News/New York Times.

Includes 3 tables showing voters' ERA stance, and candidate choice by ERA stance, by sex; and regression analysis relating ERA stance and other voter characteristics to gender differences in opposition to Reagan.

GENDER DIFFERENCES IN VOTING FOR FEMALE CANDIDATES: EVIDENCE FROM THE 1982 ELECTION

(p. 179-197) By John F. Zipp and Eric Plutzer. Article analyzing relationship between voters' gender and their support for female political candidates, based on data from exit polls conducted during 1982 elections for Governor or U.S. Senator in 5 States. Includes 6 tables showing regression analysis results for Republican, Democrat, and Independent voters.

LIKE MOTHER, LIKE DAUGHTER: INTERGENERATIONAL TRANSMISSION OF DK RESPONSE RATES

(p. 198-208) By Ronald B. Rapoport. Article exploring parent-child similarities in public opinion survey response (with regard to "don't know" answers and political attitudes), by sex. Data are from surveys conducted between Nov. 1973-Feb. 1976 in 8 countries. Includes 2 tables.

EXPECTATION/DISILLUSION AND PRESIDENTIAL POPULARITY: THE REAGAN EXPERIENCE

(p. 209-213) By Lee Sigelman and Kathleen Knight. Article, with 2 tables showing trends in public approval of Reagan and confidence in his administration's ability to reach selected policy goals; and analysis of relationship between educational attainment and Reagan support, by political party; selected months 1981-82.

Data are from national telephone surveys conducted by CBS News/New York Times.

RACISM, RATIONAL CHOICE, AND WHITE OPPOSITION TO RACIAL CHANGE: A CASE STUDY OF BUSING

(p. 214-233) By McKee J. McClendon. Article examining attitudes of Akron, Ohio, residents regarding racial discrimination and busing. Analyzes causes of busing opposition, including symbolic racism (belief that blacks are given unneeded preferential treatment), traditional prejudice, and various nonracial factors.

Data are from telephone interviews with 242 residents conducted Mar.-Apr. 1981. Includes 5 tables presenting results of statistical analyses.

FACE-TO-FACE INTERVIEWS AND MAILED QUESTIONNAIRES: THE NET DIFFERENCE IN RESPONSE RATE

(p. 234-252) By John Goyder. Article examining correlation between data collection method (interviews vs. mailed questionnaires) and response rates of public opinion surveys, based on a study of 517 published surveys from U.S. and other countries. Includes 4 tables.

THE POLLS: AMERICA'S MOST IMPORTANT PROBLEMS, PART I; NATIONAL AND INTERNATIONAL

(p. 264-274) By Tom W. Smith. Article on trends in public opinion concerning the most important national problem, including foreign affairs, economy, social control, civil rights, and government. Surveys were conducted by American Institute of Public Opinion (Gallup Poll) during 1935-84; in most years, several surveys were conducted. Includes 1 extended table showing results of each survey.

A0610–1.604: Fall 1985 (Vol. 49, No. 3)

HOW MUCH INCOME IS ENOUGH? MEASURING PUBLIC JUDGMENTS

(p. 285-299) By Steven Dubnoff. Article discussing methods for measuring income adequacy, and analyzing Boston SMSA residents' views concerning income levels associated with specific standards of living (poor to prosperous) for various types of families.

Data are from interviews with 588 Boston residents, conducted Apr.-June 1983. Includes 1 chart and 5 tables presenting survey responses, and results of statistical analyses.

'MORE FOR LESS' PARADOX: PUBLIC ATTITUDES ON TAXING AND SPENDING

(p. 310-316) By Susan Welch. Article examining public support for increased government spending on social programs, and preferred methods of funding increased spending, by level of government. Data are from telephone interviews with members of approximately 900 households in an unspecified midwestern State, conducted Feb.-Apr. 1983. Includes 2 tables.

PRAYER IN PUBLIC SCHOOLS: WHEN CHURCH AND STATE COLLIDE

(p. 317-329) By Kirk W. Elifson and C. Kirk Hadaway. Article examining characteristics of persons supporting and not supporting prayer in public schools. Data are based on responses to General Social Surveys conducted in 1974 and 1982 by National Opinion Research Center, and the 1980 American National Election Study.

Includes 3 tables showing respondents supporting required reading of Lord's Prayer/Bible and optional prayer in schools, by selected demographic and attitudinal characteristics, including political ideology, tolerance for atheists, support for sex education and Equal Rights Amendment, and religious practices and affiliation (including Protestant denominations).

VIEWER CHARACTERISTICS AND AGENDA SETTING BY TELEVISION NEWS

(p. 340-350) By David B. Hill. Article examining the impact of TV viewing behavior and selected viewer characteristics on extent to which TV news programs influence viewers' interest in selected social and political issues. Data are based on a study of national news broadcasts, and 1,204 responses to a survey of adult viewers, Sept. 1977-Jan. 1978. Includes 3 tables.

FINDING SUBGROUPS FOR SURVEYS

(p. 351-365) By Roger Tourangeau and A. Wade Smith. Article discussing effects of population subgroup sampling methodology on survey sample size, response, costs, and accuracy. Data are from a study of 2 methods used to obtain black respondents for the 1982 General Social Survey conducted by National Opinion Research Center. Includes 3 tables.

MATCHING SURVEY RESPONSES TO OFFICIAL RECORDS: AN EXPLORATION OF VALIDITY IN VICTIMIZATION REPORTING

(p. 366-380) By Peter V. Miller and Robert M. Groves. Article on the reliability of survey accuracy checks that compare self-reported responses with official records of respondent behavior. Data are based on a 1981 Peoria, Ill., study of police records and telephone interviews with 1,577 residents victimized by crime. Includes 2 tables.

EXPLAINING INFORMATION SYSTEM USE WITH SYSTEM-MONITORED vs. SELF-REPORTED USE MEASURES

(p. 381-387) By James S. Ettema. Article analyzing self-report vs. system-monitor methods of measuring videotex information system use, based on a study of farmers using a prototype system in 3 unspecified midwestern communities. Includes 2 undated tables.

RESPONSE SCALES: EFFECTS OF CATEGORY RANGE ON REPORTED BEHAVIOR AND COMPARATIVE JUDGMENTS

(p. 388-395) By Norbert Schwarz et al. Article examining how survey respondents' answers are affected by the range of response categories presented to them, based on 2 surveys in which 79-132 West Germans were questioned about their TV viewing behavior. Includes 2 undated tables.

THE POLLS: AMERICA'S MOST IMPORTANT PROBLEMS, PART II; REGIONAL, COMMUNITY, AND PERSONAL

(p. 403-410) By Tom W. Smith. Article on trends in public opinion concerning the most important regional, community, and family problems, including foreign affairs, economy, social control, civil rights, government, housing, transportation, ecology, energy, old age, and health.

Surveys were conducted by American Institute of Public Opinion (Gallup Poll) and other major polling organizations during 1945-78; in some years, more than 1 survey was conducted. Includes 3 tables showing results of each survey.

A0612
American Association of Blood Banks

A0612–1   1985 DIRECTORY OF COMMUNITY BLOOD BANKS
Biennial. 1985. ix+134 p.
SRI/MF/complete

Biennial directory, for 1985, presenting profiles of community blood banks, arranged by State and for Puerto Rico. Profiles generally include full- and part-time employees; volunteers; budget; counties, hospitals, and population served; blood draw and outdate rate; and blood products produced by type; primarily 1984.

Contains contents listing (p. v-ix); blood bank profiles (p. 1-124); and 3 appendices, with member lists for 2 major blood bank assns, and directory of American Red Cross blood service offices (p. 125-134).

This is the 4th edition of the report. For description of 3rd edition, see SRI 1984 Annual under this number.

Availability: American Association of Blood Banks, 1117 N. 19th St., Suite 600, Arlington VA 22209, members $25.00, nonmembers $35.00; SRI/MF/complete.

A0612–2   AMERICAN ASSOCIATION OF BLOOD BANKS 1984 ANNUAL REPORT
Annual. Mar. 22, 1985.
45 p.
SRI/MF/complete

Annual report, for 1984, of the American Assn of Blood Banks (AABB). Includes data on blood bank activities, including blood units drawn, transfused, and outdated, and crossmatches and other procedures performed, for regional blood centers and hospital blood banks and transfusion services; and transfusions by blood product type; 1983, generally with comparisons to 1982.

Data are based primarily on 1,890 responses of AABB institutional members to a 1984 survey.

Contains contents listing and president's message (p. 3-4); AABB financial report, with 3 tables (p. 6-11); blood bank data report, with 2 charts and 8 tables (p. 12-14); and AABB committee reports, listings of directors and members, and executive director's message (p. 15-45).

SRI coverage begins with the 1984 annual report. Prior to 1984, agency also published an interim report with updated statistical data.

Availability: American Association of Blood Banks, 1117 N. 19th St., Suite 600, Arlington VA 22209, †; SRI/MF/complete.

A0615
American Association of Colleges of Nursing

A0615–1   REPORT ON NURSING FACULTY SALARIES in Colleges and Universities, 1984/85
Annual. Jan. 1985.
iii+50 p. Institutional Data Series 85-1.
ISSN 0197-8691.
LC SC 80-284.
SRI/MF/complete

Annual report, for 1984/85, on nursing faculty and salaries in baccalaureate and graduate nursing programs, by faculty rank, region, type of school, and size of baccalaureate and masters enrollment. Data are shown for mean, and 25th, 50th, and 75th percentile salaries, for faculty with and without doctorates.

School types include public, secular private, and religious private, with detail for schools in universities and 4-year colleges, on campuses with academic health centers, with baccalaureate programs only, and with master's and doctoral programs.

Data are based on responses of 339 schools, representing 8,043 full-time positions, to an Aug. 1984 survey by the American Assn of Colleges of Nursing.

Contains contents and table listing (p. i-iii); introduction with 2 summary tables (p. 1-9); table key, and 15 detailed tables repeated for academic and calendar year-based salaries (p. 10-40); and sample questionnaire, and list of participating schools (p. 41-50).

This is the 7th annual report. Related reports on salaries of deans and administrative faculty are covered in SRI under A0615-2 and A0615-3, respectively.

Availability: American Association of Colleges of Nursing, Institutional Data System, One Dupont Circle, NW, Suite 530, Washington DC 20036, members $12.00, nonmembers $30.00; ordered with reports on salaries of deans and enrollment and graduations: members $24.00, nonmembers $50.00; SRI/MF/complete.

A0615–2   REPORT ON SALARIES OF NURSING DEANS in Colleges and Universities, 1984/85
Annual. Feb. 1985. ii+24 p.
Institutional Data Series 85-2.
ISSN 0270-8175.
LC 81-643386.
SRI/MF/complete

Annual report on salaries of nursing school deans in colleges/universities, 1984/85, with summary trends from 1978/79. Includes number of deans and salary percentiles for deans continuing in office; and for all deans, by term of appointment (academic and calendar year), region, institutional control and type, presence of academic health center, level of degrees offered, faculty size, and dean's highest degree earned, administrative title, academic rank, and tenure status.

Also includes number of deans, by length of term, whether elected by faculty, and type of formal review process.

Data are from responses of 326 nursing schools to a fall 1984 survey.

Contains contents and table listing (p. i-ii); introduction (p. 1-3); survey results, with narrative analysis, 16 tables, and 2 charts (p. 3-16); and questionnaire facsimile and list of surveyed schools (p. 17-24).

This is the 7th annual report.

Availability: American Association of Colleges of Nursing, Institutional Data System, One Dupont Circle, NW, Suite 530, Washington DC 20036, members $6.00, nonmembers $10.00; ordered with reports on salaries of faculty and nursing deans and enrollment/graduations report: members $24.00, nonmembers $50.00; SRI/MF/complete.

A0615–4   ENROLLMENT AND GRADUATIONS IN BACCALAUREATE AND GRADUATE PROGRAMS IN NURSING, Public, Private Religious, and Secular, Four Years: 1981-85
Annual. Mar. 1985. i+20 p.
Institutional Data Series 85-3.
SRI/MF/complete

Annual survey report, by Marion I. Murphy, on nursing school enrollment and graduates, by degree level, type of institution (public, secular, and religious), and region, 1981/82-1984/85. Includes detail for full- and part-time students, and for students who already are registered nurses vs. other ("generic") students.

Data are from surveys of schools belonging to the AACN. Number of schools reporting is specified for each data item. Separate data are presented for a subgroup of schools responding in every survey year.

Contains contents and table listing (p. i); narrative, with 2 summary tables (p. 1-6); and 7 detailed tables (p. 7-20).

This is the 4th annual report.

Availability: American Association of Colleges of Nursing, Institutional Data System, One Dupont Circle, NW, Suite 530, Washington DC 20036, members $6.00, nonmembers $10.00, plus 30% shipping and handling; SRI/MF/complete.

A0630
American Association of Colleges of Pharmacy

A0630–2   **DEGREES CONFERRED BY SCHOOLS AND COLLEGES OF PHARMACY for the Academic Year 1983/84**
Annual.   [1985.]   2+ii+24 p.
SRI/MF/complete

Annual report, by Steven H. Chasin, on number of pharmacy degrees conferred, by degree level and field, region, and race/ethnic group (white, black, Hispanic, Native American, Asian, and non-American), all by sex and institution, 1983/84. Data are based on responses of 72 institutions to an AACP survey.

Contains contents and table listing (2 p.); narrative summary (p. i-ii); 17 tables (p. 1-20); and AACP publications' information.

Availability: American Association of Colleges of Pharmacy, 4720 Montgomery Lane, Suite 602, Bethesda MD 20814, $5.00; SRI/MF/complete.

A0630–3   **ENROLLMENT REPORT ON GRADUATE DEGREE PROGRAMS IN PHARMACY, Fall 1984**
Annual.   [1985.]   2+ii+28 p.
SRI/MF/complete

Annual report, by Steven H. Chasin, on enrollment in pharmacy graduate programs, by institution, fall 1984. Includes data by degree level; full- or part-time status; discipline; minority group (black, Hispanic, Asian, Native, other minority American, and foreign); sex; geographic origin (same State as institution, other State, Canada, and other foreign country); and State of residence (including Puerto Rico).

Also includes aggregate data on foreign students by country of origin, and summary trends from 1970/71.

Data are based on a survey of 54 pharmacy schools, representing 3,029 graduate students, conducted by the AACP.

Contains contents and table listing (2 p.); introduction (p. i-ii); definitions (p. 1); and 20 tables (p. 2-24).

Availability: American Association of Colleges of Pharmacy, 4720 Montgomery Lane, Suite 602, Bethesda MD 20814, $10.00; SRI/MF/complete.

A0630–4   **ENROLLMENT REPORT ON PROFESSIONAL DEGREE PROGRAMS IN PHARMACY, Fall 1984**
Annual.   [1985.]   1+ii+27 p.
SRI/MF/complete

Annual report, by Steven H. Chasin, on fall 1984 full-time enrollment in pharmacy professional degree programs, by year of study, State of resi-

dence (including Virgin Islands and Puerto Rico), country of origin, and region. Most data are shown by institution and sex, with selected comparisons to fall 1983.

Also includes data on minority enrollment by institution and in predominantly minority and nonminority schools, by race/ethnicity (black, Hispanic, Asian, Native, other minority American, and foreign); and part-time and special student enrollments.

Data are based on responses of 72 institutions, comprising all accredited schools of pharmacy, to an AACP survey.

Contains contents and table listing (1 p.); narrative summary (p. i-ii); 13 tables (p. 1-22); and information on AACP publications (p. 24-26).

Availability: American Association of Colleges of Pharmacy, 4720 Montgomery Lane, Suite 602, Bethesda MD 20814, $10.00; SRI/MF/complete.

A0630–5   **FINANCIAL AID REPORT, 1984-85**
Annual.   Mar. 1985.   7 p.
SRI/MF/complete

Annual report, by Steven H. Chasin, on higher education student assistance for pharmacy professional degree programs, 1984/85. Presents average number of awards per school and award value per student, for Federal aid by program, and for nonfederal aid by source (State, college-based, and industry/foundation) and type of program; all shown for 1st professional and graduate degree assistance at private and public institutions.

Federal aid programs are Pell Grants; College Work-Study Program; National Defense, Guaranteed, and Health Professions Student Loans; Health Education Assistance Loan; veterans education benefits; and other.

Data are from responses of 72 institutions to an American Assn of Colleges of Pharmacy survey.

Contains 1 basic table repeated for Federal and nonfederal sources of aid (p. 1-7).

This is the 5th annual report. SRI coverage begins with this edition.

Availability: American Association of Colleges of Pharmacy, 4720 Montgomery Lane, Suite 602, Bethesda MD 20814, ‡; SRI/MF/complete.

A0640
American Association of Community and Junior Colleges

A0640–1   **1985 COMMUNITY, TECHNICAL, AND JUNIOR COLLEGE DIRECTORY**
Annual.   1985.
2+104 p.+addendum.
ISBN 0-87117-151-1.
SRI/MF/complete

Annual directory, for 1985, of 2-year community, technical, and junior colleges. Presents full- and part-time enrollment and faculty, community education enrollment, professional and administrative staff, and tuition/fees, by institution arranged by State and territory, primarily as of Oct. 1984, with comparisons to 1983, and selected summary trends from 1900.

Data are also shown for AACJC member colleges in British Honduras, Canada, Korea, Panama, Switzerland, and West Germany; and as aggregates for public and independent institutions, by U.S. State and territory.

Data are based on 1,183 responses to a 1984 AACJC survey of regionally accredited 2-year institutions.

Contains contents listing (1 p.); introductory material (p. 1-19); institutional directory, with narrative summary and 5 trend tables, definitions, and 4 detailed tables (p. 20-74); directory of related organizations (p. 75-81); and appendix, including AACJC constitution and bylaws and alphabetical list of member colleges (p. 82-104).

Directory has been published annually since 1928. SRI coverage begins with the 1984 directory.

Availability: American Association of Community and Junior Colleges, Publication Sales, 80 S. Early St., Alexandria VA 22304, $25.00; SRI/MF/complete.

A0700
American Association of Fund-Raising Counsel

A0700–1   **GIVING USA, 30th ANNUAL ISSUE: A Compilation of Facts and Trends on American Philanthropy for the Year 1984**
Annual.   1985.   112 p.
LC 59-1874.
SRI/MF/complete, dclaycd

Annual report on philanthropy, covering contributions by type of donor and by subject area (cause), 1984 and trends. Also includes data on tax deductions for contributions, hospital finances and operations, government support for public broadcasting, volunteers, and other topics. Selected data are shown by individual institution and/or donor.

Data are compiled from numerous government and private sources, generally identified for each table.

Contents:

a. Listing of contents, tables, and charts; introduction; and summary, with 2 tables. (p. 2-9)

b. Analyses of giving by donor type; philanthropy trends; giving by recipient area; and volunteer activity; with 6 charts and 67 tables. (p. 10-102)

c. Discussion of factors influencing philanthropy; notes on methodology, with 1 table; and definitions. (p. 103-112)

All tables, and charts with substantial statistics, are listed below.

Availability: American Association of Fund-Raising Counsel, 25 W. 43rd St., New York NY 10036, $25.00 (or $55.00 including annual subscription to *Fund-Raising Review*); SRI/MF/complete, delayed shipment in May 1986.

TABLES AND CHARTS:

[Data by source are shown for corporations, foundations, bequests, and individuals, unless otherwise noted. Recipient areas usually include education, social services, health/hospitals, arts/humanities, civic/public, religion, and other.]

A0700–1.1: Sources of Philanthropy

OVERVIEW

[1] Comparison of 1984 [contribution] totals to revised 1983 estimates. (p. 6)

[2] 1984 philanthropy [contributions by source and recipient area]. (p. 7)

INDIVIDUALS AND BEQUESTS

[3] Giving by individuals [total contributions and personal income, 1970-84]. (p. 11)

[4-5] 1983 deductions for charitable contributions [total and for] nonitemizers [by income size, showing number of tax returns and amount of deductions]. (p. 12-13)

[6] All top wealthholders with gross assets in excess of $500,000: percent of total assets by asset type, by sex, 1976 and 1982. (p. 14)

[7] Individual giving [total contributions], 1948-84. (p. 15)

[8-9] Charitable deduction for itemizers [total] amount and average contribution per return [by income size, showing number of returns and amount of deductions, tax years 1980-83]. (p. 16)

[10] Percent increase in number of wealthholders with gross assets of $300,000 or more [by sex], 1976-82 [period]. (p. 17)

[11] 1983 itemized deductions and percent change [showing number of returns and amount claimed for each deduction]. (p. 18)

[12-13] Giving by bequest [amount, 1970-84]; and large bequests [donor, amount, and recipient], 1984. (p. 19-21)

FOUNDATIONS

[14] Giving by foundations [amount, 1970-84]. (p. 21)

[15] Some leading U.S. private foundations ranked by payment of grants [and including assets and Federal excise tax liability, 1984 with comparison to grant payments for 1983]. (p. 23)

[16] Reported [amount of] grants designated for special population groups [including aged and handicapped persons, youth, alcohol/drug abusers, criminals, and minorities], 1981-84. (p. 24)

[17] Distribution of grants [number and value], by recipient organization type, 1982-84. (p. 25)

[18-20] Analysis of grantmaking foundations [number, assets, gifts received, and grants] by asset and grant [size] and type [of foundation, 1982]. (p. 26)

[21-24] Twenty-five largest community foundations, ranked according to assets, grants, and new gifts, 1984. (p. 28-29)

[25] Distribution of grants [number and value], by subject categories reported in 1983-84 volumes. (p. 30-31)

[26] Analysis of grantmaking foundations [number, assets, grants, and gifts received], by State [and for Puerto Rico, no date]. (p. 32-33)

[27] Foundation endowments [donor, amount, and recipient], 1984. (p. 33)

CORPORATIONS

[28] Giving by corporations [total contributions and pretax net income, 1970-84]. (p. 34)

[29-30] Contributions as a percent of U.S. pretax net income [number of companies, net income, and contributions, by industry group,

1983; and number of companies by income size, showing contribution] quartile rank, 1982. (p. 35-36)

[31] Summary of [cash, securities, product, and property] charitable contributions expenditures [of company foundations and direct giving programs, no date]. (p. 37)

[32] Distribution of corporate contributions [by recipient area, 1981-83]. (p. 38)

[33] Structure of corporate contributions [grants to and contributions by company foundations, and other company contributions, 1981-83]. (p. 38)

[34] Corporate contributions and corporate income before taxes [1936-84]. (p. 39)

A0700–1.2: Total Giving, and Areas of Philanthropic Opportunity

TOTAL GIVING

[1-2] Growth of philanthropy [total giving vs. GNP, 1968-84; and total giving, 1955-84. (p. 41)

[3-4] Donors [amount by source] and recipients [amount by area, 1955-84]. (p. 42-44)

RELIGION

[5] Giving to religion [amount, 1970-84]. (p. 47)

[6] Trend in religious preferences [distribution of adults by major religion, selected years 1947-84; and by selected socioeconomic characteristics, no date]. (p. 48)

[7] Church attendance [percent of Protestants and Catholics attending, selected years 1958-84]. (p. 49)

[8] Church/synagogue membership [percent of population belonging to a religious group, by selected socioeconomic characteristics, no date]. (p. 49)

[9] Number of U.S. churches, and of members, by religious groups [no date]. (p. 50)

[10-11] Church/synagogue membership and attendance [percent of population saying they are members and attending, various years 1937-84]. (p. 51)

[12] Protestant giving [total and per capita, and church membership, for 11] major denominations [1983-84]. (p. 52)

[13] Distribution of religious federation support of nonprofits [and religious federation income as percent of total income, shown by field of service, year formed, and size], 1982. (p. 53)

[14] Summary of current and noncurrent statistics [number of religious bodies and churches, membership, clergy, and Sunday/Sabbath schools and enrollment, 1983-85]. (p. 54)

[15] Some comparative U.S. church statistics [church membership as a percent of population, and change in membership from previous year, 1983-84]. (p. 54)

EDUCATION

[16] Giving to education [amount, 1970-84]. (p. 56)

[17-19] Giving to higher education [distribution by source (alumni, nonalumni, foundations, business, religion, and other)]; estimated voluntary support [of higher education], by source and purpose; and estimated total voluntary support; [various years 1972/73-1983/84]. [2 tables and 1 chart] (p. 58-61)

[20] Large gifts to education [donor, amount, and recipient], 1984. (p. 63-66)

HEALTH AND HOSPITALS

[21] Giving to health/hospitals [amount, 1970-84]. (p. 67)

[22-23] Change in general/community and voluntary nonprofit hospitals [number of hospitals, beds, admissions, and outpatient visits; average daily census and length of stay; occupancy rates; total expenses, and expenses per inpatient day; personnel; and payroll; 1979-83]. (p. 68)

[24] National health agencies [contributions and bequests received 1984, and total contributions 1983, by agency]. (p. 70-71)

[25] National health expenditures by type of expenditure and source of funds [private (including direct and insurance expenditures for consumers), and public (Federal and State/local government)], 1981-83. (p. 72-73)

[26] Personal health care expenditures by selected 3rd-party payers and type of expenditure, 1981-83. (p. 74-75)

[27] Large gifts to health/hospitals [donor, amount, and recipient], 1984. (p. 76)

SOCIAL SERVICES

[28] Giving to social services [amount, 1970-84]. (p. 76)

[29] Record of United Way campaigns in U.S./Canada [contributions received, 1970-84]. [chart] (p. 78)

[30] 25 largest United Way campaigns reported [amount raised or goal, by city], 1984. (p. 79)

[31-32] [Distribution of] sources of United Way support [by type of contributor; and of] services supported with United Way contributions [by type of service; 1983]. [charts] (p. 80-81)

[33-34] Total and increase in local/State revenues for alternative (non-United Way) funds [by type, 1983-84, and number soliciting contributions through payroll deduction]. (p. 83-85)

[35] Large gifts to social welfare [donor, amount, and recipient], 1984. (p. 86)

ARTS AND HUMANITIES

[36] Giving to arts/humanities [amount, 1970-84]. (p. 86)

[37-39] Public broadcasting income [for] public TV and radio systems, by source [including Corporation for Public Broadcasting, government funding by level, colleges/universities, foundations, business, subscribers, and auction; with aggregate income summary; various years FY73-83]. (p. 88-91)

[40] State arts agencies [total and per capita] legislative appropriations [by State and territory], FY84-85. (p. 93)

[41] Symphony orchestras 5-year financial summary [revenues and operating expenses by category, and support by source, 1979/80-1983/84]. (p. 95)

[42] National Endowment for the Arts [budget, by program, FY85]. (p. 97)

[43] Large gifts to arts/humanities [donor, amount, and recipient], 1984. (p. 98)

CIVIC/PUBLIC, AND VOLUNTEERS

[44-45] Giving to civic/public [amount, 1970-84]; and large gifts to civic/public causes [donor, amount, and recipient], 1984. (p. 99-100)

[46] Current volunteer strength of 20 national agencies [fund-raising and total volunteers, 1984]. (p. 101)

SUMMARY

[47] Total personal giving, personal income, and giving as percent of personal income, 1935-84. (p. 106)

A0775
American Association of School Administrators

A0775–3   ASBESTOS IN SCHOOLS: Inspection and Abatement
Monograph. [1985.] 17 p.
SRI/MF/complete

Report on efforts to identify and remove hazardous asbestos in public school facilities. Includes school facility inspections by type of inspector, and inspection results; asbestos hazard abatement efforts undertaken by school districts; and abatement methods, costs, and source of funds (school budget, bond issue/tax levy, and Federal and State assistance), 1984.

Also includes data on school district current and capital expenditures by function, 1983/84.

Most data are based on responses from 1,235 school districts to a summer 1984 AASA survey.

Contains narrative report, interspersed with 9 tables (p. 1-16); and questionnaire facsimile (1 p.).

Availability: American Association of School Administrators, Publications, 1801 N. Moore St., Arlington VA 22209, $5.00; SRI/MF/complete.

A0800
American Association of University Professors

A0800–1   ACADEME: The Annual Report on the Economic Status of the Profession, 1984/85
Bimonthly (selected issue).
Mar./Apr. 1985. 74 p.
Vol. 71, No. 2.
ISSN 0190-2946.
LC 79-642918.
SRI/MF/complete, delayed

Annual report on college and university faculty compensation and employment, by institution, 1984/85, with selected aggregate trends from 1970/71.

Includes average salary and compensation, with ratings based on comparison to similar institutions; benefits as a percent of salary; and number of full-time faculty and percent tenured; generally by academic rank and sex, for individual institutions arranged by State (also including Puerto Rico and Guam).

Also includes selected data for preclinical depts of medical schools; faculty salaries compared to CPI increases and to salaries in similar nonacademic occupations; and aggregate compensation data (including value of fringe benefits by type), by institution category and/or census division.

Data are based on reports of approximately 2,100 institutions, and were collected and tabulated by Maryse Eymonerie Associates.

Contains contents and table listings (p. 1-2); narrative report, with 2 charts and 16 tables (p. 3-18); listing of additional tables available, and data explanation (p. 19-21); and appendices, with 3 detailed tables (p. 22-74).

Report is published as the Mar./Apr. 1985 issue of the bimonthly *Academe: Bulletin of the AAUP,* and is the only feature of *Academe* covered in SRI.

Availability: American Association of University Professors, Academe, 1012 14th St., NW, Washington DC 20005, members †, nonmembers $30.00 (prepaid); SRI/MF/complete, delayed shipment in Jan. 1986.

A0875
American Automotive Leasing Association

A0875–1   ANALYSIS OF COSTS AND RELATED INFORMATION: Non-Finance Leasing (Closed-End), 1983-84
Annual. [1985.] 1+12 p.
SRI/MF/complete

Annual report presenting auto nonfinance leasing (closed-end) operating and administrative costs, fleet composition and disposition, and leasing and rental activities, for 14 unnamed firms, 1984, with comparisons to 1983. Data are from reports to the American Automotive Leasing Assn by member firms.

Contains table listing (front cover); 1 summary table comparing 1983-84 average per vehicle operating and general/administrative costs (p. 1); and 11 tables, listed below (p. 2-12).

Availability: American Automotive Leasing Association, 1001 Connecticut Ave., NW, Suite 1201, Washington DC 20006, †; SRI/MF/complete.

TABLES:
[Tables show data for 14 firms labeled by letters A-P, arranged by fleet size, 1984, with selected comparisons to 1983 average totals. Tables [1-6] show per unit per month costs.]

[1] Analysis of costs [depreciation, repairs/maintenance, insurance, tags/taxes, interest expense, delivery, and general/administrative]. (p. 2)

[2-3] Repairs and maintenance [by item, and including administrative salaries and annual mileage]; and insurance collision/comprehensive and umbrella liability [including salaries]. (p. 3-4)

[4-5] License tags, State/local taxes, and interest expense [including percent of car cost financed, and amortization and average simple interest rates]. (p. 5-6)

[6] General and administrative expenses [including salaries, advertising, travel/promotion, taxes, and insurance]. (p. 7)

[7] Composition of fleets [distribution of vehicles by size class, and by US make and for total imports; and percent of vehicles with air conditioning]. (p. 8)

[8] Type of customer [percent individuals, and fleets by size]. (p. 9)

[9] Used car disposition [percent reconditioned prior to sale and average cost, method of disposition including auctions, and whether sold at home office or on the road]. (p. 10)

[10-11] Leasing and rental activities [whether firm offers 6 selected options]; and record-keeping methods [by hand, mechanical, or electronic]. (p. 11-12)

A0875–2   ANALYSIS OF COSTS AND RELATED INFORMATION: Finance Leasing (Open-End), 1983-84
Annual. [1985.] 1+7 p.
SRI/MF/complete

Annual report presenting auto finance leasing (open-end) interest and administrative costs, fleet composition and used car disposition, and leasing and rental activities, for 15 unnamed firms, 1984, with comparison to 1983. Data are from reports to the American Automotive Leasing Assn by member firms.

Contains table listing (front cover); and 7 tables, listed below (p. 1-7).

Availability: American Automotive Leasing Association, 1001 Connecticut Ave., NW, Suite 1201, Washington DC 20006, †; SRI/MF/complete.

TABLES:
[Tables show data for 15 firms, labeled by letters A-P, arranged by fleet size, 1984 with selected comparisons to 1983 average totals.]

[1-2] Interest expense [including monthly costs per vehicle, and average monthly loan amortization and simple interest rate]; and general and administrative expenses per unit per month costs [including salaries, advertising, travel/promotion, taxes, and insurance]. (p. 1-2)

[3] Composition of fleets [distribution of vehicles by size class, and by US make and for total imports; and percent of vehicles with air conditioning]. (p. 3)

[4] Type of customer [percent individuals and fleets by size]. (p. 4)

[5] Used car disposition [including average months in operation and mileage per vehicle, percent reconditioned prior to sale and average cost, method of disposition including auctions, and whether sold at home office or on the road]. (p. 5)

[6-7] Leasing and rental activities [whether firm offers 6 selected options]; and record-keeping methods [by hand, mechanical, or electronic]. (p. 6-7)

A0950
American
Bankers Association

A0950–1   CONSUMER CREDIT DELINQUENCY BULLETIN
Quarterly.   6 p. folder.
SRI/MF/not filmed

Quarterly report on banks' consumer loan delinquency rates by loan type, and repossession ratios for mobile homes and autos, by State and for Puerto Rico. Loans are considered delinquent if a payment is more than 30 days overdue.

Data are compiled by the American Bankers Assn from member bank reports, and are published 6-12 weeks after quarter of coverage.

Contains brief narrative and 1 summary chart; and 2 tables showing the following data, by State and for Puerto Rico, monthly for quarter of coverage:

a.   Delinquency rates for personal, auto, property improvement, home equity/2nd mortgage, mobile home, recreational vehicle, bank card, and revolving credit loans, with accompanying trend charts.

b.   Repossession ratios for mobile homes and autos.

Prior to 2nd quarter 1984 issue, report was titled *Delinquency Rates on Bank Instalment Loans.*

Availability: American Bankers Association, Order Processing Department, 1120 Connecticut Ave., NW, Washington DC 20036, members $35.00 per yr., nonmembers $52.50 per yr.; SRI/MF/not filmed.

Issues reviewed during 1985: 3rd Qtr.1984-2nd Qtr. 1985 (D) (Bull. Nos. 429-432).

A0970
American Bar Association

A0970–1   REVIEW OF LEGAL EDUCATION IN THE U.S., FALL 1984: Law Schools and Bar Admission Requirements
Annual.   1985.   vii+84 p.
LC 36-17506.
SRI/MF/complete

Annual report on legal education, including law school enrollment, degrees, staff, and library holdings, by institution, 1984, with aggregate trends from 1963. Also includes data on female and minority students, and State bar admission requirements.

Data are compiled by the American Bar Assn (ABA) from law school deans, National Conference of Bar Examiners, and State boards of bar examiners.

Contains contents listing (p. vii); introduction, 7 tables listed below, and interspersed listings of schools not approved by ABA and of school status changes (p. 1-68); ABA statements, policy, and code (p. 69-74); tabular list of bar admission requirements, by State and for territories (p. 75-81); and directory of State bar examination administrators (p. 82-84).

Availability: American Bar Association, Legal Education and Admissions to the Bar Section, 750 N. Lake Shore Dr., Chicago, IL 60611, single copy †, additional copies $2.00 each; SRI/MF/complete.

TABLES:
[Data are shown for law schools approved by the ABA, for 1984 school year, unless otherwise noted. Data in tables [1-2] are shown by institution, arranged by State (including Puerto Rico).]

[1-2] Law schools and special program [shows full- and part-time enrollment by class level and for graduate students, and degrees awarded by type (including joint degrees), for total, women, and minority students; full- and part-time teachers and full-time deans/librarians (total, women, and minority); full- and part-time tuition/fees; selected requirements for entrance or degree; summer programs; and library hard copy and microform holdings]. (p. 4-62)

[3-4] Law school attendance figures [by class level and for graduate students]; and number of professional degrees conferred [by type; for total and female full- and part-time students]. (p. 65)

[5] Teachers [total and female full- and part-time, and total teaching deans/librarians]. (p. 66)

[6] Legal education and bar admission statistics [including enrollment of women, 1st-year enrollment, Law School Admission Test administrations, J.D. (Juris Doctor)/Bachelor of Law degrees awarded, and admissions to the bar], 1963-84. (p. 66)

[7] Survey of minority group students enrolled in J.D. programs [by class level, for blacks, Mexican Americans, Puerto Ricans, other Hispanic Americans, American Indian/Alaskan Native, Asian/Pacific Islander, and other, 1971/72-1984/85]. (p. 67-68)

A1015
American
Bowling Congress

A1015–1   ANNUAL REPORT, Fiscal Year Ended July 31, 1984: American Bowling Congress
Annual.   [1984.]   36 p.
SRI/MF/complete

Annual report of the American Bowling Congress, presenting data on finances, membership, and establishments, FY84. Data are shown by State and for Canada and other regions and areas.

Contains contents listing (inside front cover); narrative review of 89th season activities, with 1 summary table on FY84 awards, legal committee actions, bonding, and sanctioned tournaments (p. 2-3); annual convention minutes, delegate list, and ABC condensed financial report (p. 4-18); and 7 detailed tables, listed below (p. 19-36).

Availability: American Bowling Congress, 5301 S. 76th St., Greendale WI 53129, ‡; SRI/MF/complete.

TABLES:

MEMBERSHIP
[Tables [1-6] generally also include number of leagues, teams, and assns, and playing strength.]

[1-3] Summary of [membership] dues and [lane] fees, FY84 [for individual assns, by State, and for Canadian Provinces, 7 outer regions, Europe, Japan, and Pacific area]. (p. 19-35)

[4-6] Membership by [top 25] local assns and by [top 10] States [both based on playing strength, FY84]; and [annual] membership, 1895/96-1983/84. (p. 35-36)

ESTABLISHMENTS AND LANES

[7] Lane certification [including number of establishments and lanes by State, and by 4 foreign countries or outlying areas, FY84; and total establishments and lanes FY83-84, and new FY84]. (p. 36)

A1025
American
Bureau of Metal Statistics

A1025–1   NON-FERROUS METAL DATA, 1984
Annual.   1985.   149 p.
ISSN 0065-7611.
ISBN 910064-18-0.
LC 21-15719.
SRI/MF/not filmed

Annual statistical yearbook, for 1984, of nonferrous metals, including world production and consumption by country, U.S. imports and exports, and exchange prices. Also includes capacity or production data by individual company, by country. Most data are for 1980-84.

Data are from American Bureau of Metal Statistics, Bureau of Mines, World Bureau of Metal Statistics, and other government and private sources, and include selected trends from 1930.

Contains contents listing, description of ABMS functions and organization, and publications list and fees (p. 1-8); and 181 tables, described below (p. 9-149).

Previous report, for 1983, was also reviewed in SRI during 1985 under A1025-1 [Annual. 1984. 150 p. members †, nonmembers $60.00+handling].

Report for 1982 is described in SRI 1983 Annual under A1025-1.

Availability: American Bureau of Metal Statistics, 400 Plaza Dr. (Harmon Meadow), PO Box 1405, Secaucus NJ 07094-0405, members †, nonmembers $70.00+handling; SRI/MF/not filmed.

TABLES:
[Data are for U.S., 1980-84, unless otherwise noted.]

A1025–1.1: Copper

SUMMARY

a.   World mine, smelter, and refined production, and refined consumption, by country; and production, deliveries, and inventories, U.S. and outside U.S. 5 tables. (p. 9-14)

b.   Receipts, shipments, inventories, and consumption or production: for primary brass mills; and for smelters, refiners, and copper rod mills. 4 tables. (p. 14-18)

c.   Refined production from scrap, and distribution of refined deliveries by country; copper sulfate production; and monthly brass/bronze ingot deliveries. 4 tables. (p. 19-21)

COMPANY DATA

d. Production by company in U.S., Mexico, Canada, and other countries, and U.S. mine production by State; and lists of copper sellers in U.S., and producers in U.S., Canada, Mexico, and other countries. 3 tables. (p. 22-28)

e. World smelter and refinery plants and capacities, by country and company, end of 1984. 2 tables. (p. 29-35)

FOREIGN TRADE

f. U.S.: imports and exports (raw and by refined product), and imports by country of origin for 3 product types; exports and copper and brass imports by product and country, 1983-84, with imports by product only, 1980-84; and brass/bronze imports and exports by product type. 6 tables. (p. 36-40)

g. UK: imports and exports, by product type; consumption in fabricated products; and stocks. 3 tables. (p. 40-41)

MARKETS AND PRICES

h. Ultimate end-use markets for U.S. brass mill shipments, by product type in 5 consuming sectors; monthly prices for U.S., Canada, and London Metal Exchange; and refiner and dealer buying prices for No. 2 scrap. 7 tables. (p. 42-44)

A1025–1.2: Lead and Zinc

LEAD

SUMMARY

a. World mine and refined production, and refined consumption, all by country; U.S. smelter and secondary smelter/consumer stocks; primary refinery stocks, production, purchases, and shipments; primary lead smelted/refined; refined production and deliveries; secondary recoveries; mine production by State; consumption by end-use products; and monthly lead pigment shipments and imports, 1983-84. 13 tables. (p. 45-54)

COMPANY DATA

b. Capacities and plant locations of silver-lead refiners and smelting works in U.S., Canada, and Mexico, of Missouri lead smelters/refiners, and of smelting/refining works by country, all by company, end of 1984; and lead production by company in U.S., Canada, Mexico, and other countries. 5 tables. (p. 54-59)

FOREIGN TRADE AND PRICES

c. U.S. imports and exports, by type and country, various years 1980-84; and UK lead consumption, stocks, and imports and exports, by type. 6 tables. (p. 60-62)

d. Monthly prices, for U.S. producer, Canadian pig lead, London Metal Exchange, and Australia; and list of U.S. secondary smelters and refiners. 4 tables. (p. 63-64)

ZINC

SUMMARY

e. U.S. smelted and scrap supply and use, 1981-84; world mine production and refined slab zinc production and consumption, by country; production of slab zinc and concentrates by country and company; and U.S. mine and slab zinc production by State, including total slab production from domestic and foreign ore. 8 tables. (p. 65-74)

f. Slab smelter production, shipments, and stocks; slab production by material and grade, and consumption by end-use product; dust production, 1979-84; and production of distilled and electrolytic zinc. 6 tables. (p. 74-76)

COMPANY DATA

g. World electrolytic zinc plant capacity and production, by country and company, 1981-84; lists of U.S. secondary slab plants and zinc rollers, by company; rolled zinc production, imports, exports, and supply; total U.S. primary and secondary slab plant capacity and zinc fuming operations, various years 1980-84; and estimated annual capacities of world zinc smelting works, by country and company, end of 1984. 5 tables. (p. 77-82)

FOREIGN TRADE AND PRICES

h. U.S. imports and exports, by country and type; UK imports, exports, and consumption, by type, and slab zinc stocks; monthly prices, for U.S. producer, London Metal Exchange, and Australia; and monthly prices for Canada by grade, 1983-84. 12 tables. (p. 83-87)

A1025–1.3: Aluminum, Silver, and Gold

ALUMINUM

a. World production, including bauxite and alumina, and consumption, by country; U.S. consumption and wrought and cast product shipments; and world ingot production capacity, by country and company, end of 1984. 7 tables. (p. 88-97)

b. U.S. primary production, shipments, stocks, imports, and exports; Canadian production, consumption, and exports; and monthly prices, for U.S. and UK. 5 tables. (p. 98-99)

SILVER

c. World production by country, company, and mine, and consumption by end use and country; U.S. production by State and source; U.S. imports and refined exports by country; and U.S. refined production and disposition. 8 tables. (p. 99-107)

d. Monthly prices for New York and London fine silver and Canadian silver. 3 tables. (p. 107-108)

GOLD

e. World production, by country and by company; U.S. production by State and source; and London monthly final prices. 5 tables. (p. 108-112)

A1025–1.4: Antimony, Cadmium, Magnesium, and Other Metals

a. Antimony: world mine production by country; and U.S. production, imports, exports, consumption, stocks, and prices. 2 tables. (p. 113)

b. Cadmium metal: world refined production by country; refined production by company, and total refined cadmium producer inventories, production, and shipments, for Canada, Latin America, and U.S.; and U.S. imports and exports by country, and monthly producer prices. 6 tables. (p. 114-117)

c. Magnesium metal: world production by country; U.S. ingot production plant capa-

cities by company, end of 1984; and U.S. total magnesium metal production, consumption, and prices, and cast product shipments. 4 tables. (p. 118)

d. Molybdenum: world mine production by country; U.S. production by company, and concentrates production, shipments, exports, imports, consumption, and stocks; and U.S. products consumption by end use, 1983-84. 4 tables. (p. 119-120)

e. Cobalt: world mine production by country, U.S. consumption, and monthly prices. 2 tables. (p. 121)

f. Nickel: world mine production by country; U.S. consumption by type and end use; and monthly average prices. 3 tables. (p. 122-123)

g. Platinum metals: world production by country; U.S. stocks, and refiner recoveries; U.S. sales to consuming industries, 1983-84; and U.S. imports. 5 tables. (p. 123-124)

h. Selenium and tellurium: world producer inventories, receipts, production, and shipments by country of destination. 2 tables. (p. 125-126)

i. Titanium: U.S. production, shipments, imports, consumption, and mill product shipments. 3 tables. (p. 127)

j. Tin: world ore and smelter production, and consumption, by country; U.S. primary and secondary consumption, and total tin stocks, supply, imports, and exports; UK refined consumption and uses, and stocks; and monthly prices, for New York and London. 11 tables. (p. 128-133)

k. Uranium concentrates production, by country; and U.S. mine production by State, reserves, and concentrates production, imports, shipments, and inventories. 2 tables. (p. 133-134)

A1025–1.5: Miscellaneous

a. Copper, lead, and zinc production, for U.S. and world, 1930-84; and U.S. sundry mineral and metal production. 2 tables. (p. 134-135)

b. New York scrap metal prices, including monthly data for 1984; and miscellaneous metal, ore, and concentrate prices, end of 1984. 3 tables. (p. 136-137)

c. Historic and 1967 and 1984 constant prices of copper, lead, zinc, and aluminum, with comparison to various U.S. indexes; monthly average highs and lows and yearly average prices of copper, lead, zinc, and silver; and sterling exchange rate, and average annual prices for 7 principal metals; all 1930-84. 4 tables. (p. 138-141)

d. Foreign monthly exchange rates for UK and Canada; and data for various U.S. economic indicators, including industry production statistics. 3 tables. (p. 142-143)

e. Selected information lists, including conversion tables, and principal ore and metal import duties; stockpile material goals and inventories, end of FY84; and U.S. Government stockpiles of selected metals, showing objective, uncommitted inventory, amount required, and excess, by metal, various years 1950-84. 4 tables. (p. 144-149)

A1175
American Cancer Society

A1175–1   CANCER FACTS AND FIGURES, 1985
Annual.   1985.   31 p.
LC 64-6303.
SRI/MF/complete

Annual report, for 1985, on cancer. Includes cancer incidence and mortality, by State and for Puerto Rico, and by sex; survival rates by race; and death rates by foreign country and sex; all shown by type of cancer, various periods 1949-85.

Also includes data on American Cancer Society (ACS) finances, including research grants/fellowships awarded, by recipient institution, FY84; allocation of funds by function, 1983/84; and income from fund raising and legacies, 1974-83.

Data sources are the National Cancer Institute's Surveillance, Epidemiology and End Results Program (1977-81); NCHS; *World Health Statistics Annual 1980-82;* Census Bureau; and ACS.

Contains map, contents listing, and data sources (p. 1-2); narrative interspersed with 5 charts and 11 tables (p. 3-30); and directories of cancer centers and ACS divisions (p. 31 and back cover).

Availability: American Cancer Society, 90 Park Ave., New York NY 10016, †; SRI/MF/complete.

A1225
American Chamber of Commerce Researchers Association

A1225–1   INTER-CITY COST OF LIVING INDEX
Quarterly.   Approx. 25 p. var. paging.
ISSN 0740-7130.
LC sc83-2111.
SRI/MF/complete, delayed

Quarterly survey report presenting cost-of-living indexes and average retail prices for selected consumer items in approximately 250 cities. Data are based on reports filed by local chambers of commerce. Report is issued 2-3 months after quarter of coverage.

Contains overview of survey methodology, with accompanying list of consumer items priced; and 3 tables arranged in sections, as follows:

Section 1-2. ACCRA city composite index and cost-of-living index for metro cities [for all and grocery items, housing, utilities, transportation, health care, and miscellaneous goods/services; by city arranged by State and by MSA].

Section 3. Price report [average prices for selected grocery items; apartment rent, and home purchase price and monthly payment; monthly electric, other energy, and telephone bills; bus fare, tire balancing, and gasoline prices; hospital room, doctor and dentist office visits, and aspirin prices; costs

of selected fast food, personal care, clothing, washer repair, recreation, and alcoholic beverage items; and newspaper subscription prices; by city arranged by State].

Availability: American Chamber of Commerce Researchers Association, Mrs. Alice Klein, c/o Louisville Area Chamber of Commerce, One Riverfront Plaza, Louisville KY 40202, $75.00 per yr.; SRI/MF/complete, delayed until publication of subsequent *Index* issue.

Issues reviewed during 1985: 3rd Qtr. 1984-2nd Qtr. 1985 (D).

A1250
American Chemical Society

A1250–1   CHEMICAL AND ENGINEERING NEWS
Weekly.
ISSN 0009-2347.
LC A41-2413.
SRI/MF/excerpts, shipped quarterly

Weekly publication (except last week in Dec.) reporting U.S. and international developments and trends in research chemistry and the chemicals industry and in related industries using chemical processes for manufacturing purposes. Includes R&D, technology, production, trade, regulation, funding, employment, education, management, and finance.

Issues generally include news features; articles on business, international developments, government, science, technology, and science policy; book reviews; and American Chemical Society (ACS) news.

Statistical features include:

a.   "Key Chemicals," usually appearing in 1 or 2 issues each month, reporting on supply and demand outlook for selected chemicals.

b.   Articles analyzing sales and earnings of chemical and allied industries, quarterly for U.S. and semiannually for Canada.

c.   Semiannual and annual articles including features on capital and R&D spending, plant capacity utilization, chemistry degrees awarded, employment and earnings, leading chemical firms and chemicals, and worldwide chemical outlook.

d.   Annual chemical industry fact book with production, finance, employment, and trade summary for U.S. and foreign chemical and chemical processing industries.

e.   Topical articles and features containing statistical material.

All features with substantial statistical content are described, as they appear, under "Statistical Features." Nonstatistical features are not covered.

Availability: American Chemical Society, Director of Financial Operations, 1155 16th St., NW, Washington DC 20036, members †, nonmembers $37.00 per yr., single copy $3.00, annual index $35.00; SRI/MF/excerpts for all portions covered under "Statistical Features;" shipped quarterly.

Issues reviewed during 1985: Nov. 5, 1984-Oct. 28, 1985 (P) (Vol. 62, Nos. 45-52; Vol. 63, Nos. 1-43).

STATISTICAL FEATURES:

A1250–1.601: Nov. 5, 1984 (Vol. 62, No. 45)

THERMOSET PLASTICS OUTPUT ON RISE, BUT LIKELY TO SLOW: KEY POLYMERS, ANNUAL FEATURE

(p. 10-14) Annual article, by Bruce F. Greek, reporting on supply and demand outlook for 3 thermoset plastics: phenolics, polyesters, and epoxies. Includes text statistics on major end uses, foreign trade, and prices, primarily 1984.

EUROPEAN PETROCHEMICAL PRODUCERS FACE MORE MODEST GROWTH

(p. 15-16) Article, with 1 undated table showing number of producers and capacity for 4 petrochemicals, for U.S. and Western Europe. Data are from BP Chemicals International, London.

CONGRESS ENACTS IMPORTANT FUNDING BILLS

(p. 20-21) Article, with 1 table showing R&D funding for 5 Federal agencies (DOD, NIH, USDA, Interior, and DOE), by subagency or program, actual FY84, and Administration request and congressional appropriation FY85. Data are from congressional reports.

A1250–1.602: Nov. 12, 1984 (Vol. 62, No. 46)

CHEMICAL EARNINGS BRAKED SHARPLY IN THIRD QUARTER, QUARTERLY FEATURE

(p. 12-18) Quarterly article, by David Webber, analyzing sales, earnings, and profit margins for major U.S. chemical producing companies, 3rd quarter 1984.

Includes 3 tables showing top 10-11 chemical companies in sales, earnings, and profitability; sales, earnings, and profit margin, for 30 major chemical, 16 chemical-producing oil/gas, and 24 diversified chemical-producing companies; 3rd quarter and 1st 9 months 1984, with selected comparisons to 1983.

HYDROGEN PEROXIDE USE RESUMES STEADY GROWTH

(p. 19) Article, with 1 table summarizing hydrogen peroxide production, capacity, producers, principal end-use markets, and prices, primarily 1984.

A1250–1.603: Nov. 19, 1984 (Vol. 62, No. 47)

CHEMICAL TRADE SURPLUS CONTINUES TO SHRINK

(p. 12-13) Article, with 1 table showing exports and imports of chemicals by type, 1st 5 months 1984 with percent change from 1983. Data are from Census Bureau.

DRUG COMPANY EARNINGS SLOWED IN THIRD QUARTER, QUARTERLY FEATURE

(p. 14-16) Quarterly article, with 1 table showing sales, earnings, and profit margin, for 17 pharmaceutical firms, 3rd quarter and 1st 9 months 1984 with comparisons to 1983.

A1250–1.604: Nov. 26, 1984 (Vol. 62, No. 48)

PEERS RATE KEYWORTH GENERALLY HIGH AS PRESIDENT'S SCIENCE ADVISOR

(p. 8-13) By Wil Lepkowski. Article examining performance of the Reagan Administration's science advisor, George A. Keyworth, with 1 table showing Federal R&D funding by function, 1976-85. Data are from NSF.

INDUSTRIAL GASES SETTLING INTO SLOWER GROWTH PATTERN: KEY CHEMICALS, ANNUAL FEATURE

(p. 17-20) Annual article, by Bruce F. Greek, reporting on supply and demand outlook for 3 leading industrial gases: oxygen, nitrogen, and carbon dioxide. Includes text statistics on major end uses, foreign trade, and prices, primarily 1984.

For description of previous article, see SRI 1983 Annual under A1250-1.443.

A1250–1.605: Dec. 10, 1984 (Vol. 62, No. 50)

BIOTECHNOLOGY FIRMS GIRD FOR CLASH OVER PATENT CLAIMS

(p. 18-24) By David Webber. Article on biotechnology-related patent activity. Data are from OMEC International.

Includes 1 chart and 3 tables showing number of biotechnology-related patents issued, with distribution by sector, and with number issued to selected corporations and universities and to foreign-owned companies by country, all for 1st 9 months 1983-84.

A1250–1.606: Dec. 17, 1984 (Vol. 62, No. 51)

APPAREL IMPORTS SLOW FIBER INTERMEDIATES DEMAND: KEY CHEMICALS, ANNUAL FEATURE

(p. 13-16) Annual article, by Bruce F. Greek, reporting on supply and demand outlook for 3 major organic chemicals used in synthetic fiber production: dimethyl terephthalate/purified terephthalic acid (DMT/PTA), ethylene oxide, and cyclohexane. Includes text statistics on major derivatives and end uses, foreign trade, and prices, primarily 1984.

For description of previous article, see SRI 1983 Annual under A1250-1.440.

BIOTECHNOLOGY REVENUES, COSTS SURGED IN THIRD QUARTER, QUARTERLY FEATURE

(p. 17-18) Quarterly article, by David Webber, with 1 table showing revenues, earnings, and profit margin, for 14 biotechnology firms, 3rd quarter and 1st 9 months 1984, with comparisons to 1983.

WORLD CHEMICAL OUTLOOK, ANNUAL FEATURE

(p. 32-60) Annual report, for 1984, on world trends and developments in the chemical industry.

Data are from UN, government agencies, industry assns, and C&EN estimates. Includes introduction and 9 articles reporting on industry developments in the U.S. and other key countries or world areas. Articles with substantial statistical content are described below.

U.S.: AFTER A SHARP REBOUND, EXPANSION SLOWS FOR THE CHEMICAL INDUSTRY, ANNUAL FEATURE

(p. 34-36) By David M. Kiefer. Includes 1 table showing production for 34 types of inorganic and organic chemicals, and plastics and synthetic fibers, 1982-85.

FOREIGN TRADE: STRONG DOLLAR CRIMPS SURPLUS IN U.S. TRADE IN CHEMICALS, ANNUAL FEATURE

(p. 37-39) By Earl V. Anderson. Includes 3 tables showing U.S. export and import value by product category, with detail for chemicals by type and by country or world region, various years 1981-84.

WESTERN EUROPE: CHEMICAL MAKERS ARE EXPERIENCING A YEAR OF SHARPLY IMPROVED PROFITS

(p. 40-47) By Dermot A. O'Sullivan. Includes 1 table showing consumption of thermoplastics by type, for Western Europe, 1980-85 and 1990.

JAPAN: CHEMICAL BUSINESS RECOVERS, BUT GOOD TIMES MAY NOT LAST LONG, ANNUAL FEATURE

(p. 50-52) By Earl V. Anderson. Includes 1 table showing Japan's production of synthetic rubber, 40 types of inorganic and organic chemicals, and 5 types of plastics, 1983 and 1st 8 months 1983-84.

CANADA: REBOUND IN CHEMICALS MAY BE GRINDING TO AN EARLY HALT, ANNUAL FEATURE

(p. 53-54) By Earl V. Anderson. Includes 1 table showing Canada's production of 15 chemicals, 1979-84.

USSR/EASTERN EUROPE: FIVE-YEAR PLAN GOALS BEYOND REACH IN SOVIET UNION AND EASTERN EUROPE, ANNUAL FEATURE

(p. 55) By Richard J. Seltzer. Includes 1 table showing Soviet production of fertilizers by type, tires, and 7 chemicals or related products, 1983 and 1st 10 months 1984.

CHINA: SWEEPING ECONOMIC REFORMS ARE AIMED AT QUADRUPLING PRODUCTION

(p. 60) By Richard J. Seltzer. Includes 1 table showing PRC production of fertilizers by type, tires, and 10 chemicals or related products, 1981-83, 1st 10 months 1984, and targeted for 1985.

A1250–1.607: Dec. 24, 1984 (Vol. 62, No. 52)

CHEMICAL CAPITAL SPENDING TO CLIMB AGAIN IN 1985, ANNUAL FEATURE

(p. 16-17) Annual article, by William J. Storck, on 1985 capital spending plans of 14 leading U.S. chemical companies. Data are primarily from a C&EN survey. Includes 1 table showing capital spending by company, worldwide 1980-85, and in U.S. 1984-85.

BHOPAL DISASTER SPOTLIGHTS CHEMICAL HAZARD ISSUES

(p. 19-20) By Wil Lepkowski. Article discussing environmental impact of industrial plants on nearby communities, with 1 table showing emissions rate for 17 major pollutants for Union Carbide's methyl isocyanate plant in Institute, West Virginia, 1981. Data are from OSHA.

Data clarifications appear in the Mar. 25, 1985 issue (see A1250-1.618 below).

A1250–1.608: Jan. 7, 1985 (Vol. 63, No. 1)

JOB OUTLOOK IS GOOD FOR SPRING GRADS

(p. 9) Brief article, with 1 table showing average starting salaries for graduates with bachelor's and master's degrees, by field, 1984-85. Data are from Northwestern University's 1985 *Endicott Report.*

Endicott Report is covered in SRI under U3730-1.

CHEMICAL PRODUCTIVITY'S ERRATIC PATTERN CAUSING CONCERN

(p. 21-22) By William J. Storck. Article, with 1 table showing indexes of production, work hours, productivity, wages, and unit labor cost,

for chemical industry and all manufacturing, annually 1974-83 and quarterly 1982-3rd quarter 1984. Data are from Dept of Labor and Federal Reserve Board.

A1250–1.609: Jan. 14, 1985 (Vol. 63, No. 2)

R&D FUNDING PREDICTED TO RISE 11% IN 1985, ANNUAL FEATURE

(p. 7-8) Annual article forecasting R&D funding, by industry, for 1985. Data are derived from an annual report by Battelle Memorial Institute. Includes 1 table showing Federal and industry R&D funds, for 8 industry groups, 1985.

Full Battelle report is covered in SRI under R3300-1.

CHEMICAL INDUSTRY WILL SPEND 9% MORE ON R&D IN 1985, ANNUAL FEATURE

(p. 19-20) Annual article, by David Webber, on basic chemical industry planned R&D funding for 1985, based on a C&EN survey of 14 major companies. Includes 1 table showing R&D actual spending 1979-84, planned spending 1984-85, and spending as percent of sales 1983-84, all for 14 companies.

Corrected data appear in the Jan. 28, 1985 issue (see A1250-1.611 below).

A1250–1.610: Jan. 21, 1985 (Vol. 63, No. 3)

INDUSTRIAL SURFACTANTS SET FOR STRONG GROWTH

(p. 23-48) By Patricia L. Layman. Article on trends and outlook for the surfactant industry. Data are from Shell Chemical, Colin A. Houston and Associates, and C&EN estimates. Includes 3 charts and 1 table showing the following:

a. U.S. surfactant demand, 1977, 1982, and 1992; and surfactant production in U.S., Western Europe, and Japan, 1985; all with distribution by end-use category.

b. U.S. surfactant consumption by end-use industry (no date); and industrial surfactant demand, with distribution for U.S., Western Europe, and Japan, 1985.

A1250–1.611: Jan. 28, 1985 (Vol. 63, No. 4)

CORRECTIONS

(p. 4) Includes corrected data for annual article on chemical industry planned R&D funding. For description of article, see A1250-1.609 above.

EUROPEAN CONCERN ABOUT ACID RAIN IS GROWING

(p. 12-18) By Dermot A. O'Sullivan. Article on environmental effects of acid rain in Europe. Data are from UN. Includes 2 undated charts showing average deposition of sulfur on European continent, with detail for 14 countries including percent of deposition coming from other countries.

CHEMICAL STOCKS PERFORMED POORLY IN 1984, RECURRING FEATURE

(p. 20, 22) Recurring article, by William J. Storck, with 2 tables showing C&EN chemical stock index compared to 8 major stock indexes; and stock price (including 12-month high and low), price/earnings ratio, and dividend yield, for 30 chemical producers; all as of year end 1984 with selected comparisons to 1983.

BIOTECHNOLOGY-RELATED STOCKS FARED DISMALLY IN 1984, RECURRING FEATURE

(p. 21) Recurring article, with 1 table showing stock prices for 15 biotechnology firms, as of year end 1984, and 52-week high and low prices.

ENGINEERING RESIN DEMAND ROSE SHARPLY LAST YEAR

(p. 23) Article, with 3 tables showing consumption of engineering resin (thermoplastics), for U.S., Japan, Western Europe, and rest of world, 1984 and 1989, with detail by type of resin, 1984; and distribution of resin sales by end-use industry, 1984 with percent change from 1983. Data are from Celanese Corp.

A1250–1.612: Feb. 4, 1985 (Vol. 63, No. 5)

PRODUCTION SLOWS FOR NATURAL GAS-BASED PETROCHEMICALS: KEY CHEMICALS, ANNUAL FEATURE

(p. 10-14) Annual article, by Bruce F. Greek, reporting on supply and demand outlook for 4 natural gas based petrochemicals: ammonia, urea, methanol, and formaldehyde. Includes text statistics on major derivatives and end uses, foreign trade, and prices, primarily 1985.

REINFORCED PLASTICS GROWTH TO SLACKEN IN 1985

(p. 15) Article, with 1 table showing demand for reinforced plastics, by end use, 1975-85. Data are from Society of the Plastics Industry.

A1250–1.613: Feb. 18, 1985 (Vol. 63, No. 7)

FUNDS FOR R&D ARE UP 13% IN ADMINISTRATION'S BUDGET PROPOSAL, ANNUAL FEATURE

(p. 10-15) Annual article, by Janice R. Long and David J. Hanson, on R&D portion of Reagan Administration budget proposal, FY86.

Includes 12 tables showing R&D obligations and outlays by agency, for total R&D, basic research, and R&D facilities; and R&D funding for 7 agencies, by subagency, institute, program, or academic discipline, with detail for NSF science and chemistry funding; FY84-86.

CHEMICAL EARNINGS SLIPPED IN FOURTH QUARTER, QUARTERLY FEATURE

(p. 18-23) Quarterly article, by William J. Storck, analyzing sales, earnings, and profit margins for major U.S. chemical producing companies, 4th quarter 1984.

Includes 3 tables showing top 10 chemical companies in sales, earnings, and profitability; and sales, earnings, and profit margin, for 30 major chemical, 13 chemical-producing oil/gas, and 23 diversified chemical-producing companies; 4th quarter and full year 1984, with selected comparisons to 1983.

A1250–1.614: Feb. 25, 1985 (Vol. 63, No. 8)

GLOBAL OUTLOOK FOR FERTILIZER RAW MATERIALS: CAUTIOUS BUT POSITIVE

(p. 21-22) By Patricia L. Layman. Article, with 2 tables showing world current capacity, demand projected to 2000, and additional capacity and new plants required to meet demand, for nitrogen, phosphate, and potash; and potash consumption in developed, developing, and Communist countries, selected periods 1983-94. Data are from Texasgulf Inc., and Kali and Salz A.G.

SECOND HALF DEFLATES CANADIAN CHEMICALS, SEMIANNUAL FEATURE

(p. 24) Semiannual report on Canadian chemical industry performance. Includes 1 table showing net sales, net income, and profit margin, for 4 largest companies, 1984 with comparisons to 1983.

Feature previously appeared on a quarterly basis.

EPA FARES WELL AMONG '86 REGULATORY BUDGETS, ANNUAL FEATURE

(p. 28) Annual article, with 1 table showing Federal budget obligations for EPA, FDA, and OSHA, by function, FY84-85 and Administration proposal FY86. Data are from OMB.

R&D COSTS OF WEAPONS CONTINUES TO ESCALATE

(p. 29) Article, with 1 table showing R&D budget obligations for 7 weapons systems, FY84-85 and Administration proposal FY86. Data are from DOD.

A1250–1.615: Mar. 4, 1985 (Vol. 63, No. 9)

CHLOR-ALKALIES RETURN TO SLOW GROWTH PATTERN: KEY CHEMICALS, ANNUAL FEATURE

(p. 11-14) Annual article, by Bruce F. Greek, reporting on supply and demand outlook for 3 chlor-alkalies: chlorine, caustic soda, and soda ash. Includes text statistics on major derivatives and end uses, foreign trade, and prices, primarily 1985.

DRUG FIRM EARNINGS SLUGGISH IN FOURTH QUARTER, QUARTERLY FEATURE

(p. 16-19) Quarterly article, with 1 table showing sales, earnings, and profit margin, for 16 pharmaceutical firms, 4th quarter and full year 1984 with comparisons to 1983.

ASBESTOS: THE FIBER THAT'S PANICKING AMERICA

(p. 28-41) By Pamela S. Zurer. Article examining health effects of asbestos exposure. Data are from the National Research Council.

Includes 1 undated table showing estimated risk of developing mesothelioma and lung cancer from exposure to asbestos at 2 levels (approximately equivalent to levels in urban outside air and in U.S. schoolrooms with asbestos surfaces), with lung cancer detail for smokers and nonsmokers by sex.

A1250–1.616: Mar. 11, 1985 (Vol. 63, No. 10)

GLOBAL MAN-MADE FIBERS OUTPUT HITS RECORD HIGH

(p. 11-12) Article, with 2 tables showing synthetic and total man-made fiber production for U.S., Western Europe, Japan, and all others, 1980-84. Data are from Enka, the Netherlands.

A1250–1.617: Mar. 18, 1985 (Vol. 63, No. 11)

CHEMICAL INDUSTRY COOL TO PROSPECTS FOR INCREASED TRADE WITH SOVIETS

(p. 8-9) Article, with 1 table showing value of U.S. chemical exports to and imports from Soviet Union, by type of chemical, 1983-84. Data are from Census Bureau.

A1250–1.618: Mar. 25, 1985 (Vol. 63, No. 12)

CORRECTIONS

(p. 2) Includes data clarifications for article on pollutant emissions for Union Carbide methyl isocyanate plant in Institute, W.Va.

For description of article, see A1250-1.607 above.

MAJOR CHANGES COULD CONFRONT BASIC PETROCHEMICALS THIS YEAR: KEY CHEMICALS, ANNUAL FEATURE

(p. 22-27) Annual article, by Bruce F. Greek, reporting on supply and demand outlook for 5 petrochemicals: ethylene, propylene, butadiene, benzene, and p-xylene. Includes text statistics on major derivatives and end uses, foreign trade, and prices, primarily 1985.

For description of previous article, see SRI 1983 Annual under A1250-1.447.

A1250–1.619: Apr. 1, 1985 (Vol. 63, No. 13)

GROUP UPDATES ESTIMATE OF NATURAL GAS RESERVES

(p. 7-8) Article, with 1 table showing onshore and offshore natural gas resources potentially recoverable under conventional methods, for Alaska and contiguous U.S., as of Dec. 1984. Data are from Potential Gas Committee.

BIOTECHNOLOGY REVENUES SLOWED IN FOURTH QUARTER, QUARTERLY FEATURE

(p. 13) Quarterly article, with 1 table showing revenues, earnings, and profit margin, for 14 biotechnology firms, 4th quarter and full year 1984, with comparisons to 1983.

A1250–1.620: Apr. 8, 1985 (Vol. 63, No. 14)

CHEMICAL R&D: OUTLOOK FAIR FOR FEDERAL FUNDING, ANNUAL FEATURE

(p. 6) Annual article, with 2 tables showing Federal funding for chemistry R&D by agency, FY84-86. Data are from American Chemical Society.

LEAD CUT GIVES ALCOHOLS CRACK AT GASOLINE BLEND MARKET

(p. 17-18) Article on outlook for gasoline blend market following a Mar. 1985 EPA ruling on reductions in gasoline lead content. Data are from Herman and Associates. Includes 1 table showing demand for leaded and all gasoline, and consumption of lead and alcohol used in gasoline under old and/or new EPA rules, 1985-94.

Corrected table heading appears in Apr. 29, 1985 issue (see A1250-1.623 below).

A1250–1.621: Apr. 15, 1985 (Vol. 63, No. 15)

AGE DISCRIMINATION SUIT BREWING AGAINST HOFFMANN-LA ROCHE

(p. 12-14) By David Webber. Article, with 2 charts showing number of employment-related age discrimination charges closed by Federal and State/local agencies, with distribution by disposition, FY83. Data are from Equal Employment Opportunity Commission.

RUBBER CHEMICALS FACE SMALLER MARKET

(p. 33-60) By Stephen C. Stinson. Article on rubber industry outlook and trends. Data are from USITC, C&EN estimates, and Rubber Manufacturers Assn.

Includes text statistics, 3 charts, and 2 tables showing rubber-processing chemical trade, prices, commercial value, and end uses and production by type of chemical; synthetic rubber production by rubber type, and consumption with distribution by type; and tire production, and auto tire shipments (including exports), with distribution by tire type; various years 1974-88.

A1250–1.622: Apr. 22, 1985 (Vol. 63, No. 16)

BATTLE RAGES OVER IMPORTS OF FUEL ETHANOL

(p. 9-15) By Earl V. Anderson. Article, with 1 chart showing Brazilian ethanol consumption, with distribution by end use (including exports), 1984. Data are from Brazilian Ethanol Producers' Special Export Committee.

LITTLE GROWTH AHEAD FOR MAJOR MINERAL ACIDS: KEY CHEMICALS, ANNUAL FEATURE

(p. 18-20) Annual article, by Bruce F. Greek, reporting on supply and demand outlook for sulfuric and phosphoric acids. Includes text statistics on major derivatives and end uses, foreign trade, and prices, primarily 1985.

URBANA DOMINATES GRADUATE RANKINGS, ANNUAL FEATURE

(p. 57) Annual article on universities leading in number of chemistry graduates, 1983/84, based on the annual report of the ACS Committee on Professional Training, described below.

Includes 1 table showing number of chemistry graduates by degree level, for 25-27 institutions graduating the most at each degree level, 1983/84.

ACS COMMITTEE ON PROFESSIONAL TRAINING 1984 ANNUAL REPORT

(p. 58-63) Annual report on number of chemistry and chemical engineering undergraduate and graduate degrees awarded by 577 chemistry and 120 chemical engineering schools in 1983/84.

Includes 4 tables showing ACS-approved graduate programs and full- and part-time enrollment, fall 1981-83; graduates, by sex, 1984; schools reporting and graduates, 1980-84; and degrees awarded, by institution or campus, 1983/84; all by degree level.

Report also summarizes 1984 activities of the ACS Committee on Professional Training.

A1250–1.623: Apr. 29, 1985 (Vol. 63, No. 17)

CORRECTIONS

(p. 4) Includes corrected table heading for feature on gasoline blend market, appearing in Apr. 8, 1985 issue (for description, see A1250-1.620 above).

COSMETICS: SCIENCE IS REPLACING ART IN FORMULATIONS

(p. 19-46) By Patricia L. Layman. Article, with 1 chart and 1 table showing cosmetic surfactant market volume, with distribution by surfactant type, 1984; and cosmetic and toiletry market value for U.S. and 4 Western European countries, by type of product, 1983. Data are from industry and C&EN estimates.

A1250–1.624: May 6, 1985 (Vol. 63, No. 18)

C&EN's TOP 50 CHEMICAL PRODUCTS AND 100 CHEMICAL PRODUCERS, ANNUAL FEATURE

(p. 11-20) Annual report, by David Webber and William J. Storck, on chemical industry production, sales, assets, and earnings, including rankings of 50 leading chemicals and 100 chemical producers, 1984. Data are derived from Federal Government, trade assn, and industry sources, and C&EN estimates. Includes 2 charts and 4 tables showing the following:

a. Top 50 chemicals ranked by production, 1984 with comparisons to 1983, and including average annual change for selected periods 1974-84.

b. Top 100 chemical producers ranked by chemical sales, and including chemical operating profit, profit margin, assets, and return on assets, with comparisons to total sales, profits, and assets, 1984 with changes from 1983; and aggregate summary data for 1st and 2nd 50 largest company groups, and for chemical, petroleum/natural gas, diversified, and foreign-owned companies, 1984.

Data for the top 100 producers are also arranged alphabetically by company, and include sub-rankings for each of the chemical-related items.

Feature previously appeared as 2 separate articles; for description of 1983 rankings, see SRI 1984 Annual under A1250-1.525 and A1250-1.527.

A1250–1.625: May 13, 1985 (Vol. 63, No. 19)

CHEMICAL EARNINGS FELL AGAIN IN FIRST QUARTER, QUARTERLY FEATURE

(p. 8-12) Quarterly article, by David Webber, analyzing sales, earnings, and profit margins for major U.S. chemical producing companies, 1st quarter 1985.

Includes 4 tables showing top 10 chemical companies in sales, earnings, and profitability; sales, earnings, and profit margin, for 30 major chemical, 18 chemical-producing oil/gas, and 23 diversified chemical-producing companies; and chemical after-tax earnings for 7 major oil companies; 1st quarter 1985, with selected comparisons to 1984.

A1250–1.626: May 20, 1985 (Vol. 63, No. 20)

POLYMER OUTPUT REACHED NEW HIGH IN 1984, ANNUAL FEATURE

(p. 12-13) Annual article, by David Webber, with 1 table showing production of plastics, and synthetic fibers and rubber, by type, selected years 1974-84. Data are from Society for the Plastics Industry, Textile Economics Bureau, and Rubber Manufacturers Assn.

CANADIAN CHEMICAL EXECS ARE OPTIMISTIC, SEMIANNUAL FEATURE

(p. 14) Semiannual article, with 1 table showing Canada's production of 16 chemicals, 1984 and 1st 2 months 1984-85, with comparisons to 1983. Data are from Statistics Canada.

A1250–1.627: May 27, 1985 (Vol. 63, No. 21)

CHEMICAL PLANT CAPACITY USE LEVELING OUT, SEMIANNUAL FEATURE

(p. 24-29) Semiannual article, by William J. Storck and Bruce F. Greek, analyzing plant capacity utilization of basic chemical and polymer industries, 1st quarter 1985 with comparisons to previous periods. Data are based on C&EN estimates, and industry and government sources.

Includes 2 tables showing nameplate capacity, and nameplate and effective capacity utilization, for principal types of the following: petrochemicals; chlor-alkalies; acids; industrial gases; mineral-based inorganics; plastic, fiber, and adhesive/coating intermediates; pigments; solvents; plastics; and synthetic fibers; 1st quarter 1985, and 1st and 3rd quarters 1984.

A1250–1.628: June 3, 1985 (Vol. 63, No. 22)

COSTS OF INDUSTRIAL WASTE MANAGEMENT TO RISE

(p. 7-8) Article on effects of 1984 changes in Resource Conservation and Recovery Act and an expanded Superfund program on costs of industrial hazardous waste disposal. Data are from Congressional Budget Office.

Includes 1 table showing waste disposal costs, by industry, actual 1983, and projected for 1990 with and without industry waste reduction efforts.

DRUG FIRM PROFITABILITY INCREASED IN FIRST QUARTER, QUARTERLY FEATURE

(p. 12-13) Quarterly article, by David Webber, with 1 table showing sales, earnings, and profit margin, for 18 pharmaceutical firms, 1st quarter 1985 with comparisons to 1984.

U.S. PETROCHEMICAL OUTLOOK NOT SO DISMAL

(p. 14) Article, with 1 table showing world ethylene production, by feedstock, 1984, 1989, and 1994. Data are from DeWitt & Co, Inc.

PLASTICS EXPAND INTO NEW MARKETS

(p. 23-48) By Bruce F. Greek. Article, with 1 chart repeated for 8 thermoplastic and thermoset resins, showing consumption distribution by end use; and 1 chart showing plastics market shares by end use; all for 1985. Data are from Society of the Plastics Industry and C&EN estimates.

A1250–1.629: June 10, 1985 (Vol. 63, No. 23)

GROWING PAINS GIVE BIOTECHNOLOGY FIRMS MIXED RESULTS IN QUARTER, QUARTERLY FEATURE

(p. 9-10) Quarterly article, by David Webber, with 1 table showing revenues, earnings, and profit margins, for 12 biotechnology firms, 1st quarter 1985, with comparisons to 1984.

MAGNESIUM OUTLOOK CONTINUES TO BE BRIGHT

(p. 11) Article, with 2 tables showing magnesium consumption by end use and world area, 1984-85 and 1989. Data are from the International Magnesium Assn.

INTEREST HEIGHTENS IN DEVELOPMENT OF EASTERN OIL SHALE RESOURCES

(p. 17-19) By Joseph Haggin. Article, with 1 undated table showing mining area and recoverable resources of eastern oil shale, for 6 States. Data are from the Institute of Gas Technology.

FACTS AND FIGURES FOR THE CHEMICAL INDUSTRY ANNUAL REPORT

(p. 22-66) Annual fact book, for 1984, on U.S. chemical industry production, finances, performance, employment, and trade, with selected data for related industries and foreign countries.

Data are from government agency, trade assn, and manufacturers' reports, and include trends from 1974.

Includes 5 sections, with subsections for foreign countries, each presenting a narrative summary with text statistics, and the tables described below.

This is the 29th annual report.

PRODUCTION

(p. 24-31) "Production Increased Only Weakly in 1984." Includes 15 tables showing:

a. Production for 50 largest volume chemicals, 1983-84, and average annual percent change, selected periods 1974-84, by chemical ranked by volume. 1 table.

b. Industrial production indexes for manufacturing; nondurable manufacturing; chemicals, synthetic materials, and chemical products, by type; petroleum products; and rubber/plastics products; 1974-84. 1 table.

c. Production and/or consumption of minerals, including iodine and potash imports, and phosphate rock exports; and production of organic and inorganic chemicals, man-made fibers, plastics, and synthetic rubber; by detailed product, 1974-84. 6 tables.

d. Fertilizer supply and demand by type, including imports and exports; and nitrogen and phosphate production, by detailed product; various years 1974-84. 4 tables.

e. Energy use by chemical, fertilizer, and petroleum industries, by energy source, 1972 and 1981-84. 3 tables.

FINANCES

(p. 32-46) "Sales, Earnings, Profitability Up in 1984." Includes 13 tables showing:

a. Shipment value for all manufacturing, and selected chemicals/allied products and related industries; and PPI for all commodities, industrial commodities, 8 sectors of chemical/allied products industry, and rubber/plastic products; 1974-84. 2 tables.

b. Chemical sales, operating profits, profit margin, assets, and return on assets, for 100 largest chemical producers ranked by sales, 1984 with selected comparisons to 1983 and to total company operations. 1 table.

c. Selected operating ratios for 19 companies with sales over $1 billion and 19 companies with sales less than $1 billion, 1983-84. 1 table.

d. Capital spending, unspent capital funds, and foreign investment, for all manufacturing, and chemical and 2-6 other industries; and chemical industry capital and R&D spending, for 14-15 companies; various years 1974-85. 5 tables.

e. Chemical industry balance sheet, 1983-84; long-term debt, stockholders' equity, and debt/equity ratio for industrial chemicals/synthetics, chemicals/allied products, and all manufacturing, 1974-84; and cash flow by fund sources and applications, aggregated for 12 major chemical companies, 1980-84. 3 tables.

f. Company financial profiles, including net sales, net income, total assets, plant/equipment value, capital expenditures, net worth, stock data, and selected operating ratios, for 33 chemical and 16 pharmaceutical companies, 1981-84. 1 table.

Data clarification for this section appears in June 24, 1985 issue (see A1250-1.631 below).

EMPLOYMENT

(p. 47-49) "Chemical Workforce Growing Sluggishly." Includes 5 tables showing:

a. Total employees and production workers, workweek, and wages, for all manufacturing and 10 chemical industries, 1974 and 1982-84; and scientist/engineer employment, total and for 5 chemical industries, 1974-84. 3 tables.

b. Chemical employment for 23 companies, and aggregate sales per employee, 1975-84. 1 table.

c. Productivity indexes for chemicals/allied products and all manufacturing, 1974-84. 1 table.

Data correction for this section appears in Aug. 19, 1985 issue (see A1250-1.639 below).

FOREIGN TRADE

(p. 50-51) "World Chemical Trade Climbs to New Record." Includes 5 tables showing U.S. chemical exports and imports by product type; and U.S. and world chemical exports and imports, by country or world area of origin and destination; 1974 and 1982-84.

FOREIGN CHEMICAL INDUSTRIES

Western Europe

(p. 52-54) Includes 4 tables showing the following:

a. Chemical industry sales, exports, imports, capital spending, production and price indexes, and employment, for 10 countries; man-made fiber production for Benelux and 9 countries; and production by chemical, for 4 countries; various years 1980-84. 3 tables.

b. Major company net sales, net income, profit margin, capital and R&D spending, and employment, for 18 companies in 8 countries, 1981-84. 1 table.

Also includes 1 table showing European currency conversion values, by country, 1980-84.

Japan

(p. 55-56) Includes 3 tables showing the following for Japan:

a. Production indexes for all manufacturing, chemicals, and selected chemical process industries; and production of chemicals and plastics by type, and synthetic dyes and rubber; 1981-84. 2 tables.

b. Company sales, net income, profit margin, total assets, and employment, for 24 chemical companies, 1981-84. 1 table.

Canada

(p. 60-61) Includes 7 tables showing the following for Canada:

a. Company sales, net income, profit margin, capital expenditures, and employment, for 5 companies; and chemical production and trade, by chemical or product type; various years 1981-84. 5 tables.

b. Shipments and price indexes, for all manufacturing, chemicals/chemical products, and selected chemical process industries; various years 1980-84. 2 tables.

Mexico

(p. 62) Includes 3 tables showing Mexican chemical production, domestic sales, and imports, by chemical, 1981-84.

Eastern Europe

(p. 63-64) Includes 5 tables showing the following:

a. Production growth rate for all industries and chemical/rubber industry; and production of man-made fibers, agricultural chemicals, and various other chemical products; for 7 countries, various years 1980-84. 4 tables.

b. Soviet total and chemical exports and imports, 1974-84. 1 table.

Western Pacific

(p. 65-66) Includes 11 tables showing the following, mostly for 1981-84:

a. South Korea production, shipment, and inventory indexes for all manufacturing and for chemicals by product type; chemical production by product; and total and chemical exports and imports. 3 tables.

b. Australia and PRC chemical production, and total and/or chemical exports and imports, by chemical or product type. 5 tables.

c. Taiwan production indexes for all manufacturing and for chemicals by product type, production by chemical, and total and chemical exports and imports. 3 tables.

A1250–1.630: June 17, 1985 (Vol. 63, No. 24)

SCIENTIFIC MANPOWER: VOLUME COMPILES DATA, MAPS TRENDS

(p. 6) Article, with 1 table showing employment supply and demand for chemists and all scientists, and for chemical engineers and all engineers, 1983 and 1987. Data are from NSF.

U.S. CHEMICAL PRODUCERS WEIGH ANTIAPARTHEID TACK IN SOUTH AFRICA

(p. 20-22) By David Webber. Article, with 1 undated table showing the following for South African operations of 10 U.S. chemical companies: type of operation; percent of 1984 sales from South Africa; employment by race; and whether firm has signed Sullivan principles (voluntary code promoting social responsibility), and ratings of company's adherence to principles.

Data are from the International Council for Equality of Opportunity Principles.

A1250–1.631: June 24, 1985 (Vol. 63, No. 25)

CORRECTIONS

(p. 4) Includes correction of June 10, 1985 table presenting financial profiles of 33 chemical and 16 pharmaceutical companies. Presents data for 2 companies. Original table appears in the Finances section of Facts and Figures Report; for description, see A1250-1.629 above.

MINERAL-BASED INORGANICS FACE SLOWER PRODUCTION GROWTH: KEY CHEMICALS, ANNUAL FEATURE

(p. 12-16) Annual article, by Bruce F. Greek, reporting on supply and demand outlook for 4 inorganic chemicals: lime, sulfur, potash, and phosphorus. Includes text statistics on major derivatives and/or end uses, foreign trade, and prices, primarily 1985.

A1250–1.632: July 1, 1985 (Vol. 63, No. 26)

CHEMICAL INDUSTRY'S HEALTH CARE BENEFITS LIKELY TO CHANGE FURTHER

(p. 13-16) By David Webber. Article, with 1 table showing community hospital admissions, outpatient visits, occupancy rate, and average length of stay, 1983-84. Data are from the American Hospital Assn.

GLOBAL SHAKEOUT EXPECTED IN ETHYLENE GLYCOL

(p. 16-17) Article, with 2 charts showing worldwide demand for ethylene glycol, by end use (polyesters and antifreeze/industrial), by world area and country, 1984 and 1990. Data are from Union Carbide Ethylene Oxide Glycol Co.

A1250–1.633: July 8, 1985 (Vol. 63, No. 27)

BIOTECHNOLOGY STOCKS REGAIN LOST GROUND, RECURRING FEATURE

(p. 14) Recurring article, with 1 table showing stock prices for 15 biotechnology firms, as of June 28, 1984, and 52-week high and low prices.

ECONOMIC STATUS OF CHEMISTS SHOWS MODEST GAINS THIS YEAR, ANNUAL FEATURE

(p. 30-34) Annual article on chemists' employment and earnings as of Mar. 1985, with trends. Data are based on approximately 45,-000 responses to an ACS member survey.

Includes 9 tables showing employment status of chemical engineers, and of chemists by sex, highest degree, and minority status; chemists' salaries, by degree level, by years since bachelor's degree, sex, type of employer, major manufacturing group, job function and specialty, and academic rank; and chemists' unemployment rate, by most recent type of employer and job function and specialty; 1985, with selected trends from 1975.

Full ACS survey report is covered in SRI under A1250-4.

A1250–1.634: July 15, 1985 (Vol. 63, No. 28)

REAGAN PLAN TRIMS STRATEGIC MATERIALS STOCKPILE

(p. 4) Article, with 1 undated table showing recent Reagan Administration proposed goals for the national defense stockpile of 25 strategic materials.

EMPLOYMENT PATTERNS CHANGING IN CHEMICALS

(p. 13) Article, with 1 chart showing employment in the chemical industry, by sector, 1979 and 1st quarter 1985. Data are from the Labor Dept.

A1250–1.635: July 22, 1985 (Vol. 63, No. 29)

Facts and Figures for Chemical R&D, Annual Feature

(p. 28-56) Annual report, for 1985, on chemical R&D spending and employment in the Federal, industrial, and university sectors.

Most data are from NSF and from C&EN estimates based on Federal Government statistics, and include trends from selected previous years.

Includes introductory article, and 4 statistical sections, described below.

This is the 7th annual report.

SECTION 1: OVERVIEW

(p. 30-34) "Healthy Growth for R&D Outlays." Includes 5 charts and 10 tables showing the following:

a. Spending for total R&D, basic and applied research, and development, by sector, 1984; distribution of R&D outlays, by selected Federal functions, and for total nonfederal, 1966-85; and R&D funding and spending, by sector, and funding by character of research, in current and constant 1972 dollars, 1975-85. 5 charts and 7 tables.

b. Employed scientists and engineers, by type, 1983; and distribution of research papers in *Chemical Abstracts* by subject field, and number of U.S. patents granted to U.S. and foreign residents, various years 1974-84. 3 tables.

SECTION 2: FEDERAL GOVERNMENT

(p. 35-41) "Most of the Growth Focuses on Defense." Includes 9 tables showing the following Federal R&D obligations: for total R&D, basic and applied research (with detail for chemistry and physical science), development, and engineering and chemical engineering research, by dept or agency; and for total research and university total and basic research, by scientific discipline; various years FY79-85.

SECTION 3: INDUSTRY

(p. 43-49) "Industry Hiked Spending 10% Last Year." Includes 9 charts and 14 tables showing the following:

a. Federally and company funded industrial R&D, and development and basic and applied research spending, with detail for chemical and drug industries; and spending for applied R&D on chemicals, by chemical type, and on chemicals and drugs, by major manufacturing group; various years 1969-84. 8 tables.

b. R&D spending: for 15 major chemical companies, 1975-85; amount spent abroad by U.S. companies (with detail for chemical and drug industries), 1974-84; and by company employment and R&D budget size (for total industry, chemical/allied products, and industrial chemicals R&D), 1983. 8 charts and 2 tables.

c. R&D scientist/engineer employment by industry sector, cost per employee, and comparisons to total employment, with detail for selected chemical industries, various years 1971-84; and employment distribution for chemists, by industry sector and degree level, 1985. 1 chart and 4 tables.

SECTION 4: UNIVERSITIES AND COLLEGES

(p. 53-56) "Funding Shows Biggest Gain Since 1981." Includes 1 chart and 10 tables showing the following:

a. University R&D spending, by funding source and research type and field, 1974-84; top 12 universities and university R&D centers ranked by R&D spending, with detail by research field, FY83; and total and full-time university scientists and engineers, by field, 1977-78 and 1980-84. 7 tables.

b. Top 50 universities ranked by chemical R&D spending, and including federally financed spending, 1983 with comparisons to 1980-82; distribution of academic physical scientists in 1984 and physical science R&D spending in FY83, by census division; chemistry and chemical engineering degrees awarded, by level, 1965/66-1984/85; and total and full-time science and engineering graduate students, by field, 1977-83. 1 chart and 3 tables.

A1250–1.636: July 29, 1985 (Vol. 63, No. 30)

INDUSTRIAL GASES, PRODUCERS FACE MIXED DEMANDS: KEY CHEMICALS, ANNUAL FEATURE

(p. 9-13) Annual article, by Bruce F. Greek, reporting on supply and demand outlook for 4 leading industrial gases: carbon dioxide, hydrogen, nitrogen, and oxygen. Includes text statistics on major producers and end uses, foreign trade, and prices, primarily 1985.

For description of previous article, see A1250-1.604 above.

A1250–1.637: Aug. 5, 1985 (Vol. 63, No. 31)

MAJOR PIGMENTS GAIN GLOBAL COMMODITY STATUS: KEY CHEMICALS, RECURRING FEATURE

(p. 13-15) Recurring article, by Bruce F. Greek, reporting on supply and demand outlook for 2 major pigments: carbon black and titanium dioxide. Includes text statistics on end uses, foreign trade, and prices, primarily 1985.

Previous article, with data primarily through 1982, is described in SRI 1982 Annual under A1250-1.324. A similar article, with data through 1983 for titanium dioxide only, is described in SRI 1984 Annual under A1250-1.437.

CONGRESS FINALLY MOVES ON FISCAL 1986 MONEY BILLS, RECURRING FEATURE

(p. 17-18) Recurring article, by Janice R. Long, with 1 table showing R&D funding for 7 Federal agencies, by subagency, institute, or program, FY85 and Reagan Administration request and House appropriation for FY86.

Previous article, for FY84-85, is described in SRI 1984 Annual under A1250-1.531.

A1250–1.638: Aug. 12, 1985 (Vol. 63, No. 32)

CHEMICAL EARNINGS CONTINUE TO DECLINE IN SECOND QUARTER, QUARTERLY FEATURE

(p. 18-23) Quarterly article, by William J. Storck, analyzing sales, earnings, and profit margins for major U.S. chemical-producing companies, 2nd quarter 1985.

Includes 4 tables showing top 10 chemical companies in sales, earnings, and profitability; sales, earnings, and profit margin, for 30 major chemical, 15 chemical-producing oil/gas, and 25 diversified chemical-producing companies; and chemical after-tax earnings for 6 major oil companies; 2nd quarter and 1st half 1985, with selected comparisons to 1984.

DRAB FIRST HALF FOR CANADIAN CHEMICALS, SEMIANNUAL FEATURE

(p. 24) Semiannual report on Canadian chemical industry performance. Includes 1 table showing net sales, net income, and profit margin, for 4 largest companies, 1st half 1985 with comparisons to 1984.

A1250–1.639: Aug. 19, 1985 (Vol. 63, No. 33)

CORRECTION

(p. 2) Includes correction of June 10, 1985 table showing chemical industry employment. Presents data for 1 company.

Original table appears in the Employment section of Facts and Figures report; for description, see A1250–1.629 above.

EFFLUENT RULES COULD HAVE HARMFUL EFFECT ON CHEMICAL INDUSTRY

(p. 14-15) Article on impact of proposed EPA water pollution regulations on the chemical industry. Data are from an EPA survey covering approximately 1,000 plants affected by regulations.

Includes 1 undated table showing number of plants incurring compliance costs, with annual costs (total and for capital investment and operation/maintenance); median profitability and liquidity reductions, and production cost increase; plant and product line closures; and employment reductions; all for 3 possible sets of EPA guidelines.

A1250–1.640: Aug. 26, 1985 (Vol. 63, No. 34)

PLASTICS: GROWTH IS CONTINUING BUT SLOWER

(p. 4) Article, with 1 table showing shipment volume of thermoplastics and thermoset plastics, by type, 1st half 1985 with percent change from 1984. Data are from Society of the Plastics Industry.

DRUG FIRM PROFITABILITY CONTINUES TO RISE, QUARTERLY FEATURE

(p. 8) Quarterly article, with 1 table showing sales, earnings, and profit margin, for 15 pharmaceutical firms, 2nd quarter and 1st half 1985, with comparisons to 1984.

A1250–1.641: Sept. 2, 1985 (Vol. 63, No. 35)

CARBIDE RESTRUCTURES: PROBLEMS PROMPT MASSIVE CUTBACK

(p. 6-7) Article on reactor vessel eruption and resulting chemical leak at a Union Carbide plant in Institute, W. Va., on Aug. 11, 1985. Data are from Union Carbide Corp. Includes 1 table showing emissions of 23 pollutants during the accident.

A1250–1.642: Sept. 9, 1985 (Vol. 63, No. 36)

CHEMICAL COMPANIES INCREASE CASH ASSETS, RECURRING FEATURE

(p. 19) Recurring article, with 1 table showing the following for 13 chemical companies: cash/marketable security assets, current ratio, and cash ratio, 2nd quarter 1984-85 and 1st quarter 1985. Data are from a C&EN survey.

Previous article, with data for 3rd quarter 1983, is described in SRI 1984 Annual under A1250–1.509.

A1250–1.643: Sept. 16, 1985 (Vol. 63, No. 37)

PRODUCTION SLOWS FOR PLASTICS INTERMEDIATES: KEY CHEMICALS, RECURRING FEATURE

(p. 15-18) Recurring article, by Bruce F. Greek, reporting on supply and demand outlook for 3 major plastics starting materials: vinyl chloride, styrene, and toluene diisocyanate. Includes text statistics on major derivatives and end uses, foreign trade, and prices, primarily 1985.

Previous article, with data for 1981-83, is described in SRI 1983 Annual under A1250–1.431.

BULK DRUG OUTPUT MOVES OUTSIDE U.S.

(p. 25-59) By Stephen C. Stinson. Article, with 2 tables showing volume of bulk drug consumption for U.S., Western Europe, Japan, and rest of world, by drug type; and volume (total and for medicinal use) and value of drug consumption, by specific drug, aggregate for U.S., Western Europe, and Japan; 1982. Data are from SRI International.

A1250–1.644: Sept. 23, 1985 (Vol. 63, No. 38)

CANADA'S CHEMICAL INDUSTRY SPLIT OVER CANADA-U.S. FREE TRADE ISSUE

(p. 7-13) By Earl V. Anderson. Article on foreign trade performance of Canada's chemical industry. Data sources include Canadian Dept of Regional Industrial Expansion and U.S. Census Bureau.

Includes 2 tables and 4 charts showing Canada's chemical exports to and imports from U.S. and all other countries, by product type, and including comparisons to U.S. chemical trade with Canada and rest of world, 1984; and Canadian and U.S. tariff rates for petrochemicals, by product type, Jan. 1987.

BIOTECHNOLOGY FIRMS POST VARIED RESULTS IN SECOND QUARTER, QUARTERLY FEATURE

(p. 15-16) Quarterly article, by David Webber, with 1 table showing revenues, earnings, and profit margins, for 15 biotechnology firms, 2nd quarter and 1st half 1985, with comparisons to 1984.

BLEAK FUTURE PREDICTED FOR PETROCHEMICALS

(p. 17) Article, with 1 table showing ethylene consumption, by chemical end product, quinquennially 1974-94. Data are from Data Resources, Inc.

A1250–1.645: Sept. 30, 1985 (Vol. 63, No. 39)

CHEMICAL CAPITAL SPENDING UP SLIGHTLY

(p. 10) Article, with 1 table showing capital expenditures (total, full-year estimate, and as percent of annual budget), for 10 major chemical companies, 1st half 1985 with comparisons to 1984. Data are from a C&EN survey.

PAINTS AND COATINGS: THE GLOBAL CHALLENGE, ANNUAL FEATURE

(p. 27-68) Annual article, by Patricia L. Layman, on trends and outlook for the paint (coating) industry. Data sources include C&EN. Includes 1 table and 5 charts showing the following:

a. Top 15 countries ranked by paint production, generally 1984 with change from 1983; and market volume for architectural and special purpose coatings, by end use, and for original equipment manufacturer finishes, by industry sector, 1985.

b. Aggregate paint industry shipments for 4, 8, and 20 largest firms shown as percent of total industry shipments, selected years 1967-85; and distribution of production costs for a typical can of paint, by item (no date).

A1250–1.646: Oct. 14, 1985 (Vol. 63, No. 41)

CHEMICAL INDUSTRY HONES POLICY FOR UPCOMING TRADE NEGOTIATIONS

(p. 26-28) By Earl V. Anderson. Article, with 1 table showing U.S. chemical trade with industrialized and developing nations, by country or world area of origin and destination, 1984. Data are from Census Bureau.

A1250–1.647: Oct. 21, 1985 (Vol. 63, No. 42)

HURTING SYNTHETIC FIBER PRODUCERS LOOK FOR NEW CURBS ON IMPORTS: KEY POLYMERS, ANNUAL FEATURE

(p. 15-18) Annual article, by Bruce F. Greek, reporting on supply and demand outlook for 3 synthetic fibers: polyester, nylon, and acrylic. Includes text statistics on major end uses, foreign trade, and prices, primarily 1985.

A1250–1.648: Oct. 28, 1985 (Vol. 63, No. 43)

1986 EMPLOYMENT OUTLOOK, ANNUAL FEATURE

Annual compilation of articles on career planning and job market outlook for chemical professionals. Includes a brief introduction (p. 27), and the recurring statistical article described below.

DEMAND, RECURRING FEATURE

(p. 40-44) Recurring article, with 1 table showing chemistry and chemical engineering degrees awarded, by degree level, 1973/74-1983/84. Data are from NCES.

Previous article is described in SRI 1982 Annual under A1250–1.349.

A1250–2   1984 SURVEY REPORT: Starting Salaries and Employment Status of Chemistry and Chemical Engineering Graduates
Annual. 1984. v+67 p.
SRI/MF/complete

Annual report on starting salaries, employment status, and advanced study plans of 1983/84 chemistry and chemical engineering graduates, by highest degree, sex, certification status (for chemists only), and degree or planned study field.

Also includes data by professional experience, employer type, census division, citizenship status, age, number of job offers, race, and ethnicity (American Indian, Asian, and Hispanic); and various cross-tabulations. Salaries generally are shown as medians and means.

Data are from responses of 3,768 graduates to a summer 1984 survey.

Contains contents listing (p. iii); summary with 5 tables (p. 1-11); technical notes and table listing (p. 13-17); survey results, in 6 sections, with 46 tables (p. 18-63); and questionnaire facsimile (p. 65-67).

Availability: American Chemical Society, Distribution Office, 1155 16th St., NW, Washington DC 20036, $10.00; SRI/MF/complete.

A1250–3   PROFESSIONALS IN CHEMISTRY: 1983-84 A Digest of Information About the Chemical Profession

Biennial.   July 1985.
ix + 107 p.
ISSN 0732-460X.
LC SC 82-4034.
SRI/MF/complete

Biennial compilation, for 1983-84, on the chemical profession, with data on education, earnings, employment, and R&D. Includes selected trends from 1955 and projections to 2000. Data sources are identified for each table, and include NCES, American Chemical Society (ACS), and NSF.

Contains listing of contents, tables, and charts, and introduction (p. iii-ix); and report in 4 chapters, with brief narratives, 27 summary charts, and 2 charts and 51 tables listed below (p. 1-107).

This is the 8th edition of the report. For description of previous edition, see SRI 1983 Annual under this number.

Availability: American Chemical Society, Distribution Office, 1155 16th St., NW, Washington DC 20036, $29.95; SRI/MF/complete.

CHARTS AND TABLES:
[The listing below includes all tables, and selected charts presenting substantial statistics not covered in tables. Number gaps in the listing reflect omitted charts.]

A1250–3.1: Education

WOMEN AND MINORITIES IN QUANTITATIVE FIELDS

1.1.1-1.1.4. [Status of women and minorities (including data by race and for Hispanics, American Indians, and Asian Americans) in quantitative fields, by degree level, with comparisons to all persons in quantitative fields and to total age-relevant population, 1978/79.] (p. 2-5)

HIGH SCHOOL GRADUATES

1.1.5. Annual high school graduates, [aggregate for] fifty States and the District of Columbia, actuals 1975-82 and projected 1983-2000. (p. 6)

1.1.8. Pattern of projected high school graduates [percent change from 1981 in number of graduates, by region and for total U.S., selected years 1985-99]. [chart] (p. 9)

DEGREES
[Data are shown by degree level.]

1.2.1. Degrees granted by U.S. colleges: total, chemistry, chemical engineering, and biochemistry [1970-82 and projected 1983-94]. (p. 11)

1.2.2. Chemistry degrees granted to women [1955/56-1982/83]. (p. 12)

1.2.3. Estimates of chemistry degrees granted to minorities [black, American Indian, Asian/Pacific Islander, Hispanic, and non-U.S. citizen, 1973/74-1982/83]. (p. 13)

1.2.4. Chemistry and chemical engineering degrees awarded by [ACS] approved schools [by institution], 1982/83. (p. 14-18)

UNDERGRADUATE AND GRADUATE STUDY IN CHEMISTRY

1.3.1. ACS member's ratings of [selected chemistry and other] core undergraduate courses [in own and current curricula, no date]. (p. 19)

1.3.2. Postgraduation plans of chemistry and chemical engineering BS graduates, 1973-84. (p. 20)

1.4.2. Sources of [financial] support in graduate school of doctorate recipients, by sex and summary field, 1983. (p. 22)

1.4.3. Postgraduation plans of doctorate recipients entering the U.S. labor force, by field of doctorate, 1969-83. (p. 23)

A1250–3.2: Earnings

2.1.1-2.1.3. Starting yearly salaries of inexperienced full-time employed chemistry and chemical engineering graduates, by degree [level and percentile], summer 1983-84; and median starting salaries of BS inexperienced chemists in private industry, by sex, 1971-84. (p. 25-27)

2.1.6. Number and average starting monthly salary offers to inexperienced bachelor's degree candidates, by curriculum, July 1982-83. (p. 30)

2.1.7. Average starting salaries of doctoral recipients in business and industry, [by field], 1983. (p. 31)

2.2.1. Median yearly salaries of ACS member chemists, by degree [level, in current and constant (1967) dollars], 1960-84. (p. 35)

2.2.2. Median yearly salaries [starting and 20-24 years since BS] of nonacademic BS and PhD [ACS member] chemists, 1970-84. (p. 36)

2.2.3. Salary factors for industrial and academic chemists [base salaries and variance factors related to degree level, years since receiving BS, work function, academic rank, highest degree offered in dept, and private vs. public institutional control, 1984]. (p. 38-39)

2.3.1. Salaries paid nonacademic [ACS member] PhD chemists compared with a family budget for selected metropolitan areas [Mar. 1984]. (p. 40)

2.3.2. Median income of year round full-time workers 25 years or older, by years of education, 1983. (p. 41)

2.3.3. Salaries of scientists/engineers in R&D, by profession and degree level, 1982-83. (p. 42)

2.3.4. Median annual salaries of doctoral scientists/engineers, by years since PhD, field, and sex, 1983. (p. 43)

A1250–3.3: Employment and Demographic Characteristics

A-B. Employment status of chemists according to [sex and] race [minority and nonminority]; and unemployment rate of chemists by [most recent] work function; [no dates]. (p. 46)

3.1.1-3.1.2. Post-doctoral fellows as a percent of PhD recipients, 1973-83; and unemployment trends among new BS degree recipients, 1980-83; [all for chemists and chemical engineers]. (p. 53-54)

3.1.3. Age distribution of unemployed ACS members, 1980-84. (p. 55)

3.1.4-3.1.6. Scientists and engineers, by field and race [including Asian and Native Americans]: total population, total employed, and employed in science/engineering, 1982. (p. 56-58)

3.1.8. Doctorate recipients entering the U.S. labor force, by citizenship [status] and field of study, [biennially] 1959-83. (p. 60)

3.2.2-3.2.3. Projected employment in science occupations; and projected growth rates of defense and nondefense employment in major set occupations; [all by occupation, for 2 economic growth scenarios], 1982-87 [period]. (p. 62-63)

3.2.8. Supply/demand balance of scientists and engineers [by occupation], based on a net mobility supply model, 1983 and 1987. (p. 68)

3.2.9. Comparisons of projected job openings [for 4 economic growth scenarios] with projected degrees [by level] in science and engineering [by field], 1978-1990 [period]. (p. 69)

A1250–3.4: Chemistry R&D Funding

4.2.3. Federal basic and applied research funding, by field of science, 1967, 1980, and 1984. (p. 86)

4.2.5. Research time in universities [by field and sponsorship (Federal, other, and nonsponsored), for year ending Oct. 1979]. (p. 88)

4.3.1. Budget authority for basic research, by function [1982-84]. (p. 89)

4.3.2. Federal R&D funding, by budget function [1974-84]. (p. 90)

4.3.4-4.3.5. Federal obligations for R&D, by character of work, 1982-84 [chart]; and by performer [including Federal and State/local government, industry, universities/colleges, Federally Funded R&D Centers, other nonprofit institutions, and foreign], FY74 and FY82-FY84. (p. 93)

4.4.1-4.5.1. [Value of] programs supporting chemistry at NSF [by area of research; and value of] support of basic research in chemistry at DOD [by military branch; FY83-FY85]. (p. 94, 97)

4.5.2. Chemical sciences: DOE [operating expenses by area of research, and expenditures on capital equipment and construction, FY83-FY85]. (p. 98)

4.5.3-4.5.5. [Value of] programs supporting chemistry at DOE, EPA, and National Bureau of Standards, [by area of research, FY83-FY85]. (p. 99-101)

4.6.3. Estimated private R&D spending [as percent of sales, by industry group], 1979-83. (p. 104)

4.6.4. Company funds for R&D by selected industry [group], actual 1981-82 and projected 1983-84. (p. 105)

4.6.5. Distribution of company-funded foreign and domestic R&D expenditures among major R&D performing industries, 1981. (p. 106)

4.6.6. Company R&D performed by foreign affiliates of U.S. domestic companies outside the U.S., by selected industry [group], 1974-81. (p. 107)

A1275
American
College of Surgeons

A1275-1   SOCIO-ECONOMIC FACTBOOK FOR SURGERY, 1985
Annual. 1985. 106 p.
SRI/MF/not filmed

Annual fact book of the surgical profession, presenting data on surgeon supply, specialties, finances, operative procedures, and education, with comparisons to other medical specialties, various years 1950-83. Also includes data on hospital utilization, health expenditures and insurance, medical costs, and general population characteristics.

Data were compiled by the American College of Surgeons (ACS) Surgical Practice Dept from reports of medical assns, Federal agencies, and related professional sources.

Contains contents/chart/table listing (p. 3-5); statistical sections A-F, with 8 charts and 41 tables, listed below (p. 7-65); and narrative sections G-I, with descriptions of related medical commissions and boards, HHS organization chart, list of congressional committees with health jurisdiction, Federal health legislation, and ACS policy statements (p. 67-106).

Availability: American College of Surgeons, Surgical Practice Department, 55 E. Erie St., Chicago IL 60611, †; SRI/MF/not filmed.

CHARTS AND TABLES:

[Data by surgical specialty are generally shown for colon/rectal, general, neurological, orthopedic, plastic, and thoracic surgery; obstetrics/gynecology; ophthalmology; otolaryngology; and urology. All data are shown for U.S.]

A1275-1.1: Sections A-B: Medical Education and Surgical Manpower

MEDICAL EDUCATION

1-2. Number of operational medical schools, and [total and female] medical students and medical school graduates; and number of filled residency positions [total and foreign medical graduates in primary care, all specialties, and surgical specialties; selected years 1949/50-1983/84]. (p. 8-9)

3-4. Filled 1st-year surgical residency positions [by specialty], and filled 1st-year primary care residency positions [by type of practice], 1974/75-1983/84. (p. 10-11)

SURGICAL MANPOWER

[Data by major professional activity include office- and hospital-based patient care, medical teaching, administration, research, and other.]

5-6. Number of Federal/nonfederal physicians and per 100,000 population [total, surgeons, and primary care physicians, various years 1950-82. [chart and table] (p. 14-15)

7. Federal/nonfederal surgeons by specialty and major professional activity, 1982. (p. 16)

8-11. Active women surgeons and foreign medical graduates by surgical specialty and major professional activity, [1970 and 1980, and 1982]. (p. 17-20)

12-13. Annual certificates issued in surgical and nonsurgical specialties, 1974-83. (p. 21-22)

14. ACS fellowship [active and retired membership by specialty], Dec. 1983. (p. 23)

15. ACS [active] fellows and initiates [in general surgery and other specialties], 1974-83. (p. 24)

A1275-1.2: Section C: Selected Data on Hospitals and Use of Services

16-18. Total and short-term nonfederal hospitals, beds, and admissions; and short-term nonfederal hospital [outpatient visits, occupancy rate, average length of stay], assets, expenses, and personnel; [selected years 1950-83]. (p. 26-28)

19. Number of patients discharged from short-stay hospitals with and without operation [by patient age group and sex, census region, and hospital bed size group], 1982. (p. 29)

20. Rate of discharges from short-stay hospitals, by diagnostic class and age, 1982. [chart] (p. 30-31)

21. Ten most frequent operative procedures [and rate per 1,000 population] for patients discharged from short-stay hospitals, 1975-82. (p. 32-33)

22. Cardiovascular operations and procedures [by type], 1980-82. (p. 34)

23. Operative procedures [and rate per 1,000 population, and average length of stay], for patients discharged from short-stay hospitals, by patient age, 1975-82. (p. 35-36)

24. Average length of stay for selected operative procedures [and number performed], for patients discharged from short-stay hospitals, 1982. (p. 37)

25. Patient visits to office-based physicians [by specialty], 1981. (p. 38)

26. Settings used by physicians who perform ambulatory surgery [distribution among hospital-based and freestanding ambulatory surgery centers, and physician offices, by type of practice], 1982. (p. 39)

27. Percent of procedures performed on hospital outpatient basis by type of hospital [nonfederal, non-profit, and profit hospitals, by bed size and census division], 1982. (p. 40)

A1275-1.3: Section D: Medical Economics

[Tables and charts 28-36 show data for various years 1950-83.]

28-30. National health expenditures: [total, and personal health care portion financed by private and public sources; percent distribution] by object; and as percent of GNP. [1 table and 2 charts] (p. 42-44)

31-32. Percent of Federal budget outlays, by function; and percent of personal spending, by product. (p. 45-46)

33-34. Ratio of personal spending for medical care to disposable personal income and to total personal spending [and total amounts]; and sources of funds for personal health expenditures [direct consumer payments, insurance benefits, public, and other]. [1 table and 1 chart] (p. 47-48)

35-36. CPI for selected and medical care items. (p. 49-50)

37. Annual percentage change in CPI [by item, selected years 1960/61-1982/83]. (p. 51)

38. Average net income from medical practice by specialty [selected years 1970-83]. (p. 52)

39. Average physician professional expenses by specialty, 1983. [chart] (p. 53)

40. Average surgeons' fees for selected procedures and geographic areas [6 metro and 6 nonmetro areas], 1983. (p. 54)

A1275-1.4: Sections E-F: Health Insurance and Population Characteristics

HEALTH INSURANCE

41-42. Number of persons with private health insurance protection for hospital and surgical care [under Blue Cross-Blue Shield, commercial insurance, and independent plan coverage]; and benefit payments of private health insurance organizations [Blue Cross-Blue Shield/other plans, and commercial insurance companies; decennially 1950-80 and 1982]. (p. 56-57)

43. Number of persons with private health insurance protection by type of coverage and percent of population covered [for ages under 65 and 65/over], 1982. (p. 58)

44-45. Medicaid recipients and payments, and Medicare enrollment and benefit payments, [selected years 1970-83]. (p. 59-60)

POPULATION CHARACTERISTICS

46. Total resident population, and life expectancy at birth [by sex, decennially 1950-80 and 1982]. (p. 62)

47. Percentage distribution of resident population by age [decennially 1960-80 and 1982]. [chart] (p. 63)

48. Trends in death rates [including infant and maternal, and for 6 leading causes, selected years 1920-82]. (p. 64)

49. Median income for families, and [for] individuals [by sex, decennially 1950-80 and 1982]. [chart] (p. 65)

A1305
American
Correctional Association

A1305-2   PROBATION AND PAROLE DIRECTORY
Triennial. 1985.
xviii+495 p.
ISSN 0732-0965.
ISBN 0-942974-53-0.
LC 82-641863.
SRI/MF/complete

Triennial directory of Federal, State, local, Canadian Province, and 3 U.S. territory probation and parole agencies, as of Feb. 1, 1985. Presents the following data for most agencies: officials and services; annual budget; starting salaries by position; employment by position (often including volunteers and/or part-time paid employees), by sex; and adult and juvenile client caseload, by sex and case type; FY84 and/or Feb. 1985.

Also includes State summary data on agency policies, including charges to clients for services, and employee education and training requirements.

Data are from an ACA survey.

Contains contents listing, introductory material, and user guide (p. vi-xvii); directory (p. 1-454); appendices, with narrative articles, statistical summary including tabulated survey responses, and ACA organization and publications (p. 456-479); and glossary and bibliography (p. 481-492).

This is the 2nd edition. For description of previous edition, for 1981, see SRI 1982 Annual under this number.

Availability: American Correctional Association, 4321 Hartwick Rd., Suite L-208, College Park MD 20740, members $28.00, nonmembers $35.00; SRI/MF/complete.

A1305–3 1985 JUVENILE AND ADULT CORRECTIONAL DEPARTMENTS, INSTITUTIONS, AGENCIES, AND PAROLING AUTHORITIES, U.S. and Canada
Annual. 1985.
xxxviii+545 p.
ISBN 0-942974-62-X.
LC 79-1870.
SRI/MF/complete, delayed

Annual statistical directory of U.S. and Canadian correctional facilities, as of June 30, 1984.. Includes data on inmates, cost of care, personnel, and death sentences, by facility and/or State. Data are primarily from ACA surveys.

Contents:

a. Foreword and contents listing. (p. iv-viii)

b. Information summaries, with 1 map, 2 charts, 13 tables listed below, and user's guide. (p. x-xxxviii)

c. Directories of correctional facilities and parole services, by agency and type within each jurisdiction, generally including each facility's inmate capacity and average 1984 population, programs available, cost of care, and/or number of employees; grouped by State, U.S. territory, Federal agency including military branches, and for Canadian Federal institutions and by Province, as of June 30, 1984. (p. 1-467)

d. ACA organizational overview and publications list, and indexes. (p. 469-545)

This is the 45th edition of the directory.

Availability: American Correctional Association, 4321 Hartwick Rd., Suite L-208, College Park MD 20740, members $28.00, nonmembers $35.00 or 20% discount with purchase of any 2 or more Assn. directories; SRI/MF/complete, delayed shipment with SRI 1985 Annual.

TABLES:
[Tables show data as of June 30, 1984, unless otherwise noted. Data by race/ethnicity include Hispanics. Most tables show data by sex.

Tables show data by State, and variously also include D.C., Philadelphia, New York City, Cook County, Ill., Federal Bureau of Prisons, U.S. prison or parole commission, Correctional Services of Canada and/or Canada by Province, Guam, Puerto Rico, and occasionally other U.S. territories.]

[1] Fiscal information [adult and juvenile corrections operating budgets, capital expenditures, and projects]. (p. x-xi)

[2] Adult inmate population [by race/ethnicity and security level, with totals 1980-84]. (p. xii-xiii)

[3] Adult offender statistics [numbers committed but pending in county jails, committed to other States, under 18 in adult systems, over age 55, on furlough/supervised release, on work release, on escape status, and in State-operated and contract community homes by sex]. (p. xiv)

[4] Juveniles under supervision [in institutions by race/ethnicity; and in detention, diagnostic/evaluation centers, group homes, and day/foster care]. (p. xvi-xvii)

[5] Clients on probation, parole/aftercare. (p. xviii-xiv)

[6] Characteristics of adult paroling authorities [agency name, whether independent, number of board members, whether serving board full-time, and agency handling field services]. (p. xx)

[7] Personnel information [adult and juvenile system employees by race/ethnicity]. (p. xxii-xxiii)

[8] Correctional officers in adult systems [by race/ethnicity]. (p. xxiv)

[9] Adult and juvenile correctional departments/institutions under court order [including number of institutions affected]. (p. xxvi)

[10] Death sentence survey [whether death sentence exists; number of prisoners sentenced to death, by sex and race/ethnicity, including Asians/Pacific Islanders and American Indians; and intended method of execution; with summary trends from 1978]. (p. xxviii)

[11] Positions of adult and juvenile corrections in State government [State agencies assigned jurisdiction over corrections, and effective date]. (p. xxx)

[12-13] Adult and juvenile facilities and programs [listed in directory]. (p. xxxiv-xxxvi)

A1325
American
Council of Life Insurance

A1325–1 1984 LIFE INSURANCE FACT BOOK
Annual. [1984.] 128 p.
LC 47-27134.
SRI/MF/complete

Annual comprehensive fact book on the life insurance industry, including data on life insurance purchases, ownership, and benefit payments; and on insurance company reserves, income, assets, obligations, establishments, and employment; 1983, with historical trends from 1759.

Data are from American Council of Life Insurance surveys, company annual statements, commercial life insurance statistics publishers, and reports of Federal agencies.

Contains foreword and contents listing (p. 3-4); highlights, including 1 summary table and 2 charts (p. 5-8); 84 tables, listed below, accompanied by narrative summaries and illustrative charts (p. 9-105); and directory of State insurance officials, comparative mortality tables, life insurance industry chronology and listings of organizations and assns, glossary, and index (p. 107-128).

This is the 39th annual report.

Previous fact book, for 1983, is described in SRI 1983 Annual, under this number.

Availability: American Council of Life Insurance, Information and Reference Service, 1850 K St., NW, Washington DC 20006-2284, †; SRI/MF/complete.

TABLES:
[Historical data prior to approximately 1965 usually are for selected years only.]

A1325–1.1: Policy Purchases and Ownership

PURCHASES
[Tables [1-2] and [5] show data exclusive of policy revivals, increases, and dividend additions; tables [1-2] also show data exclusive of reinsurance acquired.]

[1] Purchases of ordinary life insurance by State [1977-83]. (p. 9)

[2] Life insurance purchases [ordinary, group, industrial, and total, 1940-83]. (p. 10)

[3] Analysis of ordinary life insurance purchases [by age, sex, and income of insured, and by size and detailed type of policy, 1973 and 1983]. (p. 11)

[4] Distribution of ordinary life insurance purchases by plan of insurance [1955-83]. (p. 12)

[5] Life insurance purchases in U.S. life insurance companies [ordinary, group, industrial, and total, 1921-83]. (p. 13)

OWNERSHIP SUMMARY DATA
[Tables [6-10] show data for ordinary, group, industrial, and credit policies.]

[6-9] Life insurance in force: [total, 1900-83]; by State and by [census] division, 1983; and by [policy] plan [1977 and 1981]. (p. 15-19)

[10] Average size life insurance policy in force [1920-83]. (p. 20)

[11] Life insurance and disposable personal income per family [1930-83]. (p. 21)

[12] Average amount of life insurance in force per family by State [and census division], 1983. (p. 22)

[13] Life insurance in force in U.S. life insurance companies [1900-83]. (p. 22)

ORDINARY LIFE INSURANCE
[14] Ordinary life insurance in force [in the U.S. and in U.S. life insurance companies, 1895-1983]. (p. 23)

[15] Mass-marketed ordinary life insurance in force by type and by size of insured group, 1983. (p. 24)

[16] Distribution of the amount of ordinary life insurance in force, by plan of insurance [1954-81]. (p. 25)

[17] Variable and universal life insurance in force [in U.S. companies 1976-82, and in the U.S. 1983]. (p. 26)

GROUP LIFE INSURANCE
[18] Group life insurance in force [in the U.S., and in U.S. life insurance companies, 1912-83]. (p. 27)

[19] Employee and dependent coverage under group life insurance [master policies and amount purchased and in force, by type], 1983. (p. 28)

[20] Group life insurance in force, by type and by size of insured group, 1983. (p. 29)

INDUSTRIAL AND CREDIT LIFE INSURANCE

[21] Industrial life insurance in force [in the U.S., and in U.S. life insurance companies, 1895-1983]. (p. 30)

[22] Home service life insurance in force [1970-83]. (p. 31)

[23] Credit life insurance in force [in the U.S., and in U.S. life insurance companies, 1917-83]. (p. 32)

LIFE INSURANCE AND AMERICAN FAMILIES

[Tables 24-25] show data for all, agent-marketed individual, and employee group life insurance.]

[24] Ownership of life insurance by adults [percent insured, by sex, age, and amount of coverage; and average coverage for men, women, wives, and children]; 1976. (p. 34)

[25] Ownership of life insurance by households (percent of households in which at least 1 member owns life insurance) [by household composition], 1976. (p. 34)

A1325–1.2: Annuities and Benefit Payments

ANNUITIES

[1] Individual annuities and supplementary contracts in force, 1983. (p. 35)

[2] Variable annuity plans [in force, considerations, and variable annuities in course of payment, for group and individual plans], 1983. (p. 36)

BENEFIT PAYMENTS

[3-4] Life insurance and annuity benefit payments [death payments, matured endowments, disability and annuity payments, surrender values, and policy dividends, 1940-83, and by State, 1983]. (p. 37-38)

[5-6] Payments to life insurance beneficiaries [1940-83; and] by State, 1983; [both by type, including ordinary, group, and industrial]. (p. 40-41)

[7] Analysis of payments to life insurance beneficiaries [by sex and age of insured at death, beneficiary sex and relationship to insured, policy duration, and method of payment, Apr. 1981]. (p. 42)

[8-9] Payments to life insurance policyholders and annuitants [1940-83]. (p. 43-44)

[10] Analysis of payments of matured endowments and surrender values [by sex and age of insured, policy duration, and method of payment, Apr. 1977 and Apr. 1981]. (p. 45)

[11] Use of life insurance benefits under supplementary contracts [benefits set aside and payments from accumulated funds, 1945-83]. (p. 46)

[12] Health insurance benefit payments [group and individual, paid by life insurance companies, 1948-83]. (p. 47)

A1325–1.3: Retirement Plans and Life Insurance Voluntary Terminations

PENSIONS AND RETIREMENT PROGRAMS

[1-2] Number of persons covered, and assets and reserves of major [private and government-administered, including railroad retirement and OASDI] pension and retirement programs [various years 1940-83]. (p. 49-50)

[3] Private pension plans with life insurance companies [plans and persons covered, total and separate account reserves, payments into

plans, persons receiving payment, and pension payments, by plan type, including individual retirement accounts and Keogh plans, 1981-83]. (p. 53)

TERMINATIONS

[4] Voluntary termination rate (ordinary policies in force) [less than 2 years and 2 years/more, 1951-83]. (p. 54)

A1325–1.4: Industry Financial Data

[Tables [1-2], [4-13], and [15-26] show data for U.S. life insurance companies.]

PREMIUM AND INVESTMENT INCOME

[1] Income [life, annuity, and health insurance premiums; and investment, other, and total income; 1911-83]. (p. 55)

[2] Premium receipts [life, annuity, and health insurance premiums, by type of plan, 1979-83]. (p. 56)

[3] Ratio of premiums and annuity considerations to disposable personal income [1929-83]. (p. 57)

[4] Ordinary life insurance premium receipts [1st year, single, renewal, and total, 1969-83]. (p. 58)

[5] Premium receipts by State [for life and health insurance, 1981-83]. (p. 59)

[6] Net rate of investment income [1915-83]. (p. 60)

[7] Life insurance company dollar [income and how used], 1983. (p. 61)

TAXES

[8] Taxes, licenses, and fees [by type, 1947-83]. (p. 63)

RESERVES AND OBLIGATIONS

[9] Policy reserves [total life insurance companies, 1890-1950; and for life, health, individual, and group insurance, and supplementary contracts with and without life contingencies, 1955-83]. (p. 64)

[10] Life insurance policy reserves by type [1956-83]. (p. 66)

[11] Obligations and surplus funds [by designated purpose, 1952-83]. (p. 66)

ASSETS

[12] Distribution of assets [amount and percent for government securities, corporate bonds and stocks, mortgages, real estate, policy loans, and miscellaneous assets, 1917-83]. (p. 68)

[13] Assets [1890-1983]. (p. 69)

[14] Sources of funds in the U.S. money and capital markets [14 types, including insurance companies, savings/loan assns, mutual savings and commercial banks, Federal Reserve banks, and mutual funds, selected years 1970-83]. (p. 69)

ACQUISITIONS OF INVESTMENTS

[15] Acquisitions of investments [government and corporate securities, mortgages, real estate, and policy loans, 1947-83]. (p. 71)

[16] Acquisitions and change in holdings of investments [for government and corporate securities; mortgages, including VA and FHA; real estate; policy loans; cash; and other and total assets; 1982-83]. (p. 73)

INVESTMENT HOLDINGS

[Data by State include Puerto Rico, U.S. territories/possessions, Canada, and other foreign. Several tables show data both as amounts and as percent of total assets.]

[17-18] Government securities owned [Federal, State/local, and foreign]; and corporate securities owned [U.S. and foreign bonds, and common and preferred stock; 1917-83]. (p. 75-77)

[19-21] Mortgages owned [farm, and nonfarm FHA, VA, and conventional, 1890-1983, and] by State, 1983; and gross flow of [4 types of] mortgage loans [1973-83]. (p. 79-82)

[22-23] Real estate owned [1890-1983; and] by State, 1979. (p. 83-84)

[24-25] Policy loans [1890-1983]; and miscellaneous assets [1890-1955, and by type, 1960-83]. (p. 85-86)

[26] Distribution of assets held in separate accounts [by asset type, 1967-83]. (p. 87)

A1325–1.5: Establishments and Employment Data

[1-2] Number of life insurance companies [1759-1983, and] by State, midyear 1983. (p. 88-89)

[3-4] Number of life insurance companies in business, year end 1982; and change in number of life insurance companies in business [stock, mutual, and total at start and end of year, and new and discontinued operations, 1950-83]. (p. 90)

[5] Number of persons employed in insurance [1945-83]. (p. 91)

A1325–1.6: Actuarial Data

[1-2] Expectation of life at birth [1900-82; and] at various ages, 1982; [by race and sex]. (p. 92-93)

[3] Distribution of ordinary policyholder deaths by [natural or external] cause [1945-83]. (p. 95)

[4] Death rate [age-adjusted, by sex, 1915-82]. (p. 97)

[5-6] Ordinary life insurance applications [standard and extra-risk issued/paid for and not taken by applicant, and declined by company]; and standard and extra-risk ordinary life insurance [purchased and in force; 1976 and 1980]. (p. 98-99)

A1325–1.7: Miscellaneous and Foreign Life Insurance

[1] Veterans life insurance [in force, benefit payments, supplementary contract payments, and premium income, 1941-83]. (p. 100)

[2] Fraternal and savings bank life insurance [in force and purchased, and assets, benefits, and premium income, total and for savings banks in 3 States, 1978-83]. (p. 101)

[3] Ratio of life insurance in force to national income in various countries [1977 and 1982]. (p. 102)

[4] Life insurance in force in various countries [value in local currency, 1960-83]. (p. 103)

[5] Life insurance in Canada [ordinary and group purchases and insurance in force, 7 types of benefit payments, and premium income, 1982-83]. (p. 104)

[6] Distribution of assets [of Canadian life insurance companies by asset type, 1978-83]. (p. 105)

A1325–2 1984-85 PENSION FACTS

Biennial, with supplementary
updates. [1985.] 55 p.
LC 75-39762.
SRI/MF/complete

Biennial report, with supplementary updates, on private and Government-administered retirement and pension plans, 1983 and trends. Includes data on persons covered, plan assets and reserves, employer and employee contributions, and benefits. Plans covered are private plans funded with life insurance companies, other private plans, Railroad Retirement System, OASDI, and Federal and State/local government employee plans.

Also includes survey findings on income sources for recent retirees and characteristics of Individual Retirement Account (IRA) owners.

Data are from American Council of Life Insurance, Federal agencies, and other specified sources.

Contains foreword and contents listing (p. 1-2); narrative report, with 14 tables listed below (p. 3-30); pension plan history (p. 31-36); current pension topics, including survey findings with 3 tables described below (p. 37-43); and glossary and bibliography (p. 44-55).

Full report is published biennially. An update, with statistics only, is published in intervening years; for description of most recent update, see SRI 1984 Annual under this number. Previously, full report was published annually; for description of 1982 report, see SRI 1983 Annual under this number.

Availability: American Council of Life Insurance, Information and Reference Services, 1850 K St., NW, Washington DC 20006-2284, †; SRI/MF/complete.

TABLES AND SURVEY FINDINGS:

A1325–2.1: Report Tables

1-2. Number of persons covered by, and assets and reserves of, major pension and retirement programs [by type of plan, various years 1940-83]. (p. 4, 7)

3. Pension plans with life insurance companies in force at year end [number of plans, persons receiving and not yet receiving pensions, payments, benefits, and reserves, by type of plan, selected years 1950-83]. (p. 10-11)

4. Outstanding amounts in IRAs and Keogh plans with selected [types of] financial institutions, year end [1982-83]. (p. 12)

5. Variable annuity plans [number of plans and persons, variable and other reserves and considerations, persons receiving payments, and annualized income, for group and individual plans], 1983. (p. 13)

6. Life insurance company separate accounts [number of companies, accounts, and participating contracts, and assets held, by type of account, Dec. 31, 1982-83]. (p. 14)

7. Life insurance company separate accounts used solely for group pension contracts [number of accounts and participating contracts, and assets held, by type of investment, Dec. 31, 1982-83]. (p. 15)

8. Private pension plans not funded with life insurance companies [number of persons receiving and not yet receiving pensions, employer and employee contributions, and benefits paid, quinquennially 1930-75]. (p. 17)

9. Distribution of assets of noninsured private pension funds [Government securities, corporate/foreign bonds, corporate equities, mortgages, open-market paper, deposits/currency, and miscellaneous, selected years 1952-83]. (p. 18)

10. Federal OASDI program [estimated number of persons with wage credits and insured for retirement benefits, assets, and contributions of employers, employees, and self-employed, selected years 1940-83]. (p. 20)

11. Persons receiving OASDI benefits at end of year and amount of benefits during year [shown for retired workers and dependents/survivors, selected years 1940-83]. (p. 21)

12-14. Federal civilian retirement systems [civil service, Federal Reserve Board, Foreign Service, and TVA]; Railroad Retirement System; and State/local government retirement plans; [number of persons receiving and not yet receiving benefits, employer and employee contributions, benefits paid to retired/disabled workers and dependents/survivors, and assets, various years 1930-83]. (p. 24-29)

A1325–2.2: Survey Findings

SURVEYS ON RETIREMENT INCOME SOURCES AND IRA OWNER CHARACTERISTICS

(p. 38-42) Discussion of survey results, including 3 tables with the following findings:

a. Distribution of retirement income by source, for married couples and unmarried men and women. Data are from an SSA 1982 survey of 18,599 social security recipients who started receiving benefits mid-year 1980-81.

b. Number of IRAs established, and savings or salaries as source of funds; by income level, 1982. Data are from a May 1983 survey conducted by the Census Bureau.

c. Distribution of IRAs and IRA asset value by type of financial institution, 1982. Data are from responses of 3,800 households to an Apr. 1983 survey conducted by the Life Insurance Marketing and Research Assn.

A1325–4 DATA TRACK

Series. For individual
publication data, see below.
SRI/MF/complete

Series of reports on socioeconomic topics of interest to the life insurance industry. Data are from Federal and private sources, and selected opinion surveys.

Each report covers a single topic, presenting statistical data and discussion of the implications for insurance product development, market analysis, and public relations.

Reports reviewed during 1985 are described below.

Availability: American Council of Life Insurance, Social Research Services, 1850 K St., NW, Washington DC 20006-2284, †; SRI/MF/complete.

A1325–4.7: Women and Money

[Monograph. Sept. 1984. 48 p. Data Track 13. SRI/MF/complete.]

Report on the economic status of women, 1960s-80s. Most data are from the Census Bureau, BLS, and American Council of Life Insurance. Includes the following data:

a. Income of women, including data by marital status, household composition, race, education, and income source, 1982, with trends from 1960. Tables 1-7. (p. 11-17)

b. Financial assets comparisons by sex, including adult and minor shareowners of public corporations, profile of adult shareowners, life insurance purchases, and ownership of selected savings and investment products, various years 1972-83. Tables 8-12. (p. 18-22)

c. Women's labor force participation, including full- and part-time employment by marital status; women's share of employment, by occupational group; positions held by female executives, by industry division; sole proprietors and self-employed workers, by sex; and women's preferences for staying home vs. working outside the home, and reasons for working; various years 1963-83. Tables 13-20. (p. 25-31)

d. Earnings, by occupation, education, and sex; husband-wife earner structure of families, including detail by race, for Hispanics, and by presence of children; women with children and absent father, by child-support situation; widows' standard-of-living changes since husbands' death; and poverty rates, by sex, marital status, age, race, and for Hispanics; mostly for 1981 or 1982. Tables 21-28. (p. 34-41)

e. Financial knowledge and security, and willingness to take financial risk; importance attributed to Government-insured savings; use of financial advisors; and concern for price vs. quality of financial products; all by sex, various years 1976-83. Tables 29-35. (p. 43-46)

A1325–4.8: Children

[Monograph. Dec. 1984. 35 p. Data Track 14. SRI/MF/complete.]

Report examining trends in family life, and characteristics of children under age 18, 1960s-84 with selected projections to 2000. Data are from Census Bureau, BLS, National Assn of Secondary School Principals, and other private and governmental sources. Includes the following data:

a. Children by age, decennially 1960-2000; and birth rates for unmarried women by age and race, selected years 1970-81.

b. Households by presence of children and type of household; family distribution by size; children by living arrangement and parents' marital status; labor force participation of mothers, by marital status and age of children; children by working status of parents; and child care arrangements used by working mothers; various periods 1958-84.

c. Educational enrollment rates for preschool and elementary/secondary school, and high school dropout rates, by age and/or race; Scholastic Aptitude Test verbal and math scores by sex; and expected field of study of college-bound high school seniors; various years 1960-84.

d. Income: distribution of children by family income level, and children in poverty by race (including Spanish origin), with detail for female-headed households; percent of children receiving AFDC, and percent of households with children receiving non-cash benefits by type; and cost of raising a child, including average college costs for public and private institutions; various years 1960-84, with poverty projections to 1990.

e. Drug use of youths by substance, including alcohol and cigarettes; reported cases of child maltreatment by type; and high school students' life goals, career interests, and perceptions of most important world and national problems and worst influences on youth, with selected detail by sex; various years 1972-83.

A1410
American
Council on Education

A1410–1   HIGHER EDUCATION PANEL REPORTS
Series.   For individual publication data, see below.
SRI/MF/complete

Continuing series of reports, by the Higher Education Panel, on topics of current policy interest to the higher education community and to government agencies.

Reports are based on data drawn from the panel's membership of 760 colleges and universities, stratified by type (university and 4- and 2-year college), public and private control, and size of enrollment. The panel conducts 3-5 surveys per year using the total membership or a subset.

Reports reviewed during 1985 are described below.

Availability: American Council on Education, Higher Education Panel, One Dupont Circle, Washington DC 20036-1193, †; SRI/MF/complete.

A1410–1.18: Plant Biology Personnel and Training at Doctorate-Granting Institutions
[Monograph. Nov. 1984 x+38 p. HEP Rpt. No. 62. SRI/MF/complete.]

By Charles J. Andersen. Report on graduate programs in plant biology at PhD-granting colleges/universities, 1982/83, with selected data for 1983/84. Covers program organizational structure; faculty, graduate students, and post-doctoral fellows/associates, with detail variously by sex, field of concentration, source of student financial support, and minority and citizenship status (including foreign students/fellows/associates from developing countries); and PhD recipients, by sex and minority status.

Also includes data on course requirements; faculty vacancies, and reasons for faculty recruitment; fields with personnel shortage and surplus; and financial support for plant biology research, by source.

Most data are shown for all, public, land-grant, and private institutions, and for aggregate 20 universities with largest federally financed R&D expenditures in life sciences.

Data are national estimates based on responses of 143 institutions with graduate programs in plant biology, to a fall 1982 survey.

Contains listings of contents, charts, and tables, and highlights (p. iii-x); narrative report, with 11 charts and 6 summary tables (p. 1-9); 11 detailed tables (p. 12-28); and appendices, with questionnaire facsimile, methodology, and listing of 50 colleges/universities with largest federally financed R&D expenditures in life sciences (p. 29-38).

A1410–1.19: Campus Trends, 1984
[Monograph. Feb. 1985. vi+20 p. HEP Rpt. No. 65. SRI/MF/complete.]

By Elaine El-Khawas. Report on selected policies and practices of higher education institutions, 1983/84. Presents data on the following topics, for 2-year colleges, 4-year colleges, and universities:

a. Curricular content, admissions and graduation requirements, and related administrative review activities, including selected detail for institutions with teacher-training programs.

b. Faculty matters, including hiring of women and minorities; trend in number of positions; and use of part-time faculty, early retirement, periodic evaluation, and development programs.

c. Types of student aid and tuition payment plans; areas of cooperation with business/industry; and administrators' perceptions of 5-year trend in various issues pertaining to students, faculty, and institutions.

Data are national estimates based on responses of 413 colleges and universities to a June/July 1984 survey.

Contains listings of contents, charts, and tables, with narrative highlights (p. iii-vi); methodology and narrative analysis, with 6 charts and 6 tables (p. 1-8); 10 detailed tables (p. 9-14); and 2 appendices, with questionnaire facsimile and technical notes (p. 15-19).

A1410–1.20: General Education Requirements in the Humanities
[Monograph. Oct. 1985. vii+26 p.+errata. HEP Rpt. No. 66. SRI/MF/complete.]

By Nancy Suniewick and Elaine El-Khawas. Report on general education course requirements for graduation from higher education institutions, 1984/85, with comparisons to 1979/80. "General education" encompasses courses that all undergraduates must take, regardless of major. Includes detailed data on subject areas and credit hours required, shown for public and private doctoral, comprehensive, baccalaureate, and 2-year institutions.

Also includes data on foreign language and formal library training requirements, instructional methods in humanities and expository writing courses, and plans to restructure general education requirements.

Data are national estimates based on responses of 374 colleges and universities to a July 1984 survey.

Contains listings of contents, charts, and tables (p. iii-vii); highlights, and narrative report interspersed with 5 charts and 11 tables (p. 1-12); statistical section, with 18 tables (p. 13-19); and 2 appendices, with survey facsimile and technical notes (p. 20-25).

A1410–2   1984-85 FACT BOOK ON HIGHER EDUCATION
Biennial.   1984.   10+201 p.
ISSN 0363-6720.
LC sn84-44781.
SRI/MF/not filmed

Biennial compilation, for 1984/85, of statistics pertinent to higher education, including data on finances, enrollment, institutions, faculty and staff, students, and degrees. Also includes data on population characteristics and economic indicators. Most data are shown for 1950s-85, with selected trends from 1900 and projections to 2050.

Most data are from Federal Government and private sources. Data sources appear beneath each table.

Contains contents listing, foreword, and introduction(5 p.); highlights on minorities and women in higher education, and on demographic/economic data (5 p.); 6 statistical sections, with 154 tables listed below, and accompanying charts (p. 1-199); and index (2 p.).

Previous edition, for 1981/82, is described in SRI 1982 Annual under this number, and was titled *Fact Book for Academic Administrators.*

Availability: Macmillan Publishing Co., 866 Third Ave., New York NY 10022, $39.95; SRI/MF/not filmed.

TABLES:
[Most tables show data for selected years within the range noted. Tables presenting data by State generally include totals for regions, outlying areas, and U.S. service schools.

Data by institution type are generally shown for 2- and 4-year colleges, and universities.]

A1410–2.1: Demographic and Economic Data

POPULATION

[1-2] Population by sex and race, [and age 65/over], 1900-2050; and resident population by State, 1965-90. (p. 1-3)

[3-5] College-age and 18-year-old population by sex and race, 1950-2050; and population ages 18-24, by State, 1965-90. (p. 4-7)

[6-7] Households [total and percent with husband/wife present], by State, 1965-80; and households, families, [and average members by age group], 1940-90. (p. 8-10)

[8] Births, deaths, and rates, 1910-82. (p. 11)

[9] Educational attainment of the population 25 years old/over [by State], 1980. (p. 12-13)

[10] College participation rates of 1972 and 1980 high school graduates by socioeconomic status, level of ability, and time of entry. (p. 14)

INCOME

[11-12] Median incomes by sex, race, and educational attainment, 1981; and estimated lifetime income of males and females, by educational attainment, 1956-79. (p. 15-16)

[13-16] Families by income range and race; median income (current and 1981 dollars) of families by race [including Spanish origin, and for unrelated] individuals, 1950-81; and median family income by State, 1969 and 1979. (p. 17-21)

[17-18] Income of families with college-age members, by enrollment status and race, 1979; and all families and families of 1st-time/full-time students [by institution type], by income level, 1967-81. (p. 22-23)

[19] Per capita personal income by State, 1950-81. (p. 24-25)

STATE FINANCES, ECONOMIC INDICATORS, AND EMPLOYMENT

[20-21] State/local tax capacity and tax effort, 1979; and State appropriations for higher education operating expenses, [1977/78-1982/83]; by State. (p. 26-29)

[22-23] GNP, 1946-82; and price indexes [including Higher Education Price Index], 1958-82. (p. 30-31)

[24-26] Civilian labor force by State, 1970-81; labor force and employment status, 1950-82; and labor force by age group, sex, and race, 1960-90. (p. 32-35)

[27-28] Employed persons by selected industry [division] and State, 1970 and 1980; and estimated employment in 1980, and average annual openings 1978-90 [period], in selected occupations. (p. 36-38)

[29] Supply and demand for doctorates [by field], 1976-85 [period]. (p. 39)

[30-31] Unemployment rates by sex and age group; and by race [including Hispanic] and kind of workers [including blue collar workers, and persons with lost labor force time], 1950-82. (p. 40-41)

HIGHER EDUCATION FINANCE

[32] [Total and higher public and private] education expenditures as a percentage of GNP, 1929/30-1980/81. (p. 42)

[33] Voluntary [total and per student] support of institutions of higher education, 1969/70-1981/82; [and estimated support by source, 1971/72-1981/82]. (p. 43)

[34-39] Current fund income and revenues [by source], and expenditures [by object], of institutions of higher education [including separate revenue and expenditure data for public and private institutions; 1909/10-1980/81]. (p. 44-55)

A1410–2.2: Enrollment

[Tables [2-38] show enrollment data for institutions of higher education, for the breakdowns indicated below.]

[1] Enrollment in all levels of education, 1960-85. (p. 56)

[2-8] By level of study [and institution type], 1899/1900-1990; by sex, control of institution, and State, 1950-82; and percentage of in-State students by control of institution and State, 1972 and 1975. (p. 57-67)

[9-10] Minority [students (blacks and others), number and] as a percentage of total enrollment, by State, 1972-80. (p. 68-71)

[11-14] In 4-year and 2-year institutions by sex and control of institution, 1950-82. (p. 72-75)

[15-26] By [full-time and part-time] attendance status and by control of institution [with detail by sex]; for all, 4-year, and 2-year institutions, 1962-82. (p. 76-87)

[27-34] First-time students by sex and by control of institution, for all, 4-year, and 2-year institutions, 1950-81; and by State, with percent change, for all institutions, 1970-81. (p. 88-97)

[35-36] Graduate [students] by sex and by control of institution, 1929/30-1988. (p. 98-99)

[37-38] For advanced degrees, by State, 1960-81, and by field of study, 1960-76. (p. 100-103)

[39] Elementary and secondary school enrollment, by control of school, 1899/1900-1985. (p. 104)

[40] Estimated retention rates, 5th grade through college entrance, 1924-80. (p. 105)

A1410–2.3: Institutions, Faculty and Staff, and Students

[All data are for institutions of higher education.]

INSTITUTIONS

[1-3] Number and percent distribution by highest level of [degree] offering, 1950/51-1982; and [number] by highest level of offering and State, fall 1982. (p. 106-109)

[4-5] [Number of] institutions by control, and percent distribution by [enrollment] size and region, 1950-81. (p. 110-111)

[6] Institutions by type of calendar and State, 1982/83. (p. 112-113)

FACULTY AND STAFF

[7-8] Instructional faculty by [full- and part-time] employment status; and [FTE] faculty and enrollment, 1959-88. (p. 114-115)

[9] Full-time faculty and percentage with tenure, by sex and State [including U.S. territories], fall 1981. (p. 116-117)

[10] Faculty by highest degree held and by type and control of institution, 1950/51-1972. (p. 118)

[11-12] Women as percentage of instructional faculty by [academic] rank [and institution control], 1962/63-1979/80; and selected faculty characteristics by sex, 1973; [both by] type of institution. (p. 119-121)

[13-14] Average faculty salary by type [and control] of institution, 1970/71-1982/83; and compensation (salary and benefits), 1965/66-1982/83; both by [academic] rank. (p. 122-125)

[15] Faculty with tenure as percentage of all faculty, by control of institution and State, fall 1981. (p. 126)

[16-18] Administrative salaries at all, public, and private institutions, by selected position, 1967/68-1982/83. (p. 127-129)

[19] Women college presidents by type and control of institution, 1975-82. (p. 130)

[20] Turnover rate of selected administrative positions, by type of institution, 1975/76 and 1980/81. (p. 131)

STUDENTS

[Data by race-ethnicity are for white, black, American Indian, Oriental, Mexican American/Chicano, Puerto Rican, and other.]

[21] Trends in average college costs by control of institution 1977/78-1984/85. (p. 132)

[22] National norms for selected characteristics of entering freshmen [highest degree planned, race-ethnicity, and source of financial support], by sex and type [and control] of institution [including data for predominantly black colleges], fall 1982. (p. 133-134)

[23] Selected freshman characteristics [including highest degree planned, race-ethnicity, high school grades, objectives, and planned field of study and career], by sex, 1966-82. (p. 135-136)

[24-25] Undergraduate residence and migration, by State [of residence and State in which attending college], 1958-75. (p. 137-140)

[26] Median years from baccalaureate to doctorate by field of study, 1958-81. (p. 141-142)

A1410–2.4: Earned Degrees

[Degree levels include bachelor's, 1st professional, master's, and doctor's. Tables [19-46] show degrees in sciences, engineering, and humanities by specific field of study.]

[1] Earned degrees by level, 1949/50-1984/85. (p. 145)

[2-8] Earned degrees by sex of student and control of institution [for all degrees and by degree level, with percent distribution], 1947/48-1984/85. (p. 146-152)

[9-12] Degrees by State [and level, 1949/50-1980/81]. (p. 153-160)

[13-16] Degrees by race-ethnicity [black, American Indian, Asian, Hispanic, white, and nonresident alien], academic area, [sex, and degree level], 1980/81. (p. 161-164)

[17] Bachelor's degrees by race and State, 1980/81. (p. 165-166)

[18] Percentage of earned doctorates awarded to women, by field of study, 1949/50-1980/81. (p. 167)

[19-46] Earned degrees in biological sciences, education, engineering, humanities, law, medicine and dentistry, nursing, physical sciences, and social sciences [by degree level, with selected data by sex], 1947/48-1980/81. (p. 168-195)

[47-49] Associate degrees by sex of student, by type and control of institution, and by State, 1965/66-1980/81. (p. 196-199)

A1410–5 ACCESS TO HIGHER EDUCATION: THE EXPERIENCE OF BLACKS, HISPANICS AND LOW SOCIO-ECONOMIC STATUS WHITES
Monograph. May 1985.
4+55 p.
SRI/MF/complete

By Valerie Lee. Report analyzing access to higher education for minority and low-income youths, based on a 1982 follow-up study of 1980 high school seniors. Presents comparisons of socioeconomic background, high school activities and academic performance, and activities after high school graduation, for blacks, Hispanics, low socioeconomic status (SES) whites, and high SES whites, often with detail by sex and for Hispanic subgroups.

Comparisons include family income and social class; parents' education; single-parent families; high school achievement in math, reading, and vocabulary, and coursework in math and science; proportion of time devoted to job, study, and TV; college application and enrollment status, including detail by type of institution and census division, and withdrawals for financial reasons; college coursework; high school and college grade point average; and marital and employment status after high school graduation.

Data are from the continuing national survey *High School and Beyond,* a study of 1980 high school sophomores and seniors; data in this report are compiled from the 1982 follow-up study of 11,876 former high school seniors.

Contains foreword and highlights (4 p.); introduction and narrative report (p. 1-19); 2 charts and 24 tables (p. 21-46); and appendices, with 5 tables (p. 50-55).

Availability: American Council on Education, One Dupont Circle, Washington DC 20036-1193, †; SRI/MF/complete.

A1410–6   HOW LOW-INCOME FAMILIES PAY FOR COLLEGE
Monograph.   July 1985.
2+32+App 4 p.
SRI/MF/complete

By Scott E. Miller and Holly Hexter. Report on higher education financing methods for low-income families (adjusted gross incomes below $15,000). Data are shown for dependent full-time students in public and independent institutions, 1983/84.

Includes percent of low-income aid recipients receiving Federal aid, by type of program, with detail for Pell Grant recipients by size of grant; financial aid recipients (number and as percent of all recipients) by source of aid, by income level; and value of typical aid "packages" (amount of financial assistance received from selected sources, based on income level and college cost), with comparison to actual need.

Aid sources include 5 Federal programs, State grants, family contributions, and various combinations of Federal and State programs.

Also includes distribution of student aid programs by major type (grants, loans, work), selected periods 1970-85.

Data are generally based on surveys of students receiving financial assistance during 1983/84. Surveys were conducted by National Assn of State Universities and Land-Grant Colleges, American Assn of State Colleges and Universities, American Assn of Community and Junior Colleges, and the National Institute of Independent Colleges and Universities.

Contains foreword and contents listing (2 p.); 6 narrative chapters interspersed with 6 charts and 9 tables (p. 1-32); and appendices with 7 tables (4 p.).

Availability: American Council on Education, Division of Policy Analysis and Research, One Dupont Circle, Washington DC 20036-1193, members $5.00, nonmembers $8.00; SRI/MF/complete.

A1410–7   HOW MIDDLE-INCOME FAMILIES PAY FOR COLLEGE
Monograph.   July 1985.
2+38+App 4 p.
SRI/MF/complete

By Scott E. Miller and Holly Hexter. Report on higher education financing methods for middle-income families (adjusted gross incomes of $15,-000-$35,000). Data are shown for dependent full-time students in public and independent institutions, 1983/84.

Includes middle-income recipients (number and as percent of all recipients) by source of aid, by income level; and value of typical aid "packages" (amount of financial assistance received from various sources, based on income level and college cost), with comparison to actual need.

Aid sources include 5 Federal programs, State grants, family contribution, and various combinations of Federal and State programs.

Also includes distribution of student aid programs by major type (grants, loans, work), selected periods 1970-85.

Data are generally based on surveys of students receiving financial assistance during 1983/84. Surveys were conducted by National Assn of State Universities and Land-Grant Colleges, American Assn of State Colleges and Universities, American Assn of Community and Junior Colleges, and the National Institute of Independent Colleges and Universities.

Contains foreword and contents listing (2 p.); 6 narrative chapters interspersed with 7 charts and 10 tables (p. 1-38); and appendices with 8 tables (4 p.)

Availability: American Council on Education, Division of Policy Analysis and Research, One Dupont Circle, Washington DC 20036-1193, members $5.00, nonmembers $8.00; SRI/MF/complete.

A1410–8   DISTRIBUTION OF STUDENT FINANCIAL AID: Trends Among the Postsecondary Sectors
Monograph.   June 1985.
1+16 p.
SRI/MF/complete

By Dr. John B. Lee. Report on trends in higher education student aid. Covers programs administered by the Dept of Education (including Pell Grants and campus-based aid), veterans and Social Security education benefits, and State grants.

Includes data on amount of aid distributed, number of recipients, and average or maximum award, by type of aid and institution (proprietary schools, and public and private or independent 2- and 4-year institutions); and percent of students receiving Dept of Education grants, and average award, by family income level; various years 1974-85.

Also includes higher education FTE expenditures, and expenditures for instruction and scholarships, by type of institution, 1977 and 1982.

Data are from Federal agencies, Higher Education General Information Survey, and University of California at Los Angeles Cooperative Institutional Research Program Surveys.

Contains foreword (1 p.); and narrative report interspersed with 12 tables (p. 1-16).

Availability: American Council on Education, Division of Policy Analysis and Research, One Dupont Circle, Washington DC 20036-1193, †; SRI/MF/complete.

A1475
American Dental Association

A1475–3   1984/85 ANNUAL REPORT ON DENTAL EDUCATION
Annual.   [1985.]   29 p.
SRI/MF/complete

Annual report on dental school programs, enrollment, and graduates, by institution, for the U.S. and Canada, 1984/85, with selected trends from 1975.

Also includes data on admission requirements, student expenses and financial assistance, patient care provided by students, and faculty positions; and detail by sex, race/ethnicity, and State of residence.

Report is a summary of the 18th annual survey of dental schools conducted for the Council on Dental Education of the American Dental Assn and the American Assn of Dental Schools.

Contains contents and table listing (p. 3); introduction with 2 text tables on enrollment of women, 1983/84-1984/85 (p. 5-7); and 2 charts and 17 tables, listed below (p. 8-29).

Supplements to this report are also published and are covered in SRI under A1475-4.

Availability: American Dental Association, Council on Dental Education, Educational Measurements Division, 211 E. Chicago Ave., Chicago IL 60611, †; SRI/MF/complete.

TABLES AND CHARTS:
[Data are shown for 1984/85 school year for U.S. and Canada, by institution, unless otherwise noted. Data for U.S. include Puerto Rico.]

A1475-3.1: Academic Programs, Enrollment, and Graduates

[Minority data are shown for blacks, Hispanics, American Indians, and Asians.]

1. Dental schools [directory, arranged by State and Province]. (p. 8-9)

2. Description of academic programs [type and length of term and program, length of academic year, and type of institutional support]. (p. 10)

3. Level of advanced standing at which transfer students and foreign dental graduates are admitted. (p. 11)

4-5. Level of predental education: of 1st-year students [aggregate U.S. only], 1975-84 [chart]; and of 1st-year students enrolled, 1984/85. (p. 12-13)

6. Dental school graduates, 1st-year and total enrollment [and number of dental schools (aggregate U.S. only)], 1975/76-1984/85. [chart] (p. 14)

7. Predoctoral enrollment [by sex and level]. (p. 15)

8-10. Distribution of 1st-year and all predoctoral students [by State of residence]; and 1st-year predoctoral minority enrollment [by sex; U.S. only]. (p. 16-20)

11. First-year enrollment, 1975-84. (p. 21)

12. Dental school [white and minority] graduates [by sex], 1984. (p. 22)

A1475-3.2: Educational Expenses, Dental School Programs, and Faculty

13. First-year tuition [resident and nonresident] and annual related educational expenses [general fees, and other educational costs by class level]. (p. 23)

14. Financial assistance awarded to predoctoral dental students [total and need-based applications, and number receiving assistance; percent of enrollment assisted; and amount requested and awarded; for U.S. only]; 1983/84. (p. 24)

15-16. Basic sciences instruction; and patient care [visits and screenings by predoctoral students at on-campus clinics and extramural facilities]. (p. 25-26)

17. Advanced education programs conducted, Dec. 1984. (p. 27)

18. Full- and part-time faculty positions [in biomedical and clinical depts], 1984. (p. 28)

19. Full- and part-time faculty positions according to dept [aggregate U.S. only], 1984. (p. 29)

A1475–4 SUPPLEMENTS TO DENTAL EDUCATION, 1984/85 Annual Report

Series. For individual publication data, see below. SRI/MF/complete

Annual series of supplementary statistical reports, for academic year 1984/85, on U.S. dental schools, covering minority enrollment, programs, admission policies and applicants, student attrition, finances, faculty, and related topics. Most reports present data by individual institution, including University of Puerto Rico. Selected reports also include data for Canada.

Series also includes 2 nonstatistical directories of dental school administrators and dept chairmen.

Data are primarily from the American Dental Assn's annual Survey of Predoctoral Dental Educational Institutions.

Statistical reports generally contain table listing, brief narrative summary, and varying number of tables.

Supplements for 1984/85 reviewed in 1985 are described below. Base report on 1984/85 annual survey is described under A1475-3. Supplements for 1983/84 are described below and in SRI 1984 Annual under A1475-7.

Availability: American Dental Association, Council on Dental Education, Educational Measurements Division, 211 E. Chicago Ave., Chicago IL 60611, †; SRI/MF/complete.

A1475–4.1: Dental School Administrators, 1984/85

[Annual. [1985.] 13 p. Supplement 1. SRI/MF/complete.]

Annual directory of administrators of U.S. dental schools, listed by institution, for academic year 1984/85. Also includes listings for 5 Canadian schools.

A1475–4.2: Dental School Tuition, 1984/85

[Annual. [1985.] 21 p. Supplement 13. SRI/MF/complete.]

Annual report presenting data on dental school undergraduate student expenses, including resident and nonresident tuition, mandatory fees, and costs of instruments, textbooks, and health services, by class level and institution, with selected rankings, academic year 1984/85.

Includes 14 tables.

A1475–4.3: Dental School Admission Information, 1984/85

[Annual. Feb. 1985. 14 p. Supplement 7. SRI/MF/complete.]

Annual report on dental school admissions, including applicants and 1st-year enrollment by sex; 1st-year student pre-dental grade averages, and mean scores on Dental Admission Test; admissions criteria and placement of transfer students; 1st-year fees and resident and nonresident tuition; educational costs by class level; and degree combinations offered; all by Canadian and/or U.S. institution, academic year 1984/85. Includes 9 tables.

Previous report, for 1982/83, is described in SRI 1983 Annual under A1475-4.5; no report was issued for 1983/84.

A1475–4.4: Financial Report, 1984/85

[Annual. Mar. 1985. 33 p. Supplement 4. SRI/MF/complete.]

Annual summary report presenting data on dental school revenues and expenditures by major source and function, with high, low, and mean amounts by enrollment size, all for public, private, and private State-related schools, FY84 with aggregate trends from FY82. Includes 17 tables.

A1475–4.5: Dental School Faculty, 1984/85

[Recurring (irreg.) Apr. 1985. 25 p. Supplement 10. SRI/MF/complete.]

Recurring report on dental school faculty and staff, including FTE administrative personnel, and basic and clinical science faculty (total and by dept); minority faculty (black, Hispanic, American Indian, and Asian), by sex; female administrators and faculty; and basic and clinical science FTE support personnel by position; 1984/85.

Also includes undergraduate and advanced education enrollment, and student/faculty and faculty/staff ratios, with institution rankings, and detail by type of institutional control.

All data are shown by institution. Includes 14 tables.

Previous report, for 1983/84, is described under A1475-7.8 below. Report previously was issued biennially.

A1475–4.6: Trend Analysis, 1984/85

[Annual. Apr. 1985. 1+23 p. Supplement 11. SRI/MF/complete.]

Annual report covering trends in dental school applications (total and by women); enrollment, with detail for 1st-year, nonresident, female, and minority students; total and minority graduates; and resident and nonresident tuition/fees; all by institution.

Also includes 1st-year enrollment by level of pre-dental education; attrition rates by class level; total and 1st-year enrollment and graduates of dental and nondental schools, by specialty; and graduates passing and failing licensure examination, by State.

Data are shown mostly for 1970s-84, with some earlier trends and enrollment projections through 1989. Includes 1 chart and 17 tables.

A1475–4.7: Dental Student Attrition, 1983/84

[Annual. [1985.] 9 p. Supplement 5. SRI/MF/complete.]

Annual report on dental school student attrition, covering withdrawals for personal and academic reasons, and freshman enrollment, by race/ethnicity (including American Indian, Asian/Pacific Islander, and Hispanic), with attrition detail by class level and sex; academic year 1983/84 with selected trends from 1973/74.

Includes 6 tables.

A1475–5 ANNUAL REPORT ON DENTAL AUXILIARY EDUCATION, 1984/85

Annual. Apr. 1985. 47 p. SRI/MF/complete

Annual report, for 1984/85, on dental auxiliary education, including dental assisting, hygiene, and laboratory technology programs. Covers enrollment, graduates, admission requirements, and tuition, by institution. Data are from an annual survey of accredited programs.

Contains table listing (1 p.); and 3 charts, and 12 tables listed below (p. 1-46).

Supplements to this report have been discontinued. For description of final supplements, covering 1981/82, see SRI 1983 Annual under A1475-8.

Availability: American Dental Association, Council on Dental Education, Educational Measurements Division, 211 E. Chicago Ave., Chicago IL 60611, †; SRI/MF/complete.

TABLES:

[Tables show data for 1984/85, unless otherwise noted. Tables 4-12 show data by institution, arranged by State, including Puerto Rico.]

1-3. 1st-year and total enrollment, and graduates, dental auxiliary programs [by type], 1973-84. (p. 1-2)

4. Institutions conducting dental hygiene education programs. [list] (p. 4-8)

5. Dental hygiene education program admission policies and data [award granted; term of instruction; number and length of terms; number of summer and inter-sessions; minimum educational requirement; and total cost to indistrict, out-of-district, and out-of-State students]. (p. 9-14)

6. Dental hygiene education programs [1st-year capacity, enrollment by year of study, and graduates by award granted]. (p. 15-19)

7-12. [Tables 4-6 are repeated for institutions conducting dental assisting education programs (p. 20-40) and dental laboratory technology programs (p. 41-46).]

A1475–7 SUPPLEMENTS TO DENTAL EDUCATION, 1983/84 Annual Report

Series. For individual publication data, see below. SRI/MF/complete

Annual series of supplementary statistical reports, for academic year 1983/84, on U.S. dental schools, covering minority enrollment, programs, admission policies and applicants, student attrition, finances, faculty, and related topics. Most reports present data by individual institution, including University of Puerto Rico.

Series also includes 2 nonstatistical directories of dental school administrators and dept chairmen.

Data are primarily from the American Dental Assn's annual Survey of Predoctoral Dental Educational Institutions.

Statistical reports generally contain brief narrative summary, and a varying number of tables.

Supplements reviewed in 1985 are described below. Base report on 1983/84 annual survey is described in SRI 1984 Annual under A1475-3.

Availability: American Dental Association, Council on Dental Education, Educational Measurements Division, 211 E. Chicago Ave., Chicago IL 60611, †; SRI/MF/complete.

A1475–7.7: Continuing Education in Dental Schools, 1983/84

[Biennial. Dec. 1983. 10 p. Supplement 6. SRI/MF/complete.]

Biennial report presenting data on dental school continuing education courses, enrollment, dental and nondental instructional staff, and days of instruction, for basic and clinical science and dental auxiliary courses; and types of facilities and materials available for continuing education programs; all by institution, 1982/83.

Includes 7 tables.

Previous report, for 1980/81, is described in SRI 1982 Annual under A1475-7.4.

A1475–7.8: Dental Faculty Information, 1983/84

[Biennial. [1984.] 28 p. Supplement 10. SRI/MF/complete.]

Biennial report on dental school faculty and staff, including FTE administrative personnel, and basic and clinical science faculty with detail by dept; minority faculty (black, Hispanic, American Indian, and Asian), by sex; female administrators and faculty; and basic and clinical science FTE support personnel by position; 1983/84.

Also includes undergraduate and advanced education enrollment, and student/faculty and faculty/staff ratios, with selected rankings, and some groupings by type of institutional control.

All data are shown by institution. Includes 14 tables.

Previous report, for 1981/82, is described in SRI 1982 Annual under A1475-7.6.

A1475–7.9: Dental School Curriculum: Clock Hours of Instruction, Basic Science Summary, 1983/84

[Recurring (irreg.) May 1984. 2+13 p. Supplement 15. SRI/MF/complete.]

Recurring report covering dental school instructional hours in basic science courses, by subject area and type of instruction (didactic and laboratory), and including type of instructional unit (dental school, medical school, joint dental/medical, or separate unit) for each subject area, all by institution (identified by number only), 1983/84.

Includes 13 tables. This is the 1st edition covered in SRI.

A1475–7.10: Dental School Curriculum: Clock Hours of Instruction, Clinical Science Summary, 1983/84

[Recurring (irreg.) May 1984. 2+25 p. Supplement 16. SRI/MF/complete.]

Recurring report covering dental school instructional hours in clinical science courses, by

subject area and type of instruction (didactic, laboratory, and intramural and extramural patient care), by institution (identified by number only), 1983/84.

Includes 25 tables. This is the 1st edition covered in SRI.

A1475–7.11: Dental School Curriculum: Clock Hours of Instruction, Behavioral Science Summary, 1983/84

[Recurring (irreg.) May 1984. 2+6 p. Supplement 17. SRI/MF/complete.]

Recurring report covering dental school instructional hours in behavioral science courses, by subject area and type of instruction (didactic and laboratory), by institution (identified by number only), 1983/84.

Includes 6 tables. This is the 1st edition covered in SRI.

A1475–7.12: Dental School Curriculum: Clock Hours of Instruction, Summary Report, 1983/84

[Biennial. June 1984. 3+15 p. no paging. Supplement 14. SRI/MF/complete.]

Biennial report covering dental school instructional hours in basic, clinical, and behavioral science courses, by subject area and type of instruction (didactic and laboratory), by institution (identified by number only), 1983/84. Also includes rankings of institutions by total and weekly instructional hours, with selected institutional characteristics (length and type of term, type of support, and type of program offered).

Includes 15 tables. This is the 2nd biennial report. Previous report, for 1981/82, is described in SRI 1983 Annual under A1475-7.12.

A1475–10   1984/85 ANNUAL REPORT ON ADVANCED DENTAL EDUCATION

Annual. Jan. 1985. ii+62 p. SRI/MF/complete

Annual report, for 1984/85, on advanced dental education programs offered by dental and nondental schools. Covers program characteristics, enrollment, graduates, stipends, and tuition, by institution and State.

Most data are from annual surveys of advanced dental education programs accredited by the American Dental Assn Commission on Dental Accreditation.

Contains table listing (p. i-ii); and 14 tables listed below (p. 1-62).

Annual report has been published since the late 1960s. SRI coverage begins with the 1984/85 edition.

Availability: American Dental Association, Council on Dental Education, Educational Measurements Division, 211 E. Chicago Ave., Chicago IL 60611, †; SRI/MF/complete.

TABLES:
[Most tables show data separately for dental and non-dental schools. All tables except 2, 5-6, and 13 show data by program type. Tables 7-12 and 14 show data by institution, arranged by State (including Puerto Rico). Data are for 1984 or 1984/85 school year, unless otherwise noted.]

1. Enrollment [1st year and total], and graduates. (p. 1)

2. [Dental school graduates; and 1st year enrollment in specialty, general practice, and advanced general dentistry programs; 1974-84.] (p. 1)

3. Number of accredited specialty and non-specialty programs [as of May 1980-84]. (p. 2)

4. Number of full-time and board certified directors of specialty and non-specialty programs. (p. 2)

5-6. [Directory of] schools with advanced education programs. (p. 3-9)

7-8. Enrollment [by class level] and graduates [receiving certificates and/or degrees]. (p. 10-26)

9-10. Program starting dates, application deadlines [for class entering in 1986, and program length]. (p. 27-43)

11-12. Stipends and tuitions [by class level]. (p. 44-60)

13. Institutions offering accredited oral/maxillofacial surgery programs with options for pursuing an M.D. degree. [list] (p. 61)

14. Dental school enrollment and graduates of advanced programs not accredited by the Commission on Dental Accreditation [for programs offering post-graduate certificates, and master and doctorate degrees]. (p. 61-62)

A1580
American Federation of State, County and Municipal Employees

A1580–1   THE STATES, THE PEOPLE, AND THE REAGAN YEARS: An Analysis of Social Spending Cuts
Recurring (irreg.) [1985.]
224 p. var. paging.
SRI/MF/complete

Recurring report analyzing Reagan Administration changes in Federal spending for 44 programs, by State, FY82-85. Covers Federal grants-in-aid to State/local governments for education, employment/training, health services, nutrition, income maintenance/human services, and infrastructure/economic development programs; and direct Federal payments to individuals.

Presents difference between actual funding and estimated funding needed to maintain FY81 service levels, FY82-85; and per capita totals, rank among the States, and share of Federal spending reduction, for the 4-year period; for each program, by State and for Puerto Rico, with U.S. summary.

Also includes Federal deficit changes attributed to tax reductions, defense spending increases, non-defense spending cuts, and legislative impact on interest costs, 1982-89.

Most data are estimates prepared by Fiscal Planning Services, Inc., for AFSCME.

Contains introduction, with 5 tables (34 p.); brief narrative summary and 1 table, repeated for each State (156 p.); and appendices, with sources, list of grant programs, 1 table, and methodology (31 p.).

This is the 3rd edition of the report published by AFSCME. For description of previous edition, see SRI 1984 Annual under this number.

Prior to 1983, less detailed reports were published by Coalition of American Public Employees (now disbanded).

Availability: American Federation of State, County and Municipal Employees, 1625 L St., NW, Washington DC 20036, †; SRI/MF/complete.

A1615
American Financial Services Association

A1615–2   1985 FINANCE FACTS YEARBOOK
Annual. [1985.] 89 p.
LC 61-14409.
SRI/MF/complete

Annual report on consumer finance industry lending activity and financial status; and on consumer income and expenditures, including savings and debt; 1970s-84. Also includes data on industrial banking company status in 18-20 States.

Data are derived from 110 responses to a 1983 AFSA survey of finance companies; and Federal Reserve Board, Census Bureau, and BLS reports.

Contains foreword, and listings of contents, tables, and charts (p. 2-6); 8 chapters, with narrative, 23 charts, and 40 tables listed below (p. 7-85); and references (p. 87-89).

Availability: American Financial Services Association, Publications, 1101 14th St., NW, Washington DC 20005, members, schools, libraries $10.00; others $15.00; SRI/MF/complete.

TABLES:
[Tables show data from middle or late 1970s through 1983 or 1984, unless otherwise noted.]

A1615–2.1: Consumer Characteristics

CONSUMER POPULATION

1-2. Population and number of households [by family type]; and population including armed forces abroad, by age and sex; July 1, various years 1979-2000. (p. 8, 10)

3. Labor force participation of the population 16 years of age/older. (p. 16)

4. Estimated school enrollment [by level]. (p. 17)

5. Employed civilians 16 years/over, by occupational groups, year end 1982-84. (p. 20)

CONSUMER INCOME, SPENDING, AND CAPITAL FORMATION

6. Distribution of GNP, by sector [personal consumption expenditures, private domestic investment, government purchases, and net exports]. (p. 23)

7-8. Sources and disposition of personal income. (p. 28)

9. Selected income characteristics of households [number, and mean and aggregate income, by householder sex, household size, type and tenure status of residence, metrononmetro location, and census region], 1983. (p. 30)

10. Families and unrelated individuals, by total money income in 1983. (p. 32)

11. GNP, by sector [personal consumption expenditures, for durable and nondurable goods, and services; and government purchases, domestic investment, and net exports]. (p. 34)

12. Personal income [by source] and its disposition [by object], 1984. (p. 38)

13. Capital formation [by business and consumers; and capital consumption allowances]. (p. 39)

CONSUMER SAVINGS, INVESTMENT, AND DEBT

14. Financing of government by individuals [shows Federal and State/local government receipts, total tax/nontax receipts of all governments, social insurance fund receipts, and personal income from current earnings]. (p. 42)

15. Saving and investment, by households [shows gross, net, and personal saving, and credit from government insurance; capital gains dividends; net durables in consumption; gross investment; capital expenditures; net financial investment; net acquisition of financial assets; net liability increase; and savings/investment discrepancy]. (p. 43)

16. Total credit market debt owed, by sector [public, private, and consumer]. (p. 44)

17-18. Balance sheet of the household sector, 1980-84; and consumer's asset to debt ratios. (p. 45, 47)

CONSUMER CREDIT
[Credit holders include commercial banks, retailers, gasoline and finance companies, savings/loan assns, credit unions, and mutual savings banks. Installment credit by type is shown for automobile, revolving, mobile home, and other credit.]

19. Consumer installment credit outstanding and net change during year, by type, by holder, 1980-84. (p. 51)

20. Consumer installment credit, by type and holder [year end 1983-84]. (p. 52)

FEDERAL RESERVE BOARD CONSUMER CREDIT SURVEY

21. Selected [financial and debt] characteristics of families using financial services [by type, including credit cards], 1983. (p. 54)

22-23. Distribution of consumer [credit] outstanding; and ratio of monthly installment debt payments in 1983 to family income in 1982, by selected family characteristics [age of family head and family income level]. (p. 55-56)

A1615–2.2: Consumer Finance Industry Operations

LENDING ACTIVITY

24-25. Receivables outstanding and consumer installment credit at finance companies, by [loan] type, 1980-84. (p. 60-61)

26. Growth in 2nd mortgage and other personal loans at a sample group of finance companies. (p. 64)

27. Loan laws under which finance companies operate, by State (no date). [tabular list] (p. 65)

28. Average loan sizes at finance companies, 1981-83. (p. 66)

29-30. Percentage distribution of personal loans made at finance companies by purpose, and by characteristics of borrowers [annual income level and age group], 1983. (p. 69-70)

31. Percentage distribution of U.S. household population, by annual income level and by age [group], 1983. (p. 71)

FINANCES

32. Assets of companies responding to AFSA questionnaire, Dec. 31, 1983. (p. 72)

33-34. Liabilities [and capital/surplus]; and gross income, expenses, and net income; of reporting finance companies, 1983. (p. 73-74)

35-36. Estimated overall cost of borrowing and return on equity, for finance companies by size of company [amount of consumer credit outstanding], 1983. (p. 75)

37. Relation of income to outstandings, assets, and equity, for finance companies, 1983. (p. 76)

INDUSTRIAL BANKING COMPANIES
[Tables present data for industrial banking companies in 18-20 States, as of year end 1982 or most recent fiscal year.]

38-40. [Number of companies and locations]; assets [net receivables and other]; and liabilities [deposits and thrift/investment certificates, and other]; and total capital]. (p. 78-80)

A1775
American Gas Association

A1775–1   QUARTERLY REPORT OF GAS INDUSTRY OPERATIONS
Quarterly. 6 p. folder.
SRI/MF/complete

Quarterly report on natural gas utility industry, with combined income statement for investor-owned companies; and customers, sales, revenues, and prices, for all companies, by consuming sector and census division. Also includes data on appliance shipments by type and fuel source, housing starts and completions, and mobile home shipments.

Data are compiled by AGA from company reports and from reports of government and private agencies, including Gas Appliance Manufacturers Assn. Report is issued 3-6 months after quarter of coverage.

Contains narrative analysis, usually with 12 trend charts; and 6 quarterly tables, listed below.

Availability: American Gas Association, Order and Billing, 1515 Wilson Blvd., Arlington VA 22209, †; SRI/MF/complete.

Issues reviewed during 1985: 3rd Qtr. 1984-2nd Qtr. 1985 (D).

QUARTERLY TABLES:
[Tables show data for quarter of coverage and/or year to date, with comparisons to previous year.]

[A] Investor-owned gas utility industry income statement [including operating revenues, expenses by type, net income, utility plant value, and accumulated provision for depreciation].

1-2. Gas utility industry customers, sales, and revenues, U.S. and by [census] division [by consuming sector].

[B-C] Average gas prices [by consuming sector, for U.S. and by census division].

[D] Appliance and housing statistics [appliance shipments by type of appliance and fuel source, and total and single-family housing starts, private housing completions, and mobile home shipments].

A1775–2   MONTHLY GAS UTILITY STATISTICAL REPORT
Monthly.   2 p.
SRI/MF/complete, shipped quarterly

Monthly statistical summary of natural gas prices, sales to ultimate consumers, residential appliance shipments, and related economic indicators, compiled by the American Gas Assn for the gas utility industry.

Data are derived from Federal Government and private sources, including the Gas Appliance Manufacturers Assn and BLS; sales data are based on a sample of 69 companies. Report is issued 2-3 months after month of coverage.

Contains 2 charts, and 5 tables listed below.

Availability: American Gas Association, Order and Billing, 1515 Wilson Blvd., Arlington VA 22209, †; SRI/MF/complete, shipped quarterly.

Issues reviewed during 1985: Aug. 1984-Aug. 1985 (D).

MONTHLY TABLES:
[Data by consuming sector are for residential, commercial, industrial, and electricity generation. Table [5] on average monthly gas utility prices begins with Sept. 1984 issue.]

[1] Gas utility [sales] volumes to ultimate consumers [by consuming sector and for transportation, for month of coverage, year to date, and forecast for current year, with comparisons to previous year].

[2] Residential appliance shipments [domestic ranges, clothes dryers, water heaters, warm air furnaces, and boilers, by type (gas, electric, and/or oil)], for month of coverage and same month of previous year].

[3] Economic indicators [including private housing starts; CPI for utility pipe gas, electricity, and fuel oil; index of total gas sales; gas utility prices by consuming sector; and carriage volumes, to and for ultimate consumers, and for resale; for month of coverage and same month of previous year].

[4-5] Average gas utility prices [by consuming sector, shown for each month, and for 12-month periods ending in each month, for current year through month of coverage and previous year, and for various earlier periods].

A1775–3   GAS FACTS 1983: A Statistical Record of the Gas Utility Industry
Annual.   1984.   x+218 p.
Catalog No. F10183.
LC 72-622849.
SRI/MF/complete

Annual report, for 1983, on natural gas industry, covering utility transmission, distribution, consumption, finances, prices, and personnel. Includes data by State, and trends from 1960s.

Report also covers natural gas reserves, production, supply, underground storage, appliances, and home heating; selected data for petroleum, coal, and electric and nuclear power industries; and foreign gas production, consumption, and trade.

Data are from Uniform Statistical Reports prepared annually by AGA utility company members; reports filed with regulatory commissions; financial publications; and other reports from government and private sources.

Contains contents and chart listings, introduction, and information sources (p. v-x); 17 sections, with 24 summary charts, 16 summary tables, and 156 detailed tables listed below (p. 1-192); 4 appendices, with glossary, conversion table, company listing by type, and 3 tables on gas consumption (p. 193-214); and index (p. 215-217).

Gas Data Book, an annual pocket-sized book containing brief excerpts from *Gas Facts,* is also available from AGA, but is not covered in SRI.

Availability: American Gas Association, Order and Billing, 1515 Wilson Blvd., Arlington VA 22209, members $25.00, nonmembers $30.00; SRI/MF/complete.

DETAILED TABLES:
[Unless otherwise noted, tables present trend data annually or for selected years, from 1960s or 1970s through 1982 or 1983.

Data by State usually are also shown by census division. Data by class of service are shown for total, residential, commercial, industrial, and other users.

Data by type of industry classification are shown for 27-28 industry divisions and major groups. Data by type of company generally are shown for distribution, transmission, integrated, and combination companies; and sometimes for gas holding companies or municipals.]

A1775–3.1: Industry Comparison and Reserves

INDUSTRY COMPARISON
1.1. Comparison of gas utility industry customers, sales, and revenues, by class of service, 1982-83. (p. 4)

U.S. RESERVES
[Tables show data for resources indicated below. Table titles 2.1-2.2, 2.4, and 2.7 begin "Summary of annual estimates of proved reserves..." Table titles 2.3, 2.5, and 2.8 begin "Changes in estimated proved reserves..." and show data by State, with detail for some State regions and districts, including offshore, 1983.]

2.1-2.3. Natural gas. (p. 6-11)

2.4-2.5. Natural gas liquids. (p. 13-15)

2.6. Total estimated remaining identified reserves of coal [anthracite/semianthracite, subbituminous, and bituminous] and lignite by State, as of Jan. 1, 1980. (p. 16)

2.7-2.8. Crude oil. (p. 17-19)

CANADIAN RESERVES
[Tables 2.9-2.11 show data for Canada.]

2.9. Summary of annual estimates of reserves of natural gas. (p. 20)

2.10-2.11. Estimated [amount of] and changes in established remaining marketable reserves of natural gas, by Province, 1983. (p. 21)

A1775–3.2: Supply
[Data by type of well generally are for total, gas, oil, dry, and occasionally service wells.]

GENERAL PRODUCTION AND SUPPLY
3.1-3.2. Annual production of fossil energy resources [natural gas, crude petroleum, bituminous coal/lignite, and anthracite coal] and electricity from hydropower and nuclear power. (p. 25)

3.3. Supply and disposition of gas [including imports]. (p. 26)

3.4-3.5. Gas utility industry: gas supply and disposition; and maximum and minimum day sendout by source of supply. (p. 27)

PRODUCTION, DELIVERIES, AND FOREIGN TRADE
[Tables 3.6-3.9, 3.11, and 3.14 show data by State.]

3.6-3.8. Gross, net wellhead, and marketed production of natural gas. (p. 28-30)

3.9. Production of natural gas by all interstate natural gas pipeline companies. (p. 31)

3.10. Total offshore production of natural gas and percent State/federally controlled. (p. 32)

3.11. Interstate movements and movements across U.S. borders of natural/supplemental gas, 1982. (p. 33)

3.12. Exports [total, and to Canada, Mexico, and Japan] of natural gas from the U.S. (p. 34)

3.13. Imports [total, and from Canada, Mexico, and Algeria] of natural gas to the U.S. (p. 34)

3.14. Natural gas delivered to consumers. (p. 35)

GASOLINE AND ALLIED PRODUCTS
3.15. Supplemental gas supplies [synthetic natural, propane-air, refinery, and other] by State, 1982. (p. 36)

3.16. Natural gas treated for natural gasoline and allied products, and quantities and value of products recovered. (p. 37)

WELLS
3.17-3.18. Number of producing gas wells; and new gas well completions; by State. (p. 38-39)

3.19. New-field wildcat wells drilled and proportion successful. (p. 40)

3.20. New well completions, by type of well. (p. 40)

3.21. New well completions, by type of well and State, 1983. (p. 42)

DRILLING OPERATIONS
3.22. Holes drilled and proportion successful, by type of exploration hole. (p. 43)

3.23. Wells and dry holes drilled as exploratory tests, by State and type of well, 1983. (p. 44)

3.24-3.25. [Total and] offshore drilling operations and expenditures, by type of well, 1981-82. (p. 45)

3.26. Average cost per foot by type of well, by depth classes. (p. 46)

WORLD DATA
3.27. World natural gas statistics [production, imports, exports, gross consumption, residential consumers, and miles of pipeline, for 11 countries and all others], 1982. (p. 48)

3.28. World well completions [by type and world area], 1981-83. (p. 49)

A1775–3.3: Underground Gas Storage, Transmission, and Distribution

UNDERGROUND AND LIQUEFIED NATURAL GAS STORAGE
4.1-4.2. Number of underground storage pools, number of aquifer pools, and ultimate capacity. (p. 52-53)

4.3. Liquefied natural gas storage operations as of Dec. 31, 1983. (p. 53)

15.6-15.11. [Amount, number, and] average percent cost and yield of preferred stock, bond, and debenture issues. (p. 176-181)

15.12. [Amount and number of] note issues. (p. 182)

CONSTRUCTION EXPENDITURES

16.1-16.2. Gas utility industry construction expenditures, by type of facility [total, production/storage, transmission, underground storage, distribution, and general, with forecast through 1987]; and [by purpose for production and storage, transmission, and distribution facilities]. (p. 185-186)

A1775–3.9: Personnel

17.1-17.2. Gas utility industry employees and payroll [total and] by type of payroll [operating, construction, and miscellaneous] and type of company. (p. 189-190)

17.3. Employee accident incident and severity rates of selected industries, 1982. (p. 191)

17.4. Death rates of workers, by [industry division], 1982. (p. 191)

17.5. Employee disabling injury rates, by type of gas utility. (p. 192)

A1775–4   GAS HOUSEHEATING SURVEY: 1983

Annual. 1984. iv + 59 p.
Catalog No. F00084.
ISSN 0749-6907.
LC 84-643352.
SRI/MF/complete

Annual report on natural gas residential heating market, including customers, consumption, and price compared to other fuel types, by utility, State, and census division, 1983, with trends from 1979. Also includes data on anticipated additions of gas househeating units in 1984, housing completions by heating fuel type, conversions to gas from other fuels, and conservation.

Most data are from an American Gas Assn survey of 157 gas utilities serving 88% of all residential customers, and reports of Census Bureau and appliance trade assns.

Contains introduction, and contents and table listings (ii-iv); executive summary (p. 1-2); analysis of survey findings, with 1 chart on housing start trends and 8 text tables (p. 3-15); and appendices, with brief narrative and 2 detailed tables (p. 17-59). All tables are listed below.

This is the 36th annual survey.

Availability: American Gas Association, Order and Billing, 1515 Wilson Blvd., Arlington VA 22209, members $15.00, nonmembers $18.00; SRI/MF/complete.

TABLES:

[Unless otherwise noted, tables show data for 1983.]

TEXT TABLES

1-2. Private housing completions [single- and multi-family units], 1983; and residential housing inventory, 1979-83; [all] by heating fuel [gas, electricity, oil, and other, by region]. (p. 4-6)

3-4. Residential and househeating customers of gas utilities, and househeating unit additions, by [region, census division, and] State, as of Dec. 31; and househeating conversions to natural gas by type of fuel [oil, propane, electricity, and other, by census division]. (p. 8-9)

5. 1984 anticipated additions of gas househeating units [new housing and conversions, by region, census division, and State]. (p. 11)

6. Manufacturers' shipments of residential heating equipment [gas, oil, and electric warm air furnaces; gas and oil boilers; heat pumps; and wall and floor gas furnaces], 1979-83. (p. 12)

7. Average annual gas consumption/unit by region [for single- and multi-family heating and baseload, with heating degree days compared to 30-year normal]. (p. 14)

8. Average conservation by region [and census division] (percent decline from 1973 baseline) [consumption normalized for weather from pre-embargo 1973]. (p. 15)

APPENDIX TABLES

[Tables show data by gas utility arranged by census division and State.]

1. Househeating data by company [customers, average single-family home consumption, housing unit losses, and unit additions through new construction and conversions, all shown for total residential and househeating-only customers; gas-heated homes' market share; and heating degree days; 1983, with anticipated gas-heated housing unit changes for 1984]. (p. 18-45)

2. Competitive fuel prices [per million Btu, for natural gas, No. 2 fuel oil, electricity, and propane, as of Dec. 31; principal competitive fuel; and average annual gas heating bill]. (p. 48-59)

A1865
American
Hospital Association

A1865–1   HOSPITALS

Semimonthly.
ISSN 0018-5973.
LC 43-4821.
SRI/MF/not filmed

Semimonthly trade publication on topics related to hospital operations, services and staff administration, facilities planning and utilization, and financial management.

Data are from AHA, Federal agencies, and other sources.

Issues include:

a. Recurring article with 1 table on CPI medical care component change for 1- and 12-month periods.

b. Quarterly articles on community hospital finances and operations; hospital economic forecasts; and tax-exempt health care bonds.

c. Annual statistical features, including salary surveys.

d. MULTIs, a separately paginated bimonthly magazine on multifacility health system management.

e. Special articles, occasionally with statistics; and regular depts.

All features with substantial statistical content are described as they appear, under "Statistical Features." Each issue of the journal is reviewed, but an abstract is published in SRI monthly issues only when statistical features appear.

Availability: Hospitals, American Hospital Publishing, Inc., 211 E. Chicago Ave., Chicago IL 60611, $40.00 per yr., single copy $3.50; SRI/MF/not filmed.

Issues reviewed during 1985: Nov. 1, 1984-Oct. 16, 1985 (P) (Vol. 58, Nos. 21-24; Vol. 59, Nos. 1-20) [Vol. 59, No. 6 incorrectly reads No. 4].

STATISTICAL FEATURES:

A1865–1.601: Nov. 1, 1984 (Vol. 58, No. 21)

PPOs' MARKET SHARE GAINS ASSESSED

(p. 19) Article, with 1 chart projecting market shares for health care delivery systems by type (preferred provider organizations, HMOs, and fee-for-service plans), 1995. Data are from Phillips and Associates, Inc.

HEALTH BENEFITS FORESEEN SUFFERING FROM TAX LAW CHANGE

(p. 25) Article on potential effects of requiring corporations to pay tax on employee benefit contributions. Data are from a recent survey of 502 chief executive officers conducted by William M. Mercer-Meidinger, Inc. Includes 1 table showing percent of respondents intending to decrease 6 fringe benefits if tax preferences are eliminated.

MEDICAL PRICE INCREASES SLOW: LATEST CPI FIGURES, RECURRING FEATURE

(p. 26) Recurring article, with 1 table showing 1- and 12-month percent change in CPI medical care components, Aug. 1984.

HOSPITALS CONTINUE TO SEE SHARP ADMISSION DECLINES

(p. 28-30) Article, with 1 chart showing hospital admissions, 2nd quarter 1982-84. Data are from AHA.

COST HIKE CAUSES CUTS IN STAY, BEDS, FTEs, QUARTERLY FEATURE

(p. 45-46) Quarterly article, with 1 chart showing community hospital operating and patient revenue margins, 1st half 1983-84; and 2 charts illustrating trends in selected other performance indicators, from 1981. Data are from AHA National Panel Survey.

COMPLIANCE PROBLEMS SEEN WITH JCAH NURSING STANDARDS

(p. 78) Article, with 1 table showing percent of hospitals not in compliance with 6 types of nursing service quality assurance standards set by Joint Commission on Accreditation of Hospitals (JCAH), 1982. The 6 standards shown are those with the highest rate of noncompliance. Data are from a JCAH survey of 1,155 hospitals.

SURVEY OF HOSPITAL SALARIES, ANNUAL FEATURE

(p. 80-96) Annual article, by Linda I. Collins, on hospital management/supervisory staff compensation, for year ended Mar. 1984. Presents data on salary range, and average salary as percent of president/administrator's salary, for 28 positions, by bed size category; prevalence of selected benefits; and percent change in salaries for executive, exempt, and nonexempt employees in health care and 5 other industries, with forecast for 1985.

Also includes profiles for 6 top management positions, showing the following: average and 25th and 75th percentile base salaries, salary grade midpoint, employees reporting, years of service and in position, age, and education; distribution by number of college degrees, sex, and academic specialization; percent serving on governing boards and receiving bonuses; and bonus as percent of base salary.

Data are from the 5th annual hospital management compensation survey conducted by William M. Mercer-Meidinger, Inc., in Mar. 1984. Survey responses cover approximately 5,500 positions reported by 186 hospitals. Includes 1 table on sample characteristics, and 8 tables and 5 charts on survey results.

COMPUTER HARDWARE IN THE HOSPITAL INDUSTRY

(p. 111-114) By C. L. Packer et al. Article on computer use in hospitals, based on 1984 surveys of 4,367 hospitals conducted by Shared Data Research, Inc.

Includes 7 charts showing the following for mainframe, mini, and microcomputer hardware: level of satisfaction with uptime, maintenance, expandability, price, performance, and available expertise; and prevalence of leased/rented vs. purchased equipment by bed size category, and of equipment supplied by 3 largest vendors and all others.

Article is part of a series of features on hospital computer use.

A1865–1.602: Nov. 16, 1984 (Vol. 58, No. 22)

HEALTH INDUSTRY JOB OUTLOOK GOOD: STUDY

(p. 30) Article, with 1 table showing health services industry employment, by segment (hospitals, convalescent institutions, physicians' and dentists' offices, and other), selected years 1971-83. Data are from an AFL-CIO study.

MEDIAN HEALTH SALARY RAISE OF 6.2% CITED

(p. 32) Article, with 1 chart showing average percent salary increase, for health care and 26 other industry groups, 1984 vs. 1983. Data are from a survey of 2,500 organizations in 27 industries, conducted by William M. Mercer-Meidinger, Inc.

LARGE BED SURPLUS PREDICTED IN MARYLAND BY '88: COMMISSION

(p. 36) Article, with 1 table showing Maryland hospital beds, 1983; and number of excess beds at 85% and 90% occupancy estimated under 3 assumptions of patient length of stay, 1988. Data are from Maryland Health Resources Planning Commission.

FEWER BOND ISSUES IN FIRST HALF OF 1984, QUARTERLY FEATURE

(p. 47-48) Quarterly article on tax-exempt health care bonds issued in 1st half 1984. Data are from *Credit Markets* and Securities Data Co.

Includes 2 tables showing top 10 underwriters ranked by value of issues underwritten, with total number of issues and number for which firm was senior underwriter; and 10 largest bond issues, including issuer and facility name, bond date, type, net interest charge, amount, quality rating, and senior underwriting firm; 1st half 1984.

For description of previous article, for 1983, see SRI 1984 Annual under A1865-1.524.

COMPREHENSIVE HOME CARE BENEFIT SOUGHT

(p. 74) Article, with 1 table showing the following for an average home health care agency, 1982 or FY82: total and FTE employment; FTE employment for direct patient care; salary for registered nurse, home health aide, and director/administrator; revenue, with percent change from 1980; Medicare share of revenue; service days per week; client visits and cost; and percent of referrals from hospitals and private physicians.

Data were compiled for the House Select Committee on Aging.

PRODUCTIVITY EFFORTS ON THE RISE

(p. 89-90) By Mark Harju and Frank Sabatino. Article, with 1 chart and 1 table showing importance of 5 administrative and 14 staffing areas for enhanced hospital productivity, as rated by hospital chief executive officers/administrators. Data are from 272 responses to an Aug. 1984 *Hospitals* survey.

A1865–1.603: Dec. 1, 1984 (Vol. 58, No. 23)

HOME CARE MARKET REVENUES SEEN TO SOAR

(p. 28) Article, with 1 table showing value of home health care market, by type of product and service, 1983, 1988, and 1995. Data are from Predicasts, Inc.

MEDICAL PRICE INCREASES STEADY FOR SECOND MONTH, RECURRING FEATURE

(p. 33) Recurring article, with 1 table showing 1- and 12-month percent change in CPI medical care components, Sept. 1984.

WHICH MAJOR SYSTEMS? ON WHICH TYPES OF COMPUTER?

(p. 81-82) By C. L. Packer et al. Article on computer use in hospitals, based on recent surveys conducted by Shared Data Research, Inc.

Includes 4 charts showing prevalence of micro, mini, and mainframe computer use in hospital financial and strategic management and in patient care, for eastern and western regions; and number of video display terminals and computer printers per hospital, by bed size and size of data processing budget.

Article is part of a series of features covering hospital computer use.

INVESTOR-OWNED FACILITIES TO CONSTITUTE 19 PERCENT OF NATION'S HOSPITALS BY 1990

(MULTIs, p. M10) Article, with 2 charts showing percent of nongovernment hospitals managed and owned/leased/controlled by multihospital systems, 1982 and 1995. Data are from a survey of 1,000 persons in the hospital industry conducted by Arthur Andersen and Co. and American College of Hospital Administrators.

EXPORT IN DEMAND

(MULTIs, p. M14-M18) By Jo Ellen Mistarz. Article, with 2 charts showing foreign hospitals and beds managed and owned by U.S. investor-owned hospital companies, 1978-84. Data sources include *1984 Directory, Investor-Owned Hospitals and Hospital Management Companies.*

CREDIT MARKETS FORECAST: 1985

(MULTIs, p. M20-M24) By Bruce D. Mansdorf. Article, with 3 tables showing value and

average interest rate for hospital tax-exempt bonds, 1978-84; and comparative forecasts of Treasury bond and bill annual rates, bond buyer index, and prime rate, various periods 1984-86. Data are from *Bond Buyer,* and selected financial organizations.

A1865–1.604: Dec. 16, 1984 (Vol. 58, No. 24)

MULTIS' 1984 GROWTH: SMALL IN NUMBERS, LARGE IN IMPACT

(p. 40-42) Article, with 1 table ranking top 10 multihospital systems by number of beds, and including type of ownership, as of Nov. 1984. Data are from AHA.

PPS INFORMATION NEEDS CAUSE DRAMATIC COMPUTER SURGE

(p. 67) Article on data processing (DP) expenditures of hospitals, based on a Shared Data Research, Inc. sample of 500 hospitals with 50-200 beds. Includes 1 table showing number of surveyed hospitals by level of DP expenditures, 1982 and 1984.

HOSPITAL CONSTRUCTION DOWN 7.7 PERCENT

(p. 70) Article, with 2 tables showing percent change in construction value for nonresidential, industrial, educational, and hospital structures, 1980-83; and top 10 architectural firms ranked by value of work in design/construction stage, with percent involving health care facilities, 1982. Data are from Commerce Dept and AHA.

SURVEY SHOWS CEOs' PRIORITIES ARE CHANGING

(p. 71-77) By W. Barry Moore. Part 1 of a 2-part article on concerns and expectations of hospital chief executive officers (CEOs). Data are based on responses of approximately 400 CEOs to a recent survey by American Hospital Publishing, Inc. and Kurt Salmon Associates, Inc.

Includes 5 charts showing survey response regarding principal administrative concerns, areas of expertise most important for future CEOs, and possibility of joining a multihospital system by region.

NONPHYSICIAN PRACTITIONERS MAKE SLOW HEADWAY ON STAFF PRIVILEGES

(p. 82-86) By Glenn Richards. Article, with 1 chart showing percent of podiatrists with hospital medical staff membership, other forms of privileges, and no privileges. Data are from a 1984 American Podiatric Medical Assn survey of 9,800 members.

A1865–1.605: Jan. 1, 1985 (Vol. 59, No. 1)

MEDICAL CARE PRICE INCREASES ADVANCE SLIGHTLY IN OCT., RECURRING FEATURE

(p. 21) Recurring article, with 1 table showing 1- and 12-month percent change in CPI medical care components, Oct. 1984.

LAYOFFS PLAGUE MANY ALABAMA HOSPITALS

(p. 23) Article, with 1 table showing Medicare and other patient days in Alabama hospitals, Mar.-Aug. period 1983-84. Data are from a 1984 Alabama Hospital Assn member survey.

HEALTH CARE COALITIONS, FUNDING GROWING: DUNLOP GROUP

(p. 24) Article, with 1 table showing number of health care coalitions, 1984; and number participating in selected educational and administrative activities, Sept. 1983-84. Data are from Dunlop Group of Six.

TAX-EXEMPT HOSPITAL ISSUES DROP AGAIN DURING 3rd QUARTER OF '84, QUARTERLY FEATURE

(p. 41-43) Quarterly article on tax-exempt health care bonds issued in 1st 9 months 1984. Data are from Securities Data Co.

Includes 3 tables showing top 10 senior managing and senior/co-managing underwriters ranked by value of issues underwritten, with total number of issues underwritten; and 10 largest bond issues, including issuer and facility name, bond date, type, net interest charge, amount, quality rating, and senior underwriting firm; 1st 9 months 1984.

CREATING A MARKET NICHE

(p. 62-67) By Joe M. Inguanzo and Mark Harju. Article on consumer awareness of health facility services. Data are based on approximately 950 responses to an Aug./Sept. 1984 survey conducted by Professional Research Consultants, Inc. and American Hospital Publishing Inc.

Includes 1 chart and 3 tables showing percent of respondents able to identify local hospital providing best care for selected services, by region, presence of children, and prior medical care experience.

Article begins a series of features on health care consumers.

CEOs PLAN TO EXPAND HOME HEALTH, OUTPATIENT SERVICES

(p. 74-77) By W. Barry Moore. Part 2 of a 2-part article on concerns and expectations of hospital chief executive officers (CEOs). Data are based on responses of approximately 400 CEOs to a recent survey by American Hospital Publishing, Inc. and Kurt Salmon Associates, Inc.

Includes 8 charts and 1 table showing survey response regarding plans to add/expand selected services, by region and bed size; likelihood of expanding use of prospective pricing systems; and expected changes in State medical assistance levels.

HOSPITAL ECONOMIC FORECAST, QUARTERLY FEATURE

(p. 78-82) Quarterly article, by Clifford Neely, on hospital expenditure and revenue trends and forecasts, 1980-85. Presents Hospital Inflation Expense Index (HIEI), computed by Merrill Lynch Economics Inc.

Includes 1 chart and 3 tables showing HIEI expense component weights; and percent change in HIEI, with detail for wages/salaries and 8 other HIEI components, and comparisons to CPI and other general economic indicators, 1980-85.

A1865–1.606: Jan. 16, 1985 (Vol. 59, No. 2)

MULTI AFFILIATION NOT ALL-PERVASIVE

(p. 19-21) Article, with 1 chart showing investor-owned hospitals as percent of all hospitals, by State and for Puerto Rico, 1984. Data sources include *1985 Directory, Investor-Owned Hospitals and Hospital Management Companies.*

HOSPITAL CFOs SEE DISPARITY BETWEEN CEOs' OPINIONS AND REALITY

(p. 103-108) By Maria R. Traska. Article, with 3 tables showing expectations of hospital chief executive officers (CEOs) concerning changes in operating profits and incidences of financial

failures, by hospital type with detail by bed size, through 1990; and areas cited as causing principal concern among CEOs. Data are from a 1984 survey conducted by Arthur Andersen and Co.

HISTORICAL CHANGES IN HOSPITAL COMPUTER USE

(p. 115-118) By C. L. Packer et al. Article on computer use in hospitals, based on 1981 and 1984 surveys conducted by Shared Data Research, Inc.

Includes 2 charts and 3 tables showing survey response concerning data processing (DP) budget by bed size, and primary types of DP systems and applications in use, 1981 and 1984.

Article is part of a series of features covering hospital computer use.

A1865–1.607: Feb. 1, 1985 (Vol. 59, No. 3)

MEDICAL CARE PRICE INCREASES SLOW: LATEST CPI, RECURRING FEATURE

(p. 23) Recurring article, with 1 table showing 1- and 12-month percent change in CPI medical care components, Nov. 1984.

M.D./ADMINISTRATOR GROWTH SEEN

(p. 26) Article on job-related attitudes of physicians serving as hospital administrators, including perception of whether colleagues view the position as primarily medical or administrative. Data are from responses of 150 physician/administrators to a summer 1984 survey conducted by Arthur Young and Co. Includes 1 table.

ADMISSIONS DROP AGAIN, COST PER CASE UP, QUARTERLY FEATURE

(p. 35-38) Quarterly article, with 1 table showing community hospital total and patient operating margins, by census division, 1st 9 months 1983-84; and 3 charts illustrating trends in selected other performance indicators from 1981. Data are from AHA National Hospital Panel Survey.

MEDICARE TURNS 20 AS AMERICA GRAYS

(p. 59-62) By Margaret M. Heckler. Article, with 1 chart showing Medicare expenditures, 1966-83.

ARE CONSUMERS SENSITIVE TO HOSPITAL COSTS?

(p. 68-69) By Joe M. Inguanzo and Mark Harju. Article on consumer awareness of health care costs. Data are based on approximately 950 responses to an Aug./Sept. 1984 survey conducted by Professional Research Consultants, Inc., and American Hospital Publishing, Inc.

Includes 2 charts showing survey responses concerning importance of cost in hospital selection, by region, urban/rural and marital status, sex, age, education, and income.

Article is part of a series of features on health care consumers.

THIRD ANNUAL MULTIs COMPENSATION SURVEY, ANNUAL FEATURE

(MULTIs, p. M24-M26) Annual article on executive compensation of nonprofit multihospital systems, as of June 1984. Data are from responses of 25 systems to a survey conducted by Compensation Institute of William M. Mercer-Meidinger, Inc.

Includes 3 tables and 1 chart showing mean and 25th and 75th percentile salary for 11 po-

sitions; prevalence of established salary policies (including detail for secular and religious systems), and prevalence and extent of bonuses, for 5-6 positions; and percent change in salary, with comparison to all executives and total health care sector, and forecasts for 1985.

URGENT CARE CENTERS

(MULTIs, p. M31-M34) By Dudley E. Morris. Article, with 1 chart showing number of freestanding urgent health care centers, by type of ownership (corporate, hospital, and physician entrepreneur), 1980, 1982, and 1984. Data are from APM, Inc. and National Assn for Ambulatory Care.

A1865–1.608: Feb. 16, 1985 (Vol. 59, No. 4)

1984's FLOATING-RATE DEBT HERALDS A TREND, QUARTERLY FEATURE

(p. 53-54) Quarterly article on tax-exempt health care bonds covering issuances in 1984. Data are from Securities Data Co.

Includes 3 tables showing top 10 senior managing and senior/co-managing underwriters ranked by value of issues underwritten, with total number of issues underwritten; and 10 largest bond issues, including issuer and facility name, bond date, type, net interest charge, amount, quality rating, and senior underwriting firm; 1984.

SHORT-TERM ISSUES ARE PERFECT FOR POOLING

(p. 58) Article, with list of short-term tax-exempt health care financing issues ranked by value, and including issue type, sale date, senior manager, and (if applicable) insurance type and quality ratings, 1984. Data are from Securities Data Co.

A1865–1.609: Mar. 1, 1985 (Vol. 59, No. 5)

ELDERLY 21 PERCENT OF POPULATION BY 2040

(p. 41, 44) Article, with 1 chart and 1 table showing short-stay hospital days for persons 65/older, decennially 1980-2050; and number and percent of discharges from Medicare prospective pricing system (PPS) hospitals, and average length of stay, for 10 most common diagnostic related groups (medical conditions), FY84. Data are from Federal agencies.

HOME HEALTH CARE STUDY PAVES WAY FOR FIXED HOME CARE BENEFITS

(p. 72) Article, with 1 undated chart showing distribution of home health care agency clients, by age group. Data are based on 673 responses to a House Aging Committee survey of Medicare-certified home health agencies.

MHAs AND THE NEW HOSPITAL JOB MARKET

(p. 80-86) By Janet Plant. Article on trends in entry-level employment for graduates with master's degrees in health administration. Data are from joint surveys conducted by Association of University Programs in Health Administration and Korn/Ferry International.

Includes 3 tables showing prevalence of entry-level employment, by type of institution/agency ownership, type of hospital, and position, for graduating classes of 1979, 1981, and 1983.

AUTOMATION IN THE MEDICAL RECORDS DEPARTMENT

(p. 100-104) By C. L. Packer et al. Article on computer use in hospitals, based on recent surveys conducted by Shared Data Research, Inc.

Includes 5 charts showing prevalence of and satisfaction with automated systems handling hospital medical records and diagnostic research group (DRG) applications, with detail by bed-size group and system type (in-house, turnkey, facility management, and shared services), primarily 1984.

Article is part of a series of features covering hospital computer use.

A1865–1.610: Mar. 16, 1985 (Vol. 59, No. 6)

[Issue incorrectly reads No. 4.]

TEACHING HOSPITALS OFFER VIEWS ON MULTIS

(p. 24, 29) Article on benefits and drawbacks associated with affiliating teaching hospitals and voluntary multihospital systems, as perceived by teaching hospital administrators/medical school deans. Data are from a survey of 90 administrators/deans, conducted by Robert Douglass Associates, Inc. and Marketing Research Consultants, Inc. Includes 1 undated chart.

Data clarification appears in the Apr. 16, 1985 issue (see A1865-1.612 below).

HYSTERECTOMY MOST FREQUENT SURGERY FOR UNDER AGE-65 GROUP: STUDY

(p. 70) Article, with 1 table showing top 4-5 surgical procedures ranked by number performed per 1,000 population aged 65/under, by sex, 1981. Data were compiled by Corporate Health Strategies, Inc. from an NCHS study.

BIG BUSINESS EMBRACES ALTERNATE DELIVERY

(p. 81-84) By Steve F. Gardner et al. Article reporting on corporate measures for controlling health care costs. Data are from a Jan. 1985 MarketPULSE Measurement Systems survey of 200 Fortune 500 firms. Includes 2 charts and 1 table showing survey response concerning use and perceived importance of selected cost containment strategies, 1985; and prevalence of employee participation in HMOs, 1983-84.

WHAT MAKES CONSUMERS SELECT A HOSPITAL?

(p. 90-94) By Joe M. Inguanzo and Mark Harju. Article on consumer preferences in selecting hospitals. Data are based on approximately 950 responses to an Aug./Sept. 1984 survey conducted by Professional Research Consultants, Inc., and American Hospital Publishing Inc.

Includes 2 charts and 2 tables showing survey results on whether respondents have a preferred hospital, reasons for preference, and most important factors affecting hospital selection, with detail by region, urban-rural and marital status, sex, age, education, and income.

Article is part of a series of features on health care consumers.

A1865–1.611: Apr. 1, 1985 (Vol. 59, No. 7)

LATEST CPI FINDS RISE IN MEDICAL CARE PRICES STEADY, RECURRING FEATURE

(p. 22) Recurring article, with 1 table showing 1- and 12-month percent change in CPI medical care components, Jan. 1985.

OTA WARNS PPS PRESSURE MAY ALTER ICU CARE

(p. 42, 45) Article, with 1 table showing hospital special and routine care days for Medicare discharges, with comparison to total hospital days, by diagnosis, 1980. Data are from Office of Technology Assessment and are based on a Health Care Financing Administration study covering 20% of Medicare discharges.

EXECUTIVE SUCCESSION: WHO DECIDES?

(p. 66-69) By Richard D. Gifford and Nancy Davidson. First of 2 articles comparing views of hospital and corporate chief executive officers (CEOs) concerning executive succession and hiring outlook. Data are from responses to a 1984 Russell Reynolds Associates, Inc., survey of CEOs at the 1,000 largest corporations, and from approximately 260 responses of CEOs at hospitals with 300/more beds.

Includes 2 charts showing hospital and corporate CEO responses concerning plans for naming and preparing a successor, and planned retirement activities. Also includes 1 table showing respondent distribution by age.

HOW DO CONSUMERS RECEIVE LOCAL HEALTH CARE INFORMATION?

(p. 74-76) By Joe M. Inguanzo and Mark Harju. Article on sources of health care information used by consumers. Data are based on approximately 950 responses to an Aug./Sept. 1984 survey conducted by Professional Research Consultants, Inc., and American Hospital Publishing, Inc.

Includes 2 charts and 1 table showing survey response concerning principal sources of local health care information, with detail by respondent characteristics including sex, marital status, and presence of family physician.

Article is part of a series of features on health care consumers.

HOSPITAL ECONOMIC FORECAST, QUARTERLY FEATURE

(p. 80-84) Quarterly article, by Clifford Neely, on hospital expenditure and revenue trends and forecasts, primarily 1980-86. Presents Hospital Inflation Expense Index (HIEI), computed by Merrill Lynch Economics Inc.

Includes 1 chart and 4 tables showing HIEI expense component weights; and percent change in HIEI, with detail for wages/salaries and 8 other HIEI components, and comparisons to CPI and other general economic indicators, 1980-86 with wage/salary trends from 1974.

MULTIS FORECAST PSYCHIATRIC GROWTH

(MULTIs, p. M30-M32) By Benedict J. Gentile and Jo Ellen Mistarz. Article on multihospital system plans for expanding psychiatric services and facilities. Data are from a 1983 AHA regional survey, and from 65 responses to a 1984 American Hospital Publishing, Inc., survey of multihospital systems.

Includes 3 charts and 1 table showing the following for multihospital system psychiatric services:

a. Anticipated changes in share of total business, and hospital and unit expansion plans, by type of control (Catholic, other religious, other nonprofit, and investor-owned), as of 1984.

b. Inpatient units and beds, freestanding hospitals and beds, and hospitals offering outpatient service, by census region and type of management (owned/leased/sponsored or contract managed), 1983.

HMO STOCK OUTLOOK

(MULTIs p. M33) Article, with 1 table showing the following for 7 publicly traded HMOs: date established; stock price as of Feb. 21, 1985; and shares outstanding and enrollment (no date). Data are from Salomon Brothers, Inc.

A1865–1.612: Apr. 16, 1985 (Vol. 59, No. 8)

CLARIFICATION

(p. 34) Data clarification for article on affiliations between teaching hospitals and voluntary multihospital systems.

For description of article, see A1865-1.610 above.

RISE SEEN IN LEVELS OF BENEFIT COVERAGE, USE OF DEDUCTIBLES

(p. 39) Article, with 1 table showing distribution of employees covered under group health insurance plans, by amount of maximum daily benefits allowed, 1979 and 1984. Data are from a Health Insurance Assn of America survey.

CROWDED SOFTWARE MARKET DOMINATED BY FEW

(p. 68) Article on computer software vendors for the health care industry. Data are from responses of 2,371 hospitals to a 1985 Shared Data Research survey. Includes 1 table showing top 10 vendors of financial management, patient care, and strategic management software ranked by number of client hospitals.

HOSPITAL-BASED MOBs: IMPORTANT GROWTH COMPONENT

(p. 94-95) Article on use of hospital-based medical office buildings (MOBs). Data are from 686 responses to a 1982 Washington University School of Medicine survey of nongovernment, nonprofit hospitals with 200/more beds.

Includes 1 table showing beds, admissions, occupancy rate, employment, and expenses, for hospitals operating/planning and not operating an MOB, 1972 and 1982.

WHAT HOSPITALS THINK OF APPLICATION SOFTWARE

(p. 101-104) By C. L. Packer et al. Article on computer use in hospitals, based on recent surveys conducted by Shared Data Research, Inc.

Includes 3 charts presenting data on prevalence of 6 software applications operating under, at, or over budget, with detail for financial planning and diagnostic research group (DRG) applications by system type (in-house, turnkey, facility management, and shared services); and willingness of current users to recommend each application to other hospitals; 1985.

Article is part of a series of features covering hospital computer use.

EXECUTIVE DEMAND HIGHEST IN MARKETING, INFORMATION SYSTEMS

(p. 106-112) By Richard D. Gifford and Nancy Davidson. Second of 2 articles comparing views of hospital and corporate chief executive officers (CEOs) concerning executive succession and hiring outlook. Data are from responses to a 1984 Russell Reynolds Associates, Inc., survey of CEOs at the 1,000 largest corporations, and from approximately 260 responses of CEOs at hospitals with 300/more beds.

Includes 1 chart and 2 tables showing hospital and corporate CEO forecasts of senior executive hiring levels during next 12-month and 5-year periods; and percent of hospitals with executives earning $75,000/more; all by area of management specialty.

A1865–1.613: May 1, 1985 (Vol. 59, No. 9)

MEDICAL CARE PRICE INCREASES EDGE UPWARD IN FEB.: CPI, RECURRING FEATURE

(p. 32) Recurring article, with 1 table showing 1- and 12-month percent change in CPI medical care components, Feb. 1985.

PPAs: A NEW PAYMENT SYSTEM EVOLVES

(p. 43-46) By Suzanne Powills and William Weinberg. Article on selective contracting approaches used by health care providers to facilitate arrangements with buyers of health care services. Data are from AHA. Includes 1 chart showing number of preferred provider arrangements in operation, by State, as of early 1985.

CONTRACTING HIKES OCCUPANCY IN PSYCH UNITS: STUDY

(p. 60-62) Article, with 1 undated table showing the following for hospital psychiatric units before and after implementation of contracted management: occupancy rate (with comparison to total hospital), length of stay, staff/bed ratios, inservice training hours, structured treatment and unstructured recreation hours, insurance share of revenues, and collections as percent of billings.

Data are from a 1982-83 George Mason University study of 16 psychiatric units.

INPATIENT CHEMICAL DEPENDENCY PROGRAM COSTS LOWER THAN RESIDENTIAL PROGRAMS: TWIN CITIES

(p. 63) Article, with 1 table showing cases, average length of stay, and average charge per day and per case, for hospital and free-standing residential alcoholism treatment programs in Minnesota and Minneapolis/St. Paul, 1983. Data are from Minneapolis Council of Community Hospitals.

HOSPITALS FACE STAFFING WOES FROM PT ENTRY LEVEL CHANGE

(p. 64) Article, with 2 undated charts showing percent of physical therapists employed in and out of hospitals, and percent of hospitals with physical therapy depts. Data are from AHA.

CRITICAL CARE UNDER PPS

(p. 66-68) By Glenn Richards. Article, with 2 tables showing number of hospitals; and critical care units and beds, by type of care (cardiac, pediatric, neonatal, and mixed/other); for total and community hospitals, 1979-83. Data are from AHA.

ADMISSIONS FALL, BUT MARGINS ARE UP IN '84, QUARTERLY FEATURE

(p. 70-72) Quarterly article, by Deborah Freko, with 1 table showing community hospital total and patient operating margins, by census division, 1983-84; 1 chart showing percent change in hospital expenses, cost per case, ad-

missions, length of stay, employment, and beds, 1983-84; and 2 charts illustrating selected hospital performance indicator trends from 1981. Data are from AHA National Hospital Panel Survey.

HOSPITAL-PHYSICIAN JOINT VENTURES: WHO'S DOING WHAT

(p. 74-78) By Michael A. Morrisey and Deal Chandler Brooks. Article, with 1 chart and 1 table showing percent of hospitals involved in hospital/physician joint ventures, by census division and type of venture (including HMOs, minor emergency centers, home health agencies, and medical office buildings), 1984. Data are from 3,601 responses to a 1984 AHA survey of hospitals.

CONSUMER SATISFACTION WITH HOSPITALIZATION

(p. 81-83) By Joe M. Inguanzo and Mark Harju. Article on consumer satisfaction with hospital personnel and accommodations. Data are based on approximately 950 responses to an Aug./Sept. 1984 survey conducted by Professional Research Consultants, Inc., and American Hospital Publishing, Inc.

Includes 2 charts showing survey response concerning satisfaction with nursing care, room appearance, hospital staff, food quality, and billing procedure, with detail for specific complaints.

Article is part of a series of features on health care consumers.

A1865–1.614: May 16, 1985 (Vol. 59, No. 10)

PLANS WITH DEDUCTIBLES INCREASE: SURVEY

(p. 27) Article, with 1 chart showing percent of companies using or considering 8 cost containment measures for employee health benefit plans, 1984. Data are from a Hewitt Associates survey of 1,185 companies.

SIZE OF FEC MARKET A MATTER OF OPINION

(p. 43-44) Article, with 1 chart showing number of free-standing ambulatory care centers, by State, 1985. Data are from American College of Emergency Physicians.

OUTPATIENT SURGERY UP 77 PERCENT: DATA

(p. 54) Article, with 1 table showing number of inpatient and outpatient surgical procedures performed, 1979-83. Data are from AHA.

HOME CARE AGENCIES UP 25 PERCENT SINCE '84

(p. 64, 68) Article, with 1 table showing Medicare certified home health agencies by type, including visiting nurses assns, hospital- and rehabilitation-based agencies, skilled nursing facilities, and government, proprietary, and nonprofit agencies, Feb. 1984-85. Data are from Health Care Financing Administration.

BABY BOOMERS HELP HMOs GROW TO 42 STATES

(p. 84, 88-89) Article, with 1 table showing HMO enrollment and number of plans, by type and State, June 1984. Data are from InterStudy's *1984 HMO Census Preview.*

INTEGRATION, PERFORMANCE KEY TO AMBULATORY CARE INFORMATION SYSTEMS

(p. 120-122) By C. L. Packer et al. Article on computer use in hospitals, based on recent surveys conducted by Shared Data Research, Inc.

Includes 2 charts and 2 tables presenting data on ambulatory care management systems,

including reasons for satisfaction, perceived benefits, and willingness to recommend system to other hospitals, by application, with summary comparison to satisfaction with traditional data processing systems, 1985.

Article is part of a series of features covering hospital computer use.

A1865–1.615: June 1, 1985 (Vol. 59, No. 11)

LATEST CPI SEES JUMP IN RATE OF INCREASE IN MEDICAL CARE PRICES, RECURRING FEATURE

(p. 25) Recurring article, with 1 table showing 1- and 12-month percent change in CPI medical care components, Mar. 1985.

NURSING HOME MARKET ATTRACTS MULTIS: SURVEY

(MULTIs, p. M24-M26) By Benedict J. Gentile and Jo Ellen Mistarz. Article on multihospital system plans for expanding nursing home and life care facilities. Data are from the Census Bureau, and from 65 responses to a 1984 American Hospital Publishing, Inc., survey of multihospital systems.

Includes 3 charts showing anticipated changes in nursing home and life care facility share of total multihospital system business; and projected percent change in population size and share, for persons age 65/over, by State, 1980-2000 period.

HOSPITAL SUPPLY STOCK

(MULTIs, p. M29) Article, with 2 tables showing earnings per share for 6 hospital supply companies, 1st quarter and full year 1984-85. Data are from Dean Witter Reynolds, Inc.

CREDENTIALING: SAY GOOD-BYE TO THE 'RUBBER STAMP'

(p. 50-52) By Deal Chandler Brooks and Michael A. Morrisey. Article on hospital review of physician applications for staff membership/clinical privileges. Data are from 3,601 responses to a 1984 AHA survey of hospitals. Includes 2 charts and 1 table showing average applications received, by census division; and review criteria and fees.

WHAT'S THE MARKET FOR EMERGENCY CARE?

(p. 53-54) By Joe M. Inguanzo and Mark Harju. Article on consumer satisfaction with hospital emergency dept service. Data are based on approximately 950 responses to an Aug./Sept. 1984 survey conducted by Professional Research Consultants, Inc., and American Hospital Publishing, Inc.

Includes 2 tables showing survey response concerning satisfaction with staff courtesy and promptness, and specific reasons for dissatisfaction.

Article is part of a series of features on health care consumers.

OCCUPATIONAL THERAPY USE RISES UNDER PPS

(p. 60-62) By Madelaine S. Gray. Article, with 1 table comparing hospital occupational therapy (OT) dept activities before and after Medicare's implementation of the prospective pricing system (PPS). Data are from 1,044 responses to a 1985 American Assn of Occupational Therapy survey of OT dept directors, and are shown separately for facilities that operate under PPS and those that do not.

A1865–1.616: June 16, 1985 (Vol. 59, No. 12)

MEDICAL CARE PRICE INCREASES, INFLATION RATE SLOW IN APRIL, RECURRING FEATURE

(p. 26) Recurring article, with 1 table showing 1- and 12-month percent change in CPI medical care components, Apr. 1985.

REFINANCINGS DOMINATE FIRST-QUARTER BONDS, QUARTERLY FEATURE

(p. 53-56) Quarterly article on tax-exempt health care facility bonds, covering issuances in 1st quarter 1985. Data are from Securities Data Co.

Includes 3 tables showing top 10 senior managing and senior/co-managing underwriters ranked by value of issues underwritten, with total number of issues underwritten; and 10 largest bond issues, including issuer and facility name, bond date, type, net interest charge, amount, quality rating, and senior underwriting firm; 1st quarter 1985.

HOME CARE BEARS BRUNT OF DRG SYSTEM

(p. 70-73) Article, with 1 table showing urban and rural home health, professional in-home nursing, and home health aide visits in eastern Washington State, various periods 1983-84. Data are from Eastern Washington Area on Aging.

INDIGENT CARE ISSUE FOCUSES ON FINANCING

(p. FB46-FB48) Article, with 1 table showing number of registered community hospitals, and patient revenue, bad debt, and charity care cost, all by type of control (nongovernment/not-for-profit, investor-owned, and State/local government), 1979-82. Data are from AHA.

ELDERLY REQUIRE SHIFT IN HOSPITAL RESOURCES

(p. FB53, FB58, FB63) By Janet A. Tedesco. Article, with 1 table showing number and percent of community hospitals with selected services and facilities associated with comprehensive long-term care, 1978 and 1980-83. Data are from AHA annual surveys, as reported in *Healthcare Financial Management.*

DIVERSIFICATION BOOSTS OUTPATIENT DELIVERY

(p. FB68) Article, with 1 chart showing percent of hospitals planning to add/expand various types of services in 1985. Data are based on responses of approximately 400 chief executive officers to a 1984 survey by American Hospital Publishing, Inc., and Kurt Salmon Associates, Inc.

HIS MARKET OVERVIEW PREDICTS GROWTH TO 1990

(p. 110-116) By C. L. Packer et al. Article on hospital information system (HIS) market. Data are from Shared Data Research, Inc., and are based on recent surveys of hospitals and on interviews with executives of 8 HIS vendor companies.

Includes 2 charts and 1 table showing HIS industry revenues, triennially 1981-90, with detail for 3 publicly traded vendors, 1981 and 1984; and percent of hospitals using selected software applications, 1985.

Article is part of a series of features covering hospital computer use.

A1865–1.617: July 1, 1985 (Vol. 59, No. 13)

LESS COSTLY HEALTH CARE BILLS DUE FROM BENEFIT CHANGES

(p. 19-20) Article, with 1 undated chart showing percent of corporate benefits officers and employees finding cost-saving changes in company health benefit plans acceptable. Data are from 3,013 responses to a survey conducted by Louis Harris and Associates for the Equitable Life Assurance Society of the U.S.

CHANGES LOOM FOR VETERANS' HEALTH CARE

(p. 30-32) Article, with 1 table showing VA expenditures for medical care/hospital services, medical facility construction, and medical administration/research/other, 1984-88. Also estimates savings under proposal requiring reimbursement of VA from veterans' private insurance for care of non-service-related problems, 1986-88. Data are from Budget of the U.S.

PLASTIC SURGERY UP 50% SINCE '81: SURVEY

(p. 54-56) Article, with 1 table showing number of aesthetic plastic surgery procedures performed, 1981 and 1984, and fee range, 1984, by procedure. Data are from an American Society of Plastic and Reconstructive Surgeons survey, and exclude reconstructive procedures.

MARKETING IS KEY TO PR PROFESSIONALS' ROLES

(p. 60-62) Article, with 1 table showing primary job responsibilities of hospital public relations/marketing directors, by hospital bed size group and public relations/marketing budget size. Data are based on 933 responses to a 1984 survey by American Society for Hospital Marketing and Public Relations.

MYTH OF THE CLOSED MEDICAL STAFF

(p. 75-77) By Michael A. Morrisey and Deal Chandler Brooks. Article on hospital policies closing medical staff and clinical privileges to new applications, and establishing exclusive contracts for provision of medical services. Data are based on responses of 3,601 hospitals to a 1984 AHA survey.

Includes 2 charts and 1 table showing percent of hospitals with full or partial closure to new applications, with bylaws (enacted or under consideration) providing for full closure, and with exclusive contracts for various depts and medical specialties; and probability that a hospital will have at least 1 exclusive contract, by census division; as of Jan. 1984.

HOSPITAL ECONOMIC FORECAST: INFLATION'S DOWNWARD TREND TO END IN '86, QUARTERLY FEATURE

(p. 78-81) Quarterly article, by Clifford Neely, on hospital expenditure and revenue trends and forecasts, 1980s-86. Presents Hospital Inflation Expense Index (HIEI), computed by Merrill Lynch Economics Inc.

Includes 1 chart and 4 tables showing HIEI expense component weights; inflation rates for hospital goods and services; and percent change in HIEI, with detail for wages/salaries and 8 other HIEI components, and comparisons to CPI and other general economic indicators, various years 1980-86.

HOSPITALS STILL DOMINATE EMERGENCY CARE MARKET

(p. 84-85) By Joe M. Inguanzo and Mark Harju. Article on consumer use of hospital emergency depts vs. minor emergency clinics. Data are based on approximately 950 responses to an Aug./Sept. 1984 survey conducted by Professional Research Consultants, Inc., and American Hospital Publishing, Inc.

Includes 2 charts and 1 table showing survey response concerning preferred type of minor emergency care, likelihood of using minor emergency clinics, and importance of selected factors in choosing clinics.

Article is part of a series of features on health care consumers.

A1865–1.618: July 16, 1985 (Vol. 59, No. 14)

CPI: PRICE INCREASES SLOW IN MAY FOR MEDICAL CARE COMMODITIES, RECURRING FEATURE

(p. 30) Recurring article, with 1 table showing 1- and 12-month percent change in CPI medical care components, May 1985.

MORE THAN 1,500 HOSPICE PROGRAMS ARE OPERATING IN U.S.: JCAH STUDY

(p. 70) Article, with 1 table showing home care staff/patient ratio for hospice programs, by program type (hospital, independent, and community home health agency) and staff category (registered nurse, licensed nurse, psychosocial support, and home health aide/technician), Dec. 1983. Data are from a Joint Commission on Accreditation of Hospitals survey.

REVENUE PROBLEMS TOP CFOs' WORRIES

(p. 76-81) By Maria R. Traska and Benedict J. Gentile. Article, with 2 charts showing hospital chief financial officers' ratings of selected issues by importance to the health care industry in general and to the officers' own hospitals. Data are from 209 responses to an Apr. 1985 *Hospitals* survey.

LATE RECEIVABLES SQUEEZE CASH FLOW

(p. 82-85) By Maria R. Traska and Benedict J. Gentile. Article on hospital cash flow problems. Data are from 209 responses to an Apr. 1985 *Hospitals* survey of hospital chief financial officers.

Includes 2 tables showing survey response on days elapsing before payment of accounts receivable (total and Medicare/Medicaid) and accounts payable; and incidence of cash-only arrangements with suppliers, by census division; Apr. 1985.

HOSPITAL CLOSURES REMAIN STABLE

(p. 91-94) By Ross M. Mullner et al. Article, with 3 tables showing community and non-community hospital closures and resulting bed losses, by bed size group and type of control, 1980-84. Data are from AHA.

CHANGING ENVIRONMENT SPURS NEW HIS DEMAND

(p. 99-101) By C. L. Packer et al. Article on hospital information system (HIS) market. Data are from Shared Data Research, Inc.

Includes 1 table and 1 chart showing market shares for 8 HIS vendors, 1984/85 and 1990; and earnings trends for 6 vendors, 1980-84.

Article is part of a series of features covering hospital computer use.

A1865–1.619: Aug. 1, 1985 (Vol. 59, No. 15)

RISE IN LOS MAY SIGNAL CASE-MIX CHANGES, QUARTERLY FEATURE

(p. 25-27) Quarterly article, with 1 table showing community hospital total and patient operating margins, by census division and bed-size group, years ending Mar. 1984-85; 1 chart showing percent change in hospital expenses, cost per case, admissions, length of stay, employment, and beds, 1st quarter 1984-85; and 2 charts illustrating selected hospital performance indicator trends from 1982. Data are from AHA National Hospital Panel Survey.

ADMINISTRATION A PROBLEM SOURCE, SAY PHARMACY COLLEGES

(p. 39) Article on problems between pharmacy colleges and their affiliated teaching hospitals. Data are from 1984 surveys of deans or dept chairmen at 72 colleges, and pharmacy directors at 67 affiliated hospitals, conducted by American Assn of Colleges of Pharmacy and American Society of Hospital Pharmacists.

Includes 1 table showing problems identified by college deans/dept chairmen.

SHIFTS SEEN IN BRITAIN'S HEALTH CARE

(MULTIs, p. M18-M19, M29) By Emily Friedman. Article, with 1 undated table showing hospitals and beds held in the UK by 4 major U.S. investor-owned multihospital systems.

INDIGENT CARE: WHERE THE MARKETPLACE FAILS

(p. 48-52) By Emily Friedman. Article on trends in health care for indigent population. Data are from the Robert Wood Johnson Foundation.

Includes 2 charts and 1 table showing percent of poverty/near-poverty population receiving Medicaid, selected years 1969-85; percent change in uninsured poor and in free care provided by hospitals, 1980-82 period; and physician visits per person, and hospital days per 1,000 persons, for uninsured and insured population under age 65, 1977, with percent change in uninsured/insured ratio.

WHAT'S THE MARKET FOR OUTPATIENT SURGERY?

(p. 55-57) By Joe M. Inguanzo and Mark Harju. Article on consumer experiences with outpatient surgery. Data are based on approximately 950 responses to an Aug./Sept. 1984 survey conducted by Professional Research Consultants, Inc., and American Hospital Publishing, Inc.

Includes 2 charts and 2 tables showing survey response concerning consumer use of outpatient surgery and whether performed in hospital, physician's office, or freestanding surgical center; and reasons for dissatisfaction with staff courtesy and promptness of treatment.

Article is part of a series of features on health care consumers.

EXPANDING MEDICAL STAFF: NONPHYSICIAN PRACTITIONERS

(p. 58-59) By Michael A. Morrisey and Deal Chandler Brooks. Article on hospital medical staff planning, and policies regarding nonphysician practitioners. Data are based on responses of 3,601 hospitals to a 1984 AHA survey.

Includes 1 chart and 2 tables showing average number of medical staff practitioners per hospital and percent of hospitals granting staff membership/privileges, by type of practitioner, with detail by type of membership and privilege for podiatrists, clinical psychologists, nurse midwives, and chiropractors; and distribution of hospitals with medical staff plans, by whether plans have been met.

A1865–1.620: Aug. 16, 1985 (Vol. 59, No. 16)

MEDICAL CARE PRICES UP 0.7 PERCENT IN JUNE: CPI, RECURRING FEATURE

(p. 34) Recurring article, with 1 table showing 1- and 12-month percent change in CPI medical care components, June 1985.

BAXTER'S CASH-FLOW STRENGTH MAY PROVIDE MERGER INSIGHT

(p. 90) Article highlighting health care-related companies among top 200 nonfinancial corporations ranked by cash flow, as listed in *Dun's Business Month.* Data are from Standard & Poor's Compustat data base. Includes 1 table ranking top 16 health care-related companies by cash flow, and also showing discretionary cash flow, net income, and cash flow/revenue ratio, 1984, with selected comparisons to 1983, and rank among top 200 corporations.

For description of *Dun's* article, see C8650-5.605.

SURVEY PREDICTS NURSING BUDGET CUTBACKS

(p. 116) Article, with 1 table showing distribution of full- and part-time registered nurses by highest educational degree attained, 1984. Data are from an AHA survey.

COST STRATEGIES OF CEOs AND MATERIALS MANAGERS DIVERGE

(p. 120) Article on importance of 10 hospital purchasing cost containment measures as perceived by hospital chief executive officers and materials managers. Data are from surveys conducted by American Hospital Publishing, Inc., and Medline Industries, Inc. Includes 1 undated table.

HEALTH PROMOTION PROGRAMS FLOURISHING: SURVEY

(p. 128-135) Article on hospital sponsorship of health promotion/patient education programs for 5 target population groups (in- and outpatients, hospital and corporate/business employees, and nonpatients/community groups), 1984. Data are from responses of 3,578 community and short-term Federal general hospitals to a survey conducted by AHA and Northwestern University.

Includes 2 charts and 1 table showing the following, by target group: hospitals offering programs, funding sources, and types of programs offered, 1984.

A1865–1.621: Sept. 1, 1985 (Vol. 59, No. 17)

HOSPITAL HOME IV, RT WILL SEE GROWTH SPURT

(p. 44-47) Article on hospital plans to offer alternate health care delivery programs. Data are from 168 responses to a June-July 1985 survey of hospitals conducted by Dean Witter Reynolds, Inc.

Includes 2 tables showing hospitals offering and not interested in offering programs, and

planning to offer hospital-operated and joint venture programs, for the following: diagnostic imaging, offsite primary care, and birthing centers; home respiratory and intravenous therapy; and wellness, occupational health, and alcohol/substance abuse programs.

PPAs: FEWER START-UPS BUT BETTER OPERATIONS

(p. 68-73) By Kathryn A. Schroer and Elworth Taylor. Article on preferred provider arrangements (PPAs). Most data are from a Dec. 1984 AHA survey of 115 PPAs.

Includes 4 charts showing the following, for 1984:

a. PPAs organized, 1979-84; and PPAs reporting hospitals, physician groups, insurance companies, and others as involved in initial organization and as remaining sole or co-owner.

b. Operational PPAs, by State; percent of PPAs contracting with selected groups (including employers and insurance groups); and percent using selected payment methods, and management functions (including case reviews and 2nd surgical opinions).

WHAT'S THE MARKET FOR HMOs AND PPAs?

(p. 74-75) By Joe M. Inguanzo and Mark Harju. Article on consumer acceptance and knowledge of HMOs and preferred provider arrangements (PPAs). Data are based on approximately 950 responses to an Aug./Sept. 1984 survey conducted by Professional Research Consultants, Inc., and American Hospital Publishing, Inc.

Includes 6 charts showing survey response concerning likelihood of changing physicians and hospitals for better insurance coverage from an HMO/PPA; familiarity with HMOs and PPAs; and whether in favor of joining HMOs and PPAs.

Article is part of a series of features on health care consumers.

HEALTH CARE POLICY LESSONS FROM BRITAIN

(p. 78-83) By Emily Friedman. Article on National Health Service (NHS) in the UK. Data are from the Health Service in England, and *Inequalities in Health and Health Care.*

Includes 1 chart and 1 table showing NHS funding by source, and expenditures by object/function, 1982/83; and NHS health care expenditures per person and per person reporting illness, by occupational class, 1972. Data are shown in British pounds.

PHYSICIAN INFLUENCE IN HOSPITALS: AN UPDATE

(p. 86-89) By Michael A. Morrisey and Deal Chandler Brooks. Article on prevalence of medical staff on hospital governing boards, and hospital policies regarding selection of dept chairpersons. Data are based on responses of 3,601 hospitals to a 1984 AHA survey.

Includes 1 chart and 1 table showing distribution of hospitals by number of medical staff members with voting privileges on governing boards, and by method used to choose clinical dept chairpersons/service chiefs.

A1865–1.622: Sept. 16, 1985 (Vol. 59, No. 18)

HOSPITAL PRICES UP SLIGHTLY, RECURRING FEATURE

(p. 26) Recurring article, with 1 table showing 1- and 12-month percent change in CPI medical care components, July 1985.

BOND GROWTH ANTICIPATES REAGAN TAX REFORM, QUARTERLY FEATURE

(p. 43-48) Quarterly article on tax-exempt health care facility bonds, covering issuances in 1st half 1985. Data are from Securities Data Co., and Prescott, Ball & Turben.

Includes 3 tables showing top 10 senior managing and senior/co-managing underwriters ranked by value of issues underwritten, with total number of issues underwritten; and 10 largest bond issues, including issuer and facility name, and bond date, type, net interest charge, amount, quality rating, and senior underwriting firm; 1st half 1985.

PATTERNS OF HOSPITAL USE BY THE ELDERLY VARY WIDELY BY AGE GROUP: HHS STUDY

(p. 61-62) Article on characteristics of elderly patients in hospitals. Data are from a 1970-77 study of 331 hospitals conducted by the National Center for Health Services Research and Health Care Technology Assessment.

Includes 1 table showing the following: average length of stay and number of diagnoses and procedures; patients covered by Medicare, undergoing operations, and discharged to another health facility; and female patients; all for patients aged 65-79 and 80/over at proprietary, not-for-profit, and public hospitals, 1970-77 period.

MOST BLUE CROSS/BLUE SHIELD PLANS COVER HOME CARE: STUDY

(p. 62-64) Article, with 1 table showing number of Blue Cross/Blue Shield plans that have contracts with home health agencies, and number of contracts, all by type of agency, 1984. Data are from a Blue Cross and Blue Shield Assn survey.

CONTRACTS WILL GROW IN NONCLINICAL AREAS

(p. 86-92) By Larry N. Feinberg and Maria R. Traska. Article on hospital plans to use outside management contracts for nonclinical and data processing services. Data are from 168 responses to a June-July 1985 survey of hospitals conducted by Dean Witter Reynolds, Inc.

Includes 3 tables showing the following for not-for-profit and investor-owned freestanding and multihospital system hospitals: number using and planning to use hospital staff vs. outside contracts for food service, housekeeping, laundry, materials management, plant operations/maintenance, and data processing, with detail for data processing services by bed size group and region.

CONTRACTS FOR CLINICAL SERVICES RISING

(p. 94-97) By Frank Sabatino. Article, with 1 table showing average annual growth of contract-managed clinical services in hospitals, by type of service, 1984-89 period. Data are from Frost & Sullivan, Inc.

BUSINESS NEEDS SPUR HMO, PPA GROWTH

(p. 98-101) By Suzanne Powills. Article, with 1 table showing trends in corporate enrollment in alternate health care delivery systems, 1982-84 period. Data are from a study of 115 corporations by the Business Roundtable Task Force on Health.

AUTOMATION IN THE HOSPITAL PHARMACY

(p. 106-113) By C. L. Packer et al. Article on hospital pharmacy use of computer systems. Data are from Shared Data Research, Inc., and are based on recent surveys of hospitals and pharmacists and on interviews with representatives of 8 pharmacy software vendor companies.

Includes 5 charts showing percent of hospital pharmacy systems by bed-size group, hospital's satisfaction with system integration, types of functions performed, and system benefits, all by type of system (facilities management and/or in-house, turnkey, and shared service); and market shares and number of clients, for 8 pharmacy software vendors.

Article is part of a series of features covering hospital computer use.

A1865–1.623: Oct. 1, 1985 (Vol. 59, No. 19)

MOST HOSPITAL LEGAL NEEDS TIED TO MALPRACTICE: SURVEY

(p. 28) Article, with text data and 1 chart on types of legal problems encountered by hospitals, by bed size. Data are based on responses from 675 hospitals to a 1985 survey by Witt Associates, Inc., and cover problems encountered since Dec. 1984.

EXECUTIVE COMPENSATION TRENDS

(MULTIs, p. M14-M16) By James B. Williams and Miles B. King. Article, with 1 chart showing senior executive base salary, benefits/perquisites, and annual bonus/incentive, all as percent of total compensation, for multihospital systems compared to industrial and financial corporations, 1980 and 1985. Data are from a Hay Management Consultants survey encompassing 71 multihospital systems.

NOT-FOR-PROFIT MULTIS RESPOND TO CHANGES: SURVEY

(MULTIs, p. M24-M25) By Benedict J. Gentile. Article, with 1 table and 1 chart showing percent of Catholic, other church-related, and secular not-for-profit multihealth care systems involved or planning involvement in alternate delivery programs by type, HMOs, preferred provider arrangements, and competitive medical plans (no dates). Alternate programs include home health care; wellness programs; ambulatory care, diagnostic, and birthing centers; nursing homes; and retirement housing.

Data are from a recent American Hospital Publishing, Inc. survey of 226 multihealth care systems.

NURSING HOME GROWTH

(MULTIs, p. M28) Article, with 1 table showing beds and occupancy rate for licensed nursing homes, selected years 1963-85. Data are from Beverly Enterprises.

HOSPITAL GOODS AND SERVICES TO GO UP IN '86: FORECAST, QUARTERLY FEATURE

(p. 74-78) Quarterly article, by Clifford Neely, on hospital expenditure and revenue trends and forecasts, 1980s-86. Presents Hospital Inflation Expense Index (HIEI), computed by Merrill Lynch Economics Inc.

Includes 1 chart and 4 tables showing inflation rates for hospital goods and services; HIEI expense component weights; and percent change in HIEI, with detail for wages/salaries (by month) and 8 other HIEI components, and comparisons to GNP, CPI, and other general economic indicators, various periods 1980-86.

PPA CONTRACTING: A CALIFORNIA EXPERIENCE

(p. 81-83) By John M. Edelston et al. Article, with 1 undated chart showing percent of southern California hospitals with alternate delivery system contracting, by ownership status (nonprofit, investor-owned, and government) and bed-size category. Data are from responses of 115 member hospitals to a 1985 survey conducted by the Hospital Council of Southern California.

AFFLUENT CONSUMERS MOST DISCRIMINATING: SURVEY

(p. 84-86) By Joe M. Inguanzo and Mark Harju. Article on consumer opinions concerning selected hospital-related issues. Data are based on approximately 950 responses to an Aug./Sept. 1984 survey conducted by Professional Research Consultants, Inc., and American Hospital Publishing, Inc.

Includes 4 charts showing survey response concerning whether all hospitals provide the same quality of care and charge the same fees for services; and whether hospitals should advertise services and admit potentially indigent patients.

Article is part of a series of features on health care consumers.

A1865–1.624: Oct. 16, 1985 (Vol. 59, No. 20)

HOSPITAL, OTHER MEDICAL-SERVICE PRICES DIP, RECURRING FEATURE

(p. 32) Recurring article, with 1 table showing 1- and 12-month percent change in CPI medical care components, Aug. 1985.

NEW LIFE-STYLES AMONG HEALTH CHANGES ENVISIONED BY 2002

(p. 33) Article, with 1 chart showing health care leaders' suggestions regarding changes in the health care system by the year 2002. Data are from a survey of 412 leaders conducted by Policy Research Institute, and Project HOPE Center for Health Affairs. The survey encompassed public policymakers, health care providers, third-party payers, and public health personnel.

INDUSTRIAL CLINICS REPRESENT PRIME TARGETS FOR HOSPITALS IN SETTING DIVERSIFICATION STRATEGIES, A NEW SURVEY FINDS

(p. 70) Article, with 1 table showing types of health care services offered by industrial clinics, 1985. Data are from responses of 20 clinics to a survey conducted by Rush-Presbyterian-St. Luke's Medical Center.

FORTY-FIVE MILLION AT RISK OF MEDICAL INDIGENCY: STUDY

(p. 76) Article, with 1 table showing number of hospital beds; and patient Medicaid and charity care cost, and bad debt; for public, private nonprofit, and proprietary hospitals, 1980. Data are from *Survey of Medical Care for the Poor and Hospitals' Financial Status, 1983*.

PHYSICIAN OFFICES INVADE CLINICAL LABORATORY MARKET

(p. 84-94) By Mary Gallivan. Article, with 1 chart and 1 table showing laboratory-testing market shares (no date); and percent sales growth, 1983-84 and 1985-90 periods; for hospital, physician office, and independent/reference laboratories. Data are from AHA and Boston Biomedical Consultants, Inc.

TURNKEY SYSTEMS DOMINATE HOSPITAL LAB MARKET

(p. 96-102) By C. L. Packer et al. Article on hospital laboratory use of computer systems. Data are from Shared Data Research, Inc., and are based on recent surveys of hospitals and laboratory directors and on interviews with representatives of 8 laboratory software vendor companies.

Includes 5 charts showing percent of hospital laboratory systems, by type (in-house, turnkey, facilities management, and shared service); types of functions performed and system benefits, by bed-size group; satisfaction with selected functions performed, for large and small hospitals; and market shares and number of clients, for 8 laboratory software vendors.

Article is part of a series of features covering hospital computer use.

EXECUTIVE SALARIES TO RISE 6.1 PERCENT IN '86, ANNUAL FEATURE

(p. 104-120) Annual article, by Linda I. Collins, on hospital management/supervisory staff compensation, 1985. Presents data on salary range, and average salary as percent of president/administrator's salary, for 29 positions, by bed size category; prevalence of selected benefits; and percent change in salaries for executive, exempt, and nonexempt employees in health care and 5 other industries, with forecast for 1986.

Also includes profiles for 7 top management positions, showing the following: mean and 25th and 75th percentile base salaries, salary grade midpoint, employees reporting, years of service and in position, and age; distribution by number of college degrees, sex, and academic specialization; percent serving on governing boards and receiving bonuses; and bonus as percent of base salary.

Data are from the 6th annual hospital management compensation survey conducted by William M. Mercer-Meidinger, Inc., in Mar. 1985. Survey responses cover approximately 5,500 positions reported by 186 hospitals. Includes 1 table on sample characteristics, and 9 tables and 5 charts on survey results.

For description of previous article, see A1865-1.601 above.

HOSPITAL EMERGENCY DEPTS LEARN HOW TO MAKE MONEY

(p. 122-124) By Suzanne Powills and Ted Matson. Article, with 1 chart showing patient visits to short-term community hospital emergency depts, 1979-84. Data are from AHA.

A1865–2   HAS/MONITREND DATA BOOK for Period Ending Dec. 31, 1984

Semiannual. 1985. 135 p.
AHA Catalog No. 097284.
SRI/MF/not filmed

Semiannual report presenting detailed median financial and operating indicators for hospitals, long-term care facilities, and rehabilitation facilities, July-Dec. 1984. Includes data by facility type and dept, with selected detail by census division and bed-size.

Indicators include various utilization, personnel, revenue, expense, service, and other measures (expressed primarily as ratios), shown for total facilities, nursing administration, and individual ancillary depts and support services.

Data are presented, as applicable, for general short-term hospitals, by census division, bed-size group, and case-mix intensity group (based on urban-rural status, size, and Medicare case index); teaching hospitals by census division; children's hospitals; long-term care facilities, by bed size group and whether in-hospital or separate; and rehabilitation facilities.

Report is intended to enable health care facility administrators to compare their facility performance with industry averages.

Data are based on a survey of approximately 2,000 institutions participating in the Hospital Administrative Services (HAS) MONITREND program.

Contains contents listing and introduction (p. 3-5); 6 sections, each including 1 table showing number of reporting facilities, and 1 table showing indicators (p. 7-128); and listing of States by census division (p. 129).

Report for Jan.-June 1984 was also reviewed by SRI during 1985 [Semiannual. Oct. 1984. 135 p. AHA Catalog No. 097684. $95.00].

Prior to Jan.-June 1984, report was titled *HAS/MONITREND Six-Month National Data Book.*

Explanations of methodology and reporting guidelines are provided in 2 separate publications, *Data Book Guide to Uniform Reporting* and *Data Book Calculation Reference,* available from the issuing agency for $5.00 each.

Related reports generated from HAS/MONITREND data are covered in SRI under A1865-6 and A1865-7.

Availability: AHA Services, Inc., PO Box 99376, Chicago IL 60693 (prepaid); 4444 W. Ferdinand, Chicago IL 60624 (billed), $95.00; SRI/MF/not filmed.

A1865–4   HOSPITAL STATISTICS, 1984 Edition

Annual. 1984. xxv+236 p.
AHA Catalog No. 082084.
ISSN 0090-6662.
ISBN 0-87258-424-0.
LC 72-626765.
SRI/MF/not filmed

Annual statistical report on hospital capacity, utilization, personnel, finances, facilities, and services, 1983, with trends from 1946. Data are shown by census division, State, MSA, 100 largest central cities, and outlying territories, crosstabulated variously by hospital bed size, control, and service classifications.

Data are derived from responses of 6,506 hospitals to the AHA 1983 annual survey.

Contents:

a. Contents and table listing, introduction, and definitions. (p. iii-xv)

b. Analysis of hospital trends, with 15 summary text tables; and technical notes, with 3 tables on survey response distribution. (p. xvii-xxv)

c. 14 detailed tables, listed below; index; and sample questionnaire. (p. 1-236)

Availability: American Hospital Association, PO Box 99376, Chicago IL 60693 (prepaid); 4444 W. Ferdinand, Chicago IL 60624 (billed), members $39.50, nonmembers $49.50; SRI/MF/not filmed.

DETAILED TABLES:

[Tables showing utilization, personnel, and finances generally include number of hospitals and beds; admissions, inpatient days, occupancy rate, average daily patient census, average stay, and surgical operations; emergency and other outpatient visits; bassinets and births; FTE personnel and trainees, by type; and expenses, including payroll and employee benefits.

Unless otherwise noted, tables show data by hospital classification, generally including type of control (Federal and other government, nongovernment not-for-profit, and investor-owned for-profit); major type of service (psychiatric, tuberculosis/other respiratory diseases, and general/other special); and length of stay (short-term and long-term). Many tables include further detail by bed-size and/or other special service categories.

"U.S.-associated areas" refers to 5-6 outlying territories.]

A1865–4.1: Hospital Statistics

TRENDS

1. Trends in utilization, personnel, and finances, for selected years 1946-83. (p. 4-7)

CURRENT DATA

[Tables 2A-14 show data for 1983 or most recent accounting period.]

2A-2B. Utilization, personnel, and finances in short-term and long-term hospitals. (p. 8-11)

3. Utilization, personnel per census, and finances per inpatient day. (p. 12-13)

4A-4D. Utilization of and personnel and finances in hospital units and nursing-home-type units operated by hospitals; and by community hospitals, by State [and census division (not shown by hospital classification)]. (p. 14-17)

5A-5E. Utilization, personnel, and finances: in U.S. registered hospitals, in census divisions, in States, in U.S. associated areas [aggregate, including Puerto Rico], and in Puerto Rico. (p. 22-147)

6-7. Utilization, personnel, and finances in community hospitals: by MSA [grouped by State and census division, with totals for nonmetro areas]; and for the 100 largest central cities; [not shown by hospital classification]. (p. 152-175)

8. Utilization, personnel, and finances in community hospitals affiliated with medical schools [by census division]. (p. 180-183)

9. Utilization, personnel per census, and finances per inpatient day in accredited hospitals. (p. 184-185)

10A-10B. AHA membership, approval [accreditation], and affiliation status [cancer program, residency, medical school, nursing school, Council of Teaching Hospitals, Blue Cross, and Medicare, all by hospital classification for U.S., and totals by State and individual associated area]. (p. 186-187)

11. Revenue in community hospitals [inpatient and outpatient revenues in all and nongovernment not-for-profit hospitals, by bed size for U.S., and totals by census division and State]. (p. 188)

12A-12B. Facilities and services [42 detailed types, including abortion, organ transplants, blood banks, genetic counseling, family planning, alcoholism/chemical dependency, computerized tomography scanners, and hospice, by hospital classification for U.S., and totals by census division and State]. (p. 193-204)

13A-13B. Hospitals, units, and beds, by [detailed] inpatient service area [by hospital classification for U.S., and totals by census division and State]. (p. 206-213)

14. Utilization, personnel, and finances in U.S. nonregistered hospitals. (p. 218-219)

A1865–6 HAS/MONITREND WORKED HOURS DATA BOOK for Period Ending Dec. 31, 1984
Semiannual. 1985. 53 p.
AHA Catalog No. 097843.
SRI/MF/not filmed

Semiannual report presenting median labor productivity indicators for hospitals, July-Dec. 1984. Includes data by hospital type and dept, bed-size, and census division.

Focuses primarily on worked-hour ratios (expressed as hours per patient day, procedure, visit, occupied bed, or other measure, as applicable), shown for total facilities, nursing administration, and individual ancillary depts and support services.

Data are presented for general short-term hospitals, by census division, bed-size group, and case-mix intensity group (based on urban-rural status, size, and Medicare case index); teaching hospitals by census division; and children's hospitals.

Report is intended to enable hospital administrators to compare their staff productivity levels with industry averages.

Data are based on a survey of approximately 2,000 institutions participating in the Hospital Administrative Services (HAS) MONITREND program.

Contains contents listing and introduction (p. 1-4); 4 sections, each including 1 table showing number of reporting hospitals, and 1 table showing indicators (p. 5-51); and listing of States by census division (p. 53).

This is the 2nd edition of the report. The 1st edition, for Jan.-June 1984, was also reviewed by SRI during 1985 [Semiannual. Oct. 1984. 53 p. AHA Catalog No. 097864. $95.00].

Explanations of methodology and reporting guidelines are provided in a separate publication, *Worked Hours Data Book User's Guide,* available from the issuing agency for $5.00.

Related reports generated from HAS/MONITREND data are covered in SRI under A1865-2 and A1865-7.

Availability: AHA Services, Inc., PO Box 99376, Chicago IL 60693 (prepaid); 4444 W. Ferdinand, Chicago IL 60624 (billed), $95.00; SRI/MF/not filmed.

A1865–7 HAS/MONITREND DISCHARGE BASED DATA BOOK for Period Ending Dec. 31, 1984
Semiannual. 1985. 79 p.
AHA Catalog No. 098284.
SRI/MF/not filmed

Semiannual report presenting median cost and productivity indicators for hospitals, July-Dec. 1984. Includes data by hospital type and dept, bed-size, and census division.

Focuses primarily on per-discharge ratios for total direct expenses, salary expenses, personnel, paid hours, and other measures, shown for total facilities, nursing administration, and individual ancillary depts and support services.

Data are presented for general short-term hospitals, by census division, bed-size group, and case-mix intensity group (based on urban-rural status, size, and Medicare case index); teaching hospitals by census division; and children's hospitals.

Report is intended to enable hospital administrators to compare their facility performance with industry averages, on a per-discharge basis.

Data are based on a survey of approximately 2,000 institutions participating in the Hospital Administrative Services (HAS) MONITREND program.

Contains contents listing and introduction (p. 1-4); 4 sections, each including 1 table showing number of reporting hospitals, and 1 table showing indicators (p. 5-71); and listing of States by census division (p. 73).

This is the 4th edition of the report. The 3rd edition, for Jan.-June 1984, was also reviewed by SRI during 1985 [Semiannual. Nov. 1984. 73 p. AHA Catalog No. 098684. $95.00].

Explanations of methodology and reporting guidelines are provided in a separate publication, *Discharge-Based Data Book User's Guide,* available from the issuing agency for $5.00.

Related reports generated from HAS/MONITREND data are covered in SRI under A1865-2 and A1865-6.

Availability: AHA Services, Inc., PO Box 99376, Chicago IL 60693 (prepaid); 4444 W. Ferdinand, Chicago IL 60624 (billed), $95.00; SRI/MF/not filmed.

A1880
American Humane Association

A1880–1 HIGHLIGHTS OF OFFICIAL CHILD NEGLECT AND ABUSE REPORTING, 1983
Annual. 1985. 36 p.
LC 78-102260.
SRI/MF/complete

Annual report on cases of child abuse and neglect, with data by jurisdiction, and by characteristics of cases, children, and perpetrators, 1983, with selected trends from 1976. Data are from a national study based on State and U.S. territory official reports of child protective service agencies.

Contains contents listing (1 p.); introduction (p. 1); narrative analysis, with 4 charts and 16 tables described below (p. 2-26); and appendix, with data items in the national study data base, and 1 table showing data participants by State and for Puerto Rico (p. 27-36).

More detailed data are available from the issuing agency upon request.

Availability: American Humane Association, Child Protection Division, 9725 E. Hampden Ave., Denver CO 80231, $5.00; SRI/MF/complete.

CHARTS AND TABLES:
[Data are shown for 1983, unless otherwise noted.]

a. Cases and children reported: total, 1976-83; and by State, Guam, Puerto Rico, Virgin Islands, and Mariana Islands, 1983 with comparison to 1982. Chart 1 and tables 1-2. (p. 3-5)

b. Case distribution: by case type; source of report; age, sex, and race/ethnicity (including Hispanic) of child, caretaker, and perpetrator; family characteristics, including single female household head, number of children, and public assistance status; caretaker's employment status; child's relationship to caretaker and perpetrator; type of maltreatment; case status; and protective and other services provided; with various cross-tabulations, and sexual maltreatment trends from 1976. Charts 2-4 and tables 3-16. (p. 6-26)

A1885
American Institute of Certified Public Accountants

A1885–1 SUPPLY OF ACCOUNTING GRADUATES and the Demand for Public Accounting Recruits, 1985
Annual. 1985. iv+27 p.
ISSN 0884-2310.
LC 85-64323.
SRI/MF/not filmed

Annual survey report, by Mary McInnes and James H. MacNeill, estimating supply and demand for accounting graduates by degree level, by demographic and selected other characteristics, 1983/84-1984/85, with trends from 1971/72.

Covers accounting graduates by region, sex, and institution's accreditation status with AACSB, and for public and private schools, and minorities (American Indians, Asians, blacks, and Hispanics) in traditionally minority and majority schools; and public accounting firms' employment of new graduates, by sex and minority group; most by degree level.

Also includes percent of new hires expected to hold master's degree, by firm size.

Data are from responses of 478 accredited and nonaccredited AACSB member schools, 76 nonmember schools, and 213 public accounting firms to surveys conducted during 1985.

Contains contents/table listing (iii-iv); introduction, summary, and survey results with 30 tables (p. 1-23); and 3 appendices, including questionnaire facsimiles (p. 25-27).

This is the 15th annual report.

Availability: American Institute of Certified Public Accountants, 1211 Ave. of the Americas, New York NY 10036-8775, †; SRI/MF/not filmed.

A1960
American Institute of Physics

A1960–1 EMPLOYMENT SURVEY, 1983
Annual. Sept. 1984. 8 p.
AIP Pub. No. R-282.7.
SRI/MF/complete

Annual report, by Susanne D. Ellis, on employment status of 1982/83 physics and astronomy graduates, by highest degree earned. Covers types of employment and employers, and characteristics of employed graduates and graduates continuing their studies.

Data are from a survey conducted each Dec. as a follow-up to 2 summer surveys reported in *Survey of Physics and Astronomy Bachelor's Degree Recipients* and *Graduate Student Survey*. The 1982/83 summer survey reports are described in SRI 1984 Annual under A1960-3 and A1960-4, respectively.

Contains narrative summary, 2 charts, and 10 tables listed below.

Availability: American Institute of Physics, Manpower Statistics Division, 335 E. 45th St., New York NY 10017, †; SRI/MF/complete.

TABLES:
[Data are for 1982/83 degree recipients, unless otherwise noted.

Data on work activity variously include teaching, research, computer science, data analysis, programming, research/development/design, and quality control.

Data on type of employer variously include academic institution, industry, government, and federally funded research center.

Data on occupational status generally include postdoctorate studies/student, full-time employed, part-time employed, unemployed/seeking employment, and sometimes military service or return to foreign country.]

I-II. Changes in occupational status of physics and astronomy degree recipients [by degree level] between the summer of 1983 and the following winter. (p. 2-3)

III. Occupational status of [U.S. and foreign] experimental and theoretical [doctoral] physicists by type of dissertation research, 1983/84.

IV. Characteristics [sex, age, citizenship, type of research, and subfield] of postdoctoral and full-time employed physics and astronomy doctorate recipients. (p. 4)

V. Subfield mobility of doctoral level physicists [subfield distribution of postdoctoral fellowships and employment, by dissertation subfield]. (p. 5)

VI. Factors influencing the length of postdoctoral fellowships [percent taking less or more than 2 years, by citizenship, subfield, and whether specifically sought postdoctorate], for doctoral level physicists. (p. 6)

VII. Employment with potential permanence accepted by doctorate recipients [by subfield, work activity, whether physics related, and whether interested in a job change; by type of employer]. (p. 6)

VIII-IX. Characteristics of physics masters and bachelors that influence the time required to secure employment [percent requiring various time periods, by sex, age, highest degree granted at institution last attended, type of em-

ployment, type of employer (masters only), school region (bachelors only), and type of work activity]. (p. 7-8)

X. Employment of astronomy bachelors [by work activity and type of employer, with aggregate median monthly salary]. (p. 8)

A1960–2 PHYSICS AND ASTRONOMY ENROLLMENTS AND DEGREES
Annual series. For individual publication data, see below.
SRI/MF/complete

Series of 3 annual reports, by Susanne D. Ellis, on enrollments and degrees awarded in physics and astronomy depts of U.S. colleges and universities.

Reports are based on an annual AIP survey of approximately 800 degree-granting depts.

Series consists of 1 summary analytical report showing aggregate data by institution, student, or dept characteristics; and 2 supplementary reports showing detailed survey data by institution.

Reports reviewed during 1985 are described below.

Availability: American Institute of Physics, Manpower Statistics Division, 335 E. 45th St., New York NY 10017, †; SRI/MF/complete.

A1960–2.1: Enrollments and Degrees
[Annual. June 1985. 8 p. AIP Pub. No. R-151.22. SRI/MF/complete.]

Annual summary report on physics and astronomy enrollments and degrees awarded, various academic years 1973/74-1984/85.

Contains narrative analysis, interspersed with 2 trend charts, and 1 chart and 14 tables listed below.

TABLES AND CHART:
[Data by type of institution are shown by highest degree offered. Data by region are shown for 9 census divisions. Tables II-III and XII show enrollment data through 1984/85 and degree data through 1983/84.]

PHYSICS

I. Institutions, by highest physics degree offered, 1980/81-1984/85. (p. 1)

II-III. Physics enrollments and degrees awarded; and undergraduate and graduate enrollments and degrees, by institution type; 1973/74-1984/85. (p. 2)

IV. Introductory physics enrollments in physics degree-granting institutions, by geographic region, 1980/81-1984/85. (p. 3)

V. Introductory physics enrollments [by major field of study and institution type], 1984/85. (p. 3)

Figure II. Actual and projected number of undergraduate physics majors [by level, for graduating classes of 1985-88]. (p. 4)

VI. Undergraduate physics majors [by level], by geographic region and type of institution, 1984/85. (p. 4)

VII. Trend in entering U.S. and foreign graduate physics students, 1975/76-1984/85. (p. 5)

VIII. Foreign graduate physics students, and those holding teaching assistantships [for doctorate- and masters-granting institutions, by region], 1984-85. (p. 5)

IX. Full-time and part-time graduate physics enrollment, by type of institution, 1975/76-1984/85. (p. 5)

X. Unfilled assistantships for 1st-year graduate physics students [in doctorate- and masters-granting depts, by region], Sept. 1984. (p. 6)

XI-XII. Physics degrees, by type of institution and geographic region; and number of physics degrees granted, by sex and minority group status [black, American Indian, Mexican American, Hispanic, Oriental, Asian Indian, and Arab]; 1983/84. (p. 7)

ASTRONOMY

XIII. Trend in astronomy enrollments and degrees, 1975/76-1984/85. (p. 8)

XIV. Astronomy [depts and] enrollments 1984/85, and degrees 1983/84, by type of institution. (p. 8)

A1960–2.2: Data on Physics Enrollments and Degrees: A Supplement
[Annual. June 1985. 20 p. AIP Pub. No. R-151.22A. SRI/MF/complete.]

Annual supplement to AIP survey report, presenting detailed data on physics degrees granted in 1983/84, and enrollments in 1984/85, for approximately 750 individual degree-granting colleges and universities.

Contains 1 table showing physics undergraduates by class, and total and 1st-year graduate students, 1984/85; and degrees granted, by level, 1983/84; all by institution, arranged by State.

A1960–2.3: Data on Astronomy Enrollments and Degrees: A Supplement
[Annual. June 1985. 4 p. AIP Pub. No. R-151.22B. SRI/MF/complete.]

Annual supplement to AIP survey report, presenting detailed data on astronomy degrees granted in 1983/84, and enrollments in 1984/85, for 67 individual degree-granting colleges and universities.

Contains 1 table showing enrollments in introductory astronomy courses by science and nonscience majors, number of junior and senior undergraduate majors, and total and 1st-year graduate students, 1984/85; astronomy degrees granted, by level, 1983/84; and whether dept is for astronomy only or astronomy/physics combined; all by institution, arranged by State.

A1960–3 1983/84 SURVEY OF PHYSICS AND ASTRONOMY BACHELOR'S DEGREE RECIPIENTS
Annual. Mar. 1985. 8 p.
AIP Pub. No. 211.16.
SRI/MF/complete

Annual report, by Susanne D. Ellis, on a survey of postgraduation plans and demographic characteristics of 1983/84 physics and astronomy bachelor degree recipients. Data are from an American Institute of Physics survey, conducted during summer 1984, of 4,878 physics and 137 astronomy baccalaureate recipients, 1983/84 academic year.

Contains narrative summary; 4 charts showing plans of physics and astronomy bachelors, 1984 and selected trends; and 12 tables, listed below.

Availability: American Institute of Physics, Manpower Statistics Division, 335 E. 45th St., New York NY 10017, †; SRI/MF/complete.

TABLES:
[Data by type of employer include some or all of the following: manufacturing and service industries, high school, college/university, government, military, federally funded R&D centers, and other. Data by type of institution are by highest degree offered at institution attended. Data are for 1984 or 1983/84, unless otherwise noted.]

PHYSICS GRADUATES

I. Postbaccalaureate plans [physics or other graduate study, civilian employment, military service, and undecided] of successive graduating classes of physics bachelors [and total bachelor's degrees, 1974/75-1983/84]. (p. 1)

II. Characteristics of new physics bachelors [by sex, age, citizenship, minority group (U.S. blacks and other minorities, and foreign minorities), type of institution attended, and whether double major; for graduates planning physics or other graduate study, employment, or undecided]. (p. 2)

III. Comparison between men and women physics bachelors and their high school physics backgrounds. (p. 2)

IV. Postbaccalaureate plans [physics or other graduate study, and employment] of U.S. [black, Oriental, and other] and foreign [Oriental and other] minority groups among the physics bachelors of the class of 1984. (p. 3)

V. Selected characteristics [sex, and region and type of institution attended] of minority physics bachelors [Mexican American, American and Asian Indian, Arab, and U.S. and foreign black, Hispanic, and Oriental]. (p. 3)

VI. Sources of anticipated support for 1st-year graduate study, biennially 1980-84. (p. 4)

VII. Changes in employment outlook for new physics bachelors [by number of job offers at graduation, summer] 1974-84. (p. 4)

VIII. Initial employment of physics bachelors [by type of employer, 1975/76-1983/84]. (p. 6)

IX. Starting [median] salaries of physics bachelors [by sex and type of employer]. (p. 6)

X. Full-time employment [type of work activity] of new physics bachelors [by type of employer]. (p. 6)

ASTRONOMY GRADUATES

XI. Characteristics [sex, citizenship, age, type of high school physics and type of institution attended, whether science or arts degree, and double major] of astronomy bachelors. (p. 7)

XII. Postbaccalaureate plans [astronomy or other graduate study, employment, and undecided] of successive graduating classes of astronomy bachelors [1977/78-1983/84]. (p. 7)

A1960–4   1983/84 GRADUATE STUDENT SURVEY
Annual. Sept. 1985. 12 p.
AIP Pub. No. R-207.17.
SRI/MF/complete

Annual report, by Susanne D. Ellis, on physics and astronomy graduate student and degree recipient characteristics and employment opportunities, 1983/84 academic year. Most data are

based on responses of 6,401 physics and 461 astronomy graduate students and degree recipients to a summer 1984 survey by the American Institute of Physics.

Contains narrative summary, interspersed with 5 charts showing summary data, and academic background and postdegree employment status of physics terminal master's and physics and astronomy doctorate degree recipients, 1983/84; and 14 tables, listed below.

Survey of physics graduate students has been conducted annually since early 1960s. Astronomy students were added in 1974.

Availability: American Institute of Physics, Manpower Statistics Division, 335 E. 45th St., New York NY 10017, †; SRI/MF/complete.

TABLES:
[Employer types include secondary school, 4-year college, university, industry, government/military, nonprofit organizations, and federally funded research centers. Data are for 1983/84 academic year.]

PHYSICS GRADUATE STUDENTS

I. Characteristics of the graduate physics student population [sex, citizenship, whether studied physics in high school, major of bachelor's degree, type of bachelor's and graduate institution, student status, and source of support, for all graduate students, 1st-year students, and terminal master's and doctorate degree recipients]. (p. 2)

II. Characteristics of minority group physics students [sex, degree and student status, whether studied physics in high school, FTE years of graduate study, subfield, and graduate degree recipients, for U.S. and foreign black, American Indian, Puerto Rican, Mexican American, other U.S. and foreign Hispanic, Asian Indian, U.S. and foreign oriental, and Arab]. (p. 3)

III. Number of graduate physics students, by subfield and years of graduate study completed. (p. 3)

IV. Sources of support for graduate physics students, by sex and degree status. (p. 4)

V. Number of advanced graduate physics students specializing in selected experimental or theoretical subfields, by years of graduate study completed. (p. 4)

VI. Distribution by subfield and [number of] employment offers, for doctorate [degree] recipients. (p. 5)

VII. Employment of doctoral graduates, by citizenship [for U.S. and foreign employers]. (p. 5)

VIII. Distribution by subfield [and number] of employment offers, for terminal master's [degree recipients]. (p. 7)

IX. Employment characteristics [employer type and work activity] of recipients of master's degrees. (p. 7)

X. Use of physics in potentially permanent employment of graduate degree recipients [percent of doctorate and terminal master's degree recipients reporting extensive, little, or no use of physics training with respect to method and/or subject matter, by type of employer]. (p. 9)

XI. Initial employment with potential permanence for physics doctorate [degree] recipients [by type of employer, including university tenure status, and by type of work activity]. (p. 9)

XII. Median monthly salaries paid by U.S. employers to new physics degree recipients [by type of employer, for bachelor's, terminal master's, and doctorate degree recipients]. (p. 10)

ASTRONOMY GRADUATE STUDENTS

XIII. Graduate astronomy students, by subfield and years of graduate study. (p. 10)

XIV. Characteristics of the graduate astronomy student population [same detail as in table I, but also including subfield]. (p. 11)

A1960–6   1983 SALARIES, SOCIETY MEMBERSHIP SURVEY
Annual. 1985. 4+29 p.
Pub. No. R-311.01.
ISBN 0-88318-478-8.
SRI/MF/complete

Annual report on salaries of doctoral level physicists, with some data for master's and bachelor's levels, 1983 with comparisons to 1981. Data include means, medians, and quartiles, and are shown by census division, State, selected metro area, employer type, years from degree, work activity, and sex, with selected cross-tabulations. Includes median age for most categories.

Also includes data for Canada and selected Provinces.

Employer types include universities and colleges (with detail by faculty rank), secondary schools, industry/self employed, government, federally funded R&D centers, and nonprofit organizations.

Work activities include teaching, basic and applied research, development, design/engineering, and administration.

Data are from a spring 1983 random sample survey of AIP members.

Contains contents and table listing (1 p.); introduction, with 14 charts and 28 tables (p. 1-27); and appendices with technical notes (p. 28-29).

This is the 2nd annual report.

Availability: American Institute of Physics, Manpower Statistics Division, 335 E. 45th St., New York, NY 10017, single copies †, multiple copies on request; SRI/MF/complete.

A2000
American
Iron and Steel Institute

A2000–2   ANNUAL STATISTICAL REPORT, American Iron and Steel Institute, 1984
Annual. 1985. 113 p.
LC 14-3046.
SRI/MF/complete

Annual report, for 1984, on the iron and steel industry, with trends from the 1940s. Includes data on U.S. industry production, finances, employment, shipments, and foreign trade. Also includes selected data for Canada and other foreign countries.

Data are compiled by American Iron and Steel Institute from individual companies and from other foreign and domestic sources, including U.S. Depts of Labor, Commerce, and Interior.

Contains contents listing and foreword (p. 3-5); and 66 tables, listed below (p. 8-113).

Availability: American Iron and Steel Institute, 1000 16th St., NW, Washington DC 20036, $15.00 (prepaid); SRI/MF/complete.

TABLES:

[Tables show data for U.S., unless otherwise noted. Data by grade are generally for carbon, alloy, and stainless steel.]

A2000–2.1: Financial and Employment Data

[Tables 1C-1D and 2-4A show data for total iron/steel industry and for steel industry segment, 1979-84.]

SELECTED HIGHLIGHTS

1A. Shipments, apparent supply, imports [and exports of steel mill products (with imports as percent of apparent supply by selected country/area of origin)], and employment [1975-84]. (p. 8)

1B. Raw steel data [world and U.S. production, U.S. capability, and percent U.S. production by furnace and cast types, 1975-84]. (p. 8)

1C. Income data [net sales and income, and net income as percent of stockholders' equity]. (p. 9)

1D. Cash flow data [capital expenditures, cash provided from or used for operations and financing, and change in cash/marketable securities]. (p. 9)

1E. Capital expenditures for environmental facilities [selected periods 1951-75, and annually 1976-84]. (p. 10)

FINANCIAL AND ECONOMIC STATISTICS

2-4A. Income statement [including revenues by source, and costs for employment, supplies, and taxes]; balance sheet [by major item]; and cash flow statement [with detailed operating and financial sources and dispositions]. (p. 12-17)

5. BLS: CPI, and PPI of steel prices [for steel mill products, other iron/steel products, and total industrial commodities, 1960-84 and monthly 1984]. (p. 18)

EMPLOYMENT AND WAGE DATA

[Tables 6, 7, and 10-11 show data for employees engaged in the sale and/or production of iron/steel products.]

6. Total employment cost per hour worked, wage employees [including regular pay, overtime, and other payroll costs, 1965-84]. (p. 20)

6A. Standard hourly wage rate changes and minimum wage rates (per agreement with the United Steelworkers of America) [effective dates Oct. 1, 1961-Feb. 1, 1984]. (p. 21)

7. Number of employees, hours worked, and payroll cost [for wage and salaried employees, 1965-84]. (p. 22)

8. Collective bargaining agreements with United Steelworkers of America [with effective date of agreement and periods of general steel strikes, 1946-83]. (p. 23)

9. BLS index of output per man-hour in the steel industry (all employees) [1954-84]. (p. 24)

10. Occupational injury/illness [with aggregate man-hours, deaths, and workdays lost, 1980-84]. (p. 25)

11. Wage employees classified by age and by length of service [1983-84]. (p. 25)

A2000–2.2: Shipments, Exports, and Imports

[Most tables show data by product, often with summary totals by grade. Data by market classification are shown by industry and/or use.]

SHIPMENTS OF STEEL PRODUCTS

12-13. Shipments of steel mill products, all grades and by grades, 1984. (p. 28-31)

14-15. Net shipments of steel mill products, all grades and by market classification [with aggregate detail by month, 1975-84]. (p. 32-37)

16. Shipments of steel mill products by market classification, all grades, 1984. (p. 38-40)

EXPORTS

17-18. Exports of iron and steel products [1975-84]. (p. 42-45)

19. Exports of steel mill products [by month, 1975-84]. (p. 45)

20-20A. Exports of iron and steel products by countries of destination, 1984. (p. 46-51)

IMPORTS

21-22. Imports of iron and steel products [1975-84]. (p. 52-54)

23. Imports of steel mill products [by month, 1975-84]. (p. 54)

24-25A. Imports of steel mill products [total and as percent of U.S. apparent supply, 1980-84]; and of iron and steel products, 1984; [all] by countries of origin. (p. 55-61)

26-26A. Imports of iron and steel products, by customs district [and port], 1984. (p. 62-69)

A2000–2.3: Production and Consumption

RAW STEEL PRODUCTION

27-28. Raw steel production: by type of furnace, grade, and cast [1970-84]; and by States [1980-84]. (p. 72-74)

29. Monthly and quarterly raw steel production and capability utilization [1980-84]. (p. 75)

PIG IRON AND FERROALLOYS PRODUCTION

30-32. Blast furnace production [by type of furnace]; pig iron consumption/sales; and pig iron shipments other than for own use [by type; all 1975-84]. (p. 78)

33-34. Production of ferroalloys; and ferroalloy imports for consumption; [both by type, 1980-84]. (p. 79)

35. Materials used by blast furnaces in manufacture of iron (pig/molten), 1984. (p. 80)

BASIC MATERIALS

36. Consumption of coal [by use, 1975-84]. (p. 82)

37. Consumption of fluxes [1979-83, and by use 1984, by flux type]. (p. 82)

38. Production, receipts, consumption, and shipments of coke [1980-84]. (p. 83)

39. Iron ore receipts and consumption [by original source in U.S., Canada, and all other foreign countries], 1984. (p. 84)

40-41. [U.S.] imports of iron ore by countries of origin, and iron ore shipments destined for Great Lakes [by port of origin, 1975-84]. (p. 85-86)

42. Agglomerated products [materials used, production, receipts of foreign production, and consumption in blast and steelmaking furnaces, 1980-84]. (p. 87)

43-44. Scrap: stocks, production, receipts, and consumption by manufacturers of pig iron/raw steel/castings [1975-84]; and scrap consumption by grade [including iron scrap, 1983-84]. (p. 88-89)

45. Consumption of scrap and pig iron by types of furnaces [1980-84]. (p. 90)

46-48. Consumption of electric power, oxygen, and fuels [by type, with selected data by use, 1980-84]. (p. 91-93)

49. Imports for [U.S.] consumption of manganese ore, by countries of origin [1975-84]. (p. 94)

A2000–2.4: Canadian and World Production

CANADA

[Tables 50-63 show data for Canada.]

50-51. Income, [costs], dividends, return on sales and stockholders' equity, [and employment]; and balance sheet; [reported by companies comprising 80% of Canadian raw steel production) [1982-84]. (p. 96-97)

52-54. Production of pig iron and ferroalloys; materials consumed by blast furnaces in the production of pig iron; and raw steel production [by type of steel and furnace; 1975-84]. (p. 98-99)

55. Net shipments of rolled steel products [by product type, 1975-84]. (p. 100-101)

56-57. Imports and exports of iron and steel products [by product type, 1980-84]. (p. 102-103)

58-60. Consumption of coal, coke, and fuel oil [by use, 1975-84]. (p. 104-105)

61-63. Consumption of fluxes [by type] in steelmaking furnaces [1975-84]; and consumption of oxygen and pig iron [by use, 1980-84]. (p. 105-106)

WORLD STATISTICS

64-66. World production of iron ore/concentrates/agglomerates, pig iron, and raw steel, by countries [with totals for world areas, 1980-84]. (p. 108-113)

A2010
American
Iron Ore Association

A2010–1   **IRON ORE AND IRON ORE AGGLOMERATES: U.S. and Canada**
Monthly. 2 p.
SRI/MF/not filmed

Monthly report on U.S. and Canadian iron industry, covering domestic and foreign receipts, consumption, and inventories of ore; and blast furnaces operating. Data are compiled jointly by American Iron Ore Assn and American Iron and Steel Institute. Reports are issued approximately 2 months after month of coverage.

Contains 8 tables showing the following for U.S. and Canada:

a. Great Lakes and other U.S. and Canadian ores, and total foreign ores: receipts at iron/steel plants; consumption in blast furnaces, steel furnaces, sintering plants, and miscellaneous processes; and inventory at furnace yards and at docks/plants/mines; for month of coverage and/or current year to date, with comparisons to previous year.

b. Blast furnaces: total and number in operation last day of month.

Most U.S. data are shown by region or State.

Availability: American Iron Ore Association, 1501 Euclid Ave., 514 Bulkley Bldg., Cleveland OH 44115, †; SRI/MF/not filmed.

Issues reviewed during 1985: Sept. 1984-Aug. 1985 (D).

A2010-2   SHIPMENTS OF U.S. AND CANADIAN IRON ORE from Loading Docks Destined to Great Lakes
Monthly.   1 p.
SRI/MF/not filmed

Monthly summary of Great Lakes shipments of U.S. and Canadian iron ore, by loading port of origin. Data are compiled by the American Iron Ore Assn and are for month of coverage, current year to date, and same periods of previous year. Reports are issued approximately 1-3 weeks after month of coverage.

Contains 1 monthly table showing shipments in gross tons for U.S., Canada, combined countries, and by individual Great Lakes port.

Dec. issue also includes an annual table summarizing shipment trends from 1970s.

Availability: American Iron Ore Association, 1501 Euclid Ave., 514 Bulkley Bldg., Cleveland OH 44115, †; SRI/MF/not filmed.

Issues reviewed during 1985: Oct. 1984-Sept. 1985 (D).

A2010-3   IRON ORE, 1984
Annual.   June 1985.
2 + 108 p.
LC 59-42154.
SRI/MF/not filmed

Annual report on the iron ore industry in Canada and U.S., 1984, with trends from 1975. Covers production, trade by country of destination and origin, inventories, consumption, receipts, and shipments.

Data were compiled by American Iron Ore Assn from original data collected, and from other sources, including American Iron and Steel Institute, Statistics Canada, and U.S. Dept of Interior.

Contains contents listing (1 p.); definitions (p. 1); 7 sections with explanatory notes, 3 maps, and 51 tables listed below (p. 3-90); and directory of reporting companies, and index (p. 91-108).

Availability: American Iron Ore Association, 1501 Euclid Ave., 514 Bulkley Bldg., Cleveland OH 44115, †; SRI/MF/not filmed.

TABLES:
[Iron ore originating areas are U.S. Great Lakes, western, southern, and northeastern areas; and Canadian Great Lakes, western, and eastern areas. Foreign ores are all iron ores from outside U.S. and Canada.]

A2010-3.1: 1984 Data
[Tables show data for 1984. Data by plant location are for selected groups of States.]

PRODUCTION AND SHIPMENTS
[1-2] Iron ore mine production and total shipments, U.S. and Canada [by originating area and type of ore product, including coarse, fines, pellets, and sinter]. (p. 8-9)

[3-4] Iron ore mined and shipped, U.S. Great Lakes originating area by ranges, and Canada Great Lakes originating area by districts. (p. 10-11)

INVENTORIES, RECEIPTS, AND CONSUMPTION
[5] Domestic/foreign iron ores at iron/steel plants [Jan. 1 and Dec. 31 inventory, and receipts and consumption, for] U.S. [by plant location] and Canada. (p. 12)

[6-11] U.S. and Canada iron ores [by originating area], and foreign iron ores, at iron/steel plants [Jan. 1 and Dec. 31 inventory, and receipts and consumption, for U.S. by plant location and for Canada]. (p. 13-18)

[12-14] Receipts, consumption, and [Dec. 31] inventory of iron ore at U.S. iron/steel plants [by plant location, for U.S. and Canadian Great Lakes and other originating area and for foreign ores]. (p. 19-21)

[15-16] Receipts and consumption at U.S. and Canadian iron/steel plants and inventory at furnace yards and docks/plants/mines [by month]. (p. 22-23)

A2010-3.2: Trends
[Tables show data for 1975-84, unless otherwise noted.]

SHIPMENTS AND TRADE
[1] Iron ore mine production and total shipments, U.S. and Canada [by type of ore product, by originating area], 1980-84. (p. 26-27)

[2-3] Iron ore in U.S. and Canada [shipments, exports, and imports]. (p. 28-29)

[4] Iron ore exported from U.S. [by country of destination]. (p. 30-31)

[5-6] Iron ore imports to U.S. by country of origin and by customs districts. (p. 32-35)

[7-8] Iron ore: exported from Canada [by country of destination]; and imports to Canada by country of origin. (p. 36-37)

[9-10] U.S. and Canadian iron ore shipments from loading docks destined to the Great Lakes [annually by port and dock, and total by month]. (p. 38-41)

RECEIPTS, CONSUMPTION, AND INVENTORY
[Tables [11-24] show data by the following iron ore originating areas: Great Lake areas in U.S. and Canada, other U.S. and Canadian areas, and foreign ores. Inventory data are shown as of Dec. 31.]

[11-12] Receipts and consumption of iron ore at U.S. iron/steel plants. (p. 42-43)

[13-15] Consumption of iron ore in U.S. blast and steel furnaces, and sintering plants (located at iron/steel plants). (p. 44-46)

[16-17] Inventory of iron ore at U.S. iron/steel plants, 1975-84; at U.S. docks, 1979; and at docks/plants/mines, 1980-84. (p. 47-48)

[18] Receipts of iron ore at Canadian iron/steel plants. (p. 49)

[19-22] Consumption of iron ore at Canadian iron/steel plants, blast and steel furnaces, and sintering plants (located at iron/steel plants). (p. 50-53)

[23-24] Inventory of iron ore at Canadian iron/steel plants, 1975-84; and at docks/plants/mines, 1980-84. (p. 54-55)

WORLD PRODUCTION
[25] World production of iron ore/iron ore concentrates/iron ore agglomerates, by countries. (p. 56-58)

A2010-3.3: Ore Products and Analyses
FURNACES
[1] Number of blast furnaces operating last day of month, U.S. [by State or State group], and Canada, 1984. (p. 60)

PRODUCTS
[Tables [2-6] show data for 1975-84.]

[2-3] Consumption of ore, scrap, mill cinder, limestone, and coke per net ton of pig iron produced in U.S. and Canada. (p. 61-62)

[4] Production of pig iron, U.S. [by State or State group], and Canada. (p. 63)

[5-6] U.S. and Canada steel production [by type of furnace]. (p. 64)

ANALYSES OF ORE
[7-8] Grade names and analyses [of U.S. and Canadian ore] shipped [by originating area]; and of Canada by-product ores, Great Lakes area; [by grade name and mining company], 1984. (p. 66-75)

[9] Grade classification, average analyses [and shipments], U.S. and Canada combined areas, 1980-84. (p. 79-81)

[10] Type of product, average analyses, [and shipments, for run of mine, coarse, fines, pellets, sinter, and other], U.S. and Canada combined areas [and U.S. originating areas], 1980-84. (p. 85-90)

A2050
American
Jewish Committee

A2050-1   AMERICAN JEWISH YEAR BOOK, 1985
Annual.   1984.   xi + 498 p.
Vol. 85.
ISBN 0-8276-0247-2.
LC 99-4040.
SRI/MF/excerpts

Annual compilation, for 1985, of articles on characteristics and activities of Israeli, U.S., and world Jewish community. Includes Jewish population estimates, by U.S. State and selected city, 1984, and by country, 1982.

Contains preface (1 p.); list of contributing authors, and contents listing (p. vii-xi); 2 articles on Jewish life in Latin America (p. 3-102); 5 articles on U.S. issues affecting Jews, and Jewish demography (p. 105-190); 10 articles on Jewish situation in other countries (p. 191-329); and directories, lists, necrology, calendars, and index (p. 333-498).

Articles containing substantial statistics are described below. This is the 85th annual compilation.

Availability: American Jewish Committee, American Jewish Year Book, 165 E. 56th St., New York NY 10022, $25.95; SRI/MF/excerpts for statistical articles described below.

STATISTICAL ARTICLES:

A2050-1.1: Latin American Jewry
DEMOGRAPHY OF LATIN AMERICAN JEWRY
(p. 51-102) By U. O. Schmelz and Sergio DellaPergola. Article on demographic and socio-economic characteristics of Jewish population

in Latin America, 1982 and trends, with detail for Argentina and Brazil. Data are primarily from Latin American Government censuses, and estimates by Hebrew University of Jerusalem Institute of Contemporary Jewry.

Includes 19 tables showing the following Jewish population data, with selected comparisons to the general population:

a. Population size: by Latin American region and country, with comparisons to other world regions, 1982; trends from 1895 for Argentina, including births, deaths, and migration; trends from 1940 for Brazil, by region and State; and projections through 2000, for Argentina and rest of Latin America.

b. Population characteristics: including distributions by age, sex, marital status, country of birth, educational attainment, and occupation; average number of children for married women, by woman's age, labor force status, and educational attainment; and schools and educational enrollment; primarily for Argentina, with some data for other Latin American countries and for Argentinian cities, various periods 1940s-80s.

A2050-1.2: U.S. Jewry

LABOR MARKET STATUS OF AMERICAN JEWS: PATTERNS AND DETERMINANTS

(p. 131-153) By Barry R. Chiswick. Article examining Jewish labor force status, based primarily on data from 1957 Current Population Survey and 1970 Census of Population. Includes 14 tables showing Jewish vs. non-Jewish labor force characteristics, including the following:

a. Comparisons for Jews, Protestants (with detail by race), and Catholics, including proportion living in rural areas, median income (by sex), occupational distribution, educational attainment, birth rates, and women's labor force participation; 1956, 1957, or 1970.

b. Earnings and education by race/ethnicity, with detail by parentage (native- vs. foreign-born) for Jews, blacks, and persons of Mexican origin, 1970.

RECENT JEWISH COMMUNITY POPULATION STUDIES: A ROUNDUP

(p. 154-178) By Gary A. Tobin and Alvin Chenkin. Article examining data from local Jewish population studies conducted in 16 cities during 1979-84, to indicate changes in the Jewish community since the 1970 National Jewish Population Study (NJPS).

Includes 2 tables on sampling methodology; and 18 tables showing survey findings by city (with year of study noted) and for 1970 NJPS, including Jewish population distribution by the following characteristics:

a. Household size, age, sex, marital status, educational level, occupation, household income, nativity, and moving plans.

b. Religious identification (Orthodox, Conservative, or Reformed); synagogue membership and attendance; ritual observance; Jewish organization and community center membership; travel to Israel; and Jewish charitable contributions.

JEWISH POPULATION IN THE U.S., 1984, ANNUAL FEATURE

(p. 179-190) Annual article, by Alvin Chenkin, with 3 tables showing U.S. total population and estimated Jewish population, by State, and by census region and division; and Jewish population by city for communities with a Jewish population of 100 or more; 1984.

Data are from census reports, 1970 National Jewish Population Study, and other sources.

A2050-1.3: World Jewry

CANADIAN JEWRY: SOME RECENT CENSUS FINDINGS

(p. 191-201) By Leo Davids. Article on Canadian Jewish population and demographic characteristics, primarily for 1981. Data are based on Canadian censuses.

Includes 5 tables showing Canadian Jewish population by major city, with detail for children and aged; total and Jewish population, by age and marital status; and total and Jewish married women, by age and number of children; 1981, with selected comparisons to 1961 and 1971, and estimates for 1985.

WORLD JEWISH POPULATION, 1982, ANNUAL FEATURE

(p. 324-329) Annual article, by U. O. Schmelz and Sergio DellaPergola, with 7 tables showing total population and estimated Jewish population, by continent, world region, and country, 1982, with comparisons to 1980. Data have been updated on basis of UN estimates.

A2068
American League of Professional Baseball Clubs

A2068-1   1985 AMERICAN LEAGUE RED BOOK
Annual. Feb. 18, 1985.
112 p.
LC 72-625050.
SRI/MF/complete

Annual fact book, for 1985, of the American League of Professional Baseball Clubs. Includes data on player and team performance, and game attendance, 1984 and trends. Data are compiled by the league.

Contains contents listing (p. 1) and the following:

a. Club and park information, including player rosters and 1984 performance data; and selected general information. (p. 2-48)

b. Team and player 1984 batting, pitching, and fielding performance data; 1984 leading performances, with historical data from 1893; player awards; team standings; and career records of active pitchers. (p. 49-72)

c. Historical records, including 20-game winning pitchers, 1901-84; top 10 all-time pitchers and batters in selected categories, by team; lifetime batting records and stolen bases of active players; and team win/loss performance vs. opposing clubs since 1901. (p. 73-84)

d. 1984 pennant race, by month; box scores of 1984 championship series and World Series games; results of championship series from 1969 and World Series from 1903; team standings, 1901-84; average length of 1984 games; home and road game attendance,

1983-84, and all-time attendance records, by team; league attendance trends, 1901-84; free agent roster and 1984 performance data; and selected general information. (p. 85-107)

e. 1985 spring training and regular season addresses and schedules. (p. 108-112 and back cover)

Availability: Alfred Publishing Co., PO Box CN 13150, Trenton NJ 08650, $9.95+$2.75 shipping, or $22.65 with *National League Green Book* (see A8015-1 below); SRI/MF/complete.

A2070
American
Library Association

A2070-1   ACRL UNIVERSITY LIBRARY STATISTICS, 1983/84
Recurring (irreg.) Mar. 1985.
57 p.
ISBN 0-8389-6892-9.
SRI/MF/complete, delayed

Recurring report, for 1983/84, on library resources, staff, and expenditures of universities that are not members of the Assn of Research Libraries (ARL). Report complements the ARL annual report showing similar data for ARL-member libraries, described in SRI under A3365-1.

Includes the following data, by institution: library volumes and additions, serials, microform holdings by type, interlibrary loan activity, staff (including students), and expenditures by object; PhD degrees awarded and number of fields; total and graduate student enrollment; library expenditures as percent of total university expenditures; and rankings by selected library characteristics.

Also includes library operating ratio medians and ranges.

Data are based on responses from 86 universities to an ACRL survey.

Contains contents listing (1 p.); introduction and university code guide (p. 1-1a); 22 tables, interspersed with explanatory notes (p. 2-39); facsimile questionnaire and footnotes (p. 40-56); and list of ACRL publications (p. 57).

Previous report, with data for 1981/82, is described in SRI 1983 Annual under this number.

Availability: American Library Association, Association of College and Research Libraries, 50 E. Huron St., Chicago IL 60611, members $12.00, nonmembers $15.00; SRI/MF/complete, delayed shipment in Mar. 1986.

A2072
American
Logistics Association

A2072–1 ALA 1984-85 WORLDWIDE DIRECTORY AND FACT BOOK
Annual. [1984.] 228 p.
ISBN 0-915959-00-3.
SRI/MF/complete

Annual fact book and directory, for 1984/85, of the American Logistics Assn, presenting information of interest to companies that market food and other consumer products to military resale agencies. Includes statistics on sales by product category or dept, for post exchanges and commissaries by military branch, U.S. Army Troop Support Agency, and Veterans Canteen Service, various periods FY70s-84.

Also includes sales-inflation comparisons; average sales and profits per square foot, for Army/Air Force Exchange Service; and shelf space allocations by product, for Air Force Commissary Service.

Data are based on reports from individual agencies.

Contains contents listing (p. 3); ALA information and directories, and members of military-related congressional committees (p. 6-157); information on military resale agencies, including 1-3 tables for most agencies (p. 164-224); and index to military resale agency personnel (p. 225-227).

Availability: American Logistics Association, 1133 15th St., NW, Suite 500, Washington DC 20005, members $15.00, nonmembers $35.00; SRI/MF/complete.

A2075
American
Management Association

A2075–7 1985 AMA REPORT ON INFORMATION CENTERS
Monograph. 1985.
vi+121 p.
ISBN 0-8144-3151-8.
SRI/MF/complete

Survey report on corporate information centers (ICs), which provide computer user support services for employees. Presents detailed data on ICs, including prevalence, start-up reasons and dates, staffing, and functions; number and job functions of employees served; hardware and/or software expenditures, selection criteria, purchase plans, and training methods; and personal computer brands used. Most data are shown by company sales size.

Also presents comparisons between companies with and without ICs, including industry distribution, revenue trends, number of microcomputers at work site, job functions of employees who use computers, and computer hardware "strategies" and user training methods; comparison of hardware strategies before and after IC implementation; and data on extent of computer access and use among employees.

Data are based primarily on responses from 1,296 IC managers, other data processing execu-

tives, and computer end-users, to 2 surveys conducted Dec. 1984-Feb. 1985. The surveys encompassed selected American Management Assn seminar participants and Data Processing Management Assn members.

Contains contents and table listings (p. iii-vi); 10 chapters, with narrative analysis, 39 tables, and methodology (p. 3-80); and 2 appendices, with 37 tables (p. 81-121).

Availability: American Management Association, AMA Membership Publications Division, 135 W. 50th St., New York NY 10020, members enrolled in the Information Systems and Technology and General Administrative Services Divisions †, other members and additional copies $225.00, nonmembers $250.00; SRI/MF/complete.

A2075–8 CHANGING AMERICAN WORKPLACE: WORK ALTERNATIVES IN THE '80S
Monograph. 1985. 48 p.
ISBN 0-8144-3152-6.
LC 85-11187.
SRI/MF/complete

Report on corporate managers' use of alternative working arrangements for employees. Covers 21 types of programs, classified as follows: job-related (e.g., job sharing, job enrichment, and cross-training); quality of work life (e.g., flextime, compressed work week, and labor-management committees); alternative organizational structures (e.g., project teams); and employee participation and control (e.g., employee-owned organizations or equity participation).

Includes data on use of each type of program, with detail by company employment size, unionization status, and industry, and by employee occupational category.

Data are based on 1,618 responses to an American Management Assn membership survey.

Contains contents listing (p. 5); introduction (p. 7-11); narrative report in 4 sections, with 1 chart and 4 tables (p. 12-39); bibliography (p. 40-41); and appendix, with 10 tables (p. 42-48).

Availability: American Management Association, AMA Membership Publications Division, 135 W. 50th St., New York NY 10020, members: 1st copy †, additional copies $10.00; nonmembers $13.50; SRI/MF/complete.

A2100
American Meat Institute

A2100–1 MEATFACTS, 1985
Annual. Aug. 1985. 44 p.
SRI/MF/complete

Annual statistical overview, for 1984, of the U.S. meat industry. Includes data on livestock numbers, slaughter, and meat production; farm marketing receipts; meat consumption, nutrition, and prices; foreign meat production, and trade; and meat packing industry financial and operating data; with selected trends from 1925.

Most data are from USDA, Dept of Commerce, and Labor Dept.

Contains introduction and contents listing (p. 1-2); 3 maps and 6 summary charts; and 3 charts and 46 tables, listed below (p. 3-44).

This is the 15th annual edition.

Availability: American Meat Institute, Communications Department, PO Box 3556, Washington DC 20007, members $5.00, nonmembers $10.00; SRI/MF/complete.

TABLES AND CHARTS:

A2100–1.1: Livestock and Meat Production Industry

LIVESTOCK INVENTORIES AND FINANCES

[1] Cattle, sheep, and hogs on farms, Jan. 1; and total U.S. resident population, July 1; [quinquennially 1925-50, and annually 1951-85]. (p. 3)

[2] Cattle/calves and sheep/lambs on farms, Jan. 1, 1985; and hogs, Dec. 1, 1984; by State [arranged by region]. (p. 4)

[3] Numbers of operations with livestock, by State [arranged by region] and species [cattle, milk cows, hogs, and sheep], 1983-84. (p. 5)

[4] Livestock prices received by farmers, U.S. averages for all grades [beef cattle, calves, hogs, and lambs, quinquennially 1925-50, and annually 1951-84]. (p. 6)

[5] Cash receipts from farm marketings of meat animals [cattle/calves, hogs, and sheep/lambs], by State [ranked by total cash receipts], 1984. (p. 7)

[6] Cash receipts [distribution by type, including crops, livestock, meat animals, and government payments], 1984. [chart] (p. 7)

[7] Number of feedlots and cattle marketed, by feedlot capacity [individually for 7 leading States, and aggregate for 13 leading States], 1984. (p. 8)

SLAUGHTER AND PRODUCTS

[8] Composition of commercial cattle slaughter [steers/heifers, cows, and bulls/stags], 1960-84. (p. 9)

[9] Livestock slaughter [by species] and meat production [beef, veal, lamb/mutton, and pork; quinquennially 1925-60, and annually 1961-84]. (p. 10)

[10] Livestock slaughter [number of head and average live weight, by species]; and meat production [dressed weight and average dressed weight, by type; all for federally inspected, other commercial, and farm slaughter]; 1983-84. (p. 11)

[11] [Commercial] slaughter and number of [federally inspected] plants, by species and State, 1984. (p. 12)

[12] Number of livestock slaughtering plants, by State, Jan. 1, 1984-85. (p. 14)

[13] Livestock slaughter shares by firm size [percent of total slaughter accounted for by 4-12 largest firms, and total number of firms], 1972-83. (p. 15)

[14] Federally inspected slaughter plants [and slaughter], by species and size, 1984. (p. 16)

[15] Large plants, number and slaughter [and percent of federally inspected plants and commercial slaughter, all for cattle and hogs], 1975-84. (p. 16)

[16] Top 25 packers (ranked by 1984 sales). (p. 17)

[17-18] Top 10 steer/heifer and hog slaughterers in 1984 (ranked alphabetically). (p. 17)

[19-20] Steer and hog carcass breakdown [pounds of retail meat, by cut, and other products (no date)]. (p. 18-19)

[21] Beef quality and yield graded [and total commercial beef production], 1974-81 and 1983-84. (p. 20)

[22] Hamburger and beef: [per capita] consumption and [per pound] prices, 1971-84. (p. 21)

[23-24] Meat products processed and canned under Federal inspection [by product], 1983-84. (p. 22-24)

[25] U.S. production of edible by-products, edible and inedible tallow, and lard, 1970-84. (p. 25)

[26] Cattlehides: slaughter, prices [at Chicago market], and [volume and value of] exports, 1970-84. (p. 25)

MEAT CONSUMPTION AND NUTRITION

[27-28] Per capita disappearance of red meat, carcass and retail weight basis [beef, veal, pork, and lamb/mutton]; and of red meat, poultry, and fish, retail weight basis; 1960-84. (p. 26-27)

[29] Beef and pork nutritional profiles. (p. 28)

[30-32] Red meats and fat: [fat from meat as percent of total calories in average daily diet; fat content of meats by type; and trends in animal vs. vegetable sources of fat in the diet, selected periods 1909-1981]. 1 table and 2 charts. (p. 29)

PRICES AND EXPENDITURES

[33] Livestock and wholesale meat prices [by species or product], 1977-84. (p. 30)

[34] Average retail meat prices [for beef and pork, by cut, and for poultry by type, quinquennially 1965-80 and annually 1981-84]. (p. 31)

[35] CPI [for all items, foods, and meats]; and PPI [for total finished goods, all commodities, and meats]; 1977-84. (p. 32)

[36] Per capita [disposable] income, and red meat expenditures [amount and as percent of total food expenditures], 1965-84. (p. 33)

[37] Consumer expenditures for meat, poultry, and fish in grocery stores [and total grocery store food/beverage and nonfood/general merchandise sales], 1973 and 1983. (p. 34)

INDUSTRY DATA

[38] Employment, [hourly and weekly] earnings, [and average weekly hours], for meat packing and meat processing industries, compared with all food and all manufacturing [selected years 1965-84]. (p. 35)

[39] Sales, raw materials costs, expenses, and net earnings of the meat packing industry, 1978-83. (p. 36)

[40] Breakdown of meat packers' sales dollar, by species slaughtered [cattle and hogs], 1982-83. (p. 37)

[41] Financial ratios for meat packers compared with all manufacturers, 1983. (p. 37)

A2100–1.2: Meat Foreign Trade and Consumption

[1] Meat animals, meat and meat products: value of U.S. exports and imports [by species], 1982-84. (p. 38)

[2] U.S. imports, exports, and net imports of beef/veal, pork, lamb/mutton, and total meat in relation to domestic production, 1976-84. (p. 39)

[3-4] U.S. imports of selected red meat products; and U.S. exports of selected red meat and livestock products; by major markets, 1983-84. (p. 40-41)

[5] U.S. canned ham imports by country, 1970-84. (p. 42)

[6] U.S. ham production [by type] and [canned ham] imports, 1970-84. (p. 42)

[7] World meat [beef/veal, pork, and lamb/mutton] trade in selected countries, 1984. (p. 43)

[8] Per capita meat [beef/veal, pork, lamb/mutton/goat, and poultry] disappearance in selected countries, 1984. (p. 44)

A2100–2 FINANCIAL REVIEW OF THE MEAT PACKING INDUSTRY, 1984

Annual. Sept. 1985. 27 p.
ISSN 0163-3708.
LC 78-646705.
SRI/MF/complete

Annual report presenting detailed data on meat packing industry finances and processing operations, including employment and earnings, 1984, with selected trends from as early as 1925.

Data are from a 1984 American Meat Institute (AMI) survey of 148 meat packing and processing companies, and from USDA and other Government and trade sources.

Contains contents listing (inside front cover); brief summary, with 1 chart (p. 1); 3 sections with narrative summary, 6 charts, and 33 tables (p. 2-24); and 3 appendix tables (p. 25-27). All tables, and selected charts with substantial data not covered in tables, are listed below.

This is the 60th annual report.

Availability: American Meat Institute, Communications Department, PO Box 3556, Washington DC 20007, members $7.50, nonmembers $15.00; SRI/MF/complete.

TABLES AND CHARTS:

[Data are shown for 1983-84, unless otherwise noted.]

INDUSTRY FINANCES AND EMPLOYMENT

1.1. Financial ratios of the meat packing industry, 1982-84. (p. 3)

1.2. Sales, raw material costs, expenses, and income of the meat packing industry [including employee benefit costs by type, depreciation, rent, and taxes], 1973-84. (p. 4-5)

1.3-1.6. Livestock prices [by species]; commercial meat production [by type]; meat price indices [by type]; and year-end assets, liabilities, and net worth of the meat packing industry. (p. 6-7)

1.7. Employment [total and production workers], earnings, [and weekly hours, for all manufacturing, and meat packing and processing]. (p. 8)

SURVEYED COMPANIES FINANCES

[Tables 2.2-2.4 and 2.7-2.19 generally show data by company classification: for meat processing companies, and national, regional, and local meat packing companies. All tables show data for AMI survey participants only.]

2.1. Business structure [number of cooperatives, subsidiaries, and independently incorporated companies; and number of stockholders; for meat packers and processors], 1984. (p. 9)

2.2. Percentage breakdown of the sales dollar, by company classification, 1984. (p. 10)

2.3. Earnings ratios. (p. 11)

2.4. [Percentage] breakdown of sales, by product category [fresh and processed meat, and non-meat items], 1984. (p. 11)

2.5a. Breakdown of meat packers' sales dollar, by species slaughtered [cattle and hog]. (p. 12)

2.5b. Financial ratios for [total, beef, and pork] meat packers compared with all manufacturers, 1984. (p. 12)

2.6. Breakdown of hog packer's 1984 sales dollar by percent of fresh meat sales. (p. 13)

2.7. Percentage breakdown of current assets, 1984. (p. 14)

2.8-2.9. Ratios: current assets to current liabilities; and liabilities to net worth. (p. 15)

2.10. Net worth as percent of total assets. (p. 16)

2.11-2.15b. Ratios: fixed assets to net worth; and sales to working capital, net worth, inventory, total assets, and fixed assets. (p. 16-18)

2.16-2.19. Total selling/administrative, advertising, and repairs/maintenance expenses as percent of total operating expenses; and capital expenditures. (p. 19)

EMPLOYEE EARNINGS AND BENEFITS

3.1 Employment [total and production workers], earnings, [and weekly hours] in the meat [packing and processing] industry compared with the food industry [selected years 1970-84]. (p. 20)

[A-B] Wage/salary and benefit costs [total, and] as percentage of operating expenses [for] the meat packing industry [selected years 1970-84]. (p. 21)

3.2. Average straight-time earnings and percentage distribution of production workers in the meat packing and processing industries [with earnings detail by company type (multi- and single-plant), employment size, and share of workers covered by labor contract, all by region], June 1984. (p. 22)

3.3. Average straight-time earnings in selected occupations in the meat packing industry, by company type [and employment size], June 1984. (p. 23)

3.4. Employee benefits [percent of production workers receiving insurance, retirement, and other benefits] in the meat packing industry [by company type], June 1984. (p. 24)

APPENDIX DATA

A1. Financial ratios for manufacturing industries [by major industry group]. (p. 25)

A2. Financial results of the meat packing industry [including total sales, net worth and income, and income ratios, selected years] 1925-84. (p. 26)

A3. Meat animals processed by the meat packing industry [shows number slaughtered, and live and dressed weight, for cattle, calves, sheep/lambs, and hogs, selected years] 1925-84. (p. 27)

A2200
American
Medical Association

**A2200–3   PHYSICIAN
CHARACTERISTICS AND
DISTRIBUTION IN THE U.S.,
1983 Edition**
Annual. 1984. vii+295 p.
Rpt. No. OP-180/3.
ISSN 0731-0315.
ISBN 0-89970-179-5.
LC 82-644625.
SRI/MF/complete, current & previous year reports

Annual report, by Mary Ann Eiler, on Federal and nonfederal physician characteristics and geographic distribution in the U.S. and outlying areas, 1982 and trends. Includes data on women and foreign medical graduate (FMG) physicians.

Data are derived from the AMA Physician Masterfile as of Dec. 31, 1982. The Masterfile compiles data from the Record of Physicians' Professional Activities survey and other medical field sources.

Contents:

a. Listings of contents, tables, charts, and appendices, and foreword (p. iii-vii); and introduction, data source information, reference materials, and definitions (p. 1-7).

b. Physician demographic, professional, and summary geographic characteristics, including data on trends, age and sex distribution, and certification; with narrative, 14 summary tables, 9 charts, 1 map, and 41 detailed tables described below. (p. 7-85)

c. Physician professional characteristics by detailed geographic location, with 14 tables, described below. (p. 86-277)

d. Appendices, including lists of SMSAs and census regions and divisions; county size classifications; abbreviations and definitions; list of medical specialty boards; 2 summary tables, described below; questionnaire facsimile; and index. (p. 278-295)

Previous report, for 1982, has also been reviewed and is also available on SRI microfiche under this number [Annual. 1983. vi+286 p. Rpt. No. OP-180. ISBN 0-89970-163-9. $33.00, members 10% discount]. Report is substantially similar in content and format, but also includes data for the Panama Canal Zone.

Report for 1981 is described in SRI 1982 Annual under this number.

Availability: American Medical Association, Book and Pamphlet Fulfillment OP-180/3, PO Box 10946, Chicago IL 60610, $35.00+$4.00 shipping and handling (prepaid), members 10% discount; SRI/MF/complete.

TABLES:

[Data by activity are shown for the following: office patient care (occasionally with detail for general practice, and medical, surgical, and other specialties); hospital patient care (occasionally with detail for residents and full-time staff); and other (usually with detail for medical teaching, administration, and research).

Data by specialty usually are shown for 37 categories.]

A2200–3.1: Demographic and Professional Characteristics

a. Total physicians by activity, specialty, age, and sex; FMG, women, and total office-based physicians, by specialty; nonfederal physicians by activity, by metro vs. non-metro status; and total and nonfederal physician comparison with total population, with detail by State and specialty; various years 1965-82. Tables A1-A12. (p. 18-36)

b. Total physicians by age, sex, and activity, and by specialty and board certification status; nonfederal physicians by age, sex, and specialty; FMG and women physicians by activity and specialty; FMG physicians by age, sex, and activity; and total physicians by school of graduation and graduates of Canadian and foreign schools, by year of graduation and sex; 1982. Tables B1-B17. (p. 42-65)

c. Total, Federal, and nonfederal physicians by age, sex, and State; women and FMG physicians by activity and State; and counties with no active physician in patient care, with land area and population detail; 1982. Tables C1-C12. (p. 69-82)

A2200–3.2: Detailed Geographic Distribution, and Appendix Tables

[Tables show data for 1982, by specialty and activity, unless otherwise noted. The tables include totals for U.S. and possessions, combined and/or separately, plus the additional breakdowns noted. Data by State also are shown for Puerto Rico, Virgin Islands, and Pacific Islands.]

a. All physicians. Table 1. (p. 86)

b. Federal physicians: by census region and division; and by service branch (Army, Navy, Air Force, Public Health Service, VA, and other). Tables 2-5. (p. 87-108)

c. Nonfederal physicians: by census region and division; by State; by county size group, individual county, and SMSA (all by activity only); and for all SMSAs. Tables 6-14. (p. 109-277)

d. Nonfederal physicians and civilian population, by State, selected years 1965-82. Tables C1-C2. (p. 290-291)

**A2200–5   SOCIOECONOMIC
CHARACTERISTICS OF
MEDICAL PRACTICE, 1984**
Annual. Aug. 1984.
xi+140 p. Rpt. No. OP-228.
ISBN 0-89970-176-0.
SRI/MF/complete

Annual compilation of articles and statistics on economic aspects of medical practice, 1973-83. Includes data on physicians' hours, workload, and finances, by medical specialty, type and location of practice, and physician age and employment status.

Most data are compiled by the AMA Socioeconomic Monitoring System (SMS) from quarterly telephone surveys of approximately 4,000 physicians.

Contains contents and table listings, foreword, and introduction (p. iii-xi); methodology, with 2 tables (p. 1-9); 6 articles, with 1 chart and 14 tables, described below (p. 11-34); 41 detailed tables, listed below (p. 36-113); and appendices with survey questionnaire, definitions, and computation formulas (p. 115-140).

This is the 2nd annual SMS report.

Availability: American Medical Association, Book and Pamphlet Fulfillment, PO Box 10946, Chicago IL 60610, $16.00+$3.50 shipping and handling (prepaid); SRI/MF/complete.

STATISTICAL ARTICLES AND TABLES:

A2200–5.1: Statistical Articles
[Articles are reprinted from *SMS Report,* a periodically published newsletter.]

PAYMENT FOR PHYSICIANS' SERVICES

(p. 11-14) Includes 2 tables showing distribution of physicians' patients by type of 3rd-party payor (Medicare, Medicaid, Blue Shield, other private, and pre-pay); and percent of fee for follow-up office visit covered, for Medicare, Medicaid, and Blue Shield; by region and specialty, 1979 and 1983.

CHANGING MEDICAL PRACTICE ARRANGEMENTS

(p. 15-18) Includes 4 tables showing distribution of physicians by size of practice, employment status (including self-employed, hospital, and government), and type of practice income (including fee-for-service, salary, and percent of gross or net billings); and percent of physicians in professional corporations; with selected detail by specialty and age; 1975 and/or 1983.

ROLE OF PROFIT IN MEDICINE

(p. 19-22) Includes 2 tables comparing characteristics of physicians with admitting privileges at proprietary and nonproprietary hospitals, 1983. Tables show distribution by sex, years of practice, type of practice (solo and non-solo), and region; and average income, practice expenses, weekly hours worked in office and hospital, hospital patients discharged per week, length of hospital stay, and time spent per hospital visit.

DIFFERENCES IN PRACTICE CHARACTERISTICS BETWEEN FEMALE AND MALE PHYSICIANS

(p. 23-26) Includes 2 tables comparing employment status (self-employed vs. employee), weekly hours and patient visits, and annual and hourly income, for female and male physicians, with some detail by specialty and age, various years 1972-83.

PHYSICIANS' INVOLVEMENT WITH MEDICARE

(p. 27-30) Includes 1 chart and 2 tables on Medicare patients' share of physicians' total visits, with selected detail by region and specialty and for office visits and hospital rounds, 4th quarter 1983.

PROFIT IN MEDICINE: THE IMPACT ON HOSPITAL STAFFING PATTERNS AND PHYSICIAN PRACTICE BEHAVIOR

(p. 31-34) Includes 2 tables showing the following data for proprietary and nonproprietary hospitals: total and board-certified staff physicians per 100 beds, by specialty, 1982; and percent of hospitals implementing selected cost reduction measures, 1st quarter 1984.

Data on staffing patterns are from American Hospital Assn.

A2200–5.2: Detailed Tables

[Tables show data by practice specialty, for solo and non-solo practice, and by census division, metro-nonmetro location and city size, and physician employment status (self-employed and employee) and age group.

Tables show data for various years 1973-83. Data for 1983 include detail by demographic and physician characteristics for specific practice specialties.]

WORK HOURS

1-2. Mean number of weeks practiced. (p. 36-39)

3. Mean number of hours in professional activities per week. (p. 40-41)

4-6. Mean number of hours in [total] and direct patient care activities per week. (p. 42-47)

7-11. Mean number of office hours, hours on hospital rounds, and hours in surgery per week. (p. 48-57)

WORKLOAD

12-17. Mean number of total patient visits, office visits, and visits on hospital rounds per week. (p. 58-69)

18. Mean number of surgical procedures per week. (p. 70-71)

SPECIALTY WORKLOADS

[Tables 19-22 begin "Mean patient care activities per week" and show number of cases or procedures and hours spent for the specialties noted below.]

19. Psychiatry [sessions with individual patients, and with family/nonfamily groups]. (p. 72-73)

20. Radiology [film readings, radiodiagnostic procedures, radiotherapy patients, and consultations]. (p. 74-75)

21. Anesthesiology [patients anesthetized by physician and by nurse anesthetist under physicians' supervision, and preanesthesia/other inpatient visits]. (p. 76-77)

22. Pathology [surgical consultations, examinations of surgical specimens, laboratory procedures, and autopsies]. (p. 78-79)

WAITING TIME AND HOSPITAL UTILIZATION

23-24. Mean number of days waiting time to be scheduled for an appointment; and mean number of minutes waiting time by patients arriving for an appointment. (p. 80-83)

25-26. Mean number of patients discharged from the hospital per week; and number of days for hospital stays per patient. (p. 84-87)

FINANCES

27-32. Mean fee for an office visit with an established and a new patient; and for a hospital follow-up visit. (p. 88-99)

33-36. Mean and median professional expenses of self-employed physicians. (p. 100-105)

37. Means of selected components of professional expenses [including non-physician payroll, office expenses, medical supplies and equipment, and professional liability insurance]. (p. 106-107)

38-41. Mean and median physician net income after expenses before taxes. (p. 108-113)

A2200–6 AMERICAN HEALTH CARE SYSTEM, 1984

Biennial. 1984. vi+83 p.
Rpt. No. OP-259.
ISBN 0-89970-173-6.
SRI/MF/complete, except for tables 41-47

Biennial compilation of statistics related to the health care system, primarily 1960s-82, with trends from as early as 1900. Includes data on population health status, health care expenditures and financing, medical education and personnel, and health care facilities.

Data are from AMA, NCHS, and other specified Federal and private sources.

Contains listing of contents, charts, and tables (p. iii-vi); and introduction and 7 chapters, with brief narrative overviews, 11 charts, and 47 tables (p. 1-83). All tables, and charts presenting substantial data, are listed below.

Report has been published since 1978; SRI coverage begins with the 1984 edition.

Availability: American Medical Association, Book and Pamphlet Fulfillment, PO Box 10946, Chicago IL 60610, $9.95+$3.00 shipping and handling (prepaid), members 10% discount; SRI/MF/complete, except for tables 41-47 for which reproduction permission could not be obtained.

TABLES AND CHARTS:

A2200–6.1: Vital Statistics

1-2. Late fetal and infant mortality rates, and percent of live births with low birth weight, by race [various years 1950-82]. (p. 4-5)

3. Selected notifiable disease rates [by disease, selected years 1960-81]. (p. 7)

4-5. Physician visits [by] source of place of care, and restricted-activity and bed-disability days, [both] by [patient] age, sex, and race [various years 1964-81]. (p. 8-9)

6. Life expectancy at birth [by] race and sex, selected years 1900-82. (p. 10)

7. Age-adjusted death rates for selected causes of death, selected years 1960-82. (p. 11)

A2200–6.2: Health Care Expenditures and Financing

HEALTH EXPENDITURES

Chart 4. Nation's health dollar [distribution by source and function], 1982. (p. 17)

Chart 5. Aspects of the health care industry compared to the economy as a whole, 1982. (p. 18)

8. Aggregate and per capita national health expenditures, [and GNP], selected years 1929-82. (p. 19)

9-10. National health expenditures by type of expenditure, selected years 1950-82, [with cross-tabulation] by source of funds, 1982. (p. 20-22)

11. Medicare enrollment: number of aged medicare enrollees and [average annual] percent change, by type of coverage, age, sex, and race, 1966 and 1980-81. (p. 23)

12-13. Medicare utilization and reimbursement: number of aged persons served [including persons served per 1,000 enrolled], amount reimbursed, and [average annual] percent change, by type of service, 1967 and 1980-81. (p. 24-25)

14-15. CPI and medical care component [by item], selected years 1950-83. (p. 26-27)

16. Annual percentage increases in selected components of the CPI, selected years 1972-83. (p. 28)

FINANCING MECHANISMS

17. Personal health care expenditures by selected 3rd-party payers and type of expenditure, 1982. (p. 30)

Charts 6-7. Percentage distribution of personal health care expenditures [public vs. private sources] of funds, [selected years] 1970-82; and distribution of health insurance coverage [by type], 1980. (p. 31-32)

A2200–6.3: Medical Education and Manpower

MEDICAL EDUCATION

18. [Medical school] application activity for 1st-year class [applicants, applications, acceptances, and 1st-year enrollment], selected years 1962/63-1982/83. (p. 35)

19. Students in medical/basic science schools [number of schools, total and 1st-year enrollment, and graduates], selected years 1962/63-1982/83. (p. 36)

20. Women in medical schools [applicants, 1st-year enrollment, and graduates], 1972/73-1982/83. (p. 37)

21. Percentage [and number] of minority enrollment of U.S. citizens in medical schools [1st-year and total enrollment, and graduates, by minority group (black, American Indian/Alaskan Native, Mexican American, Puerto Rican, other Hispanic, and Asian/Pacific Islander)], 1982/83. (p. 38)

22. Medical school expenditures by function, 1981/82. (p. 39)

23. Percent of funds to public and private medical schools [from Federal, State, and other sources], 1971/72 and 1981/82. (p. 40)

24. Major sources of loans and scholarship funds [number and amount by type], 1980/81-1981/82. (p. 41-42)

MEDICAL MANPOWER

25. Number of postgraduate year 1 and residency positions offered, and residents on duty, by specialty, [various years] 1981/82-1983/84. (p. 43-44)

Chart 8. Foreign medical graduates by citizenship [U.S. and other] in residency positions, 1978-82. (p. 45)

A2200–6.4: Physicians and Health Personnel

PHYSICIAN CHARACTERISTICS

[Tables 26-29 and 32 begin "Federal/non-Federal physicians..."]

26. [Compared to total] population, selected years 1900-82. (p. 48)

Charts 10-11. Percentage distribution of Federal/non-Federal physicians by age, sex, and specialty, 1982. (p. 50-51)

27-29. By major professional activity [office- and hospital-based patient care, medical teaching, administration, research, and inactive] and specialty, [various years 1963-82]. (p. 52-56)

30-31. Federal/non-Federal women physicians and foreign medical graduates, by specialty, [various years 1963-82]. (p. 57-58)

32. By specialty and corresponding board certification, 1981. (p. 59-61)

33. Non-Federal physician/population ratios and rank by State, 1982. (p. 62-64)

HEALTH PERSONNEL

34. Estimated number of persons active in selected health occupations [clinical laboratory technician, dentist, dental hygienist and assistant, dietician, registered and practical nurse, nursing aide/orderly, pharmacist, physician, psychologist, radiologic technician, and therapist], 1981. (p. 65)

35. Active registered nurses, [by full- and part-time] status and number per 100,000 population, selected years 1950-80. (p. 66)

A2200–6.5: Medical Practice and Health Care Facilities

MEDICAL PRACTICE PROFILE

[Data show mean amounts by physician specialty and age.]

36-37. Net income (income after expenses but before taxes) from medical practice, and number of hours in patient care activities per week, [various] years 1973-82. (p. 69-70)

38-40. Number of total patient visits per week, professional expenses, and fee for an office visit with an established patient, [various years 1973-82]. (p. 71-73)

HEALTH CARE FACILITIES

41. Trends in [number of] hospitals [and beds] by classification [total, Federal, short-term private nonprofit and for-profit, and short-term State/local government], 1980-82. (p. 76)

42. Short-stay hospitals and beds [by] type of ownership [Federal, non-government nonprofit and proprietary, and State/local], selected years 1960-82. (p. 77)

43. Community hospitals [by bed-size category], 1972 and 1982. (p. 78)

44. Selected measures in community hospitals [number of hospitals and beds, admissions, average daily census and length of stay, occupancy rate, surgical operations, bassinets, births, and outpatient visits], 1972 and 1981-82. (p. 79)

45. [Percent of community hospitals offering] selected facilities and services, 1981-82. (p. 80-81)

46-47. Total expenditures, and adjusted expenses per inpatient day, community hospitals [by bed-size category], 1981-82. (p. 82-83)

A2275
American Music Conference

A2275–1   MUSIC USA: 1985 Review of the Music Industry and Amateur Music Participation
Annual. 1985. 21 p.
ISSN 0197-4173.
ISBN 0-918196-10-8.
LC 80-642143.
SRI/MF/complete

Annual report, for 1985, on music industry. Presents data on retail sales volume and value for musical instruments and accessories, sheet music, and sound equipment, various years 1940-84; and foreign trade of instruments and accessories, 1982-84, with leading trading partner countries for 1984. Instrument data are shown by type.

Also includes data on number of amateur musicians, selected demographic characteristics, and percent who play regularly, with some detail by type of instrument; and percent of households with players and instruments; 1985, with selected trends from 1972.

Data are from trade assns; Federal agencies; industry estimates; and surveys conducted by the Gallup Organization in 1978 and 1985, and by National Opinion Research Center in 1972.

Contains letter from AMC president (p. 1); narrative analysis interspersed with 11 charts and 22 tables (p. 1-16); and directory of AMC directors and member companies (p. 17-21).

Availability: American Music Conference, 150 E. Huron, Chicago IL 60611, members $2.50, music profession $15.00, others $35.00; SRI/MF/complete.

A2350
American Newspaper Publishers Association

A2350–2   PRESSTIME
Monthly.
ISSN 0194-3243.
LC 79-644846.
SRI/MF/complete, shipped quarterly

Monthly trade journal reporting on newspaper publication developments, including technological advances, employee-management relations, and government decisions affecting the news industry.

Issues generally contain:

a. Articles and news briefs, occasionally with statistics; and monthly narrative editorial features.

b. Monthly "Newsprint" section, with 5 monthly tables presenting ANPA survey data on newsprint supply and demand, current to 2-3 months prior to cover date; and 1 quarterly table on paper company net income.

Annual features include articles on ANPA surveys of newspaper prices, capital expenditures, and newsprint consumption; and a report on paper mill labor contract wage increases. A semiannual subject index appears in Jan. and July issues.

May 1985 issue contains an annual insert, '85 *Facts About Newspapers,* covered separately in SRI under A2350-4.

Monthly and quarterly tables are listed below; monthly tables appear in most issues. All additional features with substantial statistical content are described, as they appear, under "Statistical Features;" page locations and latest periods of coverage for quarterly table are also noted. Non-statistical features are not covered.

Availability: American Newspaper Publishers Association, Presstime, Box 17407, Dulles International Airport, Washington DC 20041, members †, nonmembers $100.00 per yr.; SRI/MF/complete, shipped quarterly.

Issues reviewed during 1985: Nov. 1984-Oct. 1985 (P) (Vol. 6, Nos. 11-12; Vol. 7, Nos. 1-10).

MONTHLY TABLES:

[All tables show data on newsprint, for month of coverage, sometimes with data for previous 1-3 months; tables [1-4] also show cumulative data for year to date. All tables include comparisons to same periods of previous year.]

[1] Estimated consumption of all U.S. daily newspapers [by region and circulation size].

[2] Estimated consumption of all U.S. users.

[3] Production [U.S. and Canadian].

[4] Shipments [from U.S. and Canadian mills to U.S., Canada, and areas outside North America (export)].

[5] Stocks [and occasionally days' supply on hand and in transit; for U.S. publishers and Canadian and U.S. mills].

QUARTERLY TABLE:

[1] Financial report of [12-17 selected] paper companies [net income cumulative for year to date, current to approximately 3-4 months prior to cover date, and for same period of preceding year (appearance of table is contingent upon availability of data)].

STATISTICAL FEATURES:

A2350–2.601: Nov. 1984 (Vol. 6, No. 11)

HIKES AVERAGE 5%

(p. 52) Brief article, with 1 table showing number of newspaper labor contracts, and average percent increase in wage, by job category, 1984-85. Data are based on settlements received by the ANPA Human Resources Dept during 1st 7 months of 1984.

A2350–2.602: Dec. 1984 (Vol. 6, No. 12)

SPECIAL REPORT: COUPONS

(p. 13-19) By Marcia Ruth. Article, with 1 chart showing coupon distribution by media type, 1981-83. Data are from A. C. Nielsen Co.

STUDY SHOWS SHARP DECLINE IN UNION MEMBERSHIP

(p. 52) Brief article, with 1 chart showing percent of labor force in labor unions, 1970-80 and 1982. Data are from Bureau of National Affairs.

A2350–2.603: Jan. 1985 (Vol. 7, No. 1)

QUARTERLY TABLE

[1] Financial report of 15 paper companies, for 1st 9 months 1983-84. (p. 57)

NEWSPAPER ANALYSTS OPTIMISTIC ON SECOND HALF OF '80s

(p. 38) By J. Kendrick Noble, Jr. Article, with 1 table showing daily and Sunday newspapers and circulation; expenditures for retail, classified, and national advertising in newspapers; and newspaper total net revenues; selected years 1983-90. Data are from Newspaper Advertising Bureau, Census Bureau, and Paine Webber Inc.

TOP 25 U.S. NEWSPAPER ADVERTISERS (1982-83), ANNUAL FEATURE

(p. 51) Annual table showing advertising expenditures in newspapers and all media for top 25 newspaper advertisers, 1983; with rank among top 100 advertisers in all media, and comparisons to 1982. Data are reprinted from the Sept. 14, 1984 issue of *Advertising Age*.

For description of previous table, see SRI 1983 Annual under A2350-2.409. For description of *Advertising Age* issue, see SRI 1984 Annual under C2710-1.559.

A2350–2.604: Feb. 1985 (Vol. 7, No. 2)

SPECIAL REPORT: BUYING EQUIPMENT

(p. 21-27) By Paul Kruglinski. Article, with 1 table showing newspaper plant expenditures on new equipment, and number of plants reporting, 1978-84. Data are from ANPA annual survey.

MOST OF '84 LABOR PACTS HAVE 3-YEAR TERMS, ANNUAL FEATURE

(p. 47) Annual article, with 3 tables showing the following for labor contracts negotiated at pulp/paper mills in 1984: number of mills and employees affected, and weighted average wage increase, by region, 1984-86. Also includes national totals for 1983. Data are from the American Paper Institute.

For description of previous article, with data for contracts negotiated in 1982, see SRI 1983 Annual under A2350-2.404.

A2350–2.605: Mar. 1985 (Vol. 7, No. 3)

QUARTERLY TABLE

[1] Financial report of 13 paper companies, 1983-84. (p. 62).

BOTH NEWS AND ADVERTISING EXPAND AS THE NEWSPAPER GETS FATTER

(p. 8-9) By Leo Bogart. Article, with 1 table showing average number of newspaper pages, and percent of space used for editorial portion and for advertising by type, for weekday and Sunday editions, 1977 and 1983. Data are based on reports of 164 newspapers with circulation of 100,000 or more.

25 CENTS DAILY, 50 CENTS SUNDAY REMAIN PREDOMINANT NEWSPAPER PRICES, ANNUAL FEATURE

(p. 44-45) Annual article on newspaper pricing for 1984. Data are from an ANPA survey of single-copy, street sale (city zone) prices for 1,803 daily and 792 Sunday papers.

Includes 2 tables showing number of daily and Sunday papers, by price, for total U.S., each State, D.C., Canada, Bahamas, Bermuda, Guam, Puerto Rico, and Virgin Islands.

A2350–2.606: May 1985 (Vol. 7, No. 5)

DESPITE DROP IN THE NUMBER OF REPORTING NEWSPAPERS, CAPITAL-EXPENDITURE PROJECTIONS RISE, ANNUAL FEATURE

(p. 66) Annual article on newspaper industry capital expenditures and outlook, based on responses of 369 U.S. and 18 Canadian newspapers to an ANPA survey. Includes 2 tables showing U.S. and Canadian outlays for plant expansion and modernization, and for new equipment by item, 1984 and estimated 1985.

A2350–2.607: June 1985 (Vol. 7, No. 6)

QUARTERLY TABLE

[1] Financial report of 12 paper companies, 1st quarter 1984-85. (p. 85)

A2350–2.608: Aug. 1985 (Vol. 7, No. 8)

SPECIAL REPORT: JOA

(p. 16-24) By Margaret Genovese. Article, with 1 table showing the following data for newspaper joint operating agreements in 22 cities: newspapers involved, type of edition, circulation, owners, and years agreement began and expires. Data are from U.S. Justice Dept, ANPA, and Audit Bureau of Circulations.

'84 CONSUMPTION ROSE 8 PERCENT AT U.S. DAILIES, ANNUAL FEATURE

(p. 56) Annual article, with 2 tables showing newsprint consumption, by State; and number of newspapers and newsprint consumption, by census region; 1983-84. Data are based on an ANPA survey of 1,728 daily newspapers.

A2350–2.609: Oct. 1985 (Vol. 7, No. 10)

OFFSET PAPERS GAIN IN SHARE OF NEWSPAPER CIRCULATION

(p. 57) Article, with 2 undated tables showing circulation and number of daily newspapers by circulation size group, by printing category (offset, letterpress, and combination). Data are from ANPA and 1985 *Editor and Publisher Yearbook*.

A2350–3 NEWSPRINT STATISTICS, 1984
Annual. Sept. 1985. 14 p. SRI/MF/complete, current & previous year reports

Annual report presenting newsprint supply-demand statistics for the U.S. and Canada, 1984 and trends. Report is compiled by American Newspaper Publishers Assn from ANPA surveys of 1,728 daily newspapers and from reports of the American Paper Institute, Canadian Pulp and Paper Assn, and Census Bureau.

Contains 19 tables, described below, with brief interspersed narrative.

Previous report, for 1983, was also reviewed in SRI during 1985, and is also available on SRI microfiche under A2350-3 [Annual. Aug. 1984. 14 p. †].

Availability: American Newspaper Publishers Association, Newsprint and Transportation Department, The Newspaper Center, Box 17407, Dulles International Airport, Washington DC 20041, †; SRI/MF/complete.

TABLES:

[All data are for newsprint. Unless otherwise noted, data are for 1984, often with comparisons to 1983 or trends from 1980.]

CONSUMPTION

a. Consumption by U.S. daily newspapers, by month, State, and region (census divisions and Northeast); U.S. per capita consumption; and U.S. and Canadian shipments to U.S users, by user region. 6 tables. (p. 1-3)

PRODUCTION, CAPACITY, AND STOCKS

b. U.S. and Canada: production, by month; and capacity, production, operating rates, and shipments to Canada and/or U.S. and overseas. 7 tables. (p. 4-5)

c. U.S. publishers' stocks (tonnage and days of supply), and U.S. and Canadian mill stocks, by month; and U.S. and Canadian mill capacity, by company, 1984-85. 3 tables. (p. 6-10)

PRICES, IMPORTS, AND EXPORTS

d. Prices in eastern and western U.S., selected dates 1970-84; U.S. domestic supply by source, and imports; and Canadian exports to U.S. and 5 world areas. 4 tables. (p. 11-13)

A2350–4 '85 FACTS ABOUT NEWSPAPERS
Annual. Apr. 1985. 25 p. SRI/MF/complete

Annual report on newspaper publishing industry in the U.S. and Canada, including employment, circulation, advertising revenue, and newsprint consumption, various years 1946-85. Also includes data on ANPA membership. Data are from ANPA, *Editor and Publisher,* Commerce Dept, and other specified sources.

Contains 1984 highlights (p. 1); 17 tables and 7 accompanying charts, described below (p. 2-19); narrative summary with text statistics, including data on readership (p. 20-21); and description of ANPA organization and services, with 1 table showing membership by newspaper circulation size, as of Apr. 1, 1985 (p. 22-25).

Availability: American Newspaper Publishers Association, Public Affairs Department, The Newspaper Center, Box 17407, Dulles International Airport, Washington DC 20041, †; SRI/MF/complete.

TABLES AND CHARTS:

[Historical data are generally shown for selected years within date ranges noted. Data for newspapers often include breakdowns for morning, evening, and Sunday editions.]

a. Daily newspapers by circulation size, total circulation, single copy sales price, and advertising dollar volume compared to GNP, 1946-84; advertising revenue compared to other media, 1983-84; ratio of advertising to total content, 1946-83; and newsprint consumption and prices, 1970-84. 5 charts and 9 tables. (p. 2-11)

b. Newspaper employment by sex, 1960-84, and compared to U.S. total employment, 1947-84; journalism school graduates employed in non-media areas and in media by type, continuing education, and unemployed, 1983-84; weekly newspapers and circulation, 1960-85; and circulation of 20 largest newspapers, and daily and Sunday newspapers owned and circulation for 20 largest newspaper companies, as of Sept. 1984. 2 charts and 5 tables. (p. 12-16)

c. Canada: daily newspapers and circulation, 1946-84; advertising dollar volume compared to GNP, 1962-84; and advertising revenue compared to other media, 1983-84. 3 tables. (p. 17-19)

A2450
American
Optometric Association

A2450–1   1984/85 COE ANNUAL SURVEY OF OPTOMETRIC EDUCATIONAL INSTITUTIONS, Part I
Annual. [1985.]
34 p. no paging.
SRI/MF/complete, current & previous year reports

Annual report on selected characteristics of optometry school faculty, students, and libraries, 1984/85. Data are based on responses from 16 U.S. schools, 1 Puerto Rican school, and 2 Canadian schools, to a survey conducted by the Council on Optometric Education.

Contains tabulation of responses to 31 survey questions, described below, presented in 3 sections on faculty, students, and libraries.

Part II presents financial data for optometry schools, and is available to AOA members only. SRI covers only Part I.

Previous report, for 1983/84 academic year, was also reviewed by SRI during 1985, and is also available on SRI microfiche under A2450-1 [Annual. [1984.] 28 p. no paging. †].

Availability: American Optometric Association, 243 N. Lindbergh Blvd., St. Louis MO 63141, †; SRI/MF/complete, Part I.

TABLES:
[Data are shown by school for 1984/85. Minority groups are black, Spanish surname, American Indian, Asian American, and foreign national.]

FACULTY
a. FTE full-time and part-time faculty; whether full-time faculty allowed optometric practice in and outside school; and faculty salary and total compensation (high, low, and median), by academic rank. (4 questions)

STUDENTS
b. Enrollment and degrees: including full-time professional degree students by program year, sex, and minority group (with trends from 1980/81); withdrawals/dismissals, by reason and program year; degrees awarded; prior educational attainment of 1st-year students; and enrollment by program year, by permanent residence (State or Province, and foreign country). (6 questions)

c. Admissions: including students admitted under State contracts; selected admissions policies; and applications and acceptances for 1st year class. (5 questions)

d. Student finances: including scholarship and loan utilization; percent of students receiving financial aid and loans, by program year and by source (State and/or Federal); and resident and nonresident educational expenditures, and average room/board expenditure, by program year. (4 questions)

e. Other enrollment and programs: including availability of selected program types; and enrollment in part-time/special, graduate, paraoptometric, and residency programs, by sex. (3 questions)

LIBRARIES
f. Library operations: including audiovisual materials and services, annual losses, bound volumes, serial titles, annual budget by object, and other income. (9 questions)

A2470
American
Osteopathic Association

A2470–1   1984-85 YEARBOOK AND DIRECTORY OF OSTEOPATHIC PHYSICIANS
Annual. Oct. 1984. 662 p.
ISSN 0084-358X.
LC 81-10637.
SRI/MF/excerpts

Annual American Osteopathic Assn (AOA) yearbook, for 1984, including data on number and location of osteopathic physicians, osteopathic college enrollment and graduates, and physician characteristics, with selected trends and forecasts for 1932-1988/89.

Also includes directories of U.S. and Canadian osteopathic physicians, affiliated organizations, and educational programs; AOA organization and position papers; and related reference material.

Most data are from AOA records and surveys.

Contains contents listing (p. 7-8); and 46 sections, including statistical section (p. 447-460) with 20 tables listed below.

This is the 76th annual yearbook.

Availability: American Osteopathic Association, Order Department, 212 E. Ohio St., Chicago IL 60611, members $9.00, nonmembers $35.00; SRI/MF/excerpts for tables listed below.

TABLES:

OSTEOPATHIC PHYSICIANS
[1] Growth of the osteopathic profession [number of listed AOA members and nonmembers, and new graduates, 1932-84]. (p. 447)

[2-4] Distribution of listed DOs [doctors of osteopathy, AOA members and nonmembers]; and of DOs by age and by occupational status [including patient care by type of setting, intern, resident, other in-training, and retired; all by State, with totals for Canada, foreign, outlying territories (with some detail for Puerto Rico and Guam), and U.S. Public Health Service and/or military, as of Aug. 1984]. (p. 447-449)

[5] Numbers of current osteopathic certifications [by field, as of July 1984]. (p. 450)

[6] Distribution of DOs by population [size] of community [with total in foreign countries, as of Aug. 1984]. (p. 450)

INTERN AND RESIDENT TRAINING
[7-8] Growth of osteopathic intern training programs [by State]; and osteopathic interns in Federal training programs [by military branch and for Public Health Service; 1979/80-1984/85]. (p. 451)

[9-11] AOA-approved residency positions in osteopathic hospitals, and residents in AOA-approved osteopathic training and nonosteopathic programs, [all by field, 1984/85, most with trend from 1979/80]. (p. 452-454)

COLLEGE ENROLLMENT AND RESEARCH ACTIVITIES
[Tables 13-19] show data by college of osteopathic medicine.]

[12] Women in colleges of osteopathic medicine [enrollment and graduates, 1956/57-1983/84]. (p. 455)

[13] Size of graduating class, 1984 and 1985. (p. 455)

[14] Enrollment [1968/69-1988/89]. (p. 456-457)

[15-16] Actual and expected enrollment by class, 1983/84-1984/85. (p. 456-457)

[17-18] Expected enrollment of women and ethnic minorities [by class, and graduates], 1984/85. (p. 458)

[19] Survey of osteopathic research activities [number of studies and funding amounts, by funding source], 1983. (p. 459)

HOSPITAL FACILITIES
[20] Osteopathic hospitals by State [total and AOA-accredited hospitals; hospitals with AOA-approved postdoctoral training programs; total beds, bassinets, and special care beds; and hospitals by number of beds; as of June 1984]. (p. 460)

A2500
American Paper Institute

A2500–1   1984 STATISTICS OF PAPER, PAPERBOARD, AND WOOD PULP
Annual. Oct. 1984.
iii+75 p.
ISSN 0097-4730.
LC 75-640158.
SRI/MF/complete

Annual report on paper, paperboard, and wood pulp production, consumption, trade, finances, and employment, 1983, with selected historical data from 1899 and forecasts to 1986. Also includes data on recycling, wood supply, and paper industry energy use. Selected data are shown by region and State.

Data are from American Paper Institute (API), other trade assns, and Federal agencies.

Contains foreword and contents listing (i-iii); 5 sections, each with a narrative summary, interspersed with 3 illustrative charts, and 38 tables listed below (p. 1-71); and index (p. 72-75).

This is the 22nd edition of the report. Previous report, for 1982, is described in SRI 1983 Annual under this number.

Availability: American Paper Institute, 260 Madison Ave., New York NY 10016, members †, nonmembers $225.00; SRI/MF/complete.

TABLES:

A2500–1.1:   Section I: Production and Related Output Data

I-I.A. Paper/board and paper plus paperboard production, imports, exports, and new supply [and GNP, various years 1899-1983]. (p. 2-4)

II. Total paper shipments [by grade], 1959-83. (p. 6-9)

III-IV. Paperboard production; and containerboard production for domestic use [including recycled; all] by end use, 1955-83. (p. 10-13)

V. Bleached paperboard production (on machines primarily producing bleached packaging paperboard) for packaging and nonpackaging uses, 1960-83. (p. 14-15)

VI-VIII. Paperboard production: by region, 1965-83; by grade, 1968-83; and by months, 1983; [all by type for domestic use, with total exports]. (p. 16-25)

IX. Box plant consumption [of linerboard/ corrugating material and total containerboard] by months, 1983. (p. 24-25)

X. Paper and paperboard production, new supply, and new supply/real GNP [ratio, by grade], 1959-83. (p. 26-29)

XI-XII. Capacity to produce paper and board [by type]; and wood pulp capacity [by grade]; 1972-86. (p. 30-33)

XIII-XIV. Imports and exports: wood pulp, paper, paperboard, and products [by grade], 1978-83. (p. 34-37)

XV. Value of shipments of [SIC 5-digit] product classes, 1977-82. (p. 38)

A2500-1.2: Section II: Regional Data

XVI. State data [pulpwood consumption; wood pulp production; and paper, paperboard, wet machine board, and construction paper/ board production or shipments; by census division and State], 1981-82. (p. 40-41)

XVII. Capacity of paper, paperboard, and wood pulp, by census division [by grade, selected years] 1970-86. (p. 42-43)

A2500-1.3: Section III: Inputs and Related Data

XVIII. Pulp, paper, and paperboard industry estimated fuel and energy use [by type], 1972 and 1979-83. (p. 48-49)

XIX. Recyclable paper utilization and recovery [including foreign trade], 1970-83. (p. 50)

XX. Recyclable paper recovery [by grade], 1977-83. (p. 51)

XXI.A-XXI.B. Production of wood pulp and market wood pulp [by type], 1971-83. (p. 52)

XXII. Consumption of pulpwood, wood pulp, and other fibrous materials in paper/paperboard mills; and consumption of wood pulp in other mills; [by type], 1971-83. (p. 53)

XXIII. Wage rates and employment, paper and allied products industry [average earnings and hours, and total and production employees], 1965-83. (p. 54-55)

XXIV. Pulp/paper/board mills: output per man-hour, 1947-83. (p. 56)

XXV. Compensation of employees in the paper/allied products industry in the GNP accounts [employees and wages, wage supplements, capital consumption allowance, and average annual earnings per FTE employee], 1948-83. (p. 57)

XXVI. Paper and allied products [SIC 3-digit industry] capital expenditures, 1947-83. (p. 58)

XXVII.A-XXVII.B. Pulp/paper industry environmental protection capital expenditures, and paper/allied products expenditures on R&D, 1966-84. (p. 59)

XXVIII. Wood supply and demand [commercial forest land acreage, and forest industry ownership; and softwood and hardwood removals, mortality, and growth; by region, 1976]. (p. 60)

A2500-1.4: Sections IV and V: Financial Data on the Paper Industry and Supplement

XXIX. Paper/allied products industry: profit and loss data, cash inflow, and selected balance sheet data, 1950-83. (p. 62-63)

XXX. Wholesale/producers price indexes for selected subgroups and classes of wood pulp, paper, paperboard, and converted products, 1968-83. (p. 64-65)

XXXI. General statistics for the paper and allied products [SIC 4-digit] industry [total employees and payroll; production workers, hours, and wages; value added by manufacture; materials costs; shipment value; capital expenditures; and inventories]; 1981-82. (p. 66)

XXXII-XXXIII. Wet machine board and construction paper/board production, imports, exports, and consumption: census data, 1947-83. (p. 68-69)

XXXIV-XXXV. Imports and exports [of paper and paperboard, by grade], 1959-83. (p. 70-71)

A2500-2 PAPER, PAPERBOARD, AND WOOD PULP Monthly Statistical Summary
Monthly.
Approx. 12 p.+insert.
ISSN 0003-0341.
LC 76-641204.
SRI/MF/complete, shipped quarterly

Monthly report on wood pulp, paper, and paperboard industry production and trade. Also covers employment, capital expenditures, productivity, prices, inventories, orders, and consumption for selected products.

Data are from American Paper Institute's Pulp, Minerals, and Technology Group; American Pulpwood Assn; Census Bureau; and other government agencies. Data are current to 1-2 months prior to cover date.

Issues contain narrative summary with occasional summary tables; 18 summary charts, and 7 monthly tables including an industry fact sheet insert; and 2 other recurring tables.

Monthly and other recurring tables are listed below. Monthly tables appear in all issues. Recurring table [8] on sales and earnings appears in Oct. 1984, Feb. 1985, and July 1985 issues; and recurring table [9] on production, trade, and new supply appears in Feb. 1985 and June 1985 issues.

Availability: American Paper Institute, 260 Madison Ave., New York NY 10016, members †, nonmembers $255.00 per yr.; SRI/MF/complete, shipped quarterly.

Issues reviewed during 1985: Aug. 1984-July 1985 (P) (Vol. 62, Nos. 8-12; Vol. 63, Nos. 1-7) [Monthly table [7], industry fact sheet, is unavailable for the Aug.-Oct. 1984 issues].

TABLES:

MONTHLY TABLES
[Data generally are shown for previous 1-2 years, 2-4 most current months available, and current year to date.]

[1] Paper and paperboard statistics: production, shipments, and [new and unfilled] orders [for selected grades].

[2] Wood pulp statistics [production, imports, exports, and new supply, for total and market wood pulp by type].

[3] Fibrous raw materials [consumption at paper/paperboard mills; inventories by mill type; days supply of chemical paper grade market pulp; and receipts, consumption, residues, and inventories, by region].

[4] U.S. trade [imports from and exports to] Canada [by grade].

[5] Pulp, paper, and paperboard imports and exports data [by grade].

[6] PPI [by type of pulp, paper, or paperboard products].

[7] Industry fact sheet [production of paper, paperboard, and wood pulp, by grade; capacity utilization rate; and additional operating data, including employment and production worker earnings, capital expenditures, worker productivity, corporate sales and earnings and net worth, corporate depreciation, price and demand indexes, magazine advertising pages, publisher consumption, and total wholesaler sales and inventories].

OTHER RECURRING TABLES
[8] Sales and earnings [aggregated for approximately 30 paper and paper/allied product companies, quarterly through most recent quarter of current year, and same quarters of previous year; occasionally with additional data on various items, including taxes, equity, and long-term debt].

[9] Paper/paperboard [production, imports, exports, new supply, and real GNP, with selected ratios; quarterly for current year to date and previous year, and annually for 7-9 preceding years].

A2500-3 NEWSPRINT DIVISION MONTHLY STATISTICAL REPORT
Monthly+supplements.
Approx. 12 p.
SRI/MF/complete, shipped quarterly

Monthly report on U.S. and Canadian newsprint production, shipments, inventory, and plant capacity. Also covers U.S. consumption, foreign trade, publishers' stock, and newspaper circulation.

Reports are issued approximately 3-8 weeks after month of coverage. Data are from 16-17 reporting paper companies, API estimates for nonreporting companies, American Newspaper Publishers Assn (ANPA), Canadian Pulp and Paper Assn, Census Bureau, and other sources.

Contains 2 trend charts and 1 summary table; 17 detailed monthly tables, listed below; and monthly supplement table on imports and quarterly supplement table on exports, also listed below.

Monthly tables appear in all issues; import supplement is issued monthly and accompanies most issues; export supplement is issued in Jan., Mar., June, and Sept.

Availability: American Paper Institute, Newsprint Division, 260 Madison Ave., New York NY 10016, members †, nonmembers $50.00 per yr.; SRI/MF/complete, shipped quarterly.

Issues reviewed during 1985: Sept. 1984-Sept. 1985 (D) [July-Aug. 1984 issues are unavailable].

TABLES:

PRODUCTION, SHIPMENTS, AND CONSUMPTION
[Data are shown monthly for year to date and 2 previous years, unless otherwise noted.]

[1-6] [Production, shipments, end-of-month inventory, and] distribution of shipments; for North America, U.S., and Canada [including shipments to U.S. from overseas].

[7-8] Total U.S. estimated consumption [by ANPA daily newspapers and all users, unadjusted and seasonally adjusted; and seasonally adjusted total North American shipments].

[9] ANPA survey of newspapers publishers stock, end of month [unadjusted and seasonally adjusted], and end-of-month days supply [on hand/in transit].

[10] Operating rates [U.S., Canada, and North America].

[11-12] Newsprint shipments by destination [from U.S., Canada, and North America to 8 U.S. census divisions; annually for 1971 to previous year, and quarterly for previous 1-2 years and current year to date (usually quarter preceding month of publication)].

HISTORICAL AND ECONOMIC DATA

[13] Newsprint historical data [shows selected trends based on tables listed above, plus U.S. newsprint tonnage loss due to newspaper strikes, and U.S. newspaper data, including advertising as percent of total pages, and per-household circulation, all for previous 17-25 years].

[14] Forecasts of U.S. economy: GNP and industrial production index [selected estimates and projections, quarterly, current and following year].

[15] Advertising expenditures, by media, percent of total [selected years 1950 to previous 1-2 years].

[16-17] Annual capacity [actual or forecast 1966-87]; and announced capacity increases [by mill and location, by year of completion; both shown for U.S. and Canada, with summary of announced increases for rest of world by country and mill].

MONTHLY IMPORT SUPPLEMENT

[18] U.S. newsprint imports, by country of origin and port of entry [volume and value, for month prior to month of coverage and year to date; prior to 1985, table appeared quarterly].

QUARTERLY EXPORT SUPPLEMENT

[19] Exports of newsprint [from the U.S., Canada, and Scandinavia to selected countries and world areas, for year to date current to 1-3 months prior to month of coverage].

A2500-4 **EXPORTS OF KRAFT LINERBOARD AND CORRUGATING MATERIAL from Major Supplying Countries to World Markets, 1983-84**
Annual. June 1985.
33+20 p.
SRI/MF/not filmed

Annual report on containerboard exports from major supplying countries, by world area and country of destination, 1983-84, with trends from 1970. Includes data for kraft linerboard and corrugating medium.

Supplying countries covered in detail are U.S., Canada, Finland, Sweden, and Norway. Other supplying countries covered are Austria, Portugal, Spain, and Brazil.

Data are derived primarily from reports of Census Bureau, and pulp and paper assns of supplying countries.

Contains narrative analysis, interspersed with 2 illustrative charts and 19 tables (p. 1-28); and appendix and statistical note, with 3 tables (p. 29-33+20 p.).

This is the 21st annual report.

Availability: American Paper Institute, International Department, 260 Madison Ave., New York NY 10016, members †, nonmembers $75.00; SRI/MF/not filmed.

A2500-5 **EXPORTS OF PULP, PAPER, PAPERBOARD, AND CONVERTED PRODUCTS to World Markets, 1984**
Annual. June 1985.
34+App 15 p.
SRI/MF/not filmed

Annual report on volume and value of U.S. paper industry exports, by detailed product category and area or country of destination, mostly 1983-84, with trends from 1972. Covers pulp, paper, paperboard, and converted products.

Areas of destination include Western Europe, Canada, Mexico, Central America/Caribbean area/other islands, South America, Near/Middle East, Africa, Oceania/Far East, Soviet Union/Eastern Europe, Japan, and PRC.

Report is compiled by the American Paper Institute's International Dept, based on Census Bureau data.

Contains narrative analysis, with 2 summary charts and 18 tables (p. 1-34); and 2 appendices with 4 tables (15 p.).

This is the 13th annual report.

Availability: American Paper Institute, International Department, 260 Madison Ave., New York NY 10016, members †, nonmembers $75.00; SRI/MF/not filmed.

A2500-6 **PAPER, PAPERBOARD, WOOD PULP CAPACITY: Fiber Consumption, 1983-86, with Additional Data for 1987**
Annual. Nov. 1984.
29 p.+errata.
SRI/MF/complete

Annual report on paper, paperboard, and wood pulp industry capacity, by product grade and census division, 1983-87, with summary trends from 1970.

Also includes data on mills and machines shut down, new machines, and age of machines; fiber and recyclable paper consumption in manufacturing; announced capacity expansions, by company; and world capacity, by country or region.

Data are from an annual API source.

Contains contents listing (p. 1); survey commentary, with 5 summary tables (p. 3-7); 4 summary charts and 17 detailed tables (p. 8-27); and definitions (p. 28-29).

Availability: American Paper Institute, 260 Madison Ave., New York NY 10016, members †, nonmembers $250.00; SRI/MF/complete.

A2575
American Petroleum Institute

A2575-1 **WEEKLY STATISTICAL BULLETIN**
Weekly. Approx. 10 p.
ISSN 0003-0457.
SRI/MF/complete, shipped quarterly

Weekly report estimating U.S. crude oil and refined product daily average production and imports, and end-of-week stocks, by PAD district. Data are compiled by API from member reports and DOE data, and are issued approximately 1 week after week covered.

Report contains 1 summary table; 7 detailed tables, listed below, of which 6 appear weekly and 1 appears monthly (usually in the 2nd issue of the month); revisions to previously published tables; and 3 charts.

For description of API report on monthly estimates of U.S. average daily petroleum supply and demand balance, see A2575-2 below.

Availability: American Petroleum Institute, Publications and Distribution Section, 1220 L St., NW, Washington DC 20005, $50.00 per yr. (includes *Monthly Statistical Report*); SRI/MF/complete, shipped quarterly.

Issues reviewed during 1985: Nov. 2, 1984-Oct. 25, 1985 (D) (Vol. 65, Nos. 44-52; Vol. 66, Nos. 1-43).

TABLES:

WEEKLY TABLES
[All tables show data by PAD district, for week of coverage, with comparisons to previous 1-3 weeks and/or same week of previous year. Tables [1-3] also show data for subdivisions of districts 1-3.

Data on products include motor gasoline, jet fuels (naphtha and kerosene), fuel oils, liquefied petroleum gas (imports only), and other categories.]

[1] Refinery operations [daily averages for total input, crude oil runs to distillation units, input to crude oil distillation units, operable capacity, and percent operated].

[2-3] Refinery output [daily averages], and stocks [end-of-week totals], of selected products.

[4] [Daily average API and DOE latest] estimated domestic production of crude oil (including lease condensate); imports [daily average total and from Canada]; and stocks of crude oil [end-of-week total].

[5] Location of crude oil stocks.

[6] Imports of petroleum products [daily averages].

MONTHLY TABLE

[7] Estimated daily average production of crude oil/lease condensate [by State and Texas district; API data for 2 preceding months, and DOE data for latest 1-2 months available, generally 4-7 months prior to publication date].

A2575–2 MONTHLY STATISTICAL REPORT
Monthly.
Approx. 6 p. no paging.
SRI/MF/complete, shipped quarterly

Monthly report on estimated U.S. petroleum supply and demand, compiled by API from member reports and DOE data. Reports are issued 2-3 weeks following month of coverage.

Contains narrative analysis, summary tables and charts, and 1 detailed table showing:

a. Products supplied and stocks for 8-9 refined products, and exports and total domestic products supplied.

b. Supply, including domestic production and imports.

c. Refinery operations, including input to crude oil distillation units, operable capacity, refinery utilization rate, and crude oil runs.

Refined product stocks are shown for current month, previous month, and same month of preceding year. All other items are shown for current month, year to date, and same periods of preceding year. June, Sept., and Dec. issues also include quarterly data for most items.

Issues also occasionally include statistical articles or special charts. All additional features with substantial statistical content are described, as they appear, under "Statistical Features." Non-statistical features are not covered.

Availability: American Petroleum Institute, Publications and Distribution Section, 1220 L St., NW, Washington DC 20005, $10.00 per yr. (or included in subscription to *Weekly Statistical Bulletin*); SRI/MF/complete, shipped quarterly.

Issues reviewed during 1985: Oct. 1984-Sept. 1985 (D) (Vol. 8, Nos. 10-12; Vol. 9, Nos. 1-9).

STATISTICAL FEATURES:

A2575–2.601: Dec. 1984 (Vol. 8, No. 12)
ESTIMATED U.S. PETROLEUM BALANCE, RECURRING FEATURE

(9 p.) Recurring article summarizing petroleum supply and demand, 1984. Data are from DOE and American Petroleum Institute.

Includes 4 tables and 1 chart showing consumption of energy by type, distillate consumption by sector, and demand for "other oils" by type, various periods 1983-84; and import share of petroleum market, and OPEC share of imports, various periods 1978-84.

A2575–2.602: Mar. 1985 (Vol. 9, No. 3)
IMPORTS, ANNUAL FEATURE

(1 p.) Annual article, with 1 table showing top 11 countries ranked by petroleum exports to U.S., Jan. 1985, with comparison to Jan. 1984.

A2575–2.603: June 1985 (Vol. 9, No. 6)
ESTIMATED U.S. PETROLEUM BALANCE, RECURRING FEATURE

(5 p.) Recurring article summarizing petroleum supply and demand for 1st half 1985. Data are from DOE and American Petroleum Institute.

Includes 4 tables showing consumption of energy by type; residual fuel oil demand, for utilities, bunkers, and industrial/other users; products supplied (total and for 3 refined products); and total petroleum supply, crude oil production, and imports of crude oil and refined products; various periods 1984-85.

A2575–2.604: Aug. 1985 (Vol. 9, No. 8)
DISTILLATE DELIVERIES BY END-USE SECTOR, RECURRING FEATURE

(1 p.) Recurring table showing distillate deliveries by end-use sector, 1st half 1984-85. Table is usually presented in recurring article summarizing petroleum supply and demand, covered above in A2575-2.603.

For description of previous table, see SRI 1984 Annual under A2575-2.503.

A2575–3 MONTHLY COMPLETION REPORT: Report on Well Completions in the U.S.
Monthly. Approx. 5 p.
SRI/MF/complete, shipped quarterly

Monthly report on exploratory and development oil and gas well drilling in the U.S. Compiled by API from member data, report is issued approximately 3 weeks after month of coverage.

Report contains brief narrative, 1 summary chart, 3 monthly tables listed below, and footnotes.

Prior to Jan. 1985 issue, report was titled *Monthly Drilling Report,* included detail by State and subarea, and showed data for month of coverage and same month of previous year. Data by State and subarea continue to appear in *Quarterly Completion Report,* covered in SRI under A2575-6.

Availability: American Petroleum Institute, Publications and Distribution Section, 1220 L St., NW, Washington DC 20005, $10.00 per yr.; SRI/MF/complete, shipped quarterly.

Issues reviewed during 1985: Sept. 1984-Sept. 1985 (D).

TABLES:
[Tables show data by well type (oil, gas, and dry holes), monthly for current year to date and 2 previous years, and annually for 3-4 previous years.]

I-II. Cumulative number of total and exploratory wells and footage drilled by completion month and year.

III. Total number of wells and footage additions by completion month and year reported to the API.

A2575–4 SUMMARY OF OCCUPATIONAL INJURIES AND ILLNESSES in the Petroleum Industry
Annual. Aug. 1985.
26 p. no paging.
SRI/MF/complete

Annual survey report on occupational injuries and illnesses in the petroleum industry, by function and company, 1984. Presents data on employment; hours worked; recordable injury and illness cases; fatalities; cases involving lost workdays, and number of days away from work and of restricted activity; nonfatal cases without lost workdays; and selected incidence rates; by functional area, for 131 individual companies.

Data are based on company reports to API, and cover only operations subject to OSHA recordkeeping requirements.

Contains introduction (1 p.); 15 tables (23 p.); and list of respondents with identification number used in tables (2 p.).

Availability: American Petroleum Institute, Publications and Distribution Section, 1220 L St., NW, Washington DC 20005, $5.00; SRI/MF/complete.

A2575–5 API MONTHLY REPORT COVERING INVENTORIES OF NATURAL GAS LIQUIDS AND LIQUEFIED REFINERY GASES
Monthly. Approx. 3 p.
ISSN 0024-421X.
LC sc79-4044.
SRI/MF/complete, shipped quarterly

Monthly report on U.S. inventories of liquefied petroleum and liquefied refinery gases, including ethane, propane, isobutane, normal butane, pentane plus, and other stocks. Report is issued 4-5 weeks after month of coverage and is compiled by American Petroleum Institute from member reports.

Issues contain 2 trend charts; and 1 table showing total end-of-month inventories at plants/terminals/underground/refineries, by product and region; and total underground inventories, by product; for month of coverage, with comparative summary data for previous month, and same month of previous year. Issues also occasionally include revisions to previous reports.

Prior to Apr. 1985 issue, report was titled *Liquefied Petroleum Gas Report.*

Availability: American Petroleum Institute, Publications and Distribution Section, 1220 L St., NW, Washington DC 20005, $10.00 per yr.; SRI/MF/complete, shipped quarterly.

Issues reviewed during 1985: Sept. 1984-Aug. 1985 (D).

A2575–6 QUARTERLY COMPLETION REPORT
Quarterly.
ISSN 0003-5789.
SRI/MF/complete

Quarterly report on oil and gas well drilling in producing States and offshore. Includes data by well type, including exploratory and development wells.

Data are based on API estimates and member reports, and are shown for dates of well completion. Reports are issued 2-3 months after quarter of coverage, and have been published by API since 1970.

Contains contents listing, preface, and introduction; 4 statistical sections, with 21 tables listed below; and 3 appendices, including source agencies for drilling statistics and Assn of Petroleum Geologists-Committee on Statistics of Drilling district chairmen.

Fourth quarter issue also includes an additional table showing total number of year-end suspense wells, by State and State region, for year of coverage.

Prior to 1st quarter 1985 issue, report format varied substantially; detailed comparisons to previous quarters and years were omitted; report included 2 tables showing data on wells reported as multiple completions (wells equipped to produce oil and/or gas separately from more than one reservoir); report title was *Quarterly Review of Drilling Statistics for the U.S;* and data were shown for reporting rather than completion dates.

Availability: American Petroleum Institute, Publications and Distribution Section, 1220 L St., NW, Washington DC 20005, $20.00 per yr.; SRI/MF/complete.

Issues reviewed during 1985: 3rd Qtr. 1984-2nd Qtr. 1985 (D) (Vol. XVIII, Nos. 3-4; Vol. I, Nos. 1-2) [New numbering sequence begins with 1st Qtr. 1985 issue (Vol. I, No. 1)].

TABLES:

[Unless otherwise noted, tables show number and footage of U.S. wells, for total, oil, and gas wells, and dry holes. Data are shown quarterly for year-to-date, generally with annual and/or quarterly comparisons to 2-3 previous years.]

[1-2] Summary of estimated and reported completions [of exploratory/development and exploratory wells only].

[3-5] Estimated wells drilled by depth intervals [with aggregate totals for exploratory and development wells].

[6] Total well completions [including service wells; shown by State (with detail for onshore and offshore); by district for California, Louisiana, New Mexico, and Texas; for offshore Federal waters of Pacific Coast and Northern Gulf of Mexico; and for total exploratory and development wells].

[7] Well completions by depth intervals.

[8-21] [Tables [6-7] are repeated with quarterly and annual data for 2 previous years, including additional detail for strategic/core test, exploratory, development, new-field wildcat, and onshore and offshore wells; 1st quarter 1985 issue also includes additional tables showing data for 1982.]

A2575–7   U.S. CRUDE OIL DISTILLATION REFINING CAPACITY SURVEY for 1985-86
Annual.   June 1985.   3 p.
SRI/MF/complete

Annual report on crude oil distillation refining capacity changes, Mar. 1985-Mar. 1986. Includes total capacity by quarter, operable capacity shutdown, and inoperable capacity; and new and expanded capacity, by company and refinery location, by quarter; all by PAD district and/or subdivision.

Data are from an API member survey. Contains 4 tables.

Availability: American Petroleum Institute, Publications and Distribution Section, 1220 L St., NW, Washington DC 20005, ‡; SRI/MF/complete.

A2575–8   REPORTED FIRE LOSSES IN THE PETROLEUM INDUSTRY for 1984
Annual.   Aug. 1985.
5 p. no paging.
SRI/MF/complete

Annual report on petroleum industry fires and fire loss, by type of property, 1984. Data are based on reports from 76 companies responding to an annual API survey. Reporting was restricted to fires resulting in losses of $2,500 or more.

Contains 3 tables, listed below, with brief accompanying narrative (p. 1-3); and list of reporting companies (p. 4).

This is the 55th annual survey.

Availability: American Petroleum Institute, Publications and Distribution Section, 1220 L St., NW, Washington DC 20005, $5.00; SRI/MF/complete.

TABLES:

[Data by class of property are for exploration/production/drilling, gas processing, offshore portion, petrochemicals, refining, retail and wholesale marketing, and pipeline.]

1. Current replacement values, fire losses, and fire-loss ratios, by classes of property, 1984. (p. 1)

2. Number of fires reported for 1984 [by class of property for fires originating on and outside oil company property, and for 3 loss size categories]. (p. 2)

3. Tank fire experience, 1983-84: fires originating in tanks resulting in losses of $2,500 or more [by structural type of tank, by class of product (including crude oil, and liquefied natural and petroleum gases), and by type of location]. (p. 3)

A2575–9   1983 JOINT ASSOCIATION SURVEY ON DRILLING COSTS
Annual.   Nov. 1984.
vii+84 p.
SRI/MF/complete

Annual report on 1983 drilling costs for U.S. oil and gas wells and dry holes. Includes number of wells and footage drilled and estimated costs, by State, offshore location, and type of well.

Data are compiled from a Joint Assn Survey (JAS) of operator costs conducted by API, Independent Petroleum Assn of America, and Mid-Continent Oil and Gas Assn; and from the API *Quarterly Review of Drilling Statistics* (QRDS, covered in SRI under A2575-6).

Contains contents and table listing (p. v-vii), and the following:

a. Summary and survey description, with 3 text tables including summary comparisons to 1982. (p. 1-4)

b. Statistical section, with 53 tables showing number, footage drilled, and drilling cost, by depth interval, for oil and gas wells and dry holes, by State with detail for selected onshore and offshore areas and State districts, and for Appalachian region and Federal waters (total and northern Gulf of Mexico), 1983. (p. 6-59)

c. Appendix A-C, with survey questionnaire facsimile, and 1 summary table showing QRDS vs. JAS findings. (p. 62-65)

d. Appendix D-F, with 2 tables showing wells, footage, and drilling cost, for exploratory and development oil and gas wells and dry holes, and for single and multiple completion oil and gas wells, 1983; and number of JAS companies and wells, by number of wells drilled, 1979-83. (p. 66-70)

e. Appendix G-H, with 12 maps and survey methodology. (p. 71-84)

Availability: American Petroleum Institute, Publications and Distribution Section, 1220 L St., NW, Washington DC 20005, $15.00; SRI/MF/complete.

A2575–10   NEW CONSTRUCTION AND DEACTIVATION OF SERVICE STATIONS in the Petroleum Industry
Annual.   May 1985.   4 p.
SRI/MF/complete

Annual summary report on gasoline service station new construction, renovation, and deactivation, 1983-84, based on reports of 30 oil companies.

Contains 4 tables, definitions, and list of reporting companies.

Availability: American Petroleum Institute, Publications and Distribution Section, 1220 L St., NW, Washington DC 20005, $5.00; SRI/MF/complete.

A2575–11   REVIEW OF FATAL INJURIES IN THE PETROLEUM INDUSTRY for 1984
Annual.   Aug. 1985.   6 p.
LC 44-37408.
SRI/MF/complete

Annual report, for 1984, on petroleum industry accidental deaths, based on reports of 131 oil and gas companies and their subsidiaries.

Contains description of specific accidents, with 1 table showing fatalities by industry function and by cause, 1983-84.

This is the 52nd annual report.

Availability: American Petroleum Institute, Publications and Distribution Section, 1220 L St., NW, Washington DC 20005, $5.00; SRI/MF/complete.

A2575–12   IMPORTED CRUDE OIL AND PETROLEUM PRODUCTS
Monthly.   Approx. 65 p. var. paging.
SRI/MF/complete

Monthly report on U.S. imports of crude oil, residual fuel oil, finished petroleum products, and unfinished oils, by importing company. Within each company, data are further shown by port of entry, country of origin, and, as applicable, recipient company, destination, and type of product. Includes quantity and selected physical properties.

Report is compiled by API from DOE data, and is issued approximately 2 months after month of coverage.

Contains contents listing; 4 tables repeated for PAD Districts I-IV combined and V, and usually for adjusted data for previous months; and list of companies reporting no imports.

Availability: American Petroleum Institute, Publications and Distribution Section, 1220 L St., NW, Washington DC 20005, $200.00 per yr.; SRI/MF/complete.

Issues reviewed during 1985: Sept. 1984-Aug. 1985 (D).

A2575–14   BASIC PETROLEUM DATA BOOK: Petroleum Industry Statistics
3 times per year.
Approx. 300 p. no paging.
ISSN 0730-5621.
LC sn82-779.
SRI/MF/complete

Compilation of reference statistics, issued 3 times per year, on world oil and gas industry exploration, production, refining, demand, financial condition, prices, and reserves. Data are compiled from API member reports and from numerous Federal Government, trade assn, and commercial publications.

Data are most recent available as of cover date, and include trends from as early as the 1940s. Report format and table topics remain essentially the same from issue to issue. Contents of the current issue are as follows:

Contents and table listings.

Section I. Energy: summary of world supply and demand, with 14 tables.

Section II-IV. Crude oil reserves, exploration, drilling, and production, with 29 tables.

Section V-VI. Financial data and prices, with 28 tables.

Section VII-X. Demand, refining, imports, and exports, with 39 tables.

Section XI-XII. Offshore oil and gas, and transportation, with 1 chart and 24 tables.

Section XIII. Natural gas, with 10 tables.

Section XIV-XV. OPEC, and miscellaneous, with 9 tables.

Each section is preceded by a table listing. Tables and chart are listed below.

Availability: American Petroleum Institute, Publications and Distribution Section, 1220 L St., NW, Washington DC 20005, $40.00 per yr.; SRI/MF/complete.

Issues reviewed during 1985: Jan.-Sept. 1985 (D) (Vol. V, Nos. 1-3).

TABLES AND CHART:
[Data are shown for U.S., unless otherwise noted.]

A2575–14.1: Energy Supply and Demand

SECTION I: ENERGY SUMMARY

1-2. Market economies: oil consumption and production, history and projections, midprice scenario [for U.S., Canada, Japan, OECD, and OPEC, 1980-95]; and energy projections, comparison of EIA [Energy Information Administration] midprice projections with [7] other [commercial and governmental organizations'] projections for 1985, 1990, and 1995 [with 1981 actual]. (2 p.)

3-7. Selected economic, demographic, and energy indicators [1947-83]; comparison of [6] midprice energy supply/demand projections, and projections of energy demand by sector [by source], for 1990; and total gross consumption and production of energy resources, by major sources [1947-84]. (7 p.)

8-12. Total gross consumption by consuming sector; and demand for energy inputs in the industrial, household/commercial, and transportation sectors, and for electricity generation by utilities [all by energy source; 1947-84]. (10 p.)

13-14. World primary energy and coal production [by region and country, 1973-83]. (2 p.)

A2575–14.2: Oil Reserves, Exploration, Drilling, and Production

SECTION II: CRUDE OIL RESERVES

1-3. Estimated proved world reserves of crude oil, annually as of Jan. 1 [for U.S., Canada, and 8 world areas, 1948-85]; reserves [and production] of U.S. crude oil [1947-83]; and estimated world proven crude oil reserves, 20 leading nations (annually as of Jan. 1) [1975-85]. (7 p.)

4. USGS [U.S. Geological Survey] estimates of [identified and undiscovered recoverable] oil and gas resources [by onshore and offshore petroleum region (no date)]. (1 p.)

SECTION III: EXPLORATION AND DRILLING

1-3. [New-field wildcat and total] exploratory wells and footage, and development and total wells and footage [and service/stratigraphic/core tests, 1947-84]; and wells drilled by depth interval [1959-84]. (7 p.)

4-5. U.S. petroleum geophysical exploration (crew months) [by method, 1951-83]; and Free World exploration [for U.S., Canada, and 6 world areas, 1954-83]. (4 p.)

6-8. Historical record: number of new-field oil, gas, and oil/gas discoveries proved after 6 years to be of significant size [by year drilled, 1947-77]. (6 p.)

9-11. Estimated drilling costs by well classification, onshore and offshore [and total, 1959-83]. (6 p.)

12-13. Free World total and exploratory well completions [by country and world area, 1970-82]. (2 p.)

14-16. Annual average rotary rig activity, by State [number in operation, 1949-84]; total [exploratory and development] wells reported as completed, by State [1967-84]; and rotary rig census [number of contractor and oil company owned rigs, number stacked and active, and number by drilling depth capability and by type, 1967-84]. (9 p.)

17-18. Producing natural gas/condensate wells and oil wells, by State (as of Dec. 31) [various years 1947-84]. (6 p.)

19-20. Producing oil wells by State and by type [flowing and artificial lift, as of Dec. 31, 1947-84]; and in Free World (as of July 1) [by country and world area, 1970-84]. (9 p.)

SECTION IV: PRODUCTION

1-2. World crude oil production by area [for U.S., Canada, and 7 world areas, 1947-84; and for] 20 leading nations [1974-84]. (6 p.)

3. Stripper wells and stripper well production [1947-83]. (1 p.)

4-5. Crude oil production [total 1947-84], and average per well per day [1947-81], by State. (6 p.)

A2575–14.3: Finance and Prices

SECTION V: FINANCIAL DATA

[Data for "a group of petroleum companies" are aggregates for multinational corporations monitored by Chase Manhattan Bank to determine the financial condition of the petroleum industry.]

1-3. Average hourly earnings, total mining and manufacturing vs. petroleum/natural gas extraction and petroleum refining [1947-84]; number of employees, petroleum/natural gas extraction and petroleum refining [1947-84]; and sources of capital [amount from internal and external funds] of a group of petroleum companies [1947-83]. (3 p.)

4-5. Net income as a percent of net worth: petroleum, other selected industry groups, and total manufacturing, mining, [and trade, 1947-81]; and domestic and foreign net income of a group of petroleum companies [1960-83]. (4 p.)

6-7. World petroleum industry capital and exploration expenditures, U.S. vs. foreign [1947-83]; and sources and uses of working capital of a group of petroleum companies [1947-83]. (4 p.)

8-10. Domestic and foreign capital expenditures [by category] of the world petroleum industry, and estimated U.S. exploration/development expenditures of Chase Manhattan Bank and all other companies [1947-83]; and U.S. estimated expenditures for exploration, development, and production [1973-82]. (6 p.)

11. Environmental protection [total, capital, administrative/operating/maintenance, and R&D] expenditures of the petroleum industry [for air, water, and land/other, 1966-83]. (2 p.)

12-14. Summary financial data; capital expenditures [by category]; and net income as a percent of stockholders' equity; [1968-83, aggregated for] 24 leading U.S. oil companies [with comparisons to total U.S., and world] oil and nonoil companies. (5 p.)

SECTION VI: PRICES

1-2. Average annual wellhead price of crude oil and natural gas, current and constant 1967 dollars or cents [and PPI for all commodities, 1947-84]. (2 p.)

3. Refiner acquisition cost of [domestic and imported] crude oil [1968-84]. (1 p.)

4-5. Trend of wholesale prices of commodities utilized in the production of petroleum [1947-84]; and trend of regular grade gasoline prices vs. prices of other consumer goods and services [1947-84]. (4 p.)

6-7. Annual average retail price of No. 2 home heating oil [and CPI, 1956-83]; and total dollar value of crude oil and natural gas at the wellhead [including production and price, 1947-83]. (3 p.)

8-9. Average wellhead value of crude oil [1947-80], and natural gas [1947-83], by State. (5 p.)

10-11. Posted and official government selling prices of key foreign crude oils [by type and country, various dates 1970-85]. (4 p.)

12. Average retail gasoline prices [including tax] for [approximately 50] cities [decennially 1920-70, and annually 1971-77]; and [leaded and unleaded] prices for [approximately 30 SMSAs, and for census regions, 1978-84]. (3 p.)

13-14. Average price of natural gas consumed by end-use sector [1967-83]; and cost [and quantity] of petroleum imports [1970-84]. (2 p.)

A2575–14.4: Supply, Demand, Refining, and Trade

SECTION VII: DEMAND

1. Estimated world demand for refined petroleum products, by area [for U.S., Canada, and 8 world areas, 1950-84]. (2 p.)

2-6. Total supply and demand for all oils, total and motor gasoline, and distillate and residual fuel oil [including imports and exports, various years 1947-84]. (9 p.)

7-8. Deliveries of distillate and residual fuel oil to electric utilities [1947-83]; and motor gasoline consumption/sales [by State, 1962-84]. (4 p.)

9-12. Sales or deliveries of distillate and residual fuel oils, by State and by uses [1947-83]. (10 p.)

13-17. Total supply and demand [including imports and exports] for naphtha and kerosene type jet fuel [1965-84]; and for kerosene, natural gas liquids/liquefied refinery gases, and lubricants [1947-84]. (8 p.)

SECTION VIII: REFINING

1-2. Estimated worldwide crude oil refining capacity by area, as of Jan. 1 [for U.S. and 8 world areas, 1947-85]; and worldwide crude oil refinery runs [U.S., Canada, Japan, and 8 world areas, 1965-84]. (4 p.)

3-5. Crude oil refining capacity (as of Jan. 1) [1947-85]; percentage yields of refined petroleum products from crude oil [1964-84]; and crude oil refinery runs by PAD district, domestic vs. foreign [1947-82]. (6 p.)

6. Number, and capacity [by process], of [operating and idle] petroleum refineries [by PAD district and State], as of Jan. 1, 1985. (1 p.)

SECTION IX: IMPORTS

1-2. Share of imports in domestic petroleum [refined product] demand, total imports of petroleum [and products], and petroleum [and natural gas liquids] production [1947-84]. (3 p.)

3-7. U.S. crude oil imports by [world] area and country of origin [1947-84], and by PAD districts [1952-84]; and imports of residual and distillate fuel [1950-84], and of unfinished oils and refined products [1959-84], by PAD districts. (10 p.)

8-9. Total petroleum imports by source [country of origin, 1957-84]; and direct petroleum imports from members of the Organization of Arab Petroleum Exporting Countries, [monthly] Sept. 1973-Apr. 1974. (4 p.)

10. World oil movements [between country or area of origin and destination, 1972-84]. (7 p.)

SECTION X: EXPORTS

1-2. Total domestic production and exports of crude oil and its products; and exports of petroleum to selected areas [by country or world area; 1947-84]. (3 p.)

3-6. Africa and Middle East oil exports to selected areas [U.S., Western Europe, Japan, and other areas, various years 1959-84]; and the role of Middle East and African oil in Western European and Japanese consumption and in world exports [1961-84]. (4 p.)

A2575–14.5: Offshore and Transportation

SECTION XI: OFFSHORE

1-2. Estimated worldwide production of crude oil onshore vs. offshore [1969-83]; and estimated worldwide offshore production by area [for U.S., Venezuela, and 8 world areas, 1970-83]. (2 p.)

3. Production and value of crude oil/condensate onshore and offshore [cumulative to 1953, and 1954-84]. (2 p.)

4-5. Estimated worldwide production of natural gas onshore vs. offshore; and estimated worldwide offshore production by area [for U.S. and 7 world areas; 1970-82]. (2 p.)

6-8. Production and value of natural gas onshore and offshore [cumulative to 1953, and 1954-83]; and total offshore wells drilled [by type] and accumulated production [shown for] Federal and State leases [by State and offshore area], all-time to Jan. 1, 1985 [wells] and 1982 [production]. (4 p.)

9-11. Outer Continental Shelf (OCS) oil/gas lease sales [tracts and acres offered and leased, bonus, 1st-year rental, average and highest bid per acre, and State or area of tract, by sale date, to Aug. 22, 1984]; OCS revenue and production value [including royalties], percentage cumulative revenue of cumulative production value [1953-83]; and OCS oil/gas sales, total bonus vs. total amount of all bids received [and State or area of tract, by sale date, to Aug. 22, 1984]. (8 p.)

12-13. Offshore platforms/other structures [for Federal and State waters, by State], as of Dec. 31, 1983; and worldwide water depth records [for] exploratory drilling and platforms [and including company and location, selected years 1935-83]. [1 table and 1 chart] (2 p.)

14-15. Eight-year OCS blowout experience [by type of activity, and including pollution, injuries, and other major damage, total period] 1971-82; and oil spills of 50 barrels/more [and amount spilled] in Federal [Gulf of Mexico and Pacific] waters, 1970-83. (2 p.)

16-17. Historical data on leasing continental seabeds adjacent to the U.S. [by region, through Dec. 31, 1983]; and basin ranking [of] 5-year OCS oil/gas leasing program [by resource potential and exploration interest, 1979]. (2 p.)

SECTION XII: TRANSPORTATION

1. Gas utility industry miles of pipeline and main, by type [1947-83]. (1 p.)

2-4. U.S. and world tank ship fleet (actual and T2-SE-A1 equivalents) [number and characteristics, 1947-79]; and age distribution of world tank ship fleet by major flag of registry (as of Dec. 31, 1979) [by year of construction]. (4 p.)

5. Sources of oil spills and [hazardous and] other substances, 1983. (1 p.)

6-7. Total and average consumption of motor fuel, and total and average travel [mileage], by motor vehicles [and including number of vehicles registered, all by vehicle type, 1947-83]. (4 p.)

8. U.S. car sales by [car size and import] market-class comparisons [1970-84]. (1 p.)

A2575–14.6: Natural Gas

SECTION XIII: NATURAL GAS

1-3. Estimated proved world reserves of natural gas, annually as of Jan. 1 [for U.S., Canada, and 8 world areas, 1967-85]; and supply of U.S. natural gas and reserves of natural gas liquids [1947-83]. (4 p.)

4-6. World marketed production of natural gas by area [U.S., Canada, and 8 world areas, 1950-83]; salient statistics of natural gas in the U.S. [including production, exports, imports, value at wellhead, consumption, storage, and withdrawals or losses, 1947-83]; and U.S. imports of natural gas by source [Canada, Mexico, and Algeria, 1968-83]. (5 p.)

7-8. Estimated natural gas reserves (as of Jan. 1) [1975-85]; and world natural gas production [1974-83; both for] 20 leading nations. (9 p.)

9-10. Marketed production and consumption of natural gas, by State [1947-83]. (8 p.)

A2575–14.7: OPEC and Miscellaneous

SECTION XIV: OPEC

1-2. OPEC crude oil reserves, annually as of Jan. 1 [1960-85]; and production [per day, 1960-84; all by country]. (2 p.)

3-4. U.S. total petroleum and crude oil imports from OPEC nations [per day, by country of origin, 1960-84]. (2 p.)

5-7. OPEC refinery capacity, revenues from oil, and marketed production of natural gas [by country, 1965-83]. (6 p.)

SECTION XV: MISCELLANEOUS

1. Estimated average number of employees in [5] important segments of the petroleum industry [by State], 1983. (2 p.)

2. [Conversion tables.] (1 p.)

A2575–15   MONTHLY REPORT OF HEATING OIL AND OTHER MIDDLE DISTILLATES: Sales by States
Monthly.   Approx. 4 p.
SRI/MF/complete, shipped quarterly

Monthly report on nonmilitary sales of kerosene, other heating oils, and diesel oil, by State. Report is issued 1-2 months after month of coverage and is based on reports from approximately 50 companies, accounting for approximately 80% of sales.

Contains 3 tables showing gallons of No. 1 kerosene, No. 2 oil, and diesel oil sold, by State, for month of coverage, year to date, and same periods of previous year. Also usually includes revisions of previous monthly tables.

Journal has been discontinued with the Jan. 1985 issue, due to budgetary reasons. Similar data are available in DOE's *Petroleum Marketing Monthly,* described in *American Statistics Index* (a companion Congressional Information Service publication) under 3162-11.

Availability: American Petroleum Institute, Publications and Distribution Section, 1220 L St., NW, Washington DC 20005, $16.00 per yr.; SRI/MF/complete, shipped quarterly.

Issues reviewed during 1985: Sept. 1984-Jan. 1985 (D).

A2575–17   SUMMARY OF MOTOR VEHICLE ACCIDENTS IN THE PETROLEUM INDUSTRY for 1984
Annual.   Aug. 1985.
7 p. no paging.
SRI/MF/complete

Annual survey report on car, truck, and service vehicle accidents in the petroleum industry, 1984. Includes number of accidents, fleet size and miles traveled, accident rates per million miles and per 100 vehicles, and number of companies providing data, all shown by petroleum industry sector.

Data are from responses of 90 companies to an API survey.

Contains summary (1 p.); 2 tables (4 p.); and list of participating companies (1 p.).

This is the 52nd survey report.

Availability: American Petroleum Institute, Publications and Distribution Section, 1220 L St., NW, Washington DC 20005, $5.00; SRI/MF/complete.

A2575–18 WELL COMPLETIONS AND FOOTAGE DRILLED IN THE U.S., 1970-82
Monograph. Jan. 1985.
iii + 121 p.
SRI/MF/complete

Report presenting number of completions and footage drilled, for total, exploratory, and/or development oil and gas wells and dry holes, by completion month, State, and depth interval, 1970-82. Also includes completions and footage for stratigraphic/core test, service, and new field wildcat wells, by State.

Data are often shown for onshore and offshore areas, and data by State include selected detail by producing district and for Federal waters.

Data were compiled by API. Purpose of report is to present historical drilling data adjusted to reflect new reporting procedures adopted by API in Jan. 1985. Current data are published in API's *Monthly Completion Report* and *Quarterly Completion Report,* covered in SRI under A2575-3 and A2575-6, respectively.

Contains preface and contents listing (p. ii-iii); 8 extended tables presenting data by month (p. 1-15), State (p. 16-106), and depth (p. 107-119); and appendix with footnotes (p. 120-121).

Availability: American Petroleum Institute, Publications and Distribution Section, 1220 L St., NW, Washington DC 20005, $6.00; SRI/MF/complete.

A2620
American Psychological Association

A2620–1 1984/85 FACULTY SALARIES IN GRADUATE DEPARTMENTS OF PSYCHOLOGY
Annual. Jan. 1985.
44 p. no paging.
SRI/MF/complete

Annual report, by Joy Stapp et al., on faculty salaries in psychology graduate depts, 1984/85. Covers 9-month salaries in doctoral and master's depts, by faculty academic rank and years in rank, variously cross-tabulated by census division, institution control (public and private), and dept type (including educational psychology, professional school, counseling, and human development).

Also includes aggregate data for top-ranked doctoral depts (ranking based on assessments published by the National Academy of Sciences); 12-month salaries for Canadian depts; and trends from 1981/82.

Salaries are shown variously as actual distribution, means, medians, percentiles, and quartiles.

Data are based on responses of 379 graduate depts, with 6,503 full-time faculty, to a fall 1984 survey conducted jointly by American Psychological Assn and Council of Graduate Depts of Psychology.

Contains introduction, references, and table listing (5 p.); and 22 tables (38 p.).

Availability: American Psychological Association, Human Resources Research, 1200 17th St., NW, Washington DC 20036, †; SRI/MF/complete.

A2620–2 SALARIES IN PSYCHOLOGY, 1985
Annual. Aug. 1985.
76 + App 4 p.
SRI/MF/complete

Annual report, by Georgine Pion and Paul Bramblett, on doctoral and master's level psychologists' salaries and additional income, by type of position and employment setting, 1985. Most data are shown by years of experience and include actual distribution, means, medians, percentiles, and quartiles.

Types of positions include faculty by academic rank, research, direct human services, applied psychology, administration, and others.

Employment settings include colleges/universities, public school systems, government and private research organizations, various health facilities, private practice, business/industry, and others.

Data are based on 10,214 responses to an Apr. 1985 random sample survey of American Psychological Assn members employed full-time.

Contains contents listing (1 p.); introduction (p. 1-5); 15 sections, with 49 tables interspersed with narrative summaries (p. 6-76); and 2 appendices, with survey questionnaire facsimile, and 1 table showing number of respondents. (4 p.).

This is the 4th survey report. Previous report, for 1983, is described in SRI 1983 Annual under this number. No report was issued for 1984.

Availability: American Psychological Association, Human Resources Research, 1200 17th St., NW, Washington DC 20036, †; SRI/MF/complete.

A2620–3 SUMMARY REPORT OF 1984/85 SURVEY OF GRADUATE DEPARTMENTS OF PSYCHOLOGY
Annual. June 1985. 3 + 36 p.
SRI/MF/complete, current & previous year reports

Annual report, by Georgine Pion et al., on graduate psychology depts in U.S. and Canada, 1984/85. Includes data on faculty and student characteristics, faculty salaries, and student financial aid. Data are from 404 U.S. and 24 Canadian depts responding to an Oct. 1984 survey.

Contains contents listing (1 p.); highlights and methodology, with 1 table showing survey respondent characteristics (p. 1-6); survey report, with 15 tables described below (p. 7-35); and bibliography (p. 36).

Previous report, for 1983/84, has also been reviewed and is also available on SRI microfiche under A2620-3 [Annual. Mar. 1984. 23 p. †]. Report for 1983/84 is substantially similar in format and content, but also includes data on allocation of funds for faculty travel and dept operations, summer session programs, and student admissions and Graduate Record Examination scores, and omits data on student enrollment.

Report for 1982/83 is described in SRI 1983 Annual under A2620-3.

Availability: American Psychological Association, Human Resources Research, 1200 17th St., NW, Washington DC 20036, †; SRI/MF/complete.

TABLES:

[Data generally are shown for U.S. public and private and Canadian total doctoral and master programs. Data by race/ethnicity include white, black, Hispanic, Asian, and American Indian. Salaries and student aid values show median, and 1st and 3rd quartiles.]

a. Faculty, by sex, race/ethnicity, subfield specialty, academic rank and years in rank, and employment and tenure status; new appointments; faculty salaries by academic rank and years in rank; and salaries for new faculty, dept chairpersons, and administrators, with selected estimates for 1985/86. 5 tables. (p. 8-17)

b. Enrollment, by sex, race/ethnicity, full- and part-time status, and practice vs. research specialties; students receiving financial support; and amount of support, by academic level and type of assistance. 10 tables. (p. 22-35)

A2625
American Public Power Association

A2625–1 PUBLIC POWER
Bimonthly.
ISSN 0033-3654.
LC 47-36541.
SRI/MF/excerpts, delayed

Bimonthly publication reporting trends and developments affecting publicly owned electric utilities. Data are compiled from Energy Information Administration and Rural Electrification Administration (REA) reports, and from information provided by APPA members.

Issues contain feature articles, occasionally including statistics; and narrative editorial depts. Annual features include a directory of publicly owned utilities, with summary statistics; and articles on electricity costs in major cities, cost comparison for private vs. public utilities, and utility capital spending and bond financing.

Features with substantial statistical content are described, as they appear, under "Statistical Features." Each issue of the journal is reviewed, but an abstract is published in SRI monthly issues only when statistical features appear.

Availability: American Public Power Association, Circulation Manager, Public Power, 2301 M St., NW, Washington DC 20037, $35.00 per yr., single copy $5.00, Directory Issue: members $20.00, nonmembers $40.00; SRI/MF/excerpts for all portions described under "Statistical Features;" delayed shipment 3 months from issue date.

Issues reviewed during 1985: Nov./Dec. 1984-Sept./Oct. 1985 (P) (Vol. 42, No. 6; Vol. 43, Nos. 1-5).

STATISTICAL FEATURES:

A2625–1.601: Nov./Dec. 1984 (Vol. 42, No. 6)

CORRECTION

(p. 108) Corrected data for article on electric utility salaries appearing in the Sept./Oct. 1984 issue.

For description of original article, see SRI 1984 Annual under A2625-1.506.

A2625–1.602: Jan./Feb. 1985 (Vol. 43, No. 1)

PRICE OF ELECTRICITY IN MAJOR CITIES COMPARED, ANNUAL FEATURE

(p. 28-29) Annual article, with 1 chart ranking 33 largest cities by residential electricity cost per kWh, as of Jan. 1, 1984, with comparison to 1983. Data are from an APPA survey.

This is the 2nd annual survey.

PUBLIC POWER DIRECTORY, 1985, ANNUAL FEATURE

(p. D1-D96) Annual statistical directory of local publicly owned electric utilities. Also includes summary data for other types of electric power organizations, and statistical directories of publicly owned cable communication systems and major Canadian electric utilities.

Data are from APPA, Energy Information Administration, Rural Electrification Administration (REA), and other sources.

Contains contents listing (p. D2); and the following:

a. Electric utility summary statistics: number of systems (no date); and customers, revenues, net plant investment, installed capacity, and kWh sales and generation, 1982-83; for local publicly owned systems, private power companies, REA borrowers, and Federal power agencies. 2 tables. (p. D3-D4)

b. Ranking of 20 largest State/local publicly owned electric systems, by number of customers served, plant value, kWh sales, and revenues, 1983; selected electric utility trends, various years 1890-1984; and installed generating capacity of public power systems, by fuel type, 1980 and 1982-83. 4 tables and 16 charts. (p. D5-D11)

c. Directory of local publicly owned electric utilities, arranged by State and outlying area, showing year established, address, chief official, meters served, generation and capacity, wholesale power purchases or sales, and gross annual revenues; data are for various years 1981-84, specified for each utility. (p. D12-D66)

d. Directories of organizations representing local publicly owned systems. (p. D68-D75)

e. Directory of Federal power agencies, with text data on value of REA insured and guaranteed loans, FY84 and cumulative. (p. D75-D76)

f. Directory of major Canadian electric utilities, by Province, including text data on system generating capacity and customers served. (p. D78-D79)

g. Directory of publicly owned cable communication systems, arranged by State, showing address, chief official, year started, number of subscribers and channels, monthly rate, type of organizational structure and financing, and utility use. (p. D82-D85)

h. Directory of APPA members. (p. D88-D92)

i. Editorial index for 1984. (p. D92-D96)

This is the 24th annual edition of the directory.

LOCAL SYSTEMS BUDGET $5.65 BILLION FOR 1985 PLANT WORK, ANNUAL FEATURE

(p. 54-55) Annual article, by Jeannie Kilmer, on capital spending plans of local publicly owned electric utilities for 1985. Data are from an annual *Public Power* survey. Includes 1 table showing expenditures for distribution, transmission, conservation/load management, and generation by fuel type, 1984-85.

A2625–1.603: Mar./Apr. 1985 (Vol. 43, No. 2)

PUBLIC POWER BOND ISSUES TOPPED $10 BILLION IN '84, ANNUAL FEATURE

(p. 17) Annual article reviewing tax-exempt revenue bond issues by local publicly owned electric utilities, 1984. Data were compiled by Shearson Lehman Brothers, Inc. Includes 1 chart and 2 tables showing total number of issues, 1978-84 and quarterly 1982-84; and value of issues from individual joint-action power systems, 1975-84 period.

A2625–1.604: May/June 1985 (Vol. 43, No. 3)

PUBLIC POWER COSTS LESS, ANNUAL FEATURE

(p. 28-31) Annual article, by Jeannie Kilmer, comparing publicly and privately owned electric utility company sales, expenses, and costs to user. Data are from annual DOE reports.

Includes 4 tables and 4 charts showing the following, for private and public companies: residential and commercial/industrial average annual electricity consumption, revenue per kWh, and bill; and operating and managerial expenses, by type; selected years 1946-83.

PUBLIC POWER CONTRIBUTES MORE, RECURRING FEATURE

(p. 33) Recurring article, by Jeannie Kilmer, with 1 table showing State/local tax payments as a percent of gross electric operating revenue, for public and private utilities by region, 1983. Data are from reports of 191 private and 569 public utilities, and include number reporting for each region.

Previous article, for 1982, is described in SRI 1984 Annual under A2625-1.503.

A2625–1.605: July/Aug. 1985 (Vol. 43, No. 4)

NATIONAL OPINION POLL GIVES PUBLIC POWER HIGH MARKS

(p. 18-19) By Madalyn Cafruny. Article, with 4 charts showing public views on desirability of public vs. private utilities, cost-based vs. market-based rates for Federal hydroelectric power, public utilities' "first right" to Federal hydroelectric power, and repayment of Federal dam debt at original vs. current interest rate.

Data are from a Mar.-Apr. 1985 telephone survey of 1,300 adults, conducted by Hamilton & Staff for American Public Power Assn.

A2625–1.606: Sept./Oct. 1985 (Vol. 43, No. 5)

COMPARISON OF POWER SUPPLY ALTERNATIVES

(p. 34-35) Table showing the following for 30 conventional or developing technologies used in electric power generation: capacity range and factor; operating/maintenance costs; efficiency and equivalent availability rates; capital

costs for 1985; lead time and whether dispatchable; and advantages and disadvantages.

Most data are from Electric Power Research Institute and other industry sources.

A2650
American
Public Transit Association

A2650–1   TRANSIT FACT BOOK, 1985 Edition

Annual. May 1985. 80 p.
ISSN 0149-3132.
LC 75-7535.
SRI/MF/complete

Annual report, for 1985, on U.S. and Canadian urban mass transportation systems. Includes data on finances, operations, equipment, employment, energy use, and government assistance, various periods 1940-83. Covers rail systems, buses, trolley coaches, cable cars, and ferry boats.

Data are based on reports from American Public Transit Assn member systems; and from Canadian Urban Transit Assn.

Contains contents and table listing, and summary (p. 4-8); 4 report sections, with 3 charts, 33 tables listed below, and description of U.S. Urban Mass Transportation Act (p. 10-70); and glossary (p. 72-80).

This is the 38th edition of the report. For description of previous report, for 1981, see SRI 1981 Annual under this number. No reports were issued for 1982-84.

Availability: American Public Transit Association, 1225 Connecticut Ave., NW, Suite 200, Washington DC 20036, †; SRI/MF/complete.

TABLES:

[Data are for U.S., unless otherwise noted. Figures II-IV and VII-IX are numbered in sequence with charts in the report, but present tabular data or lists.]

A2650–1.1: Finances, Operations, and Passengers

[Unless otherwise noted, tables beginning "Trend of..." show data for various years 1940-83.]

SUMMARY DATA

1. Transit modal statistics at a glance [number of systems and vehicles, and summary operations and finances, for bus, heavy and light rail, trolley coach, commuter railroad, cable car, inclined plane, urban ferry, aerial tramway, and automated guideway transit, 1981-83]. (p. 10-12)

2. Transit systems classified by vehicle type [all rail, multi-mode, and all bus] and population group [city size; as of Dec. 31, 1983]. (p. 13)

3. Transit financial statement for 1981-83. (p. 14-15)

4. Publicly owned transit [systems, vehicles, mileage, and unlinked passenger trips; totals and] as a portion of all transit, [selected years 1940-83]. (p. 17)

FINANCIAL DATA

[Data by vehicle mode are shown for multi-mode systems and bus systems only.]

5A-5B. Trend of transit revenues [passenger and other operating revenues, nonoperating/auxiliary revenues, and State/local and Federal operating assistance], dollars and percent of total revenue. (p. 18-19)

Figure II. Source of revenue by transit system vehicle mode and population of area served [1979-83]. (p. 20-21)

6A-6B. Trend of transit expenses by function class [transportation, vehicle and nonvehicle maintenance, general administration, depreciation/amortization, other reconciling items], dollars and percent of operating expense. (p. 22-23)

7A-7B. Trend of transit expenses by object class [labor, services, materials/supplies, utilities, casualty/liability costs, and other], dollars and percent of operating expense, [1975-83]. (p. 24-25)

Figure III. Operating expense by transit system vehicle mode and population [size group] of area served [1979-83]. (p. 26-27)

Figure IV. Transit operating expense for 1983 classified by function and object class [including salaries/wages and fringe benefits]. (p. 28-29)

PASSENGERS

8-9. Trend of transit passenger trips [passenger rides, and unlinked transit passenger trips, for heavy and light rail, surface lines by population size group, trolley, and bus]. (p. 30, 32)

10-11. Trend of passenger miles and vehicle miles operated [for light and heavy rail, trolley, and bus]. (p. 33-34)

12. Trend of transit fares. (p. 35)

EMPLOYMENT AND FUEL CONSUMPTION

13. Trend of transit employment, compensation, and labor costs [including fringe benefit costs]. (p. 36)

14. Trend of transit employees by job category [1975-83]. (p. 37)

15. Trend of energy consumption by transit passenger vehicles [electric power, gasoline, and diesel fuel]. (p. 40)

SPECIAL TRANSIT SYSTEMS

16. Trend of commuter railroad operations [systems, revenues, expenses, linked passenger trips, vehicles, and vehicle miles, 1973-83]. (p. 41)

17. Trend of local/suburban operations by Class I intercity bus carriers [passenger revenue, passengers, and vehicle miles, 1970-83]. (p. 42)

A2650-1.2: Vehicle Characteristics and System Locations, Federal Aid, and Canada Data

VEHICLE CHARACTERISTICS AND SYSTEM LOCATIONS
[Tables 18-19 and Figure VII show data for commuter and/or light and heavy rail, trolley coach, and bus.]

18-19. Transit passenger vehicles owned/leased; and new transit passenger vehicles delivered [with detail for buses by size; various periods 1940-83]. (p. 44-45)

Figure VII. Characteristics of the urban transit fleet [vehicles owned/leased, in active service, and with major rehabilitation; average vehicle age, length, and number of seats; and vehicles with air conditioning, 2-way radios, and wheelchair accessibility; 1980-83]. (p. 46-48)

Figure VIII. Number of bus service providers [urbanized area and small urban/rural systems, and non-profit elderly/disabled services], by State [1984]. (p. 49-51)

Figure IX. Rail, trolley coach, and marine transit service in operation as of Nov. 1, 1984 [listing of organizations operating transit systems, by city]. (p. 52-54)

FEDERAL ASSISTANCE

20. U.S. Government operating grant approvals [and amount approved] for mass transportation [FY75-83]. (p. 57)

21-22. U.S. Government capital grant approvals for mass transportation by program; and by use [bus, rapid transit, commuter rail, and other; various periods FY65-83]. (p. 58, 60)

CANADA

[Tables 23-27 begin "Canadian Transit Operations:...." Data are shown for various periods 1940-83.]

23. Summary statistics [systems, passenger trips, vehicle miles, revenues, and expenses]. (p. 66)

24-25. Passenger vehicles owned/leased; and new passenger vehicle purchases; [for light, heavy, and commuter rail, trolley coach, and bus (with detail by size)]. (p. 66-68)

26-27. Fares [and average revenue per revenue passenger trip]; and employees [by job category]. (p. 69-70)

A2665
American Rental Association

A2665-1   1984 COST OF DOING BUSINESS SURVEY
Annual. Aug. 1985. 29 p. SRI/MF/complete

Annual survey report presenting financial data for the equipment rental industry, 1984, with trends from 1981. Includes financial and operating ratios, income by source and operating expenses by item, operating profit, net income before taxes, detailed assets and liabilities, and net worth.

Data are shown variously for all companies; by revenue size, rental share of total revenues, and type of equipment rented; and for 9 U.S. regions and Canada.

Data are based on responses by 376 companies to a 1984 survey, and were compiled for the American Rental Assn by Browne, Bortz, and Coddington, Inc.

Contains contents listing (inside front cover); narrative overview, with text tables and 4 charts (p. 1-3); and 5 sections, with 1 map, 1 chart, and 20 tables (p. 4-29).

Availability: American Rental Association, 1900 19th St., Moline IL 61265, $10.00; SRI/MF/complete.

A2700
American Society for Engineering Education

A2700-1   ENGINEERING EDUCATION
8 issues per year.
Approx. 60 p. per issue; cumulative pagination throughout year.
ISSN 0022-0809.
LC 73-647370.
SRI/MF/not filmed

Monthly journal (Oct.-May) reporting on engineering and technical education, including teaching methods and their evaluation, continuing and nontraditional study, college-industry relations, college enrollment and degrees, and student and faculty characteristics.

Data are from surveys by American Society for Engineering Education (ASEE) and American Assn of Engineering Societies (AAES), and from studies submitted by individual researchers.

Issues generally contain articles and special features, occasionally including statistics; and narrative editorial depts.

Annual statistical features include reports on engineering and/or engineering technology enrollment and degrees, and engineering college research and graduate study programs.

May issue includes annual author and subject index.

Features with substantial statistical content are described, as they appear, under "Statistical Features." Each issue of the journal is reviewed, but an abstract is published in SRI monthly issues only when statistical features appear. Generally, statistical data from single-institution samplings are not covered.

Availability: American Society for Engineering Education, 11 Dupont Circle, NW, Suite 200, Washington DC 20036, members †, nonmembers $32.00 per yr., students $15.00 per yr., single copy $3.00, Mar. issue $17.00; SRI/MF/not filmed.

Issues reviewed during 1985: Nov. 1984-Oct. 1985 (P) (Vol. 75, Nos. 2-8; Vol. 76, No. 1).

STATISTICAL FEATURES:

A2700-1.601: Nov. 1984 (Vol. 75, No. 2)
ENGINEERING TECHNOLOGY ENROLLMENTS, 1983, ANNUAL FEATURE

(p. 100-104) Annual article, by Patrick J. Sheridan, reporting on the annual engineering technology enrollment survey conducted by the Engineering Manpower Commission of the American Assn of Engineering Societies, 1983.

Includes 5 tables showing engineering technology enrollment by academic level, and number of schools, fall 1973-83; and enrollment detail by curriculum, by institution arranged by State, and for women and minorities (black, Hispanic, Asian/Pacific Islander, and American Indian), fall 1983. Most tables include detail for full-time and part-time students.

A2700–1.602: Dec. 1984 (Vol. 75, No. 3)

CHANGES IN ACCREDITATION, CURRENT AND FUTURE

(p. 156-158) By Richard G. Cunningham. Article on higher education accreditation activities of the Accreditation Board for Engineering and Technology (ABET). Data are from ABET. Includes 2 tables showing number of programs and institutions involved in accreditation/reaccreditation actions, 1978-83; and number of accredited disciplines and institutions with accredited programs, 1938 and 1983.

A2700–1.603: Mar. 1985 (Vol. 75, No. 6)

ENGINEERING COLLEGE RESEARCH AND GRADUATE STUDY, ANNUAL FEATURE

(p. 311-614) Annual full-issue report on engineering college research and graduate study programs, based on 218 responses to a 1984 survey of engineering colleges and schools belonging to the American Society for Engineering Education.

Contains foreword (p. 318-319); narrative article on industry support for university R&D, list of institutions responding, questionnaire facsimile, and data summary (p. 320-328); summaries for individual institutions (p. 329-580); and indexes to graduate study fields and research areas (p. 581-614).

Each institution summary includes text data and 1-6 tables showing most or all of the following, for 1983/84 or fall 1984:

a. Names of officers, total number of faculty and undergraduates, graduate degree requirements, and off-campus extension centers.

b. Number of faculty, and enrollment and degrees granted by level, by degree program; graduate students appointments made; and topics of accepted doctoral theses.

c. Personnel engaged in separately budgeted research; research expenditures, by source of support; and expenditures and number of projects, for separately budgeted research by engineering college unit, and for engineering-related research outside the engineering college by type.

This is the 19th annual survey report.

A2700–1.604: Apr. 1985 (Vol. 75, No. 7)

ENGINEERING AND ENGINEERING TECHNOLOGY DEGREES GRANTED, 1984, ANNUAL FEATURE

(p. 637-645) Annual article, by Paul Doigan, on engineering and engineering technology degrees awarded in 1984. Data are from responses of nearly all engineering schools to an annual American Assn of Engineering Societies (AAES) survey.

Includes 8 tables showing engineering and engineering technology degrees, by curriculum, and individual institution arranged by State, with summary for top 5 States and/or top 10 institutions; and engineering degrees by minority group (female, black, Hispanic, American Indian, Asian/Pacific Islander, and foreign national); all by degree level, 1984.

HOW NSF ENCOURAGES INDUSTRY-UNIVERSITY PARTNERSHIPS

(p. 646-648) By John A. Weese. Article, with 1 table showing NSF expenditures for 3 R&D programs involving interaction between industry and university sectors, FY82-85.

ENGINEERS' PLANS AND ATTITUDES TOWARD GRADUATE AND CONTINUING EDUCATION

(p. 659-664) By Carolyn M. Jagacinski et al. Article on educational attainment and plans of persons holding bachelor's degrees in engineering. Data are from over 2,600 responses to a 1981 NSF-sponsored survey of engineers obtaining bachelor's degrees during 1960-81.

Includes 1 table and 2 charts showing respondent distribution by highest degree held and planned, by date and field of bachelor's degree, race-ethnicity (white, black, Hispanic, and foreign national), and current job function; and responses concerning preferred focus of graduate programs, and desirability of engineering and management graduate work by job function.

A2700–1.605: May 1985 (Vol. 75, No. 8)

MINORITY STUDENTS: UNDERSTANDING A NEW CLIENTELE

(p. 696-700) By Diane Tarmy Rudnick. Article on recruitment and characteristics of female and minority engineering technology students. Data are based on a 1982 survey of 1,288 students at Wentworth Institute of Technology and 4 other institutions.

Includes 5 tables showing survey responses concerning reasons for choosing engineering technology field, family income, academic background and achievement, extracurricular activities and interests, and career expectations, shown separately for women, minority, Caucasian, and all student respondents.

WHAT JOB COMPETENCIES ARE REQUIRED OF ENGINEERING TECHNOLOGY ADMINISTRATORS?

(p. 701-705) By Frank A. Gourley, Jr. Article on personal characteristics and job skill requirements of administrators of engineering technology educational programs. Data are based on responses of 92 administrators to a May 1983 survey.

Includes 9 charts and 2 tables showing respondent characteristics, including type of institutional employer, degrees earned, registration as professional engineer, years in present position, sources of training, and age; and survey responses concerning job requirements and interest in professional improvement.

Also includes 1 technical table analyzing differences between selected respondent subgroups.

A2900
American Society of Association Executives

A2900–3 **1985 ASSOCIATION EXECUTIVE COMPENSATION STUDY**
Biennial. 1985. viii+68 p.
ISSN 0273-0367.
LC 80-648625.
SRI/MF/complete

Biennial report on compensation of association executives, by position, assn characteristics, and census division, 1985. Also covers assn personnel policies and benefit provisions for executives.

Data are from responses of 1,528 ASAE members, representing 6,201 executives, to a questionnaire collecting data in effect Jan. 1, 1985.

Contains foreword (p. iii); contents listing, and introduction with methodology and definitions (iv-viii); report in 4 sections, with 1 text table showing 1981 and 1983 comparative compensation data for management positions, and 48 tables described below (p. 1-63); and appendix with questionnaire facsimile (p. 61-68).

Report previously was designated as annual. For description of previous edition, with data for 1983, see SRI 1983 Annual under this number.

Availability: American Society of Association Executives, 1575 Eye St., NW, Washington DC 20005, members, $50.00, nonmembers $100.00; SRI/MF/complete.

TABLES:

[Assn categories are trade assns and professional societies. Data by assn scope are shown for national, State/regional, and local assns. Data for top executives are shown for chief and deputy chief executives only.

Salary and compensation tables show average, median, and quartile amounts. Personnel and benefit tables show survey response by assn scope.]

a. Base salary and total cash compensation of top assn executives: by assn budget, scope, and census division, shown for each assn category; by detailed assn type (industry or professional group); and for selected metro areas. Tables 1-11. (p. 4-14)

b. Total cash compensation for 24 dept head positions, by assn scope, category, budget, and census division. Tables 12-35. (p. 16-39)

c. Personnel practices: type of salary structure for all management; provision of cash bonus system for top executives and dept heads; and type and length of contract provided top executives, and provisions for early termination of contract. Tables 36-37. (p. 42-44)

d. Employment experience of top executives, by assn scope. Table 38. (p. 45)

e. Fringe benefits: detailed retirement plan and insurance provisions, for all management; and provision of selected perquisites to management personnel and/or top executives. Tables 39-44. (p. 46-53)

f. Analysis of sample characteristics. Tables 45-48. (p. 56-59)

A2940
American Society of Civil Engineers

A2940-1   ASCE SALARY SURVEY, 1983
Biennial. 1984. 3+71 p.
ISBN 0-87262-410-2.
LC 82-73522.
SRI/MF/complete

Biennial survey report on salaries and benefits of civil engineers, by employment category and ASCE professional grade, 1983, with selected summary trends from 1973. Includes salary comparisons by region. Salary data are shown variously as medians, averages, and ranges, generally with detail for entry level and maximum rate within grade. Benefit data are shown as percent of base payroll and/or average value, by benefit type.

Employment categories are consulting, construction, and design/construct firms; railroads/utilities/industries; State government depts/agencies; municipalities/counties/regional authorities; and 9/10- and 11/12-month educational contracts.

Report also includes data on academic salaries by position and type of school; employers' familiarity with ASCE *Manual 55: Guide to Employment Conditions for Civil Engineers,* comparisons of actual conditions to *Manual* recommendations, and use of ASCE grade classifications; and selected sample characteristics.

Data are from a 4th quarter 1983 ASCE survey of 575 organizations representing 25,939 employees, approximately 15-20% of U.S. civil engineers.

Contains listing of contents, tables, and charts (3 p.); narrative summary of findings, methodology, and definitions, with 9 tables (p. 1-15); and 4 appendices, with 9 charts, 28 tables, questionnaire facsimile, ASCE professional grade descriptions, and list of previous salary survey reports (p. 17-71).

This is the 17th biennial report.

Please note that the 1981 survey report, described in SRI 1983 Annual but not microfilmed during 1983, now is available on SRI microfiche (as part of the 1983 collection) under this number.

Availability: American Society of Civil Engineers, Publications, 345 E. 47th St., New York NY 10017-2398, members $9.00, nonmembers $12.00; SRI/MF/complete.

A3000
American Soybean Association

A3000-1   SOYA BLUEBOOK '85
Annual. 1985. 270 p.
ISSN 0275-4509.
LC 81-640171.
SRI/MF/complete

Annual bluebook, with data on U.S. soybean production, processing, prices, utilization, and foreign trade, various periods 1925-85. Also includes some world, Brazilian, Argentine, and Canadian data. Data are compiled from USDA and other sources, identified for each table.

Contains contents listing (p. 7); directories of soybean-related trade assns, government agencies, and companies, and buyer's guide to products and services (p. 10-192); statistical section with contents listing, 3 maps, 12 trend charts, and 42 tables described below (p. 193-250); and glossary, soybean standards, and indexes (p. 251-270).

Availability: American Soybean Association, Circulation and Sales Department, 777 Craig Rd., PO Box 27300, St. Louis MO 63141, $25.00; SRI/MF/complete.

TABLES:
[Data are for U.S., unless otherwise noted. Data are usually shown for 1984 or 1984/85, generally with trends from the 1970s or earlier, including selected trends from as early as 1925. Some tables include detail by month.]

a. Soybean planting and harvesting dates, by State; and soybean acreage, yield, and production, total and by State. 6 tables. (p. 195-203)

b. Argentine and Brazilian soybean harvested area, yield, and production, by Province or State; Canadian soybean acreage, yield, production, farm price and value, foreign trade, processing, and products; and world soybean harvested area and production, by country. 5 tables. (p. 207-211)

c. Supply and disposition data for soybeans and soybean meal and oil, including acreage, yield, stocks, production, and trade; for U.S., Brazil, and Argentina. 4 tables. (p. 215-219)

d. Soybean prices; price support operations, including Commodity Credit Corp. (CCC) activities; crop value, total and for major producing States; distribution of farm marketings by month; and product yields, prices, and value, with spread between product value and soybean price received by farmers. 6 tables. (p. 220-225)

e. Products: soybean meal and oil prices; supply and disposition data for soybean meal, soy and 3 other types of oilseed cakes/meals, soybean oil, and all edible fats and oils by type; world production of protein meals, oilseeds, and vegetable and marine oils, by detailed type; and soybean oil utilization by product type. 11 tables. (p. 226-237)

f. Foreign trade: soybean and product exports; soybean exports by port; soy and cottonseed oil exports, by type (commercial or P.L. 480) and method of payment; Brazilian soybean and product exports; and imports and exports of soybean and other types of cakes/meals; generally with export detail by country or area of destination. 10 tables. (p. 238-250)

A3035
American Symphony Orchestra League

A3035-1   AMERICAN SYMPHONY ORCHESTRA LEAGUE 1984 ANNUAL REPORT
Annual. [1985.]
28 p. no paging.
SRI/MF/complete

Annual report, for 1984, of the American Symphony Orchestra League. Includes aggregate financial trends for professional symphony orchestras, as follows: revenues, tax-supported grants, and private sector support, all by source, and operating expenses by category, 1979/80-1983/84 seasons; and total operating income/support, 1975-84.

Contains League report, with activity summary, 2 financial tables, and lists of contributors, directors, staff, and member orchestras (22 p.); and report on orchestra finances, with narrative summary, 1 table, and 9 charts (6 p.).

This is the 4th edition of the report. SRI coverage begins with this edition.

Availability: American Symphony Orchestra League, 633 E St., NW, Washington DC 20004, †; SRI/MF/complete.

A3075
American Trucking Associations

A3075-1   MONTHLY TRUCK TONNAGE REPORT
Monthly. Approx. 2 p.
SRI/MF/complete, shipped quarterly

Monthly press release summarizing truck freight tonnage carried, and comparing tonnage indexes with production, sales, and price indexes. Data are based on approximately 160 responses to a monthly survey of Class I and II motor carriers of general freight, representing approximately one-half of tonnage moved. Report is issued approximately 2 months after cover date.

Contains narrative, and 3 monthly tables as follows:

[1] Indexes and comparisons [showing tonnage index, industrial production index, retail store sales index, PPI, CPI, and total tonnage carried, for current month, previous 2 months, and same month of previous year].

[2] Adjusted monthly truck [tonnage] index, historical [current year to date and 5 previous years].

[3] Three-month moving average of adjusted truck tonnage index [monthly, for current year to date through month prior to month of coverage, and 1-2 previous years].

Report also includes 2 annual tables (Jan. 1985 issue) showing revised truck tonnage index data for previous 5 years and seasonal/trading day adjustment factors for current year, all by month.

Report price includes *Weekly Truck Tonnage Report,* not covered in SRI.

Availability: American Trucking Associations, Statistical Analysis Department, 2200 Mill Rd., Alexandria VA 22314, $35.00 per yr.; SRI/MF/complete, shipped quarterly.

Issues reviewed during 1985: Sept. 1984-Aug. 1985 (D).

A3075–4   FINANCIAL ANALYSIS OF THE MOTOR CARRIER INDUSTRY, 1984
Annual. [1985.] 47 p.
ISSN 0099-2445.
LC 75-644511.
SRI/MF/complete

Annual report, by Susan Gregg, on Class I and II motor carrier finances, 1982-83. Covers income, expenses, operating ratios, and balance sheets of general freight and special commodity carriers. Also includes data on tonnage and mileage.

Data cover 1,856 carriers and are based on financial reports filed with the ICC.

Contents:

a. Contents listing, narrative overview, study scope, and terminology, with 1 chart showing distribution of revenues by type of carrier and type of property carried, 1983. (p. 1-13)

b. Carrier group financial data, with narrative analyses, 12 summary tables, and 5 detailed tables listed below. (p. 15-40)

c. Analysis of industry performance, and comparisons to general economy, with 1 table showing percent change in selected financial and operating indicators for Class I carriers, by type of carrier and type of property carried, 1983-84. (p. 41-47)

Report was discontinued with the 1982 edition, due to funding constraints. Annual publication resumes with the 1984 edition. For description of 1982 report, see SRI 1983 Annual under this number.

Availability: American Trucking Associations, Statistical Analysis Department, 2200 Mill Rd., Alexandria VA 22314, $25.00 or $40.00 ordered with 1985 Analysis; SRI/MF/complete.

CARRIER GROUP TABLES:
[Data are for 1982-83. Tables show data in the following categories, by detailed item: income and expenses, assets, liabilities and equity, financial and operating ratios, and productivity measures (including total tonnage and miles).

Carrier groups A, B, and C are general freight carriers classified by gross revenue size. Carrier group D consists of specialized commodity carriers.]

[1] Composite carrier groups A, B, C, and D. (p. 20-21)

[2-3] Carrier groups A and B [by region]. (p. 24-25, 28-29)

[4] Carrier group C [by revenue size and length of haul]. (p. 32-33)

[5] Carrier group D [by commodity carried, including household goods, heavy machinery, petroleum products, refrigerated and agricultural products, motor vehicles, building materials, and other special commodities]. (p. 38-39)

A3075–6   INTERSTATE INFORMATION REPORT: Truck Taxes and Highway Finance
Recurring (irreg., selected issue). Feb. 1985.
10 p. no paging.
SRI/MF/complete

Annual report on trucking industry share of State and Federal highway taxes, 1983. Presents the following data for trucks compared to all motor vehicles: registrations, and State and Federal highway user taxes paid, by State, with U.S. totals by tax type and trends from 1957.

Also includes data on highway user fees and tax rates; and capital outlay and maintenance and total expenditures for State-administered highways.

Contains narrative summary, 1 chart, and 12 tables.

Interstate Information Report is a generally nonstatistical newsletter published approximately 4 times each year. The annual issue on truck taxes, usually published in the spring, is the only feature covered in SRI.

Availability: American Trucking Associations, Department of Economics and Taxation, 2200 Mill Rd., Alexandria VA 22314, †; SRI/MF/complete.

**A3225
Association for Education in Journalism and Mass Communication**

A3225–1   JOURNALISM EDUCATOR
Quarterly (selected issue).
Spring 1985. (p. 3-9, 53-60).
Vol. 39, No. 1.
ISSN 0022-5517.
SRI/MF/excerpts, current & previous year reports

Annual feature, "1984 Survey: No change in Mass Comm Enrollments," by Paul V. Peterson, on college/university enrollment and degrees awarded for journalism/mass communications programs, 1984 with comparisons to 1983 and summary trends from 1978.

Includes enrollment and degrees awarded by level, by institution and campus; with various institutional rankings and selected detail by sex and specialization. Also includes aggregate minority enrollment by sex and level, and undergraduate degrees by specialization, shown for black, Hispanic, Asian, and American Indian/Alaskan Native.

Data are based on survey responses from 180 schools, representing 78,856 students. The survey has been conducted annually for over 15 years.

Contains narrative article, with 14 tables (p. 3-9); and 1 additional table presenting detailed data by institution (p. 53-60). Data corrections appear on p. 16 of the Summer 1985 issue of *Journalism Educator,* and are also available on SRI microfiche under this number.

Survey report for 1983 has also been received and is also available on SRI microfiche under this number [Quarterly (selected issue). Spring 1984. p. 3-52 passim].

Journalism Educator is a primarily narrative periodical on developments in journalism/mass communication education. Survey report on enrollment and degrees awarded is the only feature covered in SRI.

Availability: Association for Education in Journalism and Mass Communication, University of South Carolina, College of Journalism, Columbia SC 29208, $15.00 per yr.; SRI/MF/excerpts for all portions presenting survey results.

**A3245
Association for School, College and University Staffing**

A3245–1   TEACHER SUPPLY/DEMAND, 1985: A Report Based upon an Opinion Survey of Teacher Placement Officers
Annual. Jan. 1985.
6 p. no paging.
SRI/MF/not filmed

Annual report, by James N. Akin, presenting supply/demand ratings for elementary/secondary school teachers by academic field, for contiguous U.S., 1976 and 1980-85, and by region and for Alaska and Hawaii, 1985.

Also includes average starting salaries of special education and elementary/secondary school teachers with bachelors and masters degrees, by region and for Alaska and Hawaii, 1982/83-1984/85.

Data are based on 61 responses to an Oct. 1984 survey of teacher placement officers, and previous surveys.

Contains survey background and summary (2 p.); and 3 tables (4 p.).

Availability: Association for School, College and University Staffing, PO Box 4411, Madison WI 53711, †; SRI/MF/not filmed.

**A3255
Association for University Business and Economic Research**

A3255–1   UNIVERSITY RESEARCH IN BUSINESS AND ECONOMICS: A Bibliography of 1983 Publications
Annual. [1985.] vii+315 p.
Vol. XXVIII.
ISSN 0066-8761.
ISBN 0-89527-083-8.
SRI/MF/complete, delayed

Annual bibliography listing approximately 2,000 journal articles and monographs published in 1983 by university business and economics schools and research organizations. Covers only institutions that are members of the Assn for University Business and Economic Research (AUBER) or the American Assembly of Collegiate Schools of Business.

Contains preface and contents listing (p. iii-vii); bibliography arranged by subject area (p. 3-153) and by institution and publication (p. 157-289); and author index (p. 293-315).

Availability: Association for University Business and Economic Research, Bureau of Business Research, College of Business and Economics, West Virginia University, PO Box 6025, Morgantown WV 26506-6025, $25.00; SRI/MF/complete, delayed shipment in Mar. 1986.

A3273
Association of American Medical Colleges

A3273–2 REPORT ON MEDICAL SCHOOL FACULTY SALARIES, 1984/85
Annual. Jan. 1985. ii+94 p.
LC 78-648234.
SRI/MF/complete

Annual report, by William C. Smith, Jr., on compensation of medical school full-time faculty, 1984/85 academic year, with selected comparisons to 1983/84. Includes data by dept; region; degree (M.D., other doctoral, and nondoctoral); academic rank; public or private institution control; and type of compensation (base compensation only and base/supplemental compensation); with selected cross-tabulations.

Data are shown variously as total, percentile, and mean compensation values, generally with number of faculty represented.

Data are from a survey of 122 of 127 accredited medical schools and represent 35,307 filled positions. Data are current as of Sept. 1984.

Contains contents listing (p. i-ii); scope and definitions, questionnaire facsimile, and list of participating schools (p. 1-5); and 32 tables, with accompanying key (p. 7-94).

This is the 20th annual report.

Availability: Association of American Medical Colleges, Membership and Subscriptions, One Dupont Circle, NW, Suite 200, Washington DC 20036, $8.75 (book rate), $10.00 (1st class) (prepaid); SRI/MF/complete.

A3273–3 1984 COTH SURVEY OF HOUSESTAFF STIPENDS, BENEFITS, AND FUNDING
Annual. Jan. 1985.
viii+123 p.
SRI/MF/complete

Annual report, for 1984/85 academic year, on teaching hospital house staff (interns/residents and clinical fellows) stipends, benefits, and expenditures, by region and hospital characteristics (affiliation status, ownership, and bed size).

Stipend data are shown as median, mean, and 25th and 75th percentiles amounts, by post-MD year; and also include detail for 23 cities, comparisons to 1983/84, and national trends from 1969/70.

Also includes funding distribution by source of revenue; changes in residency programs, including number of residents by specialty; ratios of residents and post-M.D. trainees to beds; minorities' share of total house staff; and summary data on clerkship fees and application policies.

Data are from 355 responses of Council of Teaching Hospitals member institutions to Assn of American Medical Colleges survey.

Contains contents and table listings, and introduction (p. iii-viii); 3 chapters, with narrative summaries, 5 charts, and 88 tables (p. 1-107); and 9 appendices, with questionnaire facsimile, 9 tables, and 1 map (p. 108-123).

Availability: Association of American Medical Colleges, Membership and Subscriptions, One Dupont Circle, NW, Washington DC 20036, $7.00 (prepaid); SRI/MF/complete.

A3273–4 COTH DIRECTORY 1985: Educational Programs and Services
Annual. [1985.] xiv+234 p.
SRI/MF/complete

Annual directory, for 1985, of teaching hospital members of the Council of Teaching Hospitals (COTH) of the Assn of American Medical Colleges. Includes data on hospital education programs, services, and operating characteristics, for institutions in States, Puerto Rico, and Beirut, Lebanon.

Data are from a COTH annual survey of member hospitals, American Hospital Assn, and Accreditation Council on Graduate Medical Education.

Contains contents listing, introduction, listings of officers and representatives, and directory data codes and abbreviations (p. i-xiv); 1 directory table, described below, presenting teaching member hospital characteristics (p. 2-221); address directory of corresponding members (p. 222-224); and index (p. 226-234).

This is the 17th annual directory.

Availability: Association of American Medical Colleges, Membership and Subscriptions, One Dupont Circle, NW, Suite 200, Washington DC 20036, $8.00; SRI/MF/complete.

DIRECTORY TABLE:
[The following items are shown for each hospital listed in the directory, arranged by State (including Puerto Rico) and city, and for Beirut, Lebanon.

Types of government and nonprofit control include State, county, city, city-county, and hospital district/authority (nonfederal); church operated and other nonprofit; and Air Force, Army, Navy, PHS, VA, Dept of Justice, and other Federal.]

a. Hospital administrator and address; and accreditation/approval and facilities/services provided, indicated by number code.

b. Type of government or nonprofit control; specialty service provided; whether average stay is short- or long-term; inpatient beds, births, and admissions; emergency room and outpatient visits; total and payroll expenses; and number of personnel.

c. Medical school affiliation; foreign medical graduates and other residents in training, 1st post-M.D. year and total; and approved graduate/undergraduate educational program residencies, by specialty.

A3273–8 JOURNAL OF MEDICAL EDUCATION
Monthly.
Cumulative pagination throughout year.
ISSN 0022-2577.
LC 52-64044.
SRI/MF/excerpts, shipped quarterly

Monthly journal reporting on issues and developments in medical education, including medical school curriculum, instruction, research, applications, enrollments, and characteristics of faculty, students, and graduates.

Issues include articles and research news briefs, many with statistics; and "Datagram" recurring statistical feature usually analyzing time series data on selected topics.

Special issues on selected topics are published occasionally, as part 2 of regular issues. These special issues are paginated separately from the regular issues.

Features with substantial broad-based statistical content are described, as they appear, under "Statistical Features." Nonstatistical features and analyses based on experience of single institutions are not covered. Each issue of the journal is reviewed, but an abstract is published in SRI monthly issues only when features with broad-based statistics appear.

Availability: Association of American Medical Colleges, Membership and Subscriptions, One Dupont Circle, NW, Suite 200, Washington DC 20036, $27.50 per yr., students $22.50 per yr., single copy $3.00, supplements $5.00; SRI/MF/ excerpts for all portions described under "Statistical Features;" shipped quarterly.

Issues reviewed during 1985: Nov. 1984-Oct. 1985 (P) (Vol. 59, Nos. 11-12; Vol. 60, Nos. 1-10) [Nov. 1984 issue is published in 2 parts].

STATISTICAL FEATURES:

A3273–8.601: Nov. 1984 (Vol. 59, No. 11, Pt. 2)

PHYSICIANS FOR THE TWENTY-FIRST CENTURY

Special issue forecasting developments and needs of medical education programs as reported by the AAMC Project Panel on the General Professional Education of the Physician and College Preparation for Medicine. Report is primarily narrative, but includes the following statistical articles:

MEDICAL EDUCATION IN THE U.S. AND CANADA

(p. 35-56) By August G. Swanson. Article on characteristics of U.S. and Canadian medical school curricula, faculties, and students, 1981/82-1983/84. Data are from AAMC and Assn of Canadian Medical Colleges.

Includes 22 tables showing the following, for various periods 1981/82-1983/84:

a. By institution: full-time faculty members in basic and clinical sciences, student enrollment, and graduates, for 127 U.S. and 16 Canadian medical schools.

b. U.S. and Canadian enrollment of medical students, basic science graduate students, residents, and clinical fellows; U.S. and Canadian medical schools by research spending level; and aggregate U.S./Canadian medical schools, by time required for preclinical curricula and clerkships by discipline, time requirements by type of instruction, and weeks available for electives in senior year.

c. U.S. aggregate medical schools: funding by source; total and accepted applicants by undergraduate major and grade point average; undergraduate colleges and medical school applicants and matriculants, by number of applications submitted from undergraduate school; medical schools by number of colleges providing matriculants; students taking various elective courses; medical schools by grading system and use of certification examinations; and graduates by career plans and perception of instructional time for selected areas.

REPORT OF THE WORKING GROUP ON ESSENTIAL KNOWLEDGE

(p. 109-123) Article, with 2 tables showing number of medical schools requiring or recommending various undergraduate courses for students planning to enter medical school, 1982/83. Data are from *Medical School Admission Requirements*, covered in SRI under A3273-10.

A3273–8.602: Dec. 1984 (Vol. 59, No. 12)

IMPACT OF WOMEN AND FOREIGN MEDICAL GRADUATES ON SPECIALTY DISTRIBUTION OF U.S. HOUSE OFFICERS

(p. 921-927) By Stephen S. Mick and Jacqueline Lowe Worobey. Article, with 2 tables showing number of U.S. and foreign medical school graduates serving as hospital house officers (excluding interns), by sex and specialty (primary care, hospital-based, medical, surgical, and psychiatry/physiatry), 1973/74 and 1979/80 training years. Data were compiled by the authors.

ASSESSMENT OF CLINICAL SKILLS IN U.S. MEDICAL SCHOOLS

(p. 957-959) By Lawrence J. Fabrey et al. Article, with 1 table showing perceived usefulness of observational checklists for evaluating medical students' performance in 15 clinical procedures, by medical specialty. Data are based on responses of 319 clinical dept heads to a 1981 survey conducted by the authors.

DELPHI STUDY TO IDENTIFY FUTURE ROLES FOR PHYSICIAN'S ASSISTANTS

(p. 962-963) By Steven R. Shelton et al. Article on likelihood of physician's assistants (PAs) playing an active role in selected types of health care and facilities and health-related occupations, as rated by 39 PA training program directors. Data are based on a 1982 survey. Includes 1 table.

DATAGRAM: FINANCIAL ASSISTANCE FOR MEDICAL STUDENTS, 1983/84, ANNUAL FEATURE

(p. 973-975) Annual article, with 3 tables showing number and value of scholarships, loans, and work study grants awarded to medical students, by general source and type, with detail for Federal aid, 1982/83-1983/84; and total value of aid, 1974/75-1983/84.

This is the 2nd annual feature. For description of previous feature, see SRI 1984 Annual under A3273-8.502.

A3273–8.603: Jan. 1985 (Vol. 60, No. 1)

HEALTH CARE DELIVERY SYSTEM CHANGES: A SPECIAL CHALLENGE FOR TEACHING HOSPITALS

(p. 1-8) By C. Thomas Smith. Article discussing impact of health care financing changes on teaching hospitals. Data are from American Hospital Assn surveys and an unpublished report of the Assn of American Medical Colleges.

Includes 2 tables showing hospitals, beds, admissions, patient days, outpatient visits, residents, net patient revenue, bad debt, and charity care expenditures, for teaching hospitals and all short-term hospitals, 1979/80; and medical school revenues, by source, 1970/71 and 1981/82.

IMPACT OF BOARD CERTIFICATION ON PHYSICIAN PRACTICE CHARACTERISTICS

(p. 9-15) By Edmund R. Becker, et al. Article, with 4 tables comparing the following for board-certified vs. total or noncertified physicians: number, 1971-81, with 1981 detail by specialty, age, and sex; and gross and net income, work time per week and year, and distribution by practice type and location (population size category), by specialty, 1981.

Data are from the American Medical Assn's 1981 Physician Masterfile, and 2nd quarter 1982 Socioeconomic Monitoring System survey.

DENTISTRY IN MEDICAL EDUCATION: RESULTS OF A COMPREHENSIVE SURVEY

(p. 16-20) By James W. Curtis, Jr., et al. Article on dentistry instruction in U.S. and Canadian medical schools, based on 115 responses to a 1982/83 survey conducted by the Dentistry Dept of Bowman Gray School of Medicine at Wake Forest University. Includes 3 tables showing survey findings on inclusion of dentistry lectures and clinical teaching in curriculum, hours alloted, topics taught, and ideal hours and topics.

DATAGRAM: INFLATION AND MEDICAL SCHOOL FACULTY SALARIES

(p. 72-74) Article, with 1 table showing medical school mean salary (in current and constant dollars) for basic and clinical science faculty, with amount required to maintain 1973 purchasing power, and comparison to CPI, 1973-83. Data are from AAMC.

A3273–8.604: Mar. 1985 (Vol. 60, No. 3)

CAREER CHOICE OF 'FIFTH PATHWAY' GRADUATES FROM NEW YORK STATE MEDICAL SCHOOLS

(p. 159-166) By Barry Stimmel and Harry Smith, Jr. Article on career plans of persons completing "fifth pathway" programs which allow graduates of foreign medical schools to enroll in U.S. clinical training programs in order to become eligible for licensure. Data are from National Board of Medical Examiners and American Medical Assn records, and cover 510 persons graduating from New York State "fifth pathway" programs in 1976-78.

Includes 5 tables showing graduates by choice of medical specialty and professional activity (academic, office, hospital, resident, and other), and number not taking and not passing State licensing exams, with selected comparisons to graduates of a traditional medical degree program in New York State, all as of June or Dec. 1981.

TIMING AND MOTIVATION IN PEDIATRIC CAREER CHOICES

(p. 174-180) By Robert Adler et al. Article on career plans of pediatric residents, based on responses from 214 3rd-year residents in 21 programs to a May 1982 survey conducted by the authors. Includes 1 table showing respondents by career choice in 1 and 5 years.

A3273–8.605: Apr. 1985 (Vol. 60, No. 4)

FINDINGS ON GERIATRIC MEDICINE AND GERONTOLOGY FROM THE NBME EXAMINATIONS

(p. 330-332) By Edmund H. Duthie, Jr., et al. Article discussing student performance on gerontology and nongerontology portions of

the National Board of Medical Examiners (NBME) examinations. Data were compiled by the authors from 1983 NBME examination results of over 12,000 student participants.

Includes 1 table showing prevalence of gerontology items, and proportion of students correctly answering gerontology and nongerontology items, by examination subject area.

A3273–8.606: May 1985 (Vol. 60, No. 5)

DATAGRAM: HOUSE STAFF EXPENDITURES IN COTH MEMBER HOSPITALS

(p. 422-424) Article on teaching hospital stipends for house staff (residents and clinical fellows), 1983/84. Data are from 355 responses of Council of Teaching Hospitals member institutions to an Assn of American Medical Colleges survey.

Includes 3 tables showing teaching hospital mean expenditures for resident stipends/benefits (actual and as percent of hospital operating budget), by region, type of affiliation and ownership, and bed size; and distribution of expenditures for residents and clinical fellows by funding source; 1983/84, with selected national trends from 1969/70.

Full survey report is covered in SRI under A3273-3.

A3273–8.607: June 1985 (Vol. 60, No. 6)

OFFICE PROCEDURAL SKILLS IN FAMILY MEDICINE

(p. 444-453) By Larry G. Heikes and Craig L. Gjerde. Article on residency training in outpatient procedural skills for family medical practice. Data are from responses of 131 residents, 34 faculty members, and 236 graduates in 9 Iowa family practice residency programs to a 1982 survey conducted by the authors.

Includes 2 tables showing survey response concerning 40 family practice skills, including which skills residency graduates should be able to perform, and experience with performing or supervising the performance of each skill as part of a residency program.

DATAGRAM: RESULTS OF THE NRMP FOR 1985, ANNUAL FEATURE

(p. 498-500) Annual article reporting on National Resident Matching Program (NRMP) participation, 1985. Includes 2 tables showing number of positions offered and matched applicants, by specialty; and unmatched participants and withdrawals; most by applicant type (U.S. senior medical students, other U.S./ Canadian citizens, and foreign graduates of foreign medical schools).

A3273–8.608: July 1985 (Vol. 60, No. 7)

PHYSICIAN SPECIALIST GROWTH INTO THE 21ST CENTURY

(p. 558-559) By David A. Kindig and Nancy Cross Dunham. Article, with 1 chart showing physicians in primary and non-primary care specialties, 1980 and 2020. Data are from authors' estimates.

DATAGRAM: FACULTY PERCEPTIONS OF CURRENT CLINICAL EVALUATION SYSTEMS

(p. 573-576) Article on medical school faculty opinions regarding student clinical evaluation programs. Data are based on responses of 490 U.S. and Canadian physicians to a Nov. 1983-June 1984 Assn of American Medical Colleges survey.

Includes 4 tables showing survey response on quality of evaluation programs, areas of greatest concern, reviews of evaluation policies and procedures, and consequences of reviews, 1983/84.

A3273–8.609: Aug. 1985 (Vol. 60, No. 8)

ACADEMIC CLINICIANS WITHOUT RESIDENCY TRAINING PROGRAMS

(p. 641-644) By Samuel H. Greenblatt and Philip L. Gildenberg. Article, with 1 table showing medical schools without closely affiliated residency training programs in each of 17 specialties, 1983/84. Data were compiled by the authors.

DATAGRAM: NET PATIENT REVENUE AT UNIVERSITY-OWNED TEACHING HOSPITALS, 1982, ANNUAL FEATURE

(p. 655-658) Annual article on university-owned teaching hospitals' funding trends, FY75-82. Data are based on responses of 66 hospitals to the 1983 13th annual survey conducted for Council of Teaching Hospitals.

Includes 4 tables showing distribution of State-funded teaching hospitals by proportion of operating revenues received from State appropriations, FY75-82; and aggregate net patient revenue of teaching hospitals, by source, for inpatient and outpatient care, and for hospitals receiving and not receiving State appropriations earmarked for patient care, FY81-82.

A3273–8.610: Sept. 1985 (Vol. 60, No. 9)

IMPACT OF MEDICAL SCHOOL CLASS RANKING SYSTEMS ON APPLICANTS' RATINGS FOR RESIDENCY POSITIONS

(p. 684-691) By Laura T. Gutman and Seymour Grufferman. Article examining medical school grading and transcript procedures and their effect on the evaluation process of a residency selection committee. Data are from applications of 106 graduates from 56 medical schools to a Duke University residency program.

Includes 4 undated tables showing medical school grading systems and transcript formats; and selection scores of applicants whose transcripts did and did not include information on class standing.

A3273–10 MEDICAL SCHOOL ADMISSION REQUIREMENTS, 1986/87, U.S. and Canada
Annual. 1985. xiv+365 p.
LC 51-7778.
SRI/MF/complete

Annual report on medical school programs, applicants, admissions, enrollment, and fees in the U.S. and Canada, 1984/85, with trends from 1976/77 and some data for 1986/87. Report is designed to assist premedical students and their advisers. Most data are from reports to the Assn of American Medical Colleges by 124 U.S. (including 3 Puerto Rican) and 16 Canadian medical schools, and are current as of Feb. 1985.

Contains contents and table listings, and alphabetical and geographical listings of medical schools (p. v-xiv); foreword (p. 1-2); and the following chapters:

U.S.

Chapter 1-2. Overview of medical education process; and premedical curriculum plan-

ning guidelines, with 2 tables showing undergraduate subjects required by 10 or more medical schools, 1986/87; and total and accepted applicants, by undergraduate major, 1984/85. (p. 3-11)

Chapter 3. Factors in deciding whether and where to apply to medical school, with 7 tables showing applicants/acceptees, by undergraduate grade average and Medical College Admission Test (MCAT) score; State residency status and sex of 1st-year entrants, by individual institution; acceptance rates, by age and sex; applicants and acceptees by sex and minority group (black, American Indian, Mexican American, and Puerto Rican), and women entrants; and total and 1st-year enrollment, by racial/ethnic category including minority groups noted above, Asian/Pacific Islanders, other Hispanics, and foreign students; various years 1980/81-1984/85. (p. 12-26)

Chapter 4-6. Information on MCAT and American Medical College Application Service; explanation of the medical school application and selection process, with 1 table (p. 33) showing applicants, applications, and new entrants, 1980/81-1984/85; and financial information, with 1 table (p. 42) showing private and public school average expenses for 1st-year students, 1984/85. (p. 27-47)

Chapter 7-9. Minority student assistance, with 3 tables showing 1st-year and total enrollment, 1976/77-1984/85, and by individual institution, fall 1984, for the 4 minority groups noted above; alternatives for applicants not admitted to medical school; and planning information for high school students. (p. 48-74)

Chapter 10. Profiles of 124 medical schools, each covering curriculum, entrance requirements, selection factors, and financial aid, with 3 tables showing application timetable, 1st-year class 1986/87; and resident and nonresident expenses, applicants, and entrants, 1st-year class 1984/85. (p. 75-329)

CANADA

Chapter 11. Information about Canadian medical schools, including 2 summary tables showing subjects required by 3 or more schools for entering class 1986/87, and expenses for 1st-year students 1984/85; and profiles of 16 individual institutions, similar to those described above for U.S. schools. (p. 330-365)

This is the 36th edition of the report.

Availability: Association of American Medical Colleges, Membership and Subscriptions, One Dupont Circle, NW, Suite 200, Washington DC 20036, $8.50 (prepaid, book rate), $10.50 (prepaid, 1st class); SRI/MF/complete.

A3275
Association of American Railroads

A3275–1 RAILROAD REVENUES, EXPENSES, AND INCOME: Class I Railroads in the U.S.
Quarterly. Approx. 4 p.
SRI/MF/complete

Quarterly report on Class I railroad freight and passenger revenues, expenses, and income, including data by railroad company and district. Data are compiled from railroad reports to the ICC and are issued 3-6 months after quarter of coverage.

Usually contains 5 tables, listed below.

Agency also issues a narrative summary, which is not covered in SRI.

Availability: Association of American Railroads, Information and Public Affairs Office, 1920 L St., NW, Washington DC 20036, $20.00 per yr., single copy $5.00; SRI/MF/complete.

Issues reviewed during 1985: 3rd Qtr. 1984-2nd Qtr. 1985 (D) (Nos. 719-722).

QUARTERLY TABLES:

[1] Railroad revenues, expenses, and income [by account item, with selected ratios, for quarter of coverage, year to date, and same periods of previous year].

[2] Rate of return on property investment [eastern, southern, and western districts, year to date and same period of previous year].

[3-4] Railroad [freight and operating] revenues, [operating] expenses, and [net railway operating and ordinary] income; by district and individual railroad, for quarter of coverage, year to date, and same periods of previous year].

[5] Total operating revenues, expenses, ordinary income, net railway operating income, revenue ton-miles, and capital expenditures [by quarter, year to date and previous 4-5 years].

A3275–2 TRENDS: Carloadings of Major Railroads
Weekly. Approx. 2 p.
SRI/MF/complete, shipped quarterly

Weekly press release on estimated major railroad freight traffic, by commodity. Data are compiled by Assn of American Railroads from reports submitted to ICC. Week of data coverage is approximately 1 week prior to publication date.

Contains narrative summary with text statistics on piggyback carloadings, and 1 table showing the following:

a. Carloadings by approximately 20 commodity groups, for week of coverage, with change from same week of previous year and preceding week.

b. Total cars loaded, for current and preceding year to date.

c. Estimated revenue ton-miles, for week of coverage and year to date of current and preceding year.

An early Jan. issue also includes 1 annual table presenting summary data for previous 2 years.

Availability: Association of American Railroads, Information and Public Affairs Office, 1920 L St., NW, Washington DC 20036, †; SRI/MF/complete, shipped quarterly.

Issues reviewed during 1985: Nov. 1, 1984-Oct. 31, 1985 (P).

A3275-3   TRENDS: Freight Cars and Locomotives Ordered and Delivered
Monthly.   2 p.
SRI/MF/complete, shipped quarterly

Monthly press release on railroad and private car line freight cars and locomotives ordered and delivered, and backlog, compiled by Assn of American Railroads and American Railway Car Institute. Data are current to 3-6 weeks prior to publication date.

Contains narrative summary, and 1 table showing:

a. New and rebuilt freight cars ordered and delivered, and locomotives delivered, for month of coverage, year to date, same periods of preceding year, and previous month.

b. Backlog orders of new and rebuilt freight cars and locomotives, usually as of 1st of cover date month, same month of previous year, and previous month, with annual averages for current and preceding year.

Table shows data for freight cars built in railroad shops and by car builders.

Availability: Association of American Railroads, Information and Public Affairs Office, 1920 L St., NW, Washington DC 20036, †; SRI/MF/complete, shipped quarterly.

Issues reviewed during 1985: Nov. 29, 1984-Oct. 23, 1985 (P) [No Feb. 1985 issue was published].

A3275-4   STATISTICS OF RAILROADS OF CLASS I IN THE U.S.
Annual, discontinued.

Annual summary report on Class I line-haul railroad finances and operations, discontinued with the 1983 report.

For description of the 1983 report, see SRI 1984 Annual, under this number. Report is replaced by *Railroad Ten-Year Trends,* described under A3275-8 below.

A3275-5   RAILROAD FACTS, 1984 Edition
Annual.   Oct. 1984.   64 p.
LC A66-7305.
SRI/MF/complete

Annual report on Class I line-haul railroad operations and finances, 1983, with selected trends from 1929. Covers passenger and freight traffic and revenues, operating expenses, mileage, and equipment. Also includes data on employment, fuel consumption, and comparisons with other transport modes.

Data are compiled by the Assn of American Railroads from original studies, individual railroad reports, ICC, and other sources.

Contains contents listing and preface (p. 1-2); narrative review and outlook, with text statistics (p. 3-8); summary table on finances, equipment, traffic, employment, and operations, 1982-83 (p. 9); 1 chart, and 54 tables listed below (p. 10-61); and index (p. 62-64).

Report has been published annually since 1965.

Previous report, for 1983, is described in SRI 1983 Annual, under this number.

Availability: Association of American Railroads, Information and Public Affairs Office, 1920 L St., NW, Washington DC 20036, †; SRI/MF/complete.

TABLES:
[Tables show data for selected years 1929-83, unless otherwise noted. Data by district are for total U.S., and eastern, western, and southern railway districts.]

A3275-5.1: Finances
REVENUES AND EXPENSES

[1] Condensed income account [1973 and 1982-83]. (p. 10)

[2] Distribution of operating revenues [for payroll and benefits, taxes, equipment/fuel, and other expenses, 1983]. (p. 11)

[3-5] Operating and freight revenues, and operating expenses [by district]. (p. 12-14)

[6] Principal categories of [maintenance and transportation] expenses. (p. 15)

TAXES, INVESTMENT, AND EQUIPMENT DEBT

[7] Taxes [payroll, Federal income, deferred, and other]. (p. 16)

[8-9] Net railway operating income and rate of return on net investment [by district]. (p. 17-18)

[10] Retained funds and capital expenditures [1956-83]. (p. 19)

[11] Net income (ordinary) [by district]. (p. 20)

[12] [Shareholders' equity and] rate of return on shareholders' equity [1961-83]. (p. 21)

[13] Net working capital [by district, Dec. 31, selected years 1958-83]. (p. 22)

[14] Equipment obligations [and average interest rate, issued and outstanding, 1951 and 1955-83]. (p. 23)

A3275-5.2: Traffic and Mileage
FREIGHT AND PASSENGER TRAFFIC

[1] Revenue carloadings, major railroads [by district]. (p. 24)

[2] Revenue carloadings by [commodity] classes, major railroads [1982-83]. (p. 25)

[3] Piggyback loadings [revenue cars by district, 1957-83; and trailers/containers, 1961-83]. (p. 26)

[4] Originated tonnage [by district]. (p. 27)

[5] Freight commodities [tons originated and revenues, 1983]. (p. 28)

[6-8] Revenue ton-miles and ton-mile revenue [by district], and revenue and distance per ton and per passenger. (p. 29-31)

[9] Volume of U.S. intercity freight and passenger traffic [by transport mode, including railroad, truck, bus, waterway, air, and oil pipeline]. (p. 32)

MILEAGE
[Tables [10-16] show data by district.]

[10-11] Freight train and freight car miles. (p. 33-34)

[12-14] Cars per average freight train, and average freight carload and train load [in tons]. (p. 35-37)

[15-16] Net ton-miles per train hour, and revenue ton-miles per car loaded. (p. 38-39)

[17-18] Revenue ton-miles per gallon of fuel consumed [1971-83] and per employee and employee hour [1969-83]. (p. 40-41)

A3275-5.3: Plant and Equipment
ROADWAYS AND ROLLING STOCK

[1-2] Miles of road and track owned [selected years 1929-82]. (p. 42)

[3] Railroad mileage operated, by States, 1982. (p. 43)

[4] Locomotives in service [by type, for diesel electric, steam, electric, and other]. (p. 44)

[5] Age of locomotives [number of locomotives by period built, selected periods pre-1960 to 1983]. (p. 45)

[6-7] Freight cars [selected years 1929-83], and types of freight equipment [1983, both for Class I and other railroads, and car companies/shippers]. (p. 46-47)

[8] Average freight car capacity. (p. 48)

[9] Cost of new freight cars [general and special service box and flat cars, and 5 types of hopper cars, 1966-83]. (p. 49)

[10] Passenger train cars [by district, and for Pullman Co. or Amtrak]. (p. 50)

[11] New and rebuilt equipment [locomotive units, freight cars, and passenger train cars, selected years 1953-83]. (p. 51)

[12-13] New rail and crossties laid. (p. 52)

[14] Weight of rail in place [1983]. (p. 53)

CAPITAL OUTLAY

[15] Railroad investment, net [by district]. (p. 54)

[16] Capital expenditures [for equipment and roadway/structures, 1953-83]. (p. 55)

A3275-5.4: Employment, Fuel Consumption, and Amtrak

[1] Employment, payroll, and [annual and hourly] earnings. (p. 56)

[2] Employment and annual wages by [occupational] classes, 1983. (p. 57)

[3] Railroad employment by States, 1983. (p. 58)

[4] Railroad cost recovery index [labor, fuel, and materials/supplies, 1967-83; with other costs, 1977-83; base year=1977]. (p. 59)

[5] Diesel fuel consumption and cost [by railway district, selected years 1953-83]. (p. 60)

[6] Statistics of National Railroad Passenger Corp. (Amtrak) [plant/equipment, traffic, operation mileage, and finances, 1982-83]. (p. 61)

A3275-6   ECONOMIC ABZ's OF THE RAILROAD INDUSTRY
Annual, discontinued.

Annual compilation of statistics on railroad finances and operations, discontinued with the 1983 report.

For description of the 1983 report, see SRI 1984 Annual, under this number. Report has been replaced by *Railroad Ten-Year Trends,* described under A3275-8 below.

A3275–7 ANALYSIS OF CLASS I RAILROADS, 1983
Annual. Sept. 1984.
iv + 204 p. + foldout. Oversized.
Series No. 6.
ISSN 0091-4894.
LC 73-643888.
SRI/MF/complete

Annual report on Class I freight and passenger railroads, covering finances, operations, and employment, by railroad company and district, 1983.

Contains contents listing and index to companies (p. i-ii); notes on accounting and reporting changes (p. iii-iv); 14 financial summary line items (p. 1-6); 764 detailed line items, described below, on finances (p. 7-66) and resources and operations (p. 67-168); 11 charts and 22 tables ranking companies by selected measures (p. 169-188); and index and data sources (p. 189-204).

Also contains 1 foldout insert (inside front cover) comparing summary financial data under depreciation accounting and retirement/replacement/betterment accounting methods, by company and district, 1983.

This is the 6th annual report.

Availability: Association of American Railroads, Information and Public Affairs Office, 1920 L St., NW, Washington DC 20036, $75.00; SRI/MF/complete.

DETAILED LINE ITEMS:
[Data are shown for total U.S., 3 railroad districts, and 30 companies, 1983.]

a. Income statement and balance sheet: operating revenues and other income, fixed charges, income taxes, assets including road and equipment, current and noncurrent liabilities, shareholders' equity, and net working capital. Lines 15-99. (p. 7-24)

b. Cash and stock dividends, investments and rate of return, sources and applications of working capital, operating and freight service expenses by function and object, railway taxes, equipment rents, and financial ratios. Lines 100-300. (p. 25-66)

c. Resources and railway operations: average employment, and total and average annual compensation, all by job function; hours worked and paid, including overtime and vacation/holiday; mileage operated; ties and rail laid; capital expenditures; locomotives and freight cars in service, owned and leased, installed, and retired; and summary of operations. Lines 301-532. (p. 67-114)

d. Traffic and operations: carloads and tons originated and gross freight revenue, all by commodity group; and operations characteristics, including loaded and empty freight car miles by car type, switching data, operating ratios, and fuel consumption and costs by fuel type and function. Lines 533-778. (p. 115-168)

A3275–8 RAILROAD TEN-YEAR TRENDS
Annual. 1984.
111 p. no paging + 4 p. addenda. Vol. No. 1.
SRI/MF/complete

Annual report on Class I railroad finances and operations, shown primarily for 1973-83. Includes data on income and expenses, balance sheets, freight traffic, employment, vehicles, fuel use, and other operations.

Data are primarily from railroad reports to ICC, and Assn of American Railroads records.

Contains preface and listing of contents/tables (5 p.); sections I-III on industry finances and operations, with 85 tables described below (87 p.); and section IV presenting brief profiles of 9 industry assns and organizations (9 p.).

This is the 1st edition of the report. This report replaces *Statistics of Class I Railroads* and *Economic ABZ's of the Railroad Industry,* which have been covered in SRI under A3275-4 and A3275-6, respectively.

Availability: Association of American Railroads, Information and Public Affairs Office, 1920 L St., NW, Washington DC 20036, members †, nonmembers new subscribers $25.00, previous subscribers to Economic ABZs of the Railroad Industry $10.00; SRI/MF/complete.

TABLES:
[Data are shown for 1973-83, unless otherwise noted.]

A3275–8.1: Overview and Finances

INDUSTRY OVERVIEW

a. Intercity freight traffic distribution, by transport mode, 1983; number of Class I and other line-haul railroads, and switching/terminal companies, selected years 1920-84; railroad mergers and consolidations since 1957; and ranking of 21 railroad systems by operating revenue, with data for subsidiaries, 1983. Table I.1-I.4.

FINANCIAL PERFORMANCE AND INDICATORS

b. Income and expenses by detailed item; adjustment indexes for major costs, 4th quarter 1980-4th quarter 1984; hourly and annual wages; fringe benefit expenses; retirement tax rates, 1974-87; diesel fuel prices; and taxes by type. Tables II.A1-II.A7.

c. Property investment; shareholder equity and stock dividends; long-term and equipment debt and interest rates; expenditures for rolling stock and roadway/structures; and rolling stock costs and lease expenditures. Tables II.B1-II.B9.

d. Return on investment and shareholder equity, with comparisons to other industries 1975-82; ICC approved cost of capital; revenue margin; capital and long-term debt; income coverage of fixed charges; assets, liabilities, working capital, and daily operating cost; operating revenue, and capital turnover rate; and income, depreciation, deferred taxes, capital expenditures, and cash flow. Tables II.C1-II.C10.

e. Stock dividend average yield, earnings per share, and price/earnings ratio, 1979-83; and Class I railroad bond ratings, 1976-84; all by company. Tables II.C11-II.C12.

A3275–8.2: Operations

a. Track mileage owned; rail and crosstie installations; rail mileage by weight range, 1983; locomotives and freight cars installed and leased, and in service by type (with some trends from 1969); locomotives and freight cars by age, as of Jan. 1, 1984; locomotive average horsepower; freight car deliveries by type, 1978-83; freight car capacity; and freight car service life and percent salvage value, by type (no date). Tables III.A1-III.A13.

b. Employment by occupation and company; total and average earnings and compensation; payroll taxes, and value of benefits; monthly employment seasonality index; hours worked and paid for; employment ratios; and railroad occupations represented, by labor union. Tables III.B1-III.B7.

c. Freight carloadings, tons, and ton-miles; intercity freight traffic share and revenues, by transport mode, various years 1969-83; quarterly revenue carloading index; tons originated 1969-83, and revenue share 1983, by commodity; coal freight tonnage and revenues compared to total production; coal tonnage of top 4 coal railroads, 1983; grain traffic by transport mode; piggyback carloadings, selected years 1957-83; and freight car types used for various commodities. Tables III.C1-III.C13.

d. Energy consumption and fuel efficiency by transportation sector or mode, various periods 1973-83; railroad consumption of diesel fuel and of electricity for motive power; and coal production and Class I railroad use, selected years 1920-83. Tables III.D1-III.D6.

e. Productivity measures of freight tonnage, train-miles, and train-hours; average length of haul and car trips; overheated journals and ratio to freight car-miles; and freight loss/damage claims. Tables III.E1-III.E13.

A3350
Association of Home Appliance Manufacturers

A3350–1 MAJOR HOME APPLIANCE FACTORY SHIPMENTS
Monthly. Approx. 2 p.
SRI/MF/complete, shipped quarterly

Monthly press release on factory shipments of major home appliances, including room air conditioners, dehumidifiers, dishwashers, disposers, compactors, refrigeration units, gas and electric ranges, microwave ovens/ranges, and laundry appliances. Most data are based on appliance manufacturer reports to Assn of Home Appliance Manufacturers. Release generally is issued 2-3 weeks after month of coverage.

Contains narrative summary; 1 monthly table showing shipments by appliance type, for month of coverage, year to date, and same periods of previous year, with quarterly summary; and an annual table (Apr. 1985 issue) showing 12-year trends and forecasts.

Availability: Association of Home Appliance Manufacturers, 20 N. Wacker Dr., Chicago IL 60606, †; SRI/MF/complete, shipped quarterly.

Issues reviewed during 1985: Oct. 1984-Sept. 1985 (D).

A3350–2 **APPLIANCE SALES BY DISTRIBUTORS, States, 1984**
Annual. [1985.]
6 p. var. paging.
SRI/MF/complete

Annual report, for 1984, on distributor sales of home laundry, refrigeration, and kitchen appliances, by State and product type. Also includes number of households, by State, 1980. Data are from AHAM and Census Bureau.

Contains 3 tables.

Availability: Association of Home Appliance Manufacturers, 20 N. Wacker Dr., Chicago IL 60606, †; SRI/MF/complete.

A3350–3 **MAJOR APPLIANCE INDUSTRY FACTS BOOK**
Annual. [1985.] 52 p.
SRI/MF/complete

Annual report on major home appliance manufacturing and market trends, various years 1920-85. Most data are from AHAM and Federal sources.

Contains contents and product listings (p. 1-2); 3 sections presenting narrative summaries, 7 charts, and 28 tables described below (p. 2-38); selected industry information, including product milestones, directory of organizations, and lists of AHAM publications and members (p. 39-49); and indexes (p. 50-52).

This is the 1st edition of the report.

Availability: Association of Home Appliance Manufacturers, 20 N. Wacker Dr., Chicago IL 60606, $15.00; SRI/MF/complete.

TABLES:
[Tables show data for major home appliances, generally by type.]

MANUFACTURING

1. Companies and plants manufacturing [no date]. (p. 2)

2. Employment [total and production workers, 1973-83]. (p. 3)

3. Average annual percentage productivity increase (output per employee hour) [with comparison to total and durable goods manufacturing, 1958-83 period]. (p. 4)

4. 1982 cost of materials/components in production. (p. 4)

5. New capital expenditures [1967-82]. (p. 5)

6. Estimated 1983 dollar sales (manufacturer dollar value). (p. 6)

MARKETING AND DISTRIBUTION

7. Ownership, number and percentage of households with product [1960, 1970, and 1982]. (p. 8-9)

8. Use in new housing [including number of appliances sold directly to home builders, with comparison to total sales, 1979]. (p. 10)

9-10. Exports and imports [1970 and 1980-83]. (p. 11-12)

11-12. Historical perspective, and trends and forecasts: factory unit shipments (domestic/export), [decennial periods 1920-79, and annually 1975-85, with 1st and record years of shipments]. (p. 13, 16-17)

13. Primary retail outlets [number of establishments by type, 1977]. (p. 19)

PRICES, ENERGY EFFICIENCY, AND CONSUMER PREFERENCES

14-17. PPI and CPI [with comparisons to nonappliance items, various years 1957-83]. (p. 22-27)

18. "Hours to earn" [number of hours average production worker must work to earn purchase price of appliances, 1968 and 1983]. (p. 28)

19. [Distribution of] residential energy consumption by end use [and percent of total U.S. consumption for each residential use] (1980). (p. 30)

20. Average energy use [1980 or 1983]. (p. 31)

21-25. Energy efficiency and consumption trends [various years 1972-83]. (p. 32-35)

26. Room air conditioner shipments by energy efficiency (EER) classification [1974, 1978, and 1980-84]. (p. 35)

27. Consumer capacity preferences [1972 and 1983]. (p. 36)

28. Percent of shipments by color [1982-83]. (p. 37)

A3354
Association of Information Systems Professionals

A3354–1 **1985 ANNUAL SALARY SURVEY RESULTS**
Annual. 1985. 115 p.
SRI/MF/complete

Annual report on word processing (wp) salaries in U.S. and Canada, by position, location, and industry, as of Feb. 1985. Data are based on a mail survey of 19,613 wp employees in 1,969 U.S. and Canadian companies.

Contains contents listing, survey methodology, job title definitions, and map of zip code regions (p. 2-7); and 1 table showing the following for each of 15 wp positions: number of companies and employees surveyed; weekly average, high, low, median, and modal salaries; and total average weekly hours for each location or industry. Table is repeated for:

a. U.S., 10 zip code regions, 36 metro areas, and total nonmetro. (p. 8-55)

b. Canada, 5 metro areas, and total nonmetro. (p. 56-62)

c. 30 U.S. industries. (p. 63-92)

d. 23 Canadian industries. (p. 93-115)

This is the 11th annual report.

Availability: Association of Information Systems Professionals, 1015 N. York Rd., Willow Grove PA 19090, members $35.00, nonmembers $60.00; SRI/MF/complete.

A3365
Association of Research Libraries

A3365–1 **ARL STATISTICS, 1983-84**
Annual. 1985.
71 p.+errata sheet.
ISSN 0147-2135.
LC 77-647280.
SRI/MF/complete

Annual report, compiled by Nicola Daval and Alexander Lichtenstein, on research library holdings, expenditures, and staff, 1983/84. Presents data for 105 university and 12 other research libraries in U.S. and Canada.

Covers total and added volumes, microform holdings, and current serials; interlibrary loan activity; operating expenditures by function, including salaries/wages; and FTE staff; all with rank order, by institution.

Also includes university library aggregate operating ratios; and library size indexes, PhD degrees awarded, and fall 1983 student enrollment, by institution.

Data are from an annual survey of ARL members.

Contains contents listing and trend chart (p. 3-4); introduction with text data and references, and library code guide (p. 5-7a); 4 tables, library size index, and 14 ranking tables (p. 8-46); and facsimile questionnaire, footnotes, and list of ARL statistical publications (p. 47-71).

Availability: Association of Research Libraries, 1527 New Hampshire Ave., NW, Washington DC 20036, members $8.00, nonmembers $10.00; SRI/MF/complete.

A3365–2 **ARL ANNUAL SALARY SURVEY, 1984**
Annual. Dec. 1984. 56 p.
ISSN 0361-5669.
LC 76-640547.
SRI/MF/complete

Annual survey report, by Gordon Fretwell, on salaries at university and nonuniversity member libraries of Assn of Research Libraries (ARL), FY85 with selected trends from FY74.

Includes the following data for university libraries: filled positions, average years of experience, and average, median, and beginning salaries, for approximately 100 individual institutions; librarians and/or average salary, by sex, position, years of experience, institutional control, staff size, census division, and for Canada, with selected detail for minority, medical, and law librarians; and minority librarians, by census division and race/ethnicity (black, Hispanic, Asian, and American Indian/Alaskan Native).

Also includes university and nonuniversity libraries, and librarians by salary range; median and beginning salaries for 11 individual nonuniversity libraries; nonuniversity library staff and salary summary; and salary index comparison to CPI.

Contains contents and table listing (p. 3-4); introduction and explanatory notes, with 1 text table (p. 5-7); 27 detailed tables (p. 9-41); and questionnaire facsimiles and footnotes. (p. 42-56)

Availability: Association of Research Libraries, 1527 New Hampshire Ave., NW, Washington DC 20036, members $8.00, nonmembers $10.00; SRI/MF/complete.

A3370
Association
of Schools and
Colleges of Optometry

A3370–1   JOURNAL OF OPTOMETRIC EDUCATION
Quarterly. Approx. 30 p.
ISSN 0098-6917.
LC 76-646768.
SRI/MF/excerpts

Quarterly journal of the Assn of Schools and Colleges of Optometry, containing feature articles and statistics on student, applicant, and school characteristics, and various academic and professional issues.

Each issue contains regular depts and feature articles. Features with substantial statistical content are described, as they appear, under "Statistical Features." Each issue of the journal is reviewed, but an abstract is published in SRI monthly issues only when statistical features appear.

Availability: Association of Schools and Colleges of Optometry, 600 Maryland Ave., SW, Suite 410, Washington DC 20024, members †, nonmembers $15.00 per yr.; SRI/MF/excerpts for all portions covered under "Statistical Features."

Issues reviewed during 1985: Fall 1984-Summer 1985 (P) (Vol. 10, Nos. 2-4; Vol. 11, No. 1).

STATISTICAL FEATURES:

A3370–1.601: Fall 1984 (Vol. 10, No. 2)

SURVEY OF OPTOMETRY GRADUATES TO DETERMINE PRACTICE PATTERNS: PART I, DEMOGRAPHY AND PRACTICE CHARACTERISTICS

(p. 15-19) By Robert L. Bleimann and Lee W. Smith. First of 2 survey articles on optometrists' demographic and professional characteristics. Data are from 2,275 responses to a 1983 ASCO survey of optometry school classes graduated during 1979-81, and from a 1978 survey of approximately 22,000 practicing optometrists conducted by American Optometric Assn.

Includes 7 tables showing number of respondents practicing optometry, by State, 1978 and 1983 surveys; and 1983 survey respondents, by sex and type of employment (self-employed, salaried in clinical and nonclinical setting, and other), and by incidence of referrals to and from selected health professionals and others, with detail for each graduating class.

A3370–1.602: Winter 1985 (Vol. 10, No. 3)

SURVEY OF OPTOMETRY GRADUATES TO DETERMINE PRACTICE PATTERNS: PART II, LICENSURE AND PRACTICE ESTABLISHMENT EXPERIENCES

(p. 15-19) By Robert L. Bleimann and Lee W. Smith. Second of 2 survey articles on optometrists' demographic and professional characteristics. Data are from 2,275 responses to a 1983 ASCO survey of optometry school classes graduated during 1979-81.

Includes text data and 5 tables on respondents' licensure and practice experience, includ-

ing number of States in which a license was sought, practice location relative to licensure attempts, reasons for licensure failures, lapsed time between graduation and licensure attempts and between initial and current practice, and graduates temporarily or permanently lost to the profession.

ANALYSIS OF PHARMACOLOGY TRAINING IN SCHOOLS OF OPTOMETRY, MEDICINE AND DENTISTRY

(p. 20-25) By Marti Waigandt and Alex Waigandt. Survey article on hours of pharmacology instruction offered in optometry, medical, and dental schools, by subject area. Data are based on responses from 41 schools in 14 States to a spring 1984 survey. Includes 1 chart and 3 tables.

ANNUAL SURVEY OF OPTOMETRIC EDUCATIONAL INSTITUTIONS, 1983/84

(p. 26-30) Annual survey report, for 1983/84 academic year, on optometry school student enrollment characteristics and financial aid. Data are from a survey of 16 schools, conducted by the Council on Optometric Education of the American Optometric Assn.

Includes 6 tables showing the following, by institution, 1983/84:

a. Entering class grade point averages and number of students; and previous higher educational attainment of 1st-year students (years of study completed or degree earned).

b. Enrolled students by sex and minority group (black, Spanish surname, American Indian, Asian American, and foreign national); percent of students receiving financial aid and student loans; and annual student expenditures; mostly by student year level.

A3372
Association of
Schools of Public Health

A3372–3   U.S. SCHOOLS OF PUBLIC HEALTH DATA REPORT on Applicants, Students, Graduates, and Expenditures, 1983/84, with Trends Analysis for 1974/75-1983/84
Annual. Sept. 1985.
vi+68 p.
SRI/MF/complete

Annual report, by Judith H. Magee, on characteristics of applicants, students (newly enrolled and total), and graduates, for accredited schools of public health, by institution, 1983/84, with trends from as early as 1958.

Includes selected detail by sex, U.S. vs. foreign citizenship, race, ethnicity (American Indian, Asian, and Hispanic), full- and part-time enrollment status, area of specialization, highest previous degree, and degree earned or planned.

Also includes data on school expenditures by object and by source of funds (including Federal grants and student aid), shown by institution code number only, FY84, with trends from FY75.

Data were compiled by ASPH Data Center from reports of all 23 accredited schools of public health.

Contains contents/table listing (p. i-ii); preface and notes (p. iii-vi); and 5 report sections, with 57 tables (p. 1-68).

Availability: Association of Schools of Public Health, 1015 15th St., NW, Suite 404, Washington DC 20005, ‡, price upon request; SRI/MF/complete.

A3376
Association of
Theological Schools
in the U.S. and Canada

A3376–1   FACT BOOK ON THEOLOGICAL EDUCATION for the Academic Year 1984/85
Annual. [1985.] xii+164 p.
SRI/MF/complete

Annual report, by William L. Baumgaertner, on U.S. and Canadian theological school enrollment, professional staff, graduates, finances, and library operations, 1984/85 and trends.

Data are from reports submitted by 197 member schools.

Contains table listing and introduction (p. ii-xii); narrative report, interspersed with 39 tables described below (p. 1-45); and appendices, with 85 tables also described below (p. 46-164).

This is the 16th annual edition of the report. SRI coverage begins with this edition.

Availability: Association of Theological Schools in the U.S. and Canada, 42 E. National Rd., PO Box 130, Vandalia OH 45377, $15.00; SRI/MF/complete.

TABLES:
[Data by race/ethnicity are generally shown for blacks, Hispanics, Pacific/Asian Americans, and Native Americans. Personnel compensation data exclude Roman Catholic schools.]

A3376–1.1: Main Report
[Data are shown for various calendar or academic years 1968-85.]

a. Enrollment by degree level and program type, by sex and race/ethnicity; women and black graduates by degree level, and women ordination degree graduates by denomination; professional and doctoral graduates, by program; and percent change in enrollment by school size. Tables 1-21. (p. 1-24)

b. Administrative personnel and part- and full-time faculty by sex, and library personnel; black and women's professional employment, by position; and personnel compensation by position and school accreditation status. Tables 22-37. (p. 25-39)

c. Revenues, expenditures, and surplus or deficit; and average revenues by source and expenditures by function, per student, by school accreditation status. Tables 38-39. (p. 42-43)

A3376–1.2: Appendix Tables
[Most data are shown by school denomination, size, university relationship (integral or independent), cluster affiliation, accreditation status, racial character (primarily black or white), and highest degree offered, and by U.S. region and for Canada.]

a. Enrollment (total and FTE) by degree program, by institution, various years 1956-84; enrollment by race/ethnicity and for women, by program, and professional and graduate enrollment, fall 1984; and total and minority students completing programs, 1983/84. Tables A-M. (p. 46-115)

b. Personnel by sex and race, by position, with full- and part-time status of faculty and library staff, fall 1984; and revenues by source and expenditures by function (total and excluding Roman Catholic schools), 1983/84. Tables O-JJ.2. (p. 116-141)

c. Library book/periodical expenditures (total and per student and faculty member); and book, periodical, and microform holdings, with detail for periodicals acquired by subscription and as gifts; 1983/84. Tables KK-MM. (p. 142)

d. Compensation averages by position, including contract salary, housing allowance, additional benefits, and pension; and total compensation ranges and averages; 1984/85. Tables NN-VV. (p. 143-157)

e. Gift/grant income ranges and averages, by type, with detail for operations and capital purposes income; 1983/84. Tables WW.1-WW.7. (p. 158-164)

A3380
Atomic Industrial Forum

A3380–1 **NUCLEAR POWER FACTS AND FIGURES**
Annual. Apr. 1985. 15 p.
LC sn85-24038.
SRI/MF/complete, current & previous year reports

Annual report on U.S. and world nuclear power industry, including data on reactors and capacity, electrical generation and costs, uranium resources, and employment, 1984 with selected trends from 1950 and projections to 2005. Also includes some comparisons to other types of energy.

Data are from DOE, Atomic Industrial Forum, Institute of Nuclear Power Operations, OECD, and International Atomic Energy Agency.

Contains 22 tables, listed below (p. 1-17).

Previous edition, published in 1984, was also reviewed during 1985 and is also available on SRI microfiche under this number [Annual. Mar. 1984. 17 p. †]. Previous edition is substantially similar in format and content, but also includes data on U.S. reactor orders.

Report has been published since 1975. SRI coverage begins with the 1984 edition.

Availability: Atomic Industrial Forum, Publications, 7101 Wisconsin Ave., Bethesda MD 20814-4805, †; SRI/MF/complete.

TABLES:

A3380–1.1: U.S. Data
[All tables except table [2] show U.S. data.]
REACTORS

[1] Status of nuclear power plants [number and capacity of reactors operable, with construction permits, and on order], as of Jan. 1, 1985. (p. 1)

[2] Status of nuclear power plants outside the U.S. [number and capacity of reactors operable, under construction, on order, and planned], as of Jan. 1, 1985. (p. 1)

[3] Nuclear milestones [text data on reactor status and generating capacity], 1984. (p. 1)

[4] Manufacturers of operating reactors [number of reactors, by type and manufacturer (no date)]. (p. 1)

OPERATING DATA

[5-6] Energy production and consumption by [type of fuel], 1950-84. (p. 2-3)

[7-8] Installed electrical generating capacity by prime mover, and generation by [type of fuel], 1950-84. (p. 4-5)

[9] Nuclear electrical capacity and generation and share of total energy production [1957-84, 1990, and 1995]. (p. 6)

[10] State and regional [census division] electrical generation by nuclear power [with rankings by nuclear share of total kWh generated], 1984. (p. 7)

[11] Average lead time for nuclear power plants [number of units, capacity, and duration of 4 pre-operational stages] by year of commercial operation, 1970-84. (p. 8)

[12] Profile of reactors going into commercial operation [units and capacity added per year and cumulative], 1984-91. (p. 8)

[13] Average electrical generating costs and power plant performance, 1983 [shows number of units, generating capacity and cost (with cost detail for capital, fuel, and operation/maintenance), and 3 performance measures, all for nuclear, coal, and oil units, by year of initial commercial operation]. (p. 9)

EMPLOYMENT

[14] Employment requirements in the nuclear power industry [by occupation], current [employment and vacancies 1984] and projected [positions 1994]. (p. 10)

[15] Employment in the nuclear energy field by occupation [for private, government, and government contract sectors], 1983. (p. 11)

URANIUM RESOURCES

[16] Forecast of domestic uranium requirements [selected years 1983-2000]. (p. 12)

[17] Uranium resources [reasonably assured and estimated additional, by recovery cost category], as of Dec. 31, 1983. (p. 12)

[18] Domestic uranium produced in [New Mexico, Wyoming, Texas, and aggregate 6 other States], 1983. (p. 12)

A3380–1.2: World Data
[Tables [1-2] and [4] show data for various years 1983-2005, and include nuclear share of total electrical capacity and/or generation.]

[1-2] World nuclear electrical capacity and generation; and nuclear electrical generation in OECD [by country]. (p. 13)

[3] World uranium resources [reasonably assured and estimated additional, by recovery cost category, by country and continent, as of Jan. 1, 1983]. (p. 14)

[4] Nuclear generating capacity outside the U.S. [by country]. (p. 15)

A3425
Bank Administration Institute

A3425–1 **1983 SURVEY OF THE CHECK COLLECTION SYSTEM**
Annual. 1984. xiii + 141 p.
Rpt. No. 6283.
LC 77-77478.
SRI/MF/complete, delayed

Annual survey report, by Michael T. Curtiss, analyzing commercial bank check collection and processing system performance and labor productivity, 1983, with comparisons from 1979.

Covers system performance measures, including incidence of rejected items, transit returns and holdovers, and free/lost, missent/miscoded, and exception items; labor productivity measures for various check collection/processing activities; and check truncation methods.

Also includes dollar value analysis of return and exception items.

Data are generally shown for 16 regions, each identified by a major city.

Data are based on responses of 138 banks to a Bank Administration Institute survey covering the week of Nov. 14-19, 1983.

Contains contents and table listings (p. v-xiii); analysis of survey results, with illustrative charts and text tables (p. 1-52); and appendices, with survey questionnaire facsimile, 62 detailed tables, and selected respondent comments (p. 53-141).

This is the 13th annual survey.

Availability: Bank Administration Institute, 60 Gould Center, Rolling Meadows IL 60008, members $24.00, nonmembers $36.00; SRI/MF/complete, delayed shipment in Feb. 1986.

A3425–2 **U.S. BANK PERFORMANCE PROFILE**
Annual. 1985.
123 p. no paging.
Rpt. No. 1204.
ISBN 1-55520-004-4.
SRI/MF/complete, delayed

Annual report presenting 70 financial and operating performance ratios for banks, by bank asset size and State, 1984. Data are based on periodic reports filed with Federal regulatory authorities by 14,464 insured banks. Number of reporting banks is specified for each asset size class and State.

Purpose of report is to enable individual banks to compare their performance with that of banks of similar size and location.

Contains introduction and methodology, 5 trend charts, and ratio definitions (8 p.); 1 table (repeated for each of 6 asset size classes, all banks, and each State) showing bottom and top percentile, median, and lower and upper quartile ratios, and 1 additional table (repeated for each State) showing median ratios for each asset size class (110 p.); and appendix, with ratio formulas (5 p.).

Both tables show ratios in the following categories: operating performance (13 ratios); yields and rates (6 ratios); asset quality (5 ratios); classified loans (6 ratios); interest sensitivity (4 ratios); liquidity (4 ratios); sources and uses of funds (21 ratios); capital position (5 ratios); growth statistics (4 ratios); and off balance sheet commitments/contingencies (2 ratios).

This series began in 1973. Customized analyses of operating ratios for individual banks or groups of banks may be ordered from the issuing agency but are not covered in SRI.

Availability: Bank Administration Institute, 60 Gould Center, Rolling Meadows IL 60008, members $50.00, nonmembers $75.00; SRI/ MF/complete, delayed shipment in Oct. 1986.

A3425–3 1983 SURVEY OF THE ELECTRONIC FUNDS TRANSFER TRANSACTION SYSTEM
Annual. [1985.]
74 p. var. paging.
Rpt. No. 6473.
LC 80-67016.
SRI/MF/complete, delayed

Annual report, by Karen Kimsey Sward, on banking industry use of electronic funds transfer, by region, 1983 and trends. Report focuses on automated clearinghouses (ACH), which move debit and credit transactions among financial institutions, and automated teller machines (ATM).

Data are from a survey of electronic transactions at 107 banks during the week of Nov. 14-20, 1983, with selected comparisons to 1980-82 surveys. Purpose of the report is to enable individual financial institutions to compare their electronic funds transfer experience with that of other institutions.

Contains contents and table listings (p. v-vii); introduction and highlights (p. 3-4); ACH and ATM findings, with 23 tables listed below (p. 5-50); and appendices A-C, with sample questionnaire, map, 1 table showing respondents by region, and respondent comments (17 p.)

This is the 6th annual survey.

Availability: Bank Administration Institute, 60 Gould Center, Rolling Meadows IL 60008, members $24.00, nonmembers $36.00; SRI/ MF/complete, delayed shipment in May 1986.

TABLES:
[Tables generally show data by 16 regions, each identified by a major city. All data are shown for 1983; most tables include comparative data for 1982 or 1980-82.]

ACH TRANSACTIONS
[All tables begin "Percent of..."]

1-3. ACH debits and credits sent and received, and items sent vs. received. (p. 6-9)

4-5. ACH items returned of items sent and received. (p. 11-12)

6-7. ACH debit transactions sent and received, by type of transaction [insurance premiums, home mortgages, telephone bill payments, and corporate and other payments]. (p. 13-16)

ATM TRANSACTIONS
[ATM transaction types include cash withdrawals from checking, savings, and credit cards; checking and savings deposits; bill payments; and balance inquiries.

Locations are main offices, branches, and off-premise. Installation types include lobby, vestibule, through-the-wall, drive-up, free-standing, university/college, shopping center, grocery/retail store, office/corporate complex, and hospital.]

8-12, A, and 13. Percent and average dollar value of proprietary and interchange ATM

transactions; total dollar value of proprietary ATM activity [not by region]; and average weekly transactions per proprietary and interchange ATM unit; [all by type of transaction]. (p. 18-33)

14-15. Number of weekly proprietary and interchange transactions per ATM unit [by] location [and installation type]. (p. 34-39)

16-17. ATM units and installation plans [percents by type of installation and location]. (p. 40-45)

18. On-line vs. off-line ATM units. (p. 46)

19-21. Service charge: [percent of institutions levying charge for ATM use]; structure of types of fees; and comparison ATM transactions and DDA [demand deposited accounting] paper items [whether charge is higher, lower, or same]. (p. 47-49)

22. Active ATM access cards [percent of proprietary annd local/regional network card-holding customers using ATM at least once a month]. (p. 50)

A3425–4 1984 BAI BANK CASH COMPENSATION SURVEY
Annual. 1984.
xiii+265 p. no paging.
Rpt. No. 4134.
ISSN 0194-0759.
LC sc85-4280.
SRI/MF/complete, delayed

Annual report, by Andrew M. Mosko, on bank employee salaries, by bank asset size and census division, 1984. Includes mean and median base salary with change from 1983, salary range, number of reporting banks and incumbents, and banks giving incentive awards and amount of average award, for 89 officer-level and other positions.

Also includes officers' mean age, years of service and in present position, and employees supervised.

Data are based on 1,758 responses to a Mar.-June 1984 survey of Bank Administration Institute member banks, ranging in asset size from under $20 million to over $1 billion.

Contains contents listing and introduction (p. v-xiii); and 1 table repeated for all banks by asset size, and by census division and asset size (265 p.).

This is the 11th survey.

Availability: Bank Administration Institute, 60 Gould Center, Rolling Meadows IL 60008, members $50.00, nonmembers $75.00; SRI/ MF/complete, delayed shipment in Dec. 1985.

A3470
Bicycle Manufacturers Association of America

A3470–1 1984 BICYCLE MARKET IN REVIEW
Annual. [1985.]
23 p. no paging.
SRI/MF/complete

Annual report on domestic shipments and imports of bicycles, by type, 1984 and trends. Presents the following data, various years 1975-84:

a. Total and import market, with detail for lightweight and 20-inch bicycles; import and domestic market shares; imports by country of origin (with average dollar value for lightweight and 20-inch models); and imports by month and quarter.

b. Domestic shipments, with detail for boys' and girls' models and by hub type, quarter, and purchaser type (national distributor, wholesaler/jobber, regional chain, other retailer/ bike shop, and discount store).

Data are from Bicycle Manufacturers Assn of America. Contains 16 charts and 3 tables.

Availability: Bicycle Manufacturers Association of America, 1055 Thomas Jefferson St., NW, Washington DC 20007, †; SRI/MF/complete.

A3675
Building Owners and Managers Association International

A3675–1 1985 BOMA EXPERIENCE EXCHANGE REPORT: Income/Expense Analysis for Office Buildings
Annual. 1985. vi+382 p.
LC 79-649602.
SRI/MF/complete, delayed

Annual report on U.S. and Canadian private sector and government office building income and expenses per square foot, by city and building characteristics, 1984. Covers income by source, including office and retail space rental; and expenses by detailed item, including utilities and payroll. Also covers space per tenant and worker, occupancy rate, and year-end rent.

Data are shown as median, average, and/or ranges, for major cities, with detail by building square footage and type of location (downtown or surburban). Also included are national analyses by building square footage, height, age, and type of location; comparisons for buildings surveyed 1980-84; and analyses for all-electric, single-purpose, medical, agency-managed, and financial buildings.

Report also includes detailed survey data on office building occupancy, by region and city, generally as of May 1, 1984.

Financial data are from a 1985 survey of 2,544 private and 544 government office buildings; other data are from an occupancy survey of 6,101 buildings.

Purpose of report is to permit building owners and managers to compare their operations with those of similar size and location.

Contents:

a. Foreword and contents listing.(p. iii-vi)

b. User information; methodology; and article on applications of report data, with 3 charts and 10 tables. (p. 1-15)

c. 4 statistical sections, each preceded by contents listing, with tabulations covering U.S. and Canadian private sector and government office buildings. (p. 15-356)

d. Appendices, including facsimile of survey questionnaire, Building Owners and Managers Assn activities, building area measurement methodology, and 1 table presenting results of office building occupancy survey. (p. 357-382)

This is the 65th annual report.

Availability: Building Owners and Managers Association International, 1250 Eye St., NW, Washington DC 20005, members $95.00, non-members $195.00, $5.00 shipping and handling; SRI/MF/complete, delayed shipment in Feb. 1986.

A3750
California Fig Institute

A3750–1 STATISTICAL REVIEW OF THE CALIFORNIA DRIED FIG INDUSTRY, 1984
Annual. [1984.]
19 p. no paging.
SRI/MF/complete

Annual report on California fig production, acreage, yield, shipments, utilization, farm value, and prices, 1983, with selected trends from 1944. Data are shown variously for fresh and/or dried figs, and include detail by variety and for merchantable and substandard production. California produces all commercial U.S. figs.

Also includes data on U.S. imports and consumption of dried figs and fig paste, by country of origin.

Data are primarily from California Crop and Livestock Reporting Service, California Dried Fig Advisory Board, and Federal agencies.

Contains contents listing (1 p.); and 18 tables (18 p.).

Availability: California Fig Institute, 1205 E. Olive, PO Box 709, Fresno CA 93712, †; SRI/MF/complete.

A3800
Carpet and Rug Institute

A3800–1 CARPET AND RUG INSTITUTE INDUSTRY REVIEW, 1983
Annual. 1985. 17 p.
SRI/MF/complete

Annual report on the carpet and rug industry, presenting data on shipments, PPI, materials consumed, and foreign trade, 1983, with trends from the 1960s. Most data are from industry sources and Census Bureau.

Contains preface, highlights, and contents listing (2 p.); 18 trend charts, including PPI from 1950 (p. 2-6); and 13 appendix tables, listed below (p. 7-17).

Availability: Carpet and Rug Institute, PO Box 2048, Dalton GA 30720, members $3.00, non-members $10.00; SRI/MF/complete.

TABLES:

[Most tables show quantity; dollar value is also frequently included. Tables show data for 1977-83, unless otherwise noted.]

1-2. Total industry shipments [by carpet type]. (p. 7)

3. Total industry shipments, quarterly analysis. (p. 8)

4-5. Total industry and broadloom shipments [1963-83]. (p. 9)

6. Carpet/rug fiber shipments [by type of material, 1980 and quarterly 1982-83]. (p. 10)

7. Carpet/rug exports and imports [1975-83]. (p. 10)

8. Carpet and total textiles balance of trade [1975-83]. (p. 11)

9-10. 1983 exports and imports of carpet/rugs by type [by country of destination and origin]. (p. 12-15)

11-12. Primary and secondary backing consumed [by carpet and material types]. (p. 16)

13. Housing starts and [shipments of] tufted roll goods/rugs larger than 6'x9' [1963-83]. (p. 17)

A3840
Chamber of Commerce of the U.S.

A3840–1 EMPLOYEE BENEFITS, 1983
Annual. Dec. 1984. 36 p.
U.S. Chamber Pub. No. 6794.
ISSN 0194-3499.
ISBN 0-89834-060-8.
LC 54-2030.
SRI/MF/complete

Annual report presenting detailed data on employee benefits, by type and industry, 1983. Includes benefit payments expressed as percent of payroll, cents per payroll hour, and dollars per year per employee; and percent of companies paying benefits; all by benefit type and industry group, with selected additional detail by region and company size (number of employees).

Also includes employee payroll deductions for insurance and pension plans, and average earnings (straight-time, overtime, holiday, shift differential, and incentive/bonus pay), generally shown as percent of payroll, by industry; and benefit trends from 1929, including actual expenditures for private pension and welfare plans.

Most data are based on survey responses of 1,454 employers, and are limited to employees covered by the Fair Labor Standards Act. Data on actual expenditures are from Commerce Dept.

Contains listings of contents, tables, and charts (p. 3); introduction and summary (p. 4-5); survey analysis interspersed with 4 charts and 21 tables (p. 6-32); and survey methodology and facsimile of survey questionnaire (p. 33-36).

This is the 22nd edition of the report; prior to 1979 reports were issued biennially. An historical overview of employee benefits for 1951-79 is described in SRI 1983 Annual under A3840-10. The historical overview is not available on SRI microfiche, but may be ordered from the issuing agency.

Availability: Chamber of Commerce of the U.S., Publications Fulfillment, 1615 H St., NW, Washington DC 20062, $17.50 (prepaid); SRI/MF/complete.

A3840–2 ANALYSIS OF WORKERS' COMPENSATION LAWS, 1985
Annual. 1985. viii+46 p.
U.S. Chamber Pub. No. 6803.
ISSN 0191-118X.
ISBN 0-89834-062-4.
LC 60-36379.
SRI/MF/complete

Annual report, for 1985, presenting detailed information on workers' compensation laws, by State, outlying area, and Canadian Province. Includes type of law (mandatory or elective), insurance requirements (including penalties for failure to insure), coverage, benefits, and claims administration.

Data are from legislative reporting services, insurance companies, and various government agencies.

Contains contents and table listing, and introduction (p. iii-viii); 3 report sections, with narrative summaries, 15 tables, and directory of workers' compensation administrators (p. 1-46); and abbreviations and methodology (p. 46).

Availability: Chamber of Commerce of the U.S., Data Processing, 1615 H St., NW, Washington DC 20062, $12.00; SRI/MF/complete.

A3840–3 1985 SURVEY OF LOCAL CHAMBERS OF COMMERCE
Biennial. [1985.]
5+53 p.+errata.
SRI/MF/not filmed

Biennial report on a survey of chambers of commerce, providing data on income, salary and benefits, organizational structure, membership, and programs, 1984. Report is intended to enable individual organizations to compare their operations with averages for other chambers in localities of similar income size and population. Data are from responses of 824 organizations to a 1985 survey.

Contains foreword and index of tables (5 p.); and report, in 2 parts, as follows:

Part I. 11 tables, listed below. (p. 1-20)

Part II. Management salaries by total income, including the following data repeated by income size group: average, median, highest, and lowest total and membership income, payroll, employees, and salaries; top 10 salaries of chief executives; and percent of organizations offering each of 10 specified benefits. Data on salaries and benefits are shown by management position. (p. 21-49)

Also includes list of organizations represented in 1985 survey.

Biennial report alternates with a less comprehensive interim report. Biennial report for 1982, and interim report for 1983, are described in SRI 1983 and 1984 Annuals respectively, under this number.

Availability: Chamber of Commerce of the U.S., Office of Chamber of Commerce Relations, 1615 H St., NW, Washington DC 20062, $30.00; SRI/MF/not filmed.

PART I TABLES:

[Tables show 1984 averages by population size group, and include number of organizations reporting. For selected items, separate averages for top 10 organizations are included.]

[1] Income: sources and average amount [including total and membership income, 5 special project sources, and special funds]. (p. 1)

[2] Income from government, services [and publications], foundations, and reserve [or contingency] funds [by source]. (p. 2)

[3] Salaries and [10] fringe benefits for [19 positions of] management level personnel [with average percent increase in salary]. (p. 3-8)

[4] Payroll, staff, and personnel procedures [including salary review, holidays, vacation, and sick leave]. (p. 8)

[5] Finance and membership [including membership rates, number and average value of membership accounts, cost of service per member, percent of accounts lost, revenue lost due to lost accounts, change in number of accounts, method of reimbursing salespeople, and member recruitment methods]. (p. 9-10)

[6] Board of directors: terms of office, election procedure, and meetings. (p. 11)

[7] Board of directors orientation [including time spent and supplies provided], and organization structure [including membership activity and meeting attendance]. (p. 12)

[8] Building and quarters [whether owned or rented, location, size, and facilities]; and data processing [arrangement (own, rent, free time, and service bureau) and functional uses]. (p. 13)

[9] Member and public relations [including methods of communication with members, and media used]. (p. 14)

[10] Program of work [how developed, members involved, and activities (including political action committees)]. (p. 15)

[11] Business classification information: dues income and membership accounts [by type of business]. (p. 16-20)

A3840–6   ECONOMIC OUTLOOK: Chamber of Commerce of the U.S.

Monthly. Approx. 20 p.
SRI/MF/complete, shipped quarterly

Monthly report (with occasional combined issues) presenting forecasts and/or recent trends for approximately 50 economic indicators. Data are from U.S. Chamber of Commerce Forecast Section.

Issues generally contain narrative summary and/or feature articles on economic outlook, often with illustrative charts or tables, and occasionally with more substantial data; and 2 monthly economic indicator tables, accompanied by forecast assumptions.

Monthly tables are described below and appear in all issues. All additional features with substantial statistical content are described, as they appear, under "Statistical Features." Non-statistical features are not covered.

Availability: Chamber of Commerce of the U.S., Forecast Section, 1615 H St., NW, Washington DC 20062, $60.00 per yr., single copy $7.50; SRI/MF/complete, shipped quarterly.

Issues reviewed during 1985: Nov. 1984-Oct. 1985 (P) [July/Aug. 1985 is a combined issue].

MONTHLY TABLES:

[Table I shows most data as percent change, annually for previous, current, and 2-3 coming years, and quarterly for 7-10 consecutive quarters, usually through 1-2 coming years. Data through quarter ending 2-4 months prior to cover date are actual; other data are forecasts.

Table II shows data for current and previous month or quarter, specified for each indicator, and same period of preceding year. Data for most indicators are current to 1-2 months prior to cover date.

Table numbers and indicators may vary from issue to issue.]

I. U.S. economic outlook [including GNP, consumption, investment, trade, Government purchases, final sales, industrial production, business inventories, car sales, housing starts, unemployment rate, compensation, productivity, labor costs, GNP deflator, selected interest rates, profits from current production, and Government receipts and outlays].

II. Trends in commerce [including population, GNP, money supply, personal income and consumption expenditures, personal savings rate, employment, earnings, purchasing power of dollar, retail sales, service employment, purchases of service, airline traffic, corporate profits, capacity utilization rate, new businesses, business costs, PPI, Federal spending and debt, and goods/services trade].

STATISTICAL FEATURES:

A3840–6.601: Nov. 1984

U.S. INDUSTRIAL OUTLOOK

(p. 4-17) By Rajni Bonnie Ohri and Graciela Testa-Ortiz. Article, with 4 tables showing percent change in employment, output, productivity, real GDP, and real plant/equipment expenditures, by industry division and/or manufacturing industry group, various periods 1961-2nd quarter 1984.

A3840–6.602: Dec. 1984

HIGH GROWTH SCENARIO IS INDEED POSSIBLE

(p. 1-2) By Richard W. Rahn and Graciela Testa-Ortiz. Article, with 3 tables primarily showing percent change in real GNP, fixed investment, consumption, government spending, and productivity, for 7 economic recovery periods 1949-84 and projected (under high growth assumptions) for 1980-89 period. Most data are from U.S. Chamber of Commerce.

A3840–6.603: Jan./Feb. 1985

POLICY CERTAINTY WOULD MAKE THE CRYSTAL BALL CLEARER

(p. 1) By Richard W. Rahn. Article, with 1 table comparing accuracy of the following GNP forecasts for 1983-84: U.S. Chamber of Commerce, consensus forecast, and average forecast of major econometric models. Data are from *Blue Chip Economic Indicators*.

GIVING FREE TRADE A BAD NAME

(p. 12-15) By Rajni Bonnie Ohri. Article, with 2 tables showing percent change in U.S. imports and exports, for selected countries and/or world areas, 1984; and value of U.S. trade with Japan and Western Europe, 1976-83. Data are from Commerce Dept.

A3840–6.604: Mar. 1985

EUROPESSIMISM: FACTORS UNDERLYING WESTERN EUROPE'S ECONOMIC DECLINE

(p. 7-11) By Graciela Testa-Ortiz. Article, with 3 tables showing unemployment rate and percent change in real GDP, for selected European and various other countries or world areas; and components of U.S. net capital inflows and outflows; various periods 1981-86, with average unemployment rate for 1970s. Data sources include OECD and Federal Reserve Bank of St. Louis.

EAST ASIA ON THE MOVE

(p. 11-15) By Rajni Bonnie Ohri. Article, with 1 chart and 2 tables showing percent change in real GDP, 1983-85; and percent change in exports to and imports from U.S., 1st 8 months 1984 vs. same period 1983; for 8 East Asian countries, with GDP comparison to selected other world areas, 1970-82 period. Data are from IMF and 3 U.S. banks.

GROWTH OF PER CAPITA PERSONAL INCOME

(p. 19) Article, with 1 chart showing average annual growth rate of per capita personal income, by region, 1978-83 period.

A3840–6.605: Apr. 1985

PRODUCTIVITY CHALLENGE

(p. 3-7) By Graciela Testa-Ortiz. Article, with 3 charts and 1 table showing U.S. GDP per worker, and percent change in tax rates, business investment, and manufacturing and general productivity, with comparisons to GDP and manufacturing productivity of 2-6 foreign countries or areas, various periods 1950-83. Data sources include BLS and U.S. Chamber of Commerce.

MYSTERY OF THE DOLLAR

(p. 7-11) By Rajni Bonnie Ohri. Article, with 1 table showing exchange rate for 6 foreign currencies vs. U.S. dollar, 1970, 1980, and Feb. 1985.

CAPITAL COST RECOVERY AND TAX REFORM

(p. 11-14) By David R. Burton. Article, with 7 tables showing structure and capital cost impact of various proposed and enacted tax reform measures affecting capital cost recovery (no dates); and investment/GNP ratio, and percent change in fixed nonresidential investment, during selected economic recovery periods 1949-82.

A3840–6.606: May 1985

BUSINESS INVESTMENT STILL THE MAINSTAY OF OVERALL ECONOMIC ACTIVITY

(p. 1-9) By Richard W. Rahn and Graciela Testa-Ortiz. Article, with 6 charts and 1 table showing employment, housing starts, mortgage interest rates, consumer confidence index, fixed investment share of GNP, refiners' price for imported crude oil, and percent change in exchange rate and trade with 6 industrial countries, various periods 1980-87.

Data sources include Commerce Dept.

ECONOMIC IMPACT OF THE WHITE HOUSE/REPUBLICAN LEADERSHIP COMPROMISE BUDGET PACKAGE

(p. 9-10) By Graciela Testa-Ortiz. Article, with 1 table forecasting effects on selected economic indicators resulting from adoption of FY86 Federal budget compromise plan supported by Reagan Administration and congressional Republican leadership, 1986-87. Data are from Data Resources, Inc.

WHEN WILL THE LIGHTS GO OUT?

(p. 13-17) By Rajni Bonnie Ohri. Article, with 1 chart comparing electricity production growth rates, as projected by 4 organizations/analysts, various periods 1982-2000. Data are from *Public Utilities Fortnightly*.

SMALL BUSINESS OPINION POLL

(p. 20) Brief article on general outlook for small businesses, based on 274 responses to a survey of persons attending the 1985 U.S. Chamber of Commerce annual meeting.

Includes text data showing survey responses concerning small business growth, major problems, and participation in political areas; whether own company maintains government contracts; consumer attitudes toward business; Federal involvement in farm commodity prices; and proposed change allowing employers to hire teenagers for summer jobs at 75% of minimum wage.

A3840–6.607: June 1985

ECONOMIC STAGNATION AND GOVERNMENT GROWTH: SOME NEW EVIDENCE

(p. 5-8) By Ronald D. Utt. Article, with 6 tables showing government spending and taxes/fees as a percent of GDP; industrial production, employment, and per capita income indexes; and GDP growth rates; generally for U.S. and 6-10 other industrial countries, various periods 1965-84.

Data are from OECD, BLS, and Commerce Dept.

BOOSTING CAPITAL FORMATION AND TAX REVENUES: THE CASE OF CAPITAL GAINS TAX RATE REDUCTION

(p. 8-11) By William Orzechowski. Article, with 3 tables showing number and value of initial public stock offerings, and new funds raised by venture capital companies; market value of corporate equities; and capital gains and tax rates and revenues; various years 1959-83.

Data are from *Going Public,* Federal Reserve Bank, and NYSE.

A3840–6.608: July/Aug. 1985

TAX REFORM

(p. 1-7) By Richard W. Rahn. Article, with 1 undated table showing capital cost impact of selected proposed and enacted tax reform measures affecting capital cost recovery.

TAX INCENTIVES AND THE RATE OF INVESTMENT

(p. 10-12) By Ronald D. Utt. Article discussing role of tax incentives in encouraging capital investment by businesses. Data sources include Commerce Dept, Machinery and Allied Products Institute, and Labor Dept.

Includes 3 tables showing producers' durable equipment categories ranked by capital investment, 1979 and 1984; manufacturing productivity change compared to 9 foreign countries, various periods 1973-84; and impact of Treasury Dept's proposed capital cost recovery system on durable equipment investment, as estimated with 3 econometric models, 1986-90.

U.S. MANUFACTURING IS ALIVE AND WELL

(p. 12-16) By Rajni Bonnie Ohri. Article, with 1 chart and 2 tables showing top 10 industries ranked by employment gains; and production index and capacity change for various manufacturing industries; various periods 1970-85. Data are from BLS and Federal Reserve.

COUNTIES THAT DEPEND ON FARMING

(p. 20) Brief article, with 1 table ranking top 20 counties by farm income as percent of total income, 1975-79 period. Data are from Agriculture Dept.

SOUTH AND WEST HAVE FASTEST GROWING METROPOLITAN AREAS

(p. 20) Brief article, with 1 table ranking top 11 MSAs by percent increase in population, 1980-84 period. Data are from Census Bureau.

A3840–6.609: Sept. 1985

REGIONAL SURVEY, ANNUAL FEATURE

(p. 5-12) Annual article, by Rajni Bonnie Ohri, with 3 tables showing personal income per capita, percent change in retail sales, and unemployment rate, by census division, various periods 1983-May 1985. Data are from Commerce Dept and BLS.

For description of previous feature, see SRI 1984 Annual under A3840-6.504.

DEVELOPING COUNTRY DEBT: WE ARE NOT OUT OF THE WOODS YET

(p. 12-21) By Graciela Testa-Ortiz. Article on economic developments affecting debt-servicing abilities of developing countries. Data are from IMF, Morgan Guaranty Bank, and other sources.

Includes 5 tables showing trend in selected economic indicators, aggregated for indebted developing countries, major borrowers, and countries with debt-servicing problems, with detail for 8 Latin American and 7 Asian developing countries; and selected measures of the impact of external economic conditions on economies of 7 Latin American countries; various periods 1964-87.

A3840–6.610: Oct. 1985

U.S. ECONOMY: BRIGHTER DAYS AHEAD

(p. 1-6) By Richard W. Rahn and Graciela Testa-Ortiz. Article, with 3 tables showing trend in 10 economic indicators during recovery periods, 3rd quarter 1982-2nd quarter 1985; and estimated impact of House Ways and Means Committee tax reform proposal on rental price of investment and on 10 economic indicators, 1-5 years after implementation.

Data sources include Washington University Macroeconomic Model.

AMERICAN AGRICULTURE AT THE CROSSROADS

(p. 6-10) By Rajni Bonnie Ohri. Article, with 1 table showing distribution of farm debt secured and not secured by real estate, by type of lender, as of Jan. 1, 1985. Data are from USDA.

1985: THE YEAR OF THE VAT?

(p. 13-15) By Terree P. Alverson. Article, with 1 chart showing EPA hazardous waste "superfund" excise tax revenues, 1986-90.

A3870
Child Welfare
League of America

A3870–2   ANNUAL SALARY STUDY AND SURVEY OF SELECTED PERSONNEL ISSUES, 1985
Annual. June 1985. 35 p.
Rpt. No. AM-19.
ISBN 0-87868-244-9.
LC 64-4651.
SRI/MF/complete, delayed

Annual survey report, by Michael Botsko and Mary Ann Jones, on salaries paid by voluntary child welfare agencies, by position, with detail by census division and for Canada, as of Jan. 1, 1985, with selected trends from 1980. Covers executives, social workers, teachers, and other professional and administrative positions.

Includes distribution of employees by salary, and median and upper quartile salary levels, with additional detail by agency staff size, social workers' and teachers' educational attainment, and teachers' work setting (day care or institutional).

Also includes number of agencies, full- and part-time employees, and staff racial/ethnic composition (black, white, and Hispanic), generally shown for voluntary agencies and for local public agencies; and median salaries for public agencies.

Report is based on a Child Welfare League of America survey of 261 member agencies. The survey drew responses from 188 voluntary and 33 local public agencies. Most salary data are for voluntary agencies only.

Contains contents and table listings (3 p.); introduction (p. 1-5); 25 tables showing survey findings, and brief discussion (p. 6-33); and appendix, with facsimile questionnaire and 1 table on participating agencies by State (p. 34-35).

This is the 19th edition of the report. No 1984 edition was published. For description of 1983 edition, see SRI 1983 Annual under this number.

Availability: Child Welfare League of America, Research Center, 67 Irving Place, New York NY 10003, $6.00+$1.50 shipping and handling; SRI/MF/complete, shipment delayed until issuance of 20th edition.

A3900
College and University Personnel Association

A3900–1   1984/85 ADMINISTRATIVE COMPENSATION SURVEY
Annual.   Mar. 1985.
xi+130 p.
ISBN 0-910402-25-6.
LC 77-83796.
SRI/MF/complete, delayed

Annual survey report, by Forest C. Benedict et al., on salaries for 99 primary and 69 secondary administrative positions in higher education, 1984/85. Salaries are generally shown as 1st and 3rd quartiles and/or medians, by position.

Shows salaries for universities and 2- and 4-year colleges, by institutional control (public and private), enrollment size, and budget size; and for private independent and religious institutions, and 2-year technical institutes.

Also includes salaries for inside vs. outside hire; salaries and years of service by minority status and by sex; salary trends, 1981/82-1984/85; and distribution of salary ranges.

Data are based on responses from 1,574 of 2,894 institutions surveyed by CUPA, and reflect salaries in effect during fall 1984.

Contains contents and table listings (p. ii-iv); introduction, with sample characteristics, methodology, and definitions (p. v-xi); 58 tables for primary positions, and list of responding institutions (p. 1-85); 8 tables for secondary positions, and list of responding institutions (p. 87-108); and questionnaire facsimile, position descriptions, and special study order form (p. 109-130)

This is the 8th annual survey. Prior to 1977, surveys were conducted biennially.

Salary data on secondary administrative positions were previously published as a biennial supplement, discontinued with 1982/83 report (for description, see SRI 1983 Annual under A3900-3).

Availability: College and University Personnel Association, 11 Dupont Circle, Suite 120, Washington DC 20036, members $25.00, nonmembers participating in study $75.00, others $150.00; SRI/MF/complete, delayed shipment in Mar. 1986.

A3900–3   ADMINISTRATIVE COMPENSATION SURVEY SUPPLEMENT
Biennial, discontinued.

Biennial survey report on salaries for 39 secondary administrative positions in higher education, discontinued with 1982/83 report (for description, see SRI 1983 Annual under this number).

Data are now included in *Administrative Compensation Survey,* covered in SRI under A3900-1.

A3900–4   1984-85 NATIONAL FACULTY SALARY SURVEY by Discipline and Rank in Private Colleges and Universities
Annual.   Mar. 1985.
ii+36 p.
ISBN 0-910402-36-11.
SRI/MF/complete, delayed

Annual report, by Richard D. Howe et al., on faculty salaries in private colleges and universities, 1984/85. Presents average, high, and low salaries, and number of faculty and institutions represented, by academic rank, for 46 disciplines.

Data are from responses of 451 private institutions, representing approximately 40,000 faculty members, to a survey conducted by CUPA in conjunction with Appalachian State University.

Contains contents listing (p. ii); introduction and survey methodology (p. 1-7); and appendices, with listings of disciplines and participating institutions, and 1 table repeated for each discipline (p. 8-36).

This is the 3rd annual survey. For description of a related report on State colleges and universities, see A3900-5.

Availability: College and University Personnel Association, 11 Dupont Circle, Suite 120, Washington DC 20036, members $10.00, nonmembers $25.00; SRI/MF/complete, delayed shipment in Mar. 1986.

A3900–5   1984-85 NATIONAL FACULTY SALARY SURVEY by Discipline and Rank in State Colleges and Universities
Annual.   Mar. 1985.
ii+45 p.
ISBN 0-910402-35-3.
SRI/MF/complete, delayed

Annual report, by Richard D. Howe et al., on faculty salaries at State colleges and universities, 1984/85. Presents average, high, and low salaries, and number of faculty and institutions represented, by academic rank, for 46 disciplines; shown for institutions with and without collective bargaining contracts.

Data are from responses of 272 public institutions, representing approximately 60,000 faculty members, to a fall 1984 survey conducted by CUPA in conjunction with Appalachian State University.

Contains contents listing (p. ii); introduction and survey methodology (p. 1-7); and appendices, with listings of disciplines and participating institutions, and 1 table repeated for each discipline (p. 8-45).

This is the 3rd annual survey. For description of a related report on private colleges and universities, see A3900-4 above.

Availability: College and University Personnel Association, 11 Dupont Circle, Suite 120, Washington DC 20036, members $10.00, nonmembers $25.00; SRI/MF/complete, delayed shipment in Mar. 1986.

A3940
College Placement Council

A NOTE ABOUT CPC SALARY SURVEY

The *CPC Salary Survey* reports, covered in SRI under A3940-1 and A3940-2, track starting salaries and jobs offered to graduating college students over a 12-month period beginning in Sept. Data are based on a survey of 187 placement offices at 163 colleges and universities.

Each report includes the following data, presented in 4-5 tables: number of job offers and average salary offered, and 10th, 50th, and 90th salary percentiles, by field of study and type of employer for bachelor and master degree candidates, and by field of study for doctoral candidates. Data for bachelor candidates are also shown by job function. Data for master degree candidates include selected detail for candidates with and without employment experience.

Employer types include business (3 categories), manufacturing/industrial (12 categories), Federal and State/local government, and nonprofit/educational institutions.

A3940–1   CPC SALARY SURVEY: National and Regional Interim Reports
Annual series.   7 p. (national reports), approx. 20 p. (regional reports).
ISSN 0196-1044 (national).
ISSN 0196-1004 (regional).
LC 79-4046.
SRI/MF/complete, delayed

Annual set of 3 national interim reports issued in Feb., Apr., and May; and interim reports for 7 regions issued 5 times per year in Feb., Mar., Apr., May, and July. Data are shown for job and salary offers made during interim period since preceding report and cumulatively from Sept. 1 through 1st or 2nd week of publication month or preceding month.

Each report contains the data described in the note above. Regional data are presented in 7 regional issues, which also include comparisons to national data, and lists of survey schools in each region.

Reports issued during 1985 are listed below.

Issuing agency also publishes preliminary and formal national job and salary offer reports, and an annual report on employer plans for hiring college graduates, described in SRI under A3940-2 and A3940-3, respectively.

Availability: College Placement Council, 62 Highland Ave., Bethlehem PA 18017, members and subscribers to the salary survey package: national issues $10.00 each, regional issues $15.00 each; others inquire at issuing agency; SRI/MF/complete, delayed shipment in Dec. 1985.

REPORTS:

A3940–1.1: National Reports
Issues reviewed during 1985: Feb.-May 1985 (P) (Nos. 1-3).

A3940–1.2: Eastern College Personnel Officers
Issues reviewed during 1985: Feb.-July 1985 (P) (Nos. 1-5).

A3940–1.3: Middle Atlantic Placement Association

Issues reviewed during 1985: Feb.-July 1985 (P) (Nos. 1-5).

A3940–1.4: Midwest College Placement Association

Issues reviewed during 1985: Feb.-July 1985 (P) (Nos. 1-5).

A3940–1.5: Rocky Mountain College Placement Association

Issues reviewed during 1985: Feb.-July 1985 (P) (Nos. 1-5).

A3940–1.6: Southern College Placement Association

Issues reviewed during 1985: Feb.-July 1985 (P) (Nos. 1-5).

A3940–1.7: Southwestern Placement Association

Issues reviewed during 1985: Feb.-July 1985 (P) (Nos. 1-5).

A3940–1.8: Western College Placement Association

Issues reviewed during 1985: Feb.-July 1985 (P) (Nos. 1-5).

A3940–2 **CPC SALARY SURVEY: A Study of 1984-85 Beginning Offers, Preliminary and Formal Reports**
Annual series. Approx. 8 p.
ISSN 0196-1004.
LC 79-4046.
SRI/MF/complete, delayed

Annual set of 5 national reports on job and salary offers to graduating college students. Set includes a preliminary report issued in Dec.; formal reports issued in Jan., Mar., and July; and summer supplement issued in Oct.

Preliminary and formal reports show data for offers made from Sept. 1 through 1st or 2nd week of publication month (prior month for July report). Summer supplement shows data for offers made from early June through late Sept. All reports include comparisons to previous year.

Each report contains the data described in the note above A3940-1, accompanied by brief narrative analysis. Reports also occasionally include additional data. July 1985 formal report includes the additional data described below.

Subscription price includes an annual report on employer plans for hiring college graduates, covered in SRI under A3940-3. Issuing agency also publishes interim national and regional job and salary offer reports, covered under A3940-1.

Availability: College Placement Council, 62 Highland Ave., Bethlehem PA 18017, members †, nonmembers $105.00 (includes *Recruiting*); SRI/MF/complete, delayed shipment in Dec. 1985.

Issues reviewed during 1985: Preliminary report (for 1984/85 graduates): Dec. 1984 (P).

Issues reviewed during 1985: Formal reports (for 1984/85 graduates): Jan.-July 1985 (Nos. 1-3).

ADDITIONAL DATA:

A3940–2.601: July 1985 (Formal Report No. 3)
DATA BY SEX

(p. 4-5) Regular tables and illustrative chart on job and salary offers to bachelor's degree candidates by field of study and job function show data by sex, for Sept. 1, 1984 through June 7, 1985 period.

A3940–3 **RECRUITING '85**
Annual. Oct. 1984. 8 p.
ISSN 0272-2259.
LC SN 80-13783.
SRI/MF/complete, delayed

Annual report on employer plans for hiring 1985 college graduates, with comparison to hires of 1984 graduates.

Presents number of hires, by academic field, degree level, and employer type (3 business categories, 12 manufacturing/industrial categories, and nonprofit/educational institutions); and number of recruiting interview schedules, and campuses scheduled for recruiting, by employer type; actual/anticipated 1984/85, and actual 1983/84.

Also includes estimated Federal Government hiring, by degree level and entry position category, FY84-85.

Data are from survey responses of 399 private sector employers to a July 1984 survey, and from U.S. Office of Personnel Management.

Contains narrative summary, with 4 tables (p. 1-7); and employer classification definitions (p. 8).

Report has been published since 1970/71. It is available separately or as part of a package that also includes an annual series of survey reports on jobs and salaries offered to graduates, described in SRI under A3940-2.

Availability: College Placement Council, 62 Highland Ave., Bethlehem PA 18017, members †, nonmembers $10.00 (or $105.00 included in *CPC Salary Survey*); SRI/MF/complete, delayed shipment in Apr. 1985.

A3940–4 **INFLATION AND THE COLLEGE GRADUATE**
Quinquennial, with annual supplements. For individual bibliographic data, see below.
LC 82-119504.
SRI/MF/complete

Quinquennial report, with annual supplements, on average actual and inflation-adjusted salary offers to new college graduates in selected fields, for current recruiting year and trends. Covers detailed business, science, and engineering fields for bachelor's and master's degree candidates, and also humanities and other social sciences for bachelor's candidates. Also includes CPI trends.

Data are from College Placement Council's *Salary Survey* reports, covered in SRI under A3940-1 and A3940-2. Inflation adjustments are based on CPI changes.

Annual supplements update all tables in the quinquennial report. Most recent supplement is described below.

Availability: College Placement Council, 62 Highland Ave., Bethlehem PA 18017, $15.00 (for base report and annual updates through 1985); SRI/MF/complete.

A3940–4.5: Inflation and the College Graduate, 1983-84 Update
[Annual. [1985.] 4 p. SRI/MF/complete.]

Contains 1 extended table showing data for recruiting year 1983/84.

A4175
Copper
Development Association

A4175–1 **ANNUAL DATA, 1985: Copper, Brass, Bronze; Copper Supply and Consumption, 1964-84**
Annual. [1985.] 20 p.
SRI/MF/complete

Annual report on supply and consumption of copper and copper alloys in the U.S., 1964-84. Includes the following data:

a. Production, for copper mines by State, smelters, and refined copper; stocks and/or foreign trade, for ore, blister and refined copper, and scrap; and copper recovery from scrap.

b. Consumption of refined copper, scrap, metals, and alloying metals; and product supply, consumption by end use market, and foreign trade; shown variously for brass mills, wire rod mills, foundries, powder plants, and aggregate other industries.

Also includes data on copper mine production and brass mill product supply, by foreign country.

Data are from Bureau of Mines, Commerce Dept, American Bureau of Metal Statistics, and other sources, identified in each table.

Contains preface, table listing, and 1 schematic chart on the flow of copper in the U.S. economy (p. 1-5); and 24 tables, arranged in 4 groups (p. 6-20).

Availability: Copper Development Association, Greenwich Office Park 2, Box 1840, Greenwich CT 06836-1840, †; SRI/MF/complete.

A4325
Council for
Financial Aid to Education

A4325–1 **CORPORATE SUPPORT OF EDUCATION, 1983**
Annual. Dec. 1984.
1+17 p.
ISSN 0270-4501.
LC 80-644000.
SRI/MF/complete

Annual report on corporate contributions to higher education, 1983 and trends. Includes data by industry and marketing area, and comparisons to total corporate contributions, education contributions from all sources, and corporate earnings and assets.

Most data are based on responses of 503 corporations to a CFAE survey.

Contains contents listing and highlights (p. 1); report, with narrative analysis, text statistics, 2 charts, and 14 tables listed below (p. 2-15); and appendix with data notes (p. 16).

Report title has changed from *Corporate Support of Higher Education.*

Availability: Council for Financial Aid to Education, 680 Fifth Ave., Suite 800C, New York NY 10019, $10.00 (prepaid); SRI/MF/complete.

TABLES:
[Data are for 1983, unless otherwise noted. Tables VI-VIII and X-XI show data by major industry group.]

I. National trends in corporate pretax net income and [total and education] contributions [1968-83]. (p. 2)

II. Corporate support of colleges/universities in relation to total voluntary support and institutional expenditures [1968/69-1983/84]. (p. 4)

III. Percentage distribution of corporate contributions [to education, health/human services, culture/art, civic activities, and other, 1980-83]. (p. 5)

IV.A-IV.B. Company gifts, by type [cash/securities, company products, and other property, 1982-83]; and gifts of company products, by [selected] industry [total 1982-83, and to education, 1983]. (p. 5)

V. Structure of corporate contributions [to company foundations and others, and from company foundations; and number of companies with foundations; 1978-83]. (p. 6)

VI-VIII. Percentage of reporting companies with corporate foundations; foundation cash flow [in-payments, earnings, and grants]; and changes in market value of corporate foundation assets. (p. 6-8)

IX. Total contributions and support of education in relation to worldwide and U.S. only pretax net income and assets [1978-83]. (p. 9)

X. Support of education, 2 survey years (347 companies participating in both surveys) [1982-83]. (p. 10)

XI. Total contributions and support of education in relation to worldwide pretax net income and assets. (p. 12-13)

XII. Contributions by manufacturing companies, by size of worldwide pretax net income and assets. (p. 14)

XIII. Support of education, [total contributions, and worldwide pretax net income, for 21] major marketing areas. (p. 15)

A4325–2   VOLUNTARY SUPPORT OF EDUCATION, 1983/84
Annual. Aug. 1985.
79 p. Oversized.
ISSN 0363-3683.
LC 81-641373.
SRI/MF/complete

Annual survey report on voluntary support to educational institutions, 1983/84 and trends. Presents amount of support, by source, purpose, and form of giving; and enrollment, total expenditures, and endowment market value; all for individual institutions grouped by type, 1983/84, with summary data by institution type, and summary comparisons to 1982/83 and trends from as early as 1949/50.

Sources of support are alumni, parents, foundations, businesses, religious organizations, and other individuals and organizations. Forms of giving are bequests and trusts/pooled income

funds/annuities; annual fund (also including number of alumni on record, solicited, and donating); property gifts (company products, and other corporate and noncorporate gifts); and corporate matching gifts (also including number of gifts matched).

Purposes are current operations and capital purposes, with detail for restricted and unrestricted funds, property/buildings/equipment, and loan funds. Summary data are shown for specific categories of current operations, including compensation, research, library, and student aid.

Types of institutions are public and private 4-year (doctoral, comprehensive, general baccalaureate, and professional/specialized) and 2-year institutions; and independent elementary/secondary schools. Selected summary data are shown for private men's, women's, and coeducational colleges, and for boys' and girls' day and boarding schools.

Data are based primarily on survey responses from 1,622 institutions, and exclude income from invested funds and government sources.

Contains contents listing and preface, with 1 table on survey sample (p. 1-2); narrative report, with 22 tables (p. 3-74); and appendix, with 6 tables (p. 75-78, and inside back cover).

This is the 25th edition.

Availability: Council for Financial Aid to Education, 680 Fifth Ave., Suite 800C, New York NY 10019, $20.00; SRI/MF/complete.

**A4500
Council on Foundations**

A4500–1   PHILANTHROPY OF ORGANIZED RELIGION
Monograph. Feb. 1985.
xx+144 p.
SRI/MF/complete

Report on nature and extent of philanthropic activities of religious organizations, 1984.

Includes data on world areas of activity; characteristics of populations served; types of services provided; social issues supported; value of charitable gifts, with comparisons to foundations and corporate giving; involvement in grantmaking and loan/investment activities; staffing levels, with detail for full- and part-time salaried and nonsalaried workers; and monetary value of services provided by volunteer staff.

Selected data are shown by type of organization (including 7 specific faiths and denominations), and for domestic vs. international activities.

Characteristics of populations served include data by race and ethnic group (Hispanic, American Indian, and Asian American), and for children, the elderly, persons in poverty, the handicapped, prisoners/ex-offenders, homeless/runaways, refugees/immigrants, women, and veterans. Types of services provided include activities relating to education, employment, economic development, housing, health, and various social needs.

Data are based primarily on responses from 485 religious groups to an Apr.-May 1984 survey conducted by The Council on Foundations.

Contains listings of contents, charts, and tables (p. i-iii); introductory material and summary (p. iv-xx); narrative report in 7 chapters, with 12

charts and 10 tables (p. 1-103); commentaries (p. 104-112); and appendices, with facsimile of survey questionnaire, project descriptions, bibliography, and list of religious organizations administering grants (p. 113-144).

Availability: Council on Foundations, 1828 L St., NW, Washington DC 20036, $15.00; SRI/MF/complete

**A4530
CPC Foundation**

A4530–3   CAREER VALUES OF THE NEW LIFESTYLE PROFESSIONALS
Monograph. 1984. 121 p.
ISBN 0-914885-05-7.
SRI/MF/complete

By Sandra E. LaMarre and David M. Hopkins. Report examining work-related attitudes, preferences, and expectations of graduating college students, by student and school characteristics, 1982. Includes data on intended job-search techniques; immediate post-graduation plans; perceived factors necessary for career success; preferred job attributes; and attitudes toward job effort and performance relative to traditional "work ethic" values.

Also includes preferred frequency of performance appraisals, basis for raises, and forms of bonuses and benefits; importance of job vs. various personal demands; views on various questions of business ethics; and expected tenure with 1st employer, and number of employers during 5 years following graduation.

Most data are shown by student and school characteristics, including student's field of study, citizenship status, sex, age, race (Caucasian, black, and Oriental), religious preference, family income, marital status, and childhood environment (rural, small town, suburban, urban), and school's region, affiliation (public, private, and church), and location (urban, suburban, and rural).

Data are from 1,930 responses to a survey of graduating seniors at 50 4-year institutions, conducted by the authors during Mar.-June 1982.

Contains preface, contents listing, introductory statements, and methodology (p. i-xviii); 9 report chapters, with narrative analysis, 1 chart, and 53 tables (p. 1-111); and 4 appendices, with questionnaire facsimile, list of participating institutions, and sample characteristics (p. 112-121).

Availability: CPC Foundation, 62 Highland Ave., Bethlehem PA 18017, $14.95; SRI/MF/complete.

A4530–4   ORGANIZATION AND SCOPE OF COLLEGE RELATIONS AND RECRUITING
Monograph. 1984. v+255 p.
ISBN 0-914885-07-3.
SRI/MF/complete

By Gary J. Scott. Report on college relations and recruiting practices of employers in 14 industries and in government/nonprofit organizations, 1982.

Includes all or most of the following data for each employer category, with selected detail by company/organization size (number of employees): college relations/recruiting staff size, titles, and activities; interviewer training programs; average cost per hire; hiring changes and problems, and changes in traits of college graduates, over past and/or next 5 years; number of campus visits, interviews, job offers, and hires, during 1981/82 recruiting year; and campus selection criteria.

Also includes data on chief executive officers' involvement in and views on recruiting.

Data are based on responses of 577 college relations/recruiting managers and 88 chief executives to a fall 1982 survey.

Contains preface and contents listing (p. iii-v); overview, methodology, and discussion of findings, with 4 tables on chief executives (p. 1-14); survey findings arranged by employer category, with narrative summaries and 18 tables repeated for most categories (p. 15-245); and 3 appendices, with questionnaire facsimile and 1 table on sample characteristics (p. 247-255).

Availability: CPC Foundation, 62 Highland Ave., Bethlehem PA 18017, $18.95; SRI/MF/ complete.

A4575
Credit Union
National Association

A4575–1   CREDIT UNION REPORT, 1984
Annual. [1985.]
6 p. no paging.
SRI/MF/complete

Annual report on credit union finances and operations, 1984 and trends. Includes selected data by State and for Puerto Rico. Covers the following:

a. Total credit unions, membership, and value of shares/deposits, loans outstanding, reserves, and assets, selected years 1935-84; and credit union distribution, types of services offered, operating ratios, and employment (full- and part-time and volunteers), by asset size, 1984.

b. Data by State and for Puerto Rico: credit unions by type of charter (State or Federal), membership and ratio to population, and value of savings, loans, reserves, assets, share drafts, real estate loans, individual retirement accounts, and certificates, 1984.

c. Credit union share composition (regular, certificates, and drafts) and average dividend on savings, 4th quarter 1980-82 and quarterly 1983-84; credit union installment loans, auto loans, and savings, compared to other types of institutions, Dec. 1983-84; and interest rates for personal and auto loans, by credit union asset size, Dec. 1980-84.

Contains brief narrative, 12 tables, and directory of credit union leagues.

Availability: Credit Union National Association, PO Box 431, Madison WI 53701, †; SRI/MF/complete.

A4620
Direct
Marketing Association

A4620–1   FACT BOOK ON DIRECT MARKETING, 1985 Edition
Annual. Mar. 1985.
xii+302 p.
ISSN 0739-9464.
ISBN 0-933641-00-1.
LC sn82-20480.
SRI/MF/complete, current & previous year reports

Annual fact book, for 1985, on trends and developments in the direct marketing industry. Includes data on direct marketing use, sales, and costs; comparisons to other advertising methods; consumer characteristics, and purchases through and attitudes toward direct mail; and other topics. Data generally are current to 1983 or 1984; some trends from 1970s or earlier are included.

Data are primarily from Direct Marketing Assn, USPS, and other industry sources; and surveys of consumers and businesses conducted by various private research organizations.

Contains listings of contents, tables, and charts (p. ix-xii); 16 narrative report chapters, interspersed with text data, 31 charts, and 58 tables (p. 1-214); 7 appendices, with 24 charts and 54 tables, directory of assns, glossary, and bibliography of related publications (p. 215-288); and index (p. 289-302).

Statistical tables and charts are described below.

This is the 8th annual edition of the report. Previous edition, for 1984, was also reviewed in SRI during 1985, and is also available on SRI microfiche under A4620-1 [Annual. Mar. 1984. xii+302 p. members $49.95, nonmembers $79.95]. Previous edition was substantially similar in format and content, but included data on consumer mail order complaints to FTC; and omitted appendix data on catalog industry operations, mailing list tests, telemarketing, consumer mail order surveys, and special markets.

For description of 1983 edition, see SRI 1983 Annual under A4620-1.

Availability: Direct Marketing Association, Publications Division, Six E. 43rd St., New York NY 10017, members $49.95, nonmembers $79.95; SRI/MF/complete.

TABLES AND CHARTS:

A4620–1.1: Narrative Report Data

a. Consumer attitudes: types of mail order problems experienced, and advantages and disadvantages of mail order shopping, as reported by consumers in 1983. 2 tables. (p. 27)

b. Direct marketing scope: direct response advertising expenditures (including data by media and leading advertiser), billings of leading direct marketing advertising agencies, and sales volume of leading direct marketers, mostly 1983-84, with selected trends from 1977; and direct mail charitable contributions, by category, 1982. 7 tables. (p. 38-45)

c. Business-to-business direct marketing: cost of average sales call and business letter, and business/industrial direct marketing ex-

penditures and sales, various years 1969-85; business executives' recall of and response to direct mailings, 1980; characteristics of direct mail advertising in office equipment, printing, and wholesale/durable goods industries, various years 1979-81; and characteristics of typical catalogs, 1983. 2 charts and 7 tables. (p. 47-56)

d. Consumers: response to direct mailings, including factors that would influence consumers to buy more, 1978; consumers purchasing mail order items in past year, by product category and selected demographic characteristics, 1983; selected market demographic and economic trends and projections, various periods 1920-2000; amount, types, and disposition of mail received by households, various years 1972-78; and attitudes toward promotional mail, by sex, 1981. 23 charts and 25 tables. (p. 58-96)

e. Media: advertising expenditures and unit costs, by media, various years 1977-84; 3rd class mail volume, by mail classification, 1983-84; direct mail volume, 1977-84, and expenditures, 1984, by mail classification; and direct mail advertising expenditures, 1937-84. 7 tables. (p. 128-132)

f. Telephone marketing: consumer and business telephones and calls, and monthly distribution of interstate and intrastate calls, 1982; and telephone marketing expenditures, 1977-83. 1 chart and 4 tables. (p. 133-136)

g. TV: selected TV market data, including households with TVs, and average hours of TV usage per day; households reached by cable networks accepting advertising; TV viewing patterns of men, women, teenagers, and children; and homes with cable TV, for 50 market areas; 1983 or 1984, with TV household and usage trends from 1950s or 1960s. 4 charts and 2 tables. (p. 141-147)

h. Production costs: costs by component for producing and mailing 3 types of direct mail pieces, 1984. 1 table. (p. 168-168C)

i. Delivery systems: pieces of mail delivered, 1983-84, and postal rates, 1960-85, by USPS mail classification; and private postal systems, revenues, and pieces of mail delivered, 1976-77 and 1981-82. 1 chart and 3 tables. (p. 174-179)

A4620–1.2: Appendix Data

a. Industry statistics: median gross profit margin for mail order houses and selected other retail industries, 1982; consumers purchasing mail order items, by product category and selected demographic characteristics, 1983; and growth opportunities and problems cited by direct marketers, 1984. 1 chart and 3 tables. (p. 216-221)

b. Catalogs: distribution of catalog purchasers (heavy, medium, and light use) and nonpurchasers, by census division, area population size, income, family size, and household type, 1982; and catalog industry operations, including type of merchandise sold, production methods, media use, merchandise prices, catalog structure, ordering and return policies, and order incentives used, mostly 1983. 12 charts and 12 tables. (p. 222-229)

c. Publications: top 50 consumer magazines ranked by advertising pages per copy, and top 20 consumer and business magazines ranked by average subscription circulation, 1983; and circulation promotion activities of publications, including method used, 1981-82. 4 tables. (p. 230-233)

d. Seasonality of direct mailings: including distribution of mailings by month, for 10 mailing categories, 1979/80-1983/84. 11 tables. (p. 234-239)

e. Mailing lists: mailing list testing by direct mailers, including number of lists tested during past year, and testing criteria, 1984; and corporate use of mailing lists, by business category, 1982, with comparison to 1981. 5 tables. (p. 240-242)

f. Fund raising: percent of consumers opening fund-raising vs. other kinds of mail, with detail by sex, age, and region, 1981; and summary of State laws regulating charitable solicitations, including bonding requirement, by State, as of Dec. 1, 1984. 4 tables. (p. 243-248)

g. Telemarketing: consumer preference for shopping by mail vs. telephone, and reasons for not ordering from TV advertisements and not shopping by mail/telephone; socioeconomic characteristics of mail/telephone shoppers; and telephone shoppers' practices, including payment method and reasons for not using credit cards; fall 1984. 2 charts and 4 tables. (p. 249-250B)

h. Coupons: distribution of coupons issued, by media and face value, various years 1978-84; and grocery coupon redemption rates, by media, 1984. 2 charts and 1 table. (p. 250C-250E)

i. Consumer mail order surveys: types of advertising mail received by households, and types of mail order problems encountered, with selected detail by household income, Oct. 1982; and characteristics of mail order purchases (including source of information, type of merchandise, price per order, and purchaser characteristics), and consumers' attitudes concerning direct marketing, July 1984. 6 tables. (p. 250F-250I)

j. Special markets (elderly, youth, and women): selected indicators, including population age 65/over, 1970, 1980, and 1990; and college students' use of mail order catalogs, reasons for using catalogs, and types of merchandise ordered, 1984. 7 charts and 4 tables. (p. 250J-250O)

A4650
Distilled Spirits
Council of the U.S.

A4650–1   ANNUAL STATISTICAL REVIEW, 1984/85, Distilled Spirits Industry

Annual. Sept. 1985.
vi+60 p.
ISSN 0066-4367.
LC 54-17193.
SRI/MF/complete

Annual report on the production and distribution operations of the distilled spirits industry, 1984. Also includes data on public revenues, retail prices, and operations in license and control States, with selected historical data from 1933.

Data are from Bureau of Alcohol, Tobacco and Firearms; Census Bureau; Internal Revenue Service; and other Federal, State, and local government and industry sources.

Contains preface, foreword, and contents listing (p. iii-vi); 53 tables, listed below, with brief summaries and 16 accompanying maps and charts (p. 1-55); and glossary and bibliography (p. 56-60).

This is the 45th annual report.

Availability: Distilled Spirits Council of the U.S., Economics and Statistics Division, 1250 Eye St., NW, Washington DC 20005, †; SRI/MF/complete.

TABLES:

[Classes of distilled spirits include whiskey, brandy, rum, gin, vodka, and others. Generally, trends from the 1930s to the 1960s are shown for selected years, and other trends are shown annually.]

A4650–1.1:   Distillation,   Shipments, Stocks, and Withdrawals

DISTILLATION AND SHIPMENTS

1-2. Distillation of whiskey, brandy, and rum, 1934-84; and by month, 1983-84. (p. 3-4)

3. Direct distillation (partial production) of gin and vodka, 1934-84. (p. 4)

4. Whiskey distillation, by [selected] State, 1983-84. (p. 5)

5. Grain/grain products used by the distilled spirits industry: by type of grain, 1946-84. (p. 5)

6. Production of distillers' dried grains, 1946-84. (p. 6)

7. Shipments of whiskey barrels in the U.S., [annually] 1933-84. (p. 6)

8. Fruit/fruit products used by the distilled spirits industry, 1955-84. (p. 6)

STOCKS AND WITHDRAWALS

9-10. Stocks of distilled spirits at distilleries, by class, year end 1934-84; and apparent whiskey stocks, distillation, and usage, 1935-84. (p. 8)

11-12. Stocks of distilled spirits in bonded storage at distilleries, by class, month end; and whiskey stocks in bonded storage, year end, by [selected] State; 1983-84. (p. 9)

13-14. Taxable withdrawals from bonded premises at $10.50 per [proof] gallon [by month]; and tax-free withdrawals of distilled spirits, by usage; 1983-84. (p. 10)

A4650–1.2: Bottling, Sales, and Shipments

BOTTLING

[Tables 15-18 begin "Bottling of..."]

15. Distilled spirits: by class, 1940-84. (p. 12)

16-17. Whiskey and other distilled spirits, by [selected] State, 1984; and whiskey by type, 1939-84. (p. 12-13)

18. Distilled spirits, by class and type, 1983-84. (p. 14)

SALES AND SHIPMENTS

19-20. Estimated distilled spirits [domestic and imported] entering U.S. trade channels, including bottled exports: by class and type, 1975-84; and [for] domestic and foreign bottling, by class and type, 1983-84. (p. 15-16)

21-22. Sales of distilled spirits [gallons] and percentage distribution: retail sales in control States, and supplier shipments in license States (shipments by distillers/rectifiers/bottlers/importers), by class and type, 1984. (p. 18-21)

23-24. Red and green strip stamps used by the distilled spirits industry, by bottle size; and distilled spirits volume represented by strip stamps, by bottle size and stamp color; FY74-84. (p. 22-23)

A4650–1.3: Foreign Trade

25. U.S. commercial exports of distilled spirits [by class], 1975-84. (p. 25)

26. U.S. commercial exports of [whiskey and other] distilled spirits, by [country of] destination, 1983-84. (p. 26-27)

27-28. U.S. shipments of distilled spirits to Puerto Rico and U.S. Virgin Islands: [by class and container type], 1983-84; and by class, 1974-84. (p. 28)

29-31. U.S. dutiable imports of distilled spirits for consumption, by class: 1934-84; and by country of origin [by container size], and bottled and bulk, 1983-84. (p. 29-34)

32. Shipments of [rum and other] distilled spirits to U.S. from Puerto Rico and U.S. Virgin Islands, 1935-84. (p. 34)

A4650–1.4: Apparent Consumption, and Public Revenues

APPARENT CONSUMPTION

33. Apparent consumption of distilled spirits: in license and control States [includes wine and per capita gallons; number of States allowing sale of distilled spirits; and aggregate resident and adult population and per capita consumption; 1934-84]. (p. 35)

34-36. Apparent consumption of distilled spirits: by month, 1983-84; by State, 1975-84; and by State, total and per capita, 1983-84. (p. 36-38)

37-38. Adult per capita and total apparent consumption of distilled spirits, wine, and beer, by State; and apparent consumption of alcohol from distilled spirits, wine, and beer, by State, total and per capita; 1984. (p. 39-40)

PUBLIC REVENUES

39. Public revenues from distilled spirits of Federal, State, and local governments, 1961-84. (p. 42)

40. U.S. Federal tax collections from distilled spirits, by tax class, 1983-84. (p. 42)

41. Import duties on distilled spirits [by class and type], 1958-85. (p. 43)

42. Federal and license State excise taxes on distilled spirits [by State], 1933-85. (p. 44-45)

A4650–1.5: Miscellaneous

ECONOMIC DATA

43. Value added per employee-hour [for] distilled spirits and all manufacturing, and supplier price indices, 1967-84. (p. 46)

44. Consumer price, industrial production, and distilled spirits indices, 1967-84. (p. 47)

45. Estimated U.S. retail expenditures on alcohol beverages by type, 1949-84. (p. 48)

46. Alcohol beverage expenditures for personal and business consumption, 1959-84. (p. 49)

47. Estimated percentage of on- and off-premise spirit sales in control States [by State], 1983-84. (p. 49)

STATE AND LOCAL CONTROLS

[Unless otherwise noted, tables show data by State, 1984. Tables 50 and 52 arrange data for license and control States.]

48. Wet and dry population for consumption of distilled spirits. (p. 51)

49. Legal age to purchase distilled spirits; and number of counties or other political subdivisions permitting and prohibiting sale. (p. 52)

50. Number of retail outlets/licenses issued for the sale of distilled spirits; number of outlets/licenses per 1,000 population; and number of persons per outlet/license; [all for on- and off-premise]. (p. 53)

51. Summary of local option changes [wet and dry status changes, and counties gained or lost for legal sales, for 3 States]. (p. 54)

52. Legal minimum age for purchases of distilled spirits, July 1985; and legal age population, [as of] July 1984. (p. 54)

53. Number of States [by] legal drinking age [for distilled spirits, table and fortified wine, and beer (3.2% and over)], 1975-85. (p. 55)

A4650–2   1984/85 PUBLIC REVENUES FROM ALCOHOL BEVERAGES
Annual.   July 1985.
viii+88 p.
ISSN 0148-0863.
LC 77-642153.
SRI/MF/complete

Annual report on Federal, State, and local revenues from the sale, taxation, or regulation of alcoholic beverages, by State, beverage type, and revenue source, 1984, with comparisons to 1983 and selected trends from 1933. Includes data on tax rates, import duties by world area of origin, and State alcoholic beverage revenue share of total tax revenues.

Also includes Federal excise tax revenue collections, and tax rates as percent of price or cost, for selected commodities or services, FY84; alcoholic beverage consumption, by State, 1984; and number of States by legal drinking age for 5 beverage types, selected years 1975-85.

Data are from Federal, State, and local alcoholic beverage regulatory units, and other sources.

Contains preface, foreword, and listing of contents, tables, and charts (p. iii-viii); Parts I-III, with brief narrative summaries, 12 charts, and 24 tables (p. 1-36); and Part IV, with introductory summary and chart, and individual State profiles each with 1 table and accompanying text (p. 37-88).

Availability: Distilled Spirits Council of the U.S., Economics and Statistics Division, 1250 Eye St., NW, Washington DC 20005, †; SRI/MF/complete.

A4700
Edison Electric Institute

A4700–1   STATISTICAL YEARBOOK OF THE ELECTRIC UTILITY INDUSTRY, 1983
Annual.   Dec. 1984.
v+99 p.   Rpt. No. 51.
ISSN 0361-3607.
LC 82-641051.
SRI/MF/complete, delayed

Annual report presenting electric utility industry financial and operating data, 1983, with selected trends from 1963. Most data are shown by State and census division for total and investor-owned electric utilities.

Covers electricity production and capacity by type of prime mover and utility ownership; fossil fuel consumption and cost for electric generation; customers, sales, revenues, and average bills, by consuming sector; investor-owned electric utility construction and other expenditures, assets, liabilities, taxes, and employment; and overhead electric line circuit miles.

Also includes electricity production and capacity of top 15 countries; index of weekly electric power output; energy supply and disposition, by type of energy; public utility long-term financing and yields, by financing method; CPI and PPI trends; and industrial electric power cost as percent of product shipment value, by SIC 2-digit industry.

Data are from Energy Information Administration, and various other government and private sources.

Contains contents listing (p. iii-v); narrative review, and 1 summary table (p. 1-5); 10 statistical sections, with 15 charts and 90 tables (p. 6-94); and glossary, index, and 2 maps (p. 95-99).

Availability: Edison Electric Institute, Publishing Department, 1111 19th St., NW, Washington DC 20036-3691, $30.00, members 20% discount; SRI/MF/complete, delayed shipment when next edition is published.

A4700–4   ELECTRIC PERSPECTIVES
Quarterly.   Approx. 50 p.
ISSN 0364-474X.
LC 80-645213.
SRI/MF/complete

Quarterly publication reporting on business, regulatory, and technological developments concerning electric utilities. Data sources include Edison Electric Institute (EEI) and Federal agencies.

Issues contain feature articles, occasionally statistical; and regular editorial depts, including the following:

a. "Financial Review" section, occasionally statistical, including quarterly data on investor-owned utility finances.

b. "Statistical Review" section, with data on varying topics including utility costs and sales, and residential energy costs.

All features with substantial statistical content are described, as they appear, under "Statistical Features." Nonstatistical features are not described.

Availability: Edison Electric Institute, Electric Perspectives, 1111 19th St., NW, Washington DC 20036-3691, members $22.00 per yr., nonmembers $27.50 per yr.; SRI/MF/complete.

Issues reviewed during 1985: Fall 1984-Spring 1985 (P).

STATISTICAL FEATURES:

A4700–4.601: Fall 1984

FINANCIAL REVIEW: EARNINGS PER SHARE INCREASE 23 PERCENT; TOTAL ASSETS HIT RECORD $353 BILLION, UP 10 PERCENT, QUARTERLY FEATURE

(p. 37-40) Quarterly article, with 2 tables showing investor-owned electric utility income by source, operating expenses by type, net income, stock dividends, earnings per share, and assets and liabilities by type, for 12- and/or 3-month periods ended Mar. 31, 1983-84.

Data are national estimates based on unaudited reports from investor-owned electric utilities accounting for approximately 95% of industry assets and revenues.

STATISTICAL REVIEW: FIRST QUARTER SALES OF ELECTRICITY UP 11.3 PERCENT

(p. 45-46) Article, with 1 table showing the following for investor-owned electric utilities: customers, electricity sales, and revenues, by consuming sector, for 12- and 3-month periods ended Mar. 31, 1983-84. Data are from EEI.

A4700–4.602: Winter 1984

FINANCIAL REVIEW: EARNINGS PER SHARE UP 11.5 PERCENT; OPERATING REVENUES AT $28 BILLION IN SECOND QUARTER, QUARTERLY FEATURE

(p. 36-39) Quarterly article, with 2 tables showing investor-owned electric utility income by source, operating expenses by type, net income, stock dividends, earnings per share, and assets and liabilities by type, for 12- and/or 3-month periods ended June 30, 1983-84.

Data are national estimates based on unaudited reports from investor-owned electric utilities accounting for approximately 95% of industry assets and revenues.

STATISTICAL REVIEW: NUCLEAR AND COAL EQUAL IN 1983 GENERATING COSTS

(p. 44-47) Article comparing electric generating costs for nuclear, oil, and coal-fired power plants. Data are from responses of 135 utilities to a 1984 survey conducted by Atomic Industrial Forum.

Includes 1 table showing the following for nuclear, oil, and coal-fired plants entering commercial operation, 1970-82: number of units; generating capacity; capital, fuel, operating/maintenance, and other costs; capacity and availability factors; and forced outage rate. Also includes listing of surveyed plants.

A4700–4.603: Spring 1985

MANDATORY WHEELING: IS COMPETITION IN THE NATION'S BEST INTEREST?

(p. 2-11) By Douglas C. Bauer and Bruce S. Edelston. Article discussing mandatory electric power wheeling (access to utility transmission lines by nonutility sellers and purchasers of power). Data are from EEI.

Includes 2 tables showing kWh of wheeled power delivered by investor-owned utilities, quinquennially 1961-81; and number of wheeling service agreements on file with FERC, by type (no date).

FOREST DECLINE IN WESTERN EUROPE

(p. 12-17) By Robert A. Beck. Article on scientific debate in Europe concerning forest damage by acid rain. Includes 1 undated table comparing annual sulfate deposition for 3 West German regions, upper New York State, and Tennessee/North Carolina.

FINANCIAL REVIEW: EARNINGS PER SHARE DECLINE 3.0 PERCENT; CONSTRUCTION WORK IN PROGRESS UP ONLY 3.1 PERCENT, QUARTERLY FEATURE

(p. 30-33) Quarterly article, with 2 tables showing investor-owned electric utility income by source, operating expenses by type, net income, stock dividends, earnings per share, shares outstanding, and assets and liabilities by type, for 12- and/or 3-month periods ended Sept. 30, 1983-84.

Data are national estimates based on unaudited reports from investor-owned electric utilities accounting for approximately 95% of industry assets and revenues.

STATISTICAL REVIEW: SALES TURNOVER

(p. 36-37) Brief article, with 2 tables comparing the following for electric utilities and selected other industries: length of time required for sales revenues to equal assets, and assets per dollar of annual revenue, FY83 or 2nd quarter 1984.

A4725
Electronic
Industries Association

**A4725–1   ELECTRONIC MARKET
DATA BOOK, 1985 Edition**
Annual. 1985.
xiii+168 p.+errata
LC 72-627504.
SRI/MF/not filmed

Annual data book on electronic industry production, sales, R&D, foreign trade, and other operating statistics, by product, generally 1975-84, with selected trends from as early as 1966. Also includes data on DOD, DOE, DOT, and NASA budgets by function or program, FY86. Data are compiled from reports of Federal agencies, and EIA estimates.

Contains foreword, and listings of contents, tables, and charts (p. iii-xiii); introduction and summary, with 2 charts, and 1 table showing factory sales by industry group, 1975-84 (p. 1-4); and 6 chapters, with 36 charts and data maps, and 91 tables (p. 5-164).

All chapter tables, and selected maps and charts with substantial statistics not included in tables, are described below.

Availability: Electronic Industries Association, Marketing Services Department, 2001 Eye St., NW, Washington DC 20006, $80.00 (prepaid); SRI/MF/not filmed.

TABLES, MAPS, AND CHARTS:
[Unless otherwise noted, data are for U.S.; sales data show factory sales volume/and or value (with some additional detail for sales to dealer volume); and shipment data show factory shipment value.]

A4725–1.1: Consumer Electronics

a. Consumer electronic product sales, and number in use, by product type, 1975-84. 2 tables. (p. 5-6)

b. Video equipment and related data, including TV broadcast stations; production and/or sales of TV receivers, projection TVs, videocassette recorders, blank videocassettes, color video cameras, and videodisc players; videocassette recorder imports; and volume of TV receiver and videocassette recorder sales to dealers, by region and census division; various years 1975-84. 3 maps and 15 tables. (p. 6-16)

c. Audio equipment, including home and auto radio sales; audio system sales, by type; portable tape equipment sales, and player and recorder imports; and blank cassette tape sales; various years 1975-84. 6 tables. (p. 21-23)

d. Foreign trade in consumer electronics, by product type, 1975-84; and CPI for 3 consumer electronic products and all items, 1967-84. 3 tables. (p. 29-33)

e. Estimates of volume of sales to dealers and value of factory sales, for home computers and software, programmable video games, video game cartridges, videodiscs, compact disc players, and telephones and answering devices; and percent of households with various types of electronic products; various years 1980-84. 6 tables. (p. 35)

A4725–1.2: Communications and Industrial Electronics

COMMUNICATIONS

a. General, including communications equipment shipment summary, by type; and communications and communications carrier equipment shipments, by class and/or detailed type; 1975-84. 4 tables. (p. 37-41)

b. Telephone installed base market for key, private branch exchange (PBX), and Centrex systems, by type of telephone company ownership, 1979-88. 2 tables. (p. 46-49)

c. Broadcasting, including TV and radio stations, by type and operating status; total TV households, and cable TV systems, subscribers, and market penetration; and public safety and special service radio stations in use, by type; various years 1966-84. 4 tables. (p. 52-61)

d. Foreign trade in communications equipment, by type, 1983-84. 1 table. (p. 63)

INDUSTRIAL ELECTRONICS

e. Computer and peripheral equipment shipments, and industrial electronic equipment shipments and sales, all by type; and value and volume of demand for disk drives in U.S. and aggregate foreign markets; various years 1975-88. 3 tables. (p. 65-74)

f. Industrial equipment, including control and processing equipment shipments, by type; volume of producer shipments of industrial robots by type, with total shipment value; robot exports, production capacity, and capacity utilization rates; and shipments of testing and measuring equipment, nuclear radiation detection and monitoring instruments, and electromedical equipment, by type; various years 1975-84. 9 tables. (p. 89-105)

g. Miscellaneous, including industrial electronic equipment foreign trade; miscellaneous electronic systems and equipment shipments; distribution of worldwide laser industry parent companies, manufacturing, and consumption, by location (Japan, Europe, North America, and other areas); and worldwide sales of commercial lasers by type and application; various years 1975-85. 2 charts and 3 tables. (p. 107-113)

A4725–1.3: Government Electronics

a. Federal budget receipts and outlays, FY84-88; DOD budget authority and outlays, by function, FY86; and electronics-related portion of DOD appropriations for R&D, procurement of weapons systems/military construction, and operation/maintenance, FY84-94. 2 charts and 2 tables. (p. 118-120)

b. NASA, DOE, and DOT budgets, by function, various years FY84-86. 2 charts and 1 table. (p. 120-122)

A4725–1.4: Electronic Components

a. Summary of component sales by type, 1975-84. 1 table. (p. 124)

b. Electron tubes, including TV picture tube sales and foreign trade, with detail for color TV tube imports by country of origin; receiving tube sales and exports; power/special purpose tube sales; and electron tube foreign trade; generally by type, various years 1975-84. 11 tables. (p. 124-132)

c. Solid state product shipments and foreign trade, by type, various years 1975-84. 2 tables. (p. 134-135)

d. Electronic parts and other components, including resistor consumption; sales of capacitors, passive networks, and TV/FM radio accessories; shipments of switches, relays, connectors, quartz crystals, filters, coils and transformers, and wires and cables; and foreign trade; all by type, various years 1970-84. 13 tables. (p. 137-145)

A4725–1.5: General Information

a. Foreign trade in electronic products, by industry sector and country of origin and destination, with detail for major trading partners; various years 1980-84. 6 tables. (p. 149-155)

b. Employment in electronic industries, including employment by occupational group; total and female employment; and production worker employment, average earnings, and average hours and overtime hours; generally by SIC 3- to 4-digit industry; various years 1980-84. 2 tables. (p. 156-158)

c. Engineer and computer specialist employment supply-demand, with detail by specialty, 1987; and employment of R&D scientists/engineers by industry sector, 1984. 1 chart and 1 table. (p. 159-162)

A4725–2   ELECTRONIC MARKET TRENDS

Monthly.   Approx. 30 p.
SRI/MF/not filmed

Monthly report on electronic industry market developments in the consumer, commercial, government, and foreign sectors. Covers new products and applications; and trends in employment, price indexes, sales, and foreign trade.

Data are compiled by the Electronic Industries Assn (EIA) from industry publications, and reports of U.S. Dept of Commerce, other Federal sources, trade assns, and research firms.

Issues generally contain contents and table listing, and the following:

a. Feature articles, occasionally with statistics, usually on selected product categories, market sectors, or foreign markets.

b. Monthly EIA Statistics, with 8 tables on sales, employment, general and industry economic indicators, and foreign trade. Month of data coverage is 3 months prior to cover date.

Monthly tables are listed below and appear in all issues. All additional features with substantial statistical content are described, as they appear, under "Statistical Features." Nonstatistical features are not covered.

Availability: Electronic Industries Association, Marketing Services Department, 2001 Eye St., NW, Washington DC 20006, $150.00 per yr., single copy $15.00, combined subscription with *Electronics Foreign Trade* $225.00 per yr.; SRI/MF/not filmed.

Issues reviewed during 1985: Aug. 1984-Sept. 1985 (P).

MONTHLY TABLES:

[Tables generally show data for month of coverage and year to date, often with comparison to previous year. Tables [1-3] include 5-year trends.]

1. Electronic industries [factory sales] trends by industry group [consumer electronics, communications equipment, computers/industrial products, and electronic components].

2. [Production workers and total] employment [for consumer electronics, communications equipment, computers, and electronic components].

3. Government economic performance indicators: GNP; prices [CPI for TV, sound equipment, and all items]; production [PPI for intermediate materials and electronic components, and industrial production index]; and interest rates.

4. Factory sales of selected electronic products [home video equipment and electron tubes, by type].

5-6. Balance of trade; [and value of] bilateral trade [with 10] major trade partners; by [electronic] product group.

7-8. [Value of] imports and exports of electronic products [by type; prior to July 1985 issue, data were presented in 1 table].

STATISTICAL FEATURES:

A4725–2.601: Aug. 1984

MARKET OPPORTUNITIES FOR KEYBOARDS AS SEPARATE PERIPHERAL EQUIPMENT

(p. 1-5) Article, with 2 charts showing shipment value of total and membrane computer keyboards, with distribution by end-use sector, 1982.

A4725–2.602: Sept. 1984

SCIENCE/ENGINEERING JOBS GREW TWICE AS FAST AS OVERALL U.S. 1982 EMPLOYMENT

(p. 3-7) Article, with 1 chart and 1 table showing employment of scientists and engineers, with detail by field and for women, blacks, and Asians, 1982. Data are from NSF.

A4725–2.603: Oct. 1984

FLEDGLING COMPETITION IN THE COMPUTER STORAGE MEDIA MARKETPLACE

(p. 4-11) Article, with 1 chart and 1 table showing shipment volume for smaller Winchester disk drives by size (full and half height 5.25 inch, and sub 5.25 inch), and for floppy, rigid, and optical disks, various years 1984-94. Data are from *Electronic News* and International Resource Development Inc.

VOICE MAIL OFFERS BROADENING APPLICATIONS FOR TELECOMMUNICATIONS

(p. 12-16) Article on market outlook for voice mail processing systems. Data are from a survey of voice mail system owners, conducted by Venture Development Corp. Includes 1 undated chart showing reasons for considering a change in voice mail supplier.

EXPLODING DEMAND TARGETING FOR DIN CONNECTORS

(p. 17-19) Article, with 1 chart showing world shipment value for printed circuit board connectors, with distribution by type (European-developed DIN, modified DIN, and other), 1983 and 1988. (DIN are the German initials for the German Institute for Standardization.) Data are from Venture Development Corp.

A4725–2.604: Jan. 1985

FOREIGN DIRECT INVESTMENT IN THE U.S.

(p. 1-2) Article, with 2 charts showing number of direct investments in the U.S., by source country, and by recipient industry sector, 1983.

EIA TEN-YEAR FORECAST, BIENNIAL FEATURE

(p. 12-16) Biennial article forecasting DOD total and electronics expenditures through FY94. Data are compiled by EIA Government Division/Requirements Committee from market studies and interviews with defense market officials.

Includes 3 tables showing DOD budget outlays for military personnel; and DOD total and electronics budget overall growth rates, and outlays by purpose (operation/maintenance, procurement, research/development/testing/evaluation, and other); various periods FY84-94.

For description of previous article, showing data for FY81-92, see SRI 1983 Annual under A4725-2.402.

A4725–2.605: Feb. 1985

OVERVIEW OF DEFENSE ENVIRONMENT

(p. 13-16) Article, with 1 chart showing number of major new defense programs submitted to Defense Resources Board, and number approved, FY83-86. Major programs are those with R&D value of $200/more million and procurement value of $1/more billion.

A4725–2.606: Apr. 1985

DEFENSE TELECOMMUNICATIONS

(p. 10-12) Article, with 1 table showing value of DOD telecommunications market, for Army, Navy, Air Force, and other Defense agencies, FY84-94. Data are an EIA study.

A4725–2.607: May 1985

HIGH TECHNOLOGY: THE PUBLIC'S VIEW

(p. 5-11) Article, with 1 undated table showing public opinion on computer applications in business offices. Data are based on responses of 1,256 members of the general public and 400 business executives, members of Congress, science editors, and school superintendents, to a Louis Harris and Associates, Inc. survey conducted for Southern New England Telephone. Table shows survey responses for each group.

CURRENT TRENDS IN COMPUTER SOFTWARE

(p. 12-15) Article, with 2 tables showing microcomputer software sales, by application, 1983-84; and global revenues of software manufacturers, for packaged, custom, and integrated systems software, 1984 with percent change from 1983. Data are from International Resource Development Inc. and International Data Corp.

A4725–2.608: June 1985

LEADING IMPORTERS OF U.S. ELECTRONICS PRODUCTS FOR 1984

(p. 6) Brief article, with 1 table showing value of U.S. electronics exports and imports, for top 10 countries of origin and destination, 1984. Data are from Commerce Dept.

CONSUMER ELECTRONICS INDUSTRY ADDS $40 BILLION TO U.S. ECONOMY

(p. 15-16) Article, with 1 table showing consumer electronics industry direct and indirect impacts on the economy in terms of value added and FTE employment, for 12 product categories, 1983. Data are from Arthur D. Little, Inc.

COMPUTER SHAKE-OUT

(p. 16) Brief article, with 1 table showing number of computer dealer business failures, and total number of personal computer manufacturers, computer magazines, and major software producers, 1983 and 1985.

COLOR TELEVISIONS: A SUCCESS STORY

(p. 17-18) Article, with 1 table comparing the following for all households, those with 1 and 2/more color TVs, and those with no color TV: household size, income level, and age of household head. Data are from a Jan.-Feb. 1985 survey of 127,000 households, conducted by Market Facts, Inc.

A4725–3   ELECTRONICS FOREIGN TRADE

Monthly.   Approx. 65 p.
ISSN 0146-9231.
SRI/MF/not filmed

Monthly report presenting data on foreign trade in electronic products, by detailed product classification and foreign country. Data are compiled by EIA Marketing Services Dept mainly from U.S. Dept of Commerce reports. Report is issued approximately 6 weeks after month of data coverage.

Contains contents listing, notes, and 8 monthly tables listed below.

Availability: Electronic Industries Association, Marketing Services Department, 2001 Eye St., NW, Washington DC 20006, $150.00 per yr., single copy $15.00, combined subscription with *Electronic Market Trends* $225.00 per yr.; SRI/MF/not filmed.

Issues reviewed during 1985: Sept. 1984-Aug. 1985 (D).

MONTHLY TABLES:

[Tables show data for month of coverage and/or year to date. Product groups are electronic parts; electron tubes; consumer electronics; and communications, industrial, and solid state products. Detailed import and export data are shown by USITC and Dept of Commerce product classifications, respectively.]

[1] Balance of trade for electronic products [value of imports, exports, and trade balance, by product group].

[2] [Import and export detail by product classification: value and unit volume.]

[3] Bilateral trade [value] by product group, major U.S. trade partners.

[4-6] Imports and exports [value] by product group, major country suppliers and markets [with value and unit volume detail by product classification].

[7-8] 806.30/807 and Generalized System of Preferences (GSP) imports, by product group, major country suppliers [shows value of imports under provisions 806.30/807 (manufactured in U.S., further processed abroad, and reimported for completion, or assembled abroad from U.S. components); and under GSP (duty free products from designated beneficiary countries)].

A4725-4 CONSUMER ELECTRONICS ANNUAL REVIEW, 1985 Edition: Industry Facts and Figures
Annual. 1985. 62 p.
ISSN 0272-894X.
SRI/MF/not filmed

Annual report on consumer electronics industry developments, including production, factory sales, and trade, by product type, 1970s-84. Data are from the Marketing Services Dept of the Electronic Industries Assn.

Contains contents listing (p. 2-4); overview and history, with 2 trend charts, and 2 tables described below (p. 5-13); narrative report, interspersed with 3 maps and 36 tables, also described below (p. 14-50); and industry chronology, lists of available publications and trade assns, and glossary (p. 51-62).

Availability: Electronic Industries Association, Marketing Services Department, 2001 Eye St., NW, Washington DC 20006, † with stamped, self-addressed envelope; SRI/MF/not filmed.

MAPS AND TABLES:

[Data are shown for 1974-84, unless otherwise noted.]

a. Overview: factory sales by product. 2 tables. (p. 5-6)

b. Video: TV production and sales to dealers, for color and monochrome portable and console sets; distribution of sales to dealers by region,

for color and monochrome TV sets and videocassette recorders, 1984; projection TV production, factory sales, and sales to dealers, and videocassette recorder, color video camera, videodisc player, blank videocassette, and videodisc factory sales and/or sales to dealer, various years 1978-84; and TV stations in operation, 1960-85. 3 maps and 14 tables. (p. 15-28)

c. Audio: factory sales of portable/table, compact, component, and console audio systems, 1975-84; imports of audio tape equipment; audio tape equipment and cassettes, and car sound equipment sales to dealers and/or factory sales, various years 1980-84; radio production, including FM-AM/FM table, clock, portable, and car units; and AM and FM broadcasting stations in operation, 1960-85. 10 tables. (p. 29-38)

d. Computers, video games, and telecommunications: sales to dealers and factory sales of personal computers and software, programmable video games, video game cartridges, telephone answering devices, and cordless, corded, and total telephones, various years 1980-84. 8 tables. (p. 41-43)

e. Foreign trade and product use: imports and exports of color and monochrome TVs, home and car radios, phonographs, and audio and video tape equipment, and imports of car tape players; and consumer electronics products in use, and household penetration as of year end 1984, by product type. 4 tables. (p. 47-50)

A4745
Family Service America

A4745-1 STATE OF FAMILIES, 1984-85
Annual. 1984. 88 p.
ISBN 0-87304-212-3.
LC 84-18792.
SRI/MF/complete

Annual report discussing family life patterns, and social and economic factors affecting families. Includes illustrative data (primarily charts) on topics relevant to the status of families, for various periods 1959-95, with selected historical trends from as early as 1890 and population projections to 2010. Data topics include the following:

a. Population demographic characteristics; life expectancy, and time spent in education, work, and retirement; poverty status of minorities; and health care, crime, and education indicators, including crime rates by city size, functional incompetency rates among adults, and educational status of labor force.

b. Government finances, including composition of Federal payments to individuals, and sources of State and local revenues; computer and robot markets; and industrial production, GNP, and personal income trends.

c. Labor force characteristics, including age composition, employment and unemployment, participation of racial minorities and females (including mothers with young children), and job opportunities in selected occupations; and economic trends, including per capita personal income by census division, households by income group, and prime interest rate.

Data are from Census Bureau, BLS, and other private and government sources.

Contains contents listing and introduction (p. 3-5); 14 narrative sections, interspersed with 57 charts and 1 table (p. 7-70); narrative results of a survey of family service agencies concerning major family problems (p. 71-77); and directory of Family Service America member agencies (p. 78-88).

This is the 1st annual report.

Availability: Family Service America, 44 E. 23rd St., New York NY 10010, member agencies $7.00, nonmembers $10.00; SRI/MF/complete.

A4775
Federation of American Hospitals

A4775-1 BACKGROUND DATA ON CHANGES IN HOSPITAL EXPENDITURES AND REVENUES
Annual, discontinued coverage.

Annual report on community hospital expenditures and revenue trends, described in SRI 1983 Annual under this number. Because this report is no longer available to the general public, SRI coverage has been discontinued.

Inquiries regarding specific data may be made to Federation of American Hospitals, 1111 19th St., NW, Suite 402, Washington DC 20036.

A4775-2 STATISTICAL PROFILE OF THE INVESTOR-OWNED HOSPITAL INDUSTRY, 1983
Annual. [1985.]
37 p. var. paging.
SRI/MF/not filmed

Annual report presenting operating and financial data for investor-owned hospitals, with selected comparisons to hospitals owned by management companies, mostly for 1982-83.

Data are from 545 responses to an FAH survey of 1,051 investor-owned hospitals, and from the FAH *Directory of Investor-Owned Hospitals and Hospital Management Companies.* Survey data are extrapolated to represent the entire industry.

Contains contents listing (1 p.); highlights (p. i-ii); narrative analysis in 8 sections, with text data, and 13 tables listed below (p. 1-18); and 3 methodological appendices, with 4 tables on respondent characteristics (13 p.).

This is the 4th edition of the report. The 3rd edition was not described in SRI. For description of the 2nd edition, for 1981, see SRI 1983 Annual under this number.

Availability: Federation of American Hospitals, 1111 19th St., NW, Suite 402, Washington DC 20036, $12.00; SRI/MF/not filmed.

TABLES:

[Tables 1-4 are for all investor-owned hospitals, including psychiatric and other special care facilities, and show data by type of ownership (multifacility and independent). Tables 5-11 are for investor-owned acute care general hospitals only. Data are for 1982-83, unless otherwise noted.]

1-2. Growth of hospital industry, by [number of] hospitals and beds [also shown for nonprofit hospitals operated under management contract], 1978-83. (p. 2-3)

3. Hospitals by bed size. (p. 5)

4. [Number] of hospitals, by State, 1983. (p. 6)

5. Number of beds, by region and bed size. (p. 8)

6. [Percent of hospitals offering] selected services, 1983. (p. 9)

7. Comparison by licensed bed size of inpatient and outpatient utilization. (p. 10)

8. Utilization by type of payor [Medicare, Medicaid, other cost-based, and all other]. (p. 11)

9. Comparison by bed size of FTE employees per adjusted daily census. (p. 13)

10-11. Summary statement of income [and expenses; total and] on a per adjusted admission basis. (p. 14-15)

12. Revenues and expenses per adjusted admission, [and total admissions and hospitals, for] comparable management company hospitals. (p. 17)

13. Acute care general hospital acquisitions by the [aggregate] 7 largest hospital management companies [number of not-for-profit, city/county government-owned, and investor-owned hospitals and beds acquired], Jan. 1980-Aug. 1984 [period]. (p. 18)

A4875
Fibre Box Association

A4875–1   FIBRE BOX INDUSTRY ANNUAL REPORT, 1984
Annual. 1985. 16 p.
LC 72-624847.
SRI/MF/complete

Annual report on fiber box industry trends, 1960-84. Includes data on shipments by geographic area and end-use industry, production, materials consumption, prices, employment, earnings, and productivity. Data are from industry reports, American Paper Institute, and BLS.

Contains contents listing (inside front cover); introduction (p. 1); statistical section with 20 illustrative charts, and 15 tables described below (p. 2-15); and definitions (p. 16).

This is the 44th annual report.

Availability: Fibre Box Association, 5725 N. East River Rd., Chicago IL 60631, $10.00; SRI/MF/complete.

TABLES:

a. Corrugated and solid fiber container shipment value and volume, and converters and sheet plant shipments, 1960-84; and monthly and quarterly total container shipment volume (actual and seasonally adjusted), and shipment distribution by SIC 2- or 3-digit end-use industry, 1982-84. 6 tables. (p. 2-7)

b. Corrugated production by type of board, and total container shipment volume by geographic area, 1960-84, with shipment quarterly and monthly detail for 1982-84. 3 tables. (p. 8-11)

c. Containerboard production for domestic use, and consumption by box plants, 1960-84; and inventory and weeks of supply at box plants and mill sites, monthly Jan. 1983-84; all by type of board. 3 tables. (p. 12-13)

d. Corrugated container quarterly price index, compared to PPI 1960-84, and by area 1982-84; and industry employment, hours, regular and overtime earnings, and productivity ratios, 1960-84. 3 tables. (p. 14-15)

A4950
Food Marketing Institute

A4950–1   1983 ANNUAL FINANCIAL REVIEW: The Annual Report of the Supermarket Industry
Annual. 1984. 20 p.
SRI/MF/complete, delayed

Annual report on supermarket industry financial ratios, 1980-83, with trends from 1974. Covers grocery and food firms with annual sales of more than $2 million.

Data are primarily from a mail survey, supplemented by SEC 10-K reports, covering 148 firms operating 10,335 stores. The survey was conducted by Gerke Economics, Inc.

Contains executive summary and contents listing (p.1-3); narrative overview and financial statements, with 15 charts and 4 tables, described below (p. 4-15); methodology, with 3 tables (p. 17-19); and definitions (p. 20).

Previous report, for 1982, is described in SRI 1983 Annual, under this number.

Availability: Food Marketing Institute, Research Division, 1750 K St., NW, Washington DC 20006, members $7.50, nonmembers $15.00; SRI/MF/complete, delayed shipment in Sept. 1985.

CHARTS AND TABLES:

a. CPI percent change for all urban consumers and food at home, average prime interest rates, and supermarket sales and net income in current and real dollars, 1974-83. 5 charts. (p. 4-5)

b. Supermarket net income after taxes as percent of sales, assets, and net worth, with and without inflation adjustments, and by size category; and effective tax rates; 1980-83. 10 charts. (p. 6-9)

c. Supermarket income statement and balance sheet, showing distribution of income, expense, asset, liability, and net worth items, including comparison of balance sheet items with and without inflation adjustments; 1980-83. 4 tables. (p. 11-15)

A4950–2   1984 FACTS ABOUT STORE DEVELOPMENT
Annual. 1985. iii+37 p.
ISSN 0732-233X.
LC 82-642410.
SRI/MF/complete, delayed

Annual report on supermarkets opened, remodeled, and closed, in U.S. and Canada, 1984, with trends from 1980. Includes data on new store size and cost, remodeling capital investments, incorporation of specialty depts, new and existing store ownership status, and lease arrangements. Most data are shown by region, other location characteristics, store type and size, and company sales range.

Data are from responses of 200 companies, representing more than 8,500 supermarkets, to a Jan. 1985 FMI survey.

Contains executive summary and contents listing (p. ii-iii); survey report, with 5 charts and 18 tables (p. 1-30); and appendix, with questionnaire facsimile (p. 32-35).

All tables are listed below. Charts generally present trend data for topics covered in tables.

Availability: Food Marketing Institute, Research Department, 1750 K St., NW, Washington DC 20006, members $10.00, nonmembers $20.00; SRI/MF/complete, delayed shipment in Sept. 1986.

TABLES:

[Tables 3-14 show data by some or all of the following: company sales range; store location in 8 U.S. regions and Canada; store size; store type (conventional, superstore, combination, limited assortment, and warehouse); and location type (community/regional, neighborhood, free standing, and other).

Data are for 1984, unless otherwise noted.]

1. Percentage of stores opened, closed, or remodeled, 1980-84. (p. 1)

2. Type and average age of supermarkets in operation on Dec. 31, 1984. (p. 2)

3-7. Typical total square feet for new stores; typical building, store equipment/fixtures/decorations, and total construction costs per square foot; and typical number of months from construction to breakeven; [showing median, middle range, and number of stores]. (p. 4-8)

8A-8D. Profile of new store construction: number of stores and medians. (p. 9-10)

9A-9B. Percent and base number of stores with specialty depts [bakery, service deli, floral, and snack bar/restaurant]. (p. 11-12)

10A-14. Number of supermarkets owned and leased; and mean rent and ownership/lease arrangement for new and existing stores [minimum rent, overages as percent of sales, expected total rent after 5 years, services provided by landlord, and store size]. (p. 12-28)

15-18. Years from 1st opening and last major remodeling to present remodeling, and capital investment per supermarket and per square foot per major remodeling [median, middle range, and number of stores, by company sales range]. (p. 29-30)

A4950–3   TRENDS: CONSUMER ATTITUDES AND THE SUPERMARKET, 1985 Update
Annual. 1985. vi+51 p.
ISSN 0163-4488.
LC 78-646718.
SRI/MF/complete, delayed

Annual survey report, for 1985, on consumer practices and attitudes affecting the supermarket industry, including general economic concerns, views on supermarket industry performance and practices, and shopping patterns. Also includes selected comparative data from previous surveys, primarily for 1980s.

Current data are from a national telephone sample survey conducted by Louis Harris and Associates in Jan. 1985, and are based on responses from 1,005 heads of household who had shopped for groceries recently. The sample was weighted to an 80% female-20% male ratio.

Contains contents and table listings (p. iii-vi); introduction and highlights (p. 1-4); 8 chapters presenting survey findings, with 41 tables described below (p. 5-47); and methodology, with 2 tables showing sample demographic profiles, weighting, and sampling error (p. 49-51).

This is the 14th report in the FMI attitude survey series.

Availability: Food Marketing Institute, Research Department, 1750 K St., NW, Washington DC 20006, members $15.00, nonmembers $30.00; SRI/MF/complete, delayed shipment in May 1986.

SURVEY FINDINGS:

[Tables show distribution of responses to questions in the areas noted below. Selected tables show data by sociodemographic breakdowns, including family type and size; income; region; race (white, black, and Hispanic); rural or urban residence; age; and sex, including data for working women.]

a. General outlook: expectations for general and personal economic situation in coming year, and for prices in next 6 months. Tables 1-5. (p. 5-8)

b. Supermarkets: views on supermarket areas of responsibility; performance assessment for supermarket usually patronized; and supermarket selection factors. Tables 6-8. (p. 9-13)

c. Economizing: methods used to lower food bills and to save time in the supermarket. Tables 9-11. (p. 15-17)

d. Shopping patterns: weekly grocery expenditures; number of supermarkets patronized, and shopping frequency, time of day, and day of week; and preferred outlet type for selected food and nonfood items. Tables 19-21. (p. 19-25)

e. Consumer activism: willingness to participate in various personal and organized consumer protest activities, and actions taken in past year. Tables 22-24. (p. 27-28)

f. Nutrition and product safety: concern about food nutritional content; behavior and views regarding food safety; reliance on self, government, or private organizations to ascertain product safety; concerns and/or awareness regarding various substances in foods, and use of irradiation to sterilize food. Tables 25-31. (p. 27-35)

g. Food consumption patterns: favorite main course items and snack foods, and reasons; frequency of purchasing microwave, generic, unpackaged/bulk, gourmet/specialty, salad bar, and delicatessen/other carry out foods at supermarket; and changes in household eating habits. Tables 32-37. (p. 37-42)

h. Age group comparisons: responses of shoppers in 4 age groups concerning selected topics noted above, with emphasis on the baby boom generation. Tables 38-41. (p. 43-47)

A4950–4 OPERATING RESULTS OF INDEPENDENT SUPERMARKETS, 1984
Annual. 1985. 5+137 p.
SRI/MF/complete, delayed

Annual report presenting detailed sales and operating ratios for independent supermarkets, 1984. Data are shown separately for conventional, super, superette, and warehouse stores, with detail for most and least profitable stores in 3 of the store categories, by region and store square footage (conventional stores only), and by sales size (conventional and super stores only).

Includes sales distribution, gross margin, and inventory turnover, by dept; sales change from 1983; average transaction size; sales per hour; operating expenses by category, and pretax profit, expressed as percent of sales; personnel productivity ratios, including payroll and benefits per labor hour; and store area, checkouts, and space productivity ratios.

Data are shown as typical (median or mean) amounts and middle ranges, and are based on responses of 192 companies to a spring 1985 survey of FMI members in U.S. and Canada. Respondents represent 292 stores; number of stores reporting is shown for each data item.

Report is intended to enable individual stores to compare their performance with that of similar stores.

Contains contents listing, foreword, and summary, with 1 table (5 p.); 4 statistical sections, with 4 basic tables repeated for each store category (p. 3-124); and appendix, with definitions, survey form facsimile, and order forms (p. 127-137).

Availability: Food Marketing Institute, Research Department, 1750 K St., NW, Washington DC 20006, members $25.00, nonmembers $50.00; SRI/MF/complete, delayed shipment in Oct. 1986.

A4950–5 FOOD MARKETING INDUSTRY SPEAKS, 1985
Annual. 2 volumes.
For individual publication data, see below.
ISSN 0190-504X.
LC 79-640398.
SRI/MF/complete, delayed

Annual survey report on food marketing industry wholesale and retail operations, sales, and productivity, for U.S. and Canada, 1984. Data are from Food Marketing Institute surveys, and various business and Federal Government publications.

Report is issued in 2 volumes: a narrative summary report, and a statistical report with detailed tabulations. Volumes are individually described below.

Availability: Food Marketing Institute, Research Department, 1750 K St., NW, Washington DC 20006, 2 volume report: members $15.00, nonmembers $30.00; summary only: members $10.00, nonmembers $20.00; SRI/MF/complete, delayed shipment in Aug. 1986.

A4950–5.1: Narrative Summary
[Annual. 1985. 18 p. SRI/MF/complete, delayed.]

Contains 1 table showing typical store performance (p. 2); contents listing (p. 3); narrative analysis with 17 charts and 14 tables, presenting summary and trend data on U.S. economic conditions and food marketing industry financial performance and operations (p. 4-15); and appendix on survey methodology, with 7 tables showing summary results and respondent characteristics (p. 17-18).

Most data in charts and tables are based on the detailed tabulations described below.

A4950–5.2: Detailed Tabulations
[Annual. 1985. xi+136 p. SRI/MF/complete, delayed.]

Contains foreword, and listings of contents, tables, and charts (p. iii-xi); 141 tables listed below, and 17 charts showing summary operating data and sales detail by supermarket type (conventional, super, combination, and warehouse) (p. 1-117); and glossary and survey questionnaire facsimiles (p. 119-136).

TABLES:
[Data are for 1984, unless otherwise noted. Data by region are shown for 8 U.S. regions and Canada. Data by affiliation are shown for chain and independent retailers, or for cooperative, voluntary, and unaffiliated wholesalers.]

Wholesale Operations
[Tables 1-5 show data by wholesaler affiliation and/or sales size class.]

1. Geographic region of wholesale headquarters. (p. 1)

2. Average percent change in wholesale sales [also shows data by region and number of supermarkets served], 1984 vs. 1983. (p. 1)

3. Percentage of annual sales volume attributed to [independent food stores, corporately owned stores, other food chains, convenience stores, hospitals, restaurants, schools, and other], summary table of means. (p. 2)

4. Average sales per retail store served, in millions of dollars. (p. 2)

5. Services provided to membership [including advertising, private and generic label, engineering, accounting, and education/training]. (p. 3)

Distribution Center Operations
SAMPLE DESCRIPTIONS
[Tables 6-13 show data for total and/or retail and wholesale companies, with selected detail by company sales size class.]

6. Profile of companies [geographic region of headquarters, with detail for wholesalers by affiliation]. (p. 3)

7-9. Percentage of companies using microcomputers in distribution centers, use of microcomputers in warehouses [by function]; and percentage of companies with majority of microcomputers operating in a network. (p. 4)

10-11. Percentage of companies offering incentives associated with work productivity; and incentive programs [by type] available to distribution center employees; [for salaried and nonsalaried employees, and truck drivers]. (p. 5)

12-13. Typical percentage of annual distribution center compensation expense alloted to incentive programs; and percentage of total distribution center incentives, cash vs. noncash. (p. 5-6)

DRY GROCERY
[Tables 14-31 show data for dry grocery distribution center/section, usually by square footage range. Some data are shown for retail and wholesale operations.]

14-17. Average total area in square feet, number of employees, and number of supermarkets served per center/section; and type of selection method [manual, select to conveyor, and automated]. (p. 6-7)

18-22. Average number of cases shipped per week, and per direct and total labor hour; and cases selected and stored/replenished per direct labor hour. (p. 7-9)

23-25. Average number of inbound truck loads and rail cars, and outbound vehicle loads, per week. (p. 9-10)

26A-28. Average number of items available, and inventory turns; and current scratch rate. (p. 10-11)

29A-29C. Average number of orders processed per week [with detail for retailers by type of selection method]. (p. 12)

30-31. Shifts per day, days per week of operation, and unionization; and average number of cases received per direct labor hour. (p. 13)

FROZEN FOODS

32-49. [Data from tables 14-31 are repeated for frozen food distribution center/sections.] (p. 14-20)

Retail Operations

[Most tables show data by geographic region of retailer's headquarters, sales size class, and retail affiliation.]

SAMPLE DESCRIPTIONS

50. Geographic region of retailers headquarters. (p. 21)

51. Average percentage of operations supplied by outside wholesalers and direct vendor deliveries. (p. 21)

52. Number of supermarkets company operates [by region only]. (p. 22)

53A-53B. Percentage of operation supplied by [own warehouse, direct vendor deliveries, and wholesalers by affiliation]. (p. 22)

SALES AND PRODUCTIVITY

54-56. Retail sales [omits data by affiliation], 1984; and typical percent change in retail sales [total and identical stores], 1984 vs. 1983. (p. 23-24)

57. Typical weekly sales per supermarket. (p. 25)

58. Trends in sales distribution [percent of store sales in grocery, meat, and produce depts, totals only, 1976-84]. (p. 25)

59A-59B. Profile by store type [average weekly sales, productivity, size, item prices, and number of items carried; for conventional, super, combination, and warehouse stores only]. (p. 26)

60-63. Typical weekly sales per square foot of selling area and per checkout; typical sale per customer transaction; and typical sales per labor hour for store employees. (p. 27-30)

64. Sales per labor hour and hourly wage rates [by dept only, 1976-84]. (p. 31)

STORE OPERATIONS AND PROMOTION

65. Store development [new, remodeled, and closed supermarkets, totals only]. (p. 31)

66. Total size of typical supermarket. (p. 32)

67A-68B. Average number of items and average price of each item carried by a typical supermarket. (p. 32-33)

69A-69B. Credit cards [percent of stores accepting credit cards for groceries and other items]. (p. 33)

70A-70C. Percentage of sales accounted for by general merchandise, HABA (health and beauty aids), and tobacco. (p. 34-36)

71A-71B. Specialty depts and services offered by supermarkets. (p. 37)

72A-72B. Percentage of total stores currently using promotional techniques [by type]. (p. 38)

73. Typical supermarket advertising costs as a percent of sales. (p. 39)

74A-74B. Percentage of advertising dollars spent [by media]. (p. 40)

SCANNING AND BULK FOODS

75A-75B. Current uses of scanning POS [point-of-sale] data. (p. 41)

76. Scanning installation update [by manufacturer and State, 1984, and summary, 1974-Mar. 1985]. (p. 42)

77A-78B. Percentage of supermarkets selling bulk foods, and average number of bulk items carried. (p. 43)

MEAT OPERATIONS

79. Percentage of sales accounted for by the meat dept. (p. 44)

80-81. Average number of employees in the meat dept; and wages/salaries/fringe benefits as percentage of meat dept sales. (p. 44-45)

82-83. Typical sales and average pounds per labor hour for meat dept employees. (p. 46-47)

84A-86B. Percent of meat sales [total] and boneless vs. bone-in, by type [of meat]; and typical number of fresh meat items carried. (p. 48-51)

87A-90B. Fresh beef: percentage of sales by [grade]; percent of cuts received at stores as [carcass, primals, subprimals, and retail cuts]; and percent of types of packaging at stores, and types of cuts sold at retail. (p. 52-54)

91A-91B. Percentage of stores selling frozen red meat. (p. 54)

92A-93B. Percentage of types of chickens and turkeys and sections received at stores. (p. 55-56)

94A-96B. Percentage of ground beef ground in store; and proportion of total ground beef sales by [grade and] packaging types. (p. 57-58)

97A-98B. Location of deli dept, and products [by type] included in typical deli dept. (p. 58-59)

99A-99B. Percent of meat supplied by [company-owned warehouse/processing plant, and packer and wholesaler direct deliver]. (p. 60)

100A-100B. Percentage of meat dept sales devoted to service and self-service meats. (p. 60)

101A-102B. Open dating practices for meat; and meat-related services available to customers. (p. 61-62)

103A-103B. Training [on- and off-the-job] programs available for meat dept employees. (p. 63)

104A-104B. Proportion of total linear feet of meat cases by case type. (p. 64-65)

105-106. Typical percentage of total selling area devoted to total meat dept, and to meat receiving/preparation/storage. (p. 66-67)

107A-107B. Average number of packer brands carried by meat dept. (p. 68)

108A-108B. Point-of-purchase displays [by type] used to promote meat products. (p. 69)

109A-109B. Scanning of meat products [percent of stores with scanning equipment which do and do not scan meat, and percent of meat products scanned]. (p. 70)

FISH AND SEAFOOD

[Tables 110A-120B show separate data for fresh and frozen seafood, unless otherwise noted.]

110A-111. Percentage of stores carrying seafood; and size in square feet of average supermarket with fresh seafood. (p. 70-71)

112A-113B. Percentage of total retail and seafood sales accounted for by frozen and fresh seafood. (p. 72-74)

114A-114B. Number of companies including seafood items as [seafood, meat, or other dept]. (p. 75)

115A-115B. Percentage of fresh seafood sections offering service and self-service. (p. 76)

116A-116C. Average gross margin of seafood section. (p. 77-79)

117A-117B. Average linear feet of food cases devoted to [seafood]. (p. 80)

118A-119B. Percentage of companies offering special training for employees handling fresh seafood; and average number of employees devoted to seafood. (p. 80-81)

120A-120B. Average number of [fresh, frozen, and other] seafood items carried. (p. 81)

121A-122B. Open dating practices and types of prepackaging used for fresh seafood items. (p. 82-83)

123A-124B. Percentage of companies offering prepared seafood dishes, and seafood-related services available to customers. (p. 84-85)

125A-125B. Types of advertising used to promote seafood products [by media]. (p. 86)

126A-126B. Use of scanners with fresh seafood products [and percent of products scanned]. (p. 87)

ELECTRONIC FUNDS TRANSFER

[Data in tables 129-135B refer to Automatic Teller Machines (ATMs).]

127A-128B. Percentage of companies and stores with ATM or other electronic banking services. (p. 88-89)

129-131B. Typical number of transactions per week per machine; owners [including banks and other financial institutions]; and type of compensation for nonsupermarket-owned equipment. (p. 90-92)

132A-133B. Mixture of transactions [including cash dispensing and deposits]; and rating [of machine use and selected operations]. (p. 93-94)

134A-135B. Effect on check and cash volume at checkout. (p. 95)

136A-137B. Percentage of companies expecting to install [an ATM or other electronic] system within next 2 and 5 years. (p. 96-99)

External Factors

[Tables 138-140 show data for 1976-84.]

138. Operating results [profit and expense percentages]. (p. 100)

139. Percent of disposable income spent on food [at home and away from home]. (p. 100)

140. CPI [all items, food at home, and food away from home]. (p. 101)

141. Historical data [average percent change in retail sales for all and identical stores, weekly store sales and sales per square foot, sales per transaction, and number of items in supermarket; various years 1974-84]. (p. 101)

A4950-6   1984-85 MANAGEMENT COMPENSATION STUDY for Wholesalers and Large Retailers

Annual. 1985. 1+391 p.
SRI/MF/complete, delayed

Annual report, prepared by Sibson and Co., on salary and bonus compensation for 48 senior executive, staff, merchandising, and store operations positions in the food marketing industry, for the year ended Mar. 31, 1985. Includes data by sales size and region. Also includes summary data on benefit programs.

Report is based on survey responses of 86 food marketers and is intended to enable individual companies to compare their compensation levels with industry averages.

Contains contents listing, introduction, and index (1 p., p. 1-5); and the following:

Part I. Participant profile, with 3 tables showing number of respondents by sales and employment size, and region; and list of responding companies. (p. 6-11)

Part II. Compensation program information, with summary analysis, and 14 tables showing types of bonus and benefit plans offered; basis for bonus awards, and employee eligibility and participation; and bonus as percent of salary; with detail by sales size, region, and position. (p. 12-30)

Part III. Percent change in compensation, with 1 table showing average change in compensation by bonus and nonbonus companies for 48 positions. (p. 31-33)

Part IV. Pay levels for survey positions, with explanation of data (p. 35-42); and 1 detailed table, further described below, usually with accompanying chart, presenting compensation data for 48 positions nationally (p. 45-265), and for 6-11 merchandising and store operations positions in 5 regions (p. 269-379).

Appendix. Survey position descriptions. (p. 382-391)

Availability: Food Marketing Institute, Research Department, 1750 K St., NW, Washington DC 20006, members $250.00, nonmembers $500.00; SRI/MF/complete, delayed shipment in Oct. 1986.

PART IV TABLE:

Table shows average bonus and salary, and salary range, for each position. Data are grouped by sales size, number of stores, or purchasing expenditures, as appropriate for each position. Table also shows number of incumbents; selected detail by position reported to; and, for national and/or regional data on store and meat dept managers, average weekly days, nights, and hours worked, annual Sundays worked, and Sunday and holiday pay policies.

A4950-7   DATA PROCESSING SURVEY, 1984

Annual. Sept. 1984.
vi+22 p.
Special Research Rpt. 36.
SRI/MF/complete, delayed

Annual report, for 1984, on retail and wholesale food marketers' data processing (DP) employment, expenses, and operations, by size of company. Data are from survey responses of 67 companies with annual sales of over $50 million.

Contains contents and table listing (p. v-vi); 22 tables, listed below (p. 1-17); and facsimile questionnaire (p. 18-22).

This is the 6th annual report. Previous report, for 1983, is described in SRI 1983 Annual, under this number.

A separate *Data Processing Directory,* providing data on hardware, software, and systems development activities of 72 food retailers and wholesalers, is also available from the issuing agency (members $30.00, nonmembers $60.00), but is not covered by SRI.

Availability: Food Marketing Institute, Research Division, 1750 K St., NW, Washington DC 20006, members $5.00, nonmembers $10.00; SRI/MF/complete, delayed shipment in Sept. 1985.

TABLES:

[Most data are shown for wholesalers and retailers by sales size, 1984.]

EMPLOYEES

1-3. Number of respondents; and average number of DP employees, and company sales per DP employee, (excluding data entry). (p. 1)

4A-4D. Proportion of DP employees (excluding data entry) in each job title [with detail for DP dept]. (p. 2-5)

5. Data entry employees. (p. 6)

FINANCES

6A-6B. Average DP expense including employee fringes. (p. 7)

7. Expected increase in DP budget next year. (p. 8)

8A-8B. DP expense budget, and actual DP expenses most recent fiscal year, as a percent of net company sales. (p. 9-10)

9A-9B. Distribution of total DP expense budget [by object], this fiscal year. (p. 11-12)

DEVELOPMENT AND ADMINISTRATION

10A-10B. Systems development activity. (p. 13)

11A-11B. Description of DP dept operation. (p. 14-15)

12A-12B. Experience with selected technologies. (p. 16)

13. Personal computers [number of companies with computers and number of units installed, currently and projected at year end, by computer manufacturer]. (p. 17)

A4950-18   CHECK AND CASH TRANSACTIONS: A Cost Analysis for the Supermarket

Monograph. 1984. 34 p.
SRI/MF/complete, delayed

Survey report on supermarket costs for handling 3 types of customer transactions: cash for payment, check for payment, and check for cash only. Includes average cost for each type of transaction, with detail for selected cost components.

Data are from responses of 77 companies to a spring 1984 survey conducted by the Food Marketing Institute. Responding companies operate 3,850 supermarkets.

Purpose of the report is to enable individual companies to compute their own check- and cash-handling costs and to compare their costs to industry averages.

Contains contents listing (1 p.); executive summary and introduction (p. 1-3); participant profile and survey findings, with 3 tables (p. 5-6); definitions and methodology (p. 7-8); and questionnaire facsimile (p. 9-34).

Availability: Food Marketing Institute, Research Department, 1750 K St., NW, Washington DC 20006, members $15.00, nonmembers $30.00; SRI/MF/complete, delayed shipment in Nov. 1985.

A4957
Footwear Industries of America

A4957-2   STATISTICAL REPORTER: Quarterly Report

Quarterly. Approx. 15 p.
SRI/MF/complete

Quarterly statistical report on the footwear industry. Covers quantity and/or value of footwear production, shipments, and trade by country of origin and destination, with detail by footwear type and material. Also covers industry employment, hours, earnings, and labor productivity; and PPI, CPI, retail sales, and personal consumption expenditures, for footwear and selected other categories.

Data are primarily from Commerce and Labor Depts, and generally are shown for quarter of coverage, year to date, and selected previous periods. Report is published 3-9 months after quarter of coverage.

Contains 8 highlight tables and 24-25 detailed tables.

Report updates and supplements annual *Footwear Manual,* covered in SRI under A4957-1.

Availability: Footwear Industries of America, Publications, 3700 Market St., Philadelphia PA 19104, members †, nonmembers $15.00 per yr. (or † with purchase of *Footwear Manual*); SRI/MF/complete.

Issues reviewed during 1985: 1st Qtr. 1984-2nd Qtr. 1985 (D).

A4965
Foreign Policy Association

A4965-1   GREAT DECISIONS '85 NATIONAL OPINION BALLOT REPORT

Annual. July 1985.
6 p. Foldout.
SRI/MF/complete

Annual report presenting results of an opinion survey on selected foreign policy topics. Data for each topic are based on responses of 3,400-4,900 participants in the Great Decisions program, a series of nationwide foreign policy seminars.

Contains summaries of respondent characteristics and survey findings, and distribution of responses to questions regarding the following:

a. Latin America: U.S. policy options in Cuba; and most important U.S. policy goal in Central America, including prevention of Communist expansion, and use of economic aid/trade to promote development.

b. U.S.-USSR relations: resumption of arms control negotiations, including U.S. and USSR use of concessions; U.S. use of economic sanctions to influence Soviet policy; and U.S. stance in diplomatic relations.

c. Iran-Iraq war: U.S. tilt toward Iran or Iraq vs. neutrality; and use of military force vs. diplomacy to secure U.S. interests in Persian Gulf.

d. U.S. budget deficit and foreign trade: effectiveness of various means of reducing deficit; and trade policy best suited to U.S. needs.

e. Philippines: U.S. policy in Philippines, including noninvolvement, support for Marcos government, and encouragement of democratic reforms.

f. Population growth: U.S. actions for curbing population growth and encouraging family planning worldwide and/or in third-world countries; and effectiveness of various methods for reducing population growth.

g. NATO: U.S. military and political policies regarding strengthening of NATO forces, nuclear weapons use, encouragement of European member financial contribution, expansion of member cooperation on non-NATO issues, and U.S. cooperation with European allies.

h. U.S. intelligence: use of covert action.

Availability: Foreign Policy Association, 205 Lexington Ave., New York NY 10016, †, 10 or more copies $1.00 each (prepaid); SRI/MF/complete.

A5040
Futures Industry Association

A5040–1   VOLUME OF FUTURES TRADING, 1960-84
Annual. [1985.]
8 p. no paging.
SRI/MF/complete

Annual report on commodity futures contracts trading volume for farm products, metals and raw materials, securities, and foreign currencies, by commodity and exchange, 1984, with detailed trends from 1980, and summary trends from 1960. Also includes ranking of exchanges by contract volume, and option contracts traded.

Contains 1 chart and 5 tables.

Report is an annual summary of a weekly report available to members only, and not covered in SRI. A monthly summary of the weekly report is covered under A5040-2.

Availability: Futures Industry Association, 1825 Eye St., NW, Suite 1040, Washington DC 20006, members †, nonmembers ◆; SRI/MF/complete.

A5040–2   MONTHLY VOLUME REPORT: Futures Contracts Traded
Monthly. 4 p.
SRI/MF/complete, shipped quarterly

Monthly summary of a weekly bulletin on volume of commodity futures contracts traded on approximately 10 exchanges, by commodity and exchange. Report, compiled by the Futures Industry Assn, is issued approximately 2 weeks after month of coverage.

Contains the following tables:

[1] Futures contracts traded [by commodity and exchange, for month of coverage, year to date, and same periods of previous year; and total contract volume for same periods of preceding 4 years].

[2] [Trading summary, by commodity group, for month of coverage, year to date, and same periods of previous year; table begins in May 1985 issue.]

[3] [Commodities having] changes of over 50,000 contracts [between month of coverage and same month of previous year, showing increase or decrease in contracts].

Prior to May 1985 issue, report differed slightly in format and usually included data on options contracts traded.

Availability: Futures Industry Association, 1825 Eye St., NW, Suite 1040, Washington DC 20006, members †, nonmembers ◆; SRI/MF/complete, shipped quarterly.

Issues reviewed during 1985: Oct. 1984-Sept. 1985 (D) [May 1985 issue incorrectly reads Apr. 1985].

A5100
Gas Appliance
Manufacturers Association

A5100–1   STATISTICAL HIGHLIGHTS
Monthly, with annual summary. 13 p.
SRI/MF/complete, shipped quarterly

Monthly report, with annual summary, on shipments of gas and electric appliances and heating equipment. Data are compiled from member reports to GAMA, and releases from Assn of Home Appliance Manufacturers, and are issued approximately 1 month after month of coverage.

Contains contents listing, and 12 monthly tables listed below.

The annual 10-year summary tables generally accompany the Mar. or Apr. issue.

Availability: Gas Appliance Manufacturers Association, 1901 N. Moore St., Suite 1100, Arlington VA 22209, †; SRI/MF/complete, shipped quarterly.

Issues reviewed during 1985: Sept. 1984-Aug. 1985 (D); and annual summary for 1975-84.

TABLES:

[Tables show total industry shipments, monthly and by quarter for current year to date and previous year, unless otherwise noted.]

[1-2] Residential gas and electric ranges [by type].

[3] LP-gas (liquefied petroleum gas) ranges [with and without ovens] for recreational vehicles, not expanded.

[4] Residential gas and electric storage water heaters, not expanded.

[5] Commercial [gas and electric] water heaters, not expanded.

[6] Central heating [gas, oil, and electric warm air] furnaces.

[7] Heating equipment [gas boilers; and oil boilers, not expanded].

[8] Gas residential [vented and direct vent system] wall furnaces.

[9] Other heating equipment, not expanded [gas recreational vehicle heating systems and gas floor furnaces].

[10] Gas unit heaters [propeller fan and blower types] and duct furnaces.

[11] Gas and electric clothes dryers.

[12] Gas grills [annual totals only, for previous 2 years].

A5120
General Aviation
Manufacturers Association

A5120–1   GENERAL AVIATION AIRPLANE SHIPMENT REPORT
Monthly, with annual summary. Approx. 4 p.
SRI/MF/complete, shipped quarterly

Monthly report, with annual summary, on general aviation aircraft shipments and billing prices, by manufacturer and model. Also includes shipments of "off-the-shelf" aircraft to the military. Data exclude helicopters.

Data are compiled by General Aviation Manufacturers Assn, and are shown for month of coverage, previous month, and current year to date. Report is issued 2-3 weeks after month of coverage.

Contains 1 extended table.

An annual summary accompanies the Dec. or Jan. issue.

Availability: General Aviation Manufacturers Association, 1400 K St., NW, Suite 801, Washington DC 20005, †; SRI/MF/complete, shipped quarterly.

Issues reviewed during 1985: Oct. 1984-Sept. 1985; and annual summary for 1984 (D).

A5120–2   GENERAL AVIATION STATISTICAL DATABOOK, 1985 Edition
Annual. [1985.] 29 p.
LC sc83-1662.
SRI/MF/complete

Annual report on general aviation operations, for 1984, covering aircraft production and active fleet, pilots and other aviation personnel, landing facilities, accidents, and fuel use, with selected trends from 1946 and forecasts to 1996. Selected data are shown by State. Data are from original studies, FAA, and National Transportation Safety Board.

Contains foreword and contents listing (p. 1-2); report in 5 sections, with 2 charts and 22 tables (p. 4-27); and directory of GAMA members, and index (p. 28-29). All tables, and 1 chart presenting data not found in the tables, are listed below.

An additional annual report, *Industry Reports,* containing forecast data on aircraft shipments, is also published by issuing agency, but is not covered by SRI.

Availability: General Aviation Manufacturers Association, 1400 K St., NW, Suite 801, Washington DC 20005, $3.00; SRI/MF/complete.

TABLES AND CHART:

[Data are for U.S. general aviation, unless otherwise noted. Data by type or class of certificate include airline transport, helicopters, and gliders.]

A5120–2.1: Aircraft

[1] Annual shipments of new aircraft by units shipped, number of companies reporting, and factory net billings [1946-84]. (p. 4)

[2-3] Aircraft shipments, by type of aircraft and by month [1962-84]. (p. 6-7)

[4-5] Aircraft exports [units and billings, 1965-84]; and by type [1972-84]. (p. 8)

[6] Type and primary use of active aircraft in 1983. (p. 10)

[7] Active aircraft, by region and State (as of Dec. 31, 1981-83). (p. 11)

[8] Estimated hours flown, by type of aircraft [as of Dec. 31, 1977-83]. (p. 12)

[9] Active aircraft and average hours annually flown per aircraft, by type [1979-83]. (p. 12)

A5120–2.2: Pilots

[All tables except table [3] show data as of Dec. 31. Data on personnel are for all types of aviation.]

[1] Active pilot [and nonpilot aviation-related] certificates held [by type of certification, 1973-84]. (p. 14)

[2] Active pilots [by type] and flight instructors, by FAA region and State (1983). (p. 15)

[3] Student pilot certificates processed, by month [1972-84]. (p. 16)

[4-5] Estimated total and instrument rated pilots, 1976-83; and estimated instrument ratings held, by class of certificates, 1982-83. (p. 17)

[6] Women actively engaged in aviation [by type of certificate, 1972-84]. (p. 18)

A5120–2.3: Miscellaneous

[Tables 1-4 show data as of Dec. 31.]

[1] Civil/joint-use airports/heliports/stolports/seaplane bases on record, by type of ownership [and by whether paved and lighted, all by FAA region and State], 1984. (p. 20-21)

[2] FAA air route facilities and services [by type, including air traffic control towers and centers, instrument landing systems, and radar], 1972-83. (p. 22)

[3-4] Estimated active aircraft by type of aircraft [1979-95]; and forecast active pilots by type of certificate [1984-95]. (p. 24-25)

[5-6] Forecast hours flown and estimated fuel consumed, by type of aircraft [FY80-96]. (p. 26)

[7] Accident rates [for total and fatal accidents], 1972-84. [chart] (p. 27)

[8] Fuel consumed, by type of aircraft, 1983. (p. 27)

A5135
German American
Chamber of Commerce

A5135–1   GERMAN-AMERICAN TRADE NEWS
Quarterly.
ISSN 0192-0103.
LC 67-5453.
SRI/MF/complete

Quarterly journal promoting trade and business relations between the U.S. and the Federal Republic of Germany. Includes reporting on investment trends, industries or individual companies, financing, and trade legislation or regulation.

Data sources include IMF, U.S. and German Government agencies, and Deutsche Bundesbank.

Issues contain feature articles, some with statistics, and news briefs and trade fair calendar.

Features with substantial statistical content are described, as they appear, under "Statistical Features." All issues are reviewed and filmed, and an abstract appears in SRI monthly issues regardless of statistical content.

Publication of this journal is suspended with the Apr./May 1985 issue.

Availability: German American Chamber of Commerce, 666 Fifth Ave., New York NY 10103, $9.00 per yr., single copy $2.50; SRI/MF/complete.

Issues reviewed during 1985: Jan.-Apr./May 1985 (P) (Vol. 39, Nos. 1-2).

STATISTICAL FEATURES:

A5135–1.601: Jan. 1985 (Vol. 39, No. 1)
FREIGHT FORWARDER AS AN ORGANIZER OF THE TRANSPORTATION OF GOODS

(p. 22-28) Article, with 2 tables showing the following for West Germany: volume of freight transported, by mode, 1960 and 1984; and percent of freight service companies performing various shipping and storage functions (no date). Data are from Bundesverband Spedition und Lagerei e.V.

NEARLY 300 AIRLINES ARE PRESENTLY AUTHORIZED TO FLY IN THE U.S.

(p. 29-32) By Hans P. Wiedeman. Article, with 3 tables showing freight traffic for 10 U.S. airlines; and passenger traffic for top 20 U.S. and top 10 German airports; 1983. Data sources include Airport Operators Council International and Flughafen Frankfurt Main AG.

100 LARGEST COMPANIES IN THE FEDERAL REPUBLIC

(p. 40) Table showing top 100 German companies ranked by 1983 sales, and also showing 1982 rank and 1983 employment. Data are from *Die Zeit* (Hamburg).

Similar data, for 1982, were published in the Jan./Feb. 1984 issue; for description, see SRI 1984 Annual, under A5135–1.502.

ECONOMIC FORECAST FOR 1985: SLOWDOWN IN GERMAN ECONOMIC GROWTH

(p. 50-53) Article, with 2 tables showing selected economic indicators for West Germany, including GNP and components, prices, employment, and national income and components, annually 1983-85 and semiannually 1984-85.

Data are from Sachverstaendigenrat zur Begutachtung der Gesamtwirtschaftlichen Entwicklung.

A5135–1.602: Apr./May 1985 (Vol. 39, No. 2)
NEW YORK'S ECONOMIC RESURGENCE

(p. 12-18) Article on NYC and its importance as an international business center. Data are from Main Hurdman, New York Chamber of Commerce and Industry, Commerce Dept, and German American Chamber of Commerce. Includes 1 table and 5 charts showing the following:

a. Foreign firms' reasons for choosing or not choosing NYC as a business location, and ratings of municipal services; and distribution of NYC foreign executive residences by borough and neighboring area, and of foreign-owned firms by nationality; (no dates).

b. Foreign direct investment in U.S., and U.S. direct investment abroad, for 6-9 countries, with investment share for principal industry sectors, 1983.

AMERICAN SUBSIDIARIES OF GERMAN FIRMS WITH MORE THAN 2,000 EMPLOYEES

(p. 20) Table ranking top 12 German companies by U.S. subsidiary employment, and also showing principal product and/or headquarters location for each subsidiary (no dates). Data are from German American Chamber of Commerce.

INSURANCE IN U.S.A.

(p. 21-28) By Henry Salfeld. Article, with 1 undated table ranking top 10 U.S. property/casualty insurance companies by net premiums written, and also showing comparative rank and amount of assets and policyholders' surplus. Data are from Frenkel and Co. Inc.

QUEST FOR A PRESIDENT (AND RETAINING HIM)

(p. 34-38) By Knut R. Fischer. Article, with 1 undated table showing total and base compensation for chief executive and chief operating officers of U.S. companies with sales under $10 million, by sales size, industry sector, and region.

STRUCTURE AND ECONOMIC ROLE OF TRANSPORTATION IN THE U.S.

(p. 60-68) By Gerhard Stebich. Article comparing transportation sectors of the U.S. and West Germany. Data are from German Federal Freight Transport Assn and Transportation Policy Associates.

Includes 3 tables showing the following for 1983:

a. West Germany and U.S.: land area; population; GNP; export and import share of GNP; length of roads, rail lines, inland waterways, and pipelines; and number of automobiles, buses, and trucks.

b. U.S.: passenger and intercity freight traffic, by transportation mode.

A5135-2   U.S.-GERMAN ECONOMIC SURVEY, 1984

Annual. Feb. 1985. 206 p.
ISSN 0147-4421.
LC 77-649637.
SRI/MF/complete

Annual compilation of articles and comparative statistics on West German and U.S. commercial and economic trends and policies, 1960s-84. Includes data on socioeconomic conditions, industrial production, finance, trade, GNP, and prices. Data are primarily from U.S. Commerce and Labor Depts, and Statistisches Bundesamt.

Contents:

a. Contents listing; preface; and 13 feature articles on economics, finance, and industrial development, with German-language summaries. (p. 7-132)

b. Narrative profiles of companies, States, German cities, and trade fair organizations purchasing advertising space. (p. 136-185)

c. Statistical review section, with 2 maps, 9 charts, and 26 tables; and information sources and index of advertisers. (p. 187-206)

Articles with statistics, and statistical review tables and charts, are described below.

This is the 10th annual edition.

Availability: Manhattan Publishing Co., PO Box 650, Croton-on-Hudson NY 10520, $12.50 (prepaid); SRI/MF/complete.

STATISTICAL FEATURES:

A5135-2.1: Statistical Articles

NEW TECHNOLOGICAL DEVELOPMENT IN THE FEDERAL REPUBLIC OF GERMANY

(p. 11-22) By Martin Bangemann. Article, with 1 chart showing the following for 3 leading countries in research expenditures: expenditure amount, and share of country's overall economic performance, 1983.

VENTURE CAPITAL: FINANCING THE NEW IDEAS OF A CHANGING WORLD, A U.S.-GERMAN PERSPECTIVE

(p. 115-120) By Charles F. Bacon. Article, with 2 text tables showing venture capital firms and funds under management, for U.S. Rocky Mountain region; and U.S. venture funds by source; 1977 and 1983. Data are from Venture Economics, Inc.

A5135-2.2: Statistical Review Tables and Charts

[Data are shown for U.S. and West Germany, various periods 1960-84.]

a. Population by sex, and State or Province; households and land area; labor force and unemployment; manufacturing hourly earnings; and CPI, PPI, and industrial production indexes. 2 maps, 4 charts, and 12 tables. (p. 188-193)

b. Manufacturing productivity and labor costs, including hourly output and compensation indexes, and production worker compensation amounts. 2 charts and 2 tables. (p. 194-195)

c. Trade and foreign investment, including bilateral trade by detailed commodity; and direct investment abroad and foreign investment in U.S. and Germany, by industry and country. 1 chart and 5 tables. (p. 196-199)

d. Economic indicators, including GNP by expenditure type, at current and constant 1972 prices; currency exchange rates; and revenues of 13 German companies, with percent ownership in U.S. affiliates. 2 charts and 7 tables. (p. 200-203)

A5145
Gold Institute

A5145-1   MODERN GOLD COINAGE, 1984

Annual. [1985.] 30 p.
ISSN 0149-4279.
LC 77-643382.
SRI/MF/complete, delayed

Annual report on gold coins issued as money in 57 countries or world areas, 1984. Includes number, gold content, and physical characteristics of coins, for 161 coin issues grouped by country. Also includes mint where coins were struck, total gold used, and total face value of coins in local currency, for each country.

Data are from ministries of finance, central banks, government and private mints, and numismatic experts.

Contains introduction (p. 1); 1 summary table (p. 2-3); 1 detailed table repeated for each country (p. 4-29); and directory of mints (p. 30).

Availability: Gold Institute, 1001 Connecticut Ave., NW, Washington DC 20036, $15.00; SRI/MF/complete, delayed shipment in Mar. 1986.

A5145-2   WORLD MINE PRODUCTION OF GOLD, 1983-87

Annual. Feb. 1985. 9 p.
SRI/MF/complete

Annual report on gold mine production from underground/surface/alluvial sources in 57 countries, 1983-87. Data are from approximately 250 mining enterprises.

Contains brief narrative (p. 1); 2 tables showing gold production by country, 1983, estimated 1984, and projected 1985-87 (p. 2-3); and list showing name and location of participating companies, arranged by country (p. 4-10).

Availability: Gold Institute, 1001 Connecticut Ave., NW, Washington DC 20036, †; SRI/MF/complete.

A5160
Guttmacher, Alan, Institute

A5160-1   FAMILY PLANNING PERSPECTIVES

Bimonthly.
Cumulative pagination throughout year.
ISSN 0014-7354.
LC 72-620943.
SRI/MF/not filmed

Bimonthly journal on family planning medical and policy issues, including contraception and abortion.

Each issue contains articles, some with statistical content; a news digest section summarizing recent developments in family planning; and book reviews. Annual subject and author indexes appear in Nov./Dec. issue.

Features with substantial statistical content are described, as they appear, under "Statistical Features." Each issue of the journal is reviewed, but an abstract is published in SRI monthly issues only when statistical features appear. Features presenting solely clinical data are not covered.

Availability: Alan Guttmacher Institute, 111 Fifth Ave., New York NY 10003, members $12.00, nonmembers $24.00; SRI/MF/not filmed.

Issues reviewed during 1985: Sept./Oct. 1984-July/Aug. 1985 (P) (Vol. 16, Nos. 5-6; Vol. 17, Nos. 1-4).

STATISTICAL FEATURES:

A5160-1.601: Sept./Oct. 1984 (Vol. 16, No. 5)

AMERICAN HOUSEHOLD STRUCTURE IN TRANSITION

(p. 205-211) By Paul C. Glick. Article on trends in household characteristics. Data are from Census Bureau. Includes 6 tables showing the following for 1960, 1970, and 1983:

a. Households and persons in households, by selected characteristics, including living arrangements, and presence of own children.

b. Single parents by sex, by householder and marital status; lone householders by sex, by age group and marital status; unmarried couples, by age group, householder status, and presence of children; and children younger than 18, by living arrangement.

EFFECTIVENESS OF FAMILY PLANNING CLINICS IN SERVING ADOLESCENTS

(p. 212-218) By Ellen Eliason Kisker. Article on the quality of service offered to teenage patients by family planning clinics. Data are from a 1981 Alan Guttmacher Institute survey of over 11,000 family planning clinic directors and patients, pharmacists, and physicians. Includes 3 tables showing the following for teenage family planning clinic patients:

a. Percent citing satisfaction or dissatisfaction with selected aspects of clinic care; and mean delay between 1st intercourse and 1st clinic visit, patient retention, and net satisfaction, by type of clinic, number of patients served by clinic, and metro status.

b. Regression analysis examining effects of changes in selected clinic characteristics on mean delay between 1st intercourse and 1st clinic visit, patient retention, and net satisfaction.

MOST AMERICANS REMAIN OPPOSED TO ABORTION BAN AND CONTINUE TO SUPPORT WOMAN'S RIGHT TO DECIDE

(p. 233-234) Article, with 1 table showing percent of adults approving of legal abortions under 6 specific circumstances and under any circumstance, selected periods 1965-84. Data are based on a Mar. 1984 survey of 1,473 adults conducted by National Opinion Research Center (NORC), and earlier NORC surveys.

For description of a similar article, with survey data for 1960s-83, see SRI 1984 Annual under A5160-1.502.

A5160–1.602: Nov./Dec. 1984 (Vol. 16, No. 6)

CONTRACEPTIVE PRACTICE AMONG AMERICAN WOMEN, 1973-82

(p. 253-259) By Christine A. Bachrach. Article on contraceptive use among U.S. women. Data are national estimates based on responses of 7,969 women aged 15-44 to Cycle III of the National Survey of Family Growth (NSFG), conducted by NCHS, Aug. 1982-Feb. 1983, with comparisons to previous NSFG findings.

Includes 9 tables showing women aged 15-44, number exposed to unintended pregnancy, and prevalence of contraceptive use, by marital status, with detail by contraceptive method, race, age group, childbearing intentions, religion (Protestant and Catholic), and poverty status, 1973, 1976, and/or 1982.

SECOND-TRIMESTER ABORTIONS IN THE U.S.

(p. 260-266) By David A. Grimes. Article, with 4 tables showing number of 2nd-3rd trimester abortions, and distribution by type of procedure, by length of gestation, 1981; and abortion-related deaths and/or rates by procedure and length of gestation, and distribution of 2nd-3rd trimester deaths by cause, 1972-81 period. Data are primarily from the Centers for Disease Control.

CONTRACEPTION: THE MORNING AFTER

(p. 266-270) By Jeanette H. Johnson. Article, with 2 tables showing failure rates of postcoital contraceptives, or "morning-after pills," based on 8 specified studies, various periods 1974-82; and reasons cited for seeking postcoital contraception by 511 patients at a family planning clinic in Avon, England, 1983.

EFFECT OF MARITAL DISSOLUTION ON CONTRACEPTIVE PROTECTION

(p. 271-274) By Larry Bumpass and Ronald R. Rindfuss. Article comparing contraceptive use among married and separated women, by method of contraception. Data are from the 1973 and 1976 National Surveys of Family Growth, conducted by NCHS. Includes text statistics and 3 tables.

LOW BIRTH WEIGHT MOST LIKELY AMONG BABIES WHO ARE BLACK, PREMATURE, HAVE BIRTH DIFFICULTIES

(p. 279-280) Article, with 1 table showing low birth weight births as a percent of all live births in hospitals to married women, by race, length of gestation, type of delivery, and infant health, 1972 and 1980. Data are based on National Natality Surveys.

TEENAGE CHILDBEARING AND WELFARE: PREVENTIVE AND AMELIORATIVE STRATEGIES

(p. 285-289) By Kristin A. Moore and Richard F. Wertheimer. Article examining potential effects of changes in fertility, family size, marriage rate, and educational attainment on use of public assistance programs by young women, projected for 1990. Data are based on computer models developed by the Urban Institute.

Includes 2 tables showing number of women aged 20-24 and 25-29 receiving AFDC, with detail for women with 1st birth before age 20; and program costs for AFDC, Medicaid, and food stamps; 1990 projected under 7 scenarios.

A5160–1.603: Jan./Feb. 1985 (Vol. 17, No. 1)

HOLY WAR

(p. 5-9) By Patricia Donovan. Article, with 1 table showing violent acts directed at abortion clinics, by type of act (including bombing, vandalism, assault, and arson), 1981-84. Data are from National Abortion Federation.

CONTRACEPTIVE USE, PREGNANCY, AND FERTILITY PATTERNS AMONG SINGLE AMERICAN WOMEN IN THEIR 20s

(p. 10-19) By Koray Tanfer and Marjorie C. Horn. Article analyzing pregnancy experience and contraceptive use among unmarried young women, 1983. Most data are from 1983 National Survey of Unmarried Women.

Includes 7 tables showing the following for never-married women aged 20-29, by race, generally 1983:

a. Contraceptives: distribution of women who have ever had sexual intercourse and women who are currently sexually active, by selected socioeconomic characteristics, with detail for contraceptive users by method used currently and at 1st and most recent intercourse.

b. Pregnancies: percent of women ever pregnant and ever having live birth, and number of pregnancies and live births per 1,000 women, by selected socioeconomic characteristics; and distribution of 1st, most recent, and all pregnancies, by whether wanted or unwanted, pregnancy outcome, and whether contraceptive was ever used and used at time of conception.

Socioeconomic characteristics include age group, educational attainment and current school status, religion and degree of religiosity, labor force status, living arrangement currently and at age 15, and metro or nonmetro residence.

LEGAL ABORTION IN ITALY: 1980-81

(p. 19-23) By Simonetta Landucci Tosi et al. Article, with 5 tables showing the following for Italy: number of abortions performed, and number per 1,000 live births and per 1,000 women age 15-49, by region and province; and distribution of abortions, by education, marital status, age group, number of prior live births, weeks of gestation, length of hospital stay, and type of facility, anesthesia, and procedure; primarily 1980-81.

A similar article, with data for 1978-79, is described in SRI 1982 Annual under A5160-1.301.

PUBLIC FUNDING OF CONTRACEPTIVE, STERILIZATION AND ABORTION SERVICES, 1983, ANNUAL FEATURE

(p. 25-30) Annual article, by Rachel Benson Gold and Barry Nestor, on publicly funded contraceptive services and abortions, FY83. Data are from various Federal and private sources.

Includes 4 tables showing public expenditures for contraceptive services, sterilizations, and abortions; and number of publicly funded abortions; by funding source and State, FY83 with selected summary comparisons to FY82.

Previous article, for FY82, is described in SRI 1984 Annual under A5160-1.505.

FAMILY PLANNING CLINIC SERVICES IN THE U.S., 1983

(p. 30-35) By Aida Torres and Jacqueline Darroch Forrest. Article on family planning services and patients, 1983 and trends. Most data are from Alan Guttmacher Institute. Includes 6 tables showing the following, 1983 with some trends from 1973:

a. Teenage and low-income women at risk of pregnancy, aggregated for metro and nonmetro counties with no family planning services; and number of metro and nonmetro counties without services.

b. Family planning agencies, clinics, and patients, by agency type (hospital, health dept, Planned Parenthood, and other), with agency and clinic summary by region; patients receiving public assistance; total patients, and low-income and teenage patients (actual and as percent of women at risk of pregnancy), by region and State; and patients by contraceptive method used.

A similar article, for 1981, is described in SRI 1984 Annual under A5160-1.502.

A5160–1.604: Mar./Apr. 1985 (Vol. 17, No. 2)

TEENAGE PREGNANCY IN DEVELOPED COUNTRIES: DETERMINANTS AND POLICY IMPLICATIONS

(p. 53-63) By Elise F. Jones et al. Article on teenage pregnancy and contraceptive use in developed countries, various periods 1976-81. Data are from Alan Guttmacher Institute.

Includes 2 charts and 2 tables presenting data on teenage pregnancy rates and outcomes (abortions, and legitimate and illegitimate births), and prevalence of contraceptive use with detail for birth control pill, for U.S., Canada, and 4 European countries; and correlation analysis of teenage birth rates and socioeconomic characteristics, aggregated for 37 developed countries; various periods 1976-81.

AVAILABILITY OF REPRODUCTIVE HEALTH SERVICES FROM U.S. PRIVATE PHYSICIANS

(p. 63-69) By Margaret Terry Orr and Jacqueline Darroch Forrest. Article on availability of reproductive health services from private physicians. Data are from 2,247 responses to a 1983 Alan Guttmacher Institute survey of private physicians.

Includes text data and 7 tables showing survey response concerning types of services provided; criteria for or reasons for not providing female sterilization, vasectomy, and abortion; willingness to provide contraceptives to minors with and without parental consent, and to accept Medicaid or reduce fees for low-income patients; and average fees charged; generally by medical specialty.

FAILURE RATE FOR SPONGE HIGHER THAN FOR DIAPHRAGM: PAROUS SPONGE USERS ARE MOST LIKELY TO CONCEIVE

(p. 80-81) Article, with 1 table showing average 12-month accidental pregrancy rate among U.S. and UK women using contraceptive sponge and diaphragm, with detail for users with and without prior live birth. Data are from Family Health International studies conducted among 1,440 U.S. and 249 UK users, various periods 1979-83.

WHO: LONG-TERM PILL USE MAY CAUSE SMALL RISE IN CERVICAL CANCER

(p. 82) Article, with 1 table showing relative risk of cervical cancer among women who have ever used oral contraceptives, by duration of use. Data are from studies of patients at 10 medical centers in 8 countries, conducted 1979-83 and sponsored by World Health Organization.

PORTRAIT OF AMERICAN WOMEN WHO OBTAIN ABORTIONS

(p. 90-96) By Stanley K. Henshaw et al. Article characterizing abortions and abortion clients, 1980-81. Data sources include Census Bureau, Centers for Disease Control, and Alan Guttmacher Institute annual surveys of abortion providers. Includes 7 tables showing the following:

a. Legal abortions, abortion rate, and/or abortions as percent of pregnancies, by abortion method and client age group, race, marital status, number of live births and prior induced abortions, and gestational period; and pregnancies and pregnancy rate, by age at conception and at birth or abortion; 1980-81.

b. Abortions by State of residence and occurrence, with detail for abortions performed for nonresidents, and resident abortion rate, 1981.

Abortion and pregnancy rates are generally per 1,000 women aged 15-44. Corrected data appear in July/Aug. 1985 issue; for description, see A5160-1.606 below.

A similar article, for 1979-80, is described in SRI 1983 Annual under A5160-1.403.

A5160–1.605: May/June 1985 (Vol. 17, No. 3)

PAYING FOR MATERNITY CARE

(p. 103-111) By Rachel Benson Gold and Asta M. Kenney. Article on pregnancy costs and medical coverage. Data are from Census Bureau and Health and Human Services Dept. Includes 2 tables showing the following:

a. Women aged 15-44, by type of medical coverage (group, individual, Medicaid, Medicare, Civilian Health and Medical Program of the Uniformed Services, and none); shown by age group, income, poverty status, race (also including Hispanic), marital status, employment status, industry of employment, and wage basis (hourly and salary); 1984.

b. AFDC and Medicaid eligibility and payments, Medicaid benefits, outpatient and physician visit limits, and median family income, by State, 1985.

NEED FOR PRENATAL CARE IN THE U.S.: EVIDENCE FROM THE 1980 NATIONAL NATALITY SURVEY

(p. 118-124) By Susheela Singh et al. Article examining levels of prenatal care by selected socioeconomic characteristics, 1980. Data are from National Natality Survey, National Survey of Family Growth, and U.S. vital statistics.

Includes text data and 6 tables showing births by trimester when prenatal care began, percent of mothers receiving inadequate prenatal care (care begun in 2nd or 3rd trimester, or no care), and risk of inadequate prenatal care, all by various socioeconomic characteristics, including metro-nonmetro status, education, age group, marital and poverty status, and race/ethnicity (black, white, and Hispanic).

WAY TO LOWER BLACK NEONATAL MORTALITY NOT SIMPLE, STUDY FINDS

(p. 129-130) Article, with 1 table comparing rates of low birthweight, prematurity, and neonatal mortality, for blacks and whites by sex, in California, 1980/81. Data are from U.S. Centers for Disease Control and University of California.

HEALTH CONSEQUENCES OF TEENAGE FERTILITY

(p. 132-139) By Carolyn Makinson. Article examining effects of teenage pregnancy on mother and infant health. Data are from NCHS and other sources.

Includes text data and 3 tables showing the following by age of mother: rates of 3 nonfatal maternal complications for NYC; U.S. maternal mortality rates by race, and distribution of mothers by period prenatal care began (including mothers with no prenatal care); and English/Welsh postneonatal death rates (total and for sudden deaths), by mother's number of previous live births; various periods 1968-78.

A5160–1.606: July/Aug. 1985 (Vol. 17, No. 4)

PROJECT REDIRECTION: EVALUATION OF A COMPREHENSIVE PROGRAM FOR DISADVANTAGED TEENAGE MOTHERS

(p. 150-155) By Denise F. Polit and Janet R. Kahn. Article evaluating program designed to promote disadvantaged teenage mothers' economic self-sufficiency and social responsibility (Project Redirection). Data are based on a sample of 305 project participants and a control group of 370 nonparticipants, at 4 project sites, during 1980-83 period.

Includes 5 tables showing the following for participants vs. nonparticipants:

a. Socioeconomic characteristics: age; educational attainment; number of pregnancies and siblings; marital and pregnancy status; race/ethnicity (including Mexican American and Puerto Rican); whether mother was a teenage parent and mother's educational attainment; and whether living in AFDC household and raised by both parents.

b. Subsequent pregnancies and births, contraceptive use, educational attainment, and employment status, all at 12 and/or 24 months after 1st project interview.

SOCIAL AND ENVIRONMENTAL FACTORS INFLUENCING CONTRACEPTIVE USE AMONG BLACK ADOLESCENTS

(p. 165-169) By Dennis P. Hogan et al. Article, with 2 tables showing contraceptive use at 1st intercourse, for black teenagers in Chicago, by sex and selected socioeconomic characteristics

(including social class, neighborhood quality, career aspirations, and parents' marital status), 1979.

Data are from responses of 348 female and 124 male black teenagers to a 1979 Chicago Urban League survey.

PARENT-CHILD COMMUNICATION AND ADOLESCENT SEXUAL BEHAVIOR

(p. 169-174) By Susan F. Newcomer and J. Richard Udry. Article on prevalence and openness of mother-daughter and mother-son discussions regarding sex and birth control, and the possible relationship to effective use of contraceptives among teenagers. Data are based on responses of 1,405 teenagers and their parents to a 1980 survey, and 1,152 responses to a 1982 follow-up survey. Both surveys were conducted by the authors.

Includes 5 tables showing survey response.

U.S. TEACHERS AND PUBLIC, STRONGLY IN FAVOR OF SEX EDUCATION IN SCHOOLS, DIFFER ON APPROPRIATE TOPICS

(p. 183-184) Article, with 1 table showing percent of teachers and general public supporting sex education in elementary and high schools, by topic. Data are from surveys conducted by the Gallup Organization for *Phi Delta Kappan,* and cover responses of 813 public school teachers to a May 1984 survey and 1,528 adults to a May 1985 survey.

RISK OF INFECTION FROM IUD USE SIMILAR IN DEVELOPING AND DEVELOPED COUNTRIES

(p. 184) Article, with 1 table showing risk of contracting pelvic inflammatory disease (PID) among intrauterine device (IUD) users who have had at least 1 child, by IUD use status (current or previous), for developing and developed countries, Mar. 1978-Dec. 1979 period. Data are from a World Health Organization Study of PID patients at 12 hospitals in 10 countries.

CORRECTION

(p. 189) Includes corrected data for article on women who obtain abortions, described under A5160-1.604 above.

A5160–2   ABORTION SERVICES in the U.S., Each State, and Metropolitan Area, 1981-82

Recurring (irreg.) June 1985.
6+ii+87 p.
LC 81-69082.
SRI/MF/not filmed

Recurring report, edited by Stanley K. Henshaw and Ellen Blaine, on abortions, 1981-82, with trends from 1973. Includes data on patient characteristics; and abortions performed and facilities providing abortions, by SMSA, State, and/or census division.

Data are primarily from approximately 3,400 responses to the 1983 Abortion Provider Survey conducted by the Alan Guttmacher Institute (AGI), and earlier surveys; and from the Centers for Disease Control.

Contains list of survey staff, acknowledgements, and contents and table listings (6 p.); introduction (p. i-ii); 8 articles, with numerous charts and tables (p. 1-49); survey methodology and facsimile questionnaires (p. 51-60); and 10 detailed tables, preceded by narrative introduction (p. 62-87).

Detailed tables are described below. Articles were originally published in the AGI *Family Planning Perspectives,* covered in SRI under A5160-1.

Availability: Alan Guttmacher Institute, 111 Fifth Ave., New York NY 10003, $10.00; SRI/MF/not filmed.

TABLES:

a. Abortions: number, rate, and as percent of pregnancies, by age, race, and marital status; and abortions by number of previous abortions and live births, weeks of gestation, and method; 1973-81. Tables 1-4. (p. 62-67)

b. Abortions and rate, providers, and percent of abortions in hospitals, by SMSA and for aggregate nonmetro areas by State; and abortions and providers, shown for hospitals, and for nonhospital facilities reporting 400/more and fewer than 400 abortions, by State; 1981 and/or 1982. Tables 5-6. (p. 68-75)

c. Abortions and/or rates: by State and census division of occurrence, 1973-82; and by State of patient's residence, 1978-81. Tables 7-10. (p. 76-87)

A5160–3 ORGANIZED FAMILY PLANNING SERVICES IN THE U.S., 1981-83
Recurring (irreg.) Dec. 1984.
5+103 p.
SRI/MF/not filmed

Recurring report on family planning services and patients, by region, State, and metro-nonmetro status, 1983, with selected comparisons to 1981 and summary trends from FY69.

Most data are estimates by Alan Guttmacher Institute and are based on data from Planned Parenthood Federation of America and other State and local reporting systems, and on surveys of service providers not included in reporting systems.

Contains listings of contents and charts/tables (3 p.); study highlights and definitions, and narrative analysis interspersed with 1 chart and 8 summary or trend tables (p. 1-36); 23 detailed tables, described below (p. 37-80); appendix on methodology, with 3 summary tables (p. 82-97); and appendix article on public funding for contraceptive, sterilization, and abortion services, with 4 tables (p. 98-103).

Appendix article is reprinted from the Jan./Feb. 1985 issue of *Family Planning Perspectives;* for description, see A5160-1.603.

Studies of family planning services and patients have been conducted annually since 1969; results are published irregularly. SRI coverage begins with the 1981-83 report.

Availability: Alan Guttmacher Institute, 111 Fifth Ave., New York NY 10003, $6.00; SRI/MF/not filmed.

TABLES:

[Unless otherwise noted, data are shown by region and State, for 1983.]

a. Total number of counties; number of counties without family planning clinics offering medical services; and number of poor and teenage females at risk of unintended pregnancy who live in counties without clinics; for all, metro, and nonmetro counties. Tables 1-3. (p. 37-42)

b. Agencies and clinic sites providing family planning services, and patients served, by type of provider (hospital, health dept, Planned Parenthood, and other), with detail for metro and nonmetro areas, 1981 and/or 1983. Tables 4-12. (p. 43-59)

c. Family planning patients (female), by poverty status, race (including Hispanic), contraception method used, and patient status (new or continuing); patients receiving welfare; patients under age 20, with summary trends from FY69; poor and teenage females at risk of unintended pregnancy, and number served by family planning providers; and family planning visits per patient. Tables 13-23. (p. 60-80)

**A5173
Health Insurance
Association of America**

A5173–1 NEW GROUP HEALTH INSURANCE
Biennial. [1985.] 16 p.
LC 75-645091.
SRI/MF/complete

Biennial summary report on coverage characteristics of new group health insurance policies written during 1st quarter 1984, with comparisons to 1979. Presents data on employees covered, by type of coverage, deductible, maximum benefit, cost containment features, employer-employee contribution arrangements, and other provisions; and employees and cases covered, by selected type of coverage and size of group.

Types of coverage include major medical, hospital, surgical, nursing home, dental, maternity, mental/nervous disorder, disability, and others.

Data are from a survey of 25 insurance companies accounting for 53.6% of group health insurance premiums written in 1983. Most data analysis is limited to plans covering 25-499 employees.

Contains methodology, and contents listing (p. 1-2); and report, with narrative analysis, text data, and 8 tables (p. 3-16).

This is the 22nd survey report. Prior to the 1984 survey, report was published annually, and consisted of a narrative summary booklet and a statistical volume showing detailed survey results. Statistical volume is no longer published. For description of previous survey report, for 1982, see SRI 1983 Annual under this number.

Availability: Health Insurance Association of America, Order Fulfillment, 1850 K St., NW, Washington DC 20006-2284, †; SRI/MF/complete.

A5173–2 SOURCE BOOK OF HEALTH INSURANCE DATA, 1984-85
Biennial. [1985.] 104 p.
LC 60-187.
SRI/MF/complete

Biennial report, for 1984-85, on health insurance coverage, benefits paid, and premium income; and health care programs, costs, use, and personnel; various years 1935-85. Also includes selected data by State.

Data are compiled from Health Insurance Assn, government agency, and hospital and medical assn reports. Data source is noted for each table.

Contains foreword, contents listing, and 1 trend table (p. 1-4); 7 chapters, with narrative summaries, 3 charts, and 57 tables (p. 5-79); appendices, with chronology of insurance industry events, and 2 tables showing number of persons covered (by type of coverage and insurer) in 1983 (p. 81-89); and glossary and index (p. 91-104).

Chapter tables, and selected chart showing substantial statistics not covered in tables, are listed below.

This report alternates with an interim report providing updated information for selected tables. For description of last previous full report, for 1982-83, see SRI 1983 Annual under this number. Prior to the 1982-83 edition, full report was published annually.

Availability: Health Insurance Association of America, Order Fulfillment, 1850 K St., NW, Washington DC 20006-2284, †; SRI/MF/complete.

CHAPTER TABLES AND CHART:
[Data by State generally include U.S. territories/possessions.]

A5173–2.1: Health Insurance
[Data shown by type of insurer include all insurers, all insurance companies, Blue Cross/Blue Shield, and, sometimes, other plans.

Data by type of policy are for group policies, and individual/family policies.]

EXTENT OF COVERAGE
[Titles for tables 1.1-1.8 begin "Number of persons..." Tables 1.1-1.6 include 1983 detail for persons under age 65 and 65/over.]

1.1. With health insurance protection, by type of coverage [hospital, surgical, physician, major medical, and dental expense, and short- and long-term disability income, selected years 1940-83]. (p. 10)

1.2-1.5. With hospital insurance, and surgical, physician's, and major medical expense protection, by type of insurer [and policy, various years 1940-83]. (p. 11-14)

1.6. With major medical expense protection with insurance companies, by type of policy [selected years 1951-83]. (p. 15)

1.7. With disability income protection, by type of [insurance] program [and policy]; selected years 1946-83. (p. 16)

1.8. With dental expense protection, by type of insurer [1967-83]. (p. 17)

BENEFIT PAYMENTS
[Titles for tables 2.1-2.2. begin "Health insurance benefit payments..." Data by type of coverage include medical and dental expenses, and loss of income.]

2.1. By type of insurer and by type of coverage [selected years 1950-83]. (p. 20)

2.2. Of insurance companies [by type of coverage, by type of policy, selected years 1945-83]. (p. 21)

2.3. Income loss and benefits paid for short-term non-occupational sickness [includes payments for individual insurance, and group benefits for private industry and government employees, selected years 1950-82]. (p. 22)

PREMIUM INCOME
[Table titles begin "Health insurance premiums..."]

3.1. And ratio to disposable personal income [by type of insurer, selected years 1940-83]. (p. 24)

3.2. Of insurance companies, by type of policy and by type of protection [loss of income and hospital/medical expenses, selected years 1935-83]. (p. 25)

A5173–2.2: Government Health Care Programs

4.1. Federal and State/local government expenditures for health/medical care [selected years 1950-83]. (p. 32)

4.2. Annual number of Medicaid recipients and benefits paid by Federal/State governments [for age 65/over, families with dependent children, and all others, FY68-83]. (p. 33)

4.3. Medicare [hospital/medical, hospital (Part A), and supplementary medical (Part B) insurance] enrollments and benefit payments [to all enrollees, and to enrollees aged 65/over, 1966-83]. (p. 34)

4.4. Medicare and Medicaid benefits [paid, and persons enrolled], by State, 1983. (p. 35)

4.5. Hospital/medical expenditures under workers' compensation [State/local and Federal, 1965-83]. (p. 36)

4.6. Public health programs of State health agencies: expenditures [by Federal, State, and other source] and persons served; [all by State], 1982. (p. 37)

A5173–2.3: Medical Care Costs

[Types of expenditure generally include health services and supplies, personal health care expenses (hospital care, physician and dental services, drug/medical sundries, and others), program administration, government public health activities, research, and construction.]

NATIONAL HEALTH EXPENDITURES AND PROJECTIONS

[A] Projected expenditures for physicians' services, hospital care, and nursing home care [with] percent distribution by [patient] age, 1978 and [projected for 2003 under constant and declining mortality rates]. [chart] (p. 42)

5.1. National health expenditures, by type of expenditure, and source of funds [public or private], 1983. (p. 45)

5.2. Comparison of [amount and] growth rates of GNP and national health expenditures [selected years 1950-84]. (p. 45)

5.3. Aggregate and per capita amount and percentage distribution of national health expenditure, by type of expenditure, selected years 1965-85. (p. 46)

5.4. National health care expenditures, by type of expenditure and [private consumers and other, and Federal and State/local public] source of funds, 1982-83. (p. 47)

PERSONAL HEALTH CARE

[Tables show data for personal health care expenditures.]

5.5 Per capita amount by age [all ages, under 65, and 65/over] and type of expenditure, 1981. (p. 48)

5.6. Factors affecting growth [distribution for prices, population, and intensity]; 12-month period ending Dec. [1979-83]. (p. 48)

5.7 By type of payer [direct and 3rd-party payment sources, including private health insurance, philanthropy/industry, and Federal and State/local governments], and type of expenditure, 1983. (p. 49)

5.8. By source of payment [including direct payments, and private health insurance, government, and philanthropy/industry payments, 1966-83]. (p. 50)

PERSONAL CONSUMPTION AND CPI

5.9. Personal consumption expenditures, by type of product, 1983. (p. 51)

5.10. Ratio of personal consumption expenditures for medical care to disposable personal income and to total personal consumption expenditures [selected years 1950-83]. (p. 52)

5.11. Personal consumption expenditures for medical care [by type, selected years 1950-83]. (p. 53)

5.12-5.13. CPI for medical care items, and annual changes in CPI [by item, for urban wage/clerical workers and all urban consumers, selected years 1947-84]. (p. 54-55)

5.14. CPI [7 general items, for urban wage/clerical workers and all urban consumers, selected years 1935-84]. (p. 56)

HOSPITAL AND OTHER COSTS

5.15. Average cost to community hospitals per patient day and per patient stay, and average length of stay in community hospitals [selected years 1946-83]. (p. 57)

5.16. Community hospital statistics [average hospital cost per day and per hospital stay, and average length of stay, by State], 1983. (p. 58)

5.17. Comparison of hospital semi-private room charges, by State, July 1984 and Jan. 1985. (p. 59)

5.18 1984 fees [high, middle, and low ranges] for surgical, [obstetrics-gynecology], and emergency medical procedures [all by specialty and/or procedure]. (p. 60)

5.19. Average dentist charges [by procedure], selected areas [total U.S. and by region], 1984. (p. 61)

5.20. Median office-visit fees, by type of [visit and] physician, 1982-84. (p. 61)

5.21. Regional variations in median physician fees [by type of visit, for general and family practitioners, and all surgical and nonsurgical specialists], 1984. (p. 62)

5.22. Total [urban and rural] medical costs of having a baby [for delivery and birthing rooms, and cesarean procedures, by region], 1982. (p. 66)

5.23. Certain costs of accidents by class [including motor vehicle, work, and home], 1983. (p. 63)

A5173–2.4: Disability, Health Care Utilization, and Health Status

ACUTE AND CHRONIC DISABILITY

[Data by type of disability day are generally shown for restricted activity, bed disability, and school- and/or work-loss days.]

6.1. Disability due to chronic and acute conditions, by social and economic characteristics [sex, family income, education, and occupation, by type of disability day], 1982 (days per person). (p. 67)

6.2. Selected health characteristics [disability days by type or physician visits per person], by geographic region, 1982. (p. 68)

6.3. Workdays lost due to [5] acute conditions [by age group and sex], 1982. (p. 69)

6.4. Days lost from school per 100 children (age 5-17) per year, due to acute conditions, by sex and [7] condition groups, 1982. (p. 70)

6.5. Percent distribution of persons with limitation of activity due to chronic conditions, by degree of limitation according to sex and age, 1982. (p. 70)

OCCUPATIONAL INJURY AND ILLNESS, AND DISABILITY INSURANCE

6.6. Number of occupational injuries and illnesses, and lost workdays, private sector, by industry division, 1983. (p. 71)

6.7. Growth in the social security disability insurance program [number insured and receiving benefits, and amount paid], 1965-84. (p. 72)

UTILIZATION TRENDS

6.8. Utilization of community hospitals [beds, average daily census, and admissions, selected years 1950-83]. (p. 73)

6.9. Rate of discharges and average length of stay for patients discharged from short-stay non-Federal hospitals, by sex [by diagnosis], 1983. (p. 74)

6.10. Rate of all listed surgical operations for patients discharged from short-stay non-Federal hospitals, by age and sex, 1983. (p. 74)

6.11. [Percent of community hospitals with] selected facilities, services, and special beds, 1983. (p. 75)

6.12. Number of physician visits per person [by age and sex], 1982. (p. 75)

A5173–2.5: Health Manpower

[Tables 7.2-7.3 show number and rate per 100,000 population.]

7.1. Estimated number of persons active in [13] selected health occupations, 1982. (p. 78)

7.2. Estimated active health professionals [physicians, dentists, and nurses, selected years 1965-83]. (p. 78)

7.3. Active [non-Federal] physicians, pharmacists, and dentists, by State, 1982. (p. 79)

A5173–3   **HEALTH AND HEALTH INSURANCE: The Public's View**
Annual, discontinued.

Annual survey report on public attitudes toward health care service and costs, medical malpractice, health insurance companies, and bioethical issues. Report is discontinued with the 1984 edition.

For description of report, see SRI 1984 Annual under this number.

A5178
Healthcare Financial Management Association

A5178–1   **HOSPITAL INDUSTRY ANALYSIS REPORT, 1979-83**
Annual. 1984. iv + 123 p.
SRI/MF/complete

Annual report, by William O. Cleverley, presenting hospital financial ratios, 1979-83. Covers 29 ratios concerning profitability, liquidity, capital structure, activity (revenue vs. assets), and other areas. Includes median and upper and lower quartile values, by region and bed size; and median values, by Standard & Poor's (S&P) bond rating, and by urban-rural status and bed size.

Also includes balance sheet and income statement summaries; median bed size, by S&P rating; and number of reporting hospitals, by region, bed size, and S&P rating.

Data are from audited financial statements of over 1,100 hospitals participating in HFMA's Financial Analysis Service.

Contains contents listing (p. iii-iv); overview and executive summary (p. 3-13); brief narrative with 2 charts, repeated for each ratio (p. 17-59); appendices A-B, with definitions of ratios and regions (p. 62-67); and appendices C-G, with 6 detailed tables (p. 71-123).

This is the 5th annual report; SRI coverage begins with this edition.

Availability: Healthcare Financial Management Association, Order Department, 1900 Spring Rd., Suite 500, Oak Brook IL 60521, $149.00; SRI/MF/complete.

A5185
Hearing Industries Association

A5185–1   QUARTERLY REPORT
Quarterly. Approx. 5 p.
SRI/MF/complete

Quarterly report on domestic- and foreign-manufactured hearing aid unit sales, by type and State. Also includes exports by country or world region of destination (with detail for Canadian Provinces), and hearing aids issued to VA clinics. Report is issued approximately 6 weeks after quarter of coverage. Data are from HIA participating companies and Federal agencies, and are compiled by Hauck & Associates, Inc.

Contains 9 quarterly tables, listed below.

Availability: Hearing Industries Association, 1800 M St., NW, Washington DC 20036, †; SRI/MF/complete.

Issues reviewed during 1985: 3rd Qtr. 1984-2nd Qtr. 1985 (D).

QUARTERLY TABLES:
[Tables A-C show data annually for previous 3-7 years. Other tables generally show data cumulatively for current year through quarter of coverage, with comparisons to previous years and selected quarterly detail. Types of hearing aids are eyeglass, behind and inside the ear, and convertible. Number and sequence of tables may vary slightly.]

[1] Unit sales: by States, domestic; and export [to Canada and other].

A. Import statistics [hearing aid units and value, and parts value].

B. Veterans Administration [hearing aids issued to VA clinics by the Federal Prosthetics Distribution Center; fiscal year data].

C. Cros [contralateral routing of offside signals] and bicros, by type [except convertible; domestic- and foreign-manufactured hearing aids sold].

D. Tinnitus maskers [unit shipments].

E. Gross exports of completed hearing aid units, by destination [Japan and 5 world regions].

F. Canadian [unit sales of U.S. companies] by Province.

G-H. Net units sold by type and origin [domestic and foreign].

A5190
Helicopter Association International

A5190–1   1985 HELICOPTER ANNUAL
Annual. Jan. 1985. 256 p.
ISSN 0739-5728.
SRI/MF/complete

Annual source book, for 1985, presenting information on helicopters used in civil aviation. Includes data on helicopter fleets, production, trade, flying hours, pilots, accidents, and landing facilities. Data are from HAI, Aerospace Industries Assn, FAA, and other sources.

Contents:

a. Contents listing. (p. 3)

b. Specifications for helicopters and for equipment used in helicopters; 5 feature articles; and world directories of helicopter operators and HAI members. (p. 7-208)

c. Statistical section, with 1 chart, 14 tables listed below, and helicopter historical highlights and record flights. (p. 210-216)

d. Directory of organizations, publications, and individuals that affect aviation policy; and information on HIA activities and organization. (p. 218-256)

This is the 3rd edition of the report. SRI coverage begins with this edition.

Availability: Helicopter Association International, 1619 Duke St., Alexandria VA 22314-3406, $35.00; SRI/MF/complete.

TABLES:
[Data are for U.S., unless otherwise noted. HAI data cover member operators worldwide.]

[1] Total helicopter fleet, by model/series [with type and number of engines, arranged by manufacturer], (as of Nov. 1984). (p. 210)

[2] Number of helicopters by manufacturer and percent total fleet (as of Sept. 1, 1984). (p. 211)

[3] Civil helicopter production [domestic and export, 1970-83]. (p. 211)

[4-5] Exports and imports of civil helicopters [units and value, by region of destination or country of origin, 1979-83]. (p. 211)

[6-7] Civil helicopter fleet [in U.S., Canada, and Mexico, 1982]; and civil helicopter operators and helicopters operated in [aggregate] North America [including] U.S., Canada, Mexico, and Puerto Rico [1965-80 and 1982; all shown for commercial, corporate/executive, and civil government agency operations]. (p. 212)

[8-9] Helicopter flying hours and accident rate, general aviation, U.S. and Canada [and accident rates for HAI members; 1972-83]. (p. 212)

[10] Accident rate comparison, piston vs. turbine [1975-80]. (p. 212)

[11] HAI reported accident rate [and flying hours, and total and fatal accidents, 1980-83]. (p. 212)

[12] Active pilots by type of certificate [1973-83]. (p. 213)

[13-14] Heliports/helistops and hospital heliports [by census division and for Puerto Rico and Canada, with total elevated facilities, selected years 1973-84]. (p. 213)

A5200
Highway Loss Data Institute

NOTE ABOUT HIGHWAY LOSS DATA INSTITUTE PUBLICATIONS:

Highway Loss Data Institute (HLDI) is a nonprofit organization supported by the Insurance Institute for Highway Safety. Publications are based on motor vehicle noncommercial insurance loss data supplied by major insurance firms, standardized for proportion of youthful operators and deductible amounts of coverage.

HLDI publications include 1 annual series on collision coverage (A5200-1); 2 annual reports on automobile theft and personal injury insurance loss experiences (A5200-2 and A5200-3); and a continuing series of special reports analyzing particular vehicles or safety features (A5200-4).

Annual reports show data by make and model series for each model year by passenger car size group (small and other subcompact and compact, and large), and body style (2-door, 4-door, station wagon, and sports/specialty); or for multipurpose vehicles by type (van, pickup, and utility).

A5200–1   AUTOMOBILE INSURANCE LOSSES: Collision Coverages
Annual series. For individual publication data, see below.
SRI/MF/complete

Annual series of reports comparing collision coverage claim frequencies and amounts for motor vehicles damaged during their 1st 1-3 years of operation, by vehicle type.

Reports reviewed during 1985 are described below. For descriptive note on HLDI publications, see A5200 above.

Availability: Highway Loss Data Institute, Watergate 600, Washington DC 20037, †; SRI/MF/complete.

A5200–1.1: Insurance Losses, Collision Coverages: Passenger Vehicles, Vans, Pickups, and Utility Vehicles. 1984 Models During Their First Year, 1983 Models During Their First Two Years, 1982 Models During Their First Three Years
[Annual. Jan. 1985. viii+52 p. Research Rpt. HLDI R84-2. ISSN 0093-0466. SRI/MF/complete.]

Annual report presenting standardized insurance claim frequencies and loss experiences for 1982-84 model passenger cars and other noncommercial vehicles, by make and series, during their 1st 1-3 years of operation.

Contains summary, and listings of contents, charts, and tables (p. v-viii); introduction and discussion of results, with 1 summary chart, and 9 tables listed below (p. 1-39); 2 appendices, with lists of vehicle classifications and definitions (p. 40-50); and list of HLDI publications (p. 51-52).

TABLES:

PASSENGER CARS

1-3. Relative average loss payments per insured vehicle year for 1982-84 model year cars with the best and worst collision coverage results. (p. 4-6)

4-6. Insurance losses, collision coverages, 1982-84 models, passenger cars [shows total insured vehicle years, relative claim frequency, and relative average loss payment per claim and per insured vehicle year, by make and model grouped by body style and size]. (p. 7-29)

OTHER NONCOMMERCIAL VEHICLES

7-9 [Tables 4-6 generally are repeated for 1982-84 model vans, pickups, and utility vehicles.] (p. 32-39)

A5200–1.2: Automobile Insurance Losses, Collision Coverages: Initial Results for 1985 Models

[Annual. July 1985. vii + 24 p. Research Rpt. HLDI R85-1. ISSN 0196-2663. SRI/MF/ complete.]

Annual report on insurance claim frequency and average loss payment for 1985 model passenger cars during their initial 6 months of operation, from Oct. 1984 through Feb. 1985. Includes data by size class, make, and series, with summary comparison to 1984 models.

Contains summary, and contents and table listings (p. v-vii); introduction and discussion of results, with 2 tables (p. 1-8); appendices, with data sources, methodology, definitions, and vehicle specifications (p. 9-22); and list of other HLDI publications (p. 23-24).

A5200–2   INSURANCE LOSSES, THEFT COVERAGES: Passenger Cars, Vans, Pickups, and Utility Vehicles. 1984 Models During Their First Year, 1983 Models During Their First Two Years, 1982 Models During Their First Three Years
Annual.   Mar. 1985.
viii + 50 p.
Research Rpt. HLDI T84-1.
ISSN 0276-4997.
SRI/MF/complete

Annual report on theft insurance claims and payments for 1982-84 model automobiles and noncommercial vans, pickups, and utility vehicles. Shows claim frequency, and average payment per claim and per insured vehicle year, by vehicle size class and/or body style, make/series, and model year.

Data are based on claims filed with 13 insurers under comprehensive coverage, and are adjusted for differences in operator age groups and deductible amounts.

Contains summary, and contents and table listings (p. v-viii); narrative report with 12 tables (p. 1-37); and appendices, with vehicle series designations, definitions, and HLDI publications list (p. 38-50).

For descriptive note on HLDI publications, see A5200 above.

Availability: Highway Loss Data Institute, Watergate 600, Washington DC 20037, †; SRI/MF/ complete.

A5200–3   INSURANCE LOSSES, PERSONAL INJURY PROTECTION COVERAGES: Passenger Cars, Vans, Pickups, and Utility Vehicles, 1982-84 Models
Annual.   Aug. 1985.
vii + 31 p.
Research Rpt. HLDI I84-1.
ISSN 0734-9017.
SRI/MF/complete

Annual report on personal injury insurance claim frequencies for 1982-84 model passenger cars, vans, pickup trucks, and utility vehicles, by domestic and foreign make and series, shown for all medical claims, and claims exceeding $250, $500, and $1,000, for the period from model's introduction through Dec. 1984.

Report is based on claims for medical expenses made under personal injury protection (PIP) coverages provided in 20 "no-fault" States. Frequency analyses are presented for all vehicles in each claim size category, and data may not be comparable for all vehicles.

Contains summary, and listings of contents, charts, and tables (p. v-vii); introduction and narrative analysis, with 1 summary chart, and 5 tables listed below (p. 1-16); appendices A-D, including list of PIP States, methodology, definitions, and list of model vehicle series designations (p. 17-28); and list of HLDI publications (p. 29-31).

For descriptive note on HLDI publications, see A5200 above.

Availability: Highway Loss Data Institute, Watergate 600, Washington DC 20037, †; SRI/MF/ complete.

TABLES:

[All tables show years of exposure and claim frequency by size of PIP claim, for 1982-84 model vehicles. Tables [2-5] show data by make and series.]

1. Claim frequencies [per 1,000 insured vehicle years; for each passenger car model year]. (p. 3)

2-3. Passenger cars with the best and worst [at least 35% better or worse than average] injury loss experience: relative injury claim frequencies. (p. 4-5)

4-5. Relative claim frequency [for passenger cars by body style, vans, pickup trucks, and utility vehicles, most by vehicle-size group]. (p. 7-12, 15-16)

A5370
Idaho Library Association

A5370–1   IDAHO LIBRARIAN
Quarterly.   Approx. 20 p. per issue; cumulative pagination throughout year.
ISSN 0019-1213.
LC SN 78-355.
SRI/MF/excerpts

Quarterly journal of Idaho library activities and operations. Covers library administration and services, technological developments, and librarian education.

Issues are primarily narrative and generally contain editorial depts and feature articles. Annual tables on academic and public library operations are included in the Jan. and Apr. issues, respectively.

Features with substantial statistical content are described, as they appear, under "Statistical Features." Each issue of the journal is reviewed, but an abstract is published in SRI monthly issues only when annual tables or other features with substantial statistical content appear.

Availability: Idaho Library Association, Editor, Idaho Librarian, University of Idaho Library, Moscow ID 83843, members †, nonmembers $10.00 per yr., single copy $2.50; SRI/MF/excerpts for all portions described under "Statistical Features."

Issues reviewed during 1985: Jan.-Oct. 1985 (P) (Vol. 37, Nos. 1-4).

STATISTICAL FEATURES:

A5370–1.601: Jan. 1985 (Vol. 37, No. 1)

STATISTICS FOR IDAHO ACADEMIC LIBRARIES, ANNUAL FEATURE

(p. 7) Annual table showing Idaho academic library holdings by type, hours of operation, professional and nonprofessional staff, and expenditures of State/institution and Federal funds, all by individual institution, as of July 1, 1984.

A5370–1.602: Apr. 1985 (Vol. 37, No. 2)

PUBLIC LIBRARY STATISTICS: 1984, ANNUAL FEATURE

(p. 43-48) Annual feature consisting of 2 tables showing Idaho public library income by source, expenditures by object, population served, borrowers, holdings, and circulation, all by library grouped by county and region, FY84.

A5425
Independent Petroleum Association of America

A5425-1   PETROLEUM
INDEPENDENT: The Oil and
Gas Producing Industry in
Your State, 1985-86
7 times per year (selected
issue). Sept. 1985. 128 p.
Vol. 55, No. 5.
LC 41-10748.
SRI/MF/complete

Annual report presenting detailed petroleum industry data for the U.S. and by producing State, 1984, with trends from the 1970s or earlier. Covers exploration and development, production, reserves, prices, and industry finances and employment. Also includes data on U.S. energy consumption, and world oil reserves.

Data are compiled from reports of industry assns and Federal and State agencies, and from other published materials.

Contains contents listing, introduction with 3 summary charts, data sources, energy conversions, and abbreviations (p. 3-9); national and State 1984 statistical profiles, described below (p. 12-91); 1 chart and 32 tables, listed below, primarily presenting trend data by State (p. 92-125); and glossary (p. 126).

Report is published as the Sept. issue of *Petroleum Independent,* a periodical issued 7 times a year. The periodical does not usually contain substantial statistics. This annual issue is the only feature covered in SRI.

Availability: Petroleum Independent Publishers, Inc., Statistics Department, 1101 16th St., NW, Washington DC 20036, members and selected institutions †, others $5.00; SRI/MF/complete.

STATISTICS:

A5425-1.1: Profiles

(p. 12-91) The following 4 tables, plus 2 trend charts and 1 map showing oil and/or gas producing areas, are repeated for total U.S. and 33 producing States.

Tables include data for crude oil, natural gas, and natural gas liquids, as appropriate.

TABLES:

[1] Historical information [including producing States or counties and acreage, and percent of acreage leased; 1st year of production; year and amount of peak production; deepest well drilled; total wells drilled as of Dec. 1984; and cumulative production and reserves, as of Dec. 1983].

[2] Value of oil and gas [including average wellhead price and wellhead value of production, severance/production taxes paid, and production employment, 1984; and cumulative wellhead value as of Dec. 1984.].

[3] 1984 industry statistics [including seismic crew months worked; rotary drilling rigs active; exploratory, development, and wildcat wells and footage drilled; producing wells; and average daily production].

[4] 1983 latest available data [including new reserves added, and total proved reserves; producing and abandoned stripper wells; stripper well production and reserves; and drilling costs].

A5425-1.2: Trends

[All tables except [17-18], [21-28], and [30-32] show data by State. Data are for 1975-84, unless otherwise noted.]

[1] Seismic exploration activity [crew months worked; also includes data for marine and undesignated land areas]. (p. 92)

[2] Acreage under lease. (p. 93)

[3] Rotary rigs active. (p. 94)

[4-7] New field wildcat, exploratory, development, and total wells drilled [also includes data for Federal waters]. (p. 95-98)

[8] Cost of drilling and equipping wells [including wells and footage drilled, and cost, with detail for onshore and offshore locations, Texas districts, selected other State subareas, Appalachian region, and 4 Federal water areas], 1983. (p. 99)

[9-10] Producing crude oil and natural gas wells [also includes data for Federal waters]. (p. 100-101)

[11-12] Crude oil and natural gas production [with U.S. average daily oil production]. (p. 102-103)

[13-14] Stripper well crude oil production, and producing crude oil stripper wells, [1974-83]. (p. 104-105)

[15-16] Crude oil and natural gas wellhead prices. (p. 106-107)

[17-18] Wholesale petroleum prices, total and east of California, [by product type, 1935-84]. (p. 108-109)

[19] Severance/production taxes paid. (p. 110)

[20] Employment in the petroleum industry [for mining, manufacturing, transportation, wholesale, and retail sectors], 1984. (p. 111)

[21] Drilling summary [including wells and footage drilled, total cost, and average depth, for oil wells, gas wells, and dry holes], 1983. (p. 112)

[22] Drilling costs [total, per well, and per foot, 1964-83]. (p. 112)

[23] Cost indices [for oil field machinery and wages, oil well casing, and carbon line pipe, 1965-84]. (p. 112)

[24] World crude oil reserves [for U.S., Canada, Communist nations, and 5 world regions]. (p. 114)

[25] Energy consumption [of crude oil/natural gas liquid, natural gas, and total energy, 1950-84]. (p. 117)

[26] Hourly earnings [for oil/gas companies compared to all manufacturing companies, 1950-84]. (p. 118)

[27] Peak year milestones [for selected petroleum industry indicators]. (p. 118)

[28] Financial data [including rates of return for oil/gas companies compared to all manufacturing companies, and exploration/development outlays for larger oil/gas companies and independents, 1960-83]. (p. 118)

[29] Consumption of petroleum products [by type], 1984. (p. 120)

[30] Crude oil production by Chase Group [of companies, aggregate compared to all other production; 1950-83, and excluding Alaska North Slope, 1977-83]. (p. 121)

[31] Gasoline retail prices [excluding taxes, tax amount, and pump price, 1969-84]. (p. 121)

[A] U.S. petroleum resources: crude oil and natural gas [measured, indicated/inferred, and undiscovered recoverable, 1981]. [chart] (p. 123)

[32] Statistical summary of the petroleum producing industry [including production, imports, total supply and demand, reserves, wells and footage drilled, and prices, with selected detail for crude oil, natural gas, natural gas liquids, and refined products, 1950-84]. (p. 124-125)

A5425-2   U.S. PETROLEUM
STATISTICS, 1985 Final
Annual. [Oct. 1985].
9 p. no paging, pocket size
foldout.
SRI/MF/complete

Annual report on U.S. oil and gas industry trends, 1965-84, including supply and demand, prices, and finances. Data are compiled by the Independent Petroleum Assn of America from member data and reports of Federal and other industry sources.

Contains 1 table showing peak year data for 14 supply indicators, and 16 other tables listed below.

Availability: Independent Petroleum Association of America, Statistics Department, 1101 16th St., NW, Washington DC 20036, †; SRI/MF/complete.

TABLES:
[Tables show data for 1965-84.]

A5425-2.1: Supply and Demand

1. Exploration activity [seismic crew count, total acres leased, active rotary rigs, and total, dry, and new field wildcat wells].

2. Drilling [oil, gas, dry, and service well completions; and total footage drilled].

3. Number of producing wells [stripper and other crude oil, and total natural gas wells].

4. Drilling costs and indices [for oil field machinery, well casings, and oil field wages; and total, per well, and per foot drilling costs].

5. New reserves added [crude oil, gas liquids, and natural gas; and amount of crude oil and natural gas per new well].

6. Proved reserves [of crude oil, gas liquids, and natural gas; and reserve/production ratios for crude oil, total liquids, and natural gas; as of Dec. 31].

7. Petroleum production [of stripper and other crude oil, with averages per well; and gas liquids].

8. Petroleum consumption [domestic petroleum demand and exports, and petroleum and natural gas shares of U.S. energy consumption].

9. Petroleum supply [crude oil and refined product imports, and total production and supply].

10. Imports by origin [OPEC, Arab OPEC, and Western and Eastern Hemispheres].

A5425-2.2: Prices and Finance

11. Natural gas [production, imports, exports, and domestic supply; and current and constant 1984 prices].

12. Composite value and prices [crude oil and natural gas wellhead value, natural gas price per barrel, and composite oil/gas price per barrel in current and constant 1984 dollars].

13. Wholesale oil prices [per gallon for motor gasoline, kerosene, and distillate and residual fuel oil; and aggregate average price per barrel].

14. Prices [for crude oil wellhead in current and constant 1984 dollars, and motor gasoline including and excluding retail fuel taxes]; and wages [for oil/gas and all manufacturing industries].

15. Financial data [rate of return for oil and all manufacturing companies, and exploration/development outlays for larger companies and independents].

16. General economic data [GNP, PPI, CPI, and crude price index].

A5600
Institute of
Real Estate Management

A5600–1   INCOME/EXPENSE ANALYSIS: APARTMENTS, 1984 Edition
Annual. 1984. 224 p.
ISSN 0194-1941.
ISBN 0-912104-77-5.
LC 79-643863.
SRI/MF/not filmed

Annual report on apartment building income and expense ratios for U.S. and Canada, 1983, with trends primarily from 1980. Covers income by source, vacancy/rent loss, and expenses by detailed item, all shown as percent of total possible income and as amount per square foot; and tenant turnover rate.

Data are shown as medians and/or ranges, by building type, for selected U.S. and Canadian metro areas, by U.S. region, and for total U.S. and Canada.

Building types are furnished and unfurnished elevator, low-rise (12-24 units and 25/more units), and garden-type. Income and expense data for unfurnished buildings also are shown by building age.

Also includes summary trends for percent of buildings with utilities/services included in rent, and for heating costs, by type of fuel; and distribution of buildings by heating fuel type and region.

Data are from a 1983 survey of 5,771 apartment buildings. Report is intended as an aid in comparing operations of similar apartment properties.

Contains contents listing, user guidelines, and map (p. 3-10); trend analysis with narrative summary, 4 charts, and 31 tables (p. 12-42); detailed tabulations of survey results, arranged by building type, with accompanying summary chart and tables (p. 44-215); and survey form facsimile, worksheet, sample characteristics, and index (p. 216-224).

Availability: Institute of Real Estate Management, Publications, 430 N. Michigan Ave., Chicago IL 60611, $65.00; SRI/MF/not filmed.

A5600–2   INCOME/EXPENSE ANALYSIS: OFFICE BUILDINGS, Downtown and Suburban, 1984 Edition
Annual. 1984. 240 p.
ISSN 0146-9630.
ISBN 0-912104-78-3.
LC 77-649065.
SRI/MF/not filmed

Annual report on downtown and suburban office building income and expenses for U.S. and Canada, 1983, with trends from 1971. Covers income by source, vacancy/rent loss, and expenses by detailed item, shown as medians and ranges, per square foot of building area and rentable office space; year-end vacancy level; percent of buildings that contract cleaning services; and average tenant alteration allowances.

Data are shown for downtown and suburban buildings, for selected U.S. and Canadian metro areas, by U.S. region, and for total U.S. and Canada, with U.S. detail by building size, age group, rental range, and number of stories.

Also includes analyses of leasing commissions, and energy consumption and cost by fuel type, by U.S. city and region, and for Canada.

Data are from a 1984 survey of approximately 2,300 office buildings. Report is intended as an aid in comparing operations of similar office building properties.

Contains contents listing (p. 3); trend analysis and summary, with 3 charts and 18 tables (p. 4-11); user guidelines and map (p. 12-18); detailed tabulations of survey results, arranged by location (p. 20-220); 4 summary charts (p. 221-222); leasing and energy consumption analyses, with detailed tabulations (p. 224-231); and survey form facsimile, worksheet, participating cities and sample characteristics, and index (p. 232-240).

Availability: Institute of Real Estate Management, Publications, 430 N. Michigan Ave., Chicago IL 60611, $65.00; SRI/MF/not filmed.

A5600–3   EXPENSE ANALYSIS: CONDOMINIUMS, COOPERATIVES, AND PLANNED UNIT DEVELOPMENTS, 1984 Edition
Annual. 1984. 160 p.
ISBN 0-912104-79-1.
LC 79-642606.
SRI/MF/not filmed

Annual report on expenses of condominiums, cooperatives, and planned unit developments (PUDs) in U.S. and Canada, by detailed item, 1983. Data are shown as medians and ranges per unit and per square foot of floor area, by building type, grouped for selected metro areas, by building age and price range, and by U.S. region and total Canada. Building types are high-rise and/or low-rise, townhouse, and combination.

Also includes data on monthly owner assessments; and percent of projects furnishing utilities and recreational facilities, by type.

Data are from a survey of 1,053 condominiums, 70 cooperatives, and 109 PUDs. Report is intended as an aid in comparing operations of similar properties.

Contains contents listing, summary with 2 charts and 13 tables, user guidelines, and map (p. 3-14); detailed tabulation of survey results for condominiums (p. 16-108), cooperatives (p. 110-128), and PUDs (p. 130-151); and survey form facsimile, worksheet, sample characteristics, and index (p. 152-160).

Availability: Institute of Real Estate Management, Publications, 430 N. Michigan Ave., Chicago IL 60611, $47.25; SRI/MF/not filmed.

A5625
Institute of
Scrap Iron and Steel

A5625–1   FACTS, 41st EDITION, 1983 Yearbook
Annual. 1984. 12 p.
ISSN 0163-3899.
LC 78-646697.
SRI/MF/complete

Annual report on ferrous scrap metal, covering production, consumption, prices, shipments, and foreign trade, 1983, with selected trends from 1963. Includes data by furnace type and grade of scrap.

Data are from American Iron and Steel Institute, *Iron Age,* Bureau of Mines, and other Federal agencies.

Contains contents listing (p. 2); and 6 summary charts, and 16 tables listed below, interspersed with brief narrative (p. 3-12).

Availability: Institute of Scrap Iron and Steel, 1627 K St., NW, Washington DC 20006, $5.00; SRI/MF/complete.

TABLES:
[Data are for 1974-83, unless otherwise noted.]

PRODUCTION, CONSUMPTION, AND RECEIPTS

[1] Facts summary [selected years 1963-83]. (p. 3)

[2-5] Ferrous scrap consumption, purchased scrap receipts, and home scrap production; and raw steel production, and steel mill and foundry castings shipments; [1974-83 and monthly 1981-83]. (p. 4-5)

[6] Trend of U.S. steel production by [type of] furnace. (p. 5)

[7] Purchased scrap receipts, home scrap production, and ferrous scrap consumption, by grade [1981-83]. (p. 6)

[8] U.S. consumption of ferrous scrap and blast furnace iron, by type of furnace. (p. 6)

[9] Iron ore [consumption, imported for consumption, and mined domestically, monthly 1981-83]. (p. 7)

FOREIGN TRADE

[10-12] U.S. exports: of carbon steel/iron scrap [monthly 1981-83]; and of ferrous scrap by country and grade [1979-83]. (p. 8-9)

[13] U.S. imports of ferrous scrap, iron ore, pig iron, and steel products. (p. 9)

PRICES

[14-16] No. 1 heavy melting steel scrap, No. 2 bundles, and finished steel composite prices [monthly]. (p. 10)

A5650
Insurance
Information Institute

A5650–1   INSURANCE FACTS: 1984-85 Property/Casualty Fact Book
Annual.   Nov. 1984.   116 p.
LC 73-2557.
SRI/MF/complete

Annual report on property/casualty insurance industry finances, operations, and losses, 1983, with trends from 1970s or earlier. Includes data on premiums written, by type of insurance and State; and insurance-related accident, disaster, and crime incidence data.

Data are compiled from Federal and State government and private sources, particularly A. M. Best Co., National Safety Council, and National Fire Protection Assn. Data source is noted under each table.

Contents:

a. 1 table showing property/casualty insurers' aggregate operating results, 1981-83 (inside front cover); and contents listing (p. 3-4).

b. 6 narrative sections, with 7 trend charts, and 2 other charts and 90 tables listed below. (p. 5-94).

c. 2 sections of background information, including a tabular summary of auto financial responsibility limits by State and Canadian Province, selected lists and directories, and definitions; and an index. (p. 95-116, inside back cover)

Availability: Insurance Information Institute, 110 William St., New York NY 10038, member companies and insurance agents $4.50, others $9.00; SRI/MF/complete.

CHARTS AND TABLES:

A5650–1.1: Overview

COMPANIES, EMPLOYMENT, AND COVERAGE

[1] Property/casualty insurance companies [home offices], by State, 1984. (p. 11)

[2] Employment in insurance, 1976-83 (annual averages). (p. 12)

[3-4] Insurance coverages reported by U.S. households; and policy understanding, kinds of losses insured persons say they are covered against; [both for renters and owners], 1984. (p. 13)

WORLD INSURANCE INDUSTRY

[5] World premium volume by [world] area in billions of U.S. dollars and percentages [including life and non-life shares], 1981-82. (p. 15)

[6] World's [10] leading insurance countries [ranked by total premium value, with value of life and non-life premiums], 1982. (p. 15)

A5650–1.2: Industry Finances and Premiums

OPERATING RESULTS AND INVESTMENTS

[1] Net premiums written, by line, 1982-83. (p. 16)

[2] Consolidated assets and policyholders' surplus, 1978-83. (p. 18)

[3] Where the premium dollar goes [distribution for property/casualty premiums by expenditure type, 1983]. [chart] (p. 18)

I-III. Underwriting results, investment income, and combined net income before taxes: property/casualty insurance business, 1959-83. (p. 19-20)

[4] Average annual rates of return on net income after taxes as percent of net worth, selected industries [1974-83]. (p. 22)

[5] Investments of property/casualty insurers [distribution of bonds, common and preferred stocks, and other, investments, by type, 1973, 1978, and 1983]. (p. 23)

PREMIUMS

[6] Total net premiums written by property/casualty insurance companies [accident/health and other], 1974-83. (p. 24)

[7] Purchases of property/casualty insurance [premiums paid by commercial and individual purchasers, by type of insurance], 1983. [chart] (p. 24)

[8-21] Auto liability and physical damage; fire and allied lines; homeowners, commercial, and farmowners multiple peril; crop-hail; general liability; medical malpractice; workers' compensation; surety and fidelity; burglary/theft; boiler/machinery; glass; and inland and ocean marine insurance; [showing premiums written and combined ratio, generally for 1974-83]. (p. 25-33)

[22] Nuclear insurance premiums [liability and property], 1957-83. (p. 34)

[23-25] Direct written premiums [total and for] selected lines, and premium taxes, by State, 1983. (p. 35-40)

GUARANTY FUNDS

[26] Guaranty fund assessments by State [and Puerto Rico], 1969-83 [period]. (p. 41)

A5650–1.3: High Risk Insurance and Factors Affecting Insurance Costs

HIGH RISK INSURANCE

[Tables [1-5] show data by State. Selected tables include data for Guam, Virgin Islands, and/or Puerto Rico.]

[1] Private passenger cars insured through the shared market mechanisms [1982-83]. (p. 43)

[2-3] Insurance provided by FAIR [Fair Access to Insurance Requirements] plans; and by beach/windstorm plans; [1983]. (p. 44-45)

[4] Flood insurance in the U.S. [number of communities, and number and value of residential and commercial policies in force; as of Dec. 31, 1983]. (p. 46-47)

[5] Federal crime insurance [residential and commercial policies and value of insurance in force, at year end], 1983. (p. 48)

INSURANCE COSTS AND COST OF LIVING

[6-7] Price indices for property and auto insurance and related items, and annual rates of change, 1974-83. (p. 49-50)

[8] Cost of operating autos [by size] and vans, 1984. (p. 51)

[9] Composition of median monthly housing expense [1979, 1981, and 1983]. (p. 51)

LIABILITY LAWSUITS

[10] Product liability cases commenced in Federal district courts [by State and outlying area], FY82-83). (p. 53)

HEALTH CARE COSTS

[11] Hospital semiprivate room rates [by State and for Puerto Rico], Jan. 1983-84. (p. 54)

A5650–1.4: Losses

FIRES

[1-2] U.S. fire losses [property value, selected years] 1875-1983; and fire deaths per 100,000 population [by age group, 1974-83]. (p. 56)

[3-4] Causes of reported [residential and non-residential] fires; and incendiary and suspicious fires in structures; [number or distribution of fires, injuries and/or deaths, and dollar loss], 1981 or 1983 estimate. (p. 57-58)

[5-6] Structural fires and civilian fire deaths, by property use, 1983 estimates. (p. 59)

[7-8] 1983 fires resulting in 10 or more deaths; and 10 [all-time] worst multiple-death fires in the U.S.; [date, place, type of structure, and number of deaths]. (p. 60)

[9-10] U.S. fires causing property damage of $5 million or more, 1983; and 15 [all-time] most costly fires; [date, place, type of property, and estimated loss]. (p. 61-62)

CIVIL DISORDERS AND DISASTERS

[Data for "most costly" events show all-time records and include dates, location, and estimated losses.]

[11] 10 most costly U.S. civil disorders. (p. 62)

[12] Catastrophe record [date, place, and estimated loss], 1983. (p. 63-64)

[13] 10 most costly U.S. earthquakes. (p. 65)

[14-15] Hurricanes [and resulting deaths] in the U.S., 1959-83; and 10 most costly insured hurricanes. (p. 66)

[16-17] Tornadoes [and resulting deaths] in the U.S., 1959-83; and 5-year totals, tornadoes [and resulting deaths and injuries] by State [and Puerto Rico], 1979-83. (p. 67)

MOTOR VEHICLE AND OTHER ACCIDENTS, AND INSURANCE CLAIMS

[18-19] Motor vehicle accidents [deaths, injuries, and economic loss], 1983; and traffic deaths [and rates], 1974-83. (p. 68)

[20] Sex of drivers involved in [all and fatal] accidents, 1974-83. (p. 69)

[21] Motor vehicle deaths and injuries, by type of accident [for urban and rural locations], 1983. (p. 70)

[22] Countrywide average paid claim costs [for bodily injury and property damage], liability insurance, private passenger cars [1974-83]. (p. 70)

[23] Measures by States to curb drunk driving [as of Aug. 1, 1984]. (p. 72-73)

[24-25] Accidental deaths [4 types], 1982-83; and numbers and types of home accident deaths, 1974-83. (p. 74)

[26] [Total number of drivers, and drivers in fatal and total] accidents, by age of drivers, 1983. (p. 75)

[27] Cost of replacing selected [auto] parts, 1982 and 1984. (p. 76)

[28-29] 1984 model 5 mph crash test repair costs; and weight and repair costs of bumper system; [for selected auto models]. (p. 77)

[30] Insurance losses, collision coverages, in years since introduction [claim frequency, and loss per claim and per insured vehicle year], 1981-83 models, passenger cars. (p. 78)

[31] Relative average loss payments per insured vehicle year for 1983 model year cars with the best and worst collision coverage loss experience [by make, series, and body style]. (p. 79)

[32-33] 1980-82 passenger cars with best and worst loss experience, relative injury claim frequencies, personal injury protection coverages [by make, series, and body style]. (p. 81)

[34] Loss experience summary by vehicle size and model year, theft losses, passenger cars [claim frequency, and loss per claim and per insured vehicle year, 1982-83]. (p. 83)

WORK ACCIDENTS AND PROPERTY CRIMES

[35-36] Work fatalities and injuries [and rates], and economic losses from work accidents, [selected years] 1960-83. (p. 84)

[37] Occupational disease experience [distribution of claims; and average indemnity, medical, and total benefits per case; by disease, Apr. 1979-Dec. 1982 period]. (p. 86)

[38-39] Crimes against property, and motor vehicle registrations and thefts, 1974-83. (p. 87-88)

[40] Motor vehicle thefts, by States, 1982-83. (p. 88)

[41] Arrests, by age [and crime], 1983. (p. 89)

AIRCRAFT AND BOATING ACCIDENTS

[42-43] Aircraft accidents in 1983 [by type]; and accidents, scheduled airlines, 1979-83; [both showing hours flown, total and fatal accidents, and fatalities]. (p. 90)

[44] Boating accidents, [fatalities, injuries, and property damage] by State [and for Puerto Rico and Virgin Islands], 1983. (p. 91)

HEALTH INSURANCE AND HOSPITAL COSTS

[45] [Health insurance benefits paid, for private insurers, Blue Cross/Blue Shield, other plans, Medicare, and Medicaid, 1981-82.] (p. 93)

[46] Cost of hospitalization [per day, average length of stay, average cost to hospital per patient stay], and health insurance benefits paid by private insurers, [all by State and outlying area], 1982. (p. 93-94)

A5750
International Association
of Ice Cream Manufacturers

A5750–2   LATEST SCOOP, 1985 EDITION: Facts and Figures on Ice Cream and Related Products
Annual. Aug. 1985.
4 + 38 p.
ISSN 0732-0620.
LC 82-641843.
SRI/MF/complete

Annual report on U.S. and foreign production of ice cream and related products, 1984 and trends. Includes data by U.S. State and region, Canadian Province, and foreign country. Also includes data on U.S. industry operations.

Data are from the Census Bureau, USDA, International Assn of Ice Cream Manufacturers surveys and estimates, and other sources.

Contains contents listing (1 p.); general information, definitions, and nutritional data (p. 1-5); and 3 charts and 27 tables, with interspersed narrative (p. 6-38).

All tables, and 1 chart showing data not covered in tables, are listed below. Report also includes 4 text tables showing selected highlights for U.S. (p. 4) and Canada (p. 29), including preliminary ice cream production for Jan.-June 1985.

Availability: International Association of Ice Cream Manufacturers, 888 16th St., NW, Washington DC 20006, members $1.50, nonmembers $7.50; SRI/MF/complete.

TABLES AND CHART:

A5750–2.1: U.S. Data

OPERATING DATA AND PRICES

[1-2] Employees, wages, and value of shipments; and capital expenditures for new plants and equipment; frozen desserts industry [selected years] 1947-82. (p. 6-7)

[3] "Real" price of ice cream [average production worker wages, average retail price, and minutes of labor required to purchase a half-gallon of ice cream], 1974-84. (p. 8)

[A] Breakdown of ice cream processor's dollar [distribution of costs among raw materials, processing/packing, and other categories; no date]. [chart] (p. 8)

PRODUCTION

[Production data generally are shown for ice cream, ice milk, sherbet, and mellorine type products, and sometimes for water ices and other frozen dairy products. Tables [4-12] show combined data for hard frozen/soft serve products.]

[4-6] Total and per capita production, [selected years] 1859-1984; and production by States and regions, and 10 leading States, 1984. (p. 9-11)

[7-8] Monthly production, 1982-84; and [aggregate monthly production of all products] as a percent of annual average, 1964 and 1984. (p. 12-13)

[9-10] Production by regions, 1984; and per capita production by regions, [selected years] 1960-84. (p. 14-15)

[11] Production of mix for frozen products, by States and regions, 1984. (p. 16)

[12] Number of plants [including and excluding counter freezers for ice cream], 1960-84. (p. 17)

[13-19] Production [total and per capita, shown separately for hard frozen and soft serve products, 1984, with detail by region and trends from 1955]. (p. 18-24)

MISCELLANEOUS

[20-21] Supermarket frozen food dept sales [volume and value], and gross profit margin, by product category, 1983/84. (p. 26)

[22] Packaging [distribution of packaged ice cream by container size, material, and shape, 1984]. (p. 27)

[23] Ice cream flavors [10-15 most popular flavors and varieties, and top 3-5 flavors in 5 variety categories, 1984]. (p. 28)

A5750–2.2: Canadian and International Data

CANADA

[1-2] Production, 1971-84; and monthly production, 1984; of ice cream and related products. (p. 30-31)

[3-4] Per capita production of ice cream, [selected years] 1970-84; and hard and soft production of ice cream, 1982-84; by Provinces. (p. 32-33)

INTERNATIONAL

[5] [Total and per capita production of ice cream and related frozen products, by type, for 55 countries, various years 1977-84]. (p. 34-38)

A5785
International
Business Forms Industries

A5785–2   PERSPECTIVE 85: The Present and Future of the North American Forms Industry
Annual. 1985. 2 + 50 p.
LC 81-161999.
SRI/MF/complete

Annual report on the business form industry, 1984, with trends from 1958 and projections through 1989. Includes data on the following:

a. Shipment value by product type, 1984-89; and capacity utilization rates, weeks of order backlog, profitability, and average order size by U.S. region and for Canada, all by company sales size, various periods 1984.

b. Installed base of office personal computers and computer printers by type, with related form revenues and distribution of paper consumption by form type, both by type of printer, various years 1983-92; and paper supplier capacity by paper type, 1983-87.

c. Distribution of raw materials used in forms manufacture (no date); change in GNP, 1985-89; and firms using selected marketing techniques, including telemarketing and conferences, by company sales size and for distribution-based and direct sellers, and by U.S. region and for Canada, 1984.

d. Census of Manufactures data, including establishments and plants (total and with 20/ more employees); employment and payroll; production workers, hours, and wages; value added; cost of materials by type; shipment value and unit sales, by product type; capital expenditures; inventories; and selected operating ratios; shown variously by employment and sales size, region, and State, with some comparisons to other industries, various years 1958-84.

Data are from IBFI member firms, and other industry and government sources.

Contains listings of contents, tables, and charts (2 p.); narrative report, interspersed with 9 charts and 15 tables (p. 1-27); and 4 appendices, with 1 map, 3 charts, and 13 tables (p. 29-50).

Availability: International Business Forms Industries, 1730 N. Lynn St., Arlington VA 22209, members $150.00, nonmembers $300.00; SRI/MF/complete.

A5785–3   1984-85 ANNUAL RATIO STUDY

Annual. 1985. 2+82 p.
SRI/MF/complete

Annual report, compiled by Feddeman, Lesche and Tate, Inc., presenting detailed balance sheet, income and expense, and operating ratios for the business forms industry, 1984. Report is intended for use by individual companies in comparing their performance to industry averages.

Ratios are shown primarily by company sales size, market (direct and indirect), product type (continuous custom, unit sets, and mixed), and average order size, with separate data for industry leaders.

Also includes absolute data on industry sales, production value, pretax net income, assets, and employment.

Data are based on survey responses from 82 International Business Forms Industries members, for the year ended Dec. 31, 1984.

Contents:

a. Contents and table listings (2 p.); introduction and summary (p. 1-5); absolute data, with 1 table (p. 8-9); and computation notes (p. 11).

b. Summary statistics, with 4 tables (p. 13-28); and special analyses (product mix, key ratio, cost of production, and value added), with 25 tables (p. 29-55).

c. Appendices, with user guide, cause-effect analysis, standard account classifications, and sample questionnaire (p. 57-82).

Availability: International Business Forms Industries, 1730 N. Lynn St., Arlington VA 22209, members $175.00, nonmembers $350.00; SRI/MF/complete.

A5800
International
City Management Association

A5800–1   MUNICIPAL YEAR BOOK, 1985

Annual. Jan. 1985.
xix+428 p.   Vol. 52.
ISSN 0077-2186.
ISBN 0-87326-960-8.
LC 34-27121.
SRI/MF/not filmed

Annual source book, for 1985, of urban data and developments, for U.S. and Canadian cities. Includes information on local government structure, public services, and intergovernmental relations.

Data are based on International City Management Assn (ICMA) surveys of local officials of 6,627 cities with over 2,500 population and 381 areas under 2,500 population; reports of the Federation of Canadian Municipalities; Census Bureau reports; and other sources. Data are primarily for 1984, with some trends from the 1970s.

Contains contents listing (3 p.) and the following:

Introduction. Includes 4 tables showing U.S. and Canadian municipalities by type, by ICMA region; number of local governments by type; and U.S. municipalities and counties, by population size, region, metro status, and form of government. (p. xi-xix)

Part A. Municipal Profiles. Annual statistical report, described below. (p. 3-66)

Part B-D. 10 annual and special reports, including 8 reports with statistical content described below. (p. 69-238)

Part E. Directories of the following: State and/or Canadian Province municipal and county leagues and assns, councils of governments, and professional organizations; local government officials in Canada and 10 other countries; and U.S. county and municipal officials, with 4 tables (p. 254, 292) showing number of officials by sex, race/ethnicity (including white, black, Mexican-American, American Indian, Oriental, and other), and position. (p. 241-381)

Part F. References. (p. 385-405)

Biographical sketches of authors, and index. (p. 409-428)

Availability: International City Management Association, 1120 G St., NW, Washington DC 20005, $63.50 (prepaid), $65.75 (billed); SRI/MF/not filmed.

STATISTICAL REPORTS:

A5800–1.1: Part A. Local Government Profiles

PROFILES OF INDIVIDUAL CITIES AND COUNTIES

(p. 3-66) Annual report, by Ross H. Hoff, on the population characteristics, and government structure, employment, and finances of 2,570 municipalities with 10,000 or more population, and 1,358 counties with 25,000 or more population, according to the 1980 census.

Includes 8 tables (p. 3-11) showing summary data on city and county revenues and expenditures, by population size group and State; and 2 extended tables (p. 12-66) showing the following for individual cities and counties, grouped by State:

a. Government form; metro status; and 1982 population.

b. Revenues: total and per capita by source, including intergovernmental sources, property and other taxes, and charges/miscellaneous sources, FY83.

c. Expenditures: total and per capita by function, including police, fire, streets, and sewers/sanitation (cities); and law enforcement, streets, hospitals, welfare, and finance/administration (counties); FY83.

d. Utility revenues and expenditures (cities only); long term public debt; and FTE personnel and average salary.

A5800–1.2: Part B. The Intergovernmental Dimension

MUNICIPAL ANNEXATION AND BOUNDARY CHANGES: 1980-83

(p. 80-84) Annual report, by Joel C. Miller, on municipal annexation and incorporation activity. Data are from Census Bureau's *Boundary and Annexation Survey.*

Includes 6 tables showing municipal annexations, and resulting population and land area changes, by city and State; and population of municipal disincorporations, mergers, boundary changes, and largest annexations and incorporations, for selected cities; various periods 1980-84, with selected comparisons to 1970 population.

A5800–1.3: Part C. Personnel Issues

SALARIES OF MUNICIPAL OFFICIALS FOR 1984

(p. 87-112) Annual report, by Ross H. Hoff, on salaries of municipal officials, as of Jan. 1, 1984. Presents data for 26 positions, based on responses of 5,106 cities to an ICMA survey. Includes 1 table on survey sample characteristics, and 3 tables showing:

a. Average salaries for 24 positions, 1978-84; and for 4 positions in central cities and suburban areas of 20 SMSAs, Jan. 1, 1984.

b. Mean, median, and 1st and 3rd quartile salaries for 26 positions, by city size category, with varying detail by region, city type, and form of government, Jan. 1, 1984.

For description of report for 1985, see A5800-2.66 below.

SALARIES OF COUNTY OFFICIALS FOR 1984

(p. 113-122) Annual report, by Amy Cohen Paul, on salaries of county officials, as of July 1, 1984. Presents data for 12 positions, based on responses of 1,792 counties to an ICMA survey. Includes 2 summary tables; and 1 detailed table showing mean, median, and 1st and 3rd quartile salaries for 12 positions by county size category, with varying detail by region and county type (metro and nonmetro).

Also includes 1 table on survey sample characteristics.

Report was also published in *Baseline Data Reports.*

POLICE, FIRE, AND REFUSE COLLECTION AND DISPOSAL DEPARTMENTS: PERSONNEL, COMPENSATION, AND EXPENDITURES

(p. 123-177) Annual report, by Gerard J. Hoetmer, on employment, compensation, and expenditures of police, fire, and refuse collection/disposal depts of 1,480 cities with over 10,000 population, as of Jan. 1, 1984.

Includes 17 summary tables showing data by city size, with detail by form of government and census region and division, and including salary trends from 1973; and 1 extended table, listing cities by size and showing the following for each dept:

a. Uniformed and total personnel, weekly hours, entrance and maximum salaries, maximum longevity pay, and number of years to maximum.

b. Expenditures for salaries/wages, contributions to employee retirement and insurance, capital outlay, and other.

For description of a related report presenting a more detailed analysis, see A5800-2.59 below.

A5800–1.4: Part D. Management Trends and Issues

LOCAL GOVERNMENT MANAGERS: PROFILE OF THE PROFESSIONALS IN A MATURING PROFESSION

(p. 181-188) By Mary A. Schellinger. Report on demographic and job mobility characteristics of chief administrators of local governments with council-manager form of government or similar administration. Data are from responses of managers in 2,131 municipalities, 144 counties, and 85 councils of governments to a summer 1984 ICMA survey.

Includes 1 table on survey sample characteristics; and 13 tables showing the following manager characteristics, generally by census region and division and/or population size:

a. Demographic: age, sex, race/ethnicity (white, black, Indian, and Asian), marital status, educational attainment, and political party preference.

b. Job tenure and mobility: years as a manager and years in current position; number of governments served; whether previous position was managerial; and previous position of managers promoted from within the same government.

For description of a similar survey, for 1980, see SRI 1981 Annual under A5800-2.25.

INTERGOVERNMENTAL SERVICE ARRANGEMENTS AND THE TRANSFER OF FUNCTIONS

(p. 194-202) By Lori M. Henderson. Report examining local government delivery of public services through the use of intergovernmental agreements. Data are from responses of chief administrative officers of 1,654 cities and 435 counties to a summer 1983 survey conducted by ICMA and the Advisory Commission on Intergovernmental Relations (ACIR).

Includes 1 summary table, and 3 tables repeated for 3 types of intergovernmental service agreement (service contracts and transfers, and joint agreements), showing survey response of cities and counties for the following:

a. Number with agreements, by population size, census region, metro status, and form of government.

b. 10 services most frequently arranged; and number of agreements, by type of service and cooperating jurisdiction or organization (including other cities and counties, school and special districts, State, regional and nonprofit organizations, and private firms).

Also includes 1 table on survey sample characteristics; and 1 table presenting summary data on cities' use of private contracting services, based on 1972 and 1982 ACIR surveys.

Report was also published in *Baseline Data Reports.*

HUMAN SERVICES IN LOCAL GOVERNMENT: PATTERNS OF SERVICE AT METROPOLITAN LEVELS

(p. 203-216) By Robert Agranoff and Alex N. Pattakos. Report on local government role in providing services for the elderly, children/youth, handicapped, and general population. Data are from responses of chief administrators in 761 cities and 112 counties to a spring 1984 ICMA survey.

Includes 1 table on sample characteristics, and 14 tables and 5 charts showing survey response of cities and counties for the following, variously by population size, census region, metro status, and government form:

a. Service delivery methods used (direct service, joint ventures, intergovernmental contracts, contracts with nongovernment groups, and financial and in-kind support), by program type, and number and/or level of services provided.

b. Administrative and organizational characteristics of human services management, including revenue sources and detail by

functions; and whether programs and people served have increased or decreased in past 3 years.

For description of related report, see A5800-2.67 below.

MOTIVATING LOCAL GOVERNMENT EMPLOYEES WITH INCENTIVES

(p. 217-238) By Amy Cohen Paul. Report on benefit plans and work incentives for local government employees (excluding police, fire, and education personnel). Data are from responses of 1,265 cities to a summer 1984 ICMA survey.

Includes 1 table on survey sample characteristics; 3 tables showing summary data on selected employee incentives and benefits, generally by city size, census division, metro status, and government form; and 1 extended table showing incidence of the following incentives and benefits for each city, arranged by State:

a. Educational: tuition reimbursement, time off with pay for course attendance, salary increase at course completion, and availability to all employees.

b. Job related: 4-day work week, flextime, task system, sick leave conversion and pooling, attendance cash bonus, early retirement, personal leave, job redesign and rotation, labor-management policy committees, and team approach to job functions.

c. Awards and extraordinary benefits: cash and nonmonetary awards for suggestions and job and safety performance; dental insurance; eye care; substance abuse programs; personal, health, financial, and legal counseling; cafeteria-type selection of benefits; and day care program.

For description of related report, see A5800-2.65 below.

A5800–2   BASELINE DATA REPORTS

Series. For individual publication data, see below.
LC 76-5644.
SRI/MF/not filmed

Continuing series of reports on municipal government activities and management. Each report covers one selected topic, including finance, employment, and government functions and structures.

Data are based on surveys of municipal officials by the International City Management Assn (ICMA), Census Bureau studies, and other sources. Many of the reports are also included in *Municipal Yearbook,* covered in SRI under A5800-1.

Reports reviewed during 1985 are described below.

Availability: International City Management Association, 1120 G St., NW, Washington DC 20005, $240.00 per yr., single report $14.75; SRI/MF/not filmed.

A5800–2.59: Police, Fire, and Refuse Collection

[Annual. July 1984. 13 p. Oversized. Vol. 16, No. 7. SRI/MF/not filmed.]

Annual report, by Gerard J. Hoetmer, on employment, compensation, and expenditures of police, fire, and refuse collection and disposal depts of cities with over 10,000 population, as

of Jan. 1, 1984. Data are based on an ICMA survey of 2,599 cities, and are shown for each type of dept.

Includes 1 chart and 19 tables, showing survey response for the following, by city population size, census region and division, and form of government, unless otherwise noted:

a. Personnel and salaries: full-time and civilian/nonuniformed personnel; and entrance and maximum base salaries, longevity pay availability, maximum salary with longevity, and number of years of service to reach maximum salary and maximum longevity, by city size only.

b. Expenditures: salaries/wages, retirement and insurance benefits (by city size only), capital outlay, other expenditures, and total personnel expenditures.

Also includes selected trends from 1973, and 1 table on sample characteristics.

For description of 1983 report, see SRI 1983 Annual, under A5800-2.49.

A5800–2.60: City Use of Citizen Surveys

[Monograph. Aug. 1984. 16 p. Vol. 16, No. 8. SRI/MF/not filmed.]

By Clarence J. Hein and Karl F. Johnson. Report on city use of citizen surveys. Data are from responses of 683 cities with populations over 25,000 to a 1982 survey conducted by the L. P. Cookingham Institute, University of Missouri at Kansas City. Includes 13 tables showing survey response on the following:

a. Use of general, special, and departmental surveys, and whether city has a citizen assistance office, shown variously by census region and division, State, form of government, and city size.

b. Use of city staff and consultants in conducting surveys and developing questionnaires; and sources of input used in surveys.

Also includes 1 table on survey sample characteristics; and a nonstatistical case study of a 1983 citizen survey conducted in Lake Oswego, Oreg., with narrative report and questionnaire facsimile.

A5800–2.61: City Employment and Payrolls

[Annual. Sept. 1984. 16 p. Vol. 16, No. 9. SRI/MF/not filmed.]

Annual report on city government employment and payrolls, as of Oct. 1983. Data are from a Census Bureau survey covering all cities with populations over 25,000 and a sampling of smaller cities. Includes 4 tables showing the following:

a. Summary: FTE and total employment, and total payroll, by detailed municipal function; and employment and payroll summary data by city size.

b. By city: population; total and FTE employment; total payroll; and payroll and FTE employment, by selected non-school function; for individual cities with population over 25,000, arranged by State.

A5800–2.62: Salaries of County Officials for 1984

[Annual. Oct. 1984. 11 p. Vol. 16, No. 10. SRI/MF/not filmed.]

Annual report, by Amy Cohen Paul, on salaries of county officials, as of July 1, 1984. Presents data for 12 positions, based on responses of 1,792 counties to an ICMA survey. Includes 2 summary tables; and 1 detailed table showing mean, median, and 1st and 3rd quartile salaries for 12 positions by county size category, with varying detail by region and county type (metro and nonmetro).

Also includes 1 table on survey sample characteristics.

A5800–2.63: Facilitating Economic Development

[Monograph. Nov./Dec. 1984. 23 p. Vol. 16, No. 11/12. SRI/MF/not filmed.]

By Cheryl Farr. Report on local government efforts to facilitate economic development. Data are from responses of 1,126 cities with populations of 10,000-250,000 to an ICMA summer 1984 survey.

Includes 21 tables showing survey response for the following, generally by city size, census region or division, metro status, and government organizational structure:

a. Organization most active in promoting economic development, including city government (with detail by organizational structure), local development corporation, and private business; whether economic development plans have been adopted, and methods used to create plans; and revenue sources for economic development activities.

b. Construction/improvements to encourage economic development, for streets/sidewalks/bridges, recreation and parking facilities, and sewage, water, and public transportation systems, all by key financing source.

c. Economic development efforts by type of activity, including the following: public information/relations to attract/retain business/industry; commercial revitalization; efforts to attract foreign business; financial incentives to encourage private investment; historic preservation and aesthetic improvement efforts; and programs to encourage minority economic development.

Also includes 5 tables on survey sample characteristics; and 1 extended table showing population, and methods used to implement adopted economic development plans, by respondent city.

A5800–2.64: Microcomputer Use and Policy

[Monograph. Jan. 1985 7 p. Vol. 17, No. 1. SRI/MF/not filmed.]

By Kenneth L. Kraemer et al. Report on municipal government microcomputer use. Data are from responses of 84 cities with population of 50,000 or more to a 1984 survey conducted by the Public Policy Research Organization at University of California, Irvine.

Includes 8 tables showing survey response on presence of microcomputers and computer information centers, and policies governing their use, by city size; microcomputer purchase plans, and use by dept/division; and selected comparisons between cities with and without microcomputers and between sample cities and all U.S. cities with similar populations.

A5800–2.65: Employee Incentives and Special Fringe Benefits, 1984

[Monograph. Feb. 1985. 24 p. Vol. 17, No. 2. SRI/MF/not filmed.]

By John M. Greiner. Report on benefit plans and work incentives for local government employees (excluding police, fire, and education personnel). Data are from responses of 1,265 cities to a spring 1984 ICMA survey, with selected comparisons to a similar 1978 ICMA survey.

Includes 4 charts and 20 tables showing survey response on incidence of the following incentives and benefits, generally by city size, census region, metro status, and form of government:

a. Educational: tuition reimbursement, time off with pay for course attendance, and salary increase at course completion.

b. Job related: sick leave conversion and pooling; attendance cash bonus; labor-management policy committees; quality circles; team approach to job functions; job redesign, rotation, and sharing; task systems; and flextime and 4-day work week.

c. Awards and extraordinary benefits: cash and nonmonetary awards for suggestions and job performance; safety incentives; deferred compensation; dental insurance; personal, health, financial, and legal counseling; eye care; substance abuse programs; sabbaticals; cafeteria-type selection of benefits; and day care program.

Also includes 1 table on survey sample characteristics.

A5800–2.66: Salaries of Municipal Officials, 1985

[Annual. Mar. 1985. 27 p. Vol. 17, No. 3. SRI/MF/not filmed.]

Annual report, by Ross H. Hoff, on salaries of municipal officials, as of Jan. 1, 1985. Presents data for 26 positions, based on responses of 4,936 cities to an ICMA survey. Includes 3 tables showing:

a. Average salaries for 24 positions, 1980-85; and for 4 positions in central cities and suburban areas of 15 MSAs, Jan. 1, 1985.

b. Mean, median, and 1st and 3rd quartile salaries for 26 positions, by city size category, with varying detail by region, city type, and form of government, Jan. 1, 1985.

Also includes 1 table on survey sample characteristics.

A5800–2.67: Local Government Human Services

[Monograph. Apr. 1985. 20 p. Vol. 17, No. 4. SRI/MF/not filmed.]

By Robert Agranoff and Alex N. Pattakos. Report on local government role in providing services for the elderly, children/youth, handicapped, and general population. Data are from responses of 761 cities and 112 counties to a spring 1984 ICMA survey.

Includes 20 tables showing survey response of cities and counties for the following, variously by population size, census region, metro status, and government form:

a. Service delivery methods used (direct service, joint ventures, intergovernmental contracts, contracts with nongovernment

groups, and financial and in-kind support), by program type, and number and level of services provided.

b. Administrative and organizational characteristics of human services management, including revenue sources and detail by functions; and whether programs and people served have increased or decreased in past 3 years.

Also includes 1 table on survey sample characteristics.

A5800–3   **SALARIES $35,000 AND OVER FOR LOCAL GOVERNMENT MANAGERS, COUNTY MANAGERS/CHIEF ADMINISTRATIVE OFFICERS, AND REGIONAL COUNCIL DIRECTORS, as of Jan. 1, 1985**
Annual. [1985.]
27 p. var. paging.
SRI/MF/not filmed

Annual compilation of data on salaries $35,000 and over paid chief appointed officials in cities, counties, and regional councils, as of Jan. 1, 1985. Data are compiled from reports submitted to Municipal Data Service of the International City Management Assn.

Contains 1 extended table showing annual salary paid and population for each municipality or area, ranked by salary, for local government managers (18 p.), county managers/chief administrative officers (2 p.), and regional council directors (7 p.).

Availability: International City Management Association, Municipal Data Service, 1120 G St., NW, Washington DC 20005, †; SRI/MF/not filmed.

A5900
International Ladies
Garment Workers Union

A5900–1   **CONDITIONS IN THE WOMEN'S GARMENT INDUSTRY**
2 issues per year.
Approx. 15 p.
SRI/MF/complete

Recurring report, published 2 times a year, on sales, production, imports, employment, and earnings in the women's and children's garment industry.

Data are from Census Bureau, BLS, and ILGWU Research Dept, and are current to 2-3 months prior to cover date.

Contains narrative analysis of industry and general economic developments, interspersed with 5 tables showing the following:

a. Retail sales of women's/children's clothing/accessories by type of outlet; unit production of selected women's/misses' garments, and value of output; and employment, man-hours, and payroll of production workers, by garment type; all for various periods of current and previous year, and annually for 4-13 previous years. 3 tables.

b. Imports of selected women's and children's garments, by type of fabric, for year to date, same period of previous year, and annually for 5 prior years; and average hourly earnings, for women's garment industry sectors and other selected industries, month of coverage and same month of 6 previous years. 2 tables.

An annual table, showing unit production and net value of shipments for women's and children's garments by detailed product, for approximately 10 previous years, is included when data become available.

Availability: International Ladies Garment Workers Union, Research Department, 1710 Broadway, New York NY 10019, †; SRI/MF/complete.

Issues reviewed during 1985: Jan. 8 and June 24, 1985 (P).

A6025
Investment Company Institute

A6025–1 **1985 MUTUAL FUND FACT BOOK**
Annual. [1985.] 104 p.
ISSN 0077-2550.
LC 80-647954.
SRI/MF/complete

Annual fact book on the mutual funds industry, presenting data on industry growth, performance, holdings, and transactions, 1984, with trends from as early as 1940. Also includes 1984 survey data on women's savings and decision-making practices, and demographic characteristics of individual retirement account (IRA) owners.

Data are compiled by the Investment Company Institute.

Contains contents listing (p. 3); narrative report interspersed with 30 charts and 17 tables (p. 5-53); glossary (p. 54-56); statistical appendix, with 39 tables (p. 57-98); and index (p. 99-104).

All tables, and selected charts with substantial statistics not covered by tables, are listed below.

Availability: Investment Company Institute, Research Department, 1600 M St., NW, Washington DC 20036, $4.00; SRI/MF/complete.

TABLES AND CHARTS:
[Investment objectives include aggressive growth, growth, growth/income, balanced, income, bond and municipal bond, option income, and money market funds.]

A6025–1.1: Text Charts and Tables

PERFORMANCE TRENDS AND PORTFOLIO COMPOSITION

[1] Number of mutual funds classified by investment objective, 1980 and 1984. [chart] (p. 9)

[2] Money market mutual funds average annual yield [1977-84]. [chart] (p. 11)

[3] Mutual fund investment performance [compared to Standard & Poor's 500 index and inflation rate], period ending Dec. 31, 1984. [chart] (p. 12)

[4-5] Dividends and reinvestment [1971-84], and capital gains and dividends distributions to shareholders [1975-84], all types of mutual funds. (p. 13)

[6-7] Money market funds asset composition [average days to maturity, and number of funds]; and portfolio composition of equity/bond/income funds; year end 1984. (p. 18)

[8-9] Diversification of mutual fund portfolios [market value of] common stock holdings, and percent of total common stock [market value held, by industry group, selected years 1974-84]. (p. 19-20)

ACCOUNTS, ASSETS, SALES, AND REDEMPTIONS

[10] Percent distribution of total net assets by type of fund, 1974 and 1984. [chart] (p. 22)

[11-13] Number [of stock/bond/income and money market/short-term municipal bond] mutual funds, and mutual fund shareholder accounts; and assets of mutual funds; [various years 1940-84]. [charts] (p. 23-24)

[14-16] Sales, redemptions, and assets: equity/bond/income funds, money market mutual funds, and short-term municipal bond funds [various years 1971-84]. (p. 25)

[17-18] Net exchanges [transfer of investment funds] by investment objective, 1984; and sales exchanges, all types of mutual funds [selected years 1974-84]. [charts] (p. 26-27)

[19-20] Percent of equity and bond/income funds sales and redemptions [by investment objective, 1983-84]. (p. 29)

[21-22] Mutual fund assets and sales classified by investment objective [1983-84]. (p. 30)

[23-24] Money market and short-term municipal bond funds assets and shareholder accounts [by fund type (general purpose, broker/dealer, and institutional), 1980 and 1984]. [charts] (p. 34)

WOMEN'S SURVEY DATA, AND MUTUAL FUND SALES

[25] Key findings by marital status [survey results based on a national sample of 2,100 women, including responses concerning savings practices and goals, responsibility for making decisions, and knowledge and ownership of mutual funds, with detail for married women by employment status]. (p. 37)

[26] Sales of load and no-load funds [percent of funds sold with and without additional sales charges], by investment objectives, 1984. [chart] (p. 39)

RETIREMENT MARKETS AND IRA OWNERS

[27] Comparative equity performance [of mutual funds, bank funds, and Standard & Poor's 500 index], 10-year total return, period ending Dec. 31, 1984. [chart] (p. 44)

[28] Total net assets held in pension/profit sharing accounts in [equity/bond/income and money market/short-term municipal bond funds], year end [1980 and] 1984. [chart] (p. 44)

[29-30] Growth in [number of accounts and assets] in mutual funds IRA and Keogh plans [1981-84]. [charts] (p. 46)

[31-32] Characteristics of households classified by IRA ownership [including data on income, age, and prevalence of higher education/degrees, fall 1984]. (p. 49-50)

[33-34] Percentage of households owning IRAs and potential market [number of households without IRAs], by [1982] household income; and ownership of different types of IRAs (percent of IRA owners by type owned); [fall 1984]. [charts] (p. 51)

[35] Estimated value of IRA plans outstanding [by type of financial institution holding funds and for self-directed accounts], Dec. 1981 and Dec. 1984. (p. 52)

A6025–1.2: Appendix Tables
[Fund characteristics include distribution methods (broker/dealer, direct selling, no-load, and other), and investment objectives.]

ACCOUNTS, ASSETS, SALES, AND REDEMPTIONS

[1-2] Shareholder accounts, total net assets, and cash position, 1965-84; and distribution of mutual fund assets [by type of investment], 1966-84; [for] equity/bond/income funds. (p. 59-60)

[3-4] Total net assets and cash position by fund characteristics, year end [1981-84]; and total net assets of mutual funds by investment objective, within method of distribution, 1980-84. (p. 61-62)

[5-7] Type of shareholder accounts [regular, contractual accumulation and single payment, and withdrawal], 1971-84; mutual funds capital changes, 1965-84; and annual repurchase (redemption) rate, 1952-84; [all for] equity/bond/income funds. (p. 63-65)

[8] Mutual funds net new money flow [and] net new money flow from individuals to savings/investment vehicles [selected years 1960-84]. (p. 66)

[9] Mutual funds' distributions to shareholders [net investment income and net realized capital gains], equity/bond/income funds, 1965-84. (p. 67)

[10] Sales and reinvested dividends, by fund characteristics, 1981-84. (p. 68-69)

[11] Sales and redemptions of equity/bond/income funds by fund characteristics [and by type of sale and redemption, 1982-84]. (p. 70)

[12-13] Sales and redemptions of mutual funds by investment objective within method of distribution, 1980-84. (p. 71-72)

GEOGRAPHIC DISTRIBUTION OF SALES

[14-15] Investor purchases of equity/bond/income fund shares by States and geographical regions [census divisions, U.S. territories/possessions, Canada, and other countries], by method of distribution, 1984. (p. 73-76)

PORTFOLIO TRANSACTIONS

[16-18] Total purchases, total sales, and net purchases of portfolio securities, common stocks, and securities other than common stocks, by mutual funds, 1963-84. (p. 77-79)

[19-22] Portfolio purchases and sales by fund characteristics [1981-84]; and sales, redemptions, and net sales due to exchanges, by investment objective, 1982-84. (p. 80-81)

MUNICIPAL BOND FUNDS

[23] Short-term municipal bond funds [sales, redemptions, net sales, number of funds, accounts outstanding, and net assets], 1980-84. (p. 82)

MONEY MARKET FUNDS

[Tables [24-27] begin "Money market fund..."]

[24] [Sales, redemptions, net sales, number of funds, accounts outstanding, average maturity, and net assets, 1974-84. (p. 83)

[25-26] Assets [1979-84]; and shareholder accounts [1982-84; shown monthly, by type of fund]. (p. 84-86)

[27] Asset composition, year end 1979-84. (p. 87)

IRA AND KEOGH ACCOUNTS

[28-29] IRA and Keogh assets and accounts [managed by mutual funds], by investment objective, year end 1984. (p. 88)

FIDUCIARY, BUSINESS, AND INSTITUTIONAL INVESTORS

[Tables [30-38] begin "Fiduciary, business, and institutional investors of..."]

[30] Mutual funds excluding money market and short-term municipal bond funds [reported assets, institutional accounts in force, and value of institutional holdings, 1954-84]. (p. 89)

[31-38] Equity/bond/income funds; money market funds [total and by type of fund (general purpose, broker/dealer, and institutional)]; and short-term municipal bond funds [all showing] number of accounts and value of holdings [by type of investor including corporations, retirement plans, insurance companies/other financial institutions, unions, churches/religious organizations, assns, hospitals/other health facilities, schools/colleges, and foundations, various years 1982-84]. (p. 90-97)

[39] Assets of major [institutions] and financial intermediaries [aggregated for commercial and mutual savings banks, credit unions, savings and loan assns, fire/casualty and life insurance companies, bank trusts, closed-end investment companies, mutual funds, and private and government pension funds, 1980-84]. (p. 98)

A6025–5   TRENDS IN MUTUAL FUND ACTIVITY
Monthly.   Approx. 10 p. no paging.
SRI/MF/complete, shipped quarterly

Monthly report presenting statistics on mutual fund sales, assets, and investments, by investment objective. Also includes data on short-term (money market and limited maturity municipal bond) funds. Report is issued 1-2 months after cover date.

Data are compiled from reports of approximately 900 mutual funds, 90 municipal bond funds, and 300 money market funds.

Issues contain 11 monthly tables, listed below.

Prior to July 1985 issue, report format and content varied slightly.

Most monthly tables appear in all issues; Sept. 1985 issue also includes an insert chart showing mutual fund sales trends from 1980.

Issuing agency also publishes a less detailed monthly news release covering mutual fund activities. News release is not covered in SRI.

Availability: Investment Company Institute, Research Department, 1600 M St., NW, Washington DC 20036, †; SRI/MF/complete, shipped quarterly.

Issues reviewed during 1985: Oct. 1984-Sept. 1985 (D).

MONTHLY TABLES:

[All data are shown for cover date month, previous month, and same month of preceding year. Tables 1-4 exclude data on short-term funds. Tables 2A-4B show data classified according to sales methods and investment objectives.

Sales method classifications are sales force, direct marketing, not offering shares, and variable annuity (or annuity products). Investment objective classifications are aggressive growth, growth, growth/income, precious metals, international, balanced, income, option/income, government, GNMA, corporate bond, long-term municipal bond, and State municipals.]

1. Monthly statistics of open-end companies [total and new sales, reinvested dividends, sales due to exchanges, share redemptions, cash/short-term security holdings, net assets, liquidity asset ratio, common stock and other security purchases and sales, and number of funds].

2A-2B. Sales and redemptions.

3A-3B. Exchanges into and out of the funds.

4A-4B. Total assets, liquid assets, and liquidity ratios.

5. Portfolio activity [common stock and other security purchases and sales], classified by investment objective.

A. Monthly statistics [of] limited maturity municipal bonds [total net assets and change during month, regular sales of shares, investment income reinvested, total redemptions, sales and redemptions due to exchanges, and number of funds].

B. Monthly statistics of money market funds [total net assets and change during month; composition of assets (including Treasury bills and other U.S. securities, repurchase agreements, 3 types of certificates of deposit, commercial paper, bankers' acceptances, and cash reserves); average portfolio maturity; and number of accounts outstanding and funds].

C. Sales and redemptions of money market funds [regular sales of shares, investment income reinvested, total redemptions, and sales and redemptions due to exchanges].

A6200
Lead Industries Association

A6200–1   ANNUAL REVIEW, U.S. LEAD INDUSTRY with Statements from Other Countries
Annual, discontinued.

Annual report on lead production, stocks, consumption, and trade, discontinued with report for 1978-79 (for description, see SRI 1981 Annual under this number).

Report has been discontinued due to budgetary constraints.

A6225
Life Insurance Marketing and Research Association

A6225–1   MONTHLY SURVEY OF LIFE INSURANCE SALES in the U.S. and Canada
Monthly, with annual supplement. 6 p.
SRI/MF/complete, shipped quarterly

Monthly report, with annual supplement, on trends in life insurance policy sales in U.S. and Canada. Presents data on reported sales of ordinary and group life insurance policies, aggregated for 126 U.S. and 35 Canadian companies (ordinary life) and for 51 U.S. and 17 Canadian companies (group life). Report is issued approximately 2 months after month of coverage.

Issues generally contain data explanation, with 1 summary table; and 6 monthly tables showing U.S. and Canadian life insurance sales results, and summary of interest rate ranges and trends.

Sales results include annualized premium, and number and face value of policies, and are shown monthly and cumulatively for current year through month of coverage, with comparisons to previous year. Interest rates are shown for month of coverage and previous month.

Data for ordinary policy sales include detail for company categories based on amount of insurance in force; further U.S. detail for ordinary and combination companies/depts; and U.S. and Canadian detail for variable and/or universal life policies. (Data for Canadian universal life and U.S. variable life policies begin with the Jan. 1985 issue.)

Annual supplement, usually issued with the Jan. report, is a list of reporting companies.

Availability: Life Insurance Marketing and Research Association, PO Box 208, Hartford CT 06141, †; SRI/MF/complete, shipped quarterly.

Issues reviewed during 1985: Sept. 1984-Aug. 1985 (D).

A6325
Manufactured Housing Institute

A6325–1   MANUFACTURING REPORT
Monthly. 9 p.
SRI/MF/complete, shipped quarterly

Monthly report on mobile/manufactured home production and estimated shipments, by State and region, and manufacturer inventory. Data are from reports to National Conference of States on Building Codes and Standards. Reports are issued approximately 2 months after month of coverage.

Contains brief analysis, and 7 monthly tables listed below.

Availability: Manufactured Housing Institute, 1745 Jefferson Davis Hwy., Suite 511, Arlington VA 22202, members †, nonmembers $55.00 per yr.; SRI/MF/complete, shipped quarterly.

Issues reviewed during 1985: Sept. 1984-Aug. 1985 (D).

MONTHLY TABLES:

[1-2] Mobile/manufactured home production and estimated shipments [monthly and cumulatively for present year to date and previous year].

[3] Manufacturer inventory [total homes, and as percent of production, monthly for present year to date and previous year].

[4-5] Mobile/manufactured home production and shipments [by State and region, for month of coverage and year to date for present and previous year].

[6] Year-to-date product mix [shipments and production of single- and multi-section homes, by State and region].

[7] Shipments of [total, and single- and multi-section] mobile/manufactured homes, by State, ranked from highest to lowest [for month of coverage].

A6325–2 MANUFACTURED HOME FINANCING IN 1984, 34th Annual Survey
Annual. Aug. 15, 1985.
32 p.
SRI/MF/complete

Annual report on mobile home consumer financing, by type of lending institution, with loan characteristics and methods of repayment, 1984 and trends. Also includes data on manufacturer shipments, by region and State, 1980-84. Document refers to mobile homes as "manufactured homes."

Data are from responses of 491 lending institutions to a Jan. 1985 survey sponsored by MHI; and from National Conference of States on Building Codes and Standards, Federal Reserve Board, and Jon Whitney Associates, Inc.

Contains contents listing (p. 3); survey report, with background, summary, 14 charts, and 32 tables (p. 8-28); and appendix, with 3 charts and 3 tables (p. 29-32).

All tables are listed below. Most charts contain aggregate trends for table topics from 1980; those presenting substantial statistics not covered in tables are also listed below.

Availability: Manufactured Housing Institute, 1745 Jefferson Davis Hwy., Suite 511, Arlington VA 22202, members $1.00, nonmembers $2.00, postage and handling $1.00; SRI/MF/complete.

CHARTS AND TABLES:

A6325–2.1: Survey Data
[Tables show data by type of institution (banks, savings and loan assns, finance companies, mortgage bankers, service companies, and credit unions), and include number of reporting institutions. Data are for 1984, unless otherwise noted.]

SUMMARY

[1] Gross dollar value of manufactured [home] retail paper outstanding and number of [outstanding] accounts of reporting institutions [1981-84]. (p. 8)

[2] Number of manufactured housing [direct and indirect] loans made in the past year [1981-84]. (p. 10)

FINANCING ARRANGEMENTS, PROFITABILITY, AND PLANS

[3] Financing of other types of housing/construction [including conventional homes/

tracts, manufactured home/modular subdivisions, and manufactured home parks]. (p. 11)

[4-6] Profitability of manufactured home lending compared to real estate, auto, and other secured loans. (p. 11)

[7] Lenders interest in a secondary market for manufactured home loans. (p. 12)

[8-9] Plans for manufactured home financing [start or discontinue financing, and change in portfolio size]; and approximate dollar volume lenders plan to commit for manufactured home loans; in 1985. (p. 13)

[10-12] Institutions currently active in manufactured home financing, number of financial locations represented, and number of States operating. (p. 14)

[13-15] Minimum acceptable down payment, and average/typical and maximum maturity, on manufactured home loans [for new and existing single- and multi-section homes]. (p. 15-17)

REPAYMENT OF LOANS AND PORTFOLIO PROTECTION

[16] Average turnover for manufactured home retail loans. (p. 20)

[17-18] Manufactured home loans involved in a transfer of equity/assumption; and disposition of manufactured home loans made in the past year. (p. 20)

[19-20] Manufactured home loans paid off by repayment/prepayment, and by repossession. (p. 21)

[21] Manufactured home consumer loan delinquencies [by number of days delinquent, 1981-84]. (p. 22)

[22] Manufactured home repossessions on hand/in process, as of Dec. 31, [1981-84]. (p. 23)

[23] Percentage of loans outstanding recovered in selling a repossessed manufactured home [by type of loan arrangement]. (p. 24)

[24-25] When repossession proceedings begin; and manufactured home portfolio protection methods [6 types, including FHA insurance and VA guaranty]. (p. 25)

[26] Insurance policies of manufactured home lenders [by type]. (p. 25)

INSTITUTIONS AND WHOLESALE FINANCING

[27] Number of years experience in manufactured home financing. (p. 25)

[28] Manufactured home loan net activity [loans advanced, repayment and repossession liquidations, and accounts outstanding at beginning and end of year, 1981-84]. (p. 26)

[29] Dollar amount outstanding of manufactured housing wholesale financing. (p. 27)

[30-31] Wholesale loan portfolio protection methods; and [number of] manufactured housing dealers/distributors represented in wholesale portfolio. (p. 27)

[32] Regional distribution of manufactured housing lenders [number of institutions by region and State]. (p. 28)

A6325–2.2: Appendix Data

SHIPMENTS

[1] Manufactured home shipment and dollar volume trends [1970-84]. (p. 29)

[2] Change in manufactured home product mix: multi-section manufactured home shipments [and share of total shipments, 1970-84]. (p. 29)

[3] Average prices of new manufactured homes [single- and multi-section, and all sizes, 1980-84]. [chart] (p. 30)

[4] Manufactured home shipments to States [by region and State, 1980-84]. (p. 31)

FINANCES

[5] Percent of manufactured homes purchased with financing (average monthly percent) [1978-84]. [chart] (p. 32)

**A6375
Menswear Retailers of America**

A6375–1 MRA ANNUAL BUSINESS SURVEY, 1984 Men's Store Operating Experiences
Annual. June 24, 1985.
59 p.
MRA Business Newsletter Section II.
SRI/MF/complete

Annual survey report on men's wear retailer operating and financial performance, 1984. Report covers firms handling men's wear only and firms also handling women's wear, and includes data by sales volume, metro population size group, and geographic region. Most data are shown as ratio medians and ranges.

Data are based on survey responses from 181 men's wear retailers, compiled by Tyson Belzer and Associates, Inc. Report is intended to permit individual retailers to compare their operations with those of similar retailers.

Contains contents listing, definitions, highlights, and sample characteristics (p. 1-9); special analyses of survey data, with 4 trend charts, and 18 tables described below (p. 10-22); merchandising and operating data, with 39 tables also described below (p. 23-56); and map and list of related publications (p. 57-58).

Availability: Menswear Retailers of America, National Clothier Corporation Division, 2011 Eye St., NW, Suite 600, Washington DC 20006, $35.00, members 20% discount; SRI/MF/complete.

TABLES:
[Data are for 1984, unless otherwise noted.]

SPECIAL ANALYSES

a. Sales distribution, initial markup, and markdown, by men's wear category, 1980-84. 3 tables. (p. 10)

b. Key business ratios, by firm sales volume, region, and metro size class. 4 tables. (p. 12-15)

c. Star performers: data for selected financial performance criteria, aggregated for firms in the upper 25% of performance criterion, by sales volume and region. 2 tables. (p. 17)

d. Number of store employees by function, by sales volume; and employee productivity and sales productivity measures, by sales volume, metro size, and region. 7 tables. (p. 18-21)

e. Compensation of store owners and alteration/tailoring personnel, by sales volume, region, and metro size. 2 tables. (p. 22)

MERCHANDISING AND OPERATING DATA
[Most tables show data for all firms, firms handling men's wear only, and firms also handling women's wear.]

f. Operating experiences, including profit levels; initial markup and shrinkage by major dept; leased dept sales as percent of total sales; and selected merchandising, productivity, and financial ratios. 5 tables. (p. 23-26)

g. By merchandise classification: distribution of sales, average inventory, and ending inventory; sales change from 1983; markdowns as percent of sales; and inventory turnover. 7 tables. (p. 27-33)

h. Stock/sales ratio at the beginning of each month; advertising expenditure distribution by media; composite operating statement; and monthly sales/publicity cost ratios. 6 tables. (p. 34-38)

i. Detailed merchandising, operating, productivity, and financial data, generally expressed as percent of sales or other ratio, by sales volume, metro size, and region, with some comparisons to 1983. 21 tables. (p. 39-56)

A6376
Metal Treating Institute

A6376–1 ANALYSIS OF NATIONAL BILLINGS: COMMERCIAL HEAT TREATERS
Monthly. 7 p. no paging.
SRI/MF/complete, shipped quarterly

Monthly press release on commercial metal heat treatment industry billings, by region. Heat treatment involves use of high temperatures to alter the properties of metals.

Data are from reports of members of the Metal Treating Institute (MTI). Release is issued 6 weeks after month of coverage.

Contains brief narrative with 1 summary table; 10 charts with monthly and cumulative trends; and 2 tables showing number of member companies and billings, for 9 MTI districts (Michigan, Canada, and 7 U.S. regions), for month of coverage, year to date, and same periods of previous year. Also occasionally includes revisions for previous issues.

Prior to May 1985, data were shown for Michigan and 8 regions, with no separate data for Canada.

Availability: Metal Treating Institute, 300 N. Second St., Suite 11, Jacksonville Beach FL 32250, participating members †, others inquire at issuing agency; SRI/MF/complete, shipped quarterly.

Issues reviewed during 1985: Oct. 1984-Sept. 1985 (D).

A6400
Morris, Robert, Associates

A6400–1 REPORT ON DOMESTIC AND INTERNATIONAL LOAN CHARGE-OFFS, 1984
Annual. 1985. 48 p.
SRI/MF/not filmed

Annual report on domestic and international loan charge-offs and recoveries by banks, 1984. Includes data by Federal Reserve district, bank asset size, and borrower type, industry, and country.

Data are from 1,120 responses to an RMA survey of member banks. Respondents represent 39% of RMA membership and approximately 59% of total gross loans outstanding in domestic offices of U.S. commercial banks as of Dec. 1984.

Purpose of the report is to enable individual banks to compare their charge-off/recovery experience with industry averages.

Contains contents and table listing, and preface (p. 3-4); and 2 sections, with explanatory notes and 21 tables listed below (p. 5-48).

This is the 14th annual report.

Availability: Robert Morris Associates, Order Department, 1616 Philadelphia National Bank Bldg., Philadelphia PA 19107, members $10.00, nonmembers $15.00; SRI/MF/not filmed.

TABLES:
[Data are for 1984, unless otherwise noted.]

DOMESTIC LOAN CHARGE-OFFS
[Tables 1-11 present data by bank asset size group and Federal Reserve district.]

1. Base data gathered from banks responding to the survey [number of banks, total assets, loans outstanding, and dollars charged off and recovered]. (p. 9)

2. Charge-off and recovery experience in percentage form [including gross and net charge-offs as percent of average loan portfolio, and recoveries as percent of charge-offs, 1982-84]. (p. 10)

3. Loan charge-offs compared to average loan portfolio in median and quartiles. (p. 11)

4-11. Reported loan and charge-off experience, by type of loan [real estate, depository institutions, securities, farming, commercial/industrial, individuals, and all other]. (p. 12-34)

12-16. Ranking of high-loss industries nationwide: by number of times SIC [number] is cited, by bank size groupings, by Federal Reserve districts, and by dollars charged off, 1984; and by probability of charge-offs in 1985. (p. 35-41)

INTERNATIONAL LOAN CHARGE-OFFS
[Tables 1-2 show data by asset and international loan portfolio size groups. Types of borrower are governments/governmental agencies/governmental banks, foreign banks, and private commercial enterprises.]

1. Base data gathered from banks responding to the survey [number of banks, total assets, international loans/deposits outstanding and charged off, and total dollars recovered]. (p. 45)

2. Charge-off and recovery experience in percentage form [gross and net charge-offs as percent of international loans/deposits outstanding, and recoveries as percent of charge-offs, 1983-84]. (p. 45)

3-5. International charge-offs: by country and type of borrower; and by type of borrower further broken down by country of borrower [with number of loans]. (p. 46-48)

A6400–2 JOURNAL OF COMMERCIAL BANK LENDING
Monthly. Approx. 65 p.
ISSN 0021-986X.
LC 75-648976.
SRI/MF/not filmed

Monthly journal on developments and issues in commercial bank lending, including analyses of lending practices and characteristic risks for selected industries, project financing, international finance, and loan sharing. Also includes reports on legislation affecting commercial lending, and on management methods.

Issues generally include contents listing; and several articles, usually by bank executives, occasionally including statistics.

Aug. issue includes an annual subject index to articles appearing in past 12 issues. Sept. issue includes an annual feature on finance company operating ratios.

Features with substantial statistical content are described, as they appear, under "Statistical Features." Each issue of the journal is reviewed, but an abstract is published in SRI monthly issues only when statistical features appear.

Availability: Robert Morris Associates, Order Department, 1616 Philadelphia National Bank Bldg., Philadelphia PA 19107, associates $14.00 per yr. (included in dues payment), others $28.00 per yr., single copy $3.00; SRI/MF/not filmed.

Issues reviewed during 1985: Nov. 1984-Oct. 1985 (P) (Vol. 67, Nos. 3-12; Vol. 68, Nos. 1-2).

STATISTICAL FEATURES:

A6400–2.601: Jan. 1985 (Vol. 67, No. 5)

APPLICATION AND EFFECTS OF IN-SUBSTANCE DEFEASANCE

(p. 19-31) By R. Brian Calvert. Article on use of in-substance defeasance to extinguish corporate bond debt. Data are from Bear Stearns and Co. Includes 1 undated table showing coupon rate, amount outstanding, and maturity date, for bond issues of 71 companies considered candidates for technique.

A6400–2.602: Apr. 1985 (Vol. 67, No. 8)

LENDING TO THE CARPET INDUSTRY

(p. 8-17) By Jane F. McNabb. Article analyzing financial developments in the carpet manufacturing industry, with 2 tables showing selected financial ratios FY84, and distribution of assets and liabilities by type for an average small manufacturer in 1983. Data are from Robert Morris Associates *Annual Statement Studies*.

MAKING ENERGY LOANS: A BLUEPRINT FOR DECISION MAKING, PART 1

(p. 24-36) By Jack L. Battle, Jr., and Peter S. Rose. Article, with 1 undated table showing energy industry use of selected risk-adjustment methods for capital budgeting decisions. Data are from a survey of 300 oil, gas, coal, and lignite companies, conducted by Texas A&M University.

This is Part 1 of a 2-part article.

INDUSTRY LEVERAGE: WARNING SIGNALS FLASH

(p. 37-43) By Frank Renaud. Article, with 3 tables showing selected financial ratios for manufacturing durable and nondurable goods industries, with detail for debt/asset ratio and debt as percent of liabilities by major industry group, 2nd quarter 1975-84. Data are from Census Bureau.

A6400–2.603: July 1985 (Vol. 67, No. 11)

ASSESSING FINANCIAL DISTRESS

(p. 39-55) By Jerry A. Viscione. Article on analysis of financial ratios as a means of determining corporate financial distress. Data are from 24 companies filing for bankruptcy between Oct. 1, 1979 and Dec. 31, 1982, obtained from SEC.

Includes 7 charts and 4 tables, primarily showing aggregate financial ratio trends for the companies prior to bankruptcy filing.

AICPA's PEER REVIEW PROGRAM: IMPLICATIONS FOR BANKERS

(p. 56-63) By Walter Kunitake and Mark Dirsmith. Article on effectiveness of peer review program for accounting firms, implemented by American Institute of Certified Public Accountants (AICPA). Data are from AICPA.

Includes 2 tables showing number of firms receiving AICPA peer review reports, by report result (unqualified, qualified, and adverse), 1977-83 period and/or 1984. Data are shown separately for members of AICPA's SEC Practice Section and Private Companies Practice Section.

A6400–2.604: Aug. 1985 (Vol. 67, No. 12)

LENDING TO HEALTH CLUBS

(p. 8-20) By Patricia Kilburg and Dev Strischek. Article examining considerations in lending to health clubs. Data are from International Racquet Sports Assn and Robert Morris Associates.

Includes text data on health club profitability and liquidity ratios, 1983; 1 table showing average club revenues by source, earnings, and membership, overall and aggregated for top 5 clubs, 1982; and 2 undated tables showing examples of equipment prices and leasehold improvement costs.

A6400–2.605: Sept. 1985 (Vol. 68, No. 1)

ANALYSIS OF FINANCE COMPANY RATIOS IN 1984, ANNUAL FEATURE

(p. 40-49) Annual article, by Raymond M. Neihengen, Jr., et al., with 2 tables showing detailed financial and operating ratios aggregated for consumer (direct cash lending) and diversified finance companies, Dec. 31, 1980-84. Tables also show total loan volume, amount outstanding, and net receivables.

Data are compiled by First National Bank of Chicago. Related reports are covered in SRI under B3700-1 and B3700-3.

A6400–3   RMA '85 ANNUAL STATEMENT STUDIES, Fiscal Year Ends June 30, 1984-Mar. 31, 1985

Annual. Sept. 1985. 416 p.
LC 72-626355.
SRI/MF/not filmed

Annual report presenting composite financial ratios and performance data for over 340 manufacturing, wholesaling, retailing, service, and contractor SIC 4-digit industries, for fiscal years ending during June 30, 1984-Mar. 31, 1985, and trends from FY81.

Most data are based on financial statements of companies with assets less than $100 million, as reported by Robert Morris Associates member banks. Data may not be representative of a given industry. Report is designed for commercial bankers and others who make lending and business decisions.

Contents:

Contents listing, introduction, definition of ratios, and descriptions of industries covered. (p. 3-40)

Part I. Manufacturing industries. Financial statements for individual industries, showing the following for each industry: number of statements received (5 types); distribution of itemized assets, liabilities, and income; 16 financial and operating ratios (upper and lower quartiles, and median); and value of net sales and total assets. Ratios include sales/receivables, cost of sales/inventory and payables, sales/working capital and total assets, debt/worth, officer compensation/sales, and others. Data are shown for 4 asset size categories, FY84 or FY85, and for 4 categories combined, FY81-85. (p. 41-184)

Part II. Wholesaling industries. Presents data as described above for Part I. (p. 185-242)

Part III. Retailing, services, and industries not elsewhere classified. Presents data as described above for Part I. (p. 243-370)

Part IV. Contractor industries. Presents data as described above for Part I, with the following variations: data are shown for 4 contract revenue size categories, with no upper limit, FY84 or FY85, and 4 categories combined, FY82-85; total contract revenues are shown in place of net sales; and statements present 13 financial and operating ratios. (p. 371-391)

Part V. Finance industry supplement. Consumer finance and diversified finance company composite lending and financial ratios, as of Dec. 31, 1982-84. Data were compiled by the First National Bank of Chicago. 2 tables. (p. 393-396)

Part VI. Sources of composite financial data: bibliography; indexes; and survey form facsimile. (p. 397-416)

This is the 63rd annual report.

Availability: Robert Morris Associates, PO Box 8500, S-1140, Philadelphia PA 19178, members 1st copy †, additional copies $10.00 each, nonmembers $32.50 (prepaid); SRI/MF/not filmed.

A6450 Mortgage Bankers Association of America

A6450–1   NATIONAL DELINQUENCY SURVEY

Quarterly.   6 p. folder.
SRI/MF/complete

Quarterly report on 1- to 4-unit residential mortgage loans with overdue installments, by loan type and State. Report is issued approximately 3 months after quarter of coverage. Data are based on a survey by the Mortgage Bankers Assn Economics Dept of approximately 500 financial institutions holding over 9 million mortgage loans.

Contains narrative summary; 1 summary trend chart; and 3 tables showing percent of all, conventional, VA, and FHA loans past due 30, 60, and 90 or more days, and percent in foreclosure, as follows:

a. Quarterly for year to date and 2 previous years; and by State (including Puerto Rico), and census division and region, for quarter of coverage (also shows total loans serviced).

b. Change from previous quarter and from same quarter of previous year, by census region.

Most tables include detail for FHA 235/237 and 245 loans.

Availability: Mortgage Bankers Association of America, Economics Department, 1125 15th St., NW, Washington DC 20005, members †, nonmembers $25.00 per yr.; SRI/MF/complete.

Issues reviewed during 1985: 3rd Qtr. 1984-2nd Qtr. 1985 (D).

A6450–2   MORTGAGE BANKING

Monthly.
ISSN 0027-1241.
LC 49-30714.
SRI/MF/excerpts, shipped quarterly

Monthly journal on mortgage market trends and developments, including real estate investment and institutional lending. Includes monthly data on housing construction and sales, lender activity, and related topics; data are current to 2-10 months prior to month of publication.

Issues contain feature articles, occasionally with statistics; narrative editorial departments; and "Mortgage Market Trends" monthly statistical feature, with narrative analysis and 13 tables listed below.

An Annual index to articles appears in the Jan. issue.

Monthly "Mortgage Market Trends" tables appear in all issues. All additional features with substantial statistical content are described, as they appear, under "Statistical Features." Non-statistical features are not covered.

Availability: Mortgage Banking, PO Box 37236, Washington DC 20013, $29.00 per yr., single copy $2.75; SRI/MF/excerpts for monthly tables and all portions described under "Statistical Features;" shipped quarterly.

Issues reviewed during 1985: Nov. 1984-Oct. 1985 (P) (Vol. 45, Nos. 2-12; Vol. 46, No. 1).

MORTGAGE MARKET TRENDS:

[Data are shown for month of coverage and 5 previous months, often with year-to-date totals, and comparisons to previous 3 years. Data by unit type generally are shown for residential 1-4 units and 5/more units, and nonresidential. Data format and content may vary slightly from issue to issue.]

HOUSING ACTIVITY

[1-2] Residential structures, by unit type and region [permits and housing starts, number and annual rate].

[3-5] Housing sales [existing homes sold, new homes sold and available for sale, and months supply of new homes at current rate]; value of new construction put in place [annual rate by unit type]; and construction status [units under construction and completed, by type].

LENDER ACTIVITY

[6-7] Long-term mortgage loans closed [by type of unit]; and long-term commitment activity [amount issued during month and outstanding]; by type of institution.

[8] Mortgage insurance [applications received, and units and amounts insured, for FHA, VA, and private mortgages].

SECONDARY MARKET, INTEREST RATES, AND YIELDS

[9] Secondary market activity [FNMA, Federal Home Loan Mortgage Corp. (FHLMC), and GNMA].

[10] Interest rates and yields [for selected types of mortgages and securities; and selected basis point spreads].

MORTGAGE BANKING ACTIVITY

[Tables [11-13] generally show data by unit type. Tables [11-12] include selected detail for FHA, VA, and conventional mortgages.]

[11] Long-term mortgage loans closed [seasonally adjusted and unadjusted].

[12] Commitment activity: long-term mortgage loans [commitments made and outstanding to borrowers and from investors; outstanding inventory; coverage; servicing volume; and notes payable].

[13] Construction and land loan activity [construction loans closed, disbursements during month, inventory, commitments to borrowers issued during month, and monthly balances].

STATISTICAL FEATURES:

A6450–2.601: Nov. 1984 (Vol. 45, No. 2)

TARGETING MARKETING FOR LENDER SUCCESS: FANNIE MAE SURVEY

(p. 33-38) By Winslow Hayward. Article on competition for residential mortgage lending among mortgage companies, thrift institutions, and commercial banks. Data are from a recent FNMA survey of 1,200 residential lenders.

Includes 2 undated tables showing percent of mortgage companies, thrifts, and commercial banks which processed over 33% of mortgage applications through non-FNMA companies, purchased whole single-family loans, and are affiliated with parent mortgage companies and realtors; and percent of mortgage companies selling loans to other mortgage companies/depositories, Federal agencies, and others, by size of servicing portfolio.

FHA EXPERIENCE

(p. 41-57) By Thomas J. Bak et al. Article examining performance of FHA-insured mortgages endorsed during mid-1970s-1982.

Includes data on number of mortgages insured, and incidence of insurance claims, with comparisons for level-payment vs. graduated-payment mortgages and for various mortgage/purchase price ratios.

Data were compiled by the authors. Includes 16 tables.

A6450–2.602: Dec. 1984 (Vol. 45, No. 3)

MORTGAGE-BACKED SECURITIES TRACK RECORD

(p. 21-26) By Michael Stamper et al. Article on recent trends in the secondary mortgage market. Data are from Federal Reserve.

Includes 3 tables showing value outstanding for mortgage pass-through security issues of Federal Home Loan Mortgage Corp., FNMA, and GNMA, with trading volume and turnover rates for GNMA and combined other pass-through securities, 1981-1st half 1984; and turnover rates for Treasury securities, 1978-83.

FEDERAL BUDGET DEFICITS AND ZERO SUM GAMES

(p. 43-58) By Edison Zayas. Article discussing alternatives for reducing Federal budget deficits. Data are from Federal sources.

Includes 4 tables showing value of Federal deficit and borrowings, national savings by source, and total funds raised by nonfinancial sector, 1976-83; Federal deficits from cyclical and structural economic causes, FY80-89; and Federal outlays by major expenditure category, FY84 and FY89.

A6450–2.603: Jan. 1985 (Vol. 45, No. 4)

MORTGAGE PREPAYMENTS: THE REGIONAL DIFFERENCE

(p. 25-38) By Michael Waldman et al. Article on geographic differences in mortgage prepayment rates, and impact on yields from mortgage pools. Data are based on a study by Salomon Bros., Inc. Includes 6 tables showing the following data, for various periods 1982-Oct. 1984:

a. Mortgage pools outstanding, prepayment and unemployment rates, and growth in personal income and housing stock, for U.S. and 4-10 States with largest amounts outstanding.

b. Outstanding amount of Federal Home Loan Mortgage Corp. (FHLMC) mortgage guarantor pools issued, and of FHLMC and FNMA mortgage pools issued to thrift and other institutions, for single- and multi-State sellers/servicers; and prepayment rates and mortgage yields for FHLMC pools maturing in 22 years, for U.S. and 2 States.

c. Prepayment rates, and mortgage pools outstanding, by State and for Puerto Rico.

BANKING ON ENERGY

(p. 41-48) By Charles V. Hardwick, Jr. Article, with 1 table comparing prices of natural gas, electricity, and No. 2 fuel oil excluding tax, most shown annually 1973-83, and monthly 1981-July 1984. Data are from Energy Information Administration.

HOUSE AS AN INVESTMENT: AS ATTRACTIVE AS EVER?

(p. 52-62) By Daniel Durning and Michael S. Salkin. Article analyzing investment potential of California housing. Includes 6 tables show-

ing internal rate of return (IRR) on median-valued house; housing price appreciation rate and outlook; and IRR on owner-occupied house vs. comparable investment under 7 inflation scenarios; various periods 1960-91.

TOMORROW'S ECONOMY

(p. 73-76) By Daniel A. Blumberg. Article, with 1 table showing years in which factory utilization rate reached 85%, and subsequent percent increase in inflation, various periods 1955-80.

A6450–2.604: Mar. 1985 (Vol. 45, No. 6)

FHA MULTIFAMILY TERMINATIONS: A REVIEW

(p. 44-50) By Glory Dixon. Article, with 3 tables showing the following for multifamily housing mortgages insured by HUD under specific sections of the National Housing Act: endorsements, claim and non-claim terminations, and contracts in force, as of Apr. 30, 1984; endorsements, 1970-83; and endorsements and claims, 1949-84.

A6450–2.605: June 1985 (Vol. 45, No. 9)

RISKY BUSINESS

(p. 9-16) By David J. Gallitano. Article on trends in the private mortgage insurance industry. Includes 2 tables comparing typical mortgage payment/income ratios and new home equity growth, 1977 and 1981; and mortgage interest and delinquency rates, mortgage insurance underwriting ratios, mortgage instrument mix, unemployment rate, and housing appreciation rate, primarily for 1960s and 1980s.

HUD: GOING BY THE NUMBERS

(p. 63-76) By Rick Calvert. Article examining trends in mortgages insured under 2 HUD programs for financing construction/rehabilitation of multifamily rental/cooperative housing. Data are from HUD's Multifamily Insured and Direct Loan Information System.

Includes 10 tables showing number of endorsements, claim and nonclaim terminations, and mortgages in force, for Sections 221(d)(3) and 222(d)(4) of the National Housing Act, various periods 1958-84. Data for 221(d)(3) are shown for market-rate and below-market-rate mortgages, by type of subsidy and mortgagor. Data for 221(d)(4) are shown for subsidized and nonsubsidized mortgages.

A6450–2.606: Aug. 1985 (Vol. 45, No. 11)

SERVICING COSTS: PUTTING THE PIECES TOGETHER

(p. 9-20) By Victor Cholewicki. Article analyzing mortgage banking loan servicing expenses and income, 1979-83. Data are from Mortgage Bankers Assn annual "cost study" surveys. Survey respondents accounted for over 30% of total dollar volume serviced by mortgage bankers during 1979-83.

Includes 4 charts and 10 tables primarily showing itemized servicing expenses and income per loan, with selected ratios and detail by dollar volume serviced, 1983, generally with trends from 1979.

A6450–2.607: Sept. 1985 (Vol. 45, No. 12)

PROLIFERATION OF MORTGAGE-BACKED SECURITIES

(p. 24-44) By Joseph Hu. Article on growth of mortgage-backed securities market. Data are from Federal and private sources. Includes 10 tables showing the following data:

a. GNMA mortgage-backed securities, FNMA pass-through certificates, and Federal Home Loan Mortgage Corp. participation certificates issued and outstanding, 1970-85.

b. Yields and basis point spreads on GNMA securities, monthly 1982-June 1985; and adjustable rate mortgage (ARM) originations, and ARMs as a percent of conventional mortgages, quarterly 1982-1st quarter 1985.

c. Collateralized mortgage obligations issued, by type of financial institution, collateral, and maturity class, with basis point spread over Treasury securities of comparable maturity, June 1983-85 period.

d. Monthly payment and buydown cost comparisons for 15- and 30-year mortgages (no dates).

A6450–3   FINANCIAL STATEMENTS AND OPERATING RATIOS for the Mortgage Banking Industry, 1983
Annual.   Oct. 1984.   43 p.
Trends Rpt. No. 34.
ISSN 0095-9308.
LC 75-640703.
SRI/MF/complete

Annual report presenting mortgage banking industry aggregate financial and operating data, 1983. Covers income and expenses, assets and liabilities, and selected operating ratios and activity indicators, by volume, type of lending activity, and type of ownership.

Data are based on responses of 167 mortgage banking firms to a Mortgage Bankers Assn survey. Report is intended to permit individual firms to compare their performance with industry averages.

Contains preface, contents and table listing, and narrative summary, with 1 trend table (p. 1-5); 5 current data sections, with 25 tables listed below (p. 8-36); 1 historical trends section, with 5 tables showing data as described below, for the average firm, 1979-83 (p. 37-42); and notes (p. 43).

This is the 20th annual report.

Availability: Mortgage Bankers Association of America, 1125 15th St., NW, Washington DC 20005, members $30.00, nonmembers $50.00; SRI/MF/complete.

TABLES:

[All data are for 1983. Each of the tables listed below is repeated for the following breakdowns: by millions of dollars of mortgage loans closed and serviced (.01-.02); by income property loans closed and serviced as a percent of total loans closed and serviced (.03-.04); and by type of ownership (.05).

Types of ownership are bank holding company controlled, service corporation for savings and loan, other controlled, and privately and publicly owned firms.

Except for data shown by type of ownership, tables show data for 6 asset groups.]

1.01-1.05. Comparative income statement [distribution]. (p. 8-12)

2.01-2.05. Income statement, average firm [amounts]. (p. 14-18)

3.01-3.05. Comparative balance sheet [distribution]. (p. 20-24)

4.01-4.05. Balance sheet, average firm [amounts]. (p. 26-30)

5.01-5.05. Selected ratios [12 profitability ratios, 5 leverage ratios, 12 banking activity and operating ratios, and 10 liquidity ratios]. (p. 32-36)

A6450–4   LOANS CLOSED AND SERVICING VOLUME for the Mortgage Banking Industry, 1983
Annual.   Dec. 1984.   31 p.
Trends Rpt. No. 35.
ISSN 0363-1710.
LC 76-644814.
SRI/MF/complete

Annual report on loans closed and serviced in the mortgage banking industry, 1983, with trends from 1976. Includes data by type of loan and investor, and also by service and origination volume.

Data are from approximately 200 member firms, FHLBB, Federal Reserve Board, and HUD.

Contains preface, contents and table listing, and narrative summary with 1 trend table (p. 1-7); 4 sections with 7 illustrative charts, and 17 tables listed below (p. 10-30); and notes (p. 31).

Availability: Mortgage Bankers Association of America, 1125 15th St., NW, Washington DC 20005, members $20.00, nonmembers $35.00; SRI/MF/complete.

TABLES:

[Tables show data for 1983, unless otherwise noted. Most tables with data by property type are for 1-4 unit and multiunit residential, and nonresidential; and data by loan type generally include FHA, VA, and conventional. Tables 9-10, 13-14, and 17 also include data for construction, land development, 2nd mortgage, mobile home, and other non-1st mortgage loan types.

Data by investor or institution generally include life insurance companies, mutual savings banks, commercial banks, savings and loan assns, Federal and/or federally sponsored credit agencies, and State finance agencies.]

MORTGAGE BANKERS' SHARE OF THE MARKET
[Data by institution include mortgage bankers and omit State finance agencies.]

1. Total mortgage originations [value and distribution], by 6 institutions [and by type of property and loan]. (p. 10)

2. Originations by mortgage bankers as a percent of originations [aggregate for] 6 institutions [for residential property by loan type], 1976-83. (p. 11)

3. Servicing by mortgage bankers as a percent of mortgage debt outstanding [by type of property and loan], 1976-83. (p. 12)

MORTGAGE BANKING HISTORICAL TRENDS
[Tables 4-8 show total value and distribution of loans, 1976-83, and begin "Mortgage bankers'..."]

4. Originations by type of loan. (p. 14)

5. Loans originated, by purchasing investor. (p. 15)

6. Originations of non-1st mortgage loans [construction, land development, 2nd mortgage, and other nonmortgage loans]. (p. 16)

7-8. Servicing: by investor, and by property and loan type. (p. 17-18)

AVERAGE SIZE LOAN

9-10. Mortgage bankers' average size loan originated and serviced, by loan type and by origination or servicing volume [loan size group]. (p. 20-21)

11. Mortgage bankers' average size loan originated for investor [types], by origination volume. (p. 22)

LOANS CLOSED AND SERVICED

12. Mortgage loans originated by type of investor by size of origination volume for mortgage bankers [and type of property and loan]. (p. 24-25)

13-14. Loans originated and loans serviced by mortgage bankers [by size of origination volume and by size of servicing portfolio; both by type of loan and investor]. (p. 26-27)

15. Share of mortgage bankers' originations by type of loan, 1978-83, by size of servicing portfolio. (p. 28)

16. Percent of mortgage loans originated, 1979-83, by type of purchasing investor, by size of mortgage bankers' servicing portfolio. (p. 29)

17. Mortgage bankers' activity, average firm [by type of loan and investor], 1977-83. (p. 30)

A6475
Motor Vehicle Manufacturers Association of the U.S.

A6475–1   MVMA MOTOR VEHICLE FACTS AND FIGURES '85
Annual.   1985.   96 p.
ISSN 0272-3995.
LC 76-649119.
SRI/MF/not filmed

Annual compilation, for 1985, of data on the motor vehicle manufacturing industry. Includes U.S. and world data on motor vehicle production, sales, registration, ownership and use, and industry economic impact, 1960s-84, with numerous trends from as early as 1900.

Data are from Motor Vehicle Manufacturers Assn, R. L. Polk and Co., American Trucking Assns, FHA, and other Federal and commercial sources, identified for each table.

Contains contents listing (p. 1); narrative overview (p. 2-3); report in 3 sections, with brief narrative descriptions, 50 charts, 5 maps, and 135 tables listed below (p. 4-93); and index (p. 94-96).

Availability: Motor Vehicle Manufacturers Association of the U.S., Communications Department, 300 New Center Bldg., Detroit MI 48202, $7.50; SRI/MF/not filmed.

TABLES:

[Tables show data for U.S., unless otherwise noted. Most tables with data for motor vehicles show separate data for passenger cars and trucks/buses.]

A6475–1.1: Production, Sales, Registrations, and Foreign Trade

PRODUCTION AND SALES

[1-5] Highest annual production years and retail sales years; record production and retail sales by month; and production milestones; [various years from 1906]. (p. 4)

[6-7] Annual motor vehicle production, factory sales, [total and domestic new car and truck] retail sales, [and dealer end-of-year stocks, various years 1900-84]. (p. 6-7)

[8] U.S. and Canada motor vehicle production [by manufacturer and make], 1982-84. (p. 8-9)

[9-10] Factory sales [total and domestic] of trucks/buses and diesel trucks by gross vehicle weight (GVW) [various years 1965-84]. (p. 10-11)

[11] Annual motor vehicle factory sales from U.S. and Canadian plants [selected years 1965-84]. (p. 11)

[12] Truck and bus factory sales by body type [1978-84]. (p. 12)

[13] Recreational vehicle shipments [by vehicle type, including travel trailer, truck camper, motor home, and camping trailer, 1965-84]. (p. 12)

[14] Motor vehicle assemblies by State [and specific plant location, 1984]. (p. 13)

RETAIL SALES

[15] Retail sales of passenger cars [domestic and imports, by domestic manufacturer], 1979-84. (p. 14-15)

[16] Retail passenger car sales [domestic; imports from Japan, Germany, and other countries; and U.S.-sponsored imports; 1972-84]. (p. 16)

[17] New car retail sales [distribution] by [size] class [1972-84]. (p. 16)

[18] Retail sales of new trucks by franchised dealers of U.S. manufacturers [by GVW and type, 1979-84]. (p. 17)

[19] Total retail sales of new trucks [domestic, by GVW; and imports, total and from Japan; 1973-84]. (p. 17)

REGISTRATIONS

[Tables [20] and [22-25] show data by State.]

[20] New registrations [1983-84]. (p. 18)

[21] Historical total [privately and privately/publicly owned] motor vehicle registrations [selected years 1900-84]. (p. 19)

[22-23] Total motor vehicle registrations, 1983-84; and [privately and privately/publicly owned] truck registrations [1980-83]. (p. 20-21)

[24-25] Motor bus [including commercial, federally owned, and school buses], trailers, truck tractors, and light truck registrations, 1983. (p. 22-23)

OPERATING AND RETIRED VEHICLES

[26-29] Average age of passenger cars and trucks in use [selected years 1941-84]; and passenger cars and trucks in use by age (as of July 1) [1970, 1975, 1980, and 1984]. (p. 24-25)

[30] Cars in operation, by model year (as of July of each year) [1972-84]. (p. 26)

[31] Motor vehicles retired from use [selected years 1955-84]. (p. 26)

[32] Trucks in operation, by model year (as of July of each year) [1972-84]. (p. 27)

[33] Passenger car and truck survival rates [by vehicle age], 1979-82 [period]. (p. 27)

WORLD PRODUCTION AND TRADE

[34] World vehicle production (in descending order of 1983 total vehicle output) [by manufacturer, with world region summary, 1982-83]. (p. 28)

[35-36] World motor vehicle production [for 25 countries], 1983-84; [and for U.S., Canada, Europe, Japan, and others, selected years 1950-84]. (p. 29)

[37] New passenger car exports by country of destination, 1984. (p. 30)

[38] Automotive exports by product, 1984. (p. 30)

[39] Automotive imports by country of origin, 1984. (p. 31)

[40] Imports of new assembled passenger cars [from 8 countries and all others, selected years 1965-84]. (p. 31)

[41] Automotive imports by product, 1984. (p. 31)

[42] Exports and imports of motor vehicles [and exports as percent of production; for U.S. and 26] selected countries, 1983. (p. 32)

[43] World motor vehicle exports [by country of origin, for U.S. and 8 countries, selected years 1970-83]. (p. 32)

CANADA

[44-45] New motor vehicle sales in Canada [selected years 1970-84]; and by Province [1983-84]. (p. 33)

[46-47] Motor vehicle registrations in Canada [selected years 1970-83]; and registrations and drivers' licenses, by Province, 1983. (p. 33)

WORLD REGISTRATIONS

[48] World motor vehicle registrations [and total, per car, and per vehicle populations, all by world area and country], 1983 [with world totals, selected years 1960-83]. (p. 34-35)

U.S. MOTOR VEHICLE PARTS AND ACCESSORIES

[49] Factory installations of selected equipment [model years 1981-84]. (p. 36)

A6475–1.2: Ownership and Usage

PRICE AND SALES TRENDS

[1] New car prices [in 1967 dollars] and consumer expenditures per new [domestic and import] car; [and median family income, and weeks of income needed to equal car expenditure and cost; with detail for cars with and without added safety/emissions equipment, 1967-84]. (p. 38)

[2] Indices of consumer costs [CPI by item, including new and used cars, and new cars with added safety/emissions equipment, selected years 1950-84]. (p. 39)

[3] Retail price increases of automobiles due to Federal [safety and emission] regulations (adjusted to 1984 dollars) [model years 1968-85]. (p. 39)

[4] Retail sales of new cars by [consuming] sector [consumer, business, and government, 1960-84]. (p. 39)

TRIPS BY PURPOSE

[5-6] Person-trips and mode of transportation; and motor vehicle trips, travel, and average trip length; [mostly shown as percent distributions], by trip purpose [1977]. (p. 40)

AUTOMOBILE OWNERSHIP AND PURCHASE CHARACTERISTICS

[Tables [7-8] show data as percent distributions, for domestic cars and imports, 1983.]

[7] Characteristics of automobile owners and drivers [by sex, age, occupation, and personal income]. (p. 41)

[8] New car purchase characteristics [by whether replacement car, model year replaced, whether financed, length of finance contract, principal use, and number of years planned to keep]. (p. 41)

[9] Passenger car operating costs [variable costs for gas/oil, maintenance, and tires; and fixed cost; selected years] 1950-84. (p. 42)

[10] Annual fixed cost of operating passenger car [for insurance by type, license/registration, depreciation, and financing, selected years] 1950-84. (p. 42)

[11] Motor vehicle ownership by selected household characteristics [vehicles per household, by household size, age of head, and annual income], 1977. (p. 43)

COMMUTING

[12] Mode of transportation to work [by State], 1980. (p. 44)

[13-14] Head of households' mode of transportation to work, by area [inside and outside SMSAs and by census region], distance, and time, [as percent distributions], 1979. (p. 45)

[15] [Percent of] households with motor vehicles available [by number of vehicles and State, 1980]. (p. 46)

TRUCK AND GOVERNMENT OWNERSHIP

[16] Compact pickup and mini-van ownership [distribution of vehicles by company or private owner, sex of owner and principal driver, whether principal vehicle owned, and usage, with detail for domestic and import pickups, 1984]. (p. 46)

[17] Characteristics of trucks owned [major use, body type, annual mileage, method of acquisition (purchased or leased), and year model, with detail by GVW, 1977]. (p. 47)

[18] Government [Federal and State/county/local] ownership of motor vehicles, by State, 1983. (p. 48)

SCHOOL BUSES

[19] School bus usage and ownership, by States [including number of pupils transported at public expense, and expenditure of public funds], 1982/83. (p. 49)

VEHICLE MILES

[20] Motor vehicle travel [vehicle-miles on urban and rural roads, number of registered vehicles, and fuel consumed, all by passenger and cargo vehicle type], 1983. (p. 50)

[21] Vehicle miles of travel and fuel consumption [by vehicle type, selected years 1940-84]. (p. 51)

[22] Vehicle miles of [urban and rural] travel [by State], 1983 [and total U.S., 1984]. (p. 52)

[23] Model year and average annual miles of household vehicles [1968/older to 1978 model years]. (p. 52)

TRANSIT INDUSTRY AND INTERCITY TRANSPORTATION

[24] Transit industry equipment and revenues [passenger vehicles owned, new equipment delivered, and passenger trips, by type of vehicle (heavy and light rail cars, trolley coaches, and motor buses); selected years 1940-83]. (p. 53)

[25] Seating capacity of new buses delivered [selected years 1945-83]. (p. 53)

[26] Intercity bus industry [number of companies, buses, employees, bus-miles, and revenue passengers, selected years 1960-83]. (p. 53)

[27] Intercity passenger miles by mode of travel [automobiles, motor coaches, railways, and airways, selected years 1960-84]. (p. 54)

[28] Intercity freight movement by mode [ton-miles for trucks, railways, inland waterways, pipelines, and domestic airways, selected years 1950-84]. (p. 55)

LICENSED DRIVERS

[29-30] Licensed drivers by States [and sex], and by age and sex, 1984. (p. 56)

A6475–1.3: Economic and Social Impact

TRANSPORTATION EXPENDITURES

[1] Personal consumption expenditures for transportation [user-operated, and purchased local and intercity, selected years 1972-84]. (p. 58)

[2] Passenger and freight transportation expenditures [by transport mode, selected years 1970-83]. (p. 59)

CORPORATE PROFITS AND GNP COMPARISON

[3] Corporate profits [motor vehicle/equipment manufacturers, total manufacturing, and total U.S., 1970 and 1972-84]. (p. 60)

[4] Motor vehicle output and trade as percent of GNP [1970 and 1972-84]. (p. 60)

CREDIT

[5] Average interest rate, maturity, value, and monthly payment of [new and used] automobile loans by finance companies [1975-84]. (p. 61)

[6] Automobile consumer installment credit [including amount extended and repaid, and amount outstanding by type of holder, 1970-84]. (p. 61)

EMPLOYMENT, PAYROLLS, AND CAPITAL EXPENDITURES

[7] Employment, payrolls, receipts, [and establishments] related to the manufacture and use of motor vehicles [for vehicle and parts manufacturing, wholesale and retail trade, services, highway construction/maintenance, petroleum, and transportation industries], 1982. (p. 62)

[8] Employment in motor vehicle and related industries, by State, 1982. (p. 63)

[9-11] Automotive [wholesale, retail, and selected service] businesses [establishments, sales or receipts, employees, and payrolls], by State, 1982. (p. 64-66)

[12] Motor vehicle/equipment manufacturing [establishments, employees, and payrolls], by State, 1982. (p. 67)

[13] Direct/indirect employment per $1 billion of final demand for motor vehicles [by industry division and selected major group], 1983. (p. 67)

[14] $34 billion automotive parts produced in other industries [automotive shipment value and employment, by non-automotive manufacturing group], 1982. (p. 68)

[15] Motor vehicle parts/accessories manufacturing industries [establishments, employees, payrolls, and shipment value], 1982. (p. 68)

[16] Motor vehicle/equipment manufacturing production workers hourly compensation in [U.S. and 14] selected countries, 1984. (p. 69)

[17] Motor vehicle/equipment manufacturing employment [and hourly earnings] (annual average) [1966-84]. (p. 69)

[18] Motor vehicles/parts manufacturers' new plant/equipment expenditures [selected years 1950-85]. (p. 70)

[19] Motor vehicle manufacturers' facilities and employment [by State], 1984. (p. 70)

[20] Truck trailer and truck/bus body manufacturers' [establishments, employees, and payrolls, by State], 1982. (p. 71)

[21] Earnings of motor vehicle/equipment [and all] manufacturing employees [by State, 1981-83]. (p. 72)

[22] Profile of new car dealers [establishments, sales, employees, and payroll, by State], 1982 [with comparisons to 1977]. (p. 73)

MATERIALS CONSUMPTION

[23] Automotive materials consumption [selected metals, cotton, and natural and synthetic rubber, 1979-83]. (p. 74)

FUEL ECONOMY AND NOISE STANDARDS

[24] Manufacturers' new car corporate average fuel economy city/highway miles per gallon (MPG) rating [by manufacturer, 1975-85]. (p. 75)

[25] New car 50-State corporate average fuel economy city/highway MPG rating [Federal standard; and rating for domestic, import, and total fleet; model years 1974-85]. (p. 75)

[26] Light truck fuel economy progress (MPG) [Federal standards, and rating for domestic and import 2- and 4-wheel drive vehicles, model years 1979-85]. (p. 76)

[27] Manufacturers' light truck corporate average fuel economy (MPG) [for 2- and 4-wheel drive vehicles by manufacturer, model years 1983-85]. (p. 76)

[28] Voluntary truck/bus fuel conservation program (millions of gallons) [for selected fuel efficiency options, 1975-83]. (p. 76)

[29] Gas guzzler tax, Energy Tax Act of 1978 [tax levied on purchases of less fuel efficient vehicles, by MPG, 1980-86]. (p. 77)

[30] Federal and [8] State motor vehicle noise standards (required of manufacturers) [1982-86]. (p. 77)

TAXES AND HIGHWAY EXPENDITURES

[Tables 31-37] show data on taxes or fees, by type.]

[31-32] State and Federal motor vehicle taxes, and special State and Federal truck taxes [receipts for selected years 1930-84]. (p. 78)

[33-35] State highway user, motor use, and truck [State and Federal highway user] tax revenues, State 1983 or 1984. (p. 79-81)

[36-37] State highway user taxes and Federal Highway Trust Fund receipts [from all motor vehicles and trucks], 1983. (p. 81)

[38-39] Highway Trust Fund receipts and disbursements [FY60 and FY64-84]. (p. 82)

[40] Receipts and disbursements for highways [1978-85]. (p. 83)

HIGHWAYS AND STREETS

[41-42] Interstate/defense highway system mileage by States, 1984; and national system [1970 and 1984; including mileage open, under construction, and planned]. (p. 84)

[43] Roads/streets [surfaced and nonsurfaced mileage under State and county/local control, selected years 1904-83]. (p. 85)

[44] Rural and urban road mileage [by State], 1983. (p. 85)

AIR POLLUTANTS AND CONTROLS

[45] Cars in operation with emission controls [by type of control, selected years 1967-84]. (p. 86)

[46] Sources of air pollutants, 1983. (p. 87)

[47-48] Automobile and light- and heavy-duty truck exhaust emissions reduction progress, Federal 49-State standards [by type of emission, for various model years through 1992]. (p. 88)

TRAFFIC ACCIDENTS AND SAFETY

[49] Federal motor vehicle safety standards. [tabular list] (p. 89)

[50] Traffic fatality rate [and deaths] by causes [5-year averages 1913-47 and annually 1950-84]. (p. 90)

[51] Traffic fatality rates [and deaths], by States [1982-83]. (p. 91)

[52-53] Traffic fatality rate and deaths in [U.S. and 13] selected countries [various years 1970-83]. (p. 92)

[54] Countries [and U.S. States and Canadian Provinces] with safety belt use laws [and effective date]. (p. 92)

MOTOR VEHICLE THEFT

[55-56] Motor vehicle registrations and thefts, 1970-83; and thefts by State, 1982-83. (p. 93)

A6475–2 WORLD MOTOR VEHICLE DATA, 1984-85 Edition
Annual. 1985. 366 p.
ISSN 0085-8307.
LC 73-640507.
SRI/MF/complete, delayed

Annual report on motor vehicle industry world production, trade, sales, and registrations, by country, mostly 1983, with trends from the early 1900s. Also includes some data on vehicles in use and scrappage. Data are compiled primarily from foreign government agencies, trade assns, private services, and the press.

Data are shown generally by type of vehicle, including passenger cars, trucks, buses, commercial vehicles, and occasionally tractors or other special vehicles. Production, sales, and registrations are generally shown by manufacturer and occasionally by model. Some foreign trade data are shown by country of origin or destination.

Contents:

a. Contents listing. (p. 5)

b. World summary: 25 tables on total and diesel production, by country; leading world manufacturers; and diesel and/or other motor vehicle registrations, exports, imports, and scrappage, all by country; various years 1900-84. (p. 7-44)

c. Country data: 1-29 tables showing production, sales, exports, imports, registrations, vehicles in use, assemblies, and scrappage, various years 1900-84, repeated as applicable for 47 countries and 4 country groups, arranged by world area, as indicated below. (p. 45-366)

Report has been published since 1964. This is the 21st edition.

Availability: Motor Vehicle Manufacturers Association of the U.S., Communications Department, 300 New Center Bldg., Detroit MI 48202, $35.00; SRI/MF/complete, delayed shipment in Oct. 1985.

COUNTRY TABLES:

A6475–2.1: Country Data

a. Africa: total continent, Morocco, Nigeria, South Africa, and Tunisia. 7 tables. (p. 46-54)

b. Asia: India, Israel, Japan, South Korea, Kuwait, Malaysia, Oman, Philippines, and Taiwan. 47 tables. (p. 56-104)

c. Europe: Austria, Belgium, Denmark, EC and Western Europe, Finland, France, West Germany, Greece, Ireland, Italy, Luxembourg, Netherlands, Nordic countries, Norway, Portugal, Spain, Sweden, Switzerland, Turkey, and UK. 136 tables. (p. 106-266)

d. Eastern Europe: Czechoslovakia, East Germany, Hungary, Poland, Soviet Union, Yugoslavia, and Eastern bloc countries (including Romania, PRC, and Bulgaria). 18 tables. (p. 268-286)

e. Oceania: Australia, New Zealand, and Papua New Guinea. 14 tables. (p. 288-301)

f. Western Hemisphere: Argentina, Brazil, Canada, Chile, Colombia, Latin American Free Trade Assn countries (including Uruguay), Mexico, Peru, Puerto Rico, U.S., and Venezuela. 52 tables. (p. 304-366)

A6485
Motorcycle Industry Council

A6485–1   **1985 MOTORCYCLE STATISTICAL ANNUAL**
Annual. 1985. 46 p.
ISSN 0149-3027.
LC 77-643309.
SRI/MF/complete

Annual report on the composition, growth, and retail sales of the motorcycle market, and on motorcycle usage, cost of operation, accidents, and registrations, 1984, with trends from 1945. Also includes a socioeconomic profile of motorcycle owners.

Data are compiled by the Motorcycle Industry Council from member dealers and other sources, identified in each table. Most data are shown by State.

Contains introduction and contents listing (p. 1-4); 43 tables and charts, listed below, each accompanied by a narrative summary with text statistics (p. 6-43); and listings of national and State motorcycle assns, and index (p. 44-46).

Availability: Motorcycle Industry Council, Research and Statistics Department, 3151 Airway

Ave., Bldg. P-1, Costa Mesa CA 92626, members †, nonmembers $25.00, educational institutions, students and motorcycle dealers $10.00; SRI/MF/complete.

TABLES AND CHARTS:
[Data are for 1984, unless otherwise noted.]

A6485–1.1: Motorcycle Market and Marketing

MOTORCYCLE MARKET

[1-2] Estimated motorcycle population: model type, engine displacement, and year [sold new]; and model type by engine displacement; [1983-84]. (p. 6-7)

[3-4] Estimated motorcycle population and penetration, by region [chart], and by State. (p. 8)

[5-6] Total motorcycle registrations, [quinquennially 1945-80 and 1984]; and by State, 1975-84. (p. 9-10)

[7] Estimated annual economic value of the motorcycle retail marketplace [and new motorcycle retail sales volume and value], by State. (p. 11)

[8] New motorcycle unit sales summary, 1969-84: retail and wholesale sales, imports, and U.S. production. (p. 12)

[9-10] U.S. motorcycle imports [and value], by country [Japan, Europe, and all others], and by engine displacement, 1978-84. (p. 13)

[11-12] New motorcycle wholesale sales: [total volume and value; and volume by model, engine type, and engine displacement, and for] 10 leading States; 1980-84. (p. 14)

[13-14] New motorcycle registrations: by State, and 10 leading brands by market share, 1979-84. (p. 15-16)

MANUFACTURERS AND DISTRIBUTORS

[15] Profile of [5] major motorcycle manufacturers/ distributors [shows brand name, address of manufacturer and distributor, year of incorporation, and other products sold]. (p. 18)

[16] Other 1985 motorcycle manufacturers/ distributors [shows primary U.S. manufacturer/distributor, and country of manufacture, for 30 brands]. (p. 19-20)

RETAIL MARKETPLACE
[Data are shown for franchised and nonfranchised outlets.]

[17] Motorcycle retail outlets, employees, and payroll [by State, 1985]. (p. 22)

[18-19] Estimated retail sales by motorcycle outlets [new and used motorcycles, parts/accessories, service, and other], and distribution of motorcycle outlets by retail sales. (p. 23)

[20-21] Motorcycle retail outlet profile [employees, payroll, years at same location and under current ownership, advertising expenditures, new and used motorcycle sales, and number of new brands carried]; and distribution of motorcycle related sales [by type] per outlet. [chart] (p. 24)

A6485–1.2: Usage and Ownership
MOTORCYCLE USAGE

[1-2] Motorcycles used on- and off-highway [by model type and] by State. (p. 26)

[3] Public land and off-highway motorcycle statistics, by State [shows acreage (total and

for Federal and State public lands); and off-highway motorcycle data, including sales, number in use, economic value of market, and market penetration]. (p. 27)

[4-6] 11.5 billion motorcycle miles traveled, on- and off-highway mileage, by model type. [charts] (p. 28-29)

[7-9] Average annual [motorcycle] mileage traveled [by model type; distribution of on- and off-highway mileage] by season, riding area, [and for] weekends and daylight; and motorcycle commuting [number used, and average days per month and roundtrip mileage]. (p. 30)

[10-11] Motorcycles retired from use/ scrapped; and operability rate [probability of operation 6 months to 11.5 years after sale, by model type; with accompanying chart]. (p. 31)

[12-13] Energy use per passenger mile [for selected transportation modes and uses, chart]; and 1985 motorcycle fuel economy figures [by model type and engine displacement]. (p. 32)

[14] Annual operating and ownership costs [by type], automobile vs. motorcycle. (p. 33)

[15-17] State motorcycle rider education programs [including number of rider education sites, graduates, and instructors, and State and Federal funding]; and 1985 State motorcycle operator licensing programs and procedures; [all by State]. (p. 35-37)

[18] Motorcycle accident statistics [including registrations, accidents reported, fatalities, and rates; all by State, 1984, with U.S. totals 1983-84]. (p. 38)

[19-20] State motorcycle equipment requirements; and off-highway motorcycle requirements; June 1985 [both by State]. [charts] (p. 39-40)

MOTORCYCLE OWNERS

[21-22] Motorcycle owner profile: number of owners and riders; [and distribution by] sex, marital status, age, education, occupation, income, and motorcycle ownership [years of regular riding, and total motorcycles ever owned; 1980 and 1985]. (p. 42-43)

A6490
Motorcycle Safety Foundation

A6490–1   **CYCLE SAFETY INFO: State Motorcycle Operator Licensing, 1985**
Annual. [1984.] 4 p.
SRI/MF/complete

Annual report, for 1985, on motorcycle operator licensing procedures of States. Includes licensing requirements, and number of testing sites and examiners, as of Sept. 1984; and number of licensed drivers and motorcycle operators, as of Dec. 31, 1983; all by State.

Data were compiled by the Motorcycle Safety Foundation from a survey of State licensing authorities.

Contains narrative summary (1 p.); and 3 tabular lists (3 p.).

This is the 9th annual report.

Availability: Motorcycle Safety Foundation, National Headquarters, PO Box 5044, Costa Mesa CA 92628, †; SRI/MF/complete.

A6490–2 MOTORCYCLE STATISTICS, 1983
Annual. [1984.] 2 p.
SRI/MF/complete

Annual report on motorcycle accidents, fatalities, and registrations, by State, 1983, with total U.S. trends from 1973. Most data are compiled from State records by Motorcycle Safety Foundation and American Motorcyclist Assn.

Contains summary, 3 charts, and 1 table.

Previous report, for 1982, is described in SRI 1983 Annual, under this number.

Availability: Motorcycle Safety Foundation, National Headquarters, PO Box 5044, Costa Mesa CA 92628, †; SRI/MF/complete.

A6520
National Association for State Information Systems

A6520–1 NASIS 1984-85 REPORT: Information Systems Technology in State Government
Annual. 1985.
154 p. var. paging.
SRI/MF/complete

Annual report on State government computer systems, including inventory, uses, and management, 1984, with selected trends from 1970s. Data are based on annual State surveys conducted by NASIS. Report is intended primarily to assist States in management and development of information systems resources.

Contents:

Contents and table listings, foreword, and NASIS description. (p. iii-viii)

Chapter 1-2. Introduction and observations. (p. 3-7)

Chapter 3. Responses of reporting States, with 21 tables and 1 chart, listed below, and accompanying narrative. (p. 11-34)

App. A. Hardware inventory, with 1 extended tabular list showing hardware information including vendor and operating system name, type of use, specifications of equipment in 6 categories, and procurement method, all for individual government agencies (excluding higher education) grouped by State (also including Alberta) and branch of government. (p. A2-A102)

App. B. NASIS prime contact directory. (p. B3-B10)

This is the 15th annual report.

Availability: National Association for State Information Systems, Iron Works Pike, PO Box 11910, Lexington KY 40578, $50.00; SRI/MF/complete.

CHART AND TABLES:
[Unless otherwise noted, tables show 1984 survey results. Tables 2 and 18 include data for Saskatchewan and/or Alberta. In tables showing data by State, States are grouped by population size.]

A6520–1.1: State Responses

COORDINATION AND INVENTORY

1-2. State agencies control summary [by population size group]; and coordination and control [by State; both showing scope of centralized information system authority, by function (planning, systems design, programming, hardware acquisitions, operations, and telecommunications)]. (p. 11-12)

3. Computers by size, 1979-84. (p. 13)

4-5. Method of procurement of computer systems [summary], 1974-84, and by [population] size, 1984. (p. 14)

6-7. Trend of computer inventories [July 1], 1979-84, and microcomputer inventories, 1984 [all by State]. (p. 15-16)

SALARIES, CONTRACTS, AND TRAINING

8. Average salary for major job classifications, by State groupings. (p. 17)

9. Contractual services [projects and cost, by area of computer application]. (p. 18)

10. Instructional methods and number of personnel attending [training programs]. (p. 19)

11. Cost of formal training, 1984-85. (p. 19)

PROBLEMS, DOCUMENTATION, FEDERAL AID, AND SOFTWARE

12-13. External and internal problems related to information systems, 1979-84. (p. 20-21)

14. Formalized documentation: State plans and policies [by State]. (p. 23)

15. Federal assistance in State information systems development [number of applications by area, and percent of costs reimbursed by Federal Government, 1983-84]. (p. 24)

16-17. Utilization of software products [specific software titles grouped by application] by State. (p. 26-29)

FUNDING, SECURITY, AND TRANSFER PROJECTS

[A]-18. [Percent of information system funds from direct appropriations and from revolving/working capital funds or applied receipts, summary 1972-84, and by State 1984]. (p. 30-31)

19. State EDP (electronic data processing) spending [distribution by object]. [chart] (p. 32)

20. Security and privacy [number of States with physical and data security plans, by plan type]. (p. 33)

21. Systems and programs transferred to or from other States, 1984/85 additions [by State, including type of application and product, year transfer began, and status as of July 1984]. (p. 34)

A6600
National Association of Barber-Styling Schools

A6600–1 RESEARCH REPORTS
Series. For individual publication data, see below.
SRI/MF/complete

Series of reports on barber schools, students, and graduates; barbers and barber shops; and licensing requirements; all by State and for Puerto Rico. Data are compiled by the National Assn of Barber-Styling Schools.

Series consists of an annual statistical report and a biennial directory. Reports issued in 1985 are described below.

Availability: National Association of Barber-Styling Schools, 304 S. 11th St., Lincoln NE 68508, †; SRI/MF/complete.

A6600–1.1: State Barber Laws; and Barber School, Barber Students, and Barber Statistics
[Annual. Apr. 1, 1985. 2 p. Research Rpt. No. 3A/6A. SRI/MF/complete.]

Two annual tables showing the following by State and for Puerto Rico, as of Apr. 1, 1985:

a. Barber laws: summary of education, residence, apprenticeship, and other requirements for barber certification, and costs of barber and apprentice license and other fees.

b. Barber schools and barbers: number of barber schools (private, vocational, and penal); students enrolled and graduating; barber shops; registered and apprentice barbers; and barber/population ratio.

A6600–1.2: Barber Schools in the U.S.A. and P.R.
[Biennial. Apr. 1985. 4 p. Research Rpt. No. 5A. SRI/MF/complete.]

Biennial directory of barber schools, by State and for Puerto Rico, as of Apr. 1985. Notes type of school (private, vocational, and institutional), and whether nationally accredited.

Previous directory, for 1983, is described in SRI 1983 Annual under this number. Biennial publication schedule began in 1981; previously, directory was issued annually.

A6635
National
Association of Broadcasters

A6635-1 1984 RADIO FINANCIAL REPORT
Annual. 1985. 102 p.
SRI/MF/complete, delayed

Annual report presenting median financial and employment data for radio broadcasting stations, by station category, program format, and market and revenue size, 1983 with summary trends from 1976. Covers revenues by source, expenditures by object, profit margin, full- and part-time employment, and selected productivity and operating ratios. Selected data are shown separately for stations reporting a profit.

Station categories are full-time AM, AM/FM, daytime, FM, and class 1A 50 kw.

Data are from 1,777 responses to a survey of all 8,099 commercial stations operating for the full calendar year 1983. Report is intended to enable radio broadcasters to compare their operations with industry medians.

Contains contents and table listing (1 p.); introduction (p. 1-2); 6 charts and 93 tables (p. 3-101); and definitions (p. 102).

Availability: National Association of Broadcasters, Publications, 1771 N St., NW, Washington DC 20036-2898, members $20.00, nonmembers $60.00; SRI/MF/complete, delayed shipment in Apr. 1986.

A6635-2 1984 TELEVISION FINANCIAL REPORT
Annual. 1984. 114 p.
SRI/MF/complete, delayed

Annual report presenting median financial and employment data for commercial TV broadcasting stations, by station category, market and revenue size, and census division, 1983. Covers revenues by source, expenditures by object, profit margin, full- and part-time employment, and selected productivity and operating ratios. Selected data are shown separately for stations reporting a profit.

Station categories are affiliate, independent, UHF, UHF affiliate and independent, VHF independent, satellite, primary and secondary market, and 1- and 2-station market.

Data are from 491 responses to a survey of all 831 commercial stations operating for the full calendar year 1983. Report is intended to enable TV broadcasters to compare their operations with industry medians.

Contains contents and table listing (1 p.); introduction (p. 1-2); 104 tables (p. 3-112); and listing of areas of dominant influence (TV markets) grouped by market size, and definitions (p. 113-114).

Availability: National Association of Broadcasters, Publications, 1771 N St., NW, Washington DC 20036-2898, members $20.00, nonmembers $60.00; SRI/MF/complete, delayed shipment in Dec. 1985.

A6635-4 GROUP AND CROSS-MEDIA OWNERSHIP OF TELEVISION STATIONS: 1985
Annual. Apr. 1985. 27 p.
SRI/MF/complete, current & previous year reports

Annual report, by Herbert H. Howard, on multiple TV station ownership, and cross-media ownership involving newspapers and TV stations, in the top 100 Arbitron Areas of Dominant Influence (ADIs), as of Jan. 1, 1985. Includes aggregate data on group and cross-media ownership; and weekly TV circulation (households reached), percent of total U.S. TV households reached, number of stations, and circulation rankings, for each of 180 group owners, 1985, with ranking comparison to 1984.

Also includes top 100 ADI markets, ranked by market share of TV households, 1984/85.

Data are from *Television Factbook,* Arbitron Co., FCC, and other sources.

Contains narrative analysis, with 1 chart and 5 tables (p. 1-16); and appendices, with 2 tables (p. 17-27).

Previous report, covering data as of Jan. 1, 1984, was also reviewed in SRI during 1985, and is also available on SRI microfiche under A6635-4 [Annual. June 1984. i+22 p., members $20.00, nonmembers $60.00]. Previous report is substantially similar in format and content, but does not include data on top 100 ADI markets.

Availability: National Association of Broadcasters, Publications, 1771 N St., NW, Washington DC 20036-2898, members $20.00, nonmembers $40.00; SRI/MF/complete.

A6650
National Association
of Business Economists

A6650-1 SALARY CHARACTERISTICS, 1984
Biennial. 1984. 8 p.
SRI/MF/complete

Biennial report on earnings of business economists, 1984 and trends. Includes data by sex, education, years of experience, industry, and location. Data are from 1,503 member responses to a spring 1984 NABE survey.

Contains survey highlights and background (p. 2-3); and narrative analysis, with 1 chart, and 14 interspersed tables listed below (p. 3-8).

This is the 9th NABE salary survey since 1964. Surveys have been conducted biennially since 1972.

Previous report, for 1982, is described in SRI 1982 Annual, under this number.

Availability: National Association of Business Economists, 28349 Chagrin Blvd., Suite 201, Cleveland OH 44122, $10.00; SRI/MF/complete.

TABLES:
[Tables show number of respondents and median income, 1984, unless otherwise noted. Some tables also show "mode" or most frequently reported income.]

1-2. Percentage distribution of base salary by income class, and base salary male and female [both for total, New York, and other]. (p. 3)

3. Additional [primary and professional secondary] compensation, male and female. (p. 3)

4-5. Base salary by income class, percent distribution; and additional [primary and professional] secondary compensation; by industry of employment. (p. 4)

6. Compensation by area of responsibility [base salary and additional primary and professional secondary income]. (p. 5)

7-10. Primary compensation, by size of firm, number of persons supervised, education [level], and years of professional experience. (p. 5-7)

11-12. Base salary: by location [for 13 selected cities], and by [census division and foreign]. (p. 7)

13. Salary trends [base salary and additional primary income, selected years 1964-84]. (p. 8)

14. Industry distribution [only], salary survey [biennially 1974-84]. (p. 8)

A6650-2 NABE NEWS: National Association of Business Economists 1984 Annual Meeting Membership Survey
Bimonthly (selected issue).
Nov. 1984. (p. 1-8). No. 48.
ISSN 0745-3205.
LC sn82-8405.
SRI/MF/excerpts

Annual *NABE News* feature, by Ben E. Laden, presenting economic forecasts and policy views of business economists, based on a 1984 sample survey of 205 NABE members. Includes narrative analysis and 7 tables showing the following:

a. Economic conditions and outlook: change in recent business conditions; forecast and recent performance of GNP, and selected economic and financial indicators; and expected growth and unemployment rates relative to total U.S., by census region; various periods 1982-85.

b. Long-term outlook: GNP, inflation, and productivity change rate, through 1988, with comparisons to previous forecasts and actual rates.

c. Policy: views on adequacy of current monetary and fiscal policy, economic policies of Reagan and Mondale, and appropriateness of selected fiscal policies for future implementation.

d. Miscellaneous: date current business cycle will peak, and reason cycle may be less than 46 months; forecast of Federal budget deficit, FY84-85; and selected investments expected to earn high return over coming 12-month period.

The survey feature appears annually in the Nov. issue of *NABE News* and is the only feature of this publication covered in SRI.

Availability: National Association of Business Economists, 28349 Chagrin Blvd., Suite 201, Cleveland OH 44122, members †, nonmembers $7.50 per issue; SRI/MF/excerpts, for annual NABE survey.

A6705
National Association of College and University Business Officers

A6705-1   COMPARATIVE FINANCIAL STATISTICS for Public Community and Junior Colleges, 1983/84
Annual.   Apr. 1985.   x+94 p.
SRI/MF/complete

Annual report, by Nathan Dickmeyer and Anna Marie Cirino, on finances and other characteristics of 2-year public community/junior colleges, FY84, with trends from FY79. Covers revenues by source, expenditures by function, and staff by function, all shown as percent distribution and as amount per student.

Also includes course distribution by class size; building replacement value, scholarships/Pell grants, and service area population, all shown as ratios to enrollment; and computer service sources, and types of computer systems used.

Data are shown for 4 enrollment size groups and for primarily vocational/technical schools. Most data are shown as median and 1st and 3rd quartile.

Data are from a sample survey of 560 colleges, conducted by NACUBO in cooperation with Assn of Community College Trustees, American Assn of Community and Junior Colleges, and NCES. Report is intended primarily to enable individual colleges to compare their financial performance with national norms for similar institutions.

Contains contents and table listings and preface (p. iii-x); report, in 4 chapters, with 6 charts and 31 tables (p. 1-71); and 4 appendices, including methodology, facsimile questionnaire, definitions, and listing of participating colleges (p. 73-94).

This is the 7th annual report.

Availability: National Association of College and University Business Officers, One Dupont Circle, Suite 500, Washington DC 20036-1178, members $25.00, nonmembers $30.00; SRI/MF/complete.

A6705-2   RESULTS OF THE 1984 NACUBO COMPARATIVE PERFORMANCE STUDY and Investment Questionnaire
Annual.   1985.   viii+179 p.
SRI/MF/complete

Annual survey report, by Bruce M. Dresner, analyzing college/university investment pool performance and endowment fund characteristics, FY84, with selected trends from FY71. Report is intended to aid administrators in evaluating their investment pools.

Presents data on investment pool rates of return and asset composition, including aggregates by pool asset size and investment objective; comparisons to Higher Education Price Index and other indexes; and detail for individual institutions, nontraditional investments (foreign securities and venture capital), and stock and bond turnover.

Also includes data on endowment fund size (total, per student, and per faculty), life income fund size, and funds held in trust, all for individual institutions; asset composition of endowment funds; and selected aspects of investment pool and endowment fund management.

Individual institutions are identified by name for fund size data, but only by code for investment pool data.

Data are based on a survey of 206 institutions representing endowment/life income funds with a market value of approximately $26.3 billion.

Contains preface and contents listing (p. iii-viii); 2 report sections, with narrative analysis, 6 charts, and 78 tables (p. 1-94); 7 supplemental exhibits, including indexes of investment managers and endowment custodians, and 12 detailed tables (p. 95-169); and 3 appendices, with methodology and definitions (p. 170-179).

Report has been published annually since 1971.

Availability: National Association of College and University Business Officers, One Dupont Circle, Suite 500, Washington DC 20036-1178, members $30.00, nonmembers $50.00 (prepaid); SRI/MF/complete.

A6755
National Association of Fleet Administrators

A6755-1   NAFA BULLETIN: The Magazine for Fleet Administrators
Monthly.
SRI/MF/excerpts, shipped quarterly

Monthly periodical reporting on topics of concern to auto fleet administrators, including fleet management, energy trends and developments, and vehicle efficiency, maintenance, and safety. Data are based on National Assn of Fleet Administrators (NAFA) surveys and other sources.

Issues contain editorial depts and feature articles. Features include annual surveys of fleet administrators regarding operating expenses; acquisition plans; personal use of fleet autos, and reimbursement for company use of personally owned autos; and disposition of used autos.

Features with substantial statistical content are described, as they appear, under "Statistical Features." Each issue of the journal is reviewed, but an abstract is published in SRI monthly issues only when statistical features appear.

Availability: National Association of Fleet Administrators, 120 Wood Ave. S., Iselin, NJ 08830, members †, nonmembers $24.00 per yr.; SRI/MF/excerpts for all portions described under "Statistical Features;" shipped quarterly.

Issues reviewed during 1985: Oct. 1984-Oct. 1985 (P).

STATISTICAL FEATURES:

A6755-1.601: Oct. 1984
EPA's 1985 ESTIMATED GAS MILEAGE FIGURES, ANNUAL FEATURE

(p. 12-17) Annual tabular listing of EPA fuel economy mileage estimates for all 1985 model year passenger cars sold in the U.S., by model arranged by size class.

For description of listing for 1984 model year cars, see SRI 1983 Annual under A6755-1.409.

NAFA's ANNUAL LAW ENFORCEMENT SEMINAR

(p. 18-20) Article, with 1 undated table showing the following for 13 unspecified State police auto fleets: fleet composition by auto and engine size class; average mileage; and operating expense per mile by auto size class.

CANADIAN FLEETS REPORT: 47% OF NEW CAR ORDERS WILL BE FOR COMPACTS

(p. 32-36) Article on new auto acquisition plans of Canadian fleets. Data are based on responses of 24 fleets operating 5,537 vehicles to a 1984 NAFA survey. Includes 1 table showing number of fleets ordering 12 items of optional equipment, by auto size class.

QUESTIONS AND ANSWERS ON THE OUTLOOK FOR U.S. MOTOR FUEL PRICES

(p. 38-40) By Jacques R. Maroni. Article, with 4 tables summarizing world oil supply and demand, various years 1973-85; and showing U.S. price per gallon for regular unleaded gasoline and diesel fuel, selected years 1981-90.

ONTARIO CHAPTER'S NEW CAR SURVEY: LITTLE GROWTH IN 1985; LEVELLING-OFF IS EVIDENT

(p. 54) Article on new auto acquisition plans, for 1985, of fleets belonging to the Ontario, Canada, NAFA chapter. Data are based on responses of 24 fleets to a membership survey. Includes 1 table.

A6755-1.602: Dec. 1984
FEWER ACCIDENTS, LOWER COSTS WITHOUT ROOF-MOUNTED LIGHTS

(p. 12-17, 35) Article comparing fuel economy, operating costs, and safety record of police patrol cars equipped with roof- and grill-mounted emergency lights, with detail for marked and unmarked cars. Data are from a 1982-84 Illinois State Police study. Includes 8 tables.

A6755-1.603: Jan. 1985
SHOULD THE U.S. CONTINUE TO LIMIT JAPANESE IMPORTS?

(p. 8-11, 41) Article, with 1 table showing Japanese share of motor vehicle market in U.S. and 8 Western European countries, 1980. Data are from *The Economist,* London.

COOPERATION, COORDINATION, AND COMMITMENT CAN SOLVE HIGHWAY, BRIDGE PROBLEMS

(p. 12-22, 30) Article, with 2 tables showing Federal funding requirements for highways, by type of project (including bridges and safety programs), 1986-95; and Federal, State, and local highway expenditures, selected years 1965-82. Data are from Federal Highway Administration.

A6755-1.604: Feb. 1985
NAFA's PERSONAL USE SURVEY REVEALS: MOST FLEETS PAY DRIVERS 20 CENTS FOR BUSINESS USE OF PERSONAL CAR, ANNUAL FEATURE

(p. 10-27) Annual survey on personal use of company fleet cars and business use of personally owned cars. Data are based on responses of 407 U.S. and Canadian fleets to a 1984 NAFA survey.

Includes 5 tables showing distribution of responses as follows:

a. Reimbursement rate for business use of personal car, and chargeback rate for personal use of fleet cars, 1980-84, for U.S. commercial fleets.

b. Number of fleets, company-owned cars, and leased cars; and policies and limitations governing personal use of fleet cars; shown for 7 industry groups, public utilities, and government (all U.S. only), and for Canada, 1984.

A6755–1.605: Mar. 1985

AVERAGE SERVICE LIFE IS 30.2 MONTHS/57,732 MILES; LEASED CARS REPLACED SOONER THAN COMPANY-OWNED, ANNUAL FEATURE

(p. 8-20) Annual article on marketing of used fleet autos. Data are from responses of 216 fleet managers to the 1984 NAFA Used-Car Marketing Survey. Respondents represent 147,281 autos.

Includes 4 tables showing number of owned and leased autos in fleet, used autos sold in 1984 by model year and marketing method, and average miles and months of service at time of sale, for 8 industry sectors, utilities and government, and Canadian fleets.

U.S. MODELS HAVE LOWEST COLLISION REPAIR COSTS, ANNUAL FEATURE

(p. 44-45, 50) Annual article, with 1 table showing index of collision coverage loss per insured vehicle year, for selected 1984 model year autos with best and worst coverage loss. Data are from Highway Loss Data Institute.

A6755–1.606: Apr. 1985

FLEET OPERATING COSTS DECLINE FOR 3rd YEAR, ANNUAL FEATURE

(p. 8-12) Annual article on fleet operating expenses in U.S. and Canada. Data are from responses of 84 fleets operating 79,669 passenger autos, to a survey conducted by NAFA.

Includes 1 chart and 3 tables showing U.S. composite fleet operating, incidental, and standing expenses, by item, and personal use credits; and operating expenses by item, and average miles per gallon and/or per month, by auto size class for U.S., and total for Canada; mostly 1982-84.

A6755–1.607: Aug. 1985

IMPORT CARS IN FLEETS GROW BY 29% IN 2 YEARS

(p. 51) Article on import autos in North American fleets. Data are from Runzheimer International surveys of U.S. and Canadian fleets conducted in 1982 (95 respondents), 1983 (532 respondents), and 1984 (506 respondents).

Includes 3 tables showing average fleet domestic vs. import composition, and percent of fleets owning imported autos and average number owned.

A6755–1.608: Sept. 1985

FOR 1986, MOST FLEET MANAGERS ARE BUYING MID-SIZE CARS, ANNUAL FEATURE

(p. 6-16) Annual survey on new auto acquisition plans of commercial fleets. Data are based on responses of 243 fleets operating 173,248 vehicles to a 1985 NAFA survey.

Includes 5 tables showing the following for U.S. commercial fleets:

a. Composite fleet summary, by auto size class, 1981-85; and distribution of new auto orders, by body style.

b. Fleet size, composition by owned or leased status and auto size class, and new auto acquisitions, 1985; planned new auto acquisitions by size class, 1986; and number of fleets ordering 12 items of optional equipment, by auto size class; all for 7 industry sectors.

Also includes 1 table showing total fleets surveyed (including government, utility, and Canadian fleets), with total acquisitions, actual 1985 and planned 1986.

OHIO BELT USE SURVEYS SHOW: DRIVERS WHO DON'T BUCKLE UP PUT COMFORT BEFORE PERSONAL SAFETY

(p. 38-43, 50) By Jack Walsh. Article on use of vehicle safety restraints among Ohio motorists, based on State Highway Patrol studies involving over 300,000 vehicle occupants, conducted 1981-84. Includes 3 undated tables showing incidence of safety restraint use, and distribution of fatal accidents, by day of week and type of vehicle and/or road.

POPULATION COVERED BY STATE SEAT BELT USE LAWS

(p. 50) Brief article, with 1 table showing the following for 14 States with seat belt use laws: date of enactment, effective date, and population. Population data are from U.S. Census Bureau.

A6755–1.609: Oct. 1985

EPA's 1986 ESTIMATED GAS MILEAGE FIGURES, ANNUAL FEATURE

(p. 10-14) Annual tabular listing of EPA fuel economy mileage estimates for all 1986 model year passenger cars sold in the U.S., by model arranged by size class.

Listing for 1985 model year is described in A6755-1.601 above.

FORD ON IMPORTS: JAPAN'S HOLD ON MARKET IS TOUGH TO BREAK

(p. 20-25, 58) Article, with 1 chart showing Japanese auto market share in U.S., 1970s-July 1985.

NEW CAR SURVEY REVEALS PURCHASING PLANS FOR PUBLIC UTILITY AND GOVERNMENT GROUPS

(p. 34, 50) Article on new auto acquisition plans for government and public utility fleets. Data are based on responses of 33 fleets operating 22,080 vehicles to a 1985 NAFA survey. Includes 1 table showing number of fleets ordering 12 types of optional equipment, by auto size class.

Data from 1984 survey appeared in annual feature covering acquisition plans of commercial fleets; for description, see SRI 1984 Annual under A6755-1.511

A6755–2   NAFA's ANNUAL REFERENCE BOOK, 1985
Annual. 1984. 132 p.
SRI/MF/excerpts

Annual automobile fleet administrator's reference book, for 1985, presenting manufacturer sales and service representative directory, service recommendations for 1982-85 automobile

makes, and features on topics of interest to fleet administrators, including vehicle fuel efficiency and specifications, safety, operating expenses, and State and Canadian Province regulations and taxes.

Data sources include National Assn of Fleet Administrators surveys, and Government reports.

Features with substantial statistical content are described below.

NAFA's Annual Reference Book is included in monthly *NAFA Bulletin* subscription price. *NAFA Bulletin* is covered in SRI under A6755-1.

Availability: National Association of Fleet Administrators, 120 Wood Ave. S., Iselin NJ 08830, members †, nonmembers $15.00; SRI/MF/excerpts for portions described under "Statistical Features."

STATISTICAL FEATURES:

A6755–2.1: Vehicle Information, Safety Survey, and Fleet Finances

a. Fuel efficiency: EPA estimated miles per gallon (MPG) for 1985 automobile models grouped by size class, with selected specifications. 1 table. (p. 6-12)

b. Canada: average fleet operating costs per mile, including running, standing, and incidental expenses, and gas prices, 1979-83 and 1st half 1984. 1 table. (p. 24)

c. Composite survey fleet: current fleet size and planned acquisitions in coming year, by vehicle size class; and total acquisitions in previous year; 1980-84 model years. 1 table. (p. 38)

d. Safety: highway accident summary aggregated for 332 fleets, including miles driven, preventable and nonpreventable accidents, injuries, and value of vehicle damage, Oct. 1983-Sept. 1984. Text statistics. (p. 44)

e. Finances and maintenance: composite fleet per car operating, incidental, and standing expenses by item, credits, and average miles per month, 1981-83, with operating expense trends from 1964; and estimates of operating cost and resale value of well maintained and nonmaintained cars (no date). 3 tables. (p. 106-108)

A6835
National Association
of Independent Schools

A6835–1   **NAIS MEMBER SCHOOL TUITION FEES, TEACHERS' SALARIES, ADMINISTRATIVE SALARIES, 1984/85**
Annual. 1984. 20 p.
ISSN 0161-1097.
LC 77-646697.
SRI/MF/not filmed

Annual report on private elementary and secondary school average tuition fees, and teacher and administration salaries, 1984/85. Includes data by type of school and by grade and U.S. region, with selected data for Canada and U.S. territories.

Data are based on responses from 778 NAIS member schools.

Contains 9 tables, listed below, with brief accompanying analysis.

Issuing agency also publishes a companion annual report on school operations and enrollment, covered in SRI under A6835-2.

Availability: National Association of Independent Schools, 18 Tremont St., Boston MA 02108, members $8.00, nonmembers $50.00; SRI/MF/not filmed.

TABLES:

[Data generally are shown for girls', boys', and coeducational day and boarding schools, 1984/85. Most tables include median and range. Several include data for Canada.]

TUITION FEES

1-3. Tuition fees [with change from 1983/84, by grade and region, and including data for coeducational day schools in Virgin Islands/Puerto Rico/Guam]. (p. 3-7)

FACULTY SALARIES

1. Cash salaries for beginning teachers with no teaching experience. (p. 8)

2. Teachers' salaries by area [(region), with detail for experienced and beginning teachers]. (p. 8-10)

3. Teachers' salaries [including increase since 1979/80]. (p. 11)

ADMINISTRATIVE SALARIES

1-3. Salary ranges for administrative officers [by position, by enrollment size of school]. (p. 12-20)

A6835-2   NAIS MEMBER SCHOOL OPERATIONS, 1983/84; NAIS MEMBERSHIP, 1984/85

Annual. 1985. 14 p.
ISSN 0160-8282.
LC 77-641437.
SRI/MF/not filmed

Annual report on private elementary and secondary school finances, and minority enrollment and faculty, by type of school, various years 1980/81-1984/85. Also includes selected data by region, and data on NAIS membership.

Data are based on responses to Sept. 1984 surveys from 568 schools belonging to NAIS.

Contains introduction, contents listing, glossary, and 1 summary table (p. 1-2); and 5 sections, with narrative summaries, and 19 tables, described below (p. 3-14).

Availability: National Association of Independent Schools, 18 Tremont St., Boston MA 02108, members $8.00, nonmembers $50.00; SRI/MF/not filmed.

TABLES:

[Most data are shown for girls', boys', and coeducational day and/or boarding schools, frequently with further detail for elementary and secondary levels. Data are for 1983/84, unless otherwise noted.]

a. Financial aid: distribution of income by source, including tuition, endowments, and gifts; schools reporting total financial aid income from single source; and students aided, amounts granted, and financial aid share of total enrollment and operating budget. Tables 1-2. (p. 3)

b. Minorities: minority student enrollment by region and for Hawaii, and teachers, all by race-ethnicity (black, Hispanic, Asian, and Native American, and also Pacific Islander for Hawaii enrollment), 1984/85, with selected trends from 1980/81. Tables 3-8. (p. 4-5)

c. Operations: number of schools where income exceeded and equaled expense, and expense exceeded income; student/teacher and teacher/other personnel ratios; and expense and income per student, by detailed item. Tables 9 and 10A-C. (p. 6-11)

d. NAIS membership analysis: number of member schools and enrollments, with summary data by membership status (active, affiliate, and new school services), and detail for active members/new school services, as of Sept. 1984; and schools and enrollment, 1980/81-1984/85. 7 tables. (p. 12-13)

A7000
National Association of Realtors

A7000-1   OUTLOOK FOR THE ECONOMY AND REAL ESTATE

Monthly. Approx. 5-15 p. SRI/MF/complete, shipped quarterly

Monthly report, by Jack Carlson, on current and projected economic conditions and trends affecting the residential, commercial, and industrial real estate markets, with detailed forecasts of housing sales and prices. Data are derived from a model developed by the National Assn of Realtors (NAR), and Data Resources, Inc.

Issues include narrative sections on aggregate economy, employment and inflation, monetary policy and interest rates, and real estate markets, occasionally including statistics; and occasional "special supplement" sections focusing on a specific topic, and usually containing statistics.

Issues also include 2 monthly tables showing the following data for quarter 1-3 quarters prior to cover date, 7 subsequent quarters, current year, and 2-3 previous and 1-2 coming years:

a. Aggregate economy, including GNP and percent change in selected components; manufacturing capacity utilization rate; auto sales; percent change in industrial production in Japan and European Common Market; trade deficit, and value of U.S. dollar; employment and unemployment rate; household income, taxes, debt, and interest payments; percent change in CPI, PPI, hourly compensation, productivity, labor costs, and other inflation measures; corporate profits and tax liability; and Federal tax receipts and expenditures.

b. Real estate markets and prices, including new and existing single-family home sales and median prices; monthly mortgage payment, and share of median family income; private single- and multi-family housing starts; mobile home shipments; housing affordability index; mortgage debt outstanding; homeowners' equity; housing inventory; rental, office, and industrial vacancy rates; and percent change in new commercial and industrial building construction.

c. Financial markets, including percent change in money supply; personal savings and rate; business and government savings; foreign current account deficits; nonresidential, residential, and inventory investment; and interest rates by type.

Prior to Jan. 1985, monthly tables also included data on consumer installment debt and commercial/industrial loans. Prior to Sept. 1985, monthly tables included data on new mortgage commitments and capital costs; and omitted data on trade deficit, value of U.S. dollar, and household debt.

Monthly tables appear in all issues. All additional features with substantial statistical content not covered in monthly tables are described, as they appear, under "Statistical Features." Nonstatistical features are not covered.

Availability: National Association of Realtors, Economics and Research Division, 777 14th St., NW, Washington DC 20005, †; SRI/MF/complete, shipped quarterly.

Issues reviewed during 1985: Nov. 1984-Oct. 1985 (P).

STATISTICAL FEATURES:

A7000-1.601: Jan. 1985

COMMERCIAL AND INDUSTRIAL REAL ESTATE MARKETS, RECURRING FEATURE

(p. 5) Includes 1 recurring table showing square footage of retail/other commercial, office, and industrial building contracts, 1981-85. Data are from Data Resources, Inc. and National Assn of Realtors.

A7000-1.602: Feb. 1985

SPECIAL SUPPLEMENT: MACROECONOMIC IMPACTS OF TAX REFORM

(p. 3-10) Article estimating the potential impact of 3 income tax reform proposals (Kemp-Kasten, Bradley-Gephardt, and Treasury) on selected economic indicators, 1986-95. Data are from National Assn of Realtors and Data Resources, Inc. Includes 15 tables.

A7000-1.603: Mar. 1985

SPECIAL SUPPLEMENT: THE CURRENT RECOVERY, WAS CONSUMPTION OR INVESTMENT RESPONSIBLE?

(p. 4-9) Article analyzing change in GNP components during the current economic recovery period (4th quarter 1982-4th quarter 1984), with comparison to average change during 6 previous periods. Includes 3 tables.

A7000-1.604: Apr. 1985

FISCAL POLICY

(p. 6-7) Article, with 1 table showing potential impact of FY86 Federal deficit reduction on selected economic indicators in 1988, 1990, and 1995. Data are from Senate testimony.

SPECIAL SUPPLEMENT: TAX REFORM PRODUCTIVITY OF TAX PROVISIONS AFFECTING COMMERCIAL REAL ESTATE

(p. 9-10) Article, with 1 table analyzing the impact of recent Treasury Dept tax reform proposals on a typical commercial real estate investment.

A7000–1.605: May 1985

REAL ESTATE MARKETS, RECURRING FEATURE

(p. 3-4) Includes 1 recurring table showing square footage of retail/other commercial, office, and industrial building contracts, 1981-85. Data are from Data Resources, Inc., and National Assn of Realtors.

SPECIAL SUPPLEMENT: THE IMPACT OF TAX REFORM ON REAL ESTATE

(p. 5-22) Article estimating the potential impact of 3 income tax reform proposals (Kemp-Kasten, Bradley-Gephardt, and Treasury) on home ownership costs and commercial real estate investment, various years 1984-86. Data are from National Assn of Realtors. Includes 8 tables.

A7000–1.606: June 1985

REAL ESTATE MARKETS, RECURRING FEATURE

(p. 3-4) Includes 1 recurring table showing square footage of retail/other commercial, office, and industrial building contracts, 1981-86. Data are from Data Resources, Inc., and National Assn of Realtors.

SPECIAL SUPPLEMENT: THE IMPACT OF THE REAGAN TAX REFORM PROPOSAL

(p. 5-14) Article estimating potential impact of 2 Reagan Administration income tax reform proposals on homeownership costs, housing value, commercial real estate investments, and selected economic indicators, various years 1986-95. Data are from National Assn of Realtors. Includes 5 tables.

A7000–1.607: Sept. 1985

REAL ESTATE MARKETS, RECURRING FEATURE

(p. 3-4) Includes 1 recurring table showing square footage of retail/other commercial, office, and industrial building contracts, 1981-86. Data are from Data Resources, Inc., and National Assn of Realtors.

A7000–2 EXISTING HOME SALES, Monthly Report
Monthly. 15 p.
SRI/MF/complete, shipped quarterly

Monthly report on sales of existing homes. Covers single-family home sales volume and value and price range by region, and median price in selected metro areas; apartment condominium/cooperative sales by region; and total sales by State. Also includes housing affordability index.

Most data are compiled by NAR from reports of over 250 local boards of realtors and multiple listing systems. Month of coverage is month prior to publication date.

Report regularly includes narrative introduction, with text statistics and summary tables; 1 table showing U.S. summary trends, including homes available for sale; and 12 detailed tables, listed below, some with corresponding charts.

Availability: National Association of Realtors, Economics and Research Division, 777 14th St., NW, Washington DC 20005, members $36.00 per yr., nonmembers $48.00 per yr.; SRI/MF/complete, shipped quarterly.

Issues reviewed during 1985: Oct. 1984-Sept. 1985 (P).

TABLES:

[Tables [1-6] and [9-10] usually show data for total U.S. and by census region. Tables [1-3] and [8-12] show data for month of coverage or quarter ending in month of coverage, with monthly or quarterly trends for preceding 12 months or 4 quarters, and annual trends mostly from 1970s.]

[1-2] Existing single-family home sales and dollar volume of sales [seasonally adjusted and unadjusted].

[3] Sales price of existing single-family homes (not seasonally adjusted) [median and mean].

[4-5] Sales of existing single-family homes, by price class (percentage distribution) [for month of coverage and same month of previous 4 years; also shows median price].

[6] Sales of existing single-family homes, by number of bedrooms (percentage distribution) [for month of coverage].

[7] Median sales price of existing single-family homes, by number of bedrooms [for month of coverage and same month of previous 4 years].

[8] Housing affordability [existing home median price, mortgage rate, monthly principal/interest payment and payment as percent of income, median family income, qualifying income, and affordability index].

[9-10] Apartment condo/co-op sales; and total existing home sales, single-family/apartment condos/co-ops (seasonally adjusted annual rates).

[11] Total existing home sales for each State, single-family/apartment condos/co-ops.

[12] Median sales price of existing single-family homes [in each of approximately 40 metro areas (not seasonally adjusted).

A7000–7 NATIONAL ASSOCIATION OF REALTORS MEMBERSHIP PROFILE, 1984
Recurring (irreg.) 1984.
63+App 6 p.
SRI/MF/complete

Recurring report on the socioeconomic and professional characteristics of real estate brokers and salespersons holding membership in the National Assn of Realtors (NAR), 1983 or 1984, with selected trends from 1963.

Presents median income and distribution of brokers and salespersons, by some or all of the following with various cross-tabulations:

a. Sex, age, education, job satisfaction, undergraduate field, participation in instructional programs, prior occupational category, full- or part-time status and whether another job is held, years of real estate licensure, years of experience in real estate and with present firm, years of NAR membership, and number of employers during real estate career.

b. Security licenses held, function within firm, business specialty, types of real estate activities, size of firm, ownership in firm, firm's franchise status and affiliation with related companies, and hours worked.

Data are based on 2,356 responses to a July-Sept. 1984 survey of NAR members.

Contains contents listing (1 p.); introduction and highlights (p. 1-7); broker profiles, with 44 tables (p. 11-36); salesperson profiles, with 39 tables (p. 39-63); and appendices on survey methodology, with 1 table and questionnaire facsimile (6 p.).

Previous report, covering 1981 survey, is described in SRI 1982 Annual under this number.

Availability: National Association of Realtors, Economics and Research Division, 777 14th St., NW, Washington DC 20005, $10.00; SRI/MF/complete.

A7015
National Association of Regulatory Utility Commissioners

A7015–1 1983 ANNUAL REPORT ON UTILITY AND CARRIER REGULATION
Annual. Nov. 30, 1984.
xvii+908 p.
LC 76-644813.
SRI/MF/complete, delayed

Annual report, for 1983, presenting detailed data on the activities, jurisdiction, finances, and employees of U.S. and Canadian Government agencies regulating the public and private utility and transportation industries. Also includes selected data on finances and operations of regulated companies.

Industry coverage includes electric, gas, telephone, telegraph, water, and sewer utilities; pipelines and cable TV services; bus, motor, and railroad carriers; and various other utilities and carriers.

Data are compiled by the National Assn of Regulatory Utility Commissioners from reports submitted by Federal, State, territorial, and Canadian provincial and national agencies.

Contents:

Preface, and contents and table listing. (p. iii-xvii)

Part I. Agency profiles and history, generally with 1 organization chart, and 1-5 tables for each agency on personnel and/or receipts and expenditures, volume of proceedings, and consumer complaints. Agencies are arranged alphabetically. (p. 1-301)

Part II. Rate cases, with 1 extended table showing rate increases requested and granted, profitability allowed, projected revenues and expenses, and capital structure and costs allowed, by company, 1983. Data are arranged by type of utility and carrier, and by individual regulatory agency. (p. 302-406)

Part III. Utility regulation, with 102 tables on scope of agency jurisdiction, and operations of regulated utilities, by type of utility. (p. 407-751)

Part IV. Transportation regulation, with 25 tables on scope of jurisdiction, by type of carrier. (p. 752-801)

Part V. Miscellaneous regulatory information, with 25 lists and tables on agency employment, salaries, budget, and administrative procedures. (p. 802-899)

Index. (p. 900-908)

Tables in Parts III-V are described below.

Availability: National Association of Regulatory Utility Commissioners, 1102 Interstate Commerce Commission Bldg., Constitution Ave. and 12th St., NW, PO Box 684, Washington DC 20044, $42.50; SRI/MF/complete, delayed shipment in Dec. 1985.

PARTS III-V TABLES:

[Data are generally shown by U.S. and Canadian regulatory agency, and are for 1983 unless otherwise noted.]

A7015–1.1: Regulatory Data

UTILITY REGULATION

a. Number of utilities and pipelines under agency jurisdiction, by State; utilities by type and ownership; scope of rate regulation; method of determining rate base, cost of service allowances, and depreciation policies; rate of return allowed and earned; and accounting, auditing, and report requirements, including management audit/study contracts and consultants. Tables 1-33. (p. 409-512)

b. Corporate transactions regulated; competitive bidding requirements; computer use and plans, budgets, and staff; safety and service requirements; certificates, licenses, and permits; and interstate compacts affecting hydroelectric developments. Tables 34-45. (p. 513-557)

c. Environmental standards; income tax provisions; billing practices; service disconnection and reconnection policies; underground utility damage prevention laws; plant abandonment cost policies; and energy conservation activities. Tables 46-52. (p. 559-588)

d. Communications services regulated, including cable TV; Bell System intrastate rate increases, 1970-83; and scope of regulation of radio common carriers, by State. Tables 53-57. (p. 590-606)

e. Telephone subscriber privacy policies, directory assistance and listing charges, rate reductions for employees, usage-sensitive pricing, rate for coin telephones, and rate policies for nonprofit groups and handicapped persons; and telephone plant value, revenues, expenditures, telephones in service, and average customers, calls, and bills. Tables 58-67. (p. 608-650)

f. State taxation of telecommunications services; accounting for telephone station connections; use of telephone directory advertising revenues in ratemaking; regulatory provisions regarding equipment for hearing impaired; and State authorization of intrastate long-distance service competition for resale and bypass. Tables 68-76. (p. 651-679)

g. Electricity, gas, and water and sewerage utility regulation, and plant value, revenues, expenses, customers, consumption, average bills, and plant investment; gas companies adding new customers; gas pipeline safety activity and expenses; average gas and competing fuel prices in selected cities; and States with higher gas prices than oil prices. Tables 77-102. (p. 684-751)

TRANSPORTATION REGULATION

h. Scope of regulation, by type of carrier; motor carriers regulated and enforcement activity; motor carrier and railroad safety investigators and earnings; truck insurance requirements; railroads regulated, and safety program participation and expenses; and railroad accident reporting requirements. Tables 103-127. (p. 753-801)

MISCELLANEOUS

i. Other functions performed by agencies, and other businesses under agency jurisdiction; terms of commissioners; time requirements for rate decisions and appeals; and commission officials and staff, including number of full-time employees and salary for key positions, 1984. Tables 128-136. (p. 804-851)

j. Costs of regulation, including agency receipts by source and expenditures by object; legal status of agencies; use of administrative law examiners; public information services; freedom of information statutory requirements; and directory of State consumer and energy offices. Tables 137-152. (p. 853-899)

A7105
National Association of Securities Dealers

A7105–1   1984 NASDAQ FACT BOOK
Annual. [1985.] 119 p.
ISSN 0741-0921.
LC sc83-1846.
SRI/MF/complete

Annual report on trading volume and price performance of 4,723 over-the-counter securities on the NASDAQ national list and national market systems, 1984, with aggregate trends from 1971. Data are compiled by NASD.

Includes number of shares traded, and high, low, and closing bid prices, by security, with summary data by industry division, and detail for 50 most active securities and market value leaders; types of securities traded; and trading volume and/or value comparisons to NYSE, AMEX, and major foreign markets.

Also includes selected financial data for typical NASDAQ domestic and foreign companies; market qualifications; number of NASDAQ companies and market makers (registered brokers), by State; data for American Depositary Receipts (ADRs) and foreign securities traded on NASDAQ, including share and dollar volume for leading securities, and number of issuers by country; listing of market makers; number of NASDAQ computer terminal installations by country; and listing of newspapers and other media covering NASDAQ.

Contains contents listing (p. 1); and report, with narrative analysis, 7 charts, and 30 tables (p. 2-119).

Availability: National Association of Securities Dealers, 1735 K St., NW, Washington DC 20006, †; SRI/MF/complete.

A7130
National Association of State Racing Commissioners

A7130–1   PARI-MUTUEL RACING, 1984
Annual. [1985.] 24 p.
SRI/MF/complete

Annual report, for 1984, on pari-mutuel horse racing in U.S., Canada, and Puerto Rico. Also covers greyhound racing and jai alai in U.S. Includes data on revenue, total races and games, attendance, and purse distribution, by State and Province.

Data are based on information provided by members of the National Assn of State Racing Commissioners, and the Canadian Ministry of Agriculture.

Contains 4 sections, with 17 tables listed below. Each section on the U.S. also includes a brief summary of related tax methods, by State.

Availability: National Association of State Racing Commissioners, Box 4216, Lexington KY 40504, $25.00; SRI/MF/complete.

TABLES:

[Tables show data for 1984, unless otherwise noted. Revenues by category are for track and/or occupational licenses, pari-mutuel taxes, breakage, admission taxes, miscellaneous, and, for jai alai only, franchise fees.]

A7130–1.1: Horse Racing

U.S.

[Tables [2-8] show data by State, for thoroughbred, harness, quarter horse, and mixed races.]

[1] Racing revenue to States by years (1934-84). (p. 2)

[2] Total horse racing days and total races. (p. 3)

[3] Attendance and daily average attendance. (p. 4)

[4] Pari-mutuel and daily average handle. (p. 5)

[5-6] Total revenue to government; and revenue to government by category. (p. 6-9)

[7] Simulcasting/telephone betting in the U.S. [pari-mutuel handle and total revenue to government; also includes data for greyhound racing]. (p. 10)

[8] Stakes/purse distribution. (p. 11)

CANADA AND PUERTO RICO

[Tables present data by Canadian Province and for Puerto Rico, for thoroughbred and harness races.]

[9] Horse racing in Canada and Puerto Rico [racing days, number of races, attendance, and daily average attendance. (p. 16)

[10] Handle [pari-mutuel and daily average], total revenue, and stakes/purse distribution. (p. 17)

A7130–1.2: Greyhound Racing and Jai Alai in U.S., and Legal Age Summary

GREYHOUND RACING

[1-2] Greyhound racing in the U.S. [total performances, number of races, attendance, daily average attendance, and pari-mutuel and daily average handle]; and revenue to government [by category], and stakes/purse distribution; [all by State and for 3 Alabama counties]. (p. 18)

[3-4] Greyhound racing revenue and total greyhound/horse racing revenue to the States (1959-84). (p. 21)

JAI ALAI

[Tables show data for Connecticut, Florida, and Rhode Island.]

[5-6] Jai alai [number of performances and games played, attendance, daily average attendance, and pari-mutuel and daily average handle]; and revenue to government [by category]. (p. 22)

LEGAL AGE

[7] Legal age to attend and wager at race track [by State]. (p. 23)

A7140
National Association
of State Scholarship
and Grant Programs

A7140-1   NASSGP 16th ANNUAL
SURVEY REPORT, 1984/85
Academic Year
Annual.   Jan. 1985.
iv+140 p.
SRI/MF/complete

Annual report on State-administered student aid for higher education, 1984/85, with selected trends from 1979/80. Includes data on number and value of awards, and characteristics of recipients, with detail by program and State. Data were compiled by NASSGP, and are based primarily on a survey of member agencies.

Contains contents/table listing (p. iii-iv); and report in 7 sections, with narrative summaries, 27 tables and lists, and NASSGP directory (p. 1-140). Tables and lists present the statistics described below, and summaries of application procedures and criteria, eligible institution and program types, agency policies, and planned changes in aid programs.

Availability: Pennsylvania Higher Education Assistance Agency, Attention: Research and Statistics, 660 Boas St., Harrisburg PA 17102-1398, $5.00; SRI/MF/complete.

STATISTICS:

[Data are estimates for 1984/85, unless otherwise noted. Most data are shown by detailed aid program, arranged by State (also including Puerto Rico).]

a. Totals: number and value of need and non-need based awards to undergraduate and graduate students, with comparisons to 1983/84; and awards, appropriation, and selection criteria, for other awards from NASSGP member agencies, and for awards from nonmember agencies (also shows administering agency). (p. 13-36)

b. Need-based undergraduate awards: number and value of awards with competitive and attendance conditions; award and award value distributions by type of institution (in-State public and private, and out-of-State); and value of State Student Incentive Grant (SSIG) program awards, with comparison to 1983/84 amount awarded and amount returned to Federal Government. (p. 37-46)

c. Program characteristics: applicants, recipients, total value of awards, and rejections due to lack of need or funds; and program starting year, maximum allowable award, and average, low, and high awards. (p. 53-68)

d. Recipients of need-based undergraduate awards, and value of awards, by selected recipient characteristics, including type of school or program attended, citizenship and residency status, whether financially independent, sex, race/ethnicity (including American Indian, Oriental, and Spanish American), age, and family income; and total value of need-based undergraduate awards, 1979/80-1984/85. (p. 122, 127-129)

A7150
National Association
of State Universities
and Land-Grant Colleges

A7150-3   APPROPRIATIONS OF
STATE TAX FUNDS for
Operating Expenses of
Higher Education, 1984/85
Annual.   Oct. 1984.   26 p.
LC 75-617890.
SRI/MF/complete

Annual report, by M. M. Chambers, on State appropriations for higher education, by institution and function, FY85. Includes appropriations for operating expenses of colleges and universities, coordinating and governing boards, student financial aid, and community colleges and vocational/technical schools. Excludes appropriations for capital outlay.

Data are collected by Center for Higher Education, Illinois State University.

Contains introduction, with 1 map (p. 1-6); 1 table showing appropriations by State, FY75, FY83, and FY85, and percent gains over the past 2- and 10-year periods (p. 7); and 1 table repeated for each State showing FY85 appropriations, by institution and function (p. 8-26).

This is the 26th edition of the report.

Availability: National Association of State Universities and Land-Grant Colleges, Office of Communications Services, One Dupont Circle, NW, Suite 710, Washington DC 20036, †; SRI/MF/complete.

A7150-4   1984/85 STUDENT
CHARGES AT STATE AND
LAND-GRANT
UNIVERSITIES
Annual.   [1985.]   1+17+6 p.
SRI/MF/complete

Annual report on State and land-grant university student charges, 1984/85, with trends from the 1960s. Covers resident and nonresident tuition/fees, room, and board, and includes data for individual institutions. Data are from survey responses of 135 NASULGC member institutions in the 50 States, D.C., Guam, Puerto Rico, and Virgin Islands.

Contains table listing (1 p.); and narrative analysis with 18 tables, listed below (p. 1-17, 6 p.).

Availability: National Association of State Universities and Land-Grant Colleges, Office of Communications Services, One Dupont Circle, NW, Suite 710, Washington DC 20036, †; SRI/MF/complete.

TABLES:

[Data are for 1984/85, unless otherwise noted. Most data are shown for undergraduate residents and nonresidents.]

1. Two-year comparison of median charges [tuition/fees, room, and board, 1983/84-1984/85]. (p. 1-2)

2. Regional comparison of median tuition/fees. (p. 3)

3. Two-year comparison of median tuition/fees for graduate and professional students [in law, medicine, veterinary medicine, and dentistry, 1983/84-1984/85]. (p. 4)

4-9. Ranges, and range of increases, for tuition/fees and total charges. (p. 6-9)

10-11. Twenty-year trend of median charges for tuition/fees [1965/66-1984/85]; and 16-year trend of median total charges [1969/70-1984/85]. (p. 11-12)

12-17. Highest and lowest charges for tuition/fees and total charges; and largest and smallest increase in tuition/fees [ranked for 10 universities]. (p. 13-16)

18. Full-time student charges [tuition/fees, room, and board; by institution, grouped by State or territory]. (6 p.)

A7310
National
Association of Wheat
Growers

A7310-1   WHEAT GROWER: 1985
Wheat Facts
Monthly (selected issue).
Sept. 1985.   (p. 17-39).
Vol. 8, No. 9.
SRI/MF/excerpts

Annual report, for 1985, by *Wheat Grower* journal, on wheat production, consumption, and foreign trade in U.S. and other major wheat growing countries. Includes data on production costs, prices received by farmers, and government wheat support programs, 1960s-85 with selected earlier trends.

Data are from USDA, National Food Review, and other sources.

Contains contents listing, and chronology of major events affecting wheat growers (p. 18-19); 2 charts, 2 maps, and 20 tables (p. 20-36); and wheat weight and measurement conversions, explanation of wheat classes, and historical and general information on wheat and agriculture (p. 37-39).

All tables, charts, and selected map presenting data not covered in tables, are listed below.

Wheat Grower is a monthly periodical reporting trends and developments in the wheat growing industry, and normally contains only narrative articles. This annual report is the only feature covered in SRI.

This is the 8th annual report.

Availability: National Association of Wheat Growers, 415 Second St., NE, Suite 300, Washington DC 20002, †; SRI/MF/excerpts for annual Wheat Facts section.

TABLES, CHARTS, AND MAP:

[Data are for U.S. unless otherwise noted.]

WHEAT PRODUCTION, SUPPLY, AND USE

[1] Annual wheat production, [acreage, and yield], 1965-85. (p. 20)

[2] Wheat production [and yield in 17 National Association of Wheat Growers] States, 1982-85. (p. 20)

[3] Marketing year wheat supply and disappearance [including beginning and ending stocks, trade, production, and domestic use], 1965/66-1985/86. (p. 21)

[4] Wheat by classes: supply and disappearance [for 5 varieties], 1984/85-1985/86. (p. 21)

[5] Wheat supply and use [acreage, yield, production, trade, domestic use, and carryover, selected years] 1930/31-1985/86. (p. 22)

[6] Use of wheat [including domestic food, feed/seed/industrial, trade, USDA Commodity Credit Corp. inventory, and reseed/farmer-owned reserve], 1965-85. (p. 22)

[7] Marketing chain for wheat used for white bread [cost components for producing average pound of bread, including transportation, processing/marketing, baking, and wholesaler handling], 1983. [chart] (p. 23)

PRICES AND FEDERAL WHEAT PROGRAM

[8-10] All wheat, monthly prices received [for 20 States] 1983-84, and monthly average prices received by farmers 1955/56-1985/86; and wheat parity prices [selected annual averages 1950-84, and monthly average, Jan. 1984-July 1985]. (p. 24-25)

[11] Wheat program summary [production, national average support/target price and price to farmers, direct payments, loan rate, farm value, participating farms, acreage allotment, acreage diversion/set aside, diversions/special grazing and hay program payments, marketing certificate/deficiency payments, and government payments], 1960-85. (p. 26-27)

FOREIGN DATA, CONSUMPTION, AND U.S. EXPORTS

[12] Wheat: world production, consumption, and net exports [for major exporters and importers, residual, and world], 1983/84-1985/86. (p. 28)

[13] Value of total domestic consumption of grain products [by product type], 1983. (p. 28)

[14] U.S. wheat exports by [ranked country or area of] destination, 1980/81-1984/85. (p. 29)

[15-16] USSR and PRC wheat and coarse grain imports [by country or area of origin], 1977/78-1984/85. (p. 30)

[17] Wheat supply and disappearance: major U.S. competitors [Canada, Australia, Argentina, and EC], 1975/76-1985/86. (p. 31)

REGIONAL EXPORT DATA AND WHEAT PRODUCTS

[18] Wheat inspected for export by class, region, and port area, June 1984-May 1985 [period]. (p. 34)

[19] Products of flour produced from 1 acre of wheat [pounds of wheat flour used by product type], 1983. (p. 34)

[20] Wheat exports by port area [interior, gulf, lakes, Atlantic, and 3 Pacific ports, 1983-84]. [map] (p. 35)

GRADING STANDARDS AND PRODUCTION EXPENDITURES

[21] Grades and grade requirements for all classes of wheat (except mixed) [no date]. (p. 36)

[22-23] Farm production expenditures [total and average per farm, with detail by sales size group]; and expenditures [by item] as a percent of total farm outlay; 1984. [table and chart] (p. 36)

A7330
National
Automobile Dealers
Association

**A7330–1   NADA DATA FOR 1985:
Economic Impact of
America's New Car and
Truck Dealers**
Annual.   [1985.]   20 p.
SRI/MF/complete

Annual report, for 1985, on franchised new car and truck dealer operations and finances. Includes data on dealerships, sales, employment, advertising, and other topics, with selected detail by State. Most data are current through 1984 and include trends from 1970s.

Data are compiled by the NADA Industry Analysis Division from original research, and from reports of Federal agencies and *Ward's Automotive Reports.*

Contains contents listing (inside front cover); introduction (p. 1); 4 charts, and 43 tables arranged in 15 sections, each usually accompanied by brief analysis with text statistics (p. 2-19); and list of NADA officials, and 1 tabular listing of industry operating highlights for 1984 (p. 20).

Sections are listed below, and tables within each section are described.

Availability: National Automobile Dealers Association, Industry Analysis Department, 8400 Westpark Dr., McLean VA 22102, $5.00; SRI/MF/complete.

TABLE SECTIONS:

[1] Average dealer profile [sales, gross, expense, and net worth; net pre-tax profit in current and constant 1967 dollars; new and used vehicle and service/parts sales; and average new vehicle selling price; 1978-84]. 1 table. (p. 2)

[2] NADA optimism index [dealer profit expectation index, various dates Apr. 1976-Jan. 1985]. 1 table. (p. 3)

[3] Number of franchised new car dealerships [for dual and exclusive domestic and imported makes, 1975-85; and total dealerships by State, as of Jan. 1, 1985]. 2 tables. (p. 4)

[4] Total dealership sales dollars [total and average franchised dealer sales, 1974-84, and by State, 1984; and number of franchised dealers and dealer sales, payroll, and employees, as percent of retail totals, by State]. 3 tables. (p. 5-6)

[5] New vehicle dept [new domestic and imported car sales volume, 1975-84; sales by month, 1983-84; and sales and market shares for 8 domestic and foreign manufacturers and all other imports, average new car sales per

dealer and vehicle selling price, and domestic and imported new car inventories and days' supplies, various years 1974-84]. 5 tables. (p. 7-8)

[6] Used vehicle dept [wholesale and retail used vehicle sales volume, and average retail selling price of used cars, for franchised dealers, 1975-84]. 2 tables. (p. 9)

[7] Service and parts depts [aggregate market value by type of service establishment, 1979-84; number of auto repair facilities by type, 1984; and franchised dealer labor and parts sales, by type, 1983-84]. 3 tables. (p. 10)

[8] Employment and payrolls [franchised dealership employees by occupation, 1984; total and average dealership employment, 1974-84, and by State, 1984; and total and average annual or weekly payroll and earnings, various years 1975-84, and by State, 1984]. 6 tables. (p. 11-12)

[9] Advertising and the franchised dealership [local advertising expenditures, including total amounts, averages per dealer and per new vehicle sold, and ratios to sales, with detail by media type and sales volume, various years 1976-84]. 4 tables. (p. 13)

[10] Consumer credit [average maturity of new car finance company loans, selected years 1970-Feb. 1985; and average finance rate on new car loans at finance companies and banks, average prime rate, total consumer and auto installment credit outstanding, and auto credit outstanding by type of lending institution, 1974-84]. 5 tables. (p. 14)

[11] Vehicles in operation and scrappage [cars and trucks/buses in operation, as of Jan. 1, 1975-85; population and cars in operation, selected years 1910-2005; and car and truck/bus scrappage, number and as percent of cars and trucks/buses in operation and new cars and trucks/buses registered, 1975-84]. 4 tables. (p. 15)

[12] Total registrations [cars and trucks/buses, by State, 1984, and totals, 1975-84]. 2 tables. (p. 16)

[13] Franchised new truck dealer [new truck sales by gross vehicle weight, 1983-84]. 1 table. (p. 17)

[14] [Domestic] truck inventories [and days' supplies, by weight class, 1983 and monthly 1984]. 1 table (p. 18)

[15] Truck dealership profile [total sales value by dept (new and used vehicle and service/parts), and new unit sales by weight class, 1983-84; and NADA American Truck Dealers Division membership by primary make and State, and for selected metro areas, Puerto Rico, American Samoa, and Canada, as of Apr. 1985]. 3 tables. (p. 18-19)

A7350
National
Business Aircraft Association

A7350–1 NBAA BUSINESS FLYING

Series. For individual
publication data, see below.
SRI/MF/complete.

Series of reports on business aircraft ownership
and use. Data generally are drawn from annual
FAA reports and privately commissioned surveys or studies.

Usually 1-3 reports are issued each year, including recurring reports on general and business
aviation.

Report reviewed during 1985 is described below.

Availability: National Business Aircraft Association, 1200 18th St., NW, Washington DC
20036, not available by subscription, member
single copy $1.00, nonmember single copy $2.00,
minimum charge $10.00; SRI/MF/complete.

A7350–1.16: Successful Team: Fortune 500 and Business Aircraft

[Recurring (irreg.) Mar. 1985. 8 p. 1985—
Section 1. SRI/MF/complete.]

Recurring report on business aircraft ownership among *Fortune* magazine's 500 largest
industrial firms, 1983 and trends. Data are
from an annual survey conducted by Aviation
Data Service, Inc.

Includes 7 tables primarily showing aggregate financial performance indicators, and
number of companies by SIC 2-digit industry,
1983, and average company employment,
1979-83, all for companies operating and not
operating aircraft; and fleet composition and
value by aircraft type, and number of companies by fleet size, 1983.

Previous report, for 1981, is described in
SRI 1983 Annual under A7350-1.14.

A7375
National
Catholic Educational
Association

A7375–1 U.S. CATHOLIC ELEMENTARY AND SECONDARY SCHOOLS, 1984/85

Annual. Mar. 8, 1985.
1+20 p.
SRI/MF/complete

Annual report, by Frank H. Bredeweg, on Catholic elementary and secondary schools, enrollment, teachers, and student characteristics,
1984/85, with trends from 1968/69.

Includes Catholic schools and enrollment by
region; schools by type of administration, type of
location, and enrollment size; enrollment distribution for Catholics and non-Catholics; top 10
States and 20 dioceses ranked by enrollment; enrollment by race/ethnicity (black, Hispanic,
Asian, American Indian, and other); pupil/
teacher ratio; teachers from religious orders, by
sex; and lay teachers. Most data are shown for
elementary and secondary schools.

Also includes data on population, births,
school-age children, and public and private
school enrollment, various years 1955-95; and
church-related private school enrollment, by religious affiliation, 1965/66, 1978/79, and 1980/
81.

Most data are shown for elementary and secondary schools.

Data are primarily from NCES and reports of
167 diocesan offices to National Catholic Educational Assn.

Contains introduction (1 p.); and report highlights and narrative, with text statistics and 16
tables (p. 1-20).

Availability: National Catholic Educational
Association, Publication Sales, Suite 100, 1077
30th St., NW, Washington DC 20007-3852,
$5.50 (prepaid), members 10% discount; SRI/
MF/complete.

A7375–2 CATHOLIC HIGH SCHOOL: A NATIONAL PORTRAIT

Monograph. 1985. x+254 p.
SRI/MF/complete

Report profiling Catholic secondary education,
including characteristics of students, teachers,
administration, facilities, curricula, parental involvement, and finances, 1983 and trends. Also
includes selected comparisons to public secondary education.

Report is based primarily on responses of 910
Catholic high school principals to a Sept. 1983
survey of 1,464 Catholic high schools, conducted
by Search Institute in collaboration with National Catholic Educational Assn.

Contains listings of contents and statistical exhibits (p. iii-vi); introduction, with 2 tables on
survey sample size and topics (p. 1-7); 16 chapters, with narrative analysis, text data, and 73
statistical exhibits, described below (p. 9-180);
notes (p. 181-187); and 4 appendices, presenting
directory of consultants, questionnaire facsimile
with tabulated responses, directory of schools
with achievements in selected areas, and additional information sources (p. 189-254).

Availability: National Catholic Educational
Association, Publication Sales, 1077 30th St.,
NW, Suite 100, Washington DC 20007-3852,
$19.75; SRI/MF/complete.

CHAPTERS:
[Data are for Catholic secondary education, with
selected comparisons to public secondary education. Data generally are shown as survey response distributions or averages, and are current
as of Sept. 1983. The descriptions below include
text tables as well as the numbered statistical
exhibits noted.

Many charts and tables show data breakdowns
by various school characteristics, including region, enrollment size, gender composition (boys,
girls, and coed), and administrative control (diocesan, parochial, interparochial, and private).
Data by race and ethnic origin are shown for
black, white, American Indian/Alaskan Native,
Asian/Pacific Islander, and Hispanic.]

A7375–2.1: Chapters 1-3: Overview, Students, and Teachers

a. Overview, including indicators of religious
emphasis; commitment to academic excellence, faith development, and community;
and school environment (morale, discipline, structure, and order). Exhibits 1.1-
1.3. (p. 9-17)

b. Student enrollment by grade, sex, race and
ethnic origin, family income and housing
tenure, and elementary school type (public,
Catholic, other private); non-Catholic enrollment; financial aid criteria, recipients,
and grants; and schools serving handicapped students, and accessibility of facilities. Exhibits 2.1-2.9. (p. 19-35)

c. Teachers by sex, age, religious identification (Catholic and non-Catholic laity, and
in religious orders), race and ethnic origin,
length of service, and education; teacher
demographic composition in 1962; 1st-
year and maximum teacher salaries;
schools offering tenure and merit pay; and
student-teacher ratios. Exhibits 3.1-3.6. (p.
37-47)

A7375–2.2: Chapters 4-9: Curricula, Environment, Administration, Facilities, and Finances

a. Academic programs, including graduation
requirements, course offerings, and student
coursework, by subject; students in college
preparatory, general, and vocational programs; special programs and co-curricular
activities offered, including driver education, drug education, gifted/talented student and foreign exchange programs;
courses taught in Spanish, clubs, musical
organizations, and sports; and student
postgraduation plans. Exhibits 4.1-4.10. (p.
49-62)

b. Religious programs, including religious
identification of religion dept faculty and
administration; availability of religious services; and importance of religion curricula
and impact on other aspects of education.
Exhibits 5.1-5.3. (p. 63-70)

c. Environment, including expulsion and suspension policies for drug and alcohol use,
aggressive behavior, and theft; seriousness
of absenteeism, alcohol and drug use,
crime, and other student behavior problems, and change from 1980; principals'
perceptions of teacher and student morale;
and student, staff, and student family attendance at school events. Exhibits 6.1-6.4.
(p. 71-79)

d. Principals and/or administrators, by religious identification, sex, race and ethnic
origin, education, years of service, and age;
relationship of lay vs. religious principal to
minority share of enrollment; full-time
teachers by age; school board meeting frequency; and person or group with decision-making authority for budgetary, personnel,
curricula, and student-related issues. Exhibits 7.1-7.4. (p. 81-89)

e. Facilities and resources by type, with comparison to 1980; facility accessibility to
handicapped; library book and periodical
holdings since 1974; and computer use by
application. Exhibits 8.1-8.3. (p. 91-99)

f. Income from tuition/fees, contributions,
subsidies, fund-raising, and other sources;
tuition by grade; per pupil expenditures;
operating expenses by object; schools with
over 5% surplus or deficit; State aid by
function; participation in 11 Federal aid
programs; and developmental/public relations activities and personnel. Exhibits 9.1-
9.7. (p. 101-112)

A7375–2.3: Chapters 10-16: Parental Involvement and Miscellaneous

a. Parent-teacher conference frequency; volunteer service areas; activities of parent organizations; and principals' perception of parental views of school goals. Exhibits 10.1-10.4. (p. 113-121)

b. Evaluations of educational trends over past 5 years (including enrollment and test scores), and of areas of school needs and achievements, including need for remedial courses; selected characteristics of schools with high concentration of low-income students, single-sex and coed schools, and schools with various types of administrative control; schools with enrollment waiting lists; student retention; student involvement in administration-related tasks; and overall index of school health. Exhibits 11.1-16.2. (p. 123-180)

A7400
National Coal Association

A7400–2 INTERNATIONAL COAL, 1985 EDITION

Annual. 1985.
4+i+106 p. var. paging.
ISSN 0146-3845.
LC 77-648257.
SRI/MF/not filmed

Annual statistical report on world coal industry, covering production, reserves, consumption, trade, and employment, by country, 1979-84 and selected historical trends. Also includes data on world energy resources. Data are compiled from reports of U.S. and foreign government agencies and private assns.

Contains contents listing (2 p.); 5 summary tables (p. i); 3 statistical sections, with 9 maps and 140 tables (p. I.1-III.42); and 2 appendices, with 1 table, 2 charts, and membership directory of U.S. Coal Exporters Assn (p. IV.1-IV.3). All nonsummary tables are described below.

Availability: National Coal Association, Publications Department, 1130 17th St., NW, Washington DC 20036-4677, members †, nonprofit organizations $95.00, others $165.00; SRI/MF/not filmed.

TABLES:

[Tables generally show data for 1979-83, with selected data for 1984-mid 1985 and trends from as early as 1926. Data by coal type are shown for bituminous, anthracite, and, occasionally, coke, lignite, and briquets.]

A7400–2.1: World and U.S. Data

a. World data: coal reserves and production, by type; coal vs. industrial production indexes; crude oil, natural gas, and raw steel production; energy consumption, by source; and mineral fuel shipments through Panama Canal, by fuel type and trade route; generally shown by country. 15 tables. (p. I.1-I.19)

b. U.S. coal supply and demand summary; number of mines, employment, and productivity, by mine or coal type; and coal consumption, by sector. 3 tables. (p. II.1)

c. U.S. trade: export and import volume and/or value, by coal type, country of destination or origin, and U.S. customs district; monthly bituminous trade; bituminous exports by use (metallurgy or steam) and by port of exit, both by destination; and quantity, cost, Btu value, and sulfur content of imported coal delivered to electric utilities, by country of origin and utility. 30 tables. (p. II.2-II.32)

d. Rail rates from mine to port of exit for U.S. export coal, by coal type, mine district, and port; U.S. rail dumpings of bituminous coal for export, by Atlantic port and railroad company; coal shipments to U.S. military forces in West Germany, by type; and ocean freight rates for selected routes. 4 tables. (p. II.33-II.35)

A7400–2.2: Data for Selected Countries

[Data for each country or area noted below include 3-8 tables, usually showing coal production, consumption by sector, trade volume and/or value by country of origin and/or destination, and, often, number of mines, year-end stocks, productivity, and employment, with selected detail by coal and mine type. Substantial additional data and exceptions are indicated below.]

a. Australia; Belgium; Canada, also including energy consumption by source, and coal imports from U.S. by transport mode; and Colombia, also including electric generating capacity by fuel source projected to 1990, and coal reserves. 29 tables. (p. III.1-III.13)

b. France; Federal Republic of Germany; Italy, showing only consumption and trade data; Japan, showing only production and trade data; Netherlands, showing only consumption and trade data; and Poland. 32 tables. (p. III.16-III.31)

c. South Africa, showing only summary coal production, domestic sales, and trade data; Spain; Sweden; UK, also including energy consumption by source; and USSR, showing only coal production, and summary consumption and trade data. 27 tables. (p. III.33-III.42)

d. EC, showing coal production, employment, colliery stocks, imports from 3rd-party countries, and deliveries. 1 table. (p. IV.1)

A7400–3 INTERNATIONAL COAL REVIEW

Monthly. Approx. 22 p. no paging.
SRI/MF/not filmed

Monthly statistical report covering U.S. and foreign coal trade. U.S. data are primarily from U.S. Dept of Commerce. Foreign data are primarily from EC, Statistics Canada, Australian Joint Coal Board, and International Iron and Steel Institute.

Issues generally contain 18 domestic and 5 foreign monthly tables, and occasional special tables. Monthly tables are listed below; most appear in all issues. All additional tables are described, as they appear, under "Statistical Features."

Prior to the Feb. 4, 1985 issue, report was published semimonthly, with separate issues for U.S. and foreign data.

Prior to the Sept. 1985 issue, report also included a monthly table on South African coal production and exports.

Availability: National Coal Association, Publications Department, 1130 17th St., NW, Washington DC 20036-4677, members †, nonmembers $150.00 per yr.; SRI/MF/not filmed.

Issues reviewed during 1985: Nov. 2, 1984-Jan. 7, 1985 (semimonthly); and Feb. 4-Oct. 1985 (monthly) (P) [No foreign issue for Jan. 1985 was published].

MONTHLY TABLES:

[Tables are numbered consecutively in each issue. Table numbering will vary when special tables are included or regular monthly tables are omitted.]

U.S. SECTION

[Month of coverage is 2 months prior to month of publication. Tables [3-16] show value and/or quantity, for month of coverage and/or year to date and generally for same periods of previous year, for U.S.]

1-2. Summary of U.S. bituminous coal exports and export prices [to Canada and overseas, monthly for current year through month of coverage and for previous year].

3-8. Exports of metallurgical and steam coal [by country of destination].

9-11. Exports of anthracite, lignite, and coke [by country of destination].

12-14. Exports of metallurgical and steam coal, by country of destination, by customs district of exit.

15. Imports of bituminous coal, coke, and briquets [by country of origin].

16. Imports of bituminous coal and coke, by country of origin, by customs district of entry.

17. Single-trip ocean freight rates per long ton of coal [for selected world routes; as of date of publication or up to 6 weeks prior to publication date].

18. Foreign exchange rates [for approximately 40 currencies vs. U.S. dollar, for month of coverage, previous 2 months, and same month of previous year].

FOREIGN SECTION

[Month of coverage is 2-6 months prior to month of publication. Table sequence and format may vary.]

19. Coal exports from Australia, by type [and country of destination; for fiscal year to date through month of coverage, and selected prior periods. Prior to Sept. 1985 issue, data were presented in 2 tables, and were shown for New South Wales, Queensland, and total Australia; and destination data were shown only for Japan and other].

20. Canadian coal production [by type], and exports [by country of destination; for month of coverage and year to date, and same periods of previous year. Prior to Sept. 1985 issue, table also showed coke production and coal and coke imports].

21. Japanese imports of [coking and steam] coal [by country of origin; for year to date and same period of previous year. Table begins in Oct. 1985 issue].

22. Crude steel production [by country and world area; for month of coverage and year to date, and same periods of previous year].

23. Coal production [by region and method], stocks [by region, domestic] consumption [by sector], and exports [by country of destination and port of exit], for New South Wales, Australia [for year to date through month of coverage, and same period of previous year].

STATISTICAL FEATURES:

A7400-3.601: Dec. 18, 1984

SPECIAL TABLE

[A] Canadian imports of bituminous coal from the U.S., by Province [via rail and water, Jan.-Sept. 1984 period, with comparison to same period of 1983; data are from the Canadian Energy, Mines, and Resources Dept]. (p. 3)

A7400-3.602: Apr. 2, 1985

SPECIAL TABLES

[Data are from EC Statistical Office.]

[A] Selected statistics: EC [hard and brown coal production; and hard coke stocks, and deliveries to electric power and coking plants; by country, various periods 1983-84].

[B] Coal imports into the EC (excludes intra-EC trade) [by country, cross-tabulated by country of origin, Oct. and 1st 10 months 1984].

A7400-3.603: July 8, 1985

SPECIAL TABLE

[A] Selected statistics: EC [hard and brown coal production; hard coke production and stocks; and hard coal deliveries to electric power and coking plants; by country, various periods 1983-84; data are from EC Statistical Office].

A7400-3.604: Oct. 1985

SPECIAL TABLE

[A] Energy Profile: The EC [coal production, stocks, exports, imports by country of origin, and deliveries by end use; coke, iron, and steel production; steel exports and imports; and electricity generation by fuel type, imports and exports, and fuel use by type; Jan.-Mar. 1984-85; data are from Eurostat].

A7400-4   COAL TRAFFIC, 1983
Annual.   1985.
92 p. var. paging.
ISSN 0069-4916.
LC 75-641344.
SRI/MF/not filmed

Annual report on transportation of coal by rail, water, truck, and pipeline, with detail by individual carrier, primarily for 1979-83, with selected trends from as early as 1900. Also includes data on origin and destination of shipments, and railroad equipment and carloadings.

Data are from Federal Government sources and private assns.

Contains foreword and contents listing, with 1 summary table (5 p.); 6 statistical sections with 3 charts, and 62 tables described below (p. I.1-VI.3); section on rail transportation contracts (p. VII.1-VII.21); and 5 appendices, including rail rate data, definitions, and Bureau of Mines coal producing districts (p. VIII.1-VIII.10).

Availability: National Coal Association, Publications Department, 1130 17th St., NW, Washington DC 20036-4677, members †, nonprofit organizations $50.00, others $75.00; SRI/MF/ not filmed.

TABLES:

[Tables generally show data for various years 1979-83, with selected trends from as early as 1900.

Data by coal district are shown for 23-24 Bureau of Mines producing districts. Data by consumer use are generally shown for coke/gas plants, electric utilities, other industrial, and residential/commercial.

Data sources are shown for each table.]

A7400-4.1: Shipments

(p. I.1-I.7) Includes 6 tables showing coal shipments as follows:

a. Total, and by consumer sector, district of origin, and destination State; for rail, water (often including breakdowns for river, Great Lakes, and Tidewater), truck, and tramway/conveyor/slurry pipeline.

b. By district of origin, by destination State and for Canada and overseas.

A7400-4.2: Railroad Traffic

[Data by rail district are shown for the 3 Class I railroad districts.]

a. Rail shipments by destination State, consumer sector, and coal district of origin; and average revenue, freight carload, and haul, for bituminous/lignite, and for total carload traffic. 5 tables. (p. II.1-II.6)

b. Total and coal revenue freight originated and revenue received, and average coal revenue per ton by railroad district, aggregate for Class I railroads, various years 1963-83; volume carried and average revenue, by major coal-hauling railroad, 1982-83; and revenue freight originated and terminated, total traffic, and gross revenue, by Class I railroad, 1983. 5 tables. (p. II.7-II.11)

c. Freight cars and carloadings: aggregate weekly carloadings; coal and total commodity carloadings; and freight cars and/or general service hopper cars, including number owned, capacity, utilization, and number installed and on-order (new and rebuilt); with detail by major coal-hauling or Class I railroad, various years 1969-84. 14 tables. (p. II.12-II.19)

d. Coal dumpings at Atlantic ports, by railroad, destined for New England, abroad, and inside capes; various years 1978-82. 2 tables. (p. II.20)

e. Locomotives owned by Class I railroads, by locomotive type and service status; and indexes for total and coal railroad freight rates vs. PPI, and coal rates by month; various years 1976-83. 3 tables. (p. II.21)

A7400-4.3: Water Traffic

[Most data for waterborne traffic are shown for 1978-82. Data by traffic type are shown for coastwise, lakewise, internal, and local traffic.]

a. Domestic inland waterway: tons of coal shipped, by shipping and receiving areas, and by origin by destination; and tons originated, terminated, and carried, by major coal-hauling river system. 4 tables. (p. III.1-III.4)

b. Coal water traffic: domestic ton-miles of water movement of coal vs. all commodities, by carrier type; average haul total and over inland waterways, with inland waterway tonnage; tonnage, by coal district of origin, and for imports, exports, and domestic shipments; coal share of all waterborne commerce; and tonnage shipped by barge; generally by traffic type. 7 tables. (p. III.5-III.7)

A7400-4.4: Truck, Great Lakes, and Pipeline Traffic

a. Truck shipments: by destination State, consumer sector, and coal district of origin. 4 tables. (p. IV.1-IV.3)

b. Great Lakes: coal tonnage and total bulk freight, 1900-83; bituminous shipments, by month and lake, and by loading port and destination for shipments from Lake Erie; railroad coal dumpings at Lake Erie ports, by port and railroad; and State of origin of Lake Erie coal. 10 tables. (p. V.1-V.5)

c. Coal slurry pipelines: pipeline systems existing and planned, showing each system's length, annual capacity, and current status. 2 tables. (p. VI.1-VI.3)

A7400–5   COAL DATA, 1984 Edition

Annual. 1985.
102 p. var. paging.
ISSN 0145-417X.
LC 76-648911.
SRI/MF/not filmed

Annual report on coal industry, including production, value, consumption, shipments, stocks, employment, safety, and machinery, with data by coal district and State, 1983 and trends. Also covers total energy production, reserves, and use; and coke production and consumption.

Data are from DOE and other Federal Government and private sources.

Contents:

a. Foreword, contents listing, and 1 summary table. (4 p., p. i)

b. 4 statistical sections, with 164 tables described below. (p. I.1-IV.9)

c. 4 appendices, covering pay provisions; wage classifications showing standard daily wage rates under National Bituminous Coal Wage Agreement for 1984, by class of labor, by quarter Oct. 1984-Jan. 1988; conversion factors; and definitions of Bureau of Mines coal producing districts. (p. IV.1-IV.12)

Report has been published since 1935.

Availability: National Coal Association, Publications Department, 1130 17th St., NW, Washington DC 20036-4677, members †, nonprofit organizations $50.00, others $75.00; SRI/MF/ not filmed.

TABLES:

[Unless otherwise noted, data are for 1979-83, with occasional monthly detail. Data by State generally are shown only for the relevant coal-bearing States.

Data by mining method are shown for underground or surface mining. Major consuming sectors generally include residential/commercial, industrial, and transportation, often with detail for industrial users (electric utilities, coke plants, and other).

Data by coal type generally are shown for bituminous, sub-bituminous, lignite, and anthracite. Each table includes extensive footnotes.]

A7400–5.1: Energy Statistics, and Bituminous Coal and Lignite

ENERGY STATISTICS

a. Supply and demand: energy production, consumption by consuming sector, and net imports, by type of energy source; deliveries of distillate and residual fuel oil, by end use; and petroleum imports by type, and from OPEC and non-OPEC countries. 11 tables. (p. I.1-I.5)

BITUMINOUS COAL AND LIGNITE

[Data by district are shown for 20-23 coal production districts defined by Bureau of Mines. Footnotes for each table define the occasional inclusion of shipments to Canada or Mexico.]

b. National summary data: bituminous/lignite supply and demand components, 1923-83; productivity indexes, PPI, and average weekly earnings, for bituminous and other selected industries; bituminous/lignite production, by mining method and region (east and west of Mississippi River); total production value; and number of mines, average annual output per mine, employment, productivity, and price indicators, all by mining method. 9 tables. (p. II.1-II.4)

c. Coal production: production of 50 largest bituminous/lignite mines, by company; weekly production, 1981-84, and for peak weeks 1960-83; production by quarter, district, State, mining method, and mining equipment type; captive production for selected industries; number of mines and production, by size of output and mining method; production, by coal type and volatility, coalbed and overburden thickness, and major coalbed; and surface acres mined and reclaimed. 27 tables. (p. II.5-II.19)

d. Number of mines, employment, output per person per day, and days worked: all by State, district, and mining method. 24 tables. (p. II.20-II.31)

e. Safety: fatal, nonfatal with and without days lost, disabling, and nondisabling injuries and incidence rates, by mining method and type of mine or other mine-related operation, with detail for fatalities by cause. 4 tables. (p. II.32-II.34)

f. Prices: average price per ton by mining method and for coal sold in the open market, by State and district. 8 tables. (p. II.35-II.38)

g. Plant and equipment: equipment units by type and mining method, with selected State detail, cleaning plant operations and methods, and clean coal as percent of total production, 1974-78; and number of processing plants by State. 9 tables. (p. II.39-II.42)

h. Supply and demand, for bituminous or bituminous/lignite: consumption; stocks and days supply at end of year or month; shipments, by mode of transport, consuming sector, district of origin, and census division and State of destination; average sulfur content of coal, by State and district, by consuming sector; exports by country of destination; and imports by country of origin. 15 tables. (p. II.43-II.55)

A7400–5.2: Electric Utilities, Coke, and Iron and Steel

a. Electric utilities: electricity production by energy source, census division, and State; fuel consumption at electric utilities and fuel deliveries at steam electric plants, by type of fuel; and electricity generated by coal and coal consumed at electric utilities. 7 tables. (p. II.56-II.59)

b. Steam electric plants: average fuel delivery price, average heating efficiency and sulfur content of fuels delivered, and fuel utiliza-

tion efficiency, by fuel type; average heating efficiency and sulfur content of coal delivered, by census division; and coal delivery volume and average price, by type of purchase (contract or spot), mining method, and census division and State. 8 tables. (p. II.60-II.63)

c. Coke and breeze production, with coke detail by State and plant type; coke imports by country, exports, producer/distributor stocks, and consumption (total and for iron furnaces); iron/steel industry coal consumption, and coke production, receipts, consumption, and shipments; characteristics of coal used at coke plants, including receipts by State; coke distribution and sales, by plant type; pig iron and raw steel capacity utilization and/or production; and selected production ratios. 19 tables. (p. II.64-II.68)

A7400–5.3: Anthracite and Energy Resources and Reserves

a. Anthracite: exports; production and average value, by mining method; consumption by consuming sector; number of mines, days worked, employees, and output per person-day; equipment use by mine type; shipments by mode of transportation; distribution by destination State; and stocks at end of year or month, by industrial consumer class. 10 tables. (p. III.1-III.3)

b. Reserves: coal resources, by coal type and State; reserve bases of coal, by coal type, State, mining method, sulfur content, and volatility; coal reserves on Indian reservations, by State; reserves and discoveries in new and old fields of crude oil, natural gas, and natural gas liquids; and number of Federal coal leases, acreage, reserves, and production, by Federal region and State; all for various years 1974-83. 13 tables. (p. IV.1-IV.9)

A7400–8   STEAM ELECTRIC MARKET ANALYSIS

Monthly. Approx. 50 p.
SRI/MF/not filmed

Monthly report presenting data on electricity generation and fuel consumption for individual steam electric plants, arranged by State. Data are compiled by the National Coal Assn. Reports are issued 2 months after month of coverage.

Contains 7 monthly tables, listed below.

Availability: National Coal Association, Publications Department, 1130 17th St., NW, Washington DC 20036-4677, members †, nonmembers $300.00 per yr.; SRI/MF/not filmed.

Issues reviewed during 1985: Sept. 1984-Aug. 1985 (D).

MONTHLY TABLES:

[Data by source are shown for coal, oil, and gas, unless otherwise noted. Tables [5-7] show data by individual plant, arranged by operating utility and State, for month of coverage, with comparisons to same month of previous year.]

[1-4] National electric production [for month of coverage and 12-23 previous months]; and electricity production by State [and census division, for month of coverage]; by source [coal, oil, gas, nuclear, oil/gas turbines, hydro, and other].

[5] Fuel consumption [for coal, oil, and gas] and [coal] stockpiles at electric utility plants.

[6] [Generation at steam electric plants, with distribution by fuel type.]

[7] Generation at nuclear steam electric plants.

A7400–9 POWER PLANT COAL DELIVERIES
Monthly. Approx. 85 p.
SRI/MF/not filmed

Monthly report on volume, cost, and quality of coal delivered to power plants, by census division, State, and plant. Also includes source mine. Data are compiled by National Coal Assn. Reports are issued 3 months after month of coverage.

Usually contains contents listing and code explanation; and 6 monthly tables, listed below.

Availability: National Coal Association, Publications Department, 1130 17th St., NW, Washington DC 20036-4677, members †, nonmembers $500.00 per yr.; SRI/MF/not filmed.

Issues reviewed during 1985: Aug. 1984-July 1985 (D).

MONTHLY TABLES:
[All tables show volume, in addition to the data described below. Tables [4-6] show data for month of coverage. Quality measures variously include average Btu per pound, sulfur and ash content as percent of coal weight, and sulfur content range.

Data by production type are for contract, spot, surface, and underground.]

[1] Steam coal prices (FOB utility plant) [by production type, for month of coverage and same month of previous year].

[2-3] Cost and quality of steam coal deliveries, by producing State [cross-tabulated by] consuming States [for month of coverage and same month of previous year]; and [cost of] steam coal deliveries by month and production type [for year to date and previous year; data begin with the Oct. or Nov. 1984 issues].

[4-5] Summary: cost and quality of coal deliveries [by production type], by State and census [division].

[6] Cost and quality of coal delivered to electric utilities [with source mine type and location, and selected summaries for contract and spot coal deliveries, all by individual plant arranged alphabetically by operating utility, and also indicating type of coal and State].

A7400–10 ELECTRIC UTILITY COAL STOCKPILES, 1984
Annual. 1985. xi+125 p.
SRI/MF/not filmed

Annual report on coal stockpiles and use, and electrical generation, of steam electric power plants, monthly 1984. Covers electrical generation, capacity, and capacity utilization and heat rates; coal consumption, stockpile, and days of supply; and type of coal used; for individual plants arranged by utility and State.

Also includes aggregate plant data by census division and North American Electric Reliability Council (NERC) region.

Contains contents listing (1 p.); index (p. i-vii); and 1 basic table repeated for each census division (p. viii-ix), NERC region (p. x-xi), and individual plant (p. 1-125).

This is the 1st edition of the report.

Availability: National Coal Association, Publications Department, 1130 17th St., NW, Washington DC 20036-4677, members †, nonmembers $50.00; SRI/MF/not filmed.

A7460
National Conference of Catholic Charities

A7460–1 NCCC ANNUAL SURVEY, 1983
Annual. Nov. 1984.
2+20 p.
ISSN 0161-4894.
LC 78-643453.
SRI/MF/complete

Annual report, for 1983, on activities and operations of the National Conference of Catholic Charities, including personnel, funding, and services. Report is based on survey responses from agencies in 118 dioceses.

Contains listings of contents, tables, and charts (2 p.); and 6 report sections arranged in 2 parts, with brief narrative, 9 charts, and 24 tables listed below (p. 1-20).

This is the 6th annual survey.

Availability: National Conference of Catholic Charities, 1346 Connecticut Ave., NW, Washington DC 20036, $7.50; SRI/MF/complete.

TABLES:
[Tables show data for 1983, unless otherwise noted.]

A7460–1.1: Administrative Information
ORGANIZATION AND PERSONNEL

1. [Organizational] structure [of reporting diocesan agencies]. (p. 1)

2. Personnel [religious and lay staff by sex, and personnel by race and ethnic group (including Hispanic and Asian), all by position]. (p. 2)

3. Volunteers [and number of agencies and institutions receiving United Way funds]. (p. 4)

FINANCES

4-5. Income and expenditures [by category]. (p. 6)

[A] Trend of major cash income sources [1978-83; table is identified as Chart 6 in document]. (p. 6)

A7460–1.2: Services and Activities
SERVICES
[Tables 6-16 show number of dioceses offering services and number of persons served, by type of service.]

6-9. Social services [by recipient category]. (p. 8-11)

10. Emergency services to the poor [including detail for men, women, and children]. (p. 12)

11-16. Health, housing, recreation, legal, employment, and education services. (p. 13-14)

LEGISLATIVE AND COMMUNITY ACTIVITIES

17. Convening [number of convenings, and dioceses and participants involved, by type of group]. (p. 16)

---

18. Influencing public policy implementation: general policy [at national, State, and local level]; Title XX comprehensive annual services plan; and community program development; [number of dioceses, activities, and/or programs, by type of activity or program]. (p. 17)

19. Activities to address conference concerns [dioceses and/or parishes involved, by type of activity and issue]. (p. 18)

PARISH PROGRAMS

20. Personnel in parish social ministry programs. (p. 19)

21-22. Parish programs; and social services delivered in parishes; [dioceses and parishes involved, by type of program or service]. (p. 19)

FAMILY LIFE PROGRAM

23. Family life relationship [including number of agencies with diocesan family life programs, and program organization and activities]. (p. 20)

A7485
National Cotton Council of America

A7485–1 COTTON COUNTS ITS CUSTOMERS: The Quantity of Cotton Consumed in Final Uses in the U.S., Revised 1982-83 and Preliminary 1984
Annual. 1985. vi+110 p.
SRI/MF/not filmed

Annual report on cotton and other material consumption in textile product manufacture, by end use, 1982-84. Covers 92 detailed product categories in apparel, home furnishing, and industrial sectors.

Data are from textile manufacturers and Census Bureau.

Contains foreword and contents listing (p. iii-vi); 2 summary tables, including rankings of 92 major end-use product categories by cotton consumption, 1984 (p. 1-19); and 1 detailed table showing production, gray cotton material requirement, and total and cotton material consumption, by detailed end use within each product category, 1982-84 (p. 20-110).

Availability: National Cotton Council of America, Economic Services, PO Box 12285, Memphis TN 38182, members †, nonmembers $50.00, 40% discount to public and educational institution libraries; SRI/MF/not filmed.

A7485–2 ECONOMIC OUTLOOK FOR U.S. COTTON, 1985
Annual. Mar. 1985.
26 p.+App 72 p.
SRI/MF/not filmed

Annual report on cotton economic performance and outlook, including production, consumption, foreign trade, acreage, crop value, prices, and production costs, various years 1959-86. Also includes data on other fibers, cottonseed and cottonseed products, world supply and demand, and general economic indicators.

Contains contents listing (1 p.); narrative report, with 35 text tables and charts (p. 1-26); and appendix, with table listing, and 68 tables described below (72 p.).

Availability: National Cotton Council of America, Economic Services, PO Box 12285, Memphis TN 38182, †; SRI/MF/not filmed.

TABLES:
[Data are for U.S., unless otherwise noted.]

a. General economic indicators, including GNP, industrial production index, unemployment rate, housing starts, retail sales (total and apparel stores), personal income, CPI (total and apparel/upkeep), WPI for finished goods, New York Federal Reserve Bank discount rate, and commercial bank prime rate; monthly and/or quarterly, 1960s-84 or 1970s-1984. Tables A.1-A.14. (14 p.)

b. Textile industry indicators, including mill inventory/shipment ratio and inventory/unfilled order ratio for cotton gray goods; and textile mill and apparel/other textile employment and average weekly hours; monthly 1965-84 or 1975-84. Tables B.1-B.5. (5 p.)

c. Mill fiber consumption, for cotton, wool, silk/wool, and man-made fibers by type; man-made fiber-producing capacity, by fiber type; denim and corduroy production and related cotton consumption; and textile imports, exports, and balance for man-made fiber, cotton, and wool; various periods 1959-86. Tables C.1-C.7 and D.1-D.9. (16 p.)

d. World and foreign fiber consumption, by fiber type; foreign cotton acreage and production, for importing and exporting countries; and U.S. and foreign cotton stocks, production, consumption, and trade; various years 1975-84. Tables E.1-E.3 and F.1-F.2. (5 p.)

e. Cotton planting intentions, by region or State, for 1985/86 crop year; and cotton planted and harvested acreage, production, and yield, by State and region, and value and harvested acreage compared to selected other crops, various years 1965/66-1984/85. Tables G.1-G.9. (9 p.)

f. Raw cotton exports by country of destination; cotton price index; mill-delivered prices of staple cotton, polyester, and rayon; spot cotton prices; and upland cotton prices received by farmers; various periods 1974/75-1984. H.1-H.2 and I.1-I.4.(6 p.)

g. Cottonseed and cottonseed product data, including production (with detail by State for seed), seed consumption and crushings, prices, value, and yield; and cotton production costs, including average gasoline and diesel fuel prices paid by farmers in Cotton Belt States; various periods 1965-84. J.1-J.10 and K.1-K.3. (13 p.)

A7505
National Council
for US-China Trade

A7505–1   CHINA BUSINESS REVIEW
Bimonthly.   Approx. 70 p.
ISSN 0163-7169.
LC 74-643476.
SRI/MF/not filmed

Bimonthly journal reporting commercial and economic information of special interest to exporters and importers engaged in U.S.-China trade. Covers developments in China's economy, U.S. Government regulations, and news of scientific, technical, and other exchanges or agreements between China and other countries.

Data are from U.S. and Chinese Government publications, press releases, private industry, and other sources.

Journal includes feature articles and editorial depts, some with statistics; and "China Business" and "China Data" sections, described below, with recurring data on China foreign business arrangements and trade, and key domestic socioeconomic indicators.

"China Business" section appears in all issues. "China Data" section appears when data are available. Additional features with substantial statistical content are described, as they appear, under "Statistical Features;" page location and latest period of coverage for "China Data" section are also noted. Nonstatistical contents are not covered.

Availability: China Business Review, PO Box 3000, Dept. W, Denville NJ 07834, $90.00 per yr., academic libraries $60.00, faculty/students $48.00, single copy $15.00; SRI/MF/not filmed.

Issues reviewed during 1985: Nov./Dec. 1984-Sept./Oct. 1985 (P) (Vol. 11, No. 6; Vol. 12, Nos. 1-5).

STATISTICAL SECTIONS:

CHINA BUSINESS
["China Business" section consists of tabular lists describing recently reported foreign business arrangements, as noted below, current to approximately 4-6 weeks prior to cover date. Lists include nature, value, and status of each arrangement, and parties involved. Lists of sales and negotiations appear in every issue. Lists of joint ventures and other arrangements appear when data are available.]

a. China's imports and exports: sales and negotiations, by type of industry or commodity.

b. Direct investment/processing/countertrade: includes joint ventures, compensation trade, licensing, coproduction, leasing, and/or processing/assembly.

CHINA DATA
["China Data" section consists of 1 extended table showing all or some of the following data, generally for 4-6 preceding years, sometimes with forecasts for current year. Table content may vary, depending on data availability.]

a. Key indicators, including GNP, population, and industrial and agricultural output; official price index; State budget revenues and expenditures; and currency in circulation.

b. Output by detailed commodity, for industry consumer goods, and agriculture.

c. Foreign trade, total and with principal trading partners; and total, foreign exchange, and gold reserves.

STATISTICAL FEATURES:

A7505–1.601: Nov./Dec. 1984 (Vol. 11, No. 6)

FOCUS ON INVESTMENT ZONES

(p. 14-40) Compilation of features examining areas of China which the government has designated as open to foreign investment. Includes a profile of each area presenting some or all of the following, generally as of 1983 or 1984:

a. Population and land area; key industries, crops, and natural resources; value of industrial output; industrial employment; usage and physical characteristics of communications systems and infrastructure (including ports, rail lines, roads, and airports); and power and water supplies.

b. Foreign investment projects, plans, and priorities, and investment values; and foreign trade values and principal commodities.

CHINA'S EXPORT PRODUCTION BASES

(p. 52-54) By Tom Engle. Article, with 1 table showing export value and/or primary commodities, for China's 29 principal exporting locations, arranged by Province, various years 1981-83. Data sources include S. Y. Ma of Hong Kong University.

A7505–1.602: Jan./Feb. 1985 (Vol. 12, No. 1)

CHINA'S OIL INDUSTRY CHARTS A NEW COURSE

(p. 14-18) By David Denny. Article, with 1 chart and 2 tables showing the following for China: petroleum demand distribution by end use, 1982; volume and value of crude oil and refined product exports, 1981-1st half 1984; and value of drilling/oil field equipment imports from U.S., 1977-84.

Data are from National Council for U.S.-China Trade, *China's Customs Statistics,* and the U.S. Commerce Dept.

A7505–1.603: Mar./Apr. 1985 (Vol. 12, No. 2)

CHINA DATA, RECURRING FEATURE

(p. 54-55) Most data are shown for 1978-84. For data description, see A7505-1 above.

SILK ROAD TO COUNTERTRADE

(p. 6-7) By Andrew S. Heyden. Article, with 1 chart showing value of U.S. imports of silk from China, including raw materials/yarn/fiber, fabric, and garments, 1979-84. Data are from Commerce Dept.

REFORMING THE DOMESTIC BANKING SYSTEM

(p. 17-23) By Daniel Brotman. Article, with 1 chart showing value of loans made by Industrial and Commercial Bank of China, by loan type (working capital, technical transformation, and consumer/private business), 1984.

Data are from Industrial and Commercial Bank of China.

REFORMING THE LABOR SYSTEM

(p. 40-44) By Tom Engle. Article, with 2 charts showing number of workers in China, as follows: for rural areas, 1983-84; for urban government-operated and collective enterprises, and self-employed, 1983; and total projected to 2000. Data are from Chinese government agencies.

A7505–1.604: May/June 1985 (Vol. 12, No. 3)

GOLD MINING AND PRODUCTION

(p. 8-11) By Michael H. Conway. Article, with 1 chart showing Chinese gold production, 1980-87. Data are from Gold Institute and author estimates.

MAJOR GOLD AND DIAMOND MINES

(p. 12) Summary of diamond and gold mines and/or deposits in China provinces, including text data on estimated gold production for some mines and provinces, various years 1979-84. Data are from Davy McKee Corp. and National Council for U.S.-China Trade.

CHINA'S STEEL INDUSTRY

(p. 20-24) By Richard E. Gillespie and Martin Weil. Article, with 1 chart and 1 table showing China's steel imports from Japan/EC, by product, 1983; and foreign steel equipment/technology purchases, including company, country, date, and contract details and/or value, July 1983-Apr. 1985, with similar information for purchases under negotiation.

RATIONALIZING STEEL OUTPUT

(p. 25-29) By Martin Weil. Article, with 1 table showing the following for 14 major steel mills in China: location, main products, production (mostly 1984 or 1985), and expansion/renovation plans.

U.S. MANUFACTURING EQUITY JOINT VENTURES IN CHINA

(p. 33-35) Table showing the following for U.S.-China manufacturing joint ventures in China, grouped by industry: venture name, location, purpose, investment value, participating companies, and participants' equity shares; date of announcement, approval, contract signing, and/or startup; and duration.

Table covers operating ventures, and ventures being considered and formalized, as of Apr. 1985.

A7505–1.605: July/Aug. 1985 (Vol. 12, No. 4)

CITIC: PACESETTING CORPORATION

(p. 6-11) By Tom Engle. Article, with 1 undated table showing China International Trust and Investment Corp. (CITIC) joint ventures with foreign companies, including venture name and location, partners, project description, and investment (including CITIC share). Data are from CITIC and National Council.

ELECTRIC POWER AND THE CHINESE ECONOMY

(p. 14-17) By David Denny. Article, with 1 chart showing Chinese electric power consumption, by sector, 1983. Data are from China Ministry of Water Resources and Electric Power.

CHINA'S NUCLEAR HISTORY

(p. 28-31) By Bradley Hahn. Article, with 1 chart showing reported Chinese nuclear weapons tests, with test date, detonation size, and test type (including tower, bomber, missile, underground, and atmospheric), 1964-84.

CHINA'S RENEWABLE ENERGIES

(p. 32-35) By David Nianguo Li. Article, with 5 tables showing China's consumption of energy from biomass, geothermal, solar, wind, and ocean sources, 1984, 1990, and 2000.

FINDING SPACE TO LIVE AND WORK IN BEIJING

(p. 36-43) By Andrew Ness. Article on available and planned hotel, apartment, and office accommodations in Beijing, China. Includes 1 undated table showing the following, as applicable, for each facility: name and size, investment company, number of rooms or apartments, room rates, number of foreign companies based in facility, rental terms, construction schedule, and expansion and renovation plans.

CHINA HEADS TOWARD 2000

(p. 48) Article, with 1 table on World Bank loans to China, showing the following for each transaction, FY85: project name and description, total cost, and loan amount. Also includes list of projects planned for FY86. Table is accompanied by a related article (p. 46-48).

For description of a similar feature, with data for FY82-86, see SRI 1984 Annual under A7505-1.502.

U.S. SERVICE EQUITY JOINT VENTURES IN CHINA

(p. 56-57) Table showing the following for U.S.-China service equity joint ventures in China, grouped by industry: venture name, location, purpose, investment value, participating companies, and participants' equity shares; date of announcement, approval, contract signing, and/or startup; and duration.

Table covers operating ventures, and ventures being considered and formalized, as of June 1985.

A7505–1.606: Sept./Oct. 1985 (Vol. 12, No. 5)

LURE OF TELEVISION

(p. 14-19) By Molly E. Wyman. Article on foreign participation in major Chinese plants producing TVs and TV-related items. Data are from National Council for U.S.-China Trade.

Includes 1 table showing plant name, products, capacity, and foreign partner, with agreement type and date, for 7 major producing cities or provinces, and other specified locations. Table also shows aggregate TV production (amount and as percent of national production) for each of 7 cities and provinces, 1984 with percent change from 1983.

TELECOMMUNICATIONS SALES TO CHINA

(p. 28-29) By A. Kelly Ho. Article, with 1 chart showing value of Chinese imports of telecommunications/audio equipment, from Japan, U.S., Hong Kong, and all others, 1984. Data are from China's Customs Statistics, and are shown in Chinese yen and U.S. dollars.

U.S. BUSINESS AND HONG KONG

(p. 45) Three charts showing value of Hong Kong exports to and imports from U.S., by type; and value of U.S. investment in Hong Kong manufacturing industry, by industry group; 1984. Data are from Hong Kong Industry Dept, Industrial Promotion Division.

Charts are accompanied by a directory of Hong Kong government offices and other organizations in the U.S.

A7540
National Council
of Savings Institutions

**A7540–1   1984 NATIONAL FACT
BOOK OF SAVINGS
INSTITUTIONS**
Annual. 1984. 44 p.
ISSN 8756-9043.
LC 85-640297.
SRI/MF/not filmed

Annual fact book presenting data on financial condition and operations of savings institutions, as of Dec. 31, 1983. Includes data by State, comparisons to other types of financial institutions, selected data for 1984, and trends from as early as 1945.

Data are from National Council of Savings Institutions, Federal Reserve Board, FHLBB, FDIC, and other private and government sources.

Contains contents listing and highlights (p. 1-4); 2 charts, and 47 tables listed below, arranged in 2 sections (p. 6-40); and glossary and subject index (p. 41-44).

This is the 24th annual fact book.

Previous report, for 1982, is described in SRI 1983 Annual under A6850-1; in Nov. 1983, the National Assn of Mutual Savings Banks and the National Savings and Loan League merged to form the National Council of Savings Institutions.

Availability: National Council of Savings Institutions, Research and Economics Department, 1101 15th St., NW, Suite 400, Washington DC 20005, $15.00; SRI/MF/not filmed.

TABLES:

[Unless otherwise noted, tables show data for savings banks and savings and loan assns, as of Dec. 31, 1983. Data for "selected financial institutions" include comparisons to commercial banks.]

A7540–1.1: Deposits and General Reserve Accounts

1. Assets and liabilities, and percentage distribution [by detailed item]. (p. 6)

2. Assets and liabilities [by item], 1975-83. (p. 7)

3-4. Membership in deposit insurance funds [by type] and FHLB system, selected year-end dates 1945-83; and total deposits, including interest, year-end dates 1973-83. (p. 8)

5. Deposit activity in regular accounts, monthly 1980-July 1984. (p. 10)

6. Net flow of investment funds, 1974-83. (p. 11)

7. Savings and time accounts in selected types of financial institutions, by type of accounts, 1979-83. (p. 12)

8. Financial saving by households [in aggregate savings institutions, by item], 1982-83. (p. 12)

9-10. Net gains in total deposits, including interest; and ratio of general reserve accounts to deposits; 1973-83. (p. 13)

A7540–1.2: Capital Market Investments

[Data by type of loan are generally for FHA, VA, conventional, and nonresidential.]

11. Mortgage debt outstanding, by type of holder, year-end dates 1973-83. (p. 13)

12. Percentage distribution of mortgage holdings by depository institutions [savings and commercial banks, savings and loan assns, and life insurance companies], by type of loan and property. (p. 14)

13-14. Gross flow of funds [by type], 1977-83. (p. 14-15)

15-16. Mortgage loans held, and net flow of mortgage funds, by type of property and loan, year-end dates 1973-83. (p. 16-17)

17. Gross flow of mortgage funds, by type of [property], 1973-83. (p. 18)

18. Home mortgage delinquency and foreclosure rates of savings banks, by type of loan, quarterly 1978-1st half 1984. (p. 19)

19. Ratios of liquid assets and borrowings to deposits of savings banks, June and Dec. 1973-83. (p. 20)

A7540–1.3: Income and Expenses

20-22. Income and expenses, and rates of return on assets held [total, mortgages, and securities]; and retained earnings as percent of total assets held by selected types of financial institutions; 1973-83. (p. 21-22)

23-24. Income [by source] and expenses; and income and expense ratios [to assets, deposits, securities held, and mortgage loans]. (p. 23)

25. Ranking of top 100 thrifts in the U.S., in order of assets. (p. 24-25)

A7540–1.4: Selected State Statistics

[All tables show data for 3-15 selected States, usually with aggregate data for remaining States.]

1S. Assets and liabilities of savings banks [by detailed item, and number of banks]. (p. 28)

2S. Deposits, number of accounts, and average size of accounts. (p. 29)

3S-4S. [Number of institutions, and] distribution according to [asset] size. (p. 30)

5S. Number of offices of depository [selected financial] institutions. (p. 31)

6S. Savings held in selected [financial institutions]. (p. 31)

7S-8S. Keogh and individual retirement accounts [and amounts outstanding] in savings banks. (p. 32)

9S. Ratio of capital/general reserve accounts to total assets, selected types of depository [financial] institutions. (p. 33)

10S. Mortgage holdings of selected types of financial institutions. (p. 33)

11S-12S. Rates of return on assets held [total, mortgages, and securities], selected years 1970-83. (p. 34)

13S. Ratio of cash/investments maturing within 1 year to deposits of savings banks, 1980-83. (p. 35)

14S-15S. Average annual rate of interest paid on deposits, 1973-83. (p. 35-36)

16S-17S. Retained earnings as percent of total assets, 1973-83. (p. 36-37)

18S-20S. Total savings bank life insurance [amounts] in force, including reinsurance programs, 1973-83; and number of savings bank life insurance policies and [amounts of ordinary and group] insurance in force [1970 and 1975-83]. (p. 37-38)

21S-22S. Number of savings banks offering [35 types of] selected services; and selected balance sheet powers and services of savings banks. (p. 39-40)

A7640
National Education Association

A7640–1   ESTIMATES OF SCHOOL STATISTICS, 1984/85
   Annual.   Mar. 1985.   43 p.
   LC 59-914.
   SRI/MF/complete

Annual report estimating enrollment, attendance, instructional staff, and finances of public elementary and secondary schools, by State, for 1984/85 school year, with revised estimates for 1983/84 and trends from 1974/75. Also includes data on school districts.

Report is compiled by NEA Research Division from Dec. 1984 estimates of State education officials.

Contains contents and table listing, foreword, and 2 summary tables (p. 1-7); narrative report, with text tables showing trends from 1974/75 (p. 9-26); 11 detailed tables, listed below, with explanatory notes (p. 27-40); and glossary (p. 41-43).

This is the 43rd edition of the report.

Availability: National Education Association, NEA Professional Library, PO Box 509, West Haven CT 06516, members $4.95 (Order No. 3100-8-00), nonmembers $12.95 (Order No. 3100-8-10); SRI/MF/complete.

TABLES:
[Tables show revised estimates for 1983/84 and preliminary estimates for 1984/85 for public elementary/and secondary schools, by State and region. Data on enrollment and classroom teachers are shown separately for elementary and secondary schools.]

1. Number of basic administrative units [operating and nonoperating school districts]. (p. 30)

2. Fall enrollment. (p. 31)

3-4. Average daily membership and average daily attendance in public elementary/secondary day schools, and number of public high school graduates. (p. 32-33)

5-6. Number of instructional staff members, by type of position [and, for classroom teachers, by sex]. (p. 34-35)

7. Average annual salaries of total instructional staff and of classroom teachers. (p. 36)

8-9. Revenue and nonrevenue receipts [from Federal, State, and local/other sources]. (p. 37-38)

10-11. Expenditures [total and per pupil current expenditures for schools, current expenditures for other programs, capital outlay, and interest on school debt]. (p. 39-40)

A7640–2   NATIONAL AND STATE STATISTICS OF FACULTY SALARIES Paid in Higher Education
   Annual, discontinued.

Annual report on faculty salaries in higher education, discontinued with report covering 1981/82 academic year (for description, see SRI 1983 Annual under this number).

NEA has established a computerized data bank. Information on the availability of statistics can be obtained from local NEA offices.

A7640–3   SALARIES SCHEDULED FOR FACULTY IN HIGHER EDUCATION
   Annual, discontinued.

Annual report on higher education faculty salary schedules, discontinued with report covering 1982/83 academic year (for description, see SRI 1984 Annual under this number).

NEA has established a computerized data bank. Information on the availability of statistics can be obtained from local NEA offices.

A7640–6   NATIONWIDE TEACHER OPINION POLL
   Annual, discontinued.

Annual survey report on public school teachers' views regarding education-related issues, discontinued with Sept. 1983 edition (for description, see SRI 1984 Annual under this number).

NEA has established a computerized data bank. Information on the availability of statistics can be obtained from local NEA offices.

A7640–7   RANKINGS OF THE STATES, 1985
   Annual.   Aug. 1985.   67 p.
   ISSN 0077-4332.
   LC 74-176052/R76.
   SRI/MF/complete

Annual report presenting State rankings pertaining to public education, including school enrollment, faculty, and finances; and population, income, and general government finances; various periods 1980-1984/85, with trends from the 1970s. Report focuses on elementary/secondary education, but also includes some data on higher education.

Data are from NEA research, Federal agencies, and *Sales and Marketing Management, Survey of Buying Power.*

Contains foreword, technical notes, and contents listing (3 p.); 8 statistical sections, with notes and narrative summaries, and 117 tables described below (p. 6-60); and bibliography, glossary, and table index (p. 61-67).

This is the 28th annual report.

Availability: National Education Association, NEA Professional Library, PO Box 509, West Haven CT 06516, members $6.00 (Stock No. 3092-3-60), nonmembers $14.95 (Stock No. 3092-3-70); SRI/MF/complete.

TABLES:
[All tables show rankings of States, with U.S. total or average, by the items noted below. Data are for public elementary/secondary schools, unless otherwise noted. Tables on revenue and expenditures include comparisons to personal income in addition to the data noted. Abbreviations: ADA (average daily attendance) and ADM (average daily membership).]

a. Population, including total, change from 1974, detail by age group, and density; and live births; various periods 1983-84. 13 tables. (p. 7-11)

b. Enrollment and attendance, including number of school districts, enrollment number and as percent of school age population, ADA, and ADM, mostly 1984/85; percent change in high school graduates and public/private participation in Federal school lunch program, various periods 1979/80-1984/85; and higher education enrollment and percent of students who are women, fall 1983, with enrollment change from 1982. 13 tables. (p. 13-17)

c. Faculty, including FTE noninstructional and/or instructional staff in local schools and public higher education institutions, Oct. 1983; pupil/teacher ratios, fall 1984; percent male teachers, 1984/85; and average salaries for teachers and instructional staff, 1983/84-1984/85, with comparison to 1974/75. 22 tables. (p. 20-27)

d. General financial resources, including total and per capita personal and disposable income; personal income per school age child and per pupil in ADA; government enterprise personal income as percent of total income; farm income; and effective buying income and retail sales per household; 1983, with selected comparisons to 1973 and 1982. 16 tables. (p. 30-35)

e. Government revenue, including State/local government general revenue; and State and/or local government total, property, income, and general sales tax revenues and/or collections; mostly shown per capita, 1983 or 1982/83. 16 tables. (p. 37-42)

f. School revenue, including amount per pupil; and percent from local, State, and Federal sources; 1983/84-1984/85. 11 tables. (p. 44-47)

g. Government expenditures and debt, including State and/or State/local government per capita expenditures for all functions, public welfare, health/hospitals, police and fire protection, highways, capital outlay, and interest on debt, 1982/83. 11 tables. (p. 50-53)

h. School expenditures, including State and State/local government per capita expenditures for higher education and local schools, and for education as percent of total expenditures, 1982/83; and per pupil expenditures, 1983/84-1984/85. 15 tables. (p. 55-59)

A7640–8 TEACHER SUPPLY AND DEMAND in Public Schools
Annual, discontinued.

Annual report on teacher supply and demand in elementary and secondary public schools, discontinued with report covering 1981/82 academic year (for description, see SRI 1983 Annual under this number).

NEA has established a computerized data bank. Information on the availability of statistics can be obtained from local NEA offices.

A7800
National Farm and Power Equipment Dealers Association

A7800–1 EQUIPMENT DEALERS 1984 COST OF DOING BUSINESS STUDY:
Agricultural, Industrial, Lawn and Garden
Annual. [1985.] 15 p.
SRI/MF/complete

Annual report presenting U.S./Canadian agricultural, industrial, and lawn/garden equipment dealers' average operating and financial data, 1984. Report is intended to enable individual dealers to compare their performance with industry averages.

Includes sales and margins for new and used equipment, parts, service, other lines, and rental/lease income; expenses by item; assets and liabilities; inventory by type; personnel by function; and financial and productivity ratios; shown for each type of dealer, with average sales and profits for aggregate dealers by region (U.S. and Canadian) and selected State.

Data for agricultural equipment dealers also include inventory turnover; investment in fixed assets by type; and detail by U.S. region and sales size group.

Data are based on 1,125 responses to a National Farm and Power Equipment Dealers Assn (NFPEDA) survey of approximately 11,000 U.S. and Canadian agricultural and industrial equipment dealers, and selected U.S. lawn/garden equipment dealers.

Contains foreword and narrative summary, with 4 text tables (p. 2-4); 6 trend charts and 6 tables (p. 5-14); 1 table showing NFPEDA membership by region (p. 14); and definitions (p. 15).
Availability: National Farm and Power Equipment Dealers Association, 10877 Watson Rd., St. Louis MO 63127, $7.50; SRI/MF/complete.

A7815
National Federation of Independent Business

A7815–1 NFIB QUARTERLY ECONOMIC REPORT FOR SMALL BUSINESS
Quarterly. Approx. 30 p.
ISSN 0362-3548.
LC 76-642389.
SRI/MF/not filmed

Quarterly report on the expectations of small business firms concerning economic conditions affecting their own business and business in general. Data are from a survey of NFIB members, conducted quarterly since 1973. Report is issued approximately 4 months after date of coverage.

Contains contents listing; narrative report with 8-12 charts and 25-30 tables on survey topics described below; and appendices, with 4 tables showing characteristics of responding firms, and facsimile survey questionnaire.

Report data are also available on computer tape; for information, contact Faculty Associates, Inc., 3633 Patrick's Point Dr., No. 2, Trinidad CA 95570.

Availability: National Federation of Independent Business, Research and Education Foundation, Capital Gallery East, Suite 700, 600 Maryland Ave., SW, Washington DC 20024, †; SRI/MF/not filmed.

Issues reviewed during 1985: July 1984-July 1985 (D) (Nos. 44-48).

TOPICS:
[For each topic noted below, 2 or more tables and/or charts are presented, showing response for current survey, usually with comparison to selected earlier surveys and occasionally with detail by industry. Sequence of topics varies.]

a. Sales and earnings levels compared to prior quarter; expected sales level for next quarter; and (usually) reasons for higher or lower earnings.

b. Employment change, current job openings, expected net labor force changes for next quarter, and (occasionally) average length of job openings.

c. Price and compensation levels compared to prior quarter, and planned changes for next quarter.

d. Inventory change during prior quarter, current adequacy, and planned change for next quarter.

e. Capital expenditures, including whether made in last 6 months, by type of expenditure; distribution, by size of expenditure; and whether expected in next 3-6 months.

f. Credit conditions and accounts receivable, including interest rate on short-term loans; interest rate and credit availability compared to prior quarter; and expected financing conditions for next quarter.

g. Outlook: expected general business conditions over next 3-6 months, and climate for small business expansion in next quarter; index of small business optimism by major component; and single most important problem (such as taxes, inflation, interest rates, and government regulation).

A7830
National Federation of State High School Associations

A7830–1 NATIONAL FEDERATION HANDBOOK, 1984/85
Annual. 1984. 119 p.
ISSN 0737-5204.
LC 77-648224.
SRI/MF/complete

Annual yearbook of the National Federation of State High School Assns, whose members govern athletic competition and other interscholastic activities. Includes data on sports participation of member schools, by State, for 1983/84.

Contents:

a. Contents listing; and Federation information, including constitution and bylaws, history, programs, recommended athletic eligibility standards, and awards. (p. 2-72)

b. Athletic competition optional limitations; types of nonathletic competition sponsored; and types of athletic competition in which State championships are determined, for boys and girls; all by State. 3 tables. (p. 73-76)

c. Sports participation survey results, showing number of schools and participants, by type of sport (total and by State), and for 10 most popular sports, 1983/84 school year; and total participants, 1971-1983/84; all for boys and girls. 6 tables. (p. 77-90)

d. Federation officers, staff, and committee members; and membership directory, including number of schools and students represented by each State, Canadian, and U.S. outlying area and military base assn. (p. 91-113)

e. Standardized calendar, and list of Federation publications and audiovisual materials. (p. 114-119)

Availability: National Federation of State High School Associations, Order Department, 11724 Plaza Circle, PO Box 20626, Kansas City MO 64195, $2.00+$2.00 handling; SRI/MF/complete.

A7830-2 NATIONAL HIGH SCHOOL SPORTS RECORD BOOK, 1985 Edition

Annual. 1985. 248 p.
ISSN 0192-978X.
LC 79-643196.
SRI/MF/complete

Annual compilation of all-time record scores and achievements for 15 interscholastic high school sports, often shown separately for boys and girls, current through 1983/84 school year. Data are from National Federation of State High School Assns members.

Contains contents listing and foreword (p. 3-4); record statistics, arranged alphabetically by sport (p. 6-245); and photo and other credits (p. 246-248).

This is the 7th edition of the *Record Book*.

Availability: National Federation of State High School Associations, Order Department, 11724 Plaza Circle, PO Box 20626, Kansas City MO 64195, $3.95+$2.00 shipping and handling; SRI/MF/complete.

A7860 National Football League

A7860-1 OFFICIAL 1985 NATIONAL FOOTBALL LEAGUE RECORD AND FACT BOOK

Annual. 1985. 326 p.
ISSN 0883-4199.
LC 85-646073.
SRI/MF/complete, current & previous year reports

Annual factbook presenting National Football League 1984 team and player performance data, all-time team and player records, and team profiles, including officials and 1985 schedule. Also includes paid attendance, 1934-84. Data are compiled by the league.

Contains contents listing (p. 3) and the following:

a. 1985 schedules, including televised games; coaches' statistics; active player statistical leaders; and selected general information. (p. 4-19)

b. Draft choices by team, 1985 and trends; team profiles, including stadium capacity, officials,

record holders, team rosters, and player and team statistics for 1984 season; 1984-85 trades; and 1984 preseason and regular season standings, team-by-team and week-by-week results, and games and attendance. (p. 20-164)

c. Player awards and all-star teams, 1984; regular and postseason games and attendance, 1934-84; all-time top 10 weekends in attendance and scoring, and top 10 televised sports events by audience rating; detailed conference, team, and player performance statistics, 1984; Hall of Fame member profiles; chronology of professional football major events, 1892-1985; annual team standings, 1921-84; and all-time team vs. team results. (p. 165-243)

d. Team, player, and/or game statistics for Super and Pro Bowls, conference and divisional championships, night and overtime games, and interconference games; No. 1 draft choices; and selected general information; various years 1933-85. (p. 244-263)

e. Player and team records, for all-time, leading performances, and postseason games and Super and Pro Bowls; and officials' roster and rules. (p. 263-326)

Previous edition, for 1983 season, was also reviewed in 1985 and is also available on SRI microfiche under A7860-1 [Annual. 1984. 318 p. $11.95]. Edition for 1982 season is described in SRI 1983 Annual under this number, and is titled *Official National Football League Record Manual.*

Availability: NFL Properties, Inc., Attention: Janice Fried, 410 Park Ave., New York NY 10022, $13.95; SRI/MF/complete.

A7870 National Forest Products Association

A7870-2 MONTHLY STATISTICS FOR THE WOOD PRODUCTS INDUSTRY

Monthly. 2 p.
SRI/MF/complete, shipped quarterly

Monthly report on lumber industry production, consumption, shipments, new and unfilled orders, gross stocks, and foreign trade, compiled by Copeland Economics Group for the National Forest Products Assn. Report is issued approximately 2 months after month of coverage.

Contains 5 monthly tables, listed below.

Report is discontinued with issue presenting Oct. 1984 data. Similar data are continued in *NFPA Economics Monthly,* described under A7870-3 below.

Availability: National Forest Products Association, 1619 Massachusetts Ave., NW, Washington DC 20036, members $5.00 per issue, nonmembers $10.00 per issue; SRI/MF/complete, shipped quarterly.

Issues reviewed during 1985: Sept.-Oct. 1984 (D).

MONTHLY TABLES:
[Data are shown for softwood and hardwood lumber, with additional detail as noted. Lumber producing regions are defined by species.]

Tables [3-4] show data for month of coverage and year to date, with percent change from previous month and/or same period of preceding year.]

[1] Estimated industry totals [production, shipments, orders received, and end-of-month unfilled orders and gross stocks, by lumber] producing region [with aggregate data on flooring and structural panels, for month of coverage, with summary comparisons to previous month and same month of preceding year].

[2] Year-to-date domestic lumber production, and trade statistics [shipments and orders received, for current and previous year].

[3] International trade statistics [imports and exports, with detail for railroad ties and for trade with Canada].

[4] Lumber consumption.

[5] Seasonally adjusted annual rates [of production and shipments, with softwood detail by lumber producing region, for month of coverage with percent change from previous month and same month of preceding year].

A7870-3 NFPA ECONOMICS MONTHLY

Monthly, with quarterly supplements.
Approx. 10 p. var. paging.
SRI/MF/complete

Monthly report, with quarterly supplements, reporting economic trends and developments in the U.S. and Canadian lumber industry. Covers production, consumption, sales, employment, foreign trade, new and unfilled orders, and gross stocks.

Data are compiled by NFPA from Federal agencies. Monthly data are current to 2-3 months prior to issue date. Quarterly data are issued 3 months after quarter of coverage.

Monthly report contains 8 trend charts, and 7 tables; and 1 or more feature articles focusing on a single topic, occasionally containing statistics. Quarterly supplement contains 4 tables. Monthly tables appear in a separately paginated section; quarterly supplement is unpaginated.

Monthly and quarterly tables are listed below. All additional features with substantial statistics on topics not covered in monthly tables are described, as they appear, under "Statistical Features." Nonstatistical features are not covered.

Report begins with the Mar. 1985 issue. Similar monthly data were published in *Monthly Statistics for the Wood Products Industry,* discontinued with issue presenting Oct. 1984 data. For description, see A7870-2 above.

Availability: National Forest Products Association, 1619 Massachusetts Ave., NW, Washington DC 20036, members $45.00, nonmembers $145.00; SRI/MF/complete.

Issues reviewed during 1985: Mar.-Sept. 1985 (P) (Vol. I, Nos. 1-7); and 4th Qtr. 1984-2nd Qtr. 1985 supplements.

TABLES:
[All tables except tables [F-G] show data for softwood and hardwood lumber. Tables [A], [C], 1-2, and 4 also show data by lumber region, defined by species (generally including southern and western pine, Douglas fir, California redwood, southern and Appalachian hardwood, and other).]

MONTHLY TABLES

[Tables [C-D] and [F-G] show data for month of coverage, with comparisons to previous month and year. Table order may vary.]

[A] Estimated industry totals [production, shipments, and orders received, for month of coverage; and unfilled orders and gross stocks as of end of month; table includes data for flooring and structural panels].

[B] Year-to-date production, shipments, and orders [received; includes data for same period of previous year].

[C] Seasonally adjusted [production and shipment] annual rates.

[D] Lumber consumption.

[E] International trade statistics [softwood lumber trade with Canada, and total imports and exports of softwood and hardwood products by type (including lumber, logs, plywood, veneer, particleboard, hardboard, and other), for month of coverage and year to date, with percent change from previous month and same period of previous year].

[F] Construction and housing statistics [new construction value, housing starts, and mobile home shipments].

[G] Employment statistics [employment in lumber, furniture, all manufacturing, and total industries].

QUARTERLY TABLES

[Data are shown quarterly for current year to date and 2 previous years, and annual averages for 8 earlier years.]

1. Estimated total regional lumber production, shipments, and new orders.

2. Estimated regional sources of domestic consumption of lumber (net imports allocated).

3. Imports [and] exports of lumber [by species, and for railroad ties and special products].

4. Estimated gross mill stocks of lumber and unfilled orders for lumber by region.

STATISTICAL FEATURE:

A7870–3.601: Sept. 1985 (Vol. 1, No. 7)

TRADE GETS THE ATTENTION IN WASHINGTON

(4 p.) Article on foreign trade issues affecting the lumber industry. Data are from Federal agencies. Includes 1 chart and 2 tables showing volume and/or value of wood product exports, by major country of destination 1984, and by product type 1980-1st 7 months 1985; and selected foreign exchange rates, Feb. and Sept. 1985.

A7900
National Funeral Directors Association of the U.S.

A7900–1 STATISTICAL ABSTRACT OF FUNERAL SERVICE FACTS AND FIGURES of the U.S., 1984 Edition
Annual. Oct. 3, 1984.
7+108 p.+erratum.
SRI/MF/complete

Annual report, by Vanderlyn R. Pine, on funeral home finances and operations, FY83. Includes data by census division and type of service.

Report is based on a 1984 survey of 671 operators reporting on 97,040 funerals.

Contains a preface with survey questionnaire facsimile, and contents listing (6 p.); and 2 maps, and 33 detailed tables listed below (p. 1-108).

Availability: National Funeral Directors Association of the U.S., 135 W. Wells St., Suite 600, Milwaukee WI 53203, nonprofit and educational institutions $10.00, others $50.00; SRI/MF/complete.

TABLES:

[Tables show data for the U.S. and by census division, FY83, unless otherwise noted. Most data are percentages or averages. Table numbers begin with 2.]

A7900–1.1: Characteristics and Income Sources of Reporting Firms

2-3A. Source of survey data: [number of firms participating and number of funerals reported, by State]; and percentage of firms reporting, average number and percentage of all services conducted, and total number for firms reporting, per volume category. (p. 2-3)

4. Form of ownership [individual proprietorships, partnerships, and public and private corporations]. (p. 4)

5. Collection procedures [allowing cash discounts, charging interest, and using sales contracts and finance plans]. (p. 4)

6. Personnel [percent of licensees among employees and owners, and firms with retirement and profit-sharing plans]. (p. 5)

7. Motor equipment [percent operating ambulance service, owning and renting all or part of motor equipment, and pooling equipment with others]. (p. 5)

8. [Average] investment [per funeral, by category]. (p. 6)

9-11. Charges as a percent of gross sales for total adult services; [average] charges and [casket] cost; and average funeral charges per firm. (p. 6-8)

12. Interment receptacle [percent usage, and average sale and cost]. (p. 8)

A7900–1.2: Operating Income, Expenses, and Price Ranges

[Table titles beginning "Operating service income" generally show percent of total reported funerals and charges, and average funeral charge and casket cost, all for the following service categories: child, welfare-adult, partial-adult (not all services provided by funeral home), and total-adult (all services provided by funeral home) by funeral charge dollar range.]

13-13.9. Operating service income. (p. 9-18)

14-14.9. Average funeral service operating expenses [for 8 items, including automobile, personnel, promotion, and taxes, by service category]. (p. 19-28)

14S. Selected expenses [employee and owner compensation, automobile, and building]. (p. 29)

15. Average margins (all services). (p. 30-31)

16-16.9. Funeral service operating income, operating expenses, and investment patterns by size category (average per all services). (p. 32-41)

17-17.9. Selected findings [including ownership, personnel, compensation, investment, and collection data]. (p. 42-51)

18-18.9. Average and percentage per service income and expense statement for all services. (p. 52-61)

19-19.9. Ranges in prices of services offered. (p. 62-66)

20A-20J. Operating service income: nonveterans; all veterans; noneligible and eligible veterans; [veterans, by period of conflict; and] other eligible veterans; [U.S. totals only]. (p. 67-76)

21-24. Charges and [casket] costs for firms using single-, bi-, tri-, and multi-unit pricing. (p. 77-79)

25A-25B. Operating service income [by sex of deceased; U.S. totals only]. (p. 80-81)

26A-26C. Operating service income, by age [and sex of deceased; U.S. totals only]. (p. 82-84)

27. Operating service income, by arrangement status [non- and pre-arranged; U.S. totals only]. (p. 85)

28-28.9. Operating service income, partial-adult services. (p. 86-90)

29-30D. Average values, by competition category and by market area [population size] category [including operating income and expenses, merchandise costs, investments, and charges per funeral; U.S. totals only]. (p. 91-96)

31A-31D. Funeral service operating income, operating expenses, and investment patterns, by size category for firms using single-, bi-, tri-, and multi-unit pricing (average per all services) [U.S. totals only]. (p. 97-100)

32A-32E. Charges and [casket] costs for funerals with final disposition burial, cremation, entombment, scientific donation, and other. (p. 101-103)

33-33.9. Balance sheet. (p. 104-108)

A7945
National Golf Foundation

A7945–1   STATISTICAL PROFILE OF GOLF in the U.S.: 1984 Annual Review

Annual.   [1985.]   11 p.
Rpt. No. ST-1.
SRI/MF/complete

Annual report on golf facilities, presenting statistics on courses by type, State, and census division, 1984 and trends. Also includes data on players, and rounds played. Data are compiled by National Golf Foundation.

Contains narrative summary, contents listing, 5 charts, and 12 tables described below.

Availability: National Golf Foundation, 200 Castlewood Dr., North Palm Beach FL 33408, $25.00; SRI/MF/complete.

TABLES:

[Data are for 1984, unless otherwise noted. Types of facilities are private, daily fee, and municipal.]

a. Facilities by type, selected years 1931-41 and annually 1946-84; and regulation, executive, and par-3 golf facilities and 9- and 18-hole courses, by facility type, State, and census division. 2 tables. (p. 5-7)

b. Population/golf course ratios: by State and census division; and 10 metro areas farthest above and below national average. 3 tables. (p. 8-9)

c. Rounds played, 1957-84, with 1984 detail by region, by facility type, and for men, women, junior players, and senior players; and number of frequent and occasional players. 7 tables. (p. 10-11)

A7945–3   DAILY FEE GOLF COURSE, OPERATIONAL DATA SURVEY

Biennial, discontinued.

Biennial report on daily-fee golf course operations and finances, discontinued with the 1982 report (for description, see SRI 1983 Annual under this number). Report has been discontinued for budgetary reasons.

A7955
National Governors' Association

A7955–1   FISCAL SURVEY OF THE STATES, February 1985 Update

Annual.   Feb. 1985.   9+13 p.
ISSN 0198-6562.
LC 79-105592.
SRI/MF/complete

Annual report on financial condition of State governments, FY83-85. Includes general fund revenues, expenditures, and balances, and budget stabilization/reserve fund balances, all by State. Data are actual for FY83-84 and estimates for FY85, and are based on a late 1984 survey of State budget officers.

Contains narrative analysis, with 1 map and 2 charts, (p. 1-9); and notes and 7 detailed tables (11 p.).

Report is published as a year-end update to the 1984 *Fiscal Survey of the States,* described in SRI 1984 Annual under A7955-2.

Availability: National Governors' Association, Public Affairs Office, Hall of the States, 444 N. Capitol St., NW, Washington DC 20001, $4.00; SRI/MF/complete.

A7955–2   FISCAL SURVEY OF THE STATES, 1985

Annual.   July 1985.   2+68 p.
ISSN 0198-6562.
LC 80-641033.
SRI/MF/complete

Annual report, for 1985, on financial condition of State governments. Includes general fund revenues, expenditures, and balances, and funds reserved for budget stabilization, by State, FY84-87. Data are actual for FY84 and estimates for FY85-87, and are based on a spring 1985 survey of State budget officers.

Also includes aggregate trends from FY78; data on State short-term borrowing, government employment (including presence of hiring and travel freezes), and employee compensation increases, all by State, various periods FY83-86; and States with tax increases and decreases, FY86.

Contains listings of contents and tables (2 p.); narrative analysis, with text statistics and 6 tables (p. 1-24); and appendix, with 14 detailed tables, listings of general fund revenue adjustments and transfers, and notes (p. 26-68).

This is the 11th annual report.

Availability: National Governors' Association, Public Affairs Office, Hall of the States, 444 N. Capitol St., NW, Washington DC 20001, $20.00+$2.50 postage and handling (prepaid); SRI/MF/complete.

A7980
National Housewares Manufacturers Association

A7980–2   EIGHTEENTH ANNUAL MARKETING RESEARCH STUDY of Housewares Manufacturers, 1984

Annual.   Apr. 1985.   16 p.
SRI/MF/complete

Annual report summarizing houseware manufacturers' sales and marketing activities, 1984, with some forecasts for 1985 and trends from 1966.

Includes data on manufacturers and sales by sales range and product category, sales to retailers and wholesalers by outlet type, consumer color preferences by product category, price changes and reasons for change, export sales and perceived importance, prevalence of immediate order fulfillment, duration of accounts receivable, and anticipated economic and operational problems.

Data are from responses of 578 manufacturers participating in the 1984 NHMA International Housewares Expositions, to a survey conducted by B. Angell and Associates, Inc.

Contains methodology, and highlights with text statistics (p. 1-3); and survey report, with 5 charts and 12 tables (p. 4-16).

Availability: National Housewares Manufacturers Association, Publication Orders, 1324 Merchandise Mart, Chicago IL 60654-1273, †; SRI/MF/complete.

A8010
National League for Nursing

A8010–3   NURSING AND HEALTH CARE

Monthly.   Approx. 55 p. cumulative pagination throughout year.
ISSN 0276-5284.
LC sc82-684.
SRI/MF/excerpts, shipped quarterly

Monthly journal (except July and Aug.) reporting on topics of interest to nurses, primarily developments in nursing service, education, and research.

Issues contain feature articles, occasionally with statistics; and regular editorial depts.

Features with substantial statistical content are described, as they appear, under "Statistical Features." Each issue of the journal is reviewed, but an abstract is published in SRI monthly issues only when statistical features appear.

Availability: Nursing and Health Care, Ten Columbus Circle, New York NY 10019-1350, members †, nonmembers $17.00 per yr., libraries and institutions $25.00 per yr.; SRI/MF/excerpts for all portions described under "Statistical Features;" shipped quarterly.

Issues reviewed during 1985: Nov. 1984-Oct. 1985 (P) (Vol. 5, Nos. 9-10; Vol. 6, Nos. 1-8).

STATISTICAL FEATURES:

A8010–3.601: Apr. 1985 (Vol. 6, No. 4)

CLINICAL NURSE SPECIALIST: IN SEARCH OF THE RIGHT ROLE

(p. 203-207) By Mary Ellen A. Wyers et al. Article on components of the clinical nurse specialist role, as perceived by nurse administrators, graduate nurse educators, and clinical nurse specialists. Data are from a national survey of 527 administrators, educators, and specialists (49% response rate), conducted by University of Texas at Arlington and Methodist Hospitals of Dallas. Includes 3 tables.

A8010–3.602: Oct. 1985 (Vol. 6, No. 8)

NURSES SCORE VICTORY ON NURSE EDUCATION ACT

(p. 418-419) By Sally B. Solomon. Article, with 1 table showing Federal funding authorizations for nursing education, by category, FY86-88.

For description of a similar article, with data for FY84-85, see SRI 1984 Annual under A8010-3.504.

A8015
National League of Professional Baseball Clubs

A8015–1 **NATIONAL LEAGUE GREEN BOOK, 1985**
Annual. 1985. 112 p.
ISSN 0736-041X.
LC sn83-419.
SRI/MF/excerpts

Annual fact book, for 1985, of the National League of Professional Baseball Clubs. Includes data on player and team performance, and game attendance, 1984 and trends. Data are compiled by the league.

Contains contents listing (p. 1) and the following:

a. Club and park information, including player rosters and 1984 performance data; all-star, championship series, and World Series data, including 1984 box scores, World Series attendance and receipts, and selected trends from 1903; and selected general information. (p. 2-45)

b. Team standings, lifetime batting and pitching records of active players, top 10 all-time batters in selected categories (by team), free agent roster and performance, and team and pitcher win/loss performance vs. opposing clubs, all for 1984 season, with selected historical trends from 1901; team and player 1984 batting, pitching, and fielding performance; other performance statistics; award winners; and 1984 game lengths. (p. 46-101)

c. Attendance at home and road games, 1983-84, and all-time attendance records, by team; league attendance trends, 1901-84; 1985 ticket prices, by team; 1985 spring training and regular season addresses and schedules; and selected general information. (p. 102-112 and back cover)

Availability: Alfred Publishing Co., PO Box CN 13150, Trenton NJ 08650, $9.95+$2.75 shipping, or $22.65 with *American League Red Book* (see A2068-1 above); SRI/MF/excerpt, p. 105 (attendance and ticket prices).

A8050
National Machine Tool Builders' Association

A8050–1 **INDUSTRY ESTIMATES: Machine Tool Orders and Shipments**
Monthly. Approx. 5 p.
SRI/MF/complete, shipped quarterly

Monthly press release on value of machine tool industry domestic and foreign orders, shipments, and cancellations, for metal cutting and metal forming tools. Data are from reports submitted to the National Machine Tool Builders' Assn, and are issued 1 month after month of coverage.

Each issue contains narrative analysis; and 4 tables showing net and gross new orders, order backlog, shipments, and cancellations, monthly and cumulatively for current year through month of coverage, with selected comparisons to previous year.

Issue for last month of each quarter includes an additional table showing quarterly orders and shipments for current and previous 5-7 years, with 3 accompanying charts showing trends from 1956. Three annual summary tables appear in the Jan. issue.

Availability: National Machine Tool Builders' Association, Publications, 7901 Westpark Dr., McLean VA 22102-4269, $25.00 per yr. (or $40.00 per yr. with *Economic Handbook*); SRI/MF/complete, shipped quarterly.
Issues reviewed during 1985: Oct. 1984-Sept. 1985 (D).

A8050–2 **1984-85 ECONOMIC HANDBOOK OF THE MACHINE TOOL INDUSTRY**
Annual. Aug. 15, 1984.
325 p. var. paging.
ISSN 0070-8550.
LC 73-646105.
SRI/MF/complete

Annual compilation of data on the machine tool industry, 1983 and trends. Report covers U.S. and world machine tool production, trade, employment, finance, and use, and also includes general economic data.

Data are compiled by National Machine Tool Builders' Assn from various Federal, international, and industry sources, identified in each table.

Contains table of contents (p. vii); 9 chapters with brief narrative reviews, 50 summary charts, and 261 detailed tables, described below (p. 1-265); and abbreviations, explanation of terms, and index (53 p.).

This is the 16th annual edition.

Availability: National Machine Tool Builders' Association, Publications, 7901 Westpark Dr., McLean VA 22102-4269, members $20.00, nonmembers $35.00; SRI/MF/complete.

TABLES:
[Data are shown for 1983 or most recent available year, generally with trends from 1970s or 1960s. Some data include historical trends from as early as 1930s. Machine tool industry data often are shown separately for metal cutting and metal forming sectors. Most production, shipment, and foreign trade data are shown as value and units.]

A8050–2.1: Economic Trends

U.S. DATA

a. Economic indicators, including GNP compared to all manufacturing and machine tool shipments, government receipts by level, and private investment; price deflators; corporate profits and tax liability; and Federal receipts and outlays. 10 tables. (p. 4-11)

b. Balance of trade for machine tools/parts and all merchandise; U.S. direct foreign investment, by country or area; and capital investment of machinery industry and all manufacturing for foreign affiliates of U.S. companies, by country or area. 3 tables. (p. 12-14)

c. Plant and equipment investments, with machine tool share; manufacturing total and equipment purchases, depreciation, net investment, and net value; new and unspent capital appropriations; gross book value of total and machinery/equipment

depreciable assets; and property/plant/equipment net value; with selected detail for major machine tool-consuming industries. 8 tables. (p. 15-22)

d. Business loan interest rates; manufacturing capacity utilization, production indexes, inventories, new and unfilled orders, and shipments, for machine tool and/or major consuming industries; business cycle leading indicators, and troughs and peaks since 1854; PPI for machine tools and components; and national defense purchases and price deflators. 26 tables. (p. 23-42)

WORLD DATA

e. GNP, fixed capital investment as percent of GNP, U.S. foreign investment, production and price indexes, export value index, foreign trade, balance of trade and payments, production worker earnings, and manufacturing productivity indexes, by selected country; Soviet trade with Communist and non-Communist countries; and U.S. trade with Communist countries. 14 tables. (p. 44-55)

f. Capital cost recovery allowances; and tax revenues as percent of GNP, by tax type including social security; all by selected country. 3 tables. (p. 56-58)

A8050–2.2: U.S. Machine Tool Industry

a. Establishments, employees, value added, and shipment value, by region and State; establishments and employees, by employment size group; materials cost and consumption; finished products, work in process, and materials inventories; and value of primary and secondary products. 14 tables. (p. 62-74)

b. Domestic and foreign shipments, new orders, and cancellations; unfilled orders; shipments, by machine value and detailed type including numerically controlled/automated; and shipments by SIC 4-digit industry and military prime contract awards, by machine type. 43 tables. (p. 77-120)

c. Foreign trade, including imports as percent of domestic consumption, by machine type; total production, trade, and domestic consumption; and imports and exports, by country of origin or destination and detailed machine type. 29 tables. (p. 126-160)

A8050–2.3: World Machine Tool Industry

a. Summary world production, consumption, and trade, by country; export market shares of major producing countries; imports and exports of EC countries, by SITC 6-digit machine tool classification; and import share of domestic consumption for U.S., Japan, UK, and West Germany. 16 tables. (p. 163-184)

b. Detailed machine tool production and/or trade for West Germany, Japan, UK, Spain, France, Italy, Sweden, Switzerland, Netherlands, Canada, Argentina, Czechoslovakia, and Soviet Union.

Also includes employment for Germany, Japan, UK, Spain, and France; productivity for Germany; shipments and orders for UK and France; hours and earnings for France; companies and employment for Sweden; sales for Netherlands; and comparisons to other industrial production for Argentina and Soviet Union. 58 tables. (p. 186-228)

c. Production for PRC and for East Europe by country, with comparisons to U.S.; and Communist bloc imports by major non-Communist country of origin, and exports by area of destination. 4 tables. (p. 229-232)

A8050–2.4: Machine Tool Employment, Finances, and Use
[Data are for U.S., unless otherwise noted.]

a. Employment and payroll; production workers, hours, earnings, overtime, and work injury rates, with selected comparisons to other industries; labor turnover; female employment; earnings, by occupation and selected city; productivity; and earnings and/or supplemental labor costs in U.S. and 7 other countries. 20 tables. (p. 235-249)

b. Financial ratios compared to other industries; gross book value of depreciable assets; capital investments; and indexes of sales, profit, depreciation, stock value, and working capital. 5 tables. (p. 253-257)

c. Use of machine tools, including number in metalworking industries, by equipment type and age, industry, and selected city; total in other industries, training, and storage/surplus; and number in 6 foreign countries. 8 tables. (p. 260-265)

A8050–3   **U.S. FOREIGN TRADE IN MACHINE TOOLS**
Monthly. Approx. 15 p. var. paging.
SRI/MF/complete, shipped quarterly

Monthly report (10-11 issues per year) on volume and value of U.S. machine tool imports and exports, by country of origin and destination, by type of machine. Data are from Dept of Commerce and National Machine Tool Builders' Assn, and are issued 2-4 months after month of coverage.

Each issue contains brief narrative analysis with 2-3 charts and 1 summary table; and 6 detailed tables showing trade data by specific type of machine tool (as defined in Tariff Schedules of the U.S.) for major trading partners, and by general category (metal cutting and forming) for other countries, for month of coverage, with selected year-to-date totals. Issues also occasionally include revised tables for previous issues.

June and Dec. issues include additional summary tables, and 6 additional detailed tables presenting trade data for the 1st half and full year, respectively. Issues for the last month of each quarter include summary data for the quarter.

Availability: National Machine Tool Builders' Association, Publications, 7901 Westpark Dr., McLean VA 22102-4269, $36.00 per yr.(prepaid); SRI/MF/complete, shipped quarterly.

Issues reviewed during 1985: Aug. 1984-July 1985 (D) [No Jan.-Feb. 1985 issues were published].

A8060
National Mass Retailing Institute

A8060–2   **6th ANNUAL STUDY OF SECURITY AND LOSS PREVENTION PROCEDURES IN RETAILING, 1984**
Annual. Dec. 1984. 50 p.
LC 77-151334.
SRI/MF/complete

Annual report on retail industry inventory "shrinkage" and control measures, including use of security personnel, programs, and devices. Data are based on a 1984 Arthur Young & Co. survey of 88 mass merchandisers, 37 department stores, and 51 specialty stores, with operations in 33,652 locations. Also includes data on food retailers.

Contains contents listing and introduction (p. 3-4); narrative report in 11 sections, with 7 charts, and 33 tables described below (p. 5-45); and appendix, with 3 tables on food retailers' shrinkage and control measures (p. 46-50).

Availability: National Mass Retailing Institute, 570 Seventh Ave., New York NY 10018, members $30.00, nonmembers $45.00; SRI/MF/complete.

TABLES:
[Most data are for 1983, with selected comparisons to 1982, and are generally shown as distributions for mass merchandisers, department stores, specialty stores, and all other respondents.]

a. Sample characteristics and inventory shrinkage: sample companies by sales size, number and urban-suburban location of stores, and shrinkage as percent of sales, with total value of shrinkage and shrinkage rates by region. Tables 1-5. (p. 5-8)

b. Shoplifting: total apprehensions, prosecutions as a percent of apprehensions, and convictions as a percent of apprehensions and prosecutions; and apprehensions of employees by job category. Tables 6-7. (p. 12-16)

c. Security practices: security expenditures as a percent of sales and by function; and security devices used on selling floor, with ratings of most and least effective methods. Tables 8-13. (p. 17-20)

d. Personnel practices: number of security/loss-prevention employees; screening methods and prior experience deemed important in hiring security personnel; methods used to screen nonsecurity personnel; polygraph test use, and reasons for not using; training programs used for security and nonsecurity personnel; and reward policies for improved loss prevention, by type. Tables 14-21. (p. 22-26)

e. Shrinkage comparisons: low vs. high shrinkage companies by sales size, security expenditure/sales ratio, use of security and nonsecurity personnel training programs, and security devices used on selling floor. Tables 22-33. (p. 30-44)

A8060–3   **COMPENSATION IN MASS RETAILING, 1983/84**
Biennial. Oct. 1984.
ii+55 p.
SRI/MF/complete

Biennial report on compensation of discount department store executives and managers, 1983-84. Presents data on average and/or median base salary 1983-84, and bonus 1983, by position, for 8 functional categories in 4 sales volume groups.

Data are based on survey responses from 53 companies with 11,457 outlets. The survey was conducted by National Mass Retailing Institute.

Contains contents listing (1 p.); introduction and explanatory notes (p. i-ii); and 4 statistical sections, with 32 tables (p. 1-55).

For description of previous report, for 1981/82, see SRI 1983 Annual under this number.

Availability: National Mass Retailing Institute, 570 Seventh Ave., New York NY 10018, members 1st copy †, additional copies $50.00 each; nonmembers $70.00, certified educational institutions $23.00; SRI/MF/complete.

A8060–5   **MASS RETAILERS' EXECUTIVE PERQUISITE REPORT, 1983**
Biennial. Nov. 1983. 28 p.
SRI/MF/complete

Biennial report on perquisites and benefits offered to retail trade executives and managers, by position, 1983. Covers headquarters, merchandising, field, and store management positions.

Data are based on survey responses from more than 73% of NMRI's retail membership.

Contains contents listing and introduction (2 p.); and 5 sections, with 1 table repeated for each position category (p. 2-24), and responses to 6 survey questions (p. 26-28).

This is the 4th biennial report. SRI coverage begins with this report.

Availability: National Mass Retailing Institute, 570 Seventh Ave., New York NY 10018, members: 1st copy †, additional copies $35.00; nonmembers $45.00; certified educational institutions $13.00; SRI/MF/complete.

A8060–6   **OPERATING RESULTS OF SELF-SERVICE DISCOUNT DEPARTMENT STORES and the Mass Retailers' Merchandising Report, 1984-85**
Annual. Aug. 1985.
xii+162 p.
ISSN 0474-2656.
LC 77-640100.
SRI/MF/complete

Annual report, by Gene A. German and Gerard F. Hawkes, providing detailed data on sales, expenses, earnings, and operating ratios of self-service discount department stores, by sales size category. Also includes "Mass Retailers' Merchandising Report" showing operating data by sales department. Data are shown for FY85, with selected trends from FY80.

Data are based on survey responses of 31 firms operating 3,475 stores with aggregate sales of $25.1 billion, and are shown separately for all firms and for 26 "identical" firms with 2 or more years of consecutive responses to the annual survey.

Report is produced by Cornell University, under sponsorship of National Mass Retailing Institute, and is intended to permit individual stores to compare their performance with industry averages.

Contents:

Foreword, contents listing, and highlights. (p. iii-xii)

Section 1, Part I. Six-year trends for all firms and identical firms. Includes 30 charts and 30 tables showing trends in 30 financial and operating indicators, including average sales per store and square foot, average sales and occupancy cost per square foot of selling area, and cumulative markup and stockturns for owned depts, mostly FY80-85. (p. 1-30)

Section 1, Part II-III. Identical and all firm analysis. Includes 1 highlights table, and 4 detailed tables listed below, repeated for identical firms (p. 32-77) and all firms (p. 31-132).

Section 2, Part I-II. Mass Retailers' Merchandising Report. Includes 7 tables showing FY85 middle range and/or FY84-85 averages for net sales by payment type, and for the following by dept: sales as percent of store total, stockturns, markup as percent of original retail, stock shortage and markdown as percent of owned dept sales, and gross margin as percent of owned dept sales; repeated for identical firms (p. 135-141) and all firms (p. 145-151).

Appendix. Includes survey methodology and questionnaire facsimiles. (p. 154-162)

This is the 21st annual report; prior to this edition, report was covered in SRI under U1380-1. Previous report is described under U1380-1, below.

Availability: National Mass Retailing Institute, 570 Seventh Ave., New York NY 10018, members $65.00, nonmembers $80.00, educational institutions $35.00; SRI/MF/complete.

DETAILED TABLES:

[Data include FY84-85 averages and FY85 middle range. All data are shown by sales size; data in tables [1] and [3-4] are also shown by gross margin, expense, and payroll levels.]

[1] Gross margin, expense[s], and earnings [as] percent of sales [including expenses for payroll, advertising, taxes/licenses, utilities, and 13 other items].

[2] Expenses for selected responsibility centers [as] percent of sales [for 12 expense categories, including advertising/promotion, accounting, data processing, employee benefits, warehousing, transportation, and other store operations].

[3] Assets [as] percent of total assets [for components of current and other assets and of property/equipment, and for total intangible assets].

[4] Liabilities and net worth [as] percent of total [for components of current liabilities, long-term debt, and net worth].

A8095
National
Network of Runaway and Youth Services

A8095-1 TO WHOM DO THEY BELONG? A Profile of America's Runaway and Homeless Youth and the Programs That Help Them
Monograph. July 1985.
37 p.
SRI/MF/complete

Survey report on the characteristics and needs of programs serving homeless and runaway youths, 1983/84. Includes data on number of youths sheltered, by sex, reason for needing shelter, and whether sexually or physically abused; youths turned away, by reason; hotline and other nonshelter services provided; success rate in helping youths; detailed program needs; trends in youths' problems; and program funding sources, staff, and use of volunteers.

Data are based on survey responses of 210 youth service programs in 50 States and Puerto Rico. Responding programs represent 312 shelters and 230 foster care homes. Survey responses are for a 1-year period during 1983/84.

Contains contents listing (1 p.); introduction and methodology (p. 1-9); narrative report, with text data (p. 10-22); policy recommendations and epilogue (p. 23-26); and bibliography, information on issuing agency, and list of respondents arranged by region (p. 27-37).

Availability: National Network of Runaway and Youth Services, 905 Sixth St., SW, Suite 411, Washington DC 20024, $4.00; SRI/MF/complete.

A8110
National
Office Products Association

A8110-1 NOPA DEALER OPERATING RESULTS, 1984
Annual. 1984. 68 p.
LC 83-111825.
SRI/MF/not filmed

Annual report presenting median financial and operating data for office product dealers, 1983, with summary trends from 1973. Most data are shown by sales volume, region, and major product (office supplies or furniture).

Includes detailed balance sheet, income and expenses, and other financial and operating ratios; average sales and profit per employee and per square foot; average inventory turns; and distribution of companies by community size, number of stores, profitability, personnel structure, type of business organization, service personnel and average salary, and selected operating characteristics.

Report is based on data from 514 NOPA members, and is intended to permit individual dealers to compare their operations with industry averages.

Contents:

a. Contents listing; and introduction, methodology, and summary, with 2 charts and 3 tables. (p. 2-5)

b. 3 basic tables, generally repeated for all dealers, by sales volume, and for dealers with branch stores (p. 6-19); by region (p. 20-35); and by major product (p. 36-50).

c. 14 important financial ratios, with definitions and 3 tables. (p. 51-59)

d. Chart of accounts and worksheet. (p. 60-68)

This is the 55th annual report.

Availability: National Office Products Association, 301 N. Fairfax St., Alexandria VA 22314, price on request; SRI/MF/not filmed.

A8140
National
Paper Trade Association

A8140-2 PAPER MERCHANT PERFORMANCE for the Year 1984
Annual. 1985.
58 p. var. paging.
SRI/MF/complete

Annual report presenting average financial and operating performance measures for paper merchants, 1984, with trends from 1974. Covers approximately 40 ratios and other measures of sales, profitability, and management performance, including employee productivity, for printing, industrial, and dual paper merchants. Includes detail by sales volume; sales emphasis (direct, indirect, warehouse); profitability category; and NPTA region.

Also includes trends in printing PPI, and sample median and total sales.

Data are based on 203 responses to a 1985 survey of NPTA members, conducted by Management Foresight, Inc. Report is intended to permit individual firms to compare their operations to industry averages.

Contains contents listing (1 p.); introduction, and narrative report in 4 chapters interspersed with 3 summary charts and 24 text tables (p. 1-25); summary table list and abbreviations (p. 26); 12 summary tables (12 p.); and 6 appendices, including 1 table on sample characteristics, and methodology and definitions (18 p.).

Availability: National Paper Trade Association, 111 Great Neck Rd., Great Neck NY 11021, 1st copy $135.00, additional copies $40.00; SRI/MF/complete.

A8140-3 NPTA MANAGEMENT NEWS
Monthly.
ISSN 0739-2214.
LC sn83-8190.
SRI/MF/complete, shipped quarterly

Monthly report on industrial and printing paper wholesale distribution business activity, with monthly sales data for 7 regions, and NYC, Chicago, and Los Angeles metro areas. Month of data coverage is 2 months prior to cover date.

Contains several regular editorial depts and feature articles, occasionally with statistics, including a quarterly feature on printing order backlog, and several annual features on paper company performance; and monthly "Paper Merchant Sales Report" section, containing 6 trend charts, and 1 table described below. May

1985 issue also includes a subject index of articles appearing in issues from mid-1983 through mid-1985.

Monthly charts and table appear in all issues (sometimes published as a separate page). All additional features with substantial statistical content are described, as they appear, under "Statistical Features." Nonstatistical features are not covered.

Availability: National Paper Trade Association, 111 Great Neck Rd., Great Neck NY 11021, $25.00 per yr.; SRI/MF/complete, shipped quarterly.

Issues reviewed during 1985: Nov. 1984-Oct. 1985 (P) (Vol. XXV, Nos. 11-12; Vol. XXVI, Nos. 1-10).

MONTHLY TABLE:

[Data are shown for industrial and printing papers, by region and for 3 metro areas.]

a. Percent change in sales activity per selling day, for month of coverage compared to previous month and to same month of previous year, and for year to date compared to same period of previous year.

b. Days outstanding for accounts/notes receivable at close of month of coverage, and calendar days' cost of ending inventory for month prior to month of coverage, both with comparisons to same month of previous year.

STATISTICAL FEATURES:

A8140–3.601: Nov. 1984 (Vol. XXV, No. 11)

[Data for the following articles are from NPTA's 1984 *Paper Merchant Performance* report; full report is covered in SRI under A8140-2.]

IS THE COMPENSATION QUESTION TEARING YOUR COMPANY APART?

(p. 10-13) Article, with 3 tables showing paper merchants' compensation and payroll as percents of gross profits and operating expenses; average compensation per employee, by position; compensation of highest paid employee; fringe benefit value, per employee and as a percent of total compensation; and personnel productivity indexes; all for printing, industrial, and dual companies, mostly for 1981-83.

SALES DEPT PERFORMANCE

(p. 19-20) Part 2 of a 2-part article on the performance of paper merchant sales depts.

Includes 1 table showing the following for printing, industrial, and dual paper merchants: median sales, compensation, profit, and number of orders and invoice lines handled, all per inside sales service employee; and expenses for inside sales service as a percent of gross profit; 1981-83.

For description of part 1 of this article, see SRI 1984 Annual, under A8140-3.510.

A8140–3.602: Dec. 1984 (Vol. XXV, No. 12)

COMPUTERIZATION OF THE INDUSTRY: A STATUS REPORT

(p. 10-14) Article on paper distribution industry's use of computers. Data are based on 170 responses to a member survey conducted by the National Paper Trade Assn in Sept. 1984.

Includes 7 charts primarily showing survey response distribution on the following: com-

puterization status and plans (own computer, service bureau, or no computer); data processing expenditures as a percent of sales, and change in expenditures for 1984 vs. 1983 and 1985 vs. 1984; personal computer use at work and at home; customer demand for computer-related services; and manufacturer of hardware used; with selected detail by type of paper company.

A8140–3.603: Jan. 1985 (Vol. XXVI, No. 1)

PRINTERS SURVEYED ON PAPER SITUATION, QUARTERLY FEATURE

(p. 8) Quarterly article, with 1 table showing the following for printing companies by type: average order backlog at beginning of 2nd-4th quarters 1984, with comparison to record high during 1980-3rd quarter 1984 period; and distribution of companies by change in backlog (more, less, or same), Oct. 1984 vs. Oct. 1983.

Data are based on over 1,000 responses to a National Assn of Printers and Lithographers survey.

For description of previous article, see SRI 1984 Annual under A8140-3.510.

A8140–3.604: Mar. 1985 (Vol. XXVI, No. 3)

PAPER DISTRIBUTION'S CHANGING INTERNATIONAL SCENE

(p. 10-14) Article, with 4 tables showing imported paper volume and/or value, by type, grade, and country of origin, various periods 1976-84. Data are from Dept of Commerce and American Paper Institute.

INDUSTRIAL PAPER: WHO'S THE COMPETITION?

(p. 20-21) Article on tobacco/confectionery distributors' diversification into paper goods and other products. Data are based on a recent survey conducted by *U.S. Tobacco and Confectionery Journal.*

Includes 2 undated tables showing warehouse space allocation by product category, and product categories with perceived sales potential, all for tobacco/confectionery distributors by sales size group.

A8140–3.605: Apr. 1985 (Vol. XXVI, No. 4)

WAREHOUSE: TRACKING EXPENSES AND PRODUCTIVITY

(p. 20-21) Article, with 6 tables showing warehouse median operating expense and productivity ratios, median sales per cubic foot, and delivery employee average salary, for printing, industrial, and dual paper merchants, 1981-83. Data are from NPTA's annual industry performance study, based on a member survey; full study report is covered in SRI under A8140-2.

PRINTERS FOUND PAPER EASIER TO GET REPORTS NAPL, QUARTERLY FEATURE

(p. 22) Quarterly article, with 2 tables showing the following for printing companies by type: paper inventory levels; average order backlog at beginning of 3rd-4th quarters 1984 and 1st quarter 1985, with comparison to record high during 1980-84 period; and distribution of companies by change in backlog (more, less, or same), Jan. 1985 vs. Jan. 1984.

Data are based on a National Assn of Printers and Lithographers survey.

A8140–3.606: June 1985 (Vol. XXVI, No. 6)

PAPER DISTRIBUTORS SEE INCREASE IN PAST DUE ACCOUNTS

(p. 4) Brief article, with 1 table showing percent of paper distributor accounts receivable that are current, and past due by number of days outstanding, quarterly 1983-84. Data are from TRW, Inc.

INDUSTRIAL PAPER MARKETS, HOW BIG?

(p. 36) Article, with 2 tables showing sales shares for 3 industrial paper categories, for industrial and dual paper merchants, 1981-83; and sanitary paper sales distribution by end-use industry, by paper type, 1977. Data are from National Paper Trade Assn.

A8140–3.607: July 1985 (Vol. XXVI, No. 7)

MERCHANTS POST HIGHEST SALES GROWTH IN 5 YEARS, ANNUAL FEATURE

(p. 10-13) Annual article, with 3 tables showing mean percent change in sales, value of average warehouse order, inventory turnover, and selected profitability and other performance measures, for printing, industrial, and dual paper merchants, 1983-84.

Data are from NPTA's *Paper Merchant Performance* report for 1984; full report is covered in SRI under A8140-2.

Previous feature is described in SRI 1984 Annual under A8140-3.507.

A8140–3.608: Aug. 1985 (Vol. XXVI, No. 8)

PRINTERS SEE PAPER INVENTORY LEVELS DROP, QUARTERLY FEATURE

(p. 10) Quarterly article, with 1 table showing the following for printing companies by type: average order backlog at beginning of 4th quarter 1984 and 1st-2nd quarters 1985, with comparison to record high during 1980-1st quarter 1985 period; and distribution of companies by change in backlog (more, less, or same), Apr. 1985 vs. Apr. 1984.

Data are based on a National Assn of Printers and Lithographers survey.

EXPECTATIONS FOR PRINTING AND PAPER DEMAND

(p. 12-15) Article, with 1 table showing printing/writing paper production capacity, by paper type, 1983-87. Data are from American Paper Institute.

ROTA, YOU VS THE INDUSTRY, ANNUAL FEATURE

(p. 22-23) Annual article, with 1 table showing expense/gross profit ratios for 8 expense items, for printing, industrial, and dual paper merchants with high and low return on assets, 1983-84.

Data are from NPTA's *Paper Merchant Performance* report for 1984; full report is covered in SRI under A8140-2.

WHITE HOUSE TAX PLAN

(p. 24) Article on impact of Reagan Administration's income tax rate reduction proposal on corporate retained earnings. Data are from National Assn of Wholesaler-Distributors. Includes 1 undated table comparing taxes and tax rates under current and proposed laws, by taxable income.

A8140–3.609: Sept. 1985 (Vol. XXVI, No. 9)

PRINTERS SHOW INCREASED PROFITS

(p. 10) Article, with 1 table showing sales, pre-tax profits, and return on investment, for average printing firm, 1980-84. Data are from Printing Industries of America.

MERCHANT INVENTORY MANAGEMENT, ANNUAL FEATURE

(p. 28) Annual article, with 1 table showing selected inventory performance measures, for industrial and printing paper merchants with median, high, and low return on assets, 1983-84. Data are from NPTA's annual financial ratio study, based on a member survey. Full study report is covered in SRI under A8140-2. Previous feature is described in SRI 1984 Annual under A8140-3.509.

A8140–3.610: Oct. 1985 (Vol. XXVI, No. 10)

PRINTERS SEE FURTHER DECLINE IN PAPER INVENTORIES, QUARTERLY FEATURE

(p. 24) Quarterly article, with 1 table showing the following for printing companies by type: average order backlog at beginning of 1st-3rd quarters 1985, with comparison to record high during 1980-2nd quarter 1985 period; and distribution of companies by change in backlog (more, less, or same), July 1, 1985 vs. July 1, 1984.

Data are based on a National Assn of Printers and Lithographers survey.

A8145
National Paperbox and Packaging Association

A8145–1   60th ANNUAL FINANCIAL SURVEY OF THE RIGID PAPER BOX INDUSTRY

Annual. [1985.] 29 p.
SRI/MF/complete

Annual report, by Robert D. Landel, on rigid paper box industry finances and operations, 1984, with trends from 1967. Includes data on billings, sales, price and production indexes, pre-tax profits, financial and operating ratios, inventory and labor turnover rates, billing collection period, employment, user industries, and new and used machinery purchases, with selected detail by region and sales size category.

Also includes selected U.S. economic indicators.

Data are based on reports from National Paperbox and Packaging Assn members, and are intended to permit individual companies to compare their performance with that of similar companies.

Contains narrative sections on management and the general economy, with 5 tables (p. 1-12); and paperbox industry report, with narrative analysis, 3 charts, and 12 tables (p. 13-29).

Availability: National Paperbox and Packaging Association, 231 Kings Hwy., E., Haddonfield NJ 08033, members $25.00, nonmembers $50.00; SRI/MF/complete.

A8175
National Planning Association

A8175–5   1983 NATIONAL ECONOMIC PROJECTIONS SERIES

Annual series. For individual publication data, see below.
SRI/MF/not filmed

Annual series of 3 reports presenting long-term national economic trends and projections based on data from Federal agencies and NPA growth model.

The series provides continuously revised projections of major indicators for the economy as a whole and for industry divisions. The same indicators are covered each year, but the distribution of the data among the reports and the analytical focus may vary.

The 1st and 3rd volumes of the 1983 series are described below; for description of the 2nd volume, see SRI 1984 Annual under this number. The 1982 series is described in SRI 1983 and 1984 Annuals under A8175-9.

Availability: National Planning Association, Center for Socio-Economic Analysis, 1616 P St., NW, Suite 400, Washington DC 20036, $900.00 per 3-volume set, $2000.00 joint subscription with Regional EPS series and all NPA publications, 50% discount for university and public libraries; SRI/MF/not filmed.

A8175–5.2: U.S. Economic Growth, 1983-2000

[Monograph. May 1984. vii+95 p. Rpt. No. 83-N-1. SRI/MF/not filmed.]

By Nestor E. Terleckyj. Report projecting economic growth indicators to 2000, based on data available as of Dec. 1983. Includes data on the following indicators, shown annually 1947-2000 or 1948-2000:

a. Population and labor force, by age and sex; and employment by sector, unemployment rate, and jobs.

b. Federal and State/local government receipts by type, purchases of goods/services (including employee compensation), and budget balances; Federal expenditures by category and for major transfer programs; and GNP by sector.

c. Private sector hours worked, output, investment, depreciation, capital, and earnings; Government and private sector R&D investment and capital, with selected ratios; personal income by component; and national income, and income and GNP deflators.

Contains listing of contents, charts, and tables (p. v-vi); preface (p. vii); narrative analysis, in 5 chapters, interspersed with 22 summary charts and text tables (p. 1-35); and 29 detailed tables (p. 38-95).

A8175–5.3: NPA Model of U.S. Economic Growth 1948-83: Description and Testing

[Monograph. Oct. 1984. vii+137 p. Rpt. No. 83-N-3. SRI/MF/not filmed.]

By Nestor E. Terleckyj et al. Report presenting technical description of NPA economic growth model, including detailed results of a test of the accuracy of model projections for 1949-83.

Contains contents listing and preface (p. v-vii); narrative description of model and listing of variables used (p. 1-19); test description and results, with 17 extended tables (p. 20-133); and narrative history of NPA projections, with 1 summary table (p. 134-137).

A8175–9   1984 NATIONAL ECONOMIC PROJECTIONS SERIES

Annual series. For individual publication data, see below.
SRI/MF/not filmed

Annual series of 3 reports presenting long-term national economic trends and projections based on data from Federal agencies and NPA growth model.

The series provides continuously revised projections of major indicators for the economy as a whole and for industry divisions. The same indicators are covered each year, but the distribution of the data among the reports and the analytical focus may vary.

The first 2 volumes of the 1984 series are described below; volume 3 has not yet been published. For description of volumes 1 and 3 of the 1983 series, see A8175-5 above; volume 2 is described in SRI 1984 Annual under the same number.

Data in this series also are available from the issuing agency on computer tape and disk and in computer printout form.

Availability: National Planning Association, Center for Socio-Economic Analysis, 1616 P St., NW, Suite 400, Washington DC 20036, $900.00 per 3-volume set, $2000.00 joint subscription with Regional EPS series and all NPA publications, 50% discount for university and public libraries; SRI/MF/not filmed.

A8175–9.1: Economic Growth Projections for the U.S.: 1984-2000

[Monograph. May 1985. vi+1+97 p. Rpt. No. 84-N-1. SRI/MF/not filmed.]

By Nestor E. Terleckyj et al. Report projecting economic growth indicators to 2000, based on data available as of Nov. 1984. Includes data on the following indicators, various years 1948-2000:

a. Population, labor force by sex, and labor force participation rates, by age and sex; employment by sector; unemployment rate; and number of jobs.

b. Federal government receipts by type, purchases of defense- and non-defense-related goods/services, expenditures by category and for major transfer programs, and budget balance; State/local government tax receipts, purchases of goods/services and employee compensation, and budget balance; and GNP by sector.

c. Private sector hours worked, output, general and fixed investment, depreciation, capital, and earnings; Government and private industry R&D investment and capital, with selected ratios; personal income by component; national income, and income and GNP deflators; and industrial production index.

Contains listing of contents, charts, and tables (p. v-vi); preface (1 p.); narrative analysis, in 5 chapters, interspersed with 20 summary charts and tables (p. 1-33); and 31 detailed tables (p. 36-97).

A8175–9.2: Sectoral Economic Growth in the U.S.: 1984-2000

[Monograph. May 1985. vii+65 p. Rpt. No. 84-N-2. SRI/MF/not filmed.]

By Nestor E. Terleckyj and Houri Ramo. Report presenting long-term economic trends and projections for industry divisions. Includes gross value of output, employment, hours, labor productivity, and earnings, by industry division and for total private business sector, various years 1947-2000.

Contains contents/table listing and preface (p. v-vii); narrative analysis, in 4 chapters, interspersed with 7 summary tables (p. 1-16); and 24 detailed tables (p. 18-65).

A8175–10   1984 REGIONAL ECONOMIC PROJECTIONS SERIES

Annual series. For individual publication data, see below.
ISSN 0090-9262.
LC 73-641587.
SRI/MF/not filmed

Annual series, by Timothy B. Sivia and Nestor E. Terleckyj, issued in 3 volumes, presenting regional, State, and local trends and projections for major economic and demographic indicators. Data are NPA estimates based on reports from Bureau of Economic Analysis (BEA), other Federal agencies, and the University of Georgia Institute for Behavioral Research.

Volumes I-III of the 1984 series are described below. For description of 1983 series, see SRI 1984 Annual under A8175-6.

Data in this series also are available from the issuing agency on computer tape and disk and in computer printout form.

Availability: National Planning Association, Center for Socio-Economic Analysis, 1616 P St., NW, Suite 400, Washington DC 20036, $1600.00 per 3-volume set, $2000.00 joint subscription with National EPS series and all NPA publications, 50% discount for university and public libraries; SRI/MF/not filmed.

A8175–10.1: U.S. Economic Growth: Regional Projections, 1984-2000. Summary Volume I: Population, Employment, Personal Income, and Per Capita Income for Nation, Regions, States, Economic Areas, Metropolitan Statistical Areas, and Counties

[Annual. Feb. 1985. viii+358+App 34 p. Rpt. No. 84-R-1. SRI/MF/not filmed.]

Presents the following data: population, employment, and total and per capita personal income, by region, State, BEA economic area, MSA, and county, quinquennially 1970-2000, with selected comparisons to 1969 and 1982. Income data are in 1972 dollars.

Also includes rankings of fastest and slowest growing MSAs by projected change in number of jobs, 1982-2000 period; and personal consumption expenditure index, 1967-82.

Contains contents and table listing and preface (p. v-viii); overview and methodology, with 8 tables (p. 1-39); 5 detailed tables (p. 42-358); and appendix, with list of counties comprising BEA economic areas and MSAs (p. A1-A34).

A8175–10.2: U.S. Economic Growth: Regional Projections, 1984-2000. Volume II: Population, Employment, and Income Detail for Nation, Regions, States, Economic Areas, and Metropolitan Statistical Areas

[Annual. Feb. 1985. xviii+288+App 34 p. Rpt. No. 84-R-2. SRI/MF/not filmed.]

Presents the following data: population, employment and earnings by industry division, and personal income by source, by region, State, BEA economic area, and MSA, quinquennially 1970-2000. Earnings and income data are in 1972 dollars.

Contains contents listing and preface (p. v-xviii); 4 statistical sections, with 556 tables (p. 1-288); and appendix, with list of counties comprising BEA economic areas and MSAs. (p. A1-A34).

A8175–10.3: U.S. Economic Growth: Regional Projections, 1984-2000. Volume III: Population by Age, Sex, and Race for U.S., Regions, States, MSAs

[Annual. Mar. 1985. viii+377+App 34 p. Rpt. No. 84-R-3. SRI/MF/not filmed.]

Presents the following data: total and white population by age and sex, by region, State, and MSA, 1970 and quinquennially 1980-2000.

Contains contents listing and preface (p. v-viii); 3 statistical sections, with 363 tables (p. 1-377); and appendix, with list of counties comprising BEA economic areas and MSAs (p. A1-A34).

A8200
National
Restaurant Association

A8200–1   NRA NEWS

Monthly. Approx. 50 p.
ISSN 0465-7004.
LC SN 78-5535.
SRI/MF/complete, shipped quarterly

Monthly trade journal (combined June/July issue) reporting on food service industry trends and developments. Covers sales, employment, customer characteristics, food prices, government regulation, and other topics of interest to food service executives.

Data are from the National Restaurant Assn (NRA) and Federal and private sources.

Each issue contains several feature articles and editorial depts, occasionally with statistics; and "Foodservice Trends" section, with the following recurring statistical features:

a. Commodity price index recurring table showing percent change in wholesale prices of approximately 15 food commodities, and in NRA food cost index and PPI (all food), for various periods current to 2-3 months prior to cover date. Table is accompanied by brief article.

b. Quarterly CREST (Consumer Reports on Eating-Out Share Trends) survey article, with 4-5 charts showing percent change in customer traffic, industry sales, and check size, by restaurant type, for quarter ending approximately 3 months prior to cover date, with comparison to previous periods; based

on data compiled by NPD Research, Inc., from records maintained by a panel of 10,000 families and 2,800 nonfamily households.

Annual statistical features include franchise restaurant sales and establishments; food service sales trends and outlook; and review of industry operations.

Articles with substantial statistical content are described, as they appear, under "Statistical Features;" page locations and latest periods of coverage for recurring table and CREST charts are also noted. Nonstatistical features are not covered.

Availability: NRA News, Publications Department, 311 First St., NW, Washington DC 20001, members †, nonmembers $125.00 per yr.; SRI/MF/complete, shipped quarterly.

Issues reviewed during 1985: Nov. 1984-Oct. 1985 (P) (Vol. 4, Nos. 10-11; Vol. 5, Nos. 1-9).

STATISTICAL FEATURES:

A8200–1.601: Nov. 1984 (Vol. 4, No. 10)

QUARTERLY CREST CHARTS

(p. 39-42) Restaurant customers, sales, and average check size, for summer 1984.

RECURRING TABLE

(p. 43) Commodity price index, for Aug. 1984.

TARGETING TODAY'S BABY BOOM MARKET

(p. 17-20) By Cecelia Niepold. Article, with 3 tables showing family visits to restaurants as percent of total visits, by restaurant type; and reasons for dining out, and restaurant qualities considered important, for consumers with children under age 13, with detail for fast food and family restaurants and selected comparisons to all consumers.

Data are based on NRA surveys conducted 1982-84.

REGIONAL MENU PRICE INCREASES FOR FIRST 6 MONTHS OF 1984

(p. 43-44) Article, with 3 tables showing percent change in prices for food at home and away from home, for 11 cities and by census region, various periods 1980-84; and menu price percent change, by census region by city population size, 1st half 1984 vs. 1st half 1983. Data are from BLS.

A8200–1.602: Dec. 1984 (Vol. 4, No. 11)

1985 NRA FORECAST: FOODSERVICE SALES TO EQUAL $178 BILLION, ANNUAL FEATURE

Annual compilation of articles on food service sales trends and outlook, with final data for 1982-83, revised estimates for 1984, and forecasts for 1985. Unless otherwise noted, data are prepared by NRA in consultation with Malcolm M. Knapp, Inc. Includes the following individual articles:

MAJOR FACTORS AFFECTING INDUSTRY GROWTH

(p. 15-19) Article, with 6 charts showing percent of consumers eating out recently, with detail for those aged 25-34, working women, households with income over $35,000, and single consumers, all by type of restaurant (no dates); and food service sales trends, 1982/83-1984/85.

FOOD SERVICE INDUSTRY IN 1985

(p. 20-26) Annual article forecasting food/drink sales for commercial, institutional, and military food services in 1985. Includes 8 tables showing sales for each food service segment and by detailed eating place type, 1982 and 1984-85.

Also includes 6 charts showing trends in restaurant traffic and number of franchise units, various periods 1970-84; and consumer survey data on nutrition-related changes among restaurant customers, and selected characteristics of customers most likely to try ethnic dishes and to take advantage of early/late dinner discounts. Chart data are from CREST, Commerce Dept, NRA, and Gallup Organization.

REGIONAL AND STATE-BY-STATE FORECAST

(p. 27-32) Annual article forecasting eating place sales, by State and census division, 1984-85; and percent change in personal income and employment, by census division, 1985 vs. 1984. Includes 1 chart and 9 tables.

FOOD AND DRINK PURCHASES PROJECTED TO REACH $72 BILLION IN 1985

(p. 33) Annual article forecasting food/drink purchases for commercial, institutional, and military food services, by detailed eating place type, 1985. Includes 1 table.

INDUSTRY SALES TO REACH $164.5 BILLION IN 1984

(p. 34) Annual article, with 1 table showing food/drink sales, by eating place type, 1983-84.

ECONOMY AFFECTS CONSUMER ABILITY TO EAT OUT

(p. 35-36) Annual article reporting on consumer satisfaction with current levels of eating-out activity, with detail by income and eating-out frequency, 1981-84. Data are from polls conducted Sept. 1981-84 by the Gallup Organization for NRA. Includes 4 charts.

A8200–1.603: Jan. 1985 (Vol. 5, No. 1)

RECURRING TABLE

(p. 41) Commodity price index, for Oct. 1984.

CURRENT AND PROJECTED EMPLOYMENT TRENDS IN THE FOODSERVICE INDUSTRY

(p. 36-39) Article, with 8 tables showing the following, generally by food service occupational category: food service industry and eating/drinking place employment, 1982 and 1995; employee replacement rates, and job openings, 1980s-90s; and employment distribution by sex, age, and weekly hours worked, 1980.

Data are from BLS and the Census Bureau.

JUICE UP YOUR PROFITS WITH ORANGE JUICE

(p. 42-43) Article, with 2 charts and 4 tables showing the following for orange juice: unit production, 1981-85; monthly PPI for frozen product, 1981-Oct. 1984; in-home consumption by age and sex, consumption in restaurants and institutional food service operations, and percent of all and 4 types of restaurants serving orange juice, 1984. Data are from Florida Dept of Citrus, USDA, and BLS.

NRA's MARKET RESEARCH GROUP DISCUSSES MARKET NICHES

(p. 44) Article, with 1 table showing percent of surveyed consumers who reported having eaten out recently, by sex, with detail for women by employment status, 1978 and 1983. Data are from the Gallup Organization.

A8200–1.604: Feb. 1985 (Vol. 5, No. 2)

QUARTERLY CREST CHARTS

(p. 37-40) Restaurant customers, sales, and average check size, with customer detail by meal period, for fall 1984.

WHAT YOU EAT MAY DEPEND ON WHERE YOU ARE

(p. 40-44) Article, with 7 tables showing number of restaurants by detailed type, and by census division for selected types, 1984.

Data are based on the 3rd annual RE-COUNT study compiled by Restaurant Consulting Group, Inc. covering approximately 80% of all restaurants as of spring 1984.

For description of article reporting on the 1st annual study, see SRI 1983 Annual under A8200-1.411.

A8200–1.605: Mar. 1985 (Vol. 5, No. 3)

DIVERSITY PROPELS FRANCHISE RESTAURANT SALES TO $38.7 BILLION IN 1983, ANNUAL FEATURE

(p. 33-43) Annual compilation of 4 articles, by Cecilia Niepold and Susan Adelman, on franchise restaurant companies, sales, and establishments. Data are from Commerce Dept's *Franchising in the Economy, 1983-85*.

Includes 5 charts, 2 maps, and 13 tables showing the following for the franchise restaurant industry:

a. Sales and establishments, with detail by type of food served, and sales comparison to total eating place industry, various years 1970-85; and companies and sales by firm size, companies by duration of franchise agreements issued and by type of food and service offered, and establishments by census division and for selected States, 1983.

b. Foreign establishments of U.S. franchisors, by country or world area and by type of food served, various years 1973-83.

A8200–1.606: Apr. 1985 (Vol. 5, No. 4)

ANNUAL CREST REPORT REVEALS RESTAURANTS PROSPERED IN 1984, ANNUAL FEATURE

(p. 36-38) Annual article analyzing trends in restaurant customer traffic. Data are from CREST surveys by NPD Research, Inc.

Includes 2 charts and 1 table showing percent change in sales, per person check size, and customer traffic; and distribution of sales and customer traffic by type of customer (adults only, adults with children under 18, and children only) and by meal period; for all, quick-service, midscale, and upscale restaurants, year ended Nov. 1984, with comparisons to same period 1982-83.

WHO SPENDS WHAT FOR RESTAURANT MEALS

(p. 38-40) Article reporting on consumer spending for food away from home, with comparisons to total food expenditures. Data are from BLS and The Conference Board. Includes 8 tables showing the following for 1980/81:

a. Expenditures for food away from home per capita and/or as percent of total food budget, for all households and by income level, region, age of household head, and meal period; per capita spending for food consumed at home; and alcoholic beverage expenditures away from home, and distribution of households and of expenditures for food away from home, by income level.

b. Single person average expenditures, for food at home, and for food away from home with detail by meal period, for all single householders and by sex and age group (over and under 35).

SPOTLIGHT ON HOTEL/MOTEL RESTAURANT PATRONS

(p. 41-44) Article on characteristics of hotel/motel restaurant customers, including prevalence of lodging guests and others, and data by age, household income and size, and use of marketing promotions, with detail for midscale and upscale establishments, and comparative data for all restaurants and for expenditures of hotel/motel restaurant customers.

Data are from Sept. 1983-Aug. 1984 CREST surveys. Includes 6 tables.

A8200–1.607: May 1985 (Vol. 5, No. 5)

QUARTERLY CREST CHARTS

(p. 42-44) Restaurant customers, sales, and average check size, for winter 1985.

MEXICAN RESTAURANTS, HOTTER THAN EVER

(p. 33-36) Article, with 4 tables showing the following for Mexican food restaurants:

a. Customer traffic percent change, 1980-84; and customers patronizing restaurants 1/more times monthly, by sex, age, and household size and income, with summary comparison to all restaurants, 1983.

b. Distribution of customer traffic and sales, by type of operation (quick service, midscale, upscale), Dec. 1983-Nov. 1984 period; and restaurants (number, and percent of total restaurants), by census division 1984.

Data are from NRA, CREST, and Restaurant Consulting Group.

EATING PLACE SALES RISE FASTEST IN THE SOUTH AND WEST

(p. 36-41) Article, with 2 tables showing sales and number of units for restaurants/lunchrooms, refreshment places (limited menu/no table service), cafeterias, and other food service operations, all by census division and State, 1982 with percent change from 1977. Data are from Census Bureau.

A8200–1.608: June/July 1985 (Vol. 5, No. 6)

FOODSERVICE INDUSTRY: A BRIEF LOOK AT 1983, ANNUAL FEATURE

(p. 37-39) Annual report on the size, scope, and growth of the food service industry, 1982-83. Data are from Malcolm M. Knapp, Inc.

Includes 1 chart and 1 table showing food service industry food/drink sales and purchases, 1983, with comparisons to 1982; and number of units (no date); all by detailed industry segment.

This is the 16th annual report.

NEW RESTAURANT CONCEPTS

(p. 40-42) Article, with 2 tables comparing consumer patronage of 15 types of specialty restaurants, based on responses of 2,069 adults to a Mar. 1985 survey conducted by the Gallup Organization for National Restaurant Assn.

Full survey report is covered in SRI under A8200-9.

HOW YOUR CUSTOMERS DECIDE WHAT TO TIP

(p. 43-44) Article, with 2 tables showing criteria used by restaurant patrons to determine amount of tip, by age group. Data are based on a Feb.-Mar. 1985 telephone survey of approximately 1,000 adults, conducted by the Gallup Organization for National Restaurant Assn.

A8200–1.609: Aug. 1985 (Vol. 5, No. 7)

QUARTERLY CREST CHARTS

(p. 42-44) Restaurant customers, sales, and average check size, for spring 1985.

CONSUMERS EAT OUT MORE IN 1985

(p. 36-38) Article reporting on consumer dining practices. Data are from responses of 6,788 households (representing 14,255 persons age 8 and over) to a Mar.-Apr. 1985 survey conducted for NRA by NFO Research, Inc.

Includes 5 tables showing the following for meals eaten during week prior to survey, with selected comparisons to 1981:

a. Number of meals consumed away from home, by meal period, sex, age, income, and women's employment status.

b. Distribution of weekly meals by whether privately or commercially prepared or skipped; and frequency of eating privately or commercially prepared meals or skipping meals, by meal period.

For description of previous survey, conducted in 1981, see SRI 1981 Annual under A8200-1.209.

LARGER RESTAURANT FIRMS MAKE INROADS

(p. 39-41) Article, with 6 tables showing the following for all eating places, restaurants/lunchrooms, and refreshment places (limited menu/no table service): distribution of companies, units, and sales, by company sales size and unit size categories, 1982, with selected comparisons to 1977.

Data are from 1977 and 1982 Censuses of Retail Trade.

A8200–1.610: Sept. 1985 (Vol. 5, No. 8)

ASIAN CUISINE: GOOD FORTUNE FOR RESTAURATEURS

(p. 38-41) Article on Asian food restaurants, with 4 tables showing the following:

a. Consumers ordering Chinese, Japanese, or other Asian food 1/more times monthly, by age, sex, household size and income, and dining out frequency, 1983; and Asian restaurants (number, and percent of total restaurants), by census division, 1984.

b. Asian restaurant sales and customer traffic shares; and distribution of meals served by place eaten (on premises or at various off-premise locations), with comparison to all restaurants; all by type of operation (quick service, midscale, upscale), Dec. 1983-Nov. 1984 period.

Data are from NRA, CREST, and Restaurant Consulting Group.

NRA REVISES 1985 FORECAST, ANNUAL FEATURE

(p. 42) Annual article, with 1 table showing revised estimates of 1984-85 food/drink sales, for commercial food service by segment, and for institutional and military food services. Data are from NRA and Malcolm M. Knapp, Inc.

For description of original 1985 forecast, see A8200-1.602, above.

WHAT CONSUMERS ARE EATING

(p. 43-44) Article, with 1 table ranking top 20 menu items by percent growth in orders, 1984 vs. 1982 (June-Nov. period). Data are from CREST surveys.

A8200–1.611: Oct. 1985 (Vol. 5, No. 9)

RECURRING TABLE

(p. 38-42) Commodity price index, for July 1985. Table is accompanied by 2 charts showing prices and production for beef and poultry, quarterly 1983-85.

YUPPIES: THEY EAT OUT OFTEN AND HAVE MONEY TO SPEND

(p. 36-38) Article reporting on restaurant patronage by "yuppies" (young urban professionals). Data are based on surveys conducted during 1985 by GDR/CREST Enterprises and National Restaurant Assn.

Includes 1 table and 1 chart showing average check size, by meal period and restaurant type; and types of specialty restaurants patronized; for yuppies, with comparison to general population.

BREAKFAST WAKES UP SALES

(p. 41-44) Article on restaurant breakfast market developments. Data are from NRA and CREST surveys.

Includes 7 tables showing consumers' breakfast habits (eating at home/friend's house, eating in restaurant or at school/work, or skipping meal), July 1985; restaurant traffic and sales trends, by meal period, 1978-84, with selected breakfast detail by restaurant type; and percent of restaurant patrons ordering various breakfast items (total and take out), various periods Dec. 1983-Sept. 1985.

A8200–2 FRANCHISE RESTAURANTS: A Statistical Appendix to Foodservice Trends
Annual. Mar. 1985.
2+71 p.
SRI/MF/complete

Annual report, for 1985, on the franchise restaurant industry, including data on establishments, sales, services, employment, ownership, and investment. Most data are for 1973-85, with selected trends from 1969. Data are from *Franchising in the Economy,* published by U.S. Dept of Commerce.

Contains contents listing (2 p.); and introduction, and 6 statistical sections with 46 tables, described below (p. 1-71). Tables in each section are preceded by highlights.

Availability: National Restaurant Association, Publications Department, 311 First St., NW, Washington DC 20001, members $12.50, nonmembers $25.00; SRI/MF/complete.

TABLES:

[Data are shown for various years 1973-85, with selected trends from 1969. Franchise types are chicken, hamburger/franks/roast beef, pizza, Mexican, seafood, pancake, steak/full menu, and sandwich/other.]

a. Total industry: companies surveyed, by franchise type; company- and franchisee-owned establishments and sales; chain companies,

establishments, and sales, by 6 size groups based on number of establishments; and chains, by type of service provided (self-service/drive-in/drive-thru and waiter/waitress), by franchise type. 10 tables. (p. 3-11)

b. Franchise types: including companies, establishments, and sales; and company- and franchisee-owned establishments and sales; all by franchise type. 9 tables. (p. 13-30)

c. Donut shops and ice cream/yogurt stores: companies and employment; and establishments and sales (company- and franchisee-owned). 4 tables. (p. 32-35)

d. Other data: franchise agreements by term of agreement, and renewals and terminations; ownership changes; minority ownership (black, Spanish surname, American Indian, and Oriental); low, high, and median cash investment and start-up cost, for company-and/or franchisee-owned establishments; franchisor sales of non-food merchandise, supplies, and food ingredients to franchisees; and company- and franchisee-owned restaurant employment. 7 tables. (p. 37-43)

e. Establishments (company- and franchisee-owned), by State and census division. 10 tables. (p. 45-64)

f. International franchising: U.S. companies and establishments in international franchising; and establishments, by country or world region; both by franchise type. 6 tables. (p. 66-71)

A8200–3 RESTAURANT INDUSTRY OPERATIONS REPORT '85 for the U.S.
Annual. 1985. 99 p.
LC sn82-20267.
SRI/MF/complete

Annual report presenting detailed financial and operating ratios for restaurants, 1984. Includes data by type of establishment, urban-rural location, region, sales size, and profit-loss status.

Data are based on reports submitted by 718 National Restaurant Assn members, compiled and analyzed by Laventhol and Horwath accountants. Report is intended to enable individual restaurant owners to compare their performance with that of the industry.

Contents:

a. Listings of contents, tables, and charts; introduction; explanatory notes; analysis, with 2 trend charts, and 1 table (p. 6) showing food service industry sales by market segment, 1984-85; and report methodology, with 1 table. (p. 1-10)

b. Survey results, with 2 charts showing income and expense distribution of restaurant industry dollar, 1984 with comparisons to 1983; 8 charts, and 25 tables listed below, generally repeated for food-only restaurants and for food/alcoholic beverage restaurants. (p. 11-87)

c. Comments on restaurant business situation in 22 metro areas, explanation of terms, and worksheet. (p. 88-99)

Availability: National Restaurant Association, Publications Department, 311 First St., NW, Washington DC 20001, members $19.00, nonmembers $38.00; SRI/MF/complete.

TABLES:

[In the listing below, the 1st page number is for food-only restaurants, the 2nd for food/alcoholic beverage restaurants. Table numbering in document skips from 14 to 17.]

All data are for 1984. Tables 2-5 and 17-27 show median, upper quartile, and lower quartile levels. Tables 4 and 9-27 show data as amount per seat and as ratio to total sales.

Restaurant types variously include full menu/tableservice, limited menu/tableservice, limited menu/no tableservice, cafeteria, coffee shop, and other. Data by location are for urban, suburban, and rural. Types of affiliation are single-unit/independent, multi-unit/company-operated, and multi-unit/franchisee-operated.]

1. Composition of participating restaurants [including distribution by years in business, restaurant type, region, location, affiliation, types of meals served, sales size class, profit vs. loss, owned or leased land/building, type of ownership, and menu theme]. (p. 12, 52)

2. Average check [by years in business, location, types of meals served, menu theme, and region, with additional detail by restaurant type for food-only restaurants]. (p. 14, 54)

3. Average daily seat turnover [by years in business, location, types of meals served, menu theme, region, and restaurant type]. (p. 15, 55)

4. Net income differential [selected financial and operating data for restaurants reporting profit vs. loss]. (p. 16-17, 56-57)

5. Earnings ratio [by years in business, location, lease or ownership of land/building, occupancy in attached or detached building, and type of restaurant]. (p. 18, 58)

6. Cost per dollar of sales [total cost of sales and payroll, with additional detail for cost of food and beverages for food/beverage restaurants, by restaurant type, location, profit vs. loss, ownership, and menu theme, and for food-only restaurants by types of meals served]. (p. 19, 59)

7. Analysis of employee data [full- and part-time employees per restaurant; FTE employees per restaurant and per 100 seats and average daily covers; sales and payroll per FTE employee; and productivity index; by restaurant type, location, and profit vs. loss]. (p. 24, 64)

8. Occupancy costs [rent, property and other taxes, and insurance], interest, and depreciation, amount per seat [by restaurant type, location, and region]. (p. 25, 65)

9-14. Cross-tabulation of profit before occupation costs and of restaurant profit, by franchise [or independent ownership] and [single- and multi-unit] organization; by location and type of restaurant; by sales [size class] and age of operation; and by menu theme and region for food/beverage restaurants only. (p. 26-28, 65-68)

17. Statement of income and expenses, all restaurants. (p. 29, 69)

18-27. Statement of income and expenses [by restaurant type, years in business, location, affiliation, sales size class, region, and menu theme]. (p. 30-49, 70-87)

A8200–6　**EXECUTIVE COMPENSATION AND BENEFITS in the Foodservice Industry, 1985 Edition**
Recurring (irreg.)　Mar. 1985.
63 p.
SRI/MF/complete

Recurring report on compensation of food service industry executives and supervisors, 1984. Includes median and upper and lower quartile salary, bonus/incentive, profit sharing, and total benefits cost, for 28 positions, by type of organization (chain, franchise, and independent), type of ownership and restaurant, scope of operation (local, regional, U.S., and international), and sales volume.

Also includes data on vacation allotment by years of service; and other types of benefits provided.

Data are from responses of 508 NRA members, employing over 134,000 workers, to a Sept. 1984 survey conducted in cooperation with Laventhol and Horwath.

Contains contents listing, background, and summary with 11 tables showing respondent characteristics (p. 1-9); 1 basic table, repeated for each position (p. 10-49); vacation and benefits summary, with 5 tables (p. 50-53); and appendices I-II, with comparative cost indexes for selected cities, and questionnaire facsimile (p. 54-63).

This is the 3rd survey. Previous survey, conducted in 1981, is described in SRI 1982 Annual under this number.

Availability: National Restaurant Association, Publications Department, 311 First St., NW, Washington DC 20001, members $20.00, nonmembers $40.00; SRI/MF/complete.

A8200–8　**CONSUMER ATTITUDE AND BEHAVIOR STUDIES**
Series.　For individual publication data, see below.
SRI/MF/complete

Continuing series of reports analyzing restaurant user characteristics and attitudes, based on results of consumer surveys. Reports are intended to aid the restaurant industry in marketing decisions.

Report reviewed during 1985 is described below.

Availability: National Restaurant Association, Publications Department, 311 First St., NW, Washington DC 20001; SRI/MF/complete.

A8200–8.5: Consumer Restaurant Behavior: A View Based on Occasion Segmentation

[Monograph. Oct. 1984. 74 p. Rpt. No. CS 982. members $25.00, nonmembers $30.00. SRI/MF/complete.]

Report examining consumers' occasions for dining out, 1984. Presents data relating types of occasions to the following: reasons for dining out; restaurant characteristics desired; type of restaurant chosen; selected characteristics of the restaurant visit, including meal period, party size, presence of children, and check size and payment method; and consumer demographic characteristics.

Occasion types are fast/inexpensive, on familiar ground, personal convenience, business/social obligation, family meal, special night out, and social fun.

Data are based on interviews with 310 recent restaurant patrons in 5 major metro areas, conducted during Mar. 1984 by Creative Research Associates, Inc.

Contains contents listing (1 p.); report purpose and overview (p. 1-5); 4 chapters, with narrative analysis and 14 tables (p. 6-47); and appendix, with lists, 17 detailed tables, and methodology (p. 48-73).

A8200–9　**CONSUMER PREFERENCES FOR NEW RESTAURANT CONCEPTS**
Monograph.　Apr. 1985.
119 p.
SRI/MF/complete

Survey report on consumer patronage of restaurants specializing in various food concepts. Presents data on consumers recently patronizing and likely to patronize 15 types of specialty restaurants, by sex, race, age, education, income, marital status, household size, employment status (for female consumers), region, and residence category (central city, suburban, and rural).

Data are from responses of 2,069 adults to a Mar. 1985 survey conducted by the Gallup Organization.

Contains contents listing (1 p.); introduction (p. 1); 2 sections with narrative analysis and 7 tables (p. 2-25); 2 detailed tables (p. 26-115); and facsimile of survey questionnaire, and sample characteristics (p. 116-118).

Availability: National Restaurant Association, Publications Department, 311 First St., NW, Washington DC 20001, members $10.00, nonmembers $20.00; SRI/MF/complete.

A8275
National
Retail Hardware Association

A8275–1　**FINANCIAL OPERATING REPORTS**
Annual series.　For individual publication data, see below.
SRI/MF/complete

Annual series of 3 reports on average financial and operating data of retail hardware stores, home centers, and lumber/building material outlets, 1983.

Reports are based on annual spring mail surveys of retailers and include analysis of results by sales volume category.

General format:

a. Contents listing and introduction.

b. Highlights and monthly sales: includes 2 tables showing annual net sales and increase over previous year, margin, net profit on sales and on investment, and stock turns, for all retailers and by sales volume size and selected other store categories; and industry average percent of sales by month.

c. Average operating results: includes income statement, balance sheet, and financial and operating ratios, for all retailers and high and low profit retailers, and by sales volume and sales floor size groups; and income statement and operating ratios only, by trade area size, store location, whether single or multiple store business, and selected other store categories.

d. Strategic profit model, with 1 chart showing computation of average rate of return on net worth for high profit store category.

e. Departmental sales and productivity: including departmental share of net sales, sales area, inventory, and cost of goods sold, for handling firms and average store; departmental sales per square feet for handling firms only; and average store gross margin return on inventory investment (GMROI), by dept.

f. New store feasibility analysis, with 1 illustrative table.

Survey size and additional breakdowns, as applicable, are described below.

Availability: National Retail Hardware Association, Research Services Department, 770 N. High School Rd., Indianapolis IN 46224; SRI/MF/complete.

A8275–1.1: 1984 Management Report for Retail Hardware Stores

[Annual. 1984. 23 p. $20.00. SRI/MF/complete.]

Presents data for retail hardware stores, 1983, based on survey responses from 744 dealers. Income statement and operating ratios are also shown by type of ownership and by census division.

A8275–1.2: 1984: The Bottom Line for Retail Home Centers

[Annual. 1984. 23 p. $20.00. SRI/MF/complete.]

Presents data for retail home center outlets, 1983, based on survey responses from 163 dealers. Income statement and operating ratios are also shown by type of origin (originally hardware, lumber/building material, or home center dealer), and outlet orientation (contractor or consumer).

A8275–1.3: 1984 Lumber/Building Materials Financial Report

[Annual. 1984. 19 p. $20.00. SRI/MF/complete.]

Presents data for retail lumber/building material outlets, 1983, based on survey responses from 291 dealers. Income statement and operating ratios are also shown by outlet orientation (contractor or consumer).

A8300
National
Retail Merchants Association

A8300–1 DEPARTMENT AND SPECIALTY STORE Merchandising and Operating Results of 1983

Annual. 1984. xxiii+225 p.
LC 72-626565.
SRI/MF/not filmed

Annual report, for 1983, presenting 16 merchandising and operating results (MOR) ratios for department and specialty stores, by sales size and detailed type of merchandise, with summary trends from 1979. Data are compiled by the National Retail Merchants Assn from cooperating companies' 1983 fiscal year financial statements. The number of companies reporting is specified for each merchandise group.

MOR ratios, shown for median and superior (highest quartile) performance, include cumulative mark-on; markdowns, stock shortages, net workroom cost, and gross margin, all as percent of net sales; stock turnover and age; returns as percent of gross sales; sales per square foot of selling space; sales promotion costs and selling salaries, both as percent of sales; and 5 others.

Contains contents listing (p. iii); and the following:

a. Explanation of MOR ratios, and listing of merchandise groups. (p. vi-xvi)

b. Department store inventory BLS price indexes, by major store dept, Jan. 1983-84 and July 1983; number of MOR reporting companies, 1983, and 1982-83 sales, by merchandise division; reporting department and specialty store sales distribution, percent of markdowns to owned sales, and stock/sales ratios, by sales size, Feb. 1983-Jan. 1984; and selected MOR ratio trends by merchandise group, for department and specialty stores with sales over $1 million, 1979-83. 6 tables. (p. xvii-xxiii)

c. Detailed MOR ratio table for department and specialty stores, by sales size and detailed type of merchandise, 1983. (p. 2-225).

This is the 59th edition of the report. Previous report, for 1982, is described in SRI 1983 Annual, under this number.

Availability: National Retail Merchants Association, Book Order Division, 100 W. 31st St., New York NY 10001, members $37.50, nonmembers $69.50; SRI/MF/not filmed.

A8300–2 FINANCIAL AND OPERATING RESULTS OF DEPARTMENT AND SPECIALTY STORES of 1983

Annual. 1984. 122 p.
ISSN 0547-8804.
LC 72-92812.
SRI/MF/not filmed

Annual report, for 1983, presenting department and specialty store financial and operating ratios, by sales volume size, with trends from 1974. Also includes sales trends by census division and in selected States and cities.

Data are based primarily on survey responses of 125 companies operating 4,072 stores, and are for the fiscal year ending nearest to Jan. 31, 1984.

Contents:

Contents listing. (1 p.)

Part I. Financial and operating trends, retail credit analysis, methodology, and selected performance results, with 23 tables listed below. (p. 1-36)

Part II. Typical and middle range operating data and ratios by store sales volume category, with 2 extended tables, described below. (p. 38-122)

Availability: National Retail Merchants Association, Book Order Division, 100 W. 31st St., New York NY 10001, members $37.50, nonmembers $69.50; SRI/MF/not filmed.

TABLES:

[Unless otherwise noted, data are shown separately for department and specialty stores, generally by 2-8 sales volume categories.]

A8300–2.1: Part I, Summary

FINANCIAL AND OPERATING TRENDS

[1-2] Department and specialty stores 10-year financial operating results [aggregate sales, gross margin, net expense, earnings from merchandising operations, other income/deductions, pretax earnings in current and 1967 constant dollars, and CPI], 1974-83. (p. 1-2)

RETAIL CREDIT OPERATING RESULTS

[Tables [3-8] show data for department stores only, for 1983 unless otherwise noted.]

[3] Analysis of respondents. (p. 3)

[4] Sales by terms of sale: comparison of cash store credit and 3rd-party credit sales. (p. 4)

[5] Average size of sales transaction, 1983 and 1982, store credit card, bank credit card, cash purchases. (p. 4)

[6] Analysis of accounts receivable results. (p. 5)

[7] Collections and bad debt results. (p. 5)

[8] New account acquisition: proprietary store credit results. (p. 6)

REPORTING COMPANIES, TRENDS, AND PERFORMANCE GUIDELINES

[9] Number of reporting companies [including aggregate and average sales volume for owned and leased departments, 1983]. (p. 7)

[10-11] Annual financial and operating trends, department and specialty stores with annual total company sales over $1 million [including percent changes and ratios for total sales; ratios for retail departments' sales, gross margin, profits, operating costs, pretax earnings, and sales by terms of sale; and actual stock turns, and sales per square foot]; 1974-83. (p. 14-17)

[12] Performance guidelines [including ratios for sales, merchandising, earnings, expenses by function, sales and buying payroll, and selected financial operating items, 1983]. (p. 20-23)

SELECTED PERFORMANCE TABLES

I. Sales and inventory price trends [annual percent change in sales, and percent change from prior year for department store inventory price index], 1974-83. (p. 26)

II-VI. Pretax earnings, percent of total store sales and of capital/surplus; stock shortage, percent of net owned retail sales; and net operating expenses and credit sales, percent of total company sales; 1974-83. (p. 26-28)

VII. Distribution of sales and sales promotion expenditures by month [aggregate all stores, for newspaper, display, radio/TV, and total], percent of total year's expenses [1983]. (p. 29)

VIII. Inward transportation [typical and middle range] percent of cost purchases [1979-83]. (p. 30)

IX. Balance sheet data, ratios [1983]. (p. 31)

SALES CHANGE BY GEOGRAPHIC DIVISION

[X-XI] Estimates of monthly retail sales [percent change from previous year for GAF stores (stores which specialize in department store type merchandise) in 18 States and 5 cities, 1981-83; and for department, apparel/accessory, and/or GAF stores, by census division, 1982-83]. (p. 35-36)

A8300–2.2: Part II, Operating Results

Two tables generally showing typical, middle range, and prior year typical sales, merchandising, earnings, and expense ratios; distribution of sales by source (owned and leased depts) and type (cash, credit, private label credit, and 3rd party credit cards); selling space as percent of total space; sales personnel as percent of total employees; average gross sale; and percent change in sales from owned and leased depts.

Ratios for stores over $1 million include itemization of expenses by detailed retail accounting classification.

Tables are repeated for sales volume categories of department stores (p. 38-102), and specialty stores (p. 104-122).

A8375
National Safety Council

A8375-1   TRAFFIC SAFETY
Bimonthly.   Approx. 30 p.
ISSN 0041-0721.
LC 28-14389.
SRI/MF/not filmed

Bimonthly publication reporting developments in traffic safety programs and trends in accident and fatality statistics.

Data are from State traffic authorities, the National Safety Council, R. L. Polk and Co., NCHS, and other sources. Month of data coverage is 3-6 months preceding publication date.

Issues contain feature articles and editorial depts, occasionally with statistics, including an annual analysis of traffic fatalities; and 3 bimonthly tables presenting traffic accident data.

Prior to July/Aug. issue, report also included a bimonthly table showing traffic deaths and rates for major cities in 9 population size classes.

Bimonthly tables are listed below; most appear in all issues. All additional features with substantial statistical content are described, as they appear, under "Statistical Features." Nonstatistical features are not covered.

Availability: Traffic Safety Magazine, PO Box 11933, Chicago IL 60611, members $12.55 per yr., single copy $2.90; nonmembers $15.75 per yr., single copy $3.65; SRI/MF/not filmed.

Issues reviewed during 1985: Nov./Dec. 1984-Sept./Oct. 1985 (P) (Vol. 84, No. 6; Vol. 85, Nos. 1-5).

BIMONTHLY TABLES:
[Tables [1] and [3] show cumulative data for current year through month of coverage; table [3] includes comparisons to the previous year or 2 years.]

[1] [Traffic fatality] reductions at the end of [month of coverage, for States and occasionally cities with reductions over same period of previous year].

[2] Motor vehicle deaths and changes, total U.S. [by month for current year through month of coverage, and previous 3 years].

[3] Traffic deaths [by State and for Puerto Rico].

STATISTICAL FEATURES:

A8375-1.601: Nov./Dec. 1984 (Vol. 84, No. 6)

TRAFFIC ACCIDENT FACTS, ANNUAL FEATURE
(p. 12-15) Annual summary, for 1983, of motor vehicle accident statistics. Includes 11 tables showing the following data:

a. Motor vehicle urban and rural deaths by type of accident; accidents and drivers involved, by severity of accident; and deaths by weekday by month; 1983.

b. Motor vehicle deaths and death rates, registered vehicles, mileage, licensed drivers, and accident costs, 1943-83; and types of improper driving reported in urban and rural accidents, and accidents and occupant fatalities by type of vehicle, 1983.

c. Deaths on major holidays, 1956-83; drivers involved in accidents, by sex, 1969-83; deaths by State, 1982-83; all drivers and those involved in accidents, by age group, 1983; and urban and rural deaths and total injuries, by victim age and accident type including pedestrian and pedalcycle, 1983.

For description of previous annual feature, for 1982, see SRI 1983 Annual, under A8375-1.404.

A8375-1.602: May/June 1985 (Vol. 85, No. 3)

OHIO BELT USE SURVEYS SHOW: DRIVERS WHO DON'T BUCKLE UP PUT COMFORT BEFORE SAFETY
(p. 14-15, 28-29) By Jack Walsh. Article on use of vehicle safety restraints among Ohio motorists, based on State Highway Patrol studies involving over 300,000 vehicle occupants, conducted 1981-84. Includes 3 undated tables showing incidence of safety restraint use, and distribution of fatal accidents, by day of week and type of vehicle and/or road.

TRAFFIC TOLL SWINGS UP IN 1984, ANNUAL FEATURE
(p. 20-24) Annual analysis, by Barbara Carraro, of motor vehicle fatalities, including location, circumstances, and victim age, 1984 and trends. Includes text statistics, and 8 tables showing the following:

a. Motor vehicle accident deaths and rates, injuries, and costs; vehicle travel mileage and registrations; and population; 1984.

b. Motor vehicle deaths, by urban population size group, rural road type, region, accident type, and victim age group, 1984 and/or percent change from 1974 and 1983.

c. National accident fatality toll, for motor vehicle accidents, public non-motor-vehicle accidents, and accidents at home and at work, with some data on injuries and costs, 1983-84.

d. States and cities (over 200,000 population) reporting decreases in traffic fatalities, and percent decrease, 1984.

A8375-2   ACCIDENT FACTS, 1984
Edition
Annual.   1984.   97 p.
Stock No. 021.64.
ISBN 0-87912-013-4.
LC 28-14389.
SRI/MF/not filmed

Annual report on accidental deaths and disabling injuries, 1983, with trends from 1865. Covers accidents occurring in the workplace, traffic, public areas, home, schools, and on farms; with

selected data for cities, States, and foreign countries. Includes analysis of accident circumstances and victim demographic characteristics.

Data are compiled from numerous government and private sources, specified for each table.

Contains contents listing (p. 1); 7 sections with brief narrative analyses interspersed with 18 charts and 96 tables, described below (p. 2-93); index (p. 94-96); and definitions (inside back cover).

This is the 63rd edition.

Availability: National Safety Council, Order Department, 444 N. Michigan Ave., Chicago IL 60611, members $9.00, nonmembers $11.25 (prepaid); SRI/MF/not filmed.

CHARTS AND TABLES:
[Tables show data for 1983, unless otherwise noted. Most tables include rates for accidents or deaths. Accidents by class are mostly for motor vehicle, work, home, and public place accidents.]

A8375-2.1: Summaries
a. Summaries by class of accident, including average annual accidental deaths and disabling injuries; costs and cost components of accidents; deaths by type of accident and victim age; leading causes of accidental and other deaths, by sex and age, 1980; and accident incidence rates. 3 charts and 8 tables. (p. 2-11)

b. Accidental deaths, by International Classification of Diseases category, 1979-1980. 1 table. (p. 12)

c. Accidental deaths: by class, age, and type, various periods 1903-83; by age, sex, month, and type, 1980; by month; by class and selected cities, and by class and State; by selected city, 1982; and State totals, 1978-80. 1 chart and 8 tables. (p. 13-19)

d. Fires and property loss, by property use; deaths and years of potential life lost, from accidents and other causes of death, 1982; and deaths from specific major disasters, by location and date, 1865-1983. 3 tables. (p. 20-21)

e. World accidental deaths: for Canadian Provinces by cause, 1982; and totals for 34 countries, latest available year, 1980-82. 2 tables. (p. 22)

A8375-2.2: Work Accidents
a. Summaries of work deaths, injuries, and accident-related time loss and costs; accidental deaths and injuries on and off the job, selected years 1945-83; parts of body injured; workers' compensation claims for wrist injuries, 1979; disability days, including data by age group and occupation, 1980; work accident death trends from 1933; and prevalence of injuries among female workers, including data by occupation, 1981; with selected detail by industry division. 2 charts and 9 tables. (p. 23-29)

b. Occupational injury/illness, lost work days, and rates, by SIC 1- to 4-digit industry, various years 1981-83; industrial safety awards, by industry group and leading company; and compensated/reported workers' compensation cases (total and for death claims), by State and Canadian Province, 1981-83. 1 chart and 7 tables. (p. 30-39)

A8375–2.3: Motor Vehicle Accidents

a. Summary, including deaths, disabling injuries, costs, mileage, registered vehicles, and licensed drivers; fatal, injury, and property damage accidents, and drivers involved; deaths and/or injuries, by accident type, day or night, urban/rural location, and victim age; type of vehicle involved in fatal accidents by roadway class, 1982; and pedalcycle use, and deaths by age, quinquennially 1940-70 and annually 1973-83. 4 charts and 6 tables. (p. 40-45)

b. Vehicle movement analysis and urban and rural accidents, various periods 1981-83; accidents, deaths, and injuries, by city population size and rural road type; types of improper driving in accidents; contributing factors in Louisiana fatal and injury accidents; and world traffic fatalities, by country, various years 1975-82. 7 tables. (p. 46-49)

c. Accidents, by day and hour; deaths by day, 1983, and month, 1974-83; distribution of North Carolina driver and pedestrian deaths by victim blood alcohol content (BAC) level, 1970-83; and accidents, by driver age, 1982, and sex, 1969-83. 1 chart and 6 tables. (p. 50-54)

d. Pedestrian deaths/injuries, by age and action, 1982, and by city size and victim age, 1981; number of vehicles involved in accidents, and occupant fatalities, by vehicle type; motorcycle rider deaths, 1974-83; motor vehicle deaths on holidays, 1972-83; and types of trucks involved in Ohio fatal, injury, and property damage accidents. 6 tables. (p. 55-57)

e. Deaths by type of accident and victim age, and accident costs, various periods 1913-83; distribution of accidents by driver State residence status; deaths by urban and rural location and accident type, selected periods 1943-83, and by age, 1983; motor vehicle deaths, and mileage rates, by State, various years 1979-83; and fleet accident rates, by vehicle type, various periods 1963-83. 3 charts and 9 tables. (p. 58-64)

f. Traffic deaths for specific cities, 1982-83; and average days between deaths, 1977-83; both by population size group. 2 tables. (p. 65-71)

A8375–2.4: Other Accidents

PUBLIC ACCIDENTS

a. Public accidental deaths, by type and victim age; deaths, by public accident type, 1950, 1955, and 1957-83; sports participation, fatalities, and injuries, by type of sport, various years 1981-83; civil and general aviation accidents and deaths, 1974-83; public transport passenger miles and deaths, by transport mode, various years 1978-83; railroad accident deaths and injuries, selected years 1933-83; and railroad crossing accidents, selected years 1943-83. 1 chart and 7 tables. (p. 72-78)

HOME ACCIDENTS

b. Home urban and farm accidental deaths and disabling injuries; deaths by type of accident and victim age; poisoning deaths by type, age, and sex, 1980; space heaters in use, and related fires, burns, and deaths, by type of unit, 1978 and 1982; and deaths by type of accident, 1950, 1955, and 1957-83. 2 charts and 4 tables. (p. 79-84)

FARM ACCIDENTS

c. Farm resident accidental deaths and disabling injuries, by class; farm work injury rates, by sex, age, and type of farm; injuries by severity and cause of accident; tractor accident fatality rates, by type of accident, 1969-82; accidental deaths, by class, 1964-83; and nontransport deaths, by type of accident, 1961-80. 6 tables. (p. 85-88)

SCHOOL ACCIDENTS

d. Accidental deaths by class, 5-14 age group; deaths by location and age (through age 24), 1980; student accident rates, by activity, location, and sex, 1980/81; and school bus accidents by type, and injuries, by State. 5 tables. (p. 89-93)

A8460
National Society
of Professional Engineers

A8460–1   PROFESSIONAL ENGINEER INCOME AND SALARY SURVEY, 1985
Annual.   June 1985   64 p.
NSPE Pub. No. 0004.
LC A55-10041.
SRI/MF/complete, delayed

Annual survey report on compensation of professional engineers, 1984. Includes data by experience, degree level, engineering field, job function, professional registration status, level of professional and managerial responsibility, industry or service of employer, organization size, region, and selected metro area, with various cross-tabulations.

Compensation data are shown as means, medians, 1st and 9th deciles, and 1st and 3rd quartiles.

Also includes data on incidence of promotions, job changes, and salary increases during 1984; and engineers' assessments of current status and outlook for their employers' economic condition and for engineering manpower levels in general.

Data are based on responses of 14,160 NSPE members to a Jan. 1985 mail survey conducted by Abbott, Langer and Associates.

Contains introduction, contents listing, highlights, definitions, and methodology (p. 2-5); report, with 1 map, 12 charts, and 21 tables (p. 6-21); and 2 appendices including sample survey form and detailed income cross-tabulations, with 22 tables (p. 22-64).

This is the 19th survey report.

Availability: National Society of Professional Engineers, 1420 King St., Alexandria VA 22314, members $30.00, nonmembers $55.00; SRI/MF/complete, delayed shipment in Oct. 1985.

A8465
National Society
of Public Accountants

A8465–1   INCOME AND FEES OF ACCOUNTANTS IN PUBLIC PRACTICE: A 1985 Survey Report
Triennial.   July 1985.
v+49 p.
SRI/MF/complete

Triennial report on public accounting firm finances and operations, by firm location and characteristics, 1984.

Includes data on income, with comparison to 1983 and expectations for 1985; income, clients, and fees charged, by type of service provided; billing base, and hourly rate by type of employee; computer functions and arrangements; office facilities, and rent paid; accountant characteristics, including education, sex, age, and qualifications; and promotional methods.

Data are shown by region, population size group, major metro area, and firm characteristics (ownership, employment and income size, primary income source, and years in operation).

Data are based on responses of 3,063 accounts to a 1985 survey conducted by the National Society of Public Accountants.

Contains highlights, contents and table listing, and foreword (p. ii-v); introduction, with 1 map (p. 1-2); 13 chapters, with narrative and 13 tables (p. 3-44); and questionnaire facsimile (p. 45-49).

This is the 6th triennial report. Previous report, for 1981, is described in SRI 1982 Annual under this number.

Availability: National Society of Public Accountants, 1010 N. Fairfax St., Alexandria VA 22314, members $25.00, nonmembers $40.00; SRI/MF/complete.

A8475
National
Soft Drink Association

A8475–1   SALES SURVEY OF THE SOFT DRINK INDUSTRY, NSDA, 1983
Annual.   [1985.]
19 p.+errata.
SRI/MF/complete

Annual report on soft drink industry bulk and package sales, 1983, showing the following for U.S. and by region: percent change in sales volume and value and in employment; and market shares by bulk or package type, outlet type including vending machines, and regular and diet flavor.

Bulk and package types are pre-mix and post-mix bulk, plastic containers by size, aluminum and bi-metal cans, and 1-way and refillable glass containers by size. Data by flavor also include aseptic drinks.

Also includes national labor productivity ratios; and wholesale value, production, and per capita consumption, decennially 1849-1939 and annually 1945-83.

Data are from an annual survey conducted by NSDA, covering assn members and other soft drink manufacturers and distributors.

Contains contents listing (1 p.); foreword (p. 1-2); national analysis, with text data, 14 charts, and 25 tables (p. 3-11); regional data, with 22 tables (p. 12-17); reconciliation of sales estimates from NSDA and U.S. Census of Manufactures (p. 18); and historical trend table (p. 19).

Availability: National Soft Drink Association, 1101 16th St., NW, Washington DC 20036, members †, nonmembers $1.50; SRI/MF/complete.

A8485
National
Sporting Goods Association

A8485–2   SPORTING GOODS MARKET in 1985

Annual. 1985. 72 p.
ISSN 0193-8401.
LC 83-645617.
SRI/MF/complete, delayed

Annual report estimating consumer purchases of sporting goods, by detailed type of product, Oct. 1983-Sept. 1984 for spring/summer products, and Jan.-Dec. 1984 for fall/winter products, with trends from 1970s. Covers clothing, footwear, and equipment.

Includes volume, value, and average price of purchases, with selected detail by type of outlet and trends from 1976; distribution of purchases, by age and sex of user, household income, education of household head, and census division; and product rankings within each census division and income group, by share of all purchases.

Also includes forecasts of sporting goods and recreational transport product sales for 1985.

Most data are projections based on a survey of approximately 80,000 households participating in the National Family Opinion, Inc., consumer panel. Survey response rate was 69%. Study was conducted by Irwin Broh and Associates, Inc.

Contains contents listing, and introduction with 1 summary table (p. 3-7); 3 basic tables repeated for each product category or type (p. 8-45); 3 additional tables (p. 48-70); and order form for brand share reports on individual product types, also available from the issuing agency but not covered in SRI.

Availability: National Sporting Goods Association, 1699 Wall St., Mt. Prospect IL 60056, members $25.00, nonmembers $95.00; SRI/MF/complete, delayed shipment in Dec. 1985.

A8510
National Urban League

A8510–1   STATE OF BLACK AMERICA, 1985

Annual. Jan. 16, 1985.
4+vi+232 p.
ISSN 0148-6985.
ISBN 0-87855-937-X.
LC 77-647469.
SRI/MF/complete, delayed

Annual compilation of papers, for 1985, on selected social, political, and economic events and conditions affecting black Americans. Papers were prepared at the invitation of the National Urban League. Data are from various Federal and private sources, and are current to the 1980s, with trends from the 1960s.

Contains author biographies and contents listing (4 p.); overview (p. i-vi); 7 papers, most with substantial statistics (p. 1-183); conclusions and recommendations, and 1984 chronology of events with implications for race relations (p. 185-223); and appendix paper on minority students (p. 225-231).

Papers with substantial statistics are described below.

Availability: National Urban League, Communications Department, Equal Opportunity Bldg., 500 E. 62nd St., New York NY 10021, $17.00; SRI/MF/complete, delayed shipment in Dec. 1985.

A8510–1.1: Papers

BLACK FAMILY TODAY AND TOMORROW

(p. 1-20) By James D. McGhee. Includes 5 tables (p. 16-20) showing the following data for various years 1960-83:

a. By race: families, by type of household head (married couple, and male and female householder with no spouse present); ratio of divorced persons to persons with spouse present; prevalence of divorced and separated persons, by sex; and median family income, with detail for married couples by wife's labor force status, and for female-headed households.

b. Selected characteristics of black female householders with no spouse present, including median age, marital status, and presence of children.

Data are from Census Bureau.

MODERN TECHNOLOGY AND URBAN SCHOOLS

(p. 37-64) By Robert E. Fullilove, III. Report on public school computer use and math education. Data are based on various surveys of schools and students, and a study of black and Hispanic students participating in a math skills development program at the University of California, Berkeley. Includes 11 tables (p. 54-64) showing the following data:

a. Schools providing computer-based instruction, computers used, average hours of use and students per computer, and use of microcomputers and terminals by instructional purpose, all shown by elementary/secondary education level, region, and metro status, spring 1982.

b. Comparison of computer availability, use, and needs, for schools receiving and not receiving Federal aid under the Title I program, spring 1982.

c. Comparison of computer availability and use, for elementary schools serving predominantly white upper, middle, and low income populations, and predominantly minority populations (no date).

d. National comparisons of math test performance and course enrollment, for black, white, and/or Hispanic students, various years 1973-82; and 1st-year calculus grades of participants in the Berkeley program, 1983/84.

BLACKENING IN MEDIA: THE STATE OF BLACKS IN THE PRESS

(p. 65-103) By Samuel L. Adams. Includes 6 charts and 3 tables (p. 96-103) showing the following data for various years 1978-84:

a. Percent of newspapers employing minority journalists, and percent with no minority news executives, by circulation size; radio/TV employees by race (with detail for blacks by sex), by occupational category; and minorities' share of news staff employment of daily newspapers.

b. TV and radio stations, and cable TV systems, by race of owner; broadcast stations owned by blacks, Asians, Native Americans, and Hispanics; "distress" sales of white-owned broadcast stations to minorities to avoid revocation of license; and tax certificates issued to owners selling stations to minorities.

Data are from American Society of Newspaper Editors and other sources.

BLACKS IN THE U.S. LABOR MOVEMENT: WORKING OR NOT?

(p. 105-126) By Lenneal J. Henderson. Includes 3 tables (p. 124-126) showing State and local government labor bargaining units, agreements, strikes, and days of idleness, 1974 and 1980; total and black/other labor force and participation rates, selected years 1960-82; and labor force by occupational category, and unemployed, by race, 1980.

Data are from the Census Bureau and other Federal sources.

POTENTIAL AND PROBLEMS OF BLACK FINANCIAL INSTITUTIONS

(p. 127-142) By William D. Bradford. Includes 6 tables showing number and assets of total and black-owned commercial banks, savings and loan assns, and insurance companies, with analysis of longevity of black-owned institutions, various years 1973-83.

Data are from *Black Enterprise Magazine* and *Federal Reserve Bulletin.*

AGED BLACK AMERICANS: DOUBLE JEOPARDY RE-EXAMINED

(p. 143-183) By Jacquelyne Johnson Jackson. Includes 12 tables showing the following data, for population age 65/over by race, unless otherwise noted:

a. Population, with distribution by marital status and type of living arrangement, and median years of education, all by sex and age, various years 1980-83; labor force participation and unemployment rates, by sex, 1981 and 1983-84; and percent of population below poverty level, 1966-83.

b. Income medians, by family type and for individuals by sex; estimated after-tax income per household member, by age of household head (for population age 15/

over, not by race); death rates by sex and age; and life expectancy at 0 years and 65 years, by sex; various years 1980-83.

c. Population, mean monthly household income, and percent of population living in households receiving Federal benefits and food stamps, for total population by race and sex, and for population age 65/over by sex, July-Sept. 1983 period.

Most data are from the Census Bureau and NCHS.

A8600
Newspaper Advertising Bureau

A8600–5   1984 DAILY NEWSPAPER READERSHIP DEMOGRAPHIC TABLES for Total U.S., Top 100 Metros, and Top 100 DMAs
Annual. [1985.] iii+34 p.
SRI/MF/complete

Annual report, for 1984, on socioeconomic characteristics of daily newspaper readers, aggregated for total U.S., top 100 MSAs, and top 100 designated market areas. Shows total adult population, and average weekday newspaper audience, gross impressions, and gross rating points, by sex, cross-tabulated by age, education, household income and size, employment and marital status, occupation, employed adults in household, race, census region, and locality type (metro central city, suburban, nonmetro).

Data are from a 1984 Simmons Market Research Bureau study.

Contains contents listing (1 p.); notes and methodology, with 1 summary table (p. i-iii); and 33 detailed tables (p. 2-34).

Summary table shows reader characteristics for local papers/*USA Today*/*Wall Street Journal* combined. Detailed tables exclude the 2 national publications.

Availability: Newspaper Advertising Bureau, Research Department, 1180 Ave. of the Americas, New York NY 10036, $3.00+postage; SRI/MF/complete.

A8600–7   NEWSPAPER READERSHIP PROJECT RESEARCH REPORTS
Series. For individual publication data, see below.
SRI/MF/complete

Continuing series of marketing research reports analyzing aspects of newspaper readership and production, including personnel profiles, management practices, and consumer behavior. Reports are intended to promote circulation and readership.

Data are based on surveys conducted or sponsored by NAB's Newspaper Readership Project, and often include breakdowns by sex, age, education, income, and other socioeconomic and demographic characteristics.

SRI covers only those reports with broad-based statistical content. Report reviewed during 1985 is described below.

Availability: Newspaper Advertising Bureau, Research Department, 1180 Ave. of the Americas, New York NY 10036; SRI/MF/complete.

A8600–7.7: Newspapers in American News Habits: A Comparative Assessment
[Monograph.   July 1985.   xvii+116 p.
$6.50+postage. SRI/MF/complete.]

Report on consumer use of news media, by media type. Covers the following topics, generally shown by audience frequency of newspaper use, and selected socioeconomic and demographic characteristics:

a. Newspaper, TV, and radio total and news exposure, including by time of day, type of newspaper and whether home delivered, TV program type, and for random vs. specific TV viewing; and household vs. individual newspaper readership.

b. Newspaper readership by primary language spoken in home, and in relation to readership of magazines, news magazines, and books; audience preferences for newspaper vs. TV news, and newspaper news vs. feature items; preferred newspaper content categories; various newspaper reading habits; effect of newspaper editorials on perception of news; and whether reader has ever written letter to editor, placed classified advertisement, or clipped coupon/other advertisement.

c. Opinions on responsibility to keep informed of news, and on most important problem facing U.S. today; interest in national/international vs. local news; recreational, social, and selected other activities; relative importance of 4 personal goals; sources for major news stories, by story type; and postponement of buying selected consumer items.

Data are based on a May 1982 survey of adults in 1,979 households, conducted by Audits & Surveys, Inc.

Contains preface, listings of contents, tables, and charts (p. v-xiii); highlights (p. xv-xvii); narrative analysis in 5 sections, interspersed with 6 charts and 65 tables (p. 1-109); and appendix on survey sample characteristics, with 1 chart and 1 table (p. 111-116).

A8600–8   RESEARCH REPORT SERIES
Series. For individual publication data, see below.
SRI/MF/complete

Continuing series of marketing research reports analyzing aspects of newspaper readership, advertising effects, and consumer behavior, either generally or in relation to a particular industry. Reports are directed to newspapers and their advertisers, and are intended to help individual companies use newspaper advertising effectively.

Data are based on surveys conducted or sponsored by NAB, and usually include breakdowns by age, sex, education, income, and other sociodemographic characteristics.

SRI covers only those reports with substantial statistical content. Reports reviewed during 1985 are described below.

Availability: Newspaper Advertising Bureau, Research Department, 1180 Ave. of the Americas, New York NY 10036; SRI/MF/complete.

A8600–8.18: Classified Advertising: Readership and Use Among Purchasers of General Merchandise and Recreation and Leisure Items, 1984

[Monograph. Nov. 1984. 2+25+App 4 p.
$3.00+postage. SRI/MF/complete.]

Report on readership of and response to classified advertisements for merchandise. Includes data on readership of all classified advertisements, by category; and purchases of general merchandise and recreation-related items by type, including whether made through dealer or private party, and use of classified advertising to find item and to contact seller. Data generally are shown by selected household characteristics.

Data are based on 11,657 responses to a Feb. 1984 preliminary survey of households; and responses to a Mar. 1984 follow-up survey of 6,987 households reporting recent general merchandise or recreation item purchases; both conducted by National Survey Panel of Paratest Marketing.

Contains introduction and overview (2 p.); report, with 9 tables and interspersed narrative (p. 1-25); and appendix, with 2 tables and questionnaire facsimiles (4 p.).

A8600–8.19: Readership of Newspaper Pages and Sections: Demographic Segments, SMRB SMM—1984
[Annual. Jan. 1984. iv+25 p. $3.00+postage. SRI/MF/complete.]

Annual report on daily newspaper readership, with data on percent of weekday audience reading entire paper and specific sections, and estimated average weekday audience, by reader sociodemographic characteristics.

Data are from *1984 Study of Media and Markets*, a Simmons Market Research Bureau report derived from interviews with a sample of over 19,000 adults.

Contains contents listing (1 p.); introduction (p. i-iv); and 25 tables (p. 1-25).

A8600–8.20: Automotive Aftermarket 1984: A Study of Primary Car Maintainers
[Monograph.   Dec. 1984.   viii+69+16 p.
$4.00+postage. SRI/MF/complete.]

Report on consumer auto maintenance practices, 1984. Includes data on maintenance regularity; service outlet selection factors and loyalty; auto parts/supplies purchases, outlet preferences, brand loyalty, installation practices, and information sources, mostly by product type; and characteristics of auto owners who do their own maintenance, with detail for women.

Also includes data on auto-buying plans (new vs. used and American vs. foreign); warranty and extended service protection coverage; and factors in auto-buying decisions.

Data often are shown by selected socioeconomic characteristics, newspaper-reading practices, involvement in do-it-yourself activity, number of autos in household, and whether a new auto was purchased during 1982-84.

Also includes general data on the auto industry, including production by leading auto manufacturers; expenditures on autos, maintenance, and fuel/oil; repair sales and facilities; parts outlets, by type; and newpaper advertising expenditures; various years 1978-83.

Consumer data are based on telephone interviews with adults responsible for auto maintenance in 1,202 households, conducted Jan.-Feb. 1984 by the Gallup Organization. Auto industry data are from reports of various industry sources.

Contains listings of contents and tables (p. v-viii); report in 7 sections, with narrative analysis and 33 tables (p. 1-61); appendix, with 4 tables (p. 65-68); and questionnaire facsimile (16 p.).

A8600–8.21: Field Experiment of the Sales Effectiveness of Direct Mail, ROP and Inserts

[Monograph. Jan. 1985. 28 p. $3.00+postage. SRI/MF/complete.]

Report comparing the cost-effectiveness of advertising campaigns using run of paper (ROP) advertisements in the pages of daily newspapers, separate inserts included with newspapers, and direct mailings of circulars.

Data are based on an experimental study involving 6 retailers in Atlanta, Ga., conducted during spring 1984.

Contains contents listing (1 p.); narrative report, interspersed with 5 tables (p. 1-22); and appendix, with narrative and 3 tables (p. 23-27).

A8600–8.22: Key Facts About Newspapers and Advertising, 1985

[Annual. Mar. 1985. iv+43 p. $2.00+postage. SRI/MF/complete.]

Annual report describing services available from NAB and presenting data on aspects of newspaper readership and advertising, with selected comparisons to other media. Includes the following data, shown primarily for 1983 or 1984, with some trends from 1970s:

a. Newspapers offering color ads, and cost comparison to black and white; and newspaper vs. TV household penetration and ad costs in top 20 markets.

b. Sociodemographic characteristics of daily and Sunday/weekend newspaper audience; newspaper audience reach and readership frequency patterns; number and circulation of newspapers, by type, for U.S. and Canada; consumer spending on newspapers; how newspapers are obtained (subscription, single-copy purchases, other); and newspaper reading habits.

c. Ad readership; audience reach of multiple ad insertions; reader response to ads, including enjoyment and believability compared to other media; advertising influence on purchases, by media; and coupon data, including distribution by media and consumer use.

d. Advertising expenditure/sales ratio for selected retail and service industries; national and local/retail advertising expenditures, by media; newspaper classified ad expenditures; and newspaper insert ad volume, revenues, circulation, and costs.

Data are from a variety of sources, specified for each table.

Contains contents listing (p. ii-iv); NAB telephone directory, and narrative report interspersed with 1 chart and 33 tables (p. 1-35); and list of NAB reports (p. 36-43).

A8600–8.23: Coupon Facts, 1985: Findings on Cents-Off Coupon Usage and Users

[Recurring (irreg.) Apr. 1985. 30 p. $2.00+postage. SRI/MF/complete.]

Recurring report on cents-off coupons issued by manufacturers. Includes data on number and face value of coupons issued; distribution media; redemption rates; extent of coupon use among households, demographic profile of users, and use characteristics (frequency, media, and minimum value redeemed); and newspaper coupon impact on sales; various years 1971-84.

Data are shown for U.S. and/or Canada, and include selected detail by product category.

Data are from Nielsen Clearing House, Simmons Market Research Bureau, and NAB-SCAN.

Contains contents and table listings (2 p.); introduction (p. 1-2); narrative report in 6 sections, with 22 tables (p. 3-26); and 2 appendices with advertising source information, and bibliography (p. 27-30).

For description of previous report, see SRI 1982 Annual under A8600-8.5.

A8600–8.24: Product and Service Users: Average Weekday and Average Sunday/Weekend Newspaper Coverage

[Recurring (irreg.) July 1985. 42 p. $3.00+postage. SRI/MF/complete.]

Recurring report presenting statistics on newspaper readership among selected categories of consumers, including users of specific types of products and services, and participants in community activities, sports, travel, and other leisure activities, 1984. Includes users/participants as a percent of total population; and percent of users/participants reached by daily and Sunday/weekend newpapers (total and in metro areas); shown for each consumer category.

Data are derived from *1984 Simmons Study of Media and Markets.*

Contains contents/table listing (2 p.), introduction (p. 1-2), and 40 tables (p. 3-42).

Previous report, presenting results from the 1981 study, is described in SRI 1983 Annual under A8600-8.6.

A8610
Newsprint
Information Committee

A8610–1   NEWSPAPER AND NEWSPRINT FACTS at a Glance, 1984-85
Annual. [1985.] 29 p.
SRI/MF/complete

Annual report on U.S. and Canadian newsprint and newspaper industry, 1984, with selected trends from 1934. Covers newsprint production, trade, capacity by mill, consumption, and prices. Also includes data on U.S. consumption by State and major newspaper, and world production and consumption.

Data are from Canadian Pulp & Paper Assn, American Paper Institute, American Newspaper Publishers Assn, Audit Bureau of Circulations, and other sources.

Contains introduction, and 12 tables listed below (p. 1-15); highlights of Canadian Newsprint Information Committee research surveys on advertising, consumer habits, and other topics, with text statistics (p. 16-25); and newsprint specifications, assn meeting information, and index (p. 26-29).

This is the 27th edition.

Availability: Newsprint Information Committee, 420 Lexington Ave., New York NY 10017, media/research organizations †, others $2.50; SRI/MF/complete.

TABLES:

NORTH AMERICA

[1] 1985 newsprint capacity, by producers [by Canadian and U.S. mill]. (p. 3-5)

[2] North American newsprint capacity, production, consumption, [and] sources of supply [selected years 1965-85]. (p. 6)

[3] Flow of North American newsprint [Canadian and U.S. production, consumption, and exports, and U.S. imports], 1984. (p. 7)

WORLD

[4] Canada leads world in newsprint production [production and percent of world total, for 10 countries, 1984]. (p. 8)

[5] U.S. is world's leading consumer of newsprint [consumption and percent of world total, for 11 countries, 1984]. (p. 8)

U.S.

[6] Price of newsprint, 1934-84. (p. 9)

[7] Newsprint as an element of total publishing cost [for daily newspapers, by circulation size, 1983-84]. (p. 9)

[8] U.S. newsprint consumption, 1954-84. (p. 10)

[9] Data on U.S. newspapers [including circulation, average pages printed, and advertising revenue, 1974 and 1983-84]. (p. 12)

[10] Largest [10] U.S. dailies [ranked by circulation, as of Mar. 31, 1985, with 1984 newsprint usage]. (p. 13)

[11] Largest [10] U.S. newspaper companies (ranked by daily circulation) [and with Sunday circulation, average for 6-months ended Sept. 30, 1984; also shows number of daily and Sunday papers]. (p. 13)

[12] Newspaper newsprint consumption, by States [and census division, 1983-84]. (p. 14-15)

A8630
North American
Electric Reliability Council

A8630–2   ELECTRIC POWER SUPPLY AND DEMAND, 1985-94
Annual. 1985. 115 p.
SRI/MF/complete

Annual report presenting detailed forecasts of U.S. and Canadian electricity supply and demand, by NERC region and subregion, various years 1984-94. Covers total electricity requirement; summer and winter peak demand; generating capacity and net electrical energy requirements, by energy source; and fossil fuel requirements, by type of fuel.

Also includes descriptive lists of planned generating unit additions and retirements, and unit conversions from oil to coal, by utility; and existing and planned transmission line mileage.

Data are based on reports of NERC regional councils.

Contains contents listing, introduction, and listing of NERC regions and subregions (p. 2-5); and 69 tables, arranged in 9 sections, with brief narrative summaries. (p. 6-115).

Availability: North American Electric Reliability Council, Research Park, Terhune Rd., Princeton NJ 08540, †; SRI/MF/complete.

A8640
North American Telecommunications Association

A8640–2 **1985 TELECOMMUNICATIONS SOURCEBOOK**
Annual. [1984.] 344 p.
SRI/MF/excerpts

Annual telecommunications industry sourcebook, including trends, product development, and directories; and statistics on telephone equipment installations and other industry operations, 1983 and trends. Data are from FCC, other Federal Government, and telephone industry sources.

Contains contents listing (p. 3-4); narrative industry overview (p. 9-58); statistical review section, with 2 charts and 14 tables, described below (p. 61-86); and product guide, directory, resource listing, index, and NATA profile (p. 89-344).

Availability: North American Telecommunications Association, 2000 M St., NW, Suite 550, Washington DC 20036, members $25.00, nonmembers $75.00+$2.00 postage and handling; SRI/MF/excerpts for "Statistical Review" section.

STATISTICAL REVIEW SECTION:

a. Manufacturers' shipments and/or installed base, for stand-alone key, private branch exchange (PBX), and centrex telephone equipment markets, by vendor segment (Bell and independent operating companies, AT&T Information Systems, and interconnect industry), 1979-88; and Bell PBX-centrex systems installed and removed, by State, 1983. 2 charts and 10 tables. (p. 67-79)

b. Interconnect industry stations, and sales and other revenue, for PBX vs. key telephone systems, 1982-88; and telephone and telephone answering machine sales volume and value, and average price, 1984-85. 2 tables. (p. 81-82)

c. Access lines for subscribers maintained by AT&T, Southern New England/Cincinnati Bell, and independent companies, by type of service; and imports and exports of telephones, and telephone switching/switchboard and other equipment, by country or world area of origin or destination; 1983. 2 tables. (p. 83-84)

A8658
Opera America

A8658–1 **PROFILE: 1984, Opera America and the Professional Opera Companies**
Annual. [1984.] 72 p.
SRI/MF/complete

Annual report, for 1984, of OPERA America, with data on professional opera company finances and operations. Data are from responses of 71 U.S. and 5 Canadian opera companies to an OPERA America membership survey.

Contents:

a. Contents listing, preface, description of OPERA America organization and activities, and review of 1982/83 opera season. (p. 1-24)

b. Opera company survey report, with 3 charts and 14 tables showing personnel and nonpersonnel expenses; income by source, with detail for Canada and for Metropolitan Opera of NYC; attendance, subscribers, productions, and performances; and percent of companies experiencing decline in attendance, and average decline, by company budget size; 1982/83, with selected trends from 1978/79. (p. 25-33)

c. Performance schedules, and photographs illustrating scenes from productions. (p. 34-48)

d. Directory of OPERA America member companies in U.S. (by State), Puerto Rico, Canada (by Province), and Venezuela, with the following data for most companies: productions and performances, ticket prices, operating budget, attendance, and broadcast audience, generally for FY84-85. (p. 49-52)

Report has been published since 1976. SRI coverage begins with this edition.

Availability: OPERA America, 633 E St., NW, Washington DC 20004, members $5.00, nonmembers $8.00, plus $1.00 postage and handling; SRI/MF/complete.

A8670
Pacific Area Travel Association

A8670–1 **ANNUAL STATISTICAL REPORT, 1983**
Annual. [1984.]
2+vi+107 p.
SRI/MF/not filmed

Annual report on visitor arrivals in Pacific Area Travel Assn (PATA) countries, by visitor travel mode, nationality, residence, sex, and purpose of visit, all by PATA country, 1983, with selected trends from 1973.

Also includes data on number of hotel rooms and occupancy rates, rooms under construction and planned (with forecasts to 1988), average length of stay, visitor expenditures, and national tourist organization budgets by function and market area, all by PATA country; and outbound travel of PATA country residents by country of destination.

Data are from reports submitted by PATA countries based on tourist embarkation/debarkation cards.

Contains contents and table listing (2 p.); introduction, summary, and table notes (p. i-vi); 6 sections, with 3 charts and 25 tables (p. 2-102); and listing of tourism R&D projects, by country, 1983-84 (p. 103-106).

This is the 16th annual report.

Availability: Pacific Area Travel Association, 228 Grant Ave., San Francisco CA 94108, members $40.00, nonmembers $65.00; SRI/MF/not filmed.

A8680
Phi Delta Kappa

A8680–1 **PHI DELTA KAPPAN**
10 issues per year.
Approx. 70 p. paginated cumulatively throughout the year.
ISSN 0031-7217.
LC 46-35485.
SRI/MF/excerpts, shipped quarterly

Monthly professional journal (published Sept.-June) presenting research results and essays on issues, trends, and policies in education and the teaching profession. Covers testing, curriculum development, teacher education, enrollment, school finance and administration, and other topics of interest to the profession. A Gallup Poll on public attitudes toward public schools appears annually.

Issues contain feature articles and essays, occasionally with supporting statistics; and regular narrative editorial features.

Features with substantial statistical content are described, as they appear, under "Statistical Features." Each issue of the journal is reviewed, but an abstract is published in SRI monthly issues only when statistical features appear.

Availability: Phi Delta Kappan, Director of Administrative Services, 8th and Union, PO Box 789, Bloomington IN 47402, $20.00 per yr., library and institution rate $25.00, single copy $2.50; SRI/MF/excerpts for all portions described under "Statistical Features;" shipped quarterly.

Issues reviewed during 1985: Nov. 1984-Oct. 1985 (P) (Vol. 66, Nos. 3-10; Vol. 67, Nos. 1-2).

STATISTICAL FEATURES:

A8680–1.601: Nov. 1984 (Vol. 66, No. 3)
STATES AND SCHOOL FINANCE: LOOKING BACK AND LOOKING AHEAD

(p. 196-201) By John Augenblick. Article on trends in State funding for education. Data were compiled by the author, from various published sources.

Includes 5 tables showing average percent change in 4 types of tax; and number of States, by whether increase or decrease in education aid per $1,000 of personal income, level of aid (low, medium, and high), percent change in number of teachers and students, level of teacher average salary and percent change in salary, and teacher salary share of expenditures and average expenditure per teacher, with selected cross-tabulations; primarily 1978/79-1983/84 period or 1983/84.

A8680-1.602: Jan. 1985 (Vol. 66, No. 5)

GALLUP POLL OF TEACHERS' ATTITUDES TOWARD THE PUBLIC SCHOOLS, PART 2

(p. 323-330) By Alec Gallup. Part 2 of a 2-part article on teachers' attitudes concerning the public school system and various education-related issues. Data are based on 813 responses to an Apr./May 1984 Gallup/Phi Delta Kappa survey. Includes 4 charts and 19 tables showing responses concerning the following:

a. Teaching as career for own child; ratings of the social benefit and prestige of selected occupations; impact of unionization on quality of public education; and support for teacher strikes, and compulsory use of an arbitrator to settle disputes.

b. Goals of education; course requirements for college-bound and other students; lengthening of school day and year; support for sex education, and subjects it should include in high school and elementary school; and responsibility for determining school curriculum and books used in schools.

Many tables show separate responses for elementary and high school teachers, and include comparisons with attitudes of the general public.

Part 1 of the survey appears in the Oct. 1984 issue (for description, see 1984 SRI Annual under A8680-1.506).

VOICES FROM THE ATTIC: CANADIAN PUBLIC OPINION ON EDUCATION

(p. 344-348) By G. E. Malcolm MacLeod. Article on Canadian public opinion concerning public schools and education. Data are based on 2,109 responses to a Mar./Apr. 1984 survey, conducted by Canadian Education Assn and Canadian Gallup Poll Ltd.

Includes 1 chart and 6 tables showing survey response related to the following: confidence in selected societal institutions; rating of public schools; major school problems; elementary and high school student workloads; and areas in which schools excel; often shown separately by whether respondent has child in school, with selected comparison to U.S. public opinion.

A8680-1.603: Feb. 1985 (Vol. 66, No. 6)

[Data for the following articles are based on studies conducted by the International Assn for the Evaluation of Educational Achievement (IEA).]

INTERNATIONAL COMPARISONS OF COGNITIVE ACHIEVEMENT

(p. 403-406) By James S. Coleman. Article comparing results of reading and science achievement tests among students of 10 countries. Data are from study results published in 1973. Includes 2 tables.

MATHEMATICS ACHIEVEMENT IN U.S. SCHOOLS: PRELIMINARY FINDINGS FROM THE SECOND IEA MATHEMATICS STUDY

(p. 407-413) By Kenneth J. Travers and Curtis C. McKnight. Article, with 8 tables presenting data on mathematics course coverage and student achievement test results by subject area, and comparisons to international median achievement scores, for 8th and 12th grade students, 1981/82 with summary comparisons to 1964.

SECOND INTERNATIONAL SCIENCE STUDY: U.S. RESULTS

(p. 414-417) By Willard J. Jacobson and Rodney L. Doran. Article, with 2 tables showing science achievement test results, for 5th, 9th, and 12th grade students, with detail by sex and for biology and physical science, 1983 with comparisons to 1970.

A8680-1.604: Mar. 1985 (Vol. 66, No. 7)

RESEARCH EVIDENCE OF A SCHOOL DISCIPLINE PROBLEM

(p. 482-488) By Keith Baker. Article on student crime and disciplinary problems in public schools. Data are from specified studies published by National Education Assn and other organizations during 1978-83.

Includes 4 tables showing study results concerning student misbehavior as related to student grades and as an interference to teaching; former teachers declining to reenter profession, by type of discipline problem experienced; and relationship between student misbehavior and experience as a victim of school crime.

A8680-1.605: Apr. 1985 (Vol. 66, No. 8)

EVIDENCE THAT GOOD EARLY CHILDHOOD PROGRAMS WORK

(p. 545-551) By Lawrence J. Schweinhart and David P. Weikart. Article analyzing results of 7 preschool education programs for the disadvantaged, including the impact on students' future scholastic achievement. Data are from recently published studies. Includes 3 tables.

An accompanying article, with 2 tables, presents further detail for 1 program, including potential monetary costs and benefits (p. 548-553).

A8680-1.606: May 1985 (Vol. 66, No. 9)

MEASUREMENT-DRIVEN INSTRUCTION: IT'S ON THE ROAD

(p. 628-634) By W. James Popham et al. Article, with 1 chart and 1 table showing percent of students passing State competency tests in reading and mathematics, for Texas 9th graders by race (including Hispanic), and for South Carolina elementary school students in selected grades, various years 1980-84.

CHRISTIAN SCHOOLS AND TEACHER LICENSING

(p. 646-647) By Bruce K. Alcorn. Article discussing teacher certification in Christian private schools. Data are from responses of 142 schools to a 1982 survey of Assn of Christian Schools International (ACSI) members in 10 midwestern States, and a survey of State education depts in the same States.

Includes 3 tables showing number of respondent ACSI schools, and number requiring and encouraging teachers to obtain State certification, by State and school type (church-related, independent, and other), 1982; and summary of State regulations concerning approval of private schools and certification of teachers, by State (no date).

A8680-1.607: Sept. 1985 (Vol. 67, No. 1)

17th ANNUAL GALLUP POLL OF THE PUBLIC'S ATTITUDES TOWARD THE PUBLIC SCHOOLS

(p. 35-47) Annual survey article, by Alec M. Gallup, on public opinion concerning public

schools. Survey covered 1,528 adults and was conducted May 17-26, 1985. Includes 2 charts and 35 tables showing survey responses related to the following:

a. Ratings of local, national, and own children's schools, and of teachers and administrators; adequacy of teacher salaries, and merit pay; teacher competency testing; course requirements for college-bound and other students; and sex education, including appropriate topics for high school and elementary courses.

b. Extracurricular activities and participation standards; coeducational sports; student homework; parent control over child's homework and TV viewing time; problems facing public schools; rights of students; right of school authorities to examine student property; solutions to student discipline problems; and provision of tax-supported child care for preschoolers and "latchkey" students who arrive home before their working parents.

c. Tax increases to support education; funding levels for special instruction; support of and standards for private schools and home-based education; government use of voucher system alloting funds to parents for child's education; and importance of college education.

Many tables show data by whether respondent has child in public or nonpublic school, or no children in school, and include comparisons to previous surveys from as early as 1969. Some tables also include detail by respondent characteristics, including sex, race, age, education, income, community size, region, and white or blue collar occupation.

A8680-1.608: Oct. 1985 (Vol. 67, No. 2)

TEACHER FLIGHT: YES OR GUESS?

(p. 148-149) By M. Gilbert Wilkins and Ann Korschgen. Article, with 2 tables showing number of Wisconsin public school districts, FTE teachers employed, and teacher resignations (total and those permanently leaving the education profession), all by district employment size, 1982/83-1983/84. Data are from 346 responses to a survey of State school districts, conducted by the authors.

A8695
Photo Marketing Association International

A8695-2   1985 CONSUMER PHOTOGRAPHIC SURVEY
Biennial. July 1985.
4+51 p.
SRI/MF/not filmed

Biennial survey report, for 1985, on consumer attitudes and purchasing behavior with regard to photographic equipment and supplies, with selected detail by consumer demographic characteristics and comparisons to 1981 and 1983 surveys.

Covers number, types, age, and/or cost of cameras and home video equipment owned, occasions and frequency of use, and type of outlet where purchased; factors influencing purchase decision and outlet choice; and future purchase intentions.

Also covers camera repairs; film purchases and processing, including costs and types of outlets used; print storage and display; response to advertising; photographic activity, interest, and skill; and use of professional photographer services.

Also includes data on video tape purchases and rentals; and conversion of prints/slides/movie film to video tape.

Data are from responses of 1,259 households to a Dec. 1984 survey, conducted by National Family Opinion (NFO) Research.

Contains contents listing and introduction (4 p.); main survey response tabulation in 15 sections, with 48 charts and 160 tables (p. 1-39); and 3 appendices, with tabulated response to survey questions, 9 tables on respondent characteristics, and explanatory notes (p. 41-51).

For description of previous report, for 1983, see SRI 1983 Annual under this number.

Availability: Photo Marketing Association International, 3000 Picture Pl., Jackson MI 49201, members $95.00, nonmembers $110.00; SRI/MF/not filmed.

A8720
Potash and
Phosphate Institute

A8720–1   STATISTICAL REPORT:
Potash Sales
Monthly.   7 p. Oversized.
SRI/MF/complete, shipped quarterly

Monthly report on potash sales by producers in U.S. and Canada, including domestic sales by State or Province, and exports by country of destination. Report is issued 3-6 weeks after month of coverage, and is one of a series on potash production and disposition (see A8720-2 through A8720-5).

Contains 7 tables, listed below.

Availability: Potash and Phosphate Institute, 2801 Buford Hwy., NE, Suite 401, Atlanta GA 30329-2199, †; SRI/MF/complete, shipped quarterly.

Issues reviewed during 1985: Aug. 1984-Aug. 1985 (D).

TABLES:

[Tables [2-7] show tonnage for current month, for North American, Canadian, and U.S. producers, by potash type, including sulphates and standard, coarse, granular, and soluble muriates. Table sequence may vary.]

[1] Total potash sales [agricultural by State and Canadian Province, and total exports; nonagricultural total U.S., Canada, and exports; and total by type; usually for current month, fertilizer year (July-June) to date, and same periods of previous year].

[2-4] Potash sales [agricultural by State and Province of destination, and total exports; and nonagricultural total U.S., Canada, and exports].

[5-7] Potash exports [agricultural and nonagricultural, by country of destination].

A8720–2   STATISTICAL REPORT:
Potash Production,
Inventory, Disappearance,
and Sales
Monthly, with quarterly and annual summaries.
4 p. Oversized.
SRI/MF/complete, shipped quarterly

Monthly report, with quarterly and annual summaries, on total potash production tonnage, inventories, disappearance, and agricultural and nonagricultural sales and exports by U.S. and Canadian producers. Report is issued monthly, with separate quarterly summaries, and annual summaries for the calendar and fertilizer (July/June) years. Report is issued 1-2 months after the period covered, and is one in a series on potash production and disposition (see A8720-1 through A8720-5).

Contains 4-13 tables, listed below.

Prior to the Jan./Mar. 1984 quarterly summary, export data in tables [5-7] were published in a separate report, covered in SRI under A8720-3. The separate report has been discontinued.

Availability: Potash and Phosphate Institute, 2801 Buford Hwy., NE, Suite 401, Atlanta GA 30329-2199, †; SRI/MF/complete, shipped quarterly.

Issues reviewed during 1985: Monthly Reports: Sept. 1984-Sept. 1985 (D).

Issues reviewed during 1985: Quarterly Summaries: July/Sept. 1984-Apr./May 1985 (D).

Issues reviewed during 1985: Annual Summaries: Calendar Year 1984 and Fertilizer Year 1984/85 (D).

TABLES:

[Tables [2-13] show data for sulphates (U.S. only) and by type of muriate. Monthly tables [1-4] show data for U.S. and Canadian producers for month of coverage and same month of previous year.

Monthly tables [1-4] also appear in quarterly and annual summaries showing data for current period of coverage and same period of previous year. Quarterly tables [5-7] also appear in calendar and fertilizer year annual summaries, showing data for current year of coverage. Tables [8-13] appear in annual reports only, and show tonnages for the fertilizer or calendar year.]

MONTHLY TABLES

[1] Potash report summary [tonnage; also including cumulative tonnage and monthly inventories, for previous and current fertilizer year to date].

[2-4] Report of potash production, inventory, disappearance, and [agricultural and nonagricultural] sales [and exports].

QUARTERLY TABLES

[5-7] North American, Canadian, and U.S. producers [agricultural and nonagricultural] potash exports [by country of destination; for current quarter of coverage].

ANNUAL TABLES

[8-13] North American, Canadian, and U.S. producers domestic potash sales [by State and Province of destination, and total exports], agricultural and nonagricultural.

A8720–3   STATISTICAL REPORT:
Potash Exports
Quarterly, discontinued.

Quarterly report on potash exports of North American producers, by type and country of destination, discontinued as a separate publication with Oct./Dec. 1983 issue. Data have been incorporated into the monthly *Statistical Report: Potash Production, Inventory, Disappearance, and Sales,* described under A8720-2.

A8720–4   STATISTICAL REPORT:
Potash Imports
Quarterly, with annual summaries.   1 p.
SRI/MF/complete

Quarterly report, with annual summaries, on U.S. potash imports, by State and country of origin. Report is issued 4-9 weeks after period covered, with annual summaries at the end of the calendar and fertilizer (July-June) years.

Contains 1 table showing data for muriate and sulphate potash and potash product, for quarter of coverage.

Report is part of a series on potash production and disposition (see A8720-1 through A8720-5).

Availability: Potash and Phosphate Institute, 2801 Buford Hwy., NE, Suite 401, Atlanta GA 30329-2199, †; SRI/MF/complete.

Issues reviewed during 1985: July/Sept. 1984-Apr./June 1985 (D); and annual summaries for calendar year 1984 and fertilizer year 1985.

A8720–5   STATISTICAL REPORT:
Press Release, Potash Sales
Quarterly.   2 p.
SRI/MF/complete

Quarterly press release on total U.S. and Canadian sales, exports, and imports of potash muriates and sulphates, with annual summaries included at the end of the calendar and fertilizer (July-June) years. Report is issued 5-6 weeks after quarter covered, and is one of a series on potash production and disposition (see A8720-1 through A8720-4).

Contains brief narrative summary, and 1 quarterly table showing U.S. and Canadian agricultural and nonagricultural sales and combined exports, and total overseas imports into U.S., by potash type, for current quarter and same quarter of previous year.

Availability: Potash and Phosphate Institute, 2801 Buford Hwy., NE, Suite 401, Atlanta GA 30329-2199, †; SRI/MF/complete.

Issues reviewed during 1985: July/Sept. 1984-Apr./June 1985 (D) (Nos. E.265-E.268).

A8740
Printing Industries of America

A8740–1   1985 FINANCIAL RATIO STUDY

Annual series. For individual publication data, see below. SRI/MF/complete, current & previous year series

Annual series of 14 reports on printing industry finances, 1985. Includes detailed financial and operating ratios, and total sales, assets, and income, shown by printing process, product specialty, sales volume range, and location.

Reports are based on operating statements and balance sheets submitted by 879 representative members of the U.S. and Canadian printing industry, and are intended to permit individual firms to compare their operations with industry averages.

Vol. I contains contents listing, user's guide for the series, and discussion of various management topics. Vol. II-XIV generally include the following:

a. Foreword; contents listing; and explanation of value-added ratios (based on sales less material costs).

b. Operations report and supporting schedules, presenting income, profit, and detailed expense ratios based on value added and/or sales.

c. Balance sheet ratios.

d. Significant facts: includes average assets, investment, sales, payroll, and profit per employee, usually including and excluding executives; sales/assets ratio; and employee distribution among factory, sales, and administrative depts.

e. Return on investment per $100 worth of sales.

f. Absolute data: number of firms reporting; and assets, sales, and income.

Data in Vol. II-XIV are shown for all firms and for profit leaders (firms earning 8% or greater pretax profits on sales); and for additional classifications, varying with each report, as indicated below.

This is the 62nd annual series. The 61st series, for 1984, has also been received; 1984 reports are also available on SRI microfiche, as indicated below. The 60th series, for 1983, is described in SRI 1983 Annual under this number.

Availability: Printing Industries of America, Financial Services, 1730 N. Lynn St., Arlington VA 22209, 1984 and 1985 series—participants: members $40.00 per book, $350.00 complete set, nonmembers $60.00 per book, $525.00 complete set; nonparticipants: members $60.00+$1.95 postage per book, $500.00+$5.00 handling per complete set, nonmembers $90.00+$1.95 postage per book, $750.00+$5.00 handling per complete set (all orders prepaid); SRI/MF/complete.

A8740–1.1: 1985 Financial Ratio Study: Volume I. Management Guide to the PIA Ratio Studies

[Annual. 1985. 82 p. SRI/MF/complete, current & previous year reports.]

Report for 1984 has also been received, and is also available on SRI microfiche under A8740-1.1 [Annual. 1984. 83 p.].

A8740–1.2: 1985 Financial Ratio Study: Volume II. All Printers by Sales Volume

[Annual. 1985. 20 p. SRI/MF/complete, current & previous year reports.]

Shows data for all printers by 6 sales volume ranges.

Report for 1984 has also been received, and is also available on SRI microfiche under A8740-1.2 [Annual. 1984. 20 p.].

A8740–1.3: 1985 Financial Ratio Study: Volume III. All Printers by Product Specialty

[Annual. 1985. 20 p. SRI/MF/complete, current & previous year reports.]

Shows data for all printers by specialty: commercial/advertising, magazine/periodical, newspaper, financial, direct mail/catalog, directory, label, and packaging.

Report for 1984 has also been received, and is also available on SRI microfiche under A8740-1.3 [Annual. 1984. 20 p.].

A8740–1.4: 1985 Financial Ratio Study: Volume IV. All Printers by Geographic Region

[Annual. 1985. 20 p. SRI/MF/complete, current & previous year reports.]

Shows data for all printers in Canada and 11 U.S. regions, including Chicago, metropolitan New York/New Jersey, and eastern Pennsylvania/Maryland/D.C. areas.

Report for 1984 has also been received, and is also available on SRI microfiche under A8740-1.4 [Annual. 1984. 20 p.].

A8740–1.5: 1985 Financial Ratio Study: Volume V. Sheetfed Printers by Size and Geographic Area

[Annual. 1985. 43 p. SRI/MF/complete, current & previous year reports.]

Shows data for sheetfed printers by 6 sales volume ranges and for Canada and 11 U.S. regions.

Report for 1984 has also been received, and is also available on SRI microfiche under A8740-1.5 [Annual. 1984. 43 p.].

A8740–1.6: 1985 Financial Ratio Study: Volume VI. Web Offset Printers—Heatset

[Annual. 1985. 42 p. SRI/MF/complete, current & previous year reports.]

Shows data for heatset web offset printers, by 4 sales volume ranges, product specialty (commercial/advertising and magazine/periodical), and percent of paper supplied.

Report for 1984 has also been received, and is also available on SRI microfiche under A8740-1.6 [Annual. 1984. 49 p.].

A8740–1.7: 1985 Financial Ratio Study: Volume VII. Web Offset Printers—Non-Heatset

[Annual. 1985. 34 p. SRI/MF/complete, current & previous year reports.]

Shows data for non-heatset web offset printers, by 5 sales volume ranges and product specialty (commercial/advertising, newspaper, book, directory, and no predominant specialty).

Report for 1984 has also been received, and is also available on SRI microfiche under A8740-1.7 [Annual. 1984. 34 p.].

A8740–1.8: 1985 Financial Ratio Study: Volume VIII. Combination Offset—Sheetfed/Web

[Annual. 1985. 48 p. SRI/MF/complete, current & previous year reports.]

Shows data for combination offset-sheetfed/web printers, by 5 sales volume ranges, product specialty (commercial/advertising, magazine/periodical, newspaper, book, and no predominant product), and percent of web sales.

Report for 1984 has also been received, and is also available on SRI microfiche under A8740-1.8 [Annual. 1984. 48 p.].

A8740–1.9: 1985 Financial Ratio Study: Volume IX. Book Manufacturers

[Annual. 1985. 42 p. SRI/MF/complete, current & previous year reports.]

Shows data for book manufacturers by 3 sales volume ranges, process specialty (sheet-fed, web-fed, and combination offset), and product specialty (printing/binding and printing only).

Report for 1984 has also been received, and is also available on SRI microfiche under A8740-1.9 [Annual. 1984. 42 p.].

A8740–1.10: 1985 Financial Ratio Study: Volume X. Large Printers

[Annual. 1985. 35 p. SRI/MF/complete, current & previous year reports.]

Shows data for printers with over $10 million in sales by 4 sales volume ranges and by product specialty (commercial/advertising, magazine/periodical, newspaper, direct mail/catalog, book, and packaging).

Report for 1984 has also been received, and is also available on SRI microfiche under A8740-1.10 [Annual. 1984. 35 p.].

A8740–1.11: 1985 Financial Ratio Study: Volume XI. Typographers

[Annual. 1985. 24 p. SRI/MF/complete, current & previous year reports.]

Shows data for typographers by 3 sales volume ranges and by market (printers/lithographers, advertising agencies, publishers, books, and direct buyers).

Report for 1984 has also been received, and is also available on SRI microfiche under A8740-1.11 [Annual. 1984. 24 p.].

A8740–1.12: 1985 Financial Ratio Study: Volume XII. Preparatory Specialists

[Annual. 1985. 30 p. SRI/MF/complete, current & previous year reports.]

Shows data for preparatory specialists, by 4 sales volume ranges, market (printers/lithographers, advertising agencies, publishers, and carton manufacturers), and type of work (black/white and color).

Report for 1984 has also been received, and is also available on SRI microfiche under A8740-1.12 [Annual. 1984. 30 p.].

A8740–1.13: 1985 Financial Ratio Study: Volume XIII. Binders

[Annual. 1985. 24 p. SRI/MF/complete, current & previous year reports.]

Shows data for binders by 3 sales volume ranges and product specialty (pamphlet, edition books, looseleaf, and no predominant specialty).

Report for 1984 has also been received, and is also available on SRI microfiche under A8740-1.13 [Annual. 1984. 24 p.].

A8740–1.14: 1985 Financial Ratio Study: Volume XIV. Quick Printers
[Annual. 1985. 16 p. SRI/MF/complete, current & previous year reports.]

Shows data for quick printers by 3 sales volume ranges.

Report for 1984 has also been received, and is also available on SRI microfiche under A8740-1.14 [Annual. 1984. 21 p.]. Report for 1984 also includes data by metro and nonmetro status.

A8755
Professional Picture
Framers Association

A8755–1   PPFA INDUSTRY PROFILE, 1984: Customers, Retailers, Wholesalers, Manufacturers
Biennial. 1985. 36 p.
SRI/MF/not filmed

Biennial report profiling picture framing industry operations, 1984 with selected trends from 1979. Data are primarily from survey responses of 765 retailer and 166 manufacturer/wholesaler members of Professional Picture Framers Assn, and 1,079 consumers who frequent member shops.

Contains contents listing, introduction, and methodology (p. 3-5); and survey results, with brief narrative highlights and 37 tables showing survey responses concerning the topics described below (p. 6-36).

This is the 3rd biennial profile report. For description of previous report, see SRI 1982 Annual under this number.

Availability: Professional Picture Framers Association, 4305 Sarellen Rd., PO Box 7655, Richmond VA 23231, members: 1st copy †, additional copies $15.00 each; nonmembers $30.00; SRI/MF/not filmed.

TABLE TOPICS:

a. Consumers: sociodemographic characteristics; purchase characteristics, including value and type of object being framed, and price of framing; shop selection factors and frequency of visits; and satisfaction with product and service. 8 tables. (p. 6-13)

b. Retailers: demographic characteristics; operations, including ownership, shop site and size, employment, equipment investment, owner and employee experience and training, sales, business mix, average ticket per customer, and perceived impact of 1982-83 recession; average price of prints, and cash/check and credit transactions; advertising media use, and impact on sales; supply purchase methods, and type of materials used; and use of computers and glass; with selected cross-tabulations by revenue group. 16 tables. (p. 14-28)

c. Manufacturers/wholesalers: operations, including sales, clientele characteristics, product lines, cost/sales ratio, employment, and employee unionization; sales staff and compensation method; sales policies; advertising media use; shipment methods and delivery

time; equipment and inventory value; material imports, and use of synthetics; and perceived impact of 1982-83 and other recessions. 13 tables. (p. 29-36)

A8755–2   PPFA OPERATING RATIO STUDY: A Guide to Improving Frame Shop Profitability
Recurring (irreg.)   Nov. 1984.
23 p.
SRI/MF/not filmed

Recurring report presenting detailed financial and operating ratios for the picture framing retail industry, with detail by type of ownership (proprietorships/partnerships and corporations/franchises) and region, 1982. Also includes data on average salaries, sales and profits per square foot, and employment, 1980 and 1983.

Most data are based on 228 responses to a Professional Picture Framers Assn survey of 4,-120 retailers, and include comparisons to earlier surveys. Report is designed to enable individual retailers to compare their performance with that of the industry.

Contains introduction and methodology (p. 5-6); and survey results, with narrative and 12 tables (p. 7-23).

For description of previous report, with data for 1979, see SRI 1981 Annual under this number.

Availability: Professional Picture Framers Association, 4305 Sarellen Rd., PO Box 7655, Richmond VA 23231, members: 1st copy †, additional copies $15.00; nonmembers $40.00; SRI/MF/not filmed.

A8770
Public Relations
Society of America

A8770–1   PUBLIC RELATIONS JOURNAL
Monthly.   Approx. 45 p.
ISSN 0033-3670.
LC 49-23911.
SRI/MF/excerpts, shipped quarterly

Monthly journal (semimonthly in Sept.) reporting on public relations practices and developments in business, nonprofit organizations, and government.

Issues generally contain articles, occasionally with statistics, and editorial depts. An annual survey of business and assn advertising expenditures appears in Nov. issue. Additional Sept. issue is a directory of members, not included in subscription for nonmembers.

Features with substantial statistical content are described, as they appear, under "Statistical Features." Each issue of the journal is reviewed, but an abstract is published in SRI monthly issues only when statistical features appear.

Availability: Public Relations Society of America, 845 Third Ave., New York NY 10022, members †, nonmembers $28.00 per yr., single copy $3.00, directory issue $95.00 to nonmember subscribers; SRI/MF/excerpts for all portions described under "Statistical Features;" shipped quarterly.

Issues reviewed during 1985: Nov. 1984-Sept. 1985 (P) (Vol. 40, Nos. 11-12; Vol. 41, Nos. 1-9).

STATISTICAL FEATURES:

A8770–1.601: Nov. 1984 (Vol. 40, No. 11)
THE IMAGE OF CORPORATE IMAGE

(p. 12-14) By Pat Botwinick. Article on corporate advertising to maintain a good public image. Data are from 3,141 responses to a *Barron's* survey of institutional and individual investors, brokers, corporate executives, and investment bankers.

Includes 1 chart and 2 tables presenting survey response concerning importance of corporate image, whether image advertising prompts investigations into companies' investment potential, best media for image advertising, and methods for evaluating advertising effectiveness, all shown separately for each type of respondent (no dates).

CORPORATE ADVERTISING COSTS, ANNUAL FEATURE

(p. 20-25) Annual survey report on business and assn advertising expenditures, by media, 1977-83, with detail for 20 leading advertisers, 1983. Data are compiled by Leading National Advertisers from Publishers Advertising Reports, Broadcast Advertising Reports, and Institute of Outdoor Advertising. Includes 4 tables. This is the 13th annual survey.

ANNUAL REPORT CREDIBILITY

(p. 31-34) Article on investor use and opinion of corporate annual reports, and annual report characteristics. Data are from a survey of 247 individual and 50 professional investors, conducted by Hill and Knowlton, Inc., and a Graphic Arts Center study of 457 annual reports from Fortune 500 corporations. Includes 3 charts and 2 tables showing the following:

a. Individual investors' use of annual reports, and views on detail, readability, and other report characteristics; and professional investors' views on importance of annual reports compared to other information sources, and weaknesses and most important sections of reports.

b. Selected physical characteristics of reports, including types of special features, cover designs, and text art/graphics used.

A8770–1.602: Dec. 1984 (Vol. 40, No. 12)
MINNESOTA SURVEY SHOWS: 'APR' A PLUS; WOMEN GAIN IN NUMBERS AND PAY

(p. 6-7) Article, with 1 table showing mean salary range (total and by sex) for public relations personnel employed in Minnesota, by years of experience, 1983. Data are from a survey of members of the Minnesota Chapter of the Public Relations Society of America, conducted by Carol Morgan Associates.

A8770–1.603: June 1985 (Vol. 41, No. 6)
SALARY SURVEY

(p. 26-29) By Celia Kuperszmid Lehrman. Article on compensation of public relations (PR) professionals in U.S. and Canada. Data are based on a *PR Reporter* survey of 4,400 professionals, and a PRSA Counselors Academy survey of 354 PR firms, both conducted in 1984.

Includes 4 charts showing median salaries and salary ranges for PR personnel in Canada, and in U.S. by major industry group, 1984; and percent of employers offering bonuses and various types of benefits, and average salaries by position, for U.S./Canadian PR counseling firms, with salary detail for U.S. by region and for NYC (no date).

A8770–1.604: Aug. 1985 (Vol. 41, No. 8)
BUYING HABITS OF PUBLIC RELATIONS PROFESSIONALS

(p. 19-22) By Celia Kuperszmid Lehrman. Article on professional buying practices of public relations practitioners. Data are based on a 1985 survey of *Public Relations Journal* subscribers conducted by Globe Research Corp.

Includes 3 charts showing percent of respondents involved in purchasing products/services/equipment, including types used/recommended/purchased in past 12 months; and areas of involvement in planning off-premises meetings; for all, public relations firm/service, and company/organizational subscribers.

A8790
Recreation Vehicle
Industry Association

A8790–1   RV FINANCIAL FACTS
Quarterly.   4 p.
SRI/MF/complete

Quarterly newsletter (combined fall/winter issue) on recreational vehicle (RV) industry market developments and general economic conditions affecting RV industry outlook. Data are from issuing agency and American Bankers Assn.

Issues contain brief narrative articles; 1 illustrative chart showing RV shipment trends; and 1 other chart showing delinquency rates on 8-10 types of bank installment loans, for quarter 2 quarters prior to cover date.

Availability: Recreation Vehicle Industry Association, PO Box 2999, 1896 Preston White Dr., Reston VA 22090, †; SRI/MF/complete.

Issues reviewed during 1985: Fall/Winter 1984/85-Spring 1985 (P) (Vol. 10, No. 3; Vol. 11, No. 1) [Fall/Winter 1984/85 is a combined issue].

A8790–2   RV CONSUMER: Current Trends and Future Prospects
Recurring (irreg.)   Apr. 1985.
14+11 p.   Rpt. No. WP21.
SRI/MF/complete

Recurring report, by Richard T. Curtin, on recreational vehicle (RV) ownership and potential market, 1984, with selected comparisons to 1980. Current data are based on a 1984 survey of 2,491 vehicle-owning households conducted by Survey Research Center at the University of Michigan. Includes survey response on the following:

a. Households owning RVs; average RV length and number of sleeping spaces; current and potential owner and rental markets; rental agreement preferences; 1st-time and replacement RV purchases; and replacement purchase plans.

b. Factors influencing next RV purchase selection and timing; willingness to buy replacement RV on credit at current interest rates; and interest rate on outstanding RV loan, perceptions of current rate, and highest rate willing to pay.

Selected data are shown by respondent age, income, and region, and by vehicle type.

Contains listings of contents and tables (2 p.); narrative analysis and survey methodology (p. 1-14); and 13 tables (11 p.).

For description of previous report, published in 1982, see SRI 1983 Annual under this number. Report is also issued by the University of Michigan as part of *Survey of Consumer Attitudes: Working Papers Series,* covered in SRI under U7475-4.

Availability: Recreation Vehicle Industry Association, PO Box 2999, 1896 Preston White Dr., Reston VA 22090, $10.00+$1.00 handling (prepaid); SRI/MF/complete.

A8790–3   RVs, AMERICA'S FAMILY CAMPING VEHICLES: A Year-End Report, 1984
Annual.   1985.   17 p.
ISSN 0734-7715.
LC 82-645488.
SRI/MF/complete

Annual report on recreational vehicle (RV) industry market, 1984 and trends. Includes data on RV shipment volume and value, shipments and/or deliveries by State and census division, and wholesale and retail value, all by vehicle type, various years 1976-84. Also includes consumer data on RV ownership and purchase intentions, and potential market by age and region, mostly 1984.

Data are from annual RVIA surveys of RV manufacturers; and Survey Research Center, University of Michigan.

Contains contents listing (inside front cover); narrative highlights (p. 1); sections on shipments and marketplace, with 22 charts and 32 tables (some with accompanying illustrative charts) (p. 2-11); section on consumers, with narrative analysis, 2 charts, and 1 table (p. 12-14); and appendix, with 3 charts and 11 tables (p. 15-17).

Availability: Recreation Vehicle Industry Association, PO Box 2999, 1896 Preston White Dr., Reston VA 22090, members one copy †, all others $5.75; SRI/MF/complete.

A8790–4   RECREATION VEHICLE FINANCING: A Survey of Lenders' 1984 Experiences
Annual.   1985.   33 p.
ISSN 0733-530X.
LC 82-644156.
SRI/MF/complete

Annual report on new and used recreational vehicle (RV) financing practices of banks, savings and loan assns, finance companies, and credit unions, 1984. Covers retail and wholesale RV loans. Also includes data on other loans, consumer market characteristics, and RV shipments.

Data are based primarily on 299 responses, representing 6,580 operating locations, to a Feb. 1985 RVIA Finance Committee survey of financial institutions. Other data sources include 1984 survey findings on RV market characteristics from Survey Research Center at the University of Michigan, and American Bankers Assn re-

ports on consumer loan delinquency. Survey Research Center findings and American Bankers Assn reports are further described in SRI under A8790-2 and A0950-1, respectively.

Contains contents listing (p. 2); narrative summary, with 5 charts and 1 text table (p. 3-6); 13 illustrative charts, and 1 chart and 54 tables described below (p. 7-27); and appendix, with descriptions and average prices of RVs by type, questionnaire facsimile, and 3 economic indicator trend charts (p. 28-33).

This is the 6th annual survey.

Availability: Recreation Vehicle Industry Association, PO Box 2999, 1896 Preston White Dr., Reston VA 22090, $5.75; SRI/MF/complete.

TABLES AND CHART:
[Unless otherwise noted, data are for 1984. Tables 1-39 show data for banks, savings and loan assns, sales installment/finance firms, and credit unions, with number of responding institutions in each category.]

a. Lender characteristics: value of all and RV loans outstanding; profitability of RV loans vs. auto and other secured loans; future plans for RV financing; number of financing locations; number of years making RV loans; and methods used to determine loan values. Tables 1-6 (p. 7-9).

b. RV retail direct and indirect loans: number and value of loans outstanding and loans made in 1984; interest accounting methods; minimum down payment required; maximum maturity, percent early payoffs, and average turnover; additional items and vehicle types financed; and portfolio protection methods (indirect loans only). Tables 7-25. (p. 10-17).

c. RV wholesale financing (floor planning): value of loans and percent of manufacturer's invoice financed; policy regarding financing for used RV units; renewal terms; percent of units financed wholesale that became retail loans; portfolio protection methods; and number of RV manufacturing firms and dealerships represented in portfolio. Tables 26-33. (p. 18-20).

d. Defaults and other loans: RV loan defaults by time in arrears; repossession activities; number and value of all direct and indirect loans outstanding; value of all wholesale loans; and financing availability for autos, airplanes, boats, motorcycles, and snowmobiles. Tables 34-39. (p. 21-23).

e. RV market characteristics, including RV ownership, number of years before planned replacement purchase, and factors influencing next purchase, by age, income, and region; and replacement purchase plans (including vehicles other than RVs), and whether current RV was replacement or 1st-time purchase, generally by vehicle type. 5 tables. (p. 24-25).

f. Bank loan delinquency rates by type of loan. 1 chart. (p. 25).

g. RV shipments, by vehicle type, 1970-84. 10 tables. (p. 26-27).

A8800
Robotic Industries Association

A8800–1   WORLDWIDE ROBOTICS SURVEY AND DIRECTORY
Annual. 1985. 2+78 p.
ISBN 0-933747-00-4.
LC 85-60726.
SRI/MF/complete

Annual worldwide robotics industry survey and directories, 1983. Includes data on robot units in operation by application and type, and value of robot units by type, year end 1983; and status of robotics industry standards; all shown for 7-15 countries.

Also includes information on multinational robotics industry agreements; directory of worldwide robot manufacturers, suppliers, and research institutes, arranged by country; and directory of RIA members, with brief profiles.

Data are based primarily on responses from representatives of robotics-related organizations in 14 countries to an RIA survey.

Contains contents listing and introduction (2 p.); survey findings, with 1 chart and 2 tables (p. 1-3); and robotics standards, agreements, directories, and list of survey respondents (p. 4-78).

This is the 3rd edition of the survey/directory.

Availability: Robotic Industries Association, PO Box 1366, Dearborn MI 48121, members $30.00 (prepaid), nonmembers $40.00 (prepaid), $1.00 shipping and handling; SRI/MF/complete.

A8810
Rubber Manufacturers Association

A8810–1   MONTHLY TIRE REPORT
Monthly. 4 p.
SRI/MF/complete

Monthly report on tire shipments, production, inventories, and trade; and inner tube shipments and imports. Data are compiled from Commerce Dept and approximately 25 tire manufacturer reports, and Rubber Manufacturers Assn estimates, and are issued approximately 2 months after month of coverage.

Contains brief narrative, 4 trend charts, methodology, and glossary; and 2 tables showing the following by vehicle type:

a. Tire shipments (original equipment, replacements, and exports), production, and inventory; and inner tube shipments; for month of coverage, year to date, and same periods of preceding year.

b. Imports of tires and inner tubes, monthly for current year (through month of coverage) and previous year; table begins in Jan. 1985 issue.

Prior to Jan. 1985 issue, format differed slightly, and report was titled *Monthly Tire and Inner Tube Report.*

Availability: Rubber Manufacturers Association, Management Information Services, 1400 K St., NW, Washington DC 20005, selected institutions †, others $200.00 per yr.; SRI/MF/complete

Issues reviewed during 1985: Sept. 1984-Aug. 1985 (D).

A8810–2   MONTHLY RUBBER CONSUMPTION REPORT
Monthly. 4 p.
SRI/MF/complete

Monthly report on rubber industry production, trade, consumption, and stocks. Data are compiled primarily from reports submitted to RMA by approximately 75 rubber manufacturers, and are published approximately 2 months after month of coverage.

Includes brief narrative; 3 summary trend charts; methodology and glossary; and 1 table showing data, as applicable, for new, natural, and synthetic rubber, by SIC 7-digit product code or code group, for month of coverage and previous month, same month of previous year, and cumulatively for current and previous year.

Prior to Jan. 1985 issue, format differed slightly, and report was titled *Industry Rubber Report.*

Availability: Rubber Manufacturers Association, Management Information Services, 1400 K St., NW, Washington DC 20005, selected institutions †, others $200.00 per yr.; SRI/MF/complete

Issues reviewed during 1985: Aug. 1984-Aug. 1985 (D).

A8818
Scientific Manpower Commission

A8818–3   TECHNOLOGICAL MARKETPLACE: SUPPLY AND DEMAND FOR SCIENTISTS AND ENGINEERS, Third Edition
Recurring (irreg.) May 1985.
3+54 p.+errata.
ISSN 0732-2631.
LC sn82-2904.
SRI/MF/complete

Recurring report, by Betty M. Vetter, analyzing supply and demand trends and outlook for scientists and engineers, by field, various years 1959-98.

Includes projected and/or actual data on college/university enrollment and degrees awarded, with degree detail for foreign nationals; immigrants; employment by sector, with detail for R&D; employment status and starting salaries of new graduates; academic employment, including tenure status of faculty by age group, and change in ability to recruit/retain faculty; R&D funding by sector; and job openings, with detail for various Federal spending assumptions.

Data generally are shown by engineering and science field, with selected detail by degree level, sex, and race-ethnicity (including Hispanic, American Indian, and Asian).

Data are from NCES, National Research Council, NSF, and numerous other sources, specified for each table and chart.

Contains contents listing (1 p.); narrative report with 19 charts and 38 tables (p. 1-47); and notes, data sources, and bibliography (p. 48-54).

Second edition of the report is described in SRI 1983 Annual under this number; SRI coverage begins with the 2nd edition. Title has changed from *Supply and Demand for Scientists and Engineers.*

Availability: Scientific Manpower Commission, 1776 Massachusetts Ave., NW, Washington DC 20036, $25.00; SRI/MF/complete.

A8825
Securities Industry Association

A8825–1   SECURITIES INDUSTRY TRENDS: An Analysis of Emerging Trends in the Securities Industry
6-8 issues per year.
Approx. 20 p. var. paging.
ISSN 0276-2749.
LC 79-3918.
SRI/MF/complete, shipped quarterly

Periodical issued approximately 6-8 times per year, presenting summary analyses of the securities industry. Includes data on securities trading activity, yields, prices, and underwriting; and revenues and expenses of securities firms.

Month of data coverage is 1-4 months prior to publication. Data are from SEC studies and reports by securities firms and other Federal and commercial sources.

Report regularly includes special feature articles, usually with statistics; securities industry statistics section, with 6 recurring tables, listed below; and book and periodical reviews.

Prior to Apr. 30, 1985 issue, report included an additional recurring table on mutual fund net sales, net purchase of common stock and other securities, and cash position.

Recurring tables appear in most issues. All additional features with substantial statistical content are described, as they appear, under "Statistical Features." Nonstatistical features are not covered.

Availability: Securities Industry Association, Research Department, 120 Broadway, New York NY 10271, members $36.00 per yr., nonmembers $60.00 per yr.; SRI/MF/complete; shipped quarterly.

Issues reviewed during 1985: Aug. 22, 1984-Aug. 26, 1985 (P) (Vol. X, Nos. 5-6; Vol. XI, Nos. 1-6).

RECURRING TABLES:
[Tables show data for month of coverage and same month of previous year, unless otherwise noted. Tables [1] and [4] also show data for year to date for current and previous year. Table sequence may vary.]

TRADING DATA

[1] [Average daily share] volume [and value of shares traded by major stock exchange, odd-lot shares purchased and sold on NYSE, and contracts traded].

[2] [Corporate and municipal bond] yields (monthly averages) [and Bond Buyer Index].

[3] [End of month] prices [averages/indices for 6 major reporting authorities].

[4] Underwriting [volume and/or value of gross new corporate stock and debt and municipal note and bond issues].

[5] Margin debt [outstanding, net change, and percent of accounts with equity under 40%].

NYSE FIRMS FINANCIAL DATA

[6] [Aggregate] financial data for NYSE firms doing a public business [revenue, expenses, net income before taxes, and percent of firms showing loss; quarter ending 3-5 months prior to cover date, usually year to date, and same periods of previous year].

STATISTICAL FEATURES:

A8825–1.601: Aug. 22, 1984 (Vol. X, No. 5)

SEC RULE 415: BENEFITS AND COSTS FOR EQUITY ISSUERS

(p. 1-13) By Gary Gray and J. Randall Wooldridge. Article analyzing effect of SEC Rule 415 on costs of issuing primary equity securities. (Rule 415 allows corporate issuers to register securities with the SEC and then continuously offer "off the shelf" sales.) Includes 4 tables presenting multiple regression analyses based on a sample of 116 securities offered on NYSE and AMEX during Mar. 3-Dec. 31, 1982 at a minimum price of $10 per share and issue size of 250,000 shares.

A8825–1.602: Oct. 12, 1984 (Vol. X, No. 6)

ANALYZING PROFITABILITY BY FIRM CATEGORY: 1983 AND 1H 1984, SEMIANNUAL FEATURE

(1-19) Second article of a 2-part semiannual feature, by Ira Epstein and Neil L. Shandalow, reviewing securities industry revenues and expenses, 1983-1st half 1984.

Contains analysis, with 14 tables showing the following data, primarily for 1983 and 1st half 1984, with some trends from 1979:

a. Industry revenues by source, expenses by function, and pre-tax net income.

b. Summaries of after-tax return on equity components, revenue sources, and major expenses, for national full-line, large investment banks, New York based regionals, and regional firms.

c. Employment and compensation averages, for national full-line firms; and aggregate revenues, commissions, and capital, for top 10 and top 11-25 firms, and rest of industry.

Part I appears in the July 30, 1984 issue; for description, see SRI 1984 Annual under A8825-1.505.

A8825–1.603: Feb. 28, 1985 (Vol. XI, No. 1)

KEYS TO A CHANGING SECURITIES INDUSTRY

(p. 1-11) Compilation of articles on outlook for the securities industry through the 1980s. Data are from a survey of over 600 securities industry professionals and customers, conducted by SIA and Arthur Andersen & Co.

Includes 4 tables showing survey response concerning factors with greatest effect on industry structure and profitability, product development, and relationships with underwriting clients.

A8825–1.604: Apr. 30, 1985 (Vol. XI, No. 2)

1984 PERFORMANCE OF THE SECURITIES INDUSTRY, SEMIANNUAL FEATURE

(p. 1-20) First article of a 2-part semiannual feature, by Ira Epstein, reviewing securities industry revenues and expenses, 1983-84.

Contains analysis, with 15 tables showing the following data, primarily for 1983-84, with some trends from 1977:

a. Industry after-tax return on equity, with detail by component; revenues by source; commission revenues by type; underwriting revenues and volume by type of security, with market shares for top 10 and top 11-25 firms, and rest of industry; and trading profits.

b. Equity sales volume, price per share, and value of shares traded, for NYSE, AMEX, and regional exchanges; indicators of net margin interest income, including broker call rate and rate charged margin customers; and industry expenses by function.

c. Employment and compensation averages; and aggregate revenues, commissions, and capital, for top 10 and top 11-25 firms, and rest of industry.

A8825–1.605: May 13, 1985 (Vol. XI, No. 3)

DELPHI STUDY: KEY FINDINGS AND IMPLICATIONS FOR FIRMS

(p. 1-17) By Edward I. O'Brien et al. Article examining outlook for securities industry through the 1980s. Data are from a survey of over 600 securities industry professionals and customers, conducted by SIA and Arthur Andersen & Co.

Includes 3 charts and 1 table showing survey response on role of account executives; and securities industry capital growth rates, sources, and concentration among top firms; various periods 1978-88.

Other findings from this survey appear in the Feb. 28, 1985 issue; for description, see A8825-1.603 above.

A8825–1.606: June 28, 1985 (Vol. XI, No. 4)

1984 PERFORMANCE OF THE SECURITIES INDUSTRY BY FIRM CATEGORY, SEMIANNUAL FEATURE

(p. 1-21) Second article of a 2-part semiannual feature, by Ira Epstein, reviewing securities industry revenues and expenses, by firm category, 1983-84.

Contains analysis, with 9 tables showing the following primarily for 1984, with comparisons to 1982-83:

a. Summaries of after-tax return on equity components, revenue sources, and major expenses, for national full-line, large investment banks, NYC-based regionals, regional firms, and discounters, with comparisons to total securities industry.

b. Industry revenues, expenses, commissions by type, and pre-tax net income.

A8825–1.607: July 31, 1985 (Vol. XI, No. 5)

INTRODUCING SIA's INVESTOR ACTIVITY REPORT

(p. 1-13) By Jeffrey M. Schaefer. Article announcing a new data series covering retail and institutional components of trading volume on NYSE and AMEX. Includes summary text data and 2 tables showing the following for NYSE and AMEX: share volume by type, sales/purchases, member trading, and activity summary, daily May 1985.

Data will be published by SIA in weekly and monthly reports.

A8825–1.608: Aug. 26, 1985 (Vol. XI, No. 6)

SUMMARY OF THE NEW YORK SECURITIES INDUSTRY: ITS CONTRIBUTION TO NEW YORK STATE AND CITY

(p. 1-15) By Allan Young and David Strongin. Article examining contributions of the securities industry to the economies of New York State and NYC. Data are from responses of 74 securities firms to a recent SIA survey, and from various other Federal, State, and industry sources. Includes 8 tables showing the following:

a. Security/commodity broker employment, for New York State and NYC, with comparisons for NYC to total private and manufacturing and services employment, various years 1958-83.

b. Securities industry: professional salaries and bonuses, in and outside NYC, for 3 job categories (no date); and mean expenses per employee, aggregate for top 10 and 11-25 firms, and by type or size of firm, 1982-83.

c. Survey response on whether firm borrowed funds to finance business activities; percent change in office space requirements, and office space occupancy expenses; and mean revenues per employee; all by firm employment size, various periods 1980-83.

A8825–2 FOREIGN ACTIVITY: An Analysis of Foreign Participation in the U.S. Securities Markets
Quarterly. Approx. 10 p.
SRI/MF/complete

Quarterly report on foreign investor purchases and sales of U.S. Treasury and corporate securities. Includes analysis of activity by Canadian, European, Mideastern, Latin American, and Asian investors, with related domestic or international economic developments, and net purchases of foreign stocks by U.S. investors.

Data are current through quarter 3-4 months prior to cover date.

Contains narrative highlights and analysis sections, interspersed with 4 quarterly tables listed below; and, occasionally, additional tables presenting summary or trend data for topics covered in quarterly tables, and special analyses.

Quarterly tables appear in all issues. All other features with substantial statistical content not covered in quarterly tables are described, as they appear, under "Statistical Features." Nonstatistical features and summary or trend tables are not described.

Availability: Securities Industry Association, Research Department, 120 Broadway, New York NY 10271, members $30.00 per yr., nonmembers $48.00 per yr.; SRI/MF/complete.

Issues reviewed during 1985: Oct. 16, 1984-Oct. 24, 1985 (P) (Vol. VII, No. 4; Vol. VIII, Nos. 1-4).

QUARTERLY TABLES:

[Tables show data by world region and selected country. Data are generally for quarter of coverage and preceding quarter. Table sequence and titles may vary.]

I. Gross activity/transactions in and net purchases of U.S. equities.

II. Gross activity/transactions in and net purchases of U.S. corporate bonds.

III. Net foreign purchases and total foreign holdings of U.S. Treasury notes/bonds.

IV. Gross activity/transactions in and net purchases of foreign stocks by U.S. investors.

STATISTICAL FEATURE:

A8825–2.601: Feb. 6, 1985 (Vol. VIII, No. 1)

FOREIGN AND INSTITUTIONAL PARTICIPATION IN U.S. EQUITIES

(p. 3) Brief article, with 1 table showing net purchases of U.S. equities by mutual and pension funds, life and property/liability insurance companies, State/local retirement systems, and foreign investors, selected years 1970-83 and 1st 9 months 1984. Data are from Federal agencies.

A8825–5   SECURITIES INDUSTRY YEARBOOK, 1985-86
Annual. 1985. 637 p.
LC 81-2046.
SRI/MF/current report delayed, previous report complete

Annual report on securities industry firms and market activity in U.S. and Canada, 1984. Includes individual firm organization, financial position, and rankings; and aggregate industry finances and market activity, with selected data for previous years and for foreign transactions.

Data are from a survey of Securities Industry Assn (SIA) member firms, accounting for approximately 90% of North American securities industry business; and other industry sources.

Contents:

a. Contents listing. (p. 5-6)

b. Tabular rankings of securities firms in terms of capital, 1984-85, and in terms of number of offices, employees, and registered representatives, 1985, all as of Jan. 1. (p. 8-48)

c. Listings of firms by type of ownership, with value of stock outstanding for publicly traded firms as of Dec. 31, 1984. (p. 50-57)

d. Directory of SIA member firms, generally presenting the following information for each: personnel; number of offices and accounts; amounts of ownership equity and subordinated liabilities; net capital requirement; and number and value of underwriting and syndication issues, by type; as of Dec. 1984. (p. 60-606)

e. Listing of firms by State, Province, and city. (p. 607-614)

f. Industry composite and market statistics with 1 illustrative chart, and 4 charts and 17 tables listed below. (p. 616-628)

g. Directories of major exchanges and SIA personnel. (p. 630-637)

This is the 6th edition of the yearbook. The 5th edition, for 1984-85, was also reviewed by SRI during 1985, and is also available on SRI microfiche under A8825-5 [Annual. 1984. 604 p. Members $45.00, nonmembers $70.00 (prepaid)]. For description of the 4th edition, see SRI 1983 Annual under A8825-5.

Availability: Securities Industry Association, Attention: Yearbook Department, 120 Broadway, New York NY 10271, members $50.00, nonmembers $85.00 (prepaid); SRI/MF/current report complete, delayed shipment in Jan. 1986; previous report complete

TABLES AND CHARTS:

[1] Revenues and expenses of NYSE firms doing a public business [by major item, and firms with profits and losses], 1982-84. (p. 616-617)

[2-4] Securities firms average after-tax return on equity; number of NYSE member firms doing a public business (at year end); and number of NASD [National Assn of Securities Dealers] member firms; [1975-84]. [charts] (p. 618)

[5-8] Market activity: NYSE, regional stock exchanges, AMEX, and NASDAQ [annual share volume and value traded, average daily volume, and average price, 1971-84; and number of listed companies for NYSE and AMEX, and number of NASDAQ quoted securities, 1976-84]. (p. 619-620)

[9-10] Performance indices [for NYSE common stocks, AMEX market value, NASDAQ composite, Dow-Jones industrial average, and Standard & Poor's and value line composite indexes], year end 1971-84. (p. 621-622)

[11] Options activity, number and value of contracts traded [by exchange], 1980-84. (p. 622)

[12] New issue information [value and number of corporate and municipal issues by type], 1983-84. (p. 623)

[13] Initial public offerings [value and number of issues], 1979-84. (p. 623)

[14] Interest rates, yields and P/E [price/earnings] ratios [including bank prime rate, money and capital market rates, State and local notes/bonds, corporate bonds, dividend/price ratio, and Dow-Jones average P/E ratio]; 1980-84 averages. (p. 624)

[15-16] Customer financing [regulated margin credit, 1975-84; and margin requirements and effective date for stock [selected dates 1968-74]. [1 chart and 1 table] (p. 625)

[17-20] Selected foreign information: discount rate of foreign central banks, and foreign exchange rate, [by country], 1982-84; and [gross activity and net purchases for] foreign transactions in U.S. equities, and U.S. transactions in foreign stocks, [by world region], 1983-84. (p. 626-627)

[21] Economic indicators [including ratio of investment to GNP, savings rate, CPI, unemployment rate, and GNP], 1975-84. (p. 628)

A8900
Shipbuilders
Council of America

A8900–2   STATISTICAL QUARTERLY
Quarterly, discontinued.

Quarterly report on civilian and naval shipyard employment, and civilian shipyard hours and earnings, discontinued with 4th quarter 1983 report (for description, see SRI 1984 Annual under this number).

Issuing agency has discontinued report in favor of *Shipbuilders Council of America Statistical Summary;* for description, see A8900-4 below.

A8900–4   SHIPBUILDERS COUNCIL OF AMERICA STATISTICAL SUMMARY
Annual. Jan. 1985. 19 p.
SRI/MF/complete

Annual report on U.S. shipbuilding activity, including merchant and naval vessel construction, orders, and deliveries, 1950s-85 with selected earlier trends. Also includes data on industry employment and earnings, offshore oil rig construction, world fleets by country, and steel shipments.

Data are from Shipbuilders Council, BLS, U.S. Maritime Administration, and other sources.

Contains listing of charts and tables (1 p.); and 7 trend charts, and 16 tables listed below (p. 1-19).

This is the 1st edition of the annual statistical summary. Similar statistics previously were presented in *Annual Report, Shipbuilders Council of America;* for description, see SRI 1983 Annual under A8900-3. Because the *Annual Report* no longer contains statistics, SRI coverage has been discontinued.

Availability: Shipbuilders Council of America, 1110 Vermont Ave., NW, Suite 1250, Washington DC 20005-3553, †; SRI/MF/complete.

TABLES:

CONSTRUCTION, ORDERS, AND DELIVERIES

[Tables [1-6] show number and total tonnage of ships weighing 1,000 tons/over or with 1,000 light displacement tons/over, for U.S. private shipyards.]

[1-2] New merchant type and naval vessels under construction/on order [by type of vessel, Jan. 1981-85]. (p. 4-5)

[3-4] New merchant type vessel contracts and [deliveries, by type of contract (construction subsidy, government account, U.S. flag no subsidy, and foreign registry), 1953-84]. (p. 6-7)

[5-6] Naval combatant and auxiliary vessels contracted for and delivered [including number of shipyards and initial contract values, 1960-84]. (p. 8-9)

[7] Offshore mobile oil rigs under construction/on order [U.S. and foreign, by rig type, Jan. 1980-85]. (p. 10)

EMPLOYMENT, EARNINGS, AND PRICE INDEXES

[8] Naval shipyard employment [total and for selected groupings of shipyards, annually 1968-83 and monthly 1983-July 1984]. (p. 11)

[9] Prevailing wages of [workers by position and grade, by naval shipyard, as of June-Sept. 1984]. (p. 12)

[10] BLS average hours and earnings for [total private, durable goods, and shipbuilding/repair] industries [annually 1974-83 and monthly 1983-July 1984]. (p. 13)

[11-12] CPI (large cities), and material index for NAVSEA [Naval Sea Systems Command] steel vessel contracts, [monthly 1978-Oct. 1984]. (p. 14)

[13] Index of straight-time average hourly earnings [aggregate] for selected shipyards, all regions, [monthly 1979-Sept. 1984]. (p. 15)

WORLD FLEET AND STEEL SHIPMENTS

[14-15] Merchant ships on order in world, and fleets of the world [number and/or tonnage of ships, by country, various periods 1964-84]. (p. 17-18)

[16] Annual shipments of finished steel to all U.S. industry and to shipbuilding/marine equipment industry [1945-84]. (p. 19)

A8902
Silver Institute

A8902-1   MINE PRODUCTION OF SILVER IN 1983 with Projections for 1984-87
Annual.   Nov. 1984.   10 p.
SRI/MF/complete

Annual report on silver mine production, worldwide and by country, 1983, with projections to 1987. Presents data for 49 designated International Trade Countries arranged by production size group, and for 9 Communist countries, all ranked by actual 1983 production.

Data are from U.S. Bureau of Mines, foreign government depts, and 246 mining enterprises headquartered in 27 countries.

Contains brief narrative (p. 1); 1 table (p. 2-3); and list of participating companies (p. 4-10).

Availability: Silver Institute, Suite 1138, 1001 Connecticut Ave., NW, Washington DC 20036, †; SRI/MF/complete.

A8902-2   MODERN SILVER COINAGE, 1984
Annual.   [1985.]   43 p.
ISSN 0149-7707.
LC 78-640559.
SRI/MF/complete, delayed

Annual report on silver coins issued as money in 77 world areas of origin, 1984. Includes number, silver content, and physical characteristics of coins, for 262 coin issues grouped by area of origin. Also includes mint where coins were struck, total silver used, and total face value of coins in local currency, for each area.

Data are from ministries of finance, central banks, government and private mints, and numismatic experts.

Contains introduction (p. 1); 1 summary table (p. 2-3); 1 detailed table repeated for each area (p. 4-41); and list of mints issuing coins in 1984 (p. 42-43).

This is the 13th annual edition.

Availability: Silver Institute, 1001 Connecticut Ave., Suite 1138, Washington DC 20036, $15.00; SRI/MF/complete, delayed shipment in Apr. 1986.

A8902-3   SILVER INSTITUTE LETTER: Information on Silver for Industry
Bimonthly.   Approx. 4 p.
ISSN 0730-8132.   LC 82-717.
SRI/MF/complete

Bimonthly newsletter reporting on worldwide refined silver production, disposition, and stocks; uses of silver; and Silver Institute activities. Data are from reports of approximately 50 silver refineries to the institute.

Contents:

a. Brief articles, occasionally with substantial statistics; and a recurring table on industrial silver consumption in Japan.

b. 2 bimonthly tables showing "999" silver production by source (primary ores/concentrates, coins, and old and new scrap), disposition (converted in plant, and shipped out), and stocks, for U.S. and foreign refiners.

Bimonthly data are shown for month 1-2 months prior to publication date, previous 1-3 months and years, and current and previous years to date. Foreign data are aggregated for all known refiners in Australia, Canada, Mexico, Peru, South Africa, Sweden, and West Germany, and some other refiners in Europe and Asia.

Bimonthly tables appear in all issues. All additional features with substantial statistical content are described, as they appear, under "Statistical Features." Nonstatistical features are not covered.

Availability: Silver Institute, 1001 Connecticut Ave., NW, Suite 1138, Washington DC 20036, †; SRI/MF/complete.

Issues reviewed during 1985: Dec. 1984-Oct. 1985 (P) (Vol. XIV, No. 6; Vol. XV, Nos. 1-5).

STATISTICAL FEATURES:

A8902-3.601: Dec. 1984 (Vol. XIV, No. 6)

MINERS PROVIDE NEEDED SILVER, ANNUAL FEATURE

(p. 2) Annual article, with 1 table showing scheduled silver mine production, for 8 countries and rest of world, 1984. Data are from the Silver Institute's *Mine Production of Silver, 1983-87.*

JAPAN USES MORE SILVER, RECURRING FEATURE

(p. 4) Recurring table showing Japanese average monthly silver consumption, 1983 and 1st 9 months 1984. Data are from Japan Mining Assn.

A8902-3.602: Apr. 1985 (Vol. XV, No. 2)

TRANSLATION OF MONEY

Article, with 1 table showing silver price per troy ounce in currencies of 34 countries, Jan. 2, 1985 and Apr. 1, 1985.

A8912
Society of Exploration Geophysicists

A8912-1   MONTHLY SEISMIC CREW COUNT
Monthly.   2 p.
SRI/MF/complete, shipped quarterly

Monthly press release on number of seismic land crews and marine vessels exploring for oil/gas in the U.S. and Canada. Data are compiled by the Society of Exploration Geophysicists and are issued approximately 2 weeks after month of coverage.

Contains brief narrative summary; 3 charts with trends from as early as the 1930s; and 2 tables showing number of seismic crews and vessels, and number of sponsors, all by type of sponsor (contractors, oil companies, and/or government), for current and previous month, with U.S. trends for 6 previous years.

Availability: Society of Exploration Geophysicists, Headquarters Office, PO Box 702740, Tulsa OK 74170-2740, †; SRI/MF/complete, shipped quarterly.

Issues reviewed during 1985: Oct. 1984-Sept. 1985 (D).

A8912-2   INTERNATIONAL SEISMIC CREW COUNT
Quarterly.   2 p.
SRI/MF/complete

Quarterly press release on seismic land crews and marine vessels exploring for oil/gas, by world area or country. Data are compiled by the Society of Exploration Geophysicists, and are issued approximately 5 months after quarter of coverage.

Contains brief summary, with 1 trend chart; and 2 tables showing number of seismic crews and vessels, and number of sponsors, all by type of sponsor (contractors, oil companies, and governments), in U.S., Canada, Mexico, Central/South America, Europe, Middle East, Africa, and Far East, for last month of current and previous quarters.

Availability: Society of Exploration Geophysicists, Headquarters Office, PO Box 702740, Tulsa OK 74170-2740, †; SRI/MF/complete.

Issues reviewed during 1985: 2nd Qtr. 1984-1st Qtr. 1985 (D).

A8912-3   SPECIAL REPORT: GEOPHYSICAL ACTIVITY IN 1984
Annual.   Oct. 1985.
p. 33-54.
ISSN 0016-8030.
LC 60-37909.
SRI/MF/complete

Annual report, by Gerald E. Montgomery, on geophysical exploration activity for energy resources, research, and other purposes in the non-Communist world, 1984. Includes data on costs, miles surveyed, survey methods, and crew months, by world area.

Data are compiled by the Geophysical Activity Committee from questionnaires sent to more than 500 institutions and companies.

Contains narrative, 7 charts, and 19 tables listed below.

Report is reprinted from the October 1985 issue (Vol. 4, No. 10) of *Geophysics: The Leading Edge of Exploration,* and is paginated from that issue.

Availability: Society of Exploration Geophysicists, Headquarters Office, PO Box 702740, Tulsa OK 74170-2740, $3.00; SRI/MF/complete.

TABLES:

[Tables show data for 1984. Expenditure data are shown in U.S. dollars. Data by area are for 6 world areas, U.S., Canada, and Mexico.

Survey objectives generally include petroleum, minerals, engineering, geothermal, groundwater, oceanography, and research. Survey types include land, marine, airborne, and drill hole.

Seismic and other exploration activities include acquisition cost, line-miles, crew-months, and various operating ratios.]

1-2. Total worldwide expenditures by survey type and area, by survey objective. (p. 33-35)

3-6. Worldwide petroleum land and marine seismic activity, and seismic line-miles by energy source [including dynamite, all by area]. (p. 36-38)

7. Worldwide average unit costs [and exploration activities] for petroleum surveys [by area, survey type, and method]. (p. 39-43)

8-10. Petroleum seismic [land and marine] activity [in U.S. and Canada by State, Province, and offshore region; and in Mexico]. (p. 44-45)

11-12. Total worldwide expenditures on gravity/magnetic and airborne surveys [by survey objective and area]. (p. 45-46)

13A-14B. Western and Eastern Hemisphere airborne and land mining activity [by survey method]. (p. 46-47)

15-16. Worldwide groundwater/engineering and geothermal activity [by survey method]. (p. 48)

17. Worldwide average unit costs [and exploration activity], by survey objective, type, and method. (p. 49-54)

A8916
Society of Industrial Realtors

A8916-1   INDUSTRIAL REAL ESTATE MARKET SURVEY
Semiannual.
Spring/Summer 1985.
viii+236 p.
ISSN 0730-0131.
LC 81-649990.
SRI/MF/complete, Fall/Winter 1984 & Spring/Summer 1985 reports

Semiannual survey report, for spring/summer 1985, on industrial real estate market conditions and outlook, including sales, construction costs, prices, and financing, by region and metro area. Also includes data for Canada, UK, and France. Based on a spring 1985 survey of 146 specialists in 99 metro areas.

Contains user's guide, glossary, contents listing, and list of survey participants (p. iii-viii); national analysis, with 9 summary tables and charts (p. 1-7); 9 basic tables listed below, repeated for 92 U.S. and 3 Canadian cities or metro market areas grouped by region (each regional section also includes 5 summary charts), and 1 English city and 3 French cities (p. 10-231); and questionnaire facsimile (p. 234-236).

This is the 11th semiannual survey. Previous report, for fall/winter 1984, was also reviewed in 1985 and is also available on SRI microfiche under this number [Semiannual. Fall/Winter 1984. viii+234 p. $50.00].

Availability: Society of Industrial Realtors, 777 14th St., NW, Washington DC 20005, $50.00 per yr.; SRI/MF/complete.

BASIC TABLES:

[The following tables are repeated for 17 northeastern metro areas, and 1 Canadian city (p. 10-47); 17 central Great Lakes metro areas, and 2 Canadian cities (p. 50-89); 26 southern metro areas (p. 92-145); 8 southwestern and 9 mid-continent metro areas (p. 148-187); 15 western metro areas (p. 190-221); and 1 English and 3 French cities (p. 224-231).

Data by category are shown for manufacturing, warehousing/distribution, and high technology.]

[1] Industrial market characteristics [square footage of available space and area vacant, for central city and suburbs].

[2] Dollar volume of sales and leases compared to a year ago [by category].

[3] Gross sales and lease prices of prime industrial buildings and sites [price per square foot, and change from previous year, for central city and suburbs].

[4] Rate of new construction compared to a year ago [by category].

[5] Construction cost of prime industrial buildings [cost per square foot, and change from previous year].

[6] Vacancy situation [and average shelf life] for prime industrial properties [by property size].

[7] Composition of absorption [of available space, by category; and inside and outside industrial parks].

[8] Mortgage financing for industrial properties [most important source, most prevalent interest rates, and money supply availability].

[9] Outlook for industrial real estate activity for next 12 months [sales and lease prices and dollar volume, construction costs, and absorption].

A8920
Society of the Plastics Industry

A8920-1   FACTS AND FIGURES OF THE U.S. PLASTICS INDUSTRY, 1985 Edition
Annual.   Sept. 1985.
3+127 p.
ISSN 0740-8420.
LC sc83-8335.
SRI/MF/complete

Annual report, for 1985, on the plastics industry, covering production, sales, markets, and foreign trade, by resin type; and industry financial and operating characteristics. Includes data by company. Most data are for 1984, with some forecasts for 1985 and trends from 1980 or earlier.

Data sources, identified for each table, include monthly statistical reports of the SPI compiled by Ernst & Whinney from company surveys, other SPI reports, and government and private sources.

Contains contents listing (2 p.); report, with 52 charts and 115 tables, interspersed with narrative (p. 1-125); and list of other sources of information (p. 126-127).

All tables are listed below. Most charts illustrate or provide long-term trends for data contained in tables; however, 1 chart (p. 20) shows plastics processing industry hourly wage index, 1968-84.

Availability: Society of the Plastics Industry, Statistical Department, 355 Lexington Ave., New York NY 10017, members $55.00, nonmembers $110.00; SRI/MF/complete.

TABLES:

[Data "by major market" are generally shown for transportation, packaging, building/construction, electrical/electronic, furniture/furnishings, consumer/institutional, industrial/machinery, adhesives/inks/coatings, exports, and other.]

A8920-1.1: Industry Overview

TRENDS

[1] Introduction of plastics resins [with date and example of use, selected years 1868-1983]. (p. 3)

[2-3] 1984 in review: production and sales/captive use [by resin]; and distribution of sales/captive use, by major market; [1983-84]. (p. 4)

[4-5] Total U.S. production and sales/captive use of plastics resin [total and by resin, various years 1959-84]. (p. 5-7)

[6] Plastics resins domestic merchant sales [quantity and value by resin, 1983-84]. (p. 9)

[7] Apparent U.S. consumption of selected plastics resins [also showing production, imports, and exports, by resin for 1984, and totals for 1976-83]. (p. 10)

[8] Plastics materials/resins: value of shipments [compared to other chemical categories and other commodities, 1980-84]. (p. 11)

[9-10] Plastics materials/resins (SIC 2821) and miscellaneous products (SIC 3079): [shipment value, employment, production workers and earnings, and trade, 1980-85, with trend from 1972]. (p. 12)

GENERAL ECONOMIC STATISTICS

[11] Commodity, balance of trade [for plastics/resins and 6 other commodity categories, 1980-84]. (p. 14)

[12] PPI [for plastics resins/materials and 5 other commodity groups, 1968-84]. (p. 17)

[13] Profile of 50 biggest [SIC 4-digit] manufacturing industries [ranked by value of shipments, and including number of plants, 1984]. (p. 18)

[14] [Plastics, chemicals, and total] sales of major plastics producing companies [1983-84, with company rankings by plastics sales for 1984]. (p. 21)

[15] Top 10 States of the plastics industry [ranked by establishments, employment, value of shipments, new capital expenditures, and payroll], 1982. (p. 23)

[16] Plastic processing industry: [detailed financial and operating ratios] by sales group, 1984. (p. 24-25)

FEEDSTOCKS AND ADDITIVES

[17-19] Plastics derived from major feedstocks [1983-84]; plastics consumption of feedstocks, 1984; and selected plastics precursors [1983-84; showing total feedstock or precursor production and portion used to manufacture plastics]. (p. 28)

[20] Consumption of additives [by type, 1980-84]. (p. 30)

A8920–1.2: Individual Resins

[Most data are shown for 1980-84, with selected trends from 1973. Tables [1-18], [25-28], [33-38], and [42-71] generally include the following data for the individual resins noted: production and sales/captive use, share of total plastics sales/captive use, domestic consumption by end use, and distribution by major market.

Lists of companies providing data are included for most resin types.]

THERMOSETTING RESINS

[1-18] Epoxy, phenolic, unsaturated polyester, urea, and melamine. (p. 37-47)

[19] Miscellaneous thermosets [production and sales, by resin]. (p. 49)

[20-21] Polyurethane foam: distribution of sales/use by major market; and domestic sales/captive use [by end use; all for flexible/semi-flexible and rigid foam]. (p. 50)

[22-24] Isocyanates, polyether polyols, and polyester polyols [production and sales/captive use]. (p. 51)

THERMOPLASTIC RESINS

[Tables [33-38] and [42-71] include capacity utilization rates, 1974-83; and manufacturing capacity estimates, by company, as of Dec. 31, 1983-84.]

[25-28] ABS [acrylonitrile-butadiene-styrene] and SAN [styrene-acrylonitrile]. (p. 53-54)

[29-31] Engineering thermoplastic resins [types manufactured, by company; production and sales/captive use; and distribution of major market]. (p. 57)

[32] Sales of fluoropolymer resins (granular type only). (p. 58)

[33-38] High density polyethylene. (p. 60-61)

[39-41] Latex materials [production distribution by product type and end use; and production, and sales/captive use by end use, for styrene butadiene/other styrene based latexes]. (p. 63)

[42-71] Low density polyethylene, nylon, polypropylene, polystyrene, and polyvinyl chloride. (p. 64-77)

[72] Polyvinyl acetate [sales/captive use of vinyl acetate monomer for polyvinyl acetate, by end use]. (p. 79)

[73] Polyvinyl alcohol [production, and domestic and export sales/captive use]. (p. 79)

[74] Other vinyl resins [production and sales/captive use]. (p. 80)

[75] Miscellaneous thermoplastics [production and sales, by type of resin]. (p. 80)

[76] Domestic sales/use of selected thermoplastics, by process grade. (p. 81-82)

A8920–1.3: Products, Markets, and Machinery

[Data are for 1980-84, unless otherwise noted.]

FABRICATED PLASTIC PRODUCTS

[1] Reinforced plastics shipments, by market [1980-85]. (p. 85)

[2-6] Shipments of thermoplastic pipe/tube/conduit and plastic fittings, by material and application. (p. 86-88)

[7-8] Plastic bottles: production [by end-use market and material, 1979-83]. (p. 89)

[9-11] Plumbing fixtures: production [of lavatories, bathtubs, and shower stalls, by material (plastics vs. metals and vitreous china), 1979-83]. (p. 90)

[12] PPI [for 30] plastics products [Dec. 1984 and percent change from 1983]. (p. 91)

MAJOR MARKETS

[13-15] Comparison of 1984 data to prior years: 5-year comparison of resin [unit] sales/use, and comparative percentage distribution [1980-84]; and percentage change in sales/use [selected periods 1979-84; all] by major market. (p. 95-96)

[16] 1984 distribution of plastic resin sales/use (captive), by major market [with detail by product category, by resin type]. (p. 114-117)

MACHINERY

[17-19] Dollar sales of plastics machinery [by type]; and shipments of single screw extrusion machinery, and of injection molding machinery [domestic and export]. (p. 124-125)

A8920–2 1984 ANNUAL LABOR SURVEY, Plastics Processing Companies
Annual. Jan. 15, 1985.
42 p.
SRI/MF/complete

Annual survey report on the plastics processing industry work force, 1984. Includes data on union representation, compensation practices, benefits, hours, turnover, and employment and wages by occupation. Data are generally shown by region and include selected comparisons to 1983.

Data are based on responses of 275 companies, employing approximately 25,400 workers, to a Sept. 1984 survey.

Contains contents listing (1 p.); highlights and 23 tables (p. 1-27); and list of participants, job classifications, and questionnaire facsimile (p. 28-42).

This is the 46th edition of the report.

Availability: Society of the Plastics Industry, Statistical Department, 355 Lexington Ave., New York NY 10017, members $50.00, non-members $100.00; SRI/MF/complete.

A8920–3 SALARY AND SALES POLICY SURVEY NO. 14, 1984, Plastics Processing Companies
Biennial. May 17, 1985.
ii+56 p.
SRI/MF/complete

Biennial report, for 1984, on plastics processing industry salaries for managers, supervisors, salespersons, and engineers, and policies pertaining to sales personnel and manufacturer's representatives.

Includes lowest, highest, and median salaries, and average number of persons supervised, for 34 positions. Data are shown for plants by census region and for all division offices, arranged by company sales size group, and include median salary comparisons to 1982 and summary trends from 1976.

Also includes data on type of sales force used; salesperson turnover rate; and company policies concerning salesperson compensation, selling costs, moving expenses, auto ownership and expense allowances, and manufacturer's representative contracts and commissions; all by company sales size group.

Data are from a survey of 197 plastics processing companies operating 249 plants and 27 division offices. Report is intended to enable individual companies to compare their salaries with industry medians.

Contains contents listing and table index (3 p.); highlights, with 6 tables (p. 1-4); salary section, with 1 table repeated for each sales size group (p. 5-34); sales policy and manufacturer's representative sections, with 20 tables (p. 35-44); and listing of participants, questionnaire facsimile, and job descriptions (p. 45-56).

Previous report, for 1982, is described in SRI 1983 Annual, under this number.

Availability: Society of the Plastics Industry, Statistical Department, 355 Lexington Ave., New York NY 10017, members $75.00, non-members $150.00; SRI/MF/complete.

A8920–4 FINANCIAL AND OPERATING RATIOS, Survey No. 23, 1984: Plastics Processing Companies
Annual. June 30, 1985.
3+vi+35 p. Survey No. 23.
SRI/MF/complete

Annual report presenting plastics processing industry financial and operating ratios, 1984. Data are from survey responses of 188 companies. Report is intended to enable individual companies to compare their performance with industry medians.

Includes itemized operating statement and balance sheet ratios, productivity and other ratios, and percent change in sales compared to 1983, generally shown by major type of processing activity, sales size class, and profitability level (more, less, or median).

Contains contents and table listings (1 p.); summary highlights, with 18 charts and 6 tables on respondent characteristics (p. i-vi); 3 extended survey result tables (p. 1-21); definitions (p. 22-23); list of survey participants (p. 24-27); and questionnaire facsimiles (p. 29-36).

Availability: Society of the Plastics Industry, Literature Sales Department, 355 Lexington Ave., New York NY 10017, members $50.00, nonmembers $100.00; SRI/MF/complete.

A8920–5   MONTHLY STATISTICAL REPORT, RESINS: Production and Sales, and Captive Use of Thermosetting and Thermoplastic Resins
Monthly, with quarterly and annual summaries.   11 p.
SRI/MF/complete, shipped quarterly

Monthly report, with quarterly and annual summaries, on plastic resin production, sales/captive use, and foreign trade, by detailed resin type and/or end use, mostly for month of coverage, year to date, and same periods of previous year.

Data are based on information from approximately 110 companies, and are compiled by Ernst and Whinney, Inc., for the SPI Committee on Resin Statistics. Report is issued approximately 3 months after period of coverage.

Monthly issues contain 1 summary trend chart and 4 tables. Issues also occasionally include a tabular list of reporting companies showing types of resins produced by each company.

Annual summary presents all report data by month for the full calendar year. Quarterly summaries contain 1 table showing domestic polyester resin summary data for quarter of coverage, year to date, and same periods of previous years; and, occasionally, revised data for previous periods. Summary for 4th quarter also includes quarterly data by month for the full year.

Availability: Ernst and Whinney, Trade Association Service Department, 153 E. 53rd St., New York NY 10022, members $300.00 per yr., nonmembers $400.00 per yr.; SRI/MF/complete, shipped quarterly.

Issues reviewed during 1985: Monthly Reports: Sept. 1984-Aug. 1985 (D) (1984 Nos. 9-12; 1985 Nos. 1-8).

Issues reviewed during 1985: Quarterly Summaries: 1st Qtr. 1984-2nd Qtr. 1985 (D).

Issues reviewed during 1985: Annual Summary: calendar year 1984 (D).

A8920–6   MONTHLY STATISTICAL REPORT, PIPE AND FITTINGS: Shipments of Thermoplastics Pipe, Tube, Conduit and Fittings
Monthly, with annual summary.   Approx. 12 p.
SRI/MF/complete, shipped quarterly

Monthly report, with annual summary, on thermoplastic pipe/tube/conduit and fittings shipment volume, by type of material and application, for month of coverage, year to date, and same periods of previous year. Also includes shipment value for fittings.

Data are compiled from approximately 80 companies by Ernst and Whinney, Inc., for the SPI Committee on Resin Statistics. Reports are issued approximately 2 months after month of coverage.

Contains 6 tables, and usually a tabular list of reporting companies showing types of products manufactured by each company.

Annual summary accompanies the Jan. issue and presents monthly data for the year.

Report is discontinued with issue presenting May 1985 data.

Availability: Ernst and Whinney, Trade Association Service Department, 153 E. 53rd St., New York NY 10022, members $50.00 per yr., nonmembers $100.00 per yr.; SRI/MF/complete, shipped quarterly.

Issues reviewed during 1985: Sept. 1984-May 1985; and annual summary for 1984 (D).

A8930
Society of Women Engineers

A8930–1   PROFILE OF THE WOMAN ENGINEER
Biennial.   1985.   13 p.
SRI/MF/complete

Biennial survey report on educational, employment, and personal characteristics of women engineers, 1983. Includes data on degree field, type of employer, job functions, supervisory responsibilities, salaries (by field and years since bachelor's degree), marital status, and region of residence.

Data are from responses of 2,112 SWE nonstudent female members to a survey conducted winter 1983/84.

Contains contents listing (p. 2); introduction and summary (p. 3); narrative report, with text data, 1 map, 9 charts, and 2 tables (p. 4-10); and facsimile of survey questionnaire (p. 11-13).

This is the 5th biennial edition of the report. For description of 1981 survey, see SRI 1983 Annual under this number.

Availability: Society of Women Engineers, United Engineering Center, 345 E. 47th St., Rm. 305, New York NY 10017, members $5.00, nonmembers $10.00; SRI/MF/complete.

A8945
Southern
Regional Education Board

A8945–6   STATE AND LOCAL TAX PERFORMANCE
Annual, discontinued.

Annual report analyzing State/local government use of taxing ability, discontinued with 1981 report (for description, see SRI 1983 Annual under this number).

A8945–8   HIGHER EDUCATION ENROLLMENT, 1982: Trends in the Nation and the South
Biennial.   1984.   iii+71 p.
SRI/MF/complete

Biennial report, by Joseph L. Marks, on black and Hispanic enrollment in higher education institutions, for 14 southern States and U.S., 1982, with trends from 1976 and comparisons to total or white enrollment. Includes data by attendance status (full- and part-time); degree level (undergraduate, graduate, and 1st-time professional); sex; and type of institution (public and private 2-year, 4-year, and predominantly black).

Also includes total enrollment for individual predominantly black and predominantly Hispanic institutions.

Data are from SREB tabulations of NCES data tapes for Higher Education General Information Surveys (HEGIS).

Contains contents listing (p. iii); brief narrative, with 10 charts and 15 summary tables (p. 2-22); 6 detailed tables, (p. 24-63); and 2 appendix tables (p. 65-71).

Report has been published biennially since 1978. For description of 1978 report, see SRI 1980 Annual under A8945-7. Report for 1980 was not received for coverage in SRI.

Availability: Southern Regional Education Board, 1340 Spring St., NW, Atlanta GA 30309, $6.00; SRI/MF/complete.

A8945–9   ANALYSIS OF TRANSCRIPTS OF TEACHERS AND ARTS AND SCIENCES GRADUATES
Monograph.   1985.
vi+108 p.
SRI/MF/complete

By Eva C. Galambos et al. Report analyzing college coursework of 1982/83 teacher education graduates of southern colleges. Presents detailed data on courses taken by graduates eligible for State teacher certification, with comparisons to arts/science graduates not eligible for teacher certification.

Data are based on a study of 6,043 transcripts from 17 colleges in 14 SREB States. Report also includes summary comparisons to a 1961 study of teacher coursework.

Contains contents and table listings (p. iii-vi); 8 chapters, with narrative analysis and 36 tables (p. 1-91); and 14 appendices, including list of participating institutions, methodology, transcript study facsimiles, and 6 tables (p. 93-108).

Issuing agency has also published the following related reports, not covered in SRI: *Teacher Preparation: The Anatomy of a College Degree,* a summary of study results; and *Improving Teacher Education: An Agenda for Higher Education and the Schools,* a companion nonstatistical report.

Availability: Southern Regional Education Board, 1340 Spring St., NW, Atlanta GA 30309, $6.50; SRI/MF/complete.

A8955
Spain-U.S. Chamber of Commerce

A8955–1   SPAIN-U.S. TRADE BULLETIN
Bimonthly.   Approx. 35 p.
ISSN 0561-5313.
SRI/MF/complete

Bimonthly journal promoting U.S./Spanish trade relations. Includes reporting on business activities, recent legislation, trade regulations, tourism, and areas of investment opportunity in both countries. Some articles are in Spanish.

Data are from U.S. Dept of Commerce, the Spanish Ministry of Commerce and Tourism, and other sources.

General format:

a. Feature articles and news brief sections, occasionally with statistics, including annual trade reviews; and bimonthly summary of recent Spanish legislation.

b. Bimonthly table on Spanish exports to U.S., for approximately 70 products grouped under 10 industry sectors, for current year through month 2-4 months prior to publication date, with change from previous year.

Bimonthly table appears in most issues. All additional features with substantial statistical content are described, as they appear, under "Statistical Features." Nonstatistical features are not covered.

Journal was published quarterly during Mar.-Dec. 1984.

Availability: Spain-U.S. Chamber of Commerce, 500 Fifth Ave., New York NY 10110, members †, others $25.00 per yr., single copy $5.00; SRI/MF/complete.

Issues reviewed during 1985: Oct./Nov./Dec. 1984-July/Aug. 1985 (P) (Nos. 135-139).

STATISTICAL FEATURES:

A8955–1.601: Oct./Nov./Dec. 1984 (No. 135)

SPANISH ECONOMY'S GROWTH EXCEEDS FORECASTS

(p. 10) Brief article, with 1 table showing value of Spanish exports, by country or trading market, 1st half 1984 and percent change from same period of 1983. Data are from Spain's commerce dept.

A8955–1.602: Jan./Feb. 1985 (No. 136)

NOTA SOBRE EL COMERCIO ENTRE ESPANA Y LOS ESTADOS UNIDOS DURANTE EL PRIMER SEMESTRE DE 1984, ANNUAL FEATURE

(p. 12-15) Annual article, by Maria Schaer, summarizing Spain-U.S. trade in the 1st half of 1984. Includes 6 tables showing total trade value, balance, and index (in pesetas); and trade value (in dollars) by commodity; 1st half 1979-84. Article is in Spanish.

A8955–1.603: May/June 1985 (No. 138)

SPAIN AND THE THIRD ENLARGEMENT OF THE EEC

(p. 5-12) By Francesc Granell. Article on the economic impact of Spain's admission to EC. Data are from OECD, Banco de Bilbao, and Spain Customs Dept. Includes 4 tables showing the following:

a. Imports, exports, and GDP per capita, 1983; and distribution of employment by sector (agriculture, industry, and services), 1960 and 1983; for Spain and 6-8 other industrialized countries.

b. Export distribution by commodity, 1964, 1975, and 1983; and value added and employment, by industry division, with value added detail by agricultural commodity and manufacturing industry group, 1981; for Spain.

A8965
Special Libraries Association

A8965–2 **SPECIAL LIBRARIES: SLA 1984 Salary Survey Update**
Quarterly (selected issue).
Oct. 1984. (p. 338-340).
Vol. 75, No. 4..
ISSN 0038-6723.
SRI/MF/excerpts

Annual article on salaries of special librarians in U.S. and Canada, 1984. Data are from responses of 1,389 SLA members to an Apr.-May 1984 survey. Includes 3 tables showing mean, median, and percentile salaries, by U.S. census division and for Canada, and aggregate for 4 job categories, as of Apr. 1984, with comparisons to 1983.

Data provide a partial update for detailed salary statistics presented in *SLA Triennial Salary Survey,* described in SRI 1984 Annual, under A8965-1.

Special Libraries is a primarily narrative periodical reporting on management, research, and other professional topics of interest to special librarians. Annual salary update is the only feature covered in SRI.

Availability: Special Libraries Association, Circulation Department, 235 Park Ave. S., New York NY 10003, members $12.00 per yr., nonmembers $36.00 per yr., single copy $9.00; SRI/MF/excerpts for annual survey article.

A8990
Steel Service Center Institute

A8990–1 **TOTAL MILL SHIPMENTS AND SHIPMENTS TO SERVICE CENTERS, 1926-83**
Recurring (irreg.) [1985.]
37 p.
SRI/MF/not filmed

Recurring report presenting detailed statistics on steel mill shipments (total and to service centers), by type of steel and product, 1920s-83. Data are compiled by American Iron and Steel Institute. Contains contents listing and 114 tables.

Previous report, with data through 1979, is described in SRI 1981 Annual under this number.

Availability: Steel Service Center Institute, 1600 Terminal Tower, Cleveland OH 44113-2229, ‡; SRI/MF/not filmed.

A8990–2 **BUSINESS CONDITIONS**
Monthly, in 2 parts.
8 p. no paging.
SRI/MF/not filmed

Monthly report, in 2 parts, on steel service center business conditions, including orders, shipments, inventories, work force, and dependence on foreign steel. (Service centers distribute steel products to manufacturers and fabricators.)

Data are from ongoing member surveys of the Steel Service Center Institute (SSCI) and the National Assn of Purchasing Management (NAPM) Steel Committee. The SSCI sample accounts for 30-40% of total industrial steel shipments.

Report is published in 2 parts, described below. Parts I and II are issued during the 1st and 3rd weeks of the month, respectively.

Part II is accompanied by a news release, not covered in SRI.

Availability: Steel Service Center Institute, 1600 Terminal Tower, Cleveland OH 44113-2229, ‡; SRI/MF/not filmed.

Issues reviewed during 1985: Part I: Nov. 6, 1984-Oct. 4, 1985 (P).

Issues reviewed during 1985: Part II: Nov. 19, 1984-Oct. 21, 1985 (P).

REPORT PARTS:
[Data are from SSCI member surveys, unless otherwise noted.]

PART I
[Most data are shown monthly for current year through month of publication, and previous year.]

a. General business conditions: expectations for general economy in next 3 months. 1 table.

b. Own business: shipment levels and customer payment promptness compared with 3 months ago; expected order levels in next 3 months; adequacy of current order levels; and whether work force is on short time/layoff. 5 tables.

c. Inventories: current inventory levels compared with 3 months ago; number of months inventory would cover current shipping levels; adequacy of current inventory levels; current receipts compared with shipments, and expected receipt and inventory levels and specific product shortages in next 3 months. 7 tables.

d. Foreign steel: foreign mills' prices compared with domestic prices, and activity in seeking U.S. business compared with 3 months ago; and expected dependence on foreign steel in next 6 months. 3 tables.

PART II
[Data are current to month prior to month of publication, unless otherwise noted.]

e. Tonnage shipments and inventories, for flat roll, stainless, and other steel, for 3 or more consecutive quarters through most current full quarter, and monthly for current year to date. 1 table.

f. NAPM survey: purchasing managers' expected steel order, backlog, and receipt levels in next 3 months, and inventory level in next 6 months; and number of months inventory would cover current shipping levels; monthly for current year through month of publication, and previous year. 5 tables.

g. Number of months' shipments on hand, and shipment and inventory summary trends, monthly for current year to date and 2 previous years. 1 chart and 1 table.

A9025
Teachers Insurance and Annuity Association

A9025–3   COLLEGE AND UNIVERSITY EMPLOYEE RETIREMENT AND INSURANCE BENEFITS COST SURVEY
Biennial.   1984.   50 p.
SRI/MF/complete

Biennial report on retirement and insurance program expenditures of higher education institutions, 1983 with trends from 1977.

Includes data on prevalence of benefits, and expenditures and payroll deductions per employee and/or as percent of payroll expense, variously cross-tabulated by benefit type, institution control (public and private) and type (university, liberal arts college, and other 4-year institution), census region, and enrollment size.

Benefit types include social security; unemployment and workers' compensation; public retirement systems; insured and noninsured pension plans; unfunded pension payments; and life, health care, travel accident, and long-term disability income insurance.

Data are based on 639 responses to a 1984 survey of degree-granting institutions with enrollment of 500 or more, and on 3 previous surveys.

Contains contents and table listings (p. 2-3); introduction and summary (p. 4-5); report with 4 charts and 26 tables (p. 6-46); and questionnaire facsimile (p. 47-50).

This is the 4th biennial survey report. SRI coverage begins with this edition.

Availability: Teachers Insurance and Annuity Association, Educational Research Division, 730 Third Ave., New York NY 10017, $4.50; SRI/MF/complete.

A9055
Television Bureau of Advertising

A9055–1   TV BASICS 28: The Television Bureau of Advertising's Report on the Scope and Dimensions of Television Today
Annual.   [1985.]
10 p. no paging.
SRI/MF/complete

Annual report on TV ownership, use, perceived credibility, and advertising expenditures, with comparisons to other media, various years 1950-85. Most data are compiled from private media research organizations.

Contains 23 tables showing the following data:

a. Color, multiset, and total TV homes, Jan. 1985; total and per home average daily viewing hours, 1984; daily viewing hours, by region and demographic characteristics, Feb. 1985; and UHF and VHF commercial TV stations, and total and summer daily viewing hours, various years 1950-84. 5 tables.

b. Advertisers and brands using network and spot TV, 1984; network and spot TV billings, and TV share of total billings, for top 10 ad-

vertising agencies ranked by total TV billings, 1984; and top 10 business categories ranked by expenditures on local TV advertising, 1983-84. 3 tables.

c. Percent of population reached by TV in an average day and week, Feb. 1982, and daily viewing hours, Feb. 1985, by sex, and for teenagers and children; and distribution of daily time spent with media, by media type, with detail for upper-income and college-educated adults, Jan. 1985. 2 tables.

d. Cable TV operating systems and subscribers, and percent of TV homes with cable, selected years 1960-85; weekly viewing of over-the-air, cable-originated, and pay cable programs, for homes with no cable, and with basic and pay cable, Feb. 1985; and total, national, and local advertising expenditures, by media, 1983-84. 5 tables.

e. Households with color TV (number, and percent of total TV households); color and monochrome TV set sales; advertising media judged most authoritative, exciting, influential, and believable; media judged source of most news; and distribution of network and non-network TV commercials by time length; various years 1959-85. 6 tables.

f. Local TV advertising expenditures; and distribution of commercials by day part, length, and month; for top 40 business categories ranked by local TV advertising expenditures, 1984. 1 table.

g. Network and spot TV advertising expenditures, for top 100 companies ranked by total TV advertising expenditures, 1984. 1 table.

Availability: Television Bureau of Advertising, ◆; SRI/MF/complete.

A9055–2   GNP, AD VOLUME, AND TV AD VOLUME, 1960-95
Recurring (irreg.)
Sept. 24, 1985.   3 p.
SRI/MF/complete, Feb., Aug., & Sept. 24, 1985 reports

Recurring report showing trends in total and TV advertising expenditures for 1960-95, with comparison to GNP. Data are from Commerce Dept and McCann-Erickson advertising agency, with estimates by TV Bureau of Advertising.

Contains 2 tables showing GNP, and value of all advertising and of network, spot, and local TV advertising, 1960-95; and value of syndication barter TV advertising, 1980-95.

Report is issued irregularly, as sufficient new data become available. Previous editions issued in Feb. and Aug. 1985 were also reviewed in SRI during 1985, and are also available on SRI microfiche under A9055-2 [Recurring (irreg.) Feb. and Aug. 1985. 3 p. ◆]. Prior to Aug. 1985 edition, report does not include data on syndication barter.

Availability: Television Bureau of Advertising, ◆; SRI/MF/complete.

A9055–3   ADVERTISING VOLUME IN THE U.S., 1948-84
Semiannual.   Aug. 1985.   6 p.
SRI/MF/complete, May & Aug. 1985 reports

Semiannual report on national and local advertising expenditures in 8 major media, 1948-84. Data are from McCann-Erickson, Inc.

Contains 1 table showing value of all advertising in newspapers; magazines; farm publications; network, spot, and local TV and radio; direct mail; business papers; outdoor; and miscellaneous; with national and local totals for selected media; 1948-84.

Previous report, issued in May 1985, was also reviewed by SRI in 1985, and is also available on SRI microfiche under A9055-3 [Semiannual. May 1985. 6 p. ◆].

Availability: Television Bureau of Advertising, ◆; SRI/MF/complete.

A9055–4   TRENDS IN TELEVISION, 1950 to Date
Annual.   Apr. 1985.   13 p.
SRI/MF/complete

Annual report on trends in TV ownership, usage, advertising expenditures, and stations, various years 1950-85. Most data are from media research organizations.

Contains contents and table listing (p. 1); and 12 tables, listed below (p. 2-13).

Availability: Television Bureau of Advertising, ◆; SRI/MF/complete.

TABLES:

[1-2] TV households [and total households]; and multi-set and color TV households [1950-85]. (p. 2-3)

[3] TV sets [in home, and average number per household and per multi-set household, 1950-85]. (p. 4)

[4] Time spent viewing, per TV home, per day [1950-84]. (p. 5)

[5] TV set sales (domestic/imports) [monochrome and color, 1950-85]. (p. 6)

[6] Commercial [UHF and VHF] TV stations [1950-85]. (p. 7)

[7-8] Advertising [dollar] volume in the U.S. [total and TV]; and TV advertising [dollar] volume [network, spot, and local; 1950-85]. (p. 8-9)

[9] Station time sales [network compensation, spot, and local, 1950-84]. (p. 10)

[10-11] Non-network and network TV commercial activity, by length of commercial [1965-84]. (p. 11-12)

[12] Number of advertisers and brands using [spot and network] TV [1970-84]. (p. 13)

A9055–5   CABLE FACTS
Recurring (irreg.)   May 1985.
21 p.
SRI/MF/complete, current & previous year reports

Recurring report on cable TV industry market developments and advertising revenues, various periods 1980-85, with some trends from 1952 and projections to 1994.

Presents data on number of operating systems and subscribers, with selected detail by subscription size category, channel capacity, and whether local advertising accepted; and cable and pay TV market penetration and households, with detail by market size and for major metro areas and cable networks.

Also includes data on advertising revenues for total and cable TV and for 4 cable networks; household viewing time for cable (with detail by network), pay, network, independent, and public

TV; top 10 cable advertisers ranked by expenditures, with comparison to expenditures for network and spot TV; cable TV and related industry mergers and suspensions; and network TV prime time audience.

Data are from A. C. Nielsen Co., Arbitron Co., Broadcast Advertisers Reports, and other industry sources.

Contains contents listing (p. 1); and 22 tables interspersed with brief narrative (p. 2-21).

Previous report, issued in Aug. 1984, was also reviewed in SRI during 1985, and is also available on SRI microfiche under A9055-5 [Semiannual. Aug. 1984. 20 p. ◆]. Note that SRI designated periodicity as semiannual in the Aug. 1984 edition.

Report has been issued since 1983. Report is issued 1-3 times per year, as sufficient new data become available. SRI coverage begins with the Aug. 1984 edition.

Availability: Television Bureau of Advertising, ◆; SRI/MF/complete.

A9055–6   TRENDS IN MEDIA: Audience, Costs, CPM's
Recurring (irreg.)   Aug. 1985.
12 p.
SRI/MF/complete, Feb. &
Aug. 1985 reports

Recurring report on trends in media advertising costs and viewership or circulation, various years 1950-85. Data are shown for network and spot TV, by day-part, in all markets or aggregate top 100 markets; for aggregate top 50 magazines in advertising revenues; and for daily newspapers.

Also includes advertising share of content in daily/Sunday newspapers.

Data are from A. C. Nielsen Co., TV Bureau of Advertising, Magazine Publishers Assn, Inc., *Editor and Publisher's International Yearbook,* and other sources.

Contains contents listing (p. 1); and 11 tables (p. 2-12).

Previous report, issued in Feb. 1985, was also reviewed by SRI during 1985, and is also available on SRI microfiche under A9055-6 [Annual. Feb. 1985. 12 p. ◆]. Note that SRI designated periodicity as annual in the Feb. 1985 edition.

Report has been published since 1982. Report usually is issued 1-2 times per year, as sufficient new data become available. SRI coverage begins with the Feb. 1985 edition.

Availability: Television Bureau of Advertising, ◆; SRI/MF/complete.

A9065
Theatre Communications Group

A9065–1   THEATRE FACTS 84: A Statistical Guide to the Finances and Productivity of the Nonprofit Professional Theatre in America
Annual.   1985.   14 p.
Vol. 11.
ISBN 0-930452-46-1.
LC 82-647014.
SRI/MF/complete, delayed

Annual report, by Robert Holley, on nonprofit professional theater finances and operations, 1980-84. Data are from Theatre Communications Group (TCG) 1984 survey of 230 member theaters.

Contents:

a. Foreword and methodology, with 1 table showing the following for the total sample: attendance, subscribers, performances, and productions; earned, contributed, and total income; total expenses and deficit; and artistic, administrative, and technical staff, and volunteers; 1984. (front cover, and p. 1-2)

b. Narrative trend analysis, with 5 charts and 5 tables showing the following for a subsample of 37 theaters: earned and contributed income by source, and expenses by category, 1980-84. (p. 3-12)

c. List of participating theaters. (p. 13-14)

This is the 11th annual survey.

Availability: Theatre Communications Group, Publications Department, 355 Lexington Ave., New York NY 10017, $3.00; SRI/MF/complete, delayed shipment in Dec. 1985.

A9075
Tobacco Institute

A9075–1   TOBACCO INDUSTRY PROFILE, 1984
Annual.   [1984.]   4 p.
SRI/MF/complete

Annual report, for 1984, presenting an overview of the tobacco industry. Includes data on tobacco crop cash receipts, by selected State; grower income per acre, for tobacco and 9 other crops; and export volume and value for tobacco leaf and cigarettes, by major custom district port; 1983.

Also includes summary data on other tobacco industry indicators, including consumption, factories and warehouses, manufacturing employment and wages, wholesalers, retail outlets, imports (leaf and products), government tax receipts, and U.S. and world production.

Data are from Federal Government and industry sources.

Contains narrative report, interspersed with text data, 1 chart, and 3 tables.

Report has been published since 1968. SRI coverage begins with this edition.

Availability: Tobacco Institute, 1875 I St., NW, Washington DC 20006, †; SRI/MF/complete.

A9075–2   TAX BURDEN ON TOBACCO: Historical Compilation, 1984
Annual.   Jan. 1985.
viii + 196 p.   Vol. 19.
ISSN 0563-6191.
LC 68-7933/r77.
SRI/MF/complete

Annual report on trends in taxation of cigarettes and other tobacco products, primarily by State, 1950s-84, with selected historical trends from as early as 1863.

Data are from State tobacco tax administrators, IRS, Dept of Agriculture, Census Bureau, and tobacco industry sources.

Contents:

a. Foreword, contents and table listing, highlights, and 1 map (p. iii-viii); and 3 trend charts (p. 1-3).

b. 17 numbered tables, listed below. (p. 4-144)

c. 1 table summarizing cigarette tax trends, primarily 1950-84; repeated for individual taxing States and for all taxing States combined. (p. 145-196)

This is the 19th edition of the report. SRI coverage begins with this edition.

Availability: Tobacco Institute, 1875 I St., NW, Washington DC 20006, †; SRI/MF/complete.

TABLES:

SUMMARY TRENDS
[Tables 1-2 and 4-5 show separate data for cigarettes and other tobacco products.]

1. Federal, State, and local tobacco taxes [FY83-84, and total since 1863]. (p. 4)

2-3. Federal tax collections on [cigarettes and all] tobacco products, and per capita [and total] consumption [of cigarettes, selected fiscal years 1865-1984]. (p. 5-6)

4-5. Number of States taxing tobacco products, and net State tobacco tax collections, 1921-84. (p. 7-8)

STATE DATA
[Tables 6-16 show data by State.]

6. State cigarette tax rate changes since July 1, 1950, through Nov. 1, 1984. (p. 9)

7-11. State cigarette tax rates; gross State cigarette taxes; net State cigarette tax collections; and State tax-paid cigarette sales [total and per capita, in packs; FY50-84]. (p. 10-29)

12-12A. States which tax both cigarettes and other tobacco products [includes gross and net collections, and other product categories taxed, FY54-84]; and State tax rates on other tobacco products, Nov. 1, 1984. (p. 30-61)

13-14. Cigarette taxes as a percentage of retail price as of Nov. 1, 1954-84, and as a percentage of weighted average price before taxes as of Nov. 1, 1984 [also includes average price, State sales tax, and State and Federal cigarette tax, all per pack]. (p. 62-93)

15. General sales or gross receipts tax applied to cigarettes [shows sales tax rate and whether applicable to cigarettes and/or inclusive of excise tax, and amount tax adds to cost of single pack and carton, as of various dates] 1957-84. (p. 94-121)

16. County and city tobacco taxes [number of jurisdictions taxing cigarettes and other tobacco products, and gross or net tax amounts, for cities and/or counties], FY63-84. (p. 122-143)

FEDERAL TAX RATES

17. History of Federal tax rates on cigarettes, 1864-1984.

A9095
Toy Manufacturers of America

A9095–1   NATIONAL STATISTICS PROGRAM: Shipments, 1983 vs. 1984
Annual. Feb. 1985. 3 p.
SRI/MF/complete

Annual report on toy shipment volume and value, by type of toy and game, including electronic games and home video systems and software, 1983-84.

Data are from survey responses of 84 toy companies, accounting for approximately 65% of industry shipments in 1983-84; and from Electronic Industries Assn and other sources. Data were compiled by The NPD Group, in conjunction with Toy Manufacturers of America.

Report consists of 1 table.

Availability: Toy Manufacturers of America, 200 Fifth Ave., New York NY 10010, †; SRI/MF/complete.

A9095–2   MONTHLY MARKET TREND REPORTS
Monthly. 3 p.
SRI/MF/complete, shipped quarterly

Monthly summary of toy shipment and order values. Data are compiled by Locker, Greenberg, and Brainin, P.C., from surveys of approximately 50 toy manufacturers. Reports are issued approximately 6 weeks after month of coverage.

Contains list of participating companies, and 2 tables showing value of toy shipments, and orders received, canceled, and on hand, monthly and cumulatively through month of coverage, for current and previous 1-2 years.

Availability: Toy Manufacturers of America, 200 Fifth Ave., New York NY 10010, †; SRI/MF/complete, shipped quarterly.

Issues reviewed during 1985: Sept. 1984-Aug. 1985 (D).

A9095–3   TOY MANUFACTURERS OF AMERICA 1983 Financial and Operating Ratio Report
Annual. [1984.] 19 p.
SRI/MF/complete

Annual report presenting toy industry financial and operating ratios, 1983, with selected trends from 1978. Also includes sales trends, advertising expenditure distribution by media type, and sales distribution by outlet type.

Most data are shown by company sales size, and for all, high-profit, public, and private companies.

Data are compiled by Profit Planning Group from survey responses of 59 toy manufacturers.

Contains executive summary and contents listing (p. 1-2); introductory profit analysis, with 1 charts and 2 tables (p. 3-6); and survey analysis and results, with 7 tables (p. 7-19).

Availability: Toy Manufacturers of America, 200 Fifth Ave., New York NY 10010, participants †, nonparticipating members $75.00, others $100.00; SRI/MF/complete.

A9150
United Bus Owners of America

A9150–1   1983-84 OPERATING TRENDS
Annual. [1985.] 4 p. Folder.
SRI/MF/complete

Annual report presenting aggregate financial and operating data for bus transportation companies, 1st half 1983-84. Covers revenues by source, expenses by item, operating ratios, mileage, employment, fleet size and age, driver wages, and fuel consumption, with selected detail for charter and regular route service.

Report was prepared by the National Transportation Consulting Group, Ernst & Whinney, based on 44 responses to a survey of UBOA members. Report is intended to enable individual companies to compare their performance with industry averages.

Contains narrative summary, with text statistics, 2 charts, and 6 tables.

This is the 1st edition of the report.

Availability: United Bus Owners of America, 1275 K St., NW, Suite 800, Washington DC 20005-4006, ◆; SRI/MF/complete.

A9275
U.S. Brewers Association

A9275–1   BREWING INDUSTRY IN THE U.S.: BREWERS ALMANAC, 1984
Annual. 1984. vi+106 p.
LC 45-51432.
SRI/MF/not filmed

Annual report presenting detailed brewing industry financial and operating data, 1983, with trends from as early as 1862, and some data for 1984. Selected data are shown by State and census division. Most data are from Treasury Dept, Census Bureau, BLS, and State alcohol beverage control agencies.

Contains listing of contents, tables, and charts (p. iii-vi), and the following:

Chapter 1-2. Industry overview, with 1 map, and 1 text table (p. 1) showing 1983 brewery production in 24 countries. (p. 1-5)

Chapter 3-6. Industry data, with 11 summary charts, 1 summary table, and 75 detailed tables listed below; each chapter includes a brief introduction. (p. 6-97)

Chapter 7. Local option and State controls as of July 1, 1984; and directory of State alcohol beverage control agencies. (p. 98-106)

Availability: U.S. Brewers Association, 1750 K St., NW, Washington DC 20006, members †, nonmembers $60.00; SRI/MF/not filmed.

DETAILED TABLES:

[Most fiscal year data are shown for year ended June 30.]

A9275–1.1: Production and Withdrawals (Brewery Sales)

1-2. Production, withdrawals, and per capita consumption of malt beverages, [various years] FY04-83. (p. 7)

3. Production, removals [taxable and tax-free withdrawals], losses, and stocks on hand June 30, and breweries operated, FY42-83. (p. 8)

4-7. Production of malt beverages; and tax removals of packaged beer, draught beer, and malt beverages; by States, FY75-83. (p. 9-12)

8. Taxpaid withdrawals of malt beverages, by [census] division, FY74-83. (p. 13)

9. Malt beverage sales by States, 1983: taxable removals, by State and combination groupings. (p. 14)

10. Production, draught and packaged sales, and total taxpaid withdrawals of malt beverages, 1936-83. (p. 14)

11. Production and withdrawals of malt beverages [by month] 1972-83, with percent change from same month of previous year. (p. 15-17)

12. Taxpaid packaged removals of malt beverages by type of container, 1976-83. (p. 18)

13. Number of breweries operated, by States, FY72-83. (p. 18)

14. Seasonal index of production and withdrawals, [monthly] 1984. (p. 19)

15. Production and withdrawals adjusted for seasonal variation, [monthly] 1979-83. (p. 22)

16. [Brewing] consumption of agricultural products [by commodity], FY57-83. (p. 25)

17-18. Shipments and production of [returnable and nonreturnable] beer bottles, [monthly] 1974-82. (p. 26)

19. Estimated production of beer cans, 1954-83. (p. 26)

A9275–1.2: Census of Manufactures Data
[Data are from Census of Manufactures and interim 1982 Annual Survey of Manufactures.]

20. General statistics for malt beverage industry [employees and payroll; number, man-hours, and wages of production workers; value added; material cost; value of shipments; and new capital expenditures; 1949-82]. (p. 27)

21. Selected general statistics, by size of establishment [establishments, employees, payroll, value added, value of shipments, and new capital expenditures, for malt and malt beverages], 1977. (p. 28)

22. Value of manufacturers' inventories [malt and malt beverages], 1972 and 1977. (p. 28)

23-25. Malt beverages: selected operating ratios [1967-72 and 1977]; and materials consumed by kind, and quantity and value of shipments by all producers [by product], 1982 and 1977. (p. 28-29)

26. General statistics [same breakdowns as in table 20, plus number of establishments, 1982; and employees and value added, 1977], by geographic areas [for] malt beverages. (p. 30)

27. Malt, general statistics [same breakdowns as in table 20, plus number of establishments, gross value of fixed assets, end-of-year inventories, specialization ratio, and coverage ratio], 1963-82. (p. 30)

A9275–1.3: Financial Data: Employment, Hours, and Earnings; and Price Indexes

FINANCIAL DATA

[A] Percent of net profit (after Federal income taxes) to gross sales/receipts from operations for the brewing industry and all manufacturing, 1954-81. (p. 31)

28-29. Comparative profit and loss statement and comparative balance sheet, for breweries submitting balance sheets [1976-81]. (p. 32-33)

30-38. Number of returns; current, other, and total assets; liabilities; net worth; gross sales/gross receipts from operations; and net profit or loss before and after Federal income/excess profits taxes; all by total assets classes for breweries submitting balance sheets [1972-81]. (p. 34-42)

EMPLOYMENT, HOURS, AND EARNINGS

39. Employment, hours, and earnings for production workers in the malt beverage, all food, and all manufacturing industries, 1966-83. (p. 43)

PRICE INDEXES

40. Wholesale and retail price indexes for malt beverages, 1962-83. (p. 44)

A9275–1.4: Shipments and Consumption

41-42. Shipments of malt beverages: by States, 1976-83; and by [census] divisions, 1974-83. (p. 46-47)

43. 1983 consumption and per capita consumption of malt beverages, distilled spirits, and wines, by [census division]. (p. 47)

44-49. Shipments 1976-83, and per capita consumption 1973-83, of malt beverages, distilled spirits, and wine; all by States. (p. 48-53)

50. 1983 population and malt beverage consumption [total and per adult and per capita, by State]. (p. 54)

51. Malt beverage shipments by States, barrels per month in 1983, with percent change from same month in 1982. (p. 55-71)

52. State per capita [malt beverage] consumption by rank, 1981-83. (p. 72)

53-54. Shipments of malt beverages [total and] adjusted for seasonal variation, by months 1977-83. (p. 73)

55. Consumer expenditures for alcohol beverages [1960-83]. (p. 74)

56. Seasonal index of shipment of malt beverages [by month], 1984. (p. 74)

A9275–1.5: Foreign Trade

57-60. U.S. exports of malt beverages (exclusive of shipments to armed forces overseas), malt extracts, malt, and hops [by country or world area of destination, various years 1973-83]. (p. 76-79)

61. U.S. exports of malt beverages, by months, 1966-83. (p. 80)

62-64. U.S. imports of malt beverages, barley malt, and hops [by country or world area of origin, various years 1973-83]. (p. 81-82)

65. Imports of malt beverages, by months, 1975-83. (p. 83)

A9275–1.6: Taxes

FEDERAL TAX

66. History of Federal excise tax on beer [1862-present]. (p. 84)

67. Internal revenue paid to U.S. Government by the distilling and brewing industries [FY10-83]. (p. 85)

68. Federal internal revenue collections from the malt beverage industry [FY34-83]. (p. 85)

69. Internal revenue collections by principal sources [alcohol, corporation income/profits, individual income, employment, estate/gift, tobacco, manufacturer's excise, and all other taxes], FY52-83. (p. 86)

STATE TAX

70. Average State excise tax per barrel, 1956-83. (p. 91)

71-72. Methods of tax collection, by States [rate, method of payment, and by whom paid]; and State taxes on malt beverages, expressed by rate; July 1, 1984. (p. 92-94)

73. Federal tax collections on malt beverages, distilled spirits, and wines, by States, FY83. (p. 95)

74. History of State excise/license tax collections [1974-83]. (p. 96)

BEER PROHIBITION

75. Post-Prohibition population in areas dry for beer, by States, 1974-83. (p. 97)

A9300
U.S. Catholic Mission Association

A9300–1   MISSION HANDBOOK, 1985-86
Annual. [1985.]   47 p.
ISSN 0095-2036.
LC 74-648018.
SRI/MF/complete

Annual handbook on U.S. Catholic clerical and lay missionaries serving abroad, by country and sponsoring religious order or organization, 1985, with trends from 1956. Includes data for Alaska, Hawaii, and selected U.S. territory missions; and directories of Catholic missionary organizations. Data are compiled by the U.S. Catholic Mission Assn.

Contains contents listing, and description of assn purpose and activities (p. 3-8); mission inventory, with 6 tables listed below (p. 10-42); and directories of mission institutes and seminars, Catholic mission-sending groups, and other assistance organizations (p. 45-47).

Availability: U.S. Catholic Mission Association, 1233 Lawrence St., NE, Washington DC 20017, $1.50+postage; SRI/MF/complete.

TABLES:

[Tables show data for U.S. Catholic personnel, 1985, unless otherwise noted. Data by country include Alaska, Hawaii, and selected U.S. territories.]

[1] Personnel serving abroad: religious priests, brothers, and sisters; diocesan priests; and lay personnel [showing number of missionaries sent abroad in each category by country served, alphabetically by sponsor]. (p. 11-23)

[2] U.S. Catholic mission fields abroad: [ranking of 113 countries by missionary population]. (p. 24-25)

[3] Overseas missionaries [same personnel types as table 1, plus seminarians; selected years] 1956-85. (p. 26)

[4] Countries abroad served by U.S. Catholic personnel [by sex, showing number of religious missionaries by sponsor and total lay missionaries, listed alphabetically by country]. (p. 27-39)

[5] Field distribution abroad of missionaries [by sex and country, arranged by world region]. (p. 40-41)

[6] Field distribution by [world] areas, [selected years] 1956-85. (p. 42)

A9330
U.S. Conference of Mayors

A9330–4   FEDERAL BUDGET AND THE CITIES: A Review of the President's Budget for FY86
Annual. Feb. 7, 1985.
viii+95 p.
LC sn82-20657.
SRI/MF/complete

Annual report analyzing the potential impact on urban areas of the Reagan Administration's Federal budget proposal for FY86. Includes data on past and proposed budgets for selected programs and agencies, mostly FY81-86.

Budget areas covered include Administration on Aging programs; National Endowments for the Arts and Humanities; HUD community development and assisted housing programs; DOD; economic and small business development programs; Labor Dept employment and training programs; selected DOE and EPA programs; and Interior Dept urban parks, land/water conservation, and historic preservation programs.

Additional areas covered include food assistance and nutrition programs; Medicare, Medicaid, Centers for Disease Control, and other health programs; community action, social service, and income security programs; DOT public transportation and Federal highway programs; and selected education, public safety, science/technology, and VA programs.

Report also includes data on Federal budget outlay distribution trends, including percent for individuals and State/local government aid, and forecasts for selected economic indicators, various years FY78-90.

Data are primarily from *U.S. Budget* and Federal agency budget highlight reports and press releases.

Contains contents listing (1 p.); preface and overview, with 1 table (p. i-viii); narrative analysis in 19 sections, interspersed with 25 tables (p. 1-90); and glossary (p. 91-95).

Availability: U.S. Conference of Mayors, Office of Information and Member Communications, 1620 Eye St., NW, Washington DC 20006, $15.00; SRI/MF/complete.

A9330–6   HOUSING NEEDS AND CONDITIONS IN AMERICA'S CITIES: A Survey of the Nation's Principal Cities
Monograph.   June 1984.
19+App 9 p.
SRI/MF/complete

Report on low-income housing conditions and assistance in large cities, 1984. Includes data on waiting periods for assisted housing for families, elderly persons, and handicapped persons; reasons for declining supply of low-income rental units; barriers to finding adequate housing; most effective public actions for eliminating substandard housing; and needed and anticipated funding for public housing modernization.

Data are based on responses from 66 cities to an Apr. 1984 survey of housing, community development, and planning officials in cities with populations of 30,000/over.

Contains summary, foreword, and methodology with 2 tables (p. 1-6); narrative analysis, interspersed with 7 tables (p. 7-19); and 3 appendices, including list of cities represented, and questionnaire facsimile (9 p.).

Availability: U.S. Conference of Mayors, Office of Information and Member Communications, 1620 Eye St., NW, Washington DC 20006, $10.00; SRI/MF/complete.

A9350
U.S. League of Savings Institutions

A9350–2   '85 SAVINGS INSTITUTIONS SOURCEBOOK
Annual.   1985.   80 p.
ISSN 0882-3197.
LC 85-641339.
SRI/MF/complete

Annual sourcebook on savings institutions' lending activities and financial condition, 1984, with trends from 1960 and selected comparisons to other types of financial institutions. Includes data on savings, mortgage lending, housing trends, savings institution operations, and Federal agencies.

Data are compiled by the U.S. League of Savings Institutions from Federal Reserve Board, Dept of Commerce, FHLBB, and other government and private sources.

Contains contents listing, preface, and narrative review (p. 3-19); 99 tables, listed below (p. 21-69); and glossary and index (p. 70-80).

This is the 2nd edition of the report.

Availability: U.S. League of Savings Institutions, Order Processing, 111 E. Wacker Dr., Chicago IL 60601, †; SRI/MF/complete.

TABLES:
[Tables show data for 1960, 1965, and annually 1970-84, unless otherwise noted. Data for savings institutions often are shown separately for savings assns and savings banks.]

A9350–2.1: Savings

1. Distribution of total personal income [including taxes, disposable income, outlays, and savings]. (p. 21)

2. Allocation of household funds [1981-84]. (p. 22)

3-4. Annual change in financial assets of households [by type of financial institution, life insurance and pension fund reserves, credit/equity instruments, and money market fund shares]; and over-the-counter savings [by type of financial institution]. (p. 22-23)

5. Average annual yield on selected investments [including savings deposits and State/local, Federal, and corporate bonds]. (p. 23)

6-7. Total savings, and number and size of accounts at all savings institutions. (p. 24)

8. Average interest rate on savings at assns [by month, 1982-84]. (p. 24)

9. Savings flows at all savings institutions. (p. 25)

10-11. Savings deposits, year end 1984; and quarterly change in savings deposits, 1984; at FSLIC-insured institutions, by type of account [including passbook and money market certificate]. (p. 26)

12. Net new savings flows at savings institutions [quarterly 1976-84]. (p. 27)

A9350–2.2: Mortgage Lending

13. Growth in selected types of credit [including residential and commercial mortgages, corporate/foreign bonds, government obligations, consumer credit, and Federal debt, 1960 and 1984]. (p. 28)

14-15. Mortgage loans outstanding: by type of property [residential (1- to 4-family and multifamily), commercial, and farm]; and by type of property and lender, year end 1984. (p. 28-29)

16. Residential mortgage loans outstanding and savings institutions' share, 1984. (p. 29)

17. Annual change in [Federal] agency-supported residential debt. (p. 30)

18-19. 1- to 4-family and multi-family mortgage loans outstanding, by [type of] lender. (p. 30-31)

20. Long-term interest rates [for conventional loans on new homes, and yields on new utility issues and corporate bonds, 1965 and 1970-84]. (p. 31)

21. Effective interest rates on conventional home mortgage loans closed [for savings institutions and all major lenders, monthly 1983-84]. (p. 32)

22. Terms on conventional mortgage loans [and average purchase price, for new and existing single-family homes, Dec. 1981-84]. (p. 32)

23. Mortgage portfolio [including value of loans outstanding for 1- to 4-family homes and other properties, total number of loans, and average balance], all savings institutions. (p. 33)

24-25. Mortgage lending activity [loans outstanding and acquired, portfolio inflows, and turnover ratio], of all savings assns; and all savings banks [1970-84]. (p. 34)

26-27. Mortgage loans acquired [including loans closed, and loans/participations purchased], all FSLIC-insured assns; and all savings banks [1970-84]. (p. 35)

28-29. Mortgage portfolio inflows [including repayments, and loans/participations sold] at FSLIC-insured assns and all savings banks [1970-84]. (p. 36)

30-31. Mortgage loans made, by purpose of loan [home purchase, home construction, and other]; and 1- to 4-family [new and existing] homes financed; all assns. (p. 37)

32. Mortgage loans made [and distribution of loans closed] by FSLIC-insured institutions, by purpose of loan [1983-84]. (p. 37)

33. Private and government mortgage insurance [and insurance as percent of home mortgage debt]. (p. 38)

34. Mortgage foreclosures by FSLIC-insured assns [including number and rate for conventional and FHA/VA loans, 1965 and 1970-84]. (p. 38)

A9350–2.3: Housing

35-36. Private and public housing starts; and private housing starts, by regions. (p. 39)

37-38. Private housing starts, by months [1982-84]; and subsidized housing starts [1965 and 1970-84]. (p. 39)

39. Annual dollar volume of [public, private, and private residential] new construction; [and GNP and private domestic investment; 1980-84]. (p. 40)

40. Private housing starts, by number of family units. (p. 40)

41. Private starts of apartments [buildings and units, 1965 and 1970-84]. (p. 41)

42-43. New 1-family homes sold, by price [1973-84]; and [number, dollar volume, and median price of] new and existing 1-family homes sold [1970-84]. (p. 41)

44. Inventory of unsold speculatively built 1-family homes, and number of months required to clear inventory [by month 1982-84]. (p. 42)

45. Mobile home shipments. (p. 42)

46. Residential construction costs and consumer prices [percent change, and Boeckh index of residential construction costs]. (p. 42)

47. Homeownership [owner- and renter-occupied units, selected years] 1890-1983. (p. 43)

48. Number of families and households. (p. 43)

49. Apartment absorption rates [quarterly 1970-3rd quarter 1984]. (p. 44)

50. Rental and homeowner vacancy rates. (p. 44)

A9350–2.4: Savings Institution Operations
[Tables show data for all savings institutions, unless otherwise noted.]

51. Total assets of financial intermediaries at year end [by type of financial institution, selected years 1960-84]. (p. 44)

52-54. Number and assets: by State [and for U.S. territories] Dec. 31, 1984; [for] savings assns, by [Federal and State] charter; and [for] savings banks, by insurance status [FDIC, FSLIC, and State funds]. (p. 45-47)

55. Distribution of savings assns by asset size, Dec. 31, 1984. (p. 48)

56. Permanent stock savings assns [number and assets, for California, Texas, Florida, and other States, Dec. 31, 1983-84]. (p. 48)

57-64. Statement of operations; total operating income and expense [distribution by source and object]; and income and expense ratios [1982-84]; all for FSLIC-insured institutions and FDIC-insured savings banks. (p. 49-51)

65. Selected significant ratios [asset utilization, profit margin, and return on equity and on average assets], for [all] federally insured savings institutions. (p. 52)

66. Minimum liquidity requirements for FHLB members [short-term and overall, selected dates 1950-80]. (p. 52)

67. Number of offices [and branches]. (p. 53)

68. Personnel [total and per $1 million of assets]. (p. 53)

69-74. Condensed statement of condition of FSLIC-insured savings institutions and FDIC-insured savings banks, as of Dec. 31, 1984; and total assets and liabilities [by item]. (p. 54-57)

A9350–2.5: Federal Agencies

75. FHLB districts. (p. 57)

76. Membership of the FHLB system [including number of federally- and State-chartered assns, savings banks, and life insurance companies, by bank district], year end 1984. (p. 58)

77. Selected operating factors of the FHLB system [including average cost of obligations, weighted average rate on advances, and number of borrowers at month end, by month 1982-Feb. 84]. (p. 58)

78. FHLB lending activity [including advances made, repaid, and outstanding]. (p. 59)

79. FHLB capital stock, member deposits, and obligations. (p. 59)

80-81. Weighted rate on advances, and dividend rates paid, by FHLB district, 1982-84. (p. 59)

82-83. FHLB combined statement of condition, and combined operating statement, [1983-84]. (p. 60)

84-85. Number of FSLIC and FDIC member institutions; and FSLIC [primary and secondary] reserves, and FDIC deposit insurance fund [both as percent of insured liability]. (p. 61)

86-89. FSLIC and FDIC comparative statements of condition, and comparative operating statements, [1982-83]. (p. 62-63)

90. FDIC regions. (p. 64)

91. Federal Home Loan Mortgage Corp. activity [mortgage purchases and sales, FHA/VA and conventional loans, and participation certificates, 1970-84]. (p. 64)

92. VA guaranteed home mortgage loans made [number and amount]. (p. 64)

93. FHA insured mortgage and other loans made. (p. 65)

94. FHA interest rate ceilings [on 1-family homes and apartments, selected dates 1970-83]. (p. 65)

95. FNMA activity [loan purchases and sales, total portfolio, and mortgage-backed securities]. (p. 66)

96-97. GNMA loan portfolio, by function [special assistance and management/liquidation, 1965 and 1970-84]; and GNMA mortgage-backed security program [value of pass-through security applications and issues, and of bonds sold, 1970-84]. (p. 66)

98-99. Major Federal laws [1932-84] and major regulatory changes [1984] affecting savings institutions. (p. 67-69)

A9360
U.S. Telephone Association

A9360–1   HOLDING COMPANY REPORT
Annual.   June 1985.
34 p. var. paging+insert.
SRI/MF/complete

Annual report, for 1984, on finances and operations of major independent telephone holding companies. Report focuses on 16 companies that control 259 of the 1,440 operating independent companies in the U.S., and 75% of the independent access lines.

Contains introduction, and the following:

a. 1 table showing aggregate operating and financial data for 16 holding companies. (1 p.)

b. Profiles for each of the 16 holding companies, including address and officers; list of operating companies, and number of stockholders, access lines, exchanges, States of operation, plant investment, operating revenues, and employment, as of Dec. 31, 1984; and construction expenditures, 1984 and estimated 1985-86. (p. 1-16a)

c. 1 table showing access lines and total operating revenues of top 25 telephone holding companies or groups, as of Dec. 31, 1984. (1 p.)

A profile of a 17th holding company is included as an insert.

Availability: U.S. Telephone Association, 1801 K St., NW, Suite 1201, Washington DC 20006, $5.00; SRI/MF/complete.

A9360–2   STATISTICS OF THE TELEPHONE INDUSTRY, 1984
Annual.   2 volumes.
For individual publication data, see below.
LC 56-19815.
SRI/MF/complete, delayed

Annual report on independent telephone company finances and operations, covering income and expenses, assets and liabilities, employment, and equipment, 1984 with trends from 1974. Includes data by FCC classification based on annual operating revenues. Also includes detail for Bell System affiliates, and data for the Rural Electrification Administration (REA).

Most data are from reports submitted to the U.S. Telephone Assn by 655 companies.

Report is issued in 2 volumes as follows:

Vol. I. Presents aggregate data for the 655 independent reporting companies, and other independents; with data on REA activities.

Vol. II. Presents data for each of the 655 independent reporting companies.

Both volumes are described below.

Phone Facts '84 containing summary highlights is also available from the assn, but is not covered by SRI.

Availability: U.S. Telephone Association, 1801 K St., NW, Suite 1201, Washington DC 20006; SRI/MF/complete, delayed shipment in Jan. 1986.

A9360–2.1: Volume I
[Annual. July 1985. 3+31 p. $10.00. SRI/MF/complete, delayed.]

Contains contents listing (p. 1); 1 summary table described below (p. 2-5); narrative highlights (p. 7); and 5 charts, and 24 tables also described below (p. 8-33).

TABLES:
[Unless otherwise noted, tables show aggregate data. Most data for reporting companies are shown for total industry, and for Bell System and/or independent only companies.]

a. Industry summary: including number of access lines, companies, and exchanges; operating revenues, employment, and total investment in plant; and daily average number of conversations; generally for independent reporting and nonreporting companies, and the Bell System, 1975-84. 1 table. (p. 2-5)

b. Independent companies: top 100 companies ranked by number of access lines, and including operating revenues, 1985; construction expenditures, 1974-84; and companies and access lines, by State, 1984. 3 tables. (p. 8-11)

c. Reporting companies' financing by type of security; assets and liabilities, with detail for investment in plant; income and expenses, with detail for operating revenues and taxes; access lines by type; average daily calls and toll messages; central offices by number of lines and type of equipment; financial ratios; employment and payroll; and operating ratios; various years 1977-84. 16 tables. (p. 12-27)

d. Comparisons for reporting companies grouped by revenue class, including number of companies and access lines; capitalization by type of investment, value of plant in service and depreciation reserve; and revenues, expenses, and net operating income, per access line; 1980-84. 3 tables. (p. 28-30)

e. REA and Rural Telephone Bank loan activities, and REA borrowers and subscribers by type, various years 1975-84. 1 table. (p. 31)

A9360–2.2: Volume II
[Annual. July 1985. 14+164 p.+errata. Reporting companies $10.00, nonreporting member companies $15.00, others $35.00. SRI/MF/complete, delayed.]

Contains foreword (1 p.); alphabetical listing of independent reporting companies, with revenue class, location, and ranking based on 1984 operating revenues (13 p.); and 1 detailed table (p. 1-164), showing the following for each of the 655 independent reporting companies, arranged in rank order, 1983-84:

a. Value of plant in service; depreciation/amortization reserves; number of exchanges and access lines; and capitalization including funded debt (bonds and other), stock, retained earnings, and maturity of long-term debt/short-term notes.

b. Revenue from local and toll service and other sources; expenses by item, including taxes; net income; deductions, including interest; and dividends.

A9385
Western
Interstate Commission
for Higher Education

**A9385–1   WICHE STUDENT
EXCHANGE PROGRAMS,
Statistical Report, Academic
Year 1984/85**
Annual.   Dec. 1984.   12 p.
Pub. No. 2A131.
SRI/MF/complete

Annual report on student exchange programs in
the 13 western member States of WICHE, 1984/
85. Includes data on enrollment, on support fees
paid by States to enable resident students to enroll in professional and graduate programs in other States when not available in their home States,
and on other exchange programs.

Contains narrative description of programs, interspersed with 7 tables listed below (p. 2-12).

Availability: Western Interstate Commission
for Higher Education, Publications, PO Drawer
P, Boulder CO 80302, †; SRI/MF/complete.

TABLES:
[Unless otherwise noted, data are for academic
year 1984/85.]

**PROFESSIONAL STUDENT EXCHANGE
PROGRAM**
[Table titles begin "Professional student exchange program..." Tables 1-2 and 5 include
out-of-region data.]

1. Summary of enrollment and fees for purposes of comparison [by field; and participating programs receiving and prepared to receive
students; various periods 1983/84-1986/87].
(p. 3)

2. Student and fee totals, all fields [students
sent and fees paid, and received in public and
private programs, by State]. (p. 4)

3-4. Enrollment and fees; and student distribution [by receiving school] and fee payments;
[all by sending State and field]. (p. 4-7)

5. Receipt of support fees by States and institutions [by field]. (p. 8-9)

OTHER PROGRAMS

6. Community College Student Exchange
Program: nonresident tuition waivers granted
[by State and institution]. (p. 11)

[7]. Mineral Engineering Program enrollments [by State and institution]. (p. 12)

**A9385–3   TUITION AND FEES IN
PUBLIC HIGHER
EDUCATION IN THE WEST,
1984/85**
Annual.   Apr. 1985   iii+34 p.
Pub. No. 2A140.
SRI/MF/complete

Annual report on public higher education tui-
tion/fees in the 14 western member States of
WICHE, 1979/80-1984/85. Data are shown by
individual institution grouped by State, and are
presented separately for resident students at
community colleges, and for resident and nonresident graduate and undergraduate students at
4-year schools. Also includes summary data by
WICHE State.

Data are from State higher education executive officers, and from *The College Cost Book,
1984-85.*

Contains acknowledgments (p. iii); introduction (p. 1-2); and statistical section, with 11 tables (p. 3-34).

This is the 5th annual report.

Availability: Western Interstate Commission
for Higher Education, Publications, PO Drawer
P, Boulder CO 80302, $5.00 (prepaid); SRI/MF/
complete.

**A9385–5   FACT BOOK ON
HIGH-TECHNOLOGY AND
ENERGY-RELATED HIGHER
EDUCATION IN THE WEST**
Monograph.   Jan. 1983.
vii+78 p.   Pub. No. 2A118.
SRI/MF/complete

Fact book compiling data on supply-demand
situation for high-technology and energy-related
manpower in the West, with comparisons to
U.S., 1970s-early 1980s. Data often include detail for western census divisions and/or States.

Includes data on high-technology and energy-
related employment, and job openings by occupation projected to 1990; engineering and
science enrollment and degrees, by level and
field, with selected detail by race/ethnicity and
for foreign nationals; college engineering faculty
and salaries; and engineer salaries, by field.

Also includes data on percent of high school
graduates with math and science courses, by sex
and race/ethnicity; and Scholastic Aptitude Test
verbal and math scores.

Data are from National Science Foundation,
Engineering Manpower Commission, NCES,
and numerous other sources.

Contents:

Contents and table listing, and foreword (p.
iii-vii); and introduction (p. 1-2).

Part I. Importance of Science and Technology
to the U.S. and the West. Includes 7 charts
and 3 tables. (p. 3-12)

Part II. Indicators of Supply and Demand. Includes 20 charts and 8 tables. (p. 13-42)

Part III. Problems Affecting Supply and Demand. Includes 6 charts and 12 tables. (p.
43-54)

Information sources (p. 55-58); and appendix,
with 21 tables (p. 59-78).

Availability: Western Interstate Commission
for Higher Education, Publications, PO Drawer
P, Boulder CO 80302, $5.00; SRI/MF/com-
plete.

**A9385–6   MINORITIES IN HIGHER
EDUCATION: The Changing
Southwest**
Series.   For individual
publication data, see below.
SRI/MF/complete

By Geoffrey Dolman, Jr., and Norman S. Kauf-
man. Series of 5 reports examining demographic
and socioeconomic trends relevant to higher
education for racial/ethnic minorities in southwestern States.

Each report covers a single State, and includes
data on population, selected years 1960-2000;
postsecondary enrollment shares, 1980; earned
degrees, by level, 1976/77-1980/81; and other
education-related trends; generally shown for
whites, blacks, Hispanics, and others (with some
detail for American Indians and Asian Americans).

Data are from Census Bureau, NCES, and other sources.

Each report contains contents listing, foreword, introduction, and summary highlights; 16-
17 charts and 1 table, interspersed with narrative;
and bibliography.

Reports are listed below.

Availability: Western Interstate Commission
for Higher Education, Publications, PO Drawer
P, Boulder CO 80302, $5.00 each, complete set
of five volumes $20.00; SRI/MF/complete.

A9385–6.1: Arizona
[Monograph. Dec. 1984. vi+34 p. Pub. No.
2A134a. SRI/MF/complete.]

A9385–6.2: California
[Monograph. Dec. 1984. vi+33 p. Pub. No.
2A134b. SRI/MF/complete.]

A9385–6.3: Colorado
[Monograph. Aug. 1984. vi+34 p. Pub. No.
2A134c. SRI/MF/complete.]

A9385–6.4: Texas
[Monograph. Sept. 1984. vi+34 p. Pub. No.
2A134e. SRI/MF/complete.]

A9385–6.5: New Mexico
[Monograph. May 1985. vi+34 p. Pub. No.
2A134d. SRI/MF/complete.]

**A9385–7   FEDERAL STUDENT AID
PROGRAMS IN THE WEST:
Funding and Distribution**
Monograph.   May 1985.
v+17 p.   Pub. No. 2A144,
Information Series No. 9.
SRI/MF/complete

Report on Federal and State student aid trends in
western States and nationwide, various years
1970/71-1984/85. Includes data on value of Pell
Grant awards in each of 14 western member
States of WICHE, by type of institution, with
each State's share of U.S. total awards, population, and higher education enrollment.

Also includes total value of student grants
awarded through State-funded programs, for
U.S. and each WICHE State; and U.S. student
aid trends, with detail by major Federal program.

Most data are from Dept of Education, and
National Assn of State Scholarship and Grant
Programs.

Contains contents and table listings, and foreword (p. iii-v); and narrative report, with 5 tables
(p. 1-17).

Availability: Western Interstate Commission
for Higher Education, Publications, PO Drawer
P, Boulder CO 80302, $5.00; SRI/MF/com-
plete.

**A9385–8   STAFF RECRUITMENT AND
RETENTION IN
COMMUNITY SUPPORT
PROGRAMS: A Ten-State
Study**
Monograph.   July 1984.
vii+65 p.   Pub. No. 3B37.
SRI/MF/complete

By J. Donald Moore. Survey report on staffing problems of community programs serving the chronically mentally ill. Includes data on types of positions difficult to fill and to keep filled, incentives used to recruit and retain staff, skills and characteristics sought in staff members, and successful recruiting methods.

Data are based on telephone interviews with administrators of 54 programs in 10 States. The sample included 43 community mental health centers, and 11 other types of programs. States surveyed were among those with NIMH-funded manpower development and community support programs. No survey date is given.

Contains contents and table listings, and preface (p. iii-vii); introduction, methodology, findings, and recommendations, with narrative and 26 tables (p. 1-43); references (p. 45); and appendices, including questionnaire facsimile (p. 47-65).

Availability: Western Interstate Commission for Higher Education, Publications, PO Drawer P, Boulder CO 80302, †; SRI/MF/complete.

A9385-10   QUALITY IN TEACHER EDUCATION: A Crisis Revisited
Monograph.   Apr. 1985.
viii+76 p.   Order No. 2A136.
SRI/MF/complete

By Erica Gosman. Report on factors affecting the quality of teaching in elementary/secondary schools. Discusses trends and developments in preservice and inservice teacher education, and teacher supply-demand.

Also presents tabular summaries of State policies on teacher training and competency testing, as of 1983 or early 1984; and selected statistical trends, including Scholastic Aptitude Test scores of education majors compared to national average, new teacher graduates, college undergraduate enrollment, percent of college freshmen planning teaching careers, and starting salaries for teachers compared to other professions, various years 1970s-80s, with graduate and enrollment projections through 1992.

Data are from NCES and independent research studies.

Contains contents and table listings, foreword, and summary (p. iii-viii); introduction and narrative analysis, interspersed with 9 tables (p. 1-56); appendix, presenting related findings of major task forces and commissions on education (p. 57-59); and bibliography (p. 61-76).

Availability: Western Interstate Commission for Higher Education, Publications, PO Drawer P, Boulder CO 80302, $10.00; SRI/MF/complete.

A9395
Western Wood Products Association

A9395-1   1984 STATISTICAL YEARBOOK OF THE WESTERN LUMBER INDUSTRY
Annual.   Aug. 1985.
3+33 p.
ISSN 0195-931X.
LC 82-640405.
SRI/MF/not filmed

Annual report on western region lumber production and sawmill operating characteristics, and lumber industry export and import trends, including data by species cut, State, county, and region, 1984, with trends from 1972.

Data are from various Federal and private sources.

Contains brief introduction (inside front cover); map of the 12-State western lumber region, and contents listing (2 p.); 24 tables, described below (p. 1-32); and additional reference sources (p. 33).

Availability: Western Wood Products Association, Economic Services Department, 1500 Yeon Bldg., Portland OR 97204, $12.50; SRI/MF/not filmed.

TABLES:

a. State commercial forest acreage and sawtimber volume, and distribution of public (including Federal and Indian) and private ownership, Jan. 1, 1977; lumber production volume and value, 1976-84; employment, 1983-84; and State sawmill operating profile, including timber source by ownership, species cut, processing, transport, markets, and distribution channels, 1984. 2 tables, repeated for 10 States and California/Nevada combined. (p. 1-11)

b. Western region commercial forest acreage and sawtimber net volume, and ownership, for region excluding and including Alaska/Hawaii, and for total U.S., Jan. 1, 1977; western region (excluding Alaska/Hawaii) lumber production and value, 1976-84, and employment, 1983-84; and regional western sawmill operating profiles, including most data described above for States, by annual production size class, 1984. 5 tables. (p. 12-15)

c. Coastal and inland region production summaries, including new and unfilled orders, shipments, and stocks, by month, 1983-84; production by region and species, 1976-84; production by State, county, and species, 1984; and total annual production by State and county, and by State and species, 1976-84. 8 tables. (p. 16-25)

d. California redwood region lumber production, by species and county, 1976-84; comparison of soft and hardwood production in U.S., and western regions, 1972-84; and lumber production, for 29 States, 1982-83. 4 tables. (p. 26-27)

e. Exports of softwood logs and lumber to all countries and to Japan and China, from 4 States; lumber exports by destination and species; lumber imports from all countries and Canada, by species; softwood consumption by demand type and supply region; and

housing starts and mobile home shipments, by U.S. region and type of structure; all 1976-84. 5 tables. (p. 28-32)

A9410
Women's College Coalition

A9410-4   '67/'77: A PROFILE OF RECENT WOMEN'S COLLEGE GRADUATES
Monograph.   Feb. 1985.
23 p. var. paging.
SRI/MF/complete

Survey report on characteristics and attitudes of women's college graduates (classes of 1967 and 1977), spring 1984.

Includes data on graduates' academic and family background; actual and preferred employment status; occupations and salaries, with salary detail by undergraduate degree field; perceived recognition in major field and expectations for the future; participation in civic, professional, and alumnae activities; and extent of involvement in college activities during undergraduate period, and relationship to current salary level.

Also includes graduates' assessments of own and all women's colleges, and opinions on women's issues.

Data are based on 4,984 responses to a spring 1984 survey of 1967 and 1977 graduates from 48 women's colleges, and generally are shown by graduating class.

Contains preface, introduction, and highlights (5 p.); survey findings, with text data, 1 chart, and 12 tables (p. 1-16); and survey methodology, and list of participating colleges (1 p.)

Availability: Women's College Coalition, 1725 K St., NW, Suite 1003, Washington DC 20006, members $5.00, nonmembers $6.00; SRI/MF/complete.

A9415
Women's International Bowling Congress

A9415-1   WOMEN'S INTERNATIONAL BOWLING CONGRESS 1983-84 ANNUAL REPORT
Annual.   [1984.]   69 p.
ISSN 0162-7147.
LC 80-643765.
SRI/MF/complete

Annual report of the Women's International Bowling Congress (WIBC). Includes data on WIBC members and leagues, by city, State, outlying area, Canadian Province, and selected foreign country and city, mostly July 31, 1984. Also includes data on charitable contributions.

Contains contents listing (inside front cover); review of activities, with 2 tables (p. 1-36); WIBC delegates by State, scores, and prizes (p. 37-55); membership statistics (p. 56-65); and financial report and personnel rosters (p. 66-69).

Availability: Women's International Bowling Congress, 5301 S. 76th St., Greendale WI 53129, †; SRI/MF/complete.

A9600
Zinc Institute

A9600–1   **U.S. MARKETS FOR ZINC
DIE CASTING, 1979-83**
Annual.   [1985.]
10 p. no paging.
SRI/MF/complete

Annual report on zinc die casting consumption,
by end-use market, 1979-83. Also includes total
die casters, and number reporting sales in each
market.

Data are based Zinc Institute surveys of die
casters. The 1983 survey drew 412 responses.

Contains narrative analysis, 2 summary charts,
and 2 charts repeated for each end use.

This is the 10th annual report.

Availability: Zinc Institute, 292 Madison Ave.,
New York NY 10017, †; SRI/MF/complete.

A9600–2   **1978-84 U.S. AUTOMOTIVE
MARKET FOR ZINC DIE
CASTING**
Annual.   [1985.]   2 p.
SRI/MF/complete

Annual report on auto industry use of zinc die
castings, 1978-84. Includes data on average
weight of castings per auto, by auto size class and
manufacturer; and casting market shares, by auto
manufacturer.

Data are from a Zinc Institute survey, and are
based in part on design data from the top 4 auto
manufacturers.

Contains narrative analysis and 13 charts.

Availability: Zinc Institute, 292 Madison Ave.,
New York NY 10017, †; SRI/MF/complete.

A9600–4   **SHIPMENTS OF HOT DIP
AFTER FABRICATION
GALVANIZED STEEL by
End-Use Industries**
Annual, discontinued.

Annual report on shipments of hot dip after fabrication galvanized steel, discontinued with report
for 1982 (for description, see SRI 1984 Annual
under this number).

A9600–5   **U.S. AUTOMOTIVE MARKET
FOR ZINC COATINGS,
1982-84**
Annual.   [1985.]   3 p.
SRI/MF/not filmed

Annual report on auto industry use of zinc coatings, 1982-84. Includes data on amount and
types of zinc-coated steel used, with detail by
auto size class and by auto manufacturer. Also
includes zinc content (coated metals and paint)
of a typical car.

Data are from an annual survey of the top 4
auto manufacturers, conducted by the Zinc Institute.

Contains narrative analysis, 5 charts, and 3
tables.

This is the 3rd annual report.

Availability: Zinc Institute, 292 Madison Ave.,
New York NY 10017, †; SRI/MF/not filmed.

B0125
Advance Mortgage Corp.

B0125-1 **U.S. HOUSING MARKETS**
Quarterly.
ISSN 0502-9716.
SRI/MF/not filmed

Quarterly report on housing markets in 17 MSAs, covering permits, construction, completions, vacancies, mortgage and loan activity, and market area employment. Includes selected data for multiple unit structures, walkup and elevator apartments, and mobile home shipments and prices.

Data are compiled from reports of private organizations and of State, local, and Federal government agencies, including U.S. Census Bureau. Report is issued approximately 3 months after quarter of coverage.

General format: contents listing, and narrative introduction with text statistics and 1 semiannual summary table; 8 quarterly tables, accompanied by 1-2 summary charts; and 7 semiannual tables, including data on mortgages.

Subscription to *U.S. Housing Markets* also includes prepublication and special releases which are primarily narrative and are covered in SRI only when they include substantial statistics.

Quarterly tables are listed below and appear in all issues. All additional features with substantial statistical content are described, as they appear, under "Statistical Features."

Beginning with the 1st Quarter 1985 issue, report is published by Lomas and Nettleton and is described in SRI under B5190-1.

Availability: U.S. Housing Markets, Publication Department, 404 Penobscot Bldg., Detroit MI 48226, $130.00 per yr., sample issue $24.95; SRI/MF/not filmed.

Issues reviewed during 1985: 3rd Qtr.-2nd Half 1985 (D).

QUARTERLY TABLES:
[Tables show data for most recent quarter available or final month of period of coverage, with selected comparisons to previous quarters, months, or years. Table sequence may vary.]

PERMITS AND COMPLETIONS
[1] Private housing permits: dwelling units in permits issued [1-family, 2- to 4-family, and 5 or more family units, and highrise and/or total apartments, for U.S. and 17 MSAs; includes U.S. housing starts].

[2] Multifamily completions: units in [walkup and elevator and/or total] buildings of 2 or more units [and units under construction; U.S. and 17-27 MSAs].

VACANCIES
[3] Distribution of U.S. vacancies [percent of housing for rent and for sale in central cities, suburbs, and outside metro areas].

[4] Vacancies in multiple units [percent of units for rent and for sale in structures with 2 or more and 5 or more units].

[5] Vacancy rates: estimated vacancies [and/or vacancy rates] in total available housing supply [for U.S. and 19-28 urban and suburban areas].

EMPLOYMENT
[6] Employment trends [total and manufacturing employment, and unemployment rate, by region and 17 MSAs].

MANUFACTURED HOUSING
[7] U.S. [single- and multi-wide] mobile home shipments [and total placements; and total and multi-section shipments for 12 States].

[8] Average price of mobile homes placed for residential use [U.S. and by region].

STATISTICAL FEATURE:

B0125-1.601: 2nd Half, 1984
SEMIANNUAL TABLES
[1] Housing starts [and/or] permits [1-family and multi-family units, for total U.S., 4 regions, 8 divisions, and 17 MSAs], 1984 vs. 1983. (p. 14)

[2] Other significant markets: housing permits [for 1-family and multi-family units], and [total] employment growth, [for 20 MSAs, various periods 1982-84]. (p. 22-23)

[3-6] Mortgage rates: long-term bond yields [Aaa corporate new issues and U.S. long term]; insured mortgage yields [rate, private market GNMA average, and FNMA mandatory]; conventional loan secondary markets [Federal Home Loan Mortgage Corp. and FNMA fixed and adjustable rate]; and conventional loan rates [for 80%, 95%, and 1-year adjustable loans, including FHLBB effective fixed rates, for 17 MSAs; all mortgage rates are shown as of selected dates, Nov. 1983-Feb. 1985]. (p. 25-26)

[7] Insured loan activity [FHA and VA applications for new 1-family and existing homes, and FHA and VA total 1-family homes insured, U.S. and 17 MSAs, quarterly 3rd quarter 1983-4th quarter 1984, and annually 1982-84]. (p. 27-29)

B0350
AT&T Communications

B0350-1 **WORLD'S TELEPHONES: A Statistical Compilation as of Jan. 1, 1983**
Annual. [1985.] 148 p.
LC 12-16862.
SRI/MF/not filmed

Annual report on world telephone operations, covering the number of telephones in service, by type, country, and city, as of Jan. 1, 1983. Also includes comparisons to population size, selected trends, and data on telephone lines and conversations. Data are compiled by AT&T Communications from survey responses of telephone administrations and operating companies worldwide.

Contains contents/table listing, introduction, notes, and description of international telephone world numbering zones (p. 3-13); 10 charts and 18 tables (p. 14-106); and listing of nonreporting countries, table notes, definitions, and index (p. 107-148). All tables, and selected charts presenting substantial data not covered in tables, are listed below.

This is the 70th annual report. Previous editions were issued by the AT&T Long Lines Dept.

Availability: AT&T Customer Information Center, Commercial Sales Representative, PO Box 19901, Indianapolis IN 46219, $19.95; SRI/MF/not filmed.

TABLES AND CHARTS:
[Tables show data as of Jan. 1, 1983, unless otherwise noted. Tables 7-17 show data for individual countries grouped by international telephone world numbering zone.]

1-3. Selected telephone statistics, totals for all zones and the world [shows total, privately operated, and automatic telephones, and total telephones per 100 population, by international world numbering zone, 1983, with summary comparison to 1978]. (p. 14)

[A-B] World population and reported world telephones, [selected years 1925-83]. [charts] (p. 15)

4-6. Business and residence telephones; automatic telephones by type of switching; and main and extension/PBX [private branch exchange] telephones; for [39] countries which have reported 1,000,000 or more telephones. (p. 17, 20-21)

7-8. Service information [number of telephones] by type of switching and type of operation [private and government]. (p. 22-27)

9-11. Main telephones by business and residence; extension/PBX telephones; business and residence telephones; and PBX telephones by business and residence. (p. 29-34, 39-41)

12. Coin box and public telephone stations [total and number capable of originating international calls]. (p. 42-44)

13. Telephone subscriber lines by business and residence. (p. 45-47)

14-16. Telephone traffic: local, long distance, and international outgoing [shows number of calls, metered pulses, and/or minutes; includes percent of international outgoing traffic with international subscriber dialing]. (p. 48-55)

17. Most frequently called countries, with percentage of total international calls. (p. 56-65)

18. Telephones in the world's principal cities: total telephones, main telephones, and population. (p. 66-105)

B0525
Arbitron Ratings Co.

B0525–3   **1984-85 UNIVERSE ESTIMATES SUMMARY**
Annual.   1984.   5+147 p.
LC sn84-10237.
SRI/MF/complete

Annual report, for 1984/85, on TV markets, presenting data on the number and geographic distribution of all contiguous U.S. households and households owning TVs, by Area of Dominant Influence (ADI), non-ADI market, county, State, and census division. ADI data are for Arbitron-defined TV market areas, and include detail on population in TV households by age and sex.

Data are from Market Statistics, Inc., Advertising Research Foundation, Census Bureau, and Arbitron surveys.

Contains contents listing (1 p.); introduction, with methodology and explanatory notes (4 p.); 10 tables, described below (p. 1-146); and calendar showing market survey dates and number surveyed (1 p.).

Availability: Arbitron Ratings Co., 1350 Ave. of the Americas, Suite 1105, New York NY 10019, †; SRI/MF/complete.

TABLES:
[Data are for 1984/85.]

a. ADI and non-ADI markets: rankings by number of TV households, and alphabetical listings; with additional data for ADI markets on total households, percent TV penetration, and percent of U.S. total TV households. 4 tables. (p. 1-8)

b. Counties in ADI markets: including TV households and population size group for individual counties, grouped by ADI market. 1 table. (p. 9-31)

c. Population in TV households: by age group and sex, for each ADI market arranged alphabetically; and by ADI market, arranged alphabetically and by ADI ranking, for each age group and sex category. 3 tables. (p. 32-95)

d. Total and TV households, by county, State, and census division, with population size category and ADI market assignment for each county. 2 tables. (p. 96-146)

B0600
Atlas Van Lines

B0600–1   **ATLAS VAN LINES 18th ANNUAL SURVEY OF CORPORATE MOVING PRACTICES**
Annual.   Apr. 1985.   13 p.
SRI/MF/complete

Annual survey report on corporate employee transfers, and relocation policies, assistance, and costs, 1984 and trends. Includes the following data, shown for 1984 unless otherwise noted:

a. Number and percent of employees moved in 1984, with change from 1983, reasons for change, and expected trend in 1985; average move frequency per employee; percent of transferred employees who are women; characteristics of frequently transferred employees (age, salary range, job categories); most common season for moves; effect of spouse employment status on employee relocation; and employees declining relocation, with trend, reasons, and career effect.

b. Company moving policies and practices, including presence and functions of centralized transportation dept, reimbursement level and types of assistance provided transferred employees, insurance coverage for transported goods, use of relocation services and carrier contracts, and carrier selection and evaluation criteria; and cost of average relocation, for van line packing/transport and other expenditures.

c. Most useful provisions of 1980 Household Goods Transportation Act; and perceived effects of deregulation on service providers and users in the airline, trucking, household goods transport, communications, and finance industries.

Also includes selected comparisons to previous surveys, 1978-83.

Data for 1984 are based on a survey of over 6,000 corporate executives.

Contains narrative analysis, with 4 summary trend charts (p. 1-4); and response data for 65 survey questions (p. 5-13).

Availability: Atlas Van Lines, 1212 St. George Rd., PO Box 509, Evansville IN 47703, ‡; SRI/MF/complete.

B0650
Bank of America

B0650–4   **CALIFORNIA AGRICULTURE OUTLOOK, 1985**
Annual.   June 1985.   10 p.
SRI/MF/complete

Annual report on financial outlook for California's agricultural sector in 1985. Includes data on farm cash receipts, with detail for 4 crop categories and livestock/livestock products; and gross farm income and production expenses; 1980-85.

Data are prepared by Bank of America.

Contains narrative overview and analysis, with 3 charts and 2 tables.

Availability: Bank of America, Banking Divisions Public Relations No. 3402, Box 37000, San Francisco CA 94137, †; SRI/MF/complete.

B0900
Bankers Trust Co.

B0900–1   **ECONOMIC BENCHMARKS**
Periodic report, discontinued.

Periodic report showing quarterly data on approximately 44 economic indicators, discontinued with Feb. 29, 1984 issue (for description, see SRI 1984 Annual under this number).

B0900–2   **CREDIT AND CAPITAL MARKETS**
Annual, discontinued.

Annual report forecasting credit expansion and capital formation activities, discontinued with 1984 report (for description, see SRI 1984 Annual under this number).

B0900–3   **CREDIT AND CAPITAL MARKETS REASSESSED**
Annual, discontinued.

Annual report presenting revised forecasts of long- and short-term capital formation activity, discontinued with 1983 report (for description, see SRI 1983 Annual under this number).

B1530
Board of Trade of
Kansas City, Missouri

B1530–1   **ANNUAL STATISTICAL REPORT, 1984, The Board of Trade of Kansas City, Missouri, Inc.**
Annual.   [1985.]   59 p.
ISSN 0193-4376.
LC 79-3226.
SRI/MF/complete

Annual report on Kansas City Board of Trade grain market activity, Jan.-Dec. 1984. Includes futures volume and prices, daily cash prices, and grain storage, receipts, and shipments, 1984; U.S. grain production by State, 1982-84; and selected trends from 1956.

Contains contents listing (p. 1); 24 tables, listed below (p. 5-58); and grain freight rate and metric conversion tables (p. 59).

Availability: Board of Trade of Kansas City, Missouri, Marketing Department, 4800 Main St., Suite 303, Kansas City MO 64112, current edition †, prior year reports $3.00; SRI/MF/complete.

TABLES:
[Tables on "grain" generally include detail for wheat, corn, sorghum, oats, rye, barley, and soybeans. Data are for 1984, unless otherwise noted.]

FUTURES VOLUME AND PRICES

[1-3] Volume of wheat futures trading [bushels and contracts, monthly 1983-84 and annually 1973-82]; and Kansas City wheat futures [high and low prices and dates set, by month of delivery]. (p. 5)

[4] Jan.-Dec. daily wheat futures prices [open, high, low, and close, by month of delivery]. (p. 17)

[5] Volume of wheat options (in contracts) [Oct.-Dec. 1984]. (p. 18)

[6] Daily closes on wheat [put and call] options trading, Oct. 30-Nov. 30, 1984. (p. 19-20)

[7] Daily cash grain prices [low and high]. (p. 23-26)

[8-9] Volume of Value Line futures contracts [by month]; and Kansas City Value Line futures contract high and low prices and dates set [by month of delivery]. (p. 27)

[10-11] Jan.-Nov. Value Line and Jan.-Dec. mini Value Line stock index futures [open, high, low, and settle, by month of delivery]. (p. 28-52)

GRAIN PRODUCTION

[12-15] Wheat and corn production [by State]; and soybean and sorghum production of leading States; [1982-84, with harvested acres and yield for 1984]. (p. 53-55)

[16] Grain production of U.S. [1956-84]. (p. 55)

GRAIN STORAGE, RECEIPTS, AND SHIPMENTS

[17] Mills, grain elevators, and operators in Kansas City, storage capacity of elevators, and daily capacity of mills, as of Dec. 31, 1984. (p. 56)

[18-19] Receipts of grain [bushels by month, and carloads by individual railroad]. (p. 57)

[20] Shipments of grain [by month, and by mode of transportation]. (p. 57)

[21-22] Stocks of grain in store, Jan. 1 and Dec. 31, 1984, public elevator stocks; and average bushels per carload. (p. 58)

[23-24] Receipts and shipments of grain at Kansas City in bushels for past 15 years [1970-84]. (p. 58)

B1582
Boeing
Commercial Airplane Co.

B1582-1 **WORLD JET AIRPLANE INVENTORY at Year-End 1984**
Annual. June 1985. 91 p.
Doc. No. Z13678.
ISSN 0736-864X.
LC sc83-3055.
SRI/MF/complete

Annual report on world commercial jet aircraft fleet, 1984 and trends. Presents detailed data by aircraft model, including announced deliveries to and orders from U.S. and non-U.S. customers, various years 1947-84; and inventories at year end 1984, by age of aircraft, individual owner/operator, and equipment type and series, and for world regions and Canada.

Also shows jet planes leased out by airlines at year end, including lessee and lessor.

Owner/operator categories are airlines, government agencies, manufacturers/brokers/leasing companies, and private operators.

Data are from Boeing's JETTRACK computerized information system containing reports from plane manufacturers and operators, governments, trade publications, and other sources.

Contains contents and table listing (p. 1); introduction and abbreviations (p. 2-3); and 47 tables, arranged in 7 sections (p. 5-91).

This is the 7th annual report.

Availability: Boeing Commercial Airplane Co., Marketing Department, PO Box 3707, Mail Stop 76-15, Seattle WA 98124, †; SRI/MF/complete.

B1900
Chase Manhattan Bank

B1900-2 **PETROLEUM SITUATION**
Recurring (irreg.)
Approx. 6 p.
ISSN 0276-5829.
LC sc80-1053.
SRI/MF/complete

Recurring report on petroleum and energy industry developments. Issues generally consist of a feature article analyzing trends or outlook for a specific energy source or industry sector.

Features with substantial statistical content are described, as they appear, under "Statistical Features."

Availability: Chase Manhattan Bank, Energy Economics, Global Petroleum Division, 7th Floor, One Chase Manhattan Plaza, New York NY 10081, †; SRI/MF/complete.

Issues reviewed during 1985: Oct. 1984 (P) (Vol. 8, No. 1).

STATISTICAL FEATURE:

B1900-2.601: Oct. 1984 (Vol. 8, No. 1)
CHANGING STRUCTURE OF THE WORLD REFINING INDUSTRY

(p. 1-5) Article, with 1 undated table showing product yields from distillation of 3 qualities of crude oil. Data are from *Oil and Gas Journal* and company reports.

B1900-3 **FINANCIAL ANALYSIS OF A GROUP OF PETROLEUM COMPANIES, 1984**
Annual. July 1985. 29 p.
ISSN 0193-8940.
LC SC 79-3306.
SRI/MF/complete, current & previous year reports

Annual report, by David J. Behling, Jr. et al., summarizing the aggregate financial performance of 19 multinational petroleum companies, 1984, with comparisons to 1983.

Data are compiled primarily from annual company reports to stockholders and to the SEC.

Contains listing of companies and foreword (p. 2-3); narrative report, interspersed with text tables and 21 charts (p. 4-20); and statistical section, with 13 detailed tables, listed below (p. 21-28).

Previous report, for 1983, was also reviewed during 1985, and is also available on SRI microfiche under B1900-3 [Annual. Dec. 1984. 29 p. †]. Previous report is substantially similar in format and content, but omits table on taxes.

Availability: Chase Manhattan Bank, Energy Economics, Global Petroleum Division, 7th Floor, One Chase Manhattan Plaza, New York NY 10081, †; SRI/MF/complete.

TABLES:

[Tables show data for 1983 and/or 1984, unless otherwise noted.]

1-2. Net crude oil production, and refinery crude runs [barrels per day, for U.S., Canada, Venezuela, other Western Hemisphere, and 4 Eastern Hemisphere regions]. (p. 22)

3-4. Income statement, and distribution of total revenue dollar, [by item]. (p. 23)

5. Rates of return [and earnings, for average capital employed, shareholders' equity, total assets, and gross operating profit; and average gross fixed assets]. (p. 24)

6. Source and use of working capital. (p. 24)

7. Expenditures for fixed assets [crude oil/natural gas exploration/production, natural gas liquids plants, pipelines, marine and other transportation, refineries/chemical plants, marketing, and other, for U.S. and other countries; and aggregate for U.S., Canada, Venezuela, other Western Hemisphere, and 4 Eastern Hemisphere regions]. (p. 25)

8. Capital and exploration expenditures [by function, for U.S. and other countries]. (p. 25)

9-10. Balance sheet [by item]; and earnings reinvested and employed. (p. 26)

11-12. Taxes [income and other, and total revenue]; and working capital. (p. 27)

13. Investment in fixed [gross and net] assets [for same breakdowns as in table 7]. (p. 28)

B1900-4 **1984 CAPITAL INVESTMENTS OF THE WORLD PETROLEUM INDUSTRY**
Annual. Sept. 1985. 24 p.
LC 72-621455.
SRI/MF/complete, current & 2 previous years reports

Annual report, by David J. Behling, Jr., et al., on oil and gas industry capital and exploration expenditures, by non-Communist country or world area, 1974-84. Data are estimates based on Chase Manhattan's review of the financial performance of major oil companies and on surveys of investor- and government-owned operators.

Contains foreword and narrative summary, with 6 summary charts (p. 3-10); and statistical appendix, with contents listing, definitions, and 6 tables listed below (p. 11-23).

Previous reports, for 1982-83, were also reviewed in SRI during 1985, and are also available on SRI microfiche under B1900-4 [Annual. Sept. 1984. 24 p. †; and Annual. Apr. 1985. 24 p. †].

Availability: Chase Manhattan Bank, Global Petroleum—Energy Economics, One Chase Manhattan Plaza, New York NY 10081, †; SRI/MF/complete.

TABLES:

[Tables 1-4 show data for crude oil/natural gas and natural gas liquids production, and pipelines, tankers, refineries, chemical plants, marketing, and other capital expenditures, for U.S., Canada, Venezuela, and 5 world areas. Tables 1 and 4 also include data for geological/geophysical expense/lease rentals.]

1. Capital and exploration expenditures, 1984. (p. 14-15)

2-3. Gross and net investment in fixed assets, Dec. 31, 1984. (p. 14-15)

4. Capital and exploration expenditures [and total foreign flag tankers, 1974-84]. (p. 16-21)

5. Exploration and production expenditures, U.S. (excludes natural gas liquids plants) [for

onshore and offshore lease acquisitions, producing wells, dry holes, geological/geophysical expense, and lease rentals], 1974-84. (p. 22)

6. Capital expenditures, Chase Group [of petroleum companies] vs. rest of industry [1975 and 1983-84]. (p. 23)

B1900-5   COAL SITUATION
Quarterly. Approx. 4 p.
LC sn82-20018.
SRI/MF/complete

Quarterly review of U.S. and world coal industry developments. Issues usually contain 1 article with statistics.

Features with substantial statistical content are described, as they appear, under "Statistical Features."

Availability: Chase Manhattan Bank, Global Mining and Metals Division, Coal Situation, 3rd Floor, One Chase Manhattan Plaza, New York NY 10081, †; SRI/MF/complete.

Issues reviewed during 1985: Oct. 1984-Sept. 1985 (P) (Vol. 4, No. 4; Vol. 5, Nos. 1-4).

STATISTICAL FEATURES:

B1900-5.601: Oct. 1984 (Vol. 4, No. 4)
NORTH AMERICAN ELECTRIC POWER SUPPLY AND DEMAND 1984-93

(p. 1-4) Article forecasting U.S. and Canada electricity supply and demand to 1993. Data are from North American Electric Reliability Council (NERC).

Includes 1 chart estimating U.S. growth rate for summer peak electricity demand, decennial periods beginning 1974-84. Also includes 5 tables showing the following for U.S. and Canada: electricity demand, and utility coal consumption, by NERC region; planned generating additions and distribution of electricity generation, by type of fuel; and utility coal supplies, by producing region; various periods 1983-93.

Full NERC report is covered in SRI under A8630-2.

B1900-5.602: Mar. 1985 (Vol. 5, No. 2)
INTERNATIONAL COAL TRADE 1985, ANNUAL FEATURE

(3 p.) Annual article analyzing factors affecting world coal trade through 1985. Includes 4 tables showing metallurgical and thermal coal (hard coal) imports and exports, 1983-84, and forecast 1985 under 3 economic growth assumptions; and EC hard coal imports from third party countries, 1982-84; all by country or world area.

B1900-5.603: June 1985 (Vol. 5, No. 3)
WORLD COAL OUTLOOK, 1985-2000

(2 p.) Article summarizing findings of *World Coal Outlook: A Reassessment.* Includes 2 tables showing world coal consumption by end use, and imports by transport mode, selected years 1983-2000.

Complete report is available from issuing source for $300.00, but is not presently covered by SRI.

B1900-5.604: Sept. 1985 (Vol. 5, No. 4)
SENSITIVITY OF WORLD COAL MARKETS TO FALLING OIL PRICES

(3 p.) Article analyzing the impact of crude oil prices on use of coal for electric power generation, in U.S., EC, and Japan. Data are from National Coal Assn, International Energy Agency, and original research. Includes 5 tables showing the following:

a. Price averages for coal (delivered or imported) vs. heavy fuel oil (HFO), by census division for U.S., and by coal source for EC and Japan; and crude oil prices required for coal-burning power plants to break even in switching from coal to HFO, for U.S., EC, and Japanese plants (new and with current oil-burning capability); various periods 1985.

b. Operating costs and ratios and capital costs, for typical coal- and oil-burning power plants scheduled for 1990 startup.

B2120
Chicago Board of Trade

B2120-1   1984 INTEREST RATE AND METALS FUTURES STATISTICAL ANNUAL
Annual. 1985. 352 p.
SRI/MF/complete, delayed

Annual compilation of statistics on futures trading in fixed-interest rate securities, precious metals, and stock market indexes on Chicago Board of Trade (CBT), Jan.-Dec. 1984, for delivery to 1987. Covers futures contracts on: GNMA Collateralized Depository Receipts (CDRs), GNMA II contracts (single-family level payment mortgage-backed certificates), long-term Treasury bonds, Treasury bond options, 10 year Treasury notes, silver, gold, and major market indexes.

Highlights of trading conditions are presented for each type of future, with the following trading data: 1984 deliveries against commitments, by delivery day; 1984 opening, high, low, and closing prices or premiums, and volume of sales and open contracts, by trading day and delivery month; and monthly price or premium range trends, generally from 1983/84 trading year, by trading and delivery month.

Contains contents listing (1 p.), and the following:

a. Introduction and discussion of interest rates and other factors affecting futures prices; record futures contract prices, for 1983-84 delivery and all-time, by contract month and trading date; date of highest volume of sales and open contracts for 27 commodities, including 90-day commercial paper and 8 types of futures noted above; and sales volume, monthly 1983-84 and annually 1979-84, and deliveries against commitments, monthly 1984, for 13-27 commodity contracts. (p. 1-12)

b. GNMA-CDR futures contracts: trading data, covering deliveries through June 1986; 8% and 9% contract prices and yields, daily 1984; registrations, monthly 1978-84; applications and securities issued, monthly 1977-84; and FNMA portfolio activities, monthly 1983-84. (p. 13-43)

c. GNMA II futures contracts: trading data, covering deliveries through Mar. 1985 (trading begins in Mar. 1984). (p. 45-57)

d. Treasury bond futures contracts: trading data, covering deliveries through Sept. 1987; and cash market quotes, and 9% contract prices and yields, daily 1984. (p. 59-87)

e. Treasury bond futures call and put options, and Treasury 10-year note futures contracts: trading data, covering deliveries through Sept. 1985 for Treasury bond options and through June 1986 for 10-year Treasury notes. (p. 89-272)

f. Silver (1,000 ounce) futures contracts: trading data, covering deliveries through Apr. 1986. (p. 273-301)

g. Gold (kilo) futures contracts: trading data, covering deliveries through Feb. 1986. (p. 303-331)

h. Major market index futures contracts: trading data, covering deliveries through June 1985 (trading begins July 1984; omits deliveries against commitments data). (p. 333-341)

i. Miscellaneous data: yields/rates for 8 types of financial instruments; prime rate; selected commodity wholesale prices; silver consumption by end use; monthly gold and silver imports, exports, production, and futures contracts registrations; CPI by expenditure category; monthly money supply; and quarterly GNP; various years 1974-84. (p. 342-347)

j. Index. (p. 349-352)

For description of CBT companion volume, see B2120-2, below.

Availability: Chicago Board of Trade, Education Publications, La Salle at Jackson, Chicago IL 60604, members and educators $16.00, others $17.00; set of both 1984 CBT annuals: members and educators $25.00, others $30.00; postage and handling $2.50 each, $3.00 per set; SRI/MF/complete, delayed shipment in Feb. 1986.

B2120-2   STATISTICAL ANNUAL, 1984, CHICAGO BOARD OF TRADE: Grains, Forest Products, Energy, and Options on Soybean Futures
Annual. 1985.
8+378 p.+errata.
ISSN 0163-5409.
LC 78-648247.
SRI/MF/complete, delayed

Annual report on grain, grain product, plywood, and crude oil futures traded on the Chicago Board of Trade (CBT), Jan.-Dec. 1984, for delivery to 1986.

Includes futures prices, volume, and open contracts, selected trading data for other exchanges, cash prices, and selected agricultural commodity shipment and disposition information, various years 1970-85.

Data are from CBT and other exchanges, USDA, and private research services.

Contains contents listing and introduction (8 p.); 4 statistical sections, described below (p. 1-359); and index (p. 361-378).

For description of CBT companion volume, see B2120-1, above.

Availability: Chicago Board of Trade, Education Publications, LaSalle at Jackson, Chicago IL 60604, members and educators $16.00, others

$18.00; set of both 1984 CBT annuals: members and educators $25.00, others $30.00; plus postage and handling $2.50 each, $3.00 per set; SRI/MF/complete, delayed shipment in Feb. 1986.

STATISTICAL SECTIONS:

B2120–2.1: Futures Prices, Sales, and Open Contracts

SUMMARY

a. CBT: futures highest and lowest prices generally for 1983-84 delivery and for all-time, and highest 1-day volume of sales and open contracts, all by trading date; dates trading began; contract sales volume, monthly 1983-84, and annually 1979-84; and monthly deliveries against futures commitments, 1984; all by commodity. (p. 2-7)

DAILY PRICES AND VOLUME

[Data shown for each commodity futures are: deliveries against futures commitments, daily 1984; and opening, high, low, and closing prices, and volume of sales and open contracts, by trading day Jan.-Dec. 1984 for delivery through the month noted.]

b. Wheat for delivery to Mar. 1986 (p. 8-26); corn for delivery to May 1986 (p. 27-52); oats for delivery to Dec. 1985 (p. 53-66); soybeans for delivery to Mar. 1986 (p. 67-92); soybean call and put options exercised, by strike price, for delivery to Nov. 1985 (trading begins Oct. 1984) (p. 93-134); soybean oil for delivery to Dec. 1985 (p. 135-160); and soybean meal for delivery to Dec. 1985 (p. 161-186).

c. Western plywood for delivery to Sept. 1984 (trading discontinued Sept. 1984) (p. 187-197); and crude oil for delivery to Dec. 1984 (trading discontinued July 1984) (p. 199-209).

MONTHLY PRICE RANGES

d. Monthly high and low prices for wheat, corn, oats, soybeans, soybean oil and meal, western plywood, crude oil, and soybean call and put options, by various trading years 1973/74-1984/85, and various delivery years 1975-86. (p. 210-257)

B2120–2.2: Cash Prices

RECORD PRICES

a. CBT record highest and lowest cash grain prices, with occurrence date, by commodity. (p. 259)

DAILY AND MONTHLY PRICES

b. Daily cash prices at selected commodity exchanges for wheat, corn, soybeans, soybean oil and meal, and coconut, cottonseed, and palm oils, 1984. (p. 260-281)

c. Monthly cash prices at selected commodity exchanges for crude soybean oil, palm oil, wheat, corn, grain sorghum, oats, barley, cottonseed and linseed meal, soybean meal, soybeans, and plywood; and price ratios for hog/corn, steer/corn, and broiler/feed; by crop years 1975/76-1984/85. (p. 282-287)

d. Monthly range of cash prices at selected commodity exchanges for loose lard, corn oil, and coconut, by crop year 1975-84. (p. 288)

HISTORICAL PRICES

e. Record highest and lowest cash prices for wheat, corn, and oats, 1893-1984, and for soybeans, 1947-84, including month of occurrence. (p. 289-292)

B2120–2.3: Receipts, Shipments, Exports, and Imports

RECEIPTS AND SHIPMENTS

a. Grain receipts and shipments at primary markets and CBT, by type of grain, weekly and/or monthly 1982-84, and annually 1975-84. (p. 294-297)

b. CBT receipts and shipments, by transport mode and grain type, 1975-84; shipments to Canadian and overseas ports, by grain type, 1983; lake shipments, largest 1-day receipts, and crop year receipts and shipments, by grain type, 1975-84; and St. Lawrence Seaway official opening and closing dates, 1975-84. (p. 298-301)

c. Western grain center receipts and shipments by center, 1982-84 (tables showing data for 1982-83 incorrectly read 1984); CBT and U.S. grain stocks, weekly 1984, and monthly 1971-84; and total and deliverable weekly stocks, for CBT and 3 grain centers, 1984; all by grain type. (p. 302-308)

EXPORTS AND IMPORTS

d. CBT exports by grain type, weekly 1984, and annually 1975-84; and U.S. grain exports by country of destination, for wheat, barley, oats, corn, sorghum, soybeans and cottonseed, and soybean and cottonseed meal and oil, various periods 1979/80-84. (p. 309-314)

e. U.S. exports and imports of flour, and grain by type, monthly 1984, and annually 1980-84; and exports of flour, and types of grain, oilseed, oil, and meal, including peanuts, crop years 1975/76-1983/84. (p. 315-316)

f. Grain inspected for export from U.S./Canada, by grain type, by country of destination, and by U.S. region and port area, 1984 with selected aggregate comparisons to 1983. (p. 317-320)

B2120–2.4: Supply, Disposition, and Miscellaneous

GRAINS, LIVESTOCK, AND PLYWOOD

a. Supply, disposition, and price summary for wheat, soybean oil, soybeans, and soybean meal; feed grain supply and disposition, and quarterly consumption; soybean product volume and value-price spread; and soybean crushings and capacity utilization; various periods 1972-85. (p. 322-332)

b. U.S. carry-over grain on and off farms, by crop year, by grain type, 1977-84; quarterly grain stocks, by grain type, 1976-84; and monthly Chicago registrations for soybean oil and meal, 1975-84, and for western plywood, 1982-84. (p. 333-335)

c. U.S. oil seeds monthly crushings, production, and stocks, by seed, with palm oil imports, 1975/76-1984/85; monthly prices received by farmers and parity prices, by type of grain, 1975/76-1984/85; and U.S. grain price support quantities, rate, and average farm prices, by grain, 1981/82-1983/84. (p. 336-342)

d. U.S. grain harvested acreage, yield, and production, by grain type, total 1975-84, and by State 1984; world grain production by grain type, by country and world area, 1982/83-1983/84; U.S. cattle/calf, hog, and chicken inventory, total 1975-84, and by State 1984 or 1985; and U.S. livestock inventory by detailed class, 1982-84. (p. 343-349)

e. Plywood inventory, production, exports, imports, new orders, and shipments, monthly 1977-84; and private housing permits, starts, and completions, and mobile home shipments, monthly 1984, and annually 1974-83. (p. 350-351)

FACILITIES

f. Listings of public grain elevators, and CBT nongrain storage facilities, by commodity, showing operator, location, and capacity; and U.S. and Canada commercial grain storage capacity, by principal grain center. (p. 352-354)

TARIFFS AND MISCELLANEOUS DATA

g. Carload tariff rates, from Chicago to 11 cities, Jan. 1985; annual precipitation, by State, 1972-84; U.S. customary and metric measurement equivalents and conversion factors; recommended seed planting dates, by U.S. region, and harvest months by foreign country; and U.S. tariff duties on cereal and farm product imports, and Canadian tariff duties on imports from U.S., by commodity, as of Jan. 1, 1979. (p. 355-359)

B2130
Chicago Mercantile Exchange

B2130–1 **INTERNATIONAL MONETARY MARKET YEAR BOOK, 1983**
Annual. [1984.] 575 p.
ISSN 0195-9980.
LC 79-644317.
SRI/MF/complete

Annual report on International Monetary Market (IMM) futures contracts trading in gold, silver, Treasury bills and notes, certificates of deposit, and 8 foreign currencies, 1983 and trends. Includes trading volume and price trends, and selected economic indicators for U.S. and 7 foreign countries. Data are compiled by the Statistical Dept of the Chicago Mercantile Exchange (CME).

Contains contents listing (p. 1); introduction, with 26 tables showing IMM membership sales, trading history and price range trends, and trading summary, various periods 1972-85 (p. 4-61); 4 statistical sections, with 328 tables, described below (p. 64-526); 1 chart section, with 33 trend charts (p. 529-561); and index (p. 563-575).

Availability: Chicago Mercantile Exchange, Office Services, 30 S. Wacker Dr., Chicago IL 60606, $10.00; SRI/MF/complete.

TABLES:

[Foreign currencies covered are: UK, Canada, West Germany, Netherlands, France, Japan, Mexico, and Switzerland. Data for foreign countries include the above except for the Netherlands.]

FUTURES

a. Contract daily price ranges, settlement prices or indexes, volume, and open interest, for contracts traded in 1983, for delivery as far as Dec. 1985, by commodity, as follows: 90-day Treasury bills (p. 64-97); 3-month domestic certificates of deposit (p. 98-117); 3-month Eurodollar time deposits (p. 118-138); gold bullion (p. 139-167); and 8 foreign currencies (p. 168-290). 12 tables. (p. 64-290)

b. Trading volume and interest: CME, IMM, and Index and Option Market monthly trading volume and month-end open interest, and IMM daily volume and open interest, 1983; and IMM volume, volume high, open interest, open interest high, and contracts delivered, by month, various years 1972-83; all by commodity. 94 tables. (p. 292-343)

CASH MARKET PRICES

c. Treasury bill auction market yields, for 13-, 26-, and 52-week bills; Federal debt, and gross public debt; daily cash market price ranges, for Treasury bills, certificates of deposit, Eurodollar, and Federal funds; Federal Reserve Bank of New York open-market operations; prime rate charged by banks; Federal Reserve Bank discount rates; and average money market rates; 1983, with selected trends from as early as 1970. 15 tables. (p. 346-374)

d. Gold and silver bullion average prices, London market, 1800s-1983; and daily prices for bullion and Krugerrands, by market, 1983. 11 tables. (p. 375-398)

e. Foreign currency: high, low, and last spot prices, monthly 1972-83 and daily 1983; and closing against U.S. dollar, forward rates, and London Euro deposit daily closings (including U.S. dollar), daily 1983; all by currency. 40 tables. (p. 399-494)

ECONOMIC INDICATORS AND FUNDAMENTALS

f. Gold: New York and Chicago depository holdings and movements, weekly 1983; non-Communist world production, fabrication, and end-use, by country or region, 1978-82; and U.S. production, imports, and exports, monthly 1976-83. 12 tables. (p. 496-498)

g. U.S. and 7 foreign countries: selected indicators, variously including GNP, national income, international transactions, and reserves (all with detail by item for U.S.); construction activity (U.S. only); population; balance of trade; government finances; personal income; money supply; production, price, sales, and earnings indexes; interest rates and bond yields; and others; shown monthly, quarterly, or annually, various years 1970-83. 144 tables. (p. 499-526)

B2130–2   CHICAGO MERCANTILE EXCHANGE YEAR BOOK, 1983
Annual. [1985.] 273 p.
SRI/MF/complete

Annual statistical yearbook of futures contracts traded on the Chicago Mercantile Exchange (CME), by commodity, 1983, with trends for 1970s or earlier. Includes daily prices, volume, open interest, and deliveries, shown by contract trading and delivery month, for live cattle and hogs, feeder cattle, and frozen pork bellies.

Also includes CME membership sales prices; all-time trading records; cash market prices and receipts in selected midwestern markets; hog- and beef/steer-corn price ratios; packer/shipper hog purchases; livestock slaughter and marketings; meat production; cattle and hog inventories by State; pork belly storage movement and stocks; and cold storage holdings.

Contains contents listing (p. 1); introduction, with summary of CME structure and trading regulations, and 12 tables (p. 2-28); 6 sections, with trading and delivery specifications, and 72 tables and 19 trend charts (p. 29-266); and index (p. 267-272).

For description of previous yearbook, for 1982, see SRI 1983 Annual under this number.

Availability: Chicago Mercantile Exchange, Office Services, 30 S. Wacker Dr., Chicago IL 60606, $10.00; SRI/MF/complete.

B2130–3   INDEX AND OPTION MARKET YEARBOOK, 1983
Annual. [1984.] 301 p.
SRI/MF/complete, current & previous year reports

Annual statistical yearbook of futures trading activity on the index and options market of the Chicago Mercantile Exchange (CME), 1983, with some trends from 1969. Includes trading volume; opening and closing range, high, low, and settlement prices; and open interest; by contract trading day and delivery month, for Standard & Poor's (S&P) 500 and 100 stock price indexes, random length lumber, and S&P's 500 call and put options.

Also includes membership sales prices for index and option markets; trading histories, including high and low records; summary trading on CME commodities and international monetary markets; daily performance of selected securities price indexes; daily stock volume on NYSE; weekly cash lumber prices; housing starts and permits; and lumber production and mill stocks. Data were compiled by CME.

Contains contents listing (p. 1); introduction, with summary of CME structure and trading regulations, and 13 tables (p. 2-48); 4 sections, with 89 tables and 16 trend charts (p. 49-294); and index (p. 296-301).

Report began publication with the 1982 edition, which has also been received and is also available on SRI microfiche under this number [Annual. [1983.] 285 p. $10.00]. The 1982 edition is substantially similar in format, but includes trading data for S&P 500 and lumber futures only, and also includes detailed economic indicator and population data.

Availability: Chicago Mercantile Exchange, Office Services, 30 S. Wacker Dr., Chicago IL 60606, $10.00; SRI/MF/complete.

B2320
Columbian Chemicals Co.

B2320–1   QUARTERLY CONSUMPTION REPORT: Carbon Black and Dry Rubber Hydrocarbons
Quarterly.   Approx. 3 p.
SRI/MF/complete

Quarterly report on carbon black and dry rubber hydrocarbon supply and demand. Reports are issued 3-6 months after quarter of coverage.

Issues include narrative summary, and 1 table and 1 chart showing carbon black production and shipments, by grade; and dry rubber hydrocarbon and carbon black domestic consumption, by type or grade; for quarter of coverage, with comparisons to selected previous periods.

Availability: Columbian Chemicals Co., 3200 W. Market St., PO Box 5373, Akron OH 44313, †; SRI/MF/complete.

Issues reviewed during 1985: 1st-2nd Qtrs. 1985 (D) [No reports for 2nd-4th Qtrs. 1984 were published].

B2360
Commercial Service Systems, Inc.

B2360–1   SHOPLIFTING in Supermarkets, Drug Stores, Discount Stores, 22nd Annual Report
Annual. Apr. 30, 1985 19 p.
SRI/MF/complete

Annual report, by Roger Griffin, on shoplifters apprehended in supermarkets, drugstores, and discount stores, 1984, with selected trends from 1973. Also includes shoplifter characteristics and circumstances, and type and value of recovered merchandise. Data are from a study of 28,296 shoplifting apprehensions at 1,043 stores located in Southern California and other western States.

Contains introduction (1 p.); contents listing, and formulas for estimating shoplifting losses for individual retailers (p. 1-5); 21 tables, listed below (p. 6-18); and sample apprehension report form (p. 19).

Availability: Commercial Service Systems, Inc., PO Box 3307, Van Nuys CA 91407, †; SRI/MF/complete, except sample apprehension report form.

TABLES:

[Most tables show data for supermarkets, drugstores, and discount stores, 1984.]

[1-4] Average number of items and value of merchandise recovered per apprehension [all cases, and for adults and juveniles by sex]. (p. 6-7)

[5-6] Number of cases in which 1 to 25 items were recovered; and value range [of] merchandise recovered. (p. 8-9)

[7-8] Shoplifters referred to police [adults prosecuted and juveniles referred, by sex]. (p. 10)

[9-14] When apprehension occurred [time of day, month, and day of week]; sex of shoplifter [adults and juveniles]; age of shoplifter; and [percent of] shoplifters under 30 years of age. (p. 11-13)

[15] Cigarettes recovered [cigarette item recoveries as percent of all cases and of all merchandise value, for 8 unnamed companies, 1982-84]. (p. 14)

[16-17] Value of merchandise recovered [total and cigarettes]; and categories of merchandise recovered. (p. 15)

[18] Methods of concealment. (p. 16)

[19-21] Shoplifting [summary] data [various years 1973-84]. (p. 17-18)

B2380
Commodity Exchange, Inc.

B2380–1 COMEX 1984 STATISTICAL YEARBOOK
Annual. For individual publication data, see below.
ISSN 0162-4970.
LC 78-645223.
SRI/MF/complete

Annual statistical yearbook of futures trading on the Commodity Exchange, Inc. (COMEX) during 1984. Covers gold, silver, copper, and aluminum; and gold and silver options. Data are compiled by COMEX.

Yearbook is issued in 2 volumes, covering metals futures and options. Volumes are individually described below.

Availability: Commodity Exchange, Inc., Four World Trade Center, New York NY 10048, $15.00+$1.50 postage and handling per volume; SRI/MF/complete

B2380–1.1: Metals Data, 1984
[Annual. 1985. 151 p. SRI/MF/complete.]
Annual report on COMEX futures trading during 1984, for delivery through Sept. or Oct. 1986. Covers gold, silver, copper, and aluminum contracts.

Contents:

a. Introduction, contents listing, trading summary, contract specifications, 1 summary table, and abbreviations key. (p. 3-10)

b. Trading data for gold (p. 12-42), silver (p. 44-73), copper (p. 76-105), and aluminum (p. 108-137), with 7 tables for each metal, showing opening, high, low, closing, and settlement prices, volume traded, and open interest, all by trading day and delivery month; and depository or warehouse stocks, and deliveries, by day.

c. Metals prices, with 7 tables showing London bullion fixing, and Handy and Harman base prices, for gold and silver; and copper prices for U.S. producers cathode, refiners scrap No. 2, and New York dealers spot cathode; all by trading day. (p. 140-150)

B2380–1.2: Options Data, 1984
[Annual. 1985. 135 p. SRI/MF/complete.]
Annual report on COMEX trading in gold and silver put and call options during 1984, for delivery through Aug. 1985 (gold) or Sept. 1985 (silver).

Contents:

a. Introduction, contents listing, trading summary, contract specifications, 1 summary table, and abbreviations key. (p. 3-11)

b. Trading data for put and call options, for gold (p. 14-105) and silver (p. 108-133), with 7 tables for each metal, showing opening, high, low, closing, and settlement prices, volume traded, and open interest, by trading day and delivery month; and options exercised during contract life and at expiration, by strike price and month.

B2975
Deutsch, Shea and Evans

B2975–1 HIGH TECHNOLOGY RECRUITMENT INDEX
Monthly. 2 p.
SRI/MF/complete, shipped quarterly

Monthly press release presenting index of demand for engineers/scientists based on recruitment advertising in approximately 40 major newspapers and technical journals (1961=base year).

Includes brief narrative, and 1 table showing high technology recruitment index for month of coverage and/or 3-month running average, current to 1-2 months prior to publication date, with comparisons to previous 11-12 months.

Availability: Deutsch, Shea and Evans, ◆; SRI/MF/complete, shipped quarterly.

Issues reviewed during 1985: Nov. 16, 1984-Oct. 22, 1985 (P).

B3075
Douglas Aircraft Co.

B3075–1 OUTLOOK FOR COMMERCIAL AIRCRAFT, 1985-99
Annual. Sept. 1985. i+46 p.
SRI/MF/complete

Annual report projecting world airline traffic and aircraft requirements to 1999, with trends from 1971. Includes passenger and cargo traffic; passenger seat capacity and load factors; passenger aircraft retirements, orders/options, deliveries, and new aircraft requirements (number and value), all by class of aircraft; and cargo fleet composition and aircraft demand, by size of aircraft.

Selected traffic data are shown by world region, and for scheduled and nonscheduled service in U.S. and elsewhere. Cargo traffic data include detail for all-cargo and passenger/cargo combined transport.

Projections are derived from econometric models for 32 International Air Transport Assn regions, and are based on data from 96 individual airlines.

Contains contents listing (p. i); introduction, and 7 report sections, with 26 charts and 2 tables (p. 1-35); and appendices, with definitions and 8 tables (p. 38-45).

Availability: Douglas Aircraft Co., Marketing Strategic Plans (18-70), 3855 Lakewood Blvd., Long Beach CA 90846, ‡; SRI/MF/complete.

B3370
Exxon Corp.

B3370–1 TURBINE-ENGINED FLEETS OF THE WORLD'S AIRLINES, 1985
Annual. 1985. 42 p.
SRI/MF/complete

Annual report on world air carrier turbine-powered fleets, covering aircraft in service and on order as of Mar. 31, 1985. Data are compiled by Aviation Data Service, Inc., from survey responses of 780 airlines, including local service/commuter airlines.

Contains narrative summary (p. 1); 2 tables showing turbine-powered aircraft and helicopters in service and on order as of Mar. 31, 1985, by manufacturer and model, arranged by propulsion type, and arranged alphabetically by airline, with airline country of operation, aircraft engine specifications, and remarks on options and leases (p. 2-41); and glossary (p. 42).

Report is issued each year as a supplement to *Air World Survey,* a narrative report not covered in SRI.

Availability: Exxon International, Commercial Department, Air World Survey, 200 Park Ave., Florham Park NJ 07932, †; SRI/MF/complete.

B3370–4 EXXON BACKGROUND SERIES
Series. For individual publication data, see below.
SRI/MF/complete

Continuing series of reports on world petroleum industry. Reports are prepared by the Exxon Corp. Public Affairs Dept and are based on data collected from private and government sources.

Reports are issued intermittently, usually once each year. Each report covers a single topic and consists of narrative analysis interspersed with a few tables and/or charts.

Report reviewed during 1985 is described below.

Availability: Exxon Corp., Public Affairs Department, 1251 Ave. of the Americas, New York NY 10020, †; SRI/MF/complete.

B3370–4.2: Middle East Oil and Gas
[Monograph. Dec. 1984. 40 p. SRI/MF/complete.]
Report presenting an overview of oil and gas supply and demand situation for the Middle East, by country, 1970s-83, with trends from as early as 1945. Includes data on oil and gas production and proved reserves; producing oil wells; gas utilization; production capacity for natural gas liquids and oil refining; domestic consumption of energy products; and land area, population, and government oil revenues.

Also includes data on Arabian light crude oil prices, and aggregate OPEC oil production; and selected comparisons to other countries and world areas.

Data are from a variety of specified Federal and private sources.

Contains listings of contents, tables, charts, and maps (2 p.); and narrative report interspersed with 3 maps, 10 charts, and 12 tables (p. 2-40).

B3500
First Hawaiian Bank

B3500–1   ECONOMIC INDICATORS,
Hawaii
Bimonthly, with annual
summary. Approx. 8 p.
ISSN 0015-2757.
SRI/MF/complete

Bimonthly report, with annual summary, reviewing Hawaii business activity, employment, population, and personal income changes. Includes selected data by county and industry. Data are compiled by the Research Dept of First Hawaiian Bank.

Period of coverage is 2-4 months prior to publication, and is specified for each data series covered. Some data are reprinted in the following issue if more recent figures are not available.

Each issue contains contents listing; feature articles, sometimes with trend charts; and 6 bimonthly tables listed below. The annual summary accompanies a spring issue (usually Mar./Apr.).

A special supplement reviewing economic issues in the Hawaii State Legislature during 1985/86 was also published and is also available on SRI microfiche under this number.

Availability: First Hawaiian Bank, Research Department, PO Box 3200, Honolulu HI 96847, †; SRI/MF/complete.

Issues reviewed during 1985: Sept./Oct. 1984-July/Aug. 1985 (P); special legislative supplement, Feb. 1985; and annual summary for 1983-84.

BIMONTHLY TABLES:
[All tables include percent change from preceding period and from same period of previous year. Some data are reported cumulatively from Jan. Table content may vary slightly from issue to issue.

Tables are repeated in annual summary, showing data for previous 2 years.]

[1] U.S. economic indicators [approximately 15 selected indicators].

[2] Business activity [tourism (includes visitors, accommodations, and hotel occupancy rate, all by county, and meeting attendance); defense expenditures; sugar production and sales value; pineapple shipments and sales value; crop and livestock production and prices for selected commodities; construction put in place, permits authorized by type and county, public contracts awarded by level of government and county, and cost indexes; housing sales and prices, by county; business sales (gross receipts, sales in 5 industry sectors, and Oahu new car sales); electricity generated, gas sales, and telephone lines in service; and Honolulu CPI].

[3] Population [by county, and for military personnel and foreign immigration]; and personal income [by industry division and type, and per capita by county].

[4] Employment and jobs [shows employment and unemployment, by county; jobs, by industry sector and/or county, and for self-employed; and unemployment insurance claims and payments].

[5] Public assistance [recipients and payments, by type of service].

[6] Banking and finance [bank total and demand deposits by county, and loans outstanding by type; Honolulu conventional home mortgage rates; savings and loan assn deposits and loans; and tax collections by county].

B3500–2   NEIGHBOR ISLAND
PROFILES
Series. For individual
publication data, see below.
SRI/MF/complete

Annual series of reports on socioeconomic conditions and trends in Hawaii, for Hawaii, Kauai, and Maui Counties. Data are prepared by the research division of First Hawaiian Bank.

Each report covers a single county and contains narrative analysis and 1 table generally showing the following data:

a. Population, per capita personal income, civilian labor force by employment status, and number of jobs.

b. Business receipts, tax collections, and bank deposits and debits to demand deposits.

c. Tourism, including number of westbound visitors with intended length of stay, and hotel inventory and occupancy.

d. Construction private permits by type of unit, and public contracts awarded by level of government; sales of single-family homes and condominiums, with average prices; electricity generated; and telephone access lines.

e. Sugar production, and value of livestock and crops.

Data for Honolulu County are not covered in this series, but are included in bimonthly *Economic Indicators* (covered in SRI under B3500-1).

Reports for 1984 on Kauai and Maui Counties, and report for 1985 on Maui County are described below; for description of 1984 report on Hawaii County, see SRI 1984 Annual under this number.

No 1983 reports were published; for description of 1982 reports, see SRI 1983 Annual under this number. Series title has changed from *Hawaii Counties Report.*

Availability: First Hawaiian Bank, Research Department, PO Box 3200, Honolulu HI 96847, †; SRI/MF/complete.

B3500–2.1: Kauai County in 1984
[Annual. Sept./Oct. 1984. 8 p. SRI/MF/complete.]

Presents data for 1979-1st 7 months 1984.

B3500–2.2: Maui County in 1984
[Annual. Nov./Dec. 1984. 8 p. SRI/MF/complete.]

Presents data for 1979-1st 9 months 1984.

B3500–2.3: Maui County in 1985
[Annual. July/Aug. 1985. 4 p. SRI/MF/complete.]

Presents data for 1980-1st 5 months 1985.
Detailed table omits data on bank deposits and debits to demand deposits, visitors intended length of stay, public contracts awarded by government level, electricity generated, and telephone access lines; and includes data on visitor expenditures and pineapple sales.

B3700
First National Bank of
Chicago

B3700–1   CONSUMER FINANCE
(DIRECT CASH LENDING)
COMPANY RATIOS
Annual. [1985.] 3 p.
SRI/MF/complete

Annual report presenting aggregate lending ratios and other financial data for consumer finance companies involved in direct cash lending, Dec. 1980-84. Data are based on a mail survey, conducted by Robert Morris Associates, of a cross-section of national and regional loan companies.

Contains 1 table showing 41 items as of Dec. 31, 1980-84, including numerous financial and lending ratios, lending volume for year, total amount outstanding, average loan size and balance, and percent delinquent accounts by days past due.

Report has been published since 1948.

Availability: First National Bank of Chicago, Group D, One First National Plaza, Suite 0084, Chicago IL 60670, †; SRI/MF/complete.

B3700–3   DIVERSIFIED FINANCE
COMPANY RATIOS
Annual. [1985.] 3 p.
SRI/MF/complete

Annual report presenting aggregate lending ratios and other financial data for diversified finance companies, Dec. 1980-84. Data are based on a mail survey, conducted by Robert Morris Associates, of a cross-section of national and regional diversified finance companies.

Contains 1 table showing 49 items as of Dec. 31, 1980-84, including numerous financial and lending ratios, lending volume for year, total amount outstanding, analysis of retail auto lending, and percent of loan balances delinquent 60 days/more.

Report has been published since 1935.

Availability: First National Bank of Chicago, Group D, One First National Plaza, Suite 0084, Chicago IL 60670, †; SRI/MF/complete.

B3900
First
Security Bank of Idaho

B3900–1   IDAHO CONSTRUCTION
REPORT: Authorized
Building Permit
Construction, 56 Major
Locations
Monthly. 5 p.
SRI/MF/complete, shipped
quarterly

Monthly report on Idaho construction activity, by location. Data are compiled by First Security Bank of Idaho. Reports are issued approximately 1 month after month of coverage.

Contains brief narrative; 1 summary table; and 4 detailed tables showing housing units constructed, building permits issued, value of new residential and nonresidential construction, and value of alterations/repairs, in approximately 55 Idaho cities and counties, for month of coverage, year to date, and same periods of previous year. *Availability:* Dr. Kelly K. Matthews, First Security Co., PO Box 30006, Salt Lake City UT 84125, †; SRI/MF/complete, shipped quarterly. *Issues reviewed during 1985:* Oct. 1984-Aug. 1985 (D) (Vol. 31, Nos. 10-12; Vol. 32, Nos. 1-8).

B3940
General Electric Mortgage Insurance Corp.

B3940-1   SURVEY OF ADJUSTABLE TYPE MORTGAGES
Annual. Aug. 1984. 74 p.
Survey No. 5.
SRI/MF/complete

Annual report on alternative mortgage lending practices of savings and loan assns (S&Ls) and other lenders, as of Aug. 1984. Focuses on adjustable rate mortgages (ARMs), and includes data by S&L asset size and region. Covers the following data topics:

a. Types of mortgages offered (conventional fixed-rate, ARMs, balloon, and growing equity-type), and each type's share of total lending; VA/FHA share of total lending; types of mortgages purchased; and whether offering second mortgages.

b. Conventional mortgages and ARMs: whether mortgages are originated for own portfolio; primary purchaser of mortgages (Freddie Mac, Fannie Mae, private investor, or other); and delinquency and foreclosure rates.

c. Conventional mortgages: maturity, prepayment penalties, interest rates, and other features of fixed-rate mortgages; plans to de-emphasize or discontinue fixed-rate mortgages; total volume of conventional mortgage originations; and percent of conventional business insured by private mortgage insurance companies.

d. ARMs: number of ARM plans offered, most popular plan, and index used for most popular plan; qualifying payment-income ratio, initial interest rates, caps, adjustment frequencies, and other features of ARMs; and methods of providing information on ARMs, and recipients of information.

Data are based on a survey of 400 S&Ls and 100 mortgage and commercial banks, conducted July 25-Aug. 3, 1984 by Research Triangle Institute. S&Ls surveyed are a representative sample; banks surveyed are those with largest mortgage servicing volume in 1984. Survey response rate was approximately 92%.

Contains introduction and highlights (p. 1-12); 1 summary table and 23 charts (p. 13-38); methodology (p. 39-42); and 59 detailed tables (p. 44-74).

Previous report, presenting results of June 1983 survey, is described in SRI 1983 Annual under this number. Report previously was issued semiannually.

Availability: General Electric Mortgage Insurance Corp., PO Box 177800, Raleigh NC 27619, $15.00, additional copies $3.00; SRI/MF/complete.

B4000
Grant, Alexander, and Co.

B4000-1   SIXTH ANNUAL STUDY OF GENERAL MANUFACTURING CLIMATES of the Forty-Eight Contiguous States of America
Annual.   June 1985.   138 p.
LC sn84-10500.
SRI/MF/not filmed

Annual report ranking manufacturing business climate factors in 48 contiguous States and 8 regions, 1984. Covers fiscal policy, State regulated employment costs, labor force availability and productivity, union employment, energy costs, environmental control, and population.

Report is intended to assist manufacturers in site selection. Data are derived from Federal Government reports, U.S. Chamber of Commerce, Insurance Technical and Actuarial Consultants Corp., and other sources.

Contains contents listing (1 p.) and the following:

a. Executive summary, with 1 map and 3 tables; and narrative analyses, background, and methodology, interspersed with 2 tables on factor weighting. (p. 1-39)

b. 22 tables on individual factors, listed below. (p. 41-85)

c. State analyses, each with an illustrative chart and 1 table showing the following: national and regional composite rank for all, government, and nongovernment factors; and rank, factor value, and national average, for each factor; all for 1984. (p. 87-135)

Availability: Manufacturing Climates Study, Alexander Grant and Co., 1700 Prudential Plaza, Chicago IL 60601, $35.00; SRI/MF/not filmed.

MEASUREMENT FACTOR TABLES:
[All tables show factor value and national and regional rank, by State, with regional averages, 1984.]

FISCAL POLICY, UNEMPLOYMENT INSURANCE, AND WORKERS' COMPENSATION

A1-A5. State/local taxes per $1,000 of personal income, and percentage change over 3 years; government general expenditure vs. general revenue growth over 3 years; and government debt and welfare expenditure, per capita. (p. 42-51)

B1-B4. Average unemployment compensation benefits paid per year, and net worth of State unemployment compensation trust fund, per covered worker; maximum weekly payment for permanent/temporary total disability under workers' compensation insurance; and weighted average workers' compensation levels per $100 of payroll [aggregated] for manufacturing classifications. (p. 52-59)

LABOR COSTS, AVAILABILITY, AND PRODUCTIVITY

C1-C4. Annual average hourly manufacturing wage, and percentage change over 3 years; and union manufacturing employment as a percent of total manufacturing employment, and percentage change over 2 years in the union manufacturing work force. (p. 60-67)

D1-D5. Government-funded vocational educational enrollment as a percentage of population 16-64 years of age; percentage of high school educated adults between 25-64 years of age; average percent of manufacturing working time lost due to work stoppages over 2 years involving 1,000 or more workers; value added by manufacturing employees per dollar of production payroll; and annual average hours worked per week. (p. 68-77)

OTHER FACTORS

E1-E4. Fuel/electric energy costs per million Btu(s) for manufacturers; net pollution abatement expenditures as a percentage of the value of manufacturing shipments; population density per square mile; and net change in population over 3 years. (p. 78-85)

B4050
Grimm, W. T., and Co.

B4050-1   MERGERSTAT REVIEW, 1984
Annual.   1985.   iv+205 p
LC sn83-11979.
SRI/MF/excerpts

Annual report on business mergers, acquisitions, and divestitures, 1984, with trends from 1963. Covers announced transfers of ownership involving at least 10% of a company's assets or equity, and divestitures with a minimum purchase price of $500,000.

Includes data on number of transactions and dollar value paid; largest transactions, with participants and price paid; methods of payment; transactions involving foreign buyers and sellers, with detail by country; outcomes of tender offers; leveraged buyouts; acquisitions of public and private companies; premiums (over market price) and price/earnings ratios paid; and terminated transactions.

Other data include transaction volume and characteristics for specific industries; and rankings of industries, companies, States, and regions by various indicators of acquisition and/or divestiture activity.

Also includes a roster of 291 individual transactions in 1984, showing date, participants, seller's line of business and annual sales, price paid, payment method, and selected other financial aspects of each transaction.

Data are from W. T. Grimm and Co. research, and other private sources.

Contains introduction and contents listing (p. i-iv), and the following:

Section I. Statistical Review and Discussion. Includes 81 tables. (p. 1-128)

Section II-III. Historical Data Checklist, and Industry Analysis. Includes 4 tables. (p. 129-146)

Section IV. Transaction Roster. (p. 147-205)

This is the 5th annual report.

Availability: W. T. Grimm and Co., 135 S. La Salle St., Chicago IL 60603, $125.00; SRI/MF/excerpts for all sections except transaction roster.

B4300
Handy and Harman

B4300–1   SILVER MARKET, 1984,
69th Annual Review
Annual. 1985. 26 p.
ISSN 0361-2732.
LC 81-649254.
SRI/MF/complete

Annual report on silver market activity in the U.S. and non-Communist world, including stocks, consumption by end use, foreign trade, and prices, 1980-84, with selected trends from 1975. Data are compiled from reports by government and private sources, and U.S. Bureau of Mines *Mineral Industry Surveys*.

Contents:

a. Highlights, contents listing, and market review for world, U.S., UK, West Germany, France, Canada, Mexico, Japan, and India, 1984; with text statistics, 3 U.S. trend charts, and 1 table showing Japan industrial silver consumption by end use, 1983-84. (p. 2-18)

b. Summary of world stocks and outlook, with 1 table showing private and U.S. Government stocks by depository, estimated total foreign government stocks, and conjectural U.S. and foreign stocks, 1983-84. (p. 19-20)

c. Statistical section, with 6 detailed tables listed below. (p. 21-26)

Availability: Handy and Harman, Advertising Department, 850 Third Ave., New York NY 10022, †; SRI/MF/complete.

TABLES:
[Data are for 1980-84, unless otherwise noted. Most data for 1984 are preliminary.]

[1-2] World silver consumption and supplies (excluding Communist-dominated areas) [including industrial uses, coinage, new production, and secondary supply sources, mostly with detail for U.S. and selected other countries]. (p. 22-23)

[3] U.S. industrial consumption of silver, by end use. (p. 24)

[4-5] Imports of silver into and exports from the U.S. [by country]. (p. 25)

[6] Silver quotations [high, low, and average New York (Handy and Harman) and London daily fixing prices, 1975-84]. (p. 26)

B4490
Heidrick and Struggles

B4490–2   PROFILE SERIES
Series. For individual
publication data, see below.
SRI/MF/complete

Continuing series of reports on selected characteristics and attitudes of corporate executives. Most data are from Heidrick and Struggles' surveys of executives in the largest U.S. industrial corporations and selected nonindustrial sectors.

Reports generally contain introduction and narrative summary of findings, and tables presenting survey response data.

Reports are updated either irregularly or annually. Reports reviewed during 1985 are described below.

Availability: Heidrick and Struggles, 125 S. Wacker Dr., Suite 2800, Chicago IL 60606; SRI/MF/complete.

B4490–2.11: Human Resources: Function in Transition
[Recurring (irreg.) 1984. 16 p. $20.00. SRI/MF/complete.]

Recurring report profiling corporate human resource depts and executives. Data are from 284 reponses to a summer 1984 survey of 894 companies among the 1,000 largest industrials/nonindustrials.

Includes 8 charts and 14 tables showing survey response concerning domestic and foreign employment size; unionization; human resource dept's budget, payroll share, staff size, functions, and program success; 3 companies with best programs; and human resource executive's title, responsibilities, compensation, perquisites, experience, workweek, place of birth (U.S. regions and foreign), sex, marital status, age, and educational background.

Most data are shown for all companies, all industrials, industrials by sales size, and all nonindustrials.

Report updates a 1977 survey. SRI coverage begins with the 1984 edition.

B4490–2.12: Changing Board
[Annual. 1985. 12 p. $35.00. SRI/MF/complete.]

Annual board profile series update, for 1984, presenting survey findings on the composition, compensation, and policies of corporate boards of directors.

Data are based on a late 1984 survey of 500 largest industrial companies and 500 leading nonindustrial companies. Survey response rate was 39.1%.

Includes 5 charts and 18 tables showing the following data, generally for all companies, all industrials, industrials by sales size, and all nonindustrials:

a. Board size and number of meetings; chairman's role in management; board composition by sex and race and whether independent or company-affiliated; and number, purposes, and membership restrictions of board committees.

b. Director compensation amount and basis; outside director perquisites, retirement policy, and expected time commitment; board procedures for evaluating chief executive officer; and primary board concerns.

c. Chairmen's views on selected aspects of board operations.

This is the 10th survey.

B4490–2.13: Mobile Manager
[Recurring (irreg.) 1985. 16 p. $20.00. SRI/MF/complete.]

Recurring report on recently appointed corporate executives, based on 545 responses to a 1985 survey of chairmen/presidents/vice-presidents whose appointments were announced in *The Wall Street Journal* during 2nd half 1984; with selected comparisons to 1979 survey.

Includes 10 charts and 16 tables showing survey response on the following, with selected detail by respondent age group:

a. Demographic characteristics (age, sex, race-ethnicity, religion, education, marital status, and spouse's employment status); title; compensation, and change with recent appointment; types of perquisites received; employer size, type, and location (5 regions and foreign); and job sources, including executive recruiter, personal contact, and newspaper advertisement.

b. Number of employers during career; willingness to relocate; weekly work hours; satisfaction with career progress; vacation weeks; planned retirement age; leadership style; experience as mentor and protege; definition of corporate loyalty; and views on selected business issues.

This is the 9th recurring report; 7th and 8th reports, for 1981-82, are described in SRI 1983 Annual under B4490-2.5 and B4490-2.6.

B4500
Hertz Corp.

B4500–2   NEW CAR OPERATING
COSTS SURVEY, 1984
Annual. Feb. 18, 1985.
4+7 p.
SRI/MF/complete

Annual press release presenting Hertz Corp. estimates, for 1984, of the per mile cost of owning and operating new U.S. model cars. Includes estimates for 1984 models, and comparative estimates from 1972-83 model years, by size category and use duration.

Contains narrative summary with text statistics (p. 1-4); 6 tables, listed below (4 p.); and methodology (2 p.).

Availability: Hertz Corp., Public Affairs Department, 660 Madison Ave., New York NY 10021, †; SRI/MF/complete.

TABLES:
[Operating costs are expressed in cents per mile. Current data may not be comparable to earlier data due to car size group changes. Car size groups include subcompact, compact, midsize, intermediate, and standard.]

IA. Estimates of 1984 new car ownership and operating costs [averages for various annual mileages and years of use, by car size group]; and historical comparisons of new intermediate-size car costs, [selected years 1925-84].

IB. Estimates of 1984 model new passenger [compact] car ownership and operating costs; and current 1984 data compact car expenses, yearly costs and mileages; [all by years of use, for constant and declining annual mileage].

II. Breakout of new car ownership and operating costs over the years [including depreciation, insurance/licenses/fees, interest, maintenance/repair, and gasoline/other service station expenses; by purchase price and years owned, for 1972-84 model intermediate cars and 1979-84 model compact cars].

III. Yearly and lifetime costs of intermediate-size car bought new in 1975, driven 10,000 miles per year and scrapped in 1984 [cost breakdowns similar to those in table II].

IV. 10-year summary of domestic auto size changes [price, wheelbase, overall length, and weight; by car size group, 1973-84 model years].

B4500–4 HERTZ '84 20-CITY CAR COST STUDY
Annual. Mar. 25, 1985.
4 p. + 10 p. no paging.
SRI/MF/complete

Annual press release presenting Hertz Corp. estimates of 1984 domestic model auto ownership and operating costs in 20 major cities. Also includes estimates for earlier models.

Contains narrative summary, with text statistics (p. 1-4); 10 tables, described below (8 p.); and explanation of cost calculations (2 p.).

Previous report, for 1983, was unavailable for review. Report for 1982, titled *Big-City Car Costs, 1982,* is described in SRI 1983 Annual under this number.

Availability: Hertz Corp., Public Affairs Department, 660 Madison Ave., New York NY 10021, †; SRI/MF/complete.

TABLES:
a. City rankings by compact auto ownership/operating cost per mile, 1979-84; 1984 model average purchase price, depreciation, maintenance/repair, and other costs; and total operating costs per mile for 5 size groups; all for autos kept 5 years at 10,000 miles per year, shown for 20 individual cities, with selected 20-city and U.S. averages. 3 tables.

b. Average auto ownership/operating costs: for 1984 models, by annual mileage, years of use, and size group, with detail for compact autos; for intermediate-size autos, selected years 1925-84; and by cost item, size group, and years of use, selected years 1972-84, with detail for 1975 intermediate-size autos. 6 tables.

c. Size and price of selected models in each size group, selected years 1973-84. 1 table.

B4500–6 MOTOR VEHICLE OPERATING COSTS AND FUEL USAGE, 1984
Annual. Aug. 12, 1985.
6 p. + 7 p. no paging.
SRI/MF/complete, current & previous year reports

Annual press release presenting Hertz Corp. estimates of the annual cost of automobile and truck ownership, operation, and fuel use, 1984, with selected trends from 1925. Also includes data on average mileages, various years 1950-84.

Data are based on records of approximately 400,000 vehicles in the Hertz lease-rental fleet, projected on the basis of national vehicle registrations and mileage statistics.

Contains narrative summary with text statistics (p. 1-6); and 7 tables, listed below (7 p.).

Previous report, for 1983, has also been received in 1985, and is also available on SRI microfiche under B4500-6 [Annual. Aug. 6, 1984. 6 p. + 7 p. no paging. †]. Report for 1982 is described in SRI 1983 Annual under this number.

Availability: Hertz Corp., Public Affairs Department, 660 Madison Ave., New York NY 10021, †; SRI/MF/complete.

TABLES:
[Tables I-III show data for passenger cars and trucks, various years 1950-84.]

I. Vehicle operating costs and fuel usage key year summaries [including total, depreciation, fuel, and other costs, per unit, per mile, and per capita; and average new vehicle purchase price; new vehicle registrations; total vehicles on road; average annual mileage, and fuel consumption, per vehicle and per capita; and fuel cost per gallon].

II. Average motor vehicle ownership and operating expenses by years [cost per unit and per mile, miles per year, and units on road].

III. Mileage traveled and fuel used, by purpose [business, essential family use, commuting, and pleasure].

4A-4B. Estimates of 1984 [model] new car [per mile] ownership/operating costs [at various annual mileages for 1-10 years of usage, by size group (subcompact, compact, midsize, intermediate, and full size); with detail for compact models].

[A]. Historical comparisons of new intermediate size car costs [average 3- and 10-year usages, at varying average annual mileages, selected years 1925-84].

[B]. Current 1984 data, compact car expenses: [yearly costs and mileages for various ownership periods].

B4500–7 CAR AND TRUCK LEASE-RENTAL STUDY
Annual. Aug. 31, 1985.
6 p. + 7 p. no paging.
SRI/MF/complete

Annual press release on the passenger car and truck lease-rental industry, including revenues, vehicles, mileage, and fuel consumption, 1984, with trends from 1950. Also presents general data on vehicle sales for personal vs. nonpersonal use, and mileage and fuel consumption by purpose of travel. Data are Hertz Corp. estimates.

Contents:
a. Narrative analysis, with text statistics. (p. 1-6)

b. 1 table showing the following for passenger cars and/or trucks: lease and rental units and revenues, with detail for lease units by whether fleet or individual car and by whether full service or financed truck; new units in lease/rental service; vehicles on the road; lease/rental units' fuel consumption and mileage; and fleet cars on the road and mileage; with selected comparisons to all vehicles, selected years 1950-84. (3 p.)

c. 2 tables showing domestic and imported fleet and individual new car sales; and mileage traveled and fuel used, for trucks and for passenger cars by purpose of travel; various years 1950-84. (3 p.)

d. 1 table showing new and used domestic and imported cars sold for personal and nonpersonal use, 1984. (1 p.)

Availability: Hertz Corp., Public Affairs Department, 660 Madison Ave., New York NY 10021, †; SRI/MF/complete.

B4550
Honeywell, Inc.

B4550–1 OFFICE AUTOMATION AND THE WORKPLACE
Series. For individual publication data, see below.
SRI/MF/not filmed

Continuing series of reports on aspects of office automation, including extent of use, effects on productivity, and attitudes of professional, managerial, and clerical workers. Data are based on surveys of office personnel, conducted or sponsored by Honeywell, Inc.

Series begins with the reports described below.

Availability: Honeywell Office Management Systems Division, 300 Concord Rd., MA 30-811A, Billerica MA 01821, †; SRI/MF/not filmed.

B4550–1.1: National Survey of Managers and Secretaries
[Monograph. Mar. 1983. 105 p. var. paging. SRI/MF/not filmed.]

Report comparing secretaries' and managers' perceptions of the impact of automation on office environment and productivity.

Includes data on principal work activities and time requirements; perceived need for typing skills among managers; methods for improving productivity; types of automated equipment in office, extent of use, and satisfaction with equipment; and principal concerns about equipment, with detail for users and non-users. Also includes job titles, length of experience, and other sample characteristics.

Data are from responses of 909 secretary/manager pairs, to a Nov. 1982-Jan. 1983 survey conducted by Response Analysis Corp.

Contains contents listing (1 p.); executive summary, with 1 text table (p. ii-vii); 3 chapters, with narrative analysis and 38 tables (75 p.); and methodology and questionnaire facsimiles (34 p.).

B4550–1.2: National Survey of Knowledge Workers
[Monograph. Nov. 1984. 92 p. SRI/MF/not filmed.]

Report on implications of office automation as perceived by administrative professionals, including administrators in marketing, purchasing, finance, design/analysis, operations, personnel, and legal services.

Includes data on overall definition of office automation; automated equipment availability, use, and training; automation effects on work activities, productivity, personnel levels, and career advancement; preferences regarding working in office or at home; software adequacy and whether purchased or developed in-house; top management expectations and support for automation; and non-user interest in computer acquisition.

Data generally cover personal computers, computer terminals, word processors, teleconferencing facilities, programmable telephones, and electronic mail and message centers. Most data include detail by demographic characteristics and area of professional expertise.

Data are from responses of 701 professionals, employed by Forbes 500 corporations, to an Aug./Sept. 1984 survey sponsored by Honeywell, Inc.

Contains contents listing, summary, and methodology (p. 1-8); narrative analysis, interspersed with 34 tables (p. 9-68); and 3 appendices, including sample characteristics, respondent job titles, and questionnaire facsimile with summary responses (p. 69-92).

B4550–2   INDOOR AIR QUALITY: A National Survey of Office Worker Attitudes
Monograph.   Feb. 1985.
54 p.
SRI/MF/complete

Survey report on opinions of workers concerning air quality in the office.

Includes data on conditions perceived as important to a productive work environment; prevalence and causes of good and poor air quality, and effect of poor air quality on workers, office environment, and productivity; concern of management about air quality, and whether management has been asked to install air cleaner; and measures actually taken to improve air quality.

Also includes data on presence and type of air clearning equipment; and presence of windows, and how often opened.

Some data include detail by worker sex, and by office characteristics including type of work area (crowded, enclosed, or open) and age of building.

Data are from responses of 600 office workers to a Sept. 1984 survey sponsored by Honeywell, Inc.

Contains contents listing, summary, and survey methodology (p. 1-7); narrative analysis interspersed with 21 tables (p. 8-39); and appendices, with 1 table on survey sample characteristics, and questionnaire facsimile with response summaries (p. 40-54).

Availability: Mary S. Sprague, Honeywell Technalysis, 380 Madison Ave., Fifth Floor, New York NY 10017, †; SRI/MF/complete.

B4675
Hughes Tool Co.

B4675–1   INTERNATIONAL ROTARY DRILLING RIG REPORT
Monthly.   7 p.
SRI/MF/complete, shipped quarterly

Monthly report on number of rotary drilling rigs in operation in 6 world areas, by country, excluding the U.S. and Canada. Data are compiled by the Hughes Tool Co. Report is issued approximately 6 weeks after month of coverage.

Contains 2 tables showing total rig count, for 6 non-Communist world areas and offshore PRC; and land and offshore rig counts for approximately 90 countries, arranged by world area; for month of coverage, previous month, and same month of preceding year.

Availability: Hughes Tool Co., ◆; SRI/MF/complete, shipped quarterly.

Issues reviewed during 1985: Oct. 1984-Sept. 1985 (D).

B4700
Industrial Relations Data and Information Services

B4700–1   U.S. UNION SOURCEBOOK: Membership, Finances, Structure, Directory
Annual.   1985.
163 p. var. paging.
ISBN 0-961392-30-4.
LC 85-14274.
SRI/MF/complete

Annual directory, by Leo Troy and Neil Sheflin, of labor organizations, presenting data on membership and finances, 1980s (generally current to 1982 or 1983), with trends from as early as 1897. Includes data by individual organization, by organization category, and by State. Also includes membership data for 10 foreign countries.

Categories include organization sector (public and private), type (trade unions and employee assns), and affiliation (AFL-CIO, independent, American Assn of Classified School Employees, and Assembly of Government Employees).

Data are from individual labor organizations, BLS, and other sources.

Contents:

Preface, and contents and table/chart listings. (p. v-ix)

Section 1-2. Highlights and Leading Events of Organized Labor. Includes narrative and 13 charts. (p. 1.1-1.4, 2.1-2.3)

Section 3-4. Membership and Finances. Includes narrative summaries, data sources and methodology, and 35 tables described below. (p. 3.1-3.23, 4.1-4.32)

Section 5. Governance and Structure. Includes narrative and 1 organizational chart. (p. 5.1-5.4)

Section 6. Directory. Includes some or all of the following for individual labor organizations, arranged by affiliation: U.S. and Canadian membership, 1981-83; start and peak membership years; current member-

ship as percent of peak membership; number of local, intermediate, and Canadian affiliates; publications, election date, and convention frequency; contact information; and compensation of highest paid officers. (p. 6.1-6.39)

Section 7. State and International Series. Includes narrative summary, data sources and methodology, and 16 tables described below. (p. 7.1-7.17)

App. A-C. Includes 3 tables showing labor organization membership (U.S. and Canadian, and by sector and affiliation), and organized labor's share of total employment and labor force, 1897-1983; U.S. and Canadian membership for 60 largest organizations, start year-1983; and listing of active and inactive organizations, including peak and 1983 membership for each. (p. A1-A3, B1-B20, C1-C9)

This is the 1st edition of the directory.

Availability: Industrial Relations Data and Information Services, PO Box 226WOB, West Orange NJ 07052, $25.00; SRI/MF/complete.

TABLES:

B4700–1.1: Labor Organization Membership Trends and Finances

a. Membership trends, including data by organization sector, type, and affiliation; fastest growing, fastest declining, and largest organizations; size distribution of organizations; membership concentration; organization starts, terminations, and mergers, and number of members involved; organized labor's share of total employment, by industry division; U.S. and Canadian membership; and public sector membership composition (Federal, State/local, post office, and education); various years 1897-1984. 30 tables. (p. 3.5-3.22)

b. Finances, including income (total and from members), expenses, assets, and liabilities, for approximately 200 parent labor organizations; and income by source, expenses by function, assets and liabilities by type, and current ratio, for AFL-CIO and 50 parent organizations with largest assets; 1982, with selected aggregate data including comparisons to 1980. 5 tables. (p. 4.3-4.32)

B4700–1.2: State and Foreign Data

a. States: labor organization membership (total, by sector, and for 10 largest organizations), and organized labor's share of total employment, with selected State rankings, various years 1939-82; labor organizations (national, intermediate, and State), 1983, and finances (total and net assets and receipts), 1982; and right-to-work law status, selected years 1953-82; all by State and/or U.S. territory (selected membership data also shown by census division). 14 tables. (p. 7.3-7.15)

b. Foreign: labor organization membership, 1948-83, and organized labor's share of total labor force, 1950-83, for 10 foreign countries. 2 tables. (p. 7.16-7.17)

B4750
Irving Trust Co.

B4750-2 **ECONOMIC OUTLOOK**
Monthly. 2 p.
SRI/MF/complete, shipped
quarterly

Monthly report analyzing major consumer, business, industrial, and government economic performance indicators. Actual data are current to 2-4 months prior to publication date.

Contains narrative analysis; and 1 table presenting actual percent changes for most recent quarter or months and year, and forecast annual or quarterly percent changes over the following year, for approximately 30 price and industry indicators.

Both actual and forecast data are revised for each monthly report to incorporate latest available data.

Availability: Irving Trust Co. customer representatives, ‡; SRI/MF/complete, shipped quarterly.

Issues reviewed during 1985: Nov. 1984-Oct. 1985 (P).

B4790
Johnson and Higgins

B4790-2 **EXECUTIVE REPORT ON LARGE CORPORATE PENSION PLANS, 1984**
Annual. 1984. 55 p.
ISSN 0192-222X.
LC 79-644875.
SRI/MF/complete

Annual report on corporate pension plan costs and benefit funding status, by industry, FY83, with comparisons to FY82. Data are based on annual reports to shareholders of 661 companies listed in *Fortune* magazine's rankings of top industrial and nonindustrial companies.

Contains contents listing (p. 3); introduction and methodology, with 1 chart (p. 4-7); 10 report sections, with narrative, 29 summary charts and tables, and 10 detailed tables listed below (p. 8-49); and appendix, with list of surveyed corporations (p. 50-54).

This is the 7th annual report.

Availability: Johnson and Higgins, National Benefits Office, 95 Wall St., New York NY 10005, †; SRI/MF/complete.

DETAILED TABLES:

[Data are for FY82-83, unless otherwise noted. Most tables show data for 5 Fortune 500 industrial ranking groups, 26 manufacturing industry groups, and 3-4 nonmanufacturing industry sectors. Most tables show average percentages and/or amounts, totals on which averages are based, and sample distribution by percentile range.]

1. About the companies surveyed [number of companies in *Fortune* directories, and number of survey participants, 1984]. (p. 9)

2-3. Change in pension expense, and pension expense as a percentage of pretax profits. (p. 14-19)

4. Change in pension expense per employee. (p. 22-23)

5. Pension expense as a percentage of compensation. (p. 26-27)

6-7. Ratio of plan assets to present value of vested benefits and total accumulated benefits, with reported interest rates, FY83. (p. 32-37)

8. Effect of interest rate assumption on unfunded vested benefits [UVB], FY83. (p. 40-41)

9-10. Ratio of UVB and unfunded total accumulated benefits to net worth, FY83. (p. 44-49)

B4950
Kent Economic and Development Institute, Inc.

B4950-1 **KEDI ECONOMIC SURVEY**
Monthly. Approx. 30 p.
SRI/MF/complete, delayed

Monthly report forecasting quarterly changes in national income and product account components, employment and unemployment, and financial sector activity, over a 10-12 quarter period. Also includes actual data for varying previous periods.

Report is based on a large-scale economic model developed by KEDI. Forecasts are made approximately 6 weeks preceding publication.

Issues generally contain:

a. Contents and table listing; and overview of current economic conditions, and explanation of forecast assumptions, with 1 highlights table showing KEDI forecasts for 15 economic indicators, usually for current, preceding, and 2-3 selected future years.

b. 11 monthly forecast tables, listed below, each accompanied by narrative summary, with occasional text tables.

c. 1 table comparing accuracy of forecasts made by KEDI and various other major forecasters for 1 or more economic indicators, selected each month; and 1 table showing historical data series sources.

Text tables presenting substantial data on topics not covered in monthly tables are described, as they appear, under "Statistical Features."

An annual assessment of the accuracy of forecasts made by major forecasters for selected previous periods is published separately, but is not covered in SRI.

Availability: KEDI Economic Survey, PO Box 99, Tallmadge OH 44278, $500.00 per yr.; SRI/MF/complete, delayed shipment 3 months from issue date.

Issues reviewed during 1985: Nov. 1, 1984-Oct. 1, 1985 (P) (Vol. 10, Nos. 2-12) [Dec. 1, 1984 and Jan. 1, 1985 issues are both numbered Vol. 10, No. 3; Vol. 10, No. 11 incorrectly reads No. 10].

MONTHLY FORECAST TABLES:

[Data usually are shown quarterly and annually for current, preceding, and following years (Jan.-May issues), or for current and 2 following years (June-Dec. issues), with additional annual totals.]

1.11-1.12. Selected indicators of real growth [including industrial production index, capacity utilization rate, housing starts, and auto

sales]; and real GNP [including personal consumption expenditures, private domestic investment, net exports, and Federal and State/local purchases].

1.21-1.22. Prices and nominal GNP [including CPI, PPI, and GNP price deflators].

1.30. Employment and labor [including labor force, total and farm employment, and unemployment rate].

1.41. Housing [including starts, building permits, home prices, and mobile home shipments].

1.42. Automobiles [shows passenger car domestic and import sales, dealer inventories, and factory shipments; and light-duty truck sales].

1.50. Federal and State/local budgets [shows personal and corporate income tax revenues, and budget surplus/deficit].

1.60. Income [including personal income and savings, corporate profits, and average weekly earnings].

1.70. Money and credit [including currency/demand deposits, time deposits, consumer credit, bank business loans, and savings and loan assn mortgages outstanding].

1.80. Interest rates, yields, and securities prices [shows prime, conventional mortgage, and Aaa corporate bond rates; 90-day Treasury bill and 20-year Government bond yields; and Standard & Poor's 500 average].

STATISTICAL FEATURES:

B4950-1.601: Aug. 1, 1985 (Vol. 10, No. 10)

TOP TEN IN PERSONAL INCOME

(p. 20) Table ranking top 10 countries by per capita income (no date). Data are from World Bank.

B4950-1.602: Sept. 1, 1985 (Vol. 10, No. 11)

[Issue incorrectly reads No. 10.]

MONEY AND CREDIT

(p. 22) Includes 1 table showing value of U.S. trade deficit, by major trading partner, 1984-85.

B5000
Korn/Ferry International

B5000-3 **BOARD OF DIRECTORS ANNUAL STUDY**
Annual series. For individual publication data, see below.
LC 78-643541.
SRI/MF/complete

Annual series of 5 reports on corporate board of director composition, compensation, and practices, 1984, with comparisons to 1980 and/or 1983. Data are presented for all boards and for boards of retail and insurance companies, companies with revenues over $1 billion, and financial institutions.

Reports generally include number of inside and outside directors; director occupational and sociodemographic characteristics, including detail for women and minorities; types of committees; director compensation, benefits, and time spent on board matters; meeting frequency; various board policies and practices; addition of new directors; and views on relative importance of various board-related issues; with selected detail by company revenue size.

Data are from responses of 633 major U.S. corporations to a 1984 Korn/Ferry International survey.

Each report contains narrative summary with text statistics, and 9-12 tables. Individual reports are listed below.

This is the 12th edition of the report series.

Availability: Korn/Ferry International, 237 Park Ave., New York NY 10017, $15.00 each; SRI/MF/complete.

REPORTS:

B5000–3.1: Board of Directors Twelfth Annual Study
[Annual. Feb. 1985. 26 p. SRI/MF/complete.]

B5000–3.2: Board of Directors Twelfth Annual Study: Billion Dollar Corporations, Supplement 1985
[Annual. [Feb. 1985.] 18 p. SRI/MF/complete.]

B5000–3.3: Board of Directors Twelfth Annual Study: Banks and Other Financial Institutions, Supplement 1985
[Annual. [Feb. 1985.] 18 p. SRI/MF/complete.]

B5000–3.4: 1985 Annual Board of Directors Study of Retail Companies
[Annual. [1985.] 21 p. SRI/MF/complete.]

B5000–3.5: 1985 Annual Board of Directors Study of Insurance Companies
[Annual. [1985.] 19 p. SRI/MF/complete.]

B5050
Laventhol and Horwath

B5050–1 **WORLDWIDE LODGING INDUSTRY, 1984 EDITION: Fourteenth Annual Report on International Hotel Operations**
Annual. 1984. 108 p.
ISSN 0361-218X.
LC 76-640982.
SRI/MF/complete

Annual report on international hotel median operating and financial performance, 1983. Includes data on occupancy, income, expenses, assets, and liabilities, with detail on sales and payroll by hotel dept.

Data are shown by world region, and are based on responses of 666 hotels to a Dec. 1983 survey.

Contents:

a. Listings of contents and exhibits; foreword; and discussion of tourism trends in various countries and world regions, with text data, and 1 table (p. 25) on U.S. hotel sales and occupancy rates, by region and selected hotel characteristics, as of Mar. 1984, and percent change from 1983. (p. 1-25)

b. Worldwide summary, with 1 summary chart, and 5 tables listed below. (p. 26-31)

c. Regional sections, each with narrative, currency conversion table, 2 summary charts, and 18 tables listed below, showing data for the region and usually for its composite countries and/or subregions, as follows: Africa/Middle East (p. 32-46), Asia/Australasia (p. 47-60), North America (p. 61-74), Europe (p. 75-88), and Latin America (p. 89-103).

d. Appendix with definitions and list of related publications. (p. 104-106)

A digest of the annual report and a narrative midyear commentary are also issued, but are not covered by SRI.

Availability: Laventhol and Horwath, Publications, 1845 Walnut St., Philadelphia PA 19103, $50.00; SRI/MF/complete.

TABLES:
[Data are for 1983, unless otherwise noted. Most data are shown as mean or median figures.]

B5050–1.1: Summary

1-2. General profile of typical contributor based on various measures of central tendency, and highlights, all hotels. (p. 27)

3. Market data [percent domestic, foreign, and repeat business; distribution of government, business, tourist, conference, and other sources of business; percent advance reservations, and distribution by type; and ratio of travel agent commissions to room sales]; 5-year trend, all hotels [1979-83]. (p. 29)

4. [Data in table 3 are repeated, with detail for Africa/Middle East, Asia/Australasia, North America, Europe, and Latin America, 1983.] (p. 30)

5. Nationality of guests [percents and rankings for 17 countries or regions of guest origin, with detail for each of the hotel regions noted in table 4, and ranking comparisons to 1982]. (p. 31)

B5050–1.2: World Regions

AFRICA AND MIDDLE EAST
[All tables show data for the total region. Tables I.3-I.18 include detail for Northern Africa, Southern Africa, and the Middle East.]

I.1-I.2. General profile of typical contributor based on various measures of central tendency; and highlights. (p. 32)

I.3-I.4. Market data and nationality of guests [with same breakdowns as in tables 3 and 5 above.] (p. 34)

I.5. Comparison of sales and profitability [sales, income before fixed charges, and net income, all per available room; ratios of income before fixed charges to room and total sales; and number of times average room rate was earned; 1982-83]. (p. 35)

I.6. Occupancy, double occupancy, [and] room rates [1982-83]. (p. 35)

I.7. Composition of sales [percent from rooms, food, beverages, telephone, minor operated dept, and rental/other]. (p. 36)

I.8. Minor operated depts and other income [and expenses] amounts per room and ratios to [total] sales. (p. 37)

I.9. Food and beverage statistics [sales, shown variously per room, per seat, and per guest; with detail by type of facility and for room service, selected ratios, average check size, and covers served per seat]. (p. 38-39)

I.10. Cash payroll, employee benefits, total payroll, and employment statistics [including sales per employee, productivity index for 1982-83, and FTE employees per 100 available rooms by dept]. (p. 40)

I.11. Analysis of undistributed operating expenses [amounts and ratios to sales, for administrative/general, marketing, energy, and property operation/maintenance, with comparative ratios for 1982]. (p. 41)

I.12. Energy costs per occupied room per day [by energy source; credit for energy sales; and net energy costs, 1982-83]. (p. 42)

I.13. Method of payment for hotel services [percent from cash, credit card, travel agent/tour operator, and other credit]. (p. 42)

I.14. Credit card commission annual cost per occupied room [and ratio to sales]. (p. 42)

I.15. Fixed charges [rent, property taxes, insurance, interest, and depreciation/amortization] amounts per room and ratio to total sales. (p. 43)

I.16. Balance sheet statistics, liquidity ratios [current assets/liabilities ratio; accounts receivable per room, and ratio to sales; and food, beverage, and operating supplies turnover and/or inventories per room]. (p. 43)

I.17. Statement of income and expenses per available rooms. (p. 44)

I.18. Ratio to total sales [for each income and expense item]. (p. 45)

ASIA AND AUSTRALASIA
II.1-II.18. [Tables I.1-I.18 are repeated for Asia/Australasia, with detail for Asia, Far East, and Pacific Basin.] (p. 47-59)

NORTH AMERICA AND CARIBBEAN
III.1-III.18. [Tables I.1-I.18 are repeated for North America, with detail for Canada, U.S., and Caribbean.] (p. 61-73)

EUROPE
IV.1-IV.18. [Tables I.1-I.18 are repeated for Europe, with detail for Continental Europe, Scandinavia, and UK.] (p. 75-87)

LATIN AMERICA
V.1-V.18. [Tables I.1-I.18 are repeated for Latin America, with detail for Mexico and Central/South America.] (p. 89-103)

B5050–2 **U.S. LODGING INDUSTRY, 1984 EDITION: 52nd Annual Report on Hotel and Motor Hotel Operations**
Annual. 1984. 83 p.
ISSN 0361-2198.
LC 76-640984.
SRI/MF/complete

Annual report on median operating results of the U.S. lodging industry, 1983, with comparisons to 1982. Also includes data on composition and sources of lodging demand.

Data are shown as the ratio of itemized operating expenditures to total and departmental revenues, and as costs and income per available room, by geographic region, urban location, and establishment size, rate group, and occupancy ratio.

Report is based on a study of hotel and motel operations, conducted by Laventhol and Horwath.

Contains contents listing (1 p.) and the following:

a. Industry summary and outlook, with 4 tables showing lodging establishments, rooms, value, employees, and annual sales, 1928 and 1984; hotels, rooms, and receipts, by style of operation; number of guest rooms, by establishment size, 1948 and 1977; and rooms, occupancy, sales, employees, and salaries/wages, 2000. (p. 2-4)

b. Discussion of lodging market trends in 48 cities and areas, with text data and 5 tables presenting summary data for selected areas. (p. 5-33)

c. Study results, with narrative analysis, 1 chart showing income and expense distributions for 1983, text data, and 40 tables listed below. (p. 34-80)

d. Explanation of terms. (p. 82-83)

Availability: Laventhol and Horwath, Publications, 1845 Walnut St., Philadelphia PA 19103, $50.00; SRI/MF/complete.

TABLES:

[Data are shown for 1983, unless otherwise noted. Most data are shown as medians or arithmetic means.

Data by establishment type are shown for some or all of the following: property age, size, room rate group, occupancy, and restaurant operation, including ratio of food/beverage sales to room sales.

Data by location are generally shown for center city, airport, suburban, highway, and resort. Data by region are shown for Northeast, Southeast, North and South Central, and Western regions. Data by market are for convention and other.]

B5050-2.1: General and Sales Data

MARKETS

1-2. General profile of typical contributor based on various measures of central tendency; and highlights. (p. 35)

3. Market data [percent domestic, foreign, and repeat business; distribution of government, business, tourist, conference, and other sources of business; percent advance reservations, and distribution by type; and ratio of travel agent commissions to room sales; all by location and market types]. (p. 37)

4. Nationality of guests [by region, U.S. and international, including ratios of 16 foreign nationalities to total international]. (p. 38)

PERFORMANCE MEASUREMENTS

[Tables 5-7 include medians for all establishments.]

5. Comparison of sales and profitability by selected criteria [by establishment type; for total sales, income before fixed charges, and net income before tax, 1982-83]. (p. 39)

6. General statistics [by establishment type; ratio of income before fixed charges to room and total sales, and number of times average rate was earned, 1982-83]. (p. 40)

7. Occupancy, double occupancy, and average rate [by establishment type, region, and total sales category; 1982-83]. (p. 41)

8. Net income differential [by dept and balance sheet item for lodging facilities reporting net income and loss, and percent change in net income]. (p. 43)

9-10. [Ratio or amounts by dept and balance sheet item, for] independent and chain affiliated [facilities, 1983], and comparison of data by location [1982-83]. (p. 44-45)

SALES ANALYSIS

11. Composition of sales [percent share by dept, by establishment type and location, with reported net income and loss]. (p. 46-47)

12. Sales per guest day [by dept, by location, market, and reported net income and loss]. (p. 46)

13-14. Rooms dept: median [revenue and expense] amounts per room and ratios to sales [by establishment size]; and expenses per occupied room per day, by occupancy. (p. 48-49)

B5050-2.2: Restaurant Operations and Minor Operated Depts

[Tables 15-17 include food/beverage sales ratios to room sales.]

15. Restaurant operations, by selected criteria [occupancy rate, establishments reporting net income and loss, and convention market, for sales and sales costs, 11 types of departmental expenses, income, and productivity index]. (p. 51)

16. Food and beverage statistics, by selected criteria [establishments size and location, and convention market; for food and beverage sales by facility, with amount per available room and per seat; and for average check, covers served, and room service sales per occupied room and per guest]. (p. 52-55)

17. Restaurant operations, cost of sales/cash payroll [1982-83]. (p. 54)

18. Minor operated depts and other income, median amounts per room and ratios to sales [by establishment size, location, and market; includes rental income and telephone costs]. (p. 56)

B5050-2.3: Payroll and Other Expenses

EMPLOYEES, PAYROLL, AND ROOM EXPENSES

19. Staffing levels and employee productivity, all establishments [employees per 100 available and occupied rooms, and sales per employee, by dept]. (p. 57)

20. Cash payroll, employee benefits, total payroll, and employment statistics, by selected criteria [by establishment type, dept, and reported net income and loss, and including 1982-83 productivity index]. (p. 58-59)

21. Payroll/related expenses per occupied room per day, by [dept and] occupancy. (p. 60)

UNDISTRIBUTED OPERATING EXPENSES

[Tables 24-26 include means for all establishments.]

22. Analysis of undistributed operating expenses, by selected criteria [costs per room, and ratios to room and total sales, for administrative/general, marketing, energy costs, and property operation/maintenance, by establishment type]. (p. 60-61)

23. Management fees, all establishments [amount per room and ratio to total sales, in lower and upper quartiles and median, 1982-83]. (p. 62)

24. How the marketing dollar was spent [payroll, sales, advertising, merchandising, public relations/publicity, fees/commissions, and other sales/promotions, with marketing cost index, by market and convention market]. (p. 62)

25. Energy costs per occupied room per day, by location [4 energy types and credit for sale, 1983, and net cost, 1982-83]. (p. 63)

26. How the property operation and maintenance dollar was spent, by [establishment] age [for 9 expense categories]. (p. 63)

B5050-2.4: Credit, Fixed Charges, and Balance Sheets

CREDIT AND COLLECTION

[Tables 27-29 include medians or means for all establishments.]

27. Method of payment for services [by establishment type and location]. (p. 64)

28. Credit card commissions, annual cost per occupied room [and ratio to total sales, by establishment type and location, 1982-83]. (p. 65)

FIXED CHARGES

29. Fixed charges: median amounts per room and ratio to total sales, by selected criteria [by establishment age, size, region, and location]. (p. 66-67)

BALANCE SHEET DATA

30. Balance sheet statistics, liquidity ratios, all establishments [accounts receivable, and food and beverage inventories, 1982-83]. (p. 66)

SPECIAL ANALYSIS

31-36. Cross tabulation of income before fixed charges and income tax, by affiliation and profitability, size and region, and room rate and occupancy, [all shown by] amount per room and ratio to total sales. (p. 67-69)

SUMMARY

[37-40] Statement of income and expenses, median amounts per available room; and ratios to total sales [for all establishments and by establishment type, including sales volume category, and region]. (p. 70-79)

B5050-3   **CALIFORNIA RESTAURANT OPERATIONS, 1984 EDITION: 9th Annual Report on Restaurant Operations in California**
Annual. 1984. 19 p.
SRI/MF/complete, current & previous year reports

Annual report presenting average financial and operating data for the California restaurant industry, by establishment characteristics, 1983. Includes data on income and expenses by detailed item, profits, average check, sales per square foot, cost of sales, full- and part-time employment, seat turnover, and labor productivity.

Data are generally industry medians; income and expense items are often shown per seat and as ratios to sales. Establishment characteristics include age, menu type (full and limited table service and other), sales size, types of beverages served (full liquor service, wine and/or beer only, and no alcohol), menu theme (steak/seafood, continental, American, and other), and location (urban, suburban, and rural).

Data are based on reponses of 105 restaurants to a Laventhol and Horwath survey. Report is designed to enable restaurant owners to compare their operations with averages for similar establishments.

Contains contents listing (1 p.); introductory comments from local areas (p. 3); narrative analysis, with 1 chart and 15 tables (p. 4-17); and definitions and comparison worksheet (p. 18-19).

Previous report, for 1982, has also been received, and is also available on SRI microfiche under this number [Annual. 1983. 23 p. $35.00].

Report for 1981 is unavailable for coverage in SRI; for description of 1980 report, see SRI 1982 Annual under this number.

Availability: Laventhol and Horwath, Publications, 1845 Walnut St., Philadelphia PA 19103, $35.00; SRI/MF/complete.

B5050-4   NATIONAL TREND OF BUSINESS: Lodging Industry
Monthly.   Approx. 8 p.
SRI/MF/complete, shipped quarterly

Monthly report on hotel and motel room sales, occupancy rates, and food and beverage sales and costs, by affiliation, region, location, size, and type. Data are based on a monthly survey of approximately 2,000 hotels and motels, and are published approximately 10 weeks after month of coverage.

Each issue generally includes 6 detailed tables showing the following data by hotel/motel affiliation, region, type of location, and lodging size and type, for month of coverage, year to date, and usually 12-month period ending in month of coverage, with comparisons to same periods of previous year:

a. Room and food/beverage sales change; total and double occupancy rates; and room and total sales per occupied room.

b. Food/beverage sales per occupied room, and average receipt per cover; food and beverage costs as percent of sales; food/beverage payroll as percent of sales and per cover; and change in number of covers served.

Each issue also includes a brief narrative analysis, with occasional charts, 2 tables showing occupancy rate projections for 3 coming months, and seasonally adjusted occupancy rates for month of coverage.

Report also includes 1 annual table, usually appearing in Dec. issue, showing occupancy rates and room sales per occupied room, by region, with detail for selected States and urban areas.

A similar report, *National Trend of Business: Economy Lodging Industry,* and lodging reports for selected metro areas are also available from the issuing agency, but are not covered in SRI.

Availability: Laventhol and Horwath, Publications, 1845 Walnut St., Philadelphia PA 19103, †; SRI/MF/complete, shipped quarterly.

Issues reviewed during 1985: Aug. 1984-June 1985 (D).

B5050-6   4th ANNUAL STUDY OF FINANCIAL RESULTS AND REPORTING TRENDS in the Gaming Industry, 1984
Annual.   1984.   27 p.
SRI/MF/complete

Annual report presenting financial data for casino/hotel operations of 17 corporations, 1983, with comparisons to 1982. Data are shown by corporation, with detail for individual casino/hotels in Atlantic City.

Data are compiled from corporate reports to shareholders and the SEC, New Jersey Casino Control Commission records, and a survey of corporations with gaming operations. The report sample represents 70% of all gaming revenues, and 100% of revenues in Atlantic City.

Contains contents listing and introduction (p. 1-3); and narrative report, with 1 chart and 8 tables listed below (p. 4-27).

Availability: Laventhol and Horwath, Publications, 1845 Walnut St., Philadelphia PA 19103, $35.00; SRI/MF/complete.

TABLES:
[Tables show data by corporation, 1982-83, unless otherwise noted.]

A. Corporations included in this study [square footage and number of guest rooms, FY83 or FY84]. (p. 4-5)

B. Consolidated corporate operating results [total revenue, income from operations, net income, and casino/hotel revenue]. (p. 8-9)

C. Gross operating profit [and casino and hotel/other revenue] of gaming operations. (p. 10-11)

D. Promotional allowance as a percentage of casino revenue. (p. 15)

E. Gaming gross operating profit as a percentage of identifiable gaming operation assets. (p. 16)

F. Corporate interest expense and depreciation/amortization. (p. 17)

G. Total corporate assets, shareholders' equity, return on shareholders' equity, and debt-to-equity ratio [1983]. (p. 18)

H. Atlantic City [aggregate] operating results [casino win, and income before income taxes, 1978-83]; and 1983 Atlantic City summary [itemized income and expenses, including table game and slot machine revenues, income taxes, and casino labor expenses; and casino revenue and income per square foot; for 9 casino/hotels]. 1 chart and 1 table. (p. 22-25)

B5050-7   LIFECARE INDUSTRY, 1984 EDITION: Fourth Annual Report on the Lifecare Industry in the U.S.
Annual.   1984.   25 p.
SRI/MF/complete

Annual report, for 1984, on "lifecare" retirement facilities, which provide both apartments for independent living and a nursing center for medical/skilled care. Includes data on facilities, finances, employment, and resident characteristics. Data are based on responses of 85 facilities to a survey conducted by Laventhol and Horwath.

Contains contents listing (p. 1); 5 topical articles, including comments from various local areas (p. 2-7); and survey results, with 23 tables described below (p. 8-25).
SRI coverage begins with this edition.

Availability: Laventhol and Horwath, Publications, 1845 Walnut St., Philadelphia PA 19103, $35.00; SRI/MF/complete.

TABLES:
[Data generally are shown for 1984, with selected trends from 1981. Most data are shown as medians and upper and lower quartiles by facility type (principally lifecare or nursing care), with various cross-tabulations by facility location (metro or nonmetro), size (under 200 or 200/over apartments), region, and age (pre-1976 or 1976/later).]

a. Facilities, including those owned by nonprofit organizations, retaining management companies, providing free transportation, and requiring waiting list deposit of under and over $1,000; total apartments and nursing

beds; acreage, and residents per acre; size of apartment complex, nursing and activity centers, and apartments by type; and nursing beds per facility, and apartments and residents per bed. Tables 1-5. (p. 9-11)

b. Pre-construction marketing, occupancy during 1st 6 months, and time elapsed before reaching 95% occupancy; entrance and monthly fees, by apartment type and/or number of occupants; nursing center daily rate for private and semiprivate room, by level of care; and rate increases for apartments and nursing centers. Tables 6-10. (p. 11-16)

c. Nursing center patient days, and beds occupied per day; average age of all and new residents by sex; residents requiring financial assistance, and with children living nearby; persons on waiting list per apartment, and average waiting period by apartment type; and residents, deaths, and permanent transfers to nursing center, by sex. Tables 11-16. (p. 17-19)

d. Finances, including salaries and employment, by position; payroll and employee ratios for dietary, housekeeping/maintenance, and total depts; expense ratios, including food, utilities, and medical costs; loss of revenue per apartment resident due to transfers to nursing facility; and reserve funds. Tables 17-23. (p. 20-25)

B5050-8   FLORIDA LODGING INDUSTRY: Ninth Annual Report on Hotel Operations
Annual.   1984.   27 p.
SRI/MF/complete, current & previous year reports

Annual report presenting financial and operating data for the Florida lodging industry, 1983, with comparisons to 1982 and some data for 1984. Includes income and expenses by detailed item, employment, occupancy rates, and balance sheet ratios. Data generally are industry medians and quartiles; income and expense items are shown per room and/or as ratios to total sales.

Also includes summary data on lodging operations in selected State areas; and selected characteristics of lodging guests (domestic vs. foreign, reason for visit, and use of advance reservations).

Data are based on information supplied by Florida hotels and motels participating in an annual Laventhol and Horwath study of the U.S. lodging industry. Report is designed to enable individual establishments to compare their operations with industry averages.

Contains contents listing (p. 1); summary of recent developments, with 1 table (p. 2-7); study results, with 2 charts and 20 tables (p. 8-25); and explanation of terms, and worksheet (p. 26-27).

Previous report, for 1982, was also reviewed during 1985 and is also available on SRI microfiche under this number. [Annual. 1983. 27 p. $35.00]. SRI coverage begins with the report for 1982.

Report on U.S. lodging industry is covered in SRI under B5050-2.

Availability: Laventhol and Horwath, Publications, 1845 Walnut St., Philadelphia PA 19103, $35.00; SRI/MF/complete.

B5050-9 TEXAS LODGING INDUSTRY: Sixth Annual Report on Texas Hotel Operations

Annual. 1984. 37 p.
SRI/MF/complete, current & previous year reports

Annual report presenting financial and operating data for the Texas lodging industry, 1983, with selected trends from 1978 and some data for 1984. Includes income and expenses by detailed item, employment, occupancy rates, and balance sheet ratios. Data generally are industry medians and quartiles; income and expense items are shown per room and/or as ratios to sales.

Also presents data on hotels and rooms operated and/or opened by individual Texas-based lodging chains, 1983; Texas hotels and rooms, by location, for individual major lodging chains, May 1984; new Dallas and Houston hotels/motels; and selected characteristics of lodging guests (domestic vs. foreign, reason for visit, use of advance reservations, and method of payment), 1981-83.

Data are based on information supplied by Texas hotels and motels participating in an annual Laventhol and Horwath study of the U.S. lodging industry. Report is designed to enable individual establishments to compare their operations with industry averages.

Contains contents listing (p. 1); summary of recent developments, with 1 chart and 6 tables (p. 2-13); study results, with 6 charts and 22 tables (p. 14-33); and explanation of terms, and worksheet (p. 34-37).

Previous report, for 1982, was also reviewed during 1985 and is also available on SRI microfiche under this number [Annual. 1983. 35 p. $35.00]. Previous report is substantially similar in format and content, but also includes data on foreign guests of Texas hotels/motels by country of origin. SRI coverage beings with report for 1982.

Report on U.S. lodging industry is covered in SRI under B5050-2.

Availability: Laventhol and Horwath, Publications, 1845 Walnut St., Philadelphia PA 19103, $35.00; SRI/MF/complete.

B5050-10 CALIFORNIA LODGING INDUSTRY: 2nd Annual Report on California Hotel Operations

Annual. 1984. 27 p.
SRI/MF/complete, current & previous year reports

Annual report presenting financial and operating data for the California lodging industry, 1983, with some comparisons to 1982. Includes income and expenses by detailed item, employment, occupancy rates, and balance sheet ratios. Data generally are industry medians and quartiles; income and expense items are shown per room and/or as ratios to sales.

Also includes data on new or proposed lodging facilities in selected areas; and characteristics of lodging guests (domestic vs. foreign, reason for visit, and use of advance reservations).

Data are based on information supplied by California hotels and motels participating in an annual Laventhol and Horwath study of the U.S. lodging industry. Report is designed to enable individual establishments to compare their operations with industry averages.

Contains contents listing (p. 1); summary of recent developments, with 7 tables (p. 2-7); study results, with 2 charts and 21 tables (p. 8-25); and explanation of terms, and worksheet (p. 26-27).

Previous report, for 1982, was also reviewed during 1985 and is also available on SRI microfiche under this number [Annual. 1984. 34 p. $35.00]. SRI coverage begins with report for 1982.

Report on U.S. lodging industry is covered in SRI under B5050-2.

Availability: Laventhol and Horwath, Publications, 1845 Walnut St., Philadelphia PA 19103, $35.00; SRI/MF/complete.

B5165
Lilly, Eli, and Co.

B5165-1 LILLY DIGEST, 1984

Annual. 1984. 55 p.
LC 50-19446.
SRI/MF/complete

Annual report presenting average operating and financial statistics for a cross-section of independent community pharmacies and their prescription depts, 1983. Includes analysis by store sales volume category, and by census division, with selected trends from 1960s.

Data are based on responses of 1,547 pharmacies to a Lilly Co. annual survey. Purpose of report is to enable pharmacies to compare their operations with industry averages.

Contains foreword, and listing of contents, tables, and charts (p. 1-3); report, with 4 charts, and 29 tables listed below, interspersed with narrative analyses (p. 4-54); and survey form facsimile (p. 55).

Availability: Eli Lilly and Co., Lilly Digest, 307 E. McCarty St., Indianapolis IN 46285, †; SRI/MF/complete.

TABLES:

[Tables show data for 1983, unless otherwise noted. Tables 1-3, 6-7, 9-14, and 18-19 include averages per pharmacy for most or all of the following operating items:]

a. Prescription, other, and total sales; cost of goods sold; gross margin; 15 types of expenses, including heat/light/power; net profit before taxes; total income of self-employed proprietor; value of inventory at cost and as percent of sales; and annual inventory turnover rate.

b. Size of area and sales per square foot; sales and net profit per dollar invested in inventory; number of new and renewed prescriptions dispensed; prescription charge; and hours per week pharmacy was open, worked by proprietor, and worked by employed pharmacist.]

OPERATIONS AND SALES

1-2. Current trends in pharmacy and prescription dept operations [1982-83]. (p. 5)

3. Summary of sales volume [by sales size class, and number of pharmacies in each class]. (p. 8-11)

4. Averages of pharmacy operations [for selected operating items], 1974-83. (p. 13)

PRESCRIPTION DEPT ANALYSIS

5. Average community pharmacy break-even data [required months and percent of total sales], 1974-83. (p. 16)

6. Summary by number of prescriptions dispensed daily. (p. 18-19)

7. Summary of prescription income [by ratio of prescription income to sales]. (p. 20-21)

8. Prescription trends in *Lilly Digest* pharmacies [for sales, ratio of prescription sales to total sales, number of prescriptions, percent renewals, prescription charge, prescription inventory, and prescription sales per dollar of prescription inventory, 1964-83]. (p. 22)

HEART OF THE LILLY DIGEST

9-14. [Operating data by annual sales size class and by number of daily prescriptions.] (p. 24-35)

NET PROFIT AND TURNOVER

15. Net profit according to sales size [1983, with 1982 totals]. (p. 36)

16. Turnover comparison (percent of sales) [for selected operating items, for fast and slow inventory turnover pharmacies]. (p. 36)

REGIONAL VARIATIONS, LOCATION, AND RENT

17. Geographic summary of average prescription charge and net profit [by census division]. (p. 37)

18-19. Summary [of averages per pharmacy for detailed operating items] by [census division], and according to location [downtown, neighborhood, shopping center, and medical office building]. (p. 38-41)

20-21. Rental percentages, by sales size; and rent correlated with various factors [average sales, rent, and square footage, by annual sales volume, prescription percent of total sales, prescriptions dispensed daily, years pharmacy has been in operation, and census division]. (p. 42-43)

BALANCE SHEET AND FINANCIAL RATIOS

22-23. Current trends in balance sheet information [as of Dec. 31, 1982-83]; and current financial ratios, by pharmacy age. (p. 46)

24-27. Balance sheet and financial ratios by pharmacy age [for 4 sales sizes], as of Dec. 31, 1983. (p. 47-50)

28. 10-year trends [in balance sheet items, 1974-83]. (p. 51)

29. Summary of [selected] operating figures in pharmacies reporting 2 years and 1 year [1982 and/or 1983]. (p. 52)

B5165-2 1984 NACDS-LILLY DIGEST: A Survey of Chain Pharmacy Operations for 1983

Annual. 1984. 41 p.
ISSN 0092-8410.
LC 74-640605.
SRI/MF/complete

Annual report presenting operating and financial statistics for chain drugstores and their prescription depts, by store characteristics and location, 1983, with selected trends from 1974.

Includes data on prescription and other sales; cost of goods sold; gross margin; 11 types of expenses; net profit before taxes; warehouse fee; value of prescription and other inventory at cost and as percent of sales; and annual inventory turnover rate.

Also includes data on size of prescription and other area, and sales per square foot; prescription and other sales and total net profit per dollar invested in inventory; number of new and renewed prescriptions dispensed; prescription charge; and weekly hours open and hours worked by manager and employed pharmacists.

Data are shown by sales size, prescription volume, prescription income as percent of sales, number of units in chain, location (downtown, neighborhood, shopping center, and medical building), and census division.

Data are based on responses of 1,203 pharmacies to an Eli Lilly and Co. annual survey. Purpose of the report is to enable pharmacies to compare their operations with industry averages.

Contains foreword, and listing of contents, tables, and charts (p. 1-3); report, with narrative analysis, 10 charts, and 16 tables (p. 4-40); and conclusion (p. 41).

This is the 14th edition of the *Digest*.

Availability: Eli Lilly and Co., NACDS-Lilly Digest, 307 E. McCarty St., Indianapolis IN 46285, †; SRI/MF/complete.

**B5165–3   LILLY HOSPITAL
PHARMACY SURVEY, 1984**
Annual.   1984.   31 p.
SRI/MF/complete

Annual report presenting average operating and financial statistics for hospital pharmacies, by hospital type (general and specialized) and bed capacity, 1983, with summary comparisons to 1982.

Includes data on pharmacy size; weekly hours open; hours worked and payroll, for pharmacists, technicians, and support personnel; special services offered; value of inventory and purchases, and inventory turnover rate, with detail for pharmacies in hospitals with medical school faculty on staff, and for pharmacies purchasing from wholesalers; and weekly volume of prescriptions and other preparations.

Also includes summary data on hospital admissions, occupancy rate, and patient days; and selected detail by census division and type of hospital control (government, Federal, profit, and private nonprofit), and for outpatient pharmacies and pharmacies with satellite services.

Data are based on responses of 2,102 hospital pharmacies to a 1984 Eli Lilly and Co. survey. Report is designed to enable pharmacies to compare their operations with industry averages.

Contains foreword, and listing of contents, charts, and tables (p. 3-5); report, with narrative analysis, 11 charts, and 15 tables (p. 6-29); and worksheet for comparative analysis (p. 30-31).

Survey has been conducted annually since 1976; SRI coverage begins with the 1984 edition.

Availability: Eli Lilly and Co., 307 E. McCarty St., Indianapolis IN 46285, †; SRI/MF/complete.

B5190
Lomas and Nettleton

B5190–1   U.S. HOUSING MARKETS
Quarterly.
ISSN 0502-9716.
LC 82-641491.
SRI/MF/not filmed

Quarterly report on housing markets in 17 MSAs, covering permits, construction, completions, vacancies, mortgage and loan activity, and market area employment. Includes selected data for multiple unit structures, walkup and elevator apartments, and mobile home shipments and prices.

Data are compiled from reports of private organizations and of State, local, and Federal government agencies, including U.S. Census Bureau. Report is issued approximately 3 months after quarter of coverage.

General format: contents listing, and narrative introduction with text statistics and 1 semiannual summary table; 9 quarterly tables, accompanied by 1-2 summary charts; and 6 semiannual tables, including data on mortgages.

Subscription to *U.S. Housing Markets* also includes prepublication and special releases which are primarily narrative and are covered in SRI only when they include substantial statistics.

Quarterly tables are listed below; most appear in all issues. All additional features with substantial statistical content are described, as they appear, under "Statistical Features."

Prior to 1st Quarter 1985 issue, report is described in SRI under B0125-1. Previous issuing agency, Advance Mortgage Corp., has been acquired by Lomas and Nettleton.

Availability: U.S. Housing Markets, Publication Department, 404 Penobscot Bldg., Detroit MI 48226, $130.00 per yr., sample issue $24.95; SRI/MF/not filmed.

Issues reviewed during 1985: 1st Qtr.-1st Half 1985 (D).

QUARTERLY TABLES:

[Tables show data for most recent quarter available or final month of period of coverage, with selected comparisons to previous quarters, months, or years. Table sequence may vary.]

PERMITS AND COMPLETIONS

[1] Private housing permits: dwelling units in permits issued [1-family, 2- to 4-family, and 5 or more family units, and highrise and/or total apartments, for U.S. and 17 MSAs; includes U.S. housing starts].

[2] Multifamily completions: units in [walkup and elevator and/or total] buildings of 2 or more units [and units under construction; U.S. and 17-27 MSAs].

VACANCIES

[3] Distribution of U.S. vacancies [percent of housing for rent and for sale in central cities, suburbs, and outside metro areas].

[4] Vacancies in multiple units [percent of units for rent and for sale in structures with 2 or more and 5 or more units].

[5] Vacancy rates: estimated vacancies [and/or vacancy rates] in total available housing supply [for U.S. and 19-28 urban and suburban areas].

EMPLOYMENT

[6] Employment trends [total and manufacturing employment, and unemployment rate, by region and 17 MSAs].

MANUFACTURED HOUSING

[7] U.S. [single- and multi-wide] mobile home shipments [and total placements; and total and multi-section shipments for 12 States].

[8] Average price of mobile homes placed for residential use [U.S. and by region].

PERMITS AND EMPLOYMENT

[9] Other significant markets: housing permits [for 1-family and multi-family units], and [total] employment growth [for 20 MSAs; prior to 1st Quarter 1985 issue, table appeared on a semiannual basis].

STATISTICAL FEATURE:

B5190–1.601: 1st Half, 1985
SEMIANNUAL TABLES

[1] Housing starts and permits [1-family and multi-family, for total U.S., 4 regions, 8 divisions, and 17 MSAs], 1st half 1985 vs. 1st half 1984. (p. 14)

[2-5] Mortgage rates: long-term bond yields [Aaa corporate new issues and U.S. long term]; insured mortgage yields [rate, private market GNMA average, and FNMA mandatory]; conventional loan secondary markets [Federal Home Loan Mortgage Corp. and FNMA fixed and adjustable rate]; and conventional loan rates [for 80%, 95%, and 1-year adjustable loans, including FHLBB effective fixed rates, for 17 MSAs; all mortgage rates are shown as of selected dates, May 1984-Aug. 1985]. (p. 25-26)

[6] Insured loan activity [FHA and VA applications for new 1-family and existing homes, and FHA and VA total 1-family homes insured, U.S. and 17 MSAs, quarterly 1st quarter 1984-2nd quarter 1985, and annually 1982-84]. (p. 27-29)

B5275
Manpower, Inc.

**B5275–1   MANPOWER, INC.
Employment Outlook Survey**
Quarterly.   6 p. + insert.
SRI/MF/complete

Quarterly report on employer hiring intentions, by industry division and region. Data are from a survey of approximately 12,000 public and private employers in over 350 cities. Survey is conducted by telephone approximately 5 weeks prior to quarter of coverage, and report is issued 1-3 weeks before the beginning of the quarter.

Contains 5 sections, covering U.S. and 4 regions, each with brief analysis, 1 trend chart, and 1 table showing distribution of employers by hiring plans (increase, no change, decrease, or undecided) for quarter of coverage, by industry division.

Report also usually includes an insert sheet, with narrative and 1 table showing comparative summary data for selected quarter or quarters of previous year.

Availability: Manpower, Inc., International Research Department, International Headquarters, 5301 N. Ironwood Rd., PO Box 2053, Milwaukee WI 53201-2053, ‡; SRI/MF/complete.

Issues reviewed during 1985: 1st-4th Qtrs. 1985 (D).

B5350
Manufacturers
Hanover Trust Co.

B5350–2   FINANCIAL DIGEST
Weekly.   4 p.
SRI/MF/complete, shipped
quarterly

Weekly report (biweekly in July and Aug.) on money and securities markets and banking activity. Most data are current to within approximately 1 week of cover date and are compiled by Manufacturers Hanover Trust Co.

Contains narrative analysis of selected aspects of the economy, usually including charts or other text statistics, and occasionally including tables or charts with substantial statistical content; and 7 regularly appearing tables showing selected weekly totals or averages for the following:

a. Selected Federal Reserve data (credit balances, U.S. Treasury deposits, currency in circulation, member bank reserves, money supply, and domestic nonfinancial debt); the New York money market; and business indicators (most recent quarter or month).

b. Short-term paper outstanding (time deposits of $100,000/more and commercial paper); commercial/industrial bank loans; securities markets; and international Eurodollar and foreign exchange rates.

Most tables include comparisons to selected previous periods, usually including same period of the previous year.

Weekly tables appear in all issues. All additional features with substantial statistical content are described, as they appear, under "Statistical Features." Nonstatistical features are not covered.

Availability: Manufacturers Hanover Trust Co., Economics Department, Financial Digest, 270 Park Ave., 17th Floor, New York NY 10017, †; SRI/MF/complete, shipped quarterly.

Issues reviewed during 1985: Nov. 5, 1984-Oct. 28, 1985 (P) (Vol. XXI, Nos. 39-45; Vol. XXII, Nos. 1-38).

STATISTICAL FEATURE:

B5350–2.601: Apr. 1, 1985 (Vol. XXII, No. 13)

WIDENING U.S. TRADE DEFICIT HELPS PUT LATIN AMERICA BACK ON THE GROWTH TRACK

(3 p.) Article, with 1 table showing merchandise trade and current account balances of 6 Latin American countries with high external debt levels, 1981 and 1984. Data are from IMF and Manufacturers Hanover Trust Co. estimates.

Volume 6, Number 1-12

B5350–3   ECONOMIC REPORT
Monthly.   Approx. 4 p.
SRI/MF/complete

Monthly report (except July and Aug.), by Irwin L. Kellner, commenting on U.S. economic developments and presenting quarterly economic forecasts.

Contains narrative articles, occasionally with substantial statistics; and 1 recurring table showing annual and quarterly levels for GNP components and selected indicators, including consumption, investment, inventory changes, net exports, government purchases, final sales, CPI, personal income (total and disposable), savings rate, employment rate, industrial production index, housing starts, domestic automobile sales, corporate profits, and net cash flow.

Table shows actual data for quarter preceding cover date month and 2-4 previous quarters, and projections for 3-5 succeeding quarters.

Each issue of the report is reviewed, but an abstract is published in SRI monthly issues only when recurring table or other statistical features appear. Recurring table appears in Feb., June, and Oct. 1985 issues. Articles with substantial additional statistics are described, as they appear, under "Statistical Features." Nonstatistical features are not described.

All issues are filmed, but microfiche is shipped only when an issue is abstracted.

Availability: Manufacturers Hanover Trust Co., Economics Department, 270 Park Ave., 17th Floor, New York NY 10017, †; SRI/MF/ complete.

Issues reviewed during 1985: Nov. 1984-Oct. 1985 (P).

STATISTICAL FEATURES:

B5350–3.601: Dec. 1984
TAIL WAGS THE DOG

Article, with 1 table showing production worker employment, trade deficit, and import share of consumption, for 7 manufacturing groups, 1979, 1983, and Aug. 1984. Data are primarily from Federal agencies and trade assns.

B5350–3.602: Mar. 1985
BUCK STOPS WHERE?

(3 p.) Article, with 1 table showing U.S. current account balance, and component inflows and outflows through direct investment, security purchases, and bank liabilities to or claims on foreigners, 1981-84. Data are from Commerce Dept.

B5350–3.603: Sept. 1985
CROWDING OUT

(3 p.) Article, with 1 table showing gross savings and private domestic investment, U.S. budget deficit, and foreign capital inflows, 1980-85. Data are from Bureau of Economic Analysis and Treasury Dept.

B6025
Merrill Lynch
Relocation Management

B6025–1   STUDY OF EMPLOYEE
RELOCATION POLICIES
Among Major U.S.
Corporations, 1985
Annual.   1985.   xv+286 p.
SRI/MF/complete

Annual report on employee relocation practices of corporations, by major industry group, 1984. Includes data on reimbursement policies for transferred homeowners, problems encountered, and expenses covered.

Data are based on telephone interviews with administrative personnel in 604 firms, conducted Jan.-Feb. 1985.

Contains listings of contents and tables (1 p.); introduction, with 2 tables showing survey sample by industry and by number of transferred homeowners, 1980-84 (p. i-ii); summary of findings, with 15 tables including selected comparisons from previous surveys as early as 1976 (p. iii-xv); and statistical section with 88 tables, described below (p. 1-286).

This is the 13th edition of the report. A separately published summary of this edition, a reprint of p. i-xv, is also available from the issuing agency for $10.00.

Availability: Merrill Lynch Relocation Management, Marketing Department, Four Corporate Park Dr., White Plains NY 10604, $25.00; SRI/MF/complete.

TABLES:

[All tables show data for 20 major industry groups and all others, and by number of transferred renters or homeowners. Tables show data for 1984, unless otherwise noted.]

a. Total and women employees transferred, expected transfers in 1985, and homeowners transferred. Tables 1-4. (p. 1-12)

b. Company policies for disposing of transferred employee's former living quarters and purchase of new house, including expenses reimbursed, limitations, and equity loans/advances; problems experienced; and aid given employees to get mortgage financing. Tables 5-27. (p. 13-83)

c. Firms having difficulties with employees accepting transfers into high cost-of-living areas, and incentives used; mortgage interest differential allowances (MIDA), including adjustable rate mortgage provisions; mortgage buy-downs and refinancing; assistance to offset additional tax liability; job placement assistance for working spouses; renter transfer assistance; reimbursement for househunting trips, temporary quarters, household goods shipment, and incidental expenses; and firms' use of outside relocation services. Tables 28-68. (p. 84-212)

d. Eligibility of new professional and new college graduate hires for same relocation benefits as current employees, and type of assistance given; domestic and international short-term transfers, and average length of stay; and provision and administration of property management assistance, for employees on short-term assignments. Tables 69-77. (p. 213-243)

e. Companies relocating groups of employees; average homeowner relocation cost; average cost per transferred employee for MIDA/ cost-of-living/mortgage assistance/tax adder allowances; and average time homes were for sale before being purchased by company/ relocation service. Tables 78-81. (p. 244-255)

f. Firms requiring relocation expense reimbursement if transferred employee leaves firm within 1 year; firms offering to move employees to another location if original move is unsuccessful; firms with flexible benefit programs for transferred employees; and recent changes in relocation policy and anticipated changes in 1985. Tables 82-88. (p. 256-286)

B6045
Metropolitan
Life Insurance Co.

B6045–1   STATISTICAL BULLETIN, Metropolitan Life Insurance Co.
Quarterly.   Approx. 20 p.
ISSN 0741-9767.
LC 31-30794.
SRI/MF/complete, delayed

Quarterly report on health and demographic topics of interest to the insurance industry, including trends in life expectancy, mortality, accidents, disease and disability, and population growth. Most data are from Census Bureau, NCHS, and other Federal agencies.

Issues contain several articles, usually statistical. Fourth quarter issue includes an index and contents list for the year.

Features with substantial statistical content are described, as they appear, under "Statistical Features."

Availability: Metropolitan Life Insurance Co., Statistical Bulletin, One Madison Ave., New York NY 10010-3690, nonprofit organizations $20.00 per yr., others $25.00 per yr.; SRI/MF/ complete, delayed shipment 3 months after abstract is published.

Issues reviewed during 1985: Jan./Mar.-July/ Sept. 1985 (P) (Vol. 66, Nos. 1-3).

STATISTICAL FEATURES:

B6045–1.601: Jan./Mar. 1985 (Vol. 66, No. 1)

RISKY FIRST YEAR OF LIFE

(p. 2-8) Article, with 1 table showing infant mortality rates, by sex and accident type, 1969/70 and 1979/80. Data are from NCHS.

CONTINUED DECLINE IN MORTALITY IN U.S., CANADA, AND WESTERN EUROPE

(p. 9-13) Article, with 2 tables showing mortality rate by sex and age group, for U.S. (with detail by race), Canada, and 10 Western European countries, 1976 and 1981. Data are from NCHS, *Statistics Canada,* and *World Health Statistics Annual.*

This is the 1st in a series of articles comparing mortality rates in selected countries.

POPULATION PROFILE: PERSONS AGED 25-64

(p. 20-24) Article, with 2 tables showing adult population as follows: by sex and age group,

selected years 1970-2050; and distribution by selected demographic characteristics, as of Apr. 1980, Mar. 1982, or Mar. 1983. Data are from Census Bureau and Labor Dept.

B6045–1.602: Apr./June 1985 (Vol. 66, No. 2)

SIGNIFICANT REGIONAL VARIATIONS IN COST OF CORONARY BYPASS SURGERY

(p. 4-9) Article, with 1 chart and 1 table showing the following for coronary bypass operations: number of cases, average length of hospital stay, physician charge, and hospital room/board and ancillary charges, by census division and for each State with 100/more cases, Jan. 1982-July 1983 period. Data cover 3,088 cases insured through Metropolitan Life Insurance Co.

CURRENT TRENDS IN INTERNATIONAL MORTALITY FROM DISEASES OF THE CIRCULATORY SYSTEM

(p. 18-23) Article, with 2 charts and 2 tables showing mortality rate from diseases of the circulatory system by sex and age group, for U.S. by race, Canada, and 10 Western European countries or subareas, with summary indexes for selected foreign countries relative to U.S., 1976 and 1981. Data are from *World Health Statistics Annual* and government reports.

This is the 2nd in a series of articles comparing mortality rates in selected countries.

ACCIDENT DEATH TOLL: 1984, ANNUAL FEATURE

(p. 24-27) Annual article, with 1 table showing number of incidents and fatalities, for catastrophic accidents resulting in 5 or more deaths, by type of accident, 1983-84. Data were compiled by Metropolitan Life Insurance Co.

B6045–1.603: July/Sept. 1985 (Vol. 66, No. 3)

MORTALITY TRENDS OF LUNG AND BREAST CANCER IN WOMEN

(p. 4-9) Article, with 2 tables showing mortality rates from breast cancer and lung cancer for women age 35-84, by age group and race, selected years 1960-82. Data are based on NCHS statistics.

VARIATIONS IN HYSTERECTOMY COSTS BY REGION

(p. 10-17) Article, with 2 charts and 3 tables showing the following for hysterectomies:

a. Occurrence rate per 1,000 women, by type of surgical procedure (abdominal or vaginal), by region, 1981 and 1983.

b. Number of cases, by type of surgical procedure; and average hospital room/board and ancillary charges, length of hospital stay, and physician charge; by census division and selected State, Jan. 1982-June 1983 period.

Occurrence rate data are from NCHS. Other data are based on analysis of 15,029 cases insured through Metropolitan Life Insurance Co.

SLIGHT GAINS IN U.S. LONGEVITY, ANNUAL FEATURE

(p. 20-23) Annual article, with 2 tables showing life expectancy at selected ages, by sex, selected periods 1900-84; and life expectancy and mortality rate, by age, sex, and race, 1982. Data are from Metropolitan Life Insurance Co. and NCHS.

POPULATION CHANGES IN THE U.S. AND CANADA

(p. 24-28) Article, with 2 tables showing population for U.S. by census division and State, and for Canada by Province, selected years 1975-85. Data are from Census Bureau, NCHS, and *Statistics Canada.*

B6045–2   METROPOLITAN LIFE SURVEY OF THE AMERICAN TEACHER, 1985
Annual.   Aug. 1985.
4+84 p.
SRI/MF/complete, current & previous year reports

Annual survey report examining views of elementary and secondary school teachers on issues concerning public education, 1985.

Presents survey responses concerning educational reform, including changes in teacher compensation; school problems; retaining, attracting, and training good teachers; improvement of school relations with business and colleges; leaving vs. staying in teaching, including reasons for both, and other occupations attracting teachers; job stress and satisfaction; quality of teaching environment; and teacher vs. school responsibility for selected educational tasks.

Data are often shown by teacher or school characteristics, including level of experience, sex, school type (elementary, junior high, and high school), region, and location type (inner city, other urban, suburban, small town, and rural).

Data are from 1,846 telephone interviews with public school teachers, conducted Apr. 25-June 8, 1985, by Louis Harris and Associates.

Contains foreword, and contents and table listings (4 p.); introduction and highlights (p. 1-6); survey report, with 4 charts and 35 tables, interspersed with brief narratives (p. 7-55); methodology, with 4 tables (p. 58-65); and interview form /facsimile/ (p. 69-85).

Previous report, for 1984, was also reviewed in SRI during 1985, and is also available on SRI microfiche under B6045-2 [Monograph. June 1984. 74 p. †]. Survey topics covered in previous report vary substantially from those described above; and previous report also included selected data shown by teacher age and labor union status. SRI coverage begins with the 1984 survey report.

Availability: The American Teacher Survey, Metropolitan Life Insurance Co., One Madison Ave., New York NY 10010-3690, †; SRI/MF/ complete.

B6110
Minneapolis Grain Exchange

B6110–1   ONE HUNDRED AND SECOND STATISTICAL ANNUAL, Year Ending Dec. 31, 1984, Minneapolis Grain Exchange
Annual. [1985.] 127 p.
ISSN 0736-1092.
LC sc82-4406.
SRI/MF/complete

Annual report, for 1984, on the grain market in northwestern States served by the Minneapolis Grain Exchange (MGE). Includes data on grain production and MGE carlot receipts, for Minnesota, North and South Dakota, and selected other States; and movement, storage, and prices; all by type of grain, with selected trends from 1912.

Data are from MGE, USDA, and Western Weighing and Railroad Inspection Bureau.

Contains contents listing, definitions, and abbreviations (p. 6-7); 35 tables listed below, accompanied by 3 summary charts (p. 8-126); and measurement conversion tables (p. 127).

Availability: Minneapolis Grain Exchange, 150 Grain Exchange Bldg., 400 S. Fourth St., Minneapolis MN 55415, $20.00+$1.35 postage, supply limited; SRI/MF/complete.

TABLES:

[Tables showing data by commodity generally include wheat, corn, oats, barley, rye, flaxseed, soybeans, and sunflower seed.

Data are shown by month for 1984, unless otherwise noted. Tables often also include totals for 1983-84.]

B6110–1.1: Production and Futures Market

[1] Crop production [harvested acreage, and yield per acre, by commodity, in Minnesota, North and South Dakota, and selected other States, annually 1978-84, and for U.S. 1983-84]. (p. 8-9)

[2] MGE spring wheat futures trading volume, [monthly] 1975-84. (p. 10)

[3-4] Daily Minneapolis futures opening, high, low, close, open contracts, and volume of trading: spring wheat; and white wheat [Sept.-Dec. 1984]. (p. 14-31)

[5-6] Spring wheat call and put options, daily Minneapolis futures opening, high, low, close, open contracts, and volume of trading Oct.-Dec. 1984. (p. 35-41)

[7-9] Daily basis: 14% protein wheat, delivered Minneapolis/Duluth; and No. 2 yellow corn and No. 1 yellow soybean, delivered Minneapolis. (p. 45-49)

B6110–1.2: Storage and Movement

[Tables [3-15] show data by commodity.]

[1-2] Elevator capacity within Duluth-Superior and Minneapolis-St. Paul switching districts [by company and elevator]. (p. 51)

[3-9] Volume of grain handled by Minneapolis-St. Paul/Red Wing/Winona and Duluth-Superior area elevators as reported to the MGE, by rail, truck, and barge or vessel; and trucks received in Minneapolis-St. Paul area terminals (including Hastings/Savage/New Ulm). (p. 52-58)

[10] Navigation season comparative final report, vessel clearances of grain out of Duluth-Superior to domestic, Canadian, and overseas ports [annually 1982-84]. (p. 58)

[11] Historic lake shipments [annually] 1951-84. (p. 59)

[12-13] Weekly stocks of grain and sunflower seed in stores in Minneapolis-St. Paul licensed public elevators; and weekly stocks of grain, sunflower seed, and flaxseed in stores in Duluth-Superior licensed public elevators. (p. 60-63)

[14] [Weekly] stocks of grain at selected elevator/terminal sites in the U.S. [omits data for flaxseed and includes sorghum]. (p. 64)

[15] [Weekly] spring wheat stocks in a deliverable position, Minneapolis-St. Paul/Duluth-Superior/Red Wing switching districts. (p. 65)

[16] Summary of primary wheat exports from Pacific Northwest/California ports. (p. 66)

B6110–1.3: Cash Markets

[Tables [6-10] show data by commodity.]

[1] Daily Minneapolis cash wheat prices, including local and diversion delivery points. (p. 68-79)

[2-3] Minneapolis [monthly] cash wheat high and low, 1912-84; and daily Minneapolis cash durum prices as reported by the USDA *Grain Market News*. (p. 80-83)

[4] Daily prices reported for Minneapolis cash coarse grain, barley, flaxseed, soybeans, and sunflowers (includes local and diversion points). (p. 84-95)

[5] Monthly average cash grain prices [for No. 1 dark northern spring wheat, No. 2 yellow corn, No. 1 yellow soybeans, No. 2 heavy oats, No. 1 flaxseed, and No. 2 rye, Minneapolis 1972-84; and for oil sunflower seed, Minneapolis and Duluth 1976-84]. (p. 96-97)

[6-7] Daily carlot receipts handled by MGE sampling dept [for Minnesota and North and South Dakota]; and monthly summary of rail cars and amounts handled [includes screenings, buckwheat, milo, and millet]. (p. 99-111)

[8-9] Daily carlot shipments reported by Western Weighing and Railroad Inspection Bureau; and monthly summary of rail cars and amounts shipped from Minneapolis-St. Paul; [includes data for screenings, flour, millstuffs, and various oils and meals]. (p. 113-125)

[10] Receipts and shipments (by rail, in bushels), 1950-84 [annually; omits data for soybeans and sunflower seeds]. (p. 126)

B6200
Morgan Guaranty Trust Co. of New York

B6200–2   WORLD FINANCIAL MARKETS
Monthly. Approx. 20 p.
ISSN 0190-2083.
LC 78-2438.
SRI/MF/complete, shipped quarterly

Monthly report on foreign exchange market developments and rates, and domestic and international economic issues affecting financial markets.

Most monthly data are current to month preceding cover date, with some data current to cover date month. Data are compiled by Morgan Guaranty Trust Co. from various private and Government sources.

Issues generally contain:

a. 1-2 feature articles, with statistics, on selected aspects of the world economy.

b. Statistical appendix section, with 15 detailed monthly tables, listed below; and irregularly recurring index key to data.

Most monthly appendix tables appear in all issues. All articles with substantial statistical content are described, as they appear, under "Statistical Features." Nonstatistical features are not covered.

Availability: Morgan Guaranty Trust Co. of New York, International Economics Department, 23 Wall St., New York NY 10015, ‡; SRI/MF/complete, shipped quarterly.

Issues reviewed during 1985: Oct./Nov. 1984-Sept./Oct. 1985 (P) [Oct./Nov. 1984, Mar./Apr. 1985, and Sept./Oct. 1985 issues are combined issues].

MONTHLY APPENDIX TABLES:

[Tables generally show data for month prior to cover date, with various trends, usually including data for several recent months and for 3-4 previous years (full year or as of Dec. 31).

Tables [1-2] and [8-15] show data for U.S. and 12-33 other countries. Table sequence and format may vary.]

[1] Nominal effective exchange rates [also includes weekly detail for cover date month and preceding month].

[2-3] Real effective exchange rates, industrial and developing countries.

[4] International banking market size [gross claims and liabilities for domestic currencies and Eurocurrencies, with detail for nonbanks and banks and for dollars and other currencies].

[5] International bond isues and bank credits [by country of borrower, bond issues by type of instrument and currency, and Eurocurrency and foreign bank credits].

[6] Eurocurrency deposit rates [prime banks' bid rates, for 6-9 Eurocurrency denominations by duration of deposit].

[7] International bond yields [on long-term issues for U.S. companies and European governments].

[8] Central bank discount rates.

[9-11] Day-to-day money rates, Treasury bill rates, and representative money market rates.

[12-15] Commercial bank deposit rates and lending rates to prime borrowers, and domestic government and corporate bond yields.

STATISTICAL FEATURES:

B6200-2.601: Oct./Nov. 1984

LDC DEBT PROBLEM: AT THE MIDPOINT?

(p. 1-11) Article analyzing major developing countries' external debt situation. Includes 11 tables showing the following:

a. 16 developing countries: current account balances; change in current account and trade balances, interest payments, merchandise imports and exports, and real GDP; percent of external debt interest payments covered by trade surplus; gross external debt; and average external debt as percent of exports; all by country, various periods 1981-85.

b. Current account balance, external debt and interest payments as percent of exports, and debt change, for Brazil, Chile, and Mexico, all based on selected economic assumptions, various periods 1982-90; and change in industrial countries' imports from developing countries, by importing country, 2nd half 1984 vs. 2nd half 1982.

B6200-2.602: Dec. 1984

HELP WANTED IN EUROPE

(p. 1-11) Article analyzing factors affecting European employment situation. Includes 12 tables showing the following for U.S., Japan, Canada, and 4-10 European countries, unless otherwise noted:

a. Unemployment rates (total and youth), change in size of labor force, labor force participation rates by sex, and workers unemployed 12/more months as percent of total unemployment; various periods 1975-84.

b. Real GNP change; inflation rate; current account balances; and general government financial and budget balances and debt, all as percent of GNP; various periods 1973-85.

c. European exports to U.S.: as percent of GNP, 1983; and change, 1st 10 months 1984 vs. same period of 1983; for 8 countries.

B6200-2.603: Jan. 1985

LOWER OIL PRICES

(p. 1-11) Article on world oil supply and demand trends, and market outlook. Includes 13 tables showing the following:

a. Consumption of oil in industrial and developing countries, with total energy consumption shares by fuel type; oil exports of Communist countries, production of OPEC and others, and inventories in industrial countries; and OPEC current account balance; with some detail by country, various periods 1973-85.

b. Prices of oil compared to OECD manufacturer prices and GNP growth and to dollar exchange rate; and non-oil export value, current account balance, change in real GDP, interest payments as percent of ex-

ports, and debt-export ratios, for 4 oil-importing and 4 oil-exporting developing countries; generally shown under 3 economic scenarios, various years 1984-90.

B6200-2.604: Feb. 1985

ARGENTINA

(p. 1-11) Article analyzing Argentine economic trends and outlook. Includes 11 tables showing the following for Argentina:

a. GDP per capita, with comparison to 4 other countries, 1984, cumulative since 1925, and annual average since 1950; actual and targeted change in consumer prices, monthly 1984; government revenues and expenditures as percent of GDP, 1982-84; and change in monetary base, industrial wages and production, and GDP components, various periods 1981-85.

b. Current account balance and total external debt, 1983-85; foreign exchange sources and uses, 1978-83 period; wheat and corn actual production, and potential production, exports, and export earnings, 1979/80-1983/84 period; industrial exports as percent of total industrial output, with comparison to 7 other countries, 1980; and petroleum production, trade, and consumption, 1982-84.

B6200-2.605: Mar./Apr. 1985

BONN SUMMIT AND THE U.S. TRADE DEFICIT

(p. 1-13) Article analyzing trends in international trade balances, with focus on the U.S. Data sources include Commerce Dept. Includes 9 tables showing the following:

a. U.S.: trade and current account balances, net foreign debt, and selected economic indicators, 1984, and estimated 1985-89 under 5 economic policy assumptions; and balance of trade in 1984 with change from 1980, and percent change in imports during 1980-84 period, by commodity and selected trading partner, with detail for trade with Japan.

b. U.S. balance of payments, changes in U.S. official and private holdings of foreign assets, and changes in foreign official and private holdings of U.S. assets; Japan's current account balance, long-term capital outflows, and external assets; and current account balances for selected world areas and countries; various periods 1980-85.

c. Production growth rate and employment shares, by selected manufacturing industry and for total U.S.; and Japan's balance of trade, and percent change in imports, by selected trading partner; various periods 1980-84.

B6200-2.606: May 1985

LATIN AMERICA'S TRADE POLICIES

(p. 1-11) Article analyzing trends and developments in Latin American export performance and trade policies. Includes 10 tables showing the following, for various periods 1960s-85:

a. Trade and current account balances; changes in exports, imports, consumer prices, and GDP; manufactured goods' share of total exports; and distribution of exports by country or area of destination; for 8 Latin American countries with high external debt, with selected comparisons to Asian developing countries.

b. Latin America's share of world exports, for 10 commodities; and value of exports of manufactured goods, for 5 Latin American countries.

B6200-2.607: June 1985

CROSSROADS EUROPE

(p. 1-9) Article analyzing trends and outlook for Europe's economic performance and policies. Also projects world economic outlook through 1989 under 3 scenarios: extended U.S. fiscal restraint with weakening world economy, moderate U.S. restraint with compensating foreign stimulus, and moderate U.S. restraint with higher European/Japanese growth.

Includes 11 tables showing the following:

a. European economic indicators, including current account balances, currency exchange rates, and changes in GNP, consumer prices, export and import prices, and exports to U.S.; for 9 European countries, with comparisons to Japan and/or U.S., various periods 1980-85.

b. World outlook under 3 scenarios: change in current account balance, for U.S., Japan, Europe, 4 European countries, and less developed countries (OPEC and non-OPEC), 1985 and 1989; and changes in U.S. trade balance, selected other U.S. economic indicators, non-U.S. OECD real GNP (with detail for Europe and Japan), and non-U.S. consumer prices, 1984-89.

B6200-2.608: July 1985

INTERNATIONAL BANK LENDING TRENDS

(p. 1-11) Article on international bank lending developments. Data sources include Bank for International Settlements, Federal Reserve Board, Bank of England, Deutsche Bundesbank, and OECD.

Includes 7 tables showing trends in international bank loan outstanding claims, by bank's parent country and by debtor country, 1983 and/or 1984; new international bond issues and bank credit commitments, 1981-1st half 1985; and U.S. and Japanese net capital flows intermediated by banks domestically and abroad, 1982-84.

B6200-2.609: Aug. 1985

THE LOWER DOLLAR

(p. 1-3) Article, with 2 tables showing 3-month Eurocurrency annual interest rates for currencies of 7 countries, as of Aug. 1985, with change from June 1984; and exchange rates for 6 foreign currencies against U.S. dollar, 1984 and as of Aug. 1985, with 1985-86 hypothetical change in strength of dollar based on exchange rates remaining at Aug. 1985 levels.

EUROPEAN MONETARY ISSUES

(p. 3-9) Article, with 7 tables showing real effective change rates, trade balances, and percent change in consumer prices and GNP, for 7 European Monetary System member countries, UK, U.S., and Japan; British monetary growth rate and target trends; and value of international bond issues, and external foreign currency assets of banks, compared for European Currency Unit and other currencies; various periods 1973-85.

B6200–2.610: Sept./Oct. 1985

STRENGTHENING THE LDC DEBT STRATEGY

(p. 1-14) Article analyzing external debt situation of developing nations. Includes 19 tables showing the following:

a. 9-10 major debtor nations: GDP and consumer price change; trade and current account balances; capital flow; external debt and interest payment ratios to exports; domestic investment and savings, and public-sector deficits and expenditures, all as percent of GDP; IMF, World Bank, and commercial bank loan activity; foreign direct investment; and OECD export credits; all by country, with aggregate comparisons to other developing nations, various periods 1977-85.

b. Change in imports of 7 major industrial countries from all developing countries, 10 major debtor nations, and Latin America, and in U.S. imports (total, from OECD, and from non-OECD Latin America and Asia), various periods 1983-85; IMF borrowings and repayments, 1979-July 1985, and repayments scheduled through 1990; and World Bank policy-based loan commitments (loans based on debtor country's improvement in certain policy areas), selected periods FY80-85.

B6625
New York Stock Exchange

B6625–1   FACT BOOK 1985
Annual.   May 1985.   i+86 p.
LC 56-10699.
SRI/MF/complete.

Annual fact book, for 1984, on NYSE activity. Includes securities trading volume, stock prices, credit data, and investor and member firm characteristics, with historical trends from as early as 1875. Also includes selected data for other U.S. exchanges and for foreign exchanges. Data are from government and private sources, and NYSE.

Contains contents listing (p. 1); narrative analysis in 10 sections, interspersed with 6 summary charts, and 83 tables described below (p. 2-65): historical section, with list of significant dates, and 25 tables listed below (p. 66-83); and index and list of NYSE publications (p. 84-86).
This is the 30th edition.

Availability: New York Stock Exchange, Publications Department, 11 Wall St., New York NY 10005, $3.70; SRI/MF/complete.

TABLES:

B6625–1.1: Text Tables
[In addition to the topics described below, tables present additional 1984 detail, including monthly trading data, for topics covered in historical section tables.]

MARKET ACTIVITY AND FUTURES EXCHANGE
[Most data are shown for 1984, with selected trends from 1970s.]

a. NYSE activity, including new records set; trading days and hours; most active stocks; trading volume for AT&T and 7 regional holding companies; market quality indicators; and shares offered by special methods. 21 tables. (p. 5-15)

b. Trading of NYSE-listed stocks on other exchanges and over-the-counter markets; and Intermarket Trading System activity. 5 tables. (p. 17-19)

c. Warrant and bond market volume on NYSE, and most active bonds; NYSE common stock yield and price/earnings ratio indexes; and New York Futures Exchange futures and options trading. 6 tables. (p. 20-26)

NYSE STOCK PRICES, LISTED COMPANIES, AND MARKET CREDIT

d. Price changes, 1980-83; and high and low prices by month for industrial, transportation, utility, and finance stocks, 1984. 4 tables. (p. 29-32)

e. Dividend longevity records for all common stocks; and companies paying annual dividends since 18th century. 2 tables. (p. 33)

f. Listing requirements, selected years 1961-84; listed securities and market value, by industry and type, 1984; and foreign securities listings and market value, by world region, 1984. 6 tables. (p. 36-39)

g. 50 leading companies in number of stockholders and in market value of stock, Dec. 31, 1984; stock list net increase, stock dividends and splits, new listings, and removals, 1975-84; and rosters of companies with new common stock listings, mergers and consolidations, name changes, listing removals, and stock splits in 1984. 9 tables. (p. 39-47)

h. Securities market credit, including initial margin rate requirements, selected periods 1934-74; and net equity status of stock margin accounts, Dec. 1983-84. 5 tables. (p. 48-51)

INVESTORS, EXCHANGE COMMUNITY, AND FOREIGN MARKETS

i. Shareholder characteristics, including highlights of 7 NYSE shareowner surveys; shareowner distribution by State, demographic characteristics, and portfolio size; and estimated holdings of selected types of institutional investors; various years 1955-83. 4 tables. (p. 52-55)

j. Public transaction study highlights, including volume distribution by type of investor, shown for NYSE and/or other markets, various periods 1952-80. 6 tables. (p. 56-57)

k. Exchange community, including NYSE seat sales, 1984; securities industry personnel in U.S., New York State, and NYC, 1975-84; NYSE member offices and registered representatives, by State, 1982-83; NYSE disbursements for customer assistance, 1963-84; Securities Investor Protection Corp. assessments and advances, 1971-84; and new securities issues, by type, 1975-84. 12 tables. (p. 58-63)

l. Foreign purchases from and sales to Americans, for U.S. and foreign stocks, 1974-84; and foreign stock exchange data, including listed companies, market value, trading activity, and stock price index, by exchange, 1984, with price index trends from 1981. 3 tables. (p. 64-65)

B6625–1.2: NYSE Activity: Trends
[Tables generally show recent trends annually and historical trends for selected years within the date range noted. Many tables note record highs and lows.]

[1] Reported volume, turnover rate, and reported trades, [1900-84]. (p. 69)

[2] Daily reported share volume: average, high, and low days [1900-84]. (p. 70)

[3] Total volume in round and odd lots, average prices [1930-84]. (p. 71)

[4] NYSE large block transactions [total and daily average, number of shares, and shares as percent of reported volume, 1965-84]. (p. 71)

[5] Reported share volume records [years, months, days, quarters, weeks, and 1st hour, 1975-Mar. 1985]. (p. 72)

[6] Largest block transactions [in NYSE history, through Mar. 29, 1985]. (p. 72)

[7] NYSE member purchases and sales in round lots [1937-84]. (p. 73)

[8] Odd-lot volume [purchase and sales shares and value, 1920-84]. (p. 73)

[9-10] [Number and] market value of shares sold on [NYSE, ASE, and other] registered exchanges [1935-84]. (p. 74)

[11] Bond volume (par value) [total, daily average, and high and low day, 1900-84]. (p. 75)

[12] NYSE common stock index (closing prices) [high and low day, and year end, 1939-84]. (p. 76)

[13-14] Cash dividends and yields [common and preferred stocks, 1929-84]; and [common] stock yields [by size of yield, 1980-84]. (p. 77)

[15] Listed companies' financial data [all U.S. vs. NYSE companies, and assets, sales or revenues, and net income, 1962-83]. (p. 78)

[16-17] All NYSE listed stocks and bonds [number of companies or issuers, issues, market or par value, and average price, 1924-84]. (p. 79)

[18] Securities industry credit [margin accounts and debt, securing collateral, credit balances, and potential purchasing power, year end 1965-74 and quarterly 1975-84]. (p. 80)

[19] Short sales [round lots for members and nonmembers, and odd lots, 1940-84]. (p. 81)

[20] Short interest [high, low, and year end, 1931-84]. (p. 81)

[21] [Partnership and corporation] member organizations, sales offices, and personnel [1899-1984]. (p. 82)

[22] Membership prices [high and low, 1875-1984]. (p. 82)

[23-24] Income and expenses and balance sheet of NYSE member firms [1971-84]. (p. 83)

[25] NYSE communication services [number of tickers/displays, and last sale and bid/ask interrogation devices, 1975-84]. (p. 83)

B6670
Nielsen, A. C., Co.

B6670–1   1985 NIELSEN REPORT ON TELEVISION
Annual. 1985. 17 p.
LC 82-20697.
SRI/MF/complete

Annual chartbook on TV viewing patterns, audience size, and leading programs, 1984, with selected trends from 1950. Data are from various Nielsen indexes.

Contains narrative, and 12 charts and 3 tables, described below.

This is the 30th edition of the report.

Availability: A. C. Nielsen Co., Corporate Communications, Nielsen Plaza, Northbrook IL 60062, †; SRI/MF/complete.

CHARTS AND TABLES:

a. TV households, distribution by number of stations and channels received, and percent with color and multiple sets; and persons in TV households, by age and sex; various periods 1950-84. 3 charts. (p. 2-4)

b. TV usage, including average daily hours, 1965/66-1983/84; and average weekly hours, by household size, income, whether cable subscriber, and presence of nonadults, and by viewer age and sex, by day-part, Nov. 1984, with comparisons to 1980. 4 charts. (p. 5-9)

c. Prime time audience by half-hour segment and evening audience by program type, both by viewer age and sex, Nov. 1984; prime time audience, by night of week, Nov. 1975 and 1984; source of prime time viewing (cable, pay cable, network, and other), by cable subscription status, 1983-84; and videocassette recorder (VCR) use, including time of day and source of recorded programs, Jan. 1985. 4 charts. (p. 10-13)

d. Prime time mini-series programming, including audience levels and network hours aired, for 1st-run and repeat broadcasts, 1976/77-1983/84. 1 chart. (p. 14)

e. Ratings of top 20 syndicated programs, top 10-11 prime time programs in U.S. and 9 metro areas, and top 15 regularly scheduled network programs by audience sex and age; Nov. 1984. 3 tables. (p. 15-17)

B6790
Nuclear Assurance Corp.

B6790–1   UPDATE: A Bimonthly Review of the Nuclear Industry
Bimonthly.
ISSN 0731-3225.
LC 82-640736.
SRI/MF/not filmed

Bimonthly report reviewing trends and developments in the nuclear power industry worldwide, and presenting data on nuclear reactor and fuel cycle operations. Most data are from NAC's Fuel-Trac computerized information service.

Each issue includes contents listing and the following sections:

a. "Industry Overview and Status," with articles on selected topics including nuclear generating capacity, and fuel conversion, fabrication, and reprocessing.

b. "Statistical Digest," with tables presenting selected data based on Fuel-Trac and on government and private sources.

c. "Focus on" special feature article.

Recurring features include data on nuclear power plant licensing and construction status, and plant capacity factors; and annual forecasts of nuclear generating capacity and uranium production.

Features with substantial statistical content are described, as they appear, under "Statistical Features." Each issue of the report is reviewed, but an abstract is published in SRI monthly issues only when features with substantial nontechnical statistics appear.

Availability: Nuclear Assurance Corp., 5720 Peachtree Pkwy., Norcross GA 30092, $250.00 per yr., single copy $80.00; SRI/MF/not filmed. *Issues reviewed during 1985:* Oct. 1984-Oct. 1985 (P) (Nos. 26-32).

STATISTICAL FEATURES:

B6790–1.601: Oct. 1984 (No. 26)

NUCLEAR POWER IN THE PEOPLE'S REPUBLIC OF CHINA

(p. 2-3) Article, with 1 table showing generating capacity, reactor type, and construction completion date, for PRC nuclear power plants scheduled for commercial operation, 1989-90s.

STATISTICAL DIGEST, RECURRING FEATURE

(p. 9-10) Includes 2 recurring tables on licensing and construction status of U.S. nuclear power plants, showing the following:

a. Nuclear reactor units licensed for commercial operations, construction permits granted and pending, reactor units on order and announced, and total units and design capacity, annually 1973-83 and monthly Jan.-May 1984.

b. Listing of nuclear generating plants under construction or planned, including utility, reactor type, planned startup date and capacity, percent complete, and licensing status (no date).

B6790–1.602: Dec. 1984 (No. 27)

STATUS OF MAJOR NUCLEAR ENERGY PRODUCING COUNTRIES IN 1984

(p. 2-4) Article, with 3 tables showing number of months of delay for individual U.S. and foreign nuclear reactors postponing commercial operation, with detail for U.S. reactors with multiple delays, as of Dec. 1984.

CANADIAN URANIUM SUPPLY

(p. 5-7) Article, with 1 undated text table showing distribution of Canadian uranium exports, by country.

DISPOSAL FEE FOR HIGH-LEVEL RADIOACTIVE WASTE AND SPENT NUCLEAR FUEL

(p. 10-11) Article, with 1 table showing nuclear power generating capacity, and industry payments made to DOE's Nuclear Waste Fund to cover disposal service costs, 1981-90.

STATISTICAL DIGEST, RECURRING FEATURE

(p. 12-17) Includes 1 recurring undated table presenting fuel cycle data for all light water nuclear reactors operating/under construction in the non-Communist world. Table shows technical data (initial core and equilibrium cycle parameters) and generating capacity for individual reactors, arranged by nuclear steam system supplier.

B6790–1.603: Feb. 1985 (No. 28)

PIPE CRACKING IN BOILING WATER REACTORS

(p. 2-3) Article, with 1 table showing worldwide incidents of intergranular stress corrosion cracking of piping in boiling water nuclear reactors, by type of piping system, 1974-Jan. 1982 period.

URANIUM SUPPLY IN SOUTHERN AFRICA

(p. 4-6) Article, with 4 undated text tables showing summary production or ownership data for 3 South African mining companies, and distribution of South African uranium oxide exports by consuming country.

STATISTICAL DIGEST, RECURRING FEATURE

(p. 8-17) Includes 3 recurring tables on U.S. and non-U.S. nuclear power plant capacity factors, showing the following:

a. U.S. reactors licensed, nuclear-based electricity generation capacity, nuclear share of total electricity generation, maximum dependable generation capacity, and capacity factor (capacity utilization percent), annually 1973-83 and monthly Jan.-Sept. 1984.

b. Capacity factor and cumulative generation for individual U.S. and non-U.S. light water reactors, various periods 1960s-84.

FOCUS ON: TMI-RELATED PLANT MODIFICATIONS

(p. 18-24) Article, with tabular list of nuclear power plant design and operational modifications mandated by NRC as a result of the Mar. 1979 incident at Three Mile Island, Pa., with number of plants required to make modifications and number completing modifications.

B6790–1.604: Apr. 1985 (No. 29)

ENRICHMENT MARKET TO 2020: DEMAND PROJECTIONS

(p. 4-6) Article, with 1 table showing world uranium enrichment capacity projections, by supplier, selected years 1985-2020.

SPENT FUEL TRANSPORTATION IN THE U.S.

(p. 7-8) Article, with 2 tables showing shipments of spent nuclear fuel, by destination category, 1964-83; and shipment activity associated with decommissioning of Nuclear Fuel Services West Valley storage facility, including shipment mode, volume, and destination, as of Apr. 1985.

STATISTICAL DIGEST, RECURRING FEATURE

(p. 9-11) Includes 2 recurring tables on licensing and construction status of U.S. nuclear power plants, showing the following:

a. Nuclear reactor units licensed for commercial operations, construction permits granted and pending, reactor units on order and announced, and total units and design capacity, annually 1973-83 and monthly Jan.-Oct. 1984.

b. Listing of nuclear generating plants under construction or planned, including utility, reactor type, planned startup date and capacity, percent complete, and licensing status as of Apr. 1985.

B6790-1.605: June 1985 (No. 30)

U.S. URANIUM IMPORTS

(p. 2-4) Article, with 1 undated text table showing distribution of U.S. uranium imports by country of origin. Data are from non-U.S. supplier contracts signed in 1983, with deliveries for 1985-2000 period.

WORLDWIDE LASER ENRICHMENT PROGRAMS

(p. 4-6) Article, with 1 table showing R&D funding for laser technology for uranium enrichment, program status, and estimated unit costs, for U.S., France, Germany, and UK, FY85-86. Data are from U.S. Budget requests and foreign sources.

FUEL FABRICATION INTERFACE WITH AVLIS TECHNOLOGY

(p. 7-8) Article, with 3 undated charts showing distribution of U.S., non-U.S., and global uranium dioxide fabrication capacity, by conversion/procurement process. Also includes tabular list of uranium dioxide conversion/procurement processes used or planned, by U.S. and foreign nuclear fuel fabricator, arranged by country.

STATISTICAL DIGEST, RECURRING FEATURE

(p. 9-14) Includes 1 recurring undated table presenting fuel cycle data for all light water nuclear reactors operating/under construction in the non-Communist world. Table shows technical data (initial core and equilibrium cycle parameters) and generating capacity for individual reactors, arranged by nuclear steam system supplier.

B6790-1.606: Aug. 1985 (No. 31)

NUCLEAR MEGAWATT FORECASTS THROUGH THE YEAR 2000, ANNUAL FEATURE

(p. 2-3) Annual article, with 1 table showing nuclear generating capacity as of year end 1984, and projected capacity selected years 1986-2000, for 26 individual countries and others. Includes utility-based and Nuclear Assurance Corp. projections.

Previous article is described in SRI 1984 Annual under B6790-1.504.

U.S. URANIUM PRODUCTION LEVEL PROJECTIONS, ANNUAL FEATURE

(p. 4-6) Annual article, with 1 chart on uranium production capacity utilization trends, biennially 1976-84; and 1 undated text table showing number of uranium production centers shut down/on standby and deferred, by previous operational status (operational, under construction, and in planning stage).

Previous article is described in SRI 1984 Annual under B6790-1.503.

STATISTICAL DIGEST, RECURRING FEATURE

(p. 9-19) Includes 3 recurring tables on U.S. and non-U.S. nuclear power plant capacity factors, showing the following:

a. U.S. reactors operable, nuclear-based electricity generation capacity, nuclear share of total electricity generation, maximum dependable generation capacity, and capacity factor (capacity utilization percent), annually 1973-84 and monthly Jan.-Mar. 1985.

b. Capacity factor and cumulative generation for individual U.S. and non-U.S. light water reactors, various periods 1960s-85.

FOCUS ON: FRENCH LASER ENRICHMENT PROGRAM

(p. 20-22) Article, with 1 text table showing R&D expenditures on advanced uranium enrichment processes by France's government-owned Commissariat a l'Energie Atomique, 1975-85. Data are shown in French and U.S. currencies.

B6790-1.607: Oct. 1985 (No. 32)

COST ANALYSIS OF THE JAPANESE PROTOTYPE ENRICHMENT PLANT

(p. 5-7) Article, with 3 tables showing Japanese Government budget allocations for uranium enrichment plant, FY79-84; and estimated capital expenditures and plant production, various years 1985-98. Financial data are shown in Japanese yen and U.S. dollars.

IN-CORE FUEL UTILIZATION TRENDS

(p. 8-9) Article, with 1 table showing world light water reactor average in-core uranium utilization (including and excluding end of cycle 1 discharges), by reactor type, 1970-84. Data are from analysis of fuel discharges of approximately 200 reactors worldwide.

STATISTICAL DIGEST, RECURRING FEATURE

(p. 10-12) Includes 2 recurring tables on licensing and construction status of U.S. nuclear power plants, showing the following:

a. Nuclear reactor units licensed for commercial operations, construction permits granted and pending, reactor units on order and announced, and total units and design capacity, annually 1973-84 and monthly Jan.-Apr. 1985.

b. Listing of nuclear generating plants under construction or planned, including utility, reactor type, planned startup date and capacity, percent complete, and licensing status as of Oct. 1985.

U.S. URANIUM SUPPLY: CURRENT STATUS AND FUTURE OUTLOOK

(p. 13-16) Article, with 4 tables showing uranium production centers and nominal capacity, by operating status and method of uranium recovery, 1983 and/or 1985; and location, ownership, capacity, and recovery method of individual production centers currently operating or expected to restart by end of 1985.

B6800
NUEXCO

B6800-1   NUEXCO MONTHLY REPORT ON THE NUCLEAR FUEL MARKET

Monthly.
Approx. 30 p.+addendum.
ISSN 0742-4582.
LC sn84-6094.
SRI/MF/complete, shipped quarterly

Monthly report on U.S. and worldwide uranium marketing and procurement activities, and other industry trends and developments. Includes data on uranium supply, demand, trade, and prices; market for uranium conversion and enrichment services; and material and labor costs relevant to uranium production in selected countries.

Data are prepared as a broker service, and are compiled from industry and government sources. Data are current to 1-4 months prior to publication date.

Contents:

a. Insert, with executive summary, "Figures of the Month" summary, and index to previous issue.

b. Contents listing.

c. Several narrative sections, and occasional special inserts, discussing developments in the uranium market, and including world regional analyses with detail for specific countries; some with statistics.

d. Statistical sections, with 18 monthly tables listed below.

Occasionally also includes tables showing current cost of enriched uranium and optimum tails assay (concentration of uranium in waste products) at various feed and work unit cost levels.

Subscription also includes occasional special reports.

Monthly tables appear in all issues. All additional features and special reports with substantial statistical content, except uranium cost and optimum tails assay tables, are described, as they appear, under "Statistical Features." Nonstatistical features are not covered.

Availability: NUEXCO, R. Wesley Miller, 3000 Sand Hill Rd., Menlo Park CA 94025, subscription price on request; back issues $25.00 each; SRI/MF/complete, shipped quarterly.

Issues reviewed during 1985: Nov. 1984-Oct. 1985 (P) (Nos. 195-206).

MONTHLY TABLES:

[Market data are current to month prior to cover date. Government data are current to 1-4 months prior to publication.]

CURRENT MARKET DATA

[Data are for month of coverage. Tables [6-11] show number of pounds or separative work units (SWUs), and delivery period, by NUEXCO reference number.]

[1] [Exchange, uranium hexafluoride, conversion, and SWU values (prices at which transactions for significant quantities of natural uranium concentrates, hexafluoride, conversion services, and SWUs could be concluded, with detail for SWUs by whether DOE or other origin); loan use charge rate (annual interest rate at which uranium loans could be conclud-

ed); and transaction value (weighted average price of uranium in recent transactions); uranium hexafluoride data begin with May 1985 issue.]

[2-5] Exchange, transaction, and conversion value [with comparison to previous month and year], SWU value [for DOE and non-DOE origin], and uranium hexafluoride value, expressed in selected producer/consumer currencies [uranium hexafluoride data begin with July 1985 issue].

[6] Recent transactions [uranium sales and loans, and secondary market conversion and enrichment services; also includes price as percent of current value, and country or world area of seller/lender and buyer/borrower group].

[7-11] Uranium, loan, conversion, and SWU supply and demand.

HISTORICAL MARKET DATA

[12] Historical exchange values [monthly from Aug. 1968].

[13] Historical transaction values [monthly from May 1976].

[14] Historical conversion values [monthly from Jan. 1981].

GOVERNMENT STATISTICS

[Most data are shown monthly for month of coverage and 12 or more previous months, with annual average for previous year. Occasionally, additional tables are included showing monthly data for several previous years.]

[15] Australia [price index for materials used in manufacturing industry, and mining wage index].

[16] Canada [industry selling price index for manufacturing, and average hourly earnings for uranium and metal mining, mines/quarries/oil wells, primary nonferrous metal, and chemicals/chemical products industry groups].

[17] Republic of South Africa [average declared working costs and cost index per metric ton of gold ore milled, CPI, PPI, and mining/quarrying industry employment and wages/salaries].

[18] U.S. [PPI for industrial and all commodities; CPI; GNP implicit price deflator; and gross average hourly earnings of production or nonsupervisory workers for metal mining, primary nonferrous metals, chemicals/allied products, and electric/electronic equipment industry groups].

STATISTICAL FEATURES:

B6800-1.601: Nov. 1984 (No. 195)

ENRICHED URANIUM AND SWUS

(p. 2-5) Article, with 1 table showing operational nuclear reactors and total electric generating capacity for reactors using uranium enrichment services, and market shares for principal enrichment service suppliers, by country, as of Nov. 1, 1984.

REPUBLIC OF SOUTH AFRICA, QUARTERLY FEATURE

(p. 21) Quarterly article on uranium-related developments in South Africa. Includes text statistics, and 1 table showing uranium production at 13 mining operations, 1st-3rd quarter 1984.

UNITED STATES

(p. 22) Article, with 1 table showing volume and average grade of reasonably assured uranium resources, by cost category, as of Dec. 31, 1983. Data are from DOE.

B6800-1.602: Dec. 1984 (No. 196)

SWEDEN

(p. 20-24) Article on nuclear power industry in Sweden. Data sources include *Swedish Nuclear News*. Includes 3 tables showing electricity generation by type of fuel, 1983; utility owner, capacity, 1983 capacity factor, reactor type, and commercial operation date, for nuclear power plants operating/under construction as of late 1984; and ownership shares in Swedish Nuclear Fuel Supply Company, 1984.

Corrected information appears in the Jan. 1985 issue (for description, see B6800-1.603).

UPDATE: URANIUM RESOURCES IN SOUTH AFRICA

(p. 26-30) Article, with 1 table showing South Africa's official assessment of reasonably assured and estimated additional uranium resources, by principal deposit or district, as of Jan. 1, 1983. Data are from Nuclear Development Corp. of South Africa.

Article updates a report appearing in the Sept. 1984 issue; for description see SRI 1984 Annual under B6800-1.512.

B6800-1.603: Jan. 1985 (No. 197)

U.S. NUCLEAR FUEL FABRICATORS

(p. 15-19) Article, with 1 undated table showing plant location, type of light-water reactor (LWR) for which fuel is produced, and production capacity, for 5 companies fabricating LWR nuclear fuel.

CORRECTION

(p. 19) Text correction for article on Swedish nuclear power industry appearing in Dec. 1984 issue.

For description of article, see B6800-1.602 above.

B6800-1.604: Feb. 1985 (No. 198)

PRIMARY MARKET CONVERTERS IN THE USA

(p. 11-14) Article, with 2 tables showing uranium hexafluoride consumption, for U.S., Europe, Far East, and all others, 1985-99; and capacity, and U.S. and world market shares, for 2 U.S. companies and all others providing uranium conversion services (no date).

REPUBLIC OF SOUTH AFRICA, QUARTERLY FEATURE

(p. 16-17) Quarterly article on uranium-related developments in South Africa. Includes 2 tables showing uranium production at 13 mining operations, 1st-4th quarter 1984; and uranium and gold prices in U.S. and South African currencies, as of Dec. 1983-84.

B6800-1.605: Mar. 1985 (No. 199)

ASSESSMENT OF TODAY'S URANIUM MARKET: STARTING TO COME OF AGE

(p. 13-19) By James E. Vaughan. Article, with 5 tables showing the following uranium market data for 1983-84:

a. Deliveries to European, U.S., and other users, and to non-users, with number of contracts, all by pricing category (fixed, negotiated, and spot).

b. Production, deliveries to users and non-users, and inventory additions, for Australia, Canada, France/Central Africa, Southern Africa, U.S., other producers, and nonproducers.

B6800-1.606: Apr. 1985 (No. 200)

PRIVATIZATION AND THE COMPETITIVENESS OF U.S. ENRICHMENT SERVICES

(p. 13-17) By Karl P. Cohen. Article examining the competitive situation for U.S. uranium enrichment services.

Includes 1 table showing U.S. uranium enrichment capacity and production, and projected domestic and foreign demand in 2000, as of 1973 and 1985. Also includes 1 chart and 2 tables on selected economic aspects of world competition for enrichment services.

JAPAN, ANNUAL FEATURE

(p. 18-19) Annual article on results of price negotiations between Japanese utilities and their major uranium suppliers, with 1 table showing negotiated price compared to *Nuexco* exchange values, FY81-86.

Previous article, covering FY81-85, is described in SRI 1984 Annual under B6800-1.508.

B6800-1.607: May 1985 (No. 201)

SOUTH AFRICA, QUARTERLY FEATURE

(p. 18) Quarterly article on uranium-related developments in South Africa. Includes 1 table showing uranium production at 13 mining operations, 4th quarter and full year 1984, and 1st quarter 1985.

B6800-1.608: June 1985 (No. 202)

NUCLEAR FUEL MARKET IN THE FEDERAL REPUBLIC OF GERMANY

(p. 15-21) Article, with 2 tables and 2 charts showing the following data for West Germany: capacity, reactor type, startup date, and completion status, for individual plants grouped by lead utility/fuel buyer; number of nuclear plants, by State, with each State's governing political party; and ownership shares for individual nuclear plants and uranium production operations, by company. No data dates are given.

UNITED STATES, RECURRING FEATURE

(p. 23-24) Recurring article on nuclear power unit licensing, construction, and startup status, as of mid-1985. Includes 2 tables showing utility, capacity, reactor type, planned or actual startup date, and construction or licensing status, for individual units entering or nearing commercial operation during 1985-86. Data are based on utility forecasts and published information.

Previous articles, with data for 1983 and 1984, are described in SRI 1984 Annual under B6800-1.505 and B6800-1.512, respectively.

B6800-1.609: July 1985 (No. 203)

BRAZIL

(p. 12-15) Article, with 1 undated table showing estimated uranium reserves in Brazil, by ore deposit or mine. Data are from NUCLAM, a joint Brazil-West German fuel cycle services company.

JAPAN, ANNUAL FEATURE

(p. 16-19) Annual article on Japan's nuclear power industry, as of mid-1985. Data sources include Japanese Ministry of International Trade and Industry.

Includes 2 tables showing capacity, startup date, utility owner, and reactor type, for nuclear reactors in operation, under construction, undergoing licensing, or planned, as of mid-1985.

Previous feature, with data as of mid-1984, is described in SRI 1984 Annual under B6800-1.513.

B6800–1.610: Aug. 1985 (No. 204)

SOUTH AFRICA, QUARTERLY FEATURE

(p. 16) Quarterly article on uranium-related developments in South Africa. Includes 1 table showing uranium production at 13 mining operations, 1st-2nd quarter 1985.

URANIUM PRODUCTION IN THE U.S.

(p. 17-22) Article, with 1 table and text data showing uranium reserves by recovery cost category, and uranium oxide sales and exchange value, selected periods 1966-2000; and uranium discoveries, status of projects, and related business activities, by company, 1981-85. Data sources include DOE.

B6800–1.611: Sept. 1985 (No. 205)

PRIMARY MARKET CONVERTERS: COMURHEX

(p. 17-22) Article, with 1 undated table showing annual uranium hexafluoride production capacity and plant location of 5 uranium conversion companies in U.S., Canada, UK, and France.

B7100
Pannell Kerr Forster

**B7100–1   TRENDS IN THE HOTEL INDUSTRY, 1984
International Edition**
Annual.   1984.   92 p.
ISSN 0278-3983.
LC 81-643956.
SRI/MF/not filmed

Annual report on operating results of international hotel industry, 1983, with comparisons to 1982. Includes data for payroll, food, beverage, telephone, laundry/dry cleaning, energy, and other income and expense items. Data are shown as ratios to total and departmental revenues, and as costs per available room per year, by world region and selected country.

Also includes average rooms per establishment, occupancy rates, room charges, and selected comparisons to U.S. hotel/motel industry; exchange rates in terms of U.S. dollar, by country arranged by world area, as of Dec. 31, 1983; and summary trends from 1977.

Report is based on a survey of 400 international hotels, conducted by Pannell Kerr Forster.

Contains contents and table listings (p. 1); and report, with narrative analysis, 3 charts, and 38 tables (p. 2-91).

This is the 11th annual report.

Availability: Pannell Kerr Forster, Trends, 262 North Belt East, Houston TX 77060, $50.00; SRI/MF/not filmed.

B7100–2   TRENDS IN THE HOTEL INDUSTRY, USA Edition, 1984
Annual.   1984.   77 p.
LC A40-3316.
SRI/MF/not filmed

Annual report on operating results of the U.S. hotel and motel industry, 1983, with comparisons to 1982. Presents detailed data for individual income and expense items, including property taxes and insurance, food and beverages, fuel and telephone use, payroll, laundry/dry cleaning, janitorial services, and employee benefit plans.

Data are shown as the ratio of itemized operating expenses to total departmental revenues, and as costs and income per available room, by geographic region, size classification, and rate group, for transient and resort hotels, and motels with and without restaurants.

Also includes occupancy rates, with monthly detail for selected cities and States; room charges; and summary trends from 1964.

Report is based on a survey of 1,000 hotels and motels, conducted by Pannell Kerr Forster.

Contains listing of contents, tables, and charts (p. 1); narrative analysis (p. 2-16); and 6 charts and 42 tables (p. 17-77).

This is the 48th annual report.

Availability: Pannell Kerr Forster, Trends, 262 North Belt East, Houston TX 77060, $50.00; SRI/MF/not filmed.

B7400
PHH Group

B7400–1   EXPENSECHECK TRENDLINES: Business Travel Expenses
Monthly.   Approx. 15 p.
SRI/MF/complete, shipped quarterly

Monthly report on business travel costs, with analysis of individual cost components. Report is published in 5 sections covering total U.S. and 4 specific industries. Industries covered are consumer products, health/beauty, medical products, and pharmaceutical.

Data are derived from actual expenses reported by approximately 20,000 corporate employees representing more than 100 companies which subscribe to the travel management services of PHH Group.

Each section contains 2 tables showing costs per traveler, for meals, lodging, public transportation, car rental, telephone/telegraph, postage/supplies, entertainment, and miscellaneous; and number and unit cost of meals and lodging nights per traveler; all for month of coverage and year to date, with percent change from previous month and year.

National section also includes a newsletter, entitled *Communique,* generally containing 1-2 news briefs or articles, occasionally with statistics, including 1 quarterly table showing index of overall business travel costs (1976 = 100) for current year through month of coverage.

Prior to Jan. 1985 issue, report also included sections for chemical and insurance industries. These sections have been temporarily suspended.

Report is published approximately 7 weeks after month of coverage.

Monthly tables appear in all issues. *Communique* quarterly table usually appears in Mar., June, Sept., and Dec. issues. All other *Communique* features with substantial statistical content are described, as they appear, under "Statistical Features." Nonstatistical features are not covered.

Report sections may be ordered separately or as a group. SRI coverage begins with the Aug. 1984 issue.

A triennial survey on corporate travel policies is also available from the issuing agency, but is not covered by SRI.

Availability: TEMS, IVI Management Systems, Inc., 400 Skokie Blvd, Northbrook IL 60062-2862, Communique and National Trendline $150.00 per yr., single industry $75.00 per yr.; SRI/MF/complete, shipped quarterly.

Issues reviewed during 1985: Aug. 1984-May 1985 (D) (National sections are numbered T.147-T.156).

STATISTICAL FEATURE:

B7400–1.601: Oct. 1984 (National Section, No. T.149)

MEAL AND LODGING ANALYSIS TOOL

(2 p.) Article, with 1 table showing number of meals and lodging nights and cost of entertainment per month, for average business traveler, 1980-1st 10 months 1984.

B8130
Salmon, Kurt, Associates

B8130–1   KSA PERSPECTIVE: TEXTILE PROFILE FOR 1984
Annual.   June 1985.   12 p.
SRI/MF/complete

Annual report presenting financial performance data for 45 publicly owned textile manufacturers in 5 industry segments, FY84 and trends. Includes sales, net income, and 9 financial and operating ratios, all by company, FY84, with rankings for each indicator, comparisons to FY83, and top performers over FY80-84 period.

Industry segments covered are finished consumer products for the home, knitted/woven fabrics, spun/textured yarn, diversified companies, and other (converters/printers/nonwovens/miscellaneous).

Also includes sales and net income of 2 multi-industry conglomerates with textile sales comprising less than half of total business; and analyses of textile industry aggregate profit and loss data and working capital flow, various years FY80-84.

Data are derived from annual reports to SEC and to company stockholders.

Contains narrative analysis interspersed with 7 charts and 6 tables.

Report is excerpted from detailed profile of industry finances, a computer print-out of approximately 400 pages. Detailed profile is available from the issuing agency for $300.00, but is not covered by SRI.

Availability: Kurt Salmon Associates, 350 Fifth Ave., New York NY 10118, †; SRI/MF/complete.

B8130-2   KSA PERSPECTIVE: APPAREL PROFILE FOR 1984
Annual.   June 1985.   8 p.
SRI/MF/complete

Annual report presenting financial performance data for 56 publicly owned apparel manufacturers in 4 industry segments, FY84 and trends. Includes sales, net income, and 9 financial and operating ratios, all by company, FY84, with rankings for each indicator, comparisons to FY83, and top performers over FY80-84 period.

Industry segments covered are women's/children's wear, men's/boys' wear, diversified, and associated fashion products.

Also includes sales and net income of 13 multi-industry conglomerates with apparel sales comprising less than half of total business; and analyses of apparel industry aggregate profit and loss data and working capital flow, various years FY80-84.

Data are derived from annual reports to SEC and to company stockholders.

Contains narrative analysis interspersed with 2 charts and 6 tables.

Report is excerpted from detailed profile of industry finances, a computer print-out of approximately 400 pages. Detailed profile is available from the issuing agency for $300.00, but is not covered by SRI.

Availability: Kurt Salmon Associates, 350 Fifth Ave., New York NY 10118, †; SRI/MF/complete.

B8130-3   KSA PERSPECTIVE: FOOTWEAR PROFILE FOR 1984
Annual.   June 1985.
6 p.+errata.
SRI/MF/complete

Annual report presenting financial performance data for 34-35 publicly owned footwear companies in 3 industry segments, FY84 and trends. Includes sales, net income, and 9 financial and operating ratios, all by company, with rankings for each indicator and comparisons to FY83.

Industry segments covered are manufacturers, retailers, and miscellaneous/multi-industry companies.

Also includes analyses of footwear industry aggregate profit and loss data and working capital flow, various years FY80-84.

Data are derived from annual reports to SEC and to company stockholders.

Contains narrative analysis interspersed with 5 charts and 5 tables.

Report is excerpted from detailed profile of industry finances, a computer print-out of approximately 200 pages. Detailed profile is available from the issuing agency for $200.00, but is not covered by SRI.

Availability: Kurt Salmon Associates, 350 Fifth Ave., New York NY 10118, †; SRI/MF/complete.

B8150
Seafirst Corp.

B8150-1   PACIFIC NORTHWEST INDUSTRIES: Seafirst Corporation Annual Review
Annual, discontinued.

Annual report on economic and industrial trends and outlook for Pacific Northwest region, with detailed data on Washington State business indicators, employment, and production. Report is discontinued with the 1984 edition (for description see SRI 1984 Annual under this number).

Similar data are available in *Pacific Northwest Executive,* a quarterly report published by the University of Washington Graduate School of Business Administration, covered in SRI under U9120-1.

B8250
Security Pacific National Bank

B8250-1   ECONOMIC REPORT: OUTLOOK SERIES
Series.   For individual publication data, see below.
SRI/MF/complete

Series of annual reports analyzing the economic outlook for California, the U.S., and world regions. Most data are based on Security Pacific Economics Dept analyses of State and Federal sources, or international statistical sources such as the OECD.

Report on California and near-term U.S. outlook is described below; the 2 other reports, on long-term U.S. and international economic outlooks, are no longer published by the issuing agency. For description of most previous editions of these 2 reports, see SRI 1984 Annual and SRI 1983 Annual under B8250-1.4 and B8250-1.1, respectively.

Availability: Security Pacific National Bank, Economics Department, H8-13, PO Box 2097, Terminal Annex, Los Angeles CA 90051, †; SRI/MF/complete.

B8250-1.1: California Economic Outlook and U.S. Economic Update
[Annual. Fall 1984. 33 p. Rpt. No. 72. SRI/MF/complete.]

Annual report on California economic trends and outlook, 1976-85; and U.S. outlook, through 1985.

Contains 4 sections, with 16 tables as follows:

California

a. Near-term outlook: GSP; total, disposable, and per capita personal income; labor force by employment status, and nonagricultural wage/salary employment by industry division; population and net migration; and taxable sales and CPI; quarterly 1984-85 or annually 1983-85. 4 tables. (p. 2-6)

b. Industry trends: bank loans and deposits by type, and loan/deposit ratio; new housing permits by type, and residential and non-residential construction value by type, 1983-85; and imports and exports, for 10

leading trading countries 1983, and 6 leading product categories 1983-1st quarter 1984. 5 tables. (p. 9-13)

c. Regional trends: selected economic indicators for 3 State regions, 1976-83. 3 tables. (p. 20-23)

U.S. Near-Term Outlook

d. GNP and deflator, 1983-85; and forecasts for selected economic and business indicators, including housing starts, auto sales, personal income, saving rate, industrial production index, employment and unemployment, PPI, CPI, GNP, personal consumption expenditures, private investments, government purchases, foreign trade, and corporate profits, quarterly 1984-85 and/or annually 1983-85. 4 tables. (p. 25-30)

B8320
Shell Oil Co.

B8320-1   NATIONAL ENERGY OUTLOOK
Recurring, discontinued.

Recurring pamphlet assessing U.S. energy outlook to 2000, discontinued with the July 1982 edition (for description, see SRI 1983 Annual under this number).

B8400
Sibson and Co.

B8400-1   ANNUAL REPORT 1985: EXECUTIVE COMPENSATION
Annual.   1984.   7+149 p.
LC 81-642136.
SRI/MF/not filmed

Annual report on top management compensation and related corporate policies, 1984. Includes data on salary and bonus levels; job evaluation techniques; prevalence and characteristics of annual and long-term incentive plans, including performance measures used for plan development, stock option plans, and incentives offered by top 200 industrial and other major corporations (shown for individual firms); perquisites offered, including retirement and insurance plans; and employment contract components and use.

Also includes selected detail by position or management level, and summary trends from 1980. Data are often shown by company sales size and/or type of industry.

Most data are from a 1984 survey of approximately 1,000 companies with sales of $10 million-$30 billion.

Contains foreword, and listings of contents and exhibits (7 p.); highlights, with 1 chart and 1 summary table (p. 1-5); narrative report, with 14 charts and 75 tables (p. 7-133); and appendix, with list of companies participating in survey (p. 135-149).

This is the 20th annual report. Additional comprehensive reports covering insurance and financial industries in detail, and cluster reports tailored to meet participant's specifications, are also available from the issuing agency, but are not covered by SRI.

Availability: Sibson and Co., 777 Alexander Rd., Princeton NJ 08540, $185.00; SRI/MF/not filmed.

B8400-2 1986 ANNUAL SALARY PLANNING SURVEY
Annual. Sept. 1985.
1+18 p.
SRI/MF/not filmed

Annual report on corporate salary administration plans for 1986. Presents data on salary range revisions and average merit increases, for officers/executives, exempt employees, and salaried and hourly nonexempt employees, shown by industry sector and region, actual 1985 and planned 1986.

Also includes data on competitive salary objectives; merit increase timing; use of bonuses and other forms of variable compensation, and of salary investment and flexible benefit plans; job evaluation methods; use of geographic differentials in establishing salaries; salary information provided employees; method of computing charges for personal use of company cars; changes in benefits provided; and use of computers in salary administration.

Data are from 1,090 company responses to a 1985 survey.

Contains introduction (1 p.); contents listing, profile of participants with 2 tables, and summary (p. 1-3); report with brief narrative analyses and 14 tables (p. 4-16); and appendix listings of industry sector components and geographic regions (p. 17-18).

This is the 12th annual survey report. A separate report on Canadian companies is also available from the issuing agency, but is not covered in SRI.

Availability: Sibson and Co., 777 Alexander Rd., Princeton NJ 08540, participants †, others ‡; SRI/MF/not filmed.

B8415
SIN Television Network

B8415-1 SPANISH USA, 1984
Recurring (irreg.) 1984.
21 p.
SRI/MF/complete

Recurring report, for 1984, on a market survey of Hispanic Americans. Covers demographic and socioeconomic characteristics, consumer buying habits, attitudes on selected social and cultural matters, language skills, and media use (total and Spanish-language). Includes selected comparisons to 1981 survey findings.

Data are based on 775 responses to a fall 1983-Apr. 1984 survey conducted by Yankelovich, Skelly, and White, Inc. Survey covered 19 of 30 cities with largest Hispanic populations.

Contains narrative report, interspersed with 18 text tables (p. 6-10); appendix, with 14 tables (p. 12-18); and methodology, with 2 tables (p. 20-21).

For description of previous report, covering a Sept. 1980-Apr. 1981 survey, see SRI 1982 Annual, under this number.

Availability: SIN Television Network, 460 W. 42nd St., New York NY 10036, †; SRI/MF/complete.

B8545
Strategy Research Corp.

B8545-1 U.S. HISPANIC MARKET, 1984
Recurring (irreg.) 1984.
4+324 p.
SRI/MF/complete, delayed

Recurring report, for 1984, presenting market characteristics of the U.S. Hispanic population. Includes data on immigration patterns, demographic profiles, language ability, media use, income, and personal consumption, with detail by age, sex, country of origin, and market area or Area of Dominant Influence (ADI). Also includes data on population of Puerto Rico. Data generally are current to 1984 or 1985, with selected trends from as early as 1790.

Report was compiled for the National Assn of Spanish Broadcasters by Strategy Research Corp., and is based on data from personal interviews, Immigration and Naturalization Service, Census Bureau, and commercial sources. Report defines "Hispanics" as persons of Spanish origin or heritage who speak Spanish.

Contains contents listing (2 p.); introductory section on report purpose and methodology (p. 1-3); 8 report sections, with narrative and 209 tables described below (p. 7-284); narrative section on Spanish media availability, with directory listings of TV and radio stations, publications, and media representatives, by State and city (p. 287-319); and conclusions (p. 323-324).

Previous report, for 1980, is described in SRI 1981 Annual under this number.

Availability: Strategy Research Corp., 100 N.W. 37th Ave., Miami FL 33125, $50.00; SRI/MF/complete, delayed until May 1986.

TABLES:
[Unless otherwise noted, data are shown for U.S. Hispanic population. Data by market area are shown for New York State, Florida, California, and Texas/Southwest. Data by country of origin generally include Mexican, Puerto Rican, Cuban, and other Hispanic origin.]

B8545-1.1: Immigration and Population Characteristics
IMMIGRATION
a. U.S. total and Hispanic immigration, by detailed country and world area of origin, various periods 1820-1981; total population and immigration trends from 1790; and top 11 languages ranked by number of native speakers worldwide, as of mid-year 1983. 11 tables. (p. 8-33).

POPULATION AND DEMOGRAPHIC PROFILE
b. Hispanic population in U.S. and Hispanic countries; and U.S. Hispanic population by country of origin, market area, region, and State, with various cross-tabulations and comparisons to total population; mostly 1985, with selected trends from as early as 1950. 12 tables. (p. 37-57)

c. Demographic characteristics: Hispanic population by age, sex, educational attainment, and urban-rural and metro-nonmetro status; median age; households by size, and average household size by market area; median family income, with detail by region; and employment by sex and occupa-

tional group; mostly by country of origin, 1985, with selected comparisons to total population and trends from as early as 1978. 9 tables. (p. 58-71)

B8545-1.2: Lifestyle and Language, and Media Habits
[Unless otherwise noted, tables show survey responses, generally as percent distributions.]
LANGUAGE PATTERNS
a. Language: 1st language learned, speaking fluency, writing and reading ability, language most comfortable speaking, and language spoken at home, work, and social functions, all shown for English and Spanish; and difficulty in understanding Hispanics of other origins; all by market area, country of origin, and age group, 1984. 37 tables. (p. 76-99)

SHOPPING PREFERENCES AND TELEPHONE OWNERSHIP
b. Consumer preferences for Spanish- and English-speaking sales people, Hispanic sales people, Spanish-language signs/advertisements, and products geared toward Hispanic tastes, by market area, country of origin, and age group; and household telephone ownership status, by selected ADI; 1984. 4 tables. (p. 100-103)

MEDIA HABITS
c. Media use: use of Spanish-language media by type, and average hours of use, by market area and age group; and average number of TV sets per household, and cable TV penetration, by selected ADI; 1984. 6 tables. (p. 107-112)

d. TV audience size and shares (among total households, and adult audience by sex), for individual stations in 6 ADIs, spring 1984. 6 tables. (p. 113-116)

B8545-1.3: Income and Expenditures, Market Profiles, and Puerto Rico
HOUSEHOLD INCOME AND PERSONAL CONSUMPTION
a. Family median income, by country of origin and region, with comparison to total population; and mean and aggregate household income, and personal consumption expenditures (with detail for durable and nondurable goods, and services), all by region. 5 tables. (p. 121-125)

MARKET BY MARKET
b. Top 30 Hispanic ADIs ranked by population, with all or most of the following shown for each: population by county, age, and sex; household telephone ownership; and number of Spanish-language TV and radio stations, and newspapers/magazines; various years 1970-85. 101 tables. (p. 129-249)

c. U.S./Mexico border market characteristics: population, by U.S. ADI and Mexican city; rank of 4 border-area SMSAs among total U.S. markets, by selected population and market indicators; and 30 largest Hispanic ADIs if Mexico border populations are included; (no dates). 3 tables. (p. 250-253)

PUERTO RICO
d. Total population of Puerto Rico and U.S., 1970, 1980, and 1985; and population of Puerto Rico by age and sex, with median age, 1980. 2 tables. (p. 257-258)

B8545–1.4: Product Usage

a. Household use indexes for Hispanics vs. non-Hispanics, for selected food and beverage, health and beauty aid, cleaning, and paper products, by type, with detail for Hispanics by market area and country of origin, 1984. 9 tables. (p. 261-280)

b. Brand loyalty (percent of consumers who use 1 brand or switch brands frequently), by market area, country of origin, and age group; and average weekly grocery expenditures, by market area; 1984. 4 tables. (p. 281-284)

B8560
Sunkist Growers, Inc.

B8560–1   CITRUS FRUIT INDUSTRY
Statistical Bulletin, 1985
Annual.   1985.   4+61 p.
ISSN 03262-014X.
LC 76-641810.
SRI/MF/complete

Annual report on citrus industry trends, 1970s-84, with focus on Arizona/California. Presents detailed data for oranges, tangerines, grapefruit, lemons, and limes. Data generally are current through 1983/84 and include trends from 1974/75 or 1979/80, with some earlier trends. Covers the following topics:

a. Citrus production, acreage, shipments by week and month, utilization (fresh or processed), prices, and production costs, for Arizona/California, with selected data also shown for Florida and Texas.

b. Total citrus production for U.S., world, and selected foreign countries; U.S. per capita consumption of citrus and other fruits and of juices; U.S. packs of canned citrus juices; U.S. exports of citrus fruits and juices, orange juice concentrate, and orange and lemon oil, by country or region of destination; and citrus fruit exports of foreign countries.

Data are compiled by Sunkist Growers Inc., from Federal and State government reports, and industry sources including California/Arizona Citrus League.

Contains table listing and introduction (4 p.); and 36 summary charts and 61 tables (p. 1-61).

Availability: Sunkist Growers, Inc., Information Systems Department, PO Box 7888, Van Nuys CA 91409, †; SRI/MF/complete.

B8990
Transportation Policy Associates

B8990–1   TRANSPORTATION IN
AMERICA
Annual (3 volumes).
3 volumes.
For individual publication data, see below.
SRI/MF/not filmed

Annual report on trends in transportation operations and finances, by transport mode, various years 1939-85. Includes data on passenger and freight traffic, revenues and costs, fuel consumption, government taxes/fees, employment and earnings, and accident fatalities. Data are from transportation assns, CAB, FAA, ICC, and other sources.

Report is issued in 3 volumes: main report, and 2 supplements with updates and corrections. Main report and 1st supplement are described below.

This is the 3rd annual edition. SRI coverage begins with this edition. Copies of the 1st and 2nd editions are available from the issuing agency for $5.00.

Similar data previously were published by Transportation Assn of America in *Transportation Facts and Trends,* discontinued with the 1981 edition (for description see SRI 1982 Annual under A9125-1).

Availability: Transportation Policy Associates, PO Box 33633, Farragut Station, Washington DC 20033, $28.00; SRI/MF/not filmed.

B8990–1.1: Main Report
[Annual. Mar. 1985. 3+46 p. SRI/MF/not filmed.]

Contains contents listing (1 p.); 29 charts and 27 tables, with interspersed narrative (p. 1-26); description of DOT and regulatory agencies and committees (p. 27-31); source data, with 2 tables (p. 32-41); and information on issuing agency (p. 42-46).

All tables, and selected charts with substantial data not covered in tables, are listed below.

TABLES AND CHARTS:
[Tables [5-16] and [19-27] show data by transport mode, generally including air, rail, truck, bus, water, pipeline, and (as appropriate) private auto. Exact categories of transport modes vary from table to table. Some tables include detail for regulated and nonregulated carriers, and by specific type of water transport. Trend data usually are shown for selected years within the ranges indicated.]

ECONOMIC TRENDS, FREIGHT, AND PASSENGERS

[1] Transportation, 20% of America [outlays for private autos, regulated carriers, non-regulated trucking, and other transport, 1983]. [chart] (p. 1)

[2] Transportation is a heavy user of other industries' products [transportation industry's share of consumption, for 8 commodities (no date)]. [chart] (p. 1)

[3] Transportation outlays [freight and passenger] vs. GNP [1960-84]. (p. 2)

[4] National economic vs. transport trends [including GNP, industrial production index, population, and intercity ton-miles and passenger-miles], 1939-84. (p. 3)

[5-6] Nation's freight and passenger bill [including purchase and operating costs for private automobiles and aircraft, costs of water freight transport by detailed type, and costs of local passenger transport by type including taxi and school bus; 1960-83]. (p. 4-5)

[7-10] Domestic intercity ton-miles, tonnage carried, travel [passenger-miles], and passengers carried, [1939-84]. (p. 6-9)

[11] Revenues of ICC, CAB, and FERC regulated carriers in domestic operation [including freight forwarders; 1947-83]. (p. 10)

[12] Transportation revenue vs. general [producer and consumer] price trends [1947-83]. (p. 11)

[13] Intercity freight federally regulated (percent of total ton-miles per mode) [1939-84]. (p. 12)

PETROLEUM TRANSPORT AND CONSUMPTION

[14] Transportation of petroleum [ton-miles 1972-83, and tons 1955-83, for crude oil and petroleum products]. (p. 13)

[15] Petroleum consumption [in transportation, including by type of highway vehicle, 1965-83]. (p. 14)

[16] Transportation demand vs. total domestic demand for petroleum [by type of petroleum product, 1955-83]. (p. 15)

GOVERNMENT EXPENDITURES, AND USER TAXES/FEES

[17] Federal and state/local government expenditures for transport facilities/ services [airways, airports, highways, rivers/harbors, rail (Amtrak), and urban mass transit, 1947-84]. (p. 16)

[18] Federal and state transport user taxes and fees [Federal taxes related to air transport and motor vehicles, and State motor fuel taxes and registration/license/mileage levies, 1947-83]. (p. 17)

EMPLOYMENT AND EARNINGS

[19-20] Employment in transportation and related industries [including government transport, and in] specialized transportation occupations, [1950-83]. (p. 18-19)

[21] Average annual earnings and total compensation per full-time employee [for 7 transportation industries compared to selected other industry sectors, 1947-83]. (p. 20)

MISCELLANEOUS

[22] Basic intercity transportation mileage within the continental U.S. [1939-83]. (p. 21)

[23] Number of privately/publicly owned transport units [by type, 1950-83]. (p. 22)

[24] Expenditures for new plant/equipment by transport and related industries [1950-85]. (p. 23)

[25] Average length of haul of domestic interstate freight and passenger modes [1947-83]. (p. 24)

[26] U.S. Government transportation research/planning/R&D outlays [by agency; and total Federal R&D outlays; 1960-83]. (p. 25)

[27] Transportation vs. total fatalities in U.S. from accidents [including detail by type of motor vehicle and aircraft, for commercial and recreational water vessels, and for gas and liquid pipelines, 1970-83]. (p. 26)

[28-29] [Domestic intercity passenger-miles handled and passengers carried by Class I railroads, including Amtrak, commuter, and other systems, 1970-84]. (p. 35-36)

B8990-1.2: Supplements, Updates, and Corrections: 1st Supplement

[Annual July 1985. 15 p. no paging. SRI/MF/not filmed.]

Contains 1 table showing percent change in traffic indicators, by transport mode, 1- to 6-month periods of 1st half 1985 vs. same periods of 1984 (1 p.); and 16 tables revising and updating main report tables [3-12], [14], [18], [20], [24-25], and [27], with data through 1984 or 1985 (12 p.).

B9300
United Van Lines

B9300-1   UNITED VAN LINES MIGRATION STUDY

Annual. Mar. 5, 1985. 5 p.
Rpt. No. 17-85.
SRI/MF/complete

Annual press release reporting 1984 interstate population migration patterns, as indicated by over 175,000 household goods shipments handled by United Van Lines.

Contains narrative analysis; 1 table showing outbound and inbound household goods shipments, by State; and 1 map illustrating migration patterns.

Availability: United Van Lines, One United Dr., Fenton MO 63026, †; SRI/MF/complete.

B9550
Young, Arthur, and Co.

B9550-1   EXECUTIVE COMPENSATION, the Twelfth Edition

Annual. 1984. 194 p.
LC 77-156190.
SRI/MF/complete

Annual report, by Edwin S. Mruk and James A. Giardina, on corporate executive compensation, 1983-84. Includes salary levels as of Dec. 1983 and Apr. 1984, bonus levels for 1983, selected comparisons to 1982, and summary trends from 1978. Data are shown by position, industry, corporation sales or asset size, and region, with detail for bonus and nonbonus companies. Separate data are presented for parent companies and subsidiaries/divisions.

Data are from survey responses of approximately 1,300 Financial Executives Institute member corporations and other companies, and represent approximately 13,500 executives in 22 top executive and senior financial management positions.

Industry classifications are manufacturing (durable and nondurable goods), nonmanufacturing, and financial services, with further detail for 25 SIC 2- or 3-digit industries.

Contains listings of contents and tables (p. 3-4); foreword, methodology, and highlights (p. 5-10); 2 report sections, covering parent companies

(p. 11-153) and subsidiaries/divisions (p. 155-181), with narrative overviews and 480 tables arranged by position and industry; and Appendix I-II, with job descriptions and industry definitions (p. 183-191).

Availability: Arthur Young and Co., PO Box 5806, Grand Central Station, New York NY 10017, $195.00; SRI/MF/complete.

B9550-4   EXECUTIVE DEMAND INDEX

Quarterly. 6 p.
SRI/MF/complete

Quarterly report presenting indexes of demand for executives, based on employment advertising in major business publications (1978=base year). Reports are issued 1-3 weeks after quarter of coverage.

Issues usually include narrative summary and definitions; and 1 chart and 7 tables showing demand index by executive function, industry sector, and region, for quarter of coverage and year to date, with comparisons to same periods of previous year, and summary trends for previous 12-28 quarters.

Data by region are shown for 5 U.S. regions and total international. Data by industry sector are shown for manufacturing, general services, and financial services.

Availability: Young, Arthur, and Co., Arthur Young Executive Resource Consultants, 277 Park Ave., New York NY 10172, †; SRI/MF/complete.

Issues reviewed during 1985: 4th Qtr. 1984-3rd Qtr. 1985 (D).

C0105
Abingdon Press

C0105-1 **YEARBOOK OF AMERICAN AND CANADIAN CHURCHES, 1985**
Annual. [June] 1985.
v+295 p.
ISSN 0195-9043.
ISBN 0-687-46640-7.
LC 16-5726.
SRI/MF/excerpts

Annual report on U.S. and Canadian churches, presenting data on denominations, membership, attendance, clergy, finances, and theological seminary enrollment. Most data are for 1983 or 1984, with selected trends for 1970s and historical data from as early as 1890. Also includes directories of religious organizations and publications.

Data are compiled by National Council of the Churches of Christ in the U.S.A. from 219 U.S. and 84 Canadian religious bodies, Census Bureau, Gallup surveys, and other sources.

Contents:

Introduction and contents listing. (p. iii-v)

Chapter I. Calendar for church use. (p. 1-3)

Chapter II. Directories of U.S. and Canadian national, regional, and local religious organizations; international confessional, interdenominational, and cooperative agencies; Christian conferences; theological seminaries and church-related colleges; religious periodicals; and service agencies. (p. 5-226)

Chapter III. Statistical and historical section, with narrative; text data, 2 maps, and 37 tables, described below; and list of depositories of historical materials in U.S. and Canada. (p. 227-286)

Index. (p. 287-295)

This is the 53rd edition of the report.

Availability: Abingdon Press, Yearbook of American and Canadian Churches, 201 Eighth Ave. S., PO Box 801, Nashville TN 37202, $15.95; SRI/MF/excerpts for statistical portions of Chapter III.

CHAPTER III STATISTICS:

C0105-1.1: Churches, Membership, and Finances

CHURCHES AND MEMBERSHIP

a. Churches, membership, pastors, total clergy, and Sunday/Sabbath schools and enrollment, shown for 219 U.S. and 84 Canadian denominations/religious bodies, 1984 or most current year reported; and percent of U.S. population with church membership, and change in membership, 1983-84. 5 tables. (p. 229-241)

b. Churches and members of major U.S. religions; churches, membership, and pastors, for religious bodies comprising National Council of the Churches of Christ in the U.S.A., 1984 or most current year reported; U.S. membership in 29 denominations, selected years 1940-83; and total membership, selected years 1890-1983. 4 tables. (p. 242-246)

FINANCES

c. Total and per member contributions and donations, for 40 U.S. and 30 Canadian Protestant denominations, 1984 or most current year reported; total U.S. charitable contributions, by donor type 1983, and by function 1955-83; Canadian per taxpayer charitable contributions, by Province, 1981; selected characteristics of U.S. and Canadian personal and family income and expenses, various years 1980-85; and denominational per member contributions, in current and constant 1967 dollars, 1961-83. 2 maps and 11 tables. (p. 248-257)

C0105-1.2: Catholic Data, Seminaries, and Selected Survey Results

a. Religious TV audience survey, 1984: trend in contributions to religious TV programs vs. local church in past 3 years; and comparisons of viewers and nonviewers of religious TV programs, including demographic characteristics, importance of religion in life, and involvement in local church. 4 tables. (p. 263-266)

b. Catholic data (U. S.): archdioceses and dioceses, and population; hierarchy and clergy; educational institutions, teachers, and students; hospitals and patients, nursing schools and enrollment, orphanages and invalid/aged homes and residents, and children cared for in foster homes; and recorded baptisms, converts, marriages, and deaths; 1984, with selected historical trends. Text data. (p. 267-269)

c. Theological seminaries and FTE enrollment (U.S./Canada combined), and total enrollment (separate U.S. and Canada data), 1978-84; and U.S. seminary enrollment of women, blacks, Hispanics, and Pacific/Asian Americans, various years 1970-84. 6 tables. (p. 270-272)

d. School prayer in U.S.: survey responses concerning prayer or Bible reading in public schools, by selected demographic and religious characteristics, and by views on selected other social issues; 1974, 1980, and 1982. 3 tables. (p. 275-278)

e. Church attendance trends in U.S. and Canada, by major denomination; and value of new construction of religious buildings; various years 1957-84. 4 tables. (p. 281-282)

C0175
American Banker, Inc.

C0175-1 **AMERICAN BANKER**
5 per week. Oversized.
ISSN 0002-7561.
LC SN 78-4624.
SRI/MF/excerpts

Daily (Mon.-Fri.) journal of the financial service industry. Covers news concerning banks and related financial institutions. Includes detailed statistics on the financial performance of individual institutions and bank investment funds.

Issues contain numerous newspaper-style news and feature articles; and several recurring depts, including technological developments in banking, and statistics on recent investment market and bank stock performance.

Statistical features include the following:

a. Annual rankings of individual financial institutions, including top commercial banks and thrift institutions, holding companies, credit unions, finance companies, and foreign- and minority-owned banks, by various criteria; and leading institutions in correspondent banking, holiday savings fund activity, trust activity, mortgage and commercial/industrial lending, and executive compensation.

b. Occasional special tables and statistical articles.

Major annual and special statistical features are described, as they appear, under "Statistical Features." Each issue of the journal is reviewed, but an abstract is published in SRI monthly issues only when such features appear.

Availability: American Banker, Inc., One State St. Plaza, New York NY 10004, $460.00 per yr., single copy $3.00; SRI/MF/excerpts for all portions covered under "Statistical Features."

Issues reviewed during 1985: Nov. 1, 1984-Oct. 31, 1985 (P) (Vol. CXLIX, Nos. 218-257; Vol. CL, Nos. 1-215).

STATISTICAL FEATURES:

C0175-1.601: Nov. 30, 1984 (Vol. CXLIX, No. 237)

AMERICAN BANKER RANKS THE TOP CORRESPONDENT BANKS, ANNUAL FEATURE

(p. 27-34, 40) Annual compilation of 5 tables on correspondent balances of commercial banks, showing the following rankings based on demand deposits: 341 largest banks in deposits due domestic banks, 57 largest banks in deposits due foreign banks, and 100 largest banks in deposits due thrift institutions, all as of June 30, 1984 with comparisons to June 30, 1983.

Also includes detail for Edge Act subsidiaries, comparative data for time/savings deposits or total correspondent balance, and summary data by Federal Reserve district.

Data are from an annual *American Banker* survey. Tables are accompanied by 3 related articles, with 3 summary tables (p. 1, 7-10).

C0175–1.602: Dec. 6, 1984 (Vol. CXLIX, No. 241)

TOP MINORITY-OWNED INSTITUTIONS

(p. 15) Data additions for compilation of 5 tables on banks and thrift institutions with at least 50% of ownership held by minorities (including women).

For description of tables, see SRI 1984 Annual under C0175-1.539.

C0175–1.603: Dec. 17, 1984 (Vol. CXLIX, No. 248)

TOP 100 CREDIT UNIONS IN THE U.S., ANNUAL FEATURE

(p. 8-10) Annual ranking of 100 credit unions with greatest assets, as of June 30, 1984. Data are from *American Banker* 7th annual survey.

Includes 7 tables showing top 100 credit unions ranked by assets, and including type of insurance, number of regular share accounts, capital/asset ratio, and value of member savings, capital, and individual retirement accounts (IRAs); with detail for 5-12 credit unions with largest IRA and capital values and gain in assets, and largest and smallest capital/assets ratio; and summary data for all credit unions; as of June 30, 1984 with comparisons to June 30, 1983.

Tables are accompanied by a related article, with 1 summary table (p. 1, 10, 13).

C0175–1.604: Dec. 19, 1984 (Vol. CXLIX, No. 250)

AMERICAN BANKER STATISTICAL GUIDE TO THE TOP 100 BANK HOLDING COMPANIES IN THE U.S., ANNUAL FEATURE

(p. 9-10, 15-16) Annual compilation of 6 tables on bank holding companies, showing the following data primarily as of Dec. 31, 1983, with comparisons to Dec. 31, 1982:

a. Alphabetical list of 100 largest companies, with total, average, and discrete assets; average value of deposits and equity capital; net, net operating, and gross trust income; return on assets and equity; change in earnings per share; market/book value ratio; total and foreign offices; and number of banks controlled; with selected rankings.

b. Rankings of top 5 companies by income, assets, return on assets and equity, and trust income.

C0175–1.605: Jan. 4, 1985 (Vol. CL, No. 3)

FINANCIAL SERVICES SCENE: AN AMERICAN BANKER SCORECARD

(p. 10-11) Table on competition among 30 major financial services companies, showing the following for each firm as of Dec. 31, 1983:

a. Assets; income; number of countries and States of operation; number of outlets; and value and/or volume of discount and full-service brokerage accounts, cash management and mutual fund accounts, annuities, individual retirement accounts, and Keogh/other retirement accounts.

b. Value of bank and thrift deposits; assets under discretionary management; life insurance in force, premiums written, and face value of new issuances; property/casualty insurance premiums written; value of loans by type; lease assets; and commercial finance company receivables.

Data are from public documents and *American Banker* surveys. Table is accompanied by a related article, with 1 chart and 6 tables showing selected rankings (p. 1, 6-8, 12-13).

C0175–1.606: Jan. 10, 1985 (Vol. CL, No. 7)

YEAREND BIG DEALS: WISCONSIN ACTIVITY QUICKENS AS INTERSTATE BANKING LOOMS

(p. 14-16) By Bart Fraust. Article on financial institution mergers and acquisitions during 1984. Includes 6 tabular lists showing companies involved in transactions, with selected detail on assets of acquiring and acquired companies, and transaction prices and ratios of premium to equity and earnings, all arranged by status of transaction as of Dec. 1984.

C0175–1.607: Jan. 11, 1985 (Vol. CL, No. 8)

AMERICAN BANKER RANKS THE TOP HOLIDAY CLUB INSTITUTIONS, ANNUAL FEATURE

(p. 7-13) Annual compilation of 6 tables showing holiday savings club accounts, payouts, rate offered, and major account type, for individual major banks, thrift institutions, and credit unions, grouped by State, 1983-84; with 1984 rankings of top 10 institutions by average payouts, and of top 50 institutions, top 25 banks and thrifts, and top 10 credit unions by total payouts.

Data are from responses of 307 institutions to an *American Banker* annual survey. Tables are accompanied by a related article, with 4 summary tables (p. 1, 14).

C0175–1.608: Jan. 15, 1985 (Vol. CL, No. 10)

FAILURE GLUT CREATES A BUYER'S MARKET, ANNUAL FEATURE

(p. 1-16, passim) Annual article, by Andrew Albert, on financial institution failures, 1984. Includes 2 tables showing number of failed banks and thrift institutions, by State and for Puerto Rico; and 3 listings of bank and thrift failures and of thrift acquisitions involving FSLIC assistance, with deposit or asset value and name of acquiring or assuming institution for each; 1984.

Data addendum, presenting aggregate trends, appears in the Jan. 16, 1985 issue (see C0175-1.609 below).

C0175–1.609: Jan. 16, 1985 (Vol. CL, No. 11)

BANK FAILURES

(p. 10) Table showing number of bank failures, by State and for Puerto Rico, 1982-84. Data are presented as an addendum to annual article on financial institution failures (for description, see C0175-1.608 above).

C0175–1.610: Jan. 17, 1985 (Vol. CL, No. 12)

GUIDE TO ON-LINE SECURITIES BROKERS, RECURRING FEATURE

(p. 6) Recurring table showing the following for 9 retail online brokerage firms, as of Jan. 16, 1985: location, hours of operation, number of online accounts, commission rates and minimum fee, and types of service provided. Data are from an *American Banker* survey.

Table is accompanied by a related article (p. 1, 6).

For description of last previous feature, see SRI 1984 Annual under C0175-1.540.

C0175–1.611: Jan. 21, 1985 (Vol. CL, No. 14)

WHO'S WHO IN HOME BANKING NATIONWIDE, RECURRING FEATURE

(p. 18) Recurring table showing number of personal identification codes issued and types of services offered, for individual financial institutions with electronic home banking services, arranged by State and for Canada, as of Jan. 18, 1985. Data are from *American Banker* surveys.

Table is accompanied by a related article (p. 1, 16).

C0175–1.612: Jan. 25, 1985 (Vol. CL, No. 18)

TOP 25 THRIFTS IN MORTGAGE-BACKED PASS-THROUGH SECURITIES

(p. 6) Table showing top 25 FSLIC-insured thrift institutions ranked by value of mortgage-backed pass-through securities, with amount in federally insured and other mortgage pools, and value of total assets, as of June 30, 1984. Data are from Data Resources, Inc.

C0175–1.613: Feb. 7, 1985 (Vol. CL, No. 27)

ESTIMATED VALUE OF IRA ASSETS

(p. 6) Table showing asset value of individual retirement accounts, by type of financial institution, as of Dec. 1983-84. Data are from Investment Co. Institute.

C0175–1.614: Feb. 21, 1985 (Vol. CL, No. 36)

AMERICAN BANKER RANKS THE FOREIGN BANKS IN THE U.S., ANNUAL FEATURE

(p. 35-54) Annual compilation of data on large foreign banks with U.S. affiliates (branches, agencies, commercial bank subsidiaries, Edge Act corporations formed by U.S. banks to engage in foreign banking, New York investment companies, and finance companies). Data are from an *American Banker* survey.

Includes 4 charts on market shares; list of representative offices by U.S. city and State; and 14 tables showing the following, as of June 1984, often with comparisons to 1983:

a. Commercial/industrial loans outstanding, assets, and deposits: for banks with more than $1 billion in loans at U.S. affiliates, with number of branch/agency offices and subsidiaries; summary by type of affiliate and for 10 leading countries; by type of affiliate by parent company, generally arranged by U.S. city and State (including Guam, Puerto Rico, and Virgin Islands); and for affiliates of all types, grouped by parent company and country, with number of offices and parent's Dec. 1983 assets.

b. Top 10 branches, agencies, and commercial and Edge bank subsidiaries, ranked by loans; and top 10 U.S. cities ranked by total foreign banking offices, with number of offices by type.

Data are accompanied by 2 related articles, with 1 map (p. 1, 58-59).

C0175–1.615: Feb. 28, 1985 (Vol. CL, No. 41)

AMERICAN BANKER RANKS THE TOP 300 THRIFTS IN THE U.S., ANNUAL FEATURE

(p. 35-43) Annual compilation of data on top 300 thrift institutions, including savings banks and savings and loan assns (S&Ls). Data are from an *American Banker* annual survey.

Includes 2 tables showing top 300 thrifts ranked by deposits, and including assets, net worth, and type of charter and insurance, with groupings by State; and top 300 thrifts ranked by assets; as of Dec. 1984, often with comparisons to 1983.

Also includes 10 tables showing summary data; aggregate deposits of top 300 thrifts, and number and deposits of all savings banks and S&Ls, 1979-84; and top 10 thrifts in net income and loss, 1984.

Tables are accompanied by a related article, with 1 summary chart (p. 1, 45, 47).

C0175–1.616: Mar. 6, 1985 (Vol. CL, No. 45)

AMERICAN BANKER DIRECTORY OF NEW FINANCIAL INSTITUTIONS, 1984

(p. 11-15, 18-22) Two tables showing the following for individual financial institutions beginning operation in 1984, arranged by State: date opened and initial capital for banks/thrifts, and date chartered and potential membership for Federal credit unions. Data were compiled by *American Banker*.

Tables are accompanied by 2 related articles, with 1 chart showing number of new commercial banks, 1980-84 (p. 1, 16-17).

100 SMALLEST INSURED COMMERCIAL BANKS IN THE U.S., ANNUAL FEATURE

(p. 32) Annual table ranking 100 smallest insured commercial banks by value of deposits, and also showing assets, equity capital, net loan value, return on assets and equity, and 5-year deposit growth, all as of June 30, 1984. Also shows year established, and net operating income for 1st half 1984.

Data are from Data Resources, Inc., and are based on bank reports submitted to Federal Government regulators. Table is accompanied by a related article with 1 summary table (p. 1, 30-31).

C0175–1.617: Mar. 15, 1985 (Vol. CL, No. 52)

AMERICAN BANKER RANKS THE TOP 300 BANKS IN THE U.S., ANNUAL FEATURE

(p. 43-52) Annual compilation of 4 tables ranking top 300 commercial banks by deposits and assets, and including the following for top 300 in deposits: groupings by State and for Puerto Rico, and amount of capital, surplus/undivided profits, and, where applicable, supplemental capital, as of Dec. 31, 1984 with comparisons to 1983.

Also includes 3 summary tables; and 2 tables showing aggregate deposit and capital trends for various subgroups of the top 300, with deposit comparisons to all other commercial banks and to all savings banks, 1960s-84 (p. 53).

Commercial bank data have been compiled annually since 1921 by *American Banker* in cooperation with *Polk's Bank Directory*. Savings bank summary data are from National Council of Savings Institutions.

Tables are accompanied by a related article, with 1 summary chart (p. 1, 58).

C0175–1.618: Mar. 18, 1985 (Vol. CL, No. 53)

TOP CORRESPONDENT BANKS, ANNUAL FEATURE

(p. 26-36) Annual compilation of 3 tables on bank correspondent balances, showing the following as of June 1984 with comparisons to 1983: banks with correspondent balances over $10 million ranked by demand deposits due all banks; and banks with interbank deposits over $10 million ranked by total deposits due all banks; with groupings by State and Federal Reserve district, and comparisons to time/savings deposits, deposits due U.S. banks, and total deposits.

Data are from an *American Banker* survey. Tables are accompanied by 2 related articles, with 1 summary table (p. 2, 6-7).

For description of a related feature on correspondent balances, see C0175-1.601 above.

C0175–1.619: Mar. 22, 1985 (Vol. CL, No. 57)

AMERICAN BANKER REVIEWS ACQUISITIONS BY THE TOP 300 BANKS, ANNUAL FEATURE

(p. 21-24) Two annual tables on 1984 merger/acquisition activities and name changes among top 300 banks in deposits, including name and location of participants, type and date of transaction, and, where applicable, value of merged deposits as of Dec. 1984; and number of acquiring and acquired banks, and deposits in acquired banks, by State and for Puerto Rico, 1983-84.

Data are from an *American Banker* survey. Tables are accompanied by a related article with 2 charts showing summary trends from 1980 (p. 1, 27).

C0175–1.620: Mar. 29, 1985 (Vol. CL, No. 62)

AMERICAN BANKER RANKS THE TOP BANK HOLDING COMPANIES BY ASSETS AND EARNINGS, ANNUAL FEATURE

(p. 11-15) Annual compilation of 3 tables showing top 100 bank holding companies ranked by assets, and including deposits, and number of banks and branches; and top 100 banks/bank holding companies ranked by net income, and including adjusted net income (with value of items used in adjustments), and returns on assets and equity; as of Dec. 1984 with comparisons to 1983.

Data were compiled by *American Banker*. Tables are accompanied by 2 related articles with 1 summary chart (p. 1, 18).

C0175–1.621: Apr. 2, 1985 (Vol. CL, No. 64)

AMERICAN BANKER RANKS THE TOP DEPOSIT TAKING INSTITUTIONS, ANNUAL FEATURE

(p. 15-25) Annual compilation of 5 tables presenting data on size and characteristics of deposits in 300 largest commercial banks and 300 largest thrift institutions. Tables show the following data, as of Dec. 1984:

a. Deposit size, national rank, annual net income, and value of negotiable order of withdrawal (NOW), super NOW, money market demand, and individual retirement accounts (IRA), for top 300 banks and 300 thrift institutions arranged by State and for Puerto Rico.

b. Rankings of top 25 deposit-taking institutions by value of all deposits, and of top 25 banks and 25 thrift institutions by value of IRA deposits, with comparisons to 1983.

Data were compiled by *American Banker*. Tables are accompanied by a related article, with 2 summary charts and 1 table (p. 1, 37-38).

Previous feature, with data for 1983, is described in SRI 1984 Annual under C0175-1.519.

C0175–1.622: Apr. 16, 1985 (Vol. CL, No. 74)

AMERICAN BANKER RANKS THE TOP BANKS AND BANK HOLDING COMPANIES IN CAPITAL, ANNUAL FEATURE

(p. 27-29) Two annual tables showing top 100 commercial banks ranked by capital funds (shareholders' equity/subordinated debt), and including assets, capital/assets ratio, and rank number based on deposits; and top 50 bank holding companies ranked by primary capital (shareholders' equity/mandatory capital notes), and including primary capital/assets ratio, shareholders' equity, capital funds, assets, and rank number based on assets; as of Dec. 1984 with comparisons to 1983.

Data were compiled by *American Banker*. Tables are accompanied by 5 summary tables (p. 30), and by a related article with 1 summary chart (p. 1, 46-47).

Previous feature, with data on top banks in 1983, is described in SRI 1984 Annual under C0175-1.520.

C0175–1.623: Apr. 30, 1985 (Vol. CL, No. 84)

AMERICAN BANKER RANKS THE TOP 5,000 BANKS IN THE U.S., ANNUAL FEATURE

(p. 27-52) Annual table showing top 5,000 commercial banks ranked by deposit value, as of Dec. 1984 with comparisons to 1983. Data are arranged by State and for Guam and Puerto Rico, with subgroupings for major cities.

Data were compiled by *American Banker* in cooperation with *Polk's World Bank Directory*. Table is accompanied by 1 summary chart, 5 summary tables, and 2 related articles (p. 1, 52-63 passim).

C0175–1.624: May 6, 1985 (Vol. CL, No. 88)

TOP 100 MORTGAGE SERVICERS AMONG BANKS AND MORTGAGE COMPANIES, ANNUAL FEATURE

(p. 26-29) Annual compilation of 6 tables on top mortgage servicers, showing the following:

a. Top 100 servicers ranked by value of permanent mortgages serviced, and including number of mortgages and GNMA and non-GNMA investors, year opened, and notes on corporate affiliations; and 10 servicers with greatest increase and decrease in servicing value among the top 100; as of Dec. 1984 with comparisons to Dec. 1983.

b. Top 25 servicers ranked by value of mortgages serviced by all subsidiaries, and including number of subsidiaries, as of Dec. 1984; and top 27 savings institutions with $1 billion or more in servicing for others ranked by value of loans serviced, and including fees and total assets, 3rd quarter 1984.

Data were compiled by *American Banker*. Feature is accompanied by a related article, with 1 table showing aggregate number of firms, and value of mortgages serviced, for bank- and thrift-related and all other institutions among the top 100 (p. 1, 12).

C0175–1.625: May 21, 1985 (Vol. CL, No. 99)

SURVEY SHOWS NEW PRODUCT OFFERINGS HAVE GOTTEN BACK TO BASICS

(p. 25) By Philip T. Sudo. Article, with 1 table showing top 16 new financial services/products based on planned introductions, for banks/thrifts with assets of $500-999 million and $1 billion or more, 1985. Data are from a Feb.-Mar. 1985 survey of 234 banks and 186 thrifts conducted by Behavioral Science Research Corp.

C0175–1.626: May 29, 1985 (Vol. CL, No. 104)

DISCOUNT BROKERAGE

(p. 6-7, 16-22) Table showing the following for individual bank holding companies offering discount brokerage services, arranged by State: assets ranking, date service began, types of services offered, and percent of customers from full-service and discount brokers and making 1st stock purchase. Data are from an *American Banker* survey of 250 bank holding companies and independent banks.

An accompanying table (p. 22) presents averages for discount brokerage services, including accounts opened, value and volume of shares traded, and value of commissions, with detail for aggregate top 50 and 100 firms and firms operating more and less than 1 year.

No data dates are given.

C0175–1.627: May 30, 1985 (Vol. CL, No. 105)

TOP 50 BANKING COMPANIES IN EXECUTIVE PAY, ANNUAL FEATURE

(p. 12-17) Annual table showing top 50 banking companies ranked by aggregate compensation of 2 highest paid executives, and including each organization's earnings and assets, and each executive's age, position, and compensation, 1984 with comparisons to 1983. Data were compiled by *American Banker*.

Table is accompanied by a related article (p. 10-11, 24) with 1 summary table; and 1 table showing compensation, age, and position, for 2 highest paid executives at 19 nonbank financial institutions, 1984 (p. 18).

C0175–1.628: June 4, 1985 (Vol. CL, No. 108)

WHO'S WHO IN VIDEO BANKING NATIONWIDE, RECURRING FEATURE

(p. 32-33) Recurring table showing number of personal identification codes issued and types of services offered, for individual financial institutions with electronic home banking services, arranged by State and for Canada, as of May 31, 1985. Data are from *American Banker* surveys.

Table is accompanied by related articles (p. 1, 31, 38).

C0175–1.629: June 6, 1985 (Vol. CL, No. 110)

UNCERTAINTY HURTING BROKERS

(p. 1, 8) By Nina Easton. Article on developments in regulation of brokered deposits in financial institutions. Data are from an FDIC survey of troubled institutions holding 5% or more of their deposits in fully insured brokered funds, as of Feb. 1985. Includes 1 table ranking top 25 suppliers of fully insured brokered funds by deposit amount.

C0175–1.630: June 14, 1985 (Vol. CL, No. 116)

TOP 100 FINANCE COMPANIES IN THE U.S., ANNUAL FEATURE

(p. 14-17) Annual compilation of 7 tables showing the following data for finance companies, as of Dec. 31, 1984 (or nearest fiscal year end), with selected comparisons to Dec. 31, 1983:

a. Capital funds rankings of top 100 companies, also showing capital/surplus, net and acquired receivables, total assets, net and deferred income, and bank credit available/in use; and capital funds rankings for finance companies below top 100, and top independent/affiliated, bank-related, and captive companies.

b. Receivables of top 10 companies in consumer, commercial/industrial, bank-related and nonbank industrial/equipment leasing, and factoring sectors; and net income ranking for top 50 companies.

Data are from an annual *American Banker* survey. Tables are accompanied by related article, with 1 summary chart and 1 summary table; 2 tables showing aggregate consumer and auto installment credit outstanding, by type of lender, 1983-84; and glossary (p. 1, 12-13, 16-17).

C0175–1.631: June 17, 1985 (Vol. CL, No. 117)

MEASURES TAKEN: SHORING THAILAND'S CREDITWORTHINESS

(p. 12-13) By Willard D. Sharpe. Article, with 2 text tables showing Thailand current account deficit (amount and as percent of GDP), and GDP growth rates, 1979-84.

C0175–1.632: June 21, 1985 (Vol. CL, No. 121)

TOP 100 COMMERCIAL BANKS IN LOANS TO BUSINESS, ANNUAL FEATURE

(p. 22-23) Annual table ranking top 100 commercial banks by total commercial/industrial lending volume, and including value of domestic business loans, and total gross loans and assets, by institution, as of Dec. 31, 1984, with comparisons to Dec. 31, 1983.

Data were supplied by Data Resources, Inc., and are based on Federal Reserve Board reports of condition and income for all insured commercial banks.

Table is accompanied by 8 summary tables ranking top and bottom 5-10 banks by change in lending volume, return on commercial/industrial loans, and ratio of business to total lending; and related articles, with 2 summary tables (p. 1, 6, 24-27).

C0175–1.633: June 25, 1985 (Vol. CL, No. 123)

1984 PERFORMANCE OF TOP U.S. BANKING COMPANIES, ANNUAL FEATURE

(p. 24-26) Annual compilation of 3 tables ranking 78 commercial banking companies with assets over $5 billion, by return on average assets and equity, percent change in earnings per share, stock market-to-book value, and year-end assets, mostly as of Dec. 31, 1984, with comparisons to 1983.

Companies are ranked within the following categories: money center institutions, and other institutions with assets of $10 billion/more and $5-10 billion. Tables also show each company's price/earnings multiple and dividend yield.

Data are from Cates Consulting Analysts, Inc. Tables are accompanied by a related article, with 3 summary tables and 1 additional table ranking selected banks by net interest margin lost (p. 1, 25, 30).

C0175–1.634: June 28, 1985 (Vol. CL, No. 126)

TOP 100 FIRMS IN DISCRETIONARY ASSETS AND TRUST INCOME, ANNUAL FEATURE

(p. 10-20, passim) Annual compilation of 3 tables on top bank and trust companies, showing the following data, by company, 1984, with selected comparisons to 1983:

a. Top 100 companies ranked by market value of discretionary assets, and also showing deposit rank and trust income rank.

b. Top 100 companies ranked by trust income, and also showing total operating income and market value of trust assets.

c. Discretionary assets of individual subsidiaries of companies ranked among top 100 in trust assets.

Data are from *American Banker* annual survey. Tables are accompanied by a related article, with 2 summary tables (p. 1, 19-20, 25).

C0175–1.635: July 23, 1985 (Vol. CL, No. 142)

LOAN-LOSS RESERVES AT THE TOP 10

(p. 14) Table showing top 10 bank holding companies ranked by total assets, and also showing loan loss reserves as a percent of total loans, as of June 30, 1984-85.

C0175–1.636: July 25, 1985 (Vol. CL, No. 144)

FLEET FINANCIAL TOPS KEEFE'S BANK 'HONOR ROLL'

(p. 3, 7) By John P. Forde. Article, with 1 table ranking 10 best and worst bank holding companies by 10-year compound growth rates in earnings per share, 1984. Data are from a Keefe, Bruyette, and Woods, Inc. annual ranking of 184 bank holding companies.

C0175–1.637: July 29, 1985 (Vol. CL, No. 146)

FOREIGN INVESTMENT IN THE U.S.

Compilation of features on foreign investments in U.S. Includes the statistical features described below.

FOREIGN PIGGY BANKS REVAMP U.S. INDUSTRY

(p. 16-18) By M. S. Mendelsohn. Article, with 2 charts showing flow of capital into U.S. from Europe, Japan, and all other foreign sources, 1983-84; and direct and portfolio assets held abroad by U.S. residents, 1981-84. Data are from Bank for International Settlements and Commerce Dept.

DEALS THAT DIDN'T GET AWAY

(p. 26-29, 60-65) Compilation of State profiles, each showing the following for the top 2-6 foreign investments in the State during the 1980s: foreign investor, U.S. subsidiary, product, investment amount, and jobs created. Data are from State economic development offices.

SCRUTINY ON BRITISH BOUNTY

(p. 41-42) By M. S. Mendelsohn. Article, with 1 chart showing net British direct investment in the U.S. (in U.S. dollars), selected years 1975-1983. Data are from U.K. Trade and Industry Dept.

AMERICAN BANKER RANKS THE TOP 500 BANKS IN THE WORLD BY DEPOSITS, ANNUAL FEATURE

(p. 67-82) Annual compilation of 12 tables on foreign and U.S. banks with largest deposits, showing the following data as of Dec. 1984 with selected comparisons to 1983:

a. World's top 1,000 banks ranked by deposits, with the following detail for the top 500: deposits in U.S. and domestic currency, ranking within each country and U.S. State, aggregate deposits and number of banks by country, and alphabetical listing with deposit and asset rank.

b. Top 10 banks ranked by 1-year deposit gain and loss; 10 countries with most deposits among top 500 banks, with number of banks; and currency exchange rates and number of banks in top 500 by quintile, by country.

Data were compiled by *American Banker*.

Tables are accompanied by a related article, with 1 chart showing share of deposits in top 500 banks, for U.S., Japan, and all other countries, 1979 and 1984 (p. 1, 89).

C0175–1.638: July 30, 1985 (Vol. CL, No. 147)

AMERICAN BANKER RANKS THE TOP 500 BANKS IN THE WORLD BY ASSETS, ANNUAL FEATURE

(p. 45-54) Annual compilation of 9 tables on foreign and U.S. banks and bank companies with largest assets, showing the following data as of Dec. 1984 with selected comparisons to 1983:

a. World's top 500 banks ranked by assets, with number of branches and employees; and top 86 banks/savings banks/bank holding companies ranked by assets, and alphabetical list of top 500 banks, both with asset and deposit rank among the top 500.

b. Top 10 banks (among the 500) ranked by 1-year assets increase and decrease; number of banks in top 500 by quintile, by country; and assets and number of banks aggregated for U.S., foreign countries, and 10 countries with greatest number of banks among the 500.

Data were compiled by *American Banker*.

Tables are accompanied by a related article, with 1 table and 1 chart showing assets of 9 banks acquired in 1984, and including acquirer; and share of assets in top 500 banks, for U.S., Japan, and all other countries, 1983-84 (p. 1, 62).

C0175–1.639: Aug. 12, 1985 (Vol. CL, No. 156)

COUNTING STANDBY LETTERS OF CREDIT WOULD HIT BIG BANKS' CAPITAL RATIOS

(p. 1, 6, 19) By Bart Fraust. Article on effects of proposals to include standby letters of credit in capital ratio calculations of bank holding companies. Data are from Keefe, Bruyette & Woods, Inc. Includes 1 table showing capital/assets ratios with and without standby letters of credit, for 10 bank holding companies with greatest standby letter value, as of year end 1984.

C0175–1.640: Aug. 16, 1985 (Vol. CL, No. 160)

TOP 100 BANKS IN LOANS TO AGRICULTURE, RECURRING FEATURE

(p. 8-9) Recurring table ranking top 100 commercial banks by value of agricultural loans, and including loans secured by farmland and for agricultural production, interest/fee income from total and agricultural loans, total loans, and net income, as of Dec. 31, 1984, with comparisons to Dec. 31, 1983.

Data were supplied by Data Resources, Inc., and are based on Federal Reserve Board reports of condition and income for all insured commercial banks.

Table is accompanied by 2 related articles, with 1 table ranking top 5 banks with greatest lending gain and loss in farm lending (p. 1-11, passim).

Previous table, for 1982, is described in SRI 1984 Annual under C0175-1.503.

C0175–1.641: Aug. 20, 1985 (Vol. CL, No. 162)

TOP 300 THRIFT INSTITUTIONS IN THE U.S., ANNUAL FEATURE

(p. 30-37) Annual midyear ranking of top 300 thrift institutions by deposit size, as of June 30, 1985. Covers mutual and stock savings and loan assns and savings banks. Data are from an *American Banker* midyear survey.

Includes 10 tables showing top 300 thrift institutions ranked by deposits and assets, and including net worth, net worth/assets ratio, and charter and insurance type, with groupings by State and for Puerto Rico, and detail for 10 institutions with greatest deposit gain and loss and with largest and smallest net worth/assets ratio; and summary of top 300 institutions by type of charter and insurer; all as of June 1985 with comparisons to June and Dec. 1984.

Tables are accompanied by a related article (p. 1, 10).

For description of year-end rankings for 1984, see C0175-1.615 above.

C0175–1.642: Aug. 22, 1985 (Vol. CL, No. 164)

WHO OPENED BANK DOORS IN FIRST HALF OF 1985

(p. 10-16) Two tables showing the following for individual financial institutions beginning operation 1st half 1985, arranged by State: date opened and initial capital for banks/thrifts, and date chartered and potential membership for credit unions. Data were compiled by *American Banker*.

Tables are accompanied by 1 summary table showing banks opened by type and State; and a related article (p. 9).

A similar article, with data for 1984, is described under C0175-1.616 above.

C0175–1.643: Aug. 23, 1985 (Vol. CL, No. 165)

TOP 300 COMMERCIAL BANKS IN THE U.S., ANNUAL FEATURE

(p. 35-42) Annual midyear ranking of top 300 commercial banks by deposit size as of June 30, 1985. Data are from *American Banker* midyear survey.

Includes 3 tables showing top 300 banks ranked by deposits, with groupings by State and for Puerto Rico, and including capital (total and primary) and assets; and detail for banks involved in acquisitions (including deposits of merged banks); primarily as of June 1985 with comparisons to June and Dec. 1984.

Tables are accompanied by a related article (p. 1, 47-48).

For description of year-end rankings for 1984, see C0175-1.617 above.

C0175–1.644: Aug. 28, 1985 (Vol. CL, No. 168)

TOP LETTER OF CREDIT BANKS

(p. 10-11) Table ranking top 100 commercial banks by value of standby letters of credit, and including assets and asset rank, as of Dec. 31, 1984 with comparisons to Dec. 31, 1983.

Data were supplied by Data Resources, Inc., and are based on Federal Reserve Board reports of condition and income for all insured commercial banks. Table is accompanied by a related article (p. 1, 10-11).

C0175–1.645: Aug. 29, 1985 (Vol. CL, No. 169)

FED DATA SHOW PRODUCTIVITY IS UP AT BANKS

(p. 3, 8) By David O. Tyson. Article, with 1 table showing the following averages for commercial banks in 3 asset-size groups, 1982-84: amount of regular savings deposits, certificates of deposit under $100,000, time open/other time deposits, and interest-bearing checking account deposits, with each deposit category's share of total time or demand deposits.

Data were compiled by Federal Reserve Board of New York from reports of 509 banks.

C0175–1.646: Sept. 6, 1985 (Vol. CL, No. 174)

THREE NY SAVINGS BANKS ARE ABOUT TO LOSE THEIR LIFERAFT

(p. 3, 7) By Mark Basch. Article on New York State savings banks with net worth certificates held by FDIC or FSLIC. Data are from New York State Banking Dept. Includes 1 table ranking 8 New York State savings banks by assets, and including 2nd quarter profit/loss, net worth, and value of net worth certificates, as of June 30, 1985.

C0175-1.647: Sept. 11, 1985 (Vol. CL, No. 177)

SURVEY FINDS WIDE BANK INTEREST IN MUTUAL FUNDS

(p. 1, 11) By Andrew Albert. Article on mutual fund activity at top U.S. banks. Data are based on responses of 240 banks to a 1985 Alliance Capital Management Corp. survey.

Includes 1 table showing respondents currently offering, not offering, and planning to offer mutual funds; and survey response on use of 1 or 2/more investment company funds, and reasons for favoring or avoiding mutual funds.

C0175-1.648: Sept. 18, 1985 (Vol. CL, No. 182)

FULL RESULTS OF SURVEY ON CASH MANAGEMENT PROFITABILITY

(p. 20-22) By Tom Ferris. Article on profitability of cash management services at top U.S. banks. Data are based on responses of 64 banks to a 1985 *American Banker* survey.

Includes 1 table showing survey response on cash management dept operations, changes in expenditures for cash management sales/marketing and product development, profitability by type of service, and reasons banks offer selected services, all with detail for respondents that are among top 25 and 26-100 banks offering cash management services.

C0175-1.649: Sept. 20, 1985 (Vol. CL, No. 184)

TOP 100 BANK HOLDING COMPANIES, SEMIANNUAL FEATURE

(p. 20-22) Semiannual compilation of 6 tables on bank holding companies, showing the following data primarily as of June 30, 1985, with comparisons to Dec. 31, 1984:

a. Ranking of top 100 companies by assets, and including deposits, number of banks and branches, primary and total capital, and net income; and ranking of top 50 companies by primary capital.

b. Alphabetical listing of companies with primary capital greater than $400 million, top 25 companies by net income, and 10 largest and smallest companies in ratio of primary capital to assets.

Tables are accompanied by a related article with 1 summary chart (p. 1, 28).

Semiannual feature updates 2 annual features on top 100 bank holding companies; for descriptions see C0175-1.604 and C0175-1.620, above.

C0175-1.650: Sept. 30, 1985 (Vol. CL, No. 190)

TOP 300 MORTGAGE COMPANIES, ANNUAL FEATURE

(p. 32-36) Annual table ranking top 300 mortgage companies by value of mortgages serviced, and including number of investors by type (GNMA pools and others) and mortgages serviced, for year ended June 30, 1985 with comparisons to previous year. Data are from the 19th *American Banker* survey of the mortgage industry.

Table is accompanied by a related article, with 2 summary tables and 1 other table showing major acquisitions of 5 mortgage companies ranked among the top 300, including company acquired, portfolio, and price (p. 1, 42-43).

C0175-1.651: Oct. 1, 1985 (Vol. CL, No. 191)

TOP 100 COMMERCIAL BANKS IN SERVICING OF PERMANENT MORTGAGES, ANNUAL FEATURE

(p. 14) Annual table ranking top 100 commercial banks by value of mortgages serviced for investors, and including number of investors by type (GNMA pools and others), number of mortgages serviced for investors, and value of mortgages serviced and owned, as of June 30, 1985, with comparative rank for June 1984. Data were compiled by *American Banker*.

Table is accompanied by a related article, with 3 summary tables, and 2 tables showing the following: top 63 savings institutions ranked by value of loans serviced for others, with loan servicing fees and total assets, as of 1st quarter 1985; and top 25 mortgage companies and commercial banks ranked by value of mortgages serviced for others, as of June 30, 1985, with comparison to June 1984, and number of subsidiaries for selected companies (p. 1, 16, 18).

C0175-1.652: Oct. 15, 1985 (Vol. CL, No. 201)

MINORITY-OWNED COMMERCIAL BANKS IN THE U.S., ANNUAL FEATURE

(p. 8, 10) Annual tabular listing of approximately 90 largest minority-owned commercial banks, grouped by State, showing the following for each institution: minority category (Asian, black, Hispanic, Native American, multi-racial, and women); deposits, assets, and net loans, as of Dec. 31, 1983-84; and net income, 1983-84. Data were compiled by *American Banker*.

Also includes related article (p. 1, 10, 12-13), with 1 summary table; and 1 table ranking top 3-10 minority-owned banks by assets and net income, and within each minority category, 1984.

Previous feature is described in SRI 1984 Annual under C0175-1.539.

C0175-1.653: Oct. 16, 1985 (Vol. CL, No. 202)

IN CASE OF BIG-BANK FAILURE...

(p. 1, 20, 22-23) By Robert Trigaux. Article, with 1 map and 1 table showing bank deposits and status of interstate banking legislation, by State, as of June 1, 1985; and number of banks and uninsured deposits as percent of total deposits, by deposit size group, as of June 30, 1984.

Data are from Federal Reserve Bank of Boston, Data Resources Inc., and Sheshunoff Data.

C0175-1.654: Oct. 23, 1985 (Vol. CL, No. 209)

EDGE BANKS USA, ANNUAL FEATURE

(p. 1A-11A) Annual feature profiling finances and operations of organizations incorporated under the Edge Act (nationally chartered organizations established to engage only in international banking and investment). Data are compiled by *American Banker*. Includes 3 charts and 8 tables showing the following:

a. Top 10 Edge Act systems ranked by assets; aggregate Edge bank offices and assets, by location (13 cities, all other U.S., and foreign); and summary statistics (offices, total assets and deposits, and business loans) for Miami, NYC, all other U.S., and foreign Edge banks; various periods Dec. 31, 1980-June 30, 1985.

b. Edge Act bank corporations, listed alphabetically, with each office's location, assets, deposits, clearing balances, business loans, and opening date; 10 largest Edge banks in Miami, ranked by deposit size and largest increases; and geographic listing of Edge offices, arranged by State, city, and foreign location, and showing each office's assets; Dec. 31, 1984, with comparisons to Dec. 31, 1983.

Also includes a directory of Edge banks, including date established, number of employees, and name, age, and title of chief executive.

Data are from *American Banker* surveys. Tables are accompanied by related articles, with 1 summary chart (p. 1, 8, 20).

C0175-1.655: Oct. 29, 1985 (Vol. CL, No. 213)

FARMERS GRATEFUL FOR BANK'S TIGHT FISTS

(p. 1, 32, 36) By Richard Ringer. Article, with 3 charts and 1 table showing Iowa farm production loans 30/more days past due as percent of total production loans; delinquent farm loans as percent of total; number of commercial bank failures; and farms foreclosed, acquired, and sold; various periods 1982-85.

Data are from Federal Reserve Board, and Iowa Depts of Banking and Agriculture.

C0175-2   HOW CONSUMER AMERICA VIEWS THE CHANGING FINANCIAL SERVICES INDUSTRY
Monograph. 1984. 16 p.
SRI/MF/complete

Compilation of survey articles presenting consumer opinions on banking industry services, innovations, operations, and government regulation. Includes survey response on the following topics:

a. Whether banks are seen more as public utilities than as private businesses; and opinions on the following, including whether government regulation of each is needed: fee/balance requirements, check-holding policies, closing of bank branches that are unprofitable or located in low-income areas, and subsidized banking services for low-income/elderly persons (with detail by source of subsidy).

b. Confidence in and health of banking/financial system, and perception of banking industry health relative to major industry problems (loans to developing countries and government aid to banks in trouble); whether banks should be able to expand into insurance/real estate sales; and whether banks are over-regulated.

c. Use of and satisfaction with banking/financial institutions or services, by type (including fully automated systems), with detail for 2-8 leading financial services firms; and personal computer ownership, and whether computer owners would consider home banking.

Data are based on responses of 1,004 adults to a July 1984 survey of households conducted by Reichman Research Inc. for *American Banker*.

Contains 16 articles, with text data, 28 charts, and 8 tables (p. 1-16).

Articles are reprinted from *American Banker* Oct. 20-29, 1984 issues.

Availability: American Banker, Inc., Attention: Gina Caputo, One State St. Plaza, New York NY 10004, $10.00; SRI/MF/complete.

C0200
American Demographics, Inc.

C0200–1 INTERNATIONAL DEMOGRAPHICS
Monthly. Approx. 15 p.
ISSN 0731-5414.
LC SN 82-940.
SRI/MF/complete, shipped quarterly

Monthly report on current topics related to international demography, with statistics on population size and characteristics for various countries, and analyses of related economic and social factors.

Data are from foreign government agencies and statistical yearbooks, U.S. Census Bureau, UN, and private sources.

Issues generally contain:

a. Several articles and brief news items, occasionally with statistics.

b. "Country Profile" monthly feature, focusing on a different country or area each month, with 1 table showing population by age group and sex, with illustrative chart; a varying number of trend charts; and often 1 or more additional tables.

c. "Regions" recurring feature, often with statistics, including updated or corrected census data for countries previously profiled in *International Demographics*.

d. Listings and descriptions of new publications and available data sources.

An annual cumulative index is published in the Dec. issue.

"Country Profile" and all other features with substantial statistical content are described, as they appear, under "Statistical Features." Nonstatistical features are not covered.

Availability: International Demographics, PO Box 68, Ithaca NY 14851, $148.00 per yr.; SRI/MF/complete, shipped quarterly.

Issues reviewed during 1985: Nov. 1984-Oct. 1985 (P) (Vol. 3, Nos. 11-12; Vol. 4, Nos. 1-10).

STATISTICAL FEATURES:

C0200–1.601: Nov. 1984 (Vol. 3, No. 11)
TEENAGERS IN EUROPE DECLINE

(p. 1-2) Article, with 1 table showing European teenage population, and share of total population, by region, selected years 1975-2000. Data are from the UN.

WEST GERMAN STUDY CONFIRMS YOUTH RETAIN BRAND LOYALTY

(p. 3, 8-10) Article on brand loyalty and other purchasing patterns among Western European youth, with focus on West Germany. Data are from 503 responses to a 1970 survey of 16 year old West Germans, and to a 1984 follow-up survey of the same group. Surveys were sponsored by Munich's Institute for Youth Research, and *Bravo* magazine.

Includes 1 table showing percent of respondents using and relying on same product brand in 1984 as in 1970, by selected product category.

COUNTRY PROFILE: SPAIN

(p. 4-7) Profile of Spain. Includes 2 tables showing population by age and sex, 1984; and population of cities over 100,000, primarily 1982. Data sources include *Polk's World Bank Directory*.

REGIONS, RECURRING FEATURE

(p. 13) Includes 1 table showing number of married women and all women in Australia who are employed, unemployed looking for full-time or part-time work, in and not in labor force, and age 15/over, 1977-82. Data are from Australian Bureau of Statistics.

C0200–1.602: Dec. 1984 (Vol. 3, No. 12)
JAPANESE WOMEN BUYERS LIKE WHAT THEY FIND

(p. 1-2, 10) Article, with 1 chart showing Japanese women age 25-69, by age group, decennially 1970-2000.

COUNTRY PROFILE: CYPRUS

(p. 4-7) Profile of Cyprus. Includes 3 tables showing population by age and sex, 1982; average household size, and distribution of households by size, for total, urban, and rural areas, 1971 and 1981; and distribution of men aged 20/over, by occupational category, 1981. Data are from Cyprus Ministry of Finance.

MISTAKEN IMPRESSION

(p. 11) Data clarification for profile of Sao Paulo, Brazil.

For description of profile, see SRI 1984 Annual under C0200-1.510.

REGIONS, RECURRING FEATURE

(p. 13) Includes 1 table showing Canadian households and/or percent of households, by size, tenure status, dwelling type, principal heating fuel, and ownership of selected consumer durable goods, 1983-84. Data are from *Statistics Canada Daily*.

C0200–1.603: Jan. 1985 (Vol. 4, No. 1)
COUNTRY PROFILE: FEDERATION OF MALAYSIA

(p. 1-8) Profile of Malaysia. Includes 1 chart and 2 tables showing percent of households owning selected consumer durable goods, by region and for urban and rural areas; population by age and sex; and population of cities over 100,000; primarily 1980. Data sources include Malaysia Dept of Statistics, and *Polk's World Bank Directory*.

Data correction appears in the Mar. 1985 issue (see C0200-1.605 below).

REGIONS, RECURRING FEATURE

(p. 10-11) Includes 1 table showing divorces and divorce rate, by Canadian Province, 1982-83. Data are from *Statistics Canada Daily*.

C0200–1.604: Feb. 1985 (Vol. 4, No. 2)
PROFILE: THE METROPOLITAN AREA OF RIO DE JANEIRO

(p. 1-9) Profile of Rio de Janeiro, Brazil, metro area. Includes 4 tables showing the following, for 1980 unless otherwise noted:

a. Rio de Janeiro and metro area population by age and sex; and metro area employment by industry division and sex.

b. Population, population density, median income, and percent of homes connected to general sewerage systems; population growth rate, 1970-80 period; and households, and percent of households with electricity and owning selected consumer durable goods; all by metro area municipality and administrative region.

Data are from the Brazilian census bureau.

INDEX OF POTENTIAL ENGLISH READERSHIP

(p. 10-11) Article, with 1 undated table estimating number of persons per 1,000 population who may purchase English-language materials, by country. Data are from *International Demographics*.

C0200–1.605: Mar. 1985 (Vol. 4, No. 3)
PROFILE: REPUBLIC OF COLOMBIA

(p. 1-8) Profile of Colombia. Includes 1 chart and 2 tables showing population, as follows: by age and sex, 1985; for urban and rural areas, quinquennially 1970-2000; and average annual growth rate, with comparison to total Latin America, 5-year periods 1950-85. Data sources include World Bank and Colombian government agencies.

EUROPE'S WOMEN AND THEIR HOUSEHOLDS

(p. 9) Article, with 1 undated table showing distribution of women by marital and employment status, with further detail for married women by husband's employment status, for total EC and 10 member countries. Data are from Commission of the European Communities.

ERRATA

(p. 9) Corrected data for profile of Malaysia.

For description of profile, see C0200-1.603 above.

REGIONS, RECURRING FEATURE

(p. 10-11) Includes 1 table showing the following for 21 Arab countries, total world, more and less developed countries, Sweden, and Japan: population and growth rate (with detail for Arab countries by type of population policy), number of years in which population will double, birth and fertility rates, total and infant mortality rates, and life expectancy, as of 1983; and population projected to 2000.

Data are from UN Fund for Population Activities.

C0200–1.606: Apr. 1985 (Vol. 4, No. 4)
PROFILE: REPUBLIC OF SENEGAL

(p. 1-8) Profile of Senegal. Includes 2 tables showing population by age and sex, 1985; and population by sex, by type or level of education, 1982. Data are from Direction de la Statistique, Dakar.

C0200–1.607: May 1985 (Vol. 4, No. 5)
PROFILE: GREATER LONDON

(p. 1-8) Profile of London, UK. Includes 4 tables showing the following:

a. Population by age and sex; and population, households, average household size, percent of households with children under age 16, and percent of households composed of single persons receiving and not receiving pensions, by borough; 1981.

b. Households; owner-occupied homes; total population; working married women age

16-59; men age 16-64; persons of pensionable age, over age 75, and under age 15; professionals and persons with higher education; and persons born outside UK; all as percent of total UK (no date).

c. Population, with distribution for Inner and Outer London, by type of neighborhood (no date).

Most data are from UK government.

USING FOREIGN-BORN POPULATIONS TO TEST FOR MARKET FEASIBILITY

(p. 9) Article, with 1 chart showing distribution of U.S. foreign-born population, and foreign-born persons as percent of U.S. population, by world area of origin, 1980. Data are from Census Bureau.

C0200–1.608: June 1985 (Vol. 4, No. 6)

PROFILE: REPUBLIC OF VENEZUELA

(p. 1-10) Profile of Venezuela. Includes 1 chart and 3 tables showing population by age and sex; distribution of male and female employment, by industry; population, households, and population density, by administrative division; and distribution of total, rural, urban, and Caracas households, by income group, with median income; 1980 or 1981, with population growth from 1971 for administrative divisions.

Data are from Venezuela Central Office of Statistics and Computation.

NEW URBAN PROJECTIONS RELEASED

(p. 5) Brief article, with 1 table showing top 35 urban areas worldwide, ranked by population, 1985 with comparisons to 1990 and 1995. Data are from the UN.

$47 GOLD MINE OF DEMOGRAPHIC INFORMATION

(p. 10-11) Article, with 2 tables showing top and bottom 20 countries, ranked by population growth rate, 1980-85 period; and top 25 countries ranked by population, 1984 and 2025. Data are from the UN.

C0200–1.609: July 1985 (Vol. 4, No. 7)

PROFILE: REPUBLIC OF AUSTRIA

(p. 1-6) Profile of Austria. Includes 4 tables showing population by age and sex, 1985; population of 5 major cities (no date); and land area, population, households, and occupied dwellings (total and by presence of various plumbing facilities and central heating), 1981 or 1983, with selected trends from 1971.

Data sources include *Polk's World Bank Directory, International Edition* and *Oesterreichischer Arbeiterkammertag, Wien.*

REGIONS, RECURRING FEATURE

(p. 10-12) Includes 2 tables showing distribution of Indonesian household expenditures by item, by region, 1978; and take-home pay as percent of gross earnings for typical manufacturing worker, for 22 OECD countries, 1983. Data are from *World Bank Working Papers* and *The OECD Observer.*

C0200–1.610: Aug. 1985 (Vol. 4, No. 8)

COUNTRY PROFILE: REPUBLIC OF BOTSWANA

(p. 1-6) Profile of Botswana. Includes 3 tables showing population by age and sex, and by urban and rural town; and employment and average monthly earnings, for citizens and noncitizens, by industry; various years 1971-1983. Data are from the Central Statistics Office, Gaborone.

CAR OWNERSHIP

(p. 7) Brief article, with 1 table showing number of cars per 1,000 persons, for U.S., Japan, and 13 European countries, 1976 and 1981. Data are from *Eurostat Review* and *Luxembourg.*

INVISIBLE BUSINESSWOMAN

(p. 9) Article on women's role in the informal business sector (small-scale trade in goods and services) in developing countries. Data are from International Labor Organization. Includes 1 undated chart showing percent of tradespersons who are women, for Haiti, Ghana, Thailand, Seychelles, Brazil, and Uruguay.

REGIONS, RECURRING FEATURE

(p. 10-12) Includes 2 tables showing population of Australia's 12 major cities, 1981 and 1983; and employment status of Norwegian women, by age group, 1970, 1975, and 1980.

Data are from Australian Bureau of Statistics; and Central Bureau of Statistics, Oslo.

C0200–1.611: Sept. 1985 (Vol. 4, No. 9)

COUNTRY PROFILE: GRAND DUCHY OF LUXEMBOURG

(p. 1-6) Profile of Luxembourg. Includes 1 chart and 3 tables showing population by age and sex, 1981; number of dogs owned by all households, 1966 and 1975; population of 10 cities, 1947, 1970, and 1981; and percent of households owning 7 major consumer goods, 1970 and 1981. Data are from the Ministere de L'Economie and *Annuaire Statistique.*

SMALLEST COUNTRIES

(p. 9) Brief article, with 1 table showing the following for U.S. and 29 World Bank member countries with populations of less than 1 million: population and life expectancy at birth, 1983; per capita GNP, 1982-83 and annual percent change for 1965-83 period; and average annual inflation rates, 1965-73 and 1973-83 periods.

Data are from World Bank Development Reports, 1984 and 1985.

REGIONS, RECURRING FEATURE

(p. 10-11) Includes 1 table showing Mauritian employment in large establishments, for 9 industries and all others, 1983.

C0200–1.612: Oct. 1985 (Vol. 4, No. 10)

AREA PROFILE: BUENOS AIRES

(p. 1-11) Profile of Buenos Aires, Argentina, metro area. Includes 4 tables showing the following, for Buenos Aires and/or greater metro area:

a. Population by age and sex; and summary population and housing characteristics, expressed as percent of total Argentina; 1980.

b. Population, density, percent age 65/over, and percent college-educated, 1980; and population annual growth rate, 1970-80 period; all by municipality and school district.

c. Employment by industry division and sex, with comparison to Argentina, 1980.

Data are from the *Censo Nacional de Poblacion y Vivienda de 1980.*

ELECTRICITY ONE KEY TO RECEPTIVE CUSTOMERS

(p. 9) Brief article, with 1 table showing electricity consumption per capita, by world area and for selected countries, 1979 and 1981. Data are from UN *Yearbook of World Energy Statistics.*

C0250
American Paint Journal Co.

C0250–1   **DECORATIVE PRODUCTS WORLD: Outlook '85—Decorative Products Industry Sidesteps Economic Consensus**
Bimonthly (selected issue).
Jan. 1985.   (p. 38-47).
Vol. 77, No. 3.
ISSN 0199-4328.
LC 82-643606.
SRI/MF/excerpts

Annual feature, by Rich Hirsch and Pamela Gerhardt, on retail operations of decorative product dealers, 1984, based on responses of over 400 *Decorative Products World* subscribers to a Sept. 1984 survey.

Covers decorative product sales and merchandising of lumber/building supply and hardware stores, home centers, independent and paint manufacturer-owned specialty stores, and other dealer types.

Includes 20 tables showing survey response on the following, by dealer type, for 1984 unless otherwise noted:

a. Sales of decorative products, with change from 1983; anticipated change in sales and in cost of goods sold, 1985; average inventory value and gross margin, by product type; sales distribution by dept and customer category; dealer types perceived as chief competition; plans to open new stores, remodel, expand, or relocate, 1985; average product display space and staff size; and percent of dealers employing a decorator.

b. Paint depts: average number of product lines carried, with detail for national, regional, and private labels; gross margin; and inventory value, with anticipated change in 1985.

c. Wallcovering depts: percent of dealers selling from sample books, stock, and self-displays; and average number of sample books, and investment and gross margin for samples and stock.

Survey is an annual feature of the monthly publication *Decorative Products World,* which generally contains only narrative articles. Annual survey is the only feature covered by SRI.

Availability: Decorative Products World, 2911 Washington Ave., St. Louis MO 63103, $18.00 per yr., single copy $2.50, Buyers' Guide $15.00; SRI/MF/excerpts for annual survey article.

C1050
Best, A. M., Co.

C1050–1   BEST'S REVIEW: PROPERTY/CASUALTY INSURANCE EDITION

Monthly.
ISSN 0161-7745.
LC 73-613400.
SRI/MF/not filmed

Monthly trade journal reporting on property/casualty insurance industry marketing trends and developments, management topics, current events, regulation, and finance.

General format:

a. Regular departmental features, including data on insurance company stocks; and "World Insurance Forum," often with statistics on foreign insurance industries.

b. Articles, often with substantial statistics, including annual data on property/casualty underwriting business by individual company, line of business, and State.

Features with substantial statistical content are described, as they appear, under "Statistical Features." Each issue of the journal is reviewed, but an abstract is published in SRI monthly issues only when statistical features appear.

Availability: Best's Review: Property/Casualty Insurance Edition, Subscription Department, Oldwick NJ 08858, $14.00 per yr., single copy $1.50; SRI/MF/not filmed.

Issues reviewed during 1985: Nov. 1984-Oct. 1985 (P) (Vol. 85, Nos. 7-12; Vol. 86, Nos. 1-6).

STATISTICAL FEATURES:

C1050–1.601: Nov. 1984 (Vol. 85, No. 7)

1983 PROPERTY/CASUALTY ASSETS STUDY, ANNUAL FEATURE

(p. 12) Annual article, with 1 chart showing value of assets and distribution by type, aggregated for top 100 property/casualty groups, 1983.

For description of previous article, for 1982, see SRI 1983 Annual under C1050-1.411.

PROPERTY/CASUALTY BOND STUDY, ANNUAL FEATURE

(p. 12) Annual article, with 1 chart showing distribution of property/casualty insurance industry bond holdings by maturity period, 1983, with detail for maturity periods showing exceptional change in size of holdings since 1982.

WORKERS' COMPENSATION AND INLAND MARINE MARKETING, 1983, ANNUAL FEATURE

(p. 32-40) Annual article, by Pamela Loos, on marketing of workers' compensation and inland marine insurance lines, 1983 and trends. Includes 2 text tables on market share of national and regional companies and direct writers, for both lines, 1979-83; and 4 tables showing the following for both lines:

a. By State: direct premiums written, and change from 1982; adjusted loss ratio; and market shares of national and regional companies, direct writers, and each of 3 leading companies; 1983.

b. For 20 leading writers: direct premiums written, 1983, and change from 1982; market share, 1980-83; and loss ratio, 1981-83.

Previous articles included data on fidelity and surety bonding insurance.

CORRECTION

(p. 32) Corrected data for article on property insurance marketing, appearing in Sept. 1984 issue.

For article description, see SRI 1984 Annual under C1050-1.511.

WORLD INSURANCE FORUM: ATHENS, ANNUAL FEATURE

(p. 98-104) Annual article, by John D. Polites, on Greek insurance industry developments. Includes 1 table showing share of insurance business for state-controlled and private insurance companies, by line of coverage, 1981 and 1983.

WORLD INSURANCE FORUM: TEL AVIV, ANNUAL FEATURE

(p. 106-108) Annual article, by Shlomo Jannai, on Israeli insurance industry developments. Data are based on a Mar.-Apr. 1984 survey by the Central Bureau of Statistics, and are shown in shekels.

Includes 1 table showing life and non-life insurance premiums written by Israeli insurance companies, 1982-83.

C1050–1.602: Dec. 1984 (Vol. 85, No. 8)

SATELLITE RESCUE ATTEMPTED

(p. 66-68) Brief insert article reporting on efforts to recover 2 satellites (Indonesia's PALAPA B2 and Western Union's WESTAR 6) from incorrect orbits. Includes 1 undated table showing reported insurance claims paid, recovery costs, and estimated sale price after recovery, for each satellite.

C1050–1.603: Jan. 1985 (Vol. 85, No. 9)

REVIEW AND PREVIEW, ANNUAL FEATURE

(p. 16-18, 76-83) Annual article, by John C. Burridge, on property-casualty insurance industry financial performance and operating results, by company type and line of coverage, 1980-84.

Data are based on information supplied by property/casualty companies representing approximately 95% of the industry.

Includes 1 table showing net premiums written; loss/loss adjustment expense, underwriting expense, and combined pre-dividend and post-dividend ratios; and underwriting gain or loss after dividend; generally for stock, mutual, reciprocal, and all companies, 1980-84. Table is repeated for the following lines:

a. All property/casualty; and auto, including commercial, private passenger, physical damage, and liability.

b. Fire, allied, homeowner and commercial multiple peril, inland marine, workers' compensation, medical malpractice, and other liability.

Also includes 3 text tables showing property/casualty industry 1984 surplus status, 1977-84 underwriting cash flow, and 1984 combined ratios compared to 1978; and 1 other table showing net premiums earned, ratios of reserves and investment income to earned premiums, and income change, 1951-84.

1985: THE BATTLES AHEAD, ANNUAL FEATURE

(p. 24-28, 84-85) Annual article, by Peter van Aartrijk, Jr., on outlook for the property/casu-

alty insurance industry. Data are based on approximately 1,000 responses to a fall 1984 membership survey by Independent Insurance Agents of America.

Includes 1 table showing percent of respondents reporting a "hardening" of the commercial insurance market; specific lines affected; and indicators of hardening, including policy cancellations and premium price increases for specific lines.

C1050–1.604: Feb. 1985 (Vol. 85, No. 10)

1984 INSURANCE STOCK TRENDS, ANNUAL FEATURE

(p. 13-15, 103-104) Annual article, by Peter van Aartrijk Jr., on the insurance stock performance of 77 major property/casualty, multiple line, life/health, and broker/agent companies, 1984. Most data are from A. M. Best Co.

Includes 3 tables showing market value, dividend, and yield, 1984; year-end prices, 1970s-84; and 10-year high and low prices; by company, with aggregate price indexes for all companies included in *Best's Insurance Industry Stock Indexes,* and comparisons to CPI and 6 major securities market indexes.

WORLD INSURANCE FORUM: PAKISTAN

(p. 94) By M.S. Chishti. Article on Pakistani insurance industry developments. Includes 1 table showing cash and stock dividend yield for 8 insurance companies, 1983.

C1050–1.605: Mar. 1985 (Vol. 85, No. 11)

INTERNATIONAL INSURANCE STUDY

(p. 10) Brief article, with 1 map showing distribution of world insurance market, by world area, 1982. Data are from Best's *On-Line Reports.*

CORPORATE CHANGES, 1984, ANNUAL FEATURE

(p. 12-14, 95-102) Annual article on property/casualty insurance company transitions, 1984. Includes lists of company formations, ownership and name changes, and retirements, 1984.

Correction appears in the May 1985 issue (see C1050-1.607 below).

WORLD INSURANCE FORUM: TOKYO

(p. 72-74) By Akira Morino. Article on Japanese non-life insurance industry developments. Includes 1 table showing the following for non-life insurance business of domestic insurers: premium income by line of coverage, total net premiums, claims, expenses, and loss and expense ratios, 1983, with comparisons to 1982.

C1050–1.606: Apr. 1985 (Vol. 85, No. 12)

WORLD INSURANCE FORUM: ZURICH

(p. 88-92) By K. G. Fletcher. Article, with 1 undated table showing Swiss consumer expenditures for insurance as percent of net earnings, by type of insurance.

C1050–1.607: May 1985 (Vol. 86, No. 1)

CORRECTION

(p. 2) Correction for article on property/casualty insurance company transitions, appearing in Mar. 1985 issue.

For article description, see C1050-1.605 above.

1984 UNDERWRITING RESULTS: AN UPDATE, ANNUAL FEATURE

(p. 14-20) Annual article on underwriting results for the property/casualty insurance industry, 1984. Data are based on information supplied by property/casualty companies representing approximately 99% of the industry.

Includes text data and 4 tables showing property/casualty premiums written and earned, losses and expenses incurred, underwriting gain or loss, policyholder dividend, operating and net investment income, and selected financial ratios, various periods 1974-84, with estimates for 1985. Data include some detail by line of coverage and for stock, mutual, and reciprocal companies.

Lines of coverage include fire, allied, homeowners and commercial multiple peril, inland marine, workers' compensation, medical malpractice, other liability, and auto liability and physical damage.

For description of article for 1983, see SRI 1984 Annual under C1050-1.507.

PROFILES IN CONVERSION

(p. 22-26, 104-107) By Henry T. Tillman, III. Article on mutual insurance company conversions to other forms of ownership. Article also appears in Apr. 1985 issue of *Best's Review: Life/Health Insurance Edition.*

For article description, see C1050-2.605 below.

C1050–1.608: June 1985 (Vol. 86, No. 2)

200 LEADING PROPERTY/CASUALTY COMPANIES AND GROUPS, ANNUAL FEATURE

(p. 14-17) Annual article on 200 largest insurance companies in property/casualty premium income, 1984. Data are from Best's Executive Data Service. Includes text statistics and 2 tables ranking companies by property/casualty premiums, 1984, with comparison to 1979 and 1983. Tables also show 1984 accident/health, life, and total premiums, and total premium rank, for top 100 companies.

LONG-AWAITED BETROTHAL

(p. 22-29) By Douglas C. Moat. Article reporting on life insurance business of independent property/casualty insurance agents. Data are based on 477 responses to a national survey of 2,500 agents conducted recently by Russell Miller, Inc.

Includes 6 tables showing survey findings on the following, generally by extent of respondents' success in selling life insurance:

a. Profit margin trends from 1977; commissions from life insurance sales, by product type; and 3-year revenue growth.

b. Factors in decision to sell life insurance; frequency of soliciting life insurance business; and percent of agency business derived from sales of personal and commercial life insurance.

WHERE WE STAND

(p. 52-58) By Joseph R. Aspland. Article on status of the reinsurance industry. Data are from *Best's Aggregates and Averages,* based on a 1984 survey conducted by the Reinsurance Assn of America.

Includes 3 charts showing combined ratio, 1974-3rd quarter 1984, and net income, 1973-83, for reinsurance industry; and change in loss reserves/loss adjustment expense reserves and paid loss, 1979-83, for total insurance industry.

ECONOMIC FACTORS IN PROPERTY/LIABILITY INSURANCE CLAIMS COSTS, ANNUAL FEATURE

(p. 80-81) Annual article, by Norton E. Masterson, on economic factors affecting insurance claim settlement costs. Includes 3 tables showing CPI (total and for auto body work), and indexes of physician fees, hospital room rates, and auto crash part costs, Dec. 1982-84; and claim settlement cost indexes for 14 lines of property and liability insurance coverage, 1976-85.

C1050–1.609: July 1985 (Vol. 86, No. 3)

INSURANCE PREMIUM DISTRIBUTION, 1984, ANNUAL FEATURE

(p. 14-16) Annual article, by Virginia Vogt, analyzing property/casualty insurance premiums written in the U.S. in 1984, including leading insurers and distribution of premiums by line of business and State.

Includes 4 tables, listed below. Tables [2-4] show data for 1984, with selected comparisons to 1983.

TABLES:

[1] Percent of property/casualty market [for national and regional agency, and direct writer insurers, 1975-84].

[2] Leading insurers and their market share [20 companies ranked by premiums written.]

[3] Premium distribution by line [showing the following for each line of business: premiums written; loss ratio; and 3 leading writers and their share of total premiums for the line, with the line's share of the top writer's total premiums].

[4] Insurance premium distribution and leading writers by State [showing the following for each State: direct premiums, ranking, share of U.S. total premiums, loss ratio, 3 leading writers and their shares of the State market, and premiums written by leading writer].

WORLD INSURANCE FORUM: AMSTERDAM, ANNUAL FEATURE

(p. 78) Annual article, by F. Schreuder, on Dutch insurance industry developments. Data are from the Dutch Chamber of Insurance. Includes 2 tables showing the following for Dutch non-life insurance companies: premiums (in guilders) by line of insurance, 1979-83; and technical balance (minus expenses), interest/other income, result, and solvency margin, all as percent of gross premiums, 1978-83.

C1050–1.610: Aug. 1985 (Vol. 86, No. 4)

AUTO INSURANCE, 1984, ANNUAL FEATURE

(p. 14-16, 21) Annual article, by Pamela Loos, analyzing the distribution and profitability of auto insurance premiums written in 1984. Includes 3 text tables on market shares of national, regional, and direct writers, 1980-84; and the following data:

a. 20 leading companies in all types of auto insurance, and in private passenger and commercial auto insurance, showing the following for each company: premiums written, 1984 and change from 1983; market share, 1981-84; loss ratio, 1982-84; and auto insurance share of company's total premiums, 1984. 3 tables.

b. State distribution of 1984 auto insurance business, showing the following for each State: premiums written, change from

1983, and national rank; loss ratio; and State market shares for national, regional, and direct writers, and for 3 leading companies. 1 table.

SECOND TIME AROUND

(p. 22-28, 89) By Franklin W. Nutter. Article discussing issues regarding medical malpractice claims. Includes 1 undated table showing number of States that have enacted various types of medical malpractice legislation, and status of legislation (whether intact, unconstitutional, or repealed/expired).

C1050–1.611: Sept. 1985 (Vol. 86, No. 5)

GENERAL LIABILITY/MEDICAL MALPRACTICE INSURANCE MARKETING, 1984, ANNUAL FEATURE

(p. 16-18, 106-109) Annual article, by Marian Freedman, analyzing general liability and medical malpractice insurance markets, by leading company and State, 1984 and trends. Includes 1 text table showing market shares for national, regional, and direct writers of liability insurance, 1980-84; and 5 detailed tables showing:

a. 20 leading companies in general liability and medical malpractice insurance and in both lines of insurance combined, showing for each company: premiums written in 1984, and change from 1983; market share, 1981-84; loss ratios, 1982-84; and liability insurance share of company's total premiums, 1984.

b. State distribution of 1984 general liability and medical malpractice insurance business, showing for each State: ranking; premiums written, and change from 1983; loss ratio; and State market shares for national, regional, and direct writers, and for 3 leading companies.

WORLD INSURANCE FORUM: TOKYO

(p. 66-69) By Akira Morino. Article on Japanese insurance industry developments. Includes 1 table showing property/casualty insurance premium income (in yen) for selected lines of coverage, 1984.

C1050–1.612: Oct. 1985 (Vol. 86, No. 6)

BEST OF BOTH WORLDS

(p. 24-28, 126-127) By Donald L. Jordan and Clifford D. Moore, III. Article, with 1 chart and 1 table showing the following data aggregated for 50 largest regional property/casualty insurance brokers:

a. Average annual revenue growth rates by revenue class, with comparison to total commercial line business, largest public brokers, and GNP, 1981-84 period.

b. Characteristics, including average revenues, employment, offices, and account size; shares of revenues from commissions and fees; types of business activity; and extent of automation; 1984.

Data are from Temple, Barker & Sloane, Inc.

PROPERTY INSURANCE MARKETING, 1984, ANNUAL FEATURE

(p. 40-48, 129-131) Annual article, by Pamela Loos, analyzing property/casualty insurance marketing data, by State and leading company, for homeowners, commercial multiple peril, fire, and allied lines, 1984 and trends. Data are from A. M. Best Co.

Includes 4 text tables showing market shares for national, regional, and direct writers, 1980-84; and 8 detailed tables showing the following for each line of insurance:

a. For each State: direct premiums, rank, and gain; loss ratio; and market shares for national, regional, and direct writers, and for 3 top companies; 1984.

b. For each of 20 leading companies: direct premiums, gain, and share of company's total premiums, 1984; company's market share, 1981-84; and loss ratio, 1982-84.

A PERMANENT CHANGE

(p. 78-80, 134) By Albert W. Davis. Article, with 1 table showing the following, aggregated for reinsurance companies and primary insurance carriers: net premiums written, surplus, and combined ratios, 1981-84. Data are from Reinsurance Assn of America.

KEMPER ISSUES MID-1985 REPLACEMENT COST STUDY, ANNUAL FEATURE

(p. 90-92) Brief annual article, with 1 table showing percent change in replacement costs for machinery/equipment by type of industry and for industrial buildings by region, semiannually 1983-1st half 1985. Data are from Kemper Group biennial surveys of North American manufacturers.

WORLD INSURANCE FORUM: ZURICH, ANNUAL FEATURE

(p. 108-110) Annual article, by K. G. Fletcher, on Swiss insurance industry developments. Data are from company annual reports, and are shown in Swiss francs. Includes 1 table showing top 7 companies ranked by value of premiums written, 1983-84.

C1050–2   BEST'S REVIEW: LIFE/HEALTH INSURANCE EDITION

Monthly.
ISSN 0005-9706.   LC 80-175.
SRI/MF/not filmed

Monthly trade journal reporting on life/health insurance industry marketing trends and developments, management topics, current events, regulation, and finance.

General format:

a. Articles, often with substantial statistics, including annual data on underwriting activity and finances of individual companies.

b. Regular departmental features, including data on insurance company stocks.

c. Monthly feature comparing life insurance policies of major insurers.

Monthly feature is described below and appears in all issues. All other features with substantial statistical content are described, as they appear, under "Statistical Features." Nonstatistical contents are not covered.

Availability: Best's Review: Life/Health Insurance Edition, Subscription Department, Oldwick NJ 08858, $14.00 per yr., single copy $1.50; SRI/MF/not filmed.

Issues reviewed during 1985: Nov. 1984-Oct. 1985 (P) (Vol. 85, Nos. 7-12; Vol. 86, Nos. 1-6) [Vol. 85, No. 11 incorrectly reads Vol. 86, No. 1].

MONTHLY POLICY COMPARISON

Monthly feature comparing life insurance policies of major insurers. Data generally are based on analysis of policies issued by 200 companies with at least $500 million in ordinary life insurance business during 1-2 previous years.

Each issue covers 1 type of policy, with updates usually appearing semiannually. Types of policies include universal life and interest sensitive whole life, participating whole life, graded premium whole life, indeterminate premium whole life and renewable term, flexible premium retirement annuities, and variable life.

Feature generally contains brief narrative and 1 table showing detailed characteristics of policies, including minimum issue amount, charges or premiums, policy loan rate, and cash value, all by company.

STATISTICAL FEATURES:

C1050–2.601: Nov. 1984 (Vol. 85, No. 7)

1983 AVERAGE POLICY SIZE, ANNUAL FEATURE

(p. 112-116) Annual article, by Carole King, reporting on average ordinary life insurance policy size for 125 companies with most insurance in force as of Dec. 31, 1983. Includes 1 summary table, and 1 table showing average size of policies issued during year and in force at end of year, by company, 1973 and 1979-83.

For description of previous article, for 1982, see SRI 1983 Annual under C1050-2.410.

C1050–2.602: Dec. 1984 (Vol. 85, No. 8)

10-YEAR DIVIDEND COMPARISONS, ANNUAL FEATURE

(p. 114-122) Annual article comparing actual and 1974-scale dividend payments for average $25,000 life insurance policies issued in 1974 to males aged 35, by 70 leading life insurance companies, 1975-84. Data are from *Best's Flitcraft Compend.* Includes 2 tables showing the following for 1975-84:

a. Top 10 insurers ranked by average yearly payment and difference, and interest-adjusted payment and surrender cost indexes, for total period.

b. Actual and 1974-scale annual and total premiums, total dividends per $1,000 of insurance and net payments, 10th-year cash value and term dividend, and payment and surrender cost indexes and rankings, by insurer.

Data addenda, for 1 company, appear in the Feb. 1985 issue (see C1050-2.603 below).

20-YEAR DIVIDEND COMPARISONS, ANNUAL FEATURE

(p. 123-130) Annual article comparing actual and 1964-scale dividends for average $10,000 life insurance policies issued in 1964 to males aged 35, by 70 leading life insurance companies, 1965-84. Data are from *Best's Flitcraft Compend.* Includes 2 tables showing the following for 1965-84:

a. Top 10 insurers ranked by average yearly payment and difference, and interest-adjusted payment and surrender cost indexes, for total period.

b. Actual and 1964-scale annual and total premiums, total dividends per $1,000 of insurance and net payments, 20th-year cash value and term dividend, and payment and surrender cost indexes and rankings, by insurer.

C1050–2.603: Feb. 1985 (Vol. 85, No. 10)

REVIEW OF 1984 AND 1985 OUTLOOK

(p. 12) Article, with 2 charts showing distribution of life/health insurance direct premiums written, and annual percent change in premiums written, by major line of coverage, 1983. Data are from A. M. Best Co.

1984 INSURANCE STOCK TRENDS, ANNUAL FEATURE

(p. 13-16, 104) Annual article, by Peter van Aartrijk, Jr., on the insurance stock performance of 77 major property/casualty, multiple line, life/health, and broker/agent companies, 1984. Article also appears in property/casualty insurance edition of *Best's Review;* for description, see C1050-1.604 above.

CONSERVATION: STEMMING THE FLOOD

(p. 40-42, 106) By Audrene Lojovich. Article reporting on a life insurance industry study involving use of aggressive and conventional techniques to retain clients who had chosen not to continue coverage under existing policies. Data are based on a program covering 835 such clients, conducted Mar-June 1984 by the Minnesota Mutual Life Insurance Co.

Includes 2 tables showing number of clients intending to drop coverage, and number persuaded to retain policies, for 8 unnamed insurance agencies using aggressive and conventional techniques.

CORRECTION

(p. 68) Addenda for annual feature on 10-year dividend comparisons, appearing in the Dec. 1984 issue. Presents data for 1 company.

For feature description, see C1050-2.602 above.

C1050–2.604: Mar. 1985 (Vol. 85, No. 11)

[Issue incorrectly reads Vol. 86, No. 1.]

INTERNATIONAL INSURANCE STUDY

(p. 12) Brief article, with 1 map showing distribution of world insurance market, by world area, 1982. Data are from Best's *On-Line Reports.*

LIFE INSURANCE COMPANY CHANGES, 1984, ANNUAL FEATURE

(p. 16-20, 126-128) Annual article on life insurance company transitions, 1984 and trends.

Includes lists of company formations, name changes, and mergers and retirements, 1984; and 2 tables showing number of new and retired companies 1975-84, and new, retired, and total companies, by State, 1984 with comparisons to 1983.

C1050–2.605: Apr. 1985 (Vol. 85, No. 12)

PROFILES IN CONVERSION

(p. 24-28, 128-130) By Henry T. Tillman III. Article on mutual insurance company conversions to other forms of ownership. Data are from A. M. Best Co.

Includes 2 tables showing the following for 27 companies involved in conversion transactions during 1968-85: headquarters State; type of company (property/casualty or life/health); year of conversion; net premiums written and premium/surplus ratio for year prior to conversion and/or 1983; and type of conversion (merger, stock, or bulk reinsurance); with current status for transactions initiated since 1982.

C1050–2.606: June 1985 (Vol. 86, No. 2)

LONG-AWAITED BETROTHAL

(p. 16-22, 128) By Douglas C. Moat. Article reporting on life insurance business of independent property/casualty insurance agents. Article also appears in June 1985 issue of *Best's Review: Property/Casualty Insurance Edition.* For article description, see C1050-1.608, above.

INDIVIDUAL AND GROUP ANNUITIES IN 1984, ANNUAL FEATURE

(p. 77-80) Annual article on annuity premium income of 221 companies with annuity writings of at least $10 million in 1984. Includes text statistics, and 1 table showing individual and group direct and total premiums and annuity fund deposits, by company, ranked by total annuity funds, 1984.

C1050–2.607: July 1985 (Vol. 86, No. 3)

500 LEADING LIFE COMPANIES IN TOTAL PREMIUM INCOME, ANNUAL FEATURE

(p. 66-69) Annual article, with 1 table showing 500 leading U.S/Canadian life/health insurance companies ranked by premium income, 1984, and including percent change from 1983, and comparative 1983 and 1974 rank.

LEADING LIFE COMPANIES IN THREE CATEGORIES, ANNUAL FEATURE

(p. 70-74) Annual article, with 3 tables showing 100 leading U.S./Canadian life insurance companies ranked by assets and insurance issued and in force; and 100 leading U.S. mutual and stock life companies ranked by assets and insurance in force; 1984 with comparisons to 1983.

C1050–2.608: Aug. 1985 (Vol. 86, No. 4)

1984 SALES RESULTS OF THE LEADING LIFE COMPANIES, ANNUAL FEATURE

(p. 70-74) Annual ranked lists, with accompanying narrative analysis, of leading U.S./Canadian life insurance companies, 1984. Includes 3 tables showing leading 100, 50, and 25 companies in sales of ordinary, group, and industrial life insurance, respectively, ranked by insurance issued and in force, and gain in insurance in force, 1984, with comparisons to 1983.

UNIVERSAL LIFE INSURANCE, 1984

(p. 76-83) Annual article, with 1 table showing universal life insurance direct and net premiums, and insurance issued and in force, for each of 314 companies, 1984, with comparisons to 1983. Data are based on responses of over 1,600 life insurance companies to a survey by A. M. Best Co.

C1050–2.609: Sept. 1985 (Vol. 86, No. 5)

LEADING WRITERS OF CREDIT LIFE INSURANCE, 1984, ANNUAL FEATURE

(p. 80-82) Annual article on top 100 U.S. and Canadian writers of credit life insurance, 1984. Includes 2 tables showing total and credit life insurance issued and in force, for each company, 1984, with credit insurance change from 1983.

Previous article, for 1982, was described in SRI 1983 Annual under C1050-2.411. No article for 1983 was published.

C1050–2.610: Oct. 1985 (Vol. 86, No. 6)

LIFE INSURANCE COMPANY ASSETS, 1984, ANNUAL FEATURE

(p. 84-88) Annual article on asset allocation and investment yields of 125 leading U.S. and Canadian life/health insurance companies, accounting for more than 83% of industry assets, 1984. Includes 2 tables showing the following:

a. Aggregate asset allocation; and change in asset value; 1983-84.

b. Asset allocation among bonds, preferred and common stock, mortgages, real estate, policy loans, cash, separate accounts, and other assets, 1984; and net yield on invested assets before Federal income tax, 1980-84; by company, ranked by total assets.

C1200
Bill Communications

C1200–1   SALES AND MARKETING MANAGEMENT

Monthly, and special annual issues.
ISSN 0163-7517.
LC 75-649980.
SRI/MF/excerpts, shipped quarterly

Monthly trade journal (with 4 additional annual survey issues) reporting on corporate sales and marketing management activities in industrial and consumer markets. Covers marketing strategies and problems; sales force performance, motivation, and compensation; analysis of market composition; selected company profiles; and personnel changes.

Data are from the Federal Government, private assns and research firms, individual companies, and the journal's own research.

Journal is published monthly, except semi-monthly in Feb., Apr., July, and Oct. These 4 additional issues are annual surveys of selling costs, industrial purchasing power, and consumer buying power (2 issues).

General format:

a. News briefs on sales or marketing topics, occasionally statistical.

b. Feature articles, some with statistics, including annual surveys of sales meeting practices and executive compensation; and narrative monthly depts.

c. S&MM Marketgraph, recurring market analysis feature, usually with charts and tables on sales and marketing opportunities in specific markets.

d. Recurring S&MM Salesgraph, usually including 1 table, with brief accompanying narrative, on sales or shipments of specific products.

All features with substantial statistical content are described as they appear, under "Statistical Features." Nonstatistical features or issues are not covered.

Availability: Sales and Marketing Management, Subscription Service Department, PO Box 1024, South Eastern PA 19398-9990, $36.00 per yr., single copy $5.00, special issue prices vary; SRI/MF/excerpts for all portions described under "Statistical Features;" shipped quarterly.

Issues reviewed during 1985: Nov. 12, 1984-Oct. 28, 1985 (P) (Vol. 133, Nos. 7-8; Vol. 134, Nos. 1-8; Vol. 135, Nos. 1-6) [Vol. 133, No. 7 incorrectly reads No. 6; Vol. 134, No. 2 incorrectly reads No. 1].

STATISTICAL FEATURES:

C1200–1.601: Nov. 12, 1984 (Vol. 133, No. 7)

[Issue incorrectly reads No. 6.]

BUCKEYE BAROMETER

(p. 16) Article, with 1 table showing population for Ohio's MSAs, 1978 and 1983. Data are from *Surveys of Buying Power.*

FOR SALESWOMEN, WHOLESALE PAYS

(p. 19) Table showing employment and median weekly earnings for sales representatives in manufacturing and wholesale trade, by sex, 1982, with percent change from 1979. Data are from BLS.

MORE DOLLARS TO DO THE JOB, ANNUAL FEATURE

(p. 80-84) Annual article on sales meeting practices. Data are based on 318 responses to an Aug. 1984 survey of S&MM corporate subscribers. Includes 12 tables showing response distribution for the following:

a. Company annual sales meeting budget; time spent planning for national and regional meetings; agenda items and preparation; meeting sites and selection factors; actual and planned use of teleconferences; suggestions for improving meetings; and meeting cost-cutting steps.

b. Company annual sales, size of sales force, and use of own sales force vs. independent representatives.

C1200–1.602: Dec. 3, 1984 (Vol. 133, No. 8)

OF COMPUTERS AND CUISINARTS

(p. 16) Article, with 1 table showing computer software sales in top 10 counties, 1983. Data are from *1984 Survey of Buying Power.*

AMERICA'S BEST AND WORST SALES FORCES

(p. 19-23) Article presenting sales executives' ratings of corporate sales forces in 11 industry sectors, 1984. Data are based on responses of 678 executives to a 1984 S&MM survey.

Includes 12 tables showing the following for each sector: 10 companies with best overall ratings; and company with best and worst rating for each of 10 sales force functions.

WHAT MAKES SALES FORCES RUN?

(p. 24-26) Article, with 1 table showing sales executives' ratings of 10 factors as very or extremely important to a successful selling operation. Data are based on responses of 678 executives to a 1984 S&MM survey.

C1200–1.603: Jan. 14, 1985 (Vol. 134, No. 1)

BIRMINGHAM BILLS vs. THE PHOENIX EAGLES

(p. 14) Article, with 1 undated table ranking 5 largest and smallest National Football League franchise cities by population, and also showing median household effective buying income. Data are from S&MM's *1984 Survey of Buying Power.*

SALES FORCE HIGHLIGHT: FOR SALESMEN, AIRCRAFT; FOR SALESWOMEN, IRON AND STEEL

(p. 25) Brief article, with 1 table showing average earnings of manufacturing sales representatives, by sex and industry group, 1979. Data are from Census Bureau.

C1200–1.604: Feb. 4, 1985 (Vol. 134, No. 2)

[Issue incorrectly reads No. 1.]

SETTING INDUSTRIAL AD BUDGETS

(p. 80) Article, with 1 undated chart showing corporate advertising expenditures per $1,000 of sales, by market share level. Data are from a study of 600 industrial businesses, conducted by Strategic Planning Institute for Cahner's Publishing Co.

C1200–1.605: Feb. 18, 1985 (Vol. 134, No. 3)

[Special issue price is $35.00.]

1985 SURVEY OF SELLING COSTS ANNUAL FULL-ISSUE FEATURE

(p. 5-127) Annual survey issue, for 1985, on trends in the component costs of selling, including costs in 86 major metro areas; compensation levels; sales meetings, training, and support; and transportation. Also includes selling costs in 6 Canadian metro areas.

Data are from S&MM survey research, Federal Government, private corporations and research firms, and trade assns.

Contents:

Contents and table listing. (p. 5-6)

Section I, features and highlights, with 3 charts and 20 tables. (p. 9-40)

Sections II-VI, covering individual sales cost components, with 7 charts and 39 tables. (p. 41-127)

All charts and tables are listed below.

CHARTS AND TABLES:

[Data generally are shown for 1984, unless otherwise noted. Data by industry are shown for various major industry groups.]

SECTION I. SURVEY FEATURES

[Data by type of salesperson are for account representative, detail salesperson, sales engineer, industrial products salesperson, and service salesperson.]

[1-2] S&MM's U.S. selling cost index [and average component costs, for food/drink, auto rental, and lodging, 1972-85]. [table and chart] (p. 11-12)

[3-4] S&MM's Canadian selling costs index [and average component costs, for food/drink and lodging, 1974-84]. [table and chart] (p. 14)

[5] Corporate [credit] cards and the industries that use them [by industry and type of card, no date]. (p. 26)

[6-7] S&MM's regional and national selling cost averages and per diem indexes; and how regional per diem costs are changing [with trends from 1982; for meals and lodging. (p. 28)

[8] Monthly business travel expenditures [by type of expense], 1980-84 (p. 31)

[9] How direct sales costs are changing [by type of salesperson, 1984 median and trends from 1974]. (p. 31)

[10] S&MM's 1985 cost per call [1980-84]. [chart] (p. 32)

[11] Cost per call by type of salesperson, 1984 median and trends from 1974. (p. 33)

[12] High-cost markets and low-cost markets [top and bottom 10-12 SMSAs ranked by per diem sales cost index]. (p. 34)

[13] Where sales costs are rising the fastest [10 SMSAs ranked by per diem increase 1983/84, with comparison to 1982/83]. (p. 35)

[14] Average travel/entertainment spending [per company and employee] by industry [no date]. (p. 35)

I.1-I.4. Typical salespeople's call patterns [average calls per day and per year, and days in field per year]; direct sales costs of salesperson's call; direct sales costs per salesperson's call; and cost per call by effective call days per week; [all by type of salesperson]. (p. 36)

I.5-I.9. [Tables illustrate computation of sales call efficiency indexes.] (p. 37-38)

SECTION II. METRO SALES COSTS: U.S. AND CANADA

II.1-II.2. Selling costs in 86 major U.S. markets and in [6] major Canadian markets [for lodging; meals; per diem total, with increase from 1983 and index; cost of 2 drinks; airport to downtown by taxi and limousine; and per diem auto rental]. (p. 42-52)

II.3. Meal and lodging tax rates by metro market [for each market included in tables II.1-II.2]. (p. 53)

SECTION III. COMPENSATION

III.1. Salespeople's annual compensation [salary and incentive pay for consumer and industrial products sectors, by salesperson level, 1983-84]. (p. 56)

III.2. Sales force selling expenses [for compensation and travel/entertainment] as a percentage of sales in major industries [1983-84]. (p. 56)

III.3. Total selling expenses as a percentage of company sales [by industry, 1983-84]. (p. 57)

III.4. Alternative sales compensation and incentive plans [distribution of companies by type of plan used, for consumer and industrial products and other industries, with total industry comparison to 1983]. (p. 57)

III.5.-III.6. How compensation for salespeople and sales-support personnel is growing [by level of authority or experience, 1978-84]. [charts] (p. 58-59)

III.7. Average earnings of experienced sales representatives: [selected years] 1952-83. [chart] (p. 62)

III.8. Benefits paid by companies [distribution of companies by type of benefit, no date]. [chart] (p. 62)

III.9. Earnings of salaried [sales] representatives by selected industries [high and low median, no date]. (p. 62)

III.10-III.11. Starting salaries [offered to] trainees with college degrees [1983-84], [and to] college graduates [to be hired [from classes of 1984-85]; [both shown for bachelor's degrees and master of business administration (MBA) degrees or candidates, by sales function and/or field]. (p. 63)

III.12. Salary statistics for MBA graduates entering marketing [average salary and range, no date]. (p. 63)

SECTION IV. SALES MEETINGS AND SALES TRAINING

[Tables IV.1-IV.3 show data by type of company: industrial products, consumer products, and services.]

IV.1. Average cost of sales training per salesperson [training/salary cost and median training period, 1983-84]. (p. 68)

IV.2. Sites most frequently used for sales training [and median length of training time]. (p. 68)

IV.3. Length of training period for new salespeople [1983-84]. (p. 69)

IV.4. Sales meeting costs [in 30 cities for lodging, food/beverage, hospitality functions, and meeting rooms]. (p. 70-84)

IV.5. Selected conference centers [facilities and rates for 15 centers]. (p. 86-88)

IV.6. Selected resort hotels [facilities, and rates by season, for 25 hotels]. (p. 90-97)

IV.7-IV.8. Selected airport hotels [for 21 cities] and budget motel chains [for 9 cities; facilities and rates]. (p. 98-100)

SECTION V. SALES SUPPORT AND INCENTIVES

V.1. Selected incentive travel destinations [air fare, lodging, meal, and group activity costs for 22 U.S. and foreign locations]. (p. 104)

V.2. Selected incentive cruises [cost per person and air fare for 4 cruise lines]. (p. 106)

V.3. Use of commission dollars by [manufacturers' representative] agencies [distribution by function]. [chart] (p. 106)

V.4. Expected increases in 1985 trade show exhibition costs [by component]. (p. 108)

V.5-V.6. Audiovisual equipment purchase and rental costs [by type of equipment, 1983-84]. (p. 108-110)

V.7. Typical trade show exhibit costs [by component]. (p. 110)

V.8. Estimated advertising percentages [of net sales] in selected industries [1983-85, and percent change from 1982]. (p. 112-113)

SECTION VI. TRANSPORTATION

VI.1-VI.2. Fleet car operating costs, by region [no date]; and 5-year forecast of fleet car costs [by component, 1985 and 1990]. (p. 116)

VI.3. Automobile fleet purchase costs [for selected models, by engine size, 1984-85]. (p. 116)

VI.4. Auto mileage reimbursement plans [distribution of consumer and industrial products companies and other companies, by type of plan used, 1983-84]. (p. 120)

VI.5-VI.6. Annual operating costs [for] manual vs. automatic transmissions [including ownership costs; and] for 1985 model cars [annual variable and fixed costs; for various models]. (p. 120)

VI.7. Breakdown of fleet car operating costs [with percent change from 1983]. (p. 120)

VI.8. Sources of autos used by salespeople [company and employee owned and leased, 1980-84]. [chart] (p. 122)

VI.9-VI.10. Operating costs in standard city, and fuel cost and consumption, by car size [1985 models]. (p. 122)

VI.11. Air fares for the 25 most traveled routes [1983-84]. (p. 122)

VI.12. Average cost of moving between selected cities. (p. 124)

VI.13. Standard and economy car rental rates [by region and city/metro area]. (p. 126-127)

VI.14. Average cost of 15 frequently made moves [between metro areas, 1984 and percent change from 1983]. (p. 127)

C1200–1.606: Mar. 11, 1985 (Vol. 134, No. 4)

S&MM SALESGRAPH

(p. 27) "Modest Expectations for Consumer Electronics." Table showing unit sales to dealers, 1985 and percent change from 1984; and household penetration (no date); for 9 leading consumer electronics products. Data are from Electronic Industries Assn.

BASIC INDUSTRIES PERK UP

(p. 36) Article, with 1 table showing top 10 SIC 4-digit industries ranked by estimated percent change in shipments, 1984/85, with comparison to 1983/84. Data are from Commerce Dept.

EPSON AMERICA'S SLY DISTRIBUTOR SWITCH

(p. 45-49) By Arthur Bragg. Article, with 2 charts showing shipments of lightweight portable computers in the $1,000-$5,000 price range, 1982-84, with shipment and revenue detail for 1 company. Data are from Dataquest and Epson America.

SALES FORCES WAVER ON LAP-TOP COMPUTERS

(p. 62-69) By Thayer C. Taylor. Article, with 1 table showing shipments and revenues for notebook and briefcase type portable computers, 1983-86. Data are from Yankee Group.

PC SOFTWARE AND THE FORTUNE 1000

(p. 120) Chart showing distribution of portable computer software units sold to Fortune 1000 firms, by application, 1984. Data are from Corporate Software.

1985 PORTABLE SHIPMENTS: THE EXPERTS DON'T AGREE

(p. 124) Table showing U.S. or world shipments of lightweight portable computers, as forecast by 4 research firms, 1985, with percent change from 1984.

C1200–1.607: Apr. 1, 1985 (Vol. 134, No. 5)

S&MM SALESGRAPH

(p. 17) "Two-Earner Couples: It Helps To Be White." Table showing median weekly earnings of all families and of 1- and 2-income married couples, for whites, blacks, and Hispanics, 4th quarter 1984, with change from 4th quarter 1983. Data are from BLS.

WOMAN'S PLACE IS ON THE SALES FORCE

(p. 34-37) By Rayna Skolnik. Article, with 1 table showing total and female salespeople, by manufacturing industry group, 1980. Data are from Census Bureau.

MURKY LIGHT ON HIRING, TRAINING COSTS

(p. 154) Article, with 1 undated table showing average cost of hiring/training salespeople, by selected industry group. Data are from McGraw-Hill.

C1200–1.608: Apr. 22, 1985 (Vol. 134, No. 6)

1985 SURVEY OF INDUSTRIAL AND COMMERCIAL BUYING POWER, ANNUAL ISSUE

Annual survey of 1984 industrial and commercial activity, as indicated by number of establishments, employment, and shipments, with industry concentration measures.

Presents data for detailed nonagricultural industries, including data by leading county for SIC 4-digit industries. Survey is intended primarily as a guide for industrial marketing. Most data are from Trinet, Inc.

Contents:

a. Contents listing. (p. 3)

b. Highlights, including narrative articles, with 1 chart showing national income in 5 industries, 1975-83; and 9 tables listed below. (p. 6-48)

c. Statistical section, with user guides, and 2 detailed tables also listed below. (p. 51-113)

TABLES:

[Tables show data for 1984. Total plants or establishments generally include only units with 20 or more employees. Large plants or establishments are units with 100 or more employees. Leading counties are counties with 1,000 or more employees in the applicable SIC 4-digit industry.]

HIGHLIGHTS TABLES

[1] Top 50 counties in [number of] manufacturing plants [and share of total U.S. shipments]. (p. 8)

[2] Summary of 2-digit major groups in this year's SICBP [total and large establishments, employment, shipments/receipts, and percent of shipments produced in large plants]. (p. 10)

[3] 50 leading metro markets in manufacturing activity [ranked by shipment value, and also showing share of U.S. shipments, and number of plants]. (p. 19)

[4] Nation's largest employers [top 5 SIC 4-digit manufacturing and nonmanufacturing industries ranked by total employment]. (p. 20)

[5] Top 25 counties in service industry activity [ranked by receipts, and also showing share of U.S. receipts]. (p. 20-21)

[6] Survey vs. Census Bureau: [comparison of] 1984 shipment totals as reported by [Trinet, Inc. vs. Census Bureau, for selected SIC 2-digit manufacturing industries]. (p. 22)

[7] Regional and State summaries of manufacturing markets [total and large plants, shipment value, share of U.S. shipments, plant index, and percent of shipments produced in large plants]. (p. 28)

[8] Top 50 counties in manufacturing activity [ranked by shipment value, and including plants, leading SIC industry and shipment value, and shipments of leading SIC industry as percent of U.S. SIC total and county's manufacturing total]. (p. 30)

[9] Profile of the 50 biggest manufacturing industries [ranked by shipment value, and including plants, shipment index, and percent of shipments produced in large plants]. (p. 32)

BY SIC 4-DIGIT INDUSTRY

[10] U.S. establishment and shipments/receipts totals for [individual] 4-digit SIC industries [total and large establishments, employment, shipments/receipts, and percent of shipments produced in large plants]. (p. 54-57)

STATE AND COUNTY DATA

[11] State and county totals for manufacturing and nonmanufacturing industries surveyed [total and large establishments, shipments/receipts, share of U.S. shipments, and percent of shipments produced in large plants, by State and county, with SIC 4-digit industry detail for leading counties]. (p. 59-113)

C1200–1.609: May 13, 1985 (Vol. 134, No. 7)

METRO WARS

(p. 16) Article, with 1 table ranking top 5 MSAs by household and effective buying income, 1984. Data are from Census Bureau.

S&MM MARKET HIGHLIGHT: HI-TECH INDUSTRIES, THE ACTION SPREADS ACROSS THE MAP

(p. 32) News brief, with 1 table showing number of high-technology firms in top 10 States and total U.S., Jan. 1985, with change from Mar. 1984. Data are from American Electronics Assn.

MARKETING MANAGERS NO STRANGERS TO THE PC

(p. 118) Article, with 1 undated chart showing prevalence of personal computer use among marketing/advertising managers, by selected application. Data are from a Trinet, Inc., survey of 200 managers at Fortune 1500 firms.

LOOSE LIPS SINK CHIPS

(p. 146) Article, with 1 table showing personal computer shipments as forecast by 4 organizations (Link Resources, Future Computing, Dataquest, and InfoCorp), 1985 with percent change from 1984.

C1200–1.610: July 1, 1985 (Vol. 135, No. 1)

GRAINING OF AMERICA

(p. 27) Article, with 1 table showing sales for restaurant/drinking places in top 20 metro areas, 1984. Data are from *1985 Survey of Buying Power.*

MANAGERS' USE OF PC BY COMPANY SIZE

(p. 122) Article, with 1 undated table showing prevalence of personal computer use among corporate managers, by selected application, and including average number of applications, all by company employment size. Data are from 645 responses to a *Fortune* survey.

CORPORATIONS TO MARRY COMPUTER, TELEPHONE

(p. 126-127) Article, with 1 chart showing installed base of computerized telephones, 1983-89. Data are from Forrester Research.

C1200–1.611: July 22, 1985 (Vol. 135, No. 2)

[Issue price is $65.00.]

1985 SURVEY OF BUYING POWER, PART I, ANNUAL ISSUE

Annual survey of population, effective buying income, and retail sales of U.S. and Canadian markets, 1984. Most data are from S&MM calculations, 1980 Census of Population and Housing, other Census Bureau reports, Dept of Labor, and Statistics Canada.

Contents:

Contents listing. (p. A5)

Section A. Feature articles on marketer use of buying power survey, with interspersed survey and market highlights tables, including 4 summary methodology tables; and S&MM Marketgraphs. (p. A7-A65)

Section B-C. National, regional, and State summaries, and metro area rankings; and metro area, county, and city data. (p. B1-B48, C1-C214)

Section D. Canadian Survey of Buying Power. (p. D1-D16)

Nonsummary statistical portions of sections are described below.

SURVEY SECTIONS:
[Data are for 1984, unless otherwise noted. Abbreviations: EBI (effective buying income) and BPI (buying power index).]

SECTION A: HIGHLIGHTS AND MARKETGRAPHS

Highlights Tables

[1] Retail store sales, survey vs. Census Bureau [by selected kind of business, 1984 and percent change from 1983]. (p. A10)

[2] The top 25: leading Hispanic metros [top 25 metro areas ranked by Hispanic population, and including Hispanics as a percent of total metro population]. (p. A24)

[3] Nuances of regional growth [population, 1984 and percent change from 1980; and share of U.S. population, 1970, 1980, and 1984; by census division and State]. (p. A28-A29)

[4] For richer or for poorer: median household EBI [for the top 10 and bottom 10 metro areas]. (p. A33)

[5] Shoulder to shoulder: [25] metro [areas] with the highest population density. (p. A50)

[6] The top 25: leading black metros [top 25 metro areas ranked by black population, and including blacks as a percent of total metro population]. (p. A54)

S&MM Marketgraphs

(p. A61) "Asians: East Meets West." Includes 1 chart and 2 tables showing top 25 metro areas and top 3 States, ranked by Asian/Pacific Islander population, with majority ethnic group share in each of top 3 States, and including comparisons to total U.S.; and distribution of U.S. Asian/Pacific Islander population by ethnic group; 1980.

(p. A62) "Old, Older, Oldest: The Maturity Market." Includes 1 chart and 2 tables showing top 25 metro areas and top 5 States, ranked by percent of population age 50/over, with median age and total population for top 5 States, and including comparisons to total U.S.; and distribution of U.S. population among persons age 65-74, 75-84, and 85/over; various years 1980-2000.

(p. A65) "Service Industries: A 70% Share of GNP." Includes 1 chart and 2 tables showing top 25 counties and top 5 States, ranked by service industry receipts, with number of service industry establishments in top 5 States, and including comparisons to total U.S.; and service industry market shares by industry group; 1982.

SECTION B: U.S., REGIONAL, AND STATE SUMMARIES; METROPOLITAN MARKET RANKINGS

(p. B1-B48) Contains table listing, 28 tables listed below, and alphabetical listing of 316

metro markets covered. Tables [1-3] show data by census division and State; titles begin "Regional and State summaries of..."

[1] Population [median age, population by age group, and households]. (p. B3)

[2] EBI [total and per capita; average and median household EBI; and households by EBI group]. (p. B5)

[3] Retail sales [total, per household, and by kind of business; and indexes of sales activity, buying power, and quality]. (p. B7)

[4-28] Metro market ranking: [by total], suburban, black, and Spanish-origin population; children under 6 and 6-17, and population 35-49 years old; total and one-person households; households with EBI $50,000/over; total, suburban, and median household EBI; BPI; total and per household retail sales; [and sales for 9 kinds of business]. (p. B9-B44)

SECTION C: METRO AREA, COUNTY, AND CITY DATA LISTED BY STATES

(p. C1-C214) Contains table listing, user guide, glossary, and the following data for each metro area, county, and city arranged by State: population (total population, median age, population distribution by age group, and households); retail sales (total and by kind of business); and EBI (total and median household EBI, household distribution by EBI group, and BPI).

SECTION D: CANADA

(p. D1-D16) Contains listings of tables and S&MM's Canadian metro markets; introductory article; and population, retail sales, and EBI data comparable to that described in Section C, shown by Province, S&MM and census metro area, city, and county. No population data by age are presented for Canada.

C1200–1.612: Aug. 12, 1985 (Vol. 135, No. 3)

ALBERTA AND THE HOUSTON SYNDROME

(p. 35) Article, with 1 table showing Canada population by Province, 1982 and 1984. Data are from *Survey of Buying Power*.

S&MM SALESGRAPH

(p. 37) "Silver Linings Among PC Market's Clouds." Shows percent of households owning or intending to purchase a personal computer (PC), and top 5 brands and top 5 types of peripheral equipment favored by PC owners and prospective buyers. Data are based on responses of 39,000 households to a Mar. 1985 survey conducted by Future Computing, Inc.

MARKETERS LINE UP FOR A 13% RAISE, ANNUAL FEATURE

(p. 52-57) Annual article, by Mark Thalenberg, reporting on 1984 compensation of 115 top sales and marketing executives at 104 companies in 24 industry groups. Data are based on an S&MM annual survey of proxy statements filed with the SEC.

Includes 1 table showing salaries/fees/bonuses/commissions, long-term gain realized, and total compensation, for each executive, with company name, sales, profit/loss, and industry group, 1984 and selected changes from 1983; and 1 table showing summary data for top 10 executives.

IS YOUR SALES FORCE PULLING ITS WEIGHT?

(p. 58-59) By Thayer C. Taylor. Article, with 2 tables showing number of sales workers and value of shipments per sales worker, by manufacturing industry group, and for top and bottom 25 SIC 3- or 4-digit manufacturing industries ranked by sales worker productivity, 1982, with percent change 1980-82 period.

Data are from BLS and Census Bureau.

PERSISTENT DEMAND KEEPS SALES HIRES STEADY

(p. 70-72) By Arthur Bragg. Article on developments in corporate recruiting of sales and marketing personnel. Data are from Northwestern University, University of Pennsylvania, and Dartnell Corp.

Includes 3 tables showing starting salaries offered bachelor's degree graduates in sales/marketing and business administration, and master of business administration (MBA) graduates with technical and nontechnical bachelor's degrees, classes of 1984-85; and average starting salary and range for MBA graduates in sales, market research, and general marketing, and high and low median earnings of salaried sales representatives in 13 industry groups (no dates).

BIG COMPANIES TO SPEND HEAVILY ON PCs

(p. 94) Article, with 1 chart showing distribution of Fortune 500 companies by number of personal computers installed, actual 1st quarter 1985, and planned 4th quarter 1985-86. Data are from Newton-Evans Research Co.

GO SOUTH, YOUNG (SALES)MAN!

(p. 116) Article, with 1 chart showing percent of companies planning to increase sales staff size, by census division, 2nd half 1985. Data are from a Sales Consultants International survey of over 1,300 executives.

C1200–1.613: Sept. 9, 1985 (Vol. 135, No. 4)

ABERRATION ACROSS THE NATION

(p. 23) Article, with 1 chart showing population in metro and nonmetro counties, 1972-74 and 1982-84. Data are from *Survey of Buying Power*.

ONLINE DATABASE INDUSTRY'S FLASHY FUTURE

(p. 147) Brief article, with 1 table showing market value for online data bases and business information services, and number of online users, 1984 and 1990. Data are from Business Communications Co.

C1200–1.614: Oct. 7, 1985 (Vol. 135, No. 5)

29% DRUNK, 96% CLEAN, 91% BORED

(p. 12) Article, with 1 table showing top 10 metro areas ranked by meal/lodging costs per diem, 1984. Data are from *Survey of Selling Costs*.

S&MM MARKET HIGHLIGHT: BOOM TIMES FOR BACKYARD DISHES

(p. 28) Article, with 1 chart showing home satellite receiving terminal sales volume and value, 1985 and 1989. Data are from Frost and Sullivan, Inc.

WHEN SALESPEOPLE TALK, DOES MANAGEMENT LISTEN?

(p. 43-45) By Don Waite. Article on views of sales representatives and managers concerning their companies' willingness to solicit their ideas, responsiveness to their concerns, and recognition of their efforts. Data are from responses of 8,288 representatives and 1,077 1st-line managers to a survey conducted by Sales Staff Survey. Includes 4 undated tables.

SMALL GAINS FOR HI-TECH SALES, MARKETING EXECS

(p. 62) Article, with 1 table showing percent change in base salary of high-technology industry executives in 3 sales and marketing job categories, and aggregate for 19 categories, 1980-85. Data are from responses of 1,095 companies to an American Electronics Assn survey.

SPECIAL SECTION: FLEET CARS, ANNUAL FEATURE

Annual compilation of articles on developments affecting commercial car fleets. Articles with statistics are described below.

READY TO HIT THE ROAD

(p. 82-88) By Arthur Bragg. Article on corporate auto fleet management trends. Data are from an Aug. 1985 S&MM survey of 60 fleet administrators and sales and marketing managers.

Includes 3 charts and 3 tables showing survey response on planned changes in fleet size; computer use by application; whether company owns and/or leases autos, and autos operated by size class, model years 1984-86; major management concerns, including costs, maintenance problems, and auto resale values; and auto replacement interval.

YES, SALESPEOPLE CAN HELP CONTROL COSTS

(p. 97-98) Article, with 2 tables showing operating and ownership costs for 1985 model autos, as follows: 10 cities ranked by annual average costs for typical mid-sized auto; and by auto size class. Data are from Runzheimer International.

C1200–1.615: Oct. 28, 1985 (Vol. 135, No. 6)

[Issue price is $35.00.]

1985 SURVEY OF BUYING POWER, PART II, ANNUAL ISSUE

Part II of a special annual survey of population, effective buying income (EBI), and retail sales of U.S. markets, 1984 and 1989. Most data are from S&MM calculations and Census Bureau reports.

Contents:

Contents listing. (p. 3)

Section A. Narrative features, and survey and market highlights, with 9 tables. (p. 5-48)

Sections B-F. Merchandise line sales; metro area market projections; and newspaper, TV, and zip code markets; with 20 tables. (p. 51-182)

Tables are listed below.

For description of Part I, see C1200-1.611 above.

TABLES:

[Abbreviations: EBI (effective buying income); ADI (area of dominant influence); BPI (buying power index).]

SECTION A. SURVEY HIGHLIGHTS

[1] Metro market outlook through 1989 [metro and nonmetro population, households, EBI, retail sales, and BPI; projected 1989 with percent change for 1984-89 period]. (p. 6)

[2] Top 50 markets in 1989 [ranked by population, 1989, with percent change for 1984-89 period and 1984 rank]. (p. 7)

[3-4] Tomorrow's fastest growing and negative-growth markets [top 25 metro markets ranked by greatest population growth and loss, 1984-89 period, with population for 1989]. (p. 8)

[5] Vying for dollars: The biggest ADIs and how they rate [top 25 ADIs ranked by population, with households, EBI, total retail sales, and rankings, 1984]. (p. 10)

[6] Most affluent markets of 1989: Bridgeport-Stamford topples Long Island [top 50 metro markets ranked by per household EBI, 1989, with percent increase for 1984-89 period]. (p. 13)

[7] Retail sales outlook, 1985-87 [sales by kind of business]. (p. 22)

[8] How good are the survey's projections? Regional and State comparisons [1984 population and retail sales (actual and as projected by 1980 Survey of Buying Power), by census division and for 10 most populous States]. (p. 28)

[9] Prospecting for retail dollars: State household spending habits in 1989 [average household EBI, and retail sales per household, by State, 1989]. (p. 42)

SECTION B. MERCHANDISE LINE SALES

[Tables [10-17] show 1984 data for the following merchandise lines: groceries/other foods, health/beauty aids, women's/girls' clothing, men's/boys' clothing, footwear, major household appliances, and furniture/sleep equipment.]

[10] Summary of merchandise line sales by [census division] and State [sales for all stores, and by store type (food, drug, apparel, department, or furniture/home furnishings/appliance stores, as applicable), for each merchandise line]. (p. 53)

[11-17] Metro market ranking [by sales, for each merchandise line]. (p. 54-60)

SECTION C. 1989 PROJECTIONS FOR U.S. METRO MARKETS

[Tables [18-19] show population, households, EBI, retail sales, and BPI, in indicated geographic detail, 1989 with comparisons to 1984.]

[18] Summary of projections by [census division] and State. (p. 63)

[19] Metro area projections [with detail by component city and county, all grouped by State]. (p. 64-98)

SECTIONS D-E. NEWSPAPER AND TV MARKETS

[Store groups are food, general merchandise, furniture/furnishings/appliances, automotive, and drugs.]

[20] Newspaper market ranking [by number of] households [1984]. (p. 101)

[21] Survey of newspaper markets [population, households, EBI, retail sales (total and by store group), and newspaper circulation related to number of households, by metro market grouped by State, 1984]. (p. 102-152)

[22] Alphabetical listing of TV markets [showing each county's share of households in the ADI]. (p. 156-159)

[23-27] Arbitron TV market (ADI) ranking [by] population, households, EBI, total retail sales, and BPI, [1984]. (p. 161-165)

[28] Survey of TV markets [population by age, households, black and Hispanic population, EBI, retail sales, and BPI, by TV ADI market grouped by State, 1984]. (p. 166-174)

SECTION F. ZIP CODE MARKETS

[29] Zip data [zip code area name and location, and summary demographic, socioeconomic, and housing data, for 6 zip code areas]. (p. 176-181)

C1200–2   SURVEY OF BUYING POWER DATA SERVICE, 1984

Annual. 1984.
920 p. var. paging.
LC 79-643867.
SRI/MF/complete

Annual survey of consumer buying power, 1983, presenting detailed market, population, household, and retail sales data, by location. Includes market data projections for 1988, and retail sales comparisons to 1977. Data are shown for total U.S. and by census division, State, MSA, county, and TV Area of Dominant Influence (ADI), with selected MSA and ADI rankings.

Data are from Sales and Marketing Management calculations, and Census Bureau reports, including 1977 Census of Retail Trade.

Market data generally include population and density, percent white population, households, effective buying income (EBI), retail sales, buying power index (BPI), and BPI for economy-, moderate-, and premium-priced products.

Population data include population by age and sex, and median age by sex.

Household data generally include number of households by age of householder, size, and EBI group; average household size; median and average household EBI; and per capita EBI.

Retail sales are shown by kind of business and selected merchandise line. Businesses generally include all food stores, supermarkets, eating/drinking places, general merchandise and department stores, apparel/accessory stores, furniture/home furnishings/appliance stores, automotive dealers, gasoline service stations, building materials/hardware dealers, and drugstores. Merchandise lines generally include groceries/other foods, drugs, health/beauty aids, major household appliances, TVs, audio equipment/musical instruments and supplies, furniture/sleep equipment, men's/boys' clothing, women's/girls' clothing, and footwear.

Contains user's guide (p. 3-12); contents listing, definitions, and addenda (p. A1-A14); and 21 separately paginated sections as follows:

Section 1-2. Maps and selected summary MSA data (103 p.); and market, population, and household data, by census division and State (5 p.).

Section 3-7. MSA rankings, by selected market and household data (47 p.); and market, population, and household data, by MSA and county, arranged by State (368 p.).

Section 8-10. Retail sales by kind of business and merchandise line, by census division and State (7 p.); metro market rankings by retail sales, by kind of business (14 p.); and retail sales by kind of business, by MSA and county, arranged by State (146 p.).

Section 11-12. MSA rankings by retail sales, by merchandise line (11 p.); and retail sales by merchandise line, by MSA and aggregate for nonmetro areas, arranged by State (43 p.).

Section 13-15. Market data projections, by census division, State, MSA, and county, with selected MSA rankings. (84 p.)

Section 16-21. ADI data, including market data and projections, and retail sales by kind of business and merchandise line, with ADI rankings. (66 p.)

Portions of this report, along with comparable data for Canada, appear in the 2nd July and Oct. issues of *Sales and Marketing Management,* covered by SRI under C1200-1.

Availability: Bill Communications, Sales and Marketing Management, Sales Builder Division, 633 Third Ave., New York NY 10017, $259.95; SRI/MF/complete.

C1200–4   INCENTIVE MARKETING

Monthly.
ISSN 0019-3364.
LC 52-41302.
SRI/MF/excerpts, shipped quarterly

Monthly journal reporting on the sales and consumer incentives market. Covers merchandise and travel incentives for salespeople and dealers; and coupons, premiums, gifts, sweepstakes/contests, and other types of consumer promotions.

Most data are from *Incentive Marketing* reader surveys covering companies that use incentive programs.

Issues generally contain several feature articles, occasionally with statistics; and numerous editorial depts. Annual statistical features include survey reports on incentive spending by industry. A nonstatistical buyer's guide usually appears in Feb.

Features with substantial statistical content are described, as they appear, under "Statistical Features." Each issue of the journal is reviewed, but an abstract is published in SRI monthly issues only when statistical features appear.

Availability: Bill Communications, Circulation Department, 633 Third Ave., New York NY 10017, $32.00 per yr., single copy $3.00, Dec. Facts issue $15.00; SRI/MF/excerpts for all portions described under "Statistical Features;" shipped quarterly.

Issues reviewed during 1985: Nov. 1984-Oct. 1985 (P) (Vol. 158, Nos. 11-12; Vol. 159, Nos. 1-10) [Vol. 159, No. 4 incorrectly reads No. 3].

STATISTICAL FEATURES:

C1200–4.601: Dec. 1984 (Vol. 158, No. 12)

FACTS '84, ANNUAL FEATURE

(p. 43-65) Annual survey report on incentive market trends. Covers merchandise and travel incentives for salespeople and dealers, business gifts, and various types of consumer promotions.

Includes detailed data on incentive expenditures by type and industry, 1983-84, and summary trends from 1967.

Data are from annual surveys of *Incentive Marketing* readers.

Contains overview article and sales, dealer, consumer, and travel incentive reports with 6 charts and 3 tables (p. 43-53); and 1 detailed table (p. 53-65).

C1200–4.602: Jan. 1985 (Vol. 159, No. 1)

INCENTIVE TRAVEL OVERVIEW

(p. 47-48) Article on corporate use of travel incentives. Includes 1 chart showing sales gain with use of incentives and incentive costs as percent of sales, 1982-84.

Also includes 2 other charts (p. 36, 45) showing top 10 user industries ranked by incentive travel expenditures, with aggregate share of all spending for travel incentives; and travel budget allocations; 1984.

Data are from a 1984 survey of incentive travel users, and from previous surveys.

C1200–4.603: Feb. 1985 (Vol. 159, No. 2)

INCENTIVE OVERVIEW

(p. 56-58) Article summarizing incentive market trends, 1983-84. Data are from a 1984 *Incentive Marketing* survey. Includes 1 chart and 1 table showing incentive expenditures, by type, 1983-84; and top 10 industries ranked by consumer premium expenditures, 1984.

C1200–4.604: Mar. 1985 (Vol. 159, No. 3)

LIFE STYLE MARKETING

(p. 27-34) By Pat Seelig. Article on categorization of consumer lifestyles for the purpose of determining marketing strategies and incentive programs. Data are from a 1981 Values and Life Styles (VALS) survey conducted by SRI International.

Includes 1 undated table showing median age and household income, prevalence of women and whites, and mean educational attainment, for 9 life-style groups.

C1200–4.605: Apr. 1985 (Vol. 159, No. 4)

[Issue incorrectly reads No. 3.]

DEALER INCENTIVES, ANNUAL FEATURE

(p. 49-54) Annual article on dealer incentive programs. Data are from responses of 194 companies to a Feb.-Mar. 1985 survey, and from previous surveys. Includes text data and 4 charts showing survey response on the following, various years 1980-85:

a. Sales gain with use of incentives, and incentive costs as percent of sales gain; types of dealers earning incentives; and spending plans, suppliers, and average cost per award, for merchandise and travel programs.

b. Dealer incentive objectives; methods used to promote incentive programs; types of incentives used most often and considered most effective; and means of obtaining and delivering awards.

C1200–4.606: May 1985 (Vol. 159, No. 5)

CONSUMER PROMOTION, ANNUAL FEATURE

(p. 43-59) Annual article reporting on use of consumer premiums, 1984, based on responses of 184 companies to a 1985 survey by *Incentive Marketing.*

Includes 2 charts and 2 tables showing expenditures on consumer premiums, by premi-

um type and for top 10 user industries, 1984; median number of consumer responses per 1,-000 advertising exposures, by premium type and advertising/distribution method (no date); and types of premiums considered most and least effective in achieving selected objectives, 1985.

Previous article, covering 1984 survey, is described in SRI 1984 Annual under C1200-4.506.

C1200–4.607: July 1985 (Vol. 159, No. 7)

WORLD TRAVEL SURVEY: SETTING SIGHTS ON SALES, ANNUAL FEATURE

(p. 28-43, 87) Annual article on corporate use of travel incentives for salespeople, dealers, and distributors. Data are from 252 responses to a 1985 survey of companies that use travel incentives, and from previous surveys.

Includes 4 charts and 2 tables showing top 10 industry groups ranked by incentive travel expenditures, 1984; and trip starts by month, trip costs, trip arrangement methods, travel budget allocation, and destination preferences, 1985.

C1200–4.608: Sept. 1985 (Vol. 159, No. 9)

CORPORATE GIFT-GIVING, ANNUAL FEATURE

(p. 31-46) Annual article reporting on business gift-giving practices. Data are based on 256 responses to a May-June 1985 survey of companies that use gift incentives. Includes text data, and 7 tables showing gift sources and delivery and presentation methods, use of personalized gifts, and most popular gifts.

C1200–4.609: Oct. 1985 (Vol. 159, No. 10)

SALES INCENTIVES: ANTIDOTES FOR INACTION, ANNUAL FEATURE

(p. 33-44, 99) Annual article reporting on use of incentive programs for salespeople. Data are from responses of 231 sales incentive users to a July 1985 survey, and from previous surveys.

Includes text data and 6 charts showing sales incentive objectives, sales gain with use of incentives, percent of sales force earning awards, sales incentive expenditures of top 10 user industries, types of awards used, methods of obtaining awards, incentive campaigns launched by month, and incentive costs as percent of sales, various years 1978-85.

Previous article is described in SRI 1984 Annual under C1200-4.509.

C1200–5   RESTAURANT BUSINESS

18 issues per year.
ISSN 0097-8043.
LC 74-644389.
SRI/MF/excerpts, shipped quarterly

Trade journal (published 18 times a year) of the restaurant and food service industry, including company and market profiles, and articles on product line merchandising and promotion, equipment, and management.

Most data are from the journal's own research, Federal Government, and private research assns.

Issues generally contain narrative special features or articles; and regular editorial depts, including "Trade Quotes" section presenting selected stock data for approximately 80 food service companies.

Annual statistical features include franchise restaurant operations summary; restaurant advertising expenditures; food service operations of supermarkets; and restaurant growth index.

Features with substantial statistical content are described, as they appear, under "Statistical Features." Each issue of the journal is reviewed, but an abstract is published in SRI monthly issues only when statistical features appear.

Availability: Restaurant Business, 633 Third Ave., New York NY 10017, quaiified subscribers †, others $63.00 per yr., single copy $5.00; SRI/MF/excerpts for all portions described under "Statistical Features;" shipped quarterly.

Issues reviewed during 1985: Nov. 1, 1984-Oct. 10, 1985 (P) (Vol. 83, Nos. 16-18; Vol. 84, Nos. 1-15).

STATISTICAL FEATURES:

C1200-5.601: Nov. 1, 1984 (Vol. 83, No. 16)

BEHIND THE GOURMET BURGER BOOM

(p. 121-137) By Jacque Kochak. Article, with 2 tables showing number of units as of mid-summer 1984, average sales per unit 1983, and growth outlook, for 12 full service and 6 self-service gourmet hamburger chains.

C-STORES VIE FOR FAST FOOD MARKET

(p. 140-150) By Cynthia Amorese. Article, with 1 table showing top 10 companies owning convenience store chains ranked by number of units operated, and including names of chains owned, number of States of operation, and geographic area of concentration, 1984.

EXPANDING EUROPEAN MARKETS

(p. 152-161) By Priscilla Andreiev. Article, with 2 tables showing U.S. franchise restaurant establishments, by country or world area, 1975-82; and total units, units outside U.S., countries of operations, and growth plans, for 28 U.S. restaurant chains, as of June 1984 or latest available quarter.

C1200-5.602: Dec. 10, 1984 (Vol. 83, No. 18)

ITALIAN MARKET GROWS WITH FRESH APPROACH TO PASTA

(p. 105-120) By Jacque White Kochak. Article, with 1 chart showing Italian food restaurants and market share, by region, 1983. Data are from Restaurant Consulting Group, Inc.

C1200-5.603: Jan. 20, 1985 (Vol. 84, No. 2)

BROADER MENUS SPICE UP CHICKEN SALES

(p. 97-112) By Tom Strenk. Article, with 1 chart and text data showing restaurants specializing in chicken, by census division and as percent of total restaurants, 1984. Data are from Restaurant Consulting Group, Inc.

C1200-5.604: Mar. 1, 1985 (Vol. 84, No. 4)

REGIONAL CHAINS DOMINATE BARBECUE SEGMENT

(p. 97-111) By Jacque White Kochak. Article, with 1 chart and 1 table showing total and barbecue restaurants, by State and census division, 1984. Data are from Restaurant Consulting Group, Inc.

C1200-5.605: Mar. 20, 1985 (Vol. 84, No. 5)

RESTAURANT FRANCHISING IN THE ECONOMY, ANNUAL FEATURE

(p. 165-182) Annual feature, by Andrew Kostecka, analyzing developments in franchising generally and for restaurants and other specific industries. Data are from Commerce Dept. Includes 1 chart and 11 tables showing the following for restaurant franchising:

a. Franchise company-owned and franchisee-owned units and sales: by type of food served, 1979 and 1983-85; for 30 leading systems, 1983-84; and by State, 1983.

b. Franchise companies, 1983; franchisor sales of products/services to franchisees, by sales category, 1983-85; franchise and all other restaurant sales, 1979 and 1984; and companies with international franchises, and units by country or world area, by type of food served, 1983.

C1200-5.606: May 1, 1985 (Vol. 84, No. 7)

UP FRONT: FAST FOOD AD SPENDING, ANNUAL FEATURE

(p. 48, 53) Annual article, with 1 table showing top 20 fast food restaurants ranked by radio advertising expenditures, 1984, with comparisons to 1983. Data are from Radio Advertising Bureau.

FOODSERVICE 2000

(p. 207-238) Compilation of articles discussing market outlook for the food service industry to 2000. Data are from *American Demographics,* Data Resources, Inc., Census Bureau, National Planning Assn, and BLS. Includes 6 charts and 1 table showing the following:

a. Population and/or percent change, by age group and region; median income of families and single persons; and percent of households with husband and wife present, and headed by men and women with no spouse present; various periods 1978-2000.

b. Population, households, effective buying income, and retail sales, 1986 and 1996, for top 30 metro areas ranked by 1996 population.

c. Employment in total food service industry and in eating/drinking places, by occupation, 1982 and 1995.

C1200-5.607: May 20, 1985 (Vol. 84, No. 8)

FAST FOOD PHENOMENON IN EUROPE

(p. 124-128) By Charles Fessel. Article, with 3 undated tables showing 10 European countries ranked by fast food share of consumer spending on food away from home; market share for 6 leading fast food chains in Europe; and top 18 fast food chains in UK ranked by number of establishments, with comparison to aggregate privately owned/new concept establishments.

SWEET PARADOX PROVES PROFITABLE

(p. 135-142) By Jacque White Kochak. Article, with 2 charts showing number of donut and ice cream restaurants, by census division, and as percent of total U.S. restaurants, 1984. Data are from Restaurant Consulting Group, Inc.

C1200-5.608: June 10, 1985 (Vol. 84, No. 9)

TAKING MONEY OUT OF YOUR FIRM

(p. 108) By Irving L. Blackman. Article, with 1 table showing average personal income tax deductions claimed, by type and income level, 1983. Data are from IRS.

CHAINS BOOST TV AD EXPENDITURES, ANNUAL FEATURE

(p. 152, 158) Annual article, with 1 table showing network and spot TV advertising expenditures, for top 15 fast food restaurants ranked by total TV advertising expenditures, 1984 with comparisons to 1983. Data are from TV Bureau of Advertising, based on Broadcast Advertisers Reports.

ANALYZING SHIFTS IN RESTAURANT GROWTH

(p. 200-204) Article, with 3 tables showing number of restaurants by detailed type and census division, 1984; with percent change for restaurant types and States with growth rates farthest above and below average for 1983-84 period.

Data are based on the 3rd annual RE-COUNT study compiled by Restaurant Consulting Group, and are current to spring 1984.

C1200-5.609: July 1, 1985 (Vol. 84, No. 10)

SEAFOOD OPERATORS TAKE A FRESH APPROACH

(p. 93-108) By Jacque White Kochak. Article, with 1 chart showing number of fish/seafood restaurants, by census division, spring 1984. Data are from Restaurant Consulting Group.

C1200-5.610: July 20, 1985 (Vol. 84, No. 11)

ODDS OF THE AUDIT GAME

(p. 86) By Irving L. Blackman. Article, with 1 table showing probability of an IRS income tax audit, by personal income, noncorporate business income, and corporate asset level, 1984.

C1200-5.611: Aug. 10, 1985 (Vol. 84, No. 12)

FOOD STORE COUNTERATTACK, ANNUAL FEATURE

(p. 209-216) Annual article, by Jacque White Kochak, on supermarket competition with restaurants. Data sources include *Progressive Grocer.*

Includes 2 tables showing the following for supermarkets: sales and number of stores for top 20 chains ranked by sales, 1984, with comparisons to 1983; and total industry sales and number of stores, and percent of stores offering selected special services including delicatessens, catering, bakeries, salad bars, sit-down restaurants, and store-made pizza and pasta, 1973-84.

Previous article is described in SRI 1984 Annual under C1200-5.509.

C1200-5.612: Sept. 20, 1985 (Vol. 84, No. 14)

NEW PRODUCTS DELIVER QUALITY AND FRESHNESS

(p. 101-116) By Jacque White Kochak. Article, with 1 table and 1 chart showing the following for pizza restaurants: top 10 chains ranked by 1984 sales, with number of units and growth outlook; and total units by census division, spring 1984. Data sources include Restaurant Consulting Group, Inc.

LIQUOR LEGISLATION: STATE BY STATE ANALYSIS

(p. 122-126) Article, with tabular list summarizing status of liquor liability laws affecting food/beverage establishments, by State, 1985. Data are from National Restaurant Assn.

18th ANNUAL RESTAURANT GROWTH INDEX, ANNUAL FEATURE

(p. 133-260) Annual report on food service sales, by major market segment, 1983-84, with projections to 1989. Also includes selected demographic data; and restaurant sales, and restaurant activity and growth indexes (RAI and RGI), by geographic area.

Major market segments are separate eating/drinking places, hotel/motel, retail, business/industrial, health care, student, leisure, and transportation. Geographic breakdowns include census divisions, States, MSAs, and TV areas of dominant influence (ADIs).

RAI is based on an area's eating place-food store sales ratio. RGI is a measure of restaurant supply-demand in an area.

Data are from RBI Research, Malcolm M. Knapp Inc., Census Bureau, and BLS.

Contents:

a. Summary article, with 2 tables showing food service industry sales, sales growth rate, and purchases, for commercial/contract, institutional/internal, and military markets, and by major market segment, 1982-83, with number of units for 1983, and sales growth rate projections to 1989. (p. 133-135)

b. Major market segment analyses, each with 1 table showing the sales, growth rate, purchase, and unit data described above, for the total segment and 3-8 subsegments; and narrative analysis of military market. (p. 136-178)

c. "18th Annual Restaurant Growth Index," by Jeffrey Hall. Article with narrative analysis, definitions, explanation of RGI computation, and 4 tables showing average sales and employees per establishment and sales and payroll per employee, for selected food service industry segments, 1982; distribution of households by income, 1968 and 1983; and average household income, and distribution of householders and workers, by major occupational category, various years 1982-85. (p. 183-197)

d. List of MSAs covered in RGI. (p. 200-204)

e. 3 tables showing population, average household size, eating/drinking place sales, eating place sales and units, sales and market share for fast food establishments and restaurants, RAI, and RGI, all by census division, State, MSA, nonmetro portion of State, and ADI, 1984. (p. 206-244)

f. 8 tables ranking top 100 MSAs and ADIs by eating place, restaurant, and fast food total and per capita sales, and by RAI and RGI, 1984. (p. 246-260)

C1555
Blue Sky Marketing

C1555–1   MINNESOTA POCKET DATA BOOK, 1985-86

Biennial.   1985.   9+384 p.
ISSN 0094-3983.
ISBN 0-911493-03-4.
LC 74-645305.
SRI/MF/complete

Biennial compilation, for 1985-86, of detailed social, economic, and governmental statistics for Minnesota. Data are primarily for 1970s-84, with population trends from 1900.

Report is designed to present a comprehensive overview of the State. Extensive geographic, economic, and demographic breakdowns are shown, as applicable, for most topics. These breakdowns include data by city, county, MSA, urban-rural status, State region, commodity, government agency, industry, occupation, age, marital status, race, and sex. Comparisons to total U.S. and neighboring States are also often included.

Most data are from Federal and State government sources.

Contains introduction and contents listing (8 p.); and the following:

a. 13 topical sections, with 180 maps and charts, and 183 tables. (p. 2-242)

b. 3 geographic sections, with 4-6 tables repeated for each State region and county; and 1 table on population by city. (p. 244-358)

c. Data source listing and subject index. (p. 360-384)

All tables and charts with substantial statistics are described below. This is the 2nd biennial edition.

Availability: Blue Sky Marketing, PO Box 17003, St. Paul MN 55117, $29.95; SRI/MF/complete.

CHARTS AND TABLES:

C1555–1.1: Population

(p. 2-22) Contains 14 maps and charts, and 16 tables. Includes population and density since 1900; migration and population change; population of largest cities, and fastest and slowest growing cities; households; births; total, infant, and fetal deaths; marriages; and divorces/annulments.

C1555–1.2: Health

(p. 24-34) Contains 6 maps and charts, and 13 tables. Includes physicians, nurses, dentists, and chiropractors; hospitals, beds, staff, utilization, and costs; overweight population; nursing license renewals; nursing home beds and patients; HMO enrollment, costs, and utilization; deaths by cause; infant mortality; abortions; and chemical dependency treatment admissions.

C1555–1.3: Social Services

(p. 36-46) Contains 10 charts and 9 tables. Includes public assistance recipients, cases, and payments, by program; AFDC payment levels by State; and value of food coupon books issued.

Also includes mentally ill and retarded, and chemically dependent institutional populations; State nursing home expenditures; State

hospital expenditures, revenues, and patients; children under State guardianship, and adoptions; and veterans benefit payments.

C1555–1.4: Housing and Media

(p. 48-66) Contains 10 maps and charts, and 9 tables. Includes property values; manufactured homes built/shipped to State; residential building permits and public housing contract awards; and State housing agency loan financing.

Also includes newspapers and periodicals; cable TV revenues, systems, and subscribers; TV and AM-FM radio stations; and TV households.

C1555–1.5: Business/Employment

(p. 68-90) Contains 16 maps and charts, and 19 tables. Includes new incorporations; retail, wholesale, and service industry payroll, and sales or receipts; commercial forest land, and forest products harvested and manufactured; travel-related expenditures, payroll, employment, and tax receipts; wholesale establishments; and manufacturing employment and payroll.

Also includes forest industry, Indian reservation, State government, and occupational employment; unemployment compensation claims; personal and family income; and wages.

C1555–1.6: Government

(p. 92-112) Contains 9 maps and charts, and 17 tables. Includes revenues by level of government; sales and income tax collections; and State rankings by State/local tax, property tax, personal and corporate income tax, sales tax collections, per capita State/local expenditures, and per capita personal income.

Also includes general fund, State/local, and city revenues by source and expenditures by function; State agency budgets; State legislators; National Guard personnel, State and Federal funding, and military training at Camp Riley; Air National Guard aircraft; and State consumer service activities and complaints received.

C1555–1.7: Energy

(p. 114-122) Contains 3 charts and 8 tables. Includes energy consumption and prices, by consuming sector and/or fuel type.

C1555–1.8: Education

(p. 124-148) Contains 18 maps and charts, and 29 tables. Includes minimum length of school year and day, by State; educational enrollment; public school staff, salaries, and expenditures; nonpublic schools and enrollment; high school graduation rates; and educational attainment of adult population.

Also includes higher education enrollment, degrees, and State funding; tuition/fees in community colleges and public universities in selected States; higher education revenues by source and expenditures by function; vocational-technical enrollment and revenues; and public library facilities, staff, holdings, and finances.

C1555–1.9: Transportation/Shipping

(p. 150-172) Contains 20 maps and charts, and 15 tables. Includes highway mileage and maintenance expenditures, by State; public transit program mileage, passengers, and costs; motor vehicle registrations; trucks and freight transportation; and rail abandonment and total track mileage.

Also includes Mississippi River lockages; freight tonnage handled by river and Lake Superior ports; Duluth-Superior port domestic and international trade and vessels; and aircraft by type and primary use.

C1555–1.10: Geography/Recreation

(p. 176-204) Contains 32 maps and charts, and 18 tables. Includes land use and ownership; mining acreage, and mineral production; frost dates; sources of sulfur dioxide and nitrogen oxide emissions, and potential ground water contamination; State environmental quality control expenditures; and metro area sewage system operations.

Also includes recreational activity participation and facilities; fishing and hunting licenses, participation, and expenditures; game harvested; major rivers and length; and shoreland housing.

C1555–1.11: Public Safety

(p. 206-224) Contains 28 maps and charts, and 14 tables. Includes crimes by offense; arrests; stolen property value; offenses cleared; outcomes of criminal procedure; correctional facility population, costs, and expenditures; probation and parole; juvenile court processing and placements; juvenile cases without legal representation; and child maltreatment.

Also includes traffic accident injuries and fatalities, economic impact, and restraint device use and savings; major disaster declarations and counties affected; and flood damage assessment.

C1555–1.12: Agriculture

(p. 226-242) Contains 14 maps and charts, and 16 tables. Includes farms and farmland; agricultural export value; farm income and production expenses; crop prices and production; acreage planted and harvested; wild rice acreage and production; cropland erosion and prevention costs; farmland value; grain warehouses and capacity; State agriculture dept expenditures and revenues.

C1555–1.13: Regions and Counties

(p. 244-348) Contains 4-6 tables repeated for each of 13 State regions and 87 counties. Includes population and migration; land area; land use (counties only); educational enrollment; property values and taxes (counties only); and public assistance payments and recipients.

C1555–1.14: Cities

(p. 350-358) Contains 1 table showing population by city.

C1560
Boating Industry, Inc.

C1560–1   BOATING INDUSTRY
Monthly.
ISSN 0006-5404.
LC 74-647999.
SRI/MF/excerpts, shipped quarterly

Monthly trade journal of the recreational boating industry, reporting on sales trends, marketing strategies, trade shows, new products, and other topics of interest to marinas and marine product dealers and manufacturers. Covers power boats and sailboats; boat motors, materials, and accessories; and water skis and other water sports equipment.

Data are from industry sources, Federal agencies, and *Boating Industry* surveys.

Issues generally contain feature articles, occasionally with statistics; and numerous regular depts.

Annual features include boating industry statistics (Jan.); sailing industry market overview (May); and a nonstatistical marine buyer's guide (Dec.).

A 2nd issue published in Feb. is a nonstatistical annual supplement sponsored by Marine Retailers Assn of America.

Features with substantial statistical content are described, as they appear, under "Statistical Features." Journal is reviewed every month but an abstract is published in SRI monthly issues only when features with substantial statistical content appear.

Availability: Boating Industry, Circulation Department, 850 Third Ave., New York NY 10022, qualified subscribers $20.00 per yr., single copy $4.00, Buyer's Guide $25.00, Jan. and Sept. issues $5.00; SRI/MF/excerpts for all portions described under "Statistical Features;" shipped quarterly.

Issues reviewed during 1985: Nov. 1984-Oct. 1985 (P) (Vol. 47, Nos. 11-12; Vol. 48, Nos. 1-10).

STATISTICAL FEATURES:

C1560–1.601: Jan. 1985 (Vol. 48, No. 1)
BOATING BUSINESS, 1984, ANNUAL FEATURE

(p. 33-48) Annual compilation of recreational boating industry statistics, 1984 and trends. Data sources include *Boating Industry* surveys, trade assns, U.S. Coast Guard, and U.S. Chamber of Commerce.

Includes text statistics, 14 charts, 1 map, and 6 tables, with substantial data for the following:

a. Retail sales: total, outboard boat and motor, inboard/outdrive boat, and trailers, with average values, various years 1977-84.
b. Boat export and import value, 1975-83; dollar volume for top 8 countries of destination and top 11 competing countries, 1983; and forecasts of top 12 countries of destination ranked by U.S. export growth rate.
c. Outboard boat sales and average length; and boating accidents, boats involved in accidents, fatalities, nonfatal injuries, and fatality rate; various years 1969-84.

d. Registered boats, population, inland water area, miles of coastal shoreline, and 1983 effective buying income, by State and outlying territory; and registered boats by region.
e. Water ski and trailer sales; average trailer retail cost; and sailboat sales and average retail cost (non-powered, and auxiliary-powered by size); various years 1973-84.

C1560–1.602: May 1985 (Vol. 48, No. 5)
SAIL REGROUPS, ANNUAL FEATURE

(p. 36-40) Annual article, by Peter Morton Coan, presenting sailing industry statistics for 1984. Data are from various industry sources. Includes text statistics on sailboats and persons sailing, sales by vessel type, sailboat manufacturers, and sailing instruction facilities associated with marinas/boat dealers and schools/sailing assns.

Feature for 1984 was nonstatistical; for description of feature for 1983, see SRI 1983 Annual under C1560-1.402.

C1560–1.603: Sept. 1985 (Vol. 48, No. 9)
IMPORTS UP/EXPORTS DOWN

(p. 66-67, 234) By Bob Moyat. Article, with 2 tables showing volume and value of recreational boat imports and exports, by type of vessel and country of origin and destination, 1983-84. Data were compiled by National Marine Manufacturers Assn.

C1575
Bobit Publishing Co.

C1575–1   SCHOOL BUS FLEET
Bimonthly.
ISSN 0036-6501.
LC SN 79-9218.
SRI/MF/excerpts

Bimonthly journal on school bus fleet management and operating trends and developments. Journal is primarily narrative, but occasionally includes features with substantial statistical content. An annual factbook issue is published in Dec./Jan.

Features with substantial statistical content are described, as they appear, under "Statistical Features." Each issue of the journal is reviewed, but an abstract is published in SRI monthly issues only when statistical features appear.

Availability: School Bus Fleet, Subscription Manager, 2500 Artesia Blvd., Redondo Beach CA 90278-3296, qualified subscribers †, others $12.00 per yr., single copy $2.00, Fact Book $20.00; SRI/MF/excerpts for all portions covered under "Statistical Features."

Issues reviewed during 1985: Dec. 1984/Jan. 1985-Oct./Nov. 1985 (P) (Vol. 29, No. 6; Vol. 30, Nos. 1-5).

STATISTICAL FEATURES:

C1575–1.601: Dec. 1984/Jan. 1985 (Vol. 29, No. 6)
SCHOOL BUS INDUSTRY STATISTICS, ANNUAL FEATURE

(p. 5-11) Annual compilation of statistics on school bus pupil transportation, accidents, and costs, by State, various years 1960/61-1982/83. Data are from reports of the National Safety Council, National Assn of State Directors of Pupil Transportation Services, State education and highway depts, and other sources. Includes 2 summary charts and the following tables:

[1] School transportation [pupils transported at public expense, vehicles used by type and ownership, buses, and transportation expenditures/capital outlay, all by State and for Manitoba, Guam, Puerto Rico, and Saipan], 1982/83. (p. 5)

[2] [School bus] accidents by State [includes mileage, accidents by type, and total and pupil injuries, primarily 1982/83]. (p. 8)

[3] Growth of school transportation in the U.S. [pupils transported, vehicles used, and expenditures, 1960/61-1982/83]. (p. 11)

Feature is part of the annual factbook issue.

C1575–1.602: Feb./Mar. 1985 (Vol. 30, No. 1)

SBF SURVEY LOOKS AT THE DANGER ZONE

(p. 14-18) Article, with 1 table showing number of States by status of school bus safety equipment requirements (mandatory, not mandatory, optional, or legislation pending) for selected types of equipment. Data are from 47 responses to a Dec. 1984 *School Bus Fleet* survey of State pupil transportation directors.

SCHOOL BUS MAINTENANCE PRACTICE SURVEYED

(p. 51-56) Article, with 2 charts showing per bus maintenance budget and inventory value, for contractor and district school bus fleets, by fleet size, 1984. Data are from 207 responses of school bus fleet managers to a Dec. 1984 *School Bus Fleet* survey.

C1575–1.603: June/July 1985 (Vol. 30, No. 3)

KIDS NEED TO BE WATCHED TOO, ANNUAL FEATURE

(p. 32-35) First of 2 annual articles, by Roscoe Bernard, with 3 charts showing number of children killed during school bus loading/unloading, various periods 1969-83. Includes deaths caused by school buses and by other vehicles. Data are from Kansas Dept of Transportation, and cover total U.S.

Full report is covered in SRI under A3040-2.

Previous article is described in SRI 1984 Annual under C1575-1.504.

C1575–1.604: Aug./Sep. 1985 (Vol. 30, No. 4)

SURVEY REVEALS SUBTLE CHANGES IN PROCUREMENT PRACTICES, RECURRING FEATURE

(p. 14-18) Recurring article on school bus fleet characteristics. Most data are based on responses of 187 readers to a 1985 *School Bus Fleet* survey.

Includes 4 charts showing distribution of respondents by job title, and survey response on months in which bus specifications are written (with comparison to 1983 survey); average annual expenditures for replacement parts, by type of part; and value of maintenance parts inventory.

Previous survey article, for 1983, is described in SRI 1983 Annual under C1575-1.402.

INSURANCE: CRISIS IN THE INDUSTRY

(p. 20-23) Article, with 1 table showing school bus mileage, number of vehicles, and accidents (total and involving property damage only), 1974-83. Data are from National Safety Council (NSC) *Accident Fact Book*.

Full NSC report is covered by SRI under A8375-2.

SBF's TOP 25, ANNUAL FEATURE

(p. 24) Annual article, with 1 table showing top 25 school districts ranked by number of school buses. Data are based on responses of 34 State directors of pupil transportation to a 1985 *School Bus Fleet* survey.

This is the 1st annual survey.

C1575–1.605: Oct./Nov. 1985 (Vol. 30, No. 4)

SAFETY OF OUR CHILDREN, ANNUAL FEATURE

(p. 38-45) Second of 2 annual articles, by Lee Comeau, with 1 table showing number of children killed during school bus loading/unloading, by purpose of travel and whether child was in front or back of bus, and for deaths caused by other vehicles, 1980-83. Data are from Kansas Dept of Transportation, and cover total U.S.

Full report is covered in SRI under A3040-2.

C1575–2   AUTOMOTIVE FLEET
Monthly.
ISSN 0005-1519.
LC 68-2155.
SRI/MF/excerpts, shipped quarterly

Monthly report on trends and developments in automobile and light truck fleet management and operations, with data on fuel prices and used car auction prices.

Issues generally contain feature articles, occasionally statistical; editorial depts, including news columns and industry personnel developments; and 2 monthly tables, listed below.

Monthly tables appear in all issues. All additional features with substantial statistical content (except vehicle specifications) are described, as they appear, under "Statistical Features." Non-statistical features are not covered.

Availability: Automotive Fleet, Subscription Manager, 2500 Artesia Blvd., Redondo Beach CA 90278-9984, qualified subscribers †, others $24.00 per yr., single copy $2.00, Fact Book $25.00; SRI/MF/excerpts for monthly data and all portions covered under "Statistical Features;" shipped quarterly.

Issues reviewed during 1985: Nov. 1984-Oct. 1985 (P) (Vol. 24, Nos. 1-12; and Vol. 24 Supplement).

MONTHLY TABLES:

[1] Gas prices [for unleaded gasoline (full- and self-serve) in approximately 15 cities, as of a selected date during month 1-2 months prior to cover date; data are from Runzheimer International].

[2] Used cars [average auction prices by year, make, and model, by region, usually for week 1-4 weeks prior to cover date; data are from *Automotive Market Report*].

STATISTICAL FEATURES:

C1575–2.601: Dec. 1984 (Vol. 24, No. 2)

U.S. LIGHT TRUCK STATISTICS, ANNUAL FEATURE

(p. 21-30) Annual compilation of statistics on light truck/van fleets, sales, and registrations. Includes 3 charts and 9 tables showing the following:

a. Light truck total and fleet sales or registrations, by domestic and import manufacturer; and light truck retail sales, by gross vehicle weight and body type; various years 1976-84.

b. Truck and bus factory sales, by gross vehicle weight and body type, with detail for diesel trucks, various periods 1969-83; and operating and ownership expenses for a 1984 model year passenger van over a 3-year period, by item.

c. Top 25 business/commercial and utility light truck/van fleets, ranked by number of vehicles, 1984 with comparisons to 1983.

FLEET STUDY: NO 'MAXI' MOVE TOWARD MINIVANS

(p. 79) Article on corporate fleet planned acquisitions of minivans in 1985, based on a Runzheimer and Co. survey of 30 fleets. Includes 1 table.

C1575–2.602: Jan. 1985 (Vol. 24, No. 3)

MANUALS COST $206 LESS PER YEAR, RUNZHEIMER SAYS

(p. 22-24) Brief article, with 1 table comparing annual operating and ownership costs of automatic and manual transmission versions of four 1984 auto models. Data are from Runzheimer and Co.

LEASING: TWELFTH BIENNIAL SURVEY UNVEILS CHANGING INDUSTRY PARAMETERS

(p. 29-35) Biennial article on fleet characteristics of the auto and truck lease/rental industry. Data are from responses of 401 *Automotive Fleet* readers to a 1984 survey. Includes 1 table showing the following, biennially 1964-84:

a. Survey response rate; respondent distribution, by whether affiliated with new auto dealer, and by type of lease used (finance/management, fixed, and full/partial maintenance); and average age at replacement and annual mileage for leased and rented cars and trucks.

b. Fleet composition, by auto size class; percent of autos leased and rented; average auto value and per month revenue; and percent of trucks leased and rented, by weight class.

For description of previous article, see SRI 1983 Annual under C1575-2.403.

NATION ON THE MOVE

(p. 92-94) Article on business travel characteristics, based on a recent Hertz Corp. survey. Includes 1 undated table showing survey response on the following: whether job involves business travel; number of local, regional, and long-distance business trips, and total miles traveled, by transport mode; business travel expenditures; and foreign business trips.

C1575–2.603: Mar. 1985 (Vol. 24, No. 5)

CONTROLLING CAR RENTAL COSTS THROUGH NEGOTIATION

(p. 34-40) Article on strategies for corporate negotiations with car rental firms, with 1 undated table showing number of States and locations served and corporate negotiation policies of 10 car rental companies. Data are from Runzheimer and Co.

COMPETITIVE INTERNATIONAL DAILY-RENTAL MARKET

(p. 44-50) Article on world car rental market. Data are from *Canadian Automotive Fleet* magazine and *Automotive Fleet* research. Includes 2 charts and 3 tables showing the following for various years 1978-84:

a. Canada: on-airport market shares and fleet size, for 4 major and all other companies; and total on- and off-airport revenues and fleet size.

b. Western Europe: market shares for 5 major and all other companies.

c. U.S.: on-airport market shares, fleet size, and revenues, for 5 major and all other companies; off-airport revenues, and fleet size for 12 major and all other companies; and average rental car mileage, revenue, and months of service at time of replacement.

SURVEY FINDS INCREASE IN PERSONAL-USE CHARGES REPORTED AS INCOME, ANNUAL FEATURE

(p. 64-73) Annual survey article on personal use of company fleet cars and business use of personally owned cars. Data are based on responses of 407 U.S. and Canadian fleets to a 1984 National Assn of Fleet Administrators (NAFA) survey.

Includes 3 tables showing survey response for the following: number of fleets, and company-owned and leased cars, shown for 7 industry groups, public utilities, and government (all U.S. only), and for Canada, 1984; and reimbursement rate for business use of personal car, 1980-84, for U.S. commercial fleets.

For description of full NAFA survey report, see A6755-1.604 above.

C1575–2.604: Apr. 1985 (Vol. 24, No. 6)

OPERATING COSTS RISE 13 PERCENT ON CLOSED-END LEASED VEHICLES

(p. 30-31) Article on nonfinanced (closed-end) leased auto costs and fleet composition. Data are from a recent American Automotive Leasing Assn (AALA) survey of member firms.

Includes 4 tables showing the following for nonfinanced fleets: general/administrative costs and operating costs by item, per unit per month, 1984 vs. 1983, and by fleet size, 1984; total costs per month and average annual mileage and months in operation, 1977-84; and distribution of fleet autos by make and size class, and percent with air-conditioning, with comparisons to open-end fleets, 1983-84.

Full AALA report is covered by SRI under A0875-1.

CLASS III, REVISITED

(p. 32-38) Article, with 2 tables showing domestic truck sales by gross vehicle weight, and imported truck sales (total and Japanese), 1971-84. Data are from Motor Vehicle Manufacturers Assn.

NAFA's ANNUAL USED-CAR MARKETING SURVEY, ANNUAL FEATURE

(p. 45-51) Annual article on marketing of used fleet autos. Data are from responses of 216 fleet managers to the 1984 National Assn of Fleet Administrators (NAFA) Used-Car Marketing Survey. Respondents represent 147,281 autos.

Includes 1 table showing number of owned and leased autos in fleet, and used autos sold in 1984 by model year and marketing method, for 8 industry sectors, utilities and government, and Canadian fleets.

For description of full NAFA survey report, see A6755-1.605, above.

C1575–2.605: Fact Book (Vol. 24 Supplement)

Annual *Automotive Fleet* fact book presenting data on fleet car and light truck sales and registrations, make and size of cars, types of ownership and leasing arrangements, and operating costs.

Data are from *Automotive Fleet* Research Dept, American Automotive Leasing Assn (AALA), National Assn of Fleet Administrators (NAFA), and other sources.

Contents:

a. Statistical sections, with 5 charts and 23 tables listed below. (p. 9-30, 161-170)

b. Fleet directories, including fleet sales and marketing personnel, by motor vehicle manufacturer and selected makes (p. 33-50); lease/rental companies (p. 60-119); and fleet dealers by make, disposal/salvage companies, and consultants (p. 121-160).

c. Reference section, including *Automotive Fleet* editorial index, June 1984-Mar. 1985; directories of National Auto Auction Assn members and tire industry fleet experts; 1985 model year auto and truck specifications, by make and model; State auto insurance, registration, and tax requirements; and directory of related assns. (p. 172-214)

Only the statistical sections are available on SRI microfiche.

Light truck statistics were previously published separately from the *Fact Book* issue. For description of previous feature, see SRI 1984 Annual under C1575-2.501.

TABLES AND CHARTS:

AUTO STATISTICS

[Types of fleets include business fleets, by ownership or leasing arrangement; and government, utilities, police, taxi, daily rental, and driver school fleets.]

[1] Fleet figures by type and size [and selected data for leasing by individuals, and leased vs. owned trucks], as of Jan. 1, 1985. (p. 9)

[2-3] Fleet registrations by month and year; and new fleet vehicles registered [cars and trucks: renting/leasing, commercial, and government; 1975-84]. (p. 10)

[4-6] Daily rental market profile [number of cars, 1984 revenue, and 1983-84 airport market shares, for each of top 5 companies and all others; and number of cars for off-airport rental fleets, with aggregate 1984 revenue; with 1 chart showing average age of cars at replacement, revenue per month, and yearly mileage, selected years 1978-84]. (p. 12)

[7] Cars in fleets by type of business [and individually leased cars, other fleets by type, and daily truck rentals, 1975-84]. (p. 14)

[8] Composition of *Automotive Fleet* fleet/leasing market [by fleet type, with average annual mileage and trade-in time, no date]. [chart] (p. 14)

[9] 1984 model year registrations, fleet vs. retail [by model]. (p. 16)

[10] Fleet registrations [by make], 1978-84 model years. (p. 20)

[11] Net change of fleet sales, by [motor vehicle] manufacturer, 1982-84 model years. [chart] (p. 20)

[12] Size and model cars purchased, by major leasing companies [distribution], 1984 vs. 1983. (p. 22)

[13] AALA fleet costs survey for closed-end leases [monthly operating costs, by item, 1983-84; and total monthly costs, average months in operation, and average annual mileage, 1977-84]. (p. 24)

[14] Composition of the AALA fleet [distribution by size and make, and percent with air conditioning, 1977-84]. (p. 24)

[15] [AALA] used car disposition [distribution to dealers, auctions, and lessee employees; and percent and average expenditure of AALA members doing reconditioning; 1977-84]. (p. 24)

[16] Fleet car operating costs by region [no date]. (p. 26)

[17-20] NAFA personal use and used car data [commercial fleet distribution by reimbursement rates for business use of personal car, 1980-84; used autos sold in 1984 by model year and marketing method; and average miles and months in service at time of sale]. (p. 26)

[21-23] NAFA survey of operating expenses [by item, composite and by auto size class; with summary personal use credits, and average miles per month and per gallon; 1981-83. Includes summary chart.] (p. 28)

LIGHT TRUCK STATISTICS

[24] 1981-84 light truck fleet sales by maker, plus percent of retail [market]. [chart] (p. 161)

[25-26] U.S. and import light truck market statistics [new Class I/II registrations (national and fleet totals), by make, 1976-1984]. (p. 162-164)

[27-28] Top 25 utility and business/commercial light truck/van fleets [ranked by number of vehicles, 1984, and rank in 1983]. (p. 166-170)

C1575–2.606: May 1985 (Vol. 24, No. 7)

NEW ENTRIES TO LIVEN UP COMPACT PICKUP MARKET

(p. 95-100) Article, with 1 table showing compact pickup truck sales, by model, 1984 and 1987. Data are from J. D. Power and Associates.

Also includes 2 tables showing compact pickup truck specifications.

C1575–2.607: June 1985 (Vol. 24, No. 8)

AUTOMOTIVE FLEET'S SIXTH ANNUAL TOP 100, ANNUAL FEATURE

(p. 24-40) Annual *Automotive Fleet* ranking of 100 largest corporate auto and light truck/van fleets, 1985. Includes 1 table showing the following for each company, ranked by total fleet size: headquarters and fleet contact person; whether vehicles are owned or leased, and name of lessor or use of in-house leasing; number of autos and trucks/vans; and comparative rank order for 1984.

ASSESSMENT OF BANK INVOLVEMENT IN VEHICLE LEASING

(p. 48-60) Article on financial institution involvement in motor vehicle leasing. Data are based on 219 responses to a Consumer Bankers Assn 1985 membership survey, and *Automotive Fleet* research. Includes 10 tables showing the following:

a. Number and value of leases, portfolio balances, types of leases offered (with average term and capital cost for each type), use of depreciation tax deductions, method of handling investment tax credit, and availability of used car leases; with detail by portfolio size and/or region, 1984, with selected trends from 1981.

b. Top 30 banks ranked by number of auto leases in portfolio (no date).

FLEET OPERATING COSTS DECLINE FOR THIRD YEAR, ANNUAL FEATURE

(p. 72-76) Annual article on fleet operating expenses in U.S. and Canada. Data are from a National Assn of Fleet Administrators (NAFA) survey of 84 fleets operating over 79,000 passenger autos.

Includes 1 chart and 2 tables showing composite fleet operating, incidental, and standing expenses, by item, and personal use credits; and operating expenses by item, and average miles per month and per gallon, by auto size class; 1982-84.

Previous article, for 1983, is described in SRI 1984 Annual under C1575-2.506. For description of full NAFA survey, see A6755-1.606 above.

TOP FLEET DEALERS HONORED BY AUTOMOTIVE FLEET'S NINTH ANNUAL DEALER AWARDS, ANNUAL FEATURE

(p. 131-132) Annual tabular list of *Automotive Fleet* fleet dealer award recipients, showing dealership name and location, and number of units sold, for top 3 dealers for each of 13 makes, 1984.

ANALYSIS OF '84's MOST POPULAR CAR AND LIGHT-TRUCK COLORS

(p. 165-167) Article, with 3 charts and 3 tables showing color popularity rankings of passenger autos and trucks, by size class, 1983-84. Data are from the DuPont Co.

C1575–2.608: July 1985 (Vol. 24, No. 9)

FLEET CAR REGISTRATIONS

(p. 40-42) Table and 4 charts showing fleet auto registrations, by model arranged by size class; and distribution of fleet auto sales, by manufacturer and size class; full year and/or 1st half 1984-85 model years. Data are from *Automotive Fleet* Research Dept.

C1575–2.609: Aug. 1985 (Vol. 24, No. 10)

WHAT LEADING LESSORS RECOMMEND FOR '86

(p. 33-34, 49-52) Article, with 1 table showing new auto acquisition cost, operating cost per mile, and resale value, for selected 1986 auto models. Data are from Gelco Corp.

Also includes model recommendations of selected leasing companies.

FLEET-CAR ACCESSORIES: WEIGHING ALL THE OPTIONS

(p. 54-56) Article, with 1 chart showing percent of fleet autos with 10 accessories/options, 1983 and 1985. Data are from surveys by Runzheimer International.

C1575–2.610: Sept. 1985 (Vol. 24, No. 11)

GASOLINES FOR TODAY AND TOMORROW

(p. 25-34) By Peter Dorn. Article, with 1 table showing market share and customer satisfaction rating, for leaded regular, unleaded regular, and unleaded premium gasoline, 1985.

WHY TIRE COSTS CONTINUE TO DECLINE

(p. 118-125) Article, with 1 table showing market shares for light truck replacement tires, by company, 1981-85. Data are from *Modern Tire Dealer.*

C1575–2.611: Oct. 1985 (Vol. 24, No. 12)

REVENUES FROM VEHICLE LEASING AND RENTAL

(p. 19) Brief article, with 1 table showing auto and truck leasing and rental revenues and units in service, with number of individual auto leases, 1974 and 1983-84. Data are from Hertz Corp.

NAFA's NEW-CAR ACQUISITION SURVEY, ANNUAL FEATURE

(p. 87-101) Annual article on corporate auto fleet composition in 1985, and planned acquisition of 1986 models. Data are based on responses of 243 fleets operating 173,248 vehicles to a 1985 National Assn of Fleet Administrators (NAFA) survey.

Includes 3 tables showing fleet composition by owned or leased status and auto size class, and new car acquisitions, 1985; planned acquisitions by auto size class, 1986; and number of survey respondents, 1983-85; for 7 industry sectors, with selected composite trends from 1981.

Complete NAFA survey is described under A6755-1.608 above.

C1575–3   METROPOLITAN: 1984 Fact Book

Bimonthly (selected issue).
1984.   142 p.
Vol. 80, No. 6.
ISSN 0162-6221.
SRI/MF/excerpts

Annual fact book issue of *Metropolitan,* presenting funding data for urban mass transit systems, generally for FY65-Sept. 1983. Issue also includes directory of equipment and service suppliers. Data are from American Public Transit Assn and Urban Mass Transportation Administration (UMTA).

"Industry Statistics" section of the fact book includes 1 illustrative chart, and 6 other charts and 2 tables listed below.

Metropolitan is a bimonthly periodical reporting on trends and developments in the mass transport industry. Journal does not usually contain substantial statistics. Only the annual fact book and an annual feature on the top 50 urban bus transit systems are covered in SRI.

For description of annual feature on top transit systems, see C1575-4 below.

Availability: Metropolitan, Subscription Manager, 2500 Artesia Blvd., Redondo Beach CA 90278-3296, qualified subscribers †, others $12.00 per yr., single copy $2.00, Fact Book $20.00; SRI/MF/excerpts for statistical portions described below.

TABLES AND CHARTS:

[1] Capital grants [for Section 3, Section 5 Capital, Urban Systems, and Interstate Transfer programs, FY65-73 total, and annually FY74-Sept. 1983]. (p. 121)

[2] UMTA funded rail vehicles [distribution by type, FY65-82]. [chart] (p. 122)

[3] Transit buses delivered [distribution by size, 1983]. [chart] (p. 122)

[4] UMTA transit bus commitments by size [distribution, FY65-83 period]. [chart] (p. 123)

[5-7] [Selected findings from a spring 1984 survey of transit equipment vendors, concerning maintenance materials and problems, and warranties.] [charts] (p. 124)

[8] Approved Federal transit capital grants [and number of projects] by State [Feb. 1965-FY83]. (p. 125)

C1575–4   METRO MAGAZINE: Top 50 Transit Fleets

Bimonthly (selected issue).
Sept./Oct. 1985.   (p. 62-67)
Vol. 81, No. 5.
ISSN 0162-6221.
SRI/MF/excerpts

Annual feature ranking top 50 urban bus transit systems by fleet size, and including number of articulated buses and buses over and under 35 feet in length, and average age of buses, 1985 with selected comparisons to 1984. Data are from American Public Transit Assn and Bobit Publishing Research.

Includes brief narrative and 1 extended table. This is the 2nd annual feature.

Metro Magazine is a bimonthly periodical reporting on trends and developments in the mass transport industry. Journal does not usually contain substantial statistics. Only the top 50 fleet feature and an annual fact book issue are covered in SRI. *Metro Magazine* previously was titled *Metropolitan.*

For description of annual fact book issue, see C1575-3 above.

Availability: Metro Magazine, Subscription Manager, 2500 Artesia Blvd., Redondo Beach CA 90278-3296, $12.00 per yr., single copy $2.00, Fact Book $20.00; SRI/MF/excerpts for annual top 50 fleet feature.

C1650
Bowker, R. R., Co.

C1650–1 LIBRARY JOURNAL
Semimonthly.
ISSN 0363-0277.
LC 76-645271.
SRI/MF/not filmed

Semimonthly trade journal (monthly in Jan., July, Aug., and Dec.) of the library and information services professions, focusing primarily on public libraries. Covers book, periodical, and equipment selection; government activities affecting libraries; information technology; facilities design; and personnel, salaries, and professional development topics.

Most data are from the journal's own research, or are based on news and research reported by library systems and individuals.

Issues generally contain news briefs; feature articles, some with statistics; and narrative depts. Annual statistical features cover automated circulation systems, periodical prices, placements and salary levels of library school graduates, and public and academic library construction projects.

Features with substantial statistical content are described, as they appear, under "Statistical Features." Each issue of the journal is reviewed, but an abstract is published in SRI monthly issues only when statistical features appear.

Availability: R. R. Bowker Co., Library Journal, Subscription Department, PO Box 1427, Riverton NJ 08077, $64.00 per yr., single copy $3.50, Spring and Fall Announcement Issues $4.95; SRI/MF/not filmed.

Issues reviewed during 1985: Nov. 1, 1984-Oct. 15, 1985 (P) (Vol. 109, Nos. 18-20; Vol. 110, Nos. 1-17).

STATISTICAL FEATURES:

C1650–1.601: Dec. 1984 (Vol. 109, No. 20)

LIBRARY BUILDINGS IN 1984, ANNUAL FEATURE

(p. 2224-2234) Annual feature, by Bette-Lee Fox, on academic and public library construction and renovation. Includes 8 tables showing costs, size, and book and seating capacity of individual projects, FY84, with selected aggregate trends for academic libraries from FY74 and for public libraries from FY79.

Individual project data are shown by institution or community, and include projects in Canada. Public library data also include funding by source.

C1650–1.602: Feb. 15, 1985 (Vol. 110, No. 3)

LIBRARIANS IN ALTERNATIVE WORK PLACES

(p. 108-110) By Betty-Carol Sellen and Susan J. Vaughn. Article on salaries and placements of library school graduates in nonlibrary information jobs. Data are from responses of 487 graduates to a 1981/82 survey.

Includes 4 tables showing placements in various types of private and public sector organizations; salary ranges for full- and part-time workers by type of employment; and methods used to acquire position.

CREATING THE LIBRARY HABIT

(p. 111-114) By Barbara Will Razzano. Article on library use patterns, based on 1,240 responses to a Mar./Apr. 1982 survey of adult patrons of 28 upstate New York libraries serving populations of 25,000 or less. Includes 1 table showing purpose of library visits, for respondents (currently and in their youth) and for respondents' children.

C1650–1.603: Apr. 1, 1984 (Vol. 110, No. 6)

UNRELENTING CHANGE: THE 1984 AUTOMATED LIBRARY SYSTEM MARKETPLACE, ANNUAL FEATURE

(p. 31-40) Annual article, by Joseph R. Matthews, on the library market for automated systems, 1984. Includes 2 charts and 5 tables showing total and new turnkey automated systems in operation, by vendor and system size (number of terminals), 1984 with summary trends from 1973; and library- and vendor-developed microcomputer systems available and software price.

C1650–1.604: May 1, 1984 (Vol. 110, No. 8)

LIBRARY COMPUTING

(p. 91-130) Compilation of articles on microcomputer use in libraries. Data are from The Bowker National Library Microcomputer Usage Study, 1984.

Includes 8 tables showing the following for public, college/university, high school, elementary school, and special libraries, generally for mid-year 1984:

a. Total libraries, and number using microcomputers; microcomputer units installed (number and brands), purchase plans, and availability for on-site use by public/students.

b. Software availability to public/students, including on- and off-site use, number of packages, and most requested titles; and library use of software, including types of functions and suppliers.

C1650–1.605: June 15, 1984 (Vol. 110, No. 11)

MANAGING PUBLIC LIBRARY INVESTMENTS

(p. 23-26) By Don Sager. Article on investments as source of income for public libraries. Data are from surveys of public libraries conducted by NCES in 1977/78 (8,456 responses) and by Public Library Assn in June 1984 (271 responses).

Includes text data on investment practices of public libraries, based on 1984 survey; and 2 tables showing number of libraries in each survey, and percent of revenues from nongovernmental sources reported in 1977/78 survey, by size of population served.

C1650–1.606: Aug. 1985 (Vol. 110, No. 13)

PRICE INDEXES FOR 1985: U.S. PERIODICALS, ANNUAL FEATURE

(p. 53-58) Annual article, by Judith G. Horn and Rebecca T. Lenzini, on trends in library subscription prices for periodicals, 1977-85. Data are based on a study of 3,731 periodical titles.

Includes 6 tables showing number of periodical titles, average prices, and price index, by subject category, various periods 1977-85. This is the 25th annual survey.

C1650–1.607: Oct. 1, 1985 (Vol. 110, No. 16)

COST IS NOT EVERYTHING

(p. 52-55) Russell T. Clement. Article on automated turnkey systems for libraries. Data are based on responses of 21 libraries to a survey conducted by the author (respondents had recently purchased automated turnkey systems).

Includes 1 undated text table showing librarians' ratings of selected factors affecting purchasing decisions for automated turnkey systems.

PLACEMENTS AND SALARIES 1984: NO SURPRISES, ANNUAL FEATURE

(p. 59-65) Annual report, by Carol L. Learmont and Stephen Van Houten, on placements and salaries for 1984 graduates of accredited library school programs in U.S. and Canada. Data are from survey responses of 57 schools.

Includes 12 tables showing placements and salary averages and ranges, by region, graduating school, and type of employing library, with selected historical trends from the 1950s; and comparative salary data for graduates with and without previous experience. Most data are shown by sex; data by region include totals for Canada.

This is the 34th annual report.

C1650–1.608: Oct. 15, 1985 (Vol. 110, No. 17)

NCLIS LIBRARY STATISTICAL SAMPLER

(p. 35-38) Article presenting library statistics frequently requested from the National Commission on Library and Information Science (NCLIS). Most data are from NCES and R. R. Bowker Co.

Includes 4 charts and 10 tables showing libraries and budgets, by type of library; public libraries by population served; library funding by source, and expenditures by category; and sources of funds for library networks/cooperatives and State library agencies; various periods 1977-85, with historical trend in number of public libraries from 1776.

C1650–2 PUBLISHERS WEEKLY
Weekly.
ISSN 0000-0019.
LC 1-15589.
SRI/MF/not filmed

Weekly trade journal (except last week in Dec.) reporting on U.S. and foreign publishing and bookselling, marketing, design, manufacturing, and foreign trade. Occasionally includes data on business and finance, and on book sales, production, and consumer expenditures. Data are based on original surveys and other commercial and Federal sources.

General format:

a. Narrative features and editorial depts, including book reviews and bestseller lists; and annual articles reporting book trade statistics.

b. Irregularly recurring table, entitled "A Look at the Books," showing financial performance of 1-10 publishing companies, generally for most recent quarter reported and year to date, with comparisons to same periods of previous year.

c. Monthly "Gallup Survey," by Leonard A. Wood, on book purchasing habits and consumer characteristics, based on surveys conducted by the Gallup Organization.

d. Quarterly article on book publishing industry sales and consumer expenditures on books.

A semiannual index is published in Feb. and Aug. issues.

All features with substantial statistical content are described, as they appear, under "Statistical Features;" page locations and latest periods of coverage for recurring table are also noted. Non-statistical features and issues are not covered.

Availability: R. R. Bowker Co., Publishers Weekly, Subscription Department, PO Box 1428, Riverton NJ 08077-9964, $84.00 per yr., single copy $2.00, announcement issues $4.95; SRI/MF/not filmed.

Issues reviewed during 1985: Nov. 2, 1984-Oct. 25, 1985 (P) (Vol. 226, Nos. 18-25; Vol. 227, Nos. 1-26; Vol. 228, Nos. 1-17) [Vol. 226, No. 22 incorrectly reads No. 21; Vol. 228, No. 1 incorrectly reads Vol. 227, No. 27].

STATISTICAL FEATURES:

C1650–2.601: Nov. 9, 1984 (Vol. 226, No. 19)

RECURRING TABLE

(p. 16) Look at the books, for 9 months or quarter ended Aug. 31 or Sept. 30, 1984.

C1650–2.602: Nov. 23, 1984 (Vol. 226, No. 21)

RECURRING TABLE

(p. 18) Look at the books, for quarter and 9 months ended Sept. 30, 1984.

GALLUP SURVEY, MONTHLY FEATURE

(p. 19) Monthly survey article, with 2 tables showing responses concerning influence of author familiarity on book purchases, and incidence of recent book purchases, by sex, education, and subject category. Surveys were conducted 1983-84.

INFORMATION STORAGE AND RETRIEVAL: A WEALTH OF NEW CHOICES EMERGES

(p. 36-42) By Steven Sieck. Article, with 1 table showing top 20 online information system companies ranked by revenue, and also including number of subscribers, 1983 with comparisons to 1982. Data are from LINK Resources Corp.

PC SOFTWARE AND ONLINE DATABASES: TODAY, THEY'RE THE MIDDLE OF THE ACTION

(p. 44-48) By Haines B. Gaffner. Article on growth of microcomputer software and online database markets. Data are from LINK Resources Corp. Includes 1 chart and 1 table showing total software and online database revenues, and revenues or market share by application, various years 1983-89.

C1650–2.603: Nov. 30, 1984 (Vol. 226, No. 22)

[Contents page incorrectly reads No. 21.]

THIRD QUARTER SALES: SLUGGISH AND DISAPPOINTING, QUARTERLY FEATURE

(p. 34) Quarterly article, by John P. Dessauer, on book industry sales in 3rd quarter 1984. Includes 2 tables showing estimated net sales quantity and value by type of book, and consumer expenditures on books by type of sales outlet, 3rd quarter and 1st 9 months 1983-84.

COMMUNICATIONS TRENDS STUDY PREDICTS SOFTWARE SALE INCREASES IN BOOKSTORES

(p. 56) By Martha Moutray-Kinney. Article, with 1 table forecasting bookstore sales of microcomputer software vs. total sales, 1984-85. Data are from Communications Trends, Inc.

C1650–2.604: Dec. 7, 1984 (Vol. 226, No. 23)

RETAILING OF COMPUTER MAGAZINES, 1984

(p. 56-57) By Efrem Sigel. Article, with 2 tables showing circulation and single-copy sales of 8 leading computer magazines, 1st-2nd half 1983 and 1st half 1984. Data were compiled by Communications Trends from Audit Bureau of Circulation and other sources.

C1650–2.605: Dec. 14, 1984 (Vol. 226, No. 24)

PUBLISHING LAGS IN COMMUNICATIONS INDUSTRY, INVESTMENT REPORT SAYS

(p. 14) Brief article, with 3 tables showing top 10 publishing companies ranked by revenues and growth rate 1983, and by compound annual growth rate for 1979-83 period. Data are from Veronis, Suhler & Associates.

GALLUP SURVEY, MONTHLY FEATURE

(p. 18) Monthly survey article, with 4 tables showing responses concerning incidence of book purchasing, by age and subject category 1984, with projections for 1990 by age. Survey covered over 9,000 adults and was conducted Jan.-Sept. 1984.

C1650–2.606: Jan. 4, 1985 (Vol. 227, No. 1)

LONGEST-RUNNING HARDCOVER AND PAPERBACK BESTSELLERS FOR 1984, ANNUAL FEATURE

(p. 36-37) Two annual lists of bestselling books in rank order, showing title, author, publisher, price, number of weeks on the 1983 and 1984 bestseller lists, and date published, for fiction and nonfiction hardcover, and mass market and trade paperback books.

NO PAPER SHORTAGES SEEN FOR 1985 AS CAPACITY GROWS

(p. 41, 44) Article, with 1 table showing paper, paperboard, and wood pulp capacity additions, by grade, 1975-84 and 1985-87 periods. Data are from American Paper Institute.

C1650–2.607: Jan. 18, 1985 (Vol. 227, No. 3)

RECURRING TABLE

(p. 30) Look at the books, for quarter and 6 or 9 months ended Sept. 30 or Oct. 31, 1984.

C1650–2.608: Feb. 8, 1985 (Vol. 227, No. 6)

GALLUP SURVEY, MONTHLY FEATURE

(p. 31) Monthly survey article, with 3 tables showing responses concerning incidence of paperback book purchasing by price range, number of purchases and average price paid, and share of purchases made at discount prices, by subject category; and share of hardcover books purchased at discount prices; 1984 with some quarterly detail. Surveys were conducted monthly during 1984 and covered a total of 12,386 adults.

C1650–2.609: Feb. 15, 1985 (Vol. 227, No. 7)

VIDEOCASSETTE BUSINESS: IS THERE A VCR IN YOUR FUTURE?

(p. 36-51, passim) By Linda Sunshine. Article, with 2 text tables showing number of households with TVs and videocassette recorders, and value of videocassette retail sales and rentals, various years 1982-88. Data are from F. Eberstadt & Co. and *Video Marketing Newsletter.*

C1650–2.610: Mar. 1, 1985 (Vol. 227, No. 9)

RECURRING TABLE

(p. 25) Look at the books, for quarter and year ended Dec. 31, 1984.

C1650–2.611: Mar. 15, 1985 (Vol. 227, No. 11)

RECURRING TABLE

(p. 21) Look at the books, for various periods ending Nov. 30, 1984-Jan. 31, 1985.

1984: THE YEAR IN REVIEW, ANNUAL FEATURE

Annual collection of articles reviewing publishing industry trends, for 1984. Articles containing substantial statistics are described below.

HARDCOVER BESTSELLERS, ANNUAL FEATURE

(p. 32-36) Annual article, by Daisy Maryles, with 1 list showing title, publisher, and copies sold, for top 15 fiction and 15 nonfiction hardcover bestsellers, 1984. Covers books published in 1983 or 1984.

PAPERBACK TOP SELLERS, ANNUAL FEATURE

(p. 36-42) Annual article, by Sally A. Lodge, with 4 lists showing title, publisher, and copies in print, for mass market paperbacks with over 1 million copies in print; mass market titles issued or reissued in conjunction with TV or movie productions; trade paperbacks with shipments of over 50,000 copies; and almanacs, atlases, and annuals; 1984. Covers paperbacks published or reprinted in 1983 or 1984.

TITLE OUTPUT AND AVERAGE PRICES: 1984 PRELIMINARY FIGURES, ANNUAL FEATURE

(p. 52-55) Annual article, by Chandler B. Grannis, on book production and prices, by book type and subject area, 1984 and trends. Data are derived from computer analysis of listings in *Paperbound Books in Print* and *Weekly Record/American Book Publishing Record,* published by R. R. Bowker.

Includes 9 tables showing hardbound and paperbound new books and new editions published, imported titles, total value, and average price, by subject area, various years 1972-84.

C1650–2.612: Mar. 29, 1985 (Vol. 227, No. 13)

GALLUP SURVEY, MONTHLY FEATURE

(p. 24) Monthly survey article, with 3 tables showing responses concerning incidence of book purchasing via book clubs and mail order, by book type, nonfiction subject category, and purchaser characteristics, 1984. Surveys were conducted monthly during 1984 and covered a total of 12,386 adults.

FOURTH QUARTER 1984 SALES: A WEAK FINISH, QUARTERLY FEATURE

(p. 26) Quarterly article, by John P. Dessauer, on book industry sales in 4th quarter 1984. Includes 2 tables showing estimated net sales quantity and value by type of book, and consumer expenditures on books by type of sales outlet, 4th quarter and full year 1983-84. Data are from *Book Industry Trends.*

C1650–2.613: Apr. 26, 1985 (Vol. 227, No. 17)

RECURRING TABLE

(p. 21) Look at the books, for various periods ending Dec. 31, 1984-Feb. 28, 1985.

C1650–2.614: May 17, 1985 (Vol. 227, No. 20)

GALLUP SURVEY, MONTHLY FEATURE

(p. 26) Monthly survey article, with 5 tables showing responses concerning incidence of book purchasing, by outlet type and fiction subject category, and for religious books; and average price paid, and share of purchases made at discount prices; all by region, 1984. Surveys were conducted monthly during 1984 and covered a total of 12,386 adults.

BOOK BUYING BARELY UP IN SCHOOL LIBRARIES

(p. 32) Brief article, with 1 undated table showing total and per pupil median and mean expenditures for books, periodicals, and audiovisual materials in school library media centers, by educational level. Data are from 1,093 responses to a recent survey published by *School Library Journal.*

SOFTWARE ADVERTISING: THE END OF THE BIG BUDGET?

(p. 53-58, passim) By Efrem Sigel. Article, with 5 tables showing retail and wholesale computer software sales for total and home applications; revenues, and advertising budgets with some detail by media, for 5 leading business and home computer software companies; and advertising pages in 5 general computer magazines; various periods 1982-85. Data are from Communications Trends, Inc.

C1650–2.615: June 7, 1985 (Vol. 227, No. 23)

FIRST QUARTER SALES ERRATIC, QUARTERLY FEATURE

(p. 34) Quarterly article, by John P. Dessauer, on book industry sales in 1st quarter 1985. Includes 2 tables showing estimated net sales quantity and value by type of book, and consumer expenditures on books by type of sales outlet, 1st quarter 1984-85.

C1650–2.616: June 14, 1985 (Vol. 227, No. 24)

RECURRING TABLE

(p. 30) Look at the books, for quarter ended Mar. 31, 1985.

GALLUP SURVEY, MONTHLY FEATURE

(p. 40) Monthly survey article, with 3 tables showing responses concerning socioeconomic characteristics of frequent book buyers, and subject categories purchased. Surveys were conducted monthly during 1984 and covered a total of 12,386 adults.

C1650–2.617: June 28, 1985 (Vol. 227, No. 26)

ESTIMATED BOOK PUBLISHING INDUSTRY SALES, ANNUAL FEATURE

(p. 21) Annual table showing book publishing industry sales revenues, by type of publisher, 1972, 1977, and 1982-84. Data are from Assn of American Publishers (AAP).

Previous feature is described in SRI 1984 Annual under C1650-2.523. Full AAP report, *Industry Statistics,* is covered by SRI under A3274-2.

C1650–2.618: July 26, 1985 (Vol. 228, No. 4)

GALLUP SURVEY, MONTHLY FEATURE

(p. 96) Monthly survey article, with 2 tables showing responses of mothers of preschool-age children concerning frequency of borrowing children's books from public library, by mother's education and by age of oldest preschool child; and age to begin reading to a child, by mother's education. Survey was conducted May 2-15, 1985, and included responses from 792 mothers.

This is the first in a series of 3 articles on children's books. For description of the 2nd article, see C1650-2.624.

C1650–2.619: Aug. 9, 1985 (Vol. 228, No. 6)

RECURRING TABLE

(p. 21) Look at the books, for quarter and 6 months or year ended Apr. 30 or June 30, 1985.

C1650–2.620: Aug. 23, 1985 (Vol. 228, No. 8)

RECURRING TABLE

(p. 21) Look at the books, for 3 months ended May 31, 1985, and quarter and 6 months ended June 30, 1985.

TITLE OUTPUT AND AVERAGE PRICES: 1984 FINAL FIGURES, ANNUAL FEATURE

(p. 41-44) Annual article, by Chandler B. Grannis, on book production and prices, 1984 and trends. Data are derived from *Paperbound Books in Print, Publishers Weekly,* and *Weekly Record,* all published by R. R. Bowker Co.

Includes 9 tables showing hardbound and paperbound new books and new editions published, and total and average prices, by subject area or Dewey Decimal classification, with selected detail for mass market and trade paperbacks, and imported titles, various years 1977-84.

Sept. 6, 1985 issue includes data corrections; for description see C1650-2.621, below.

C1650–2.621: Sept. 6, 1985 (Vol. 228, No. 10)

CORRECTION

(p. 13) Includes corrected data for annual article on book production and average prices, described under C1650-2.620.

SECOND QUARTER SALES SHOW LITTLE IMPROVEMENT, QUARTERLY FEATURE

(p. 24) Quarterly article, by John P. Dessauer, on book industry sales in 2nd quarter 1985. Includes 2 tables showing estimated net sales quantity and value by type of book, and consumer expenditures on books by type of sales outlet, 1st-2nd quarters 1984-85.

C1650–2.622: Sept. 13, 1985 (Vol. 228, No. 11)

U.S. EXPORTS, IMPORTS, UNESCO REPORTS, ANNUAL FEATURE

(p. 96-98) Annual article, by Chandler B. Grannis, with 4 tables showing volume and/or value of U.S. book exports and imports, by book category and principal country; and title output, by country; various years 1980-84. Data are from Commerce Dept, UNESCO, and R. R. Bowker Co.

C1650–2.623: Sept. 20, 1985 (Vol. 228, No. 12)

GALLUP SURVEY, MONTHLY FEATURE

(p. 63-64) Monthly survey article, with 7 tables showing responses concerning cookbook ownership, recent purchases, and price paid, by type of cookbook and respondent characteristics. Survey was conducted June 24-July 21, 1985, and included responses from 792 women.

C1650–2.624: Oct. 4, 1985 (Vol. 228, No. 14)

RECURRING TABLE

(p. 18) Look at the books, for quarter ended June 30, or July 31, 1985.

GALLUP SURVEY, MONTHLY FEATURE

(p. 21) Monthly survey article, with 2 tables showing responses of mothers of preschool-age children concerning types of books read to children and use of familiar vs. newer/modern books; shown by mother's age and education, age of oldest preschool child, region, and/or frequency of reading to child. Survey was conducted May 3-12, 1985, and included responses from 792 mothers.

This is the second in a series of 3 articles on children's books. For description of the 1st article, see C1650-2.618, above.

C1650–3   BOWKER ANNUAL OF LIBRARY AND BOOK TRADE INFORMATION, 30th Edition, 1985

Annual. 1985. xii+768 p.
ISSN 0068-0540.
ISBN 0-8352-1975-5.
LC 55-12434.
SRI/MF/not filmed

Annual compilation of articles and statistics relating to library, book trade, and information industry activities during 1984. Also includes directories of library and related organizations. Data are from R. R. Bowker Co., NCES, *American Library Directory,* library assns, and other Federal and private research services.

Contents:

Contents listing and preface. (p. v-xii)

Part 1. Reports from the Field. 35 articles on industry news, library services, Federal agencies and libraries, and activities of national assns. (p. 3-230)

Part 2. Legislation, Funding, and Grants. 9 articles on legislation affecting information science and publishing; and on Federal and foundation funding to libraries. (p. 233-314)

Part 3. Library/Information Science Education, Placement, and Salaries. 7 articles on placement and salaries of librarians, lists of accredited library schools, and library scholarship sources and awards. (p. 317-395)

Part 4. Research and Statistics. 16 articles and statistics on number and types of libraries, library operations and building construction, and book publishing and distribution. (p. 399-499)

Part 5-6. Reference Information and Directory of Organizations. Includes bibliographies; 1984 book awards and best-sellers; directory of library, book trade, and related organizations; calendar of 1985/86 library activities; and index. (p. 503-768)

Articles with statistics are described below.

Availability: R. R. Bowker Co., PO Box 1385, Ann Arbor MI 41806, $69.95; SRI/MF/not filmed.

STATISTICAL ARTICLES:
[Data by State generally include D.C. and outlying areas.]

C1650–3.1: Part 1: Reports from the Field

a. "Federal Library and Information Center Committee (FLICC)," by James P. Riley. Includes 1 table showing number of interagency agreements for Federal library/information center use of online information retrieval services, by service, FY80-84. The agreements involve participants in the Federal Library and Information Network (FEDLINK). (p. 140-146)

b. "National Agricultural Library," by Eugene M. Farkas. Includes 1 table showing additions to collection, and technical and service activities, FY84-86. (p. 155-159)

c. "National Library of Medicine," by Robert B. Mehnert. Includes 1 table showing holdings, titles received and cataloged, circulation and interlibrary loan transactions, and computer searching activities, FY84. (p. 159-163)

C1650–3.2: Part 2: Legislation, Funding, and Grants

LEGISLATION

a. "Legislation and Regulations Affecting Libraries in 1984," by Eileen D. Cooke and Carol C. Henderson. Includes 3 tables showing appropriations for Federal library and library-related programs, FY84-85; Library Service and Construction Act funding authorization levels, FY84-89; and status of library legislation, as of Oct. 12, 1984. (p. 233-247)

FUNDING AND GRANTS

b. "Council on Library Resources, Inc.," by Jane A. Rosenberg. Includes listing of grants awarded to CLR supported projects, showing amount, recipient, and type of program, FY83-84. (p. 265-271)

c. "U.S. Dept of Education Library Programs, 1984," by Ray M. Fry. Includes 12 tables on library programs administered by Dept of Education, showing the following: available funds, by program; literacy and research/demonstration projects and funding; library career training fellowships (number and amount), by institution, with summary by academic level and total institutions recruiting minorities; and research library grants, by institution and type of activity; various fiscal or academic years 1966-84. (p. 271-298)

d. "Education Consolidation and Improvement Act of 1981, Chapter 2: Year Three," by Phyllis Land Usher. Includes 1 table showing ECIA Chapter 2 allotments, by State, FY86. (p. 299-301)

e. "National Endowment for the Humanities Support for Libraries, 1984." Includes 1 table showing amount, institution, and subject of 8 NEH library awards, Dec. 1984. (p. 301-308)

f. "National Science Foundation Support for Research in Information Science and Technology, 1984," by Charles N. Brownstein. Includes text data showing amount, recipient, and subject of library-related research sponsored by NSF, FY84. (p. 309-310)

g. "Foundation Grants to Libraries, 1984." Includes 3 tables showing number and amount of grants awarded by 12 leading library funders; and largest grants to libraries and leading recipients, 1982-83. (p. 311-314)

C1650–3.3: Part 3: Library/Information Science Education, Placement, and Salaries

a. "Alternative Careers for Librarians," by Betty-Carol Sellen and Susan J. Vaughn. Includes 9 tables on characteristics of graduate librarians working outside libraries, including type of employer and work activity, salary, method of job acquisition, and academic background. Data are based on 487 responses to a 1981 survey. (p. 331-337)

b. "Placements and Salaries, 1983: Catching Up," by Carol L. Learmont and Stephen Van Houten. Includes 13 tables showing the following data, by sex, for 1983 graduates of library schools in U.S. and Canada: employment status as of spring 1984, by U.S. region; placements and salary ranges, by placing school, type of library, and U.S. region, with summary trends from 1950s; special placements, by type; and salaries with and without previous experience. (p. 356-371)

c. "Jobs Gone Begging: Personnel Needs and Youth Services," by Richard Ashford. Includes 2 charts and 4 tables showing New England job vacancies in library/information science, by specialization and type of employer; average advertised salary, by type of employer; and demand for librarians by library function; 1980-83. (p. 371-381)

d. "Library Scholarship and Award Recipients, 1984." List of awards showing amount, purpose, donor, and recipient, by award name. (p. 387-395)

C1650–3.4: Part 4: Research and Statistics

LIBRARY RESEARCH AND STATISTICS

a. "Analysis of Library Data Collection and Development of Plans for the Future: A Project Summary," by Mary Jo Lynch. Includes 1 undated table showing types of public library operating data collected by State library agencies. (p. 405-411)

b. "NCES Survey of Public Libraries, 1982," by Robert A. Heintze. Includes 9 tables showing the following for public libraries: service outlets by type; libraries, professional and other staff, attendance, and circulation, by size of population served; professional staff by degree level; receipts by source and expenditures by category; computer use; days open by urban-rural status; and volumes held and added; mostly for 1982. (p. 412-417)

c. "Academic Research Libraries: Recent Studies," by Kendon L. Stubbs. Includes 1 table ranking 181 academic libraries by a score indicating their qualification as research facilities, 1978/79. The score is based on several quantitative variables, including collection and staff size. (p. 417-425)

d. "Bowker National Library Microcomputer Usage Study, 1984," by Terri Mitchem. Includes 10 tables showing number of libraries using microcomputers; microcomputers installed, and market share by brand; microcomputer purchase plans, and availability for public/student use; software lending to public/students, including on- and off-site use, number of packages, and most requested titles; and library use of software, including types of functions and suppliers; all by type of library, generally for midyear 1984. (p. 426-434)

e. "Selected Characteristics of the U.S. Population," by W. Vance Grant. Table showing resident population in U.S. and outlying areas, and armed forces serving abroad; population by age, education, and metro-nonmetro and employment status; public and private school enrollment, by level; and higher education faculty and students; 1984 or latest available date. (p. 434-435)

f. "Number of Libraries in the U.S. and Canada." Table showing number of libraries in the U.S., U.S.-administered areas, and Canada, by detailed type, 1984. (p. 435-437)

g. "Public and Academic Library Acquisition Expenditures, 1983/84." Includes 2 tables showing public and college/university library acquisition expenditures by type, and number of libraries, by State, 1983/84. (p. 437-442)

h. "Price Indexes for School and Academic Library Acquisitions," by D. Kent Halstead. Includes 2 tables showing average prices and price indexes for elementary and secondary, and college/university library materials, by type, FY75-84. (p. 442-446)

i. "Library Buildings in 1984," by Bette-Lee Fox. Includes 7 tables showing new construction and renovation costs, square footage, capacity, and architect, for public libraries by city (arranged by State and Canada Province), and academic libraries by institution, with funding by government level and from gift sources for public libraries; FY84 and summary trends from 1974. (p. 446-458)

BOOK PUBLISHING STATISTICS

j. "Book Title Output and Average Prices, 1984 Preliminary Figures," by Chandler B. Grannis. Includes 9 tables showing number of domestic and imported new books and editions, paperback titles, and average hardcover and paperback prices, mostly by subject, various years 1977-84; and average book prices from *Publishers Weekly* fall announcement ads, 1972-84. (p. 459-468)

k. "Book Sales Statistics: Highlights from Assn of American Publishers, 1983," by Chandler B. Grannis. Includes 1 table estimating book publishing sales, by industry segment, selected years 1972-83. (p. 469-470)

l. "Prices of U.S. and Foreign Published Materials," by Dennis E. Smith. Includes 15 tables showing average prices and/or price indexes for U.S. periodicals and serial services, hardcover books, paperbacks, nonprint materials, library microfilm, college books, and newspapers; and for total North American academic books, and books published in UK, Germany, and 26 Latin American countries and areas; with selected detail by subject area, various years 1977-84. (p. 471-488)

m. "U.S. Book Exports and Imports and International Title Output," by Chandler B. Grannis. Includes 4 tables showing quantity and/or value of U.S. book imports and exports, by type and country; and book production, by country; various years 1979-83. (p. 489-492)

n. "British Book Production, 1984." Includes 3 tables showing UK book title output, by subject, 1983-84, with summary trends from 1947. (p. 493-497)

o. "Number of Book Outlets in the U.S. and Canada." Includes 2 tables showing bookstores by type, and general and paperback wholesalers, for the U.S. and Canada, 1984. (p. 497-498)

p. "Book Review Media Statistics." Table showing number of books reviewed by specific publications, 1983-84. (p. 499)

C1750
Broadcasting Publications

C1750–1 **BROADCASTING**
Weekly.
ISSN 0007-2028.
LC 33-14221.
SRI/MF/excerpts, shipped quarterly

Weekly trade journal (combined issue at year end) of the radio and TV broadcasting industry, presenting news, feature articles, and statistics on broadcaster financial condition, network and program ratings, advertising investment, Government regulation, and other topics.

Data are from Federal Government, private research firms, advertising agencies, individual companies, and the journal's own research.

Each issue contains narrative articles, occasionally with statistics; and numerous editorial depts, including stock and earnings data for broadcasting-related companies. Recurring statistical features include the following:

a. Weekly table on TV program ratings, usually in "Programming" section, showing network, rating, and share, for all prime time TV programs for week ended 1 week preceding publication.

b. Weekly "Summary of Broadcasting" table, usually in "For the Record" section, showing stations licensed/on the air and with construction permits, and total authorized, by type of station, for most recent date reported by FCC; data for same dates frequently appear in more than 1 weekly issue.

c. Other features, including recurring articles on prime time audience of commercial TV networks, and advertising on independent TV stations; and numerous annual features, including advertising billings and expenditures, and broadcasting industry finances.

Weekly tables appear in most issues. All additional features with substantial statistical content are described, as they appear, under "Statistical Features." Nonstatistical features are not covered.

Availability: Broadcasting, 1735 DeSales St., NW, Washington DC 20036, $65.00 per yr., single copy $2.00, special issues $3.50; SRI/MF/excerpts for weekly tables and all portions covered under "Statistical Features;" shipped quarterly.

Issues reviewed during 1985: Nov. 5, 1984-Oct. 28, 1985 (P) (Vol. 107, Nos. 19-26; Vol. 108, Nos. 1-25; Vol. 109, Nos. 1-18).

STATISTICAL FEATURES:

C1750–1.601: Nov. 19, 1984 (Vol. 107, No. 21)
VS&A RANKS FINANCIAL HEALTH OF MEDIA

(p. 72, 75-76) Article, with 1 table showing growth in revenues, operating income, cash flow, and assets, and other financial ratios, for the broadcasting industry, also including rank among 10 selected segments of the communications industry, 1979-83 period and/or 1983. Data are from Veronis, Suhler and Associates.

C1750–1.602: Nov. 26, 1984 (Vol. 107, No. 22)
BUSY YEAR

(p. 54) Brief article, with 5 tables showing advertising expenditures as follows: for network and spot TV, by day part, 3rd quarter and 1st 9 months 1983-84; and by major network, 1st 3 quarters 1984. Data are from TV Bureau of Advertising, based on data from Broadcast Advertisers Reports, Inc.

TRACKING INDIES, RECURRING FEATURE

(p. 56-57) Recurring article, with 3 tables showing independent TV stations' share of spot advertising expenditures, for top 20-25 advertisers and product categories ranked by total spot advertising expenditures, and for top 25 advertisers ranked by expenditures with independent stations, 1st 9 months 1984.

Data were compiled by Assn of Independent TV Stations, based on data from Broadcast Advertisers Reports, Inc. Data correction appears in the Dec. 3, 1984 issue (see C1750-1.603 below).

C1750–1.603: Dec. 3, 1984 (Vol. 107, No. 23)
ERRATA

(p. 24) Data correction for recurring article on independent TV stations' share of advertising expenditures. Article appears in the Nov. 26, 1984 issue (for description, see C1750-1.602 above).

C1750–1.604: Jan. 7, 1985 (Vol. 108, No. 1)
CBS WINS; NBC POSTS BIG GAIN IN NOV. SWEEPS, RECURRING FEATURE

(p. 51-53) Recurring article, with 1 table comparing prime time audience of the 3 commercial TV networks, by Arbitron area of dominant influence (ADI), Nov. 1984. Table shows results of Arbitron sweep reports as compiled by NBC.

CABLE STOCKS TURNING IN STRONG PERFORMANCE

(p. 164-174, passim) Article, with 2 tables showing the following for 7 major cable TV multiple system operators: stock owned by institutional investors (amount and as percent of shares outstanding), as of Sept. 30, 1984, with percent change from Dec. 31, 1983; and stock prices, (with comparison to Standard & Poor's 500), May 31, 1984 and Jan. 2, 1985. Data are from CDA Investment Technologies, and *Broadcasting*.

C1750–1.605: Jan. 28, 1985 (Vol. 108, No. 4)
CHANGING HANDS 1984: BROADCAST STATION SALES TOP $2 BILLION; ACTIVE YEAR FOR CABLE TRANSACTIONS, ANNUAL FEATURE

(p. 45-75) Annual report on broadcasting ownership changes in 1984. Contains narrative summary of individual transactions, including stations, owners, and dollar amounts involved; and 1 table (p. 46) showing total transaction value and number of stations involved in ownership changes, for radio, TV, and combined radio/TV, 1954-84.

Corrected data appear in the Feb. 4 and Feb. 11, 1985 issues (see C1750-1.606 and C1750-1.607 below).

EXPLORING THE OPTIONS OF 12/25%

(p. 91-92) Article, with 1 undated table showing the following for 10 major TV station owners: number of VHF and UHF stations owned, and stations' aggregate share of total TV households. Data are from *Broadcasting* and Arbitron Co.

C1750–1.606: Feb. 4, 1985 (Vol. 108, No. 5)
ERRATA

(p. 23) Includes data correction for annual feature on broadcasting ownership changes.

For description of feature, see C1750-1.605 above.

TOP 50 FIFTH ESTATE AGENCIES POST 15% BILLINGS RISE IN '84, ANNUAL FEATURE

(p. 39-49) Annual report on top 50 advertising agencies ranked by broadcast/cable billings, 1984. Data are based on a *Broadcasting* survey.

Contains narrative summary; brief profile of each agency; and 1 table showing each agency's broadcast billings (total, for cable TV, and for network and spot TV and radio), and broadcast billings as percent of all billings, 1984 with selected comparisons to 1983.

This is the 33rd annual report.

C1750–1.607: Feb. 11, 1985 (Vol. 108, No. 6)
ERRATA

(p. 25) Includes data correction for annual feature on broadcasting ownership changes.

For description of feature, see C1750-1.605 above.

YEAR-END RESULTS

(p. 64) Table showing network radio advertising billings, monthly 1983-84. Data are from Radio Network Assn, based on figures supplied by Ernst and Whinney.

C1750–1.608: Feb. 18, 1985 (Vol. 108, No. 7)

ABC, CBS REPORT DROP IN EARNINGS IN FOURTH QUARTER

(p. 56) Article, with 1 table showing operating profit margins for the 3 major network broadcasting companies, 1979-84. Data are from company reports.

Correction appears in the Feb. 25, 1985 issue (see C1750-1.609 below).

C1750–1.609: Feb. 25, 1985 (Vol. 108, No. 8)

ERRATA

(p. 33) Correction for article on profits of 3 major broadcasting companies. For description of article, see C1750-1.608 above.

TOP 10 STATS, RECURRING FEATURE

(p. 66) Recurring brief article, with 1 table showing spot radio advertising billings, by market size group, 1983-84. Data are from Radio Expenditure Reports, Inc.

C1750–1.610: Mar. 4, 1985 (Vol. 108, No. 9)

BASEBALL 1985, ANNUAL FEATURE

(p. 43-62) Annual article on payments by radio and TV networks and stations for the rights to broadcast major league baseball games. Includes 1 table showing TV and radio rights holders, number of affiliates, and broadcast rights payments for 1984-85, by baseball team, arranged by league and division.

C1750–1.611: Mar. 18, 1985 (Vol. 108, No. 11)

BATES SURVEY SHOWS MEDIA COSTS OUTPACING INFLATION, ANNUAL FEATURE

(p. 48-49) Annual article on media advertising price trends. Data are from Ted Bates Advertising. Includes 3 tables showing advertising cost and national expenditure indexes, by media, with comparison to CPI, 1976-84 or 1976-85.

INTV LOGS SPOT DOLLARS OF TOP ADVERTISERS, RECURRING FEATURE

(p. 50) Recurring article, with 3 tables showing independent TV stations' share of spot advertising expenditures, for top 20-25 advertisers and product categories ranked by total spot advertising expenditures, and for top 25 advertisers ranked by expenditures with independent stations, 1984.

Data were compiled by Assn of Independent TV Stations, based on data from Broadcast Advertisers Reports, Inc.

C1750–1.612: Mar. 25, 1985 (Vol. 108, No. 12)

UNCERTAIN WORLD OF REGIONAL CABLE SPORTS NETWORKS

(p. 42-50) Article, with 1 undated table showing the following for 15 regional cable TV sports networks: startup date, type of service, number of affiliates and subscribers, and professional teams covered.

C1750–1.613: Apr. 1, 1985 (Vol. 108, No. 13)

FEB. SWEEP NUMBERS SHOW STRIDES NBC HAS MADE, RECURRING FEATURE

(p. 72-74) Recurring article, with 1 table comparing prime time audience of the 3 commercial TV networks, by Arbitron area of dominant influence (ADI), Feb. 1985. Table shows results of Arbitron sweep reports as compiled by CBS.

C1750–1.614: Apr. 8, 1985 (Vol. 108, No. 14)

TV AD TALLY, ANNUAL FEATURE

(p. 140) Annual brief article, with 2 tables showing top 25 network and national/regional spot TV advertisers ranked by 1984 expenditures, with comparison to 1983. Data are from TV Bureau of Advertising, based on Broadcast Advertisers Reports data.

For description of 1983 rankings, see SRI 1984 Annual under C1750-1.510 and C1750-1.512.

'WHEEL OF FORTUNE' WIDENS LEAD IN CASSANDRA REPORT, RECURRING FEATURE

(p. 148-149) Recurring article, with 1 table ranking syndicated TV programs broadcast in 25/more markets by rating, and including number of markets, Feb. 1985 with comparison to Nov. and Feb. 1984. Data are from A. C. Nielsen Co.

C1750–1.615: Apr. 15, 1985 (Vol. 108, No. 15)

STEREO ON THE POTOMAC

(p. 146-147) Brief article, with 1 undated table showing TV stations equipped for broadcasting in multichannel stereo sound, including stereo start-up date and hours per week broadcast in true stereo.

C1750–1.616: Apr. 22, 1985 (Vol. 108, No. 16)

RAB REVIEWS

(p. 100) Brief article, with 1 table showing radio billings for top 10 advertising agencies ranked by radio share of total billings, 1984. Data are from Radio Advertising Bureau.

C1750–1.617: May 6, 1985 (Vol. 108, No. 18)

TOP 100 COMPANIES IN ELECTRONIC COMMUNICATIONS, ANNUAL FEATURE

(p. 47-53) Annual report on revenues and earnings of 100 largest publicly owned companies in broadcasting and related electronic communication fields, 1984. Data are from Broadcasting.

Includes 1 table showing the following, by company: total revenues and earnings, profit margin, earnings per share, price/earnings ratio, electronic communication share of total revenues, and rankings for total and electronic communication revenues, 1984 with selected comparisons to 1983.

C1750–1.618: May 13, 1985 (Vol. 108, No. 19)

ERRATA

(p. 22) Includes title correction for weekly table on TV program ratings appearing in the May 6, 1985 issue.

SPACE WARC PRIMED TO MAKE HISTORY

(p. 82-90) Article on preparations for an international conference on fixed communications satellite services. Data are from International Telecommunications Union and other sources. Includes 2 tables showing number of satellites in orbit, announced, and being coordinated, all by type and orbital slot, 1984.

C1750–1.619: May 27, 1985 (Vol. 108, No. 21)

KEEPING SCORE AS THE BIG GET BIGGER

(p. 35-36) Article, with 1 table ranking top 20 TV station companies by total market share, and also showing the following for each station owned: share of U.S. market, metro area of operation, and the area's rank among Arbitron's Areas of Dominant Influence; 1985. Data were compiled by Broadcasting, and reflect proposed mergers and sales.

C1750–1.620: June 3, 1985 (Vol. 108, No. 22)

STEREO SOUND STILL A QUESTION MARK FOR CABLE

(p. 59-60) Article on cable TV systems' ability to carry stereo broadcasts. Data are primarily from Arbitron Co. Includes 1 table showing the following for TV market areas with stations broadcasting in stereo: market rank among Areas of Dominant Influence, 1983/84; call letters and network affiliation of stations with stereo (no date); and number of cable TV households, May 1985.

BROADCASTING'S TOP 50 MSOs, ANNUAL FEATURE

(p. 76) Annual table on the top 50 cable multiple system operators (MSOs), showing the following for each operator: basic subscribers, homes passed, basic penetration, pay subscriptions, and total homes in franchised areas, mostly as of Apr. 30, 1985.

Additional data appear in June 17, 1985 issue (see C1750-1.622 below)

C1750–1.621: June 10, 1985 (Vol. 108, No. 23)

FIFTH ESTATERS SORT OUT TAX PROPOSAL

(p. 110-113) Article, with 1 table showing effective income tax rates (statutory rate less deductions/credits), for 17 major communications industry corporations, 1984.

C1750–1.622: June 17, 1985 (Vol. 108, No. 24)

ERRATA

(p. 23) Includes additional data for annual table on top 50 multiple system operators.

For table description, see C1750-1.620 above.

RADIO LISTENING PROFILES

(p. 59) Two charts showing FM and AM radio audience shares among persons age 12/over, by age group and day-part, spring 1985. Data were compiled by NBC Radio Research, based on data from Statistical Research Inc.

C1750–1.623: June 24, 1985 (Vol. 108, No. 25)

INTV 1st-QUARTER UPDATE, RECURRING FEATURE

(p. 52) Recurring article, with 3 tables showing independent TV stations' share of spot advertising expenditures, for top 20-25 advertisers and product categories ranked by total spot advertising expenditures, 1st quarter 1985 with comparison to 1984.

Data were compiled by Assn of Independent TV Stations, based on data from Broadcast Advertisers Reports, Inc.

C1750–1.624: July 1, 1985 (Vol. 109, No. 1)

NETWORK'S UPFRONT SALES OFF AND RUNNING

(p. 29) Article, with 1 table showing estimated cost for a 30-second advertising spot on selected TV network programs, 1985/86 season.

C1750–1.625: July 8, 1985 (Vol. 109, No. 2)

SATELLITE SUPPLY AND DEMAND LAWS BENEFITING USERS

(p. 46-50) Article, with 1 table showing the following for 23 orbiting communications satellites, arranged by corporate owner: number of transponders by type, orbital slots, and launch dates. Covers launchings from June 1978-May 1985.

Corrected data appear in the Aug. 5, 1985 issue (see C1750-1.628 below).

C1750–1.626: July 15, 1985 (Vol. 109, No. 3)

'WHEEL OF FORTUNE' CONTINUES CASSANDRA DOMINANCE, RECURRING FEATURE

(p. 36-38) Recurring article, with 1 table ranking syndicated TV programs broadcast in 25/ more markets by rating, and including number of markets, May 1985 with comparison to Feb. 1985, and Nov. and May 1984. Data are from A. C. Nielsen Co.

C1750–1.627: July 22, 1985 (Vol. 109, No. 4)

OPTIMISM ON THE RADIO NETWORK FRONT, ANNUAL FEATURE

(p. 46-50) Annual article, with 1 undated table showing number of affiliates for 16 major radio networks.

SHAKEOUT AFTER THE CHR GOLDRUSH, ANNUAL FEATURE

(p. 54-58) Annual article, with 1 table ranking top 17 radio formats by number of stations using format full-time, as of July 1985. Data are from the Radio Information Center.

STUDY PROJECTS BARTER, CABLE ADVERTISING TO TAKE BITE FROM THREE NETWORKS

(p. 97) Article, with 1 table showing distribution of revenues from network TV advertising and from TV barter syndication, by daypart or program type, 1985. Barter syndication involves a program cost reduction/advertising time control tradeoff between the syndicator and the TV station.

C1750–1.628: Aug. 5, 1985 (Vol. 109, No. 6)

ERRATA

(p. 18) Includes data correction for article on orbiting communications satellites, appearing in the July 8, 1985 issue.

For article description, see C1750-1.625 above.

SPECIAL REPORT: FOOTBALL 1985, ANNUAL FEATURE

(p. 32-40) Annual article on payments and rights to broadcast collegiate and professional football games on radio and TV, 1985.

Includes text data on payments and rights; and 2 tabular lists showing National Football League local/regional coverage by team, including broadcast originator, number of stations, games scheduled, and rights holder, for radio broadcasts of preseason and regular season games and for TV broadcast of preseason games; 1985.

C1750–1.629: Sept. 9, 1985 (Vol. 109, No. 11)

TOP OF THE TOWNS IN RADIO, ANNUAL FEATURE

(p. 35-38) Annual article, with 1 table showing program format and average listening audience of the 10 most popular radio stations in the top 50 markets, based on Arbitron spring 1985 survey.

C1750–1.630: Sept. 16, 1985 (Vol. 109, No. 12)

FALL BRINGS NEW SYNDICATED SHOWS, ANNUAL FEATURE

(p. 52) Annual article, with 1 table showing the following for 28 syndicated TV programs premiering in fall 1985: syndicator and producer, number of TV markets carrying the program and share of TV households, number of original and repeat episodes, and premiere date.

For description of previous feature, see SRI 1984 Annual under C1750-1.529. Additional data appear in the Sept. 30, 1985 issue (see C1750-1.631 below).

C1750–1.631: Sept. 30, 1985 (Vol. 109, No. 14)

ERRATA

(p. 26) Includes additional data for annual feature on syndicated TV programs, appearing in Sept. 16, 1985 issue.

For feature description, see C1750-1.630 above.

C1750–1.632: Oct. 21, 1985 (Vol. 109, No. 17)

FROM 1 TO 214: U.S.A.'s NEW TV MARKETS, ANNUAL FEATURE

(p. 33-35) Annual article, with 1 table ranking 214 areas of dominant influence (ADIs) by number of TV households, 1985/86, with 1984/85 rank. Data are from Arbitron Co.

Previous feature is described in SRI 1984 Annual under C1750-1.531.

CHAPTERS SEVEN AND ELEVEN

(p. 82) Brief article, with 1 table showing number of business failures, and liabilities of failed businesses, for radio and TV industries, 1983-84 and 1st half 1984-85. Data are from Dun and Bradstreet.

C1750–2   BROADCASTING/CABLE CASTING YEARBOOK, 1985

Annual. 1985.
1326 p. var. paging.
LC 71-649524.
SRI/MF/excerpts, delayed

Annual broadcasting industry directory and statistical source book, 1985. Covers regulation, station ownership and operations, broadcast markets, cable TV (CATV), advertising agencies and other broadcast-related businesses, equipment, professional awards and assns, and broadcast education.

Most data are from Federal agencies and private research firms.

Contents:

Preface, editorial and advertiser indexes, and glossaries. (p. i-xvi)

Section A. Fifth Estate. Includes broadcast finance and operation highlights (p. A2); and text data (p. A34-A62) on owners of multiple-station and cross-media holdings. (p. A1-A62)

Section B. Radio. Includes 1 table listed below; and text data (p. B405-B408) on world radio and TV facilities, including number of receivers and transmitters, by country. (p. B1-B408)

Section C. TV. Includes 4 tables listed below; U.S. and Canada station directory, with text data (p. C1-C77) on cable subscribers and advertising rates; and text data (p. C96-C133) on ownership and finances of stations with pending applications, and on sale prices of station transfers. (p. C1-C216)

Section D. Cable. Includes 4 tables listed below; operation and finance highlights (p. D3); and directories of U.S. and Canadian CATV systems and multiple system operators (MSOs), with various text data (p. D7-D340) on personnel, area served, subscribers and charges, homes passed, stations carried, advertising revenue, and ownership. (p. D1-D344)

Section E-F. Satellites and Programming. Includes text data (p. E1-E8) on satellite broadcasting, including cable systems and subscribers served. (p. E1-E8, F1-F104)

Section G-I. Advertising, Marketing, Technology, and Professional Services. Includes 10 tables listed below. (p. G1-G16, H1-H72, I1-I80)

U.S. directories generally include U.S. territories. Sections A-B and E-I also include nonstatistical narratives on broadcasting history and regulations; directories of U.S. and foreign broadcast stations, and selected broadcast assns, schools, suppliers of equipment and other services, and other broadcast-related businesses; and a buyers' guide and bibliography.

Availability: Broadcasting Publications, 1735 DeSales St., NW, Washington DC 20036, $75.00 (prepaid), $85.00 (if billed); SRI/MF/excerpts, for highlights, text data, and tables listed below; delayed shipment in Dec. 1985.

TABLES:

C1750–2.1: Broadcasting Data

RADIO AND TV MARKETS

[B1] Radio city of license, with county or market population [alphabetical list of cities with commercial radio station, by State]. (p. B334-B348)

[C1] ADI market atlas [for 1984/85, for each of 211 markets listed alphabetically, showing: rank; TV households in ADI, by county; TV stations; and accompanying map]. (p. C134-C208)

[C2] Markets ranked by size [number and percent of U.S. total TV households; and men, women, teens, and children, by ADI; for 1984/85 season (table incorrectly reads 1983/84)]. (p. C209-C212)

[C3] TV markets by Nielsen Marketing Research Territory [including the following for 10 regional markets and component designated market areas (DMA): TV households, market size (distribution among DMAs and as percent of total U.S.), and rank, as of Jan. 1985]. (p. C212-C213)

[C4] How network delivery varies by market [TV households, with share of total U.S.; and prime-time audience share and performance index, for 3 major networks; all by ADI, as of May 1984]. (p. C213-C216)

CABLE TV

[D1] Cable penetration [and households, by DMA, as of July 1983]. (p. D342-D343)

[D2] Top 50 DMAs ranked by % cable penetration. (p. D343)

[D3] Cable penetration and projected households [in top 50 DMAs]. (p. D343)

[D4] Top 50 MSOs [ranked by number of basic subscribers, with numbers of homes passed, market penetration, pay subscriptions, and unpassed homes in franchise area]. (p. D344)

AUDIENCE

[G1] Trend of radio and TV ownership [1949-84]. (p. G16)

[G2] TV usage per home per week in hours and minutes [by time of day for weekday periods, Saturdays, and Sundays, Nov. 1984.] (p. G16)

[G3] Types of [prime-time] network TV shows and their audiences [number of programs, percent of average audience, and percent share of programming, by program type], Feb. 1983. (p. G16)

[G4] TV audience composition [percent of homes using TV, number of viewers per 1,000 viewing homes, and audience distribution among men, women, teens, and children, by day-part, Nov. 1984]. (p. G16)

RADIO AND TV TRENDS AND SALES

[H1-H2] Growth of broadcasting, and comparable record of station growth since TV began [TV and AM and FM radio stations authorized and operating; AM stations licensed and under construction; and experimental FM stations; various periods 1922-84]. (p. H54-H55)

[H3-H4] Sales of TV receivers and radio sets [volume and value, by type, 1958-1983]. (p. H56)

[H5] 31 years of station transactions [number of stations changing hands, and transaction value, for radio, TV, and combined radio/TV stations, 1954-84]. (p. H72)

ADVERTISING AGENCIES

[I1] Broadcasting's top 50 advertising agencies [ranked by total broadcast/cable billings, with detail for network and spot TV and radio, and cable TV; and broadcast share of agency's total billings; 1984 with percent change in broadcast billings from 1983]. (p. I80)

C1800
Business News Publishing Co.

C1800–1 **AIR CONDITIONING, HEATING, AND REFRIGERATION NEWS: 1985 Statistical Panorama**
Weekly (selected issue).
Apr. 8, 1985. 132 p.
Vol. 164, No. 14, Serial No. 2922.
ISSN 0002-2276.
SRI/MF/complete

Annual heating/cooling industry review and outlook issue, by Gordon D. Duffy and Thomas A. Mahoney, presenting data on shipments of air conditioning, refrigeration, home heating, and related products, 1984, with selected forecasts for 1985 and trends. Also includes energy use patterns, new housing characteristics, selected foreign trade data, and 1980 housing and market profiles by metro area and State.

Data sources include Census Bureau, Air Conditioning and Refrigeration Institute, National Assn of Home Builders, and an *Air-Conditioning and Refrigeration Wholesalers* member survey.

Contains contents listing (p. 5); and numerous brief articles and market profiles as follows:

a. Forecasts and perspective, with 6 charts showing various air conditioning, heating, and refrigeration product shipments, 1984; and annual percent change in shipments of selected products, and in housing starts and passenger car sales, various years 1964-84. (p. 14-27)

b. Shipments of air conditioning, refrigeration, heating, and related products, including air pollution control equipment; with 22 charts and 5 tables showing shipments of 22 products, and distribution of selected products by type and/or capacity, various years 1970-84. (p. 28-39, 92-103)

c. State markets, with 1 table ranking States by number of all-year housing units and by number of units with various types of cooling equipment, heating systems, and fuels used, 1980. (p. 41-51)

d. Market profiles, with 1 table repeated for 105 medium and small metro areas showing number of housing units, distribution by type of heating system and fuel used, and percent of housing units with central or room air conditioning, 1980. (p. 55-90)

e. Housing and construction characteristics, with 1 table and 1 chart showing number of single- and multi-family homes completed, by type of heating system and/or space-heating fuel, and by presence of air conditioning, all by region, 1983-84; and conventional housing starts, selected years 1975-84. (p. 103-118)

f. International trade, with 1 table and text data showing air conditioning/refrigeration imports and exports by product type and major country or world area of origin or destination; various years 1980-84. (p. 118-121)

g. Wholesalers, with 2 tables showing air conditioning and refrigeration equipment unit shipments by detailed product type, 1974-83; and results of a wholesaler survey, showing expectations for sales change by product, by U.S. region and for Canada, 1984-85. (p. 121-126)

Air Conditioning, Heating, and Refrigeration News is a weekly publication reporting trends and developments in the heating/cooling industry, and normally contains only limited statistical data. The annual statistical panorama is the only feature of ACH&RN covered by SRI.

This is the 20th annual statistical panorama report.

Availability: Business News Publishing Co., PO Box 2600, Troy MI 48007, $15.00; SRI/MF/ complete.

C1850
Cahners Publishing Co.

C1850–1 **PACKAGING**
Monthly.
ISSN 0746-3839.
LC 84-644682/r85.
SRI/MF/not filmed

Monthly trade journal, with annual special issue, reporting on developments and trends in the packaging industry. Covers manufacturing, R&D, marketing, and consumption. Most data are from Cahners Economics Dept, U.S. Dept of Commerce, and individual company reports.

General format:

a. Feature articles, occasionally with statistics, and narrative depts, placed throughout.

b. Monthly "Packaging Economics" feature, with 1 monthly table, further described below, presenting packaging PPI trends and forecasts; and, occasionally, additional charts and tables.

c. Annual *Packaging Encyclopedia & Yearbook* special issue, containing material and process information, technical specifications, and industry statistics.

Oct. issue is usually a nonstatistical buyer's guide.

Monthly table appears in most issues. All additional features with substantial statistical content are described, as they appear, under "Statistical Features." Nonstatistical features are not covered.

Availability: Packaging, 270 St. Paul St., Denver CO 80206-5191, qualified subscribers †, others $45.00 per yr., single copy $5.00, Packaging Encyclopedia $30.00, Annual Buyers Guide $25.00; SRI/MF/not filmed.

Issues reviewed during 1985: Nov. 1984-Oct. 1985; and Packaging Encyclopedia & Yearbook 1985 (P) (Vol. 29, Nos. 12-13; Vol. 30, Nos. 1-11).

MONTHLY TABLE:

Table shows PPI for selected packaging materials and products (grouped as plastic, paper, and wood/metal/glass), for quarter ending 2-4 months prior to cover date, and forecast for 3-4 subsequent quarters. One group is covered in each issue.

STATISTICAL FEATURES:

C1850–1.601: Jan. 1985 (Vol. 30, No. 1)
MATERIALS FORECAST: DEMAND TO PUSH PLASTIC, PAPER COSTS

(p. 42-44) By Kate Bertrand. Article, with 2 tables showing capacity, production, and price, for 6 thermoplastic resins, selected years 1983-88; and market volume for 4 polyethylene films, 1981 and 1986. Data are from Chemical Data, Inc. and American Hoechst Corp.

C1850–1.602: Packaging Encyclopedia and Yearbook 1985 (Vol. 30, No. 4)

PLASTIC PACKAGING: THE TREND ACCELERATES

(p. 10-11) Article, with 1 chart showing distribution of rigid containers, by type of material, 1981 and 1991. Data are from Du Pont de Nemours and Co.

PACKAGING'S 1985 SALARY SURVEY, BIENNIAL FEATURE

(p. 22-29) Biennial article on income, other characteristics, and opinions of packaging industry professionals. Data are based on a 1985 *Packaging* survey.

Includes text data, 2 charts, and 1 table showing respondents' industry sector, income by age group and experience, and perceptions concerning the packaging function's importance and outlook.

Previous report, for 1983, is described in SRI 1983 Annual under C1850-1.406.

PACKAGING ECONOMICS: A LOOK AT COST TRENDS

(p. 31-35) By Edmund A. Leonard. Article on market outlook for glass, plastic, and other containers. Data are from Census Bureau, Commerce Dept, and Dun and Bradstreet. Includes 3 tables showing the following:

a. Glass containers: value of industry and product shipments, and of product imports and exports; and industry value added, employment, establishments (total and number with 20/fewer employees), and shipment shares of 5 leading States and aggregate 4 largest companies; 1983.

b. Plastic bottle unit sales, by end-use market, 1973, 1978, and 1983; and net sales and 2 profitability measures, for 13 packaging-related SIC 4-digit industries, FY84.

OUTLOOK FOR MATERIALS: ADEQUATE SUPPLIES, RISING PRICES

(p. 39-41) Article, with 2 tables showing capacity, production, and price, for 6 thermoplastic resins, selected years 1983-88; and market volume for 4 polyethylene films, 1981 and 1986. Data are from Chemical Data, Inc. and American Hoechst Corp.

Data also appeared in feature described under C1850-1.601, above.

STATISTICS OF PACKAGING, ANNUAL FEATURE

(p. 302-307) Annual article, by Susan R. Friedman, on container and packaging material production and marketing, 1984, with selected trends 1960-89. Data sources include Charles H. Kline and Co., Commerce Dept, and Chemical Specialties Manufacturers Assn.

Includes 15 tables showing:

a. Shipments and/or market share, and growth rate, for paperboard, metal, plastic, paper, glass, wood, and textile packaging materials, selected years 1973-89.

b. Consumption of polyethylene and shrink/stretch films, aerosol containers, and extrusion coatings, by end use; distribution of cellophane shipments by end use; consumption of films and plastics for packaging, by material type; and shipments of blow-molded plastic bottles; various years 1960-84.

c. Packaging material value, consumer and shipping container production, and end-use distribution of containers, all by detailed material or container type, various years 1960-85.

C1850–1.603: May 1985 (Vol. 30, No. 6)

POLYMER BLENDS AND ALLOYS WILL UPGRADE FOOD PACKAGING

(p. 59-62) By Peter R. Lantos. Article, with 2 tables showing consumption of polymer plastic blends, by type, 1982.

C1850–1.604: June 1985 (Vol. 30, No. 7)

CONSUMER SURVEY

(p. 28-50) By Karen Beagley. Article reporting on consumer views and attitudes regarding product packaging. Data are based on 1,559 responses to a National Family Opinion Research survey. Includes 17 charts and 11 tables showing survey response on the following:

a. Factors influencing product purchase decisions, including package types; opinions on suitability, cost, and weight of various package types; nutritional value of canned vs. frozen vegetables; importance and effectiveness of child-resistant and tamper-proof packaging; and use and comprehension of nutrition information on food product labels and literature accompanying pharmaceutical items.

b. Receptiveness to new brands and food products; price comparison practices; coupon use; reading of advertisements for sale information; and microwave oven use.

Some data include detail for 9 age/lifestyle groupings.

C1850–1.605: Sept. 1985 (Vol. 30, No. 10)

NEW BEVERAGE PACKAGE BIG SUCCESS IN TAIWAN

(p. 56-58) By James R. Russo. Article, with 1 undated chart showing volume of pasteurized milk sales in Taiwan, by type of container (glass, plastic bottle, gable-top carton, and new "Tetra King" polystyrene package).

C1850–2 ELECTRONIC BUSINESS

Semimonthly.
ISSN 0163-6197.
LC 78-648318.
SRI/MF/not filmed

Semimonthly trade journal (monthly in Dec.) reporting on U.S. and world business trends in the electronics industry, including marketing, new products, management, and other nontechnical industry topics. Data are based on Cahners Economic Dept forecasts, BLS and Commerce Dept studies, individual company reports, and other sources.

Issues contain feature articles, often with statistics; regular editorial depts; and 3 recurring statistical depts (semimonthly "Business Barometer," monthly "Leadtime Index," and recurring "Market Spotlight"), described below.

Annual statistical features include electronic components/equipment market forecasts, rankings of top 200 electronics companies, data on leading companies in various electronics industry sectors, and military electronics market.

Semimonthly "Business Barometer" appears in all issues. Monthly "Leadtime Index" usually appears in 1st issue of each month. "Market

Spotlight" appears on an irregular basis, as explained below. All additional features with substantial statistical content are described, as they appear, under "Statistical Features." Nonstatistical features are not covered.

Availability: Electronic Business, 270 St. Paul St., Denver CO 80206-5191, qualified subscribers †, others $40.00 per yr., single copy $4.00, plant site issue $10.00; SRI/MF/not filmed.

Issues reviewed during 1985: Nov. 1, 1984-Oct. 15, 1985 (P) (Vol. 10, Nos. 17-19; Vol. 11, Nos. 1-20).

STATISTICAL DEPTS:

SEMIMONTHLY DATA

a. "Business Barometer," including narrative analysis with several charts, most showing trends and outlook for various electronics industry indicators.

MONTHLY DATA

b. "Leadtime Index," with 1 table indicating number of weeks required to build/ship orders, by detailed type of electronic component, as of publication month. Data are based on responses to an electronic business survey by "Purchasing" magazine.

IRREGULARLY RECURRING DATA

c. "Market Spotlight," including narrative analysis, usually with 1-2 charts, on leadtime trends and outlook for a selected electronics product category. "Market Spotlight" appeared in May 15, June 15, Aug. 1, and Aug. 15, 1985 issues. Prior to May 15, feature was titled "Leadtime Forecast" and appeared on a monthly basis.

STATISTICAL FEATURES:

C1850–2.601: Nov. 1, 1984 (Vol. 10, No. 17)

CAPACITOR INDUSTRY HOLDS POWER, CONTROLS GROWTH, ANNUAL FEATURE

(p. 112-116) Annual article, by Michael Seither, on capacitor market developments and leading manufacturers, 1983. Data are from Electronic Industries Assn and Gnostic Concepts Inc.

Includes 3 charts showing capacitor sales volume and value, by capacitor type, 1973 and/or 1982-83; and top 10 capacitor manufacturers ranked by U.S. shipment value, 1983 with comparison to 1982.

C1850–2.602: Nov. 15, 1984 (Vol. 10, No. 18)

PATENT NONSENSE: THE FIGHT OVER FIBER OPTICS

(p. 24-26) Article, with 1 chart showing fiber optic cable market shares by manufacturer, 1983. Data are from Kessler Marketing Intelligence.

'YEAR OF SURVIVAL' IN THE U.S. ATM INDUSTRY

(p. 31-32) Article, with 2 charts showing automated teller machine shipments, 1980-84; and market shares by manufacturer, 1984. Data are from Linda Fenner Zimmer and Datapro Research Corp.

BURROUGHS TRIES TO INCREASE ITS MARKET SHARE IN JAPAN

(p. 32) Article, with 1 chart showing volume and/or value of computer mainframe shipments in Japan, 1982-83.

C1850–2.603: Dec. 10, 1984 (Vol. 10, No. 19)

LASER PRINTERS: HP RUSHES IN WHERE IBM FEARS TO TREAD

(p. 36-38) Article, with 1 chart showing estimated revenues for the laser printer market, 1983, 1985, and 1988. Data are from C. A. Pesko Associates.

DEC, INTEL & MOTOROLA FIGHT TO BE THE BUS DRIVER

(p. 148-151) By William Arnold. Article, with 2 charts showing worldwide shipment value of single-board computers, by type, 1983 and 1988. Data are from Gnostic Concepts Inc.

CAD FOR PRINTED CIRCUIT BOARDS GROWS BY DESIGN

(p. 154-156) By David Card. Article, with 2 charts showing top 8 printed circuit board/computer-aided design (CAD) equipment manufacturers ranked by revenue, 1983; and revenues for CAD systems by design type, 1984 and 1988. Data are from Dataquest, Inc.

TAIWAN COMPANIES MOUNT A LARGE SCALE VLSI EFFORT

(p. 160-162) By Charles Hintermeister. Article, with 3 charts showing Taiwan's export and import values, for semiconductors/integrated circuits in 1st half 1983-84, and for electronic components by type in 1982-83.

MILITARY ELECTRONICS, ANNUAL FEATURE

Annual compilation of articles on the military market for electronic products. Includes the following statistical articles:

MILITARY ELECTRONICS RIDE ON DEFENSE SPENDING CREST, ANNUAL FEATURE

(p. 196-202) Annual article, by Michael Seither, on forecasts of military spending for electronic products. Data are from Electronic Industries Assn and Henderson Ventures.

Includes 3 charts and 1 table showing electronics content of DOD budget for R&D, procurement, and operations/maintenance, with detail for procurement budget by sector, FY85; and production value of military electronic equipment by type, 1983-86.

HIGH FRONTIER YIELDS HIGH ELECTRONICS FUNDING

(p. 228-230) By Jack Cushman. Article, with 2 charts showing DOD total and space system procurement budgets, with total budget distribution by general purpose, and electronic share of space systems procurement, FY85. Data are from Electronic Industries Assn.

C1850–2.604: Jan. 1, 1985 (Vol. 11, No. 1)

GENERAL MOTORS MAKES ELECTRONICS ITS BUSINESS

(p. 71-82) By Norman Alster. Article, with 2 tables showing transaction value for General Motors' (GM) acquisition of Electronic Data Systems and for 6 other electronic industry mergers proposed/completed during 1984; with summary financial and operating data for GM.

OUTLOOK 1985, ANNUAL FEATURE

Annual compilation of articles forecasting market trends for electronics equipment and components, 1985. Articles with substantial statistical content are described below.

1985: A YEAR OF GROWTH, BUT ON A SLOWER TRACK

(p. 88-93) By Alden M. Hayashi. Article, with 3 illustrative charts, and 1 chart showing GNP and value of electronic equipment production (in current and constant 1982 dollars), 1984-85. Data are from Gnostic Concepts Inc.

PERIPHERALS: ONLY THE STRONG WILL SURVIVE IN 1985, ANNUAL FEATURE

(p. 130-137) Annual article, by Mary Jo Foley, on computer peripherals market. Data are from specified industry sources. Includes 5 charts showing market volume and/or value for terminals, printers, and micro input and communications equipment; and worldwide shipment value for original equipment manufacturers, with market share by disc type; 1985.

IC MAKERS CALL THE TUNE FOR EQUIPMENT SUPPLIERS, ANNUAL FEATURE

(p. 150-154) Annual article, by Mark Mehler, with 1 table showing electronics equipment purchasing plans of electronics manufacturers, 1985. Data are based on an *Electronic Business* survey of purchasing managers.

IN '85 TEST AND MEASURE WILL MEET THE CAE LINK, ANNUAL FEATURE

(p. 158-163) Annual article, by Mary Ann Murphy, with 3 charts showing the following for electronic test/measurement equipment: worldwide sales, growth rate by equipment type, and market share for 2 leading manufacturers and all others, 1984 or 1984-85. Data are from Prime Data, Inc.

COMPUTER-AIDED WAVE WILL CONTINUE IN 1985

(p. 164-171) By David Card. Article, with 2 charts showing computer-aided design/computer-aided manufacturing sales and market share, for 10 leading companies, 1984. Data are from Daratech, Inc.

FORECAST OF U.S. OEM ELECTRONIC COMPONENT PURCHASES, ANNUAL FEATURE

(p. 184-199) Annual article, with 4 tables showing value of original equipment manufacturers' purchases of electronic components, 1983-85, and expected change in prices 1985, by product type with detail by application. Data are from an *Electronic Business* survey of purchasing managers.

C1850–2.605: Jan. 15, 1985 (Vol. 11, No. 2)

TEKTRONIX TESTS AND MEASURES JAPAN THROUGH A SONY PARTNERSHIP

(p. 94-95) By Mary Jo Foley. Article, with 2 charts showing value of electronic test/measurement equipment market in Japan, 1983, and estimated annual growth for next 5 years, by equipment type. Data are from Prime Data, Inc.

LIFE IN THE FAST LANE: SUPERGROWTH COMPANIES

(p. 98-103) By Linda Stallmann. Article, with 12 tables ranking top 100 electronics companies by 5-year compound sales growth, and including sales, profit margin, reporting period, and headquarters location; with rankings and compound profit margin in 10 industry segments; all as of latest available fiscal year (specified for each company). Most data are from company financial reports.

SHIELDED MARKET GETS A STRONG FINANCIAL COATING

(p. 110-113) By Michael Seither. Article on the electromagnetic interference (EMI) shielding market. Data are from Business Communications Co. and Strategic Analysis. Includes 2 charts showing percent of plastic enclosures shielded, and EMI shielding market value, 1982 and 1987; and recent shielding prices by type.

C1850–2.606: Feb. 1, 1985 (Vol. 11, No. 3)

PATIENCE PAYS OFF FOR NEC AMERICA

(p. 56-62) By Tim Mead. Article, with 2 charts showing top 10 communications companies ranked by North American sales; and U.S. shipment volume and value for private branch exchanges and key systems, with market shares by company; 1983. Also includes sales data for NEC Corp. and NEC America.

Data are from Arthur D. Little Inc., Eastern Management Group, and Dataquest, Inc.

PROTOCOL CONVERTORS: BOARDS BEAT BOXES

(p. 70-72) By Anne Hyde. Article, with 2 charts showing market value for computer stand-alone protocol converters, with market share by manufacturer, various years 1984-88. Data are from International Data Corp.

PCB INDUSTRY SALES TO REACH $6.8 BILLION IN '88

(p. 89-93) Article, with 1 chart showing printed circuit board sales, with market share by end use and board type, 1983. Data are from Frost and Sullivan, Inc.

C1850–2.607: Feb. 15, 1985 (Vol. 11, No. 4)

COMPUTER AND ELECTRONICS INDUSTRY EMBRACES THE TRIAD

(p. 30-36) Article, with 1 chart showing investment flow among U.S., Japan, and EC, FY82. Data are from Bank of Japan.

NEW FACTS IN THE FRACTIOUS FLAP OVER THE FLAT TAX

(p. 67-68) Article, with 1 chart showing public investment in companies with net worth of under $5 million, during periods of increasing and decreasing capital gains taxes, 1972-83. Data are from Capital Publishing Corp.

HIGH-END WINCHESTERS: A CROWDED, VOLATILE MARKET

(p. 68-69) Article, with 1 table showing worldwide shipments and revenues for U.S. and foreign manufacturers of 5.25-inch Winchester disk drives with 30-100 megabyte capacity, by type of manufacturer, 1983-87. Data are from Disk/Trend, Inc.

STANDARD CELLS ENJOY SPECIFIC BUSINESS GROWTH

(p. 128-130) By Shelley Tsantes. Article, with 3 charts showing worldwide market value 1984 and 1990, and annual growth rate during 1981-90 period, for application-specific integrated circuits by type. Data are from Integrated Circuit Engineering Corp.

CIM IS NO PASSING FAD IN SEMICONDUCTOR FAB

(p. 148-153) By Mark Mehler. Article, with 2 charts showing growth rate for sales of computer-integrated manufacturing equipment used in semiconductor and all industries, by application, 1983-88 period. Data are from VLSI Research Inc.

COMPANIES ARE BUILDING, EQUIPPING AT A MODEST CLIP

(p. 190-204) Article, with 12 tables showing capital expenditures 1981-84 with 3-year compounded growth rate, and sales with 5-year compounded growth rate (no date), for 143 electronics companies arranged alphabetically and by specialty. Data were compiled by *Electronic Business*.

C1850–2.608: Mar. 1, 1985 (Vol. 11, No. 5)

GCA WORKS HARD TO PUT ON A JAPANESE FACE

(p. 30-38) Article, with 1 chart showing value of demand for semiconductor production equipment in Japan, by type, 1983 and 1986. Data are from Nomura Research Institute.

SEMI GEAR: THE OUTLOOK, ONCE BRIGHT, IS NOMURA

(p. 38-39) Article, with 1 table showing the following for semiconductor production equipment in Japan: market value, 1983 and 1986; and major suppliers and share of 1983 market; by equipment type. Data are from Nomura Research Institute.

LOCAL LOWDOWN: FAST TIMES ON LAN LANE

(p. 104-113) By Anne Hyde. Article, with 1 chart showing local area network market share, by application, 1984. Data are from L. F. Rothschild, Unterberg, Towbin.

FAST FORWARD: THE ACCELERATING TEMPO OF TECHNOLOGY

(p. 120-122) Article, with 1 chart showing U.S. vs. Japanese technological leadtime or lag, for transistors, microprocessors, and 5 semiconductors developed during 1948-83.

SEMI TOUGH SCENE FOR THE CHIP KINGS, ANNUAL FEATURE

(p. 138-144) Annual article, by Michael Seither, on world semiconductor market performance, 1984. Data are from Integrated Circuit Engineering Corp. and Semiconductor Industry Assn.

Includes 3 charts and 1 table showing world semiconductor and integrated circuit production value and/or consumption, by leading manufacturer and/or for U.S., Europe, Japan, and rest of world, 1984 with some data for 1983.

TEXAS INSTRUMENTS: READY FOR A 256k BRAWL

(p. 148-149) Article, with 2 charts showing top 10 integrated circuit manufacturers ranked by production value, 1984; and Texas Instruments' semiconductor sales by product line, 1983-84. Data are from Integrated Circuit Engineering Corp. and Montgomery Securities.

BETTING ON THE EUROPEAN COMBINATION

(p. 154-155) Article, with 1 chart showing top 9 European integrated circuit manufacturers ranked by production value, 1984. Data are from Integrated Circuit Engineering Corp.

NEC CORP.: LEADING THE JAPANESE CHARGE

(p. 155-156) Article, with 1 chart showing top 10 Japanese integrated circuit manufacturers ranked by production value, 1984. Data are from Integrated Circuit Engineering Corp.

PORTABLE COMPUTER SALES TO TOP $17 BILLION IN 1989

(p. 180-181) Article, with 2 charts showing portable computer sales, worldwide by type, and for U.S. by end-use sector, 1983 and 1989. Data are from Creative Strategies Inc.

C1850–2.609: Mar. 15, 1985 (Vol. 11, No. 6)

DO SUPERCOMPUTER USERS WANT IBM COMPATIBILITY?

(p. 32-33) Article, with 2 charts showing volume and value of supercomputer shipments, with market share by end-use sector and manufacturer, 1984 and 1990. Data are from Hambrecht and Quist.

QUICK LOOK AT KOREA'S TOP ELECTRONICS COMPANIES

(p. 38-42) Article, with 2 charts showing the following for South Korean electronics industry: value of production and exports, with distribution by product group, 1979 and 1983; and top 16 manufacturers ranked by sales, 1st half 1984 with percent change from 1983. Data sources include Dong Suh Securities Co., Ltd.

DISK DUPLICATORS DON'T DOUBT DUPLICATION DEMAND

(p. 46, 51) Article, with 1 chart showing shipments of disk-duplication machines, with market share for desktop and industrial units, 1982, 1984, and 1986. Data are from Dataquest, Inc.

REASSESSING THE CARIBBEAN INITIATIVE

(p. 56-58) By Mary Jo Foley. Article, with 1 table showing value of U.S. imports from 6 Caribbean countries with considerable electronics investment, under 4 tariff provisions, 1st 9 months 1984. Data are from Caribbean Basin Business Information Center.

JAPAN'S COMPUTERS: FAST GROWTH IN A HOT MARKET

(p. 110-116) Article, with 3 charts showing top 10 Japanese computer companies ranked by sales (in yen) 1983, and by sales increase (in yen) and growth rate 1983 vs. 1982. Data are from *Computopia*.

C1850–2.610: Apr. 1, 1985 (Vol. 11, No. 7)

MSX IN THE U.S.: STRIKING WHILE THE IRON IS COLD

(p. 34-35) Article, with 1 chart showing volume and value of home computer shipments, 1983-85. Data are from Future Computing, Inc.

RUST VALLEY: HOME OF RED INK AND IRON OXIDE

(p. 43-44) Article, with 1 chart showing North American market volume of rigid disk drives, 1983, 1985, and 1987. Data are from Dataquest, Inc.

DIGITIZERS: THE MOUSE THAT ROARED

(p. 49-50) Article, with 2 charts showing market volume of computer-aided design/computer-aided manufacturing (CAD/CAM) workstations, with distribution by type, 1983 and 1988; and revenues for personal computer-based CAD/CAM/computer-aided engineering systems, with market shares by vendor, 1984. Data are from Dataquest, Inc. and Daratech, Inc.

MODEMS: FROM THE BENCH TO THE PLAYING FIELD

(p. 70-73) By Anne Hyde. Article, with 4 charts showing microcomputer modem shipments and sales, with shipment distribution by speed type and vendor, and sales distribution by design type; and distribution of computer modem shipments by sales method; various years 1983-88. Data are from Creative Strategies International and International Data Corp.

STANDARDS: A SWITCH IN TIME FOR SUPPLIES

(p. 74-78) By Mark Mehler. Article, with 1 chart showing market value for electronic (ac/dc) switching power supplies by type, 1984-85. Data are from Salzer Technology Enterprises, Inc.

WILL COLOR MONITORS PROFIT FROM SLIDING CHIP PRICES?

(p. 114-116) By Alden M. Hayashi. Article, with 1 chart and 1 table showing color monitor and color display system sales, by end-use sector (business, industrial, and consumer), with some detail by application, various years 1984-90. Data are from International Competitive Assessments.

C1850–2.611: Apr. 15, 1985 (Vol. 11, No. 8)

8-BIT WARS: U.S. AND JAPAN CROSS SWORDS AGAIN

(p. 26-28) Article, with 2 charts showing market supply of 4- and 8-bit microcontrollers and 8- and 16-bit microprocessors, with share for U.S. and Europe and/or Japan, 2nd quarter 1983-84. Data are from Dataquest, Inc.

VCRs: JAPAN INC. MEETS KOREA LTD.

(p. 34-36) Article, with 2 charts showing distribution of U.S. videocassette recorder market, by price range and manufacturer, 1984; and distribution of Japanese consumer electronics production, by product type and destination, including U.S., Europe, and Japan (no date). Data are from Video Marketing and Henderson Electronics Market Forecast.

LOGICAL MOVES OF WILFRED CORRIGAN

(p. 53-78) By Shelley Tsantes. Article, with 1 chart showing distribution of semiconductor gate/linear array market worldwide, by end-use sector, 1984 and 1990. Data are from Integrated Circuit Engineering Corp.

CONNECTOR MAKERS WAIT FOR AN UPTURN TO PLUG IN, ANNUAL FEATURE

(p. 92-101) Annual article, by Torrey Byles, on market performance of electronic and telecommunication connectors and interconnection devices, 1984. Data are from Gnostic Concepts, Inc. and Merrill Lynch Capital Markets Group.

Includes 2 charts showing connector/socket production value, 1983-85; and top 11 connector/interconnection suppliers, ranked by value of shipments, 1983-84.

DETROIT PRESSES MERCHANTS TO ACCELERATE IN ELECTRONICS

(p. 109-114) By David Card. Article, with 2 charts showing distribution of semiconductor functions in 1984 model year autos, by application; and value of electronic parts in average motor vehicle, quinquennially 1970-95. Data are from Dataquest, Inc. and Ford Motor Co.

LOCAL HEROES: DISTRIBUTORS UNDER THE GIANTS' SHADOWS

(p. 120-128) By Norman Alster. Article, with 3 charts showing electronic sales (total and distributors' share); and total and industrial distributor sales, with detail for computer distributors and by revenue group; 1984. Also includes listing of industrial distributors with annual sales between $10-25 million.

Data are from National Electronic Distributors Assn.

ISLAND HOPPING: HANDLERS ARE THE MISSING LINK

(p. 131-136) By David Card. Article, with 1 chart showing sales of handling devices for integrated circuits, with market share by manufacturer, 1983. Data are from VLSI Research Inc.

C1850–2.612: May 1, 1985 (Vol. 11, No. 9)

ELECTRONIC SHOPPING: WELCOME ONE AND MALL

(p. 46-50) Article, with 2 charts showing installations of electronic shopping computer terminals in retail stores/shopping malls, with share of terminals allowing direct payment for purchase, 1985 and 1989. Data are from Touche Ross and Co.

UNREGULATED GROWTH IN A REGULATED MANNER

(p. 62-72) By Mary Jo Foley. Article, with 2 charts showing top 10-12 vendors of mini and supermini computers ranked by worldwide shipment revenues, 1984. Data are from International Data Corp.

COMPLEMENTARY MARKETS: CMOS FINDS ITS WAY

(p. 94-106) By Alden M. Hayashi. Article, with 3 charts showing value of world consumption of integrated circuits, with distribution by type, 1984 and 1990; share of memory market for complementary vs. negative-channel metal-oxide semiconductors, by memory type, 1982 and 1988; and summary data on costs savings associated with complementary metal-oxide semiconductors.

Data are from Integrated Circuit Engineering Corp., Harris Corp., and Dataquest, Inc.

CUSTOM AND SEMICUSTOM VLSI IS THE ONLY WAY TO GO

(p. 158-160) By Carol Suby. Article, with 1 chart showing estimated market value of application-specific integrated circuits, with share by type, 1986 and 1990. Data are from Electronic Trend Publications.

C1850–2.613: May 15, 1985 (Vol. 11, No. 10)

LEAN, MEAN AND HUNGRY: HERE COME THE KOREANS

(p. 44-50) Article, with 1 table showing capital investment, products made/planned, production status, and location, for 8 South Korean semiconductor manufacturers, 1983/84 with some investment estimates for 1985 and 1989. Data are from Integrated Circuit Engineering Corp.

ECL, OR THE WAR IN HIGH-END SUPERMINIS

(p. 60-62) Article, with 1 chart showing worldwide sales of superminicomputers, with market share by manufacturer, 1984. Data are from Yankee Group, Inc.

SEMICONDUCTOR MANUFACTURING

Compilation of features on market conditions for semiconductor equipment. Statistical features are described below.

EQUIPMENT MAKERS LOOK FOR A EUROPEAN RECOVERY

(p. 105-106) By Mark Mehler. Article, with 1 chart showing top 11 semiconductor equipment manufacturers ranked by value of worldwide shipments, 1984. Data are from VLSI Research Inc.

SEMICONDUCTOR FABRICATION

(p. 112-113) Chart showing worldwide semiconductor equipment sales, and top 2 vendors ranked by worldwide sales, by equipment type, 1984. Data are from VLSI Research Inc.

MATERIALS GROW WITH SEMICONDUCTOR VOLUME

(p. 116) By David Card. Article, with 1 table showing worldwide production value for wafer fabrication materials, by type, 1984-87. Data are from Rose Associates.

C1850–2.614: June 1, 1985 (Vol. 11, No. 11)

DISTRIBUTORS' VITAL SIGNS: STABLE, BUT WEAK, ANNUAL FEATURE

(p. 79-88) Annual article, by John Kerr, on market outlook for electronics distributors. Data sources include Hambrecht and Quist Inc., and *Electronic Business*.

Includes 2 charts and 2 tables showing the following:

a. Electronic distributors' sales of semiconductors, systems, connectors, and other passive components, 1984-85; and electronic component shipment value, for manufacturers and distributors, 1982-86.

b. Sales distribution by product, operating profit as percent of sales, sales per employee, number of stocking locations, and field sales employment, for top 15 industrial electronics distributors ranked by total sales, calendar or fiscal year 1984, with quarterly sales detail for 6 distributors and comparisons to 1983.

ROBOTS DO EVERYTHING BUT MAKE MONEY FOR VENDORS

(p. 93-98) By Anne Hyde. Article, with 3 charts showing robot sales as follows: by manufacturer (with detail for light-assembly robots), 1984; and by application, 1983 and 1990. Data are from Prudential-Bache Securities Inc. and International Data Corp.

ROBOTS: THE SYSTEM IS THE SOLUTION

(p. 106-107) By John Kerr. Article, with 1 chart showing revenues of robot systems manufacturers, by system price range, 1984. Data are from Dataquest, Inc.

PRINTED WIRING BOARD BUSINESS HITS $9 BILLION

(p. 122-124) By Carol Suby. Article, with 2 undated charts showing distribution of costs by item, for producing and assembling printed wiring boards. Data are from responses of 129 original equipment manufacturers and independent companies to a summer 1984 survey conducted by the Institute for Interconnecting and Packaging Electronic Circuits.

C1850–2.615: June 15, 1985 (Vol. 11, No. 12)

MINICOMPUTERS AND THE BATTLE OVER OA

(p. 30-33) Article, with 1 chart showing installed base of office automation software packages, by vendor, 1984 and 1989. Data are from The Yankee Group.

SMCs CHALLENGE PCB EQUIPMENT MAKERS

(p. 121-126, 133-134) By Mark Mehler. Article, with 2 charts showing printed circuit board (PCB) production value, and PCB insertion equipment sales, both by board type, 1984. Data sources include Institute for Interconnecting Packaging Electronic Circuits and Don Brown Associates.

CAE: THE DASH TO THE DESK TOP GAINS SPEED

(p. 138-142) By Alden M. Hayashi. Article, with 3 charts showing top 11 vendors of computer-aided engineering (CAE) systems ranked by revenues, 1984; consumer opinions on factors discouraging CAE system purchases (no date); and percent of electrical engineers and layout designers using computer-aided design/manufacturing/engineering systems, 1983 and 1988.

Data sources include Daratech, Inc., and Dataquest, Inc.

C1850–2.616: July 1, 1985 (Vol. 11, No. 13)

BIT OF A BATTLE IN MICROPROCESSORS

(p. 26-28) Article, with 2 charts showing 8-bit microprocessor market shares, by type (no date); and top 10 microprocessor suppliers ranked by sales, 1984. Data are from Dataquest Inc. and Integrated Circuit Engineering Corp.

LTX SEEKS DIGITAL WATERS AS LINEAR SEAS SWELL

(p. 48-60) By David Card. Article, with 2 charts showing market shares for very large scale integration (VLSI) testing equipment, by manufacturer, 1983; and sales of linear semiconductor test equipment, by manufacturer, 1984. Data are from VLSI Research Inc. and Prudential-Bache Securities.

GROWTHBUSTERS: THE LOWDOWN ON THE SLOWDOWN

(p. 64-67) By Carol Suby. Article, with 1 chart showing value of U.S. electronics exports to and imports from Japan and Europe, 1984. Data are from Commerce Dept.

PERIPHERAL DARWINISM: TO THE STRONG GO THE SALES

(p. 72-74) By John Kerr. Article, with 1 chart showing worldwide revenues for computer disk cartridges/packs, and hard-disks by capacity, 1983 and 1987. Data are from Disk/Trend, Inc.

SOFTWARE: TOO MANY FIRMS CHASING TOO FEW DOLLARS

(p. 76-81) By Mary Jo Foley. Article, with 2 charts showing worldwide market value for systems and applications software, by price range, 1984. Data are from InfoCorp.

BIG CHIP SLIP ALSO HITS T&M

(p. 92-93) By David Card. Article, with 2 charts showing electronic test/measurement equipment (T&M) sales worldwide, 1984-85; and T&M market growth rate, by equipment type, 1983/84 and 1984/85 periods. Data are from Prime Data.

CHIP MAKERS GO BOTTOM FISHING IN THE SEMI SLUMP

(p. 94, 97) By Shelley Tsantes. Article, with 1 chart showing semiconductor market shares, for U.S., Europe, Japan, and rest of world, 1974, 1980, and 1984.

C1850–2.617: July 15, 1985 (Vol. 11, No. 14)

LIFE IN THE FAST LANE: ARRAYS SHIFT INTO HIGH GEAR

(p. 76-80) By John Kerr. Article, with 6 charts showing worldwide market value of electronic gate arrays (total and for high-performance gate arrays), with total market by gate type and by number of gates per array, 1984 and 1990. Data are from Integrated Circuit Engineering Corp. and industry estimates.

HARD TIMES: WINCHESTER WARRIORS COUNT THEIR DEAD

(p. 85-89) By Frank Catalano. Article, with 1 chart showing estimated market value for micro-Winchester disk drives, by type, 1984-85. Data are from Shearson Lehman Brothers, Inc.

MAINFRAMES: OPPORTUNITY KNOCKS. IS ANYONE HOME?

(p. 95-100) By Mary Jo Foley. Article, with 1 chart showing market value of large-scale mainframe computers, by manufacturer, 1984. Data are from International Data Corp.

ELECTRONIC BUSINESS 200, ANNUAL FEATURE

(p. 106-170) Annual compilation of articles on financial performance of top 200 electronics companies, ranked by electronics sales during 1984. Data are primarily from company financial reports.

Includes 1 detailed table (p. 112-125) showing each company's electronics sales and rank; total sales and net income, with amounts per employee and 5-year growth rates; and selected financial and operating ratios.

Also includes 15 summary tables showing the following for 1984 with selected comparisons to 1983: aggregate data for top 200 companies; top 6-15 companies in 12 industry segments ranked by sales per employee, with selected financial ratios; and top 10 and bottom 5 companies ranked by selected measures covered in detailed table.

Corrected data appear in the Oct. 1, 1985 issue; for description, see C1850-2.622 below.

C1850–2.618: Aug. 1, 1985 (Vol. 11, No. 15)

HEWLETT-PACKARD FOCUSES ON THE OFFICE SPECTRUM

(p. 46-55) By Frank Catalano. Article, with 1 chart showing office personal computer market shares, by manufacturer, 1984. Data are from Future Computing, Inc.

MOTOR MAKERS FORCED TO OVERHAUL STRATEGIES

(p. 64-69) By Carol Suby. Article, with 1 chart showing production value for direct current permanent magnet motors used in computer/office equipment, by source (captive, import, U.S.-based/foreign-manufactured, and U.S.-based/U.S.-manufactured), 1982 and 1987. Data are from Electronicast Corp.

BYPASS BONANZA SPURS VENDORS' MARKETING EFFORTS

(p. 72-77) By Anne Hyde. Article, with 1 undated chart showing distribution of telecommunication bypass system technologies by type (microwave, satellite, cable, and other), with and without regulations preventing local exchange carriers from bypassing public-switched networks. Data are from L. F. Rothschild, Unterberg, Towbin.

IBM CASTS A LONG BLUE SHADOW IN CAD/CAM/CAE

(p. 92-93) By Carol Suby. Article, with 1 table showing revenues for computer-aided design/manufacturing/engineering system vendors (total and for 9 leading vendors), 1985, with change from 1984. Data are from Daratech, Inc.

C1850–2.619: Aug. 15, 1985 (Vol. 11, No. 16)

REAGAN'S TAX PROPOSAL: THE AGE OF THE ENTREPRENEUR

(p. 39-42) Article analyzing impact of Reagan Administration tax reform proposals on electronics industry. Data are from E. F. Hutton Corp. Includes 1 undated table showing the following for 10 electronics companies, 1984: reported net income, adjustments under 3 proposed tax changes (dividend credit, low statutory tax rate, and elimination of investment tax credit), and net income after adjustments.

ATE TESTERS: BACK TO ASICs

(p. 50) Article, with 1 chart showing worldwide sales for application-specific integrated circuits, by type, 1984 and 1990. Data are from Integrated Circuit Engineering Corp.

UNIX: THIS YEAR PROMISES MAY MATCH REALITY

(p. 76-78) By Mary Jo Foley. Article on market outlook for Unix systems (operating software developed by Bell Laboratories). Data are from Yates Ventures. Includes 2 charts showing number of Unix systems sold, by vendor, 1984; and worldwide shipments of Unix-based systems, by category, 1985.

BEST ETCH: GOOD GROWTH IN A DRY MARKET

(p. 90-92) By Mark Mehler. Article, with 2 charts showing worldwide market value for integrated circuit dry etching systems, by type, 1984 and 1988; and square inches of dry film etched, by application type, 1984. Data are from Salzer Technology Enterprises and VLSI Research Inc.

APPLE COMPUTER: LOOKING FOR A EUROPEAN STRATEGY

(p. 101-106) By Jack Gee. Article, with 2 charts showing top 3 personal computer manufacturers ranked by market shares in each of 4 European countries, 1984; and shipments of personal computers (business use only) in Europe, by vendor, 1984. Data are from Intelligent Electronics.

AND VISIONS OF GaAs DANCED IN THEIR HEADS

(p. 138-139) By Mary Jo Foley. Article, with 2 charts showing Federal budget for Strategic Computing Program (DOD computer research program), by participating sector and function, 1984. Data are from Defense Advanced Research Projects Agency.

C1850–2.620: Sept. 1, 1985 (Vol. 11, No. 17)

GOVERNMENT DP MARKET: IN MIPs WE TRUST

(p. 82-90) By Mary Jo Foley. Article, with 1 chart showing Federal Government purchases of large- and small-scale data processing systems, by purchasing agency and vendor, FY84. Data are from GSA.

RESISTOR MAKERS PREPARE FOR A LONG COLD WINTER

(p. 92-98) By John Kerr. Article on market outlook for resistors. Data are from Electronic Trend Publications and Gnostic Concepts Inc.

Includes 5 charts showing resistor consumption value (total and for original equipment manufacturers), by application or component type; resistor market value as percent of total electronics equipment market; and percent of printed circuit board components (total and resistors) that are surface mounted; various years 1984-90.

MITEL'S FORMULA: BRITISH CASH PLUS ISDN CHIPS

(p. 100-108) By Anne Hyde. Article, with 1 chart showing approximate installations of telephone digital subscriber lines (central office and private branch exchange lines), 1984, 1988, and 1991. Data are from Intel Corp.

PRINTED CIRCUITS, ANNUAL FEATURE

Annual compilation of articles on printed circuit board (PCB) industry outlook, including data on manufacturers, production, and materials. Statistical articles are described below.

FLAT YEAR FORECAST FOR INDEPENDENT PCB MAKERS, ANNUAL FEATURE

(p. 112-120) Annual article, by David Card, on market outlook for PCB industry. Data are from Gnostic Concepts Inc. and International Technology Group.

Includes 3 charts showing value of worldwide PCB production, by type, 1984 and 1989; top 10 independent PCB manufacturers ranked by sales, 1984, with sales projections for 1985; and PCB sales, by industry group, 1984 and 1989.

Previous feature is described in SRI 1984 Annual under C1850-2.515.

CROWDED WORLD OF PCB CAD VENDORS

(p. 124-128) By David Card. Article, with 1 chart showing world sales of PCBs for computer-aided design (CAD) systems, for top 13 vendors and aggregate for all other vendors with sales over $15 million, 1984. Data are from Dataquest, Inc.

PCB MAKERS: LIVING IN A MATERIALS WORLD, ANNUAL FEATURE

(p. 132) Annual article, with 1 chart showing market value for materials used in PCB production, by end use, 1984. Data are from Strategic Analysis, Inc.

Previous feature is described in SRI 1984 Annual under C1850-2.515.

Other Article

INS AND OUTS OF IC CROSS-LICENSING AGREEMENTS

(p. 150-151) By Carol Suby. Article, with 1 table showing number of U.S. patents granted to 10 major semiconductor companies, 1982-84. Data are from a report by E. J. Kuuttila & Associates.

C1850–2.621: Sept. 15, 1985 (Vol. 11, No. 18)

HEAD FOR THE HILLS, HERE COME THE CAE GIANTS

(p. 26-32) Article, with 2 charts showing sales of top 10 computer-aided engineering system vendors and all others, 1984; and shipments and revenues for 3 types of computer-aided design workstations, 1984 and 1989. Data are from Dataquest, Inc.

SHAKEOUT CONTINUES IN IBM PC-COMPATIBLES

(p. 32-38) Article, with 2 charts showing personal computer (PC) sales to business, by type of distributor, 1985; and IBM PC-compatible market volume, by manufacturer, 1984-85. Data are from Future Computing, Inc.

MICRO SYSTEMS OPEN UP ARCHITECTURES

(p. 38-40) Article, with 1 chart showing world sales of microprocessor development systems, 1983-88. Data are from Prime Data.

IF YOU CAN'T BEAT 'EM, IMPORT FROM 'EM

(p. 46-53) By Mary Jo Foley. Article, with 4 charts and 3 tables showing consumer electronic product sales, 1983-86, and market growth in next 3-4 years (no dates), all by product type. Data are from EIA Consumer Electronics Group, and Frost and Sullivan, Inc.

JAPAN'S TOP 10 ELECTRONICS COMPANIES: BIGGER NOT RICHER

(p. 56-57) By Paula Doe. Article on financial performance of top 10 Japanese electronics companies ranked by electronics sales, FY84 or FY85. Data are from *Electronic Business* and Nomura Securities, and are generally shown in Japanese yen and U.S. dollars.

Includes 3 tables showing selected financial data for each of the top 10 companies, FY84 or FY85, with some detail for subsidiaries, and selected comparisons to financial performance of leading U.S. electronics companies. Financial data include electronics and total sales, operating earnings, net income, sales and income per employee, return on equity and investment, and export ratio.

PRIMAL SCREEN: WHERE'S MY FLAT PANEL DISPLAY?

(p. 70-72) By Fred McGrail. Article on computer terminal displays market. Data are from Stanford Resources, Inc. Includes 2 charts showing world market value for flat panel screens by type and for cathode ray tubes, 1983-90.

WHY COMMERCIAL DISTRIBUTORS BECOME MILITARY MINDED

(p. 78-84) By Carol Suby. Article, with 1 chart showing military semiconductor market value, for 3 types of components, 1983-85. Data are from Dataquest, Inc.

NO LAYOFFS: A BET ON THE FUTURE

(p. 138) By Albert Socolovsky. Article, with 1 chart showing electronics sales per employee, for 3 major companies, FY80-84.

C1850–2.622: Oct. 1, 1985 (Vol. 11, No. 19)

LETTERS: ELECTRONIC BUSINESS 200

(p. 20) Includes corrected data for 1 company covered in feature on financial performance of 200 leading electronics companies.

For description of feature, see C1850-2.617 above.

DATA CONVERSION: A BUOYANT REAL WORLD BUSINESS

(p. 98-100) By Shelley Tsantes. Article, with 2 charts showing the following for linear integrated circuits, by type: revenues, 1984, and revenue growth rate, 1984-90 period. Data are from Dataquest, Inc.

WILL LATCH-UP LOCK UP A WHOLE NEW CMOS MARKET?

(p. 104-105) By Mark Mehler. Article, with 1 chart showing worldwide sales of epitaxial silicon wafers (total and for complementary metal-oxide semiconductors), 1984 and 1990. Data are from *Electronics Materials Report.*

TOP 40 EUROPEAN ELECTRONICS COMPANIES, ANNUAL TABLE

(p. 112-113) Annual table showing sales, assets, and profits per employee; selected financial and operating ratios; and headquarters country; for top 40 electronics companies operating in Europe, ranked by electronics sales; for most recently completed fiscal year as of mid-1984. Data are from Mackintosh International.

Table is accompanied by a related article (p. 110-111).

VARs: A VERTICAL MARKET VICTORY

(p. 136-137) Article, with 1 chart showing sales of office personal computers, by type of distributor, 1985 and 1990. Data are from Future Computing, Inc.

C1850–2.623: Oct. 15, 1985 (Vol. 11, No. 20)

SATELLITES: HIGH TECH, HIGH PROFILE AND HIGH RISK

(p. 24-32) Article on market outlook for communications satellite industry. Data are from International Resource Development Inc., Dataquest Inc., and Office of Technology Assessment.

Includes 3 charts and 1 table showing transponders in use, by type of transmission; market value for satellite-based private networks; earth station sales (total and for direct broadcast satellites); and launches of commercial communications satellites, by company, with headquarters country; various periods 1965-93.

CROWDED WORLD OF 32-BIT MICROPROCESSORS

(p. 63-66) By Shelley Tsantes. Article, with 1 chart showing worldwide revenues for 32-bit microprocessors, 1984-90. Data are from Dataquest Inc.

BOOM AND BUST IN THE IC EQUIPMENT INDUSTRY

(p. 72) By Mark Mehler. Article, with 1 chart showing top 11 semiconductor equipment manufacturers ranked by worldwide shipment value, 1984. Data are from VLSI Research Inc.

JAPAN LEADS THE LIST OF TOP FOREIGN FIRMS IN THE U.S.

(p. 85-87) By Carol Suby and Linda Stallmann. Article, with 1 table showing electronics sales in U.S., total sales, currency conversion value, types of products, and headquarters country, all for top 31 foreign electronics companies ranked by electronics sales in U.S., for most recently completed fiscal year as of mid-1985.

LONG LEADTIMES FOR MILITARY CYLINDRICAL CONNECTORS

(p. 106) Article, with 1 chart showing market value for military cylindrical connectors, 1982-85 and 1989. Data are from The Fleck Group Inc.

C1850–3   RESTAURANTS AND INSTITUTIONS

Biweekly.
ISSN 0273-5520.
LC 81-641204.
SRI/MF/not filmed

Biweekly trade journal of the food service industry, reporting on finances and operations, customer attitudes and characteristics, marketing techniques, food preparation, and individual companies and establishments. Includes data on sales, costs, employment, salaries, and menus. Covers full-service and fast-food restaurants, and hotel, school, retail store, transportation, health care, military, and employee dining facilities.

Data are primarily from the journal's own or other private research.

Issues generally contain:

a. Articles, some with statistics.

b. "Reconnaissance" section with several regular depts, including monthly charts or tables on food service sales and profits, managerial and hourly job openings, labor and food cost indexes, and prices of selected menu items; and recurring chart on food service equipment dealer sales.

Annual statistical features include industry trends and outlook; leading independent restaurants; menu census; franchise establishments; top 400 food service operations; growth chains; and consumer eating out patterns. A recurring jobs survey report, covering personnel developments, is also presented.

Journal also includes an annual buyer's guide; and several full-issue cookbooks.

Substantial monthly statistics are described below. All additional features with substantial statistical content are described, as they appear, under "Statistical Features." Nonstatistical features are not covered.

Availability: Restaurants and Institutions, 270 St. Paul St., Denver CO 80206-5191, qualified subscribers †, others $70.00 per yr., single copy $5.00, Buyers Guide $25.00, other special issue prices vary; SRI/MF/not filmed.

Issues reviewed during 1985: Nov. 7, 1984-Oct. 30, 1985 (P) (Vol. 94, Nos. 22-26; Vol. 95, Nos. 1-22).

MONTHLY STATISTICS:

[Data on profits, managerial openings, and food cost index generally appear within one issue; remaining data appear in the alternate issue.

Data on profits, sales, and job openings are based on surveys of food service operators, conducted 1-3 months prior to cover date.]

PROFITS AND SALES

Two charts showing change in food service profits and sales, for survey month and 6-month outlook, in commercial and institutional establishments. Charts appear in "Business Confidence Index" dept.

JOB OPENINGS

Two charts showing change in food service job openings for managerial and hourly positions, for survey month compared to previous year average. Chart appears in "Human Resources" dept.

FOOD COST INDEX

Table showing wholesale prices for approximately 20 food items, generally for month of publication, previous month, same month of prior year, and selected other months.

LABOR COST INDEX

Table showing salaries for 7-8 food service industry positions, by region and for commercial and institutional establishments, generally for month prior to month of publication. Data are based on a monthly survey of 160 food service operators. Table appears in "Human Resources" dept.

MENU SELLING PRICES

Table showing average selling price for selected menu items, by census region and type of restaurant, generally for month 1-2 months prior to month of publication. Data are based on surveys of approximately 75 restaurants. Table appears in "Menu Concepts" dept.

STATISTICAL FEATURES:

C1850–3.601: Nov. 7, 1984 (Vol. 94, No. 22)

DEALER SALES FOR THE 3 MONTHS ENDED AUG. 31, 1984, RECURRING FEATURE

(p. 78) Recurring chart showing trend in dealer sales of 4 types of food service equipment, for 3-month period ended Aug. 31, 1984 vs. preceding 3-month period. Shows percent of dealers reporting increase, decrease, and no change. Data are from *Foodservice Equipment Specialist* Dealer Business Index.

DOLLARS WORTH

(p. 89-98) By Elizabeth Faulkner. Article, with 1 undated table showing cost per case and per week for most frequently ordered food items in small, medium, and large food service operations in 6 market segments. Data are based on a *Restaurants and Institutions* survey, and are intended to permit individual operators to compare their costs with similar establishments.

GOURMET HAMBURGER

(p. 103-128) By Maureen Pratscher. Article, with 1 table showing the following for 20 gourmet hamburger chains: year founded; number of units, average check size and sales per unit, and alcoholic beverage share of total sales, primarily 1984; and selected ownership detail. Also includes chain profiles.

Data correction appears in the Jan. 9, 1985 issue; for description, see C1850-3.605 below.

C1850–3.602: Nov. 21, 1984 (Vol. 94, No. 23)

MEALS FOR THE ELDERLY GET 3-YEAR EXTENSION, FUNDING BOOST

(p. 24) Article, with 1 table showing the following for elderly persons receiving government-supported meals at congregate meal sites and at home: average age, income and health characteristics, selected welfare benefits received, and degree of self-sufficiency, 1983. Data are from U.S. Administration on Aging.

FROZEN FOODS GUIDE

(p. 105-109) Article reporting on food service industry use of frozen foods. Data are from a *Restaurants and Institutions* survey of approximately 1,400 food service operators.

Includes 1 table and 3 charts showing survey response on use of selected frozen food items; reasons for purchasing frozen foods, with detail for baked goods; and use of frozen vs. fresh items for selected entrees and baked goods.

C1850–3.603: Dec. 5, 1984 (Vol. 94, No. 24)

PRESSURE BUILDS FOR RESTAURANT WARNINGS ON SULFITING AGENTS

(p. 30) Article, with 1 undated table showing estimated content level and per capita daily consumption, for sulfiting agents (additives used to preserve and freshen food) in 11 food categories. Data are from Federation of American Societies for Experimental Biology.

TASTES OF AMERICA, ANNUAL FEATURE

(p. 99-140) Annual feature on consumer eating out practices and preferences, 1984, with comparisons to 1980-83. Data are based on responses of approximately 1,400 households to the 5th annual *Restaurants and Institutions* consumer survey conducted May-June 1984 by NFO Research, Inc. Contains 4 sections with the following statistics:

a. "Eating Out." Includes favorite dining companion; expectations for buying power and eating out frequency in 1985; complaints about restaurants, with comparison to 1980; type of restaurant patronized in past month, with detail for strongest and weakest regional markets; purchases of food for consumption away from purchase place, by type of operation, with comparison to 1983; and factors influencing restaurant choice. 4 charts and 2 tables. (p. 100-105)

b. "Food Ordering." Includes menu items ordered more and less frequently than in past; and various food items ranked by ordering frequency, with detail for selected regions and customer age groups. 2 charts and 2 tables (p. 111-114)

c. "Best Customers." Includes selected health food preferences of consumers likely to try new restaurants; and factors influencing restaurant choice, weekly spending for eating out (with comparison to 1982-83), and main sources of irritation in restaurants, for frequent patrons, heaviest spenders, those most likely to try new restaurants, and business diners. 1 chart and 3 tables. (p. 127-131)

d. "Life Stages." Includes percent of consumers ordering alcoholic beverages with lunch by type of drink and age category, and older customers' favorite chain restaurants, main sources of irritation in restaurants, and eating out practices and preferences, all for single persons, couples, and parents; and percent of meals eaten and food dollar spent for food at and away from home, by age category. 1 chart and 4 tables. (p. 137-140)

This is the 1st of 2 features comprising the annual report.

C1850–3.604: Dec. 19, 1984 (Vol. 94, No. 25)

TASTES OF AMERICA, ANNUAL FEATURE

(p. 105-142.H) Annual feature on consumer eating out practices and preferences, 1984, with comparisons to 1980 and 1983, and detail for restaurant chains.

Data are based on responses of approximately 1,400 households to the 5th annual *Restaurants and Institutions* consumer survey conducted May-June 1984 by NFO Research, Inc. Contains 3 sections with the following statistics:

a. "The People's Choice." Includes popularity rankings for top 4-29 restaurant chains, grouped by market segment; consumer awareness and patronage of 25 chains generally concentrated in specified regions; satisfaction index ratings for top 3 chains in each census region, and for 16 chains with high popularity potential based on current patronage; and 10 most patronized chains; with selected comparisons to 1983. 7 tables. (p. 106-112)

b. "Chain Profiles." Includes sociodemographic characteristics, food preferences, and other restaurants patronized, for typical customers of leading chains in 8 market segments. Text statistics. (p. 115-136)

c. "Thirsts of America." Includes percent of customers ordering alcoholic beverages in restaurants, by meal period, type of beverage, census region, income level, and customer type (heaviest spenders, business diners, and those most likely to try new restaurant); with selected comparisons to 1980. 4 charts and 1 table. (p. 142.A-142.H)

This is the 2nd of 2 features comprising the annual report.

C1850–3.605: Jan. 9, 1985 (Vol. 95, No. 1)

CORRECTION

(p. 92) Corrected data for article on gourmet hamburger restaurant chains, appearing in Nov. 7, 1984 issue.

For article description, see C1850-3.601, above.

100 RICHEST INDEPENDENT RESTAURANTS IN AMERICA, ANNUAL FEATURE

(p. 97-112) Annual article, for 1985, profiling the top 100 restaurants with independent owners, ranked by total annual sales. Profiles include text data on annual sales and customers. Also includes listing of top 60 restaurants with independent owners and annual sales between $3 million and $4.5 million. Data are compiled by *Restaurants and Institutions*.

C1850–3.606: Jan. 23, 1985 (Vol. 95, No. 2)

1985 ANNUAL REPORT

(p. 111-200) Annual report, for 1985, on food service industry trends and outlook. Presents data on food and alcoholic beverage sales, number of establishments, employment, and food sales market shares, 1983-85, with total 1982 sales; and comparisons of 3 sales growth forecasts, 1985; all by detailed industry segment. Also includes employment trends by industry.

Industry segments covered include full-service and fast food restaurants, health care, elementary/secondary schools, business/industry, colleges, hotel/motel, retail stores, convenience/grocery stores, military, recreation, and transportation.

Also includes data on school lunch and breakfast program participation; convenience store fast food item sales and profit indicators; and airline food service costs; various periods 1978-84.

Data are from Cahners Bureau of Foodservice Research, Technomics Consultants, National Restaurant Assn, USDA, GDR/CREST Enterprises, Air Transport Assn, and other sources.

Contains overview and 12 segment reports, with narrative analysis, 14 charts, and 17 tables. This is the 10th annual report.

C1850–3.607: Feb. 6, 1985 (Vol. 95, No. 3)

PLAYING FOR KEEPS

(p. 105-108) By Howard Schlossberg. Article, with 1 table showing top 15 restaurant chains ranked by TV advertising expenditures, 1st 9 months 1984 with comparisons to same period of 1983. Data are from TV Bureau of Advertising and Broadcast Advertisers Reports.

C1850–3.608: Feb. 20, 1985 (Vol. 95, No. 4)

DEALER SALES FOR THE 3 MONTHS ENDED OCT. 31, 1984, RECURRING FEATURE

(p. 78) Recurring chart showing trends in dealer sales of 4 types of food service equipment, for 3-month period ended Oct. 31, 1984 vs. preceding 3-month period. Shows percent of dealers reporting increase, decrease, and no change. Data are from *Foodservice Equipment Specialist* Dealer Business Index.

1985 MENU CENSUS, ANNUAL FEATURE

(p. 95-124) Annual article, for 1985, reporting on food service menu survey. Presents detailed data on popularity of individual food and beverage menu items, including percent of food service operators offering each item, and percent rating each item a good seller by region, with additional detail by type of food service operation.

Data are from responses of over 2,300 food service operators to a *Restaurants and Institutions* survey.

Contains narrative analyses with text data, and 10 charts and 17 tables.

NEW GDR CREST SURVEY TRACKS CUSTOMER BEHAVIOR IN NON-CAPTIVE INSTITUTIONAL MARKET

(p. 143-145) By Elizabeth Faulkner. Article on institutional food service customers. Data are from RACER (Restricted Access Consumer Eatings Report), a data base compiling records from a panel of 5,000 households. RACER is maintained by GDR/CREST Enterprises and excludes hospital patients, military personnel, and other "captive" institutional food service customers.

Includes 1 table and 5 charts showing institutional food service patronage, and average expenditure, by meal period and/or type of setting; availability of microwave ovens and refrigerators at school/work, by consumer age group; and usual source of main meal. No dates are given.

This is the 1st in a series of articles based on RACER findings.

USE THE OL' BEAN TO GRIND OUT FRESH IDEAS

(p. 163-166) By Kathleen Marshall. Article reporting on coffee marketing in food service operations. Data are from *Restaurants and Institutions* 1985 Menu Census, and a Gallup Organization 1983 survey of 505 restaurants that serve coffee, with comparison to previous surveys.

Includes 2 charts and 1 table showing percent of food service operators offering regular and decaffeinated coffee, by type of operation, 1985; and restaurant customer complaints about coffee, 1980-83.

C1850–3.609: Mar. 20, 1985 (Vol. 95, No. 6)

SURVEY REVEALS GROWTH OF ENTREPRENEURIAL FOODSERVICE ACTIVITY, ANNUAL FEATURE

(p. 74-75) Annual article on franchise food service establishments and sales. Data are from Commerce Dept's *Franchising in the Economy.*

Includes 1 table and 2 charts showing company- and franchisee-owned establishments and sales, 1983-85; sales distribution by type of food served (no date); and number of franchise establishments owned by minorities, selected years 1978-83.

Previous article is described in SRI 1984 Annual under C1850-3.507.

C1850–3.610: Apr. 3, 1985 (Vol. 95, No. 7)

INVESTING IN RESTAURANT FUTURES

(p. 107-114) By Shelley Wolson. Article on food service industry equipment buying practices. Data are based on 4,486 responses to a *Restaurants and Institutions* 1983-84 survey.

Includes 2 charts and 2 tables showing percent of operators buying new equipment, for industry segments with greatest and least purchasing activity; principal reasons for purchases; and estimated manufacturers' sales 1985, and percent change 1984-85; all by type of equipment.

Also includes 1 table on survey respondent characteristics.

C1850–3.611: Apr. 17, 1985 (Vol. 95, No. 8)

COEX '85 ALSO LOOKS AT STRATEGY AND PURCHASING

(p. 22-23, 28) Article on planning and purchasing practices of food service companies. Data are from over 100 responses to recent GDR/CREST surveys of food service executives.

Includes 2 undated tables showing present and projected frequency of strategic business plan development, for small, medium, and large chains; and views of corporate and purchasing officers on relative importance of purchasing function, and on degree of interaction between purchasing and other departments.

SURVEY GIVES COEX A PICTURE OF CHAIN COMPUTER USE

(p. 72) Article, with 1 undated table showing percent of small, medium, large, and all restaurant chains using computer systems, by function. Data are from responses of 106 chains to a GDR/CREST survey.

DEALER SALES FOR THE THREE MONTHS ENDED DEC. 31, 1984, RECURRING FEATURE

(p. 80) Recurring chart showing trend in dealer sales of 4 types of food service equipment, for 3-month period ended Dec. 31, 1984 vs. preceding 3-month period. Shows percent of dealers reporting increase, decrease, and no change. Data are from *Food Service Equipment Specialist* Dealer Business Index.

C1850–3.612: May 1, 1985 (Vol. 95, No. 9)

SURVEY SHOWS 86% OF CHAINS USING POINT-OF-SALE SYSTEMS

(p. 70-71) Article on most popular features of electronic cash register systems used in restaurants. Data are based on approximately 95 responses to a GDR/CREST survey of restaurant chains. Includes 1 undated table.

C1850–3.613: May 15, 1985 (Vol. 95, No. 10)

MERGERS AND ACQUISITIONS: DEALING A WINNING HAND IN HIGH-STAKES GAME

(p. 179-182) By Howard Schlossberg. Article, with 1 chart and 1 table showing distribution of restaurant industry acquisitions by reason for acquisition (no date); and number of food industry acquiring companies, total acquisitions, and acquisitions involving similar businesses, by type of company, 1984 with comparisons to 1983.

Data sources include *Restaurants and Institutions* and Food Institute.

COEX '85 TACKLES FINICKY EATERS, PICKY BANKERS

(p. 186-187) Article, with 1 table and 1 chart showing restaurant customer expenditures and traffic by meal period as percent of total expenditures and traffic, for all and quick service, midscale, and upscale restaurants, Dec. 1983-Nov. 1984 period; and distribution of meals eaten away from home by source (commercial restaurant, noncommercial/noncaptive, food brought from home, and other, no date).

Data are from GDR/CREST Enterprises.

BROWN BAGGER: NEW RESEARCH PROBES THE RELUCTANT CONSUMER'S BEHAVIOR

(p. 291-294) By Elizabeth Faulkner. Article discussing consumer sources of meals. Data are from RACER (Restricted Access Consumer Eatings Report), a data base compiling records from a panel of 5,000 households. RACER is maintained by GDR/CREST Enterprises.

Includes 5 undated charts showing distribution of meals by source, with detail for lunch and for persons frequently bringing food from home; distribution of meals brought from home, by meal period; and index measuring likelihood of bringing food from home, by income, sex, occupational group (blue or white collar), and community population size.

Article is part of a series of features based on RACER findings.

TAKEOUT BUSINESS BOOSTS DISPOSABLE PRODUCTS USE

(p. 325-327) Article, with 2 tables and 1 chart showing prevalence of disposable product use in food service industry, by reason, service area, and industry segment, 1983 with selected comparisons to 1972. Data are from responses of 1,007 food service operators to a Cahners Bureau of Foodservice Research survey.

C1850–3.614: May 29, 1985 (vol. 95, No. 11)

EXCLUSIVE JOB$ SURVEY REVEALS UPBEAT MOOD, RECURRING FEATURE

(p. 93-100) Recurring article, by Maureen Pratscher, on food service industry personnel developments, focusing on executives' characteristics, salaries, and attitudes. Data are from responses of approximately 1,850 food service executives to a 1985 *Restaurants and Institutions* survey.

Includes 9 charts and 3 tables showing survey results on the following:

a. Food service management employee average weekly hours, annual salaries, years in food service industry and in present job, and turnover rates, all by position, with some comparisons to the 1984 survey.

b. Executives' satisfaction with last raise; and views on various issues related to serving alcoholic beverages, including support for national minimum drinking age and sanctions against beverage operators allowing patrons to overdrink, and methods for reducing drunken driver incidents.

C1850–3.615: June 12, 1985 (vol. 95, No. 12)

DEALER SALES FOR THE THREE MONTHS ENDED FEB. 28, 1985, RECURRING FEATURE

(p. 78) Recurring chart showing trend in dealer sales of 4 types of food service equipment, for 3-month period ended Feb. 28, 1985 vs. preceding 3-month period. Shows percent of dealers reporting increase, decrease, and no change. Data are from *Food Service Equipment Specialist* Dealer Business Index.

C1850–3.616: June 26, 1985 (Vol. 95, No. 13)

1985 GROWTH CHAINS, ANNUAL FEATURE

(p. 91-138) Annual feature, by Elizabeth Faulkner et al., on food service organizations with outstanding growth prospects, 1985. Data are from *Restaurants & Institutions* and company estimates.

Includes profiles of approximately 80 such organizations grouped by type, presenting headquarters location, establishments as of Jan. 1, 1985, food/drink sales for 1984 or 1985, owners and/or top executives, and summary of current activities and outlook.

C1850–3.617: July 10, 1985 (Vol. 95, No. 14)

RESTAURANT TV SPENDING CONTINUES TO SKYROCKET

(p. 24) Article, with 1 table showing TV advertising expenditures, 1983-84, for top 15 restaurant advertisers ranked by 1984 expenditures. Data are from TV Bureau of Advertising, based on Broadcast Advertisers Reports.

KNOWING LEAD TIMES CAN FACILITATE PLANS FOR EQUIPMENT PURCHASES

(p. 70) Article, with 1 table showing time elapsed between purchase and delivery of food service equipment, by detailed type of equipment, Apr. 1985, with comparisons to Feb. 1985. Data are from *Food Service Equipment Specialist* Dealer Lead Times Index survey.

'400' PART I: BUSINESS AND FINANCE, ANNUAL FEATURE

(p. 91-257) Annual ranking of top 400 food service/lodging organizations based on food service sales in 1984 with comparison to 1983, and including headquarters location, industry segment, and number of units as of Jan. 1, 1984-85.

Industry segments covered include fast food and full-service restaurants, franchise and diversified operations, schools, employee feeding, colleges, military, transportation, health care, retail, recreation, lodging, and government institutions.

Also includes sales trends for total food service industry and the top 400, 1964-84; list of companies new to the top 400; food service stock price trends, 1976-85, with 1983-84 prices for selected companies; and rankings of top 25 companies in food service/lodging sales and in food service sales growth, top 100 lodging companies in room sales (with number of properties and rooms), and top 50 restaurant chains in sales, 1984 or 1985, with comparisons to previous year.

Data are from *Restaurants & Institutions* and company estimates.

Contains analysis, with 2 charts (p. 91-101); ranked listing of the top 400 (p. 102-128); profiles of companies and industry segments, interspersed with 1 chart and 4 tables (p. 132-235); ranked listings of top lodging organizations and restaurant chains, with narrative summaries (p. 236-250); and alphabetical listing of the top 400 (p. 253-257).

This is Part I of the 21st annual report.

C1850–3.618: July 24, 1985 (Vol. 95, No. 15)

'400' PART II: MENU CONCEPTS AND OPERATIONS, ANNUAL FEATURE

(p. 99-222) Annual report on operations of top 400 food service/lodging organizations, 1984. Presents profiles of menu and promotional developments for individual organizations grouped by concept or market segment, with each organization's sales, sales ranking, and number of units.

Concepts and market segments covered include various food themes, coffee shops/family restaurants, retail and recreation, theme and dinner houses, cafeterias, transportation, lodging, schools, and contract operations.

Also includes data on expansion, alcoholic beverage sales, franchising developments, and advertising budgets and expenditures, for various individual organizations; distributor services desired by food service operators; and number of foreign and domestic units for leading international food service organizations.

Data are from *Restaurants & Institutions* and company estimates.

Contains analyses interspersed with company profiles, 4 charts and 1 table (p. 99-204); ranked listing of the top 400, by census division (p. 209-212); and alphabetical listing of the top 400 (p. 215-222).

This is Part II of the 21st annual report.

C1850–3.619: Aug. 7, 1985 (Vol. 95, No. 16)

DEALER SALES FOR THE THREE MONTHS ENDED APR. 30, 1985, RECURRING FEATURE

(p. 86) Recurring chart showing trend in dealer sales of 4 types of food service equipment, for 3-month period ended Apr. 30, 1985 vs. preceding 3-month period. Shows percent of dealers reporting increase, decrease, and no change. Data are from *Food Service Equipment Specialist* Dealer Business Index.

EQUIPMENT CENSUS SHOWS USAGE CHANGING WITH MENUS

(p. 197-198) Article, with 1 table showing percent of chain, independent, and institutional food service operators using various types of kitchen equipment; and average number in use; all by detailed type of equipment. Data are from *Restaurants and Institutions* 1985 Equipment Census.

C1850–3.620: Aug. 21, 1985 (Vol. 95, No. 17)

AMERICANS EATING MORE POULTRY, FISH, FATS

(p. 24) Article, with 1 table showing per capita food consumption, by commodity, selected periods 1960-84. Data are from USDA.

JOB$ SURVEY FINDS TIP REPORTING STILL A TOUCHY SUBJECT, RECURRING FEATURE

(p. 145-152) Recurring feature, by Maureen Pratscher, on food service industry personnel attitudes and characteristics. Data are from a 1985 survey of food service executives by *Restaurants and Institutions*. Includes 2 charts and 5 tables showing the following:

a. Employee views on tip reporting regulations, compared to a year ago; and whether tip reporting procedure presents problems for food service operators, and types of problems encountered.

b. Respondent eating habits, assessment of own vices, and involvement in various types of community services and plans for coming year; and major career concerns, by age group.

MEAL SKIPPERS: WHO ARE THEY AND WHY AREN'T THEY EATING

(p. 185-188) Article on characteristics of persons who skip meals/snacks at least 3 times a week. Data are from RACER (Restricted Access Consumer Eatings Report), a data base compiling records from a panel of 5,000 households. RACER is maintained by GDR/CREST Enterprises.

Includes 2 undated charts showing distribution of meals skipped, by meal period; and index measuring likelihood of an adult skipping breakfast meal, by sex, age, and household size.

Article is part of a series of features based on RACER findings.

C1850–3.621: Sept. 18, 1985 (Vol. 95, No. 19)

BREAKFAST PROVIDES NUTRIENTS, OPPORTUNITY FOR OPERATORS

(p. 64-65) Article, with 1 undated chart showing distribution of daily calorie intake, by meal period. Data are from General Mills, Inc.

WHAT FOODSERVICE BUYS

(p. 119-126) Article, with 1 undated table repeated for 20 food service menu items, showing the following: percent of operators using and not using item; and percent of operators classified as heavy, medium, and light users, by industry segment.

Industry segments covered are full service and fast food restaurants, hotel/motel, retail/recreation, health care, school/college, and employee feeding.

Data are from a Simmons Market Research Bureau study.

C1850–3.622: Oct. 2, 1985 (Vol. 95, No. 20)

NRA-GALLUP SURVEY FINDS ADVENTUROUS CONSUMERS

(p. 26-27) Article, with 2 tables showing 13 types of specialty restaurants ranked by percent of adults recently patronizing or likely to patronize the type of restaurant. Data are based on responses of over 2,000 adults to a Mar. 1985 survey conducted by the Gallup Organization for National Restaurant Assn.

Full survey report is covered in SRI under A8200-9.

DEALER SALES FOR THE THREE MONTHS ENDED JULY 24, 1985, RECURRING FEATURE

(p. 80) Recurring chart showing trend in dealer sales of 4 types of food service equipment, for 3-month period ended July 24, 1985 vs. preceding 3-month period. Shows percent of dealers reporting increase, decrease, and no change. Data are from *Food Service Equipment Specialist* Dealer Business Index.

DEEP-FREEZE ITEMS GET WARM RECEPTION

(p. 106-110) By Maureen Pratscher. Article, with 1 undated table showing 38 frozen food items ranked by percent of chain restaurants using item, with comparison to total restaurant industry use.

C1850–3.623: Oct. 30, 1985 (Vol. 95, No. 22)

FEDERAL DATA CENTER MEASURES GOVERNMENT FOODSERVICE PROCUREMENT

(p. 32) Article, with 1 chart showing Federal expenditures for food service equipment, by equipment category, 1984. Data are from Federal Procurement Data Center.

MILLION MEALERS: 50 TOP INSTITUTIONS

(p. 117-120) By Laura Pokrzywa. Article on leading food service operations in institutional market segments, as ranked by value of food purchases, 1984. Data are from *Restaurants and Institutions* and company estimates.

Includes 3 tables showing headquarters location, value of food/beverage purchases, and number of units, for top 10 operations in military and contract market segments and for top 40 operations in nonmilitary segment, 1984.

C1865
Cash Management Institute

C1865–1   DONOGHUE'S MUTUAL FUNDS ALMANAC, 16th Annual Edition, 1985-86
Annual. 1985. 134 p.
ISSN 0737-0369.
ISBN 0-913755-02-8.
LC 72-622174.
SRI/MF/complete

Annual almanac presenting information on the investment objectives, characteristics, and financial performance of over 850 mutual funds, 1984 and trends. Includes the following data for individual money and equity/bond funds, grouped by objective:

a. All funds: percent gain or loss per share, 1975-84; growth of $10,000 investment over 1980-84 and 1975-84 periods; total assets, 1983-84; minimum purchase; and date organized.

b. Money funds only: availability of checking and wire redemption services, check return, exchange privileges, and IRA and Keogh plans, with minimum check amount and wire fee.

c. Equity/bond funds only: maximum sales charge; dividend and capital gains distributions, 1984; percent yield, 1984; and availability of withdrawal and retirement plans.

Also includes alphabetical listings of funds and distributors; rankings of top funds in yield, gain per share, and investment growth; and listings of new and changed funds.

Contains contents listing and user guide (p. 3-5); 6 narrative sections presenting investment information (p. 6-21); 7 tables and lists (p. 22-126); and glossary (p. 127-134).

Availability: Donoghue's Mutual Funds Almanac, PO Box 540, Holliston MA 01746, $23.00; SRI/MF/complete.

C2000
Chase, Dana, Publications

C2000–1   APPLIANCE
Monthly.
ISSN 0003-6781.
LC 78-1694.
SRI/MF/not filmed

Monthly trade journal of the appliance industry. Covers trends and developments in production, engineering, purchasing, and management, for producers of consumer, commercial, and business appliances.

General format:

a. Feature or special report articles, occasionally with statistics; and regular narrative depts, placed throughout.

b. Monthly "Appliance Statistics" table showing factory unit shipments for approximately 40 appliances, including major appliances, air conditioner and heating systems, TVs, and home video equipment, for month 3 months prior to cover date, year to date, and same periods of previous year.

Major annual features include statistical forecast of appliance sales and shipments, and industry purchasing directory (Jan. issue); 10-year statistical review of appliance shipments (Apr. issue); and industry portrait with directories (Sept. issue).

Monthly table appears in all issues. All additional features with substantial statistical content are described, as they appear, under "Statistical Features." Nonstatistical contents are not covered.

Availability: Appliance, Circulation Department, 1000 Jorie Blvd., CS 5030, Oak Brook IL 60521, qualified subscribers †, others $40.00 per yr., single copy $4.00, Jan. issue $20.00; SRI/MF/not filmed.

Issues reviewed during 1985: Nov. 1984-Oct. 1985 (P) (Vol. 41, Nos. 11-12; Vol. 42, Nos. 1-10) [Nov. 1984, and Apr., June, and Aug. 1985 issues are published in 2 sections].

STATISTICAL FEATURES:

C2000–1.601: Dec. 1984 (Vol. 41, No. 12)

APPLIANCE PRODUCTION IN WEST GERMANY

(p. 13) Table showing West German household appliance production, imports, exports, and unit sales, by type, 1980-83. Data are from the West German household appliance producers' assn.

C2000–1.602: Jan. 1985 (Vol. 42, No. 1)
[Issue price is $15.00.]

APPLIANCE 33rd ANNUAL FORECASTS

Annual *Appliance* forecast report, for 1985, consisting of articles analyzing the outlook for appliance industry sales and shipments through 1990. Articles with substantial statistical content are described below.

1985: A VERY GOOD YEAR, ANNUAL FEATURE

(p. 41-45) Annual article, by David E. Simpson, forecasting appliance sales and industry developments to 1990. Data for 1983 are from Commerce Dept; other data are *Appliance* forecasts.

Includes 3 tables showing unit shipments of major appliances, and of water heating, comfort conditioning, electric housewares, and business and/or outdoor appliances; and distributor unit sales of consumer electronic products; all by detailed product type, 1983-90, with selected comparisons to 1973.

HOLDING STEADY IN '85, ANNUAL FEATURE

(p. 48) Annual article, by Harry Paynter, presenting Gas Appliance Manufacturers Assn industry forecast for 1985. Includes 1 table showing unit sales of selected gas appliances, with some comparative data for electric and oil products, 1983-85.

C2000–1.603: Apr. 1985 (Vol. 42, No. 4)
[Issue is published in 2 parts.]

PART 1

32nd ANNUAL APPLIANCE STATISTICAL REVIEW

(p. 41-44) Annual *Appliance* 10-year review of unit shipments for major, comfort conditioning, consumer electronic, personal care, electric houseware, outdoor, and business appliances; vending machines; and plumbing appliances/fixtures; 1975-84.

Data are from trade assns, *Appliance* estimates, *Merchandising*, and Commerce Dept.

Contains 1 summary table, and 9 detailed tables showing shipments of specified products in each of the categories noted above, 1975-84. (Table for consumer electronics shows distributor unit sales, rather than shipments.)

C2000–1.604: June 1985 (Vol. 42, No. 6)
[Issue is published in 2 parts.]

PART 1

INCREDIBLE VALUE STORY

(p. 41-48) By James Stevens. Article, with 1 chart and 5 tables showing selected home appliance industry trends, including labor productivity, PPI and CPI, hours of work required to earn appliance purchase price, and energy use reductions, by type of appliance, various periods 1957-83. Data are from Federal agencies and industry sources.

AUTOMATING FOR QUALITY AND EFFICIENCY

(p. 50-52) By James Stevens. Article, with 2 tables showing market saturation levels for 8 appliances (no date), and microwave oven unit sales, 1980-84, all for France.

C2000–1.605: Sept. 1985 (Vol. 42, No. 9)

PORTRAIT OF THE U.S. APPLIANCE INDUSTRY, ANNUAL FEATURE

(p. 41-60) Annual article presenting overview of appliance industry. Data are from *Appliance* surveys and estimates, and other sources.

Includes 4 tables showing the following by appliance type: percent of homes with various appliances, selected years 1963-84; low, high, and average life expectancy, and number of units to be replaced in 1985-86; and market shares by manufacturer, and retail market value, 1984.

Also includes a directory of U.S. appliance companies and principal executives, with types of appliances produced.

C2000-1.606: Oct. 1985 (Vol. 42, No. 10)

TAIWAN ELECTRONIC APPLIANCE TRADE

(p. 25) Two tables showing Taiwan's exports and imports of electronic products, by product type and world area, 1984.

C2130
Chicago Sun-Times

C2130-1   POCKET GUIDE TO THE CHICAGO MARKET, 1985
Annual. [1985.]
119 p. Pocket-size.
SRI/MF/complete

Annual compilation of statistics on population, income, economic, and retail trade characteristics of the Chicago market. Data are shown primarily for 1980-83, with selected trends from 1935 and projections to 2005. Data sources include Federal Government, *Sales and Marketing Management* magazine, private assns and research firms, and *Chicago Sun-Times* research.

The Chicago market is defined variously as Chicago city, Northeastern Illinois Counties Area (NICA, formerly the Chicago SMSA), Chicago city/retail trading zone, Chicago-Gary-Lake County Consolidated MSA, Chicago ADI, and NICA/Gary-Hammond Primary MSA.

Report is designed to present a comprehensive overview of the Chicago market. Extensive socioeconomic, demographic, and geographic breakdowns are shown, as applicable, for most topics. These breakdowns include data by community area, county, commodity, income, industry, age, marital status, and sex. Comparisons to other U.S. metro areas are also occasionally included.

Contains contents and table listing (p. 3); and 3 sections, with 49 tables described below, interspersed with brief narrative highlights, and lists of Chicago area zip codes (p. 5-119).

Availability: Chicago Sun-Times, National Advertising, 401 N. Wabash Ave., Chicago IL 60611, †; SRI/MF/complete.

TABLE SECTIONS:

C2130-1.1: Section 1: Understanding and Defining the Chicago Market

(p. 5-28) Contains 12 tables. Includes population, households, effective buying income (EBI), and retail sales, with projections to 1988; housing units by tenure and household size; employment; newspaper circulation; gross metropolitan product; personal income; wages/salaries; bank clearings; manufactured

products gross sales; industrial activity index; electric power sales; steel production; industrial building/land investment; and air traffic.

C2130-1.2: Section 2-3: Measuring and Selling the Chicago Market

(p. 29-119) Contains 35 tables. Includes population and households, projected to 2005; median household income; marriages, births, and deaths; new car sales; building permits; median home value and contract rent; weather averages and extremes; retail establishments and sales, with sales comparisons to Cook County and State; and NICA population, households, EBI, and retail sales compared to greater NYC.

Also includes CPI and PPI, with detail for food; size and location of regional shopping centers; comparison of Chicago *Sun-Times* and *Tribune* newspapers, including net reach and advertising costs; selected appliance ownership; and adults purchasing clothes in past year.

Also includes the following U.S. data: population of 64 MSAs, including inside and outside central cities; EBI of 44 MSAs; and retail sales of top 10 MSAs.

C2140
Child and Waters

C2140-1   TRAVEL INDUSTRY WORLD YEARBOOK: The Big Picture, 1985
Annual. 1985. 136 p.
Vol. 29.
ISBN 0-9611200-2-9.
ISSN 0738-9515.
SRI/MF/not filmed

Annual report, by Somerset R. Waters, for 1985, on U.S. and world tourist travel trends and markets. Includes data on travel industry, travel destinations, accommodations, and transportation. Data are generally for 1982-83, with selected trends from 1960s and projections to 1990.

Data are from various sources, including Federal Government, OECD, private companies, foreign governments, World Tourism Organization (WTO), and other trade organizations.

Contains contents listing and geographic index (p. 2-3); narrative analysis interspersed with 1 map, 10 charts, and 55 tables, described below (p. 4-124); 11 supplemental tables, also described below (p. 125-134); and glossary and references (p. 135-136).

This is the 29th annual edition.

Availability: Child and Waters, 516 Fifth Ave., New York NY 10036, $49.00+$3.00 postage; SRI/MF/not filmed.

TABLES AND CHARTS:

C2140-1.1: World Tourism Summary

a. Travel trends: tourist arrivals, receipts, and/or expenditures, by country or world region, various years 1981-83; 20 countries ranked by tourism expenditures and receipts, 1982; and tourism spending and jobs generated, for U.S., Europe, Canada/Pacific, and rest of world, 1983. 5 tables. (p. 5-11)

b. Comparison of U.S. and world tourism before and after 1973 oil embargo; and revenues generated from U.S. and world tourism, compared with GNP and world gross product and trade, 1983 and 1990. 2 tables. (p. 14-15)

C2140-1.2: U.S. Domestic and International Travel

a. Travel summary: change in U.S. travel receipts by kind of business, traffic by mode, national park use, and gasoline demand, 1st 9 months 1984 vs. 1983; and domestic travel price index, with change in selected components, 1979-83. 2 tables. (p. 18-20)

b. Paid vacation time of average U.S. worker, by years of service (no date); State appropriations for tourism and the arts, with rankings, by State, FY84; and travel industry advertising expenditures of top 25 magazine advertisers and top 20 TV advertisers, 1983, with ranking comparison to 1982. 1 chart and 3 tables. (p. 21-25)

c. Tourism spending in U.S., by expenditure category and by State; total foreign visitor spending; and jobs generated from tourism, by State; 1982. 2 tables. (p. 28-31)

d. Domestic trip characteristics, including transportation mode, reason, distance, duration, region of origin and destination, and number and demographic characteristics of travelers, 1977; and top 10 States ranked by travel promotion budgets, 1984/85. 2 tables. (p. 33-43)

e. Foreign travel by U.S. citizens and U.S. travel by non-U.S. citizens: detailed data including traveler and trip characteristics, origins and destinations, and expenditures; and U.S. travel account balance of payments; various periods 1979-84. 1 chart and 10 tables. (p. 52-60)

C2140-1.3: World Regional Travel Summary

a. Canadian and Mexican tourist arrivals in U.S., 1981-84; and tourist arrivals and expenditures in the Caribbean, by country and/or region, various years 1970-83. 2 charts and 2 tables. (p. 61-70)

b. Western European unemployment rate, by country, 1979 and 1984; international tourism changes, including arrivals and receipts, by country or world area, 1982-83; establishments, rooms, and countries of operations, for major European hotel chains, 1983; and bed-nights spent by foreign tourists in lodging establishments, by country, 1983, with trend from 1980. 5 tables. (p. 75-82)

c. U.S. citizen business and pleasure travel, and total border entries, to Soviet Union, 1972-83; visitor arrivals in the Pacific region, with detail by area, 1973-83; and Africa visitor arrivals and receipts from tourism, 1982, and per capita income, 1980. 1 map, 2 charts, and 3 tables. (p. 83-103)

C2140-1.4: Travel Agents, Hotels, and Food Service
[Data are for U.S. unless otherwise noted.]

a. Travel agent share of total travel industry bookings, by travel mode and for hotels and packaged tours (no date); distribution of travel agency dollar volume by trip purpose, 1983; number of travel agents, and value of airline ticket sales, selected years 1966-84; and travel agency home, branch, and independent offices, by State, 1983. 1 chart and 3 tables. (p. 106-108)

b. International hotels: market data including source of business, composition of clientele, incidence of repeat business, and use of advance reservations; and industry financial and operating trends; generally by world area, various years 1982-84. 3 tables. (p. 109-110)

c. Lodging industry: distribution of rooms by type of locale and by room rate, 1984; hotel market data and financial and operating trends, by region, various years 1982-84; and top 25 hotel chains, generally ranked by number of rooms, selected years 1975-82. 2 charts and 3 tables. (p. 111-113)

d. Food service industry sales by type of establishment, 1983; and distribution of expenses for food-only restaurants, by expense category, 1981-82. 1 chart and 1 table. (p. 114-115)

C2140–1.5: Transportation

a. Passenger car registrations, by world region, 1970 and 1982; U.S. passenger transportation expenditures, by travel mode, 1981-82; vehicle miles traveled, for all U.S. roads/streets, 1974-84; U.S. rental car fleet size and rental locations, by company, 1982-84; and passenger capacity and ownership, for 9 new cruise ships, 1983-85. 5 tables. (p. 116-119)

b. World airline passenger traffic 1974-83, with detail for North Atlantic route; International Air Transport Assn (IATA) member airlines' passenger traffic and load factors, 1983; and passenger traffic, revenues, and profit, aggregated for U.S. airlines, 1979-83. 4 tables. (p. 120-123)

C2140–1.6: Supplemental Data

a. U.S. passport recipients, by sex and age, selected SMSA, object of travel, State and region of residence, and occupation, various years 1979-83. 5 tables. (p. 125-128)

b. Top 50 world hotel/motel chains ranked by number of rooms, and including number of establishments, 1981-82; population and auto registrations, by world area and country, 1981, with aggregate trends from 1960; number of travel agencies and population per agency, by State, 1983; top 50 world airports ranked by passenger traffic, 1983; foreign visitors to U.S. by country or world area of origin, 1977 and 1983; and Federal Government per diem foreign travel allowance by country or city, 1983-84. 6 tables. (p. 129-134)

C2150
Chilton Co.

C2150–1   CHILTON'S DISTRIBUTION for Traffic and Transportation Decision Makers
Monthly.
ISSN 0273-6721.
LC 80-643825.
SRI/MF/excerpts, shipped quarterly

Monthly trade journal on technical, regulatory, and financial aspects of the physical distribution of industrial goods, including management of inventory control, materials handling, and traffic.

General format:

a. Editorial depts; and feature articles, occasionally with statistics.

b. "Dialogue" feature, usually with statistics, based on results of reader surveys.

c. Quarterly "Forecast" section, with 5 tables and 1 chart.

July issue is an annual nonstatistical index to transportation and distribution services. Dec. issue includes annual editorial index.

Quarterly forecast tables and chart are listed below. All additional features with substantial statistical content are described, as they appear, under "Statistical Features;" page locations and latest period of coverage for quarterly forecast tables and chart are also noted. Nonstatistical features are not covered.

Availability: Chilton's Distribution, PO Box 2105, Radnor PA 19089, qualified subscribers †, others $40.00 per yr., single copy $2.00, Distribution Guide $20.00; SRI/MF/excerpts for all portions covered under "Statistical Features;" shipped quarterly.

Issues reviewed during 1985: Nov. 1984-Oct. 1985 (P) (Vol. 83, Nos. 11-12; Vol. 84, Nos. 1-10).

QUARTERLY FORECAST TABLES AND CHART:
[Data are forecasts and are usually shown for 3 quarters following month of publication. Table order varies.]

[1-2] General economic indicators; and diesel [full- and self-serve] fuel prices.

[3] Distribution index [truck, rail, air, and water shipments; warehouse space utilization; and inventory valuation; based on survey responses of approximately 100 shippers/warehousers].

[4] Purchasing managers' composite index [of purchasing activity]. [chart]

[5-6] Transportation tonnage and cost indexes [for rail, truck, and barge traffic].

STATISTICAL FEATURES:

C2150–1.601: Nov. 1984 (Vol. 83, No. 11)
DIALOGUE: PUBLIC APPEAL

(p. 7-8) Article reporting shippers' opinions on public warehousing. Data are from a reader survey. Includes 1 table.

THIS YEAR'S TRAIL TO THE TOP DISTRIBUTION CAREERS, ANNUAL FEATURE

(p. 57-67) Annual survey article, by Bernard J. LaLonde and Larry W. Emmelhainz, on industrial distribution executives' career patterns, work responsibilities, and industry outlook, 1984. Data are based on responses from 139 National Council of Physical Distribution Management members to an Aug. 1984 survey conducted by Ohio State University Logistics Research Group.

Includes 11 charts and 4 tables showing respondents' organizational position, job functions, educational background and needs, age distribution, compensation, and expectations for the 1980s, including computer use, impact of deregulation, and economic outlook.

C2150–1.602: Dec. 1984 (Vol. 83, No. 12)
DIALOGUE: STANDARDS GAIN FAVOR

(p. 7-8) Article reporting shippers' opinions on packaging management and need for Federal packaging standards. Data are from a reader survey. Includes 1 table.

OCEAN/AIR FINANCIAL REPORTS

(p. 17-20) Article on trends and outlook for the air and ocean freight industries. Data are from Air Transport Assn (ATA), International Air Transport Assn (IATA), and other specified sources. Includes 8 tables showing the following:

a. Top 30 air carriers ranked by freight ton miles, 1983; and international and domestic freight and airmail traffic for aggregate IATA airlines, 1983 with percent change from 1982.

b. Cargo ton miles and operating and net profit/loss for 26 U.S. and 2 Canadian ATA airlines, 1983; and value of freight ton-miles, freight revenue, profit and income, and return on investment, for aggregate scheduled airlines, 1973-83.

c. Market shares, capacity, revenues, earnings, and other financial data, for 3 leading U.S.-flag ocean containership operators, with detail by trade region; and aggregate containership load factors by trade region; various years 1983-86.

For description of a similar article showing data on air freight industry only, see SRI 1984 Annual, under C2150-1.502.

C2150–1.603: Jan. 1985 (Vol. 84, No. 1)
QUARTERLY FORECAST FEATURE

(p. 24-25) For 1st-4th quarters 1985.
For data description, see C2150-1 above.

DIALOGUE: CUSTOM-MADE FOR SHIPPERS?

(p. 7-8) Article reporting shippers' opinions on import and export regulations and enforcement authority. Data are from a reader survey. Includes 1 table.

C2150–1.604: Feb. 1985 (Vol. 84, No. 2)
DIALOGUE: SHIPPERS DECLINE RAILS' POLICIES

(p. 7-8) Article reporting shippers' opinions on railroad liability rates and practices. Data are from a reader survey. Includes 1 table.

C2150–1.605: Mar. 1985 (Vol. 84, No. 3)
QUARTERLY FORECAST FEATURE

(p. 56-57) For 2nd quarter 1985.
For data description, see C2150-1 above.

DIALOGUE: PAYING FOR 'YOUR' MISTAKES

(p. 7-8) Article on shippers' problems with freight overpayments and duplicate billings. Data are from a reader survey. Includes 1 table.

C2150–1.606: Apr. 1985 (Vol. 84, No. 4)

DIALOGUE: A MESSAGE TO YOUR CONGRESSMAN

(p. 7-8) Article on shippers' opinions regarding trucking industry deregulation. Data are from a reader survey. Includes 1 table.

MIXED EMOTIONS ABOUT MICROS

(p. 43-45) Article on microcomputer use in the warehousing industry. Data are from responses of 162 warehousers to a recent survey conducted by 3 industry analysts. Includes 4 undated charts showing survey response on current and planned microcomputer applications, level of satisfaction with equipment performance and value, and reasons for not using microcomputers.

C2150–1.607: May 1985 (Vol. 84, No. 5)

DIALOGUE: EVALUATING THE VENDORS' OUTPUT

(p. 7-8) Article reporting shippers' computer software needs, sources of information, vendor selection criteria, and feasibility of in-house development. Data are from a reader survey. Includes 1 table.

DISTRIBUTION'S CARRIER PORTFOLIO, QUARTERLY FEATURE

(p. 34-35) Quarterly article, with 1 chart and 1 table showing *Distribution's* carrier stock index vs. Dow Jones industrial index, 2nd quarter 1984-1st quarter 1985; and operating ratios, net income, profit margin, and return on equity, for 39 carrier companies arranged by type, for quarters ending Jan. and Apr. 1985. Carrier types are airlines, container lessors, common carriers, railroads, and air carriers/forwarders.

Data are prepared by Nordby International, Inc. This is the 1st quarterly feature.

C2150–1.608: June 1985 (Vol. 84, No. 6)

QUARTERLY FORECAST FEATURE

(p. 46-47) For 3rd quarter 1985-1st quarter 1986.

For data description, see C2150-1, above.

DIALOGUE: CONRAIL AT THE CROSSROAD

(p. 7-8) Article reporting shippers' opinions on the proposed sale of Government-owned Conrail to Norfolk Southern. Data are from a reader survey. Includes 1 table.

SOME BIG NUMBERS GET BELITTLED, ANNUAL FEATURE

(p. 51-58) Annual article, by Kurt Hoffman, on motor carrier financial performance, 1984 and trends. Includes 4 charts summarizing carrier performance trends, 1980-84; and 1 table showing operating revenues and income, net income, revenue tons hauled, operating ratio, and return on equity, for 15 large Class I household goods carriers, 1983-84.

Data for top 100 Class I carriers, usually included in this feature, were unavailable for publication. Missing data appear in Sept. 1985 issue, described under C2150-1.610 below.

C2150–1.609: Aug. 1985 (Vol. 84, No. 8)

DIALOGUE: OCEAN SHIPPERS SOAPBOX

(p. 7-8) Article reporting shippers' opinions on Trans-Pacific Westbound Rate Agreement, and other topics concerning marine freight shipment rates. Data are from a reader survey. Includes 1 table.

ONCE A FROG, ALWAYS A FROG?

(p. 70-78) By Peter T. Bower. Article on railroad industry trends and outlook. Includes 1 table showing the following for 11 railroad holding companies: return on assets; and business mix (percent rail, barge/truck/air, coal/oil/gas/uranium, forestry, hotels/real estate/construction, and data processing/telecommunication); 1980 and 1984.

DISTRIBUTION'S CARRIER PORTFOLIO, QUARTERLY FEATURE

(p. 88-89) Quarterly article, with 1 table showing operating ratios, net income, profit margin, and return on equity, for 39 carrier companies arranged by type, for quarters ending Apr. and July 1985. Carrier types are airlines, container lessors, common carriers, railroads, and air carriers/forwarders.

Data are prepared by Nordby International, Inc.

C2150–1.610: Sept. 1985 (Vol. 84, No. 9)

QUARTERLY FORECAST FEATURE

(p. 24-25) For 4th quarter 1985-2nd quarter 1986.

For data description, see C2150-1, above.

DIALOGUE: IS DEREGULATION HAZARDOUS TO YOUR HEALTH?

(p. 7-8) Article reporting shippers' opinions on causes of highway accidents involving shippers, and effect of transportation industry deregulation on highway safety. Data are from a reader survey. Includes 1 table.

HOW GREAT ARE THE 48? ANNUAL FEATURE

(p. 50-55) Annual article, by Cathy Coffman and Bruce Heydt, summarizing State taxes, fees, highway regulations, and other State data of interest to distributors, 1985. Data were compiled by *Distribution* from various sources, including an Alexander Grant and Co. business climate study (covered in SRI under B4000-1).

Includes 1 extended table (undated) showing the following, for contiguous U.S. by State:

a. Motor fuel tax rates; highway motor vehicle size and weight limits; State/local taxes per $1,000 of personal income; and State government general expenditure vs. general revenue growth over 3 years, and per capita debt.

b. Average manufacturing wages, energy costs, labor force density per square mile, and union manufacturing employment as a percent of total manufacturing employment.

Selected data include 2- and 3-year trends for unspecified periods.

HIT (AND MISS) PARADE, ANNUAL FEATURE

(p. 59-62) Annual article, by Joseph V. Barks and Cathy Coffman, with 6 tables on the financial performance of freight trucking companies, showing the following: operating revenues and income, net income, revenue tons hauled, operating ratio, and return on equity, for each of 111 leading Class I carriers, 1983-84.

Data are usually included in annual feature on motor carrier financial performance, appearing in June 1985 issue (for description, see C2150-1.608 above).

C2150–1.611: Oct. 1985 (Vol. 84, No. 10)

DIALOGUE: IN SEARCH OF CUSTOMER SERVICE

(p. 7-8) Article reporting shippers' awareness of and opinions on current management theories, including innovations in customer service. Data are from a reader survey. Includes 1 table.

GRAND SCHEME OF THINGS, ANNUAL FEATURE

(p. 84-92) Annual article on international business practices of U.S. companies, focusing on international distribution functions. Data are from an undated survey of companies involved in international business, conducted by *Distribution* and Logistics International.

Includes 6 charts showing survey response on planning and organization of international distribution activities, including use of computer modeling and consultants.

This is the 3rd annual survey.

C2150–2   CHILTON'S IRON AGE: Metals Producer
Semimonthly.

SRI now covers this publication under C2150-9.

C2150–3   CHILTON'S AUTOMOTIVE INDUSTRIES
Monthly.
ISSN 0273-656X.
LC 80-644280.
SRI/MF/excerpts, shipped quarterly

Monthly trade journal of the automotive and automotive supplier industries, presenting news and analyses of manufacturing, materials, and supply and demand trends and developments.

Journal also includes *Chilton's Truck and Off-Highway Industries*, a separately paginated bimonthly insert covering the heavy-duty truck and off-highway equipment industry.

Issues are primarily narrative, but occasionally present articles with substantial statistics. Annual features include a compilation of vehicle engine specifications (Apr.) and a supplier directory (June).

All features with substantial statistical content, except vehicle and equipment specifications, are described, as they appear, under "Statistical Features." Each issue of the journal is reviewed, but an abstract is published in SRI monthly issues only when statistical features appear.

Availability: Chilton's Automotive Industries, Circulation Department, PO Box 1441, Riverton NJ 08077-0455, qualified subscribers †, others price on request; SRI/MF/excerpts for all portions described under "Statistical Features;" shipped quarterly.

Issues reviewed during 1985: Nov. 1984-Oct. 1985 (P) (Vol. 164, Nos. 11-12; Vol. 165, Nos. 1-10).

STATISTICAL FEATURES:

C2150–3.601: Nov. 1984 (Vol. 164, No. 11)

[Includes *Truck and Off-Highway Industries.*]

Automotive Industries

TOMORROW'S NEW CAR BUYERS SURVEYED: ARE AUTOMAKERS ON TARGET?

(p. 28-34) By Lindsay Brooke and Jennifer G. Mintzer. Article on consumers' auto buying practices. Data are from a recent *Automotive Industries* survey of a random sample of 18-30 year olds. Includes 12 charts showing survey response on the following:

a. Preferred auto options, transmission type, engine size, and body style; importance of selected factors when purchasing new auto, including fuel economy, price, and length of warranty; and expected price of next new auto.

b. Ratings of domestic vs. Japanese import autos; seat belt use; preference for passive restraint vs. seat belts in new autos; domestic and imported makes ranked by consumer preference; and main sources of consumer information on autos.

QUALITY GOES IN BEFORE THE PART COMES OUT

(p. 51-52) By John McElroy. Article comparing productivity of U.S. and Japanese auto engine plants. Data are from *Automotive Industries.*

Includes 1 undated table showing plant characteristics including size, employment, production rate and productivity, inventory, absenteeism rate, hourly wage, and number of robots, for Toyota Kamigo plant, Chrysler Trenton plant, and Ford Dearborn plant.

C2150–3.602: Dec. 1984 (Vol. 164, No. 12)

ANALYSTS FORESEE LUXURY CAR UPSWING, RECURRING FEATURE

(p. 68-69) Recurring article, by Jennifer G. Mintzer, with 1 table showing auto and light truck production and import/domestic sales forecasts of 11 research organizations, 1985. Table also shows each organization's opinion on whether auto trade restraint agreement between U.S. and Japan will be continued in 1985.

TARGET MARKETING AND NICHE PLAYERS

(p. 79) By Thomas F. O'Grady. Article, with 1 table showing motor vehicle sales and market shares, by domestic and import manufacturer, 1984 model year.

C2150–3.603: Jan. 1985 (Vol. 165, No. 1)

WHO BUILDS CARS BEST?

(p. 32-38) By Lance A. Ealey. Article on auto industry performance and developments, as viewed by 1,132 manufacturing and production managers responding to a recent worldwide survey conducted by *Automotive Industries.* Includes 8 charts and 5 tables showing survey response on the following:

a. Auto companies with best records for vehicle reliability, integration of design/engineering/manufacturing functions, and manufacturing efficiency; and countries with best records for auto engineering problem solving, design, and production engineering.

b. Ease of manufacturing autos today vs. 10 years ago, and expectations for change; effectiveness of computer-aided-design/computer-aided-manufacturing (CAD/CAM); importance of automation and other factors in quality control; and whether plant manager bonuses should be based on plant quality performance.

Corrected data appear in the Feb. 1985 issue (see C2150-3.604 below).

BIG GROWTH FORECAST FOR ZINC-COATED SHEET

(p. 65-66) By Peter J. Mullins. Article, with 1 table showing auto industry consumption of galvanized steel (total and per auto), by steel type, 1983-89.

C2150–3.604: Feb. 1985 (Vol. 165, No. 2)

[Includes *Truck and Off-Highway Industries.*]

Automotive Industries

CORRECTION

(p. 15) Data correction for Jan. 1985 article on auto industry performance and developments.

For description of article, see C2150-3.603 above.

UAW STUDY SEES $2,600 JAPANESE ADVANTAGE

(p. 23-24) By John McElroy. Brief article, with 1 undated table showing average cost advantage of Japanese imported autos over domestic makes, by item. Data are from a recent United Auto Workers study.

C2150–3.605: Mar. 1985 (Vol. 165, No. 3)

JAPANESE IN AMERICA: BUILDING AN EMPIRE

(p. 26-30) By John McElroy. Article, with 1 chart and 1 table showing Japanese autos produced in U.S., and in Japan for U.S. market, by manufacturer, 1990; and total Japanese autos produced in U.S., 1983-88 and 1990. Data are from *Automotive Industries* and Daiwa Securities Co., Ltd.

C2150–3.606: Apr. 1985 (Vol. 165, No. 4)

[Includes *Truck and Off-Highway Industries.*]

Automotive Industries

FIRST ANNUAL INDUSTRY REPORT CARD, ANNUAL FEATURE

(p. 22-25) Annual article, by John McElroy, comparing business performance trends of 4 major auto manufacturers. Data sources include J. D. Power and Associates. Includes 1 table, repeated for each manufacturer, showing consumer quality rating, market share, sales return, production per employee, inventory turns, long-term debt, and working capital, selected years 1973-84.

END OF THE QUOTAS AND THE U.S. ECONOMY

(p. 78) By Thomas F. O'Grady. Article, with 1 table showing GNP in current and constant 1972 dollars, and foreign trade deficit, with estimated changes resulting from a specified relaxation of the Voluntary Restraint Agreement covering imports of Japanese motor vehicles, quarterly 1985-87.

C2150–3.607: May 1985 (Vol. 165, No. 5)

AS YOU SEE IT: TOP 40 CARS THROUGH HISTORY

(p. 107-109) By Jennifer G. Mintzer and Mary Ann Angeli. Article reporting results of an *Automotive Industries* reader survey on top 40 auto models and 10 most significant advances in automotive design/engineering and manufacturing, 1885-1985 period. Includes 1 tabular listing and 2 charts.

C2150–3.608: June 1985 (Vol. 165, No. 6)

[Includes *Truck and Off-Highway Industries.*]

Automotive Industries

THE ENVELOPE, PLEASE

(p. 17) Brief article, with 1 table showing limits on Japanese auto exports to the U.S. under the Voluntary Restraint Agreement, by manufacturer, 1984-85. Data are from *Asahi Shimbun* newspaper.

AI's TOTAL CAR COEFFICIENT, ANNUAL FEATURE

(p. 68-69) Annual article, by Lindsay Brooke, on total car coefficient (TCC), a measurement of auto quality based on interior volume, gas mileage, acceleration capability, and price. Includes 1 table showing auto models ranked by TCC, grouped by price range.

C2150–3.609: July 1985 (Vol. 165, No. 7)

GUIDED TOUR OF AUTOMAKER PURCHASING DEPTS

(p. 23-30) By Joseph M. Callahan. Article, with 3 charts ranking 9 major companies manufacturing autos in the U.S., by purchasing staff size, number of suppliers used, and value of purchases, 1985. Data are from company executives.

C2150–3.610: Aug. 1984 (Vol. 165, No. 8)

[Includes *Truck and Off-Highway Industries.*]

Automotive Industries

MIRROR MARKETING: WHEN YOUR NAME IS YOUR UNIQUE FEATURE, ANNUAL FEATURE

(p. 26-29) Annual article, by Lance Ealey and Lindsay Brooke, with 1 chart showing 31 domestic and imported auto makes ranked by customer satisfaction index, 1984. Data are from J. D. Power and Associates.

Previous article is described in SRI 1984 Annual under C2150-3.502.

PIRELLI UNBAGS SUPER TIRES

(p. 54-55) By Peter J. Mullins. Article, with 1 undated table showing global tire market, by vehicle type and world region or country.

Truck and Off-Highway Industries

FYI: WORLD HEAVY-DUTY TRUCKMAKERS '84

(p. T5) Chart showing 5 largest heavy-duty truckmakers ranked by units produced, 1984.

C2150–3.611: Sept. 1985 (Vol. 165, No. 9)

I CAN'T GET NO SATISFACTION, ANNUAL FEATURE

(p. 14) Annual article, with 1 chart showing 29 domestic and imported auto makes ranked by customer satisfaction index, 1985. Data are from J. D. Power and Associates.

Previous article is described under C2150-3.610 above.

GLOBAL MERGERS NET HARDWARE FOR U.S.; SURVIVAL FOR EUROPE

(p. 54-59) By Peter J. Mullins. Article, with 2 charts showing top 10 motor vehicle producing countries ranked by number of vehicles, 1984; and joint ventures in auto and auto parts production involving companies in U.S., Japan, Korea, and Europe, with participants, type of venture, and equity shares (no dates).

BOOM TIMES FOR ELECTROGALVANIZED STEEL

(p. 76-79) By George J. McManus and Bryan H. Berry. Article, with 1 table showing location, capacity, cost, and suppliers, for 5 electrogalvanizing steel plants scheduled for startup in 1986.

INCENTIVES KICK SMALL CAR SALES

(p. 94) By Thomas F. O'Grady. Article, with 1 chart showing reduced financing programs of 4 major U.S. auto manufacturers, including autos covered, dates of programs, and financing rates, 1985.

C2150–3.612: Oct. 1984 (Vol. 165, No. 10)

[Includes *Truck and Off-Highway Industries.*]

Truck and Off-Highway Industries

JAPANESE TRUCKS MAKE US BEACHHEAD

(p. T4-T5) By Joseph M. Callahan. Article, with 1 table showing sales of imported medium-duty trucks, with detail for 6 manufacturers, 1983-84 and 1st quarter 1985. Data are derived from State registrations.

C2150–4   CHILTON'S COMMERCIAL CARRIER JOURNAL

Monthly.
ISSN 0734-1423.
LC 82-4905.
SRI/MF/excerpts, shipped quarterly

Monthly trade journal on commercial truck and other vehicle fleet management, maintenance, finances, and operations. Most data are from industry sources and Federal agencies.

Issues generally contain feature articles, occasionally with statistics; and narrative editorial depts and columns. Annual features include nonstatistical fleet reference guide (Apr.) and buyer's guide (Oct.); and a statistical review of industry financial and operating performance (July).

Features with substantial statistical content are described, as they appear, under "Statistical Features." Each issue of the journal is reviewed, but an abstract is published in SRI monthly issues only when statistical features appear.

Availability: Chilton's Commercial Carrier Journal, Circulation Department, PO Box 2045, Radnor PA 19089, qualified subscribers †, others $35.00 per yr., single copy $5.00, special issues $10.00; SRI/MF/excerpts for all portions described under "Statistical Features;" shipped quarterly.

Issues reviewed during 1985: Nov. 1984-Oct. 1985 (P) (Vol. 141, Nos. 11-12; Vol. 142, Nos. 1-10).

STATISTICAL FEATURES:

C2150–4.601: June 1985 (Vol. 142, No. 6)

HEALTHY INDEPENDENT BROKERAGES THRIVE

(p. 64-67) By Parry Desmond. Article, with 1 table showing distribution of motor freight brokers, by revenue level, 1983. Data are based on responses of members of the Transportation Brokers Conference of America to an Iowa State University survey.

C2150–4.602: July 1985 (Vol. 142, No. 7)

1984's TOP 100: EXPENSES, ELUSIVE KEY TO PROFITABILITY, ANNUAL FEATURE

(p. 89-105) Annual article, by Carl Glines and Eileen Nase, on the financial and operating performance of 100 largest for-hire freight carriers, and financial performance of 2nd 100 largest carriers, 1984 and trends. Data are from American Trucking Assns.

Includes 2 tables showing the following data by company, 1984, with selected comparisons to 1983 and aggregate trends from 1982:

a. Top 100: gross revenue and rank, expenses, and net aftertax income; profit margin, return on equity, assets/liability ratio, and long-term debt/equity ratio; trucks, truck/tractors, and trailers owned; vehicles leased/rented; maintenance employees; maintenance and insurance expenses by type; owned, leased, and intermodal vehicle mileage, and linehaul cost per mile; number and tonnage of shipments; and operating ratio and rank.

b. 2nd 100: gross revenue and rank, expenses, net aftertax income, and operating ratio.

Tables also show each company's location and types of shipments handled.

INDUSTRY TRENDS AND STATISTICS, ANNUAL FEATURE

(p. 107-116) Annual compilation, by Jerry Standley and Margaret Roman-Slavin, of trucking industry statistics, including number of carriers, carrier finances, and truck factory sales, 1984 and trends. Data are from Motor Vehicle Manufacturers Assn, American Trucking Assns, *Commercial Carrier Journal,* and other sources. Includes 9 tables showing the following:

a. Private/for-hire fleets, and vehicles by type, all by fleet size and operator category (including common/contractor carriers, lease/rental companies, governments, 6 industry categories, sanitation/refuse, schools, and bus operators), Apr. 1985.

b. For-hire carriers, by ICC class, 1978-84; and Class I/II common carriers, operating revenues, expenses by type, net income and profit margin, operating ratio, vehicle mileage, and tons handled, 1983-84.

c. Factory sales of trucks by gross vehicle weight, with detail for diesel trucks, and by truck and diesel engine make; and trailer shipments, by type; various periods 1970-84.

PRIVATE FLEETS, ANNUAL FEATURE

(p. 119-140) Annual statistical compilation, by Rich Cross, on characteristics of vehicle fleets operated by businesses and government agencies, 1984, with comparisons to 1983. Data are from responses of 519 private fleets to an A. T. Kearney, Inc. survey sponsored by Private Truck Council of America, and from GSA. Includes 22 tables showing the following:

a. Private fleet survey findings, including fleet mileage, drivers, vehicles, average vehicle age and miles per gallon, union status, operating costs (by region and for Canada), driver and mechanic wages, and selected ratios; response to questions on single-source and trip leasing, transportation subsidiaries, and intercorporate hauling; and private fleets with and applying for authority to also operate as for-hire carriers; generally shown for straight truck/van, mixed, and tractor/trailer fleets, 1983-84.

b. Fleet vehicles, by type, for individual large fleet operators grouped by category (general industry, lease/rental, food, public utilities, city and State governments, petroleum, and Federal government), with mileage and leased vehicles for most operators, 1984.

C2150–4.603: Aug. 1985 (Vol. 142, No. 8)

IS DIESEL EXHAUST DEADLY?

(p. 62-67) By Rich Cross. Article on health effects of diesel exhaust emissions, with 1 chart showing estimated diesel particulate urban emissions without Federal diesel particulate standards, by vehicle or engine type, 1984, 1995, and 2000. Data are from EPA.

C2150–6   CHILTON'S FOOD ENGINEERING

Monthly.
ISSN 0193-323X.
SRI/MF/excerpts, shipped quarterly

Monthly trade journal of the food and beverage product manufacturing industry. Covers processing methods and equipment, packaging, new products, industry finances, Government regulation, and related topics.

Data are from journal surveys, Federal Government, and other sources.

Issues contain regular editorial depts; and feature articles, occasionally with substantial statistics.

Annual statistical features include a "state-of-the-industry" report, with sales and profit data for individual companies; and reports on plant construction, new products, capital spending, and management salaries.

Features with substantial statistical content are described, as they appear, under "Statistical Features." Each issue of the journal is reviewed, but an abstract is published in SRI monthly issues only when statistical features appear.

Availability: Chilton's Food Engineering, Circulation Department, Chilton Way, Radnor PA 19089, qualified subscribers $24.00 per yr., academic community/college students $12.00 per yr., others $36.00 per yr., single copy $3.00; SRI/MF/excerpts, for all portions described under "Statistical Features;" shipped quarterly.

Issues reviewed during 1985: Nov. 1984-Oct. 1985 (P) (Vol. 56, Nos. 11-12; Vol. 57, Nos. 1-10) [Vol. 56, No. 11 incorrectly reads Vol. 55].

STATISTICAL FEATURES:

C2150–6.601: Nov. 1984 (Vol. 56, No. 11)

[Contents page incorrectly reads Vol. 55.]

CAPITAL EXPENDITURES REPORT, ANNUAL FEATURE

(p. 93-106) Annual article, by Bill Drennan, on top 50 food/beverage manufacturers, based on 1983 capital expenditures. Data are from journal's survey.

Includes 1 table showing capital expenditure ranking for each company, 1983, with comparisons to 1979-82; and 1 table repeated for each company, showing capital expenditures, net sales, and net earnings, 1982-83, with estimated expenditures for 1984.

This is the 6th annual survey.

KING SUGAR: STILL No. 1, BUT LOSING GROUND

(p. 108-110) Article, with 2 charts showing sugar price per pound, 1980/81 and 1982/83; and per capita consumption of sweeteners, by type, 1975 and 1983. Data are from a study conducted by Economic Perspectives, Inc.

C2150–6.602: Dec. 1984 (Vol. 56, No. 12)

1984 SALARY SURVEY, ANNUAL FEATURE

(p. 61-68) Annual article, by Bill Drennan, on salaries of management employees at food/beverage manufacturing companies, based on approximately 1,600 responses to a 1984 journal survey of employees.

Includes 7 tables showing respondent distribution by position and salary range; and median salary, by position, product specialty, educational attainment, years of experience, region, and company employment size; 1984.

TOMORROW THE WORLD!

(p. 71-76) Article on export market outlook for U.S. food companies. Data are based on a 1984 journal survey of processed food exporters.

Includes 8 text tables showing respondent distribution by product specialty, major region for exports, level of recent and anticipated sales change, major obstacle for increased exports, and region and product category with greatest growth potential.

C2150–6.603: Feb. 1985 (Vol. 57, No. 2)

GROWING FOOD BANK NETWORK

(p. 92-93) Article reporting on Second Harvest Food Banks, a nonprofit organization that distributes food industry surplus products to charities. Includes 1 chart showing amount of food distributed by Second Harvest, 1979-84.

C2150–6.604: Mar. 1985 (Vol. 57, No. 3)

WILL ADVERTISING REMEDY THE AILING CANNED FOODS MARKET?

(p. 23-24) By Dianne L. Taylor. Article, with 2 tables showing annual change in advertising expenditures, for selected SIC 3- and 4-digit food/kindred product industries, 1985; and number of food cans manufactured, 1978 and 1982-85. Data are from Schonfeld and Associates, Inc. and the Commerce Dept.

DEREGULATION: IS IT WORKING?

(p. 104-109) Article examining impact on trucking industry of deregulation as mandated under the Motor Carrier Act of 1980. Data are from Private Truck Council of America and Census Bureau.

Includes 4 tables showing private fleet tractor/trailer annual mileage, cost per mile, and empty miles as percent of total mileage, 1981-83; delivery/route worker and truck driver employment, 1980-83; and backhaul operations of Borden, Inc. before and after deregulation, by region and metro area.

C2150–6.605: May 1985 (Vol. 57, No. 5)

FOOD IN THE YEAR 2000

(p. 90-120) Article on food industry market outlook, with 3 tables showing population by age group, various years 1980-2040; and families by household income level, quinquennially 1980-95. Data are from Census Bureau, *American Demographics,* Data Resources, Inc., and SSA.

C2150–6.606: June 1985 (Vol. 57, No. 6)

COMPUTERS: ACCEPTED AT LAST!

(p. 56-67) By Jim Wagner. Article on food industry use of computers. Data are from responses of 220 companies to an Apr. 1985 survey conducted by *Food Engineering.*

Includes 6 charts showing survey response on the following: types of computer/automation equipment used, and applications; views on equipment performance and extent of computer use in the food industry; actual and desired level of automation in own company; and planned spending for computers, 1985.

C2150–6.607: Aug. 1985 (Vol. 57, No. 8)

SELECTING A NEW PLANT SITE? CENTRAL STATES MAY OFFER MORE

(p. 29-30) By Dianne L. Taylor. Article, with 1 undated table comparing operating costs in 8 locations, for a hypothetical 295-worker snack food plant. Data are from Boyd Co. Location Consultants.

STATE OF THE INDUSTRY: ACQUISITIONS STILL MOLD THE INDUSTRY, ANNUAL FEATURE

(p. 67-87) Annual feature on developments in the food manufacturing industry. Data are from E. F. Hutton and Co. and Federal and industry sources. Includes 4 tables and 5 charts showing the following:

a. Tax reform impact: income, taxes, tax rate, and estimated earnings per share, for latest fiscal year and under proposed tax reform measures; shown for 19 food processing companies.

b. Market trends: beer shipment volume, for 6 major brewers, 1983-84; seafood consumption and import records, 1984, with selected detail by product category, and comparison to previous records; per capita consumption of dairy products, wine, meat (beef, pork, other), and poultry, various years 1975-84; frozen prepared food shipment volume, 1979-84; snack food sales, 1983-85; and cookie/cracker shipment value, 1982-84.

LACTOSE PERMEATE-TO-PROTEIN PROJECT MAY GIVE DAIRIES A 'FREE' FEED SOURCE

(p. 118) Article reporting on technology designed to convert lactose permeate (a by-product of milk filtration process) to a high-quality feed. Data are from California Milk Advisory Board and Dairy Research, Inc. Includes 1 undated table estimating costs and income for a conversion facility.

C2150–6.608: Sept. 1985 (Vol. 57, No. 9)

CHEMICAL CONFUSION

(p. 72-73) By A. Elizabeth Sloan. Article reporting on consumer concerns regarding chemical additives in food. Data are based on a May 1984 *Good Housekeeping* survey. Includes 1 table showing percent of consumers expressing concern about selected food ingredients and additives.

TRACKING THE NEW FOOD PLANTS, ANNUAL FEATURE

(p. 77-87) Annual listing, for 1985, of new construction and expansion projects involving food plants, generally showing the following for each project: company, location, primary product, type of project and/or square footage, estimated cost, employees, and planning/completion status and date.

This is the 8th annual listing. Includes brief accompanying article (p. 76).

C2150–6.609: Oct. 1985 (Vol. 57, No. 10)

BEATING THE MEATPACKER BLUES WITH VALUE-ADDED PROCESSING

(p. 25-26) Article, with 1 chart showing per capita consumption of beef, 1977-85.

NEW PRODUCT ANALYSIS, ANNUAL FEATURE

(p. 65-88) Annual article, by Kevin Hannigan, on new product introductions. Also includes analysis of food product trends and developments. Data are from food industry sources. Includes 6 tables and 1 chart showing the following:

a. Top 20 companies ranked by total new product introductions, 1980-84; wine cooler shipment value and/or volume, various years 1983-90; and percent change in sales of presweetened powdered soft drink mixes by sweetener type, Jan. 1985, with market shares for sugar- and aspartame-sweetened mixes, Jan. 1983-85.

b. Consumer patronage of 15 types of specialty restaurants (no date); market shares, and sales change from previous year, for selected frozen dessert specialities, 1984; and types of ethnic food served at home and prepared most often by consumers, 1984.

This is the 5th annual analysis.

C2150–7   CHILTON'S JEWELERS' CIRCULAR/KEYSTONE
Monthly.
ISSN 0194-2905.
SRI/MF/not filmed

Monthly trade journal (with an additional issue midyear) reporting on trends in jewelry and watch manufacturing and marketing. Covers retail and wholesale operations, product development, prices, and trade. Data are from Jewelers Board of Trade (JBT), American Watch Assn, original research, and other sources.

General format:

a. Feature articles and editorial depts, some with statistics.

b. 6 monthly tables on marketing trends, listed below.

c. Irregularly recurring features, including diamond and colored gemstone retail price indexes, wholesale trends, and text table showing quarterly sales and earnings of 2-10 varying jewelry companies.

d. Annual and semiannual features, including semiannual table on watch imports; jewelers' statistical almanac and directory (midyear); sales outlook; and editorial index.

Monthly tables appear in most issues. All additional features with substantial statistical content are described, as they appear, under "Statistical Features." Nonstatistical features are not covered.

Prior to the June 1985 issue, journal included an additional monthly table on jewelry and watch production workers' employment and earnings.

Subscription price includes several additional issues published throughout the year. These issues, providing nonstatistical information for specific trade shows, are mailed on a regional basis. SRI does not cover these regional issues.

SRI coverage of this publication begins with the Oct. 1984 issue.

Availability: Jewelers' Circular/Keystone, Chilton Way, Radnor PA 19089, industry subscribers $24.00 per yr., single copy $4.00, Directory $12.00; others $45.00 per yr., single copy $5.00, Directory $24.00.; SRI/MF/not filmed.

Issues reviewed during 1985: Oct. 1984-Oct. 1985 (P) (Vol. CLV, Nos. 10-12; Vol. CLVI, Nos. 1-12) [Vol. CLVI, No. 11 is issued in 2 parts].

MONTHLY TABLES:

[Data generally are shown for latest available month (ranging from 1 to 8 months prior to cover date), with comparisons to same month of previous year. Tables [2-4] also show data for year to date and percent change from same period of previous year. Tables [4-6] are occasionally shown as text statistics.]

[1] JBT economic report [new jewelry businesses and failures, by business type and/or region; firms receiving increase and decrease in JBT credit ratings; number and average value of credit claims placed with JBT for collection; and number of jewelry retailers, wholesalers, and manufacturers].

[2-3] Imports and exports dollar value [for watches/clocks, gemstones by type, pearls, finished jewelry, and (imports only) synthetic and imitation stones].

[4] Vital statistics [births, deaths, marriages, and divorces].

[5] Monthly sales trends [retail jewelers' sales; shows percent change only].

[6] Metal prices [New York market prices for gold, silver, and platinum; also shows price ranges for previous month; table title may vary].

STATISTICAL FEATURES:

C2150–7.601: Oct. 1984 (Vol. CLV, No. 10)

PEARLS: THE REAL THING

(p. 100-108) Article, with 1 text table showing customs value of natural pearl imports, by country of origin 1983-1st half 1984, and total 1982. Data are from Commerce Dept.

DISTRIBUTORS REPORT FIRST HALF SALES, RECURRING FEATURE

(p. 236) Recurring summary of jewelry wholesale trends, with 1 table showing percent change in sales of jewelry by major category, June and 1st half 1984. Data are from American Jewelry Distributors Assn.

C2150–7.602: Nov. 1984 (Vol. CLV, No. 11)

WATCH IMPORTS FELL IN FIRST HALF: AWA, SEMIANNUAL FEATURE

(p. G) Semiannual article, with 1 table showing watch import volume and value, by type, 1983-1st half 1984. Data are from American Watch Assn.

C2150–7.603: Dec. 1984 (Vol. CLV, No. 12)

WATCHES, FLATWARE PACE WHOLESALERS, RECURRING FEATURE

(p. 111) Recurring summary of jewelry wholesale trends, with 1 table showing percent

change in sales of jewelry by major category, Sept. and 1st 9 months 1984. Data are from American Jewelry Distributors Assn.

C2150–7.604: Jan. 1985 (Vol. CLVI, No. 1)

SELLING COLOR

(p. 50-52) By Helene Huffer. Article, with 4 undated tables showing the following for colored gemstone jewelry, by type of stone: sales distribution, with detail by type of jewelry; ranges of stone size, jeweler cost, and retail price; sales share for pieces with diamond accents and for items purchased by jeweler as finished pieces; and prevalence in jeweler inventory.

Data are based on recent sales reported by over 50 jewelry stores participating in the *Jewelers' Circular/Keystone* Retail Jeweler Panel.

JEWELERS LOOK AT 1985: IT COULD BE A VERY GOOD YEAR, ANNUAL FEATURE

(p. 114-116) Annual article, by George Holmes, on jewelry sales outlook for 1985. Data are from a fall 1984 survey of *Jewelers' Circular/Keystone* Retail Jeweler Panel.

Includes 1 chart and 1 table showing survey response concerning expected sales and profit changes, and most popular pieces and price range for 4 jewelry categories, 1985.

C2150–7.605: Feb. 1985 (Vol. CLVI, No. 3)

SALARIES JEWELERS PAY

(p. 170-174) By Nena Baker. Article, with 2 undated charts showing the following for jewelry store employees: prevalence of selected benefits, including paid vacation and sick leave, health and life insurance, profit sharing, pensions, and stock options; and median compensation, for salespeople by sex (with detail for women by age), and for 4 other positions.

Data are from a survey of *Jewelers' Circular-Keystone* Retail Jewelers Panel.

JBT AT 100: INTO THE COMPUTER AGE

(p. 314-318) By William George Shuster. Article, with 1 table showing jewelry business failures, and credit inquiries received by Jewelers Board of Trade (JBT), selected years 1933-84. Data are from JBT.

WATCHES CONTINUE TO LEAD AJDA SALES, RECURRING FEATURE

(p. 339) Recurring summary of jewelry wholesale trends, with 1 table showing percent change in sales of jewelry by major category, Oct. and 1st 10 months 1984 (table incorrectly reads January-June 1984). Data are from American Jewelry Distributors Assn.

C2150–7.606: Apr. 1985 (Vol. CLVI, No. 6)

WATCHES, FLATWARE MAKE WHOLESALERS' YEAR, RECURRING FEATURE

(p. 224) Recurring summary of jewelry wholesale trends, with 1 table showing percent change in sales of jewelry by major category, Dec. and full year 1984. Data are from American Jewelry Distributors Assn.

C2150–7.607: May 1985 (Vol. CLVI, No. 7)

AWA: WATCH IMPORTS HIT 147.4 MILLION, SEMIANNUAL FEATURE

(p. 90) Semiannual article with text data and 1 table showing watch import volume and value by type, 1983-84, and total volume, 1980-84. Data are from American Watch Assn and Commerce Dept.

CHARGE CARDS: PLASTIC THAT'S FOR REAL

(p. 100-102) By Nena Baker. Article on credit card policies and use among jewelry retailers. Data are from a recent survey of *Jewelers' Circular-Keystone* Retail Jewelers Panel.

Includes 3 charts and 1 table showing responses concerning preferred credit cards (including store accounts), length of period between sale and customer payment, methods for advertising credit card policies, and perceived effectiveness of store accounts vs. 2 major bank cards, (no dates).

AJDA SALES DIPPED SLIGHTLY IN JAN., RECURRING FEATURE

(p. 172) Recurring summary of jewelry wholesale trends, with 1 table showing percent change in sales of jewelry by major category, Jan. 1985. Data are from American Jewelry Distributors Assn.

C2150–7.608: June 1985 (Vol. CLVI, No. 8)

DIAMOND JEWELRY: QUALITY SELLS

(p. 202-203) Article, with 4 tables showing diamond jewelry purchased and value, by type of jewelry; and average price paid for diamonds; shown variously by sex and marital status, and for young women; various years 1978-84. Data are from Diamond Promotion Service.

C2150–7.609: June 21, 1985 [1985 Almanac]

JEWELERS' CIRCULAR/KEYSTONE 1985 ALMANAC

Annual fact book, for 1985, presenting detailed jewelry industry statistics and a related directory. Covers sales, marketing trends, prices, trade, shipments, and employment, including data by product and business type and location. Also includes consumer characteristics.

Data are compiled from *Jewelers' Circular/Keystone* Retail Jewelers Panel and consumer surveys, and from numerous Federal and industry sources.

Contains contents listing and narrative summary (p. 922-928); and 13 sections with numerous articles, 137 tables, and directory of jewelry assns (p. 929-983).

Tables with substantial statistical content are described below.

TABLES:

INDUSTRY DATA

a. Jewelry companies, establishments or stores, sales, and employment, shown variously by sales, employment, and establishment size categories, for selected metro areas, and by month and State, various years 1972-84; and imports and exports by product type and country of origin and destination, 1982-84. 14 tables. (p. 929-935)

b. Jewelry manufacturers outlook for 1985, and policy regarding service/interest charges on past-due accounts; number of production workers by month, 1981-84; and number of establishments and paid employees, and annual payroll, for 3 industry segments, by State and for Puerto Rico, 1981-82. 5 tables. (p. 935-938)

c. Jewelry wholesale sales change; and distribution of weddings and jewelry sales, by month; generally 1983-84. 3 tables. (p. 938-939)

JEWELRY BUSINESSES, AND CONSUMER CHARACTERISTICS

d. Jewelry stores, sales, and employment, by type of ownership, 1982; jewelry industry establishments and failures by type of business, with detail by region, 1983-84; type of insurance carried by jewelers, and jewelers' ratings of insurance agents, Oct. 1984; employee benefits offered by jewelers, and jewelry store average salary by position and sex (with detail by age for women), Feb. 1985; and selected U.S economic indicators, various periods 1983-85. 8 tables. (p. 940-941)

e. Population, marriages, births, effective buying income (EBI), and percent of population living in metro areas, generally by State and census division, with State rankings; population distribution by age, for U.S. and by census division; 10 States with greatest and least population change; top 50 market areas ranked by household EBI, with population size; and percent of households in selected EBI categories, by location; generally 1983, with comparisons to 1982 and selected trends from 1960. 8 tables. (p. 942-946)

DIAMOND AND GEMSTONE JEWELRY

f. Diamond jewelry market, including consumer acquisitions, sales volume and value, and average price paid, generally by type of jewelry and recipient characteristics, various years 1974-84; engagement ring sales distribution by diamond clarity and weight, selected years 1973-84; diamond price trends from 1949; diamond production by country and for selected mines, various years 1980-83; and volume and value of diamond imports and exports by country of origin and destination, various years 1973-83. 24 tables. (p. 955-962)

g. Colored gemstones and pearl market including jewelers' cost and selling price by type of gemstone and for pearls, Jan. 1985; and value and/or volume of jewelry imports and exports, by product type and country of origin and destination, 1983 with comparisons to 1982. 16 tables. (p. 963-966)

PRECIOUS METAL AND FASHION JEWELRY, WATCHES AND CLOCKS, TABLEWARES, AND METALS

h. Precious metal and fashion jewelry, watches/clocks, and tableware industry data, including employment, payroll, production workers, production hours and wages, value added, cost of materials, shipment value by product category, year-end inventories, capital expenditures, and PPI; and volume and/or value of exports and imports by detailed product type and country of destination and origin. 44 tables. (p. 967-979)

i. Gold, silver, and platinum monthly prices and/or price ranges, and consumption by industry or end-use; gold supply and demand; U.S. and world gold production, with detail for major producing States and countries; exports and imports of gold bullion and silver, by country of destination and origin; silver mined, for U.S. and by major producing State; and world silver consumption by country and use, and supply by country and source; various years 1970-87. 15 tables. (p. 980-983)

C2150–7.610: July 1985 (Vol. CLVI, No. 9)

JEWELERS PREDICT THEIR CHRISTMAS BEST-SELLERS

(p. 110-111) By Debbie Holmes. Article on jewelry sales outlook for fall/Christmas 1985. Data are from a survey of *Jewelers' Circular/Keystone* Retail Jeweler Panel.

Includes 2 tables showing survey response concerning jewelry sales expectations, by major category including repair services, fall/Christmas, 1985; and most popular pieces and price range for 4 jewelry categories, with selected detail by type, 2nd half 1985.

WATCH SERVICE: IMPORTANT BUT NOT IN-HOUSE

(p. 186-188) By Jane Victoria Smith. Article on watch sales and servicing. Data are from a survey of *Jewelers' Circular/Keystone* Retail Jeweler Panel.

Includes text data and 4 tables showing survey response concerning watch sales and repair as a share of total sales; repair service location (in-house, trade shop, factory), mark-up percentage, and turnaround time; major problems associated with service; and brands with best and worst factory service.

DISTRIBUTORS' SALES DIP IN QUARTER, RECURRING FEATURE

(p. 254) Recurring summary of jewelry wholesale trends, with 1 table showing percent change in sales of jewelry by major category, Mar. 1985 and 1st half 1984. Data are from American Jewelry Distributors Assn.

C2150–7.611: Aug. 1985 (Vol. CLVI, No. 10)

DE BEERS LOOKS AT RETAIL MARKET

(p. 432) Article, with 4 undated tables showing the following for diamond jewelry, by type of retail outlet: distribution of sales volume and value, and of purchases by customer income level and category (premarital, female family heads, single women, men, and teenage girls); and average jewelry price. Data are from a survey conducted by De Beers' Diamond Information Center.

C2150–7.612: Sept. 1985, Part I (Vol. CLVI, No. 11)

REPORT FROM THAILAND: MORE HEAT FOR THE AMERICAN MARKET

(p. 148-161) By George Holmes. Article, with 3 tables showing value of Thailand gemstone exports, by type of stone; and ruby, blue sapphire, gemstone, and jewelry exports to 8-10 leading and all other countries of destination; various years 1981-84. Data are from Thailand Government depts.

C2150–7.613: Sept. 1985, Part II (Vol. CLVI, No. 11)

[Issue price is $12.00.]

PRODUCTION: MORE OF THE SAME

(p. 13-18) By Russell Shor. Article, with 1 table showing natural diamond production in 19 leading countries, 1983. Data are from U.S. Bureau of Mines.

COMPETITION KNOWS MORE

(p. 135-140) By Martin Gruber. Article, with 1 table showing value of precious/costume jewelry imports into U.S., for 13 leading and all other countries of origin, 1984. Data are from U.S. Commerce Dept.

C2150–7.614: Oct. 1985 (Vol. CLVI, No. 12)

GEM IMPORTS: CUT DIAMONDS, PEARLS SOAR

(p. 152) Brief article, with 1 table showing volume of rough and cut diamond imports (in carats) and average value per carat, 1978-84. Data are from Dept of Interior.

AJDA: JEWELRY UP VOLUME DOWN, RECURRING FEATURE

(p. 248) Recurring summary of jewelry wholesale trends, with 1 table showing percent change in sales of jewelry by major category, July 1985 and 1st 7 months 1985. Data are from American Jewelry Distributors Assn.

GEM DIAMOND PRODUCTION JUMPS

(p. 272-273) By Russell Shor. Article, with 1 table showing world production of gem and industrial natural diamonds, by country, 1980-84. Data are from U.S. Bureau of Mines.

C2150–8   CHILTON'S IRON AGE: Manufacturing Management
Semimonthly.
ISSN 0747-6310.
SRI/MF/excerpts, shipped quarterly

Semimonthly trade journal of metalworking management, reporting on trends and developments in metal producing and metalworking industries. Covers materials availability and prices, production, technology, marketing, and industry general economic condition.

Most data are from American Iron and Steel Institute, company annual reports and other industry sources, *Iron Age* research, and the Federal Government.

Issues contain news and feature articles, some with statistics; regular editorial depts; and 4 semimonthly and 3 monthly tables, listed below.

Annual statistical features include a forecast of metalworking orders and shipments in 23-29 industries, updated quarterly; a review of metals prices and production; and financial and operating data for individual metals companies. A quarterly sales and earnings summary for metals companies is also included.

SRI coverage of this journal begins with the Nov. 5, 1984 issue. Most recurring features also appear in *Chilton's Iron Age: Metals Producer,* described in SRI under C2150-9.

Semimonthly tables appear in all issues. All additional features with substantial statistical content are described, as they appear, under "Statistical Features;" page locations and latest periods of coverage for monthly tables are also noted. Nonstatistical features are not covered.

Availability: Chilton's Iron Age: Manufacturing Management, Circulation Manager, PO Box 2040, Radnor PA 19089, qualified subscribers †, selected others $42.00 per yr., single copy $2.50; SRI/MF/excerpts for semimonthly tables and all portions covered under "Statistical Features;" shipped quarterly.

Issues reviewed during 1985: Nov. 5, 1984-Oct. 18, 1985 (P) (Vol. 227, Nos. 21-24; Vol. 228, Nos. 1-20).

SEMIMONTHLY TABLES:

[Tables [1-4] generally show data as of week 2-4 weeks prior to cover date. Tables [1-3] include selected comparisons to prior periods.]

[1] Price and production data [steel production by district, and prices for iron ore at Lake Superior].

[2] Steel production, composite prices [net production, capability utilization rate, selected composite prices, and scrap prices; also includes year-to-date data].

[3] Nonferrous prices [for primary metal, Straits tin, and scrap by type].

[4] Ferrous scrap prices [by type, in 17 cities].

MONTHLY TABLES:

[1] Steel prices [by product type and producer, and by product type in 24 steel service center cities; for month prior to cover date].

[2] Order trends [capital expenditures for manufacturing and mining, for quarter ending 1-3 months prior to cover date, or projected for current or next quarter; and durable goods new orders, shipments, inventories, and unfilled orders, and metalworking new orders by industry group, for month 2-3 months prior to cover date; all with comparative data for selected previous periods].

[3] Price trends [price indexes for approximately 20 metalworking product lines including equipment, automobiles, trucks, and containers; for month 2 months prior to cover date, with change from previous month and year].

STATISTICAL FEATURES:

C2150-8.601: Nov. 5, 1984 (Vol. 227, No. 21)

MONTHLY TABLE

[1] Steel prices [Oct. 1984]. (p. 67-68)

HOW MATERIAL USE IS CHANGING UNDER THE HOOD

(p. 51-57) By Bryan H. Berry. Article, with technical data, and 1 table showing consumption of glass fiber thermoset composites, by auto and truck component, 1982-88. Data are from Owens-Corning Fiberglas Corp.

C2150-8.602: Nov. 19, 1984 (Vol. 227, No. 22)

MONTHLY TABLE

[3] Price trends [Sept. 1984]. (p. 108)

MEGA-DEALS NOW RULE MERGERS

(p. 28) By John D. Baxter. Article, with 1 chart showing number of corporate mergers/acquisitions and aggregate dollar value paid, 1st half 1983-84. Data are from W. T. Grimm and Co.

MERGERS: WHAT YOU SHOULD KNOW BEFORE YOU BUY

(p. 67-75) By Edwin W. Bowers. Article, with 1 table showing merger cases submitted to the Federal Government, with cases investigated further and cases approved, FY79-84. Also includes 1 table showing pre- and post-merger operating data for 2 companies.

3rd QUARTER EARNINGS: PRODUCERS ARE STILL WAITING FOR AN UPTURN, QUARTERLY FEATURE

(p. 77-82) Quarterly article, by George J. McManus and Robert J. Regan, with 2 tables showing earnings/loss and sales for 20 steel and 22 nonferrous companies, 3rd quarter 1983-84. Also shows earnings per share for 12 steel companies, 1984.

For description of previous article, see SRI 1984 Annual under C2150-2.520.

C2150-8.603: Dec. 3, 1984 (Vol. 227, No. 23)

MONTHLY TABLES

[1] Steel prices [Nov. 1984]. (p. 88-89)

[2] Order trends [3rd quarter or Sept. 1984]. (p. 92)

PLANT SPENDING TURNS INSIDE OUT

(p. 26) By John D. Baxter. Article, with 1 table showing capital spending (in 1972 dollars) for goods produced by basic industries, and for office/computing/accounting equipment, 1980 and 1983. Data are from Commerce Dept.

C2150-8.604: Dec. 17, 1984 (Vol. 227, No. 24)

MONTHLY TABLE

[3] Price trends [Oct. 1984]. (p. 64)

C2150-8.605: Jan. 4, 1985 (Vol. 228, No. 1)

MONTHLY TABLE

[1] Steel prices [Dec. 1984]. (p. 108, 112)

1985 FORECAST: HOW INDUSTRY WILL HOLD UP THIS YEAR, ANNUAL FEATURE

(p. 26-57) Annual article, by John D. Baxter, presenting Iron Age forecast of business conditions for 29 metal-intensive industries, 1985.

Includes 4 charts showing selected general economic indicators, various periods 1982-85; and 29 charts showing shipment levels, sales, or orders, by metal-intensive industry, 1981-85.

For description of previous article, see SRI 1984 Annual under C2150-2.505.

LOOKING BACK IN 1984

(p. 88-93) Article, with 1 table showing retail auto sales for 6 U.S. manufacturers, quarterly 1984. Data are from Motor Vehicle Manufacturers Assn.

ANNUAL STATISTICAL REVIEW

(p. 94-101) Annual statistical review, for 1984, of metal prices and production, with selected trends from 1953. Contains 28 tables, listed below:

Steel Production

[1] World steel production [by country, 1974-84]. (p. 94)

[2] U.S. yearly raw steel production [by method, 1953-84]. (p. 94)

[3] U.S. monthly raw steel production, net tons [1959-84]. (p. 95)

[4] U.S. raw steel production, rate of capability utilization [monthly, 1966-84]. (p. 95)

Steel Prices

[5-6] Composite prices by periods [1978-84]; and Iron Age finished steel composite price [monthly 1965-84]. (p. 95)

[7-14] Galvanized and cold-rolled sheets, structural steel shapes, special quality bars, steel plates, hot-rolled sheet and strip, and tinplate [monthly prices, various years 1973-84]. (p. 96)

Iron Ore

[15] Pig iron, production [by type 1973-84]. (p. 96)

[16] U.S. iron ore supply [domestic shipments, exports, and imports, 1975-84]. (p. 97)

Steel Scrap

[17-18] Scrap composites: average of Iron Age scrap prices [at] Pittsburgh/Chicago/Philadelphia [and separately at each city, for No. 1 heavy melt and No. 2 bundles, monthly 1979-84]. (p. 97)

Nonferrous Production and Prices

[19-25] U.S. production of primary aluminum, refined copper, slab zinc, and refined lead; [and prices for] aluminum 99.5% ingot, electrolytic copper, and Straits tin; [monthly, various years 1973-84]. (p. 98-99)

[26-28] [Prices for] zinc, common grade lead, and electrolytic nickel [most shown monthly, various years 1973-84]. (p. 101)

For description of previous article, see SRI 1984 Annual under C2150-2.505.

C2150-8.606: Jan. 18, 1985 (Vol. 228, No. 2)

MONTHLY TABLE

[3] Price trends [Nov. 1984]. (p. 60)

ADMINISTRATION OBTAINS STEEL TRADE ACCORDS WITH 7 NATIONS

(p. 17) Article, with 1 table showing U.S. steel imports from EC, 7 countries with voluntary trade agreements, and 5 countries and all others with no agreements, with market share data for selected countries, 1st 9 months 1984.

DO ROBOTS HAVE A MIND OF THEIR OWN?

(p. 29-34) By Robert E. Harvey. Article, with 1 table showing robot sales, 1981-84 and 1990. Data are from Iron Age estimates and Robotic Industries Assn.

CAN COPPER BOUNCE BACK AFTER BEING FLOORED?

(p. 38-40) By Robert J. Regan. Article, with 1 table showing imports of copper from Chile, Canada, and all others, monthly 1983-Oct. 1984. Data are from American Bureau of Metal Statistics.

C2150-8.607: Feb. 1, 1985 (Vol. 228, No. 3)

MONTHLY TABLES

[1] Steel prices [Jan. 1985]. (p. 60-61)

[2] Order trends [3rd quarter or Nov. 1984]. (p. 64)

C2150-8.608: Feb. 15, 1985 (Vol. 228, No. 4)

MONTHLY TABLE

[3] Price trends [Dec. 1984]. (p. 76)

C2150-8.609: Mar. 1, 1985 (Vol. 228, No. 5)

MONTHLY TABLES

[1] Steel prices [Feb. 1985]. (p. 78-80)

[2] Order trends [4th quarter or Dec. 1984]. (p. 84)

NATION'S R&D BUDGET IS EXPECTED TO GO UP AGAIN IN 1985

(p. 19) Article, with 1 chart showing R&D expenditures, and distribution by sector (Federal Government, industry, universities, and other nonprofit institutions), 1985. Data are from Battelle Memorial Institute.

Full Battelle report is covered in SRI under R3300-1.

C2150–8.610: Mar. 15, 1985 (Vol. 228, No. 6)

MONTHLY TABLE

[3] Price trends [Jan. 1985]. (p. 22)

4th QUARTER EARNINGS: STEEL BATTERED; NONFERROUS DEALT SETBACK, QUARTERLY FEATURE

(p. 47-51) Quarterly article, by George J. McManus and Robert J. Regan, with 2 tables showing earnings/loss and sales for 6-19 steel and 18 nonferrous companies, full year and/or 4th quarter 1983-84. Also shows earnings per share for 12 steel companies, 1984.

COMPUTERS IN MANUFACTURING

(p. 52-59) By Robert E. Harvey. Article, with 1 table showing value of manufacturing automation market, by type of equipment, 1985, 1990, and 1995. Data are from Honeywell, Inc.

C2150–8.611: Apr. 5, 1985 (Vol. 228, No. 7)

MONTHLY TABLES

[1] Steel prices [Mar. 1985]. (p. 72-73)

[2] Order trends [4th quarter 1984 or Jan. 1985]. (p. 76)

MANUFACTURING FORECAST: CLEAR SAILING AHEAD, QUARTERLY FEATURE

(p. 26-46A4) First and 2nd quarter 1985 update of *Iron Age* annual forecast of business outlook for 25 metal-intensive industries. Most data are from industry assns and Commerce Dept. Includes 3 charts on general economic indicators; and 25 charts showing quarterly trends in shipments, sales, or orders, by industry, 1st quarter 1984-2nd quarter 1985.

C2150–8.612: Apr. 19, 1985 (Vol. 228, No. 8)

MONTHLY TABLE

[3] Price trends [Feb. 1985]. (p. 80)

C2150–8.613: May 3, 1985 (Vol. 228, No. 9)

MONTHLY TABLES

[1] Steel prices [Apr. 1985]. (p. 107-108)

[2] Order trends [4th quarter 1984 or Feb. 1985]. (p. 110)

ANNUAL STEEL/NONFERROUS FINANCIAL ANALYSIS

(p. 35-40) Annual article, by Michael Marley and Robert J. Regan, presenting financial data for 20 steel and 12 nonferrous metals companies, 1983-84.

Includes 2 tables showing the following for each company, 1983-84: net sales/revenues, profit, invested and working capital, funded debt, capital expenditures, stockholders' equity and outstanding stock, earnings and dividends per share, and selected operating ratios. Tables also show:

a. For steel companies: production, shipments, employment costs, depreciation/depletion/amortization, provision for Federal income taxes, net income, interest expense on funded debt, common stock value and price range, and stock price/earnings ratio.

b. For nonferrous metals companies: U.S./foreign income tax, extraordinary income, and net and retained earnings.

For description of previous article, see SRI 1984 Annual under C2150-2.513.

C2150–8.614: May 17, 1985 (Vol. 228, No. 10)

MONTHLY TABLE

[3] Price trends [Mar. 1985]. (p. 60)

C2150–8.615: June 7, 1985 (Vol. 228, No. 11)

MONTHLY TABLE

[1] Steel prices [May 1985]. (p. 161-164)

C2150–8.616: June 21, 1985 (Vol. 228, No. 12)

MONTHLY TABLE

[3] Price trends [Apr. 1985]. (p. 60)

FASTEST RISING STAR IN A HOT TECHNOLOGY

(p. 19-26) By Robert E. Harvey. Article, with 1 table showing revenues from assembly robot shipments to U.S. companies and worldwide, 1979-88. Data are from Dataquest, Inc.

C2150–8.617: July 5, 1985 (Vol. 228, No. 13)

MONTHLY TABLES

[1] Steel prices [June 1985]. (p. 64-65)

[2] Order trends [1st quarter 1985 or Apr. 1985]. (p. 68)

3rd QUARTER MANUFACTURING FORECAST: CAN SHAKEN BUSINESS RECOVERY SURVIVE? QUARTERLY FEATURE

(p. 19-42A4) Third quarter 1985 update of *Iron Age* annual forecast of business outlook for 25 metal-intensive industries. Most data are from industry assns and Commerce Dept. Includes 3 charts on general economic indicators; and 25 charts showing quarterly trends in shipments, sales, or orders, by industry, 2nd quarter 1984-3rd quarter 1985.

1st QUARTER EARNINGS: STEEL IN THE RED; NONFERROUS OFF, QUARTERLY FEATURE

(p. 50A2-50A4) Quarterly article, by George J. McManus and Robert J. Regan, with 2 tables showing earnings/loss and sales for 20 steel and 25 nonferrous companies, 1st quarter 1984-85. Also shows earnings per share for 9 steel companies, 1985.

C2150–8.618: July 19, 1985 (Vol. 228, No. 14)

MONTHLY TABLE

[3] Price trends [May 1985]. (p. 52)

CASH SHORTAGE NEED NOT STOP EXPANSION

(p. 28-34) By George A. Weimer. Article, with 1 table showing business fixed investment for structures and producers' durable equipment, and selected sources of borrowed funds, 1980-84. Data were compiled by Brimmer and Co. from private and Federal sources.

TUNGSTEN BATTERED FROM ALL DIRECTIONS

(p. 36-38) Article, with 1 table showing tungsten imports from 4 leading countries and all other countries, 1975-84. Data are from Bureau of Mines and industry sources.

C2150–8.619: Aug. 2, 1985 (Vol. 228, No. 15)

MONTHLY TABLES

[1] Steel prices [July 1985]. (p. 103-104)

[2] Order trends [2nd quarter or May 1985]. (p. 108)

C2150–8.620: Aug. 16, 1985 (Vol. 228, No. 16)

MONTHLY TABLE

[3] Price trends [June 1985]. (p. 76)

MAKING A CASE FOR FMS

(p. 31-56) By Robert E. Harvey and James B. Pond. Article, with 1 chart showing estimated flexible manufacturing system units installed, 1984-1990. Data are from the Yankee Group, Inc.

C2150–8.621: Sept. 6, 1985 (Vol. 228, No. 17)

MONTHLY TABLES

[1] Steel prices [Aug. 1985]. (p. 112-113)

[2] Order trends [3nd quarter or June 1985]. (p. 116)

LEASING IS TOPS IN CAPITAL INVESTMENT

(p. 26) By John D. Baxter. Article, with 1 chart showing leasing as a percent of capital equipment investment, 1978 and 1983. Data are from Commerce Dept.

ANNUAL FINANCIAL SCOREBOARD: WAS YOUR COMPANY A PERFORMANCE LEADER?

(p. 33-50) By John D. Baxter. Annual article on financial performance of approximately 260 companies in 14 metal producing and metalworking industry groups, 1984. Data are primarily from company annual reports.

Includes 1 table repeated for each industry group showing the following, by company: revenues, operating profits, and net earnings, FY84; and average annual percent change in revenues, operating profits, net earnings, and return on invested capital, equity, and sales, FY80-84 period.

Companies are ranked within each industry group by average annual return on invested capital, FY80-84 period.

Previous article is described in SRI 1984 Annual under C2150-2.521.

2nd QUARTER EARNINGS: STEEL HANGS ON; NONFERROUS SLIPS, QUARTERLY FEATURE

(p. 85-88) Quarterly article, by George J. McManus and Robert J. Regan, with 2 tables showing earnings/loss and sales for 20 steel and 26 nonferrous companies, 2nd quarter 1984-85. Also shows earnings per share for 15 steel companies, 1985.

C2150–8.622: Sept. 20, 1985 (Vol. 228, No. 18)

MONTHLY TABLE

[3] Price trends [July 1985]. (p. 76)

C2150–8.623: Oct. 4, 1985 (Vol. 228, No. 19)

MONTHLY TABLES

[1] Steel prices [Sept. 1985]. (p. 96-97)

[2] Order trends [3rd quarter or July 1985]. (p. 100)

DIRECTORS SEE SHIFT IN CRITICAL ISSUES

(p. 24) By John D. Baxter. Article, with 1 undated chart showing views of corporate directors on relative importance of 3 corporate issues (financial results, strategic planning, and managerial succession), currently and in 5 years. Data are from a 1984 Korn/Ferry International survey of approximately 600 major corporations.

Full survey report is covered in SRI under B5000-3.

4th QUARTER MANUFACTURING FORECAST: SLOWER BUT STILL GOING, QUARTERLY FEATURE

(p. 28-49) Fourth quarter 1985 update of *Iron Age* annual forecast of business outlook for 23 metal-intensive industries. Most data are from industry assns and Commerce Dept. Includes 3 charts on general economic indicators; and 23 charts showing quarterly trends in shipments, sales, or orders, by industry, 3rd quarter 1984-4th quarter 1985.

C2150–8.624: Oct. 18, 1985 (Vol. 228, No. 20)

MONTHLY TABLE

[3] Price trends [Aug. 1985]. (p. 68)

PLEASE, NO MORE MYTHS ABOUT THE DECLINE OF U.S. MANUFACTURING

(p. 22-28) By John D. Baxter. Article on manufacturing industry trends and outlook. Data are from Commerce and Labor Depts.

Includes 6 charts showing manufacturing employment as percent of all nonagricultural employment, manufacturing value added as percent of GNP, productivity growth for manufacturing and all nonagricultural industries, manufactured goods trade balance, value of imports, and growth in value of U.S. dollar, various periods 1960-85.

ALUMINUM FLOWING FREELY

(p. 33-38) By Robert J. Regan. Article, with 1 table showing U.S. imports and exports of aluminum ingot and mill products, 1975-84. Data are from Commerce Dept and Aluminum Assn.

C2150–9   CHILTON'S IRON AGE: Metals Producer
Monthly.
ISSN 0747-6329.
LC 80-642133.
SRI/MF/excerpts, shipped quarterly

Monthly trade journal of metalworking management, reporting on trends and developments in metal producing and metalworking industries. Covers materials availability and prices, production, technology, marketing, and industry general economic condition.

Most data are from American Iron and Steel Institute, company annual reports and other industry sources, *Iron Age* research, and the Federal Government.

Issues contain news and feature articles, some with statistics; regular editorial depts; and several regularly recurring features.

Most recurring features also appear in *Chilton's Iron Age: Manufacturing Management*, covered in SRI under C2150-8. All features that appear in both journals are described and filmed for *Manufacturing Management* only.

All *Metals Producer* features with substantial statistical content not included in *Manufacturing Management* are described, as they appear, under "Statistical Features." Each issue of the journal is reviewed, but an abstract is published in SRI monthly issues only when such statistical features appear.

Prior to the Nov. 5, 1984 issue, journal was described in SRI under C2150-2. Prior to the Jan. 4, 1985 issue, journal was published semimonthly.

Availability: Chilton's Iron Age: Metals Producer, Circulation Manager, PO Box 2040, Radnor PA 19089, qualified subscribers †, selected others $24.00 per yr., single copy $2.50; SRI/MF/excerpts for all portions described under "Statistical Features;" shipped quarterly.

Issues reviewed during 1985: Nov. 5, 1984-Oct. 4, 1985 (P) (Vol. 227, Nos. 21-24; Vol. 228, Nos. 1-19) [Beginning with Vol. 228, issues are numbered with odd numbers only].

STATISTICAL FEATURES:

C2150–9.601: Nov. 19, 1984 (Vol. 227, No. 22)

NICKEL PRODUCERS EXPECT DEMAND TO BE IN BALANCE WITH SUPPLY DURING 1985

(p. 23) Brief article, with 1 table showing nickel consumption for U.S., Japan, Europe, and all others, quarterly 1984. Data are from Falconbridge, Ltd.

C2150–9.602: Dec. 3, 1984 (Vol. 227, No. 23)

PUSHBUTTON AGE ARRIVES IN STEEL

(p. 57-62) By George J. McManus. Article, with 2 undated charts showing distribution of computer use in the Japanese steel industry, by function (for head office and steelworks); and Japanese computer expenditures as a percent of sales, for 6 industries. Data are from Japan Iron and Steel Foundation and other industry sources.

ALCOA DEFENDS ITS HOME TURF

(p. 65-67) By Robert J. Regan. Article, with 1 table showing shipments of sheet, plate, foil, and other aluminum products, 1974-83. Data are from Aluminum Assn.

C2150–9.603: Dec. 17, 1984 (Vol. 227, No. 24)

RESTORING ORDER TO WORLD STEEL

(p. 37-48) By George J. McManus. Article on world steel consumption and production outlook. Data are from International Iron and Steel Institute (IISI) and Bethlehem Steel Corp. Includes 9 tables showing the following, various periods 1975-95:

a. Steel production, aggregate for IISI members in U.S., EC, Japan, and other countries; and apparent steel consumption for Western and Communist world, and Western liquid steelmaking capacity, by country, country grouping, or world region.

b. Percent of crude steel continuously cast, and finished steel products as percent of crude steel production, for U.S., EC, and Japan.

c. Sales, profits, and crude steel production, aggregate for selected steel companies in U.S., EC, Japan, and Canada.

C2150–9.604: Feb. 1, 1985 (Vol. 228, No. 3)

ELECTRIC FURNACE REPORT: A PIPELINE FULL OF TECHNOLOGY

(p. 28-32B5) By George J. McManus. Article, with 1 table showing world steel production using hot metal and electric furnace processes, 1975-84. Data are from Airco Carbon.

C2150–9.605: May 3, 1985 (Vol. 228, No. 9)

IRON AGE'S 1984 TOP 50 WORLD STEEL PRODUCERS, ANNUAL FEATURE

(p. 72-82) Annual article, by James B. Pond, on production and operations of world's 50 largest steel producers, 1984. Data are from an *Iron Age: Metals Producer* survey.

Includes 6 summary tables showing 9-12 producers with highest labor productivity and gain in production, greatest employment decrease, and highest and lowest capacity utilization; and 1 extended table showing top 50 producers ranked by crude steel production, and including maximum capability, exports as percent of shipments, employment, labor productivity, and capital expenditures; 1984 with comparisons to 1983.

For description of previous article, see SRI 1984 Annual under C2150-2.512.

C2150–9.606: July 5, 1985 (Vol. 228, No. 13)

STEEL IN THE THIRD WORLD

(p. 23-31) By George J. McManus. Article, with 3 tables showing developing countries' foreign debt and debt service (amount and as percent of exports), 1980-85; world liquid steelmaking capacity, with detail for Western Europe, North America, Japan, and all developing countries, selected years 1974-90; and steel consumption in developing countries, by world region, 1984-85.

Also includes tabular list of world direct reduction ironmaking plants installed/under construction, with start-up date, company, location (city and country), number of units, fuel type, process, and capacity, various years 1957-88.

C2150–9.607: Aug. 2, 1985 (Vol. 228, No. 15)

LEVINSON TAKES ON A NEW ROLE

(p. 65-67) By George J. McManus. Article, with 2 charts showing steel shipments (total and for steel service centers), 1983-85.

C2150–9.608: Sept. 6, 1985 (Vol. 228, No. 17)

NOT BY CASH FLOW ALONE

(p. 7) By Gene Beaudet. Article, with 1 table showing steel industry earnings, cash flow, plant spending, and shortfall between cash generated and expenditures, 1982-84. Data reflect steel operations of 83% of American Iron and Steel Institute members.

C2150–9.609: Oct. 4, 1985 (Vol. 228, No. 19)

INDIRECT TRADE: THE UNCOUNTED STEEL IMPORTS

(p. 63-67) By George J. McManus. Article, with 2 tables showing value of domestic shipments, exports, and imports of selected metal products, 1984; and volume of exports and imports of steel products, by type, 1982. Data are from Commerce Dept and International Iron and Steel Institute.

C2175
Chronicle of Higher Education, Inc.

C2175–1   CHRONICLE OF HIGHER EDUCATION

Weekly. Oversized.
ISSN 0009-5982.
LC 80-1055.
SRI/MF/excerpts, shipped quarterly

Weekly journal (except last 2 weeks in Aug. and Dec.) presenting news and opinion articles on trends and developments in higher education in the U.S. and foreign countries; and including data on higher education enrollment, funding levels and sources, and student and faculty characteristics.

Data are from various Federal and State agencies, private organizations, and surveys conducted for the journal by John Minter Associates.

Issues generally contain:

a. Articles, generally narrative, but occasionally including substantial statistics.

b. "Fact-File" and "Chronicle Survey" sections on varying subjects, each usually containing 1 or more tables with accompanying article.

c. Regular editorial depts, including weekly listings of grant awards, gifts, and bequests; notes on status of Federal legislation affecting education; Federal agency rulings; and recurring current awareness tables or charts illustrating trends in stock market performance of endowment or faculty pension funds, faculty pay compared to CPI, and best selling titles in campus bookstores.

Last issue of each volume includes an article index.

All features with substantial statistical content, including "Fact-File" and "Chronicle Survey" sections, are described, as they appear, under "Statistical Features." Nonstatistical features are not covered.

Availability: Chronicle of Higher Education, Subscription Department, PO Box 1955, Marion OH 43305, $48.00 per yr., single copy $1.75; SRI/MF/excerpts for all portions described under "Statistical Features;" shipped quarterly.

Issues reviewed during 1985: Nov. 7, 1984-Oct. 30, 1985 (P) (Vol. XXIX, Nos. 11-24; Vol. XXX, Nos. 1-24; Vol. XXXI, Nos. 1-9).

STATISTICAL FEATURES:

C2175–1.601: Nov. 21, 1984 (Vol. XXIX, No. 13)

U.S. FUNDS SOUGHT FOR OLDER STUDENTS AND PART-TIMERS

(p. 1, 18) By Donna Engelgau. Article, with 1 chart showing percent change in college enrollment, by age group, and for female and full- and part-time students, primarily 1973-83 period. Data are from NCES.

CHRONICLE SURVEY: COLLEGE PRESIDENTS' VIEWS ON TRENDS AND ISSUES ON THEIR CAMPUSES

(p. 14) Table showing college presidents' assessments of the status of their institutions, including trends and 5-year outlook for academic and financial condition, and student services; and perceived change in level of financial support by source, and areas posing greatest concern and placing greatest demands on president's time, 1983/84. Data are shown by type of public and private institution.

Data are from responses of 338 college/university presidents to a survey conducted by John Minter Associates. Includes accompanying article (p. 1, 15).

C2175–1.602: Nov. 28, 1984 (Vol. XXIX, No. 14)

CORPORATIONS GAVE A RECORD $1.29 BILLION TO EDUCATION IN 1983, DESPITE LOW PROFITS, ANNUAL FEATURE

(p. 22) Annual article, by Paul Desruisseaux, with 1 table showing corporate contributions to higher education (amount, as percent of pretax net income, and as percent of total giving), 1968-83.

Data are from an annual report of the Council for Financial Aid to Education. Full report is covered in SRI under A4325-1.

C2175–1.603: Dec. 5, 1984 (Vol. XXIX, No. 15)

FACT FILE: MINORITY ENROLLMENTS AT MORE THAN 3,100 COLLEGES AND UNIVERSITIES

(p. 13-24) Brief article, with 1 extended table showing higher education enrollment, with distribution by ethnicity/citizenship (American Indian/Alaskan Native, Asian/Pacific Islander, black, Hispanic, white, and foreign), for over 3,100 institutions arranged by State and U.S. territory, fall 1982. Data were compiled by Dept of Education and published by NCES.

C2175–1.604: Dec. 12, 1984 (Vol. XXIX, No. 16)

FACT-FILE: ENROLLMENT, STIPENDS, AND DEGREES AT 239 GRADUATE SCHOOLS, FALL 1984, ANNUAL FEATURE

(p. 14) Annual table showing total and 1st-time graduate enrollment; applications received; graduate assistants and fellows; chemistry, economics, electrical engineering, and English dept teaching assistant stipends; and master's and PhD degrees awarded; all by institution type and/or control, fall 1984 and change from fall 1983.

Data are from Council of Graduate Schools in the U.S. and Graduate Record Examinations Board. Includes accompanying article (p. 1, 14).

For data correction, see C2175-1.610 below.

CHRONICLE SURVEY: FACULTY SALARIES, 1984/85 ESTIMATES, ANNUAL FEATURE

(p. 24) Annual table showing average faculty salaries by academic rank, by institution type and control, 1984/85. Data are based on responses of 1,866 faculty members to a random sample survey conducted by John Minter Associates. Includes accompanying article (p. 1, 24).

MATCH-UPS FOR THIS YEAR'S FOOTBALL BOWL GAMES, ANNUAL FEATURE

(p. 28) Annual table estimating payments to college football bowl participating teams, by game, 1984 season.

C2175–1.605: Jan. 9, 1985 (Vol. XXIX, No. 17)

GOVERNMENT'S CHART OF STATE EDUCATION STATISTICS MAKES UNFAIR COMPARISONS, EDUCATORS CHARGE

(p. 25-26) By Jean Evangelauf. Article, with 1 table showing American College Test or Scholastic Aptitude Test average scores and 2-year change, with percent of high school graduates taking test, by State, 1984. Data are from Dept of Education.

COLLEGE ENDOWMENTS LOSE 2.8 PCT. IN 1984, ANNUAL FEATURE

(p. 36) Annual article, by Jean Evangelauf, with 1 table showing investment return rate for higher education institutions' endowment funds, by level of investment and equity, with comparisons to selected general investment indexes, CPI, and Higher Education Price Index, for selected periods ended June 30, 1984.

Data are from preliminary results of a recent survey of 155 investment funds, conducted by the National Assn of College and University Business Officers (NACUBO). Full NACUBO survey report is covered in SRI under A6705-2.

C2175–1.606: Jan. 16, 1985 (Vol. XXIX, No. 18)

FACT-FILE: FRESHMAN CHARACTERISTICS AND ATTITUDES, ANNUAL FEATURE

(p. 15-16) Two annual tables presenting data on college freshman characteristics, activities, and attitudes, based on responses of 182,370 freshmen at 345 colleges and universities to a fall 1984 survey. Data are from *American Freshman: National Norms for Fall 1984;* full report is covered in SRI under U6215-1.

Tables show response distributions for questions on students' socioeconomic background; academic and career plans; methods of financing education; and work- and recreation-related activities, political views, attitudes on a variety of current issues, and personal objectives, with detail by sex and by type of school including Catholic, Protestant, and predominantly black colleges.

Includes accompanying article (p. 1, 14).

BLACK STUDENTS' AVERAGE APTITUDE-TEST SCORES UP 7 POINTS IN A YEAR

(p. 17) By Lawrence Biemiller. Article, with 2 tables showing average verbal and mathematics scores on Scholastic Aptitude Test, by race/ethnicity (American Indian, Asian American, black, Mexican American, Puerto Rican, white, and other), 1976-84, and by family income for white and black students, 1984. Data are from the College Board.

C2175–1.607: Jan. 23, 1985 (Vol. XXIX, No. 19)

4 YEARS' CHANGE IN STUDENT AID, ANNUAL FEATURE

(p. 20) Annual table showing value of higher education student aid in current and constant 1982 dollars, by program, 1980/81-1984/85. Data are from the College Board.

FACT-FILE: ESTIMATED STATE STUDENT AID, 1984-85, ANNUAL FEATURE

(p. 21) Annual table showing number and value of undergraduate and graduate/professional student aid awards for needy and non-needy students, by State and for Puerto Rico, 1984/85. Data are based on a survey conducted by the National Assn of State Scholarship and Grant Programs; full survey report is covered in SRI under A7140-1.

Includes accompanying article (p. 1, 20).

FACT-FILE: FALL 1983 ENROLLMENT, ANNUAL FEATURE

(p. 22) Annual table showing full- and part-time student enrollment by type and control of institution, and academic level, by sex; and public and private institution enrollment by State and U.S. territory; fall 1983. Data are from NCES.

For description of previous feature, for fall 1982, see SRI 1983 Annual under C2175-1.404.

C2175–1.608: Jan. 30, 1985 (Vol. XXIX, No. 20)

SCORES ON GRADUATE ADMISSION TESTS FELL FROM 1964 TO 1982, NIE STUDY FINDS

(p. 18) By Jean Evangelauf. Article, with 1 table showing test results relative to national average scores, by undergraduate discipline, for Law School Admissions Test, Graduate Management Admissions Test, and verbal and quantitative portions of Graduate Record Examination, 1981/82. Data are from the National Institute of Education.

C2175–1.609: Feb. 6, 1985 (Vol. XXIX, No. 21)

RATE OF DEFAULT DECLINES ON LOANS TO STUDENTS, VARIES WIDELY AMONG STATES

(p. 26) Article, with 1 chart and 1 table showing Guaranteed Student Loan default rates, by State, FY83, with percent change from FY81. Data are from Pennsylvania Higher Education Assistance Agency.

C2175–1.610: Feb. 13, 1985 (Vol. XXIX, No. 22)

FACT-FILE: ENROLLMENT, STIPENDS, AND DEGREES AT 239 GRADUATE SCHOOLS, FALL 1984

(p. 3) Correction for annual table on graduate enrollment and related data, appearing in the Dec. 12, 1984 issue.

For description of original table, see C2175-1.604 above.

FACT-FILE: HIGHER EDUCATION FUNDS IN PRESIDENT REAGAN'S 1986 BUDGET, RECURRING FEATURE

(p. 32) Recurring table showing FY84 actual, FY85 estimated, and FY86 requested Federal funds for higher education programs in Education Dept and other Federal agencies, by detailed program.

Includes related article (p. 31, 33-38).

C2175–1.611: Feb. 20, 1985 (Vol. XXIX, No. 23)

BENNETT AND STOCKMAN, BACKING AID CUTS, RAP STUDENTS AND PRESIDENTS, DRAW COLLEGES' FIRE

(p. 21, 24-25) By Donna Engelgau. Article, with 1 chart showing percent of student finan-

cial aid recipients with family incomes above and below $30,000, by type of aid, primarily FY83. Data are from the College Board.

C2175–1.612: Mar. 6, 1985 (Vol. XXX, No. 1)

COLLEGE OFFICIALS SAY U.S. UNDERSTATED AID CUTS FOR NEEDY STUDENTS

(p. 26) Article, with 1 table showing average Pell Grant award, by family income level and college attendance cost, 1986/87, as estimated by student aid officers and by U.S. Dept of Education. Data are from National Assn of Student Financial Aid Administrators.

C2175–1.613: Mar. 13, 1985 (Vol. XXX, No. 2)

6 IN 10 COLLEGES PROBING QUALITY OF CURRICULA

(p. 1, 15) By Jean Evangelauf. Article, with 1 table showing curriculum reforms under consideration by higher education institutions, and selected admissions and graduation requirements, by institution type, 1983/84. Data were compiled by the American Council on Education from reports of 413 colleges and universities.

POPULARITY OF 'EARLY' SEMESTER CALENDAR GAINS; 71 COLLEGES SWITCH THIS YEAR

(p. 14) By Jean Evangelauf. Article, with 1 table showing percent of higher education institutions using the quarter system, early and traditional semester, and 4-1-4 academic calendars, 1984/85. Data were compiled by the National Assn of College Stores from reports of 3,102 colleges and universities.

C2175–1.614: Mar. 20, 1985 (Vol. XXX, No. 3)

FACT-FILE: MEDIAN SALARIES OF ADMINISTRATORS, 1984/85, ANNUAL FEATURE

(p. 31) Annual table showing median salaries for college/university administrators in approximately 100 positions, by type of institution, 1984/85, with percent change from 1983/84. Data are from responses of 1,594 institutions to a College and University Personnel Assn survey. Includes accompanying article (p. 1, 31).

Full survey report is covered in SRI under A3900-1.

C2175–1.615: Mar. 27, 1985 (Vol. XXX, No. 4)

ALUMNAE GIVE HIGH MARKS TO WOMEN'S COLLEGES IN SURVEY

(p. 16) Article, with 1 table showing distribution of women's college graduates (classes of 1967 and 1977) by occupation, 1984. Data are from a Women's College Coalition (WCC) survey of graduates from 48 women's colleges.

Full WCC survey report is covered in SRI under A9410-4.

FACT FILE: MEDIAN SALARIES OF ADMINISTRATORS IN 'SECONDARY' POSITIONS, 1984/85, ANNUAL FEATURE

(p. 22) Annual table showing median salaries of college/university administrators in approximately 70 positions classified as "secondary," by type of institution, 1984/85. Data are based on responses of 1,277 institutions to a College and University Personnel Assn survey.

No data were collected for 1983/84. For description of data for 1982/83, see SRI 1983 Annual under C2175-1.417.

C2175–1.616: Apr. 3, 1985 (Vol. XXX, No. 5)

FACT-FILE: AVERAGE FACULTY SALARIES BY RANK AND TYPE OF INSTITUTION, 1984/85, ANNUAL FEATURE

(p. 24) Annual table showing average faculty salary, by academic rank and institution type (including church-related institutions), 1984/85 and percent change from 1983/84. Data are from an annual survey by the American Assn of University Professors.

Includes accompanying article (p. 1, 24) with 1 chart and 1 text table showing annual percent change in faculty salaries 1974/75-1984/85, and average salary by rank and sex 1984/85.

Full survey report is covered in SRI under A0800-1.

C2175–1.617: Apr. 10, 1985 (Vol. XXX, No. 6)

CHRONICLE SURVEY: CHANGES IN NUMBERS OF FRESHMAN APPLICANTS, ANNUAL FEATURE

(p. 16) First of 2 annual tables tracking monthly freshman applicant trends for fall 1985/86 classes. Data are based on a sample of 331 4-year colleges and universities with enrollment over 500.

Table shows percent of public and private 4-year institutions reporting increases or decreases in freshman applicants, by curriculum type, region, and enrollment size, Mar. 1985 compared to Mar. 1984. Includes accompanying article (p. 1, 16).

Tables tracking applicants for fall 1982/83 classes are described in SRI 1983 Annual (beginning with C2175-1.414). No tables were published for 1983/84 classes.

EACH OF 250,000 STUDENTS FROM POOR FAMILIES SEEN LOSING $1,160 IN AID UNDER REAGAN PLAN

(p. 19) By Cheryl M. Fields. Article, with 1 table showing number of low-income, minority, single female parent, and all female students who would lose student aid under the proposed Reagan Administration FY86 budget, by income group. Data are from American Assn of State Colleges and Universities.

C2175–1.618: Apr. 17, 1985 (Vol. XXX, No. 7)

FRESHMAN MERIT SCHOLARS, ANNUAL FEATURE

(p. 2) Annual table showing top 50 higher education institutions ranked by number of National Merit Scholars enrolled in freshman class, with number of scholarships sponsored by each institution, 1984. Data are from National Merit Scholarship Corp.

For description of previous feature, see SRI 1984 Annual under C2175-1.520.

NUMBER OF COLLEGES AND UNIVERSITIES BY ENROLLMENT IN FALL, 1983

(p. 3) Table showing number of private and public universities, other 4-year institutions, and 2-year institutions, by enrollment size, fall 1983. Data are from NCES.

FACT-FILE: VALUE OF 206 ENDOWMENTS ON JUNE 30, 1984, ANNUAL FEATURE

(p. 12) Annual table showing market value of endowments of 206 higher education institutions, as of June 30, 1983-84. Data are from National Assn of College and University Business Officers (NACUBO).

Includes accompanying article (p. 13) with 1 table showing average return rates of college endowments vs. selected financial indexes, CPI, and Higher Education Price Index, FY84.

Detailed annual NACUBO report is covered in SRI under A6705-2.

C2175–1.619: Apr. 24, 1985 (Vol. XXX, No. 8)

FACT-FILE: AVERAGE SALARIES FOR FULL-TIME FACULTY MEMBERS THIS YEAR AT MORE THAN 1,700 U.S. COLLEGES AND UNIVERSITIES, ANNUAL FEATURE

(p. 27-30) Annual table showing average higher education faculty salaries, by academic rank, for over 1,700 institutions arranged by State (and including Guam and Puerto Rico), with summary percentile data by type of institution, 1984/85.

Data are from a survey conducted for American Assn of University Professors (AAUP) by Maryse Eymonerie Associates.

Full AAUP report is covered in SRI under A0800-1.

Additional data appear in the June 5, 1985 issue (see C2175-1.624 below).

C2175–1.620: May 1, 1985 (Vol. XXX, No. 9)

HIGHER SALARIES GO TO PROFESSORS IN FACULTY UNIONS

(p. 1, 30) By Jean Evangelauf. Article, with 1 text table showing average salary for unionized and nonunionized higher education faculty in public institutions, by academic rank, 1984/85. Data are based on salaries of 60,831 faculty members at 272 public institutions covered in a survey conducted by College and University Personnel Assn.

FACT-FILE: AVERAGE FACULTY SALARIES BY RANK IN SELECTED FIELDS, 1984/85, ANNUAL FEATURE

(p. 30) Annual table showing higher education faculty average salary at public and private institutions, by academic rank and detailed discipline, 1984/85. Data are from 723 responses to a College and University Personnel Assn survey of public and private institutions.

C2175–1.621: May 15, 1985 (Vol. XXX, No. 11)

FACT-FILE: 1983/84 HOLDINGS OF RESEARCH LIBRARIES IN U.S., CANADA, ANNUAL FEATURE

(p. 12) Annual table showing the following for leading U.S. and Canadian university and other research libraries: total and added volumes, current serials, and spending for materials and salaries, by institution or library, 1983/84. Data are from an Assn of Research Libraries report, covered in SRI under A3365-1. Includes related article (p. 12).

C2175–1.622: May 22, 1985 (Vol. XXX, No. 12)

28 Pct. IN SURVEY SAY ALCOHOL PROBLEMS HAVE DECREASED

(p. 3) By Zoe Ingalls. Article on higher education administrators' opinions concerning student alcohol use. Data are from responses of officials at 202 colleges to a 1985 survey conducted jointly by Ohio and Radford Universities, and from a similar 1979 survey.

Includes 1 table showing responses concerning prevalence of alcohol education and abuse programs and selected alcohol-related policies, and whether alcohol abuse on campus has increased or decreased, 1979 and 1985; and potential impact of raising legal drinking age to 21 on selected student behavior patterns associated with alcohol consumption, 1985.

DIVESTMENTS BY 42 INSTITUTIONS OF HIGHER EDUCATION

(p. 16) Article on higher education institution divestment of stocks in corporations conducting business in South Africa. Data are from American Committee on Africa. Includes 1 table showing value and/or year of divestment, by institution, for full and partial divestments completed during 1976-85.

Includes related articles (p. 16-17).

C2175–1.623: May 29, 1985 (Vol. XXX, No. 13)

[Data for the following features are from an annual report by American Assn of Fund-Raising Counsel; full report is covered in SRI under A0700-1. Features are accompanied by 2 related articles (p. 1, 15-17).]

FACT-FILE: LARGEST GIFTS AND BEQUESTS TO COLLEGES AND UNIVERSITIES IN 1984, ANNUAL FEATURE

(p. 16) Annual table showing amount, donor, and recipient, for 162 largest gifts/bequests to higher education institutions, 1984.

FACT FILE: 55 LARGE FOUNDATIONS RANKED BY GRANTS MADE IN 1984, ANNUAL FEATURE

(p. 17) Annual table ranking top 55 foundations by value of grants awarded, and also showing foundation assets, 1984 with grant comparison to 1983.

C2175–1.624: June 5, 1985 (Vol. XXX, No. 14)

SUPPLEMENTAL DATA ON SALARIES FOR FACULTY MEMBERS IN 1984-85

(p. 26) Additional data for Apr. 24, 1985 annual table on average higher education faculty salaries. Includes data for 41 institutions arranged by State.

For description of original table, see C2175-1.619 above.

DEATHS AND CATASTROPHIC INJURIES IN FOOTBALL ARE DECLINING IN HIGH SCHOOLS AND COLLEGES, RECURRING FEATURE

(p. 27) Recurring article, with 1 table showing high school/college football player deaths directly and indirectly attributable to participation in football, and permanent cervical cord injuries, with direct deaths and permanent injuries per 100,000 participants, 1977-84.

Data are based on surveys conducted by researchers at the University of North Carolina and National Federation of State High School Assns.

Previous article, with data for 1977-83, is described in SRI 1984 Annual under C2175-1.536.

C2175–1.625: June 12, 1985 (Vol. XXX, No. 15)

CHRONICLE SURVEY: FACULTY MEMBERS' VIEWS OF TRENDS IN THEIR DEPTS, 1983 TO 1984, ANNUAL FEATURE

(p. 22) Annual table showing faculty perceptions concerning trends in their depts, including course offerings, enrollment, library services, and budget, all by dept discipline.

Data are based on 1,866 responses to a sample survey of faculty members teaching during fall 1983-84. Includes accompanying article (p. 21).

C2175–1.626: June 19, 1985 (Vol. XXX, No. 16)

6 IN 10 AMERICANS THINK COLLEGE SPORTS ARE OVEREMPHASIZED, SURVEY FINDS; 187 PRESIDENTS ARE EXPECTED AT NCAA MEETING THIS WEEK TO WEIGH REFORMS

(p. 1, 28) Article presenting public opinion on collegiate athletics, based on 1,402 responses to a May 1985 Media General, Inc. survey.

Includes text data showing survey response on the following: frequency and nature of own betting on college games, and opinion on whether and how often spectator gambling encourages athletes to cheat; awareness of recent incident involving indictments for college basketball game-fixing, and opinion on school's response; and opinions on degree to which schools emphasize sports, whether coaches should have job security regardless of team's record, and athlete academic standards and remuneration.

FACT-FILE: U.S. FUNDS FOR COLLEGES AND UNIVERSITIES, ANNUAL FEATURE

(p. 20) Annual table ranking top 100 higher education institutions by Federal funding obligations, total and for R&D, FY83. Data are from NSF.

C2175–1.627: June 26, 1985 (Vol. XXX, No. 17)

PANEL ANALYZES EDUCATION GRADUATES' COLLEGE TRANSCRIPTS, FINDS WEAK GROUNDING IN LIBERAL ARTS, URGES 25 REFORMS

(p. 11) By Jean Evangelauf. Article examining the adequacy of education curricula, with 1 table showing percent of students majoring in education and arts/sciences with no credit hours in selected disciplines. Data are from a Southern Regional Education Board review of transcripts of 6,000 students earning baccalaureate degrees from 17 southern institutions in 1982-83.

Full report is covered in SRI under A8945-9.

C2175–1.628: July 10, 1985 (Vol. XXX, No. 19)

CHRONICLE SURVEY: CHANGES IN NUMBERS OF FRESHMAN APPLICANTS, ANNUAL FEATURE

(p. 11) Second of 2 annual tables tracking monthly freshman applicant trends for fall 1985/86 classes. Data are based on a sample of 331 4-year colleges and universities with enrollment over 500.

Table shows percent of public and private 4-year institutions reporting increases or decreases in freshman applicants, and percent of freshman applicants paying deposits, all by curriculum type, region, and enrollment size, June 1985 compared to June 1984.

Tables tracking applicants for fall 1982/83 classes are described in SRI 1983 Annual (beginning with C2175-1.414). No tables were published for 1983/84 classes.

FACT-FILE: TOP NON-PROFIT DEFENSE CONTRACTORS, ANNUAL FEATURE

(p. 16) Annual table showing top 112 colleges, universities, and nonprofit organizations ranked by value of DOD contract awards for research/development/testing/evaluation, with rank among top 500 DOD contractors, FY84. Data are from DOD.

C2175–1.629: July 17, 1985 (Vol. XXX, No. 20)

FACT-FILE: VOLUNTARY SUPPORT OF HIGHER EDUCATION, 1983/84, ANNUAL FEATURE

(p. 10-11) Two annual tables showing higher education voluntary support, by institution type and control, and purpose and source of support, 1983/84; and enrollment, CPI, higher education price index, and total and per student institutional expenditures and voluntary support, selected years 1949/50-1983/84. Data are from Council for Financial Aid to Education.

Includes accompanying article (p. 1, 11) with 1 table ranking top 20 institutions by voluntary funds received, with data for 2 multiple-unit systems, 1983/84.

Full survey report is covered in SRI under A4325-2.

CHRONICLE SURVEY: FACULTY MEMBERS' SUMMER-SCHOOL EARNINGS, 1984, ANNUAL FEATURE

(p. 25) Annual table showing percent of faculty members reporting summer-school earnings, with average amount and earnings as percent of base salary, by discipline, academic rank, and institution type and control, 1984. Data are based on responses of 1,866 faculty members to a weighted sample survey of faculty teaching courses in fall 1983-84.

Includes accompanying article (p. 23, 25) with 1 table showing percent of faculty members reporting outside earnings excluding summer-school pay, and average amount, by discipline, 1983/84.

Previous feature is described in SRI 1984 Annual under C2175-1.523.

C2175–1.630: July 31, 1985 (Vol. XXX, No. 22)

FACT-FILE: COLLEGE AND UNIVERSITY ENROLLMENTS, 1970-93

(p. 13) Table showing higher education enrollment, by institution type and control, and student sex, age group, academic level, and full- and part-time status, selected years 1970-93. Data are from NCES.

C2175–1.631: Aug. 7, 1985 (Vol. XXX, No. 23)

LIBERAL-ARTS COLLEGES RANK HIGH IN PRODUCTION OF PHDs

(p. 3) Article on bachelor degree recipients going on to earn doctoral degrees. Data are based on a Great Lakes Colleges Assn comparison of doctoral degree recipients, 1951-80 period, and bachelor degree recipients, 1946-76 period, at 1,500 institutions.

Includes 1 table showing top 50 higher education institutions ranked by percent of bachelor degree recipients going on to earn doctoral degrees, and including number of doctoral degree recipients, by institution, shown for humanities, sciences, and all fields.

Data clarification appears in Sept. 11, 1985 issue; for description, see C2175-1.634 below.

C2175–1.632: Aug. 14, 1985 (Vol. XXX, No. 24)

TUITION AND STUDENT FEES AT 2,600 COLLEGES AND UNIVERSITIES, 1985/86, ANNUAL FEATURE

(p. 13-18) Annual table showing tuition/fees 1984/85-1985/86, and added out-of-State tuition 1985/86, for 2,600 institutions, arranged by State and for Puerto Rico.

Includes accompanying article with 3 tables showing distribution of institutions by tuition charges, and average on-campus expenses by item, both for 2- and/or 4-year public and private institutions; and top 10 public and private institutions ranked by total charges; 1985/86 (p. 1, 12).

Data were compiled by the College Board.

Corrected data appear in Oct. 2, 1985 issue; for description, see C2175-1.637 below.

C2175–1.633: Sept. 4, 1985 (Vol. XXXI, No. 1)

HIGHER EDUCATION 1985/86

Special report on issues and developments in higher education, 1985/86 and trends. Report is interspersed throughout the issue and contains numerous articles, including interviews with students, faculty, and administrators. Features with substantial statistical content are described below.

NEW ACADEMIC YEAR: SIGNS OF UNEASINESS AMID CALM AND STABILITY ON MANY CAMPUSES

(p. 1-3) By Robert L. Jacobson. Article on general outlook for higher education, 1985/86. Data sources include the College Board, NCES, and the Gallup Organization. Includes 6 tables showing the following:

a. Higher education institutions, by type (2- and 4-year) and control (public and private), with enrollment for each, fall 1985; average tuition/fees by institution type and control, 1985/86 with percent change from 1984/85; and degrees conferred by level and sex, 1985/86.

b. Survey response of 258 college presidents on anticipated challenges (including finances, campus morale, and academic quality), and political outlook for education by governmental level, 1985/86; and public opinion on importance of college education, 1978 and 1985.

VOYAGES EARTHLY AND CELESTIAL: FROM COLUMBUS TO THE COMET

(p. 16-17) Article, with 1 undated table showing higher education research funds by source and object (basic research and applied R&D). Data are from NSF.

WHAT THEY'RE READING, WEARING, JOINING, APPLAUDING, PROTESTING

(p. 30-32) Article on characteristics of higher education students. Data are from various education organizations. Includes 1 chart, 1 table, and text statistics showing the following:

a. Distribution of students by distance between home and college (no date); students by sex, age (over and under 25), and full- and part-time status, 1985/86; and foreign student enrollment in U.S. institutions, for top 10 countries of origin, 1983/84.

b. Most and least popular academic major and career choices of college freshmen (no date); and fraternity and sorority chapters, and Army ROTC enrollment, various academic or calendar years 1964-85.

ACADEMIC 'LEADERS,' JAZZ, DEADLINES, RUNNING, AND MORE

(p. 47-48) Article on characteristics of higher education faculty and administrators. Data are from NCES, American Assn of University Professors, and College and University Personnel Assn.

Includes 1 table showing faculty by full- and part-time status and institution type and control, 1985/86; average faculty salary, and median salaries for chief academic officers and chief executives of systems and single institutions, 1984/85; and total and administrative/support staff employment (no date).

IN WASHINGTON AND THE STATES: COURT'S AGENDA, HEARINGS, REGULATIONS, REPORTS, AND STUDIES

(p. 62-65) Article, with text statistics showing number of Federal grant applications and awards, by selected Federal agency and private organization, 1984 or FY85; and State appropriations for education, by State, 1985/86, with percent change from 1983/84. Data are from Federal and State agencies.

Other Article

STUDENTS AT LIBERAL-ARTS COLLEGES DIFFER FROM THOSE AT OTHER INSTITUTIONS IN THEIR OUTLOOK ON EDUCATION

(p. 29, 37) By Elizabeth Greene. Article on opinions of students at liberal arts vs. other 4-year higher education institutions concerning general vs. liberal education, administrator- and faculty-student relations, and classroom activities. Data are from a spring 1984 Carnegie Foundation survey of 5,000 undergraduates. Includes 1 table.

C2175–1.634: Sept. 11, 1985 (Vol. XXXI, No. 2)

CORRECTIONS

(p. 3) Includes data clarification for feature on bachelor and doctoral degree recipients, appearing in Aug. 7, 1985 issue.

For feature description, see C2175-1.631 above.

C2175–1.635: Sept. 18, 1985 (Vol. XXXI, NO. 3)

$37-MILLION FROM BASKETBALL CHAMPIONSHIP HELPS NCAA BALANCE ITS BIGGEST BUDGET, ANNUAL FEATURE

(p. 38) Annual article, with 1 table showing National Collegiate Athletic Assn (NCAA) revenues by source and expenses by function/object, actual 1984/85 and budgeted 1985/86. Data are from NCAA.

C2175–1.636: Sept. 25, 1985 (Vol. XXXI, No. 4)

TWO-THIRDS OF PUBLIC SAYS COLLEGE IS VERY IMPORTANT

(p. 3) Article, with text statistics showing public opinion on whether selected advantages result from a college education, including better job opportunities, and higher income and social status. Data are from 1,528 responses to a 1985 survey sponsored by Phi Delta Kappa and conducted by the Gallup Organization, Inc.

C2175–1.637: Oct. 2, 1985 (Vol. XXXI, No. 5)

CORRECTION

(p. 3) Includes data correction for feature on tuition and fees, appearing in Aug. 14, 1985 issue.

For feature description, see C2175–1.632 above.

SCORES CONTINUED TO RISE LAST YEAR ON SAT, ACT TEST

(p. 33, 37) Annual article, by Lawrence Biemiller, with 2 tables showing average verbal and mathematics Scholastic Aptitude Test scores, by race/ethnicity (Indian, Asian American, Mexican American, Puerto Rican, black, white, and other) and sex; and by State, with percent of students taking test; all 1984-85. Data are from College Board.

For descriptions of related articles, see C2175–1.606 and C2175–1.607 above, and C2175–1.536 in SRI 1984 Annual.

C2175–1.638: Oct. 9, 1985 (Vol. XXXI, No. 6)

FACT-FILE: DEGREES CONFERRED BY U.S. COLLEGES AND UNIVERSITIES, 1982/83, ANNUAL FEATURE

(p. 22) Annual table showing higher education degrees conferred, by field, sex, and level, for public and private institutions, 1982/83, with comparisons to earlier periods. Data are from NCES.

For description of previous feature, see SRI 1984 Annual under C2175–1.508.

FACT-FILE: FOREIGN STUDENTS IN U.S. INSTITUTIONS, 1984/85, ANNUAL FEATURE

(p. 34) Four annual tables showing 76 institutions ranked by number of foreign students, with percent of total enrollment; number of foreign students, by discipline and State; and 64 foreign countries, ranked by number of students in U.S. colleges; 1983/84 and/or 1984/85. Data are from Institute of International Education.

Includes accompanying article (p. 31, 34).

C2175–1.639: Oct. 16, 1985 (Vol. XXXI, No. 7)

HARVARD, YALE LEAD COLLEGES IN PRODUCING EXECUTIVES

(p. 2) Article, with 2 undated tables showing top 12 higher education institutions ranked by number of undergraduate and graduate degree recipients who became corporate executives. Data are from a 1985 Standard & Poor's Corp. survey of 70,000 executives.

C2175–1.640: Oct. 23, 1985 (Vol. XXXI, No. 8)

40 Pct. OF ADULTS WANT FURTHER EDUCATION, BUT MOST SAY THEY WOULD NEED STUDENT AID

(p. 17) Article, with 1 undated table showing public opinion concerning Federal aid to higher education institutions for academic research by area, and for low- and middle-income students. Data are from a 1985 Opinion Research Corp. survey of 1,004 adults.

C2175–1.641: Oct. 30, 1985 (Vol. XXXI, No. 9)

UNIVERSITIES RECEIVED $34-MILLION FOR RESEARCH ON 'STAR WARS'

(p. 5, 10) By Kim McDonald. Article, with 1 table showing top 30 universities or university-managed laboratories ranked by value of DOD contract awards for research on a space-based defense system (Strategic Defense Initiative), FY85. Data are from DOD.

FACT-FILE: STATE APPROPRIATIONS FOR HIGHER EDUCATION IN 1985/86 AND CHANGES OVER 2 YEARS, ANNUAL FEATURE

(p. 12-14) Two annual tables showing State higher education appropriations, by institution and for student aid, arranged by State, 1985/86 and 2-year percent change; and State rankings by 1985/86 appropriation total amount, amounts per capita and per $1,000 personal income, and 2- and 10-year percent change with and without inflation.

Data were compiled by M. M. Chambers and Edward R. Hines for the National Assn of State Universities and Land-Grant Colleges. Tables are accompanied by a related map (p. 1) and article (p. 1, 14).

Full report is covered in SRI under A7150-3.

C2400
Commodity Research Bureau

C2400–1   1985 CRB COMMODITY YEAR BOOK
Annual. May 1985. 302 p.
ISSN 0010-3241.
ISBN 0-910418-17-9.
LC 39-11418.
SRI/MF/complete, current & previous year reports

Annual yearbook, through Apr. 1985, on trends in over 110 basic commodities of world commerce, including production, consumption, supply, foreign trade, and prices. Includes data by country, State, and end use.

Data are compiled from government, commodity exchange, trade assn, and other private agency reports.

Contents:

a. Introduction and contents listing; 1984-85 price trend analysis, with 46 trend charts and 1 table showing CRB monthly futures price index for 1981-Apr. 1985; and 4 articles, with illustrative statistics, discussing trends affecting Eurodollar futures, soybean oil supply and demand vs. other oils and fats (including detailed statistics by commodity and country), guidelines for corporate trading of commodities, and CRB price forecasting. (p. 2T-58T)

b. Futures trading highlights, with 2 tables showing exchange volume rankings, 1983-84; and total contracts traded, by commodity and exchange, 1980-84. (p. 59T-62T)

c. Measurement conversion factors. (p. 64T-66T)

d. Commodity sections, arranged alphabetically, most with brief narrative analysis, price trend charts, and 2-33 tables described below. (p. 1-302)

Data are updated in Oct., Jan., and Apr. following publication of *Commodity Year Book*. Updates are covered by SRI as they appear, under C2400-2.

Previous yearbook, for 1984, has also been reviewed by SRI in 1985, and is also available on SRI microfiche under C2400-1 [Annual. May 1984. 385 p. ISBN 0-910418-16-0. $39.95]. Previous yearbook is substantially similar in content and format, with the following exceptions: topics covered in articles differ; and commodity sections include data on hard fibers and safflower oil, and omit data on gasoline, currencies, Eurodollars, U.S. Treasury notes, and certificates of deposit.

Availability: Commodity Research Bureau, 75 Montgomery St., Jersey City NJ 07302, yearbook only $46.95, combined subscription with abstract service $96.95 (prepaid); SRI/MF/complete.

COMMODITY TABLES AND CHARTS:

C2400–1.1: Commodities

Data generally are shown for 1970s-84; some data are shown through early 1985. U.S. data frequently include monthly detail.

Data for each commodity usually include production by country or world area; spot, average, and/or wholesale prices in selected countries, world areas, and/or cities; and U.S. detail, including stocks, consumption by end use, foreign trade, sales/shipment volume and value, futures trading, supply, disappearance, acreage, yield, and prices, as applicable.

Also includes U.S. data on livestock slaughter; pasture and range condition; coal industry mines, employment, and productivity; crop price support; steel production capacity utilization; wheat Government loan program; fuel consumption for electric power generation; natural gas reserves; gas utility sales and revenues by class of service; and uranium supply and demand of utilities.

Other U.S. data include cold storage holdings; cotton purchases reported by exchanges, and government production forecasts compared to actual crop; feed-price ratios; aluminum and lead recovered from scrap; PPI; CPI; money supply; GNP and income; futures trading for Treasury bonds, notes, and bills, and for GNMAs, Eurodollars, certificates of deposit, and stock indexes; residential construction contracts; motor vehicle registrations; and selected production, consumption, and livestock data, by State.

Other world data include consumption, trade, processing, utilization, stocks, livestock inventories, and crop acreage and yield, for selected commodities, most with detail by country or world area; futures trading in selected world currencies; currency exchange rates; and trade-weighted dollar exchange rates for selected commodities.

C2400–2   COMMODITY YEAR BOOK
Statistical Abstract Service
3 per year.   75 p.
ISSN 0010-3241.
SRI/MF/complete

Periodic report, issued 3 times yearly, presenting updated supply-demand statistics for basic commodities covered in annual *CRB Commodity Year Book.*

For description of *Year Book,* see C2400-1 above.

Reports present various data for each commodity, including prices, production (with occasional detail by State or country), stocks, exports and imports, futures trading, and other indicators as applicable. Data are the most recent available as of publication date, and generally include 2-3 year trends.

Data are from government, commodity exchange, trade assn, and other private sources.

Each report contains contents listing (p. 2); 2 sections presenting monthly update tables and annual update tables for individual commodities; and 1 section presenting trend charts. Page locations of detailed data appearing in *CRB Commodity Year Book* are noted in parentheses following the commodity name in the update tables. Commodities are arranged alphabetically.

Reports are issued in Oct., Jan., and Apr. following publication of *CRB Commodity Year Book.* Reports for Jan. and Apr. 1985 update the 1984 *Yearbook;* report for Oct. 1985 updates the 1985 *Yearbook.*

Reports for Apr. 1983-Oct. 1984 were not covered in SRI. For description of Oct. 1982-Jan. 1983 reports, see SRI 1983 Annual under C2400-2.

Availability: Commodity Research Bureau, 75 Montgomery St., Jersey City NJ 07302, $65.00 per yr.; SRI/MF/complete.

Issues reviewed during 1985: Jan.-Oct. 1985 (P) (Vol. 22, Nos. 2-3; Vol. 23, No. 1).

C2425
Communication Channels

C2425–1   PENSION WORLD
Monthly.
ISSN 0098-1753.
LC 75-642816.
SRI/MF/excerpts, shipped
quarterly

Monthly journal on pension fund and employee benefit plan investment and administration, including news and feature articles on pension fund investment strategies, regulatory compliance, legislative developments, and other topics.

Issues contain feature articles, occasionally with statistics; and editorial depts.

Annual statistical features include directories of real estate investment management companies, and master and directed trust services.

Features with substantial statistical content are described, as they appear, under "Statistical Features." Each issue of the journal is reviewed, but an abstract is published in SRI monthly issues only when statistical features appear.

Availability: Pension World, Circulation Department, 6255 Barfield Rd., Atlanta GA 30328, $41.00 per yr., single copy $3.50; SRI/MF/excerpts for all portions described under "Statistical Features;" shipped quarterly.

Issues reviewed during 1985: Nov. 1984-Oct. 1985 (P) (Vol. 20, Nos. 11-12; Vol. 21, Nos. 1-10).

STATISTICAL FEATURES:

C2425–1.601: Dec. 1984 (Vol. 20, No. 12)

7th ANNUAL REAL ESTATE PORTFOLIO MANAGER DIRECTORY: UPDATE

(p. 54-55) Table updating 7th Annual Real Estate Portfolio Manager Directory.

For description of directory, see SRI 1984 Annual, under C2425-1.509.

9th ANNUAL DIRECTORY OF MASTER AND DIRECTED TRUST SERVICES

(p. 57-83) Annual directory, for 1984, of banks and trust companies offering master and/or directed trust services.

Includes 1 table showing the following for 76 firms: address and principal contact; number of separate master and directed trust clients; value of master, directed, and custodial and total employee benefit assets managed; number of portfolios maintained; average account workload of managers and supervisors; and selected operating characteristics, including type of accounting system and short-term instruments used, reporting and credit timeliness, services provided, and fee structure.

C2425–1.602: Jan. 1985 (Vol. 21, No. 1)

TOP CORPORATIONS SUPPORT 401(k) PLANS

(p. 30-34) By Alan D. Entine. Article on corporate use of tax-deferred salary reduction (401(k)) plans. Data are based on 64 responses to a survey of Fortune 200 companies conducted in Aug.-Sept. 1984.

Includes list of responding companies, and 7 tables showing survey findings on the following aspects of 401(k) plans: monthly contributions by employees and employers, and percent of salary deferred, for profit-sharing and savings plans; plan participation, by employee age group; and methods of distributing information to employees and of staying current with changes in Federal laws and regulations.

C2425–1.603: Feb. 1985 (Vol. 21, No. 2)

HOW DO MUTUAL FUND MANAGERS MAKE INVESTMENT DECISIONS?

(p. 24-27) By John M. Cheney and E. Theodore Veit. Article on investment considerations and portfolio management criteria of mutual fund managers. Data are from responses of 73 managers to a Dec. 1982 survey conducted by the authors.

Includes 6 tables showing survey responses concerning importance of various timing methods, rate of return attributable to successful timing vs. selection, self-imposed diversification requirements, methods of evaluating portfolio performance, and performance evaluation of own fund in past 5 years.

C2425–1.604: Apr. 1985 (Vol. 21, No. 4)

401(k) EXPLOSION CONTINUED IN 1984

(p. 22) Brief article, with 1 chart showing percent of companies sponsoring, developing, or considering a tax-deferred salary reduction (401(k)) plan, 1982-84. Data are from *Hay/Huggins Bulletin on Employee Benefits and Actuarial Services.*

C2425–1.605: Aug. 1985 (Vol. 21, No. 8)

BEFORE YOU START...WHAT ARE OTHER COMPANIES DOING?

(p. 24-28 passim) By Duane C. Bollert. Article discussing corporate 401(k) tax-deferred salary reduction plans for employees. Data are from a Hewitt Associates survey of 200 plans. Includes 3 undated tables showing distribution of plans by employer match per $1 employee contribution, types of vesting offered, and maximum employee contribution.

CURRENT ISSUES IN PLAN DESIGN: STATE EMPLOYEE HEALTH BENEFIT PLANS ARE ZEROING IN ON COST CONTAINMENT

(p. 43-50) By John P. Mackin. Article, with 3 tables showing the following for State employee health insurance plans, by State (and for Virgin Islands): monthly cost to employee and to State, by type of coverage (employee only, employee/family, and retiree only), 1984-85. Data are from a 1985 survey by Martin E. Segal Co.

C2425–1.606: Sept. 1985 (Vol. 21, No. 9)

1985 REAL ESTATE PORTFOLIO MANAGER DIRECTORY, ANNUAL FEATURE

(p. 67-79) Annual directory, for 1985, of 97 companies providing real estate investment management services for pension funds. Companies listed responded to a 1985 survey of 536 U.S. and Canadian firms offering some form of real estate service.

Includes the following information for each company: name, address, contact person, value of all and pension fund real estate assets managed, number of pension fund real estate clients, composition of real estate holdings, type of participation offered, geographical diversification, minimum investment, return on investment, and fee.

C2425–2   TRUSTS AND ESTATES
Monthly.
ISSN 0041-3682.
LC 76-646521.
SRI/MF/excerpts, shipped
quarterly

Monthly journal (semimonthly in Dec.) of professional trust fund administration and estate planning services. Includes analyses of trends in portfolio management, investment in selected industries or equities, and outlook for the general economy.

Issues contain feature articles, occasionally with statistics; and editorial depts. Additional Dec. issue is an annual directory of trust institutions.

Features with substantial statistical content are described, as they appear, under "Statistical Features." Each issue of the journal is reviewed, but an abstract is published in SRI monthly issues only when statistical features appear.

Availability: Trusts and Estates, Circulation Department, 6255 Barfield Rd., Atlanta GA 30328, $49.00 per yr., single copy $3.75, Directory issue $24.50; SRI/MF/excerpts for all portions described under "Statistical Features;" shipped quarterly.

Issues reviewed during 1985: Nov. 1984-Oct. 1985 (P) (Vol. 123, Nos. 11-12; Vol. 124, Nos. 1-10); and 1985 Directory of Trust Institutions (Dec. 15, 1984).

STATISTICAL FEATURES:

C2425–2.601: Dec. 1984 (Vol. 123, No. 12)

RELATIONSHIP MANAGEMENT FOR ESTATE PLANNING CUSTOMERS

(p. 48-50) Article, with 2 tables comparing types of financial services used and sources of financial information and advice, for users and nonusers of estate planning services, 1983. Data are from a national survey of 500 households with income or liquid assets of $15,000/more, conducted Aug. 1983 by Synergistics Research Corp..

C2425–2.602: 1985 Directory of Trust Institutions (Dec. 15, 1984)

1985 DIRECTORY OF TRUST INSTITUTIONS

(p. 41-213) Annual directory of trust institutions. Presents list of over 5,000 bank trust depts in the U.S. (arranged by State and city, and including Puerto Rico and Virgin Islands) and Canada (arranged by Province and city), with the value of managed trust assets, 1984, shown for most institutions.

This is the 23rd annual directory.

C2425–2.603: Feb. 1985 (Vol. 124, No. 2)

INVESTMENT OPPORTUNITIES IN AGRICULTURAL REAL ESTATE

(p. 41-45) By George E. Schwab. Article, with 1 table showing annual rate of return and relative volatility of investments in agricultural and commercial real estate, common stocks, and corporate bonds, with comparison to compound inflation rate, 1960-83 period.

C2425–2.604: May 1985 (Vol. 124, No. 5)

EQUITY PERFORMANCE STUDY SHOWS BANKS COMING ON STRONG

(p. 19-20) By Michael C. Baker. Article, with 2 tables comparing annualized rate of return for equity funds managed by banks, insurance companies, mutual fund groups, and investment advisors, for 3-, 5-, and 10-year periods ended Dec. 1984, and for recession and expansion periods during 1981-84.

Data are from a study of 880 equity funds with aggregate assets of over $300 million, conducted by CDA Investment Technologies, Inc. Also includes 1 table showing funds and assets included in the study, by type of manager.

C2425–2.605: Sept. 1985 (Vol. 124, No. 9)

BANKS VERSUS COUNSELORS: THE RACE CONTINUES, ANNUAL FEATURE

(p. 45-48) Annual article, by Donald H. Korytowski and Carolyn Mainguene, comparing investment performance and market share of equity portfolios managed by bank/trust companies vs. investment counselors, various periods 1980-84. Data are based on analysis of over 4,000 tax-exempt funds comprising SEI Corp.'s Funds Evaluation Services data base. Includes 7 tables.

C2425–3   AMERICAN CITY AND COUNTY
Monthly.
ISSN 0149-337X.
LC 75-647619.
SRI/MF/excerpts, shipped quarterly

Monthly journal for local government officials, reporting on trends and technological developments in public works engineering and management.

Issues contain articles, occasionally with statistics; regular editorial depts; and "Municipal Cost Indexes" section, with 1 chart and 2 tables showing the following data:

a. Cost indexes for approximately 60 types of equipment, construction materials, fuel, and other products used by local governments; CPI and PPI; and *American City and County* municipal cost and construction aggregate cost indexes; for month of publication, with comparison to previous month and year.

b. Municipal finance trends, including total receipts, Federal grants, expenditures by category, budget surplus, and employment; for most recent available quarter, with comparison to previous periods.

"Municipal Cost Indexes" section appears in all issues. All additional features with substantial nontechnical statistical content are described, as they appear, under "Statistical Features." Nonstatistical and technical specification features are not covered.

Availability: American City and County, Circulation Department, 6255 Barfield Rd., Atlanta GA 30328, qualified subscribers †, others $41.00 per yr., single copy $3.50; SRI/MF/excerpts for monthly cost indexes and all portions described under "Statistical Features;" shipped quarterly.

Issues reviewed during 1985: Nov. 1984-Oct. 1985 (P) (Vol. 99, Nos. 11-12; Vol. 100, Nos. 1-10).

STATISTICAL FEATURES:

C2425–3.601: Nov. 1984 (Vol. 99, No. 11)

WHAT ARE THE ISSUES FOR 1985?

(p. 46-50) By Ken Anderberg. Article, with 1 table showing infrastructure funding needs and resources, for highways/bridges, other transportation, water supply/distribution, and wastewater collection/treatment, 1983-2000 period. Data are from a study commissioned by the Joint Economic Committee of Congress.

C2425–3.602: July 1985 (Vol. 100, No. 7)

AC&C's 1985 SALARY AND BENEFITS SURVEY, ANNUAL FEATURE

(p. 58-60) Annual article, by Ken Anderberg, on salaries and benefit plans for local government employees. Data are from responses of 431 city/county financial officers to a 1985 survey conducted by *American City and County.*

Includes 2 tables and 3 charts showing mean salaries for 9-12 positions, by community population size and region; and survey response on frequency of employee performance reviews, and incidence of employee medical and dental insurance coverage, with detail by payment method (employer or employee paid).

COMPARABLE WORTH EMERGING AS WOMEN'S ISSUE OF THE '80s

(p. 62-64) By Cathy Dombrowski. Article, with 1 table showing average earnings of white, black, Hispanic, and all women as percent of earnings of all men, by employment sector, 1980. Data are from Census Bureau.

C2500
Congressional Quarterly, Inc.

C2500–2   CONGRESSIONAL QUARTERLY ALMANAC: 98th Congress, 2nd Session, 1984
Annual. 1985.
1066 p. var. paging. Vol. XL.
ISBN 0-87187-346-X.
LC 47-41081.
SRI/MF/not filmed

Annual review of the organization and major legislative actions of the Congress, covering the 98th Congress, 2nd session, 1984. Includes data on committee, floor, and conference activities; Administration budget requests and final appropriations; and member characteristics and voting records.

Contents:

Contents listing, glossary, and description of the legislative process. (p. vii-xxviii)

Chapter 1. 98th Congress, 2nd Session. Overview of organization and activity, with 4 tables. (p. 3-29)

Chapter 2. Defense, with 1 table. (p. 33-68)

Chapter 3. Foreign Policy, with 1 table. (p. 69-125)

Chapter 4. Economic Policy, with 8 tables. (p. 127-177)

Chapter 5. Congress and Government. (p. 179-212)

Chapter 6. Law Enforcement/Judiciary, with 2 tables. (p. 213-268)

Chapter 7. Transportation/Commerce/Consumers. (p. 269-301)

Chapter 8. Environment/Energy. (p. 303-357)

Chapter 9. Agriculture. (p. 359-366)

Chapter 10. Appropriations, with 18 tables. (p. 367-447)

Chapter 11. Health/Education/Welfare, with 1 table. (p. 449-504)

App. A-F, including special reports; political report and voting studies, with 43 tables; lobby registrations; presidential messages, with 2 tables; and public laws enacted. (p. 1A-18F)

App. S and H. Senate and House Roll-Call Votes and Index. (p. 1S-131H)

Index. (29 p.)

All tables noted above are described below. Report also includes scattered text tables or less substantial tables; these are not described. Most described tables showing final budget authorizations or appropriations also include amount passed by the House and Senate and/or requested by the Administration.

Availability: Congressional Quarterly, Inc., Order Division, 1414 22nd St., NW, Washington DC 20037, $135.00; SRI/MF/not filmed.

TABLES:

C2500–2.1: Legislative Action

98th CONGRESS, 2nd SESSION

a. Senate cloture votes, 1984; vetoes cast by President Reagan, 1981-84; public laws enacted, 1967-84; and House and Senate recorded vote totals, 1972-84. 4 tables. (p. 5-10)

DEFENSE AND FOREIGN POLICY

b. DOD authorizations, by function, FY85; and military and economic aid to El Salvador, FY81-85. 2 tables. (p. 40, 77)

ECONOMIC POLICY

c. Federal budget authority, revenues, outlays, and deficit, with detail by function, agency, and resolution stage, various years FY79-87; Reagan Administration assumptions for selected economic indicators and Federal pay raises, 1982-89; and Administration proposed budget compared to House and Senate resolutions and to conference agreements, FY84-87, with detail for FY85 budget targets by function. 8 tables. (p. 129-159)

LAW ENFORCEMENT/JUDICIARY

d. Refugee admissions, by world region of origin, FY81-85; and female, black, and Hispanic judicial nominees as percent of all nominees for U.S. court of appeals and district court, for Reagan Administration and 4 preceding Administrations. 2 tables. (p. 238, 244)

APPROPRIATIONS

e. Appropriations for Federal depts, independent agencies, and military construction, by detailed agency or program, FY85; supplemental appropriations, FY84; and foreign aid appropriations by program, FY85, with detail for security assistance to 21 countries, FY84-85. 18 tables. (p. 368-441)

HEALTH/EDUCATION/WELFARE

f. Budget requests and allocations for family planning, maternal/child health, and food assistance, by program, FY81-85. 1 table. (p. 466-467)

APPENDICES

g. Presidential landslide victories since 1828; election returns for presidential, gubernatorial, and congressional races, by party, candidate, and State, 1984; number of terms served by House incumbents defeated in 1984; and partisan composition of U.S. and State legislatures, and governorships, 1985 with detail for freshman Senators since 1914. 9 tables. (p. 4B-32B)

h. Democratic Convention delegate voting results for major platform issues and presidential candidate, by State and territory, 1984. 2 tables. (p. 67B-68B)

i. Annual analysis of congressional support of President, including annual percent of presidential victories in voting, 1953-84; composite presidential support and opposition scores for House and Senate, by party and region, 1983-84; and House and Sen-

ate outcome of recorded votes on which President took a position, highest scores in support of and opposition to President, and score of each member, 1984. 10 tables. (p. 12C-25C)

j. Annual analyses of party unity, member voting participation, and conservative coalition voting, by party and region, with highest, lowest, and individual scores, 1984 with selected trends from 1965. 22 tables. (p. 27C-42C)

k. Report of President Reagan to Congress on Lebanon conflict, with 2 tables showing multinational force (MNF) expenses for Marine Corps and Navy, by activity, FY84; and military casualties since MNF deployment in Sept. 1982, by participating country. 2 text tables. (p. 17E-18E)

C2700
Crain Automotive Group

C2700–1   AUTOMOTIVE NEWS
Weekly. Oversized.
ISSN 0005-1551.
LC 77-618337.
SRI/MF/excerpts

Weekly trade journal of the automotive industry, presenting news and statistics on motor vehicle production, sales, registrations, R&D, dealership and promotional developments, and related industry topics.

Most data are from journal staff surveys, motor vehicle manufacturer and trade assns, R. L. Polk & Co. Motor Statistical Division, and Data Resources Inc. Period of coverage is 2-10 days prior to cover date for weekly data, 1-3 months prior to cover date for monthly data.

General format:

a. Newspaper style articles and news briefs, occasionally with statistics; and special topic inserts, appearing several times each year, usually including some statistics.

b. 29 regularly recurring weekly, monthly, and quarterly tables, each usually accompanied by a summary article with text statistics.

c. Recurring *Automotive News* World Outlook feature, generally appearing 2-4 times per year, with varying motor vehicle trend and forecast data by country and region.

A special additional market data book issue is published in Apr. Issue for Sept. 30, 1985 is a nonstatistical special edition commemorating the 100th anniversary of the auto.

Regularly recurring tables are listed below. All additional features with substantial statistical content, including recurring World Outlook feature, are described, as they appear, under "Statistical Features;" page locations and latest periods of coverage for recurring tables are also noted. Nonstatistical features and features presenting only vehicle technical or specification data are not covered.

Availability: Automotive News, Circulation Department, 740 Rush St., Chicago IL 60611, $45.00 per yr., single copy $1.00, Market Data Book $22.50; SRI/MF/excerpts for all portions covered under "Statistical Features."

Issues reviewed during 1985: Nov. 5, 1984-Oct. 30, 1985 (P) (Nos. 5047-5099) [Both the Market Data Book and the Apr. 29 issues read No. 5072].

TABLES:

WEEKLY TABLES

[1-2] Auction averages: model breakdown [average price for 8 model years, for month of coverage, and previous 2 months]; and used car sales [average price for month of coverage, previous month, and same month of previous year].

[3-6] U.S. and Canadian truck and car production [by manufacturer, with U.S. car detail by make and model, for week of cover date, previous week, and current month and year to date, with selected comparisons to previous year].

[7] Domestic car sales [by make and manufacturer, for 10-day period ended approximately 2 weeks prior to cover date, current and previous years. Table presenting data for 3rd period of each month also shows data for entire month and year to date, and includes detailed breakdown by model. Table appears approximately 3 times a month].

MONTHLY TABLES

[Tables show data for month 1-3 months prior to month of publication, year to date, and same periods of previous year, unless otherwise noted.]

[8] Light-duty [truck] sales [by domestic and import model and/or manufacturer].

[8A] Major [truck] manufacturers [sales of light-, medium-, and heavy-duty trucks, for 3 leading manufacturers; table begins in the May 13, 1985 issue].

[9-10] Truck and heavy-duty registrations [number and market shares, by make; cumulative for current and previous years to date].

[11] New truck sales [or registrations], by make and GVW [gross vehicle weight] class.

[12] Auto market in [month prior to month of publication, sales by size group and total import sales].

[13] New car stocks [days supply, by manufacturer, make, and model, for month of publication, previous month, and same month of preceding year].

[14] Import stocks [days supply, by manufacturer with totals for Japanese, German, and other car models; and days supply of imported trucks by manufacturer; for month of publication, previous month, and same month of preceding year].

[15] New car market shares in U.S. [registrations and market share by domestic make and manufacturer, and total imports].

[16] *Automotive News* analysis of new car registrations [by detailed model].

[17] Market shares [by domestic and import make, and total registrations, year to date of current and previous years].

[18] Import registration shares in U.S. [number and market share by make; accompanying article usually includes text tables showing import registrations by country of origin, and imported truck registrations by make].

[19] Service index [percent change in profits, repair orders written, and sales of labor, shop parts, and all parts/accessories].

[20-21] Imported car sales, and U.S. car sales by marketing unit [both by make only].

[22] Import sales by model.

[23] Top cars [number of registrations by make, ranked for year to month of coverage, present and previous years.].

[24-25] Overseas production, registrations, and sales [for cars and/or trucks/buses, by make, for year through varying months, for selected countries including France, UK, Spain, Japan, Argentina, Switzerland, and West Germany].

QUARTERLY TABLES

[26] U.S. car outlets [number of dealerships active as of 1st day of current and selected preceding quarters, by domestic manufacturer].

[27] U.S. franchises [number of domestic franchises active as of 1st day of current and selected preceding quarters, by make].

[28] Auto makers' financial results [sales and/or net profits/loss for 4 largest U.S. manufacturers, for quarter ending 1-2 months prior to month of publication and usually year to date of current and previous year].

STATISTICAL FEATURES:

[Page numbers for recurring tables include accompanying articles.]

C2700–1.601: Nov. 5, 1984 (No. 5047)

WEEKLY TABLES

[1-2] Auction averages, for Nov. 1984. (p. 62)

[3-6] Production, for week ended Nov. 3, 1984. (p. 68)

[7] Domestic car sales, omitted.

MONTHLY TABLES

[24] Overseas production in Brazil and France, through Aug. 1984; Japan, through July 1984; and Spain, through June 1984. (p. 37)

[25] Overseas registrations in UK and Sweden, through Sept. 1984; West Germany, Austria, and Denmark, through Aug. 1984; Japan and Switzerland, through July 1984; and France, through June 1984. (p. 37)

REAGAN REELECTION WILL PROLONG AUTO ACCESS TO WHITE HOUSE

(p. 1, 66) By Helen Kahn. Article, with 2 tables showing the following for 5 auto manufacturers: unit sales and profits, 1st 9 months 1980 and 1984; and hourly employees and layoffs, as of Nov. 1, 1980 and 1984.

DEALERS SPEND HEAVILY FOR SPOT TV

(p. 6) By Joseph Bohn. Article, with 1 table showing spot TV advertising expenditures of 23 domestic and foreign auto manufacturers, 1st half 1983-84. Data are from TV Bureau of Advertising based on Broadcast Advertisers Reports data.

FORD'S ON TOP, RECURRING FEATURE

(p. 37-38) Recurring article on new auto sales in Western Europe. Includes 2 tables showing sales by country and manufacturer, and for all Japanese autos sold in Europe, 1st 8 months 1983-84.

C2700–1.602: Nov. 12, 1984 (No. 5048)

WEEKLY TABLES

[1-2] Auction averages, for Nov. 1984. (p. 57)

[3-6] Production, for week ended Nov. 10, 1984. (p. 74)

[7] Domestic car sales [by model], for Oct. 21-31, 1984. (p. 6, 68)

MONTHLY TABLES

[12] Auto market, for Oct. 1984. (p. 6, 68)

[13] New car stocks, for Nov. 1, 1984. (p. 3, 73)

[15-16] New car market shares and registrations, for Aug. 1984. (p. 26, 52)

[19] Service index, for Sept. 1984. (p. 4)

[20-21] Import sales, and U.S. car sales by marketing unit, for Oct. 1984. (p. 6, 68)

[22] Import sales by model, for Sept. 1984. (p. 46)

QUARTERLY TABLES

[26-27] U.S. car outlets and franchises, for Oct. 1, 1984. (p. 3, 72)

[28] Auto makers' financial results, for 3rd quarter 1984. (p. 38)

290 U.S. MODELS OFFERED FOR '85, ANNUAL FEATURE

(p. 4, 67) Annual article, by John K. Teahen, Jr., reviewing 1985 domestic car body styles. Includes 3 tables showing number of 1985 models offered, by manufacturer, model, and size class, all by body style, with summary comparisons to 1984; and total models offered, 1942 and 1946-85.

BRIGHT DAYS FOR LIGHT TRUCKS

(p. E27-E28) By Jack Walsh. Article, with 1 table showing sales of domestic and imported light trucks, 1978-84 model years.

FLEETS 'WAIT AND SEE' ON MINIVANS

(p. 65) By Francis J. Gawronski. Article on corporate fleet planned acquisitions of minivans in 1985, and ownership of station wagons and mini- and full-size vans (no date). Data are from a Runzheimer and Co. survey of 30 fleets. Includes 2 text tables.

C2700–1.603: Nov. 19, 1984 (No. 5049)

WEEKLY TABLES

[1-2] Auction averages, for Nov. 1984. (p. 40)

[3-6] Production, for week ended Nov. 17, 1984. (p. 55)

[7] Domestic car sales, for Nov. 1-10, 1984. (p. 8)

MONTHLY TABLES

[8] Truck sales, for Oct. 1984. (p. 16, 36)

[14] Import stocks, for Nov. 1, 1984. (p. 1, 53)

[17] Market shares, for 1st 8 months 1984. (p. 49)

[18] Import registration shares, for Aug. 1984. (p. 49)

[23] Top cars, for 1st 8 months 1984. (p. 49)

C2700–1.604: Nov. 26, 1984 (No. 5050)

WEEKLY TABLES

[1-2] Auction averages, for Nov. 1984. (p. 55)

[3-6] Production, for week ended Nov. 24, 1984. (p. 63)

[7] Domestic car sales, omitted.

MONTHLY TABLES

[9-11] Truck and heavy-duty registrations, and new truck sales, through Sept. 1984. (p. 16, 40, 44)

STEEL-PRODUCING OUTLOOK CHARTED

(p. 24) Article, with 2 tables showing growth in apparent steel consumption, for selected countries or country groups, and steel making

capacity for industrial and less developed countries, various periods 1979-95. Data are from Chase Econometrics Associates.

STICK SHIFT CALLED $206 CHEAPER

(p. 28) By Francis J. Gawronski. Article, with 2 tables comparing annual operating and ownership expenses of automatic and manual transmission versions of four 1984 auto models. Data are from Runzheimer and Co.

MARKET WILL KEEP POPPIN'

(p. E1-E2) By Al Fleming. Article on van conversion industry outlook, based on an *Automotive News* fall 1984 survey. Includes 1 chart showing survey response on conversion company operations, including prices, types of conversions offered (with detail by van make), and whether warranties are offered.

JAPANESE VEHICLE PRODUCTION INCREASES 7 Pct. FOR MONTH, RECURRING FEATURE

(p. 56) Recurring article, with 3 tables showing the following for Japan: auto, truck, and bus production and new registrations; and auto production by size class; 1st 8 months 1983-84. Data are from Japan Mini-Vehicle Assn, Japan Automobile Dealers Assn, and Japan Automobile Manufacturers Assn.

C2700–1.605: Dec. 3, 1984 (No. 5051)

WEEKLY TABLES

[1-2] Auction averages, for Nov. 1984. (p. 51)

[3-6] Production, for week ended Dec. 1, 1984. (p. 65)

[7] Domestic car sales, for Nov. 11-20, 1984. (p. 2)

MONTHLY TABLES

[24] Overseas production in France, through Sept. 1984; and Japan, UK, and Spain, through Aug. 1984. (p. 34)

[25] Overseas registrations in West Germany and Austria, through Sept. 1984; Switzerland and Japan, through Aug. 1984; and France, through July 1984. (p. 34)

TOO CLOSE TO CALL IN EUROPE, RECURRING FEATURE

(p. 33) Recurring article on new auto sales in Western Europe. Includes 2 tables showing sales and/or market shares by country and manufacturer, and for all Japanese autos sold in Europe, 1st 9 months 1983-84.

C2700–1.606: Dec. 10, 1984 (No. 5052)

WEEKLY TABLES

[1-2] Auction averages, for Dec. 1984. (p. 37)

[3-6] Production, for week ended Dec. 8, 1984. (p. 50)

[7] Domestic car sales [by model], for Nov. 21-30, 1984. (p. 8)

MONTHLY TABLES

[12] Auto market, for Nov. 1984. (p. 8)

[20-21] Import sales, and U.S. car sales by marketing unit, for Nov. 1984. (p. 8)

C2700–1.607: Dec. 17, 1984 (No. 5053)

WEEKLY TABLES

[1-2] Auction averages, for Dec. 1984. (p. 38)

[3-6] Production, for week ended Dec. 15, 1984. (p. 50)

[7] Domestic car sales, for Dec. 1-10, 1984. (p. 2)

MONTHLY TABLES

[13] New car stocks, for Dec. 1, 1984. (p. 1, 49)

[19] Service index, for Oct. 1984. (p. 1)

C2700–1.608: Dec. 24, 1984 (No. 5054)

WEEKLY TABLES

[1-2] Auction averages, for Dec. 1984. (p. 20)

[3-6] Production, for week ended Dec. 22, 1984. (p. 31)

[7] Domestic car sales, omitted.

MONTHLY TABLE

[14] Import stocks, for Dec. 1, 1984. (p. 2, 30)

C2700–1.609: Dec. 31, 1984 (No. 5055)

WEEKLY TABLES

[1-7] Omitted.

MONTHLY TABLES

[9-10] Truck and heavy-duty registrations, through Oct. 1984. (p. 14)

[24] Overseas production in Italy, UK, and Japan, through Sept. 1984. (p. 20)

[25] Overseas registrations in West Germany, UK, Sweden, and Denmark, through Oct. 1984; Norway, Holland, Italy, Switzerland, Austria, and Japan, through Sept. 1984; and France, through Aug. 1984. (p. 20, 22)

'84 MODEL-RUN OUTPUT UP 44 Pct., ANNUAL FEATURE

(p. 17) Annual article, by Louise Kertesz, on domestic car production trends for 1984 model year. Includes 1 table showing production by manufacturer, make, and model, 1983-84 model years.

C2700–1.610: Jan. 7, 1985 (No. 5056)

WEEKLY TABLES

[1-2] Auction averages, omitted.

[3-6] Production, for week ended Jan. 5, 1985. (p. 54)

[7] Domestic car sales, for Dec. 11-20, 1984. (p. 6)

MONTHLY TABLES

[8] Truck sales, for Nov. 1984. (p. 22, 27)

[22] Import sales [by model], for Oct. 1984. (p. 20)

POWER EQUIPMENT OPTIONS ON 1984 U.S. MODELS, ANNUAL FEATURE

(p. 38) Annual table showing power equipment installations on 1984 model autos, by equipment type and auto manufacturer, make, and model. Includes number of installations, and percent of total auto output.

C2700–1.611: Jan. 14, 1985 (No. 5057)

WEEKLY TABLES

[1-2] Auction averages, for Jan. 1985. (p. 47)

[3-6] Production, for week ended Jan. 12, 1985. (p. 62)

[7] Domestic car sales [by model], for Dec. 21-31, 1984. (p. 2, 60)

MONTHLY TABLES

[12] Auto market, for Dec. and full year 1984. (p. 2, 60)

[13] New car stocks, for Jan. 1, 1985. (p. 1, 58)

[17] Market shares, for 1st 9 months 1984. (p. 42)

[18] Import registration shares, for Sept. 1984. (p. 42)

[20-21] Import sales, and U.S. car sales by marketing unit, for Dec. 1984. (p. 2, 60)

[23] Top cars, for 1st 9 months 1984. (p. 42)

ECONOMIC FORECAST '85

Compilation of features presenting economic forecasts for the motor vehicle industry, primarily 1985. Statistical features are described below.

WHEN IS THE BOOM ENDING? IT'S A TOSS-UP

(p. E1-E4) By Michelle Krebs. Article presenting auto and truck sales and general economic indicator forecasts of chief economists at 3 major auto companies, 1985. Includes 1 table.

JUST HOW GOOD WILL 1985 BE? ANNUAL FEATURE

(p. E4-E5) Annual survey article, by Michelle Krebs, with 1 table showing import and domestic auto and total truck sales, as forecast by 10 auto market analysts, 1985.

For description of previous article, see SRI 1983 Annual under C2700-1.450.

'AUTOMOTIVE NEWS' WORLD OUTLOOK, RECURRING FEATURE

(p. E5) Recurring table showing auto and truck production and registrations, by selected country and/or world region, 1983-90. Data are from Data Resources, Inc.

Includes accompanying article, with 1 table on U.S. general economic indicators 1984-85 (p. E5, E12).

SHOOT-OUT IN WILD WESTERN EUROPE

(p. E8) By Michelle Krebs. Article, with 1 table showing percent change in GDP or GNP, consumption, investment, and inflation, and unemployment rate, for 6 Western European countries, 1984-85. Data are from *Economic Forecasts: A Worldwide Survey*.

Other Article

ELECTRONIC OPTIONS ON 1984 U.S.-BUILT MODELS, ANNUAL FEATURE

(p. 34) Annual table showing installations of speed control, digital clock, and electronic instrument panel options in 1984 model autos, by auto manufacturer, make, and model. Includes number of installations, and percent of total auto output.

C2700–1.612: Jan. 21, 1985 (No. 5058)

WEEKLY TABLES

[1-2] Auction averages, for Jan. 1985. (p. 55)

[3-6] Production, for week ended Jan. 19, 1985. (p. 71)

[7] Domestic car sales, for Jan. 1-10, 1985. (p. 2, 68)

MONTHLY TABLES

[8] Truck sales, for Dec. 1984. (p. 18, 46)

[11] New truck sales, through Oct. 1984. (p. 50)

[14] Import stocks, for Jan. 1, 1985. (p. 3)

[15-16] New car market shares and registrations, for Sept. 1984. (p. 44, 66)

[19] Service index, for Nov. 1984. (p. 1)

EARLY COUNT HAS FORD AS WINNER IN EUROPE, RECURRING FEATURE

(p. 8) Recurring article, by Richard Feast, on new auto sales in Western Europe. Includes 2 tables showing sales and/or market shares by country and manufacturer, and for all Japanese autos sold in Europe, 1984 with comparisons to 1983.

BRAZILIANS ARE EXPORT EXPERTS

(p. 41-42) Article, with 4 tables showing the following for Brazil, 1st 9 months 1984: auto and commercial vehicle sales, production, and exports, by manufacturer; and sales of leading 2-6 models in 4 size classes. Data are from Brazilian Manufacturers Assn.

C2700–1.613: Jan. 28, 1985 (No. 5059)

WEEKLY TABLES

[1-2] Auction averages, for Jan. 1985. (p. 247)

[3-6] Production, for week ended Jan. 26, 1985. (p. 264)

[7] Domestic car sales, for Jan. 11-20, 1985. (p. 6)

TIRE OPTIONS ON 1984 MODEL CARS, ANNUAL FEATURE

(p. 162) Annual table showing tire installations on 1984 model autos, by tire type and auto manufacturer, make, and model. Includes number of installations, and percent of total auto output.

SUNROOF OPTIONAL EQUIPMENT, ANNUAL FEATURE

(p. 232) Annual table showing roof option installations on 1984 model year autos, by option type and auto manufacturer, make, and model. Includes number of installations, and percent of total auto output.

ENGINE OPTIONS ON 1984 U.S. MODELS, ANNUAL FEATURE

(p. 244) Annual table showing engine installations on 1984 model year autos, by engine type and auto manufacturer, make, and model. Includes number of installations, and percent of total auto output.

Table title incorrectly reads 1983.

C2700–1.614: Feb. 4, 1985 (No. 5060)

WEEKLY TABLES

[1-2] Auction averages, for Feb. 1985. (p. 39)

[3-6] Production, for week ended Feb. 2, 1985. (p. 54)

[7] Domestic car sales, omitted.

MONTHLY TABLES

[9-11] Truck and heavy-duty registrations, and new truck sales, through Nov. 1984. (p. 16, 27, 34)

[15-16] New car market shares and registrations, for Oct. 1984. (p. 22, 53)

INDUSTRY CAN COMPETE, COMMERCE DEPT SAYS

(p. 1, 49) By Jake Kelderman. Article, with 1 table showing aggregate working capital and selected operating ratios for 4 largest U.S. auto manufacturers, as of Dec. 31, 1978 and 1983 and Sept. 30, 1984. Data are from Commerce Dept.

C2700–1.615: Feb. 11, 1985 (No. 5061)

WEEKLY TABLES

[1-2] Auction averages, for Feb. 1985. (p. 38)

[3-6] Production, for week ended Feb. 9, 1985. (p. 54)

[7] Domestic car sales [by model], for Jan. 21-31, 1985. (p. 3, 50)

MONTHLY TABLES

[12] Auto market, for Jan. 1985 (p. 3, 50)

[17] Market shares, for 1st 10 months 1984. (p. 47)

[18] Import registration shares, for Oct. 1984. (p. 47)

[20-21] Import sales, and U.S. car sales by marketing unit, for Jan. 1985. (p. 3, 50)

[22] Import sales [by model], for Dec. 1984. (p. 35)

[23] Top cars, for 1st 10 months 1984. (p. 47)

QUARTERLY TABLES

[26-27] U.S. retail car outlets [dealerships and exclusive and multiple] franchises, for Jan. 1, 1984-85 [data are combined in a single table and include franchise data by manufacturer]. (p. 1, 32)

DOMESTIC DEALER TOTAL UP FOR SECOND YEAR IN ROW, ANNUAL FEATURE

(p. 1, 32) Annual article, by John K. Teahen, Jr., with text statistics and 1 table showing number of auto dealerships handling domestic makes, Jan. 1, 1947-85, and quarterly Jan. 1, 1984-Jan. 1, 1985. Data are from *Automotive News*.

SEAT OPTIONS ON 1984 U.S. MODELS

(p. 48) Table showing seat option installations on 1984 model year autos, by option type and auto manufacturer, make, and model. Includes number of installations, and percent of total auto output.

C2700–1.616: Feb. 18, 1985 (No. 5062)

WEEKLY TABLES

[1-2] Auction averages, for Feb. 1985. (p. 39)

[3-6] Production, for week ended Feb. 16, 1985. (p. 54)

[7] Domestic car sales, for Feb. 1-10, 1985. (p. 3)

MONTHLY TABLES

[8] Truck sales, for Jan. 1985. (p. 18, 32)

[13] New car stocks, for Jan. 1, 1985. (p. 1, 49)

[19] Service index, for Dec. 1984. (p. 1)

BIG THREE SET PROFIT RECORD OF $9.8 BILLION

(p. 8) Brief article, with 1 table showing profits of 3 largest U.S. auto manufacturers, 1983-84.

C2700–1.617: Feb. 25, 1985 (No. 5063)

WEEKLY TABLES

[1-2] Auction averages, for Feb. 1985. (p. 59)

[3-6] Production, for week ended Feb. 23, 1985. (p. 74)

[7] Domestic car sales, omitted.

MONTHLY TABLES

[9-10] Truck and heavy-duty registrations, through Dec. 1984. (p. 16, 56)

[14] Import stocks, for Feb. 1, 1985. (p. 2)

[24] Overseas production in UK and Brazil, through Nov. 1984; and Spain, Japan, and France, through Oct. 1984. (p. 40, 42)

[25] Overseas registrations in Italy, Austria, UK, and Sweden, through Dec. 1984; Switzerland, Denmark, and West Germany, through Nov. 1984; France and Japan, through Oct. 1984; and Belgium, through Sept. 1984. (p. 40, 42)

1984 DIESEL SALES TOP 1.2 MILLION

(p. 41) Article, with 1 table showing diesel auto sales in Europe (total and as percent of all auto sales), by country, 1st 9 months 1983-84.

AIR CONDITIONING INSTALLATIONS, ANNUAL FEATURE

(p. 52) Annual table showing air conditioning unit installations on 1983-84 model year autos, by auto manufacturer, make, and model. Includes number of installations, and percent of total auto output.

SALES OF DIESEL-POWERED NEW CARS IN THE U.S.

(p. 68) Table showing diesel auto sales by import and domestic manufacturer or make, and total auto sales, 1980-84.

C2700–1.618: Mar. 4, 1985 (No. 5064)

WEEKLY TABLES

[1-2] Auction averages, for Feb. 1985. (p. 39)

[3-6] Production, for week ended Mar. 2, 1985. (p. 54)

[7] Domestic car sales, for Feb. 11-20, 1985. (p. 3)

TRANSMISSION OPTIONS ON 1984 U.S. MODELS, ANNUAL FEATURE

(p. 39) Annual table showing transmission installations on 1984 model year autos, by transmission type and auto manufacturer, make, and model. Includes number of installations, and percent of total auto output.

C2700–1.619: Mar. 11, 1985 (No. 5065)

WEEKLY TABLES

[1-2] Auction averages, for Mar. 1985. (p. 38)

[3-6] Production, for week ended Mar. 9, 1985. (p. 54)

[7] Domestic car sales [by model], for Feb. 21-28, 1985. (p. 6, 50)

MONTHLY TABLES

[12] Auto market, for Feb. 1985. (p. 6, 50)

[15-16] New car market shares for Nov. 1984, and new car registrations for Dec. 1984. (p. 24, 53)

[17] Market shares, for 1st 11 months 1984. (p. 20)

[18] Import registration shares, for Nov. 1984. (p. 20)

[20-21] Imported car sales, and U.S. car sales by marketing unit, for Feb. 1985 [also includes import sales for 1983-84]. (p. 6, E44, 50)

[23] Top cars, for 1st 11 months 1984. (p. 20)

IMPORT WORLD

Compilation of features on imported auto and truck trends and developments. Statistical features are described below.

IMPORT PRICES RISE SHARPLY, ANNUAL FEATURE

(p. E14-E20) Annual article, by John K. Teahen, Jr., with 1 table showing average new car transaction price, for domestics and imports, 1967-84. Data are from U.S. Bureau of Economic Analysis.

Also includes accompanying text data showing prices for new imports by detailed model, as of Mar. 1, 1985.

IMPORT MODEL COUNT IS ON A ROLL, ANNUAL FEATURE

(p. E26) Annual article, by John K. Teahen, Jr., reviewing 1984 imported auto body styles offered in U.S. Includes text statistics and 1 table showing number of 1985 models offered by all domestic manufacturers and 29 import manufacturers, for 4 body styles, as of Mar. 1985 with summary comparisons to 1984; and total import models offered, Mar. 1978-83.

MUSCLING IN ON MEDIUM TRUCKS

(p. E32-E36) By Arthur Flax. Article, with 4 tables showing imported truck sales (total, Japanese, and domestic-sponsored), and domestic truck sales by gross vehicle weight, 1971-84; and value of motor vehicles/parts trade, worldwide and with Canada, and as a percent of GNP and all merchandise trade, 1970-83.

Data are from Motor Vehicle Manufacturers Assn, Census Bureau, and Statistics Canada.

TV AD SPENDING CLIMBS, ANNUAL FEATURE

(p. E42) Annual brief article, with 1 table showing network and spot TV advertising expenditures, for 13 foreign auto/truck manufacturers ranked by aggregate network/spot expenditures, 1984 with comparisons to 1983. Data are from TV Bureau of Advertising based on Broadcast Advertisers Reports.

Other Article

IMPORT-U.S. BUYER PROFILES STEADY

(p. 39) By Matt DeLorenzo. Article examining demographic characteristics of new-auto buyers. Data are from J. D. Power and Associates.

Includes 2 tables showing the following for 1984 new-auto buyers: percent male, married, and from 2-income households; and median household income, age, and price paid for car; all by domestic, Japanese, and European auto make, with summary comparisons to total driving-age population and persons intending to buy a new auto, including percent college graduates.

C2700–1.620: Mar. 18, 1985 (No. 5066)

WEEKLY TABLES

[1-2] Auction averages, for Mar. 1985. (p. 47)

[3-6] Production, for week ended Mar. 16, 1985. (p. 63)

[7] Domestic car sales, for Mar. 1-10, 1985. (p. 8)

MONTHLY TABLES

[8] Truck sales, for Feb. 1985. (p. 16, 22, 24)

[13] New car stocks, for Mar. 1, 1985. (p. 1, 57)

IMPORT-CAR DEALS CLIMB TO 12,427; CHEVY IS REASON, SEMIANNUAL FEATURE

(p. 1, 62) Semiannual article, by John K. Teahen, Jr., reviewing import auto dealership trends. Includes 3 tables showing import franchises by nationality and make, and outlets handling imports only (exclusives and duals) and import-domestic duals, Jan. 1 1984-85; and import outlets, Jan. 1, 1957-85.

DEALER TOTAL, U.S. AND IMPORT, STEADY FOR YEAR

(p. 62) Brief article, with 1 table showing total (domestic/import) new auto outlets, Jan. 1, 1957-85.

C2700–1.621: Mar. 25, 1985 (No. 5067)

WEEKLY TABLES

[1-2] Auction averages, for Mar. 1985. (p. 54)

[3-6] Production, for week ended Mar. 23, 1985. (p. 70)

[7] Domestic car sales, omitted.

MONTHLY TABLES

[14] Import stocks, for Mar. 1, 1985. (p. 2, 65)

[16] New car registrations, for Nov. 1984. (p. 55)

[19] Service index, for Jan. 1985. (p. 2)

[24] Overseas production in West Germany, France, and Brazil, through Dec. 1984; and Spain and Japan, through Nov. 1984. (p. 42)

[25] Overseas registrations in West Germany, Spain, Holland, Belgium, Austria, Denmark, and Norway, through Dec. 1984; and France and Japan, through Nov. 1984. (p. 42)

SALES PER OUTLET CLIMB; JAPANESE WIN TOP 4 SPOTS, SEMIANNUAL FEATURE

(p. 1, 65) Semiannual article, by Jenny L. King, reviewing auto dealer sales volume in 1984. Includes 3 tables showing sales per outlet, by make, 1975-84; and by model nameplate for 5 size groups, 1983-84; with selected rankings.

C2700–1.622: Apr. 1, 1985 (No. 5068)

WEEKLY TABLES

[1-2] Auction averages, for Mar. 1985. (p. 52)

[3-6] Production, for week ended Mar. 30, 1985. (p. 59)

[7] Domestic car sales, for Mar. 11-20, 1985. (p. 55)

MONTHLY TABLES

[9-10] Truck and heavy-duty registrations, Jan. 1985. (p. 18, 36)

[15-16] New car market shares and registrations, for Dec. 1984. (p. 28, 35)

[17] Market shares, for full year 1984. (p. 30)

[18] Import registration shares, for Dec. 1984. (p. 30)

[22] Import sales [by model], for Feb. 1985. (p. 52)

[23] Top cars, through Dec. 1984. (p. 30)

SALES BY NAMEPLATE

(p. 20) Table showing auto sales by model, ranked for 1984 with comparisons to 1983.

C2700–1.623: Apr. 8, 1985 (No. 5069)

WEEKLY TABLES

[1-2] Auction averages, for Apr. 1985. (p. 42)

[3-6] Production, for week ended Apr. 6, 1985. (p. 51)

[7] Domestic car sales [by model], for Mar. 21-31, 1985. (p. 1, 46)

MONTHLY TABLES

[11] New truck sales, for Jan. 1985. (p. 32)

[12] Auto market, for Mar. 1985. (p. 1, 46)

[20-21] Imported car sales, and U.S. car sales by marketing unit, for Mar. 1985. (p. 1, 46)

[22] Import sales [by model], for Jan. 1985. (p. 14)

C2700–1.624: Apr. 15, 1985 (No. 5070)

WEEKLY TABLES

[1-2] Auction averages, for Apr. 1985. (p. 62)

[3-6] Production, for week ended Apr. 13, 1985. (p. 78)

[7] Domestic car sales, omitted.

MONTHLY TABLES

[8] Truck sales, for Mar. 1985. (p. 16, 59)

[13] New car stocks, for Apr. 1, 1985. (p. 1, 74)

[15-16] New car market shares and registrations, for Jan. 1985. (p. 3, 77)

[19] Service index, for Feb. 1985. (p. 2)

[24] Overseas production in France and Brazil, through Jan. 1985; and Spain, Japan, and UK, through Dec. 1984. (p. 44)

[25] Overseas registrations in UK and Sweden, through Feb. 1985; and France, Switzerland, Finland, Ireland, and Japan, through Dec. 1984. (p. 44)

C2700–1.625: Apr. 22, 1985 (No. 5071)

WEEKLY TABLES

[1-2] Auction averages, for Apr. 1985. (p. 35)

[3-6] Production, for week ended Apr. 20, 1985. (p. 51)

[7] Domestic car sales, for Apr. 1-10, 1985. (p. 2)

MONTHLY TABLES

[14] Import stocks, for Apr. 1, 1985. (p. 1, 49)

[17] Market shares, for Jan. 1985. (p. 32)

[18] Import registration shares, for Jan. 1985. (p. 32)

[23] Top cars, through Jan. 1985. (p. 32)

PETERBILT, MACK LEAD

(p. E18) Brief article, with 1 table showing medium/heavy-duty truck retail outlets and average registrations per outlet, by manufacturer, 1983-84.

C2700–1.626: Apr. 24, 1985 (No. 5072)

WEEKLY TABLES

[1-7] Omitted.

1984 MARKET DATA BOOK ISSUE

Annual auto industry market data book, covering production, sales, registrations, prices, option installations, manufacturers, dealers, and selected other topics, 1984 and trends. Also includes detailed specifications for 1985 model autos and trucks. Book focuses on U.S. auto industry, but also presents data on imports and on production in Canada and other countries.

Data are from original surveys, and reports of Motor Vehicle Manufacturers Assn, R. L. Polk & Co., and other industry sources.

Includes contents listing (p. 1); 9 statistical sections, with 17 charts and 141 tables interspersed with narrative and text data, and industry directories (p. 3-196); and index (p. 198).

Tables, charts, and substantial text data are described below. Industry directories (p. 83-193) are not included on SRI microfiche.

TABLES, CHARTS, AND TEXT DATA:

[Data are for U.S., unless otherwise noted. Most data are shown for various periods 1984, generally with comparison to 1983 or trends from 1970s. Also includes selected historical trends from as early as 1946 and projections to 1990.]

a. Production: world motor vehicle production, for autos and trucks by manufacturer, world region, and country, and for top 12 manufacturers; U.S. and Canadian auto and truck production by manufacturer, with detail by make and/or model; and U.S. factory sales (domestic and export) of special trucks by type, and auto production by size class and State. 24 tables. (p. 3-18)

b. Sales/registrations: Canadian auto and truck registrations; auto registrations by make, and sales of Japanese autos, for 15 Western European countries; U.S. auto and truck sales and registrations, with detail by State and for Federal Government, by size class, and by domestic and import manufacturer, make, and model; and U.S. domestic and import diesel auto sales by make, and total recreational vehicle shipments by type. 28 tables. (p. 19-36)

c. Specifications, prices, and options: detailed specifications and EPA fuel economy mileage estimates for domestic and import autos and trucks; number of domestic and import auto models offered, and retail prices; used auto average auction prices; and number of option installations by option type; with detail by body style and manufacturer, make, and model. Text data and 20 tables. (p. 37-70)

d. Manufacturers: net sales, profit/loss, and other financial and operating data, for 4 major manufacturers and ancillary finance companies; income and sales for 7 leading Japanese auto manufacturers; auto and truck production and registrations to 1990, by selected country and/or world region; general economic indicators and vehicle sales; and capital expenditures, production value and index, employment, exports, and capacity utilization, for motor vehicle and parts industries, with comparisons to all manufacturing. 18 tables. (p. 71-74)

e. Dealers: domestic and import auto and truck retail outlets and auto franchises, by manufacturer and make; domestic and import auto and truck sales and/or registrations per outlet, with detail by body size and manufacturer, make, and model; used vehicle sales by new auto/truck dealers; *Automotive News* service index; and average dealership financial performance trends. 1 chart and 13 tables. (p. 75-78)

f. Suppliers: injection molding polyurethane consumption, and machine tool and reinforced plastic shipments, by end use; rubber consumption and magnesium production and shipments, by world region; auto and truck color selections; sales and earnings for 7 tire companies; tire imports and exports, by country; industrial robots in U.S. and 3 other countries, and average cost, shipments, and orders; glass fiber composite consumption in vehicle manufacturing; and amount of zinc and aluminum in typical auto. 3 charts and 24 tables. (p. 79-82)

g. Et Cetera: auto inventories and days supply, motor vehicle advertising expenditures by media and manufacturer, and new auto buyer demographic characteristics by auto make, all with detail for import and domestic vehicles; Japanese motor vehicle exports, by country and world region; autos and trucks in use and scrapped; U.S. and Canada cross-border shipments, by manufacturer, make, and model; and motor vehicle/parts trade with Canada and rest of world. 14 tables. (p. 194-196)

C2700–1.627: Apr. 29, 1985 (No. 5072)

WEEKLY TABLES

[1-2] Auction averages, for Apr. 1985. (p. 37)

[3-6] Production, for week ended Apr. 27, 1985. (p. 51)

[7] Domestic car sales, for Apr. 11-20, 1985. (p. 8)

MONTHLY TABLES

[9-11] Truck and heavy-duty registrations, and new truck sales, through Feb. 1985. (p. 16, 30)

AUTO INDUSTRY BOOSTS TV SPENDING

(p. 24, 32) By Edward Lapham. Article, with 3 tables showing network and spot TV advertising expenditures, for 18 foreign and domestic auto/truck manufacturers ranked by aggregate network/spot expenditures; and top 20 auto dealer assns and 15 auto dealers ranked by TV advertising expenditures; 1984 with comparisons to 1983.

Data are from TV Bureau of Advertising based on Broadcast Advertisers Reports.

'AUTOMOTIVE NEWS' WORLD OUTLOOK, RECURRING FEATURE

(p. 50) Recurring table showing auto and truck production and registrations, by selected country and/or world region, 1983-90. Data are from Data Resources, Inc.

Includes accompanying article, with 1 table showing the following for 9 Japanese auto manufacturers: production, domestic sales, and sales to North America, Europe, and rest of world, 1984, 1986, and 1990 (p. 1, 50).

C2700–1.628: May 6, 1985 (No. 5073)

WEEKLY TABLES

[1-2] Auction averages, for Apr. 1985. (p. 48)

[3-6] Production, for week ended May 4, 1985. (p. 62)

[7] Domestic car sales, omitted.

MONTHLY TABLES

[15-16] New car market shares and registrations, for Feb. 1985. (p. 26, 60)

QUARTERLY TABLES

[26-27] U.S. car outlets and franchises, for Apr. 1, 1985. (p. 1, 57)

[28] Auto makers' financial results, for 1st quarter 1985. (p. 3)

C2700–1.629: May 13, 1985 (No. 5074)

WEEKLY TABLES

[1-2] Auction averages, for May 1985. (p. 61)

[3-6] Production, for week ended May 11, 1985. (p. 77)

[7] Domestic car sales [by model], for Apr. 21-30, 1985. (p. 6, 58)

MONTHLY TABLES

[8-8A] Light-duty and major manufacturer [truck] sales, for Apr. 1985. (p. 24)

[12] Auto market, for Apr. 1985. (p. 6, 58)

[13] New car stocks, for May 1, 1985. (p. 1, 76)

[17] Market shares, for 1st 2 months, 1985. (p. 55)

[18] Import registration shares, for Feb. 1985. (p. 55)

[20-21] Import sales, and U.S. car sales by marketing unit, for Apr. 1985. (p. 6, 58)

[22] Import sales by model, for Mar. 1985. (p. 56)

[23] Top cars, for 1st 2 months 1985. (p. 55)

C2700–1.630: May 20, 1985 (No. 5075)

WEEKLY TABLES

[1-2] Auction averages, for May 1985. (p. 51)

[3-6] Production, for week ended May 18, 1985. (p. 66)

[7] Domestic car sales, for May 1-10, 1985. (p. 8)

MONTHLY TABLES

[9-11] Truck and heavy-duty registrations, and new truck sales, through Mar. 1985. (p. 50, 60)

[14] Import stocks, for May 1, 1985. (p. 1, 64)

[19] Service index, for Mar. 1985. (p. 3, 65)

[24] Overseas production in France, Japan, and Brazil, through Feb. 1985; and Netherlands, through Dec. 1984. (p. 38)

[25] Overseas registrations in West Germany, UK, and Sweden, through Mar. 1985; and Belgium, Austria, and Japan, through Feb. 1985. (p. 38)

UNO IS EUROPE'S No. 1 SELLER, ANNUAL FEATURE

(p. 35-37) Annual article, with 1 table showing top 10 auto models ranked by sales, and total auto sales, for 14 Western European countries, 1984 (with comparative rank for 1983). Data are from an *Automotive News* survey.

FORD EDGES FIAT FOR EUROPEAN SALES LEADERSHIP, ANNUAL FEATURE

(p. 35-37) Annual article, with 1 table showing new car market volume and market share, by manufacturer and for all Japanese imports, for 16 European countries, 1983-84. Data are from *Automotive News* and are based primarily on government statistics.

Previous article, for 1982-83, is described in SRI 1984 Annual under C2700-1.525.

JAPANESE THANK WEST GERMANS, ANNUAL FEATURE

(p. 37) Annual article, with 1 table showing sales by manufacturer, and aggregate market share, for Japanese autos sold in Europe by country, 1984 with comparisons to 1983.

Previous article, for 1983, is described in SRI 1984 Annual under C2700-1.525.

U.S. QUOTAS LISTED FOR JAPANESE AUTO MAKERS

(p. 50) Brief article, with 1 table showing limits on Japanese auto exports to the U.S. under the Voluntary Restraint Agreement, by manufacturer, for the years beginning Apr. 1, 1984-85. Data are from *Japan Economic Journal.*

C2700–1.631: May 27, 1985 (No. 5076)

WEEKLY TABLES

[1-2] Auction averages, for May 1985. (p. 32)

[3-6] Production, for week ended May 25, 1985. (p. 47)

[7] Domestic car sales, for May 11-20, 1985. (p. 42)

MONTHLY TABLES

[15-16] New car market shares and registrations, for Mar. 1985. (p. 6, 46)

U.S. STUDY GIVES IMPORTS 36 Pct. OF 1988 MARKET

(p. 1, 42) By Geoff Sundstrom. Article, with 1 table showing U.S. sales of auto imports from Japan (captive and noncaptive), Europe, South Korea, and all other countries, and of U.S.-built Japanese autos and Canadian-built U.S. autos, 1984-88. Data are from Commerce Dept.

C2700–1.632: June 3, 1985 (No. 5077)

WEEKLY TABLES

[1-2] Auction averages, for May 1985. (p. 54)

[3-6] Production, for week ended June 1, 1985. (p. 70)

[7] Domestic car sales, omitted.

MONTHLY TABLES

[17] Market shares, for 1st 3 months 1985. (p. 14)

[18] Import registration shares, for Mar. 1985. (p. 14)

[22] Import sales by model, for Apr. 1985. (p. 48)

[23] Top cars, for 1st 3 months 1985. (p. 14)

PERSONAL-USE FLAT RATE GAINS POPULARITY

(p. E4-E10) Article on personal use of company fleet cars. Data are based on responses of 407 U.S. and Canadian fleets operating 264,-905 passenger autos, to a 1984 National Assn of Fleet Administrators (NAFA) survey.

Includes 1 table showing distribution of responses on number of fleets, and policies and limitations governing personal use of fleet cars; for 7 industry groups, public utilities, and government (all U.S. only), and for Canada, 1984.

Full NAFA survey is described under A6755-1.604, above.

FLEET OPERATING EXPENSES CONTINUE TO EBB

(p. E10-E12) Article on fleet operating expenses in U.S. and Canada. Data are from responses of 84 fleets operating 79,669 passenger autos, to a NAFA survey.

Includes 3 tables showing U.S. composite fleet operating, incidental, and standing expenses, by item, and personal use credits; and operating expenses by item, and average miles per gallon and/or per month, by auto size class for U.S., and total for Canada; mostly 1982-84.

Full NAFA survey is described under A6755-1.606, above.

REDUCING EXCESS MAINTENANCE

(p. E26) Article reporting opinions of corporate auto fleet managers on dealing with excessive vehicle maintenance problems. Data are based on responses of over 200 managers to a recent Runzheimer International survey. Includes 1 table.

IMPORT FLEET IS ON THE RISE

(p. E27) Article on import autos in North American fleets. Data are from Runzheimer

International surveys of U.S. and Canadian fleets conducted in 1982 (95 respondents), 1983 (532 respondents), and 1984 (506 respondents).

Includes 1 table showing average fleet domestic vs. import composition, and percent of fleets owning imported autos and average number owned.

UNLEADED GAS PRICES TO RISE

(p. E28) Brief article, with 1 table showing self-serve unleaded gasoline prices, monthly Jan. 1984-Apr. 1985. Data are from Runzheimer International.

GAS PRICES FELL AGAIN IN '84

(p. E28) Brief article, with 1 table showing average price per gallon of regular and unleaded gasoline, 1974-84. Data are from American Automobile Assn surveys of approximately 6,000 service stations.

C2700–1.633: June 10, 1985 (No. 5078)

WEEKLY TABLES

[1-2] Auction averages, for June 1985. (p. 43)

[3-6] Production, for week ended June 8, 1985. (p. 59)

[7] Domestic car sales [by model], for May 21-31, 1985. (p. 6, 54)

MONTHLY TABLES

[12] Auto market, for May 1985. (p. 6, 54)

[20-21] Import sales, and U.S. car sales by marketing unit, for May 1985. (p. 6, 54)

C2700–1.634: June 17, 1985 (No. 5079)

WEEKLY TABLES

[1-2] Auction averages, for June 1985. (p. 51)

[3-6] Production, for week ended June 15, 1985. (p. 66)

[7] Domestic car sales, for June 1-10, 1985. (p. 2, 61)

MONTHLY TABLES

[8-8A] Light-duty and major manufacturer [truck] sales, for May 1985. (p. 44)

[13] New car stocks, for June 1, 1985. (p. 1, 61)

[19] Service index, for Apr. 1985. (p. 1, 61)

[22] Import sales by model, for May 1985. (p. 26)

[24] Overseas production in France and Brazil, through Mar. 1985; and UK and Spain, through Feb. 1985. (p. 38)

[25] Overseas registrations in UK and Sweden, through Apr. 1985; Austria and Denmark, through Mar. 1985; Switzerland and France, through Feb. 1985; and sales in Italy, through Mar. 1985. (p. 38)

C2700–1.635: June 24, 1985 (No. 5080)

WEEKLY TABLES

[1-2] Auction averages, for June 1985. (p. 41)

[3-6] Production, for week ended June 22, 1985. (p. 55)

[7] Domestic car sales, omitted.

MONTHLY TABLES

[9-10] Truck and heavy-duty registrations, through Apr. 1985. (p. 16, 32)

[11] New truck sales, Dec. 1984 and Apr. 1985. (p. 24, 50)

---

[14] Import stocks, for June 1, 1985. (p. 2, 54)

[15-16] New car market shares and registrations, for Apr. 1985. (p. 30, 36)

C2700–1.636: July 1, 1985 (No. 5081)

WEEKLY TABLES

[1-2] Auction averages, for June 1985. (p. 29)

[3-6] Production, for week ended June 29, 1985. (p. 42)

[7] Domestic car sales, for June 11-20, 1985. (p. 6)

C2700–1.637: July 8, 1985 (No. 5082)

WEEKLY TABLES

[1-2] Auction averages, for July 1985. (p. 48)

[3-6] Production, for week ended July 6, 1985. (p. 63)

[7] Domestic car sales [by model], for June 21-30, 1985. (p. 1, 58)

MONTHLY TABLES

[12] Auto market, for June 1985. (p. 1, 58)

[20-21] Import sales, and U.S. car sales by marketing unit, for June 1985. (p. 1, 58)

[24] Overseas production in Japan, UK, and Spain, through Mar. 1985; and France, through Apr. 1985. (p. 36)

[25] Overseas registrations in UK and Sweden, through May 1985; West Germany, Austria, and Denmark, through Apr. 1985; and Japan, Switzerland, and Norway, through Mar. 1985. (p. 36)

RECORD NUMBER OF VEHICLES BUILT IN SPAIN

(p. 34) By Richard Feast. Article, with 1 table showing auto production in Spain, by make, 1980-84.

C2700–1.638: July 15, 1985 (No. 5083)

WEEKLY TABLES

[1-2] Auction averages, for July 1985. (p. 36)

[3-6] Production, for week ended June 13, 1985. (p. 51)

[7] Domestic car sales, omitted.

MONTHLY TABLES

[8-8A] Light-duty and major manufacturer [truck] sales, for June 1985. (p. 18, 26)

[13] New car stocks, for July 1, 1985. (p. 1, 50)

[17] Market shares, for 1st 4 months 1985. (p. 30)

[18] Import registration shares, for Apr. 1985. (p. 30)

[19] Service index, for May 1985. (p. 1, 49)

[23] Top cars, for 1st 4 months 1985. (p. 30)

SERVICE PROFITS, ANNUAL FEATURE

Annual compilation of articles on auto dealer service and parts business. Includes the annual statistical articles described below.

OUTLOOK FOR SERVICE STILL UPBEAT

(p. E1-E2, E6) Annual survey article, by Colleen Belli, on auto dealer service dept operations and profit outlook, based on responses of service managers to a 1985 *Automotive News* survey. Includes 1 table showing survey response on the following, 1983-85:

---

a. Sales outlook for dealer and auto industry; and dealer service dept profit potential, advertising/promotion adequacy, responsibility for hiring mechanics and buying service equipment, new service equipment buying plans, profitability of service on new vs. older autos, hours open per week, number of employees, most profitable service operation, and profitability of new auto warranty work and extended service contracts.

b. Respondent characteristics: age, previous job, years in current position, compensation level and composition, and whether salary/benefits are commensurate with experience.

DEALERS REAP $30.7 BILLION IN SERVICE

(p. E16) Annual article, by Jack Walsh, on auto dealer parts and service sales. Data are from the National Automobile Dealers Assn.

Includes 3 tables showing value of service/parts market, 1979-84, and number of auto repair facilities, 1984, by type of service establishment; and franchised new auto dealer labor and parts sales, by type, 1983-84.

Other Article

EXECUTIVE PAY UP 15 Pct., ANNUAL FEATURE

(p. 1, 48-49) Annual article, by Michelle Krebs, on motor vehicle industry executive compensation. Data are from company proxy statements.

Includes 2 tables showing total income of 2 top executives of 4 auto manufacturing companies; and salary/bonus of 170 highest paid executives of vehicle manufacturing and supplier companies; 1983-84.

C2700–1.639: July 22, 1985 (No. 5084)

WEEKLY TABLES

[1-2] Auction averages, for July 1985. (p. 39)

[3-6] Production, for week ended July 20, 1985. (p. 54)

[7] Domestic car sales, for June 1-10, 1985. (p. 6)

MONTHLY TABLES

[9-10] Truck and heavy-duty registrations, through May 1985. (p. 34)

[12] Auto market, for 1st half 1985. (p. 48)

[14] Import stocks, for July 1, 1985. (p. 1, 52)

[15-16] New car market shares and registrations, for May 1985. (p. 30, 32)

DOE ANALYSIS DETECTS MOVE TO SMALLER CARS

(p. 2, 53) By Jake Kelderman. Article, with 1 table showing fuel economy estimates for new domestic and import autos and light trucks, 1st 6 months, model years 1978-85. Data are from DOE.

C2700–1.640: July 29, 1985 (No. 5085)

WEEKLY TABLES

[1-2] Auction averages, for July 1985. (p. 41)

[3-6] Production, for week ended July 27, 1985. (p. 57)

[7] Domestic car sales, for July 11-20, 1985. (p. 3)

MONTHLY TABLES

[11] New truck registrations, for May 1985. (p. 38)

[17] Market shares, for 1st 5 months 1985. (p. 20)

[18] Import registration shares, for May 1985 [table incorrectly reads Apr.]. (p. 20)

[22] Import sales by model, for June 1985. (p. 31)

[23] Top cars, for 1st 5 months 1985. (p. 20)

HOW DEALERSHIPS DIFFER IN JAPAN

(p. 49) By Lawrence D. Dietz. Article, with 1 undated table showing Japanese auto distributors, branches, and market shares, for 6 leading manufacturers and all others. Data are from Alec Group.

Also includes 1 additional table with data on Nissan dealerships.

C2700–1.641: Aug. 5, 1985 (No. 5086)
WEEKLY TABLES

[1-2] Auction averages, for July 1985. (p. 60)

[3-6] Production, for week ended Aug. 3, 1985. (p. 66)

[7] Domestic car sales, omitted.

MONTHLY TABLES

[19] Service index, for June 1985. (p. 1, 8)

[24] Overseas production in Japan, Brazil, UK, and Spain, through Apr. 1985; and France, through May 1985. (p. 40)

[25] Overseas registrations in UK and Sweden, through June 1985; West Germany, Austria, and Denmark, through May 1985; Italy, Switzerland, and Japan, through Apr. 1985; and France and the Netherlands, through Mar. 1985. (p. 40)

QUARTERLY TABLES

[26-27] U.S. car outlets and franchises, for July 1, 1985. (p. 1, 61)

[28] Auto makers' financial results, for 1st half and 2nd quarter 1985. (p. 2, 8)

REPORT CARD TIME FOR EUROPE'S AUTO MAKERS

(p. 38-39) By Richard Feast. Article, with 1 table showing Western Europe auto sales, net profit/loss, production, and employees, all by manufacturer, 1984.

C2700–1.642: Aug. 12, 1985 (No. 5087)
WEEKLY TABLES

[1-2] Auction averages, for Aug. 1985. (p. 45)

[3-6] Production, for week ended Aug. 10, 1985. (p. 59)

[7] Domestic car sales [by model], for July 21-31, 1985. (p. 7)

MONTHLY TABLES

[12] Auto market, for July 1985. (p. 7)

[13] New car stocks, for Aug. 1, 1985. (p. 1, 58)

[20-21] Import sales, and U.S. car sales by marketing unit, for July 1985. (p. 7)

C2700–1.643: Aug. 19, 1985 (No. 5088)
WEEKLY TABLES

[1-2] Auction averages, for Aug. 1985. (p. 33)

[3-6] Production, for week ended Aug. 17, 1985. (p. 46)

[7] Domestic car sales, for Aug. 1-10, 1985. (p. 2, 45)

MONTHLY TABLES

[8-8A] Light-duty and major manufacturer [truck] sales, for July 1985. (p. 14, 24)

[9-11] Truck and heavy-duty registrations, and new truck registrations, through June 1985. (p. 14, 26)

[14] Import stocks, for Aug. 1, 1985. (p. 1, 45)

VW GROUP SNARES LEAD IN EUROPE, RECURRING FEATURE

(p. 1, 45) Recurring article, by Richard Feast, on new auto sales in Western Europe. Includes 2 tables showing market shares and/or sales, by country and manufacturer, and for all Japanese autos sold in Europe, 1st half 1984-85.

CASH REGISTERS KEEP JINGLING AT DEALERSHIPS, ANNUAL FEATURE

(p. E1-E2) Annual article, by Colleen Belli, on profit expectations of new car/truck dealers. Data are from National Automobile Dealers Assn surveys. Includes 1 table showing profit expectation index, and percent of dealers expecting increased, decreased, and unchanged profits, Apr. 1976-Apr. 1980 and quarterly Jan. 1981-Jan. 1985.

Previous article, with data for 1979-84, is described in SRI 1984 Annual under C2700-1.543.

SELLING CARS FROM THE INSIDE OUT

(p. E10-E12) By Arthur Flax. Article, with 2 charts showing percent of domestic and imported new autos with standard or optional radios, and percent that can be ordered without radios ("deletable") or that must be ordered with standard radios, 1984-85. Data are from Car Audio Specialists, Inc.

C2700–1.644: Aug. 26, 1985 (No. 5089)
WEEKLY TABLES

[1-2] Auction averages, for Aug. 1985. (p. 43)

[3-6] Production, for week ended Aug. 24, 1985. (p. 59)

[7] Domestic car sales, omitted.

MONTHLY TABLES

[15-16] New car market shares and registrations, for June 1985. (p. 50-51)

[22] Import sales by model, for July 1985. (p. 36)

C2700–1.645: Sept. 2, 1985 (No. 5090)
WEEKLY TABLES

[1-2] Auction averages, for Aug. 1985. (p. 41)

[3-6] Production, for week ended Aug. 31, 1985. (p. 47)

[7] Domestic car sales, omitted.

C2700–1.646: Sept. 9, 1985 (No. 5091)
WEEKLY TABLES

[1-2] Auction averages, for Sept. 1985. (p. 53)

[3-6] Production, for week ended Sept. 7, 1985. (p. 67)

[7] Domestic car sales, for Aug. 11-20, 1985; and [by model], for Aug. 21-31, 1985. (p. 1, 24, 66)

MONTHLY TABLES

[12] Auto market, for Aug. 1985. (p. 1, 66)

[17] Market shares, for 1st half 1985. (p. 61)

[18] Import registration shares, for June 1985. (p. 61)

[19] Service index, for July 1985. (p. 2)

[20-21] Import sales, and U.S. car sales by marketing unit, for Aug. 1985. (p. 1, 66)

[23] Top cars, through June 1985. (p. 61)

[24] Overseas production in Brazil, Japan, and France, through June 1985; and UK and Spain, through May 1985. (p. 38)

[25] Overseas registrations in UK and Sweden, through July 1985; West Germany, the Netherlands, Belgium, Austria, Denmark, and Japan, through June 1985; Switzerland, through May 1985; and France and Ireland, through Apr. 1985. (p. 38)

C2700–1.647: Sept. 16, 1985 (No. 5092)
WEEKLY TABLES

[1-2] Auction averages, for Sept. 1985. (p. 41)

[3-6] Production, for week ended Sept. 14, 1985. (p. 54)

[7] Domestic car sales, omitted.

MONTHLY TABLES

[8-8A] Light-duty and major manufacturer [truck] sales, for Aug. 1985. (p. 14, 32)

[13] New car stocks, for Sept. 1, 1985. (p. 1, 50)

C2700–1.648: Sept. 23, 1985 (No. 5093)
WEEKLY TABLES

[1-2] Auction averages, for Sept. 1985. (p. 61)

[3-6] Production, for week ended Sept. 21, 1985. (p. 74)

[7] Domestic car sales, omitted.

MONTHLY TABLES

[14] Import stocks, for Sept. 1, 1985. (p. 1, 73)

[15-16] New car market shares and registrations, for July 1985. (p. 70-71)

[22] Import sales by model, for Aug. 1985. (p. 49)

1986: THE YEAR OF THE CREATIVE INCENTIVE, ANNUAL FEATURE

(p. E8-E9) Annual survey article, by Michelle Krebs, reporting on new motor vehicle sales projections by 13 market analysts. Includes 1 table showing new car and truck sales projections (total and import) by each analyst, 1986-88.

OVERSEAS TOURIST DELIVERY IS HERE TO STAY

(p. E10) By Richard Feast. Article, with 1 table showing direct factory auto deliveries to tourists by 7 European manufacturers, 1st 8 months 1984-85.

LEADING 1984 AUTO ADVERTISING SPENDERS, ANNUAL FEATURE

(p. E40-E42) Annual article analyzing domestic and import automobile industry advertising expenditures in 1984. Data are from *Advertising Age*. Includes 1 table showing advertising expenditures by media, repeated for 8 domestic and import manufacturers (with detail by division), 1983-84.

C2700–1.649: Sept. 30, 1985 (No. 5094)
WEEKLY TABLES

[1-2] Auction averages, for Sept. 1985. (p. 39)

[3-6] Production, for week ended Sept. 28, 1985. (p. 51)

[7] Domestic car sales, for Sept. 1-10 and 11-20, 1985. (p. 2, 35)

MONTHLY TABLES

[9-11] Truck and heavy-duty registrations, and new truck registrations, through July 1985. (p. 16, 20, 30)

[17] Market shares, for 1st 7 months 1985. (p. 32)

[18] Import registration shares, for July 1985. (p. 32)

[23] Top cars, through July 1985. (p. 32)

C2700-1.650: Oct. 7, 1985 (No. 5095)

WEEKLY TABLES

[1-2] Auction averages, for Oct. 1985. (p. 49)

[3-6] Production, for week ended Oct. 5, 1985. (p. 63)

[7] Domestic car sales, for 1985 model year; [and by model], for Sept. 21-30, 1985. (p. 1, 60)

MONTHLY TABLES

[12] Auto market, for Sept. 1985. (p. 1, 60)

[20-21] Import sales, and U.S. car sales by marketing unit, for Sept. 1985. (p. 1, 60)

[24] Overseas production in UK, through June 1985; and Brazil, through July 1985. (p. 36)

[25] Overseas registrations in UK and Sweden, through Aug. 1985; West Germany, Austria, and Denmark, through July 1985; Italy and Switzerland, through June 1985; and France, through May 1985. (p. 36)

VW GOLF STILL HOT IN EUROPE, ANNUAL FEATURE

(p. 34) Annual article, with 1 table showing top 10 auto models ranked by sales for 10 European countries, 1st half or 1st 5 months 1985.

CHARTING CAFE SINCE LAW BEGAN

(p. 58) Brief article, with 1 table showing corporate average fuel economy (CAFE) standards for autos, 1978-87 model years.

C2700-1.651: Oct. 14, 1985 (No. 5096)

WEEKLY TABLES

[1-2] Auction averages, for Oct. 1985. (p. 40)

[3-6] Production, for week ended Oct. 12, 1985. (p. 50)

[7] Domestic car sales, omitted.

MONTHLY TABLES

[8-8A] Light-duty and major manufacturer [truck] sales, for Sept. 1985. (p. 32)

[13] New car stocks, for Oct. 1, 1985. (p. 1, 8)

[19] Service index, for Aug. 1985. (p. 1, 8)

C2700-1.652: Oct. 21, 1985 (No. 5097)

WEEKLY TABLES

[1-2] Auction averages, for Oct. 1985. (p. 45)

[3-6] Production, for week ended Oct. 19, 1985. (p. 58)

[7] Domestic car sales, for Oct. 1-10, 1985. (p. 3)

MONTHLY TABLES

[14] Import stocks, for Oct. 1, 1985. (p. 1, 56)

[22] Import sales by model, for Sept. 1985. (p. 28)

IMPORT DEALERSHIPS UP 25 Pct., SEMIANNUAL FEATURE

(p. 1, 54) Semiannual article, by Dan McCosh, reviewing import auto dealership trends. Includes 3 tables showing import franchises by nationality and make, and outlets handling imports only (exclusives and duals) and import-domestic duals, Jan. 1 and July 1, 1985; and import outlets, Jan. 1, 1957-85 and July 1, 1985.

OVERSEAS

Compilation of features on overseas motor vehicle production and sales, and industry financial performance. Features with substantial statistical content are described below.

JAPANESE CHALK UP ANOTHER RECORD YEAR, ANNUAL FEATURE

(p. E7) Annual article, by Michelle Krebs, analyzing financial performance of Japanese motor vehicle industry. Includes 1 table showing sales and net income (in yen and dollars), and unit sales (total and overseas), for 7 manufacturers, various 12-month periods 1984-85, with percent change from previous period.

COMPETING IN SOUTH AFRICA'S TOUGH MARKET

(p. E8) By Jeremy Sinek. Article, with 4 tables showing the following for South Africa: 10 best-selling autos/commercial vehicles, and market share, by make, various periods 1983-85 (table showing data for 1983-84 incorrectly reads 1st half 1984-85); and top 10 auto models and makes ranked by sales, 1st half 1984-85.

VW-AUDI HOLDS LEAD AS SALES SWELL IN EUROPE, RECURRING FEATURE

(p. E10) Recurring article, by Richard Feast, on new auto sales in Western Europe. Includes 2 tables showing market shares and/or percent sales change, by country and manufacturer, and for all Japanese autos sold in Europe, various periods 1984-85.

EUROPEAN AUTO INDUSTRY EYES RECORD SALES

(p. E12) By Richard Feast. Article, with 2 tables showing new auto market shares, by manufacturer and for all Japanese imports, aggregate for 16 European countries, 1978-1st half 1985; and highest and lowest auto sales years, for 14 European countries, 1976-83.

C2700-1.653: Oct. 28, 1985 (No. 5098)

WEEKLY TABLES

[1-2] Auction averages, for Oct. 1985. (p. 31)

[3-6] Production, for week ended Oct. 26, 1985. (p. 43)

[7] Domestic car sales, for Oct. 11-20, 1985. (p. 41)

MONTHLY TABLES

[9-11] Truck and heavy-duty registrations, and new truck registrations, through Aug. 1985. (p. 20, 24)

FOUR JAPANESE MAKES LEAD SALES-PER-DEALER RANKING, SEMIANNUAL FEATURE

(p. 1, 42) Semiannual article, by Jenny L. King, reviewing auto/truck dealer sales volume in 1985. Includes 3 tables showing auto sales per outlet, by make and by model nameplate for 5 size groups; and auto/truck sales per outlet, with selected rankings, various periods 1976-1st half 1985.

EPA MILEAGE RATINGS FOR '86 MODELS, ANNUAL FEATURE

(p. 28-29) Annual tabular listing of EPA fuel economy mileage estimates for all 1986 model year passenger cars, pickup trucks, vans, and specialty vehicles sold in U.S., by model arranged by size group.

C2710
Crain Communications

C2710-1   ADVERTISING AGE

Semiweekly, and special annual issues. Oversized.
ISSN 0001-8899.
LC 42-47059.
SRI/MF/excerpts

Semiweekly trade journal (weekly for 1st week of Jan. and July and 4th week of Nov. and Dec.) of the advertising and marketing industry. Includes data on advertising expenditures, finances of advertising agencies and media companies, magazine advertising pages, consumer awareness of advertisements, and other advertising/marketing-related topics. Most data are from individual company reports, trade assns, and private research or consulting firms.

General format:

a. Numerous news briefs and feature articles, some with statistics, including 2 weekly charts showing stock performance trends for aggregate leading advertisers and media companies; and weekly "Special Report" section focusing on a selected topic, and usually containing some statistics.

b. 1 monthly table and 1 quarterly table on advertising pages; and 2 irregularly recurring tables on newspaper advertising investment and linage, based on data from Media Records Inc.; all listed below.

c. Monthly "adWatch" feature, by Scott Hume, measuring consumer recall of advertising, based on a monthly random survey of approximately 1,250 adults by SRI Research Center, Inc.; usually with text data and 1 chart.

Four special issues, including annual features on leading advertising agencies, media companies, and advertisers, are also published.

Monthly "adWatch" feature and all articles with substantial statistical content are described, as they appear, under "Statistical Features;" page locations and latest periods of coverage for monthly, quarterly, and other recurring tables are also noted. Nonstatistical features are not covered.

Availability: Advertising Age, Circulation Department, 740 Rush St., Chicago IL 60611, $55.00 per yr., Monday single copy $1.25, Thursday single copy $0.75, special issue prices vary; SRI/MF/excerpts for all portions covered under "Statistical Features."

Issues reviewed during 1985: Nov. 1, 1984-Oct. 31, 1985 (P) (Vol. 55, Nos. 74-89; Vol. 56, Nos. 1-85).

RECURRING TABLES:

MONTHLY TABLE

[1] Consumer magazine ad linage, advertising pages for U.S., Canadian, and [other] foreign consumer publications [by publication; for month of cover date or 1-3 months prior, year to date, and same periods of previous year].

IRREGULARLY RECURRING TABLES

[Data are for month 3-5 months prior to cover date, and same month of previous year.]

[1] Flash report: newspaper advertising investment [by 16 product or service categories].

[2] Newspaper advertising MRCS/SAU [Media Records Conversion System/Standard Advertising Unit] inches [shows advertising linage costs for selected newspapers in approximately 60 cities]; prior to Apr. 1, 1985 issue, table was titled "Newspaper ad linage."

QUARTERLY TABLE

[1] Ad pages in [U.S. and Canadian] farm publications [by publication, for quarter ending 1 month prior to cover date, year to date, and same periods of previous year].

STATISTICAL FEATURES:

C2710–1.601: Nov. 1, 1984 (Vol. 55, No. 74)

SURVEY RESULTS POSITIVE

(p. 22-23) By Jack J. Honomichl. Article on developments in the survey research industry, based on membership surveys conducted by the Council of American Survey Research Organizations. Includes 1 table showing prevalence of selected data collection techniques, 1981-83.

PLOTTING STRUCTURAL CHANGES IN INDUSTRY

(p. 34-39) By Eileen Cole. Article on trends and developments in market research industry worldwide. Data are from Research International and *Advertising Age*.

Includes 2 tables showing world's top 10 market research companies ranked by sales, and also including number of countries with company offices, 1982; and expenditures for market research, by world area, 1977, 1979, and 1983.

C2710–1.602: Nov. 5, 1984 (Vol. 55, No. 75)

IRREGULARLY RECURRING TABLE

[1] Flash report: newspaper advertising investment for Aug. 1984. (p. 88)

TAMBRANDS SURVIVES IN MARKET 'JUNGLE'

(p. 4, 74) By Sherry Siegel. Article, with 1 chart showing sales and market shares for leading sanitary napkin and tampon manufacturers, 1983. Data are from Daniel Meade of First Boston Research.

C2710–1.603: Nov. 8, 1984 (Vol. 55, No. 76)

CHAINS DIAGNOSE NEED FOR IMAGE CAMPAIGNS

(p. 12-13) By Esther Fritz Kuntz. Article, with 1 table showing top 10 centrally managed multihospital chains ranked by number of beds, 1983. Data are from *Modern Healthcare*.

MARKETING STAFFS GIVE HOSPITALS A SHOT IN ARM

(p. 14-17) By M. Lynn Folse. Article, with 1 chart showing distribution of former hospital patients by whether patient or physician was responsible for hospital selection, 1984. Data are from a survey conducted by SRI Research Center, Inc.

HMOs KEEP PROFESSION ON ITS TOES

(p. 20-22) By Elizabeth Chappell White. Article, with 2 tables showing top 10 HMO plans and chains ranked by enrollment, 1983 with chain comparison to 1982. Data are from InterStudy.

C2710–1.604: Nov. 12, 1984 (Vol. 55, No. 77)

IRREGULARLY RECURRING TABLE

[2] Newspaper ad linage, Aug. 1984. (p. 57)

AGENCIES CHEER VOTE: 'CONSUMERS WILL SPEND'

(p. 2, 111) Article, with 1 table showing Reagan and Mondale shares of votes cast in 1984 presidential election, with comparison to 7 major pre-election polls. Data are from *Advertising Age*.

NO DOLDRUMS FOR PUBLIC SHOPS, QUARTERLY FEATURE

(p. 114) Quarterly article, by Stewart Alter, on finances of publicly owned advertising agencies. Data are from agency reports. Includes 1 table showing income and revenues for 8-9 agencies, 3rd quarter and 1st 9 months, 1983-84.

C2710–1.605: Nov. 15, 1984 (Vol. 55, No. 78)

BUSINESS COMPUTER MARKETING: DESIGNING THE OFFICE OF THE FUTURE

(p. 11-13) By Ed Fitch. Article, with 2 charts showing market shares for top 7 and all other telephone private branch exchange (PBX) manufacturers, 1987; and number of white collar workers, and personal computer work stations, 1980 and 1990. Data are from Gartner Group and *New York Times*.

SOFTWARE LINKS BIG AND SMALL

(p. 16-18) By Richard Edel. Article, with 1 table showing worldwide sales for U.S. vendors of hardware and software for mainframe/mini and micro computers, biennially 1983-89. Data are from InfoCorp.

TAKING THE NEXT LOGICAL STEP

(p. 21-23) By Kurt Hoffman. Article on artificial intelligence research and marketing. Data are from International Resource Development, Inc. Includes 1 chart showing sales for the "knowledge engineering" market segment, mainly composed of computers equipped with human knowledge and reasoning capability, 1985 and 1993.

CHIPS ARE DOWN FOR SEMICONDUCTOR INDUSTRY

(p. 22-25) By Cathy Curtis. Article, with 1 table showing worldwide sales of semiconductor chips, 1983-87. Data are from Semiconductor Industry Assn.

INDUSTRY GIANTS CROSS LINES

(p. 24-25) By Cara S. Trager. Article, with 1 table and 1 chart showing market shares for top 7 and all other personal computer manufacturers, 1982-84; and revenues for IBM and aggregate top 100 data processing companies, 1980-84. Data are from Future Computing and Gartner Group.

C2710–1.606: Nov. 19, 1984 (Vol. 55, No. 79)

MONTHLY TABLE

[1] Consumer magazine ad linage, advertising pages for U.S., Canadian, and [other] foreign consumer publications, Oct. or Nov. 1984. (p. 79-80)

'NEW YORK TIMES' TOPS DESIGNERS' LIST

(p. 3, 36-39) By Michael Emery. Article, with 3 undated tables showing top 10-20 daily newspapers in use of color and overall design as rated by 170 respondents to a survey of members of the Society of Newspaper Design. Survey was conducted by Media Research Institute for *Advertising Age*.

RADIO STATIONS FOSTER LOYALTY IN DETROIT

(p. 46) By Pat Strnad. Article, with 2 undated charts on black radio listeners, showing percent listening to AM vs. FM and percent listening at specific times of day. Data are from Arbitron.

C2710–1.607: Nov. 26, 1984 (Vol. 55, No. 80)

FORD AD BUY FUELS SUPER BOWL FILLUP

(p. 1, 76) By Verne Gay. Article, with 1 table showing TV advertising costs for a 30-second spot, and audience ratings, for the Super Bowl game, 1975-85. Data are from Lord, Geller, Frederico, Einstein and J. Walter Thompson USA.

MONTHLY adWATCH FEATURE

(p. 3, 54) "Ads Offer Less Bang for Buck." Covers Oct. 1984 survey. Includes 1 chart showing advertisers with the greatest increase or decrease in consumer awareness; and text data on awareness of advertising in 5 product categories.

GENERICS SMOKE OUT COMPETITION, ANNUAL FEATURE

(p. 28) Annual article, by John C. Maxwell, Jr., on cigarette market volume and share, by company and brand. Data were compiled by the author.

Includes 2 tables showing domestic and export market volume and domestic market share, for 6 major companies; and market volume and share, for 10 leading brands arranged by company; 1983-84.

C2710–1.608: Nov. 29, 1984 (Vol. 55, No. 81)

MEDIA BUDGETING NEEDS CREATIVE TOUCH

(p. 3, 46-47) By Herb Zeltner. Article, with 1 table showing advertising cost indexes, by media, 1984-85. Data were compiled by the author.

PRICE INCREASES TO MODERATE IN 1985, ANNUAL FEATURE

(p. 11-13) Annual article, by Robert J. Coen, on advertising media price trends. Data are from McCann-Erickson, Inc., Broadcast Advertisers Reports, Inc., A. C. Nielsen Co., and Commerce Dept.

Includes 4 tables showing indexes of cost per 1,000 exposures and per unit, by media, with comparison to selected other economic indicators, 1981-85; and network TV advertising time available, minutes sold, revenues, costs, and homes and adults reached, 1973 and 1983.

AD-SUPPORTED MEDIA GROW MORE ROBUST

(p. 22-30) By John S. Suhler and David C. Lamb. Article on financial trends of 5 advertising-supported segments of the communications industry. Data are from Veronis, Suhler and Associates.

Includes 11 tables showing revenues, operating income, assets, cash flow, profit margin, and other financial ratios, for consumer and business magazine publishing, cable/pay TV, radio/TV broadcasting, and newspaper segments, with aggregate comparison to segments not relying on advertising, various periods 1979-83.

INTERCONNECTS MAY BE CABLE'S LINK TO AD GROWTH

(p. 36) By Kevin Brown. Article on cable TV "interconnects," cooperative groups of franchises in a major market formed to sell local advertising time.

Includes 1 table showing the following for top 25 cable TV systems, ranked by subscribers as of various months 1983-84: operator; advertising-supported networks carried and whether local advertising is sold on those networks; and "interconnect" membership, with number of systems involved and total subscribers reached.

C2710–1.609: Dec. 3, 1984 (Vol. 55, No. 82)

IRREGULARLY RECURRING TABLE

[2] Newspaper ad linage, Sept. 1984. (p. 66)

ADVERTISING AGE'S GLOBAL MEDIA LINEUP

(p. 50-51) Table showing the following for 16 leading periodicals marketed worldwide: circulation by world area, as of June 1984; advertising costs per page and per 1,000 exposures, 1985; and lists of printing plants used for international editions, and of top 5 worldwide advertisers during 1984.

Data were compiled by *Advertising Age*.

C2710–1.610: Dec. 6, 1984 (Vol. 55, No. 83)

COMMUNITY CHANNELS CAUSE CONTROVERSY

(p. 12) By Don Veraska. Article, with 1 table showing audience shares and weekly minutes viewed per cable TV household, for cable, superstation, pay, and network TV, 1st half 1983-84. Data are from A. C. Nielsen Co.

LOCAL ADS HIT THE SPOT FOR OPERATORS

(p. 13) By Sharon Donovan. Article, with 1 chart showing advertising sales for 4 cable TV networks, 1983-84. Data are from Broadcast Advertisers Reports, Inc.

C2710–1.611: Dec. 10, 1984 (Vol. 55, No. 84)

IRREGULARLY RECURRING TABLE

[1] Flash report: newspaper advertising investment for Sept. 1984. (p. 68)

BUCKS BALLOON IN BIG BURGER BATTLE, RECURRING FEATURE

(p. 2, 82) Recurring article, by Scott Hume, with 1 table showing network and local TV advertising expenditures, for top 15 fast food chains ranked by network/local expenditures, and for total fast food industry, 1st 9 months 1984 with comparison to 1st 9 months 1983. Data are from TV Bureau of Advertising and Broadcast Advertisers Reports.

C2710–1.612: Dec. 17, 1984 (Vol. 55, No. 86)

NET TV AD SLOWDOWN SEEN, ANNUAL FEATURE

(p. 4) Annual article, by Stewart Alter, on advertising sales trends and outlook by media. Data are from Robert Coen of McCann-Erickson, Inc. Includes 1 table showing national, local, and cable TV advertising revenue forecast for 1985, with detail for national print and broadcast.

QUICK, EASY MEALS SEE SALES COOKING, ANNUAL FEATURE

(p. 46) Annual article, by John C. Maxwell, Jr., on consumer fast-food purchasing habits. Data are from Commerce Dept. Includes 2 tables showing top 10 fast-food chains ranked by sales, with comparison to total fast-food sales, 1979-83; and sales by type of fast food, 1981-84, with number of companies for each type.

For description of last previous article, see SRI 1984 Annual, under C2710-1.503.

C2710–1.613: Dec. 20, 1984 (Vol. 55, No. 87)

OUTDOOR BOARDS GET DOWN TO BUSINESS

(p. 16-21) By Kurt Hoffman. Article, with 1 table showing sales of outdoor advertising, by advertiser retail category, 2nd quarter 1983-84. Data are from Institute of Outdoor Advertising.

SANTA WILL BE CARRYING A BIG BAG OF TOYS

(p. 30) By Peter Francese. Article, with 1 chart showing toy shipments, 1977-83. Data are from *American Demographics*.

C2710–1.614: Dec. 24, 1984 (Vol. 55, No. 88)

MONTHLY TABLE

[1] Consumer magazine ad linage, advertising pages for U.S., Canadian, and [other] foreign consumer publications, Nov. or Dec. 1984. (p. 35-36)

Corrected data appear in the Jan. 21, 1985 issue (see C2710-1.620 below).

MONTHLY adWATCH FEATURE

(p. 2, 37) "Coke Scores Extra Point in Cola Ad Wars." Covers Nov. 1984 survey. Includes 1 chart showing advertisers with the greatest increase or decrease in consumer awareness; and text data on awareness of advertising in soft drink and 3 other product categories.

C2710–1.615: Dec. 31, 1984 (Vol. 55, No. 89)

HOT NEW ITEMS LIGHT FIRE IN FOOD, HAIRCARE

(p. 2, 26) By Alan B. Miller, Jr. Article, with 1 table showing food store sales increase for 5 product types with greatest growth in 3 food and 2 nonfood categories, year ended Nov. 9, 1984. Data are from Selling Areas Marketing Inc.

C2710–1.616: Jan. 7, 1985 (Vol. 56, No. 1)

IRREGULARLY RECURRING TABLES

[1] Flash report: newspaper advertising investment for Oct. 1984. (p. 30)

[2] Newspaper ad linage, Oct. 1984. (p. 44)

C2710–1.617: Jan. 10, 1985 (Vol. 56, No. 2)

LIVING AND SUCCEEDING BY THE RULES OF THE GAME

(p. 14-15) By John Campbell Collins. Article on the marketing of syndicated TV programs. Data sources include A. C. Nielsen Co. and *The Complete Directory to Prime Time Network TV Shows*.

Includes 1 chart and 1 table showing adult audience shares for aggregate independent and network affiliate stations, 1972 and 1984; and rating and network, for top-rated program of the TV season, 1950/51-1983/84.

C2710–1.618: Jan. 14, 1985 (Vol. 56, No. 3)

QUARTERLY TABLE

[1] Ad pages in [U.S. and Canadian] farm publications, 4th quarter 1984. (p. 64)

NEW YEAR LEAVES TOP EXECS BASKING IN HAPPY PAY DAZE

(p. 1) By Stewart Alter. Article, with 2 tables showing average salary, salary range, and bonus percentage or value, for 5-6 top executive positions with corporate advertisers and advertising agencies, 1984 with selected comparison to 1983. Data are from Judd-Falk Inc.

AD SPENDING HIKE PREDICTED FOR '85

(p. 40-42) Article, with 1 chart showing percent change in advertising expenditures, for 7 foreign countries, 1983-85. Data are from *Advertising Age*.

C2710–1.619: Jan. 17, 1985 (Vol. 56, No. 4)

RESEARCH, MARKETING SHORTCHANGED

(p. 16-19) By Sherry Siegel. Article on advertising in magazines marketed for a specific city or region. Data are from *Advertising Age*. Includes 1 table showing top 25 city/regional magazines ranked by advertising linage, 1984 with comparison to 1983.

Corrected data appear in the Jan. 28, 1985 issue (see C2710-1.622 below).

C2710–1.620: Jan. 21, 1985 (Vol. 56, No. 5)

MONTHLY TABLE

[1] Consumer magazine ad linage, advertising pages for U.S., Canadian, and [other] foreign consumer publications, Dec. 1984 or Jan. 1985. (p. 75-76)

CORRECTIONS AND CLARIFICATIONS

(p. 6) Includes corrected data for monthly table on consumer magazine ad linage.

For original table, see C2710-1.614 above.

C2710–1.621: Jan. 24, 1985 (Vol. 56, No. 6)

LOOKING AT SOME SUNDAY STATISTICS

(p. 24) By Kevin Brown. Article, with 1 table showing top 25 Sunday edition newspapers ranked by circulation, for 6-month period ended Sept. 30, 1984. Data are from Audit Bureau of Circulations.

SUNDAY MAGAZINES FEEL AD PINCH

(p. 28-30) By William F. Gloede. Article, with 2 charts and 1 table showing the following for 3 major Sunday newspaper magazine inserts: circulation, 1980-83; and aggregate advertising pages and revenues, by product category (no date). Data are from Publishers Information Bureau.

Corrected data appear in the Jan. 28, 1985 issue (see C2710-1.622 below).

C2710–1.622: Jan. 28, 1985 (Vol. 56, No. 7)

APPLE FAILS TO REGISTER: VIEWERS FLUNK QUIZ ON 'LEMMINGS'

(p. 1, 98) By Joseph M. Winski. Article on TV viewer awareness of advertising during 1985 Super Bowl game. Data are from telephone interviews with 300 viewers age 18/over, conducted Jan. 22-23, 1985, by SRI Research Center, Inc. Includes 2 tables showing advertisements recalled, and number of respondents recalling no specific advertisements.

CORRECTIONS AND CLARIFICATIONS

(p. 6) Includes data correction for table on city/regional magazine circulation (see C2710-1.619 above).

AGENCIES SEEK TIE WITH U.S. SHOPS

(p. 62-63) By Valerie Mackie. Article, with 2 tables showing India's top 10 advertising agencies ranked by billings, and also including major clients and foreign agency affiliates, 1984 with percent change from 1983; and top 11 advertisers in India ranked by advertising budget, 1984. Data are from *Advertising Age*.

CIRCULATION: SUNDAY MAGAZINES IN THE 1980s

(p. 97) Corrected table for feature on Sunday newspaper magazines inserts (see C2710-1.621 above).

C2710–1.623: Feb. 4, 1985 (Vol. 56, No. 9)

IRREGULARLY RECURRING TABLE

[2] Newspaper ad linage, Nov. 1984. (p. 52)

Corrected data appear in the Feb. 18, 1985 issue (see C2710-1.627 below).

COLGATE'S DRILLING HITS ANOTHER NERVE AT P&G

(p. 1, 70) By Nancy Giges. Article, with 1 chart showing toothpaste market shares, for top 5 brands and all others, June and Dec. 1984. Data are from *Advertising Age*.

MONTHLY adWATCH FEATURE

(p. 4, 28) "Consumers' Advertising Recall Was All Wet over the Holidays." Covers Dec. 1984 survey. Includes 1 chart showing advertisers with the greatest increase or decrease in consumer awareness; and text data on awareness of advertising in 6 product categories, and top 10 advertisements recalled.

LIQUOR SALES STILL DOWN, ANNUAL FEATURE

(p. 48) Annual article, by John C. Maxwell, Jr., on liquor sales trends. Data were compiled by the author. Includes 1 table ranking 38 leading brands by case sales, 1983-84. Table also shows company for each brand.

C2710–1.624: Feb. 7, 1985 (Vol. 56, No. 10)

PERSONAL COMPUTER MARKETING: RETAILERS KEY IN ON NICHES

(p. 13-15) By Betsy Gilbert. Article on personal computer marketing outlook. Data are from Future Computing, and a *Fortune* survey of 2,800 subscribers.

Includes 2 charts and 3 tables showing top 10 computer retail chains ranked by number of stores, 1984; survey responses concerning outlet chosen for business purchases of personal computers (no date); and number of computer specialty retail stores, and software and hardware sales by type of outlet, 1984 and 1989.

Data correction appears in the Mar. 4, 1985 issue (see C2710-1.630 below).

C2710–1.625: Feb. 11, 1985 (Vol. 56, No. 11)

AD PRESSURE MOUNTS FOR EUROPEAN TV

(p. 3, 64) By Laurel Wentz. Article, with 1 undated table showing number of national TV channels (total and with advertising), and average minutes of advertising per day, for U.S. and 16 European countries.

BEER ADS: HOORAY FOR THE RED, WHITE & BREW

(p. 84) By Scott Hume. Article, with 1 table showing beer shipments for 5 major brewers, 1982-84. Data are from company reports.

Corrected data appear in the Feb. 18, 1985 issue (see C2710-1.627 below).

C2710–1.626: Feb. 14, 1985 (Vol. 56, No. 12)

BABY FOOD BECOMES MORE THAN A MATTER OF TASTE

(p. 17-18) By Cara S. Trager. Article, with 1 undated chart showing baby food market shares for 3 major companies. Data are from Selling Areas Marketing Inc.

PARENTS DON'T JUST WANT TO HAVE FUN TOYS

(p. 24-25) By Cara S. Trager. Article, with 1 table showing infant toy market shares for top 5 and all other manufacturers, 1983. Data are from NPD Group and Fisher-Price.

DIAPER SERVICES UNWRAPPING MARKET POTENTIAL

(p. 26-27) By Laurie Freeman. Article, with 1 undated chart showing household use and annual sales of disposable and cloth diapers. Data are from National Institute of Infant Services.

DISPOSABLES TRY TO STOP LEAKAGE

(p. 26-27) Article, with 1 undated chart showing disposable diaper market shares, for top 3 and all other manufacturers. Data are from First Boston Corp.

FOR-PROFIT CENTERS OPEN DOORS TO DAYCARE

(p. 30, 32-33) By Margaret LeRoux. Article, with 1 undated chart showing distribution of working parents by type of child day care arrangement (own or another home, group center, at-work center, and other). Data are from Census Bureau.

MEDIA FOR BRINGING UP BABY

(p. 34) Table showing the following for 10 parent-oriented magazines: percent of readers who are pregnant or have children under age 2; and paid or controlled circulation; (no dates). Data are from magazine reports.

Corrected data appear in the Feb. 25, 1985 issue (see C2710-1.628 below).

C2710–1.627: Feb. 18, 1985 (Vol. 56, No. 13)

MONTHLY TABLE

[1] Consumer magazine ad linage, advertising pages for U.S., Canadian, and [other] foreign consumer publications, Jan. or Feb. 1985. (p. 75-76)

Corrected data appear in the Feb. 25, 1985 issue (see C2710-1.628 below).

MONEY-LOSING ACCOUNTS DOG AD AGENCIES

(p. 3, 74) By Stewart Alter. Article on profitability of accounts at small/medium-sized advertising agencies. Data are from studies conducted by BCS/Profit Index Systems, Inc., among 51-102 of its client agencies.

Includes 1 table showing the following for profitable and unprofitable accounts: gross income, operating profit or loss, number of accounts, time spent on accounts, and cost per hour, 1976/77, 1981/82, and 1983/84.

CORRECTIONS AND CLARIFICATIONS

(p. 6) Includes data corrections for recurring table on newspaper advertising linage, and for article on shipments of major brewers (see C2710-1.623 and C2710-1.625 above, respectively).

C2710–1.628: Feb. 25, 1985 (Vol. 56, No. 15)

IRREGULARLY RECURRING TABLE

[1] Flash report: newspaper advertising investment for Nov. and Dec. 1984; [includes 2 tables]. (p. 76)

MONTHLY adWATCH FEATURE

(p. 4, 68) "Cola, Wine Makers Race to Bottleneck." Covers Jan. 1985 survey. Includes 1 chart showing advertisers with the greatest increase or decrease in consumer awareness; and text data on top 10 advertisements recalled, and awareness of advertising in 6 product categories.

CORRECTIONS AND CLARIFICATIONS

(p. 6) Includes data corrections for table on parent-oriented magazines, and for monthly table on consumer magazine advertising linage (see C2710-1.626 and C2710-1.627 above, respectively).

C2710–1.629: Feb. 28, 1985 (Vol. 56, No. 16)

BATTLE FOR SHELF SPACE

(p. 16) By Laurie Freeman. Article, with 1 chart showing number of new products introduced into food/drugstores, 1980-84. Data are from Dancer Fitzgerald Sample's *New Product News*.

C2710–1.630: Mar. 4, 1985 (Vol. 56, No. 17)

IRREGULARLY RECURRING TABLE

[2] Newspaper ad linage, Dec. 1984. (p. 82)

CORRECTIONS AND CLARIFICATIONS

(p. 6) Includes data correction for article on personal computer marketing, appearing in Feb. 7, 1985 issue.

For article description, see C2710-1.624 above.

MAGAZINES REACT TO SINGLE-COPY SALES SLUMP, SEMIANNUAL FEATURE

(p. 66) Semiannual article, by Stuart J. Elliott, with 1 table showing top 10 magazines ranked by circulation, 2nd half 1983-84. Data are from Audit Bureau of Circulations.

C2710–1.631: Mar. 7, 1985 (Vol. 56, No. 18)

DIRECT MARKETING: TAKING THE BEST OF BOTH SCENES

(p. 13, 16) By Len Strazewski. Article, with 3 undated tables presenting summary data on consumers' reactions to telemarketing and direct mail programs. Data are from a Simmons Market Research Bureau survey.

COMPANIES FIND MARKETING ANSWER IN TELEPHONE

(p. 14-15) By Richard Edel. Article, with 1 chart showing number of toll-free (800) telephone numbers in use, 1984; and number of calls made to 800 numbers, selected years 1967-84. Data are from AT&T.

AT&T DIALS ITS OWN SERVICE

(p. 14) Article, with 1 chart showing long distance telephone service sales and market shares for AT&T, MCI Telecommunications, and all others, 1984. Data are from MCI Telecommunications.

C2710–1.632: Mar. 11, 1985 (Vol. 56, No. 19)

BIG MAC SERVES UP BIG TV AD BILL FOR '84, RECURRING FEATURE

(p. 6) Recurring article, by Scott Hume, with 1 table showing network and local TV advertising expenditures, for top 15 fast food chains ranked by network/local expenditures, and for total fast food industry, 1984 with comparison to 1983. Data are from TV Bureau of Advertising and Broadcast Advertisers Reports.

ROLE OF PR IN PROXY FIGHTS, TENDER OFFERS

(p. 36-39) By Jack Bernstein. Article, with 1 table showing top 20 public relations firms ranked by net fee income, 1984 with percent change from 1983. Data are from *O'Dwyer's Directory of Public Relations Firms*.

BEER AD BAN WON'T HURT NETS

(p. 74) By Verne Gay. Article, with 2 tables showing the following for 26 companies that purchase substantial advertising time during network TV sports programs: rankings by company's share of TV networks' total sports advertising revenues, and by sports advertising's share of company's total TV advertising expenditures, 1983. Data are from L. F. Rothschild, Unterberg, Towbin.

DDB A WINNER IN UP-&-DOWN 4th QUARTER, QUARTERLY FEATURE

(p. 90) Quarterly article, by Stewart Alter, on finances of publicly owned advertising agencies. Data are from agency reports. Includes 1 table showing income and revenues for 9 agencies, 4th quarter and full year, 1983-84.

Corrected data appear in the Mar. 18, 1985 issue (see C2710-1.633 below).

C2710–1.633: Mar. 18, 1985 (Vol. 56, No. 21)

MONTHLY TABLE

[1] Consumer magazine ad linage, advertising pages for U.S., Canadian, and [other] foreign consumer publications, Feb. or Mar. 1985. (p. 91-92)

Corrected data appear in the Apr. 1, 1985 issue (see C2710-1.637 below).

CORRECTIONS AND CLARIFICATIONS

(p. 6) Includes data correction for quarterly article on advertising agency finances appearing in the Mar. 11, 1985 issue; for description, see C2710-1.632 above.

DIRECT-MARKETING AGENCIES REGISTER STRONG '84 GAINS

(p. 76) Article, with 2 tables showing top 42 direct marketing companies, and top 14 direct marketing/related business companies, ranked by billings, 1984 with comparison to 1983. Data are from Direct Marketing Assn.

For description of a related article presenting revised rankings, see C2710-1.638 below.

TV SPOT TESTING FLAT FOR '84

(p. 88) Article, with 2 charts showing distribution of market research expenditures, for consumer magazines by type of study, and for metro newspapers by whether study handled in-house or through outside agency, 1982-84, with summary indexes based on 1982 expenditures. Data were compiled by Advertising Research Foundation.

C2710–1.634: Mar. 21, 1985 (Vol. 56, No. 22)

TOURING THE TOP 10 U.S. HISPANIC MARKETS

(p. 14-43) Compilation of articles on 10 metro areas with highest Hispanic population. Includes 10 undated tables showing the following for each metro area: Spanish-language newspapers and publishing frequency; and Spanish-language radio and TV stations, with hours broadcast in Spanish per day or week.

C2710–1.635: Mar. 25, 1985 (Vol. 56, No. 23)

MONTHLY adWATCH FEATURE

(p. 6, 113) "P&G Ad Awareness Scores Fit To Be Tide." Covers Feb. 1985 survey. Includes 1 chart showing advertisers with the greatest increase or decrease in consumer awareness; and text data on top 10 advertisements recalled, and awareness of advertising in laundry-product and 6 other product categories.

C2710–1.636: Mar. 28, 1985 (Vol. 56, No. 24)

[Issue price is $3.00.]

U.S. ADVERTISING AGENCY PROFILES, 1985 EDITION (ANNUAL ISSUE)

(p. 1-112) Annual special issue on income, accounts, and employees of 619 advertising agencies, 1984. Includes narrative profiles of each agency, grouped by region and/or income, each showing most or all of the following data: U.S. and worldwide gross income and billings, with detail for U.S. billings by type and media; accounts lost and gained; number of employees and offices; and subsidiaries, 1984, with comparisons to 1983.

Also includes profiles of 4 major holding companies (p. 112) whose subsidiaries are principally advertising agencies.

Issue also contains results of the 1st recurring survey of corporate advertising directors' opinions on top agencies and agency attributes, conducted in 1984, with 2 charts and 4 tables (p. 6); and an additional 2 charts and 26 tables, listed below.

Most data are from individual agency reports. This is the 41st annual feature. Data corrections and addenda appear in the Apr. 8, Apr. 15, Apr. 22, and May 13, 1985 issues (see C2710-1.638, C2710-1.640, C2710-1.642, and C2710-1.647 below).

CHARTS AND TABLES:

[Unless otherwise noted, tables show data by agency, in rank order. Tables [9-15] and [17-26] show data for agencies with gross income of $5 million/over. Data on media billings are based on a subgroup of 144 reporting agencies.]

[1-4] Top 10 agencies in world income, U.S. income, world billings, and non-U.S. billings [1983-84]. (p. 1)

[5-6] Agencies [with over] $15 million and $5-15 million in gross income [shows world and U.S. gross income and billings, U.S. capitalized fees, and total employees, 1983-84]. (p. 14-20)

[7-8] Agencies [with] $1-5 million and less than $1 million in gross income, [1983-84]. (p. 20-24)

[9-15] Top 10 agencies by percent change in world and U.S. income and billings; U.S. capitalized fees as a percent of U.S. billings; productivity [world billings per employee]; and foreign billings as a percent of world billings; [all for 1984, generally with comparison to 1983]. (p. 30-50 passim)

[16] PR's [public relations] influence on top 10 [shows top 10 agencies in world gross income ranked by income exclusive of public relations fees, 1984]. (p. 51)

[17-24] Top 10 agencies by newspaper, magazine, spot and network TV, radio, cable, outdoor, and direct mail billings, [1984; table [24] incorrectly reads direct marketing billings]. (p. 64-80, passim)

[25] Advertising concentration by city [shows aggregate agency billings for 10 leading cities (no date)]. [chart] (p. 106)

[26] 1984 media breakdown of U.S. billings [not by agency]. [chart] (p. 108)

[27] 1984 composite statistics in 41st agency report [number of agencies, and aggregate capitalized fees, U.S. billings, and employment, for 4 gross income groups]. (p. 112)

[28] Agency groups lead top agencies [worldwide and U.S. gross income for 3 top holding companies compared to top advertising agencies, 1984 with percent change from 1983]. (p. 112)

C2710–1.637: Apr. 1, 1985 (Vol. 56, No. 25)

IRREGULARLY RECURRING TABLE

[2] Newspaper advertising MRCS/SAU inches, Jan. 1985. (p. 70)

Corrected data appear in the Apr. 22, 1985 issue (see C2710-1.642 below).

CORRECTIONS AND CLARIFICATIONS

(p. 6) Includes corrected data for monthly table [1] on consumer magazine advertising linage.

For original table, see C2710-1.633 above.

DPZ: A BRIDESMAID, BUT NEVER A BRIDE

(p. 54, 56) By Roberto Duailibi. Article, with 1 table showing top 5 advertisers in Brazil ranked by expenditures, 1984. Data are from A. C. Nielsen Co.

C2710–1.638: Apr. 8, 1985 (Vol. 56, No. 27)

CORRECTIONS AND CLARIFICATIONS

(p. 6) Includes data corrections for Mar. 28, 1985 annual special issue profiling U.S. advertising agencies.

For issue description, see C2710-1.636 above.

SOME SHOPS QUARREL WITH DMA BILLINGS REPORT

(p. 70) By Paul L. Edwards. Article, with 1 table showing revised ranking of top 10 direct marketing agencies by billings, 1984 with comparison to 1983. Data are from Direct Marketing Assn.

For description of previous rankings, see C2710-1.633 above.

C2710–1.639: Apr. 11, 1985 (Vol. 56, No. 28)

MARKETING IN CANADA

(p. 16) Three tables showing top 10 advertisers in Canada ranked by expenditures, 1983; top 10 Canadian advertising agencies ranked by billings, 1984; and top 10 U.S. magazines ranked by circulation in Canada (no date). Data are from *Advertising Age*, Audit Bureau of Circulations, and publishers' reports.

C2710–1.640: Apr. 15, 1985 (Vol. 56, No. 29)

QUARTERLY TABLE

[1] Ad pages in [U.S. and Canadian] farm publications, 1st quarter 1985. (p. 78)

COORS PORES OVER PLANS TO EXPAND

(p. 4, 58) By Scott Hume. Article, with 1 chart showing shares of market shipments for 3 major brewers, 1978-84. Data are from R. S. Weinberg and Associates.

CORRECTIONS AND CLARIFICATIONS

(p. 6) Includes data correction for Mar. 28, 1985 annual special issue profiling U.S. advertising agencies.

For issue description, see C2710-1.636 above.

AGENCY PROFILE REPORT ADDENDUM

(p. 87) Table showing gross income and billings for 16 advertising agencies omitted from the annual special issue profiling U.S. agencies.

For issue description, see C2710-1.636 above.

C2710–1.641: Apr. 18, 1985 (Vol. 56, No. 30)

GROCERY MARKETING: SUPERMARKETS EVOLVING TO AVOID EXTINCTION

(p. 15-17) By Mary McCabe English. Article, with 1 chart showing prevalence of households using coupons, and distribution of coupon redemptions by retail outlet type, 1984. Data are from Simmons Market Research Bureau.

ALTERNATIVES GAIN ON PRICE AND PRINT ADS

(p. 18) By Russell Shaw. Article, with 1 chart showing distribution of grocery industry advertising expenditures by media, 1982-83. Data are from Food Marketing Institute.

CONVENIENCE OUTLETS EXPANDING CUSTOMER BASE

(p. 36-39) By Faye Brookman. Article, with 2 charts showing convenience stores' share of grocery sales, 1974-84; and convenience store industry sales, 1979-83. Data are from *C-Store Business* and National Assn of Convenience Stores.

SPECIALIZING IN GOURMET TASTES

(p. 43-45) By Joanne Y. Cleaver. Article, with 2 charts showing percent of specialty food stores stocking or planning to add selected types of products (no date); and number of food stores, and specialty stores by type of food sold, 1982. Data are from a 1984 Gourmet Retail Market Report, and Census Bureau.

C2710–1.642: Apr. 22, 1985 (Vol. 56, No. 31)

IRREGULARLY RECURRING TABLE

[1] Flash report: newspaper advertising investment for Jan. 1985. (p. 40)

MONTHLY TABLE

[1] Consumer magazine ad linage, advertising pages for U.S., Canadian, and [other] foreign consumer publications, Mar. or Apr. 1985. (p. 125-126)

'NEW' ATARI TRIES TO BRING BACK OLD GROWTH

(p. 4, 112) By Cleveland Horton. Article, with 1 chart showing market shares for 6 major home computer manufacturers and all others, 1983-84. Data are from Future Computing, Inc.

CORRECTIONS AND CLARIFICATIONS

(p. 6) Includes data corrections for Mar. 28, 1985 annual special issue profiling U.S. advertising agencies; and for irregularly recurring table on newspaper advertising linage.

For description of annual special issue, see C2710-1.636 above; for recurring table, see C2710-1.637 above.

FOREIGN AGENCY INCOME REPORT, ANNUAL FEATURE

(p. 58-82) Annual report, by Dennis Chase, on income, billings, and employees of 892 advertising agencies in 72 foreign countries. Data are from a 1984 *Advertising Age* survey.

Includes 4 tables showing world's top 50 agencies and top 15 agency groups ranked by gross income, with billings; and individual agencies ranked within each country by gross income, with billings, employment, and number of offices; 1984, with selected comparisons to 1983. Monetary values are shown in U.S. and domestic currencies for agency rankings within countries.

Corrected data for Australia appear in the Apr. 29, 1985 issue (see C2710-1.643 below); and additional data corrections appear in the May 20 and July 15, 1985 issues (see C2710-1.649 and C2710-1.662 below).

SURVEY BAD RAPS MEDIA

(p. 118) Article, with 1 undated chart showing public ratings of honesty/ethical standards of 10 occupations. Data are based on over 1,000 responses to a survey conducted by Minnesota Opinion Research for American Society of Newspaper Editors.

Article incorrectly identifies the survey source as Media Opinion Research (see C2710-1.645 below for correction).

IT PAYS TO RUN BBDO, OGILVY

(p. 132) By Stewart Alter. Article, with 1 table showing cash compensation of 25 highest-paid executives at publicly owned advertising agencies, 1984. Data were compiled by *Advertising Age* from agency proxy statements.

C2710–1.643: Apr. 29, 1985 (Vol. 56, No. 33)

MONTHLY adWATCH FEATURE

(p. 4, 99) "Lionel Roars for Pepsi." Covers Mar. 1985 survey. Includes 1 chart showing advertisers with the greatest increase or decrease in consumer awareness; and text data on top 10 advertisements recalled, and awareness of advertising in soft drink and 4 other product categories.

CORRECTION

(p. 94) Includes corrected data for annual feature on foreign agency income (see C2710-1.642 above).

C2710–1.644: May 2, 1985 (Vol. 56, No. 34)

PRIZES BECOME MORE SOPHISTICATED

(p. 46) Article, with 2 charts showing corporate expenditures on travel and merchandise incentives for salespeople/dealers, and on total incentives/consumer premiums, various years 1982-84. Data are from *Incentive Marketing* and *Premium/Incentive Business*.

C2710–1.645: May 6, 1985 (Vol. 56, No. 35)

IRREGULARLY RECURRING TABLE

[2] Newspaper advertising MRCS/SAU inches, Feb. 1985. (p. 76)

FAS-FAX HAS GOOD READING FOR BIG DAILIES

(p. 3, 94) By William F. Gloede and Gary Levin. Article, with 1 table showing circulation for daily and Sunday editions of 16 major newspapers, for 6-month period ended Mar. 31, 1985 with percent change from previous year. Data are from Audit Bureau of Circulations.

CORRECTIONS AND CLARIFICATIONS

(p. 6) Text corrections for article presenting data on public ratings of occupational honesty/ethical standards appearing in Apr. 22, 1985 issue.

For article description, see C2710-1.642 above.

FINAL FIGURES: 1984 AD SPENDING UP 16%, ANNUAL FEATURE

(p. 47) Annual article, by Robert J. Coen, with 2 tables showing actual value and monthly index of advertising expenditures by media, 1983 and/or 1984. Data are from McCann-Erickson, Inc.

C2710–1.646: May 9, 1985 (Vol. 56, No. 36)

AUTO MAKERS USE SOFT SELL TO MOVE SOFT RIDE

(p. 20-24) By Ralph Gray. Article, with 1 table showing top 7 metro areas ranked by German luxury auto shares of new car registrations, 1983. Data are from Claritas Corp. and R. L. Polk and Co.

TOASTING WEALTH WITH SPARKLING WINES

(p. 30-32) By Len Strazewski. Article, with 1 chart showing top 5 States ranked by champagne sales volume, 1983. Data are from *Wine Marketing Handbook* (covered in SRI under C4775-2).

RESEARCHERS, BUSINESSES STRIKE GOLD WITH DATA

(p. 50) By Peter Francese. Article, with 1 chart showing research company sales of consumer market data, quinquennially 1975-90. Data are from *American Demographics*.

C2710–1.647: May 13, 1985 (Vol. 56, No. 37)

CORRECTIONS AND CLARIFICATIONS

(p. 6) Includes data correction for Mar. 28, 1985 annual special issue profiling U.S. advertising agencies.

For issue description, see C2710-1.636 above.

1st QUARTER NOT BAD OMEN, QUARTERLY FEATURE

(p. 12) Quarterly article, by Stewart Alter, on finances of publicly owned advertising agencies. Data are from agency reports. Includes 1 table showing income and revenues for 9 agencies, 1st quarter 1984-85.

SILICON VALLEY SHOPS SEEK INJECTION OF HOPE

(p. 44) By Cleveland Horton and Jennifer Pendleton. Article, with 1 table showing top 12 California advertising agencies serving the high-technology industry, ranked by billings, with percent of billings that are computer-related, 1985 with comparison to 1984. Data are from *Advertising Age*.

PRIVATE-LABEL, GENERIC FOOD SALES DROP

(p. 96) Article, with 2 tables showing private label and generic product shares of food store sales, by product category, for year ended Mar. 29, 1985 with comparison to previous year. Data are from Selling Areas Marketing Inc.

C2710–1.648: May 16, 1985 (Vol. 56, No. 38)

MUFFLER SHOPS SEARCH FOR GOLDEN TOUCH

(p. 15) By Len Strazewski. Article, with 1 undated chart showing distribution of auto muffler/exhaust system replacement market, by retail outlet type. Data are from *Muffler Digest*.

MASS-OUTLET RETAILERS GEAR UP AUTOMOTIVE SECTIONS

(p. 22-24) By Faye Brookman. Article, with 1 table showing number and percent of retail outlets selling auto parts/supplies, by outlet type, 1980 and 1983. Data are from Automotive Parts and Accessories Assn.

DO-IT-YOURSELFERS BUILD PARTS MARKET

(p. 30-32) By Cathy Curtis. Article, with 1 chart showing sales for auto parts/supply stores, 1980-86. Data are from Dun and Bradstreet.

SECURITY MARKETERS STRIVE FOR LOCK ON AWARENESS

(p. 36) By Frank Vizard. Article, with 1 undated chart showing wholesale value of auto security devices sold through retail outlets, by outlet type. Data are from *Installation News*.

C2710–1.649: May 20, 1985 (Vol. 56, No. 39)

MONTHLY TABLE

[1] Consumer magazine ad linage, advertising pages for U.S., Canadian, and [other] foreign consumer publications, Apr. or May 1985. (p. 93-94)

Additional data appear in the May 27, 1985 issue (see C2710-1.651 below).

SEVEN-UP STANDS UP TO COLA'S CHALLENGE

(p. 4, 92) By Scott Hume. Article, with 2 undated charts showing soft drink market shares by company and flavor. Data are from John Maxwell and *Beverage Industry*.

CORRECTIONS AND CLARIFICATIONS

(p. 6) Includes data corrections for annual feature on foreign agency income; further data corrections appear in July 15, 1985 issue (see C2710-1.662 below).

For description of original annual feature, see C2710-1.642 above.

C2710–1.650: May 23, 1985 (Vol. 56, No. 40)

TAMPA IS TOPS: AA POLL RANKS FLORIDA AIRPORT BEST IN U.S., WHILE CHICAGO'S O'HARE LEADS LIST OF LOSERS

(p. 2) By Robert Goldsborough. Article, with 1 table showing 10 most and 5 least favorite airports as rated by approximately 200 *Advertising Age* readers responding to a Mar. 21, 1985 survey.

RESEARCH BUSINESS REVIEW: THE NATION'S TOP 40 MARKETING/ADVERTISING RESEARCH COMPANIES, ANNUAL FEATURE

(p. 15-38) Annual report, by Jack J. Honomichl, on marketing/advertising research industry. Data are from *Advertising Age*.

Includes 1 chart and 2 tables showing research industry nominal and real revenue growth trends, 1975-84; and top 40 research companies ranked by total research revenue (and also including foreign revenues), and worldwide and U.S. revenues for aggregate top 40 research companies and top 40 advertising agencies, 1984, with comparisons to 1983.

Also includes brief profile of each ranked company, including business description and employment data.

C2710–1.651: May 27, 1985 (Vol. 56, No. 41)

IRREGULARLY RECURRING TABLE

[1] Flash report: newspaper advertising investment for Feb. 1985. (p. 60)

MONTHLY adWATCH FEATURE

(p. 3, 87) "Survey: Coors Is the One, 'Beer Talk' Scores." Covers Apr. 1985 survey. Includes 1 chart showing advertisers with the greatest increase or decrease in consumer awareness; and text data on top 10 advertisements recalled, and awareness of advertising in beer and 2 other product categories.

CORRECTIONS AND CLARIFICATIONS

(p. 6) Includes additional data for monthly table [1] on consumer magazine ad linage.

For original table, see C2710-1.649 above.

SMOKELESS TOBACCO SALES UP DURING '84, ANNUAL FEATURE

(p. 64) Annual article, by John C. Maxwell, with 2 tables showing smokeless tobacco sales

volume by product type, by company and brand, 1982-84. Data were compiled by the author.

C2710–1.652: May 30, 1985 (Vol. 56, No. 42)

CABLE TV: SERVING VARIED HOME ENTERTAINMENT MENU

(p. 13-15) By Mark Trost. Article, with 1 chart showing total persons and cable TV subscribers owning stereo components, videocassette recorders, and personal computers, 1984. Data are from Simmons Market Research Bureau.

VIDEOCASSETTE RECORDERS IN OPERATORS' ARSENALS

(p. 24-25) By Sharon Donovan. Article, with 1 table showing top 10 cable TV multiple system operators ranked by basic subscribers, various months 1983-84. Data are from Cabletelevision Advertising Bureau.

CHANNELS ANSWER INTERACTIVE CALL

(p. 26) By Sallie Rose Hollis. Article, with 1 table showing top 10 cable TV advertisers ranked by expenditures, 1st 9 months 1984. Data are from Cabletelevision Advertising Bureau, based on 4 cable networks covered by Broadcast Advertiser Reports.

INDUSTRY'S DEREGULATED FORECAST IS ROSY

(p. 27) By Don Veraska. Article, with 1 chart showing advertising revenues for spot/network cable TV, 1981-86, 1990, and 1993. Data are from Cabletelevision Advertising Bureau.

C2710–1.653: June 3, 1985 (Vol. 56, No. 43)

IRREGULARLY RECURRING TABLE

[2] Newspaper advertising MRCS/SAU inches, Mar. 1985. (p. 82)

CIGAR SALES DECLINE ACROSS BOARD DURING 1984, ANNUAL FEATURE

(p. 49) Annual article, by John C. Maxwell, Jr., with 1 table showing cigar sales volume, by company and brand, 1982-84. Data were compiled by the author.

ILL WIND BLOWS DRUG MARKETERS GOOD

(p. 65) By Nancy Giges. Article, with 1 table showing market shares for the top 10 over-the-counter cold remedy brands, and also including manufacturer and advertising agency, winter 1984/85. Data are from *Advertising Age*.

C2710–1.654: June 6, 1985 (Vol. 56, No. 44)

LICENSING: STARRING ON MARKETING TEAM

(p. 15-16) By Joanne Y. Cleaver. Article on sales and marketing of merchandise bearing a licensed image or trademark. Data are from *The Licensing Letter* and publishers' reports.

Includes 2 charts showing sales distribution of licensed merchandise, by product category, 1984; and publishing data for 6 licensing trade periodicals, including circulation and number of advertising pages (no date).

Data clarifications for the licensing trade periodicals appear in the June 17, 1985 issue (see C2710-1.656 below).

C2710–1.655: June 13, 1985 (Vol. 56, No. 46)

[Issue price is $3.00.]

SECOND 100 LEADING NATIONAL ADVERTISERS (SPECIAL ISSUE)

(p. 1-68) Special issue on 1984 media expenditures of the 2nd 100 largest U.S. advertisers, including summary firm profiles. Each profile includes all or most of the following: U.S. and worldwide sales, with detail by product dept; worldwide net income; and U.S. operating profits and advertising expenditures by media; 1984 with comparisons to 1983.

Data are based on reports from individual companies, statistical services, and trade assns.

Issue contains an introductory article; 100 profiles, arranged alphabetically; and listing of the top 100 advertisers and 11 tables listed below, interspersed throughout the issue.

TABLES:

[Unless otherwise noted, tables show data by company, for 1984.]

[1] 2nd 100 leading national advertisers [ranked by advertising expenditures]. (p. 1)

[2] Media spending by the 2nd 100 leading national advertisers [for newspapers, magazines, network cable, spot and network TV and radio, outdoor, and farm publications, 1983-84]. (p. 10-11)

[3] 2nd 100 leading advertisers [grouped by industry], with U.S. sales [and advertising expenditures, and worldwide sales and earnings]. (p. 14)

[4-10] Top 25 advertisers [ranked] by percent change [in expenditures for] magazine, network cable, spot and network TV and radio, and outdoor [advertising, with 1983-84 expenditures and media shares of total 1984 advertising expenditures]. (p. 16-58, passim)

[11] 2nd 100's [and all advertisers' aggregate] advertising spending by medium [1983-84]. (p. 68)

C2710-1.656: June 17, 1985 (Vol. 56, No. 47)

MONTHLY TABLE

[1] Consumer magazine ad linage, advertising pages for U.S., Canadian, and [other] foreign consumer publications, May or June 1985. (p. 79-80)

CORRECTIONS AND CLARIFICATIONS

(p. 6) Includes data clarification for article on sales and marketing of licensed merchandise appearing in June 6, 1985 issue (see C2710-1.654 above).

C2710-1.657: June 24, 1985 (Vol. 56, No. 49)

BETTER THE SECOND TIME AROUND

(p. 3, 99) By Keith L. Reinhard. Article on the International Advertising Film Festival in Cannes, with 1 table showing number of "Gold Lion" awards for excellence in TV/cinema advertising won by representatives from U.S. and 6 other countries, 1980-84. Data are from *Advertising Age*.

MONTHLY adWATCH FEATURE

(p. 14) "Newsmakers Harvest Consumer Awareness." Covers May 1985 survey. Includes 1 chart showing advertisers with the greatest increase or decrease in consumer awareness; and text data on top 10 advertisements recalled, and awareness of advertising in 4 product categories.

INTERNATIONAL AGENCY/CLIENT REPORT, ANNUAL FEATURE

(p. 42-60) Annual article profiling 29 advertising agencies with multinational clients accounting for over $3 million of business. Data are compiled by *Advertising Age* from individual company reports.

Includes text data on agencies' total and non-U.S. gross income and billings, and number of affiliated agencies, 1984 with comparison to previous years. Each profile also includes tabular list of multinational clients, showing countries in which they advertise.

Previous feature, with data for 1983, is described in SRI 1984 Annual under C2710-1.541.

C2710-1.658: June 27, 1985 (Vol. 56, No. 50)

[Issue price is $3.00.]

100 LEADING MEDIA COMPANIES, ANNUAL FEATURE (SPECIAL ISSUE)

(p. 1-64) Annual special issue on 1984 finances and activities of the 100 companies with highest revenues from media properties, including summary firm profiles. Data are from individual company reports and *Advertising Age* estimates.

Contents:

a. Introductory article and 1 summary table ranking top 100 companies by media revenues, 1984. (p. 1-2)

b. Company profiles, with lists of media properties owned, and total and media sales, with detail by media; and 7 interspersed tables, showing the following for selected profiled companies: net income; total and media revenues, with detail by media; and, as applicable, circulation of top newspaper, advertising revenues of top magazine, number of radio and TV stations owned, and cable subscribers; mostly for 1984 with comparison to 1983. (p. 4-64)

Also includes return on sales for top 100 publicly held companies, 1983-84 (p. 63); and a summary of print and broadcast property purchases by top 100 companies during 1984-85, including buyer, seller, property, and price (p. 18-19).

This is the 5th annual report. Corrected data appear in the Aug. 5 and 19, 1985 issues (see C2710-1.667 and C2710-1.671, below).

C2710-1.659: July 1, 1985 (Vol. 56, No. 51)

IRREGULARLY RECURRING TABLES

[1] Flash report: newspaper advertising investment for Mar. 1985. (p. 28)

[2] Newspaper advertising MRCS/SAU inches, Apr. 1985. (p. 44)

C2710-1.660: July 8, 1985 (Vol. 56, No. 52)

READY TO REBOUND: TV SPORTS MARKET DECLINE ENDS

(p. 1, 64) By Robert Raissman. Article, with 1 table showing TV advertising costs for 30-second spots on 12 network sports programs, 1984-85. Data are from *Advertising Age*.

C2710-1.661: July 11, 1985 (Vol. 56, No. 53)

BREAKING THE LANGUAGE BARRIER

(p. 26) By John Parry. Article on cable TV in Europe. Data are from CIT Research. Includes 1 undated table showing percent of households with cable TV, and cable ownership and operating regulations, for 13 European countries.

PEOPLE PATTERNS: 'TYPICAL' AMERICAN FAMILY A DYING BREED

(p. 29) By Peter Francese. Article, with 1 chart showing male population age 18-54, and number with children under age 18 living with them, for 1970, 1980, and 1984. Data are from Census Bureau.

C2710-1.662: July 15, 1985 (Vol. 56, No. 54)

QUARTERLY TABLE

[1] Ad pages in [U.S. and Canadian] farm publications, 2nd quarter 1985. (p. 76)

CORRECTIONS AND CLARIFICATIONS

(p. 6) Includes data correction for annual feature on foreign agency income. Data were incorrectly reported in a previous correction appearing in the May 20, 1985 issue (see C2710-1.649 above).

For description of original annual feature, see C2710-1.642 above.

SCHONFELD TRACKS AD SPENDING, ANNUAL FEATURE

(p. 39) Annual article, with 1 table showing advertising expenditure growth rates, and expenditures as percent of sales and of gross margin, for 250 industries (primarily SIC 4-digit), 1984. Data are from an annual study by Schonfeld and Associates, based on 10-K Reports filed with the SEC.

COFFEE GRINDS TO A HALT, DECAFFEINATES STAY HOT, ANNUAL FEATURE

(p. 62) Annual article, by John C. Maxwell, Jr., with 1 table showing regular and instant coffee market shares, by company and brand, 1980-84. Data were compiled by the author.

C2710-1.663: July 18, 1985 (Vol. 56, No. 55)

LIQUOR MARKETING: DISTILLERS TRY TACTICS TO BRAKE SALES SLIDE

(p. 13-14) By Ed Fitch. Article, with 2 charts showing the following for distilled spirits: percent change in sales, 1981-84; and per capita consumption, selected years 1970-84. Data are from *Impact*.

C2710-1.664: July 22, 1985 (Vol. 56, No. 56)

MONTHLY TABLE

[1] Consumer magazine ad linage, advertising pages for U.S., Canadian, and [other] foreign consumer publications, June or July 1985. (p. 55-56)

COEN BACKS OFF ON '85

(p. 3, 59) By Stewart Alter. Article, with 1 table showing advertising expenditure forecasts by media, including national and local media totals, 1985. Data are from Robert Coen of McCann-Erickson, and update annual forecasts appearing in the Dec. 17, 1984 issue.

For description of annual forecasts, see C2710-1.612 above.

MONTHLY adWATCH FEATURE

(p. 6) "Marketers Find Bad News Does Some Good." Covers June 1985 survey. Includes 1 chart showing trends in awareness of advertising for Coca-Cola and Pepsi-Cola; and text data on awareness of advertising in soft drink and 5 other product categories.

C2710–1.665: July 25, 1985 (Vol. 56, No. 57)

DELTA FLIES WHILE EASTERN GETS GROUNDED IN AA POLL

(p. 2) By Robert Goldsborough. Article, with 1 table showing 10 most and 7 least favorite U.S. airlines as rated by approximately 200 *Advertising Age* readers responding to a May 23, 1985 survey.

NEWSPAPERS: INDUSTRY DELIVERS SOLUTION TO BAD NEWS

(p. 15-16) By William F. Gloede. Article, with 1 chart showing percent of adults who read newspapers, selected periods 1974-84. Data are from Simmons Market Research Bureau/ Value and Life-Style surveys.

RIVALS BATTLE FOR AD AND PROMOTION SCOOPS

(p. 18, 20) By Alan Radding. Article, with 1 table showing circulation of 17 major newspapers in 8 cities, for 6-month period ended Mar. 31, 1985, with percent change from same period 1984. Data are from Audit Bureau of Circulations.

AGGRESSIVE STANCE TRANSFORMS CLASSIFIED AD SALES

(p. 44-45) By Van Wallach. Article, with 1 chart showing newspaper revenues from classified advertising sales, 1979-84. Data are from Newspaper Advertising Bureau.

C2710–1.666: July 29, 1985 (Vol. 56, No. 58)

NEWSPAPER AUDIENCE STUDY DRAWS CONTROVERSY

(p. 44-45) By William F. Gloede. Article, with 2 tables showing readership and circulation data for individual newspapers in top 50 and 6 other Areas of Dominant Influence (ADIs), 1984 or 1985. Data are from a 1985 Simmons-Scarborough study, based on telephone interviews with over 73,000 ADI residents; and Audit Bureau of Circulations.

C2710–1.667: Aug. 5, 1985 (Vol. 56, No. 60)

IRREGULARLY RECURRING TABLE

[2] Newspaper advertising MRCS/SAU inches, May 1985. (p. 52)

CORRECTIONS AND CLARIFICATIONS

(p. 6) Includes data correction for annual feature on 100 leading media companies, appearing in June 27, 1985 issue.

For feature description, see C2710-1.658 above.

COLD CEREALS HEATING UP, ANNUAL FEATURE

(p. 42) Annual article, by John C. Maxwell, Jr., with 2 tables showing market shares (volume and value) for cold cereals, by company and brand, 1982-84.

C2710–1.668: Aug. 8, 1985 (Vol. 56, No. 61)

ADVERTISING: JOIN IT AND SEE THE WORLD

(p. 3, 33) Article, with 1 undated table showing advertising employment opportunities for Americans abroad, and average salaries, by position, for 10 countries. Data are from *Advertising Age*.

C2710–1.669: Aug. 12, 1985 (Vol. 56, No. 62)

IRREGULARLY RECURRING TABLE

[1] Flash report: newspaper advertising investment for Apr. 1985. (p. 34)

OGILVY, FCB ESCAPE POOR QUARTER TREND, QUARTERLY FEATURE

(p. 3, 74) Quarterly article, by Stewart Alter, on finances of publicly owned advertising agencies. Data are from agency reports. Includes 1 table showing income and revenues for 8 agencies, 2nd quarter and 1st half 1984-85.

CATS TRIGGER PET-FOOD GAINS, ANNUAL FEATURE

(p. 31) Annual article, by John C. Maxwell, Jr., with 4 tables showing pet food sales by brand and product type, and sales and market share by manufacturer, 1983-84. Data were compiled by the author.

Data clarification appears in the Sept. 2, 1985 issue (see C2710-1.675 below).

C2710–1.670: Aug. 15, 1985 (Vol. 56, No. 63)

SALES PROMOTION: MARKETING IMAGE PLOTS TURNAROUND

(p. 15-16) By Curt Schleier. Article, with 1 chart and 1 table showing coupon distributions and redemptions, 1980-84; and average coupon redemption rates for grocery products, by distribution media and coupon type, 1982 and 1984. Data are from A. C. Nielsen Co.

TRADE WARS THREATEN FUTURE PEACE OF MARKETERS

(p. 18, 20) By Richard Edel. Article, with 2 charts showing manufacturer expenditures for sales promotion and advertising, for all merchandise, biennially 1974-82, and for package goods, with detail for consumer and trade promotion, 1984. Data are from Marketing Communications and Majers Corp.

PROMOTIONS ADD FIZZ IN SOFT DRINK BUSINESS

(p. 24-26) By Sally Fennell Robbins. Article, with 1 table showing expenditures for sales promotions by type (coupon, point of purchase, and promotional/advertising space), 1983-84. Data are from Marketing and Communications.

C2710–1.671: Aug. 19, 1985 (Vol. 56, No. 64)

MONTHLY TABLE

[1] Consumer magazine ad linage, advertising pages for U.S., Canadian, and [other] foreign consumer publications, July or Aug. 1985. (p. 59-60)

CORRECTIONS AND CLARIFICATIONS

(p. 6) Includes data correction for annual feature on 100 leading media companies, appearing in June 27, 1985 issue.

For feature description, see C2710-1.658 above.

C2710–1.672: Aug. 22, 1985 (Vol. 56, No. 65)

TRAVEL AND TOURISM: INDUSTRY TAKES ROAD TO RECOVERY IN 1985

(p. 15-16) By Joanne Y. Cleaver. Article, with 3 tables showing number of person-trips originating in and received by 8 regions; and selected traveler socioeconomic characteristics, and percent of travelers owning credit cards, for all, pleasure, and business/convention travelers, with comparisons to total adult population; 1984. Data are from U.S. Travel Data Center.

MARKETING ENTERS AIRLINES' FLIGHT PLANS

(p. 19, 23) By Richard Edel. Article, with 1 table and 1 chart showing top 16 commercial airlines ranked by number of passengers, revenue passenger miles, and operating revenues, 1984; and index of airline fares vs. CPI, 1982-84. Data are from Air Transport Assn.

C2710–1.673: Aug. 26, 1985 (Vol. 56, No. 66)

MONTHLY adWATCH FEATURE

(p. 3, 57) "Coke Ads Score Again." Covers July 1985 survey. Includes text data on top 10 advertisements recalled, and awareness of advertising in soft drink and 19 other product categories.

SINGLE-COPY MAGAZINE SALES STILL WEAK, SEMIANNUAL FEATURE

(p. 42) Semiannual article, by Stuart J. Elliott, with 1 table showing top 10 magazines ranked by circulation, 1st half 1984-85. Data are from Audit Bureau of Circulations.

C2710–1.674: Aug. 29, 1985 (Vol. 56, No. 67)

NEW FORMATS GAIN FREQUENCY ON AM BAND

(p. 18-19) By Janice Steinberg. Article, with 1 table showing number of radio stations and average audience shares, by station format type, 1984 and/or 1985. Data are from *American Radio,* and are based on 173 Arbitron markets with 2,865 stations.

Full *American Radio* report is described in SRI under C3165-1.

PEOPLE PATTERNS: HOUSEHOLDS CHANGING CONSTANTLY

(p. 32) By Peter Francese. Article, with 1 chart showing median number of years people live in 4 types of household arrangements (married with children, single living alone and with children, and cohabitating), 1968-80 period. Data are from a Rand Corp. study of 10,000 household interviews conducted by University of Michigan's Institute for Survey Research.

C2710–1.675: Sept. 2, 1985 (Vol. 56, No. 68)

IRREGULARLY RECURRING TABLE

[2] Newspaper advertising MRCS/SAU inches, June 1985. (p. 54)

CORRECTIONS AND CLARIFICATIONS

(p. 6) Includes data clarification for annual feature on pet food sales, appearing in Aug. 12, 1985 issue.

For feature description, see C2710-1.669 above.

C2710–1.676: Sept. 9, 1985 (Vol. 56, No. 70)

IRREGULARLY RECURRING TABLE

[1] Flash report: newspaper advertising investment for May 1985. (p. 104)

ADVERTISERS POLISHING IMAGE-AD BUDGETS

(p. 125, 128) By Thomas G. Garbett. Article, with 1 table showing advertising billings and income, employment, and number of offices, for top 50 agencies handling corporate advertising ranked by business-to-business billings, 1984, with billing comparisons to 1983. Data are from *Business Marketing*.

C2710–1.677: Sept. 16, 1985 (Vol. 56, No. 72)

IRREGULARLY RECURRING TABLE

[1] Flash report: newspaper advertising investment for June 1985. (p. 65)

AVERAGE PRIME TIME 30: $118,840

(p. 1, 124) By Verne Gay and Craig Reiss. Article, with 1 table showing costs for 30-second advertising spots on each prime time network TV program, 1985/86 season. Data were compiled by *Advertising Age* from agency and network sources.

RAYOVAC BACK ON BEAM IN BATTERY MARKET

(p. 47) By Laurie Freeman. Article, with 1 table showing battery market shares, sales, and advertising budget, for 3 leading brands, 1985.

CHINESE MEDIA A QUAGMIRE FOR OUTSIDERS

(p. 75, 78) By Lynne Reaves. Article, with 3 undated tables showing PRC coverage or circulation, and advertising rates, for 5-11 leading Chinese TV stations, newspapers, and magazines.

A related article, with 1 table showing leading foreign advertisers in China, also appears (p. 74, 78).

C2710–1.678: Sept. 19, 1985 (Vol. 56, No. 73)

GROCERY MARKETING: CATERING TO DIFFERENT SEGMENTS

(p. 15-19) By Mary McCabe English. Article, with 2 tables showing top 10 food/beverage corporations ranked by sales, 1984; and number of adults who do major household food shopping, by sex, 1981-84. Data are from *Food Processing* and Simmons Market Research Bureau.

STORES SKEW STYLES TOWARD SHOPPERS' NEEDS

(p. 22-28) By Debra Kent. Article, with 1 chart and 1 table showing percent of supermarkets offering selected special services, and top 10 supermarket chains ranked by sales, 1984. Data are from *Progressive Grocer*.

ETHNIC PRODUCTS SATISFY CRAVING FOR SOMETHING NEW

(p. 46-48) By Sewell Whitney. Article, with 1 table showing frequency of Hispanic, Italian, and Oriental style food consumption in and away from home, 1973 and 1984. Data are from Market Research Corp. of America.

C2710–1.679: Sept. 23, 1985 (Vol. 56, No. 74)

MONTHLY TABLE

[1] Consumer magazine ad linage, advertising pages for U.S., Canadian, and [other] foreign consumer publications, Aug. or Sept. 1985. (p. 83-84)

Additional data appear in the Oct. 14, 1984 issue (see C2710-1.684 below).

C2710–1.680: Sept. 26, 1985 (Vol. 56, No. 75)

[Issue price is $3.00.]

100 LEADING NATIONAL ADVERTISERS (ANNUAL ISSUE)

Annual special issue on 1984 media expenditures of the 100 largest U.S. advertisers, including summary firm profiles. Each profile includes most or all of the following: U.S. and/or worldwide sales, with detail by product division; worldwide net income; and U.S. operating profits and advertising expenditures by media; 1984 with comparisons to 1983.

Data are based on reports from individual companies, statistical services, and trade assns.

Issue contains an introductory article; 100 profiles, arranged alphabetically; and 16 tables listed below, interspersed throughout the issue.

TABLES:

[1] 100 leading national advertisers by rank, [by total advertising expenditures, 1984]. (p. 1)

[2] Media spending by the 100 leading national advertisers [for newspapers, magazines, network cable TV, spot and network TV and radio, outdoor, farm publications, and all other media, all by company, 1983-84]. (p. 10-11)

[3] 100 leading national advertisers with U.S. sales [and advertising expenditures, and worldwide sales and earnings, for advertisers grouped by type of product or service, 1983 and/or 1984]. (p. 16)

[4-13] Top 25 advertisers in newspapers, magazines, business/industrial [publications], spot and network TV and radio, outdoor, farm publications, and network cable [TV, all showing advertising expenditures, by company, 1983-84]. (p. 28-66 passim)

[14] Second 100 leading national advertisers by rank, [by advertising expenditures, 1984]. (p. 146)

[15] All advertisers' total 1984 ad spending by media and product category. (p. 154-155)

[16] Top 200 advertisers' spending as % of all advertisers' [media expenditures, for aggregate top 100, 2nd 100, and all advertisers, for 9 media, 1983-84]. (p. 156)

C2710–1.681: Sept. 30, 1985 (Vol. 56, No. 76)

MONTHLY adWATCH FEATURE

(p. 12, 88) "BK Sees Ad Awareness Slipping Away." Covers Aug. 1985 survey. Includes 1 chart showing advertisers with the greatest increase or decrease in consumer awareness; and text data on top 10 advertisements recalled, and awareness of advertising in fast food and 4 other product categories.

C2710–1.682: Oct. 3, 1985 (Vol. 56, No. 77)

MAGAZINES: VIEWING THE FUTURE IN A NEW LIGHT

(p. 15-16) By Belinda Hulin-Salkin. Article, with 1 chart and 3 tables showing number of magazine titles published, quinquennially 1965-85; and single-copy sales volume (with share of total circulation), for leading personality, computer, and women's magazines, 6-month period ending June 30, 1985, with percent change from same period of previous year.

Data are from *Ayer Directory of Publications* and Audit Bureau of Circulations.

MIND-BOGGLING SUCCESS

(p. 36) Table showing consumer magazine industry advertising revenues, quinquennially 1950-80 and 1984. Data are from Publishers Information Bureau.

CHEAPER BY THE SUBSCRIPTION

(p. 38) Chart showing average single-copy and 1-year subscription prices for aggregate top 50 magazines in advertising revenues, selected years 1965-84. Data are from Magazine Publishers Assn.

MEN'S SOPHISTICATE TITLES FEEL CIRCULATION PINCH

(p. 52-53) By Gary Levin. Article, with 1 table showing single-copy sales volume (with share of total circulation), for 6 leading men's magazines, 6-month period ended June 30, 1985, with percent change from same period of previous year. Data are from Audit Bureau of Circulations.

C2710–1.683: Oct. 7, 1985 (Vol. 56, No. 78)

IRREGULARLY RECURRING TABLE

[2] Newspaper advertising MRCS/SAU inches, July 1985. (p. 78)

STAGE SET FOR AGENCY REVIEWS AT P&G-VICKS

(p. 1, 92) By Nancy Giges. Article, with 1 table showing advertising budgets for 6 corporations involved in major retailer mergers in 1985. Data are from *Advertising Age*.

WINE MARKET RIDES 'COOL' BREEZE, ANNUAL FEATURE

(p. 45) Annual article, by John C. Maxwell, Jr., with 1 table showing wine shipments and market shares for 34 leading domestic wine companies, all other domestic companies, and total imports, 1982-84, with 1983-84 rankings. Data were compiled by the author.

HERD OF MOUSSE SELLERS STAMPEDES MARKET

(p. 68-70) By Pat Sloan. Article, with 1 table showing market shares for leading hair care mousse brands, and percent change in sales of total and selected brands, 1983-84 and 1st 2 quarters 1985. Data are from Salomon Brothers, Inc.

C2710–1.684: Oct. 14, 1985 (Vol. 56, No. 80)

IRREGULARLY RECURRING TABLE

[1] Flash report: newspaper advertising investment for July 1985. (p. 52)

QUARTERLY TABLE

[1] Ad pages in [U.S. and Canadian] farm publications, 3rd quarter 1985. (p. 98)

JWT, OGILVY STILL ON TOP, RECURRING FEATURE

(p. 3, 92) Recurring article, by Joseph M. Winski, on corporate advertising directors' opinions on top advertising agencies and agency attributes. Data are based on an SRI Research Center survey of 300 directors from companies with sales of at least $25 million located in the top 20 market areas.

Includes 1 chart and 2 tables showing respondent ratings of leading advertising agencies, 2nd quarter 1985, with comparisons to Oct. 1984-June 1985 period.

Previous article is included in the annual issue on advertising agency profiles, described above under C2710-1.636.

CORRECTIONS AND CLARIFICATIONS

(p. 6) Includes additional data for monthly table [1] on consumer magazine advertising linage, appearing in Sept. 23, 1985 issue.

For original table, see C2710-1.679 above.

To-FITNESS HOPES FOR INSTANT YOGURT SUCCESS

(p. 74-76) By Julie Franz. Article, with 1 table ranking top 5 yogurt brands by market share, with 1984 advertising expenditures and advertising agency for each. Data are from A. C. Nielsen Co. and Leading National Advertisers.

C2710–1.685: Oct. 17, 1985 (Vol. 56, No. 81)

DIRECT MARKETING: ALTERNATIVE MEDIA TRY TO GET THEIR FEET IN THE DOOR

(p. 15, 58) By Eileen Norris. Article, with 1 table showing distribution of consumers' direct response merchandise orders, by type of advertising media, July 1984. Data are from a consumer survey conducted in Oct. 1984 by Simmons Market Research Bureau and Rapp & Collins.

C2710–1.686: Oct. 21, 1985 (Vol. 56, No. 82)

MONTHLY TABLE

[1] Consumer magazine ad linage, advertising pages for U.S., Canadian, and [other] foreign consumer publications, Sept. or Oct. 1985. (p. 93-94)

SOFT-DRINK GIANTS SQUEEZE INTO CITRUS SODA SEGMENT

(p. 3, 103) By Nancy Giges and Gary Levin. Article, with 1 table showing market shares for 6 major citrus-flavored soft drink brands, with brand manufacturer and advertising agency for each, as of June/July 1985. Data are from *Advertising Age.*

C2710–1.687: Oct. 24, 1985 (Vol. 56, No. 83)

DINE OUT IN JAKARTA, WORK IN NEW YORK, LIVE IN LISBON, AND YOU MAY BREAK EVEN

(p. 9) Article, with 4 undated tables showing wage/salary and consumer price indexes, and typical prices for a restaurant meal and hotel room, in 10 major cities of the world. Data are from a survey report published by Union Bank of Switzerland.

HYATT'S THE PLACE: AA READERS RANK MARRIOTT, WESTIN NEXT BEST

(p. 12) By Robert Goldsborough. Article, with 1 table showing 10 best hotel/motels as rated by approximately 150 *Advertising Age* readers responding to an Aug. 1985 survey.

HEALTHCARE MARKETING: PRODUCT MANAGEMENT IS IN THE AIR

(p. 15, 18-19) By Richard Edel. Article, with 3 undated tables showing advertising media used by hospital marketers; and impact of Medicare's diagnostic related groups (DRG) reimbursement system on hospital operations and on purchasing decisions of hospital personnel by type.

Data are from an Allied Research Associates survey, and Gordon DRG Report.

SHORTER PATIENT STAYS DICTATE NEW GAME PLAN

(p. 31-32) By Beverly Montgomery-Karp. Article, with 1 table showing hospital administrative goals as cited by hospital marketers, 1984-85. Data are from an Allied Research Associates survey.

DRUG COMPANIES REACH INTO MIXED MARKETING BAG

(p. 35-36) By Jaan Kangilaski. Article, with 1 undated chart showing consumer willingness to ask their doctor for specific advertised prescription drug brands. Data are from Ruder Finn & Rotman 1985 Health Care Survey report.

C2710–1.688: Oct. 28, 1985 (Vol. 56, No. 84)

MIGHTY URGE TO MERGE: BIG NAME BUYERS BAG BRANDS

(p. 1, 38-46) Article on 4 recent major retailer mergers and their impact on advertising. Data are primarily from Mark S. Albion of Harvard University, and Marketing Intelligence Service.

Includes text data, 3 charts, and 3 tables showing number of new product introductions; cost for launching a new product; and advertising expenditures and agency, for leading brands owned by 6 merging retailers; selected years 1975-86.

MONTHLY adWATCH FEATURE

(p. 4, 98) "Cherry Coke Takes Fizz Out of Sister Brands." Covers Sept. 1985 survey. Includes 1 chart showing advertisers with the greatest increase or decrease in consumer awareness; and text data on top 10 advertisements recalled, and awareness of advertising in soft drink and 5 other product categories.

C2710–1.689: Oct. 31, 1985 (Vol. 56, No. 85)

NBA PRACTICES FULL-COURT PRESS IN MARKETING

(p. 26-28) By Mark Bittman. Article, with 1 chart showing attendance at professional basketball games, 1980/81-1984/85, with 1984/85 season average attendance per game. Data are from National Basketball Assn.

C2710–2 PENSIONS AND INVESTMENT AGE

Biweekly. Oversized.
ISSN 0273-5466.
LC 74-648522.
SRI/MF/excerpts, shipped quarterly

Biweekly journal reporting on trends and developments in the management and investment of institutional pension, employee benefit, profit-sharing, and other tax-exempt funds. Covers corporate, State and local government, Taft-Hartley, and other major funds.

Data are from *Pensions & Investments Performance Evaluation Report (PIPER),* original surveys, and other sources.

Issues include numerous news and feature articles, occasionally with statistics; summaries of new security issues and corporate cash management activities; and narrative editorial depts. Recurring statistical features include the following:

a. Monthly table presenting Payden & Rygel index of short-maturity assets, described below. Table, which begins with Apr. 15, 1985 issue, alternates with a monthly illustrative chart on the Payden & Rygel index; chart is not covered in SRI.

b. Quarterly reviews of performance of bank and insurance company pooled equity and fixed-income funds, and pooled special equity and international funds, described below.

c. Semiannual article on cash/short-term holdings of Fortune 100 corporations.

d. Annual statistical features, including ranking of 1,000 largest employee benefit funds (Jan.); analysis of pension fund and financial data for Fortune 100 companies (Aug.); and profiles and directories of investment management firms; and others.

Features with substantial statistical content are described, as they appear, under "Statistical Features;" page locations and latest periods of coverage for monthly table and quarterly fund performance reviews are also noted. Each issue of the journal is reviewed, but an abstract is published in SRI monthly issues only when statistical features appear.

Availability: Pensions and Investment Age, Circulation Department, 740 Rush St., Chicago IL 60611, $75.00 per yr., single copy $4.00, special issue prices vary; SRI/MF/excerpts for all portions covered under "Statistical Features;" shipped quarterly.

Issues reviewed during 1985: Nov. 12, 1984-Oct. 28, 1985 (P) (Vol. 12, Nos. 23-26; Vol. 13, Nos. 1-23) [Vol. 13, No. 4 incorrectly reads No. 6].

MONTHLY TABLE

Monthly Payden & Rygel index of short-maturity assets, showing the following: total returns for 90- and 180-day Treasury bills and certificates of deposit (domestic and Eurodollar), and for 1- and 2-year Treasury notes, for selected periods (current to month prior to month of publication), with yield level change (discrepancy between simple yields and total returns) for each instrument.

QUARTERLY REVIEWS:

FUND PERFORMANCE

Quarterly reviews of investment performance for bank and insurance company pooled equity and fixed-income funds, and pooled special equity and international funds, through quarter ending 2-3 months prior to publication date. Data are from PIPER which ranks the performance of approximately 230 funds.

Includes 1-2 charts and 1-4 tables showing rates of return for each type of fund, as follows: high, low, median, and 1st and 3rd quartile rates; and rates for top 10 funds in 4 asset size groups and/or for individual funds in top quartile (with rankings); with selected comparisons to Standard & Poor's 500 and, occasionally, other indexes; generally for 3-month and 1-, 3-, 5-, and 10-year periods ending with last month of quarter of coverage.

Feature on 4th quarter performance of pooled equity and fixed-income funds includes 2 additional tables showing rates for all funds.

Features include 1-3 accompanying articles.

STATISTICAL FEATURES:

C2710–2.601: Nov. 12, 1984 (Vol. 12, No. 23)

POOLED EQUITY AND FIXED-INCOME FUNDS, QUARTERLY FEATURE

(p. 13-20) For quarter ended Sept. 30, 1984. For data description, see C2710-2 above.

C2710–2.602: Nov. 26, 1984 (Vol. 12, No. 24)

POOLED SPECIAL EQUITY AND INTERNATIONAL FUNDS, QUARTERLY FEATURE

(p. 29-31) For quarter ended Sept. 30, 1984. For data description, see C2710-2 above. Data corrections appear in the Jan. 7, 1985 issue (see C2710-2.605 below).

TWO MET LIFE POOLS TAKE PIPER LEAD, QUARTERLY FEATURE

(p. 44-46) Quarterly article on investment performance of pooled real estate funds, with 2 tables showing rate of return, primarily for 5 open-end and closed-end funds with highest and lowest performance, variously for 3-month, and 1-, 3-, and 5-year periods ended June 30, 1984.

Data are from *Pensions and Investments Performance Evaluation Report* (PIPER).

C2710–2.603: Dec. 10, 1984 (Vol. 12, No. 25)

GROWTH OF FUTURES FUNDS SLOWS

(p. 27-29) By Barry B. Burr. Article, with 1 table showing trading volume for stock index futures contracts of Standard & Poor's 500 companies, 1982-1st 10 months 1984. Data are from Chicago Mercantile Exchange.

C2710–2.604: Dec. 24, 1984 (Vol. 12, No. 26)

DEDICATIONS, IMMUNIZATIONS SOAR, RECURRING ARTICLE

(p. 8) Recurring article, by Barry B. Burr, on use of bond portfolio dedications and immunizations to enhance pension fund profitability during periods of volatile interest rates. Includes 1 table showing the following for 24 pension funds dedicated or immunized in 1984: investment strategy, annualized yield, portfolio value and pension assets share, and portfolio manager.

For description of previous article, see SRI 1984 Annual under C2710-2.522.

C2710–2.605: Jan. 7, 1985 (Vol. 13, No. 1)

[The 5 articles described below present rankings of the top 10 investment management companies in various categories of new business, for the Jan. 1-Nov. 15, 1984 period. Data are based on a *Pensions and Investment Age* survey.]

FUNDS ACTIVE IN PASSIVE STYLE

(p. 3, 26) By Trudy Ring. Article, with 3 tables ranking top companies in new tax-exempt business, for 3 asset-size categories.

MANAGERS OF INDEX FUNDS REPORT LARGEST GAINS

(p. 4, 26) By Trudy Ring. Article, with 3 tables ranking top companies in new equity business, for 3 asset-size categories.

DEDICATION, IMMUNIZATION ATTRACT LARGE FUNDS

(p. 4, 26) By Trudy Ring. Article, with 3 tables ranking top companies in new fixed-income business, for 3 asset-size categories.

CORRECTIONS

(p. 9) Includes corrected data for feature on performance of international funds for periods ending Sept. 30, 1984.

Feature appeared in the Nov. 26, 1984 issue, and is covered under C2710-2.602.

REALTY ADVISERS REPORT NEW-BUSINESS GAINS

(p. 13) Brief article, with 2 tables ranking top companies in new real estate business, for 2 asset-size categories.

Data correction appears in the Feb. 4, 1985 issue (see C2710-2.607 below).

GIC SALES BOOM

(p. 26) By Chuck Paustian. Article, with 1 table ranking top companies in new guaranteed investment contract business.

Data correction appears in the Feb. 18, 1985 issue (see C2710-2.608 below).

C2710–2.606: Jan. 21, 1985 (Vol. 13, No. 2)

[Issue price is $5.00.]

TOP 1,000 FUNDS, ANNUAL FEATURE

Annual compilation of articles, profiles, and tables on the investment activities and performance of major nonfederal employee benefit funds, including pension, profit-sharing, and savings/thrift plans, for year ended Sept. 1984, with summary comparisons to 1983. Covers corporate, public, union, and miscellaneous plans.

Data are from *Pensions and Investment Age* surveys, and *1985 Money Market Directory*. Includes the following statistical portions:

a. "Pension Asset Growth Stunted in 1984." Article, with 1 chart showing aggregate asset mix of top 200 funds by type of fund, 1983-84. (p. 3, 14)

b. Aggregate asset mix of top 200 and 201-1,000 funds, 1983 and/or 1984; and aggregate asset value of top 1,000 funds, and of top 200 by type of fund, 1982-84. 3 charts. (p. 13, 30)

c. Top 1,000 funds/sponsors, ranked by asset size, 1984. 2 tables. (p. 16, 25-28)

d. Aggregate assets of top 25-1,000 funds and top 200 pension funds; and selected aggregate data for top 200 funds, including total contributions, benefits paid, and number

and/or assets of funds with internal management, indexing, and various types of investments; 1983-84. 1 table. (p. 32)

e. Profiles of the top 200 funds, each with 1 table showing asset value by type of plan, employer contributions, and benefit payments, 1984; and brief description of investment portfolio and management. (p. 32-90) (Feb. 4, 1985 issue includes corrected data for 1 profile; see C2710-2.607 below).

f. Asset size and/or rank, 1984, for: top 25 profit-sharing and 25 pension plans; top 10-25 corporate, public, union, and miscellaneous funds; funds with various types of investments (guaranteed investment contract, dedicated bond portfolio, equity real estate, mortgage, mortgage-backed security, overseas, oil/gas, and venture capital); sponsors with internally managed pension funds; and funds with indexed assets. 16 tables. (p. 40-76, passim)

g. Listings of funds using futures and options. 2 tables. (p. 62)

C2710–2.607: Feb. 4, 1985 (Vol. 13, No. 3)

CORRECTIONS

(p. 6) Includes corrected data for article on top investment companies in new real estate business, and for 1 company profiled in annual feature on top 1,000 funds.

Real estate article appears in the Jan. 7, 1985 issue (for description, see C2710-2.605 above). Annual feature appears in the Jan. 21, 1985 issue (for description, see C2710-2.606 above).

TOP UNDERWRITER CAPTURES QUARTER OF MARKET IN 1984, ANNUAL FEATURE

(p. 11-16) Annual compilation of articles, by Marci Baker, on securities underwriting activity by brokerage firms, 1984. Data are from IDD Information Services, Inc.

Includes 14 tables showing number and value of issues underwritten, as follows: aggregate issues, by type of security; top 25 firms ranked by total underwriting value; and top 5 firms ranked by underwriting value under full-credit and bonus-credit systems, for all issues, common stock, and convertible and nonconvertible preferred stock and debt; 1984, generally with comparison to 1983.

Previous article, with data for 1983, is described in SRI 1984 Annual under C2710-2.506.

C2710–2.608: Feb. 18, 1985 (Vol. 13, No. 4)

[Issue incorrectly reads No. 6.]

POOLED EQUITY AND FIXED-INCOME FUNDS, QUARTERLY FEATURE

(p. 13-26) For quarter ended Dec. 31, 1984.

For data description, see C2710-2 above. Data corrections appear in the Mar. 4, 1985 issue (see C2710-2.609 below).

CORRECTIONS

(p. 8) Includes corrected data for article on top investment companies in new guaranteed investment contract business.

Article appeared in the Jan. 7, 1985 issue; for description, see C2710-2.605 above.

SWINGS IN RETURNS HIGHLIGHT APPRAISAL STRATEGY, QUARTERLY FEATURE

(p. 29-30) Quarterly article, by Mark Westerbeck, on investment performance of pooled real estate funds, with 2 tables showing rate of return, primarily for 5 open-end and closed-end funds with highest and lowest performance, variously for 9-month and 3- and 5-year periods ended Sept. 30, 1984.

Data are from Evaluation Associates Inc.

CHANGE IN INTERNATIONAL INVESTMENT

(p. 43) Table showing percent of corporate pension plans with international investments, by plan asset size, 1979-84. Data are from Greenwich Research Associates. Related article appears on p. 44.

C2710–2.609: Mar. 4, 1985 (Vol. 13, No. 5)

POOLED SPECIAL EQUITY AND INTERNATIONAL FUNDS, QUARTERLY FEATURE

(p. 41-44) For quarter ended Dec. 31, 1984.
For data description, see C2710-2 above.

SALARY SURVEY NOTES DISPARITY

(p. 1, 49) By Rose Darby. Article, with 1 undated table showing mean and median salary for corporate pension executives and public pension fund officials, by asset size group. Data are from 1,076 pension executives and 260 public fund officials responding to a recent Greenwich Research Associates survey.

CORRECTIONS

(p. 42-43) Corrected data for feature on performance of pooled equity and fixed-income funds for periods ending Dec. 31, 1984.

Feature appeared in the Feb. 18, 1985 issue, and is covered under C2710-2.608.

C2710–2.610: Mar. 18, 1985 (Vol. 13, No. 6)

DEFINED BENEFIT PLAN USE UP

(p. 3, 51) By Joel Chernoff. Article on impact of Reagan Administration guidelines, issued in May 1984, covering asset reversions in pension plan terminations. Data are from Pension Benefit Guaranty Corp.

Includes 1 table showing number of defined benefit and defined contribution successor plans and participants, for plans adopted Jan.-May 1984 and June 1984-Jan. 1985 periods.

C2710–2.611: Apr. 1, 1985 (Vol. 13, No. 7)

INDEX FUNDS SHOW SIGNIFICANT GROWTH

(p. 1, 53) By Trudy Ring. Article, with 1 table showing top 19 investment firms ranked by assets managed in index funds, as of Dec. 31, 1984 with comparison to 1983. Data are based on a recent survey by *Pensions and Investment Age.*

MANAGERS STEP UP BIDS FOR UNION FUND ASSETS

(p. 27, 32) By Fred Williams. Article, with 1 table showing assets ranking for union pension funds included among the 1,000 largest employee benefit funds, 1984.

For description of feature on 1,000 largest funds, see C2710-2.606 above.

COMPANIES EXTEND INTEREST IN NOTES

(p. 49-50) By Barry B. Burr. Article, with 3 tables showing number and value of extendible corporate debt issues, annually 1982-84, 1st

quarter 1982-85, and for top 5 underwriters and top 5 issuers during 1982-1st quarter 1985 period. Data are from IDD Information Services, Inc.

C2710–2.612: Apr. 15, 1985 (Vol. 13, No. 8)

MONTHLY TABLE

(p. 27, 30) Payden & Rygel index of short-maturity assets, selected periods 4th quarter 1984-Mar. 1985. Includes accompanying article.

DOMESTIC ISSUES LAG FOREIGN IN 1st QUARTER, RECURRING FEATURE

(p. 73, 76) By Marci Baker. Recurring article, with 2 tables showing volume and value of U.S. new securities issues, by type; and top 10 investment firms ranked by value of U.S. and foreign new securities underwritten; 1st quarter 1985. Data are from IDD Information Services, Inc.

C2710–2.613: Apr. 29, 1985 (Vol. 13, No. 9)

FUNDS TAKE ACTIVE INTEREST IN PASSIVE STRATEGIES, RECURRING FEATURE

(p. 2, 34) Recurring article, by Trudy Ring, with 2 tables showing top 5-10 investment firms ranked by new accounts and new assets managed, 1st quarter 1985. Data are from a recent *Pensions and Investment Age* survey.

C2710–2.614: May 6, 1985 (Vol. 13, No. 10)

[Special issue price is $5.00.]

12th ANNUAL PROFILES: MANAGERS OF AMERICA'S WEALTH

(p. 3-128) Annual full-issue feature profiling assets and operations of 874 investment management organizations, including commercial banks, insurance companies, and investment counselors, as of Jan. 1, 1985.

Data are from a survey by *Pensions and Investment Age.*

Contents:

a. Narrative summaries, with 9 charts presenting data on asset size or mix, by type of management organization, and for aggregate top 100 and 200 organizations, with selected comparisons to Jan. 1982-84. (p. 3-6)

b. Ranking of all organizations by tax-exempt assets managed, and of top 100 organizations by total assets managed. 2 tables. (p. 8-16)

c. Profiles of individual organizations, each with 1 table showing some or all of the following: assets managed (total and by type, including tax-exempt, fully discretionary tax-exempt, real estate, and international); minimum and types of accounts managed; and number of tax-exempt clients, portfolio managers, and research personnel. (p. 19-126)

d. Summary data, including average number of stocks followed, and number of managers using options, stock index futures, and fixed-income futures; top 25 banks/trust companies, insurance companies, investment counselors, and real estate and international managers, and top 60 Canadian investment managers, ranked by assets

managed; top 25 managers of guaranteed income contracts and 401(k) plans ranked by value; and top 25 managers ranked by new business value. 10 tables. (p. 19-34, 88-122, passim)

e. List of organizations by location. (p. 126-128)

Data corrections for top 25 real estate managers appear in the May 27, 1985 issue; see C2710-2.616 below. Additional data appear in the Aug. 19, 1985 issue; for description see C2710-2.622 below.

C2710–2.615: May 13, 1985 (Vol. 13, No. 11)

MONTHLY TABLE

(p. 39) Payden & Rygel index of short-maturity assets, 1st quarter and Apr. 1985.

POOLED EQUITY AND FIXED-INCOME FUNDS, QUARTERLY FEATURE

(p. 13-19) For quarter ended Mar. 31, 1985.
For data description, see C2710-2 above.
Data clarification appears in the May 27, 1985 issue (see C2710-2.616 below).

COPLEY WINS AGAIN IN '84, QUARTERLY FEATURE

(p. 22-23) Quarterly article, by Mark Westerbeck, on investment performance of pooled real estate funds, with 2 tables showing rate of return for individual open-end and closed-end funds (with rankings), variously for 1-, 3-, 5-, and 10-year periods ended Dec. 31, 1984, with comparisons to CPI.

Data are from *Pensions and Investments Performance Evaluation Report* (PIPER).

C2710–2.616: May 27, 1985 (Vol. 13, No. 12)

POOLED SPECIAL EQUITY AND INTERNATIONAL FUNDS, QUARTERLY FEATURE

(p. 37-38) For quarter ended Mar. 31, 1985.
For data description, see C2710-2 above.

CORRECTIONS

(p. 4) Includes data clarification for quarterly feature on fixed-income fund performance (see C2710-2.615 above).

MERRILL LEADS '84 CAPITAL RANKINGS

(p. 15-16) By Marci Baker. Article, with 1 table ranking top 20 investment banking firms by aggregate value of shareholder's equity and subordinated debt, as of Jan. 1, 1985, with comparisons to Jan. 1984. Data are from Securities Industry Assn.

MASTER TRUST DIRECTORY, ANNUAL FEATURE

(p. 19-33) Annual feature profiling 36 U.S. and Canadian master trust/master custodial banks, with assets of $1 billion or more, for year ended Mar. 31, 1985. Data are from a *Pensions & Investment Age* survey.

Profiles include all or most of the following data: value of master trust and master custodial assets; number of clients and account managers/supervisors; smallest and largest clients' asset size; type of services offered; accounting and reporting practices; and fee structure.

Feature also includes several related articles; and 2 tables (p. 28-29) ranking profiled banks by master trust/master custodial assets.

Data corrections appear in the June 10, 1985 issue; for description see C2710-2.617 below.

CORRECTIONS

(p. 43) Data correction for ranking of real estate managers originally appearing in annual feature on investment management organizations; for description of feature, see C2710-2.614 above.

CORPORATE LIQUIDITY DROPS, SEMIANNUAL FEATURE

(p. 51, 53) Semiannual article, by Richard J. Gillespie, on cash holdings (cash/short-term investments) among Fortune 100 largest industrial companies, as of Dec. 31, 1984. Data are compiled by Wright Investors' Service.

Includes 3 tables showing holdings as of Dec. 1983-84, for 10 companies with largest current holdings, and with largest increases and decreases.

C2710–2.617: June 10, 1985 (Vol. 13, No. 13)

CORRECTIONS

(p. 4) Includes data corrections for annual master trust directory, appearing in the May 27, 1985 issue; for description, see C2710-2.616 above.

CONTRIBUTORY PLANS GAIN IN POPULARITY

(p. 17) Article, with 1 table showing pension plan enrollment by plan type (defined benefit and defined contribution), 1974-84. Data are from Labor Dept, Internal Revenue Service, and Employee Benefit Research Institute estimates.

C2710–2.618: June 24, 1985 (Vol. 13, No. 14)

MONTHLY TABLE

(p. 47) Payden & Rygel index of short-maturity assets, selected periods Jan.-May 1985.

FEAR OF INTERVENTION BY CONGRESS MIGHT FORCE FIRMS' HANDS

(p. 3, 58) By Joel Chernoff. Article on corporate termination of overfunded pension plans and reversion of terminated plans' surplus assets, with 1 undated table showing the following for 10 largest reversions: company name, type of successor plan (spinoff or defined contribution), and amount of reversion.

Data are from company estimates supplied to Pension Benefit Guaranty Corp., and other company data.

INTERNATIONAL DIRECTORY, ANNUAL FEATURE

(p. 13-24) Annual profiles of 83 U.S.- and foreign-based investment management firms controlling more than $15.9 billion in international market investments by U.S. tax-exempt institutions, as of Mar. 31, 1985. Data are from a *Pensions and Investment Age* survey.

Profiles generally include text statistics on all or some of the following: total and tax-exempt assets managed; tax-exempt assets invested overseas, by type of instrument (foreign stocks and bonds, and cash equivalents); number of clients; countries of investment concentration; minimum account size; and investment approach.

Also includes 2 related articles; and 2 tables ranking management firms by tax-exempt assets invested overseas (for 83 firms) and by new business (for 52 firms).

C2710–2.619: July 8, 1985 (Vol. 13, No. 15)

GOOD RETURNS A CATCH-22?

(p. 3, 25) By Chuck Paustian. Article, with 2 tables ranking completed and pending pension plan terminations by value of reverted assets, and including sponsor institution and termination date for each, June 1981-May 1985. Data are from Pension Benefit Guaranty Corp.

C2710–2.620: July 22, 1985 (Vol. 13, No. 16)

SURVEY SHOWS SHIFTS IN MANAGEMENT FEES

(p. 3, 44) By Chuck Paustian. Article on investment management fees, 1984. Data are from a survey of 165 management organizations, conducted by SEI Corp.

Includes 1 table showing high, median, low, and 25th and 75th quartile fees, for large and small counselors and banks/trust companies, by fund size and type (balanced, equity, and fixed), 1984. Data are in basis points.

Similar article, with data for 1982, is described in SRI 1983 Annual under C2710-2.408.

FIELD DEFINING INDEPENDENT ROLE, ANNUAL FEATURE

(p. CM3-CM22) Annual directory, by Richard J. Gillespie, of U.S. and Canadian banks, assns, and other institutions providing cash management services, including types of services offered, number of clients, and size of professional staff, 1985. Data are from a *Pensions and Investment Age* survey. Includes 1 table and individual profiles.

Additional data appear in the Aug. 19, 1985 issue; for description see C2710-2.622 below.

PICKING A DISBURSEMENT BANK

(p. CM26-CM27) By Steven F. Maier and Larry A. Marks. Article examining factors in cash managers' selection of banks for controlled disbursement of funds. Data are from a Phoenix-Hecht, Inc., 1985 survey of banks.

Includes 3 tables showing number of controlled disbursement bank sites, by State, 1985; and check clearing time and "slippage" (difference between time actually needed to clear a check and time elapsed before depositor is granted access to funds), for 8-10 cities, Mar. 1981 and Jan. 1985.

FIXED-RATE ISSUES TOP DRAW, RECURRING FEATURE

(p. 29, 32) Recurring article, by Marci Baker, with 4 tables showing net underwriting proceeds and volume, for domestic issues by type; and top 10 investment management firms ranked by proceeds from domestic, Eurobond, and total underwritings; 1st half 1985. Data are from IDD Information Services, Inc.

C2710–2.621: Aug. 5, 1985 (Vol. 13, No. 17)

MONTHLY TABLE

(p. 27) Payden & Rygel index of short-maturity assets, selected periods Jan.-June 1985.

TERMINATION GOLD IS MINED

(p. 3, 43) By Barry B. Burr. Article on role of pension fund terminations in corporate acquisitions. Data are from Pension Benefit Guaranty Corp., and W. T. Grimm and Co.

Includes 1 table showing the following for 12 recent acquisitions of companies with terminated pension plans: name of acquiring and target company, takeover value, and value of reverted assets from terminated plan.

C2710–2.622: Aug. 19, 1985 (Vol. 13, No. 18)

MONTHLY TABLE

(p. 13) Payden & Rygel index of short-maturity assets, selected periods Jan.-July 1985.

POOLED EQUITY AND FIXED-INCOME FUNDS, QUARTERLY FEATURE

(p. 33-39) For quarter ended June 30, 1985. For data description, see C2710-2 above.

WORLD BANK DOUBLES PROFITS

(p. 1, 79) By Richard J. Gillespie. Article, with 1 chart showing World Bank net income, FY81-85.

REPORT FOOTNOTES GIVE BOOT TO FASB's RULES, ANNUAL FEATURE

(p. 3, 44-45, 74) Annual article, by Barry B. Burr and Rick Rosenfeld, analyzing pension fund and corporate financial data for Fortune 100 companies, 1984. Data were compiled by Wright Investors' Service from company annual financial reports.

Includes 1 detailed table showing the following for each company: pension fund total and vested benefits, assets, vested funding status, and expenses; rate of return assumed in computing pension benefits; corporate net worth, assets, and operating income; and selected ratios; 1984, with selected comparisons to 1983.

This is the 3rd annual article.

CASH MANAGEMENT: WACHOVIA, CITIBANK, CHEMICAL TOP CASH SURVEY, ANNUAL FEATURE

(p. 13-14) Annual article on corporate cash managers' ratings of bank cash management services. Data are from a 1985 *Pensions & Investment Age* survey of 1,300 managers belonging to regional cash management assns; the survey drew 12% response.

Includes 3 tables showing top 6-12 banks in ratings for 3 service categories (lockbox, disbursement, and concentration).

Also includes an accompanying article on survey methodology (p. 16).

This is the 5th survey. For description of previous article, see SRI 1984 Annual under C2710-2.520.

CASH MANAGEMENT ADDENDUM

(p. 20-22) Addendum to annual directory of institutions providing cash management services, presented in the July 22, 1985 issue. Presents profiles of 29 additional banks. For description of original feature, see C2710-2.620 above.

GROWTH OF PENSION PLANS PROJECTED

(p. 30) Article, with 1 table showing value of private pension fund assets in U.S., 9 other countries, and rest of world, as of Dec. 31, 1984 and projected for 1990. Data are from InterSec Research Corp.

MONEY MANAGERS' ADDENDUM

(p. 66-72) Addendum to annual feature profiling assets and operations of investment management organizations, appearing in the May 6, 1985 issue. Presents profiles of 37 additional organizations. For description of original feature, see C2710-2.614 above.

C2710-2.623: Sept. 2, 1985 (Vol. 13, No. 19)

POOLED SPECIAL EQUITY AND INTERNATIONAL FUNDS, QUARTERLY FEATURE

(p. 31-32, 43-44) For quarter ended June 30, 1985.

For data description, see C2710-2 above.

TOP FUNDS FOR YEAR ALSO LEAD IN QUARTER, QUARTERLY FEATURE

(p. 19-22) Quarterly article, by Alan Krauss, on investment performance of pooled real estate funds, with 2 tables showing rate of return for individual open-end and closed-end funds (with rankings), shown variously for quarter and 1- and 3-year periods ended Mar. 31, 1985, with comparisons to CPI.

Data are from *Pensions and Investments Performance Evaluation Report* (PIPER) and Evaluation Associates.

ESOPs HEADED FOR CHANGE

(p. 37) By Rick Rosenfeld. Article on proposed restructuring of employee stock ownership plans (ESOPs). Data are from the National Center for Employee Ownership.

Includes 1 table showing number of employees, and percent of stock owned by employees, for 19 companies with ESOPs, May 1985. Table covers companies with 66%/more stock owned by employees.

DREXEL STRONGER IN PLACEMENTS

(p. 42) Article, with 1 table showing top 10 investment firms ranked by value of private placements, 1984 and 1st half 1985. Data are from IDD Information Services, Inc.

C2710-2.624: Sept. 16, 1985 (Vol. 13, No. 20)

MONTHLY TABLE

(p. 47) Payden & Rygel index of short-maturity assets, selected periods ended Aug. 30, 1985.

REAL ESTATE DIRECTORY, ANNUAL FEATURE

(p. 13-35) Annual directory, for 1985, of top 100 real estate investment advisors, showing the following for each advisor: address, total and tax-exempt real estate assets managed and equity, number of tax-exempt real estate clients, executive contact, and occasionally book vs. market value of property holdings, asset distribution by property type, assets in equity vs. hybrid debt, and major clients.

Also includes 4 tables ranking top 100 advisors by total assets; and ranking top 10 advisors by tax-exempt new business assets, and by tax-exempt mortgages and real estate equity.

Data are from a *Pensions and Investment Age* annual survey.

C2710-2.625: Sept. 30, 1985 (Vol. 13, No. 21)

INVESTORS FAVORED SALOMON IN SURVEY, ANNUAL FEATURE

(p. 3, 17) Annual article, by Alan Krauss, on institutional investment managers' evaluations of brokerage firms, based on 104 responses to a *Pensions and Investment Age* survey. Includes 2 tables showing the following:

a. Brokerage commissions paid, trading costs per share, and number of firms used; and top 6 brokerage firms ranked by fees received from respondents; 1984.

b. Survey response on best firms overall, in equity research and trading, and in fixed-income research and execution; and best stock market technicians, Wall Street economists, and regional brokerage firms.

This is the 5th annual survey.

100 LARGEST INVESTMENT INSTITUTIONS AND SUBSIDIARIES

(p. 27) Table ranking 100 largest investment institutions by assets, and including assets of selected subsidiaries, as of Mar. 31, 1985 for most institutions. Also includes related article (p. 28).

SOME EQUITY MANAGERS GO WITH GROWTH STOCKS

(p. 52) Article, with 1 undated table showing 77 investment firms incorporating emerging growth stocks into their portfolios, ranked by tax-exempt assets managed. Data are from a recent *Pensions and Investment Age* survey.

FEW MANAGERS EMPLOY QUANTITATIVE ANALYSIS

(p. 54) Article, with 1 undated table showing 53 investment firms using quantitative methods to evaluate stocks, ranked by tax-exempt assets managed. Data are from a recent *Pensions and Investment Age* survey.

CONSULTANTS' CLIENTS ASKED TO BACK 401(K)

(p. 57) Article, with 1 table showing percent of eligible employees participating in 401(k) salary reduction plans and individual retirement accounts, by income level, 1983. Data are from The Wyatt Co.

C2710-2.626: Oct. 14, 1985 (Vol. 13, No. 22)

MONTHLY TABLE

(p. 43) Payden & Rygel index of short-maturity assets, selected periods ended Sept. 30, 1985.

INDEXING LURES MOST NEW MONEY, RECURRING FEATURE

(p. 3, 56) Recurring article, by Trudy Ring, with 2 tables showing top 6-13 investment firms ranked by new accounts and new assets managed, 3rd quarter 1985. Data are from *Pensions and Investment Age*.

DATA BASE, ANNUAL FEATURE

(p. 16-34) Annual directory of investment service data bases and software systems offered for microcomputers, showing the following for each system: address, system description, access requirements, and occasionally number of clients, data base size, and access fees.

Data are from a recent *Pensions and Investment Age* survey. Also includes accompanying article (p. 15, 34). For description of previous directory, see SRI 1984 Annual under C2710-2.523.

DOMESTIC ISSUES TOP 1984 LEVEL, RECURRING FEATURE

(p. 37-38) Recurring article, by Marci Baker, with 2 tables showing top 10 investment management firms ranked by underwriting issues and value, for mortgage-related and initial public offerings; and for all, bond, and stock issues, by type; 1st 9 months 1985. Data are from IDD Information Services, Inc.

CURRENT ACCOUNTS, QUARTERLY FEATURE

(p. 54-56) Quarterly tabular list of new institutional investment accounts recently acquired by approximately 150 investment management firms, showing for each: client name, type of fund, and amount managed. Data are compiled by *Pensions and Investment Age*.

This is the 1st quarterly feature. Similar information previously was published on a monthly basis, but was not covered in SRI.

C2710-2.627: Oct. 28, 1985 (Vol. 13, No. 23)

FUNDING OF SYSTEMS IS BETTER THAN EXPECTED

(p. 19-20) By Chuck Paustian. Article, with 1 table showing State employee retirement system funded ratios (assets as percent of accrued liabilities), and interest and salary contribution rates, by State, various dates June 30, 1982-Oct. 1, 1984.

Data are from Martin E. Segal Co., and a survey conducted by National Assn of State Retirement Administrators.

MANAGERS PUT MARKET TIMING IN USE

(p. 64) Article, with 1 undated table showing tax-exempt assets managed by each of 26 investment firms using market timing (shifting of assets based on market outlook) as a management method. Data are from a recent *Pensions and Investment Age* survey.

FEW CHOOSE PASSIVE PATH

(p. 66) Article, with 1 undated table showing tax-exempt assets managed by each of 22 investment firms using passive management (investment in index funds). Data are from a recent *Pensions and Investment Age* survey.

C2825
Daily Racing Form, Inc.

C2825-1   1984 SURVEY ON SPORTS ATTENDANCE
Annual. Mar. 1985.
8 p. no paging.
SRI/MF/complete

Annual report on attendance at horse races and other spectator sports, 1984, with trends from 1940. Data are from sports assns and publications.

Includes 4 tables showing thoroughbred and harness/trotting race attendance, compared to 10 other sports nationwide and to major league baseball in 8 cities, 1984 with change from 1983; and thoroughbred racing days and/or attendance, annually 1940-84, and by State for 1984.

Availability: Daily Racing Form, Inc., Ten Lake Dr., Hightstown NJ 08520, †; SRI/MF/ complete.

C2950
Decisions Publications

C2950–3   MARKETING AND MEDIA DECISIONS

Monthly, and special annual issues.
ISSN 0195-4296.
LC 80-640244.
SRI/MF/excerpts, shipped quarterly

Monthly journal (with 3 annual special issues) covering topics related to advertising media selection. Includes recurring data on advertising costs and expenditures, by media and/or brand.

Data are from private research firms, advertising agencies, Federal Government, and individual companies.

Issues generally contain:

a. Feature articles, often with statistics; and editorial depts.

b. "Media Cost Index" monthly feature, with 7-11 charts on costs of purchasing specified units of advertising time or space, for nighttime and daytime network and spot TV, spot and network radio, national supplements, consumer magazines, daily newspapers, business publications, and outdoor advertising. Data are excerpted from industry published sources (identified for each chart), and are shown for month 4-5 months prior to cover date, with illustrative comparisons to previous months and year.

c. "Brand Report" feature article, evaluating recent advertising expenditures and strategies of selected products or industries, usually including 1-3 tables.

Annual statistical features include surveys of advertising expenditures by leading brands, and media costs.

Monthly "Media Cost Index" feature appears in all regular issues. All additional features with substantial statistical content are described, as they appear, under "Statistical Features." Non-statistical features are not covered.

Availability: Marketing and Media Decisions, 1140 Ave. of the Americas, New York NY 10036, qualified subscribers †, others $40.00 per yr., single copy $3.00; SRI/MF/excerpts for cost index charts and all portions covered under "Statistical Features;" shipped quarterly.

Issues reviewed during 1985: Nov. 1984-Oct. 1985; and Business Marketing, Spring, and Fall Special Issues for 1985 (P) (Vol. 19, Nos. 14-15; Vol. 20, Nos. 1-13).

STATISTICAL FEATURES:

C2950–3.601: Nov. 1984 (Vol. 19, No. 14)

SELLING BUSINESS INFORMATION TO U.S. BUSINESSES

(p. 25) Article, with 1 table showing business expenditures on information, by category, 1983 with change from 1982. Data are from Cox, Lloyd Associates.

MINING THOSE LOCAL AD NUGGETS

(p. 57-59, 108-112) Article, with 1 table showing cable TV local advertising revenue, and subscribers in advertising systems (number and as percent of total subscribers), for 15 major multiple system operators, 1983 and/or 1984. Data are from Paul Kagan Associates, Inc.

"DAILY NEWS" TRIES TO FIND ITS WAY

(p. 64-65, 168-174) Article, with 3 tables comparing weekday circulation and advertising linage for 3 leading NYC daily newspapers, various periods 1979-84. Data are from Audit Bureau of Circulation, and Media Records.

Additional data appear in the Jan. 1985 issue (see C2950-3.603 below).

BRAND REPORT 104: SOFTWARE

(p. 143-154) Article, with 2 tables showing computer software sales value, by home and business market segment, 1982-84 and 1989; and most prevalent microcomputer software applications among Fortune 1000 firms (no date). Data are from Future Computing and Newton-Evans.

C2950–3.602: Dec. 1984 (Vol. 19, No. 15)

INVESTORS DISTRUST ANNUAL REPORTS

(p. 8) Article, with 1 table showing investors' ratings of importance for 13 sections of corporate annual reports. Data are from a recent Hill and Knowlton survey of 247 individual investors and 50 security analysts. Includes 1 table.

NO DECLINE IN CO-OP FUNDING

(p. 28) Brief article, with 1 undated table showing average cooperative retail advertising expense reimbursements by top 20 manufacturers. Data are from Multi-Ad Services, Inc.

MRI CABLE STATS

Article, with 1 table presenting the following data for viewers of 16 cable TV networks, for subscribers to cable, pay, and subscription TV, and for the total population: number, median age, and median income, by sex, fall 1984. Data are from surveys conducted by Mediamark Research, Inc., during 1983-84.

SIMMONS CHARTS DIRECT MARKETING SURGE

(p. 33) Article, with 1 undated table ranking top 10 advertising media by share of retail sales orders generated. Data are from Simmons Market Research Bureau.

EUROPE'S HIGH TECH GLAMOUR

(p. 62-66, 84-86) Article, with 1 table showing number of TV households, basic cable TV market penetration and revenues, and direct broadcast satellite market penetration, for 8 European countries, selected years 1982-95. Data are from *Marketing and Media Decisions* and other private sources.

ARE OUR PRINT MEDIA GOING GLOBAL?

(p. 70-72, 136) Article, with 3 tables showing international advertising revenues and top product categories, and circulation by world area, for international editions of 8-16 U.S. magazines; and percent of Europeans reporting poor/no familiarity with English, by country. Advertising data are for 1983; other data are undated. Data sources include *Rome Reports* and the Pan European survey.

BRAND REPORT 105: CIGARETTES

(p. 99-106) Article, with 2 tables showing cigarette advertising expenditures by media, 1983; and market shares, 1st half 1984, by manufacturer and brand. Data are from Leading National Advertisers, Media Records, and Laidlaw Ansbacher.

C2950–3.603: Jan. 1985 (Vol. 20, No. 1)

SOME SETBACKS, BUT OVERALL, CABLE GAINS

(p. 22) Article, with 1 table showing average primetime and full-day household viewership for 9 advertiser-supported cable TV networks, 2nd-3rd quarters 1984, with rankings by viewership for 3rd quarter 1984. Data are from A. C. Nielsen Co.

ADDENDA

(p. 33) Additional data for Nov. 1984 article on weekday circulation and advertising linage for 3 NYC daily newspapers. Includes 1 table on Sunday and/or weekday advertising linage for each newspaper, 1st half 1983-84 with change from 1st half 1982.

For description of original article, see C2950-3.601 above.

ADVERTISERS FLOCK TO AD-SUPPORTED SYNDICATION

(p. 57-66) Article, with 6 tables showing the following for syndicated TV programs arranged by type: distributor, number of episodes available, and minutes of local and/or national advertising time allotted and whether available on barter or cash/barter terms, generally for programs available as of Sept. 1985. Data sources include Petry TV.

MAGAZINE ADVERTISING EXPENDITURES

(p. 76-77) By Debbie Solomon. Article, with 2 tables showing top 20 magazines ranked by advertising expenditures, with amount spent for network and spot TV; and advertising expenditure per 1,000 copies sold, and readers per copy, for 20 magazines with highest circulation; 1983. Data are from Leading National Advertisers, Inc.

BRAND REPORT 106: FAST PALATE-PLEASERS TEMPT BABY BOOMERS

(p. 83-90) Article, with 1 table showing advertising expenditures by media type, for top 2-3 restaurant chains in each of 5 food categories, ranked by total advertising expenditures, 1st half 1984. Data are from Leading National Advertisers and the Radio Advertising Bureau.

C2950–3.604: Feb. 1985 (Vol. 20, No. 2)

LONG-TERM MEDIA OUTLOOK

(p. 20) Article, with 1 chart showing advertising cost index, by media, 1989 and trends. Data are from D'Arcy MacManus Masius.

BATTLE OF THE INSERTS—NEWSPAPERS vs. MAILBOX

(p. 62-68, 124) Article, with 1 chart showing grocery and health/beauty aids coupon distribution, by media type, 1983. Data are from A. C. Nielsen Co.

CABLE AD SCORECARD, ANNUAL FEATURE

(p. 76-84) Annual feature profiling the top 20 agencies in cable TV advertising, 1984-85. Data are from individual company reports. Each profile includes data on cable TV billings by agency, 1984-85.

BRAND REPORT 107: THE "NOUVELLE" PET FOOD MARKET

(p. 115-123) Article, with 4 tables showing pet food advertising expenditures, by company and media, 1st half 1984; pet food market shares, by company and type of food, 1983; and percent of households owning dogs and cats, by income level (no date).

Data are from *Petfood Industry,* Leading National Advertisers, Radio Advertising Bureau, and American Veterinary Medical Assn.

C2950-3.605: Mar. 1985 (Vol. 20, No. 3)

GAUGING SOCIAL EFFECT OF WORKING WOMEN

(p. 36-38) Article on public perceptions regarding working women. Data are from an R. H. Bruskin Associates survey of 1,000 adults. Includes 1 undated table showing response distribution concerning whether working women have positive, negative, or no effect on selected aspects of the economy, personal relationships, and childrearing, by sex.

LICENSED PRODUCTS PASS $40 BILLION MARK

(p. 40) Article, with 1 table showing licensed product sales by product category, 1984. Data are from *The Licensing Letter.*

GREENING OF THE MATURITY MARKET

(p. 72-80, 146-152) Article, with 2 charts and 1 table showing per capita income and discretionary income share, 1980 or 1981; and percent change in population, decennially 1990-2020; by age. Data are from Census Bureau and Conference Board.

CONTEMPORARY HIT RADIO BANDWAGON

(p. 112-114) By Paul Thury. Article, with 1 undated table showing share of audience aged 12/over, for radio stations with contemporary hit formats in top 10 radio market cities. Data are from Arbitron Co.

BRAND REPORT 108: IMPORTED CARS

(p. 117-128) Article, with 3 tables showing top 5 Japanese and European auto manufacturers ranked by U.S. sales in 1984, and including advertising expenditures by media during 1st half 1984; and buyer characteristics (percent men, married persons, college graduates, and professionals), for all, Japanese, and European 1984 model year autos.

Most data are from Leading National Advertisers, and J. David Power Associates.

C2950-3.606: Apr. 1985 (Vol. 20, No. 5)

55 COMPUTER BOOKS 'BYTE' THE DUST

(p. 8) Article, with 1 chart showing computer magazine startups and failures, 1975/prior and 1976-84. Data are from *Marketing Technology.*

EFFECTS OF SMOKING ON PRODUCTIVITY

(p. 32) Article, with 1 undated table showing supervisors' perceptions of smoking's effect on productivity, by industry division. Data are based on interviews with approximately 1,500 supervisors, conducted by Response Analysis Corp. in a study commissioned by the Tobacco Institute.

FINANCIAL CABLE NETS MEAN BUSINESS

(p. 60, 64-65, 156-157) Article, with 3 tables presenting selected audience and/or advertising cost data for specific business/financial programs on cable TV, 5 leading business/financial periodicals, and 5 network news programs, various periods 2nd half 1984-1st quarter 1985. Data are from A. C. Nielsen Co., Audit Bureau of Circulations, Mediamark Research, and Paul Kagan Associates.

SPECIAL REPORT: RADIO

(p. 83-120) Compilation of articles on radio advertising. Data are from Radio Expenditure Reports, and Broadcast Advertisers Reports, Inc.

Includes 4 tables ranking top 100 companies and top 30 product categories by national spot and network radio advertising expenditures for 1984, with 1983 comparison for companies, and expenditures for top 3 brands within each product category.

OVERVIEW OF THE SCIENCE MAGAZINE CATEGORY

(p. 124, 128) By John Camilleri. Article, with 1 undated table presenting selected comparisons of 5 leading science magazines, including circulation, selected reader demographics, subscription/single copy sales ratio, advertising/editorial page ratio, and policy on tobacco advertisements.

MEDIA COSTS ADD UP TO MARKETING OPPORTUNITIES

(p. 132-134) By Larry Kelley. Article, with 1 undated table ranking 10 highest and 10 lowest markets by index of TV advertising cost per capita. Data are from *Media Market Guide.*

BRAND REPORT 109: AIRLINES

(p. 141-154) Article, with 3 tables showing airline advertising expenditures, by carrier and media type, 1st half 1984; passenger and total revenues, and operating income and expenses, for major, national, and new entrant carriers, 1979-85; and passengers at top 10 airports, 1983.

Data are from Leading National Advertisers, L. F. Rothschild Unterberg Towbin, and Air Transport Assn of America.

Additional data appear in the May 1985 issue (see C2950-3.607 below).

C2950-3.607: May 1985 (Vol. 20, No. 6)

AIRLINE AD DOLLARS IN NEWSPAPERS FOR 1984

(p. 24) Table showing newspaper advertising expenditures of 14 airlines, 1984. Data are from Media Records.

Table is an addendum to Brand Report 109 on airlines; for description, see C2950-3.606 above.

REAL BABY BOOMERS

(p. 30) Article, with 1 chart showing distribution of adult population by age group, 1984. Data are from Simmons Market Research Bureau.

ECONOMIC OUTLOOK FROM BUSINESS PRESS

(p. 32-33) Article, with 1 table showing forecast value or annual percent change for 12 economic indicators, selected periods 1984-86, with actual year-end totals for 1984. Data are from Cahners Publishing Co.

WISHBONE OFFENSE: BRANDING A COMMODITY

(p. 80-84, 176) Article, with 1 chart showing market share for 3 chicken products (whole, parts, and processed), 1979 and 1984. Data are from National Broiler Council.

NEWSPAPER RATE DIFFERENTIALS

(p. 101, 104) By Debbie Solomon. Article, with 3 tables showing percent difference in rates charged to national vs. local newspaper advertisers, by circulation size 1982 and 1984,

and aggregate for selected years 1933-84; with detail for rates charged by 10 leading newspapers, 1984. Data are from American Assn of Advertising Agencies.

TUNING IN TO VCR USAGE

(p. 119-120) By Betsy Frank. Article, with text data showing average TV use in households with and without videocassette recorders (VCR); with detail for VCR households, including use of TV to play taped material, and whether TV programs are viewed during taping; by day part, Dec. 1984. Data are from A. C. Nielsen Co.

BRAND REPORT 110: BEER

(p. 123-138) Article, with 3 tables showing advertising expenditures of 5 leading domestic brewers, by media, 1st 9 months, 1984; market shares for top 9 brewers, selected years 1979-84; and market shares and production for top 10 brands, 1984. Data are from *Beverage Industry,* and advertising industry sources.

C2950-3.608: June 1985 (Vol. 20, No. 8)

RADIO'S TOP 10

(p. 24) Article, with 2 tables ranking top 10 advertising agencies by percent and amount of billings spent on radio advertisements, 1984. Data are from Radio Advertising Bureau.

COMBINED NETWORK SHARE DROPS 4%

(p. 24) Article, with 1 table showing top 12 TV specials ranked by household audience ratings, 1984. Data are from Arbitron Co.

ABC's NEWSPAPER FAS-FAX

(p. 33) Article, with 1 table showing percent of newspapers with increasing, decreasing, and unchanged circulations, by size group, for morning, all-day, evening, and Sunday papers, 6-month period ending Mar. 1985. Data are from Audit Bureau of Circulations.

SNIFF THIS VCR

(p. 42) Article, with 1 chart showing market shares worldwide for Betamax vs. VHS videocassette recorders, 1975 or 1976 and 1983. Data are from Communications Studies and Planning Inc.

COMPUTER MAGAZINES: A PERSPECTIVE

(p. 66-73, 188) Article, with 1 chart and 3 tables showing computer magazine mergers/failures since 1984, by magazine category; distribution of computer advertising expenditures, by media (no date); and computer magazine 1st quarter advertising revenues and/or pages, by publication, 1984 and/or 1985. Data are from specified published sources.

RESTORING JAGUAR'S ROAR

(p. 75-79, 192) Article, with 2 charts and 1 table showing sales volume for 9 makes of luxury cars, 1982-84; and luxury car market shares by category (new-luxury, world class, and traditional), 1984 and 1990. Data are from J. D. Power and Associates.

PEPSI LOBS WILSON OUT OF BOUNDS

(p. 88-94, 186) Article, with 2 tables showing sales volume and value for tennis rackets, tennis balls, and golf clubs (individual and sets), 1976-84 or 1983-84. Data are from an annual survey by the National Sporting Goods Assn.

Full survey report is covered in SRI under A8485-2.

1984 BRAND LEADERS IN NEWSPAPERS, ANNUAL FEATURE

(p. 101-136) Annual article on national newspaper advertising expenditures, by service or product type and leading brands and companies, 1984 and trends. Data are from Media Records.

Includes 5 tables showing national newspaper advertising expenditures for the following:

a. Automobile companies, top 25 makes, with detail for pickup/camper, factory, dealer assn, and local dealer ads, 1984; and top 20 cigarette brands, 1982-84.

b. 100 leading advertisers, 1983-84; 3 leading brands or companies in selected product/service categories, 1980-84; and by detailed product/service category, 1983-84.

Detailed survey report is available for $1,125 from Media Records, 370 Seventh Ave., New York NY 10001. Individual product reports are also available, for $115-$325.

C2950–3.609: July 1985 (Vol. 20, No. 9)

BOOM CONTINUES FOR VCR's

(p. 6) Article, with 2 tables on market outlook for videocassette recorders (VCRs) and other home electronic media. Includes homes with VCRs (number, and as percent of TV households), 1985-94; and installed base, shipments, and revenues, for VCRs and home computers, and selected market indicators for cable TV and telephones, 1984 and 1989.

Data are from Paul Kagan Associates and Link Resources.

ROCKY TIMES FOR MICROS

(p. 8) Article, with 1 table showing top 7 microcomputer software suppliers and top 8 microcomputer manufacturers ranked by revenues, 1st quarter 1985, with comparisons to 1st quarter 1984, and including net income for each company, 1st quarter 1984-85. Data are from Digital Information Group.

NEWSPAPERS SET NEW RECORDS IN 1984

(p. 22) Article, with 1 chart showing circulation for Sunday, morning, and evening newspapers, selected years 1946-84. Data are from '85 Facts About Newspapers, compiled by American Newspaper Publishers Assn.

For description of full report, see A2350-4.

14th ANNUAL REPORT: THE TOP 200 BRANDS

(p. 45-122) Annual report on advertising expenditures, by media, for top 200 advertised brands, 1984 and trends. Data are from various media research organizations, including Leading National Advertisers Inc., Media Records, Broadcast Advertisers Reports, and Radio Expenditure Reports. Includes the following:

a. Index of brand profiles; narrative summary; list of brands added to and dropped from the top 200 in 1984; and 1 table showing top 200 brands ranked by advertising expenditures, 1984, with comparisons to 1981-83. (p. 48-58)

b. Profiles for top 200 advertised brands, each including parent company; marketing and advertising executives; advertising agencies and executives; and 1 table showing advertising expenditures, by media, 1983-84. (p. 60-122)

WHO'S SQUEEZING WHOM IN THE LEMON-LIME WARS?

(p. 125-127, 166) Article, with 2 tables comparing the following for 7-Up and Sprite soft drink brands: advertising expenditures, by media, 1983-84; and market shares and case sales, 1982-84. Data are from industry sources.

MAXXUM CLICKS FOR MINOLTA

(p. 138-142, 168) Article, with 1 table showing shipments of lens shutter/range finder and single-lens reflex 35mm cameras, 1975-84. Data are from The Wolfman Report.

MESSAGE OR MEDIUM?

(p. 146-149) By Stephen Martin. Article, with 1 undated table showing public opinion on credibility of advertising in 5 media. Data are from 1,001 responses to a survey conducted by Opinion Research Corp. for the Newspaper Advertising Bureau.

CABLE BUYING POWER

(p. 150, 156) By Beverly O'Malley. Article, with 2 text tables showing selected characteristics of cable TV viewers, including product usage by product type, 1984. Data are from Simmons Market Research Bureau.

C2950–3.610: Aug. 1985 (Vol. 20, No. 10)

ATTITUDES TOWARD ADS: SOME CHANGE THEIR MINDS

(p. 8) Article, with 1 table showing consumer attitudes toward advertising, including perceived quality and product claim credibility, 1974 and 1985. Data are from a Jan. 1985 survey of 800 persons conducted by Ogilvy & Mather, and a similar survey conducted by American Assn of Advertising Agencies in 1974.

PAY TV SEES ITS GROWTH SLOW DOWN

(p. 22) Article, with 1 table showing new cable TV subscriptions for pay services, 1975-84. Data are from Paul Kagan Associates.

BIG PLANS FOR MEDIA PLANNING

(p. 24) Article, with 1 undated table showing importance of selected advertising industry concerns, including cost control, compensation, and government restrictions, as rated by advertising executives. Data are from a recent Vitt Media survey of 101 senior-level executives.

INDIES GAIN

(p. 30) Article, with 1 table showing spot TV expenditures for top 25 advertisers, and including independent station shares, 1st quarter 1985. Data are from Broadcast Advertisers Reports.

FROM FAN LOYALTY TO BRAND LOYALTY

(p. 42-45, 83-85) Article, with 2 tables showing TV advertising revenues from sports programming, for 3 major networks, 1979-84; and subscribers or date of startup, owner, sector and/or area covered, and market areas represented, by cable TV sports service (no date). Data are from Broadcast Advertisers Reports, and QV Publishing Inc.

INFLUENCING THE INFLUENTIALS

(p. 56-60, 116) Article, with 2 tables showing newspaper advertising expenditures, for 30 selected companies; and top 15 magazines ranked by corporate/assn advertising pages, with revenues generated; 1984. Data are from Media Records and Publishers Information Bureau.

DEMOGRAPHIC EROSION: PROBLEM FOR FOOTBALL SPONSORS?

(p. 74-77) By Ed Papazian. Article, with 1 table showing percent of adult population watching Monday night professional football telecast, by sex, age, race, and educational attainment, fall 1977 and 1984. Data are from Simmons Market Research Bureau.

BRAND REPORT 113: LIQUOR

(p. 88-104 passim) Article, with 4 tables showing the following for distilled spirits: consumer distribution by sex, and market shares, both by detailed product type; adult per capita consumption, with comparisons to beer and wine; and advertising expenditures, by media; various years 1970-84.

Data are from Simmons Market Research Bureau, Impact Databank, Leading National Advertisers, and Media Records.

C2950–3.611: Sept. 1985 (Vol. 20, No. 11)

WOMEN ADOPT THE SPORTING LIFE

(p. 20) Article, with 1 table showing adults participating in selected sports activities on 1 occasion in past 12-month period and all year long, with detail for female total and new participants, all by activity, 1984. Data are from American Sports Data, Inc.

CABLE'S REACH INTO THE TOP MARKETS

(p. 38) Article, with 1 table showing the following for the 10 largest areas of dominant influence: cable and total TV households, and households with cable TV available, 1983-84; and ranking in number of cable TV households, 1984. Data are from Paul Kagan Associates.

YUPPIE WAY OF THINKING

(p. 42) Article, with 1 undated table showing prices that the general population, and "yuppie" (young upwardly-mobile professional) and "non-yuppie" baby boomers (persons born 1945-60 period) are willing to pay for selected commodities. Data are from a Market Facts study of 1,385 consumers, including 412 baby boomers.

VCRs: THE SAGA CONTINUES

(p. 83-88, 156-158) Article on home video equipment market. Data are from Electronic Industries Assn and Paul Kagan Associates. Includes 2 tables showing the following:

a. Unit sales to retailers of videocassette recorders (VCRs), color video cameras, and TVs by type, June and 1st half 1984-85.

b. VCR shipments to dealers, unit sales to institutions, and obsolete unit replacements; and VCRs per household, new VCR households, and total VCR and TV households; 1985-94.

IS BIGGER BETTER?

(p. 111-113) By Allen Banks. Article comparing selected audience characteristics for top-rated and average-rated TV programs, including attentiveness, loyalty, and advertising recall among female viewers aged 18-49. Includes 9 undated tables.

LATE NIGHT TV'S FLICKERING PICTURE

(p. 114-118) By Donna Campanella. Article, with 5 tables showing ratings for 4 late night network TV programs, by sex and age group, various periods 1982-85. Data are from A. C. Nielsen Co.

NATIONAL SUNDAY MAGAZINES

(p. 118-120) By Debbie Solomon. Article, with 1 undated table showing the following for 5-6 Sunday newspaper magazines: distribution of readers by sex; median age and household income of readers; and newspapers carrying magazine, aggregate circulation, and advertising costs. Data are from Leo Burnett.

BRAND REPORT 114: HOME ELECTRONICS

(p. 125-142, 146-150) Article, with 1 table showing color TV advertising expenditures by media, for 5 color TV manufacturers, 1984 and 1st quarter 1985. Data are from Leading National Advertisers and Media Records.

C2950-3.612: Fall 1985 (Vol. 20, No. 12)

MEDIA COSTS, ANNUAL ISSUE

Annual special issue on media advertising costs. Includes the annual statistical features described below.

FORECAST 1986: RATES WILL RISE BUT CAUTION WILL RULE, ANNUAL FEATURE

(p. 8-12) Annual article on media cost outlook for 1986, based on a *Marketing and Media Decisions* survey of media directors. Includes 3 tables showing actual and anticipated changes in media unit cost, audience, and cost-per-thousand, by media, various years 1981-86.

This is the 15th annual forecast.

ECONOMY'S BIG CHILL: ADVERTISERS AND MEDIA AWAIT A WARMING TREND, ANNUAL FEATURE

(p. 15-20, 99) Annual article, with 1 table showing forecasts of 5 economists for 4 economic indicators, 2nd half 1985-1st half 1986.

Previous article is described in SRI 1984 Annual under C2950-3.513.

TED BATES REVIEWS A DECADE AT THE RACES, ANNUAL FEATURE

(p. 25-30) Annual article on media cost trends, 1976-85. Data are from Ted Bates Advertising. Includes 5 tables showing advertising cost-per-thousand indexes, and total and national advertising expenditures, with detail by media and comparisons to CPI and GNP, various periods 1976-85.

TELEVISION PRICES MAY GO SKY HIGH, DESPITE THE CLOUDY PICTURE, ANNUAL FEATURE

(p. 33-41, 100) Annual article, with 1 table showing network and spot TV advertising expenditures for top 10 TV advertisers ranked by total TV advertising expenditures, 1984. Data are from Television Bureau of Advertising.

Previous article is described in SRI 1984 Annual under C2950-3.513.

CABLE PUTS A LID ON RISES AS IT REDEFINES ITS BASE, ANNUAL FEATURE

(p. 43-48, 97-98) Annual article on developments in cable TV advertising. Data are from Paul Kagan Associates, Inc. and Broadcast Advertisers Reports. Includes 4 tables showing the following:

a. Cable network subscribers, May 1984-85; and audience ratings and advertising cost estimates, by programming category (no date); for top 11 networks ranked by number of subscribers.

b. Top 10 cable advertisers ranked by 1984 expenditures, with comparison to 1983.

c. Homes with TVs, and cable TV homes available to advertising-supported cable networks, both with adjustments for number of homes actually viewing TV; and revenues for major broadcast networks and advertising-supported cable networks; 1984-94.

d. Subscribers and advertising revenues, for 15 advertising-supported cable networks, 1984-85.

Previous article is described in SRI 1984 Annual under C2950-3.513.

RADIO MAY BE HOT, BUT ITS RATE HIKES ARE NOT, ANNUAL FEATURE

(p. 51-54, 101-102) Annual article, with 2 tables showing top 10 radio advertisers ranked by spot and network advertising expenditures, 1984. Data are from Broadcast Advertisers Report, and Radio Expenditures Reports.

Previous article is described in SRI 1984 Annual under C2950-3.513.

AGENCIES TO MAGAZINES: KEEP IT CLOSE TO 7%, ANNUAL FEATURE

(p. 57-62, 103-104) Annual article on consumer magazine advertising and rate setting, 1985. Data are from Magazine Publishers Assn. and James B. Kobak.

Includes 4 tables showing consumer magazine advertising, subscription, and single copy shares of total revenue, and expenses and profit as percent of revenues, various years 1970-85; and top 10 magazine and Sunday magazine advertisers ranked by expenditures, 1984.

'ONE MORE TIME' FOR THE BUSINESS PRESS, ANNUAL FEATURE

(p. 65-71, 95) Annual article on business magazine advertising and rate setting, 1985. Data are from J. Walter Thompson and James B. Kobak.

Includes 3 tables showing the following for business magazines: aggregate revenues of 100 publications, by publication category, 1974 and 1984; advertising revenues for 6 individual publications, 1980, 1983, and 1984; and advertising and subscription shares of total revenues, selected years 1970-85.

NEWSPAPERS HAVE A SURPRISE FOR AGENCIES, ANNUAL FEATURE

(p. 73-78) Annual article, with 1 table and 1 chart showing top 10 newspaper advertisers ranked by expenditures, 1984, with comparison to 1983; and newspaper advertising general rate index, 1980-84 and Jan.-June 1984. Data are from Media Records and Newspaper Advertising Bureau.

Previous article is described in SRI 1984 Annual under C2950-3.513.

OUTDOOR'S RATE FORECAST: A COOL 6%-TO-7% RISE, ANNUAL FEATURE

(p. 80-83) Annual article on outdoor advertising costs. Data are from Leading National Advertisers and the Institute of Outdoor Advertising. Includes 2 tables showing top 10 outdoor advertisers ranked by expenditures, 1984; and poster panel costs aggregated for top 50 metro markets, monthly Jan. 1977-Sept. 1985.

DIRECT MARKETERS SEEK TO STEADY RATES, ANNUAL FEATURE

(p. 91-94) Annual article on direct marketing costs. Most data are from Direct Marketing Assn. Includes 2 tables showing top 10 direct

market advertisers ranked by expenditures, 1983-84; and direct mail advertising costs by component, 1984.

Previous article is described in SRI 1984 Annual under C2950-3.513.

C2950-3.613: Oct. 1985 (Vol. 20, No. 13)

MORE ON THE CD MARKET

(p. 14) Article on market outlook for compact disc (CD) players. Data are from a *Newsweek* survey.

Includes 1 undated chart showing sources of information on stereo equipment cited by all respondents and by those intending to purchase a CD player.

LIVABLE ALTERNATIVES

(p. 20) Article, with 1 undated table showing 25 most and least livable MSAs, as rated by *American Demographics,* with comparison to Rand McNally ratings.

SCIENCE BOOKS SEARCH FOR THE RIGHT FORMULA

(p. 53-57, 144-150) Article, with 2 tables showing science magazine advertising pages and revenues, 1984-85; and advertising rate base and cost-per-thousand, and reader median age and household income, generally 1st half 1985; all for 6 science magazines. Data are from Publishers Information Bureau and Simmons Market Research Bureau.

BRAND REPORT 126: CIGARETTES

(p. 104-118) Article, with 1 table showing cigarette advertising expenditures by media, for 15 leading brands, 1984. Data are from Leading National Advertisers and Media Records.

C3150
Dun and Bradstreet

C3150-1   **MONTHLY BANK CLEARING REPORT**
Monthly. 5 p.
ISSN 0027-0199.
SRI/MF/complete, shipped quarterly

Monthly report on bank check clearings in NYC and 25 other major cities, compiled from Federal Reserve Bank records. Report is issued approximately 2 months after month of coverage.

Contains narrative summary, and 3 tables showing the following:

a. Comparisons of clearings, by city, for current month, preceding month, and same month of preceding year; and cumulatively for current year to date and same period of previous 2 years. 2 tables.

b. Total clearings for 26 cities, NYC, and 25 cities excluding NYC, monthly for year to date and preceding 3-4 years. 1 table.

Table showing cumulative data begins in Mar. 1985 issue.

Availability: Dun and Bradstreet, Economic Analysis Department, 299 Park Ave., New York NY 10171, price on request; SRI/MF/complete, shipped quarterly.

Issues reviewed during 1985: Aug. 1984-July 1985 (D).

C3150–2   MONTHLY FAILURES
Monthly. Approx. 4 p.
SRI/MF/complete

Monthly report on business failures and aggregate liabilities of failed companies. Report is compiled by Dun and Bradstreet and is issued approximately 15 months after month of coverage; publication time may vary according to data availability.

Contains narrative summary; and 7 tables showing business failures and liabilities, by census division, State, industry division and major group, and liability size group, and for 25 largest cities. Also includes adjusted and unadjusted indexes based on number of failures per 10,000 enterprises listed in *Dun & Bradstreet Reference Book.* Data are shown for month of coverage or year to date, with comparisons to previous year.

Report was suspended following the issue presenting data for July 1982 (for description, see SRI 1983 Annual under C3150-2). Report resumes with a special cumulative issue presenting data for Jan.-Dec. 1983.

A similar quarterly report with data by detailed industry is also covered by SRI, under C3150-6.

Availability: Dun and Bradstreet, Economic Analysis Department, 299 Park Ave., New York NY 10171, $18.00 per yr.; SRI/MF/complete.

Issues reviewed during 1985: Cumulative Jan.-Dec. 1983 (D) (K-25, Nos. 1-12).

C3150–3   NEW BUSINESS
INCORPORATIONS
Monthly. Approx. 5 p.
SRI/MF/complete, shipped
quarterly

Monthly report on new business incorporations, by census division and State. Report is compiled by Dun and Bradstreet and generally is issued 3-8 months after month of coverage.

Contains narrative summary; and 1-3 tables showing unadjusted new business incorporations by census division and State, for month of coverage and year to date, and same periods of previous year, with comparison to month prior to month of coverage. Also shows seasonally adjusted totals for month of coverage and selected prior periods.

Prior to the Jan. 1984 issue, report was designated *Monthly New Incorporations.*

Availability: Dun and Bradstreet, Economic Analysis Department, 299 Park Ave., New York NY 10171, $18.00 per yr.; SRI/MF/complete, shipped quarterly.

Issues reviewed during 1985: Jan. 1984-Apr. 1985 (D).

C3150–4   BUSINESS EXPECTATIONS
Quarterly.
SRI/MF/complete

Quarterly report on business executives' expectations for sales, profits, selling prices, inventory levels, employment, and new orders. Shows executives expecting increase, decrease, and no change in each indicator for current quarter compared with same quarter of previous year. Includes detail for durable and nondurable goods manufacturers, wholesalers, and retailers.

Data are from surveys of approximately 1,400 executives conducted approximately 6 weeks prior to quarter of coverage. Report is issued 2-4 weeks after beginning of quarter covered.

Contains narrative summary of survey findings, with 1 table and generally 1-3 trend charts.

Availability: Dun and Bradstreet, Economic Analysis Department, 299 Park Ave., New York NY 10171, $23.00 per yr.; SRI/MF/complete.

Issues reviewed during 1985: 3rd Qtr. 1984-2nd Qtr. 1985 (D).

C3150–6   BUSINESS FAILURES:
QUARTERLY FAILURE
REPORT
Quarterly. Approx. 4 p.
SRI/MF/complete

Quarterly report containing 1 table showing business failures, and aggregate liabilities of failed companies, by detailed industry group, quarterly for year to date. Report is compiled by Dun and Bradstreet, and is usually issued 6-12 months after quarter of coverage.

Report was suspended following the issue presenting data through 2nd quarter 1982 (for description, see SRI 1983 Annual under C3150-6). Report resumes with the issue presenting data through 4th quarter 1983.

Prior to the 4th quarter 1983 issue, report was designated as *Dun's Statistical Review: Quarterly Failure Report, Detailed Divisions of Industry.*

A similar monthly report with data by geographic location is also covered by SRI, under C3150-2.

Availability: Dun and Bradstreet, Economic Analysis Department, 299 Park Ave., New York NY 10171, $23.00 per yr.; SRI/MF/complete.

Issues reviewed during 1985: 4th Qtr. 1983 (D).

C3150–7   BUILDING PERMITS
Monthly.
SRI/MF/complete

Monthly report on value of building permits issued in the 200 most populous cities. Data are compiled by Dun and Bradstreet. Report is issued 5-10 months after period of coverage, depending on availability of data.

Contains narrative summary; and 2 tables showing building permit value for 200 largest cities ranked by population size and/or percent change in permit value, for period of coverage, with comparison to previous year. Also includes detail for 5 NYC boroughs.

Report was suspended following the issue presenting data for Jan. 1982 (for description, see SRI 1983 Annual under C3150-7). Report resumes with the issue covering 1st quarter 1984, and will temporarily continue on a quarterly schedule.

Availability: Dun and Bradstreet, Economic Analysis Department, 299 Park Ave., New York NY 10171, $18.00 per yr.; SRI/MF/complete.

Issues reviewed during 1985: 1st-3rd Qtrs. 1984 (D).

C3150–8   1982-83 BUSINESS
FAILURE RECORD, DUN
AND BRADSTREET
Annual. 1985. 15 p.
SRI/MF/not filmed

Annual report on business failures, 1982-83, with trends from 1926. Includes number and/or liabilities of failed businesses, by industry, cause, length of operation, and location. Failures are defined as business discontinuances with court proceedings, or voluntary actions involving loss to creditors.

Data are compiled by Dun & Bradstreet's Economic Analysis Dept.

Contains contents listing, and definitions (p. 1-2); and 12 tables, listed below (p. 3-15).

Previous report, published in 1983, is described in SRI 1983 Annual, under this number. No report was published in 1984.

Availability: Dun and Bradstreet, Economic Analysis Department, 299 Park Ave., New York NY 10171, †; SRI/MF/not filmed.

TABLES:

[1] Failure trends since 1926 [number, rate, and total and average liabilities; annually through 1983]. (p. 3)

[2-3] Failures [and rates] by States and [census divisions, 1970 and 1980-83]. (p. 4-5)

[4] Failures [and liabilities] in 25 cities [1980-83]. (p. 6)

[5] Failure distribution by liability size [1945-83]. (p. 7)

[6] Business failures [and liabilities, by major industry group, selected years 1940-83]. (p. 8-9)

[7] Failure distribution [and average liability], by [industry] sector [1970 and 1980-83]. (p. 10)

[8] Failures [rates] in specific retail and manufacturing lines [1982-83]. (p. 11)

[9] Failures [as percent of total failures] by age of business [1950-83]. (p. 12)

[10] Failures [by industry sector, distributed by] age of business [1982-83]. (p. 13)

[11-12] Causes of business failures [by industry sector], 1982-83. (p. 14-15)

C3165
Duncan, James H., Jr.

C3165–1   AMERICAN RADIO: Spring
1985 Report
Semiannual. Aug. 1985.
269 p. var. paging.
Vol. X, No. 1.
SRI/MF/complete, Fall 1984 &
Spring 1985 reports

Semiannual report, by James H. Duncan, Jr., on radio broadcast industry, spring 1985, presenting detailed data on station formats and audiences, broadcast market characteristics, and broadcast-related businesses, with selected trends from 1976.

Includes numerous station and market rankings based on various listenership measures, with detail by station type (including public/noncommercial stations) and program format; station trading activity, including transaction price; leading radio representatives based on stations covered; station and listenership measures for leading ownership groups; and audience characteristics, including age and sex composition, for individual stations grouped by format.

Also includes Arbitron and other market reports for 168 individual market areas, with data on population, consumer spendable income, and retail sales; aggregate radio revenue; FM market share; average audience and audience shares for individual stations and program formats; and other station data, including audience age and sex composition, market share trends from 1983, frequency, power authorization, and advertising rates.

Data are from Arbitron Co. and other private research firms, Birch monthly reports, *Broadcast Week, Broadcasting Yearbook,* and original research.

Contains introduction, highlights, and index (5 p.); section A, with rankings, broadcast-related data, and format detail (A1-A49); and section B, with market report data (216 p.)

Report generally is issued in Feb. (fall edition) and Aug. (spring edition). This is the 19th edition.

Previous report, for fall 1984, was also reviewed by SRI in 1985 and is also available on SRI microfiche under C3165-1 [Semiannual. Feb. 1985. 230 p. var. paging. Vol. IX, No. 2. $55.00].

Availability: James H. Duncan, Jr., Duncan's American Radio, Inc., Box 2966, Kalamazoo MI 49003, $60.00; SRI/MF/complete.

C3250
Editor and Publisher Co.

C3250–1 **1985 EDITOR AND PUBLISHER MARKET GUIDE**
Annual. 1985.
603 p. var. paging.
ISBN 9-9916233-1-0.
LC 45-44873.
SRI/MF/complete, delayed

Annual market guide, for 1985, presenting detailed sociodemographic and economic characteristics for MSAs, counties, and communities with a daily newspaper, in the U.S., Puerto Rico, and Canada.

Includes location, population, disposable income and other household characteristics, transportation, principal industries, utilities, and retail sales and outlets. Also includes summary State and Province data.

Report is based on *1977 Census of Retail Sales,* 1980 U.S. census, and other U.S. Government agency reports; Statistics Canada censuses; *Editor and Publisher* estimates; and other sources.

Retail sales data by kind of business are shown for lumber/hardware, general merchandise, food, automotive dealers, gasoline stations, apparel, furniture, eating/drinking places, and drugstores.

Contents:

Section I. Introduction: index, definitions, and notes; alphabetical listing of MSAs and Consolidated Metropolitan Statistical Areas; market rankings of MSAs and leading counties and cities, 1985, in terms of population, disposable personal income, total retail and food sales, and disposable income per household; and directory of newspaper representatives in U.S. and Canada. 5 tables. (p. I.1-I.44)

Sections II-III. Surveys of daily newspaper cities: city profiles with text data, described below, arranged by State including Puerto Rico, and Canadian Province. (p. II.1-II.386, III.1-III.21)

Section IV. Population, income, and retail sales tables: population; number of households; disposable personal income; income per capita and per household; number of farms, and crop and livestock values; and total retail sales and number of stores, by

kind of business; all by State, Province, MSA and Canadian metro area, county, and city, with U.S. and Canadian totals; various years 1977-86. 2 tables. (p. IV.1-IV.151)

Index to advertisers. (1 p.)

Market guide has been published annually since 1924.

Availability: Editor and Publisher Co., 11 W. 19th St., New York NY 10011, $50.00 (prepaid); SRI/MF/complete, delayed shipment in Dec. 1985.

NEWSPAPER MARKET SURVEYS:

C3250–1.1: Text Data

a. For each State and Province: population by age group, and retail sales by kind of business, various years 1970-85. 2 tables.

b. For each metro area: location; transportation facilities by type; population; households; number of financial institutions and deposits, by type of institution; passenger autos; electric and gas utility meters; principal industries, generally with employment and worker weekly earnings; climate; tap water characteristics; shopping centers and retail outlets; and newspaper circulation.

C3400
Fairchild Publications

C3400–1 **FAIRCHILD FACT FILE**
Series. For individual publication data, see below.
SRI/MF/complete

Series of fact file reports presenting production and retail marketing data for selected consumer goods industries, including apparel, home textiles, major household appliances, and home electronic products. Series also includes special reports on aspects of manufacturing and marketing and the U.S. economy.

Reports generally are updated annually or biennially and are compiled by the Market Research Division from sources such as consumer surveys, BLS, BEA, Census Bureau, trade assns, Target Group Index, and *Sales and Marketing Management.*

General format for reports on specific industries includes a narrative summary of industry and market trends, and the following data:

a. General industry statistics, including companies, establishments, total and production employment, hours and earnings, payroll, value added, shipments value, and capital expenditures; establishments and employment, by employment size and leading State; and industry concentration and financial data, including key business ratios; all for 1-10 SIC 4-digit industries.

b. Production and shipments data, generally including quantity and/or value by item, fabric/material, and leading State; raw materials consumption; production indexes and/or PPI; and selected wholesale price data.

c. Foreign trade, including quantity and value of imports by product type and leading country of origin, and exports by item.

d. Retail market, including product target market population by sex and/or age group projected to 2000 or beyond; stores, product sales, and operating ratios for selected outlet types, including department stores; newspaper advertising linage monthly distribution; CPI; and, occasionally, monthly sales distribution.

e. Consumer buying habits, variously including selection criteria; expenditure data; selected survey results; and purchase distributions by price level, type of outlet, month, and individual item.

Reports that basically follow the general format are described briefly, as they appear; periods of coverage, data omissions, and additional data are noted. Reports issued in special format are described in detail, as they appear.

Reports reviewed during 1985 are described below.

Availability: Fairchild Fact Files, Fairchild Books, Seven E. 12th St., New York NY 10003, single copy $15.00; SRI/MF/complete.

C3400–1.67: Home Textiles
[Biennial. 1984. 38 p. ISBN 87005-486-4. SRI/MF/complete.]

Biennial report on home textiles and drapery hardware/blinds/shades industries, various periods 1970-84. Report basically follows general format, but omits data on manufacturing employment by employment size; production and shipments by leading State; wholesale prices; projected market population; stores by outlet type; newspaper advertising linage; monthly purchase distribution and sales; and consumer selection criteria.

Additional data include value added by leading State; cost of raw materials; household composition, marriages, and private housing activity; drapery/upholstery stores, employment, and payroll, by employment size; sales of 25 top retailers; purchase distribution by region; and purchasing plans of teenage female students.

Includes 41 tables.

Report updates a 1982 report; for description, see SRI 1983 Annual, under C3400-1.44.

C3400–1.68: Dresses (Women's, Misses', and Juniors')
[Biennial. 1984. 31 p. ISBN 87005-487-2. SRI/MF/complete.]

Biennial report on women's dress industry, various periods 1972-84, with population projections to 2005. Report basically follows general format, but omits data on manufacturing employment by employment size; establishments, employment, production, and shipments, by leading State; industry concentration and financial ratios; raw materials consumption; and monthly sales distribution.

Additional data include establishments and shipment value by leading county; monthly production; exports by leading country of destination; adult female population by height and weight; labor force by age to 1995, and employment by occupation; marriages and births; women's ready-to-wear stores and employment by employment size; and purchasing habits and expenditures of female teenagers.

Includes 36 tables.

Report updates a 1982 report; for description, see SRI 1983 Annual, under C3400-1.46.

C3400–1.69: Retailing/Merchandising Trends

[Monograph. 1984. 52 p. ISBN 87005-488-0. SRI/MF/complete.]

Report on trends in retail trade and developments in merchandising techniques, various years 1972-84. Covers retail sales by outlet type, census division, and leading metro area; gross margin and value of purchases or sales, by outlet type and merchandise line; employment and establishments by outlet type; and sales of licensed goods by category.

Also includes sales and number of stores for 7 multi-division operators and 5 chains; and sales rankings for top 10 department stores and top 10 specialty chains, with headquarters location, parent company, and number of units.

Report, which varies from the general format for the series, contains contents listing (1 p.); and narrative, in 3 parts, interspersed with 18 text tables (p. 1-49).

C3400–1.70: Department Store Sales

[Annual. 1984. 51 p. ISBN 87005-489-9. LC sn83-11364. SRI/MF/complete.]

Annual report summarizing data on retail sales of department stores and leading apparel specialty stores, 1983. Data are based on company financial statements and trade source estimates.

Report, which varies from the general format for the series, contains contents/table listing (1 p.), introduction (p. 1), and the following tables showing data by company, generally for 1983 or the latest available fiscal year:

[1] Summary of available sales [revenues and units operated] for department stores [arranged by headquarters location]. (p. 2-30)

[2] Department store volume leaders [ranking by sales, with number of units, headquarters location, and parent company]. (p. 31-37)

[3] Major national/regional chains [sales, with detail for subsidiaries]. (p. 38-41)

[4] Traditional department stores and apparel stores operated by conglomerate corporations [listing, with 1983-85 status changes]. (p. 42-48)

C3400–1.71: Consumer Market Developments

[Annual. 1984. 65 p. ISBN 87005-490-2. SRI/MF/complete.]

Annual report presenting demographic and economic data relevant to consumer market conditions, various periods 1970-2005. Most data are from Census Bureau and BLS.

Report, which varies from the general format for the series, contains contents listing (1 p.); and 11 sections, with narrative analysis and the following tables:

a. Births, and birth and fertility rates, by race, 1972-83, with detail by census division for 1982; birth rate for women 18-44, by age group, June 1980 and June 1983; and distribution of births, by age of mother, birth order, and month, various years 1972-83. 6 tables. (p. 2-6)

b. Population by age, sex, race/ethnicity (white, black, American Indian/Eskimo/ Aleut, Asian/Pacific Islander, and Hispanic), census region and division, State, and metro status, with data on median age, various years 1970-2005; population mobility rates, 1960s-83; and rankings of top 10 metro markets by black population, top 5 States by Hispanic population, and top 10 Consolidated MSAs by total population, various years 1980-83. 13 tables. (p. 7-20)

c. Marriages and rates, selected periods 1980-83; and distribution of single (never married) population, by age group and sex, selected years 1970-84. 2 tables. (p. 21-22)

d. Households, with distribution by composition; average number of children and adults per household; and total number of children by race/ethnicity (includes Hispanic), young adults (age 18-34), and elderly (age 65/over), with distribution by living arrangement; various years 1970-84. 4 tables. (p. 25-27)

e. School enrollment of persons age 3-34 by academic level, and educational attainment of persons age 25/over by race/ethnicity (includes Hispanic), with detail by age and sex, various years 1970-83. 4 tables. (p. 27-31)

f. Labor force by employment status and age, and employment by full- and part-time status and occupation group, by sex, various years 1975-95 with selected summary trends from 1950; employment by class of worker (self-employed, wage/salary, and unpaid family), families and median income by number of wage earners, and employment by household composition, various years 1975-84. 12 tables. (p. 32-41)

g. Earnings by sex, age, race/ethnicity (includes Hispanic), occupation, industry division, and class of worker (self-employed and wage/salary employment), various years 1982-84. 3 tables. (p. 41-43)

h. Personal income by source, sex, age, region, and selected Consolidated MSA; income disposition; persons age 14/over by sex, families and unrelated persons by age of householder, and population by age, with median income and distribution by income level; decile distribution of family income; families and median income, by family type and census region; and top 10 metro areas ranked by median household effective buying income; various years 1976-84. 10 tables. (p. 44-51)

i. Housing trends including distribution of nonfarm families by housing status (home renter or owner, mobile home resident, and other); distribution of home owners by value of house and equity; and mean and median equity and percent of families owning homes, by income level, and age and race (white or nonwhite/Hispanic) of family head; 1983, with selected comparisons to 1970 and 1977. 3 tables. (p. 52-53)

j. Consumer and mortgage debt outstanding and financial assets, and percent of families with debt and owning financial assets, all by age of family head, with asset detail by type and by family income level; distribution of families by current and inflation-adjusted net worth; and actual net worth and family distribution, by age of family head with detail by marital and labor force status; 1983, with selected comparisons to 1977. 5 tables. (p. 54-57)

k. Personal consumption expenditures by product category, with detail by age of household head and household income level, comparisons to pre-tax and disposable income, and summary data on household size and other characteristics, various periods 1980-84. 5 tables. (p. 58-62)

C3400–1.72: Women's Inner Fashions: Nightwear, Daywear, and Loungewear

[Biennial. 1985. 39 p. ISBN 87005-520-8. SRI/MF/complete.]

Biennial report on women's lingerie industry, various periods 1977-84, with population projections to 2005. Report basically follows general format, but omits data on key business ratios and production by leading State.

Additional data include apparent consumption; payroll and capital expenditures, by leading State; women age 16/over, by height and weight group; and purchasing habits and expenditures of female teenagers.

Includes 40 tables.

Report updates a 1983 report; for description see SRI 1983 Annual, under C3400-1.55.

C3400–1.73: Fashion Accessories (Men's and Women's)

[Biennial. 1985. 46 p. ISBN 87005-521-6. SRI/MF/complete.]

Biennial report on fashion accessory industry, various periods 1972-84, with population projections to 2005. Report basically follows general format, but omits data on employment by leading State, key business ratios, raw materials consumption, wholesale prices, imports by country of origin, and CPI.

Additional data include marriages by month, and purchasing habits and expenditures of female teenagers.

Includes 43 tables.

Report updates a 1983 report; for description see SRI 1983 Annual, under C3400-1.49.

C3400–1.74: Men's Furnishings and Work Wear

[Biennial. 1985. 44 p. ISBN 87005-526-7. SRI/MF/complete.]

Biennial report on men's furnishings and work wear industries, various periods 1977-85, with population projections to 2005. Furnishings industry encompasses a variety of apparel items other than suits and sports jackets. Furnishings and work wear data are presented in 2 separate sections; each section basically follows the general format, with data omissions and additions as follows:

a. Furnishings industry data omit industry concentration and financial data, production by leading State, wholesale prices, imports by country of origin, and consumer expenditures; and include data on male population age 18-74, by height and weight.

b. Work wear industry data omit industry concentration and financial data, production by leading State, wholesale prices, foreign trade, population projections, retail stores and operating ratios by outlet type, newspaper advertising linage, CPI, and most consumer buying habit data; and include data on employment by sex and occupational group.

Includes 53 tables.

Previous report, for 1983, is described in SRI 1983 Annual under C3400-1.48.

C3400-1.75: Infants', Toddlers', Girls', and Boys' Wear

[Biennial. 1985. 49 p. ISBN 87005-522-4. SRI/MF/complete.]

Biennial report on children's clothing industries, various periods 1975-85, with population projections to 2000. Report basically follows general format, but omits key business ratios, production by leading State, wholesale prices, imports by product type and country, and consumer expenditures.

Additional data include shipment value by establishment employment size; births, and birth and fertility rates; families by number of children and household earners; children by employment status of mother; percent of children enrolled in school, by age and sex; and projected child population by region.

Includes 52 tables.

Previous report, for 1983, is described in SRI 1983 Annual under C3400-1.50.

C3400-1.76: Textile/Apparel Industries

[Biennial. 1985. 56 p. ISBN 87005-531-3. SRI/MF/complete.]

Biennial report on textile and apparel industries, various periods 1974-85. Report basically follows general format for sections on general industry statistics, production and shipments, and foreign trade, but omits data on production and shipments by leading State, wholesale prices, and imports by country of origin. Report also omits sections on retail market and consumer buying habits.

Additional data include shipment value and/or value added, by leading State and employment size; cost of materials, by industry; leading industry groups ranked by value added and shipments value; leading publicly owned textile and apparel companies ranked by sales, with profits; fiber/yarn production, shipments, and consumption; apparel sales and cost of goods sold, projected to 1995; textile mill capital expenditures and equipment; and textile machinery industry statistics.

Includes 54 tables.

Previous report, for 1983, is described in SRI 1984 Annual under C3400-1.57.

C3400-1.77: Women's Coats, Suits, Rainwear, and Furs

[Biennial. 1985. 38 p. ISBN 87005-523-2. SRI/MF/complete.]

Biennial report on women's coat, suit, rainwear, and fur industries, various periods 1977-85, with population and labor force projections to 2005. Coats/suits/rainwear and fur data are presented in 2 separate sections; each section basically follows the general format, with data omissions and additions as follows:

a. Coats/suits/rainwear industry data omit employment by leading State, industry financial data, production by leading State, wholesale prices, imports by country of origin, and exports by item; and include data on shipment value by employment size, value added by leading State, monthly production distribution by item, female labor force by age, and female population age 16/over by height and weight.

b. Fur industry data omit production worker hours and earnings, employment by leading State, industry financial data, production data and indexes, raw materials consumption, wholesale prices, all foreign trade data except import value by country of origin, target market population projections, CPI, and consumer buying habits; and include data on value added by employment size.

Includes 42 tables.

Previous report is described in SRI 1983 Annual under C3400-1.51.

C3400-2 FAIRCHILD'S FINANCIAL MANUAL OF RETAIL STORES, 1984

Annual. 1984. 8+228 p.
ISBN 87005-471-6.
LC 59-4791.
SRI/MF/complete, delayed

Annual report presenting financial and operating data for approximately 300 publicly owned retail companies, various years 1978-84. Most data are from annual company reports to shareholders.

Contents:

a. Summary statistics for 115 leading food, drug, shoe, department store, specialty, mass merchandisers, discounter, and other retailers; showing the following for each company: sales, net and pretax income or profits, and shareholders' equity, and ratios, 1982-83; and aggregate trends from 1974. 19 tables. (6 p.)

b. Individual company organizational and financial data, including number of stores; net sales and income; common stock shares outstanding, earnings per share, equity, and cash and stock dividends; income, assets, and liabilities, by type; and statistical summary (working capital, shareholders' equity, and 3-5 operating ratios); various years 1978-84. (p. 1-212)

c. Index of companies and subsidiaries. (p. 223-239)

This is the 57th annual edition.

Availability: Fairchild Books, Seven E. 12th St., New York NY 10003, $60.00; SRI/MF/complete, delayed shipment in Oct. 1985.

C3400-4 ELECTRONIC NEWS FINANCIAL FACT BOOK and Directory, 1984

Annual. 1984. 4+525 p.
ISBN 87005-469-4.
LC 62-19605.
SRI/MF/complete, delayed

Annual directory of approximately 650 publicly owned electronic companies, with business and financial information, various years 1977-83. Data are from annual company reports to shareholders and *Electronic News.*

Contents:

a. Summary data for 51 leading companies in electronic sales, showing the following for each company: total and electronic sales, 1984; stock prices, June 30, 1983-84; and earnings per share, price/earnings ratio, and sales, 1983-84. 2 tables. (2 p.)

b. Individual firm organizational and financial data, generally including divisions and subsidiaries; number of employees; plant area; net sales and income; revenues by line of business; common stock shares outstanding, earnings per share, equity, and cash and stock dividends; income, assets, and liabilities; and working capital, shareholders' equity, and 4-5 operating ratios; various years 1977-84. (p. 1-499)

c. Index of electronic companies and subsidiaries. (p. 501-525)

This is the 23rd annual edition.

Availability: Fairchild Books, Seven E. 12th St., New York NY 10003, $125.00; SRI/MF/complete, delayed shipment in Oct. 1985.

C3400-5 FAIRCHILD'S TEXTILE AND APPAREL FINANCIAL DIRECTORY, 1984

Annual. 1984. 9+162 p.
ISBN 87005-470-8.
SRI/MF/complete, delayed

Annual directory of approximately 175 publicly owned textile and apparel companies, with business and financial information, various years 1977-84. Most data are from annual company reports to shareholders.

Contents:

a. Industry summaries including shipment, export, and import values; and employment, production workers and earnings, capital expenditures, sales, profits, and selected operating ratios; for apparel and/or textile fiber/mill product industries, various periods 1979-84. 7 tables. (5 p.)

b. Sales, net and pretax income, and shareholders' equity, for 53 leading fiber/textile and apparel manufacturers, 1982-83. 2 tables. (2 p.)

c. Individual firm organizational and financial data, including business activities; divisions and subsidiaries; net sales and income; revenues by line of business; common stock shares outstanding, earnings per share, equity, and cash and stock dividends; income, assets, and liabilities, by type; and statistical summary (working capital, shareholders' equity, and 2-5 operating ratios); various years 1977-84. (p. 1-132)

d. Indexes of textile trademarks, and divisions and subsidiaries. (p. 133-162)

This is the 11th annual edition.

Availability: Fairchild Books, Seven E. 12th St., New York NY 10003, $50.00; SRI/MF/complete, delayed shipment in Oct. 1985.

C3400-6 SN DISTRIBUTION STUDY OF GROCERY STORE SALES, 1985

Annual. 1985. 4+313 p.
ISBN 87005-501-1.
SRI/MF/complete, delayed

Annual report, for 1985, on sales, store units, and market shares of food store chains, voluntary/cooperative groups, convenience stores, and independents, for 302 metro markets in U.S. and Canada. Data are from various newspaper organizations, Federal agencies, Food Marketing Institute, and *Sales & Marketing Management.*

Contents:

Overview, contents listing, and introduction. (4 p.)

Section 1. Statistical profiles of the top 50 SMSAs ranked by supermarket sales, showing the following: number of stores, market share, and principal supplier, for leading stores arranged by type; and retail food store and supermarket sales, number of food stores, households by size, population by age of household head, net effective buying income (EBI), and households by EBI group, all for total SMSA, central city, and U.S.; 1983, with EBI changes projected to 1988. (p. 1-101)

Section 2. Other markets' retail grocery store profiles, showing number of stores, market share, and principal supplier, for leading stores grouped by type, and arranged alphabetically by State, SMSA or city, and Canadian Province and city. (p. 103-266)

Section 3. Profiles of 31 leading publicly owned food chains, including number of stores, market areas covered, and retail sales; with 1 table (p. 268) showing sales, net and pretax income, and shareholder's equity, by chain, 1982-83. (p. 267-289)

Section 4. Grocery store statistical profile, with 13 tables listed below. (p. 291-302)

Section 5. Calendar of industry conventions and annual meetings for 1985, and directories of food assns and newspapers/representatives. (p. 303-313)

Availability: Fairchild Books, Seven E. 12th St., New York NY 10003, $40.00; SRI/MF/ complete, delayed shipment in Apr. 1986.

SECTION 4 TABLES:

[Data are for grocery stores, unless otherwise noted.]

[1] Firms, [stores, and sales], by sales size, 1977. (p. 292)

[2] Concentration of sales, [stores, and payroll] among [4-50] major firms, 1977. (p. 292)

[3] Firms, number of stores operated, and sales [by store units per firm], 1977. (p. 293)

[4-5] Stores [and sales] by sales size; and stores with payroll and sales, by type of merchandise; 1972 and 1977. (p. 294-295)

[6-7] [Total and chain] grocery stores and supermarkets: estimated number of stores and sales, 1973-83. (p. 296)

[8-9] Distribution of sales and per capita sales, by geographic region [1980-83]. (p. 297)

[10] Sales by months, 1979-83. (p. 298)

[11] Distribution of the U.S. resident population, personal income, and supermarket sales, by State and [census division], 1983. (p. 299-300)

[12] Per capita consumption of major food commodities [by commodity, 1979-81]. (p. 301)

[13] CPI [1980-83]. (p. 302)

C3475
Fieldmark Media

C3475–1   SUPERMARKET BUSINESS

Monthly.   Oversized.
ISSN 0196-5700.
LC 79-649274.
SRI/MF/excerpts, shipped quarterly

Monthly trade journal of the retail and wholesale grocery industry, covering product sales and merchandising, technology, store operations and design, finance, advertising and sales promotion, and personnel management. Most data are from Federal Government, Selling Areas Marketing Inc., and journal surveys of industry executives and individual companies.

General format:

a. Feature articles, occasionally with statistics; regular narrative depts; and scattered news briefs and analyses of current grocery trends.

b. Monthly table, with accompanying article, showing percent change in health/beauty aids sales in food stores, by product type, for 2-3 consecutive 4-week periods ended approximately 6-11 weeks prior to cover date, compared to same periods of previous year.

Annual features include report on consumer use of supermarket products (June); survey of supermarket deli and bakery operations (July); study of household spending for products sold through grocery stores (Sept.); supermarket chain sales and income report (Oct.); directory of equipment suppliers (Nov.); and subject index (Dec.).

Journal occasionally includes *Instore Business* or other separately paginated supplements.

Monthly table appears in all issues. All additional features with substantial statistical content are described, as they appear, under "Statistical Features." Nonstatistical features are not covered.

Availability: Fieldmark Media, Supermarket Business, 25 W. 43rd St., New York NY 10036, industry subscribers †, others $35.00 per yr., single copy $3.50, Sept. issue $20.00; SRI/MF/excerpts for monthly table and all portions covered under "Statistical Features;" shipped quarterly.

Issues reviewed during 1985: Nov. 1984-Oct. 1985 (P) (Vol. 39, Nos. 11-12; Vol. 40, Nos. 1-10) [Vol. 40, No. 4 incorrectly reads No. 3 on contents page].

STATISTICAL FEATURES:

C3475–1.601: Mar. 1985 (Vol. 40, No. 3)

THE CHANGING WHOLESALER/INDEPENDENT RELATIONSHIP: WHAT MAKES A RETAILER SWITCH?

(p. 19-24) Article comparing perceptions of grocery wholesalers and independent retailers regarding factors most important to their own industries and to the wholesaler/retailer business relationship. Data are from responses of approximately 85 wholesalers and 290 retailers to a survey conducted by *Supermarket Business* and National American Wholesale Grocers Association. Includes 8 undated tables.

C3475–1.602: Apr. 1985 (Vol. 40, No. 4)

NEW PRODUCT INTRODUCTIONS AVERAGE TWO PER DAY

(p. 11) Article, with 1 table showing number of new food products introduced, 1980-84, for top 20 manufacturers ranked by cumulative introductions during 1980-84 period. Data are from Dancer Fitzgerald Sample.

C3475–1.603: May 1985 (Vol. 40, No. 5)

PUTTING SOME SPARKLE INTO THE WINE MARKET

(p. 57-66) By Kevin Coupe. Article, with 1 table showing consumption of domestic, imported, sparkling, dessert, and table wines, and of carbonated wine drinks and vermouth, 1982-84. Data are from Wine Institute.

PUTTING SOME PUNCH INTO PRODUCE DEPARTMENTS

(p. 106-109) By Herman Roberts, Jr. et al. Article, with 1 chart and 1 table showing supermarket and produce dept managers' perceptions concerning effect of "farm-fresh look" marketing method on customer satisfaction and produce sales (no date). Data are based on 680 responses to a survey of Southern California supermarkets conducted by the authors.

C3475–1.604: June 1985 (Vol. 40, No. 6)

2ND ANNUAL PRODUCT PREFERENCE STUDY: HOW FIVE GROUPS BUY SUPERMARKET PRODUCTS

(p. 27-73 passim) Annual feature, by Robert Dietrich, presenting consumer use data for supermarket products, 1984. Focuses on upper-income ($20,000/more) consumers in 5 groups: blacks, 1-person households, age 65/ older, age 35-44, and working women.

Most data are based on a Mediamark Research Inc. survey of over 40,000 adults.

Contents:

a. Methodology; user guide; and 3 tables showing demographic comparisons to total population, product use summary, and zip codes/cities with population concentrations, for all or most of the consumer groups noted above.

b. Use profiles for 18 product categories, each with several tables showing use of specific products among the consumer groups noted above and among all homemakers or adults.

HBA PRODUCT PERFORMANCE

(p. 9B-20B) Article on top-selling products' contribution to total sales and gross margins in each of 37 health/beauty aid product categories. Includes 1 table, repeated for each product category, showing the following for each of 5 item classifications based on dollar sales: percent gross margin, percent of total category sales (units and dollars), and percent of total category margin.

Also includes 2 summary tables. No data dates or sources are given.

C3475–1.605: July 1985 (Vol. 40, No. 7)

TAKING OFF: THIRD ANNUAL OPERATIONS REPORT

(Supplement, p. 1A-42A) Annual article on supermarket deli and fresh bakery dept operations, 1984 and selected trends. Data are based on a *Supermarket Business* survey drawing responses from industry executives responsible for over 10,000 supermarkets.

Includes bakery and deli sections, with a total of 20 charts and 33 tables showing survey response on the following:

a. Number and percent of supermarkets with each type of dept; dept size and sales, with comparison to total store, and sales change from 1983 and expected for 1985; gross margins; percent of supermarkets with combined deli and bakery depts; number of employees; labor costs as percent of sales; and sales per square foot and per employee.

b. Types of equipment, suppliers, and promotional methods used, and services or facilities offered; sales shares, by product type; percent of store customers who shop dept, and average amount spent; preferred location for dept; items most frequently added/increased; preparation methods, by product (bakery only); and hours spent on preparation and service (deli only).

C3475–1.606: Sept. 1985 (Vol. 40, No. 9)

38th ANNUAL CONSUMER EXPENDITURES STUDY

(p. 55-226, passim) Annual report on consumer expenditures for food and selected nonfood items in grocery stores, by product and store type, 1984, with trends from 1964. Also includes comparisons of grocery store vs. total market, by product type. Data are from Federal Government and *Supermarket Business* research.

Contents:

a. Contents listing, and narrative report and methodology, with 5 charts and 10 tables listed below. (p. 55-80)

b. Summary: 6 tables showing the following for perishables, food and nonfood dry groceries, health/beauty aids, and general merchandise, by detailed product type: value of consumption, expenditures in grocery stores, share of store sales, and grocery share of total market, 1983-84; and expenditures in supermarkets, share of supermarket sales, and supermarket dollar and percent margins, 1984. (p. 83-110)

c. Product category profiles: primarily narrative sales reviews presented for 20 product categories, interspersed with 7 tables showing general merchandise and health/beauty aids sales trends, by product, mostly 1983-84. (p. 113-226)

Report Charts and Tables:

[Tables [1-7] and [12] show data by product category or detailed product type.]

[1] Total grocery store sales [distribution, 1984 with comparison to 1983]. [chart] (p. 70)

[2] Weekly spending in grocery stores per household and per capita [1983-84]. (p. 70)

[3] How an average household doles out its dollars in grocery stores each week [1983-84]. (p. 71)

[4-5] Categories that increased and decreased in sales in 1984 [largest increases and decreases in dollar sales, with percent change in sales, sales share of total store volume, and selected detail on percent change in retail price and tonnage, 1984 vs. 1983]. (p. 73)

[6] Some significant shifts over 20 years [market shares, 1964 and 1984]. [chart] (p. 74)

[7] 15-year perspective on how food products sell in grocery stores [sales value, selected years 1969-84]. (p. 74)

[8] Little real sales growth seen [percent change in aggregate food store prices, 1975-84]. [chart] (p. 76)

[9-10] Food store sales by store [sales] volume and affiliation [1983-84]. (p. 76)

[11] Service and size pull in shoppers [market share by food store type, 1984 with comparison to 1983]. [chart] (p. 78)

[12] The year supermarket prices leveled off [percent price changes, 1983-84]. (p. 78)

[13] Dining out keeps ahead of eating at home [share of food dollar 1983-84, and percent change in dollar sales, prices, and tonnage, 1984 vs. 1983, for restaurants and grocery stores]. [chart] (p. 80)

[14] Ranking of retail sales [for 12 outlet types] by trade [value, 1984 with percent change from 1983]. (p. 80)

[15] Grocery store sales trends [number of grocery stores and sales, with detail by sales size and for chain stores], 1984. (p. 80)

C3475–1.607: Oct. 1985 (Vol. 40, No. 10)

TOP PUBLIC CHAINS, ANNUAL FEATURE

(p. 20-25) Annual article, by Norman Bussel, on sales and profitability of the 44 leading publicly owned supermarket chains, 1984.

Includes 7 tables showing sales, net income or loss, and stores operated, for top 44 chains ranked by sales; with additional groupings for top 10 chains ranked by profit margin and growth in sales and earnings, and 15 chains with earnings decline; 1984 with comparisons to 1983.

LOOK AT SUPERMARKET STOCK PERFORMANCE, RECURRING FEATURE

(p. 30-31) Recurring article, with 2 tables showing stock price (recent, and 52-week high and low), price/earnings ratio, and annual dividend rate and yield, for 43 retail supermarket chains and 9 wholesalers; and supermarket business chain and wholesaler stock indexes compared to 4 major stock indexes. Recent stock prices and indexes are shown as of the beginning of the 2 months prior to month of publication. Other data are undated.

Data are prepared by Nordby International, Inc. This is the 1st recurring feature.

LEADING WHOLESALERS

(p. 32-33) By Norman Bussel. Article on sales of the 11 leading publicly owned food wholesalers, 1984. Data are from a *Supermarket Business* survey.

Includes 2 tables showing sales, net income, and stores serviced and operated, for top 11 wholesalers ranked by sales; 1984 with comparisons to 1983.

C3935
Folio Publishing Corp.

C3935–1   FOLIO: The Magazine for Magazine Management

Monthly.
ISSN 0046-4333.
LC 72-626840.
SRI/MF/excerpts, shipped quarterly

Monthly trade journal (2 issues in Oct.) of the magazine publishing industry, reporting developments in management techniques, circulation, advertising, sales, graphics, and production. Includes announcements of new magazines, mergers and acquisitions, and closings.

Data are from Audit Bureau of Circulations, trade assns, private sources, and the journal's own research.

Includes:

a. Editorial sections and feature articles, occasionally with statistics; and regular editorial depts.

b. Annual Folio 400 ranking of top consumer and business magazines (2nd Oct. issue).

c. Other annual features, including data on advertising pages and revenues, profitability, magazine paper demand, and publications most popular in college bookstores; and an editorial index (Feb.).

d. Quarterly features on investment performance of individual publishing stocks, and periodical delivery times by selected city.

e. Other recurring statistics on magazine circulation, personnel compensation, overseas sales, advertising revenues, and freelance writing.

Quarterly table on periodical delivery time is described below. Other features with substantial statistical content are described, as they appear, under "Statistical Features;" page locations and latest periods of coverage for quarterly table are also noted. Each issue of the journal is reviewed, but an abstract is published in SRI monthly issues only when quarterly table or other statistical features appear.

Availability: Folio, PO Box 4006, 125 Elm St., New Canaan CT 06840-4006, $58.00 per yr., single copy $6.00, May issue $10.00, Folio 400 issue $25.00, back issues $8.00; SRI/MF/excerpts for all portions covered under "Statistical Features;" shipped quarterly.

Issues reviewed during 1985: Nov. 1984-Oct. 1985 (P) (Vol. 13, Nos. 11-12; Vol. 14, Nos. 1-10); and Folio 400 issue [Jan.-Feb. 1985 issues omit volume and issue numbers].

QUARTERLY TABLE:

[1] Publication delivery box score: monthly 2nd class publications [shows percent of publications delivered early, on-time, and late in relation to USPS service standard, by selected city, for quarter ending 4-5 months prior to cover date].

STATISTICAL FEATURES:

C3935–1.601: Nov. 1984 (Vol. 13, No. 11)

302 OF FOLIO 400 MAGAZINES SHOW REVENUE GAINS

(p. 14-15) Article, with 1 chart showing aggregate subscription, newsstand, and advertising revenues of Folio 400 magazines, 1983.

MAGAZINE EMPLOYMENT INCREASES BY 36% WHILE RECEIPTS SOAR

(p. 19-20) Article, with 1 table showing receipts of specialized and general/consumer periodicals from single-copy sales and/or subscriptions and advertising, 1977 and 1982. Data are from Census Bureau.

PRINT BUYERS RATE PRODUCTION QUALITY AS HIGHEST CRITERION

(p. 28) Brief article on criteria rated most important by magazines when choosing and retaining a printer. Data are from responses of 185 magazine print buyers to a Webb Co. survey conducted by Mid-Continent Research, Inc. Includes 2 undated tables.

64% OF CONSUMER MAGAZINES GAIN CIRC IN FIRST HALF OF 1984, SEMIANNUAL FEATURE

(p. 44-48) Semiannual article on magazine circulation, 1st half 1984. Data are from Audit Bureau of Circulations. Includes 1 table showing top 20 magazines ranked by average circulation per issue, 1st half 1984 with comparison to 1st half 1983.

55% OF MAGAZINES REPORT SINGLE-COPY SALES DECLINES, SEMIANNUAL FEATURE

(p. 59-60) Semiannual article on single-copy magazine sales, 1st half 1984. Data are from Audit Bureau of Circulations. Includes 1 table showing top 20 magazines ranked by single-copy sales, 1st half 1984 with comparison to 1st half 1983.

C3935–1.602: Dec. 1984 (Vol. 13, No. 12)

CLOSING INDUSTRIAL SALE TAKES AVERAGE 5.5 CALLS

(p. 25) Article, with 1 table showing average cost for closing an industrial sale, and distribution of closed sales, by number of sales calls made, 1981 and 1983. Data are from McGraw-Hill surveys.

TOP 10 AMERICAN MAGAZINES IN ANNUAL FOREIGN SINGLE-COPY SALES, SEMIANNUAL FEATURE

(p. 32) Semiannual article on U.S. magazines with highest single-copy sales overseas. Data are full-year 1983 estimates from Boarts International, Inc., based on Audit Bureau of Circulations report for Dec. 31, 1983.

Includes 1 table ranking top 10 magazines by foreign sales value, and showing foreign and U.S. issues sold, cover price, and issue frequency, 1983.

SEVEN MAGAZINES OVERSTATE CIRCULATION BY 2 PERCENT OR MORE, RECURRING FEATURE

(p. 44) Recurring brief article, with 1 table showing publisher vs. Audit Bureau of Circulations (ABC) estimates of circulation, for magazines for which the 2 estimates vary by more than 2%. Data are from ABC audit report for 3rd quarter 1984.

PAPER CHASE

(p. 68-76) By Diane Reese. Article, with 2 charts and 1 table showing average price for coated groundwood paper; and freesheet/groundwood coated paper import volume, production capacity, and demand; various years 1978-86. Data sources include St. Regis Corp. and Federal Government.

C3935–1.603: Jan. 1985 (Vol. 14, No. 1)

MAGAZINE REVENUE UP 8.7% OVER 5 YEARS; BELOW COMMUNICATIONS GROUP AVERAGE

(p. 8) Brief article, with 1 chart showing aggregate pre-tax operating income margins for business and consumer magazines, 1979-83. Data are from Veronis, Suhler and Associates.

9-MONTH REVENUES UP 18%, RECURRING FEATURE

(p. 25) Recurring article on advertising revenues and pages of Publishers Information Bureau magazines. Includes 2 tables ranking top 10 magazines in advertising pages and revenues, 1st 9 months 1984 with comparisons to 1983.

FOREIGN PAPER IS ABUNDANT

(p. 52) Article, with 1 table showing volume of coated paper shipments, imports, and exports, 1982 and 1984. Data are from American Paper Institute.

PRODUCTION: WHO GETS PAID HOW MUCH

(p. 77-92) By Barbara Love. Article on salaries of magazine production staffs. Data are from 437 responses of magazine production managers and staff members to a Sept. 1984 *Folio* survey.

Includes 33 tables, primarily showing distribution of respondents by salary range and availability of deferred compensation, by title, variously cross-tabulated by sex, years of experience, number of magazines handled (and circulation and page size of largest), region, and number of employees supervised.

C3935–1.604: Feb. 1985 (Vol. 14, No. 2)

[Volume and issue numbers are omitted.]

FIRST QUARTER RESULTS SET UPWARD TREND IN AD REVENUES FOR '85

(p. 8) Brief article, with 1 table showing expenditures for local advertising, and for national advertising by media, 1985 with percent change from 1984. Data are from McCann-Erickson, Inc.

LIBEL LOSS RATE DROPS 35%

(p. 30-31) Article, with 1 table showing number of libel cases brought against the mass media and average initial award; and percent of cases lost by all media (with detail for jury and non-jury trials) and lost by magazines, newspapers, and broadcasters; 1980-82 and 1982-84 periods. Data are from Libel Defense Resource Center.

CORRECTIONS TO THE FOLIO 400/1984

(p. 38) Article presenting corrections and additions to 1984 Folio 400 annual ranking of the magazine publishing industry.

For description of original feature, see SRI 1984 Annual under C3935-1.512.

BUSINESS PUBS' REVENUES UP 6.9% IN 1983

(p. 42-44) Article on financial performance of business magazine publishing industry. Data are from Veronis, Suhler and Associates.

Includes 2 tables showing selected business publishing financial ratios, including operating margins and growth rates for revenues, pre-tax operating income, assets, and cash flow, with ranking among 10 communication industry segments and detail for 3 leading publishers, various periods 1979-83.

CONSUMER MAGAZINES MAKE EFFICIENT USE OF ASSETS

(p. 48-49) Article on financial performance of consumer magazine publishing industry. Data are from Veronis, Suhler and Associates.

Includes 2 tables showing selected consumer publishing financial ratios, including operating margins and growth rates for revenues, pre-tax operating income, assets, and cash flow, with ranking among 10 communication industry segments and detail for 3 leading publishers, various periods 1979-83.

C3935–1.605: Mar. 1985 (Vol. 14, No. 3)

QUARTERLY TABLE

[1] Publication delivery, by selected city, 3rd quarter 1984. (p. 51)

SLOWER BUT HEALTHY GROWTH FOR MAGAZINES FOR '85, SAYS COMMERCE DEPT

(p. 8) Brief article, with 1 chart showing percent growth in gross receipts and employment for periodicals, 1983-85. Data are from Commerce Dept.

2% TO 4% AD PAGE INCREASE FOR 1985, COEN PREDICTS, ANNUAL FEATURE

(p. 31-34) Annual article on magazine advertising pages and revenue. Data are from Robert Coen of McCann-Erickson, Inc. Includes 2 tables showing national advertising revenue by media, 1984 with percent change from 1983; and percent change in expenditures for network and spot TV, and magazine advertising, by product category, 1st 9 months 1983-84.

EIGHT MAGAZINES AMONG INC. 500, ANNUAL FEATURE

(p. 35-36) Annual article, with 1 table showing sales revenues of 8 leading small, privately held magazine publishers, 1979 and 1983. Data are from INC. magazine.

C3935–1.606: Apr. 1985 (Vol. 14, No. 4)

SEVEN OF NINE PIB CATEGORIES SHOW AD GAINS, RECURRING FEATURE

(p. 24-25) Recurring article on advertising revenues and pages of Publishers Information Bureau magazines. Includes 2 tables ranking top 10 magazines in advertising pages and revenues, 1984 with comparisons to 1983.

4% GROWTH THROUGH '89?

(p. 33) Article, with 1 chart showing average annual growth rate for publishing industry revenues, by sector (magazines, newspapers, books, and miscellaneous), 1985-89 period. Data are from Commerce Dept.

COATED PAPER CAPACITY ON THE RISE

(p. 35-37) Article, with 1 chart showing production capacity for coated groundwood and free sheet paper, 1983-87. Data are from American Paper Institute.

A similar article, for 1979-86, is described in SRI 1984 Annual under C3935-1.506.

McCALL'S STILL TOP FREELANCE MARKET, RECURRING FEATURE

(p. 40, 45) Recurring article on best magazines for freelance writers, based on *Writer's Digest* criteria. Data are from a *Writer's Digest* survey of several hundred magazines.

Includes 1 table showing number of manuscripts purchased per year, minimum and maximum word rate, percent of payment made for stories commissioned but not used, type of rights bought, and whether author is shown galleys, for 10 best magazines, 1985.

Previous article, appearing in Aug. 1984 issue, is described in SRI 1984 Annual under C3935-1.509.

COSMO: TOP SELLER AT COLLEGES, ANNUAL FEATURE

(p. 47) Annual article, with 1 table showing 10 most popular magazines in college bookstores, based on a 1985 *College Store Executive* survey of bookstore managers.

TOP U.S. MAGAZINES IN ANNUAL FOREIGN NEWSSTAND SALES, SEMIANNUAL FEATURE

(p. 52) Semiannual article on U.S. magazines with highest single-copy sales overseas. Data are 1st half 1984 estimates from Boarts International, Inc., based on Audit Bureau of Circulations report for June 1984.

Includes 1 table ranking top 10 magazines by foreign sales value, and showing foreign and U.S. issues sold, cover price, and issue frequency, 1st half 1984.

1984: A BILLION DOLLAR YEAR FOR ACQUISITIONS

(p. 82-95) By James B. Kobak. Article on 10 major magazine acquisitions in 1984, presenting transaction price for each acquisition, and some or all of the following for 8 magazines or magazine groups sold: working capital requirements, revenue, pre-tax profit, and price/earnings ratio, primarily 1983.

Also includes operational profiles for 20 Ziff-Davis publications included in transactions, with related market size indicators for the automotive, bridal, photography, audio, boating, travel agency, and meeting/convention markets, various years 1974-84.

Most data are from specified industry sources.

Contains narrative analysis, 1 chart and 8 tables on major acquisitions, and 23 tables on Ziff-Davis publications and related markets.

C3935–1.607: May 1985 (Vol. 14, No. 5)

60% OF CONSUMER MAGAZINES POST CIRCULATION INCREASES, SEMIANNUAL FEATURE

(p. 23, 26) Semiannual article on magazine circulation, 2nd half 1984. Data are from Audit Bureau of Circulations. Includes 2 tables showing top 10 magazines ranked by total circulation and by percent increase in circulation, 2nd half 1984 with comparisons to 2nd half 1983.

Article is accompanied by 1 chart showing percent of consumer magazines increasing subscriptions, single-copy sales, and total circulation, 2nd half 1984 vs. 2nd half 1983 (front cover).

TAX REFORMS UP DEMAND FOR FLEXIBLE BENEFITS

(p. 29-30) Article, with 1 chart showing number of companies offering flexible programs for employee selection of benefit plans, 1978-85.

FOLIO: TRACKS PUBLISHING COMPANIES' FINANCIAL PERFORMANCE, QUARTERLY FEATURE

(p. 46) Quarterly article, with 1 chart and 1 table showing magazine publishing stock index compared with Dow Jones Industrial Average, Oct. 1984-Mar. 1985; and stock price, price/earnings ratio, earnings per share, dividend rate and yield, and 52-week high and low prices, for 17 leading magazine publishers, primarily as of Mar. 14, 1985. Data sources include Nordby International, Inc.

This is the 1st quarterly article.

C3935–1.608: June 1985 (Vol. 14, No. 6)

HAVE NEWSSTAND SALES BOTTOMED OUT?

(p. 34-35) Article, with 1 table showing magazine newsstand sales as percent of total circulation, by magazine category, 1983-84. Data are from Council for Periodical Distributors Assn.

AGENCY USE OF SYNDICATED DATA

(p. 44) Article, with 1 undated table showing advertising agencies' reasons for adjusting magazine circulation data from syndicated research services. Data are from responses of 109 agencies to a Magazine Publishers Assn survey.

HELLO, SUBSCRIBER

(p. 87-92) By Ted Scala. Article, with 1 chart showing percent of magazine publishers using telemarketing for new and renewed subscriptions, fall 1984 and spring 1985. Data are from *Capell's Circulation Report,* and are based on semiannual surveys of approximately 100 consumer magazines.

C3935–1.609: July 1985 (Vol. 14, No. 7)

FORTUNE 500: PUBLISHING IS BEST TOTAL ROI INDUSTRY

(p. 22) Article, with 1 table showing sales and net income of 11 magazine publishing companies in Fortune 500, 1984, with 1983-84 sales rank.

REGIONALS GO AFTER MORE NATIONAL ADS

(p. 25) Article, with 1 table showing total adult audience and market penetration rate, ranked for 14 leading periodicals and all city/regional magazines, spring 1985. Data are from Mediamark Research, Inc. and City and Regional Magazine Assn.

POOR FOLLOW-UP ON READER INQUIRY

(p. 36) Article, with 1 undated table showing average time taken by industrial advertisers to respond to business magazine ad inquiries. Data are from a recent study conducted by E. S. Advertising Services, Inc.

EDITORS' AVERAGE SALARY: $34,623, RECURRING FEATURE

(p. 68-84) Recurring article, by Barbara Love and Jean Angelo, on compensation paid magazine editorial personnel. Data are based on 484 responses to a spring 1985 *Folio* survey.

Includes 7 charts and 8 tables showing the following for editorial management, art directors, and general, managing/executive, senior/associate, and copy editors:

a. Salary averages: by publication type (business vs. consumer), average annual editorial pages produced, frequency, circulation, and number of editors on staff; and by region and respondent sex, years in business, and whether responsible for 1 or more magazines.

b. Bonus averages by region, circulation size, and sex; and percent of respondents receiving bonus and deferred compensation, by publication type and circulation size.

This is the 2nd salary survey. Previous survey is described in SRI 1982 Annual under C3935-1.310.

C3935–1.610: Aug. 1985 (Vol. 14, No. 8)

QUARTERLY TABLE

[1] Publication delivery, by selected city, 1st quarter 1985. (p. 56)

6% HIKE IN PAPER USE EXPECTED IN '85-'86, ANNUAL FEATURE

(p. 36-37) Annual article forecasting consumer magazine publishing industry paper demand through 1986. Data are based on responses of 99 publishers to a 1985 Magazine Publishers Assn survey. Includes 2 tables showing paper demand by grade, with distribution by basis weight, 1984-86.

FOR-PROFITS BENEFITING FROM NONPROFIT POSTAGE BREAKS

(p. 42) Article, with 1 table showing appropriations under revenue-foregone postal subsidy, by class of mail, FY85. Data are from General Accounting Office.

C3935–1.611: Sept. 1985 (Vol. 14, No. 9)

AD SALES EXPECTED TO REMAIN FLAT, ANNUAL FEATURE

(p. 19, 25-26) Annual article presenting revised forecasts of advertising revenues by media, 1985. Data are prepared by Robert J. Coen of McCann-Erickson, Inc. Includes 1 table.

For description of original forecast, see C3935-1.605 above.

PRE-TAX PROFITS GROW TO 11.29%, ANNUAL FEATURE

(p. 19-20) Annual article on magazine publishing revenues and expenses, 1984. Data are from responses of 172 magazines to a survey conducted by Price Waterhouse for Magazine Publishers Assn, and from previous surveys.

Includes 2 tables showing aggregate revenues by source, costs by item, and pre-tax profits, all as percent of total revenues, 1982-84, with 1984 pre-tax profit detail by circulation size and advertising revenue range.

MORE EMPLOYEES RELOCATED

(p. 44) Article, with 1 table showing corporate employee relocation assistance policies of publishing/printing vs. all companies, 1984. Data are based on a survey conducted by Merrill Lynch Relocation Management, Inc.

Full Merrill Lynch survey is covered in SRI under B6025-1.

DISTURBING FORCES IN SINGLE-COPY SALES

(p. 122) By Nigel P. Heaton. Article, with 1 chart showing average newsstand sales of magazines reporting to Audit Bureau of Circulations, selected years 1973-83. Data are from Curtis Circulation Co.

C3935–1.612: Oct. 1985 (Vol. 14, No. 10)

QUARTERLY TABLE

[1] Publication delivery, by selected city, 2nd quarter 1985. (p. 54)

60.4% OF ABC MAGAZINES' CIRCULATION UP 1ST HALF, SEMIANNUAL FEATURE

(p. 25, 49-51) Semiannual article on magazine circulation, 1st half 1985. Data are from Audit Bureau of Circulations. Includes 2 tables showing top 10 magazines ranked by percent annual increase in circulation, and by total circulation, 1st half 1985.

MAGAZINES OVERSTATING CIRCULATION BY 2% OR MORE, RECURRING FEATURE

(p. 58) Recurring brief article, with 1 table showing publisher vs. Audit Bureau of Circulations (ABC) estimates of circulation, for magazines for which the 2 estimates vary by more than 2%. Data are from ABC audit report released 2nd quarter 1985.

TOP U.S. MAGAZINES IN ANNUAL FOREIGN NEWSSTAND SALES, SEMIANNUAL FEATURE

(p. 64-65) Semiannual article on U.S. magazines with highest single-copy sales overseas. Data are 2nd half 1984 estimates from Boarts International, Inc., based on Audit Bureau of Circulations report for Dec. 1984.

Includes 1 table ranking top 10 magazines by foreign sales value, and showing foreign and U.S. issues sold, cover price, and issue frequency, 2nd half 1984.

61% OF WEEKLY PUBLICATIONS DELIVERED LATE, SEMIANNUAL FEATURE

(p. 66) Semiannual table on USPS delivery efficiency for weekly priority publications. Data are from Red Tag News Publications Assn, Inc. Table shows percent of on-time, 1 day late, and later deliveries in approximately 40 cities, 1st half 1985.

CIRCULATION DIRECTOR'S AVERAGE SALARY 68% HIGHER THAN A MANAGER'S

(p. 100-105) By Barbara Love and Jean Angelo. Article on compensation paid to magazine circulation managers and directors. Data are based on 263 responses to a recent *Folio* survey.

Includes 2 charts and 5 tables showing the following for circulation directors and managers:

a. Salary averages: by publication type (business vs. consumer), by region, size and type of circulation, whether magazine is audited, number of magazines under respondent's responsibility, and respondent sex, employees under supervision, and years in business.

b. Bonus averages by region, circulation size, and sex; percent of respondents receiving deferred compensation, by publication type and circulation size; and job responsibilities.

This is the 1st circulation salary survey.

C3935–1.613: Folio 400/1985

[Issue price is $25.00]

(383 p., special issue) Annual ranking of top 400 magazines for 1984, based on revenues, advertising pages, and circulation. Covers consumer and business publications, and includes data on multipublication companies. Data are compiled by the magazines and analyzed by *Folio*.

Contents:

a. Contents listing (p. 6-10); and introduction, with user's guide, 2 summary tables, and 7 summary charts, including 1980-84 performance summary for the Folio 400 (p. 13-30).

b. Folio 400 table (p. 33-46); and consumer and business magazine sections, with 78 tables, and magazine profiles (p. 50-356).

c. Indexes (p. 359-383).

Folio 400 table, consumer and business magazine tables, and magazine profiles are described below.

This is the 7th annual ranking.

TABLES AND PROFILES:

FOLIO 400

(p. 33-46) Table shows the following for each of the top 400 magazines, ranked by total revenue: total, advertising, subscription, and newsstand revenues; percent change in revenues; advertising pages; and average subscription and newsstand circulation; 1984 with 1983 total revenue ranking.

CONSUMER AND BUSINESS MAGAZINE TABLES, AND MAGAZINE PROFILES

(p. 50-278, 281-356) Tables show 1984 rankings of magazines by numerous performance criteria, including items in the Folio 400 table, plus subscription prices, editorial vs. advertising pages per copy, other ratios, and growth categories. Rankings are shown for top magazines overall, for fastest growing and/or new magazines, and for magazines grouped by detailed market segment, including various industry, occupation, consumer interest, humanities and science, and demographic groups.

Profiles of individual magazines include publisher directory information and summary of editorial content or focus.

C3950
Forbes, Inc.

C3950–1   FORBES
Biweekly.
ISSN 0015-6914.   LC 76-149.
SRI/MF/excerpts, shipped quarterly

Biweekly journal (with 3 additional special issues) reporting on domestic and foreign business and investment trends. Presents articles on corporate developments, money and securities markets, taxes, banking, Federal Government policies, and investment strategies.

Includes occasional articles with substantial data on securities, corporations, or industry sectors, grouped for analytical purposes. Also includes annual features presenting stock performance forecasts, financial data on major corporations and mutual funds, results of a corporate executive compensation survey, and profiles of 400 wealthiest persons/families.

Issues contain feature articles, occasionally with substantial statistics; regular editorial depts; and the following biweekly statistical features:

a. "Forbes Index," with 10 charts showing trends in *Forbes* composite economic index since 1970; and 8 component economic indicators for latest 13-14 months, ending 2-3 months prior to cover date.

b. "Forbes/Wilshire 5000 Review," prepared by Wilshire Associates, with 11 charts and 3 tables showing trends in Wilshire 5000 equity index since mid-1970s; selected other stock performance indexes, including percent change by industry sector for 2- and 52-week periods ending approximately 4 weeks prior to cover date; and securities analysts' current estimates of annual earnings per share by industry sector, with rankings based on recent changes in estimates.

Biweekly "Forbes Index" and "Forbes/Wilshire 5000 Review" appear in all regular biweekly issues. All additional features with substantial statistical content are described, as they appear, under "Statistical Features." Nonstatistical features are not covered.

Availability: Forbes, Subscription Services Manager, 60 Fifth Ave., New York NY 10011, $42.00 per yr., single copy $3.00, special issues $4.00; SRI/MF/excerpts for "Forbes Index" and "Forbes/Wilshire 5000 Review," and for all portions covered under "Statistical Features;" shipped quarterly.

Issues reviewed during 1985: Nov. 5, 1984-Oct. 28, 1985 (P) (Vol. 134, Nos. 11-15; Vol. 135, Nos. 1-13; Vol. 136, Nos. 1-11).

STATISTICAL FEATURES:

C3950–1.601: Nov. 5, 1984 (Vol. 134, No. 11)

WHAT IT TAKES TO STAY ON TOP, ANNUAL FEATURE

(p. 128-174) Annual article, by Steve Kichen, presenting tabular list of small companies with sales of less than $250 million, average return on equity of at least 14.3% over the past 5 years and 10% over the last 12 months, and debt not exceeding equity, as of 1984. Data are from Standard & Poor's, William O'Neil & Co., *The Unlisted Market Guide,* and *Forbes.*

List shows the following for 300 such companies, ranked by 5-year return on equity: 5-year average and latest 12-month returns on equity; earnings per share in last 12 months, and 5-year growth rate; latest fiscal year sales and profits; recent stock price and percent change in 1984; price/earnings ratio in last 12 months; book value per share, and long-term debt/equity ratio.

Also includes alphabetical listing, with market value and selected rankings for each company.

Previous article, for 1983, is described in SRI 1983 Annual, under C3950-1.426.

C3950–1.602: Nov. 19, 1984 (Vol. 134, No. 12)

WHAT'S AROUND THE CORNER IN 1985? ANNUAL FEATURE

(p. 84-160) Annual article, by Steve Kichen and Leslie Pittel, forecasting 1985 stock performance for 1,000 large corporations, each with a market capitalization of over $70 million. Data are from Lynch, Jones, and Ryan's Institutional Brokers Estimate System.

Includes 1 extended table showing the following for each stock: recent price; earnings per share, 1983 and estimated 1984-85; and estimated price/earnings ratio, 1985, with number of analysts contributing estimates, and confidence factor indicating level of agreement among analysts.

M.B.A. MILLS

(p. 316-326) By John A. Byrne. Article, with 1 table showing full- and part-time enrollment in master of business administration programs at 10 institutions with largest enrollment, 1983/84. Data are from American Assembly of Collegiate Schools of Business.

C3950–1.603: Dec. 3, 1984 (Vol. 134, No. 13)

SHOPPING AT HOME, RECURRING FEATURE

(p. 86) Recurring article, by Leslie Pittel, on potentially undervalued stocks. Covers stocks with poor performance record during 1984, likelihood of being sold for tax write-off in Dec. 1984, and potential for improved performance in 1985. Data are from Wilshire Associates, Standard & Poor's, and *Forbes*.

Includes 1 table showing the following for 25 such stocks: recent price and 52-week range; latest 12-month earnings per share and price/earnings ratio; and yield, return on equity, and price/book and debt/equity ratios.

A similar article is described in SRI 1983 Annual, under C3950-1.403.

PSRs REVISITED

(p. 273-274) By Steve Kichen. Article on debt-adjusted market price/sales ratio (PSR) as a measure of stock performance. Data are from ISYS Corp.

Includes 2 undated tables showing the following data for 60 stocks with debt-adjusted PSR significantly lower or higher than unadjusted PSR: recent price and 52-week range; debt-adjusted and unadjusted PSR; earnings per share and price/earnings ratio for latest 12 months; current, cash flow/debt, and debt/equity ratios; and book value.

C3950–1.604: Dec. 17, 1984 (Vol. 134, No. 14)

DREAM DELAYED, DREAM DENIED

(p. 36-37) By Robert Teitelman. Article, with 1 undated table showing the following for 10 biotechnology companies: initial offering and recent stock prices, equity, debt, and value of R&D limited partnerships. Data are from Whale Securities, Inc.

GREAT TIMBER BAILOUT OF 1984

(p. 162-165) By Kathleen K. Wiegner. Article on Federal law permitting forest product companies to buy out of Forest Service timber-cutting contracts. Data are from Salomon Brothers and Timber Data Co.

Includes 1 table showing the following for 14 companies: net worth; and volume of unharvested timber under contract, potential financial loss associated with contract, buyout timber volume, potential loss removed, buyout cost, and remaining potential loss. Volume and loss data are as of June or Aug. 1984.

C3950–1.605: Dec. 31, 1984 (Vol. 134, No. 15)

YEN FOR NEW MARKETS

(p. 46-47) By Richard Phalon. Article, with 1 table showing the following for 4 largest Japanese and 4 largest U.S. brokerage firms: net worth, Sept. 1984; and estimated revenues and net income, FY84. Data are from Japanese companies and Lipper Analytical Services.

C3950–1.606: Jan. 14, 1985 (Vol. 135, No. 1)

**37th ANNUAL REPORT
ON AMERICAN INDUSTRY**

(p. 46-271) Annual feature presenting "Forbes Yardsticks 1984," on the profitability, growth, and stock market performance of approximately 1,000 publicly owned corporations

with revenues in excess of $450 million. Includes comparisons of return on equity, sales and earnings, and financial and operating ratios, for individual firms, overall and within industry groups.

Contains introduction (p. 46-47); industry rankings, with 42 tables, described below (p. 50-214); financial performance rankings, with accompanying narrative, and 3 tables also described below (p. 216-259); industry median summary table (p. 260-262); and alphabetical index of companies covered (p. 264-271).

TABLES:

COMPANY RANKINGS WITHIN EACH INDUSTRY
[For each industry sector noted below, tables show corporate sales and profits shares generated within each industry; 5-year average and latest 12-month returns on equity and sales, and percent change in earnings per share; debt/equity ratio; and net profit margin; all by company, with industry medians.]

a. Aerospace/defense; air freight and passenger transport; apparel and shoes; auto/truck manufacturing and suppliers; banks (multinationals and by region); beverages (alcoholic and soft drink); broadcasting; building (commercial and residential); and building materials (cement/gypsum, lumber, equipment, and other). 10 tables. (p. 50-117)

b. Chemicals; coal; computers; consumer products (appliances, home furnishings, and household and personal products); diversified companies and conglomerates; electrical equipment; electric utilities by region; electronics; financial services; food processors; health care; heavy equipment; industrial machinery; and insurance. 14 tables. (p. 118-166)

c. Leisure/recreation; metals (nonferrous and steel); natural gas utilities; office equipment; oilfield drillers/services; packaging; paper; petroleum; publishing; retailers (general and specialty). 11 tables. (p. 168-197)

d. Services (fast food chains, food distributors, and industrial and office services); supermarket chains; surface transportation (railroads, trucks, and other); telecommunication; textiles; thrift institutions; and tobacco. 7 tables. (p. 198-214)

OVERALL RANKINGS
[Data are shown by company.]

e. Growth rankings: percent growth in sales and earnings per share, 5-year average and latest 12 months. 1 table. (p. 216-229)

f. Stock market performance rankings: recent price, 5-year change, and range 1980-84; book value per share and recent price/book value ratio; latest 12-month earnings per share, and price/earnings and price/sales ratios; and annual dividend and current yield. 1 table. (p. 232-251)

g. Profitability rankings: return on equity, 5-year average and latest 12 months. 1 table. (p. 254-259)

C3950–1.607: Jan. 28, 1985 (Vol. 135, No. 2)

MANY HAPPY RETURNS

(p. 31-32) By James Cook. Article, with 1 table comparing estimated construction costs to

cash on hand, for 17 publicly owned utilities, 1984-86. Data are from Salomon Brothers, Inc.

MAKING MONEY THE SLOW WAY, ANNUAL FEATURE

(p. 112-117) Annual article, by Laura R. Walbert, on the investment performance of open-end mutual funds in 2nd half 1984. Data are from CDA Investment Technologies, Inc.

Includes 2 tables showing rates of return for top 10 funds, 2nd half 1984; and assets as of Sept. 30, 1984, and rates of return during 6-month and 10-year periods ended Dec. 31, 1984, for 317 funds.

C3950–1.608: Feb. 11, 1985 (Vol. 135, No. 3)

NUCLEAR FOLLIES

(front cover, p. 82-100) By James Cook. Article, with 1 table (foldout) showing the following data for 36 nuclear reactors under construction as of Jan. 1, 1984: ownership shares, by utility; architect/engineer, construction manager, and reactor supplier; total expected cost, net capacity, cost per kilowatt, and allowance for funds under construction as percent of cost; year ordered and expected to enter service; and estimated impact on utility rates. Plants are ranked by cost per kilowatt. Data are from individual utilities and other sources.

FORBES/TUCS INSTITUTIONAL PORTFOLIO REPORT, QUARTERLY FEATURE

(p. 184-185) Quarterly article on pension fund participation in stock market activity, 4th quarter 1984. Data are based on over 3,000 pension funds monitored by Trust Universe Comparison Service of Wilshire Associates.

Includes 7 tables showing selected financial ratios for pension fund portfolios, and portfolio composition by type of investment; and pension fund investment shares, for 5-10 most popular stocks (overall and in 9 industry groups), 10 with greatest increase and decrease, and 10 most overweighted and underweighted relative to Wilshire 5000; 4th quarter 1984 with some comparisons to 3rd quarter 1984.

This is the 1st quarterly article.

C3950–1.609: Feb. 25, 1985 (Vol. 135, No. 4)

AS GOOD AS THEIR WORD

(p. 52-53) By Barry Stavro. Article, with 1 table showing the following data for 13 banking institutions without Federal deposit insurance which failed in the July 1982-Sept. 1984 period: State, date of failure, number of depositors, and amounts insured and repaid to date.

FAT, WIRED CATS

(p. 84-89) By Alex Ben Block. Article on investment potential of cable TV companies. Data are from Paul Kagan Associates.

Includes 1 undated table showing the following data for 15 cable TV companies: basic subscribers, homes passed, and penetration rate; earnings, cash flow, and long-term debt per share; cable TV revenues as percent of total company revenues; and recent stock price and liquidation value per share. Data are from Paul Kagan Associates.

C3950-1.609   Forbes, Inc.

ON INSIDERS' COATTAILS

(p. 174-176) By Steve Kichen and Leslie Pittel. Article on investment potential of companies in which inside management owns substantial stock. Data are from Computer Directions Advisers, *Value Line Investment Survey,* Standard & Poor's, and *Forbes.*

Includes 1 undated table showing the following data for 37 companies with 10-40% of stock owned by inside management: percent insider holdings, recent price, latest 12-month earnings per share and price/earnings ratio, yield, current and debt/equity ratios, book value per share, and sales.

C3950-1.610: Mar. 11, 1985 (Vol. 135, No. 5)

WHAT'S IN A NAME?

(p. 112-117) Article, with 1 table ranking top 10 New York and top 4 regional investment banking firms by capital raised in initial public offerings during Jan. 1, 1984-Jan. 31, 1985, and showing number of issues underwritten, and average price change between offering date and Feb. 1985. Data are from Securities Data Co. and CompuServe.

WHY IS NO ONE SAFE?

(p. 134-140) By Allan Sloan. Article on recent corporate acquisition trends. Data are from W. T. Grimm & Co. Includes 1 chart showing transaction participants and price, for corporate acquisitions exceeding $1 billion, 1969-84.

SMART DARTS REVISITED

(p. 204-211) By Leslie Pittel. Article comparing performance of randomly chosen stocks with performance of stocks chosen on basis of selected criteria. Data are from Wilshire Associates, Standard & Poor's Corp., *Forbes,* and Lynch, Jones, and Ryan.

Includes 5 tables showing stock price (recent and as of July 30, 1984), latest 12-month earnings per share and price/earnings ratio, yield and book value (no date), and estimated earnings per share for 1985; all for computer-generated portfolios of 24-25 stocks in each of the following categories: randomly chosen, lowest price/earnings and price/book value ratios, and highest proven and anticipated sales/earnings growth.

Article updates a similar feature which appeared in the July 30, 1984 issue; for description, see SRI 1984 Annual under C3950-1.520.

TAKE YOUR PICK

(p. 224) By Stanley W. Angrist. Article on soybean futures trading. Includes 1 table showing soybean futures price spreads for Nov.-July, and profit or loss, 1968-84.

C3950-1.611: Mar. 25, 1985 (Vol. 135, No. 6)

THE PARTS AND THE WHOLE

(p. 264-268) By Leslie Pittel. Article on the investment performance of stocks involved in corporate spinoffs (distribution of shares in a company's subsidiary to the company's shareholders). Includes 3 tables showing the following:

a. Spinoff date; and parent and spinoff company name, stock price as of spinoff date, and recent stock price; for 35 spinoffs during 1981-84.

b. Parent company name, principal business, possible spinoff business, and sales and earnings in latest fiscal year, for 15 potential spinoffs.

C3950-1.612: Apr. 8, 1985 (Vol. 135, No. 7)

OUTGUESSING THE GUESSERS, ANNUAL FEATURE

(p. 172-178) Annual lists, with accompanying analysis by Steve Kichen and Michael Ozanian, of 56 companies predicted by security analysts to post significant earnings gains or losses during 1985, and of 49 companies with earnings estimates revised substantially since Aug. 1984.

Data are from Lynch, Jones, and Ryan's Institutional Brokers Estimate System, representing estimates by approximately 2,000 security analysts.

Includes 4 tables showing the following data for each company: recent stock price; earnings per share, 1984 and estimated 1985; price/earnings ratio based on 1985 estimates; number of estimates received; and level of agreement among estimates. Tables on companies with revised estimates include both Aug. 1984 and current estimates.

C3950-1.613: Apr. 29, 1985 (Vol. 135, No. 9)

[Issue price is $4.00.]

FORBES 500s, ANNUAL FEATURE

(p. 158-364) Annual feature, for 1984, ranking the top 500 publicly owned corporations by selected measures, and presenting employment and stock market data for each ranked company. Data are from *Forbes,* William O'Neil & Co., and Lynch, Jones, and Ryan's Institutional Brokers Estimate System.

Contains brief overview, with 1 summary table (p. 158-159); and 8 detailed tables, most with brief accompanying narrative and summary data, as follows:

a. Top 500 companies ranked by sales (p. 162-170), net profits with accompanying data on cash flow (p. 174-188), assets (p. 192-200), and market value (p. 205-212); and all 785 companies included among the top 500 lists ranked by employment, with accompanying data on per-employee sales, profits, and assets (p. 231-242); 1984, with selected comparisons to 1983. 5 tables.

b. Alphabetical list of all 785 companies, with financial data and rankings repeated for each company. 1 table. (p. 244-266)

c. Stock market data for each of the 785 companies (arranged alphabetically), including stock price, performance relative to overall market, price/earnings and price/sales ratios, profit margin, earnings per share, dividend rate and anticipated growth, dividend payout ratio, and shares outstanding and percent held by institutions, all shown for latest available date, with some estimates for 1985 and comparisons to latest 5-year and 12-month periods. 1 table. (p. 268-307)

d. Directory of ranked companies, including address, telephone number, chief executive, and industry group. 1 table. (p. 308-364)

This is the 17th annual feature.

C3950-1.614: May 20, 1985 (Vol. 135, No. 11)

FIT TO FIGHT

(p. 230-232) By Ellen Benoit. Article, with 1 chart comparing 1944 and 1985 prices for selected uniform and equipment items issued to field combat soldiers.

FORBES/TUCS INSTITUTIONAL PORTFOLIO REPORT, QUARTERLY FEATURE

(p. 254-255) Quarterly article on pension fund participation in stock market activity, 1st quarter 1985. Data are based on over 4,000 pension funds monitored by Trust Universe Comparison Service of Wilshire Associates.

Includes 7 tables showing selected financial ratios for pension fund portfolios, and portfolio composition by type of investment; and pension fund investment shares, for 5-10 most popular stocks (overall and in 9 industry groups), 10 with greatest increase and decrease, and 10 most overweighted and underweighted relative to Wilshire 5000; 1st quarter 1985 with some comparisons to 4th quarter 1984.

YOU GET WHAT YOU PAY FOR

(p. 256) By Michael Ozanian. Article on investment potential of stocks currently selling at a price less than 6.4 times estimated 1986 earnings. Data are from Institutional Brokers Estimate System, Standard & Poor's Corp., and *Forbes.*

Includes 1 table showing the following for 20 such stocks: recent prices, book value, value/price and debt/equity ratios, and yield; and earnings and price/earnings ratio, for latest 12-month period and estimated for 1986.

C3950-1.615: June 3, 1985 (Vol. 135, No. 12)

WHO GETS THE MOST PAY, ANNUAL FEATURE

(p. 114-153) Annual article, by John A. Byrne, on compensation paid to chief executive officers (CEOs) of 785 corporations, 1984. Includes 1 table showing the following data by company: chief executive name, age, tenure with firm (total and as CEO), background, and compensation (salary/bonus, stock gains, and other), with overall and industry compensation rank.

Also includes 2 charts and 3 summary tables showing number of CEOs and median compensation, by tenure, age group, business background, and company sales volume; and highest- and lowest-paid CEOs, median compensation, and number of companies represented, by industry.

BITTER PILLS

(p. 203-206) By Francesca Lunzer. Article, with 1 undated table showing the following for 10 most-prescribed drugs for people over age 65: best-selling brand name and manufacturer; availability of generic substitute; cost per 100, for brand name and generic; dosage per day; and type of condition treated. Data are from Arthur D. Little and American Assn of Retired Persons.

FREE AS THE AIR

(p. 208-212) By Anne McGrath. Article, with 1 undated table showing membership criteria and benefits for frequent flier promotional programs of 13 major airlines.

CHERCHEZ LA CASH

(p. 234-236) By Leslie Pittel. Article on investment potential of companies with favorable ratio of stock price to 'free cash flow' (pretax income plus depreciation, minus capital outlays). Data are from Standard & Poor's Compustat Services and *Forbes*.

Includes 1 undated table showing the following for 50 such companies: current stock price, and 12-month high and low; free cash flow per share; free cash flow/price, debt/free cash flow, and debt/equity ratios; and earnings per share and price/earning ratio, for latest 12 months.

C3950–1.616: June 17, 1985 (Vol. 135, No. 13)

WILL IT RAIN IN AUGUST?

(p. 224) By Stanley W. Angrist. Article, with 1 table showing trends in December wheat vs. corn price spread, and potential commodity investment profit, 1973-84.

C3950–1.617: July 29, 1985 (Vol. 136, No. 3)

$26 BILLION SOLUTION

(p. 40-41) By Howard Gold. Article on effect of deregulation on telephone industry depreciation accounting. Includes 1 table showing the following for individual Bell local and regional operating companies, and for 3 largest independent telephone companies, as of Dec. 31, 1984: depreciation reserve (percent of plant depreciated); composite depreciation rate (currently allowed by State regulators); estimated reserve deficiency; and date of next scheduled adjustment in depreciation rate.

STATES' FIGHTS

(p. 132-133) By Laura Saunders. Article on impact of eliminating State/local tax deductions under Federal income tax reform proposal. Data are from Census Bureau.

Includes 1 map and 1 table showing the following data, by State: State/local taxes as percent of personal income, 1982, and estimated per capita change in State/local taxes under proposed reform; and highest marginal income tax rate, and percent of State/local revenues from individual income, property, sales, and other taxes, 1983.

SPECIAL REPORT: SPOTLIGHT ON INTERNATIONAL BUSINESS, ANNUAL FEATURE

(p. 161-192) Annual compilation of 4 tables presenting selected financial data for the 500 largest foreign companies, 100 largest foreign investments in U.S. and U.S. multinational corporations, and 100 foreign stocks traded in U.S., primarily 1984. Each table is preceded by a brief narrative summary. Tables show the following data:

a. Foreign companies ranked by revenue, with net income, assets, market value of common stock, corporate headquarters, industry, and employees.

b. Foreign investors in U.S. ranked by revenues, with names of companies involved, and each U.S. company's foreign ownership share, revenue, net income, assets, and primary industry.

c. U.S. multinational corporations ranked by foreign revenue, and including total revenue, and foreign and total operating profit and assets.

d. Stocks of foreign companies traded in U.S, including exchange, primary industry, headquarters country, recent and 52-week high and low stock prices, earnings per share in last 12-month period, price/earnings ratio, dividend per share, and yield rate.

C3950–1.618: Aug. 12, 1985 (Vol. 136, No. 4)

READY FOR TAKEOFF

(p. 30-31) By Howard Banks. Article, with 1 chart showing airline revenue passenger miles, and market shares aggregated for top 4, 5th-12th largest, and all other airlines, 1970, 1975, and 1st half 1985. Data are from Air Transport Association.

FORBES/TUCS INSTITUTIONAL PORTFOLIO REPORT, QUARTERLY FEATURE

(p. 132-133) Quarterly article on pension fund participation in stock market activity, 2nd quarter 1985. Data are based on over 4,000 pension funds monitored by Trust Universe Comparison Service of Wilshire Associates.

Includes 7 tables showing selected financial ratios for pension fund portfolios, and portfolio composition by type of investment; and pension fund investment shares, for 5-10 most popular stocks (overall and in 9 industry groups), 10 with greatest increase and decrease, and 10 most overweighted and underweighted relative to Wilshire 5000; 2nd quarter 1985 with some comparisons to 1st quarter 1985.

C3950–1.619: Aug. 26, 1985 (Vol. 136, No. 5)

BUYING ON BAD NEWS

(p. 150-151) By Ben Weberman and Matthew Schifrin. Article, with 1 undated table showing percent stock ownership in individual savings institutions held by 10 investment companies with 5%/more of their portfolios comprised of savings institution stocks. Data were compiled by Paine Webber from statements filed with Government agencies.

C3950–1.620: Sept. 9, 1985 (Vol. 136, No. 6)

LORD, MAKE ME CHASTE, BUT NOT JUST YET

(p. 56) By Laura Saunders. Article, with 1 undated table ranking top 10 banks by value of mandatory convertible notes outstanding, with note value as percent of primary capital. Mandatory convertible notes are ordinary long-term borrowings that banks promise to replace with equity within 12 years. Data are from Salomon Brothers, and Keefe, Bruyette & Woods.

HAVE ANOTHER CUP, PLEASE

(p. 156) By Stanley W. Angrist. Article, with 1 table showing world coffee production, imports, domestic usage, exports, supply, and beginning and ending stocks, for years ended Sept. 30, 1982-86. Data are from USDA.

C3950–1.621: Sept. 16, 1985 (Vol. 136, No. 7)

[Issue price is $4.00]

1985 ANNUAL MUTUAL FUNDS SURVEY

Annual compilation of features on mutual fund performance and investment results. Includes the statistical features described below.

HONOR ROLL

(p. 80-81) Article, with 1 table showing assets as of June 30, 1985, and selected characteristics and investment performance indicators, for 23 most consistently high-performing mutual funds.

IF YOU WANT TO SELL AMERICA SHORT

(p. 90) By Christopher Power. Article, with 1 undated table comparing rates of return for 13 global mutual funds (portfolios include U.S. securities) and 13 international funds (foreign securities only), latest 12-month period.

A PRICE ON YOUR HEAD

(p. 92-93) By Mary Kuntz. Article, with 1 table showing the following for 5 publicly traded companies whose primary business is mutual fund management: recent stock price, earnings per share over latest 12-month period, price earnings ratio (no date), assets under management (no date), and 1984 revenues.

1985 FUND RATINGS

(p. 98-174) Annual feature presenting investment performance data for approximately 1,000 individual mutual funds, 1985. Data are from CDA Investment Technologies, Inc.

Contains 5 tables showing *Forbes* ratings in rising and declining markets; average annual total return, 1976-85; total and income dividend returns in latest 12 month period; assets as of June 30, 1985, with change from 1984; annual expenses per $100 investment; and maximum sales charge; all by fund grouped by type (stock, balanced, bond/preferred stock, municipal bond, and money market).

Also includes listing of fund distributors, showing address, exchange privileges, and fund names and types.

C3950–1.622: Sept. 23, 1985 (Vol. 136, No. 8)

LOSERS, KEEPERS

(p. 214-216) By Leslie Pittel. Article on investment potential of stocks in companies with large tax-loss carryforwards. Includes 2 tables showing the following:

a. 42 companies with operating losses and large carryforwards in 1981: stock price percent change, 1981-85 period.

b. 24 companies with recent large carryforwards: stock price (recent and 52-week range); earnings per share, for latest 12-month period; and tax loss per share, cash, sales, and current ratio (no dates).

OIL SLICK

(p. 236) By Stanley W. Angrist. Article, with 1 table showing oil production and consumption in selected countries and world regions, 1979-85. Data are from *British Petroleum Statistical Review*.

C3950–1.623: Oct. 21, 1985 (Vol. 136, No. 10)

CHIEFS AND INDIANS

(p. 8) Article, with 1 undated chart showing chief executive compensation in 9 countries as percent of U.S.

DO YOU REALLY WANT TO BE YOUR OWN BOSS?

(p. 86-96) By Richard Greene. Article, with 1 table showing business failure rate, 1983, and percent change in employment, Oct. 1983-Oct. 1984, each for 10 industry sectors dominated by small businesses. The sectors covered are those with the lowest failure rates and greatest employment growth. Data are from SBA.

C3950–1.624: Oct. 28, 1985 (Vol. 136, No. 11)

[Issue price is $4.00.]

FORBES 400

(p. 108-330) Annual feature, by Jeff Bloch et al., profiling the 400 wealthiest individuals and families in the U.S., 1985. Data are based on *Forbes* research.

Includes introductory articles, and individual profiles presenting most or all of the following: name, age, locality, background, and lifestyle of individual or family; total net worth; type and source of earnings/assets (including inheritance); and charitable activities and contributions.

Profiles are arranged in descending order by net worth.

Also includes profiles of 64 former *Forbes* 400 members not on 1985 list, and 7 individuals who nearly made the list; and an alphabetical index.

Also includes text tables on *Forbes* 400 members' educational attainment (p. 172), top 14 metro areas (p. 178) and top 5 States (p. 182) of residence, age distribution (p. 202), and top 12 colleges/universities attended (p. 234).

C3975
Freeman, Miller, Publications

C3975–1   FOREST INDUSTRIES
Monthly.
ISSN 0015-7430.
LC 63-26965.
SRI/MF/excerpts, shipped quarterly

Monthly trade journal reporting developments and trends in logging, pulpwood and forest management, and manufacture of lumber, plywood, board, and pulp. Includes data on U.S. and Canadian paper/forest product companies' sales and earnings, and occasionally data on U.S. and Canadian lumber mill production. Data are from USDA, forestry assns, lumber companies, and other sources.

Issues generally contain:

a. Articles, occasionally with statistics; and regular editorial depts.

b. Monthly "FI Stock Index" feature (beginning with the June 1985 issue), with 1 chart and 2 tables showing stock price (including 52-week high and low), price/earnings ratio, and annual dividend rate and yield, for 35 U.S. and 10 Canadian forest product companies; and U.S. and Canadian forest product indexes compared to 4 major stock indexes; all as of a specified date for month previous to month of publication, with comparisons to previous periods; feature is compiled by Nordby International, Inc.

c. Quarterly feature (beginning with the June 1985 issue), with 2 tables on income results (sales and earnings) of approximately 25 U.S. and Canadian paper/forest product companies, for quarter ending 3 months prior to cover date, with percent change from previous year.

Monthly "FI Stock Index" appears in all issues. All additional features with substantial statistical content are described, as they appear, under "Statistical Features;" page location and latest period of coverage for quarterly table are also noted. Nonstatistical features are not covered.

Availability: Forest Industries, Circulation Department, 500 Howard St., San Francisco CA 94105, qualified subscribers †, others $35.00 per yr., single copy $3.50; SRI/MF/excerpts for monthly stock index feature and all portions covered under "Statistical Features;" shipped quarterly.

Issues reviewed during 1985: Nov. 1984-Oct. 1985 (P) (Vol. 111, Nos. 11-12; Vol. 112, Nos. 1-10).

STATISTICAL FEATURES:

C3975–1.601: Nov. 1984 (Vol. 111, No. 11)

GOOD POTENTIAL SEEN FOR HARDWOOD EXPORTS

(p. 34-36) By Philip A. Araman. Article, with 2 charts and 2 tables showing export distribution for 4 hardwood products, by world area and species (no date); distribution of sawtimber, sawmill logs, and lumber yields, by grade (no date); and hardwood lumber demand index, for U.S., world, and non-U.S. importers, decennial periods 1970-2000. Data sources include National Forest Products Assn.

C3975–1.602: Jan. 1985 (Vol. 112, No. 1)

CANADIAN LUMBER: FREE MARKET OR UNFAIR EDGE?

(p. 28) Article, with 1 table showing softwood lumber production, and imports from Canada and other countries, 1975-83 and 1st 7 months 1984. Data are from Northwest Independent Forest Manufacturers.

STUMPAGE FORMULAS: DIFFERENT, YES; SUBSIDY, NO.

(p. 29-30) Article, with 2 tables showing softwood lumber imports from Canada and other countries, by species, with total imports by selected country of origin, 1978-83; and Canadian share of softwood lumber market in eastern portion of U.S., by State, 1982. Data are from the Census Bureau and Southern Forest Products Assn.

C3975–1.603: Mar. 1985 (Vol. 112, No. 3)

FOR FORESTRY FIRMS, '84 RESULTS LOOK GOOD

(p. 11) Article, with 1 table showing sales and earnings for 16 forest product companies, 4th quarter and full year 1984, with change from 1983.

C3975–1.604: Apr. 1985 (Vol. 112, No. 4)

ANOTHER RECORD YEAR FOR STRUCTURAL PANELS, ANNUAL FEATURE

(p. 16-17) Annual article, with 1 table showing wood panel production by grade, 1974-84. Article appears in "1985 Panel Review," an annual review for the panel sector of the lumber industry.

C3975–1.605: May 1985 (Vol. 112, No. 5)

LOW PRICES DEPRESSED '84 CORPORATE EARNINGS

(p. 22-25) By David A. Pease. Article, with 5 tables showing sales, earnings, and building product share of total sales, for selected major U.S. and Canadian forest product companies, with sales and earnings rankings for top 20 companies, 1984 with comparisons to 1983. Data are based on company reports.

CAN U.S. EXPAND FOREST PRODUCTS EXPORTS TO JAPAN?

(p. 36-37) By Roger A. Sedjo. Article, with 2 tables showing volume of wood product imports for Japan and total world; and value of Japan's wood product consumption, total imports, and imports from U.S.; by product, 1980. Data are from Commerce Dept and UN Food and Agricultural Organization.

C3975–1.606: June 1985 (Vol. 112, No. 6)

QUARTERLY TABLES

(p. 13) Paper/forest products income results, 1st quarter 1985.

C3975–1.607: July 1985 (Vol. 112, No. 7)

1985 ANNUAL LUMBER REVIEW: OVERALL ECONOMY LOOKS OKAY, BUT LUMBER'S WOES PERSIST, ANNUAL FEATURE

(p. 24-31) Annual article on U.S. and Canadian lumber production and mills, 1984 and trends. Data are from National Forest Products Assn, Statistics Canada, and responses of approximately 470 U.S. and Canadian firms to a survey conducted by *Forest Industries*. Includes 4 tables showing the following:

a. U.S. softwood and hardwood consumption, and production by region; Canadian softwood/hardwood production, for British Columbia and all other Provinces; and production, mills, and number of companies producing over 1 billion board feet, aggregated for top 100 producers; 1975-84.

b. Production ranking of 418 leading companies, with headquarters location, number of mills, and hardwood and softwood production, 1984, with production comparisons to 1983.

C3975–1.608: Sept. 1985 (Vol. 112, No. 9)

QUARTERLY TABLES

(p. 11) Paper/forest products income results, 2nd quarter 1985.

C3975–1.609: Oct. 1985 (Vol. 112, No. 10)

ANALYZING LOGGING INJURIES: WHO GETS HURT AND WHY?

(p. 32-33) Article, with 2 tables showing percent of logging industry injuries, for selected job categories and activities, 2nd quarter 1982. Data are from BLS.

FOREIGN TRADE LIFTS FINLAND'S ECONOMY

(p. F3) Article, with 1 table showing value of Finnish forest industry exports, by country and world area of destination, 1983. Data are from Finland's Board of Custom Statistics and are shown in finnmarks.

C3975–2   PULP AND PAPER

Monthly.
ISSN 0033-4081.
LC 79-6885.
SRI/MF/excerpts, shipped
quarterly

Monthly trade journal (semimonthly in Nov.) reporting on U.S. and Canadian paper, pulp, and board manufacturing industries, including production, engineering/maintenance, management, and marketing.

Most data are from the Commerce Dept, American Paper Institute, Paperboard Packaging Council, and Canadian Pulp and Paper Assn.

General format:

a. "Month in Statistics" section, with 1 chart and 1 table, described below.

b. "News Scan" section, including occasional statistical items, and 1 quarterly table on income results (sales and earnings) of approximately 40 U.S. and Canadian paper/forest product companies, for quarter ending 3 months prior to cover date, with percent change from previous year; prior to the Jan. 1985 issue, section was titled "News Roundup."

c. "Grade Profile" section, appearing in most issues, providing annual data on a selected industry sector or product type, with text statistics on outlook and prices, and 2 tables showing total production, capacity, and consumption, and frequently capacity utilization rate and foreign trade, for current and previous 2 years for that sector or product, and current annual capacities and capacity share for major producing companies; for U.S. and occasionally for Canada.

d. "Chemical Report" section, appearing in most issues, providing annual supply-demand data for a selected chemical or mineral used in the paper industry, for U.S. and Canada. Prior to the Sept. 1985 issue, section was titled "Chemical Markets."

e. Editorial depts and feature articles, some with statistics, including annual statistical features on industry outlook and capital spending plans (Jan.); world production and marketing developments (Aug.); and a chemical supply survey (Oct. or Nov.).

The additional Nov. issue is a nonstatistical buyer's guide. An annual index is included in the Dec. issue.

"Month in Statistics" section appears in all issues. Articles with substantial nontechnical statistical content are described, as they appear, under "Statistical Features;" page locations, topics, and latest periods of coverage for "Grade Profile" and "Chemical Report" sections and quarterly "News Scan" table are also noted. Nonstatistical features are not covered.

Availability: Pulp and Paper, Circulation Department, 500 Howard St., San Francisco CA 94105, industry subscribers †, others $45.00 per yr., single copy $4.00, Buyers Guide $25.00; SRI/MF/excerpts for "Month in Statistics" and all portions covered under "Statistical Features;" shipped quarterly.

Issues reviewed during 1985: Nov. 1984-Oct. 1985 (P) (Vol. 58, Nos. 11-12; Vol. 59, Nos. 1-10) [Nov. 15 and Dec. 1984 issues are both numbered Vol. 58, No. 12].

MONTH IN STATISTICS:

Includes U.S. paper and paperboard production, by type; wood pulp production, and wastepaper and pulpwood consumption; corrugated box shipments, and containerboard inventories; total paper imports, and imports of Canadian newsprint; and exports of paper, linerboard, and wood pulp.

Also includes Canadian newsprint and other paper/board shipments, newsprint operating rate and inventories held by U.S. consumers, and wood pulp exports and operating rate; and (beginning in Jan. 1985 issue) North American/Scandinavian pulp inventories and operating rate.

Data are shown for month 3 or 4 months prior to cover date, and year to date, with comparisons to previous year.

STATISTICAL FEATURES:

C3975–2.601: Nov. 1984 (Vol. 58, No. 11)

MONTHLY SECTION

Grade Profile: Unbleached Kraft Paper

(p. 13) Presents industry data for 1982-84, and company capacity data for 1984.

CORRECTION

(p. 25) Data correction for monthly Grade Profile table appearing in the Sept. 1984 issue.

For table description, see SRI 1984 Annual under C3975-2.511.

U.S. CAPITAL SPENDING FORECAST LOWERED

(p. 33) Article, with 1 table showing capital spending of U.S. and Canadian pulp/paper companies, 1983-84, and annualized by quarter 1984. Data are from Commerce Dept and Statistics Canada.

PULP/PAPER CHEMICAL USE, PRICES CONTINUE TO STRENGTHEN IN 1984-85, ANNUAL FEATURE

(p. 77-85) Annual report, by Barry Shockett, on price and availability of chemicals used in processing pulp and paper. Report is based on *Pulp and Paper* surveys of chemical producers in U.S. and Canada.

Includes 4 charts, and profiles of specific chemicals for each of the 2 survey countries. Profiles generally cover uses, availability, demand, sources, and prices, various years 1978-84, and market forecast, 1985.

CONTAINERBOARD QUALITY CHANGES AS PACKAGING MAKES NEW DEMANDS

(p. 120-123) By K. Flinkman and T. Willner. Article, with 1 table showing tonnage distribution (no date), and percent tonnage increase for 1981-86 period, for unprinted and 1-4 color printed corrugated board in UK, West Germany, and France.

C3975–2.602: Dec. 1984 (Vol. 58, No. 12)

MONTHLY SECTION

Grade Profile: Newsprint

(p. 13) Presents industry data for 1983-85, and company capacity data for 1984.

NEWS ROUNDUP QUARTERLY TABLE

(p. 31, 33) Paper/forest products income results, 3rd quarter 1984.

IP TO PERMANENTLY CLOSE CAMDEN KRAFT MILL

(p. 23) Article, with 1 table showing owner, capacity, and announcement date, for 10 mills

ceasing production of unbleached kraft paper during 1978-85. Data are *Pulp and Paper* estimates.

SECOND SALARY SURVEY: MEDIAN INCOME UP 7% FROM LAST YEAR, ANNUAL FEATURE

(p. 76-82) Annual article, by Kenneth E. Smith, on salaries and benefits of pulp/paper professionals, based on an Aug. 1984 survey of an unspecified number of *Pulp and Paper* readers.

Includes 3 charts and 19 tables showing survey response concerning respondent age and years of experience; type and value of employee benefits; and compensation level, by employer type and sales size, job function, supervisory responsibility, years of experience, number of jobs held, years with current employer, and degree level and field; with selected detail for Canadian respondents only.

C3975–2.603: Jan. 1985 (Vol. 59, No. 1)

MONTHLY SECTIONS

Grade Profile: Linerboard

(p. 13) Presents industry data for 1983-85, and company capacity data for 1985.

Data correction appears in the Feb. 1985 issue (see C3975-2.604 below).

Chemical Markets: Titanium Dioxide

(p. 207) Presents industry data for 1981-84.

OUTLOOK '85, ANNUAL FEATURE

Annual compilation of articles on paper industry outlook in U.S. and Canada for 1985, based on American Paper Institute and Canadian Pulp and Paper Assn estimates, and other sources. Includes 4 articles with substantial statistics, as follows:

U.S. PAPER INDUSTRY RECOVERY EXPECTED TO CONTINUE IN 1985, ANNUAL FEATURE

(p. 57-65) Includes 2 tables showing changes in real GNP and housing starts and in paper industry production, operating rates, prices, costs, and profits, as forecast by 9 analysts, 1985; and growth in wood pulp, paper, and paperboard capacity, by grade, 1975-84 and 1985-87 periods.

CANADIAN INDUSTRY: MORE SILVER LININGS THAN CLOUDS AHEAD FOR CANADA'S TROUBLED MILLS, ANNUAL FEATURE

(p. 66-75) Includes 2 tables showing the following for newsprint: U.S. consumption and demand, U.S. supply by source (Canada, Europe, and domestic), and Canadian shipments by destination (domestic, U.S., and overseas), 1984-85; and operating rates for U.S. and Canada, 1984-86.

LABOR: MODERATION IN DEMANDS, ANNUAL FEATURE

(p. 75-77) Includes 1 table showing major contracts on U.S. paper industry bargaining calendars, including companies, mill locations, unions, contract expiration dates, and number of employees affected, by region, 1985.

CAPITAL SPENDING, ANNUAL FEATURE

(p. 109-116) Annual article, by Carl Espe and Stephanie Pollitzer, on U.S. and Canadian pulp and paper firms' capital spending plans through 1987. Data are from an annual survey by *Pulp and Paper*. Includes the following data, generally shown for U.S. and Canada:

a. Capital expenditures for production and environmental quality: trends 1979-85; and by State, Province, type of facility, and U.S. census division or Canadian region, total 1984-86 or later. 6 tables.

b. Capital expenditures for individual companies spending $100 million or more, various periods 1982-86; and "greenfield" mills and new paper machines (including capacity and startup date), and major modernization/expansion project expenditures, by mill. 8 tables.

The complete survey results are available from *Pulp and Paper* for $85.00.

Other Articles

U.S. PAPER INDUSTRY TO LIFT CAPACITY BY 1.6%/YEAR OVER NEXT THREE YEARS

(p. 117-118) By Willard E. Mies. Article, with 4 tables showing wood pulp and paper capacity additions, 1975-84 and 1985-87 periods; share of capacity, by census region, 1984-87 period; and annual capacity, 1984-87; all by grade. Data are from the American Paper Institute.

1984 SAW BUDWORM POPULATION FALL, BUT 13-YEAR INFESTATION ISN'T OVER YET

(p. 136-139) By Nancy J. Larsen. Article, with 1 table showing acreage infested by budworms, for Maine and selected Canadian Provinces, 1983-84.

C3975–2.604: Feb. 1985 (Vol. 59, No. 2)

MONTHLY SECTIONS

Grade Profile: Tissue

(p. 13) Presents industry data for 1983-85, and company capacity data for 1985.

Chemical Markets: Chlorine

(p. 195) Presents 2 tables showing chlorine capacity, production, imports, exports, and consumption (total and paper industry), for U.S. and Canada, 1981-84.

CORRECTION

(p. 13) Data correction for monthly Grade Profile table appearing in the Jan. 1985 issue. For table description, see C3975-2.603 above.

IP LABOR PACT TRIGGERS MAJOR CONVERSION AT PINE BLUFF

(p. 29-31) Article, with 1 table showing company owner, capacity additions, and completion date, for individual coated groundwood mills with expansion plans announced or under study as of early 1985. Data are from *Pulp and Paper*.

EEC FINES PRODUCERS IN PULP CARTEL CASE; APPEALS EXPECTED

(p. 35-37) Article on results of an EC investigation of price-fixing among pulp suppliers, with 1 table showing fines imposed on major bleached sulfate market pulp producers and 1 trade assn in U.S., Canada, Finland, and Sweden, Dec. 1984.

WAGE SETTLEMENTS: A DOWNWARD SPIRAL

(p. 43) By Julian M. Kien. Article, with 1 chart showing percent increase in 1st year wages for collective bargaining settlements in paper and all manufacturing industries, 1980-84. Data are from Conference Board.

CROSS-DIRECTION CONTROL IS STILL TOP PROCESS AUTOMATION TREND

(p. 72-76) By Kenneth E. Smith. Article, with 1 table and 4 charts showing unit sales for 3 types of paper machine cross-direction (CD) control systems, and potential operational benefits of CD control, various years 1973-84. Data are from equipment suppliers.

C3975–2.605: Mar. 1985 (Vol. 59, No. 3)

MONTHLY SECTION

Grade Profile: Coated Free Sheet Papers

(p. 13) Presents industry data for 1983-85, and company capacity data for 1985.

NEWS SCAN QUARTERLY TABLE

(p. 25) Paper/forest products income results (U.S. data only), full year 1984.

WASTE-TO-ENERGY INCINERATION PLANTS MAY CUT FUTURE WASTEPAPER SUPPLIES

(p. 114-117) By Michael J. Ducey. Article reporting on State actions affecting wastepaper disposal. Most data are from a *Pulp and Paper* survey of industry and government officials. Includes 1 chart showing wastepaper prices by grade, 1980-84; and 3 undated tables showing resource recovery plants operating and planned, wastepaper burned, recycling paper mills and wastepaper consumption, and characteristics of resource recovery regulations, by State, with summary operational data by type of resource recovery plant.

PAPER INDUSTRY SALARY INCREASES OUTPACED BY 4.6% INFLATION IN 1984

(p. 118-119) By Deborah S. Sollosi. Article, with 1 table showing engineers' median salaries, for 17 major industry groups including paper and lumber/wood products, 1983-84. Data are from annual surveys of approximately 650 organizations, conducted by American Assn of Engineering Societies.

SLOW CAPACITY GROWTH SHOULD KEEP LINER MARKET TIGHT

(p. 150-154) By Willard E. Mies. Article on supply and demand trends and outlook for the linerboard industry, including production, consumption, trade, and capacity, for Western Europe and/or U.S., various years 1982-86. Data are from Morgan Stanley and Co., and ASSI Kraftliner. Includes 2 tables.

RECYCLING: MORE SUPPLIERS MEETING INDIVIDUAL MILL SPECIFICATIONS

(p. 265) By Michael J. Ducey. Article, with 1 table showing consumption of 5 chemicals used in papermaking recycling processes, with comparison to consumption in total pulp/paper and all industries, 1984.

C3975–2.606: Apr. 1985 (Vol. 59, No. 4)

MONTHLY SECTION

Grade Profile: Uncoated Printing/Writing Free-Sheet Papers

(p. 13) Presents industry data for 1983-85, and company capacity data for 1985.

NEWS SCAN QUARTERLY TABLE

(p. 31) Paper/forest products income results (Canada data only), full year 1984.

SCOTT SLATES SECOND COATED MACHINE AT MILL

(p. 23) Article, with 1 table showing company owner, capacity additions, project type, and completion date, for individual coated free-sheet mills with expansion plans announced or under study as of early 1985. Data are from *Pulp and Paper*.

PULP AND PAPER INDUSTRY SAFETY PERFORMANCE IMPROVES IN U.S. SOUTH

(p. 247) Article, with 2 tables showing pulp/paper industry fatalities, and injury/illness incidence rate by type of mill, for southern U.S., 1980-84; and number of mills and hours worked, and injury/illness cases and rates, for selected western States, 1984.

Data are from Southern Pulp and Paper Safety Assn, and Pacific Coast Assn of Pulp and Paper Manufacturers.

C3975–2.607: May 1985 (Vol. 59, No. 5)

MONTHLY SECTION

Grade Profile: Coated Groundwood Paper

(p. 13) Presents industry data for 1983-85, and company capacity data for 1985.

U.S. MILLS GENERATED 55% OF THEIR ENERGY IN '84

(p. 33-35) Article, with 1 chart showing paper industry shipment value, and expenditures for energy, 1972-84. Data are from Census Bureau and American Paper Institute.

U.S. PULP/PAPER DEMAND EXPECTED TO SHOW EVEN FURTHER GROWTH

(p. 94-99) Article, with 3 tables showing U.S. uncoated free-sheet and coated paper shipments by grade and total supply, and exports and mill consumption of wastepaper by type, 1984 with comparisons to 1983; and summary data on European paper manufacturing projects and changes in capacity and demand, by paper type, primarily 1984-87 period.

Data are from American Paper Institute and European Paper Institute.

C3975–2.608: June 1985 (Vol. 59, No. 6)

MONTHLY SECTION

Grade Profile: Corrugating Medium

(p. 13) Presents industry data for 1983-85, and company capacity data for 1985.

NEWS SCAN QUARTERLY TABLE

(p. 27) Paper/forest products income results (U.S. data only), 1st quarter 1985.

U.S. PAPER COMPANIES TO TRIM CAPITAL SPENDING PLANS

(p. 33) Article, with 1 table showing capital spending plans for 23 U.S. and 2 Canadian paper companies, 1984-85. Data are from recent company statements and annual reports.

P&P EXCLUSIVE SURVEY: TRENDS IN BLEACHING EQUIPMENT, CHEMICAL USE, ANNUAL FEATURE

(p. 56-58, 66) Annual article, by Michael J. Ducey, on chemical use in pulp bleaching plants. Data are based on a 1985 *Pulp and Paper* survey involving 70 U.S. and Canadian mills/bleach plants.

Includes 4 tables showing Canadian sample characteristics, technical data, and number of mills using various bleaching chemical substitutes.

This is the 3rd annual survey report.

C3975–2.609: July 1985 (Vol. 59, No. 7)

MONTHLY SECTION

Grade Profile: Recycled Paperboard

(p. 13) Presents industry data for 1983-85, and company capacity data for 1985.

NEWS SCAN QUARTERLY TABLE

(p. 33) Paper/forest products income results (Canada data only), 1st quarter 1985.

FEW GREENFIELD MARKET PULP MILLS SEEN FOR THE 80s, ANNUAL FEATURE

(p. 37) Annual article, with 1 table showing world location, startup date, capacity, product grade, and company, for 14 market pulp mills initiating operations in 1984-86. Data are from Jaakko Poyry.

Previous feature, for 1984-85, is described in SRI 1984 Annual under C3975-2.510.

INDUSTRY COMMITMENT TO REFORESTING PRIVATE LANDS IS CRUCIAL TO THE FUTURE

(p. 72-74) By R. Scott Wallinger. Article, with 1 undated chart showing distribution of softwood sawtimber inventory vs. harvest, by land ownership class. Data are from the National Forest Products Assn.

U.S. PULPWOOD COST OUTLOOK IS GOOD, REGIONAL SUPPLIES APPEAR ADEQUATE

(p. 92-95) Article on factors affecting pulpwood costs. Data sources include American Pulpwood Assn. Includes 6 tables showing the following by region:

a. Forestland distribution, by land ownership class (no date); and cost of delivered wood as a percent of pulp cost, 1973 and 1983.

b. Consumption of softwood and hardwood; and distribution of delivered roundwood cost by component, and of wood supply (roundwood and chip) by land ownership class or controlled vs. open market; (no dates).

BLEACHING: CHEMICAL SUBSTITUTES, EQUIPMENT INCREASE EFFICIENCY

(p. 201) Article, with 1 table showing consumption of 4 chemicals used in the bleaching of chemical pulp, for all industries and for pulp/paper industry (total and bleaching process segment), 1984, with 2nd quarter 1985 prices.

C3975–2.610: Aug. 1985 (Vol. 59, No. 8)

MONTHLY SECTION

Grade Profile: Bleached Paperboard

(p. 13) Presents industry data for 1983-85, and company capacity data for 1985.

CRUDE TALL OIL: TIGHT SUPPLY OF CTO DISRUPTING TOFA PRICE, SUPPLY

(p. 43) Article, with 1 chart showing crude tall oil production, with detail by product type, 1980-84.

U.S. LED WORLD PULP AND PAPER PRODUCERS TO A RECORD YEAR IN 1984, ANNUAL FEATURE

(p. 55-64) Annual article, by John Pearson et al., reviewing world pulp and paper/paperboard capacity, production, and consumption, 1984. Data were compiled by *Pulp and Paper International*. Includes 4 tables showing the following, generally for pulp and paper/paperboard:

a. Production and per capita consumption for 20 leading producing and consuming countries, 1984 with percent change from 1983; and production, by continent, selected years 1960-84.

b. Mills, capacity, production, and total and per capita consumption, for 147 countries and 9 world areas; and summary profiles,

including capacity, operating rate, production, imports, and exports, with chemical woodpulp production and trade detail, for 27 leading producing countries; 1983 and/ or 1984.

ITT RAYONIER'S PRESIDENT AND CEO TALKS ABOUT SPECIALTY PULP MARKETS

(p. 108-110) By Willard E. Mies. Article, with 1 table showing production of dissolving pulp, for U.S. and Canada, selected years 1950-84. Data are from American Paper Institute and Canadian Pulp & Paper Assn.

MAINTENANCE IS NO PRIZE ASSIGNMENT

(p. 149) By Matthew J. Coleman. Article on opinions of paper mill engineers and other personnel regarding operations of mill engineering and maintenance depts, including role of engineers in maintenance depts. Data are from an Apr. 1985 *Pulp & Paper* reader survey. Includes 1 table.

C3975–2.611: Sept. 1985 (Vol. 59, No. 9)

MONTHLY SECTION

Grade Profile: Uncoated Groundwood Paper

(p. 13) Presents industry data for 1983-85, and company capacity data for 1985.

Chemical Report: Sulfur

(p. 43) Presents 2 charts showing trends in sulfur consumption, sulfite pulp production, and sulfur and sulfite pulp prices, for U.S. and Canada, 1980-84.

NEWS SCAN QUARTERLY TABLE

(p. 21) Paper/forest products income results (U.S. data only), 2nd quarter 1985.

GROWTH AHEAD FOR CANADIAN DOMESTIC PAPER DEMAND

(p. 37) Article, with 1 table showing Canadian consumption of paperboard, wrapping paper, newsprint, culture paper, and building boards, 1990, 1995, and 2000. Data are from Canadian Forestry Service.

ENGINEERS: LOSING THE CAREER GAME?

Compilation of articles on pulp and paper industry engineering education, employment, and salaries. Includes the statistical articles described below.

TODAY'S PULP AND PAPER SCHOOLS STRESS HIGH-TECH SPECIALIZATION

(p. 56-58) By Deborah S. Sollosi. Article, with 1 undated table showing academic credit hours required for undergraduate degree in pulp and paper programs, by subject area and degree program, for 7 institutions. Data are from a *Pulp and Paper* survey.

MIAMI U CURRICULUM GETS HIGH MARKS FROM ALUMNI, EMPLOYERS

(p. 61-64) By Robert D. Fraik. Article presenting results of surveys conducted by Miami University to evaluate its paper science/engineering curriculum. Data are from survey responses of 242 Miami alumni and 74 paper industry employers.

Includes 9 undated tables presenting selected survey findings, including alumni employment characteristics, views of alumni and employers on importance of various courses, and employers' anticipated demand for paper science graduates.

HIGHEST PAID ENGINEERS FOUND IN MANAGEMENT AND MARKETING

(p. 81-85) By Kenneth E. Smith. Article on engineer salaries, with selected comparisons to other professions. Data are from surveys by *Pulp and Paper,* BLS, and the National Society of Professional Engineers.

Includes 4 tables and 3 charts showing income of pulp/paper professionals with bachelor degrees, by educational field, job function, and supervisory responsibility; income of all professional engineers, by job function, employer type (including specific industries), and supervisory responsibility; and salaries for selected engineering, science, and legal occupations; 1984, with pulp/paper income comparisons to 1983.

For description of article on *Pulp and Paper* survey, see C3975-2.602, above.

PAPER INDUSTRY ENGINEERS NOT HAPPY WITH IMAGE OR PROSPECTS

(p. 86-89) By Matthew J. Coleman. Article, with 1 undated chart showing percent of pulp and paper engineers desiring additional education in selected subject areas. Data are from a *Pulp and Paper* survey.

ENGINEERS RISE TO THE CORPORATE LEVEL VIA PRODUCTION AND SALES

(p. 111-113) By Michael J. Ducey. Article, with 1 table showing new hires of engineering, science, and nontechnical graduates of higher education institutions offering and not offering pulp/paper curricula, by degree level, 1980-84 period. Data are from a survey conducted by the Technical Assn of the Pulp & Paper Industry (TAPPI), covering 37 TAPPI member firms.

C3975–2.612: Oct. 1985 (Vol. 59, No. 10)

MONTHLY SECTION

Grade Profile: Paper-Grade Chemical Market Pulp

(p. 13) Presents industry data for 1983-85, and company capacity data for 1985.

NEWS SCAN QUARTERLY TABLE

(p. 27) Paper/forest products income results (Canada data only), 2nd quarter 1985.

SPENDING FOR R&D SOARS, BUT PAPER LAGS BEHIND

(p. 35) Article, with 1 table showing paper industry R&D expenditures (total, per employee, and as percent of sales), by company, 1984, with selected comparisons to 1983. Data are from *Business Week*.

WORLD PAPER/BOARD CAPACITY EXPECTED TO GROW ONLY 1.4%/YEAR DURING 1984-89, ANNUAL FEATURE

(p. 37-39) Annual article, with 2 tables showing world woodpulp and paper/paperboard capacity, by country or world area, 1984 and 1989, with trends from 1979. Data are from the UN Food and Agriculture Organization.

For description of previous article, see SRI 1984 Annual, under C3975-2.512.

CHEMICALS HELP TO IMPROVE QUALITY AND EFFICIENCY IN U.S. PAPER MILLS

(p. 81-86) By Michael J. Ducey. Article, with 3 tables showing market volume for selected paper coating binders and latexes, 1980-84; and consumption of 4 chemicals used in recycled papermaking, shown for all industries and for pulp/paper industry (total and in recycling process), 1984, with prices for 1985. Data are from *Pulp & Paper* survey.

CANADIAN PULP AND PAPER INDUSTRY INCREASES CHEMICAL USES IN 1984-85

(p. 86-90) By Michael J. Ducey. Article, with 2 tables showing Canadian market volume for selected paper coating binders and latexes, 1980-84. Data are from Polysar Latex.

C4040
Gallup Poll

C4040–1   GALLUP REPORT

Monthly.   Approx. 30 p.
ISSN 0731-6143.
LC sc81-3017.
SRI/MF/not filmed

Monthly report (with occasional combined issues) on opinion surveys conducted by the Gallup Poll concerning contemporary political, social, and economic issues, trends, and policies. Data generally are current to 2-4 weeks prior to publication date. Report usually is issued several months after publication date.

Most issues contain survey results on approximately 6 topics, each generally including narrative summary of survey background and response, text summary tables, and 1-10 tables showing survey response, by detailed sociodemographic breakdowns. Survey results for some topics may also include additional tables on responses to follow-up questions, and text statistics on opinion trends from previous surveys.

Issues also generally contain description of polling and survey interpretation techniques, with 2-4 tables showing sample size and methodology for estimating sampling error. A table on national election prediction accuracy since 1936 is included on a space available basis.

Sociodemographic breakdowns are based on a sample size of at least 1,500 persons, and generally show response distribution by sex, age, region, race, educational attainment, political affiliation, occupation, income, religious preference, and labor union status.

All features with substantial statistical content are described, as they appear, under "Statistical Features." Nonstatistical contents are not covered.

Availability: Gallup Report, PO Box 628, Princeton NJ 08542, academic institutions $45.00 per yr., others $75.00 per yr., single copy $10.00, Religion in America issue $25.00; SRI/MF/not filmed.

Issues reviewed during 1985: Aug./Sept. 1984-Aug. 1985 (P) (Nos. 227/228-239) [Aug./Sept. 1984 and Jan./Feb. 1985 are combined issues; Aug/Sept. 1984 issue incorrectly reads Nos. 228/229].

STATISTICAL FEATURES:

C4040–1.601: Aug./Sept. 1984 (Nos. 227/228)

POLL RESULTS

Opinion and attitude polls covered in the Aug./Sept. 1984 issue are as follows:

a. Female vs. male president capability for handling foreign policy, Soviet relations, situation in Central America, unemployment, the economy, and quality of life; willingness to vote for female candidates for mayor, governor, Congress, and President; and perceived effect of increase in women officeholders on the government. Conducted July 1984; with 11 tables, and trends from 1937. (p. 2-14)

b. Presidential election 1984: preferences between Reagan/Bush and Mondale/Ferraro tickets; and perceived capability of Reagan vs. Mondale in handling selected U.S. problems, including inflation, the economy, foreign and Soviet relations, unemployment, Central America, budget deficit, threat of war, the environment, conditions of the poor and minorities, and women's rights. Conducted Aug. 10-13 and Sept. 7-10, 1984; with 10 tables. (p. 15-26)

c. Family situation and world safety, perceived change from 1980; political party affiliation; and personal financial situation, perceived change from 1 year ago, and expected change for next year. Conducted June-July 1984; with 8 tables, and trends from 1937. (p. 28-38)

d. Olympics: world support for holding games in different countries vs. establishing a permanent site in Greece. Conducted June-July 1984 in 19 countries; with 2 tables, including responses by country and sociodemographic detail for U.S. (p. 39-41)

SPECIAL SURVEY: 16th ANNUAL GALLUP POLL OF THE PUBLIC'S ATTITUDES TOWARD THE PUBLIC SCHOOLS

(p. 42-57) Special reprint of annual survey article reviewing trends in public opinion concerning public schools. Article was originally published in Sept. 1984 issue of *Phi Delta Kappan.* Survey covered 1,515 adults and was conducted May 18-27, 1984. Includes 5 charts and 38 tables showing survey responses related to the following:

a. Education's importance to America's future; ratings of public schools, staff, and officials, and of students' parents; tax increases to support education; 1984 presidential candidates' support for education; lengthening of school day and year; student workloads; course requirements for college-bound and other students; special instruction and extracurricular activities; examination-based graduation; and raising college entrance requirements.

b. Teacher examinations and career ladders; teacher compensation, including adequacy of current levels, higher salaries for math/science/vocational teachers, and merit pay; teaching as career for own child; school prayer; schools without traditional grade level systems; credit for community service; school problems, including student discipline; education goals; and responsibility for determining school curriculum.

Many tables show data by whether respondent has child in school and/or in public or nonpub-

lic school; and by respondent sex, race, age, community size, education, and region. Selected tables also include comparisons to previous years, from as early as 1969.

Article is also described in SRI 1984 Annual, and is available on SRI microfiche, under A8680-1.505.

C4040–1.602: Oct. 1984 (No. 229)

Opinion and attitude polls covered in the Oct. 1984 issue are as follows:

a. Support for nuclear weapons freeze, ban on abortions, tax increases to reduce Federal deficit, prayer in public schools, reduced defense spending, tuition tax credits, Equal Rights Amendment, increased spending for social programs, relaxing pollution controls to reduce costs to industry, and maintaining cost-of-living increases on social security benefits. Conducted Sept. 28-Oct. 1, 1984; with 10 tables. (p. 3-13)

b. Presidential election 1984: candidate perceived better for peace, prosperity, and Soviet relations; and whether Reagan Administration defense policies have brought U.S. closer to war or peace. Conducted Sept. 28-Oct. 1, 1984; with 4 tables, and trends from Jan. 1984. (p. 14-18)

c. National problem perceived as most important, including threat of war, international tensions, unemployment, cost of living, budget deficit, economy, moral decline in society, poverty/hunger, crime, and dissatisfaction with government; general satisfaction with Nation's situation; and awareness of and support for Mondale's tax policy, and its perceived effect on economy. Conducted Sept.-Oct. 1984; with 4 tables, and trends from 1935. (p. 19-26)

d. Perceived major failings of parents in raising children; and teenagers' views on major problems facing adolescents. Conducted Oct. 26-29, 1984; with 3 tables, and trends from 1977. (p. 27-28)

C4040–1.603: Nov. 1984 (No. 230)

Opinion and attitude polls covered in the Nov. 1984 issue are as follows:

a. Presidential elections: preference for Reagan vs. Mondale, and for candidates in preceding 8 elections; reasons for not voting, and for voting for Reagan and Mondale; whether voted for candidates from 1 political party or different parties; Ferraro's effect on likelihood of voting for Mondale; and support for change in the political campaign system. Conducted mostly Oct.-Nov. 1984; with 9 tables, and trends from 1952. (p. 3-19)

b. Voter turnout and registration, and political party affiliation (Republican, Democrat, or Independent). Conducted various months 1984; with 4 tables, and trends from 1946. (p. 20-26)

C4040–1.604: Dec. 1984 (No. 231)

Opinion and attitude polls covered in the Dec. 1984 issue are as follows:

a. Ten most admired men and women, 1946-84. 2 annual tabular lists. (p. 3-7)

b. Presidential performance ratings for Reagan, with summary comparisons to previous Presidents. Conducted Nov.-Dec. 1984; with 1 chart and 2 tables, and trends from 1940s. (p. 8-11)

c. Economic outlook for personal finances, general economy, housing values, interest rates, and personal income vs. prices; and market condition for purchases of home furnishings/appliances. Conducted Nov. 30-Dec. 3, 1984; with 9 tables, and trends from 1976. (p. 12-21)

d. International: annual world report on public expectations for 1985, including general outlook by country; and U.S. outlook concerning peace, labor disputes, and chance of world war in next 10 years. Conducted Nov.-Dec. 1984 in 24 countries; with 3 charts and 4 tables, and trends from 1960. (p. 22-29)

C4040-1.605: Jan./Feb. 1985 (Nos. 232/233)

POLL RESULTS

Opinion and attitude polls covered in the Jan./Feb. 1985 issue are as follows:

a. Death penalty: support for death penalty or life imprisonment for convicted murderers; whether death penalty is a deterrent for murder, and public support as affected by hypothetical evidence showing death penalty is and is not a deterrent; perceived bias against blacks and poor in awarding death penalty; and form of execution perceived as most humane. Conducted Jan. 11-14, 1985; with 8 tables, and selected trends from 1936. (p. 3-11)

b. Vigilantism: whether justifiable; and awareness of NYC "subway vigilante" incident. Conducted Jan. 25-28, 1985; with 2 tables. (p. 12-14)

c. Reagan's presidential performance, expected historical assessment. Conducted Jan. 25-28, 1985; with 1 table. (p. 15-16)

d. Illegal aliens: whether hiring illegal aliens should be illegal; support for mandatory identification cards; and whether illegal aliens should be eligible for permanent resident status if they have lived in U.S. since 1982. Conducted June-July 1984; with 3 tables, and trends from 1977. (p. 17-20)

e. Political party perceived best for serving interests of businessmen/professionals, average citizen, small business, farmers, retired, unemployed, women, labor union members, blacks, and white collar, skilled, and unskilled workers. Conducted Nov. 30-Dec. 3, 1984; with 13 tables, and trends from 1947. (p. 21-34)

SPECIAL SURVEY: PHI DELTA KAPPA/GALLUP POLL OF TEACHERS' ATTITUDES TOWARD THE PUBLIC SCHOOLS

(p. 35-51) Special reprint of survey article on teachers' attitudes concerning public schools and education. Article was originally published in 2 parts in Oct. 1984 and Jan. 1985 issues of *Phi Delta Kappan*. Data are based on responses from 813 teachers to an Apr./May 1984 survey. Includes 52 tables showing responses concerning the following:

a. Ratings of own and local schools, local teachers and school officials, students' parents, and own educational training; 1984 presidential candidates' support for education; support for school prayer amendment;

reasons teachers leave education profession; and own school's difficulty in attracting and retaining good teachers.

b. Compensation adequacy; higher salaries for science/math/technical/vocational teachers; and merit pay, including reasons for support or opposition, responsibility and criteria for awarding, and percent of teachers warranting.

c. School problems, including discipline; standard examinations for grade promotion and graduation; remedial instruction; raising college entrance requirements; and teacher examinations.

d. Teaching as career for own child; impact of unionization on quality of public education; support for teacher strikes, and compulsory use of an arbitrator to settle disputes; and ratings of the social benefit and prestige of selected occupations.

e. Course requirements for college-bound and other students; support for sex education, and subjects it should include in high school and elementary school; goals of education; lengthening of school day and year; and responsibility for determining school curriculum and books used in schools.

Many tables show separate responses for elementary and high school teachers, and include comparisons with attitudes of the general public.

Survey is also described in SRI 1984 and 1985 Annuals under A8680-1.506 and A8680-1.602, respectively. Survey is available on SRI microfiche under those numbers.

C4040-1.606: Mar. 1985 (No. 234)

Opinion and attitude polls covered in the Mar. 1985 issue are as follows:

a. Government: appropriateness of current level of Federal spending on defense and social programs; and approval of Reagan's general performance and handling of economy, foreign policy, Soviet relations, and disarmament negotiations. Conducted Jan. 11-14 and 25-28, 1985; with 7 tables, and selected trends from 1960. (p. 3-11)

b. Space-based defense system (Strategic Defense Initiative or "Star Wars"): awareness of and support for development, and perceived effect on world security and future arms agreement with Soviet Union. Conducted Jan. 25-28; with 4 tables. (p. 12-16)

c. Cost of living: annual survey of perceived income needs for family of 4 and respondent's own family; and average weekly food expenditures. Conducted Jan. 11-14 and 25-28, 1985; with 2 tables, and trends from 1937. (p. 17-20)

d. Poverty: perceived increase or decrease in number of poor; personal lack of effort vs. circumstances as cause for poverty; fairness of distribution of wealth; and involvement in charitable activities. Conducted Dec. 7-10 1984; with 4 tables, and selected trends from 1977. (p. 21-26)

e. Birth control pills: whether use involves health risk, and types of risks perceived, including detail by marital status and presence of children (no dates). 2 tables. (p. 27-29)

C4040-1.607: Apr. 1985 (No. 235)

Opinion and attitude polls covered in the Apr. 1985 issue are as follows:

a. Reagan Administration: perceived effect of Reagan policies on selected national issues, including inflation, defense, unemployment, foreign respect for U.S., energy, world peace, reduction of Federal Government size and personal taxes, balanced budget, nuclear disarmament, and environment. Conducted Feb. 15-18, 1985; with 12 tables, and comparison to 1982. (p. 3-15)

b. Nuclear weapons: perceived nuclear superiority of U.S. vs. Soviet Union; and whether arms build-up or imbalance of power poses greater war threat. Conducted Feb. 15-18, 1985; with 2 tables, and trends from 1982. (p. 16-18)

c. National problem perceived as most important, including threat of war/international tensions, unemployment, government spending/deficit, cost of living/taxes, economy, poverty, crime, drug abuse, moral decline in society, and problems of the elderly. Conducted Jan. 25-28, 1985; with 1 table, and trends from 1983. (p. 19-21)

d. Political party perceived best able to handle major problems, and party perceived best for peace and prosperity. Conducted Jan. 25-28 and Mar. 8-11, 1985; with 5 tables, and trends from 1939. (p. 22-27)

e. Euthanasia: public approval of court rulings allowing the withholding of life-sustaining medical treatment for terminally ill patients. Conducted Jan. 25-28, 1985; with 1 table. (p. 28-29)

C4040-1.608: May 1985 (No. 236)

[Price for this issue is $25.00.]

Special May 1985 issue features full reprint of annual *Religion in America, 50 Years: 1935-85*. Report is covered in SRI under R8780-2, and is available on SRI microfiche under that number.

C4040-1.609: June 1985 (No. 237)

Opinion and attitude polls covered in the June 1985 issue are as follows:

a. Government: perceived seriousness of budget deficit, and approval of spending cuts in defense and social programs, income tax increase, and entitlement program cuts; approval of Reagan's general performance and visit to Bitburg cemetery, and awareness and approval of Nicaragua trade embargo, and support for presidential election regional primaries. Conducted Apr.-May 1985; with 10 tables, and selected trends from 1982. (p. 2-14)

b. Handguns: approval of handgun registration, and sale/possession bans by local communities; and gun ownership, including type of gun owned. Conducted Apr. 12-15, 1985; with 4 tables, and trends from 1972. (p. 15-19)

c. Subminimum wage for youth summer employment, awareness of and support for proposals; and seat belt use, and support for law fining nonusers. Conducted Apr. 12-15, 1985; with 4 tables, and selected trends from 1973. (p. 20-25) *d.* UN performance ratings by US public, with summary comparison to ratings in 16 foreign countries; acceptability of premarital sex; and approval of labor unions. Conducted Feb. 15-18, or Apr. 12-15, 1985; with 3 tables, and trends from 1936. (p. 26-31)

C4040–1.610: July 1985 (No. 238)

Opinion and attitude polls covered in the July 1985 issue are as follows:

a. Societal institutions: ratings of public confidence in church/organized religion, military, Supreme Court, banks/banking, public schools, Congress, newspapers, big business, TV, and organized labor. Conducted May 17-20, 1985; with 11 tables, and trends from 1973. (p. 2-13)

b. Tax reform proposal of Reagan Administration: expected effect on own taxes, taxes of wealthy, middle income, and poor families, and taxes of large and small companies; perceived fairness and simplicity; appraisal of specific features, including taxing employer-provided health insurance and eliminating State/local tax deduction; tax return preparation by self vs. professional; and overall support for reform proposal. Conducted June 7-10, 1985; with 15 tables. (p. 14-30)

C4040–1.611: Aug. 1985 (No. 239)

Aug. 1985 issue presents results of 2 opinion and attitude polls, as described below.

HONESTY AND ETHICAL STANDARDS, RECURRING FEATURE

(p. 2-28) Recurring survey on public perception of honesty/ethical standards of persons in 25 occupations, as follows:

a. Clergy, druggists/pharmacists, physicians, dentists, college teachers, engineers, police, bankers, TV reporters/commentators, funeral directors, journalists, newspaper reporters, and lawyers.

b. Business executives, Senators, stockbrokers, building contractors, Congressmen, State and local political officeholders, realtors, labor union leaders, advertising practitioners, and insurance and car salesmen.

Survey was conducted July 12-15, 1985. Includes 26 tables, and summary trends from 1976. For description of previous poll, see SRI 1984 Annual, under C4040-1.501.

RELOCATION PLAN

(p. 29-30) Survey on public support for proposed plan to relocate unemployed persons from large cities to areas with better employment opportunities, including provision of Federal housing vouchers to pay for family rent. Survey was conducted June 7-10, 1985. Includes 1 table.

C4170
Gordon Publications

C4170–1 MART
Monthly. Oversized.
ISSN 0025-4061.
LC 58-40314.
SRI/MF/excerpts, shipped quarterly

Monthly trade journal reporting on marketing developments and trends of interest to retailers of consumer electronic products and home appliances. Covers sales, management, new products, store operations, promotional techniques, and consumer buying attitudes.

Data are primarily from manufacturers and trade assns., and from the journal's own research.

Issues contain numerous articles, occasionally with statistics. Annual statistical features include consumer electronics market trends and outlook, and a survey of retail personnel compensation.

Features with substantial statistical content are described, as they appear, under "Statistical Features." Each issue of the journal is reviewed, but an abstract is published in SRI monthly issues only when original surveys, or other features with statistics not already described and filmed in other sources, appear.

Availability: Mart, Circulation Manager, PO Box 1952, Dover NJ 07801-0952, qualified subscribers †, others $30.00 per yr., single copy $3.00; SRI/MF/excerpts for all portions covered under "Statistical Features;" shipped quarterly.

Issues reviewed during 1985: Nov. 1984-Oct. 1985 (P) (Vol. 31, Nos. 3-12; Vol. 32, Nos. 1-2).

STATISTICAL FEATURES:

C4170–1.601: Nov. 1984 (Vol. 31, No. 3)

NATION'S LEADING RETAILERS OF HOME ELECTRONICS AND MAJOR APPLIANCES

(p. 9, 12-13) Article, with 1 table showing total sales 1983, and number of stores as of Dec. 1984, for 15 electronics/appliance retailers with greatest market impact as rated by *Mart.*

C4170–1.602: Dec. 1984 (Vol. 31, No. 4)

'85 ECONOMY: WHAT CAN RETAILERS EXPECT?

(p. 6-8) Article, with 2 tables showing factory sales of aggregate consumer electronic products, 1980-85; and household penetration of selected electronic products (no date). Data are from Electronics Industries Assn/Consumer Electronics Group.

C4170–1.603: Jan. 1985 (Vol. 31, No. 5)

SURVEY SHOWS RETAILERS DISCOVERING HOME SECURITY PHONE SYSTEMS

(p. 60-61) Article on retail market for systems integrating telephones and home security devices. Data are from a recent *Mart* survey of retailers. Includes 4 undated tables showing response distribution concerning most important manufacturer service, average profit margin, most popular price range, and sales relative to previous year.

MICROWAVE OVENS: WHAT DO CONSUMERS LIKE? WHY DO THEY BUY AND WHERE?

(p. 80-85) Article on consumer buying practices in purchasing microwave ovens and accessories. Data are based on 293 responses to a *Mart* survey of recent purchasers of microwave ovens.

Includes 25 undated tables showing responses concerning number of microwave ovens owned, and satisfaction with product; purchasing characteristics, including outlet type, extent of shopping, price range, factors affecting buying decision, and reaction to salesperson, with some detail for microwave accessories; source of interest in microwave cooking, frequency of use, and satisfaction with results; and whether outlet offered cooking classes, and whether attended.

C4170–1.604: Feb. 1985 (Vol. 31, No. 6)

1984 WAS THE BEST YEAR YET FOR CONSUMER ELECTRONICS, EIA STATISTICS REPORT, ANNUAL FEATURE

(p. 34, 44) Annual article, with 15 tables showing percent of households owning consumer electronic products, as of Jan. 1985; and volume of sales to dealers, and value of factory sales, various years 1980-85; all by product type, including videocassette recorders, TVs, audio systems, telephones, and computers. Data are from Electronic Industries Assn.

C4170–1.605: June 1985 (Vol. 31, No. 10)

MART'S ANNUAL COMPENSATION SURVEY

(p. 6-8) Annual article on retail store personnel salaries and benefits. Data are from a recent *Mart* survey of over 1,000 owners, presidents, and managers of selected types of retail operations (appliance/TV, home electronics, electronic specialty, and department stores, and mass merchandisers).

Includes 2 undated tables showing average salary for 7 positions, for total U.S. and by region; and survey response on whether selected benefits are offered.

Previous feature is described in SRI 1984 Annual under C4170-1.504.

C4170–1.606: Aug. 1985 (Vol. 31, No. 12)

VSDA SURVEY: RENTALS STILL THE BACKBONE

(p. 10) Article on home video product retail market shares. Data are from *TV Digest* and a Video Software Dealers Assn (VSDA) survey of video retail outlets.

Includes 5 charts showing market shares for videocassette sales vs. rentals, and for all video products by type (no dates); distribution of prerecorded videocassettes, by producer for 1984, and by film type (no date); and VSDA convention attendance, 1982-85.

C4170–1.607: Sept. 1985 (Vol. 32, No. 1)

KIDVID DELUGE SENDS PRICES TUMBLING

(p. 28) Article, with 1 table showing top 6 home video software producers ranked by market share, 1st half 1985. Data are from *Video Week.*

C4170–1.608: Oct. 1985 (Vol. 32, No. 2)

RESEARCH STUDY SHOWS CD OWNERSHIP DOUBLING WITHIN YEAR

(p. 12) Article, with 1 chart showing 13 compact disc (CD) player manufacturers ranked by familiarity among consumers who intend to buy CD players. Data are from an Apr. 1985 survey of 1,045 households with stereos, conducted by ASK Associates, Inc., for *Newsweek.*

APPLIANCE POWER USE PLUMMETS, BUT BILLS STAY HIGH

(p. 28) Article, with 1 chart showing home appliance energy use reductions, for 5 major appliances, 1972-84 period. Data are from Assn of Home Appliance Manufacturers.

C4200
Gralla Publications

C4200–1   MERCHANDISING
     Monthly. Oversized.
     ISSN 0362-3920.
     LC 76-641228.
     SRI/MF/excerpts, shipped
     quarterly

Monthly trade journal reporting on marketing developments and trends in consumer electronics, housewares, and major appliances. Covers retail sales, consumer buying attitudes, store operations, new products, and promotional techniques.

Data are based on original surveys of consumers and retailers, and manufacturer reports of shipment estimates.

Issues generally contain regular narrative depts and feature articles, some with statistics. Recurring statistical features include the following:

a. Prerecorded videocassette industry news, with 1 monthly table showing the following rankings: top 30 videocassettes in rentals; and top 10 videocassettes, top 5 laserdiscs, and top 5 alternative (nontheatrical) programs, in sales; all for current and previous month, and indicating number of months included among top.

b. Annual statistical and marketing reports on sales, retail value, and trade of consumer electronics, housewares, and major appliances; and an annual national consumer attitude survey.

Nov. issue includes an annual directory of products, services, and suppliers.

Monthly table appears in all issues. All additional features with substantial statistical content are described, as they appear, under "Statistical Features." Nonstatistical features are not covered.

Availability: Merchandising, Circulation Department, Rm. 930, 1501 Broadway, New York NY 10036, qualified subscribers †, others $33.00 per yr., single copy $4.00, Mar. and Sept. issues $15.00 each; SRI/MF/excerpts for monthly table and all portions covered under "Statistical Features;" shipped quarterly.

Issues reviewed during 1985: Nov. 1984-Oct. 1985 (P) (Vol. 9, Nos. 11-12; Vol. 10, Nos. 1-10).

STATISTICAL FEATURES:

C4200–1.601: Nov. 1984 (Vol. 9, No. 11)

MICROWAVE OVENS SHOULD ACCOUNT FOR GAINS IN DOLLAR VOLUME OF 21.9 PERCENT IN 1984

(p. 43, 46) By Nancy Markov. Article on retailers' microwave oven sales and marketing. Data are from responses of 129 retailers, representing 566 stores, to a 1984 *Merchandising* survey.

Includes 10 tables showing sample characteristics, and survey response concerning microwave oven sales value, type and size of units sold, number of brands and models carried, best-selling price range, customer demand for selected features, and new and replacement sales shares, various years 1982-84.

C4200–1.602: Dec. 1984 (Vol. 9, No. 12)

RETAILERS PREDICT THAT VCRs, REFRIGERATORS, MICROWAVE COOKWARE WILL LEAD SALES IN '85

(p. 12B-13) By Lee Rath. Article on retailer outlook for consumer electronics, major appliance, and houseware sales and profits in 1985. Data are from a 1984 *Merchandising* survey of retailers representing 543 outlets.

Includes 12 tables showing survey response concerning products expected to generate greatest increase in sales and profits, 1985 and expected increase over 1984.

TOUGH TIMES MAY BRIGHTEN FOR DIEHARD COMPUTER DEALERS

(p. 26-27) By Frank Cavaliere. Article on computer dealer inventory outlook for 1985. Data are from responses of 199 retailers to a 1984 *Merchandising* survey.

Includes 4 tables showing survey response concerning retail outlet types, computer brands carried, and average price and gross profit margin for leading models, primarily 1983-85.

PHONE OWNERSHIP IS RISING, ACCORDING TO RESEARCH STUDY

(p. 30) By Frank Cavaliere. Article on residential telephone ownership, based on a June 1984 survey of 1,008 persons conducted by Yankee Group. Includes 1 chart showing percent of respondents owning, intending to purchase, and not intending to purchase a telephone.

C4200–1.603: Mar. 1985 (Vol. 10, No. 3)

63rd ANNUAL STATISTICAL AND MARKETING REPORT

(p. 79-102) Annual report on shipments and retail sales, including foreign trade, of major household appliances, consumer electronic products, and housewares, 1980-84. Also includes market profiles by State for 1984. Data are from Federal and private sources.

Contains narrative analysis, and 136 tables showing the following:

a. Shipments and retail value, 1980-84, and change in shipments by product characteristics, and in sales by outlet type, 1983-84; all by product, for major appliances (p. 80-87), home and auto electronic products (p. 88-94), and housewares (p. 95-99). 126 tables.

b. Export and import shipments and manufacturer's value/freight/insurance, by product, 1981-84. 9 tables. (p. 100-101)

c. Market profiles: residential and farm residential electrified homes, total housing permits, and personal income, by census division and State, 3rd quarter or full-year 1984, with percent change from 1983. 1 table. (p. 102)

C4200–1.604: Apr. 1985 (Vol. 10, No. 4)

ANNUAL VCR SHIPMENTS SHOULD HIT 10 MILLION BY 1987

(p. 31, 54) By Marilyn Sibirski. Article, with 1 undated chart showing subject category preferences of prerecorded videocassette rental customers. Data are from Venture Development Corp.

C4200–1.605: Aug. 1985 (Vol. 10, No. 8)

RETAIL ELECTRONICS SALES TO HIT $34 BILLION IN '86, ANNUAL FEATURE

(p. 14) Annual article, by Lee Rath, on market outlook for consumer electronics. Data are from Electronics Industries Assn/Consumer Electronics Group. Includes 1 table showing volume of sales to dealers, for consumer electronics by product type, 1985 with percent change from 1984.

Article presenting data for 1984 is described in SRI 1984 Annual under C4200-1.508.

C4200–1.606: Sept. 1985 (Vol. 10, No. 9)

HOME HEALTHCARE PRODUCTS STAND OUT IN 1985

(p. 11) By Regina Eisman. Article, with 1 table showing percent growth in houseware sales, by product type, 1985. Data are from a *Merchandising* survey of houseware manufacturers.

THIRTEENTH ANNUAL CONSUMER SURVEY

(p. 12-30) Annual report on consumer purchase plans for 21 categories of electronic products, major appliances, and housewares, with profiles of prime marketing targets; 1985. Data are from responses of 1,201 consumers to a survey conducted by Home Testing Institute for *Merchandising*.

Includes 66 tables showing survey response on the following for each product category: current ownership, purchase plans, and outlet preferences, for specific types of products; and household characteristics of most likely purchasers, for a selected product within each category.

Also includes 4 tables showing respondent characteristics.

C4215
Graves, Earl G.,
Publishing Co.

C4215–1   BLACK ENTERPRISE
     Monthly.
     ISSN 0006-4165.
     LC 74-25061.
     SRI/MF/not filmed

Monthly journal reporting on topics of interest to blacks, including career opportunities, black-owned businesses, and economic, social, and political issues. Data sources include Federal agencies and the journal's own research.

General format:

a. Feature articles and regular narrative depts.

b. "Facts and Figures" section, with 1-4 charts or tables often including data on various indicators of black socioeconomic standing.

Annual statistical features include financial performance of top 100 black-owned businesses and of black-owned financial institutions; and attitudes of blacks on current issues.

Features with substantial statistical content are described, as they appear, under "Statistical Features." Data in "Facts and Figures" section usually are described only when shown by race or for blacks or all minorities. Each issue of the journal is reviewed, but an abstract is published in SRI monthly issues only when statistical features appear.

Availability: Black Enterprise, PO Box 3009, Harlan IA 51537, $15.00 per yr., single copy $1.95, June issue $3.00; SRI/MF/not filmed.

Issues reviewed during 1985: Dec. 1984-Nov. 1985 (P) (Vol. 15, Nos. 5-12; Vol. 16, Nos. 1-4).

STATISTICAL FEATURES:

C4215–1.601: Dec. 1984 (Vol. 15, No. 5)

FACTS AND FIGURES

(p. 49) Includes 1 table showing black families, income, and expenditures by category, 1973 and 1982. Data are from Census Bureau, BLS, and Black Enterprise Research.

C4215–1.602: Jan. 1985 (Vol. 15, No. 6)

FACTS AND FIGURES

(p. 43) Includes 2 charts showing daily newspapers' total and minority employment, 1978-84; and percent of black female and male heads of household receiving income from selected sources (no date).

Data are from American Society of Newspaper Editors and National Urban League.

BLACK ENTERPRISE ANNUAL ECONOMIC OUTLOOK: SEEKING A FOUNDATION FOR STABILITY

(p. 46-60) Annual article, by Derek T. Dingle, summarizing views of leading black economists serving on *Black Enterprise* Board of Economists. Also includes 2 charts showing total and black unemployment rates, Sept. 1983-Sept. 1984; and distribution of all, married-couple, and female householder (no husband present) black families, by income level, 1982.

Data are from BLS, Census Bureau, and Black Enterprise Research.

C4215–1.603: Feb. 1985 (Vol. 15, No. 7)

DESIGNS FOR THE FUTURE

(p. 57-64) By Edmund Newton. Article, with 1 table showing employment 1982, and employment increase 1982-95 period, for 11 engineering disciplines with substantial growth. Data are from BLS.

WORKING ON THE HILL

(p. 77-80) By Robert Calvert, Jr. Article, with 1 table showing the following for 14 congressional staff positions: salary range, and average salary paid in Senate and House of Representatives, 1983/84 or 1984; with description of position duties. Data are from Congressional Management Foundation.

CAREERS AND OPPORTUNITIES 1985

(p. 87-92) By Edmund Newton. Article, with 3 charts showing black work force in 6 occupational categories with significant growth in black employment, 1983-84; distribution of college graduates by type of occupation, including jobs not requiring a degree, 1982-95 period; and entry-level salary of fastest growing professions, 1982/83. Data are from BLS.

PAVING THE WAY FOR BIG MONEY CONTRACTS

(p. 119-122) By Sam Fulwood. Article, with 1 table showing value of government contracts awarded to all and minority firms, FY78-3rd quarter FY84. Data are from Commerce Dept.

C4215–1.604: Mar. 1985 (Vol. 15, No. 8)

FACTS AND FIGURES

(p. 37) Includes 1 undated chart ranking States by number of black households. Data are from Census Bureau.

C4215–1.605: May 1985 (Vol. 15, No. 10)

FACTS AND FIGURES

(p. 35) Includes 1 table showing population, and labor force by employment status and race, all by sex for persons age 20/older, Jan. 1985. Data are from Brimmer and Co.

NO TRESPASSING!

(p. 37-44) Article on housing discrimination. Data are from Census Bureau and a University of Wisconsin 1983 survey of 28 cities. Includes 1 table showing total and black population, and 3 measures of racial residential segregation, for 15 cities with black population over 100,000 and a high incidence of residential segregation, 1980 with some comparisons to 1970.

C4215–1.606: June 1985 (Vol. 15, No. 11)

FACTS AND FIGURES

(p. 80) Includes 1 chart showing number of self-employed workers by race, 1972 and 1982. Data are from *The State of Small Business.*

1985 ANNUAL REPORT ON BLACK BUSINESS

(p. 85-184) Annual feature on black-owned businesses and financial institutions, including lists of the top 100 businesses ranked by 1984 sales, and of all banks, savings and loan assns, and insurance companies, ranked by 1984 assets. Lists also show location, chief executive, year started, employment, and the following: type of business and 1983 sales rank, for top 100; deposits and loans, for banks and savings and loan assns; and insurance in force, and premium and net investment income, for insurance companies.

Top 100 list is accompanied by an analytical article, with 3 charts and 3 tables showing sales and number of companies by industry group, and number of companies in cities with black mayors, 1984; companies new to list in 1985; top 10 companies in sales growth and employment, 1984 with comparison to 1983; and aggregate number and employment of information system companies on list, 1980-84.

Financial institution lists also are accompanied by analytical articles, each with 1 table showing aggregate employment and financial data for 1983-84.

Feature also includes several articles on outstanding companies; 1 article on black-owned hair care/cosmetic businesses, with 1 table showing number and aggregate employment of firms on the top 100 list, 1978-84; and 1 article on economic outlook, with 1 table showing labor union membership by industry division and race, 1984 with summary trends from 1956.

This is the 13th annual feature.

C4215–1.607: July 1985 (Vol. 15, No. 12)

FACTS AND FIGURES

(p. 39) Includes 1 undated chart comparing 4 socioeconomic issues of most concern to blacks and whites, based on a Roper Organization Survey of 1,989 adults.

C4215–1.608: Aug. 1985 (Vol. 16, No. 1)

FACTS AND FIGURES

(p. 20) Includes 2 charts and 1 table on job outlook through 1995, including 1982 and 1985 employment in selected fast-growing occupations. Data are from *Career Opportunities News* and BLS.

SOLDIERS IN THE CORPORATE WORLD

(p. 42-44) Article, with 1 table showing black percent of DOD enlisted personnel and officers, by service branch, 1985.

B.E. READERS SPEAK OUT, ANNUAL FEATURE

(p. 95-102) Annual article summarizing results of a Mar. 1985 opinion and attitude survey of *Black Enterprise* readers. The survey drew approximately 4,000 responses.

Includes 1 table on respondent characteristics, and 1 table showing distribution of responses to questions on the following topics:

a. Personal finances: black economic status compared to 5 years ago; criteria for middle class status; whether respondent is 1st generation in own family to attain middle class status; incidence of 2-income households, and of family members receiving public assistance; and belief that lending institutions discriminate against blacks.

b. Business: whether government is supportive of black business development; existence of black businesses in own neighborhood; efforts to patronize black businesses; problems facing black businesses; and own potential sources of start-up capital.

c. Employment: job opportunity trend for blacks in past decade; reason hired for present position (qualifications vs. employer's quota); affirmative action's effectiveness, and necessity in 10 years; most effective actions against companies that discriminate on basis of race; and whether a black ever will head a Fortune 500 company.

d. Politics: whether significant differences exist between major parties; party supported; whether blacks should form their own party; voting effect on black welfare; responsiveness of black elected officials; whether black mayors have improved city government; and likelihood of a black President/Vice-President in 20th Century.

e. Leadership: own efforts to further black progress in past decade, and obligation to help disadvantaged blacks; need for strong black leader, and effectiveness of existing leadership; individuals and organizations best representing black aspirations; and whether blacks can achieve equality without alliances with whites.

f. Race: prevalence of racism today compared to last decade; own ability to cope with racism in various situations, and most effective means of coping; whether blacks are overly sensitive about race; and own experience as victim of racism, and effect on feelings toward other ethnic groups.

g. Media portrayal of blacks: fairness in movies, magazines, newspapers, TV, advertising, and radio; and whether media portrayal affects public image of blacks.

For description of last survey results covered by SRI, see SRI 1982 Annual under C4215-1.309. Survey results published in 1983 contained only text statistics, and no survey was published for 1984.

C4215-1.609: Oct. 1985 (Vol. 16, No. 3)

SHORTFALL IN BLACK INCOME REFLECTED IN TAX PATTERN

(p. 39) Article, with 1 table showing the following by race: taxpaying and non-taxpaying households; household money income before and after taxes; and tax payments by type (Federal and State income, Social Security, Federal retirement, property, and sales/excise); 1983. Data are from Brimmer & Co. and the Census Bureau.

FACTS AND FIGURES

(p. 41) Includes 1 table showing broadcast media total and black employment, with detail for blacks by sex, all by job category, 1983. Data are from FCC.

COST OF RAISING A CHILD

(p. 43) Article, with 1 undated table showing child-rearing expenses by category (groceries, dining out, clothing, housing, medical, education, transportation, and other), by child age group. Data are from USDA.

C4215-1.610: Nov. 1985 (Vol. 16, No. 4)

CHANGING PATTERN IN U.S. HOUSEHOLD ASSETS

(p. 34) Article, with 1 table showing percent of households owning 6 types of financial assets (checking and savings accounts, money market accounts and funds, certificates of deposit, and IRA/Keogh plans), 1977 and 1983. Data are from *American Demographics*.

FACTS AND FIGURES

(p. 41) Includes 2 tables showing the following:

a. Black percent of total population, for 44 major cities with 30%/more black population, 1980. Data are from the Census Bureau.

b. Characteristics of households owning credit cards, including income and liquid assets, and household head's age and occupation (blue or white collar worker, other), with detail by type of card (no date). Data are from *American Demographics*.

C4300
Hanley-Wood

C4300-1   BUILDER

Monthly.
ISSN 0744-1193.
LC 82-642608/r83.
SRI/MF/not filmed

Monthly journal of the National Assn of Home Builders (NAHB), reporting on housing construction and market developments. Covers construction and remodeling activities, design, marketing techniques, financing, new products, and economic and governmental developments affecting the housing industry.

Issues generally contain:

a. News and feature articles, occasionally with statistics.

b. Regular editorial depts, including monthly "Outlook" section, by Michael Sumichrast, presenting 6 charts showing summary housing trends; 3 charts showing builder ratings for present new housing sales and 6-month sales outlook; and 1-2 additional tables or charts.

c. Quarterly feature on housing starts, by census region and for 90-95 MSAs, with 5 tables.

Annual features include a survey of prospective homebuyer characteristics, and ranking of top 100 builders.

Monthly "Outlook" charts appear in all issues. All other statistical features, including quarterly housing starts, and additional "Outlook" tables and charts with substantial statistical content, are described, as they appear, under "Statistical Features."

Please note that, prior to the Aug. 1985 issue, excerpts from this publication (monthly charts and all portions described under "Statistical Features") were available on SRI microfiche.

Availability: Circulation, Builder Magazine, PO Box 1434, Riverton NJ 08077, NAHB members †, others $25.00 per yr., single copy $5.00; SRI/MF/not filmed.

Issues reviewed during 1985: Nov. 1984-Oct. 1985 (P) (Vol. 7, Nos. 11-12; Vol. 8, Nos. 1-10).

STATISTICAL FEATURES:

C4300-1.601: Dec. 1984 (Vol. 7, No. 12)

OUTLOOK: TAPERING OFF

(p. 11-14) Includes 1 table showing cumulative increase in housing starts, by month, 1984 vs. 1983. Data are from NAHB Economics Division.

DESPITE RECOVERY S&Ls ARE IN TROUBLE

(p. 32-33) Article, with 2 tables showing mortgage yield, cost of funds rate, and rate of return on assets, for FSLIC-insured savings institutions, 1979-1st half 1984. Data are from FHLBB.

ECONOMISTS FORECAST A GOOD YEAR AHEAD

(p. 36) Article, with 1 table showing single- and multi-family housing starts by census region, and total mobile home shipments, 1984-85. Data are from NAHB.

GYPSUM PRICES WILL KEEP ON RISING

(p. 42, 46) Brief article, with 1 table showing percent change in PPI, for all commodities,

construction materials, and selected building materials, Sept. 1984 vs. Sept. 1983. Data are from BLS.

HOME PRICES FALL

(p. 50, 54) Article, with 1 table showing average sales price for new/existing homes in 10 MSAs, 3rd quarter 1983-84. Data were compiled by NAHB.

C4300-1.602: Jan. 1985 (Vol. 8, No. 1)

STARTS WILL LEVEL OFF IN THE FIRST QUARTER, QUARTERLY FEATURE

(p. 78-84) Quarterly article, with 5 tables showing housing starts, by census region and for 95 MSAs, quarterly 1984-1st quarter 1985. Data are from NAHB.

This is the 1st appearance of the feature.

ARMs CUSHION FALL OF RESALES

(p. 112) Brief article, with 1 table showing existing home sales, 3rd quarter 1984 with percent change from 3rd quarter 1983, for each State reporting sales increase during the period. Data are from National Assn of Realtors.

ROLE REVERSAL

(p. 194-199) By Carol Anderson. Article on involvement of savings and loan assns (S&Ls) in real estate development. Data are from a recent survey of 372 S&Ls, conducted by Robert Charles Lesser & Co. Includes 3 undated charts showing respondent distribution by type of current and planned real estate activity.

C4300-1.603: Feb. 1985 (Vol. 8, No. 2)

OUTLOOK: PROBLEMS AHEAD

(p. 11-13) Includes 1 table showing impact of the Treasury Dept's tax proposal and 2 other tax plans on housing starts, 1986-95. Data are from Data Resources, Inc.

LIFE AFTER SECTION 8

(p. 110-17) By Penelope Lemov. Article, with 1 table showing construction starts for rental units subsidized by HUD's Section 8 program, 1976-85. Data are from HUD.

C4300-1.604: Mar. 1985 (Vol. 8, No. 3)

OUTLOOK: ROLLING ON

(p. 11-13) Includes 1 table showing trends and forecasts for selected economic indicators, 1983-86. Data compiled by NAHB Economics Division.

MOVE-UP HOUSING MADE ITS MOVE LAST YEAR

(p. 62) Article, with 1 chart showing repeat and 1st-time buyers' shares of the new housing market, 2-year periods 1975-84. Data are from NAHB Economics Division.

PROPOSED BUDGET CUTS SUBSIDIZED HOUSING

(p. 70-74) Article, with 1 table showing number of housing units subsidized under HUD Section 8 and other programs, FY80 and FY85-86. Data are from HUD.

FIVE-YEAR LOCAL FORECAST

(p. 94-105) By Penelope Lemov. Article, with 1 table showing average annual single- and multi-family housing starts, in 94 metro areas arranged by region, 5-year periods 1970-89. Data are from NAHB Forecasting Service.

NAHB ANNOUNCES 20 BIGGEST HBAs

(p. 123) Brief article, with 1 table showing top 20 home builder assns ranked by membership, as of Oct. 1, 1984.

C4300–1.605: Apr. 1985 (Vol. 8, No. 4)

TEXAS: AFTER THE RISE A VERY BIG FALL

(p. 42-44) Article, with 1 table showing single- and multi-family housing starts, for Texas, Dallas-Fort Worth area, and Houston, 1981-85. Data are from NAHB Forecasting Service.

ARMs, INCOME GAINS BOOST AFFORDABILITY

(p. 50-54) Article, with 1 table showing average household income and home price, and mortgage payment as percent of income, for 14 metro areas, 1983-84. Data are from Lomas and Nettleton Co.

NORTHEAST TOPS RESALE REBOUND

(p. 58) Article, with 1 table showing top 10 States ranked by existing home sales, 4th quarter 1984 with percent change from 4th quarter 1983. Data are from National Assn of Realtors.

COMPENSATION UP 27% FOR BUILDER EXECS

(p. 68, 72) Article, with 1 table showing home building industry average salary and bonus, for 3 top executive positions, 1980 and 1984. Data are from NAHB's *Builders Cost of Doing Business Study,* 1984.

HOT BUTTONS, ANNUAL FEATURE

(p. 88-107) Annual article, by Leslie Ensor Stockman et al., on new-home shopper characteristics and buying intentions, 1985. Data are from 1,819 responses to a recent survey of prospective buyers in 7 market areas, conducted by George A. Fulton Research and Consulting.

Includes 11 tables presenting survey data on value, square footage, and equity or down payment, of current home and planned home purchase; and buyers' age, household income and composition, reasons for buying new home, and interest in selected design options; all by expected home purchase price range.

C4300–1.606: May 1985 (Vol. 8, No. 5)

OUTLOOK: RENTAL DILEMMA

(p. 11-13) Includes 1 table showing housing starts by type (single-family, total multifamily, and multifamily with 5/more rental units), 1975-86. Data are from Census Bureau, HUD, and NAHB.

U.S. WON'T TURN INTO NATION OF RENTERS

(p. 72-74) Brief article, with 1 chart showing consumer willingness to purchase housing if interest portion of monthly mortgage were not deductible. Data are from responses of 3,130 single-family home buyers to a Dec. 1984 survey conducted by Harvard-MIT Joint Center for Urban Studies.

STARTS STRONG THROUGH SECOND QUARTER, QUARTERLY FEATURE

(p. 100-112) Quarterly article, with 5 tables showing housing starts, by census region and for 91 MSAs, 2nd quarter 1984-2nd quarter 1985. Data are from NAHB.

BUILDER 100, ANNUAL FEATURE

(p. 142-167, 200) Annual feature, by Penelope Lemov, presenting top 100 home construction companies ranked by unit production, and also including the following for each company: production by type (detached and attached for-sale, and rental); gross revenues; whether public or privately held; and top executives, principal State markets, and diversified enterprises; primarily 1984, with comparative 1983 rank.

Also includes data on top 100 construction activity by detailed type of structure, general outlook for 1985 housing market, and summaries of data included with the rankings; and comparison to single- and multi-family housing production of all builders, 1984.

Data were compiled by *Builder.*

Contains narrative overview, brief profiles of selected companies, 10 charts and 10 tables, detailed ranked list, and index of companies.

This is the 2nd annual feature.

C4300–1.607: June 1985 (Vol. 8, No. 6)

OUTLOOK: SPLIT PERSONALITY

(p. 11-13) Includes 1 table showing housing starts, by type of dwelling and region, selected quarters 1984-85. Data are from Census Bureau and NAHB.

TAX PROPOSALS: TOUGH PILLS TO SWALLOW

(p. 43-46) Article, with 1 table estimating impact of recent Treasury Dept tax reform proposals on depreciation allowances for the purchase of a $1 million commercial building, for 18 consecutive years from purchase. Data are from Seidman and Seidman/BDO.

REITs STAGE COMEBACK AMONG INVESTORS

(p. 50-54) Article, with 1 table showing capital invested in real estate investment trusts, 1971-1st quarter 1985. Data are from National Assn of Securities Dealers.

PENSION FUNDS STILL COOL IN MORTGAGES

(p. 62) Article, with 1 chart showing distribution of mortgage-related investments of private pension funds, by type, as of Sept. 1984. Data are from HUD.

RETIREMENT HOUSING: A MATURING MARKET

(p. 70-91) By Leslie Ensor Stockman and June Fletcher. Article on market outlook for retirement housing. Data are from Census Bureau. Includes 1 table and 3 charts showing the following:

a. Population aged 55/over, decennially 1970-2000; and population aged 65/over, with share of total population, by State, 1983.

b. Estimated housing purchase/rental market among persons aged 65-74 and 70-84, computed from 1980 data on population and households, living arrangements, household composition, income level (above or below $18,500), and household moves.

C4300–1.608: July 1985 (Vol. 8, No. 7)

OUTLOOK: BALANCING ACT

(p. 11, 13) Includes 1 table showing housing starts, by region and for single- and multi-family units, 1st 4 months 1984-85. Data are from Census Bureau.

SINGLE-FAMILY SURGE SOFTENS CONDO FALL

(p. 38-39) Article, with 2 tables showing single-family detached housing starts, monthly Mar. 1984-Apr. 1985; and condominium starts, 1974-85. Data are from Census Bureau and *U.S. Housing Markets.*

POLL: DON'T MEDDLE WITH HOME DEDUCTION

(p. 50) Article, with 1 undated table showing public support for 3 Federal income tax reform proposals eliminating deductions for property taxes and for mortgages on primary and second homes. Data are based on 1,500 responses to a survey conducted by Decision Making Information for NAHB.

S&Ls: LEADING SOURCE OF PERMANENT FINANCING

(p. 50, 54) Article, with 1 table showing distribution of permanent financing for commercial/apartment real estate development projects, by type of lender, 2nd half 1984. Data are based on an Urban Land Institute survey covering 477 projects with a total value of $8.3 billion.

Similar article, with data for 4th quarter 1983-1st quarter 1984 period, is described in SRI 1984 Annual under C4300-1.512.

C4300–1.609: Aug. 1985 (Vol. 8, No. 8)

MANY BIG BUILDERS FACING HARD TIMES

(p. 38-39) Article, with 1 table comparing single-family new home price and CPI trends, 1980-1st quarter 1985. Data are from Census Bureau and BLS.

HOUSING STARTS TO LEVEL OFF IN THIRD QUARTER, QUARTERLY FEATURE

(p. 58-64) Quarterly article, with 5 tables showing housing starts, by census region and for approximately 90 MSAs, 3rd quarter 1984-3rd quarter 1985. Data are from NAHB.

C4300–1.610: Sept. 1985 (Vol. 8, No. 9)

BUDGET CUTS RURAL HOUSING, HUD FUNDS

(p. 35-38) Article, with 1 table showing number of HUD-assisted housing units funded, by program, under FY85 appropriations and FY86 Administration request and House appropriation. Data are from House Appropriations Committee and NAHB.

COMMERCIAL BREAK

(p. 76-89) By Penelope Lemov. Article on residential builders' involvement in commercial construction. Data are from a recent *Builder* survey of 500 builders.

Includes 1 chart and 4 tables showing survey response on involvement in commercial projects during 1984, including square footage and value of projects built; and reasons for starting commercial activity, types of projects built, and future plans; all by builder size group (based on number of houses built annually).

Also includes income, expenses, and development costs, by item, for 6 commercial projects completed by residential builders.

C4300–1.611: Oct. 1985 (Vol. 8, No. 10)

LOOSER RULES ENHANCE APPEAL OF FHA LOANS

(p. 45, 48) Article, with 1 table showing number of single-family mortgages insured by FHA vs. private insurers, quarterly 1984-2nd quarter 1985. Data are from NAHB Mortgage Finance Division.

RESALE RATES, PRICES UP IN SECOND QUARTER

(p. 60, 66) Brief article, with 1 table showing top 10 States ranked by existing home sales, 2nd quarter 1985 with percent change from 2nd quarter 1984. Data are from National Assn of Realtors.

Similar article is described under C4300-1.605, above.

THEY'RE BIGGER, TALLER AND SOMEWHAT COSTLIER

(p. 70, 72) Brief article, with 1 table showing distribution of new single-family homes by sales price range, 1983-84. Data are from Census Bureau and HUD.

STANDOUT MARKETS FOR NEW HOME SALES

(p. 78) Table showing 10 leading metro areas ranked by new single-family home sales, and including total home sales, 1984. Data are from Chicago Title Insurance Co.

C4380
Harcourt Brace Jovanovich

C4380–1   QUICK FROZEN FOODS
Monthly.
ISSN 0033-6408.
LC 44-46818.
SRI/MF/not filmed

Monthly trade journal of the frozen food industry. Covers retail and food service sales, storage and transportation developments, Government regulation, processing, and merchandising and promotion. Data are primarily from the journal's own or other private research.

Issues generally contain feature articles and narrative depts; and the following recurring statistical features:

a. "Retail Reports" (occasionally titled "Regional Reports"), a series of articles on frozen food sales and consumption in specific market areas.

b. Recurring "Data File" feature, with 1-2 tables variously showing frozen food production, consumption, exports, and cold storage holdings, by product type.

Annual statistical features include refrigerated warehouse and trucking surveys; frozen foods almanac, with data on production, storage capacity, and trade; and expansion plans for supermarkets and frozen food distributors and packers.

Recurring "Data File" tables, "Retail Reports," and all articles with substantial statistical content are described as they appear, under "Statistical Features." Each issue of the journal is reviewed, but an abstract is published in SRI monthly issues only when statistical features appear.

Availability: Quick Frozen Foods, Circulation Department, One E. First St., Duluth MN 55802, $20.00 per yr., single copy $2.00; SRI/MF/not filmed.

Issues reviewed during 1985: Nov. 1984-Oct. 1985 (P) (Vol. 47, Nos. 4-11; Vol. 48, Nos. 1-3) [Vol. 47, No. 8 incorrectly reads No. 3; no July 1985 issue was published].

STATISTICAL FEATURES:

C4380–1.601: Nov. 1984 (Vol. 47, No. 4)

STATE OF THE INDUSTRY: FROZEN FOOD PRODUCTION NEARS $33 BILLION IN 1983, ANNUAL FEATURE

(p. 45-58, 79-81) Part 1 of a 2-part annual article, by Ross Chamberlain, on frozen food production. Includes 1 table showing frozen food production volume and value, for retail and institutional sectors, by product type, 1983 with percent change from 1982.

1984 FROZEN FOODS ALMANAC, ANNUAL FEATURE

(p. 61-76) Annual report on frozen food production, storage capacity, and foreign trade, 1983 and trends. Data are from *Quick Frozen Foods,* Depts of Commerce and Agriculture, and industry sources. Contains 20 tables showing the following:

a. Production value and/or volume, by frozen food product type, 1983, with selected trends from as early as 1939, and detail for retail and institutional sectors and for selected product types (seafood, breaded and processed products, fruits, juices, vegetables, meat and poultry); and volume and value of purchases for USDA child nutrition program, 1983/84. 15 tables. (p. 62-72)

b. Freezer storage capacity: by type of warehouse, biennially 1941-83; and by State and census division, Oct. 1, 1983. 3 tables. (p. 73)

c. Import and export volume and value, by frozen food commodity, with fresh/frozen totals for some commodities, and imports of food processing and agricultural machinery, 1979-83. 2 tables. (p. 74-76)

For description of previous report, see SRI 1983 Annual under C4380-1.411.

C4380–1.602: Dec. 1984 (Vol. 47, No. 5)

STATE OF THE INDUSTRY: 1983 POULTRY, BEVERAGES UP; FRUITS AND VEGETABLES FALL, ANNUAL FEATURE

(p. 32-44) Part 2 of a 2-part annual article, by Ross Chamberlain, on frozen food production. Data are from Depts of Commerce and Agriculture, industry sources, and *Quick Frozen Foods.* Includes 6 tables showing frozen food total and per capita consumption and sales, 1942-83; and production volume and value, for vegetables, fruits, juice concentrates, and poultry, by product, 1982-83, with summary data for retail and institutional sectors.

C4380–1.603: Jan. 1985 (Vol. 47, No. 6)

REGIONAL REPORT: INDIANAPOLIS CARTS RACING FOR FRUIT, PUDDING AND PIES

(p. 38-41) Article on frozen food sales and consumption by product type, in Indianapolis, Ind. Data are from Selling Areas Marketing Inc. (SAMI). Includes 4 tables showing per household consumption indexes for product types with highest and lowest indexes, including Indianapolis' rank among 48 SAMI markets, for an unspecified period.

Article is part of a series covering specific market areas.

C4380–1.604: Feb. 1985 (Vol. 47, No. 7)

SOME BRIGHT SPOTS EXPECTED IN JUICE CONCENTRATES BUSINESS, ANNUAL FEATURE

(p. 18-22, 60) Annual article on Florida citrus industry conditions, with data on frozen concentrated orange juice (FCOJ) sales. Data are from Florida Citrus Processors Assn, Florida Citrus Mutual, and *Quick Frozen Foods.*

Includes 2 tables showing Florida FCOJ retail, institutional, and bulk sales value and volume, 1959/60-1983/84.

FROM THE LAND OF FISH 'N CHIPS: ENGLAND SWINGS FROZEN'S WAY

(p. 38-40) Article, with 1 table showing UK seafood landings, imports, exports, consumption in households and by type of foodservice operation, and nonhuman consumption, with some detail for fresh and frozen tonnage, 1983.

DATA FILE, RECURRING FEATURE

(p. 42P-42Q) Includes the following tables:

[1] Cold storage holdings [frozen vegetables, potatoes, fish and other seafood, fruits, juices, poultry, and eggs, all by type, selected months Nov. 1983-Nov. 1984].

[2] U.S. exports of frozen foods [volume for meat, poultry, fish, other seafood, vegetables, fruits, and fruit juices, all by type, May-Aug. 1984, with cumulative volume and value, Jan.-Aug. 1984].

C4380–1.605: Mar. 1985 (Vol. 47, No. 8)
[Issue incorrectly reads No. 3.]

PACKERS BUILDING FF STORAGE; PLANTS UNDER RENOVATION, ANNUAL FEATURE

(p. 34-42, 51-53) Annual article, by Ross Chamberlain, on frozen food packers' expansion plans for 1985. Data are from a *Quick Frozen Foods* survey.

Includes 2 charts and 6 tables showing percent of packers planning construction or renovation for plant, warehouse, office, and other areas; and percent planning purchases of equipment and supplies by detailed type; 1985, and various trends 1981-84.

FF DISTRIBUTORS BUILDING TRUCK FLEETS AND WAREHOUSES, ANNUAL FEATURE

(p. 44-47) Annual article, by Ross Chamberlain, on frozen food distributors' expansion plans for 1985. Data are from a *Quick Frozen Foods* survey.

Includes 5 tables showing percent of distributors planning construction or renovation for warehouse, office, and other areas; and percent planning purchases of equipment and warehouse insulation, by type; 1985, and various trends 1982-84.

SLICING OFF A BIGGER PIECE OF THE PREPARED FROZEN PIE

(p. 50F-50G) Article, with 1 table showing foodservice industry revenues by type of operation, for commercial, contract, and institutional sectors, 1984, with percent change from 1983. Data are from the National Restaurant Assn.

C4380–1.606: Apr. 1985 (Vol. 47, No. 9)

RETAIL REPORT: RALEIGH CONSUMERS ARE SWEET ON BEEF PIZZA, MERINGUE PIE

(p. 36-40) Article on frozen food sales and consumption by product type, in Raleigh/Greensboro/Winston-Salem, N.C. Data are from Selling Areas Marketing Inc. (SAMI). Includes 4 tables showing per household consumption indexes for product types with highest and lowest indexes, including Raleigh/Greensboro/Winston-Salem's rank among 48 SAMI markets, for an unspecified period.

Article is part of a series covering specific market areas.

FOOD INDUSTRY MERGERS STILL A STRONG TREND

(p. 51) Article, with 1 chart showing food industry mergers/acquisitions, 1975-84. Data are from the Food Institute.

C4380–1.607: May 1985 (Vol. 47, No. 10)

BIGGER FF DEPARTMENTS IN STORE FOR 1985-86, ANNUAL FEATURE

(p. 30-40, 60) Annual article on anticipated supermarket chain business and expansion plans, with emphasis on frozen foods (FF), 1985. Data are from 45 responses to a Mar. 1985 *Quick Frozen Foods* survey, and from earlier surveys.

Includes 10 tables showing survey responses on planned new store openings and FF dept expansions; number of stores served; weekly sales per store; FF sales as percent of total sales; FF case buying plans, by type of case; FF warehouse construction, expansion, and renovation plans; FF products with greatest sales growth and decline; and FF-related equipment purchase plans, by type of equipment; 1985 with trends from 1983.

Data are shown for corporate chains, voluntaries, and cooperatives.

RETAIL REPORT: VEGETABLES, ENTREES TOPS IN BIG APPLE

(p. 42-46) Article on frozen food sales and consumption by product type, in NYC. Data are from Selling Areas Marketing Inc. (SAMI). Includes 4 tables showing per household consumption indexes for product types with highest and lowest indexes, including NYC's rank among 48 SAMI markets, for year ended June 22, 1984.

Article is part of a series covering specific market areas.

C4380–1.608: June 1985 (Vol. 47, No. 11)

ANNUAL WAREHOUSING SURVEY: EQUIPMENT TOPS CONSTRUCTION IN ZERO STORAGE 1985 PLANS

(p. 28-34) Annual survey article, by Ross Chamberlain, on public refrigerated warehouse construction and equipment purchase plans, and services provided, 1985, with comparisons to previous surveys. Current data are from responses of 78 warehouse executives to a spring 1985 *Quick Frozen Foods* survey.

Includes 4 tables showing survey response on planned new warehouse construction, and warehouse additions and renovations; planned equipment purchases, by type (including computers); computer applications; and types of services provided; various years 1981-85.

ANNUAL TRUCKER SURVEY: FF TRANSPORTATION ACTIVITY EASES UP, TRUCKERS CUT BACK

(p. 36-40) Annual survey article on refrigerated trucking industry equipment buying and leasing plans and frozen food haulage, 1985, with comparisons to previous surveys. Current data are from responses of 35 industry executives to a spring 1985 *Quick Frozen Foods* survey.

Includes 3 tables showing survey response on frozen food haulage increases and decreases, whether refrigerated storage facilities are owned or rented, plans to build/add and rent more refrigerated storage space, plans to buy or lease selected types of equipment (including computers), and computer applications, 1983-85.

C4380–1.609: Aug. 1985 (Vol. 48, No. 1)

FROZEN PIES DECLINE SLOWING; CHEESECAKE, TURNOVERS RISE, ANNUAL FEATURE

(p. 26-29) Annual article, by Ross Chamberlain, with 12 charts showing market shares for frozen sweet goods and pies, by type, for total U.S. and top 5 market areas, 1984. Data are from Selling Areas Marketing Inc.

SELLING UNDERUTILIZED SEAFOOD NEEDN'T BE FISHING EXPEDITION

(p. 36A-36E) Article on consumer familiarity with nontraditional seafood, based on a University of Massachusetts survey. Includes 4 undated tables showing traditional and nontraditional fish prices (whole fish and fillets), and consumer awareness and opinion of nontraditional seafoods, all by seafood type.

IMAGINATIVE MARKETERS PAINT NEW PICTURE OF FROZEN PIZZA

(p. 38-42) By Heidi Parsons. Article, with 1 chart showing frozen pizza sales volume, 1979-83 and for year ending Sept. 14, 1984. Data are from Selling Areas Marketing Inc.

FROZEN PIZZA SALES STILL SOFT AS BILLION DOLLAR MARKET HOLDS, ANNUAL FEATURE

(p. 72-76) Annual article, with 1 chart showing frozen pizza market shares, by topping, repeated for 8 leading market areas, 1984. Data are from Selling Areas Marketing Inc.

BIG SUPERS GET MORE SUPER IN AMERICAN RETAIL MARKETING

(p. 78-79) Article, with 2 charts and 1 table showing top 20 supermarket chains ranked by sales, and including units operated; aggregate sales for top 20 chains vs. all other grocery stores; and percent gain in sales, for top 20 chains, other large operators, and all grocery stores; 1984, with selected comparisons to 1983. Data are from the Food Institute.

C4380–1.610: Sept. 1985 (Vol. 48, No. 2)

FROZEN POULTRY NEARS BILLION DOLLAR MARK AS RED MEAT LOSES MUSCLE, SAYS SAMI EXEC

(p. 6-7) Article, with 4 tables showing frozen poultry retail sales, by product type, selected periods Oct. 1983-May 1985. Data are from Selling Areas Marketing Inc.

HIGH TECH PACKAGING PUTS FF ON HIGH ROAD

(p. 10-15) Article on trends in frozen food packaging. Data are from Assn of Home Appliance Manufacturers and Technomic Consultants. Includes 1 chart and 2 tables showing microwave oven shipments, 1972-85; and frozen food retail market volume, by container type, 1983 and 1988.

MICROWAVES AND FROZENS: GOOD MARRIAGE OF CONVENIENCE

(p. 20-21) Article on variety and location in grocery stores of foods that can be prepared in microwave ovens, based on a recent *Quick Frozen Foods* consumer survey. Includes 2 undated charts showing survey response.

ANY WAY YOU SLICE THEM, POTATOES NEED MORE PUSH

(p. 26-30) By Heidi Parsons. Article, with 1 chart showing frozen potato retail sales volume, 1979-Sept. 1984. Data are from Selling Areas Marketing Inc.

PER CAPITA DINING OUT BILL RISES AS FF's SHARE HITS $19 BILLION

(p. 34A-34B) Article, with 1 map showing per capita spending at eating/drinking places, by census division or region, 1984. Data are from Food Institute.

MATURE FOOD ADDITIVE BUSINESS CHARACTERIZED BY BIG CHANGES

(p. 44) Article, with 1 table showing food additive sales, by type, selected years 1980-94. Data are from Business Communications Co.

BREADED SEAFOODS RIDING FLAT, BUT BATTERED TAKES A BEATING, ANNUAL FEATURE

(p. 50-53) Annual article, with 3 tables showing production volume and value for frozen shrimp, fish sticks, and fish portions, by product type, for retail and institutional markets, 1983-84. Data are from Commerce Dept and *Quick Frozen Foods*.

Data on fish and shrimp were previously reported separately. Previous articles are described in SRI 1984 Annual under C4380-1.509 and C4380-1.510.

C4380–1.611: Oct. 1985 (Vol. 48, No. 3)

1985 FROZEN FOODS ALMANAC, ANNUAL FEATURE

(p. 31-52) Annual report on frozen food production, storage capacity, and foreign trade, 1984 and trends. Data are from *Quick Frozen Foods,* Commerce and Agriculture Depts, and industry sources. Contains 8 charts and 18 tables showing the following:

a. Frozen food production value and volume, for retail and institutional sectors and by detailed product type (including seafood, breaded and prepared products, fruits, juices, vegetables, meats, and poultry), 1984 with selected trends from as early as 1939. 8 charts and 13 tables. (p. 32-48)

b. Freezer storage capacity: by type of warehouse, biennially 1941-83; and by State and census division, Oct. 1, 1983. 3 tables. (p. 49)

c. Import and export volume and value, by frozen food commodity, with fresh/frozen totals for some commodities, and imports of food processing and agricultural machinery, 1980-84. 2 tables. (p. 50-52)

For description of previous report, see C4380-1.601 above.

C4380–2   HOME AND AUTO
Monthly. Oversized.
ISSN 0162-8801.
LC 70-612942.
SRI/MF/not filmed

Monthly trade journal (semimonthly in July) of the automotive aftermarket industry, reporting on do-it-yourself (DIY) sales, marketing, and product trends and developments. Data are primarily from the journal's own research.

Issues generally contain news and feature articles, occasionally with statistics; and regular depts, including price comparisons for selected automotive products in various chains and locations, and occasionally stock exchange averages or recent financial results for selected retail chains.

Annual statistical features include car care survey of automotive aftermarket sales (Apr.), non-automotive chain aftermarket sales survey (June), and automotive DIY survey (Oct.). The 2nd July issue is an annual buyer's guide.

Features with substantial statistical content are described, as they appear, under "Statistical Features." Each issue of the journal is reviewed, but an abstract is published in SRI monthly issues only when features with substantial statistical content appear.

Availability: Home and Auto, Circulation Department, One E. First St., Duluth MN 55802, $25.00 per yr., single copy $2.50, July Buyer's Guide $8.00; SRI/MF/not filmed.

Issues reviewed during 1985: Nov. 1, 1984-Oct. 1, 1985 (P) (Vol. 94, Nos. 11-12; Vol. 95, Nos. 1-10).

STATISTICAL FEATURES:

C4380–2.601: Dec. 1, 1984 (Vol. 94, No. 12)

"BACK TO BASICS" BOOSTS CAR WAX SALES

(p. 40) Article, with 3 charts showing retail inventory turns, and total and chain sales, for auto wax/polish products, primarily 1980-84. Data are from *Home and Auto 1984 Car Care Center* survey.

C4380–2.602: Jan. 1, 1985 (Vol. 95, No. 1)

FIGHTING OIL'S STATUS QUO

(p. 18) By Ron Stevens. Article on retail marketing of motor oil, including importance of product rebates and other promotion methods, and preferred types of manufacturer incentives. Data are based on a recent *Home and Auto* survey of aftermarket retailers and suppliers. Includes 4 undated tables.

C4380–2.603: Apr. 1, 1985 (Vol. 95, No. 4)

CAR CARE CENTER, ANNUAL FEATURE

(p. 27-69) Annual survey report on auto aftermarket retail sales, 1984, with trends from 1980. Data are based on the performance of 63 retail aftermarket chains representing approximately 35,000 outlets in the U.S. and Canada.

Contains sections on 21 auto repair and maintenance product groups, each with narrative analysis including 1985 sales forecasts, and 5 charts showing the following: aftermarket sales, annual inventory turns, average gross margin, and car care promotion's share of sales, for retail chains; and total aftermarket sales; primarily 1980-84.

This is the 11th annual survey.

C4380–2.604: May 1, 1985 (Vol. 95, No. 5)

PUTTING THE LESSONS TO WORK

(p. 19-22) Article on automotive parts/supplies aftermarket retailer participation in supplier racing promotions. Data are from a *Home & Auto* survey of retail aftermarket chains.

Includes 4 charts showing survey response concerning retailer use of in-store promotions and employee sales contests in connection with racing promotions, and overall awareness of supplier promotion programs and willingness to increase chain participation, 1981-85.

Article is accompanied by several related articles comprising the Seventh Annual *Home & Auto* Racing Merchandising Section. Section appears annually but usually does not include substantial statistics.

C4380–2.605: June 1, 1985 (Vol. 95, No. 6)

1984 WAS PAUSE TO CONSOLIDATE, ANNUAL FEATURE

(p. 1, 41) Annual article on auto aftermarket sales by nonautomotive retailers. Data are from a survey of 50 retail chains conducted by *Home and Auto,* and other industry sources.

Includes 2 charts and 1 table showing the following for nonautomotive retail chains: distribution of aftermarket sales, and sales as percent of total aftermarket sales, by product group, 1980-84; and aftermarket sales by food, drug, hardware, and home center chains, 1984.

Also includes text data on nonautomotive retailers' degree of commitment to auto product sales (no date) and average gross margins, 1982-84, both by type of outlet; and planned change in auto aftermarket products carried by retail chains, by product category, 1983.

MERCHANDISING TRANSMISSION AND OIL COOLERS: A CASE OF APPLES AND PEARS

(p. 38) By Alex DeBarr. Article, with 2 charts showing sales of transmission/oil coolers in total and retail chain auto aftermarkets, 1984; and transmission/oil cooler sales distribution by retail outlet type (no date).

Data are from *Home and Auto's* annual survey on auto aftermarket sales; for description of complete survey, see C4380-2.603 above.

C4380–2.606: July 1, 1985 (Vol. 95, No. 7)

IT'S THERE FOR THE ASKING, ANNUAL FEATURE

(p. 24-25, 32) Annual article on import auto aftermarket, with import auto registration trends. Data are from automotive industry sources, and *Home and Auto* surveys of aftermarket chains and 32 aftermarket hard parts manufacturers. Includes 5 charts and 1 table showing the following:

a. Aftermarket hard parts manufacturer survey findings, including percent of respondents manufacturing replacement parts for import autos, 1980, 1982, and 1985; and import share of auto registrations by State, 1982-84.

b. Aftermarket chain survey findings, including percent of respondents selling import parts and using various merchandising practices, 1983-85.

This is the 3rd annual survey.

C4380–2.607: Aug. 1, 1985 (Vol. 95, No. 8)

IN-HOUSE PUBLICATIONS BOOST PRODUCTIVITY

(p. 27) By Maggie Kelch. Article on use of employee newsletters by aftermarket retail chains, based on a *Home & Auto* survey of 45 chains. Includes 1 undated table showing survey response on newsletter objectives.

C4380–2.608: Sept. 1, 1985 (Vol. 95, No. 9)

COMFORT IS KEY TO SELLING CLIMATE CONTROL

(p. 10-11, 30) By Jeff Solomon-Hess. Article, with 1 chart showing percent of do-it-yourselfers (DIYers) maintaining own auto air conditioning systems, 1980-84. Data are based on a recent *Home & Auto* survey of DIYers.

C4380–2.609: Oct. 1, 1985 (Vol. 95, No. 10)

DIYers STEP BACK FROM UNDER THE HOOD, ANNUAL FEATURE

(p. 37-45) Annual survey report, for 1985, on automotive do-it-yourself (DIY) activity in U.S. and Canada, with trends from 1981. Data are based on responses by DIY customers to questionnaires distributed by 26 retail chains.

Includes 3 charts and 11 tables showing survey response on under hood, under chassis, electrical, and cosmetic DIY activity, by specific type of work; and DIYer profile, including level of experience, age, reasons for doing own work, type of retail outlet preferred, auto repair schooling, unplanned purchases made, sources of assistance and advertising, and number of vehicles owned; all for U.S. and Canadian respondents, various years 1981-85.

This is the 11th annual survey.

C4385
Harcourt Brace Jovanovich: Energy Publications

C4385–1   **PIPELINE AND GAS JOURNAL**
Monthly.
ISSN 0032-0188.
LC 76-612862.
SRI/MF/not filmed

Monthly trade journal reporting developments in international pipeline and natural gas utility design, construction, and operations.

Issues generally contain regular news and editorial depts; and feature articles, occasionally with statistics.

Annual statistical features include reports on pipeline construction, finances and operations of 500 largest gas distribution utilities and pipeline companies, and capital expenditures of distribution utilities.

Features with substantial statistical content are described, as they appear, under "Statistical Features." Each issue of the journal is reviewed, but an abstract is published in SRI monthly issues only when features with substantial statistical content appear.

Prior to the June 1985 issue, microfiche status for this publication was SRI/MF/excerpts (for all portions covered under "Statistical Features"). Harcourt Brace Jovanovich has cancelled all outside microfilming arrangements.

Availability: Pipeline and Gas Journal, One E. First St., Duluth MN 55802, industry subscribers $12.00 per yr., nonindustry subscribers $40.00 per yr., single copy $3.00; SRI/MF/not filmed.

Issues reviewed during 1985: Nov. 1984-Oct. 1985 (P) (Vol. 211, Nos. 13-14; Vol. 212, Nos. 1-10).

STATISTICAL FEATURES:

C4385–1.601: Dec. 1984 (Vol. 211, No. 14)

[Data for the following 2 articles are based on P&GJ's 19th annual survey of 350 gas utility executives.]

DISTRIBUTION PIPING FORECAST, ANNUAL FEATURE

(p. 14-15) Annual article, by Jim Watts, forecasting gas distribution utilities' expenditures for expansion and maintenance in 1985. Includes 3 charts showing capital expenditure shares for construction and maintenance, 1971-85; and miles of new/replacement mains and service lines, actual 1984 and planned 1985.

UTILITIES FINDING NEW APPLICATIONS FOR PLASTIC PIPE, ANNUAL FEATURE

(p. 16) Annual article, by Jim Watts, with 1 chart showing plastic pipe share of total installations, for gas distribution systems, 1984-85.

C4385–1.602: Jan. 1985 (Vol. 212, No. 1)

PIPELINE CONSTRUCTION FORECAST, ANNUAL FEATURE

(p. 12-13) Annual report, by Dean Hale, on U.S. and Canadian pipeline projects planned or under construction, for 1985, based on P&GJ annual construction survey.

Includes 2 tables showing U.S. and Canadian pipeline mileage planned/proposed and expected to be completed, by type, 1985; and tabular list of 20 major pipeline projects by type and company, showing mileage, size, and points of origin and destination.

C4385–1.603: May 1985 (Vol. 212, No. 5)

NATURAL GAS CAN PLAY ROLE IN DEVELOPING NEEDED CONTINENTAL ENERGY POLICY

(p. 14-15) By Dale W. Steffes. Article on potential benefits of a continental energy policy covering U.S., Canada, and Mexico. Data are from World Bank, and Planning and Forecasting Consultants.

Includes 2 tables showing per capita energy consumption and other summary socioeconomic characteristics of the 3 countries; and total energy consumption, and reserves and production by fuel type, for U.S. and aggregated for Mexico/Canada, 1985.

C4385–1.604: Aug. 1985 (Vol. 212, No. 8)

OUTSIDE DAMAGE MAIN CAUSE OF ACCIDENTS

(p. 8) Article, with 2 charts showing hazardous liquids/gas pipeline leaks/failures and pipeline-related fatalities, 1973-83. Data are from Materials Transportation Bureau.

5th P&GJ 500: DIMENSIONS OF 500 LEADING ENERGY PIPELINE COMPANIES, ANNUAL FEATURE

(p. 12-42) Annual article, by Jim Watts and Dean Hale, presenting data on the finances and operations of the 500 largest gas distribution utilities, gas transmission/gathering pipeline companies, and liquids pipeline companies, 1984. Data are from a P&GJ survey.

Contains review of survey findings, with 14 summary tables ranking top 10-15 companies in each category (including some separate rankings for integrated gas and combination gas/electric utilities) by value of plant additions, revenues, sales, miles of mains or pipelines, deliveries, and/or number of customers, 1984 (p. 12-16); and 3 detailed tables, listed below (p. 19-42).

All tables show comparative rank order for previous year.

TABLES:

[Tables show operating revenues, net income, value of plant additions and/or property, and additional data noted below, by company, 1984.]

[1] 300 leading gas distribution utilities [ranked by number of customers, and including sales and miles of mains and services].

[2] 100 leading gas pipelines [ranked by total pipeline miles, and including sales, and miles of transmission, field/gathering, and storage pipelines].

[3] 100 leading liquid pipelines [ranked by total delivery volume, and including volume of crude oil and product deliveries, and miles of pipeline (gathering, crude trunk, and products trunk)].

C4385–1.605: Sept. 1985 (Vol. 212, No. 9)

CONSTRUCTION UP 65%, ANNUAL FEATURE

(p. 12-16) Annual article, by Dean Hale, on pipeline construction mileage planned or underway outside the U.S., 1985.

Includes 4 tables showing pipeline mileage planned and under construction, by country or world area, and mileage completed during 1985, all by type of pipeline, as of Aug. 1, 1985.

DANISH LINES NEARLY COMPLETE

(p. 40-44) Article, with 1 undated table showing location, length, and construction status, for Danish natural gas pipeline projects.

C4385–2 PETROLEUM ENGINEER INTERNATIONAL
Monthly.
ISSN 0164-8322.
SRI/MF/not filmed

Monthly trade journal (semimonthly in July) reporting trends and developments in world oil and gas drilling activity and production technology.

Journal includes feature articles and recurring editorial depts, occasionally with statistics; and the following regularly appearing statistical features:

a. Monthly rotary rig drilling activity feature (p. 3), with 1 table showing number of rigs in operation by State (including land and offshore totals for some States), Texas district, and land and offshore Canada, for week 2-3 weeks prior to cover date and 3 preceding weeks.

b. Recurring international rotary rig report, with 1 table showing total and offshore rotary rigs in operation, by country and world region, for month 3 months prior to cover date, previous month, and same month of preceding year.

c. Semiannual list of land and offshore contract drilling rigs, by State subregion, Canadian Province, and foreign country.

d. Annual deep well drilling report, usually in Mar. issue; annual articles on drilling costs and well servicing activity; and a nonstatistical review of new products (2nd July issue).

Monthly and other recurring rig data are from Hughes Tool Co. reports.

Monthly drilling activity feature appears in most issues. All additional features with substantial statistical content are described, as they appear, under "Statistical Features;" page location and latest period of coverage for recurring international rig report are also noted. Nonstatistical features and technical data are not covered.

Prior to the June 1985 issue, microfiche status for this publication was SRI/MF/excerpts (for monthly table and all portions covered under "Statistical Features"). Harcourt Brace Jovanovich has canceled all outside microfilming arrangements.

Availability: Petroleum Engineer International, One E. First St., Duluth MN 55802, qualified subscribers $18.00 per yr., others $50.00 per yr., single copy $3.00; SRI/MF/not filmed.

Issues reviewed during 1985: Nov. 1984-Oct. 1985 (P) (Vol. 56, Nos. 13-15; Vol. 57, Nos. 1-11).

STATISTICAL FEATURES:

C4385–2.601: Nov. 1984 (Vol. 56, No. 13)

OFFSHORE ACTIVITY TO INCREASE IN 1985

(p. 10-14) Article, with 1 chart showing offshore rig supply and demand, Aug. 1983-84. Data are from Offshore Data Services, Inc.

C4385–2.602: Nov. 15, 1984 (Vol. 56, No. 14)

WHAT STRUCTURES TO EXPECT FOR DEEPWATER DEVELOPMENTS

(p. 32-44) By W. B. Bleakley. Article on investment and structural requirements for deepwater drilling operations. Includes 3 tables showing number of deepwater wells, 1970-83; and cost summaries for deepwater structure and offloading system.

FALL 1984 INTERNATIONAL WORLD RIG LOCATOR, SEMIANNUAL FEATURE

(p. R1-R39) Semiannual tabular list showing operating specifications for contract rotary land and offshore drilling rigs, by contractor, arranged by State, Canadian Province, and country arranged by world region, with contractor directories, fall 1984.

C4385–2.603: Dec. 1984 (Vol. 56, No. 15)

RECURRING TABLE

(p. 46-48) International rotary rig report, for Sept. 1984.

SHALLOW WELLS AREN'T ALWAYS SIMPLE

(p. 36-42) By Steven D. Moore. Article, with 1 table showing shallow inland oil wells and footage drilled, and cost, for Illinois, Indiana, Appalachian Region, and total U.S., 1982.

C4385–2.604: Jan. 1985 (Vol. 57, No. 1)

STRIPPER WELL OUTPUT UP BY 20 MILLION BBL, ANNUAL FEATURE

(p. 64) Annual article, with 1 table showing number, production, and abandonments of stripper wells, 1974-83. Data are from *National Stripper Well Survey,* prepared by Interstate Oil Compact Commission and National Stripper Well Assn.

C4385–2.605: Mar. 1985 (Vol. 57, No. 3)

NORTH SEA SURVEY COUNTS 1,300 DIVERS

(p. 14-16) Brief article, with 1 text table showing diving and offshore support personnel working in the North Sea, as of July 1984. Data are from Assn of Offshore Diving Contractors.

ANNUAL DEEP WELL REPORT

Annual report, by Rich McNally and Laura Jacobus, on deep oil/gas well drilling activities in the U.S., 1982-84, presenting data on wells drilled to 15,000 feet or deeper. Data are derived from various industry sources, including contract drilling and operating companies and Petroleum Information Corp.

Contains 3 statistical articles, described below; and 2 foldouts (p. 29-32), with list of deep well operators, 1 map, and 5 charts showing selected deep well drilling trends, 1978-84.

This is the 41st annual report.

U.S. DRILLERS COMPLETE 614 DEEP WELLS IN 1984, ANNUAL FEATURE

(p. 21-26, 35) Annual article on drilling activity for wells drilled to 15,000 feet or deeper, 1982-84 and trends. Includes 2 tables showing the following:

a. Number of wells; average well depth and cost, mud cost, and number of bits; average tubular goods tonnage and cost; total, wildcat, and development well success ratios; total costs for mud, drilling, and completion; and total costs and footage; 1982-84, repeated for U.S., 13 States (with land and offshore detail for selected States), and offshore Atlantic Coast.

b. Total, exploratory, and producing wells completed; average number of bits, and mud and well costs; footage drilled; and record depths; 1938-84.

CONTRASTING MARKS IN ULTRADEEP DRILLING, ANNUAL FEATURE

(p. 26) Annual article on characteristics of wells drilled to 20,000 feet or deeper, 1982-84. Includes 1 table repeating data described in paragraph a. of preceding article abstract, for ultradeep land and offshore well completions in U.S., with completion totals by State, 1982-84.

OPERATORS REMAIN OPTIMISTIC ABOUT DEEP WELLS

(p. 37) Article on well operators' outlook for deep well drilling in 1985. Data are from a *Petroleum Engineer International* survey. Includes 8 charts showing well operator responses concerning deep well drilling plans, rig contract rates, and overall drilling costs, 1985; types of rig contracts used in 1984; and major technological problems.

Other Features

DRILLING COSTS ROSE IN 1984, ANNUAL FEATURE

(p. 76) Annual article, with 1 table showing onshore drilling costs index 1982-84, and actual costs 1984, by well depth. Data are from Energy Information Administration.

SPRING 1985 INTERNATIONAL WORLD RIG LOCATOR, SEMIANNUAL FEATURE

(p. R1-R39) Semiannual tabular list showing operating specifications for contract rotary land and offshore drilling rigs, by contractor, arranged by State and subarea, Canadian Province, and country arranged by world region; with contractor directories, spring 1985.

C4385–2.606: May 1985 (Vol. 57, No. 5)

SHAKEOUT PREDICTED FOR SERVICE INDUSTRY

(p. 88) Article, with 1 table showing oil/gas wellhead revenue, reinvestment share of revenue, drilling expenditures and footage, and active rigs, 1981-85. Data are from American Petroleum Institute and E. F. Hutton.

C4385–2.607: June 1985 (Vol. 57, No. 6)

THIRD LEASING PROGRAM CALLS FOR 43 OFFERINGS

(p. 10-14) Article, with 2 tables showing Outer Continental Shelf oil/gas resource estimates, as of July 1986, and lease sale schedule through June 1991, both by planning area.

INTERNATIONAL DEEP WELL REPORT, ANNUAL FEATURE

(p. 21-26) Annual article, by Rich McNally, on oil/gas deep well drilling activity in non-Communist world outside the U.S., 1984 and trends. Covers wells drilled to 15,000 feet or deeper. Data are from a *Petroleum Engineer International* survey. Includes 9 tables showing the following:

a. Wells completed; average depth and costs; average number of bits; success ratio for wildcat and development wells; total costs by category (mud, drilling, and completion); and total footage; all for Canada and 6 world regions, 1982-84.

b. Wells completed and average depth, for 27 countries, 1984.

Also includes alphabetical listing of international deep well operators.

U.S. GAS RESOURCES ESTIMATED TO BE 784 Tcf

(p. 68) Brief article, with 1 table showing estimates of onshore and offshore gas resources in contiguous U.S. and Alaska, by depth level, 1984. Data are from Potential Gas Committee of Colorado School of Mines.

Full Potential Gas Committee report is covered in SRI under R8765-1.

C4385–2.608: July 1985 (Vol. 57, No. 7)

INTERNATIONAL REPORT: PETROLEOS MEXICANOS

(p. 18b) News brief, with 1 table showing Mexico's proven reserves of crude oil, condensate, and dry gas, by region, as of Dec. 31, 1984. Data are from Petroleos Mexicanos.

WELL SERVICING ACTIVITY SHOWS NEW LIFE, ANNUAL FEATURE

(p. 20-32) Annual article, by Steven D. Moore, presenting detailed data on oil and gas well servicing activities, 1984. Data are based on responses from over 100 independent and integrated companies to a *Petroleum Engineer International* survey.

Includes 1 map and 4 tables showing the following, for total U.S. and 11 oil/gas producing regions:

a. Total wells, well completions/recompletions, artificial lifts, lift installations and repairs, tubular repairs, fracturing/acid stimulations, and servicing expenditures, 1984; and estimated servicing budget, 1985.

b. Total oil and gas wells, new oil and gas exploration and development wells completed, wells recompleted in same and new zone, and abandoned wells, as of Jan. 1, 1985.

c. Service jobs, by type, 1984.

C4385–2.609: Aug. 1985 (Vol. 57, No. 9)

RECURRING TABLE

(p. 56) International rotary rig report, for May 1985.

C4385–2.610: Oct. 1985 (Vol. 57, No. 11)

DEEPWATER ACTIVITY INTENSIFIES IN GULF

(p. 10-14) By Jeff Littleton. Article, with 2 tables ranking 31 companies by number of offshore oil/gas drilling platforms operated in Gulf of Mexico, and including detail by water depth for 9 companies, as of May 17, 1985. Data are from Minerals Management Service.

FALL 1985 INTERNATIONAL WORLD RIG LOCATOR, SEMIANNUAL FEATURE

(p. R3-R36) Semiannual tabular list showing operating specifications for contract rotary land and offshore drilling rigs, by contractor, arranged by State, Canadian Province, and country arranged by world region; with contractor directories, fall 1985.

C4390
Harcourt Brace Jovanovich: Magazines for Industry

C4390–1   BEVERAGE INDUSTRY, 1985 Annual Manual
Annual. 1984. 308 p.
ISSN 0148-6187.
SRI/MF/excerpts

Annual directory and statistical compilation for the beverage industry, 1983-84, with selected trends from as early as 1849. Covers soft drinks, coffee, milk, powdered drinks, tea, wine, beer, fruit juice, liquor, and bottled water. Includes data on sales, consumption, and operations.

Most data are from Federal Government, private research organizations, and *Beverage Industry* surveys.

Contents:

Contents listing. (p. 3-5)

Section 1. Annual Statistics. Narrative articles, with 9 charts and 62 tables, described below; and descriptive listing of restrictive packaging and litter/recycling laws. (p. 7-136)

Section 2. New Products, Services, Literature. (p. 137-150)

Section 3. Manual of Operations. Operating information and directories. (p. 153-212)

Section 4. Comprehensive Buyer's Guide. (p. 213-308)

Availability: Book Sales, HBJ Publications, One E. First St., Duluth MN 55802, $45.00; SRI/MF/excerpts for all statistical tables and charts described below and accompanying articles.

TABLES AND CHARTS:

C4390–1.1: Beverage Consumption and Soft Drink Sales Trends

a. Beverage consumption by type, including imputed water consumption, 1965-83; consumption prevalence by consumer age group, by beverage type, 1981; population projections by region for 3 under-34 age groups, through 1990; tea sales,1978-83; and domestic and imported wine consumption, 1977-83. 1 chart and 6 tables. (p. 8-14)

b. Soft drinks: sales volume and advertising expenditures, by company and brand, with sales rankings for top brands; manufacturing plants, by State; production volume and value, and per capita consumption; and selected demographic characteristics of households using soft drinks, by type of drink; various years 1973-84, with production and consumption trends from 1849. 9 tables. (p. 18-36)

C4390–1.2: Alcoholic Beverages

a. Beer market shares for top 9 and all other brewers; beer wholesale price index; selected demographic characteristics of beer drinkers, by type of beer; beer production and advertising expenditures, by company and brand; market shares for top 10 light beer brands; and malt liquor sales volume, by brand; various periods 1972-84. 8 tables. (p. 38-45)

b. Wine sales volume, by leading company, and for total domestic and imported wine, selected years 1978-83, with 1982-83 rankings. 1 table. (p. 47)

c. Distilled spirits consumption by type, with detail for domestic and imported whiskeys; and sales volume for top 36 brands; 1982-83. 2 tables. (p. 52-54)

C4390–1.3: Production, Packaging, and Vending Machines

a. Beverage producers' opinions on importance of selected equipment features, major machinery problems, expected investment return on capital equipment, and factors affecting investment return, all by beverage type, 1984. 3 tables. (p. 56-60)

b. Packaging: sales volume by package type, for soft drinks and beer, 1982-84; and distribution of packaged soft drink and beer production by type of material used for secondary packaging (no date). 4 tables. (p. 64-70)

c. Vending machine shipment volume and value, 1982-83, and number of manufacturers, for all vending machines, and for beverage machines by type; and bulk soft drink sales volume, 1972-83. 2 tables (p. 72-74)

d. Juice production costs, summary comparison for aseptic, glass, and can containers (no dates). 6 charts. (p. 94)

C4390–1.4: Miscellaneous

a. Sweetener break-even price analysis, for high fructose corn syrup (no date). 1 chart and 1 table. (p. 98)

b. Fruit juice and drink sales volume and value by type, including frozen and ready-to-serve by container type, 1982-83. 1 table. (p. 106)

c. Drink mixes: retail sales volume for instant breakfast and other powdered mixes by brand; and institutional sales volume for powdered mixes by brand and for syrups; with aggregate data on sales value; 1980-83. 3 tables. (p. 108-110)

d. Bottled water per capita consumption, and consumption by type including imports, 1976-83. 3 tables. (p. 112-113)

C4390–1.5: Distribution Costs, Expansion Plans, and Market Profiles

a. Beverage distribution: cost per case; cost changes and components; computer use; and truck and van fleet profiles, including

number of vehicles, percent owned and leased, average vehicle age and miles per gallon, and average deliveries per day; generally shown for beer wholesalers, soft drink plants and warehouses, and bottled water plants, 1983 and/or 1984. 1 chart and 7 tables. (p. 114-119)

b. Beverage firms' equipment purchase plans for 1984, including level of spending (with comparison to 1983), and types of equipment, all by type of beverage. 5 tables. (p. 120-123)

c. Beverage market profiles for Milwaukee, Wis., Phoenix, Ariz., Houston, Tex., and St. Louis, Mo., with various data generally including beer and/or soft drink brand market shares (no dates). 7 tables. (p. 124-129)

C4390–2   BEVERAGE INDUSTRY

Monthly. Oversized.
ISSN 0148-6187.
LC 73-640297.
SRI/MF/not filmed

Monthly journal of the beverage industry, reporting on trends in marketing, sales, consumption, and product/equipment development for soft drinks, beer, bottled water, juice, wine, beverage powders, and spirits.

Most data are from industry sources, the Federal Government, and *Beverage Industry* research.

Contents:

a. News and feature articles, including coverage of beverage market trends; company profiles; and annual features with data on consumption and sales of various beverage types, soft drink industry structure, salaries of executives/managers, and other topics.

b. "Beverage Business Indicators" monthly feature, with 3 tables and 3 charts showing the following: beverage CPI and PPI, by beverage type; imports and domestic removals of beer, wine, and spirits; and shipments of closures by type; for various months ranging from 4-10 months prior to cover date, generally with comparison to prior month and previous year.

Monthly "Beverage Business Indicators" feature appears in all issues. All additional features with substantial statistical content are described, as they appear, under "Statistical Features." Non-statistical features are not covered.

Prior to the June 1985 issue, microfiche status for this publication was SRI/MF/excerpts (for "Beverage Business Indicators" and all portions covered under "Statistical Features"). Harcourt Brace Jovanovich has canceled all outside microfilming arrangements.

Availability: Beverage Industry, One E. First St., Duluth MN 55802, qualified subscribers †, others $35.00 per yr., single copy $2.00; SRI/MF/not filmed.

Issues reviewed during 1985: Nov. 1984-Oct. 1985 (P) (Vol. 75, Nos. 11-12; Vol. 76, Nos. 1-10; Whole Nos. 990-1001) [Oct. 1985 issue incorrectly reads Whole No. 1000].

STATISTICAL FEATURES:

C4390–2.601: Nov. 1984 (Vol. 75, No. 11, Whole No. 990)

269 FIRMS CONTROL 75% OF INDUSTRY VOLUME, ANNUAL FEATURE

(p. 4, 28-29) Annual article on soft drink industry concentration, 1983. Data are from Beverage Marketing Corp.

Includes 3 tables showing number of headquarter companies (multi-plant owners) and distribution plants owned; wholesale sales of headquarter and headquarter/other companies; and manufacturing plants owned by headquarter and other companies; all by wholesale sales range, 1983. Also includes list of leading headquarter companies by sales size.

For description of previous feature, for 1982, see SRI 1984 Annual under C4390-2.502.

STUDY: DIET BEVERAGE MARKET TO GROW 60% BY '90

(p. 7) Article, with 1 table showing retail sales of reduced calorie food and beverages, and reduced caffeine beverages, with detail by beverage type, selected years 1982-90. Data are from Frost and Sullivan, Inc.

SD CAN SHIPMENTS UP 13.2% IN 1984

(p. 13-14) Article, with 2 tables showing shipments of cans for soft drinks and beer, 1982-1st half 1984; and distribution of soft drink sales by container type, 1983-84. Data are from Can Manufacturers Institute, and A. C. Nielsen Co.

SMALLER, BUT WISER INDUSTRY FIGHTS BACK WITH SINGLE SERVICE

(p. 16-24, 162) By Paul E. Mullins. Article on the glass container manufacturing industry. Data were compiled by *Beverage Industry.* Includes list of glass plants closed, 1980-84; 1 table showing number of glass plants, and tank and feeder units, as of Jan. 1, 1980-85; and 1 chart showing distribution of glass container shipments, by end-use category, 1983.

BI SURVEY: BOTTLERS TO BUY MORE EQUIPMENT IN '85

(p. 36-38) Article on beverage bottlers' equipment purchase plans for 1985, based on 131 responses to a 1984 survey conducted by Market Data Communications.

Includes 4 tables showing percent of respondents planning purchase of new and used materials handling and production equipment in 1985, and average amount budgeted, by equipment type; and perceived importance of selected machinery problems and technological advances.

BOTTLERS BUDGET $.5 MILLION FOR NEW EQUIPMENT

(p. 36) Article on beverage bottlers' plans for purchasing vending machines in 1985, based on 111 responses to a 1984 survey of vending managers conducted by Market Data Communications. Includes 1 table showing average budget and number of machines to be purchased, by machine type, 1985.

BOTTLERS EARMARK OVER $1 MILLION FOR FLEETS IN '85

(p. 38) Article on beverage bottlers' plans for purchasing trucks in 1985, based on 160 responses to a 1984 survey of fleet managers conducted by Market Data Communications. Includes 1 table showing average budget and number of purchases planned, for trucks, truck bodies, trailer/tractors, and trailers, 1985.

BOTTLERS LOOK TO COLD MARKET TO AID SALES

(p. 47-49) Article, with 1 undated table showing costs by type, for packaging and merchandising juice drinks in aseptic, glass, and steel containers. Data are from Frost and Sullivan, Inc.

STUDY SAYS SDs NO BIG SALT SOURCE

(p. 136) Article, with 1 undated table showing total and added sodium levels in soft drinks by type. Data are from Miles Laboratories.

C4390–2.602: Dec. 1984 (Vol. 75, No. 12, Whole No. 991)

STUDY: INDUSTRY TO REACH 5.13 BIL. CASES BY 1993

(p. 4, 58) Article, with 1 table showing sales volume of packaged soft drinks, selected years 1967-93. Data are from Commerce Dept and Business Trend Analysts.

CONSUMERS FEEL LESS IS BEST IN SDs TODAY

(p. 22-23) By Jeffrey Schussler. Article, with 1 chart showing bottled water gallonage and per capita consumption, selected years 1977-90. Data are from Beverage Marketing Corp.

C4390–2.603: Jan. 1985 (Vol. 76, No. 1, Whole No. 992)

BEER CONSUMPTION DOWN .6% IN '84, ANNUAL FEATURE

(p. 1, 68-73) Annual article, by Gary A. Hemphill, with 6 tables showing production and capacity of 9 leading brewers and all others, with detail by brand including ranking of top 10 brands; malt liquor sales volume for 10 brands and all others; imports, consumption, and tax-free exports of brewery products; and imported beer market volume for top 36 brands and all others; various years 1972-84.

Data are from John C. Maxwell and Laidlaw Ansbacher Inc.

COUPON USE JUMPS 18%

(p. 4) Article, with 1 chart showing percent of coupons issued in/on product and through selected media, 1979-83. Data are from A. C. Nielsen Co.

RETAILERS, INDUSTRY FORM FLORIDA BIRP

(p. 40) Article, with 1 table showing the following for 4 State recycling programs sponsored by the beverage industry: year program started; number of centers operated and jobs created; and pounds of material recycled (with detail by material type), and amount paid to the public; various periods 1971-84. Data are from Florida Beverage Industry Recycling Program.

PURCHASING DECENTRALIZING, BUT TOP TITLES STILL CALL SHOTS

(p. 49-51) By Paul E. Mullins. Article on personnel responsible for purchasing decisions in the beer wholesaling and soft drink manufacturing industries. Data are based on 1,495 responses to a recent Beverage Industry survey.

Includes 7 tables showing survey response on whether executives have sole responsibility for purchasing decisions or have authority to specify/recommend products, by position category, with detail by type of equipment and company ownership.

C4390–2.604: Feb. 1985 (Vol. 76, No. 2, Whole No. 993)

SOFT DRINKS, JUICE, BOTTLED WATER PACE GAINS, ANNUAL FEATURE

(p. 1, 38-42) Annual article on beverage consumption, 1984 and trends. Data are from various Federal and private sources.

Includes 7 charts and 2 tables showing per capita consumption by beverage type (including water), with percent change for domestic and imported wine; and sales volume for iced and hot tea; various years 1964-84.

C4390–2.605: Mar. 1985 (Vol. 76, No. 3, Whole No. 994)

ANNUAL SOFT DRINK SALES REPORT: COLAS, FLAVORS PUSH 6.1% GAIN

(p. 1, 17-23, 68) Annual article, by Michelle Palmer, on soft drink consumption, 1984 and trends. Data are from Laidlaw Ansbacher Inc.

Includes 1 chart and 7 tables showing soft drink consumption and market shares, by company and brand, and by flavor, with detail for diet drinks and caffeine-free cola/pepper drinks, various years 1971-84; and per capita soft drink consumption, 1963-84.

NATIONAL BRANDS DOMINATE, BUT REGIONALS ALSO THRIVE

(p. 28-32) Article on beverage industry use of aseptic packaging (flexible containers that do not require refrigeration). Data are from Laidlaw Ansbacher Inc., and Dupont.

Includes 2 tables showing per capita consumption of juice, 1975-84; and production and marketing costs, by type, for juice packaged in aseptic, glass, and steel containers (no date).

LIQUOR SALES DROP AGAIN; OFF 1.2% IN '84, ANNUAL FEATURE

(p. 59) Annual article, with 2 tables showing consumption of domestic and imported distilled spirits by type, with detail for Canadian and Scotch whiskey; and case sales and producing company, for top 38 distilled spirit brands; 1983-84. Data are from Laidlaw Ansbacher Inc.

C4390–2.606: Apr. 1985 (Vol. 76, No. 4, Whole No. 995)

CANS, PET LEAD PACKAGING GAINS, ANNUAL FEATURE

(p. 1, 30-32) Annual article, with 2 charts and 2 tables showing soft drink and beer total sales volume, and packaged sales volume by container type, 1983-85. Data are from Arthur M. Stupay of Prescott, Ball and Turben.

For description of last previous feature, see SRI 1984 Annual under C4390-2.505.

PAPER, PLASTIC BATTLE IT OUT, ANNUAL FEATURE

(p. 4, 35) Annual article on developments in beverage industry secondary and tertiary packaging (packaging used to hold together several containers). Data are from Beverage Industry. Includes 2 tables showing distribution of marketed soft drink and beer volume by type of secondary/tertiary packaging material, by type of container, 1984.

For description of last previous feature, see SRI 1984 Annual under C4390-2.505. June 1985 issue includes corrected tables (see C4390-2.608 below).

C4390–2.607: May 1985 (Vol. 76, No. 5, Whole No. 996)

FIRMS SEEK DURABLE, SAFE AND EASY TO MAINTAIN FORK LIFT TRUCKS

(p. 10) Article, with 1 chart showing percent of beverage manufacturers increasing, decreasing, and maintaining same level of purchases of fork lift trucks, 1984 vs. earlier years. Data are from a survey of manufacturers conducted for Beverage Industry.

NSDA SURVEY DISCOVERS START OF GROWTH TRENDS, ANNUAL FEATURE

(p. 18) Annual article on the soft drink market in 1983, based on 292 responses to a National Soft Drink Assn industry survey. Includes 3 charts showing soft drink market shares, for bulk and packaged products, and by flavor (including decaffeinated); and distribution of packaged soft drinks by container type; 1983.

Previous article, for 1982, is described in SRI 1983 Annual under C5250-2.416.

C4390–2.608: June 1985 (Vol. 76, No. 6, Whole No. 997)

HIGHER VOLUME, COSTS EXPECTED IN '85, ANNUAL FEATURE

(p. 1, 25-27) Annual article, by Arthur W. Zimmerman, on beverage industry distribution costs and fleet operations. Data are based on a Beverage Industry survey of soft drink and beer distributors and warehouses.

Includes 5 charts and 2 tables showing survey responses concerning distribution volume and cost changes, 1985 vs. 1984; expected 1985 distribution costs; and distribution shares of total operating costs by component (no date); mostly shown separately for soft drink and beer respondents.

Previous article is described in SRI 1984 Annual under C4390-2.508.

HFCS DOMINATES MARKET; LOW-CAL OPTIONS ON THE RISE

(p. 1, 56-60) By Michelle Palmer. Article, with 2 charts showing beverage sweetener volume and/or share, for high fructose corn syrup, sugar, low-calorie sweeteners, and glucose/dextrose, various years 1970-90. Data are from USDA.

BOTTLED WATER POSTS A RECORD YEAR FOR CONSUMPTION

(p. 6, 45) Article on bottled water industry. Data are from Beverage Marketing Corp.

Includes 2 charts and 1 table showing shares of total bottled water plants and wholesale market, for independently owned and headquarter company-owned plants (no date); and number of headquarter companies, and manufacturing and distributing plants, by headquarter company sales size, 1984.

OJ SALES GAIN MERE 2%; LOW SUPPLY BOOSTS PRICES

(p. 20) Article, with 1 chart showing sales volume of fruit juices and drinks, with detail for orange and grapefruit juice, 1983-84. Data are from Florida Dept of Citrus.

UNIFORMS HELP REFLECT COMPANY AND EMPLOYEE PERSONALITIES, ANNUAL FEATURE

(p. 40) Annual article, with 1 undated table showing distribution of employee uniforms sold to the beverage industry, by occupational category. Data are from a Beverage Industry survey of major suppliers.

Previous article is described in SRI 1984 Annual under C4390-2.508.

LIGHTWEIGHT HAND TRUCKS NEED SOLID CONSTRUCTION

(p. 41) Article, with 1 undated table showing selected hand truck features considered important by beverage industry equipment purchasers. Data are from a *Beverage Industry* survey.

JAPANESE BEVERAGES MARK 22% INCREASE

(p. 61) Article, with 2 tables showing shipments of non-alcoholic beverages in Japan, by type, for 10 major suppliers, 1983; and soft drink shipments in Japan, 1979-84. Data are from Yamasaki International.

CORRECTION

(p. 65) Two corrected tables for annual feature on beverage industry secondary and tertiary packaging.

For feature description, see C4390-2.606 above.

C4390–2.609: July 1985 (Vol. 76, No. 7, Whole No. 998)

WHY IMPORT SALES ARE BOOMING

(p. 1, 47-50) By Gary A. Hemphill. Article, with 1 chart showing top 5 imported beer brands ranked by market share, 1984. Data are from John C. Maxwell Jr. of Furman, Selz, Mager, Dietz and Birney.

AD SPENDING JUMPS BY 14.4%; TV AND RADIO POST MAJOR GAINS

(p. 4, 29-30) Article on beverage industry media advertising expenditures. Data are from Leading National Advertisers, Inc. and Broadcast Advertisers Reports.

Includes 2 charts and 2 tables showing percent change in soft drink advertising expenditures, by media, 1984 vs. 1983; regular and diet shares of soft drink TV advertising expenditures, 1983-84; and top 10 soft drink and beer brands ranked by total advertising expenditures, with expenditures by media, 1984.

FASTER LINES SPUR EFFICIENT, DURABLE CASERS, UNCASERS

(p. 10) Article on beverage industry purchasing of casing and uncasing equipment. Data are from a 1985 *Beverage Industry* survey of beverage producers. Includes 1 undated chart showing survey response concerning the importance of selected caser/uncaser features.

C4390–2.610: Aug. 1985 (Vol. 76, No. 8, Whole No. 999)

ANNUAL SALARY SURVEY: HOW DO YOU STACK UP?

(p. 5, 18) Annual article, by Gary A. Hemphill, on salaries of executives/managers in soft drink bottling, brewery, and beer wholesale industries. Data are from 902 responses to a survey conducted by Market Data Communications for *Beverage Industry*.

Includes 1 chart and 3 tables showing average salaries by position, company employment size, and years experience, for aggregate and/or each industry (no dates).

Previous feature is described in SRI 1984 Annual under C4390-2.510.

IN SEARCH OF THE ASEPTIC ADULT MARKET

(p. 5, 14-16) By Michelle Palmer. Article on marketing of beverages in aseptic packaging (flexible containers that do not require refrigeration). Data are from A. C. Nielsen Co.

Includes 2 charts showing percent of fruit juice packaged in aseptic containers, with detail by flavor (no date); and aseptic product retail sales shares, for Capri Sun brands and all other producers, 1983-85.

POWDERED DRINK MARKET DRY; SALES DECLINE 6.3% IN 1984, ANNUAL FEATURE

(p. 6, 41) Annual article, with 1 table showing the following for powdered drink mixes, 1979-84: sales value; and sales volume, by company and brand and for private label/others. Data are from John C. Maxwell, Jr.

Previous feature, with data for 1974-83, is described in SRI 1984 Annual under C4390-2.510.

DECLINING WATER QUALITY DRIVES BOTTLERS TO BIGGER INVESTMENTS

(p. 24-25) Article on beverage industry purchasing of water treatment equipment. Data are from a *Beverage Industry* survey of beverage producers. Includes 1 undated chart showing survey response concerning the importance of selected water treatment system features.

C4390–2.611: Sept. 1985 (Vol. 76, No. 9, Whole No. 1000)

BEVERAGES JUMP 1.3% TO ALL-TIME HIGH

(p. 4, 20) Article, with 2 charts showing consumption of beverages by type, 1960 and 1984. Data are from M. Shanken Communications, Inc.

BOTTLERS LOOK FOR QUALITY IN LABELER/CODERS

(p. 46) Article on beverage industry purchasing of labeling and coding equipment. Data are from a survey of beverage bottlers conducted for *Beverage Industry* by Market Data Communications. Includes 1 undated chart showing survey response on the importance of selected labeling equipment features.

C4390–2.612: Oct. 1985 (Vol. 76, No. 10, Whole No. 1001)

[Issue incorrectly reads Whole No. 1000.]

HEALTH AWARENESS, FLAVORS ADD UP TO $1.3 BILLION BOTTLED WATER BUSINESS

(p. 4, 22-26) By Michelle Palmer. Article, with 2 charts and 1 table showing percent growth in bottled water market, market shares, and shares of wholesale sales, all by type of water (non-sparkling, sparkling, and club/seltzer and/or imported); and wholesale sales for top 18 and all other bottled water brands; 1984. Data are from Beverage Marketing Corp.

COMPUTERS GIVE USERS A COMPETITIVE EDGE

(p. 47) Article on beverage industry purchasing of data processing equipment. Data are from a survey of beverage producers conducted for *Beverage Industry* by Infometrics. Includes 1 undated chart showing survey response on the importance of selected data processing equipment features.

C4390–3   PAPERBOARD PACKAGING
Monthly.
ISSN 0031-1227.
LC 62-38067.
SRI/MF/not filmed

Monthly trade journal reporting on trends and developments in the paperboard packaging industry, including production, marketing, technological developments, international news, and management. Data are from National Paperbox and Packaging Assn, American Paper Institute, industry reports, and other sources.

General format:

a. Monthly "Industry Statistics" feature, with news briefs and 3 charts showing average weekly paperboard production, fiber box shipments, and composite tube/core sales, for month 2 months prior to cover date with cumulative year-to-date totals and averages.

b. Feature articles and regular editorial depts, occasionally with statistics.

Annual statistical features include an industry equipment status report (Jan.) and trend review (Sept.).

Monthly "Industry Statistics" feature appears in all issues. All additional features with substantial nontechnical statistical content are described, as they appear, under "Statistical Features." Nonstatistical features are not covered.

Prior to the June 1985 issue, microfiche status for this publication was SRI/MF/excerpts (for monthly charts and all portions covered under "Statistical Features"). Harcourt Brace Jovanovich has canceled all outside microfilming arrangements.

Availability: Paperboard Packaging, One E. First St., Duluth MN 55802, $18.00 per yr., single copy $2.00; SRI/MF/not filmed.

Issues reviewed during 1985: Nov. 1984-Oct. 1985 (P) (Vol. 69, Nos. 11-12; Vol. 70, Nos. 1-10).

STATISTICAL FEATURES:

C4390–3.601: Jan. 1985 (Vol. 70, No. 1)

EQUIPMENT STATUS REPORT: WHAT'S ON-LINE? ANNUAL FEATURE

(p. 34-44) Annual article, with 1 extended table showing plants in operation, and equipment in use by type, for corrugated (including sheet plants) and folding carton industries, by census division and for Canada, as of Jan. 1985. Data are from a *Paperboard Packaging* survey of box plant managers.

This is the 1st annual article. Feature replaces annual buying forecast formerly appearing in Jan. issues.

EUROPEAN BOXBOARDS FACE MARKET FIGHT

(p. 46-56) By Rowena Mills. Article, with 1 table showing UK consumer food expenditures as percent of total expenditures, selected years 1960-83. Data are from the UK Central Statistics Office.

C4390–3.602: Feb. 1985 (Vol. 70, No. 2)

PAPERBOARD 1985 OUTLOOK IS BULLISH

(p. 44-50) By John R. Curtin. Article, with 1 table showing cartonboard production, by country or world area, 1970, 1980, and 1990. Data are from SRI International.

C4390–3.603: Apr. 1985 (Vol. 70, No. 4)

SALES OF FOLDING CARTONS ON THE RISE

(p. 38-43) Survey article presenting business outlook and capital equipment plans of executives in the folding carton sector of the paperboard packaging industry. Data are from a 1984 Infometrics survey of folding carton plant executives. Includes 16 charts and 18 tables showing survey response on the following:

a. Employment size, importance of training for selected functions, and satisfaction with manufacturers' training programs; and actual and forecast sales levels, with detail by product category.

b. Importance of various materials, technological processes, and types of equipment, including degree of current and/or anticipated use; and disposition of aged equipment, and frequency of retrofit operations.

C4390–3.604: July 1985 (Vol. 70, No. 7)

CENSUS '85 SHOWS ROBUST INDUSTRY, ANNUAL FEATURE

(p. 18-22) Annual article on major equipment and materials purchasing plans of corrugated and folding carton sectors of the paperboard packaging industry. Data are from surveys of operations at 1,377 corrugated converting plants and 613 folding carton plants in the U.S. and Canada, conducted by Infometrics.

Includes 20 charts and 3 tables showing number of plants planning major equipment purchases within next year, by equipment type; distribution of adhesives, cutting dies, and inks used, by type; and average and total expenditures for selected materials; primarily 1985, with material expenditure data for 1984.

C4390–3.605: Aug. 1985 (Vol. 70, No. 8)

COVER YOUR REAR, AND THEIRS

(p. 38-40) By Susan R. Geier. Article on employee job safety in the paperboard industry. Data are from BLS and HHS.

Includes 3 charts and 1 table showing average accident rates per 100 employees, for general merchandising and paperboard container/box industries, with detail for paperboard industry by company size, as of Apr. 1984; and worker compensation costs (total and per covered employee), selected years 1960-82.

C4390–3.606: Sept. 1985 (Vol. 70, No. 9)

STATISTICS: BOTH DELIGHTFUL AND DISMAL, ANNUAL FEATURE

(p. 26-46, 99-102) Annual report, by Fred Sharring, reviewing paperboard packaging industry trends. Data are from Commerce Dept, American Paper Institute, Fibre Box Assn, and other sources. Includes 25 tables with the following data, generally for 1954, 1964, and annually 1974-84, with selected trends from as early as 1944 and some data for 1985:

a. Paper and paperboard total and per capita production; average annual and daily paperboard packages used, by type; and converted paperboard shipment value, by product type. Tables A1-A4. (p. 28-30)

b. Pulp production, foreign trade, and net supply, by grade; pulp consumption for board/paper and other uses; and North American pulp prices, by grade. Tables B1-B3. (p. 30-32)

c. Paperstock mill receipts, trade, recovery, and recovery ratio; paperstock consumption in board/paper production compared to consumption of other materials; and paperstock prices, by grade and region. Tables C1-C3. (p. 36)

d. Paperboard mill production, by grade; board mill capacity and utilization; and capacity outlook, by paperboard grade, through 1986. Tables D1-D3. (p. 38-40)

e. Fiber box production, and fiber shipment volume and value, all for corrugated and solid fiber; corrugated board production, and corrugated and solid fiberboard consumption, by grade; and fiber box plants, equipment, companies, capital investment, and production workers. Tables E1-E5. (p. 40-44)

f. Folding boxboard production by grade, consumption, and shipment volume and value; and folding carton plants, equipment, companies, capacity, employment, and capital investment. Tables F1-F3. (p. 46, 99)

g. Composite fiber can and other product production. Table G. (p. 99)

h. Fiber drum production, value, and average price. Table H. (p. 99)

i. Rigid box sales, and distribution by end use. Tables I1-I2. (p. 100)

C4390–3.607: Oct. 1985 (Vol. 70, No. 10)

SALES AND PRODUCTION SOUND OFF

(p. 37-40) Article comparing opinions of corrugated container industry sales and production managers concerning interdepartmental relations. Data are from a survey conducted by *Paperboard Packaging* and the Infometrics division of Harcourt Brace Jovanovich.

Includes 7 undated charts showing characteristics of good salespersons, as perceived by sales and production managers; sales managers' responses concerning areas of customer complaints, sales dept ability to handle complaints, and computer use in serving customers; and production managers' complaints about sales personnel, and practices regarding meeting with customers.

Feature is included with the 2nd annual "Corrugated Industry Report."

C4485
Hayden Publishing Co.

C4485–1   **COMPUTER DECISIONS**
Biweekly.
ISSN 0010-4558.
LC 70-9210.
SRI/MF/excerpts, shipped quarterly

Biweekly journal reporting on data processing management trends and developments, including outlook for new products, user evaluation of equipment, personnel practices, and activities of top manufacturers.

Issues contain articles, occasionally presenting statistics; and editorial depts, including coverage of new data processing products on the market, and tabular summaries of product specifications and prices.

Annual statistical features include a survey of data processing managers' salaries and benefits, and a report on the financial performance of the top 100 data processing vendors.

Features with substantial statistical content other than product specifications and prices are described, as they appear, under "Statistical Features." Each issue of the journal is reviewed, but an abstract is published in SRI monthly issues only when statistical features appear.

Prior to Jan. 15, 1985 issue, journal was published monthly.

Availability: Computer Decisions, PO Box 1417, Riverton NJ 08077, qualified subscribers †, others $40.00 per yr.; SRI/MF/excerpts for all portions described under "Statistical Features;" shipped quarterly.

Issues reviewed during 1985: Nov. 1984-Oct. 22, 1985 (P) (Vol. 16, Nos. 14-16; Vol. 17, Nos. 1-21).

STATISTICAL FEATURES:

C4485–1.601: Jan. 15, 1985 (Vol. 17, No. 1)

SURVIVORS OF 1990, ANNUAL FEATURE

(p. 74-78) Annual article, by Miriam Lacob, rating 39 office-automation equipment vendors' likelihood of surviving as suppliers to large companies through 1990. Data are based on responses of 33 Office Automation Society International members to a 1984 *Computer Decisions* survey, and include comparisons to 1982-83 surveys. Includes 1 table.

This is the 1st of 2 articles. The 2nd article appears in the Feb. 12, 1985 issue (for description, see C4485-1.602 below).

C4485–1.602: Feb. 12, 1985 (Vol. 17, No. 3)

SINGLE-SITE SURVIVORS, ANNUAL FEATURE

(p. 60-64) Annual article, by Miriam Lacob, rating 39 office-automation equipment vendors' likelihood of surviving as suppliers to small (single computer) companies through 1990. Data are based on responses of 32 Office Automation Society International members to a 1984 *Computer Decisions* survey, and include comparisons to 1982-83 surveys. Includes 1 table.

This is the 2nd of 2 articles. The 1st article appears in the Jan. 15, 1985 issue (for description, see C4485-1.601 above).

SALARY SURVEY: DID YOU RAISE THE ANTE IN '84? ANNUAL FEATURE

(p. 98-105) Annual article, by David Whieldon, reporting on compensation of management information system/data processing (MIS/DP) managers, 1984. Data are from 1,328 responses to a survey of *Computer Decisions* readers, conducted in Aug. 1984 by Abbott, Langer and Associates.

Includes 4 charts and 2 tables showing the following:

a. Median salaries of top MIS/DP officers and data processing managers: by region and for selected metro areas and States; by selected industry group; for manufacturing and nonmanufacturing sectors by sales size; and by company employment and MIS/DP budget size.

b. Percent of managers receiving selected types of benefits and perquisites, with comparisons to 1983.

This is the 1st of 2 articles reporting survey findings.

C4485–1.603: Feb. 26, 1985 (Vol. 17, No. 4)

SALARY SURVEY: HOW MUCH IS ENOUGH FOR STAFF? ANNUAL FEATURE

(p. 116-120) Annual article, by David Whieldon, reporting on compensation of management information system/data processing (MIS/DP) employees in nonmanagerial positions, 1984. Data are from 1,328 responses to a survey of *Computer Decisions* readers, conducted in Aug. 1984 by Abbott, Langer and Associates.

Includes 2 tables showing median salary for 21 positions, by region and for selected metro areas and States, and by selected industry group.

This is the 2nd of 2 articles reporting survey findings.

C4485–1.604: Apr. 9, 1985 (Vol. 17, No. 7)

MINIS REACH MIDDLE GROUND

(p. 62-64) Article, with 1 chart showing distribution of office work groups using minicomputer integrated automation packages, by work group size, June 1984 and year end 1986. Data are from Yankee Group, Inc.

C4485–1.605: Apr. 23, 1985 (Vol. 17, No. 8)

SMALLER MICRO MAKERS CLAIM STRENGTH

(p. 28-30) Article, with 1 chart showing value of microcomputer market, with distribution by vendor, 1982-84. Data are from Future Computing, Inc.

DP SECURITY: A DELICATE BALANCE

(p. 104-114, 140) By James Miskiewicz. Article, with 1 undated chart showing prevalence of employee involvement in computer-related crimes, by employee position. Data are from 179 responses to an American Bar Assn survey of government agencies and Fortune 500 companies.

C4485–1.606: June 4, 1985 (Vol. 17, No. 11)

1984: THE GOOD NOT-SO-OLD DAYS, ANNUAL FEATURE

(p. 66-84) Annual article, by Lee Keough, analyzing performance of leading data processing (DP) vendors, 1984. Data are from *Computer Decisions*. Includes 2 charts and 4 tables showing the following for 1984, with selected comparisons to 1983:

a. DP rankings: top 100 companies, by revenues; top and bottom 20 companies, by revenue growth rate; and top 15 fast-growth companies by revenue growth rate, and including principal business and revenues.

b. Aggregate revenues of top 100 companies by product segment; and top 100 company revenue shares, for International Business Machines Corp. vs. aggregate other top 10 and top 100 companies.

C4485–1.607: Oct. 8, 1985 (Vol. 17, No. 20)

PORTABLE ALLEGIANCES

(p. 24) Table ranking 17 vendors of portable computers by consumer purchase plans, 1985, with comparisons to 1983-84. Data are from a *Computer Decisions* reader survey.

SURVEY: MSA DOMINATES MAINFRAME APPLICATIONS

(p. 26) Brief article, with 1 chart showing market shares for 6 categories of mainframe applications software, by vendor, 1985. Data are compiled from a Mar. 1985 survey of approximately 11,000 IBM and plug-compatible mainframe sites, conducted by Computer Intelligence Inc.

C4590
Hitchcock Publishing Co.

C4590–1   **INFOSYSTEMS: The Magazine for Information Systems Management**
Monthly.
ISSN 0364-5533.
LC 72-625717.
SRI/MF/excerpts, shipped quarterly

Monthly trade journal reporting developments and trends in the data processing and information systems management industries. Journal is primarily narrative, but occasionally contains statistical articles, including annual features on micrographics use, and data processing employment, salaries, and budgets.

Features with substantial statistical content are described, as they appear, under "Statistical Features." Each issue of the journal is reviewed, but an abstract is published in SRI monthly issues only when statistical features appear.

Availability: Hitchcock Publishing Co., Circulation Department, Infosystems, PO Box 3007, Wheaton IL 60189-9933, qualified subscribers †, others $65.00 per yr., single copy $6.00; SRI/MF/excerpts for all portions covered under "Statistical Features;" shipped quarterly.

Issues reviewed during 1985: Nov. 1984-Oct. 1985 (P) (Vol. 31, Nos. 11-12; Vol. 32, Nos. 1-10).

STATISTICAL FEATURES:

C4590–1.601: Nov. 1984 (Vol. 31, No. 11)

CLERICALS, PROFESSIONALS VIE FOR MARKET

(p. 18) Brief article, with 1 chart showing computer workstation shipments, with market share by user's occupational category, 1988. Data are from Advanced Resources Development.

C4590–1.602: Jan. 1985 (Vol. 32, No. 1)

HOW DO YOU COMPARE TO 1,000 OTHER COMPANIES?

(p. 86) By Darryl Landvater. Brief article on corporate use of materials requirement planning and manufacturing resources planning systems. Data are from survey responses of over 1,800 companies. Includes 4 undated text tables presenting survey results concerning implementation and benefits of the systems.

C4590–1.603: Mar. 1985 (Vol. 32, No. 3)

MIS/DP TIGHTENS GRIP ON SYSTEMS, ANNUAL FEATURE

(p. 30-34) Annual article, by Chuck Cozette and Ray Winkler, reporting on the data communications roles of management information systems/data processing (MIS/DP) managers. Data are from 1,160 responses to a Jan. 1985 Hitchcock Research Services survey of 4,000 MIS/DP managers.

Includes 7 tables showing survey response concerning the following: use of selected products and services, job title and role in purchase of data communications equipment/services, current and planned geographic extent of data base system (local, metro, and long distance), and position title of supervisor and person responsible for data communications.

C4590–1.604: Apr. 1985 (Vol. 32, No. 4)

ADAPSO GOES AFTER PC PIRATES

(p. 13) Article on unauthorized duplication of computer software, based on a recent Future Computing, Inc. survey. Includes 1 undated chart showing percent of authorized vs. unauthorized software, by type.

SIZING UP MICROGRAPHICS, ANNUAL FEATURE

(p. 54-59) Annual survey article, by Chuck Cozette, on micrographics use by businesses. Data are based on 1,560 responses to a recent survey conducted by Hitchcock Marketing and Research Services, and earlier surveys.

Contains narrative analysis, and 11 tables showing survey response on the following, for 1980-85:

a. Dept or staff supervising micrographic operations, designing systems, recommending equipment, and approving expenditures; and expenditures on micrographics.

b. Plans to use micrographics, and current use by application, including in-house computer-output micrographics and computer-assisted retrieval systems; and how micrographics needs are handled (in-house vs. service organization), and types of services used.

This is the 15th annual survey.

C4590–1.605: June 1985 (Vol. 32, No. 6)

27th ANNUAL DP SALARY SURVEY: PROSPERITY CONTINUES

(p. 27-38) Annual article, by Chuck Cozette, on salaries of data processing (DP) staff by detailed position. Data are from responses of 790 firms reporting salaries for 8,863 employees to a 1985 *Infosystems* survey. Includes 1 chart and 4 tables showing:

a. Distribution of DP budget by function; and average total and DP employees, by DP equipment rental range.

b. Average weekly salary, by census division, equipment rental range, and industry; and lowest, highest, quartile, average, median, and mean weekly salaries; all by detailed DP position, as of Mar. 1985 with summary comparisons to 1984.

NEW ECONOMICS OF COMPUTERS

(p. 66-68) By C. Warren Axelrod. Article, with 1 table showing shipment value for 7 types of computer equipment, 1982 and 1987. Data are from International Data Corp.

C4590–1.606: July 1985 (Vol. 32, No. 7)

"RISING STAR" INSTILLS BOREDOM

(p. 66) Article on managerial delegation of computer-oriented tasks to support staff, based on an Omni Group survey of 3,000 computer users employed by Fortune 1000 companies. Includes 1 undated chart showing survey response on incidence of task delegation, with detail by type of task.

C4670
Huebner Publications

C4670–1   PURCHASING WORLD

Monthly.
ISSN 0093-1659.
LC 73-642852.
SRI/MF/excerpts, shipped quarterly

Monthly trade journal of industrial purchasing management, reporting trends and developments in wholesale purchasing, commodity prices and availability, economic indicators, and purchasing strategies.

Data are from journal surveys of industrial corporations; private research organizations, including Data Resources, Inc. (DRI); BLS and other Federal Government sources; the National Assn of Purchasing Managers; and industry trade assns. Data in regular statistical features are presented for trend purposes rather than for currency, but are usually current to 1-3 months prior to cover date.

Journal includes feature articles, occasionally with statistics, including surveys of purchasing managers' views on business conditions, DRI and Wharton economic forecasts, narrative editorial depts, and the following regular statistical sections:

a. "PW Predicts" section covering market, supply and demand, and price outlook for approximately 15 varying commodities, with narrative analysis and text statistics, and trend charts or tables for 4 or more selected commodities, some including price projections for next 6 months.

b. "Business Datatrak" section, with monthly charts and tables, described below; occasional special charts or tables; and accompanying narrative analyses.

"PW Predicts" and most monthly "Datatrak" statistics appear in all issues. All additional features with substantial statistical content are described, as they appear, under "Statistical Features." Nonstatistical features are not covered.

Availability: Purchasing World, 6521 Davis Industrial Pkwy., Solon OH 44139, qualified subscribers †, others $46.00 per yr.; SRI/MF/excerpts for monthly statistical sections, and all portions covered under "Statistical Features;" shipped quarterly.

Issues reviewed during 1985: Nov. 1984-Oct. 1985 (P) (Vol. 28, Nos. 11-12; Vol. 29, Nos. 1-10).

BUSINESS DATATRAK:

[1] Key economic trends [with 3 or more charts showing selected economic indicator trends, varying in each issue; and 1 chart showing National Assn of Purchasing Managers (NAPM) "business barometer"].

[2] Current prices [with 3 or more charts, and 1 table showing price levels for approximately 50 industrial products, for month of coverage, and percent change from previous month and year].

[3] Steel scene [with 6 charts showing selected steel industry trends, including comparison of import and domestic steel prices, based on surveys by the NAPM Steel Buyers Committee and the Steel Service Center Institute; may not appear in every issue].

[4] Procurement status [with 4 charts showing selected business purchasing indicator trends; and text data on leadtimes for selected commodities in Chicago, Cleveland, Houston, Los Angeles, Philadelphia, and Pittsburgh; prior to Sept. 1985 issue, feature also included a table on leadtime trends in 8 industry sectors].

[5] Raw material price barometer [with 1 trend chart, and 1 table showing spot market prices for materials in 8 categories including scrappage, for month of coverage, previous month, and same month of previous year].

STATISTICAL FEATURES:

C4670–1.601: Nov. 1984 (Vol. 28, No. 11)

INDUSTRIAL PRICE TRENDS, QUARTERLY FEATURE

(p. 16) Quarterly DRI economic forecast article presenting price forecasts for basic industrial commodities into 1986. Includes 1 table comparing 3rd quarter prices for 30 commodities grouped as raw materials/energy, metals, components, construction products, and machinery, shown as annual percent change 1983/84-1985/86.

IMPORT SURGE CONTINUES

(p. 49) Article on purchasing manager plans for importing activity, based on a survey of *Purchasing World* readers. Includes 2 undated charts showing change in importing activity and perceived import price advantage.

Results of a similar survey appear in the Apr. 1984 issue; for description, see SRI 1984 Annual under C4670-1.506.

TRANSPORTATION DEREGULATION IS PAYING OFF

(p. 50, 59) By Thomas F. Dillon. Article on transportation deregulation impact on industrial purchasing, based on a *Purchasing World* reader survey. Includes 5 undated charts showing respondents' opinions on transportation costs, quality of service, change in number and type of carriers used, and other operating trends since deregulation.

MRO DEMAND BOUNCING BACK

(p. 68) Article, with 2 charts showing percent change in demand and price indexes for maintenance, repair, and operation items supplied by industrial distributors, 1979-85. Data are from National and Southern Industrial Distributors Assns (NIDA-SIDA) and *Purchasing World* estimates.

BUSINESS DATA FILE, ANNUAL FEATURE

(p. 84-88) Second of 2 features comprising 1984 annual buyers guide to office equipment. Data are from company reports.

Contains 1 extended table showing microcomputer model names, specifications, and prices; company annual sales; and number of sales and service locations; all by company.

Part 1 of buyers guide appears in Oct. 1984 issue and covers electronic typewriters, copiers, and facsimile equipment. For description, see SRI 1984 Annual under C4670-1.512.

C4670–1.602: Dec. 1984 (Vol. 28, No. 12)

IMPORT PRICE BARGAINS GOING STRONG, RECURRING FEATURE

(p. 20) Recurring brief article, with 1 table showing percent change in import prices for 12 product categories, 3rd quarter 1984 vs. 3rd quarter 1983. Data are from BLS.

Table previously appeared on a quarterly basis; for last quarterly appearance, see SRI 1983 Annual under C8650-2.407.

NO SWEAT ON THE INDUSTRIAL PRICE FRONT, SEMIANNUAL FEATURE

(p. 38) Semiannual article, with 3 charts showing purchasing managers' outlook for change in industrial prices, overall and in 5 sectors, 1984-85. Data are from a *Purchasing World* national survey.

RATE HIKE PROJECTIONS TONED DOWN, QUARTERLY FEATURE

(p. 50) Quarterly article, with 1 chart showing revised freight shipping rate increases, 1978-86. Data are from Wharton Econometric Forecasting Associates.

BUYERS STILL CALLING SHOTS IN PLASTICS INDUSTRY

(p. 58) Article, with 3 charts showing percent change in plastic resin supply, demand, and prices, 1981-86. Data are from BLS, Society for the Plastics Industries, and *Purchasing World*.

C4670–1.603: Jan. 1985 (Vol. 29, No. 1)

TURNING THE SCREWS ON CREDIT

(p. 20) Brief article, with 1 chart showing vendor credit policy outlook through mid-1985. Data are from a member survey of National Assn of Credit Management.

FORECAST '85
ANNUAL FEATURE

Annual compilation of economic forecast articles. Those with substantial statistics are described below.

SIGNALS MIXED IN NAPM COMMITTEE EYES, ANNUAL FEATURE

(p. 62, 64) Annual article presenting 1985 economic predictions of members of National Assn of Purchasing Management's Business Survey Committee. Includes text statistics and 4 charts showing expected trends in prices, inflation, business conditions, and capital spending.

TOP EXECUTIVES ARE STILL BULLISH, ANNUAL FEATURE

(p. 64, 66) Annual article on corporate executives' business outlook for 1985, based on a McGraw-Hill survey of executives in over 550 leading companies. Includes 2 tables showing expected change in prices and real demand, by industry group, 1985.

Previous article, for 1984, was nonstatistical.

MODELS AGREE ECONOMY WILL GROW, BUT SLOWER, ANNUAL FEATURE

(p. 66, 68) Annual article, with 1 table comparing 4 major econometric consulting firms' forecasts for real GNP, industrial production, GNP price deflator, PPI, CPI, prime interest rate, and unemployment rate, 1985-86.

SOME PRODUCT LINES IN FOR HEFTY PRICE BOOSTS, QUARTERLY FEATURE

(p. 68, 70) Quarterly DRI economic forecast article presenting price forecasts for basic industrial commodities through 1986. Includes 1 table comparing 4th quarter prices for 30 commodities grouped as raw materials/energy, metals, components, construction products, and measuring, shown as annual percent change, 1984/85-1985/86.

Other Article

PMs AREN'T 'BUYING' TALK OF RECESSION, ANNUAL FEATURE

(p. 80) Annual article on purchasing managers' business outlook for 1985, based on a survey of *Purchasing World* readers. Includes text statistics and 4 charts showing respondents' expectations about procurement costs, business activity, inventories, and delivery performance, 1985.

C4670–1.604: Feb. 1985 (Vol. 29, No. 2)

PACKAGING PRICES ON THE RISE, ANNUAL FEATURE

(p. 52) Annual article on purchasing managers' outlook for packaging prices in 1985, based on a survey of *Purchasing World* readers. Includes 2 charts.

C4670–1.605: Mar. 1985 (Vol. 29, No. 3)

RATE SLOWDOWNS SEEN FOR 1985, QUARTERLY FEATURE

(p. 54-55) Quarterly article, with 1 chart showing revised freight shipping rate increases, 1978-86. Data are from Wharton Econometric Forecasting Associates.

TRANSPORTATION BUYERS ENJOY ENVIABLE POSITION, SEMIANNUAL FEATURE

(p. 58-60) Semiannual article reporting on purchasing managers' perceptions of direction and degree of change in overall freight costs, 1984-85. Data are based on a *Purchasing World* survey. Includes 3 charts.

MOST INDUSTRIAL GROWTH SOLID, BUT SOME LOSSES SEEN

(p. 84-85) Article, with 1 table showing percent change in demand for 68 commodities, 1985 vs. 1984. Data are from Commerce Dept's *1985 U.S. Industrial Outlook*.

C4670–1.606: Apr. 1985 (Vol. 29, No. 4)

INDUSTRIAL PRICE TRENDS, QUARTERLY FEATURE

(p. 16) Quarterly DRI economic forecast article presenting price forecasts for basic industrial commodities through 1987. Includes 1 table comparing 1st quarter prices for 30 commodities grouped as raw materials/energy, metals, components, construction items, and machinery, shown as annual percent change, 1984/85-1986/87.

OFFSHORE BARGAINS UNABATED, RECURRING FEATURE

(p. 20) Recurring brief article, with 1 table showing percent change in import prices for 12 product categories, 4th quarter 1984 vs. 4th quarter 1983. Data are from BLS.

QUALITY TOPS LIST ON SURVEY OF AUTOMOTIVE PURCHASING

(p. 66-69) By Jon Lowell. Article discussing auto industry purchasing managers' profes-

sional concerns, including business relationships with parts suppliers. Data are from a 1985 survey of over 100 managers, conducted by *Ward's Auto World*.

Includes 1 table showing survey response concerning most important factors in supplier selection; estimated change in number of suppliers and reliance on imports, and foreign countries/areas anticipated as major sources, through 1990; job satisfaction; and developments in inventory and purchasing policies and practices.

PMs SEE PRICE DISCOUNTING CONTINUING

(p. 70) Article on discount price trends, based on a *Purchasing World* reader survey. Includes 3 undated charts showing prevalence of off-price purchases.

C4670–1.607: May 1985 (Vol. 29, No. 5)

WOMEN MAKE THEIR MARK IN PURCHASING

(p. 46-58) By Caroline Reich. Article examining professional and demographic characteristics of women employed in industrial purchasing. Data are from a *Purchasing World* survey of women in corporate purchasing depts.

Includes 1 chart and 1 table showing survey response on whether salaries of men and women are equitable; and distribution of respondents by job title, age, education and major area of study, years of experience, principal product/service of current facility, company and facility employment size, employees supervised and in purchasing dept, and salary level; (no dates).

IT'S A ONE WORLD ECONOMY

(p. 118) Article, with 1 chart showing percent change in average monthly value of imports, 1982-84; and purchasing executives' anticipated level of change in import prices (no date). Data are from Commerce Dept, and a recent *Purchasing World* survey of purchasing executives.

C4670–1.608: June 1985 (Vol. 29, No. 6)

FREIGHT BILL AT $275 BILLION; TO CLIMB IN '85

(p. 20) Brief article, with 2 charts showing freight share of GNP, selected years 1970-84; and billings distribution by transport mode (no date). Data are from Transportation Policy Associates.

PACKAGING IS ONE OF YEAR'S BETTER BUYS, ANNUAL FEATURE

(p. 50-58) Annual article, by Robert S. Reichard, with 5 charts summarizing packaging industry market trends, including percent change in container output, 1978-84. Data sources include BLS and Federal Reserve Board.

For description of previous article, see SRI 1984 Annual under C4670-1.507.

KIND OF YEAR(S) A SHIPPER CAN LIVE WITH, QUARTERLY FEATURE

(p. 90) Quarterly article, with 1 chart showing revised freight shipping rate increases, 1978-87. Data are from Wharton Econometric Forecasting Associates.

C4670–1.609: July 1985 (Vol. 29, No. 7)

ROBOTS

(p. 14) Brief article, with 1 chart showing shipments, and value of billings and order backlog, for robots, 1983-84. Data are from Robotic Industries Assn.

SEMICONDUCTORS

(p. 19) Article, with 2 charts showing semiconductor market shares for U.S., Japan, Europe, and rest of world, 1984-85. Data are from Semiconductor Industry Assn.

MIDYEAR ECONOMIC REPORT, ANNUAL FEATURE

Annual compilation of midyear economic forecast articles. Those with substantial statistics are described below.

CONCERN CLOUDS PM's POSITIVE LOOK ON ECONOMY, ANNUAL FEATURE

(p. 38-40) Annual article on purchasing managers' business outlook for 1985, based on surveys of *Purchasing World* readers and members of National Assn of Purchasing Management's Business Survey Committee. Includes text statistics and 3 charts showing respondents' expectations regarding market growth, price trends, inventory strategies, and capital outlays, 1985.

PRICES TO REMAIN IN CHECK, QUARTERLY FEATURE

(p. 40-42) Quarterly DRI economic forecast article presenting price forecasts for basic industrial commodities into 1987. Includes 1 table comparing 2nd quarter prices for 24 commodities grouped as raw materials/energy, metals, components, construction supplies, and machinery, shown as annual percent change 1984/85-1986/87.

DOUBT GROWS AS ECONOMY SLOWS, ANNUAL FEATURE

(p. 44-45) Annual article on corporate executives' business outlook for 1985, based on a McGraw-Hill survey. Includes 1 chart showing expected percent increase in prices, by selected manufacturing industry group, 1985.

Previous article, for 1984, did not contain substantial statistics.

MODELS PRESENT BULLISH VIEW OF ECONOMY, ANNUAL FEATURE

(p. 45) Annual article, with 1 table comparing 4 major econometric consulting firms' forecasts for GNP, GNP price deflator, industrial production, PPI, CPI, prime interest rate, and unemployment rate, 1985-86.

C4670–1.610: Aug. 1985 (Vol. 29, No. 8)

PORTABLE COMPUTERS

(p. 20) Brief article, with 1 chart and 1 table showing portable computer sales growth rates, 1985-89; and market share by product type, 1985. Data are from Frost and Sullivan, Inc.

OFFICE SPACE COSTLY, RISING HIGHER

(p. 26) Brief article, with 1 chart showing percent change in office space rental rates, 1984-85, and 1975-85 period. Data are based on a survey of 15 cities, conducted by Howard Ecker & Co.

NEW TOYS IN YOUR ELECTRONIC FUTURE

(p. 62) By James A. Lorincz. Article, with 4 tables showing biomedical and information product market revenues by segment; and artificial intelligence and total computer industry and employment; various years 1984-2000. Data are from Arthur D. Little, Inc.

C4670–1.611: Sept. 1985 (Vol. 29, No. 9)

CHECK'S IN THE MAIL

(p. 22) Article, with 2 undated charts showing vendors' plans regarding use of tighter credit policies and more collection placements to deal with account payment problems. Data are from National Assn of Credit Management.

NONFERROUS MARKETS CONFOUND THE EXPERTS

(p. PW20-PW23) By Robert S. Reichard and Thomas F. Dillon. Article, with 1 chart showing nonferrous metal price changes, 1981-86. Data are from BLS and *Purchasing World* estimates.

RATE FAVORS SHIPPERS TODAY, NEXT YEAR, QUARTERLY FEATURE

(p. 84) Quarterly article, with 1 chart showing revised freight shipping rate increases, 1978-87. Data are from Wharton Econometric Forecasting Associates.

C4670–1.612: Oct. 1985 (Vol. 29, No. 10)

ANOTHER DIP IN OFFSHORE QUOTES, RECURRING FEATURE

(p. 24) Recurring article, with 1 table showing percent change in import prices for 14 product categories, 1st quarter 1985 vs. 1st quarter 1984. Data are from BLS.

SOUTH AFRICAN UNREST JEOPARDIZES SUPPLY OF STRATEGIC METALS

(p. 46.PW1) Article, with 2 undated tables on dependence of U.S. and total Free World on South Africa as source of 5 metals critical to steel/aerospace/defense/electronics industries. Tables show South African supply as percent of total. Data are from Commerce Dept and Shearson Lehman Bros.

PRODUCER PRICES: THREE ACTS, SAME SCENARIO THROUGH 1987, QUARTERLY FEATURE

(p. 92) Quarterly DRI economic forecast article presenting price forecasts for basic industrial commodities into 1987. Includes 1 table comparing 3rd quarter prices for 25 commodities grouped as raw materials/energy, metals, components, construction supplies, and machinery, shown as annual percent change 1984/85-1986/87.

C4680
Hunter Publishing Co.

C4680–1   NATIONAL PETROLEUM NEWS
Monthly.
ISSN 0149-5267.
LC 55-3942.
SRI/MF/excerpts, shipped quarterly

Monthly publication (semimonthly in June or July) reporting on U.S. petroleum product marketing, R&D, sales, regulation, and finance. Includes data on oil jobbers, service stations, convenience stores with gasoline sales, and fuel oil and liquefied petroleum gas dealers. Also presents periodic data on gasoline prices, petroleum product stocks, and oil company earnings.

Issues generally contain brief articles on regional and general developments and trends, and topical articles and features, occasionally with statistics; and monthly editorial features.

Regular statistical features include the following:

a. 2 monthly tables on gasoline prices and petroleum stocks ("Marketplace at a Glance").

b. Quarterly article on oil company earnings, annual NPN Factbook issue (mid-June or July), and annual outlook feature for marketers (Dec. or Jan.).

Monthly tables are listed below and appear in most issues. All additional features with substantial statistical content are described, as they appear, under "Statistical Features." Nonstatistical features are not covered.

Availability: National Petroleum News, Circulation Department, 950 Lee St., Des Plaines IL 60016, qualified subscribers $46.00 per yr., others $61.00 per yr., single copy $4.50, Fact Book $35.00; SRI/MF/excerpts for monthly tables and all portions described under "Statistical Features;" shipped quarterly.

Issues reviewed during 1985: Nov. 1984-Oct. 1985 (P) (Vol. 76, Nos. 11-12; Vol. 77, Nos. 1-10); and NPN 1985 Fact Book.

MONTHLY TABLES:

[1] Average gasoline prices in the U.S. [by grade of gasoline and region, with U.S. city average, generally for month 2-3 months prior to cover date; data are from BLS].

[2] Stocks [total and unleaded gasoline, jet kerosene, distillates, and residual fuels, generally as of 4-7 weeks prior to cover date, and for same date of previous year; data are from American Petroleum Institute].

STATISTICAL FEATURES:

C4680–1.601: Nov. 1984 (Vol. 76, No. 11)

DOE: ECONOMIC SURGE LIFTS '84 DEMAND, PRICES, BUT '85 PRODUCT PICTURE TO RESUME FLAT COURSE, RECURRING FEATURE

(p. 35-37) Recurring article analyzing short-term forecast of Energy Information Administration. Includes 2 tables showing energy demand and prices, by fuel type, 1983-85 with quarterly detail.

NPRA: IMPORTED GASOLINE INFLUX REAL; SOME REFINERS SEEK FED RESTRICTIONS

(p. 37) Brief article, with 1 table showing gasoline imports of top 10 importing companies, 1st half 1984. Data are from National Petroleum Refiners Assn.

C4680–1.602: Dec. 1984 (Vol. 76, No. 12)

MAJORS' THIRD-QUARTER PROFITS SHRINK, REFLECTING 'QUITE LOUSY' PUMP PRICES, QUARTERLY FEATURE

(p. 33) Quarterly article on trends in oil company earnings. Includes 1 table showing earnings for 23 companies, 3rd quarter and 1st 9 months 1983-84.

LATEST STATION COUNT 21.4% BELOW 1977; FUEL OIL DEALER POPULATION FALLS 17.5%

(p. 34-36) Article, with 2 tables showing establishments, sales, payroll, and employment, for service stations and fuel oil dealers, by State, 1982 with comparisons to 1977. Data are from Census Bureau.

ANOTHER PICKENS RAID?

(p. 43) Brief article, with 1 table showing top 5 oil companies in sales and earnings, and top 5 ranked by assets, gasoline gallonage and market share, and number of service stations and branded jobbers, primarily 1983.

HEATING OIL'S ROUGH ROAD TO CONTINUE, STUDY SAYS

(p. 52) Brief article, with 2 tables showing new and total single-family housing, and distribution by type of heating energy used, by census region, various years 1974-83. Data are from Petroleum Industry Research Foundation.

C4680–1.603: Jan. 1985 (Vol. 77, No. 1)

INTEREST FADES IN ATLANTIC WATERS AS POSSIBLE SOURCE OF OIL OR GAS

(p. 22-23) By J. Richard Shaner. Article, with 1 table showing oil/gas wells drilled along Atlantic Coast and estimated cost, by company and site, 1978-84 period.

SLIDE IN STATION COUNT EBBING; SURVIVORS START TO GET FITTER, ANNUAL FEATURE

(p. 28-29) Annual article reporting on U.S. Dept of Commerce forecasts of gasoline service station establishments and sales, 1985. Includes 2 tables showing total service station establishments, 1972-85; and number and sales of company- and franchisee-owned establishments, 1983-85.

C-STORES' 'GAS' SHARE STILL GROWING, ANNUAL FEATURE

(p. 31) Annual article on convenience store gasoline marketing, 1983. Data are from John F. Roscoe surveys of small food store industry and gasoline marketing.

Includes 1 table showing total convenience stores and number selling gasoline, gasoline units added, gallons sold, profit margin per gallon, and gasoline sales as percent of total sales, for 11 individual chains, 1983.

Full survey reports are covered in SRI under C8115-1 and C8115-2.

OUTLOOK '85: ANOTHER TOUGH YEAR AHEAD, ANNUAL FEATURE

(p. 34-41) Annual article, by J. Richard Shaner, on oil industry marketing outlook, for 1985. Data are from the Independent Petroleum Assn of America and DOE. Includes 2 tables and 1 chart showing the following:

a. Domestic demand for 6 petroleum products; total exports; domestic production of crude oil and natural gas liquids; imports of crude oil and 6 products; other supply; closing stocks for 6 products, unfinished oils, natural gas liquids, and crude oil; and crude runs to stills; 1984 and quarterly 1985.

b. Demand, prices, and supply, for various petroleum products, 1982-85 and/or quarterly 1984-85.

C-STORES TO REPEAT '84 SUCCESS PATTERN THIS YEAR, ANNUAL FEATURE

(p. 51) Annual article reporting on U.S. Dept of Commerce forecasts of convenience store establishments and sales, 1985. Includes 1 table showing number and sales of company- and franchisee-owned establishments, 1983-85.

C4680–1.604: Feb. 1985 (Vol. 77, No. 2)

WHY IMPORTS COMPOUND U.S. REFINER WOES

(p. 38) Article, with 2 tables showing number of refineries by capacity range, and number shut down; and crude oil distillation capacity and utilization; 1980-84. Data are from DOE and American Petroleum Institute.

C4680–1.605: Mar. 1985 (Vol. 77, No. 3)

18 REFINERIES SHUT IN '84, FEWER THAN IN PREVIOUS YEAR, ANNUAL FEATURE

(p. 16) Annual article, with 1 text table showing owner, location, and distillation capacity, for refineries closed in 1984. Data are from Energy Information Administration.

YEAR-END EARNINGS REPORTS YIELD SURPRISES: EXXON, SHELL, STANDARD (IND.) SET RECORDS, QUARTERLY FEATURE

(p. 31-32) Quarterly article on trends in oil company earnings. Includes 3 tables showing earnings for 19 companies, with selected detail for earnings from domestic and foreign refining/marketing operations, 4th quarter and full year 1983-84; and annual earnings of top 3 companies, 1979-84.

TAX EVASION AND MISLABELING RIP-OFFS

(p. 38-44) By J. Richard Shaner. Article, with 1 table showing State tax rates on gasoline, diesel fuel, and gasohol, by State, as of Jan. 1, 1985. Data are from National Highway Users Federation.

C4680–1.606: Apr. 1985 (Vol. 77, No. 4)

MOST OHIO JOBBERS FAVOR BELOW-COST SELLING BILL: SURVEY

(p. 26) Article on Ohio petroleum wholesalers' support for State involvement in jobber-related issues, including actions affecting pricing, labeling, tax credits, divestiture, and other industry practices. Data are from 115 responses to a Nov./Dec. 1984 member survey conducted by Ohio Petroleum Marketers Assn. Includes 1 table.

DOE's SHORT-TERM ENERGY OUTLOOK: BASICALLY MEDIOCRE, RECURRING FEATURE

(p. 33) Recurring article analyzing short-term energy forecast of Energy Information Administration. Includes 1 table showing prices and supply for various petroleum products, and aggregate product import volume, 1983 and quarterly 1984-2nd quarter 1986.

PREMIUM OCTANES CONTINUE STEADY UPWARD CLIMB, RECURRING FEATURE

(p. 33) Recurring article on gasoline octane ratings. Data are from National Institute for Petroleum and Energy Research. Includes 1 table showing octane ratings for leaded and unleaded gasoline, summer 1982-84 (with 1984 detail by region) and winter 1982/83-1983/84.

C4680–1.607: May 1985 (Vol. 77, No. 5)

ARCO ENDS CHINESE PRODUCT IMPORTS; MORE LEFT FOR INDIES TO TOUGHEN UP

(p. 26-29) By Mark Emond. Article, with 2 charts and 1 table showing West Coast gasoline imports, from all sources and from PRC 1982-84, and by month 1982-Feb. 1985. Data are from Pacific West Oil Data.

HOW 1984 MERGERS ALTERED RETAIL RANKINGS

(p. 35) Brief article, with 2 tables ranking top 21 oil companies by number of gasoline service stations owned, and also showing number of States serviced, 1984 with comparisons to 1983. Data are from an NPN survey.

SMALL JOBBERS UNDER SIEGE

(p. 42-45) By Marvin Reid and Tim Grace. Article on trends in petroleum product marketing, with 1 table showing number of jobber and agent distributors for 19 major oil companies, Jan. 1981 and 1984. Data are from NPN Factbook.

For description of a similar article, for 1972 and 1983, see SRI 1984 Annual under C4680-1.504.

C4680–1.608: June 1985 (Vol. 77, No. 6)

CHEVRON, TEXACO '84 MARKET SHARE CHAMPS, ANNUAL FEATURE

(p. 27-28) Annual article on gasoline sales performance of major oil companies, 1984. Data are from company annual reports and Federal Highway Administration.

Includes 2 charts and 2 tables showing top 12 oil companies ranked by volume of gasoline sales, 1983-84; and highway and off-highway gasoline consumption, 1978-84.

For description of previous article, presenting 1982 data, see SRI 1983 Annual under C4680-1.408. No article appeared in 1984.

FIRST-QUARTER EARNINGS SLUMP, BUT MOST MADE SOME MONEY

(p. 31) Quarterly article on trends in oil company earnings. Includes 1 table showing corporate and/or downstream (refining/marketing) earnings for 20 companies, 1st quarter 1984-85. Downstream earnings are worldwide.

C4680–1.609: July 1985 (Vol. 77, No. 7)

ARCO DATA SHOWS MARKET SHARE GAIN FROM LOW-BALLING MAY HAVE LIMITS

(p. 20) By Mark Emond. Article, with 1 table showing shares of California gasoline retail market, for 7 individual leading companies, and for aggregate major and independent companies, 1982-85. Data are from Lundberg Survey.

PRIVATE FLEET SURVEY: TANK TRUCKS COST MORE

(p. 52) Brief article, with 1 table comparing operating data for tank trucks vs. averages for all types of private truck fleet vehicles, 1983-84. Includes cost per mile, vehicles per fleet, mileage per year and per trip, percent of mileage run empty, and vehicle age. Data are from an A. T. Kearney survey for the Private Truck Council of America.

C4680–1.610: NPN 1985 Fact Book Issue

[Issue price is $35.00.]

Annual fact book presenting detailed petroleum industry statistics and related directories. Covers finances, supply and demand, marketing, prices, and employment, including data by product, company, and State, various years 1950-85. Also includes selected data for Canada and other foreign countries, and data on vehicle registrations and sales of tires, batteries, and accessories.

Data are compiled from NPN surveys and numerous Government and industry sources, identified for each table.

Contains introduction, contents listing, and index (p. 4-10); statistical sections, generally including narrative summaries, with 44 maps and charts, and 162 tables (p. 13-167); and directories of trade assns, oil marketing companies and executives, and Federal energy-related officials (p. 169-209).

All tables, and charts presenting data not covered in tables, are listed below.

TABLES AND CHARTS:

[Data are for U.S., unless otherwise noted.]

ANNUAL REPORTS

[1] Ranking the top [19 major oil] marketing companies [by total assets and sales, net income, and net sales among *Fortune* 500 companies, 1983-84]. (p. 13)

[2] Oil company annual reports [gross sales, net income, and total assets, 1983-84, with percent change from 1979; and net income as percent of average stockholder equity, crude oil and refined product imports, net domestic and foreign crude oil production and refinery runs, and domestic refined product sales, 1983-84; for 21 companies]. (p. 14-15)

[3-4] Quarterly and full year earnings, 1984 vs. 1983; and how they fared in 1983 vs. 1982; [for 21-22 major oil companies]. (p. 16)

ADVERTISING

[5-6] Spot and network TV spending [on advertising, for 13-20 oil companies, 1983-84]. (p. 18)

[7] How some oil companies split their [advertising] budgets [expenditures by media, for 4 major companies, 1983-84]. (p. 18)

AUTOMOTIVE

[8] Current automotive registrations [of cars, trucks/buses, and motorcycles, by State, 1983-84]. (p. 20)

[9] Estimated licensed drivers, by sex and States, 1983-84. (p. 21)

[10] Passenger car energy indicators [average and total fuel consumption and mileage, and registrations, 1967 and 1970-84]. (p. 22)

[11] Mileage and consumption data [and registrations, by vehicle type, including trucks and commercial and school buses; and average travel mileage by road type]; 1983. (p. 22)

[12] 1983 relationships by population and drivers [population; licensed drivers and registered motor vehicles per 1,000 persons; fuel consumption per vehicle; and miles per gallon of gas, per vehicle, and per driver; all by State]. (p. 23)

BRAND NAMES

[13] Brand names of gasoline and motor oil [by company]. (p. 26-29)

CAPITAL SPENDING

[14] Capital spending in the oil industry: a 20-year overview at home and abroad [shows U.S. and foreign capital expenditures, by oil industry function, 1965-84]. (p. 31)

DISTRIBUTION, OUTLETS, AND EMPLOYMENT

[15] How oil companies handle product distribution [total branded retail outlets; number of States where gasoline brand is marketed; and number and selected operating characteristics of branded service stations, branded jobbers/commission agents, bulk plants, and terminals; all shown for over 200 oil companies and jobbers, undated]. (p. 35-43)

[16] Branded retail outlets [by State, for approximately 200 companies, undated]. (p. 44-51)

[17] Average number of employees [for oil/gas extraction, and petroleum manufacturing, transportation, wholesale, and retail industries, by State], as of Jan. 1, 1984. (p. 53)

[114] [Number of convenience stores, and value of in-store and gasoline sales, with comparison to number of supermarkets, households, and population, all by census division and State], 1983. (p. 121)

[115-117] Sales by C-stores [total and gasoline], number of C-stores [total and selling gasoline], and average annual per store volume [total and in-store sales, various years] 1973-84. [charts] (p. 122)

MARKET SHARE

[118] Gasoline consumption: on- vs. off-highway use, [1978-84]. (p. 124)

[119] Gasoline market: by gross gallonage and relative shares [of top 12 oil companies, 1980-84]. (p. 124-125)

SUPPLY AND DEMAND

[120-122] Stocks of motor gasoline, distillate fuel oil, and residual fuel oil, [by region, monthly 1983-84]. (p. 128)

[123] Refinery and bulk terminal stocks [by product type] by States and PAD regions, 1984. (p. 130)

[124-125] Petroleum products supplied and imported [by type, monthly 1982-84]. (p. 132)

[126] Crude oil production [by State and PAD district], 1974-83. (p. 133)

[127] Domestic supply trend [by type of refined product, selected years 1960-84]. (p. 135)

[128-130] Estimated petroleum balance [supplies of crude oil and refined products, including domestic and imported supplies and data by product type]; refinery operations [input to distillation units, capacity and percent utilized, and crude oil runs]; and crude and product inventories [including data by product type; all for 1983-84, with detail for 2nd-4th quarters]. (p. 135)

[131] Role of imports in domestic demand [selected years 1950-84]. (p. 136)

[132] Petroleum product consumption [by product type and State], 1983. (p. 137)

[133-34] Crude oil imports, and domestic supply of oil products, [1975-84]. [charts] (p. 138)

[135] Unleaded gasoline: the growth by years [annually 1973-84 and monthly 1984]. (p. 138)

[136] Supply and demand, principal products [domestic supply, production, and imports, 1983-84]. (p. 138)

[137-140] Oil imports [crude, residual fuel oil, and other products]; origins of oil imports [OPEC, Arab OPEC, and western and eastern hemispheres]; and total well completions, proved reserves, and supply; [1982-84]. (p. 138)

[141] IPAA (Independent Petroleum Assn of America) '85 forecast [domestic demand and production, imports, exports, and closing stocks, with detail for crude oil, natural gas liquids, and refined products; and crude runs to stills; annually 1984-85 and quarterly 1985]. (p. 140)

[142] All-time total [oil, gas, and dry] wells drilled [by State and PAD district, and in Federal waters, as of Jan. 1, 1984]. (p. 143)

[143] [Average yield (gallonage) of 1 bbl. of crude oil, by refined product type, undated]. (p. 144)

STORAGE CAPACITY

[144-145] Primary storage capacity [in operation, under construction, and idle]; and primary minimum operating inventories [in PAD districts 1-4 combined and 5; all for crude oil and by refined product type, 1983, with comparison to 1978 or 1979]. (p. 147)

[146-150] Estimated storage capacity and inventory in the petroleum distribution system [for crude oil and/or refined products by type, by system sector (primary, bulk plants, motor fuel outlets, and specific end-user categories)], as of Mar. 31, 1983. (p. 148)

TAXES

[151-152] State tax collections [from motor fuel taxes, by State, 1983-84, with 1984 tax rate]; and Federal [collections from gasoline, diesel/special fuels, and lube oil taxes, 1970-84]. (p. 150)

TIRES, BATTERIES, AND ACCESSORIES (TBA) AFTERMARKET

[153-154] Outlook for tires and batteries at stations [shipments, and total and per-station unit sales]; and battery shipments improve [replacement and original equipment; 1970s-84]. (p. 152)

[155] Where batteries are sold [private and manufacturer brand shipments, by distribution channel, 1983-84]. (p. 152)

[156-157] Auto, truck, and farm tire shipments [original equipment, replacement, and export, 1983-84]. (p. 153)

[158] Where consumers get tune-ups [distribution among service stations, car dealers, repair shops, and do-it-yourself, 1981-84]. [chart] (p. 153)

[159-160] Ethylene glycol-base antifreeze sales [civilian and government bulk and packaged], 1983-84. (p. 153)

[161] Automotive products/services [establishments and sales, for company- and franchisee-owned establishments, 1983-85]. (p. 154)

[162-164] 1985 crankcase drain intervals and recommended oil; automatic transmission/transaxle drain intervals and recommended fluids; and chassis lubrication intervals; [by manufacturer]. (p. 154)

[165] Exclusive 1984 service job analysis [number of jobs performed in service stations, independent repair shops, and new car/truck dealers, by detailed type of service]. (p. 156-157)

REFINERIES

[166] Refineries and capacities by States [listing of refineries (identified by company and location), arranged by State; with operable capacity, and capacity shut down but capable of startup within 90 days, for each refinery and State, as of Jan. 1, 1984; coverage also includes selected State subregions, Puerto Rico, Virgin Islands, and Guam]. (p. 159-161)

[167] Lubricating oil and wax capacities of U.S. [and Canadian] refineries [by company, with location and crude oil capacity, 1984]. (p. 161)

[168] Refineries and capacities, by companies [ranked by total capacity, with capacity for each refinery location], as of Jan. 1, 1984. (p. 163-165)

[169] Refinery closings [and resulting capacity reduction, for individual refineries grouped by PAD district, with refinery owner, location, dates of last operation and shutdown, and years in operation], 1981-84. (p. 166-167)

C4680–1.611: Aug. 1985 (Vol. 77, No. 8)

BOXSCORE: 24 REFINERIES GONE, CAPACITY OFF 600,420 B/D, ANNUAL FEATURE

(p. 33) Annual article, with 2 tables showing refineries by crude oil distillation capacity, 1981-85; and owner, location, and years of operation and/or capacity, for refineries closed and started up/reactivated during 1984, grouped by PAD district. Data are from the Energy Information Administration.

IPAA: DEMAND UP AGAIN, WILL INCREASE 1% IN 1985

(p. 37) Article, with 1 table showing domestic demand, imports, and closing stocks for selected petroleum products; crude oil imports; domestic production of crude oil and natural gas liquids; other supply; and crude runs to stills; quarterly 1985. Data are from Independent Petroleum Assn of America.

TO STAY IN OR SELL OUT: A BIG DECISION FOR JOBBERS

(p. 44-48) By Marvin Reid. Article, with 1 undated table showing number of oil jobber businesses and percent of jobbers going out of business, as forecast by oil marketers, refiners, assn executives, and industry observers, over the next 2, 5, and 10 years. Data are from Petroleum Marketers Assn of America.

BATTERY 'FEEDERS' HELP MAJORS PUT MORE 'B' BACK INTO TBA

(p. 50-53) By Mark Emond. Article, with 1 table showing battery shipments, by outlet type, 1980-84. Data are from Battery Council International.

C4680–1.612: Sept. 1985 (Vol. 77, No. 9)

SEARCH FOR NEW 'EDGE' DRIVES OCTANE INCREASES FOR LEADED, UNLEADED, RECURRING FEATURE

(p. 36) Recurring article on gasoline octane ratings. Data are from National Institute for Petroleum and Energy Research. Includes 1 table showing octane ratings for leaded and unleaded gasoline, winter 1983/84-1984/85.

EARNINGS REFLECT RESTRUCTURING, FEW MAJORS REPORT FIRST-HALF PROFITS, QUARTERLY FEATURE

(p. 36) Quarterly article on trends in oil company earnings. Includes 1 table showing earnings for 20 companies, 2nd quarter and 1st half 1984-85.

EXCLUSIVE SERVICE JOB ANALYSIS SHOWS STATION TBA/REPAIR REVIVAL

(p. 49-52) By Don Smith. Article on motor vehicle service/repair market shares of service stations, repair shops, new vehicle dealers, and self-serviced fleets. Data are from a Hunter Publishing Co. survey covering approximately 329,000 service outlets.

Includes 2 charts and 1 table showing sales, triennially 1972-84; and number of outlets, and jobs performed by detailed type, 1984; all by type of outlet.

C-STORE SALES UP, GASOLINE GAINS SLOW

(p. 60-62) Article, with 1 table showing the following for convenience stores, 1983-84: total and/or average gasoline and nongasoline sales, and pre-tax profits; and investment per new store, and average square footage, for urban and rural locations.

Data are based on responses of 131 companies to a National Assn of Convenience Stores survey.

C4680–1.613: Oct. 1985 (Vol. 77, No. 10)

CAN OPEC PRODUCT FORCE ITS WAY INTO U.S.?

(p. 44-46) Article, with 1 table showing OPEC refined oil product exports, by world area of destination, 1984 and high and low forecasts for next 2-3 year period. Data are from Petroleum Industry Research Foundation.

'85-'86 PRICE FORECAST: NO IMPROVEMENT, RECURRING FEATURE

(p. 48) Recurring article analyzing short-term forecast of Energy Information Administration. Includes 1 table showing energy prices and supply, by fuel type, 1984 and quarterly 1985-86.

C4680–2   FUEL OIL NEWS: The Oil Heat Industry—1984

Monthly (selected issues).
For individual publication data, see below.
SRI/MF/excerpts

Annual survey report, by George Schultz, on fuel oil dealers' fuel and heating/cooling equipment operations, 1984. Survey was conducted by *Fuel Oil News.*

Survey results are reported in the Dec. 1984 and Jan. 1985 issues of *Fuel Oil News,* and include 46 tables listed below.

Dec. 1984 issue is the annual source book issue, and also includes directories of petroleum trade assns and suppliers.

Fuel Oil News is a monthly publication containing primarily narrative material. The annual source book/dealer survey is the only feature covered in SRI. This is the 7th source book.

Availability: Fuel Oil News, PO Box 360, Whitehouse NJ 08888, $19.00 per yr., single copy $2.00; SRI/MF/excerpts for survey report.

TABLES:

[Tables show data by region, mostly as percents or averages.]

C4680–2.601: Dec. 1984 (Vol. 49, No. 12)

PART I

FUEL SALES

1. Type of petroleum sold [fuel oil and gasoline]. (p. 54)

2. Sources of business income [retail and bulk fuel oil and gasoline sales]. (p. 54)

3. Petroleum revenue as a percent of total. (p. 56)

4. Petroleum products sold [No. 2 fuel oil, gasoline, and other product categories]. (p. 56)

5. Average size of business [number of residential fuel oil accounts and commercial/industrial customers; distillate, residual, and gasoline volumes; and employees]. (p. 56)

6. Annual heating oil sales by types of customers [private homes, apartments, and educational, hospital, commercial, and industrial facilities]. (p. 58)

7-8. Total annual company dollar revenues, and pre-tax earnings. (p. 58)

COMPUTERS AND TRUCKS

9. EDP [electronic data processing] usage [and number of units]. (p. 58)

10. Computer applications [in use]. (p. 58)

11. Trucks per marketer [average number and capacity], and engines and truck tanks by type [in use and preferred]. (p. 62)

12. Average age of trucks, and percent buying [new truck or tank] this year. (p. 62)

13. Average drop [delivery] in gallons [for 275- and 550-gallon tanks]. (p. 64)

14. Percent [of dealers] using 2-way radios. (p. 64)

HEATING AND COOLING EQUIPMENT OPERATIONS

15. Percent of fuel oil dealers that sell/install/service all types of heating/cooling equipment. (p. 64)

16. Trends of equipment sales, past 12 months [for residential and commercial sectors]. (p. 64)

17. Sources of business income [wholesale, retail, air conditioning, and other sales]. (p. 64)

18-20. Percent of fuel oil dealers that sell/install/service selected heating and cooling equipment [residential and commercial, by type of equipment]. (p. 64, 66-67)

21. Average number of units installed in past 12 months [residential and commercial burners, boilers, and furnaces]. (p. 68)

22. Service dept [percent of dealers with depts; percent with profitable depts; and average calls per year, parts/inventory value, and number of technicians]. (p. 68)

CONVERSIONS TO GAS

23-24. Percent of dealers: losing customers to gas heat [and average number of customers lost]; and indicating gas conversions are a major threat to their business, [taking steps to combat conversions, and making conversions from oil to gas]. (p. 72)

C4680–2.602: Jan. 1985 (Vol. 50, No. 1)

PART II

MISCELLANEOUS

25. Percent recommending furnace/boiler replacement under [selected] conditions. (p. 31)

26. Brand name specifications (percentage of dealers who recommend equipment replacements by brand) [and percent of customers following recommendations]. (p. 31)

27. Percent indicating [selected] factors in brand selection. (p. 31)

28A-K. Issues affecting the industry: [importance of] government controls/interference, ability to hire/retain good people, reduced number of suppliers, reduction in company overhead, competition from majors and utilities, computer systems/strong internal controls, ability to increase sales, high interest rates, financial payment systems, and theft control of all products. (p. 32, 34)

29. Type of business entity [corporation, subchapter corporation, and proprietorship]. (p. 34)

30. How goods are computed: percent of dealers using [selected] methods. (p. 34)

31. Value exchanges at end of reporting period [by method]. (p. 34)

32. Percent of dealers trading on the futures markets. (p. 33)

33-36. Number of retail gasoline outlets, average gasoline volume per station, services offered at retail outlets, and trend in [increasing] retail outlets in past 2 years. (p. 33)

37. Industry publication most helpful to dealers in operating their fuel oil business. (p. 33)

C4687
Inc. Publishing Co.

C4687–1   INC.

Monthly.
ISSN 0162-8968.
LC 79-643168.
SRI/MF/excerpts, shipped quarterly

Monthly journal reporting trends in business activity and management of smaller corporations. Covers company finance, accounting, marketing, regulatory developments, personnel practices, and prominent firms and executives.

Issues generally contain feature articles, occasionally with substantial statistics; and editorial depts, including monthly "Investing in Growth Companies" section presenting selected stock market data for small corporations.

Annual statistical features include rankings of fastest growing privately and publicly held small corporations; survey of executive or management compensation at small corporations; and analysis of States' small business conditions, with ratings.

Features with substantial statistical content are described, as they appear, under "Statistical Features." Each issue of the journal is reviewed, but an abstract is published in SRI monthly issues only when statistical features appear.

Availability: INC. Magazine, PO Box 2538, Boulder CO 80322, $24.00 per yr., single copy $3.00; SRI/MF/excerpts for all portions described under "Statistical Features;" shipped quarterly.

Issues reviewed during 1985: Nov. 1984-Oct. 1985 (P) (Vol. 6, Nos. 11-12; Vol. 7, Nos. 1-10).

STATISTICAL FEATURES:

C4687–1.601: Dec. 1984 (Vol. 6, No. 12)

INC. 500: AMERICA's FAST-GROWING PRIVATE COMPANIES, ANNUAL FEATURE

Annual compilation of articles and statistics on the fastest growing small privately held companies. The INC. private 500 companies had sales of $100,000 to $25 million in 1978, and are ranked by 1979-83 sales growth. Includes the statistical features described below.

INSIDE THE INC. 500

(p 52-53) By Curtis Hartman. Narrative analysis, with composite profile of the INC. private 500, and 3 tables ranking top 10 companies by total and per-employee sales, 1983; and by number of new employees, 1979-83 period. Includes accompanying introduction (p. 51).

INC. 500

(p. 107-136, passim) Ranked listing of INC. private 500, showing the following for each company: percent sales growth 1979-83, and rank; sales, profit range, and employees, 1979 and 1983; number of acquisitions during 1979-83; business description; and founding date.

Data are from individual companies, and are accompanied by alphabetical index (p. 54-55) and selection criteria (p. 136).

This is the 4th annual ranking.

C4687–1.602: Apr. 1985 (Vol. 7, No. 4)

HOT SPOTS

(p. 18) Brief article, with 1 table ranking top 10 retail market areas by percent change in sales, 1983 vs. 1982, and also showing actual sales for 1983. Data are from *Adweek*.

HEALTH CARE STOCKS: 90% CONFUSION AND 10% OPPORTUNITY

(p. 171-172) Article, with 2 tables showing percent change in value for 5 best and worst performing health care stocks in 1984. Data are from Whale Securities, Inc.

C4687–1.603: May 1985 (Vol. 7, No. 5)

1985 INC. 100, ANNUAL FEATURE

(p. 57-67) Annual article on the 100 fastest growing publicly held companies with sales of $100,000-$25 million in 1980, ranked by percent increase in sales during 1980-84 period. Data sources include company annual reports and SEC disclosure forms, business publications, and journal telephone interviews.

Contains analysis of findings and description of survey methodology; index of companies; and the following statistics:

a. Composite profile of the top 100; top 10 companies ranked by total and per employee sales, employment growth, and net income compared to sales, 1984; and number of top 100 companies by State, 1984-85. 6 tables.

b. Ranking of the top 100, including the following for each: percent change in sales, and number of acquisitions, 1980-84 period; sales, net income, and employment, 1980 and 1984; equity value and share held by chief executive officer, 1984; and date of incorporation and 1st public offering, type of business, and comparative 1984 rank. 1 extended table.

This is the 7th annual survey.

GRIN AND BEAR IT, ANNUAL FEATURE

(p. 83-84) Annual article, by Robert A. Mamis, analyzing the stock performance of the 1985 INC. 100 fastest growing publicly held small companies. Includes 2 tables showing INC. 100 companies ranked by Mar. 1985 value of a $100 investment made in Mar. 1984; and including stock price for each company, and comparison to industrial averages of 4 major stock indexes, Mar. 1984-85.

C4687–1.604: June 1985 (Vol. 7, No. 6)

SCORECARD: TAKE IT AWAY, MOM AND POP

(p. 22) Brief article, with 1 table ranking 20 kinds of small businesses (annual sales under $1 million) by number of establishments, 1984, with change from 1979. Data are from Dun & Bradstreet.

C4687–1.605: July 1985 (Vol. 7, No. 7)

WALKING UNDER LADDERS

(p. 23) Brief article, with 1 undated table ranking top 10 product categories by liability insurance cost as percent of sales revenue. Data are from Insurance Services Office, Inc.

C4687–1.606: Sept. 1985 (Vol. 7, No. 9)

SCORECARD: NO FREE LUNCH

(p. 12) Brief article, with 1 undated table showing breakfast, lunch, and dinner costs in 10 most expensive U.S. cities ranked by total daily business meal expenses. Data are from Laventhol and Horwath.

TAKE AT THE TOP, ANNUAL FEATURE

(p. 66-74) Annual article, by Tim Smart, analyzing executive compensation in small/medium sized companies, 1985. Data are from responses of 516 companies to a Feb. 1985 survey of INC. subscribers, conducted by INC. and Peat, Marwick, Mitchell & Co.

Includes 3 charts and 3 tables showing characteristics of respondent companies and their chief executive officers; percent of companies changing various compensation policies or methods; and average salaries of chief executives, and chief operating, financial, and marketing officers, by sales volume, industry, and region.

This is the 7th annual compensation survey.

C4687–1.607: Oct. 1985 (Vol. 7, No. 10)

SMALL-TIME JUSTICE

(p. 22) Article, with 1 table showing Federal antitrust caseloads (total and for top 9-11 industries affected), 1980 and 1984. Data are from *Trade Regulation Reports*, published by Commerce Clearing House, Inc.

REPORT ON THE STATES, ANNUAL FEATURE

(p. 90-93) Annual report, by Nell Margolis, rating States according to social, economic, and governmental conditions affecting small business activity. Data are primarily from Federal and State agencies.

Includes 1 table showing the following indicators for 50 States, ranked by overall rating:

a. Bank loans as percent of bank assets; commercial/industrial loans and Small Business Investment Co. investments per capita; availability of direct loans, loan and bond guarantees, and venture capital; average weekly wage; percent of labor force unionized and high school graduates; and value added per worker.

b. Taxes per $1,000 personal income; types of small business support programs and agencies available; percent change in population 1980-84, employment 1982-84, and personal income 1981-83; businesses per 1,000 population; and number of INC. 100 companies, 1979-85 period.

Trend periods noted are the only data dates provided. Accompanying narrative analysis includes rankings of top 10 States for selected indicators.

This is the 5th annual report.

C4710
Information for Industry

C4710–1 **MERGERS AND ACQUISITIONS: The Journal of Corporate Venture**
Quarterly.
ISSN 0026-0010.
LC 66-9930.
SRI/MF/excerpts

Quarterly journal, with annual "Index and Almanac," on corporate mergers and acquisitions. Data are compiled by Information for Industry. Quarter of data coverage is 1 quarter prior to cover date.

General format:

a. Regularly recurring features, including reports on recent merger, divestiture, and joint venture activity; and articles, occasionally with statistics.

b. Quarterly "Rosters" section, containing the following: narrative review of selected transactions; "Data Base Report" article, often with statistics; 1 table on top 25 transactions; 3 rosters; and 7 "Profile" tables.

Annual "Almanac and Index" issue is usually published in spring, and includes "Profile" section with annual summary of quarterly data; cross-index of acquiring and acquired companies; and previous year article index.

Quarterly tables and rosters are listed below. All additional features with substantial statistical content are described, as they appear, under "Statistical Features."

Prior to Fall 1984 issue, quarter of data coverage was 2 quarters prior to cover date. Fall 1984 issue contains quarterly rosters and tables for both 2nd and 3rd quarters 1984.

Beginning with the 1985 Almanac and Index issue, SRI covers this journal under C6050-1. Issuing agency name has changed to MLR Enterprises.

Availability: Mergers & Acquisitions, 229 S. 18th St., Philadelphia PA 19103, $129.00 per yr.; SRI/MF/excerpts for quarterly tables and rosters and portions described under "Statistical Features."

Issues reviewed during 1985: Fall 1984-Winter 1985 (Vol. 19, Nos. 3-4).

QUARTERLY TABLES AND ROSTERS:
[All tables and rosters show data for quarter of coverage.]

TOP TRANSACTIONS

[1] Top 25 transactions by dollar volume [shows value of transaction, acquiring and acquired/merged companies, and investment advisors].

ROSTERS

[1-3] U.S. mergers and acquisitions, foreign investment in U.S., and U.S. investment abroad [arranged by SIC 2- or 3-digit industry, generally showing the following for each transaction: name, location, sales or revenues, net income or loss, and type of business activity, for acquiring and acquired companies; and transaction terms and effective date].

PROFILE

[1] Merger and acquisition activity [number and value of transactions, for U.S. and foreign mergers/acquisitions by U.S. companies, and

U.S. mergers/acquisitions by foreign companies, with comparison to previous 2-4 quarters].

[2-7] [Ranking of top acquiring companies by number of transactions, and of top acquiring and divesting industries by number and value of transactions; and number of transactions, by form of payment.]

STATISTICAL FEATURES:

C4710-1.601: Fall 1984 (Vol. 19, No. 3)

DATA BASE REPORT: CALIFORNIA IS M&A LEADER

(p. R153) Article, with 2 tables ranking 7 regions and 10 most populous States by number of corporate mergers/acquisitions during 1st 3 quarters 1984, with comparison to same period of 1983.

C4710-1.602: Winter 1985 (Vol. 19, No. 4)

LEADING DEALMAKERS OF 1984, ANNUAL FEATURE

(p. 20) Annual article, with 1 table ranking top 21 investment companies by number of mergers/acquisitions/related transactions, and including number of transactions initiated and exceeding $100 million, 1984 with comparisons to 1983. Data were compiled from *Wall Street Journal* advertisements.

This is the 2nd annual ranking.

REDIRECTION OF POWER IN AMERICAN BANKING

(p. 48-53) By Michael C. Connor. Article, with 1 table showing the following for 20 interstate acquisitions of banks, 1981-84 period: names and assets of acquiring and target banks, date announced, and target price.

IN LBOs THE BASICS COUNT

(p. R90) Article, with 1 table showing showing top 10 industry groups ranked by number of leveraged buyouts, 1984. Data are from *Mergers and Acquisitions*.

C4712
Information Publications

C4712-1   **ALMANAC OF THE 50 STATES: Basic Data Profiles with Comparative Tables**
Annual. 1985. xiii+446 p.
ISBN 0- 931845-02-5 (pbk.).
ISBN 0- 931845-03-3 (library).
LC 85-171664.
SRI/MF/complete

Annual almanac, for 1985, presenting social, economic, and governmental statistical profiles of each of 50 States and D.C. Data are shown for various years 1970s-85, with population projections to 2000.

Report is designed to present overviews of the States for comparative analysis. Socioeconomic breakdowns are shown, as applicable, for many topics. These breakdowns include data by urban-rural status, commodity, income, industry, occupation, age, educational attainment, marital status, race, and sex.

Most data are from *Statistical Abstract of the U.S.: 1984* and its supplements, and other Federal sources.

Contains contents listing and introduction (p. v-xiii); an 8-page profile for each State, D.C., and total U.S., containing statistics in 13 categories as described below (p. 3-418); and 52 tables presenting selected State rankings based on statistics from the profiles (p. 421-446).

This is the 1st edition of the *Almanac.*

Availability: Information Publications, PO Box 1536, Burlington VT 05402-1536, $35.00 (pbk.), $42.50 (library edition); SRI/MF/complete.

PROFILE STATISTICS:

a. **State Summary:** includes highlights from the other 12 categories.

b. **Geography and Environment:** includes land and water area, and percent federally owned; topographic features; population of capital and largest city; number of urban and rural places by size class; national forest acreage; and State park acreage, visitors, and expenditures.

c. **Demographics and Population Characteristics:** includes population trends from 1970 and projections to 2000, migration, families and households, and foreign-born population by country or world area of birth, and period of immigration.

d. **Vital Statistics and Health:** includes births (total and to teenagers), abortions, deaths by leading cause, marriages, divorces, physicians, dentists, hospitals, and nursing facilities.

e. **Education:** includes public and private schools, enrollment, and high school graduates; public school teachers, and State receipts and expenditures; and higher education institutions, enrollment, and tuition and fees.

f. **Social Insurance and Welfare Programs:** includes social security beneficiaries and payments; Medicare enrollment; Medicaid recipients; AFDC and SSI recipients and payments; workers compensation payments; and unemployment insurance initial claims, weeks compensated, beneficiaries, and net benefits.

g. **Housing and Construction:** includes housing units, occupancy and structural characteristics, and median value or rent; value of residential construction; and number and value of housing units authorized by building permits.

h. **Government and Elections:** includes State officials; executive, legislative, and local government structure; State employees and payroll; voting age population, voter registration, and voter turnout; presidential election results; and congressional representation.

i. **Governmental Finance:** includes Federal, State, and local revenues; State expenditures by function; and Federal aid by program.

j. **Crime, Law Enforcement, and Courts:** includes Part I offenses and rates; number of police agencies; arrests (total and juvenile); total prisoners and number under death sentence, parolees, and probationers; members and terms for highest State court; and general and limited/special jurisdiction court judges and population per judge.

k. **Labor and Income:** includes civilian labor force by employment status, unemployment and labor force participation rates, and insured unemployment by reason; hours and earnings of manufacturing production workers; organized labor membership; work stoppages, workers involved, and days idle; median household and family incomes; per capita personal income; and poverty rates.

l. **Agriculture, Business, and Industry:** includes business establishments and payroll; farms, acreage, value, income, debt/asset ratio, and crop and livestock marketings; fish catch and value; forest acreage; fuel and nonfuel mineral production value; residential and nonresidential construction contracts; manufacturing shipments; commercial banks and savings and loan assns, and assets; and retail stores by kind of business.

m. **Communication, Energy, and Transportation:** includes telephones, daily newspapers, and radio and TV stations; energy consumption, by source and end-use sector; installed kWh capacity; gas customers, sales, and revenues; nuclear plants; highway mileage; vehicle registrations and mileage; licensed drivers; traffic fatalities; aircraft facilities and registrations; active pilots; and railroads and track mileage.

C4721
International Currency Analysis

C4721-1   **1984 WORLD CURRENCY YEARBOOK**
Annual. 1985. 958 p.
ISBN 0-917645-00-6.
ISSN 0743-5363.
SRI/MF/not filmed

Yearbook, edited by Philip P. Cowitt, on world monetary trends and developments, presenting detailed data by country on currency in circulation, official and black market currency exchange rates, and gold prices, various years 1973-83. Also includes data on Eurocurrency interest rates, gold supply and demand, foreign trade, and selected economic indicators.

Data are from central banks, ministries of finance, *Pick World Currency Report*, and currency dealers.

Contents:

a. Contents listing, abbreviations, and glossary. (p. 3-11)

b. Currency overview, including narrative analyses; lists of currency and trade areas, and currency ownership restrictions by country; 8 tables, listed below; and currency information and exchange rates for 49 small countries. (p. 14-39)

c. Profiles of 112 currencies, generally including the following for each: narrative review of currency history, transferability, developments, and administration; lists of currency varieties and/or areas where used; and 6-8 tables, also listed below. (p. 41-852)

e. Gold review, including narrative analysis; list of gold ownership and trading restrictions by country; 3 summary or trend charts; and 14 tables, also listed below. (p. 862-879)

f. Profiles of 37 gold-trading countries, each including narrative analysis and 2-3 tables showing monthly prices of gold bullion and coins and (where applicable) gold futures contracts, mostly 1974-83. (p. 880-933)

g. Directory of central banks; and subject index. (p. 936-958)

This is the 23rd edition. Previous yearbook, entitled *Pick's Currency Yearbook,* was published by Pick Publishing Corp., and was described in SRI 1981 Annual under C7550-2.

Availability: International Currency Analysis, 7239 Ave. N, Brooklyn NY 11234, $225.00; SRI/MF/not filmed.

TABLES:

C4721-1.1: Currency Overview

[Tables [1] and [3-8] show data by country, with selected rankings.]

[1] Destruction of paper money [percent decline in purchasing power, increase in cost of living, and change in free/black market value of currency, 1950-82 period]. (p. 23)

[2] Age of currencies [years and months elapsed since original issuance, most recent revaluation, or floating, for 112 currencies], at Dec. 30, 1983. (p. 25)

[3-6] Currency circulation, money supply, government debt, and GNP, per capita [shown (as applicable) in national currency units, free/black market or official rate of U.S. dollar, constant 1940 U.S. dollars, and/or as percent increase in cost of living], at end of 1982. (p. 27-33)

[7] Foreign trade [value of exports and imports] per capita, 1982. (p. 35)

[8] Black market premiums/discounts for the U.S. dollar, based on official rate or effective rate, end of Dec. 1983. (p. 37)

C4721-1.2: Currency Profiles

[Currency profiles are arranged alphabetically by country or area. Most profiles include tables [1-6]. U.S. profile also includes tables [7-8].]

[1] Population, 1979-82.

[2] Ten-year currency record [change in monetary circulation, domestic purchasing power, and free market value; and number of devaluations; selected periods Dec. 1972-Dec. 1983].

[3] Currency in circulation, [1973-82 or most current years available].

[4] Currency circulation per capita [in national units, U.S. dollars at black or free market rate, and/or constant 1940 U.S. dollars; 1979-82 or most current years available].

[5] Official, [effective, and/or other Government approved] exchange rates [for U.S. dollar, 1974-83].

[6] Black or free market rates of U.S. dollars [or local currency] and/or unlicensed/nonbank transfers abroad, [monthly 1974-83].

[7] Purchasing power of the U.S. dollar [in cents per dollar of 1940 value, 1973-82].

[8] U.S. Treasury gold stock [1973-82].

C4721-1.3: Gold Review

[Tables [1-2], [6-7], [11], and [13] show data in U.S. dollars; tables [3-4] and [9-10] show data in metric tons. Tables [5] and [8] show both dollars and tons.]

SUPPLY

[1] Holdings of SDRs [Special Drawing Rights or "paper gold," by country or world area, 1974-82]. (p. 863)

[2] Average London gold price, [monthly 1978-82]. (p. 864)

[3] International gold production [in U.S., South Africa, Canada, and other noncommunist countries, 1973-82]. (p. 864)

[4] World market supply [world gold production, official sales, and disinvestment; and Soviet and satellite country sales; 1981-82]. (p. 865)

[5] [Official gold holdings of selected countries and international agencies, 1981-82.] (p. 865)

[6] Estimated private gold hoards [in France and by world area, 1974-82]. (p. 866)

SALES AND TRADE

[7] Approximate private gold sales in all international markets, [monthly 1973-82]. (p. 868)

[8] British international gold trade, [1970-82]. (p. 871)

[9-10] British gold exports and imports [by country of destination or origin, 1980]. (p. 871-872)

[11] [Gold futures contract prices for 1-year delivery, at 5 trading centers, Dec. 1974-82.] (p. 874)

[12] [British gold coins minted and official sales, 1974-82.] (p. 875)

[13] Percentage premiums of [12] gold coins over their gold content in Zurich, [1980-82]. (p. 876)

[14] IMF and U.S. Treasury Dept gold auctions [amounts and prices, various periods Jan. 1978-May 1980]. (p. 878-879)

C4722
International
Thomson Communications
Inc.

C4722-1   CABLEFILE/85
Annual. Jan. 1985.
1301 p. var. paging.
ISSN 0363-1915.
LC 76-645575.
SRI/MF/excerpts

Annual directory, for 1985, of cable TV system operators, programming services, and equipment distributors. Also presents selected cable industry statistics, including subscription and financial trends, and operating profiles of individual systems. Data are compiled from FCC reports and original research.

Contents:

Section I. Contents listing and foreword. (p. I.3-I.6)

Section II. Directory of cable TV assns; and glossary. (p. II.3-II.18)

Section III. Programming services. Includes directories of basic and pay cable, and other service companies, with satellite and transponder, start-up date, number of subscribers and affiliated stations, programming hours, and subscription price for each company, as of July 1984, with selected trends from 1981; and 1 table showing TV households, homes passed, and basic and pay cable subscribers, 1975-83 and estimated 1984-90. (p. III.3-III.26)

Section IV. Financial data. Includes directory of top 50 companies with cable interests, accompanied by descriptions of cable and communications affiliates or subsidiaries; 1 table showing top 50 companies ranked by total revenues, with net income, cable-related revenues and operating income, total and cable-related assets, and stock prices, 1982-83; and directory of financial analysts specializing in the cable industry. (p. IV.3-IV.26)

Sections V-VI. Catalogs of suppliers, services, and equipment. (p. V.3-V.111, VI.3-VI.62)

Section VII. Multiple system operators (MSOs). Includes 1 tabular list showing top 100 MSOs ranked by subscribers; and directory, including number of operating systems, basic and pay subscribers, and homes passed for most MSOs; as of most recent available month, generally Aug.-Oct. 1984. (p. VII.3-VII.45)

Section VIII. Industry statistics. Includes 5 tables showing top 250 cable systems ranked by number of subscribers, with number of homes passed, as of various months 1982-84; number of systems and subscribers, by subscriber size category, channel capacity, and number of pay services carried, as of Oct. 1984; and systems, number of communities served, basic and pay subscribers, and homes passed, by State and for 4 U.S. territories (no date). (p. VIII.3-VIII.8)

Section IX. System profile. Includes profiles of operating systems arranged alphabetically by community served, by State, each generally including MSO, franchise expiration dates, turn-on date, population, homes passed, miles of cable, channel capacity, earth stations, basic and/or pay rates, programming tiers and services available, and pay and basic subscribers; as of most recent available month, generally Apr.-Sept. 1984. (p. IX.3-IX.836)

Section X. Callbook. Directory of executives of cable and related companies. (p. X.3-X.161)

Previous edition was issued in 2 volumes, and was described in SRI 1984 Annual under C8920-1. Issuing agency has changed from Titsch Communications, Inc. This is the 10th annual directory.

Availability: International Thomson Communications Inc., PO Box 5208-TA, Denver CO 80217-5208, $124.95 (prepaid), $129.95 (if billed); SRI/MF/excerpts for directories containing statistics, and all tables, tabular lists, and profiles.

C4722-2   CABLEVISION
Weekly.
ISSN 0361-8374.
LC 76-642520.
SRI/MF/excerpts, shipped quarterly

Weekly trade journal of the cable TV industry, covering developments in cable systems, programming services, satellites, equipment, and government regulation. Includes subscriber data for individual cable systems and programming services, current to 1-3 months prior to publication. Also includes data on cable franchising and construction activity, and finances.

Data sources include FCC, A. C. Nielsen Co., Arbitron Co., International Communications Research, and the journal's own research.

Issues generally contain several news and feature articles, occasionally statistical; numerous editorial depts, including 1 weekly table showing current stock performance of cable TV operating, service/finance, and manufacturing/distributing companies; and "Cable Stats" feature, with occasional special tables, and the following recurring tables and lists:

a. 6 semimonthly and monthly tables, listed below.

b. Recurring lists, most appearing monthly, showing films carried on cable TV, including film title, distributor, and carrying network; franchising status of core cities in top 50 markets; cable networks listed by transponder number for orbiting satellites; and national advertisers' contract status.

Issues also include an annual statistical feature on cable construction.

Features with substantial statistical content are described, as they appear, under "Statistical Features;" page locations and latest periods of coverage for monthly and semimonthly "Cable Stats" tables are also noted. Nonstatistical features are not covered.

Prior to Nov. 5, 1984 issue, journal was covered in SRI under C8920-2. Issuing agency name has changed from Titsch Communications, Inc.

Availability: CableVision, PO Box 5208-TA, Denver CO 80217-5208, $64.00 per yr., single copy $3.00; SRI/MF/excerpts for "Cable Stats" feature and all portions covered under "Statistical Features;" shipped quarterly.

Issues reviewed during 1985: Nov. 5, 1984-Oct. 28, 1985 (P) (Vol. 10, Nos. 10-54; Vol. 11, Nos. 1-6) [July 22/29, 1985 is a combined issue].

CABLE STATS:

[Tables are included on a space-available basis. Tables [1-2] and [6] are generally current to 1-5 months prior to publication date.]

SEMIMONTHLY TABLES

[1-2] Top MSOs and systems [20-100 multiple system operators and cable systems ranked by number of basic subscribers].

MONTHLY TABLES

[3] Cable industry growth chart [TV households, homes passed by cable, and basic and pay subscribers, 1975-90].

[4] Cable barometer [TV households, homes passed by cable, and basic and pay subscribers, as of Aug. 31, 1984].

[5] Cable services subscriber count [number of affiliates and subscribers, by service, for national satellite and non-satellite fed, and regional entertainment services, by service type; and expected starting dates for announced services; as of most recent available date, with occasional comparisons to previous year].

[6] Franchising calendar [status of franchises, including homes passed, by city for selected States].

STATISTICAL FEATURES:

C4722-2.601: Nov. 5, 1984 (Vol. 10, No. 10)

CABLE STATS

Monthly Table

[5] Cable services subscriber count [most recent available date]. (p. 102)

C4722-2.602: Nov. 12, 1984 (Vol. 10, No. 11)

CABLE STATS

Semimonthly Tables

[1-2] Top 20 MSOs and systems [various months Dec. 1983-Oct. 1984]. (p. 49)

C4722-2.603: Nov. 19, 1984 (Vol. 10, No. 12)

CABLE STATS

Monthly Table

[6] Franchising calendar [primarily for Jan.-Sept. 1984]. (p. 44-45)

Special Tables

[A-B] Percent of systems [and subscribers] by channel capacity, and percent of systems by subscriber size, [as of May 31, 1983-84]. (p. 44)

C4722-2.604: Nov. 26, 1984 (Vol. 10, No. 13)

CABLE STATS

Semimonthly Tables

[1-2] Top 100 MSOs and systems [various months June 1983-Oct. 1984]. (p. 88)

Monthly Tables

[3] Cable industry growth chart [1975-90]. (p. 86)

[4] Cable barometer [as of Aug. 31, 1984]. (p. 86)

C4722-2.605: Dec. 3, 1984 (Vol. 10, No. 14)

CABLE STATS

Monthly Table

[5] Cable services subscriber count [most recent available date]. (p. 52)

DECLINE OF NETWORK DOMINANCE: GENIUS CHALLENGES THE ESTABLISHMENT

(p. 30-39) By Louis Chunovic. Article, with 1 chart and 1 table showing percent of TV households with and without cable watching network TV, 1979/80-1982/83; and audience shares and weekly minutes viewed per household, for cable, superstation, pay, network, independent, and public TV, 2nd quarter and 1st half 1983-84. Data are from A. C. Nielsen Co.

C4722-2.606: Dec. 10, 1984 (Vol. 10, No. 15)

CABLE STATS

Semimonthly Tables

[1-2] Top 20 MSOs and systems [various months Dec. 1983-Oct. 1984]. (p. 154)

C4722-2.607: Dec. 17, 1984 (Vol. 10, No. 16)

CABLE STATS

Monthly Table

[6] Franchising calendar [primarily for Jan.-Nov. 1984]. (p. 52-53)

CABLE, PAY TV LEAD THE PACK IN GROWTH RATE

(p. 36-39) Article, with 1 table showing revenues, operating income, assets, cash flow, profit margin, and other financial ratios, for cable/pay TV industry, also including rank among 10 segments of the communications industry, primarily 1979-83. Data are from Veronis, Suhler and Associates.

C4722-2.608: Dec. 24, 1984 (Vol. 10, No. 17)

CABLE STATS

Semimonthly Tables

[1-2] Top 100 MSOs and systems [various months June 1983-Dec. 1984]. (p. 37)

Monthly Tables

[3] Cable industry growth chart [1975-90]. (p. 36)

[4] Cable barometer [as of Aug. 31, 1984]. (p. 36)

C4722-2.609: Dec. 31, 1984 (Vol. 10, No. 18)

CABLE STATS

Monthly Table

[5] Cable services subscriber count [most recent available date]. (p. 36)

AD SALES & INTERCONNECTS: GETTING THE GRAVY TRAIN ON TRACK

(p. 20-25) By Cecilia Capuzzi. Article on cable TV advertising sales. Data were compiled by Cable Networks Inc.

Includes 3 tables showing sales of spot TV advertising, for national and local TV, cable TV, and among the top 50 TV markets; and cable subscribers and household penetration, and market share of aggregate top 15 multiple system operators, for top 20 TV markets; various years 1975-84.

C4722-2.610: Jan. 7, 1985 (Vol. 10, No. 19)

CABLE STATS

Semimonthly Tables

[1-2] Top 20 MSOs and systems [various months Dec. 1983-Nov. 1984]. (p. 37)

COMPANIES PLAN REDUCTIONS IN TRADE SHOW ATTENDANCE

(p. 9, 20-21) Article, with 1 table showing attendance and number of exhibitors, for 7 major cable TV industry conventions, 1983-84.

PRUDENTIAL-BACHE ANALYST: CABLE INDUSTRY WILL ENJOY MODERATE GROWTH

(p. 11) Article, with 3 tables showing market share, subscriber rate, and revenue, for the 4 major pay TV networks, 1984-86. Data are from Prudential-Bache Securities Inc.

C4722-2.611: Jan. 14, 1985 (Vol. 10, No. 20)

CABLE STATS

Monthly Table

[6] Franchising calendar [primarily for Apr.-Dec. 1984]. (p. 44-45)

C4722-2.612: Jan. 21, 1985 (Vol. 10, No. 21)

CABLE STATS

Semimonthly Tables

[1-2] Top 100 MSOs and systems [various months June 1983-Jan. 1985]. (p. 45)

Monthly Tables

[3] Cable industry growth chart [1975-90]. (p. 44)

[4] Cable barometer [as of Aug. 31, 1984]. (p. 44)

C4722–2.613: Jan. 28, 1985 (Vol. 10, No. 22)

CABLE STATS

Monthly Table

[5] Cable services subscriber count [most recent available date]. (p. 62)

C4722–2.614: Feb. 4, 1985 (Vol. 10, No. 23)

CABLE STATS

Semimonthly Tables

[1-2] Top 20 MSOs and systems [various months Dec. 1983-Jan. 1985]. (p. 49)

C4722–2.615: Feb. 11, 1985 (Vol. 10, No. 24)

CABLE STATS

Monthly Table

[6] Franchising calendar [primarily for Feb. 1984-Jan. 1985]. (p. 48-49)

C4722–2.616: Feb. 18, 1985 (Vol. 10, No. 25)

CABLE STATS

Semimonthly Tables

[1-2] Top 100 MSOs and systems [various months Apr. 1984-Feb. 1985]. (p. 49)

Monthly Tables

[3] Cable industry growth chart [1975-90]. (p. 48)

[4] Cable barometer [as of Aug. 31, 1984]. (p. 48)

CABLE BROKERS' REPORT: '84 SYSTEM SALES PACE CONTINUING IN '85

(p. 28-32) By Victoria Gits. Article on cable system sales and market outlook, as reported by industry brokerage firms.

Includes 8 tables showing number and value of cable system sales, and value of cable debt/equity placement, 1983-84; and cable system location, buyer, seller, subscribers, and homes passed, for each sales transaction handled in 1984; all for 7-8 major brokerage firms.

Additional data appear in the Mar. 4, 1985 issue (see C4722-2.618 below).

C4722–2.617: Feb. 25, 1985 (Vol. 10, No. 26)

CABLE STATS

Monthly Table

[5] Cable services subscriber count [most recent available date]. (p. 44)

NOTICE FOR PROPOSED RULEMAKING SLATED FOR EEO PROVISIONS

(p. 17) Article, with 1 table showing cable TV industry full-time employment, by race and sex, 1983-84. Data are from FCC.

'84 CABLE RATINGS REPORT, RECURRING FEATURE

(p. 18) Recurring article, with 1 table showing the following for 10 cable TV networks: audience rating and share, and number of households viewing, 4th quarter and full year 1984. Data are from A. C. Nielsen Co.

C4722–2.618: Mar. 4, 1985 (Vol. 10, No. 27)

CABLE STATS

Semimonthly Tables

[1-2] Top 20 MSOs and systems [various months Oct. 1984-Feb. 1985]. (p. 65)

CORRECTION

(p. 22) Includes additional data for feature on cable system sales reported by brokerage firms, appearing in Feb. 18, 1985 issue.

For description of original feature, see C4722-2.616 above.

SLOW BUT STEADY: THE NEW ERA IN CATV CONSTRUCTION, ANNUAL FEATURE

(p. 30-43) Annual article, by Fred Dawson and Cecilia Capuzzi, on cable TV construction activity and expenditures. Data are based on a *CableVision* survey of cable system operators and manufacturers. Includes 1 table showing new and replacement aerial and underground plant construction miles, and new and replacement costs by type of equipment or function, 1984-85.

This is the 10th annual survey.

C4722–2.619: Mar. 11, 1985 (Vol. 10, No. 28)

CABLE STATS

Monthly Table

[6] Franchising calendar [primarily for Feb. 1984-May 1985]. (p. 48-49)

C4722–2.620: Mar. 18, 1985 (Vol. 10, No. 29)

CABLE STATS

Semimonthly Tables

[1-2] Top 100 MSOs and systems [various months Apr. 1984-Mar. 1985]. (p. 45)

Monthly Tables

[3] Cable industry growth chart [1975-90]. (p. 44)

[4] Cable barometer [as of Aug. 31, 1984]. (p. 44)

C4722–2.621: Mar. 25, 1985 (Vol. 10, No. 30)

CABLE STATS

Monthly Table

[5] Cable services subscriber count [most recent available date]. (p. 56)

NIELSEN ESTIMATES 44.6 PERCENT PENETRATION

(p. 12) Article, with 1 table showing top 25 designated market areas ranked by number of cable TV households, Feb. 1985. Data are from A. C. Nielsen Co.

C4722–2.622: Apr. 1, 1985 (Vol. 10, No. 31)

CABLE STATS

Semimonthly Tables

[1-2] Top 20 MSOs and systems [various months Oct. 1984-Feb. 1985]. (p. 57)

C4722–2.623: Apr. 8, 1985 (Vol. 10, No. 32)

CABLE STATS

Monthly Table

[6] Franchising calendar [primarily for Feb. 1984-May 1985]. (p. 48-49)

C4722–2.624: Apr. 15, 1985 (Vol. 10, No. 33)

CABLE STATS

Semimonthly Tables

[1-2] Top 100 MSOs and systems [various months Apr. 1984-Apr. 1985]. (p. 57)

Monthly Tables

[3] Cable industry growth chart [1975-90]. (p. 56)

[4] Cable barometer [as of Aug. 31, 1984]. (p. 56)

LIFETIME GAINS NIELSEN SLOT, NICK SETS RECORD, RECURRING FEATURE

(p. 25) Recurring article, with 2 tables showing the following for 10 basic cable TV networks: audience rating and share, and number of households receiving, Feb.-Mar. 1985. Data are from A. C. Nielsen Co.

C4722–2.625: Apr. 22, 1985 (Vol. 10, No. 34)

CABLE STATS

Monthly Table

[5] Cable services subscriber count [most recent available date]. (p. 48)

C4722–2.626: Apr. 29, 1985 (Vol. 10, No. 35)

CABLE STATS

Semimonthly Tables

[1-2] Top 20 MSOs and systems [various months Oct. 1984-Feb. 1985]. (p. 57)

FRUSTRATION IN CANADA: SOCIAL ENGINEERING vs. MARKETPLACE IMPERATIVES

(p. 32-44) By Simon Applebaum. Article, with 2 tables showing the following for Canada: cable TV subscribers by network, including selected networks originating in U.S., as of Feb. 28, 1985; and total TV households, and cable TV operating systems, homes passed, subscribers, plant miles, and operating revenues, selected years 1978-84.

Data are from Mediastats Toronto Inc., Statistics Canada, and Canadian Cable TV Assn.

C4722–2.627: May 6, 1985 (Vol. 10, No. 36)

CABLE STATS

Monthly Table

[6] Franchising calendar [primarily for Feb. 1984-May 1985]. (p. 48-49)

C4722–2.628: May 13, 1985 (Vol. 10, No. 37)

CABLE STATS

Semimonthly Tables

[1-2] Top 100 MSOs and systems [various months Apr. 1984-Apr. 1985]. (p. 49)

Corrected data appear in May 20, 1985 issue (see C4722-2.629 below).

Monthly Tables

[3] Cable industry growth chart [1975-90]. (p. 48)

[4] Cable barometer [as of Aug. 31, 1984]. (p. 48)

C4722–2.629: May 20, 1985 (Vol. 10, No. 38)

CABLE STATS

Monthly Table

[5] Cable services subscriber count [most recent available date]. (p. 72)

CORRECTIONS

(p. 17) Includes corrected data for semimonthly tables on top 100 MSOs and systems.
For original tables, see C4722-2.628 above.

C4722–2.630: May 27, 1985 (Vol. 10, No. 39)

CABLE STATS

Semimonthly Tables

[1-2] Top 20 MSOs and systems [various months Dec. 1984-Apr. 1985]. (p. 45)

NETWORK TV VIEWING DOWN 6.8 Pct.

(p. 20) Article, with 1 table showing audience shares and weekly minutes viewed per cable TV household, for satellite network, superstation, advertising-supported cable, pay, network, independent, and public TV, 1st quarter 1983-85. Data are from A. C. Nielsen Co.

C4722–2.631: June 3, 1985 (Vol. 10, No. 40)

CABLE STATS

Semimonthly Tables

[1-2] Top 100 MSOs and systems [various months Apr. 1984-Apr. 1985]. (p. 149)

Monthly Table

[5] Cable services subscriber count [most recent available date]. (p. 148)

DESTINY OF PAY TV

(p. 78-80, 90) By Victoria Gits. Article, with 1 table showing audience shares and weekly minutes viewed per cable TV household, for satellite network, superstation, advertising-supported cable, pay, network, independent, and public TV, 1st quarter 1983-85. Data are from A. C. Nielsen Co.

C4722–2.632: June 10, 1985 (Vol. 10, No. 41)

CABLE STATS

Monthly Table

[6] Franchising calendar [primarily for Feb. 1984-June 1985]. (p. 56-57)

C4722–2.633: June 17, 1985 (Vol. 10, No. 42)

CABLE STATS

Semimonthly Tables

[1-2] Top 100 MSOs and systems [various months Apr. 1984-Apr. 1985]. (p. 49)

Monthly Tables

[3] Cable industry growth chart [1975-90]. (p. 48)

[4] Cable barometer [as of Aug. 31, 1984]. (p. 48)

C4722–2.634: June 24, 1985 (Vol. 10, No. 43)

CABLE STATS

Monthly Table

[5] Cable services subscriber count [most recent available date]. (p. 48)

C4722–2.635: July 1, 1985 (Vol. 10, No. 44)

CABLE STATS

Semimonthly Tables

[1-2] Top 20 MSOs and systems [various months Dec. 1984-May 1985]. (p. 49)

C4722–2.636: July 8, 1985 (Vol. 10, No. 45)

CABLE STATS

Monthly Table

[6] Franchising calendar [primarily for Feb. 1984-Apr. 1985]. (p. 48-49)

C4722–2.637: July 15, 1985 (Vol. 10, No. 46)

CABLE STATS

Semimonthly Tables

[1-2] Top 100 MSOs and systems [various months Apr. 1984-June 1985]. (p. 41)

Monthly Tables

[3] Cable industry growth chart [1975-90]. (p. 40)

[4] Cable barometer [as of Aug. 31, 1984]. (p. 40)

C4722–2.638: July 22/29, 1985 (Vol. 10, No. 47)

CABLE STATS

Monthly Table

[5] Cable services subscriber count [most recent available date]. (p. 100)

C4722–2.639: Aug. 5, 1985 (Vol. 10, No. 48)

CABLE STATS

Semimonthly Tables

[1-2] Top 20 MSOs and systems [various months Dec. 1984-July 1985]. (p. 49)

WTBS, USA MAINTAIN LEADS ON NIELSEN LIST, RECURRING FEATURE

(p. 28) Recurring article, with 2 tables showing the following for 8-11 basic cable TV networks: audience rating and share, and number of households receiving, Feb. and May 1985. Data are from A. C. Nielsen Co.

C4722–2.640: Aug. 12, 1985 (Vol. 10, No. 49)

CABLE STATS

Semimonthly Tables

[1-2] Top 100 MSOs and systems [various months Apr. 1984-July 1985]. (p. 49)

Monthly Tables

[3] Cable industry growth chart [1975-90]. (p. 48)

[4] Cable barometer [as of Aug. 31, 1984]. (p. 48)

C4722–2.641: Aug. 19, 1985 (Vol. 10, No. 50)

CABLE STATS

Monthly Table

[6] Franchising calendar [primarily for Feb. 1984-Aug. 1985]. (p. 40-41)

VIEWERSHIP OF AD-SUPPORTED CABLE SURGING, SURVEY SAYS

(p. 22) Article, with 2 tables showing TV audience shares among total, cable, and pay cable TV households, for the following services: advertising-supported basic cable and superstations, and pay, network, independent, and public TV, for 6-month period ended Mar. 1984-85. Data are from A. C. Nielsen Co. and Cabletelevision Advertising Bureau.

C4722–2.642: Aug. 26, 1985 (Vol. 10, No. 51)

CABLE STATS

Semimonthly Tables

[1-2] Top 100 MSOs and systems [various months Apr. 1984-July 1985]. (p. 57)

Monthly Tables

[3] Cable industry growth chart [1975-90]. (p. 56)

[4] Cable barometer [as of Aug. 31, 1984]. (p. 56)

C4722–2.643: Sept. 2, 1985 (Vol. 10, No. 52)

CABLE STATS

Semimonthly Tables

[1-2] Top 20 MSOs and systems [various months Dec. 1984-July 1985]. (p. 49)

C4722–2.644: Sept. 9, 1985 (Vol. 10, No. 53)

CABLE STATS

Monthly Table

[5] Cable services subscriber count [most recent available date]. (p. 40)

C4722–2.645: Sept. 16, 1985 (Vol. 10, No. 54)

CABLE STATS

Semimonthly Tables

[1-2] Top 100 MSOs and systems [various months Apr. 1984-Aug. 1985]. (p. 65)

Monthly Tables

[3] Cable industry growth chart [1975-90]. (p. 64)

[4] Cable barometer [as of Aug. 31, 1984]. (p. 64)

C4722–2.646: Sept. 23, 1985 (Vol. 11, No. 1)

CABLE STATS

Monthly Table

[6] Franchising calendar [primarily for Feb. 1984-Sept. 1985]. (p. 56-57)

C4722–2.647: Sept. 30, 1985 (Vol. 11, No. 2)

NIELSEN FIGURES REVEAL SWITCH-ON OPPORTUNITIES

(p. 11) Article, with 2 undated tables showing percent of cable system subscribers and signal-processing facilities (headends) receiving more than 1 station affiliated with each of the 3 major networks, and more than 1 independent and educational station, all by system channel capacity. Data are from A. C. Nielsen Co.

C4722–2.648: Oct. 7, 1985 (Vol. 11, No. 3)

CABLE STATS

Monthly Table

[5] Cable services subscriber count [most recent available date]. (p. 40)

C4722–2.649: Oct. 14, 1985 (Vol. 11, No. 4)

CABLE STATS

Semimonthly Tables

[1-2] Top 100 MSOs and systems [various months Apr. 1984-Oct. 1985]. (p. 57)

Monthly Tables

[3] Cable industry growth chart [1975-90]. (p. 56)

[4] Cable barometer [as of Aug. 31, 1984]. (p. 56)

SYSTEM VALUES MAY WAVER, PANELISTS SAY

(p. 44) Article, with 1 chart showing sales of cable TV systems, and system market values as measured by cash flow multiples, 1977-84. Data are from Paul Kagan Associates, Inc.

C4722–2.650: Oct. 21, 1985 (Vol. 11, No. 5)

CABLE STATS

Monthly Table

[6] Franchising calendar [primarily for Feb. 1984-Oct. 1985]. (p. 40-41)

C4725
Intertec Publishing Corp.

**C4725–1   IMPLEMENT AND
TRACTOR**
Monthly.
ISSN 0019-2953.
LC 46-31380.
SRI/MF/excerpts, shipped
quarterly

Monthly trade journal (semimonthly in Jan. and Mar.) reporting trends and developments in the farm and industrial equipment industry, covering retail and wholesale management and operations, engineering and product information, foreign trade, and news of meetings, expositions, and other industry events.

The 2nd Jan. issue is a nonstatistical directory of dealers, product brand names, equipment distributors, and exporters/importers, with subject index to articles published in the previous year; the 2nd Mar. issue (Red Book) presents equipment specifications and performance data.

Data are from the Farm and Industrial Equipment Institute (FIEI), Food and Agriculture Organization, dealer reports, original surveys, and Commerce Dept.

General format:

a. Editor's introduction, occasionally with text statistics on production, sales, or exports.

b. Articles, usually focusing on aspects of tractor or large equipment distribution operations, frequently with statistics, including an annual market statistics report in the Nov. issue.

c. "Manufacturers Edition" section, with articles and features aimed at manufacturers of farm, construction, and lawn/garden equipment, occasionally including statistics; section is separately paginated and only included in industry subscriptions.

d. 2 monthly tables, listed below, on farm equipment auction prices and retail sales.

Monthly tables appear in most issues. All additional features with substantial statistical content are described, as they appear, under "Statistical Features." Nonstatistical features are not covered.

Availability: Implement and Tractor, Circulation Department, PO Box 12901, Overland Park KS 66212-0930, qualified subscribers $10.00 per yr., others $34.00 per yr., single copy $2.00, Annual Statistical Number $4.00, Product File and Red Book issues $5.00; SRI/MF/excerpts for monthly tables and all portions covered under "Statistical Features;" shipped quarterly.

Issues reviewed during 1985: Nov. 1984-Oct. 1985 (P) (Vol. 99, Nos. 13-14; Vol. 100, Nos. 1-12).

MONTHLY TABLES:

[1] Unit retail sales [text table showing summary totals for farm 2- and 4-wheel-drive tractors by horsepower, combines, balers, forage harvesters, and mower conditioners, for month 2 months prior to cover date, year to date, and same periods of previous year; table occasionally includes data for Canada].

[2] Auction prices of used equipment [showing farm equipment manufacturer, model, and condition, and prices paid, at national wholesale auctions of selected dealers conducted during month 2-3 months prior to cover date].

STATISTICAL FEATURES:

C4725–1.601: Nov. 1984 (Vol. 99, No. 13)

47th MARKET STATISTICS ISSUE, ANNUAL FEATURE

(p. 22-47) Annual compilation of farm equipment market statistics. Most data are from Farm and Industrial Equipment Institute and dealer reports, or from Commerce Dept and Census of Agriculture reports. Includes 9 tables, as follows:

a. Motor vehicles and specified machines on farms; wheel tractors' wholesale prices; and principal machines on farms, by State and region; various years 1951-84. 2 tables. (p. 24-36)

b. Retail sales volume for farm wheel tractors by horsepower, 1980-83, and for self-propelled combines and 7 other types of equipment, 1982-83, all by State and for Federal Government purchases and miscellaneous. 2 tables. (p. 38-40)

c. Farm equipment import and export quantity and/or value, by country of origin or destination and by product type, with detail for wheel tractor imports, various periods 1979-1st half 1984. 5 tables. (p. 42-47)

Shipment data usually included in annual compilation appear in Dec. 1984 issue; for description, see C4725-1.602, below.

MEASURING THREE INDUSTRIES: MATERIALS CONSUMED IN 1982 AND 1977

(p. ME2-ME8) Article, with 3 tables showing quantity and value of materials, parts, containers, and supplies consumed in the farm equipment, lawn/garden equipment, and construction machinery industries, by item, 1977 and 1982. Data are from the Census of Manufactures.

C4725–1.602: Dec. 1984 (Vol. 99, No. 14)

FARM EQUIPMENT SHIPMENTS, ANNUAL FEATURE

(p. 18-22) Three annual tables showing shipment value for wheel tractors, farm machinery, and garden equipment, including attachments and parts; and unit shipments of farm machines and equipment; all by type of unit, 1979-83. Data are from Census Bureau.

Tables usually are included in the annual market statistics issue (see C4725-1.601, above).

ITALIAN EQUIPMENT ON THE U.S. MARKET: A GROWING PRESENCE

(p. I4-I6) Article, with 1 table showing tractor imports from Italy, 1980-1st half 1984. Includes import volume and value, with detail for wheel tractor volume by horsepower. Data are from Commerce Dept.

C4725–1.603: Jan. 1985 (Vol. 100, No. 1)

CAN PARTS PRODUCE PROFIT?

By Scott Nesbitt. Article, with 1 table comparing parts distribution costs and sales, average number of plants/warehouses, and percent of delivery costs paid by customers, for manufacturers of farm equipment, industrial parts, and transportation equipment, 1984. Data are from a 1984 survey by Herbert W. Davis and Co.

C4725–1.604: Feb. 1985 (Vol. 100, No. 3)

FORECASTERS' VIEW OF 1985: NOT MUCH CHANGE, SEMIANNUAL FEATURE

(p. 14-16) Semiannual article, by Bill Fogarty, forecasting farm equipment retail sales through 1986. Forecast is based on a Farm and Industrial Equipment Institute survey conducted in Dec. 1984.

Includes 2 tables showing actual and/or forecast unit retail sales or percent change in sales, by equipment type, various periods 1983-86.

SURVEY FINDS IH/CASE MERGER IS WELCOMED

(p. 26, 44) By Scott Nesbitt. Article, with 1 table showing farm equipment dealers' and others' expectations regarding business impact of proposed merger between International Harvester and J. I. Case. Data are from 316 responses to a Dec. 1984 *Implement and Tractor* reader survey, and are shown for dealers by equipment brand, and for repair shop operators, manufacturers, sales representatives, and farmers.

DEALERS SEE BETTER YEAR IN 1985

(p. 34-35) Article, with 1 table showing farm equipment dealers' business expectations for 1985, including sales trends for specific depts and equipment categories. Data are from 66 responses to a Nov.-Dec.1984 survey by *Implement and Tractor.*

C4725-1.605: Mar. 31, 1985 (Vol. 100, No. 5)

NEBRASKA TRACTOR TESTS, ANNUAL FEATURE

(p. 86-143) Annual report on results of tractor performance tests conducted 1984, under University of Nebraska direction, to verify advertising claims of new tractors offered for sale. Tests show power take-off and drawbar performance, fuel consumption, and sound level, by manufacturer and model, under specified test conditions.

Contains contents listing (p. 86); explanation of test law and conditions (p. 87); results of approximately 30 tests, 1984 (p. 88-134); and summary of 1974-84 tests, by tractor manufacturer and model (p. 136-143).

Report is included in 69th annual *Implement & Tractor Red Book Issue,* which presents detailed specifications for agricultural tractors and equipment, hydraulic components, and ground loading transport equipment.

C4725-1.606: Apr. 1985 (Vol. 100, No. 6)

1984 RETAIL SALES OF FARM WHEEL TRACTORS BY PTO HORSEPOWER, ANNUAL FEATURE

(p. 12-13) Annual table showing unit sales of 2- and 4-wheel drive farm tractors by horsepower, by State and to the Federal Government, 1984. Data are from Farm and Industrial Equipment Institute (FIEI).

RETAIL SALES OF SELECTED FARM EQUIPMENT, ANNUAL FEATURE

(p. 26) Annual table showing unit sales of combines, corn heads, hay balers, windrowers, grinder-mixers, forage harvesters, and mower conditioners, by State and to the Federal Government, 1983-84. Data are from FIEI.

C4725-1.607: May 1985 (Vol. 100, No. 7)

PARTS RETAILING: WHO'S GETTING THE BUSINESS?

(p. 10-14) By Richard A. Edwards. Article, with 1 undated table on farmers' outlet preferences for purchases of tractor/implement parts and supplies, based on a Texas Agricultural Extension Service survey of 1,400 Texas farmers. Table includes type of outlet preferred and reason for preference, by type of item.

C4725-1.608: June 1985 (Vol. 100, No. 8)

SHORT-LEASH BENEFIT, SPENDING THE AD BUCKS

(p. 16-17) By Scott Nesbitt. Article, with 2 tables showing farm equipment dealers' views on when a customer account is considered past due, and distribution of advertising expenditures by dealership dept. Data are from responses of 55-60 dealers to Jan.-Feb. 1985 surveys conducted by *Implement and Tractor.*

UPDATING THE SALES FORECAST: SLOWER 1985, BETTER 1986, SEMIANNUAL FEATURE

(p. 18-20) Semiannual article, by Bill Fogarty, forecasting farm equipment retail sales through 1986. Forecast is based on a Farm and Industrial Equipment Institute survey conducted in May 1985.

Includes 2 tables showing actual and/or forecast unit retail sales or percent change in sales, by equipment type, 1984-86 or 1985-86.

FARM EQUIPMENT IMPORTS, EXPORTS: SCANNING 1984 PERFORMANCE

(p. 22-23) By Bill Fogarty. Article on U.S. farm equipment export and import values, by leading country of destination and origin, 1984, with summary trends from 1979. Data are from Commerce Dept. Includes text statistics and 1 table.

C4725-1.609: Aug. 1985 (Vol. 100, No. 10)

WHERE THE TRAINING DOLLARS GO

(p. 26) Article on farm equipment dealership employee training emphasis and cost. Data are from responses of 25 dealers to a May 1985 survey conducted by *Implement and Tractor.*

Includes 4 tables showing the following for general and service managers, and sales, service, and parts dept personnel: annual training costs and man-days per employee, and percent of employees receiving training on product features and in sales or technical skills.

C4725-1.610: Sept. 1985 (Vol. 100, No. 11)

SERVICE DEPT LOSSES GOT WORSE IN 1984

(p. 18-21) By Richard A. Edwards. Article, with 1 table showing farm equipment dealership service dept average gross margin, overhead expenses, and net losses, 1976-84. Data are from National Farm and Power Equipment Dealers Assn *Cost of Doing Business Study,* covered in SRI under A7800-1.

C4725-1.611: Oct. 1985 (Vol. 100, No. 12)

PARTS MANAGER WAGES REVEALED

(p. 14-15, 27) Article, with 1 table showing average base wage and incentive compensation, for parts dept managers at farm equipment dealerships, by parts sales size, 1985. Data are from responses of 40 dealers to a July 1985 survey conducted by *Implement and Tractor.*

C4725-2   LAWN AND GARDEN MARKETING

10 issues per year.
ISSN 0091-4665.
LC 73-643478.
SRI/MF/excerpts, shipped quarterly

Periodical, published 10 times per year, reporting on trends and activities in the lawn and garden industry.

Periodical is primarily narrative, but also includes a quarterly statistical report on product seasonal movements, annual market data articles, and other statistical features. An annual index of articles appears in the Nov./Dec. issue.

Features with substantial statistical content are described, as they appear, under "Statistical Features." Each issue of the journal is reviewed, but an abstract is published in SRI monthly issues only when statistical features appear.

Availability: Lawn and Garden Marketing, Circulation Department, PO Box 12901, Overland Park KS 66212-0930, qualified subscribers †, others $24.00 per yr., single copy $2.00, back issues $3.00, plus postage and handling; SRI/MF/excerpts for portions described under "Statistical Features;" shipped quarterly.

Issues reviewed during 1985: Nov./Dec. 1984-Oct. 1985 (P) (Vol. 23, No. 10; Vol. 24, Nos. 1-9).

STATISTICAL FEATURES:

C4725-2.601: Nov./Dec. 1984 (Vol. 23, No. 10)

NEW GALLUP DATA: CONSUMERS BUY 21 PERCENT MORE IN '84

(p. 4-6) Article, with 3 tables and 1 chart showing retail sales of lawn/garden products, by category, 1983-84; and percent of households participating in gardening, by detailed type of activity, 1981-84, with summary data by region for 1984. Data are from a Gallup Organization survey conducted for Gardens for All.

PRODUCT MOVEMENT REPORT, SUMMER 1984, QUARTERLY FEATURE

(p. 14) Quarterly article on lawn and garden product seasonal retail sales. Data are from a *Lawn and Garden Marketing* survey of retailers.

Includes 1 table showing percent of retailers reporting increased, steady, and decreased sales, by product type and census region; and walk-behind mower median inventory; summer 1984.

EQUIPMENT SHIPMENTS AT $2.38 BILLION

(p. 16-18) Article, with 1 table showing volume and value of lawn and garden equipment shipments, by detailed item, 1977 and 1982. Data are from the Census of Manufactures.

RETAILERS SEE BIG '85 INCREASE

(p. 24, 41) Article, with 1 chart and text data showing 1985 sales outlook for lawn/garden products, by type of retail outlet and for distributors. Data are from a *Lawn and Garden Marketing* survey.

C4725-2.602: Jan. 1985 (Vol. 24, No. 1)

MANUFACTURERS' SHIPMENTS UP 12.8 PERCENT, ANNUAL FEATURE

(p. 34) Annual article on lawn and garden power equipment industry shipments, 1983-84. Data are from Outdoor Power Equipment Institute. Includes 1 table showing shipment volume and value for walk-behind power mowers, lawn tractors/riding mowers, riding garden tractors, and rotary tillers, 1983-84.

CHEMICALS, FERTILIZERS: $1.5 BILLION MARKET

(p. 36) Article, with 1 chart and 1 table showing lawn/garden/houseplant chemical retail sales, by type, 1984 and 1989; and aggregate sales distribution by type of outlet, 1984. Data are based on a recent survey by C. H. Kline and Co.

CORRECTION

(p. 40) Corrections for data on household gardening activity appearing in Nov./Dec. 1984 issue.

For article description, see C4725-2.601, above.

C4725-2.603: Feb. 1985 (Vol. 24, No. 2)

PRODUCT MOVEMENT REPORT, FALL 1984, QUARTERLY FEATURE

(p. 30) Quarterly article on lawn and garden product seasonal retail sales. Data are from a *Lawn and Garden Marketing* survey of retailers.

Includes 1 table showing percent of retailers reporting increased, steady, and decreased sales, by product type and census region; and chain saw median inventory; fall 1984.

C4725–2.604: Mar. 1985 (Vol. 24, No. 3)

TARGET MARKETING IS THE GAME

(p. 6-12) By Scott R. Nesbitt. Article, with 1 table showing shipments of ride-on lawn mowers (rear engine), lawn tractors (front engine), and garden tractors, 1973-85. Data are from Outdoor Power Equipment Institute.

CHEMICAL DEBATES YIELD NEW CROP OF PRODUCTS

(p. 14-24) By Steve Trusty. Article, with 1 table showing percent of consumers using selected types of products for lawn/garden pest control, 1982-84. Data are from a Gardens for All/Gallup Organization survey.

NEW HYPE FOR SUMMER GARDENING?

(p. 30) Article on retail marketing of bedding plants, with 1 table showing average price increase per flat and per pack, 1982-84. Data are from Bedding Plants Inc. annual surveys.

C4725–2.605: Apr./May 1985 (Vol. 24, No. 4)

PRODUCT MOVEMENT REPORT, WINTER 1984-85, QUARTERLY FEATURE

(p. 6) Quarterly article on lawn and garden product seasonal retail sales. Data are from a *Lawn and Garden Marketing* survey of retailers.

Includes 1 table showing percent of retailers reporting increased, steady, and decreased sales, by product type and census region; winter 1984/85.

FALL'S BEST SELLERS

(p. 8-12, 43) Compilation of 2 articles, with 2 charts and 3 tables showing percent of retailers carrying various lawn and garden products, and reporting increased or decreased sales of selected items; all by type of retail outlet (multi-dept, garden center, and hardware/homecenter), fall 1984. Data are from a *Lawn and Garden Marketing* survey of retailers.

PANEL OF GARDENERS REPORT PURCHASES

(p. 20-22) Article, with 1 table showing percent of households participating in various gardening activities, fall 1982-84. Data are from 427 responses to a *Better Homes and Gardens* survey.

HOW HOME CENTERS RANK LAWN AND GARDEN

(p. 59) Article, with 1 chart showing the following for home center stores: lawn/garden dept share of net sales, sales area, inventory, and cost of goods sold, 1984. Data are based on 163 responses to a National Retail Hardware Assn (NRHA) survey of home center dealers. Full NRHA survey report, *The Bottom Line,* is covered in SRI under A8275-1.2.

C4725–2.606: June 1985 (Vol. 24, No. 5)

WINTER SALES REPORT

(p. 14-16) Article, with 1 chart and 1 table showing percent of lawn/garden retailers carrying arts/crafts products, and percent reporting increased or decreased snowthrower and replacement part sales, by type of outlet, winter 1984/85. Data are from a *Lawn and Gar-*

den Marketing survey of multi-dept stores, garden centers, hardware/home centers, and power equipment dealers.

C4725–2.607: Aug. 1985 (Vol. 24, No. 7)

OPE SHIPMENTS TO PASS 5 YEAR RECORD, ANNUAL FEATURE

(p. 16-24) Annual article, for 1985, presenting the Outdoor Power Equipment Institute forecast of lawn and garden equipment shipments. Data are based on a survey of 23 manufacturers conducted by Bolens Corp.

Includes 3 charts showing shipments of commercial turf care mowers (walk-behind rotary, and riding rotary turf and reel); and total industry shipments of tractors (rear-engine riding, front-engine lawn, and garden) and walk-behind tillers, snowthrowers, and rotary mowers; various years ending Aug. 31, 1981-90.

PRODUCT MOVEMENT REPORT, SPRING 1985, QUARTERLY FEATURE

(p. 76) Quarterly article on lawn and garden product seasonal retail sales. Data are from a *Lawn and Garden Marketing* survey of retailers.

Includes 1 table showing percent of retailers reporting increased, steady, and decreased sales, by product type and census region, spring 1985.

C4725–2.608: Sept. 1985 (Vol. 24, No. 8)

PLANNING '86 MERCHANDISING STRATEGIES

(p. 8-26, 81, 83) Article on merchandising and advertising plans of lawn and garden equipment dealers. Data are from a spring 1985 *Lawn and Garden Marketing* survey.

Includes 2 charts and 6 tables showing advertising plans for 1986 compared to 1985 (more, less, or same overall, and use of cooperative advertising); advertising spending (amount and as percent of sales), 1985; plans for advertising of specific types of products in 1986; lawn/garden display space, 1985-86; and personnel training plans for 1986; by type of outlet (multi-dept, garden center, hardware/home, and power equipment).

C4740
Irving-Cloud Publishing Co.

C4740–1   **JOBBER TOPICS: Fifty-first Anniversary Marketing Directory Issue**
Monthly (selected issue).
July 1985.
(p. 62-67, 95, 1S-50S).
Vol. 128, No. 6.
SRI/MF/excerpts

Annual marketing directory issue, for 1985, presenting automotive parts wholesale industry directories and statistics, including data on wholesaler financial performance, motor vehicle production and registrations, and related topics. Data are compiled from numerous trade assns and other sources, identified for each table.

Issue includes the following annual statistical features:

a. "'How's Business' Query Brings Mixed Signals From Jobber Panel." By Bill Ellis. Sur-

vey article on jobber business conditions during 1st quarter 1985. Includes 6 tables showing survey response on trends in unit and dollar sales, cash position, and collections; retail trade group most responsible for improved sales; and general economic trends; all by region, 1st quarter 1985 vs. 1st quarter 1984. (p. 62-67, 95)

b. "Automotive Statistics" section, with index, and 7 charts and 61 tables, listed below. (p. 1S-50S)

Jobber Topics is a monthly magazine, generally narrative in content, but also including monthly survey statistics on jobber business conditions, and Dept of Commerce data on automotive equipment wholesaler sales and inventories. Monthly issues also include occasional original survey articles. The 2 annual features noted above are the only features covered in SRI.

The annual marketing directory issue also includes directories of trade assns, warehouse distributors, parts remanufacturers, manufacturers' agents, jobbers, and parts manufacturers; and a buyer's guide.

Availability: Jobber Topics, 7300 N. Cicero Ave., Chicago IL 60646, $20.00 per yr., single copy $2.50, directory $35.00; SRI/MF/excerpts for business conditions survey article and "Automotive Statistics" section.

AUTOMOTIVE STATISTICS SECTION:
[Unless otherwise noted, data are for U.S., 1983.]

C4740–1.1: Wholesaler Market, Financial, and Operating Data

[1] Automotive wholesalers among largest in 1984 [branches, sales personnel, and shops, of top 42 companies listed alphabetically]. (p. 4S)

[2] Scope of the automotive service industry: in brief [automotive service establishments, including motor vehicle and parts manufacturers, service and repair firms, new and used car dealers, fleets, farm/garden equipment wholesalers, and trade assns; and automotive parts/supplies wholesale and retail sales; various years 1977-84]. (p. 5S)

[3] Total parts and service market [revenues, by retail outlet type], 1979-84. (p. 5S)

[4] State by State look at the wholesaler's market [vehicle registrations and dealers, wholesale outlets, service stations, and repair shops; selected years 1982-84]. (p. 6S-7S)

[5-8] ASIA [Automotive Service Industry Assn median] wholesaler: costs, income, and profit as percentage of sales; quick profile [of sales and productivity]; how his profits scored [as percent of sales, assests, net worth, and net working capital]; and balance sheet [percentages]. (p. 8S-10S)

[9] Leading [26] merchandise items as reported by ASIA wholesalers. (p. 11S)

[10] Employee pay [by position] as percent of sales, based on median ASIA jobber. (p. 11S)

[11] ASIA Jobber's operating costs as percent of gross margin. (p. 12S)

[12] Leading [23] product groupings as reported by ASIA wholesalers. (p. 12S)

[13] PBE [Paint, body, and equipment] wholesalers' cost of doing business [net sales and operating expenses shown as percent of total sales, by item; and median sales, inventory turnover, and employees] as reported by ASIA. (p. 13S)

[14] Expense item statement for median ASIA jobber [as percent of net sales]. (p. 14S)

[15] Battery shipments [replacement and original equipment], 1981-84. (p. 14S)

[16-17] ASIA's median wholesaler: how well he managed his assets [including inventory turnover, and financial and other] key business ratios. (p. 15S)

[18] Productivity measures for staff of ASIA jobber [average non-shop employees, with sales, gross margin, and operating expense, per employee; and payroll and total compensation, as percent of sales]. (p. 15S)

C4740–1.2: Wholesaler Financial and Operating Data

[1] Relative size of State and regional wholesaler assns [assn membership in 34 States and 4 regions, 1984, with rankings for 1983-84]. (p. 16S)

[2] ASIA wholesaler's shop profit as percent of labor sales. (p. 16S)

[3-4] 1985 jobber [customer and employee training] clinic study: percent holding clinics, 1985 compared to 1981; and median cost per clinic; [both by sales size group]. [2 charts] (p. 17S)

[5] How jobbers manage inventory [inventory management and average sales, by inventory method (no date)]. (p. 17S)

[6] Number of workers, by [occupational] category of median ASIA wholesaler [no date]. (p. 18S)

[7] Where jobbers sell selected items [outlets for brake parts, paint/body supplies, and service/repair equipment (no dates)]. (p. 18S)

[8] Leading [8 products which are] profitmakers among PBE products [no date]. (p. 18S)

[9] Establishments handling automotive products [distribution by outlet type], 1980 compared to 1983. [chart] (p. 19S)

[10] MEMA [Motor and Equipment Manufacturers Assn] "composite" wholesaler [assets, liabilities and net worth, financial and operating ratios, and profit or loss; most shown as percentages, 1981-83]. (p. 20S)

[11] Unit sales [per month] by median jobbers of selected product lines [no date]. (p. 21S)

C4740–1.3: Distributors, Vehicle Data, and Miscellaneous

[1] Model run output [domestic passenger car production and production ranking, by model, arranged by size class], 1984 compared to 1983. (p. 22S-23S)

[2-3] Jobber affiliations [distribution among franchises, chains, and independents (chart)]; and sales per square foot, by geographic area [based on zip code prefixes; no dates]. (p. 24S)

[4] How jobbers advertise [distribution of average advertising dollar by media type (no date)]. [chart] (p. 25S)

[5] Average miles per vehicle [by vehicle type, 1978-83]. (p. 25S)

[6] U.S.-Canadian trade in automotive products [autos, trucks, parts, and tires/tubes], 1983-84. (p. 26S)

[7] Jobber sales per square foot compared to total sales volume [no date]. (p. 26S)

[8] Performance measures for ASIA warehouse distributors (WD) [including sales and various operating ratios, 1984]. (p. 27S)

[9] MEMA's profile of average WD [assets, liabilities and net worth, financial and operating ratios, and profit or loss; most shown as percentages, 1981-83]. (p. 28S)

[10] Motor bus registrations [by type (including school buses) and ownership, by State]. (p. 29S)

[11] Operating costs [by item] of average WD, as percent of net sales: AWDA [Automotive Warehouse Distributors Assn, 1984]. (p. 30S)

[12] Balance sheet [percentages] of median AWDA distributor, 1984. (p. 31S)

[13] AWDA figures for WD net profit, turnover, [and] sales per employee [by company sales size (no date)]. (p. 31S)

[14] Number of automobile dealers, 1947-84. (p. 32S)

[15] MEMA members forecast overall 1985 sales increase [by product group and company sales size]. (p. 33S)

[16] Car production by model year, 1959-84. (p. 33S)

[17] Latest financial rankings of publicly-owned automotive [parts] firms [ranked by revenues, net income, profit margin, and return on capital]. (p. 34S-35S)

[18] How ASIA's heavy-duty distributor measured up in sales, profits, [and other financial and operating measures]. (p. 36S)

[19] Milestones in production of motor trucks/buses [selected years 1938-79]. (p. 36S)

[20] Productivity of [non-shop] people working for ASIA heavy-duty distributors [including selected sales, profit, and expense productivity measures]. (p. 37S)

[21] Annual factory sales of [autos and trucks/buses] from U.S. plants, [1970-84]. (p. 37S)

[22-24] Jobber services provided to wholesale and retail trade, and percentage of jobbers selling specified PBE lines [no dates]. (p. 38S)

[25] Imported new car sales [by make], 1979-84. (p. 39S)

[26] Five leading vehicle producers worldwide [ranked by production], 1982-84. (p. 39S)

[27] Car production [by manufacturer, make, and model], 1984 compared to 1983. (p. 40S-41S)

C4740–1.4: Trade Shows, Vehicle Production, and Miscellaneous

[1-2] Yearly statistics of international and regional automotive [trade] show [exhibitors, booths, and attendance, various years 1933-85]. (p. 42S-43S)

[3] Milestones in production of cars [selected years 1912-79]. (p. 43S)

[4] What it costs to own [and] operate average car in 1985 [by item]. (p. 44S)

[5] Vehicle production milestones (cars/trucks/buses) [selected years 1906-82]. (p. 44S)

[6] Automotive wholesaler failures [and liabilities. 1946-83]. (p. 45S)

[7] Parts, service sales of franchised new car dealerships: $30.6 billion [sales by type, 1983-84]. (p. 45S)

[8] Motor truck registrations by State, [1982-83]. (p. 46S)

[9-10] How jobbers fight retail competition [by marketing technique]; and jobbers' strongest retail competitors [by type; no dates]. [2 charts] (p. 47S)

[11] Profile of establishments influenced by *Jobber Topics* [number of establishments by type, by State and for Puerto Rico (no date)]. (p. 48S-49S)

[12] U.S. van and light truck production, 1984 vs. 1983. (p. 50S)

C4775
Jobson Publishing Corp.

C4775–1   LIQUOR HANDBOOK, 1985
Annual. 1985. 314 p.
ISSN 0459-4843.
LC sc79-3655.
SRI/MF/not filmed

Annual report presenting detailed statistics pertaining to the liquor industry, 1984, with selected projections to 1994 and trends from as early as 1922. Covers sales, consumption, foreign trade, advertising expenditures, consumer characteristics, distillery operations, government regulation and taxation, and other topics. Includes selected data by product type, company, brand, census division, State, and metro area.

Data were compiled by Steve L. Barsby and Associates, Inc., from Federal agencies, Distilled Spirits Council of the U.S., original estimates, and other sources. Data sources are noted beneath each table.

Contains contents listing, user note, and foreword (p. 8-14); indexes (p. 16-25); 8 report sections, with 52 charts and 397 tables, interspersed with brief narratives (p. 29-305); and list of advertisers (p. 309-314).

All tables, and selected charts with substantial statistics not covered by tables, are described below.

This is the 32nd annual edition of the report. Previous report, for 1984, was also reviewed in SRI during 1985 [Annual. 1984. 304 p. $49.95]. Previous report is organized differently, but is substantially similar in content. Previous report omits data on other beverage types, and on Hispanics and college students; and also includes data on illegal liquor activities, liquor store owner opinions, and consumer purchases by retail outlet type.

Availability: Jobson Publishing Corp., 352 Park Ave., S., New York NY 10010, $59.95; SRI/MF/not filmed.

TABLES AND CHARTS:

[Unless otherwise noted, data pertain to distilled spirits, and are shown for U.S. Data by State often include subtotals for license States (with distribution regulated by tier system of licensing) and control States (with State monopoly over distribution). Data generally are current to 1984 and include comparisons to 1983 or trends from 1960s or 1970s, with some historical trends (from as early as 1922) and projections (as noted below).

Product types generally include whiskey varieties, gin, rum, vodka, tequila, brandy, cordials and liqueurs, and prepared cocktails.]

C4775-1.1: Consumption, Markets for Major Product Types, and Foreign Trade

[Data on sales volume include selected projections to 1989.]

CONSUMPTION TRENDS

a. Consumption and/or sales volume, by State, census division, leading brand, product type, month, and major metro area, including comparisons to personal income and population; number of new product introductions, and gallons entering trade channels, by product type; consumer spending, with detail for alcohol and beverages; and gallonage bottled by month and product type. 10 charts and 30 tables. (p. 29-80)

MARKETS FOR MAJOR PRODUCT TYPES, AND FOREIGN TRADE

b. Whiskey sales volume and consumption trends by variety, shown variously by State, month, metro area, price class, and leading brand; whiskey gallonage bottled by month and selected State, and distilled spirits bottled output by product type; and whiskey advertising expenditures by media and brand. 7 charts and 48 tables. (p. 82-111)

c. Foreign trade by product type and country of origin or destination; imported whiskey bottling and sales, by month; distilled spirits stocks, by product type and State, and for Kentucky distillers; U.S. customs duties and duty reductions; and bourbon import duties of selected countries. 17 tables. (p. 111-120)

d. Market profiles for specific product types: variously including consumption and/or sales volume by State, leading brand, month, price class, and metro area; bottled gallonage by month; advertising expenditures by media and brand; imports, mostly by country of origin; metric measurements; production and stock data; and consumer preferences (for cordials only). 22 charts and 136 tables. (p. 122-205)

C4775-1.2: Advertising and Promotion, and Supplier Performance

ADVERTISING AND PROMOTION

a. Distilled spirits advertising expenditures by media, with detail by leading brand, product type, month, and company, and comparison to consumption; magazine and newspaper circulation data, including magazine rankings by subscriber income and home ownership, and top newspaper publications, owners, and market areas; and liquor store advertising expenditures in newspapers. 3 charts and 32 tables. (p. 206-228)

b. December holiday share of total annual sales. 1 table. (p. 228)

SUPPLIER SALES AND ADVERTISING

c. Supplier sales generated by leading brands; sales value and volume, market shares, and average selling prices, by supplier and/or product type; and advertising expenditures of individual suppliers spending over $250,000. 3 charts and 12 tables (p. 231-237)

C4775-1.3: National and International Market Characteristics

NATIONAL LIQUOR MARKET

a. Population size and characteristics, including projections to 1994; distilled spirits sales volume in aggregate top 50 markets, by product type; consumer expenditures; alcohol consumption patterns among affluent adults; legal drinking age population by State; and major metro market and regional population profiles. 13 tables (p. 238-247)

b. Consumer expenditures for distilled spirits (total and per capita), with amount for Federal/State taxes, and comparisons to disposable income and to expenditures for all alcoholic beverages; population, income, and distilled spirits consumption trends; economic indicators, including alcoholic beverage PPI and CPI; strip stamp and closure purchases; imports of bitters by country of origin; and summary of State laws on couponing. 13 tables (p. 250-256)

c. Licensing: control State mark-up percentages; retail licenses for on- and off-premise consumption; distribution of sales by price classes, by product type; number of wholesalers/importers/distributors by alcoholic beverage type; number of counties permitting and prohibiting sales; Federal permits for alcoholic beverage operations, and wholesale liquor operations in license States; and State laws concerning samples for retailers; mostly by State. 8 tables. (p. 257-262)

d. Taxation, including Federal excise rates; tax revenue from alcoholic beverages, by type; and State tax rates since repeal of Prohibition. 3 tables. (p. 263)

e. Price structure: alcohol consumption patterns of adults, by beverage type; sales margin of distillers compared to general manufacturing; supplier price index, by product type; and retail prices of 8 leading brands, and sales restrictions placed on grocery, drug, and liquor stores regarding alcoholic and nonalcoholic beverages and accessories, by license and control State. 5 tables. (p. 264-267)

f. Socioeconomic characteristics of alcoholic beverage consumers, with detail by product type; drinking and purchasing habits, including brand selection factors, and product type most often purchased, with detail for selected market groups including college students; and black and Hispanic population characteristics, and alcohol consumption patterns. 32 tables. (p. 268-283)

INTERNATIONAL MARKET

g. Alcohol and distilled spirits consumption, with detail by product type; and retail bottle prices for 5 selected U.S. brands; all by country. 2 charts and 6 tables. (p. 284-287)

C4775-1.4: Distillery Operations

a. Production: number of distillery and bottling operations, by State; whiskey used in redistillation, and whiskey production, by selected States; grain and malt consumption at distilleries, by commodity; whiskey barrel shipments; usage of tax-free withdrawals; and production by product type. 7 tables. (p. 288-291)

b. Storage and use, including stocks by product type and selected State; Kentucky whiskey stocks, by distiller; and tax-paid withdrawals by month. 5 tables. (p. 292-294)

c. Bottling trends, including bottled output by product type; and gallonage bottled by month, product type, and major State. 4 tables. (p. 294-296)

C4775-1.5: Other Beverages

a. Consumption of beverages, including use of soft drinks and juices as mixers; retail spending and sales; grocery store shares of beverage market; soft drink market shares by flavor; advertising expenditures for top brands; sales of leading beverage companies and brands; and beverage CPI; mostly shown by beverage type, with detail by variety. 5 charts and 18 tables. (p. 297-303)

b. Beer sales volume and/or consumption, by beer type and for top 10 domestic and imported brands; advertising and marketing data for leading imported brands; and top 10 brewers ranked by production. 7 tables. (p. 304-305)

C4775-2   WINE MARKETING HANDBOOK, 1985
Annual. 1985. 156 p.
ISSN 0364-5738.
LC 72-626221/r83.
SRI/MF/not filmed

Annual report presenting detailed statistics pertaining to the wine industry, 1984 and trends. Covers sales, consumption, production, foreign trade, advertising expenditures, consumer characteristics, taxation, and other topics. Includes selected data by product type, company, brand, State, and metro area.

Data are compiled by Jobson Publishing Corp., from Federal agencies, Wine Institute, and other sources. Data sources are noted beneath each table.

Contains contents listing, foreword, and index (p. 6-18); 28 charts and 160 tables, with accompanying narrative, arranged in 6 sections (p. 21-154); and index of advertisers (p. 155-156). Tables and charts are described below.

This is the 15th annual edition of the report. Previous report, for 1984, was also reviewed in SRI during 1985 [Annual. 1984. 144 p. $39.95]. Previous report is substantially similar in content, but also includes data on New York State wine production by product type, and on wine bottle shipments.

Availability: Jobson Publishing Corp., 352 Park Ave., S., New York NY 10010, $49.95; SRI/MF/not filmed.

TABLES AND CHARTS:
[Unless otherwise noted, data pertain to wine and are shown for U.S. Data generally are current to 1984 and include comparisons to 1983 or trends from 1960s or 1970s, with some historical trends from as early as 1934 and projections as noted below.

Product types generally include vermouth, and table, dessert, and champagne/sparkling wines; data often are shown separately for domestic and imported products. Data by State are arranged according to whether license or control State.]

C4775–2.1: Sections 1-4: Wine Market, Market for Major Wine Types, Advertising and Promotion, and Other Beverages

a. Consumption and/or sales volume, by product type, imported brand, month, State (including sales volume projections for 1989), and top 5-50 metro areas; consumption per capita by State; consumption projections for 1989; consumer expenditures; selected population trends; and sales for off-premise consumption, by product type, for 5 metro areas. 11 charts and 30 tables. (p. 21-50)

b. International market: total and/or per capita consumption for selected countries, with detail by product type (including fortified and fruit wines), and comparisons to U.S.; and production by top 10 producing countries. 2 charts and 6 tables. (p. 51-53)

c. Wineries: sales volume for 10 leading wineries and all others; case prices and sales volume for major domestic and imported brands; and top 10 wineries ranked by value of sales. 3 tables. (p. 53-54)

d. Market profiles for specific product types (including wine coolers), variously including consumption and/or sales volume, by month, State, leading metro area, and price class; imports by country of origin; sales of leading imports by brand; consumer preferences by variety, and retail availability by outlet type and State (for table wines only); taxable withdrawals; and advertising expenditures by media and brand. 13 charts and 73 tables. (p. 55-93)

e. Advertising expenditures by media, company and brand, product type, wine assn, and winery/importer. 2 charts and 31 tables. (p. 94-111)

f. Market profiles for other beverages (including beer, distilled spirits, and various types of nonalcoholic beverages), including retail spending, consumption, grocery store market share, CPI, and advertising expenditures of top 10 brands; with additional detail, including sales volume and value, for beer, soft drink, bottled water, and fruit/fruit drink product categories, brands, and/or companies. 5 charts and 24 tables. (p. 112-118)

C4775–2.2: Sections 5-6: Market Data and Statistics, and Production and Inventories

a. Consumer expenditures and savings; PPI and CPI for alcoholic beverages; population and median income, by region and for metro and nonmetro areas; disposable income; GNP; money income of persons age 14/over, by sex; wine consumption per capita and per $1 million income, by State; employment, and unemployment rate; and families and income, by race and for Hispanics. 3 charts and 12 tables. (p. 119-123)

b. Socioeconomic characteristics of alcoholic beverage consumers, with detail by wine and other beverage type; wine and/or other alcoholic beverage consumption habits, including types of beverages used, frequency of drinking, wine gift-giving occasions, and use by college students, with selected socioeconomic breakdowns; legal drinking age, and population of legal drinking age, by State; and selected population and socioeconomic trends and projections. 4 charts and 31 tables. (p. 124-135)

c. Distribution and taxation: mark-up percentages by State or county with control of alcohol sales; wholesale licenses, and retail licenses for on- and off-premise consumption, by State; number of alcohol-related operating permits by type of holder; wine market shares by price class; U.S. customs duties on wine; Federal wine excise tax collections and excise rates; and State exise rates by product type. 10 tables. (p. 135-140)

d. Foreign trade: imports and exports, by product type and/or country of origin or destination; U.S. market shares for French and Spanish wines, by detailed type; and U.S. balance of trade for wine. 1 chart and 9 tables. (p. 141-144)

e. Production, taxable and tax-free withdrawals, and stocks, with selected detail by product type, State, and month; California storage cooperage and inventories by product type (with comparisons to total U.S.); wine cellar consumption of fruits and juices/concentrates; bonded wine cellars and taxpaid bottling houses, by State; domestic and imported gallonage entering trade channels; and State laws concerning wine tasting and off-premise sales. 3 charts and 18 tables. (p. 145-154)

C4825 · Journal Publications

C4825–3   **SEAFOOD BUSINESS REPORT: Pacific Packers' Report, Annual Feature**
Bimonthly (selected issue).
Mar./Apr. 1985. (p. 62-101).
Vol. 4, No. 2.
ISSN 0733-0464.
LC SN 82-4231.
SRI/MF/excerpts

Annual issue of *Seafood Business Report* on Pacific Coast seafood industry, 1984, with selected trends from 1940. Most data are shown for Alaska, Washington State, Oregon, California, and/or British Columbia.

Covers landings; processing, including canned packs and fresh and frozen poundage and/or values, with some detail by company; and prices; shown variously for salmon, shellfish, bottomfish, and/or tuna, by species.

Also includes data on Alaska salmon harvest forecasts for 1985, and joint venture and foreign bottomfish catch; U.S. tuna packs, including data for selected non-Pacific Coast areas, and imports of frozen tuna; and salmon hatchery releases, by agency, including data for Idaho.

Data are compiled from reports of State, Federal, and Canadian agencies responsible for fisheries management, and industry trade assns.

Includes 28 tables (p. 62-101).

Seafood Business Report is a bimonthly, generally narrative periodical reporting trends and developments in the seafood industry. "Pacific Packers' Report" is the only feature described by SRI.

Availability: Seafood Business Report, Circulation Department, 21 Elm St., Camden ME 04843, qualified subscribers †, others $12.00 per yr.; SRI/MF/excerpts for annual feature described.

C4850 Judge, Edward E., and Sons

C4850–1   **ALMANAC OF THE CANNING, FREEZING, PRESERVING INDUSTRIES, 1985**
Annual. 1985. 662 p.
LC 72-622383.
SRI/MF/excerpts

Annual almanac, for 1985, of the food processing industries. Includes detailed data on fruit and vegetable crops, and frozen and canned food packs and international trade, by commodity, 1970s-84, with selected trends from the 1800s. Also includes detailed data on food processing company operations, taken from the 1982 Census of Manufactures; and food consumption and prices, government purchases, technical and regulatory information, and a buyer's guide.

Most data are from USDA, Commerce Dept, National Food Processors Assn, American Frozen Food Institute, and other industry assns and publications.

Contents:

Index to contents, and list of assn presidents and convention cities since 1890. (p. 3-15)

Section I-II. Assn and FDA Personnel; and Food Law and Regulations. (p. 16-83)

Section III. Labeling and Packaging. Includes 3 tables (p. 159-161) showing can prices, by type and size, 1931-84; metal can shipments, by product category, 1977-84; and glass container shipments, by type, 1975-83. (p. 84-165)

Section IV-V. Emergency Permits, Unavoidable Contaminants, and Good Manufacturing Practice Regulations; and Food and Drug Standards of Identity, Quality, and Fill. (p. 166-330)

Section VI. USDA Quality Grade Standards: Canned, Glass, and Frozen Foods. (p. 331-483)

Section VII. Raw Product Statistics. Contains 57 tables showing harvested acreage, yield, production, and value, for 15 vegetable crops (also including prices and sales for mushrooms), by State, 1975-84; and 14 tables generally showing utilized production, use, price, and value, for apples and 8 other fruit crops by type, by State, various years 1975-84. (p. 484-519)

Section VIII. U.S. Pack Statistics. Includes 158 tables on commodity packs, described below; and 1982 Census of Manufactures industry and product statistics, with 10 tables, also described below. (p. 520-589)

Section IX. International Trade and World Packs. Includes 10 tables showing value or volume for the following: U.S. canned and frozen food exports and imports (including exports of canned fruits and vegetables, by country or world area of destination); world canned fruit and vegetable imports, for selected countries by country of origin; and world fruit and vegetable packs, by country; all by commodity, various years 1975-84. (p. 590-607)

Section X. Canned Food Prices. Contains 1 table showing high and low canner spot selling prices for canned vegetables, fruits, and fish, by commodity, 1978/79-1984/85. (p. 608-614)

Section XI. Appendix. Includes 12 tables (p. 618-623) showing Government frozen and/or canned food purchases for military, and for child nutrition and domestic feeding programs, various years 1975-85; and civilian per capita consumption of fresh, canned, and frozen products, various periods 1909-83; all by commodity. (p. 615-625)

Section XII. Buyer's Guide for Machinery, Supplies, and Services. (p. 627-659)

This is the 70th annual edition. A detailed directory of companies and assns is also available from the issuing agency, but is not covered by SRI.

Availability: Edward E. Judge and Sons, PO Box 866, Westminster MD 21157, $32.50; SRI/MF/excerpts for nontechnical statistical tables in Sections III and VII-XI.

SECTION VIII TABLES:

C4850–1.1: U.S. Pack and Industry Statistics

a. Canned vegetable, fruit, and juice packs (total and by region or State and container size), with some detail by product style, and for carryover, stock, shipments, exports, and Government purchases, all by commodity, generally 1975-84, with summary pack trends from 1899; and tomato product, mayonnaise, and salad dressing packs and value, by product type, selected years 1967-82. 104 tables. (p. 521-552)

b. Canned seafood pack and value, and packing plants, (total and by State and type); salmon and tuna packs, by State or area, variety, and/or container size; and per capita consumption of canned fishery products; generally 1975-84, with summary pack trends from 1927. 9 tables. (p. 552-556)

c. Canned meat packs, 1975-84; and canned and frozen specialty product pack and value, selected years 1967-82; all by product type. 2 tables. (p. 557-559)

d. Frozen vegetable and fruit packs (total and by State or region, and container size class and/or product style); and packer supply, shipments, and stocks; all by commodity, generally 1975-84, with summary pack trends from 1942. 40 tables. (p. 560-573)

e. Frozen citrus juice concentrate production, by type; noncitrus concentrate/juice production; and frozen fruit supply, disappearance, and stocks, by commodity; various years 1948/49-1984. 3 tables. (p. 574-575)

f. Industry data: number of companies and establishments, employees, payroll, production workers, hours of labor, wages, value added by manufacture, cost of materials, production value, capital expenditures, value of fixed assets, operating ratios, and inventories; and consumption of fuels and other materials, by type, and electricity; all for 8 SIC 4-digit industries, with selected detail by State and employment size, mostly 1982, with selected trends from 1958. 10 tables. (p. 578-589)

C4950
Kenedy, P. J., and Sons

C4950–1   OFFICIAL CATHOLIC DIRECTORY, 1985
Annual. 1985.
xxxii+1517+foldout.
ISSN 0078-3854.
ISBN 0-87217-974-5.
LC 1-30961.
SRI/MF/excerpts

Annual directory, for 1985, of the Catholic Church, listing Vatican officials and offices; U.S. dioceses and archdioceses, national organizations, territorial and foreign missions, religious orders, churches, institutions, clergy, and deceased hierarchy and clergy; and Canadian and Mexican dioceses and officials. Includes statistics on churches, institutions, clergy, and religious orders, for dioceses in U.S. and territories.

Contains contents listing and general information (p. iii-viii); directory listing for Vatican (p. ix-xvi); directory listings for U.S., Canada, and Mexico, including statistical summaries for dioceses and religious orders (p. xvii-xxxii, 1-1517); and 1 extended table (oversized foldout) showing the following items by census division, State, archdiocese, and diocese, 1985, with totals for 1975 and 1984:

OFFICIALS, CLERGY, AND CHURCHES

a. Cardinals, archbishops, bishops, abbots, diocesan and religious priests, total priests, permanent deacons, brothers, and sisters.

b. Parishes, resident and nonresident pastors, missions, stations, and chapels.

SEMINARIES

c. Diocesan and religious seminaries and students, diocesan students in other seminaries, and total seminarians.

SCHOOLS, STUDENTS, AND TEACHERS

d. Colleges/universities, diocesan/parochial and private high schools and elementary schools, and protective institutions, with number of students for each type of institution; released-time high school and elementary pupils; and total students under Catholic instruction.

e. Teaching priests, scholastics, brothers, and sisters; lay teachers; and total teachers.

HOSPITALS, NURSING HOMES, AND INSTITUTIONS

f. General and special hospitals, with bed capacity and patients treated annually for each type of hospital; and nursing schools and students.

g. Orphanages/asylums and resident children; children in foster homes; total dependent children; and homes for the aged, with number of guests.

MISCELLANEOUS STATISTICS

h. Infant baptisms, converts, total baptisms, marriages, deaths, Catholic population, and total population (as of Jan. 1).

This is the 153rd edition.

Availability: Official Catholic Directory, P. J. Kenedy and Sons, 866 Third Ave., New York NY 10022, $90.75; SRI/MF/excerpts for oversized foldout table.

C5150
Lebhar-Friedman

C5150–2   DRUG STORE NEWS
Biweekly, and annual special issue. Oversized.
ISSN 0191-7587.
LC 79-642712.
SRI/MF/excerpts

Biweekly trade journal (monthly in Dec. and an additional annual issue in Apr.) of the retail and wholesale drug industry, covering drugstore operations and finances, wholesale distribution, Government regulation, and pharmaceutical and health/beauty aid (H&BA) sales, manufacture, and merchandising. Data are from private research firms, individual companies, and the journal's own research.

Issues contain news articles, often including statistics; "Financial" section, generally with 1 table showing stock market performance and financial position of leading drugstore chains and drug wholesalers and manufacturers; and "Merchandiser" section on product merchandising and management.

Annual statistical features include pharmacy practice reference special issue, with marketing data for selected prescription drugs; TV advertising expenditures of leading chains; chain drug industry financial performance and marketing operations; "Triple-A Product Study" on sales of leading drugstore products; and Nielsen review of drugstore sales and merchandising trends.

Stock market performance feature appears in most issues. All additional features with substantial statistical content are described, as they appear, under "Statistical Features." Nonstatistical features are not covered.

Availability: Drug Store News, Subscription Department, 305 Madison Ave., Suite 535, New York, NY 10165-0079, qualified subscribers $19.50 per yr., others $39.00 per yr., single copy $2.00; selected articles are also available as reprints; SRI/MF/excerpts for stock performance feature and all portions described under "Statistical Features."

Issues reviewed during 1985: Nov. 12, 1984-Oct. 28, 1985 (P) (Vol. 6, Nos. 24-26; Vol. 7, Nos. 1-23) [Apr. 29, 1985 issue cover incorrectly reads Apr. 28].

STATISTICAL FEATURES:

C5150–2.601: Nov. 12, 1984 (Vol. 6, No. 24)

WHERE THE TOP 25 STAND WITH NATURALS, ANNUAL FEATURE

(1 p.) Annual tabular listing of 25 leading drugstore chains, showing number of stores and types of natural products carried (no date).

Feature is part of an annual insert section (following p. 20) on natural product sales and marketing. For description of previous annual feature, see SRI 1984 Annual under C5150-2.502.

SPECIAL REPORT: ETHNIC PRODUCTS

(p. 43-52) By Gail Appleson. Compilation of articles on drugstore merchandising of ethnic-oriented health/beauty aid products. Data sources include Business Trends Analysis, A. C. Nielsen Co., and American Health & Beauty Aids Institute.

Includes 5 charts showing ethnic product sales 1980-83 and 1993, with distribution by product type 1983; sales volume and value distribution for ethnic hair care products, by type of product and outlet (drugstores, food stores, and mass merchandisers), 1983; and detail for 1 major drugstore chain.

PHARMACISTS: GENERIC SCRIPTS ARE ON THE RISE

(p. 67) Article, with 1 undated chart showing percent of prescriptions that are filled with generic drugs, for total, chain, and independent drugstores. Data are based on a 1984 survey of 575 pharmacists, conducted by Lebhar-Friedman Research.

C5150–2.602: Dec. 10, 1984 (Vol. 6, No. 26)

POPAI/DU PONT DRUG STORE SHOPPER STUDY

(p. 11-29) Compilation of articles on consumer shopping and purchasing habits in drugstores, by product category. Data are based on interviews with 12,131 shoppers at 258 drugstores in 40 markets, conducted in 1983 by Point-of-Purchase Advertising Institute/Du Pont.

Includes 16 tables showing share of total drugstore purchases; number of purchases per 100 shoppers; and percent of purchases that are planned, unplanned, substitutions for originally planned items, and resulting from decisions made in the store; all for 40 product categories, with detail by product type.

PHARMACY: VALIUM 5mg STAYS ON TOP OF TRANQUILIZER MARKET; ATIVAN A DISTANT SECOND, ANNUAL FEATURE

(p. 45) Annual article on market performance of leading tranquilizers. Data are from Decision Data, Inc. Includes 1 table showing manufacturer, retail market share, average quantity and price per prescription, and percent retail margin, for top 15 products, mostly June 1983-84.

For description of previous article, see SRI 1983 Annual under C5150-2.423.

C5150–2.603: Jan. 7, 1985 (Vol. 7, No. 1)

CHAIN EXECS' ECONOMIC PREDICTIONS: MOSTLY SUNNY SKIES WITH A CHANCE OF SHOWERS

(p. 33, 36) Article, with 1 table showing percent of drugstore executives believing economic recovery will continue in 1985. Data are from a fall 1984 *Drug Store News* survey of executives from chain and independent drugstores and drug wholesaling companies, and are shown separately for each group.

INDUSTRY FORECAST 1985, ANNUAL FEATURE

(p. 33, 36-37) Annual compilation of articles on drugstore industry operations and outlook, based on a *Drug Store News* survey of chain and independent drugstore executives. Includes 1 table showing percent of independent drugstores using or planning to use selected types of computerized equipment, 1984-86.

This is the 1st annual survey.

C5150–2.604: Jan. 21, 1985 (Vol. 7, No. 2)

NEW LAW SHOULD SPAWN FLURRY OF GENERIC DRUGS

(p. 43-46) Article, with 1 table showing 1983 sales for 25 drug brands whose generic equivalents will be eligible for marketing on Jan. 1, 1985. Data are from Mabon, Nugent and Co.

C5150–2.605: Mar. 18, 1985 (Vol. 7, No. 6)

COUGH/COLD TOPS DOCTORS' RECOMMENDATIONS

(p. 44-46) Article on over-the-counter drug and other products recommended by pediatricians, by brand. Data are based on a survey of 100 pediatricians conducted by Market Measures, Inc. Includes 7 undated tables.

C5150–2.606: Apr. 1, 1985 (Vol. 7, No. 7)

BEST-SELLING OTCs: COUGH/COLD DOMINATES TOP 100 OTC LIST, ANNUAL FEATURE

(p. 31-40) Annual article on over-the-counter (OTC) health product sales, based on a *Drug Store News* study of 1984 warehouse withdrawal data from major retail drug chains.

Includes 24 lists and 3 charts showing rank order for top 100 OTC products based on unit and dollar sales and profitability, with breakdowns for 8 product categories, including product category shares of top 100; and 1 table showing average prices for selected top products.

C5150–2.607: Apr. 1985 Special Issue (Vol. 7, No. 8)

1985 REFERENCE FOR PHARMACY PRACTICE, ANNUAL FEATURE

Annual special issue presenting detailed business and clinical reference information for pharmacists, including supplier directories, and marketing and clinical data for selected prescription drugs. Data are from Market Measures, U.S. Poison Control Center, and journal's own research.

Includes the following marketing and clinical data:

a. Product rankings for 200 leading prescription drugs in number of prescriptions, dollar volume, and dollar margin; arranged alphabetically by manufacturer and in rank order. 2 tables. (p. 6-14)

b. Dispensing profiles for selected prescription drug brands, including average prescription quantity, price, and gross margin; refills as percent of total prescriptions; and selected comparative data for 10 dispensing quantity categories, with profitability ranking for each category. 24 charts and 21 tables. (p. 16-21)

c. Bulk buying guide for 100 leading prescription drugs, showing manufacturer, size and price for small and bulk purchases, and savings by buying in bulk. 1 table. (p. 22-23)

d. Generic drugs: top 20 drug categories based on number of prescriptions, 1984, with comparison to 1982-83; distribution of pharmacist substitutions, by drug category, Sept. 1984; and listing of selected regulations concerning drug substitution, by State (no date). 1 chart and 2 tables. (p. 42-44)

e. Drugs and other potentially poisonous substances ranked by seriousness of medical consequences caused by misuse, with percent of cases requiring treatment at a health care facility, 1983; and retail drugstore new and refill prescription volume, 1984. 2 tables. (p. 66, 94)

C5150–2.608: Apr. 15, 1985 (Vol. 7, No. 9)

DRUG CHAIN TV ADVERTISING BUDGETS GROWING, ANNUAL FEATURE

(p. 24) Annual article, with 1 table showing top 15 drugstore chains ranked by local TV advertising expenditures, 1984 with comparison to 1983. Data are from TV Bureau of Advertising.

Previous feature is described in SRI 1984 Annual under C5150-2.515.

C5150–2.609: Apr. 29, 1985 (Vol. 7, No. 10)

[Cover incorrectly reads Apr. 28, 1985.]

1985 ANNUAL REPORT OF THE CHAIN DRUG INDUSTRY

(p. 61-203, passim) Annual compilation of articles on chain drugstores' financial performance and marketing operations, including sales, stores, product merchandising, and industry concentration, various years 1975-85.

Data are from *Drug Store News*, A. C. Nielsen Co., Chain Store Guides, Media General, and company reports.

Contains contents listing (p. 64) and the following sections:

a. Performance: news articles and features, with 1 summary chart, and 22 tables on drugstore finances and operations. (p. 61-121)

b. Products: articles on new products, and sales and operations of 14 depts, with 10 summary charts, 1 tabular listing of new drugs introduced in 1984, and 27 tables. (p. 124-166)

c. Profiles: for 22 leading drugstore chains, each with narrative analysis and generally 1-2 charts, mostly showing number of outlets, and/or sales and earnings trends, various periods 1980-85; corrected data for 1 company appear in the May 27, 1985 issue (see C5150-2.611 below). (p. 168-203)

All tables are listed below. A related chart showing industry sales trends appears on p. 1.

TABLES:

[Data are for 1984, unless otherwise noted, and often include comparisons to 1983.]

[1-3] 10-year sales, sales share, [and number of stores, for chain and independent stores, 1975-84]. (p. 64, 77)

[4] Top 50 drug chains [ranked by sales, with number of stores]. (p. 79)

[5] Evolving character of the chain drug industry [showing chain companies and stores operated, by chain size group, 1974 and 1984]. (p. 79)

[6] Chain store remodels [number of stores remodeled, by chain, 1984-85]. (p. 80)

[7] 10-year drug store share trends [chain and independent shares of total stores, 1975-84]. (p. 80)

[8] Top 50 chains [ranked by] store totals. (p. 80)

[9] Diversification areas for major drug chains [number of stores owned by type (excluding non-discount drugstores), by chain]. (p. 83)

[10] Chain drug stock performance [high, low, and last stock prices, 1984; year-end price/earnings ratios, 1983-84; and price as of Mar. 25, 1985; for 14 chains]. (p. 83)

[11] Top drug chains in warehousing [number of warehouse facilities and total square footage]. (p. 84)

[12] Combination store leaders [number of food/drug combination stores owned, for major drug or food chain companies]. (p. 87)

[13-20] [Top 14-15 drug chains ranked by] corporate sales, sales per average store, drug store units, net income, gross margin, expense and net-to-sales ratios, and return on investment, [1984 with comparisons to 1980-83]. (p. 88, 113)

[21] Status of pharmacy computers in chain drug stores [number of stores using computers in prescription depts, and share of total stores, by chain, 1984-85]. (p. 115)

[22] Deep-discount drug stores (operated by traditional drug chains) [number of stores in operation, average size, and sales per store, by chain]. (p. 116)

[23] Breakout of chain drug sales, [sales shares, gross margins, and average number of inventory turns, all by dept]. (p. 124)

[24] Prescription dept summary [including sales, prescriptions dispensed (total and per store per year), average prescription price, and number of stores with prescription depts, all for total and chain drugstores]. (p. 135)

[25] Chains expand into home health care [number of home health care centers operated, by chain]. (p. 136)

[26-49] Proprietaries, cosmetics, toiletries, stationery, food/liquor, housewares, photo, candy, tobacco, do-it-yourself, toy, and general merchandise dept productivity and highlights [showing the following for each dept: sales, and share of dept or total industry sales, with detail by product category; typical gross margin; gross profit yield from 1983; and average number of inventory turns]. (p. 139-166, passim)

C5150–2.610: May 13, 1985 (Vol. 7, No. 11)

ETHNIC ITEMS OUTSHINE GENERAL H&BA

(p. 15-19) Article, with 1 chart showing distribution of population by race/ethnicity (white, black, Hispanic, and other), decennially 1970-90. Data are from Census Bureau.

U.S. BLACK POPULATION IS SHIFTING TO SUBURBS

(p. 22) Brief article, with 1 chart showing percent of black population living in central cities, metro areas outside central cities, and nonmetro areas, 1970 and 1980. Data are from Census Bureau.

C5150–2.611: May 27, 1985 (Vol. 7, No. 12)

BUYERS EYEING COMPUTER ACCESSORY POTENTIAL

(p. 15-17) Article, with 1 chart showing personal computer sales volume, 1983-85. Data are from Electronic Industries Assn.

RETAILERS RACE CLOCK TO SELL LOW-PRICED FASHION WATCHES

(p. 15-17) Article, with 1 chart showing distribution of watch sales by price range, 1984. Data are from Timex Corp.

NEW PRODUCT PERFORMANCE, RECURRING FEATURE

(p. 19) Recurring table showing the following for 10 new product brands introduced during various periods 1984-85: manufacturer, average retail price, test markets, percent increase in product category sales, market share, and advertising budget. Data are from a *Drug Store News* survey of over 500 manufacturers.

This is the 1st appearance of the feature.

CORRECTION

(p. 50) Data correction for profile section of annual feature on chain drug industry appearing in Apr. 29, 1985 issue. Correction covers 1 company.

For feature description, see C5150-2.609 above.

C5150–2.612: June 10, 1985 (Vol. 7, No. 13)

CHECKSTAND MERCHANDISING STUDY

(p. 17-32) Compilation of articles on drugstore checkout area sales and merchandising. Data are based on telephone interviews with 30 executives from leading drug chains, conducted Jan. 23-29, 1985 by Lebhar-Friedman Research.

Includes 1 table and 6 charts showing survey responses concerning average number of registers per checkout area; checkstand share of sales; and checkstand merchandising, including type of checkout used, merchandise selection factors and sources of information, and positions responsible for merchandising decisions.

Also includes tabular listings of most profitable product categories and brands.

C5150–2.613: June 24, 1985 (Vol. 7, No. 14)

CHAINS WAGE BATTLE FOR COSMETICS MARKET, ANNUAL FEATURE

(p. 15-21) Annual article, by Marjorie Shaffer, with 2 charts showing distribution of color cosmetics and eye makeup sales by type of outlet (food, drug, and mass merchandise stores), 1983-84. Data are from A. C. Nielsen Co.

C5150–2.614: July 8, 1985 (Vol. 7, No. 15)

DIFFERING PLANS USED TO RAISE FEMININE HYGIENE SALES

(p. 13, 15) Article, with 1 chart showing sales distribution of sanitary napkins and douches among drug, grocery, and mass merchandise stores, 1984. Data are from A. C. Nielsen Co.

C5150–2.615: July 22, 1985 (Vol. 7, No. 16)

TRIPLE-A PRODUCT STUDY, ANNUAL FEATURE

(p. 29-66 passim) Annual compilation of articles on top-selling products in chain drugstores, 1984. Data were compiled by *Drug Store News* based on drug chain warehouse withdrawal figures.

Includes 42 tables showing top 100 products in health and beauty aid/over-the-counter and general merchandise product categories, and top 2-18 products in each of 14 detailed categories, mostly ranked by sales volume and value, and by profitability. Tables are listings only and do not include actual values for the rankings.

C5150–2.616: Aug. 19, 1985 (Vol. 7, No. 18)

BULK LAXATIVE SALES GROW, BUT STIMULANTS LEAD

(p. 15, 17) Article, with 1 chart showing laxative sales distribution among drug, food, and mass merchandise stores, 1984. Data are from A. C. Nielsen Co.

ANTACIDS REMAIN 'PROFIT CENTER'

(p. 15, 18) Article, with 1 chart showing antacid sales distribution among drug, food, and mass merchandise stores, 1984. Data are from A. C. Nielsen Co.

SPECIAL REPORT: HMO'S

(p. 29-31) Compilation of articles on the growth of HMOs and their competition with retail pharmacies. Data are from National Assn of Chain Drug Stores. Includes 1 table showing HMO enrollment as a percent of State population, by State, 1983.

C5150–2.617: Sept. 2, 1985 (Vol. 7, No. 19)

OTC BUYERS DETAIL THEIR DISSATISFACTION WITH MANUFACTURERS' REPS

(p. 38-42) Article on drugstore buyers' attitudes concerning over-the-counter (OTC) product manufacturer representatives and services. Data are based on a summer 1985 survey of OTC buyers from independent and chain drugstores, conducted by Lebhar-Friedman Research.

Includes 5 tables showing survey response regarding types of manufacturer services desired, dissatisfaction with services provided, preferred frequency of representatives' visits, average size of OTC dept inventory, percent of sales generated by OTC products, and frequency of OTC product advertising, all shown separately for independent and chain buyers.

C5150–2.618: Sept. 16, 1985 (Vol. 7, No. 20)

COMBO OPERATORS ACCELERATE GROWTH PLANS

(p. 29) Article, with 1 table showing number of combination food/drug stores, and average store square footage, for 23 retail chain companies, with location of corporate headquarters and detail for selected subsidiaries, 1984-86. Data are from *Drug Store News*.

C5150–2.619: Oct. 14, 1985 (Vol. 7, No. 22)

ETHNIC H&BA: $2.3 BILLION AND GROWING

(p. 71-72) Article, with 2 charts showing percent change in drugstore sales of hair care products for blacks, and of aggregate 25 health/beauty aid products, 1976-84. Data are from A. C. Nielsen.

HISPANIC PRODUCTS: BIG POTENTIAL, SLOW SALES

(p. 74) Article, with 1 undated table showing percent of Hispanic and non-Hispanic consumers using selected health and beauty aid products. Data are from Strategy Research Corp.

1985 NIELSEN REVIEW OF RETAIL DRUGSTORE TRENDS, ANNUAL FEATURE

(20 p., insert) Annual review, for 1985, of aggregate drugstore sales and merchandising trends. Includes data by market area and product type. Data were compiled by A. C. Nielsen Co. from various sources.

Includes 8 charts and 17 tables showing the following:

a. Sales by kind of retail business, CPI by item, disposable income, and cost-of-living index; sales for chain and independent drugstores, with detail by sales size; and population and drug store sales, by Nielsen marketing area; various periods 1975-85.

b. Health and beauty aid products: drugstore sales, price, inventory, and space allocation trends, generally by product category, with selected detail for chain and independent stores and comparisons to food and mass merchandise stores; distribution flow for typical new product; and consumer spending index for drug and combined food/drug stores; various periods 1980-85.

This is the 49th annual review.

AUTOMATED FUTURE TO EASE RETAIL Rx OPERATIONS

(p. 95-102) Article on drugstore pharmacy use of computers and computerized point-of-sales (POS) systems. Data are from a *Drug Store News* survey of drugstore chain executives.

Includes 4 charts and 7 tables showing the following, generally as of Apr. 1985, with some estimates for Apr. 1986:

a. Number and/or percent of stores using computers, POS registers, and scanning equipment, and stores linking in-store computers with POS system, all by chain.

b. Distribution of chains by percent of pharmacies equipped with computers and POS terminals; retailer satisfaction with and/or perceived importance of selected computer and scanning functions; nonpharmacy computer use; and percent of chains using and not using scanning equipment.

C5150–2.620: Oct. 28, 1985 (Vol. 7, No. 23)

DEEP DISCOUNTING: 3% OF INDUSTRY SALES

(p. 1, 17) Article, with 1 table showing number of deep-discount drugstores by sales size group, 1985. Data are from *Drug Store News*.

COSMETICS BIZ BOOMING, BUT FRAGRANCES OFF

(p. 13) By Marjorie Shaffer. Article, with 1 undated table showing top-selling brands of make-up, skin treatment products, and men's and women's fragrances, as ranked by drugstore buyers. Data are from a survey of buyers at chain and independent stores, conducted by Goldman Sachs and Co. Surveyed buyers are responsible for over 3,000 outlets.

DETAILING VISITS TO DRUG CHAINS INCREASE BY 20%, ANNUAL FEATURE

(p. 42-44, 50) Annual article on pharmacist attitudes concerning pharmaceutical manufacturers' representatives and services. Data are from a survey of chain and independent drugstore pharmacists, conducted by Lebhar-Friedman Research.

Includes 6 undated tables showing responses concerning actual and desired frequency of representatives' visits, manufacturers whose representatives are seen most frequently, visits from representatives for 10 new drug brands, and types of information desired and received from manufacturers, all for chain and independent stores.

C5150–3   DISCOUNT STORE NEWS

Biweekly.   Oversized.
ISSN 0012-3587.
LC 63-52555.
SRI/MF/excerpts

Biweekly journal of the full-line and specialty discount department store industry, covering financial and marketing developments, merchandise line sales and profitability, and consumer and economic trends. Journal is published every 3rd week in Sept., and once in Dec.

Data are from industry sources, including store chains, wholesalers, and National Mass Retailing Institute; media research firms; and the journal's own research.

General format:

a. News articles, occasionally with statistics; and narrative editorial depts.

b. Recurring features on stock price and earnings trends for discount store chains and retailers; and on advertised prices for varying brand name products sold by discount chains. Beginning with June 10, 1985 issue, stock feature appears biweekly.

c. Product Movement Audit (PMA) recurring feature, with narrative and usually 1 table, based on data from a leading wholesale distributor, presenting unit movement, average retail price, and total sales value, for top-selling products in selected categories, for 3-week to 12-month periods.

Annual features include a discount store census (July issue) presenting store sales and earnings by dept, with selected data by company, State, and metro area.

All articles with substantial statistical content are described, as they appear, under "Statistical Features;" page locations and period of coverage for recurring PMA tables are also noted. Non-statistical features are not covered.

Availability: Discount Store News, Subscription Department, 305 Madison Ave., Suite 535, New York NY 10165-0079, retailers $12.00 per yr., others $20.00 per yr., single copy $2.00, census issue $20.00; SRI/MF/excerpts for all portions covered under "Statistical Features."

Issues reviewed during 1985: Nov. 12, 1984-Oct. 28, 1985 (P) (Vol. 23, Nos. 22-24; Vol. 24, Nos. 1-21).

STATISTICAL FEATURES:

C5150–3.601: Nov. 12, 1984 (Vol. 23, No. 22)

TOP BRANDS ANALYSIS, ANNUAL FEATURE

(p. 15-78) Annual compilation of articles on market penetration of national brand name products in the discount store industry. Data are from a 1984 survey of 299 store managers conducted by Leo J. Shapiro and Associates. Includes 15 charts and 49 tables showing survey response for the following:

a. Depts with greatest increase in name brands, and reasons name brands contribute to sales growth, by discounter type (conventional and upscale).

b. Top-selling brands by region and/or discounter type and leading chain, repeated for 16 product categories; and increase in brands carried by region, by selected product category, 1983/84.

C5150–3.602: Nov. 26, 1984 (Vol. 23, No. 23)

DISCOUNTER NET TOPS IN LAST FISCAL YEAR

(p. 1, 29) Article on discount store chain operations and financial performance. Data are from National Mass Retailing Institute (NMRI) *Operating Results of Self-Service Discount Department Stores, 1983-84.*

Includes 4 tables showing gross margin, income, earnings, income taxes, and expenses by item, all as percent of sales, with detail for major expenses in 11 categories of chain operation; average sales per store and per square foot of selling area; and markup, stock turns and shortages, and other operating ratios; 1982/83-1983/84.

Full NMRI report is covered in SRI under U1380-1.

C5150–3.603: Dec. 10, 1984 (Vol. 23, No. 24)

MARKDOWNS INCREASE AS CHAINS KEEP UP STRONG PROMO STANCE, ANNUAL FEATURE

(p. 1, 69) Annual article comparing discount and department store merchandising performance by product category. Data are from National Mass Retailing Institute (NMRI) *Operating Results of Self-Service Discount Department Stores, 1983-84* and National Retail Merchants Assn (NRMA) *Department and Specialty Store Merchandising and Operating Results of 1983.*

Includes 1 table showing markup, markdown, stock shortage, gross margin, stock turns, and share of total sales, for 17 product categories in discount and department stores.

Full NMRI and NRMA reports are covered in SRI under U1380-1 and A8300-1, respectively.

3rd-QTR. SALES: DISCOUNT STORES OUTGAIN OLD-LINE DEPT STORES, QUARTERLY FEATURE

(p. 2) Quarterly article, with 1 table showing retail sales, and sales distribution by outlet type or retailer group, for durable and nondurable goods, 3rd quarter and 1st 9 months 1983-84. Data are from Lebhar-Friedman research and Dept of Commerce.

This is the last quarterly feature. For description of previous feature see SRI 1984 Annual under C5150-3.522.

HIGH-TECH SECURITY DEVICES GET BIGGER PLAY, ANNUAL FEATURE

(p. 3, 70) Annual article on discount store theft losses and measures taken to prevent inventory "shrinkage." Data are from responses of 176 retailers to a 1983 survey conducted by Arthur Young and Co. for National Mass Retailing Institute. Includes 1 table showing use and perceived effectiveness of various security devices for controlling shrinkage.

INDUSTRY INNOVATORS

(p. 15-69, passim) Compilation of articles profiling discount chain executives. Data are primarily from company annual reports. Includes 9 tables showing all or most of the following, for 9 leading discount chains: sales, earnings, income, return on assets or equity, and stores, various periods 1971-85.

C5150–3.604: Jan. 21, 1985 (Vol. 24, No. 2)

PRODUCT MOVEMENT AUDIT (PMA) TABLE

(p. 52, 57) Automotive accessories, Feb.-Nov. 1984.

DISCOUNTERS, OLD-LINERS HOISTED PRETAX NET IN LAST FISCAL YEAR

(p. 2, 72) Article, with 3 tables showing selected financial and operating ratios for discount and department stores (mostly shown as percents of sales), including expenses by item, average sales per square foot, and stock turns, 1983 or FY84.

Data are from reports published by National Mass Retailing Institute and National Retail Merchants Assn. Full reports are covered in SRI under U1380-1 and A8300-1, respectively.

BIGGER MARKET SHARE IS SEEN FOR TOY CHAINS

(p. 18, 28) Article, with 1 table showing top 10 toy discount chains ranked by sales, FY84, and including average store size, and number of stores as of Jan. 1984-86. Data are from *Discount Store News*.

C5150–3.605: Feb. 4, 1985 (Vol. 24, No. 3)

PRODUCT MOVEMENT AUDIT (PMA) TABLE

(p. 36) Sporting goods, 4th quarter 1984.

WOMEN'S JEANS BUYERS MORE APT TO ADD SKU'S

(p. 15) Brief article on retail merchandising of jeans. Data are based on responses of 37 clothing buyers and merchandise managers to a *Discount Store News* survey.

Includes 3 undated tables showing survey response on reasons for selling jeans, brands carried, and likelihood of increasing jean inventory, all shown separately for buyers of men's, women's, and children's clothing.

TOP BRASS'S SALARIES FAIRLY CONSTANT FROM '83 TO '84

(p. 49) Article, with 4 tables showing average or median salaries of discount store executives and managers, by position; and store manager average base salary and bonus; all by store sales size, 1983 and/or 1984.

Data are from National Mass Retailing Institute biennial compensation survey. Full survey is covered in SRI under A8060-3.

C5150–3.606: Feb. 18, 1985 (Vol. 24, No. 4)

PRODUCTIVITY JUMPS MAY NOT BE REPEATED, ANNUAL FEATURE

(p. 65) Annual article, with 1 table showing discount store toy dept average size, annual inventory turns, sales per square foot, percent markup, and gross margins, 1974 and 1979-84. Data are from *Discount Store News*.

Previous feature is described in SRI 1984 Annual under C5150-3.506.

SNUFF PRODUCTION GAINS DESPITE INDUSTRY PINCH

(p. 83) Article, with 1 table showing production of tobacco products by type, 1980-84. Data are from USDA.

C5150–3.607: Mar. 4, 1985 (Vol. 24, No. 5)

DISCOUNTERS STRENGTHEN THEIR HOLD ON SHOPPERS, SEMIANNUAL FEATURE

(p. 1, 14-15) Semiannual article on consumer shopping habits for discount-priced products.

Data are based on a Dec. 1984 survey of approximately 450 households, conducted by Leo J. Shapiro & Associates.

Includes 3 tables showing percent of consumers paying less than full price for merchandise, and indicating a preference for selected retail outlet types, all for 8 product categories, Mar. and/or Dec. 1984.

Previous feature is described in SRI 1984 Annual under C5150-3.516.

CHAINS CONCERNED OVER 1ST HALF, DESPITE FISCAL-YEAR SALES GAINS, ANNUAL FEATURE

(p. 2) Annual article, with 1 table showing sales for 10 major discount chains or parent companies, Jan. 1984-85 and FY84-85. Data are from company reports.

Previous feature is described in SRI 1984 Annual under C5150-3.508.

CHAINS PLAN MORE $$ FOR KEY MIS AREAS

(p. 2, 85, 87) Article on retailer use of computerized management information systems (MIS). Data are based on a survey of 111 retailers conducted by Arthur Young and Co.

Includes 5 tables showing survey response on MIS costs (total and payroll) as percent of sales, 1981-83; and retailer use and planned installation of point-of-sales scanning technology by type, use of microcomputers, average number of computers in use, and MIS dept planning policies (no dates); all with detail by retail sales size group and outlet type.

STORES' HEIGHTENED YULE PROMO ACTIVITY DIDN'T CHANGE SHOPPER BUYING PATTERNS

(p. 15, 85) Article, with 1 undated table showing consumer sources of information about sales promotions, by selected retail outlet type. Data are from Leo J. Shapiro & Associates.

C5150–3.608: Apr. 1, 1985 (Vol. 24, No. 7)

PRODUCT MOVEMENT AUDIT (PMA) TABLE

(p. 51-73, passim) Housewares, Nov. 1, 1984-Jan. 31, 1985 and Jan 1-Feb. 4, 1985 periods.

COFFEE GAINS, STIMULATED BY BREWED DECAF, ANNUAL FEATURE

(p. 79) Annual article on coffee consumption trends, based on a winter 1984 survey of approximately 7,500 coffee drinkers conducted by the International Coffee Organization.

Includes 1 chart and 2 tables showing distribution of coffee consumption, by coffee type, 1984; cups of regular and soluble coffee consumed per person per day, 1962 and 1981-84; and percent of consumers using 7 coffee-making products, 1975 and 1981-84.

1984 IMPORTS UP IN ALMOST ALL CATEGORIES

(p. 85) Article, with 1 table showing imports of home and auto consumer electronics products by detailed type, 4th quarter and full year 1983-84. Data are from Commerce Dept.

C5150–3.609: Apr. 15, 1985 (Vol. 24, No. 8)

CHAINS' '84: PROFITS GENERALLY BLEAK DESPITE HEAVY BIZ, SEMIANNUAL FEATURE

(p. 2, 61) Semiannual article, with 1 table showing sales and earnings of 22 major discount chains or parent companies, 1983-84. Data are from *Discount Store News*.

ANNUAL PMA: '84 BEST-SELLERS AND PROJECTIONS

(p. 19-52) Annual Product Movement Audit of leading items sold in 7 discount store depts, 1984. Data are based on reports from wholesale distributors.

Includes 7 tables showing sales rank, 1983 and/or 1984; and unit movement, average retail price, and total sales value, 1984; for top-selling items in consumable goods, hardware, automotive, health and beauty aids, toys, sporting goods, and housewares depts.

C5150–3.610: Apr. 29, 1985 (Vol. 24, No. 9)

PRODUCT MOVEMENT AUDIT (PMA) TABLE

(p. 18) Ethnic health and beauty aids, 1984.

C5150–3.611: May 13, 1985 (Vol. 24, No. 10)

PRODUCT MOVEMENT AUDIT (PMA) TABLES

(p. 142-160 passim) Stationery and housewares, 1984.

DISCOUNTERS' HOUSEWARES SALES LEAD WIDENS, ANNUAL FEATURE

(p. 127-130) Annual article, with 2 tables showing houseware manufacturers' sales, with detail by retail outlet type and for all wholesale outlets, various years 1974-84.

Data are from the National Housewares Manufacturers Assn annual survey of manufacturers; full study report is covered in SRI under A7980-2.

SPOT TV USE BY FULL-LINE DISCOUNTERS SOARED IN '84, ANNUAL FEATURE

(p. 134) Annual compilation of articles on TV advertising expenditures of discount store chains. Data are from TV Bureau of Advertising, based on Broadcast Advertisers Reports data.

Includes 5 tables showing expenditures of top 10 discount department store chains in single market spot advertising, and of top 15 discount/cataloger chains in spot advertising; network and spot expenditures of 4 major chains; and local expenditures by retail outlet type and major chain company; 1983-84.

FAST CHECKOUT, STRONG IN-STOCK, BROAD MIX SEEN SURVIVAL KEYS

(p. 140, 146) Article, with 1 table showing discount store retail sales by product category, for 1980, and forecast for 1990 under 2 scenarios. Data are from Marketing Science Institute.

C5150–3.612: June 10, 1985 (Vol. 24, No. 12)

TOP CE CHAINS ON A ROLL; SWELL NET, BIZ, STORES, TURF, ANNUAL FEATURE

(p. 1, 74) Annual article, with 1 table showing top 10 consumer electronics discount chains ranked by sales for most recently completed fiscal year, and including average store size, and number of stores as of Jan. 1984-86. Data are from *Discount Store News*.

Previous feature is described in SRI 1984 Annual under C5150-3.514

CE CHAINS BOOSTED TV-AD OUTLAY LAST YEAR, ANNUAL FEATURE

(p. 43) Annual article, with 1 table showing top 10 consumer electronics discount chains ranked by TV advertising expenditures, 1984 with comparisons to 1983. Data are from TV Bureau of Advertising, based on Broadcast Advertisers Reports data.

Previous feature is described in SRI 1984 Annual under C5150-3.514.

C5150–3.613: June 24, 1985 (Vol. 24, No. 13)

AHAM SEES MICROWAVES AS No. 1 AGAIN THIS YEAR

(p. 18) Article, with 1 table showing shipments of major household appliances by type, 1983-85. Data are from Assn of Home Appliance Manufacturers.

C5150–3.614: July 8, 1985 (Vol. 24, No. 14)

PRODUCT MOVEMENT AUDIT (PMA) TABLE

(p. 8) Hair care mousses, Jan. 1-May 17, 1985.

C5150–3.615: July 22, 1985 (Vol. 24, No. 15)

DISCOUNTERS ADD PATRONS, PARTICULARLY FOR APPAREL, SEMIANNUAL FEATURE

(p. 1, 4B) Semiannual article on consumer shopping habits for discount-priced products. Data are based on a survey of 2,250 households, conducted by Leo J. Shapiro & Associates.

Includes 6 tables showing percent of consumers shopping discount stores and paying less than full price, for selected product categories; and survey response regarding benefits of shopping discount stores, retail outlet preferences, and sales shopping, mostly for Jan. or Mar. 1984-85.

'85 DISCOUNT STORE CENSUS, ANNUAL FEATURE

(p. 1, 15-123, passim) Annual statistical feature on discount store sales and productivity by dept, and stores and sales by company, State, and metro area, 1985, with selected projections for 1986 and trends from 1962.

Data are from the journal's own research, *Sales and Marketing Management* magazine, and other sources.

Contains introductory article, with 1 summary chart showing sales by discounter outlet type (p. 1, 15); industry summaries, interspersed with 14 tables described below (p. 17-61); profiles of top 10 individual discount chains, each with 1 summary table on sales, earnings, and number of outlets (p. 62-88); and merchandising profiles for 17 depts, interspersed with 17 charts and 17 tables also described below (p. 91-123).

CHARTS AND TABLES:

a. Top 100 chains ranked by general merchandise sales, with net earnings, for most recent fiscal year with comparison to previous fiscal year; stores and square footage as of Jan. and Dec. 1985; and scheduled store additions, 1986. 1 table. (p. 17)

b. Historical trends: discount department store sales, stores, square footage, sales per square foot, average sales per store, and average store size, 1962-85. 1 table. (p. 20)

c. Stores and square footage, by region, Dec. 1985; and stores by square footage range, Dec. 1984-85. 2 tables. (p. 25-26)

d. Stores, square footage, and sales, for all discounters and discount department stores, in top 50 metro market areas and by State; population, households, and effective buying income, for top 50 metro market areas;

and discount store square footage per person and total retail sales, by State; primarily 1985. 2 tables. (p. 31, 47)

e. Specialty discount chains: top 25 ranked by sales, FY84 with comparison to FY83, with stores and square footage as of Jan. 1985-86. 1 table. (p. 50)

f. Catalog showroom chains: top 10 ranked by sales, and including income, for most recent fiscal year with comparisons to previous fiscal year; and showrooms as of Jan. and Dec. 1985, and scheduled showroom additions for 1986. 1 table. (p. 59)

g. Off-price apparel chains, top 10 ranked by FY84 sales, with stores as of Jan. 1984-86; and top 10 membership warehouse clubs ranked by sales for most recent fiscal year with comparisons to previous fiscal year, with stores and square footage as of Jan. 1985-86. 2 tables. (p. 59)

h. Discount chains (automotive, toy, consumer electronics, and sporting goods), top 10 ranked by sales, FY84 or most recently completed fiscal year, with stores as of selected months 1984-86. 4 tables. (p. 60)

i. Merchandising profiles showing the following for 17 depts: sales, for discount department stores, specialty discounters, and catalog showrooms; and discount department store sales, sales per store and square foot, average dept size, annual inventory turns, initial markup, and gross margin; 1985. 17 charts and 17 tables (p. 91-123)

C5150–3.616: Aug. 5, 1985 (Vol. 24, No. 16)

SPORTING GOODS OUTLOOK BRIGHT AS SPECIALTY DISCOUNTERS EXPAND, ANNUAL FEATURE

(p. 3, 33) Annual article, with 1 table showing top 10 sporting goods chains ranked by sales, FY84; and including number of stores as of Jan. 1984-86, and average store size. Data are from *Discount Store News*.

Previous feature is described in SRI 1984 Annual under C5150-3.521.

C5150–3.617: Aug. 19, 1985 (Vol. 24, No. 17)

PRODUCT MOVEMENT AUDIT (PMA) TABLES

(p. 25-27, 62-64, passim) Hardware and automotive accessories, Feb.-June 1985.

CLOSEOUT STORES CLOSE IN ON 780 TOTAL, ANNUAL FEATURE

(p. 1, 82) Annual article, by Arthur Markowitz, on "closeout" retailers (those specializing in surplus or salvage merchandise). Data are from *Discount Store News*. Includes 1 table showing top 30 chains ranked by sales, most recent fiscal year with comparison to previous fiscal year; and also including number of stores as of Jan. and Dec. 1985, and planned store additions for 1986.

Corrected data appear in the Oct. 28, 1985 issue (see C5150-3.620 below).

DISCOUNTERS TRY TO REDUCE SWELLING HEALTH CARE COSTS

(p. 3, 82) By Beth A. Sexer. Article, with 1 chart showing percent change in health care expenditures for total U.S., 1979-84. Data are from *Health Care Financing Review*.

SPECIALTY CHAINS GET BACK ON EXPANSION TRACK IN '85, ANNUAL FEATURE

(p. 53, 66) Annual article, with 1 table showing top 10 automotive chains ranked by sales for most recently completed fiscal year, and including number of stores as of Jan. 1984-86. Data are from *Discount Store News*.

Previous feature is described in SRI 1984 Annual under C5150-3.515.

C5150–3.618: Sept. 9, 1985 (Vol. 24, No. 18)

SHOWROOM INDUSTRY CONSOLIDATION SNOWBALLS, ANNUAL FEATURE

(p. 19) Annual article, with 1 table showing top 35 catalog showroom chains ranked by sales, for most recent fiscal year, with comparison to previous fiscal year; and including number of showrooms as of Jan. and Dec. 1985, and showroom additions planned for 1986. Data are from *Discount Store News*.

OTC DRUGS' GROWTH PACED BY ANALGESICS

(p. 29) Article, with 1 chart and 1 table showing manufacturers' sales of nonprescription drug products by type, 1983-84. Data are from Charles H. Kline and Co.

C5150–3.619: Oct. 14, 1985 (Vol. 24, No. 20)

HEAT IS ON AS RIVALRY SPREADS, ANNUAL FEATURE

(p. 49) Annual article, by Karen Paxton, with 1 table showing top 14 off-price apparel chains ranked by sales, for most recent fiscal year; and including average store size, number of stores as of Jan. 1984-86, and planned store additions for 1986. Data are from *Discount Store News*.

Previous feature is described in SRI 1984 Annual under C5150-3.508.

MOST CHAINS USING TV HIKE OUTLAY IN FIRST 6 MONTHS

(p. 60) Article, with 1 table showing top 12 off-price apparel chains ranked by TV advertising expenditures, 1st half 1985 with comparison to 1st half and full year 1984. Data are from TV Bureau of Advertising based on Broadcast Advertisers Reports data.

TOP BRANDS, ANNUAL FEATURE

(p. 81-153) Annual compilation of articles on market penetration of national brand name products in the discount store industry. Data are from a 1985 survey of 341 store managers conducted by Leo J. Shapiro and Associates. Includes 15 charts and 56 tables showing survey response on the following:

a. Depts with increase in name brands, by discounter type (conventional and upscale); and change in amount of national brands carried; 1983-85.

b. Top-selling brands by region, discounter type, and leading chain; and regions with increase in brands carried, 1985 vs. 1984; generally repeated for 17 product categories.

Previous feature is described under C5150-3.601, above.

C5150–3.620: Oct. 28, 1985 (Vol. 24, No. 21)

DISCOUNTERS BOOST NET TO 2.54% IN '84-'85, THEIR HIGHEST EVER, ANNUAL FEATURE

(p. 1, 34) Annual article, with 2 tables showing discount chain store selected operating and financial ratios (mostly as percents of sales), including expenses by item, FY84-85. Data are from report published by National Mass Retailing Institute (NMRI); full NMRI report is covered in SRI under U1380-1.

Previous feature is described under C5150-3.604, above.

CORRECTION

(p. 11) Includes data correction for article on leading closeout discount chains, appearing in Aug. 19, 1985 issue (see C5150-3.617, above).

C5150–4   CHAIN STORE AGE, EXECUTIVE

Monthly.
ISSN 0193-1199.
LC 45-30011.
SRI/MF/excerpts, shipped quarterly

Monthly trade journal of the retail chain store and shopping center industries. Retail chain types include department store, discount, general merchandise, specialty, drug, and supermarket operations. Covers merchandising, finances, new construction, technology, store design, Federal Government regulation, and economic developments that affect retail trade.

Data are from Federal Government, store chains, private research assns, and the journal's own research.

Issues contain articles, occasionally with statistics; regular editorial depts, including a descriptive list of new stores and shopping centers; and "retail technology" section (sometimes published as a 2nd separate section), with feature articles on retail use of electronic technology.

Annual statistical features include reports on capital expenditures of leading retail chains; chain store expansion and physical support systems; and activities of chains with sales over $100 million.

Features with substantial statistical content are described, as they appear, under "Statistical Features." Each issue of the journal is reviewed, but an abstract is published in SRI monthly issues only when statistical features appear.

Availability: Chain Store Age, Executive, Subscription Department, 305 Madison Ave., Suite 535, New York, NY 10165-0079, qualified subscribers †, others $20.00 per yr.; SRI/MF/excerpts for all portions described under "Statistical Features;" shipped quarterly.

Issues reviewed during 1985: Nov. 1984-Oct. 1985 (P) (Vol. 60, Nos. 11-12; Vol. 61, Nos. 1-10)[May and Oct. issues are published in 2 sections].

STATISTICAL FEATURES:

C5150–4.601: Nov. 1984 (Vol. 60, No. 11)

MEMBERSHIP RETAILING TREND TAKING OFF

(p. 17-20) Article on wholesale membership clubs (companies offering wholesale-priced goods to retailers in exchange for a membership fee, and marketing bulk goods slightly above wholesale prices to private groups). Data are from *Chain Store Age Executive.*

Includes 1 undated table showing the following for 13 membership clubs: outlets by location, proposed expansion, membership fees, and retail markup.

BIG BUILDERS: RETAIL CONSTRUCTION LOOMS LARGE IN 1984, ANNUAL FEATURE

(p. 26-44) Annual feature on expansion and capital expenditures of leading retail chains. Data are from individual chains, and *Chain Store Age Executive* estimates. Includes the following:

a. Summary, with 3 tables showing top 25 chains ranked by capital expenditures, and gross and net square footage added, 1984 with comparison to 1983. (p. 26-27)

b. Profiles of 10 chains' capital expenditures, each with 1 table showing stores in operation at end of year, stores and square footage added, stores closed, and total capital expenditures, 1983-84. (p. 30-44)

SURVEY SHOWS DISPARITY IN MIS USE BY CHAINS

(p. 59, 62) Article, with 1 undated table showing percent of general merchandise retail chains using computerized management information systems (MIS), by selected function and system type. Data are from a survey of 26 general merchandise chains conducted by Touche Ross and Co.

C5150–4.602: Jan. 1985 (Vol. 61, No. 1)

SURVEY: 35% DON'T COMPLY WITH 1984 TAX REFORM ACT

(p. 39-41) Article on retailer compliance with provisions of the Tax Reform Act of 1984 requiring that the same merchandise discounts be offered to both executive and nonexecutive employees. Data are from a survey of 150 executives from 5 types of retail outlets, conducted by Arthur Young and Co. for *Chain Store Age.*

Includes 1 chart and 3 tables showing survey response on discounts offered to all employees or to executives and nonexecutives, need and plans for current discount policy changes, and familiarity with new regulations, with detail by retail outlet type (no dates).

TAKING A CONSERVATIVE STANCE, ANNUAL FEATURE

(p. 45-48) Annual article, with 1 table showing percent change in GNP, CPI, general merchandise prices, and consumer spending for durables, nondurables, and services; and annual housing starts and unemployment rate; 1980-85. Data are from Morgan Stanley Research.

Previous feature is described in SRI 1984 Annual under C5150-4.503.

CHAINS STILL SLASHING PRICES TO LOWER HIGH INVENTORIES, RECURRING FEATURE

(p. 53-56) Recurring article, with 1 table showing leading retail chain companies ranked by sales, with earnings per share, for general merchandise, supermarket/convenience, drug, and specialty store outlet types, 3rd quarter 1984 with comparison to 3rd quarter 1983. Data are from *Chain Store Age, Executive.*

NEW CENTERS PACE INDUSTRY UPSWING, ANNUAL FEATURE

(p. 61-66) Annual article reporting on expansion plans of shopping center developers. Data are based on a *Chain Store Age, Executive* survey.

Includes 6 tables showing survey responses on increases in gross leasable area (GLA), with percent share from new construction, expansion of existing centers, and new acquisitions; types of centers owned/managed; main sources of financing; and average GLA of new centers; with detail for regional malls and neighborhood/convenience/community centers, various years 1984-86.

Previous feature, for 1984, is described in SRI 1984 Annual under C5150-4.503.

C5150–4.603: Feb. 1985 (Vol. 61, No. 2)

TAKING THE HIGH-TECH APPROACH TO PILFERAGE

(p. 55-56) Article on retail inventory "shrinkage" and control measures. Data are from a survey of 176 retailers conducted by Arthur Young and Co. for National Mass Retailing Institute.

Includes 3 tables showing survey response regarding shrinkage rate by region, and security devices used and perceived as most effective by retailers, 1982 and/or 1983.

Full National Mass Retailing Institute report is covered by SRI under A8060-2.

C5150–4.604: Mar. 1985 (Vol. 61, No. 3)

RETAILING'S GRANDE DAME: CLOAKED IN NEW STRATEGIES

(p. 18-20) Article, with 1 chart showing return on shareholders' equity for 4 major corporations owning department stores, 1983. Data are from *Chain Store Age, Executive.*

SPENDING UP DESPITE SHRINKING LABOR COSTS

(p. 96-103) Article on retailer investment in computerized management information services (MIS). Data are from 111 responses to a recent survey of retailers conducted by Arthur Young and Co.

Includes 2 undated tables showing survey response regarding MIS system development/improvement plans for near future, and use of microcomputers by application, all by retail outlet type.

C5150–4.605: Apr. 1985 (Vol. 61, No. 4)

REMODELING PAYS OFF IN HIGHER PROFITS

(p. 27-29) Article on retail chain store remodeling activity. Data are from a *Chain Store Age, Executive* survey of 180 supermarket, drugstore, discount/mass merchandiser, home center, apparel, and department store chain companies.

Includes 2 charts and 2 tables showing average percent increase in sales and profits after remodeling, 1984; expected life spans of 4 store structural components (no date); average remodeling costs per square foot, 1983-84; and average respondent number of units and annual dollar volume (no dates); all by retail outlet type.

CHAINS OPTIMISTIC ABOUT 1985 DESPITE DISAPPOINTING QUARTER, RECURRING FEATURE

(p. 72) Recurring article, with 1 table showing leading chain companies ranked by sales, with earnings per share, for general merchandise, supermarket/convenience, and drugstore chains, 4th quarter 1984 with comparison to 4th quarter 1983. Data are from *Chain Store Age, Executive.*

C5150–4.606: May 1985 (Vol. 61, No. 5)

SECTION 1

ADULT BOOM: THE AGING OF THE WUNDERGENERATION

(p. 27-30) Article on retail marketing strategies directed toward the "baby boom" generation. Data are from *People Weekly* and Marketing Science Institute.

Includes 2 charts and 2 tables showing selected characteristics of population over age 18, by age group (no date); births, 1946-64 period; and retail sales, and sales per capita among persons age 18/over, for TV/audio equipment/musical instruments and electronics product categories, 1967, 1980, and 1990.

CATALOG OPTIONS: MAIL-ORDER OR STORE TRAFFIC?

(p. 31-33) Article, with 2 charts showing number of retail catalogs mailed, and consumer sales through direct mail, 1981-83. Data are from Direct Marketing Assn.

SURVEY DISCLOSES SHIFTS IN SHOPPING CENTER CHOICES

(p. 68-78) Article on consumer shopping patterns and shopping center preferences. Data are based on a *Chain Store Age* survey of consumers in 5 major market areas, and are shown separately for large enclosed malls and neighborhood strip shopping centers.

Includes 7 tables showing survey responses regarding factors influencing shopping center choice; sources of information about sales/special events; shopping time and frequency, with frequency detail for off-price centers; and travel time to center shopped most frequently; 1985 with selected comparison to 1981.

For description of similar survey, conducted in 1981, see SRI 1981 Annual under C5150-4.209.

SECTION 2

TESTING MERCHANDISING CONCEPTS

(p. 5-11) Article on supermarket use of computerized point-of-sale scanning data, including the application of direct product profit (DPP) margins (calculated by figuring allowances and handling costs into gross profit margin). Data are from Case and Co. Includes 1 chart and 1 table comparing typical gross profit and DPP margins, for selected product categories (no dates).

C5150–4.607: June 1985 (Vol. 61, No. 6)

SEARS LOOKING TO DISCOVER CREDIT CARD CONSUMER MARKET

(p. 17-18) Article, with 1 chart showing number of credit cards issued, and billings, for 4 major credit card companies, 1984. Data are from *The Nilson Report*.

COMBOS TAKE THE LEAD IN PERFORMANCE RACE

(p. 20-26) Article, with 4 charts and 2 tables showing selected measures of supermarket productivity, including sales per transaction and square foot, profit margin, and labor costs as a percent of sales, all by store type (conventional, superstore, combination, and warehouse), 1984-85 with comparison to 1983.

Data are from a *Chain Store Age, Executive* survey of supermarkets.

C5150–4.608: July 1985 (Vol. 61, No. 7)

INDUSTRY PROFILES, ANNUAL FEATURE

(p. 15-31) Annual compilation of articles on expansion activities of supermarket, department, home center, specialty, discount, and drug retail chains. Data are from *Chain Store Age, Executive* research.

Includes 6 tables showing mean total and selling space for stores opened during and prior to 1984/85, and mean shell construction costs within recent 12-month period, for each type of chain.

PHYSICIAL SUPPORT SYSTEMS, ANNUAL FEATURE

(p. 34-81) Annual compilation of articles profiling retail chain physical support systems (store equipment) by type. Data are from a *Chain Store Age, Executive* survey of retailers.

Includes 22 undated tables showing equipment costs and/or type of equipment/materials in use, and equipment life spans, for 10-11 support system categories, by type of retail chain.

Corrected data appear in the Aug. 1985 issue (see C5150-4.609 below).

C5150–4.609: Aug. 1985 (Vol. 61, No. 8)

CORRECTION

(p. 7) Includes data correction for annual feature on ˙retail physical support systems, appearing in July 1985 issue (see C5150-4.608 above).

$100 MILLION CLUB, ANNUAL FEATURE

(p. 21-38) Annual feature on retail chains with sales of $100 million or more, 1984. Data are from companies, and *Chain Store Age, Executive* estimates.

Includes 2 tables showing the following for 294 chains ranked by sales: sales, earnings, return on equity, and number of stores, 1984 with selected comparisons to 1983; and stores to be added in 1985; with selected detail for divisions of conglomerate chains. Also includes alphabetical index of companies covered.

Corrected data appear in the Sept. 1984 issue (see C5150-4.610 below).

PROJECT FUNDING EASES IN PLACID FINANCIAL SEAS

(p. 43-46) Article on financing methods used by shopping center developers. Data are from a recent *Chain Store Age, Executive* survey of major developers.

Includes 4 tables showing survey response concerning sources of long- and short-term financing, factors expected to affect the availability of financing in 1985, and interest rates paid on short-term loans, all shown separately for developers of neighborhood strip shopping centers and regional malls.

C5150–4.610: Sept. 1985 (Vol. 61, No. 9)

CLARIFICATION

(p. 10) Includes data correction for annual $100 million dollar club feature (see C5150-4.609 above).

SHOPLIFTING DYNAMICS: WHO, WHAT, WHEN, WHERE AND HOW?

(p. 79-80) Article, with 1 table showing methods of concealment used by shoplifters apprehended in supermarkets, drugstores, and discount stores, 1984.

Data are from the annual survey report *Shoplifting in Supermarkets, Drug Stores, and Discount Stores* published by Commercial Service Systems. Full report is covered in SRI under B2360-1.

C5150–4.611: Oct. 1985 (Vol. 61, No. 10)

SECTION 2: RETAIL TECHNOLOGY

SHOPPING BY TV OR PC: IS IT VIABLE?

(p. 8-14) Article on consumer willingness to make purchases through in-home electronic shopping systems. Data are based on a recent *Chain Store Age, Executive* survey of 500 adult consumers with access to cable TV and personal computers in 5 major cities.

Includes 6 undated charts showing survey response regarding likelihood of using existing or possible future cable TV and personal computer shopping systems, and product types most likely to be purchased through each system.

C5150–5   NATION'S RESTAURANT NEWS
Weekly. Oversized.
ISSN 0028-0518.
LC SN 78-6256.
SRI/MF/excerpts, shipped quarterly

Weekly trade journal (no issues published last 2 weeks in Dec.) reporting on financial and marketing trends in the food service industry. Covers sales, construction and expansion, promotion, menu development, food trends, and government activities and other general news of interest to the food service industry.

Data are from the journal's own research, trade assns, company reports, Dept of Commerce, and other government and private sources.

Issues contain mostly news articles, occasionally with statistics; narrative editorial depts; and the following recurring statistical features:

a. "Price Movement at a Glance" recurring table, with brief accompanying narrative, showing prices for 5-11 food commodities usually for a selected date approximately 2 weeks prior to cover date, and same day of previous month and/or year.

b. "Wall Street Update" weekly feature, with 4 tables showing recent stock price and trading trends, and income data for latest available quarter and year to date, for approximately 100 food service chains, hotels/motels/casinos, and other companies with food service operations; with top 10 stocks in trading volume and in price increase and decrease.

Journal also includes "NRN Focus," containing articles on a selected food service-related topic, frequently with statistics. Annual statistical features include a forecast of food service industry sales and market developments, and a detailed report on top 100 food service chains.

Weekly "Wall Street Update" feature appears in all issues. "Price Movement" table appears in alternate issues. All other features with substantial statistical content are described, as they appear, under "Statistical Features." Nonstatistical features are not covered.

Availability: Nation's Restaurant News, Subscription Department, 305 Madison Ave., Suite 535, New York NY 10165-0079, $18.00 per yr., single copy $1.00; SRI/MF/excerpts for weekly tables, and all portions covered under "Statistical Features;" shipped quarterly.

Issues reviewed during 1985: Nov. 5, 1984-Oct. 28, 1985 (P) (Vol. 18, Nos. 25-31; Vol. 19, Nos. 1-44) [Vol. 19, Nos. 28-30 incorrectly read Nos. 27-29, respectively].

STATISTICAL FEATURES:

C5150–5.601: Nov. 5, 1984 (Vol. 18, No. 25)

MARKET SEGMENTATION SHIFTING IN GROWING LODGING INDUSTRY

(p. 73) By Joe Edwards. Article, with 1 table showing number of properties and rooms, occupancy rate, and average charge per room, for 9 major lodging chains, generally 1983. Data are from company reports and Smith Barney Research.

LODGING INDUSTRY REBOUNDS FROM FOUR YEAR SLUMP

(p. 74-76) Article, with 2 charts and 2 tables showing lodging industry income and expense distributions, 1982-83; average occupancy rate, 1968-85; and annual percent change in room and food/beverage sales, June 1984. Data are from Laventhol and Horwath, Smith Barney Research, and Commerce Dept.

C5150–5.602: Nov. 12, 1984 (Vol. 18, No. 26)

AVERAGE CHECKS UP 8%-16% NATIONWIDE

(p. 9) Article with 1 table showing average check size for restaurants not serving alcoholic beverages, by establishment age, location (urban, suburban, and rural), types of meals served, menu theme, census region, and type of operation, 1983. Data are from Laventhol and Horwath and National Restaurant Assn.

C5150–5.603: Nov. 19, 1984 (Vol. 18, No. 27)

STUDY: DRUNK DRIVING-PRODUCED DROP IN ALCOHOL SALES STABLE, BUT STILL THERE, ANNUAL FEATURE

(Insert, p. 38-40) Annual article reporting on trends in restaurant alcoholic beverage sales. Data are from a 1984 NRN survey of alcoholic beverage operations. Includes 3 charts showing percent of operators reporting increase or decrease in sales during past 12-month period; and sales share; all by type of beverage.

Article is included in "Bar Management" insert section of issue.

C5150–5.604: Nov. 26, 1984 (Vol. 18, No. 28)

NRA PREDICTS FIFTH STRAIGHT GROWTH YEAR

(p. 3, 14) Compilation of articles forecasting food service industry sales, 1985. Data are from National Restaurant Assn. Includes 2 charts and 1 table showing food service sales by type of operation for commercial and institutional market segments, and by State and census division for restaurant segment, 1985 and/or percent change from 1984.

NRN FOCUS: NONALCOHOLIC BEVERAGE SALES RISE

(p. F3-F8) By Charles Forman. Article reporting on trends in restaurant nonalcoholic beverage sales. Data are from a 1984 NRN survey of leading chain restaurants.

Includes 1 chart and 9 tables showing sales share, recent and planned menu additions, and sales change in past year, all by type of nonalcoholic beverage; soft drink serving sizes offered and recent price trends; nonalcoholic beverage sales as percent of total sales; and past and anticipated changes in restaurant hours of operation; all for dinnerhouse, fast food, and family restaurants.

C5150–5.605: Dec. 3, 1984 (Vol. 18, No. 29)

CONSUMERS CLAMOR FOR ETHNIC FOOD

(p. 1, 83) Article, with 1 chart showing consumer preferences for specific types of ethnic food in restaurants. Data are from a 1983 National Restaurant Assn study.

For description of study, see SRI 1984 Annual under A8200-8.4.

C5150–5.606: Dec. 10, 1984 (Vol. 18, No. 30)

INDUSTRY-RELATED INJURIES, ILLNESSES UP IN 1983

(p. 45) Article, with 2 tables showing injury and injury/illness incidence rate for cases with and without lost workdays, and number of lost workdays, for restaurant/tavern workers, 1980-83. Data are from Labor Dept.

C5150–5.607: Dec. 17, 1984 (Vol. 18, No. 31)

TINY BURGERS, HUGE VOLUME

(p. 1, 9) By Paul Frumkin. Article, with 1 table showing number of units and value of sales, for White Castle and 3 other fast-food restaurant chains, 1984.

C5150–5.608: Jan. 2, 1985 (Vol. 19, No. 1)

**NRN FOCUS:
FORECAST AND TRENDS
WHAT'S AHEAD FOR '85,
ANNUAL FEATURE**

Annual forecast, in 3 parts, of food service industry sales and market developments for 1985. Part 1 includes the statistical feature described below. Part 2 is nonstatistical. Part 3 appears in the Jan. 14, 1985 issue, and is described under C5150-5.609.

1985 OFF TO A SLOW START, ECONOMY MAY GET BETTER

(p. F5) By Rick Telberg. Article, with 1 table showing food service industry growth rate and percent change in sales and menu prices, Jan.-Oct. 1984 vs. same months of 1983. Data are from NRN research.

C5150–5.609: Jan. 14, 1985 (Vol. 19, No. 3)

'CHICKEN WAR' ESCALATES

(p. 1, 59) By Joe Edwards. Article, with 1 chart showing top 9 restaurant chains specializing in chicken entrees, ranked by sales, 1984. Data are from NRN estimates and company reports.

CONSUMER GROUP URGES BAN ON 3 FOOD DYES

(p. 19) By Judith Packer. Article, with 1 table showing the following for 7 synthetic food dyes: volume certified by FDA, 1984; and main uses, links to specified medical problems, and world areas prohibiting use. Data are from Public Citizen Health Research Group.

NRN FOCUS: MORE ON WHAT'S AHEAD IN '85, ANNUAL FEATURE

Annual forecast, in 3 parts, of food service industry sales and market developments for 1985. Part 1 appears in the Jan. 2, 1985 issue and is described under C5150-5.608. Part 2 is nonstatistical. Part 3 includes the following statistical feature:

ADVERTISING WILL PLAY PIVOTAL ROLE FOR CHAINS IN '85

(p. F14) By Ken Frydman. Article, with 1 chart showing TV advertising expenditures during 1st 9 months 1984, for top 5 fast food chains ranked by percent change in spending from same period of 1983. Data are from TV Bureau of Advertising.

Other Article

SALES RISE 6.5% TO $10.1B SIGNALING INDUSTRY REBOUND, RECURRING FEATURE

(p. 62) Recurring article, with 1 table showing annual percent change in food service industry sales and menu prices, as of Dec. 1983-Nov. 1984. Data are from Commerce Dept, Dept of Labor, and NRN.

C5150–5.610: Jan. 28, 1985 (Vol. 19, No. 5)

CHEF SEARCH: HIRING THE BEST KITCHEN HANDS GETS TOUGHER, MORE EXPENSIVE

(p. 1, 12) Article, with 1 table showing low, median, and high salary ranges for chefs in hospitality industry and restaurant/fast food operations, by position, 1984. Data are from Roth Young Personnel Service, Inc.

INITIAL PUBLIC OFFERINGS: FEWER, BUT BIGGER, ANNUAL FEATURE

(p. 4, 10) Annual article, by Don Jeffrey, with 1 table showing the following for food service companies making initial public stock offerings in 1984: headquarters location, type of food service, date of offering, and initial and recent stock price. Data are from NRN research.

C5150–5.611: Feb. 11, 1985 (Vol. 19, No. 7)

CHAINS, INDEPENDENTS CARVE UP PIZZA MARKET

(p. 1, 3, 63) By Don Jeffrey. Article, with 1 chart showing sales of 6 major and all other pizza restaurant chains, 1984. Data are from NRN research.

NRN FOCUS: HEALTH CARE FEEDING, A GROWING SEGMENT

(p. F3-F4) By Peter Romeo. Article, with 1 chart showing health care food service sales for contract and in-house operations, 1982-85. Data are from National Restaurant Assn.

C5150–5.612: Feb. 18, 1985 (Vol. 19, No. 8)

BREAKFAST MARKET WAR ACCELERATES

(p. 1, F3) By Rick Telberg. Article, with 1 chart and 1 table showing the following for restaurant breakfast operations: market share by restaurant type, 1979 and 1984; and average check size (no date), and 1983-84 sales as percent of total sales, for 8 restaurant chains. Data are from National Restaurant Assn and Restaurant Trends, Inc.

SEA SCALLOP SUPPLY SHORT

(p. 3, 107) By Don Jeffrey. Article, with 1 chart showing Atlantic sea scallop catch, 1977-84. Data are from National Marine Fisheries Service.

CLOSER LOOK AT '84 INDUSTRY SALES, RECURRING FEATURE

(p. 110) Recurring table showing percent change in restaurant industry sales, by region and type of operation (full-sevice, fast food, and tavern), 1st 11 months 1984 vs. same period 1983. Data are from Census Bureau.

C5150–5.613: Feb. 25, 1985 (Vol. 19, No. 9)

WINTER WEATHER CHILLS INDUSTRY SALES, RECURRING FEATURE

(p. 1-2, 47) Recurring article, by Rick Telberg, with 1 chart showing eating/drinking place sales change from previous year, Feb. 1984-Jan. 1985. Data are from the Commerce Dept.

C5150–5.614: Mar. 11, 1985 (Vol. 19, No. 11)

MENU PRICE HIKES SLOW IN JAN., RECURRING FEATURE

(p. 1) Recurring chart showing annual percent change in menu prices, as of Jan. 1984-Jan. 1985. Data are from the Labor Dept.

NRN FOCUS: 2nd TIER CHAINS, ANNUAL FEATURE

(p. 1, F1-F34) Annual compilation of articles on sales and marketing strategies of regional food service chains. Data are from an NRN survey of food service chains with annual sales under $162 million.

Includes 1 table and 1 chart showing average unit sales, 1983-84; average check size by meal period, number of existing and new units, advertising expenses, and employment, 1984; percent of chains making major menu changes, raising prices (with average increase), serving alcoholic beverages, advertising to consumers, and noting decline in bar sales, 1984; and plans for additional units and for changes in menus and advertising spending, 1985.

Also includes 1 table repeated for 8 food service market segments, generally showing the following for 3-10 chains: sales or revenues, number of units or accounts, average check size, and menu price percent change, with some detail by region and type of operation, various periods 1983-85.

Market segments covered are Mexican-style chicken, gourmet hamburger, hotels, contract feeders, chicken, dinner house, fast food, and family restaurants.

C5150–5.615: Mar. 25, 1985 (Vol. 19, No. 13)

TRUCK STOPS BOLSTER FOOD

(p. 1, 33) Article, with 1 undated chart showing percent of truck drivers and of other highway travelers patronizing "truck stop" food service facilities. Data are from the National Assn of Truck Stop Operators.

SALES SLUMP AGAIN IN FEB., RECURRING FEATURE

(p. 1) Recurring table showing annual percent change in food service sales, as of Feb. 1984-Feb. 1985. Data are from the Commerce Dept.

C5150–5.616: Apr. 8, 1985 (Vol. 19, No. 15)

CONVERSIONS MOUNT AS SITES GROW SCARCE

(p. 1, 52) By David Zuckerman. Article reporting on restaurant industry recent acquisitions activity. Includes 1 undated table showing the following for 3 companies: chains acquired and number of units, and company-owned chains expanded as a result of acquisitions.

C5150–5.617: Apr. 15, 1985 (Vol. 19, No. 16)

NRN FOCUS: C-STORES—NEW ROUTES TO FAST-FOOD PROFITS, ANNUAL FEATURE

(p. F5-F7) Annual article, by Mark Schoifet, with 1 undated table ranking top 8 convenience store companies by number of units, 1984, and also showing headquarters location and chains owned. Data are from NRN research. For description of last previous article, with data for 1982, see SRI 1983 Annual under C5150-5.404.

C5150–5.618: Apr. 22, 1985 (Vol. 19, No. 17)

NRN FOCUS: WINE, BEER, AND SPIRITS, ANNUAL FEATURE

(p. 1, F1-F32) Annual compilation of articles on restaurant alcoholic beverage merchandising practices. Data are from an NRN telephone survey of 131 operations, conducted Mar. 1985.

Includes 21 charts presenting data on alcoholic beverage sales relative to previous year and to total sales; popularity of selected alcoholic beverages, with detail for best selling brands; and stocking and promotion practices, including prevalence of complimentary snack foods by type; often with detail for chain and independent restaurants and hotel chains.

MAR. SALES REBOUND, HIT 3.6% ANNUAL GROWTH RATE, RECURRING FEATURE

(p. 3) Recurring article, with 1 chart showing eating/drinking place sales change from previous year, 1st quarter 1984-1st quarter 1985. Data are from Commerce Dept.

C5150–5.619: May 6, 1985 (Vol. 19, No. 19)

McD 1st IN U.S. TO GET NEW COKE

(p. 1, 75) Article, with 1 chart showing Coca-Cola Co. and PepsiCo Inc. share of total and food service soft drink market, various years 1980-84. Data are from soft drink industry reports.

SURVEY: TRENDS IN DESIGN

(Insert, p. 13) Article on restaurant decor. Data are from an NRN survey of 50 restaurant operators. Includes 3 charts showing operators' responses concerning importance of decor, flexibility of own restaurant decor, and need for professional designers.

Article is included in "Restaurant Interiors" insert section of issue.

MAR. 'REAL' SALES OFF 0.3%, SHOW GAIN OVER FEB., RECURRING FEATURE

(p. 78) Recurring article, with 1 chart showing annual percent change in food service sales, as of Oct. 1984-Mar. 1985. Data are from Commerce and Labor Depts.

C5150–5.620: May 20, 1985 (Vol. 19, No. 21)

VALUES AND LIFE STYLES GIVE MADISON AVE. NEW TARGET

(p. 25) By D. M. Levine. Article on categorization of consumer lifestyles for the purpose of determining marketing strategies. Data are from the Values and Life-Styles (VALS) program of SRI International. Includes 1 undated chart showing population distribution by 9 lifestyle categories.

C5150–5.621: May 27, 1985 (Vol. 19, No. 22)

SURGE IN EUROPEAN TRAVEL AIDS U.S. CHAINS ABROAD

(p. 1, 12) By Marilyn Alva. Article, with 1 chart showing number of U.S. citizens traveling to Europe, 1984-85; and 4 largest U.S. fast food chains in Europe, based on number of units, 1985. Data are from NRN research.

SALES INCREASE AT SLUGGISH ANNUAL RATE OF 3%, RECURRING FEATURE

(p. 4) Recurring article, with 1 chart showing annual percent change in eating/drinking place sales, as of Jan.-Apr. 1985. Data are from Commerce Dept.

NRN FOCUS: BLAZING PATHS TO RAISE CAPITAL

(p. F5-F8) By Rick Telberg. Article, with 1 chart showing value of restaurant industry public debt/equity offerings, 1979-84. Data are from J. C. Bradford and Co.

C5150–5.622: June 3, 1985 (Vol. 19, No. 23)

WORKER SHORTAGE GROWS

(p. 1, 163) By Peter Romeo. Article, with 1 chart showing workforce age 16-24, and eating/drinking place employment, 1970, 1985, and 1990. Data are from BLS.

PIZZA DELIVERY 'HOT': NRA

(p. 2, 88) By Peter Romeo. Article, with 2 tables showing 12 types of speciality restaurants ranked by number of adults recently patronizing or intending to patronize these restaurants. Data are based on a Feb.-May 1985 survey conducted by the Gallup Organization for National Restaurant Assn.

Full survey report is covered in SRI under A8200-9.

C5150–5.623: June 10, 1985 (Vol. 19, No. 24)

SALES LAG WORSENS, RECURRING FEATURE

(p. 1, 4) Recurring article, by Rick Telberg, with 1 chart showing food service sales change from previous year, quarterly 3rd quarter 1982-2nd quarter 1985. Data are from Commerce and Labor Depts.

TEN CASINOS POST $157G LOSS

(p. 50) By Peter Romeo. Article, with 1 table showing operating profit or loss for 10 Atlantic City casinos, 1st quarter 1984-85. Data are from the New Jersey Casino Control Commission.

C5150–5.624: June 17, 1985 (Vol. 19, No. 25)

FORECAST FUELS FEAR OF LABOR SHORTAGE

(p. 1, 4) By Linda Breggin. Article, with 1 table showing food service employment by detailed occupation, 1982 and 1995. Data are from BLS.

C5150–5.625: July 1, 1985 (Vol. 19, No. 27)

WENDY'S ENTERS BREAKFAST ARENA

(p. 1, 59) By David Zuckerman. Article, with 1 undated chart showing average breakfast sales per unit, and breakfast sales as percent of total unit sales, for 5 leading fast-food chains. Data are from NRN research.

STUDY: FREQUENT TRAVELERS DINE IN HOTELS MORE OFTEN

(p. 20) By Peter Romeo. Article, with 1 table showing frequent travelers' reasons for initially choosing a hotel and for not returning for a 2nd stay. Data are based on 1,055 responses to a 1985 survey conducted by American Hotel and Motel Assn.

COMPUTER USAGE, ANNUAL ARTICLE

(Insert, p. 5-11) Annual article on computer use in the restaurant industry. Data are from an NRN survey of approximately 160 restaurant operations.

Includes 2 charts and 3 tables showing the following, generally by type of restaurant (fast-food, family, and dinnerhouse chains, and independent establishments): computer functions in use/planned for POS/ECR (point of sale/electronic cash register) and "back-of-the-house" systems; types of computer systems installed, and planned for next 2 years; and incidence of POS/ECR interface with other computer systems.

Article is included in "Restaurant Technology" insert section of issue.

For description of previous article, see SRI 1984 Annual under C5150-5.511.

C5150–5.626: July 8, 1985 (Vol. 19, No. 28)

[Issue incorrectly reads No. 27.]

RESTAURATEURS SAY THEY'LL STICK TO IMPORTED PASTA DESPITE TARIFF

(p. 3, 67) By Paul Frumkin. Article, with 1 chart showing import volume for all and Italian pasta, 1975-84. Data are from Census Bureau and National Pasta Assn.

NRN FOCUS: COMPENSATION STUDY—DINNERHOUSES LEAD PACK, ANNUAL FEATURE

(p. F1-F4, F13) Annual compilation of articles reporting on food service industry executive compensation. Data are based on telephone interviews conducted in spring 1985 with 151 executives of major chains.

Includes 2 charts and 5 tables showing the following by type of chain (fast food, family, and dinnerhouse): average annual salary and bonus, for selected regional and unit level positions; methods for calculating bonuses; percent of regional executives receiving bonuses, by position; and types of benefits provided; 1985.

For description of previous article, see SRI 1984 Annual under C5150-5.512.

C5150–5.627: July 22, 1985 (Vol. 19, No. 30)

[Issue incorrectly reads No. 29.]

MERCHANDISING SEAFOOD IN THE 1980s

(p. 1) Table showing sales and units for 6 seafood restaurant chains, FY85. Data are from NRN research and company reports.

C5150–5.628: July 29, 1985 (Vol. 19, No. 31)

STORE-LEVEL SALES UP 6% AT BIGGEST CHAINS, RECURRING FEATURE

(p. 3) Recurring article, with 1 chart showing sales change from previous year for all eating/drinking places (as reported by Commerce Dept), and aggregated for 17 leading chains (as reported by Restaurant Trends, Inc.), May-June 1985.

C5150–5.629: Aug. 12, 1985 (Vol. 19, No. 33)

STUDY: WESTERN FOOD-ONLY UNITS OUTSELL OTHERS

(p. 3) By Peter Romeo. Article, with 1 table showing average profit per seat for food only and food/alcoholic beverage restaurants, by census region, 1983-84. Data are from Laventhol & Horwath and National Restaurant Assn.

NRN FOCUS: CHAIN ANALYSIS PART I: THE TOP 100, ANNUAL FEATURE

(p. F1-F62) Annual report on financial and operating results of top 100 food service chains and top 100 chain companies ranked by estimated sales or revenue, primarily FY85. Data are from NRN Research, and are shown for fiscal years. Includes the following:

a. Narrative overview, with index of the top 100 chains; 4 summary trend charts; and 1 chart showing major industry segments ranked by sales change, for current and previous year. (p. F3-F4)

b. Top 100 chains ranked by estimated sales for current year, and including sales for 2 previous years, share of industry sales, headquarters location, type of chain, and name of parent company. 1 table. (p. F6-F7)

c. Top 100 chain companies ranked by estimated revenue for current year, and including revenue for 2 previous years, headquarters location, and types or names of chains owned. 1 table. (p. F8-F9)

d. Top 100 chains ranked by number of units and by sales per unit, for current year with comparisons to 2 previous years. 2 tables. (p. F11)

e. Industry segment analysis, generally with 3-4 tables ranking top 2-10 chains in each segment by sales, number of units, and sales per unit, with average check size and menu price increase over previous year, all for current year with comparisons to 2 previous years. (p. F17-F62)

A summary chart, and 1 table showing 5 fastest growing chains based on increase in sales, are also included (p. 1).

C5150–5.630: Aug. 19, 1985 (Vol. 19, No. 34)

VENDORS HIT HARD BY SHORT WALK

(p. 3) By Ken Frydman. Article reporting on Aug. 1985 baseball strike's effect on stadium concessionaires. Data are from NRN Research. Includes 1 table showing number of catering employees laid off, average caterer loss per day, and total number of games missed.

SALARIES OF PROFESSIONAL-LEVEL HOSPITALITY WORKERS ON THE RISE, ANNUAL ARTICLE

(p. 45) Annual article, with 1 table forecasting median salaries for restaurant/food service and lodging industry executives, by position, 1985. Data are from Roth Young Personnel Service, Inc. *1985 U.S. Salary Outlook Survey.*

For description of previous article, see SRI 1984 Annual under C5150-5.503

NRN FOCUS: CHAIN ANALYSIS PART II, ANNUAL FEATURE

(p. F1-F8) Annual report on food service chain finances, customer characteristics, and menu items, 1985, with trends from 1980. Data are from NRN Research. Contains 14 tables showing the following:

a. CPI for food away from home, and WPI for food, monthly 1980-June 1985.

b. Burger and family restaurant/coffee shop chains: average check size, sales per unit, cost/sales ratios, profit margin, and menu price increase, 1982-85; food and labor cost increases, customer age and income distribution, and sales distribution by meal period, 1983-85; average weekly sales, items sold, and prices, by menu item, 1984-85; and cost distributions, for food, supplies, labor, and 7 other items, 1984-85.

C5150–5.631: Aug. 26, 1985 (Vol. 19, No. 35)

FOOD SERVICE SALES SOFTEN IN JULY, RECURRING FEATURE

(p. 3) Recurring article, by Rick Telberg, with 1 chart showing food service sales change from previous year, Jan.-July 1985. Data are from the Commerce Dept.

SURVEY: WHAT'S HOT, WHAT'S NOT

(Insert, p. 7-11) Article on restaurant operators' views regarding kitchen design. Data are based on an NRN survey of 162 operators. Includes 3 undated charts showing survey response on factors considered extremely/very important in purchase of kitchen equipment, use of selected energy saving measures, and availability of energy conservation training programs for employees.

Article is included in "Kitchen Design" insert section of issue.

C5150–5.632: Sept. 9, 1985 (Vol. 19, No. 37)

'SUDDENLY, CHEAP IS CHIC'

(p. 1, 69) By Rick Telberg. Article, with 1 chart showing annual percent change in average restaurant check size and in number of discount meal purchases, selected quarters 1984-1985. Data are from GDR/Crest Enterprises.

C5150–5.633: Sept. 16, 1985 (Vol. 19, No. 38)

TAX ON CANADIAN FISH COULD AFFECT ENTREE PRICES

(p. 34) Article, with 1 table showing tariff rates on fish, by species, 1985. Data are from NRN research.

STUDY SHOWS 'FOOD-ONLY' PROFITS DOWN PER DOLLAR

(p. 61) Article, with 3 charts showing average check size for food-only and food/beverage restaurants, by census region and type of operation, 1984. Data are from Laventhol & Horwath.

C5150–5.634: Sept. 23, 1985 (Vol. 19, No. 39)

SLUGGISH SALES SEEN FOR INDUSTRY: IMFA

(p. 4) By Rick Telberg. Article, with 1 table showing food service sales, 1986, with nominal and real percent change from 1985, all by industry segment. Data are from International Foodservice Manufacturers Assn.

C5150–5.635: Sept. 30, 1985 (Vol. 19, No. 40)

SCALLOP CROP IS DESTROYED

(p. 2, 113) Article, with 1 table showing scallop imports and production by type (bay, sea, and calico), 1979-84. Data are from Marine Fisheries Service.

RESTAURANTS POST FLAT AUGUST SALES, RECURRING FEATURE

(p. 4) Recurring article, with 1 chart showing food service sales change from previous year, Jan.-Aug. 1985. Data are from the Commerce Dept.

C5150–5.636: Oct. 7, 1985 (Vol. 19, No. 41)

McD UPS AD BUDGET

(p. 1, 243) By Mark Schoifet. Article, with 1 table showing top 6 fast food chains, ranked by TV advertising expenditures, Jan.-June 1985 period, with comparisons to previous year. Data are from TV Bureau of Advertising.

C5150–5.637: Oct. 14, 1985 (Vol. 19, No. 42)

TAKEOVER FRENZY RESHAPING INDUSTRY

(p. 1, 53) By Charles Bernstein. Article with 1 table showing acquiring and acquired company, price, and transaction date, for 4 recent acquisitions of food companies. Data are from NRN research.

HOUSE ALTERNATIVE TAX PLAN OFFERS NO RELIEF TO INDUSTRY

(p. F8) By Ken Rankin. Article, with 1 undated table showing tax deduction allowed for business meals under current law and under changes proposed by Reagan Administration and by House of Representatives, all by meal price. Data are from NRN research.

C5150–5.638: Oct. 21, 1985 (Vol. 19, No. 43)

NEW COMPETITION FACES U.S. FAST FEEDERS ABROAD

(p. 106) Article, with 4 tables showing fast-food sales (total and/or per capita) and outlets, and inflation rate, various periods 1984-90; and maximum outlets; all by country or world area. Data are from Euromonitor.

C5150–5.639: Oct. 28, 1985 (Vol. 19, No. 44)

CATFISH GAINS IN POPULARITY

(p. 1, 9) By David Zuckerman. Article, with 1 chart showing catfish production, selected years 1970-85. Data are from Catfish Farmers of America.

INDUSTRY SALES CLIMB 5.1 % IN SEPTEMBER, RECURRING FEATURE

(p. 4) Recurring article, with 1 chart showing food service sales change from previous year, Apr.-Sept. 1985. Data are from the Commerce Dept.

C5150–6   NATIONAL HOME CENTER NEWS

Biweekly.   Oversized.
ISSN 0192-6772.
LC 79-6811.
SRI/MF/excerpts

Biweekly journal (monthly in Dec.) of the home center (retail building materials/hardware/home improvement) industry. Covers financial and marketing developments, merchandise line sales, store expansion, sales promotion, lumber and construction industry trends, and relevant legislation and government activities.

Data are from industry sources, including store chains and trade assns; private research firms; Federal sources; and the journal's own research.

Issues contain numerous news articles and regular depts, some with statistics, including recently advertised prices of selected brand-name products; and the following regularly recurring statistics:

a. "Financial News" feature, with 4-6 tables showing stock market performance and financial position of leading home center industry retailers, wholesalers, and manufacturers, as of most recent available date (specified for each company); and comparison of industry performance to Standard & Poor's 500 index. Feature begins in the Jan. 1, 1985 issue; prior to Jan. 1985, journal included sales and earnings data only for leading retailers.

b. Lumber report, generally including 1-2 charts showing 4-year quarterly price trends for total or selected types of lumber and plywood, through quarter of cover date, or previous quarter; 1 table showing futures trading activity; and occasional additional charts or tables.

c. "U.S. Housing Starts" feature with text data, 5 charts, and 1 table showing total and single-family housing starts and permits for month 2 months prior to cover date and selected previous months, with detail by region; prior to Jan. 14, 1985 issue, feature was titled "Home-Building Activity."

d. "Existing Single-Family Home Sales" feature with text data and 4-5 charts showing trends in existing single-family home sales, including median sale price by region for month 2-3 months prior to cover date and 3 previous months.

Annual statistical features include an industry census, metro market outlook, home improvement consumer attitudes survey, and brands report.

"Financial News" tables appear in each issue; other recurring features appear in at least 1 issue each month. Annual features, additional lumber report tables, and other articles with substantial statistical content are described, as they appear, under "Statistical Features." Nonstatistical features are not covered.

Availability: National Home Center News, Subscription Department, 305 Madison Ave., Suite 535, New York NY 10165-0079, qualified subscribers †, others $25.00 per yr., single copy $2.00, census and consumer attitude issues $15.00; SRI/MF/excerpts for recurring "Financial News" tables, lumber report, "U.S. Housing Starts" feature, "Existing Single-Family Home Sales" feature, and all portions covered under "Statistical Features."

Issues reviewed during 1985: Nov. 5, 1984-Oct. 21, 1985 (P) (Vol. 10, Nos. 23-25; Vol. 11, Nos. 1-22) [Vol. 11, No. 8 incorrectly reads No. 7].

STATISTICAL FEATURES:

C5150–6.601: Nov. 5, 1984 (Vol. 10, No. 23)

4,029 FIRMS OWN 11,509 HOME CENTERS; WAREHOUSE STORES INCREASE: NEW GUIDE

(p. 42-44) Article, with 2 tables showing the following for home center/hardware/specialty chains: number of chains selling each of 49 product types; and number of companies and stores, by type of chain; 1983 and/or 1984. Data are from *Chain Store Guide: Home Center Operators and Hardware Chains* directory.

C5150–6.602: Nov. 19, 1984 (Vol. 10, No. 24)

BRITISH HOME CENTERS EYE YANKEE KNOW-HOW

(p. 58) By Elizabeth Brent. Article, with 2 tables showing number of UK stores selling do-it-yourself or home improvement merchandise, by store type, with selected detail for chain and independent stores; and sales and stores for 9 leading UK home center chains; 1983 or 1984. Data are from Euromonitor, Management Horizons, and *National Home Center News.*

C5150–6.603: Dec. 17, 1984 (Vol. 10, No. 25)

SMOOTH SAILING AHEAD FOR '85 INDUSTRY SALES EXPANSION

(p. 5, 128) By Laura Liebeck. Article, with 1 chart showing retail sales for the building material/hardware/supply industry, monthly Sept. 1983-Sept. 1984. Data are from Commerce Dept.

CORRECTIONS

(p. 8) Includes data correction for an article on residential building permits, appearing in Oct. 22, 1984 issue.

For description of article, see SRI 1984 Annual, under C5150-6.512.

CRISP ASSET MANAGEMENT SUPPORTS MOVE TO DIY RETAILING

(p. 115, 121) Article, with 1 table showing sales, profit margin, earnings per share, and return on equity, for 6 selected home center chains, 1984-85. Data are from Value Line, Inc.

C5150–6.604: Jan. 1, 1985 (Vol. 11, No. 1)

NHCN's 1985 METRO MARKET OUTLOOK, ANNUAL FEATURE

(p. 1, 20-42) Annual compilation of articles on housing construction and building materials/hardware sales trends in leading metro markets. Data are from *Sales and Marketing Management,* National Assn of Home Builders, National Assn of Realtors, and NHCN.

Includes 1 table showing top 100 SMSAs ranked by retail building material/hardware sales, 1983; and profiles of 7 SMSAs, each with 4 tables showing summary demographics, total retail and building material/hardware sales, total and single-family housing starts, median sales price of existing single-family homes, and number of home center chain stores, by chain, various periods 1978-88.

C5150–6.605: Jan. 28, 1985 (Vol. 11, No. 3)

USA HOUSING OUTLOOK

(p. 19-37) Compilation of articles on recent trends in housing construction and building material use. Data are from National Assn of Home Builders.

Includes 13 tables showing total and single-family housing starts, by census region and for 14-18 major metro areas within each region, quarterly 4th quarter 1983-1st quarter 1985, and annually 1983-85, with percent changes from previous years; and market shares for various building materials within 7 categories, and distribution of houses by number of fireplaces, 1982 with percent change from 1974.

Corrected data appear in the Feb. 25, 1985 issue (see C5150-6.607 below).

CONSUMERS' CRIME FEARS SPUR HIGH-END LOCKSET SALES

(p. 39, 44-45) Article, with 1 table showing number of households equipped with security devices, and median retail price and total market value, for do-it-yourself and professionally installed devices by price range, summer 1983. Data are from Frost and Sullivan, Inc.

TV BECOMES SCENE OF BATTLE FOR MARKET SHARE, QUARTERLY FEATURE

(p. 53) Quarterly article, with 1 table showing top 17 home center chains ranked by TV advertising expenditures, with detail for selected subsidiaries, 1st 9 months 1984, with comparison to 1st 9 months 1983. Data are from TV Bureau of Advertising analysis of Broadcast Advertisers Reports data.

C5150–6.606: Feb. 11, 1985 (Vol. 11, No. 4)

RETAILERS INCREASING MIS FUNDS

(p. 65) Article on retailer use of microcomputers. Data are based on 111 responses to an Arthur Young and Co. survey of retailers. Includes 2 undated tables showing percent of respondents using microcomputers, and planning system development/improvement within next 2 years, by application.

C5150–6.607: Feb. 25, 1985 (Vol. 11, No. 5)

CLARIFICATIONS

(p. 5) Includes data corrections for feature on recent trends in housing construction.

For feature description, see C5150-6.605 above.

SECURITY SPENDING RISES IN '84; HIGH TECH DEVICES GAIN POPULARITY

(p. 77) Article, with 1 undated chart showing most effective security devices, as cited by 176 retailers responding to an Arthur Young and Co. survey.

Full survey report is covered in SRI under A8060-2.

C5150–6.608: Mar. 11, 1985 (Vol. 11, No. 6)

DIY VIDEOTEX USE POISED FOR DRAMATIC INCREASE

(p. 148) Article on potential retail use of videotex terminals to provide information for customers. Data are from a Frost and Sullivan survey of 18 major chain retailers and 15 system suppliers.

Includes 2 tables showing number of potential locations, actual installations, and hardware and advertising/information costs, for terminals installed in building materials/hardware/garden supply stores, 1985-88; and installations, and videotex industry revenues, for terminals in retail outlets and related locations, 1983/84, 1986, and 1988.

C5150–6.609: May 6, 1985 (Vol. 11, No. 10)

TOP 10 CARRY TOP 100 TO $17B IN '84 SALES

(p. 1, 129) Article, with 1 table showing top 10 home center chains ranked by sales, 1984. Data are from *National Home Center News.*

NHCN ANNUAL REPORT ON THE HOME CENTER INDUSTRY

(p. 21-128, passim) Annual compilation of articles on home center industry, including sales trends, stores, company rankings, and operating and marketing developments, 1984. Data sources include company reports, industry assns, journal's own research, and Commerce Dept.

Includes brief company profiles (p. 74-96), each with 1 chart showing sales, 1983-84; and 8 charts and 31 tables showing the following:

a. Company rankings: top 100 companies ranked by do-it-yourself (DIY) and total sales, with number of stores (including forecast for 1985) and/or selling area, and detail for selected subsidiaries, 1984 with comparison to 1983; and top 10 companies ranked by total sales, with stores and DIY sales share, 1975-83. 1 chart and 12 tables. (p. 22-31, 106-117)

b. Warehouse stores: number by region and State; and number by chain company, with markets covered, and average inventory volume and square footage; various years 1982-85. 6 charts and 1 table. (p. 33-35)

c. Product marketing: average sales per square foot, gross margin, sales-to-inventory ratio, and gross margin return on investment, for 9 product depts in retail home centers and lumber/building material outlets, 1984. 9 tables. (p. 45-71)

d. Residential repair and remodeling expenditures by type of project, 1982-84; and 10 companies with greatest dollar and percent increase in total and DIY sales, and decrease in total sales, 1984. 1 chart and 7 tables. (p. 96-99)

e. Buying cooperatives: top 17 hardware/lumber/building material cooperatives ranked by sales, and including dealer stores and home centers, warehouses and square footage, inventory value and volume, and employment; and top 7 wholesaler cooperatives ranked by sales, and including warehouses, inventory volume and value, employment, advertising expenditures, and number of wholesalers, affiliated dealers, and customers; 1984 with comparisons to 1983. 2 tables. (p. 101-102)

Additional data for top 100 ranking appear in June 17, 1985 issue (see C5150-6.611 below).

This is the 11th annual report.

C5150–6.610: May 20, 1985 (Vol. 11, No. 11)

COMPUTERS REVOLUTIONIZE KITCHEN DESIGN; 'IF COMPETITION HAS IT, YOU'D BETTER HAVE IT TOO'

(p. 29-30) Article, with 1 undated table showing the following for 8 computerized kitchen design systems: date of 1st retail installation, total retail and home center stores with systems installed, and software and hardware prices.

C5150–6.611: June 3, 1985 (Vol. 11, No. 12)

FEDERAL DEFICIT COULD KILL ENERGY TAX CREDIT EXTENSION BILLS

(p. 3, 35-36) Article on proposed extension of homeowner energy conservation tax credits. Includes 1 table showing tax credits and maximum allowable expenditures, for use of renewable energy resources by type, and for energy conservation improvements, actual 1985 and as proposed for 1986-90 in legislation before the House of Representatives.

CORRECTIONS

(p. 5) Includes additional data for annual report on the home center industry appearing in May 6, 1985 issue. Shows data for 1 company omitted from ranking of top 100 companies.

For description of original feature, see C5150-6.609, above.

INDUSTRY COMPENSATION STUDY

(p. 21-29) Compilation of articles on home improvement industry employee compensation. Data are based on responses from 160 home center, lumber/building materials, and hardware retailers to a 1985 survey conducted by Lebhar-Freidman Research.

Includes 1 chart and 5 tables showing survey response on change in payroll, with average increase and decrease reported; median salaries and bonuses, by position; benefits offered to management and store level personnel; and awarding of bonuses by position and region; for all and/or home center respondents, with selected detail by sales size group.

COMMUNICATION SYSTEMS SEE RAPID CHANGES

(p. 53) Article on corporate plans for improving telecommunications systems. Data are based responses of 348 companies to a Conference Board survey. Includes 2 undated tables showing survey response on planned changes in telecommunications systems and budgets.

For description of complete Conference Board report, see R4105-29.51.

HOME CENTER SHRINKAGE UP 12.2% IN '84

(p. 53) Article on retail inventory "shrinkage." Data are based on a survey of 80 retailers, conducted by *Peter Berlin Report*. Includes 1 table showing percent increase in sales and shrinkage, 1984 with comparison to 1983.

C5150–6.612: July 1, 1985 (Vol. 11, No. 14)

REMODELERS, REALTORS AGREE: STRONG '85 GAINS

(p. 10) Article, with 1 undated table showing average costs for 10 types of housing remodeling projects. Data are from a 1st quarter 1985 survey of professional contractors conducted by National Assn of Home Builders.

LUMBERYARDS, WAREHOUSES FACE ZONING HASSLES

(p. 19-21) By John Caulfield. Article, with 1 undated table showing home center construction costs per square foot, by component, in Chicago, Philadelphia, and Houston. Data are from American Appraisal Associates, Inc.

C5150–6.613: July 15, 1985 (Vol. 11, No. 15)
[Issue price is $15.00.]

NHCN's 1985 CONSUMER ATTITUDE SURVEY: ATTRACTING THE DIY CONSUMER, ANNUAL FEATURE

(p. 19-32, 45-52) Annual compilation of articles on home improvement consumer shopping practices and retail outlet preferences, in 7 major market areas, 1985 with selected comparisons to 1984.

Includes data on consumer shopping patterns for home improvement products, including preferences for and perceived strengths and weaknesses of retail outlet types; home center store use and awareness of new home centers; and awareness of home improvement advertising and preferred advertising media; with selected detail by product type and market area.

Also includes data on number of households by market area; and additional detail for Phoenix market area, including home center chain stores, with consumer shopping preferences by chain, and consumer home improvement plans and expenditures.

Data are based on a 1985 telephone survey of 1,858 households, conducted by Leo J. Shapiro and Associates.

Includes 14 charts and 12 tables.

C5150–6.614: July 29, 1985 (Vol. 11, No. 16)

INTERNATIONAL REPORT

(p. 1, 19-56) Compilation of articles focusing on the home center industry and do-it-yourself (DIY) sales in Australia, Japan, UK, and EC. Data were compiled by *National Home Center News* from company reports, Japan DIY Industry Assn, Frost and Sullivan, Inc., and other sources.

Includes 1 chart and 4 tables showing DIY sales in the 3 countries, EC, and U.S., 1986; stores and sales for leading home improvement chains in Australia and Japan, various years 1983-85; and DIY sales, for EC by product type, and for 9 European countries, 1982, 1986, and 1988.

NAR HOUSING OUTLOOK OPTIMISTIC FOR NEAR FUTURE

(p. 10) Article, with 1 table showing existing single-family home sales, housing starts, and existing and new home median prices, 1985-87. Data are from National Assn of Realtors.

NEW MANUFACTURER STUDIES SHOW INSULATION MARKET NOT SATURATED

(p. 67) Article, with 1 undated chart showing distribution of homes by level of attic insulation. Data are from a survey of 80,000 homeowners conducted by National Family Opinion, Inc.

C5150–6.615: Aug. 12, 1985 (Vol. 11, No. 17)

GAMBLING ON THE STORE OF THE FUTURE

(p. 27-44 passim) By John Caulfield. Article on hardware store prototypes and remodeling plans designed by leading wholesale cooperatives to improve store performance. Data are based on reports from individual cooperatives.

Includes 5 tables showing data on operations and plans of 5 hardware wholesale cooperatives, generally including number of hardware dealers served, sales in 1984, number of stores remodeled/built based on cooperative designs through Apr. 1985, expected additional store remodels/construction by 1986 or beyond, and remodeling costs per square foot.

ALLIED BACKS BAN ON CLOSED MARKET COUNTRIES

(p. 147) Article, with 4 tables showing value of imports and exports of hand and power tools, 1977-84, with detail for 1983-84 by country of origin and destination. Data are from Commerce Dept.

JAPANESE HOME CENTERS UNVEIL GROWTH PLANS

(p. 154) Article, with 1 table showing Japanese home center industry sales and number of home center stores, 1973-85. Data are from Japan Do-It-Yourself Industry Assn.

RETAILERS OPEN TO MEET PUBLIC SHOPPING NEED

(p. 163) Article, with 1 undated table showing distribution of home center retailers by hours of store operation per day during weekdays and on Saturdays, for contractor and consumer oriented retailers. Data are from a Lebhar-Friedman Research survey of 160 retailers.

PAYLESS OUTSPENDS PACK IN 1Q TV ADVERTISING, QUARTERLY FEATURE

(p. 186) Quarterly article, with 1 table showing top 15 home center chains ranked by TV advertising expenditures, with detail for selected subsidiaries, 1st quarter 1985, with comparison to 1st quarter 1984. Data are from TV Bureau of Advertising analysis of Broadcast Advertisers Reports data.

C5150–6.616: Aug. 26, 1985 (Vol. 11, No. 18)

FEDS TIGHTEN LENDING RULES, BUT AFFORDABILITY UP

(p. 10) Article, with 1 table showing index of housing affordability and its 3 components (mortgage interest rates, median household income, and median home prices), selected months 1972-85. Data are from National Assn of Realtors.

LUMBER REPORT: STRUCTURAL WOOD PANEL SALES RISE; TECHNOLOGY CUTS PRODUCTION COST

(p. 16, 66) Includes 1 table showing number of lumber mills producing nonveneer composite structural wall panels, with capacity and production volume, 1980-90. Data are from American Plywood Assn.

STRONG SALES SPUR DEALERS TO FILL IN MOWER LINES

(p. 34-35) Article, with 1 table showing lawn mower shipments from manufacturers, by mower type, 1983-86. Data are from Outdoor Power Equipment Institute.

C5150–6.617: Sept. 9, 1985 (Vol. 11, No. 19)

RESILIENT FLOORING GROWING AS FASHIONABLE PRODUCT FOR THE ENTIRE HOME

(p. 35-36) Article, with 1 table showing market shares for floor coverings by type, 1984-85. Data are from Retail Floor Covering Institute.

C5150–6.618: Sept. 23, 1985 (Vol. 11, No. 20)

REPAIR SPENDING TOPS $83B IN 1Q

(p. 3) By Laura Liebeck. Article, with 1 table showing homeowner expenditures for residential maintenance/repair, additions/alterations, and major structural replacements, 1st and 4th quarters 1984 and 1st quarter 1985. Data are from Census Bureau.

HARDWARE STORE SHOPPING HABITS CHALLENGING HOME CENTERS' COLUMBUS ENTRY

(p. 3, 80) By Phillip M. Perry. Article on consumer shopping habits and the home center industry in Columbus, Ohio. Data are from a survey of consumers in 7 major market areas, conducted by Leo J. Shapiro Associates.

Includes 3 undated tables showing survey response on preferred outlet type (discount and home center stores) for purchasing hardware products by type, and preference for longer advertising brochures, shown for Columbus, Ohio, with comparisons to aggregate 7 or selected other markets.

EXPERT FORECASTS 27% RISE IN L&G SPENDING

(p. 24) Article, with 1 table showing sales of lawn and garden products, by type, 1985. Data are from Greenidge and Associates.

C5150–6.619: Oct. 7, 1985 (Vol. 11, No. 21)

LUMBER REPORT: NEW FOE BUGS SOUTHERN LUMBER; BEETLES GNAW 800M BOARD FEET

(p. 3, 16) Includes 1 undated table showing amount of lumber destroyed by southern pine beetles on federally owned land in 4 southern States. Data are from U.S. Forest Service.

TV SPENDING LEAPS 43% IN FIRST HALF OF '85, QUARTERLY FEATURE

(p. 21, 24) Quarterly article, with 1 table showing top 14 home center chains ranked by TV advertising expenditures, with detail for selected subsidiaries, 1st half 1985, with comparison to 1st half 1984. Data are from TV Bureau of Advertising analysis of Broadcast Advertisers Reports data.

1985 NHCN CONSUMER TOP BRANDS STUDY, ANNUAL FEATURE

(p. 29-75) Annual compilation of articles on home improvement product brands. Articles focus on consumers' attitudes concerning national brands, and awareness of specific brand names. Data are from an Aug. 1985 survey of 424 consumers purchasing at least $40 worth of home improvement products over a 12-month period. Survey was conducted by Leo J. Shapiro and Associates.

Includes 6 charts and 38 tables showing responses concerning the following:

a. Willingness to pay more for brands, importance of product value vs. brand name, characteristics associated with brand name products, quality of brand name vs. private label products, and sources of brand awareness, all shown by type of retail outlet shopped (home center, hardware store, Sears/Wards, and other).

b. Consumer awareness rankings for specific brand names in selected home improvement product categories, and rankings of product categories by extent of brand awareness among consumers.

This is the 3rd annual feature. Previous features focused on surveys of retailers' views and practices concerning national brands.

RETAIL VIDEODISC USE FALLS SHORT OF PROJECTION

(p. 77) Article on retailer use of video interactive merchandising systems providing electronic shopping aids for consumers. Data are from Yankee Group, Inc. Includes 1 table showing installations of transactional and non-transactional video interactive systems, 1984-87.

C5150–6.620: Oct. 21, 1985 (Vol. 11, No. 22)

HOME CENTERS OUT-HARDWARE HARDWARE STORES

(p. 47, 56) Article on finances and operations of retail outlets selling hardware. Data are based on 1985 surveys of home centers, do-it-yourself lumberyards, and hardware stores, conducted by National Retail Hardware Assn.

Includes 1 chart and 1 table showing home center net sales distribution by product category, 1984; selected measures of hardware dept performance and profitability in each outlet type, including sales per square foot, 1983-84; and summary respondent characteristics.

Full survey reports are covered in SRI under A8275-1.

C5150–7   CHAIN STORE AGE, GENERAL MERCHANDISE TRENDS

Monthly.
ISSN 0193-1350.
LC sn79-4345.
SRI/MF/excerpts, shipped quarterly

Monthly trade journal of the general merchandise retail chain industry. Chain types covered include general merchandise discount, department, variety, and catalogue stores; and apparel and other specialty stores. Includes reporting on finances and operations, merchandise lines, consumer trends, management development, and new products.

Most data are from industry sources and the journal's own research.

Issues contain news and feature articles, some with statistics; and the following recurring statistical features:

a. "Marketrends" monthly features on buying plans of consumers for electronic and houseware products, with 1 chart repeated for 12 products in each category showing percent of consumers planning to purchase items in coming year; and 2-3 charts or tables showing additional detail regarding consumer shopping practices for selected products. Data are from surveys conducted for *Chain Store Age* by Leo J. Shapiro and Associates, and are shown for current month, usually with comparisons to prior months and/or years.

b. Licensed toy products market monthly feature, with rankings for 5 top-selling products and 5 products with greatest decline in sales, for month 3 months prior to issue date with comparison to previous month. Data are based on surveys of toy buyers from 100 largest retail chains.

c. Retail chain sales: monthly table showing sales for approximately 25 general merchandise chains, for month 2 months prior to cover date, cumulative year to date, and same periods of previous year; and number of stores in each chain, for current and previous year.

d. Retail chain earnings: quarterly table showing earnings or loss for approximately 25 general merchandise and specialty chains, generally for quarter ending 4-5 months prior to cover date, cumulative year to date, and same periods of previous year.

Journal also includes annual features on financial performance of leading retail chains, and departmental sales and productivity.

Monthly "MarkeTrends" and licensed toy features begin in the Jan. 1985 issue and appear in most issues. Monthly retail chain sales table appears in all issues. All additional features with substantial statistical content are described, as they appear, under "Statistical Features;" page locations and latest period of coverage for quarterly table are also noted. Nonstatistical features are not covered.

Availability: Chain Store Age, General Merchandise Trends, Subscription Department, 305 Madison Ave., Suite 535, New York NY 10165-0079, retailers $12.00 per yr., others $20.00 per yr., single copy $2.00; SRI/MF/excerpts for monthly table, and for all portions covered under "Statistical Features;" shipped quarterly.

Issues reviewed during 1985: Nov. 1984-Sept. 1985 (P) (Vol. 60, Nos. 11-12; Vol. 61, Nos. 1-9).

STATISTICAL FEATURES:

C5150–7.601: Dec. 1984 (Vol. 60, No. 12)

SURVEY REVEALS EFFECTS OF UPGRADING

(p. 51-71) Article, with 1 table showing outlet choice for purchase of selected types of apparel, by outlet type and for K mart stores, 1980 and 1984. Data are from Leo J. Shapiro and Associates surveys conducted for *Chain Store Age.*

Also includes 1 chart and 6 tables showing respondent opinions regarding K mart stores.

C5150–7.602: Jan. 1985 (Vol. 61, No. 1)

QUARTERLY TABLE

(p. 116) Retail chain earnings, 3rd quarter 1984.

CEOs GIVE MIXED REVIEWS TO STAFFS

(p. 20-23) Article on views of chief executive officers (CEOs) concerning company policies and own job. Data are based on responses from 66 CEOs of 5 types of chains to a *Chain Store Age* survey.

Includes 2 tables and 1 chart showing CEOs' ratings of own company on selected measures, with comparisons to ratings given by lower-ranking retail managers; perceptions of major responsibilities; and ratings of performance of lower-ranking retail managers.

PROCESSING WARS: GMers FIGHT BACK

(p. 29) Article, with 1 chart showing photo processing market shares by retail outlet type, 1984. Data are from Berkey Film Processing.

SPORTING GOODS

(p. 95-98) Compilation of 2 articles on exercise/health care market. Data are from a *Chain Store Age/Better Homes and Gardens* survey, conducted Sept. 1983-84. Includes 1 table and 1 chart showing percent of respondents owning selected exercise and health care products, and percent interested in purchasing selected health care appliances, 1983-84.

C5150–7.603: Feb. 1985 (Vol. 61, No. 2)

DISCOUNTERS GET CONSUMERS' VOTES

(p. 65-68) Article, with 1 table showing retail outlet or outlet type preferred by consumers, for planned purchases by detailed product category, 1983-84. Data are from *Chain Store Age/Better Homes and Gardens* surveys of *Better Homes and Gardens* subscribers, conducted Aug. 1983-84, with responses from 416 households in 1983 and 423 households in 1984.

SOFTWARE SHIFTS TO EDUCATE ADULTS

(p. 78) Brief article, with 1 chart showing unit shipments of educational computer software, 1984-90. Data are from Venture Development Corp.

SHOPPERS SEEK QUALITY AT BEST PRICE

(p. 130-143) Article, with 2 tables showing outlet type preferred by consumers, and factors influencing choice of outlet, for toy purchases, 1983-84. Data are based on *Chain Store Age/Better Homes and Gardens* surveys.

NEW ATTITUDES HELP SPUR BTS SPENDING

(p. 149-151) Article reporting on consumer spending for back-to-school (BTS) items. Data are from 425 responses to *Chain Store Age/Better Homes and Gardens* surveys of *Better Homes and Gardens* subscribers, conducted 1983-84.

Includes 1 chart and 1 table showing percent of respondents with school-age children, and distribution of respondents by amount spent on BTS purchases, for all respondents and by income level, 1983-84.

Data corrections appear in the Mar. 1985 issue (see C5150-7.604 below).

C5150–7.604: Mar. 1985 (Vol. 61, No. 3)

CUSTOMERS PREFER QUALITY TO SALES

(p. 9) Brief article, with 1 undated chart showing main reasons cited by consumers for choosing a store, and recall of store characteristics most emphasized in advertising. Data are from a survey of 4,000 apparel shoppers conducted by TracABC, a research facility of ABC-TV.

CORRECTION

(p. 10) Includes data corrections for article on consumer spending for back-to-school items, appearing in Jan. 1985 issue; for description, see C5150-7.603 above.

PHOTO/CAMERA

(p. 93-103) Compilation of 2 articles reporting on retail camera market. Data are from *Chain Store Age* research and Leo J. Shapiro and Associates.

Includes 1 chart and 4 tables showing percent of photo dept buyers stocking 6 types of cameras, with detail by model; income, occupation, and education of consumers planning camera purchase, and reasons for choosing selected outlets or outlet types; and autofocus camera purchase price expectations; 1984, with comparisons to 1983.

TRENDY STYLES BRIGHTEN SUNGLASS SALES

(p. 107) Article, with 1 chart showing sunglass market shares by retail outlet type, 1985. Data are from Bausch & Lomb, Inc.

HOME OFFICES GROW BY AT LEAST 9%

(p. 108-109) Article, with 3 tables and 1 chart showing age group and income level of persons shopping for 3 types of office equipment for home use; outlet or type of outlet preferred for home office purchases; and consumers with and without offices in home, and future plans, with detail by selected demographic and socioeconomic characteristics.

Data are from a *Chain Store Age/Better Homes and Gardens* survey.

C5150–7.605: Apr. 1985 (Vol. 61, No. 4)

CONSUMER ELECTRONICS

(p. 30) Table showing types of outlets preferred by consumers for purchases of portable headphone stereos, home stereos, and videocassette recorders, 1982 and 1985. Data are from *Chain Store Age*/Leo J. Shapiro and Associates.

DISC FINDS NICHE UNDER AUTOFOCUS

(p. 88) Article, with 1 chart showing disc camera profit margins reported by store photo dept buyers, 1983-84. Data are from *Chain Store Age* research.

C5150–7.606: May 1985 (Vol. 61, No. 5)

QUARTERLY TABLE

(p. 107) Retail chain earnings, 4th quarter 1984.

CSA VALUE STUDY

(p. 13-59) Compilation of articles on consumer perceptions of value, and impact on retail outlet selection. Data are based on a *Chain Store Age*/Leo J. Shapiro and Associates telephone survey of 1,008 consumers in 5 market areas.

Includes 12 tables and 1 chart showing survey response on importance of selected factors in choice of store and product; ratings of major

outlets in each market area surveyed, by selected product category and outlet characteristic (including quality of service, merchandise, and customer relations); and acceptable profit margins, by importance attributed to 8 store selection factors.

PACKAGING ADDS A SHINE TO BETTER GLASSWARE

(p. 73-74) Article, with 1 undated table showing consumer outlet choice for latest purchase of glassware, by outlet type. Data are from a *Chain Store Age*/Leo J. Shapiro and Associates survey.

C5150–7.607: June 1985 (Vol. 61, No. 6)

STATE OF THE INDUSTRY, 1984, ANNUAL FEATURE

(p. 11-19) Annual article on financial performance of leading retail chains, 1984. Data are from *Chain Store Age* and company reports. Includes 1 chart and 5 tables showing the following:

a. Sales and earnings, 1983-84, for top 15 retail chains ranked by 1984 sales.

b. Sales and operating income percent change and value per square foot, average sales per store, and selected profitability ratios, 1984; and compound sales and operating income percent change, 1977-84 period; all for 23 major discount and department store chains.

c. Sales and number of stores, 1983-84, for top 100 retail chains ranked by 1984 sales (with detail for subsidiaries); and aggregate sales distribution by type of outlet, 1984.

CSA OUTLOOK, ANNUAL FEATURE

(p. 21-63) Annual compilation of articles analyzing financial performance of 30 leading retail chain stores. Data are from *Chain Store Age*. Each article covers an individual chain and includes 1 table showing sales, profits, and number of stores, 1980-84.

BATTERY VENDORS LOOK TO CHARGE SALES

(p. 72) Article, with 1 table showing types of outlets chosen by consumers for purchases of batteries, 1971 and 1984. Data are from National Family Opinion Research, Inc.

PHONES ON HOLD, WIRING IS HOT

(p. 88) Article, with 1 chart showing telephone unit sales, 1982-85. Data are from AT&T.

C5150–7.608: July 1985 (Vol. 61, No. 7)

QUARTERLY TABLE

(p. 79) Retail chain earnings, 1st quarter 1985.

MARKETPOWER, ANNUAL FEATURE

(p. 33-73, passim) Annual compilation of articles on space allocation and operating performance for store merchandise depts, 1984. Also includes survey findings regarding consumer purchase decisions. Data are based on *Chain Store Age* research.

Includes the following data:

a. Consumer ratings for importance of 12 factors influencing purchase decision, by selected demographic and socioeconomic characteristics, by product category, and for 5 metro areas. 3 tables.

b. Top 20 merchandise depts ranked by sales, 1984, with comparison to 1983. 1 table.

c. Market share, sales per square foot, annual turnover, and gross margin, all by type of outlet, 1984, for the following depts: accessories; automotive; hardware; home textiles; consumer electronics; lawn/garden; photo/camera; computers; nonelectric and electric housewares; hosiery; toys; sporting goods; women's, children's, and men's wear; health and beauty aids; sewing; footwear; hobby/crafts; and stationery. 1 chart and 1 table repeated for each dept.

HOME COMPUTER MARKET ALIVE, BUT KICKING

(Insert, p. 3-4) Article, with 2 undated charts showing consumer ownership/buying intentions regarding selected types of computer equipment, and type of outlet preferred for purchase of computer software programs. Data are based on 421 responses to a *Chain Store Age/Better Homes and Gardens* survey.

Article is included in "Special Report" insert section of issue.

C5150–7.609: Aug. 1985 (Vol. 61, No. 8)

VACUUMS GET A JOLT WITH GADGETRY

(p. 37-39) Article, with 2 undated charts showing consumer opinion regarding vacuum cleaner purchases, including types of outlets and equipment preferred. Data are from a *Chain Store Age/Better Homes and Gardens* survey.

FLANNEL SHEETS ARE COZY TO CONSUMERS

(p. 50-52) Article, with 2 tables on consumers' recent purchases of bed sheets, including type of outlet (by income level) and size of sheet. Data are based on a *Chain Store Age/Better Homes and Gardens* survey of 417 consumers, conducted in Apr. 1985.

C5150–7.610: Sept. 1985 (Vol. 61, No. 9)

CITIZEN BAND RADIOS POISED FOR COMEBACK

(p. 29-33) Article, with 1 table showing characteristics of consumers intending to purchase CB radios in 1985, including sex; primary use (communications or safety-related); and whether first time buyers, white collar workers, or high school graduates. Data are from Midland Co.

VIDEO CUSTOMERS WANT BETTER SOUND, TOO

(p. 34) Article, with 2 charts showing stereo video industry sales, by type of product, 1985 and 1990. Data are from Venture Development Corp.

CLOCKS: FASHIONABLE OR FUNCTIONAL?

(p. 47-48) Article, with 1 undated chart showing types of outlets chosen by consumers for purchases of wall clocks. Data are from Spartus/Waltham Co.

GIFT WRAP GOES FOR THE GLITTER

(p. 93-94) Article, with 1 chart showing distribution of Christmas gift wrap purchases by month. Data are from Gibson Greeting Cards, Inc.

C5150–8   APPAREL MERCHANDISING

Monthly.
ISSN 0746-889X.
SRI/MF/not filmed

Monthly trade journal of the retail clothing industry, including reports on marketing developments and trends, and consumer buying patterns. Most data are from industry sources and the journal's own research.

Issues contain news and feature articles, some with statistics, including recurring features on consumer buying practices for specific types of clothing as reported through surveys conducted by the Gallup Organization.

Features with substantial statistical content are described, as they appear, under "Statistical Features." Each issue of the journal is reviewed, but an abstract is published in SRI monthly issues only when statistical features appear.

Availability: Apparel Merchandising, Subscription Department, 305 Madison Ave., Suite 535, New York NY 10165-0079, retailers $18.00 per yr., others $30.00 per yr., single copy $4.00; SRI/MF/not filmed.

Issues reviewed during 1985: Nov. 1984-Oct. 1985 (Vol. 3, Nos. 11-12; Vol. 4, Nos. 1-10).

STATISTICAL FEATURES:

C5150–8.601: Nov. 1984 (Vol. 3, No. 11)

BODYWEAR

(p. 16-19) Article on merchandising of exercise and dance apparel ("bodywear"). Data are from Market Research Corp. of America, and a Lebhar-Friedman survey of buyers for 30 department and 18 discount stores.

Includes 6 tables showing bodywear sales value and volume, 1983; percent of bodywear purchased at regular price, and mean profit margin, for department and discount stores, 1983; and buyer responses concerning topselling brands, dept location of bodywear, space allocation plans, expected increase in sales volume, and sales distribution by clothing type, for department and discount stores.

CONSUMER WATCH: 11-14-YEAR-OLDS

(p. 20-23) Article on clothing shopping habits of youths age 11-14. Data are from a Gallup survey.

Includes 1 chart and 4 tables showing survey responses concerning sources of fashion information, recognition of top brands, factors influencing purchase decisions, retail outlets shopped, and problems with clothing fit, with selected detail by sex and age (no dates).

KLEIN'S COTTON LINE PUTS SNAP BACK IN PANTIES

(p. 31-32) Article, with 1 chart and 1 table showing sales distribution of women's underwear, by retail outlet type, with detail by fabric, 1983. Data are from Market Research Corp. of America.

C5150–8.602: Dec. 1984 (Vol. 3, No. 12)

TODAY'S TEENS RATE OPPOSITE SEX

(p. 9) Article on teenage boys' and girls' attitudes toward the opposite sex, based on a Gallup survey of teenagers age 13-18. Includes 1 undated table showing girls' opinions (like, dislike, and no difference) on selected clothing and personal habits of boys.

C5150–8.603: Jan. 1985 (Vol. 4, No. 1)

TODAY'S CHILDREN'S WEAR SHOPPER: DIVERSE BUT PARTICULAR

(p. 26) Article, with 1 undated table showing changes in retail outlet preferences of children's clothing shoppers, by outlet type. Data are from a 1984 study conducted by Childrenswear Manufacturers Assn and Walter Levy Associates.

C5150–8.604: Feb. 1985 (Vol. 4, No. 2)

GALLUP: THE COAT OUTLOOK

(p. 26-31) Article on women's plans for purchasing coats. Data are from a Gallup survey.

Includes 1 chart and 7 tables showing survey responses concerning planned expenditures and month of purchase, intention to shop for sale price, and retail outlet preferences, primarily 1985 or 1985-87 period; and estimated sales volume based on survey responses, 1985; all for full- and short-length coats, with detail by fabric or type.

APPAREL SOURCING FOR '85

(p. 36-38) Article on developments in retailer importing of clothing. Data are based on a survey of department and discount store executives, conducted by Lebhar-Friedman Research.

Includes 7 tables showing survey responses concerning top import source countries/world areas; import shares of private label and other merchandise; whether imports are handled inhouse or through selected outside organizations; private label share of stock; and importance of selected clothing categories in import market; all for department and discount stores, mostly 1984-85.

C5150–8.605: Mar. 1985 (Vol. 4, No. 3)

GALLUP: YOUNG MEN'S, SPLITTING IMAGES

(p. 36-38) Article on clothing shopping habits of young men. Data are from a Gallup survey of men age 15-24.

Includes 1 chart and 9 tables showing survey responses concerning expenditures for sportswear and dress clothes; sources of clothing information; reasons for store selection and retail outlet preferences; expected prices, and most frequent purchases, by clothing type; shopping frequency; use of label information; and most and least important factors in buying decision; generally shown separately for men age 15-19 and 20-24 (no dates).

C5150–8.606: Apr. 1985 (Vol. 4, No. 4)

ARE TWO SIZES TABOO?

(p. 15-19) Article on pantyhose shopping patterns of women age 18/over, based on a Gallup survey. Includes 2 charts and 3 tables showing survey responses concerning importance of selected pantyhose characteristics, including availability of multiple sizes, with detail by age; brands preferred; and brand loyalty; (no dates).

GALLUP: SMALL SIZE, BIG TICKET

(p. 32-35) Article on consumer purchases of girl's dresses. Data are based on a recent Gallup survey of mothers.

Includes 1 chart and 8 tables showing survey responses concerning number of dresses purchased per year, with 1985 plans; factors influencing purchases, including advertising and child's preferences; retail outlet preferences; and price expectations; with selected detail by clothing size and type (school or special occasion), and respondent income. Except for 1985 purchasing plans, no data dates are given.

HOW THE SPECIALISTS FARED IN '84

(p. 40) Article, with 4 tables showing percent change in sales of 4 best- and worst-selling types of clothing in women's and men's specialty stores, by region, 1984 vs. 1983. Data are from Retail Merchandising Service Automation Inc.

C5150–8.607: May 1985 (Vol. 4, No. 5)

GREAT EXPECTATIONS

(p. 14-16) Article on merchandising of women's sportswear in discount stores. Data are from a Lebhar-Friedman survey of 20 discount chains. Includes 1 chart and 4 tables showing survey responses concerning topselling brands; and inventory share, and expected percent increase in sales of selected clothing types, for basic and fashion merchandise; 1984 and/or 1985.

GALLUP: HOOKED ON BRANDS

(p. 23-25) Article on shopping patterns of women buying brassieres, based on a Gallup survey. Includes 5 charts and 5 tables showing survey responses concerning whether purchases made at regular or sale price, and preferred type of discount; prices paid; style and brand preferences; retail outlets shopped; and whether separate items bought for everyday and special occasions; with selected detail by age group (no dates).

C5150–8.608: June 1985 (Vol. 4, No. 6)

SPECIALTY STORES REFINE THEIR FORMULAS

(p. 17-19) Article, with 1 table showing sales and stores for the top 20 apparel specialty store companies ranked by sales, with detail for subsidiary chains, 1984 with comparison to 1983. Data are from *Apparel Merchandising*.

OFF-PRICERS' PARTY IS OVER

(p. 21-22) Article, with 1 table showing sales and stores for the top 19 off-price apparel specialty store chains ranked by sales, 1984 with comparison to 1983. Data are from *Apparel Merchandising*.

C5150–8.609: July 1985 (Vol. 4, No. 7)

HOSIERY TAKES TO THE TUBE

(p. 14-15) Article, with 1 table showing top 5 hosiery manufacturers ranked by TV advertising expenditures, with detail for network and spot advertising, 1984 with comparison to 1983. Data are from TV Bureau of Advertising based on data from Broadcast Advertisers Reports, Inc.

C5150–8.610: Aug. 1985 (Vol. 4, No. 8)

WHO'S MAKING THE DECISIONS?

(p. 30-33) Article on clothing buyer vs. management responsibility for merchandising decisions. Data are based on 196 responses to an *Apparel Merchandising* survey of retail clothing buyers and divisional merchandise managers.

Includes 12 undated tables showing survey response regarding involvement in various merchandising decisions, and frequency of market visits, generally for buyers, divisional merchandise managers, and general merchandise managers.

DRESS SHIRTS II, ANNUAL FEATURE

(p. 48-53) Annual article, for 1985, on consumer purchases of men's dress shirts. Data are from a Gallup survey conducted for *Apparel Merchandising*.

Includes 2 charts and 6 tables showing survey responses concerning frequency of purchases; purchase plans or preferences for specific styles, brands, patterns, and fabrics; prices paid, and frequency of buying shirts on sale; and retail outlet preferences; with selected detail by age, sex, region, and income, 1984-85.

Previous feature is described in SRI 1984 Annual under C5150-8.509.

C5150–8.611: Sept. 1985 (Vol. 4, No. 9)

GALLUP: HOW WOMEN SUIT UP

(p. 10-16) Article on swimwear shopping habits of women. Data are from a Gallup survey of over 1,500 women.

Includes 2 charts and 6 tables showing survey response on whether purchases made at regular or sale price, swimsuit size and fit, price expectations, retail outlet preferences, number of suits purchased per year, and frequency and month of purchases, with detail by respondent age, income, and region (no dates).

KNIT REVIVAL SPRINGS FORTH

(p. 40-44) Article, with 1 chart and 1 table showing men's knit shirt market shares, by retail outlet type, 1st quarter 1984-85; and retail sales of men's clothing (total and by type of shirt), 1980-84. Data are from Market Research Corp. of America.

C5150–8.612: Oct. 1985 (Vol. 4, No. 10)

NOVELTIES ON THE LOOSE

(p. 24-26) Article, with 1 chart showing sales distribution of men's woven sport shirts, by retail outlet type, 1st half 1984-85. Data are from Market Research Corp. of America.

GALLUP: THE CONTEMPORARY MALE

(p. 40-43) Article on clothing shopping habits of men age 25-35, based on a recent Gallup survey.

Includes 9 undated tables showing survey response on retail outlet and brand preferences; shopping frequency; clothing expenditures per year; impulse buying, and most frequent purchases, by clothing type; frequency of buying clothing on sale; and sources of style information; with selected detail by income group, clothing type, and region.

C5175
Lippincott and Peto

C5175–1 **RUBBER WORLD**
Monthly.
ISSN 0035-9572.
LC 54-54214.
SRI/MF/excerpts, shipped quarterly

Monthly trade journal of the rubber industry, reporting on technical developments, market activity, and related topics. Covers tire, hose, carbon black, and other major rubber and rubber chemical industry sectors.

Issues contain articles, primarily narrative or technical in nature, but occasionally including market statistics; regular news and editorial depts; and 2 monthly tables and 1 irregularly recurring table.

Monthly and irregularly recurring tables are listed below. Monthly tables appear in most issues. All additional features with substantial statistical content are described, as they appear, under "Statistical Features;" page location and latest period of coverage for irregularly recurring table are also noted. Nonstatistical features are not covered.

Availability: Rubber World, PO Box 5485, 1867 W. Market St., Akron OH 44313, $23.00 per yr., single copy $3.00; SRI/MF/excerpts for monthly tables and all portions covered under "Statistical Features;" shipped quarterly.

Issues reviewed during 1985: Nov. 1984-Oct. 1985 (P) (Vol. 191, Nos. 2-6; Vol. 192, Nos. 1-6; Vol. 193, No. 1).

RECURRING TABLES:

MONTHLY TABLES

[Tables generally show data cumulatively for current year through month 4-5 months prior to cover date, with comparisons to same period of previous year. Detail may vary.]

[1] Rubber Manufacturers Assn (RMA) industry rubber report [supply and demand data, usually including natural rubber imports, exports, and consumption; and synthetic rubber production, imports, exports, and consumption, by type of rubber].

[2] RMA monthly tire report [shipments (original equipment, replacement, and export) and production, for all and radial passenger car and truck/bus tires].

IRREGULARLY RECURRING TABLE

[1] Carbon black industry in the U.S. [production and shipments by product type, and total domestic shipments, generally for quarter ending 4-7 months prior to cover date and/or cumulative for year to date, with change from same period of previous year; data are from Columbian Chemicals Co. *Quarterly Consumption Report,* covered in SRI under B2320-1].

STATISTICAL FEATURES:

C5175–1.601: Feb. 1985 (Vol. 191, No. 5)

MARKETS, NEWS: IISRP NORTH AMERICAN AND WESTERN EUROPE NEW RUBBER CONSUMPTION FORECAST, ANNUAL FEATURE

(p. 9-12) Annual article, with 2 tables showing consumption of new natural rubber, and synthetic rubber by type, for North America and Western Europe, 1983-85 and 1989. Also includes tire rubber consumption for North America.

Data are from International Institute of Synthetic Rubber Producers, Inc.

CUSTOM MIXERS ANTICIPATING GROWTH, ANNUAL FEATURE

(p. 17-22) Annual article reporting on activities of companies that custom mix rubber polymers. Data are based on a *Rubber World* survey. Includes 2 charts showing mixed polymer capacity and production 1982-84, with 1984 production distribution by polymer type.

Also includes directory of companies, with capacity data.

C5175–1.602: May 1985 (Vol. 192, No. 2)

MARKETS, NEWS

(p. 7) Article, with 1 chart showing distribution of latex polymer sales volume, by polymer type, 1984.

C5175–1.603: July 1985 (Vol. 192, No. 4)

PROCESSING MACHINERY IMPORTS INCREASING

(p. 8, 11) Article, with 6 tables showing U.S. import and export value for rubber processing machinery, by machinery type and country of origin or destination, various periods 1979-1st quarter 1985. Data are from Commerce Dept.

C5175–1.604: Aug. 1985 (Vol. 192, No. 5)

RECURRING TABLE

[1] Carbon black industry in the U.S. [1st quarter 1985]. (p. 8)

C5175–1.605: Oct. 1985 (Vol. 193, No. 1)

MARKETS, NEWS

(p. 8) Brief article, with 1 table showing value of hose, flat belting, and V-belt shipments, 1985-90. Data were compiled by Rubber Manufacturers Assn from information supplied by 70 companies.

C5225
Maclean Hunter Media, Inc.

C5225–1 **PROGRESSIVE GROCER**
Monthly.
ISSN 0033-0787. LC 80-858.
SRI/MF/not filmed

Monthly trade journal of the supermarket/grocery store industry, covering food retailing, advertising and sales promotion, new products, merchandising trends, finance, technology, store design, product use and sales, and Federal Government regulation.

Data are from Federal Government, *Progressive Grocer* Data Center and surveys, private publishers, and research assns.

General contents:

a. "Seasonal Best Sellers" monthly table, showing index of supermarket items with high seasonal sales, for cover date or month 1-3 months subsequent, based on average sales for same month of 2-5 previous years; data are from Selling Areas Marketing, Inc.

b. Feature articles on current industry topics, and regular editorial depts, occasionally with statistics.

Annual statistical features include Nielsen review of retail grocery trends, a comprehensive report on the grocery industry, and reports on supermarket product movement and consumer use. Jan. 1985 issue also includes an index to articles appearing in 1984.

"Seasonal Best Sellers" table appears in most issues. All additional features with substantial statistical content are described, as they appear, under "Statistical Features." Nonstatistical contents are not covered.

Availability: Progressive Grocer, 1351 Washington Blvd., Stamford CT 06902, $44.00 per yr., single copy $7.50, Apr. Annual Report issue $20.00, July Sales Manual $15.00; SRI/MF/not filmed.

Issues reviewed during 1985: Nov. 1984-Oct. 1985 (P) (Vol. 63, Nos. 11-12; Vol. 64, Nos. 1-10).

STATISTICAL FEATURES:

C5225–1.601: Nov. 1984 (Vol. 63, No. 11)

MAJOR WHOLESALERS: SERVICE AND SIZE BREED SUCCESS

(p. 20-42) Compilation of articles on sales and operations of 5 leading food wholesalers. Data were compiled by *Progressive Grocer*.

Includes 1 table showing revenues, wholesale and retail sales, earnings, number of stores served and percent that are supermarkets, number of retail food stores owned, return on equity and assets, 5-year growth rate, employment, and number of distribution centers, all for 5 wholesalers, FY83 or FY84.

Also includes wholesaler profiles, each with 1 table showing retail food stores owned and/or stores served, primarily FY79-84.

MEET TODAY'S PRODUCE SHOPPER: HOW, WHAT, HOW MUCH AND WHERE THEY BUY

(p. P1-P2) By Lee W. Dyer. Article on produce purchases and expenditures of supermarket shoppers. Data are from a survey of household food shoppers, conducted by Leo J. Shapiro and Associates.

Includes 3 charts and 2 tables showing percent of respondents with increase, decrease, or no change in fresh produce consumption from the previous year, and percent purchasing selected vegetables and fruits by type; and respondent distribution by amount spent for produce and all items during weekly and "fill-in" shopping trips; (no dates).

C5225–1.602: Dec. 1984 (Vol. 63, No. 12)

GREAT SACK RACE

(p. 51-54) By Robert E. O'Neill. Article, with 2 undated charts showing cost shares for labor, material, and other costs involved in bagging groceries; and average labor costs for packing groceries in paper vs. plastic bags. Data are from a cost-analysis study conducted by Case and Co. for the American Paper Institute.

ANALGESICS EXPLOSION

(p. 87-90) Article on sales and consumer use of over-the-counter (OTC) analgesic products. Data are from A. C. Nielsen Co., and a consumer survey conducted by Simmons Market Research Bureau.

Includes 2 charts and 1 table showing average shelf space, average sales per linear foot per month, and inventory turns, for analgesics in drug, mass merchandise, and food stores; percent of consumers using analgesics, by health problem; and analgesic seasonal sales index; primarily 1983.

C5225–1.603: Jan. 1985 (Vol. 64, No. 1)

MANAGER CHALLENGES FOR 1985 AND BEYOND

(p. 22-24) Article on developments in food store management recruitment and responsibilities. Data are based on 52 responses to a 1984 survey of senior executives of major food retailing companies, conducted by Arthur D. Little Inc. for the Coca-Cola Retailing Research Council.

Includes 1 chart and 2 tables showing survey responses concerning current and future sources of store management personnel (in-house promotion, and recruitment of college graduates and personnel from other companies); store manager responsibilities; and future eligibility for bonus/incentive pay, for store management personnel by position and all store employees.

FORECAST FOR 1985: NO TRUCE AHEAD IN THE BATTLE FOR BUSINESS

(p. 43-48) By Lee W. Dyer. Article on food store merchandisers' expectations for 1985. Data are from a survey of *Progressive Grocer's* Merchandising Advisory Council, which includes executives from over 90 food retail companies, and from a similar 1983 survey.

Includes 10 charts showing survey responses concerning changes in merchandising and consumer shopping activity, promotional and merchandising methods, store manager responsibilities, quantity and value of merchandising deals/allowances, consumer brand and store loyalty, and quality and quantity of manufacturers' promotional materials.

C5225–1.604: Feb. 1985 (Vol. 64, No. 2)

PRODUCE SHOPPER TRENDS

(p. 73-74) Article on fresh produce consumption and purchasing patterns, based on a consumer survey conducted by Leo J. Shapiro and Associates, Inc.

Includes 4 charts and 1 table showing survey responses concerning frequency of serving and eating salads, with selected detail by sex and race (including Hispanic); and reasons for eating fresh fruits/vegetables, and factors influencing purchases. No dates are given.

HOW GROCERS FEEL ABOUT THEIR CUSTOMERS

(p. 103) Article on grocers' perceptions of customers' shopping behavior and attitudes. Data are from responses of 210 grocers to a 1984 survey conducted by Joseph Smith. Includes 1 table.

C5225–1.605: Mar. 1985 (Vol. 64, No. 3)

SUPERS STEP UP ETHNIC HBA EFFORTS

(p. 107-120) By Glenn Snyder. Article, with 3 charts showing the following for hair care products marketed for blacks: sales value, and unit sales distribution, by retail outlet type (food stores, drugstores, and mass merchandisers), various years 1977-83; and sales shares by product type, 1983. Data are from A. C. Nielsen Co.

C5225–1.606: Apr. 1985 (Vol. 64, No. 4)

52nd ANNUAL REPORT OF THE GROCERY INDUSTRY

(p. 23-98) First part of a 2-part annual report on all facets of the grocery industry, 1984. First part focuses on store finances and operations, and outlook for 1985.

Most data for the report are based on responses to *Progressive Grocer* surveys of chain and independent supermarket owners and managers, and chain and wholesaler executives.

Contains introduction (p. 23-25); and 45 charts and 26 tables described below, presented in 6 sections, with interspersed narrative (p. 27-98).

TABLES AND CHARTS:

[Data generally show survey responses or response distribution, with detail for independent and chain stores and/or chain and wholesale executives, on the topics described below. Most data are for 1984, occasionally with 1-3 year trends; other dates are noted below.

Selected outlook, competition, cost, and operating data are shown by some or all of the following store characteristics: region, county size classification, sales level, selling area, and format (superstore, conventional, economy, and combination).]

a. Overview: includes industry sales, and percent of consumer income spent for food, 1970s-84; sales and stores, for supermarkets by sales size, convenience stores, and other stores; wholesaler firms, branches/divisions, and sales, by wholesaler type; chain store opening/closing summary by chain size, and expected openings in 1985; and views on effects of inflation, industry concentration, and predatory pricing. 9 charts and 2 tables. (p. 28-34)

b. Outlook: expectations and plans for 1985, including problem areas; general economic conditions, price stability, grocery profits, and personal financial situation; levels of sales, labor costs, competition, and other operating factors; and impact of inflation vs. recession. 11 charts and 2 tables. (p. 38-48)

c. Competition: includes use of various competitive tactics and promotion techniques; media distribution of advertising budget and use; prospects for and/or perceived competition from grocery and other stores by type; and competitor closings. 4 charts and 7 tables. (p. 53-60)

d. Costs and prices: includes change in marketing costs by item; CPI for food away from home, and food at home by commodity; average equipment expenditures, 1976-84; types of equipment purchased; store age, and remodeling and energy costs; unionization status and wage rates for clerks and meat cutters; wage expense ratios, and gross margin; change in wholesaler productivity and employee turnover; and wage increases for 1985. 7 charts and 8 tables. (p. 64-72)

e. Store operations: includes net profit margin; sales productivity measures; store selling area and inventory; scanner use, weekly transactions, and checkouts; employment; store hours; special services and product lines offered; food stamp share of sales; type of warehouse used; product availability measures, including out-of-stock rate; employee turnover; and use of store-level computerized information. 7 charts and 6 tables. (p. 77-90)

f. Manufacturer relations: includes views on retailer/manufacturer relations, deal/allowance offers and frequency of sales visits, and quality and use of manufacturer services and supplies including display material. 7 charts and 1 table. (p. 95-98)

Other Feature

DRUGSTORES RAISE THE ANTE

(p. 101-109) By Glenn Snyder. Article on drugstore industry competition with supermarkets. Data are from A. C. Nielsen Co., *Progressive Grocer, Forbes,* and National Assn of Chain Drug Stores.

Includes 5 tables showing drugstore and grocery store sales, 1974-84; average return on equity, profit margin, and earnings per share, for aggregate leading drugstore and supermarket chains, over unspecified 5-year and 12-month periods; and average sales and operating data for aggregate large pharmacy drugstores, 1983.

C5225–1.607: May 1985 (Vol. 64, No. 5)

DOUBLE COUPON DILEMMA: ANY WAY OFF THE COMPETITIVE TREADMILL?

(p. 44-46, 55) By Michael Sansolo. Article, with 1 chart showing number of coupons distributed, selected years 1974-89. Data are from Nielsen Clearing House and American Can Co.

COUPON FOR EVERY CONSUMER

(p. 58) Article, with 1 undated table showing percent of coupons distributed, by media or other method of distribution. Data are from Nielsen Clearing House.

JAPANESE SUPERS TAKE THE LEAD IN PERISHABLES

(p. 65-68) By Gene A. German. Article, with 1 undated table showing sales distribution and gross profit margin, by product category, for supermarkets in Japan and U.S. Data are from author's estimates and *Progressive Grocer.*

52nd ANNUAL REPORT OF THE GROCERY INDUSTRY

(p. 77-96) Second part of a 2-part annual report on all facets of the grocery industry, 1984. Part 2 focuses on consumer behavior and wholesaler and chain operations.

Most data are based on responses to a survey of households conducted by Home Testing Institute, 111 responses to a *Progressive Grocer* survey of wholesalers, and 46 responses to a Cornell University survey of grocery chains.

Contains introduction (p. 77); and 5 charts and 9 tables, described below, presented in 2 sections, with interspersed narrative (p. 79-96).

CHARTS AND TABLES:

[Consumer data generally show survey response distribution for the topics listed below. Wholesaler types are voluntary, cooperative, and unaffiliated. Unless otherwise noted, data are for 1984 with selected comparisons to 1983.]

a. Consumers: includes perceptions of economic situation, price changes for all items and for food by product category, change in food spending, and supermarket profits; primary food shopper by sex, shopping times by employment status, and shopping frequency and expenditures by store type; cost-saving methods used with comparison to store managers' perceptions; grocery shopping planning; and ranking of importance of 43 supermarket characteristics/services. 5 charts and 6 tables. (p. 79-88)

b. Operating data: wholesaler employment and unionization, wages, distribution centers, stock turnover, sales productivity, profit, business shares by retail store type and for generic and brand label products, and selected other financial and operating ratios, by wholesaler type and sales size; sales and earnings of public chains and wholesalers by company; and composite chains' gross margin, expenses by item, earnings, stock turns, and selected other operating ratios, 1978/79-1983/84. 3 tables. (p. 92-96)

Other Feature

NEW EQUIPMENT ADDS COMPETITIVE MUSCLE

(p. 117-118) By Robert E. O'Neill. Article on food store equipment purchases in 1984. Data are from a *Progressive Grocer* survey. Includes 2 tables showing percent of chain and independent stores purchasing equipment by type; and distribution of independent store purchasers by amount spent, with average expenditures; all by store sales size, 1984.

C5225–1.608: June 1985 (Vol. 64, No. 6)

FIVE YEAR'S WORTH OF PRODUCT INTROS

(p. 18-19) By Martin J. Friedman. Article, with 1 table showing top 20 food industry corporations ranked by number of new products introduced, 1980-84 period. Data are from *New Product News.*

BUYER'S BEST FRIEND

(p. 21-26) Article on grocery merchandise buyers' views concerning their jobs, with focus on role of computers. Data are from a recent *Progressive Grocer* survey, and are shown separately for chain and wholesale buyers.

Includes 6 undated charts showing survey response concerning time spent in specific job activities, with comparison to 5 years prior; buying arrangements used; use of personal computers; and impact of computers on the buying process.

CLOUDS ON THE UNION HORIZON

(p. 60) Article, with 1 chart showing percent of workers who are union members, for public and private sectors, with private sector detail for goods and service industries, 1980 and 1984. Data are from BLS.

WHAT'S HAPPENING IN DELI/BAKERY MERCHANDISING: INDEPENDENTS AND CHAINS TELL HOW THEY'RE BUILDING SALES

(p. A1-A12) By Lee W. Dyer. Article on food store bakery and delicatessen dept merchandising. Data are based on a *Progressive Grocer* survey of store managers and executives, and generally are shown for independent and chain stores.

Includes 4 charts and 4 tables showing survey response on delicatessen and bakery ser-

vices offered; promotional activities, including types of promotions used, foods promoted, and emphasis given to selected special events and holidays; advertising media use; services desired from manufacturers; and source of display materials, including quality of manufacturer-supplied materials. No data dates are given.

C5225–1.609: July 1985 (Vol. 64, No. 7)

LIFE IN THE FAST LANE

(p. 39-46) By Michael Sansolo. Article, with 1 table showing top 10 fast food restaurant chains ranked by sales value, with sales volume, for chain's most recent fiscal year (unspecified). Data are from *Nation's Restaurant News.*

1985 SUPERMARKET SALES MANUAL, ANNUAL FEATURE

(p. 49-236) Annual compilation of articles on supermarket industry sales and profits, by product category and detailed type, 1984. Data are from *Progressive Grocer.*

Includes 1 summary table (p. 50); and 34 product category profiles, each with 1-13 tables showing supermarket sales, profit and profit margin, and warehouse assortment, usually by detailed product type, 1984, with selected comparison to 1983.

Some profiles also include data on weekly unit movement for a typical supermarket.

This is the 2nd annual feature.

C5225–1.610: Aug. 1985 (Vol. 64, No. 8)

WHAT'S NEW IN EFT

(p. 59-66) By Robert E. O'Neill. Article, with 4 undated charts on automatic teller machines (ATMs) in supermarkets, showing customer use by transaction type, effect on check and cash volume, methods of compensation for supermarket participation in ATM networks, and supermarket operators' ratings of ATM performance.

Data are from an annual survey of supermarkets conducted by Food Marketing Institute. Full survey report is covered in SRI under A4950-5.

C5225–1.611: Sept. 1985 (Vol. 64, No. 9)

EVOLVING MANAGER: MORE COMPLEX THAN EVER

(p. 24-28) By Michael Sansolo. Article, with 1 chart and 1 table showing supermarket manager views concerning important future job skills, and areas of responsibility over which managers need more control, with detail by store sales volume (no dates). Data are from a *Progressive Grocer* survey.

1985 GUIDE TO PRODUCT USAGE, ANNUAL FEATURE

(p. 49-150) Annual report on supermarket product movement, consumer use, and user characteristics, 1984. Data are primarily from Simmons Market Research Bureau survey of approximately 20,000 consumers, and Selling Areas Marketing Inc. (SAMI) monitoring of withdrawals from food chain and wholesaler warehouses in 54 market areas.

Contents:

a. Introduction, explanation of data, and data sources. (p. 49-51) *b.* "Winners and Losers." 1 table showing percent change in sales value and tonnage for all and private label/generic products, by supermarket product category, year ended Mar. 29, 1985 vs. previous 12-month period. (p. 54)

c. "Usage of Supermarket Products." 1 table ranking detailed products within supermarket depts, by percent of surveyed consumers using, and also showing percent of consumers using daily and using 1 brand exclusively. (p. 55-57)

d. Index to product profiles (p. 58)

e. Profiles for 24 product categories, each with 4-18 tables showing most or all of the following by product type: percent change in sales value and tonnage, percent of consumers using and using heavily, heavy users' share of consumption, and demographic characteristics of heavy users compared to average. (p. 60-148)

Report also includes a related article (p. 153-170) on GM/HBA (general merchandise and health/beauty aid) products, with 1 table presenting data as described above for "Usage of Supermarket Products," and profiles for 5 GM/HBA product categories.

1985 NIELSEN REVIEW OF RETAIL GROCERY STORE TRENDS, ANNUAL FEATURE

(p. 197-216) Annual report on trends in grocery store sales, space allocations, and new product development, various periods 1978-88. Data are primarily from A. C. Nielsen Co.

Data by geographic region are shown for New England, NYC, Middle Atlantic, East Central, Chicago, West Central, Southeast, Southwest, Los Angeles, and Pacific.

Contains 7 sections, with 17 charts and 11 tables showing the following:

a. Grocery sales, with detail by region and distributions by chain and independent store sales size; CPI for selected components; retail sales by kind of business; food-away-from-home expenditures by establishment type; and sales shares for branded, controlled, and generic products; various periods 1979-85. (p. 198-202)

b. Product movement trends, including percent changes in sales value and tonnage, prices, inventories, and average annual turns, all by product type; and new items and brands introduced, with new brand detail by product category; various periods 1978-85. (p. 204-206)

c. Health and beauty aids: percent change in sales value and volume, and prices, by product category and outlet type; and sales shares by outlet type, for specific product types; various years 1981-84. (p. 208-210)

d. Supermarket product average shelf space, annual inventory turns, and sales per month per foot of shelf space, by product type, for aggregate chains with annual sales over $1 million, various years 1982-84. (p. 211)

e. Coupons distributed and redeemed, for all products, with distribution detail by media; and grocery coupons distributed by face value, and redemption rates by media; various years 1980-84. (p. 212-214)

f. Scanning-equipped stores, average new scanning stores per month, and scanning stores' share of all grocery sales, 1979-88, with selected 1984 detail by major market area. (p. 216)

This is the 3rd annual report.

WHAT'S HAPPENING IN MEATS...AND WHAT TO EXPECT IN 1990

(p. 219-223) Article, with 3 tables showing per capita consumption of poultry and red meat by type, 1970-83 and 1990; and production of poultry, and red, canned, and processed meats by type, 1983-90 period. Data are from American Can Co.

C5800
McGraw-Hill

C5800–2   ENGINEERING NEWS-RECORD
Weekly.
ISSN 0013-807X.
LC 1-16396.
SRI/MF/not filmed

Weekly publication (except final week of year) reporting developments and trends in the U.S. construction industry, including costs, materials prices, bidding, contracts, wages, and new construction plans; top design firms and executives; and U.S. participation in world markets.

Most data are derived from *Engineering News-Record* (ENR) surveys and field reports.

Issues contain articles and other items on management, labor, and recent industry developments and trends; and regular editorial features. The following statistics are presented:

a. Weekly "Market Trends" section on costs, bidding, plans, capital, machinery sales, contract failures, wage rates, and materials prices; with 2-3 varying charts, and 4 weekly and 11 monthly tables.

b. Weekly "Unit Prices" section on contract bidding, with 1-2 tables.

c. Weekly "Materials Prices" section, with 12 monthly tables on prices in 22 selected cities for representative items in 28 materials categories, and on wage rates for key building construction trades.

d. 1-2 monthly tables on construction new plans and bidding volume.

e. Monthly "Stock Track" table tracing stock and financial performance of selected U.S. companies, and quarterly "International Stock Track" table showing corresponding data for selected foreign companies.

f. Quarterly "Cost Roundup" compilation of statistical articles on cost trends in major construction sectors.

g. Annual statistical articles, including an industrywide report and forecast, and articles on performance of top construction and design firms and specialty contractors, foreign contract awards, top executive earnings, and other industry interests.

h. Occasional statistical articles.

Weekly and monthly tables are listed below. All additional features with substantial statistical content are described, as they appear, under "Statistical Features;" page locations and latest periods of coverage for weekly and monthly tables are also noted. Nonstatistical features are not covered.

Availability: Engineering News-Record, Fulfillment Manager, PO Box 2026, Mahopac NY 10541, qualified subscribers $38.00 per yr., single copy $2.00; SRI/MF/not filmed.

Issues reviewed during 1985: Nov. 1, 1984-Oct. 31, 1985 (P) (Vol. 213, Nos. 18-25; Vol. 214, Nos. 1-26; Vol. 215, Nos. 1-18).

WEEKLY TABLES:

C5800–2.1: Market Trends, Weekly Tables

[Tables [2-4] show data for week prior to or week of publication, and for year to date with percent change from previous year to date. An annual article explaining ENR cost indexes appears in a Mar. issue.]

[1] Cost indexes [for construction, building, common labor, skilled labor, and materials; for week prior to publication, with percent change from previous month and year, based on a sampling of 20 cities; 1913=base year].

[2] Bidding volume [value for heavy/highway, nonresidential building, and multi-unit housing construction].

[3] New plans [value for approximately 20 types of heavy and highway, nonresidential building, and multi-unit housing (excludes 1-2 family) construction].

[4] New construction capital [corporate securities and State/municipal totals, with subtotals for housing and for other building/heavy construction].

C5800–2.2: Unit Prices

Weekly feature consisting of 1-2 brief articles each on the bidding of a significant construction project. Each article includes 1 table showing total bids of top competitors, and unit prices of individual items included in the accepted bid.

MONTHLY TABLES:

[All tables appear at 4-5 week intervals, but week of publication may vary from month to month.]

C5800–2.3: Market Trends, Monthly Tables

[Most tables show data for most recent available month, generally month of publication or previous month. Most also show comparative data for previous month and/or same period of previous year.]

COSTS

[An annual article explaining ENR cost indexes appears in a Mar. issue.]

[1] Wage rates, 20 cities' average [for common and skilled laborers, bricklayers, structural ironworkers, and carpenters].

[2] Material prices, 20 cities' average [for 16 materials].

[3] ENR index review [indexes for construction and building costs, and for skilled and common labor wage rates (1913 and 1967=base years), for month of publication and previous 12 months].

[4] ENR cost indexes in 22 cities [construction and building costs, by city; 1913=base year].

[5] ENR wage, materials, and cost indexes, 20 cities [for common and skilled labor wages, materials prices, and construction and building costs, by city; 1967=base year].

CONSTRUCTION TRENDS

[6] New construction planning backlog [value of total private, State/municipal, and Federal backlogs; and of 7 types of public and 3 types of private backlog].

[7] New industrial plans and contracts [value, for approximately 15 types, including manufacturing plants for 9 industry groups].

[8] New orders and construction bidding volume indexes [construction bidding volume (actual and seasonally adjusted), and fabricated structural steel bookings, 1967=base year].

[9] Construction machinery distributor sales indexes, reported by Associated Equipment Distributors [sales and inventories, surveys of 194-280 dealers; and inventory-sales ratio in months].

BOND SALES

[10] State/municipal bond sales for construction [for 3 types of buildings, 8 types of heavy and highway construction, and general improvement/unclassified].

CONTRACTOR FAILURES

[11] Contractor failures [and liabilities], reported by Dun & Bradstreet [for general building, other general, and special trade contractors, current to approximately 36 months prior to month of publication].

C5800-2.4: Materials Prices Tables

[All tables except table [8] show monthly market quotations by ENR field reporters for representative items within the category indicated by the table title. All tables except table [4] show data for 22 cities (all cities generally are not covered for all materials). All data are current as of cover date.]

[1] Cement, aggregate, ready mixed concrete: f.o.b. city.

[2] Asphalt, road oil: f.o.b. city.

[3] Iron and steel products: f.o.b. warehouse, per 100 lb., base price.

[4] Mill base price: carlot quantities [steel; for selected mill areas].

[5] Plumbing, heating, sewer pipe, and tubing: delivered carload lots.

[6] Lumber, timber, plywood, piles, ties.

[7] Window glass, explosives.

[8] Wage rates for key building construction trades: total of union base rate plus fringes [for 18 types of common and skilled building labor, equipment operators, and truck drivers].

[9] Building board, lath, and insulation: quoted in trucklots, delivered to job.

[10] Structural clay building tile, brick, and lime: quoted in carlots, delivered to job.

[11] Plaster, light weight aggregate and metal sheets: quoted in trucklots, delivered; building sheets are f.o.b. warehouse.

[12] Paint and roofing: quoted in carlots, delivered to job.

C5800-2.5: New Plans and Bidding Volume Tables

1-2 tables showing value of new plans and bidding for heavy construction (12 types), nonresidential building (9 types), and multi-unit housing (total and apartments); for month prior to cover date and year to date, with percent change from previous month and year.

C5800-2.6: Stock Track Table

Table showing stock price, revenue, earnings, and profitability ratios, for approximately 40 publicly owned companies (grouped as design firms, general and specialty contractors, and conglomerates). Most data are shown for latest available 12 months (identified by company).

STATISTICAL FEATURES:

C5800-2.601: Nov. 1, 1984 (Vol. 213, No. 18)

WEEKLY TABLES

a. Market trends, for week ended Oct. 25, 1984. (p. 126)

b. Unit prices, for Wyoming highway reconstruction contract. (p. 115)

MONTHLY TABLES

a. Materials prices, tables [8-9] for Nov. 1, 1984. (p. 100-101)

ENR REGIONAL MARKETS: MEDICAL BUILDINGS

(p. 126) Two charts showing value of new plans and bidding, for medical building construction, by region, 1st 9 months 1984 with comparisons to 1st 9 months 1983. Data are from ENR. Charts appear in "Market Trends" section.

TOUGH TIMES TRIMMED TRADES

(p. 129) Article, with 1 table showing paid membership in 15 building trade unions, selected periods 1955-1st half 1983. Data are from a survey of 216 unions, conducted by Bureau of National Affairs.

C5800-2.602: Nov. 8, 1984 (Vol. 213, No. 19)

WEEKLY TABLES

a. Market trends, for week ended Nov. 1, 1984. (p. 59)

b. Unit prices, for Maryland highway interchange construction contract. (p. 55)

MONTHLY TABLES

a. Market trends, tables [1-3] for Oct. or Nov. 1984. (p. 59)

b. Materials prices, tables [1-2] for Nov. 8, 1984. (p. 44-45)

PLANT BUILDING TO STAY HIGH

(p. 12) Article, with 1 table showing estimated capital expenditures for durable and nondurable goods industries, by type, 1984-85. Data are from Rinfret Associates, Inc. and Commerce Dept.

C5800-2.603: Nov. 15, 1984 (Vol. 213, No. 20)

WEEKLY TABLES

a. Market trends, for week ended Nov. 8, 1984. (p. 61)

b. Unit prices, for California highway reconstruction and sewer construction contracts. (p. 48)

MONTHLY TABLES

a. Market trends, tables [4-5] for Nov. 1984. (p. 61)

b. Materials prices, tables [3-5] for Nov. 15, 1984. (p. 42-43)

c. New plans and bidding volume, for Oct. 1984. (p. 37)

d. Stock track, for various periods, identified by company. (p. 25)

C5800-2.604: Nov. 22, 1984 (Vol. 213, No. 21)

WEEKLY TABLES

a. Market trends, for week ended Nov. 15, 1984. (p. 53)

b. Unit prices, for Indiana highway construction contract. (p. 40)

MONTHLY TABLES

a. Market trends, tables [6-7] for Oct. 1984. (p. 53)

b. Materials prices, tables [6-7] for Nov. 22, 1984. (p. 34-35)

JOBSITE SAFETY DECLINING SLIGHTLY, ANNUAL FEATURE

(p. 54) Annual article, with 1 table showing injuries with and without lost workdays, and number of lost workdays, per 100 employees, for private sector, construction industry, and 3 contractor types, 1982-83. Data are from BLS.

C5800-2.605: Nov. 29, 1984 (Vol. 213, No. 22)

WEEKLY TABLES

a. Market trends, for week ended Nov. 22, 1984. (p. 55)

b. Unit prices, for NYC bridge construction contract. (p. 51)

MONTHLY TABLES

a. Market trends, tables [8, 10] for Oct. 1984, [9] for June 1984, and [11] for 1982. (p. 55)

b. Materials prices, tables [8-12] for Nov. 29, 1984. (p. 46-47)

PAY TALLIED FOR NONUNION LABOR, SEMIANNUAL FEATURE

(p. 21) Semiannual article, with 1 undated table showing high and low nonunion wage rates in 15 cities, for common labor and journeyman carpenter, and for helper and journeyman bricklayer, plumber, and electrician. Data are from ENR.

This is the 1st semiannual survey.

C5800-2.606: Dec. 6, 1984 (Vol. 213, No. 23)

WEEKLY TABLES

a. Market trends, for week ended Nov. 29, 1984. (p. 55)

b. Unit prices, for Kentucky highway reconstruction contract. (p. 51)

MONTHLY TABLES

a. Market trends, tables [1-3] for Nov. or Dec. 1984. (p. 55)

b. Materials prices, tables [1-2] for Dec. 6, 1984. (p. 44-45)

INTERNATIONAL STOCK TRACK: FOREIGN FIRMS SEE STAGNANT 1985, QUARTERLY FEATURE

(p. 25) Quarterly article on recent financial performance of 43 publicly owned international construction companies. Includes 1 table showing stock price, revenue, earnings, and profitability ratios, for 43 companies based in UK, France, West Germany, Netherlands, Japan, and Canada. Data are for latest 12 months or latest closing date.

Data sources are Datastream, London, England; Financial Post Investment Databank, Toronto, Canada; and WestLB (Boursys), Duesseldorf, West Germany.

LIABILITY INSURANCE IN TURMOIL, ANNUAL FEATURE

(p. 64) Annual article on construction design firm insurance liability and claims. Data are from responses of 1,613 firms to an American Consulting Engineers Council survey. Includes 1 chart showing number of professional-liability claims filed against construction design firms, 1980-84.

JOBS BLOOM IN SMALL FIRMS

(p. 66) Article, with 1 table showing number of jobs for 10 construction industry sectors in which firms with under 500 workers account for 60% or more of employment, Nov. 1982 and July 1984. Data are from SBA.

C5800-2.607: Dec. 13, 1984 (Vol. 213, No. 24)

WEEKLY TABLES

a. Market trends, for week ended Dec. 6, 1984. (p. 57)

b. Unit prices, for Maryland highway reconstruction contract. (p. 53)

MONTHLY TABLES

a. Market trends, tables [4-5] for Dec. 1984. (p. 57)

b. Materials prices, tables [3-5] for Dec. 13, 1984. (p. 42-43)

c. New plans and bidding volume, for Nov. 1984. (p. 18)

C5800-2.608: Dec. 20, 1984 (Vol. 213, No. 25)

WEEKLY TABLES

a. Market trends, for week ended Dec. 13, 1984. (p. 141)

b. Unit prices, for North Carolina, California, and Idaho highway reconstruction contracts. (p. 93)

MONTHLY TABLES

a. Market trends, tables [6-7] for Nov. 1984. (p. 141)

b. Materials prices, tables [6-7] for Dec. 20, 1984. (p. 132-133)

c. Stock track, for various periods, identified by company. (p. 130)

QUARTERLY COST ROUNDUP

(p. 63-95) Quarterly report, for 4th quarter 1984, on construction industry cost trends and outlook. Data sources include Federal and State agencies, private organizations, and ENR surveys, and are identified on most tables and charts.

Contains introduction and 14 articles. Statistical contents of individual articles are described below.

a. "Forecast: Moderate Cost Trends To Prevail." Includes 3 tables showing building and construction cost indexes (total and for 20 cities), common and skilled labor wage rates and indexes, materials price index, and prices for 3 primary products, Dec. 1984-85 and percent change from 1983. (p. 68-69)

b. "Forecast: DRI, Price Moderation To Be '85 Theme." Includes 1 table showing percent change in prices for 26 types of construction material and equipment, 1983-87. (p. 70)

c. "Machinery: Prices Ignore Sales Increase." Includes 2 tables showing estimated percent change in sales for 7 types of construction equipment, 1985; and price indexes for 38 types of construction equipment, Apr. July, and Oct. 1984 and percent change from Oct. 1983. (p. 73)

d. "Money: Borrowers Gain a Brief Respite." Includes 1 chart showing value of new State/municipal construction bond sales, with distribution by type of construction, 1st 11 months 1984. (p. 79-80)

e. "Wages: Recovery Gets Labor-Cost Break." Includes 1 table showing construction wage indexes for common and skilled labor, equipment operators, electricians, and mechanical trades, for 20 cities, 1983-84. (p. 83)

f. "Parameter Costs: Far East Costs Trail U.S." Includes 1 undated table showing high-rise bank construction costs by major item, for steel- and concrete-framed buildings, in 3 Far Eastern and 3 U.S. cities. (p. 84)

g. "World Costs: Industrial Growth Boosts Costs." Includes 1 table showing replacement cost indexes for industrial buildings and machinery, for 7 foreign countries, Jan. and/or July 1981-85 and annually 1972-80. (p. 87)

h. "Treatment Plants: Small Plant Costs Accelerate." Includes 3 tables showing cost indexes, total and by cost component, for 5 and 50 million gallons per day municipal wastewater treatment plants, and for complete urban sewer systems, for 25 cities, 3rd quarter 1984 and change from 3rd quarter 1983. (p. 89)

i. "Water and Power: Minor Cost Hikes Cap BuRec Cost Escalation." Includes 1 table showing Bureau of Reclamation cost indexes for water and power related construction, including dams, pumping plants, hydroelectric power plants, and transmission lines, Oct. 1978-84. (p. 90)

j. "Utility Costs: Powerplant Costs Head Higher." Includes 1 chart and 1 table showing value of electric utility construction contracts, 1981-1st 9 months 1984; and construction cost indexes for steam, nuclear, and hydroelectric power plants, by region, July 1976-84. (p. 91)

k. "Builders' Indexes: Indexes Show Cost Hikes Slowing." Includes 1 table showing 19 indexes of builders' construction costs, 1981-83 and monthly Dec. 1983-Dec. 1984. (p. 92)

l. "Highways: Surfacing Bids Spark Rising Highway Costs." Includes 2 tables showing highway bid price indexes, for 20 States and for Federal-aid excavation, surfacing, and structure projects; 3rd quarter 1984 with quarterly trends from 1980 or 1981, and annual trends from 1975 (Federal projects only). (p. 94-95)

C5800-2.609: Jan. 3, 1985 (Vol. 214, No. 1)

WEEKLY TABLES

a. Market trends, for week ended Dec. 27, 1984. (p. 45)

b. Unit prices, for Oklahoma highway reconstruction contract. (p. 39)

MONTHLY TABLES

a. Materials prices, tables [8-12] for Jan. 3, 1985. (p. 30-31)

ENR REGIONAL MARKETS: TRANSPORTATION

(p. 45) Two charts showing value of new plans and bidding, for transportation projects, by region, 1st 11 months 1984 with comparisons to 1st 11 months 1983. Data are from ENR. Charts appear in "Market Trends" section.

DESIGNERS TO GET PAY HIKE

(p. 48) Article, with 1 undated table showing median salary for architects and civil engineers, by position. Data are from a survey of 162 firms, conducted by Personnel Administration Services, Inc.

C5800-2.610: Jan. 10, 1985 (Vol. 214, No. 2)

WEEKLY TABLES

a. Market trends, for week ended Jan. 3, 1985. (p. 59)

b. Unit prices, for California highway construction contract. (p. 49)

MONTHLY TABLES

a. Market trends, tables [1-3] for Dec. 1984 or Jan. 1985. (p. 59)

b. Materials prices, tables [1-2] for Jan. 10, 1985. (p. 40-41)

WAGE HIKES HIT ROCK BOTTOM, RECURRING FEATURE

(p. 60) Recurring article, with 1 chart showing 1st-year wage/benefits change for construction industry collective bargaining settlements, by region, 1984. Data are from Construction Labor Research Council.

C5800-2.611: Jan. 17, 1985 (Vol. 214, No. 3)

WEEKLY TABLES

a. Market trends, for week ended Jan. 10, 1985. (p. 57)

b. Unit prices, for Tennessee bridge construction and Utah highway reconstruction contracts. (p. 51)

MONTHLY TABLES

a. Market trends, tables [4-5] for Jan. 1985. (p. 57)

b. Materials prices, tables [3-5] for Jan. 17, 1985. (p. 40-41)

c. New plans and bidding volume, for Dec. 1984. (p. 23)

d. Stock track, for various periods, identified by company. (p. 34)

C5800-2.612: Jan. 24, 1985 (Vol. 214, No. 4)

WEEKLY TABLES

a. Market trends, for week ended Jan. 17, 1985. (p. 115)

b. Unit prices, for Montana bridge construction and Vermont highway reconstruction contracts. (p. 111)

MONTHLY TABLES

a. Market trends, tables [6-7] for Dec. 1984. (p. 115)

b. Materials prices, tables [6-7] for Jan. 24, 1985. (p. 102-103)

ENR OUTLOOK '85, ANNUAL FEATURE

(p. 44-83) Annual construction industry overview, with 6 articles analyzing trends and outlook for the industry as a whole and for its major subdivisions, 1983-86. Includes introductory article (p. 45-54), with 1 chart and 4 tables showing the following:

a. Value of contracts, by type (excluding homebuilding), 1983-86; and Federal spending for public works, by type of project and agency or program, FY84-85 and FY89.

b. Value of new plans and bidding for heavy/ highway and nonresidential building construction, by region and State, and for top 10 States in 9 construction categories, 1984 with comparions to 1983.

Data are from ENR and OMB.

WEST COAST DESIGNERS BEST PAID

(p. 124) Article, with 1 undated table showing average hourly billing rates of construction design firms by employee position, by U.S. region and for Canada, and aggregated for U.S./Canada by firm size and type and by client type (private, government, mixed). Data are from a survey of 474 firms, conducted by Design Management Consulting, Inc.

C5800–2.613: Jan. 31, 1985 (Vol. 214, No. 5)

WEEKLY TABLES

a. Market trends, for week ended Jan. 17 or Jan. 24, 1985. (p. 57)

b. Unit prices, for California highway construction contract. (p. 40)

MONTHLY TABLES

a. Market trends, tables [8, 10] for Dec. 1984, [9] for June 1984, and [11] for 1982. (p. 57)

b. Materials prices, tabies [8-12] for Jan. 31, 1985. (p. 36-37)

C5800–2.614: Feb. 7, 1985 (Vol. 214, No. 6)

WEEKLY TABLES

a. Market trends, for week ended Jan. 31, 1985. (p. 51)

b. Unit prices, for North Carolina highway grading contract. (p. 41)

MONTHLY TABLES

a. Market trends, tables [1-3] for Jan. or Feb. 1985. (p. 51)

b. Materials prices, tables [1-2] for Feb. 7, 1985. (p. 34-35)

BUDGET GIVES CONSTRUCTION LIGHT LIFT

(p. 10-11) Article, with 1 table showing Federal spending for public works projects, by type (excluding defense-related), FY84-85 and Administration proposal FY86.

FAILURES UP, BUT SIGNS BRIGHT, ANNUAL FEATURE

(p. 57-58) Annual article, with 1 chart showing construction contractor failures, 1979-84. Data are from Dun & Bradstreet Corp.

C5800–2.615: Feb. 14, 1985 (Vol. 214, No. 7)

WEEKLY TABLES

a. Market trends, for week ended Feb. 7, 1985. (p. 93)

---

b. Unit prices, for Michigan highway reconstruction contract. (p. 91)

MONTHLY TABLES

a. Market trends, tables [4-5] for Feb. 1985. (p. 93)

b. Materials prices, tables [3-5] for Feb. 14, 1985. (p. 76-77)

UNION WORKERS PAID BEST

(p. 114) Article, with 1 table showing construction industry labor union membership (number and as a percent of work force), and union and nonunion mean weekly earnings, 1977, 1980, and 1984. Data are from BLS.

C5800–2.616: Feb. 21, 1985 (Vol. 214, No. 8)

WEEKLY TABLES

a. Market trends, for week ended Feb. 14, 1985. (p. 43)

b. Unit prices, for California highway construction contract. (p. 37)

MONTHLY TABLES

a. Market trends, tables [6-7] for Jan. 1985. (p. 43)

b. Materials prices, tables [6-7] for Feb. 21, 1985. (p. 32-33)

c. Stock track, for various periods, identified by company. (p. 19)

OMB REPORT DUBIOUS ON FUTURE SPENDING

(p. 10-11) Article, with 1 table showing Federal spending for public works projects, by type, actual FY84 and estimated FY85-88 and FY94. Data are from OMB.

C5800–2.617: Feb. 28, 1985 (Vol. 214, No. 9)

WEEKLY TABLES

a. Market trends, for week ended Feb. 21, 1985. (p. 47)

b. Unit prices, for North Carolina highway construction contract. (p. 41)

MONTHLY TABLES

a. Market trends, tables [8, 10] for Jan. 1985, [9] for June 1984, and [11] for 1982. (p. 47)

b. Materials prices, tables [8-12] for Feb. 28, 1985. (p. 36-37)

c. New plans and bidding volume, for Jan. 1985. (p. 27)

C5800–2.618: Mar. 7, 1985 (Vol. 214, No. 10)

WEEKLY TABLES

a. Market trends, for week ended Feb. 28, 1985. (p. 53)

b. Unit prices, for Atlanta rapid transit system construction contract. (p. 50)

MONTHLY TABLES

a. Market trends, tables [1-3] for Feb. or Mar. 1985. (p. 53)

b. Materials prices, tables [1-2] for Mar. 7, 1985. (p. 42-43)

INTERNATIONAL STOCK TRACK: FOREIGN FIRMS' FUTURES UNCERTAIN, QUARTERLY FEATURE

(p. 24) Quarterly article on recent financial performance of 29 publicly owned international construction companies. Includes 1 table showing stock price, revenue, and earnings, for

---

29 companies based in Canada, France, West Germany, Japan, Netherlands, Norway, Spain, Sweden, Switzerland, and UK. Data are for latest 12 months or latest closing date.

Data are from *Capital International Perspective,* Geneva, Switzerland.

C5800–2.619: Mar. 14, 1985 (Vol. 214, No. 11)

WEEKLY TABLES

a. Market trends, for week ended Mar. 7, 1985. (p. 57)

b. Unit prices, for California highway reconstruction contract. (p. 51)

MONTHLY TABLES

a. Market trends, tables [4-5] for Mar. 1985. (p. 57)

b. Materials prices, tables [3-5] for Mar. 14, 1985. (p. 40-41)

c. New plans and bidding volume, for Feb. 1985. (p. 31)

C5800–2.620: Mar. 21, 1985 (Vol. 214, No. 12)

WEEKLY TABLES

a. Market trends, for week ended Mar. 14, 1985. (p. 157)

b. Unit prices, for California water pipeline, California highway bridge, and Arkansas dam construction contracts. (p. 80)

MONTHLY TABLES

a. Market trends, tables [6-7] for Feb. 1985. (p. 157)

b. Materials prices, tables [6-7] for Mar. 21, 1985. (p. 150-151)

c. Stock track, for various periods, identified by company. (p. 107)

QUARTERLY COST ROUNDUP

(p. 65-105) Quarterly report, for 1st quarter 1985, on construction industry cost trends and outlook. Data sources include Federal and State agencies, private organizations, and ENR surveys, and are identified on most tables and charts.

Contains introduction and 10 articles. Statistical contents of individual articles are described below.

a. "Money: Credit Costs Walk a Tightrope." Includes 1 chart showing potential impact of a Treasury Dept tax proposal and 2 other tax plans on single-family homeownership costs, by income level. (p. 73-74)

b. "World Costs: Costs Rise in Europe Despite Slow Economy." Includes 1 chart showing steel and concrete prices in 6 European cities, as of Mar. 1, 1985. (p. 76)

c. "Parameter Costs: Study Compares European Costs." Includes 1 undated table showing high-rise apartment construction costs by major item, for steel- and concrete-framed buildings, in 6 European cities. (p. 77)

d. "Machinery: Equipment Inflation Held to 1.7%." Includes 1 table showing price indexes for 37 types of construction equipment, July and Oct. 1984, and Jan. 1985 with percent change from Jan. 1984. (p. 83)

e. "Highways: Late '84 Surge Hits Road Costs." Includes 2 tables showing highway bid price indexes, for 20 States and for Fed-

---

eral-aid excavation, surfacing, and structure projects, 4th quarter 1984 with quarterly trends from 1980 or 1981, and annual trends from 1975 (Federal projects only). (p. 86-87)

f. "Water and Power: BuRec Costs Edge Higher Again." Includes 1 table showing Bureau of Reclamation cost indexes for water and power related construction, including dams, pumping plants, hydroelectric power plants, and transmission lines, Jan. 1979-85 with percent change for Oct. 1984-Jan. 1985 period. (p. 89)

g. "Market Survey: Recovery Brings Some Shortages." Includes 1 chart and 1 table summarizing construction productivity and work force changes, and incidence of work stoppages, Feb. 1984-Feb. 1985 period; and reports of labor shortage for selected trades and delivery delays for selected products, for 20 cities, Aug. 1984-Feb. 1985 period. (p. 90)

h. "Builders' Indexes: Building Costs Remain Moderate." Includes 1 table showing 19 indexes of builders' construction costs, 1982-84 and monthly Mar. 1984-Mar. 1985. (p. 92, 95)

i. "Wages: Stable Costs Face Spring Test." Includes 1 table showing construction wage indexes for common and skilled labor, equipment operators, electricians, and mechanical trades, for 20 cities, Mar. 1984-85. (p. 97)

INDEX HISTORY: CONSTRUCTION COSTS TRACKED FOR U.S., ANNUAL FEATURE

(p. 98-105) Annual article explaining ENR indexes of construction-related costs, and presenting historical trends in the indexes. Includes 3 tables, based on a 20-city sampling, showing building and construction cost indexes (1913 base year) as follows: total U.S., annually 1906 or 1913 to 1984, and monthly 1966-Mar. 1985; and for 20 cities, annually 1959-74, and last month of each quarter Mar. 1975-Mar. 1985.

Also includes 2 charts showing index components. Feature appears in the "Quarterly Cost Roundup" section.

MORE WAGE MODERATION SEEN, RECURRING FEATURE

(p. 160-161) Recurring article, with 1 table showing construction industry labor contracts scheduled for collective bargaining in 1985, and including workers covered, and deferred labor cost increase, all by region. Data are from Construction Labor Research Council.

C5800–2.621: Mar. 28, 1985 (Vol. 214, No. 13)

WEEKLY TABLES

a. Market trends, for week ended Mar. 21, 1985. (p. 47)

b. Unit prices, for Utah highway construction contract. (p. 41)

MONTHLY TABLES

a. Market trends, tables [8, 10] for Feb. 1985, [9] for Aug. 1984, and [11] for 1984. (p. 47)

b. Materials prices, tables [8-12] for Mar. 28, 1985. (p. 34-35)

C5800–2.622: Apr. 4, 1985 (Vol. 214, No. 14)

WEEKLY TABLES

a. Market trends, for week ended Mar. 28, 1985. (p. 77)

b. Unit prices, for New Jersey highway construction contract. (p. 57)

MONTHLY TABLES

a. Market trends, tables [1-3] for Mar. or Apr. 1985. (p. 77)

b. Materials prices, tables [1-2] for Apr. 4, 1985. (p. 54-55)

CONTRACTOR SALARIES ON THE RISE

(p. 78) Article, with 1 undated table showing construction industry average base salary for 6 management positions, by type of construction performed. Data are from a recent survey of 175 contractors and construction managers, conducted by Personnel Administration Services, Inc.

For description of a similar article, presenting data as of Mar. 1984, see SRI 1984 Annual under C5800-2.537.

C5800–2.623: Apr. 11, 1985 (Vol. 214, No. 15)

WEEKLY TABLES

a. Market trends, for week ended Apr. 4, 1985. (p. 51)

b. Unit prices, for Tennessee highway reconstruction contract. (p. 43)

MONTHLY TABLES

a. Market trends, tables [4-5] for Apr. 1985. (p. 51)

b. Materials prices, tables [3-5] for Apr. 11, 1985. (p. 38-39)

c. New plans and bidding volume, for Mar. 1985. (p. 30)

C5800–2.624: Apr. 18, 1985 (Vol. 214, No. 16)

WEEKLY TABLES

a. Market trends, for week ended Apr. 11, 1985. (p. 105)

b. Unit prices, for Virginia bridge construction contract. (p. 97)

MONTHLY TABLES

a. Market trends, tables [6-7] for Mar. 1985. (p. 105)

b. Materials prices, tables [6-7] for Apr. 18, 1985. (p. 90-91)

c. Stock track, for various periods, identified by company. (p. 44)

EXPORTERS BRING BIG BUCKS HOME

(p. 17-18) Article, with 1 chart showing foreign revenue of U.S. design/construction firms, and direct and indirect impact of foreign revenue on U.S. construction salaries/fringe benefits, corporate and personal taxes, and jobs, 1983.

Data are from responses of 266 construction/design firms to a survey conducted for International Engineering and Construction Industries Council.

TOP 400 CONTRACTORS, ANNUAL FEATURE

(p. 46-79) Annual report, for 1984, on new construction contract awards of leading companies, based on an ENR survey of 2,500 contractors. Includes the following data, shown for individual companies unless otherwise noted, 1984 with selected comparisons to 1983:

a. Firms reporting over $1 billion in contracts; value of total and foreign contracts, construction management contracts as percent of total, and specialty, for top 400 construction firms; and aggregate foreign contract value and number of firms among the top 400, by world area and contract type (design/construction, design only, and construction management). 3 tables.

b. Total contract value, value of all domestic and design/construction contracts, number of firms, and profit and loss; and value of management contracts, with detail for domestic at risk and fee only contracts and firms; for aggregate groups of 40 companies among the top 400. 2 tables.

c. Design construction contract value, with detail for foreign, design only, and design/construction management contracts; and specialty; for top 50 design/construction firms. 1 chart and 1 table.

d. Management contract value (total and foreign) for top 75 program/construction managers; value of domestic contracts for top 50 general building contractors; and domestic contract value and specialty for top 50 heavy contractors. 3 tables.

e. Location of foreign contracts, by country and firm. 2 tabular lists.

This is the 22nd annual report.

C5800–2.625: Apr. 25, 1985 (Vol. 214, No. 17)

WEEKLY TABLES

a. Market trends, for week ended Apr. 18, 1985. (p. 55)

b. Unit prices, for Maryland highway construction contract. (p. 47)

MONTHLY TABLES

a. Market trends, tables [8, 10] for Mar. 1985, [9] for Oct. 1984, and [11] for 1984. (p. 55)

b. Materials prices, tables [10-12] for Apr. 25, 1985. (p. 28-29)

C5800–2.626: May 2, 1985 (Vol. 214, No. 18)

WEEKLY TABLES

a. Market trends, for week ended Apr. 25, 1985. (p. 39)

b. Unit prices, for Texas highway reconstruction contract. (p. 37)

MONTHLY TABLES

a. Materials prices, tables [8-9] for May 2, 1985. (p. 30-31)

FUNDS FOR DEVELOPMENT GROWING

(p. 10-11) Article, with 1 table showing value of project loans to developing countries, for 25 world development banks and funds, 1985-89; with aggregate amount designated for construction, 1985-89 period. Data are from Development Bank Associates, Inc.

ENR REGIONAL MARKETS: MANUFACTURING

(p. 39) Two charts showing value of new plans and bidding, for manufacturing facility construction, by region, 1st quarter 1985 with percent change from 1st quarter 1984. Data are from ENR. Charts appear in "Market Trends" section.

For description of a similar feature, for 1984, see SRI 1984 Annual under C5800-2.526.

C5800–2.627: May 9, 1985 (Vol. 214, No. 19)

WEEKLY TABLES

a. Market trends, for week ended May 2, 1985. (p. 45)

b. Unit prices, for West Virginia highway grading and drainage contract. (p. 37)

MONTHLY TABLES

a. Market trends, tables [1-3] for Apr. or May 1985. (p. 45)

b. Materials prices, tables [1-2] for May 9, 1985. (p. 32-33)

OWNERS LAX ON PROJECT CONTROL

(p. 48) Article on project owners' methods for controlling construction quality and scheduling, including use of retainage (witholding portions of progress payments). Data are from responses of 493 owners to a survey commissioned by Wagner-Hohns-Inglis, Inc.

Includes 1 undated chart showing responses on retainage use; whether retainage reduces job problems and raises job costs; and average retainage level; for all respondents, and for developers, public/private corporations, universities/hospitals, and local/State government.

C5800–2.628: May 16, 1985 (Vol. 214, No. 20)

WEEKLY TABLES

a. Market trends, for week ended May 9, 1985. (p. 113)

b. Unit prices, for Washington State bridge construction contract. (p. 97)

MONTHLY TABLES

a. Market trends, tables [4-5] for May 1985. (p. 113)

b. Materials prices, tables [3-5] for May 16, 1985. (p. 92-93)

c. Stock track, for various periods, identified by company. (p. 77)

TOP 500 DESIGN FIRMS: DESIGN BILLINGS GAIN 12% IN 1984, ANNUAL FEATURE

(p. 36-66) Annual report on top 500 architectural and engineering design firms based on 1984 billings. Data are from an ENR survey. Report covers domestic and foreign billings, and includes 4 articles interspersed with the following data for 1984:

a. Billings distribution by type of firm and project; and total and net billings per staff member, for 5 professional positions; for aggregate top 500 firms. 3 charts.

b. Top 500 design firms based on total billings, shown in rank order grouped by billings size, and including type of firm, billings distribution by type of project, and whether construction management (CM) and foreign work is performed, with accompanying list of affiliates and subsidiaries. 2 lists.

c. Top 50 firms based on CM billings, with CM share of total billings; foreign billings by country or world area for aggregate top 500 firms, with comparison to 1983, and countries of operation for individual firms; and top 20 firms based on net billings. 1 chart and 3 lists.

This is the 21st annual report.

OPEN SHOP PLANS 3.8% RAISES, RECURRING FEATURE

(p. 121) Recurring article, with 1 table showing employment, hourly wage, and benefits as a percent of wages, for nonunion workers by selected craft, 1985. Data are based on responses of 380 nonunion contractors to a survey conducted by Personnel Administration Services, Inc.

Previous article, for 1983, is described in SRI 1984 Annual under C5800-2.525.

C5800–2.629: May 23, 1985 (Vol. 214, No. 21)

WEEKLY TABLES

a. Market trends, for week ended May 16, 1985. (p. 42)

b. Unit prices, for NYC road reconstruction contract. (p. 41)

MONTHLY TABLES

a. Market trends, tables [6-7] for Apr. 1985. (p. 42)

b. Materials prices, tables [6-7] for May 23, 1985. (p. 34-35)

c. New plans and bidding volume, for Apr. 1985. (p. 28)

C5800–2.630: May 30, 1985 (Vol. 214, No. 22)

WEEKLY TABLES

a. Market trends, for week ended May 23, 1985. (p. 82)

b. Unit prices, for Connecticut bridge reconstruction contract. (p. 85)

MONTHLY TABLES

a. Market trends, tables [8, 10] for Apr. 1985, [9] for Dec. 1984, and [11] for 1st quarter 1985. (p. 82)

b. Materials prices, tables [8-12] for May 30, 1985. (p. 64-65)

A-Es ON ECONOMIC REBOUND, RECURRING FEATURE

(p. 109) Recurring article, with 1 undated table showing number of executives and median compensation at architectural/engineering design firms, by position. Data are from a recent survey of 403 design firms, conducted by Design Management Consulting, Inc. for *Professional Services Management Journal*.

Previous article, for 1983-84, is described in SRI 1984 Annual under C5800-2.528.

C5800–2.631: June 6, 1985 (Vol. 214, No. 23)

WEEKLY TABLES

a. Market trends, for week ended May 30, 1985. (p. 53)

b. Unit prices, for Wyoming highway reconstruction contract. (p. 43)

MONTHLY TABLES

a. Market trends, tables [1-3] for May or June 1985. (p. 53)

b. Materials prices, tables [1-2] for June 6, 1985. (p. 36-37)

INTERNATIONAL STOCK TRACK: CHEERLESS FUTURE FOR FOREIGN FIRMS, QUARTERLY FEATURE

(p. 32) Quarterly article on recent financial performance of 33 publicly owned international construction companies. Includes 1 table showing stock price, revenue, and earnings, for 33 companies based in Canada, France, West Germany, Japan, Netherlands, Norway, Spain, Sweden, Switzerland, and UK. Data are for latest 12 months or latest closing date.

Data are from *Capital International Perspective*, Geneva, Switzerland.

FREEZES FASHIONABLE IN '85, RECURRING FEATURE

(p. 54-55) Recurring article, with 1 table showing construction industry collective-bargaining settlements, workers covered, and average 1st-year wage change, by region, 1st 5 months 1985. Data are from Construction Labor Research Council.

C5800–2.632: June 13, 1985 (Vol. 214, No. 24)

WEEKLY TABLES

a. Market trends, for week ended June 6, 1985. (p. 44)

b. Unit prices, for Kansas bridge construction contract. (p. 43)

MONTHLY TABLES

a. Market trends, tables [4-5] for June 1985. (p. 44)

b. Materials prices, tables [3-5] for June 13, 1985. (p. 38-39)

C5800–2.633: June 20, 1985 (Vol. 214, No. 25)

WEEKLY TABLES

a. Market trends, for week ended June 13, 1985. (p. 149)

b. Unit prices, for California and Montana highway reconstruction contracts, and Vermont highway construction contract. (p. 97)

MONTHLY TABLES

a. Market trends, tables [6-7] for May 1985. (p. 149)

b. Materials prices, tables [6-7] for June 20, 1985. (p. 142-143)

QUARTERLY COST ROUNDUP

(p. 63-94) Quarterly report, for 2nd quarter 1985, on construction industry cost trends and outlook. Data sources include Federal and State agencies, private organizations, and ENR surveys, and are identified on most tables and charts.

Contains introduction and 13 articles. Articles with substantial statistical content are described below.

a. "Highways: Costs Stable Despite Market Gain." Includes 1 chart and 3 tables showing contract cost by item, for rural vs. urban projects; and highway bid price indexes, for Federal-aid projects by State, for State highway projects in 20 States, and for Federal-aid excavation, surfacing, and structure projects; various periods 1976-1st quarter 1985. (p. 68-72)

b. "Machinery: Competition Keeps Lid on Prices." Includes 1 table showing price indexes for 35 types of construction equipment, Oct. 1984, and Jan. and Apr. 1985 with percent change from 1984. (p. 75)

c. "Wages: Union Pay Gains Still in Retreat." Includes 1 table showing construction wage indexes for common and skilled labor, equipment operators, electricians, and mechanical trades, for 20 cities, June 1984-85. (p. 76)

d. "Water and Power: BuRec Project Costs Hold Steady." Includes 1 table showing Bureau of Reclamation cost indexes for water and power related construction, including dams, pumping plants, hydroelectric power plants, and transmission lines, Apr. 1979-85 with percent change for Jan.-Apr. 1985 period. (p. 81)

e. "Treatment Plants: Big Plants Post Biggest Rise." Includes 3 tables showing cost indexes (total and by cost component), for 5 and 50 million gallons per day municipal wastewater treatment plants, and for complete urban sewer systems, for 25 cities, 1st quarter 1985 and change from 1st quarter 1984. (p. 83)

f. "Parameter Costs: Study Compares UK Costs." Includes 1 undated table showing construction costs (in U.S. dollars) by item, for steel- and concrete-framed buildings, by type, in London, England. (p. 85)

g. "Water Utility: Inflation Keeps a Low Profile." Includes 1 table showing construction cost indexes for water utility equipment by type, by region, Jan. 1977-85. (p. 86)

h. "Builders' Indexes: Inflation Stays in Low Gear." Includes 1 table showing 19 indexes of builders' construction costs, 1982-84 and monthly June 1984-June 1985. (p. 87)

i. "Materials Prices: A Buyer's Market Pacifies Prices." Includes 1 table showing average prices for selected construction materials including pipe (4 types), asphalt paving, portland cement, ready-mix concrete, and crushed stone, aggregated for 20 cities, 2nd quarter 1985 with percent change from 1st quarter 1985 and 2nd quarter 1984. (p. 88)

j. "UK Costs: Budget Cutbacks Hamper Recovery." Includes 1 chart showing materials prices (in U.S. dollars) by item, for the UK, as of May 31, 1985. (p. 89)

k. "Electric Utility: Costs for Powerplants Contained." Includes 1 table showing construction cost indexes for steam, nuclear, and hydroelectric power plants, by region, Jan. 1977-85. (p. 90)

C5800–2.634: June 27, 1985 (Vol. 214, No. 26)

WEEKLY TABLES

a. Market trends, for week ended June 20, 1985. (p. 59)

b. Unit prices, for Colorado tunnel construction contract. (p. 57)

MONTHLY TABLES

a. Market trends, tables [8, 10] for May 1985, [9] for Jan. and Feb. 1983, and [11] for 1st quarter 1985. (p. 59)

b. Materials prices, tables [8-12] for June 27, 1985. (p. 40-41)

c. New plans and bidding volume, for May 1985. (p. 30)

d. Stock track, for various periods, identified by company. (p. 29)

C5800–2.635: July 4, 1985 (Vol. 215, No. 1)

WEEKLY TABLES

a. Market trends, for week ended June 27, 1985. (p. 74)

b. Unit prices, for Texas highway construction contract. (p. 73)

MONTHLY TABLES

a. Market trends, tables [1-3] for June or July 1985. (p. 74)

b. Materials prices, tables [1-2] for July 4, 1985. (p. 54-55)

EXECUTIVE COMPENSATION, ANNUAL FEATURE

(p. 28-32) Annual report on construction industry executive compensation for 1984, based on a survey covering 289 executives at 61 publicly owned design firms, general and specialty contractors, conglomerates, and builders and developers. Data were collected for ENR by The Hay Group.

Includes 2 tables showing salary/bonus and long-term compensation, position, and company, for 10 most highly paid executives; and net profit, and position and salary/bonus and long-term compensation for each surveyed executive, by company arranged by type of firm; 1984 with comparisons to 1983.

Corrected data appear in the Sept. 12, 1985 issue; for description, see C5800-2.645 below.

C5800–2.636: July 11, 1985 (Vol. 215, No. 2)

WEEKLY TABLES

a. Market trends, for week ended July 4, 1985. (p. 59)

b. Unit prices, for Virginia highway construction contract. (p. 60)

MONTHLY TABLES

a. Market trends, tables [4-5] for July 1985. (p. 59)

b. Materials prices, tables [3-5] for July 11, 1985. (p. 46-47)

C5800–2.637: July 18, 1985 (Vol. 215, No. 3)

WEEKLY TABLES

a. Market trends, for week ended July 11, 1985. (p. 80)

b. Unit prices, for Minnesota highway reconstruction and flood control project. (p. 78)

MONTHLY TABLES

a. Market trends, tables [6-7] for June 1985. (p. 80)

b. Materials prices, tables [6-7] for July 18, 1985. (p. 70-71)

c. Stock track, for various periods, identified by company. (p. 33)

TOP INTERNATIONAL CONTRACTORS, ANNUAL FEATURE

(p. 34-59) Annual report on foreign contract awards to world's largest international construction contractors, 1984. Presents ENR industry survey data on 250 firms. Includes the following data, for 1984 with selected trends from 1980:

a. Foreign contract awards and number of firms (total and for projects in 6 world regions), by firms' country; and profit margin for foreign and domestic contracts, by total value of foreign and domestic contracts. 2 charts and 8 tables.

b. Top 250 firms ranked by foreign contract awards, with total contract awards and construction specialty. 1 table.

c. List showing contract work locations by country and firm.

This is the 7th annual survey. Corrected data appear in the Aug. 22, 1985 issue; for description, see C5800-2.642 below.

C5800–2.638: July 25, 1985 (Vol. 215, No. 4)

WEEKLY TABLES

a. Market trends, for week ended July 18, 1985. (p. 43)

b. Unit prices, for North Carolina bridge reconstruction contract. (p. 40)

MONTHLY TABLES

a. Market trends, tables [8, 10] for June 1985, [9] for Mar. 1984, and [11] for 1st quarter 1984-85. (p. 43)

b. Materials prices, tables [10-12] for July 25, 1985. (p. 36-37)

c. New plans and bidding volume, for June 1985. (p. 20)

C5800–2.639: Aug. 1, 1985 (Vol. 215, No. 5)

WEEKLY TABLES

a. Market trends, for week ended July 25, 1985. (p. 59)

b. Unit prices, for Bureau of Reclamation conduit construction contract in California, and for Washington State highway reconstruction contract. (p. 57)

MONTHLY TABLES

a. Materials prices, tables [8-9] for Aug. 1, 1985. (p. 46-47)

TOP INTERNATIONAL DESIGN FIRMS, ANNUAL FEATURE

(p. 26-39) Annual report on foreign contract billings of 200 largest international construction design firms, 1984. Data are based on an ENR survey and include the following, shown for 1984 with selected trends from 1980:

a. Foreign billings and number of firms, with detail for projects in 6 world regions; and percent of firms planning to increase and reduce domestic and foreign staff; all by firms' country. 3 charts and 8 tables.

b. Ranking of 200 firms grouped by size of foreign billings, showing foreign billings as percent of total company billings, type of company, and design specialties. 1 table.

c. List of contract work locations by country and firm.

This is the 7th annual survey.

ENR REGIONAL MARKETS: MULTI-UNIT HOUSING

(p. 59) Two charts showing value of new plans and bidding, for multi-unit housing construction, by region, 1st half 1985 with comparisons to 1st half 1984. Data are from ENR. Charts appear in "Market Trends" section.

C5800–2.640: Aug. 8, 1985 (Vol. 215, No. 6)

WEEKLY TABLES

a. Market trends, for week ended Aug. 1, 1985. (p. 43)

b. Unit prices, for Wyoming highway reconstruction contract. (p. 57)

MONTHLY TABLES

a. Market trends, tables [1-3] for July or Aug. 1985. (p. 43)

b. Materials prices, tables [1-2] for Aug. 8, 1985. (p. 36-37)

C5800-2.641: Aug. 15, 1985 (Vol. 215, No. 7)

WEEKLY TABLES

a. Market trends, for week ended Aug. 8, 1985. (p. 37)

b. Unit prices, for construction contract of airport runway in North Carolina. (p. 38)

MONTHLY TABLES

a. Market trends, tables [4-5] for Aug. 1985. (p. 37)

b. Materials prices, tables [3-5] for Aug. 15, 1985. (p. 32-33)

c. Stock track, for various periods, identified by company. (p. 19)

DESIGNER PROFITS REBOUNDING, BUT STILL TRAIL 1980 LEVELS

(p. 53) Article, with 1 table showing median profit margin and overhead rate, for construction design firms overall, and by staff size and firm type, 1984. Data are from a survey of 334 design firms, conducted by Design Management Consulting, Inc.; for *Professional Services Management Journal.*

C5800-2.642: Aug. 22, 1985 (Vol. 215, No. 8)

WEEKLY TABLES

a. Market trends, for week ended Aug. 15, 1985. (p. 98)

b. Unit prices, for California highway reconstruction contract. (p. 96)

MONTHLY TABLES

a. Market trends, tables [6-7] for July 1985. (p. 98)

b. Materials prices, tables [6-7] for Aug. 22, 1985. (p. 86-87)

CORRECTION

(p. 9) Corrected and additional data for annual article on foreign contract billings of 200 largest international construction contractors.

For description of article, see C5800-2.637 above.

1984 TOP SPECIALTY CONTRACTORS: COMPETITION PUTS A TIGHT SQUEEZE ON '84 REVENUES, ANNUAL FEATURE

(p. 44-63) Annual article on revenues and new contracts for largest specialty construction contractors, with comparative data for all specialty contractors, 1984. Data are from an ENR industry survey covering 7 specialty areas. Includes the following data:

a. Revenues by type of work, aggregated for mechanical, electrical, and other contractors; and value of contracts and revenues from renovation, aggregated for largest mechanical and electrical contractors; various years 1980-84. 6 charts.

b. Rankings by total revenues, with revenue from foreign work and percent from renovation, value of new contracts, and types of specialties, for 100 largest mechanical and electrical contractors, and for 13-30 largest roofing/sheet metal, demolition/wrecking, steel erection, glazing/curtain wall, and excavation/foundation contractors, 1984. 7 tables.

This is the 8th annual survey.

A-Es' TAX BILL COULD GROW

(p. 114) Article analyzing impact of Reagan Administration tax reform proposals on construction design firms. Data are from a survey of 334 design firms, conducted by Design Management Consulting, Inc., for *Professional Services Management Journal.*

Includes 1 table showing the following by firm staff size: median accumulated deferred taxes, annual tax increase, and median cash on hand, all based on 1984 tax data.

C5800-2.643: Aug. 29, 1985 (Vol. 215, No. 9)

WEEKLY TABLES

a. Market trends, for week ended Aug. 22, 1985. (p. 45)

b. Unit prices, for North Carolina highway construction contract. (p. 39)

MONTHLY TABLES

a. Market trends, tables [8, 10] for July 1985, [9] for Apr. 1984, and [11] for 2nd quarter 1984-85. (p. 45)

b. Materials prices, tables [8-12] for Aug. 29, 1985. (p. 34-35)

c. New plans and bidding volume, for July 1985. (p. 20)

CONTRACTING OUT IS CHEAPER

(p. 15-16) Article, with 1 undated table showing the following for asphalt paving work by private contractor vs. local government: labor costs as percent of total costs, average monthly wage of laborers, volume of asphalt placed per full-time employee, cost per ton of asphalt placed, operator experience, and crew size.

Data are from a HUD study of 8 municipal services in 20 cities near Los Angeles.

ENGINEERS GET 6.4% RAISE

(p. 54) Article, with 1 chart showing engineers' median income from salary/fees/cash bonuses/commissions, by engineering field or job function, 1984. Data are based on approximately 12,800 responses to a National Society of Professional Engineers membership survey.

Full survey report is covered by SRI under A8460-1.

C5800-2.644: Sept. 5, 1985 (Vol. 215, No. 10)

WEEKLY TABLES

a. Market trends, for week ended Aug. 29, 1985. (p. 46)

b. Unit prices, for Utah highway construction contract. (p. 45)

MONTHLY TABLES

a. Market trends, tables [1-3] for Aug. or Sept. 1985. (p. 46)

b. Materials prices, tables [1-2] for Sept. 5, 1985. (p. 36-37)

INTERNATIONAL STOCK TRACK: CHEERLESS FUTURE FOR FOREIGN FIRMS, QUARTERLY FEATURE

(p. 21) Quarterly article on recent financial performance of 34 publicly owned international construction companies. Includes 1 table showing stock price, revenue, and earnings, for 34 companies based in Canada, France, West Germany, Italy, Japan, the Netherlands, Norway, Spain, Sweden, Switzerland, and UK. Data are for latest 12 months or latest closing date.

Data are from *Capital International Perspective,* Geneva, Switzerland.

CONSTRUCTION PAY HIKES LAG

(p. 61) Article, with 1 table showing top and bottom 5 States, ranked by average construction wages, with comparison to total U.S., 1984. Data are from BLS.

C5800-2.645: Sept. 12, 1985 (Vol. 215, No. 11)

WEEKLY TABLES

a. Market trends, for week ended Sept. 5, 1985. (p. 43)

b. Unit prices, for California highway construction contract. (p. 41)

MONTHLY TABLES

a. Market trends, tables [4-5] for Sept. 1985. (p. 43)

b. Materials prices, tables [3-5] for Sept. 12, 1985. (p. 36-37)

INCORRECT COMPENSATION DATA

(p. 9) Letter to the Editor, with data correction for annual article on construction industry executive compensation. For description of article, see C5800-2.635 above. Includes corrected data for 1 company.

C5800-2.646: Sept. 19, 1985 (Vol. 215, No. 12)

WEEKLY TABLES

a. Market trends, for week ended Sept. 12, 1985. (p. 157)

b. Unit prices, for California highway and Alaska airport runway reconstruction contracts, and for Vermont bridge construction contract. (p. 90)

MONTHLY TABLES

a. Market trends, tables [6-7] for Aug. 1985. (p. 157)

b. Materials prices, tables [6-7] for Sept. 19, 1985. (p. 154-155)

c. Stock track, for various periods, identified by company. (p. 48)

QUARTERLY COST ROUNDUP

(p. 59-95) Quarterly report, for 3rd quarter 1985, on construction industry cost trends and outlook. Data sources include Federal and State agencies, private organizations, and ENR surveys, and are identified on most tables and charts.

Contains introduction and 11 articles. Articles with substantial statistical content are described below.

a. "Wages: Labor Continues Long Climb Back." Includes 4 tables showing hourly construction wage by detailed trade in 32 U.S. and 2 Canadian cities, Aug. 1, 1985, and for 5 trades in 78 cities arranged by region, May 1984; and construction wage indexes in 20 cities, 1984-85, and open-shop wage rates (high and low) in 14 cities, Aug. 1985, both for common labor and 4 trades (with detail for journeyman and/or helper). (p. 62-73)

b. "Insurance: Insurance Costs Spiral Higher." Includes 3 tables showing construction workers' compensation insurance rates by detailed type of work, for 44 States; and average rates for 5 high and low cost States; July 1985. (p. 74-75)

c. "Highways: Bid Prices Continue To Climb." Includes 2 tables showing highway bid price indexes, for 20 States and for Federal-aid excavation, surfacing, and structure projects, 2nd quarter 1985 with quarterly trends from 1980 or 1982, and annual trends from 1974 (Federal projects only). (p. 76-77)

d. "Parameter Costs: Far East Building Costs Studied." Includes 1 undated table showing construction costs (in U.S. dollars) by item, for steel- and concrete-framed buildings, by type, in Hong Kong and in Jakarta, Indonesia. (p. 78)

e. "Machinery: Equipment Prices Change Little." Includes 1 table showing price indexes for 34 types of construction equipment, Jan., Apr., and July 1985 with percent change from 1984. (p. 84)

f. "Builders' Indexes: Cost Movements Still Small." Includes 1 table showing 19 indexes of builders' construction costs, 1982-84 and monthly Sept. 1984-Sept. 1985. (p. 89)

g. "Market Survey: Backlogs and Employment Grow." Includes 1 table and 3 charts showing labor shortages and delivery delays for specified trades and products in 20 cities, as reported by general contractors responding to an ENR survey; and survey response on changes in backlogs, delivery time, and materials prices. (p. 92)

h. "Materials Prices: Summer Price Hikes Post Modest Advance." Includes 1 table showing average prices for selected construction materials, aggregated for 20 cities, 3rd quarter 1985 with percent change from 2nd quarter 1985 and 3rd quarter 1984. (p. 94)

i. "Water and Power: BuRec Costs Increase Moderately." Includes 1 table showing Bureau of Reclamation cost indexes for water and power related construction, including dams, pumping plants, hydroelectric power plants, and transmission lines, July 1979-85 with percent change for Apr.-July 1985 period. (p. 95)

SALES BEST IN PRIVATE FIRMS

(p. 160) Article, with 1 table showing annual percent change in sales, income, cash flow, return on sales, and selected ratios, for publicly vs. privately held companies (total and for construction industry), 1982-84 period. Data are from a Geneva Corp. study of 24 industries.

C5800–2.647: Sept. 26, 1985 (Vol. 215, No. 13)

WEEKLY TABLES

a. Market trends, for week ended Sept. 19, 1985. (p. 46)

b. Unit prices, for 2 Alaska airport runway reconstruction contracts. (p. 52)

MONTHLY TABLES

a. Market trends, tables [8, 10] for Aug. 1985, [9] for May 1984, and [11] for July 1985. (p. 46)

b. Materials prices, tables [10-12] for Sept. 26, 1985. (p. 44-45)

c. New plans and bidding volume, for Aug. 1985. (p. 28)

CONSTRUCTION IN VIRGINIA ENJOYS STRONG RECOVERY

(p. 28) Article, with 1 table showing value of Virginia construction market, by type of structure, 1st half 1985 with percent change from 1984. Data are from ENR Construction Economics Dept.

A-E INSURANCE RISES 14%

(p. 71) Article on construction design firm insurance liability and cost. Data are based on 1,745 responses to an American Consulting Engineers Council Aug. 1985 survey of member firms. Includes 1 table showing insurance premium cost as percent of gross billings (total and by firm type), 1983 and 1985.

A similar article, for 1980-81, is described in SRI 1982 Annual under C5800-2.316.

C5800–2.648: Oct. 3, 1985 (Vol. 215, No. 14)

WEEKLY TABLES

a. Market trends, for week ended Sept. 26, 1985. (p. 53)

b. Unit prices, for Utah and California highway reconstruction contracts. (p. 44)

MONTHLY TABLES

a. Materials prices, tables [8-9] for Oct. 3, 1985. (p. 38-39)

ENR REGIONAL MARKETS: PUBLIC PROJECTS

(p. 53) Two charts showing value of new plans and bidding, for public projects construction, by region, 1st 7 months 1985 with percent change from 1984. Data are from ENR. Charts appear in "Market Trends" section.

C5800–2.649: Oct. 10, 1985 (Vol. 215, No. 15)

WEEKLY TABLES

a. Market trends, for week ended Oct. 3, 1985. (p. 69)

b. Unit prices, for North Carolina highway grading and draining project. (p. 70)

MONTHLY TABLES

a. Market trends, tables [1-3] for Sept. or Oct. 1985. (p. 69)

b. Materials prices, tables [1-2] for Oct. 10, 1985. (p. 62-63)

C5800–2.650: Oct. 17, 1985 (Vol. 215, No. 16)

WEEKLY TABLES

a. Market trends, for week ended Oct. 10, 1985. (p. 52)

b. Unit prices, for New Jersey bridge reconstruction contracts. (p. 51)

MONTHLY TABLES

a. Market trends, tables [4-5] for Oct. 1985. (p. 52)

b. Materials prices, tables [3-5] for Oct. 17, 1985. (p. 48-49)

c. Stock track, for various periods, identified by company. (p. 29)

CONSTRUCTION GROWTH WEAKENS, ANNUAL FEATURE

(p. 30-34) Annual article on 1984-86 construction industry trends and outlook, based on a fall 1985 ENR survey of 231 design firms.

Includes 1 table and 1 chart showing contract value for all construction (excluding homes), and for heavy, nonresidential building, and multi-unit residential construction, by type, 1984 and forecast 1985-86; and value of new plans and bidding volume, by region, 1st 9 months 1984-85.

C5800–2.651: Oct. 24, 1985 (Vol. 215, No. 17)

WEEKLY TABLES

a. Market trends, for week ended Oct. 17, 1985. (p. 45)

b. Unit prices, for Utah and Idaho landslide repair projects. (p. 36)

MONTHLY TABLES

a. Market trends, tables [6-7] for Sept. 1985. (p. 45)

b. Materials prices, tables [6-7] for Oct. 24, 1985. (p. 32-33)

c. New plans and bidding volume, for Sept. 1985. (p. 26)

SCHOOL CONSTRUCTION MARKETS TO HIT $8.4 BILLION IN 1986

(p. 26) Article presenting design firms' expectations of change in the value of educational facility construction in 1986, based on an ENR survey of 231 firms. Includes 1 chart showing survey response.

C5800–2.652: Oct. 31, 1985 (Vol. 215, No. 18)

WEEKLY TABLES

a. Market trends, for week ended Oct. 24, 1985. (p. 46)

b. Unit prices, for California bridge reconstruction contract. (p. 45)

MONTHLY TABLES

a. Market trends, tables [8, 11] for Aug. 1985, [9] for June 1984, and [10] for Sept. 1985. (p. 46)

b. Materials prices, tables [8-12] for Oct. 31, 1985. (p. 34-35)

HIGHWAY SPENDING ROARS AHEAD, ANNUAL FEATURE

(p. 30-31) Annual article on State highway construction plans, 1986. Data were compiled by ENR Construction Economics Dept. Includes 1 table showing planned highway spending for new construction, resurfacing/restoration/rehabilitation/reconstruction, and maintenance, with selected detail for interstate and other highways, by State, 1986 with percent change from 1985.

C5800–3   MCGRAW-HILL ANNUAL SPRING AND FALL SURVEYS OF BUSINESS' PLANS FOR NEW PLANTS AND EQUIPMENT

Series. For individual publication data, see below.
SRI/MF/complete

Series of 2 annual reports on planned capital investment for plants and equipment in approximately 25 industry groups. Data are from annual spring and fall surveys conducted by McGraw-Hill Economics Dept. Companies surveyed account for approximately 28% of all U.S. capital spending.

Reports present previous year actual, current year planned or estimated, and future 2-3 years preliminary planned capital spending data, and also include data on expectations for sales, prices, and industry growth. Spending data are national estimates based on the survey sample.

Reports generally contain narrative analysis, methodolgy, and 10-15 tables. Reports for fall 1984 and spring 1985 are described below.

Availability: McGraw-Hill, Economics Department, 1221 Ave. of the Americas, 37th Floor, New York NY 10020; SRI/MF/complete.

C5800–3.1: 31st Annual McGraw-Hill Fall Survey of Preliminary Plans for New Plants and Equipment, 1984-86

[Annual. Nov. 1984. 29 p. $125.00. SRI/MF/complete.]

Annual report on capital spending, 1983-86, based on a fall 1984 survey of approximately 550 business firms. Includes 1983 actual, 1984 estimated, and 1985-86 planned spending, by industry division and group, with detail by spending function for the petroleum industry.

Also includes expectations for sales and for change in plant/equipment and product prices, by industry division and manufacturing industry group, 1984-85; actual spending compared to survey projections, 1955-83; and selected indicators of short-term equipment and construction capital spending, various periods 1982-3rd quarter 1984.

C5800–3.2: 38th Annual McGraw-Hill Spring Survey of Business' Plans for New Plants and Equipment, 1985-88

[Annual. May 1985. 35+12 p. $125.00. SRI/MF/complete.]

Annual report on capital spending, 1984-88, based on a spring 1985 survey of approximately 520 business firms. Includes 1984 actual, 1985 estimated, and 1986-88 planned spending, by industry division and group, with detail by spending function for the petroleum industry.

Also includes percent of capital spending for expansion, replacement/modernization, buildings, motor vehicles, and machinery/equipment; capacity expansion index and operation rates; expectations for sales and for change in plant/equipment and product prices; and sample firms' percent of total capital spending; all by industry division and manufacturing industry group, various years 1983-86.

Also includes actual spending compared to survey projections, 1965-84; and selected indicators of short-term equipment and construction capital spending, various periods 1982-1st quarter 1985.

C5800–4   AVIATION WEEK AND SPACE TECHNOLOGY
Weekly.
ISSN 0005-2175.
LC 18-14054.
SRI/MF/not filmed

Weekly trade journal reporting on developments in air transport, space technology, aeronautical and missile engineering, business flying, avionics, and military aviation.

Data are from individual airline reports, NASA, I. P. Sharp Associates, and other sources, and are current to 1-6 months prior to publication date.

Contents:

a. Articles and news items, occasionally containing substantial statistics.

b. 1 monthly and 3 quarterly tables on airline traffic, income, and expenses; and aircraft operating and cost data; by airline.

c. 1 monthly table on business and utility aircraft shipments.

d. Semiannual subject index to articles and features.

e. Annual features, including marketing directory to products and services in the aerospace industry (Dec.); aerospace industry forecast and inventory; Federal aerospace budget proposals; and ranked list of top 100 DOD contractors.

Monthly and quarterly tables are listed below. All additional features with substantial statistical content are described, as they appear, under "Statistical Features;" page locations and latest periods of coverage for monthly and quarterly tables are also noted. Nonstatistical features and issues are not covered.

Availability: Aviation Week and Space Technology, PO Box 1505, Neptune NJ 07753, qualified subscribers $51.00 per yr., selected others $65.00 per yr., single copy $4.50, special issues $10.00; SRI/MF/not filmed.

Issues reviewed during 1985: Nov. 5, 1984-Oct. 28, 1985 (P) (Vol. 121, Nos. 19-26; Vol. 122, Nos. 1-26; Vol. 123, Nos. 1-17).

MONTHLY TABLES:
[Tables may not appear every month.]

AIRLINE STATISTICS

[1] Airline traffic [number of revenue miles, enplaned passengers, revenue passenger miles, available seat miles, passenger load factor, and total and freight revenue ton-miles, for over 30 major domestic and international, national, large regional, Alaskan, Hawaiian, and all cargo airlines, for month of coverage].

AIRCRAFT SHIPMENTS STATISTICS

[2] Business and utility aircraft shipments [number of aircraft shipped by manufacturers, by model, for month of coverage and year to date; total factory billings, by manufacturer, for month of coverage; and total and export shipments and billings for all manufacturers during month of coverage, year to date, and same periods of previous year].

QUARTERLY TABLES:
[Data are shown for quarter of coverage.]

[1] Wide-body aircraft operating costs [shows the following items for 5 major wide-body aircraft models, by carrier:

a. Scheduled passenger service: revenue, revenue passenger, and available seat miles; average passenger load and seat capacity; and passenger load factor.

b. All services: selected operating data, including revenue, revenue ton, and available ton miles; average ton load and capacity, and overall load factor; nonrevenue miles as percent of revenue; revenue and nonrevenue hours; average aircraft and utilization; departures; average flight length and duration; and fuel and oil use.

c. Operating expenses: for crew, fuel/oil/taxes, insurance, aircraft maintenance, and other operations; and write-off for rentals and flight depreciation].

[2] Airline income and expenses [shows operating revenues from passengers, freight, and charters; total operating expense; and net profit/loss; for over 30 major domestic and international, national, large regional, Alaskan, and Hawaiian carriers].

[3] Narrow-body aircraft direct expenses [shows operating and cost data similar to that described in quarterly table [1] above, for 5 narrow-body models, by carrier].

STATISTICAL FEATURES:

C5800–4.601: Nov. 5, 1984 (Vol. 121, No. 19)

MONTHLY TABLE

[2] Business and utility aircraft shipments, for Sept. 1984. (p. 75)

QUARTERLY TABLE

[2] Airline income and expenses, 2nd quarter 1984. (p. 41)

FY85 DEFENSE DEPT AUTHORIZATION AND APPROPRIATION

(p. 52) Table showing Reagan Administration funding requests and congressional authorizations and appropriations, for defense procurement, RDT&E (research, development, test, and evaluation), and operation/maintenance, arranged by military branch, FY85.

C5800–4.602: Nov. 12, 1984 (Vol. 121, No. 20)

INTERNATIONAL AIR TRANSPORT, ANNUAL FEATURE

Annual collection of features on international air transport operations and finances. Data are primarily from International Air Transport Assn (IATA). Features with substantial statistical content are individually described below.

FUEL COST INDEX OF U.S. MAJORS AND NATIONALS

(p. 47) Table showing U.S. major/national domestic airline fuel costs, gallons issued, cost index, and percent of total operating expenses, annually 1970-80 and quarterly 1981-2nd quarter 1984. Table is accompanied by 1 chart on major domestic airline yields (cents per revenue passenger mile), selected dates 1983-84.

IATA AIRLINES' PASSENGER TRAFFIC, 1983

(p. 50) Table and accompanying chart showing IATA airline passenger traffic, passenger kilometers flown, available seat kilometers, and load factor, for international and domestic service, 1983.

PASSENGER COMMUTER AIRLINES GROWTH

(p. 55) Two charts showing commuter passenger carriers, aircraft, airports served, and traffic, 1978 and 1983; and commuter airline share of commuter air traffic, 1983. Data are from Regional Airline Assn.

TRAFFIC GAINS, FARES STABILIZE ON NORTH ATLANTIC ROUTES

(p. 63-83, passim) By Michael Feazel. Article on transatlantic air passenger traffic. Includes 8 tables showing passengers, seating capacity, available seat miles, and/or load factors on North Atlantic, South Atlantic, and Mid-Atlantic routes, by North and South American and European carrier, 1st half 1982-84.

SPECIAL CHARTS

(p. 108) Two charts showing percent of adults who have flown, total and by age group, 1971 and 1984. Data are from a survey conducted by Air Transport Assn and Gallup Poll.

TRANSPACIFIC TRAFFIC FORECAST

(p. 112) Chart showing projected annual growth in transpacific air passenger traffic, 1990.

ANNUAL TABLE

(p. 165) Annual table showing aggregate IATA member airlines' operating revenues and expenses, net interest payable, and result after interest payments, 1979-86.

C5800–4.603: Nov. 19, 1984 (Vol. 121, No. 21)

MONTHLY TABLE

[1] Airline traffic, for Aug. 1984. (p. 45)

C5800–4.604: Nov. 26, 1984 (Vol. 121, No. 22)

MAJOR AIRLINES ALL REPORT PROFITS IN THIRD QUARTER, QUARTERLY FEATURE

(p. 41-44) Quarterly article, by Carole A. Shifrin, on finances of major and other domestic carriers in 3rd quarter 1984. Includes 1 table showing revenues, expenses, and net profit or loss, for 11 major and 13 other carriers, 3rd quarter 1984 with comparisons to 3rd quarter 1983.

C5800–4.605: Dec. 3, 1984 (Vol. 121, No. 23)

MONTHLY TABLE

[2] Business and utility aircraft shipments, for Oct. 1984. (p. 132)

THANKSGIVING HOLIDAY TRAFFIC LIVES UP TO STRONG FORECASTS, RECURRING FEATURE

(p. 29-30) Recurring article, by Carole A. Shifrin, with 1 table showing revenue passenger miles, available seat miles, and load factor, for 11 major airlines and 15 other carriers, Oct. 1984 with comparison to Oct. 1983.

FY84 COMPETITIVE PROCUREMENT STATISTICS

(p. 149) Brief article, with 1 table showing value of Navy procurement (total and for spare parts) awarded under competitive procurement program, with comparisons to total awards and contractor support services, 1982-84.

C5800–4.606: Dec. 10, 1984 (Vol. 121, No. 24)

U.S. TALLIES COST TO SOVIETS OF TECHNOLOGY TRANSFER RULES

(p. 67-69) By Paul Mann. Article, with 1 table showing value of U.S. defense trade with 12 NATO countries, 1983.

C5800–4.607: Dec. 17, 1984 (Vol. 121, No. 25)

USAF, NASA DISCUSS SHUTTLE USE FOR SATELLITE MAINTENANCE

(p. 14-16) By Craig Covault. Article, with 1 table showing Air Force reconnaissance satellite launches, by type, 1970-84.

C5800–4.608: Jan. 14, 1985 (Vol. 122, No. 2)

MONTHLY TABLE

[1] Airline traffic, for Sept. 1984. (p. 39)

WORLD AIRLINES FACE BOOSTS IN HULL, LIABILITY INSURANCE

(p. 28-30) By James Ott. Article, with 2 tables showing expenditures for traffic liability and general insurance, for 11 major U.S. airlines, 1st-3rd quarter 1984. Data are from CAB.

C5800–4.609: Jan. 21, 1985 (Vol. 122, No. 3)

MONTHLY TABLE

[2] Business and utility aircraft shipments, for Nov. 1984. (p. 99)

QUARTERLY TABLES

[1] Wide-body aircraft operating costs, for 3rd quarter 1984. (p. 46-47)

[2] Airline income and expenses, 3rd quarter 1984. (p. 56)

JAPAN NEARS 7% GAIN IN DEFENSE BUDGET, ANNUAL FEATURE

(p. 19) Annual table showing aircraft and surface weapons requested and approved for procurement in Japan, for air, ground, and maritime self-defense forces, by manufacturer and model, FY85 with comparison to FY84. Includes brief narrative.

STRONG DEC. TRAFFIC GIVES MAJOR AIRLINES ANNUAL GAIN, RECURRING FEATURE

(p. 27-28) Recurring article, by Carole A. Shifrin, with 2 tables showing revenue passenger miles, available seat miles, and load factor, for 11 major airlines and 13 other carriers, Dec. and full year 1984 with comparisons to same periods of 1983.

FOUR EUROPEAN NATO MEMBERS EXCEED 3% GOAL

(p. 109) Brief article, with 1 table showing inflation rate and percent increase in defense spending, for 14 NATO member countries, 1982/83-1983/84. Data are from NATO and OECD.

LAVI CONTRACTS WITH U.S. COMPANIES DETAILED

(p. 112) Table on U.S. contracts awarded by Israel Aircraft Industries for construction of Lavi fighter aircraft, showing contractor, plant location, component involved, and contract value, for each award (no date). Includes brief narrative.

C5800–4.610: Jan. 28, 1985 (Vol. 122, No. 4)

MONTHLY TABLES

[1] Airline traffic, for Oct. 1984. (p. 48)

[2] Business and utility aircraft shipments, for Dec. 1984. (p. 85)

FARE WAR FEARS DEPRESS AIRLINE STOCKS, BUT ONLY TEMPORARILY

(p. 30-31) Article, with 1 table showing high, low, and year-end closing prices of airline stock, for 12 major and 21 other carriers, 1984. Data are from NYSE, AMEX, and National Assn of Securities Dealers.

GENERAL AVIATION MANUFACTURERS FORECASTING STATIC DELIVERIES

(p. 79-84) By David M. North. Article, with 1 chart showing general aviation aircraft deliveries and value of billings, 1972-84. Data are from General Aviation Manufacturers Assn.

C5800–4.611: Feb. 4, 1985 (Vol. 122, No. 5)

QUARTERLY TABLE

[3] Narrow-body aircraft direct expenses, 3rd quarter 1984. (p. 48-49)

JAPAN PLANS 1985 AIRCRAFT EXPENDITURES, ANNUAL FEATURE

(p. 22) Annual table showing number, unit price, and total cost of aircraft budgeted for defense procurement in Japan, by model, FY85, with FY84 price comparison. Includes brief narrative.

For description of previous table, with data for FY83, see SRI 1983 Annual under C5800-4.407.

C5800–4.612: Feb. 11, 1985 (Vol. 122, No. 6)

SPECIAL REPORT: FISCAL 1986 AEROSPACE BUDGETS, ANNUAL FEATURE

Part 1 of an annual collection of articles analyzing FY86 Federal aerospace budget proposals. Articles with substantial statistical content are individually described below.

NATIONAL DEFENSE BUDGET, ANNUAL TABLE

(p. 17) Annual table showing DOD budget authority and outlays for military programs, atomic energy defense, and defense-related activities, FY84-88.

DEFENSE DEPT REQUEST REFLECTS REDUCTIONS MADE IN PAST YEAR, ANNUAL FEATURE

(p. 18-20) Annual article, by Robert R. Ropelewski, analyzing DOD budget requests for FY86. Includes text data, and 1 table showing quantity and value of reductions in approximately 50 major weapons systems, FY86.

STATION STRETCH, ORBITAL VEHICLE HIGHLIGHT NASA's FUND BID, ANNUAL FEATURE

(p. 25-28) Annual article, by Craig Covault, on NASA proposed budget for FY86. Includes 1 table showing NASA budget requests, by program component, FY84-86.

C5800–4.613: Feb. 18, 1985 (Vol. 122, No. 7)

SPECIAL REPORT: FISCAL 1986 AEROSPACE BUDGETS, ANNUAL FEATURE

Part 2 of an annual collection of articles analyzing FY86 Federal aerospace budget proposals. Articles with substantial statistical content are individually described below.

SPECIAL TABLES

(p. 49, 57) Three tables showing Federal deficit, DOD outlays, and change in deficit resulting from lower receipts and from outlay change, FY85-86; DOD budget authority by service branch, FY84-86; and revisions in DOD budget authority and outlays, FY86.

FISCAL 1986 MAJOR WEAPON SYSTEM SPENDING DESCRIBED BY MILITARY SERVICE, ANNUAL FEATURE

(p. 54-55) Annual listing of Air Force, Navy, and Army funding requests for aircraft and missiles, showing manufacturer and model, budget request, and number to be procured or developed, FY86.

C5800-4.614: Feb. 25, 1985 (Vol. 122, No. 8)

MONTHLY TABLE

[2] Business and utility aircraft shipments, for Jan. 1985. (p. 107)

MAJOR AIRLINE TRAFFIC RISES 11.7% IN JAN., RECURRING FEATURE

(p. 30-31) Recurring article, with 1 table showing revenue passenger miles, available seat miles, and load factor, for 12 major airlines and 12 other carriers, Jan. 1985, with comparisons to Jan. 1984.

U.S. MAJOR CARRIERS RECORD BEST EARNINGS SINCE 1978, QUARTERLY FEATURE

(p. 32-34) Quarterly article, by Carole A. Shifrin, on finances of major domestic carriers in 4th quarter and full year, 1984. Includes 1 table showing revenues, expenses, and operating and net income or loss, for 12 major carriers, 4th quarter and full year 1984, with comparisons to 1983.

C5800-4.615: Mar. 4, 1985 (Vol. 122, No. 9)

MONTHLY TABLE

[1] Airline traffic, for Nov. 1984. (p. 45)

C5800-4.616: Mar. 11, 1985 (Vol. 122, No. 10)

U.S. MILITARY ACCIDENT RATES CONTINUE TO IMPROVE IN 1984, ANNUAL FEATURE

(p. 60-63) Annual article, with 2 tables showing Navy and Air Force flight hours, accidents, and accident rates, by aircraft model, with summaries for Air Force Commands and Marine Corps, 1984.

C5800-4.617: Mar. 18, 1985 (Vol. 122, No. 11)

AEROSPACE FORECAST AND INVENTORY, ANNUAL FEATURE

(p. 10-292) Annual feature forecasting aerospace industry sales growth and technology development, and air travel, primarily for the 1980s. Includes detailed analyses of defense and space programs, by country; R&D; and commercial sector traffic and finances. Also includes aircraft and spacecraft specifications.

Data are from a variety of government and private sources.

Contains numerous articles, summary and trend charts, and the following more substantial statistics:

a. Sales by aerospace industry sector, 1984-87; and U.S. and European defense and space budget procurement requests, by manufacturer and model (U.S. data based on FY86 budget requests). Text data. (p. 10-19)

b. Military: U.S. strategic airlift, military rotorcraft, and deep strike weapons system funding, by manufacturer/model or program, and Strategic Defense Initiative Organization budget by program, FY84-87; NATO defense spending, by country, 1983-84; and DOD R&D budget by program, FY84-86. 1 chart and 6 tables. (p. 27-73)

c. Air transport: world market value, and shares for U.S. and multinational Airbus Industrie consortium, 1980-84; number and value of short-, medium-, and long-

range aircraft, 1998; aircraft deliveries by world area, Airbus Industrie market value, and aircraft retirements, 1985-2004 period; passenger traffic of top 15 U.S. regional airlines, 1984; and North Atlantic passenger traffic and capacity, by North American and European airline, 1983-84. 6 charts and 2 tables. (p. 199-228)

d. Business flying: Canadian commercial helicopters (no date). 1 chart. (p. 289)

C5800-4.618: Mar. 25, 1985 (Vol. 122, No. 12)

MONTHLY TABLE

[2] Business and utility aircraft shipments, for Feb. 1985. (p. 101)

JAPAN FORECASTS 4.9% AEROSPACE MANUFACTURING GAIN, ANNUAL FEATURE

(p. 81) Annual table showing value of Japanese aircraft and engine production and overhaul, and parts/components and equipment production, FY84-85. Data are from Society of Japanese Aerospace Companies.

C5800-4.619: Apr. 8, 1985 (Vol. 122, No. 14)

DEFENSE AGENCY LISTS FOREIGN CONSULTANT FEES

(p. 66-67) Article, with 1 tabular list of foreign consultant fees billed to DOD by General Dynamics Corp., by subcontractor, 1982. All fees were challenged by the Defense Contract Audit Agency (DCAA). List was prepared by DCAA.

C5800-4.620: Apr. 15, 1985 (Vol. 122, No. 15)

MONTHLY TABLE

[1] Airline traffic, for Dec. 1984. (p. 35)

C5800-4.621: Apr. 22, 1985 (Vol. 122, No. 16)

SMALLER U.S. AIR CARRIERS MARK MIXED FINANCIAL RESULTS IN 1984, ANNUAL FEATURE

(p. 39-41) Annual article, by Carole A. Shifrin, on finances of nonmajor domestic carriers. Includes 1 table showing revenues, expenses, and operating and net income or loss, for 17 nonmajor carriers, 4th quarter and full year 1984, with comparisons to 1983.

C5800-4.622: Apr. 29, 1985 (Vol. 122, No. 17)

MONTHLY TABLES

[1] Airline traffic, for full year 1984. (p. 65)

[2] Business and utility aircraft shipments, for Mar. 1985. (p. 235)

LONG-TERM STRATEGIC PROGRAM BEGINNING TO SHOW RESULTS

(p. 84-96) By Robert R. Ropelewski. Article on Strategic Air Command weapons modernization programs. Includes 5 charts showing age of Minuteman and Titan missiles, and Minuteman support facilities; and actual vs. required funding for spare parts, fully mission capable rates, and spare parts cannibalization rates, for FB-111 and/or B-52 aircraft; various periods 1980-85.

WARSAW PACT ARMS AGREEMENTS NEARLY DOUBLED IN VALUE IN 1983, ANNUAL FEATURE

(p. 213) Annual article, with 2 tables showing Soviet and Eastern European personnel in 5 less developed world regions, 1983; and Warsaw Pact arms sales to Communist and non-Communist developing countries, 1980-83. Data are from NATO.

For description of previous article, see SRI 1984 Annual under C5800-4.521.

C5800-4.623: May 6, 1985 (Vol. 122, No. 18)

EUROPEAN CHARTER CARRIERS UNITE TO PROVIDE MORE SCHEDULED SERVICE

(p. 51) Article, with 1 table showing revenue passenger kilometers for 14 privately owned European airlines, 1983-84. Data are from Assn des Compagnies Aeriennes de la Communaute Europeene.

C5800-4.624: May 13, 1985 (Vol. 122, No. 19)

MONTHLY TABLE

[1] Airline traffic, for Jan. 1985 (p. 50)

STRONG TRAFFIC, COST CURBS BOOST FIRST-QUARTER AIRLINE EARNINGS, QUARTERLY FEATURE

(p. 45-49) Quarterly article, by Carole A. Shifrin, on finances of major and other domestic carriers in 1st quarter 1985. Includes 1 table showing revenues, expenses, and net profit or loss, for 12 major and 11 other carriers, 1st quarter 1985 with comparisons to 1st quarter 1984.

MCDONNELL DOUGLAS LEADS DEFENSE DEPT CONTRACTORS IN FY84, ANNUAL FEATURE

(p. 67) Annual table showing top 100 defense contractors ranked by value of DOD contract awards, and including awards as percent of all DOD contract expenditures, FY84.

C5800-4.625: May 20, 1985 (Vol. 122, No. 20)

AIRLINES LINK 13.5% TRAFFIC GAIN TO HOLIDAYS, DEEP DISCOUNTS, RECURRING FEATURE

(p. 36) Recurring article, with 1 table showing revenue passenger miles, available seat miles, and load factor, for 12 major airlines and 14 other carriers, Apr. 1985 with comparison to Apr. 1984.

C5800-4.626: May 27, 1985 (Vol. 122, No. 21)

MONTHLY TABLES

[1] Airline traffic, for Feb. 1985. (p. 56)

[2] Business and utility aircraft shipments, for Apr. 1985. (p. 111)

QUARTERLY TABLES

[1] Wide-body aircraft operating costs, for 4th quarter 1984. (p. 42-43)

[2] Airline income and expenses, 4th quarter 1984. (p. 41)

C5800-4.627: June 10, 1985 (Vol. 122, No. 23)

1984 MARKS SECOND CONSECUTIVE YEAR OF PROFITS FOR EUROPEAN AIRLINES

(p. 41-43) By Michael Feazel. Article on operations and profitability of Assn of European Airline members, 1984.

Includes 4 tables showing intra-European, North Atlantic, and total passenger capacity and traffic; revenue passenger kilometers, load factor, and dollar yield per revenue passenger kilometer, for each of 20 member airlines; and percent of passengers using promotional fares, and promotional fares as percent of normal fares, by travel region; 1984, with selected trends from 1978.

C5800–4.628: June 17, 1985 (Vol. 122, No. 24)

QUARTERLY TABLE

[3] Narrow-body aircraft direct expenses, 4th quarter 1984. (p. 40-41)

C5800–4.629: July 8, 1985 (Vol. 123, No. 1)

MONTHLY TABLE

[1] Airline traffic, for Mar. 1985. (p. 43)

C5800–4.630: July 15, 1985 (Vol. 123, No. 2)

MANY CARRIERS CREDIT JUNE TRAFFIC GAINS TO UNITED PILOTS' STRIKE, RECURRING FEATURE

(p. 32-35) Recurring article, by Carole A. Shifrin, with 1 table showing revenue passenger miles, available seat miles, and load factor, for 12 major airlines and 13 other carriers, June 1985 with comparison to June 1984.

C5800–4.631: July 22, 1985 (Vol. 123, No. 3)

MONTHLY TABLE

[2] Business and utility aircraft shipments, for May 1985. (p. 56)

C5800–4.632: July 29, 1985 (Vol. 123, No. 4)

MONTHLY TABLE

[2] Business and utility aircraft shipments, for June 1985. (p. 60)

TRAFFIC GROWTH IN EUROPE, ATLANTIC SPURS WORLD AIRLINE PROFITS IN 1984, ANNUAL FEATURE

(p. 39-41) Annual article, by Michael Feazel, on world airline operations and finances in 1984.

Includes 1 table showing aggregate International Air Transport Assn member airline profit, aircraft, average fleet age, revenues, expenses, revenue passenger kilometers, load factor, passenger fatality rates, and employees, 1980-84.

C5800–4.633: Aug. 12, 1985 (Vol. 123, No. 6)

MONTHLY TABLE

[1] Airline traffic, for Apr. 1985. (p. 41)

QUARTERLY TABLE

[2] Airline income and expenses, 1st quarter 1985. (p. 39)

INQUIRY FOCUSES ON WIND SHEAR AS CAUSE OF DELTA L-1011 CRASH

(p. 16-18) By James Ott. Article, with 1 tabular listing of U.S. airline crashes/incidents involving wind shear, June 1975-June 1984, showing the following for each: date and location, airline and aircraft model involved, number of fatalities, and flight phase. Data are from National Transportation Safety Board.

HOUSE CONSIDERS APPROPRIATIONS FOR MILITARY AND ECONOMIC AID

(p. 28-29) By James K. Gordon. Article, with 1 table showing foreign military and economic security aid requested by Reagan Administration, and congressional action taken, FY86, and comparison to appropriations authorized, FY85, all by type of funding.

UNITED STRIKE, COST CONTAINMENT SPUR SECOND-QUARTER PROFIT INCREASES, QUARTERLY FEATURE

(p. 36-38) Quarterly article, by Carole A. Shifrin, on finances of major and other domestic carriers in 2nd quarter 1985. Includes 1 table showing revenues, expenses, and operating and net income or loss, for 12 major and 12 other carriers, 2nd quarter 1985 with comparisons to 2nd quarter 1984.

SILENTKNIGHT HUSH KIT IS INSTALLED ON ZANTOP INTERNATIONAL DC-8-62

(p. 44-49) By Stanley W. Kandebo. Article, with 1 undated table showing orders and options for aircraft engine noise reduction equipment, for 10 airlines/aviation service companies. Data are from Aeronautic Development Corp., Ltd.

C5800–4.634: Aug. 19, 1985 (Vol. 123, No. 7)

QUARTERLY TABLE

[3] Narrow-body aircraft direct expenses, 1st quarter 1985. (p. 42-43)

C5800–4.635: Aug. 26, 1985 (Vol. 123, No. 8)

MONTHLY TABLE

[1] Airline traffic, for May 1985. (p. 39)

C5800–4.636: Sept. 2, 1985 (Vol. 123, No. 9)

CURRENTLY FUNDED SDIO CONTRACTORS NAMED

(p. 20-21) Brief article, with 1 tabular list showing 22 DOD contractors working on space-based Strategic Defense Initiative, ranked by contract awards, FY85.

C5800–4.637: Sept. 9, 1985 (Vol. 123, No. 10)

MONTHLY TABLE

[2] Business and utility aircraft shipments, for July 1985. (p. 80)

QUARTERLY TABLE

[1] Wide-body aircraft operating costs, for 1st quarter 1985. (p. 50-51)

C5800–4.638: Sept. 16, 1985 (Vol. 123, No. 11)

MONTHLY TABLE

[1] Airline traffic, for June 1985. (p. 51)

C5800–4.639: Sept. 23, 1985 (Vol. 123, No. 12)

AFFORDABILITY TO TAKE PRIORITY IN USAF ADVANCED FIGHTER DESIGN

(p. 14-16) By Robert R. Ropelewski. Article, with 4 charts showing the following for U.S. Air Force Tactical Air Command (TAC) aircraft: mission-capable and utilization rates, and percent inoperative due to supply shortages and maintenance problems, FY80-85.

DROP IN U.S. AIRCRAFT EXPORTS RAISES CONCERNS ABOUT PRODUCTION SECTOR

(p. 91-96) By James K. Gordon. Article, with 1 table showing general aviation aircraft exports and imports (number and value), by engine type and size, 1984-1st half 1985. Data are from Commerce Dept.

C5800–4.640: Sept. 30, 1985 (Vol. 123, No. 13)

MONTHLY TABLE

[2] Business and utility aircraft shipments, for Aug. 1985. (p. 74)

C5800–4.641: Oct. 7, 1985 (Vol. 123, No. 14)

MONTHLY TABLE

[1] Airline traffic, for July 1985. (p. 41)

JAPAN DEFENSE FORCE DETAILS FIVE-YEAR PLAN

(p. 78) Table showing Japan's proposed 5-year plan for weapons procurement, by self-defense unit and weapon type, FY85-90 period.

C5800–4.642: Oct. 14, 1985 (Vol. 123, No. 15)

QUARTERLY TABLE

[3] Narrow-body aircraft direct expenses, 2nd quarter 1985. (p. 42-43)

C5800–4.643: Oct. 21, 1985 (Vol. 123, No. 16)

MONTHLY TABLE

[2] Business and utility aircraft shipments, for Sept. 1985. (p. 155)

C5800–5 COAL AGE
Monthly.
ISSN 0009-9910.
LC GS 12-841.
SRI/MF/not filmed

Monthly publication reporting on developments and trends in the U.S. coal industry, including production, processing, marketing, technology, employment, management, regulation, and finance. Data are from various Federal Government, private, and industry sources.

Contains news brief sections; feature articles, occasionally with statistics; and monthly "Economic Scene" section, with 1 table described below.

Annual features include a statistical industry outlook (Feb.), articles on top producers and longwall operations, and nonstatistical equipment and services buyers guide (Sept.) and editorial index (Dec.).

Monthly "Economic Scene" table appears in all issues. All additional features with substantial statistical content are described, as they appear, under "Statistical Features." Nonstatistical features are not covered.

Availability: Coal Age, Fulfillment Manager, PO Box 1513, Neptune NJ 07753, qualified subscribers †, others $20.00 per yr., single copy $4.00, Sept. Buyer's Guide $5.50; SRI/MF/not filmed.

Issues reviewed during 1985: Nov. 1984-Oct. 1985 (P) (Vol. 89, Nos. 11-12; Vol. 90, Nos. 1-10) [Vol. 90, No. 6 incorrectly reads No. 5 on contents page].

ECONOMIC SCENE TABLE:

Shows bituminous/lignite and anthracite coal production; coal consumption and inventories at utilities; coal exports, operating rate, employment, and average hours and earnings; electricity output; raw steel production; blast furnace/steel mill new orders; and No. 6 fuel oil price.

Data generally are shown for month and/or year to date ending 2-4 months prior to cover date, with comparisons to previous periods.

Prior to the Feb. 1985 issue, table also included data on coal production workers and railroad carloadings.

STATISTICAL FEATURES:

C5800–5.601: Nov. 1984 (Vol. 89, No. 11)

FEW OF TOP 50 OPERATORS PLAN MINE EXPANSIONS

(p. 56-60) Article, with tabular listing of new and expanded coal mines and preparation plants under construction or planned, as of Sept. 1983. Includes name, location, type, capacity, and beginning and completion dates, for individual projects arranged by company. Data are based on 42 responses to a *Coal Age* survey of top 50 coal-producing companies.

A related article reporting on a survey conducted in late 1981 appeared in the Feb. 1982 issue of *Coal Age* and is described in SRI 1982 Annual, under C5800-5.304.

MINE SAFETY SLOWLY IMPROVES

(p. 71-73) Article, with 1 table and 1 chart on mine accidents and safety research, showing the following: total coal mines, fatalities, and fatality and injury rates, by mine employment size, 1980-83; and Bureau of Mines funds for in-house and contract research on mine health and safety, FY79-84. Data are from Mine Safety and Health Administration, and Bureau of Mines.

C5800–5.602: Jan. 1985 (Vol. 90, No. 1)

NCA PREDICTS UPS AND DOWNS FOR COAL IN '85

(p. 15) Brief article, with 1 table showing coal domestic consumption by market; steam and metallurgical exports to Canada and overseas; production by region; stock change; and imports; 1983-85. Data are from National Coal Assn.

BURNING LOW-SULFUR COAL SELECTIVELY CAN CONTROL ACID RAIN

(p. 23) Article summarizing a Massachusetts Institute of Technology study of acid rain conditions in northeastern U.S. and Canada. Includes 1 undated table showing percent of sulfate deposited in New England originating from 15 States or U.S. and Canadian regions.

C5800–5.603: Feb. 1985 (Vol. 90, No. 2)

NEW DELHI CONFERENCE: U.S. WILL REMAIN TOP COAL NATION

(p. 19) Article, with 1 chart ranking top 10 countries by coal exports, 1980 and 2000. Data are from UN.

OUTLOOK 1985: HEAVY STOCKPILES SQUEEZE PRICES, ANNUAL FEATURE

(p. 50-60) Annual article, by Joseph F. Wilkinson, on coal industry national and regional review and outlook, 1984-85. Data are from State mining depts, DOE, Keystone, and other energy forecasters.

Includes 2 tables showing bituminous/lignite exports, and domestic consumption by end use, 1984, and 1985 forecasts of 9 organizations; and deep and strip mine production, for bituminous/lignite by State, and for Pennsylvania anthracite (also shows bank and refuse production), 1984.

C5800–5.604: Apr. 1985 (Vol. 90, No. 4)

NUMBERS ARE HIGH, PROSPECTS LOW FOR TOP COAL COMPANIES, ANNUAL FEATURE

(p. 15-19) Annual article, with 1 table ranking top 15 coal companies by production, and also showing revenue and earnings, 1984 with comparisons to 1983. Data are from individual companies.

Previous article, with 1983 rankings, is described in SRI 1984 Annual under C5800-5.504.

C5800–5.605: Aug. 1985 (Vol. 90, No. 8)

U.S. SEES MARKED GROWTH IN NEW LONGWALLS IN 1985, ANNUAL FEATURE

(p. 47-65) Annual article, by Paul C. Merritt, on longwall operations in coal mines, 1985. Data are from a *Coal Age* census.

Includes 1 table showing capacity, year of initial installation, operational characteristics, seam name, and mine and location, for operating longwall installations, arranged by company, as of June 1985.

Previous feature, with data for 1984, is described in SRI 1984 Annual under C5800-5.505.

LONGWALL PRODUCTIVITY IN U.S. MINES CONTINUES TO CLIMB, ANNUAL FEATURE

(p. 68-69) Annual article, by Cecil V. Peake, with 3 tables showing the following for longwall operations in coal mines: average, high, and low cutting height, panel size, output, shifts, and labor productivity, by height of installation, 1983-84. Data are from results reported by 44-68 longwall operations.

Previous feature, with data for 1983, is described in SRI 1984 Annual under C5800-5.505.

C5800–5.606: Sept. 1985 (Vol. 90, No. 9)

COAL COMPANIES MAY HAVE TO PAY REGULATORS

(p. 11-13) Article on potential impact on coal companies of proposed coal operator fees covering costs of Federal regulatory activities. Includes 1 undated table showing cost estimates of Office of Surface Mining vs. Consolidated Coal Co. for mine permit reviews and environmental impact statements.

C5800–6   **AMERICAN MACHINIST**
Monthly.
ISSN 0002-9858.
LC 39-6898.
SRI/MF/not filmed

Monthly trade journal reporting on developments in the metalworking industry, including equipment, production, trade, and finance. Data are from McGraw-Hill Economics Dept, National Machine Tool Builders' Assn, Dept of Commerce, and other sources. Data are current to 3-6 months prior to cover date.

General format:

a. Monthly "Metalworking Trends" section containing news briefs and text statistics on industry outlook, labor, government regulation, equipment and materials, and plant operations; 3 monthly tables with corresponding charts; and 1 quarterly table on foreign trade.

b. Feature articles on machine tool technology, new products, processing, and R&D, occasionally with statistics.

c. Special reports section, usually covering an industrial process or technological development, some with statistics.

d. Narrative editorial depts.

Annual features include industry outlook, and world tool production and trade. September issue includes a nonstatistical buyer's guide.

Monthly and quarterly tables are listed below. Monthly tables appear in all issues. All additional features with substantial statistical content are described, as they appear, under "Statistical Features;" page location and latest period of coverage for quarterly table are also noted. Nonstatistical features are not covered.

Availability: American Machinist, Fulfillment Manager, PO Box 430, Hightstown NJ 08520, qualified subscribers †, others $40.00 per yr., single copy $6.00, Buyers' Guide $15.00; SRI/MF/ not filmed.

Issues reviewed during 1985: Nov. 1984-Oct. 1985 (P) (Vol. 128, Nos. 11-12; Vol. 129, Nos. 1-10).

MONTHLY TABLES:

[Tables appear in "Metalworking Trends" section. Month of data coverage is 3 months prior to cover date. Tables show data for month of coverage, previous month, and same month of preceding year.]

[1] Key metalworking indexes [production and price indexes and operating rate for selected metalworking industry sectors].

[2] Machine tool orders and shipments [including net new and export orders, total and export shipments, backlogs, and cancellations; and new orders indexes for builders and distributors (1978-80=100)].

[3] *American Machinist* materials price index [total and for plastics and 7 metals categories].

QUARTERLY TABLE:

[1] U.S. trade in machine tools [export and import values, for 10 leading customer and supplier countries, cumulative for current year through quarter ended approximately 6 months prior to cover date].

STATISTICAL FEATURES:

C5800–6.601: Nov. 1984 (Vol. 128, No. 11)

QUARTERLY TABLE

[1] U.S. trade in machine tools [by country], 1st half 1984. (p. 45)

C5800–6.602: Jan. 1985 (Vol. 129, No. 1)

1985 OUTLOOK: SETTLING FOR SLOWER GROWTH, ANNUAL FEATURE

(p. 83-90) Annual article forecasting 1985 metalworking industry production, shipments, and finances, with comparisons from 1970s. Data are from Federal agencies, National Machine Tool Builders' Assn, and McGraw-Hill Economics Dept. Includes 23 charts and 10 tables showing:

a. Shipment values, 1974-85; production and price indexes, monthly 1980-Oct. or Nov. 1984; and preferred operating rates (no date); for SIC 2- and 3-digit metalworking industries.

b. GNP by major sector, including net exports, 1980-85; and capital spending, for SIC 2- and 3-digit metalworking industries, other manufacturing, and nonmanufacturing, 1982-86.

c. Industrial goods production index and consumer durable goods production, by commodity, 1980-85; and nonelectrical machinery new orders, and cutting and forming machine tool shipments and net new orders, quarterly 1983-85.

C5800–6.603: Feb. 1985 (Vol. 129, No. 2)

QUARTERLY TABLE

[1] U.S. trade in machine tools [by country], 1st 9 months 1984. (p. 25)

WORLD MACHINE-TOOL OUTPUT UP 6%, ANNUAL FEATURE

(p. 69-73) Annual article, by Anderson Ashburn, with 2 tables showing value of cutting and forming tool production, and of total machine tool exports, imports, and consumption, for U.S. and 24-35 foreign countries, 1983-84. Data were compiled by *American Machinist.*

C5800–6.604: May 1985 (Vol. 129, No. 5)

QUARTERLY TABLE

[1] U.S. trade in machine tools [by country], full year 1984. (p. 45)

TOP CAD/CAM SUPPLIERS

(p. 61) Article, with 1 table showing top 12 manufacturers of computer-aided design/computer-aided manufacturing (CAD/CAM) equipment ranked by CAD/CAM revenues, 1984. Data are from Dataquest, Inc.

HOW ROBOTS AND OTHER AUTOMATION CHANGE THE NATURE OF THE WORK FORCE

(p. 128-131) By Steven M. Miller. Article, with 1 table showing wage/salary manufacturing employment, 1980, with long-term assessment of whether employment will increase or decrease (no date), all by occupation. Data are from Office of Technology Assessment.

C5800–6.605: Sept. 1985 (Vol. 129, No. 9)

QUARTERLY TABLE

[1] U.S. trade in machine tools [by country], 1st quarter 1985. (p. 25)

C5800–7   BUSINESS WEEK

Weekly.
ISSN 0007-7135.
LC 31-6225.
SRI/MF/not filmed

Weekly news journal (year-end combined issue) of current developments in domestic and foreign business and investments.

Issues generally contain news briefs; numerous articles, occasionally with substantial statistical content; and the following weekly statistical features:

a. "Business Week Index," with 2 charts showing aggregate production indicator trends.

b. "Figures of the Week," with 2 tables, further described below, presenting weekly and monthly data on prices, and production and economic indicators.

c. "Financial Figures of the Week," with 1 table showing selected money market rates; monetary indicators including M1 money supply, bank business loans and free reserves, and value of commercial paper issued by nonfinancial corporations; bond rates; stock index averages and NYSE volume; and prime interest rates and currency exchange rates, for 7 countries; generally for week 2 weeks prior to publication, and preceding week, month, and year, with averages for 1974 or 1975.

Additional statistical features include quarterly Corporate Scoreboard, also described below; recurring reports on *Business Week*-sponsored Louis Harris & Associates opinion surveys of general public and corporate executives; and annual features, often presenting detailed financial data for individual companies.

Prior to Dec. 1984, journal also included a monthly table on personal income by State and census division.

Weekly features appear in all issues. All additional features with substantial statistical content are described, as they appear, under "Statistical Features;" page locations and latest period of coverage for quarterly Corporate Scoreboard are also noted. Nonstatistical features are not covered.

Availability: Business Week, PO Box 430, Hightstown NJ 08520, $39.95 per yr., single copy $2.00, special issues $2.50; SRI/MF/not filmed.

Issues reviewed during 1985: Nov. 5, 1984-Oct. 28, 1985 (P) (Nos. 2867-2918) [Nos. 2884 and 2885 incorrectly read Nos. 2883 and 2884, respectively].

FIGURES OF THE WEEK TABLES:

[Tables include comparisons to previous week and/or month, same period of previous year and 1967 average.]

[1] Figures of the week [*Business Week* production index, and production in 9-10 major industry sectors; economic indicators including *Business Week* leading index, corporate bond yield, business failures, money supply (M2), real estate loans, unemployment insurance initial claims, and stock and industrial materials price indexes; and prices for 6-7 commodities; shown for week 2-4 weeks prior to cover date].

[2] Monthly figures [for 4-5 different economic indicators each week, including composite leading indicators, CPI, manufacturing operating rates, construction spending, employment,

---

unemployment rate, inventories, weekly pay, exports and imports, personal income, housing starts, PPI, retail sales, industrial production index, and durable goods orders; shown for month 1-3 months preceding cover date month].

QUARTERLY CORPORATE SCOREBOARD:

Quarterly feature reviewing financial performance of approximately 900 companies in 39 industries for quarter ending 6-10 weeks prior to issue date. Data are from Standard & Poor's Compustat Services, Inc. Generally includes:

a. Narrative analysis with 2 charts showing 3-4 year aggregate trends in profits and margins; and 3-4 tables ranking top industries and companies by various indicators of financial performance.

b. Listing of companies grouped by industry, showing the following for each: sales and profits for quarter of coverage and cumulative for year to date, with percent change from previous year; and return on equity, earnings per share, and price/earnings ratio for varying recent 12-month periods.

c. Index of companies.

Feature for 4th quarter covers 1,200 companies and also includes full-year data.

STATISTICAL FEATURES:

C5800–7.601: Nov. 12, 1984 (No. 2868)

INTERSTATE BANKING: THE BIG GAMBLE THAT CONGRESS WILL MAKE IT LEGAL

(p. 142-143) Article, with 1 data map showing number of requests filed with the Comptroller of the Currency to establish consumer banking subsidiaries, by State, as of Oct. 15, 1984. Data are from the Comptroller of the Currency.

C5800–7.602: Nov. 19, 1984 (No. 2869)

CORPORATE SCOREBOARD, QUARTERLY FEATURE

(p. 96-130) Corporate financial performance of 900 companies, for 3rd quarter 1984. For data description, see C5800-7, above.

MANDATE THAT WILL HAVE ITS LIMITS

(p. 36-37) Article, with 1 table showing 1984 presidential election exit poll results, by sex, and for whites, Catholics, union households, and Hispanics. Data are from responses of approximately 9,000 voters in 47 States to an ABC News poll.

CONGRESS WON'T BE A RUBBER STAMP FOR REAGAN

(p. 40) Article, with 1 table showing political composition of U.S. Senate and House of Representatives, 1983-85 and 1985-87 terms.

C5800–7.603: Nov. 26, 1984 (No. 2870)

PERSONAL INCOME FOR JULY

(p. 185) Monthly table showing personal income, by State and census division, July and year-to-date 1984, with comparisons to 1983. This is the final appearance of the monthly table.

C5800–7.604: Dec. 3, 1984 (No. 2871)

BUSINESS WEEK/HARRIS POLL: THE PUBLIC SEES THE LITTLE GUY AS THE LOSER

(p. 89) Article on public opinion of telephone service since AT&T reorganization. Data are from a Nov. 1984 survey of 1,247 adults conducted by Louis Harris and Associates for *Business Week*. Includes 1 chart showing percent of respondents viewing AT&T reorganization as a good or bad idea.

SURPRISE! MA BELL'S BABIES ARE STEALING THE SHOW

(p. 104-116) Article, with 1 chart showing the following for 7 regional holding companies created by AT&T reorganization: net income for 1st 9 months 1984 (amount and as percent of total net income forecast for 1984). Data are from *Business Week*.

C5800–7.605: Dec. 10, 1984 (No. 2872)

NRC IS FEELING THE HEAT FROM A NEW SOURCE

(p. 128) Article, with 1 chart showing number of nuclear reactors in commercial use, and generating capacity, 1980-84. Data are from the Atomic Industrial Forum.

C5800–7.606: Dec. 17, 1984 (No. 2873)

BUSINESS WEEK/HARRIS POLL: TAXPAYERS ARE ALL FOR REFORM—IN THEORY

(p. 31) Article on public opinion regarding the Federal tax system. Data are from a Nov. 1984 survey of 1,255 adults conducted by Louis Harris and Associates for *Business Week*. Includes 1 table showing respondents' willingness to eliminate various tax deductions in exchange for a simplified tax system with lower basic tax rates.

CIGARETTE MAKERS HAVE MET THE BAD NEWS HEAD ON, ANNUAL FEATURE

(p. 56-57) Annual article reporting on cigarette sales, 1984. Includes 2 tables showing sales volume and market share, for 6 manufacturers and top 20 brands, 1982-84.

DEATH OF MINING

(p. 64-70) Article, with 1 table showing net earnings, debt, debt as percent of capitalization, and return on equity, aggregated for 10 leading metals mining companies, 1979-83. Data are from company financial reports.

FAST-GROWING FLOCK OF OVERNIGHT MAIL SERVICES

(p. 111) Brief article, with 1 chart showing estimated revenues from overnight document/package deliveries, for USPS and 5 private companies, 1984. Data are from Legg Mason Wood Walker, Inc.

C5800–7.607: Dec. 24, 1984 (No. 2874)

PAYCHECKS WON'T GET MUCH FATTER, ANNUAL FEATURE

(p. 20-21) Annual article reporting on issues in labor negotiations, 1985. Data are from the Labor Dept and *Business Week*. Includes 1 table showing the following for labor contracts expiring in 1985: union, expiration date, employer, and number of workers covered.

UNION CARBIDE FIGHTS FOR ITS LIFE

(p. 52-56) Article, with 1 undated table showing the following for 6 major personal injury liability lawsuits against corporations: company involved, number of claims, basis of suit, and cost.

C5800–7.608: Dec. 31, 1984/Jan. 7, 1985 (No. 2875)

BUSINESS WEEK/HARRIS POLL: UNION CARBIDE'S GOOD NAME TAKES A BEATING

(p. 40) Article on public opinion regarding Union Carbide following industrial accident in Bhopal, India. Data are from a Dec. 1984 survey of 1,254 adults conducted by Louis Harris and Associates for *Business Week*. Includes 1 table showing respondents' ratings of Union Carbide's handling of the incident.

INVESTMENT OUTLOOK, 1985, ANNUAL FEATURE

(p. 61-163, passim) Annual feature on outlook for personal and institutional investment, 1985. Contains 5 sections, with narrative analyses; numerous charts, most showing trends and/or outlook for selected economic indicators and types of investment; and the following tables and charts:

a. Economists' forecast: annual table showing forecasts by 26 economists and 14 econometric services of real GNP and price changes and unemployment rate, various periods 1984-85. (p. 67)

b. Executives' investment plans: annual table and 1 chart, based on Louis Harris and Associates Nov.-Dec. 1984 survey of over 600 executives, showing percent of executives with current and/or planned personal investments, by investment type; and views on effect of Treasury Dept's proposed tax reform on selected investment strategies. (p. 79)

c. Mutual funds: annual table showing 10 best and worst performing mutual funds, for 11-month and 5-year periods ended Nov. 30, 1984. (p. 112)

d. Stock index options: 1 chart showing number of stock index options traded on 4 exchanges, 1st 11 months 1984. (p. 116)

e. Real estate: 1 chart showing change in value of nonleveraged income-producing properties by type (retail, industrial, office, and apartment), 1978-84 period. (p. 118)

f. Investment outlook scoreboard: annual listing of approximately 900 companies, showing each company's stock price, book value, price/earnings ratio, dividend rate, yield, shares outstanding, market value change, shares held by institutions, and stock turnover, 1984, and actual or estimated earnings per share, 1983-85; with accompanying table showing 10 industry sectors with best and worst earnings per share, 1984-85. (p. 139-163)

Scoreboard data are primarily from Standard & Poor's Compustat Services, Inc. Other data are from Lipper Analytical Services, Inc., AMEX, NYSE, and various sources.

C5800–7.609: Jan. 14, 1985 (No. 2876)

1985 INDUSTRY OUTLOOKS, ANNUAL FEATURE

(p. 77-114) Annual feature forecasting market conditions and business performance for 16 industries in 1985. Data are from a variety of specified sources, including industry assns, Federal agencies, and *Business Week* estimates.

Contains introduction (p. 77-78) with 2 tables showing manufacturing output change and share of total output, with comparisons to

service and all other industries, various years 1970-90; and 4 sections presenting the following data, accompanied by narrative analyses and illustrative charts:

a. "Basic Manufacturing." Includes 1 chart showing import share of steel market, 1983-85. (p. 79-84)

b. "Natural Resources." Includes 1 chart showing prices for 6 nonferrous metals, 1984-85. (p. 86-94)

c. "High Technology." Includes 3 charts showing hardware and software share of computer industry R&D spending, 1981 and 1985; number of new drugs approved by FDA, 1982-85; and value of telephone/telegraph equipment imports, 1983-85. (p. 96-106)

d. "Services and Consumer Products." Includes 4 charts showing number of movies released, and tickets sold, 1983-85; hospital admissions, 1982-85; and personal care product sales (in 1972 dollars), 1981-85. (p. 108-114)

C5800–7.610: Jan. 21, 1985 (No. 2877)

HELL HATH NO FURY LIKE A SURPRISED STOCK ANALYST

(p. 98) Article on effect of financial analysts' forecasts on stock prices. Data are based on Lynch, Jones and Ryan's Institutional Brokers Estimate System surveys of 1,800 analysts, and on *Business Week* estimates. Includes 1 table showing the following for 10 companies: percent of earnings forecasts differing significantly from average forecast, and change in stock price from yearly high, 1984-85.

HOW $20 CRUDE WOULD BATTER BIG OIL'S BALANCE SHEETS

(p. 106) Article, with 1 table showing earnings per share estimates for 5 major oil companies, based on 2 crude oil price scenarios, 1985. Data are from forecasts compiled by Lynch, Jones and Ryan; Kidder, Peabody and Co.; Salomon Bros.; Morgan Stanley; and Sanford C. Berstein.

C5800–7.611: Jan. 28, 1985 (No. 2878)

MORE CAPITAL FOR BANKS: THE CURE MAY BE WORSE THAN THE DISEASE

(p. 54) Article, with 1 table showing assets, and primary capital as percent of total assets, for 10 major banks, as of Sept. 30, 1984, with comparisons to 1983. Data are from Keefe, Bruyette, and Woods Inc.

C5800–7.612: Feb. 11, 1985 (No. 2880)

OPEC STILL HASN'T FACED UP TO REALITY

(p. 29) Article, with 1 table showing current account deficit, and change in real GNP, industrial output, and consumer prices, under 2 crude oil price scenarios, 1985. Data are estimates from Data Resources, Inc.

SCREWS ARE TIGHTENING ON U.S. COMPANIES

(p. 38-40) Article, with 1 undated table ranking top 12 U.S. companies in South Africa by number of employees. Data are from *Business Week* and Investor Responsibility Research Center.

BUSINESS WEEK/HARRIS POLL: FIGHT APARTHEID, BUT DON'T CLOSE UP SHOP

(p. 39) Article on public opinion regarding U.S. policies toward South Africa. Data are from a Jan. 1985 survey of 1,254 adults conducted by Louis Harris and Associates for *Business Week*.

Includes 1 chart showing respondents' support or opposition concerning U.S. pressure on South Africa to give blacks more freedom/government participation, and 4 possible U.S. economic sanctions against South Africa.

COMING AVALANCHE OF 15-SECOND TV ADS

(p. 80) Article with 1 chart showing percent of viewers correctly recalling brand advertised in last TV commercial seen, 1965, 1974, and 1981. Data are from SSC&B:Lintas USA and Newspaper Advertising Bureau.

C5800–7.613: Feb. 18, 1985 (No. 2881)

REAGAN TAKES A SWING AT BUSINESS

(p. 30-32) Article, with 1 table showing savings from 8 Reagan Administration budget proposals affecting business, FY86 and FY88. Data are from *Business Week*.

REGULATION MAY TURN THE THRIFTS INTO RAIDERS' PREY

(p. 40) Article, with 1 undated table showing the following for 9 Sun Belt savings institutions considered potential takeover candidates: location, date converted to public ownership, capital raised from conversion, and recent stock price. Data are from FHLBB and Bunker Ramo Information Systems.

WHY CARMAKERS WILL MOURN IF EXPORT QUOTAS DIE

(p. 46-47) Article, with 1 table showing auto production, and U.S. retail sales as percent of production, for 8 Japanese automakers, 1984. Data are from *Ward's Automotive Reports* and *Business Week*.

REMODELING: THE TIME IS RIGHT

(p. 156-158) Article, with 1 undated table showing cost range, typical cost, and percent of cost recovered upon sale of home within 5 years, for 7 types of home improvement projects. Data are from *Remodeling World*.

C5800–7.614: Feb. 25, 1985 (No. 2882)

HUNT FOR ARTIFICIAL SWEETENERS IN EARNINGS STATEMENTS

(p. 86) Article, with 1 table showing the following for 11 major companies: tax benefits deriving from 1984 Tax Reform Act provisions, and operating profits, 1984. Data are from company annual reports, *Quality of Earnings Report*, and *Business Week*.

SOBERING OF AMERICA: A PUSH TO PUT DRINKING IN ITS PLACE

(p. 112-113) Article on alcohol consumption patterns. Data are from a Feb. 1985 survey of 1,254 adults conducted by Louis Harris and Associates for *Business Week*, and earlier surveys.

Includes 1 chart showing percent of respondents drinking more than, less than, or about the same as 5 years ago, 1971 and 1985; and percent personally acquainted with an excessive drinker, 1974 and 1985.

C5800–7.615: Mar. 4, 1985 (No. 2883)

THE RAIDERS

(p. 80-90) Article reporting on trends in hostile corporate takeovers. Data are from Kidder, Peabody and Co., company reports, and *Business Week*. Includes 1 table showing the following for 5 companies: "unwanted" shareholder who has acquired controlling interest with intent to take over company, amount above market value paid by company for shareholder's stock, date of transaction, and company situation after payment.

C5800–7.616: Mar. 11, 1985 (No. 2884)
[Issue incorrectly reads No. 2883.]

TALKS WITH JAPAN NEAR THE FLASH POINT

(p. 34-35) Article, with 1 chart showing percent change in imports of Japanese cars if voluntary restraints are lifted, as forecast by 5 organizations for year beginning Apr. 1, 1985. Data were compiled by *Business Week*.

PHONE MARKET: JAPAN KEEPS HANGING UP ON THE U.S.

(p. 67) Article, with 1 chart showing sales of telecommunications equipment in Japan, 1984-86. Data are from Jardine Fleming Securities Ltd.

BOOM TIMES IN A BARGAIN-HUNTER'S PARADISE

(p. 116-120) Article on warehouse membership clubs (companies offering wholesale-priced goods to small businesses or selected consumer groups). Data are from Goldman, Sachs and Co. Includes 1 chart showing number of outlets for 4 leading warehouse clubs, 1984-85.

C5800–7.617: Mar. 18, 1985 (No. 2885)
[Issue incorrectly reads No. 2884.]

BUSINESS WEEK/HARRIS POLL: A VOTE FOR CBS OVER SENATOR HELMS

(p. 30) Article on public opinion regarding efforts of Senator Jesse Helms to promote a takeover of CBS Inc. Data are from a Mar. 1985 survey of 1,256 adults conducted by Louis Harris and Associates for *Business Week*. Includes 1 chart showing percent of respondents rating CBS performance as good or bad, and percent favoring or opposing takeover of CBS by conservative political groups.

MONEY LAUNDERING

(p. 74-82) Article, with 1 table showing amount of currency received by Federal Reserve banks above or below amount sent out to commercial banks, for 8 cities, 1980 and 1984. (A substantial surplus of currency received above amount sent out is regarded by authorities as an indicator of money laundering.) Data are from the Federal Reserve Board.

SOFTWARE FOR THE COMMON MAN

(p. 94-100) Article, with 1 chart showing value of worldwide purchases of computer software, biennially 1981-1989. Data are from Infocorp.

MORE JAPANESE CARS: HOW MUCH WILL THEY HURT?

(p. 117-120) Article, with 1 chart showing Japanese share of U.S. auto market, 1980-86. Data are from *Ward's Automotive Reports* and Merrill Lynch Economics Inc.

ATLANTIC CITY IS NO LONGER ON A HOT STREAK

(p. 124-128) Article, with 1 table showing Atlantic City, N.J., casinos ranked by gross revenues, 1984 with comparisons to 1983. Data are from New Jersey Casino Control Commission.

MAGAZINE MADNESS: THE STORY BEHIND THE BUYOUT BINGE

(p. 149-150) Article, with 1 table showing the following for 6 recent magazine acquisition transactions: buyer and number of publications owned, seller and number of publications sold, and transaction price. Data are from *Business Week*.

C5800–7.618: Mar. 22, 1985 (No. 2886)

SCOREBOARD ANNUAL ISSUE

Annual compilation of articles and statistics providing detailed information on the performance of corporations and industries in the U.S. and foreign countries.

Most of the statistical material has appeared in similar or identical form in previous issues of *Business Week*, primarily as annual features in the magazine's regular Corporate Scoreboard series.

These features have been described in SRI as they have appeared. This issue serves as a detailed compilation of these features, generally covering individual companies grouped by industry, for various periods 1979-84.

Issue also includes quarterly Corporate Scoreboard feature, described below.

CORPORATE SCOREBOARD, QUARTERLY FEATURE

(p. 15-68) Corporate financial performance of 1,200 companies, 4th quarter and full year 1984.

For data description, see C5800-7 above. Also includes the following for each company: profit margins, quarterly 1984; share value, Feb. 28, 1984; dividend yield, and book value per share, 1984; and growth in earnings per share and common equity, 1980-84 period.

C5800–7.619: Mar. 25, 1985 (No. 2887)

BUSINESS WEEK/HARRIS POLL: A BLAST AT THE DEFENSE ESTABLISHMENT

(p. 73) Article on public opinion regarding alleged overcharges by defense contractors. Data are from a Mar. 1985 survey of 1,254 adults conducted by Louis Harris and Associates for *Business Week*. Includes 1 chart showing respondents' views on prevalence of overcharging and on appropriate government penalties for companies that overcharge.

C5800–7.620: Apr. 1, 1985 (No. 2888)

TREMORS FROM OHIO'S BANK RUN

(p. 28-30) Article, with 1 table showing the following data for FDIC, FSLIC, and 10 States with nonfederal insurance funds backing deposits in savings institutions or industrial banks: number of insured institutions, maximum coverage per account, insurance fund size, and total deposits insured; as of Dec. 31, 1984. Data are from FDIC and FSLIC.

AUDITORS OWN UP TO THE COST OF THEIR ERRORS

(p. 34) Article, with 1 table showing amount paid in settlement of audit-related lawsuits since 1980, for 8 major accounting firms. Data are from SEC.

C5800–7.621: Apr. 8, 1985 (No. 2889)

BUSINESS WEEK/HARRIS POLL: RESENTMENT OF JAPAN IS DEEPENING

(p. 53) Article on public opinion regarding U.S. relations with Japan. Data are from a Mar. 14-17, 1985 survey of 1,253 adults, conducted by Louis Harris and Associates for *Business Week*. Includes 1 chart showing respondents' views on reasons for success of Japanese products, and for poor sales of American products in Japan.

DOUBLE STANDARD THAT'S SETTING WORKER AGAINST WORKER

(p. 70-71) Article on labor contracts with 2-tier wage systems, in which new employees are paid lower wages than current employees in the same job. Data are from Bureau of National Affairs, Inc., and *Business Week*.

Includes 1 table showing number of workers covered under 2-tier contracts, and industries involved, for 6 unions.

HOW INVENTORIES COULD BURY 1985 COMPUTER PROFITS

(p. 82-83) Article, with 1 table showing the following for 10 computer manufacturers: number of days of product inventory on hand and value, and pretax profits, 1984. Data are from *Business Week*.

WHAT'S IN A NAME? MILLIONS, IF IT'S LICENSED

(p. 97-98) Article, with 1 chart showing licensed product sales, by category, 1984. Data are from *Licensing Letter*.

DO VENTURE CAPITALISTS REALLY NEED A TAX BREAK?

(p. 100-101) Article, with 1 chart showing venture capital received from pension funds, foreign investors, individuals, corporations, insurance companies, and endowments/foundations, 1984. Data are from Venture Economics Inc., and *Politics and Markets*.

BANK SCOREBOARD: THE YEAR THAT BANKERS STOPPED LAUGHING, ANNUAL FEATURE

(p. 105-114) Annual article, for 1984, on the financial performance of the 200 largest banks. Data are from Standard & Poor's Compustat Services, Inc.

Includes narrative analysis, with 1 summary table showing 3-5 best and worst banks in securities trading, operating efficiency, and loan-loss provisions; and ranked listing of 200 banks, showing the following for each bank:

a. Year-end assets and rank; year-end deposits, and percent interest-bearing, noninterest-bearing, and foreign; and loans outstanding at year end, loan loss provision, and chargeoffs as percent of loans outstanding.

b. Operating and net income, return on assets, leverage, return on equity, net interest income, and 5-year growth in earnings per share.

Data are shown for 1984, with selected changes from 1983.

This is the 13th annual *Bank Scoreboard*.

C5800–7.622: Apr. 15, 1985 (No. 2890)

PORK WORKERS' BEEF: PAY CUTS THAT PERSIST

(p. 74-76) Article, with 1 undated table showing average hourly pay and number of workers at 5 major meat packing companies. Data are from United Food and Commercial Workers Union.

C5800–7.623: Apr. 22, 1985 (No. 2891)

BRINGING UP BABY: A NEW KIND OF MARKETING BOOM

(p. 58-65) Article, with 1 undated table showing typical costs of rearing a child through age 5 in midwest U.S., by major item. Data are from USDA.

C5800–7.624: Apr. 29, 1985 (No. 2892)

HOW EUROPE COULD DERAIL THE WORLD RECOVERY

(p. 42-43) Article, with 1 chart showing percent change in GNP for U.S. and 4 European countries, 1984-86. Data are from Data Resources Inc.

FIRE ON CAMPUS, TREMORS IN THE BOARDROOM

(p. 98-99) Article on college divestment of stocks in companies doing business in South Africa. Data are from *Business Week* and Social Investment Forum. Includes 1 undated table showing names and total amounts of stocks sold by 5 universities.

C5800–7.625: May 6, 1985 (No. 2893)

EXECUTIVE PAY: WHO MADE THE MOST, ANNUAL FEATURE

(p. 78-100) Annual survey reporting on compensation paid to top executives of 259 major companies in 36 industries, 1984 and trends. Also presents pay performance index, based on compensation compared to shareholder returns. Data are from Sibson and Co. and Standard & Poor's Compustat Services, Inc. Includes the following:

a. 2 summary tables on 25 highest paid executives and 10 executives with best and worst pay performance index.

b. Executive scoreboard: salary/bonus and long-term compensation, 1984, with salary/bonus change from 1983; and compensation as percent of industry standard, and pay performance index, 1984 and 1982-84 period; generally shown for top 2 executives in each company, grouped by industry.

Executive scoreboard also shows each company's sales and return on equity, 1984; and return on equity and shareholder return, both as percents of industry standards, 1984 and 1982-84 period.

WHY UNION BOSSES ARE ALSO-RANS IN THE BIG-BUCKS DERBY, ANNUAL FEATURE

(p. 102-103) Annual article on compensation of top labor union officials, 1984. Data are from Dept of Labor, Bureau of National Affairs, *Business Week,* and Teamsters for a Democratic Union. Includes 1 table showing salary and allowance paid to top 1-3 officials, and union membership, all for each of 39 unions, 1984.

C5800–7.626: May 13, 1985 (No. 2894)

ANOTHER JAPANESE-STYLE TRADE GAP

(p. 45-46) Article, with 1 chart showing U.S. and South Korea bilateral exports, 1980-85. Data are from the Commerce Dept and *Business Week*.

AFTER THE BELL BREAKUP: 'A DIFFERENT BALL GAME' FOR UNIONS

(p. 50-52) Article, with 1 chart showing number of employees represented by Communica-

tions Workers of America (CWA), for American Telephone and Telegraph Co. (AT&T) and for 7 regional companies created by AT&T divestiture, 1985. Data are from CWA.

LIQUOR MAKERS TRY THE HARD SELL IN A SOFTENING MARKET, ANNUAL FEATURE

(p. 56-60) Annual article on liquor industry market trends. Data are from *Business Week* and Clark Gavin Associates, Inc. Includes 2 tables showing market shares by type of distilled spirit, and total liquor consumption, 1974 and 1983-84; and liquor brands ranked by retail sales volume, 1982-84, with growth rate for 1980-84 period.

C5800–7.627: May 20, 1985 (No. 2895)

CORPORATE SCOREBOARD, QUARTERLY FEATURE

(p. 123-150) Corporate financial performance of 900 companies, for 1st quarter 1985.

For data description, see C5800-7 above. Also includes the following for each company: return on invested capital for recent 12-month period; growth in common equity and earnings per share, 1975-85 period; and market value of shares outstanding, as of Apr. 30, 1985.

C5800–7.628: May 27, 1985 (No. 2896)

SMALL IS BEAUTIFUL

(p. 88-104) Special report on top 100 growth companies with annual sales of under $150 million, ranked by a weighted formula based on selected measures of profitability and growth. Data are from a *Business Week* survey of 4,200 publicly owned corporations monitored by Standard & Poor's Compustat Services, Inc.

Includes ranked listing showing the following for each company: headquarters location, type of product or service, and fiscal year ending date; earnings, sales, debt as percent of capital, stock price, and price/earnings ratio, 1985; and sales and profit changes and return on capital, 1983-85 period.

Also includes 1 chart showing estimated new jobs available, with distribution by company employment size, 1985.

IT'S GETTING HARDER FOR COMPUTER GURUS TO SOUND WISE

(p. 108-110) Article, with 1 table showing the following for 9 computer industry market research corporations: headquarters location, company founder and start-up date; revenues, and number of clients and employees (no dates); and specialty. Data are from *Business Week*.

HOW TO REFORM THE PENTAGON'S WASTEFUL WAYS

(p. 144-149) Article, with 2 charts showing DOD expenditures for weapons, FY80-84; and number of defense contractors suspended/debarred for improper practices, 1980-84. Data are from DOD.

C5800–7.629: June 3, 1985 (No. 2897)

HOW UTILITIES ARE PLUGGING INTO NEW PROFITS

(p. 71-72) Article, with 1 table showing 10 major electric utility companies ranked by cash remaining after dividend payments/construction expenses, 1985, with amount per share, and stock price for May 21, 1985. Data are from Salomon Brothers.

C5800–7.630: June 10, 1985 (No. 2898)

WHAT MAKES CORPORATE TAXES A TARGET FOR REFORM

(p. 96-99) Article, with 2 tables ranking 31 industries by effective tax rate (Federal tax divided by pretax income) and top 50 companies by investment tax credit, and also showing each industry's sales, pretax income, Federal tax, and tax credits/deferrals, and each company's sales and net income, 1984. Data are from Standard & Poor's Compustat Services.

BALANCE SHEET BUSTER FROM THE FASB

(p. 107) Article, with 1 table showing debt ratios under current and proposed Financial Accounting Standards Board rules, for 11 major corporations, 1984. Data are from company reports and *Business Week*.

C5800–7.631: June 17, 1985 (No. 2899)

WIDENING TRADE GAP: IS TOKYO CALLING CONGRESS' BLUFF?

(p. 50-51) Article, with 1 table ranking 8 Japanese auto manufacturers by exports to U.S., Apr. 1985, with change from Apr. 1984. Data are from *Business Week*.

BUSINESS WEEK/HARRIS POLL: LET BUSINESS BEAR THE BURDEN

(p. 130) Article on public opinion regarding tax reform. Data are from a spring 1985 survey conducted by Louis Harris and Associates for *Business Week*. Includes 1 table showing percent of respondents favoring or opposing various provisions of the Reagan Administration tax plan.

NEW WAR BETWEEN THE STATES WILL BE FOUGHT OVER TAXES

(p. 132-133) Article with 1 undated chart showing total and per capita income tax changes under Reagan Administration proposal, for 8 most populous States. Data are from Advisory Commission on Intergovernmental Relations and *Business Week*.

C5800–7.632: June 24, 1985 (No. 2900)

COMPUTER SLUMP

(p. 74-79) Article, with 1 table showing reasons cited by corporate data processing managers for current reductions in computer purchasing/leasing. Data are from a June 1985 survey of 601 managers conducted by Louis Harris and Associates for *Business Week*.

CORPORATE BALANCE SHEET SCOREBOARD, ANNUAL FEATURE

(p. 108-130) Annual table showing selected balance sheet data for approximately 900 nonfinancial corporations in 36 industries, generally FY84 with selected comparisons to FY83.

Table includes the following: assets; short-term and long-term debt; current and fixed charge coverage ratios, and 5-year cash flow as percent of growth needs; common equity as percent of total investment capital; and stock price as percent of book value, and Standard & Poor's quality rating, as of May 31, 1985.

Data are from Standard & Poor's Compustat Services.

Also includes accompanying article and index of companies.

C5800–7.633: July 1, 1985 (No. 2901)

SPLITTING UP

(p. 50-55) Article, with 1 table showing the following data for 25 largest corporate divestitures announced since 1983: seller, unit sold, buyer, and year and price of transaction. Data are from W. T. Grimm and Co. and *Business Week*.

C5800–7.634: July 8, 1985 (No. 2902)

BUSINESS WEEK/HARRIS POLL: CONFIDENCE IN UNIONS IS CRUMBLING

(p. 76) Article on public opinion concerning most important aspect of own job. Data are from a May-June 1985 survey conducted by Louis Harris and Associates for *Business Week*. Includes 1 table.

R&D SCOREBOARD: REAGAN AND FOREIGN RIVALRY LIGHT A FIRE UNDER SPENDING, ANNUAL FEATURE

(p. 86-106) Annual feature on R&D expenditures and financial performance of 820 companies in 32 industries, 1984. Data are compiled by Standard & Poor's Compustat Services, Inc., from SEC Form 10K filings.

Contents:

a. Narrative analysis, with 4 tables showing percent growth in R&D spending in 8 industries with most growth, and rankings of R&D spending for 15 leading companies, 1984; and glossary. (p. 86-88)

b. List of companies grouped by industry, showing the following for each: sales, profits, and R&D total and per employee expenditures, 1984, generally with change from 1980 and 1983; and average annual change in employment, 1980-84. (p. 88-104)

c. Index of companies. (p. 104-106)

C5800–7.635: July 15, 1985 (No. 2903)

BUSINESS WEEK/HARRIS POLL: AMERICANS GET QUEASIER ABOUT AIR TRAVEL

(p. 37) Article on public opinion regarding safety of air travel. Data are from a June 1985 survey conducted by Louis Harris and Associates for *Business Week*. Includes 1 table showing percent of respondents viewing hijacking, on-board bombs, poor maintenance, and pilot error as sources of concern.

EPA GIVES A LITTLE ON GAS MILEAGE

(p. 38) Article on impact of recent EPA revisions in auto corporate average fuel economy (CAFE) standards. Data are from EPA and the National Highway Traffic Safety Administration. Includes 1 table showing standard CAFE rating originally mandated, and ratings for top 3 automakers under original vs. revised CAFE standards, 1978-85.

NEW COMPUTER WARS

(p. 96-104) Article, with 1 table showing minicomputer market shares, for top 10 and all other manufacturers, 1984-85. Data are from InfoCorp.

BOOMS, BUSTS, AND AMBITIONS: HOW ONE SMALL-TOWN BANK FELL

(p. 112-113) Article, with 1 chart showing average assets of failed banks, 1980-June 1985. Data are from FDIC.

C5800–7.636: July 22, 1985 (No. 2904)

CARMAKERS BET THAT THE BEARS ARE WRONG

(p. 64) Article, with 1 chart showing production and sales of U.S.-built autos, 1984-85. Data sources include *Ward's Automotive Reports* and Merrill Lynch Economics.

INTERNATIONAL CORPORATE SCOREBOARD: 1984 PROFITS PUSHED ALOFT BY THE SUPERDOLLAR, ANNUAL FEATURE

(p. 150-176) Annual feature on sales, profits, equity, and earnings per share of 1,046 foreign corporations in 57 countries, 1984. Data are compiled by Standard & Poor's Compustat Services, Inc.

Contains brief introduction, with 1 summary table showing net sales and profits of 20 largest foreign corporations, 1984; and International Scoreboard table, showing the following data by company, arranged by country and world region:

a. Sales and profits, 1984 with percent change from 1983; profit margins, 1983-84; and earnings per share, 1984.

b. Book value and rate of return, and market value of shares outstanding, 1984.

This is the 13th annual article.

C5800–7.637: July 29, 1985 (No. 2905)

BUSINESS WEEK/HARRIS POLL: REAGAN'S TAX-REFORM PLAN COULD DIE OF BOREDOM

(p. 35) Article on public opinion regarding tax reform. Data are from a June 1985 survey conducted by Louis Harris and Associates for *Business Week*. Includes 2 charts showing survey response on support of Reagan Administration tax simplification plan, and whether plan would be fair to 6 economic groups.

C5800–7.638: Aug. 5, 1985 (No. 2906)

INVESTORS ARE HOT FOR FLORIDA THRIFTS

(p. 62-63) Article, with 1 table showing the following for 8 Florida savings and loan assns perceived as likely acquisition targets: assets, book value per share, and recent stock price (no date); and earnings per share, 1984. Data are from Raymond, James, and Associates, Inc.

HEALTH CARE: NO SHOT IN THE ARM FOR PROFITS

(p. 74-75) Article reporting on corporate acquisitions of medical products/services companies. Data are from *Business Week*. Includes 1 table showing the following for 17 transactions: acquiring company, name and business of acquired company, acquisition year and price, and sales (no date).

C5800–7.639: Aug. 12, 1985 (No. 2907)

A MARKET OF THE FUTURE GETS AHEAD OF ITSELF

(p. 29) Article, with 1 chart showing circuit miles of fiber-optic network installed, 1984 and 1988, with detail for 1988 by company. Data are from Yankee Group, Inc.

BASEBALL'S BIG LEAGUE BLUES

(p. 40-48) Article, with 1 table showing salaries of 12 prominent baseball players, selected years 1907-68, with 1985 dollar equivalent amount. Data are from University of Illinois.

For description of more detailed data on prominent baseball players' salaries, see U6910-1.604 below.

BUSINESS WEEK/HARRIS POLL: BOOS FROM THE BLEACHERS

(p. 48) Article on public opinion regarding professional baseball. Data are from a July 1985 survey of approximately 1,200 adults conducted by Louis Harris and Associates for *Business Week*. Includes 1 chart showing survey response on whether fans' interests are better served by baseball players or club owners in summer 1985 dispute over free-agent system.

WHAT'S POWERING THE REITs ROCKET

(p. 66) Article, with 1 table showing sales of publicly offered real estate investment programs, by type (unleveraged, leveraged, mortgage-loan, and real estate investment trusts), 1st half 1984-85. Data are from Robert A. Stanger and Co.

PENSION FUND SCOREBOARD: THE HUGE PENSION OVERFLOW COULD MAKE WAVES IN WASHINGTON, ANNUAL FEATURE

(p. 71-75) Annual article on the financial condition of corporate pension funds, 1984. Includes 1 table showing the following pension fund data for each of the 200 largest companies in terms of sales: total and vested benefits, assets, vested funding position, net worth, assumed rate of return, and expense, 1984, with selected comparisons to 1983.

Also includes 2 tables showing total pension assets and amount scheduled to revert to company, for 10 companies planning to terminate pension plans; and 10 corporate pension funds with largest unfunded liabilities.

C5800–7.640: Aug. 19, 1985 (No. 2908)

DETROIT'S CREDIT ARMS ARE GETTING A LOT LONGER

(p. 84-85) Article, with 1 table showing the following for 3 major auto manufacturer finance companies: assets as of Dec. 31, 1984; and traditional business, and companies recently acquired. Data are from company reports.

GAME FOR THE RICH GIVES REGULATORS THE WILLIES

(p. 87-88) Article reporting on "private placement" investments (procurement of investment capital through private sources not registered with the SEC). Data are from SEC.

Includes 1 undated table showing type of investment and value of initial offering for 13 "private placement" organizations grouped by type (partnerships, stock, and debt).

FANNIE MAE TIGHTENS THE SCREWS ON MORTGAGES

(p. 88) Article reporting on changes in FNMA home financing requirements. Data are from National Assn of Realtors. Includes 1 table showing the following for the purchase of a median-priced home: cost of home, income needed to qualify for federally guaranteed mortgage, and mortgage rate, 1983-85, with 1985 detail for income requirements under old and new FNMA policies.

CORPORATE SCOREBOARD, QUARTERLY FEATURE

(p. 91-108) Corporate financial performance of 900 companies, for 2nd quarter 1985. For data description, see C5800-7 above.

C5800–7.641: Aug. 26, 1985 (No. 2909)

BUSINESS WEEK/HARRIS POLL: SURE, JAPAN IS A PROBLEM, BUT NOT MINE

(p. 68) Article on business executives' views concerning Japanese competition. Data are from responses of 301 executives to a July-Aug. 1985 survey conducted by Louis Harris and Associates for *Business Week*. Includes 1 chart showing survey response on measures likely to be taken by own company to combat Japanese competition.

C5800–7.642: Sept. 2, 1985 (No. 2910)

MIGHTY SEARS TESTS ITS CLOUT IN CREDIT CARDS

(p. 62-63) Article, with 1 table showing number of cards outstanding, for 5 major credit card companies, 1985. Data are from *Nilson Report* and *Business Week*.

SO YOU WANT A WEEKEND FARM

(p. 90-91) Article, with 1 table showing farm real estate value per acre, for 15 States, 1985. Data are from USDA.

C5800–7.643: Sept. 9, 1985 (No. 2911)

LOTTERIES: HOPING THE LUCK WILL LAST

(p. 39) Article, with 1 chart showing total revenues from State lotteries, FY70-85. Data are from Public Gaming Research Institute, Inc.

TWO WAYS TO DUCK THE HIGH COST OF DEBT

(p. 70) Article on utility companies' practice of buying back their own high-yield securities before normal redemption date. Data are from Salomon Brothers.

Includes 1 table showing the following for 9 utility companies: security issues offered for early redemption, long-term debt retired (amount and as percent of issues' value) as a result of redemption, and premium paid over market price for securities, 1985.

C5800–7.644: Sept. 16, 1985 (No. 2912)

WALKING WOUNDED

(p. 26-27) Article, with 1 table showing cumulative net losses for 20 major companies with consistent losses since 1981-82 recession, generally for 1983-1st half 1985 period. Data are from Standard & Poor's Compustat Services, Inc.

HEATING OIL PRICES ARE RISING BEFORE THE MERCURY DROPS

(p. 36) Article, with 1 chart showing refiners' inventories of distillate fuel oil, as of Aug. 1980-85. Data are from Data Resources, Inc.

'FOUR TIGERS' FALL PREY TO THE HIGH-TECH SLUMP

(p. 44-45) Article, with 1 chart showing percent change in exports, for Hong Kong, Taiwan, Singapore, and South Korea, 1st 7 months 1984-85. Data are from Data Resources, Inc. and *Business Week* estimates.

SECONDARY MORTGAGE MARKET'S CRISIS OF CONFIDENCE

(p. 112-113) Article, with 1 table showing the following for 13 leading private insurers of mortgage-backed securities: Standard & Poor's rating, parent company, and value of premiums written in 1984. Data are from Mortgage Insurance Cos. of America and Standard & Poor's Corp.

CAN A DOWN MONTH BE GOOD NEWS?

(p. 113-116) Article examining theory that stock price decline in Sept. indicates a strong market for the following year. Data are from Hirsch Organization, Inc. Includes 1 table showing percent change in stock prices, for Sept. and following year, selected years 1960-85.

C5800–7.645: Sept. 23, 1985 (No. 2913)

HOW COSMETICS MAKERS ARE TOUCHING UP THEIR STRATEGIES

(p. 66-73) Article, with 1 chart showing retail sales of cosmetics, for drug/department stores, mass merchandisers/food stores, and door-to-door companies, 1980 and 1984. Data are from Maybelline Co.

C5800–7.646: Sept. 30, 1985 (No. 2914)

CREDIT CRISIS ISN'T STAYING DOWN ON THE FARM

(p. 90-91) Article, with 1 chart and 1 table showing percent of farmers experiencing financial distress, and farm debt share, both by farm sales size, Mar. 1985; and farms with debt/asset ratio of 40%/higher (amount and as percent of all farms), by type of operation (no date). Data are from USDA.

C5800–7.647: Oct. 7, 1985 (No. 2915)

WASHINGTON TURNS UP THE HEAT ON BANKING A LA BERT LANCE

(p. 78-79) Article, with 1 table showing the following for 6 banks closed as a result of alleged violations of Federal banking laws: closing date, assets, violations charged, and disposition of charges. Data are from FDIC, House Government Operations Committee, and R. L. Polk and Co.

THE STREET'S HALFHEARTED HURRAH FOR A LOWER DOLLAR

(p. 86) Article, with 1 table showing total operating income, and foreign income as percent of total, 1984; and recent stock price; for 15 multinational companies with largest proportion of foreign earnings. Data are from company reports and *Business Week*.

PROTECTIONISM ISN'T SUCH A DIRTY WORD ANYMORE

(p. 95-96) Article, with 1 chart showing import shares of total U.S. market, for 24 product categories, 1972 and 1984. Data are from Commerce Dept., A. Gary Shilling and Co., and *Business Week*.

C5800–7.648: Oct. 14, 1985 (No. 2916)

DETROIT RAISES THE ANTE FOR PARTS SUPPLIERS

(p. 94-97) Article, with 1 chart showing percent of new car components procured from suppliers outside the auto industry; import share of total components; and number of domestic suppliers of components; 1985, 1990, and 1995. Data are from Arthur Andersen and Co.

WHAT'S INVISIBLE AND WORTH $55 BILLION?

(p. 132-134) Article, with 1 table showing value of goodwill, and goodwill as percent of net worth, for 20 companies with high goodwill values, 1984. Data are from company reports and *Business Week*.

C5800–7.649: Oct. 21, 1985 (No. 2917)

STIFF UPPER LIP AT BELEAGUERED BURROUGHS

(p. 43-44) Article, with 1 table showing computer disk drive sales for 6 major manufacturers, 1982 and 1984. Data are from *Disk/Trend Report.*

CAN THE GINNIE MAE FUNDS DELIVER ALL THEY PROMISE?

(p. 96-97) Article, with 1 table showing sales charge, rate of return for 1st 9 months 1985, and assets as of June 30, 1985, for 9 GNMA mutual funds. Data are from Lipper Analytical Services Corp.

NEW? IMPROVED? THE BRAND-NAME MERGERS

(p. 108-110) Article, with 1 table showing the following for 12 corporate acquisitions involving established brands: acquiring and acquired companies, transaction price and date, and brands acquired.

C5800–7.650: Oct. 28, 1985 (No. 2918)

INTEL'S NEW CHIP MAY LIGHT A FIRE UNDER COMPUTER SALES

(p. 34) Article, with 1 table showing unit sales of 32-bit computer chips, by type of application, 1985 and 1990. Data are from Dataquest, Inc.

BASKETBALL: BUSINESS IS BOOMING

(p. 72-82) Article, with 1 chart showing professional basketball revenues, 1980/81-84/85, with 1984/85 detail by revenue source (gate receipts, network and local TV, and other). Data are from National Basketball Assn.

C5800–8   CHEMICAL ENGINEERING
Biweekly.
ISSN 0009-2460.
LC 11-12192.
SRI/MF/not filmed

Biweekly publication reporting developments and trends in chemical engineering and in basic chemicals and chemical process industries. Includes articles on plant and project management, process technology, R&D, government regulation and funding, and personnel training and management; and regularly appearing data on chemical plant and equipment costs and output.

Most data are from Federal Government sources, McGraw-Hill Economics Dept, or private research and consulting firms, and are compiled and analyzed by *Chemical Engineering.*

Issues generally contain:

a. Three monthly "Economic Indicators" tables, showing indexes of chemical plant and equipment costs, output, and operating rate, with 5 accompanying charts.

b. Articles, generally narrative or technical in nature, but occasionally including broad based industry statistics; and narrative editorial depts.

Statistical features include a semiannual list of major chemical process industry construction projects; and a recurring feature on capital spending plans of chemical process industries. Annual subject and author indexes appear in the last issue in Dec.

Monthly tables are listed below and appear in every other issue. All additional features with substantial nontechnical statistical content are described, as they appear, under "Statistical Features." Nonstatistical features are not covered.

Availability: Chemical Engineering, Fulfillment Manager, PO Box 1482, Riverton, NJ 08077-9990, industry subscribers $27.50 per yr., single copy $6.00; SRI/MF/not filmed.

Issues reviewed during 1985: Nov. 12, 1984-Oct. 28, 1985 (P) (Vol. 91, Nos. 23-26; Vol. 92, Nos. 1-22).

MONTHLY TABLES:
[Tables usually appear on p. 7 of issue.]

[1] Plant cost index [total, for 7 types of chemical engineering equipment, machinery, and supports, and for construction labor, buildings, and engineering/supervision; for month 1-3 months prior to cover date, 2 previous months, and same month of previous year; and annual total index for 11 previous years].

[2] Equipment cost index [total and for 12 chemical process and related industries; for quarter 1-2 quarters prior to cover date, and 2 previous quarters; and annual total index for 11 previous years].

[3] Current business indicators [chemical process industry output index, value of output, and operating rate; and indexes of construction costs, industrial chemicals producer prices, industrial activity, and chemicals/allied products hourly earnings and productivity; variously for week, month, or quarter 1-5 months prior to cover date, previous 2 periods, and same period of previous year].

STATISTICAL FEATURES:

C5800–8.601: Dec. 10, 1984 (Vol. 91, No. 25)

CPI CAPITAL SPENDING IN U.S. TO STAY HEALTHY IN 1985, RECURRING FEATURE

(p. 27) Recurring article, with 1 table showing capital spending for 10 chemical process industries, 1983-86. Data are from the fall survey of business spending plans, conducted by McGraw-Hill's Dept of Economics.

C5800–8.602: Jan. 7, 1985 (Vol. 92, No. 1)

JOB FORECAST FOR THE 1990s

(p. 26-29) Article on engineering job outlook, with 1 table and 1 chart showing employment for chemical engineers by industry (with detail by chemical process industry), and for all engineers by field, 1982 and 1995. Data are from BLS.

C5800–8.603: Jan. 21, 1985 (Vol. 92, No. 2)

BOOM IN FUEL ETHANOL BEGETS NEW CAPACITY AND RESEARCH

(p. 38-41) Article, with 1 table showing the following for 7 fuel ethanol projects: company, and plant location, capacity, feedstock, construction firm, cost, and status as of 1984.

ARE YOU READY FOR THAT OVERSEAS TRIP?

(p. 123-126) By Thomas Garcia-Borras. Article, with 1 (undated) table showing inflation rate, and cost-of-living index relative to NYC, for U.S. executives in 30 major world cities. Data are from Business International Corp.

C5800–8.604: Mar. 4, 1985 (Vol. 92, No. 5)

RESEARCH BRIGHTENS FUTURE OF ENHANCED OIL RECOVERY

(p. 25-31) Article, with 1 undated chart showing potential crude oil production using 3 enhanced recovery methods (thermal recovery, chemical flooding, and miscible flooding). Data are from National Petroleum Council.

C5800–8.605: Apr. 1, 1985 (Vol. 92, No. 7)

FUTURE FERTILIZER PLANTS: WHAT WILL THEY BE LIKE?

(p. 21-25) Article, with 2 tables showing the following world data for nitrogen, phosphate rock, phosphate, and potash: current capacity; demand projected to 2000; and additional capacity, new plants, cost per plant, and capital expenditures required to meet demand. Data are from Texasgulf, Inc.

C5800–8.606: Apr. 15, 1985 (Vol. 92, No. 8)

CE ALERT: NEW CONSTRUCTION, SEMIANNUAL FEATURE

(p. 77-86) Semiannual tabular list of major chemical process industry projects in the planning stage, under construction, or completed, in U.S., Canada, Mexico, and Trinidad and Tobago, announced from late summer 1984 to early 1985.

List shows project product, location, plant capacity, and construction status, frequently with costs, by company for approximately 160 projects in 9 chemical process industries.

This is the 60th semiannual tabulation.

ARE CHEMICAL ENGINEERS LOSING FINANCIAL GROUND? ANNUAL FEATURE

(p. 99-104) Annual article, by Ken McNaughton, on salaries of chemical engineers. Data are from BLS, and surveys conducted by American Institute of Chemical Engineers, Engineering Manpower Commission, and College Placement Council.

Includes 5 tables presenting summary results from the surveys, including salary levels and job and salary offers, with detail by sex, industry, census division, and highest degree earned, and also including selected comparisons to other occupations, 1984 with comparisons to 1983.

C5800–8.607: Apr. 29, 1985 (Vol. 92, No. 9)

CE COST INDEXES SET SLOWER PACE

(p. 75-76) By Jay Matley. Article examining trends in plant and equipment cost indexes covered in monthly tables [1-2], 1975-84. Includes 3 tables.

For description of monthly tables, see C5800-8 above.

C5800–8.608: June 10, 1985 (Vol. 92, No. 12)

CPI CAPITAL SPENDING PLANS REMAIN GENEROUS IN 1985, RECURRING FEATURE

(p. 27) Recurring article, with 1 table showing capital spending for all manufacturing and 10 chemical process industries, 1983-88. Data are from the spring survey of business spending plans, conducted by McGraw-Hill's Dept of Economics.

C5800–8.609: Sept. 16, 1985 (Vol. 92, No. 19)

CHEMICAL ENGINEERS SPEAK OUT ON HAZARDOUS-WASTE MANAGEMENT

(p. 58-69) By Nicholas Basta et al. Article on chemical engineers' views regarding hazardous waste management issues. Data are from responses of 1,970 *Chemical Engineering* readers to a Mar. 1985 survey.

Includes 6 illustrative charts; 1 chart and 2 tables on selected sample characteristics; and 11 tables showing survey response on the following, with occasional detail by respondent sex, age group, and involvement of firm in hazardous waste management:

a.   Familiarity with hazardous waste regulations; funding methods preferred for waste site cleanup; reasons cited for changes in hazardous waste volume; and quality of work done by hazardous waste management firms vs. general chemical firms.

b.   Use and acceptability of hazardous waste disposal methods; desirability of having various industrial facilities near home, and compensation for having facility there; and preference for greater economic growth vs. environmental protection.

C5800–9   THIRTY-THREE: METAL PRODUCING
Monthly.
ISSN 0149-1210.
LC 77-641061.
SRI/MF/not filmed

Monthly trade journal reporting on operating, financial, and technological developments and outlook in the U.S. and world primary metal manufacturing industries (SIC major group 33): iron and steel, aluminum, copper, lead, zinc, and other nonferrous metals. Primary emphasis is on steel.

Includes data from McGraw-Hill surveys and publications, U.S. Government reports, and industry assns.

Issues generally contain:

a.   Narrative articles, often with text statistics on individual companies; and regular editorial depts.

b.   Monthly "Steel Performance Trends" table, showing steel output per worker-hour, and production and consumption indexes (1977=base year) with detail for 6 major consuming industries, for month 2-3 months prior to cover date, with comparisons to previous month and year.

An annual statistical report on steel and nonferrous metals industry outlook is included in the Dec. issue. Aug. issue includes a nonstatistical new product buyer's guide.

Prior to the Jan. 1985 issue, journal also included 2 monthly tables on steel industry operating, production, and financial indicators.

Monthly table appears in all issues. All additional features with substantial statistical content are described, as they appear, under "Statistical Features." Nonstatistical features are not covered.

Availability: 33 Metal Producing, Fulfillment Manager, PO Box 695, Hightstown NJ 08520, industry subscribers †, others $35.00 per yr., single copy $3.00; SRI/MF/not filmed.

Issues reviewed during 1985: Nov. 1984-Oct. 1985 (P) (Vol. 22, Nos. 11-12; Vol. 23, Nos. 1-10).

STATISTICAL FEATURES:

C5800–9.601: Nov. 1984 (Vol. 22, No. 11)

PILEUP IN ELECTROGALVANIZING IS JUST BEGINNING

(p. 43-47) By Walter Jacob. Article, with 2 tables showing location, line operating data, capacity, and cost, for 4 galvanized steel plants scheduled for startup in 1986; and auto sales (total and domestic) forecasts of 4 organizations, with Japanese and/or total import market shares, 1985 and 1990.

BENEATH THE RITUAL, A PREOCCUPATION WITH TRADE, ANNUAL FEATURE

(p. 48-51) Annual article, by John J. Dwyer, Jr., on world steel consumption and production outlook. Data are from International Iron and Steel Institute. Includes 4 tables showing the following for various years 1973-95:

a.   Steel consumption for Western and Communist world, and Western steelmaking capacity, by country, country grouping, or world region.

b.   Finished steel products as percent of crude steel production, and percent of crude steel continuously cast, for U.S., EC, and Japan.

ENERGY GAME: MOUNTING AN OFFENSIVE AT MID-STREAM

(p. 56-59) Article, with 2 tables showing steel mill energy consumption by fuel type (total and per ton of steel), and continuous casting and electric furnace mills as percent of all mills, 1972 and 1983; and technical data on heat loss during aluminum melting. Data are from American Iron and Steel Institute.

C5800–9.602: Dec. 1984 (Vol. 22, No. 12)

OUTLOOK '85: AFTER THE LEAN YEARS, ANNUAL FEATURE

(p. 37-52) Annual analysis of steel and nonferrous metals industry economic outlook for 1985, with trends from 1983. Includes several articles, and 6 tables showing the following:

a.   Raw steel production, net shipments, foreign trade, and apparent consumption; and steel and aluminum market volume by end-use sector, including aluminum exports; 1983-84, and forecast for 1985 under 3 growth assumptions.

b.   Steel and nonferrous metals capital investment by purpose; and prices for selected types of raw materials and energy, and for 6 metals; 1983 and/or 1984-85.

C5800–9.603: Jan. 1985 (Vol. 23, No. 1)

DIVISION IN THE ANTI-QUOTA RANKS

(p. 21) Article, with 1 chart showing distribution of steel imported by members of American Institute for Imported Steel (AIIS), by source (Europe, Japan, and rest of world or developing countries), late 1960s and 1984. Data are from AIIS.

STEEL IMPORT FRAUD: CLOAKS, DAGGERS, AND A CACHE OF SMOKING GUNS

(p. 42-44) By Joseph J. Innace. Article, with 1 table showing top 10 ports ranked by steel import volume, 1984 with comparisons to 1983. Data are from American Iron and Steel Institute.

NEEDED: A NEW APPETITE FOR ALUMINUM

(p. 47) Article, with 1 table showing aluminum consumption by end use, for U.S., Japan, and Western Europe, 1970, 1979, and 1983, with 1979 detail on consumption resulting from general economic conditions and from aluminum market changes.

C5800–9.604: Mar. 1985 (Vol. 23, No. 3)

WHY THE OIL 'GLUT' IS GOOD NEWS TO AMERICA'S MILLS

(p. 56-57) By Michael J. Kountze. Article, with 3 tables showing steel production, exports, and imports; steel and aluminum shipments by end-use industry; and aluminum exports; all estimated under 3 OPEC crude oil price scenarios, 1985. Data are from McGraw-Hill Economics.

C5800–9.605: Apr. 1985 (Vol. 23, No. 4)

WHY BANKERS AREN'T RETURNING MINI-STEEL'S PHONE CALLS

(p. 62-63) By Zoltan J. Acs. Article on developments in financing for steel mini-mills (primarily mills employing fewer than 1,000 workers). Data are from a recent survey of 55 mini-mills, conducted by the author.

Includes 1 table showing survey response concerning form of original operating company; startup capital amount and sources, and difficulty raising capital; employment; expansion plans; expansion and new technology financing sources and/or major obstacles; impact of current interest rates and credit availability; and future financing strategies.

C5800–9.606: May 1985 (Vol. 23, No. 5)

NEW TEMPO IN TEEMING

(p. 43-47) By Jo Isenberg-O'Loughlin. Article, with 1 chart showing production of continuous cast steel as a percent of total steel production, 1974-83. Data are from the International Iron and Steel Institute.

C5800–9.607: June 1985 (Vol. 23, No. 6)

IN PURSUIT OF PARITY: 'NO MORE. AND NO LESS.'

(p. 67-69) Article, with 1 table showing steel shipments and production workers, for 4 major companies, 1984. Also includes 2 tables showing U.S. Steel workforce by plant and shipments, 1981 and 1984.

WAITING GAME IN ALUMINUM

(p. 75) Article, with 1 table showing primary aluminum production capacity, by plant arranged by company, Dec. 1984-85 and June 1985-86. Data are from Aluminum Assn.

C5800–9.608: July 1985 (Vol. 23, No. 7)

HIDDEN COST OF HIGH INTEREST RATES

(p. 21) Article, with 1 undated table showing production costs for conventional and continuously cast hot-rolled steel sheet, under 3 interest rate scenarios. Data are from Congressional Research Service.

OTHER SIDE OF OUTSIDE SOURCING

(p. 39-41) By Joseph J. Innace. Article examining impact of semifinished steel imports on U.S. production of finished steel. Data are from American Iron and Steel Institute.

Includes 4 tables showing semifinished and sheet/strip steel exports and/or imports, raw steel production and shipments, raw steel from foreign and domestic sources available for finishing, and steel production percent yield with and without semifinished imports, 1980-84 and 1st 4 months 1985.

C5800–9.609: Sept. 1985 (Vol. 23, No. 9)

CONTROVERSIAL PLAN TO PARE THE STOCKPILE

(p. 37) Article, with 1 undated table showing current volume and value of national defense stockpile, and additions recently proposed by Reagan Administration, all for 11 categories of strategic materials.

LOOK AHEAD IN ALUMINUM

(p. 50-51) By Michael J. Kountze. Article, with 1 table showing aluminum shipments, by end-use market and for exports, under 3 economic scenarios, 1985. Data are from DRI/McGraw-Hill.

C5800–9.610: Oct. 1985 (Vol. 23, No. 10)

FUTURE OF DRI IN THE DEVELOPED WORLD

(p. 35-39) By Joseph J. Innace. Article, with tabular list of world direct reduction ironmaking plants (active, idled, and undetermined capacity) installed/under construction, generally with startup date, company, country, number of units, fuel type, process, and capacity, various years 1957-88; and iron production, by developing country and aggregate for developed countries, 1984.

C5800–10 U.S. BUSINESS OUTLOOK, Long-Term

Annual. Aug. 1985. 31 p.
SRI/MF/complete, current & previous year reports

Annual forecast of U.S. business activity and the performance of the economy to 1995, with trends from 1950. Presents forecasts based on 3 alternative assumptions about economic indicators. Data are based on Federal Government and McGraw-Hill Economics Dept sources.

Contains narrative report, interspersed with 15 trend charts, and 2 tables described below (p. 1-25); and 3 detailed tables, also described below (p. 26-31).

Previous report, for 1984, was also reviewed by SRI during 1985, and is also available on SRI microfiche under C5800-10 [Annual. Aug. 1984. 26 p. $50.00]. Previous report is substantially similar in format and content, but also includes data on manufacturing investment cyclical trends, capital goods/R&D spending, money supply, and Federal deficit; and omits data on GNP components and GDP.

Report for 1983 is described in SRI 1983 Annual under this number.

Availability: McGraw-Hill, Economics Department, 1221 Ave. of the Americas, 37th Floor, New York NY 10020, $50.00; SRI/MF/complete.

TABLES:

a. GNP average annual change, by major component, selected periods 1949-84, with alternative forecasts for 1984-95 period; and GDP by industry division, with detail by major manufacturing group, 1984-95. 2 tables. (p. 11, 22)

b. Detailed trends and forecasts: GNP, personal consumption expenditures, and nonresidential fixed investment, in current and constant 1972 dollars; GNP deflator; industrial production index; population; housing starts; and civilian employment; 1950, 1960, 1970-84, and alternative forecasts for 1985-95. 3 tables. (p. 26-31)

C5800–11 U.S. BUSINESS OUTLOOK, Short-Term

Quarterly. Approx. 15 p.
SRI/MF/complete

Quarterly analysis of factors affecting the general business climate, and expected performance of the economy over the next 4-6 quarters. Includes consumer spending, capital investment, and fiscal and monetary policy. Data are compiled by the McGraw-Hill Economics Dept, and are current to quarter ended 2 months prior to publication.

Contains narrative analysis, with text statistics and usually trend tables and charts on various aspects of the economy; and 1 table showing the following, for quarter of coverage and forecast for following 4-6 quarters, with annual summary:

a. National Product Accounts, including GNP, consumer spending, fixed investment, inventory change, government purchases, and net exports.

b. Key economic indicators, including housing starts, auto sales, unemployment rate, CPI, industrial production index, 90-day Treasury bill rate, corporate bond yield, and personal income.

Availability: McGraw-Hill, Economics Department, 1221 Ave. of the Americas, 37th Floor, New York NY 10020, $60.00 per yr.; SRI/MF/complete.

Issues reviewed during 1985: Nov. 1984-Aug. 1985 (P).

C5800–12 MODERN PLASTICS

Monthly.
ISSN 0026-8275.
LC 42-3582.
SRI/MF/not filmed

Monthly trade journal (2 issues in Oct.) reporting on developments and trends in plastics manufacturing, management, R&D, marketing, and consumption. Includes data on plastics production capacity, output, sales, and prices; and production in plastics-using industries. Data are from McGraw-Hill Economics Dept, petroleum and chemical companies, BLS, and other sources.

General format:

a. Monthly "Barometer" feature, with 1 table showing production trends in 9-10 major plastics end-use markets for month approximately 4 months prior to cover date, previous month, and same month of previous year; and 2 charts summarizing price and production trends for plastics; prior to the Jan. 1985 issue, feature presented forecast rather than actual data.

b. Regular editorial depts and feature articles, occasionally with substantial nontechnical statistics.

An annual *Modern Plastics Encyclopedia,* published as 2nd issue in Oct., contains material and process information, technical specifications, and a directory of suppliers.

Monthly "Barometer" feature appears in all issues except special encyclopedia issue. All additional features with substantial nontechnical statistical content are described, as they appear, under "Statistical Features." Nonstatistical contents are not covered.

Availability: Modern Plastics, Fulfillment Manager, PO Box 430, Hightstown NJ 08520, qualified subscribers $30.00 per yr., selected others $34.00 per yr., single copy $5.00, encyclopedia $36.95 (library edition); SRI/MF/not filmed.

Issues reviewed during 1985: Nov. 1984-Oct. 1985 (P) (Vol. 61, Nos. 11-12; Vol. 62, Nos. 1-10A).

STATISTICAL FEATURES:

C5800–12.601: Nov. 1984 (Vol. 61, No. 11)

WINDOW PROFILE SEMINAR CITES MARKET POTENTIAL

(p. 106-108) Article, with 1 undated table showing polyvinyl chloride (PVC) share of window production in 6 European countries or areas. Data are from Krauss Maffei.

C5800–12.602: Dec. 1984 (Vol. 61, No. 12)

COMPOUNDING TAKES OFF IN NEW DIRECTIONS

(p. 16, 20) Article, with 1 chart showing market growth of plastic compounds and all plastics, selected years 1979-88. Data are from R. M. Kossoff & Associates.

PACK EXPO '84 HERALDS A BIG YEAR FOR PLASTICS PACKAGING: 1985

(p. 92-94) Article, with 1 table showing market volume for 2 plastic materials (OPP and cellophane) used in packaging, selected years 1984-95. Data are from Mobil Chemical Films Division.

C5800–12.603: Jan. 1985 (Vol. 62, No. 1)

MATERIALS '85, ANNUAL FEATURE

(p. 49-71) Annual report, for 1985, on plastics industry technological and market developments, including data on sales, use, and prices, and U.S. and Canadian production capacity. Data were compiled by *Modern Plastics* from industry contacts and from Society of the Plastics Industry reports.

Contains introduction, and 8 narrative articles on market outlook of industry sectors; and industry statistics section (p. 61-71) presenting the following data on resins by type:

a. Sales summary, 1983-84; prices, 3rd quarter 1981-4th quarter 1984; and sales, by type of market (including exports), manufacturing process, and end use (including appliances, building materials, electrical/electronics, furniture, housewares, packaging, toys, and transportation), with various cross-tabulations, 1983-84. 40 tables. (p. 61-69)

b. Production capacity in U.S. and Canada, by company, as of Jan. 1, 1985, and planned additions for 1985/later; and Canadian domestic demand and foreign trade, 1983-84. 7 tables. (p. 70-71)

C5800–12.604: Feb. 1985 (Vol. 62, No. 2)

1984 WAS GREAT FOR ENGINEERING PLASTICS; 1985 WILL BE EVEN BETTER, ANNUAL FEATURE

(p. 12) Annual brief article, with 1 table showing U.S. and foreign consumption of engineering thermoplastics, by resin, 1984. Data are from Celanese Engineering Resins.

C5800–12.605: Apr. 1985 (Vol. 62, No. 4)

OIL-PRICE DROP, SUPERDOLLAR, KEEP RESIN COSTS DOWN, RECURRING FEATURE

(p. 18) Recurring table showing market price for crude oil and 10 resins and feedstocks, 4th quarter 1981-1st quarter 1985. Includes accompanying article (p. 18-20).

NEWEST PC SUPPLIER OFFERS MORE THAN 100 GRADES—PLUS COPOLYMERS

(p. 24) Brief article, with 1 table showing current and planned capacity of 3 polycarbonate producers, 1985 and 1988. Data are from industry estimates.

AUTOMATION: NOW IT'S FLEXIBLE AND AFFORDABLE, ANNUAL FEATURE

(p. 59-73) Annual report on recent developments in plastics processing equipment, 1983-84. Data are from industry estimates, *Modern Plastics* studies, Commerce Dept, and Society of the Plastics Industry.

Includes introduction and 5 articles, with 3 tables (p. 73) showing sales of machinery by type, and shipments of 2 types of machinery, with some detail for foreign trade, 1983-84.

C5800–12.606: May 1985 (Vol. 62, No. 5)

COMPOUNDERS EXPAND ROLE IN DEVELOPMENT OF NEW THERMOPLASTICS

(p. 66-69) By Roland R. MacBride. Article, with 1 undated table showing production capacity, plant location, and specialty, for 29 independent suppliers of hopper-ready thermoplastic compounds.

HOW TO CALCULATE THE ECONOMICS OF COMPOUNDING SYSTEMS

(p. 74-76) By Asmut Kahns. Article, with 2 undated tables showing typical capital investment and operating cost requirements for a plastics compounding system, and incidence of unscheduled shutdowns by system component.

BEAD MOLDERS OF ALL TYPES TAKE PART IN PUSH FOR NEW BUSINESS

(p. 84-87) By Robert Leaversuch. Article, with 2 tables showing expandable polystyrene (EPS) bead actual or planned capacity, for 12 U.S. and Canadian suppliers, as of early 1985; and Canadian EPS consumption by grade, 1984. Data are from EPS suppliers.

C5800–12.607: July 1985 (Vol. 62, No. 7)

COST OF POLYETHYLENE IS DOWN; HIKES ON OTHER RESINS EXPECTED TO HOLD, RECURRING FEATURE

(p. 12) Recurring table showing market price for crude oil and 10 resins and feedstocks, 1st quarter 1982-2nd quarter 1985. Includes accompanying article (p. 12-14).

FILLERS AND REINFORCEMENTS, ANNUAL FEATURE

(p. 47-55) Annual compilation of 3 articles on fillers and reinforcements used in the plastics industry. Data are from industry sources. In-

cludes 2 tables showing sales of fiber reinforcements by type; and consumption of extenders, enhancers, and nonfiber reinforcements, by type; various years 1983-86.

BLOW MOLDED ENGINEERING PLASTICS HOLD KEY TO MIDDLE VOLUME MARKETS

(p. 61-63) By George Smoluk. Article, with 1 undated table comparing cost of manufacturing a specified type of panel using steel and 4 plastic processes. Data are from General Electric Co.

C5800–12.608: Sept. 1985 (Vol. 62, No. 9)

TIGHT TITANIUM DIOXIDE SUPPLY KEEPS PRICES FIRM

(p. 20-22) Article, with 1 table showing the following for titanium dioxide: world capacity, utilization rate, and demand (with demand detail for U.S., Canada, and Western Europe), 1984 and 1986; and U.S. capacity and trade, 1984. Data are from Ampacet Corp.

CHEMICALS AND ADDITIVES, ANNUAL FEATURE

(p. 59-87) Annual feature on chemicals and additives used in the plastics industry. Includes 11 tables showing consumption of colorants, flame retardants, catalysts, stabilizers, lubricants, plasticizers, and 7 other product categories, by type or end use, primarily 1983-85.

C5800–12.609: Oct. 1985 (Vol. 62, No. 10)

STABILITY PERSISTS IN VOLUME RESIN COSTS, RECURRING FEATURE

(p. 20) Recurring table showing market price for crude oil and 10 resins and feedstocks, 2nd quarter 1982-3rd quarter 1985. Includes accompanying article (p. 20-22).

WHAT'S AT STAKE FOR USERS IN THE CHANGING PVC SUPPLY PICTURE

(p. 66-69) By Susan Avery. Article, with 2 tables showing polyvinyl chloride (PVC) resin production capacity by company (no date); and PVC effective capacity, imports, domestic sales, and utilization rates, 1984-88. Data are from *Modern Plastics* interviews with major PVC suppliers.

IMPORTS: TOUGH PROBLEM FOR U.S. PROCESSORS

(p. 70-72) By Robert Leaversuch. Article, with 2 tables showing imports of selected plastics and plastic-containing products, 1983-85, with major supplying countries and estimated domestic business lost. Data are from Commerce Dept, Data Resources Inc., and other sources.

C5800–13 TEXTILE WORLD
Monthly.
ISSN 0040-5213.
LC 8-32834.
SRI/MF/not filmed

Monthly trade journal reporting on trends and developments in the textile industry. Covers yarn manufacturing, fabric formation, chemical treatment and finishing, management, marketing, and other topics of interest to the textile industry. Month of data coverage is 1-3 months prior to cover date.

Issues generally contain feature articles, occasionally with statistics; and regular editorial depts, including the following monthly statistical features:

a. "Activity Indicators," with 1 trend chart, and 1 table showing index of textile manufacturing activity for month of coverage, with estimates for 2-3 subsequent months and comparisons to prior periods; and 1 "Figures of the Month" table, showing 22-24 textile industry indicator indexes or amounts, including employment, earnings, hours worked, PPI, sales, inventories, operating rate, shipments, and trade, and selected national economic indicators, for month of coverage, previous month, and same month of previous year.

b. "Market Outlook," with narrative analysis, 1 trend chart, and 1 table showing textile mill products price index for month of coverage, with estimates for subsequent month and comparisons to prior periods.

Other statistical features include a quarterly table on sales and earnings of selected textile companies; a quarterly feature on industry financial ratios; and annual reports on industry trends and outlook, carpet manufacturers, and financial performance of leading firms. An annual buyer's guide appears in the July issue.

"Activity Indicators" and "Market Outlook" appear in all issues. All additional features with substantial statistical content are described, as they appear, under "Statistical Features." Nonstatistical features are not covered.

Availability: Textile World, Circulation Department, PO Box 523, Hightstown, NJ 08520, qualified subscribers †, textile students $18.00 per yr., others $36.00 per yr., single copy $11.00, Buyer's Guide $15.00; SRI/MF/not filmed.

Issues reviewed during 1985: Nov. 1984-Oct. 1985 (P) (Vol. 134, Nos. 11-12; Vol. 135, Nos. 1-10).

STATISTICAL FEATURES:

C5800–13.601: Nov. 1984 (Vol. 134, No. 11)

QUARTERLY TABLE

(p. 27) Sales and earnings for 13 textile companies, for various quarter-ending dates Aug. 4, 1984-Sept. 30, 1984.

C5800–13.602: Dec. 1984 (Vol. 134, No. 12)

MESSAGE TO THROWSTERS: THINK INDUSTRIAL FABRICS

(p. 73) Article, with 1 table showing textile fiber consumption by industrial end use, 1982 and 1992. Data are from Textile Economics Bureau and Celanese Corp.

C5800–13.603: Jan. 1985 (Vol. 135, No. 1)

BALANCE SHEET RATIOS OF U.S. TEXTILE COMPANIES, QUARTERLY FEATURE

(p. 32) Quarterly article analyzing textile industry financial trends. Data are from Census Bureau. Includes 1 table showing textile industry selected financial ratios, 3rd quarter 1983, and 2nd-3rd quarters 1984.

U.S. TEXTILE ECONOMY FOR 1985: A LOT OF 'IFS', ANNUAL FEATURE

(p. 42-53) Annual report on textile industry trends and outlook, 1980-85.

Covers mill fiber consumption, by fiber type; production indexes; employment, hours, and earnings, with selected detail by type of mill;

expenditures for pollution control, employee health/safety, and R&D; foreign trade; mill inventory value, inventory/sales ratio, and operating rate; and WPI, by textile category.

Also includes apparel and nondurable goods retail sales, disposable personal income, housing starts, and new car sales.

Data are from a McGraw-Hill Dept of Economics/Data Resources Inc. survey, Federal sources, and American Textile Manufactures Institute.

Contains narrative analysis, with 4 illustrative charts and 24 tables.

GERMAN TEXTILE MACHINERY: WORLD VOLUME LEADER

(p. 55-70) Article, with 3 tables showing the following for German textile machinery equipment: export value, with detail for shipments to Canada and U.S., by product type; and market share for industrialized and developing countries and for State trading companies; various periods 1982-84.

Data are from the Fachgemeinschaft Textilmaschinen (VDMA).

EUROPEAN FINISHERS LEARN U.S. TECHNIQUES

(p. 79-80) Article, with 1 undated table showing government regulations regarding concentration of formaldehyde in the workplace, for U.S., Denmark, Germany, and USSR, with proposed revision for U.S. levels. Data are from Sun Chemical Corp.

C5800–13.604: Mar. 1985 (Vol. 135, No. 3)

QUARTERLY TABLE

(p. 28) Sales and earnings for 14 textile companies, for various quarter-ending dates Nov. 3, 1984-Dec. 31, 1984.

C5800–13.605: Apr. 1985 (Vol. 135, No. 4)

RETAILERS PICK AMERICAN GOODS, IF PRICE IS RIGHT

(p. 29) Article, with 1 table showing factors that would induce retail merchants to buy U.S.-manufactured products. Data are from a Jan. 1985 survey of 116 members of the National Retail Merchants Assn, conducted by Carl Byoir and Associates for Crafted with Pride in U.S.A. Council.

C5800–13.606: May 1985 (Vol. 135, No. 5)

BALANCE SHEET RATIOS OF U.S. TEXTILE COMPANIES, QUARTERLY FEATURE

(p. 32) Quarterly article analyzing textile industry financial trends. Data are from Census Bureau. Includes 1 table showing textile industry selected financial ratios, 4th quarter 1983, and 3rd-4th quarters 1984.

SALES AND MERCHANDISING: NEXT CARPET GROWTH AREA, ANNUAL FEATURE

(p. 37-38) Annual article, by Frank C. Wilson, describing characteristics of successful carpet manufacturing firms, with outlook for 1986. Data are from Commerce Dept and International Management. Includes 1 table showing industry shipments by carpet type, 1980-86 with quarterly detail for 1984.

C5800–13.607: June 1985 (Vol. 135, No. 6)

INVENTORIES BLOCK INDUSTRY'S GROWTH, ANNUAL FEATURE

(p. 23-27) Annual article on textile manufacturers' financial performance, 1984. Data are from Kurt Salmon Associates 14th annual performance profile of textile companies.

Includes 2 tables showing top 12 textile companies ranked by return on total equity and net aftertax income on sales, 1984, with 1984 sales and comparative 1983 rankings.

For description of Salmon Associates profile, see B8130-1.

C5800–13.608: Aug. 1985 (Vol. 135, No. 8)

BALANCE SHEET RATIOS OF U.S. TEXTILE COMPANIES, QUARTERLY FEATURE

(p. 32) Quarterly article analyzing textile industry financial trends. Data are from Census Bureau. Includes 1 table showing textile industry selected financial ratios, 1st quarter 1983, and 1st and 4th quarters 1984.

HOW CARPET PLANTS CAN CUT SAMPLING COSTS

(p. 49-50) Article, with 1 table showing number of weaving machines in operation, by type, worldwide and for U.S., 1984. Data are from Adolph Saurer, Ltd.

C5800–13.609: Oct. 1985 (Vol. 135, No. 10)

BALANCE SHEET RATIOS OF U.S. TEXTILE COMPANIES, QUARTERLY FEATURE

(p. 32) Quarterly article analyzing textile industry financial trends. Data are from Census Bureau. Includes 1 table showing textile industry selected financial ratios, 2nd quarter 1984, and 1st-2nd quarters 1985.

C5800–14   ELECTRONICS

Weekly.
ISSN 0748-3252.
LC 36-15816.
SRI/MF/not filmed

Weekly journal reporting trends and developments in the U.S. and international electronics industry. Covers R&D, technology, new products, marketing, and business activity. Includes data on general economy, and electronics shipments, employment, PPI, and trade. Data are from reports of Federal agencies, McGraw-Hill Economics Dept, and other private sources.

Issues generally contain numerous articles, occasionally with statistics; and regular editorial features, including a weekly business activity section, with 1 weekly table showing electronics industry composite index current to cover date, and 7 monthly tables presenting general economic and electronics industry data current to 2-3 months prior to cover date month. Weekly and monthly tables are listed below.

An annual forecast of worldwide electronics markets appears in a Jan. issue.

Prior to June 17, 1985 issue, journal title was *Electronics Week*.

Weekly table appears in all issues. Each monthly table generally appears in 1 issue each month; sequence of appearance varies. All additional features with substantial statistical content are described, as they appear, under "Statistical Features." Nonstatistical features are not covered.

Availability: Electronics, Circulation Manager, CN 807, Martinsville NJ 08836, industry individuals $32.00 per yr., industry companies $40.00 per yr., single copy $3.00, nonindustry rates available on request; SRI/MF/not filmed.

Issues reviewed during 1985: Nov. 5, 1984-Oct. 28, 1985 (Vol. 57, Nos. 30-36; Vol. 58, Nos. 1-43) [No issues were published for the last 2 weeks of Dec. 1984 and for Jan. 28, 1985].

TABLES:

WEEKLY TABLE

[1] *Electronics Week* index [electronics industry composite index (1982=base year), generally for week of publication, previous week, and same week of preceding year].

MONTHLY TABLES

[Table format may vary. Data are shown for month of coverage, previous month, and same month of preceding year.]

[1] Electronics production index [for 5 electronics sectors].

[2-3] Electronics industry shipments [and production workers, for 4 sectors].

[4] General economic indicators [index of leading indicators, Federal budgeted outlays (total and DOD), industry operating rate and production index, and housing starts].

[5] Electronics imports and exports [for 8 product categories].

[6] Electronic components PPI [for 7 components].

[7] General economic indicators [prime rate, retail sales, and unemployment rate].

STATISTICAL FEATURES:

C5800–14.601: Nov. 12, 1984 (Vol. 57, No. 31)

SPERRY MAPS PUSH INTO AI

(p. 34-36) Article, with 1 table showing value of artificial intelligence market, by product segment, 1983, 1987, and 1990.

C5800–14.602: Nov. 26, 1984 (Vol. 57, No. 33)

CMOS MEMORIES REPLACING n-MOS IN MEGABIT STORAGE CHIPS

(p. 53-61) By Bernard Conrad Cole. Article comparing memory market outlook for complimentary metal oxide semiconductors (CMOS) and metal oxide semiconductors (MOS). Data are from Montgomery Securities. Includes 1 table on CMOS specifications; and 1 table showing value of MOS memory market, by memory type, 1979, 1984, and 1989.

C5800–14.603: Dec. 10, 1984 (Vol. 57, No. 35)

PROTOCOL-STANDARDS FIGHT WILL BE WON IN THE MARKET

(p. 25) Article, with 1 table showing market value for local loop data-communication system, by transmission rate, 1983-89. Data are from LINK Resources Corp.

C5800–14.604: Jan. 1, 1985 (Vol. 58, No. 1)

BRIGHT GAINS IN 1985 FOR MAJOR MARKETS, ANNUAL FEATURE

(p. 61-82) Annual compilation of articles on electronics industry market conditions and outlook worldwide and for U.S., Europe, and Japan. Data are based on an annual *Electronics Week* survey and other industry sources.

Includes 1 chart and 8 tables showing the following data, generally as dollar values, for various years 1983-90:

a. Worldwide: production of electronic equipment, by region; semiconductor market, total and for selected devices; top 10 semiconductor companies ranked by production, and including headquarters location; and share of semiconductor consumption, for U.S., Japan, Europe, and all others.

b. By country: U.S. data processing equipment market, and U.S. and Japanese communications equipment market, by equipment category; and 5 European countries with largest communications equipment markets.

C5800–14.605: Jan. 7, 1985 (Vol. 58, No. 2)

FOR EUROPE, YEAR LOOKS FLAT

(p. 28-29) By John Gosch et al. Article, with 2 tables showing Western European unit sales of color TV sets and videocassette recorders, for 5 individual countries and all others, 1983-85. Data are from Grundig AG.

C5800–14.606: Jan. 14, 1985 (Vol. 58, No. 3)

DRAM MAKERS GIRD FOR 256-K

(p. 13-17) By J. Robert Lineback. Article, with 1 table showing worldwide shipment value for dynamic random-access memory chips, by memory size, 1983-85. Data are from Integrated Circuit Engineering Corp.

C5800–14.607: Feb. 4, 1985 (Vol. 58, No. 5)

DOD VEXES IC MAKERS

(p. 63-68) By Ed Macaruso. Article, with 1 table showing DOD expenditures for all electronics and for microcircuits, 1984-88. Data are from Electronic Industries Assn.

C5800–14.608: Feb. 11, 1985 (Vol. 58, No. 6)

BUDGET BOUQUET FOR ELECTRONICS

(p. 30-32) By Alexander Wolfe. Article, with 1 table showing Air Force, Navy, and Army procurement funds for aircraft and/or missiles, by model, actual FY85 and requested FY85-86. Data are from DOD.

C5800–14.609: Feb. 25, 1985 (Vol. 58, No. 8)

DOD SPENDING SPURS MARKET

(p. 55-58) By Mark T. Spence. Article, with 2 tables and 1 chart showing value of electronic equipment production by end-use application, with detail for defense-oriented passive and active components by type; and distribution of defense consumption of components, by type; various years 1983-88.

C5800–14.610: Mar. 18, 1985 (Vol. 58, No. 11)

QUIET PRINT INVADES OFFICE

(p. 59-63) By Robert Rosenberg. Article, with 1 chart showing market revenue for electronic nonimpact printers, 1983, 1985, and 1988. Data are from C. A. Pesko Associates.

C5800–14.611: Apr. 1, 1985 (Vol. 58, No. 13)

STRATEGIC C3, MORE IS LESS

(p. 18-21) By Alexander Wolfe. Article, with 1 table showing estimated budget for selected programs of the military's strategic command/control/communications system, with some detail by service branch, 1985-87. Data are from Frost and Sullivan, Inc.

C5800–14.612: Apr. 8, 1985 (Vol. 58, No. 14)

COMPONENTS FOR SMA ARRIVE

(p. 49-53) By Jerry Lyman. Article, with 1 table showing number of electronic components available in surface-mounted form, by component type, 1984-85. Data are from Don Brown Associates, Inc.

C5800–14.613: Apr. 15, 1985 (Vol. 58, No. 15)

KOREANS TRY FOR VCR REPLAY

(p. 22-23) By Michael Berger. Article, with 1 table showing value of videocassette recorder market, for U.S., Japan, and all others, 1983-86. Data are from Prudential-Bache Far East Research.

C5800–14.614: Apr. 22, 1985 (Vol. 58, No. 16)

N.Y. TRISTATE REGION MAKES BID TO BECOME TOP ELECTRONICS CENTER

(p. 31-32) By George Leopold. Article, with 1 undated chart showing top 4 States ranked by number of electronics/information technology companies. Data are from a recent American Electronics Assn survey.

C5800–14.615: Apr. 29, 1985 (Vol. 58, No. 17)

GAME STILL ISN'T OVER

(p. 50-55) Article, with 1 table showing value of U.S.-Japan trade in electronic-based products, by type, 1980-84. Data are from Commerce Dept.

C5800–14.616: May 6, 1985 (Vol. 58, No. 18)

ASIA: THE FOUR DRAGONS RUSH TO PLAY CATCH-UP GAME

(p. 48-56) By Karen Berney. Article, with 5 tables showing value of production and exports, for South Korea's electronics industry, 1981-86; and value of trade in electronic products by major category, between U.S. and South Korea, Singapore, Taiwan, and Hong Kong, 1980-84. Data are from Electronics Industries Assn of Korea and Commerce Dept.

C5800–14.617: May 13, 1985 (Vol. 58, No. 19)

STAR WARS IS THE FORCE DRIVING WEAPONS RESEARCH

(p. 28-32) By Alexander Wolfe. Article, with 1 table showing Federal budget for Strategic Defense Initiative, by function, allocated FY85, and proposed FY86. Data are from DOD.

FIELD SERVICE BOOMS DESPITE SHORTAGE OF TECHNICIANS

(p. 54-58) By Howard Bierman. Article, with 1 chart showing value of electronic product service market, by category (information processing, telecommunications, and diverse applications), 1983 and 1990. Data are from Arthur Andersen and Co.

C5800–14.618: May 20, 1985 (Vol. 58, No. 20)

SLUMP STILL PLAGUES U.S. SEMICONDUCTOR MARKET

(p. 18-19) Article, with 1 chart showing ratio of semiconductor orders to billings, aggregated for U.S., Japan, and Europe, Apr. 1984-Apr. 1985. Data are from Semiconductor Industry Assn.

SALES TO CHINA ARE A BRIGHT SPOT FOR COMPUTER BUSINESS

(p. 32-34) By Robert Rosenberg. Article, with 1 chart showing value of U.S. electronics exports to PRC, by major category, 1983-85.

ACQUISITIONS BOLSTER LORAL'S TECHNICAL BASE

(p. 46-47) Article, with 1 table showing military expenditures for research/development/testing/evaluation and procurement of electronic weapons systems, by service branch, FY83-88. Data are from Frost and Sullivan, Inc.

C5800–14.619: May 27, 1985 (Vol. 58, No. 21)

NEW HIGH-SPEED CMOS CHIPS VIE WITH FAST TTL

(p. 19-20) Article, with 1 table showing sales of standard-logic integrated circuits, by type, 1983, 1985, and 1989. Data are from Dataquest, Inc.

AT&T PACT COULD SIGNAL SURGE IN CORPORATE BYPASS

(p. 35-36) By George Leopold. Article, with 1 chart showing telephone company revenue losses resulting from consumer use of long-distance services that bypass local exchanges, by type of service (microwave radio, satellite, digital termination, and other), 1984-85 and 1989. Data are from Dataquest, Inc.

SOUTH KOREAN IC MAKER SEEKS WORLD MARKETS

(p. 46-47) Article, with 1 table showing value of worldwide and South Korean integrated circuit production, 1984-88. Data are from Dataquest, Inc.

ENDING FOURTH DECADE, CHIP MAKERS FACE DOUBT AND UPHEAVAL

(p. 50-55) By J. Robert Lineback. Article, with 1 chart and 2 tables showing number of semiconductor memory bits for personal, mini, and mainframe computers; sales of nonstandard integrated circuits, by type; and summary data on specifications and cost of memory chips; various years 1980-95. Data sources include Texas Instruments, Inc. and Integrated Circuit Engineering Corp.

C5800–14.620: June 3, 1985 (Vol. 58, No. 22)

CROWD OF HOPEFULS WARMS UP FOR 32-BIT MICROPROCESSOR RACE

(p. 50-55) By Bernard Conrad Cole. Article, with 1 chart showing 32-bit microcomputer market shares by application, 1985 and 1990. Data are from Dataquest, Inc.

C5800–14.621: June 10, 1985 (Vol. 58, No. 23)

APPLE TRIES AGAIN TO BLAST OFF IN JAPAN

(p. 34-35) Article, with 1 table showing computer shipments in Japan, for top 7 companies and all others, 1983-84. Data are from Dataquest Japan, Ltd.

C5800–14.622: June 24, 1985 (Vol. 58, No. 25)

BATTERED INDUSTRY LOOKS TO 1986 FOR SIGNS OF AN UPTURN

(p. 32-37) Compilation of articles, with 3 charts and 2 tables showing worldwide sales of semiconductors by type; U.S. production value of passive components; and U.S. sales of data processing systems, for single-user and by price range; 1984 (actual) and 1985 (Jan. and June forecasts). Data are from *Electronics* and Dataquest, Inc.

C5800–14.623: July 8, 1985 (Vol. 58, No. 27)

IBM GETS A PARTNER AND UNLOADS A PROBLEM WITH MCI DEAL

(p. 24-25) By Robert J. Kozma. Article, with 1 undated chart showing long-distance telephone service market shares for 3 telecommunications companies and all others. Data are from Northern Business Information Inc.

C5800–14.624: July 15, 1985 (Vol. 58, No. 28)

GAO RAPS PENTAGON ON VHSIC SPENDING

(p. 18, 22) Article, with 1 table showing DOD expenditures for the VHSIC (very high-speed integrated circuits) program, by category, 1981 and FY85 (approved and revised estimate). Data are from a May 1985 General Accounting Office report.

CAN U.S. CHIP MAKERS SUCCEED IN THE JAPANESE MARKETPLACE?

(p. 30-33) By Michael Berger. Article, with 1 chart showing U.S. surplus or deficit in integrated circuits trade with Japan, 1975-84. Data are from Japanese Finance Ministry.

C5800–14.625: July 22, 1985 (Vol. 58, No. 29)

GAME COULD BE OVER IN JAPAN MARKET FOR U.S. CHIP-EQUIPMENT MAKERS

(p. 26-27) By Michael Berger. Article, with 1 table showing the following for the integrated circuit equipment market in Japan: projected market value, 1986; and market shares by company, 1984; all by type of equipment. Data are from Nomura Research Institute.

CHIP BUSINESS THAT IS STILL GROWING

(p. 40-45) By Bernard Conrad Cole. Article, with 1 chart showing worldwide market value for application-specific integrated circuits, by type, 1980 and 1990. Data are from Dataquest, Inc.

C5800–14.626: July 29, 1985 (Vol. 58, No. 30)

IBM's ENTRY INTO CAE WORRIES RIVALS

(p. 53-54) Article, with 1 table showing top 12 vendors of computer-aided engineering systems, ranked by revenues, 1984 with comparisons to 1983. Data are from Daratech, Inc.

C5800–14.627: Aug. 19, 1985 (Vol. 58, No. 33)

JAPANESE CLAIM U.S. GETS FAIR SHAKE IN IC MARKET

(p. 15-16) Article, with 1 table comparing U.S. industry assn and Japanese Government data for 1984 on integrated circuit market size in Japan and U.S., and each country's market share. Table also includes Japanese data on integrated circuit bilateral trade and sales, for Japan and U.S. Data are from Semiconductor Industry Assn and Japanese Ministry of International Trade and Industry.

APPLIED DATA RESEARCH UPGRADES ITS MARKETING

(p. 22-23) Article, with 1 chart showing data base software market shares, for 3 major vendors and all others, with detail by software type for 1 vendor, 1983-84. Data are from International Data Corp.

C5800–14.628: Sept. 2, 1985 (Vol. 58, No. 35)

OPTICAL FIBER MAKES MOVE IN DATA COMMUNICATIONS

(p. 30-31) By J. Robert Lineback. Article, with 1 table showing fiber-optics sales, by user category, 1985 and 1990. Data are from Electronicast Corp.

C5800–14.629: Sept. 9, 1985 (Vol. 58, No. 36)

FAST SRAMs POINT WAY TO IMPROVED PROCESSES

(p. 16-17) Article, with 1 table showing sales and average selling price, for static and dynamic random-access memories (with sales detail for CMOS and n-MOS static memories), selected years 1980-90. Data are from Dataquest, Inc.

C5800–14.630: Sept. 23, 1985 (Vol. 58, No. 38)

WHY THE OUTLOOK IS DIMMING FOR U.S.-MADE SOLAR CELLS

(p. 32-33) By Karen Berney. Article, with 1 table projecting the following with and without repeal of energy tax credits: shipments of photovoltaic modules used in solar energy systems, by application, 1990 and 1995. Data are from Photovoltaics Energy Systems Inc.

JAPANESE PARTNER IS TOP PRIORITY FOR ATEQ

(p. 40-41) Article, with 1 chart showing semiconductor-processing equipment market value, and shares for U.S., Japan, and rest of world, 1984-85. Data are from VLSI Research Inc.

C5800–14.631: Sept. 30, 1985 (Vol. 58, No. 39)

AUSTRALIA'S MAJOR DOUBTS OVER ITS HIGH-TECH PROWESS

(p. 36-37) By Craig Addison. Article, with 1 table showing top 15 computer manufacturers ranked by value of market share in Australia, 1984, with forecasts for 1985. Data are from International Data Corp. Australia.

C5800–14.632: Oct. 7, 1985 (Vol. 58, No. 40)

TOSHIBA SET TO ENTER POWER MOS FET MARKET

(p. 15-16) Article, with 1 chart showing world market shares for power MOS FETs (metal oxide semiconductor field effect transistors), for 6 suppliers and all others, 1984. Data are from Integrated Circuit Engineering Corp.

C5800–14.633: Oct. 14, 1985 (Vol. 58, No. 41)

HP TRIES TO GET ITS CAE ACT TOGETHER

(p. 40-41) By Eve Bennett. Article, with 1 table showing top 10 vendors of computer-aided design/engineering/manufacturing systems, ranked by worldwide revenues (with detail by system application), 1984. Data are from International Data Corp.

C5800–14.634: Oct. 21, 1985 (Vol. 58, No. 42)

BIG BUCKS IN SDI ARE GETTING SMALLER

(p. 45-46) By Larry Waller. Article, with 1 chart showing distribution of Strategic Defense Initiative spending by program category, 1985-89 period. Data are from Electronic Industries Assn.

C5800–15   ARCHITECTURAL RECORD
Monthly. Oversized.
ISSN 0003-858X.
LC 12-17303.
SRI/MF/not filmed

Monthly publication (semimonthly in Apr. and Sept.) reporting developments in the architectural field, including building design and technology, new projects, and finances.

Contains narrative editorial depts and articles, occasionally with statistics; and recurring statistical features, including annual construction economy outlook (Nov. issue) with 2 updates (Apr. and Sept. issues), and quarterly metro area building cost indexes. Recurring statistical features present data derived from McGraw-Hill Information Systems Co. reports.

All features with substantial statistical content are described, as they appear, under "Statistical Features." Each issue of the journal is reviewed, but an abstract is published in SRI monthly issues only when quarterly or other statistical features appear.

Availability: Architectural Record, Subscription Department, PO Box 2023, Mahopac NY 10541, $35.00 per yr., single copy $6.00; SRI/MF/not filmed.

Issues reviewed during 1985: Nov. 1984-Oct. 1985 (P) (Vol. 172, Nos. 13-14; Vol. 173, Nos. 1-12).

STATISTICAL FEATURES:

C5800–15.601: Nov. 1984 (Vol. 172, No. 13)

DODGE/SWEET'S 1985 CONSTRUCTION OUTLOOK: THE BUILDING CYCLE FACES MID-LIFE CRISIS, ANNUAL FEATURE

(p. 37-45) Annual article on construction activity, 1984, with forecasts for 1985. Includes 2 tables showing residential and nonresidential building construction contract value and floor area, new dwelling units, and nonbuilding contract value, all by construction type, with contract value detail by region, and total contract value index; 1984-85.

COSTS: IN THIS BEST OF ALL WORLDS, WE HAVE STABILITY EVEN WHILE HAVING PROSPERITY, QUARTERLY FEATURE

(p. 49) Quarterly article on metro area building cost indexes, 1977-84. Includes 2 tables showing number of metro areas and percent increase in construction costs, by region, for 1977-July 1984 period and 3- and 12-month periods ending July 1984; and average nonresidential construction cost indexes for 21 MSAs, 1977-82, and 1st quarter 1983-2nd quarter 1984.

An explanation of methodology used to develop indexes appeared in the Jan. 1984 issue; for description, see SRI 1984 Annual, under C5800-15.502.

C5800–15.602: Feb. 1985 (Vol. 173, No. 2)

COSTS: CAN IT BE THAT STABILITY IS STABLE? BEST OF ALL WORLDS CONTINUES, QUARTERLY FEATURE

(p. 45) Quarterly article on metro area building cost indexes, 1977-84. Includes 2 tables showing number of metro areas and percent increase in construction costs, by region, for 1977-Oct. 1984 period and 3- and 12-month periods ending Oct. 1984; and average nonresidential construction cost indexes for 21 MSAs, 1977-82, and 1st quarter 1983-3rd quarter 1984.

An explanation of methodology used to develop indexes appeared in the Jan. 1984 issue; for description, see SRI 1984 Annual, under C5800-15.502.

C5800–15.603: Apr. 1985 (Vol. 173, No. 4)

CONSTRUCTION ECONOMY UPDATE: THE VOLUME IS REACHING FOR ITS PEAK, ANNUAL FEATURE

(p. 35-39) Annual article, by George A. Christie, on construction activity, 1984, with forecasts for 1985. Includes 2 tables showing residential and nonresidential building construction contract value and floor area, new dwelling units, and nonbuilding contract value, all by construction type, with contract value detail by region, and total contract value index; 1984-85, updated as of Mar. 1985.

Article updates annual Dodge/Sweet's construction outlook. For description, see C5800-15.601 above.

C5800–15.604: Mid-Apr. 1985 (Vol. 173, No. 5)

COSTS: YES, STABILITY CONTINUES TO BE STABLE, BUT WATCH OUT FOR LABOR, QUARTERLY FEATURE

(p. 37) Quarterly article on metro area building cost indexes, 1977-84. Includes 2 tables showing number of metro areas and percent increase in construction costs, by region, for 1977-Jan. 1985 period and 3- and 12-month periods ending Jan. 1985; and average nonresidential construction cost indexes for 21 MSAs, 1977-82, and quarterly 1983-84.

An explanation of methodology used to develop indexes appeared in the Jan. 1984 issue; for description, see SRI 1984 Annual under C5800-15.502.

C5800–15.605: May 1985 (Vol. 173, No. 6)

COMPUTERS: WHERE ARE WE AND WHERE ARE WE GOING ON PCs?

(p. 47-49) By Eric Teicholz and Dan Smith. Article, with 1 table showing shipments of personal computers with computer-aided design/drafting capabilities, cumulatively and annually 1983-88. Data are from Dataquest, Inc.

C5800–15.606: June 1985 (Vol. 173, No. 7)

HOW ARE FIRMS WITH COMPUTERS FARING, AND WHAT ARE THE NONUSERS WAITING FOR?

(p. 37-41) Article on computer use by architecture firms. Data are based on a recent *Architectural Record* reader survey, which drew responses from 376 firms using and 148 firms not using computers.

Presents text data on characteristics of user vs. nonuser firms; nonusers' reasons for not investing in a computer system; characteristics of users' systems, including year of 1st investment, startup experiences, system expansion, applications, cost, hardware and software vendors, and benefits; and other survey findings.

C5800–15.607: July 1985 (Vol. 173, No. 8)

COSTS: ONCE AGAIN, STEADY ON, QUARTERLY FEATURE

(p. 49) Quarterly article on metro area building cost indexes, 1977-85. Includes 2 tables showing number of metro areas and percent increase in construction costs, by region, for 1977-Apr. 1985 period and 3- and 12-month periods ending Apr. 1985; and average nonresidential construction cost indexes for 21 MSAs, 1977-83, and 1st quarter 1984-1st quarter 1985.

An explanation of methodology used to develop indexes appeared in the Jan. 1984 issue; for description, see SRI 1984 Annual under C5800-15.502.

C5800–15.608: Sept. 1985 (Vol. 173, No. 10)

CONSTRUCTION ECONOMY UPDATE: THE VOLUME CYCLE GETS UNEXPECTED LIFE, ANNUAL FEATURE

(p. 27-31) Annual article, by George A. Christie, on construction activity, 1984, with forecasts for 1985. Includes 2 tables showing residential and nonresidential building construction contract value and floor area, new dwelling units, and nonbuilding contract value, all by construction type, with contract value detail by region, and total contract value index; 1984-85, updated as of July 1985.

Article updates annual Dodge/Sweet's construction outlook. For description, see C5800-15.601 above.

C5800–15.609: Oct. 1985 (Vol. 173, No. 12)

COSTS: STEADY PROSPECTS FOR THE REST OF '85, QUARTERLY FEATURE

(p. 39) Quarterly article on metro area building cost indexes, 1977-85. Includes 2 tables showing number of metro areas and percent increase in construction costs, by region, for 1977-July 1985 period and 3- and 12-month periods ending July 1985; and average nonresidential construction cost indexes for 21 MSAs, 1977-83, and 1st quarter 1984-2nd quarter 1985.

An explanation of methodology used to develop indexes appeared in the Jan. 1984 issue; for description, see SRI 1984 Annual under C5800-15.502.

C5800–16   ENGINEERING AND MINING JOURNAL
Monthly.
ISSN 0095-8948.
LC 21-7292.
SRI/MF/not filmed

Monthly publication reporting on worldwide exploration, mining, milling, smelting, refining, and processing of metals and nonmetallic minerals, except coal, oil, and stone.

Contents:

a. Feature articles and news briefs, occasionally with statistics.

b. Regular editorial depts, including "Markets" monthly feature presenting price quotations for selected metals, ores, concentrates, ferroalloys, and nonmetallic minerals, for month prior to cover date, based on data from *Metals Week,* Handy & Harman, London Metal Exchange, and other sources.

Annual features include surveys of international mine and plant expansions, and mineral commodities outlook; and a nonstatistical buyer's guide.

Monthly "Markets" feature appears in most issues. All additional features with substantial statistical content are described, as they appear, under "Statistical Features." Nonstatistical contents are not covered.

Availability: Engineering and Mining Journal, Fulfillment Manager, PO Box 1516, Neptune NJ 07753, industry subscribers $20.00 per yr., others $38.00, single copy $3.50, Sept. issue (Buyers Guide) $5.50; SRI/MF/not filmed.

Issues reviewed during 1985: Nov. 1984-Sept. 1985 (P) (Vol. 185, Nos. 11-12; Vol. 186, Nos. 1-9).

STATISTICAL FEATURES:

C5800–16.601: Jan. 1985 (Vol. 186, No. 1)

MINING INVESTMENT 1985, ANNUAL FEATURE

(p. 25-42) Annual E&MJ international survey of plans for new and expanded mines and plants through the early 1990s. Includes brief narrative and the following:

a. Table showing mineral industry capital investment plans (number of projects and amount of investment) for 6 metals by world area, and totals for 15 other metals and nonmetals. (p. 25)

b. Tabular list of projects arranged by metal or nonmetallic mineral, and country or world area, showing the following data by company or operator: location, type of project, planned and/or current capacity, investment, starting year, stage of project development, and notes on special features. (p. 26-42)

C5800–16.602: Feb. 1985 (Vol. 186, No. 2)

GOLD DEBATE: DIFFERING VIEWS OF COSTS RELATED TO GOLD MINES IN NORTH AMERICA

(p. 50-51) Two letters to the editor, discussing an article on gold discovery costs in U.S. and Canada. Includes 1 table showing gold reserves, grade, contained gold, and discovery date, for 5 currently producing Canadian gold mines discovered during 1960s and 1970s.

Original article appeared in the Oct. 1984 issue of *Engineering and Mining Journal;* for description, see SRI 1984 Annual under C5800-16.510.

C5800–16.603: Mar. 1985 (Vol. 186, No. 3)

116th ANNUAL SURVEY AND OUTLOOK FOR WORLD MINERAL COMMODITIES

(p. 33-130) Annual survey, for 1984, of metals prices and U.S. and worldwide supply and demand situation and outlook for 42 metals and nonmetallic minerals. Data are derived from *Metals Week* price quotations, and Government and industry sources.

Contents:

a. Average annual prices of 16 major, minor, and precious metals, ferroalloys, and light metals, by trading exchange, 1983, and 1984 high and low; and average prices for 5 major metals, silver, and mercury, weekly 1984, and annually 1925-84. 3 tables. (p. 33-37)

b. Market analyses, including short-term outlook for 42 metals and nonmetallic minerals, generally presenting the following for each: text statistics and 1-6 tables showing supply and demand, for U.S., and worldwide by country or area; and, for some commodities, prices and foreign trade; 1984, with selected forecasts and trends, 1977-90. (p. 38-130)

C5800–16.604: Apr. 1985 (Vol. 186, No. 4)

INDIA'S NALCO READIES NEW BAUXITE MINE AND ALUMINA REFINERY

(p. 52-57) By N. K. Choudhary. Article, with 1 undated table showing Indian bauxite reserves (measured, indicated, and inferred), for 13 Indian States.

Also includes 3 technical tables presenting data on operations and aluminum ore assays of India's National Aluminium Co., Ltd.

C5800–16.605: May 1985 (Vol. 186, No. 5)

NEW AND RECENTLY OPENED MINES FUEL AUSTRALIAN GOLD BOOM

(p. 11-13) Article, with 1 table showing location, production status, gold reserves and production, and other operating data, for Australian gold mines opened during 1984-Apr. 1985 or scheduled to open by mid-1985. Data are from Australian Bureau of Mineral Resources.

MARKETING COGENERATED SMELTER ACID

(p. 31-33) Article, with 1 table showing acidic sulfur dioxide emissions, by source, for U.S. and Canada, 1975.

C5800–16.606: July 1985 (Vol. 186, No. 7)

INCRA PLANS A GLOBAL STRATEGY FOR COPPER

(p. 18) By Joan C. Todd. Article, with 1 table showing copper consumption in Japan/U.S./Western Europe, by end-use sector, selected years 1964-90. Data are from International Copper Research Assn and Brook Hunts and Associates, Ltd.

C5800–16.607: Sept. 1985 (Vol. 186, No. 9)

FMC's TRONA MINING PROFILE

(p. 31-35) Article, with 1 table showing soda ash production capacity from natural sources, by company and location, 1984.

MINING IN TRANSITION

(p. 63-64) By R. M. Hays et al. Article, with 1 table showing U.S. and world production and U.S. consumption of copper, raw steel, iron ore, and phosphate; and U.S. production of sand/gravel/crushed stone, gold, and coal; 1974, 1979, and 1984.

C5800–17 ELECTRICAL WHOLESALING
Monthly.
ISSN 0013-4430.
LC 22-6962.
SRI/MF/not filmed

Monthly trade journal reporting trends and developments in electrical equipment sales and marketing. Most data are compiled by McGraw-Hill Publications Research Dept.

Issues contain articles, occasionally with statistics; and regular editorial depts. Recurring statistical features include a biennial article presenting operating data for the largest wholesale distributors, an annual regional fact book (Nov. issue), and an annual industry outlook feature (Aug. issue).

Features with substantial statistical content are described, as they appear, under "Statistical Features." Each issue of the journal is reviewed, but an abstract is published in SRI monthly issues only when statistical features appear.

Availability: Electrical Wholesaling, Subscription Manager, PO Box 430, Hightstown NJ 08520, qualified subscribers $10.00 per yr., single copy $5.00; selected others $30.00 per yr., single copy $10.00; SRI/MF/not filmed.

Issues reviewed during 1985: Nov. 1984-Oct. 1985 (P) (Vol. 65, Nos. 11-12; Vol. 66, Nos. 1-10).

STATISTICAL FEATURES:

C5800–17.601: Nov. 1984 (Vol. 65, No. 11)

HOW TO WRITE A BUSINESS PLAN

(p. 41-62) By Andrea J. Herbert. Article explaining basic components of business plans, with worksheets, and 1 table showing aggregate financial and operating ratios for the electrical wholesaling industry, 1983. Data are from Electrical Manufacturers' Credit Bureau.

REGIONAL FACTBOOK, ANNUAL FEATURE

(p. 85-98) Statistical section of 6th annual "Market Planning Guidebook," presenting electrical wholesaler market area characteristics. Data are from *Electrical Wholesaling,* BLS, and Census Bureau.

Includes 3 national summary tables; and 4 tables repeated for each census division, showing the following for electrical wholesalers: product and customer distribution by type (no date); sales by State and SMSA, 1981-85; and employment, with comparative data for related industries and selected industry divisions, by State and SMSA, 1983-84.

C5800–17.602: Dec. 1984 (Vol. 65, No. 12)

INDISPENSABLE WHOLESALERS

(p. 16) By Paul E. Bowers. Article, with 1 table showing employment, and average hours and earnings, for production/nonsupervisory workers in wholesaling and all industry, 1947 and 1984.

C5800–17.603: Feb. 1985 (Vol. 66, No. 2)

MANUFACTURERS HAVE A SHOT AT MAKING MORE IN '85 THAN IN '84

(p. 44-46) By Joseph N. Spiers. Article, with 1 table showing sales and profits for 12 leading electrical equipment manufacturers, 1st 9 months 1984 with percent change from 1983. Data are from Standard & Poor's.

REPS SPEAK OUT

(p. 55-66) Article reporting electrical equipment independent sales representatives' views on developments in the electrical industry. Data are from responses of 189 independent representatives to a Dec. 1984 survey conducted by *Electrical Wholesaling.*

Includes 6 tables showing responses regarding major professional problems; and perceived value of distributor buying groups, high-tech product lines, buy/sell arrangements, do-it-yourself market, and foreign-made products.

C5800–17.604: Mar. 1985 (Vol. 66, No. 3)

ELECTRONIC WIRE AND CABLE

(p. 42-44) Article, with 1 table showing value of electronic wire and cable shipments, by type of product, 1984. Data were compiled by *Electronic Week.*

CONNECTORS

(p. 45) Article, with 1 table showing value of electronic connector shipments, by type of product, 1984. Data are from *Electronic News.*

TAPPING INTO HIGH-GROWTH NICHE MARKETS FOR PROCESS CONTROLS

(p. 86-88) By Liza Pazer. Article, with 1 table showing capital expenditures by 7 industries that are major users of automated process control equipment, 1972-85. Data are from Commerce Dept and McGraw Hill Economics.

C5800–17.605: Apr. 1985 (Vol. 66, No. 4)

TALL SALES IN TEXAS

(p. 53-65) By Lorraine Smith. Article, with 1 table showing top 5 States ranked by electrical equipment sales, 1982. Data are from Commerce Dept.

C5800-17.606: May 1985 (Vol. 66, No. 5)

REPORT CARD ON SUPPLIER PERFORMANCE

(p. 134-140) Article presenting electrical distributors' ratings of manufacturers' performance in 12 marketing and support categories, for 30 product lines. Data are from 1983/84 National Distributor Opinion Survey, conducted by *Electrical Wholesaling*. Includes 1 extended table.

C5800-17.607: June 1985 (Vol. 66, No. 6)

WHO BUYS TOOLS WHERE

(p. 50) Article on tool buying habits of 393 electrical contractors and facilities personnel responding to a recent survey conducted by *Electrical Construction and Maintenance* magazine. Includes 2 undated tables showing average tool purchase and rental value; and tool purchases and average expenditures, by supplier type.

GROWING TRADE DEFICIT IN ELECTRICAL PRODUCTS SHOULD CAUSE CONCERN

(p. 72-74) By Joseph N. Spiers. Article, with 2 tables showing trade balance for electrical equipment by product type and for all merchandise, 1st 11 months 1979 and 1983-84; and wire/cable and lighting fixture imports, total and by selected country, 1979 and 1984. Data are from Census Bureau.

C5800-17.608: July 1985 (Vol. 66, No. 7)

PICKUP IS SEEN, DESPITE A SAD FIRST QUARTER

(p. 88-89) By Joseph N. Spiers. Article, with 1 chart showing value of electrical equipment shipments, 1981-86. Data are from Census Bureau and McGraw-Hill Economics.

C5800-17.609: Aug. 1985 (Vol. 66, No. 8)

1985 MID-YEAR OUTLOOK: SLOWER GROWTH AHEAD, ANNUAL FEATURE

(p. 43-50) Annual article, by Joseph N. Spiers, on economic outlook for the electrical supply wholesaler industry, 1985-86. Data are from McGraw-Hill Economics Dept; Data Resources, Inc.; and an *Electrical Wholesaling* analysis of 249 companies. Includes the following:

a. Key economic indicators: GNP; housing starts; nonresidential construction value; industrial production index (with detail for electrical and nonelectrical machinery); new car sales; CPI percent increase; 90-day Treasury bill rate; and unemployment rate; 3rd quarter 1985-3rd quarter 1986, and annually 1984-86. 1 table.

b. Nonresidential construction expenditures, by structure type, 1984-86; top 10 manufacturing industries ranked by production growth rate, 1985-86 period, with comparison to 1984-85 and to total industry; and electrical wholesalers' sales, by census division and for 24 MSAs, 1983-85, with 1986 percent change for census divisions. 6 tables.

C5800-17.610: Sept. 1985 (Vol. 66, No. 9)

LIGHTING'S CHANGING PLAYERS

(p. 10-12) By George Ganzenmuller. Article, with 1 table showing the following for commercial/industrial lighting fixtures industry: companies; establishments (total and with 20/

more employees); employment and payroll; production workers, hours, and wages; cost of materials; and shipments value; 1972, 1977, and 1982.

Data are from Census Bureau quinquennial Census of Manufactures.

C5800-17.611: Oct. 1985 (Vol. 66, No. 10)

WILL SLUGGISH SALES AND PROFITS CONTINUE THROUGHOUT '85?

(p. 94-96) By Joseph N. Spiers. Article, with 1 table showing sales and profits for 12 leading electrical equipment manufacturers, 1st half 1985 with percent change from 1984. Data are from Standard & Poor's.

Similar article, with data for 1st 9 months 1984, is described in C5800-17.603 above.

C5800-18   13th ANNUAL MCGRAW-HILL SURVEY OF INVESTMENT IN EMPLOYEE SAFETY AND HEALTH
Annual.   June 1985.   10 p.
SRI/MF/complete

Annual survey report on planned business expenditures for employee safety/health, 1985-86, with actual expenditures for 1972-84. Includes safety/health spending amount, and as percent of total capital spending, shown by industry division and selected manufacturing group.

Data are national estimates based on a McGraw-Hill survey.

Contains narrative summary, with 3 charts; table listing; and 4 tables.

Availability: McGraw-Hill, Economics Department, 1221 Ave. of the Americas, 37th Floor, New York NY 10020, $20.00; SRI/MF/complete.

C5800-19   30th ANNUAL MCGRAW-HILL SURVEY OF BUSINESS' PLANS FOR RESEARCH AND DEVELOPMENT EXPENDITURES, 1985-88
Annual.   May 1985.
22 p.+errata sheets.
SRI/MF/complete

Annual survey report on planned industry expenditures for R&D, 1985 and 1988, with actual expenditures for 1953-84. Includes R&D spending amount, and as percent of sales and of total capital spending, shown for all industry, all manufacturing and nonmanufacturing industry, and by manufacturing group.

Most data are national estimates based on responses of approximately 500 companies to a Mar./Apr. 1985 McGraw-Hill survey. Historical expenditure trends are from NSF.

Contains narrative analysis with 3 charts (p. 1-7); table listing (p. 8); and 7 detailed tables (p. 9-22). Report is accompanied by data revisions.

Availability: McGraw-Hill, Economics Department, 1221 Ave. of the Americas, 37th Floor, New York NY 10020, $45.00; SRI/MF/complete.

C5800-20   18th ANNUAL MCGRAW-HILL SURVEY OF POLLUTION CONTROL EXPENDITURES, 1984-86
Annual.   May 1985.   23 p.
SRI/MF/complete

Annual survey report on planned industry expenditures for pollution control, 1985-86, with actual expenditures for 1967-84. Covers expenditures for air, water, and solid waste pollution control, shown by industry division and selected manufacturing group. Also includes pollution control share of all capital expenditures.

Data are national estimates based on responses of over 400 companies to a Mar./Apr. 1985 McGraw-Hill survey.

Contains narrative, with 3 charts and 1 text table (p. 1-6); table listing (p. 7); and 8 tables (p. 8-23).

Availability: McGraw-Hill, Economics Department, 1221 Ave. of the Americas, 37th Floor, New York NY 10020, $75.00; SRI/MF/complete.

C5800-24   27th ANNUAL MCGRAW-HILL SURVEY of Overseas Operations of U.S. Industrial Companies, 1985-87
Annual.   Aug. 1985.   16 p.
SRI/MF/complete

Annual survey of planned overseas capital investment expenditures of foreign affiliates of U.S. industrial companies, 1985-87, with actual expenditures for 1984. Includes expenditures by major type, industry, and world region. Also includes foreign affiliate expected sales and profit margin levels.

Most data are based on a July-Aug. 1985 survey of manufacturing and petroleum companies accounting for approximately 35% of all foreign capital spending in 1984. Dollar amounts for overseas capital expenditures are extrapolated to represent all companies.

Contains narrative report, with 2 trend charts (p. 1-6); and 6 tables listed below (p. 7-16).

Availability: McGraw-Hill, Economics Department, 1221 Ave. of the Americas, 37th Floor, New York NY 10020, $35.00; SRI/MF/complete

TABLES:

[Unless otherwise noted, tables show data for 6 manufacturing industries, petroleum, and all manufacturing and industry.]

I-III. Overseas capital expenditures: [total]; for property, building, and machinery/equipment; and by [7 world] regions [and Canada; 1984-87]. (p. 7-13)

IV-V. Expected profit margins on sales [higher, lower, same]: overseas subsidiaries vs. U.S. [1985-86; and annual change], 1984-85 and 1985-86. (p. 14-15)

VI. Expected sales of foreign affiliates [annual change, 1984-85 and 1985-86]. (p. 18)

C5800–26   1985 DODGE/SWEET'S CONSTRUCTION OUTLOOK

Annual. 1984. 8 p.
SRI/MF/complete

Annual forecast of construction activity in non-residential, residential, and nonbuilding sectors, 1985, with comparisons to 1984.

Contains narrative analysis, with 5 trend charts, and 3 text tables showing quarterly trends in building contract values by sector and type of construction, 1984-85; and 2 detailed tables, listed below.

Data are updated in spring and summer following publication of *Dodge/Sweet's Construction Outlook*. Updates are covered by SRI, as they appear, under C5800-29.

Availability: McGraw-Hill Information Systems Co., F. W. Dodge Division/Sweet's Division, 1221 Ave. of the Americas, New York NY 10020, †; SRI/MF/complete.

TABLES:

[Tables show 1984 preliminary and 1985 forecast data.]

[1] National estimates [nonresidential and residential building construction contract values and floor area, number of residential units, and nonbuilding contract value, all by type; and all construction contract value and Dodge index]. (p. 3)

[2] Regional estimates [contract value for nonresidential, residential, and nonbuilding construction, by type and region]. (p. 7)

C5800–27   CAPITAL SPENDING CHECK-UP SURVEY

Annual. Mar. 1985. 32 p.
SRI/MF/complete

Annual survey report on capital spending intentions and business outlook of manufacturing and nonmanufacturing industries through 1986, including inflation expectations. Also includes industrial production and income indicators by major industry group.

Most data are from a Jan.-Feb. 1985 McGraw-Hill survey of over 500 firms representing 22.9% of all capital expenditures. Dollar amounts are extrapolated to represent all companies.

Contains narrative analysis, with 10 trend charts and 4 text tables listed below (p. 1-14); table listing, and 9 tables also listed below (p. 15-25); and questionnaire facsimiles (7 p.).

Availability: McGraw-Hill, Economics Department, 1221 Ave. of the Americas, 37th Floor, New York NY 10020, $125.00; SRI/MF/complete.

TABLES:

[Unless otherwise noted, tables I-IX show data by major manufacturing group and for selected nonmanufacturing industries.]

1. Capital goods inflation [percent change in deflator for nonresidential fixed investment and PPI for capital goods, with comparison to survey forecasts, 1981-85]. (p. 3)

2-4. Nondurable and durable manufacturing indicators [including operating rate, shipment values, and after-tax profit/loss]; and nonmanufacturing indicators [including various indicators of production and/or income; by major industry group, quarterly 1984 and annually 1982 and/or 1983-84]. (p. 7-9)

I. Plans for capital spending [estimated 1984 and planned 1985-86]. (p. 16)

II. Inflation expectations [percent change expected in plant/equipment prices and real capital spending, 1984/85]. (p. 17)

III-VII. Capital spending on computers/other office equipment, manufacturing equipment, autos/trucks, and factories and office buildings [construction, 1984-85]. (p. 18-22)

VIII. Detailed industry capital spending [expected percent change by industry group, 1984/85-1985/86]. (p. 23-24)

IX. Survey sample size [percent of total capital spending represented by surveyed firms]. (p. 25)

C5800–28   ELECTRICAL WORLD

Monthly.
ISSN 0013-4457.
LC 12-32507.
SRI/MF/not filmed

Monthly trade journal reporting on electric utility industry developments in technology and management; power generation, transmission, and distribution activities of public and private utilities; and financing, regulation, and rates.

Data are from *Electrical World* surveys of utilities, and reports of Federal Government agencies, the Edison Electric Institute, and other private research organizations.

Issues generally include articles and recurring editorial features, occasionally with statistics; and the following regularly appearing statistical features:

a. Monthly electric power generation feature, with 1 table showing electricity output, by region, for final week of month prior to publication date, calendar year to date, and 52 weeks to date, with percent change from same periods of previous year, and total output for 4 prior weeks; and 1 chart showing weekly output trends for current and previous years; all appearing in "News" section.

b. Annual statistical report on U.S. and Canadian utility industry operations, and annual or biennial reports on capacity additions, transmission and distribution construction, facilities maintenance, steam station design and operations, union negotiations, salaries for engineers, and industry outlook.

A nonstatistical directory of technical papers and a nonstatistical buyer's guide appear annually in the June issue.

Monthly table appears in all issues. All additional features with substantial nontechnical statistical content are described, as they appear, under "Statistical Features." Nonstatistical features are not covered.

Availability: Electrical World, Fulfillment Manager, PO Box 2034, Mahopac NY 10541, qualified executives †, industry individuals $13.00 per yr., others $38.00 per yr., single copy $5.00, special issues $10.00; SRI/MF/not filmed.

Issues reviewed during 1985: Nov. 1984-Oct. 1985 (P) (Vol. 198, Nos. 11-12; Vol. 199, Nos. 1-10).

STATISTICAL FEATURES:

C5800–28.601: Nov. 1984 (Vol. 198, No. 11)

18th STEAM STATION DESIGN SURVEY, BIENNIAL FEATURE

(p. 49-53) Biennial report on design characteristics of 8 steam-powered electric-generating units recently entering planning or construction phases. Data are from an *Electrical World* survey and Edison Electric Institute.

Includes 1 table showing units with and without extraction technology, by fuel sulfur level; and 3 tables showing itemized design characteristics, by unit, for the following categories:

a. General characteristics, including generating capacity and principal fuel, fuel handling, steam generator design, ash control and disposal, piping, and valves.

b. Fans, pumps, heat-cycle apparatus, turbine, condenser, condenser cooling system, and generator and excitation system.

c. Control instrumentation, station auxiliary power, digital information and controls, emergency power system, outgoing substation, buses, and cable.

Also includes 1 table showing number and capacity of all steam units currently under construction/on order, by capacity range.

For description of the 17th survey report, see SRI 1983 Annual under C5800-28.401.

C5800–28.602: Dec. 1984 (Vol. 198, No. 12)

NEMA: 1984 SALES OUTPACE ESTIMATES, ANNUAL FEATURE

(p. 100) Annual article presenting results of a business outlook survey of National Electrical Manufacturers Assn members. Includes 1 table showing respondents' expected annual percent change in shipments, by industry group, 1984-85.

C5800–28.603: Jan. 1985 (Vol. 199, No. 1)

ANNUAL GENERATION CONSTRUCTION SURVEY

(p. 49-60) Annual report on electric plants planned or under construction as of Dec. 31, 1984. Covers nuclear, fossil, and hydroelectric powered plants. Data are from an *Electrical World* survey of utilities, and from the National Electric Reliability Council (NERC).

Includes the following, repeated for each NERC region within the above plant categories, as applicable:

a. List of plants planned or under construction, showing owner, capacity, equipment type and/or manufacturer, architect/engineer, builder, service date, and project status.

b. NERC and/or *Electrical World* forecasts of total summer generating capacity, 1984-90.

This is the 5th annual survey.

ECONOMY OF SCALE STILL HOLDS TRUE

(p. 62-64) Article, with 2 tables on electric power plant capital costs, showing average annual percent change in cost of steam plant and selected equipment, 1980-84 period; and initial and extension costs for high-sulfur coal-fired units, by generating capacity (no date). Data are from Data Resources Inc., and a 1980 study by Sargent & Lundy.

C5800–28.604: Feb. 1985 (Vol. 199, No. 2)

WAGE FREEZES MARRED 1984 BARGAINING, ANNUAL FEATURE

(p. 18-19) Annual article on contract negotiations between electric utilities and the International Brotherhood of Electrical Workers during 1984. Includes 2 tables showing number of contracts negotiated, and average percent wage increase, by type of utility ownership; and lineman wage rate and percent increase, by company; 1984, with selected comparisons to 1983.

C5800–28.605: Mar. 1985 (Vol. 199, No. 3)

IEEE/PES WINTER POWER MEETING

(p. 72-75) Article, with 1 undated chart showing percent of electric utilities using selected methods of training dispatcher operators. Data are based on responses from 40 utilities employing 738 operators, to a survey by the Dispatcher Training Working Group.

HOW MUCH DO U.S. POWERPLANTS COST?

(p. 87-88) Article on maintenance costs and capital expenditures for coal-fired electric power plants. Data are from the University of Tennessee's Construction Research Analysis group (CRA) survey of 491 coal-fired units.

Includes 1 undated table showing the following by plant classification and CRA region: number of stations and units; generating capacity; and average age, temperature, pressure, maintenance cost, and capacity cost.

HOW DO UTILITY ENGINEERS' SALARIES COMPARE? ANNUAL FEATURE

(p. 94-95) Annual article on salaries of electric utility engineers. Data are from a 1984 survey by the Engineering Manpower Commission of the American Assn of Engineering Societies.

Includes 2 illustrative charts and 1 table showing engineers' median starting salaries, salaries after 10 years, and median supervisor salaries, by industry including gas and electric utilities, 1984.

Full survey report is covered in SRI under A0685-3.

C5800–28.606: Apr. 1985 (Vol. 199, No. 4)

NUCLEAR OPTION: PUTTING THE GENIE BACK IN THE BOTTLE

(p. 12-14) Article, with 1 chart ranking top 13 countries by percent of total electricity generated by nuclear power, 1985. Data are from Edison Electric Institute.

1985 ANNUAL STATISTICAL REPORT

(p. 53-76) Annual report on electric utility industry finances, sales, capability, and capital projects, 1984-85 and trends. Data are from an *Electrical World* survey of U.S. and Canadian utilities, and from Edison Electric Institute, DOE, and various other industry and Federal sources.

Contains introduction, with 1 table showing size and composition of survey sample; and 7 statistical sections, with narrative analyses and 28 tables listed below.

This is the 81st annual survey.

TABLES:

[Data by region are generally shown for 9 National Electric Reliability Council regions, 4

subregions, contiguous U.S., and Alaska/Hawaii. Data "by ownership" are shown for investor-owned utilities, municipal/State/power district systems, cooperatives, and Federal agencies.

Expenditure types are generally generation, transmission, distribution, and miscellaneous. Types of prime mover include some or most of the following: fossil, combustion or gas turbine, nuclear, conventional hydro, steam, pumped storage, and internal combustion.]

CAPITAL EXPENDITURES

[1] Total electric power system capital expenditures [by type, for total industry and investor-owned utilities, 1974-85]. (p. 54)

[2] Electric power system spending, by ownership [and by expenditure and prime mover types, 1984-85]. (p. 55)

[3-5] 1984-85 electric utility capital spending [by region, ownership, and prime mover and expenditure types]. (p. 56-58)

TRANSMISSION AND DISTRIBUTION CONSTRUCTION

[6-9] 1984-85 new expenditures for lines and substations, and new lines and substations energized, [shown for overhead and underground transmission and primary distribution lines, and transmission and distribution substations, all by region and ownership]. (p. 60-63)

CAPABILITY

[10] Electric power industry capability [by prime mover, as of Dec. 31, 1984, and planned additions 1984/beyond]. (p. 65)

[11-12] Consumption and energy generated, by type of fuel [1974-84, and by month and region, 1984]. (p. 65)

[13] Future generating capacity additions, by regions [and by prime mover, 1984-87 and 1988-90 period]. (p. 66)

[14-15] Installed generating capacity, by type of ownership [1974-84]; and by States [and census division, cross-tabulated by prime mover, with number of plants], (Dec. 31, 1984). (p. 67-68)

SALES

[16-20] Electric customers, revenue, and energy sales, and average annual use and bill [generally for residential, small and large light/power, and other customers, 1974-84]. (p. 69-70)

INVESTOR-OWNED UTILITY FINANCES

[21] Distribution of electric revenue [by expense category, 1980-84]. (p. 71)

[22-23] Electric rate increases [granted and pending at year end] and decreases [number of actions and amounts, 1974-84]. (p. 71)

[24] Offerings of securities by investor-owned electric utilities [value of long-term debt, common and preferred stock, and total financing by purpose and type, 1978-84]. (p. 72)

[25-26] Investor-owned electric utility income [and expenses] and combined balance sheets, [1980-84]. (p. 72-73)

CANADA

[27] Electric plant construction [spending, by prime mover and expenditure types]; and line and substation construction and energized [with detail similar to tables [6-9]; all by Province, 1984-85]. (p. 74-75)

COOPERATIVES

[28] Annual statistics of Rural Electrification Administration-financed systems [including loans by source and purpose, advances, active borrowers, total and residential consumers served, energy sold, revenue, energy cost, and average annual use, 1982-84]. (p. 76)

Other Article

UNCOLLECTED FINAL BILLS CAN BE REDUCED

(p. 93-94) Article, with 1 chart showing value of uncollected final utility bills written off as bad debt, 1978-87.

C5800–28.607: May 1985 (Vol. 199, No. 5)

3rd ANNUAL MAINTENANCE SURVEY, ANNUAL FEATURE

(p. 79-85) Annual article on actual and planned maintenance expenditures of U.S. and Canadian electric utilities, 1984-85. Data are from an *Electrical World* survey of utilities.

Includes 6 tables showing maintenance expenditures on labor and materials, for generation by prime mover, and for transmission and distribution; all for contiguous U.S. by North American Electric Reliability Council region and subregion (shown by type of ownership) and for Alaska/Hawaii, Puerto Rico, and each Canadian Province, 1984-85. Includes some detail for noncapitalized equipment upgrading.

Also includes 1 table on summary characteristics of survey sample relative to total U.S. utilities.

ENGINEERS' SALARIES ARE UP, CPI AND UNEMPLOYMENT DOWN, RECURRING FEATURE

(p. 96-97) Recurring article, with 2 tables showing salaries of electrical/electronics engineers, by industry and area of expertise, as of Feb. 1, 1985. Includes mean, median, 1st and 3rd quartile, and 1st and 9th decile salaries. Data are based on over 11,000 responses to a 1985 Institute of Electrical and Electronics Engineers member survey.

Previous article, for 1983, is described in SRI 1984 Annual under C5800-28.503.

C5800–28.608: June 1985 (Vol. 199, No. 6)

CASH-RICH UTILITIES: GEARING UP FOR NEW SPENDING?

(p. 17-18) Article, with 1 table and 1 chart showing value of investor-owned electric utility security offerings by type and purpose, 1st 3 months 1984-85; and number of utility bond ratings upgraded and downgraded, 1980-84. Data are from Ebasco Services Inc. and Standard & Poor's Corp.

C5800–28.609: July 1985 (Vol. 199, No. 7)

DOE BALKS AT UTILITY PITCH TO CONGRESS FOR $2-BILLION IN CLEAN-COAL RESEARCH

(p. 27-28) Article on DOE recommendations to Congress concerning Federal R&D funds sought by utilities for clean-coal technology (reduction of coal sulfur content for pollution control). Data are from DOE. Includes 1 undated table showing funds sought for 36 clean-coal projects arranged by technology type, with utility name and project description for each.

CIVILIZING COAL: GETTING THE DIRT OUT

(p. 65-72) By Louis Iwler. Article, with 1 chart showing volume of coal mechanically cleaned to reduce sulfur content for electric utility industry, 1978-84. Data are from DOE.

SMALL SCADA SYSTEMS POISED FOR TAKEOFF

(p. 75-77) Article on automated power distribution systems (supervisory control and data acquisition systems, or SCADAs) used by electric utilities. Data are from responses of approximately 300 electric utilities to a recent survey conducted by Newton-Evans Research Co.

Includes 13 charts and 2 tables showing the following:

a. SCADA market value, with detail by vendor; typical SCADA price; and value of SCADA shipments to utilities; all by system type, various years 1984-90.

b. Survey response on current or planned use of computer-based systems, importance of computer make, transfer of SCADA data to other computer systems, maximum acceptable downtime for remote terminal units, level of system back-up needed, type of software required, and sources of custom software.

C5800–28.610: Aug. 1985 (Vol. 199, No. 8)

20th ANNUAL T&D CONSTRUCTION SURVEY

(p. 59-66) Annual article presenting data on electric utility transmission and distribution (T&D) construction activity and outlook, 1978-91. Data are based on an *Electrical World* survey. Respondents represent 74% of total generating capacity and 70.4% of total customers in contiguous 48 States.

Includes 10 tables showing number, mileage, and/or voltage capacity of actual and/or planned T&D equipment installations, including transformers, circuit breakers, capacitors, substation banks, and overhead and underground lines, various periods 1978-91; and construction activity and number of customers serviced, by North American Electric Reliability Council region, 1984.

CUSTOMERS ARE KEY TO BEATING COMPETITION

(p. 76-78) Article on opinions of residential electric utility customers on electric costs/controls over costs, and utility policies and operations. Data are from responses to a recent survey conducted by Cambridge Reports Inc. for Edison Electric Institute. Includes 10 charts showing survey response.

"THE FIRE UNLEASHED": TV IGNORES REALITY

(p. 81-85) Article, with 3 undated charts showing opinions of adults (total, college-educated, and politically active) on nuclear energy. Data are from a recent survey of 1,500 adults conducted by Cambridge Reports Inc.

WESTERN WORLD: FACING CAPACITY CRISIS IN 1990s?

(p. 84-85) Article projecting electric power demand worldwide. Data are from the International Energy Agency. Includes 1 table showing high and low estimates of the following for U.S. and 5 other industrialized countries: peak demand, available capacity, and percent in reserve, 1990 and 1995, with annual growth rates to 1990 and 1995.

C5800–28.611: Sept. 1985 (Vol. 199, No. 9)

"GENERATION IN THE '90s WILL NEED MORE THAN '80s TECHNOLOGY"—OTA

(p. 22) Article, with 1 table showing the following for major electric power plants using developing technologies, installed or under construction as of May 1985: type of technology, capacity, location, and funding source.

36th ANNUAL ELECTRIC UTILITY INDUSTRY FORECAST

Annual report on electric utility trends and forecasts, 1974-2000, including kWh sales, revenues, generating capacity, and capital expenditures. Also includes selected general economic indicators. Data are from reports of DOE, industry assns, *Electrical World,* and McGraw-Hill Economics Dept, and are generally shown for 1974-90, 1995, and 2000. Contains the following annual articles:

OUTLOOK FOR ELECTRICITY SALES STAYS STRONG FOR THE REMAINDER OF THE DECADE

(p. 51-55) Includes 5 tables showing the following:

a. Electric utility kWh sales by sector, including industrial, residential, commercial, street/highway lighting, other public authority, railroad, and interdepartmental; and GNP and GNP deflator.

b. Industrial sector: electricity used in manufacturing, in primary aluminum production, by DOE for uranium enrichment, and for all industrial purposes; electricity generated by industrial plants; industrial production index; and aluminum production.

c. Residential sector: mid-year customers; housing starts; and electricity use per customer, revenue (total and per kWh), average annual bill, and heating kWh sales.

CONTINUING GROWTH DRIVING THE INDUSTRY TO COMBUSTION TURBINES

(p. 55-58) Includes 3 tables showing electric utility kWh sales and output; peak load and percent growth, capability at peak, and reserve and capacity margins; capacity additions, by type of generation; and capital expenditures for generation, transmission, distribution, and other.

C5800–29 DODGE/SWEET'S CONSTRUCTION OUTLOOK, Updates

2 per year. 4 p.
SRI/MF/complete

Periodic report, issued twice yearly, updating annual *Dodge/Sweet's Construction Outlook.* For description of 1985 *Outlook,* see C5800-26 above.

Updates contain narrative analysis, and 2 tables showing national and regional estimates of construction contract value, by detailed construction type; and national estimates of nonresidential and residential building floor area, number of residential units, and all construction contract value and Dodge index. Data are actual for previous year and forecasts for current year.

Availability: F. W. Dodge Division/Sweet's Division, McGraw-Hill Information Systems Co., 1221 Ave. of the Americas, New York NY 10020, †; SRI/MF/complete.

Issues reviewed during 1985: 1984 Outlook, Second Update (July 1984); and 1985 Outlook, First Update (Mar. 1985) and Second Update (July 1985).

C6050
MLR Enterprises

C6050–1 MERGERS AND ACQUISITIONS: The Journal of Corporate Venture

Quarterly.
ISSN 0026-0010.
LC 66-9930.
SRI/MF/excerpts

Quarterly journal, with annual "Almanac and Index," on corporate mergers and acquisitions. Data are compiled by MLR Enterprises. Quarter of data coverage is 1 quarter prior to cover date.

General format:

a. Regularly recurring features, including reports on recent merger, divestiture, and joint venture activity; and articles, occasionally with statistics.

b. Quarterly "Rosters" section, containing the following: narrative review of selected transactions; "Data Base Report" article, often with statistics; 1 table on top 25 transactions; 3 rosters; and 7 "Profile" tables.

Annual "Almanac and Index" issue is usually published in spring, and includes "Profile" section with annual summary of quarterly data; cross index of acquiring and acquired companies; and previous year article index.

Quarterly tables and rosters are listed below. All additional features with substantial statistical content are described, as they appear, under "Statistical Features."

Prior to the 1985 Almanac and Index issue, journal is described in SRI under C4710-1. Issuing agency name has changed from Information for Industry.

Availability: Mergers & Acquisitions, 229 S. 18th St., Philadelphia PA 19103, $129.00 per yr.; SRI/MF/excerpts for quarterly tables and rosters and portions described under "Statistical Features."

Issues reviewed during 1985: 1985 Almanac and Index-Summer 1985 (Vol. 19, No. 5; Vol. 20, Nos. 1-2).

QUARTERLY TABLES AND ROSTERS:

[All tables and rosters show data for quarter of coverage.]

TOP TRANSACTIONS

[1] Top 25 transactions by dollar volume [shows value of transaction, acquiring and acquired/merged companies, and investment advisers].

ROSTERS

[1-3] U.S. mergers and acquisitions, foreign investment in U.S., and U.S. investment abroad [arranged by SIC 2- or 3-digit industry, generally showing the following for each transaction: name, location, sales or revenues, net income or loss, and type of business activity, for acquiring and acquired companies; and transaction terms and effective date].

PROFILE

[1] Merger and acquisition activity [number and value of transactions, for U.S. and foreign mergers/acquisitions by U.S. companies, U.S. mergers/acquisitions by foreign companies, and aggregate divestitures and leveraged buyouts; with comparison to previous 2-4 quarters].

[2-7] [Ranking of top acquiring companies by number of transactions, and of top acquiring and divesting industries by number and value of transactions; and number of transactions, by form of payment.]

STATISTICAL FEATURES:

C6050–1.601: Almanac and Index 1985

1984 PROFILE, ANNUAL FEATURE

(p. 25-44) Fourth annual compilation of charts, lists, and tables profiling merger activity in the U.S. and by U.S. firms abroad, 1984. Data are from quarterly tables and rosters. Includes the following data, shown for 1984 unless otherwise noted:

a. Merger/acquisition completions and transaction value by SIC 2-digit industry, for U.S. and foreign acquisitions in the U.S. and for U.S. acquisitions abroad, with summary trends from 1975; divestiture and leveraged buyout completions and transaction value, 1983-84; ranking of regions, and top 10 acquirers and States, by number of transactions; and top 100 transactions ranked by value. 7 tables.

b. Transactions and divestitures by form of payment and/or price range; 10 most active industries ranked by number and value of transactions; and 25 largest divestitures ranked by price. 6 tables.

c. 25 largest foreign acquisitions in the U.S. ranked by price; number of transactions for 6 countries most active in U.S. acquisitions and for 6 industries attracting most foreign buyers; 25 largest merger cancellations, including reason, ranked by price; and number of acquired companies by sales range. 5 tables.

C6050–1.602: Spring 1985 (Vol. 20, No. 1)

DEALMAKERS CUT FAILURE RATE

(p. 23) Article, with 1 table showing number of terminated mergers/acquisitions, by reason, 1984. Data are from *Mergers and Acquisitions.*

CAPITALIZING ON TAX BREAKS OF LEVERAGED ESOPs

(p. 39-46) By Stephen L. Key et al. Article, with 1 table showing sales, principal industry, and transaction price and effective date, for 12 leveraged buyouts financed through employee stock ownership plans during 1982-85. Data are from Kelso & Company and *Mergers and Acquisitions.*

HEIGHTENED PROSPECTS FOR RADIO-TV ACQUISITIONS

(p. 47-53) By Christopher Shaw. Article, with 1 table showing number and value of sales of radio and TV stations, 1980-84.

TENDER OFFER UPDATE: 1985, ANNUAL FEATURE

(p. 67-69) Annual article, by Douglas V. Austin and Craig D. Bernard, analyzing tender offer activity, 1978-84. Data are from SEC filings.

Includes 7 tables showing number of offers, by type, success level, contested or uncontested status, and premium level, with selected cross-tabulations and aggregate offer value, 1978-84; and price, buyer, and target company, for 10 largest offers, 1984.

C6050–1.603: Summer 1985 (Vol. 20, No. 2)

M&A IMPACT ON STOCK MARKET

(p. 21) Article, with 2 tables showing number and aggregate purchase price of acquisitions involving publicly held companies listed on NYSE, AMEX, and over-the-counter and regional exchanges, 1984. Data are from *Mergers & Acquisitions.*

SIZING UP YOUR COMPANY'S TAKEOVER VULNERABILITY

(p. 42-49) By Albert V. Bruno et al. Article on development of an index evaluating takeover vulnerability of corporations.

Includes 2 undated tables showing index factors; and index ratings, by factor, for 11 companies that were acquired by hostile or friendly offer, 4 that successfully averted hostile offers, 2 that were open for bids, and 2 that received no bids.

WINDS OF CHANGE STIMULATE COMPUTER INDUSTRY DEALS

(p. 56-61) By Barry J. Tarasoff. Article on computer industry merger/acquisition activity. Data are from Wertheim and Co., Inc. Includes 2 tables showing the following:

a. Acquiring and acquired companies, transaction price, stock price per share at transaction and 4 weeks before announcement, earnings and book values per share (no dates), and percent premium over stock price paid, for acquisitions of 30 computer-related companies, 1984-85 period.

b. Computer industry pretax profit margin and return on assets, and asset turnover ratio, 1977-84.

C6240
Murdoch Magazines

C6240–1   WEEKLY OF BUSINESS AVIATION
Weekly.   Approx. 10 p. cumulative pagination throughout volume.
SRI/MF/excerpts, shipped quarterly

Weekly publication reporting on developments in general aviation, commuter airlines, and aviation-related Federal regulation. Includes monthly statistics on business/personal aircraft shipments.

Issues contain numerous brief news articles; recent Federal airworthiness directives and regulatory exemption activities; 1 monthly table and 2 other recurring tables, listed below; and occasional special tables and articles with statistics. A quarterly subject index is published separately.

Monthly table usually appears in 2nd or 3rd issue of the month. All additional features with substantial statistical content are described, as they appear, under "Statistical Features;" page

locations and latest periods of coverage for other recurring tables are also noted. Nonstatistical features and issues are not covered.

Prior to the Mar. 4, 1985 issue, publication was described in SRI under C9700-3. Issuing agency has changed from Ziff-Davis Publishing Co.

Availability: Weekly of Business Aviation, 1156 15th St., NW, Washington DC 20005, $230.00 per yr., $138.00 per 6 months; SRI/MF/ excerpts for monthly table and all portions covered under "Statistical Features;" shipped quarterly.

Issues reviewed during 1985: Mar. 4-Oct. 28, 1985 (P) (Vol. 40, Nos. 9-25; Vol. 41, Nos. 1-18) [Vol. 40, Nos. 16-17 incorrectly read No. 15].

RECURRING TABLES:

MONTHLY TABLE

[1] Business/personal aircraft industry unit shipments [by model, for each of approximately 20 manufacturers, for month prior to cover date and calendar year to date, with 3-year trends by manufacturer, and some manufacturers' exports and/or net billings for current month].

OTHER RECURRING TABLES

[Month of coverage is 2-3 months prior to cover date.]

[1] Regional commuter carriers traffic [passengers, load factor, revenue passenger miles, and available seat miles, by commuter airline, for month of coverage].

[2] Airport and Airway Trust Fund status [balance, receipts by source, expenditures by function, and usually assets, liabilities, and equity, for month of coverage and fiscal year to date; data are from U.S. Treasury Dept].

STATISTICAL FEATURES:

C6240–1.601: Mar. 11, 1985 (Vol. 40, No. 10)

RECURRING TABLE

[2] Airport and Airway Trust Fund status, Dec. 31, 1984. (p. 79-79a, 80a)

C6240–1.602: Mar. 18, 1985 (Vol. 40, No. 11)

REGIONAL/COMMUTER AIRLINES, ANNUAL FEATURE

(p. 82a-86a) Annual article on regional/commuter airline fleets and operations. Data are from Regional Airline Assn. Includes 4 tables showing the following for 1984, with some comparisons to 1983:

a. Top 50 airlines ranked by passengers, and top 50 aggregate revenue passenger miles (RPMS).

b. Industry-wide: passenger and cargo carriers operating, aircraft in service, and hours flown in revenue service; passenger and freight traffic, and RPMs; North American airports with any and exclusive service, with comparison to major/national airlines; aircraft in use by manufacturer, and total cargo aircraft, by type; and top 11 aircraft models ranked by share of seating capacity, with number in service and flying hours.

C6240–1.603: Apr. 8, 1985 (Vol. 40, No. 14)

RECURRING TABLE

[2] Airport and Airway Trust Fund status, Jan. 31, 1985. (p. 111a)

C6240–1.604: May 6, 1985 (Vol. 40, No. 18)

RECURRING TABLE

[2] Airport and Airway Trust Fund status, Feb. 28, 1985. (p. 144a)

C6240–1.605: June 10, 1985 (Vol. 40, No. 23)

RECURRING TABLE

[2] Airport and Airway Trust Fund status, Mar. 31, 1985. (p. 183a)

C6240–1.606: July 1, 1985 (Vol. 41, No. 1)

RECURRING TABLE

[2] Airport and Airway Trust Fund status, Apr. 30, 1985. (p. 7a)

C6240–1.607: Aug. 19, 1985 (Vol. 41, No. 8)

RECURRING TABLE

[2] Airport and Airway Trust Fund status, May 31, 1985. (p. 63a)

C6240–1.608: Aug. 26, 1985 (Vol. 41, No. 9)

RECURRING TABLE

[2] Airport and Airway Trust Fund status, June 30, 1985. (p. 71a)

C6240–1.609: Sept. 9, 1985 (Vol. 41, No. 11)

RAA: LARGE AIRCRAFT CLAIM GROWING SHARE OF COMMUTER TRAFFIC

(p. 83, 83a) Brief article, with 2 tables showing aircraft in commuter/regional airline passenger service, with share of total revenue passenger miles and percent manufactured in U.S., all by seating capacity, various years 1978-85. Data are from Regional Airline Assn.

C6240–1.610: Sept. 23, 1985 (Vol. 41, No. 13)

RECURRING TABLE

[2] Airport and Airway Trust Fund status, July 31, 1985. (p. 103a)

C6585
Naval Stores Review

C6585–1   NAVAL STORES REVIEW, 1984 International Yearbook
Annual.   July 1, 1985.   28 p.
SRI/MF/not filmed

Annual report on world production, consumption, and trade of rosin, turpentine, tall oil, and other wood-derived chemicals (naval stores), 1984, with trends from the 1970s.

Contains contents listing and 1 table showing naval stores producer's prices, by commodity, 1980-84 (p. 1-3); and the following sections presenting data for various years 1975-84:

Section 1-4. U.S. naval stores production, stocks, domestic sales or use, foreign trade by country of origin and destination, and average export prices, all by commodity; and capacity of world tall oil fractionating companies. 15 tables. (p. 5-19)

Section 5-6. Foreign naval stores production, consumption, and/or trade, by commodity and country. 30 tables. (p. 21-27)

Previous edition, for 1983, was also received in 1985 [Annual. June 10, 1984. 28 p. $30.00]. The 1983 edition is substantially similar in format and content, but does not include U.S. export prices, and detailed data on U.S. rosin exports to New Zealand. Prior to the 1983 edition, report was available on SRI microfiche. For description of 1982 edition, see SRI 1983 Annual under this number.

Availability: Naval Stores Review, PO Box 2406, New Orleans LA 70176, $32.00; SRI/MF/not filmed

C6615
New Jersey Associates

C6615–1   NEW JERSEY MUNICIPAL DATA BOOK, 1985 Edition
Annual.   1985.   xiii+595 p.
ISSN 0277-9218.
ISBN 0-911273-07-7.
LC 81-649215.
SRI/MF/complete

Annual compilation of general socioeconomic and governmental statistics for New Jersey municipalities and counties. Data are shown for various years 1980-83, with population from 1970.

Most data are from reports of State and Federal agencies. Report is edited by Edith R. Hornor.

Contains contents listing, introduction, and bibliography (p. iii-xiii); and 1 data page repeated for each municipality (p. 3-569) and county (p. 575-595), with listings of selected officials and the following statistics:

a. **Demographic and land area:** population, by age, sex, and race/ethnicity; median age; high school graduates as percent of population; per capita income; population density; total area; and (for counties only) land and water area.

b. **Public services and crime:** administrative officials and form of government; police employees; total and violent crime rates; library holdings; and (for municipalities only) volunteer and paid fire fighters, and residential properties served by piped-in water and sanitary sewers.

c. **Real property:** housing units; number of property parcels and percent of total valuation, by property type; and single-family and total residential building permits issued.

d. **Government finances:** total and per capita debt; bond ratings; general tax rate; taxable net valuation, and equalized value and ratios; revenues by major source, and expenditures by object; and tax levy per capita and (for municipalities only) percent collected.

e. **Schools:** teachers; school board officials and superintendents; enrollment; revenues, expenditures, and per pupil cost; and (for municipalities) buildings owned and classrooms used, and (for counties) number of school districts.

Report also includes list of municipalities, by county (p. 572-574).

Availability: New Jersey Associates, Box 505, Montclair NJ 07042, $67.50; SRI/MF/complete.

C6615–2   NEW JERSEY ECONOMIC ALMANAC, 1985
Annual.   Nov. 1984.
xii+374 p.
ISBN 0-911273-06-9.
SRI/MF/complete

Annual compilation, for 1985, of detailed social, governmental, and economic statistics for New Jersey. Data are shown primarily for 1970s-early 1984, with population projections to 2000.

Report is designed to present a socioeconomic overview of the State. Extensive socioeconomic, demographic, and geographic breakdowns are shown, as applicable, for most topics. These breakdowns include data by city, county, SMSA, urban-rural status, commodity, income, industry, occupation, age, educational attainment, marital status, race, and sex. Comparisons to total U.S. are also often included.

Most data are from Federal and State agencies. Data sources appear beneath each table.

Contains contents listing (p. v); introduction (p. ix-xii); 201 tables arranged in 20 sections, described below (p. 3-367); and index (p. 371-374).

This is the 3rd edition.

Availability: New Jersey Associates, Box 505, Montclair NJ 07042, $35.00; SRI/MF/complete.

TABLE SECTIONS:

C6615–2.1: Profile

(p. 3) Contains 1 table. Includes summary data on land area, population characteristics, labor force and employment, personal and family income, business incorporations and failures, business telephone gains, farms and acreage, educational enrollment, and property value.

C6615–2.2: Population

(p. 7-28) Contains 19 tables. Includes population projected to 2000; households and families; housing units, occupancy, and structural and financial characteristics; personal and disposable income; total, illegitimate, and plural births; deaths by cause; crimes by offense; and police employment.

C6615–2.3: Labor Force

(p. 31-53) Contains 27 tables. Includes labor force by employment status; part-time employment; hours worked; production worker hours and earnings; insured unemployment, and initial claims and exhaustions; characteristics of the unemployed; labor union and employee assn membership; and work stoppages, workers involved, and days idle.

C6615–2.4: Agriculture

(p. 57-95) Contains 25 tables. Includes State ranking in agricultural production, and farm taxes and value; crop acreage, yield, production, prices, and value; livestock, dairy, and poultry inventory, value, marketings, and production; and bee colonies, and honey and beeswax production and prices.

Also includes farm production costs, income, and cash receipts from marketings; nurseries and acreage in stock; cut flower and mushroom production, area, sales, value, and prices; farms, acreage, property value, taxes levied, and sales; fertilizer consumption; and agricultural service employment, payroll, and establishments.

C6615–2.5: Banking, Finance, and Insurance

(p. 99-126) Contains 20 tables. Includes number of State-regulated and other financial institutions, and financial data including assets and liabilities; savings and loan assns, membership, and deposits; mortgage transactions; consumer complaints against financial institutions; operating and financial data for federally insured savings and loan assns, Federal credit unions, and life insurance companies; and banking and insurance employment, payroll, and establishments.

C6615–2.6: Communication

(p. 129-130) Contains 5 tables. Includes newspapers and circulation; radio and TV stations; and residential and business telephones and selected operating data.

C6615–2.7: Construction

(p. 133-146) Contains 10 tables. Includes construction establishments, proprietors/working partners, employment, receipts, and payroll; residential and nonresidential construction contracts awarded; and housing permits issued.

C6615–2.8: Education

(p. 149-165) Contains 16 tables. Includes elementary and secondary enrollment and schools, including schools for handicapped and vocational schools; dropouts; high school graduates and postgraduate activities; expenses per pupil; higher education enrollment by State-assisted institution and for others, and degrees conferred; and educational services employment, payroll, and establishments.

C6615–2.9: Energy

(p. 169-175) Contains 8 tables. Includes retail prices for gasoline, diesel fuel, and fuel oil; natural gas and electricity sales and retail prices by utility, by consuming sector; fuel types used by electric utilities; and sales of gasoline, diesel fuel, gasohol, and liquefied petroleum gas.

C6615–2.10: Fishing and Forestry

(p. 179-185) Contains 5 tables. Includes commercial fish landings and value; fish processing and wholesale plants and employment, and fishery product plants; forest products harvest and value; and forestry and lumber and wood products employment, payroll, and establishments.

C6615–2.11: Government

(p. 189-199) Contains 7 tables. Includes State and local government revenues by source, expenditures by function, indebtedness, and cash/security holdings; and State/local revenues and expenditures per $1,000 of personal income.

C6615–2.12: Manufacturing

(p. 203-242) Contains 6 tables. Includes manufacturing establishments, employment, and payroll; production workers and hours and wages; and value added, materials cost, shipments value, capital expenditures, and end-of-year inventories.

C6615–2.13: Mining

(p. 245-251) Contains 7 tables. Includes nonfuel mineral production and value; sand/gravel and crushed stone sold/used; number of sand/gravel producing companies; and mining employment, payroll, and establishments.

C6615–2.14: Real Estate

(p. 255-261) Contains 2 tables. Includes taxable property values; and real estate employment, payroll, and establishments.

C6615–2.15: Recreation

(p. 265-282) Contains 12 tables. Includes State forests, parks, recreation and natural areas, and historic sites, and attendance and/or acreage; fish hatcheries and game farms, and acreage and production; and harvests of deer and small game by species.

Also includes thoroughbred and harness racing days, wagers, and attendance, by track; casino revenues, taxes, table games and slot machines, employment, capital investment, and related facilities including hotel rooms and convention space, all by casino; and casino industry licensing activity, labor organizations registered, and gaming schools.

C6615–2.16: Service Industries

(p. 285-302) Contains 3 tables. Includes service industry establishments, receipts, sole proprietorships, partnerships, payroll, and employment.

C6615–2.17: Taxation

(p. 305-321) Contains 9 tables. Includes State and local tax collections; local property tax revenues; State tax rates; sales and use tax collections, and receipts and deductions, including for exempt organizations; State and Federal income tax returns, exemptions, and collections, and taxable income by source; and State and local taxes per capita and as percent of personal income.

C6615–2.18: Transportation

(p. 325-338) Contains 12 tables. Includes aircraft facilities by ownership, and abandon-

ments; pilots, flight instructors, and nonpilot aviation personnel; domestic and international aircraft departures, passengers, and revenue tonnage; general aviation aircraft and hours flown; and air transportation employment, payroll, and establishments.

Also includes railroad operating data; motor vehicle registrations and average gasoline consumption; traffic on 2 major toll roads; highway fund receipts, disbursements, and bond obligations; road/street and vehicle mileage; and traffic activity at Port Authority of New York-New Jersey bridges, tunnels, airports, and bus and marine terminals.

C6615–2.19: Wholesale and Retail Trade

(p. 341-367) Contains 7 tables. Includes wholesale and retail trade establishments, sales, payroll, and employment; wholesale trade inventories and operating expenses; retail trade proprietorships and partnerships; and central business district retail stores, sales, payroll, and employment.

C6885
Our Sunday Visitor, Inc.

C6885–1   1985 CATHOLIC ALMANAC
Annual. 1984. 588 p.
ISSN 0069-1208.
ISBN 0-87973-255-5.
LC 73-641001.
SRI/MF/excerpts, current & previous year reports

Annual compilation of facts on characteristics and activities of the U.S. and world Catholic community, 1984, with selected trends from the 1960s. Includes special reports on issues of current interest to Catholics; narrative historical reviews of Church leadership, administrative structure, doctrine, and liturgy; data on clergy, membership, and Catholic institutions; and relations with other religious organizations.

Data sources include the U.S. Catholic Mission Assn; *Annuario Pontificio, 1984*; *Statistical Yearbook of the Church, 1981*; *Directory of the Canadian Conference of Catholic Bishops, 1984*; and *The Official Catholic Directory, 1984*.

Contains contents listing and subject index (p. 3-30); and articles, directories, and lists, interspersed with the following statistics:

a. Church organization and membership by country, including archdioceses, dioceses, cardinals, archbishops, bishops, parishes, priests, seminarians, deacons, brothers, sisters, baptisms, and Catholic and total populations; and selected world and regional totals, including Catholic marriages, schools and students, and health facilities; generally as of Dec. 31, 1982. 2 statistical lists. (p. 346-379)

b. Canadian Roman and Eastern rite dioceses, including diocesan and religious priests, deacons, brothers, sisters, parishes, and total and Catholic populations, all by Province and/or diocese, and for total military vicariate, 1984, with totals for 1983. 2 tables. (p. 390-392)

c. U.S. diocesan and religious priests, deacons, brothers, sisters, parishes, total and Catholic populations, infant baptisms, and converts, all by census division, State, and diocese, and for total military ordinariate, as of Jan. 1, 1984, with totals for 1974 and 1983. 3 tables. (p. 434-442)

d. U.S. statistical summary, including total ecclesiastical jurisdictions, clergy by rank, seminarians, marriages, deaths, schools by type, teachers, hospitals, homes for the aged, and orphanages, 1984. 1 statistical list. (p. 442-443)

e. World membership of major male religious orders, as of Jan. 1, 1983; U.S. missionaries in foreign countries, by category (priests, religious brothers and sisters, seminarians, and lay persons) and world region, selected years 1960-84; and U.S. missionaries by sex, number of countries served, and country with largest group, by world region and/or sponsoring organization, 1984. 1 statistical list and 3 tables. (p. 486-487, 508-510)

f. U.S. Catholic universities/colleges, elementary and high schools, and students, by census division, State, and diocese, as of Jan. 1, 1984, with totals for 1974 and 1983; teachers by type, and enrollment at individual Catholic universities/colleges, as of Jan. 1, 1984; and seminaries and students, 1962-84. 2 tables and 2 statistical lists. (p. 515-524, 526)

g. U.S. Catholic facilities for retired/aged and handicapped persons, including capacity of individual facilities grouped by type and State. 2 statistical lists. (p. 531-545)

The 1984 almanac has also been received by SRI, and excerpts are also available on SRI microfiche under this number [Annual. 1984. 588 p. ISBN 0-87973-254-7. $12.95+postage]. The 1983 almanac is described in SRI 1983 Annual, under this number.

Availability: Our Sunday Visitor, Inc., Book Department, 200 Noll Plaza, Huntington IN 46750, $13.95; SRI/MF/excerpts for statistical portions described.

C6985
PennWell Publishing Co.

C6985–1   OIL AND GAS JOURNAL
Weekly.
ISSN 0030-1388.
LC 79-3435.
SRI/MF/not filmed

Weekly publication reporting developments and trends in the U.S. petroleum and natural gas industries, including exploration, processing, production, distribution, and finance. Also covers U.S. and worldwide supply and demand, reserves, and construction.

Data are from the American Petroleum Institute (API), American Gas Assn, and other industry and Government sources.

Issues contain numerous articles and regular editorial features. The following statistics are presented:

a. Weekly industry scoreboard table on fuel supply and demand.

b. Weekly industry statistics section, on oil and gas production, stocks, prices, and imports; with 8 weekly and 8 monthly tables.

c. 3 monthly tables on well completions and on Nelson indexes for refinery operating and equipment costs.

d. Quarterly features on refinery cost indexes, oil industry profits, pipeline cost indexes, drilling activity by technological level, and investment funds.

e. Annual and semiannual features, including world oil and gas industry outlook and review; U.S. and Canadian refining operations; offshore drilling; construction; gas processing; pipeline economics; drilling activity; petrochemical processing; financial data for top 400 oil and gas companies; and worldwide report on reserves, production, and refining capacity.

Weekly and monthly tables are described below. All additional features with substantial nontechnical statistical content are described, as they appear, under "Statistical Features;" page locations and latest periods of coverage for weekly and monthly tables are also noted. Nonstatistical features are not covered.

Availability: Oil and Gas Journal, Circulation Services Manager, PO Box 1260, Tulsa OK 74101, industry subscribers $34.00 per yr., others $82.00 per yr., single copy $3.00; SRI/MF/ not filmed.

Issues reviewed during 1985: Nov. 5, 1984-Oct. 28, 1985 (P) (Vol. 82, Nos. 45-53; Vol. 83, Nos. 1-43).

WEEKLY TABLES:

C6985–1.1: Industry Scoreboard Table

Table showing demand for gasoline, distillate, jet fuel, residual fuel oils, and other products; crude oil and natural gas liquids production, crude and product imports, and other supply; refinery crude runs to stills, input to crude stills, and utilization rate; stocks of crude, gasoline, distillate, jet fuel, and residual fuel oils; and rotary rigs in operation.

Data are current to approximately 10 days prior to cover date; and are shown for latest week and previous week or for latest 4-week and year-to-date average, with comparisons to previous year.

Prior to the Mar. 4, 1985 issue, table varies slightly from this description.

C6985–1.2: Industry Statistics, Weekly Tables

[Tables [1-8] appear in most issues; most tables show data for previous week and same period of previous year. Data are from API, DOE, Smith International, Inc., and Hughes Tool Co. Table sequence may vary.]

PRODUCTION AND STOCKS

[1] O&GJ production report [crude oil/lease condensate by selected States].

[2] API refinery report [input, crude runs, and operable capacity and utilization; and average daily output by product; by PAD district and subarea].

[3] Hughes rig count [rotary rigs in operation, by State, selected State districts or regions including offshore, and land and offshore Canada].

[4] API crude and product stocks [by PAD district].

[5] Smith rig count [and percent of rigs under footage contracts, by proposed well depth interval; and total inland, land, and offshore rigs].

PRICES AND IMPORTS

[6] Refined product and world crude prices [New York and Rotterdam spot prices for gasoline, No. 2 heating oil, and No. 6 residual fuel oil; and world crude oil prices (total, OPEC, non-OPEC, and U.S. imports)].

[7] API imports of crude and products [Canadian and other foreign crude, and products by type, for total U.S. and PAD Districts 1-4 and 5].

[8] Gasoline prices [price excluding tax, and pump prices, for approximately 45 major cities, and by PAD district].

MONTHLY TABLES:

C6985–1.3: Industry Statistics, Monthly Tables

[1] Total U.S. land and marine seismic crews [generally for previous 2 months, and for corresponding previous month of prior year; data are from Society of Exploration Geophysicists].

[2] Worldwide crude oil and gas production [crude daily average and gas total, current and previous month, and current and/or previous year to date; for 60-75 countries, OPEC, and Western Hemisphere, Western Europe, Middle East, Asia/Pacific, Africa, and Communist world areas; data are current to 2-3 months prior to date of publication].

[3] Selected U.S. and world crude prices [for 25-30 major producing U.S. regions and States, and countries; most prices are current to month of publication; data are from O&GJ, DOE, and Alaska Dept of Natural Resources].

[4] Active rigs abroad [in approximately 70 countries arranged by world region, land and offshore rigs, for month 1-2 months prior to cover date, and total rigs for same month of previous year; data are from Hughes Tool Co.].

[5-6] Smith rig count [and average proposed well depth], by State and [rig type (inland, land, and offshore); and land rig count and average depth, by contract type (daywork or footage); for week ended 10 days prior to publication date, with comparisons to previous week and/or same period of previous year, and year-to-date totals].

[7] Gulf Coast refining margins [averages and ranges of refinery product revenues, feedstock and operating costs, and gross and cash operating margins, for month approximately 3 months prior to cover date, with summary comparisons to previous and subsequent month; data are from Wright, Killen, and Feldman, Inc. Table begins with Jan. 21, 1985 issue (an article introducing the table appears in the Nov. 19, 1984 issue)].

[8] Spot gas prices [median bids for natural gas purchases from approximately 10 pipeline systems at specified receipt points in 3 southwestern States, for month current to cover date; data are from U.S. Natural Gas Clearinghouse. Table begins with Apr. 15, 1985 issue (an article introducing the table appears in the Mar. 11, 1985 issue)].

C6985–1.4: API Monthly Well Completions

Monthly table showing new oil, gas, and dry wells and footage drilled in U.S. Data are shown for month 1-3 months prior to cover date, with U.S. totals for same month of previous year and for current and previous years to date.

Prior to the Apr. 22, 1985 issue, feature was titled "U.S. Wells Drilled," and included 2 tables showing total and exploratory wells and footage drilled, by type, with detail by State, State area (including offshore), and Federal offshore region.

C6985–1.5: Nelson Cost Indexes

[Tables appear in the 1st issue of each month and show data for the most recent month available (approximately 5 months prior to date of publication), previous month, same month of previous year, and selected earlier years.]

[1] Refinery construction [cost indexes for pumps/compressors, electrical machinery, internal combustion engines, instruments, heat exchangers, miscellaneous equipment, materials component, and labor component; and refinery inflation index] (1946=base year).

[2] Refinery operating [cost indexes for fuel, labor, wages, productivity, investments/maintenance, and chemicals; and operating indexes for refinery and process units] (1956=base year).

STATISTICAL FEATURES:

C6985–1.601: Nov. 5, 1984 (Vol. 82, No. 45)

WEEKLY TABLES

a. Industry scoreboard, for Oct. 26, 1984. (p. 4)

b. Industry statistics, as of Oct. 19-31, 1984. (p. 141-142)

MONTHLY TABLES

a. Nelson Cost Indexes, for June 1984. (p. 98)

b. Industry statistics: worldwide crude oil and gas production, for Aug. 1984. (p. 143)

OPEC REDUCES CEILING ON PRODUCTION

(p. 58-61) Article, with 1 table showing new oil production quotas and effective reduction for 13 OPEC member countries, as of Nov. 1, 1984.

WORLD WELL COMPLETIONS, 1983, ANNUAL FEATURE

(p. 138) Annual table showing wells and footage or meters drilled, by country arranged by world region, 1983. Includes varying detail by type of well (oil, gas, dry, development, and wildcat). Data are from American Assn of Petroleum Geologists and American Petroleum Institute.

C6985–1.602: Nov. 12, 1984 (Vol. 82, No. 46)

WEEKLY TABLES

a. Industry scoreboard, for Nov. 2, 1984. (p. 4)

b. Industry statistics, as of Oct. 26-Nov. 7, 1984. (p. 197-198)

MONTHLY TABLE

a. U.S. wells drilled (exploratory only), for Aug. 1984. (p. 192)

INDUSTRY BRACES FOR NEW ROUND OF MAJOR OIL FIRM MERGERS

(p. 57-60) By Marcia A. Parker. Article, with 1 table showing acquisition price, and U.S. and foreign oil and gas reserves and discounted future net cash flow from reserves, for 3 largest 1984 petroleum industry mergers. Data are from Arthur Andersen and Company.

ANNUAL API ISSUE

Annual compilation of articles discussing world and U.S. petroleum industry developments and market outlook. Statistical articles are individually described below.

CAPITAL NEEDS AND AVAILABILITY FOR WORLD OIL

(p. 94-98) By David J. Behling, Jr. Article, with 2 charts on petroleum industry capital expenditure shares by country or world region, 1940s-90; and 2 tables showing world petroleum industry capital spending for a group of companies monitored by Chase Manhattan Bank and for rest of industry, and onshore and offshore rig activity by country or world region, various years 1981-84.

Most data are from Chase Manhattan Bank.

STATE OF THE WORLD OIL MARKET: WHERE IT'S HEADED IN THE SHORT TERM

(p. 99-102) By Constantine S. Nicandros. Article, with 1 chart on oil revenues and loss from price cuts, 1984; and 1 table showing world oil supply and demand, 1979 and 1983-86.

SHORT-TERM OUTLOOK FOR OIL PRICES

(p. 103-106) By William H. Brown, III. Article, with 2 tables showing outlook for OPEC oil production and revenues under current economic conditions and deep recession, by member country, 1984-86. Data are from Kidder, Peabody and Co.

FOREIGN UPSTREAM OPERATIONS MORE PROFITABLE

(p. 116-125) By Philip L. Dodge. Article comparing U.S. and foreign operations of 4 major oil companies, 1983. Data are from company annual reports. Includes 6 tables showing U.S. and foreign net investment, earnings, rate of return, production and earnings margins, proved reserves, production, expenditures, and future cash flow, by company, 1983.

Sii-DAC DRILLING ACTIVITY: DRILLING REBOUND PAUSES AS THIRD-QUARTER Sii-DAC REFLECTS LACKLUSTER ACTIVITY, QUARTERLY FEATURE

(p. 150-152) Quarterly report, by Randy Hall, on oil and gas drilling activity for 3rd quarter 1984. Data are presented in terms of the Smith International, Inc. Drilling Activity Correlator, which distinguishes 3 types of drilling activity on the basis of technological sophistication.

Includes 3 tables showing wells and footage drilled by type, 1983-3rd quarter 1984, and by region 1st 9 months 1983-84.

C6985–1.603: Nov. 19, 1984 (Vol. 82, No. 47)

WEEKLY TABLES

a. Industry scoreboard, for Nov. 9, 1984. (p. 4)

b. Industry statistics, as of Nov. 2-14, 1984. (p. 197-198)

MONTHLY TABLE

a. U.S. wells drilled (total only), for Aug. 1984. (p. 184)

SURVEY SHOWS GAS PRICE DECLINE IN CANADA, U.S.

(p. 50) Article, with 1 table showing natural gas burnertip prices in U.S. and 8 foreign countries, as of Sept. 1, 1984 with average prices during preceding 12 months. Data are from National Utility Service, Inc.

REFINERY MARGIN SERIES WILL BE FEATURED EACH MONTH IN OGJ

(p. 110-115) By James A. Dudley et al. Article introducing an O&GJ analysis of Gulf Coast refinery profitability. Data were prepared by Wright, Killen & Feldman, Inc.

Includes 6 tables showing averages and/or ranges of refinery capacity, yield, crude oil acquisition costs, processed product prices and revenues, and operating margin, various periods 1983-84; and average refining margins, annually 1975-83 and quarterly 3rd quarter 1983-3rd quarter 1984.

C6985–1.604: Nov. 26, 1984 (Vol. 82, No. 48)

WEEKLY TABLES

a. Industry scoreboard, for Nov. 16, 1984. (p. 4)

b. Industry statistics, as of Nov. 9-21, 1984. (p. 131-132)

SECOND STRAIGHT INCREASE SEEN FOR U.S. WINTER FUEL DEMAND, ANNUAL FEATURE

(p. 35-40) Annual article, by Robert J. Beck and Glenda E. Smith, on fuel oil and natural gas supply and demand outlook for winter 1984/85. Data are from DOE, API, and O&GJ.

Includes 3 tables showing the following:

a. Middle distillate and residual fuel demand (domestic and export), supply (refined, imports, and from stocks), and end of season stocks; and natural gas demand, by sector; winter 1982/83-1984/85.

b. Distillate and residual fuel stocks as of Sept. 30, and winter daily average demand, 1974-84.

THIRD QUARTER SLUMP TRIMS OIL PROFITS, QUARTERLY FEATURE

(p. 50-51) Quarterly article on U.S. oil industry profits, 1st 9 months 1984. Includes 2 tables ranking 24 oil companies by net profits, and also showing revenues for each company, and capital/exploration expenditures for 11 companies, 1st 9 months 1984, with comparisons to 3rd quarter 1984 and to same periods of 1983.

PIPELINE ECONOMICS, ANNUAL FEATURE

Annual feature, for 1984, on oil and natural gas pipeline system capital investment and construction costs. Most data are from FERC permit applications and cost reports filed by pipeline companies. Includes the following statistical features:

U.S. INTERSTATE PIPELINE SYSTEM CONTRACTS IN 1983 AS CONSTRUCTION COSTS FLATTEN, ANNUAL FEATURE

(p. 63-90) Annual article, by Warren R. True, reviewing pipeline traffic and construction cost trends, 1983. Includes 8 summary charts and the following tabular data:

a. Interstate gas and liquids pipeline mileage, 1972-83; crude and product pipeline investments, by detailed expenditure category for 5 major unnamed companies, 1983; and onshore pipeline construction costs for right-of-way, materials, labor, and other expenditures, and cost range per mile, by pipe diameter, FY75-84. 3 tables. (p. 64-65)

b. Current pipeline costs, by pipe size and State; current compressor station costs, by State; costs for stations completed during 1982, by station type and State; and summary for gas pipeline/compressor construction, 1976-82. Current projects are those with construction permits filed June 1983-May 1984. Data are shown for on- and offshore projects, by expenditure category, with pipeline mileage and station horsepower. 4 tables. (p. 66-73)

c. Interstate gas transmission pipelines: operation and maintenance expenses, mileage, and value of sales, 1982. 1 table. (p. 73)

d. Project costs for 52 selected on- and offshore pipeline projects, compressor stations, and metering/measuring facilities, by cost item. 52 tables. (p. 74-83)

e. Liquids pipelines, showing mileage by line type, crude oil and products deliveries and trunk-line traffic, value of carrier property and annual change, operating revenue, and net income, all by company, 1983, with totals for 1982-83. 1 table. (p. 84-88)

f. Gas pipelines, showing mileage by line type, transmission and other compressor stations, total sales, value of gas plant and additions, operating revenues, and net income, all by company, 1983, with totals for 1982-83. 1 table. (p. 88-90)

OGJ-MORGAN OIL PIPELINE COST INDEX: FIRST-QUARTER 1984 OIL-PIPELINE CONSTRUCTION SLOWS; COSTS INCHED HIGHER, QUARTERLY FEATURE

(p. 90-92) Quarterly article, by Joseph M. Morgan, presenting oil pipeline construction cost indexes for 1st quarter 1984 (1974=base year). Includes 1 table showing indexes for 18 cost components, 1978-83 and 1st quarter 1984.

C6985–1.605: Dec. 3, 1984 (Vol. 82, No. 49)

WEEKLY TABLES

a. Industry scoreboard, for Nov. 23, 1984. (p. 4)

b. Industry statistics, as of Nov. 16-26, 1984 (table [8] is omitted). (p. 151-153)

MONTHLY TABLES

a. Nelson Cost Indexes, for July 1984. (p. 122)

b. Industry statistics: active rigs abroad, for Oct. 1984; Smith rig count, for Nov. 23, 1984; and selected U.S. and world crude prices, for Dec. 1984. (p. 152-153)

PROPOSED TAX JUGGLING TO HIT OIL, GAS

(p. 46-49) Article, with 1 table estimating Federal tax receipts from major changes proposed in oil and gas taxation, FY86-90. Data are from Treasury Dept.

BRAZIL AIMS FOR 600,000 b/d PRODUCTION

(p. 56-58) Article, with 1 table showing Brazilian oil production onshore and offshore, by Brazilian State, July and 1st 7 months 1983-84.

C6985–1.606: Dec. 10, 1984 (Vol. 82, No. 50)

WEEKLY TABLES

a. Industry scoreboard, for Nov. 30, 1984. (p. 4)

b. Industry statistics, as of Nov. 23-Dec. 5, 1984. (p. 137-138)

MONTHLY TABLE

a. Industry statistics: total U.S. land and marine seismic crews, for Oct. 1984. (p. 134)

OIL ACTIVITY IN MANITOBA

(p. 123-134) By Andrew W. Galarnyk et al. Article, with 1 chart showing total oil production in Manitoba, Canada, and distribution by field, 1983. Data are from O&GJ.

C6985–1.607: Dec. 17, 1984 (Vol. 82, No. 51)

WEEKLY TABLES

a. Industry scoreboard, for Dec. 17, 1984. (p. 4)

b. Industry statistics, as of Nov. 30-Dec. 12, 1984. (p. 138-139)

MONTHLY TABLE

a. Industry statistics: worldwide crude oil and gas production, for Sept. 1984. (p. 140)

DISPUTE OVER AREA-WIDE LEASING CENTRAL TO OIL INDUSTRY ACCESS TO OCS ACREAGE

(p. 41-46) By Patrick Crow. Article examining effects of tract withdrawal on Outer Continental Shelf (OCS) lease sales. Data are from National Oil Industries Assn and Minerals Management Service.

Includes 1 chart and 1 table showing average bid per acre for 11 Gulf of Mexico nomination or area-wide lease sales, 1979-84; and OCS acreage in plan area, studied, offered, and leased, for 12 lease sales, 1984-Sept. 1985.

U.S. DRILLING OUTLAY DOWN 36.3% IN '83, ANNUAL FEATURE

(p. 48-50) Annual article on energy drilling activity and costs, 1983. Data are from a joint survey by 3 industry assns.

Includes 3 tables showing number, footage, and cost of wells drilled, by depth interval and well type (oil, gas, and dry), 1982-83; and by State with detail for selected onshore and offshore areas and State districts, and for Appalachian region and Federal waters, 1974-83.

Full *Joint Association Survey* is covered in SRI under A2575-9.

MODIFIED TURNKEY APPROACH CAN CUT COST OF MARSH AND SHALLOW-WATER PROJECTS

(p. 71-77) By Kenneth E. Arnold. Article, with 3 undated tables showing typical bids and estimated construction costs for oil drilling operations in shallow water. Data are from Paragon Engineering Services, Inc.

C6985–1.608: Dec. 24, 1984 (Vol. 82, No. 52)

WEEKLY TABLES

a. Industry scoreboard, for Dec. 14, 1984. (p. 4)

b. Industry statistics, as of Dec. 7-19, 1984. (p. 72-73)

PRODUCERS, PIPELINES POISED FOR PARTIAL GAS PRICE DECONTROL

(p. 17-23) By Rick Hagar. Article on potential effects of decontrol of natural gas prices. Data are from an O&GJ survey. Includes 1 table showing shut-in gas volume, by region and price control classification, as of Nov. 1984.

EIA DRILLING COSTS: DISCOUNTS DROP; DRILLING COSTS REGAIN '82 LEVELS, ANNUAL FEATURE

(p. 39-48) Annual article, By Ted Anderson and Velton T. Funk, presenting Energy Information Administration estimates of oil and gas drilling costs, 1982-84.

Includes 4 tables showing active rigs and well completions, 1978-84; and contiguous U.S. onshore composite oil/gas well drilling costs 1984, and cost indexes 1982-84 (1976=100), by well depth and region.

Article is Part 1 of a 2-part series.

C6985–1.609: Dec. 31, 1984 (Vol 82, No. 53)

WEEKLY TABLES

a. Industry scoreboard (omitted).

b. Industry statistics, as of Dec. 14-26, 1984 (tables [2], [4], [5], and [7] are omitted). (p. 185)

OUTLOOK FUZZY FOR WORLD OIL PRICES DURING 1985

(p. 41-44) By Roger Vielvoye. Article, with 1 chart showing world crude oil prices, various periods 1982-84. Data are from Energy Information Administration.

ALABAMA COALBED GAS OUTPUT RISING

(p. 50-51) Article, with 1 table showing Alabama natural gas wells and production, by coal field, as of Nov. 1, 1984. Data are from Alabama Oil and Gas Board.

MODERATE GROWTH SEEN FOR U.S. CHEMICAL SECTOR

(p. 58-60) Article on chemical industry market trends. Data are from Census Bureau and Chemical Manufacturers Assn. Includes 3 charts and 1 table showing chemical industry capital spending, utilization rate, and value of shipments, exports, and imports, 1974-84.

WORLDWIDE REPORT, ANNUAL FEATURE

(p. 71-149) Annual feature reporting results of O&GJ survey of world petroleum reserves, production, and refining capacity, 1984.

Contains narrative summary with text statistics, and the following 4 tables showing data by country:

[1] Worldwide oil and gas at a glance [estimated oil and gas proved reserves, Jan. 1, 1985; producing oil wells as of July 1, 1984; estimated daily oil production, 1984 and change from 1983; and refineries, and capacity by process, Jan. 1, 1985; all data are also shown by world region]. (p. 74-75)

[2] Worldwide production [discovery date, depth, number of wells by type, and 1st half 1984 cumulative and average daily production, for specified producing fields, grouped by company]. (p. 80-114)

[3] Survey of operating refineries worldwide (capacities as of Jan. 1, 1985) [number of plants, average daily input of crude, and capacity by type of process and product]. (p. 116-117)

[4] Worldwide refining [same input and capacity data as in table [3], shown for specified refineries, grouped by company]. (p. 118-149)

Corrected data appear in the Jan. 14, 1985 issue (see C6985-1.611 below).

EIA DRILLING COSTS: SHALLOW GAS, OIL WELLS INCREASE, ANNUAL FEATURE

(p. 156-162) Annual article, By Ted Anderson and Velton T. Funk, presenting Energy Information Administration estimates of oil and gas drilling costs, 1982-84.

Includes 6 tables showing contiguous U.S. onshore oil and gas well drilling costs 1984, and cost indexes 1982-84 (1976=100), by well depth and region.

Article is Part 2 of a 2-part series.

C6985–1.610: Jan. 7, 1985 (Vol. 83, No. 1)

WEEKLY TABLES

a. Industry scoreboard, for Dec. 21, 1984. (p. 4)

b. Industry statistics, as of Dec. 21, 1984-Jan. 2, 1985 (tables [6] and [8] are omitted). (p. 119-120)

MONTHLY TABLES

a. Nelson Cost Indexes, for Aug. 1984. (p. 86)

b. U.S. wells drilled (total only), for Sept. 1984. (p. 116)

c. Industry statistics: active rigs abroad, for Nov. 1984; and selected U.S. and world crude prices, for Jan. 1985. (p. 120)

INDEPENDENT PRODUCERS TAPPING NEW SOURCES OF CAPITAL

(p. 43-48) By Marcia A. Parker. Article on fund raising strategies of independent oil and gas companies. Data are from Census Bureau, Robert Stanger & Co., and other sources.

Includes 2 tables showing drilling external funding by source (investment companies/banks and public/private funds), drilling expenditures, and performance of public oil/gas fund sales, primarily 1981-84.

NO BIG JOLT SEEN FROM NEW PETROCHEM ENTRANTS

(p. 68) Article, with 1 table showing company, startup date, and major products and capacity, for 8 Saudi Arabian petrochemical projects beginning commercial operation during 1983-85.

QUARTERLY COSTIMATING: HOW INDEXES HAVE RISEN

(p. 98-99) Quarterly feature, by Gerald L. Farrar, on Nelson indexes of refinery operating, construction labor, and equipment and material costs. Includes 2 tables showing cost indexes for 7 equipment types, quarterly 1980-83; and cost indexes by itemized component, and indexes of refinery inflation, operation, and process operation, selected years 1954-83 and Aug. 1984.

IMPROVED ECONOMICS PROMPT ANOTHER LOOK AT FRANCE'S PARIS BASIN

(p. 105-112) By Herbert L. Brewer. Article, with 1 table showing oil wells and footage drilled, and reserves added, for U.S. (excluding Prudhoe Bay) and Paris basin in north central France, 1959-74 period.

C6985–1.611: Jan. 14, 1985 (Vol. 83, No. 2)

WEEKLY TABLES

a. Industry scoreboard, for Jan. 4, 1985. (p. 4)

b. Industry statistics, as of Dec. 21, 1984-Jan. 9, 1985. (p. 115-116)

MONTHLY TABLES

a. Industry statistics: total U.S. land and marine seismic crews, for Nov. 1984; and worldwide crude oil and gas production, for Oct. 1984. (p. 113, 117)

CORRECTION

(p. 113) Data correction for annual feature on world petroleum reserves, production, and refining capacity, appearing in Dec. 31, 1984 issue. Shows corrected data for Qatar.

For description of feature, see C6985–1.609 above.

C6985–1.612: Jan. 21, 1985 (Vol. 83, No. 3)

WEEKLY TABLES

a. Industry scoreboard, for Jan. 11, 1985. (p. 4)

b. Industry statistics, as of Jan. 4-16, 1985. (p. 98-100)

MONTHLY TABLES

a. Industry statistics: Smith rig count, for Jan. 11, 1985; and Gulf Coast refining margins, for Oct. 1984. (p. 100)

PIPELINE CONSTRUCTION TO DECLINE IN NON-COMMUNIST AREAS IN 1985, ANNUAL FEATURE

(p. 25-32) Annual article, by Rick Hagar and Warren R. True, on pipeline construction planned or underway in the non-Communist world, 1985 and beyond. Data are from an O&GJ survey and industry projections.

Includes map and 2 tables showing mileage to be completed for gas, crude, and product pipelines in the U.S., Canada, and 5 world areas, by diameter of line, 1985 and 1985/later.

MORE STATES TO MULL MOTOR FUEL TAX HIKES IN 1985

(p. 41-42) Article, with 1 tabular list on types of fuel and severance taxes and public land restrictions under consideration in State legislatures, by State, 1985. Data are from Highway Users Federation.

OGJ-MORGAN GAS PIPELINE COST INDEX: ACTIVITY, COSTS UP IN COMPETITIVE MARKET, QUARTERLY FEATURE

(p. 81-83) Quarterly article, by Joseph M. Morgan, presenting gas pipeline construction cost indexes for 1st quarter 1984 (1976=base year).

Includes 4 tables showing indexes for 13 cost components, and composite index, 1978-83 and 1st quarter 1984; and onshore and offshore gas pipeline projects, length, and cost, by pipe size, 1st quarter 1984.

C6985–1.613: Jan. 28, 1985 (Vol. 83, No. 4)

WEEKLY TABLES

a. Industry scoreboard, for Jan. 18, 1985. (p. 4)

b. Industry statistics, as of Jan. 11-21, 1985 (table [8] is omitted). (p. 188-189)

MONTHLY TABLES

a. Industry statistics: total U.S. land and marine seismic crews, for Dec. 1984; and active rigs abroad, for Dec. 1984. (p. 158, 189)

b. U.S. wells drilled, for Sept. (exploratory wells), and for Nov. (total wells), 1984. (p. 172, 180)

U.S. LISTS ADVANCE IN 1984 TOTAL ENERGY DEMAND

(p. 68) Article, with 1 table showing oil, gas, coal, and other energy consumption, 1983-84. Data are from American Petroleum Institute.

FORECAST/REVIEW, ANNUAL FEATURE

(p. 87-116) Annual survey, for 1984-85, of oil and gas industry supply and demand, including exploration, production, imports, and exports.

Includes 3 articles with text statistics and tables, some accompanied by charts. All tables are listed below.

TABLES:

SUPPLY AND DEMAND FORECASTS

[1] U.S. energy demand [for oil, natural gas, coal, hydroelectric/geothermal, and nuclear power, 1983-85]. (p. 89)

[2] U.S. natural gas supply, demand [natural gas production in Texas, Louisiana, and all other States; imports from Canada and Mexico; liquefied natural gas imports from Algeria; supplemental gas; losses; exports; and stock change; 1982-85]. (p. 89)

[3] O&GJ forecast of U.S. supply and demand [domestic demand, by refined product; product exports; supply of crude oil/lease condensate and of natural gas liquids/other hydrocarbons; imports and stocks of crude oil and products; processing gains/losses; refining capacity and utilization; crude runs to stills; and Strategic Petroleum Reserve (SPR) stocks; most shown for PAD Districts 1-4 and 5; annually 1984-85, and quarterly 1985]. (p. 90)

[4] Crude and products prices fall; gas steady [crude oil average U.S. wellhead and import prices, natural gas average wellhead price, and regular motor gasoline pump and No. 2 heating oil retail prices, 1971-84]. (p. 92)

[5] U.S. energy efficiency improves again [energy consumption compared to GNP, 1973-85]. (p. 92)

TRENDS

[Tables [6-14] show annual data for 1975-84.]

[6] U.S. production of crude oil/lease condensate [by PAD district and State or geographic area, with cumulative data for 1859-1984]. (p. 93)

[7] Supply and demand for crude in the U.S. [imports and production; refinery runs, direct use/loss, exports, and use for SPR; stock change; and primary and SPR stocks]. (p. 93)

[8] Rotary rig activity by States [and selected State regions including offshore, and for onshore and offshore Canada, with 1984 low and peak numbers]. (p. 98)

[9] [Marketed production of natural gas, by State, and total imports and exports]. (p. 99)

[10] Refinery runs by [PAD] districts [and geographic subdivisions; and refinery capacity utilization for 1984]. (p. 100)

[11] U.S. refined products [by type], natural gas liquids, and crude stocks. (p. 104)

[12] Crude imports by country of origin. (p. 106)

[13-14] Imports of refined products, and exports of refined products and crude [with detail by product type]. (p. 106)

WELL FORECAST

[15] The majors' score [total wells (1983-85) and wildcat wells (1984-85) drilled, by State and major producing State regions including offshore]. (p. 107)

[16] O&GJ well forecast for 1985 [total, wildcat, and/or field wells, and total footage drilled, 1984-85, by State and major producing State region including offshore, and for west Canada by Province, and offshore east coast Canada]. (p. 108)

[17] Quarter-century record of U.S. well completions [total wells, footage, and wildcat wells, 1959-1984]. (p. 109)

[18] Big independent operators' score [total and wildcat wells drilled in 1984 and planned for 1985, by State and major producing State region including offshore]. (p. 109)

MAJOR OIL FIELD PRODUCTION

[19] [Production, 1984; cumulative production, as of Jan. 1, 1985; and estimated reserves and wells; for major oil fields, arranged by State.] (p. 115-116)

Other Articles

METHANOL CANNOT ECONOMICALLY DISLODGE GASOLINE

(p. 119-124) By Laurence H. Cohen and Herman L. Muller. Article on methanol costs and supply, and competitive potential in gasoline market. Data are from Amoco Oil Co.

Includes 1 chart and 8 tables showing methanol onstream and total U.S. capacity, with distribution by company; world capacity and utilization; manufacturing and capital costs for production from coal, natural gas, and remote gas; and methanol vs. gasoline costs; 1984 and/or 1985.

INTERNATIONAL SEISMIC CREW COUNT, RECURRING FEATURE

(p. 158) Recurring table showing land and marine seismic crews, for U.S., Canada, Mexico, and 5 world areas, Mar. and June 1984. Data are from Society of Exploration Geophysicists.

DOMESTIC CRUDE OIL PRODUCTION PROJECTED TO 2000 ON BASIS OF RESOURCE CAPABILITY

(p. 159-166) By Joseph P. Riva, Jr. Article, with 10 tables showing crude oil production, reserves, and fields, by producing region and/or field size, with detail for Alaska; and estimated undiscovered resources; various years 1964-2000. Data are from American Assn of Petroleum Geologists, DOE, and other sources.

C6985–1.614: Feb. 4, 1985 (Vol. 83, No. 5)

WEEKLY TABLES

a. Industry scoreboard, for Jan. 25, 1985. (p. 4)

b. Industry statistics, as of Jan. 18-30, 1985. (p. 84-85)

MONTHLY TABLES

a. Nelson Cost Indexes, for Sept. 1984. (p. 67)

b. U.S. wells drilled, for Oct. (total wells), and for Nov. (exploratory wells), 1984. (p. 81-82)

c. Industry statistics: worldwide crude oil and gas production, for Nov. 1984. (p. 86)

AMOCO TOP BIDDER IN UK NINTH ROUND

(p. 38) Brief article on a UK sale of North Sea oil and gas lease tracts, with 1 undated table showing winning bidder and cash bonus bid by tract. Data are from UK Dept of Energy.

PUBLIC PROGRAMS' 1984 SALES SHOW SHARP DROP

(p. 39) Article on oil industry income from sales of limited partnerships in public oil and gas programs, 1984. Data are from RPI Publications, Inc. Includes 2 tables showing drilling and nondrilling capital raised, by type of program; and capital raised by top 20 fund-raising companies; various years 1982-84.

C6985–1.615: Feb. 11, 1985 (Vol. 83, No. 6)

WEEKLY TABLES

a. Industry scoreboard, for Feb. 1, 1985. (p. 4)

b. Industry statistics, as of Feb. 1-6, 1985 (table [6] is omitted). (p. 133-135)

MONTHLY TABLES

a. Industry statistics: selected U.S. and world crude prices, for Feb. 1985; Smith rig count, for Feb. 1, 1985; and Gulf Coast refining margins, for Nov. 1984. (p. 134-135)

C6985–1.616: Feb. 18, 1985 (Vol. 83, No. 7)

WEEKLY TABLES

a. Industry scoreboard, for Feb. 8, 1985. (p. 4)

b. Industry statistics, as of Feb. 1-13, 1985. (p. 141-142)

MONTHLY TABLES

a. U.S. wells drilled, for Dec. 1984. (p. 136, 138)

ADOPTION OF TREASURY'S TAX PLAN WOULD DEAL CRIPPLING BLOW TO INDUSTRY

(p. 41-49) Article discussing a Treasury Dept proposal for changes in oil industry taxation policies, with 1 table showing potential impact on oil production and reserves, various periods 1986-91. Data are from Interstate Oil Compact Commission.

OPERATORS IN PERU TRIM 1985 E&D DRILLING PROGRAMS

(p. 50) Article, with 1 table showing new wildcat, development, and secondary recovery oil wells in Peru, by company and drilling location, 1982-85. Data are from Petroleos del Peru, SA.

For description of a similar article, presenting data through 1984, see SRI 1984 Annual under C6985-1.513.

SCOTTISH AGENCY PREDICTS BIG GAINS IN OFFSHORE OUTLAY

(p. 56) Article, with 1 chart showing world oil/gas industry expenditures for offshore equipment/services, with distribution by country or world area, 1984 and 1988. Data are from Scottish Development Agency.

Sii-DAC DRILLING ACTIVITY: SECOND-MOST-PRODUCTIVE DRILLING YEAR STUMBLES WITH FOURTH-QUARTER DROOP IN ACTIVITY, QUARTERLY FEATURE

(p. 98-104) Quarterly report, by Randy Hall, on oil and gas drilling activity for 4th quarter 1984. Data are presented in terms of the Smith

International, Inc. Drilling Activity Correlator, which distinguishes 3 types of drilling activity on the basis of technological sophistication.

Includes 4 tables showing wells and footage drilled, by type quarterly 1977-84, and by region 3rd-4th quarter 1984 and full year 1983-84.

C6985–1.617: Feb. 25, 1985 (Vol. 83, No. 8)

WEEKLY TABLES

a. Industry scoreboard, for Feb. 15, 1985. (p. 4)

b. Industry statistics, as of Feb. 8-20, 1985. (p. 136-137)

MONTHLY TABLE

a. Industry statistics: total U.S. land and marine seismic crews, for Jan. 1985. (p. 133)

TAX, MARKET QUESTIONS CUT 1985 U.S. OIL INDUSTRY SPENDING PLANS, ANNUAL FEATURE

(p. 45-48) Annual article on U.S. oil industry capital spending plans for 1985, including exploration/drilling, production, Outer Continental Shelf lease bonuses, refining, petrochemicals, marketing, and pipelines. Data are from O&GJ.

Includes 2 tables showing planned or actual spending for domestic and foreign operations, by function, 1983-85.

CANADIAN INDUSTRY TO BOOST CAPITAL SPENDING, ANNUAL FEATURE

(p. 48) Annual article on Canadian oil industry capital spending plans for 1985, including exploration/drilling, production, refining, petrochemicals, marketing, and pipelines. Includes 1 table showing planned or actual capital spending for domestic operations, by function, 1983-85.

OGJ-MORGAN PIPELINE COST INDEX, OIL: LOWER LABOR COSTS FLATTEN CONSTRUCTION INDEX CURVE, QUARTERLY FEATURE

(p. 92-94) Quarterly article, by Joseph M. Morgan, presenting oil pipeline construction cost indexes for 2nd quarter 1984 (1974=base year). Includes 1 table showing indexes for 18 cost components, 1978-83 and 1st-2nd quarters 1984.

C6985–1.618: Mar. 4, 1985 (Vol. 83, No. 9)

WEEKLY TABLES

a. Industry scoreboard, for Feb. 22, 1985. (p. 4)

b. Industry statistics, as of Feb. 15-25, 1985 (table [8] is omitted). (p. 155-156)

MONTHLY TABLES

a. Nelson Cost Indexes, for Oct. 1984. (p. 120)

b. Industry statistics: active rigs abroad, for Jan. 1985. (p. 156)

IMPORTS WEAKEN U.S. PRODUCT MARKETS

(p. 50-51) Article, with 1 chart and 1 table showing refinery export capacity for 4 OPEC countries, Dec. 1984 and forecast Dec. 1987; and U.S. imports of gasoline and gasoline blending components, for 5 leading countries of origin and all others, 1984. Data are from Energy Information Administration.

IEA SPELLS OUT EXPLORATION TARGET

(p. 52-54) Article, with 1 table showing oil production, reserves/production ratio, and additional reserve requirements needed to meet demand (total and as a percent of potential resources), by country or world area, various years 1983-2000. Data are from International Energy Agency.

AGENCY SEES 1986 SLUMP IN TEXAS DRILLING

(p. 66) Brief article, with 1 table showing Texas oil prices and number of rigs, various years 1983-87. Data are from Texas Comptroller's Office.

C6985–1.619: Mar. 11, 1985 (Vol. 83, No. 10)

WEEKLY TABLES

a. Industry scoreboard, for Mar. 1, 1985. (p. 4)

b. Industry statistics, as of Mar. 1-6, 1985 (table [6] is omitted). (p. 163-164)

MONTHLY TABLES

a. U.S. wells drilled (exploratory only), for Oct. 1984. (p. 161)

b. Industry statistics: selected U.S. and world crude prices, for Mar. 1985; and worldwide crude oil and gas production, for Dec. 1984. (p. 164-165)

WORLD CRUDE, CONDENSATE FLOW IN '84 LOGS FIRST INCREASE SINCE '79, ANNUAL FEATURE

(p. 41-44) Annual article, by Bob Beck and Mike Obel, reviewing world oil production, 1984. Includes 2 charts and 1 table showing oil production for U.S., Canada, and individual OPEC countries, and by world region including Communist and non-Communist areas, 1984, with comparisons to 1983.

U.S. SPOT GAS MARKET PRICE LESS THAN $3/MMBTU

(p. 58) Article introducing monthly table on spot prices for natural gas purchases. Data are from U.S. Natural Gas Clearinghouse monthly surveys of industrial users and local distribution companies in Louisiana, Texas, and Oklahoma.

Includes 1 table showing median bid prices for natural gas purchases from approximately 10 pipeline systems at specified receipt points, Mar. 1985.

EXPLORATION/DEVELOPMENT ACTIVITY DUE LITTLE CHANGE IN U.S. THIS YEAR

(p. 71-74) Article, with 1 table showing oil production and number of fields, by field category (large fields placed on production in 1973/earlier, fields placed on production in 1974/later, and unclassified fields), 1982. Data are from Energy Information Administration.

C6985–1.620: Mar. 18, 1985 (Vol. 83, No. 11)

WEEKLY TABLES

a. Industry scoreboard, for Mar. 8, 1985. (p. 4)

b. Industry statistics, as of Mar. 1-13, 1985 (p. 174-176)

MONTHLY TABLES

a. U.S. wells drilled, for full year 1984. (p. 171-172)

b. Industry statistics: Smith rig count, for Mar. 8, 1985; and Gulf Coast refining margins, for Dec. 1984. (p. 176)

API SPELLS OUT LOSS IN TAX PROPOSAL

(p. 54-57) Article discussing a Treasury Dept proposal for changes in oil industry taxation policies, with 2 tables showing potential impact on oil and gas production and on total and exploratory drilling, 1986, 1990, and 1995. Data are from American Petroleum Institute.

ANNUAL REFINING REPORT

Annual report, for 1984-85, on U.S. oil refinery operations and outlook, presented in 6 articles. Articles with substantial nontechnical statistics are described below.

U.S. REFINING CAPACITY RESUMES DECLINE, ANNUAL FEATURE

(p. 89-91) Annual article, by Richard A. Corbett, on developments in oil refining capacities, based on an O&GJ industry survey.

Includes 4 tables showing refining capacity, Jan. 1, 1984-85, and scheduled for completion in 1985-86; 18 largest companies ranked by capacity, with number of refineries (no date); and number of refining companies, refineries, and capacity, by capacity size group, Jan. 1, 1984-85. Capacity data include varying detail for specific refining processes.

REFINERS MULL NO-LEAD OPTIONS

(p. 108-114) By S. F. Culberson et al. Article examining options available to refiners for conversion to unleaded gasoline production to comply with EPA standards. Data are from Pace Co. Includes 7 undated tables showing investment requirements and capacity for selected processes, and price margins by gasoline and distillate grade.

ANNUAL REFINING SURVEY

(p. 122-137) Annual report, by Aileen Cantrell, on processing capacities of oil refineries, based on an O&GJ industry survey. Includes 2 tables showing crude capacity, and charge and production capacities by process, for individual operating refineries grouped by company and State, Jan. 1, 1985. Also includes listing of inactive refineries, with capacity and location for each.

C6985–1.621: Mar. 25, 1985 (Vol. 83, No. 12)

WEEKLY TABLES

a. Industry scoreboard, for Mar. 15, 1985. (p. 4)

b. Industry statistics, as of Mar. 8-18, 1985 (table [8] is omitted). (p. 150-151)

MONTHLY TABLE

a. Industry statistics: active rigs abroad, for Feb. 1985. (p. 151)

ORDERS FOR SEMISUBMERSIBLES PACE OFFSHORE RIG CONSTRUCTION

(p. 41-46) By Rick Hagar. Article, with 1 list of world offshore rigs under construction by type, showing contractor, shipyard, and delivery date, as of early 1985. Data are from *Ocean Oil Weekly Report.*

ESTIMATE OF POTENTIAL U.S. GAS RESOURCE DECLINES, BIENNIAL FEATURE

(p. 50-51) Biennial article, with 1 table showing onshore and offshore probable, possible, and speculative natural gas resources at vari-

ous depths, by region, as of Dec. 31, 1984. Data are from Potential Gas Agency of the Colorado School of Mines.

Previous article, presenting data as of Dec. 1982, is described in SRI 1983 Annual under C6985–1.419.

END OF U.S. GAS BUBBLE, DRILLING REBOUND SEEN

(p. 52-54) Article, with 3 tables showing estimated gas consumption and production, and drilling activity required to meet demand under 3 consumption scenarios, various years 1984-90. Data are from Morgan Stanley and Co.

ANNUAL PETROCHEMICAL REPORT

Annual compilation of articles, for 1985, discussing trends and outlook for petrochemical processes, plant construction, feedstocks, and products. Articles containing nontechnical statistics are described below.

SAUDI PETROCHEM COMPLEXES MAKE DEBUT

(p. 71-76) By Ted Wett. Article, with 1 undated table showing capacity of Saudi Arabian petrochemical plants, by company, and including foreign partner, feedstocks, and products.

STOP-AND-GO RECOVERY TEMPERS PETROCHEMICAL CONSTRUCTION

(p. 80-86) By Ted Wett. Article, with 3 tables showing U.S. petrochemical production by detailed product, Nov. and 1st 11 months 1983-84; and petrochemical plants under construction/planned, by country and major product, arranged by world region, various years 1975-84. Data are from National Petroleum Refiners Assn and O&GJ.

Other Article

OGJ-MORGAN GAS PIPELINE COST INDEX: CONSTRUCTION ACTIVITY INCREASES; PRICES HOLD, QUARTERLY FEATURE

(p. 126-129) Quarterly article, by Joseph M. Morgan, presenting gas pipeline construction cost indexes for 2nd quarter 1984 (1976=base year).

Includes 2 tables showing indexes for 13 cost components, and composite index, 1979-83 and 1st-2nd quarters 1984; and principal costs for onshore and offshore gas compressor station projects, identified by size, 2nd quarter 1984.

C6985–1.622: Apr. 1, 1985 (Vol. 83, No. 13)

WEEKLY TABLES

a. Industry scoreboard, for Mar. 22, 1985. (p. 4)

b. Industry statistics, as of Mar. 15-27, 1985. (p. 163-164)

MONTHLY TABLES

a. Nelson Cost Indexes, for Nov. 1984. (p. 115)

b. Industry statistics: total U.S. land and marine seismic crews, for Feb. 1985; and worldwide crude oil and gas production, for Jan. 1985. (p. 160, 165)

INDUSTRY RESTRUCTURING KEY FACTOR IN OGJ GROUP'S 1984 PROFITS DIP, QUARTERLY FEATURE

(p. 41-46) Quarterly article, by Robert J. Beck, on U.S. oil industry profits, 1984. Includes 3 tables ranking 24 oil companies by net profits, and also showing revenues for each company; capital/exploration expenditures for 12 companies; and rates of return measures for 6 companies; 4th quarter and/or full year 1984, with comparisons to 1983.

KEY OPERATIONS SEEN CRITICAL TO U.S. OIL RESERVES

(p. 56-57) Article, with 1 table estimating oil reserve additions due to growth of conventional reserves, discovery of new fields in the contiguous U.S. and Alaska, and use of enhanced recovery methods, 1976-85 vs. 1986-2000 periods. Data are from Bureau of Economic Geology, University of Texas at Austin.

OTA: DIVERSIFY U.S. NATURAL GAS SUPPLY BASE

(p. 65) Article, with 1 table comparing natural gas production forecasts of Office of Technology Assessment (OTA), oil companies, and other public and private sources, 1985, 1990, and 2000. Data are from OTA.

QUARTERLY COSTIMATING: HOW NELSON INDEXES HAVE RISEN

(p. 116-117) Quarterly feature, by Gerald L. Farrar, on Nelson indexes of refinery operating, construction labor, and equipment and material costs. Includes 2 tables showing cost indexes for 7 equipment types, quarterly 1980-83; and cost indexes by itemized component, and indexes of refinery inflation, operation, and process operation, selected years 1954-83 and Nov. 1984.

C6985–1.623: Apr. 8, 1985 (Vol. 83, No. 14)

WEEKLY TABLES

a. Industry scoreboard, for Mar. 29, 1985. (p. 4)

b. Industry statistics, as of Mar. 22-Apr. 3, 1985 (table [6] is omitted). (p. 137-138)

MONTHLY TABLE

a. Industry statistics: selected U.S. and world crude prices, for Apr. 1985. (p. 138)

MODEL FOR U.S. LAND-RIG EFFICIENCY AIDS FORECASTS

(p. 67-73) By William J. Gresham. Article on econometric model for forecasting drilling rig efficiency. Model was developed by National Supply Co. Includes 2 methodological tables; and 1 table showing wells, footage, total and active rigs, and rig efficiency, 1983-85.

C6985–1.624: Apr. 15, 1985 (Vol. 83, No. 15)

WEEKLY TABLES

a. Industry scoreboard, for Apr. 5, 1985. (p. 4)

b. Industry statistics, as of Mar. 29-Apr. 10, 1985. (p. 92-94)

MONTHLY TABLES

a. Industry statistics: spot gas prices, for Apr. 1985; Smith rig count, for Apr. 5, 1985; and Gulf Coast refining margins, for Jan. 1985. (p. 92, 94)

C6985–1.625: Apr. 22, 1985 (Vol. 83, No. 16)

WEEKLY TABLES

a. Industry scoreboard, for Apr. 12, 1985. (p. 4)

b. Industry statistics, as of Apr. 5-17, 1985. (p. 142-143)

MONTHLY TABLE

a. API monthly well completions, for Jan.-Feb. 1985. (p. 138)

WORLDWIDE CONSTRUCTION, SEMIANNUAL FEATURE

(p. 96-128) Semiannual list, by Aileen Cantrell, of worldwide construction for refineries, petrochemicals, sulfur, gas processing, related fuels, and pipelining projects, showing the following data, where available, for each: capacity, contractor, estimated costs, and completion date. Listings are by company arranged by country, for each project type.

C6985–1.626: Apr. 29, 1985 (Vol. 83, No. 17)

WEEKLY TABLES

a. Industry scoreboard, for Apr. 19, 1985. (p. 4)

b. Industry statistics, as of Apr. 12-22, 1985 (table [8] is omitted). (p. 127-128)

MONTHLY TABLES

a. Industry statistics: total U.S. land and marine seismic crews, for Mar. 1985; and active rigs abroad, for Mar. 1985. (p. 125, 128)

SLUMP IN U.S. ONSHORE DRILLING, COMPLETION COSTS SEEN AT AN END

(p. 41-46) Article, with 2 tables showing West Virginia gas well drilling costs by component, and Hartzog Draw, Wyoming oil/gas wells drilled and average costs, various years 1980-85. Data are from Cities Service Oil & Gas Corp. and other sources.

DEBT LOADS CALLED KEY TO ACTIVITY OF BIG FIRMS

(p. 62-64) Article, with 1 table showing debt share of capital, percent change in earnings, and capital expenditures, for 5 largest multinational oil companies, 1984-88. Data are from Salomon Bros., Inc.

C6985–1.627: May 6, 1985 (Vol. 83, No. 18)

WEEKLY TABLES

a. Industry scoreboard, for Apr. 26, 1985. (p. 4)

b. Industry statistics, as of Apr. 19-May 1, 1985. (p. 274-275)

MONTHLY TABLES

a. Nelson Cost Indexes, for Dec. 1984. (p. 204)

b. Industry statistics: worldwide crude oil and gas production, for Feb. 1985. (p. 276)

PETROBRAS: CAMPOS BASIN OIL STRIKE MAY BE A GIANT FIELD

(p. 90) Article, with 1 table and 1 chart showing the following for Brazil: onshore and offshore oil production, by State, 1st 2 months 1984-85; and average daily oil production of offshore Campos Basin, 1977-84 and monthly 1984. Data are from Petroleo Brasileiro SA.

EMPLOYMENT, SECURITY LOSSES SEEN FROM TAX PLAN

(p. 91) Article, with 1 undated table showing potential job losses in 5 functional areas of oil industry resulting from enactment of Reagan Administration tax reform proposals. Data are from American Petroleum Institute.

OFFSHORE REPORT: OFFSHORE DRILLING REBOUNDS, PROMPTS NEW CONSTRUCTION, ANNUAL FEATURE

(p. 103-106) Annual article, by W. D. Moore III, summarizing world offshore drilling activity. Data are from O&GJ and Hughes Tool Co.

Includes 1 chart and 2 tables showing mobile rigs by type, and idle and working mobile rigs by world area, 1985; active rigs by world area, 1982-85; and rig utilization rate, by rig type and world area, as of May 1980-85, with overall utilization rate, 1975-85.

INTERNATIONAL SEISMIC CREW COUNT, RECURRING FEATURE

(p. 262) Recurring table showing land and marine seismic crews, for U.S., Canada, Mexico, and 5 world areas, June and Sept. 1984. Data are from Society of Exploration Geophysicists.

C6985–1.628: May 13, 1985 (Vol. 83, No. 19)

WEEKLY TABLES

a. Industry scoreboard, for May 3, 1985. (p. 4)

b. Industry statistics, as of May 3-8, 1985 (table [6] is omitted). (p. 149-150)

MONTHLY TABLE

a. Industry statistics: selected U.S. and world crude prices, for May 1985. (p. 150)

Sii-DAC DRILLING ACTIVITY: DEEPER DRILLING BOOSTS FOOTAGE TOTALS; WELL COUNTS ARE FLAT, QUARTERLY FEATURE

(p. 117-119) Quarterly report, by Jack Knowlton, on oil and gas drilling activity for 1st quarter 1985. Data are presented in terms of the Smith International, Inc. Drilling Activity Correlator, which distinguishes 3 types of drilling activity on the basis of technological sophistication.

Includes 3 tables showing wells and footage drilled, by type quarterly 1983-1st quarter 1985, and by type and region 4th quarter 1984-1st quarter 1985.

OGJ-MORGAN PIPELINE COST INDEX, OIL: LOWER LABOR COSTS HELPED HOLD OIL PIPELINE-BUILDING INDEX TO SLIGHT INCREASE, QUARTERLY FEATURE

(p. 120-127) Quarterly article, by Joseph M. Morgan, presenting oil pipeline construction cost indexes for 3rd quarter 1984 (1974 = base year). Includes 2 tables showing indexes for 18 cost components, 1951-83 and 1st-3rd quarters 1984.

FUTURE OF GAS LIES IN CONVENTIONAL SOURCES

(p. 133) By John C. McCaslin. Article, with 1 table projecting U.S. and world natural gas recoverable resources and production, for conventional sources, and for unconventional sources by type, 2000.

C6985–1.629: May 20, 1985 (Vol. 83, No. 20)

WEEKLY TABLES

a. Industry scoreboard, for May 10, 1985. (p. 4)

b. Industry statistics, as of May 3-15, 1985 (p. 99-101)

MONTHLY TABLES

a. Industry statistics: total U.S. land and marine seismic crews, for Apr. 1985; spot gas prices, for May 1985; Smith rig count, for May 10, 1985; and Gulf Coast refining margins, for Feb. 1985. (p. 96, 99, 101)

RESTRUCTURING HELPS TAKE SLICE OUT OF OGJ GROUP EARNINGS, ANNUAL FEATURE

(p. 25-32) Annual article, by Robert J. Beck and Glenda E. Smith, on financial condition and operations of 24 major and 20 smaller oil firms, 1984. Includes 1 summary table, and 3 detailed tables showing assets ranking and the following data by company, 1984 with comparisons to 1983:

a. Major companies: net profits, revenues, working capital, funds from operations, capital/exploration expenditures, percent return on stockholders' equity, assets, liquids and natural gas production and estimated reserves (with detail for reserve components), net wells drilled, crude runs to stills, and refined product sales.

b. Smaller companies: net profits, revenue, percent return on stockholders' equity, and assets.

C6985–1.630: May 27, 1985 (Vol. 83, No. 21)

WEEKLY TABLES

a. Industry scoreboard, for May 17, 1985. (p. 4)

b. Industry statistics, as of May 10-20, 1985 (table [8] is omitted). (p. 133-134)

MONTHLY TABLES

a. API monthly well completions, for Mar. 1985. (p. 129)

b. Industry statistics: active rigs abroad, for Apr. 1985. (p. 134)

U.S. IN NO RUSH TO RESCUE SMALL REFINERS HURT BY PRODUCT IMPORTS

(p. 25-30) By Patrick Crow. Article, with 1 chart showing oil refinery capacity and utilization, various periods 1980-86. Data are from Independent Refiners Coalition.

DEEP WATER, MOBILE BAY TRACTS SPARK SALE 98

(p. 46-50) Article reporting results of a Federal sale of Outer Continental Shelf oil and gas lease tracts in central Gulf of Mexico, held May 22, 1985. Includes 1 table showing winning bidder and cash bonus bid, for top 20 tracts.

SURVEYS SHOW MORE ENERGY REDUCTION STILL POSSIBLE

(p. 65-77) By Roger O. Pelham and Richard D. Moriarty. Article on oil refinery fuel consumption, and potential fuel and cost savings through selected conservation methods. Data are from results of over 70 energy studies of refining and petrochemical industries, conducted by Profimatics, Inc.

Includes 6 undated tables presenting data on typical refinery energy consumption, losses, and possible recovery; fuel gas yield by processor type; energy savings as percent of consumption, by process; and refinery capacity and cost savings using optimized steam system, for 20 unamed refineries.

C6985–1.631: June 3, 1985 (Vol. 83, No. 22)

WEEKLY TABLES

a. Industry scoreboard, for May 24, 1985. (p. 4)

b. Industry statistics, as of May 17-29, 1985. (p. 91-92)

MONTHLY TABLES

a. Nelson Cost Indexes, for Jan. 1985. (p. 77)

LEAD PHASEDOWN SEEN HIKING NAPHTHA OPTIONS

(p. 47) Article on outlook for light straight run (LSR) naphtha market following EPA ruling on reductions in gasoline lead content. Data are from Chem Systems, Inc. Includes 1 table showing LSR naphtha use in gasoline and as olefin feedstock, 1984-85, 1990, and 1995.

DISTRIBUTION OF WORLD OIL RESOURCES

(p. 86-90) By Stephen Tanzil. Article, with 3 tables showing world oil resources, production, proved reserves, and ultimate recovery, by world area and/or country, various years 1960-84. Data are from World Energy Conference, UN, and O&GJ.

C6985–1.632: June 10, 1985 (Vol. 83, No. 23)

WEEKLY TABLES

a. Industry scoreboard, for May 31, 1985. (p. 4)

b. Industry statistics, as of May 31-June 5, 1985 (table [6] is omitted). (p. 172-173)

MONTHLY TABLES

a. Industry statistics: selected U.S. and world crude prices, for June 1985; and worldwide crude oil and gas production, for Mar. 1985. (p. 173-174)

LESS DEVELOPED COUNTRIES PUSH CAMPAIGNS TO TAP NATURAL GAS

(p. 57-62) By Marcia A. Parker. Article, with 1 table showing natural gas production, consumption, and reserves in 35 developing countries in Latin America, Africa, and the Far East, 1984. Data are from World Bank.

PROFITS SLIDE FOR OGJ GROUP OF FIRMS, QUARTERLY FEATURE

(p. 72-73) Quarterly article, by Robert J. Beck and Glenda E. Smith, on U.S. oil industry profits, 1st quarter 1985. Includes 2 tables ranking 24 oil companies by net profits, and also showing revenues for each company; and net income and capital/exploration expenditures for 12 companies; 1st quarter 1985, with comparisons to 1984.

INDEPENDENTS TACKLE TAX, GAS ISSUES

(p. 78-80) Article, with 1 chart and 1 table showing consumer and wellhead natural gas price trends, various years 1973-84. Data are from Natural Gas Supply Assn.

IPAA PINPOINTS DECLINE IN U.S. DRILLING COSTS, SEMIANNUAL FEATURE

(p. 82-83) Semiannual article presenting cost indexes for drilling and equipping oil/gas wells, by component, 1978-84. Data are from Independent Petroleum Assn of America. Includes 2 tables.

IPAA: U.S. 1985 OIL, GAS DEMAND TO RISE SLIGHTLY, SEMIANNUAL FEATURE

(p. 83-84) Semiannual article presenting Independent Petroleum Assn of America forecast for crude oil and petroleum product supply and demand situation through 4th quarter 1985. Includes 3 tables showing the following:

a. Domestic demand for 6 petroleum products; total exports; domestic production for crude oil and natural gas liquids; imports of crude oil and 6 products; other supply; closing stocks of 6 products, unfinished oils, natural gas liquids, and crude oil; and crude runs to stills; quarterly 1985.

b. Energy consumption: by type of energy, 1984-85; and per unit of GNP, 1970-85.

IADC TALLY SHOWS DECLINE IN ROTARY RIG FLEET SIZE

(p. 84) Brief article, with 1 table showing U.S. and foreign rotary rig fleet owned by members of International Assn of Drilling Contractors, and member contracting firms, 1980 and 1982-85.

C6985–1.633: June 17, 1985 (Vol. 83, No. 24)

WEEKLY TABLES

a. Industry scoreboard, for June 7, 1985. (p. 4)

b. Industry statistics, as of May 31-June 12, 1985 (p. 155-156)

MONTHLY TABLE

a. API monthly well completions, for Apr. 1985. (p. 152)

PROJECTIONS UP FOR TOTAL ENERGY DEMAND BY IEA NATIONS IN 1990

(p. 57-63) By Roger Vielvoye. Article, with 1 chart showing annual oil production forecast for International Energy Agency member countries (aggregate data), selected years 1979-2000.

TANKER CASUALTY LIST LENGTHENS IN IRAN/IRAQ WAR

(p. 68) Article, with tabular list of tanker ships damaged in Persian Gulf during Iran/Iraq war and scrapped or sold for scrappage during 1984-85. Includes vessel name, year built, deadweight, and date of demolition or sale. Data are from Drewry Shipping Consultants Ltd.

U.S. EXPLORATION/PRODUCTION BUDGETS TRIMMED

(p. 73-74) Article, with 1 table showing exploration/production budgets of 20 major oil companies, 1984-85. Data are from Salomon Bros., Inc.

INCREASING VOLUMES OF CANADIAN GAS SEEN U.S. BOUND

(p. 83) Brief article, with 1 table showing U.S. natural gas supply from domestic production and imports (including percent from Canada), selected years 1984-90. Data are from Data Resources of Canada.

OGJ-MORGAN GAS PIPELINE COST INDEX: GAS-PIPELINE CONSTRUCTION COSTS RISE FRACTIONALLY, QUARTERLY FEATURE

(p. 92-94) Quarterly article, by Joseph M. Morgan, presenting gas pipeline construction cost indexes for 3rd quarter 1984 (1976=base year).

Includes 1 table showing indexes for 13 cost components, and composite index, 1979-83 and 1st-3rd quarters 1984.

BIG REFINING BOOSTS SET FOR OAPEC COUNTRIES

(p. 101-109) By S. Akashah and A. M. Abushihada. Article on oil and gas reserves, production, and refining trends in Organization of Arab Petroleum Exporting Countries (OAPEC).

Includes 6 tables showing world vs. OAPEC oil reserves and production; oil and gas reserves, and refining capacity of operating and planned refineries, by OAPEC country; and OAPEC oil consumption, and production and demand for oil and 6 refined products; various years 1970-95.

NIGERIAN REFINERIES STRIVE FOR PRODUCT BALANCE

(p. 110-117) By P. A. Obuasi. Article, with 2 tables showing capacity of 4 Nigerian refineries, by process; and average annual change in consumption rates for 10 petroleum products, selected periods 1971-83. Data are from Nigerian National Petroleum Corp. and other sources.

C6985–1.634: June 24, 1985 (Vol. 83, No. 25)

WEEKLY TABLES

a. Industry scoreboard, for June 14, 1985. (p. 4)

b. Industry statistics, as of June 7-17, 1985 (table [8] is omitted). (p. 126-128)

MONTHLY TABLES

a. Industry statistics: spot gas prices, for May 1985; active rigs abroad, for May 1985; Smith rig count, for June 14, 1985; and Gulf Coast refining margins, for Mar. 1985. (p. 126-128)

CHEVRON SEES VERY SLOW RISE IN OIL CONSUMPTION

(p. 48-49) Article, with 6 charts projecting non-Communist world oil and natural gas supply-demand outlook through 2000. Includes oil and gas production and oil consumption, by world area or country; and U.S. net oil imports, and energy consumption by fuel type; all shown as percent change, various periods 1985-2000. Data are from Chevron Corp.

FUTURE OIL DISCOVERIES OF NON-U.S. FREE WORLD

(p. 120-121) by L. F. Ivanhoe. Article, with 1 chart showing discoveries of recoverable oil reserves in U.S. and in non-Communist areas outside U.S., and average annual footage drilled, 1982-2000 period. Data are based on annual reports of DeGolyer & MacNaughton, Inc., and American Assn of Petroleum Geologists.

C6985–1.635: July 1, 1985 (Vol. 83, No. 26)

WEEKLY TABLES

a. Industry scoreboard, for June 21, 1985. (p. 4)

b. Industry statistics, as of June 14-26, 1985. (p. 77-78)

MONTHLY TABLES

a. Nelson Cost Indexes, for Feb. 1985. (p. 55)

b. Industry statistics: total U.S. land and marine seismic crews, for May 1985. (p. 75)

COMPETITION, PARTIAL DECONTROL POSE CHALLENGE TO U.S. NATURAL GAS INDUSTRY

(p. 19-23) By Rick Hagar. Article, with 1 chart showing distribution of 1985 interstate contracts for natural gas wellhead purchases, by the following price-stability categories: price controlled; and decontrolled (market responsive, subject to price "flyup," and stable price). Data are from Interstate Natural Gas Assn of America.

STUDY ASSESSES REGION TO BE OPENED TO EXPLORATION IN CHINA

(p. 34-35) Article on estimates of PRC oil and natural gas production based on comparisons with U.S. regions with similar geologic characteristics. Data are from East-West Center. Includes 2 tables showing oil and natural gas production value, total and per square kilometer, by PRC Province (with U.S. State geologic analog), through 1980 or 1982.

QUARTERLY COSTIMATING: HOW INDEXES HAVE RISEN

(p. 48-49) Quarterly feature, by Gerald L. Farrar, on Nelson indexes of refinery operating, construction labor, and equipment and material costs. Includes 2 tables showing cost indexes for industrial electric power, fuel oil transport, natural gas at wellhead, and overall refinery fuel, quarterly 1980-84; and cost indexes by itemized component, and indexes of refinery inflation, operation, and process operation, selected years 1954-84 and Feb. 1985.

C6985–1.636: July 8, 1985 (Vol. 83, No. 27)

WEEKLY TABLES

a. Industry scoreboard, for June 28, 1985. (p. 4)

b. Industry statistics, as of June 28-July 3, 1985 (table [6] is omitted). (p. 78-79)

MONTHLY TABLES

a. Industry statistics: selected U.S. and world crude prices, for June 1985; and worldwide crude oil and gas production, for Apr. 1985. (p. 79-80)

INCREASES IN SOVIETS' REVENUE FROM OIL EXPORTS TAPERING OFF, ANNUAL FEATURE

(p. 23) Annual article, with 1 table showing value of Soviet oil and gas exports, by Communist and non-Communist country of destination, 1983-84 (table incorrectly reads 1982-83).

Previous feature, with data for 1982-83, is described in SRI 1984 Annual under C6985-1.540.

ARGENTINA SEEKS TAKERS FOR ONSHORE, OFFSHORE ACREAGE

(p. 28) Article, with 1 undated table showing area of Argentine onshore and offshore oil lease tracts available for contract, and area of onshore tracts reserved for government owned Yacimentos Petroliferos Fiscales (YPF). Data are from YPF.

EXPLORATION AND DEVELOPMENT: GULF COAST TERTIARY, 1983

(p. 68-73) By William C. Eisenhardt and Harry T. Holzman. Article, with 3 charts showing wells drilled in the Tertiary geologic formation of the Gulf Coast, by district and well type, 1982-83. Data are from American Petroleum Institute.

C6985–1.637: July 15, 1985 (Vol. 83, No. 28)

WEEKLY TABLES

a. Industry scoreboard, for July 5, 1985. (p. 4)

b. Industry statistics, as of June 28-July 10, 1985. (p. 154-156)

MONTHLY TABLES

a. Industry statistics: spot gas prices, for July 1985; Smith rig count, as of July 5, 1985; and Gulf Coast refining margins, for June 1985. (p. 154, 156)

GAS PROCESSING REPORT, ANNUAL FEATURE

Annual report on worldwide developments in the natural gas processing industry. Includes the annual statistical features described below.

NUMBERS POSITIVE FOR 1984 GAS PROCESSING

(p. 71-76) Annual article, by Ted Wett, on trends in world natural gas and natural gas liquids (NGL) processing, 1970s-85. Includes 6 tables showing the following:

a. Gas throughput and proven reserves, and NGL production, for U.S., Canada, and rest of non-Communist world; and U.S. gas processing plants, throughput, capacity, and NGL production, by State; 1983 and/ or 1984, with proven reserves as of Jan. 1, 1985.

b. World gas processing plants under construction/planned 1984-85, gas production 1977-84, and gas reserves as of Jan. 1, 1985, all by country or world area; and top 20 countries ranked by gas production, 1984.

WORLDWIDE GAS PROCESSING

(p. 90-123) Annual tabular presentation, compiled by Aileen Cantrell, of world gas processing facilities as of Jan. 1, 1985. Includes 2 summary tables; and 1 extended table showing gas capacity, throughput, process method, and average daily production by type of product, all by company and plant, arranged by U.S. State, Canadian Province, and 38 other countries.

C6985–1.638: July 22, 1985 (Vol. 83, No. 29)

WEEKLY TABLES

a. Industry scoreboard, for July 12, 1985. (p. 4)

b. Industry statistics, as of July 5-17, 1985. (p. 136-137)

MONTHLY TABLE

a. API monthly well completions, for May 1985. (p. 134)

FOREIGN INVESTORS HIKE FLOW OF CAPITAL TO U.S. OPERATIONS

(p. 41-44) By Marcia A. Parker. Article, with 2 charts showing number and value of foreign investments in the U.S. petroleum industry, by type, 1980-84. Data are from Commerce Dept.

INDUSTRY AWAITS INCENTIVES, ACREAGE IN MALAYSIA

(p. 48-49) Article, with 1 table showing Malaysia offshore oil industry expenditures (in Malaysian dollars), seismic survey line kilometers, and wells drilled by type, with detail for wells drilled by Malaysia's national oil company, 1981-84. Data are from Petroliam Nasional Bhd.

FISHER SEES STABLE TEXAS OIL OUTPUT

(p. 50-51) Article, with 4 tables showing Texas oil reserve additions, production status, and reserve-to-production ratios, with selected detail by State region, various periods 1973-84.

C6985–1.639: July 29, 1985 (Vol. 83, No. 30)

WEEKLY TABLES

a. Industry scoreboard, for July 19, 1985. (p. 4)

b. Industry statistics, as of July 12-22, 1985 (table [8] is omitted). (p. 191-192)

MONTHLY TABLE

a. Industry statistics: active rigs abroad, for June 1985. (p. 192)

THREE NATIONS ACCUSED OF DUMPING OCTG

(p. 85) Article on charges of unlawful trade practices in the oil country tubular goods (OCTG) market brought by 2 U.S. companies against Canada, Taiwan, and Argentina. Data are from Lone Star Steel Co. Includes 1 table showing antidumping duties sought on OCTG imports from each country; and each country's share of U.S. OCTG market, 1979 and current.

1985 MIDYEAR FORECAST AND REVIEW, ANNUAL FEATURE

Annual feature, for 1985, on oil and gas industry supply-demand situation, covering exploration, production, imports, exports, and prices. Most data are from journal surveys and DOE. Includes the following annual statistical articles:

U.S. OIL DEMAND RISE DUE IN '85 AFTER REBOUND IN SECOND HALF

(p. 89-102) Annual article, by Robert J. Beck, on U.S. and worldwide oil supply and demand situation and outlook, 1970s-85. Includes 12 tables showing the following:

U.S. Data

a. Domestic demand, exports, and stocks, for crude oil and/or 7-8 refined products; crude oil and refined product domestic supply, imports by country of origin, and stock change; and total energy demand by fuel type; with selected detail for PAD Districts 1-4 combined and District 5, various periods 1983-85.

b. Refinery crude runs, input to distillation units, capacity, and utilization rate; crude/condensate production by PAD district and State; and refiner crude oil acquisition cost, and retail gasoline and residential heating oil prices; various periods 1976-85.

c. GNP compared to total and oil energy consumption, selected years 1929-85.

Worldwide Data

d. Production by country, with detail for OPEC ceilings; and official crude oil prices of 7 OPEC and 5 non-OPEC countries; various periods 1982-85.

U.S. DUE ANOTHER DROP IN NUMBER OF ACTIVE RIGS

(p. 106-118) Annual article, by John C. McCaslin, forecasting oil and gas well drilling activity in U.S. and Canada, by State and Province, 1984-85.

Includes 4 tables showing field and wildcat wells and total footage to be completed, by State and Canadian Province; U.S. wells drilled and planned by leading independent and major oil companies (aggregate data); and rotary rig peak, low, and average activity, by State and for Canada; all with detail for selected geographic subdivisions, including offshore, various periods 1984-85.

Other Article

CHANGE SEEN KEY TO INDONESIAN OIL OUTLOOK

(p. 162-175) By Stephen Tanzil. Article on Indonesian oil supply and demand outlook, and economic impact of oil industry. Data are from IMF, DOE, O&GJ, and other sources. Includes 8 tables showing the following, for Indonesia unless otherwise indicated:

a. Current account balance by component, including exports and imports of goods, net payments for services, and investment income, 1974-83; and Indonesian vs. world oil production and reserves, various years 1960-84, with detail by world region and Indonesian basin.

b. Oil production since 1893; percent change in oil consumption by sector, annual average for 1970-80 period, and annually for 1981-83; and projected demand for oil, and commercial energy consumption by fuel type, various years 1980-2000.

C6985–1.640: Aug. 5, 1985 (Vol. 83, No. 31)

WEEKLY TABLES

a. Industry scoreboard, for July 26, 1985. (p. 4)

b. Industry statistics, as of July 19-31, 1985. (p. 127-128)

MONTHLY TABLES

a. Nelson Cost Indexes, for Mar. 1985. (p. 102)

b. API monthly well completions, for June 1985. (p. 124)

c. Industry statistics: total U.S. land and marine seismic crews, for June 1985. (p. 124)

CANADIAN INDUSTRY RESPONDS TO ABOUT-FACE ON ENERGY POLICY

(p. 25-28) Article, with 1 chart showing Canadian oil/gas revenues, with Provincial and Federal government and industry shares, 1983-84. Data are from Canadian Petroleum Monitoring Agency.

PUBLIC FUND SALES DECLINE SHARPLY IN FIRST HALF OF 1985, QUARTERLY FEATURE

(p. 40) Quarterly article on performance of oil industry limited partnership investment funds. Data are from Robert A. Stanger & Co. Includes 1 table showing public fund sales, by type, 1st half 1984-85.

This is the 1st quarterly feature.

RESOURCE ESTIMATE FALLS FOR FEDERAL AREAS OFF THE U.S.

(p. 42) Article, with 1 table showing estimated offshore oil and gas resources in Federal areas of the Outer Continental Shelf, by area, 1981 and 1984. Data are from U.S. Geological Survey and Minerals Management Service.

COGENERATION GAS MARKET CONTINUES TO GROW

(p. 50-51) Article, with 2 tables showing cogeneration plant certification applications and electrical capacity, by fuel type, 1980-84 and 1st quarter 1985, with detail by company for natural gas-fired plants (and including plant location), 1st quarter 1985. Data are from FERC.

INTERNATIONAL SEISMIC CREW COUNT, RECURRING FEATURE

(p. 124) Recurring table showing land and marine seismic crews, for U.S., Canada, Mexico, and 5 world areas, Sept. and Dec. 1984. Data are from Society of Exploration Geophysicists.

C6985–1.641: Aug. 12, 1985 (Vol. 83, No. 32)

WEEKLY TABLES

a. Industry scoreboard, for Aug. 2, 1985. (p. 4)

b. Industry statistics, as of Aug. 2-7, 1985 (table [6] is omitted). (p. 126-127)

MONTHLY TABLES

a. Industry statistics: selected U.S. and world crude prices, for Aug. 1985; and worldwide crude oil and gas production, for May 1985. (p. 127-128)

AGA: U.S. TO HOLD EDGE IN AMMONIA PLANT COSTS

(p. 51) Article, with 1 undated table estimating capital, production, and shipping/terminal costs involved in production of ammonia in new plants in U.S. and 9 foreign countries or regions. Data are from American Gas Assn.

BANKERS TRUST SEES REBOUND IN U.S. DRILLING AFTER 1986

(p. 54-57) Article, with 1 table showing oil and gas price forecasts under stable and declining price scenarios, selected years 1984-95. Data are from Bankers Trust Co.

THREE GATHERING NETWORKS COMPRISE NORTHERN NORTH SEA GAS SYSTEM

(p. 84-90) By George W. Crayston and P. A. Philpot. Article on operations of the Northern Associated Gas System, a gas gathering, processing, and distribution system operating among 8 fields in the North Sea. Includes 2 undated tables showing the following for the system:

a. Reserves, and plateau production or exports, for oil, gas, and natural gas liquids; date of 1st oil and gas export; capital cost; number of platforms; and operating company; all by field.

b. Pipeline length, size, content, and capacity, by segment.

OGJ-MORGAN PIPELINE COST INDEX, OIL: COSTS ADVANCE SLOWLY DESPITE BUILDING REBOUND, ANNUAL FEATURE

(p. 97-101) Annual article, by Joseph M. Morgan, presenting oil pipeline component and construction cost summary for 1984, with cost index trends from 1980. Includes 4 tables showing the following:

a. Pipeline cost indexes for 18 cost components, and total composite index, annually 1980-83, and quarterly 1984; and steel line pipe inventory mileage and tonnage, purchased tonnage, mill price, and average cost, by pipe diameter, 1984, with average cost comparisons to 1974.

b. Onshore and offshore pipeline construction projects, length, cost range, and total cost, by pipe diameter; and number of steel storage tanks erected, capacity, weight, and cost, by tank type; all for 1984.

C6985–1.642: Aug. 19, 1985 (Vol. 83, No. 33)

WEEKLY TABLES

a. Industry scoreboard, for Aug. 9, 1985. (p. 4)

b. Industry statistics, as of Aug. 2-14, 1985. (p. 148-150)

MONTHLY TABLES

a. Industry statistics: spot gas prices, for July 1985; Smith rig count, for Aug. 9, 1985; and Gulf Coast refining margins, for May 1985. (p. 148, 150)

LEASE SALE OFF TEXAS DRAWS WEAK RESPONSE

(p. 56-57) Article reporting results of a Federal sale of Outer Continental Shelf oil and gas lease tracts in western Gulf of Mexico, held Aug. 14, 1985. Includes 1 table showing winning bidder and cash bonus bid, for top 20 tracts.

Sii-DAC DRILLING ACTIVITY: GAINS ACROSS CENTRAL U.S., DEEPER WELLS LIFT DRILLING TOTALS, QUARTERLY FEATURE

(p. 116-118) Quarterly report, by Jack Knowlton, on oil and gas drilling activity for 2nd quarter 1985. Data are presented in terms of the Smith International, Inc. Drilling Activity Correlator, which distinguishes 3 types of drilling activity on the basis of technological sophistication.

Includes 3 tables showing wells and footage drilled, by type, quarterly 1983-2nd quarter 1985, and by type and region, 1st-2nd quarter 1985.

C6985–1.643: Aug. 26, 1985 (Vol. 83, No. 34)

WEEKLY TABLES

a. Industry scoreboard, for Aug. 16, 1985. (p. 4)

b. Industry statistics, as of Aug. 9-19, 1985 (table [8] is omitted). (p. 92-93)

MONTHLY TABLE

a. Industry statistics: active rigs abroad, for July 1985. (p. 93)

TRANSMISSION LINES STEP UP CONTRACT CARRIAGE

(p. 36) Article, with 1 table showing contract carriage natural gas shipments by pipelines, for distributors and end users, 1982-83 and quarterly 1984-1st quarter 1985. Data are from Interstate Natural Gas Assn of America.

C6985–1.644: Sept. 2, 1985 (Vol. 83, No. 35)

WEEKLY TABLES

a. Industry scoreboard, for Aug. 23, 1985. (p. 4)

b. Industry statistics, as of Aug. 16-28, 1985. (p. 95-96)

MONTHLY TABLES

a. Nelson Cost Indexes, for Apr. 1985. (p. 76)

b. Industry statistics: total U.S. land and marine seismic crews, for July 1985. (p. 92)

RESTRUCTURING IN SECOND QUARTER KEY PART OF FIRST-HALF PROFIT SLUMP, QUARTERLY FEATURE

(p. 17-21) Quarterly article, by Robert J. Beck, on U.S. oil industry profits, 1st half 1985. Includes 3 tables ranking 25 oil companies by net profits, and also showing revenues for each company; and capital/exploration expenditures, liquids and natural gas production, refinery runs, and petroleum product sales, for selected companies; 2nd quarter and/or 1st half 1985, with comparisons to 1984.

SALOMON BROS. PINPOINTS HIKE IN CANADIAN NETBACKS

(p. 26) Article, with 1 table showing top 20 Canadian companies ranked by production of crude oil/natural gas liquids and natural gas, 1984. Data are from Salomon Bros., Inc.

TOTAL 1984 U.S. EARNINGS DROP FOR CHASE GROUP

(p. 34-35) Article, with 6 charts and 1 table showing aggregate financial trends for major oil companies, including distribution of revenues by source and expenditures (U.S. and rest of world) by type, 1983 and/or 1984. Data are from an annual Chase Manhattan Bank report, covered in SRI under B1900-4.

ETHYLENE REPORT, ANNUAL FEATURE

Annual compilation of articles on trends in world ethylene supply and demand, and processing technology. Statistical articles are described below.

NEW CAPACITY FORCES ETHYLENE PRODUCERS TO AIM FOR LOWER COST, FLEXIBILITY, ANNUAL FEATURE

(p. 39-44) Annual article, by Ted Wett, on world ethylene production capacity, 1985 and trends. Data are from DeWitt & Co., Inc. and other sources.

Includes 3 tables showing world ethylene capacity, by country and world area, as of June 1983-85; production by feedstock, 1984, 1989, and 1994; and ethylene and co product capacity and feedstocks, by plant arranged by company and country, and including plant location, as of June 1985.

POLYMER DEMAND COULD QUICKLY SOAK UP NEW OLEFIN OUTPUT

(p. 44-45) By Ted Wett. Article, with 1 table forecasting ethylene trade lost by exporters in U.S., Western Europe, and Japan, to new exporters in Canada, Saudi Arabia, Southeast Asia, and Latin America, 1987. Data are from DeWitt & Co., Inc.

Other Feature

INTERNATIONAL SEISMIC CREW COUNT, RECURRING FEATURE

(p. 92) Recurring table showing land and marine seismic crews, for U.S., Canada, Mexico, and 5 world areas, Dec. 1984 and Mar. 1985. Data are from Society of Exploration Geophysicists.

C6985–1.645: Sept. 9, 1985 (Vol. 83, No. 36)

WEEKLY TABLES

a. Industry scoreboard (omitted).

b. Industry statistics, as of Aug. 23-Sept. 4, 1985 (tables [2], [4-5], and [7] are omitted). (p. 196)

MONTHLY TABLES

a. API monthly well completions, for July 1985. (p. 192)

b. Industry statistics: worldwide crude oil and gas production, for June 1985. (p. 197)

FIRST HALF WORLD OIL FLOW FAILS TO SUSTAIN 1984 INCREASE, ANNUAL FEATURE

(p. 59-62) Annual article reviewing world crude oil production trends through 1st half 1985. Includes 1 map, 1 chart, and 1 table showing oil production by world area, including aggregate Communist countries, and detail for OPEC by country, 1st half 1985 with percent change from 1st half 1984.

ENHANCED RECOVERY BOOSTS U.S. CRUDE RESERVES, ANNUAL FEATURE

(p. 64) Annual article on Energy Information Administration oil and gas reserve estimates through 1984. Includes 1 table showing proved reserves, reserve adjustments and additions (including discoveries), and production, for crude oil, natural gas, and natural gas liquids, various years 1976-84.

OGJ 400, ANNUAL FEATURE

(p. 89-127) Annual article presenting financial and operating data for top 400 oil and gas producing companies, with rankings. Data are for 1984 company fiscal year, and are compiled by O&GJ. Contains narrative report and the following:

a. Top 10 companies ranked by rates of return on assets, revenues, and stockholders' equity. 3 charts. (p. 90)

b. Name changes from 1984 O&GJ 400; and top 10 companies ranked by amount of new reserves, with percent increase in reserves from previous year. 1 list and 1 chart. (p. 91-92)

c. Top 20 companies ranked by each of the 14 categories listed below. 7 tables. (p. 92-99)

d. Top 400 companies ranked by assets, and also showing revenue, net income, stockholders equity, capital/exploratory spending, worldwide and U.S. liquids and natural gas production and reserves, and U.S. net wells drilled, all with rankings. 1 table. (p. 102-125)

e. Alphabetical index of companies. (p. 126-127)

This is the 3rd annual feature.

PETROLEUM GEOLOGY OF THE REPUBLIC OF GUINEA-BISSAU

(p. 180-191) By Michel A. Dumestre and Francisco F. Carvalho. Article, with 1 map showing onshore and offshore exploratory wells drilled in Guinea-Bissau during the 1960-84 period, including the following for each: location, depth, completion date, and production status.

C6985–1.646: Sept. 16, 1985 (Vol. 83, No. 37)

WEEKLY TABLES

a. Industry scoreboard, for Sept. 6, 1985. (p. 4)

b. Industry statistics, as of Sept. 6-11, 1985 (table [6] is omitted). (p. 134-136)

MONTHLY TABLES

a. Industry statistics: spot gas prices, and selected U.S. and world crude prices, for Sept. 1985; Smith rig count, for Sept. 6, 1985; and Gulf Coast refining margins, for June 1985. (p. 134-136)

FLOW OF DEVELOPMENT PROJECTS SLOWS OFF UK

(p. 65-66) Article, with 1 undated table showing minimum reserve base (oil or oil equivalent) for North Sea oil fields at 4 oil price levels (in British pounds), by field size/drilling platform type.

API STUDY SHOWS OIL COMPANIES' HIGH U.S. TAX RATE

(p. 76) Article, with 1 table comparing Federal tax burden of oil vs. nonoil companies (shown as percent of net income with and without windfall profit tax), 1980-84. Data are from American Petroleum Institute.

OGJ-MORGAN GAS PIPELINE COST INDEX: PLANNED CONSTRUCTION ACTIVITY LEAPED, COSTS CREPT AHEAD, QUARTERLY FEATURE

(p. 101-106) Quarterly article, by Joseph M. Morgan, presenting gas pipeline construction cost indexes for 4th quarter 1984 (1976=base year).

Includes 5 tables showing indexes for 13 cost components, and composite index, 1980-83 and quarterly, 1984; steel pipe inventory and estimated cost in 1984, and average cost in 1976, by pipe size; and onshore and offshore gas pipeline projects, length, and cost, with cost comparison detail by pipe size, 1984.

WORLD SULFUR DERIVED FROM OIL AND GAS, ANNUAL FEATURE

(p. 117-121) Annual feature, by Ailleen Cantrell, on worldwide petroleum-based sulfur recovery plant production and capacity. Contains 1 extended table showing sulfur source material and daily production and capacity, by plant arranged by company and country, as of Jan. 1985.

C6985-1.647: Sept. 23, 1985 (Vol. 83, No. 38)

WEEKLY TABLES

a. Industry scoreboard, for Sept. 13, 1985. (p. 4)

b. Industry statistics, as of Sept. 6-18, 1985. (p. 174-175)

U.S. REFINERS BANK 3.3 BILLION G OF LEAD RIGHTS

(p. 58) Article, with 1 table showing production and imports of leaded and unleaded gasoline, 1st quarter 1984-85. Data are from EPA.

DRILLING FACES FAIR YEAR FOR WELLS AND FOOTAGE, ONLY MEDIOCRE FOR RIG DEMAND, ANNUAL FEATURE

(p. 71-75) Annual article, by W. D. Moore III, with 2 tables showing rig count, wells and footage drilled, average well depth, and wells and footage per rig (with detail for wells over 2,500 ft. deep), various years 1971-86.

C6985-1.648: Sept. 30, 1985 (Vol. 83, No. 39)

WEEKLY TABLES

a. Industry scoreboard, for Sept. 20, 1985. (p. 4)

b. Industry statistics, as of Sept. 13-23, 1985 (table [8] is omitted). (p. 80-81)

MONTHLY TABLES

a. Industry statistics: total U.S. land and marine seismic crews, and active rigs abroad, for Aug. 1985. (p. 72, 81)

U.S. GEOTHERMAL RETRENCHING FROM PERIOD OF VIGOROUS EXPANSION

(p. 17-21) By Bob Williams. Article, with 1 table showing geothermal wells and footage drilled, and development wells as percent of total, 1975-84. Data are from Republic Geothermal, Inc.

MORE FLAK HITS FERC RESTRUCTURING PLAN

(p. 26-28) Article, with 1 chart showing potential reduction of natural gas drilling under FERC's proposed block billing pricing system, with comparisons to actual gas wells drilled in 1984. Data are from Natural Gas Supply Assn.

C6985-1.649: Oct. 7, 1985 (Vol. 83, No. 40)

WEEKLY TABLES

a. Industry scoreboard, for Sept. 27, 1985. (p. 4)

b. Industry statistics, as of Sept. 20-Oct. 2, 1985. (p. 157-158)

MONTHLY TABLES

a. Nelson Cost Indexes, for May 1985. (p. 142)

GAS ROLE IN EUROPE TIED TO COMPETITIVE PRICING

(p. 48-49) By Helga Steeg. Article, with 4 charts showing aggregate energy requirements of European OECD countries, by fuel type, selected years 1960-84 and projected to 2000. Data are from International Energy Agency.

CHINA'S 1990 OIL OUTPUT GOAL SEEN ATTAINABLE

(p. 50-51) Article, with 3 tables showing PRC crude oil production and petroleum product exports; crude oil and gasoline exports, by country of destination; and refinery output for 6 products; various years 1972-84, with refinery output projected for 1990. Data are from East-West Center.

TEST SALE OF 1.1 MILLION BBL PLANNED FROM SPR

(p. 57) Article on test drawdown and sale of Strategic Petroleum Reserve crude oil. Data are from DOE. Includes 1 table showing volume of oil scheduled for sale, Nov. 18, 1985-Jan. 17, 1986 period, with storage and delivery site, delivery method, and oil specifications.

QUARTERLY COSTIMATING: HOW INDEXES HAVE RISEN

(p. 114-115) Quarterly feature, by Gerald L. Farrar, on Nelson indexes of refinery operating, construction labor, and equipment and material costs. Includes 2 tables showing cost indexes as follows: by major construction and operating component, monthly 1983-84; and by itemized component, with indexes of refinery inflation, operation, and process operation, selected years 1954-84 and May 1985.

C6985-1.650: Oct. 14, 1985 (Vol. 83, No. 41)

WEEKLY TABLES

a. Industry scoreboard, for Oct. 4, 1985. (p. 4)

b. Industry statistics, as of Oct. 4-9, 1985 (table [6] is omitted). (p. 153-154)

MONTHLY TABLES

a. API monthly well completions, for Aug. 1985. (p. 149)

b. Industry statistics: selected U.S. and world crude prices, for Oct. 1985; and worldwide crude oil and gas production, for July 1985. (p. 154-155)

ASHLAND FORESEES PERSISTENT SLIDE IN PRICES FOR CRUDE OIL

(p. 59-60) Article, with 2 tables showing outlook for non-Communist world crude oil supply, including exports from Communist world; demand (total and for U.S.); and prices under 3 pricing scenarios; various years 1982-95. Data are from Ashland Oil, Inc.

C6985-1.651: Oct. 21, 1985 (Vol. 83, No. 42)

WEEKLY TABLES

a. Industry scoreboard, for Oct. 11, 1985. (p. 4)

b. Industry statistics, as of Oct. 4-16, 1985. (p. 128-130)

MONTHLY TABLES

a. Industry statistics: spot gas prices, for Oct. 1985; Smith rig count, for Oct. 11, 1985; and Gulf Coast refining margins, for July 1985. (p. 128, 130)

ADMINISTRATION TAX PLAN SEEN HURTING SMALL FIRMS

(p. 44) Article, with 1 undated table showing potential impact of Reagan Administration tax reform proposal on typical independent oil company finances. Data are from Touche Ross and Co.

WORLDWIDE CONSTRUCTION, SEMIANNUAL FEATURE

(p. 85-113) Semiannual list, by Ailleen Cantrell, of worldwide construction for refineries, petrochemicals, sulfur, gas processing, related fuels, and pipelining projects, showing the following data, where available, for each: capacity, contractor, estimated costs, and completion date. Listings are by company arranged by country, for each project type.

C6985-1.652: Oct. 28, 1985 (Vol. 83, No. 43)

WEEKLY TABLES

a. Industry scoreboard, for Oct. 18, 1985. (p. 4)

b. Industry statistics, as of Oct. 11-21, 1985 (table [8] is omitted). (p. 157-158)

MONTHLY TABLE

a. Industry statistics: active rigs abroad, for Sept. 1985. (p. 158)

MASTER LIMITED PARTNERSHIPS SET FUND SALE PACE, QUARTERLY FEATURE

(p. 59) Quarterly article on performance of oil industry limited partnership investment funds. Data are from Robert A. Stanger & Co. Includes 1 table showing oil industry public and private fund sales by type, 1st half or 1st 9 months 1985 with change from 1984.

LAST YEAR'S ECONOMIC RECOVERY FOR U.S. INDEPENDENTS FIZZLES IN FIRST HALF OF '85, ANNUAL FEATURE

(p. 71-75) Annual article, by Jim West, on financial condition and operations of independent oil and gas drilling companies. Data are from company reports and O&GJ. Includes 4 tables showing the following:

a. Net profits and revenues for 209 independent companies ranked by profits, 1st half 1985 with percent change from 1984.

b. Natural gas and crude oil average production and prices, and crude oil windfall profits tax, shown for 12-40 independent companies, 2nd quarter and/or 1st half 1984-85.

WORLD WELL COMPLETIONS, 1984, ANNUAL FEATURE

(p. 153) Annual table showing oil, gas, and dry wells drilled, by country (with detail for North Sea wells), 1984. Data are from American Assn of Petroleum Geologists and American Petroleum Institute.

C6985–2   OFFSHORE
Monthly.
ISSN 0030-0608.
LC 67-3959.
SRI/MF/not filmed

Monthly trade journal reporting on offshore oil and gas exploration, production, transportation, and finance. Also includes trends in related scientific research, engineering and construction, and equipment manufacturing.

Data are from *Offshore* surveys of producers and operators, Electronic Rig Stats, and private and Federal sources.

Issues generally contain feature articles, often focusing on a single industry aspect or area, and occasionally including statistics; narrative editorial depts; and monthly offshore rig report, with the following statistics:

a. Number of mobile rigs working, idle, and en route, by country or world area; and rigs under construction, by type. 1 table.

b. Top 5 petroleum companies ranked by number of working rigs; rigs in use by water depth; and rig utilization rates, by rig type (beginning with July 1985 issue). 3 charts.

Rig report data are current to month prior to cover date; table includes comparisons to previous year.

Annual statistical features include tabulations of offshore platform construction projects, offshore drilling support vessels, deepwater drilling activity, and worldwide drilling and production trends.

Monthly offshore rig report appears in all issues. All additional features with substantial statistical content are described, as they appear, under "Statistical Features." Nonstatistical features are not covered.

Availability: Offshore, Circulation Services Manager, PO Box 1260, Tulsa OK 74101, qualified subscribers †, selected others $45.00 per yr., back issues $4.00; SRI/MF/not filmed.

Issues reviewed during 1985: Nov. 1984-Oct. 1985 (P) (Vol. 44, Nos. 12-13; Vol. 45, Nos. 1-10).

STATISTICAL FEATURES:

C6985–2.601: Nov. 1984 (Vol. 44, No. 12)

DAY RATE ASSUMPTIONS, RECURRING FEATURE

(p. 15) Recurring table showing day rate ranges for offshore mobile rigs in moderate and severe environments, by rig type, 1980/ 81, 1984, and 1987, and also showing day rates required for optimum return on new rig investment. Data are from Smith Barney, Harris Upham and Co.

For description of previous feature, see SRI 1984 Annual under C6985-2.509.

TWELVE YARDS WORKING ON MOBILE RIGS

(p. 17) Table showing mobile rigs under construction by type, by construction yard arranged by country, 1984 with aggregate comparison to 1980.

PLATFORM CONSTRUCTION ACTIVITY DOWN SLIGHTLY, ANNUAL FEATURE

(p. 75-83) Annual *Offshore* survey report on offshore oil and gas platform projects under construction, planned, and under study worldwide, 1984. Includes brief narrative, and 1 detailed list showing platform name, location, fabricator, type, design characteristics, status, and installation date, by operating company arranged by world area.

C6985–2.602: Dec. 1984 (Vol. 44, No. 13)

GAS PRODUCERS FIND RELIEF IN MARKETING

(p. 51-56) By Jim Redden. Article, with 2 tables showing gas production in Gulf of Mexico, Jan.-Apr. 1983-84; and offshore gas wells completed and shut-in, and production, 1979-83. Data are from Minerals Management Service.

FORECAST 85

Compilation of articles forecasting offshore oil and gas activity and market conditions in 1985. Statistical articles are described below.

MARKET BALANCES MIDEAST CAPACITY

(p. 79-85) Article, with 1 chart and 2 tables showing OPEC and non-OPEC share of oil supply, 1983 and 2000; crude oil reserves and production, 1983; and OPEC crude oil shut-in capacity, with detail for 5 countries (no date). Data sources include Conoco Inc.

PRODUCTION GAINS WON'T OFFSET DIPS ELSEWHERE

(p. 102-107) Article, with 2 tables showing U.S. offshore production of oil, condensate, and gas, in State and Federal waters, by State, 1984; and world offshore crude oil production, by country or area, 1979-83. Data are from Petroleum Information Corp., Petroconsultants S. A., and other sources.

WORLDWIDE DRILLING, DESPITE PROBLEMS, SHOWS STRENGTH

(p. 109-112) Article, with 1 table showing offshore exploration/appraisal and development well completions, by country and world area, 1984-85.

C6985–2.603: Mar. 1985 (Vol. 45, No. 3)

MARINE TRANSPORTATION, ANNUAL FEATURE

Annual compilation of articles on marine support services used by offshore oil and gas industry in exploration, construction, and production. Articles with substantial statistical content are described below.

SERVICE BOAT INDUSTRY CHANGES WITH TIMES

(p. 43-45) By Tim Cornitius. Article, with 3 tables showing the following for offshore drilling support vessels: daily charter rates in North Sea and Gulf of Mexico, and North Sea fleet by utilization status, by vessel type and size, various periods 1981-Jan. 1985. Data sources include Petrodata.

BOAT OPERATORS ACT TO MEET SPECIALIZED DEMANDS, ANNUAL FEATURE

(p. 46-62) Annual listing, for 1985, of worldwide offshore drilling support vessels in operation, presenting fleet size and design specifications by vessel type, by company. Data are from an *Offshore* survey. Listing is accompanied by a brief narrative summary, and 1 table showing top 10 companies ranked by fleet size.

C6985–2.604: Apr. 1985 (Vol. 45, No. 4)

WORLD OFFSHORE

(p. 15-17) Article, with 1 table showing installation date and number of platforms, for probable North Sea exploratory oil/gas projects in UK and Norwegian sectors, by field arranged by operating company, as of early 1985. Data are from Petrodata.

ROV SURVEY, ANNUAL FEATURE

(p. 63-64) Annual listing of contractors supplying remotely operated vehicles (ROVs) for use in offshore oil/gas exploration, with number of ROVs in fleet and in use, and planned additions, by model for each contractor, 1985, with aggregate comparisons to 1984.

Contractor listing is included among a compilation of features covering developments in ROV use and technology. Previous listing is described in 1984 SRI Annual under C6985-2.511.

C6985–2.605: May 1985 (Vol. 45, No. 5)

WORLDWIDE EXPLORATION, ANNUAL FEATURE

Annual compilation of articles on offshore oil and gas exploration, development, and production, for selected countries or world areas. Articles with substantial statistical content are described below.

1984 PRODUCTION JUMPS, WHILE EXPLORATION DROPS, ANNUAL FEATURE

(p. 112-116) Annual article, with 2 tables showing offshore daily average oil production and number of wells, by world area and/or country, 1979-84.

GULF OF MEXICO: OPERATORS SET TORRID PACE IN U.S. GULF, ANNUAL FEATURE

(p. 118-119) Annual article, by Leonard Leblanc, with text data showing total or wildcat and exploratory wells drilled by type (oil and gas wells, and dry holes), for Gulf of Mexico waters off Louisiana, Texas, and Mississippi/ Alabama/Florida, 1984 with changes from 1983. Data are from Offshore Oil Scouts Assn.

ATLANTIC COAST: FIRST OFFSHORE PRODUCTION FINALLY WITHIN SIGHT

(p. 139) By Roger Tanner. Article, with 1 table showing high, low, and median projections of oil/gas drilling activity off the Canadian Atlantic Coast, 1985-90. Data are from Canadian Petroleum Assn.

SOUTH AMERICA: BRAZIL IS THE EXCEPTION TO DRILLING DECLINE

(p. 142) Article, with 1 undated table showing depth and test capacity, for 7 wells recently striking crude oil in deepwater areas off Brazil.

C6985–2.606: June 1985 (Vol. 45, No. 6)

GREATER DEPTHS MAY BE CONTRACTOR SALVATION

(p. 58-59) By Guy Dedmon. Article, with 2 tables and 1 chart showing offshore tracts available for oil/gas lease in UK (no date), and deepwater tracts leased in Gulf of Mexico, 1983-84, both by water depth; and distribution of deepwater rigs by world region (no date). Most data are from Sonat Offshore.

DEEPWATER WELLS SURVEY, ANNUAL FEATURE

(p. 75-88) Annual list of worldwide deepwater wells drilled or planned, 1983-86, with operator and rig name, contractor, and well location and depth.

Also includes 1 summary table showing number of deepwater wells by water depth, 1983-86.

C6985–2.607: July 1985 (Vol. 45, No. 7)

WORLD OFFSHORE: INDIA

(p. 11-12) Article on oil industry development objectives of India's 7th 5-year plan, 1985-90 period. Includes 1 text table showing offshore exploratory drilling activity (rig years, wells, and footage) projected under the plan, for ONGC (the state oil company) and Oil India Ltd.

MOBILE RIG UPDATE: JACKUP NUMBERS DICTATE UTILIZATION RATE

(p. 15) Brief article, with 1 undated chart showing distribution of offshore drilling rigs worldwide, by rig type.

INDUSTRY SLUMP CATCHES UP WITH PIPELINERS

(p. 43-44) By Roger Tanner. Article, with 1 undated table showing subsea oil/gas pipeline mileage planned, by world area. Data are from an *Offshore* survey.

C6985–2.608: Aug. 1985 (Vol. 45, No. 8)

OPEC TO DOMINATE

(p. 5) Brief article, with 1 chart showing OPEC vs. non-OPEC shares of the world's oil supply, 1984 and 2000. Data are from Conoco, Inc.

WORLD PLATFORM FABRICATION RECORD

(p. 21) Table showing offshore drilling platform construction, by world area, 1983-85.

LARGE STRUCTURES WILL BE COSTLY TO REMOVE, SCRAP

(p. 60) Article, with 1 map showing number of offshore drilling platforms, by world area; and 1 table showing estimated cost of removing platforms in mild and severe environments, by water depth. No data dates are given. Data are from Oil Industry International Exploration and Production Forum.

C6985–2.609: Oct. 1985 (Vol. 45, No. 10)

ARGENTINA PREPARING FOR OFFSHORE PRODUCTION

(p. 65-66) By Gustavo Pena. Article, with 1 undated table showing oil and gas production test results from 12 offshore wells in Argentina.

C6985–3   INTERNATIONAL PETROLEUM ENCYCLOPEDIA, 1985

Annual. 1985. 394 p.
ISBN 0-87814-282-7.
LC 77-76966.
SRI/MF/excerpts

Annual compilation, for 1985, of information on the world petroleum industry. Includes detailed data on oil exploration, production, refining, reserves, consumption, and industry finances. Also includes data on natural gas and pipelines.

Most data are shown by country, with selected detail for individual U.S. States, Canadian Provinces, companies, and fields. Data are shown primarily for 1970s-85, with selected historical trends, and projections to 1990.

Data are based primarily on reports of industry trade assns and major companies, and government agencies.

Contents:

a. Contents listing and subject index (p. 4-6); and special analysis on PRC energy outlook, with 2 tables. (p. 7-33).

b. Atlas section, detailing oil industry developments by world region and country; with narrative, text data, maps of exploration and production activity, 20 charts, and 9 tables. (p. 34-239).

c. Articles on oil industry seismic activity, offshore operations, mergers, pipelines, tankers, and other topics, interspersed with statistical sections on world oil production, oil rigs and wells, consumption, refining, and major company finances; with conversion measures, 12 charts, and 40 tables. (p. 240-383).

d. Directory of foreign and U.S. oil agencies and trade assns, by country; and statistical section on gas processing, with 1 table. (p. 384-392).

All tables, and charts presenting substantial data not covered in tables, are described below.

This is the 18th edition of the *Encyclopedia*.

Availability: PennWell Publishing Co., PO Box 1260, Tulsa OK 74101, $75.00; SRI/MF/excerpts for all tables and charts described below.

TABLES AND CHARTS:

C6985–3.1: Special Analysis and Atlas

SPECIAL ANALYSIS

a. PRC heavy oil areas, and coal/lignite reserves by region (no date). 2 tables. (p. 14, 30)

ATLAS

U.S.

b. Federal receipts from proposed changes in oil and gas tax incentives for individuals and corporations, including oil depletion allowance, FY86-90; and actual windfall profit tax collections and net effect on Budget of U.S., FY80-83, and estimated collections, 1980-90. 3 tables. (p. 35, 38)

c. Reserve additions from enhanced oil recovery methods (no date). 1 chart. (p. 48)

Canada and Latin America

d. Canada: oil industry revenues, expenses, and net income, and well completions and depth drilled, by Province, 1982-83; and estimated expense distribution of gas revenues, 1984. 1 chart and 2 tables. (p. 80, 85)

e. Latin America: Brazil onshore and offshore oil production by State; energy demand in Colombia, and production in Mexico, by energy source; and Peru exploration/development spending, and crude oil production and reserves, with data for major contractors; various periods 1976-90. 1 chart and 4 tables. (p. 148, 150, 158-159)

C6985–3.2: Seismic Activity, and Worldwide Production and Consumption

a. Land and marine seismic crews operating, by country or world area, 1978-84. 1 table. (p. 241)

b. World oil and gas proven reserves, and crude oil refining capacity by process, Jan. 1, 1985; oil producing wells, July 1, 1984, and average daily production, 1984 and change from 1983; and number of refineries (no date); all by country and world region. 1 table. (p. 258-259)

c. Foreign field discovery dates; depth; number of wells by type; and cumulative and average daily production, 1st half 1984; all by field and company, arranged by country. 1 table. (p. 260-279)

d. U.S. field discovery dates; number of wells; cumulative and annual production, 1984; and estimated remaining reserves; by field grouped by State. 1 table. (p. 280-281)

e. USSR field discovery dates; depth; and cumulative and annual production, 1984; by field. 1 table. (p. 282)

f. Total energy production, 1973-83, and distribution by fuel type, cumulative 1983; by country and world region. 1 table. (p. 282)

g. Rigs active, total 1977-84, and land and offshore 1982-84; and well completions (total and wildcat oil, gas, and dry wells, and total footage), 1983; by country and world region. 2 tables. (p. 283-285)

h. Gas production, by country and world region, 1984. 1 table. (p. 286)

C6985–3.3: Offshore Operations and Industry Mergers

OFFSHORE OPERATIONS

a. Alabama offshore footage drilled and flow rate, by well (no date). 1 chart. (p. 299)

b. Rig operating status worldwide and in Gulf of Mexico, by rig type, as of Dec. 1984. 2 tables. (p. 301)

c. Worldwide offshore average oil production and wells, by world area and/or country; and total offshore production vs. world demand; various years 1970-85. 3 tables (p. 307-309)

MERGERS

d. U.S. oil company merger activity, including average stock market price for oil reserves; merger transaction participants and values; and average capital cost of reserve additions, by company; various periods 1978-84. 1 chart and 2 tables. (p. 311, 314-315)

C6985–3.4: Production Trends, Refining Capacity, and Prices

a. Oil average daily and annual production, selected years 1940-84, and consumption, 1981-83, by country and world region. 2 tables. (p. 316-320) *b.* Refining average capacities, by country and world region, selected years 1940-85; heavy oil resources in place and recoverable, and reserves, by location (no date); U.S. heavy oil steam recovery projects, date started, wells, and total and enhanced production, by company; and plants operating, and crude oil, catalytic cracking, and catalytic reforming capacities by refinery, arranged by company, U.S. State, and Canadian Province, as of Jan. 1, 1985; and refinery oil throughputs, by world region, 1973-83. 8 tables. (p. 321-357)

c. Price of gasoline, diesel fuel, heavy fuel oil for industrial use, and light fuel oil and natural gas for household and industrial uses; for 8-10 counties, 1978-83. 1 table. (p. 364)

C6985–3.5: Industry Finances, Pipelines, Tankers, and Gas Processing

a. Financial condition and operations of 26 major and 20 smaller U.S. oil companies ranked by assets, including net profits, revenues, and return on stockholders' equity; and (for major companies only) working capital, funds from operations, capital/exploration expenditures, liquids and natural gas production and reserves, wells drilled, crude runs to stills, and refined product sales; 1983 with selected comparisons to 1982. 4 tables. (p. 365-368)

b. Pipeline construction in non-Communist world, for gas, crude, and product pipelines by size, by country or world area, 1985 and planned; U.S. interstate gas and liquids pipeline mileage, 1972-83; liquids pipeline investment by item, for 5 unnamed companies, 1983; and U.S. construction costs, by category, for onshore pipelines by size, FY75-84, and for onshore and offshore pipelines by location, 1983/84. 6 tables. (p. 370-377)

c. Tanker fleet requirements for OPEC oil at 3 production levels, by world region (no date); tankers, combination carriers, and dry cargo vessels sold for scrap, by country, 1984; U.S. tanker demand by tonnage size, 1982 and 1990; and existing fleet worldwide by year built and tonnage, as of Jan. 1, 1984. 2 charts and 4 tables. (p. 378-383)

d. Gas plants, capacity, and throughput, as of Jan. 1, 1984; and average daily production by product type, 1983; by country, and selected U.S. State and Canadian Province. 1 table. (p. 392)

C7000
Penton/IPC

C7000–1   PRECISION METAL: 1984 State of the Industry Report
Monthly (selected issue).
Nov. 1984.   (p. 15-66)
Vol. 42, No. 11.
ISSN 0032-714X.
SRI/MF/excerpts

Annual survey report, by Randolph Gold et al., on metalforming industry trends and outlook, including product consumption by end-use market, shipments, and equipment orders, 1970s-85.

Includes data on the value of precision metal products consumed, by type, in the aircraft, automotive, oil field machinery, farm equipment, home appliance, electronic computing, shelving, and vending machine industries, 1977, 1982, and 1985; and shipments of major home appliances, by type, 1980-85.

Also includes operating data for 7 metalforming industries, including product shipments, orders and/or shipments of capital equipment, and business conditions and outlook; variously shown for die casting, extrusion, forging, investment casting, powder metallurgy, roll forming, and stamping industries, various periods 1979-85.

Data are from Census Bureau, Predicasts, Inc., *Precision Metal* annual industry surveys, and industry assns.

Contains introduction (p. 15); and narrative reports on end-use markets (p. 16-35) and individual metalforming industries (p. 36-66), with text data and 17 interspersed tables.

Precision Metal is a monthly periodical reporting trends and developments in metalworking industries and does not normally contain substantial statistics. The annual industry survey is the only feature described by SRI.

Availability: Precision Metal, PO Box 95795, Cleveland OH 44101, qualified subscribers †, others $30.00 per yr., single copy $4.00; SRI/MF/excerpts covering annual survey article.

C7000–2   FOUNDRY MANAGEMENT AND TECHNOLOGY
Monthly.
ISSN 0360-8999.
LC 75-642185.
SRI/MF/not filmed

Monthly trade journal reporting on trends and developments in foundry metalcasting industry, including production, management, and marketing. Data are based on studies by American Metal Market, Foundry Equipment Manufacturers Assn, BLS, and other sources. Month of data coverage is 4-6 months prior to cover date.

General format:

a. News briefs and other depts, including new products, upcoming events, environmental protection, and government regulation.

b. Feature articles on processing technology, materials, labor trends, occupational health and safety, and other subjects relating to foundries, including annual outlook articles.

c. Monthly statistical section, "Foundry Statistics," with 10 monthly tables.

d. 2 monthly and 2 quarterly price tables.

An annual buyer's guide appears in Sept. issue. Dec. issue is a nonstatistical catalog of suppliers.

Monthly and quarterly tables are listed below; monthly tables appear in all issues, except Dec. catalog issue. All additional features with substantial statistical content are described, as they appear, under "Statistical Features;" page locations and latest periods of coverage for quarterly tables are also noted. Nonstatistical features are not covered.

Availability: Foundry Management and Technology, Circulation Department, Penton Plaza, Cleveland OH 44114, industry subscribers †, others $35.00 per yr., single copy $4.00; SRI/MF/not filmed.

Issues reviewed during 1985: Nov. 1984-Oct. 1985 (P) (Vol. 112, Nos. 11-12; Vol. 113, Nos. 1-10).

MONTHLY AND QUARTERLY TABLES:
[Tables [1-13] appear monthly; tables [14-15] appear quarterly.]

FOUNDRY STATISTICS

[1-8] [Shipments: total and/or for sale, for gray iron, steel, malleable iron, aluminum, and copper- and zinc-base castings, with shipment detail by casting type; and for magnesium castings and ductile iron; for month of coverage, previous 12 months, and 2-3 prior years; prior to May 1985 issue, tables included data on unfilled orders.]

[9] Index of foundry equipment orders [monthly for 4 years through month of coverage].

[10] Production workers: estimated number [for ferrous and nonferrous industry workers], and average weekly hours and earnings [for gray iron, malleable iron, steel, and nonferrous industry workers; for month of coverage, previous month, and same month of previous year].

PRICES OF FOUNDRY METAL AND COKE
[Tables show data as of end of 1st or 2nd week of month prior to cover date month.]

[11-13] Foundry coke and pig iron [prices in approximately 5 cities; and price of silvery iron in Keokuk, Iowa].

[14-15] Nonferrous ingot, and iron and steel scrap [prices of 5 types of ingot, and of 7 types of scrap in 15 cities; tables appear quarterly].

STATISTICAL FEATURES:

C7000–2.601: Jan. 1985 (Vol. 113, No. 1)
QUARTERLY TABLES

[14-15] Nonferrous ingot, and iron and steel scrap [prices as of Dec. 10, 1984]. (p. 22)

1985 OUTLOOK: 14.7% MORE CASTINGS, ANNUAL FEATURE

(p. 28-32) Annual survey article on expected foundry industry growth, 1983-89. Data are from responses of 748 foundry managers to a *Foundry Management and Technology* survey. Includes 12 tables showing the following:

a. Perceived major industry problems, 1984-85; planned equipment purchases by type, total and for diecasters, 1985; average capacity utilization, 1984; and percent of companies with capital improvement plans for 1985 and long-term.

b. Expected changes (increase, same level, or decrease) in casting shipments and production, capital expenditures, and capacity, various periods 1984-89.

Most data are shown by major metal and by plant employment size.

C7000–2.602: Feb. 1985 (Vol. 113, No. 2)

1985 LABOR OUTLOOK: LITTLE CHANGE, ANNUAL FEATURE

(p. 61-62) Annual article, by Charles T. Sheehan, on major labor union settlements in the foundry industry, 1970s-84. Includes 2 tables showing average value of labor contract adjustments, for 1st-year of all contracts, and for each year of 3-year contracts, with detail on number and value of settlements with and without cost-of-living increases, primarily 1974-84.

C7000–2.603: Apr. 1985 (Vol. 113, No. 4)

QUARTERLY TABLES

[14-15] Nonferrous ingot, and iron and steel scrap [prices as of Mar. 14, 1985]. (p. 20)

LABOR SCENE

(p. 16) By Charles T. Sheehan. Brief article, with 1 table showing number of foundry industry labor contracts with wage and benefit adjustments due in 1985, and average value of adjustments, for 2- and/or 3-year contracts negotiated in 1983-84. Data are from National Foundry Assn.

C7000–2.604: May 1985 (Vol. 113, No. 5)

LABOR SCENE

(p. 14) By Charles T. Sheehan. Brief article, with 1 table showing average hourly compensation costs for manufacturing production workers, for U.S. and 17 other countries, 1975 and 1984. Data are from BLS.

COLLECTIVE BARGAINING MOVES BACK TO THE SHOP, ANNUAL FEATURE

(p. 67-69) Annual article, by Robert C. Rodgers, with 1 table showing total labor contract settlements at foundries, and number preceded by strikes, 1976-84. Data are from National Foundry Assn.

Previous article, for 1976-83, is described in SRI 1984 Annual under C7000-2.503.

C7000–2.605: June 1985 (Vol. 113, No. 6)

FOUNDRYMEN REPORT ON SAFETY PRODUCTS

(p. 81) Brief article, with 1 table showing responses to a *Foundry Management and Technology* reader survey on costs and types of safety equipment supplied to foundry workers, and also including respondents by position and foundry employment size.

C7000–2.606: July 1985 (Vol. 113, No. 7)

QUARTERLY TABLES

[14-15] Nonferrous ingot, and iron and steel scrap [prices as of June 10, 1985]. (p. 16)

C7000–2.607: Oct. 1985 (Vol. 113, No. 10)

QUARTERLY TABLES

[14-15] Nonferrous ingot, and iron and steel scrap [prices as of Sept. 16, 1985]. (p. 20)

C7000–3   INDUSTRY WEEK

Biweekly.
ISSN 0039-0895.
LC 73-640505.
SRI/MF/not filmed

Biweekly journal (monthly in Dec.) of industrial management, reporting current business and economic news, corporate production and marketing strategies, labor-management practices, developments in major industries, and profiles of prominent executives. Includes detailed business and economic trends and forecasts.

Data are from journal analyses, trade assns, BLS, Federal Reserve System, and Commerce Dept.

Issues contain feature articles, occasionally with statistics; news briefs and editorial depts; and 2 statistical features, "Economic Trends" and "Business Trends/Analysis," with narrative analysis, charts, and 13 recurring tables listed below. Most data are current to 1-3 months prior to cover date.

Recurring tables appear as explained below. All additional features with substantial statistical content are described, as they appear, under "Statistical Features;" page location and latest periods of coverage for monthly table are also noted. Nonstatistical features are not covered.

Availability: Industry Week, Penton Plaza, 1111 Chester Ave., Cleveland OH 44114, qualified executives †, other professionals $25.00 per yr., others $50.00 per yr., single copy $2.00; SRI/MF/not filmed.

Issues reviewed during 1985: Oct. 29, 1984-Oct. 28, 1985 (P) (Vol. 223, Nos. 3-6; Vol. 224, Nos. 1-6; Vol. 225, Nos. 1-7; Vol. 226, Nos. 1-7; Vol. 227, Nos. 1-2).

BIWEEKLY TABLES:

[Tables [1-10] show data annually for selected years from mid-1970s to coming year, and quarterly for current and coming years. Actual data are current to 1-2 quarters preceding cover date; all other data are *Industry Week* forecasts. Tables appear in varying order; not all tables appear in every issue.

Tables [11-12] show data for latest available week, month, or quarter, identified for each item, with comparisons to previous periods. Data generally are current to 2-5 weeks or 1-3 months prior to cover date. Tables appear in every issue.]

ECONOMIC TRENDS

[1-6] GNP [in current and 1972 dollars, occasionally with detail by component]; industrial production [index]; consumer and producer price indexes; capital spending; prime interest rate; and housing starts.

[7-10] Unemployment [rate]; profits; retail sales; and income and savings [rate].

[11] Mood of the economy [building permits issued, business failures, unemployment, consumer confidence and help-wanted indexes, industrial building cost index and vacancy rate, index of leading indicators, manufacturers' new orders, PPI, and weekly workhours in manufacturing].

[12] Business barometers [including aluminum, automobile, oil refinery, electric power, and raw steel output; prime interest rate; coal, lumber, and paperboard production; railroad revenue ton-miles; appliance and aircraft shipments; recreational vehicle deliveries; housing starts; freight car, industrial supplies/machinery, and machine tool orders; manufacturers' inventories; and retail sales].

MONTHLY TABLE:

BUSINESS TRENDS/ANALYSIS

[1] Manufacturing shipments [value for 20 SIC 2-digit industries, including percent change from previous month and year, accompanied by chart showing summary data for year to date for current and previous years. Data are current to 2-3 months prior to cover date].

STATISTICAL FEATURES:

C7000–3.601: Oct. 29, 1984 (Vol. 223, No. 3)

MONTHLY TABLE

[1] Manufacturing shipments, for Aug. 1984. (p. 23)

ROBOTS ARE READY, BUT WHERE ARE THE FACTORIES OF THE FUTURE?

(p. 43-48) By John Teresko. Article, with 1 table ranking top 10 and all other industrial robot manufacturers, by market shares, 1982 and 1984. Data are from Prudential-Bache Securities Inc.

C7000–3.602: Nov. 12, 1984 (Vol. 223, No. 4)

CASHING IN ON THE FITNESS BOOM

(p. 54-56) By Lad Kuzela. Article, with 1 table showing participation in 10 exercise and recreational activities, 1983, with change from 1981. Data are from *Sporting Goods Dealer* magazine.

C7000–3.603: Nov. 26, 1984 (Vol. 223, No. 5)

MONTHLY TABLE

[1] Manufacturing shipments, for Sept. 1984. (p. 28)

CEOs FORESEE A LEVELING OFF IN 1985, ANNUAL FEATURE

(p. 45-54) Annual survey article, by Dale W. Sommer, on chief executive officers' (CEOs) economic expectations for 1985. Data are based on a fall 1984 *Industry Week* survey of over 800 CEOs.

Includes 8 charts showing distribution of responses to questions on business conditions (better, worse, unchanged, or don't know) in past year and in next 6 and 12 months; and expected changes in company sales, capital spending, operating costs, employment needs, and inventories, 1985.

This is the 13th annual survey.

C7000–3.604: Dec. 10, 1984 (Vol. 223, No. 6)

U.S. MANAGERS HAVE HEALTHY ATTENDANCE MARKS

(p. 26) Brief article on health-related absenteeism among corporate executives and their subordinates, based on a recent Research & Forecasts, Inc. survey conducted for *Industry Week*. Includes 1 undated table.

C7000–3.605: Jan. 7, 1985 (Vol. 224, No. 1)

MONTHLY TABLE

[1] Manufacturing shipments, for Oct. 1984. (p. 29)

R&D 1985: EXECS SAY IT'S TOO IMPORTANT TO LEAVE TO RESEARCHERS

(p. 24-25) By John Teresko. Article, with 1 table showing Federal and industry R&D funding for 18 industry groups, 1985. Data are from Battelle Memorial Institute.

Full Battelle report is covered in SRI under R3300-1.

WHO OWNS U.S. INDUSTRY?

(p. 30-34) By John S. McClenahen. Article on foreign direct investments in U.S., 1970s-83. Data are from Commerce Dept and International Trade Administration.

Includes 2 charts and 3 tables showing value of foreign investment as follows: by country or world region of origin, 1974 and 1983; by recipient industry division, 1983; for 13 industry groups and 10 States with highest investment receipts, 1981 or 1983; and for individual transactions in excess of $200 million, with names of companies involved, and headquarter country of foreign investor, 1977-83.

POLISHING THE CORPORATE APPLE

(p. 61-62) By William Pat Patterson. Article, with 1 table showing personal computer sales of top 4 firms (ranked by 1983 sales) and all others, 1979-83. Data are from Dykstra Consultants, Inc.

C7000–3.606: Jan. 21, 1985 (Vol. 224, No. 2)

MONTHLY TABLE

[1] Manufacturing shipments, for Nov. 1984. (p. 20)

STUMBLING BLOCKS BEYOND 1985?

(p. 15-16) By Dale W. Sommer. Article, with 1 table showing amount of outstanding installment consumer credit, and credit as a percent of income, 1976-84. Data are from Federal Reserve Board and Commerce Dept.

C7000–3.607: Feb. 4, 1985 (Vol. 224, No. 3)

CHEMICALS' REACTION: THE RACE TO LAUNCH NEW PRODUCTS

(p. 41-42) By Lad Kuzela. Article, with 1 table showing average annual market growth for 9 types of specialty chemicals, 1982-87 period. Data are from Charles H. Kline and Co.

C7000–3.608: Mar. 4, 1985 (Vol. 224, No. 5)

MONTHLY TABLE

[1] Manufacturing shipments, for Dec. 1984. (p. 37)

C7000–3.609: Mar. 18, 1985 (Vol. 224, No. 6)

1984 FINANCIAL ANALYSIS OF INDUSTRY AND A PREVIEW OF 1985, ANNUAL FEATURE

(p. 59-77) Annual article, by Dale W. Sommer, reporting on the financial condition of approximately 300 companies in 24 industries, 1984.

Contains introduction, with 1 summary table; and analyses of 24 industries, each including 1 table showing revenues, net income or loss, and profit margin, by company, 1984 with comparisons to 1983. Companies are ranked by revenues.

This is the 13th annual analysis.

C7000–3.610: Apr. 1, 1985 (Vol. 225, No. 1)

MONTHLY TABLE

[1] Manufacturing shipments, for Jan. 1985. (p. 22)

OFFICES IN THE SKY

(p. 28-31) By James Braham. Article, with 1 table showing top 20 corporate aircraft fleets ranked by size, with number of aircraft by type (including helicopters), as of year end 1983. Data are from Aviation Data Service, Inc.

C7000–3.611: Apr. 29, 1985 (Vol. 225, No. 3)

MONTHLY TABLE

[1] Manufacturing shipments, for Feb. 1985. (p. 28)

C7000–3.612: May 27, 1985 (Vol. 225, No. 5)

MONTHLY TABLE

[1] Manufacturing shipments, for Mar. 1985. (p. 28)

MARRIAGE BROKER

(p. 30-31) By Marilyn Much. Article, with 1 table showing transaction value of corporate mergers handled by 10 leading investment banks, 1983-84.

VINTAGE YEAR FOR CEOs, ANNUAL FEATURE

(p. 37-39) Annual article, by Mark L. Goldstein, on compensation paid top corporate executives, 1984. Data are from statements filed with the SEC.

Includes 1 table showing the following for 50 highest paid executives: company, executive's name and title, and cash/cash equivalent compensation, 1984, with change from 1983.

C7000–3.613: June 10, 1985 (Vol. 225, No. 6)

'FREE TRADE' SET

(p. 23-25) By John S. McClenahen. Article, with 1 table showing value of U.S. exports to and imports from Israel, 1984. Data are from Commerce Dept.

FOUNTAINS OF EMPLOYMENT

(p. 57-60) By Brian S. Moskal. Article, with 1 table showing service industry employment, by industry group, as of Jan. 1985, with jobs added since Jan. 1981. Data are from Labor Dept.

C7000–3.614: June 24, 1985 (Vol. 225, No. 7)

MONTHLY TABLE

[1] Manufacturing shipments, for Apr. 1985. (p. 28)

SO NEAR, YET SO FAR

(p. 67) By Mark L. Goodstein. Article, with 1 table showing home computers in use, 1981-85 and 1990. Data are from Future Computing, Inc.

C7000–3.615: July 8, 1985 (Vol. 226, No. 1)

NEW GLOBAL GAME

(p. 34-38) By William Pat Patterson. Article on international marketing developments. Data are based on responses of 120 marketing

executives to a 1985 survey conducted by Peterson Blyth Cato Associates and Cheskin & Masten.

Includes 1 table showing 14 product categories cited by respondents as most appropriate for "global marketing" (same marketing strategy used worldwide).

LABOR IN RETREAT

(p. 54-57) By Paul G. Engel. Article, with 1 table showing membership for 9 labor unions, 1983, with peak membership year and membership loss between peak year and 1983. Data are from *Union Sourcebook*.

C7000–3.616: July 22, 1985 (Vol. 226, No. 2)

MONTHLY TABLE

[1] Manufacturing shipments, for May 1985. (p. 22)

C7000–3.617: Aug. 19, 1985 (Vol. 226, No. 4)

MONTHLY TABLE

[1] Manufacturing shipments, for June 1985. (p. 20)

C7000–3.618: Sept. 16, 1985 (Vol. 226, No. 6)

ARE U.S. STRATEGIES ON TARGET?

(p. 68-70) By Perry Pascarella. Article comparing management priorities of senior managers in North America, Japan, and Europe. Data are based on over 600 responses to a 1985 survey conducted by Boston University School of Management.

Includes 3 tables showing survey response concerning priorities for production improvements (current and future) and competition, 1985, with comparison to 1983.

C7000–3.619: Sept. 30, 1985 (Vol. 226, No. 7)

MONTHLY TABLE

[1] Manufacturing shipments, for July 1985. (p. 32)

C7000–3.620: Oct. 30, 1985 (Vol. 227, No. 2)

MONTHLY TABLE

[1] Manufacturing shipments, for Aug. 1985. (p. 29)

CADILLAC FACES NEW FOES AND A STIFFER FIGHT

(p. 16-17) By Charles R. Day. Article, with 1 table showing sales of 7 luxury auto makes, 1st 9 months 1984-85. Data are from *Ward's Automotive Reports*.

C7000–4   AIR TRANSPORT WORLD
Monthly.
ISSN 0002-2543.
LC 66-98382.
SRI/MF/not filmed

Monthly trade journal of U.S. and foreign commercial air transport industry, including statistics on passenger, cargo, and commuter traffic, financial and operating performance, and costs. Most statistics are compiled from airline reports. Data are generally current to 3-4 months prior to cover date.

Issues usually contain a special report section, with articles on a single topic, often with data from surveys by *Air Transport World;* feature articles, often focusing on specific airlines; editorial depts; and the following regular statistical features:

a. "Facts and Figures," with 6 monthly tables and 2 irregularly recurring tables on traffic levels and cost and consumption of fuel, and 1 quarterly table on financial performance.

b. "Aircraft Operating Data," with 1 monthly table showing data for different aircraft each month, on a quarterly basis for some aircraft.

c. "Commuter/Regional Statistics," with 1 monthly table.

Annual statistical features include reports on maintenance/engineering expenditures, traffic and financial forecasts, advertising expenditures, U.S. and world airline operations, and travel agent commissions from airlines.

Monthly, irregularly recurring, and quarterly tables are described below. Monthly tables appear in most issues. All additional features with substantial statistical content are described, as they appear, under "Statistical Features;" page locations and latest periods of coverage for irregularly recurring tables, quarterly table, and "Aircraft Operating Data" are also noted, as are aircraft covered in "Aircraft Operating Data." Nonstatistical features are not covered.

Availability: Air Transport World, PO Box 95759, Cleveland OH 44101, qualified subscribers †, others $35.00 per yr., single copy $4.00; SRI/MF/not filmed.

Issues reviewed during 1985: Nov. 1984-Oct. 1985 (P) (Vol. 21, Nos. 11-12; Vol. 22, Nos. 1-10).

TABLES:

[Most tables include percent change from same period of previous year. Tables showing data for individual airlines generally include rankings.

The following abbreviations are used: RPK (revenue-passenger-kilometers), FTK (freight-ton-kilometers), RPM (revenue-passenger-miles), ASM (available-seat-miles).]

FACTS AND FIGURES

Monthly Tables

[1] World airline traffic [passengers, RPKs, and FTKs, by foreign airline, year to date].

[2] Freight traffic (U.S. airlines) [transatlantic, transpacific, and Latin America FTKs, by airline, year to date and same period of previous year].

[3] U.S. airline system traffic [passengers, RPKs, and FTKs, by airline, year to date].

[4-5] U.S. national and large regional carriers and major carriers scheduled domestic operations [passengers, RPMs, ASMs, load factors, and average trip length, by carrier, month of coverage].

[6] Fuel cost and consumption [for scheduled and nonscheduled domestic and international flights, month of coverage; table may not appear in every issue].

Irregularly Recurring Tables

[1] North Atlantic traffic [east- and west-bound passengers, freight and mail tonnage, passenger load factor, and passenger and cargo flights, for scheduled and charter services, year to date].

[2] International scheduled services of Assn of European Airlines (AEA) member airlines [intra-European and intercontinental passenger and freight air traffic, year to date; table title and format may vary].

Quarterly Table

[1] U.S. airlines financial performance [operating revenues, expense, profit or loss, and net income or loss, for approximately 40 national, major, and regional carriers, quarter ending month of coverage; data are shown for 1 or more carrier types, in 1 or more tables, as space permits].

AIRCRAFT OPERATING DATA

Selected aircraft, 12- or 3-months' data [including fleet size, revenue miles and hours flown, fuel use, average speed and passengers per mile, and operating and maintenance expenses, for 1-6 aircraft models, year or quarter ending 2-8 months prior to month of coverage].

COMMUTER/REGIONAL STATISTICS

U.S. large regional and small regional/commuter carrier traffic [passengers, load factors, RPMs, and/or pounds of freight, by carrier, year to date; prior to Apr. 1985 issue, data for cargo commuter carriers (now combined with data for small regional carriers) were reported separately].

STATISTICAL FEATURES:

C7000–4.601: Nov. 1984 (Vol. 21, No. 11)

FACTS AND FIGURES RECURRING TABLES

[1] North Atlantic traffic, 1st 7 months 1984. (p. 107)

[2] International scheduled services of AEA member airlines, 1st 6 months 1984. (p. 106)

AIRCRAFT OPERATING DATA

(p. 108) For Fairchild Metro, de Havilland Dash 7, Fokker F28, British Aerospace 146, and McDonnell Douglas DC-9-30, DC-9-50, and DC-9-80 aircraft, quarter ended Mar. 31, 1984.

COMMUTER/REGIONAL AIRFRAMES AND ENGINES: INDUSTRY FACES PRODUCTIVE BUT TURBULENT YEAR, ANNUAL FEATURE

(p. 66-93) Annual article, by Lou Davis, describing equipment suitable for commuter/regional airline operations. Covers airplanes, helicopters, and engines. Descriptions are arranged alphabetically by manufacturer, and show some or all of the following for each model: development and FAA certification summary, specifications, and price; delivery start date; and aircraft delivered, on order, and on option (no dates).

C7000–4.602: Dec. 1984 (Vol. 21, No. 12)

FACTS AND FIGURES RECURRING TABLE

[2] International scheduled services of AEA member airlines, 1st 7 months 1984. (p. 106)

SPECIAL TABLE

(p. 9) Table showing yields (revenue per revenue passenger mile), by U.S. major and other airline, 3rd quarter 1983-84.

C7000–4.603: Jan. 1985 (Vol. 22, No. 1)

FACTS AND FIGURES RECURRING TABLES

[1] North Atlantic traffic, 1st 9 months 1984. (p. 93)

[2] International scheduled services of AEA member airlines, 1st 8 months 1984. (p. 92)

FACTS AND FIGURES QUARTERLY TABLE

[1] Financial performance, for major and national carriers, 3rd quarter and 1st 9 months 1984. (p. 96-97)

AIRCRAFT OPERATING DATA

(p. 98) For Lockheed L-1011, Boeing 767, 747, Airbus A300B4, and McDonnell Douglas DC-10-10 aircraft, quarter ended June 30, 1984.

1985 FORECAST: ANOTHER GOOD YEAR, BUT GROWTH RATES MAY LESSEN, ANNUAL FEATURE

(p. 16-29) Annual outlook article, by Danna K. Henderson, on world airline traffic and financial performance in 1985. Data sources include approximately 80 responses to an *Air Transport World* survey of U.S. and foreign carriers.

Includes 7 tables showing world and U.S. passenger and freight traffic, and world revenues and expenses, 1976-85; world traffic and financial forecasts, by airline, 1985, with comparisons to 1983-84; and world fleet acquisitions and disposals of specific aircraft models, by airline, 1984-85 and later.

C7000–4.604: Feb. 1985 (Vol. 22, No. 2)

FACTS AND FIGURES RECURRING TABLES

[1] North Atlantic traffic, 1st 10 months 1984. (p. 102)

[2] International scheduled services of AEA member airlines, 1st 9 months 1984. (p. 99)

AIRCRAFT OPERATING DATA

(p. 105) For Boeing 737-200, and McDonnell Douglas DC-9-10, DC-9-30, DC-9-50, and DC-9-80 aircraft, quarter ended June 30, 1984.

C7000–4.605: Mar. 1985 (Vol. 22, No. 3)

FACTS AND FIGURES RECURRING TABLE

[2] International scheduled services of AEA member airlines, 1st 10 months 1984. (p. 101)

AIRCRAFT OPERATING DATA

(p. 104) For McDonnell Douglas DC-8-61F and DC-8-63F, and Boeing 727-100F, 747-100F, and 747-200F aircraft, quarter ended Sept. 31, 1984.

C7000–4.606: Apr. 1985 (Vol. 22, No. 4)

FACTS AND FIGURES RECURRING TABLES

[1] North Atlantic traffic, full year 1984. (p. 97)

[2] International scheduled services of AEA member airlines, 1st 11 months 1984. (p. 93)

AIRCRAFT OPERATING DATA

(p. 98) For Fairchild Metro, de Havilland Dash 7, Fokker F28, and British Aerospace 146 aircraft, quarter ended Sept. 30, 1984.

DOT SEEKS END TO EAS BY '86

(p. 74-75) By Dave Higdon. Article analyzing impact of proposal to terminate Essential Air Service airline subsidy program in 1986. Data are from DOT. Includes 3 tables showing total and per passenger subsidies, with detail for Alaska and contiguous U.S. locations having highest and lowest subsidies, various fiscal or calendar years 1981-85.

FOOD IS $1-BILLION EXPENSE FOR U.S. MAJORS, NATIONALS

(p. 101) Brief article, with 4 tables showing passengers, food service expenditures, and food share of total operating expenses, for 11 major and 7 national airlines, individually 3rd quarter 1984, and aggregate 1978-83.

C7000–4.607: May 1985 (Vol. 22, No. 5)

FACTS AND FIGURES RECURRING TABLE

[2] International scheduled services of AEA member airlines, full year 1984. (p. 227)

AIRCRAFT OPERATING DATA

(p. 233) For Boeing 757, 767, and 727-200 aircraft, quarter ended Sept. 30, 1984.

1984 MARKET DEVELOPMENT REPORT, ANNUAL FEATURE

(p. 37-156) Annual review, for 1984, of U.S. and foreign airline operations. Data are from DOT, International Air Transport Assn, International Civil Aviation Organization, and airline reports.

Includes data on passenger and cargo traffic, financial performance, fleet size, employment, fuel consumption, and operating ratios, shown primarily by airline, 1984 often with comparative data for 1983, and occasionally with data for prior years.

Contents:

a. "U.S. Majors Lead Financial Surge in '84." Includes 4 tables showing top 25 world airlines in passengers, revenue passenger kilometers, cargo, fleet size, employees, and operating revenues and profits; financial results for 50 non-U.S. carriers; North Atlantic passenger and freight traffic; and U.S. carrier fuel consumption and per gallon cost, by type of service. (p. 38-51)

b. "World Airline Statistics, 1984." Presents 1 extended table showing passenger and freight traffic, load factor, employees, and fleet size, for approximately 300 U.S. and foreign carriers. (p. 52-56)

c. "Africa, Asia/Pacific, Canada, Europe, Latin America/Caribbean, and Middle East." Brief profiles of individual airlines in each world area. (p. 58-84)

d. "U.S. Majors." Brief profiles of 11 major airlines, with 5 tables showing the following, by airline: financial results, traffic (total system, domestic, and international), and load factors, with rankings. (p. 88-101)

e. "Piedmont, Aloha Receive Fewest Passenger Complaints." Article, with 1 table showing 11-18 U.S. major and national carriers ranked by complaints filed per 100,-000 passengers. (p. 102)

f. "U.S. Nationals, Cargo Carriers, Large Regionals, and Small Regionals/Commuters." Brief profiles of individual airlines, with 6 tables showing financial results and traffic for national and cargo carriers; load factors for national carriers; and financial results for large regional carriers. (p. 104-140)

g. "World Airline Fleets." Presents 2 tables showing number of jet, turboprop, piston, and helicopter aircraft in fleet and on order, by model; and number of aircraft in fleet/on order, by model and airline. (p. 142-156)

This is the 22nd annual report.

C7000–4.608: June 1985 (Vol. 22, No. 6)

AIRCRAFT OPERATING DATA

(p. 100) For Boeing 737-200, and McDonnell Douglas DC-9-10, DC-9-30, DC-9-50, and MD-80 aircraft, quarter ended Sept. 30, 1984.

U.S. MAJORS AND NATIONALS ADVERTISING ANALYSIS, 1984 VS. 1983, ANNUAL FEATURE

(p. 97-98) Three annual tables showing advertising and sales promotion expenditures compared to passengers and passenger revenues, for 12 major and 14 national carriers, 1984 with change from 1983. Presents separate data for major carriers' domestic and international operations, with detail for Atlantic, Latin American, and Pacific international flights.

C7000–4.609: July 1985 (Vol. 22, No. 7)

FACTS AND FIGURES RECURRING TABLES

[1] North Atlantic traffic, Jan. 1985. (p. 125)

[2] International scheduled services of AEA member airlines, 1st 2 months 1985. (p. 123)

FACTS AND FIGURES QUARTERLY TABLE

[1] Financial performance, for major carriers, 1st quarter 1985. (p. 126)

M&E EXPENDITURES STILL ON THE RISE, BUT COST-CUTTING MEASURES HELPING, ANNUAL FEATURE

(p. 63-66) Annual article, by Danna K. Henderson, on maintenance and engineering (M&E) activities and expenditures of 47 U.S. and foreign airlines in 1984, based on an *Air Transport World* survey. Includes 4 tables showing the following, by airline, for 1984 unless otherwise noted:

a. M&E facility/equipment spending planned for 1985/86; M&E spending, with change from 1983 and forecast for 1985; and in-house and contract shares of M&E spending, and 3 highest-cost M&E items, with notes on 5-year trends.

b. M&E employment, and share of total company employment; and types of services offered to other airlines.

C7000–4.610: Aug. 1985 (Vol. 22, No. 8)

FACTS AND FIGURES RECURRING TABLES

[1] North Atlantic traffic, 1st 4 months 1985. (p. 103)

[2] International scheduled services of AEA member airlines, 1st 5 months 1985. (p. 102)

FACTS AND FIGURES QUARTERLY TABLE

[1] Financial performance, for national carriers, 1st quarter 1985. (p. 104)

AIRCRAFT OPERATING DATA

(p. 105) For McDonnell Douglas DC-8-61F and DC-8-63F, and Boeing 727-100F, 747-100F, and 747-200F aircraft, quarter ended Dec. 31, 1984.

SPECIAL REPORT: 90% OF AIRLINES ENGAGE IN ANCILLARY ACTIVITIES

(p. 45-49) By Danna K. Henderson. Article on non-transportation activities of 66 U.S. and foreign airlines in 1984, based on an *Air Transport World* survey. Includes 2 tables showing the following data, by airline:

a. Revenues and net profit from ancillary activities, 1984; and ancillary revenues as percent of total, 1984 vs 5 years ago, and anticipated change in next 2 years.

b. Ancillary activities performed by type, including aircraft, engine, and component maintenance; ramp/line, security, and catering services; flight and ground crew training; reservations and other computer services; aircraft leasing and charter; lodging, restaurant, travel/tour, surface transport, and car rental operations; technical assistance; commuter airline aid; and other; with rankings of 3 most important activities for each airline.

C7000–4.611: Sept. 1985 (Vol. 22, No. 9)

FACTS AND FIGURES RECURRING TABLES

[1] North Atlantic traffic, 1st 5 months 1985. (p. 116)

[2] International scheduled services of AEA member airlines, 1st 4 months 1985. (p. 115)

AIRCRAFT OPERATING DATA

(p. 120) For Boeing 767 and 757-200, and Airbus A300B2 and A300B4 aircraft, quarter ended Dec. 31, 1984.

U.S. MAJORS ARE CONTROLLING PASSENGER SERVICE EXPENSES

(p. 56) Annual article on airline passenger handling operations of U.S. major carriers, 1984. Data are from CAB and DOT.

Includes 3 tables showing passenger service and food expenses, enplaned passengers, passengers denied boarding and receiving compensation, passengers voluntarily "bumped," and expenses resulting from boarding denials and "bumping," for 11-12 major U.S. airlines, 1984 with selected comparisons to 1983.

C7000–4.612: Oct. 1985 (Vol. 22, No. 10)

FACTS AND FIGURES RECURRING TABLE

[1] North Atlantic traffic, 1st 6 months 1985. (p. 139)

AIRCRAFT OPERATING DATA

(p. 140) For Fairchild SA-226 Metro, Beech 99, Fokker F27, de Havilland Dash 7, and Convair 580 aircraft, quarter ended Dec. 31, 1984.

IATA DG CONCERNED ABOUT FINANCIAL WOES OF SOME MEMBER AIRLINES, ANNUAL FEATURE

(p. 74-91) Annual article on International Air Transport Assn (IATA), presenting data on airline financial results for various periods 1980-1st half 1985. Includes 4 summary charts, and 9 tables showing the following:

a. Traffic distribution by world region; and North Atlantic operations, including number of airlines, scheduled and charter flights, passengers by class of service, passenger load factor, and freight; 1980-84.

b. IATA traffic data for 71 airlines, Jan.-June 1985, and for 112 airlines, 1984 with percent change from 1983; and IATA airline estimated traffic, fleet size, and operating revenues and expenses, with comparisons to International Civil Aviation Organization (includes USSR), 1980-84.

c. Top 20 nations in scheduled revenue-passenger-kilometers (RPKs) and percent change in airline traffic; and top 10 IATA airlines ranked by passengers, passenger-kilometers, passenger load factor, freight, and charter RPKs (total and as percent of all RPKs); 1984 with comparisons to 1983.

IATA MEMBERS CONTINUE PRODUCTIVITY GAIN, ANNUAL FEATURE

(p. 92-97) Annual analysis of per-employee productivity for IATA member airlines, 1984. Includes 4 tables showing the following:

a. Aggregate IATA airline employment and total and per employee revenue-ton-kilometers, passengers, revenue-passenger-kilometers (RPKs), and operating revenues, 1980-84 with percent change from previous year.

b. Employment, ton-kilometers, and per-employee ton-kilometers, passenger boardings, RPKs, and freight-ton-kilometers, for 112 IATA airlines; and rankings of top 10 airlines for each productivity measure; 1984 with selected comparisons to 1983.

AIRLINE DEPENDENCE ON TRAVEL AGENTS RISING, ANNUAL FEATURE

(p. 98-103) Annual article on airline use of travel agents. Data are based on responses of 40 airlines to an *Air Transport World* survey. Includes 3 tables showing the following:

a. Travel agent commissions paid (total and as percent of passenger revenues); average revenues per passenger; domestic, international, and override commission rates; percent of revenues generated by travel agents; and percent of passengers using discount fares; for 39-40 U.S. and foreign airlines, 1st half 1985 with comparisons to various periods 1980 and 1984-85.

b. Passenger revenues and commissions paid, for international and domestic services of 9-12 U.S. major carriers, 1983-84 and 1st half 1985, and for 8 national carriers, 1982-83 and 1st half 1984.

C7000–5   LODGING HOSPITALITY: Lodging's 400 Top Performers
Monthly (selected issue).
Aug. 1985.   (p. 46-85).
Vol. XLI, No. 8.
ISSN 0148-0766.
LC 77-640897.
SRI/MF/excerpts

Annual feature, for 1985, presenting financial and operating data for the 400 leading lodging facilities in 5 categories: center city, resort, suburban, highway, and airport. Data are from survey responses of *Lodging Hospitality* subscribers, and Laventhol and Horwath.

Contains narrative report, with 22 charts and 7 tables showing the following (no data dates given):

a. Affiliation, years in operation, types of services offered, automation, chain reservation system use, business booked through reservation systems, and growth plans: distributions for aggregate 400 leading performers.

b. Occupancy rate; sales and payroll expenses per room; employees per 100 rooms; sales per employee; and distribution of sales from guest rooms, food/beverage, and other: aggregates for 400 leading performers compared to total industry, with selected detail for each facility category.

c. Top 400 facilities: guest rooms/suites, total sales, room and food/beverage sales, other revenues, and average occupancy rate and employees, with selected rankings; shown for individual facilities arranged by category.

d. Top 25 lodging chains: U.S. and foreign properties and rooms; and status of properties (including company-owned, franchised/licensed, and management contract); shown for individual hotel/motel systems grouped by chain.

This is the 9th annual feature. *Lodging Hospitality* is a monthly publication reporting on developments in the lodging industry, and generally does not include substantial statistics. Annual features on management salaries and top 400 performance are the only features described in SRI. Feature on management salaries is covered under C7000-6.

Availability: Lodging Hospitality, PO Box 95759, Cleveland OH 44101, $40.00 per yr., single copy $4.00; SRI/MF/excerpts for annual feature described.

C7000–6   LODGING HOSPITALITY: Annual Salary Survey
Monthly (selected issue).
Sept. 1984.   (p. 54-56).
Vol. XL, No. 9.
ISSN 0148-0766.
LC 77-640897.
SRI/MF/excerpts

Annual survey article on salaries of management personnel in the lodging industry, by position, 1984. Data are from responses to a survey of 2,000 *Lodging Hospitality* subscribers, and responses of approximately 650 employers to a survey conducted by Roth Young Personnel Service, Inc.

Contains narrative report, and 5 tables showing mid- quartile salary range for 14 positions; and distribution of respondents by salary range, by property size and type (center city, resort, suburban, highway, and airport), for general and assistant/resident managers, and sales/marketing and food/beverage directors.

This is the 1st annual survey report.

Lodging Hospitality is a monthly publication reporting on developments in the lodging industry, and generally does not include substantial statistics. Annual reports on management salaries and performance of leading establishments are the only features described in SRI. Report on leading establishments is covered under C7000-5.

Availability: Lodging Hospitality, PO Box 95759, Cleveland OH 44101, $40.00 per yr., single copy $4.00; SRI/MF/excerpts for annual article described.

C7600
Pit and Quarry
Publications

C7600–1   CONCRETE: 1984 Review, 1985 Outlook
Monthly (selected issue).
Jan. 1985.   (p. 12-24).
Vol. 48, No. 9.
ISSN 0279-4705.
LC 59-37674.
SRI/MF/excerpts

Annual compilation of articles reviewing concrete industry production and operating trends and expectations, by sector, 1984-85. Also summarizes construction industry trends.

Data are from Census Bureau, Portland Cement Assn, and *Concrete* annual survey of industry producers.

Contains introductory article summarizing survey findings (p. 12); and 6 statistical articles described below, interspersed with brief narrative articles by industry assn leaders (p. 13-24).

Concrete is a monthly periodical reporting trends and developments in the cement industry, and normally contains primarily narrative articles. The annual concrete industry review and outlook feature is the only feature of *Concrete* covered in SRI.

Availability: Concrete, Circulation Department, One E. First St., Duluth MN 55802, $12.00 per yr., single copy $3.00; SRI/MF/excerpts for features described.

STATISTICAL ARTICLES:

1984 CONSTRUCTION GAINS TO SLOW IN FIRST HALF OF '85

(p. 13-15) By Jim G. Kostka. Article, with 1 table showing construction value of new housing units, and nonresidential buildings and public projects, by type, 1979-85.

READY MIXED CONCRETE, ANNUAL FEATURE

(p. 18-19) Annual survey article, by Patricia Murphy, with 1 table on ready mixed concrete, showing responses concerning changes during 1984 in production volume (total and by region), prices, and wages and other operating costs; and expected change in business, and capital expenditure plans, 1985.

MASONRY PRODUCTION UP AGAIN IN 1984, ANNUAL FEATURE

(p. 20-21) Annual survey article, by Patricia Murphy, with 2 tables on concrete masonry, showing industry survey data similar to data described above for ready mixed concrete. Also includes changes in product mix, and selected comparisons to 1983 survey.

PRECAST CONCRETE, PRESTRESSED CONCRETE, AND CONCRETE PIPE, ANNUAL FEATURES

(p. 21-24) Three annual articles, by Eric Schroder, with 3 tables on precast and prestressed concrete and concrete pipe, showing industry survey data similar to data described above for ready mixed concrete.

C7600–2   PIT AND QUARRY
Monthly.
ISSN 0032-0293.
LC 80-1511.
SRI/MF/not filmed

Monthly journal reporting U.S. and worldwide trends and developments in the stone products, cement, and other nonmetallic mineral industries. Covers exploration, production, technical developments, R&D, plants and equipment, working conditions, management, government regulation, and finance.

Journal includes feature articles, occasionally statistical; and regular editorial depts.

Annual statistical features include industry review and outlook, and world cement report, both in the Jan. issue.

Prior to June 1985 issue, journal also included 1 monthly table on contract values for nonresidential and residential building, and nonbuilding construction.

Monthly table appears in most issues prior to June 1985. All additional features with substantial statistical content are described, as they appear, under "Statistical Features." Nonstatistical features are not covered.

Prior to the June 1985 issue, microfiche status for this publication was SRI/MF/excerpts (for monthly table and all portions covered under "Statistical Features"). Harcourt Brace Jovanovich, publisher of *Pit and Quarry*, has canceled all outside microfilming arrangements.

Availability: Pit and Quarry Publications, Circulation Department, PO Box 6380, Duluth MN 55806-9914, $12.00 per yr., single copy $3.00; SRI/MF/not filmed.

Issues reviewed during 1985: Nov. 1984-Oct. 1985 (P) (Vol. 77, Nos. 5-12; Vol. 78, Nos. 1-4) [Vol. 77, Nos. 9-11 incorrectly read Nos. 8-10].

STATISTICAL FEATURES:

C7600–2.601: Nov. 1984 (Vol. 77, No. 5)

NCSA CONFERENCE EXPLORES TRENDS IN PAVEMENT DESIGN, MATERIAL SPECS

(p. 60-62) By Don Michard. Article, with technical data and 1 table showing manufactured stone sand production, selected years 1938-82.

C7600–2.602: Jan. 1985 (Vol. 77, No. 7)

1984 REVIEW AND 1985 OUTLOOK, ANNUAL FEATURE

Annual collection of articles reviewing U.S. cement, construction aggregate, and other nonmetals production and operating trends, and construction industry activity for 1984, with forecasts for 1985.

Data sources include Census Bureau, Bureau of Mines, Portland Cement Assn, and *Pit and Quarry* annual aggregate industry survey. Statistical articles are described below.

1984 CONSTRUCTION GAINS TO SLOW IN FIRST HALF OF '85

(p. 30-32) By Jim G. Kostka. Article, with 1 table showing construction value of new housing units, and nonresidential buildings and public projects, by type, 1979-85.

PORTLAND CEMENT IN THE U.S.: STATUS AND PROJECT SURVEY, ANNUAL FEATURE

(p. 40-46) Annual article, by Sandy Herod, on portland cement industry developments in 1983-84. Includes text data on 7 modification or expansion projects, by company, 1984-85; and 5 tables showing the following:

a. Cement production, mill shipments, trade, clinker and finish grinding capacity, kilns in use with detail by fuel source, average kiln capacity, and number of plants; 1979-83.

b. Clinker capacity of 15 largest cement companies; cement consumption, by type, 1979-85; and average mill value of all, portland, and prepared masonry cement, 1979-83.

ANNUAL AGGREGATES SURVEY SHOWS INDUSTRIES' GAINS, ANNUAL FEATURE

(p. 46-48) Annual survey article, by Sandy Herod, with 1 table showing the following, for sand/gravel, crushed stone, and lightweight aggregates:

a. Reported change in production, prices, wages, maintenance costs, fuel/energy costs, and productivity, 1984.

b. Anticipated change in production; and percent of respondents reporting plans for new plants, plant expansion, and new equipment; 1985.

This is the 29th annual survey.

OTHER MAJOR NONMETALS, ANNUAL FEATURE

(p. 48-49) Annual article, by Sandy Herod, profiling other major nonmetal industries, including agstone/aglime, barite, feldspar, gypsum, lime, phosphate rock, talc/pyrophyllite, and potash. Profiles include text data on production value and/or volume, consumption distribution by end use, and occasionally imports, generally for 1983, with some data for 1984 and selected comparisons to 1982.

INTERNATIONAL CEMENT SCENE: PLANT AND PRODUCTION UPDATE ANNUAL FEATURE

(p. 57-67) Annual report, by Don Michard, on world cement production, 1980-1983. Data are from the Bureau of Mines and company reports.

Includes 2 tables showing world cement production summary, and production of 20 leading countries, various years 1980-1983; and country profiles, with text data on capacity and start-up dates for new and planned plants and plant expansions, and cement production, 1982-1983, by country arranged by world area.

C7600–2.603: Mar. 1985 (Vol. 77, No. 9)
[Contents page incorrectly reads No. 8.]

ACCIDENT PREVENTION: WHERE TO START?

(p. 65) Article on incidence of pit/quarry accidents, with 1 undated table showing percent of accidents and of worker compensation costs involving vehicles, falls, conveyers/crushers, and manual material handling. Data are from Liberty Mutual Insurance.

C7600–2.604: Apr. 1985 (Vol. 77, No. 10)
[Issue incorrectly reads No. 9.]

IT'S NOT TOO EARLY FOR SUMMERTIME MAINTENANCE

(p. 20-22, 58) Article, with 1 undated chart showing prevalence of selected maintenance activities performed by motor vehicle fleet operators during regularly scheduled battery inspections. Data are from responses of 150 fleet operators to a survey conducted by GNB Batteries, Inc.

C7600–2.605: May 1985 (Vol. 77, No. 11)
[Issue incorrectly reads No. 10.]

FLUIDIZED BED COMBUSTION OFFERS POTENTIAL MARKETS FOR LIMESTONE

(p. 62-63) By Jay R. Read. Article, with 1 table showing fluidized bed boiler unit sales and total steam capacity, 1973/75-1985/87, and for an unspecified period. Data are condensed from Feb. 1985 issue of *Power*.

C7715
Polk, R. L., and Co.

C7715–1   POLK STATISTICS: Standard Services, Motor Statistical Division
Recurring (irreg.)   Feb. 1984.
iv + 131 p.
SRI/MF/complete

Catalog of reports available from R. L. Polk and Co. on U.S. registrations of domestic and import cars and trucks, light trucks, recreational vehicles, motorcycles, and trailers. Report data are compiled from State records, and are shown variously by make/model, gross vehicle weight, State, county, major city, post office town, and TV Area of Dominant Influence.

Catalog contains contents listing (p. i-iv); and brief description and sample tables illustrating data available in approximately 35 monthly, quarterly, and annual reports (p. 1-131).

For description of previous catalog, see SRI 1983 Annual, under this number.

Availability: R. L. Polk and Co., Motor Statistical Division, 431 Howard St., Detroit MI 48231, †; SRI/MF/complete.

C7715–2   PASSENGER CAR AND TRUCK SCRAPPAGE AND GROWTH in the U.S.
Annual.   Apr. 17, 1985.   6 p.
SRI/MF/complete

Annual press release presenting number of motor vehicles in use as of 1st and last day of year, and new vehicles registered and vehicles scrapped during year, for cars and trucks, years ended June 30, 1947-84. Data are compiled from State records.

Contains narrative summary and 3 tables.

Availability: R. L. Polk and Co., Motor Statistical Division, 431 Howard St., Detroit MI 48231, †; SRI/MF/complete.

C7715–3   POCKET SUMMARY OF REGISTRATIONS: New Cars, New Trucks
Monthly.   5 p.
SRI/MF/complete, shipped quarterly

Monthly report on new passenger car and truck registrations, by make and/or model, including imports.

Data are compiled from State records. Reports are issued approximately 2 months after month of coverage.

Contains 8 tables, listed below.

Availability: R. L. Polk and Co., Motor Statistical Division, 431 Howard St., Detroit MI 48231, †; SRI/MF/complete, shipped quarterly.

Issues reviewed during 1985: Sept. 1984-July 1985 (D).

TABLES:

[1-3] New passenger car registrations [by domestic make and model, and total imports]; and new truck registrations [by domestic and import make; all for month of coverage, year to date, and same periods of previous year].

[4] Trucks by weight groups, year to date [and total for previous year, by domestic and import make].

[5-7] New imported cars, and new imported and domestic light trucks, leading makes [year to date, current and previous year].

[8] New vehicle registrations, U.S., calendar year totals [cars and trucks, for previous 10 years].

C7800
Prentice-Hall, Inc.

C7800–1   ALMANAC OF BUSINESS AND INDUSTRIAL FINANCIAL RATIOS, 1985 Edition
Annual. [1985.]
xxvii+373 p.
ISBN 0-13-022930-X.
LC 72-181403.
SRI/MF/not filmed

Annual report, by Leo Troy, presenting composite operating and financial ratios for corporations in approximately 200 SIC 2- to 4-digit industries, for fiscal year ended June 30, 1981. Data are aggregated for all corporations within each industry, and for those operating at a profit.

Data are based on the latest IRS tax return statistics available and are presented for corporations in 12 asset size categories, from zero to $250 million/over.

Contains introduction, methodology, and definitions (p. vii-xvii); contents listing (p. xix-xxvii); statistics arranged by industry (p. 2-363); appendix (p. A1-A7); and index. (p. 369-373).

Statistics are presented in table I (for all corporations) and table II (for profitable corporations), showing: number of reporting establishments and total receipts; 12 operating factors as percent of net sales or of total receipts; and, as applicable, 6 financial ratios, and 4 financial factor percentages; all by corporation asset size, FY81. Tables are repeated for each detailed industry, arranged as follows:

a.   Agriculture, forestry, and fishing; mining, including oil/gas extraction; and construction. (p. 2-33)

b.   Manufacturing. (p. 34-175)

c.   Transportation; communication; electric, gas, and sanitary services; and wholesale and retail trade. (p. 176-267)

d.   Banking; credit agencies other than banks; security and commodity brokers, and allied services; insurance; real estate; and holding and other investment companies. (p. 268-317)

e.   Service industries, including medical, legal, and other services. (p. 318-363)

Availability: Prentice-Hall, Inc., Mail Order Sales, Old Tappan NJ 07675, $35.00; SRI/MF/ not filmed.

C7875
Production Publishing Co.

C7875–1   PRODUCTION
Monthly.
LC 48-13360.
SRI/MF/excerpts, shipped quarterly

Monthly trade journal reporting on developments in metalworking industry operations, including production processes, new equipment and materials, and management methods. Publication is directed to engineers and managers responsible for improving manufacturing efficiency, costs, and quality.

Issues include feature articles, occasionally with statistics; regular narrative depts, including news briefs, production tips, and lists of new literature and equipment; and monthly "Manufacturing Outlook" feature, usually presenting brief summaries of economic developments in or affecting manufacturing industries, and also occasionally including statistics. An annual directory of manufacturing computer suppliers appears in the Oct. issue.

Features with substantial statistical content are described, as they appear, under "Statistical Features." Each issue of the journal is reviewed, but an abstract is published in SRI monthly issues only when statistical features appear.

Availability: Production, PO Box 101, Bloomfield Hills MI 48303-0101, qualified subscribers †, others $35.00 per yr., single copy $4.00, Planbook $7.50; SRI/MF/excerpts for all portions covered under "Statistical Features;" shipped quarterly.

Issues reviewed during 1985: Nov. 1984-Oct. 1985 (P) (Vol. 94, Nos. 5-6; Vol. 95, Nos. 1-6; Vol. 96, Nos. 1-4).

STATISTICAL FEATURES:

C7875–1.601: Jan. 1985 (Vol. 95, No. 1)

1985 CAPITAL SPENDING UP 13%, ANNUAL FEATURE

(p. 38-40) Annual article, by Edward D. McCallum, Jr., on equipment capital spending forecasts for metalworking industries, 1985, presenting highlights from annual survey responses of 1,834 plants.

Includes 3 charts and 3 text tables showing expenditures by type of equipment; typical expenditures by plant employment size; reasons for investment; and current and planned use of robots and computers, by function; 1985, with selected comparisons to 1980-84 period.

For description of complete survey, see C7875-1.602 below.

C7875–1.602: Mar. 1985 (Vol. 95, No. 3)

Annual "Manufacturing Planbook" issue. Includes narrative articles and buyers guide, and the statistical features described below.

INDUSTRY TO SPEND $80 BILLION FOR R&D, ANNUAL FEATURE

(p. 21) Annual brief article, with 2 charts showing distribution of R&D funding and performance among Federal Government, industry, universities, and other nonprofit institutions, 1985. Data are from Battelle Memorial Institute.

Full Battelle report is covered in SRI under R3300-1.

CAPITAL SPENDING, 1985-86, ANNUAL FEATURE

(p. 53-59) Annual article, by Edward D. McCallum Jr., on capital equipment spending forecasts for metalworking industries, 1984, based on responses of 1,834 plants to a *Production* survey.

Includes 2 charts and 15 tables showing the following for various periods 1985-87, with some trends from 1980:

a.   Equipment spending amount; and equipment spending as a percent of total capital expenditures in selected SIC 3-digit industries; all by equipment type.

b.   Typical expenditures by plant employment size; reasons for investment; and percent of respondents using and planning to use computerized data systems and robots, by production function.

c.   Percent of respondents planning to purchase the following: manufacturing cells and systems, lasers, and electrical discharge machines, by selected SIC 2- to 4-digit industry; and computer numerical control equipment by type.

For description of related article, see C7875-1.601 above.

C7875–1.603: May 1985 (Vol. 95, No. 5)

FLEXIBLE MANUFACTURING'S FUTURE

(p. 17) Brief article, with 1 chart showing market volume for flexible manufacturing systems, 1984-90. Data are from the Yankee Group, Inc.

C7875–1.604: July 1985 (Vol. 96, No. 1)

TECHNOLOGICAL SUPERIORITY OVERSEAS

(p. 15) Article, with 1 chart showing ratings by Japanese companies of Japanese vs. U.S. technological capacity, 1980, 1985, and 1990. Data are from responses of 1,623 Japanese companies to a recent Japanese Economic Planning Agency survey published in *Japan Economic Journal*.

C7975
Providence Journal Co.

C7975–1   1985 JOURNAL-BULLETIN RHODE ISLAND ALMANAC, 99th Annual Edition
Annual. 1985. 292 p.
ISSN 0364-2909.
LC 84-640369.
SRI/MF/excerpts

Annual compilation, for 1985, of reference information and statistics for Rhode Island, including history, economy, government, and social composition. Data are primarily for various years 1980-83, with selected historical trends from as early as 1730.

Report is designed to present a comprehensive overview of the State. Various socioeconomic, demographic, and geographic breakdowns are shown, as applicable, for selected topics. These breakdowns include data by city, county, school district, urban-rural status, industry, occupation, age, and race/ethnicity. Comparisons to total U.S. are also often included.

Most data are from State and Federal government reports.

Contains contents listing (1 p.); and the following:

a. Calendars; astronomical, climatological, and historical information; State and city/town organization, depts, officials, personnel, and finances including selected salaries; bridges and airports; elections; and miscellaneous information; interspersed with text data and 17 tables. (p. 1-156)

b. Education, including selected data for individual colleges and universities; libraries; population, housing, and employment characteristics; selected business data; health facilities and capacity; newspapers; civic and service organizations; villages; radio and TV stations; highways; disasters, including damages and lives lost; and sports information; interspersed with text data and 35 tables. (p. 157-279)

c. Subject index. (p. 280-292)

All tables are described below.

Availability: Providence Journal Co., Providence Journal-Bulletin Almanac, 75 Fountain St., Providence RI 02902, $3.75; SRI/MF/excerpts for text data and statistical portions described below.

TABLES:

C7975-1.1: Statistics

a. **Finances:** selected taxation, expenditure, and social indicators, with Rhode Island rank among the 50 States; State officials' salaries; State revenues by source, and expenses by function and agency; State debt; and assessed property value and taxes levied. 10 tables. (p. 27, 58-60, and 113)

b. **Elections:** votes cast in 1983-84 elections, by office and candidate, with popular and electoral voting results for U.S. President by State; and referenda approvals and rejections. 7 tables. (p. 122-141)

c. **Education:** superintendents and salaries; educational finances, including school transportation costs; average daily membership and attendance; enrollment; staff and minimum salary; and number of buildings. 5 tables. (p. 169-171)

d. **Market and population data:** population; manufacturing share of employment; retail sales; occupied housing units; U.S. population by State and for 100 largest cities; Rhode Island and Providence population, from 1730; and population and housing characteristics. 9 tables. (p. 175-181)

e. **Employment and earnings:** labor force, by employment status; unemployment insurance claims; wages; manufacturing employment, hours, and earnings; personal income by source; housing units; financial institution operating data; business firms, employment, and payroll; residential building permits; and U.S. CPI by item. 14 tables. (p. 182-191)

f. **Highways and miscellaneous:** newspaper circulation; churches and membership, by denomination; highway distances from Providence for selected U.S. cities; and State highway mileage and fatalities. 7 tables. (p. 212-213, 225, 254-256)

C8111
Rodale Press

C8111-1   CORNUCOPIA PROJECT REPORTS
Series. For individual publication data, see below.
SRI/MF/complete

Continuing series of reports evaluating current U.S. food system and presenting recommendations for future development. Covers environmental concerns and aspects of production, marketing, and finance. Includes data on individual States' dependence on food imports from out of State, by commodity.

Data are collected for the Rodale Press Cornucopia Project from Federal and State agencies and various private sources.

Series includes reports on individual States and occasional special reports. Special reports are covered in SRI only when they include substantial statistical content.

State reports generally include detailed narrative analysis, and a food imports table showing the most recently available data for the following, by commodity: quantity and retail value of the State's production and consumption; value of shipments to and from the State; and amount of land required to meet total State consumption.

Reports reviewed in 1985 are listed below; data omissions and additional data accompanying narrative analyses are noted.

Availability: Cornucopia Project, Publications Department, 33 E. Minor St., Emmaus PA 18049, single copy $4.00 + postage and handling; SRI/MF/complete.

REPORTS:

C8111-1.22: Food in Minnesota: Regenerating Local Systems
[Monograph. 1984. 53 p. SRI/MF/complete.]
By Shirley D. Hoffman. Report also includes acres of cropland used in production, by commodity; and directory of Minnesota food organizations.

C8111-1.23: South Carolina Food System: Does It Have a Future?
[Monograph. 1985. 66 p. SRI/MF/complete.]
By John Madera. Report also includes a directory of South Carolina food organizations, and 1 table showing the following for 13 vegetables that the State imports but could grow itself: amount consumed, and import share; and economic consequences of importing, in terms of farm value lost and transportation costs; 1982.

C8115
Roscoe, John F.

C8115-1   14th ANNUAL DOLLARS PER DAY SURVEY of the Small Food Store Industry and What the 12 Largest Oil Companies Said About Gasoline Marketing in 1984
Annual. [1985.] 194 p.
SRI/MF/complete

Annual survey report covering financial condition and operations of the 11 largest publicly held convenience store chains in the small food store industry, and gasoline marketing operations and finances of top 12 oil companies, 1970s-84.

Most data are based on annual surveys of corporate annual reports, proxy statements, and 10-K reports filed with the SEC. The surveyed convenience store chains represent approximately 34% of all convenience stores; the surveyed oil companies account for approximately 66% of all gasoline sales.

Report is intended in part to permit convenience store operators to compare their operations with those of the surveyed chains.

Contents:

a. Contents listing (1 p.); and introduction, methodology, and 3 summary tables (p. 1-8).

b. Convenience store chain analysis, including narrative survey article, excerpts from corporate annual reports, and summaries of previous surveys, interspersed with 9 charts, and 68 tables described below. (p. 9-128)

c. Oil company analysis, including excerpts from corporate annual reports, and overview of domestic fuel consumption and related data, with 1 chart and 29 tables described below. (p. 129-184)

d. Survey editorial, with accompanying text data on cigarette production, tax collections, and sales, primarily 1980-84. (p. 185-193)

Prior to this edition, the oil company analysis was published as a separate report and was covered in SRI under C8115-2.

Availability: Dollars per Day Survey, PO Box 886, Benicia CA 94510, $100.00 1st copy, $20.00 each additional copy; SRI/MF/complete.

TABLES:

C8115-1.1: Convenience Store Chains
[Data are for 1970s-84. Most data are shown for 11 leading chains, often on a dollars per day per store basis, with selected rankings. Some data include comparisons to other chains.]

a. Stores; sales and profit/loss, with comparison to CPI; stores purchased, opened, closed/sold, planned, and owned vs. leased; compensation and stock ownership of top executives and board of directors; stock performance and holdings, including shares held by largest stockholders, and return on shareholder equity; and inventory valuation methods. 46 tables. (p. 14-109, passim)

b. Electricity cost analysis for headquarters cities; data on gasoline operations, including stores selling, sales volume and value, and share of total gasoline sales; and summaries from various earlier surveys. 22 tables. (p. 111-126)

C8115–1.2: Oil Companies

[Data by company are shown for 12 leading oil firms.]

a. Sales; earnings; employment; return on equity; domestic gasoline sales as percent of worldwide sales; annual financial report characteristics; percent of stock owned by corporate officers/directors; number of service stations owned; and gasoline product sales volume; all by company, primarily 1980-83. 13 tables. (p. 129-166)

b. Refining/marketing profit or loss, refining capacity utilization, and operational summaries including per station gallonage and profits, by company; and domestic energy consumption by fuel type, operable refineries by capacity size group, and top 20-25 refiners ranked by capacity and number of service stations; various periods 1979-84. 1 chart and 11 tables. (p. 168-181)

c. Motor vehicle fuel consumption, travel mileage, registrations, and sales; and highway and non-highway gasoline consumption; various years 1950-84. 5 tables. (p. 182-184)

C8115–2   WHAT DO THE 25 LARGEST OIL COMPANIES HAVE TO SAY ABOUT GASOLINE MARKETING?

Annual, discontinued.

Annual report on gasoline marketing operations and finances of leading oil companies, discontinued as a separate report with the 1983 edition (for description, see SRI 1984 Annual under this number).

Report has been incorporated in *Annual Dollars per Day Survey of the Small Food Store Industry and What the 12 Largest Oil Companies Said About Gasoline Marketing,* covered in SRI under C8115-1.

C8130
Schwartz Publications

C8130–1   DISCOUNT MERCHANDISER

Monthly.
ISSN 0012-3579.
LC 66-93756.
SRI/MF/not filmed

Monthly trade journal reporting on general merchandise retail stores selling at low margins, with minimum annual revenue of $500,000 and minimum size of 10,000 sq. ft. Covers management, sales, space allocation, discount customers and their shopping habits, and major categories of merchandise.

Data are from studies by the National Mass Retailing Institute, reports from individual retail stores, *Discount Merchandiser* (DM) annual census of stores, and other sources.

Issues generally contain the following:

a. Monthly "Scoreboard" table, showing sales and net earnings after taxes of approximately 40 individual retail companies. Data are for various periods, identified for each company, and include percent change during specified period.

b. Editorial depts; and news and feature articles, occasionally with substantial statistics.

Annual statistical features include a 2-part survey on discount chain store operations (May and June issues), with extensive statistics and profiles of leading discount store chains; and report on growth of combination stores in the supermarket and drug industries.

Monthly "Scoreboard" table appears in most issues, on a space available basis. All additional features with substantial statistical content are described, as they appear, under "Statistical Features." Nonstatistical features are not covered.

Availability: Discount Merchandiser, Circulation Department, Two Park Ave., New York NY 10157, $30.00 per yr., single copy $3.50, special issues $20.00; SRI/MF/not filmed.

Issues reviewed during 1985: Mar. 1984-Oct. 1985 (P) (Vol. 24, Nos. 3-12; Vol. 25, Nos. 1-10).

STATISTICAL FEATURES:

C8130–1.601: Mar. 1984 (Vol. 24, No. 3)

RETAIL FORECAST: SALES AND PROFITS UP, MORE DISCOUNTING

(p. 18) Article, with 1 table showing operating profits per gross square foot, for 11 discount chain stores, 1980-82 and estimated 1983. Data are from Morgan Stanley and Co.

MOTOR OIL GETS HIGH MARKS, ANNUAL FEATURE

(p. 56-65) Annual article, with 1 chart showing motor oil sales in discount stores, 1977-83.

NRMA's 1982 FINANCIAL REPORT

(p. 88) Brief article, with 1 table presenting summary financial ratios including sales, gross margins, profits, and expenses, for department stores with annual sales over $1 million, 1981-82.

Data are from an annual report of National Retail Merchants Assn. Full report is covered in SRI under A8300-2.

C8130–1.602: Apr. 1984 (Vol. 24, No. 4)

RESURGENCE IN HOUSEWARES

(p. 30-58) Article, with 1 table showing houseware sales in discount stores, by product type, 1982. Data are DM estimates.

CAMERA BUYERS PLAY THE WAITING GAME

(p. 59-76) Article on recent trends in photographic equipment market. Data are from 1983 Photo Marketing Assn (PMA) consumer survey. Contains 9 tables showing consumer shopping practices for cameras and accessories by type, including outlet preference and cost expectations.

Complete PMA biennial survey report is covered in SRI under A8695-2.

LICENSING SUPPLEMENT, ANNUAL FEATURE

(p. 78-80) Annual article, with 2 charts showing retail sales of licensed products 1978-83, with distribution by product category 1983. Data are from *The Licensing Letter.*

C8130–1.603: May 1984 (Vol. 24, No. 5)

BRIDGING THE GAP TO HIGHER PUBLICATION SALES

(p. 51-62) Article examining wholesalers' and discounters' views on the marketing of publications. Data are from DM.

Includes 3 charts and 1 table showing publication market shares and average sales, by type of retail outlet; and magazine and paperback sales per square foot (with comparison to selected other products), total sales, space allotment, profits, turnover, inventory, and selected ratios, for a typical discount store; primarily 1982.

TRUE LOOK OF THE DISCOUNT INDUSTRY PART I: MARKETING, ANNUAL FEATURE

(p. 65-118, 128-146) Annual discount retail trade market statistical feature, for 1983. Data are from DM store census, special surveys, trade assn sources, and Commerce Dept.

Includes highlights and statistical section, with 6 charts and 45 tables (p. 65-118); and discount chain profile section (p. 128-146). Sections are described below.

This is the 24th annual study. For description of the 23rd study, see SRI 1983 Annual under C8130-1.406.

STATISTICAL SECTION

[Data are shown for discount chain stores, 1983, unless otherwise noted.]

a. Stores, sales, and square footage, by census division and State with detail for general merchandise, and aggregate trends from 1960; operational summary for all and new stores, 1980-83; stores and sales, by store size; and stores, sales, and companies, by company size. 3 charts and 6 tables. (p. 70-80)

b. Sales by department; "model store" weekly sales and gross margin, floor space allocation, and weekly and annual sales per square foot, all by department; average gross margin, earnings, and expenses by object, shown as percent of sales, 1981/82-1982/83; and stores and sales by census division, 1977 and 1983. 1 chart and 6 tables. (p. 82-88)

c. Combination supermarkets, combination drugstores, and catalog showrooms: number of stores, total and departmental sales, and profiles of average stores including sales and square footage, with selected comparisons to conventional stores and selected catalog showroom trends from 1975. 1 chart and 8 tables. (p. 90-94)

d. Sales by type of retail outlet: aggregated for retailers with at least $1 billion in sales; and for 21 merchandise categories. 22 tables. (p. 96-112)

e. Households: average expenditures in discount stores, by type of merchandise; and number of households, households per store, and general merchandise expenditures per household, by census division and State, with selected summary trends from 1961. 1 chart and 2 tables. (p. 114-116)

f. Top 70 companies ranked by sales, with number of stores. 1 table. (p. 117-118)

PROFILE SECTION: $100 MILLION CLUB

g. Profiles of 48 discount store chains with sales of $100 million or more during 1983, each with a narrative summary of operating characteristics, and 1 table showing stores and sales, 1981-83. (p. 128-146)

C8130–1.604: June 1984 (Vol. 24, No. 6)

TRUE LOOK OF THE DISCOUNT INDUSTRY, PART II: MERCHANDISING THE MAJOR DEPARTMENTS, ANNUAL FEATURE

(p. 36-77) Part 2 of the annual discount retail trade market statistical feature for 1983, covering discount store sales by department. Data are DM estimates; averages represent allocations in a "model" store.

Includes narrative, and the following 2 tables, repeated for automotive, hardware, camera/photo, health/beauty aids, consumer electronics, housewares, toys, and sporting goods departments, 1983:

a. Vital statistics, including average sales and selling space per store with share for general merchandise, sales per square foot, gross margin, and annual turnover.

b. Total discount store sales, by detailed product category.

Vital statistics table is also repeated for traffic (small electrical) appliances, jewelry, stationery, tobacco and candy, garden supplies, records/tapes, domestics, women's and children's/infants' wear, men's/boys' wear, and magazines and books departments.

For description of report for 1982, see SRI 1983 Annual under C8130-1.407.

C8130–1.605: July 1984 (Vol. 24, No. 7)

VENDOR THRUST

(p. 68-78) Article, with 1 chart showing high and low sales estimates for decorative adhesive stickers, 1983-84.

C8130–1.606: Aug. 1984 (Vol. 24, No. 8)

COSMETICS: SEEKING THE DEPARTMENT STORE IMAGE

(p. 76-84) Article on discount chains' marketing of cosmetics. Data are from a 1982 *Redbook* magazine survey of women age 18/over. Includes 1 table showing retail outlet preferences for 4 types of health/beauty aids.

C8130–1.607: Sept. 1984 (Vol. 24, No. 9)

LAWN & GARDEN SHOPPER

(p. 50) Article, with 1 table showing consumer retail outlet preferences, for selected types of lawn/garden supplies. Data are from a 1983 *Better Homes and Gardens* survey.

C8130–1.608: Dec. 1984 (Vol. 24, No. 12)

BED AND BATH SUPPLEMENT: PART 2, VENDORS COORDINATE WITH RETAILERS ON BED & BATH

(p. 55-64) Article, with 1 table showing sales volume and value, by type of bed and bath linen product, 1978 and 1983. Also includes profiles of selected textile companies.

Part 1 of this feature appears in the Nov. 1984 issue and presents nonstatistical profiles of unnamed retailers.

APPAREL OPERATIONS PER DISCOUNT STORE

(p. 68) Table showing average discount store apparel sales, and selected operating and financial ratios, by type of apparel, 1983. Data are DM estimates.

C8130–1.609: Feb. 1985 (Vol. 25, No. 2)

WHO'S WHO IN THE COMBO BUSINESS, ANNUAL FEATURE

(p. 42-44) Annual feature on growth of combination stores in the supermarket and drug industries. Includes 2 tables showing total and combination stores in 1984, number of new combination stores planned for 1985/86, and typical size of new stores, for approximately 100 drug and supermarket companies. This is the 4th annual feature.

C8130–1.610: Mar. 1985 (Vol. 25, No. 3)

MOTOR OIL: "IT'S PRICE ALL THE WAY!" ANNUAL FEATURE

(p. 48-56) Annual article, with 1 chart showing motor oil sales in discount stores, 1978-84.

For description of previous article, see C8130-1.601, above.

PHOTOGOODS SUPPLEMENT: DISCOUNTERS TRY HARDER FOR PHOTOGOODS GAINS

(p. 85-98) Article on recent trends in photographic equipment market. Most data are from Photo Marketing Assn (PMA) and *American Photographer* magazine.

Includes 2 charts and 3 tables showing minilabs (compact photo processing systems) in operation; camera sales to retailers, by camera type; and photo processing market shares, camera/accessories sales volume and market shares, photographic sales as percent of total sales, and consumer plans for purchasing 35mm cameras, all by outlet type; various years 1980-84.

ETHNIC HAIR-CARE BONANZA

(p. 115-118) Article, with 1 chart showing distribution of ethnic hair care product sales volume and value, by product type, 1983. Data are from American Health and Beauty Aids Institute.

C8130–1.611: Apr. 1985 (Vol. 25, No. 4)

KIDSWEAR SUPPLEMENT

(p. 58-64) Article, with 1 undated chart showing infants' and children's wear market shares, by retailer type.

MIS COSTS UP 18 PERCENT IN '83

(p. 66-68) Article on retailer use of computers. Data are based on 111 responses to an Arthur Young and Co. survey of retailers. Includes 1 undated table showing percent of combination/grocery and discount store respondents using management information systems and microcomputers, by application.

C8130–1.612: May 1985 (Vol. 25, No. 5)

TRUE LOOK OF THE DISCOUNT INDUSTRY PART I: MARKETING, ANNUAL FEATURE

(p. 54-137) Annual discount retail trade market statistical feature, for 1984. Data are from DM store census, special surveys, trade assn sources, and Commerce Dept.

Includes highlights and statistical section, with 8 charts and 47 tables (p. 65-116); and discount chain profile section (p. 118-137). Sections are described below.

This is the 25th annual study. For description of the 24th study, see C8130-1.603 above.

STATISTICAL SECTION

[Data are shown for discount chain stores, 1984, unless otherwise noted.]

a. Stores, sales, and square footage, by census division and State with detail for general merchandise, and aggregate trends from 1960; operational summary for all and new stores, 1981-84; stores and sales, by store size; and stores, sales, and companies, by company size. 3 charts and 6 tables. (p. 58-70)

b. Sales by department; "model store" weekly sales and gross margin, floor space allocation, and weekly and annual sales per square foot, all by department; average gross margin, earnings, and expenses by object, shown as percent of sales, 1982/83-1983/84; and stores and sales by census division, 1977 and 1984. 1 chart and 6 tables. (p. 72-78)

c. Combination supermarkets, combination drugstores, and catalog showrooms: number of stores, total and departmental sales, and profiles of average stores including sales and square footage, with selected comparisons to conventional stores and selected trends from 1976; and wholesale membership club stores and sales, by company, 1984-85. 3 charts and 9 tables. (p. 80-90)

d. Households: average expenditures in discount stores, by type of merchandise; and number of households, households per store, and general merchandise expenditures per household, by census division and State, with selected summary trends from 1961. 1 chart and 2 tables. (p. 92-94)

e. Top 77 companies ranked by sales, with number of stores. 1 table. (p. 96-98)

f. Sales by type of retail outlet: aggregated for retailers with at least $1 billion in sales; and for 22 merchandise categories. 23 tables. (p. 100-116)

PROFILE SECTION: $100 MILLION CLUB

g. Profiles of 45 discount store chains with sales of $100 million or more during 1984, each with a narrative summary of operating characteristics, and 1 table showing stores and sales, 1982-84. (p. 118-137)

Corrected data on wholesale membership club stores and sales appear in the June 1985 issue (see C8130-1.613 below).

LICENSING SALES TOP $40 BILLION, ANNUAL FEATURE

(p. 137) Annual article, with 1 chart and 1 table showing retail sales of licensed products, total 1980-84, and by product category 1984. Data are from *The Licensing Letter*.

For description of previous article, for 1978-83, see C8130-1.602 above.

C8130–1.613: June 1985 (Vol. 25, No. 6)

WHOLESALE CASH-AND-CARRY WAREHOUSE CLUBS

(p. 22) Correction of May 1985 table on wholesale membership club stores and sales. Presents reprint of table with corrections. Original table appears in Part 1 of annual survey of discount store operations; for description, see C8130-1.612 above.

TRUE LOOK OF THE DISCOUNT INDUSTRY, PART II: MERCHANDISING THE MAJOR DEPARTMENTS, ANNUAL FEATURE

(p. 34-80) Part 2 of the annual discount retail trade market statistical feature for 1984, covering discount store sales by department. Data are DM estimates; averages represent allocations in a "model" store.

Includes narrative, and the following 2 tables, repeated for automotive, hardware, camera/photo, health/beauty aids, tobacco, candy, stationery, housewares, consumer electronics, toys, and sporting goods departments, 1984:

a. Vital statistics, including average sales and selling space per store with share for general merchandise, sales per square foot, gross margin, and annual turnover.

b. Total discount store sales, by detailed product category.

Vital statistics table is also repeated for traffic (small electrical) appliances, jewelry, garden supplies, domestics, men's/boys' wear, women's and children's/infants' wear, records/tapes, and magazine and book departments.

For description of report for 1983, see C8130-1.604 above.

BED AND BATH SUPPLEMENT

(p. 98-105) Article, with 1 table showing bed/bath linen sales by type of retailer, 1984.

C8130-1.614: Aug. 1985 (Vol. 25, No. 8)

HARDWARE: MORE PROMOTABLES COMING OUT OF LEFT FIELD

(p. 77-98) Article, with 1 undated chart showing discount store hardware market shares, by product type.

C8130-1.615: Sept. 1985 (Vol. 25, No. 9)

CURRENT MUDDLE IN APPAREL

(p. 64-76) Article, with 1 undated chart showing distribution of discount store sales volume and gross margin, by merchandise category. Data are from Retail Planning Associates.

Article is part 2 of a special report on women's apparel. Part 1 appeared in the July 1985 issue, and was nonstatistical.

DESPITE WHAT THEY SAY, WOMEN CHOOSE BRAND NAMES

(p. 80) Article, with 4 undated tables showing women's views regarding manufacturers' vs. store brand sleepwear, including perceived quality and styling, and purchase preferences; and factors considered important in purchasing sleepwear. Data are from a J. C. Penney study of 500 women.

SUPERCHARGED COMPETITION IN DRUGS AND COSMETICS

(p. 82-94) Article, with 1 table showing health and beauty aid sales in discount stores, by product type, 1984. Data are DM estimates.

STUDY ASSESSES DEEP-DISCOUNT IMPACT

(p. 86) Article, with 4 undated tables presenting selected findings from a study of deep-discount drug stores' impact on other retailers. Includes market share loss to deep-discount stores by traditional drug stores, supermarkets, and general merchandise discounters. The study, which encompassed 3 deep-discount stores, was conducted by Willard Bishop Consulting Economists.

C8130-1.616: Oct. 1985 (Vol. 25, No. 10)

TODAY'S TEENS: ARE THEY CLOTHES CRAZY?

(p. 22-24) Article, with 1 table showing teenage girls' expenditures for clothing (outer- and inner-wear, footwear, accessories, and general merchandise), fall 1984. Data are from Seventeen magazine.

REWARDS IN SWEETS & SMOKES

(p. 72-82) Article on candy and tobacco sales in discount stores. Most data are from Ralph Head & Affiliates, and DM estimates.

Includes 2 charts and 3 tables showing candy dept sales and shelf space distribution, by candy type (no dates); discount store tobacco sales by product type, and operating profiles of typical candy and tobacco depts, 1984; and cigarette sales and market share, for 10 leading brands, 1st quarter 1984-85.

IN HOUSEWARES: WHERE THINGS STAND FOR RETAILERS AND VENDORS

(p. 88-100) Article, with 1 undated chart showing houseware sales in discount stores, for top 10 product types. Data are DM estimates.

C8400
Simmons-Boardman Publishing Corp.

C8400-1   RAILWAY AGE
Monthly.
ISSN 0033-8826.
LC 52-38523.
SRI/MF/excerpts, shipped quarterly

Monthly trade journal reporting on trends and developments in railroads and rail rapid transit industry operations, finances, traffic, equipment, new technology, and regulation. Includes data from U.S. Railway Assn, Assn of American Railroads (AAR), ICC, individual company reports, and other sources.

General format:

a. News briefs, editorial depts, and articles, occasionally with substantial statistical content, including annual outlook and review features.

b. Monthly "Market Outlook" feature, including 1 chart showing rail freight traffic trends, and 3 monthly tables listed below; and "Lines on Labor" feature, including 1 monthly table also listed below.

c. Quarterly table on rail company revenues and expenses, compiled by AAR from reports submitted to ICC.

Most monthly tables appear in all issues. All additional features with substantial statistical content are described, as they appear, under "Statistical Features;" page location and latest period of coverage for quarterly table are also noted. Nonstatistical features are not covered.

AAR weekly and monthly reports, from which quarterly revenue and expense data are derived, are covered in SRI under A3275-2 and A3275-3, respectively.

Availability: Railway Age, Subscription Department, PO Box 530, Bristol CT 06010, qualified subscribers $12.00 per yr., others $30.00 per yr., single copy $3.00+postage and handling; SRI/MF/excerpts for monthly tables and all portions covered under "Statistical Features;" shipped quarterly.

Issues reviewed during 1985: Nov. 1984-Oct. 1985 (P) (Vol. 185, Nos. 11-12; Vol. 186, Nos. 1-10).

RECURRING STATISTICS:

MONTHLY TABLES

[1-2] Revenue freight carloadings [by commodity], and piggyback loadings, [for various weeks 3-7 weeks prior to cover date, with percent change from previous year, and year-to-date freight revenue ton-miles and piggyback loadings].

[3] Freight cars [and locomotives ordered and delivered, and on order/undelivered as of 1st day of month, for month 1-3 months prior to cover date, previous month, and year to date, with comparisons to previous year; prior to Feb. 1985 issue, data on locomotives were reported in a separate table].

[4] Class 1 railroad employment [by occupation or industry sector, as of mid-month 2-3 months prior to cover date, with percent change from previous month and same month of previous year; table begins in the Apr. 1985 issue].

QUARTERLY TABLE

[1] Revenues and expenses of railways [shows operating revenues and expenses, operating ratio, income after fixed charges, net operating income, and net income, for approximately 30 railroad companies, for quarter and year to date, ending 3-4 months prior to cover date, and same periods of previous year].

STATISTICAL FEATURES:

C8400-1.601: Nov. 1984 (Vol. 185, No. 11)

RATE OF RETURN REACHES 5.5% AS EARNINGS SOAR, RECURRING FEATURE

(p. 21) Recurring article, with 1 table showing Class I railroad operating revenues and expenses, rate of return on investment, and net revenues and ordinary income by railway district, 2nd quarter and/or 1st half 1983-84. Data are from AAR.

SEARCH FOR PRODUCTIVITY

(p. 31-34) By Gus Welty. Article on trends in railroad productivity. Data are from AAR, Transportation Assn of America, and other sources.

Includes 4 tables showing intercity freight revenue distribution by transport mode (rail, truck, oil pipeline, other); rail freight revenue per ton-mile, with adjustments for inflation; railroad productivity index; and prime interest rate; 1972-82 or 1972-83.

C8400-1.602: Dec. 1984 (Vol. 185, No. 12)

INVESTMENT TRENDS

(p. 14) Brief article, with 1 table showing railroad capital investments for rolling stock and roadway/structures, 1973-83. Data are from AAR.

C8400-1.603: Jan. 1985 (Vol. 186, No. 1)

QUARTERLY TABLE

[1] Revenues and expenses of railways, 3rd quarter 1984. (p. 8-9)

C8400-1.603# C8400–1.603 Simmons-Boardman Publishing Corp.

REGAN TAX REFORMS WOULD BE COSTLY FOR THE RAILROADS

(p. 19) Article, with 1 table showing current and accrued Federal income tax rates for 5 major railroads, 1981-83. Data are from Congressional Joint Committee on Taxation, and Goldman Sachs Research.

KEEPING WHEELS IN SHAPE

(p. 39-43) By John H. Armstrong. Article, with 1 chart and 1 table showing distribution of railcar wheel repair billings by reason for repair, and value of property damage from railroad accidents due to wheel and all equipment failures, various years 1977-83. Data are from Federal Railroad Administration and Assn of American Railroads.

PASSENGER-CAR MARKET AT A GLANCE, ANNUAL FEATURE

(p. 56) Annual feature on rail passenger industry outlook for 1985. Includes 2 charts and 4 tables showing passenger car delivery and backlog trends from 1977; passenger cars delivered and on order, by purchaser, type, and builder, 1984; and passenger car order outlook, by purchaser and type, 1985 and 1986-90 period.

C8400–1.604: Apr. 1985 (Vol. 186, No. 4)

QUARTERLY TABLE

[1] Revenues and expenses of railways, 4th quarter and full year 1984. (p. 84-85)

TRUTH ABOUT THAT 'GOLDEN AGE'

(p. 6) By Luther S. Miller. Brief article, with 1 table showing percent return on investment for 25 railroads, arranged by district, for year ending Sept. 30, 1984. Data are from ICC.

C8400–1.605: July 1985 (Vol. 186, No. 7)

QUARTERLY TABLE

[1] Revenues and expenses of railways, 1st quarter 1985. (p. 16)

CASE OF THE BLAHS, AND WORSE, RECURRING FEATURE

(p. 6) Recurring article, by Luther S. Miller, with 1 table showing average, median, low, and high forecasts for railroad freight car orders and deliveries, 1985-86. Data are from responses of 17 carbuilders and component suppliers to an American Railway Car Institute survey.

Previous surveys, for 1984-85, are described in SRI 1984 Annual under C8400-1.503 and C8400-1.508.

EARNINGS DOWN 30% ON 4.6% TRAFFIC DECLINE, RECURRING FEATURE

(p. 36) Recurring article, with 1 table showing Class I railroad operating revenues and expenses, rate of return on investment, and net revenues and ordinary income by railway district, 1st quarter 1984-85. Data are from AAR.

MIXED SIGNALS AT MIDYEAR, ANNUAL FEATURE

(p. 38-39) Annual article, by Luther S. Miller, on railroad performance in 1st half 1985, with 1 chart showing railroad capital investments for roadway and equipment, 1984-86. Data are from Kidder, Peabody and Co.

C8400–1.606: Aug. 1985 (Vol. 186, No. 8)

WATCHING WASHINGTON: RED HERRINGS AND HYPOCRISY

(p. 19) Article, with 1 table showing rates of return on equity for electric utilities, railroads, and all industry, 1979-83. Data are from Assn of American Railroads.

C8400–1.607: Sept. 1985 (Vol. 186, No. 9)

WOULD A 5% RETURN TURN ON A UTILITY?

(p. 6) Brief article, with 1 table showing percent return on investment for 22 railroads, grouped by railway district, for year ending Mar. 31, 1985. Data are from ICC.

WATCHING WASHINGTON: GNP GROWS FASTER THAN TON-MILES

(p. 19) Article, with 1 table showing freight outlays by transport mode, and GNP, 1980 and 1984. Data are from Transport Policy Associates.

For description of complete report, see B8990-1.

C8400–1.608: Oct. 1985 (Vol. 186, No. 10)

QUARTERLY TABLE

[1] Revenues and expenses of railways, 2nd quarter 1985. (p. 76-77)

FUEL: STILL RUNNING SCARED

(p. 6) By Luther S. Miller. Brief article, with 1 table showing railroad revenue ton-miles, diesel fuel consumption, and ton-miles and fuel price per gallon, 1974-84.

RATE OF RETURN DROPS BELOW 5%, RECURRING FEATURE

(p. 23) Recurring article, with 1 table showing Class I railroad operating revenues and expenses, rate of return on investment, and net revenues and ordinary income by railway district, 1st half 1984-85. Data are from Assn of American Railroads.

C8400–2 PLANT LOCATION, 1985
Annual. 1985. 256 p.
SRI/MF/complete

Annual report compiling economic, labor force, and other data relevant to the selection of industrial plant sites, for each U.S. State and Canadian Province and for Puerto Rico. Data generally are current to 1983 or 1984, and include the following:

a. Financial assistance programs available to industries; tax rates; higher education and medical facilities; high school graduates; percent unionized workers; population, by SMSA or Canadian Census Metropolitan Area; and population and climate data, by major city.

b. Labor force and unemployment, by SMSA; manufacturing employment, hours, and earnings, by industry and SMSA; manufacturing earnings, for selected occupations and SMSAs; railroad, airline, and utility services; nonfuel mineral production, by type; and listing of industry-related government agencies.

Data are from a variety of public and private sources, primarily U.S. Census Bureau, BLS, and Statistics Canada.

Contains contents listing (p. 5); 4 narrative articles on aspects of plant location (p. 6-22); directories of railroads, port authorities, and U.S. foreign trade zones (p. 26-34); statistical profiles

of States (arranged by region), Puerto Rico, and Provinces, with narrative overviews for each region and for Canada (p. 36-243); and directory of foreign development offices (p. 244-248).

Availability: Plant Location, 508 Birch St., Bristol CT 06010, qualified subscribers †, others $40.00+postage and handling; SRI/MF/complete.

C8450
Sosland Publishing Co.

C8450–1 MILLING AND BAKING NEWS: (CENSUS REPORTS)
Weekly (selected issues).
For individual publication data, see below.
ISSN 0091-4843.
LC 73-647058.
SRI/MF/excerpts

Two *Milling and Baking News* features presenting Census of Manufactures findings for bread/cake/related products industry (SIC 2051), and for flour/other grain mill products industry (SIC 2041) and blended/prepared flour industry (SIC 2045), 1982, with trends from 1954. Features are further described below.

Data are from Census Bureau quinquennial Census of Manufactures and annual surveys of manufacturers.

Milling and Baking News is a weekly journal reporting on marketing developments in the milling/baking industry. Articles do not usually contain statistics other than individual company and USDA data, stocks and futures quotations, and prices for ingredients/materials. Only reports on Census of Manufactures findings, which are published quinquennially, are covered in SRI.

Journal also publishes 3 annual directory/buyer's guides: *Grain Directory* and *Milling Directory* are described in SRI under C8450-2 and C8450-3 respectively. Nonstatistical *Baking Directory* is not covered in SRI.

Availability: Sosland Publishing Co., PO Box 29155, Shawnee Mission KS 66201, $55.00 per yr., single copy $2.00; SRI/MF/excerpts.

C8450–1.1: Baking Census Report
[June 25, 1985 (Vol. 64, No. 17). (p. 1A-24A)]

Compilation of articles, with 1 map, 5 charts, and 20 tables showing the following for bread/cake/related products industry, 1982, with trends from 1954:

a. Companies; establishments; employment and payroll for production, transportation, and other workers; production workers, hours, and wages, with selected monthly or quarterly detail; value added; cost of materials including fuel and electricity; shipment volume and value; capital expenditures by type; end-of-year inventories; and selected operating ratios; with detail by type of bakery, plant employment size, product, census division, and State.

b. Product average price per pound, by type of product; and consumption and delivered cost of ingredients/materials by type, with aggregate detail by plant employment size.

Previous baking census report, covering 1977 census findings, is described in SRI 1980 Annual under C8450-1.

C8450–1.2: Milling Census Report

[July 23, 1985 (Vol. 64, No. 21). (p. 1A-11A)]

Compilation of articles, with 2 charts and 5 tables showing the following for flour/other grain mill products industry and blended/prepared flour industry, 1982, with trends from 1967:

a. Companies; total establishments, and establishments with 20/more employees; employment and payroll; production workers, hours, and wages; cost of materials, value added, and shipments value; new capital expenditures; end-of-year inventories; and operating ratios; with selected detail by establishment employment size.

b. Companies with shipments of $100,000/ over, and shipment volume and value, by detailed product type; and consumption and delivered cost of ingredients/materials, by type.

SRI coverage of the milling census report begins with the report presenting 1980 census findings.

C8450–2   MILLING AND BAKING NEWS: 1985 Grain Directory/Buyer's Guide

Annual.   1984.   119 p.
SRI/MF/excerpts

Annual *Milling and Baking News* directory and buyer's guide, for 1985, listing U.S. and Canadian multiple facility grain companies and cooperatives, and grain equipment and services, including storage elevator capacity by type and company. Data are compiled by *Milling and Baking News.*

Contents:

a. Contents listing. (p. 5)

b. Top 101 North American multiple facility grain companies and cooperatives ranked by storage capacity, with number and locations of storage facilities (p. 9-22); and port, river, terminal, subterminal, and floating elevator companies, with capacity (p. 24-56).

c. Directories of Canadian terminal and transfer elevator companies, with capacity and number of elevators or berths (p. 57-59); directory of U.S. grain exporting companies (p. 60); and 2 tables, listed below (p. 61).

d. Directory of grain transporting railroads and buyer's guide (p. 62-82); alphabetical listings of manufacturers, distributors, and service companies (p. 83-102); index to companies and executives (p. 103-116); and 2 tables, listed below (p. 117).

Milling and Baking News is a weekly journal reporting on marketing developments in the milling/baking industry. Reports on Census of Manufactures findings appearing in the weekly journal are covered by SRI under C8450-1.

Milling and Baking News publishes 2 other directories: *Milling Directory,* covered in SRI under C8450-3; and *Baking Directory,* which is nonstatistical.

Availability: Milling and Baking News, PO Box 29155, Shawnee Mission KS 66201, $20.00; SRI/MF/excerpts for all portions except buyer, manufacturer, and product guides.

TABLES:

[Data are derived from information gathered for the 1985 directories and from USDA.]

[1-2] U.S. regional grain marketing cooperatives [with headquarters, storage capacity, and number of port, river, terminal, subterminal, and country elevators, for each cooperative]. (p. 61)

[3-4] Number and capacity of off-farm grain storage facilities [by State, 1983-84]; and top 10 States [ranked by storage capacity, 1984]. (p. 117)

C8450–3   MILLING AND BAKING NEWS: 1985 Milling Directory/Buyer's Guide

Annual.   Nov. 1984.   132 p.
SRI/MF/excerpts, current and previous year reports

Annual *Milling and Baking News* directory and buyer's guide, for 1985, listing U.S., Canadian, Central American, and Caribbean area flour milling companies. Directory entries include locations, milling and storage capacity, company officers, and, often, product brand names.

Contains contents listing (p. 5); and the following:

a. U.S. statistical summaries, with 2 maps and 6 tables showing number and capacity of mills for the following: wheat flour, durum, rye flour, and buckwheat, by State; 15 largest wheat/durum/rye milling companies; and wheat flour, by capacity size group. (p. 7-9)

b. Directories, including U.S. and Canadian multi-unit companies, grain mills by type, family flour packaging plants, mix manufacturers, specialty mills, and corn refiners (U.S. only), arranged alphabetically or by State (including Puerto Rico) and Canadian Province; and Central American and Caribbean flour mills, by country. (p. 13-74)

c. Buyer's guide to products, services, and manufacturers; alphabetical listings of companies and personnel; breadstuffs calendar of events; and index to advertisers. (p. 75-132)

Previous directory and buyer's guide, for 1984, has also been reviewed by SRI, and is also available on SRI microfiche, under C8450-3 [Annual. Nov. 1983. 134 p. $20.00]. For description of 1983 edition, see SRI 1983 Annual under this number.

Milling and Baking News is a weekly journal reporting on marketing developments in the milling/baking industry. Reports on Census of Manufactures findings appearing in the weekly journal are covered by SRI under C8450-1.

Milling and Baking News publishes 2 other directories: *Grain Directory,* covered in SRI under C8450-2; and *Baking Directory,* which is nonstatistical.

Availability: Milling and Baking News, PO Box 29155, Shawnee Mission KS 66201, $20.00; SRI/MF/excerpts for U.S. statistical summaries, and directories.

C8650
Technical Publishing Co.

C8650–1   DATAMATION

Semimonthly.
ISSN 0011-6963.
LC 58-24546.
SRI/MF/excerpts, shipped quarterly

Semimonthly trade journal reporting developments and trends in the computer, data processing (DP), and information management industries. Covers equipment, technology, costs, uses, and marketing. Data are generally based on *Datamation* surveys and other commercial sources.

Issues contain feature articles, occasionally with statistics; regular editorial depts; and news items.

Annual statistical features include minicomputer/microcomputer and computer mainframe market surveys; users' ratings of software packages; DP salaries; and financial performance of the top 100 DP companies worldwide, and the top DP companies operating in Europe.

Features with substantial statistical content are described, as they appear, under "Statistical Features." Each issue of the journal is reviewed, but an abstract is published in SRI monthly issues only when statistical features appear.

Availability: Datamation, Subscription Department, 875 Third Ave., New York NY 10022, qualified subscribers †, others $50.00 per yr., qualified students and public and school libraries $38.00 per yr., single copy $3.00; SRI/MF/excerpts for all portions described under "Statistical Features;" shipped quarterly.

Issues reviewed during 1985: Nov. 1, 1984-Oct. 15, 1985 (P) (Vol. 30, Nos. 18-21; Vol. 31, Nos. 1-20).

STATISTICAL FEATURES:

C8650–1.601: Nov. 1, 1984 (Vol. 30, No. 18)

DEALING WITH DOLLARS

(p. 136.3-136.8) By John Lamb and Paul Tate. Article, with 2 tables showing top 10 U.S. data processing companies ranked by European revenue, and also showing worldwide revenue, 1983; and exchange rates for U.S. dollar and 3 European currencies, 1980-84. Data are from *Datamation* and Economist Intelligence Unit.

C8650–1.602: Nov. 15, 1984 (Vol. 30, No. 19)

UPSTARTS OUTSHINE THE STARS, ANNUAL FEATURE

(p. 34-52) Annual article, by John W. Verity, on mini/microcomputer use by business/other organizations. Data are based on responses of 6,264 users to a 1984 survey by *Datamation* and Cowen and Co., and cover recent and planned equipment purchases.

Includes the following survey response data, generally shown by equipment supplier, with comparison to previous surveys:

a. Top 12 minicomputer systems, based on number of respondents acquiring systems and number of units acquired, with estimated value; whether substantial price concession received with last minicomputer purchase; minicomputer vendor and personal computer selection criteria; and personal computer supplier choice for new users. 2 tables and 4 charts.

b. Personal computer current and planned supplier, with detail for leading brands or systems; and microprocessor purchases. 6 charts.

BUSINESS GRAPHICS TRENDS

(p. 119-122) By John A. Lehman et al. Survey article on developments in the computer graphics market. Data are from responses of approximately 200 data processing managers, to a survey conducted by *Datamation*.

Includes 12 charts showing survey response on various topics, including the following:

a. Major factors influencing purchase of graphics technology; depts expressing need for computer graphics; prevalence of computer graphics experience among information system users; and use of graphics as decision support tool.

b. Hardware and software user satisfaction; anticipated growth of computer graphics for business applications; and major growth area for graphics use.

C8650–1.603: Dec. 1, 1984 (Vol. 30, No. 20)

SYSTEMS SOFTWARE SURVEY: USERS' FAVORITE DISKS, ANNUAL FEATURE

(p. 85-138) Annual report presenting users' ratings of 135 systems-oriented software packages. Data are based on 5,415 responses to a July 1984 Data Decisions, Inc. survey of data processing dept managers.

Includes tabular list of mean ratings; and 1 chart, repeated for all packages, 9 package types, and each individual package, showing ratings on overall satisfaction with product and support services, performance, vendor support, and operations.

Correction appears in the Dec. 15, 1984 issue (see C8650-1.604 below).

C8650–1.604: Dec. 15, 1984 (Vol. 30, No. 21)

ERRATA

(1 p. following p. 32) Corrected data for annual survey of systems-oriented software packages. For description of survey, see C8650-1.603 above.

C8650–1.605: Feb. 1, 1985 (Vol. 31, No. 3)

REAL COST OF OA

(p. 82-94) By Paul A. Strassmann. Article, with 1 table showing technology and labor cost for a typical computer workstation, 1970, 1980, 1990. Data are from *Information Systems News*.

JAPANESE DP

(p. 112-118) By Andrew Friedman and Joan Greenbaum. Article on personnel and management developments for Japanese corporate data processing (DP) depts. Data are from responses of 37 Japanese and 294 European and U.S. DP managers, to a survey conducted by International Computer Occupations Network.

Includes 2 undated charts showing survey responses concerning DP manager's involvement in DP staffing and salary decisions, and years of experience in current position, for Japan, U.S., and Europe.

For description of similar reports focusing on U.S. and Europe, see SRI 1984 Annual under C8650-1.514 and C8650-1.515, respectively.

C8650–1.606: Feb. 15, 1985 (Vol. 31, No. 4)

MICRO TO M'FRAME BLUES

(p. 43-59) By Paula S. Stone. Article, with 1 table showing corporate use of micro-to-mainframe computer links, for all and large companies, by software vendor. Data are from responses of 642 companies to a Dec. 1984 *Datamation* survey.

C8650–1.607: Mar. 1, 1985 (Vol. 31, No. 5)

MAKING THE NETWORK CONNECTION

(p. 72.2-72.8) By Paul Tate. Article, with 1 chart showing local area computer network market share, for France, Italy, West Germany, UK, and rest of Europe, 1988. Data are from Frost and Sullivan, Inc.

HANDICAPPING LANs

(p. 96-102) By Martin Pyykkonen. Article, with 2 charts showing local area computer network market shares, by product type, 1987 and 1992. Data are from Arthur D. Little, Inc.

C8650–1.608: Mar. 15, 1985 (Vol. 31, No. 6)

1985 DP BUDGET SURVEY, ANNUAL FEATURE

(p. 74-78) Annual article, by John W. Verity, on corporate spending for data processing (DP). Data are from responses of 642 DP managers to a 1984 *Datamation* survey.

Includes 3 tables showing DP budget distribution by component, 1984-85, and mean DP spending outside of budget by item (no date), both for Fortune 1000 and all firms; and percent change in DP budgets, by selected industry, 1985 vs. 1984.

C8650–1.609: May 1, 1985 (Vol. 31, No. 9)

APPLICATIONS SOFTWARE SURVEY, ANNUAL FEATURE

(p. 118-138) Annual article presenting users' ratings of 99 applications-oriented software packages. Data are based on 4,020 responses to an Aug. 1984 survey designed by Data Decisions, Inc.

Includes tabular list of mean ratings; and 1 chart repeated for all packages, 3 package types, and each individual package, showing ratings on overall satisfaction, performance, vendor support, operations, and input/output.

C8650–1.610: May 15, 1985 (Vol. 31, No. 10)

UP, UP, AND AWAY, ANNUAL FEATURE

(p. 32-42) Annual survey report, by John W. Verity, on computer mainframe user equipment use and expansion plans, with detail for major vendors' products. Data are based on responses of 4,346 users to a Feb. 1985 survey by Cowen & Co. and *Datamation*.

Includes 7 charts showing 1985 survey responses concerning the following, with selected comparisons to previous surveys:

a. Preferred vendors for IBM-compatible mainframe disk add-on procurements and database management software, and for personal computer and host-based systems and local area networks.

b. Most likely vendor choice for changes at large and small system sites; preferred personal computer software package; and incidence of procurement changes following introduction of IBM Sierra system.

TOO LITTLE, TOO LATE?

(p. 48-52) By Robert J. Crutchfield. Article, with 1 table showing likelihood of vendor change among computer mainframe users of 4 major vendors, 1983-85. Data are from a recent study by Cowen & Co. and *Datamation*.

C8650–1.611: June 1, 1985 (Vol. 31, No. 11)

DATAMATION 100: A GLOBAL INDUSTRY, ANNUAL FEATURE

(p. 36-182) Annual report, by Pamela Archbold and John W. Verity, analyzing financial performance of the top 100 data processing (DP) companies worldwide, as ranked by DP revenues in 1984.

Contents:

a. Narrative summary, with 9 tables showing the following for companies worldwide: revenues of top 10 companies in 4 industry segments; revenue changes for 10 best and 7 worst performing companies; top 10 companies by revenue per employee; earnings loss for 9 companies that lost money; and revenues of 28 foreign companies (in national currencies), ranked by revenue change; 1984 with selected comparisons to 1983. (p. 37-46)

b. Ranked listing of the top 100 world companies, showing the following for each company: total and DP revenues (includes revenues in local currency for foreign companies), employment, R&D expenditures, and net income, all for 1984, with rank and selected other comparisons to 1983. (p. 50-53)

c. Ranked listing of top 100 U.S. companies, by DP revenues, 1984. (p. 54)

d. Profiles of developments in each company, with 1 chart repeated for each of the top 50 companies showing DP revenues by product segment, 1984. (p. 58-182)

Corrected data appear in the July 15, 1985 issue; for description, see C8650-1.614 below.

C8650–1.612: June 15, 1985 (Vol. 31, No. 12)

EXODUS UP CLOSE

(p. 42) Article on Operation Exodus, the U.S. Customs Service program for intercepting illegal high-technology exports to Eastern Bloc countries. Data are from Customs Service.

Includes 2 tables showing the following for Operation Exodus: number of shipments seized and detained, and shipment value, FY82-85; and cases accepted for prosecution, indictments, arrests, and convictions, Oct. 1981-Sept. 1984 period.

C8650–1.613: July 1, 1985 (Vol. 31, No. 13)

IBM BOUNCES BACK

(p. 32-42) By Tom McCusker. Article, with 1 table showing database management system market shares, for 8 systems and all others, 1985-86. Data are from a study conducted by Cowen & Co. and *Datamation*.

FRENCH MICRO LESSONS

(p. 119-120) By James Etheridge. Article, with 1 undated table showing unit sales of professional and home microcomputers to the French school system, by French vendor and for all foreign vendors.

COMPUTER ADVERTISING, 1985: THE $2.1 BILLION PRIZE

(p. 147-152) By Efrem Sigel. Article on computer industry advertising expenditures. Data are from Communication Trends Inc. and SEC. Includes 5 tables showing the following:

a. Expenditures for worldwide advertising, total computer revenues, and selling/general/administrative costs, all aggregated for 101 major computer companies, with selected comparisons to total computer industry, various years 1981-85.

b. Aggregate computer industry expenditures for personal and other computer advertising, 1982-84; and top 10 computer companies ranked by advertising budget, with budget as percent of computer revenues, 1984.

C8650–1.614: July 15, 1985 (Vol. 31, No. 14)

CORRECTIONS

(p. 23) Includes data corrections for annual feature on the financial performance of the top 100 data processing companies worldwide, appearing in the June 1, 1985 issue (for description, see C8650-1.611 above).

HEDGING BETS IN THE OEM MARKET, ANNUAL FEATURE

(p. 48.3-48.16) Annual article, by Edith Holmes, on 1984 market performance of original equipment manufacturers (OEMs)/systems houses, organizations that develop customized computer systems for resale using components from various manufacturers. Data are from a Sentry Database Publishing survey of 2,011 OEMs and systems houses.

Includes 12 tables showing respondents' unit sales of minicomputers, personal computers, and various peripheral products, with selected market share detail by company; and shipments and percent change in sales by systems application; various years 1980-84.

C8650–1.615: Aug. 1, 1985 (Vol. 31, No. 15)

EUROPE'S 1984 VINTAGE, ANNUAL FEATURE

(p. 56.5-56.11) Annual article, by Paul Tate and Linda Runyan, on top 25 data processing (DP) companies ranked by western European DP revenues, 1984. Data are from a survey compiled by *Datamation*.

Includes 2 summary tables, and 1 table showing the following for each company: headquarters country, DP revenues (total and European), total revenues, domestic revenues as percent of total DP revenues, employees, and net income, CY84 or FY84, with selected comparisons to 1983.

EXPLORING THE OLTP REALM

(p. 60-68) By Omri Serlin. Article on market outlook for on-line transaction processing (OLTP) applications (common database available to interactive terminal users for inquiries and updates). Data are from ITOM International Co.

Includes 1 table showing worldwide OLTP shipment value, by manufacturer or system, 1982-84 and 1989, with detail for fault-tolerant system vendors.

C8650–1.616: Aug. 15, 1985 (Vol. 31, No. 16)

SUPERMICROS ASCEND TO 32 BITS

(p. 64.2-64.6) By Lamont Wood. Article, with 1 table showing super microcomputer revenues and unit shipments, for top 10 and all other vendors, 1984. Data are from Dataquest.

TOP 10 VARS

(p. 64.11-64.16) By Edith Holmes. Article, with 1 undated table showing the top 10 value-added remarketers (companies that repackage hardware for resale with software and other services), ranked by value of systems sold. Also includes computer types sold, company location, and whether company is national or international.

Data are from a recent survey of systems houses and computer original equipment manufacturers, conducted by Technical Publishing Co.

THE DP PSYCHE

(p. 103-110) By Michael L. Lyons. Article analyzing the personalities and work preferences of computer professionals. Data are from responses of 1,229 employees in approximately 100 companies in the U.S., UK, and Australia, to a recent NT Systems Corp. survey.

Includes 4 undated tables showing respondents by age group, educational level, years in computing, job type, and personality type, all shown by sex. Personality types were assessed using the Myers-Briggs Type Indicator.

C8650–1.617: Sept. 1, 1985 (Vol. 31, No. 17)

JAPAN'S TOP 10

(p. 64.4-64.14) By Thomas Murtha and Linda Runyan. Article on top 10 data processing (DP) companies in Japan, ranked by Japanese DP revenues, 1984. Data are from a survey by *Datamation*.

Includes 2 summary tables, and 1 table showing the following for each company: ownership (U.S. or Japanese), total and Japanese DP revenues and employment, total revenues, and net income, 1984 with selected comparisons to 1983.

C8650–1.618: Sept. 15, 1985 (Vol. 31, No. 18)

BRIDGING THE GAP

(p. 84.2-84.12) By Edith Holmes. Article, with 1 table showing office automation system installations, for 12 manufacturers and all others, 1983-89. Data are from the Yankee Group.

1985 DP SALARY SURVEY, ANNUAL FEATURE

(p. 89-100) Annual article on data processing (DP) salaries, 1985. Data are based on 589 responses, primarily from DP managers, to a June 1985 *Datamation* survey.

Includes 5 tables showing DP salary percent increase, and professional staff turnover rates, with detail for 18 metro areas; types of benefits and perquisites available to DP management and staff; and average DP salary by detailed position, for 11 industry categories, 2 DP budget size categories, and 18 metro areas; 1985, with selected comparisons to 1984.

Complete survey report is available from the issuing agency for $100.00.

C8650–1.619: Oct. 1, 1985 (Vol. 31, No. 19)

S. AFRICA: PULLING THE PLUG

(p. 22-28) By Willie Schatz. Article on the computer industry in South Africa. Data are from John Aczel. Includes 2 charts and 5 tables showing the following for South Africa:

a. Computer hardware value supplied by 6 leading countries; percent change in new business imports, for 4 countries of origin; and mainframe and minicomputer installations, by company; various periods 1979-84.

b. Import value of Japanese computers, by type, 1981-84; value of data processing imports, 1980-84; and information processing market value, by category, 1985 and 1990.

ENTERING THE EASTERN ZONE

(p. 64.2-64.6) By David Hebditch and Heikki Auvinen. Article, with 1 table showing value of computer hardware exports to USSR and all other Eastern Bloc countries, for 9 countries of origin, 1982-84. Data are from John Aczel.

EUROPE'S SOFTWARE SCENE

(p. 64.19-64.24) By John Lamb. Article, with 2 tables showing the following for Western Europe: computer software/services market value, by sector; and European data processing revenues of 5 leading companies; 1984. Data are from *Datamation* and European Computing Assn.

C8650–1.620: Oct. 15, 1985 (Vol. 31, No. 20)

MINING THE AFTERMARKET

(p. 80.2-80.8) By Esther Surden. Article on the computer aftermarket (peripherals, supplies, and upgraded systems). Data are from a March 1985 survey of 1,189 aftermarket retailers conducted by The Yankee Group.

Includes 1 table showing percent of value-added reseller customers buying 1 system at time of initial purchase, and returning within 2 years for additional system or upgrade, by aftermarket item.

COMPUTERS IN THE SCHOOLS

(p. 80.13-80.24) By Edith Holmes. Article, with 2 tables showing number of microcomputers in elementary/secondary schools, 1981-89; and computer hardware educational market shares for 6 companies and all others, as of June 1984. Data are from Talmis, a subsidiary of International Data Corp.

DO YOU TELECOMMUTE?

(p. 129-132) By Margrethe H. Olson. Survey article on telecommuting (working at home by using computer terminals). Data are from 958 responses to a winter 1984/85 *Datamation* reader survey.

Includes 11 tables showing respondent occupation, whether self-employed or employed by outside company, and household income; and survey response on various work characteristics, including type of computer equipment used in home, reasons for telecommuting, and opinions on advantages and disadvantages of telecommuting.

C8650-3   RESEARCH AND DEVELOPMENT

Monthly.
ISSN 0746-9179.
LC 84-642292.
SRI/MF/excerpts, shipped quarterly

Monthly publication (semimonthly in Feb.) reporting trends and developments in industrial design and quality assurance. Covers R&D funding, management, and new product developments and applications.

Issues contain regular editorial depts, including a recurring "Opinion Poll" reader survey feature; news articles on scientific and technological developments; and feature articles, occasionally statistical.

Annual features include an R&D funding forecast; surveys of R&D professionals' salaries, and the use and planned purchase of instruments and equipment; and subject and author indexes. Second Feb. issue is an annual industry telephone directory.

Features with substantial statistical content are described, as they appear, under "Statistical Features." Each issue of the journal is reviewed, but an abstract is published in SRI monthly issues only when statistical articles appear, or when "Opinion Poll" data are on topics pertaining to the R&D sector.

Availability: Research and Development, Circulation Department, PO Box 5365, New York NY 10150, qualified subscribers †, others $36.00 per yr.; SRI/MF/excerpts for all portions described under "Statistical Features;" shipped quarterly.

Issues reviewed during 1985: Nov. 1984-July 1985 (P) (Vol. 26, Nos. 11-12; Vol. 27, Nos. 1-7).

STATISTICAL FEATURES:

C8650-3.601: Nov. 1984 (Vol. 26, No. 11)

USE OF ELECTRICAL AND ELECTRONIC INSTRUMENTS, ANNUAL FEATURE

(p. 114-117) Annual article, by C. J. Mosbacher, with 1 table showing use of and plans to acquire electrical and electronic instruments and equipment, by type, for engineers, life/medical scientists, and physical scientists. Data are from responses of 898 subscribers to a May 1984 *Research and Development* survey.

OPINION POLL RESULTS: REPUBLICANS, POLITICAL ACTIVISM GET VOTE IN SURVEY OF READERS

(p. 221) Brief article reporting results of recent *Research and Development* reader survey on politics and R&D, including responsiveness of major political parties to R&D interests, and whether scientists/engineers should be involved in politics.

Includes text data showing distribution of responses from approximately 1,800 readers.

C8650-3.602: Jan. 1985 (Vol. 27, No. 1)

R&D FUNDING WILL RISE TO $110 BILLION IN 1985, ANNUAL FEATURE

(p. 68-70) Annual article, by C. J. Mosbacher, forecasting R&D funding and expenditures. Data are from NSF. Includes 1 chart showing amount of R&D money to be provided and spent by the Federal Government, industry, and other sectors, 1985.

OPINION POLL RESULTS: POLLUTION PROBLEMS DECLINE, AIDED BY R&D STAFF EFFORTS

(p. 158) Brief article reporting results of recent *Research and Development* reader survey on involvement of R&D personnel in pollution research or control, and on severity of pollution near work place.

Includes text data showing distribution of responses from approximately 2,000 readers.

C8650-3.603: Feb. 1985 (Vol. 27, No. 2)

USE OF ANALYTICAL INSTRUMENTS AND EQUIPMENT, 1985, ANNUAL FEATURE

(p. 174-177) Annual article, by C. J. Mosbacher, with 2 tables showing 33 analytical instruments ranked by growth in current or planned use, 1984-85; and use of and plans to acquire analytical instruments and equipment, by type, for engineers, physical scientists, and life/medical scientists. Data are from responses of 1,261 subscribers to a fall 1984 *Research and Development* survey.

C8650-3.604: Mar. 1985 (Vol. 27, No. 3)

1984 WAS A GOOD YEAR FOR R&D SALARIES, ANNUAL FEATURE

(p. 67-70) Annual article, by Robert R. Jones, analyzing trends in salaries of R&D professionals, by discipline. Data are from approximately 3,700 responses to an annual *Research and Development* reader survey, 1985, and earlier surveys.

Includes 24 charts and 14 tables presenting medians and ranges for salary, years with present employer, age, and years of experience; and respondent distribution by range of salary percent increase; all by scientific discipline, 1985 survey, with selected comparisons to 1981-84 surveys.

This is the 1st of 2 articles reporting the salary survey findings. For description of 2nd article, see C8650-3.605 below.

C8650-3.605: May 1985 (Vol. 27, No. 5)

R&D INCOME WINNER: MALE PhD IN INDUSTRY, ANNUAL FEATURE

(p. 100-104) Annual article, by Robert R. Jones, examining relationship of professional R&D salary levels to sex, experience, education, and type of employer. Data are from approximately 3,700 responses to an annual *Research and Development* reader survey, 1985, and earlier surveys.

Includes 5 tables showing median salary by degree level, and by sex by type of employer; and respondent distribution by salary level, past year's salary increase (with detail by sex), years with present employer, age, years of experience, highest degree, profession, type of employer, and sex; 1985 survey, with selected comparisons to surveys from 1980.

This is the 2nd of 2 articles reporting the salary survey findings. For description of 1st article, see C8650-3.604 above.

C8650-4   ELECTRIC LIGHT AND POWER

Monthly. Oversized.
ISSN 0013-4120.
LC 27-16630.
SRI/MF/excerpts, shipped quarterly

Monthly trade journal covering developments in electric utility management, technology, regulation, and operations. Data are from journal surveys, and reports of private firms and DOE.

Issues generally contain numerous news and feature articles, occasionally with statistics, and regular editorial depts. Annual statistical features include rankings of top 100 electric utilities in financial and operating performance.

Features with substantial statistical content are described, as they appear, under "Statistical Features." Each issue of the journal is reviewed, but an abstract is published in SRI monthly issues only when statistical features appear.

Availability: Electric Light and Power, Circulation Department, PO Box 1030, Barrington IL 60010, qualified subscribers †, others $38.00 per yr., single copy $4.00+postage; SRI/MF/excerpts for all portions covered under "Statistical Features;" shipped quarterly.

Issues reviewed during 1985: Nov. 1984-Oct. 1985 (P) (Vol. 62, Nos. 11-12; Vol. 63, Nos. 1-10).

STATISTICAL FEATURES:

C8650-4.601: Dec. 1984 (Vol. 62, No. 12)

TOTAL UTILITY FINANCING DROPS IN 3rd QUARTER

(p. 9) Brief article, with 1 table showing electric utility long-term debt and preferred and common stock financing, 1st 9 months 1983-84. Data are from Ebasco Business Consulting Co.

ELECTRICITY BILLS SURVEYED BY NARUC

(p. 22) Article, with 1 table showing operating utility name and residential electricity rate, for 10 cities with highest and lowest rate, Dec. 1983-Feb. 1984 period. Data are from National Assn of Regulatory Utility Commissioners.

C8650-4.602: Jan. 1985 (Vol. 63, No. 1)

'85 CAPITAL SPENDING TO FALL, FINANCING AND REGULATORY NEEDS CHANGING, ANNUAL FEATURE

(p. 11-14) Annual article, by Robert A. Lincicome et al., with 3 tables showing electric utility capital spending, by function and North American Electric Reliability Council region, 1985-89. Data are national estimates based on an EL&P survey of 200 electric utility organizations, conducted Oct.-Nov. 1984.

MOST EFFICIENT, LOWEST COST PLANTS IDENTIFIED

(p. 19) Brief article, with 1 table showing top 20 steam plants ranked by heat rate (Btu/kWh), and also showing primary fuel type, startup year of first and latest unit, capacity, net generation, and operator, 1982. Data are from Utility Data Institute.

NUCLEAR POWER INDUSTRY BEGINS DECOMMISSIONING OLD REACTORS

(p. 21-35 passim) By Robert Smock. Article, with 2 tabular lists showing date and method of decommissioning, for 7 nuclear reactors decommissioned since 1968; and startup date, reactor type, capacity, and technical data, for 13 reactors eligible for decommissioning. Data are from DOE.

C8650–4.603: Feb. 1985 (Vol. 63, No. 2)

FOUR NEW NUCLEAR PLANTS ENTER COMMERCIAL SERVICE

(p. 18) Article, with 1 table showing the following for 4 nuclear power plants entering commercial operation in 1984: generating capacity, reactor type, utility owner, date of construction permit and operating license, commercial operation date, and construction duration. Data are from Washington Public Power Supply System.

C8650–4.604: Mar. 1985 (Vol. 63, No. 3)

KWh SALES PER REAL GNP: THE SLIDE CONTINUES

(p. 1, 6) Article, with 1 table showing ratio of electricity generation to real GNP, 1976-84. Data are from Energy Information Administration of DOE.

C8650–4.605: Apr. 1985 (Vol. 63, No. 4)

UNCERTAINTIES ERODE 'BUSINESS AS USUAL,' REPORT FINDS

(p. 3) Article, with 1 table estimating electricity supply and planned capital investments for 1993, and additional capacity and capital required for 1995 under 4 demand assumptions. Data are from Congressional Research Service.

RESCUE NUCLEAR, BOLSTER INDUSTRY, EEI URGES

(p. 16, 18) By Dan Utroska. Article, with 1 table showing the following for individual nuclear power plants with construction permits as of Feb. 20, 1985: capacity, estimated completion date and percent completed at year end 1980 and 1984, and utility owner. Data are from Edison Electric Institute and *Nuclear News*.

C8650–4.606: June 1985 (Vol. 63, No. 6)

20th ANNUAL TOP 100 ELECTRIC UTILITIES REPORT: MOST UTILITIES BETTERED '83 RECORDS LAST YEAR AND IMPROVED THE QUALITY OF THEIR EARNINGS

(p. 11-14) Annual article, by Robert A. Lincicome, presenting operating and financial performance rankings for 100 largest investor-owned electric utilities, 1984.

Includes 3 summary tables; and 4 detailed tables showing earnings per share, kWh sales and distribution by customer type, long-term debt percent change and ratio to net plant value, net income, revenue, interest coverage ratio, high and low share prices, electric and gas customers and revenues, and after-tax income, all by company with rankings for most items, 1984 and/or percent change from 1983.

Also includes average annual sales growth, 1979-84 period.

EEI DETAILS UTILITY DIVERSIFICATION IN NEW REPORT

(p. 18) Article on electric utility involvement in other business ventures. Data are based on 296 responses to a recent Edison Electric Institute survey of 120 member utilities. Includes 1 undated table showing distribution of business ventures, by type.

CAN ALTERNATE ENERGY LIVE WITHOUT TAX CREDITS?

(p. 38-40) By Robert Smock. Article, with 4 tables showing shipments of photovoltaic modules used in solar energy systems, world-wide and for U.S., Japan, and Europe, 1983-84. Includes detail for U.S. by application (3rd party-financed, exports, off-grid residential and industrial/commercial, and Government projects); and for U.S. and Japan by manufacturer.

Data are from a paper delivered at the 12th Energy Technology Conference.

C8650–4.607: Aug. 1985 (Vol. 63, No. 8)

GROWING BUSINESS RISKS CHALLENGE UTILITY CREDIT

(p. 6) Article, with 1 table showing electric utility industry key credit measures, including interest coverage ratio, and ratios of debt to capital and of cash flow to construction and capital, selected years 1970-84. Data are from Standard & Poor's Corp.

TOP 100 ELECTRIC UTILITIES' 1984 OPERATING PERFORMANCES, ANNUAL FEATURE

(p. 17-21) Annual article, by Robert Smock, presenting operating data for 100 leading investor-owned electric utilities, 1984 with selected comparisons to 1983. Data are based on Uniform Statistical Reports filed by the utilities.

Includes 3 summary tables; 1 table showing top 20 generating units ranked by heat rate (Btu/kWh) and including capacity and utility owner, and top 10 utilities using only fossil-fueled boilers ranked by heat rate; and 4 detailed tables presenting the following data for each utility:

a. Heat rate and ranking; consumption of coal, oil, and gas; peak demand; total system and owned capacity and reserve rate; and load factor.

b. Electricity production, by type of generating power; and transmission and distribution line mileage and additions, with detail for underground and overhead distribution lines.

Corrected data for 2 companies appear in Sept. 1985 issue; for description, see C8650-4.608 below.

C8650–4.608: Sept. 1985 (Vol. 63, No. 9)

TOP 100 CORRECTION

(p. 4) Includes corrected data for 2 companies covered in annual feature presenting operating data for 100 leading investor-owned electric utilities.

For description of annual feature, see C8650-4.607 above.

COAL PRODUCTION TO SOAR OVER NEXT 10 YEARS

(p. 19) Article, with 3 tables showing coal production by region (East and West), exports, storage withdrawals, and consumption by end-use sector; electric utility fuel consumption, by fuel type; and coal-fired electric power capacity and capacity additions; various periods 1975-95. Data are from DOE.

C8650–4.609: Oct. 1985 (Vol. 63, No. 10)

SLOW SECOND QUARTER GROWTH BLAMED ON MILDER WEATHER

(p. 1, 3) Article, with 1 table showing revenues and earnings per share, for 29 investor-owned electric utilities, 2nd quarter 1984-85. Data are from an EL&P survey.

C8650–5   DUN'S BUSINESS MONTH

Monthly.
ISSN 0279-3040.
LC 81-646138.
SRI/MF/excerpts, shipped
quarterly

Monthly magazine reporting developments of interest to corporate executives. Covers government policy and legislation, the economy, finance, specific companies and industries, labor relations, management, marketing, technological innovations, news media, and world affairs.

Data are from Dun & Bradstreet surveys, FHLBB, and private sources.

Issues generally contain news briefs; numerous articles, occasionally with statistics; editorial depts, including brief summaries of recent surveys and studies; and the following statistical features:

a. "Investment Update" monthly table, appearing in "Personal Finance" section, showing recent price or yield, and value and percent change, for $10,000 invested 1 month and 1 year earlier for 6 types of investment (unnamed common stock index fund, 30-year Treasury bond paying $11\frac{3}{4}\%$, unnamed money market fund, gold Krugerrands, and existing and new houses).

b. Annual features on the executive job market, corporate dividend growth and cash flow, and corporate vehicle fleets.

c. Series of business trend articles based on surveys of the Dun & Bradstreet 5000, a representative sample drawn from a data base covering over 5 million companies.

"Investment Update" table appears in all issues. All additional features with substantial statistical content are described, as they appear, under "Statistical Features." Nonstatistical features are not covered.

Availability: Dun's Business Month, Subscription Department, 875 Third Ave., New York NY 10022, qualified subscribers †, others $30.00 per yr., single copy $3.00; SRI/MF/excerpts for "Investment Update" and all portions described under "Statistical Features;" shipped quarterly.

Issues reviewed during 1985: Nov. 1984-Oct. 1985 (P) (Vol. 124, Nos. 5-6; Vol. 125, Nos. 1-6; Vol. 126, Nos. 1-4).

STATISTICAL FEATURES:

C8650–5.601: Nov. 1984 (Vol. 124, No. 5)

CURRENT JOB OPENINGS, ANNUAL FEATURE

(p. 92-108) Annual list of current job openings for executives in 13 functional areas, showing position title, industry, region, and salary, 1984. Data are from 20 leading executive recruiters participating in *Dun's Business Month's* 10th annual survey.

Also includes list of participating recruiters, and a related article (p. 52-54).

C8650–5.602: Dec. 1984 (Vol. 124, No. 6)

DIVIDEND ACHIEVERS DECLINE FOR SECOND YEAR, ANNUAL FEATURE

(p. 77-91) Annual listing of 403 U.S. and Canadian corporations that have consistently increased dividend payments over the last 10 years. Data were compiled by Moody's Investors Service.

Includes introduction and 1 extended table showing the following for each company: current and 1974 dividends, and 10-year growth rate and rank; recent stock price, current yield, latest earnings per share, and 1983 payout; and annual sales, net income, return on sales, stockholders' equity, and return on equity.

This is the 6th annual listing.

C8650–5.603: Apr. 1985 (Vol. 125, No. 4)

FALLOFF IN BUSINESS FAILURES

(p. 69) Article, with 2 charts showing percent change in business failures, by industry and census division, Jan./Feb. 1985 vs. Jan./Feb. 1984. Data are from Dun & Bradstreet.

C8650–5.604: June 1985 (Vol. 125, No. 6)

DUN'S 5000: BUSINESS PURCHASES OF PCs TO SLOW DOWN

(p. 39) Survey article, with 1 table showing percent of businesses using personal computers, by employee size group, 1985 vs. 1983.

Article is part of a series based on surveys of the Dun & Bradstreet 5000.

C8650–5.605: July 1985 (Vol. 126, No. 1)

CASH FLOW: THE TOP 200, ANNUAL FEATURE

(p. 44-50) Annual article, with 1 table ranking top 200 nonfinancial corporations by cash flow, and also showing net income, discretionary cash flow, revenues, return on equity, and debt/equity and cash flow/revenue ratios, 1984, with selected comparisons to 1983. Data are from Standard & Poor's Compustat data base.

Also includes a related article (p. 40-41).

For description of previous article, see SRI 1984 Annual under C8650-5.509.

C8650–5.606: Aug. 1985 (Vol. 126, No. 2)

STRENGTH IN SMALL BUSINESS

(p. 35) Article, with 1 chart comparing number of business failures for small businesses (fewer than 100 employees) vs. all businesses, Jan. 1984, Jan. 1985, and June 1985. Data are from Dun & Bradstreet Corp.

C8650–5.607: Sept. 1985 (Vol. 126, No. 3)

U.S. CAPITAL GAP: A GROWING BURDEN

(p. 37) Article, with 1 chart showing capital flow into and out of the U.S., 1982-84.

C8650–5.608: Oct. 1985 (Vol. 126, No. 4)

FLEET MANAGEMENT: UPDATE '86, ANNUAL FEATURE

(p. 15-40) Annual compilation of articles on developments in corporate motor vehicle fleet management and operations. Data are from Runzheimer International.

Includes 1 table (p. 25) showing ownership and operating costs, and specifications, for ten 1986 auto makes/models.

REAL ESTATE LOAN CRUNCH

(p. 48) Article, with 1 table showing the following for 7 Texas bank holding companies: value of nonperforming real estate loans (amount and as percent of all nonperforming loans), and real estate loans as percent of total loan portfolio, as of 2nd quarter 1985. Data are from bank reports.

COMPANIES CUT BACK ON BENEFITS: WHAT IT'S COSTING EMPLOYEES

(p. 64-68) By Daniel Forbes. Article on reductions in corporate health care benefits. Data are based on responses of 150 companies to a recent *Dun's Business Month* survey.

Includes 1 chart showing percent of companies transferring more health care costs to employees, overall and by raising deductibles, reducing proportion of medical bills covered, and increasing employee contribution to premium payments.

C8650–6   INDUSTRIAL DISTRIBUTION
Monthly.
ISSN 0019-8153.
LC 13-8201.
SRI/MF/excerpts, shipped quarterly

Monthly trade journal reporting on management, marketing, and operating strategies for distributors of general and special line industrial supplies.

General format:

a. "Industry News" briefs, including a monthly "Indicators" section with business activity index data.

b. "Regional Report" monthly statistical feature, with 1 chart, and 2 tables on industrial supplies sales and receivables outstanding, by census division.

c. Feature articles, occasionally with statistics, including annual surveys of distributors' operations; semiannual article index; and narrative editorial depts.

d. Quarterly inflation index feature, with 2 tables.

Monthly and quarterly statistical features are described below. Monthly statistics appear in all issues. All additional features with substantial statistical content are described, as they appear, under "Statistical Features;" page locations and latest periods of coverage for quarterly feature are also noted. Nonstatistical features are not covered.

Both the 1983 and 1984 issues of *Industrial Distribution* are numbered Vol. 73 to correct an earlier error in volume numbering.

Availability: Industrial Distribution, Circulation Department, PO Box 1063, Barrington IL 60010, qualified subscribers †, others $50.00 per yr., single copy $6.00; SRI/MF/excerpts for all monthly statistics and for portions described under "Statistical Features;" shipped quarterly.

Issues reviewed during 1985: Nov. 1984-Oct. 1985 (P) (Vol. 73, Nos. 11-12; Vol. 74, Nos. 1-10).

MONTHLY STATISTICS:
[Month of coverage is 3 months prior to cover date, for most data.]

INDUSTRY NEWS

"Indicators" section, with text statistics on approximately 8 manufacturer and distributor assn business activity indexes; for month of coverage, with selected comparisons to previous month or year.

REGIONAL REPORT

[Data are shown for general and special line industrial supplies, for U.S. and by census division.]

[1] Receivables [average days outstanding, for month of coverage and same month of previous year].

[2] Sales by regions (percent change) [usually for month of coverage vs. selected previous periods; also includes detail for selected States, groups of States, and metro areas].

QUARTERLY INFLATION INDEX:

Quarterly feature, usually with narrative analysis and 2 tables showing *Industrial Distribution* inflation index (1967 = 100) for approximately 35 product categories, for quarter ending 3-4 months preceding cover date and year to date, with comparisons to selected previous periods, and summary comparisons to 7-8 other inflation indexes. Data are prepared by Alan Silver and Associates from BLS statistics.

STATISTICAL FEATURES:

C8650–6.601: Nov. 1984 (Vol. 73, No. 11)

RMA FORECASTS HOSE AND BELTING GROWTH TO SLACKEN

(p. 7) Brief article, with 1 table showing demand value for rubber/plastic industrial hose, flat-belting, and v-belts, 1984-89. Data are from Rubber Manufacturers Assn.

PRODUCTIVITY REPORT CONFIRMS SALES DOWN IN 1983

(p. 71-74) Article on industrial distributor sales and financial condition, 1983 and trends. Data are from *The Distributor Productivity Report,* based on approximately 200 responses to a membership survey by National and Southern Industrial Distributors Assns.

Includes 3 tables showing expenses by item, profit, asset management measures, productivity ratios, and other performance measures, all as percent of sales and/or gross margin, by company sales volume, 1983, with selected trends from 1979.

SALES, CONFIDENCE REBOUND IN TOOLS AND FASTENERS, ANNUAL FEATURE

(p. 93-94) Annual article on tool/fastener distributor sales and financial condition, based on a Specialty Tools and Fasteners Distributors Assn member survey. Includes 1 table showing average sales, profit as percent of sales, inventory turnover, days outstanding for accounts receivable, and selected financial and operating ratios, 1979-83.

For description of previous article, see SRI 1983 Annual, under C6185-2.407.

C8650–6.602: Dec. 1984 (Vol. 73, No. 12)

DISTRIBUTORS PREPARED FOR SLOWER GROWTH

(p. 46-47) Article, with 1 table showing estimated capital spending, by manufacturing industry group, 1984-85. Data are from Commerce Dept and Rinfret Associates, Inc.

C8650–6.603: Jan. 1985 (Vol. 74, No. 1)

QUARTERLY INFLATION INDEX

(p. 71-72) For 3rd quarter 1984. For data description, see C8650-6 above.

1985: NEW MARKETS, NEW TECHNOLOGIES, NEW CHALLENGES

(p. 43-46) By Milton J. Ellenbogen. Article, with 2 tables showing percent change in GNP, consumer prices, and industrial production, quarterly 1985; and expenditures for new industrial plants/equipment, 1983-85. Data sources include McGraw-Hill Economics.

C8650–6.604: Mar. 1985 (Vol. 74, No. 3)

QUARTERLY INFLATION INDEX

(p. 63-64) For 4th quarter 1984. For data description, see C8650-6 above.

UNIFORM PRODUCT LIABILITY LAWS URGED BY JOINT LIABILITY TASK FORCE

(p. 7) Article, with 1 chart showing number of product liability suits filed in Federal district courts, biennially 1974-84. Data are from Administrative Office of U.S. Courts.

C8650–6.605: Apr. 1985 (Vol. 74, No. 4)

INDUSTRY MARKETS GOODS THROUGH DUAL CHANNELS SAYS MCGRAW-HILL STUDY

(p. 15) Brief article, with 1 undated chart showing distribution of manufacturers by sales method (direct to industry, through intermediaries, or both), by selected industry group. Data are from a survey conducted by McGraw-Hill Laboratory of Advertising Performance.

VMA FORECASTS 3% INCREASE IN 1985 VALVE SHIPMENTS

(p. 19) Brief article, with 1 chart showing distribution of industrial valve shipments by end-use industry, 1985. Data are from a member survey conducted by Valve Manufacturers Assn.

SECOND-HALF DISTRIBUTOR SALES SEEN BETTER THAN ANTICIPATED, ANNUAL FEATURE

(p. 45) Annual article, with 1 chart forecasting percent change in sales of machine tools by type, 1985. Data are from National Tooling and Machining Assn.

Previous forecast, for 1984, is described in SRI 1984 Annual under C8650-6.508.

PRODUCT SHOWCASE REVIEW: FASTENERS

(p. 51-53) Article, with 1 table showing consumption value for industrial fasteners by type, 1985-87. Data are from Frost and Sullivan, Inc.

C8650–6.606: May 1985 (Vol. 74, No. 5)

DISTRIBUTOR PRODUCTIVITY REPORT

(p. 87-89) Article, with 4 tables showing the following for industrial distributors: percent change in sales, gross margin and payroll per employee, payroll expenses as percent of gross margin, and inventory turnover, 1979-84; and sales and inflation indexes, 1977-84. Data are from membership surveys of the National and Southern Industrial Distributors Assns (NIDA/SIDA).

C8650–6.607: June 1985 (Vol. 74, No. 6)

SUPER SALESMAN

(p. 29-32) Article, with 1 undated table showing compensation of industrial distributors' top salespeople, for 10 metro areas. Data are from an *Industrial Distributor* survey of a random sample of distributors.

HOW TO SELL SAFETY EQUIPMENT AND SUPPLIES

(p. 41-44) Article, with 1 table showing safety equipment sales distribution, by product category, 1984. Data are from a Safety Equipment Distributors Assn member survey.

C8650–6.608: July 1985 (Vol. 74, No. 7)

QUARTERLY INFLATION INDEX

(p. 67-68) For 1st quarter 1985. For data description, see C8650-6 above.

JUST-IN-TIME INVENTORY NOT LIVING UP TO ITS POTENTIAL, SAYS APICS ECONOMIST

(p. 13) Article, with 1 chart showing interest rates for long-term corporate bonds in U.S. and 6 foreign countries, Mar. 1985. Data are from American Production and Inventory Control Society.

SLOW PAYMENT AND BUSINESS FAILURES VEX CREDIT EXECS

(p. 14) Brief article, with 1 table showing credit executives' views on extent to which selected situations pose problems for their businesses. Data are from a National Assn of Credit Management member survey conducted Apr. 1985.

39th ANNUAL SURVEY OF DISTRIBUTOR OPERATIONS: '84 SALES SHOW SHARP GAINS; PROFITS UP

(p. 43-53) Annual report on industrial distributor sales, profits, and operations, 1984. Most data are based on an annual *Industrial Distribution* industry survey.

Includes 2 maps, 35 charts, and 1 table, showing distributor sales compared to Industrial Production Index, 1975-84; sales and price forecasts, by region, 1985; and financial and operating data, with selected detail for general line and specialist distributors, for 5 regions, and for combination distributors selling nonindustrial as well as industrial goods, primarily 1983-84.

Financial and operating data include profits, sales, expenses, inventory value and method of valuation, stock turns, receivables value, total and sales employees, branch locations, compensation, computer use, various operating ratios, and (for combination distributors) types of nonindustrial goods sold.

C8650–6.609: Aug. 1985 (Vol. 74, No. 8)

MAINTENANCE, REPAIRS BIGGEST AUTO PROBLEMS SAYS NEW STUDY

(p. 14) Brief article, with 1 table showing distribution of auto fleet operating problems most often cited by fleet managers, biennially 1977-85. Most recent data are from a survey of 1,422 managers conducted by Runzheimer International.

THE MARKET: PROFIT AND POTENTIAL

(p. M5) Article, with 1 chart showing aggregate expenditures on manufacturing maintenance/repair, 1973-85, 1990, and 1993. Data are from Technical Publishing Co.

C8650–6.610: Sept. 1985 (Vol. 74, No. 9)

NEW TRADE ASSOCIATION STUDIES SHED LIGHT ON INDUSTRIAL DISTRIBUTORS, ANNUAL FEATURE

(p. 7-12) Annual article on tool/fastener distributor sales and financial condition, based on Specialty Tools and Fasteners Distributors Assn surveys. Includes 1 table showing survey response on sales volume and change, inventory level change, days outstanding for accounts receivable, and selected financial and operating ratios, 1980-84.

For description of previous article, see C8650-6.601 above.

THE MARKET: AN OPEN END

(p. S14-S15) Article, with 1 chart and 1 table showing value of industrial fastener consumption, by fastener type and for aircraft/aerospace, 1985-87; and power tool sales to construction industry, by type, 1980 and 1990. Data are from Frost and Sullivan, Inc.

MECHANIC'S HAND TOOLS: PRODUCT SHOWCASE REVIEW

(p. 144-149) Article, with 1 chart and 1 table showing value of U.S. hand tool exports and imports; and manufacturer sales of mechanic's hand tools, by tool type; various years 1967-84. Data are from Commerce Dept and Business Trend Analysts.

C8650–6.611: Oct. 1985 (Vol. 74, No. 10)

1985 SPENDING ON HEALTH AND SAFETY TO INCREASE 25.4%

(p. 16) Article, with 1 table showing expenditures for employee safety/health, by durable goods manufacturing industry group, 1984 and planned 1985-86. Data are from a 1985 McGraw-Hill survey of 400 companies.

Full survey report is covered in SRI under C5800-18.

DON'T CUT THAT PRICE!

(p. 55-61) Article, with 1 chart showing industrial distributors' views concerning price-cutting policies. Data are from a recent *Industrial Distribution* survey.

POWER TRANSMISSION REVIEW

(p. 65-73) Article, with 1 table showing sales of antifriction bearings/components, in current and 1967 dollars, selected years 1958-93. Data are from Commerce Dept and Business Trend Analysts.

C8700
Telephony Publishing Corp.

C8700–1 TELEPHONY
Weekly.
ISSN 0040-2656.
LC 12-20223.
SRI/MF/excerpts, shipped quarterly

Weekly trade journal (only 3 issues in Dec.) of the telephone industry. Covers developments and trends in international telecommunications, including digital technology, communication satellites, management, government regulation, and operating costs.

Publication is primarily narrative and is intended to serve telephone engineering and management personnel. Data are from *Telephony* surveys, American Telephone and Telegraph Co. (AT&T), and other sources.

Issues contain feature articles, occasionally with statistics; and regular editorial depts. Annual statistical features include industry review and forecast (Jan.), and world telecommunications construction forecast (Feb.).

Features with substantial nontechnical statistical content are described, as they appear, under "Statistical Features." Each issue of the journal is reviewed, but an abstract is published in SRI monthly issues only when statistical features appear.

Availability: Telephony, Circulation Department, 55 E. Jackson Blvd., Chicago IL 60604, $33.00 per yr., single copy $3.00; SRI/MF/excerpts for all portions described under "Statistical Features;" shipped quarterly.

Issues reviewed during 1985: Nov. 5, 1984-Oct. 28, 1985 (P) (Vol. 207, Nos. 20-27; Vol. 208, Nos. 1-25; Vol. 209, Nos. 1-18) [Feb. 11 issue is published in 2 parts; Vol. 209, Nos. 9 and 18 incorrectly read No. 8 and No. 17, respectively].

STATISTICAL FEATURES:

C8700-1.601: Nov. 19, 1984 (Vol. 207, No. 22)

CHASING A RURAL CELLULAR RAINBOW

(p. 32-55) By LeRoy T. Carlson Jr. et al. Article on feasibility of cellular radio telephone service for rural areas. Data are from an Aug. 1984 study of 7 non-MSA markets, conducted by Telephone and Data Systems, Inc.

Includes 6 tables showing cellular demand; plant investment requirements; and estimated operating costs, income, and return on investment.

C8700-1.602: Nov. 26, 1984 (Vol. 207, No. 23)

POST-DIVESTITURE TOLL MARKETS: A LOOK AT THE SHAPE AND SIZE

(p. 72-78) By Kenneth R. Dunmore. Article on local access and transport area (LATA) organization and telephone services as affected by the AT&T divestiture. Data are from Bell System, Bell operating companies, and AT&T Communications. Includes 2 tables showing volume and value of intrastate and interstate toll messages carried in intra- and inter-LATA markets, Dec. 1983 or 1st quarter 1984.

C8700-1.603: Dec. 3, 1984 (Vol. 207, No. 24)

BEFORE BYPASSING, BEWARE!

(p. 88-172, passim) By Anthony Badalato. Article, with 1 chart showing revenue of local high-speed telecommunication services, 1980, 1985, and 1990. Data are from Gnostic Concepts Inc.

BREAKUP OF AT&T: ONE INDEPENDENT'S VIEW

(p. 96-171, passim) By Michael B. Esstman. Article on effect of AT&T divestiture on independent telephone companies. Data are from FCC and National Exchange Carrier Assn (NECA). Includes 3 tables on rates of return for independent companies, showing rates as forecast in May 1984 by FCC and NECA, and actual rates for June-Aug. 1984 as reported by NECA members.

LONG HAUL TRANSMISSION: A COST COMPARISON

(p. 130-142) Article on costs associated with long haul telecommunication systems, with technical data and 1 table showing costs per kilometer for installation of a fiber optics system, 1984. Data are from Future Systems, Inc.

C8700-1.604: Jan. 14, 1985 (Vol. 208, No. 2)

TELECOMMUNICATIONS CARRIERS TO SPEND $23.634 BILLION IN 1985, ANNUAL FEATURE

(p. 34-56) Annual state-of-the-industry feature, by Del Myers and Czatdana Inan, with

data on independent telecommunication company and regional Bell operating company (RBOC) construction spending, equipment, and operations, various years 1981-86. Also includes activities of interexchange carriers and cellular mobile radio service providers.

Data are from company reports and *Telephony* surveys of 150 business users of telecommunication services.

Includes 10 tables showing the following:

a. Construction expenditures of independent telephone companies, RBOCs, and interexchange carriers, with detail by company for RBOCs and top 20 independents, 1981-86; (RBOC data are adjusted to reflect AT&T divestiture).

b. Interexchange carrier revenues, installed switches, construction expenditures, total customers and business share, and employees, for 5 major companies, various years 1982-84.

c. RBOC local and toll revenues, with distribution by type of service; toll and wide-area telecommunications service messages; and operating and maintenance expenditures, by company; various years 1981-84.

d. Independent telephone company revenues, expenses, and plant investment, for top 20 companies; and RBOC and aggregate top 5 independent company equipment installations, removals, and expenditures, by equipment type, with expenditure rankings for top 5 independents; various years 1981-86.

e. Cellular mobile radio service in top 30 MSAs, as of 1983-85 startup, with companies providing services, and manufacturer and model of switching equipment used.

f. Business user evaluation of services, costs, and structure of major interexchange carriers.

C8700-1.605: Jan. 28, 1985 (Vol. 208, No. 4)

JAPANESE TELECOMMUNICATIONS TAKES ON A BRAND NEW LOOK

(p. 42-45, 81) By Etsuzo Masuda. Article on recent developments in Japanese telecommunications industry. Data are from responses of 569 companies to a survey conducted by *Nikkei Business* magazine. Includes 1 undated table showing percent of respondents interested in using and investing in various new telecommunications services.

C8700-1.606: Feb. 11, 1985 (Vol. 208, No. 6; Part 1)

STABILIZING THE VOLATILE TELEPHONE INSTRUMENT MARKET

(p. 126-132) By Richard A. Lindenmuth. Article, with 1 table showing wholesale sales volume and value, for cordless and corded telephones and for telephone answering devices, 1982-85. Data are from Electronic Industries Assn, Frost & Sullivan, and other private sources.

DOLLARS IN THE BYPASS DILEMMA

(p. 136-144) By Carl Thorsen. Article on long distance telephone rate structures, and impact of access fees and bypass technology. Includes 5 undated tables showing access fees, toll rates, and average revenue generated per call and per minute, for various rate periods and mileage bands.

C8700-1.607: Feb. 25, 1985 (Vol. 208, No. 8)

1985 WORLD TELECOM SPENDING: A STRUGGLE TO STAY EVEN, ANNUAL FEATURE

(p. 38-51) Annual article, by Czatdana Inan and Del Myers, forecasting world telecommunication developments, 1985. Data are from *Telephony* surveys and world telecommunication authorities. Includes 2 charts and 3 tables showing the following telecommunications industry data:

a. Capital spending, by world region and country, 1983-85, with comparison to 1984-85 forecasts assuming 6% budget growth; and access lines and percent in service as of Jan. 1984, by country; with some detail by company.

b. Funding distribution by source, and new/replacement lines, for Korea, Taiwan, and/or Thailand, various periods 1982-90.

Corrected data appear in the Apr. 22, 1985 issue (see C8700-1.611 below.)

C8700-1.608: Mar. 25, 1985 (Vol. 208, No. 12)

TELECOM SYSTEMS FOR SMALL BUSINESSES HAVE A BRIGHT FUTURE IN EUROPE

(p. 44-51) By Brian D. Simmons. Article on telecommunications growth in France, Italy, UK, and West Germany.

Includes 3 tables showing the following for each country: microcomputers installed, by application (commercial, home, and special), 1983; number of private automatic branch exchange (PABX) and key telecommunication systems for small businesses (no date); and population, and percent employed in agriculture, industry, and other sectors, 1981.

C8700-1.609: Apr. 1, 1985 (Vol. 208, No. 13)

INTEREXCHANGE CARRIERS: THE VIEW FROM WALL STREET

(p. 34-40) By Roger P. Favale. Article, with 1 undated table showing market share rankings for top 11 companies that rent wide-area telecommunications service and foreign exchange lines in bulk from AT&T and sell the services at discount prices on the retail market.

C8700-1.610: Apr. 8, 1985 (Vol. 208, No. 14)

INTERNATIONAL SURVEY COMPARES TELECOM COSTS AROUND THE WORLD, ANNUAL FEATURE

(p. 32-33) Annual article, with 1 table showing telephone and telex charges for local, long distance, and/or international service, for U.S., Canada, and 5 Western European countries, Jan. 1984-85. Data are from an annual survey conducted by National Utility Service, Inc., based on prices paid by the company's clients at 750,000 business locations worldwide.

C8700-1.611: Apr. 22, 1985 (Vol. 208, No. 16)

CORRECTION

(p. 13) Data correction for annual article forecasting world telecommunications developments, appearing in Feb. 25, 1985 issue.

For article description, see C8700-1.607 above.

BIG ENOUGH TO SERVE MANY BUT TOO SMALL TO SERVE ALL

(p. 36-40) By T. H. Chowdary. Article on India's telecommunications industry, with 1 table showing investment (in rupees) of the national telecommunications administration, and percent of investment raised through internal resources, 5-year periods 1951-85.

C8700–1.612: July 15, 1985 (Vol. 209, No. 3)

REGULATION AND COMPETITION, CANADIAN STYLE

(p. 56-63) By Marc Winfield and Percy von Lipinski. Article, with 1 undated table showing Canadian telephone service market shares, by company, and including regulatory agency with jurisdiction over each company.

C8700–1.613: Aug. 5, 1985 (Vol. 209, No. 6)

BIG BUSINESS EQUALS BIG BUCKS IN TELECOMMUNICATIONS

(p. 32-48) By Czatdana Inan. Article on developments in the corporate telecommunications market. Data are from a *Telephony* study of 140 *Fortune*-rated companies, Northern Business Information, and other sources.

Includes 4 charts and 2 tables showing rate of return of *Fortune*-rated companies, by industry division or major group (no date); private branch exchange (PBX) and key system shipments, and market shares by manufacturer, 1984; sales of top 9 independent interconnect companies, 1983-85; PBX shipments by manufacturer, 1984, and linkage with interconnect companies; and corporate structure for purchase of telecommunication equipment (no date).

C8700–1.614: Sept. 16, 1985 (Vol. 209, No. 12)

TIME DIVISION DIGITAL SWITCHES: A PROGRESS REPORT ON INSTALLATIONS IN NORTH AMERICA, ANNUAL FEATURE

(p. 68-71) Annual article, by Amos E. Joel, Jr., with 8 tables showing North American telecommunication time division digital switching equipment in service or on order, by system, with selected detail for largest offices/installations within each system, 1981-84.

C8700–2   TELEPHONY'S DIRECTORY AND BUYERS' GUIDE, 1984
Annual. 1984. 716 p.
ISSN 0196-139X.
LC 79-644663.
SRI/MF/excerpts

Annual directory, for 1984, of U.S. and Canadian telephone equipment distributors, assns and organizations, regulatory and other government agencies, and companies. Also includes listings of international telephone operations, and selected telephone industry statistics. Data are compiled from FCC, BLS, and telephone company reports.

Contents:

a. Contents listing; and directories of products and services, manufacturers and suppliers, and customer premise equipment (CPE) companies (firms that sell or lease terminal equipment for interconnection to telephone company lines), with text data on CPE company employment. (p. 5-435)

b. Independent telephone companies in U.S., with 1 table (p. 438) showing number of companies classified by number of access lines, by State and Canadian Province; and directory entries for individual companies arranged by city and State, most with selected operating data. (p. 437-610)

c. AT&T and Bell System company directories with 1 table (p. 640) showing operating revenues, expenses, and income, total assets and equipment and property shares, construction expenditures (including detail for cellular mobile), and employment, for 7 regional Bell companies, 1984, with selected trends from 1978. (p. 613-644)

d. Directories of special carriers, independent telephone investment and holding companies, U.S. and Canadian telephone assns, and U.S. regulatory and other government agencies; with selected operating data for some investment/holding companies. (p. 647-672)

e. Directories of international telephone operation organizations and record carriers; 1 table classifying foreign countries by number of telephones; and directory of telephone administrations in foreign countries, including number of telephones for each. (p. 675-690)

f. Canadian telephone information, including directory entries for individual telephone companies arranged by city and Province, most with selected operating data; and Bell system operating data. (p. 691-696)

g. Statistical article on world telephone capital investment and equipment, with 4 tables, described below. (p. 697-703)

h. Directory of domestic and international schools and universities offering telecommunications training programs. (p. 705-713)

Operating data variously include number of access lines by type; cable mileage and other plant statistics; and financial data, including plant investment, operating revenues, and construction budget. Revenues and budgets are shown for various years 1982-84, with some 1985 budgets; other data are undated.

This is the 89th annual edition.

Availability: Telephony Publishing Corp., Circulation Department, 55 E. Jackson Blvd., Chicago IL 60604, manufacturers $18.00, others $50.00; SRI/MF/excerpts for statistical portions.

STATISTICAL ARTICLE:

C8700–2.1: International Data

WORLD TELECOM 1984 SPENDING TO LEVEL OUT AT $78.8 BILLION

(p. 697-703) Annual article, by Del Myers and Czatdana Inan, on world telecommunication capital investment. Data are based primarily on a *Telephony* annual survey. Includes 4 tables showing the following:

a. U.S. and foreign telecommunication investment, 1979-84; and Western European business communications equipment, including private branch exchange systems, modems, and telex (no date), and startup dates for selected data transmission services, by country and selected company.

b. World telephone access lines, local switches by type, and plant investment by category, by country arranged by world area, with some detail by company or region,

1982; and population and telephones in 26 developing African countries, 1983, with planned telephones and investment to 2000.

C8850
Textile Economics Bureau

C8850–1   TEXTILE ORGANON
Monthly. Approx. 15 p. per issue; cumulative pagination throughout year.
ISSN 0040-5132.
LC 32-5553.
SRI/MF/complete, shipped quarterly

Monthly report providing current data on man-made fibers and manufactures, and on raw and manufactured cotton and wool, with some data on silk. Covers U.S. domestic production and shipments, consumption, stocks, and imports and exports. Also includes data on international textile industry.

Data are drawn primarily from Dept of Agriculture and Census Bureau sources, and are shown in detail by fiber and manufactured fabric.

Report includes a monthly review of fiber shipment and/or production levels during the previous month, usually with 1-2 summary tables; notes on developments of interest to the industry; 5 monthly and 3 quarterly tables, listed below; and special, annual, or other recurring features, usually containing statistics.

Annual statistical features include U.S. textile fiber end-use survey; world natural fiber review and man-made fiber trade supplement; overview of the textile industry; U.S. fiber consumption, and import-export review; world man-made fiber survey, with directory of producers; and hosiery production.

Issues also include a semiannual report on U.S. man-made fiber industry production and capacity, and a quarterly update of apparel imports. An annual index is published in the Dec. issue.

All tables are numbered consecutively within each issue. Therefore, the numbers assigned below to monthly and quarterly tables do not correspond to numbers appearing in the reports.

Monthly tables appear in all issues. All additional features with substantial statistical content are described, as they appear, under "Statistical Features;" page locations and latest periods of coverage for quarterly tables are also noted. Nonstatistical features are not described.

Prior to the Dec. 1984 issue, report also included 2 other quarterly tables on U.S. textile trade.

Availability: Textile Economics Bureau, Textile Organon, 101 Eisenhower Pkwy., Roseland NJ 07068, $140.00 per yr., schools and nonprofit institutions $50.00 per yr., single copy $25.00; June and Sept. issues $40.00; SRI/MF/complete, shipped quarterly.

Issues reviewed during 1985: Oct. 1984-Oct. 1985 (P) (Vol. 55, Nos. 9-11; Vol. 56, Nos. 1-10) [June 1985 issue omits volume and issue numbers; July/Aug. 1985 is a combined issue].

MONTHLY TABLES:

[Unless otherwise noted, data are usually shown monthly for year to date, current to 1-2 months prior to cover date, and cumulatively for current and previous year to date. Tables 1-2 begin in the Feb. 1985 issue. Sequence of tables varies from issue to issue.]

[1] Man-made fiber monthly trade balance detail [for cellulosic and noncellulosic yarn/ monofil/strips, staple+tow, and waste; for 14 consecutive months ending 2 months prior to cover date].

[2] U.S. exports of man-made fibers [by cellulosic and noncellulosic fiber type, and for textile glass fiber].

[3] U.S. man-made fiber imports for consumption [by cellulosic and noncellulosic fiber type, and for other fiber tops, yarn, and thread].

[4] Selected U.S. man-made fiber imports for consumption by country of origin [for cellulosic and noncellulosic yarn/monofil/strips and staple+tow].

[5] Selected U.S. monthly textile fiber data [man-made fiber shipments and end-of-month stocks for yarn+monofilaments and staple+-tow+fiberfill, by type of fiber; and wool and cotton consumption].

QUARTERLY TABLES:

[Tables show data quarterly, for 5-12 quarters ending 1-2 quarters preceding publication.]

[1] Quarterly man-made fiber data [shows production, domestic and export shipments, ending stock, and imports for 4 types of yarns+monofilaments and 5 types of staple+-tow, and for textile glass fiber].

[2-3] Filament yarn and staple and tow domestic shipments [by end product type (hosiery and other knits, carpets, tires, cordage, and others); and by product group (apparel, home furnishings, and industrial); also includes annual data for 4 previous years].

STATISTICAL FEATURES:

C8850-1.601: Oct. 1984 (Vol. 55, No. 9)

QUARTERLY TABLES

[1] U.S. exports of man-made fibers [2nd quarter 1984]. (p. 187)

[2] U.S. imports, exports, and balance of man-made fiber and manufactures, cotton manufactures, and wool manufactures [2nd quarter 1984]. (p. 186)

U.S. MAN-MADE FIBER TEXTILE TRADE BALANCE: AN OVERVIEW, ANNUAL FEATURE

(p. 180-183) Annual article, with 5 tables showing imports and exports of aggregate man-made fibers and fiber manufactures including and excluding garments; annually 1970-83 and semiannually 1983-1st half 1984.

For description of previous article, see SRI 1984 Annual under C8850-1.502.

SELECTED U.S. EXPORTS BY COUNTRY OF DESTINATION, ANNUAL FEATURE

(p. 184-185) Annual table showing exports of cellulosic yarn/monofil/strips; noncellulosic textile yarn and industrial yarn/monofil/ strips; and cellulosic and noncellulosic staple+tow; all by country of destination, 1982-83 and 1st half 1984.

For description of previous table, see SRI 1984 Annual under C8850-1.503.

U.S. EXPORTS AND IMPORTS OF MAN-MADE FIBERS, ANNUAL FEATURE

(p. 188-189) Two annual tables showing export and import volume and value for man-made fibers by type, 1980-1st half 1984.

For description of previous tables, see SRI 1984 Annual under C8850-1.502.

C8850-1.602: Nov. 1984 (Vol. 55, No. 10)

QUARTERLY TABLES

[1] U.S. exports of man-made fibers [3rd quarter 1984]. (p. 203)

[3] Quarterly man-made fiber data [3rd quarter 1984]. (p. 204-205)

1984 DIRECTORY OF U.S. MAN-MADE FIBER PRODUCERS, ANNUAL FEATURE

(p. 196-202) Annual directory of U.S. man-made fiber producers, updating listings appearing in the Nov. 1983 and June 1984 issues. Also includes 1 undated table showing number of producing plants, by fiber type, State, and region.

C8850-1.603: Dec. 1984 (Vol. 55, No. 11)

QUARTERLY TABLES

[4-5] Filament yarn and staple+tow domestic shipments [3rd quarter 1984]. (p. 220-221)

WORLD NATURAL FIBER SURVEY, ANNUAL FEATURE

(p. 212-216) Annual report on world raw cotton and wool industry, with 7 tables as follows:

[1] World [U.S. and foreign] production, consumption, exports, and carryover of raw cotton [5-year averages 1950-79, and annually 1970-84]. (p. 212)

[2] World raw cotton production [by world region and for 10 countries, same periods as table [1]]. (p. 213)

[3] Supply and distribution of domestic and foreign raw cotton in the U.S. for the seasons beginning Aug. 1 [1973-84]. (p. 214)

[4] U.S. calendar year imports and exports of raw cotton and cotton products [1968-83]. (p. 214)

[5] U.S. cotton acreage, [production], and yield [1964-84]. (p. 215)

[6] World raw wool production by the principal producing countries [and Eastern Europe/ PRC and all others, 5-year averages 1935-79 and annually 1965-84]. (p. 215)

[7] Disappearance of wool in the U.S. [includes mill consumption, imports, and exports, by type of product, 1970-83]. (p. 216)

NOV. 1984 CAPACITY SURVEY ANALYSIS, SEMIANNUAL FEATURE

(p. 217-219) Report on semiannual survey of U.S. man-made fiber production and capacity, Nov. 1984, with trends from 1970 and projections to 1986. Includes 2 tables showing the following:

a. Actual production of cellulosic and noncellulosic yarn+monofilaments and staple+-tow, and textile glass fibers, 1970-83.

b. Actual and projected capacity for production of same fibers, with additional detail for noncellulosic fibers, Nov. 1970-86 and May 1985-86.

C8850-1.604: Jan. 1985 (Vol. 56, No. 1)

CAPACITY UTILIZATION REVIEW, ANNUAL FEATURE

(p. 4-9) Annual report on man-made fiber industry, with 6 tables showing production, capacity, and capacity utilization rate, for cellulosic and noncellulosic yarn+monofilaments and staple+tow, and for textile glass fibers, 1970-84.

IMPORT UPDATE, QUARTERLY FEATURE

(p. 10-15) Quarterly report on apparel imports, with summary charts and text data, and 2 tables showing the following: imports of apparel yarn and fabric, imports and exports of garments, and supply available for domestic consumption, for cotton, wool, and man-made fibers; cotton and wool fabric from U.S. mills; and man-made fiber domestic shipments for apparel, and exports of semimanufactured products; 1980-83 and quarterly 1983-3rd quarter 1984.

ANNUAL SHIPMENT SUMMARY

(p. 16-17) Brief article, with 1 table showing man-made fiber shipments for yarn+monofilaments and staple+tow+fiberfill, by type of fiber, 1981-84.

C8850-1.605: Feb. 1985 (Vol. 56, No. 2)

QUARTERLY TABLE

[3] Quarterly man-made fiber data [4th quarter 1984]. (p. 34-35)

TRADE BAROMETER

(p. 24-29, passim) Article, with 4 tables showing raw fiber equivalent of imports, exports, and balance, for cotton, man-made fiber, and wool manufactures, by type of product; monthly 1984, with comparisons to 1983.

C8850-1.606: Mar. 1985 (Vol. 56, No. 3)

QUARTERLY TABLES

[4-5] Filament yarn and staple+tow domestic shipments [4th quarter 1984]. (p. 58-59)

1984: A YEAR IN PERSPECTIVE, ANNUAL FEATURE

(p. 40-46) Annual article on textile industry fiber production, trade, and consumption, 1984 and trends. Includes 11 tables, as follows:

Tables:

[Tables show data for 1960s-84 or 1970s-84. Data on man-made fiber usually include detail by fiber type.]

[1] Mill consumption by fiber. (p. 40)

[2] U.S. mill consumption of [total] man-made fiber, cotton, and wool. (p. 40)

[3-4] Man-made fiber production; and noncellulosic fiber production detail. (p. 42)

[5] Man-made fiber distribution [domestic and export shipments, imports, and domestic consumption]. (p. 43)

[6] U.S. mill consumption of fiber and domestic consumption of fiber/products [man-made, cotton, wool, and silk, with detail for imports and exports]. (p. 44)

[7] Raw fiber equivalent of imports and exports of man-made fiber, cotton and wool manufactures [by type of product]. (p. 45)

[8] Filament yarn domestic shipments by denier [acetate, polyester and nylon textile, and nylon carpet]. (p. 46)

[9] Producers' waste shipments [of rayon and noncellulosic fiber]. (p. 46)

[10-11] Raw cotton consumption and raw silk deliveries [monthly]. (p. 46)

INTERNATIONAL TRADE SUPPLEMENT, ANNUAL FEATURE

(p. 47-51) Annual report on world man-made fiber trade, with 5 tables as follows:

[1] 1984 man-made fiber production, import, export, and net available supply [of cellulosic

and noncellulosic yarn and staple+tow] by country (except olefin and textile glass). (p. 48)

[2-5] Trade detail: cellulosic fiber [yarn by type and total staple]; tire cord [rayon and noncellulosic] and spun yarn [cellulosic and noncellulosic]; and noncellulosic yarn and staple [by type]; [all showing imports and exports by country, 1982-83]. (p. 49-51)

Data corrections appear in the June 1985 issue (see C8850-1.609, below).

Previous report is described in SRI 1984 Annual under C8850-1.504.

SELECTED U.S. MONTHLY TEXTILE FIBER DATA, ANNUAL FEATURE

(p. 57) Annual table presenting revised data for monthly table [3] on textile fiber shipments and stocks, 1983 and monthly 1984.

C8850–1.607: Apr. 1985 (Vol. 56, No. 4)

1984 IMPORT/EXPORT REVIEW, ANNUAL FEATURE

(p. 64-72) Annual report on U.S. exports and imports of man-made fibers and products, 1984 and trends. Includes 3 charts with selected summary trends from 1977, and 7 tables as follows:

[1] U.S. imports of selected man-made fiber manufactures [amount and value for various types of knit fabric in the piece, and broad woven fabrics, 1980-84. (p. 64)

[2] U.S. general imports of man-made fiber apparel [by country of origin, 1978-84]. (p. 66)

[3] Selected U.S. man-made fiber imports by country of origin [noncellulosic staple+tow and yarn-singles, cellulosic and noncellulosic waste and spun yarns, and textile glass, 1983-84]. (p. 67)

[4] Selected U.S. man-made fiber and manufactures imports for consumption, by country of origin [broad woven fabrics, knit fabric in the piece, and fibers, 1980-84]. (p. 68)

[5] U.S. exports of man-made fibers [amount and value for various types of cellulosic and noncellulosic fibers, and textile glass fiber, 1980-84]. (p. 69)

[6] Selected U.S. exports by country of destination [amount and value for cellulosic yarn/monofil/strips, noncellulosic textile yarn, noncellulosic industrial yarn/monofil/strips, and cellulosic and noncellulosic staple+tow, 1983-84]. (p. 70-71)

[7] U.S. imports of man-made fibers [amount and value for various types of cellulosic and noncellulosic fibers, and other man-made fiber tops, yarn, and thread, 1980-84]. (p. 72)

IMPORT UPDATE, QUARTERLY FEATURE

(p. 73-78) Quarterly report on apparel imports, with summary charts and text data, and 2 tables showing the following: imports of apparel yarn and fabric, imports and exports of garments, and supply available for domestic consumption, for cotton, wool, and man-made fibers; cotton and wool fabric from U.S. mills; and man-made fiber domestic shipments for apparel, and exports of semimanufactured products; 1980-84 and quarterly 1983-84.

C8850–1.608: May 1985 (Vol. 56, No. 5)

QUARTERLY TABLE

[3] Quarterly man-made fiber data [1st quarter 1985]. (p. 101-102).

1984 PER CAPITA CONSUMPTION REVIEW, ANNUAL FEATURE

(p. 87-91) Annual article, with 8 tables as follows:

Tables:

[Unless otherwise noted, tables show data for 1970-84.]

[1] U.S. population, GNP (goods produced), and per capita GNP. (p. 89)

[2-3] U.S. average annual [man-made, cotton, and wool] fiber available for consumption [per capita], including textile/nontextile glass fiber and excluding nontextile glass fiber [and also showing population, various periods 1920-84]. (p. 89)

[4] Domestic consumption of [man-made, cotton, and wool] fiber/products. (p. 89)

[5] Mill consumption by [type of man-made] fiber [and for cotton and wool]. (p. 90)

[6] Percent analysis of population, per capita GNP (goods produced), and per capita consumption of man-made fiber, cotton and wool. (p. 90)

[7-8] Raw fiber equivalent of imports of man-made fiber, cotton, and wool manufactures [1979-84]; and per capita consumption of imports of man-made fiber, cotton, and wool manufactures as compared to per capita consumption of [all] man-made fiber, cotton, and wool [1978-84]. (p. 91)

MAY 1985 CAPACITY SURVEY ANALYSIS, SEMIANNUAL FEATURE

(p. 92-95) Report on semiannual survey of U.S. man-made fiber production and capacity, May 1985, with trends from 1970 and projections to 1987. Includes 2 tables showing the following:

a. Actual production of cellulosic and noncellulosic yarn+monofilaments and staple+tow, and textile glass fibers, 1970-84.

b. Actual and projected capacity for production of same fibers, with additional detail for noncellulosic fibers, Nov. 1970-86 and May 1984-87.

C8850–1.609: June 1985 (Vol. 56, No. 6)

[Issue omits volume and issue numbers.]

QUARTERLY TABLES

[4-5] Filament yarn and staple+tow domestic shipments [1st quarter 1985]. (p. 141-142)

WORLD MAN-MADE FIBER SURVEY, ANNUAL FEATURE

(p. 104-140) Annual report on world man-made fiber production, capacity, and plants, by country and world region, 1970s-86. Data are in metric tons, and will be repeated in millions of pounds in the July/Aug. 1985 issue.

Includes 10 tables, listed below (p. 104-117, 140); directory of world man-made fiber producers by country, with plant sites and type of fiber produced (p. 118-137); and list of producer affiliations, with headquarters country, owning company, company owned, and percent of capital ownership (p. 138-139).

Tables:

[Tables generally show production data for 1978-84, and capacity data for 1985-86. Tables [2-10] show data by country or world region.]

1. World production of certain textile fibers [total cellulosic fibers, noncellulosic fibers except olefin, and cotton, wool, and silk]. (p. 104)

2A-3B. World noncellulosic fiber (except olefin) and cellulosic fiber production and producing capacity. (p. 107-114)

4. Rayon vs. acetate filament yarn production and producing capacity. (p. 115)

5. World noncellulosic fiber production and producing capacity, [for yarn+monofilaments and staple+tow+fiberfill] by fiber (except olefin) [acrylic+modacrylic, nylon+aramid, polyester, and other fibers]. (p. 116)

6. World glass fiber production and producing capacity. (p. 117)

7. Estimated world cigarette tow production. (p. 117)

8. World acetate staple production and capacity. (p. 117)

9. World olefin fiber production. (p. 117)

10. Number of man-made fiber producing plants (except olefin) [cellulosic, noncellulosic, and textile glass; no date]. (p. 140)

Corrections appear in the Sept. and Oct. 1985 issues (see C8850-1.611 and C8850-1.612, below).

CORRECTION

(p. 139) Corrected data for International Trade Supplement, appearing in Mar. 1985 issue. For description, see C8850-1.606 above.

C8850–1.610: July/Aug. 1985 (Vol. 56, No. 7/8)

QUARTERLY TABLE

[3] Quarterly man-made fiber data [2nd quarter 1985]. (p. 173-174)

WORLD MAN-MADE FIBER SURVEY, ANNUAL FEATURE

(p. 151-166) Annual report repeating in millions of pounds most of the data presented in metric tons in the 1984 world man-made fiber survey article appearing in the June 1985 issue.

For description of June 1985 article, see C8850-1.609 above.

U.S. PRODUCTION OF HOSIERY, 1971-84, ANNUAL FEATURE

(p. 172) Annual table showing production of women's, men's, and children's hosiery, by type, 1971-84. Data are from National Assn of Hosiery Manufacturers.

C8850–1.611: Sept. 1985 (Vol. 56, No. 9)

QUARTERLY TABLES

[4-5] Filament yarn and staple+tow domestic shipments [2nd quarter 1985]. (p. 201-202)

TEXTILE FIBER END USE SURVEY, ANNUAL FEATURE

(p. 176, 179-195) Annual survey report on U.S. textile fiber consumption by end use, with comparisons to European Economic Community, generally 1978-84. Includes 10 tables as follows:

Tables:

[Unless otherwise noted, tables show data for 1978-84. All tables except 1 and 5 show data for man-made fibers (usually by type), cotton, and wool.]

1. End use summary changes [for total and man-made fiber]. (p. 176)

2. U.S. end use summary. (p. 180)

3. Mill consumption+semimanufactured imports. (p. 181)

4. End use vs. available supply. (p. 181)

5. Summary of man-made fiber and semimanufactured imports [by type]. (p. 182)

6-8. Apparel, home furnishings, and industrial/other consumer-type products [consumption of fibers by type of product]. (p. 183-188)

9. Exports of domestic products [by type of product]. (p. 189)

10. Textile mill consumption main end uses [aggregated] for 7 European Economic Community countries [1977-82]. (p. 193)

CORRECTION

(p. 204-205) Corrected data for World Man-Made Fiber Survey, appearing in June 1985 issue. For description, see C8850-1.609 above.

C8850–1.612: Oct. 1985 (Vol. 56, No. 10)

U.S. MAN-MADE FIBER TEXTILE TRADE BALANCE: AN OVERVIEW, ANNUAL FEATURE

(p. 211-214) Annual article, with 5 tables showing imports and exports of aggregate man-made fibers and fiber manufactures including and excluding garments; and garment trade balance; 1971-84 or 1971-1st half 1985.

For description of previous article, see C8850-1.601 above.

SELECTED U.S. EXPORTS BY COUNTRY OF DESTINATION, ANNUAL FEATURE

(p. 217-218) Annual table showing exports of cellulosic yarn/monofil/strips; noncellulosic textile yarn and industrial yarn/monofil/strips; and cellulosic and noncellulosic staple+tow; all by country of destination, 1983-84 and 1st half 1985.

For description of previous table, see C8850-1.601 above.

U.S. EXPORTS AND IMPORTS OF MAN-MADE FIBERS, ANNUAL FEATURE

(p. 219-220) Two annual tables showing export and import volume and value for man-made fibers by type, 1981-1st half 1985.

For description of previous tables, see C8850-1.601 above.

CORRECTION

(p. 218) Correction for World Man-Made Fiber Survey, appearing in June 1985 issue. For description see C8850-1.609 above.

C8900
Time, Inc.

C8900–1   **FORTUNE**
Biweekly.
ISSN 0015-8259.
LC 31-7716.
SRI/MF/excerpts, shipped quarterly

Biweekly magazine (with additional Fall issue in Oct.) on business and industry, presenting the annual Fortune 500 directory of the 500 largest industrial corporations, other major annual directories, and feature articles on corporate developments and outlook, domestic and foreign economic conditions, investment prospects, Government regulation, taxes, and financial markets.

General format:

a. Feature articles, often with a few summary charts or "Investors Snapshot" profiles of selected companies, and sometimes with more extensive statistics.

b. Regular editorial depts, including "Fortune Forecast" on outlook for selected economic indicators, and "Personal Investing," each usually including 1-3 supporting charts or tables.

c. Annual statistical directory features presenting financial and employment data for the 500 largest industrial companies; 500 largest nonindustrial companies; 50 leading exporters; 50 largest industrial companies worldwide; and 500 largest industrial and 100 largest commercial banking companies outside the U.S.

Features with substantial statistical content are described, as they appear, under "Statistical Features." Each issue of the magazine is reviewed, but an abstract is published in SRI monthly issues only when statistical features appear.

Availability: Fortune, Circulation Department, Time-Life Bldg., 541 N. Fairbanks Ct., Chicago IL 60611-3333, $42.00 per yr., single copy $3.50; SRI/MF/excerpts for all portions described under "Statistical Features;" shipped quarterly.

Issues reviewed during 1985: Nov. 12, 1984-Oct. 28, 1985 and Fall 1985 (P) (Vol. 110, Nos. 10-13; Vol. 111, Nos. 1-13; Vol. 112, Nos. 1-10).

STATISTICAL FEATURES:

C8900–1.601: Nov. 12, 1984 (Vol. 110, No. 10)

FRONTIER INVESTING

(p. 143-144) Article, with 1 table showing stock market performance data for 10 developing countries, 1976-83 period. Includes average annual rate of return, and return in best and worst year. Data are from International Finance Corp.

C8900–1.602: Nov. 26, 1984 (Vol. 110, No. 11)

TAX STUDY BUSINESS DOESN'T LIKE

(p. 33) Article, with 1 table showing the following for 15 companies paying no Federal income tax during 1981-83 period: profits reported to stockholders, amount of tax refunds/credits, and effective tax rate, for the 3-year period. Data are from Citizens for Tax Justice.

HOW COMPANIES ARE COPING WITH THE STRONG DOLLAR

(p. 116-124) By Carol J. Loomis. Article, with 1 table showing currency translation loss (due to effect of strong U.S. dollar on earnings from foreign operations and value of foreign assets), and common stockholders' equity adjusted for loss, for 5 companies with greatest loss, 1983.

C8900–1.603: Dec. 10, 1984 (Vol. 110, No. 12)

INVESTMENT BETS FOR 1985

(p. 191-194) By John J. Curran. Article, with 1 table showing estimates of growth in real GNP and corporate profits, and inflation and long-term interest rates; and types of investments recommended; for 5 major brokerage firms, 1985.

C8900–1.604: Jan. 7, 1985 (Vol. 111, No. 1)

AMERICA'S MOST ADMIRED CORPORATIONS, ANNUAL FEATURE

(p. 18-30) Annual article, by Patricia Sellers, on business community's ratings of 250 companies in 25 industries. Data are from responses of approximately 4,000 corporate executives/outside directors/financial analysts to a 1984 *Fortune* survey.

Includes 3 tables showing ratings for 3-10 most and least admired companies overall and in 8 performance categories; and ratings for each company within 25 industry groups.

Also includes brief insert article with 1 table showing 10 companies with greatest gain and loss from 1983 ratings.

COMING GLUT OF PHONE LINES

(p. 96-100) By William B. Johnston. Article, with 1 table showing the following for 12 long distance telephone companies: ownership; region served; and expenditures, circuit and route miles, and scheduled completion date for planned fiber-optic systems. Data are based on Hudson Institute estimates.

C8900–1.605: Jan. 21, 1985 (Vol. 111, No. 2)

DEALS OF THE YEAR, ANNUAL FEATURE

(p. 126-130) Annual list, with narrative analysis, by H. John Steinbreder, of the 50 largest U.S. corporate financial transactions, 1984, ranked by value of transaction, and showing value (actual and as percent of book value), date, and type of transaction; companies involved and type of industry; and financial intermediary and fee charged.

List covers mergers, acquisitions, and debt and equity offerings.

C8900–1.606: Feb. 4, 1985 (Vol. 111, No. 3)

GREAT PLASTIC CARD FIGHT BEGINS

(p. 18-23) By Monci Jo Williams. Article, with 1 table showing the following for 4 major credit cards, and for credit cards issued by Citicorp: number issued, 1984 billings, and features. Data sources include the *Nilson Report.*

C8900–1.607: Mar. 18, 1985 (Vol. 111, No. 6)

AMERICA'S NEW ABSTINENCE

(p. 20-23) By Stratford P. Sherman. Article, with 5 charts showing per capita consumption of alcoholic beverages, bottled water, diet soda, caffeinated and decaffeinated coffee, cigarettes, sugar, chicken, and pork, 1984, with trends from 1980. Data are from *Maxwell Report* and other sources.

C8900-1.608: Apr. 1, 1985 (Vol. 111, No. 7)

MONEY LAUNDERING: MORE SHOCKS AHEAD

(p. 34-39) By Anne B. Fisher. Article, with 1 chart showing estimated amount of laundered money originating in illegal drug transactions, 1974 and 1984.

C8900-1.609: Apr. 29, 1985 (Vol. 111, No. 9)

BEATING THE MARKET BY BUYING BACK STOCK

(p. 42-48) By Carol J. Loomis. Article, with 1 chart and 1 table showing average annual rate of return to stockholders, aggregated for companies repurchasing large quantities of their own stock and for Standard and Poor's 500 stock index companies, 1974-83 period; and percent decline in shares outstanding of 24 companies making major stock repurchases, 1984. Data are from *Fortune*.

FORTUNE DIRECTORY OF THE LARGEST U.S. INDUSTRIAL CORPORATIONS, ANNUAL FEATURE

(p. 252-316) Annual directory presenting sales, income, other financial data, and employment, for the 500 largest U.S. industrial corporations ranked by total sales in 1984.

Contents:

a. Narrative summary, with 1 table showing selected aggregate performance measures for the Fortune 500, 1983-84. (p. 252-265)

b. Ranked listing of the Fortune 500, showing sales, assets, net income, stockholders' equity, employees, and net income as percent of sales and equity, 1984; earnings per share, 1974 and 1983-84; and return to investors, 1984 and annual average 1974-84 period; rankings for most items; and major industry group. (p. 266-285)

c. Eleven analytical tables showing the best and/or worst performing companies, and industry medians, for selected financial performance and productivity measures; companies with operating losses ranked by amount; and arrivals to and departures from the Fortune 500 list. (p. 286-292)

d. Summary rankings among Fortune 500 for 14 measures, by company arranged by industry group. (p. 294-312)

e. Alphabetical index to corporations, and notes. (p. 314-316)

This is the 31st annual directory.

C8900-1.610: May 13, 1985 (Vol. 111, No. 10)

EYEING THE LETTERS

(p. 88) Article reporting on standby letters of credit through which banks guarantee payment of a customer's debt to a third party. Includes 1 table showing value of standby letters of credit outstanding (actual and as percent of stockholders' equity), for 5 major banks, 1984, with comparisons to 1983.

C8900-1.611: May 27, 1985 (Vol. 111, No 11)

HAVE TAKEOVERS GONE TOO FAR?

(p. 20-24) By Aloysius Ehrbar. Article, with 1 chart showing total amount paid in corporate takeovers of publicly held companies, 1981-84.

C8900-1.612: June 10, 1985 (Vol. 111, No. 12)

ARE SERVICE JOBS GOOD JOBS?

(p. 38-43) By Richard I. Kirkland, Jr. Article, with 1 chart showing total number of new jobs available, with detail for 7 occupations, 1982-95 period. Data are from BLS.

FORTUNE SERVICE 500: DIRECTORY OF THE LARGEST U.S. NON-INDUSTRIAL CORPORATIONS, ANNUAL FEATURE

(p. 175-204) Annual directory presenting financial and employment data for the 100 largest companies in diversified service, commercial banking, and diversified financial services; and for the 50 largest companies in life insurance, retailing, transportation, and utilities; 1984.

Contents:

a. Ranked listings of the 100 or 50 largest companies in each industry, generally showing assets, net income, stockholders' equity, employment, earnings per share, return to investors, and, as applicable, sales, deposits, loans, revenues, and insurance in force, 1984, with selected comparisons to 1974 and/or 1983, and rankings for most items. (p. 175-195)

b. 11 analytical tables showing the best and/or worst performing companies, and industry medians, for selected financial performance measures; companies with operating losses ranked by amount; and arrivals to and departures from the Fortune Service 500 list. (p. 196-200)

c. Notes, and alphabetical index to corporations. (p. 200-204)

Directory is accompanied by a narrative article (p. 166-172) reviewing 1984 financial performance of the Fortune Service 500.

C8900-1.613: July 22, 1985 (Vol. 112, No. 2)

IS BUSINESS TAKING ON TOO MUCH DEBT?

(p. 82-85) By Kenneth Labich. Article, with 3 tables on corporate debt burden, 1984 and trends. Tables show liabilities as percent of assets, for 15 industry sectors (based on Fortune 500), 1974 and 1984, and for 5 most and 5 least debt-burdened Fortune 100 companies, 1984.

C8900-1.614: Aug. 5, 1985 (Vol. 112, No. 3)

50 LEADING EXPORTERS, ANNUAL FEATURE

(p. 60-61) Annual listing, with accompanying article, ranking 50 leading companies by export sales, 1984, with comparison to 1983 and to total sales, and summary of major products.

C8900-1.615: Aug. 19, 1985 (Vol. 112, No. 4)

FORTUNE INTERNATIONAL 500, ANNUAL FEATURE

Annual compilation of articles on world economic trends, with directories of 500 largest industrial corporations and 100 largest commercial banks outside the U.S., and 50 largest industrial corporations worldwide. Statistical articles and directories are described below.

WORLD SHIFTS TO A SLOWER TEMPO, ANNUAL FEATURE

(p. 170-175) Annual article analyzing world economic trends. Includes numerous charts illustrating selected trends, including GNP growth aggregated for OECD member countries, 1972-81 period and 1982-86; and U.S. current account balance, 1984-86. Data are from OECD.

WORLD'S LARGEST INDUSTRIAL CORPORATIONS, ANNUAL FEATURE

(p. 178-179) Annual listing, with accompanying article, ranking 50 largest industrial companies worldwide, by sales, 1984, with sales rank for 1983, net income for 1984, industry, and headquarters.

INTERNATIONAL 500: FORTUNE DIRECTORY OF THE LARGEST INDUSTRIAL CORPORATIONS OUTSIDE THE U.S., ANNUAL FEATURE

(p. 182-211) Annual directory, presenting financial and employment data for the 500 largest industrial corporations outside the U.S., 1984. Includes narrative analysis and the following:

a. Ranked listing of companies, showing for each: sales rank, 1983-84; country; industry code; total return to investors in local currency and in U.S. dollars, year ended May 31, 1985, and 5-year average; and sales, assets, net income, stockholders' equity, and employees, 1984.

b. 9 analytical tables showing 10 best and worst performing companies in terms of sales and profit changes and returns to investors, with industry medians and country medians (investor returns only); companies that lost money; companies new/returned to and departed from the 500 list; and distribution of listed companies by country.

c. Alphabetical index.

LARGEST COMMERCIAL BANKS OUTSIDE THE U.S., ANNUAL FEATURE

(p. 214-217) Annual listing, with accompanying article, ranking the 100 largest commercial banks outside the U.S., by assets, 1984. Also shows assets and rank, 1983; percent change in assets (in U.S. dollars and local currency); deposits and rank, loans, net income, stockholders' equity, offices, and employees, 1984; and country.

C8900-1.616: Sept. 16, 1985 (Vol. 112, No. 6)

GOOD NEWS, BAD NEWS, AND AN 'INVISIBLE CEILING'

(p. 29) Article, with 1 table showing percent of business officials/managers and professionals who are white women, black women, and black men, 1976, 1980, and 1984. Data are from Equal Employment Opportunity Commission.

C8900–1.617: Oct. 14, 1985 (Vol. 112, No. 8)

INSURANCE THAT'S NOT SO SURE

(p. 153-156) By Gary Hector. Article, with 1 chart showing value of privately insured mortgages outstanding, 1980 and 1985. Data are from Mortgage Insurance Companies of America.

STOCK MARKET UPHEAVAL IN EUROPE

(p. 158-164) By Richard I. Kirkland, Jr. Article, with 1 table showing value of shares traded on stock exchanges of 6 European countries, rest of Europe, Japan, and U.S., early 1984. Data are from Capital International Perspective, SA.

C8900–1.618: Fall 1985 (Vol. 112, No. 10)
[The following features are part of the 1986 Investor's Guide special issue. Special issue price is $3.95.]

INVESTMENT STRATEGY AND VEHICLES

(p. 25-64) Compilation of articles, with 1 chart and 4 tables showing rates of return or yields for selected categories of stocks, bonds, stock and bond mutual funds, and short-term investments, various periods 1979-85. Data are from financial analysts.

BANKS SHINE AT MANAGING MONEY

(p. 161) Article, with 1 chart showing annual rate of return on common stock funds managed by bank trust depts, insurance companies, mutual funds, and investment advisors, 1982-84 period. Data are from CDA Investment Technologies.

C8910
Times Journal Co.

C8910–1   MILITARY MARKET
Monthly.
ISSN 0026-4067.
LC sn79-2666.
SRI/MF/excerpts, shipped
quarterly

Monthly trade journal on retail grocery and department store operations of the military commissary and post exchange systems in the U.S. and overseas. Includes features on merchandising trends, advertising and sales promotion techniques, and new products.

Data are from official military and civilian supermarket industry sources.

General format:

a. Articles, occasionally with statistics on sales of single departments or products; and regular news and editorial depts.

b. "Military Market Index," monthly table showing commissary and exchange systems sales, by service branch, domestic and overseas, for month 3-4 months preceding cover date, year to date, and same periods of previous year.

c. "Military Market Survey," monthly feature, usually reporting on a survey of 20-50 military commissary and exchange managers concerning purchasing and marketing issues, with text data on survey response.

Annual features include an almanac and directory issue (July), with statistics on military personnel and compensation, and commissary and exchange sales; and a nonstatistical buyer's guide (Jan.).

Monthly "Military Market Index" appears in all issues. All additional features with substantial statistical content are described, as they appear, under "Statistical Features;" "Military Market Survey" topics are also noted. Nonstatistical contents are not covered.

Availability: Military Market, Subscription Department, Springfield VA 22159-0210, qualified subscribers †, others $20.00 per yr., single copy $2.00, Jan. and July issues $5.00; SRI/MF/excerpts for monthly market index feature and all portions described under "Statistical Features;" shipped quarterly.

Issues reviewed during 1985: Nov. 1984-Oct. 1985 (P) (Vol. 35, Nos. 11-12; Vol. 36, Nos. 1-10) [Vol. 36, Nos. 2-4 incorrectly read Vol. 35].

STATISTICAL FEATURES:

C8910–1.601: Nov. 1984 (Vol. 35, No. 11)

MILITARY MARKET SURVEY: WAREHOUSES, MONTHLY FEATURE

(p. 6) Covers survey responses on warehouse operations of exchange systems.

WAREHOUSES: MAKING DO WITH WHAT YOU'VE GOT

(p. 16-21) By Jay Blucher. Article on distribution center operations of the Army/Air Force Exchange Service, with 2 charts and 1 table showing value of closing inventory, container shipments outside continental U.S. by destination, and data on order fulfillment time from Oakland center, primarily FY83.

BED, BATH & LINEN: IN SEARCH OF THE WELL-DRESSED BED

(p. 33-35) By Jay Blucher. Article, with 1 table showing retail sales, and market share by type of retailer, for 6 product groups in the bed/bath/linen category, 1982. Data are from *Home Furnishings Daily* and Bath, Bed and Linen Assn.

C8910–1.602: Dec. 1984 (Vol. 35, No. 12)

MILITARY MARKET SURVEY: DAILY DIRECT-STORE DELIVERY, MONTHLY FEATURE

(p. 6) Covers survey responses on implementing daily direct-store delivery.

C8910–1.603: Jan. 1985 (Vol. 36, No. 1)

MILITARY MARKET SURVEY: MILREPS LOOK AHEAD TO 1985, MONTHLY FEATURE

(p. 8) Covers survey responses of military representatives concerning their dealings with military resale systems, and opinions of selected military exchange policies.

C8910–1.604: Feb. 1985 (Vol. 36, No. 2)
[Issue incorrectly reads Vol. 35.]

MILITARY MARKET SURVEY: SALVAGE, NO PROBLEM, MONTHLY FEATURE

(p. 5) Covers survey responses on salvage handling and disposition in military commissaries.

C8910–1.605: Mar. 1985 (Vol. 36, No. 3)
[Issue incorrectly reads Vol. 35.]

MILITARY MARKET SURVEY: CREDIT CARDS IN EXCHANGES, MONTHLY FEATURE

(p. 5) Covers survey responses on potential authorization of credit card use in post exchanges.

C8910–1.606: Apr. 1985 (Vol. 36, No. 4)
[Issue incorrectly reads Vol. 35.]

MILITARY MARKET SURVEY: REPS SOUND OFF, MONTHLY FEATURE

(p. 6) Covers survey responses of military representatives concerning their dealings with military resale systems.

C8910–1.607: May 1985 (Vol. 36, No. 5)

MILITARY MARKET SURVEY: AAFES EXCHANGE MANAGERS AGREE, MONTHLY FEATURE

(p. 7) Covers survey responses concerning use of electronic checkout scanners in post exchanges.

THEY DO IT DIFFERENTLY UP NORTH

(p. 36-40, 43) By Jay Blucher. Article, with 1 table showing Canadian Armed Forces Exchange System (CANEX) sales (in Canadian dollars), by region and exchange, FY84. Data are from CANEX.

MARINE CORPS COMMISSARY SERVICE BRANCH

(p. 41-42) By Anne Roketenetz. Article, with 1 table showing percent change in Marine Corps commissary sales, by commissary and organizational unit (West and East Coast complexes, and independent stores), 1st quarter FY85 vs. 1st quarter FY84. Data are from Marine Corps Commissary Service Branch.

C8910–1.608: June 1985 (Vol. 36, No. 6)

MILITARY MARKET SURVEY: COMMISSARY MOBILITY PROGRAM, MONTHLY FEATURE

(p. 6) Covers survey responses of Navy commissary civilian employees concerning recently adopted Navy policy requiring new employees and requesting current employees to agree to relocate upon request as a condition of employment.

SODA SALES FOAM, BUT BEER SALES ARE FLAT

(p. 25-28) By Anne Roketenetz. Article, with 1 table showing beer sales in domestic and overseas post exchanges and clubs/package stores, with per capita sales and military population, 1980-83.

EYES AND EARS OF GOOD MANAGEMENT

(p. 31-33) By Jay Blucher. Article profiling potential Army/Air Force Exchange Service (AAFES) customers. Data are from AAFES. Includes 4 tables showing the following:

a. Army/Air Force active duty, civilian, and retired personnel and dependents, reserve personnel, and survivors; and active duty personnel, by world area and by and sex; 1985.

b. Army and Air Force enlisted personnel by educational attainment, as of Sept. 1983.

C8910–1.609: July 1985 (Vol. 36, No. 7)

MILITARY MARKET SURVEY: COMMISSARY SALVAGE, MONTHLY FEATURE

(p. 6) Covers survey responses on salvage handling and disposition in military commissaries.

26th ANNUAL ALMANAC

(p. 33-52) Annual review of commissary/exchange system developments during 1984, with data on sales and military population characteristics. Includes the following tables and charts:

Military Community

[1] Reserve forces in paid status [officers and enlisted personnel, by service branch, as of Sept. 30, 1984]. (p. 34)

[2] Population of the military community [active duty, retired, and reserve personnel and dependents, as of Mar. 31, 1985]. (p. 34)

[3] Age breakdown of active duty military [by sex, as of Sept. 30, 1984]. (p. 34)

[4-5] Age distribution of dependent children and wives of active duty military personnel [as of Mar. 31, 1985]. (p. 35)

[6] Race breakdown of active duty military [including Hispanic, as of Mar. 31, 1985]. (p. 35)

[7] Active duty military personnel by sex [as of Sept. 30, 1980-84]. (p. 35)

[8] Active duty military personnel by rank, sex, and service [as of Sept. 30, 1984]. (p. 36)

[9] Income of the military community [for active duty, retired, and reserve personnel, by income source], FY85. (p. 37)

[10-11] FY85 active duty military average compensation [by component, and total FY78-85]. (p. 37)

Military Sales

[12-19] [Domestic and overseas sales, by product and system type, 1984; and total worldwide sales, various years 1977-84; for exchanges and commissaries.] [6 tables and 2 charts] (p. 38-41)

[20-21] Largest [10] department/variety store and supermarket chains [including domestic and worldwide commissaries and exchanges, ranked by sales, 1984 with comparisons to 1983]. (p. 42)

[22-23] Combined commissary and exchange sales [1977-84], and [separate commissary and exchange sales, 1984]. (p. 42)

[24] 1984 Coast Guard exchange sales [with exchange, grocery, and other sales, by domestic and overseas unit]. (p. 46)

C8910–1.610: Aug. 1985 (Vol. 36, No. 8)

MILITARY MARKET SURVEY: COMMISSARY RESETS, MONTHLY FEATURE

(p. 6) Covers survey responses of brokers/vendor sales representatives concerning their participation in setting up commissary stock displays.

C8910–1.611: Sept. 1985 (Vol. 36, No. 9)

MILITARY MARKET SURVEY: DISTRIBUTORS AND DIRECT-STORE DELIVERY, MONTHLY FEATURE

(p. 6) Covers survey responses of commissary distributors concerning their participation in direct-store delivery programs.

MORE DATA ON DOD COMMISSARY TEST OF RESERVIST PRIVILEGES

(p. 20) Brief article on DOD testing of commissary use by military reserve personnel to determine whether their shopping privileges should be expanded. Includes 2 undated tables showing monthly commissary utilization rates and sales, for 3 test locations.

MCX: ON THE SAME WAVELENGTH

(p. 24-27) By Jay Blucher. Article, with 3 tables showing financial performance and/or inventory shrinkage of Army/Air Force, Navy, and Marine Corps exchange services and com-

mercial operations, various years 1979-84; and individual Marine Corps exchanges ranked by total sales, 1984.

C8910–1.612: Oct. 1985 (Vol. 36, No. 10)

MILITARY MARKET SURVEY: THE AMERICAN LOGISTICS ASSN, MONTHLY FEATURE

(p. 6, 86) By Nancy Tucker. Covers survey responses of military brokers concerning effectiveness of the American Logistics Assn (ALA), with detail for ALA member and nonmember broker responses.

WILL PLANOGRAMS BRING CHANGES?

(p. 46) Article, with 1 table ranking top 5 cosmetics producers by advertising expenditures for print/radio/TV, 1984. Data are from Leading National Advertisers, Inc.

TOBACCO: FLAT SALES DRAG ON

(p. 48-56) By Anne Roketenetz. Article on cigarette use among military personnel, and on-base sales trends.

Includes 9 tables showing the following for the military, generally by area of operation (domestic, overseas, and world), with selected comparisons to total U.S. adult population: per capita cigarette use; total and per capita cigarette sales, with detail by outlet type (club, commissary, and exchange); and sales of cigarettes vs. 5 other leading product categories, with rankings; various years 1970-84.

MILITARY RETIREES: MARKETERS FIND LOTS OF GOLD IN THE GRAY

(p. 72-76) By Jay Blucher. Article on income and shopping habits of retired military personnel. Data are from DOD, and 1,888 responses to a 1984 Army/Air Force Exchange Service customer survey covering 14 exchanges.

Includes 4 tables showing type of store preferred by retired military personnel for 22 product categories, 1984; and number of retired enlisted personnel and officers, with average pay levels, by age, pay grade, and years of service, as of Sept. 1984.

AAFES DATA ON SPACE PRODUCTIVITY

(p. 80) Brief article, with 2 tables showing Army/Air Force Exchange Service stores, average monthly sales and gross profit, and total and sales space, for continental U.S., Europe, and Pacific region, with detail by store class and U.S. region, total and average, FY84.

C8920
Titsch Communications, Inc.

C8920–1   CABLEFILE/85

Annual.

SRI now covers this publication under C4722-1.

C8920–2   CABLEVISION

Weekly.

SRI now covers this publication under C4722-2.

C8950
TL Enterprises

C8950–2   RV BUSINESS

Monthly.
ISSN 0744-9569.
SRI/MF/excerpts, shipped quarterly

Monthly trade journal on the recreational vehicle (RV) industry, covering production, marketing, servicing, and management trends and developments for dealers in vehicles, parts, and accessories, and for campgrounds.

Data are from Recreation Vehicle Industry Assn (RVIA), publisher surveys of dealers and manufacturers, and other sources. Month of data coverage is 2-3 months prior to cover date.

Issues contain:

a. Special articles and regular features, occasionally with statistics.

b. Monthly "Perspective" section, with 2 tables on RV sales by a sample of Dealer Advisory Board member dealers.

c. Monthly "Shipments" section, with 1 monthly table on total RV shipments, and quarterly survey data on performance of RV/mobile home distributors.

An annual directory and buyer's guide is also included in subscription.

Monthly tables are listed below and appear in all issues. All additional features with substantial statistical content, including quarterly distributor survey, are described, as they appear, under "Statistical Features." Nonstatistical features are not covered.

Availability: RV Business, Circulation Department, 29901 Agoura Rd., Agoura CA 91301, qualified subscribers †, others $24.00 per yr., single copy $2.00, Directory and Buyer's Guide $9.95; SRI/MF/excerpts for monthly tables and portions described under "Statistical Features;" shipped quarterly.

Issues reviewed during 1985: Nov. 1984-Oct. 1985 (P) (Vol. 35, Nos. 8-12; Vol. 36, Nos. 1-7).

MONTHLY TABLES:

[All tables show data for month of coverage, year to date, and same periods of previous year.]

PERSPECTIVE

[1-2] [Unit sales of new and used RVs, total and for motorhomes, travel trailers, fifthwheels, truck campers, and camping trailers; and total sales value.]

SHIPMENTS

[3] RVIA [shipments of travel and folding camping trailers, park models, fifth-wheels, truck campers, multi-use vehicles, motorhomes, van campers, and mini-motorhomes].

STATISTICAL FEATURES:

C8950–2.601: Jan. 1985 (Vol. 35, No. 10)

WDA QUARTERLY SALES FIGURES

(p. 32) Quarterly table showing percent change in sales volume for members of Warehouse Distributors Assn for Leisure and Mobile Products, by region, 3rd quarter 1984. Data are from an assn survey.

C8950–2.602: Apr. 1985 (Vol. 36, No. 1)

WDA QUARTERLY SALES FIGURES

(p. 30) Quarterly table showing percent change in sales volume for members of Warehouse Distributors Assn for Leisure and Mobile Products, by region, 4th quarter 1984. Data are from an assn survey.

C8950–2.603: May 1985 (Vol. 36, No. 2)

NEW STUDY REVEALS RVs AS ECONOMICAL TRAVEL MEANS

(p. 77) Article, with 1 table showing travel expenditures for a family of 4 by type of transportation/accommodation, by duration of trip, 1984. Data are from a summer 1984 Pannell Kerr Forster study using a hypothetical travel party of 2 adults and 2 children traveling between 38 city pairs.

C8950–2.604: June 1985 (Vol. 36, No. 3)

FOLDING CAMPING TRAILERS

(p. 60-72) By Sheryl Davis. Article, with 1 chart showing shipments of folding camping trailers and all recreational vehicles, 1975-84. Data are from Recreation Vehicle Industry Assn.

C8950–2.605: July 1985 (Vol. 36, No. 4)

WDA QUARTERLY SALES FIGURES

(p. 34) Quarterly table showing percent change in sales volume for members of Warehouse Distributors Assn for Leisure and Mobile Products, by region, 1st quarter 1985. Data are from an assn survey.

C8950–2.606: Oct. 1985 (Vol. 36, No. 7)

FACTS CONCERNING THE RECREATIONAL VEHICLE INDUSTRY IN INDIANA

(p. 25) Table showing the following for Indiana: recreational vehicle (RV) plants, retailers, employment, production, retail sales volume, and retail value of production and sales; van conversion plants; and campgrounds/RV resorts; 1984 or Apr. 1985, with selected comparisons to U.S.

Data are from Recreation Vehicle Indiana Council.

WDA QUARTERLY SALES FIGURES

(p. 26) Quarterly table showing percent change in sales volume for members of Warehouse Distributors Assn for Leisure and Mobile Products, by region, 2nd quarter 1985. Data are from an assn survey.

C9050
Trinc Transportation Consultants

C9050–1   TRINC'S BLUE BOOK OF THE TRUCKING INDUSTRY, 1984 Edition

Annual. Sept. 1984.
272 p.+errata sheet, var. paging.
LC 60-2693.
SRI/MF/not filmed

Annual yearbook, presenting trucking industry financial and operating data for Class I and II motor carriers of property, by company, region, and freight commodity, 1983. Data are from annual carrier reports filed with the ICC in Apr. 1984.

Financial and operating data are shown for 1983, and include: operating ratios; assets, liabilities, income, and expenses, by type, including workmen's compensation, fuel/oil taxes, insurance, and license fees; employment and payroll; cost of owned equipment; number of owned and leased vehicles; revenue freight tons; and mileage.

Contains contents listing, summary explanation of report coverage and format, and listings of ICC and Trinc regions (p. iii-ix); and the following sections:

Section I. Industry Summaries and Statistics. Financial and operating data for intercity general freight carriers by region, special carriers by commodity group, and common and contract special carriers; local special and general freight carriers; and local and intercity household goods carriers; with separate data for firms with revenues over and under $5 million. (p. S1-S8)

Section II. Management and Control. Alphabetical directory of carriers, showing company name and address; type of ownership; shares of common stock outstanding, and shares controlled by principal stockholders; officers and directors; and subsidiaries. (p. 1-39)

Section III-IV. Basic Accounts and Statistics. Financial and operating data by individual company: for general freight carriers arranged by Trinc region (p. 1-84A); for household goods carriers (p. 85-94); and for other special carriers arranged by commodity group including petroleum, refrigerated, and agricultural products, and motor vehicles and building materials (p. 95-198); and carrier consolidated statements (p. 199-206).

Section V. Index of carriers. (p. 207-216)

This is the 40th annual yearbook. Yearbook is discontinued with this edition. Under Federal deregulation of the trucking industry, information is no longer available from ICC.

Previous report, for 1982, is described in SRI 1983 Annual under this number.

Availability: Trinc Transportation Consultants, 8200 Greensboro Dr., Suite 303, McLean VA 22102, 1st copy $265.00, additional copies $140.00; SRI/MF/not filmed.

C9380
Variety, Inc.

C9380–1   VARIETY

Weekly.
ISSN 0042-2738.
SRI/MF/not filmed

Weekly trade journal of the entertainment industry, covering developments in film, TV, radio, music, and stage. Includes reporting on production activity, finances, marketing, attendance, and related topics; and data on film and stage boxoffice receipts, and entertainment industry stock quotations.

Data are primarily from *Variety* and other industry sources.

Issues contain numerous newspaper-style news and feature articles; occasional statistical articles and special tables; recurring lists of current top U.S. recordings and radio songs, and occasionally of top British and Australian recordings; and the weekly and monthly data described below.

Most weekly data appear in all issues. Statistical articles and special tables are described, as they appear, under "Statistical Features;" page locations and latest periods of coverage for monthly data are also noted. Nonstatistical features are not covered.

Availability: Variety, Inc., 154 W. 46th St., New York NY 10036, $75.00 per yr., single copy $1.75, special issues $2.75; SRI/MF/not filmed.

Issues reviewed during 1985: Nov. 7, 1984-Oct. 30, 1985 (P) (Vol. 317, Nos. 2-13; Vol. 318, Nos. 1-13; Vol. 319, Nos. 1-13; Vol. 320, Nos. 1-13; Vol. 321, No. 1).

WEEKLY DATA:

FILM

["U.S. Boxoffice Report" presents *Variety* national estimates and "50 Top-Grossing Films" presents actual sample data. Both features are based on data compiled by Standard Data Corp. from a sampling of approximately 2,000 theaters in 20 markets, representing approximately 11% of U.S. theaters.]

a. "U.S. Boxoffice Report" table showing receipts for week ended approximately 1 week prior to publication, year to date, and same periods of previous 2 years.

b. "Weekend Film Boxoffice Reports" table showing national receipts and number of screens for individual films grossing over $1 million during weekend prior to publication, with previous weekend comparison, total days in release, and cumulative receipts.

c. "50 Top-Grossing Films" table showing individual film receipts and rank, number of cities playing, and 1st run and showcase screens, for week ended 1 week prior to publication date, with receipts and rank for previous week, total weeks in top 50, and cumulative receipts; and including selected totals for all other films currently in release.

d. "Film Production" or "Production Update" feature showing major film production starts announced during current year through cover date, with comparisons to previous year, by company.

e. Articles with text data on recent boxoffice receipts for specific films and theaters in key U.S. cities, and for selected films in London, Paris, Australia, and, occasionally, other foreign locations.

STOCK MARKET

f. "Amusement Stock Quotations," showing NYSE, AMEX, and over-the-counter stock trading data for selected entertainment corporations, for week prior to publication.

STAGE

g. "Season Boxoffice Totals" table showing number of shows, value of receipts, and total playing weeks, aggregated for shows on Broadway and on the road, with Broadway attendance and new shows; all for week prior to publication date and/or theater season to date, for current season, and seasons 1, 10, and 20 years previous.

h. Articles with text data on recent boxoffice receipts of specific plays and theaters, for Broadway shows in New York and on the road, and for regional theaters. Occasionally includes similar text data for other types of stage productions on tour.

MONTHLY DATA:

i. "Variety Boxoffice Index" table presenting seasonally adjusted index of film receipts (1980=100) for month prior to publication, previous month, and same month of previous year; data are national estimates, as in "U.S. Boxoffice Reports."

STATISTICAL FEATURES:

C9380–1.601: Nov. 7, 1984 (Vol. 317, No. 2)

MONTHLY DATA

(p. 3) *Variety* Boxoffice Index, for Oct. 1984.

ENTERTAINMENT UNION PENSION PLANS CONTAIN SOME $2-BILLION IN ASSETS

(p. 6, 36) By David Robb. Article, with 1 table showing assets of 10 entertainment industry labor union pension funds, 1974 and 1984.

UK VID BREAKDOWN

(p. 48) Table showing UK market shares for home video software, by company, based on Feb. 13-Aug. 17, 1984 rentals. Data are from Gallup Organization.

TOP 25 PICS IN WEST GERMANY

(p. 52) Table showing top 25 films in West Germany ranked by tickets sold, and including distributor and country of origin for each, June 1980-Dec. 1983 period.

C9380–1.602: Nov. 14, 1984 (Vol. 317, No. 3)

DOMESTIC BOXOFFICE, RECURRING FEATURE

(p. 3) Recurring table showing 10 major film distributors ranked by market share, for 1984 through Nov. 11.

C9380–1.603: Nov. 21, 1984 (Vol. 317, No. 4)

2,000,000 VCRs SEEN IN CANADA BY YEAR'S END, ANNUAL FEATURE

(p. 109) Annual article, with 1 table showing videocassette recorders in use in Canada, 1979-83. Data are from Statistics Canada.

C9380–1.604: Dec. 5, 1984 (Vol. 317, No. 6)

MONTHLY DATA

(p. 3) *Variety* Boxoffice Index, for Nov. 1984.

C9380–1.605: Dec. 12, 1984 (Vol. 317, No. 7)

WARNERS, PAR IN CLOSE RACE FOR B.O. MARKET SHARE, RECURRING FEATURE

(p. 3) Recurring table showing 10 major film distributors ranked by market share, for 1984 through Dec. 2.

HALF-SEASON KEY CITY BOXOFFICE TOTALS

(p. 130) Table showing theater playing weeks, shows played, and boxoffice receipts, for cities with receipts over $1 million, full season 1983/84 and half season 1983/84-1984/85.

MOUNTING COSTS ZAP DISTRIBS' PROFITS

(p. 3, 138-139) By Richard Gold. Article on financial performance of entertainment programming and distribution companies. Data are from Veronis, Suhler and Associates.

Includes 10 tables showing pre-tax operating income and margins, revenues, assets, and cash flow and margins, with selected operating ratios, all for selected entertainment industry sectors, with detail for leading companies (including various rankings), various periods 1979-83. Comparisons to total communications industry are also included.

C9380–1.606: Dec. 26, 1984 (Vol. 317, No. 9)

MAJORS TRIM BUDGETS FOR '85 PIX, ANNUAL FEATURE

(p. 1, 60) Annual article, by Lawrence Cohn, on films with budgets of $14 million or more scheduled for 1985 release. Includes 1 table showing 1985 big-budget films ranked by estimated budget, and also showing distributor for each film.

C9380–1.607: Jan. 2, 1985 (Vol. 317, No. 10)

U.S. RELEASES CLIMBED 13% DURING 1984, RECURRING FEATURE

(p. 3, 6) Recurring article, by Lawrence Cohn, with 1 table showing motion picture releases by type of distributor or film, 4th quarter and full year 1982-84.

For description of previous article, see SRI 1984 Annual under C9380-1.541.

INDIES HAVE PROGRAMMING ON THE MIND

(p. 25, 128) By John Dempsey. Article, with 2 tables showing licensing fees paid by independent and network-affiliated TV stations for syndicated TV programs, 1975-90; and spot/local TV advertising sales of all and independent stations, 1975-84. Data are from FCC, Assn of Independent Television Stations, and other industry sources.

KATZ GUIDE TO NOV. NIELSENS

(p. 58-64) Table showing the following for 21-50 TV programs with highest audience share on independent stations in aggregate top 100 markets: number of stations broadcasting; and audience share, with detail for adults by sex and for youths; all by day part (prime access, late night, early fringe, and daytime), Nov. 1984 with comparisons from Nov. 1983.

Data were compiled by Katz Programming from A. C. Nielsen reports.

INDIE TV GUIDE TO OFF-NETWORK SHOWS, RECURRING FEATURE

(p. 92, 98) Recurring table showing distributor and number of episodes available, for syndicated TV programs arranged by type (no date). Data are from Katz Programming.

C9380–1.608: Jan. 9, 1985 (Vol. 317, No. 11)

[Special issue price is $2.50.]

NATPE CONVENTION ISSUE

MONTHLY DATA

(p. 5) *Variety* Boxoffice Index, for Dec. 1984.

MPAA RATED FEWER PICTURES DURING '84, ANNUAL FEATURE

(p. 7, 20-22) Annual article, by Todd McCarthy, with 1 table showing number of films released, by Motion Picture Assn of America audience-type rating, for aggregate 13 major/minor production companies and for all independent companies, years ended Oct. 1969-84.

1984 DOMESTIC FILM BOXOFFICE MARKET SHARES, RECURRING FEATURE

(p. 30) Recurring table showing 10 major film distributors ranked by market share, for year ended Jan. 1, 1985 with comparative rank for Dec. 1984. Includes accompanying article (p. 5, 30).

TOP GROSSERS IN SPAIN

(p. 37) Table showing top 15 films in Spain ranked by boxoffice gross, 1st half 1984.

GERMAN BOXOFFICE: JUNE-OCTOBER

(p. 39) Table showing top 10 films in West Germany ranked by boxoffice gross, June-Oct. 1984, and including film distributor.

KATZ GUIDE TO NOV. NIELSENS

(p. 62, 68) Table showing the following for 10-42 TV programs with highest audience share on network-affiliated stations in aggregate top 50 markets: number of stations broadcasting; and audience share, with detail for adults by sex and for youths; all by day part (prime access, early fringe, late night, and daytime), Nov. 1984 with comparisons from Nov. 1983.

Data were compiled by Katz Programming from A. C. Nielsen reports.

SYNDICATION AT A GLANCE, RECURRING FEATURE

(p. 91, 154) Recurring table showing distributor and number of episodes available, for syndicated TV programs arranged by type, 1985-87. Data are from Katz Programming.

C9380–1.609: Jan. 16, 1985 (Vol. 317, No. 12)

[Special issue price is $2.50.]

79th SHOW BUSINESS ANNUAL

HALF OF MEGABUCK PICS WIN MAXI B.O., ANNUAL FEATURE

(p. 7, 58, 62) Annual article, by Lawrence Cohn, on production of films with budgets of $14 million or more. Includes 1 table showing estimated budget, domestic rentals to date, producer, distributor, and month of release, for big-budget movies released 1980-84. Data are from *Variety*.

ITALIAN FILM PRODUCTION

(p. 11) Table showing films produced through Italian and combined Italian/other country ventures, 1st 11 months 1980-84.

BIG RENTAL FILMS OF 1984, ANNUAL FEATURE

(p. 16, 78, 90) Annual table showing value of U.S./Canadian rentals; name of director, producer, and distributor; and month of release; for films with rentals of $1 million or more during 1984, in rank order. Data are from *Variety.*

PAR TAKES TOP SPOT IN '84 PIC RENTALS, ANNUAL FEATURE

(p. 17, 26) Annual article, by A. D. Murphy, with 1 table showing value of U.S./Canadian film rentals as percent of total market, for 9 major U.S. distributors, 1980-84.

ALL-TIME FILM RENTAL CHAMPS, ANNUAL FEATURE

(p. 28, 50-74, passim) Annual table showing value of U.S./Canadian rentals; name of director, producer, and distributor; and year of release; for all films with all-time rentals of $4 million or more, in rank order. Data are from *Variety.*

U.S. & CANADA THEATER CIRCUITS RANKED BY SIZE, ANNUAL FEATURE

(p. 38, 76) Annual table showing 80 motion picture theater companies in U.S. and Canada ranked by total number of screens as of Dec. 1984, and also showing headquarters, number of theaters, drive-in screens, States or Provinces of theater locations, year company was founded, and number of screens added in 1981-85. Data are from *Variety.*

ADMISSIONS BY AGE GROUP

(p. 94) By Jack Valenti. Article, with 3 tables showing distribution of film admissions and frequency of film attendance, by educational attainment and/or age group, 1982-84. Data are from Opinion Research Corp. surveys commissioned by the Motion Picture Assn of America.

'84 UK PICS WENT FOR LAFFS

(p. 109) By James Park. Article, with 1 table showing estimated budget, production company, producer, screenwriter, and director, for UK films made in 1984.

ITV PROGRAMMING BREAKDOWN, ANNUAL FEATURE

(p. 125) Annual table showing average weekly broadcasting time by type of program, for UK independent TV stations, 1984.

HOW BBC DIVVIES ITS LICENSE MONEY

(p. 125) Brief article, with undated text statistics showing British Broadcasting Corp. expenditures, by TV and radio network and operation. Data are shown in UK pounds.

BBC-TV PROGRAMMING BREAKDOWN, ANNUAL FEATURE

(p. 126) Annual table showing British Broadcasting Corp. TV broadcast hours, by type of program, for year ended Mar. 1984.

GLOBAL PRICES: TV FILMS, RECURRING FEATURE

(p. 154) Recurring table showing price range for TV half-hour episodes and feature films exported from U.S., by purchasing country (no date).

1984-85 NETWORK 'SECOND SEASON' NEW SHOWS AT A GLANCE, ANNUAL FEATURE

(p. 161) Annual table showing day and hour of appearance, episode length, supplier, production principals, cast, and estimated production fee per episode, for all "second season" prime time TV series from 3 major networks, 1984/85 season.

HIT MOVIES ON U.S. TV SINCE '61

(p. 166-167, 170) Table showing top feature films broadcast on TV ranked by Nielsen rating, for all films receiving 24.0/higher rating, and including network, air date, and audience share, 1961-Aug. 1984 period. Data are from *Variety,* based on A. C. Nielsen Co. reports.

'84 RIAA VIDEO AWARDS, ANNUAL FEATURE

(p. 190-194) Annual list of videocassettes/videodisks receiving platinum and gold awards for high sales, 1984. Shows title, producer/rights owner, and date of award. Data are from Recording Industry Assn of America.

50 BEST SELLING POP SINGLES AND 40 TOP SELLING LPs/TAPES OF '84, ANNUAL FEATURE

(p. 196, 198) Two annual tables showing weeks on best selling list, highest position reached, production label, artist, and record title, for 40-50 best selling LPs/tapes and singles, 1984. Data are from *Variety* sampling of retail sales in top 25 markets.

CASINO GAMING TOPS $5-BILLION, DOUBLE GROSS REVENUES OF 1979

(p. 201, 211) By Saul F. Leonard. Article, with 1 table showing casino gaming gross revenues, for Clark County and rest of Nevada and for Atlantic City, N.J., 1983-85. Data are from Laventhol and Horwath.

For description of similar article with data for 1981-83, see SRI 1983 Annual under C9380–1.407.

BROADWAY LONG RUNS, ANNUAL FEATURE

(p. 212) Annual table showing all stage shows playing over 1,000 performances on Broadway ranked by number of performances as of Jan. 13, 1985, and also including type of show and season of 1st performance.

C9380–1.610: Jan. 30, 1985 (Vol. 318, No. 1)

PIC RELEASE PACE POURS OVER INTO '85, RECURRING FEATURE

(p. 3, 33) Recurring article, by Lawrence Cohn, with 1 table showing motion picture releases by type of distributor or film, Jan. 1982-85 and full year 1982-84.

C9380–1.611: Feb. 6, 1985 (Vol. 318, No. 2)

MONTHLY DATA

(p. 3) *Variety* Boxoffice Index, for Jan. 1985.

C9380–1.612: Feb. 13, 1985 (Vol. 318, No. 3)

YOUTH BAROMETER TRACKS PATTERNS OF ENTERTAINMENT HABITS, SPENDING

(p. 2, 38) Article examining media use habits of youths aged 14-29. Data are from "The Youth Barometer," a continuing research survey conducted by Crossley Youth/Student Surveys.

Includes 5 undated tables showing survey response on participation in leisure time activities, including film attendance, record/tape and radio listening, and TV viewing, by sex and for high school and college students and those not in school, with detail for college students by whether living at home or away.

GERMAN SURVEY, ANNUAL FEATURE

(p. 57-104, passim) Annual compilation of features on West German socioeconomic trends

and film and homevideo industry developments. Data were compiled by *Variety.* Includes 13 tables showing the following for West Germany, various years 1979-85:

a. Film: market shares, by country of origin and distributor; all-time top domestic films in rental income; distribution receipts, for domestic, U.S., and all films; number of screens and population for 7 cities; top grossing films; theaters, ticket sales and prices, and foreign and domestic releases; and employment for 3 major distributors in 5 cities. (p. 59-89, passim)

b. Homevideo: videocassette recorder sales; cassette rental distribution and number of releases, by subject; market share for top 5 video distributors; and volume and value of blank cassette sales. (p. 61-62, 73, 96)

c. Socioeconomic: population, labor force and unemployment, households, income, inflation rate, GNP, TV sets, and radios. (p. 74)

U.S. PICS CROSS HALFWAY MARK IN SHARE OF SWISS THEATRICAL BIZ

(p. 61, 102) By Ted Clark. Article, with 2 tables showing the following for Switzerland: film attendance and releases, for top 6 countries of origin ranked by attendance, 1983; and boxoffice gross (in Swiss francs), admissions, theater screens and seats, and TV sets in homes, 1970 and 1975-83.

C9380–1.613: Feb. 27, 1985 (Vol. 318, No. 5)

JAPAN'S TOP 10 PICS FOR '84

(p. 41) Table ranking top 10 films in Japan by rental income, and including film distributor, 1984.

C9380–1.614: Mar. 6, 1985 (Vol. 318, No. 6)

[Special issue price is $2.50.]

5th AMERICAN FILM MARKET EDITION

MONTHLY DATA

(p. 7) *Variety* Boxoffice Index, for Feb. 1985.

DOMESTIC BOXOFFICE, RECURRING FEATURE

(p. 7) Recurring table showing 9 major film distributors ranked by market share, for 1985 through Feb. 24. Includes accompanying article (p. 7, 339).

NEW U.S. FEATURE FILM RELEASES, RECURRING FEATURE

(p. 13) Recurring table showing motion picture releases by type of distributor or film, 1st 2 months 1970 and 1982-85, and full year 1970 and 1982-84.

C9380–1.615: Mar. 13, 1985 (Vol. 318, No. 7)

FLORIDA RANKS AS NUMBER FOUR IN CONCENTRATION OF PIC THEATERS; ANOTHER 179 SCREENS COMING UP

(p. 43, 70) By Jim Robbins. Article, with 1 table ranking 6 major Florida theater chains by number of screens, and including number of locations, 1984. Data are from National Assn of Theater Owners.

FLORIDA FILM & TV STATISTICS

(p. 44) Table showing the following for film/TV feature and music/TV advertisement productions in Florida: number produced, and in-State production budget and employment, various years 1975-84. Data are from Florida Commerce Dept.

C9380–1.616: Mar. 20, 1985 (Vol. 318, No. 8)

MAJORS UP OUTPUT OF IN-HOUSE PICS, ANNUAL FEATURE

(p. 3, 26-27) Annual article, by Lawrence Cohn, on film production and distribution activity of major distributors, 1985.

Includes 1 chart and 1 table showing number of new film releases produced in-house and through independent/affiliated companies, classic films re-released, and films shelved, for 10 major distributors, 1980-85; and aggregate major companies' film production cost and domestic rental value, and number of films produced and released by production budget range, 1984.

10th FOCUS ON LATIN AMERICAN AND U.S. HISPANIC MARKETS, ANNUAL FEATURE

Annual compilation of features on Latin American and U.S. Hispanic entertainment industry developments. Statistical features are described below.

COLOMBIA'S TOP GROSSERS, ANNUAL FEATURE

(p. 47) Annual table showing top 9 films in Colombia ranked by attendance, 1984.

MAJOR'S BRAZIL BILLINGS, ANNUAL FEATURE

(p. 47) Annual table showing receipts from film rentals in Brazil, for 7 major U.S. distributors, 1984. Data are shown in cruzeiros.

'84 COLOMBIAN MARKET SHARES

(p. 47) Table showing film rental receipts and market shares in Colombia, for 8 major distributors and for all majors and independents, 1984. Receipts are shown in Colombian pesos.

VENEZUELA'S TOP GROSSERS, ANNUAL FEATURE

(p. 52) Annual table showing top 12 films in Venezuela ranked by net billings (in bolivares), 1984.

BRAZIL'S TOP GROSSERS, PIC PRODUCTION, '84 PIC STATS, PICS ON WEBS, AND CINEMAS IN '80S

(p. 52, 56-57) Five tables showing the following for Brazil: top 10 films ranked by attendance, year ended Nov. 1984; number of feature films produced, 1971-84; gross billings (in cruzeiros) and tickets sold, for domestic and foreign films, 1984; total and U.S. feature films shown on TV, by network, 1984; and number of film theaters, 1980-84.

TOP '84 PERU GROSSERS, ANNUAL FEATURE

(p. 54) Annual table showing top 10 films in Peru ranked by rentals value, 1984.

VENEZUELA RELEASES

(p. 54) Table showing number of films released in Venezuela by country of origin, 1984.

GROSS BILLINGS IN PERU

(p. 63) Table showing gross billings (in soles) from films released in Peru, for 4 major U.S. distributors, 1984.

HISPANIC TV MARKETS IN U.S.

(p. 65) Table showing the following for 16 principal Hispanic TV markets: Hispanic households and population age 2/over, and share of total U.S. Hispanic households and population. Data are from the 1983-84 Arbitron Ethnic Population Book.

For description of similar article showing population data for 1980, see SRI 1984 Annual under C9380-1.513.

C9380–1.617: Mar. 27, 1985 (Vol. 318, No. 9)

MONTHLY DATA

(p. 3) *Variety* Boxoffice Index, for Mar. 1985.

C9380–1.618: Apr. 3, 1985 (Vol. 318, No. 10)

RELEASE SKED LIGHTENED UP IN MARCH, RECURRING FEATURE

(p. 3, 37) Recurring article, by Lawrence Cohn, with 1 table showing motion picture releases by type of distributor or film, 1st quarter 1970 and 1982-85, and full year 1970 and 1982-84.

C9380–1.619: Apr. 17, 1985 (Vol. 318, No. 12)

[Special issue price is $2.50.]

16th INTERNATIONAL TV ANNUAL

SYNDICATION RUNDOWN, ANNUAL FEATURE

(p. 50, 86) Annual table ranking syndicated TV programs by Nielsen rating, and also including number of markets broadcasting, audience share, and rating among men and women aged 18-49 and 25-54, Feb. 1985. Table covers programs broadcast in 30/more markets and rated 3.0/higher. Data are from A. C. Nielsen Co.

For description of previous table, see SRI 1984 Annual under C9830-1.516.

GLOBAL PRICES FOR TV FILMS, RECURRING FEATURE

(p. 86) Recurring table showing price range for TV half-hour episodes and feature films exported from U.S., by purchasing country (no date).

ITALIAN EXPORTS OF FILMS, TV MOVIES, AND SERIES

(p. 123) Table showing number and aggregate value of films and TV episodes exported from Italy, by purchasing country, 1983-84. Data are from Italian Ministry of Foreign Commerce.

NON-CANADIANS: FUND'S HIGHEST ROLLERS, ANNUAL FEATURE

(p. 169, 214) Annual article, by Sid Adilman, on operations of Canada's Broadcast Fund, a Government-sponsored funding source for TV productions administered by Telefilm Canada. Includes 1 table showing number of funded projects, and total budget and Telefilm investment (in Canadian dollars), for contracted, accepted, and pending French- and English-language projects, by program type, July 1983-Feb. 1985 period.

TVB IS STILL RATINGS CHAMP IN HONG KONG

(p. 188, 194) By Harold Myers. Article, with 1 table showing Hong Kong's top 10 TV programs ranked by average rating, and also showing audience share and broadcasting channel, 1984.

C9380–1.620: Apr. 24, 1985 (Vol. 318, No. 13)

AUSTRALIAN FACTS, ANNUAL FEATURE

(p. 71) Annual table showing the following for Australia: population, inflation and unemployment rates, number of film theaters, and average weekly wage and top film admission price (in Australian dollars). No data dates are given.

'84 AUSSIE RELEASES DROP OFF

(p. 72) Table showing 8 leading film distributors in Australia ranked by number of releases, 1984.

ALL-TIME AUSSIE RENTAL CHAMPS, ANNUAL FEATURE

(p. 74, 76) Annual table showing release date, distributor, and rental value, for all films with total Australian rentals of more than $500,000 (Australian dollars), in rank order as of Jan. 1, 1985. Includes accompanying brief article.

AUSSIE TV VIEWING PATTERNS, ANNUAL FEATURE

(p. 106) Two annual tables showing Australian TV households; families viewing TV; average viewing time aggregated for 6 capital cities, with detail by sex and age group; and top 10 TV programs (title and network) ranked by aggregate audience size in 5 cities. No data dates are given. Data are from McNair Anderson Associates.

C9380–1.621: May 1, 1985 (Vol. 319, No. 1)

[Special issue price is $2.50.]

28th INTERNATIONAL FILM ANNUAL

MONTHLY DATA

(p. 5) *Variety* Boxoffice Index, for Apr. 1985.

ALL-TIME FILM RENTAL CHAMPS, ANNUAL FEATURE

(p. 109-185, passim) Annual table showing value of U.S./Canadian rentals; name of director, producer, and distributor; and year of release; for films with all-time rentals of $4 million or more as of Dec. 1984, arranged in alphabetical order. Data are from *Variety*.

L.A. STILL FAR AND AWAY U.S. PRODUCTION CENTER

(p. 291) By David Robb. Article, with 1 table showing average number of employees working in film/TV production, for U.S., California, and Los Angeles County, Calif., 1974-84. Data are from California Employment Development Dept and BLS.

TOP 10 ITALIAN GROSSERS

(p. 301) Table ranking top 10 films in Italy by boxoffice gross, and also showing film director, distributor, and country of origin, 1984-Apr. 1985 period.

ITALIAN FILM PRODUCTION, ANNUAL FEATURE

(p. 302) Annual table showing films produced through Italian and combined Italian/other country ventures, 1980-84. An accompanying table shows investment value and number of films financed through Banca Nazionale del Lavoro, 1978-84.

For description of previous annual table, for 1979-83, see SRI 1984 Annual under C9380-1.520. For description of a similar table, with data through Nov. 1984, see C9380-1.609 above.

ALL-TIME GERMAN RENTAL CHAMPS

(p. 362) Table showing all-time top 10 films in West Germany ranked by earnings, and including film distributor, as of early 1985.

TOP 10 FILMS IN AUSTRALIA, 1984, ANNUAL FEATURE

(p. 379) Annual table showing top 10 films in Australia ranked by rental income (in Australian dollars), and including film distributor, 1984.

Previous table, for 1983, is described in SRI 1984 Annual under C9380-1.520.

TOP HONG KONG-MADE PICS IN '84 AND TOP GROSSING HONG KONG IMPORTS, RECURRING FEATURE

(p. 394, 397) Two recurring tables showing Hong Kong's top 10 domestic and imported films ranked by boxoffice gross (in Hong Kong dollars), and also showing film distributor, 1984.

JAPAN vs. U.S., ANNUAL FEATURE

(p. 395) Annual table showing the following for Japan and the U.S.: film boxoffice gross, attendance, average ticket price, and number of screens and releases; and population and TV households; primarily 1984 with comparisons to 1983. Data are from Motion Picture Assn of America and Eiren, Japan.

Previous table, for 1983, is described in SRI 1984 Annual under C9380-1.520.

JAPAN FILM DISTRIBUTION, ANNUAL FEATURE

(p. 395) Annual table ranking 12 leading film distributors in Japan by rental income, and also showing number of films released and theaters owned/operated, 1984 with rental comparisons to 1983. Data cover Japanese film companies and importers, and U.S. distributors. Includes accompanying article (p. 395, 456).

SPAIN: ALL-TIME B.O. CHAMPS, TOP 1984 FILMS, AND 1984's TOP GROSSERS, ANNUAL FEATURES

(p. 410-414) Three annual tables showing the following for Spain: all-time top 22 films as of Dec. 1984, and top 10 domestic and top 15 domestic/imported films in 1984, all ranked by boxoffice gross and including release dates.

Previous tables, for 1983, are described in SRI 1984 Annual under C9380-1.520.

BRITAIN'S DEPRESSED HOMEVIDEO MARKET FACES ROUGH FUTURE

(p. 437, 439, 459) By Bert Baker. Article, with 3 tables showing the following for UK: percent of TV homes with videocassette recorders (VCR), VCR market share by format and unit sales, and home videocassette sales and rentals (in British pounds), various years 1979-87.

Similar data, for various periods 1981-83, are described in SRI 1984 Annual under C9380-1.507.

HOW MANY VCRs? ANNUAL FEATURE

(p. 437) Annual table showing videocassette recorders in use in Canada, 1979-84. Data are from Statistics Canada.

For description of previous feature, for 1979-83, see C9380-1.603 above.

GERMANS GO FOR LOTS OF ACTION, ANNUAL FEATURE

(p. 438) Annual table showing number of prerecorded videocassette titles available on the West German market, by film type, 1983/84 and 1985. Data are from the German Video Institute.

Previous table, for 1983, is described in SRI 1984 Annual under C9380-1.520.

1984-85 REGULAR SERIES RATINGS, ANNUAL FEATURE

(p. 468) Annual table showing regularly scheduled TV series ranked by average rating, Sept. 24, 1984-Apr. 21, 1985 period, with comparisons to 1983/84 season.

C9380–1.622: May 22, 1985 (Vol. 319, No. 4)

DISTRIBS PLAYING IT SAFE THIS SUMMER

(p. 3, 40) By Lawrence Cohn. Article, with 1 table showing distribution of film rentals by type of film, 1971/72-1983/84. Data are from *Variety*.

C9380–1.623: May 29, 1985 (Vol. 319, No. 5)

DOMESTIC FILM B.O. MARKET SHARES, RECURRING FEATURE

(p. 3) Recurring table showing 10 major film distributors ranked by market share, and also including high and low shares (with dates), for 1985 through May 19.

FILM RENTALS OF U.S. MAJORS IN JAPAN

(p. 51) Table showing 4 major U.S. film distributors ranked by rental income in Japan, 1st quarter 1985, with percent change from 1st quarter 1984.

JAPAN B.O. vs. ATTENDANCE: 1968-84

(p. 53) Chart showing Japanese film attendance, and boxoffice gross and average admission price (in yen), 1968-84. Data are from Japanese industry sources and *Variety*.

C9380–1.624: June 5, 1985 (Vol. 319, No. 6)

MONTHLY DATA

(p. 3) *Variety* Boxoffice Index, for May 1985.

MORE U.S. RELEASES HUNT FEWER BUCKS, RECURRING FEATURE

(p. 3, 24) Recurring article, by Lawrence Cohn, with 1 table showing motion picture releases by type of distributor or film, 1st 5 months 1970 and 1982-85, and full year 1970 and 1982-84.

B'WAY BLAHS AS '84-'85 SEASON DRAWS TO CLOSE, ANNUAL FEATURE

(p. 1, 84, 88) Annual article reviewing characteristics of the 1984/85 theater season for Broadway and road performances.

Includes 4 tables showing Broadway attendance and average ticket price, 1975/76-1984/85; Broadway and road total playing weeks and boxoffice receipts, and shows playing and receipts for biggest week, 1948/49-1984/85; and playing weeks, shows played, and boxoffice receipts, for cities with receipts over $1 million, 1983/84-1984/85.

B'WAY PRODUCTION RECORD, 1899-1985, ANNUAL FEATURE

(p. 86) Annual table showing the following for Broadway: new plays and musicals, and revivals, 1899/1900-1984/85; and return shows and pre-opening flops, 1972/73-1984/85.

C9380–1.625: June 12, 1985 (Vol. 319, No. 7)

GLOBAL PIC RENTALS TUMBLED 8% IN '84

(p. 3, 31) By A. D. Murphy. Article, with 1 table showing percent change in rentals of U.S. films in 15 leading countries (for U.S. and local currency), 1984 vs. 1982-83.

BROADWAY THEATER MANAGEMENTS, BOOKINGS, GROSSES; ANNUAL FEATURE

(p. 84) Annual table showing managing company, number of weeks lighted, list of shows played, and total boxoffice receipts, for individual Broadway theaters, 1984/85 season, with selected comparisons to 1983/84 season.

Previous article, for 1983/84 season, is described in SRI 1984 Annual under C9380-1.524.

C9380–1.626: June 19, 1985 (Vol. 319, No. 8)

INDIES IN STRONG PRODUCTION COMEBACK

(p. 7, 31) By Todd McCarthy. Article, with 3 tables showing number of films released, for all sources and for independent companies, years ended May 1969-85; and 12 independent companies ranked by number of releases, 1984/85. For independent releases, tables include detail by Motion Picture Assn of America (MPAA) rating for type of audience. Data are from MPAA.

SWISS ADMISSIONS DROPPED AGAIN IN '84: U.S. PICS BIGGEST DRAW

(p. 47) By George Mezofi. Article, with 1 table showing film attendance and screenings for top 20 films shown in Switzerland, 1984.

C9380–1.627: June 26, 1985 (Vol. 319, No. 9)

KATZ GUIDE TO MAY NIELSENS

(p. 65, 74-78) Table showing the following for 20-63 TV programs with highest audience share on network-affiliated and independent stations in aggregate top 100 markets: number of stations broadcasting; designated marketing area share and household rating; and audience share, with detail for adults by sex; all by day part (prime access, daytime, early fringe, and late night), May 1985 with comparisons from Nov. 1984.

Data were compiled by Katz Programming from A. C. Nielsen reports.

For description of similar articles, with Nov. 1984 ratings, see C9380-1.607 and C9380-1.608 above.

C9380–1.628: July 3, 1985 (Vol. 319, No. 10)

DOMESTIC BOXOFFICE MARKET SHARES, RECURRING FEATURE

(p. 3) Recurring table showing 9 major film distributors ranked by market share, 1st half 1985, with detail for May 22-June 30 period.

NEW RELEASES UP TO RECENT-YEAR HIGH, RECURRING FEATURE

(p. 3, 81) Recurring article, by Lawrence Cohn, with 1 table showing motion picture releases by type of distributor or film, 1st half and 2nd quarter 1970 and 1982-85, and full year 1970 and 1982-84.

C9380–1.629: July 10, 1985 (Vol. 319, No. 11)

MONTHLY DATA

(p. 3) *Variety* Boxoffice Index, for June 1985.

C9380–1.630: July 17, 1985 (Vol. 319, No. 12)

NEW ENGLAND NUMBERS AT A GLANCE

(p. 78) Table showing the following for 6 New England States: indoor and drive-in theater screens and total and TV households (no dates), and population with U.S. rank, 1983. Data are from *Information Please Almanac,* Arbitron, and National Assn of Theater-Owners.

Table is accompanied by a related article (p. 79, 90).

8 NEW ENGLAND MARKETS MAKE ARBITRON'S ADI LIST

(p. 93) Table showing total and TV households for 8 New England metro areas, and including Arbitron Area of Dominant Influence (ADI) rank (no date).

C9380–1.631: July 24, 1985 (Vol. 319, No. 13)

BIGGEST DOMESTIC B.O. WEEKENDS IN HISTORY, ANNUAL FEATURE

(p. 30) Annual table showing top 58 all-time weekend boxoffice gross earnings for individual films, with film title, distributor, and number of screens for each weekend, through July 1985.

Also includes 1 summary table showing number of original and sequel films listed, and top weekends by season, both by distributor.

Previous feature, for 1978-early 1984 period, is described in SRI 1984 Annual under C9380-1.520.

C9380–1.632: Aug. 14, 1985 (Vol. 320, No. 3)

MONTHLY DATA

(p. 3) *Variety* Boxoffice Index, for July 1985.

C9380–1.633: Aug. 21, 1985 (Vol. 320, No. 4)

DOMESTIC B.O. MARKET SHARES, RECURRING FEATURE

(p. 3) Recurring table showing 9 major film distributors ranked by market share, Jan.-Aug. 11, 1985, with detail for summer season.

C9380–1.634: Aug. 28, 1985 (Vol. 320, No. 5)

N.J. STANDS OUT FOR CONSISTENCY IN LURING PRODUCTIONS TO STATE

(p. 40, 114) By Dan Gilroy. Article, with 1 table showing number of New Jersey film productions, by category (including feature films, TV series and movies, short subjects, music videos, and commercials), 1983-84.

C9380–1.635: Sept. 4, 1984 (Vol. 320, No. 6)

TOP-GROSSING SUMMER RELEASES, ANNUAL FEATURE

(p. 3) Annual table showing top 12 films ranked by boxoffice gross, May 22-Sept. 2, 1985 period. Includes accompanying articles (p. 3, 33).

Previous feature is described in SRI 1984 Annual under C9380-1.537.

RELEASE PACE TORRID IN AUGUST; YEAR TOTAL LOOKS TO BEAT '84, RECURRING FEATURE

(p. 3, 33) Recurring article, with 1 table showing motion picture releases by type of distributor or film, Aug. and 1st 8 months 1982-85.

C9380–1.636: Sept. 11, 1985 (Vol. 320, No. 7)

MONTHLY DATA

(p. 3) *Variety* Boxoffice Index, for Aug. 1985.

DOMESTIC FILM BOXOFFICE MARKET SHARES, RECURRING FEATURE

(p. 91) Recurring table showing 10 major film distributors ranked by market share, Jan.-Sept. 2, 1985, with detail for summer season.

C9380–1.637: Sept. 18, 1985 (Vol. 320, No. 8)

MOTION PICTURE TV AD BUYS UP 6% FOR 1ST HALF OF '85; U TOPS LIST

(p. 3, 89) By Bill Daniels. Article, with 1 table showing motion picture distributors' expenditures for TV advertising, by distributor, 1st half 1984-85.

C9380–1.638: Sept. 25, 1985 (Vol. 320, No. 9)

1985-86 NETWORK PRIMETIME SEASON AT A GLANCE, ANNUAL FEATURE

(p. 50-55, 100-102) Annual table showing day and hour of appearance, episode length, supplier, production principals, cast, and estimated production fee per episode, for all prime time TV series from 3 major networks, 1985/86 season.

THEATRICAL MOVIE RANKINGS FOR 1984-85, ANNUAL FEATURE

(p. 59) Annual table showing made-for-theater movies broadcast on TV ranked by rating, and including network, date of appearance, and audience share, Sept. 1, 1984-Aug. 31, 1985 period.

MADE-FOR-TV MOVIE RATINGS FOR 1984-85, ANNUAL FEATURE

(p. 62-94, passim) Annual table showing made-for-TV movies ranked by rating, and including network, date of appearance, supplier, and audience share, Sept. 1, 1984-Aug. 31, 1985 period.

SYNDICATION AT A GLANCE, RECURRING FEATURE

(p. 66-67, 96) Recurring table showing distributor and number of episodes available, for syndicated TV programs arranged by type, 1985-88. Data are from Katz Programming.

PBS SPECIALS: FALL '85 SEASON

(p. 76, 110) Table showing number of episodes and length, producer, underwriter, and cost per episode, for public broadcasting TV specials, fall 1985 season.

1984-85 PRIMETIME SPECIALS RATINGS, ANNUAL FEATURE

(p. 82-106, passim) Annual table showing prime time TV specials ranked by audience rating, and including network, date of appearance, and audience share, Sept. 1, 1984-Aug. 31, 1985 period.

1984-85 SEASON MINISERIES RATINGS, ANNUAL FEATURE

(p. 90) Annual table showing TV miniseries ranked by average rating, and also showing average audience share, Sept. 1, 1984-Aug. 31, 1985 period.

C9380–1.639: Oct. 2, 1985 (Vol. 320, No. 10)

[Special issue price is $2.50.]

SIXTH HOME VIDEO ANNUAL

ILLINOIS PRODUCTION AFIRE AND UNIONS CAN'T TAME IT

(p. 22) By Frank Segers. Article, with 1 table showing number of motion picture/TV productions filmed in Illinois, expenditures, and local residents hired; and number of productions sought by State film office; 1976-84. Data are from Illinois Film Office.

HOW DUTCH VCR SALES GROW

(p. 42) Table showing the following for the Netherlands: unit sales of videocassette recorders, and household audience, 1978-87.

JAPAN VIDEO STATS

(p. 45, 48) Brief article, with 5 tables showing the following for Japan: videocassette and videodisk software rentals and/or sales, with detail for videocassettes by film type and cassette running time; and videocassette recorder use habits; various years 1980-84. Data are from Japan Video Assn and Tohokushinsha Film Co.

Also includes Japanese vs. U.S. average cost components and prices for foreign prerecorded videocassettes (no date).

UK VCR FORMAT SHARE, BLANK TAPE SALES, DISTRIBUTORS SHARES OF PRE-RECORDED VIDTAPE MARKET, AND VCR GROWTH

(p. 45, 53, 77) Four tables showing UK videocassette recorder (VCR) market shares by format, unit sales of blank VCR tapes, VCRs in use, and percent of TV homes with VCRs, various years 1983-88; and market shares for prerecorded videocassettes, by company (no date). Includes accompanying article (p. 45, 94).

Similar data, for various years 1979-87, are described under C9380-1.621 above.

HOLLAND: ADMISSIONS; ALL-TIME CHAMPS; PIX MARKET SHARE; CINEMA STRUCTURE; AND SCREEN TIME; ANNUAL FEATURES

(p. 99-100, 105, 107) Annual compilation of 1 chart and 4 tables on the motion picture industry in the Netherlands. Includes the following data for various years 1974-84:

a. Film admissions in 9 individual cities and aggregate for 53 cities; and all-time top 20 domestic films ranked by tickets sold, and showing year of release.

b. Dutch films as a percent of total films released in the Netherlands; number of theater screens and seats; and distribution of movie screen time and boxoffice receipts, for domestic films and for foreign films by country of origin.

Includes accompanying articles (p. 99-117, passim).

RATINGS OF 1985 SUMMER SERIES, ANNUAL FEATURE

(p. 120) Annual table showing prime time TV series ranked by average rating, Apr. 22-Sept. 22, 1985 period. Table incorrectly reads 1984.

C9380–1.640: Oct. 9, 1985 (Vol. 320, No. 11)

MONTHLY DATA

(p. 3) *Variety* Boxoffice Index, for Sept. 1985.

INDIE FOREIGN SALES BILLION $ BUSINESS

(p. 3, 40) By Hy Hollinger. Article, with 2 tables showing overseas sales of U.S. independently produced theatrical, TV, and video films, by country or world region and for 3 major markets (AFM, Cannes, and Mifed), 1984. Data are from an American Film Marketing Assn survey of approximately 20 member companies.

GLOBAL PRICES FOR TV FILMS, RECURRING FEATURE

(p. 66) Recurring table showing price range for TV half-hour episodes and feature films exported from U.S., by purchasing country (no date).

PUBLIC BROADCASTING SERVICE PRIMETIME SERIES

(p. 108) Table showing number of episodes and length, producer, underwriter, and cost per episode, for public broadcasting TV prime time series, fall 1985 season.

C9380–1.641: Oct. 16, 1985 (Vol. 320, No. 12)

[Special issue price is $2.50.]

ELEVENTH MIFED FILM MARKET REVIEW

THIRD QTR. RELEASE PACE ALMOST EVEN WITH '84; SEE 430 FOR YEAR, RECURRING FEATURE

(p. 72, 235) Recurring article, by Lawrence Cohn, with 1 table showing motion picture releases by type of distributor or film, 3rd quarter and 1st 9 months 1970 and 1982-85, and full year 1970 and 1982-84.

BRAZIL: PIC ATTENDANCE

(p. 182, 205) Two tables showing the following for Brazil: domestic and foreign film releases and attendance, with attendance for 20 leading titles; and total film attendance for 7 major cities; 1st half 1985 and/or 1984.

TOP 30 ALL-TIME JAPANESE FILM RENTAL CHAMPS, ANNUAL FEATURE

(p. 336) Annual table showing Japan's all-time top 30 foreign and domestic films ranked by rental income (no date), and including release date and distributor for each.

Previous feature is described in SRI 1984 Annual under C9380-1.512.

HONG KONG: ALL-TIME CHAMPS; TOP GROSSING CANTONESE PICS AND FOREIGN FILMS; AND TOP LOCAL 10; RECURRING FEATURE

(p. 337-339) Four recurring tables showing Hong Kong's top 10-13 domestic and imported films for various periods 1985, and all-time top films, ranked by boxoffice gross (in Hong Kong dollars), and including distributor and/or release date for each film.

Includes accompanying article (p. 337, 412).

YANK MAJORS' RENTALS IN JAPAN, AND JAPAN MAJORS' RENTALS, ANNUAL FEATURES

(p. 337, 350) Two annual tables showing rental income for 5 major U.S. film distributors in Japan, 1975-84 and 1st half 1985, and for 4 major Japanese film companies, 1st 8 months 1984-85. Includes accompanying articles (p. 337, 350, 413).

TOP JAPAN GROSSERS

(p. 338) Table showing Japan's top 20 foreign and domestic films ranked by rental income, 1st half 1985.

JAPAN '84 FILM STATS

(p. 339) Table showing the following for Japan: number of theaters, with number playing domestic and foreign films only; number of films in release, for independent and major domestic companies and all foreign companies; admissions, pre-tax boxoffice receipts, and average ticket price; and foreign and domestic film billings; all for 1984 with percent change from 1983.

JAPAN FILM IMPORTER RENTALS, ANNUAL FEATURE

(p. 339) Annual table showing 4 Japanese film importing companies ranked by rental income, 1st half 1985 with percent change from 1st half 1984.

Previous feature is described in SRI 1984 Annual under C9380-1.544.

'84 FRENCH 1-MIL CLUB

(p. 366) Table showing France's top 44 domestic and foreign films with over 1 million admissions, ranked by admissions, and including release date and film distributor, 1984.

C9380–1.642: Oct. 30, 1985 (Vol. 321, No. 1)

MAJORS HELD PROD. COSTS FLAT FOR '85, ANNUAL FEATURE

(p. 3, 27) Annual article, by Lawrence Cohn, with 1 table showing production budget and number of films, by film budget size, aggregate for 9 major film distributors, for 1984-85 releases and 1986 scheduled releases as of Nov. 1985.

Previous feature is described in SRI 1984 Annual under C9380-1.502.

MAJOR DISTRIBS' NEW RELEASES, ANNUAL FEATURE

(p. 3) Annual table showing the following for 9 major film distributors: number of new film releases produced in-house and acquired from outside sources, and aggregate number of classic films re-released, 1984-86.

Previous feature is described in SRI 1984 Annual under C9380-1.525.

C9470
Vending Times, Inc.

C9470–1   VENDING TIMES: Census of the Industry, 1985
Monthly (selected issue).
July 1985.   74 p.
Vol. 25, No. 7-A.
ISSN 0042-3327.
LC SC 76-332.
SRI/MF/not filmed

Annual *Vending Times* report, for 1985, on the vending industry. Includes sales of vended products and number of machines, by product type; and operating ratios; various years 1974-84. Also includes data on coffee service, music, and game equipment. Data are from a survey of operating companies and manufacturers.

Contents:

a. Contents listing, introduction, analysis, and 1 summary table. (p. 6-14)

b. Vended product sales, with 16 tables listed below. (p. 19-51)

c. Fleet vehicles, and coffee service, with 3 tables listed below. (p. 52-55)

d. Operating patterns, with 1 table showing total operating companies, and distribution by number of full-time employees, 1983-84. (p. 56)

e. Music and games, including text data and 1 chart (p. 65) on coin-operated phonographs; and 8 tables listed below. (p. 58-68)

f. Operating ratio study, with 4 tables showing National Automatic Merchandising Assn members' composite average operating ratios, and profit and sales analysis by product, 1982-84. (p. 72-73)

This is the 39th annual report. *Vending Times* is a monthly journal reporting on vending industry trends and developments, and normally does not contain statistics. The annual industry census is the only feature covered by SRI.

Availability: Vending Times, Inc., 545 Eighth Ave., New York NY 10018, $25.00 per yr., census issue $10.00, single copy $3.00; SRI/MF/not filmed.

TABLES:

C9470–1.1: Vending Sales

[Tables [1-11] and [13] are for vended products, and generally show total dollar and unit sales, weekly unit sales, and number of machines on location, 1974 and 1982-84; and sales distribution by vended price and/or product categories, 1982-84 or 1984.

Manual sales data are for vending machine operators who also serve food manually.]

[1-4] Hot drinks; and bottle, can, and cup cold drinks. (p. 19-22)

[5-6] Confections/snacks and pastries. (p. 24, 27)

[7-8] Cigarettes and cigars [price/product category data omitted for cigars]. (p. 30)

[9-10] Milk and ice cream. (p. 35-36)

[11] Hot canned foods. (p. 43)

[12] Vending and manual locations [number of sites, 1983-84, and sales value, 1984, by type of location]. (p. 44)

[13] All-purpose food vendors. (p. 46)

[14] Vended food service/commissary operations [including percent of food service operators with own commissary and with outside food sources; percent using microwave ovens; and sales distribution of commissary-prepared foods by product and of vended foods by type of location, 1984]. (p. 49)

[15] Manual food service [distribution of manual food sales by type of location and product, 1982-84; and of operator expansion into manual foods, by period service started]. (p. 50)

[16] Bulk vending [machines on location, and dollar sales, by product type, 1983-84; and sales distribution by vended price, 1982-84]. (p. 51)

C9470–1.2: Fleet Vehicles, Coffee Service, and Amusement Equipment

VEHICLES

[1] Truck and van use [vending operator fleet vehicles by type, 1982-84]. (p. 52)

COFFEE SERVICE

[Tables [2-3] show data for 1980 and 1982-84.]

[2] Coffee service, equipment [average accounts and purchases, and percent of firms using approximately 15 types of coffee brewing and noncoffee equipment]. (p. 54)

[3] Coffee service, product [average purchase for 3 types of coffee and 6 related products, average sales dollar volume, cup purchases, and distribution of firms by sales volume range]. (p. 55)

AMUSEMENT EQUIPMENT

[Tables [5-11] show data for 1980 and 1982-84. Tables [6-11] show annual and weekly average dollar volume, and number of units on location.]

[4] 1984 review and outlook [reported and anticipated income percent change, by equipment type; and types of locations served]. (p. 58)

[5] Amusement equipment dollar volume [for 8 types of games and rides]. (p. 60)

[6-9] Video games, flipper [pinball] games, pool tables, and shuffle alleys. (p. 62, 66)

[10-11] Soccer tables, and arcade games (specialized). (p. 68)

C9700
Ziff-Davis Publishing Co.

C9700–2   BUSINESS AND COMMERCIAL AVIATION
Monthly (selected issues).
ISSN 0191-4642.
LC 84-642861.
SRI/MF/excerpts

Monthly periodical on general aviation and commuter aircraft operations, with detail for corporate activities. Periodical is primarily narrative, but also includes 2 annual statistical features on corporate aviation personnel salaries (Sept. or Oct. issue) and corporate aircraft operation among Fortune 500 companies (Dec. issue). Annual features are individually described below, under "Annual Statistical Features."

Periodical is abstracted in SRI only when these 2 features appear.

Availability: Business and Commercial Aviation, PO 5850, Cherry Hill NJ 08034, $30.00 per yr., single copy $4.00; SRI/MF/excerpts for all portions covered under "Annual Statistical Features."

ANNUAL STATISTICAL FEATURES:

C9700–2.601: Sept. 1984 (Vol. 55, No. 3)

1984 B/CA SALARY SURVEY, ANNUAL FEATURE

(p. 55-59) Annual article, by David W. Almy, on salaries for business aircraft pilots and maintenance personnel employed by corporate aviation depts, 1984. Data are from an annual *Business and Commercial Aviation* telephone survey of 113 depts covering 682 employees.

Includes 3 tables showing salary median and range, by position; and aircraft utilization measures, including hours flown; all by aircraft type and/or model, 1984, with salary comparison to 1983.

This is the 11th annual salary survey. Previous survey, for 1983, has also been received, and is also available on SRI microfiche under C9700-2 [Monthly (selected issue). Oct. 1983. (p. 55-58). $3.50]. Previous survey is substantially similar in format and content, but omits data on aircraft utilization. For description of 9th annual survey, see SRI 1983 Annual under C9700-2.401.

C9700–2.602: Dec. 1984 (Vol. 55, No. 6)

BUSINESS AVIATION WITHIN THE FORTUNE 500, ANNUAL FEATURE

(p. 50-53) Annual article, by David W. Almy, on business aircraft ownership and financial performance of Fortune 500 industrial corporations, 1983. Data are from Aviation Data Service, Inc.

Includes 1 chart and 2 tables showing number of firms, employment, net sales and income, assets, stockholders' equity, and selected operating ratios, for companies operating and not operating business aircraft; number of firms by aircraft fleet size; and number of aircraft operated; with selected detail by major industry group; 1983.

Previous feature, for 1982, has also been received, and is also available on SRI microfiche under C9700-2 [Monthly (selected issue). Dec. 1983. (p. 52-56). $3.50]. Previous feature is substantially similar in format and content, but includes data on fleet value by type of aircraft. For description of feature for 1981, see SRI 1983 Annual under C9700-2.402.

Beginning with the 1982 edition, SRI films the reprinted version of this feature. In addition to the data described above, the reprint also includes 1 extended table showing number of aircraft by type, for individual corporations. Reprint is also available from the issuing agency.

C9700–3   WEEKLY OF BUSINESS AVIATION
Weekly.   Approx. 10 p. cumulative pagination throughout volume.
SRI/MF/excerpts, shipped quarterly

Weekly publication reporting on developments in general aviation, commuter airlines, and aviation-related Federal regulation. Includes monthly statistics on business/personal aircraft shipments.

Issues contain numerous brief news articles; recent Federal airworthiness directives and regulatory exemption activities; 1 monthly table and 2 other recurring tables, listed below; and occasional special tables and articles with statistics. A quarterly subject index is published separately.

Monthly table usually appears in 2nd or 3rd issue of the month. All additional features with substantial statistical content are described, as they appear, under "Statistical Features;" page locations and latest periods of coverage for other recurring tables are also noted. Nonstatistical features and issues are not covered.

Beginning with the Mar. 4, 1985 issue, publication is described in SRI under C6240-1.

Availability: Ziff-Davis Publishing Co., Business Publications Division, 1156 15th St., NW, Washington DC 20005, $210.00 per yr., $125.00 per 6 months; SRI/MF/excerpts for monthly table and all portions covered under "Statistical Features;" shipped quarterly.

Issues reviewed during 1985: Nov. 5, 1984-Feb. 25, 1985 (P) (Vol. 39, Nos. 19-27; Vol. 40, Nos. 1-8).

RECURRING TABLES:

MONTHLY TABLE

[1] Business/personal aircraft industry unit shipments [by model, for each of approximately 20 manufacturers, for month prior to cover date and calendar year to date, with 3-year trends by manufacturer, and some manufacturers' exports and/or net billings for current month].

OTHER RECURRING TABLES

[Month of coverage is 2-3 months prior to cover date.]

[1] Regional commuter carriers traffic [passengers, load factor, revenue passenger miles, and available seat miles, by commuter airline, for month of coverage].

[2] Airport and Airway Trust Fund status [balance, receipts by source, expenditures by function, assets, liabilities, and equity, for month of coverage and fiscal year to date; data are from U.S. Treasury Dept].

STATISTICAL FEATURES:

C9700–3.601: Nov. 5, 1984 (Vol. 39, No. 19)

RECURRING TABLE

[2] Airport and Airway Trust Fund status, Aug. 31, 1984. (p. 151, 151a)

C9700–3.602: Dec. 10, 1984 (Vol. 39, No. 24)

RECURRING TABLE

[2] Airport and Airway Trust Fund status, Sept. 30, 1984. (p. 189, 189a)

C9700–3.603: Jan. 7, 1985 (Vol. 40, No. 1)

FY85 BUDGET TAGS $4.8 BILLION FOR HELO PROGRAMS

(p. 3-3a) Brief article, with 1 table showing DOD appropriations for helicopter-related programs, by system and/or purpose (procurement, modifications, and R&D), by manufacturer and military service branch, FY85.

C9700–3.604: Jan. 14, 1985 (Vol. 40, No. 2)

RECURRING TABLE

[2] Airport and Airway Trust Fund status, Oct. 31, 1984. (p. 15a)

C9700–3.605: Jan. 21, 1985 (Vol. 40, No. 3)

FORECAST CALLS FOR STRONG REGIONAL CARRIER GROWTH THROUGH 1995

(p. 18a-19a, 20a) Article, with 3 charts showing passenger traffic and revenue passenger miles on all and propeller aircraft, 1995; and number of propeller aircraft by seating capacity, 1983 and 1995; all for U.S. regional airlines. Data are from de Havilland Aircraft of Canada and FAA.

C9700–3.606: Jan. 28, 1985 (Vol. 40, No. 4)

GENERAL AVIATION MANUFACTURERS ASSOCIATION

(p. 30-30a, 31a) Brief article, with 1 chart and 1 table showing shipment volume and value for general aviation aircraft, 1972-84, with detail by engine type (single- and multi-engine, turboprop, and jet), 1984. Data are from General Aviation Manufacturers Assn.

C9700–3.607: Feb. 11, 1985 (Vol. 40, No. 6)

RECURRING TABLE

[2] Airport and Airway Trust Fund status, Nov. 30, 1984. (p. 48a)

R2110
American Enterprise Institute for Public Policy Research

R2110-1 PUBLIC OPINION

Bimonthly. Approx. 60 p.
ISSN 0149-9157.
LC 78-642154.
SRI/MF/excerpts

Bimonthly journal reporting results of recent public opinion surveys conducted by major polling organizations on U.S. and foreign attitudes toward current social, political, and economic issues.

Issues generally contain original articles, occasionally with substantial statistics; and an "Opinion Roundup" section with current opinion data from the Roper Organization, Gallup Organization, and other polling organizations.

Bimonthly "Opinion Roundup" and all additional features containing substantial, specifically identified survey or other data are described, as they appear, under "Statistical Features." Nonstatistical features are not covered.

A special compilation of *Public Opinion* articles concerning the role of media in the 1984 elections has also been published in 1985 and is available from the issuing agency, but is not covered in SRI.

Availability: American Enterprise Institute for Public Policy Research, Public Opinion, Circulation Department, 1150 17th St., NW, Washington DC 20036-9964, $26.00 per yr., single copy $5.00; SRI/MF/excerpts for all portions described under "Statistical Features."

Issues reviewed during 1985: Oct./Nov. 1984-Aug./Sept. 1985 (P) (Vol. 7, Nos. 5-6; Vol. 8, Nos. 1-4).

STATISTICAL FEATURES:

R2110-1.601: Oct./Nov. 1984 (Vol. 7, No. 5)

RECENT FABLES ABOUT RONALD REAGAN

(p. 6-9) By William C. Adams. Article, with 1 table showing public approval of President Reagan and his policies, various months 1982-84. Data are from ABC News/*Washington Post* surveys.

AMERICAN ATTITUDES TOWARD RACE RELATIONS

(p. 14-15, 50-53) By Tom W. Smith and Paul B. Sheatsley. Article on trends in public attitudes toward racial integration. Data are from surveys conducted by the National Opinion Research Center and other private organizations.

Includes 12 tables showing percent of white respondents approving of racial integration in schools and neighborhoods, and equal employment opportunities; indexes of overall racial tolerance among whites, by region (North and South), religious affiliation, education, income level, age, and urban-rural status; support among whites for Federal aid to blacks and all minorities; and support for busing among blacks/whites; various years 1942-84.

MITTERAND AT MIDPOINT

(p. 16, 41) By Everett Carll Ladd. Article on French public opinion concerning the Socialist government, and future voting intentions. Data are from a June 17, 1984 survey of 7,500 voters conducted by Brule Ville Associes.

Includes 1 table showing voting intentions in the next legislative election, by political party, cross-tabulated by voter sex, age, occupation, and vote cast in the last presidential election.

OPINION ROUNDUP

(p. 17-40) Compilation of 67 charts and 2 tables presenting results of recent public opinion surveys by major U.S. and French polling organizations. Data are generally from surveys conducted during the 1980s. Data on ethnic groups and attitudes are shown for total U.S. and by detailed race/ethnic group. Topics include the following:

a. U.S. ethnic group profiles, including whether born in U.S. or abroad; personal and father's education; occupational group; family income; census region of residence; number of children; religious affiliation; socioeconomic category; whether language other than English is spoken at home, by age group (under and over 18); political party affiliation and ideology; and satisfaction with life, marriage, and family financial situation.

b. U.S. ethnic group attitudes: approval of violence in certain situations; alcohol use; trustworthiness of others; belief in life after death; importance of work; Federal Government responsibility for national problems, poverty relief, improving blacks' standard of living, and assisting with medical costs; appropriateness of Federal income tax level; position on social issues, including gun control, death penalty, abortion, and premarital sex; and agreement with various statements on social structure and opportunity in the U.S.

c. French public opinion on the Socialist government; President Mitterand; potential presidential candidates; best political party for the legislature; Prime Minister Fabius; Communist ministers' departure from Mitterand's government; amount of power held by government, labor unions, and corporate directors; government structure; best Fifth Republic president; responsibility for educating children; and public and private schools; with selected detail by political party.

d. Political preferences for 1984 presidential candidates.

GENERALLY SPEAKING: SURVEYING THE MILITARY'S TOP BRASS

(p. 42-45) By Andrew Kohut and Nicholas Horrock. Article on opinions and attitudes of top military officers. Data are based on a June 1984 survey of 257 generals and admirals from the 4 branches of the military, conducted by Gallup Organization for *Newsweek*.

Includes 1 table showing percent of respondents holding aggressive, cautious, and mixed attitudes toward nuclear war and the justifiability of a 1st strike, with detail by age group (under and over 50), rank, military branch, whether graduate of service academy, political ideology, and career satisfaction.

BRITAIN EVALUATES RONALD REAGAN

(p. 46-49) By Ivor Crewe. Article on UK public opinion of the U.S. and its Presidents. Data are from surveys conducted by Social Surveys (Gallup Poll) Limited.

Includes 3 tables showing response distributions concerning presidential performance of Carter and Reagan; U.S. world standing, peace, and U.S.-UK relations as affected by elections of Nixon, Carter, and Reagan; and confidence in ability of U.S. to deal with world problems under past 4 Presidents; various periods 1970-84.

R2110-1.602: Dec. 1984/Jan. 1985 (Vol. 7, No. 6)

AS THE REALIGNMENT TURNS: A DRAMA IN MANY ACTS

(p. 2-7) By Everett Carll Ladd. Article analyzing political implications of the 1984 presidential election. Data sources include the National Opinion Research Center.

Includes 2 tables showing percent of voters identifying themselves as Democrats, Republicans, or Independents, by age group, 1983/84; and campaign receipts (total and from political action committees) of Democratic vs. Republican incumbents, challengers, and open-seat candidates for U.S. House of Representatives, Jan. 1, 1983-Oct. 17, 1984.

REFERENDUMS AND INITIATIVES 1984

(p. 15-17) By Austin Ranney. Article, with 1 extended table showing voter turnout and election results for 1984 State referenda on various social and governmental issues, including political reforms, gambling, lotteries, fiscal measures, environment, hospital cost regulation, shelter for the homeless, civil liberties/rights, and nuclear weapons freeze, all shown by State.

OPINION ROUNDUP

(p. 23-42) Compilation of 112 charts and 9 tables presenting election results, and results of public opinion surveys conducted by major polling organizations, 1984 with trends from 1932. Data by party are for Democratic and Republican, unless otherwise noted. Topics include the following:

a. Election results for presidential and congressional elections, including for individual Senate candidates; voter turnout; total, women, and black U.S. Representatives and Senators, and Governors and State legislators; party control of State legislatures, by census region; and number of States with Governor and legislature of same party; generally by party.

b. Voters: timing of voting decisions; prevalence of ticket splitting; and party of chosen candidate, and own party identification, by voter characteristics including sex, race/ethnicity, region, income, age, education, religion, occupation, and labor union membership.

c. Issues: perceived change in U.S. economy, by income; index of public satisfaction with personal/national situation; capabilities of presidential candidates; support for legal abortion and constitutional amendment banning abortion; and attitudes toward Republican and Democratic parties, including party perceived better for peace and prosperity.

d. Chosen candidate, by voter race (including Hispanic), income, and sex, for U.S. Senate elections in 4 southern States; and factors influencing presidential voting decision.

GENERAL ELECTION COVERAGE: PART I

(p. 49-54, 59) By Maura Clancey and Michael J. Robinson. Article analyzing TV coverage of the 1984 presidential election. Data are from a study of 790 TV news items broadcast Sept.-Nov. 1984.

Includes 2 charts and 2 tables showing time spent on favorable and unfavorable items concerning Reagan, Mondale, Bush, and Ferraro; ranking of 29 journalists and 3 networks by proportion of unfavorable vs. favorable new items about the campaign; and top 20 campaign issues ranked by number of news items reported.

R2110–1.603: Feb./Mar. 1985 (Vol. 8, No. 1)

TAX ATTITUDES

(p. 8-10) By Everett Carll Ladd. Article, with 2 tables showing tax burdens for average and upper income families, 1953, 1966, and 1980; and public opinion concerning effectiveness of selected methods IRS can use to reduce tax nonpayment.

Data are from Advisory Commission on Intergovernmental Relations, and a May-July 1984 survey conducted for the IRS by Yankelovich, Skelly, and White.

TAX ETHICS: SOCIAL VALUES AND NONCOMPLIANCE

(p. 11-14) By Madelyn Hochstein. Article, with 1 table showing percent of taxpayers who admit cheating on income taxes, by level of acceptance of tax deception. Data are based on a May-July 1984 survey of 2,200 taxpayers age 18/over, conducted for the IRS by Yankelovich, Skelly, and White.

OPINION ROUNDUP

(p. 19-42) Compilation of 117 charts and 9 tables presenting results of recent public opinion and population surveys conducted by various private and government organizations. Unless otherwise noted, data are from surveys conducted during the 1980s, with trends from the 1970s. Some data also include selected breakdowns by respondent socioeconomic characteristics. Topics include the following:

a. Budget of U.S.: support for spending cuts by program; approval of defense budget and spending level; preferred methods of reducing deficit; support for constitutional amendment requiring balanced budget; perceived government waste and responsibilities; and appropriateness of 1985 budget.

b. Taxation: most serious threats to national and personal economies; satisfaction with taxes paid and tax system, including fairness of corporate taxation; type of tax considered worst; approval and prevalence of various methods of tax deception, and punishments IRS should impose; use of tax forms and preparation assistance; and perceived IRS auditing practices.

c. Tax reform: willingness to forfeit tax cuts and accept tax increase to balance Federal budget, including types of taxes preferred for increases; whether Reagan is responsible for budget deficit; awareness and approval of flat tax rate proposals; and acceptance and use of selected income tax deductions and exemptions.

d. Elderly population share; life expectancy, for elderly and by sex; average social security benefits; Federal spending for elderly; and selected population characteristics including poverty and suicide rates, educational attainment, marital status, socioeconomic status, whether mother worked outside the home, household size, and church attendance, shown for elderly or by age group; various periods 1950-84, with population and life expectancy trends from early 1900s and population projection to 2030.

e. Generational differences in selected attitudes, including personal satisfaction, income adequacy and concerns, health condition, civil rights, abortion, pornography, communism, interracial relations, government assistance, social class structure, personal achievement, trustworthiness of others, women's employment in selected occupations, cohabitation without marriage, discrimination, violence, and outlook for next generation.

MEDIA IN CAMPAIGN '84: PART II, WINGLESS, TOOTHLESS, AND HOPELESS

(p. 43-48) By Michael J. Robinson. Article analyzing TV coverage of presidential candidates during the 1984 election. Data are from Patrick Caddell and Cambridge Survey Associates. Includes 1 table measuring TV broadcasting references to Reagan's abilities and reelection potential, weekly Sept.-1st week Nov. 1984.

URBAN BLIGHT: THE DEMOCRATS' ERODING METROPOLITAN BASE

(p. 49-51) By James A. Barnes and John C. Weicher. Article, with 2 tables showing share of votes cast for Democratic and Republican presidential candidates in the 25 largest metro areas, 1976, 1980, and 1984; and top 25 metro areas' share of all votes cast, arranged by State, 1984. Data are from Census Bureau, Elections Research Center, and other sources.

STATE ELECTIONS: WHAT 1984 MEANS FOR 1986

(p. 52-55) By John F. Bibby. Article on effect of 1984 election on political party composition of governorships and State legislatures. Data are from National Conference of State Legislatures and other sources.

Includes 3 tables showing the following for Democratic and Republican Parties: number of governorships held and legislatures controlled before and after 1984 election; governorships up for election, incumbents reelected and defeated, and open seats won, 1984; and correlation between President's party and party control, 1950-84 period.

R2110–1.604: June/July 1985 (Vol. 8, No. 3)

HARD TIMES: THE PUBLIC ON POVERTY

(p. 2-7, 59-60) By I. A. Lewis and William Schneider. Article presenting public opinion on poverty issues. Data are based on 2,444 responses to a *Los Angeles Times* survey conducted Apr. 20-25, 1985.

Includes text statistics; and 1 extended table showing distribution of responses by race, sex, and poverty status, to detailed questions concerning causes of poverty, conditions and characteristics of poor persons, welfare and anti-poverty programs, responsibility for solving poverty problem, and related topics.

FOLLOWING THE LEADERS: HOW RONALD REAGAN AND MARGARET THATCHER HAVE CHANGED PUBLIC OPINION

(p. 16-19, 55-58) By David R. Gergen and Anthony King. Compilation of 2 articles examining political opinion in U.S. and UK. Data are from surveys conducted by major U.S. polling organizations, and Social Surveys (Gallup Poll) Limited.

Includes 9 tables showing distribution of responses to questions on the following topics, various months 1947-85:

a. U.S.: political ideology; trust in Government; reduction in spending for social programs; level of spending for military/defense programs; and military strength of U.S. vs. USSR.

b. UK: Government focus on inflation vs. unemployment, on opportunities for self-advancement vs. guaranteed job/standard of living, and on tax reductions vs. Government services.

OPINION ROUNDUP

(p. 21-40) Compilation of 72 charts and 13 tables presenting results of recent public opinion surveys conducted during the 1980s by major polling organizations. Some data also include selected breakdowns by respondent socioeconomic characteristics. Topics include the following:

a. President Reagan performance and approval ratings, with detail for selected States.

b. Poverty: attitudes concerning poverty, including trend in level of poverty, Government responsibility for poor, reasons for poverty, effects of welfare benefits, poverty solutions and programs, welfare fraud, poverty outlook, level of government responsible for various essential services, political party best for protecting poor, President Reagan's impact on poverty, and other topics.

c. Defense: U.S. vs. USSR military and nuclear superiority; future importance of military strength; nuclear inequality vs. arms race as greater threat to peace; whether USSR would adhere to future arms agreements; impact of Reagan administration and Republican vs. Democratic congress on defense; impact of defense spending cuts on national security; and military spending level.

d. School prayer: approval of religious observances in schools; and support for constitutional amendments permitting organized and voluntary prayer in schools.

e. Death penalty: support for death penalty or life imprisonment for convicted murderers; whether blacks and poor are more likely to receive death penalty; whether death penalty is a deterrent for murder, and public support as affected by hypothetical evidence showing death penalty is and is not a deterrent; and form of execution perceived as most humane.

f. Social behaviors and products perceived as in and out of fashion.

COMPARING CHIEF EXECUTIVES

(p. 50-51, 54) By George C. Edwards. Article on public approval of President Reagan during his 1st term of office. Data are from surveys conducted by CBS News/*New York Times* and other polling organizations.

Includes 3 tables showing average approval rating of Reagan during 1st term, by respondent socioeconomic characteristics; share of vote, and approval rating in 1st post-inaugural poll, for Reagan vs. 5 preceding Presidents; and Reagan approval ratings, various months Jan. 1980-81.

LIFE QUALITY INDEX

(p. 52-53) By Gordon S. Black. Article on Life Quality Index (LQI), a measure of satisfaction with job/financial security, health, marriage/family, environment/safety, and social life. Data are based on 1,504 responses to a recent survey conducted for *USA Today*.

Includes 2 undated tables showing LQI, by component and respondent socioeconomic characteristics; and LQI scores associated with 28 life events.

R2110–1.605: Aug./Sept. 1985 (Vol. 8, No. 4)

VIEWS ON THE NEWS

(p. 6-11, 58-59) By William Schneider and I. A. Lewis. Article examining the attitudes of journalists as compared to the general public, and public opinion on news media. Data are based on 1985 surveys of 2,993 members of the general public and 2,703 newspaper journalists, conducted by *Los Angeles Times;* and a Dec. 1984-Jan. 1985 newspaper credibility survey conducted by MORI Research, Inc.

Includes 7 tables showing survey responses for public and journalists regarding the following topics:

a. Political ideology, support for President Reagan, and stand on selected economic, foreign affairs, and social issues, including own view vs. perceived view of newspaper read, with comparison to opinions of college-educated professionals; and ratings of performance and quality of local newspaper, local and network TV news, and news media in general, with selected detail for public by educational attainment.

b. Journalism's ethics and handling of power; support for selected government and legal controls over the press; news media fairness in treatment of government, church, and business activities, and of Presidents Reagan and Carter; and quality and public role of news media vs. selected other societal institutions.

AMERICANS TAKE STOCK OF BUSINESS

(p. 12-15) By Burns W. Roper and Thomas A. W. Miller. Article on public attitudes toward business. Data are based on 1985 surveys conducted by the Roper Organization.

Includes 1 chart and 3 tables showing survey responses regarding favorable attitudes toward selected societal institutions, and toward large and small business, with selected trends from 1978; government regulation of business, including impact on product safety, prices, and pollution; and appropriateness of court decisions made in recent criminal cases, including fine imposed on E. F. Hutton Corp. for fraud.

HEALING THE HEALTH CARE SYSTEM

(p. 16-20, 60) By Humphrey Taylor. Article discussing developments in health care provision, and public attitudes toward the health care system. Data are from surveys of the public, and of corporate benefit officers and employees, conducted by Louis Harris and Associates.

Includes 2 charts and 6 tables showing survey responses regarding public use of physicians, by race and income level; low-income and other persons covered by 3rd-party medical insurance; performance of overall health care system; recent changes in corporate health plans, with perceived effectiveness and employee acceptance; attitude concerning euthanasia for the terminally ill; use of cigarettes, by sex; and support for treatment vs. preventive health care emphasis; primarily 1984 or 1985, with selected trends from 1970s or earlier.

OPINION ROUNDUP

(p. 21-40) Compilation of 80 charts and 3 tables presenting results of public opinion surveys conducted by major polling organizations during the 1980s, with selected trends from as early as the 1950s. Data are shown for the U.S. public, unless otherwise noted. Topics include the following:

a. Quality of life: perceived national condition and outlook; indexes of consumer sentiment and confidence; satisfaction with personal life and marriage; current vs. past level of opportunity offered by society; and past, current, and expected future condition of personal life.

b. South Africa: attitudes toward South African government, apartheid, and U.S.-South African relations; awareness of events in South Africa; support for U.S. pressure on South African government to abandon apartheid, including preferred methods for encouraging change; and role of U.S. business investments in South African society; all shown separately for total and black respondents.

c. Tax reform proposal of Reagan Administration: support for proposal, and for specific changes in deductions; expected effect on own taxes, and benefits for selected population groups; perceived fairness and simplicity; importance of selected tax reform goals; and political party perceived best for making taxes fair and holding down level of taxes.

d. Space-based defense system (strategic defense initiative): support for development, including agreement with selected arguments used for and against system.

e. Pakistani public opinion on foreign relations issues, including recognition of current government in Afghanistan, support for Afghan refugees, aid agreements with U.S., U.S. vs. USSR superiority, and war with India.

f. West German public opinion on foreign relations issues and U.S., including attitudes toward President Reagan and his visit to Germany, moral superiority of U.S. vs. USSR foreign policy, alliances with other nations, and disarmament.

g. South African public opinion on government and apartheid, including support for and impact of economic sanctions by other nations, support for President Botha's reform proposals, possibility of interracial joint government, justifiability of violence over apartheid, whether dispute over government will end in civil war, release of imprisoned black leader Nelson Mandela, and acceptance of interracial marriage in own family, mostly shown separately for black and white respondents.

WHO SPEAKS FOR BLACK AMERICA?

(p. 41-44, 58) By Linda S. Lichter. Article on attitudes of black civil leaders vs. general black public. Data are based on telephone surveys of 105 leaders of black civil rights organizations and 600 black members of the general public, conducted May-July 1985 by Lawrence Johnson and Associates and Metro Research Services, Inc.

Includes 1 table showing black leader and/or public survey responses regarding selected social and political issues, including racial discrimination, interracial marriage, preferential treatment for minorities, political party interest in helping blacks, President Reagan's performance, role of U.S. corporations in South Africa, and other race-related issues; and membership in civil rights organizations, and representativeness and role of black leaders.

WHAT'S BIG ON CAMPUS

(p. 49-53) By Terry W. Hartle and John Taylor. Article discussing trends in political attitudes of college students. Data are based on surveys conducted by Gallup Organization, NBC News, and University of California for American Council on Education.

Includes 5 tables showing survey responses regarding presidential candidate support during last 4 elections, by age group; political ideology; future career field; and agreement with liberal and conservative views on selected social and political issues; various years 1970-84.

POLITICAL WOMAN: GENDER INDIFFERENCE

(p. 54-56) By Harmon Zeigler and Keith Poole. Article, with 3 tables showing women's attitudes toward the role of women in society (equal to men vs. more traditional place in home), shown separately for employed women and housewives, with detail by educational attainment and for supporters of President Reagan, biennially 1972-84 or 1984.

Data are from University of Michigan national election surveys.

R2110–5 VITAL STATISTICS ON CONGRESS, 1984-85 Edition

Biennial. 1984. xxiii+262 p.
AEI Studies 410.
ISBN 0-8447-3560-4 (cloth).
ISBN 0-8447-3564-7 (pbk.).
LC 84-20401.
SRI/MF/complete

Biennial compilation of statistics, by Norman J. Ornstein et al., on the U.S. House of Representatives and Senate, primarily 1950s-83 with trends from as early as 1855. Includes data on membership, elections, campaign finances, committees, staff, operating expenses, workload, appropriations, and voting.

Most data are shown for each chamber, often with detail by political party.

Data are from a variety of specified sources including congressional reports, Federal Election Commission, and Congressional Quarterly, Inc., publications.

Contains listing of contents/tables/charts, and foreword (p. vii-xxii); 8 statistical sections, each with narrative introduction, 16 summary charts, and 109 tables listed below (p. 1-197); and appendix on individual members, with 4 detailed tables also listed below (p. 198-261).

Previous report, for 1981, is described in SRI 1983 Annual, under this number.

Availability: American Enterprise Institute for Public Policy Research, Publications, 1150 17th St., NW, Washington DC 20036-9964, $19.95 (cloth), $9.95 (pbk.); SRI/MF/complete.

TABLES:

[Tables show data for selected periods within the ranges noted. Data by party are shown for Democratic and Republican Parties.]

R2110–5.1: Members

[Data are shown for House and Senate, unless otherwise noted.]

1.1. Apportionment of [House] seats, by region and State, 1910-80. (p. 7-8)

1.2-1.5. Democratic Party strength [and number of seats, by party], by region, 1924-82. (p. 10-17)

1.6-1.7. [Number of members, by length of service, 83rd-98th Congresses], 1953-83. (p. 18-20)

1.8-1.13. Prior occupations of [members, by party], 83rd-98th Congresses, 1953-83. (p. 21-27)

1.14-1.15. Religious affiliations of [members, by party], 88th-98th Congresses, 1963-83. (p. 28-29)

1.16. Blacks in Congress [by party], 41st-98th Congresses, 1869-1983. (p. 30)

1.17. Women in Congress [by party], 65th-98th Congresses, 1917-1983. (p. 31)

1.18. [Number of Democratic, Republican, other, and vacant seats], 34th-98th Congresses, 1855-1985. (p. 32-35)

R2110–5.2: Elections

2.1. Turnout in presidential and House elections, 1930-82 (percent of voting age population). (p. 40)

2.2. Popular vote and House seats won, by party, 1946-82. (p. 41-42)

2.3. Net party gains in House and Senate seats, general and special elections, 1946-82. (p. 43)

2.4. [House and Senate] losses by President's party in midterm elections, 1862-1982. (p. 44)

2.5-2.6. House and Senate seats that changed party [for incumbent losses and open seats, by party], 1954-82. (p. 45-47)

2.7-2.8. House and Senate incumbents reelected, defeated [in primary and general elections], or retired, 1946-82. (p. 49-51)

2.9. House and Senate retirements, by party, 1930-82. (p. 52)

2.10. House elections won by [incumbents with at least] 60% [of the vote], 1956-82. (p. 53)

2.11. Senate elections won by [incumbents with at least] 60% [of the vote, for total U.S., North, and South], 1944-82. (p. 54)

2.12. Marginal races among [House and Senate] members of the 98th Congress [number ever winning with 60% and 55% and less], 1982. (p. 54)

2.13. Means of election to the [House and Senate among members of the] 98th Congress [by party], 1982. (p. 55)

2.14. Ticket splitting between presidential and House candidates [number of districts with split results], 1900-80. (p. 56)

2.15. [Congressional] district voting for President [number of districts carried by President, and districts where President ran ahead of and behind his party's House candidate], 1952-80. (p. 57)

2.16. Shifts in Democratic vote in congressional districts, 1956-80. (p. 57)

2.17. Party-line [voters, defectors, and pure independents] in presidential [Senate and House] elections, 1956-82 (as a percentage of all voters). (p. 58-59)

R2110–5.3: Campaign Finance

[Data by type of political action committee (PAC) include corporate, labor, trade/membership/health, nonconnected, cooperative, and corporation without stock.]

3.1-3.4. House and Senate campaign expenditures [total, and mean expenditures by party, for all candidates, incumbents, challengers, and open seats]; and House candidates who spent more than $200,000 and $500,000, by party; 1974-82. (p. 65-70)

3.5-3.6. [Mean] campaign expenditures of House and Senate incumbents and challengers [by party], by election outcome, 1974-82. (p. 71-77)

3.7. Funding sources [percent from nonparty PACs, party, individuals, and other] for [House and Senate] candidates in general elections, by party, 1974-82. (p. 78-79)

3.8 Campaign funding sources for general election candidates in House and Senate elections [by party for incumbents, challengers, and open seats, by PAC type], 1982. (p. 80-81)

3.9. Political party financial activity [receipts, disbursements, and contributions to and expenditures for candidates, by party and party organizational unit], 1976-82. (p. 82-83)

3.10. Party contributions and coordinated expenditures [for Senate and House candidates], by party, 1976-82. (p. 84)

3.11. Number of registered PACs [by type], 1974-82. (p. 86)

3.12-3.14. Financial activity of PACs [includes receipts]; and adjusted expenditures of PACs and contributions to congressional candidates [by PAC type], 1972-82. (p. 87-90)

3.15. Types of PACs contributing to presidential, Senate, and House campaigns [with number of PACS contributing, by PAC type, 1978, 1980, and 1982]. (p. 91)

3.16-3.21. PAC contributions to House and Senate candidates [by PAC type, with distribution by incumbent, challenger, and open seat candidates, by party], 1977/78, 1979/80, and 1981/82. (p. 92-97)

3.22-3.23. [Mean] PAC and total receipts of House and Senate incumbents and challengers, by election outcome [incumbent winning with more or less than 60%, or defeated; with number of candidates], 1982. (p. 98-99)

3.24-3.26. Timing of PAC and non-PAC contributions to congressional election campaigns [by PAC type and for all other contributors], 1977/78, 1979/80, and 1981/82. (p. 100-102)

3.27. Independent expenditures in House, Senate, and presidential election campaigns [for and against Democrats and Republicans], 1977-82. (p. 103)

R2110–5.4: Committees, Staff, and Operating Expenses

COMMITTEES

[Data range for tables 4.1-4.7 is 1955-84 (84th-98th Congresses), with data shown for House and Senate.]

4.1-4.3. Number and type of committees [and subcommittees]. (p. 108-110)

4.4-4.5. [Mean number of] assignments [to standing committees, subcommittees of standing committees, and other]. (p. 111)

4.6-4.7. Majority party [members and number chairing all and standing committees/subcommittees; House majority members with 2 or more chairmanships; and average number of committees chaired by Senate majority members]. (p. 112-113)

4.8. Southern chairmanships of standing committees [and southerners as percent of majority membership], 1955-83. (p. 114)

4.9. [Total and] closed committee meetings, 1953-75. (p. 115)

STAFF AND EXPENSES

5.1. Congressional staff [for House and Senate, by general assignment, joint committees, and support agencies, 1979, 1981, and 1983]. (p. 120)

5.2. Staffs of members of the House and the Senate, 1891-1983. (p. 121)

5.3-5.4. House and Senate staff based in [home] offices, 1970s-83. (p. 123)

5.5. Staffs of House and Senate standing committees, 1891-1983. (p. 124)

5.6-5.7. Staffs of [individual] House and Senate standing committees, 1947-83. (p. 125-126)

5.8. Staffs of congressional support agencies, 1946-83. (p. 127)

5.9-5.10. Legislative branch appropriations: and the CPI, 1946-84; and by category [Senate, House, joint items, and support agencies], 1980-84. (p. 128-130)

5.11-5.13. Costs of official mail, 1971-84; and allowances for Representatives and Senators [by item], 1970-83. (p. 131-135)

R2110-5.5: Workload and Appropriations

WORKLOAD

[Date range for tables 6.1-6.4 is 1947-83 (80th-98th Congresses).]

6.1-6.2. House and Senate workload [bills introduced and passed, time in session, and committee/subcommittee meetings]. (p. 143-146)

6.3. Recorded votes in the House and Senate. (p. 148)

6.4. Congressional workload [number and pages of public and private bills enacted]. (p. 150)

6.5. Pages in the *Federal Register,* 1936-83. (p. 151)

6.6. Congressional mailings, FY54-83. (p. 152)

APPROPRIATIONS

7.1-7.2. House and Senate votes on adoption of budget resolutions, by party, FY76-84. (p. 158-159)

7.3. Budgeted and actual revenues, budget authority, outlays, and deficits, FY76-83. (p. 160-161)

7.4. Relatively uncontrollable Federal outlays under present law, FY67-84. (p. 162-163)

7.5 President's budget requests and congressional appropriations, 1968-82. (p. 164)

7.6. Supplemental appropriations [bills, and amount of budget authority], FY64-83. (p. 165)

7.7. House [total and adopted] amendments to appropriation bills, 1963-82. (p. 166)

7.8. Continuing appropriations, FY72-84. (p. 167)

7.9-7.10. Budget-related roll call votes in the House and Senate [by measure], 1955-82. (p. 168)

7.11. Rescissions and deferrals [number and amount], FY75-84. (p. 169-170)

R2110-5.6: Voting Patterns and Appendix

VOTING

[Data are shown for House and Senate.]

8.1. Presidential victories on votes, 1953-83. (p. 177-178)

8.2. Voting in support of the President's position [for all and southern Democrats, and Republicans], 1954-83. (p. 180-181)

8.3. Party unity/polarization in voting, 1953-83 (percentage of all votes). (p. 182)

8.4. Party support/unity in voting [from all and southern Democrats, and Republicans], 1954-83. (p. 183)

8.5-8.6. Conservative coalition votes and victories; and voting in support of the conservative coalition [for northern and southern Democrats, and Republicans]; 1957-83. (p. 185-186)

8.7-8.8. Committee support of the conservative coalition [by party and individual committee], 1959-83. (p. 187-195)

APPENDIX

A1-A4. House of Representatives and Senate, 1982-83 [97th-98th Congresses, showing the following for each member, arranged by State: party, years of service, age, percent of vote in most recent primary and general elections, and voting ratings from Americans for Democratic Action, Americans for Constitutional Action, and others]. (p. 199-261)

R2110-6   CHANGING UTILIZATION OF FIXED CAPITAL: An Element in Long-Term Growth

Monograph. 1984.
xv+128 p.
AEI Studies No. 407.
ISBN 0-8447-3559-0.
LC 84-9206.
SRI/MF/complete

By Murray F. Foss. Report analyzing trends in weekly hours of operation for fixed capital in manufacturing and nonmanufacturing industries, 1929-76.

Includes number or index of weekly hours, by industry division, by manufacturing industry group, and for coal and metal mining, general merchandise/apparel/furniture stores, and self-employed persons in retail trade (by kind of business).

Also includes percent of manufacturing production workers on late shifts by census region, late-shift wage differentials, and other shiftwork trends; manufacturing work hours and shifts, by value added classification; and single-unit firms' share of manufacturing value added, retail sales, and total manufacturing and retail firms.

Also includes data on value and/or hours of use for computers and other office equipment in the private sector, and for owned and leased computers in the Federal Government and in State/local governments.

Most data are derived by the author, and are based on published and unpublished Federal sources and on scholarly articles.

Contains listings of contents, tables, and charts (p. iii-viii); foreword and preface (p. ix-xv); 5 chapters, with narrative analysis, text data, and 52 tables (p. 1-108); and appendices, including text data, 1 chart, and 4 tables (p. 109-128).

Report is a sequel to *Changes in the Workweek of Fixed Capital: U.S. Manufacturing, 1929 to 1976,* covered in SRI 1982 Annual under R2110-3.

Availability: American Enterprise Institute for Public Policy Research, Publications, 1150 17th St., NW, Washington DC 20036, $14.95; SRI/MF/complete.

R2110-7   WEST BANK DATA PROJECT: A Survey of Israel's Policies

Monograph. 1984. xi+97 p.
ISBN 0-8447-3545-0 (cloth).
ISBN 0-8447-3544-2 (pbk.).
LC 84-2984.
SRI/MF/complete

By Meron Benvenisti. Report examining sociodemographic structure and planned development of the Israel-occupied West Bank territory, 1920s-80s, with selected projections to 2010. Includes data on population, land use, housing, settlement plans, and capital investments, with comparisons to the Gaza Strip, Tel Aviv, Jerusalem, and other areas.

Data are from Israeli government agencies, World Zionist Organization, and other specified sources.

Contains listings of contents, tables, and maps, and foreword and preface (p. iii-x); narrative report, in 7 sections, interspersed with 30 tables described below (p. 1-69); and 13 maps (p. 71-97).

Availability: American Enterprise Institute for Public Policy Research, Publications, 1150 17th St., NW, Washington DC 20036-9964, $25.00 (cloth), $15.00 (pbk.); SRI/MF/complete.

TABLES:

[Unless otherwise noted, data are shown for the West Bank, with selected detail by region. Data by ethnic group are shown for Jewish and Arab populations.]

a. Population, average annual growth rate of Arab population, and net migration, with comparisons to Gaza Strip and Israel, various years 1922-82. Tables 1-3. (p. 2-4)

b. Land (irrigated and rain-fed) used for agriculture, with detail by crop; land area designated for industrial development; existing and planned land use, by function and ethnic group; and public and private construction starts and completions, and apartments built; with comparisons to Gaza Strip, various periods 1966-83 and industrial development projections to 2010. Tables 4-11. (p. 13-22)

c. Housing units, families, and settlements, by settlement type (urban, rural/semiurban, and paramilitary), 1982; and settlement expenditures of World Zionist Organization, 1974-83. Tables 12-14. (p. 50-51)

d. Matei Binyamin region population characteristics, including distribution of household heads by location of employment, and distribution of resident and nonresident workers by industry sector, 1982; and families and single persons in 2 Central Massif settlements, selected years 1968-83. Tables 15-18. (p. 53-54)

e. Capital investment value and projects, by type; number and cost of housing units built, by type of settlement (urban, communal, and rural); and investment in water resource development in Jordan Valley and Judea/Samaria; various periods 1968-86. Tables 19-22. (p. 55-56)

f. Urban population, and net migration, for Tel Aviv and surrounding communities; investment and number of persons/units involved in settlement plans for Rift, Massif, and metro areas, by type of project; existing and planned settlements, and population by ethnic group, for Jerusalem and Tel Aviv metro areas; and Jewish population; various periods 1961-91. Tables 23-30. (p. 57-62)

R2800
American Productivity Center

R2800-1 MULTIPLE INPUT PRODUCTIVITY INDEXES
Quarterly.
ISSN 0741-6490.
SRI/MF/complete

Quarterly report, tracking quarterly and annual productivity changes for major sectors of the private economy and for industry groups. Data are current to 2 quarters or 1-2 years prior to cover date, and include trends from 1948.

Report focuses on the multiple input productivity index, which relates weighted labor and capital inputs to price adjusted value-added output.

Indexes are computed from BLS and Bureau of Economic Affairs data, and are updated according to latest benchmark revisions. Indexes are based on 1977 reference year.

Issues generally contain a summary of recent productivity developments; and all or some of the following recurring data, which are continuously revised and updated:

a. Productivity change rates: average annual rate of change in indexes and index components, by economic sector, sometimes with detail by industry, selected periods 1948-current year.

b. Productivity indexes: total factor, labor, capital, and capital/labor ratio indexes, by economic sector; shown for current quarter and 4-7 prior quarters.

c. Productivity levels: labor productivity (real output per hour) in 1972 constant dollars, by economic sector, selected years 1948-current year.

Data by economic sector usually are shown for private business economy, goods producing and service producing sectors, farming, manufacturing and nonmanufacturing industry, and nonfinancial corporate business. Data by industry are shown by industry division and manufacturing industry group.

Presentation of recurring data varies from issue to issue. The 1st issue of the volume year is a base issue, and includes productivity index trends from earlier years, plus detail by industry for productivity change rates and indexes.

Due to lack of funding, report has been indefinitely suspended with the Nov. 1984 issue.

Availability: American Productivity Center, 123 N. Post Oak Lane, Houston TX 77024, $50.00 per yr., 1st issue of volume year $25.00; SRI/MF/complete.

Issues reviewed during 1985: Nov. 1984 (P) (Vol. 5, No. 2).

R2800-2 PRODUCTIVITY PERSPECTIVES, 1985 Edition
Annual. Jan. 1985. 21 p.
ISSN 0741-6458.
LC 84-641816.
SRI/MF/complete

Annual report, for 1985, analyzing productivity trends and outlook for U.S. and other industrial countries. Presents data on productivity levels and changes, and productivity-related economic indicators. Data are primarily for various periods 1970s-83, with some 1984 data, and selected projections and earlier trends as noted below.

U.S. data include capital and "total factor" productivity change by economic sector; productivity changes during economic recovery periods since 1954; and labor productivity by economic sector and major manufacturing industry group, with comparisons to compensation and inflation.

Other U.S. data include capital stock growth with detail for computer equipment; distribution of R&D activity by funding and performing sector, 1960 and 1984; Federal Government and private borrowing as percent of GNP; inflation rates for selected items; percent of production workers covered by various incentive plans; impact of foreign trade on jobs in selected industries; and U.S.-Japan trade summary.

Data shown for U.S. and 4-11 foreign countries include productivity levels and growth; trade balances; exports in selected high-technology industries; GNP growth, and inflation and unemployment rates; R&D as percent of GNP, selected periods 1961-81; savings as percent of disposable personal income; capital formation and current receipts as percent of GNP; and hours worked per employee, selected years 1929-81.

Also presents selected economic growth indicators for U.S. and 5 Asian countries, including projected labor force change through 2000; distribution of Japan's direct overseas investment by locale (U.S., 3 world regions, and other), 1951-81 period and 1982; and U.S., Japan, and EC shares of manufacturing exports, decennially 1962-82.

Data are from American Productivity Center, BLS, U.S. Dept of Commerce, OECD, Japanese government agencies, and other government and private sources.

Contains listings of contents, charts, and tables (2 p.); introduction (p. 1); and narrative analysis in 3 sections, interspersed with 19 charts and 20 tables (p. 2-21).

Productivity Perspectives has been published since 1980. For description of the 1983 edition, see SRI 1984 Annual under this number. No 1984 edition was published.

Availability: American Productivity Center, Information Services, 123 N. Post Oak Lane, Houston TX 77024, members $15.00, nonmembers $25.00; SRI/MF/complete.

R3300
Battelle Memorial Institute

R3300-1 PROBABLE LEVELS OF R&D EXPENDITURES IN 1985: Forecast and Analysis
Annual. Dec. 1984. 20 p.
SRI/MF/complete

Annual report analyzing R&D funding and expenditure outlook for 1985, with trends from 1960 and preliminary estimates for 1986. Data are shown by funding and performing sector, including Federal Government, industry, colleges/universities, and other nonprofit institutions, with selected detail by Federal agency and function and by manufacturing industry group.

Also includes index of R&D cost per scientist/engineer, by performing sector.

Data are from NSF, McGraw-Hill surveys, and Battelle Memorial Institute estimates.

Contains summary (p. 1-2); analysis and forecast, with text statistics, 4 charts, and 6 tables (p. 2-19); and technical appendix, with definitions (p. 20).

Availability: Battelle Memorial Institute, Columbus Division, Publications, 505 King Ave., Columbus OH 43201-2693, †; SRI/MF/complete.

R3840
Children's Defense Fund

R3840-2 CHILDREN'S DEFENSE BUDGET: An Analysis of the President's FY86 Budget and Children
Annual. 1985.
viii+310 p.+errata.
ISSN 0736-6701.
ISBN 0-938008-40-4.
LC 84-642525.
SRI/MF/complete

Annual report analyzing the impact of Reagan Administration budget proposals on low-income families. Includes actual and proposed funding levels for Federal programs affecting children and families, FY81-86.

Also includes expenditures on defense vs. low-income aid programs, FY80-90; and rates of infant mortality, low birth-weight births, and prenatal care use, by race, 1982, with average annual change for 1978-82 period and needed to meet Surgeon General's goals for 1990.

Also includes children and families in poverty; profits and taxes of 17 major corporations; impact of recent and proposed income tax reforms; number of additional households assisted by Federal housing programs; median weekly earnings and family income; child recipients of Medicaid and AFDC; and unemployment rates; with selected detail by income, age, race-ethnicity, sex, and educational attainment, various periods 1959-84.

Also includes the following data by State, with selected rankings: percent of births to teenage mothers (total and illegitimate), of low birth weight, and to mothers receiving early prenatal care; percent of poor children not receiving Medicaid; infant mortality rates; AFDC payments as percent of poverty level income; AFDC maximum benefits and standards; State allocations for education programs; and child recipients of Title XX funded child care; various years 1978-85.

Data are compiled by Children's Defense Fund (CDF) from Budget of the U.S., and other Federal and private sources.

Contains contents listing (p. iii-vii); 18 narrative chapters, with text statistics, 4 charts, and 16 tables (p. 1-247); and 3 appendices, with 23 tables, congressional committee rosters and budget-related timetables, and lists of data sources and CDF publications (p. 250-310).

This is the 4th annual report.

Availability: Children's Defense Fund, 122 C St., NW, Suite 400, Washington DC 20001, $12.95; SRI/MF/complete.

R3850
Commission on Professional and Hospital Activities

R3850–1   LENGTH OF STAY, BY DIAGNOSIS AND OPERATION, 1983
Annual series.   For individual publication data, see below.
LC 73-173193.
SRI/MF/complete, delayed

Annual series of 14 reports presenting detailed data on short-term hospital admissions and length of stay, by diagnosis and type of operation, for all patients in the U.S., each census region, and Canada, and for geriatric and pediatric patients in the U.S., 1983.

Data are primarily from records submitted by 1,499 U.S. and 206 Canadian nonfederal hospitals participating in the Professional Activity Study (PAS) of the Commission on Professional and Hospital Activities.

Each report contains the following:

a. Contents listing; and data explanation, with 1 table showing hospitals and beds, by hospital capacity and census division or Province, for all short-term nonfederal hospitals and for PAS participants, 1983.

b. Length of stay data, with 1-2 summary tables; and 1 detailed table, repeated for 398 diagnosis and/or 264 operation categories in International Classification of Diseases (ICD) order, showing number of patients, average length of stay, and length of stay by percentile, all shown by patient age, single and multiple diagnosis status, and (for diagnosis only) whether surgically treated, 1983.

c. Appendix of ICD codes, and index.

Reports covering all patients present diagnosis and operation data separately in 2 volumes for each geographic area. Reports covering geriatric and pediatric patients combine diagnosis and operation data in single volumes.

Series began in 1963. Reports for 1983 are listed below. Data are also available from issuing agency on computer-readable magnetic tape.

Availability: Commission on Professional and Hospital Activities, 1968 Green Rd., PO Box 1809, Ann Arbor MI 48106, $40.00 per volume, $70.00 per region+$3.00 handling per order; SRI/MF/complete, delayed shipment in Dec. 1985.

REPORTS:

R3850–1.1: By Diagnosis: U.S., 1983
[Annual. Oct. 1984. v+258 p. SRI/MF/ complete, delayed.]

R3850–1.2: By Operation: U.S., 1983
[Annual. Oct. 1984. v+116 p. SRI/MF/ complete, delayed.]

R3850–1.3: By Diagnosis: U.S., North Central Region, 1983
[Annual. Oct. 1984. v+258 p. SRI/MF/ complete, delayed.]

R3850–1.4: By Operation: U.S., North Central Region, 1983
[Annual. Oct. 1984. v+116 p. SRI/MF/ complete, delayed.]

R3850–1.5: By Diagnosis: U.S., Northeastern Region, 1983
[Annual. Oct. 1984. v+258 p. SRI/MF/ complete, delayed.]

R3850–1.6: By Operation: U.S., Northeastern Region, 1983
[Annual. Oct. 1984. v+116 p. SRI/MF/ complete, delayed.]

R3850–1.7: By Diagnosis: U.S., Southern Region, 1983
[Annual. Oct. 1984. v+258 p. SRI/MF/ complete, delayed.]

R3850–1.8: By Operation: U.S., Southern Region, 1983
[Annual. Oct. 1984. v+116 p. SRI/MF/ complete, delayed.]

R3850–1.9: By Diagnosis: U.S., Western Region, 1983
[Annual. Oct. 1984. v+258 p. SRI/MF/ complete, delayed.]

R3850–1.10: By Operation: U.S., Western Region, 1983
[Annual. Oct. 1984. v+116 p. SRI/MF/ complete, delayed.]

R3850–1.11: By Diagnosis: Canada, 1983
[Annual. Oct. 1984. v+258 p. SRI/MF/ complete, delayed.]

R3850–1.12: By Operation: Canada, 1983
[Annual. Oct. 1984. v+116 p. SRI/MF/ complete, delayed.]

R3850–1.13: Geriatric Length of Stay by Diagnosis and Operation, U.S., 1983
[Annual. Oct. 1984. v+355 p. SRI/MF/ complete, delayed.]

R3850–1.14: Pediatric Length of Stay by Diagnosis and Operation, U.S., 1983
[Annual. Oct. 1984. v+355 p. SRI/MF/ complete, delayed.]

R4105
Conference Board

R4105–3   STATISTICAL BULLETIN
Monthly.   15 p.
ISSN 0010-5554.
LC 73-644166.
SRI/MF/complete, shipped quarterly

Monthly report on selected U.S. business, consumer, industrial, and government economic performance indicators.

Most data are from Conference Board analyses of Dept of Commerce, BLS, and other Federal or industry source reports, and are current to 1-2 months or 1-2 quarters preceding cover date.

Contains contents listing; narrative analysis, with 1-2 summary charts; and 11 tables, described below, interspersed with 13 charts illustrating selected economic trends.

Availability: Conference Board, 845 Third Ave., New York NY 10022, associates only, price on request; SRI/MF/complete, shipped quarterly.

Issues reviewed during 1985: Oct. 1984-Sept. 1985 (P) (Vol. 17, Nos. 10-12; Vol. 18, Nos. 1-9).

MONTHLY TABLES:

a. Status (rising, level, or declining) of approximately 20 leading economic indicators, including capital investment commitments, housing permits, inventory investment and purchasing, selected financial flows, profitability, average workweek, and unemployment claims; for the latest available month, with percent change over latest 3 months and from same month of previous year. 1 table.

b. Conference Board diffusion indexes: 12 indexes for latest available month, 3 previous months, and same month of previous year. 1 table.

c. Business executives' expectations: appraisal of current economic conditions compared with 6 months ago, and expectations for the economy and for own industry 6 months ahead; for selected months of current year and/or previous 2-3 years. 1 table.

d. Conference Board estimates of capital appropriations and expenditures, by 1,000 largest manufacturers and by investor-owned utilities, for quarter of coverage and previous 6 quarters. 1 table.

e. Economic forecasts by 8 leading forecasting institutions, for level and percent change of GNP (current and constant dollars), GNP deflator index, and unemployment rate; mostly as of month preceding cover date, with actual data for quarter preceding cover date and forecast data for 8-9 following quarters. 1 table.

f. Federal budget perspective: receipts by source, outlays by function, deficit, and (beginning in Sept. 1985 issue) underlying economic assumptions, generally shown as estimates of Congress and the Administration for current and/or 2-3 future fiscal years. 2 tables.

g. Conference Board help-wanted advertising indexes for 51 newspapers, by city arranged by census division, with advertising rate comparisons to unemployment rates; for month 2 months prior to cover date, previous 2 months, and same month of previous year. 1 table.

h. Conference Board indexes of consumer confidence and buying plans, monthly for 2 previous years and current year to date. 1 table.

i. Conference Board estimates of discretionary purchasing power, saving, and spending, for 17 consecutive quarters ending approximately 3 years prior to publication date. 1 table.

j. Conference Board estimates of new auto sales, by 10-day periods, for previous 3-4 years to latest available period. 1 table.

R4105–4   CONSUMER ATTITUDES AND BUYING PLANS
Monthly.   2 p.
ISSN 0547-7204.
LC SC 79-4258.
SRI/MF/complete, shipped quarterly

Monthly report, by Fabian Linden, on consumer expectations of business conditions, and intended durable goods purchases and travel during the next 6 months. Data are current to month prior to cover date, and are based on monthly surveys conducted by NFO Research, Inc.

Contains brief narrative analysis with 2 trend charts, and 1 table showing survey responses for current month (preliminary data), and 12 previous months, as follows:

a. Composite index series: consumer confidence (present situation and expectations) and buying plans.

b. Appraisal of present situation: business conditions (good, bad, or normal); and employment (plentiful, not so plentiful, or hard to get).

c. Expectations for next 6 months: business conditions (better, worse, or same); employment (more or fewer jobs, or same); and personal income (increase, decrease, or same).

d. Plans to buy within 6 months: auto (yes, and new, used, or uncertain); home (yes, and new, lived in, or uncertain); major appliances (total plans and for 8 appliances); and carpet.

e. Vacation intended within 6 months (in home State, other States, or foreign country); and travel mode (auto, airplane, or other); for every other month.

Availability: Conference Board, 845 Third Ave., New York NY 10022, associates only, price on request; SRI/MF/complete, shipped quarterly.

Issues reviewed during 1985: Oct. 1984-Sept. 1985 (P).

R4105–5   ECONOMIC ROAD MAPS

Series. For individual
publication data, see below.
LC 82-20303.
SRI/MF/complete

Continuing series of brief reports presenting summary data, primarily charts, on business and economic trends, developments, and issues. Series includes a recurring report on income, inflation, and tax trends; and a subject index, published annually in the spring.

Data are compiled by the Conference Board's Business Conditions Analysis Dept from Federal Government and private sources.

Approximately 12 reports are issued annually, each focusing on a specific topic. Reports reviewed during 1985 are described below.

Availability: Conference Board, 845 Third Ave., New York NY 10022, price on request; SRI/MF/complete.

R4105–5.74: Who Votes and How Much Does it Cost?

[Monograph. Sept. 1984. 4 p. Rpt. Nos. 1980-1981. SRI/MF/complete.]

Report on trends in voter participation and election campaign finances, 1930s-84. Includes data on 1980 presidential campaign spending, and funding by source, for Republican and Democratic Parties.

Contains analysis and 10 charts.

R4105–5.75: Regional and State Personal Income

[Monograph. Oct. 1984. 4 p. Rpt. Nos. 1982-1983. SRI/MF/complete.]

Report on regional trends in personal income, 1958-83. Includes per capita income growth rates by region, 1958-78 and 1978-83 periods; and total U.S. personal income by source, 1958 and 1983.

Contains analysis and 19 charts.

R4105–5.76: Post-World War II Trends in Strike Activity

[Monograph. Nov. 1984. 4 p. Rpt. Nos. 1984-1985. SRI/MF/complete.]

Report on trends in strike activity, union membership, and collective bargaining settlements, with selected comparisons to other industrialized countries.

Includes distribution of work stoppages by issue involved and number of workers idled, and distribution of idled workers and days idle, by size of stoppage (number of workers involved), 1977-81 period; and percent of collective-bargaining settlements with increased, decreased, and unchanged 1st-year wage adjustments, 1978 and 1983.

Contains analysis and 14 charts.

R4105–5.77: Taxes in Industrial Countries

[Monograph. Dec. 1984/Jan.1985. 4 p. Rpt. Nos. 1986-1987. SRI/MF/complete.]

Report on tax trends in industrial nations, various periods 1965-82. Includes average annual change in tax receipts for 16 nations, selected periods 1972-82, with actual 1982 tax receipts for U.S.; and tax revenues as percent of GDP, for U.S. and aggregate OECD and EC countries, 1965, 1975, and 1982.

Contains analysis and 12 charts.

R4105–5.78: Capital/Labor Ratio: U.S.-Japan Comparison

[Monograph. Feb. 1985. 4 p. Rpt. Nos. 1988-1989. SRI/MF/complete.]

Report comparing capital and labor input trends in U.S. and Japan. Includes the following for each country: fixed capital value and number of hours worked, with manufacturing and nonmanufacturing shares, 1983, with trends from 1970; and capital/labor ratio for selected major industries, 1972 and 1983.

Contains analysis and 10 charts.

R4105–5.79: Union Membership

[Monograph. Mar. 1985. 4 p. Rpt. Nos. 1990-1991. SRI/MF/complete.]

Report on labor union membership, including trends from 1930. Includes nonagricultural work force and union membership, with distribution for government and goods and services producing industries, 1984. Contains brief analysis and 15 charts.

R4105–5.80: Economic Road Maps 1984 Index

[Annual. [1985.] 2 p. SRI/MF/complete.]

Index to 1984 *Economic Road Maps* reports, arranged by subject and report numbers.

R4105–5.81: Two-Way Squeeze, 1985

[Annual. Apr. 1985. 2 p. Rpt. No. 1992. SRI/MF/complete.]

Annual report on inflation, income, and tax trends. Includes pretax income needed to equal 1970 after-tax purchasing power, with Federal income and social security taxes, and amount to cover inflation, for 5 income levels, 1975 and 1984-85. Contains brief analysis, 5 charts, and 1 table.

R4105–5.82: Trouble in the Farm Business

[Monograph. May 1985. 4 p. Rpt. Nos. 1993-1994. SRI/MF/complete.]

Report on trends in economic condition of agriculture. Includes the following data, shown for various years 1960-84:

a. Farm employment distribution among family members and hired workers; distribution of family farms by size; farms, average acreage, and value of buildings and land; average net farming income (in current and constant 1967 dollars); distribution of farm assets and production expenses, by type or item; and farms and value of farm products sold, by type of farm ownership.

b. Farm debt outstanding, by lender type; interest on farm debt as percent of all debt, with average delinquency rate; and government farm payments by program, with average payment per farm by value of sales.

Contains analysis, 30 charts, and 1 table.

R4105–5.83: International Dimensions of the Farm Business

[Monograph. June 1985. 4 p. Rpt. Nos. 1995-1996. SRI/MF/complete.]

Report on trends in world agricultural trade. Includes agricultural and manufacturing sector shares of U.S. exports and GNP; value of agricultural imports (total and from U.S.), for 7 countries/world areas; and value of U.S. agricultural exports, by commodity, and by country and world area of destination; various years 1979- 84.

Contains brief analysis and 13 charts.

R4105–5.84: Over 50 Generation

[Monograph. Oct. 1985. 4 p. Rpt. Nos. 1997-1998. SRI/MF/complete.]

Report on financial situation of persons over age 50. Includes data on household size, income (before and after taxes), net worth, and financial assets, all by age of household head, mostly 1983 or 1984; home ownership among persons over and under age 50 (no date); and income sources (no date), and percent of population receiving Social Security benefits, selected years 1950-83, for persons age 65/over.

Contains narrative analysis and 17 charts.

R4105–6   INTERNATIONAL ECONOMIC SCOREBOARD

Monthly. 4 p.
ISSN 0270-045X. LC 80-429.
SRI/MF/complete, shipped
quarterly

Monthly report presenting comparable economic indexes for the U.S., Canada, UK, West Germany, France, Italy, Japan, Australia, and Taiwan (beginning in Feb. 1985 issue).

Data are prepared by the Center for International Business Cycle Research at Columbia University, from composites of approximately 65 economic indicators, and are generally current to 2-3 months prior to cover date.

Contains narrative analysis, with several charts and 1 summary table; and 1 detailed table showing composite economic performance index and leading business cycle index for each country (and various countries combined), monthly for year to date and selected previous months, with percent changes from same months of preceding year, and with 10-year annual growth rate for period ending approximately 7 years prior to year of coverage.

A more detailed report, presenting economic time series data, is covered in SRI under U1245-1.

Availability: Conference Board, 845 Third Ave., New York NY 10022, price on request; SRI/MF/complete, shipped quarterly.

Issues reviewed during 1985: Oct. 1984-Sept. 1985 (P).

R4105-7   CORPORATE DIRECTORS' COMPENSATION, 1985 Edition
Annual. 1984. vi+18 p.
Rpt. No. 862.
ISBN 0-8237-0303-7.
SRI/MF/complete

Annual report, by Jeremy Bacon, on compensation of corporate outside directors, 1984 with comparison to 1983. Covers forms and amounts of payments made to directors who are not company employees, for regular board and committee service.

Includes data by industry category (manufacturing, financial, and nonfinancial services); major industry group; company sales or asset size; and committee type.

Also covers number of board and committee meetings held per year; number of committees; and insurance and other benefits provided, including liability insurance coverage limits.

Data are based on responses of 963 companies to a May-June 1984 survey.

Contains contents and table listings, highlights, and methodology (p. ii-vi); 4 chapters, with narrative analysis and 29 tables (p. 1-18); and list of related publications (inside back cover).

Prior to current edition, report was published biennially, and also included data for employee directors.

Availability: Conference Board, 845 Third Ave., New York NY 10022, price on request; SRI/MF/complete.

R4105-8   ANNUAL SURVEY OF CORPORATE CONTRIBUTIONS, 1985 EDITION (An Analysis of Survey Data for the Calendar Year 1983)
Annual. 1985. vi+37 p.
Rpt. No. 869.
ISBN 0-8237-0310-X.
LC 76-24946.
SRI/MF/complete

Annual report, by Linda Cardillo Platzer, on corporate philanthropic gifts to charitable and public interest organizations and activities, 1983, with comparisons to the 1970s and trends from 1936. Covers charitable tax-deductible contributions, and corporate assistance (financial and other donations not deductible for tax purposes).

Includes value of charitable contributions and corporate assistance, by type; contributions per employee, by employment size group; company foundation income and contributions; contributions relative to pre-tax income, by size of contributions, income, assets, and employment; contributions by recipient category (health/human services, education, culture/art, and civic/

community), by major industry; and contributions targeted for minorities, women, youth, and elderly, within each recipient category.

Also includes top 75 unnamed companies ranked by charitable contributions and social expenditures, with pre-tax income for each; trends in contributions and in income before and after taxes, 1936-83; and survey sample characteristics.

Data are based on Apr. 1984 survey responses of approximately 500 corporations.

Contains listings of contents, tables, and charts, and introduction (p. iii-vi); narrative report, with 6 charts and 4 tables (p. 1-13); 31 detailed tables (p. 15-34); and appendix, with methodology and 5 tables (p. 35-37).

This is the 18th edition of the report.

Availability: Conference Board, 845 Third Ave., New York NY 10022, price on request; SRI/MF/complete.

R4105-9   FINANCIAL INDICATORS AND CORPORATE FINANCING PLANS: A Semiannual Survey
Semiannual. Apr. 1985. 3 p.
SRI/MF/complete, Oct. 1984 & Apr. 1985 reports

Semiannual report on corporate financial executives' general economic expectations and past and planned sources for corporate financing. Data are based on responses of 40 corporate financial executives to a semiannual survey conducted Apr. 1985.

Contains narrative review of results, and 4 tables showing survey responses regarding the following:

a. Inflation outlook to 1990, with comparison to previous surveys; and new Aaa industrial bond and prime interest rates, Dow Jones Industrial Average, and real GNP and GNP deflator rates of change, June 1985 and Sept. 1985, and annually 1985-86.

b. Corporate finance: percent raised/generated from bond issues, private placements, net new equity, bank term and short-term loans, commercial paper, and other external sources, and from internal funds; for past 12 months, with expected change in coming 12 months.

c. Foreign exchange rate changes for 4 currencies against U.S. dollar, and change in price of gold, June and Sept. 1985 (based on responses from companies with international operations).

This is the 18th semiannual survey.

Previous report, covering survey conducted Oct. 1984, was also reviewed in 1985 and is also available on SRI microfiche, under this number [Semiannual. Oct. 1984. 3 p. price on request].

Availability: Conference Board, 845 Third Ave., New York NY 10022, price on request; SRI/MF/complete.

R4105-11   UTILITY INVESTMENT STATISTICS: Utility Appropriations
Quarterly. 3 p.
ISSN 0360-523X.
LC 75-648802.
SRI/MF/complete

Quarterly report on investor-owned electric and gas utility company capital appropriations and expenditures.

Data are compiled from surveys of electric companies accounting for approximately 95% of all investor-owned companies' plant investment and sales; and from gas companies accounting for approximately 50% of revenues of all investor-owned gas utilities. Usually includes preliminary data for quarter of coverage, and revised data for previous quarters.

Reports are published 3-5 months after end of quarter covered.

Contains 3 trend charts, narrative summary, and 1 table showing unadjusted and seasonally adjusted amounts for opening and closing backlogs, appropriations, canceled appropriations, and capital expenditures, for all, electric, and gas utilities, for quarter of coverage and previous 8-9 quarters.

Data in this report are available on-line through Conference Board Data Base.

Availability: Conference Board, 845 Third Ave., New York NY 10022, price on request; SRI/MF/complete.

Issues reviewed during 1985: 2nd Qtr. 1984-1st Qtr. 1985 (D).

R4105-12   CAPITAL APPROPRIATIONS and Capital Investment and Supply Conditions
Quarterly. Approx. 10 p.
SRI/MF/complete

Quarterly report on manufacturing industry capital appropriations and expenditures, and on manufacturers' assessments of adequacy of capital facilities and availability of external capital funds.

Data are from Conference Board quarterly surveys of 1,000 largest manufacturers. Surveys are conducted the month following each quarter. Report is issued approximately 3 months after quarter of coverage.

Contains 1 trend chart, narrative analysis with occasional summary tables and additional charts, and 7 quarterly tables listed below.

Prior to early 1985 issues, report included 3 additional tables (on proportion of appropriations for plant, percent change in appropriations and expenditures, and external supply shortages).

Availability: Conference Board, 845 Third Ave., New York NY 10022, price on request; SRI/MF/complete.

Issues reviewed during 1985: 3rd Qtr. 1984-2nd Qtr. 1985 (D).

QUARTERLY TABLES:

[Tables show data for all manufacturing and for durable and nondurable goods. Tables 1-3 also include breakdowns by industry group, with selected totals for all manufacturing excluding petroleum.]

APPROPRIATIONS AND EXPENDITURES

1-2. Capital appropriations and expenditures [including appropriation backlogs, new approvals, and cancellations]; and percent changes in capital appropriations and expenditures; [seasonally adjusted, for current and 2-3 previous quarters].

3. Capital appropriations and expenditures, annual totals [for previous 3-4 years].

CAPITAL INVESTMENT AND SUPPLY CONDITIONS

[Tables 4-5 and 7 show responses for current and 9 previous survey months.]

4. Adequacy of capital facilities [inadequate, sufficient, or more than adequate].

5. Change in capital facilities expected from current spending programs [expansion, no change, or reduction].

6. Anticipated sources of funds for capital expenditures [internal and external sources, for 9-10 half-year periods, through 1st or 2nd half of current year].

7. Availability of external capital funds compared with 3 months earlier [easier, same, or tighter].

R4105–17   WORLDBUSINESS PERSPECTIVES

Series. For individual publication data, see below. ISSN 0084-1455. LC 77-252. SRI/MF/complete

Series of bimonthly and occasional special reports discussing issues and developments in world business, trade, and financial markets. Data are compiled by the Conference Board from original surveys and research, private financial publications, and Federal agency reports.

Each report focuses on a specific subject, including semiannual (June and Dec.) reports on U.S. manufacturers' foreign capital investment intentions; and recurring reports on implications of U.S. balance of trade position and activities of U.S. multinational corporations.

Reports reviewed during 1985 are described below.

Availability: Conference Board, 845 Third Ave., New York NY 10022, price on request; SRI/MF/complete.

R4105–17.32: World Trade: Reversing the Decline

[Monograph. Oct. 1984. 4 p. No. 82. SRI/MF/complete.]

Report analyzing trends in world trade volume and balance. Includes 2 charts and 1 table showing value of world exports, with distribution by world region or country grouping of destination, 1975 and 1983; and merchandise exports as a percent of GNP, 1974 and 1983, and percent of imports from industrial and developing countries (no date), both for U.S., Japan, and various other industrialized countries.

R4105–17.33: Foreign Capital Expenditures by U.S. Companies: Continued Expansion in 1985

[Semiannual. Dec. 1984. 2 p. No. 83. SRI/MF/complete.]

Semiannual report on a survey of U.S. manufacturing company capital spending plans for foreign affiliates in 1985, as of Oct. 1984. Data are based on responses of 243 companies to an Oct. 1984 Conference Board survey, and include comparisons to previous surveys. Includes 3 charts showing respondents anticipating more, less, or same level of spending.

R4105–17.34: Credit Flows and the U.S. Economy: An Early Warning

[Monograph. Feb. 1985. 4 p. No. 84. SRI/MF/complete.]

Report analyzing effects of private borrowing and debt on the U.S. economy. Data are from

specified Federal and private sources. Includes 1 chart and 1 table showing executives' outlook for inflation through the 1980s; and percent change in net private credit flow and real economic activity, 1970-84.

R4105–17.35: U.S. Foreign Trade in 1984: America's Other Deficit

[Annual. Apr. 1985. 4 p. No. 85. SRI/MF/complete.]

Annual report analyzing selected measures of U.S. trade balance. Includes 1 table showing percent change in GNP and gross domestic purchases, 1982-84.

R4105–17.36: Foreign Capital Expenditures by U.S. Companies: Unchanged Expectations for 1985

[Semiannual. June 1985. 2 p. No. 86. SRI/MF/complete.]

Semiannual report on a survey of U.S. manufacturing company capital spending plans for foreign affiliates in 1985, as of Apr. 1985. Data are based on responses of 239 companies to an Apr. 1985 Conference Board survey, and include comparisons to previous surveys. Includes 3 charts showing respondents anticipating more, less, or same level of spending.

R4105–17.37: Foreign Investment in the U.S.: The Year of the Japanese

[Annual. Aug. 1985. 4 p. No. 87. SRI/MF/complete.]

Annual report on direct investment in U.S. by foreign manufacturers, 1984. Includes text data and 4 charts showing investment trends.

R4105–19   TOP EXECUTIVE COMPENSATION, 1985 Edition

Annual. 1984. vi+73 p. Rpt. No. 854. ISBN 0-8237-0296-0. LC 73-151220. SRI/MF/complete

Annual report, by Harland Fox, on compensation of top executive positions in manufacturing, retail trade, gas/electric utilities, commercial banking, insurance, and construction, 1983, with trends from 1973. Covers total compensation, base salary, and bonus awards, shown generally as median and/or as middle 50% range, often with regression analyses relating sales volume or comparable business measures to compensation levels.

Data are shown for each of 5 highest paid positions in each industry division. Manufacturing industry data include further detail by major industry group.

Also presents data on use of various incentives, including restricted stock, long-term performance, and stock option plans.

Data are from a 1984 survey of 1,053 companies.

Contains contents listing (p. ii-iii); highlights and report rationale (p. iv-vi); and survey report in 8 chapters, with narrative analysis, 36 charts, and 158 tables (p. 1-73).

This is the 22nd survey report.

Availability: Conference Board, 845 Third Ave., New York NY 10022, price on request; SRI/MF/complete.

R4105–29   RESEARCH BULLETIN

Series. For individual publication data, see below. SRI/MF/complete

Continuing series of reports on topics relevant to corporate management, including aspects of domestic and international economic development. Each report covers one topic.

Reports generally summarize Conference Board surveys and forums. SRI describes only those reports containing substantial statistics.

Reports reviewed during 1985 are described below.

Availability: Conference Board, 845 Third Ave., New York NY 10022, price on request; SRI/MF/complete.

R4105–29.44: Corporate Contributions Outlook, 1984

[Monograph. 1984. 23 p. No. 168. SRI/MF/complete.]

By Anne Klepper et al. Report on corporate philanthropic contributions to charitable and public interest organizations and activities, 1983, with trends from 1936. Presents preliminary findings from the Conference Board's annual survey of contributions. Data are based on survey responses of 503 corporations, accounting for approximately 46% of all U.S. giving during 1983.

Includes 19 tables showing the following:

a. Value of contributions, by type and recipient category; comparison of company foundation income and spending; total and educational support contributions relative to company assets and pretax income; and total contributions and pretax income, by major industry group; various years 1979-83.

b. Top 75 unnamed companies ranked by charitable contributions and social expenditures, with pretax income for each, 1983; and trends in contributions and in income before and after taxes, 1936-83.

Full survey report is covered in SRI under R4105-8.

R4105–29.45: 1985 International Economic Outlook: Views of U.S. Corporate Planners

[Annual. 1984. 15 p. No. 169. SRI/MF/complete.]

Annual report, by John Hein, on 1985 world economic outlook as forecast by 12 corporate analysts responding to a 1984 Conference Board survey. Data are primarily from OECD and the surveyed analysts.

Includes text data and 2 tables showing real GNP and GNP deflator change rates forecast by OECD for member countries; and panelists' forecasts for changes in real GNP and industrial production for 4-5 major countries or world areas, and in real GNP and consumer prices for 14 small industrial and major developing countries; various periods 1984-89, with actual industrial production change comparisons for selected periods 1978-83.

This is the 9th annual report.

R4105–29.46: Impact of Technological Change on Corporate and R&D Management: A Survey

[Monograph. 1984. 13 p. No. 170. SRI/MF/complete.]

By James K. Brown. Report analyzing effect of technological change on corporate management, particularly with regard to R&D activities. Data are based on responses of senior executives in 242 companies to a 1984 survey.

Includes 8 tables showing survey findings on corporate activities affected by technological developments, and R&D management changes resulting from technological developments, during past 12 months and/or expected during next 1-3 years.

Also includes text data on sample characteristics.

R4105–29.47: Labor Outlook, 1985
[Annual. 1984. 15 p. No. 171. SRI/MF/complete.]

Annual report, by Audrey Freedman et al., on employment and wage/benefit outlook for 1985, presenting opinions of participants in the Conference Board Labor Outlook Panel, convened Nov. 8, 1984. The 8 panel members are primarily corporate employee-relations executives and labor union leaders.

Includes 1 table showing panelists' forecasts (median and range) of quarterly unemployment rate, and of percent increase in CPI, wage/benefits during 1st year of major union contracts, average hourly earnings, and manufacturing labor costs per output unit, 1985.

Also includes text data on percent of workers receiving wage increases, freezes, or decreases during 1st year of major union contracts covering 1,000/more workers, with mean changes, 1983-84; list of selected major union contract expirations, identifying company, union, and industry, monthly 1985; and brief insert article with 1 table showing survey findings of 6 consulting firms on corporate percent salary increase in 1984 and planned for 1985.

R4105–29.48: 1985 U.S. Economy: No Crisis, No Comfort
[Annual. 1984. 19 p. No. 172. SRI/MF/complete.]

Annual compilation of articles examining U.S. economic trends and outlook. Articles were prepared by participants in the Conference Board Economic Forum, convened Nov. 30, 1984.

Includes 2 trend charts, and 3 tables showing the following:

a. GNP and deflator, corporate profits, unemployment rate, and commercial bank prime rate, 1983-85; and Federal deficit, FY84-86.

b. Nominal, real, and real after-tax interest rates, for 3-month Treasury bills, prime rate, and 4 types of loans, selected periods 1955-84; and rate of return for Standard & Poor 500 stocks during 3-, 6-, and 12-month periods following Federal Reserve discount rate cuts, 1953-84.

R4105–29.49: U.S. Regional Economies: An Updated View of 1984-85
[Annual. Dec. 1984. 14 p. No. 174. SRI/MF/complete.]

Annual compilation of articles updating regional economic trends and outlook as originally presented in *U.S. Regional Outlook, 1984-85*. Articles were prepared by participants in the Conference Board Regional Economic Forum, held in Feb. 1984. Includes 8 tables presenting various economic indicators for individual regions, with some comparisons to total U.S., various periods 1980-85.

For description of *U.S. Regional Outlook, 1984-85*, see SRI 1984 Annual under R4105-29.40.

R4105–29.50: Top Executive Compensation in U.S.-Based Multinationals
[Monograph. 1985. 9 p. No. 173. SRI/MF/complete.]

By Harland Fox. Report on compensation of top executive positions in multinational manufacturing firms, 1983. Data are from a study of 126 manufacturers, listed on NYSE or AMEX, with sales of $100 million or more.

Includes 2 charts and 14 tables presenting data on median amount and middle range of total compensation, base salaries, and bonus awards as percent of base salary; and prevalence of annual bonus awards, long-term performance plans, and stock option and restricted stock plans; with regression analyses relating sales volume to compensation levels. Most data are shown for the 5 highest paid positions.

R4105–29.51: Current Issues in Corporate Telecommunications
[Monograph. 1985. 10 p. No. 176. SRI/MF/complete.]

By Nathan Weber. Report examining factors affecting corporate selection of telecommunications systems following the divestiture of AT&T. Data are from 348 companies with sales greater than $10 million (excluding telecommunications firms) responding to a Conference Board survey.

Includes 5 charts and 6 tables showing survey response on planned changes in telecommunication systems and budgets, and most important factors in selection of new systems; principal indicators of successful telecommunication management; evaluation of service since AT&T divestiture; savings required to justify systems bypassing local exchanges, and preferred bypass technologies; and major allocations in 1983 telecommunications budget.

R4105–29.52: Summer Youth Employment: 1985 Edition
[Annual. 1985. 6 p. No. 178. SRI/MF/complete.]

Annual report, by Nathan Weber, on summer youth employment programs coordinated by private-public sector coalitions, based on a Conference Board review of programs in 14 major cities.

Includes 3 tables showing total placements, 1982-84; and placements in private and public sectors, and by type of job, 1984; for programs in each city.

Previous report, for 1983, is described in SRI 1984 Annual under R4105-29.37.

R4105–29.53: Corporate Financial Assistance for Child Care
[Monograph. 1985. 39 p. No. 177. SRI/MF/complete.]

By Dana Friedman. Report on employer-sponsored child care financial assistance programs for employees. Includes the following data for 4 types of programs (voucher, discount, flexible benefits, and flexible spending account/salary reduction): estimated number of companies with programs; average yearly assistance and costs per employee; and participation, costs, and features of programs offered by selected companies.

Also includes data on costs for 4 types of child care in 7 cities, as of Jan. 1985; and use of dependent care Federal tax credit (number of claims and credit received), 1982.

Data are from responses of 38 companies to a Conference Board survey of 113 companies known to provide child care assistance; a study of 20 other company programs; cost estimates based on data from city information/referral agencies; and IRS.

Includes 10 tables.

R4105–29.54: 1985-86 U.S. Regional Outlook
[Annual. 1985. 19 p.+erratum. No. 181. SRI/MF/complete.]

Annual compilation of articles examining regional economic trends and outlook. Articles were prepared by participants in the Conference Board Regional Economic Forum, held in Feb. 1985.

Includes 6 charts and 7 tables showing selected economic indicators for individual regions, with some comparisons to total U.S., various periods 1965-85.

R4105–29.55: Business in the Community: Where Vanguard Companies Are Focusing
[Monograph. 1985. 9 p. No. 185. SRI/MF/complete.]

By Leonard Lund. Report on corporate involvement in community development. Data are from responses of public and community affairs officers in 140 major corporations to a Conference Board survey. Includes 2 tables showing survey response on community issues of greatest concern to corporations.

R4105–37   BUSINESS EXECUTIVES' EXPECTATIONS
Quarterly. 2 p.
SRI/MF/complete

Quarterly report on chief executive officers' expectations concerning the general economy and conditions in their own industries. Data are based on Conference Board surveys conducted in the 2nd month of each quarter.

Contents:

a. Narrative summary and 4 trend charts.

b. Quarterly table showing executives' assessment of current conditions compared with 6 months ago, and expectations 6 months ahead, for the general economy and for their own industries (by industry division and major manufacturing group); and overall measure of business confidence; all for current and 5-13 previous quarters.

c. 1-4 other tables covering a different survey topic each quarter, with updates appearing annually.

Quarterly table appears in all issues. Other tables are described, as they appear, under "Statistical Features."

Availability: Conference Board, 845 Third Ave., New York NY 10022, price on request; SRI/MF/complete.

Issues reviewed during 1985: 4th Qtr. 1984-2nd Qtr. 1985 (D).

STATISTICAL FEATURES:

R4105–37.601: 4th Qtr. 1984

PROFIT EXPECTATIONS, ANNUAL FEATURE

Annual table showing chief executives' expectations for profits (substantially or moderately better or worse, or same) during coming year, as of Oct. 1976 and Nov. 1977-84. Data are from Conference Board surveys.

R4105–37.602: 1st Qtr. 1985

EMPLOYMENT EXPECTATIONS, ANNUAL FEATURE

Two annual tables showing chief executives' expectations for employment in their own industries during current year, as of 1st quarter 1978-85. Tables show expected trend in employment (no change, and up or down 1-3% or 3%/more); and expected difficulty finding qualified employees, for all industries and in manufacturing. Data are from Conference Board surveys.

R4105–37.603: 2nd Qtr. 1985

INVESTMENT PLANS RELATIVELY UNCHANGED, ANNUAL FEATURE

Two annual undated tables showing distribution of companies by capital investment changes (none, and increase or decrease of more or less than 10%), by industry division; and reasons for upward or downward revisions. Data are from Conference Board surveys.

R4105–38   CENTRALLY PLANNED ECONOMIES: Economic Overview, 1984
Annual. 1984. 72 p.
Rpt. No. 857.
SRI/MF/complete

Annual report for 1984, by Josef Adamek, presenting a narrative overview of economic development in centrally planned economies, by country. Includes text data on growth rates of selected economic indicators (actual for 1983 and national plan forecasts for 1984 and 1981-85 five-year period). Indicators include national income, industrial and agricultural production, standard of living, investment, military expenditures, and foreign trade.

Data are from official sources, and from estimates by the Conference Board and other organizations.

Contains contents listing, foreword, and introduction (p. 3-8); 25 country overviews, arranged in 4 sections (p. 9-66); and 4 appendices, with definitions, sources, official country names, and abbreviations (p. 67-72).

This is the 2nd annual edition of the report.

Availability: Conference Board, 845 Third Ave., New York NY 10022, price on request; SRI/MF/complete.

R4105–41   REGULATING INTERNATIONAL DATA TRANSMISSION: The Impact on Managing International Business
Monograph. 1984. v+23 p.
Rpt. No. 852.
ISBN 0-8237-0293-6.
SRI/MF/complete

By James R. Basche, Jr. Report discussing worldwide government regulation of international data transmission, and the impact on corporate management. Includes countries and world areas in which corporations have encountered obstacles to international data transmission, and types of obstacles encountered.

Data are from responses of 240 corporate executives in 16 countries to a summer 1983 Conference Board survey.

Contains contents listing (p. iii); introduction (p. v); 4 narrative sections, with 2 tables (p. 1-18); and 2 appendices (p. 19-23).

Availability: Conference Board, 845 Third Ave., New York, NY 10022, price on request; SRI/MF/complete.

R4105–42   MANAGING NATIONAL ACCOUNTS
Monograph. 1984. iv+35 p.
Rpt. No. 850.
ISBN 0-8237-0291-X.
SRI/MF/complete

By Linda Cardillo Platzer. Survey report examining corporate methods for promoting efficiency in the sale and servicing of contracts with major customers ("national accounts"). Includes data on assignment of various national account activities to specialized vs. general personnel, organizational level with primary responsibility for coordinating national account efforts, and factors affecting national account program success.

Data are primarily from responses of approximately 130 national account executives to a Conference Board survey.

Contains contents listing (p. ii-iii); and narrative report, with 3 charts and 1 table (p. 1-35).

Availability: Conference Board, 845 Third Ave., New York, NY 10022, price on request; SRI/MF/complete.

R4105–43   INTERNATIONAL PATTERNS OF INFLATION: A Study in Contrasts
Monograph. 1984.
ix+278 p. Rpt. No. 853.
ISBN 0-8237-0294-4.
SRI/MF/complete

Report comparing economic developments associated with inflation experiences of U.S., Japan, UK, Canada, Switzerland, France, West Germany, and Italy, 1950s-83.

Includes data on all or most of the following, for each country: industrial production and productivity, GNP or GDP, CPI, WPI, employment, money supply, foreign trade, earnings, and labor costs.

Also includes data on Japan's foreign exchange account contributions to money supply, government revenues by source and expenditures by program, government security and other money market activities, personal financial assets, and distribution of corporate surplus fund investments.

Also includes data on UK assets of public and private sectors (with detail for insurance companies and pension funds), and household borrowings; West German banking shares by type of institution; and Italy's gross fixed investments as percent of GDP.

Data are from U.S. Federal Reserve System and Dept of Commerce, OECD, IMF, and other U.S. and foreign governmental and private sources.

Contains contents listing, and introduction (p. v-ix); essay on the U.S. economy and its global impact, interspersed with 5 tables (p. 1-67); individual essays for 7 other countries, interspersed with 6 charts and 23 tables (p. 71-261); and statistical appendix, with 10 tables and notes on data sources (p. 265-278).

Availability: Conference Board, 845 Third Ave., New York NY 10022, price on request; SRI/MF/complete.

R4105–44   FEDERAL BUDGET DEFICITS AND THE U.S. ECONOMY
Monograph. 1984. iv+60 p.
Rpt. No. 855.
ISBN 0-8237-0295-2.
SRI/MF/complete

Compilation of papers analyzing Federal budget deficit outlook and implications. Includes data on Federal revenues by source, outlays by category, and deficit, various years FY65-2025, with alternative projections under a budgetary freeze and under various assumptions regarding GNP growth, inflation, unemployment, and interest rates.

Also includes 6 alternative deficit measures, 1983-88; and trends in private and public sector borrowing, and composition of saving and private investment, various periods 1970-85.

Papers were prepared by participants in the Conference Board Economic Policy Forum, convened Nov. 28, 1983. Data sources include Congressional Budget Office, Federal Reserve System, Commerce Dept, and OMB.

Contains listings of contents, tables, and charts, and preface (p. i-iv); 10 papers, with 11 charts and 21 tables (p. 1-58); bibliography (p. 59-60); and list of forum participants (inside back cover).

Availability: Conference Board, 845 Third Ave., New York NY 10022, price on request; SRI/MF/complete.

R4105–45   MANAGING OLDER WORKERS: Company Policies and Attitudes
Monograph. 1984. x+38 p.
Rpt. No. 860.
ISBN 0-8237-0301-0.
SRI/MF/complete

By Shirley H. Rhine. Survey report on corporate retirement policies and attitudes regarding older workers in manufacturing, gas/electric utility, insurance, banking, and retail industries.

Includes data on prevalence of mandatory retirement, and share of workers aged 55-64 and older, by employment size and/or industry; age and service requirements for full pension benefits, and average retirement age, for all companies and those offering early retirement; reasons for offering early retirement, and resultant problems; perceptions regarding older workers, by worker occupational category and respondent age; and prevalence of selected programs for upgrading job skills.

Data are from 363 responses to a recent Conference Board survey of corporate human resource executives.

Contains listings of contents, tables, and charts (p. iii-v); introduction, with 3 tables on sample characteristics (p. vi-ix); report in 2 parts, with text statistics, 6 charts, and 8 tables (p. 1-34); appendix with 3 charts (p. 35-38); and list of related publications (inside back cover).

Availability: Conference Board, 845 Third Ave., New York NY 10022, price on request; SRI/MF/complete.

R4105–46   MANAGING INTERNATIONAL PUBLIC AFFAIRS
Monograph. 1985. vi+34 p.
Rpt. No. 861.
ISBN 0-8237-0302-9.
SRI/MF/complete

By Seymour Lusterman. Report on foreign public affairs activities of multinational corporations. Includes data on countries in which U.S.-based and other companies operate, and countries that are focus of public affairs activities; public affairs staffing level relative to total and foreign sales and to extent of foreign operations; autonomy of local public affairs managers; and public affairs planning and coordination activities, with 5-year trend and outlook.

Data are from 54 U.S.-based and 28 other companies responding to a Conference Board survey. No survey date is given.

Contains listings of contents, tables, and charts (ii-iii); highlights and report rationale (p. iv-vi); 4 chapters, with narrative analysis, text data, and 5 tables (p. 1-29); case studies (p. 30-34); and list of related Conference Board reports (inside back cover).

Availability: Conference Board, 845 Third Ave., New York NY 10022, price on request; SRI/MF/complete.

R4105–47   NEW LOOK IN WAGE POLICY AND EMPLOYEE RELATIONS
Monograph. 1985. vi+33 p.
Rpt. No. 865.
ISBN 0-8237-0305-3.
SRI/MF/complete

By Audrey Freedman. Survey report on corporate wage-setting and employee-relations policies, 1983, with comparisons to 1978. Includes data on the following:

a. Factors influencing employee-relations management in general; and primary objective of labor negotiations (achieving best bargaining result vs. keeping company nonunion), by extent of unionization.

b. Factors influencing wage/benefit objectives, with detail by industry division and bargaining structure (company-wide vs. plant-by-plant); number, type, and outcome of management and union proposals for contract changes prior to expiration date; and non-wage objectives in bargaining.

c. Nonunion employee relations practices; quality of union-management relationship, and criteria used for evaluation; and corporate officers responsible for various human-resource functions.

Data are based on responses from 504 companies to a 1983 Conference Board survey, and on a similar survey conducted in 1978. The 1983 respondents include 302 union and 42 nonunion companies also surveyed in 1978.

Contains listing of contents, exhibits, tables, and charts (p. ii-iii); highlights and report rationale (p. iv-vi); and 5 chapters, with narrative analysis, 4 charts, and 13 tables (p. 1-33).

Availability: Conference Board, 845 Third Ave., New York NY 10022, price on request; SRI/MF/complete.

R4105–48   U.S. ECONOMY TO 1990
Monograph. 1985. 1+21 p.
Rpt. No. 864.
ISBN 0-8237-0307-X.
SRI/MF/complete

By Lora S. Collins. Report examining U.S. economic trends and outlook. Includes data (primarily illustrative charts) on a variety of indicators, including GNP, population, labor force, employment, productivity, R&D spending, inflation, capital investment, consumer spending, household composition and income, and higher education enrollment, various periods 1948-90. Selected data for 1990 include projections for optimistic and pessimistic scenarios.

Data are from Federal sources, NSF, and the Conference Board.

Contains report rationale (1 p.); and narrative analysis interspersed with 1 map, 85 charts, and 3 tables (p. 1-21).

Availability: Conference Board, 845 Third Ave., New York NY 10022, price on request; SRI/MF/complete.

R4105–49   CHIEF EXECUTIVES VIEW THEIR JOBS
Monograph. 1985. ix+94 p.
Rpt. No. 871.
ISBN 0-8237-0312-6.
SRI/MF/complete

By Harold Stieglitz. Report on views and characteristics of chief executive officers (CEOs) in industrial nations, 1984. Most data are shown for U.S., Europe, and rest of world (with some additional detail for Latin America and Canada/Australia/New Zealand).

Includes data on aspects of CEOs' business strategy for the next 3-5 years; probability that next CEO will come from within the company; and CEOs' own strengths, strengths sought in successors, priorities and primary role, approach to major decisions, views on board involvement in decisions, and views on optimum length of time to serve as CEO.

Also includes data on CEOs' current age, and age when appointed to present position; years in position and with present company; career history; number of board memberships held; and educational background.

Data are based primarily on responses of 287 CEOs to a Conference Board survey.

Contents:

Listing of contents, tables, and charts; highlights; and report rationale. (p. iii-ix)

Part I. The CEO: A Composite Picture. Includes methodology, with 1 table; and narrative analysis in 5 chapters, with 9 interspersed charts. (p. 1-33)

Part II. Some Individual CEOs. Includes comments from 20 CEOs. (p. 34-91)

Part III. Profile of the CEOs. Includes brief narrative and 1 table. (p. 92-94)

Availability: Conference Board, 845 Third Ave., New York NY 10022, price on request; SRI/MF/complete.

R4500
East-West Center: East-West Population Institute

R4500–1   PAPERS OF THE EAST-WEST POPULATION INSTITUTE
Series. For individual publication data, see below.
ISSN 0732-0531.
SRI/MF/complete

Continuing series of reports on economic, social, psychological, and environmental aspects of population in Asian and Pacific countries and the U.S.

Reports are based on original field studies sponsored by the Institute, the UN, individual countries, and U.S. agencies and universities.

Most reports include contents listing, summary, narrative analysis with a varying number of charts and tables, and bibliography.

Reports are usually statistical but occasionally consist of narrative analyses only. All reports are described in SRI.

Report reviewed during 1985 is described below.

Availability: East-West Center: East-West Population Institute, Publications Office, 1777 East-West Rd., Honolulu HI 96848, $12.00 per yr., single copies † to those engaged in demographic research or programs, single copies for others vary in price according to length; SRI/MF/complete.

R4500–1.35: Profile of Hawaii's Elderly Population
[Monograph. Aug. 1984. vii+39 p. Rpt. No. 91. $3.00. ISBN 0-86638-059-0. LC 84-18686. SRI/MF/complete.]

By Eleanor C. Nordyke et al. Report on characteristics of Hawaii's elderly (age 65/over) population, 1980, with decennial trends and projections 1900-2000. Data are from Federal and State agencies, and other specified sources.

Includes 7 charts and 15 tables showing the following for elderly Hawaiians: population by county, marital status, and education; population growth rate; median age; life expectancy; deaths and death rate; residence relative to 5 years previous (Hawaii, different State, and abroad); population sex ratio; and labor force, unemployment rate, and median and mean income.

Most data include detail by age, sex, and race/ethnicity (including white, black, Hawaiian, Chinese, Filipino, Japanese, and Korean), and comparisons to all Hawaii residents. Some data include comparisons to total U.S. and selected other countries.

R4800
Editorial
Projects in Education

R4800–2   EDUCATION WEEK
Weekly. Oversized.
ISSN 0277-4232.
LC sn81-1539.
SRI/MF/excerpts, shipped
quarterly

Weekly journal (issued 42 times per year) reporting on developments in elementary/secondary education. Covers public and private schools; regular, special, vocational, and adult education programs; and, in less detail, higher education.

Data are primarily from NCES, other Federal agencies, and professional assns.

Issues generally contain numerous news and feature articles, occasionally with substantial statistics; and regular departmental features, including "Databank" statistical section usually with several tables and/or charts on such topics as educational enrollment, finance, and staffing.

Features with substantial statistical content are described, as they appear, under "Statistical Features." Each issue of the journal is reviewed, but an abstract is published in SRI monthly issues only when statistical features appear.

Journal suspends publication during 1st week of Jan., last week of June through 2nd week of Aug., and last 2 weeks of Dec.

Availability: Education Week, PO Box 1939, Marion OH 43305, $39.94 per yr., back issues $2.00; SRI/MF/excerpts for all portions covered under "Statistical Features;" shipped quarterly.
Issues reviewed during 1985: Nov. 7, 1984-Oct. 30, 1985 (P) (Vol. IV, Nos. 10-42; Vol. V, Nos. 1-9).

STATISTICAL FEATURES:

R4800–2.601: Nov. 7, 1984 (Vol. IV, No. 10)

DATABANK: U.S. EDUCATION BUDGET, ANNUAL FEATURE

(p. 14-15) Annual table showing Federal education appropriations by purpose, final FY84, and Administration, House, and Senate recommendations FY85.

Includes related article (p. 13).

R4800–2.602: Nov. 14, 1984 (Vol. IV, No. 11)

PENTAGON REPORTS TOP-NOTCH RECRUITS

(p. 2) Brief article, with 1 table showing percent of new military recruits with high school diplomas, by military branch and for total DOD, FY80-84. Data are from DOD.

EDUCATION-RELATED BALLOT RESULTS

(p. 6) Listing of Nov. 1984 voting results on education-related referenda in 15 States.

Includes related articles (p. 1, 6-7).

R4800–2.603: Nov. 21, 1984 (Vol. IV, No. 12)

DATABANK: CLASS OF 1980, TWO YEARS LATER

(p. 12-13) Article on postsecondary activities of the high school class of 1980 during 2 years following graduation. Presents data on percent of students enrolling in postsecondary educa-

tional institutions, with detail by academic field and for those receiving financial aid; and employment status and average earnings of graduates, and prevalence of military service, marriage, and parenthood.

Most data include detail by sociodemographic characteristics including sex, race/ethnicity (Hispanic, black, white, Asian American, and American Indian), economic status, cognitive test performance, high school program type, and region or urban-rural status.

Data are shown for various periods 1980-82, and are from NCES follow-up surveys of 12,000 high school students graduated in 1980. Includes 4 charts and 3 tables.

R4800–2.604: Jan. 9, 1985 (Vol. IV, No. 16)

DATABANK: STATE EDUCATION STATISTICS, ANNUAL FEATURE

(p. 12-13) Annual table presenting the following education-related data by State, with State rankings, various years 1980-84:

a. Performance outcomes: American College Test or Scholastic Aptitude Test scores, with percent of high school seniors taking test; high school graduation rate; and test score and graduation rate gains needed to meet Federal goals for 1985 and/or 1990.

b. Resource inputs: pupil/teacher and pupil/staff ratios, average teacher salary, Federal funds as percent of school revenues, and education expenditure per pupil and as percent of per capita income.

c. Population characteristics: per capita income, percent of 5-17 year olds in poverty, median educational attainment, and minority and handicapped students' enrollment shares.

Data were compiled by Dept of Education and are from State education agencies, NCES, and other Federal and private sources. Includes accompanying article and notes (p. 10, 14).

R4800–2.605: Feb. 6, 1985 (Vol. IV, No. 20)

STATES LAUNCHING BARRAGE OF INITIATIVES, SURVEY FINDS

(p. 1, 11-31) Article on recent State enactments and proposals concerning educational and related reforms. Data are from a Jan. 1985 *Education Week* survey of State officials.

Includes 2 tabular summaries of reform activities; and 1 table showing total and education budget, budget surplus or deficit, tax changes, and whether school finance formula changes have been enacted or proposed, various periods 1983-1985/86; all by State.

For data correction, see R4800-2.610 below.

R4800–2.606: Feb. 13, 1985 (Vol. IV, No. 21)

DATABANK: PROPOSED 1986 BUDGET FOR EDUCATION, ANNUAL FEATURE

(p. 12-13) Annual table showing Federal appropriations, FY84-85; and President's FY86 budget request; all by education function and program.

Table is accompanied by 2 related articles (p. 1, 12-13, 16).

R4800–2.607: Feb. 20, 1985 (Vol. IV, No. 22)

SHAPE OF JAPANESE SCHOOLING: A STATISTICAL PROFILE

(p. 28-30) Compilation of 2 charts and 10 tables showing the following for Japan, with some comparisons to U.S., generally for various periods 1980-84:

a. Elementary and secondary schools, colleges and universities, enrollment and personnel by sex, instructional computer use, graduate degrees conferred, and education expenditures (including government appropriations and summary trends from 1950), all by school level and/or type of control.

b. Population; length of school year; average elementary class size; school completion rates; teacher average salary; high school seniors' extra-curricular activities and weekly hours spent on homework, by sex; and standard number of credits in upper secondary schools, and teaching hours in elementary and lower secondary schools, by subject.

Data are from NCES, and Japanese Ministry of Education, Science, and Culture.

Data are included in Part 1 of a 3-part series on educational developments in Japan.

For data correction, see R4800-2.611 below.

R4800–2.608: Feb. 27, 1985 (Vol. IV, No. 23)

[Articles are included in Part 2 of a 3-part series on educational developments in Japan.]

EXAMINATION HELL

(p. 12-14, 16-18) By Sheppard Ranbom. Article, with 4 tables showing Japanese junior high and high school students graduating, continuing education and vocational training, and entering employment, selected years 1955-81, with 1982 detail by program and school type; Japanese junior high school students' views on preparation for entrance examinations, 1982; and Japanese and U.S. high school students' perceptions of self-worth, control over own lives, and importance of selected life and work values, 1980.

Most data for 1980-82 are shown by sex. Data are from NCES, and Japanese government sources including 2,448 responses to a survey of students.

'NEW' MINDS FOR BUSINESS

(p. 20-23) Article, with 3 undated tables showing Japanese business firms with adult education programs, and participation rates by type of position and for new employees and those hired in mid-career, by company employment size; and prevalence of Tokyo University graduates among business leaders by industry group, and among high government officials by agency. Data are from the Japanese Ministry of Labor and *Business Community*.

R4800–2.609: Mar. 6, 1985 (Vol. IV, No. 24)

[Articles are included in Part 3 of a 3-part series on educational developments in Japan.]

LITTLE POWER, MANY DEMANDS

(p. 16-18) By Sheppard Ranbom. Article, with 3 tables showing the following for Japan: minimum credits required for teacher certification in general education, and teaching specialty and methods courses, by school level and class of certificate (no date); and distribution of teachers by degree level, and average public school teaching hours per week, both by school level, 1980.

Data are from the Japanese Ministry of Science, Education, and Culture, and National Institute for Educational Research.

HIDDEN LAW

(p. 19-22) Article, with 1 table showing total and women principals and vice principals in Japanese schools, by school type and/or level, 1982. Data are from the Japanese Ministry of Science, Education, and Culture.

R4800–2.610: Mar. 13, 1985 (Vol. IV, No. 25)

CORRECTION

(p. 3) Correction for article on recent State enactments of educational reforms, appearing in the Feb. 6, 1985 issue.

For description of original article, see R4800-2.605 above.

R4800–2.611: Mar. 20, 1985 (Vol. IV, No. 26)

U.S. LEADS DEVELOPED NATIONS IN RATE OF TEENAGE PREGNANCY

(p. 1, 13) Article, with 1 chart comparing teenage pregnancy rates and outcomes (births in and out of wedlock, and abortions), for U.S. and 5 other developed countries, 1980/81. Data are from Alan Guttmacher Institute.

CORRECTION

(p. 2) Correction for feature on educational developments in Japan, appearing in Feb. 20, 1985 issue.

For description of original feature, see R4800-2.607 above.

R4800–2.612: Apr. 17, 1985 (Vol. IV, No. 30)

HARD-WON ENROLLMENT GAINS ARE QUIETLY DETERIORATING

(p. 1, 12-15) Article, with 1 table showing average inflation-adjusted value of student aid awards, for all students and by race/ethnicity (white, black, and Hispanic), by institution type (total, 2- and 4-year public, and all private), 1978 and 1983. Data are from American Assn of State Colleges and Universities.

R4800–2.613: Apr. 24, 1985 (Vol. IV, No. 31)

DATABANK: TEACHER SUPPLY/DEMAND BY FIELD AND REGION, ANNUAL FEATURE

(p. 12-13) Annual compilation of 3 tables presenting indexes of elementary/secondary teacher shortage/surplus, by instructional field, 1976 and 1980-85; and average salaries for beginning elementary/secondary and special education teachers with bachelor's and master's degrees, 1982/83-1984/85; with detail by contiguous U.S. region and for Alaska and Hawaii.

Data are based on a survey of 60 university teacher-placement officials conducted by Assn for School, College, and University Staffing.

R4800–2.614: May 8, 1985 (Vol. IV, No. 33)

PARENTAL INVOLVEMENT IN RELATION TO SELF-REPORTED STUDENT ACHIEVEMENT

(p. 3) Table relating high school students' grades to parental involvement in the students' education, as reported by the students. Data are from Mar. 1985 NCES *Bulletin,* and represent survey responses of 1980 sophomores still attending the same school in 1982.

HEAD START AT 20

(p. 15-22) Article, with 1 table showing student enrollment and Federal appropriations for the Head Start project, FY65-85 and forecast FY86. Data are from HHS.

R4800–2.615: May 29, 1985 (Vol. IV, No. 36)

JOBS AND EDUCATION

(p. 23) By Bill Honig. Article, with 2 tables showing employment by occupational group, 1982; and new and replacement openings, 1982-95 period; shown separately for jobs requiring high and low levels of education. Data are from BLS and the author's estimates.

R4800–2.616: June 12, 1985 (Vol. IV, No. 38)

DISTRICTS RECEIVING ASBESTOS-ABATEMENT FUNDS

(p. 12, 22) Tabular list showing EPA grants and loans to individual school districts under the Asbestos School Hazard Abatement Act of 1984, by State. Includes accompanying article (p. 1, 12).

R4800–2.617: Aug. 21, 1985 (Vol. IV, No. 40/41)

PUBLIC FAVORS PAY RAISES, COMPETENCY TESTING FOR TEACHERS, N.E.A./GALLUP POLL INDICATES

(p. S2) Article presenting public opinion on teaching and other professions. Data are from 1,501 responses to an Apr.-May 1985 survey conducted by the Gallup Organization, Inc. for the National Education Assn. Includes 2 charts showing survey response on factors limiting ability of public schools to attract good teachers, and whether teaching and 8 other occupations are prestigious and demanding.

20 LARGEST CITIES, BY POPULATION

(p. S14) Table showing population of 20 largest cities, Apr. 1980, July 1982, and July 1984, with selected rankings. Data are from Census Bureau.

R4800–2.618: Aug. 28, 1985 (Vol. IV, No. 42)

GIVING TO INDEPENDENT SCHOOLS INCREASES

(p. 6) Table showing the top 10 independent schools ranked by annual/capital giving and by corporate support; and top 10 day/boarding and boarding/day schools ranked by alumni giving; 1983/84. Data are from Council for Financial Aid to Education (CFAE).

Similar feature, with data for 1982/83, is described in SRI 1984 Annual under R4800-2.525.

Full CFAE report, *Voluntary Support of Education,* is covered in SRI under A4325-2.

R4800–2.619: Sept. 18, 1985 (Vol. V, No. 3)

DATABANK: A TALLY OF PUBLIC SCHOOLS

(p. 4) Three tables showing public schools by type (special education, vocational/technical, regular, and other), grade span, and State, fall 1982-83. Data are from NCES.

R4800–2.620: Oct. 2, 1985 (Vol. V, No. 5)

UPWARD SURGE

(p. 1) Chart showing mean verbal and mathematics Scholastic Aptitude Test scores, 1975 and 1985. Data are from the College Board. Includes accompanying article (p. 5, 16).

SOUTHERN PUPILS' TEST SCORES TOP U.S. AVERAGE

(p. 5) By Lynn Olson. Article, with 1 chart showing average reading proficiency scores of 11th grade students on the National Assessment of Educational Progress (NAEP) test, for U.S., southeastern U.S., Virginia, Florida, and Tennessee, 1983/84. Data are from the Southern Regional Education Board.

R4925
Free Congress Research and Education Foundation

R4925–4   **EVANGELICAL VOTER: Religion and Politics in America**
Monograph. 1984. v+176 p.
LC 84-82043.
SRI/MF/complete

By Stuart Rothenberg and Frank Newport. Survey report on evangelical Christians' views regarding selected governmental, social, political, and religious topics, 1983. Topics covered include the following:

a. Nuclear freeze; defense spending; U.S. involvement in Central America; school prayer; private school tuition tax credits; ERA; birth control information in schools; Acquired Immune Deficiency Syndrome (AIDS); and abortion.

b. Political party, ideology, and voting behavior, including party or candidate supported in 1980, 1982, and 1984 elections; involvement in political activities; and awareness of and support for Moral Majority, National Conservative Political Action Committee, National Education Assn, and National Organization of Women.

c. Religious leaders' role in politics; own minister's political activity, and impact on own voting decision; and religious TV programs, including viewing frequency and opinion of Jerry Falwell.

Data, shown by various demographic, political, and religious characteristics, are based on telephone interviews with a national sample of 1,000 evangelical Christians. The interviews were conducted by Tarrance and Associates during July 1983.

Contains contents listing (p. iii); 9 chapters presenting introductory discussion, survey findings, and conclusions, with 44 interspersed tables (p. 3-151); 3 appendices, including respondent religious denominations, and survey instrument (p. 153-169); and bibliography (p. 170-176).

Availability: Free Congress Research and Education Foundation, Institute for Government and Politics, 721 Second St., NE, Washington DC 20002, $5.95; SRI/MF/complete.

R4925–5   SOLIDARITY AND DISSENT: Union Member Attitudes and the Political Process
Monograph.   1984.   x+65 p.
LC 84-82115.
SRI/MF/complete

By Peter Keisler. Report on labor union members' opinions concerning selected economic, social, and political issues. Data are based on telephone interviews with 1,000 union members age 18/over, conducted in Apr. 1984 by V. Lance Tarrance and Associates.

Includes responses to questions concerning most important national problem; Government budget policies including defense spending; tuition tax credits; teacher competency tests; affirmative action programs; "comparable worth" concept concerning equal pay for occupations requiring similar skills and training; and amnesty for illegal aliens living in U.S. 6/more years.

Also includes voting behavior (support for political parties vs. individual candidates); approval of President Reagan; 1984 presidential candidate preferences; perceptions of national union leaders' representativeness, and political ideology and policies; personal political ideology; and knowledge of the president of the AFL/CIO.

Selected data are shown by race, religious affiliation, occupational level (upper and lower white and blue collar), education, union affiliation, whether union activist, sex, employment status, and age.

Contains contents listing, preface, and introduction (p. iii x); 5 chapters, with narrative analysis and 59 interspersed tables (p. 1-60); and appendix, with survey methodology and notes (p. 61-65).

Availability: Free Congress Research and Education Foundation, Institute for Government and Politics, 721 Second St., NE, Washington DC 20002, $3.50; SRI/MF/complete.

R5025
Group of Thirty

R5025–3   POLICY LESSONS OF THE DEVELOPMENT EXPERIENCE
Monograph.   1985.   27 p.
Occasional Paper No. 16.
LC 85-7989.
SRI/MF/complete

By Helen Hughes. Report analyzing economic growth of developing countries. Includes data on population; average annual GDP growth rates (total, per capita, and per labor force unit); savings and investment as percent of GDP; foreign aid/investment/borrowing as percent of gross domestic investment; and CPI; various periods 1960-83.

Data are generally shown for low and middle income developing countries, and high and/or middle income oil importers and exporters, with detail by world area or country. Also includes selected comparisons to all industrial countries.

Data are from IMF and World Bank.
Contains narrative analysis interspersed with 6 tables (p. 1-22); and notes (p. 23-24).
Availability: Group of Thirty, 725 Park Ave., New York NY 10021, $10.00; SRI/MF/complete.

R5025–4   JAPAN AS CAPITAL EXPORTER AND THE WORLD ECONOMY
Monograph.   1985.   32 p.
Occasional Paper No. 18.
LC 85-8034.
SRI/MF/complete

By Masaru Yoshitomi. Report examining factors contributing to Japan's emergence as an exporter of capital. Includes data on Japan's balance of payments, including external reserves and current and capital accounts (in dollars); savings and investment as percent of GNP, by sector; average annual growth rate in exports, imports, and GNP; and contribution of external surplus to GNP growth; 1960s-83.

Data are from the Bank of Japan and the Japanese Economic Planning Agency.
Contains contents listing (1 p.); narrative analysis (p. 1-26); and 4 tables (p. 27-29).
Availability: Group of Thirty, 725 Park Ave., New York NY 10021, $10.00; SRI/MF/complete.

R5250
High/Scope Educational Research Foundation

R5250–1   EARLY CHILDHOOD DEVELOPMENT PROGRAMS IN THE EIGHTIES: The National Picture
Monograph.   1985.   iv+38 p.
SRI/MF/complete

By Lawrence J. Schweinhart. Report examining the status of early childhood education and child care during the 1980s. Presents related data on children, preprimary enrollment, child care, and government program funding and participation, with selected detail by State. Most data pertain to children age 3-5, and are shown for various calendar or fiscal years 1979-85. Data topics include the following:

a. Children (total, poor, and handicapped), by State; preprimary education enrollment, by child's age, program type, family demographic characteristics, and mother's labor force status; public kindergarten and nursery school enrollment, by State, with comparison to 1st grade enrollment; child care enrollment rates among employed mothers, by type of care; and handicapped children in special education programs, by type of disability.

b. Funding amount and children subsidized, for 9 federally funded early childhood development programs; Head Start funding (Federal and local) and children served (total and/or poor), by State and U.S. territory and for Indian and migrant children; and funding amounts and children served, for social services block grants allotted to child care and for State-funded prekindergarten programs, by State.

Data are from Census Bureau, NCES, and other sources.
Contains listings of contents and tables, and foreword (p. i-iv); executive summary (p. 1-3); narrative report, interspersed with 20 tables (p. 4-36); and bibliography (p. 37-38).
Availability: High/Scope Educational Research Foundation, 600 N. River St., Ypsilanti MI 48197, $6.00; SRI/MF/complete.

R5300
Hispanic Policy Development Project

R5300–1   HISPANIC ALMANAC
Biennial.   1984.   164 p.
ISBN 0-918911-00-1.
SRI/MF/complete, delayed

Biennial report on Hispanic demographic and socioeconomic characteristics and voting patterns, primarily 1979 or 1980, with some trends from 1960 and projections to 1990.

Covers Hispanic population by State, age, sex, occupational group, education, and English and Spanish language use and ability; and families by income level, and median family income; with detail for 20 SMSAs with highest Hispanic population, and for similar Areas of Dominant Influence (Arbitron markets based on media audience estimates), with some data by component county.

Also includes Hispanic voting age population, eligible and registered voters, and voter turnout; voting patterns by selected socioeconomic characteristics, region, and candidate or party affiliation; and prevalence of Hispanic elected officials; generally for total U.S. and for 9 States with highest Hispanic populations.

Data often include detail by ethnic background (Mexican, Puerto Rican, Cuban, and other), and comparisons to non-Hispanic racial/ethnic groups.

Data are primarily from Census Bureau and Comprehensive Technologies International analyses of census results.

Contains listings of contents, tables, maps, and charts (p. 7-14); report in 4 sections, with 37 maps/charts and 14 tables showing general data, and 3 charts and 5 tables repeated for 20 SMSAs (p. 16-152); lists of sources and Hispanic organizations (p. 154-157); and appendix, with data notes and 1 table (p. 160-164).

This is the 1st edition of the report.

Section on voters and voting patterns is also issued as a separate publication, *The Hispanic Electorate,* and is available from the issuing agency for $3.00.

Availability: Hispanic Policy Development Project, 1001 Connecticut Ave., NW, Suite 310, Washington DC 20036, nonprofit organizations $49.95, others $97.65; SRI/MF/complete, delayed shipment in Dec. 1985.

R5300–2   POLLS OF ELECTED AND APPOINTED OFFICIALS
Monograph.   2 volumes.
For individual publication data, see below.
SRI/MF/complete

Survey report, in 2 volumes, on principal concerns of Hispanic Americans in the 1980s as viewed by Hispanics serving in government positions.

Includes survey responses related to Hispanics' prospects in general, most serious problems, obstacles to job advancement, effectiveness of affirmative action programs, status of undocumented workers, prevalence of school dropouts and low voter participation, value of bilingual and parochial education, outlook for cultural retention, institutions and organizations best serving needs, and status of U.S. relations with Cuba and Puerto Rico.

Data are from telephone interviews with 448 elected and appointed Hispanic officials, conducted May-July 1983 by Public Agenda Foundation.

Each volume contains introduction, contents listing, and survey methodology with 2 tables (5 p.); narrative analysis, interspersed with 2-5 tables (8-9 p.); appendix, with sample characteristics, questionnaire facsimile, and survey results (p. i-v); and directory of Hispanic organizations (p. vi-vii). Full survey results are included in each volume.

Price includes an additional report presenting narrative summaries of recent Hispanic opinion surveys. All 3 reports are listed below.

Availability: Hispanic Policy Development Project, 1001 Connecticut Ave., NW, Suite 310 Washington DC 20036, $3.50 for the set; SRI/MF/complete.

REPORTS:

R5300-2.1: Vol. I: Moving into the Political Mainstream
[Monograph. Feb. 1984. 16+vii p. SRI/MF/complete.]

R5300-2.2: Vol. II: Moving Up to Better Education and Better Jobs
[Monograph. Feb. 1984. 17+vii p. SRI/MF/complete.]

R5300-2.3: Recent Hispanic Polls: A Summary of Results
[Monograph. Feb. 1984. 12 p. SRI/MF/complete.]

R5300-3   MAKE SOMETHING HAPPEN: Hispanics and Urban School Reform
Monograph. 2 volumes.
For individual publication data, see below.
ISBN 0- 918911-03-6 (in two volumes). SRI/MF/complete

Report of the National Commission on Secondary Schooling for Hispanics. Includes reform proposals for urban schools, and related socioeconomic data on Hispanic Americans. Report is in 2 volumes, described below.

Availability: Hispanic Policy Development Project, 1001 Connecticut Ave., NW, Suite 310, Washington DC 20036, $12.50; SRI/MF/complete.

R5300-3.1: Volume I
[Monograph. 1984. 56 p. ISBN 0-918911-01-X. SRI/MF/complete.]

Presents findings and recommendations of the National Commission on Secondary Schooling for Hispanics.

Contains contents listing and introduction (p. 7-11); summary (p. 13-15); narrative analysis in 3 sections, with 2 charts (p. 19-45); and methodology, notes, and references (p. 49-56).

R5300-3.2: Volume II
[Monograph. 1984. 107 p. ISBN 0-918911-02-8. SRI/MF/complete.]

Presents background information relevant to secondary education for Hispanics, including data on Hispanic population characteristics and educational status. Data are derived from surveys conducted by NCES and National Institute for Work and Learning, and from 1980 census.

Data are shown for Hispanic Americans, with occasional comparisons to whites, blacks, and/or national sample. Additional detail for Hispanic subgroups (Mexican, Cuban, Puerto Rican, and other) are often included.

Contains contents listing and foreword (p. 7-9); and 3 sections, as follows:

Section 1. Hispanic Profiles. Narrative interspersed with 28 maps/charts and 14 tables showing population, by State, major Hispanic metro area, sex, age, occupational group, Spanish and English use, and education; median family income; and rates for poverty, labor force participation, unemployment, female headed households, and homeownership, in 5 major SMSAs; mostly for 1979 or 1980, with selected population trends from 1970 and projections to 1990. (p. 13-51)

Section 2. Graphics, "High School and Beyond." Brief introduction; and 6 charts and 6 tables showing high school dropout rates and reasons by sex and/or census division, grade averages, enrollment rates by program (including vocational and remedial education and Spanish courses), and achievement test scores by subject area, 1980 and/or 1982. (p. 55-65)

Section 3. Reflections. 5 narrative reports; and "Hispanics in Fast Food Jobs," by Ivan Charner and Bryna Shore Fraser, with 10 tables on fast food employee characteristics, reasons for taking and quitting job, fringe benefits, training received, skills acquired, assessment of management, family/other approval of job, and general work attitudes. (p. 69-107)

R5650
Japan Economic Institute

R5650-1   YEARBOOK OF U.S.-JAPAN ECONOMIC RELATIONS in 1983
Annual. Oct. 1984.
7+129 p
SRI/MF/complete

Annual report on trends in Japanese economy and economic relations with U.S., 1979-83. Includes data on industrial production, employment, prices, finances, and trade. Also includes data on election results. Data are primarily from Japanese ministries, Bank of Japan, and U.S. Dept of Commerce.

Contains contents listing (6 p.); narrative report in 6 parts, with 20 charts (p. 1-71); appendix A on election results in Japan, with 4 tables (p. 73-74); and appendix B, with 44 tables (p. 77-129). All tables are described below.

This is the 6th annual edition. Previous edition is described in SRI 1983 Annual under this number.

Availability: Japan Economic Institute, 1000 Connecticut Ave., NW, Washington DC 20036, $6.00; SRI/MF/complete.

TABLES:
[Data are for Japan, unless otherwise noted. Most data on Japanese economy and U.S.-Japan economic relations are shown for 1979-83, often with monthly detail for 1982-83.]

ELECTION RESULTS

a. Number of candidates, seats won, and share of vote won, for lower house elections, 1983, with trends from 1976; Liberal Democratic Party (LDP) members in lower and upper house, by faction, before and after 1983 election; and listings of cabinet members and LDP officials, including age and faction. 4 tables. (p. 73-74)

JAPANESE ECONOMY

b. GNP in yen, by sector; interest rates; and money supply in yen. Tables 1-3. (p. 77-80)

c. Industrial indexes: production, producers' inventories of finished goods, consumption and inventories of materials, and manufacturing operating rates, all by industry sector; and production, by end-use classification. Tables 4-9. (p. 81-89)

d. Residential construction starts, including public and private housing, and owner-built, developer-built, and rental units. Table 10. (p. 90)

e. Working-age population; labor force, by employment status; job openings/applications ratio; and indexes of employment, wages, and labor productivity, by industry sector. Tables 11-14. (p. 91-97)

f. WPI, by industry sector and for domestic and exported products by type; CPI by item; and export and import yen-based price indexes. Tables 15-19. (p. 98-103)

g. Balance of payments in dollars, by account; foreign trade in dollars and yen; trade volume index; and trade in dollars, by country and commodity. Tables 20-27. (p. 104-112)

U.S.-JAPAN ECONOMIC RELATIONS

h. Japanese dollar- and yen-based trade with U.S.; yen-dollar exchange rates; and U.S. international transactions. Tables 28-32. (p. 113-115)

i. U.S. foreign trade: total, and by country, commodity, and with Japan by commodity. Tables 33-40. (p. 116-127)

j. U.S. direct investment abroad, by country and in Japan by industry sector; and foreign direct investment in U.S., by country and Japanese industry sector. Tables 41-44. (p. 128-129)

R5650-2   JEI REPORT
Weekly, in 2 parts.
Approx. 10 p. var. paging.
ISSN 0744-6489.
LC SN 82-20877.
SRI/MF/excerpts, shipped quarterly

Weekly report, published in 2 sections, on Japanese economic and political issues and developments, and relations with U.S. Data are generally from Japanese Government and private sources and U.S. Government agencies.

General Format:

Section A. Analysis of a selected topic, frequently including statistics.

Section B. Several brief news and feature articles, occasionally containing statistics, including reports on U.S.-Japanese competition in specific industries; statistical supplement, with 2 irregularly recurring tables; and 1 quarterly table.

Report also includes semiannual or quarterly subject indexes.

Annual statistical features include articles on U.S.-Japanese trade, Japanese economy, foreign investment by and in Japan, and other topics.

Irregularly recurring and quarterly tables are listed below. Irregularly recurring tables appeared in Nov.-Dec. 1984 and Jan., May, and July-Aug. 1985 issues. All additional features with substantial statistical content are described, as they appear, under "Statistical Features;" page locations and latest period of coverage for quarterly table are also noted. Nonstatistical features are not covered.

Availability: Japan Economic Institute, 1000 Connecticut Ave., NW, Washington DC 20036, $40.00 per yr.; SRI/MF/excerpts for monthly tables, and all portions covered under "Statistical Features;" shipped quarterly.

Issues reviewed during 1985: Nov. 2, 1984-Oct. 25, 1985 (P) (1984 Nos. 42-48; 1985 Nos. 1-41) [No issues were published for Nov. 23 and Dec. 28, 1984, and Jan. 4 and May 31, 1985].

TABLES:

IRREGULARLY RECURRING TABLES

[Data are shown for month 2-3 months prior to cover date, 2 previous months, current and previous years to date, and 2 previous full years.]

[1] Trade and payments data [Japanese balance of payments detail, and trade balance including detail for automobile and steel exports and crude oil imports; yen-dollar exchange rate; and U.S.-Japan trade balance for industrial supplies, capital and consumer goods, food/feed, and automotive products; most shown in dollars].

[2] Japanese economic indicators [job openings/applications ratio, and percent change from previous year for 12 indicators].

QUARTERLY TABLE

[1] Japan's real GNP at constant prices (1975 prices) [personal consumption spending, private residential construction and fixed nonresidential investment, change in business and government inventories, government current expenditures and fixed investment, and exports and imports; data are shown in yen, for quarter ending 3-5 months prior to cover date, 3 previous quarters, and usually 2 previous fiscal years].

STATISTICAL FEATURES:

R5650–2.601: Nov. 2, 1984 (No. 42A)

JAPANESE BANKS IN THE U.S.: AN OVERVIEW

(20 p.) Article, with 5 tables showing name or type of U.S. offices of Japanese banks, with location, and detail on number of overseas and domestic branches, arranged by Japanese parent company (no date); and value of assets, deposits, and outstanding business loans, for

domestic/foreign, total foreign, and total Japanese banks in the U.S., June 1981-83, with detail by Japanese parent company and U.S. office, June 1980-83.

Data are from *American Banker* and company annual reports. Corrected data appear in the Nov. 9, 1984 issue (see R5650–2.604 below).

R5650–2.602: Nov. 2, 1984 (No. 42B)

ENERGY CONSUMPTION IN JAPAN REBOUNDS

(p. 7-9) Article, with 3 tables showing Japan's energy supply, and demand by consuming sector, by energy type, FY83; and total supply and demand, FY79-83. Data are from Japanese Ministry of International Trade and Industry.

R5650–2.603: Nov. 9, 1984 (No. 43A)

TRILATERAL RELATIONS: A TILT TO THE PACIFIC?

(p. 1-9) Article, with 2 tables showing defense expenditures as percent of GNP and percent change in defense spending, for U.S. and 13 NATO members, various years 1979-83. Data are from NATO and DOD.

R5650–2.604: Nov. 9, 1984 (No. 43B)

CORRECTIONS

(p. 12) Corrected data for article on Japanese banks with offices in U.S. For description of article, see R5650-2.601 above.

R5650–2.605: Nov. 16, 1984 (No. 44B)

BILATERAL TRADE DEFICIT HEADED FOR $36 BILLION LEVEL

(p. 3-5) Article, with 2 tables showing value of U.S. exports to and imports from Japan, by commodity, 1st 9 months 1983-84.

R5650–2.606: Nov. 30, 1984 (No. 45A)

CORPORATE TAX DEBATE IN JAPAN AND THE U.S.

(18 p.) Article discussing corporate tax rates and reforms in U.S. and Japan. Most data are from Japanese and U.S. government agencies. Includes 13 tables showing the following for U.S. and Japan:

a. Statutory corporate tax rates, and depreciation allowances or accelerated cost recovery schedules; and estimated revenue effects of various corporate tax measures and reforms; 1983 or 1984.

b. Total tax and corporate tax revenues; subnational corporate taxes (total and as percent of national corporate taxes); number of corporations or returns, and value of sales or receipts, total and net taxes, and taxable income, by capital or asset size; and number of corporations or returns, and value of taxable income and net taxes, by industry group; various years 1950-84.

Most data are for fiscal years.

R5650–2.607: Dec. 7, 1984 (No. 46A)

IMPORT QUOTAS AND THE AUTOMOBILE INDUSTRY: THE COSTS OF PROTECTIONISM

(16 p.) By Robert W. Crandall. Article on the effects of Japanese import quotas on the U.S. automobile industry. Data are from *Consumer Reports,* and motor vehicle industry and Federal sources. Includes 8 tables showing the following data, for the U.S. unless otherwise noted, various periods 1960-83:

a. Domestic and import car registrations; after-tax rate of return on equity, for motor vehicle and all manufacturing industries; safety and emissions equipment cost per car; and *Consumer Reports* aggregate quality rating for Japanese imports and 3 major U.S. motor vehicle manufacturers.

b. Wages for motor vehicle and all manufacturing industries in U.S. and Japan; motor vehicle/equipment producers' gross investment expenditures (current and 1972 dollars); estimated effect of Japanese car quotas on U.S. car prices, with comparison to CPI; and motor vehicle industry pre-tax profits and profit per vehicle (current and/or 1972 dollars).

R5650–2.608: Dec. 14, 1984 (No. 47B)

QUARTERLY TABLE

[1] Japan's GNP [3rd quarter 1984]. (p. 2)

R5650–2.609: Dec. 21, 1984 (No. 48A)

U.S.-JAPAN COMPETITION IN MOTOR VEHICLE PARTS

(14 p.) Article, with 4 tables showing the following for U.S. motor vehicle parts/accessories industry: exports and imports, by principal country of destination and origin; exports to and imports from Japan, by product type; and list of Japanese-affiliated manufacturers, including name and ownership share for Japanese parent companies; various periods 1979-1st 9 months 1984.

Data are from USITC and Census Bureau.

R5650–2.610: Jan. 11, 1985 (No. 1B)

JAPANESE GOVERNMENT SEES 4.6 PERCENT GNP GROWTH IN FY85

(p. 7-9) Article forecasting changes in various economic indicators for Japan, with 2 tables showing actual changes FY81-83, government forecasts FY84-85, and forecasts of 14 private organizations FY85.

R5650–2.611: Jan. 18, 1985 (No. 2B)

YEN: A LOOK BACKWARD AND FORWARD

(p. 3-5) Article, with 2 tables showing yen-dollar exchange rate, and average daily trading volume (in dollars), monthly 1984; and exchange rates for dollar vs. 7 foreign currencies, selected periods Dec. 30, 1983-Jan. 1, 1985. Data sources include Tokyo and NYC interbank spot markets.

R5650–2.612: Jan. 25, 1985 (No. 3A)

NEW RISING SUN: JAPAN'S OPTOELECTRONICS INDUSTRY

(p. 1-10) Article, with 2 tables showing the following for Japan's optoelectronics industry: sales (in yen) for components, equipment, and systems, various years FY81-2000; and volume of demand, by detailed product, 1983 and 1988 with annual growth rate. Data are from Japan's Optoelectronic Industry and Technology Development Assn.

R5650–2.613: Feb. 1, 1985 (No. 4A)

RECENT TRENDS IN JAPANESE IMPORTS: A STUDY BY THE BANK OF JAPAN

(p. 1-19) Article examining structural changes in Japan's import purchases, with supporting data on trends in real household expenditures for goods and services, import price elasticities, export market vs. domestic demand, import volume and value for selected food commodities, and other aspects of import activity, 1970s-83. Data are from a Bank of Japan study. Includes several charts and 5 tables.

R5650–2.614: Feb. 15, 1985 (No. 6A)

JAPAN'S EXPANDING U.S. MANUFACTURING PRESENCE: 1984 UPDATE, ANNUAL FEATURE

(p. 1-22) Annual article on Japanese investment in U.S. industry, 1984. Data are from a survey by Japan Economic Institute. Includes alphabetical list of Japanese owned or affiliated manufacturing companies in U.S., in operation or under construction as of Dec. 31, 1984, showing the following for each: plant locations and year opened/acquired, parent company and ownership share, whether new or acquired, SIC 4-digit industry, and number of employees.

Also includes list of companies arranged alphabetically by State; list of companies arranged by SIC 4-digit industry; and list of sales, mergers, closings, and other changes since 1980-83 surveys.

R5650–2.615: Feb. 22, 1985 (No. 7B)

AWASH IN RED INK: THE 1984 U.S. TRADE ACCOUNT

(p. 4-7) Article, with 2 tables showing value of U.S. exports to and imports from Japan, by detailed commodity, 1983-84.

R5650–2.616: Mar. 1, 1985 (No. 8A)

ARMS CONTROL TALKS: AN INTERVIEW WITH THE DIRECTOR OF THE U.S. ARMS CONTROL AND DISARMAMENT AGENCY

(p. 1-8) Article, with 1 table showing number of troops and aircraft, and number and tonnage of vessels, for Japan's armed forces, and for armed forces of 6 countries deployed near Japan (including U.S. 7th Fleet and forces in South Korea), primarily 1983. Data are from Japan Defense Agency and U.S. State Dept.

R5650–2.617: Mar. 1, 1985 (No. 8B)

JAPAN'S 1984 BALANCE OF PAYMENTS SETS RECORDS, ANNUAL FEATURE

(p. 6-7) Annual article, with 1 table showing Japan's balance of payments, by component, 1980-84.

RESTRAINTS ON JAPANESE-MADE CARS COMING TO AN END?

(p. 7-9) Article, with 1 table showing U.S. retail sales volume, for imported Japanese autos by manufacturer, and for all imported and domestic autos, 1980-84. Data are from *Automotive News.*

R5650–2.618: Mar. 8, 1985 (No. 9A)

NEW HORIZONS FOR JAPAN'S NEW MATERIALS INDUSTRY

(p. 1-13) Article on Japan's new materials industry. New materials are used in manufacturing and include recently developed products in the categories of metals, ceramics, plastics, fibers, composites, glass/crystals, and coatings/adhesives. Data are from Japan's Ministry of International Trade and Industry (MITI) and are shown in yen.

Includes 2 charts and 1 table showing value of Japan's new materials market, with detail by category and market component, 2000; and MITI's new materials R&D budget by general purpose, actual FY84, and requested FY85.

Corrected data appear in the Mar. 22, 1985 issue (see R5650-2.621 below).

R5650–2.619: Mar. 8, 1985 (No. 9B)

THE YEN: WHEN IT RAINS, IT POURS

(p. 2-4) Article, with 1 table showing value of Japan's liabilities to foreigners, and of purchases of foreign assets, by type, 1981-83 period and 1984. Data are from Bank of Japan.

R5650–2.620: Mar. 22, 1985 (No. 11A)

INTEGRATION OF DOMESTIC AND INTERNATIONAL FINANCIAL MARKETS: THE JAPANESE EXPERIENCE, PART I

(p. 1-23) By Sena Eken. Article on Japanese financial and capital market trends, 1970s-82. Data sources include Bank of Japan and Japanese Ministry of Finance.

Includes 10 tables showing the following for Japan, primarily in yen:

a. Change in selected financial indicators, with comparisons to U.S. and West Germany; percent of central government debt outstanding, by type of creditor institution; value of bonds issued, outstanding, and traded, by type of issuer; number and value of foreign yen bonds by type (Samurai bonds and private placements); and outstanding balances by type of money market; various periods 1969/70-82.

b. Stock exchange trading volume and value; number and value of new stock shares traded at market and par prices; foreign purchases and sales of stocks; value of spot, forward, and swap transactions in Tokyo foreign exchange market; and turnover value and outstanding balance in Tokyo dollar call market; various years 1970-82.

This is the 1st of 2 articles reprinted from IMF's *Staff Papers.* For description of 2nd article, see R5650-2.622 below.

R5650–2.621: Mar. 22, 1985 (No. 11B)

CORRECTIONS

(p. 8) Corrected data for article on Japan's new materials market. For description of article, see R5650-2.618 above.

R5650–2.622: Mar. 29, 1985 (No. 12A)

INTEGRATION OF DOMESTIC AND INTERNATIONAL FINANCIAL MARKETS: THE JAPANESE EXPERIENCE, PART II

(p. 1-17) By Sena Eken. Article on Japanese financial and capital market trends, 1970s-82. Data sources include Bank of Japan, OECD, and IMF.

Includes 5 tables showing the following, for various years 1970-82:

a. Yen deposits of nonresidents in Japan, and in Euromarket by type of institutional depositer; and share of Eurobond and total international bond issues, and share of official holdings of foreign exchange, for yen and 4-5 other currencies.

b. Gross value of bond and share issues, and foreign bond issues/placements as percent of world total, for Japan and 3-4 major capital markets; and number of listed domestic and foreign companies, and value of listed and traded stocks, for Tokyo and 3 other stock exchanges.

This is the 2nd of 2 articles reprinted from IMF's *Staff Papers.* For description of 1st article, see R5650-2.620 above.

R5650–2.623: Mar. 29, 1985 (No. 12B)

QUARTERLY TABLE

[1] Japan's GNP [4th quarter 1984]. (p. 4)

SINO-JAPANESE TRADE BOOMS

(p. 7-9) Article, with 2 tables showing value of Japan's exports to and imports from PRC, 1979-84, with detail for various major commodities, 1982-84. Data are from Japan Tariff Assn.

R5650–2.624: Apr. 5, 1985 (No. 13A)

JAPAN AND LATIN AMERICA: ECONOMIC AND POLITICAL RELATIONS

(p. 1-14) Article, with 10 tables showing value of Japan's export and import trade with Latin America (actual and as percent of Japanese and Latin American total trade), by country and type of product; and Japan's direct investment in and aid to Latin America, by country; various periods FY79-1984.

R5650–2.625: Apr. 26, 1985 (No. 16A)

JAPANESE ECONOMY IN 1984, ANNUAL FEATURE

(p. 1-13) Annual article, with 2 tables showing Japanese GNP and components, 1983-84 and quarterly 1984; and capital investment (in yen), by industry division and selected major group, FY83-84. Data are from Japanese Economic Planning Agency.

R5650–2.626: May 3, 1985 (No. 17A)

U.S. EXPORTS TO JAPAN: A REVIEW OF 1984 SALES, ANNUAL FEATURE

(9 p.) Annual article, with 1 table showing volume and/or value of U.S. exports to Japan, 1983-84; and Japan's share of all U.S. exports, 1984; by detailed commodity. Data are from U.S. Commerce Dept.

R5650–2.627: May 3, 1985 (No. 17B)

JAPANESE WORKERS HARVEST HIGHER WAGES FROM SPRING NEGOTIATIONS, ANNUAL FEATURE

(p. 6-7) Annual article on results of wage contract negotiations in Japan, with 1 table showing amount and percent of average monthly increase 1984-85, and new monthly standard wage 1985, by company size (large and small) and for 14 major industry groups. Data are from *Nihon Keizai Shimbun.*

Previous article, for 1983-84, is described in SRI 1984 Annual under R5650-2.529.

R5650–2.628: May 17, 1985 (No. 19A)

JAPANESE DEFENSE: OUT OF THE CLOSET

(p. 1-14) Article, with 2 tables showing Japan's actual defense budget and amount proposed by Japan Defense Agency, by funded group; and top 10 companies ranked by value of defense contracts; FY84 with comparisons to FY83. Data are from Japan Defense Agency and *Nihon Keizai Shimbun,* and are shown in yen.

R5650–2.629: May 17, 1985 (No. 19B)

FY85 CAR EXPORT QUOTA ALLOCATED

(p. 5-7) Article, with 1 table showing Japan's unofficial quotas on auto exports to U.S., by manufacturer, FY81-83 period, FY84, and tentative FY85.

R5650–2.630: May 24, 1985 (No. 20A)

TAKING FROM PETER TO PAY PAUL: 1985 JAPANESE FISCAL POLICY

(12 p.) Article, with 7 tables showing Japanese Government general account expenditures by function and revenues by source, with detail for fiscal investment/loan program outlays, FY80-85; summary of budgeted payments and receipts, FY84-88; and estimated revenue effects of FY83-85 tax reforms.

Data are from Japanese Ministry of Finance, and are shown in yen.

For description of a similar article, with data through FY84, see SRI 1984 Annual under R5650-2.521.

R5650–2.631: May 24, 1985 (No. 20B)

BEIJING CONCERNED OVER BOOMING TRADE WITH TOKYO

(p. 3-6) Article, with 1 table showing value of exports to PRC, for 4-11 leading Japanese companies in each of 7 industry sectors, FY83-85. Data are from *Nihon Keizai Shimbun*.

R5650–2.632: June 7, 1985 (No. 21A)

HIGH-TECH INDUSTRIES AND THE STRUCTURE OF FOREIGN TRADE

(p. 1-10) By Michiaki Kawano. Article, with 4 tables showing industrial production indexes for Japan, and value of exports for Japan, U.S., and West Germany, with detail for selected industries, various years 1970-84; and high-technology capital investment growth rate and share of overall capital investment and growth in Japan, for all, materials, processing/assembly, and nonmanufacturing industries, 1984.

Data sources include Japanese Ministry of International Trade and Industry, Bank of Japan, and Japan Development Bank.

R5650–2.633: June 7, 1985 (No. 21B)

DETERIORATING U.S. TRADE ACCOUNT: IS THE WORST OVER?

(p. 10-12) Article, with 2 tables showing value of U.S. exports to and imports from Japan, by commodity, 1st quarter 1984-85.

R5650–2.634: June 14, 1985 (No. 22A)

U.S. IMPORTS FROM JAPAN: A REVIEW OF 1984 SALES, ANNUAL FEATURE

(p. 1-13) Annual article, with 1 table on U.S. imports from Japan, showing volume and value, 1983-84, and percent of all U.S. imports, 1984, by detailed commodity. Data are from U.S. Commerce Dept.

R5650–2.635: June 21, 1985 (No. 23B)

JAPAN'S ODA DISBURSEMENTS REACH RECORD LEVELS, ANNUAL FEATURE

(p. 4-5) Annual article, with 1 table showing Japanese net official development assistance (ODA) disbursements, by type of assistance, 1981-84. Data are from Japanese Ministry of Foreign Affairs.

For description of previous article, see SRI 1984 Annual under R5650-2.527.

U.S. SEMICONDUCTOR MAKERS FILE TRADE COMPLAINT AGAINST JAPANESE RIVALS

(p. 10-12) Article, with 1 table showing capital expenditures (in yen), for 9 major Japanese semiconductor manufacturers, FY81-85. Data are from *Nihon Keizai Shimbun*.

R5650–2.636: June 28, 1985 (No. 24B)

QUARTERLY TABLE

[1] Japan's GNP [1st quarter 1985; table is accompanied by narrative summary]. (p. 10-12)

R5650–2.637: July 12, 1985 (No. 26B)

SURGING CAPITAL OUTFLOW PUTS JAPAN NEAR TOP CREDITOR POSITION

(p. 5-7) Article, with 2 tables showing the following for Japan: net outflow of long-term capital, including portfolio investment, direct investment, loans, and capital balance, with detail for dealings with U.S. and EC; and external assets and liabilities, by category, for private and government sector; 1983-84.

JAPAN'S TELECOMMUNICATIONS MARKET HEATS UP

(p. 8-11) Article, with 1 table showing all or most of the following for 5 Japanese telecommunications companies licensed in June 1985: capital (in yen), major shareholders and percent of company owned, services offered, service locations, start-up date, type of transmission equipment, and number of circuits.

R5650–2.638: July 19, 1985 (No. 27A)

JAPAN-ASEAN TRADE RELATIONS

(p. 1-12) Article, with 4 tables showing Japan's exports to and imports from Assn of Southeast Asian Nations (ASEAN), by product category and country of destination or origin; and Japan's direct foreign investment in Asia, with detail for ASEAN member nations; various periods 1979-85. Data are from the Japan Tariff Assn and the Japanese Ministry of Finance.

R5650–2.639: July 26, 1985 (No. 28A)

U.S. AGRICULTURAL EXPORTS TO JAPAN: A REVIEW OF 1984 SALES, ANNUAL FEATURE

(14 p.) Annual article, with 14 tables showing the following for agricultural trade: value of U.S. exports, by importing country; volume and value of U.S. exports to Japan, by detailed commodity; and, for 6 commodities, volume and value of U.S. exports by importing country, and volume of Japan's imports by country of origin; various years 1980-84.

Data are from USDA and Japanese Ministry of Finance.

R5650–2.640: Aug. 2, 1985 (No. 29A)

FOREIGN LAWYERS IN JAPAN: AN INTERVIEW WITH JAMES V. FEINERMAN OF HARVARD LAW SCHOOL

(p. 1-13) Article, with 2 tables showing the following for Japan: number of persons involved in legal work, by type of work, 1982; and number of students taking and passing national legal examination for admission to law school, selected years 1949-84.

R5650–2.641: Aug. 2, 1985 (No. 29B)

JAPANESE FOREIGN DIRECT INVESTMENT CONTINUES TO BOOM, ANNUAL FEATURE

(p. 4-8) Annual article, with 2 tables showing Japan's direct foreign investment, by country or world area, and by industry sector, annually FY80-84 and total as of Mar. 31, 1985.

For description of previous article, see SRI 1984 Annual under R5650-2.536.

JAPANESE INVESTMENT IN U.S. AUTOMOTIVE ASSEMBLY FACILITIES

(p. 15) Undated table showing capacity, employment, investment, startup date, product line, and plant location, for U.S. subsidiaries of 6 Japanese auto manufacturers.

R5650–2.642: Aug. 9, 1985 (No. 30A)

JAPAN-CANADA RELATIONS

(p. 1-9) Article, with 1 table showing Japan's exports to and imports from Canada, by commodity, 1980-84. Data are from Japan Tariff Assn.

R5650–2.643: Aug. 9, 1985 (No. 30B)

CABINET ADOPTS STRINGENT FISCAL 1986 BUDGET GUIDELINES

(p. 10-11) Article, with 1 table showing changes in Japan's general account budget, by function, FY85-86. Data are from Japanese Ministry of Finance and are shown in yen.

R5650–2.644: Aug. 16, 1985 (No. 31A)

FOREIGN DIRECT INVESTMENT IN JAPAN: 1985 UPDATE, ANNUAL FEATURE

(p. 1-10) Annual article, with 3 tables showing number and value of direct foreign investments in Japan, as follows: by type (new firm, existing firm, and expanded holdings), shown by investing country or world area and for investments from individuals and subsidiaries, 1983 and 1984; and by industry division and major group, 1984.

Data are from Japanese Ministry of Finance and are shown in yen.

For description of previous article, see SRI 1984 Annual under R5650-2.526.

R5650–2.645: Aug. 23, 1985 (No. 32A)

COSTS AND BENEFITS OF PROTECTION: A STUDY BY THE ORGANIZATION FOR ECONOMIC COOPERATION AND DEVELOPMENT

(p. 1-12) Article summarizing results of an OECD study on the effects of protectionist trade policies. Includes 3 tables showing the following:

a. For 5 East Asian countries: value of exports to OECD countries, for manufactured goods subject to trade restrictions, 1980 and 1983, with 1980 comparison to exports of all manufactured goods; and value of total imports by all OECD countries and by U.S., 1979-84.

b. For 8 less developed countries with high external debt: value of OECD imports affected by nontariff trade barriers (amount and as percent of all imports), for manufactured goods and agricultural products, 1982.

R5650–2.646: Aug. 23, 1985 (No. 32B)

RISING TRADE DEFICIT EXERTING LESS DRAG ON U.S. GROWTH, ANNUAL FEATURE

(p. 4-7) Annual article, with 2 tables showing value of U.S. exports to and imports from Japan, by commodity, 1st half 1984-85.

For description of previous article, see SRI 1984 Annual under R5650-2.537.

TRENDS IN FOREIGN INVESTMENT INCOME

(p. 7-8) Article, with 2 tables showing current account balances for U.S. and Japan, with detail for merchandise trade, services, and investment income, annually 1981-84, and 1st 2 quarters 1984-85. Data are from Bank of Japan and U.S. Commerce Dept.

UPDATE ON JAPAN'S VENTURE CAPITAL INDUSTRY

(p. 12-14) Article, with 2 tables showing number and value of venture capital investments in Japan, by type and industry, and for foreign investments, 1983-84. Data are from Japanese Ministry of International Trade and Industry, and are shown in yen.

R5650-2.647: Aug. 30, 1985 (No. 33B)

JAPAN'S TRADE ENGINE DOWNSHIFTS TO LOW GEAR

(p. 1-4) Article, with 2 tables showing value of Japan's exports and imports, by world region and economic or political grouping, and by commodity, 1st half 1984-85. Data are from Japanese Ministry of Finance.

R5650-2.648: Sept. 6, 1985 (No. 34A)

JAPAN'S POLICIES FOR DECLINING INDUSTRIES: AN OVERVIEW

(p. 1-7) Article, with 1 table on Japanese Government plans for disposal of excess capacity in declining industries. Table shows the following data by industry and product: plan approval date and completion target date; capacity to be decommissioned, and percent of capacity affected; and capacity decommissioned (scrapped and mothballed) through June 1985.

R5650-2.649: Sept. 6, 1985 (No. 34B)

JAPAN-KOREA COOPERATION

(p. 4-5) Article, with 1 table showing foreign investment in South Korea, for Japan, U.S., Europe, and all others, 1962-81 period and annually 1982-84. Data are from Korean Ministry of Finance.

R5650-2.650: Sept. 13, 1985 (No. 35A)

FISCAL POLICY AND THE TRADE DEFICIT

(p. 1-9) Article, with 2 tables showing the following, as percent of GNP:

a. For U.S.: personal and business savings; private investment; Federal and State/local balances; and current account; 1970 and 1975-84.

b. For Japan: household and business savings; private investment; balances for central government, social security, and local government; and current account; FY70 and FY75-83.

Data are from U.S. Council of Economic Advisers and Japanese Economic Planning Agency.

R5650-2.651: Sept. 13, 1985 (No. 35B)

JAPAN'S EXPORTS TO MIDDLE EAST OIL-EXPORTING COUNTRIES

(p. 7-8) Article, with 1 table showing value of Japan's exports to U.S. and 7 OPEC member countries, with OPEC and U.S. shares of total exports, 1981-1st half 1985. Data are from Japan Tariff Assn.

PARTY CONTRIBUTIONS NEAR RECORD, ANNUAL FEATURE

(p. 8-10) Annual article, with 2 tables showing aggregate major donations (in yen and dollars) to Japan's political parties, by party, FY83-84; and donations (in yen) to 5 major factions of the Liberal Democratic Party, FY82-84. Data are from Japan's Ministry of Home Affairs.

R5650-2.652: Sept. 20, 1985 (No. 36A)

EDUCATIONAL REFORM: PRINCIPLES AND POLITICS

(p. 1-12) Article on Japan's educational system. Data are from *Japan Statistical Yearbook, 1984.*

Includes 2 tables showing number of institutions, teachers, and students, by type of educational institution, 1983; and rates of advancement, from lower secondary level to upper secondary level and to workforce, and from upper secondary to college (with detail by sex) and to workforce, selected years 1950-83.

R5650-2.653: Sept. 20, 1985 (No. 36B)

JAPAN CONSIDERS SOUTH AFRICAN SANCTIONS

(p. 7-9) Article, with 1 table showing Japan's exports to and imports from South Africa, annually 1980-84 and 1st half 1984-85. Data are from Japan Tariff Assn.

JAPAN-TAIWAN TRADE

(p. 9-10) Article, with 1 table showing Japan's exports to and imports from Taiwan and PRC, annually 1982-84 and 1st half 1984-85. Data are from Japan Tariff Assn.

R5650-2.654: Sept. 27, 1985 (No. 37A)

1985 UPDATE ON JAPAN'S ENERGY PROFILE: CONSERVATION

(p. 1-17) Annual article on Japan's energy industry. Data sources include Petroleum Assn of Japan, and Japan's Ministries of Finance and of International Trade and Industry. Includes 12 tables showing the following for Japan:

a. Energy supply, and consumption by sector, by energy type, FY83 and/or FY84.

b. Crude oil production, throughput, operating rate, and inventories; imported crude oil volume and value; imports and consumption of non-crude oil energy, by energy type and industry sector; electric utility output, by fuel type; electricity consumption for light and power (with detail by industry); and household energy consumption, by energy type; annually 1980-83 and monthly 1984-Mar. 1985.

c. Energy consumption, by energy type and industry sector, quarterly 1983-1st quarter 1985; industrial energy efficiency index, FY79-84; and industrial energy consumption change components, FY80-84.

R5650-2.655: Oct. 4, 1985 (No. 38B)

QUARTERLY TABLE

[1] Japan's GNP [2nd quarter 1985; table is accompanied by narrative summary]. (p. 3-4)

R5650-2.656: Oct. 18, 1985 (No. 40A)

JAPAN'S POLICIES FOR DECLINING INDUSTRIES: TWO CASE STUDIES

(p. 1-12) Article, with 2 tables showing Japan's production, imports, and exports, for 8 petrochemicals and aluminum, with selected import detail by country of origin, 1973-84. Data are from Japanese Ministry of International Trade and Industry, and Japan Tariff Assn.

R5650-2.657: Oct. 25, 1985 (No. 41A)

JAPAN-KOREA ECONOMIC RELATIONS

(p. 1-11) Article on trends in economic relations between Japan and South Korea. Data are from IMF, Japan Tariff Assn, Korean Economic Planning Board, and Korean Ministry of Finance. Includes 4 tables showing the following for Korea:

a. Trade balance overall, and trade with Japan, 1965-84, with detail for 1984 Japanese trade by commodity; and foreign investment from Japan, U.S., Europe, and all others, 1962-81 period and annually 1982-84.

b. Balance of payments; foreign exchange holdings; and real growth rates for GNP, agricultural production, mining/manufacturing, consumption, investment, exports, and imports; 1983-2nd quarter 1985.

Similar article is described in SRI 1983 Annual under R5650-2.435.

R5650-2.658: Oct. 25, 1985 (No. 41B)

JAPAN-EUROPEAN COMMUNITY TRADE

(p. 9-11) Article, with 1 table showing Japan's trade with EC, by country of origin and destination, annually 1982-84 and 1st 8 months 1984-85. Data are from Japan Tariff Assn.

R5685
Joint Center
for Political Studies

R5685-1   **BLACK ELECTED OFFICIALS: A National Roster, 1985**
Annual. June 1985.
ix+440 p. No. 5064-JCP202.
ISSN 0882-1593.
LC 84-51421.
SRI/MF/complete, delayed

Annual report, for 1985, on black elected officials, presenting statistical summary and roster of officials by State. Covers Federal, State, regional, county, municipal, judicial/law enforcement, and educational offices.

Data are from surveys of officials included in the Joint Center's data base, telephone inquiries, a newspaper clipping service, Census Bureau, and various State officials.

Contents:

a. Listings of contents, tables, and charts; preface; overview; and explanatory notes. (p. v-ix, 1-7)

b. Statistical summary, with 1 chart and 9 tables showing total and female black elected officials, by detailed office and State, and by office category and census division; and racial composition of congressional districts represented by blacks, of State legislatures, and of cities with black mayors; mostly as of Jan. 1985, with summary trends in number of black officials from 1970. (p. 8-21) *c.* References. (p. 22)

d. State rosters, each including the following: overview, with description of governmental organization and data on total and black population, voting age population, and registered voters; and list of black elected officials, grouped by office, showing title, jurisdiction, address, and term expiration date. (p. 23-401)

e. Alphabetical index to officials. (p. 403-440)

Data by State and rosters also include D.C. and Virgin Islands.

This is the 14th edition of the report.

Report is published and distributed for the Joint Center by UNIPUB, a division of R. R. Bowker Co.

Availability: UNIPUB, PO Box 1222, Ann Arbor MI 48106, $29.50+$2.50 postage and handling; SRI/MF/complete, delayed until Dec. 1985.

R5685–4   FOCUS

Monthly. Approx. 8 p.
ISSN 0740-0195.
LC 73-643826.
SRI/MF/complete

Monthly newsletter (combined Nov./Dec. issue) focusing on topics of concern to blacks, including black political participation, and economic and social issues. Data are from Federal and private sources and the Center's own research.

Issues contain feature articles, some with statistics; and narrative depts. Recurring features include summary data from the Center's annual survey of black elected officials. An annual index is published in the Nov./Dec. or Jan. issue.

Articles with substantial statistics are described, as they appear, under "Statistical Features." Each issue of the publication is reviewed, but an abstract is published in SRI monthly issues only when statistical features appear.

All issues are filmed, but microfiche is shipped only when an issue is abstracted.

Availability: Focus, 1301 Pennsylvania Ave., NW, Suite 400, Washington DC 20004, $12.00 per yr., single copy $1.25; SRI/MF/complete.

Issues reviewed during 1985: Nov./Dec. 1984-Sept. 1985 (P) (Vol. 12, No. 11/12; Vol. 13, Nos. 1-9).

STATISTICAL FEATURES:

R5685–4.601: Jan. 1985 (Vol. 13, No. 1)

MINORITIES AND MILITARY RECRUITMENT

(p. 3-4) By James R. Daugherty. Article, with 1 table showing male population 18 years of age, and number unqualified and unavailable for military service by reason; and number of military recruits required; 1981-83 and 1991-95 periods.

Data are from a Brookings Institution publication.

URBAN COMMUTER

(p. 5-6) By William P. O'Hare. Article, with 1 table showing distribution of urban area residents by location (central city and inner suburb), with cross-tabulation by commuting pattern (traveling to a central business district (CBD), a central city outside a CBD, and areas outside a central city), all by race, 1970 and 1980.

Data are from the Census Bureau.

R5685–4.602: Mar. 1985 (Vol. 13, No. 3)

REAGAN'S JUDICIAL APPOINTMENTS

(p. 4-5) By Sheldon Goldman. Article, with 3 tables showing the following for U.S. District and Appeals Courts: number of appointments by President Reagan during 1st term and by 4 preceding Presidents, with distribution by sex and race/ethnicity (white, black, Hispanic, and Asian); and number of appointments by Reagan during 1st term, and by Carter during 96th Congress, with distribution by appointee's net worth.

Data sources include Senate Judiciary Committee.

SELECTED U.S. SENATE RACES IN 1986

(p. 8) Table showing the following for 15 States having Senate elections in 1986, and for which reliable estimates of unregistered black voters are available: incumbent and party, victory margin in 1980, and Congressional Education Associates rating of voting record on issues of concern to minorities; and unregistered black voting-age population and black percent of total voting-age population, 1984. Data are from the Joint Center for Political Studies.

R5685–4.603: Apr. 1985 (Vol. 13, No. 4)

CARING FOR YOUNG MOTHERS

(p. 4-5) By Marian Wright Edelman. Article, with 1 table showing births to teenage mothers as percent of all births, for total and nonwhite population, by State, 1982. Data are from the Children's Defense Fund *Data Book.*

R5685–4.604: May 1985 (Vol. 13, No. 5)

6.2% MORE BEOs IN 1985, ANNUAL FEATURE

(p. 4-5) Annual article, with 1 table showing number of black elected officials by office, by State and for the Virgin Islands, as of Jan. 1985. Offices are grouped by category (Federal, State, substate/regional, county, municipal, judicial/law enforcement, and education). Data are from Joint Center for Political Studies.

For description of previous article, see SRI 1984 Annual under R5685-4.502.

WHO LIVES IN PUBLIC HOUSING?

(p. 6, 8) Article, with 2 undated tables showing distribution of persons living in public housing and those on waiting lists, by race/ethnicity (white, black, Hispanic, Asian, other), for total U.S. and by region. (Northeast region data exclude NYC.)

Data are based on responses of 64 public housing authorities managing a total of 477,-355 units (40% of U.S. public housing stock), to a May 1984 survey conducted by the Citizens Housing and Planning Assn.

R5685–4.605: July 1985 (Vol. 13, No. 7)

BLACK WOMEN IN THE MILITARY

(p. 3) By James R. Daugherty. Article, with 1 table showing total and black enlisted women, by service branch, 1974, 1979, and 1984. Data are from Defense Manpower Data Center.

R5685–11   ELECTION '84

Series. For individual publication data, see below.
SRI/MF/complete

Series of reports examining black participation in the 1984 presidential election process, and presenting trend data on black political activity. Data sources include JCPS, Gallup Organization, Federal agencies, selected publications, and voting place exit polls conducted by various media organizations.

Each report focuses on a specific topic. Series begins with the reports described below.

Availability: Joint Center for Political Studies, 1301 Pennsylvania Ave., NW, Suite 400, Washington DC 20004, complete series $25.00; SRI/MF/complete.

R5685–11.1: Impact of the Black Electorate

[Monograph. Jan. 1984. v+30 p. Rpt. No. 1. $4.95. ISBN 0-941410-44-7. LC 83-187197. SRI/MF/complete.]

By Thomas E. Cavanagh. Report on the black electorate, including trends in voter registration and turnout, party affiliation, and voting patterns, various years 1912-83.

Contains contents and table listings, and foreword (p. iii-v); narrative analysis (p. 1-7); and 16 tables, listed below (p. 8-28).

TABLES:

[Most trend data are shown for election years within the ranges noted.]

1-2. Black voting age population, by State, Nov. 1982; and top 50 cities ranked by black voting age population, 1980; [with comparisons to total voting age population]. (p. 8-9)

3. Congressional districts in which blacks comprise 20% or more of the voting age population [including 1982 congressional incumbent, percent of vote received by incumbent, and rating of incumbent's voting on minority issues]. (p. 10-12)

4-6. Reported black voter registration and turnout [in U.S. and the South]; and voter participation as a percent of those registered to vote and of voting age population [for congressional and presidential elections], by region and race; [various years 1964-82]. (p. 13-15)

7-8. Black party identification, 1937-80; and black support for Democratic presidential nominees, 1936-80. (p. 16-17)

9-10. Number of blacks in selected categories of elected officials, 1970-83; and [black population share in] cities with black mayors (1980 population over 50,000). (p. 18-19)

11-14. [Black representation at Democratic and Republican National Conventions, similar to data in Reports 3 and 4 (see below).] (p. 20-25)

15-16. Black voter registration [in 27 States ranked by number of unregistered blacks, 1982, with comparison to Reagan 1980 victory margin]; and presidential victory margins, 1960-80, and black percent of voting age population [1982]. (p. 26-28)

R5685–11.2: Jesse Jackson's Campaign: The Primaries and the Caucuses

[Monograph. 1984. 3+28 p. Rpt. No. 2. $4.95. ISBN 0-941410-45-5. SRI/MF/complete.]

By Thomas E. Cavanagh and Lorn S. Foster. Report analyzing the 1984 presidential candidacy of Jesse Jackson, and presenting related data on the black electorate and on Jackson campaign expenditures.

Contains contents listing and foreword (2 p.); narrative analysis (p. 1-14); and 7 tables, listed below (p. 16-27).

TABLES:

1. Southern voter registration [by race and State], 1980 and 1984. (p. 16)

2. Turnout changes [State total, and aggregate for predominantly black precincts], 1980-84; and 1984 1st-time voters in Democratic presidential primaries [as percent of total voters, by race; all for 13 States]. (p. 17)

3. Congressional districts in which blacks comprise 20% or more of the voting age population [selected information for each district, including black and Hispanic shares of voting age population (no date), and black median family income in 1979]. (p. 18-23)

4-6. 1984 Democratic presidential primary voting [shows candidate choices reported by voters in polling place exit surveys, as follows: by race, for 13 States; for blacks by age group (under 50 and 50/over), for 6 States; and for blacks by age, sex, income, and political ideology, for Alabama and Georgia]. (p. 24-26)

7. Jesse Jackson for President Campaign Committee disbursements [by function], Oct. 1, 1983-Apr. 30, 1984. (p. 27)

R5685–11.3: Blacks and the 1984 Democratic National Convention: A Guide

[Monograph. July 1984. 3+74 p. Rpt. No. 3. $4.95. ISBN 0-941410-46-3. SRI/MF/complete.]

Report on black participation in the 1984 Democratic National Convention. Includes data on total and black delegates, by State and territory, 1984, with black delegate trend from 1972 and black population share for 1980; and total and black delegates, and black alternates, 1932-84.

Also includes data on black voter registration and turnout, by age and sex, 1980; and repeats selected data presented in Report 1 of this series.

Contains contents listing and foreword (2 p.); narrative analysis (p. 1-3); convention information, including directories of black committee members, delegates, and alternates (p. 4-67); and 6 tables (p. 68-74).

R5685–11.4: Blacks and the 1984 Republican National Convention: A Guide

[Monograph. Aug. 1984 v+26 p. Rpt. No. 4. $4.95. ISBN 0-941410-51-X. SRI/MF/complete.]

Report on black participation in the 1984 Republican National Convention. Data are similar to data in Report 3 on the Democratic National Convention (see above), except that trends in total and black delegates and black alternates are shown from 1912.

Contains contents listing and foreword (2 p.); narrative analysis (p. 1); convention information, including directories of black delegates and alternates (p. 3-17); and 6 tables (p. 19-25).

R6000
National Academy of Sciences:
National Research Council

R6000–6 **SCIENCE, ENGINEERING, AND HUMANITIES DOCTORATES IN THE U.S.: 1983 Profile**
Biennial. 1985. v+155 p.
ISSN 0095-0750.
LC 74-645526.
SRI/MF/complete

Biennial survey report, for 1983, presenting labor force, compensation, and demographic characteristics of science/engineering and humanities PhDs graduated during 1940-82 period.

Includes data on PhD labor force by employment status and median salary, shown variously by sex, census division (and aggregate for U.S. territories), type of employer, primary work activity, and years since PhD, with detail for academic sector employment by position, tenure status, and age.

Also includes correlation between field of employment and field of degree; PhD recipients by sex, race-ethnicity (including Hispanic, Asian, and American Indian), age in 1983, year of PhD, and citizenship; and summary employment trends from 1973-81 surveys.

All data are shown by field of doctorate, and are presented separately for science/engineering and humanities PhDs.

Data are based on responses of 44,277 PhDs to a 1983 National Research Council survey. Responses are weighted to represent 515,259 PhDs.

Contains listings of contents, charts, and tables (p. iii-v); summary and introduction, with 6 charts (p. 1-13); narrative analysis in 2 chapters, interspersed with 2 maps and 30 tables (p. 15-93); and appendices A-H, with questionnaire facsimile and 42 summary or methodological tables (p. 99-155).

This is the 6th biennial survey. For description of previous survey, for 1981, see SRI 1982 Annual under this number.

Availability: National Academy of Sciences—National Research Council, Office of Scientific and Engineering Personnel, Survey of Doctorate Recipients, Rm. JH634, 2101 Constitution Ave., NW, Washington DC 20418, †; SRI/MF/complete.

R6000–15 **HUMANISTS ON THE MOVE: Employment Patterns for Humanities PhDs**
Monograph. 1985.
viii+69 p.
SRI/MF/complete

By Mary Belisle and Betty D. Maxfield. Report on employment patterns for humanities PhDs graduated during 1940-82 period, by field mobility status (employed in or out of PhD field), 1983.

Includes employment by PhD field, age, sex, minority group (Hispanic, black, Asian/Pacific Islander, American Indian/Alaskan Native), full- vs. part-time employment status, primary work activity, type of employer, publishing activity, and additional training and degrees; all by field mobility status, with selected cross-tabulations.

Also includes employment by detailed field; correlation between employment field and PhD, with trends from 1977; and median salary by field mobility status, by type of employer and PhD field.

Data are based on responses of 7,733 humanities PhDs to a 1983 National Research Council survey.

Contains preface, definitions, and listings of contents, charts, and tables (p. ii-viii); narrative in 6 sections, interspersed with 3 charts and 17 tables (p. 1-44); and appendices A-E, with questionnaire facsimile and 9 tables (p. 47-69).

Availability: National Academy of Sciences—National Research Council, Office of Scientific and Engineering Personnel, Survey of Doctorate Recipients, Rm. JH634, 2101 Constitution Ave., NW, Washington DC 20418, †; SRI/MF/complete.

R6000–16 **MORTALITY OF NUCLEAR WEAPONS TEST PARTICIPANTS**
Monograph. May 1985.
98 p. var. paging.
SRI/MF/complete

By C. Dennis Robinette et al. Report comparing actual vs. expected deaths through 1982 among participants in nuclear weapons tests during the 1950s, by cause of death. Most data are shown for 2 Nevada and 3 Pacific (Bikini/Enewetak atolls) weapons test series, during which 68 detonations occurred.

Includes number of test participants; radiation doses experienced; and actual vs. expected deaths by cause, with detail for leukemia and other cancer types, and including cross-tabulations by radiation dose and time since weapons test. Standard U.S. mortality rates are the basis for expected deaths.

Also includes data on all announced atmospheric nuclear weapons test series, including location, number of participants, and whether participant radiation exposure was measured, 1946-62.

Data sources include DOD and VA records on 46,186 participants used for mortality comparisons.

Contains list of abbreviations (2 p.); summary and contents listing (4 p.); introduction and methodlogy, with 1 table (p. 1-19); study results, with text statistics and 1 table (p. 20-44); references (p. 45-47); 27 tables (29 p.); and appendices, with 3 tables (14 p.).

Availability: National Academy of Sciences—National Research Council, Medical Follow-up Agency, 2101 Constitution Ave., NW, Washington DC 20418, †; SRI/MF/complete.

R6000–17 **LABOR-MARKET CONDITIONS FOR ENGINEERS: IS THERE A SHORTAGE?**
Monograph. 1984.
vii+159 p.
SRI/MF/complete

Report presenting the proceedings of a Feb. 1984 NAS symposium on labor market outlook for engineers. Includes data on supply and/or demand for engineers and other technical personnel, with detail by occupation, region, and industry, and for selected forecasting methodologies, 1980s-95 with trends from 1960.

Also includes data on electronics industry employer methods for estimating employment needs; impact of defense contracts and spending on engineer demand, and on selected economic indicators; and engineer salaries in government-owned laboratories vs. Naval Research Laboratory, by position and for new PhDs; various years 1983-87.

Most data are based on forecasting models developed by American Electronics Assn, BLS, NSF, and Business-Higher Education Forum.

Contains foreword, and listings of contents, tables, and charts (p. i-vii); symposium proceedings interspersed with 9 charts and 15 tables, and including overview and introduction, 4 papers presenting forecasting models, commentaries, summaries of other sessions, and closing remarks (p. 1-144); and 2 appendices, with symposium agenda and list of attendees (p. 147-159).

Availability: National Academy of Sciences—National Research Council, 2101 Constitution Ave., NW, Washington DC 20418, †; SRI/MF/complete.

R6300
National Center for Charitable Statistics

R6300-1 NON-PROFIT SERVICE ORGANIZATIONS: 1982
Monograph. 1985.
xiv+276 p.
LC 85-71551.
SRI/MF/complete

Report on Census of Service Industries' findings for organizations exempt from Federal income tax, by industry and locale, 1982, with comparisons to 1977 Census findings. Although organizations are nonprofit entities, they are classified according to Standard Industrial Classification (SIC) categories. Data are shown by selected SIC 2- to 4-digit service industry.

Covers establishments, revenue, expenses, annual and 1st quarter payroll, employment, and revenues and expenses per establishment and per employee, for total U.S. and by State, with selected detail for individual standard consolidated statistical areas (SCSAs) and SMSAs (including SMSA ranking by revenues), and for aggregate nonmetro areas of each State.

Coverage of the 1982 Census excludes hospitals, elementary/secondary schools, labor unions/similar organizations, political organizations, and passenger transportation arrangement services; these categories are included in 1977 Census. Both Censuses exclude religious organizations, private households, and governmental organizations elsewhere classified.

Contains preface, foreword, introduction, and listing of contents and tables (p. iii-xiv); report in 2 sections, with lists of data items covered, 7 U.S. tables, and 5 tables repeated for each State (p. 1-232); and appendices, with methodology, definitions, facsimile of Census questionnaires, lists of SIC service industries and codes, composition of SCSAs and SMSAs, 2 summary tables, and acknowledgements (p. 233-276).

Availability: National Center for Charitable Statistics, 1828 L St., NW, Washington DC 20036, $25.00; SRI/MF/complete.

R6400
National Center for Higher Education Management Systems

R6400-1 HIGHER EDUCATION FINANCING IN THE FIFTY STATES: Interstate Comparisons, FY82
Annual. Nov. 1984.
xviii+562 p.
LC 78-21570.
SRI/MF/complete, delayed

Annual report, by Marilyn McCoy and D. Kent Halstead, on higher education finances for each State, by institution control and type, FY82. Also includes data on student enrollment, State expenditures and tax collections by type, and faculty salaries.

Data are from NCES, Census Bureau, and other government and private sources.

Contents:

Contents and table listings, foreword, preface, and user guide. (p. v-xviii)

Chapter 1. Introduction and General Trends. Includes narrative summary with 7 text tables; and 56 detailed tables showing State rankings and indexes based on U.S. averages, for most of the data items covered in Chapter 3. (p. 1-75)

Chapter 2. Methodology. (p. 77-86)

Chapter 3. State by State Reports. Includes narrative summary, and 11 charts and 15 tables described below, repeated for U.S. average and each State. (p. 87-503)

Appendix A-B. Includes listing of institutions by State arranged by type, and data sources and definitions. (p. 505-562)

This is the 4th edition of the report.

Availability: National Center for Higher Education Management Systems, Publications Department, PO Drawer P, Boulder CO 80302, $29.95+$0.50 shipping and handling; SRI/MF/complete, delayed shipment in Nov. 1985.

TABLES AND CHARTS:

R6400-1.1: State by State Reports
[Tables and charts for U.S. and each State cover the data topics described below. Data are generally shown for 1981 or FY82, with selected trends from FY78.

Most data are shown separately for public and independent institutions, with selected detail for all and research universities with and without medical programs, and for comprehensive, baccalaureate, 2-year, and health and other professional/specialized institutions.]

a. State/local expenditures per capita and distribution by function, with detail for higher education including student aid; population and FTE enrollment; in-State and out-of-State enrollment, and high school graduates and number entering higher education, per 1,000 population; and State/local potential and collected revenues by tax type.

b. Institutional revenues, including State/local appropriations, tuition, private gifts/grants, and government grants/contracts; and expenditures for instruction, academic support, research, and public service; generally shown per student or faculty member.

c. Faculty size, and average salary by academic rank; number and mean size of institutions; and enrollment distribution by class level, including graduate students.

R8490
Northeast-Midwest Institute

R8490-8 STATE ENERGY FACTBOOK
Monograph. Jan. 1984.
iv+62 p.
SRI/MF/complete

By Jonathan Perman et al. Report presenting an overview of energy supply and demand, by State and region, 1980 or 1981, with some comparisons to 1970. Covers energy expenditures, prices, production, and consumption, with detail by end-use sector and/or energy type; energy self-sufficiency index; electricity cross-border delivery balance; electric utility sales and generation-associated energy losses, relative to total energy consumption; and household distribution by type of heating fuel.

Data are primarily derived from Energy Information Administration reports.

Contains contents and table listings (p. iii-iv); introduction and users guide, with 4 charts (p. 1-12); report, with 19 tables (p. 13-57); and methodology and glossary (p. 58-62).

Availability: Northeast-Midwest Institute, Publications Office, 218 D St., SE, Washington DC 20003, $15.00; SRI/MF/complete.

R8490-9 PENTAGON TILT: Regional Biases in Defense Spending and Strategy
Monograph. 1985. vii+84 p.
SRI/MF/complete

By Virginia Mayer. Report analyzing DOD regional spending patterns, FY83, with selected trends from as early as 1949.

Presents the following data, by State and/or region: DOD expenditures by function, including payroll and retirement pay; value of DOD prime, R&D, and construction contract awards; DOD military and civilian personnel, military installations, and base closure rates; population, and per capita DOD expenditures; and ratio of Federal defense and nondefense spending to Federal tax contributions.

Also includes data on DOD budget by service branch, category, and region, FY85; top 20-25 contractors ranked by value of R&D and prime contract awards, FY83; and per capita spending projections by category and region, 1989.

Contains listings of contents, charts, and tables (p. iii-v); introduction, with 2 summary charts and 1 summary table (p. 1-7); narrative report with text data, 3 maps, 3 charts, and 24 tables (p. 9-79); and data sources and bibliography (p. 81-84).

A similar report, with data for 1950-79, is described in SRI 1981 Annual under R8490-1.

Availability: Northeast-Midwest Institute, Publications Office, 218 D St., SE, Washington DC 20003, $10.00; SRI/MF/complete.

R8750
Population Reference Bureau

R8750–1   POPULATION TODAY
Monthly.   12 p.
ISSN 0749-2448.
LC sc84-7804.
SRI/MF/complete, shipped
quarterly

Monthly review (combined issue for July/Aug.) of current topics related to international population size and growth, including birth rates and fertility, migration trends, contraception and family planning, and health conditions.

Data are from foreign government agencies and statistical yearbooks; NCHS; books, journal articles, and research papers; and the bureau's own research.

Issues contain narrative articles, some with statistics; book reviews; and regular departmental features, including the following:

a. "Speaking Graphically" feature on population trends or projections for selected countries, generally presenting summary charts only, but occasionally including more substantial data.

b. "Demographer's Page" article, usually including 1 or more tables.

c. "Population Update" monthly data showing U.S. vital statistics for 12-month period ending approximately 5 months prior to cover date, with 3-4 year trends; U.S. population estimates for month 4-5 months prior to cover date, and same month of previous year; and world population and annual growth estimates, as of cover date month.

d. "Spotlight" profile of a country or country subarea, including population, land area, and summary vital statistics and economic data.

A subject index appears in the Dec. issue.

"Population Update" monthly data appear in all issues. All additional features with substantial statistical content are described, as they appear, under "Statistical Features." Nonstatistical features are not covered.

Availability: Population Reference Bureau, 777 14th St., NW, Washington DC 20005, members †, back issues $2.00; SRI/MF/complete, shipped quarterly.

Issues reviewed during 1985: Nov. 1984-Sept. 1985 (P) (Vol. 12, Nos. 11-12; Vol. 13, Nos. 1-9).

STATISTICAL FEATURES:

R8750–1.601: Nov. 1984 (Vol. 12, No. 11)
DEMOGRAPHER'S PAGE: THE DYNAMICS OF POPULATION MOMENTUM
(p. 6-7) By Murray Gendell. Article, with 1 table showing the following for the Philippines: crude birth, natural increase, and fertility rates; and women age 15-49 as percent of all women; 5-year periods 1950-2025. Data are from UN.

Data correction appears in the Dec. 1984 issue (see R8750-1.602 below).

CORRECTION
(p. 14) Data correction for "Spotlight" article on Mexico. For description of article, see SRI 1984 Annual under R8750-1.508.

SPOTLIGHT: JAPAN
(p. 16) Profile of Japan. Includes population, land area, birth and death rates, population growth rate, and value of major exports and imports, various years 1982-84.

R8750–1.602: Dec. 1984 (Vol. 12, No. 12)
STERILIZATION, BREASTFEEDING ON THE RISE
(p. 2, 8) Article, with 1 table showing prevalence of contraceptive use among women by method, by age group and race, 1982. Data are from responses of 7,969 women to an Aug. 1982-Feb. 1983 survey, conducted for the National Survey of Family Growth.

CORRECTION
(p. 5) Data correction to "Demographer's Page" table on Philippine birth and fertility rates. For description of table, see R8750-1.601 above.

DEMOGRAPHER'S PAGE: QUEBEC, THE EMPTY CRADLE
(p. 6-7) By Andre Lux. Article, with 2 tables showing the following for Quebec Province, Canada: fertility rate with comparison to rest of Canada, selected years 1851-1983; and population distribution by age group, 1981, and projected under 2 growth assumptions, 2001 and 2051. Data are from Statistics Canada.

SPOTLIGHT: NIGERIA
(p. 16) Profile of Nigeria. Includes population, birth and death rates, infant mortality rate, life expectancy, land area, and value of major exports and imports, 1983 or 1984.

R8750–1.603: Jan. 1985 (Vol. 13, No. 1)
HOW MANY PEOPLE CAN THE WORLD FEED?
(p. 2, 8-9) Article on potential for agricultural self-suffiency among developing countries. Data are from UN Food and Agriculture Organization.

Includes 2 tables showing ratio of population to agriculturally supportable population, 1975 and 2000; and population in excess of home country's supportable population, 2000; for aggregate developing countries by region, estimated at 3 levels of agricultural sophistication.

DEMOGRAPHER'S PAGE: THE MIGRATION TURNAROUND, END OF A PHENOMENON?
(p. 6-7) By Anthony Agresta. Article, with 2 tables showing annual average percent change in metro and nonmetro population, by region and census division, 1970-80 and 1980-82 periods; and net migration rates for nonmetro areas, by age and sex, 1975-76 and 1982-83 periods. Data are from Census Bureau.

SPOTLIGHT: SRI LANKA
(p. 12) Profile of Sri Lanka. Includes population and growth rate; birth, death, and infant mortality rates; land area; aggregate value of major exports and imports; and GNP per capita; various years 1980-84.

R8750–1.604: Feb. 1985 (Vol. 13, No. 2)
SPEAKING GRAPHICALLY
(p. 5) Chart showing population of Africa, Latin America, and South Asia, 1980, and projected (low, medium, and high) 2100. Data are from UN.

DEMOGRAPHER'S PAGE: 1980 RATES OF EMIGRATION TO THE U.S.
(p. 6-7) By Morton D. Winsberg. Article, with 1 table showing rate of immigration to the U.S., by world area and country of origin, 1979-81 period. Data are from U.S. Immigration and Naturalization Service and Population Reference Bureau, Inc.

SPOTLIGHT: AUSTRALIA
(p. 12) By Alice T. Day. Profile of Australia. Includes total population with growth rate and percent in urban areas; aboriginal population; birth, death, and infant mortality rates; land area; major exports and imports; and GNP per capita; various years 1981-84.

R8750–1.605: Mar. 1985 (Vol. 13, No. 3)
30 MILLION MAY HAVE DIED IN CHINA'S 1958-61 FAMINE
(p. 7) Article, with 1 table showing PRC population, and birth and death rates, 1955-64. Data are from *Population and Development Review.*

SPOTLIGHT: NEVADA
(p. 12) Profile of Nevada. Includes population, birth and death rates, land area, percent of population aged 65/over and 18/under, population ranking among the States, and lifetime residents as percent of population, various years 1960-84.

R8750–1.606: Apr. 1985 (Vol. 13, No. 4)
WORLD OF 4,845,000,000 PEOPLE
(p. 2, 8) Article, with 1 table showing world highs and lows (country and number) for selected vital statistics, as of early 1985. Data are from PRB's *World Population Data Sheet,* covered in SRI under R8750-5.

SPEAKING GRAPHICALLY
(p. 5) Includes 1 chart showing distribution of world land area among forest/woodland, permanent pasture, arable land/permanent crops, and other land. Data are from *Food and Agriculture Organization Production Yearbook, 1983.*

DEMOGRAPHER'S PAGE: URBAN PRIMACY IN DEVELOPING COUNTRIES, THE CASE OF MALI
(p. 6-7) By Ousmane Sokona. Article, with 1 table showing Mali's top 13 cities ranked by population, 1976. Data are from Bureau Centrale de Recensement.

SPOTLIGHT: BURMA
(p. 12) Profile of Burma. Includes population and annual growth rate, birth and death rates, land area, infant mortality rate, percent of population in urban areas, and per capita GNP, generally 1983 or 1985.

R8750–1.607: May 1985 (Vol. 13, No. 5)
SPOTLIGHT: COSTA RICA
(p. 12) Profile of Costa Rica. Includes population and growth rate; percent of population in urban areas; birth, death, and infant mortality rates; land area; aggregate value of major exports and imports; and per capita GNP; various years 1982-85.

R8750–1.608: June 1985 (Vol. 13, No. 6)
SPOTLIGHT: LOUISIANA
(p. 12) By Edward O'Boyle. Profile of Louisiana. Includes population, birth and death rates,

land area, percent of population aged 18/under and 65/over, and percent of persons born in Louisiana now living there, various years 1980-84.

R8750–1.609: July/Aug. 1985 (Vol. 13, No. 7/8)

SPOTLIGHT: PAKISTAN

(p. 16) Profile of Pakistan. Includes population; birth, death, and infant mortality rates; land area; percent of population aged 15/under and 65/over; population rank in world; life expectancy; and GNP per capita; various years 1983-85.

R8750–1.610: Sept. 1985 (Vol. 13, No. 9)

DEMOGRAPHER'S PAGE: POPULATION ARTICLES IN POPULAR MAGAZINES

(p. 6-7) By David Yaukey. Article, with 1 table showing number of magazine articles on demography, by magazine type, Apr. 1984-85 period. Data are from author's computer search of *Reader's Guide to Periodical Literature.*

SPOTLIGHT: PERU

(p. 12) By Leon Yacher. Profile of Peru. Includes population; birth, death, and infant mortality rates; land area; percent of population aged 15/under and 65/over; life expectancy; major exports and imports; GNP per capita; and population of capital city; various years 1982-85.

R8750–2   POPULATION BULLETIN
Series. For individual
publication data, see below.
ISSN 0032-468X.
LC 52-19281.
SRI/MF/complete

Continuing series of reports examining selected aspects of world and U.S. demography, including population growth in developed and developing countries, fertility, child development, and family planning.

Each issue focuses on a specific topic or country, and contains approximately 40 pages of narrative analysis with interspersed charts and tables.

Reports are issued 4 times yearly, in varying months. Reports reviewed during 1985 are described below.

Availability: Population Reference Bureau, 777 14th St., NW, Washington DC 20005, distributed to all PRB members (varying membership rates), or single copy $4.00; SRI/MF/complete.

R8750–2.28: Delayed Childbearing in the U.S.: Facts and Fictions
[Monograph. Nov. 1984. 43 p. Vol. 39, No. 4. SRI/MF/complete.]

By Wendy H. Baldwin and Christine Winquist Nord. Report examining implications of delayed childbearing. Data are from NCHS, the Census Bureau, and other specified sources. Includes 6 summary charts, and 3 charts and 8 tables showing the following data, for the U.S. unless otherwise noted:

a. Total and 1st births, by age of mother, various years 1950-82; and percent of women born during 1940-54 who were mothers by age 25 and 30, by race and educational attainment.

b. Percent of population never married, by age and sex, decennially 1890-1980 and 1983; interval between marriage and 1st birth, by age of mother, selected periods 1940-79; and occupational distribution of white women having 1st birth in 1980, by age.

c. Labor force participation rates of married women, by presence and age of children, 1984; child care arrangements of married mothers working full time, by age of mother and youngest child, 1982; and mean age at 1st birth projected for women born in 1950, and percent remaining childless, for U.S. and 5 European countries.

R8750–2.29: Understanding U.S. Fertility: Findings from the National Survey of Family Growth, Cycle III
[Monograph. Dec. 1984. 43 p. Vol. 39, No. 5. SRI/MF/complete.]

By William F. Pratt, et al. Report examining U.S. fertility and marriage patterns and contraceptive use. Data are based on responses of approximately 8,000 women aged 15-44 to Cycle III of the National Survey of Family Growth (NSFG), conducted by NCHS, Aug. 1982-Feb. 1983, with comparisons to previous NSFG findings.

Includes 19 charts and 15 tables showing the following data, generally with detail by various demographic characteristics (including age, race, Hispanic/non-Hispanic, religion, labor force status, education, and region):

a. Distribution of ever-married women by number of children born and number expected, average number of children wanted, and percent of actual births that were wanted, 1973 and 1982; and percent of all and never-married women who have had sexual intercourse, marital status of women, percent of 1st marriages still intact, and incidence of 1st marriage dissolutions and of remarriage, 1982.

b. Contraceptive failure and discontinuation rates, by method, 1970-75 period; contraceptive use, at 1st intercourse and currently (with detail by childbearing plans), by method, various years 1965-82; and use of family planning services by type, 1982.

c. Infertility rates among married couples, selected years 1965-82; breastfeeding patterns, selected years 1970/71-1980/81; pregnancy outcomes, and percent of births unwanted or mistimed, various periods 1960s-82; and timing of 1st birth in relation to marriage, 1982.

Also includes 1 table showing standard error computations for survey sample.

R8750–2.30: Sub-Saharan Africa: Population Pressures on Development
[Monograph. Feb. 1985. 47 p. Vol. 40, No. 1. SRI/MF/complete.]

By Thomas J. Goliber. Report examining the impact of population growth on social and economic development of sub-Saharan Africa, 1950s-84, with projections to 2060. Data are from UN, World Bank, and other specified sources. Includes 8 charts and 8 tables showing the following for sub-Saharan Africa, generally by country:

a. Population; land area; birth, death, fertility, and infant mortality rates; life expectancy;

per capita GNP; urban population growth rate, and share of total population; number of cities with 500,000/over population; percent of urban population living in largest city; and number of refugees, and primary countries of origin; various periods 1960-84.

b. Projections: population under 3 fertility rate assumptions; South Africa population distribution by race; level of agricultural self-sufficiency; and labor force; various years 1975-2060.

c. School enrollment as a percent of school-aged population, for primary, secondary, and higher education, 1960 and 1981; urban population, 1950, 1980, and 2010; and percent of population in rural areas, 1982, and percent of labor force in agriculture, 1980.

d. Fertility rate, average desired family size, and percent of women aware of modern contraception and using modern and traditional methods, for currently married women age 15-49, various years 1979-1982; Kenya population, 1950, 1975, and 2000; and strength of national family planning efforts, 1982.

R8750–2.31: Adolescent Fertility: Worldwide Concerns
[Monograph. Apr. 1985. 51 p. Vol. 40, No. 2. SRI/MF/complete.]

By Judith Senderowitz and John M. Paxman. Report examining worldwide trends and patterns in adolescent fertility. Data are from UN, Census Bureau, NCHS, and other specified sources. Includes 2 charts, and 11 tables showing the following for various countries and world areas, various years 1950-2020:

a. Female population aged 15-19; percent of male and female adolescents who have had premarital sexual intercourse; percent of females aged 15-19 ever married, mean age at 1st marriage, and fertility rates; median age at 1st birth, for women aged 20-24 and 40-44; and percent of total births occuring to women 20/under.

b. Percent of currently married women aged 15-19 and 15-49 using contraceptives; contraceptive use among adolescents; percent of all legal abortions obtained by women aged 20/under, and abortion rates for women aged 20/under and 20-24; and laws and policies on sex education/information, and contraceptive- and abortion-related health care for adolescents.

R8750–5   1985 WORLD POPULATION DATA SHEET
Annual. Apr. 1985.
1 p. Foldout. Oversized.
SRI/MF/complete

Annual data sheet, for 1985, on population size and characteristics, GNP per capita, and cultivated land area, shown for approximately 170 countries arranged by world region, with aggregate data for developing countries. Data are most recent available as of mid-1985, and are from UN, World Bank, Census Bureau, and official country publications. Data dates and sources are specified in table footnotes.

Contains 1 table showing the following:

a. Population: estimated mid-1985, projected to 2000 and 2020, annual percent natural increase, "doubling time" at current rate, percent under age 15 and over age 64, and percent urban.

b. Birth, death, infant mortality, and fertility rates; life expectancy at birth; per capita GNP, 1983; and total land area and percent cultivated.

This is the 23rd data sheet.

Availability: Population Reference Bureau, 777 14th St., NW, Washington DC 20005, $2.00; SRI/MF/complete.

R8750–12   POPULATION TRENDS AND PUBLIC POLICY

Series. For individual publication data, see below.
ISSN 0736-7716.
SRI/MF/complete

Series of reports analyzing demographic and population issues of concern to policymakers.

Reports reviewed during 1985 are described below.

Availability: Population Reference Bureau, 777 14th St., NW, Washington DC 20005, $3.00 each; SRI/MF/complete.

R8750–12.3: Population Change, Resources, and the Environment

[Monograph. Dec. 1983. 16 p. Rpt. No. 4. SRI/MF/complete.]

Report examining the impact of world population growth on environmental quality and the availability of natural resources. Includes data on global population increase, quinquennially 1950-2000; population increase for 20 countries with natural increase under 1%, 1983; and population and average number of children per family, for world regions and countries with average 5/more children per family (no date).

Data are from Population Reference Bureau.

Contains introduction (inside front cover); narrative analysis, with 5 charts and 3 tables (p. 1-15); and footnotes (p. 16).

R8750–12.4: Death and Taxes: The Public Policy Impact of Living Longer

[Monograph. Sept. 1984. 16 p. Rpt. No. 5. SRI/MF/complete.]

Report discussing effects of longer life expectancy on current public programs for the elderly. Includes data on life expectancy increases at age 65, and resulting increases in Federal outlays for the aged, both for each of 4 scenarios in which a major cause of death had been eliminated as of 1983. Data are based on PHS estimates.

Contains summary (p. 1); narrative analysis, with 5 charts and 1 table (p. 3-16); and footnotes, references, and photo credits (inside back cover).

R8750–12.5: Graying of the Sunbelt: A Look at the Impact of U.S. Elderly Migration

[Monograph. Oct. 1984. 16 p. Rpt. No. 6. SRI/MF/complete.]

By Jeanne C. Biggar. Report examining the impact of elderly migration on the Sunbelt States. Includes data showing interstate migrants received (total and age 60/over), for 12 Sunbelt States and total U.S.; and demograph-

ic and socioeconomic characteristics (including living arrangements) of migrants to non-Sunbelt and Sunbelt regions, with detail for 5 major Sunbelt States; all for 1975-80 period.

Data are based on Census Bureau estimates.

Contains summary (p. 1); narrative analysis, with 3 maps and 4 tables (p. 3-16); and footnotes, references, bibliography, and photo credits (inside back cover).

R8765
Potential Gas Committee

R8765–1   POTENTIAL SUPPLY OF NATURAL GAS IN THE U.S. (Dec. 31, 1984)

Biennial. June 1985.
xii + 161 p. + maps.
ISSN 0147-8842.
LC 76-649233.
SRI/MF/complete

Biennial report presenting estimates of potential natural gas reserves, for 7 regions, as of Dec. 31, 1984, with biennial trends from 1964.

Includes data on onshore and offshore natural gas supply (probable, possible, and speculative), by depth, region, and detailed geological area; and natural gas production, proved reserves, potential supply, and ultimately recoverable resource, with production and reserve detail for selected States and major gas fields.

Data are based primarily on Potential Gas Committee estimates, and reports of American Gas Assn and DOE.

Contains:

a. Introductory material; and listings of contents, charts, and tables. (p. iii-xii)

b. Potential Gas Committee report, with narrative summary, definitions and estimation procedures, 5 maps/charts, and 10 tables. (p. 1-24)

c. Regional reports, each with narrative description of detailed geological areas, 1 table, and generally 2-11 text tables with data by State and/or gas field. (p. 25-132)

d. Policy guidelines and membership listings for Potential Gas Committee and Potential Gas Agency (p. 133-161); and maps of natural gas reserves (back cover pocket).

Previous report, for 1982, is described in SRI 1984 Annual under this number.

Availability: Potential Gas Agency, Colorado School of Mines, Golden CO 80401, $25.00; SRI/MF/complete.

R8780
Princeton
Religion Research Center

R8780–1   EMERGING TRENDS

Monthly. Approx. 6 p.
LC 82-20489.
SRI/MF/complete, shipped quarterly

Monthly report (except July and Aug.) presenting results of surveys conducted by Gallup International on varied religious and social issues, including prevalence of religious beliefs and practices, and perceptions of organized religion in society and personal life.

Each issue contains articles on several topics; some topics recur annually or several times per year. Articles include text statistics characterizing poll results, and usually tables and/or charts showing response distribution for specific survey questions, sometimes shown by respondent characteristics. June and Sept. 1985 issues also include a subject index to articles appearing during 1979-84.

Tables and charts are described, as they appear, under "Statistical Features."

Availability: Princeton Religion Research Center, Publications Department, 53 Bank St., PO Box 310, Princeton NJ 08542, $30.00 per yr.; SRI/MF/complete, shipped quarterly.

Issues reviewed during 1985: Oct. 1984-Sept. 1985 (P) (Vol. 6, Nos. 8-10; Vol. 7, Nos. 1-7).

STATISTICAL FEATURES:

[Unless otherwise noted, data are shown for U.S. and are based on recent surveys; and data by religion are shown for Catholics and Protestants.]

R8780–1.601: Oct. 1984 (Vol. 6, No. 8)

Contains distribution of responses concerning the following:

a. Church/state separation: public awareness of 1st Amendment clause on religion; opinions on religious organization involvement in politics, clergy expression of political beliefs in sermons, and political candidate expression of religious beliefs; and whether own clergy has endorsed a presidential candidate in 1984; with detail by race, region, religion, and church membership status. 7 tables.

b. Evangelical Christians' prevalence, as measured by 3 criteria (born-again experiences, encouraging others to accept Jesus Christ, and literal view of the Bible), with trends from 1976. 4 tables.

c. Teenagers' opinions on most important personal qualities, by sex, age group, region, and religion. 1 table.

d. Influence of religion on American life: whether influence is increasing or decreasing, with detail for those perceiving an increase by sex, age, and religion, and trends from 1957. 2 tables.

R8780–1.602: Nov. 1984 (Vol. 6, No. 9)

Contains distribution of responses concerning the following:

a. Support among evangelical Christians and others for tax increases to reduce Federal deficit, prayer in public schools, reduced defense spending, tuition tax credits, ban on abortions, Equal Rights Amendment, increased spending for social programs, nuclear weapons freeze, relaxing pollution controls to reduce costs to industry, and maintaining cost-of-living increases on social security benefits. 10 tables.

b. Canadians' attitudes toward ordination of homosexuals as ministers/priests, by religion (including those with no religious preference), sex, age, and education. 1 table.

c. Societal institutions: confidence in church/organized religion, military, banks/banking, Supreme Court, public schools, newspapers, organized labor, Congress, big business, and TV, with trends from 1973 and detail for confidence in church/organized religion, by sex, age, education, region, and race. 2 tables.

d. Relevance of religion to modern problems, and perceived importance of religion in personal life, with detail by age, religion (including selected Protestant denominations), education, and sex, and trends from 1952. 9 tables.

R8780–1.603: Dec. 1984 (Vol. 6, No. 10)

Contains distribution of responses concerning the following:

a. Church/synagogue attendance and membership, with selected detail by sex, age, region, religion (including Jewish and selected Protestant denominations), race (including Hispanic), and education, and trends from 1937. 4 tables.

b. Ten most admired men and women; perceived major failings of parents in raising children; and teenagers' views on major problems facing adolescents, with trends from 1977. 3 tables.

c. Evangelical vs. other Christians' vote in 1984 presidential election by race, and political party affiliation. 2 tables.

R8780–1.604: Jan. 1985 (Vol. 7, No. 1)

Contains distribution of responses concerning the following:

a. Religious preference (Protestant, Catholic, Jewish, other, and none), with detail by age, sex, region, race (including Hispanic), and education, and trends from 1947. 2 tables.

b. Public support for ban on abortions, prayer in public schools, tax increases to reduce Federal deficit, relaxing pollution controls to reduce costs to industry, maintaining cost-of-living increases on social security benefits, reduced defense spending, tuition tax credits, nuclear weapons freeze, increased spending for social programs, and Equal Rights Amendment, all by religion (including Southern Baptist and Methodist). 10 tables.

c. Voluntarism: participation in volunteer activities, with detail by age, religion (including Southern Baptist and Methodist), and sex, and trends from 1977. 2 tables.

d. UK public and clergy belief in Christ's bodily resurrection, gospel miracles, and the Virgin Birth, and support for church involvement in political issues, shown for

general public, assistant/suffragen bishops, full-time clergy, and persons attending Church of England, Catholic, and Non-Conformist churches. 4 tables.

e. Catholic support for return of Latin mass, and willingness to attend Latin masses. 2 tables.

R8780–1.605: Feb. 1985 (Vol. 7, No. 2)

Contains distribution of responses concerning the following:

a. Reasons for joining, not joining, and not rejoining the Catholic church, among persons presently not attending church; Canadian public degree of confidence in church/organized religion, with comparison to 1979; and public agreement with selected religious tenets and practices. 5 tables.

b. Teenager opinions on importance of selected factors in choosing a career, and working environment preferences by sex; frequency of Bible reading among general public and among persons reading Bible/devotional works regularly; and teacher support for constitutional amendment allowing prayer in public schools, with detail for elementary and high school teachers. 4 tables.

R8780–1.606: Mar. 1985 (Vol. 7, No. 3)

Contains distribution of responses concerning the following:

a. Prayer/meditation practice in U.S. and 13 other countries, 1981; and Americans' prayer habits, including frequency, purpose, personal benefits, and time of prayer, with selected detail by respondent sex, age, race, education, and religion (Protestants, Catholics, all and Southern Baptists, and Methodists), with trends from 1948. 10 tables.

b. Teenagers: percent attending church/synagogue during previous week, with trends from 1977. 1 table.

R8780–1.607: Apr. 1985 (Vol. 7, No. 4)

Contains distribution of responses concerning the following:

a. Influence of religion on American life: whether influence is increasing or decreasing, with detail for those perceiving an increase by sex, age, and religion, and trends from 1957. 2 tables.

b. Beliefs of public concerning Jesus Christ's identity, divinity, and resurrection, with selected comparisons to beliefs of clergy, various years 1952-83. 11 tables.

c. Relevance of religion to modern problems, with detail by age, religion, education, and sex, and trends from 1957; and percent of population doing volunteer work for churches/religious organizations, in U.S. and 13 other countries. 3 tables.

R8780–1.608: May 1985 (Vol. 7, No. 5)

Contains distribution of responses concerning the following:

a. Spiritual experiences: personal awareness of a spiritual presence, with detail by sex, age, region, education, religion (including Southern Baptist, Methodist, and Lutheran), and importance of religion in life; type

of spiritual presence felt and effect on life; and whether church adequately meets people's spiritual needs, for U.S. and 13 other countries, 1981. 4 tables.

b. Premarital sex acceptability, by sex, age, religion, education, region, and importance of religion in life, with comparison to 1973 and 1969 surveys. 3 tables.

c. Church attendance within past year, by religion (including total and Southern Baptist, and Methodist), sex, age, region, race (including Hispanic), education, income group, and importance of religion in life; and whether religion provides comfort/strength, for U.S. and 12 other countries, 1981. 2 tables.

d. Media use of teenagers vs. parents, by teenagers' age, sex, academic ability, and region, all by media, 1984. 2 tables.

R8780–1.609: June 1985 (Vol. 7, No. 6)

Contains distribution of responses concerning the following:

a. God: belief in God/universal spirit, for U.S. and 13 other countries, 1981, with U.S. trends from 1944; importance of God in personal life, for U.S. and 14 other countries, with detail for blacks and Hispanics in U.S. and for blacks and whites in South Africa, 1981; and adjectives used to describe God, 1983. 4 tables.

b. Social and personal values considered very important in life, by age group, 1981; belief in the devil, for U.S. and 13 other countries, 1981; and perceived characteristics of the devil, 1978. 3 tables.

c. Teenagers' views on major problems facing teenagers, 1977, 1983, and 1985; and teenager acquaintance with someone who has attempted suicide, by sex, age group, region, and urban-rural status, 1985. 2 tables.

R8780–1.610: Sept. 1985 (Vol. 7, No. 7)

Contains distribution of responses concerning the following:

a. Societal institutions: confidence in church/organized religion, military, Supreme Court, banks/banking, public schools, Congress, newspapers, big business, TV, and organized labor, with trends from 1973. 1 table.

b. Ratings of honesty/ethical standards of persons in 25 occupations. 1 table.

c. Canada church/synagogue attendance, with detail for Protestants and Catholics, and trends from 1957. 1 table.

d. Pope John Paul II public ratings, with detail by religion and comparisons to 2 previous Popes, 1960-85 surveys. 2 tables.

e. Belief in life after death, for U.S. and 12 other countries, 1981, with U.S. trends from 1944; belief in heaven and hell, 1952, 1965, and 1980; and membership in top 10 non-Catholic denominations, 1983. 5 tables.

R8780-2 RELIGION IN AMERICA, 50 Years: 1935-85

Annual. May 1985. 57 p.
Gallup Rpt. No. 236.
SRI/MF/complete

Annual report, for 1985, presenting Gallup Poll findings pertaining to religion in America. Covers opinion data on influence of religion on American life, relevance of religion to modern problems, confidence in church/organized religion and other institutions, importance of religion in own life, and extent of commitment to selected religious beliefs and practices.

Also includes data on religious denomination preferences, and member sociodemographic profiles; Evangelical Christians' prevalence (those reporting born-again experiences, encouraging others to accept Jesus Christ, and holding literal view of Bible); church/synagogue membership and attendance; frequency of prayer and Bible reading; and beliefs concerning a deity, Christ's divinity, afterlife, and heaven and hell, with selected comparisons to beliefs held in other countries.

Most data are based on Gallup Polls conducted in 1984-85, with trends from as early as 1937, and include detail by respondent sociodemographic characteristics.

Contents:

a. Contents listing (p. 2); and analysis of trends in religious survey responses during past 50 years (p. 4-14).

b. General survey findings in 5 parts, with 17 charts and 47 tables. (p. 16-54).

c. Methodology, with 3 tables (p. 55-56); and 3 charts showing survey responses concerning knowledge of selected biblical facts, 1954 and 1982 (inside back cover).

This is the 7th annual report. Report is also usually published as an issue in the monthly *Gallup Report,* covered in SRI under C4040-1.

Availability: Princeton Religion Research Center, PO Box 628, Princeton NJ 08540, $25.00; SRI/MF/complete.

R8850 Public Policy Institute

R8850-1 IMPACT OF MIGRATION ON NEW YORK STATE

Monograph. Sept. 1984.
123 p. var. paging.
SRI/MF/not filmed

By Richard D. Alba and Michael J. Batutis. Report analyzing New York State population migration, 1975 80 period. Covers migration into, out of, and within the State. Includes data on migrant characteristics cross-tabulated by points of origin and destination, including the following: New York State regions; U.S. States, regions, and outlying areas; and world regions.

Migrant characteristics include birthplace, age, sex, race-ethnicity (white, black, and Hispanic American), family characteristics, education, employment status (with detail by industry division), occupation, poverty status, and household income.

Data are from the Public Use Microdata Samples of the 1980 census.

Contains contents and table listings (3 p.); narrative analysis, with 1 summary table and 6 charts (p. 1-54); and 35 tables (64 p.)

Availability: Public Policy Institute, 152 Washington Ave., Albany NY 12210, $6.00; SRI/MF/not filmed.

R9050 Tax Foundation

R9050-3 TAX FEATURES

Monthly. Approx. 4-8 p.
ISSN 0047-8040. LC 76-229.
SRI/MF/complete, shipped quarterly

Monthly publication, with several combined issues each year, presenting news and analytical articles on taxation and government spending at the Federal, State, and local level. Data are compiled by Tax Foundation, Inc., from government sources.

Issues contain an editorial column; and articles and occasional insert supplements, often with statistics. Recurring statistical features include articles on Tax Foundation, Inc. tax index trends; and trends in State/local general tax revenues, Federal tax dollar allocations, Federal aid costs to States, taxpayer purchasing power, and government spending.

All articles with substantial statistics are described, as they appear, under "Statistical Features." Each issue of the publication is reviewed, but an abstract is published in SRI monthly issues only when statistical features appear.

Prior to Aug./Sept. 1984 issue, publication was titled *Monthly Tax Features.*

Availability: Tax Foundation, One Thomas Circle, NW, Suite 500, Washington DC 20005, members, educators, and libraries †; SRI/MF/complete, shipped quarterly.

Issues reviewed during 1985: Nov./Dec. 1984-Aug. 1985 (P) (Vol. 28, No. 8; Vol. 29, Nos. 1-7) [No Oct. 1984 issue was published; Nov./Dec. 1984 and June/July 1985 are combined issues].

STATISTICAL FEATURES:

R9050-3.601: Nov./Dec. 1984 (Vol. 28, No. 8)

INDEXING STARTS JAN. 1, LOW EARNERS HELPED MOST

(p. 1-2) Article, with 1 table comparing Federal income tax payments with and without indexing, at 9 income levels, for 1985 tax year. Comparison is for a married couple, with 1 earner and 2 children, filing a joint return.

STATE-LOCAL PENSION ASSETS AT RECORD LEVEL

(p. 3) Article, with 1 table showing State/local employee retirement systems' aggregate assets, and receipts by source (employee and government contributions, and investment earnings), FY60, FY65, and FY70-83.

BUDGET WILL GROW FOR PUBLIC EDUCATION DURING NEXT DECADE

(p. 4) Article, with 1 table showing public elementary and secondary school enrollment and teachers, 1972/73, 1982/83, and 1992/93.

R9050-3.602: Feb. 1985 (Vol. 29, No. 2)

6.9% STATE-LOCAL TAX GROWTH MARKS 2nd SMALLEST RISE SINCE 1963, ANNUAL FEATURE

(p. 1-2) Annual article, with 1 table showing State/local tax collections per capita and per $1,000 of personal income, by State, FY73 and FY83, with State rankings for FY83.

PROPERTY TAXES STAGE COMEBACK IN '83

(p. 3-4) Article, with 1 table showing State/local property tax collections per capita and per $1,000 of personal income, by State, FY73 and FY83, with State rankings for FY83.

R9050-3.603: Mar. 1985 (Vol. 29, No. 3)

TAX ACTION IN '82-'84 HAS HALVED TAX CUTS PROMISED FOR '85 BY ERTA

(p. 1, 6-7) Article, with 1 table showing 1985 Federal tax receipts estimated under rates and structure in effect Jan. 1981 and 1985, with changes attributable to 9 statutory provisions instituted during the 1981-85 period.

SALES TAX REVENUES SINGLE BIGGEST SOURCE OF FUNDS FOR STATES, ANNUAL FEATURE

(p. 1-2) Annual article, with 1 table showing rates for major State taxes, by State, as of Jan. 1985. Previous article, presenting rates as of Jan. 1984, is described in 1984 SRI Annual under R9050-3.503.

FRINGE BENEFITS LOOM AS MAJOR TARGET FOR REVENUE HUNGRY UNCLE SAM IN 1985

(p. 3-4) Article, with 1 table showing value of employer contributions to 4 types of employee benefit plans (actual and as percent of wage/salary payments), selected years 1952-83.

LOCALITIES OUTPACE STATES AND WASHINGTON IN RAISING OWN-SOURCE TAX/NONTAX REVENUES, ANNUAL FEATURE

(p. 5-6) Annual article, with 1 table showing local government general revenues, by source, selected years FY02-83.

R9050-3.604: Apr. 1985 (Vol. 29, No. 4)

APR. 30 IS TAX FREEDOM DAY! ANNUAL FEATURE

(p. 1, 4) Annual article, with 2 tables showing allocation of average workday by time spent earning money to pay taxes and other living expenses, 1980-85; and date average worker finishes working to pay for taxes (Tax Freedom Day), selected years 1930-85.

CA, NY, TX, TOP PAYERS OF FEDERAL TAX BILL, ANNUAL FEATURE

(p. 2, 4) Annual article comparing States' Federal tax burdens, FY84-86. Includes text data and 1 table showing total and per capita Federal tax collections, by State, FY84-86, with rankings for FY85.

$6,346 FEDERAL TAX BILL FOR $26K EARNER, ANNUAL FEATURE

(p. 3-4) Annual article, with 1 table allocating Federal tax dollar expenditures by function, total and for an average worker (sole supporter of a 4-person family earning $26,000 per year), FY85.

R9050-3.605: May 1985 (Vol. 29, No. 5)

HIGHEST EARNING HALF OF POPULATION PAYS 90% OF ALL FEDERAL INCOME TAXES, ANNUAL FEATURE

(p. 1) Annual article, with 1 table showing income level, and Federal income tax revenue share and average tax payment, for highest and/or lowest 5, 10, 25, and 50% taxpayer income categories, 1978 and 1983.

Previous article, with data for 1981 and 1982, is described in SRI 1984 Annual under R9050-3.506.

NATION'S TAX BILL NOW MEASURES NEARLY FIVE TIMES '67 LEVEL, RECURRING FEATURE

(p. 1-2) Recurring article analyzing tax index trends through 4th quarter 1984. Includes 1 table showing tax index by level of government compared to GNP (current and constant prices) and implicit price deflator indexes, quarterly 1982-84, and 1975-84.

PACE OF FEDERAL GRANTS SLOWS SHARPLY SINCE '81, ANNUAL FEATURE

(p. 3-4) Annual article comparing States' tax payment for and receipts from Federal grant-in-aid programs, FY84. Includes 1 table showing payments and receipts, and rankings by tax burden per dollar of aid, all by State.

R9050–3.606: June/July 1985 (Vol. 29, No. 6)

GOVERNMENT SPENDING TOPS $1.58 TRILLION; NOW TOTALS $18,310 FOR EACH U.S. HOUSEHOLD, ANNUAL FEATURE

(p. 1, 4) Annual article on trends in government spending, with 1 table showing per-household and per-capita expenditures aggregated for all government levels, and Federal and State/local government total expenditures, FY50-85.

"INCOME SECURITY" CLAIMS 1/3 OF ALL PUBLIC DOLLARS SPENT, ANNUAL FEATURE

(p. 1, 4) Annual article, with 1 table showing distribution of Federal/State/local tax dollar expenditures by function, selected years FY60-83.

TAXES HEAVIEST FOR TOP EARNERS DESPITE '81 CUTS; FEW HIGHER EARNERS TURN TO TAX AVOIDANCE SCHEMES

(p. 2, 4) Article, with 2 tables showing the following data for Federal tax returns on incomes of $200,000/over: number and percent of returns with no taxable income, 1973-82; and number of returns, average tax payment and effective tax rate (excluding and including foreign taxes), and distribution of returns by effective tax rate (excluding foreign taxes), 1982.

Data are shown for adjusted gross incomes and/or "expanded" incomes (includes tax preference items subject to minimum tax) of $200,000/over.

TAX REFORM AND REAGAN I

(Insert, 4 p.) Article, with 2 tables estimating revenue changes that would result from selected provisions of tax reforms proposed by the Reagan Administration ("Reagan I") and the Treasury Dept ("Treasury I"), FY90 or FY86-90 period.

INDIVIDUAL INCOME TAXES REMAIN CHIEF $ SOURCE, ANNUAL FEATURE

(p. 3-4) Annual article, with 1 table showing distribution of Federal/State/local tax revenue dollar by tax and nontax sources, selected years FY60-83.

R9050–3.607: Aug. 1985 (Vol. 29, No. 7)

'81 TAX CUT AND SLOW INFLATION BOOST U.S. FAMILY'S BUYING POWER, ANNUAL FEATURE

(p. 1) Annual article estimating the impact of inflation and Federal tax increases on family

purchasing power, 1975-85. Includes 1 table showing median family income, Federal income and social security tax payments, and after-tax income in current and 1985 dollars, 1975-85.

BUSINESS TAX BURDENS

(Insert, 2 p.) Article, with 2 tables showing corporate pre-tax profits; Federal and State/local corporate income tax accruals and effective tax rates; corporate payroll taxes; and income/payroll taxes as percent of corporate profits; selected periods 1949-84.

PER CAPITA PROPERTY TAXES JUMP 40% FROM '76 TO '83

(p. 3-4) Article, with 1 table showing per capita property tax, and property taxes as percent of local revenues, for 40 most populous SMSAs and aggregate for 75 major SMSAs, FY83 with comparisons to FY76.

R9285
Urban Land Institute

R9285–1   **DOLLARS AND CENTS OF SHOPPING CENTERS, 1984: A Study of Receipts and Expenses in Shopping Center Operations**
Triennial. 1984. ix+341 p.
ULI Catalog No. D-40.
ISBN 0-87420-653-7.
LC 70-81240.
SRI/MF/not filmed

Triennial report, for 1984, presenting aggregate financial and operating results for shopping centers in U.S. and Canada, based primarily on 1982 data. Report is intended to permit individual shopping centers to compare their performance with industry averages.

Covers total and unowned occupancy area; operating receipts and expenses, by type; and tenant leased area, sales, rent, and common area charges, by detailed type of tenant.

Data are shown for U.S. super-regional, regional, community, and neighborhood centers, with detail for 6 regions and by center age; and for Canadian regional, community, and neighborhood centers.

Data by type of tenant are shown by SIC 4-digit classification and operating category (national chain, local chain, and independent). Data generally are shown as medians and upper and lower percentiles, per square foot of leasable area.

Also includes operating result comparisons to 1978 and 1981 surveys and to capital costs; tenant data for new leases entered into after Jan. 1, 1981, and for "food courts"; energy distribution and cost-recovery methods; merchant assn/promotional fund activities; parking facilities; and selected other aspects of shopping center operations.

Data are based on responses of 954 shopping centers to a 1983 Urban Land Institute survey.

Contains listings of contents and tables (p. iv-ix); introduction, highlights, and user's guide, with 13 tables (p. 1-16); 6 statistical sections, with 175 tables and accompanying narrative (p. 18-330); and 3 appendices, including methodology, survey sample analysis, bibliography, and lists of tenant classifications and codes (p. 332-341).

This is the 9th edition of the report. For description of 8th edition, see SRI 1982 Annual under this number.

Availability: Urban Land Institute, Publication Sales, 1090 Vermont Ave., NW, Washington DC 20005, members $85.00, others $115.00; SRI/MF/not filmed.

R9372
U.S. Committee for Refugees

R9372–1   **WORLD REFUGEE SURVEY, 1984**
Annual. 1984. 65 p.
ISSN 0197-5439.
ISBN 0-9365-4805-3.
LC 80-644592.
SRI/MF/complete, delayed

Annual report reviewing developments in world refugee movement, resettlement, and aid contributions, by country of origin and/or asylum, 1983.

Contains contents listing and glossary (p. 1-2); 21 articles on international refugee problems and policies, including 1 article with statistics (p. 3-36); world refugee statistics (p. 37-41); summary reports on refugee situation in selected countries and world areas (p. 42-58); and directory of international and U.S. refugee assistance agencies, and data sources (p. 59-64).

Sections with substantial statistical content are described below.

Availability: U.S. Committee for Refugees, 20 W. 40th St., New York NY 10018, $8.00; SRI/MF/complete, delayed shipment in Dec. 1985.

STATISTICAL SECTIONS:

GEOGRAPHIC VARIATIONS IN THE ECONOMIC ADJUSTMENT OF SOUTHEAST ASIAN REFUGEES IN THE U.S., ANNUAL FEATURE

(p. 7-8) Annual article, by Robert L. Bach et al., on the economic condition of Southeast Asian refugees living in the U.S. Most data are from a 1983 HHS survey of 1,239 households.

Includes 1 table showing the following for Southeast Asian refugees in California, Texas, and rest of U.S.: labor force participation and unemployment rates; mean weekly wages; and percent living in households receiving public cash assistance and food stamps, and percent of such households with at least 1 employed member; fall 1983.

1984 WORLD REFUGEE STATISTICS, ANNUAL FEATURE

(p. 37-41) Annual compilation of data on worldwide refugee populations. Most data are from UN High Commissioner for Refugees, and U.S. State Dept. Includes 1 map, 1 chart, and 7 tables showing the following:

a. Refugees in need of protection/assistance, by asylum country and world region (no date); and refugees entered/resettled, by resettlement country and world region, 1975-83 period; with detail by refugee source country or area, rankings of top 15-20 asylum and resettlement countries by ratios of refugees to local population, and per capita GNP for top asylum and resettlement countries.

b. Voluntarily repatriated refugees, with countries involved, 1982-84 period; and internally displaced persons, by country (no date).

c. Top 20 countries ranked by per capita and total contributions to international refugee aid agencies, with population and GNP comparisons; and total EC contributions; 1983.

R9375
U.S. Travel Data Center

R9375–1   TRAVEL PRINTOUT
Monthly.   4 p.
ISSN 0744-6233.
LC SN 82-2592.
SRI/MF/complete, shipped quarterly

Monthly newsletter on travel/tourism industry developments, including summary data on travel indicators. Data are from a variety of public and private sources, and are current to 2-4 months preceding publication date.

Contains brief narrative reviews of travel-related developments, usually with 1-2 charts and/or tables; and 2 monthly tables, listed below. Monthly tables appear in all issues. Additional features with substantial statistics are described, as they appear, under "Statistical Features." Nonstatistical features are not covered.

Availability: U.S. Travel Data Center, 1899 L St., NW, Suite 610, Washington DC 20036, $49.00 per yr.; SRI/MF/complete, shipped quarterly.

Issues reviewed during 1985: Oct. 1984-Sept. 1985 (P) (Vol. 13, Nos. 10-12; Vol. 14, Nos. 1-9).

MONTHLY TABLES:

[1] Monthly and annual rates of change in the travel price index and components [for month of coverage compared to previous month and to same month of previous year].

[2] Current travel indicators [receipts/sales for eating/drinking places, hotels/motels, and gas stations; commercial lodging demand and/or hotel occupancy rate; highway traffic; air and rail passenger traffic; travel price index; total and vacation person-trips; national park visits and overnight stays; foreign arrivals from and U.S. departures to overseas and Canada; and motor gasoline demand; for month of coverage, with percent change from previous month, same month of previous year, and beginning of current year; prior to June 1985 issue, table also included bus passenger traffic].

STATISTICAL FEATURES:

R9375–1.601: Mar. 1985 (Vol. 14, No. 3)

FOREIGN VISITORS CONTRIBUTE OVER 12% OF 1983 U.S. TOURISM RECEIPTS

(p. 1, 3) Article, with 1 table ranking top 10 States by foreign tourism receipts, with percent of total tourism receipts, 1983. Data are from Commerce Dept.

R9375–1.602: June 1985 (Vol. 14, No. 6)

TRAVEL SPENDING INCREASED 6% IN 1983

(p. 1, 3) Article, with 1 table ranking top 10 States by domestic/foreign travel expenditures, 1983. Data are from Travel Data Center's *Impact of Travel on State Economies, 1983.* For description of full report, see R9375-7.

R9375–2   SURVEY OF STATE TRAVEL OFFICES, 1984-85
Annual.   Jan. 1985.   i+96 p.
ISSN 0361-8307.
LC 74-191723.
SRI/MF/complete

Annual report on administration, promotional activities, budgets, and research of State travel development agencies, various years 1983-FY85. Data are from a June-Dec. 1984 survey of agencies in each State, D.C., and selected U.S. territories.

Contains contents listing (1 p.); preface (p. i); summary and analysis, with 3 summary tables (p. 1-11); and 7 extended tables showing the following for individual travel development agencies:

a. General administration: directory information; name and length of service of director and assistant; full- and part-time staff size; and organization characteristics. 1 table. (p. 13-22)

b. Advertising: characterization of staff and organization, advertising agency, and advertising objectives; and handling of inquiries, including number received in 1983. 1 table. (p. 23-33)

c. Budget: total budget and State rank, funding sources other than State general revenue, general and promotion budget allocations by function, advertising budget by medium, number of travel shows in which participated, foreign advertising budget allocations by medium and country, and foreign promotion and press/public relations budget by country, FY84 and/or FY85. 1 table. (p. 35-61)

d. General promotion, press/public relations, and research: characteristics of current programs; press/travel writer tours in 1983 and planned for 1984; and cost of research conducted by university faculty member and private research group. 3 tables. (p. 63-87)

e. Package tours: characteristics and status of program development; catalogues published in 1983; and number of package tours offered in 1983-84. 1 table. (p. 89-92)

This is the 12th annual report.

Availability: U.S. Travel Data Center, 1899 L St., NW, Suite 610, Washington DC 20036, $55.00; SRI/MF/complete.

R9375–3   NATIONAL TRAVEL SURVEY
Quarterly.   Approx. 90 p.
ISSN 0737-2620.
SRI/MF/complete

Quarterly report on the number, region, purpose, and transportation mode of trips by U.S. adults. Data are from monthly telephone interviews of a national probability sample of approximately 1,400 persons, conducted by RL Associates.

Contains contents listing, introduction, and narrative summary with text tables; and appendices, with approximately 60 tables listed below, glossary, and methodology.

Report usually is issued 3-6 months after quarter of coverage. Travel Data Center also publishes an annual report supplementing the quarterly data, described under R9375-5.

Availability: U.S. Travel Data Center, 1899 L St., NW, Suite 610, Washington DC 20036, $65.00 per issue; SRI/MF/complete.

Issues reviewed during 1985: 2nd-4th Qtrs. 1984 (D).

TABLES:

[Destination and residence areas are large and small MSAs and non-MSA; destination area also includes outside U.S.]

TOTAL TRAVEL

[Tables 1A-1J show data for quarter of coverage and same period of previous year.]

1A. Monthly average number and percent of U.S. adults taking trips, by major trip characteristics.

1B. Number of trips and person-trips for major trip characteristics.

1C-1J. Percent distribution of total trips [and/or] person-trips by round trip distance and mode of transport, duration of trip and type of lodging, purpose and type of trip, travel party size and structure, family income and age, destination region, region of trip origin, and area of destination and residence.

BY MODE AND PURPOSE

2A-7H. [Tables 1C-1J are repeated for air, auto/truck/recreational vehicle, business/convention, pleasure, vacation, and weekend trips, for current quarter only.]

YEAR TO DATE

8A-8B. [Repeats tables 1A-1B, showing data quarterly for year to date. Not included in 1st quarter report.]

R9375–5   1984 NATIONAL TRAVEL SURVEY, Full Year Report
Annual.   1985.
119 p. var. paging.
ISSN 0737-2620.
LC 83-641929.
SRI/MF/complete

Annual report, for 1984, summarizing results of the monthly National Travel Survey on the number, region, purpose, and transportation mode of trips by U.S. adults. Data are from monthly telephone interviews of a national probability sample of approximately 1,500 persons, conducted by RL Associates.

Contents:

a. Executive summary; contents listing; introduction; report guide; and brief narrative on travel factors, with 1 table showing selected economic indicators for 1983-84. (2 p., p. 1-7)

b. Narrative overview, with 3 tables correlating travel regions of origin and destination; and 2 tables and usually 1 chart showing average persons, miles, and nights per trip, and selected traveler characteristics (including credit card ownership), repeated for all, air, auto/truck/RV, business/convention, pleasure, vacation, and weekend travel, 1983 and/or 1984. (p. 9-33)

c. Appendix A, with 65 tables listed below. (p. A1-A65)

d. Appendices B-F, with glossary, survey methodology, questionnaire facsimile, and notes on sampling error. (p. B1-F3)

Availability: U.S. Travel Data Center, 1899 L St., NW, Suite 610, Washington DC 20036, $100.00; SRI/MF/complete.

TABLES:

[Tables 1A-1K show data for 1983-84; all other tables show 1984 data only. Destination and residence areas are large and small MSAs and non-MSA; destination areas also include outside U.S.]

TOTAL TRAVEL

1A. Monthly average number and percent of U.S. adults taking trips, by major trip characteristics. (p. A1)

1B. Number of trips and person-trips for major trip characteristics. (p. A2)

1C-1K. Percent distribution of total trips and person-trips by: round-trip distance and mode of transport; duration of trip and type of lodging; purpose and type of trip; travel-related services; travel party size and structure; family income and [individual traveler] age; destination region; region of origin; and area of destination and residence. (p. A3-A11)

BY MODE AND PURPOSE

2A-7I. [Tables 1C-1K are repeated, with applicable data, for air, auto/truck/RV, business/convention, pleasure, vacation, and weekend travel.] (p. A12-A65)

R9375–6 TOURISM'S TOP TWENTY: Fast Facts on Travel and Tourism

Recurring (irreg.) 1984.
xiii+109 p.
ISBN 0-89478-108-1.
SRI/MF/complete

Recurring report presenting a series of top 20 rankings of States, cities, foreign countries, business establishments, and other entities, based on a variety of travel and tourism related measures, various years 1980-84. Includes data on advertising, transportation, lodging, parks, passports, recreation, and travel expenditures and receipts.

Data are from Federal Government, U.S. Travel Data Center, trade assns, media organizations, and other private sources.

Contains listings of contents and tables, and introduction (p. iii-xiii, 1-4); 93 tables, described below (p. 5-97); appendices, with directory of sources (p. 98-100); and index (p. 102-109).

For description of previous report, published in 1980, see SRI 1980 Annual under this number.

Availability: U.S. Travel Data Center, 1899 L St., NW, Suite 610, Washington DC 20036 or Business Research Division, Campus Box 420, University of Colorado, Boulder CO 80309, $25.00; SRI/MF/complete.

TABLES:

[Tables show top 20 rankings, unless otherwise noted.]

a. Advertising: States by travel office budgets; foreign countries by Government expenditures on tourism development; States, U.S. destinations, foreign countries, world steamship lines, and U.S. airlines, by advertising expenditures in U.S. media; magazines by travel advertising pages, with detail by travel sector; and travel advertisers by expenditures in 5 media. Tables 1-13. (p. 5-17)

b. Air travel: U.S. cities by charter and U.S. citizen departures to international destinations, and by foreign visitor arrivals; foreign countries by passengers flying to/from U.S. on scheduled and chartered service, and by U.S.

citizen arrivals; and U.S. air routes by passenger miles and passengers. Tables 14-23. (p. 18-27)

c. Airlines: U.S. and world airlines by passengers, operating revenues, departures, and employment; U.S. airlines by revenue passenger miles, number of planes, and value of travel agency commissions; and world airlines by pasenger kilometers (international and domestic), passenger load factor, and North Atlantic passengers and load factor. Tables 24-41. (p. 28-45)

d. Airports and GNP: U.S. and world airports by passengers; FAA-operated traffic control towers by aircraft operations; and foreign countries by total and per capita GNP. Tables 42-46. (p. 46-50)

e. Auto and bus travel: States by interstate highway mileage, licensed drivers, auto registrations, and expenditures of intercity bus companies/passengers; countries by auto registrations and production; and world auto companies by production. Tables 47-53. (p. 51-57)

f. Lodging and parks: world hotel/motel chains and consortia by number of properties and rooms; National Park Service areas by acreage, recreation visits, and overnight stays; and States by recreation visits to National Park Service areas, and by State parks/recreation areas, acreage, and visitors. Tables 54-64. (p. 58-68)

g. Passports and resorts: SMSAs, States, and occupational groups, by passports received; States by recreational vehicle deliveries; U.S. resorts by occupancy rate, and total and per room sales; restaurant types by number of units; and U.S. ski resorts by skier visits and vertical transport feet per hour. Tables 65-75. (p. 69-79)

h. Sports and recreation: sports by participants; top 9 spectator sports by attendance; States by fishing and hunting licenses issued and revenues; and North America theme parks by attendance. Tables 76-82. (p. 80-86)

i. Expenditures and travel impact: countries by international tourism expenditures and receipts; foreign countries by residents visiting U.S., and by expenditures of U.S. visitors; and States by number of travel agencies, travel expenditures (total and per resident), and travel-generated employment (and share of total employment), payroll, and tax revenues. Tables 83-93. (p. 87-97)

R9375–7 IMPACT OF TRAVEL ON STATE ECONOMIES, 1983

Annual. May 1985.
62 p. var. paging.
ISSN 0730-9813.
LC 81-644365.
SRI/MF/complete

Annual report estimating the economic impact of domestic travel on each State and on selected industries, 1983. Includes estimates of travel-related expenditures, business receipts, payroll, employment, and tax revenues. Also includes summary estimates for combined domestic/foreign visitor impact.

Estimates are based on economic model analysis of data from public and private sources.

Contains summary and contents listing (2 p.); introduction, and 6 sections with 13 tables listed

below (p. 1-45); and 4 appendices, presenting description of the model, glossary, list of States showing SIC 2-digit industries providing more jobs than travel-related industries, and data sources (p. A1-D2).

A related report, *Impact of Foreign Visitors on State Economies, 1983,* is described under R9375-11.

Availability: U.S. Travel Data Center, 1899 L St., NW, Suite 610, Washington DC 20036, $55.00; SRI/MF/complete.

TABLES:

[Tables show data for 1983. Most data are shown by State, and (except for tax revenues, expenditure and employment rank, and domestic/foreign visitor impact) by selected U.S. industry category including public and automobile transportation, lodging, food, entertainment/recreation, incidental purchases, general retail trade, and travel arrangement; with totals for U.S. territories and foreign visitor spending.]

1-3. Travel expenditures in the U.S.; and domestic travel expenditures for all trips, with State ranking, share [of U.S. total travel], and percent change [from 1982]. (p. 3-11)

4-7. Travel-generated business receipts and payroll. (p. 13-25)

8-10. Travel-generated employment; and share of total employment and rank among private [sector] industries. (p. 27-36)

11-12. Travel-generated tax receipts and revenues [by level of government]. (p. 37-41)

13. Domestic/foreign visitor economic impact [expenditures, payroll, employment, and tax revenue, by State only]. (p. 44-45)

R9375–9 1983-84 ECONOMIC REVIEW OF TRAVEL in America

Annual. 1984. 3+75 p.
ISSN 0733-642X.
LC 82-644321.
SRI/MF/complete

Annual report, for 1983/84, on the economic impact of the travel industry, including data on travel characteristics and expenditures; industry receipts, prices, employment, taxes generated, and energy use; and international and regional travel. Data are shown for various years 1973-84.

Data are from the U.S. Travel Data Center, Federal agencies, World Tourism Organization, Amtrak, and American Bus Assn.

Contents:

Executive summary and contents listing. (2 p.)

Chapter I-II. Introduction, and Travel Activity and Industry Trends. Includes change in selected economic indicators; travel volume and nights away from home, by trip purpose; U.S. expenditures on domestic and foreign travel; foreign expenditures on U.S. travel; travel receipts compared to 4 other industries; and payroll income, employment, and Federal, State, and local tax revenues generated by travel; mostly 1982 and/or 1983. 7 charts and 7 tables. (p. 1-19)

Chapter III-V. Travel Price Inflation, Travel and Employment, and Travel and Energy. Includes minority and women's shares of travel employment and total employment, 1983. 8 charts and 2 tables. (p. 21-33)

Chapter VI-VIII. International Travel Trends, Regional Travel Patterns, and Conclusions. Includes payroll income, employment, and Federal, State, and local tax revenues generated by foreign visitors; number and expenditures of foreign travelers in U.S. and U.S. travelers abroad, by country of origin or destination; and trips, travel expenditures, and travel-generated employment, by destination region; 1983. 8 charts and 5 tables. (p. 35-51)

App. A-B. Basic Travel Data, and Resources. Includes 14 tables, listed below; and bibliography. (p. 55-75)

For description of previous report, for 1982/83, see SRI 1983 Annual, under this number.

Availability: U.S. Travel Data Center, 1899 L St., NW, Suite 610, Washington DC 20036, $45.00; SRI/MF/complete.

APPENDIX TABLES:

[Unless otherwise noted, tables show data for U.S., 1973-84. Travel industry sectors include air, bus, and rail transportation; lodging; food service; and entertainment/recreation. Table numbering begins with 2A.]

2A-2B. Business receipts of selected travel industry sectors [compared to GNP, in current and 1972 dollars]. (p. 55-56)

2C. Domestic intercity transportation activity [passenger-miles, by mode]. (p. 57)

2D. Travel agency locations, airline sales, airline commissions, [and airline passenger revenue], 1977-83. (p. 58)

2E. Small business firms and total firms [by travel industry sector], 1977. (p. 59)

3A. Travel price index and its components [compared to CPI]. (p. 60)

4A-4B. Payroll employment for selected travel industry sectors, 1973-83, and monthly 1981-83. (p. 61-64)

5A-5B. Travel/tourism transportation consumption of petroleum [by mode, compared to other consuming sectors]; and domestic consumption of energy [total, motor gasoline, and for travel/tourism, local, and all transportation]; 1982-83. (p. 65-66)

6A-6C. U.S. international travel and passenger fare receipts, payments, and balance; and U.S. and world international travel receipts and arrivals; 1973-83. (p. 67-69)

6D. National Government expenditures on tourism development, by top 37 countries, 1983. (p. 70)

7B-7C. Travel expenditures by U.S. and foreign visitors; and employment generated by U.S./foreign travel expenditures [both by U.S.] travel region, 1982. (p. 71-72)

R9375–11 IMPACT OF FOREIGN VISITORS ON STATE ECONOMIES, 1983
Monograph. Apr. 1985.
65 p. var. paging.
SRI/MF/complete

Report estimating the impact of foreign visitors on State and regional economies, 1983. Includes foreign visitor expenditures, by country or world area of residence, expenditure category, and trip purpose; and payroll income, employment, and tax revenues generated by foreign visitors, with detail by industry sector and/or government level.

Most data are shown by State, census division, and/or travel region. Industry sectors are transportation, lodging, food service, entertainment, and retail trade.

Estimates are based on data from the U.S. Travel and Tourism Administration (USTTA) Survey of International Air Travelers (covering 8.3 million air visitors from Mexico and overseas); Statistics Canada (covering 12 million Canadian visitors); and U.S. Commerce Dept (covering 1.4 million Mexican visitors). Report was prepared for USTTA by the U.S. Travel Data Center.

Contains contents listing (1 p.); preface and introduction (p. i-iv); narrative analysis interspersed with 14 tables (p. 1-23); and 6 appendices, with methodology and 10 tables (p. A1-F1).

A related annual report, estimating the economic impact of domestic travel, is covered in SRI under R9375-7.

Availability: U.S. Travel Data Center, 1899 L St., NW, Suite 610, Washington DC 20036, $30.00; SRI/MF/complete.

R9380
Utah Foundation

R9380–1 STATISTICAL REVIEW OF GOVERNMENT IN UTAH, 1985 Edition
Annual. 1985. iv+101 p.
LC 64-55439.
SRI/MF/complete, current & previous year reports

Annual report, for 1985, presenting detailed data on Utah State and local government finances, including revenues by source and expenditures for education, welfare services, and transportation; and selected demographic and economic data. Also includes selected data for the U.S.

Data are shown primarily for 1983-84, with trends from as early as 1900, and are from State and Federal agency reports.

Contains contents listing, review of State activities, and 1 summary table showing State social, economic, and governmental indicators, selected years 1960-84 (p. ii-iv); Parts A-J, presenting 11 summary charts, and 78 tables listed below (p. 1-99); and index (p. 100-101).

Previous report, for 1984, was also reviewed by SRI during 1985, and is also available on SRI microfiche under R9380-1 [Annual. 1984. iv+101 p. $10.00]. For description of the 1983 edition of the report, see SRI 1983 Annual under this number.

Availability: Utah Foundation, 308 Continental Bank Bldg., Salt Lake City UT 84101, $10.00; SRI/MF/complete.

TABLES:
[Data are for Utah, unless otherwise noted. Trend data often are shown only for selected years within the ranges noted.]

R9380–1.1: Part A: Social and Economic
POPULATION AND VITAL STATISTICS

[1] [Resident population, for U.S. by State, 1980 and 1984]. (p. 1)

[2-3] Population [1900-84]; and illustrative projection of population [1985-2010]. (p. 2)

[4-5] Population [decennially 1940-80 and July 1984 estimate]; and natural increase [live births and deaths], 1983; by counties. (p. 3)

[6] Population of incorporated cities and towns, 1970, 1980, and 1982. (p. 4-5)

[7] Vital statistics: births, deaths, marriages, divorces [with Utah and U.S. rates, 1950-84]. (p. 6)

RETAIL SALES, PERSONAL INCOME, AND CPI

[8] Summary of sales and purchases subject to Utah sales and use tax laws, by type of establishment, 1978-83. (p. 7)

[9] Personal income by counties [total and per capita, 1970-83]. (p. 7)

[10] Personal income [total and per capita] in Utah and the U.S. [and Utah rank in per capita income, 1929-84]. (p. 8)

[11] Personal income in Utah and the U.S. by major source [salary income by industry division and government level, and nonsalary income by type], Utah, 1960, 1970, 1980, and 1983, and U.S., 1983. (p. 9)

[12-13] BLS CPI [for U.S., 1913-84, with detail by major component and by month for recent years]. (p. 10-11)

MINERAL PRODUCTION AND FARM FINANCES

[14] Value of nonfuel mineral production [total and for 10 products, 1950-84]. (p. 12)

[15] Gross farm income [by source] and expenditures [1950-83]. (p. 12)

EMPLOYMENT

[16] Composition of labor force [by industry group, 1950-Sept. 1984]. (p. 13)

[17] Number of nonagricultural employees by counties and by major industrial classification, Sept. 1984. (p. 14)

R9380–1.2: Part B: All Governments

[1-2] Total revenue and expenditures of all governmental units in the U.S., by source or function and level of government, FY83. (p. 16-17)

[3] Federal, State, and local expenditures in the U.S. [total and per capita], FY02-83. (p. 18)

[4] Total taxes (Federal, State, and local) charged in Utah, [amount per capita, and taxes by government level as percent of personal income, FY40-84]. (p. 19)

[5] Number of government employees [for U.S.] by State [and level of government], Oct. 1983. (p. 20)

R9380–1.3: Part C: Federal Government

[1] Analysis of 1982 Federal income tax returns filed for Utah residents by county and by selected communities [including gross income and Federal taxes paid]. (p. 22)

[2] Federal and State income taxes collected in Utah as related to adjusted gross incomes, tax years 1970-82. (p. 23)

[3] Federal tax returns filed [and adjusted gross income and Federal taxes paid] in Utah by filing status and type of deduction, 1981 tax year. (p. 23)

[4] Analysis of Federal income tax returns in Utah, by gross income class, 1982 tax year. (p. 23)

[5] Federal budget receipts, expenditures, and debt [in U.S.], FY60-84. (p. 24)

[6-7] 1985 pay schedule for Federal white collar workers; and [salaries for] typical Federal positions. (p. 25)

[8] Federal expenditures [total and per capita, by expenditure category], in Utah and the U.S., FY83 [with aggregate trends from 1970]. (p. 26)

R9380–1.4: Part D: Utah State Government

[1-2] Salary ranges for State employees, 1975/76, 1980/81, and 1985/86; and salary levels of principal State [elected and appointed] officials [1984/85-1985/86]. (p. 28-29)

[3-4] State revenue [by source] and expenditures [by function, 1950-84]. (p. 30)

R9380–1.5: Part E: Local Government

[1] Taxable sales and local option sales tax collections by local units [county and city], year ended Aug. 31, 1984. (p. 32-33)

[2] Finances of local governments [revenues, expenditures, and debt, by unit of government], FY83. (p. 34)

R9380–1.6: Part F: General Finances

[1-2] General revenue [by source] and expenditures [by function] of State/local governments in Utah and the U.S., FY60, FY70, FY80, and FY83. (p. 36-37)

[3] State and local tax burden in the U.S., FY83 [includes State and local taxes paid, FY83; and population (total and in 21-64 age group), households, and personal income, 1980 or 1982; all by State]. (p. 38)

[4] Trends in principal State/local tax collections in Utah [total, per capita, and per $1,000 of personal income, by type of tax, FY50-84]. (p. 39)

[5-6] State personal income tax data [tax rates and personal exemption/credit amounts], and State/local tax rates for major taxes [corporation income, sales, motor fuel, and cigarette; all for U.S. by State], as of Jan. 1, 1985. (p. 40-41)

[7] Tax structure of Utah [tax name, legal citation, year enacted, item taxed, rate, and function], Jan. 1985. (p. 42)

R9380–1.7: Part G: Education

[1] Percent of personal income expended for public education [for U.S. by State], 1982/83. (p. 43)

[2] Expenditures for public education [public school maintenance/operations, bond interest, capital outlay, and school lunch expenditures; and total higher education and other expenditures; FY50-84]. (p. 44)

[3] Public school expenditures by school district [instructional, other operating, bond interest, maintenance/operations, and capital outlay expenditures], 1983/84 [with State totals from 1949/50]. (p. 45)

[4] Pupil/teacher ratios, school expenditures per pupil, [and average daily attendance and number of teachers], by school district, 1983/84 [and State totals from 1949/50]. (p. 46)

[5] Fall enrollments in public schools [by school district, 1965-84]. (p. 47)

[6] Salary levels for classroom teachers in school districts [by degree level], 1984/85 [and State averages from 1949/50]. (p. 48)

[7] Education and general finances of institutions of higher education [total and per student revenues by source, and expenditures by type, by institution], 1983/84 (p. 49)

[8] Enrollment at collegiate institutions of higher education [by public and private institution, 1964/65-1984/85]. (p. 50)

R9380–1.8: Part H: Social Welfare

[1] Aid to dependent children recipients per 10,000 population in U.S. [and number of families and total recipients, by State], June 1983. (p. 51)

[2-3] State public assistance expenditures by program [FY50-84]; and number of persons receiving public assistance [by program, June 1950-84]. (p. 52-53)

[4] Medicaid services provided [expenditures by type of service], 1969/70-1983/84. (p. 54)

[5] Food stamp program [participating households and persons, and value of food stamps], FY72-84. (p. 54)

[6] Social service and health expenditures [by type of service], FY80-84. (p. 54)

[7] Labor force, unemployment, payroll, employing units, unemployment benefits, and average wage, by counties, 1983 [and State totals, 1950-82]. (p. 55)

[8] Number of persons [by category] receiving OASDI (social security) benefits in the U.S. [1940-84]. (p. 56)

[9] Finances of [U.S.] old age and survivors insurance (social security) trust fund [FY40-84]. (p. 56)

R9380–1.9: Part I: Transportation

[1] Passengers carried by the Utah Transit Authority [1935-84]. (p. 57)

[2] Expenditures for State highways [FY50-84]. (p. 58)

[3-4] Motor and aviation fuel refined and consumed [FY50-84]. (p. 58)

[5] Distribution of highway-user revenues [by source and allocation], FY82-84. (p. 59)

[6] Receipts and expenditures of State and local governments for highway and related purposes [by source or object, FY83-84 or 1983]. (p. 60)

[7] Mileage of all roads and streets by surface type and [governmental] unit, as of Dec. 31, 1983. (p. 61)

[8] Air traffic at the Salt Lake City International Airport [aircraft, passenger, mail, and freight movements, 1950-84]. (p. 62)

R9380–1.10: Part J: Property Tax
LEVIES BY STATE, COUNTY, AND CITY

[1-2] Property taxes charged [by purpose, and total assessed valuation]; and average property tax mill levies [by level of government; 1950-84]. (p. 64)

[3] Assessed valuations by counties [decennially 1960-80 and 1984]. (p. 65)

[4] Total property taxes charged by all taxing units within counties [1950-84]. (p. 66)

[5] Assessed valuation and property taxes charged by class of property, 1984. (p. 67)

[6] Property taxes charged by class of property, 1960-84. (p. 68)

[7] Property taxes charged by counties [school, county, city/town, and special district taxes], 1984. (p. 69)

[8] Indicated average assessment levels of locally-assessed real property by counties [1970-82, and by type of property 1984]. (p. 70)

[9] Property tax levies in principal cities [1984 tax mill levy, by purpose; and levy totals, 1960-83]. (p. 71)

LEVIES BY LOCAL TAXING UNITS

[10] Property tax data by local units of government [taxes levied by all taxing jurisdictions including school districts, arranged by county, showing assessed valuation, mill levy, and taxes charged, 1984; and total tax levies, 1960-84]. (p. 72-99)

R9385
West Virginia
Research League

R9385–1   WEST VIRGINIA RESEARCH LEAGUE 1984 STATISTICAL HANDBOOK
Annual. [1984.] 80 p.
ISSN 0091-6102.
LC 73-643039.
SRI/MF/complete

Annual compilation, for 1984, of social, governmental, and economic statistics for West Virginia. Data are shown mostly for calendar or fiscal years 1974-83, and are primarily from Federal and State agency reports.

Report is designed to present an overview of the State. Socioeconomic and geographical breakdowns are shown, as applicable, for selected topics. These breakdowns include data by county, government agency, income, and industry. Comparisons to total U.S. are also occasionally included.

Contains contents and table listing (p. 3-6); 62 tables, described below (p. 7-78); and listing of State research studies conducted by the issuing agency (p. 80).

Availability: West Virginia Research League, 1107 Charleston National Plaza, Charleston WV 25301, $5.63; SRI/MF/complete.

TABLES:
[Data source is given beneath each table.]

R9385–1.1: Economic Summary

(p. 7) Contains 1 table. Includes summary population, personal income, employment, and earnings.

R9385–1.2: State Government Finances, Welfare Caseloads, and Work Accidents

(p. 8-28) Contains 18 tables. Includes State tax rates and fees; State fund receipts and disbursements, net revenues by source, and expenditures by function; and bonds outstanding.

Also includes general revenue, State road, human services, and workers' compensation fund cash flow; motor vehicle registrations; welfare caseloads; and worker's compensation fatal and nonfatal accidents reported.

R9385–1.3: Unemployment Insurance

(p. 29-31) Contains 3 tables. Includes unemployment compensation payments, weeks compensated, and claims; and covered employment.

R9385–1.4: Education

(p. 32-42) Contains 11 tables. Includes general school fund balances, receipts by source, and expenditures by function; and public school buildings, enrollment, attendance, per capita cost, and teachers.

Also includes higher education operating revenue and expenditures of State-supported institutions; and enrollment and degrees conferred, by public and private institutions.

R9385–1.5: Property Taxes

(p. 43-51) Contains 7 tables. Includes property assessed valuation, taxes levied, and tax rates.

R9385–1.6: Federal Data, Personal Income, and Local Government Finances

(p. 52-67) Contains 15 tables. Includes Federal aid payments and tax collections; Federal income tax returns filed and tax liability; personal income by source, including transfer payments; per capita income; and population.

Also includes State/local revenues and expenditures per capita and per $1,000 personal income; and local government revenue by source, expenditures by function, and indebtedness.

R9385–1.7: Natural Resources, Banking, and Economics

(p. 68-78) Contains 7 tables. Includes State park and forest attendance; underground and surface mine coal production; and crude petroleum and natural gas production.

Also includes State and national financial institutions, deposits, and loans; retail sales; and U.S. PPI, CPI, and price deflator index.

S0090   ALABAMA
Department of
Agriculture and Industries

S0090–1   ALABAMA AGRICULTURAL STATISTICS, 1982 Revised, 1983 Preliminary
Annual.   Sept. 1984.   52 p.
Bull. No. 26.
LC 54-63111.
SRI/MF/complete

Annual report on Alabama agricultural production, marketing, and income, 1982 and preliminary 1983, with selected trends from the 1970s. Data generally are shown by commodity and/or county and district.

Report covers production, prices, sales and/or value, and, as applicable, acreage, yield, or inventory, for field crop, potato, fruit and nut, livestock, dairy, and poultry sectors.

Report also includes data on number and acreage of farms; farm income by source; cash receipts from farm forest products and nonfarm commercial timber; and value of USDA Payment-in-Kind program support, by county.

Data are from surveys of farmers and agricultural businesses conducted by Alabama Crop and Livestock Reporting Service, and reports by Alabama Cooperative Extension Service and USDA.

Contains foreword and contents listing (p. 4-5); and report, with 12 maps and 47 tables, interspersed with narrative (p. 6-52).

This is the 26th edition of the report.

Availability: Alabama Crop and Livestock Reporting Service, PO Box 1071, Montgomery AL 36192, †; SRI/MF/complete.

S0110   ALABAMA
Department of
Banking

S0110–1   ANNUAL REPORT OF SUPERINTENDENT OF BANKS of the State of Alabama, for the Fiscal Year Ending Sept. 30, 1984
Annual.   Jan. 29, 1985.
34 p.
SRI/MF/complete

Annual report, for FY84, on financial condition of Alabama State-chartered financial institutions, presenting consolidated balance sheet data and/or income and expenses for commercial banks, small loan licensees, consumer credit agencies, and credit unions, as of Dec. 31, 1983, or Sept. 30, 1984, with selected comparisons to the previous year.

Also includes assets of individual banks, savings and loan assns, and credit unions, arranged by city or rank; deposits of individual banks;

small loan licensee and consumer credit agency operations, with detail for delinquent account legal actions; and credit union membership, loan operations, and earnings distribution.

Contains lists of Banking Dept officials (p. 1-5); and 3 report sections, with lists of bank status changes, narrative summaries, and 26 tables (p. 6-34).

Availability: Alabama Department of Banking, 651 Administrative Bldg., 64 N. Union St., Montgomery AL 36130, †; SRI/MF/complete.

S0118   ALABAMA
Administrative
Office of the
Courts

S0118–1   ALABAMA JUDICIAL SYSTEM ANNUAL REPORT, FY84
Annual.   [1985.]   3+93 p.
LC 82-645231.
SRI/MF/complete

Annual report on Alabama judicial system, including trial and appellate court caseloads and case dispositions, FY84, with trends from FY80. Covers supreme, appeals, circuit, and district courts. Includes trial court data by case type, judicial district, county, and selected major city.

Case types shown are civil, criminal, traffic, small claims, domestic relations, and juvenile cases.

Also includes data on State tax fund for fair trials; number and cost of jury trials; and judicial dept finances.

Contains contents listing (1 p.); narrative report with 1 map, 3 charts, and 11 tables (p. 1-24); lists of judicial assignments (p. 25-33); and 3 appendices with 22 tables (p. 36-93).

Availability: Alabama Administrative Office of the Courts, 817 S. Court St., Montgomery AL 36130-0101, †; SRI/MF/complete.

S0119   ALABAMA
Criminal Justice
Information Center

S0119–1   1984 CRIME IN ALABAMA
Annual.   [1985.]   i+153 p.
LC 84-644818.
SRI/MF/complete

Annual report on Alabama crimes and arrests, by offense, 1984, with trends from 1980. Includes data by county, city, MSA, and reporting law enforcement agency, and by offender age, sex, and race. Also includes law enforcement employment, and assaults on officers.

Report focuses on 8 Index offenses: murder, rape, robbery, aggravated assault, burglary, larceny/theft, motor vehicle theft, and arson. Arrests are also shown for numerous non-Index offenses.

Data are from State and local agency reports submitted under the Uniform Crime Reporting Program.

Contains preface (p. i); introduction, explanation of data collection, and glossary (p. 1-13); 61 charts and 68 tables, accompanied by brief narrative summaries with text data (p. 14-138); and 2 appendix tables (p. 139-153).

All tables and charts are described below.

This is the 9th annual report.

Availability: Alabama Criminal Justice Information Center, Statistics Analysis Center, 858 S. Court St., Montgomery AL 36130-5201, ‡; SRI/MF/complete.

TABLES AND CHARTS:
[Data are for 1984, unless otherwise noted. Although arson is classified as an Index offense, arson data generally are not included in tables showing data by Index offense.]

S0119–1.1: Index Offenses and Non-Index Arrests

INDEX OFFENSES, STATE DATA
[Summary and sections on individual offenses include data on offenses and clearances, adult and juvenile arrests, and arrests by race and/or sex, 1980-84; and the additional data described below.]

a.   Summary: also including crime rate trends from 1980, offenses by month, and arrests by age, all by offense; value of stolen/damaged property, by detailed offense classification; and value of stolen and recovered property, by property type. 14 charts and 12 tables. (p. 15-31)

b.   Homicide: also including offenses by victim and offender race, sex, and relationship, and by type of weapon and circumstance. 7 charts and 6 tables. (p. 33-36)

c.   Rape: also including offenses by victim and offender race and relationship, and by type of weapon and location. 6 charts and 7 tables. (p. 38-41)

d.   Robbery: also including offenses by type of weapon and premises. 6 charts and 4 tables. (p. 43-45) *e.* Assault: also including offenses by type of weapon. 5 charts and 3 tables. (p. 47-49)

f. Burglary, larceny, and motor vehicle theft: also including burglaries by type of entry; residential and nonresidential burglaries (day and night); larceny offenses and value stolen, by type of theft and property value; and motor vehicle thefts by type of vehicle, and vehicles stolen and recovered locally and in other jurisdictions. 16 charts and 13 tables. (p. 51-61)

g. Arson: also including reported and unfounded offenses, total clearances, clearances involving juveniles, offenses involving uninhabited/abandoned structures, and value of property damage, all by property classification. 4 charts and 3 tables. (p. 63-65)

INDEX OFFENSES BY LOCATION

h. Index crimes, 1983-84, and clearances, 1984, by city arranged by population size group, and by State university and county; and offenses and rate per 100,000 population, by MSA, 1980-84; all by offense, with selected summaries. 7 tables. (p. 66-117)

NON-INDEX OFFENSE ARRESTS

i. Arrests, by age and non-Index offense; and adult and juvenile arrests for drug sale and possession, by substance, sex, and race. 3 charts and 3 tables. (p. 121-124)

S0119–1.2: Police Employment and Assaults

a. Full-time sworn and civilian employees by sex, for sheriffs' offices and by city population size group, MSA, university campus, and agency. 5 tables. (p. 125-134)

b. Assaults on police, by injury status, weapon, type of assignment and activity, and time of day; and clearances, by type of activity. 5 tables. (p. 135-138)

S0119–1.3: Appendices

(p. 139-153) Two tables showing Index crimes by offense, and population, by law enforcement agency and county; and adult and juvenile arrests aggregated for Index and non-Index offenses, by agency.

S0121   ALABAMA
Department of Economic and Community Affairs

S0121–1   ALABAMA ECONOMIC OUTLOOK, 1985
Annual.   Mar. 1985.
xi+91 p.
LC 83-622264.
SRI/MF/complete

Annual report, for 1985, analyzing economic trends and outlook for Alabama, with selected comparisons to the U.S., 1971-90.

Indicators covered include GSP, employment, wage rates, wage/salary income, labor productivity, and capital investment, by industry division and selected major group; population; unemployment rate; personal income by source; retail sales by kind of business; financial sector,

including bank deposits, savings, life insurance sales, and mortgage and other interest rates; tax collections by type; and energy consumption and prices, by fuel (including gasoline) and consuming sector.

Data are from the Alabama Econometric Model of the University of Alabama.

Contains listings of contents, charts, and tables, and preface (p. v-xi); narrative report, with 23 charts (p. 1-53); and Econometric Model table section, with 38 tables (p. 54-91).

Previous report, for 1983, is described in SRI 1983 Annual under this number. No report was published for 1984.

Availability: Alabama Department of Economic and Community Affairs, State Planning and Federal Programs Office, Economic Development Section, PO Box 2939, Montgomery AL 36105, $20.00; SRI/MF/complete.

S0121–2   ALABAMA COUNTY DATA BOOK, 1984
Annual.   Dec. 1984.   92 p.
Unique Rpt. No. ALA-ADECA- EDA-04-25-01358-60.
LC 84-643971.
SRI/MF/complete

Annual data book presenting general economic, social, and governmental statistics for Alabama counties, and including summary data for municipalities. Data are shown primarily for 1980s-84, with population projections to 2000.

Report is designed to present an overview of the State. Municipal data are shown by city; all other data are shown by county. Socioeconomic and demographic breakdowns are shown, as applicable, for selected topics. These breakdowns include industry division, age, and urban-rural status.

Data are from Federal, State, and private sources, noted beneath each table.

Contains contents listing (p. 1); 52 tables and 20 maps arranged in 13 sections (p. 2-89); and index and notes (p. 90-92).

All tables and selected maps are described below.

This is the 9th annual report.

Availability: Alabama Department of Economic and Community Affairs, State Planning and Federal Programs Office, State Capitol, Montgomery AL 36130, $4.00; SRI/MF/complete.

DATA SECTIONS:

a. **General government:** voter registration and participation in general elections; property value, tax rate, and debt limit; local government revenues from local, State, and Federal sources, and from property, sales, and all taxes; and revenue sharing program receipts. 5 tables. (p. 3-13)

b. **Education:** population age 25/over, and percent high school and college graduates, and enrolled in private schools; and public elementary/secondary school expenditures, enrollment, and teachers. 3 tables. (p. 14-17)

c. **Transportation, communication, and utilities:** highway mileage; licensed airports and runway lengths; radio and TV stations; daily and weekly newspapers; and circulation and location of largest newspapers. 4 tables. (p. 18-28)

d. **Natural resources, recreation, and culture:** land area and use; farms and acreage; farm

cash receipts; timber production; oil, gas, and coal production; nonfuel mineral production value; recreational areas and attractions; alcoholic beverage restrictions; and public library appropriations and book stocks. 6 tables and 2 maps. (p. 29-43)

e. **Public safety:** violent and property crimes; juvenile court case referrals; traffic accidents, injuries, and fatalities; and motor vehicle registrations. 4 tables. (p. 44-47)

f. **Health and social services:** births; total and infant death rates; physicians, pharmacists, and registered nurses; hospital and nursing home beds and bed/population ratio; public assistance expenditures by program; and Federal outlays by function or object. 6 tables. (p. 48-53)

g. **Economics:** retail sales; manufacturing establishments and value added; covered employment and wages; commuting patterns; and labor force and unemployment. 9 tables. (p. 54-66)

h. **Housing and population:** housing units, and selected occupancy and structural characteristics; housing median value; population projected to 2000; land area; nonwhite population; and net migration. 9 tables. (p. 67-76)

i. **Income and banking:** median family income and percent of families in poverty; farm and nonfarm earnings; personal income by source; per capita income; and commercial bank assets, and time and demand deposits. 5 tables. (p. 77-81)

j. **Municipal data:** total and black population; median family income; and high school graduates and persons in poverty as percent of population. 1 table. (p. 84-89)

S0124   ALABAMA
Department of Education

S0124–1   STATE OF ALABAMA DEPARTMENT OF EDUCATION ANNUAL REPORT, 1983: Statistical and Financial Data for 1982/83
Annual.   [1985.]   115 p.
Bull. 1983—No. 2.
SRI/MF/complete

Annual report, for 1982/83, on Alabama public schools, covering enrollment, staff, finances, and transportation, by school system. Includes data on services for crippled children and vocational rehabilitation, with trends from FY79, and some data for FY83.

Data are compiled by the Division of Administrative and Financial Services.

Contains listings of contents and school systems (p. 4-6); and 4 sections, with 29 tables listed below (p. 8-115).

Availability: Alabama Department of Education, State Office Bldg., 501 Dexter Ave., Montgomery AL 36130-3901, †; SRI/MF/complete.

TABLES:

[Most financial data are for FY83; other data are for the school year ended June 30, 1983, unless otherwise noted.]

S0124–1.1: Sections I-II: Funds Handled by the State Department of Education, and Student Information

SOURCE AND DISPOSITION OF FUNDS

[1-2] Source and disposition of [State, Federal, and trust] funds handled by the State Dept of Education [including dispositions to higher education]; and distribution of departmental expenditures. (p. 8-15)

[3] Finance: vocational education [State and Federal] funds available [and expenditures by type]. (p. 16)

CRIPPLED CHILDREN AND VOCATIONAL REHABILITATION

[Tables show caseload data and Federal and State/local funding, FY79-83.]

[4] Crippled children service. (p. 17)

[5-6] Vocational rehabilitation. (p. 18)

STUDENT INFORMATION

[Data are shown by school system.]

[7-10] Revenues [State, Federal, local, and other] and expenditures [by type]: per student enrolled and per student ADA [average daily attendance]. (p. 20-27)

[11-13] Ninth month enrollment, by grade [and race]. (p. 28-33)

[14-15] Number of high school graduates; and number of dropouts [by grade level; all by sex and race]. (p. 34-37)

[16] ADA and average daily membership by grade group [kindergarten, elementary, junior high, and senior high]. (p. 38-39)

[17] Percent ADA by grade. (p. 40-41)

[18] Miscellaneous information: [number and ADA of transported students, and enrollment by sex and race]. (p. 42-43)

S0124–1.2: Sections III-IV: Professional Personnel, and Revenues and Expenditures

[All tables, except table [8], show data by school system.]

PROFESSIONAL PERSONNEL

[1-5] FTEs and average salaries of teachers and principals [by position], and of regular program teachers and all certified personnel by rank of certificate; and FTEs of [certified personnel other than regular teachers, by position]. (p. 46-55)

REVENUES AND EXPENDITURES

[6] Selected information from 1983/84 annual school budgets: budgeted salary and travel for superintendent; [and minimum and maximum] teacher salary schedules [by rank of certificate]. (p. 58-59)

[7] Revenue summary [State, Federal, local, and other]. (p. 60-61)

[8] Expenditures and other fund uses [total for counties, cities, and State, by object]. (p. 62-65)

[9] Revenues and other financing sources: beginning balance; State, Federal, local, and other revenues; and other financing sources; [all by detailed source]. (p. 66-103)

[10] Expenditures and other fund uses [by object]. (p. 104-109)

[11] Local funds reported by principals: receipts, expenditures, and balances; and budgetary breakdown of expenditures; [by object]. (p. 110-115)

S0129   ALABAMA
Department of Finance

S0129–1   STATE OF ALABAMA ANNUAL REPORT, Fiscal Year Ending Sept. 30, 1984
Annual.   [1984.]
4+286 p. Foldouts.
LC 40-28377.
SRI/MF/complete

Annual report on financial condition of Alabama State government, for FY84, presenting receipts by source, disbursements by function and object, and fund balances, by detailed fund, dept, and agency.

Also includes State bank deposits by institution; assessed property valuation and tax revenues, by county; property inventory and value, by State agency; detail on composition of investments and State bonded debt; and bank and insurance company securities on deposit.

Contains contents listing (1 p.); State comptroller's report, with 6 charts and 10 exhibits (p. 1-107); State auditor's report, with 27 schedules (p. 108-203); State treasurer's report, with 12 tables (p. 204-233); and report of bonded indebtedness, with 72 schedules (p. 234-286).

Availability: Alabama Department of Finance, State Comptroller, 119 State Capitol Bldg., Montgomery AL 36130-4401, †; SRI/MF/complete.

S0155   ALABAMA
Department of Industrial Relations

S0155–1   ANNUAL PLANNING INFORMATION, STATE OF ALABAMA
Annual, discontinued.

Annual planning report identifying Alabama population groups most in need of employment services, discontinued with report published in Sept. 1983 (for description, see SRI 1983 Annual under this number).

Report is discontinued due to budgetary restrictions.

S0160   ALABAMA
Department of Insurance

S0160–1   1984 ALABAMA INSURANCE REPORT: Business of 1983, Company Directory
Annual.   Oct. 29, 1984.
129 p.
LC 63-63468.
SRI/MF/complete

Annual report on Alabama insurance industry financial condition and underwriting activity, by company and type of insurance, 1983. Covers assets, liabilities, premiums written and/or earned, capital/surplus, losses incurred, and life insurance premium/annuity considerations and insurance in force.

Data are shown, as applicable, for fire/casualty, life, title, and fraternal insurance companies; and mutual aid assns.

Data for selected types of insurance include breakdowns by detailed line of coverage, including homeowner, medical malpractice, accident/health, workers compensation, automobile, and surety.

Also includes number of licensed companies; and Insurance Dept receipts by source and disbursements.

Data are from annual statements filed by individual companies.

Contains contents listing (p. 2); Insurance Dept report, with 1 table, and lists of company admissions, status changes, and licensed motor clubs and rating organizations (p. 8-20); directory of companies, with summary financial data (p. 21-36); 20 company financial tables (p. 37-125); listings of pre-paid legal and dental corporations (p. 126); and Fire Marshal's Office annual report, with text statistics (p. 127-129).

Availability: Alabama Department of Insurance, 135 S. Union St., Montgomery AL 36130-3401, †; SRI/MF/complete.

S0170   ALABAMA
Department of Pensions and Security

S0170–1   STATISTICS, Alabama Department of Pensions and Security
Monthly.   Approx. 40 p.
LC 40-28378.
SRI/MF/complete, shipped quarterly

Monthly report on Alabama public welfare cases, recipients, and payments, by county and program. Includes data on old age pensions, Aid to Blind, Aid to Permanently and Totally Disabled, aid to dependent children, aid to refugees, social services including foster and day care, food stamps, and child support.

Contains contents listing, and 22 tables listed below.

Only reports for the last month in each quarter are distributed to the agency's mailing list. However, the report is available in agency offices, and on SRI microfiche, on a monthly basis. Report is issued approximately 3 months after month of data coverage.

An annual report, presenting fiscal year totals for each monthly table, and additional data on public welfare funding and expenditures, is available from the public information office of the issuing agency. Annual report is not covered in SRI.

Availability: Alabama Department of Pensions and Security, Data Analysis and Reporting Division, 64 N. Union St., Montgomery AL 36130-1801, †; SRI/MF/complete, shipped quarterly.

Issues reviewed during 1985: Sept. 1984-July 1985 (D).

TABLES:

[Tables show data by county for month of coverage, unless otherwise noted. Tables 1-8 show number of cases or recipients, and average or total payment.]

STATE SUMMARY

1. Cases under care: Pensions and Security [State totals, by program, for month of coverage, previous month, and same month of previous year].

FINANCIAL ASSISTANCE

2. Number of cases receiving financial assistance and average amount of payments to these cases.

3-5. State supplementation: old age pensions, Aid to Blind, and Aid to Permanently and Totally Disabled.

6. Family assistance: aid to dependent children.

7-8. Special assistance: individual and family grants [in presidentially declared disasters, as they occur, State total]; and aid to refugees.

9-11. Cases receiving financial assistance through county depts of pensions and security; cases approved as categorically related and eligible for Title XIX, but receiving no money payment; and applications which were in process of investigation by county depts; [all for programs covered in tables 3-6].

SOCIAL SERVICES

12. Number of primary clients open for service.

13. Aid to children receiving day care [children and payments, for day care centers and homes, and in-home care].

14-15. Adult day care and foster care [recipients and payments, by eligibility category, with State totals for emergency shelter care].

16-17. Foster care maintenance payments, and aid to children in foster care [children and average payment].

18. Number of children in the legal custody of the State Dept of Pensions and Security [State totals].

19. Number of individuals certified as currently eligible for medical assistance under Title XIX by the Dept of Pensions and Security to Alabama Medicaid Agency [State totals, by eligibility category].

CHILD CARE FACILITIES

20. Children under care of public and private facilities [and number of facilities, by facility type; State totals].

FOOD STAMPS AND CHILD SUPPORT

21. Food stamp program [households, recipients by public assistance status, and value of stamps issued].

22. Child support cases [by AFDC status] and collections [for most recent full quarter].

S0175   ALABAMA
Department of Public Health

S0175-2   ALABAMA'S VITAL EVENTS for 1983
Annual. [1984.]   vii+261 p.
ISSN 0095-3431.
LC 84-648227.
SRI/MF/complete

Annual report, for 1983, on Alabama vital statistics, covering population, births, deaths by cause, marriages, and divorces. Includes data by county and Public Health Area (PHA), selected U.S. comparisons, and trends from 1940. Also includes data on Vital Statistics Bureau operations.

Data are primarily from records filed with the State registrar of vital statistics. Population data are from Census Bureau and estimates by University of Alabama Center for Business and Economic Research.

Contains listings of contents, charts, and tables (p. iii-vii); introduction (p. 3-6); 6 statistical sections, with brief narrative, illustrative charts, and 111 tables listed below (p. 8-254); and technical appendix, with data sources, notes, and definitions (p. 256-261).

Availability: Alabama Department of Public Health, Vital Statistics Bureau, Special Services Administration, State Office Bldg., Montgomery AL 36130, $10.00; SRI/MF/complete.

TABLES:

[Tables show data for Alabama, 1983, unless otherwise noted. Data by attendant usually are shown for physician, midwife, other, and none.]

S0175-2.1: Summary Data, Vital Statistics Bureau Activities, and Population
[Tables 2.2-2.11 refer to activities of the Alabama Bureau of Vital Statistics.]

2.1. Vital events [summary], 1973 and 1982-83. (p. 9)

2.2-2.3. Pieces of mail and fees received [by month], 1980-83. (p. 10-13)

2.4-2.5. Expenditures from all funds FY80-83, and by source of funds FY83, by purpose of expenditure. (p. 14)

2-6-2.7. Certified copies issued and sold at service counter [by month], 1980-83. (p. 16-17)

2.8-2.9. Birth amendments and delayed [birth] certificates filed, 1973-83. (p. 18-19)

2.10-2.11. Reports of adoption [of persons born in and out of Alabama], and legitimations, 1973-83. (p. 20-21)

2.12. Vital statistics summary, 1982-83. (p. 22)

3.1. Live births, deaths, and natural increase, selected years 1940-83. (p. 25)

3.2. Population by county, PHA, and race, midyear 1983. (p. 29)

3.3-3.4. Population of [40] selected cities, census data [by race], 1980; and estimated population by race, sex, and age groups, midyear 1983. (p. 30-31)

S0175-2.2: Natality
[Most tables show data by race.]

4.1-4.2. Live births and live birth rates, and age-sex-adjusted birth rates, Alabama and U.S., selected years 1940-83. (p. 35-37)

4.3. Resident births with birth rates, by county and PHA. (p. 39-40)

4.4-4.6. Live births: by month of occurrence; and by sex and area of residence [urban and rural], by age of mother. (p. 41-42)

4.7-4.8. Live births: by live birth order and age of mother; and by plurality and sex [by PHA]. (p. 43-44)

4.9-4.10. Live births by birth weight: by age of mother and period of gestation. (p. 45-46)

4.11-4.13. Live births by Apgar score: by sex; at 1 and 5 minutes; and at 1 minute by age of mother. (p. 47-48)

4.14-4.16. Live births: by legitimacy, total birth order, and month prenatal care began; all by education of mother. (p. 49-51)

4.17. Live births, by age of mother and number of prenatal visits. (p. 52)

4.18. Live births by attendant [in and not in hospital] and PHA. (p. 53)

4.19-4.21. Immature births and immaturity ratios: [total] 1960-83; and by county, PHA, and age of mother, 1983. (p. 54-58)

4.22-4.23. Illegitimate births and illegitimacy ratios: selected years 1940-83; and by county and PHA, 1983. (p. 60-63)

4.24. Live births, illegitimate births, and illegitimacy ratios [by age of mother]. (p. 64)

4.25. Illegitimacy ratios, by age of mother, 1981-83. (p. 64)

4.26. Fertility rates [and age-specific birth rates], selected years 1940-83. (p. 66)

4.27-4.28. Fertility rates [and age-specific birth rates] for white females and all other females, 1966-83. (p. 67)

4.29. Live births, by county, PHA, and age of mother. (p. 68-73)

4.30. Resident births in [32] selected cities, by age of mother. (p. 74-76)

4.31. Live births by county and PHA, by number of prenatal visits. (p. 77-82)

4.32. Live births, by [county and] hospital of occurrence, and sex. (p. 83-87)

4.33. Births [total and] by selected characteristics [under 3 prenatal visits, birth malformations, low weight births, maternal age under 20, midwives out of hospital, and illegitimate, by county and PHA]. (p. 88-93)

S0175-2.3: Mortality
[Causes of death are coded in accord with *International Classification of Diseases, 9th Revision, Adapted.* Many tables show both number of deaths and rates, by race.]

5.1-5.2. Mortality rates, and age-adjusted mortality rates, Alabama and U.S., selected years 1940-83. (p. 97-99)

5.3. Resident deaths and death rates, by county and PHA. (p. 101-102)

5.4. Important causes of death. (p. 103)

5.5-5.6. Leading causes of death: [total] and by age group. (p. 105-107)

5.7. Major causes of death by age group. (p. 108)

5.8-5.9. Resident deaths: by month of occurrence, 1981-83; and by sex and attendant, 1983. (p. 110)

5.10. Mortality and age-specific mortality rates, 1981-83. (p. 111)

5.11-5.12. Resident deaths, by age group and by selected cities. (p. 111-112)

5.13. Heart disease mortality by age [and sex]. (p. 114)

5.14. Malignant neoplasms mortality [by sex and primary site of neoplasm]. (p. 115)

5.15. Comparative accidental death rates, Alabama and U.S., selected years 1940-83. (p. 118)

5.16. Accidental mortality, by age. (p. 119)

5.17-5.18. Accidental deaths: by type of accident; and by type and age group, occurrence data [including work accidents by industry division]. (p. 120-121)

5.19-5.20. Infant mortality rates: Alabama and U.S., selected years 1940-83; and by county and PHA, 1983. (p. 125-128)

5.21. Infant mortality by cause. (p. 129)

5.22-5.23. Neonatal mortality, by county, PHA, and cause. (p. 130-132)

5.24-5.25. Infant mortality, by age, county, and PHA. (p. 134-136)

5.26. Perinatal deaths, by county and PHA. (p. 137-138)

5.27-5.36. Fetal deaths: Alabama and U.S., selected years 1945-83; and by county, PHA, cause, age of mother, sex, number of previous deliveries, weight and gestational age of fetus, and attendant [with selected cross-tabulations], 1983. (p. 140-148)

5.37-5.40. Maternal mortality: Alabama and U.S., selected years 1940-83; and by county, age group, and cause, 1983. (p. 150-153)

5.41-5.42. Selected causes of death [by county and PHA]. (p. 154-226)

S0175–2.4: Marriage and Divorce

6.1-6.2. Marriages [and/or] marriage rates: Alabama [by race] and U.S., selected years 1940-83; and by county and PHA [by race], 1983. (p. 229-232)

6.3. Marriages and marriage rates by month of occurrence. (p. 233)

6.4-6.6. Marriages: by previous marital status; by official performing ceremony; and by age and race of bride and groom. (p. 234-235)

6.7-6.8. Previous marriages by age of bride and groom. (p. 236-237)

6.9-6.11. Marriages: by age and previous marital status [of bride and groom]; by age of bride by age of groom; and by State of residence of bride and groom. (p. 238-241)

7.1. Comparative [divorces and/or] rates, Alabama and U.S., selected years 1940-83. (p. 245)

7.2. Divorces and annulments, by county and PHA. (p. 247-248)

7.3-7.5. Divorces and annulments, by duration of marriages and number of minor children. (p. 249-251)

7.6. Divorces and [annulments, and total] rates, by month. (p. 252)

7.7-7.9. Divorces and annulments: by party to whom granted; by number of this marriage [for husband and wife]; and by legal grounds for decree. (p. 253-254)

S0175–3   ALABAMA DEPARTMENT OF PUBLIC HEALTH 1984 Annual Report

Annual.   June 1985.
vi+188 p.
ADPH-P-A-15/Rev. 6-85.
LC 68-65946.
SRI/MF/complete, current & previous year reports

Annual report, for 1984, on Alabama Dept of Public Health activities and programs. Includes data on finances and employment; health facilities; diagnostic testing; communicable disease incidence and immunization; and summary vital statistics.

Contains contents listing (p. i-iii); and narrative summaries for each Dept division, with text data and interspersed maps, charts, and tables. Charts and tables presenting substantial statistics are described below.

Report for 1983 has also been reviewed in 1985, and is also available on SRI microfiche under S0175-3 [Annual. Oct. 1984. iv+192 p. †]. Previous report is substantially similar in format and content. However, previous report also includes data on population with fluoridated water systems, hypertension program care costs, and teenagers participating in family planning program; and omits data on Public Health Dept State and county employment, and infant mortality rates.

Report for 1982 is described in SRI 1983 Annual under this number.

Availability: Alabama Department of Public Health, Primary Prevention Bureau, State Office Bldg., Montgomery AL 36130, †; SRI/MF/complete.

TABLES AND CHARTS:

S0175–3.1: Public Health Service Activities

[Data are shown for 1984 or FY84, unless otherwise noted. Data often are shown by county or public health area.]

ADMINISTRATION, PUBLIC HEALTH AREAS, AND BUREAU OF AREA HEALTH SERVICES

a. Dept receipts and disbursements by source of funds, and disbursements by program and object; county and State health service employees; environmental activities, clinic services, and vital statistics for selected counties; and county health dept activities. 3 charts and 7 tables. (p. 4-38)

CLINICAL LABORATORY ADMINISTRATION

b. Rabies identifications by carrier and month; syphilis examinations; neonatal hypothyroid screenings and results, 1978-84; and serology, metabolic, bacteriology, and mycology tests performed, with selected detail by type of test and laboratory. Text data and 10 tables. (p. 42-64)

BUREAU OF DENTAL HEALTH, AND ENVIRONMENTAL AND FACILITY STANDARDS ADMINISTRATION

c. Dental health education, mobile unit, and fluoride program participation; and types of services provided by Bureau, with detail for mobile units; with selected trends from 1977. 4 charts and 10 tables. (p. 67-77)

d. Hearing aid dealer testing and licensure; bird encephalitis testing; sanitation plan review activity and number of approved sep-

tic tank manufacturers; food inspections and ratings; radioactive material licenses; and X-ray machine registrations and inspections; with selected trends from 1958. 5 charts and 10 tables. (p. 81-97)

e. Health care facilities participating in Medicare and Medicaid; and health care facility inspections, licenses, beds, and construction/expansion project review, by facility type. 4 tables. (p. 98-101)

BUREAU OF EPIDEMIOLOGY/CONSULTATION, AND FAMILY HEALTH ADMINISTRATION

f. Communicable disease cases, by month, race, age, and sex, for 30-35 diseases, with trends from 1974; laboratory-confirmed cases of rabies in animals, 1950s-84; and participants in cancer detection, family planning, maternity and well child clinic, and women/infants/children (WIC) supplemental food programs. 1 chart and 9 tables. (p. 105-128)

BUREAUS OF PREVENTIVE HEALTH SERVICES AND PUBLIC HEALTH NURSING

g. Immunization data for students, 1983-84; day care center immunization survey results; and vaccine usage by disease, 1975-84. 3 tables. (p. 134-136)

h. Tuberculosis: new cases and rates, by race, sex, and age; new cases by source of 1st report; and hospital admissions, discharges, length of stay, and costs, by facility; with comparisons to U.S. and trends from 1960. 10 charts and 8 tables. (p. 137-148)

i. Gonorrhea and syphilis cases, by age, sex, and reporting source, with comparison to U.S. and trends from 1974; gonorrhea tests and results; and patient counseling by sex. 13 charts and 9 tables. (p. 150-164)

j. Home health care patients and visits under Medicare, Medicaid, and disease/disability programs, FY80-84; public health nursing personnel, and ratio of registered nurses to population. 3 charts and 2 tables. (p. 170-174)

SPECIAL SERVICES ADMINISTRATION

k. Printing dept workloads and costs, by month; record service and vital statistic summaries, including leading causes of death, 1983-84; and infant mortality trends with comparisons to total U.S., 1974-84. 1 chart and 3 tables. (p. 180-187)

S0180   ALABAMA
Public Library Service

S0180-1   ALABAMA PUBLIC LIBRARY SERVICE Annual Report, 1983
Annual. [1984.]   36 p.
LC 78-645263.
SRI/MF/complete

Annual report on Alabama public libraries, including finances, resources, circulation, staff, and population served, by county or State region and library, FY83.

Contents:

a. Contents listing; and narrative report, with 2 summary charts, and text statistics on Library Services and Construction Act project funding and construction grants, library operations summary, and blind/physically handicapped program readers and materials. (p. 1-12)

b. Definitions. (p. 13)

c. 1 table showing population served, weekly hours open, FTE staff, volumes held and added, nonbook holdings by type, book and nonbook circulation, receipts by source, and expenditures by function; all by public library, FY83. (p. 14-19)

d. Directories, staff listing, and organizational chart. (p. 20-36)

Availability: Alabama Public Library Service, 6030 Monticello Dr., Montgomery AL 36130, †; SRI/MF/complete.

S0185   ALABAMA
Department of Public Safety

S0185-1   ALABAMA ACCIDENT SUMMARY, STATEWIDE ACCIDENTS, 1984
Annual. [1985.]
33 p. no paging+errata.
SRI/MF/complete

Annual report on Alabama traffic accidents, injuries, and fatalities, by vehicle and accident type, location, time, and other circumstances; and driver and victim characteristics; 1984.

Also includes data on alcohol involvement and safety device use in accidents, and hazardous cargo accidents by cargo type.

Report contains contents listing and 31 tables.

Prior to 1984, report was entitled *Summary of Motor Vehicle Traffic Accidents, Alabama.*

A summary of rural traffic accidents is also available from the issuing agency, but is not covered in SRI.

Availability: Alabama Department of Public Safety, Highway Patrol Division, PO Box 1511, Montgomery AL 36192, †; SRI/MF/complete.

S0275   ALASKA
Department of Administration

S0275-1   ANNUAL FINANCIAL REPORT for the Fiscal Year July 1, 1983-June 30, 1984, State of Alaska
Annual. Dec. 6, 1984.
17+224 p.
ISSN 0098-9916.
LC 75-646776.
SRI/MF/complete

Annual report on financial condition of Alaska State government, for FY84, presenting assets, liabilities, fund equities, and reserves; revenues by source; and expenditures by function; for all, general, special revenue, debt service, capital projects, enterprise, intragovernmental service, and trust and agency funds. Most data are shown by specific State agency, institution, program, or project.

Also includes actual vs. budgeted revenues and expenditures; bonded indebtedness; and selected general data, including property valuation, State employees, voters, fire depts and personnel, educational enrollment and staff, highway and ferry mileages, air carrier traffic, public recreation areas, correctional institution inmates, population by age, and personal income, mostly for 1970s-84.

Data were compiled by the Director of Finance.

Contains contents listing (5 p.); introduction, including summary text tables (p. i-ix); 72 financial statements and schedules, with accompanying notes (p. 1-195); and statistical data section, with 17 tables (p. 197-224).

Availability: Alaska Department of Administration, Finance Division, Pouch C, Juneau AK 99811, †; SRI/MF/complete.

S0280   ALASKA
Department of Commerce and Economic Development

S0280-2   COMPARATIVE STATEMENT OF ASSETS, LIABILITIES, AND CAPITAL ACCOUNTS of Alaska Banks
Quarterly. 2 p.
SRI/MF/complete

Quarterly report on the financial condition of Alaska State-chartered commercial and mutual savings banks, and national banks, by institution and type. Report is compiled by the Division of Banking, Securities, Small Loans, and Corporations, and is issued 3-9 months after end of quarter covered.

Contains 2 tables showing:

a. Comparative statement of assets, liabilities (including deposits by type), and equity capital, by central institution, as of end of quarter covered.

b. Comparative consolidated statement of condition (assets, liabilities, and equity capital), by bank type as of end of quarter covered, with totals for same date of previous year.

Availability: Alaska Department of Commerce and Economic Development, Banking, Securities, Small Loans, and Corporations Division, State Office Bldg., Pouch D, Juneau AK 99811-0800, $10.00 per yr.; SRI/MF/complete.

Issues reviewed during 1985: Sept. 30, 1984-June 30, 1985 (D).

S0280-3   INSURANCE REPORT, 1984: 46th Annual Report to the Governor of Alaska and Legislature
Annual. [1985.]   iv+116 p.
ISSN 0149-4864.
LC 60-62888.
SRI/MF/complete

Annual report on Alaska insurance industry underwriting activity and investments, by company and type of insurance, 1983. Covers investments by type; premiums written and earned; benefits paid or losses incurred; and insurance in force, issued, and terminated; for companies headquartered in Alaska and elsewhere.

Data are shown, as applicable, for life, property/casualty or fire/casualty, and surplus line insurance companies, with underwriting detail by line of coverage, including accident/health, medical malpractice, auto, surety, and workers compensation; and for title insurance companies, fraternal benefit societies, and health care service organizations.

Title insurance company data also include assets, liabilities, capital, net income, and surplus.

Also includes data on Insurance Division fees and taxes collected, expenditures, and licensing activity, for FY82-84; trends in Division finances and company underwriting activity, from as early as 1937; and finances of Insurance Guaranty Assn on behalf of insolvent companies.

Contains contents listing (p. iii-iv); Insurance Division report, with 6 tables (p. 1-26); and 16 company financial tables (p. 27-116).

Availability: Alaska Department of Commerce and Economic Development, Insurance Division, Pouch D, Juneau AK 99811, $10.00; SRI/MF/complete.

S0280-4   ALASKA PUBLIC UTILITIES COMMISSION FIFTEENTH ANNUAL REPORT to the Alaska Legislature for the Fiscal Year Ending June 30, 1984
Annual. Feb. 25, 1985.
2+73 p.
LC 73-648959.
SRI/MF/complete

Annual report presenting Alaska public utility financial and operating data, by company and utility type, 1983 and FY84, with trends from 1980. Utility types covered in detail are electric, gas, refuse collection, sewer, telecommunications, and water.

Regulatory data include certifications, rate increases, complaints, and hearings and proceedings of the Alaska Public Utilities Commission (APUC), FY84 with trends from 1981. Financial and operating data include revenues, net income, plant value, users, and rates by community.

Also includes data on APUC finances, FY83-84; oil pipeline property value, revenues, and throughput, by company; electric utility sales to residential and commercial/other sectors; and telephone facilities.

Data are from APUC records and company reports.

Contains contents listing (1 p.); introductory material (p. 1-3); 2 sections on APUC activities, with narrative, 7 charts, and 8 tables (p. 4-30); utility statistics, with 15 tables and interspersed lists of companies (p. 31-64); and appendix, with narrative and 2 tables (p. 65-73).

Availability: Alaska Department of Commerce and Economic Development, Public Utilities Commission, 420 L St., Suite 100, Anchorage AK 99501, $5.00; SRI/MF/complete.

S0285   ALASKA
Department of Community and Regional Affairs

S0285–1   ALASKA TAXABLE, 1984
Annual. Jan. 1985. 125 p.
Vol. XXIV.
ISSN 0147-2348.
LC 75-649634.
SRI/MF/complete

Annual report, for 1984, on Alaska State and locally determined property values and taxes, public debt, and tax exemption provisions, with trends from 1970s.

Contents:

a. Contents and table listing. (2 p.)

b. 4 report chapters, with description of property tax regulations; overview of valuation, population, and bonded debt, with 6 summary tables; explanation of assessment ratios; and 11 numbered tables, listed below, usually preceded by explanatory notes. (p. 2-66)

c. Appendices A-G, including background legislative texts; 7 tables, also listed below; and directory of oil/gas property tax jurisdictions. (p. 69-125)

This is the 22nd annual report.

Availability: Alaska Department of Community and Regional Affairs, Municipal and Regional Assistance Division, Pouch BH, Juneau AK 99811, †; SRI/MF/complete.

TABLES:
[Most tables show data by municipality (borough and/or city).]

S0285–1.1: Values, Taxes, and Public Debt

I. Valuation, population, and G.O. [general obligation] bonded debt [summary, 1974-84; and by municipality, 1984]. (p. 9-11)

II. Local assessment policy [type of assessment and exemption status, for 6 property categories]. (p. 18)

III.A-III.B. Statistical evaluation table, real property only [assessment/sales ratios and number of sales], 1984; and cross-correlation of cost per parcel vs. coefficient of dispersion vs. weighted mean ratio and assessment cycle. (p. 20-21)

IV. Local assessments vs. full value [for real and personal property]. (p. 23-24)

V-VI.B. Full value determination [locally and State assessed]: Jan. 1, 1984; comparison, 1980-84; and summary, 1974-84. (p. 26-31)

VII-VIII. Real property staff statistics [number of appraisers and real parcels, jurisdiction area, assessment budget, and assessment cycle]; and contract revaluation costs [by contract]; 1984. (p. 33-34)

IX-X. Municipal property and sales tax rates [by detailed local area and type of service including administration, schools, police, fire, and others, as applicable, 1982-84]. (p. 37-63)

XI.A-XI.B. Estimated property [by type] and sales tax revenue recap: assessed values and revenues, 1984. (p. 65-66)

S0285–1.2: Appendix Tables
DEFERRED FARM TAXES

[B] Farm use land assessment [applicants, acres, value, and deferred tax; statewide, FY78-84, and by municipality, FY84]. (p. 72)

SENIOR CITIZEN EXEMPTIONS

[C1-C2] Senior citizen homeowner exemption [applications approved, assessed value exempt, total revenue reimbursement, and average value and tax per application; statewide, FY77-84, and by municipality, FY84]. (p. 77-78)

[C3] Senior citizen renter payment program summary [applications approved, and annual rent and payment], FY84. (p. 83)

[D1] Senior citizen sewer/water assessment deferment, 5-year performance summary [applications approved, reimbursement, accounts with liens, and revenue collections, FY80-84]. (p. 89)

[E1-E2] Senior citizen motor vehicle registration tax program [affidavits and reimbursement; statewide, FY80-84, and by municipality, FY84]. (p. 94-95)

S0290   ALASKA
Court System

S0290–1   ALASKA COURT SYSTEM 1984 Annual Report
Annual. [1984.]
169 p. var. paging.
LC 78-645480.
SRI/MF/complete

Annual report, for FY84, on Alaska judicial system, including trial and appellate court caseloads and case dispositions. Covers supreme, appeals, superior, and district courts. Includes trial court data by case type and court location, and trends from FY81.

Case types shown are criminal and civil for most courts, with some additional detail for probate cases, including adoption, estate, guardianship, and sanity hearings; and domestic relations, juvenile, small claims, administrative review, and traffic cases. Criminal cases are occasionally shown by offense.

Report also includes data on appellate case processing time; State court system finances and personnel, including employees by sex and race-ethnicity (Caucasian, Alaskan Native, black, Asian/Pacific Islander, and other); and police, lawyers, and judges compared with population, by city and judicial district.

Data are from reports submitted to the State by judicial officers and court clerks.

Contains table of contents (p. i-iii); report with 30 summary charts and tables (p. 1-83); and statistical supplement, with foreword and table listing (p. Si-Siv), and 68 tables (p. S3-S78).

Availability: Alaska Court System, 303 K St., Anchorage AK 99501, †; SRI/MF/complete.

S0295   ALASKA
Department of Education

S0295–1   EDUCATION IN ALASKA: A Report to the People, 1983/84
Annual. [1985.] 56 p.
LC 79-643587.
SRI/MF/complete

Annual report on public elementary/secondary education in Alaska, for school year 1983/84 or FY83. Covers enrollment, attendance, staff, and finances, by school district, for Regional Education Attendance Area (REAA) and city/borough schools.

Contains contents/table listing (1 p.); narrative report (p. 1-25); and 20 tables, listed below (p. 27-56).

Availability: Alaska Department of Education, Pouch F, Juneau AK 99811, †; SRI/MF/complete.

TABLES:
[Tables show data by school district, grouped for city/borough and REAA schools, for 1983/84 or FY83, unless otherwise noted.]

S0295–1.1: Enrollment
[Tables include totals for centralized correspondence schools.]

[1-2] Final enrollment by grade. (p. 27-30)

[3-4] Final average daily membership, [high school] graduates, and [professional and certified] personnel. (p. 31-32)

S0295–1.2: Staff, Finances, and Summary
PROFESSIONAL PERSONNEL

[1-2] Professional personnel [by position and sex]. (p. 33-36)

[3-4] Professional personnel salaries [minimum and maximum]. (p. 37-38)

FINANCES

[5-6] Audited district revenues [by source; table 6, showing data for REAAs, incorrectly reads "expenditures"]. (p. 39-42)

[7-8] Food service, pupil activity, and special revenue funds [expenditures and/or revenues]. (p. 43-46)

[9-10] State aid for retirement of school construction debt [entitlements paid]; and cigarette tax distribution; [for city/borough districts only], FY84. (p. 47-48)

[11-12] Audited district expenditures [by function, including vocational and special education, plant operation/maintenance, and pupil transport]. (p. 49-52)

[13-14] District fund balances. (p. 53-54)

CERTIFIED PERSONNEL

[15] Certified personnel by sex by ethnic origin [white, black, Hispanic, Asian, American Indian, and Alaskan Native; by position]. (p. 55)

SUMMARY

[16] Statistical summary, all schools [student and staff data aggregated for public schools by type; and enrollment for Bureau of Indian Affairs and private/denominational schools]. (p. 56)

S0315   ALASKA
Department of
Health and Social Services

S0315–1   ALASKA VITAL STATISTICS
Annual Report, 1983
Annual. 1985. xiv + 160 p.
Rpt. No.
AK/DHSS/DOP/85/8.
ISSN 0277-6200.
LC 81-642531.
SRI/MF/complete, current & previous year reports

Annual report on Alaska vital statistics, covering population, births, deaths by cause, marriages, divorces, and adoptions, 1983, with trends from 1976. Includes data by State census area and Native Regional Corporation (NRC), with selected detail by demographic characteristics. Data are primarily from State Bureau of Vital Records.

Contains introduction, contents and table listing, and definitions (p. i-viii); summary section, with 2 maps, and 4 tables listed below (p. ix-xiv); overview, with methodology, narrative analysis, 13 charts, and 21 tables listed below (p. 1-34); statistical section, with 76 tables also listed below (p. 1-145); and 2 appendices, with disease classifications and report form facsimiles (p. 146-160).

Previous report, for 1982, has also been received by SRI, and is also available on SRI microfiche, under S0315-1 [Annual. 1985. xv + 107 p. + errata. †]. Previous report is substantially similar in format and content, but does not include overview section. For description of report for 1981, see SRI 1983 Annual under S0315-1.

Availability: Alaska Department of Health and Social Services, Planning Division, Pouch H-01A, Juneau AK 99811, †; SRI/MF/complete.

TABLES:
[Data are for Alaska, 1983, unless otherwise noted. Most tables specify data as place of residence or place of occurrence. Data by race are shown for white, black, Native, and other.

Tables lettered with "A" show data by State census area; tables lettered with "B" show data by NRC.]

S0315–1.1: Census Areas, Population, Summary Data, and Overview

CENSUS AREAS

1.1-1.2. Census areas within single and multiple NRCs and health service areas. [lists] (p. xi)

POPULATION AND SUMMARY

1.3. Population by census area, 1979-83. (p. xii)

1.4. Summary of vital events: births, deaths, marriages, divorces/annulments, [and population, all by census area]. (p. xiii-xiv)

OVERVIEW

1.5. Fertility rates [and women of child-bearing age, by race]. (p. 8)

1.6-1.9. Age-specific death rates; and number and rates of deaths by age, sex, and race; [Alaska and/or U.S.]. (p. 15-17)

1.10-1.14. Age-, sex-, race-, and race/sex-specific death rates, by cause of death [with 1981-83 averages for selected age-specific causes; Alaska and/or U.S.]. (p. 20-26)

1.15-1.16. Accidental death rates by age and sex [by cause]. (p. 27-29)

1.17. Age-specific rates for homicide and suicide, Alaska and U.S. (p. 31)

1.18-1.19. Native and white suicide rates by age and sex [Alaska and/or U.S.]. (p. 31)

1.20. Marriages and divorces, 1976-83. (p. 33)

1.21. Marriages by race of bride and groom. (p. 34)

S0315–1.2: Births and Deaths

BIRTHS

2.1A. Births, estimated population, and birth rates [Alaska, with U.S. birth rates], 1979-83. (p. 35-36)

2.2A. By month. (p. 37)

2.3. By race and age of mother [statewide], 1980-83. (p. 38)

2.4A. By race of mother and sex of child. (p. 39-40)

2.5A-2.6A. By age and marital status, and race and education, of mother. (p. 41-44)

2.7A-2.8A. By race of mother, 1980-83; and by race of mother and place of occurrence [hospital, outpatient, other, and unknown]. (p. 45-48)

2.9A. By race of mother and type of attendant [including midwives]. (p. 49-50)

2.10A. To unwed mothers by race and education. (p. 51-52)

2.11A-2.12A. By age and race of mother. (p. 53-55)

2.13. [By] birth weight by race and age of mother [statewide]. (p. 57-58)

2.14A-2.15A. Low birth weight births: by birth weight; and frequency and rate; 1979-83. (p. 59-62)

2.16A-2.18A. Low birth weight births: by birth weight, by race and age of mother; [and frequency and rate, by race]. (p. 63-68)

2.1B. Resident births, 1979-83. (p. 69)

2.2B-2.18B. [Tables 2.2A, 2.4A-2.12A, and 2.14A-2.18A are repeated for NRCs. Table numbering skips 2.3B and 2.13B.] (p. 70-84)

DEATHS

3.1A-3.2A. By occurrence and residence, 1979-83. (p. 86-88)

3.3A-3.4A. By race and sex, and age, of decedent. (p. 89-92)

3.5. Leading causes of death by age group [statewide]. (p. 93-94)

3.6A. [By] selected causes of death. (p. 95-96)

3.7. Rates and percentages of 15 leading causes of death, Alaska and U.S. (p. 98)

3.8A. Suicide and homicide deaths by race and sex of decedent. (p. 99-100)

3.9A-3.10A. Suicide deaths by age and sex of decedent, for natives and whites. (p. 101-102)

3.11A-3.12A. By type of accident. (p. 103-104)

3.13A-3.14A. Neonatal and infant mortality rates [Alaska and U.S.], 1979-83. (p. 105-108)

3.15A. Neonatal and postneonatal mortality rates by race of child. (p. 109-110)

3.16-3.17. Rate of infant mortality from selected causes: native and non-native and Alaska and U.S., 1979-83. (p. 111-112)

3.18. Cause of neonatal and postneonatal deaths by race. (p. 113)

3.1B-3.12B. [Tables 3.1A-3.4A, 3.6,A, and 3.8A-3.15A are repeated for NRCs. Table numbering skips 3.5B and 3.7B.] (p. 115-128)

S0315–1.3: Marriages, Divorces, and Adoptions

4.1A-4.2B. Marriages [and/or rates] by month 1983, and year 1979-83 (p. 130-134)

5.1A-5.2B. Divorces [and/or rates] by month 1983, and year 1979-83. (p. 135-140)

6.1A-6.1B. Adoptions by age and race of child; and adoption rates [census area data only], 1979-83. (p. 142-145)

S0320   ALASKA
Department of
Labor

S0320–1   ALASKA ECONOMIC
TRENDS
Monthly. Approx. 35 p.
ISSN 0160-3345.
LC 78-640712.
SRI/MF/complete, shipped quarterly

Monthly report presenting estimates of Alaska nonagricultural employment, labor force, and average hours and earnings, by industry and/or locale. Month of data coverage is 2-3 months preceding cover date.

Issues contain narrative summaries of labor market conditions, interspersed with employment trend charts and 9 monthly tables; and usually 1 or more feature articles, frequently containing statistics.

Issues also often contain additional tables showing trends, forecasts, or geographic or other detail for data topics covered in the monthly tables.

Monthly tables are listed below and appear in all issues. All additional features with substantial statistics on topics not covered in monthly tables are described, as they appear, under "Statistical Features." Nonstatistical features are not covered.

Availability: Alaska Economic Trends, PO Box 25501, Juneau AK 99802-5501, †; SRI/MF/complete, shipped quarterly.

Issues reviewed during 1985: Nov. 1984-Oct. 1985 (P) (Vol. 4, Nos. 11-12; Vol. 5, Nos. 1-10).

MONTHLY TABLES:
[Data are shown for month of coverage and previous month, with comparison to preceding year.]

[1-7] Nonagricultural wage/salary employment by place of work [industry division and selected major group] for Alaska, Anchorage,

---

Anchorage-MatSu, Fairbanks, interior, gulf coast, and southeast Alaska, [and often for 1-3 additional subareas].

[8] Labor force [by employment status] by region and census area [of Alaska].

[9] Alaska hours and earnings for selected industries.

STATISTICAL FEATURES:

S0320–1.601: Nov. 1984 (Vol. 4, No. 11)

HIGH TECH: ALASKA'S BOOM INDUSTRY?

(p. 1-5) By John Van Houten. Article, with 2 undated tables showing high-technology business firms as percent of total firms, by State; and Alaska high-technology firms and employment, by SIC 3-digit industry. Includes classifications based on proportion of scientific/technical workers, ratio of R&D expenditures to sales, and a combination of these 2 criteria. Data are from BLS.

GRAPHIC FACTS

(p. 6-17) By Jeff Hadland. Article, with 18 charts illustrating selected socioeconomic trends for Alaska and/or other States. Includes per capita personal income and median family income, 1983, and percent of population born in State of residence, 1980, all by State; and Alaska employment distribution by labor market area, 1983. Data are from Census Bureau and Alaska Dept of Labor.

ALASKA: CONSTRUCTION

(p. 18-21) By Edward Eboch. Article, with 5 tables showing Alaska housing units authorized, by month, location, and type of unit; rental vacancy rates in 3 cities; and value of publicly awarded construction contracts, by category; various dates 1983-84. Data are from HUD, Alaska Dept of Commerce and Economic Development, and *Alaska Construction and Oil.*

CENSUS OF RETAIL TRADE, PART II: A COMPARISON—ANCHORAGE, ALASKA, AND U.S.

(p. 24-25, 27-28) By Greg Huff. Article, with 3 tables showing Anchorage share of Alaska's retail business firms, sales, and employment; and retail sales and employment, for Alaska and Anchorage; all by kind of business, 1982, with selected trends from 1977 and comparisons to U.S. Data are from Census Bureau.

For description of Part I, see SRI 1984 Annual, under S0320-1.511.

S0320–1.602: Dec. 1984 (Vol. 4, No. 12)

VILLAGE NATIVE CORPORATIONS

(p. 1-8) By Edward Eboch. Article on operations of Alaska's village native corporations established under the Alaska Native Claims Settlement Act. Data are from Alaska Dept of Labor unemployment insurance files, and survey responses from over 50% of corporations.

Includes 5 tables showing village and/or regional native corporation employment, by State region and industry division, various periods 1980-1st quarter 1984.

For description of a similar article on Alaska regional native corporations, see SRI 1984 Annual, under S0320-1.507.

S0320–1.603: Jan. 1985 (Vol. 5, No. 1)

ALASKA'S ECONOMIC OUTLOOK

(p. 1-10) By Edward Eboch. Article, with 5 tables showing Alaska employment trends and forecast, by major industry group, 1983-1st half 1986; and population for Alaska and selected communities, 1982-84. Data are from Alaska Dept of Labor.

FAIRBANKS RETAIL TRADE SECTOR

(p. 17-19) By Neal Fried. Article, with 1 table showing retail sales for Alaska, Fairbanks, and U.S., by kind of business, 1982. Data are from Census Bureau.

S0320–1.604: Feb. 1985 (Vol. 5, No. 2)

FISH HARVESTING AND FISH PROCESSING IN ALASKA, 1982

(p. 1-8) By Kathleen Thomas. Article, with 2 tables showing Alaska fish/seafood industry employment, for processing, and for harvesting by species and type of operation, all by region, 1981-82.

S0320–1.605: Mar. 1985 (Vol. 5, No. 3)

WOMEN AND THE ALASKAN CIVILIAN LABOR FORCE

(p. 1-6) By Kathryn Lizik. Article, with 2 tables showing Alaska labor force by race/ethnicity (white, black, American Indian/Eskimo/Aleut, Asian/Pacific Islander, and Hispanic), employment by earnings level, and median and mean earnings, all by sex and occupational category, 1980.

IMPACT OF STATE EXPENDITURES ON EMPLOYMENT

(p. 14-17) By Edward Eboch. Article, with 2 tables showing Alaska State revenues from top 5 sources, FY84; and number of contract construction jobs created for every $1 million of State spending, by project type (no date). Data are from State Revenue Dept and University of Alaska.

S0320–1.606: Apr. 1985 (Vol. 5, No. 4)

COST OF DOING BUSINESS AND THE COST OF LIVING IN ALASKA

(p. 1-10) By Kathleen Thomas and John Boucher. Article on cost of living and doing business in Alaska as compared with contiguous U.S. Data are from Federal, State, and private sources.

Includes 7 tables showing per capita and median family income; wage rates for selected occupations; and costs of selected business and personal items, including lodging, office and heavy equipment rental, residential and commercial utilities, freight shipment, housing, transportation, taxes, medical care, and fast food; primarily for 3 major Alaska cities, Seattle, Wash., and Washington, D.C., various periods 1981-84.

ANCHORAGE LABOR TURNOVER

(p. 15-19, passim) By Greg Huff. Article, with 1 table showing hiring and termination rates for Anchorage, by industry division, quarterly 1983-1st quarter 1984, and 1983 average.

S0320–1.607: May 1985 (Vol. 5, No. 5)

ALASKA'S AVERAGE MONTHLY EARNINGS GROW SLOWLY

(p. 1-11) By Neal Fried and Greg Huff. Article, with 2 tables showing Alaska average monthly earnings, by industry division and selected major group, and by Alaska census area, biennially 1970-84.

GROWTH IN STATE GOVERNMENT EMPLOYMENT

(p. 12-15) By Edward Eboch. Article, with 2 tables showing Alaska State government employment by dept and region, 1982 and 1984.

HOURS AND EARNINGS

(p. 32-35) By Kathleen Thomas. Article, with 2 tables showing average monthly wages of Alaska State government employees, by dept and region, July 1984 and Feb. 1985.

S0320–1.608: June 1985 (Vol. 5, No. 6)

ALASKA'S MINING INDUSTRY

(p. 1-12) By Edward Eboch. Article, with 1 table showing volume and value of Alaska's mineral production, for 4 metals, sand/gravel, crushed stone, coal, and other, 1982-84. Data are from Alaska Office of Mineral Development and Division of Geological and Geophysical Surveys.

GOVERNMENT'S ROLE IN FAIRBANKS' ECONOMY

(p. 22-25) By Neal Fried. Article, with 1 table showing Federal employment, and State and local educational and noneducational employment, as percent of total government employment in Fairbanks, Alaska, 1984. Data are from Alaska Dept of Labor.

GULF COAST FISHERY

(p. 26-28) By Neal Fried. Article, with 1 table showing Alaska Gulf Coast annual average fish processing employment, 1980-84.

S0320–1.609: July 1985 (Vol. 5, No. 7)

HOURS AND EARNINGS: URBAN VERSUS RURAL MONTHLY WAGES

(p. 26-27, 29) By Kathleen Thomas. Article, with 1 table showing Alaska urban vs. rural average monthly wages, with detail for 4 urban boroughs and 5 rural regions, 1983.

S0320–1.610: Aug. 1985 (Vol. 5, No. 8)

RESIDENT AND NONRESIDENT EMPLOYMENT IN ALASKA

(p. 1-17) By John Boucher. Article, with 5 tables showing Alaska employment and wages covered by unemployment insurance, for Permanent Fund recipients and nonrecipients, by industry division and major group and by State region and census area, quarterly 1984. Permanent Fund recipients must be Alaska residents. Data are intended to provide a measure of resident vs. nonresident employment in Alaska.

ECONOMIC OUTLOOK

(p. 18-20) By Edward Eboch. Article, with 3 tables showing Anchorage CPI; housing units authorized by building permits/public contracts, for Alaska and 3 largest cities; and Alaska population by borough and State census area; various periods 1983-85. Data are from State and Federal sources.

S0320–1.611: Sept. 1985 (Vol. 5, No. 9)

RURAL VERSUS URBAN EMPLOYMENT GROWTH, 1980-1984

(p. 1-10) By Neal Fried and Greg Huff. Article, with 2 charts and 3 tables showing Alaska urban and rural employment, by industry division and geographic area, various years 1980-84.

ALASKA'S AREA COSTS

(p. 13) Article, with 1 undated table showing cost-of-living differentials (Anchorage = 1.00) for 18 Alaska communities and Seattle, Wash.

INTERIOR'S INCOME STANDINGS

(p. 20-24) Article, with 1 chart and 1 table showing per capita income for Alaska, 4 census areas in Alaska, and U.S., 1973 and 1983. Data are from U.S. Bureau of Economic Analysis.

RETAIL TRADE ON THE KENAI PENINSULA

(p. 25-27) Article, with 1 table showing retail employment, by kind of business, for Kenai Peninsula Borough, 1984. Data are from Alaska Dept of Labor.

S0320–1.612: Oct. 1985 (Vol. 5, No. 10)

POPULATION GROWTH AND MIGRATION IN ALASKA

(p. 1-10) By Greg Williams. Article, with 1 table showing Alaska population and components of change (births, deaths, natural increase, and net migration), FY46-84. Data are from Alaska Dept of Labor.

GROWTH IN ESTABLISHMENTS

(p. 12-13) By Edward Eboch. Article, with 1 table showing Alaska business establishments by industry division, 4th quarter 1981-84.

ANCHORAGE BUSINESS SERVICES

(p. 16-19) By Greg Huff. Article, with 1 table showing Anchorage business services establishments and employment, by selected 3- and 4-digit SIC code, 1980 and 1984. Data are from Alaska Dept of Labor.

S0320–5   ALASKA PLANNING INFORMATION

Annual.   Feb. 1985.
6 + 105 p. + errata.
SRI/MF/complete

Annual planning report, for 1984, analyzing Alaska labor supply and demand. Includes data on population, labor force, employment, cost of living, income, and characteristics of unemployment insurance claimants, with selected detail by industry, occupation, and census location, and comparisons to U.S. Data are generally current to 1984, and include selected trends from the 1930s and forecasts to 1989.

Data are from Alaska Dept of Labor, BLS, and the Census Bureau.

Contains listing of contents, tables, and charts (4 p.); map (1 p.); 8 chapters with narrative analyses, interspersed with 3 charts and 56 tables (p. 1-73); glossary (p. 74-76); and appendix, with 15 tables (p. 78-105). All tables are listed below.

Availability: Alaska Department of Labor, Research and Analysis Section, PO Box 25501, Juneau AK 99802-5501, †; SRI/MF/complete.

TABLES:

[Data and census classifications are for Alaska, unless otherwise noted. Data by industry are generally shown by nonagricultural industry division, often with additional detail for selected major industry groups.]

S0320–5.1: Area and Population

I.1.-I.2. Conversion of 1980 census areas to corresponding 1970 census divisions, and of 1970 census divisions to 1980 census areas. [tabular lists] (p. 2-3)

I.3. Total land area and population, by census area, 1983. (p. 4)

II.1.-II.2. Population characteristics [including births, deaths, and net migration, by census area, with some detail for whites and Natives, various periods 1970-83]. (p. 6-7)

II.3.-II.4. Population distribution by age and sex, 1970 and 1980, and [total] July 1982. (p. 7-8)

S0320–5.2: Labor Force, Employment, and Unemployment Insurance Claimants

LABOR FORCE

III.1. Current Population Survey: labor force participation and unemployment rates, 1983 annual average [and population, all by sex, race, and marital status, with selected detail for youth]. (p. 12)

III.2. Alaska and U.S.: labor force characteristics, 1980 Census of Population [including total and female labor force, by employment status, with selected detail for women by age group of children, 1980, and by duration of employment and unemployment, 1979; employment by class of worker, occupation, and industry, 1980; and families by number of workers, 1979]. (p. 13-14)

III.3-III.4. Labor force [by employment status], by State [and census division], 1983 annual average; and unemployment [rates] ranked by State [1982-83]. (p. 15-17)

III.5. Civilian labor force, employment, unemployment, and unemployment rate, statewide [by month], Jan. 1976-[Sept.] 1984. (p. 18-20)

III.6. Labor force [by employment status, and unemployment rate] by [State] region and census division, 1978-83. (p. 21-22)

NONAGRICULTURAL EMPLOYMENT

IV.1. Types of employment measures [tabular description of 3 measures]. (p. 24)

IV.2-IV.8. Nonagricultural wage/salary employment by [industry and] place of work for State, Anchorage/MatSu, Anchorage, Fairbanks, interior, Gulf Coast, and southeast, 1983. (p. 25-28)

IV.9-IV.18. Industry employment forecast [average employment, with detail for number of jobs, by industry, for State, Anchorage, Fairbanks, and southeast, various periods 1984-1st half 1986]. (p. 30-37)

OCCUPATIONAL EMPLOYMENT FORECAST

V.1. Estimated employment by occupation [1984-85 and 1989, and average annual job openings due to growth and separations, 1984-89 period]. (p. 40-48)

UNEMPLOYMENT INSURANCE CLAIMANTS

[Table titles begin "All claimants benefit year beginning 1983..."]

VI.1-VI.6. Number and percent within industry and occupation distributed by local office; and percent within local office distributed by industry and occupation. (p. 50-53)

VI.7. Occupation categories containing over 100 claimants. (p. 54)

S0320–5.3: Cost of Living and Income Measures

COST OF LIVING

VII.1. Cost of living measures [tabular description of 4 measures]. (p. 59)

VII.2. CPI, urban wage earners/clerical workers [only, for] U.S., Seattle, and Anchorage [1967-83]. (p. 60)

VII.3. Cost of selected items [food at home, electricity, heating oil, gasoline, and lumber] in [selected] Alaskan communities [Mar. or June 1984]. (p. 61)

VII.4-VII.5. Annual total [low, intermediate, and high] budget for a 4-person family [for urban U.S., Anchorage, and Seattle/Everett; and] lower budget for a family of 4 [by item, for U.S. and Anchorage]; autumn 1981. (p. 62)

INCOME MEASURES

VIII.1. Income measures [tabular description of 8 measures.] (p. 66)

VIII.2. Average earnings, UI [unemployment insurance] covered employment by [selected] industry, 1983. (p. 67)

VIII.3. Number of workers, employment, and income levels in UI covered employment [by industry division], 1983. (p. 67)

VIII.4. Hours and earnings for selected industries, 1983 annual average. (p. 68)

VIII.5. OMB poverty guidelines for Alaska, effective date 1984; and [aggregate] for all States except Alaska/Hawaii, 1983; [all by family size]. (p. 68)

VIII.6-VIII.7. Lower living standard income level, effective Aug. 1983, metropolitan and nonmetropolitan Alaska [table VIII.7 incorrectly reads "metropolitan Alaska."] (p. 68-69)

VIII.8. Personal income [total and per capita, U.S. and by Alaska] census division, 1982 [and percent change from 1981]. (p. 69)

VIII.9. Total and per capita personal income, Alaska and U.S., 1970-83. (p. 70)

VIII.10-VIII.11. 1983 per capita [U.S.] personal income, [and] estimated 1983 median income of 4-person families, [both] ranked by State. (p. 70-71)

VIII.12. Alaska and U.S. income and poverty status in 1979: 1980 census [results, including households, families, and unrelated individuals, by income type and/or level; mean and per capita income, with detail by type and number of workers in family; and family characteristics, including composition and poverty status, with detail for female householders and older persons]. (p. 72-73)

S0320–5.4: Appendix Tables

A.1.-A.6. [Table III.5 is repeated for Anchorage/Matanuska/Susitna, Gulf Coast, interior, northern, southeast, and southwest regions, Jan. 1980-Sept. 1984.] (p. 78-83)

A.7.-A.13. [Tables IV.2-IV.8 are repeated for 1978-82.] (p. 84-100)

A.14. Insured employment by major industry division, 1938-62. (p. 101)

A.15. Nonagricultural wage/salary employment [statewide, by industry division, monthly 1963-77]. (p. 102-105)

S0337   ALASKA
Office of the
Lieutenant Governor

**S0337–1   STATE OF ALASKA
OFFICIAL RETURNS, by
Election Precinct, General
Election, Nov. 6, 1984**
Biennial. [1985.] 2+68 p.
LC 83-622022.
SRI/MF/complete

Biennial report presenting results of the Alaska
general election held Nov. 6, 1984. Shows voting
for President/Vice President, U.S. Senator and
Representatives, State legislators, judges, and 4
State ballot and bonding propositions.

Also shows voter registration and turnout,
election recounts, and party affiliation of candidates.

Data generally are shown by legislative district
and precinct.

Previous report, covering 1982 general election, is described in SRI 1983 Annual under this
number.

Availability: Alaska Office of the Lieutenant
Governor, Elections Division, Community
Bldg., Pouch AF, Juneau AK 99811-9974, †;
SRI/MF/complete.

S0450   ARIZONA
Department of
Administration

**S0450–1   STATE OF ARIZONA
ANNUAL FINANCIAL
REPORT, 1983-84**
Annual. Nov. 1, 1984.
1+54 p.
ISSN 0098-9924.
LC 75-646570.
SRI/MF/complete

Annual report on financial condition of Arizona
State government, for FY84, presenting assets,
liabilities, and fund balances; revenues by source;
and expenditures (appropriated and actual) variously by agency, function, or object; for general,
special revenue, trust and agency, enterprise, internal service, and debt service funds; with selected comparisons to FY83.

Also includes property taxes receivable, by
year of levy and county.

Data are compiled from records of the Finance
Division.

Contains contents listing (p. 1); and 14 financial statements (p. 2-54).

Availability: Arizona Department of Administration, Finance Division, State Capitol, Rm.
809, 1700 W. Washington, Phoenix AZ 85007, †;
SRI/MF/complete.

S0460   ARIZONA
Banking Department

**S0460–1   CONDENSED STATEMENT
OF REPORTS FOR STATE
AND FEDERAL SAVINGS
AND LOAN ASSOCIATIONS,
Arizona**
Quarterly. 5 p.
SRI/MF/complete

Quarterly report on assets, liabilities, and equity
capital of Arizona State and Federal savings and
loan assns. Data are based on reports by assns to
the Superintendent of Banks. Report is issued 2-3
months after quarter of coverage.

Contains 1 table showing assets, liabilities, and
equity capital, by item; and number of branch
offices; all by institution, as of end of quarter
covered.

Availability: Arizona Banking Department,
3225 N. Central Ave., Century Plaza, Suite 815,
Phoenix AZ 85012, †; SRI/MF/complete.

Issues reviewed during 1985: Sept. 30, 1984-June
30, 1985 (D).

**S0460–2   CONDENSED STATEMENT
OF REPORTS OF STATE
AND NATIONAL BANKS of
Arizona**
Quarterly. Approx. 2 p.
SRI/MF/complete

Quarterly report on assets, liabilities, and equity
capital of Arizona State and national banks. Data
are based on bank reports to the Superintendent
of Banks. Report is issued 2-3 months after quarter of coverage.

Contains 2 tables showing the following:

a. By institution: loans, deposits, resources,
equity capital, and number of branch offices,
with ranking by total resources, for year ending with quarter covered.

b. Aggregate assets, liabilities, and equity capital, by item, for State and national banks, as
of end of quarter covered.

Both tables include comparisons to previous
year.

Prior to Mar. 31, 1985 edition, report consisted of 1 table showing number of branches, and
itemized assets, liabilities, and equity capital, all
by institution.

Availability: Arizona Banking Department,
3225 N. Central Ave., Century Plaza, Suite 815,
Phoenix AZ 85012, †; SRI/MF/complete.

Issues reviewed during 1985: Sept. 30, 1984-June
30, 1985 (D).

**S0460–3   ANNUAL REPORT OF THE
CONSUMER FINANCE
COMPANIES, 1983-84,
Arizona**
Annual. [1985.] 13 p.
LC 71-618077.
SRI/MF/complete

Annual report, for FY84, on the financial condition of consumer finance companies licensed to
operate in Arizona. Presents composite balance
sheet; income and expenses; and analysis of small
loan activity, delinquent accounts, recovery
suits, wage assignments, and chattel activity.
Also includes small loan trends from FY73.

Contains listings of licensees by city and type
of license, and new and surrendered licenses (p.
1-5); and 8 financial schedules and 1 table (p.
7-13).

Availability: Arizona Banking Department,
3225 N. Central Ave., Century Plaza, Suite 815,
Phoenix AZ 85012, $2.50; SRI/MF/complete.

S0465   ARIZONA
Department of
Economic Security

**S0465–1   ARIZONA LABOR MARKET
NEWSLETTER**
Monthly. Approx. 20 p.
ISSN 0743-5657.
LC sn84-2852.
SRI/MF/complete, shipped
quarterly

Monthly report (with annual special issue) on
Arizona labor market trends, including employment by county and industry, unemployment insurance activities, and production worker hours
and earnings. Data are compiled by the Arizona
Dept of Economic Security from various sources.
Month of coverage is 2-3 months prior to cover
date.

Issues generally contain articles, often with
statistics; summary data on Arizona unemployment rates and Phoenix CPI, with comparisons
to U.S., and U.S. PPI; and 5 monthly tables, listed below, with accompanying analysis.

The annual special issue, published for the 1st
time in Feb. 1985, is a nonstatistical chronology
of employment-related developments in Arizona
during the previous year.

Monthly tables appear in all issues. All addi-
tional features with substantial statistics on
Arizona are described, as they appear, under
"Statistical Features." Nonstatistical features,
and articles which contain only widely available
U.S. statistics, are not described.

Availability: Arizona Department of Economic
Security, Labor Market Information Publications, Site Code 733A, PO Box 6123, Phoenix
AZ 85005, †; SRI/MF/complete, shipped quarterly.

Issues reviewed during 1985: Nov. 1984-Oct.
1985 (P) (Vol. VIII, No. 11-12; Vol. IX, Nos.
1-10) [Vol. VIII, No. 12 incorrectly reads Vol.
VII; Vol. IX, No. 1 incorrectly reads Vol. VIII;
Vol. IX, Nos. 3-4 incorrectly read Vol. X]; and
annual special issue, Feb. 1985 (P).

MONTHLY TABLES:
[All data are shown for Arizona, for month of
coverage. Tables [1] and [4-5] also show data for
previous month and same month of previous
year. Table order may vary from month to
month.]

[1] Labor force and employment; and nonagricultural wage/salary employment, by [in-
dustry division and selected major group; all
for State and Maricopa and Pima Counties].

[2] Nonmetro counties labor force and employment [by industry division, by county].

[3] Labor force and employment, for [consid-
eration in] economic assistance programs [by
county].

[4] Estimated hours and earnings of production workers in selected industries.

[5] Unemployment insurance activities [claimants served, benefits paid, average number of weeks unemployed, and unemployment trust fund balance].

STATISTICAL FEATURES:

S0465–1.601: Nov. 1984 (Vol. VIII, No. 11)

IN AND OUT OF POVERTY

(p. 1-4) Article, with 2 tables showing the following for Arizona, by race:

a. Population, median family income, and total and female labor force (by employment status) and persons not in labor force, 1970 and 1980.

b. Families and persons below poverty level, including detail for female householders with children and for persons age 65/older, 1969 and 1979.

Data are from Census Bureau.

S0465–1.602: Feb. 1985 (Vol. IX, No. 2)

AFDC IN ARIZONA: HOW DO WE COMPARE?

(p. 13-14) Article, with 5 tables showing U.S. and Arizona AFDC average monthly payment and percent of population receiving payments, and annual AFDC recipient and expenditure growth rates, all with Arizona's ranking among States, various years 1979-82.

S0465–1.603: Mar. 1985 (Vol. IX, No. 3)

[Issue incorrectly reads Vol. X.]

ARIZONA OUTLOOK, ANNUAL FEATURE

Annual compilation of articles forecasting Arizona employment through 1987. Articles containing substantial statistics are described below.

Feature appears in each Mar. issue. For description of last previous compilation presenting substantial data for Arizona, see SRI 1983 Annual under S0465-1.405.

ARIZONA IN 1984

(p. 2-3) Article, with 1 table showing total Arizona wage/salary employment, by industry division, 1983-84.

EMPLOYMENT FORECASTS FOR 1985-87

(p. 3-8, 14-15) Compilation of 4 articles on employment in Arizona, and Maricopa, Pima, and nonmetro counties, each with 1 table showing labor force by employment status, and employment by industry division, 1984-87.

S0465–1.604: Apr. 1985 (Vol. IX, No. 4)

[Issue incorrectly reads Vol. X. The following articles are based on an Aug. 1984 survey of Maricopa and Pima County businesses employing fewer than 100 workers.]

LABOR COSTS IN PHOENIX AND TUCSON

(p. 4-6) Article, with 9 text tables showing the following for employees of small businesses in Maricopa and Pima Counties: average hourly wage, by occupation and occupational group, Aug. 1984; and percent change in wages, by occupational group and industry division, 1984 vs. 1983.

AREA AND INDUSTRY DIFFERENCES CAN MEAN PAY DIFFERENCES

(p. 6-8) Article, with 1 table comparing small business hourly wages in Maricopa County, by occupation and industry division, Aug. 1984.

S0465–1.605: May 1985 (Vol. IX, No. 5)

LABOR TURNOVER UPDATE

(p. 1-7) Article, with 5 tables showing the following for Arizona:

a. Employment, new hires, rehires, and separations, by industry division and selected major group, by county, and for total metro, nonmetro, northern, and southern areas, 2nd quarter 1984 with quarterly summary from 1982.

b. Employment and job opportunities by occupation, for automotive repair service/garage industry, annually or aggregate 1985-86.

NEW DEVELOPMENTS: CONSTRUCTION

(p. 13) Brief article, with 1 table showing top 7 Arizona cities ranked by percent increase in home sales, 1984. Data are from Arizona State University Bureau of Business and Economic Research.

S0465–1.606: June 1985 (Vol. IX, No. 6)

AVERAGE FACULTY SALARIES

(p. 9-10) Article, with 1 table showing average higher education faculty salaries, by academic rank, for selected institutions in Arizona and 5 neighboring States, 1984/85. Data are from the Apr. 24, 1985 issue of *The Chronicle of Higher Education*.

For description of complete salary report, see C2175-1.619 above.

EMPLOYMENT IN ARIZONA: WHAT WILL HAPPEN IF...?

(p. 16-20) By David Sinclair. Article illustrating 2 national economic scenarios and their impact on employment in Arizona. Data are based on author's model of the Arizona economy.

Includes 3 tables showing the following under recession and growth scenarios, various years 1984-88: U.S. GNP growth rate, average prime rate, housing starts, unemployment and inflation rates, and auto sales; and Arizona labor force by employment status, and employment by industry division.

S0465–1.607: July 1985 (Vol. IX, No. 7)

ARIZONA ECONOMY: PERSONAL INCOME IN 1984

(p. 1-5) Article, with 2 tables showing total and per capita personal income for 10 States with largest growth rate in total income (including Arizona), and Arizona per capita personal income by county, all with comparisons to U.S., various years 1981-84. Data are from Commerce Dept.

LARGEST PRIVATELY OWNED FIRMS IN ARIZONA BY 1983 REVENUES

(p. 15-17) Brief article, with 1 table showing number of employees, location, and type of industry, for Arizona's 100 largest privately owned companies in terms of annual revenues, 1983. Data are from Arthur Andersen and Co.

S0465–1.608: Aug. 1985 (Vol. IX, No. 8)

ARIZONA EMPLOYMENT: PEAKS AND TROUGHS, 1979-84

(p. 1-7) Article, with 5 tables showing dates of Arizona employment peaks and troughs, and percent changes, Aug. 1979-Dec. 1984 period; and employment for trough 1982-83 and peak 1984 periods; all by industry division, with detail by selected major industry group, and including selected industry rankings and comparisons to total U.S.

Data are from Arizona Dept of Economic Security and BLS.

UNEMPLOYMENT INSURANCE: THE GOLDEN ANNIVERSARY

(p. 8-10) Article, with 1 table showing the following for Arizona's unemployment insurance program: benefits paid, employer contributions, change in trust fund balance, and net income added to State economy, 1975-84. Data are from Arizona Dept of Economic Security.

S0465–1.609: Sept. 1985 (Vol. IX, No. 9)

FORECAST UPDATE: EMPLOYMENT IN ARIZONA, ANNUAL FEATURE

(p. 1-7) Annual article, with 4 tables showing labor force by employment status, and employment by industry division, for Arizona, Maricopa and Pima Counties, and aggregate nonmetro counties, 1984-87.

EMPLOYER 'CONTRIBUTION' RATE FOR UNEMPLOYMENT INSURANCE, STATE-BY-STATE COMPARISONS

(p. 14-16) Brief article on tax rates for employer contributions to State unemployment trust funds. Data are from Labor Dept.

Includes 2 tables showing the following, by State and for Puerto Rico and Virgin Islands: taxable wage base, various years 1982-85; employer contribution tax rates, 1983-85; and amount outstanding on Federal loans to fund State unemployment benefits, as of May 31, 1985.

SERVICES

(p. 17) Brief article, with 1 undated table showing top 25 educational users of personal computers, ranked by installed base. Table includes school districts and higher education institutions.

S0465–1.610: Oct. 1985 (Vol. IX, No. 10)

ARIZONA EDUCATION: A STATISTICAL OVERVIEW

(p. 34-38) Compilation of 13 tables presenting statistics on education in Arizona. Data sources include Arizona Dept of Education, Board of Regents, and Commission for Postsecondary Education. Includes the following for Arizona, various periods 1980-86:

a. Educational attainment of population age 25/over; and school status (enrolled, high school graduate, not enrolled/not high school graduate, or in armed forces) of population age 16-19; by county, with comparisons to total State and U.S.

b. State appropriations for higher education, with selected State rankings; general fund appropriations; and funds received from State trust lands; generally for 3 universities, with some data for community colleges.

c. Elementary/secondary education: public and private schools and enrollment, public school teachers by sex, expenditures, average cost per pupil and teacher salary, and distribution of revenues by source.

d. Public university and community college enrollment (total and FTE), and faculty and average salaries, by academic rank and/or sex, all by institution; and public university resident and nonresident fees, with aggregate comparisons to other Western States and major State universities.

Includes related articles (p. 2-33, passim).

S0465–2   ARIZONA OCCUPATIONAL PROFILES
Series. For individual publication data, see below.
LC 84-623175.
SRI/MF/complete

Series of triennial reports, each presenting data on Arizona employment and job opening outlook in a selected industry division, by detailed occupation and county. Data are from Occupational Employment Statistics (OES) surveys of over 700 occupations. Surveys are conducted in 3-year cycles. Reports are published 1-2 years after survey year.

Each report includes the following:

a. Industry and occupational information sections, with narrative analyses, summary charts and tables, and varying additional data, all pertaining to the industry under study.

b. Detailed table, repeated for Arizona and each county, showing estimated employment for year of OES survey, projected employment for year 4 years after survey, and job openings expected during the 4-year period, by detailed occupation, for the industry under study.

Reports reviewed during 1985 are described below.

Availability: Arizona Department of Economic Security, Labor Market Information Publications, Occupational Employment Statistics, Site Code 733A, PO Box 6123, Phoenix AZ 85005, †; SRI/MF/complete.

S0465–2.13: Transportation, Communications, and Public Utilities
[Triennial. July 1984. 1+47 p. Rpt. No. DES-5140. SRI/MF/complete.]

Covers employment in transportation, communications, and public utilities industries, 1982-86. Data are based on a survey of 726 firms.

For description of previous report on this topic, see SRI 1981 Annual under S0465-2.7.

S0465–2.14: Government
[Triennial. July 1984. 1+81 p. Rpt. No. DES-5281. SRI/MF/complete.]

Covers employment in Federal and State/local government, 1982-86. Data are from the Civil Service Commission, and a survey of State and local government agencies.

Additional data include 2 tables showing Federal and State government employment by major agency, with detail for all or selected counties, May 1982.

For description of previous report on this topic, see SRI 1981 Annual under S0465-2.5.

S0465–2.15: Trade
[Triennial. Sept. 1984. 1+49 p. Rpt. No. DES-5301. SRI/MF/complete.]

Covers wholesale/retail trade industry employment, 1982-86. Data are based on a survey of 5,861 firms.

Additional data include 5 tables showing number of establishments and employment, for motor vehicle-related and wholesale trade businesses, with aggregate wholesale trade data by county, 1982; retail trade employment per 1,000 population by county, 1982; and retail trade employment growth, 1971-80 and 1978-82 periods; all by type of business.

For description of previous report on this topic, see SRI 1981 Annual under S0465-2.6.

S0465–2.16: Hospitals
[Triennial. Feb. 1985. 49 p. Rpt. No. PA-332. SRI/MF/complete, current & previous report.]

Covers employment in hospitals, 1983-87. Data are primarily based on survey responses from all Arizona hospitals.

Additional data include 2 charts and 2 tables showing number of Arizona hospitals by type and ownership, by county, May 1983; and distribution of U.S. registered and licensed practical nurses, and nursing aides/orderlies/attendants, by type of employer, 1980 or 1982.

Previous report, covering 1980-84, has also been received, and is also available on SRI microfiche under this number [Triennial. Dec. 1981. 39 p. Rpt. No. DES-5376. †]. Previous report does not include the additional data described above.

S0465 2.17: Manufacturing
[Triennial. Apr. 1985. 59 p. Rpt. No. PA-340. SRI/MF/complete.]

Covers employment in Arizona manufacturing industry, 1983-87. Data are based on a survey of 1,860 firms, with 93% response rate.

Additional data include 1 table showing number of Arizona manufacturing establishments and employment, by county, 1983.

Previous report, for 1980-84, is described in SRI 1982 Annual under S0465-2.8.

S0465–4   STATISTICAL BULLETIN, Arizona Department of Economic Security
Monthly, with annual supplement. 13 p. no paging.
SRI/MF/complete, shipped quarterly

Monthly report, with annual supplement, on Arizona public assistance cases, recipients, and payments, by program, county, and district. Covers AFDC, general and emergency assistance, tuberculosis control, supplemental payments, and food stamp programs. Report is issued 1-2 months after month of coverage.

Contains narrative summary, approximately 20 trend charts, and 6 monthly tables listed below.

Annual supplement presents fiscal year monthly averages for most data covered in monthly tables.

Availability: Arizona Department of Economic Security, Family Assistance Administration, Site Code 960A, PO Box 6123, Phoenix AZ 85005, †; SRI/MF/complete, shipped quarterly.

Issues reviewed during 1985: Sept. 1984-Aug. 1985; and FY83-85 annual supplements (D).

TABLES:
[Unless otherwise noted, data are shown by State district and county, for month of coverage, with change from previous month and same month of previous year. Tables 1-2 and 4-5 show cases and/or recipients and payments.]

1. AFDC [for adult and child recipients; also includes (in footnotes) State totals for cases, recipients, and payments to Navajo/Hopi Indians, children in foster homes, and refugee resettlement program].

2. General assistance [including (in footnotes) refugee resettlement program].

3. Emergency assistance [number and value of payments].

4-5. Tuberculosis control; and supplemental payments program.

6. Food stamp program [households, persons, and coupon issuance value].

S0470   ARIZONA
Department of Education

S0470–1   ANNUAL REPORT OF THE SUPERINTENDENT OF PUBLIC INSTRUCTION, Statistical Section, for FY84, Arizona
Annual. Nov. 1984. 291 p.
ISSN 0095-5310.
LC 74-647146.
SRI/MF/complete

Annual report on Arizona public school enrollment characteristics, administration, facilities, and finances, by school district and county, with comparative enrollment data for private schools, 1983/84 or FY84. Data are from unaudited reports submitted to the State Dept of Education by school officials.

Contains contents listing (p. 5); 10 tables, listed below (p. 9-283); appendices, with data variances and omissions (p. 285-287); and index (p. 289-291).

Availability: Arizona Department of Education, 1535 W. Jefferson, Phoenix AZ 85007, $5.69+$2.50 postage and handling; SRI/MF/complete.

TABLES:
[Data are for 1983/84 or FY84, and are shown for public schools, unless otherwise noted. Data by grade include special education.]

[1] Statistics in education [public and private schools and enrollments; public school average daily membership (ADM), and number of superintendents, principals, and teachers; and total and operating school districts]. (p. 9)

[2] District expenditures [by function] and percentage of total expenditures [and revenues by source]. (p. 9-10)

[3] State summary, by grade of pupil enrollment [enrollment by race and ethnic group including Hispanic, American Indian/Alaskan Native, and Asian/Pacific Islander; dropouts; and graduates]. (p. 13)

[4] State summary of number and type of schools [and school districts, by county]. (p. 14)

[5] Private schools statistics [enrollment by grade; and schools and enrollment by county]. (p. 15)

[6] Food services information [meals served, value of donated commodities, and expenditures, by county and school district]. (p. 16-21)

[7-8] Business and financial services, State-appropriated funds and Federal grants-in-aid: statement of revenues or grants, and expenditures. (p. 24-29)

[9] Summary: annual financial report of the county school superintendent [expenditures, special county school reserve fund operations, and disbursements, by county]. (p. 32-35)

[10] Arizona school district, county, and State summary [ADM 1981/82-1983/84; enrollment; staff and staff/student ratio, by type of position; and detailed revenues by source and expenditures by function, including finances for teacher salaries, retirement, special education programs by type, and pupil transportation; repeated for each school district and county, and for the State]. (p. 40-283)

S0480   ARIZONA
Department of Health Services

S0480-1   1983 ARIZONA VITAL HEALTH STATISTICS
Annual. [1984.]
3+45 p.+errata.
ISSN 0160-9610.
LC 78-642237.
SRI/MF/complete

Annual report on Arizona vital statistics, by county, 1983. Covers births, deaths, marriages, divorces/annulments, and abortions. Includes data by sex, race/ethnicity, age, and education, with trends from 1950 or earlier, and comparisons with U.S. Data are from documents filed in Vital Records Section prior to Mar. 15, 1984.

Contains introduction and table listing (3 p.); methodology and definitions (p. 1); and 44 tables, described below (p. 2-45).

Availability: Arizona Department of Health Services, Research and Statistical Analysis Section, Information Services Office, 1740 W. Adams St., Phoenix AZ 85007, †; SRI/MF/complete.

TABLES:
[Data are shown for Arizona, 1983, unless otherwise noted. Trends from 1950 generally are shown quinquennially 1950-70 and annually 1971-83. Most data are shown by county of residence and/or occurrence. Data are shown as numbers and/or rates. Data by race usually include American Indian and Asian.]

POPULATION AND BIRTHS
a. Population, decennially 1930-80 and 1981-83. Table 1.1. (p. 2)
b. Low birth weight births: 1970-83; and by child's race and sex, and mother's age group, 1983. Tables 2.1-2.4. (p. 3-6)

c. Births: to unwed mothers and total, by mother's age group, race, and education; trends from 1950; by month, selected years 1970-83, and by child's race (including Hispanic) and sex, 1983; and with congenital anomalies, by type of anomaly and child's race and sex, 1983. Tables 2.5-2.17. (p. 7-19)

DEATHS
d. Deaths: trends from 1950; by month, selected years 1970-83; and by race and sex, 1983. Tables 3.1-3.5. (p. 20-24)
e. Fetal deaths: trends from 1950; and by child's race and sex, 1983. Tables 3.6-3.8. (p. 25-27)
f. Infant mortality: by child's age and selected cause, child's race and sex, and whether neonatal or postneonatal; and total and neonatal trends from 1950. Tables 3.9-3.15. (p. 28-34)
g. Deaths, by selected cause and age group. Tables 3.16-3.18. (p. 35-37)

MARRIAGES, DISSOLUTIONS, AND ABORTIONS
h. Marriages and dissolutions, monthly 1983, 1950, and annually 1955-83. Tables 4.1-4.6. (p. 38-43)
i. Abortions: by in-State vs. out-of-State residence, type of facility and procedure, weeks of gestation, existence of complications, reasons for termination, and women's age group, marital status, race, education, and previous live births and abortions, 1979-83; and total, 1977-83. Tables 5.1-5.2. (p. 44-45)

S0483   ARIZONA
Department of Insurance

S0483-1   71st ANNUAL REPORT OF THE DEPARTMENT OF INSURANCE, State of Arizona
Annual.   Sept. 15, 1984.
370 p.
LC 17-14279.
SRI/MF/complete

Annual report on Arizona insurance industry financial condition and underwriting activity, by company and/or type of insurance, 1983, with summary comparisons to 1982. Covers assets, liabilities, capital, surplus, and Arizona premium income, for companies with headquarters in Arizona and elsewhere.

Data are shown for life/disability, property/casualty, mortgage guaranty, and title insurance companies, and for various types of health services organizations, with income-loss analysis for top property casualty companies.

Also includes Dept finances, with trends from 1964; and company status changes.

Contains contents listing (1 p.); Insurance Dept report, including activity summary, 20 tables on top property/casualty companies, directory of personnel, 4 tables on dept finances, and lists of status changes (p. 1-32); company directory and financial profiles, and selected lists (p. 33-366); and 4 summary tables (p. 367-370).

Availability: Arizona Department of Insurance, Administrative Division, 801 E. Jefferson, Phoenix AZ 85034, $10.00; SRI/MF/complete.

S0495   ARIZONA
Department of Library, Archives and Public Records

S0495-1   ARIZONA PUBLIC LIBRARY STATISTICS, 1983-84
Annual.   1985.   1+16 p.
LC 84-622072.
SRI/MF/complete

Annual report, for FY84, on Arizona public library operations. Covers population served; FTE staff (volunteers, support, and with masters of library science degrees); hours; collection and circulation; income by source; and expenditures by object, including salaries and materials.

Data are shown by library and county.

Contains explanatory notes (1 p.); and 2 extended tables (p. 1-16).

Report previously included a directory, now published separately. The directory is not covered in SRI.

Availability: Arizona Department of Library, Archives and Public Records, Library Extension Division, Capitol Bldg., 3rd Floor, 1700 W. Washington, Phoenix AZ 85007, †; SRI/MF/complete.

S0497   ARIZONA
Department of Mines and Mineral Resources

S0497-1   PRIMARY COPPER INDUSTRY OF ARIZONA in 1983
Annual.   Jan. 1985.   72 p.
Special Rpt. No. 8.
SRI/MF/complete

Annual report, by Clifford J. Hicks, on Arizona copper industry, 1983, with selected trends from as early as 1948. Includes data on volume of copper ore mined and milled, recoverable copper and molybdenum, production capacity, and reserves, by mine and company, with selected rankings; production volume and value for copper and other nonfuel minerals; and copper industry employment, hours, wages, and productivity, with comparison to U.S.

Also includes U.S. copper production by State and company, exports, and imports by country of origin; copper smelter capacity in U.S., Canada, and Mexico, by company and plant; U.S. and world stocks of refined copper; underground and surface copper mining costs in U.S. and other countries; and average price for electrolytic copper wirebar.

Data are derived primarily from reports of the Arizona Depts of Mines and Mineral Resources and Economic Security, U.S. Bureau of Mines, Census Bureau, American Bureau of Metal Statistics, Inc., and company annual reports.

Contains contents and table listing (2 p.); introduction, summary, highlights of copper company operations, and tax descriptions (p. 1-27); and 23 tables (p. 28-72).

Availability: Arizona Department of Mines and Mineral Resources, Mineral Resources Bldg., Fairgrounds, Phoenix AZ 85007, $3.50; SRI/MF/complete.

S0500
Oil and Gas Conservation Commission
ARIZONA

S0500–1   OIL, GAS, AND HELIUM PRODUCTION, State of Arizona
Monthly. 4 p. Oversized.
SRI/MF/complete, shipped quarterly

Monthly report on Arizona oil, natural gas, and water production from 4-5 fields in Apache County accounting for total State oil and gas production. Report also includes total helium production to date; there is no current production. Report is compiled by the Arizona Oil and Gas Conservation Commission and is issued approximately 2 months following month of coverage.

Contains 1 table showing production by field, operator, and well, for month of coverage, year to date, and all-time cumulative production. Also shows gas distribution (flared/vented, used on lease, sold, and lost), for month of coverage.

Availability: Arizona Oil and Gas Conservation Commission, 1645 W. Jefferson, Suite 420, Phoenix AZ 85007, †; SRI/MF/complete, shipped quarterly.

Issues reviewed during 1985: Sept. 1984-Aug. 1985 (D).

S0515
Department of Revenue
ARIZONA

S0515–1   ARIZONA DEPARTMENT OF REVENUE Annual Report, 1983-84
Annual. [1985.] 2+48 p.
ISSN 0362-9627.
LC 76-644453.
SRI/MF/complete

Annual report on Arizona State tax revenues, by source, FY84, with trends from FY80. Covers tax rates, assessments, and collections, and distribution of funds to local governments.

Contains transmittal letter and contents listing (2 p.); report in 7 sections, with text statistics and 25 tables listed below (p. 1-36); and review of 1984 tax legislation (p. 37-48).

Availability: Arizona Department of Revenue, Management Services, 1700 W. Washington St., Phoenix AZ 85007, †; SRI/MF/complete.

TABLES:
[Data are for Arizona, FY80-84, unless otherwise noted.]

REVENUE SUMMARY, INCOME TAXES, AND REVENUE SHARING

1. Gross collections of audit assessments and delinquent tax [by Phoenix and Tucson division offices], FY83-84. (p. 1)

2-3. Gross revenue collected, and net revenue [deposited] to State general fund [both by tax source]. (p. 11-12)

4. Income tax collections [from wage withholding, individual/fiduciary, and corporation sources]. (p. 14)

5. Exemptions, deductions, and credits indexed to inflation [1977-83 tax years]. (p. 15)

6. Selected individual income tax credits [and claimants for energy conservation, property tax, and renter's credits, FY81-84]. (p. 16)

7-8. Distribution of income tax as urban revenue sharing to municipalities, FY84; and urban revenue sharing [total amount distributed], FY75-84. (p. 17)

SALES, SEVERANCE, AND LUXURY TAXES

9-10. Gross sales, use, and severance tax collections [by source]; and distribution of sales tax collections [by recipient government level], FY84. (p. 20)

11. Sales and severance tax rates [by type of taxable activity or industry classification], FY84. (p. 21)

12. Net taxable sales, by sales tax [industry] classification. (p. 22)

13-14. State sales tax distribution to counties and municipalities [for transaction privilege tax and food tax reimbursement], FY84. (p. 23-24)

15-16. Municipal sales tax collection program: collections [and tax rates] by city, FY84; and [total collections and number of cities in program], FY75-84. (p. 25)

17. Luxury tax collections [by type of tobacco and alcoholic beverage product]. (p. 27)

ESTATE AND PROPERTY TAXES

18-19. Estate tax collections [by source]; and distribution of estate tax collections [by fund], FY84. (p. 29)

20. Dept of Revenue property tax collections [flight and private rail car property taxes, and nuclear plan assessment, selected years FY75-84]. (p. 31)

21. Net assessed valuation by county [1982-84]. (p. 32)

22. Property assessment responsibility [by county], 1984. (p. 33)

23. Average property tax rates [by taxing entity (school district, county, State, city, community college, or special district), 1981-84]. (p. 34)

24-25. Summary of primary and secondary tax levies [by taxing entity, by county], 1984-85. (p. 35-36)

S0520
Office of the Secretary of State
ARIZONA

S0520–1   STATE OF ARIZONA OFFICIAL CANVASS, General Election, Nov. 6, 1984
Biennial. Nov. 26, 1984.
15 p. Oversized.
SRI/MF/complete

Biennial report presenting results of the Arizona general election held Nov. 6, 1984. Includes voting for President/Vice President, U.S. Representatives, State senators and representatives, judges, and other State officials; and for 15 propositions, including several constitutional amendments and several measures pertaining to

health care cost containment. Data are shown by county and/or district, and include party affiliation of presidential and legislative candidates.

Also includes voter registration by county.

Previous report, covering 1982 election, is described in SRI 1983 Annual under this number.

Availability: Arizona Office of the Secretary of State, Capitol West Wing, Phoenix AZ 85007, †; SRI/MF/complete.

S0525
Supreme Court
ARIZONA

S0525–1   ARIZONA COURTS: 1984 Caseload, Financial, and Personnel Report
Annual. [1985.] 211 p.
LC 85-641995.
SRI/MF/complete

Annual report, for 1984, on Arizona judicial system, including trial and appellate court caseloads, case dispositions, personnel, and finances, with selected trends from 1975. Covers supreme, appeals, superior, justice of the peace, and municipal courts. Includes data by case type, county, and municipality.

Case types shown are criminal and civil, for most courts, with some additional detail for habeas corpus, unemployment insurance, juvenile, domestic relations, probate, adoption, torts, medical malpractice, contract, eminent domain, small claims, and traffic case types.

Report also includes data on case processing time; probation activity, including offender characteristics, restitution, and public service work hours; judicial system budget for FY85; petitions for domestic violence protection orders; and mental health hearings.

Data are from reports submitted to the supreme court by individual lower courts, surveys of court finances and personnel, and budget statements compiled by the Arizona League of Cities and Towns.

Contains contents listing, judicial organization, and introduction (p. 1-6); and report in 5 sections, with 1 map, 15 charts, and 360 tables (p. 7-211).

This is the 6th annual report.

A companion volume, *1984 Annual Judicial Report,* presenting narrative analysis with summary data, is also available from the Arizona Supreme Court but is not covered by SRI.

Availability: Arizona Supreme Court, Administrative Office of the Courts, State Capitol, 211 W. Wing, Phoenix AZ 85007, †; SRI/MF/complete.

S0632 ARKANSAS
Bank Department

S0632–1   SEVENTIETH REPORT OF THE BANK COMMISSIONER of the State of Arkansas, for the Year Ended June 30, 1984
Annual. Aug. 23, 1984.
221 p.
ISSN 0149-6107.
LC 38-18983.
SRI/MF/complete

Annual report on financial condition of Arkansas State-chartered banks, trust companies, and industrial loan institutions, presenting assets, liabilities, and equity capital, as of June 30, 1984. Data are shown by institution, with aggregate trends from FY50.

Also includes State Bank Dept receipts and disbursements, FY84; number of State and national banks and branches by county; and capital as percent of assets, by bank.

Contains lists of banking officials and facilities interspersed with 7 summary tables (p. 1-28); and 1 balance sheet table repeated for each financial institution, arranged by institution type, alphabetically by city (p. 29-221).

Availability: Arkansas Bank Department, One Capitol Mall, 6D-305, Little Rock AR 72201-1093, †; SRI/MF/complete.

S0652 ARKANSAS
Crime Information Center

S0652–1   CRIME IN ARKANSAS, 1984
Annual. May 1985.
3+103 p.
LC 82-642805.
SRI/MF/complete

Annual report on Arkansas crimes and arrests, by type of offense, 1984, with summary trends from 1975. Includes data by county and reporting agency, and by offender age, sex, and race. Also includes law enforcement employment, and assaults on officers.

Report focuses on 8 Index offenses: murder, rape, robbery, aggravated assault, burglary, larceny/theft, motor vehicle theft, and arson. Arrests are also shown for numerous non-Index offenses.

Data are from State and local agency reports submitted under the Uniform Crime Reporting (UCR) Program.

Contains contents listing (1 p.); description of UCR program, and glossary (p. 1-10); and 7 statistical sections, with 17 charts and 61 tables described below (p. 11-103).

Availability: Arkansas Crime Information Center, Research and Statistics Division, One Capitol Mall, Little Rock AR 72201, †; SRI/MF/complete.

CHARTS AND TABLES:
[Data generally are shown for 1984, unless otherwise noted.]

CRIME SUMMARY
a. Trends in UCR, 1975-84; Index crimes by offense, and number of reporting and contributing agencies, by month; and population of 5 largest metro law enforcement jurisdictions, and aggregate Index crimes vs. State totals. 8 charts and 7 tables. (p. 12-18)

STATE TOTALS
[In addition to the data described below, each individual offense section includes 2 tables and 1 chart showing number of offenses, offense rate per 100,000 population, and clearance rate, 1980-84; most and least frequent month of occurrence and other characteristics; and offenses by month, 1983-84.]

b. Murders by weapon type, circumstance, and victim/offender relationship; and number of victims by age, sex, and race. 1 chart and 7 tables. (p. 22-25)

c. Rapes and attempted rapes; robbery offenses by weapon type, and offenses and value stolen by site; and aggravated assaults by weapon type. 3 charts and 13 tables. (p. 28-37)

d. Burglary offenses and value stolen by classification (day and night, residence and nonresidence), and offenses by type of entry; theft offenses by type and value stolen; motor vehicle thefts by vehicle type, and recoveries by location (same jurisdiction as theft, or other); and arson offenses, clearances, and damaged property value, by property type. 4 charts and 18 tables. (p. 40-54)

BY REPORTING AGENCY
e. Index crimes by offense, total crime rates, and percent cleared, by county and reporting agency. 1 table. (p. 56-61)

STOLEN PROPERTY VALUES
f. Value of property stolen and/or recovered: by property type, 1980-84; by Index offense, with detail by type of robbery, burglary, and theft; and by county and reporting agency. 3 tables. (p. 64-71)

ARRESTS
g. Arrests for Index offenses and 23 other crimes, by offense: by age; by race and sex; summary, 1983-84; and by county and reporting agency. 4 tables. (p. 74-89)

PERSONNEL
h. Sworn and civilian employees by sex, by county and reporting agency. 1 table. (p. 92-97)

i. Officers assaulted, by type of activity, assignment, month, time of assault, injury status, and weapon used; and clearances; with selected comparisons to 1983. 1 chart and 7 tables. (p. 100-103)

S0660 ARKANSAS
Department of Education

S0660–1   STATISTICAL SUMMARY FOR THE PUBLIC SCHOOLS of Arkansas, 1982-84
Annual. Apr. 1985. 95 p.
LC sn 85-23420.
SRI/MF/complete

Annual report on Arkansas public school enrollment, graduates, staff, and finances, 1983/84, with trends from FY03, and selected projections to 1988/89. Also includes data on transportation and food service.

Contains listing of tables and maps (p. 3-4); 1 map, and 38 tables listed below (p. 5-36); and 1 extended table showing pupil enrollment by grade and for special education, and number of teachers, all by school and school district, arranged by county, Oct. 1, 1984 (p. 37-95).

Availability: Arkansas Department of Education, School Statistics and Fiscal Services Office, Administrative Services Division, Four Capitol Mall, Education Bldg., Rm. 202-A, Little Rock AR 72201, †; SRI/MF/complete.

TABLES:
[Tables show Arkansas data for 1982/83-1983/84, unless otherwise noted.]

S0660–1.1: County and Student Data
[Tables [2], [4-5], [7], and [11] include data for special education.]

[1] Selected information pertaining to schools, by county: [enrollment; average daily attendance (ADA); high school graduates; per-child assessed valuation, revenue, and expenditures; and average teacher and administrator salaries]; 1983/84. (p. 5)

[2-3] Public and nonpublic school enrollment data [by grade and county; graduates by county; and nonpublic schools and teachers by grade level (State totals)]; 1983/84. (p. 6-7)

[4-5] Average number belonging and ADA [transported and nontransported, by grade]. (p. 9)

[6] Pupil enrollment trends [by grade, and graduates], 1973/74-1988/89. (p. 10)

[7-8] Enrollment, average number belonging, and ADA; by type of school. (p. 11)

[9] Fall enrollment [by grade and race], 1983-84. (p. 12)

[10-11] High school graduates, and enrollment by grades, [by sex]. (p. 13)

S0660–1.2: Administrative and Transportation Data
[1] Length of school term in days. (p. 13)

[2-3] Number of professional (certificated) positions and average salaries in school districts [by sex]; and nonteaching (noncertificated) positions and average salaries; [regular and Federal, by position]. (p. 14-16)

[4-5] School losses [buildings destroyed/damaged by cause, estimated loss, and insurance coverage], and value of school property [and total insurance coverage, 1983/84]. (p. 17)

[6] School bus accidents [including injuries, deaths, and property damage]. (p. 18)

[7] Selected statistics on transportation [school districts providing busing; buses; pupils transported; expenditures; transportation personnel average salary; and amount of aid from transportation fund]. (p. 19)

[8-10] Number of school districts: based on area; by number of certificated personnel; and by ADA and type of program operated. (p. 20-21)

[11] Number of schools by type of organization. (p. 21)

[12] Number of school districts according to status of professional administration. (p. 22)

[13] Office staff of county board of education [by position]. (p. 22)

S0660–1.3: Finances and Historical Trends

[1] County school administration [receipts and expenditures]. (p. 23)

[2] Free textbook fund [receipts and expenditures, by grade level]. (p. 24-25)

[3] School food service program [receipts and expenditures]. (p. 26)

[4] Building fund [receipts and expenditures] of local school districts. (p. 27)

[5] Net receipts of local school districts [by detailed local, State, Federal, and nonrevenue sources, with balances by fund]. (p. 28)

[6] Expenditures of local school districts [by fund, function, and object]. (p. 29)

[7] Expenditures for elementary/secondary education [by source of funds, 1957/58-1984/85]. (p. 30)

[8-9] Permanent school revolving loan fund and revolving loan certificate proceeds account [balance sheets]. (p. 31)

[10] Public school indebtedness [by type, as of June 30, 1983-84]. (p. 32)

[11-12] Public school grants and aid account and Dept of Education operations account: [statements of receipts and disbursements, FY84]. (p. 33-34)

[13-14] Summary of pertinent school information: [receipts by source, total and per child expenditures, average teacher salaries, per capita apportionment, and number of school districts, FY15-84; and assessed valuation, enumeration by race, enrollment, ADA, length of school term, and teaching positions, generally FY03-84]. (p. 35-36)

S0700   ARKANSAS
Department of Human Services

S0700–1   **SOCIAL SERVICES DIVISION OF DEPARTMENT OF HUMAN SERVICES**
Annual Report, July 1, 1983-June 30, 1984, Arkansas
Annual.   [1984.]   5+123 p.
LC 73-646186.
SRI/MF/complete

Annual report on Arkansas public assistance program case activity, services, recipient characteristics, and payments, by program, FY84, with selected data by county and trends from 1937. Includes data on AFDC, medical and social services, and food programs.

Contains organizational charts and contents listing (4 p.); expenditure and cost summaries, with 3 charts and 4 tables (p. 1-4); and program narrative summaries, with 11 charts and 55 tables (p. 5-123).

All tables, and charts presenting data not covered in tables, are listed below.

Availability: Arkansas Department of Human Services, Social Services Division, Research and Statistics, Seventh and Main Sts., PO Box 1437, Little Rock AR 72203, †; SRI/MF/complete.

CHARTS AND TABLES:

[Data are for Arkansas, FY84 or as of June 30, 1984, unless otherwise noted. Data by county usually include totals for 5 State areas. Several tables show separate data for child and adult recipients.

Recipient categories include Aid to the Aged, Blind, and Disabled; AFDC; foster care children; and persons under age 18.]

S0700–1.1: Expenditures and Cost Summary, AFDC, and Child Support Enforcement

EXPENDITURES AND COSTS

[Tables [1-4] show State and Federal expenditures or costs.]

[1-2] Statement of expenditures [assistance and administration, by program]; and total expenditures [by program type and for administration]. (p. 1-2)

[3-4] Total program assistance and administrative costs; and administrative cost by program. (p. 3-4)

AFDC

[5] Monthly average of cases, persons, and payment. (p. 7)

[6-7] Families receiving money payments, and total amount of payment, FY84; and families and grant amounts, June 1984; [both by county]. (p. 8-11)

[8] Distribution of money grant payments [by grant amount and number of children in case]. (p. 12)

[9-12] Children and adults receiving and deemed eligible for AFDC, by age group [and sex, by county]. (p. 13-20)

[13] Applications for assistance [received, approved, and denied, by county]. (p. 21-22)

[14] Reasons for closing cases. (p. 23)

[15] Average monthly number [of] families receiving money payment and average monthly payment per case, FY38-84. (p. 24)

[16] Cases and grant amount, FY80-84. [chart] (p. 25)

CHILD SUPPORT ENFORCEMENT

[17] Cases and collections [by AFDC status; and State share of collections and expenditures, and net revenue to State; quarterly]. (p. 29)

S0700–1.2: Medical Services

PAYMENTS AND RECIPIENTS

[Tables [1-4] show data by type of medical service, generally by recipient category.]

[1] Medical vendor payments. (p. 32)

[2-3] Recipients of Medicaid services; and recipients of medical services, by age and sex. (p. 33-34)

[4] Services for medical needy [recipients and payments]. (p. 35)

[5] Medical services: expenditures by service, monthly average [by county]. (p. 36-38)

[6] Distribution of Medicaid expenditures by type of service, FY80-84. [chart] (p. 39)

[7] Number using [selected] medical services, FY80 and FY84. [chart] (p. 40)

[8-9] Medical expenditures, and number of medical eligibles and number receiving medical services, FY80-84. [charts] (p. 41-42)

ELIGIBILITY

[10] Percent of population eligible for medical services [and number eligible and population, by county]. (p. 44-45)

[11-12] Medical eligibles [SSI/no grant and medically needy, for Aid to the Aged, Blind, and Disabled; grant and medically needy for AFDC; and persons under age 18, and foster care children; all by county]. (p. 46-49)

MISCELLANEOUS

[13] Third party liability collections [FY80-84]. [chart] (p. 51)

[14] Average cost per [drug] prescription [July 1978-83]. [chart] (p. 55)

[15] Crippled children's services [including cases, clinics, hospital days, and expenditures by object, FY83-84]. (p. 57)

[16] [Long-term care rates for level of patient care by facility classification, 1st and 2nd half FY84.] (p. 58)

[17] [Long-term care Medicaid and non-Medicaid facilities and beds, and Medicaid recipients, by facility classification.] (p. 59)

[18-19] Long-term care cases and vendor payments [by recipient category, monthly; and by level of care, facility classification, and county]. (p. 62-72)

[20] Applications for long-term care [received, approved, and denied, by selected recipient category, by county]. (p. 73-75)

S0700–1.3: Food and Social Services, and Miscellaneous

FOOD STAMP PROGRAM

[1-2] Applications for assistance [received, approved, and denied]; and participation [cases and persons, and value of coupons issued; by county]. (p. 77-80)

[3] Participation, average number [of] cases and persons per month, FY75-84. [chart] (p. 82)

COMMODITY DISTRIBUTION AND CHILD NUTRITION PROGRAMS

[4-5] Commodity distribution: school and institution participation [amount and dollar value by commodity, with total schools, school districts, and institutions served, and participants]. (p. 84-85)

[6-7] Child nutrition programs: [State administrative expenses and program funds, institutions and facilities involved, and meals provided, by program]. (p. 86-87)

SOCIAL SERVICES SUMMARY

[8-9] Purchased services: [recipients and cost, total and for selected recipient categories, medical and income eligibles, and without regard to income, all by service type]. (p. 89-91)

[10-11] Direct services [recipients, total and for persons not identified as active service cases, selected recipient categories, Medicaid and income eligibles, child welfare service, and without regard to income, all by service type]. (p. 92-94)

SUBSTITUTE CARE SERVICES FOR CHILDREN

[12] Characteristics of children in foster care [race (including American Indian, Spanish American, Oriental, Indo-Chinese, and other/ unknown); length of time in foster care; age; legal status; location; reason for entry; and sex]. (p. 95)

[13] Number of children for whom board payments were made, by source of funds [State and Title IV-E, monthly]. (p. 96)

[14] Reasons for discharge from foster care [1982-84]. (p. 96)

INTERSTATE COMPACT ACTIVITIES

[15] Report [on Interstate Compact on Juveniles activities involving runaways and juvenile offenders]. (p. 97)

[16] Interstate Compact on the Placement of Children: [activities including placements in- and out-of-State]. (p. 98)

SUPPORTIVE SERVICES

[17] [Recipients of supportive services to children and families in their own homes.] (p. 99)

[18] [Comprehensive maternity care services for unmarried parents, including infants released for adoption.] (p. 100)

CHILD DEVELOPMENT UNIT

[19] [Child Care Licensing Unit/Child Care Facility Review Board licensing activities.] (p. 106)

HOME ENERGY ASSISTANCE PROGRAM

[20] [Households served and benefit expenditures, by season.] (p. 108)

[21-23] Home energy assistance summer and winter programs [denials, approvals, and persons served, by county]. (p. 109-114)

MISCELLANEOUS

[24] Categorical assistance cases [by selected recipient category], Jan. 1937-84. (p. 116)

[25] Total State population [by county, 1980]. (p. 117)

[26] Percentages by race of recipient population [by county and selected recipient category]. (p. 118-123)

S0712 ARKANSAS
Insurance Department

S0712-1 103rd ANNUAL REPORT, 1983, State of Arkansas Insurance Department
Annual. [1985.]   259 p.
SRI/MF/complete

Annual report on Arkansas insurance industry financial condition and underwriting activity, by company and type of insurance, 1983. Covers assets, liabilities, capital, and surplus; investment income; premiums written, earned, and/or received; insurance in force; losses incurred or claims paid; loss- and expense-premium ratios; and operating and underwriting profit/loss; for companies based in Arkansas and elsewhere.

Data are shown, as applicable, for stock and mutual fire/casualty insurance companies; reciprocals/inter-insurance exchanges; farmers mutual aid assns; Lloyds underwriters; title insurance, stock life insurance, stipulated premium plan, mutual assessment, and prepaid legal insurance companies; nonprofit hospital/medical service corporations; fraternal benefit societies; and life/ accident/health and property/liability insurance companies.

Data on property/liability insurance include additional breakdowns by detailed line of coverage, including medical malpractice, workers compensation, automobile, and surety.

Also includes data on Insurance Dept activities and finances, including companies licensed, Guaranty Fund assessments and payments to insolvent companies, company and agent sanctions and penalties imposed, detailed receipts and disbursements, and firemen and police officer relief/pension fund tax premiums and payments by city, various periods 1979-84.

Contains contents listing (p. 3); Insurance Dept activities, with 8 tables (p. 4-60); and 17 company financial tables including 2 with directories (p. 61-259).

Availability: Arkansas Insurance Department, 400 University Tower Bldg., Little Rock AR 72204, †; SRI/MF/complete.

S0715 ARKANSAS
Judicial Department

S0715-1 REPORT OF THE JUDICIAL DEPARTMENT OF ARKANSAS, FY84
Annual. [1985.]   ii+134 p.
LC 67-63796.
SRI/MF/complete

Annual report on Arkansas judicial system, including trial and appellate court caseloads and case dispositions, FY84. Covers supreme, appeals, circuit, chancery, probate, and limited jurisdiction courts. Includes data by case type and court location, and selected trends from the 1970s.

Case types shown are criminal and civil, for most courts, with some additional detail for domestic relations, juvenile, guardianship, adoption, commitment, illegitimacy, small claims, and traffic case types.

Also includes data on case processing time; judges; public defender caseloads; costs assessed and fines collected in limited jurisdiction courts; and judicial system appropriations for FY85.

Data are from dept records.

Contains contents listing (p. ii); and foreword and narrative report, interspersed with 2 maps, 9 charts, 51 tables, and personnel directories (p. 1-134).

Previous report was entitled *Six Month Transition Report from Calendar Year to Fiscal Year Annual Reporting, Jan. 1-June 30, 1983;* for description, see SRI 1984 Annual under this number.

Availability: Arkansas Judicial Department, Justice Bldg., Little Rock AR 72201, †; SRI/ MF/complete.

S0720 ARKANSAS
Department of Labor

S0720-1 ARKANSAS LABOR FORCE STATISTICS: Annual Averages, State and Areas, 1975-84
Annual. July 1985.
vi+36 p.
LC 84-623119.
SRI/MF/complete

Annual report on Arkansas civilian labor force, by employment status and locale, 1975-84. Includes total employment and unemployment; agricultural employment; domestic service/self-employed/unpaid family workers; and nonagricultural manufacturing and nonmanufacturing wage/salary employment; by MSA, county, and labor area. Data were compiled by the Arkansas Labor Dept.

Contains introduction, contents listing, and definitions (p. ii-vi); and 1 map, and 1 table repeated for State and each locale (p. 1-36).

Availability: Arkansas Department of Labor, Employment Security Division, Research and Analysis Section, PO Box 2981, Little Rock AR 72203-2981, †; SRI/MF/complete.

S0720-3 ANNUAL PLANNING INFORMATION, FY85-86, Arkansas
Annual. May 1985.
xix+237 p.
LC 80-643449.
SRI/MF/complete

Annual planning report, for FY85-86, identifying Arkansas population groups most in need of employment services. Includes data on population and labor force characteristics, personal income, part-time workers, unemployment insurance claimants and exhaustees, economically disadvantaged, and vocational school enrollment; by Service Delivery Area (SDA), MSA, and county, various years 1980-86. Also includes data on job service applicants, and veteran population.

Data are primarily from State Employment Security Division, Lawrence Berkeley Laboratory, and Census Bureau.

Contains listings of contents and tables (p. iii-xix); State report, with 18 tables (p. 1-23); SDA reports, with 143 tables (p. 24-187); MSA reports, with 40 tables (p. 188-227); and appendix, with 6 tables (p. 231-237). All tables are listed below.

Availability: Arkansas Department of Labor, Employment Security Division, Research and Analysis Section, PO Box 2981, Little Rock AR 72203-2981, †; SRI/MF/complete.

TABLES:
[Data are shown for Arkansas, FY85-86, unless otherwise noted. Data by race often include American Indian, Asian, and Spanish origin or Hispanic.]

S0720–3.1: State Data

POPULATION, INCOME, AND LABOR FORCE

1-4. Civilian and total population, 1980; and projected civilian population, 1985-86; by race, sex, and age groups. (p. 2-4)

5. Civilian labor force [and unemployment] by race, age groups, and sex, FY80 and FY85-86. (p. 5)

6. Civilian labor force status by race and sex, 1980. (p. 6)

7. Total personal and per capita income, 1980 and projections for 1985-86. (p. 7)

8. Workers employed part-time for economic reasons [and long-term and total unemployed, all by sex and race]. (p. 8)

9. Veteran population [total and Vietnam era], 1980 and 1985-86. (p. 9)

10. Population potentially eligible for JTPA [Job Training Partnership Act] programs by age group, race, and sex. (p. 10)

ECONOMICALLY DISADVANTAGED

11. Poverty guidelines for economically disadvantaged, continental U.S., FY85. (p. 11)

12. Economically disadvantaged population by age groups. (p. 12)

13-14. Total civilian and economically disadvantaged populations by age groups, race, and sex; and by target groups [including veterans, ex-offenders, welfare recipients, school dropouts, unemployment insurance claimants, handicapped, and single head of household with dependent children]. (p. 13-14)

JOB SERVICE APPLICANTS AND EDUCATION

15. Characteristics of job service applicants active any time during the fiscal year [by age, race, sex, and education], as of June 30, 1984. (p. 15)

16. Years of school completed, persons 25 years of age and over [by educational attainment], by race, 1980. (p. 16)

17-18. Secondary and State school vocational/technical enrollment and completions [by detailed occupational program], school year 1983/84. (p. 17-23)

S0720–3.2: SDAs and MSAs

SDAs
[Tables 19-33 show data for Little Rock SDA.]

19-30. [Tables 1-8, 10, and 12-14, described above, are repeated.] (p. 25-35)

31. Unemployment insurance exhaustees, 1983. (p. 36)

32-33. [Tables 16-17, described above, are repeated.] (p. 37-40)

34-48. [Tables 19-33 are repeated for Central SDA, with selected additional detail by county.] (p. 42-58)

49. [Table 18, described above, is repeated for Central SDA.] (p. 59)

50-161. [Tables 34-49 are repeated for 7 additional SDAs.] (p. 61-187)

MSAs
162-201. [Tables 1-5, 7-8, 12, 16, and 31 are repeated for 4 MSAs, with selected detail by county.] (p. 189-227)

S0720–3.3: Appendix Tables
[Tables 1-3 show data by county; tables 4-5 show data by SDA.]

1-2. Civilian and veteran population, 1980 and 1985-86. (p. 231-233)

3. Estimated number of individuals without high school diploma or equivalency. (p. 234)

4-5. Persons below poverty level by race, and educational status of unemployed youth [high school graduates and nongraduates, by age group], 1980. (p. 235-236)

6. Job openings and active applicants by occupational category, [by] employment security division local offices, June 30, 1984. (p. 237)

S0727 **ARKANSAS**
State
Library

S0727–1 **ARKANSAS PUBLIC LIBRARY STATISTICS**
Annual. 1983. iii+71 p.
LC 84-622202.
SRI/MF/complete

Annual report on Arkansas public library finances, holdings, circulation, and staff, by system, FY82 and/or FY83.

Presents library income by source (county and city millage and other income, State aid, gifts/donations, revenue sharing, and grants) and expenses by function (salaries/benefits, maintenance/operation, and library materials), FY83; and hours of operation, stationary and mobile units, full- and part-time staff, FTE staff, items owned, and circulation, FY82-83; all by regional and local system, arranged by population size and taxing authority.

Also includes 1980 population for each system and for 3 counties with no library service.

Data are from reports of library administrators and 1980 census.

Contains contents listing (1 p.); introduction with text statistics and 1 map (p. i-iii); directory of public library headquarters (p. 1-5); 2 statistical sections, with 3 tables (p. 8-19); and directory of public library board members (p. 23-71).

This is the 1st edition of the report.

Availability: Arkansas State Library, Extension Services, One Capitol Mall, Little Rock AR 72201, †; SRI/MF/complete.

S0737 **ARKANSAS**
Oil and Gas Commission

S0737–1 **ARKANSAS OIL AND GAS**
Statistical Bulletin
Monthly. Approx. 15 p.
LC 52-35586.
SRI/MF/complete, shipped quarterly

Monthly report on Arkansas crude oil and natural gas production and disposition, and in-State refining stocks, receipts, products manufactured, and residue disposition. Data are compiled by the Arkansas Oil and Gas Commission from monthly field reports.

Report usually is issued approximately 10 months after month of coverage. Publication was temporarily suspended following the report for Dec. 1983; report for Jan. 1984 was issued in Sept. 1985.

Contains narrative summary, and 8 monthly tables listed below.

Availability: Arkansas Oil and Gas Commission, 314 E. Oak St., El Dorado AR 71730, †; SRI/MF/complete, shipped quarterly.

Issues reviewed during 1985: Dec. 1983-Jan. 1984 (D) (Vol. 44, No. 12; Vol. 45, No. 1).

MONTHLY TABLES:
[Unless otherwise noted, data are shown for month of coverage.]

[1] Consolidated review [crude oil/condensate production, pipeline runs, natural gas reported, gas pipeline and gasoline plant intake, and products manufactured; average daily totals for month of coverage and same month of preceding year.]

[2] South Arkansas oil and gas report [production by field].

[3] Oil pipeline report [receipts, stocks, imports, and deliveries].

[4] Disposition of gas [lease use, pipelines, vented, injected, and gasoline plants].

[5] Refinery report [including stocks, receipts, and dispositions].

[6] Gasoline plant report [gas received by source, products manufactured, and disposition of residue].

[7-8] North Arkansas gas report [production by field]; and disposition of gas [pipelines and drilling purposes].

S0757   ARKANSAS
Public Service Commission

**S0757–1   ARKANSAS PUBLIC
SERVICE COMMISSION
Fiftieth Annual Report, Year
Ending Dec. 31, 1984**
Annual.   Jan. 31, 1985.
2+35 p.
LC 52-26080.
SRI/MF/complete

Annual report presenting Arkansas public utility
regulatory data for 1984, and financial and operating data for 1983, by utility type and company. Utility types are electric, gas, water/sewer,
and telephone.

Includes data on Arkansas Public Service
Commission Utilities Division staff, complaints
received, finances, and regulatory orders issued;
and utility revenues, plant investment, and customers and sales by consuming sector.

Data are from commission records and company reports.

Contains contents listing (1 p.); introduction,
and commission activities report, with text statistics and 3 tables (p. 1-16); and utility company
statistics, with 8 tables (p. 17-35).

Availability: Arkansas Public Service Commission, Utilities Division, 1000 Center Bldg., PO
Box C-400, Little Rock AR 72203, ‡; SRI/MF/
complete.

S0780   ARKANSAS
Office of the
Treasurer

**S0780–1   BIENNIAL REPORT OF THE
TREASURER OF STATE of
the State of Arkansas for
the Biennial Period
Beginning July 1, 1982, and
Ending June 30, 1984**
Biennial.   Jan. 14, 1985.
xviii+378 p.
LC 82-646964.
SRI/MF/complete

Biennial report on financial condition of Arkansas State government for FY83-84, presenting
fund balances, receipts by source, interfund
transfers, and disbursements, for over 300 institutional, departmental, and other funds arranged
alphabetically. Includes county and municipal
aid fund revenues by locality.

Also includes data on State government bank
deposits and investments, by type and institution; and safekeeping account holdings.

Data are compiled by the State Treasurer's Office.

Contains index (p. viii-xv); 20 tables (3 p., p.
1-89); and 1 extended table covering activity of
each fund (p. 90-378).

For description of previous report, see SRI
1983 Annual under this number.

Availability: Arkansas Office of the Treasurer,
State Capitol, Rm. 220, Little Rock AR 72201,
†; SRI/MF/complete.

S0815   CALIFORNIA
Office of the
Controller

**S0815–1   ANNUAL REPORT OF THE
STATE OF CALIFORNIA for
the Fiscal Year Ended June
30, 1984**
Annual.   [1985.]
A33+615 p.
LC 10-11500.
SRI/MF/complete

Annual report on financial condition of California State government, presenting assets,
liabilities, reserves, and fund balances; revenues
by source; and expenditures; for general, governmental cost, professions and vocations, working
capital and revolving, public service enterprise,
bond, retirement, and trust and agency funds;
FY84 with selected trends from FY75.

Also includes detailed appropriations and expenditures, by agency and function, for general
and all other governmental cost funds.

Also includes data on State investments by
type; bonded debt; bank and/or savings and loan
assn account balances outside of State treasury
system; highway users tax apportionment; and
receipts from Federal Government, by State
agency.

Contains contents listing and transmittal letter
(p. A2-A3); introduction (p. A4-A5); notes, 4
summary statements, and 5 trend charts and tables (p. A8-A33); 4 sections, with 33 financial
statements (p. 2-604); and index (p. 606-615).

Availability: California Office of the Controller, Accounting Division, PO Box 1019, Sacramento CA 95805, †; SRI/MF/complete.

S0830   CALIFORNIA
Employment
Development Department

**S0830–1   CALIFORNIA LABOR
MARKET BULLETIN**
Monthly.   4 p.
SRI/MF/complete, shipped
quarterly

Monthly report on California employment and
unemployment, earnings, and hours. Data, compiled by the State in cooperation with the U.S.
Labor Dept, are shown variously by age group,
race, sex, industry, and county. Report is issued
2-6 months after month of coverage.

Contains narrative summary; and 5 monthly
tables, listed below.

Availability: California Employment Development Department, Employment Data and Research Division, Estimates and Economic
Research Group, 800 Capitol Mall, Sacramento
CA 95814, †; SRI/MF/complete, shipped quarterly.

Issues reviewed during 1985: Sept. 1984-July
1985 (D).

MONTHLY TABLES:
[Most tables show data for month of coverage,
previous 1-2 months, and same month of previous year.]

1. Employment and unemployment [and
civilian labor force; seasonally adjusted and
unadjusted].
2. Employment status of the working age
population [by age group (16-19 and 20/over),
sex, and race].
3. Earnings and hours of production/related
workers in manufacturing.
4. Monthly wage/salary employment analysis
[by industry group].
5. Monthly labor force data [by employment
status] for counties.

S0835   CALIFORNIA
Board of
Equalization

**S0835–1   ANNUAL REPORT, 1983-84:
California State Board of
Equalization**
Annual.   Dec. 31, 1984.
80+App 44 p.
ISSN 0068-5801.
LC 10-11499.
SRI/MF/complete

Annual report, for FY84, on operations of the
California Board of Equalization, established to
equalize property assessments among counties.
Covers board revenue by source and expenditures by function, sales/use tax by kind of business and county, other tax revenues, and revenue
distributions to counties and cities. Also covers
assessed property values and tax exemptions for
FY85. Selected data are also shown by company.

Data are compiled from board records.

Contents:

a. Contents listing and 1 map. (p. 2-4)

b. Narrative report in 8 chapters with 1 illustrative chart, 8 summary tables, and the following: 2 tables (p. 44) showing business tax field
audits, costs, and amounts recovered, by type
of tax; and 1 table (p. 72) showing new auto
and truck registrations, and taxable sales of
new car dealers; FY84 and trends. (p. 5-80)

c. Statistical appendix, with contents listing,
and 34 detailed tables listed below. (p. iii,
A1-A42)

This is the 135th report.

Availability: California Board of Equalization,
PO Box 1799, Sacramento CA 95808, †; SRI/
MF/complete.

DETAILED TABLES:

S0835–1.1: Administrative Data
[Tables 1-3A begin "Summary of..."]
1. Expenditures of the board [by function,
FY83-84]. (p. A1)
2. Revenues from taxes administered by the
board, [selected years] FY74-84. (p. A2)
3A-3B. Total costs of performing board functions [by program]; and revenues and ratios of
board expenditures and total costs to revenues
from assessments made by the board [by tax
type]; FY83-84. (p. A3)

S0835–1.2: Property Taxes

[Tables show data for FY85, unless otherwise noted. Tables 5-10 and 14-15 show data by county.]

4. Summary of assessed values of property subject to local general property taxes, assessment ratios, and average tax rates [by assessment agency and type of property], FY75-85. (p. A4)

5-7. Assessed value of State- and county-assessed property subject to general property taxes, inclusive of homeowners' exemption, by class of property. (p. A5-A7)

8. Number of veterans' exemptions and exempt value of veterans', college, church, religious, and welfare exemptions. (p. A8-A9)

9. Gross assessed value of State- and county-assessed property, number of homeowners' exemptions, exempt value by type of exemption, and net assessed value subject to general property taxes. (p. A10)

10. Net State- and county-assessed value of property subject to general property taxes on the secured and unsecured rolls. (p. A11)

11. Assessed value of State- and county-assessed property subject to general property taxes, inclusive of homeowners' exemption, by incorporated cities. (p. A12-A14)

12A-12B. Assessed value of property assessed by the State Board of Equalization: by type of company; and subject to local taxation, by company. (p. A15-A17)

13. [Temporarily suspended.]

14. FY84 general property tax levies as compiled for computation of the average tax rate. (p. A19)

15. FY83 general property tax dollar [distribution among city, county, school, and other districts]. (p. A20)

16. [Discontinued.]

17A. Assessed value of private cars [rolling stock of companies that are not railroads], assessed by the State Board of Equalization and subject to exclusive State taxation, by company. (p. A21)

17B. Private car tax assessments, tax rates, and tax levies [and average number of cars, selected periods] FY38-85. (p. A22)

S0835–1.3: Sales/Use Taxes

[Tables 19-21B show data for FY84.]

18. State sales/use tax collections and number of permits, FY33-84. (p. A23)

19-20. State sales/use tax statistics [taxable transactions, State sales tax, and number of permits], by type of business; and [taxable sales of retail stores and all outlets, State tax, and number of permits], by county. (p. A24-A25)

21A. Revenues distributed to cities and counties from local sales/use taxes and the State cigarette tax [by county and city]. (p. A26-A28)

21B. Revenues distributed to counties from county transportation tax [by county]. (p. A29)

21C. Local sales/use tax rates imposed by California cities on July 1, 1984 [by county and city]. (p. A29)

22. Local sales taxes, distributions, and administrative charges to cities and counties, FY57-84. (p. A30)

S0835–1.4: Highway Taxes

23. Gasoline and jet fuel tax statistics [taxable distributions, revenue, and, for gasoline only, refunds and tax-paying distributors], FY23-84. (p. A31)

24. Taxable distributions of gasoline and tax assessments, by distributor, FY83-84. (p. A32)

25. Diesel fuel and liquefied petroleum gases statistics [taxable distributions, total tax, self-assessed taxes, active permits, and tax paid at reduced rate by transit districts], FY37-84. (p. A33)

26. [Discontinued.]

S0835–1.5: Alcoholic Beverage and Cigarette Taxes

27. Beer, wine, and distilled spirits excise tax collections, FY32-84. (p. A34)

28-29. Apparent and per capita consumption of beer, wines, and distilled spirits, FY35-84. (p. A35-A36)

30A-30B. Cigarette tax revenue [including amount set aside for cities/counties]; and cigarette distributions and per capita consumption; FY60-84. (p. A37)

S0835–1.6: Insurance Taxes and Total Tax Collections

INSURANCE TAXES

31. 1983 taxable insurance premiums and total taxes assessed in 1984, by company. (p. A38-A39)

32. Summary of insurance taxes assessed in 1983-84 against companies authorized to do business in California, by type of insurer. (p. A40)

33. Insurance tax assessments against licensed insurers, tax rate, taxes on premiums, local property tax credits allowed, taxes on ocean marine business, and total taxes assessed, 1911-84. (p. A41)

TOTAL TAXES

34. Federal, State, and local tax collections, FY51-84. (p. A42)

S0840   CALIFORNIA
Department of
Finance

S0840–1   CALIFORNIA ECONOMIC INDICATORS
Bimonthly. Approx. 25 p.
ISSN 0364-2895.
LC 76-646945.
SRI/MF/complete

Bimonthly report on California economic indicators and developments. Most data are current to 1-2 months preceding cover date, and are from reports of State and Federal agencies, professional assns, and financial institutions.

Issues generally contain:

a. Narrative review of recent economic developments; 18 trend charts; 2 bimonthly economic indicator tables, listed below; and occasionally, additional charts or text tables showing revised data for indicators.

b. Chronology of significant economic events, 1969 to month of publication; and list of data sources.

c. Bimonthly table (beginning in Jan. 1985 Issue) showing U.S. business cycle peak and trough dates, and duration of expansion and contraction periods, 1854-1982.

An annual article on economic outlook for U.S. and California usually appears in the Jan. issue.

Annual economic outlook article is described, as it appears, under "Statistical Feature." Non-statistical features are not covered.

Availability: California Department of Finance, Financial Research Unit, PO Box 151, Sacramento CA 95801, $8.00 per yr.; SRI/MF/complete.

Issues reviewed during 1985: Nov. 1984-Sept. 1985 (P).

TABLES:
[Table [1] shows data monthly for 4 consecutive months ending 1-2 months prior to cover date, and for 2 latest months in same period of previous year. Table [2] generally shows data monthly for current year ending 1-2 months prior to cover date, and for 3-4 previous years.]

[1] Current California economic data [including employment by industry division and unemployment; manufacturing hours and earnings; retail sales and new auto registrations; new incorporations; CPI for State and 3 largest cities; petroleum, cement, steel, and redwood mill production; and authorized residential construction volume and nonresidential construction value].

[2] Basic data for California economic series [approximately 20 indicators, including help-wanted advertisements in Los Angeles area; manufacturing hours, overtime, and employment; insured unemployment initial claims and average duration; personal income; wages/salaries for mining/manufacturing/construction; taxable sales; DOD prime contract value; net new savings in savings and loan assns; and electricity production].

STATISTICAL FEATURE:

S0840–1.601: Jan. 1985

ECONOMIC OUTLOOK FOR 1985-86, ANNUAL FEATURE

(p. 1-2) Annual article on U.S. and California economic outlook through 1986. Data were prepared for Governor's FY86 budget. Includes 1 table showing the following for 1985-86:

a. U.S. real GNP and major components (personal consumption expenditures, gross private domestic investment, net exports, and government purchases of goods/services), current dollar GNP, GNP deflator, and CPI.

b. California and U.S. personal income, pretax corporate profits, wage/salary employment and unemployment rate, housing starts or units authorized, new car sales or registrations; and California labor force by employment status, and total taxable sales.

S0840–2   CALIFORNIA STATISTICAL ABSTRACT, 1984
Annual. [1985.] viii+229 p.
LC 58-63807.
SRI/MF/complete

Annual compilation of detailed social, governmental, and economic statistics for California. Data are for various years 1970s-83, with population trends from 1940.

Report is designed to present a comprehensive overview of the State. Extensive socioeconomic, demographic, and geographic breakdowns are shown, as applicable, for most topics. These breakdowns include data by city, county and other sub-State area, MSA, urban-rural status, commodity, government agency, income, industry, occupation, age, marital status, race/ethnicity, and sex. Comparisons to total U.S. are also occasionally included.

Most data are from reports of State and Federal agencies, public utilities, and financial institutions. Data sources appear beneath each table.

Contains contents listing, introduction, and list of MSAs (p. v-viii); 164 tables arranged in 15 sections, described below (p. 1-219); and appendix, with list of data sources, and index (p. 221-229). Each section begins with a summary description of data sources.

This is the 25th edition of the *Abstract*.

Availability: California Department of Finance, Financial, Economic, and Demographic Research Unit, 1025 P St., Rm. 83, Sacramento CA 95814-5790, †; SRI/MF/complete.

TABLE SECTIONS:

S0840–2.1: Section A: Area, Geography, and Climate

(p. 1-10) Contains 6 tables. Includes land and water areas; acreages of Federal real property, and national and State parks and other recreation areas; and elevations and climatological data, by weather station.

S0840–2.2: Section B: Population

(p. 11-20) Contains 4 tables. Includes births, deaths, and migration; and population since 1940.

S0840–2.3: Section C: Labor Force and Employment

(p. 21-51) Contains 21 tables. Includes labor force by employment status; nonfarm employment, with detail for women; manufacturing, State government, and agricultural employment; employment covered by unemployment insurance code; production worker employment, and average and overtime hours and earnings; and workers compensation underwriting data including covered disabling work injuries/illnesses.

Also includes employment service applicant characteristics; registered apprentices; union membership; work injury/illness incidence; and work stoppages, workers involved, and days idle.

S0840–2.4: Section D: Income and Cost-of-Living

(p. 53-62) Contains 9 tables. Includes personal and corporate income tax returns filed, taxes assessed, and taxable income; personal income by source; and CPI by item.

S0840–2.5: Section E: Health and Welfare

(p. 63-85) Contains 25 tables. Includes live births, marriages, and dissolutions; deaths by cause and notifiable disease cases; licensed health facilities and bed capacity; rehabilitated client characteristics, and rehabilitation benefits and costs, by disability; institutionalized narcotic addict population received and released, offenses, and outpatient status; and State mental hospital admissions, population, deaths, and discharges, by institution.

Also includes adoptions; general home relief, AFDC, foster care, and food stamp program participants and expenditures; disability and unemployment insurance activity; employment, establishments, and wages covered under unemployment insurance code; unemployment fund transactions and balance; and Medi-Cal program and SSI caseloads and payments.

S0840–2.6: Section F: Education

(p. 87-93) Contains 6 tables. Includes higher education enrollment and degrees; public school apportionments and revenues by source; public and private schools, enrollment, personnel, and graduates; and libraries, expenses, staff, books, and operations.

S0840–2.7: Section G: Resource Industries

(p. 95-143) Contains 30 tables. Includes irrigated acreage and reservoir storage capacity; major dams and reservoirs, and specifications; municipal water supply; State Water Project water deliveries and power plant generation; agricultural prices received, cash receipts, and production; farms and farmland, harvested acreage, value, and yield; value of leading farm exports; and livestock and poultry inventories.

Also includes timber production; sawtimber volume; forest land ownership and acreage managed by U.S. Forest Service; fishing and hunting licenses; commercial fish landings; mineral production and value; mineral industry establishments, employees, value added, and capital expenditures; and oil and gas wells, and oil, gas, and water production.

S0840–2.8: Section H: Manufacturing

(p. 145-154) Contains 8 tables. Includes manufacturing firms, employment, payroll, value added, capital expenditures, and production workers, hours, and wages; aerospace industry employment; DOD prime contracts to California firms; and energy purchases and use by manufacturers.

S0840–2.9: Section I: Construction

(p. 155-160) Contains 6 tables. Includes new housing units authorized and value; nonresidential valuation; housing units by value or rent; and general housing occupancy characteristics.

S0840–2.10: Section J: Transportation and Public Utilities

(p. 161-172) Contains 13 tables. Includes State highway and public road mileage; taxable motor, jet, and diesel fuel gallonage; motor vehicle registrations; licensed drivers and accident involvement; traffic accidents, injuries, and fatalities; total and airborne export and import values; electric power production; and telephones, and average monthly gas, electric, and telephone bills.

S0840–2.11: Section K: Trade and Services

(p. 173-181) Contains 7 tables. Includes taxable retail sales; alcoholic beverage consumption; wholesale and retail trade establishments, sales, and payrolls; retail trade employment; and licensed professional and vocational personnel.

S0840–2.12: Section L: Banking and Finance

(p. 183-185) Contains 2 tables. Includes commercial banks and savings and loan assns, and, as applicable, assets, loans, deposits, branches, savings, and net worth.

S0840–2.13: Section M: Public Finance

(p. 187-205) Contains 18 tables. Includes Federal aid payments, revenues, expenditures, and tax collections; State bonds outstanding, revenues by source, and expenditures by function; and receipts, payments, and bonded indebtedness, by type of local jurisdiction.

Also includes assessed property value, and property tax allocations, levies, average rate, and distribution by type of local jurisdiction; and senior citizen property tax and rental assistance.

S0840–2.14: Section N: Law Enforcement

(p. 207-211) Contains 5 tables. Includes felons received, by offense; and prison population and juvenile wards received and released, and parole status.

S0840–2.15: Section O: Elections

(p. 213-219) Contains 4 tables. Includes voter registration by party; and votes cast, by office and candidate.

S0840–3   ECONOMIC REPORT OF THE GOVERNOR, 1985, California
Annual.   Apr. 15, 1985.
ix+66+App 48 p.
LC 64-63853.
SRI/MF/complete

Annual report, for 1985, on the economic condition of California. Covers population, employment and earnings, income, government finances, and business activity. Data are generally current to 1982-84, with selected data for 1985-86, and trends from the 1960s.

Data are compiled from reports of Census Bureau, State agencies, and private sources.

Contains highlights and contents listing (p. iv-ix); overview (p. 1-2); narrative report in 8 sections, with text data and 40 tables described below, and 16 charts (p. 1-66); and statistical appendix, with table listing, and 38 tables listed below (p. A3-A48).

Availability: California Department of Finance, Financial, Economic, and Demographic Research Unit, 1025 P St., Rm. 325, Sacramento CA 95814, †; SRI/MF/complete.

TABLES AND TEXT DATA:
[Data are shown for California, unless otherwise noted.]

S0840–3.1: Narrative Report

a. Employment: by industry division and selected major group, including service industry employment by kind of business, and State and local education and other government employment (with detail by local government type), mostly 1983-84; unemployment rates for top 9-10 urban and rural counties, Sept. 1984; labor force by employment status, 1983-84; and occupations ranked by projected change in employment, 1980-90 period. Text data and 8 tables. (p. 4-13)

b. Collective bargaining: union membership by economic area, 1983; and major wage negotiations, with industries and workers involved, monthly 1985. 2 tables. (p. 14-15)

c. Inflation: CPI changes, by item, and monthly changes, for 3 California SMSAs compared to State and/or U.S.; and percent change in selected measures of U.S. inflation, including personal consumption expenditures; various years 1972-86. Text data and 3 tables. (p. 19-21)

d. Income and trade: personal income by major source, 1983-86; per capita personal income by county, 1982; number, assets, and net worth of millionaires and wealthholders, with selected detail by sex and asset type, 1982; and taxable and/or retail sales, by type of business, and for 4 SMSAs, 1983-84. 6 tables. (p. 24-31)

e. Construction: number and value of residential construction permits authorized, and housing vacancy rates in 23 selected MSAs or primary MSAs, by type of structure; new residential units built in top 10 counties; subdivision application filings; existing home median sales prices by State region, and sales distribution by price range; nonresidential construction value, by type of structure; and office space trends for selected cities and total U.S.; various periods 1980-84. 8 tables. (p. 34-42)

f. Resources: farm receipts by source, 1983; agricultural production value by leading commodity, 1982-83; timber harvest from public and private lands, employment in forest products industries, prices of selected wood products, and average stumpage prices for sawtimber in national forests (by selected species), 1980-84; natural gas prices and change in electricity sales, by consuming sector, various periods 1960-85; and electricity costs, 1970 and 1982-87. 9 tables. (p. 47-53)

g. Tourism and foreign trade: foreign visitors by country; travel-related expenditures, payroll, employment, and tax receipts, with selected detail by county; travel-related expenditures by item and employment by industry; trade balance in aggregate customs districts; and value of imports and exports; various years 1960-84. Text data and 4 tables. (p. 57-64)

S0840–3.2: Statistical Appendix

POPULATION AND LABOR FORCE

1-2. Population of U.S. and California, and components of change in California's civilian population [natural increase, net migration, and gains from military], 1960-84. (p. A5-A6)

3. Total population of counties, Jan. 1, 1984. (p. A7)

4. Civilian labor force [by employment status, annually 1967-84, and monthly 1983-84]. (p. A8)

EMPLOYMENT, EARNINGS, AND HOURS

5-6. Wage/salary workers in nonagricultural establishments [annually 1972-84; and in 17 MSAs], 1983-84; [all] by major industry division. (p. A9-A11)

7. Wage/salary workers in manufacturing [by industry group], 1979-84. (p. A12-A14)

8. Aerospace employment [by industry group, annually] 1960-84 [and monthly 1984]. (p. A15)

9-10. Average weekly and hourly earnings and average hours worked per week: production and related workers in manufacturing, California and U.S., 1960-84; and in selected California nonmanufacturing industries, 1984. (p. A16-A17)

PERSONAL INCOME, TAXES, AND CPI

11-12. Personal income, total and per capita; [and total] by major sources; 1960-84. (p. A18-A19)

13. Disposable personal income [total and per capita], 1960-83. (p. A20)

14. Industrial sources of earnings, California and U.S., 1981-83. (p. A21)

15. Number of personal income tax returns, adjusted gross income, taxable income, and tax assessed, 1960-82. (p. A22)

16. Personal income tax statistics [adjusted gross income, total and joint returns and median income, and tax assessed], by county, 1982 income year. (p. A23-A24)

17. CPI [for] U.S., California, Los Angeles, San Francisco, and San Diego, 1960-84. (p. A25)

AGRICULTURE

18. Cash farm receipts, production expenses, and income, 1960-83. (p. A26)

19-20. Cash farm receipts: all crops, livestock/poultry, miscellaneous, and government payments; and from crops [all, fruit/nut, vegetable, and field]; 1960-83. (p. A27-A28)

21. Agricultural employment [in production and services, annually] 1972-84 [and monthly 1984]. (p. A29)

BUSINESS AND COMMERCE

22. Corporate profits from operations [number of corporations with net income and net loss, and with no income/loss; and total net income and losses], 1960-82. (p. A30)

23. Bank and corporation franchise tax returns [totals, and those] reporting net income subject to State taxation [number and amounts], by industry [group, 1981-82]. (p. A31-A32)

CONSTRUCTION AND TRADE

24. Building permit activity: nonresidential valuation by selected types of construction [commercial, industrial, other, and additions/alterations], 1963-84. (p. A33)

25. Residential housing units authorized by permits [number of single and multiple units, and additions/alterations, and total value authorized], 1963-84. (p. A34)

26. Taxable transactions [value, all outlets and retail stores], and outstanding sales tax permits by type of outlet [retail, personal service, and other], 1960-84. (p. A35)

27. Taxable transactions [value] by type of business, 1979-84. (p. A36)

FINANCE

28-29. Demand and time deposits; and gross loans by major categories [real estate, commercial/industrial, agricultural, personal, and other]; all insured commercial banks, 1960-83. (p. A37-A38)

30. [Mortgage loans closed and net new savings during year, and year-end mortgages outstanding and savings capital], savings and loan assns, 1960-84. (p. A39)

31-32. Selected data on federally- and State-chartered credit unions [number of institutions, membership, assets, shares, and loans outstanding], 1960-83. (p. A40-A41)

33-34. Selected data on finance companies [number and amount of consumer/commercial loans]; and on industrial loan companies [total assets, investment certificates, and number and amount of consumer, commercial, and premium finance agency loans]; 1971-83. (p. A42-A43)

35. Summary of State tax collections [general and special funds collected and taxes per capita and per $100 of personal income, FY61-86]. (p. A44)

36. Comparative yield of State taxes [including sales/use, personal income, inheritance/gift, horse racing, fuel, and selected excise taxes, and motor vehicle fees], FY61-86. (p. A45)

37. Assessed value of tangible property, tangible property tax levies, and average tax rate [FY61-85]. (p. A46)

38. Allocations of general property tax levies [by type of local jurisdiction including school districts] as compiled for computation of the average tax rate, by county, FY84. (p. A47-A48)

S0840–5   HOUSEHOLD PROJECTIONS FOR CALIFORNIA COUNTIES: 1980-2000
Monograph.   Aug. 1984.
10 p. no paging.
Rpt. No. 84 P-2.
SRI/MF/complete

Report presenting projections of California households and population living in households, by county, quinquennially 1985-2000, with actual data for 1980.

Projections are prepared by Dept of Finance and are based on the 1980 census.

Contains projection methodology (2 p.); and 1 basic table (8 p.).

Availability: California Department of Finance, Population Research Unit, 1025 P St., Sacramento CA 95814-4998, †; SRI/MF/complete.

S0850   CALIFORNIA
Department of Food and Agriculture

S0850–1   CALIFORNIA AGRICULTURAL STATISTICS
Annual series.   For individual publication data, see below.
SRI/MF/complete

Series of annual reports presenting California agricultural statistics. Includes production, marketing, and other data by commodity, reporting district, and county; trends from 1970s or earlier; and selected comparisons to U.S. and other States.

Series includes an overview; individual reports on major commodity groups; and a 2-volume report on exports.

Data sources include California Crop and Livestock Reporting Service, USDA, State and local agencies, grower assns, shippers, and processors.

Reports are described in order of receipt. Reports reviewed during 1985 are described below.

Prior to 1985, abstracts for these reports were grouped according to period of data coverage. For descriptions of reports covered in 1984, see SRI 1984 Annual under S0850-1 and S0850-2.

Issuing agency also publishes the following related reports, not covered in SRI: *Grape Acreage Bulletin, Grape Crush Bulletin,* and *Fruit and Nut Acreage Bulletin.*

Availability: California Crop and Livestock Reporting Service, PO Box 1258, Sacramento CA 95806; SRI/MF/complete.

S0850–1.1: California Dairy Industry Statistics, 1983

[Annual. [1984.] 63 p. $3.00. LC 65-63180. SRI/MF/complete.]

Annual report on California dairy production and marketing, 1983, with selected trends from 1963. Data are shown by product, and by county, district, and/or marketing area. Covers production; farm cash receipts; average and minimum producer prices; utilization; and sales volume, with detail for milk by type of trade and container size and type.

Also includes comparisons to U.S. and other States; and data on California dairy cattle inventories and productivity, and per capita consumption of selected products.

Contains contents listing and foreword (p. 2-5); and 68 tables, interspersed with brief narrative summaries (p. 6-63).

S0850–1.2: California Livestock Statistics, 1984

[Annual. July 1985. 3+25 p. $2.00. ISSN 0361-9095. LC 75-64945. SRI/MF/complete.]

Annual report on California livestock production and marketing, mostly for 1975-84, with some data for 1985. Data are shown by species.

Report covers production, income, prices, value, inventory by county, slaughter, and shipments into California by State of origin, for cattle, sheep, and hogs.

Also includes comparisons to U.S.; California rangeland condition, milk cow inventory and production, number of farms by type, and wool production; and U.S. livestock on farms, by species and State.

Contains foreword and table listing (3 p.); and 42 tables (p. 1-25).

S0850–1.3: California Agriculture, 1984

[Annual. July 1985. 19 p. $2.00. SRI/MF/complete.]

Annual summary report presenting data on California agricultural production, 1984, with some data for 1985 and selected trends from 1950. Data are generally shown by commodity; selected data are shown by district and county.

Report covers production, value, national rank, and, as applicable, acreage, for individual commodities. Price data are also included for selected commodities.

Report also includes data on land value by irrigation status and type of use, number and acreage of farms, and rainfall by weather station; and top 20 States ranked by agricultural cash receipts.

Contains contents listing and narrative summary (p. 1-3); 12 tables (p. 4-17); and listings of State agriculture officials (p. 18 and inside back cover).

S0850–1.4: California Fruit and Nut Statistics, 1973-84

[Annual. May 1985. ii+33 p. $2.00. SRI/MF/complete.]

Annual report on California fruit and nut production, marketing, and income, 1983 and preliminary 1984, with trends from 1973. Data are shown by commodity and/or variety.

Report covers acreage, production, value, utilization, average grower returns, and price, for grapes, tree nuts, citrus fruits, and deciduous and semitropical tree fruit.

Contains foreword and contents listing (p. i-ii); and user notes, and 10 tables with footnotes (p. 1-33).

S0850–1.5: California Vegetable Crops, 1978-84

[Annual. July 1985. iv+14 p. $2.00. SRI/MF/complete.]

Annual report on California vegetable production and marketing, 1983-84, with summary trends from 1975. Data are shown by commodity and/or variety, use category, and county.

Report covers production, acreage, yield, value, prices, and sales, for vegetables, berries, and melons.

Contains foreword, contents and table listings, and 1 chart (p. i-iii); and brief narrative summary and 8 tables (p. iv, 1-14).

S0850–1.6: California Dairy Industry Statistics, 1984

[Annual. [1985.] 63 p. $3.00. LC 65-63180. SRI/MF/complete.]

Annual report on California dairy production and marketing, 1984, with selected trends from 1964. Data are shown by product, and by county, district, and/or marketing area. Covers production; farm cash receipts; average and minimum producer prices; utilization; and sales volume, with detail for milk by type of trade and container size and type.

Also includes comparisons to U.S. and other States; and data on California dairy cattle inventories and productivity, and per capita consumption of selected products.

Contains contents listing and foreword (p. 2-5); and 68 tables, interspersed with brief narrative summaries (p. 6-63).

Previous report, for 1983, is described above, under S0850-1.1.

S0850–1.7: Field Crops Statistics, California, 1980-84

[Annual. Sept. 1985. 3+28 p. $2.00. SRI/MF/complete, current & previous year reports.]

Annual report on California field crop production, 1980-1984, with summary trends from 1950. Data are shown by commodity, variety, and county. Covers acreage, yield, production, value, and prices.

Contains contents listing, foreword, and 1 map (3 p. and inside front cover); and 18 tables (p. 1-28).

Previous report, for 1979-83, was also received in 1985, and is also available on SRI microfiche under S0850-1.7 [Annual. Dec. 1984. 3+28 p. $2.00]. Report for 1981-82 is described in SRI 1983 Annual, under S0850-2.2.

S0855   CALIFORNIA Franchise Tax Board

S0855–1   STATE OF CALIFORNIA FRANCHISE TAX BOARD Annual Report, 1983

Annual. [1984.] 102 p.
LC 51-62397.
SRI/MF/complete

Annual report on California individual and corporate income tax returns, for 1982 tax year. Includes data on filings and assessments; individual income by source, and tax credits and deductions; and bank/corporate franchise income, by major industry group. Selected data are shown by adjusted gross income (AGI) class and county.

Also includes trends from as early as 1929, and data on property tax assistance for aged and blind/disabled homeowners and renters.

Contents:

a. Listing of contents, tables, and charts. (p. 2-3)

b. 5 narrative sections, interspersed with 16 charts and 21 tables presenting summary data, general fund collections by source 1982-83, and solar and energy conservation personal and corporate tax credits claimed 1970s-82. (p. 4-34)

c. Statistical appendices, with 3 tables summarizing tax law changes affecting rates, exemptions, and deductions since 1929; and 23 detailed tables listed below. (p. 35-102)

Availability: California Franchise Tax Board, Attention: Research and Statistics, Sacramento CA 95867, †; SRI/MF/complete.

TABLES:

[In addition to data noted below, tables on personal and corporate taxes show number of returns, and tables on homeowner and renter assistance show number of claimants.]

S0855–1.1: Personal Income Tax

[Unless otherwise noted, data are for 1982. Table titles begin "Personal income tax statistics..."]

1-3. Comparison by income years, 1935-82; by AGI class, 1979-82; and by AGI class, percentages cumulated, 1982; [generally showing AGI, taxable income, and tax assessed]. (p. 40-42)

4A-4G. Comparison by AGI class: State totals [with detail for income sources, credits, and deductions]; and single, separate, joint, head of household, surviving spouse, and joint head of household returns; [all including AGI, deductions, taxable income, computed tax, and tax credits]. (p. 43-62)

5. Comparison by major industry [business/professional and partnership net profit and loss, by industry division]. (p. 63)

6. Comparison by county [including AGI (with detail for joint returns), tax assessed, and population]. (p. 64)

7. County data by AGI class [all, joint, renters credit, and taxable returns; and dependents, AGI, and tax assessed]. (p. 65-80)

8. Taxes paid by high income individuals [including tax liability, and number of returns by size of liability and average tax rate, all for 4 income size groups within 4 income concept classes]. (p. 81-82)

S0855–1.2: Bank/Corporation Tax

[Table titles 1-4 begin "Bank/corporation franchise tax statistics..."]

1-2. Comparison by income years [income reported for State taxation], 1936-82; and comparison by State net income class, [net income less net loss, 1982; both also including tax assessed]. (p. 86-87)

3-4. Comparison by [major industry group], 1981-82; and by accounting period [including tax assessed, 1982; both showing corporations reporting, amount of net income subject to State taxation, and all reporting corporations' net income less net loss]. (p. 88-89)

S0855–1.3: Homeowner and Renter Assistance

[Unless otherwise noted, data are for 1983.]

HOMEOWNER ASSISTANCE

[Table titles 1-6 begin "Homeowners property tax assistance statistics..." Tables 1-4 show number of claimants paid, household income, property tax paid, and amount of assistance.]

1. Comparison by calendar years 1968-83 [includes homeowner's property tax exemption]. (p. 92)

2-4. Comparison by county, size of household income, and year of birth. (p. 93-95)

5. [Number of claimants, by] household income by amount of property taxes paid. (p. 96)

6. Major sources of household income [including social security, interest/dividends, pensions/annuities, public assistance, and net rental and business income, by household income class]. (p. 97)

RENTER ASSISTANCE

[Table titles 7-10 begin "Renters' property tax assistance statistics..."]

7-9. [Tables 2-4 are repeated for renters' assistance.] (p. 98-100)

10. [Table 6 is repeated for renters' assistance.] (p. 101)

CLAIMANTS

11. Homeowners' [and] renters' property tax assistance statistics: types of claimants [senior citizens and blind/disabled], by size of household income. (p. 102)

S0865   CALIFORNIA
Department of
Health Services

S0865–1   VITAL STATISTICS OF CALIFORNIA, 1982
Annual.   Mar. 1985.
ix + 320 p. + 2 microfiche sheets.
ISSN 0094-0356.
LC 74-636455.
SRI/MF/complete

Annual report on California vital statistics, covering population, births, and deaths by cause, 1982 with selected trends from 1950. Includes data by race, age, sex, and county, with selected comparisons to total U.S. Data are from documents registered with the Dept of Health Services.

Contents:

a. Contents listing, and highlights. (p. iv-ix)

b. 5 sections, each preceded by listing of tables and charts, with 2 maps, 11 charts, and 54 tables described below. (p. 1-288)

c. Description of data gathering procedures, and analysis of data quality. (p. 289-300)

d. Appendix, with definitions, report form facsimiles, and 2 summary tables. (p. 301-320)

e. 2 microfiche with 3 extended tables showing deaths, by detailed cause (classified according to the 9th Revision of the International Classification of Diseases), by age group and sex (110 p.); and live births by sex, race/ethnicity, age of mother, and previous live births, by county (64 p.). Data by race/ethnicity include Mexican American, American Indian, Chinese, Japanese, and Filipino.

Printed copies of the microfiched tables are available from the issuing agency for $16.00.

Availability: California Department of Health Services, Health Data and Statistics Section, 714 P St., Rm. 1476, Sacramento CA 95814, †; SRI/MF/complete.

TABLES:

[Data are for California, 1982, unless otherwise noted. Most tables specify data as place of residence or place of occurrence.

Data by race/ethnicity generally include some or all of the following: American Indian, Cambodian, Chinese, Eskimo/Aleut, Filipino, Indian, Japanese, Korean, Pacific Islander, Thai, Vietnamese, other Asian, black, white, other, and not stated. Breakdowns by Spanish/Hispanic origin are shown for Cuban, Mexican, Puerto Rican, and other or Hispanic, non-Hispanic, and not stated.]

S0865–1.1: Review of Vital Statistics

1.1 Population, deaths, live births, infant deaths, fetal deaths, and maternal deaths, 1950-82. (p. 13)

1.2 Deaths, live births, fetal deaths, maternal deaths, and infant deaths by age [by county]. (p. 15)

1.3-1.4. Total population and population density, and intercensal estimates of total population; [by county], July 1, [various years] 1970-82. (p. 16-20)

S0865–1.2: Live Births

FERTILITY AND LIVE BIRTH RATES

2.1. Number and percent of women of childbearing age, by age group, California and U.S., 1980-82. (p. 23)

2.2-2.3. General fertility rate: total fertility rate and age-specific live birth rates; and live birth rates by live birth order; California and U.S., 1970-82. (p. 24-26)

2.4. General fertility rate, and age-specific live birth rates by live birth order, 1970 and 1979-82. (p. 28)

CHILD AND MOTHER CHARACTERISTICS

[Tables 2.5-2.22 begin "Live births..."]

2.5-2.6. By race/ethnicity of child and Spanish/Hispanic origin of mother: by age of mother. (p. 29)

2.7-2.10. By race/ethnicity of child and Spanish/Hispanic origin of mother: by previous live births and age of mother, [for total State and by county]. (p. 30-177)

2.11. By age of mother [by county]. (p. 178)

2.12-2.13. By race/ethnicity of child and Spanish/Hispanic origin of mother: by sex of child [by county]. (p. 179-198)

2.14-2.19. By race/ethnicity of child and Spanish/Hispanic origin of mother: birth weight and weeks of gestation; plurality of delivery and sex; and with 1 or more congenital anomalies and congenital anomalies reported by type and sex. (p. 199-218)

2.20. By month prenatal care began and age of mother. (p. 219)

2.21. By month of birth [by county]. (p. 220)

·2.22. By type of hospital [county, private, other, unknown; by county]. (p. 221)

2.23. Total live births and estimated live births to unmarried women, by race and age of mother and live birth order. (p. 222-223)

2.24-2.26. Number of live births by estimated marital status, and estimated live births to unmarried women as a percent of total live births; [all by] race and age of mother, selected years 1966-82. (p. 224-226)

2.27. Total live births and estimated number and percent of live births to unmarried women by race of mother [by county]. (p. 227)

S0865–1.3: Fetal and Infant Deaths

FETAL DEATHS

[Tables 3.1-3.6 and 3.8-3.11 begin "Fetal Deaths..."]

3.1-3.2. By race/ethnicity of child and Spanish/Hispanic origin of mother: by age of mother. (p. 230)

3.3. Number, ratio, and percent distribution [of fetal deaths], by age of mother. (p. 231)

3.4. By age of mother [by county]. (p. 232)

3.5-3.6. By race/ethnicity of child and Spanish/Hispanic origin of mother: by birth weight and weeks of gestation. (p. 233-235)

3.7. Number and percent of fetal deaths, by weeks of gestation. (p. 236)

3.8-3.11. By race/ethnicity of child and Spanish/Hispanic origin of mother: by plurality of delivery and sex; and each cause. (p. 237-244)

INFANT DEATHS

4.1. Percent distribution of infant deaths, by age and sex. (p. 246)

4.2. Infant, neonatal, and postneonatal death rates, 1960-82. (p. 247)

4.3. Age-adjusted perinatal and infant mortality rates among single total births, by race of child, 1960 and 1965-82. (p. 248)

4.4. Infant, neonatal, and postneonatal deaths from selected causes by age. (p. 250-251)

S0865–1.4: Deaths

GENERAL

5.1. Ten leading causes of death, 1981-82. (p. 254)

5.2. Five leading causes of death, by sex and age. (p. 256-257)

5.3. Age- and sex-specific death rates and percent change, 1980-82. (p. 258)

5.4-5.5. Deaths by sex, race, and age, [total and by county]. (p. 259-273)

5.6. Deaths by month of death [by county]. (p. 274)

BY DETAILED CAUSE

[Tables begin "Deaths..."]

5.7. From selected external causes of injury and poisoning [by county]. (p. 275-276)

5.8. From selected causes [by county]. (p. 277-288)

S0900 CALIFORNIA
Department of Insurance

S0900–1   **ONE HUNDRED AND SIXTEENTH ANNUAL REPORT OF THE INSURANCE COMMISSIONER of the State of California, for the Year Ended Dec. 31, 1983**
Annual.   Aug. 1, 1984.
204 p.
LC 45-33033.
SRI/MF/complete

Annual report on California insurance industry financial condition and underwriting activity, by company and type of insurance, 1983. Covers assets, liabilities, capital/surplus, underwriting and investment gain or loss, dividends, premiums collected or earned, and losses or benefits paid and/or incurred, for companies with headquarters in California and elsewhere.

Data are shown for life/disability, fire/marine/casualty/miscellaneous, and real estate title insurers.

Also includes data on Insurance Dept receipts and disbursements, employees, securities on deposit, licensing activity, fraudulent claim enforcement activities, and consumer complaints; finances of companies in conservation or liquidation; and trends from 1974.

Data are compiled from annual statements filed by all licensed insurers, and dept internal records.

Contains contents listing (p. 3); Dept report, with 21 tables (p. 7-58); liquidation and conservation report, with 1 table repeated for each company (p. 59-171); and 3 company financial tables (p. 175-204).

Availability: California Department of Insurance, 100 Van Ness Ave., San Francisco CA 94102, †; SRI/MF/complete.

S0905 CALIFORNIA
Judicial Council

S0905–1   **1985 ANNUAL REPORT, JUDICIAL COUNCIL OF CALIFORNIA**
Annual.   Jan. 1, 1985.
xiv+267 p.+insert.
LC 67-65214.
SRI/MF/complete

Annual report on the California judicial system, including trial and appellate court caseloads and case dispositions, mostly for FY83-84. Covers supreme, appeals, superior, municipal, and justice courts. Includes trial court data by case type, county, and judicial district, and selected trends from FY75.

Case types shown are criminal and civil, for all courts, with some additional detail for probate/guardianship, eminent domain, family, juvenile, mental health, habeas corpus, traffic, and small claims case types.

Also includes data on judicial finances and personnel, average sentence for selected crimes, attorney disciplinary proceedings, and appeals court case processing time.

Contains contents listing and introduction (p. iii-xiv); Judicial Council report in 12 chapters, with text statistics, 1 chart, and 9 tables (p. 3-53); Administrative Office report in 2 chapters, with 26 charts and 57 tables (p. 57-169); 50 appendix tables (p. 173-264); and glossary (p. 265-267).

Availability: California Judicial Council, Administrative Office of the Courts, 3154 State Bldg., 350 McAllister St., San Francisco CA 94102, †; SRI/MF/complete.

S0910 CALIFORNIA
Department of Justice

S0910–1   **CRIME AND DELINQUENCY IN CALIFORNIA, 1984**
Annual.   June 1985.
2+156 p.
LC 67-63443.
SRI/MF/complete, current & previous year reports

Annual report on California crimes, arrests, and criminal justice system, 1984, with trends from 1974. Includes data on crimes and arrests, by detailed offense; demographic characteristics of persons arrested; arrest dispositions, including specific sentences; correctional facility population; and probation and parole caseloads. Also includes criminal justice expenditures and personnel.

Data are from reports of State and local criminal justice agencies, including filings submitted under the Uniform Crime Reporting Program.

Contains contents listing, introduction, and highlights (p. 1-3); report sections, with narrative summaries, text data, 103 charts, and 2 tables (p. 4-91); appendix, with methodological information and glossary (p. 94-100); and data section, with table listing and 59 tables (p. 102-156).

Report section tables show law enforcement officers killed in the line of duty, and justifiable homicides by law enforcement officers, 1975-84 (p. 10); and citizens' complaints against officers, 1984 (p. 91). Data section tables are described below.

Previous report, for 1983, was also reviewed in SRI during 1985, and is also available on SRI microfiche under S0910-1 [Annual. June 1984. 134 p. †]. SRI coverage begins with the 1983 report.

Report is supplemented by a statewide criminal justice profile, covered in SRI under S0910-2. A series of county criminal justice profiles is also published, but is not covered in SRI.

Availability: California Department of Justice, Criminal Statistics and Special Services Bureau, 4949 Broadway, PO Box 13427, Sacramento CA 95813, †; SRI/MF/complete.

DATA SECTION TABLES:

[Data are shown for California, 1984, generally with trends from 1974 or 1979, unless otherwise noted. Data by race/ethnicity include Hispanic.]

S0910–1.1: Crimes, Arrests, and Dispositions

CRIMES

[Data by Index offense are shown for willful homicide, forcible rape, robbery, aggravated assault, burglary, motor vehicle theft, and larceny/theft, with summary totals for violent and property crimes.]

a. Index crimes and rates, by offense, with comparison to total U.S. Tables 1-2. (p. 104-105)

b. Homicides, robberies, and assaults, by type of weapon; rapes and attempted rapes; robberies by location; burglaries by category (forced entry and no force, residence and nonresidence, and day and night); motor vehicle thefts by type of vehicle; and larceny/theft offenses, by type and value of property stolen. Tables 3-10. (p. 105-109)

c. Value of stolen and recovered property by type; and arson offenses and value of property damage, by property type. Tables 11-13. (p. 110-111)

ARRESTS AND DISPOSITIONS

d. Adult and juvenile arrests, and arrests by offender sex, age, and race/ethnicity, by detailed Index and non-Index offense. Tables 14-34C. (p. 112-137)

e. Dispositions of arrests: releases; complaints denied and filed; and lower and superior court dismissals, acquittals, convictions, and sentences by type; all shown by Index offense and for drug law violations and all other offenses. Tables 35-41. (p. 138-143)

S0910–1.2: Corrections, and Criminal Justice Expenditures and Employment

f. Correctional system data, including adults in State institutions and in city and county jails; parole and probation caseloads; adults removed from probation, by reason; adults committed to correctional facilities, by facility type; new referrals to probation depts, by source and sex; juvenile court dispositions of petitions; status of active juvenile cases; and juvenile population in county detention facilities, by sex. Tables 42-53. (p. 144-152)

g. Criminal justice expenditures (fiscal year data), and employment by personnel category, all by type of agency (law enforcement, prosecution, public defense, courts, and corrections); and adult and juvenile population. Tables 54-59. (p. 153-156)

S0910–2 CRIMINAL JUSTICE PROFILE, 1984, Statewide, California

Annual. Oct. 1985.
iii+123 p.
LC 80-649518.
SRI/MF/complete, current & previous year reports

Annual statistical profile of the California criminal justice system, including data by county, 1984 with trends from 1975.

Covers crimes, crime rate, and clearances, primarily by Index offense; adult and juvenile arrests, dispositions by type, and probation caseloads, with detail by Index and non-Index offense, and by offender age, sex, and race/ethnicity; criminal justice expenditures by function, and employment by agency and occupational group; and adults and juveniles held under local supervision, by type of facility.

Most data (except expenditures, employment, and local supervision) are shown by county. Index crimes are homicide, rape, robbery, assault, burglary, theft, motor vehicle theft, and arson. Data by race/ethnicity include white, black, Hispanic, American Indian, Chinese, Japanese, and Filipino.

Data are from State records.

Contains contents and table listing (p. i-iii); introduction (p. 1); 51 tables (p. 5-113); and methodology and glossary (p. 114-123).

Report is part of a series of criminal justice profiles, covering the State and each county. Report is designed to supplement *Crime and Delinquency in California*, covered in SRI under S0910-1. Individual county profiles are not covered in SRI.

Previous report, for 1983, was also reviewed in SRI during 1985, and is also available on SRI microfiche under S0910-2 [Annual. Oct. 1984. iii+117 p. †].

Availability: California Department of Justice, Criminal Statistics and Special Services Bureau, 4949 Broadway, PO Box 13427, Sacramento CA 95813, †; SRI/MF/complete.

S0930 CALIFORNIA
Public Utilities Commission

S0930–1 PUBLIC UTILITIES COMMISSION, State of California, Annual Report, FY83

Annual. Dec. 1, 1983. 70 p.
LC 9-14670.
SRI/MF/complete

Annual report presenting California public utility and transportation regulatory activities, FY83; and utility financial and operating data for 1982 with trends from 1973, by utility type. Some data are shown by company. Utility types are gas, steam, electric, telecommunications, and water.

Covers regulatory caseloads and dispositions, including rate changes by company; utility operating revenues, plant value, and customers; typical gas, electric, and telephone bills in 25 largest U.S. cities; public motor carriers regulated, insured, licensed, and investigated; rail crossing accidents, injuries, and fatalities, and automatic protection device installations by county; railroad safety program funding; and number of utilities and carriers regulated, by type.

Contains contents listing (1 p.); summary of commission membership and activities, with 4 tables and 20 charts (p. 1-53); and statistical section and appendix, with 31 tables (p. 54-70).

Previous report, for 1982, is described in SRI 1983 Annual under this number.

Availability: California Public Utilities Commission, Attention: Cashier, Rm. 3239, 350 McAllister St., San Francisco CA 94102, $10.50; SRI/MF/complete.

S0934 CALIFORNIA
Office of the Secretary of State

S0934–1 STATEMENT OF VOTE, General Election, Nov. 6, 1984, California

Biennial. 2 volumes.
For individual publication data, see below.
LC 29-27012.
SRI/MF/complete

Biennial report presenting results of California general election held Nov. 6, 1984. Report is issued in 2 volumes, individually described below.

Availability: California Office of the Secretary of State, Elections Division, Public Market Bldg., 1230 J St., Sacramento CA 95814, †; SRI/MF/complete.

S0934–1.1: Main Report

[Biennial. Dec. 1984. ix+35 p. SRI/MF/complete.]

Shows voting for President/Vice President; U.S. Representatives; State senators and assembly members; judges; and 16 propositions, including tax reform, State lottery, language of voting materials, campaign funds, and public welfare measures. Data are shown by county and/or district and include party affiliation of most candidates.

Also includes voter registration by party, and turnout, by county, with selected trends from 1912.

For description of previous report, covering the 1982 election, see SRI 1983 Annual under S0934-1.

S0934–1.2: Supplement

[Biennial. [1984.] 194 p. SRI/MF/complete.]

Shows votes cast for President/Vice President and 16 propositions, by county, city, and various political districts.

SRI coverage of the supplement begins with this edition.

S0980 COLORADO
Department of Administration

S0980–1 COMPREHENSIVE ANNUAL FINANCIAL REPORT for the Year Ended June 30, 1984, State of Colorado

Annual. Oct. 31, 1984.
ii+77 p.
LC 80-648197.
SRI/MF/complete

Annual report on financial condition of Colorado State government, for FY84, presenting assets, liabilities, and fund equity and balances; revenues by source; and expenditures by function, object, and/or agency; for all, general, current restricted, special revenue, debt service, capital project, enterprise, internal service, trust, loan, and agency funds. Includes selected trends from FY75.

Also includes budgeted vs. actual revenues and expenditures; data on State government employment; appropriations and expenditures by institution; bonded debt; and socioeconomic trends, including population, personal income, sales, assessed property values, labor force and employment by industry division, and unemployment, with selected comparisons to the U.S.

Financial data are from the State Controller's unaudited records.

Contains contents listing (p. i-ii); introduction, with 2 text tables and 10 charts (p. 1-11); financial section, with 33 financial statements and accompanying notes (p. 13-67); and statistical section, with 12 tables (p. 69-77).

Availability: Colorado Department of Administration, Accounts and Control Division, 1525 Sherman St., Rm. 706, Denver CO 80203, †; SRI/MF/complete.

S0985 COLORADO
Department of Agriculture

S0985–1 1985 COLORADO AGRICULTURAL STATISTICS

Annual. July 1985. 162 p.
Bull. 1-85.
LC 52-62059.
SRI/MF/complete

Annual report on Colorado agricultural production, marketing, and finances, 1970s-84, with some data for 1985 and selected trends from as early as 1940. Data are generally shown by commodity and/or district and county, with some comparisons to other States and total U.S.

Report covers production, prices, disposition, value, and, as applicable, acreage, yield, or inventory, for field crop, fruit, vegetable, flower, livestock, dairy, and poultry sectors.

Also includes data on number and acreage of farms; irrigation use; fertilizer consumption; precipitation; farm income and production expenses; pasture/range feed condition; cattle and sheep shipments into Colorado from selected States and foreign countries; and U.S. per capita consumption of major food and beverage products.

Data are compiled by the Colorado Crop and Livestock Reporting Service in cooperation with USDA.

Contains contents listing (p. 1); 15 maps, 4 charts, and 181 tables grouped into 4 sections, each including brief narrative (p. 2-158); and index (p. 159-162).

Availability: Colorado Crop and Livestock Reporting Service, PO Box 17066, Denver CO 80217, †; SRI/MF/complete.

S1000 COLORADO
Department of Education

S1000–2 STATISTICAL SERIES: Colorado Department of Education
Annual series. For individual publication data, see below.
SRI/MF/complete

Series of 2 annual reports on Colorado public elementary and secondary education, 1984. Reports cover certificated personnel and enrollment, and revenues and expenditures, generally by county and/or school district.

Most data are compiled from reports filed by school districts with the State Dept of Education.

Prior to 1984 reports, data on certificated personnel and enrollment were published separately.

Reports are individually described below.

A detailed report on Colorado public school finances is also available from the issuing agency, but is not covered in SRI.

Availability: Colorado Department of Education, School Finance, Office of Management Services, 303 W. Colfax Ave., 6th Floor, Denver CO 80204; SRI/MF/complete.

S1000–2.1: Certificated Personnel Salaries, Pupil Membership, and Related Information, Fall 1984
[Annual. Apr. 1985. v+128 p. $5.00. LC 82-646775. SRI/MF/complete.]

Contains contents and table listing, and introduction (p. iii-v); 19 tables listed below (p. 1-122); and data sources, definitions, and listing of school districts (p. 123-128).

TABLES:
[Tables show data for fall 1984, unless otherwise noted. Data by setting are shown for urban, suburban, outlying city, rural mountainous, and rural agricultural. District size is based on average daily attendance entitlement. Data by setting and size often include number of districts in each group. Tables 3-4, 7, and 10-16 show data by individual school district and county.]

PERSONNEL AND SALARIES

1-2. Average salaries [and number] of classroom teachers, other and total certificated personnel, superintendents, principals, and assistant superintendents and principals, by size and setting. (p. 1-2)

3-4. Classroom teachers and total certificated staff FTE, average salary, average experience [in district and total], and percent [with] masters or higher degree, by setting and size. (p. 3-16)

5-6. Certificated personnel summary: average salaries, FTE, average age, and average experience, by position and sex; and average salaries by position, sex, and college preparation. (p. 17-30)

[A] Comparison of Colorado and national classroom teachers' average salaries [and number of teachers, 1975/76-1984/85]. (p. 31)

7. Certificated personnel by ethnic group [American Indian, black, Asian American, Hispanic, and other]. (p. 32-41)

8-9. Types of certificates held by certificated personnel, and college preparation of certificated [instructional and other] personnel, fall 1979 and 1983-84. (p. 42-43)

10. Summary of school district [certificated and noncertificated] staff by [position]. (p. 44-52)

[B] Summary of the average pupil/staff ratios by setting and size. (p. 53)

ENROLLMENT AND GRADUATES

11. Fall pupil membership in each grade [including special education], as of Oct. 1, 1984. (p. 58-63)

12. Comparison of pupil membership, by size of district, fall 1983-84. (p. 64-66)

13. Summary of selected school district data [including number of schools by level, FTE classroom teachers and non-certificated and certificated staff, enrollment, pupil/teacher ratio, and discontinuance rate]. (p. 67-75)

14. Fall, closing day, and average daily membership, and average daily attendance entitlement [1975/76-1984/85]. (p. 76-98)

[C] Comparison of first grade and total fall membership, fall 1975-89. (p. 99)

15. Fall membership by ethnic group [American Indian, Asian/Pacific Islander, black, white, and Hispanic]. (p. 100-109)

16. Public high school graduates [by sex, 1979/80-1983/84]. (p. 110-122)

S1000–2.2: Revenues and Expenditures, Calendar Year 1984
[Annual. June 1985. 101 p. $5.00. SRI/MF/complete.]

Contains contents listing and explanations of data categories (p. 1-3); and 3 extended tables, showing the following data by school district grouped by county, with totals for boards of cooperative services, 1984:

a. Revenues by local, State, and Federal source, for all funds except building fund; and building fund bond receipts. Table I. (p. 4-31)

b. Revenues and expenses, for building fund, capital reserve, bond redemption, pupil activity, food service, insurance reserve, general fund, and other funds; and total current expense, including and excluding transportation. Table II. (p. 32-73)

c. Expenditures, by detailed category, including salaries, benefits, transportation, and food services. Table III. (p. 74-101)

Includes total amounts, and amounts per Oct. 1983 average daily attendance entitlement.

S1010 COLORADO
Department of Health

S1010–1 1982 ANNUAL REPORT OF VITAL STATISTICS, Colorado
Annual. [1985.] iii+4+94 p.
ISSN 0588-456X.
LC 75-646408.
SRI/MF/complete

Annual report on Colorado vital statistics, covering population growth, births, deaths by cause, marriages, and divorces, for the State and by county, health service area (HSA), and planning region, 1982, with historical trends from 1860. Also includes data on adoptions.

Data are from certificates of vital events registered in the Dept of Health prior to Apr. 15, 1983.

Contains preface, with 1 summary table (p. i-iii); listing of contents, tables, and charts (4 p.); narrative report in 9 sections, interspersed with 3 charts and 41 tables (p. 1-41); and appendices A-F, with 3 maps and 14 tables, and disease classification list, definitions, available tabulation reports, sample certificates, and life expectancy analysis (p. 42-94).

All tables are listed below.

Availability: Colorado Department of Health, Health Policy, Planning and Statistics Division, Health Statistics Section, 4210 E. 11th Ave., Denver CO 80220, $5.00; SRI/MF/complete.

TABLES:
[Unless otherwise noted, data are for Colorado, 1982. Data by race are usually shown for Anglo and Spanish surname white; black, Indian, and other nonwhite; and Spanish and non-Spanish origin.]

S1010–1.1: Population and Summary Data

1. Vital statistics [summary]: State residents [by occurrence in and out of State] and occurrences [to residents and nonresidents]. (p. i)

2. Population by age and sex, 1980 and 1982. (p. 4)

3. Population, population growth, natural increase and net in-migration with median age, [decennially] 1860-1980. (p. 5)

4-5. Population, births, and illegitimate births; and [total], infant, neonatal, and maternal deaths; Colorado residents [number and rates] and U.S. rates, [decennially 1910-50 and annually 1950-82]. (p. 6-7)

6. Total births and deaths [1975-82, and population, 1982], for selected incorporated cities (1980 population above 2,500), by city of residence [and for balance of State]. (p. 9)

7. Summary vital statistics by month of occurrence, Colorado residents and occurrence [includes resident deaths by cause]. (p. 10)

8a-8b. Population and vital events [live births by sex, low birth weight births, and illegitimate births; deaths and infant deaths by sex; and neonatal, fetal, and perinatal deaths; all] by race, Colorado residents. (p. 11)

9-10. Total pregnancies, live births, induced abortions, and spontaneous fetal deaths, for all women and women under 20 years of age: Colorado occurrence, 1970-82; and by legitimacy, Colorado residents and occurrence, 1982. (p. 12)

S1010–1.2: Births, Deaths, Adoptions, and Marriages

BIRTHS

[Tables 12-18 show data for Colorado residents.]

11. Birth and fertility rates, Colorado residents and U.S. rates [and Colorado population and women aged 15-44], selected years 1940-82. (p. 13)

12. Age-specific [births, women, and] total fertility rates, 1970 and 1982. (p. 14)

13. Selected birth statistics, 1970-82. (p. 14)

14. Live births by education of mother, other living children, and month in which prenatal care began. (p. 15)

15-16. Live births by race of child, birth weight, prenatal visits, and age of mother. (p. 16)

17. Live births, low birth weight births, and illegitimate births by single year age of mother. (p. 17)

18. Congenital anomalies reported on birth certificate. (p. 18-19)

DEATHS

[Tables 19-23 show data for Colorado occurrences; tables 24-36 show data for Colorado residents.]

19. Fetal deaths by age of mother, length of gestation, and race of fetus. (p. 20)

20-21. Induced abortions by age and race of patient, and by type of procedure and length of gestation. (p. 21)

22-23. Infant deaths by trimester in which prenatal care began and age of mother at birth, and by birth weight. (p. 22)

24-25. Infant, [neonatal, 1st week, and 1st day] deaths: from leading causes by age, and by race and sex. (p. 23)

26-27. Leading causes of death: and death rates for Colorado residents and U.S.; and by underlying cause by total mentions. (p. 24-25)

28-29. Total number of causes of death, and leading causes of death by sex, by age. (p. 25-26)

30. Deaths and death rates from leading causes [and ranking of top 10 causes], selected years 1940-82. (p. 28-29)

31. Age-specific mortality rates [and deaths and persons], 1980 and 1982. (p. 30)

32-33. Deaths from leading causes by age, sex, and race. (p. 31-32)

34. Deaths by race, [sex], and age. (p. 33)

35. Violent deaths by age and sex, [and cause]. (p. 34-35)

36. Reported cases and deaths from selected notifiable diseases, selected years 1940-82. (p. 36-37)

ADOPTIONS, MARRIAGES AND DISSOLUTIONS, AND CERTIFICATES

37. Adoptions processed, 1980-82, by year of decree [selected periods 1970-82]. (p. 38)

38-39. Type of adoption [both parents, step and single parent, legitimation, relative, and adjudication], and sex and age of child, for all processed adoptions. (p. 39)

40. Marriages and marriage dissolutions (divorces/annulments), Colorado occurrence [and rates] and U.S. rates, 1970-82. (p. 40)

41. Certified copies of birth/death certificates [issued, FY41 and FY51-83]. (p. 41)

S1010–1.3: Appendix Tables

[All data are shown by county, planning region, and HSA. Birth and death data are for Colorado residents, unless otherwise noted.]

POPULATION

A1. Estimated population, population growth [from 1981], and population density, with ranks. (p. 46-47)

A2. Population and median age by sex; percent population by race; and number of families, households, and persons in group quarters. (p. 48-49)

A3. Population by age group. (p. 50-51)

BIRTHS AND DEATHS

A4-A6. Live, low birth weight, and illegitimate births; and total, infant, neonatal, fetal, and perinatal deaths, with rates; Colorado residents and/or occurrences, 1982 and/or 1978-82 period. (p. 52-57)

A7. Birth, fertility, and pregnancy rates, with selected birth statistics [including induced abortions, and percent of women giving live birth with 12/more years education]. (p. 58-59)

A8-A9. Live births: by age group of mother; and by race and sex of child. (p. 60-65)

A10. Total deaths and death rates by sex, and percent of deaths by sex and selected age group. (p. 66-67)

A11-A12. Deaths: by age group at death; and by race and sex. (p. 68-73)

A13. Deaths and death rates for 10 leading causes. (p. 74-75)

MARRIAGES AND DISSOLUTIONS

A14. Marriages, marriage dissolutions, and separate maintenance, Colorado occurrences. (p. 76-77)

S1035   COLORADO
Judicial Department

S1035–1   **ANNUAL REPORT OF THE COLORADO JUDICIARY, July 1, 1983-June 30, 1984**
Annual. 2 volumes.
For individual publication data, see below.
ISSN 0094-7504.
LC 74-646050.
SRI/MF/complete

Annual report, for FY84, on Colorado judicial system, including trial and appellate court caseloads and case dispositions. Covers supreme, appeals, district, and county courts. Includes trial court data by case type, judicial district, and county; and trends from FY65.

Case types include civil and criminal for most courts, with additional detail for domestic relations, probate, juvenile, mental health, small claims, traffic, and other case types.

Data are from reports filed with the Office of the State Court Administrator.

Report is presented in 2 volumes, individually described below.

Availability: Colorado Judicial Department, State Court Administrator's Office, Two E. 14th Ave., Denver CO 80203, $6.00; SRI/MF/complete.

S1035–1.1: Main Report

[Annual. [1985.] ii+122 p. SRI/MF/complete.]

Report on Colorado court organization and activities, FY84. Includes data on supreme and appellate court caseloads by case type, with trends from 1960s or 1970s; and trial court caseloads by court type, district, and county, with summary trends from FY80.

Also includes data on judges, water court cases, indigent aid applications and dispositions, Judicial Dept finances, adult and juvenile probation activities, restitution paid by probationers, and community correction programs.

Contains listing of contents and tables (p. i-ii); introductory materials (p. 1-3); and 9 report sections, with narrative, 18 charts, and 38 tables (p. 5-122).

S1035–1.2: Statistical Appendix

[Annual. Feb. 15, 1985. 37 p. SRI/MF/complete.]

Statistical appendix on Colorado court caseloads, FY84. Includes trial court data on case filings and terminations, with civil filings by money amount, all shown by detailed case type, district, and county.

Also includes caseload trends for supreme court and court of appeals.

Contains table listing (2 p.); and 22 tables (p. 3-37).

S1040   COLORADO
Department of
Labor and Employment

S1040–3   **ANNUAL PLANNING INFORMATION REPORT, FY86, Colorado**
Annual. Feb. 1985.
9+iii+315 p.+errata.
SRI/MF/complete

Annual planning report, for FY86, identifying Colorado population groups most in need of employment services. Includes data on population, labor force, and personal income, by county and service delivery area (SDA); and employment by industry and occupation; for various periods FY83-87, with trends from the 1970s and projections to 1990.

Data are primarily from U.S. Dept of Labor and State Division of Employment and Training.

Contains contents and table listing (9 p.); preface and 2 maps (p. i-iii); narrative sections on national and State economic outlook, with 4 charts and 1 table (p. 1-21); statistical sections, with 13 charts and 110 tables, listed below (p. 25-298); and appendices, with methodology, poverty guidelines, job service center locations, and glossary (p. 301-315).

Availability: Colorado Department of Labor and Employment, Employment and Training Division, Labor Market Information Section, 251 E. 12th Ave., Denver CO 80203, †; SRI/MF/complete.

CHARTS AND TABLES:

[Data are shown for Colorado, unless otherwise noted. Data by race or race/ethnicity generally include Hispanics and often Indians, Indians/Eskimos, or Asian/Pacific Islanders.]

S1040–3.1: Population and Labor Force

[1-2] Estimated labor market data summary [including population]; and individuals requiring employability services [total and long-term unemployed, and persons in poverty, by race]; FY84-87. (p. 25-26)

[3] Estimated [labor force by] employment status, by race/ethnic group and sex, FY85 annual average. (p. 27)

[4] Population by age, sex, and race/ethnicity, Apr. 1980 and FY86-87. (p. 28)

[5] Population estimates by county for [Apr. 1980 and] FY85-87. (p. 29-30)

[6] Estimate of youth population and labor force [by employment status, with detail for disadvantaged youth, all by county, and selected labor market area (LMA), SMSA, or SDA], FY85 annual average. (p. 31-33)

[7] Veteran [and Vietnam era veteran] population [and total civilian population age 16/over], by county, 1980 census. (p. 34-35)

[8-9] Labor force estimates [by employment status, by county and selected SMSA, LMA, or city, 1st 11 months 1983-84]. (p. 36-37)

[10] Annual average unemployment rate [1970-84]. [chart] (p. 38)

[11] Estimated youth labor force, by race and Spanish origin [for selected counties, SMSAs, LMAs, and SDAs], FY85 annual average. (p. 39-45)

S1040–3.2: Employment and Wages by Industry, Income, and CPI

[1] Estimated industry employment by [industry division, 1985 and 1990, with annual average openings due to growth]. (p. 46)

[2] Major industry group forecasts (employment), FY85-87. (p. 47-51)

[3] Estimated total new hires [due to growth and turnover], by selected major industry groups, FY86. (p. 52-54)

[4] Average weekly wage, by [SIC] 2-digit industry, 1st quarter 1984. (p. 55-57)

[5-6] Per capita personal income, by county and JTPA (Job Training Partnership Act) SDA, 1977-82. (p. 58-60)

[7] CPI, all items, all urban consumers, U.S. and Denver-Boulder area, [monthly or bimonthly] 1978-84. (p. 61)

S1040–3.3: Employment Services and Local Area Data

STATE DATA

[Tables [2-4] show data for Colorado Employment and Training Division.]

[1] Over-the-year change analysis of services to individuals [participation in services performed for all, female, youth, veteran (total and Vietnam era), minority, and migrant/seasonal farmworker applicants], FY83-84. (p. 62)

[2] Job service applicants by occupation [total and female applicants by race/ethnicity, with detail by age group and educational attainment and for veterans and handicapped], 1st 9 months FY84. (p. 63-68)

[3] Operating report data [caseloads and services performed] for ES [Employment Services] programs [by job service center, 1st 9 months FY83-84]. (p. 69-71)

[4] Field operations [job placement] goals for [planning year] 1984, ES grants only [by job service center]. (p. 72)

[5] Characteristics of the insured unemployed [including industry division and group, occupation, sex, race/ethnicity, unemployment duration, age, and county and selected metro area, and for interstate claimants, with selected cross-tabulations], annual average 1984. (p. 73-87)

DENVER/BOULDER LABOR MARKET AREA

[6] Compound growth rate comparisons [average annual new jobs, by industry division], (for 5-year period, 1979-83) [based on 4th quarter data]. [chart] (p. 91)

[7] Major industry division forecasts [of employment], FY85-87 [and actual employment, FY84]. (p. 92)

[8-11] [Tables [1-4] listed above under S1040-3.1 are repeated for Denver/Boulder LMA.] (p. 93-96)

[12] Estimated annual number of new hires (selected [SIC 2-digit] industry groups), FY86. (p. 97-98)

[13] [Table [2] listed above under S1040-3.3 is repeated for Denver/Boulder LMA.] (p. 99-104)

SERVICE DELIVERY AREAS

[14-103] [Repeats the following for each of 10 JTPA SDAs: chart and tables [6-13] as described for Denver/Boulder LMA; and 1 table showing average monthly number of dislocated workers provided services by type of service, by age, sex, educational attainment, race/ethnicity, and for veterans, handicapped, welfare recipients, migrant and seasonal workers, and economically disadvantaged, with some detail by SDA region, 1984.] (p. 109-298)

S1040–4   COLORADO LABOR FORCE REVIEW

Monthly, with annual supplement. Approx. 15 p. SRI/MF/complete, shipped quarterly

Monthly report (not published in Dec.), with annual supplement, on Colorado employment and unemployment, earnings, hours, and economic indicators comprising the Colorado Business Composite (CBC). Includes selected data by industry and locale, and comparisons to neighboring States and U.S. Also includes Denver CPI.

Data are from State, Federal, and private sources. Report is issued 2 months after month of data coverage.

Contains contents listing; Colorado and Denver/Boulder narrative reviews; occasional special articles, some with statistics; CBC feature, with trend charts, 2 monthly tables, and quarterly employment summary; statistical section, with 7 monthly tables; and quarterly feature on insured unemployment, with 2 tables.

Annual statistical features on Colorado labor market developments and outlook appear in the Jan. Data Supplement and Oct. issue, respectively.

Monthly and quarterly tables are listed below. Monthly tables appear in all issues. All additional features with substantial statistical content are described, as they appear, under "Statistical Features;" page locations and latest periods of coverage for quarterly tables are also noted. Nonstatistical features are not covered.

Availability: Colorado Department of Labor and Employment, Employment and Training Division, Labor Market Information Section, 251 E. 12th Ave., Denver CO 80203, †; SRI/MF/complete, shipped quarterly.

Issues reviewed during 1985: Sept. 1984-Aug. 1985 (D) (Vol. XXI, Nos. 9-11; Vol. XXII, Nos. 1-8); and Jan. 1985 Data Supplement (P).

TABLES:

MONTHLY TABLES

[Tables [3-8] show data for month of coverage, usually with comparison to previous 1-2 months and same month of previous year.]

[1-2] CBC, and data series for leading indicators comprising CBC [including State stock market index, bank deposits, housing permits, and business formation index, monthly for current year to date and approximately 10 previous years].

[3] Seasonally adjusted labor force data [total employment, unemployment, and nonagricultural wage/salary jobs by industry division, for State and Denver/Boulder labor market area (LMA)].

[4] Denver area CPI by component [in alternate months presents data for all items and for food at home].

[5] State and Denver/Boulder LMA [unemployment, agricultural and nonagricultural employment, wage/salary employment by major industry group, and labor disputants].

[6] Colorado labor force estimates [employment and unemployment, by county and MSA and for Denver/Boulder LMA].

[7] Hours and earnings for selected industries [State and Denver/Boulder LMA].

[8] Selected monthly activities, Division of Employment [unemployment insurance claims and benefits, and employment service applications and placements; State and Denver area].

[9] Area labor force comparisons [unemployment and employment, for U.S., Colorado, and 6 neighboring States; previous month].

QUARTERLY TABLES

[1-2] Characteristics of the insured unemployed [industry, occupation, age, weeks unemployed, and sex, usually for quarter ending 1 month after month of coverage, previous quarter, and same quarter of previous year; with detail for current quarter, including data by race, for Hispanics, and for major LMAs].

[3] Colorado quarterly [employment] summary [average employment for current and previous 4 quarters].

STATISTICAL FEATURES:

S1040–4.601: Sept. 1984 (Vol. XXI, No. 9)

QUARTERLY TABLE

[3] Colorado quarterly employment summary, for 3rd quarter 1984. (p. 6)

S1040–4.602: Oct. 1984 (Vol. XXI, No. 10)

COLORADO LABOR MARKET OUTLOOK, ANNUAL FEATURE

(p. 10-11) Annual article on labor market outlook, based on projections by over 60 business and government leaders attending the 20th annual Business-Economic Outlook Forum, held

S1040–4.602   Colorado

Dec. 1984. Includes 1 table showing unemployment and rate, employment by type, and wage/salary employment by industry division, 1983-85.

S1040–4.603: Nov. 1984 (Vol. XXI, No. 11)

QUARTERLY TABLES

[1-2] Characteristics of the insured unemployed, for 4th quarter 1984. (p. 8-11)

S1040–4.604: Jan. 1985 Data Supplement

LABOR MARKET DEVELOPMENTS DURING 1984, ANNUAL FEATURE

(p. 3-4) Annual article, with 1 table showing average annual growth or loss in employment, including changes in poorest and best years, by industry division, various periods 1974-84.

REVISED STATISTICS, ANNUAL FEATURE

(p. 5-30) Annual data revisions, with 23 tables showing trends or revisions for selected topics covered in monthly tables, various years 1977-84.

S1040–4.605: Feb. 1985 (Vol. XXII, No. 2)

QUARTERLY TABLES

[1-2] Characteristics of the insured unemployed, for 1st quarter 1985. (p. 8-11)

S1040–4.606: Mar. 1985 (Vol. XXII, No. 3)

QUARTERLY TABLE

[3] Colorado quarterly employment summary, for 1st quarter 1985. (p. 5)

COLORADO ANNUAL PLANNING INFORMATION, ANNUAL FEATURE

(p. 9-15) Annual article, by Kenneth McNulty, with 1 table showing Colorado employment by industry division, actual FY84 and forecasts for FY85-87.

For description of previous article, for FY83-86, see SRI 1984 Annual under S1040-4.508.

S1040–4.607: Apr. 1985 (Vol. XXII, No. 4)

COLORADO PERSONAL INCOME GROWTH SLOWS TO 6.6 PERCENT DURING 1983

(p. 7-9) Annual article, with 2 tables showing Colorado personal income by industry division (with detail for Federal civilian and military employees), and per capita income, all by county, with summary change from 1978 and 1982 compared to U.S. Data are from Commerce Dept.

S1040–4.608: May 1985 (Vol. XXII, No. 5)

QUARTERLY TABLES

[1-2] Characteristics of the insured unemployed, for 2nd quarter 1985. (p. 7-10)

S1040–4.609: June 1985 (Vol. XXII, No. 6)

QUARTERLY TABLE

[3] Colorado quarterly employment summary, for 2nd quarter 1985. (p. 4)

NEOPLAN USA's ECONOMIC IMPACT ON PROWERS COUNTY, COLORADO

(p. 9-10) By David L. Larson. Article on economic impact of fall 1980 start-up of Neoplan USA (a major bus manufacturer) in Prowers County, Colorado. Data are from Colorado Labor Dept. Includes 1 table showing Prowers

County labor force by employment status, covered employment by industry division, wages, population, total and per capita personal income, and retail sales, 1978-84.

Data are from Colorado Dept of Labor and Employment.

S1040–4.610: Aug. 1985 (Vol. XXII, No. 8)

QUARTERLY TABLES

[1-2] Characteristics of the insured unemployed, for 3rd quarter 1985. (p. 12-15)

COLORADO AMONG FORTUNATE FEW TO GAIN MANUFACTURING JOBS DURING LAST FIVE YEARS

(p. 9) Article, with 1 table showing manufacturing jobs, by State, 1979 and 1984.

OCCUPATIONAL OUTLOOK

(p. 10-11) By Helen Rubenstein. Article, with 1 chart showing Colorado employment distribution by major occupational category, 1985-90 period.

S1055   COLORADO
Department of Local Affairs

S1055–3   STATE OF COLORADO, 1984: Fourteenth Annual Report, Division of Property Taxation
Annual.   June 12, 1985.
3+213 p.
SRI/MF/complete

Annual report on Colorado assessed property valuations, tax levies, and tax revenues, including data by property class, county, and local improvement and service district, mostly 1983-84. Property classes include residential, commercial, industrial, agricultural, pollution control, natural resource, and public utility properties.

Contents:

Section I-II. Table of contents, lists of dept officials and county assessors, and administrative information. (2 p., p. 1-7)

Section III. Assessed valuation: total, 1870-1984; and by property class and type, 1983 and/or 1984. 3 tables. (p. 10-12)

Section IV. Property tax revenue, by jurisdiction type, selected years 1930-84. 1 chart and 2 tables. (p. 14-15)

Section V. Public utility assessed valuation, by county, utility type, and company, 1983-84. 4 tables. (p. 18-31)

Section VI-VIII. Property and improvement assessed valuation, and number of taxable units, by detailed property class; exempt property and improvement valuation, by type (including government, religious, private school, and charities); and assessment summary; all by county, mostly 1983-84. 105 tables. (p. 35-99)

Section IX. Listing of municipal governments, and local districts. (p. 102-110)

Section X. Property tax levy and revenues for bond redemption and other funds, and assessed valuation, by purpose, city/town, and/or local district, by county, as of Jan. 1, 1985. 3 tables repeated for each county. (p. 112-208)

Section XI. Revenue and levy summary, 1983-84; and disposition of property tax petitions, 1982-84; by county. 3 tables. (p. 210-213)

Availability: Colorado Department of Local Affairs, Property Taxation Division, 1313 Sherman St., 623 State Centennial Bldg., Denver CO 80203, ‡; SRI/MF/complete.

S1068   COLORADO
Department of Public Safety

S1068–1   CRIME IN COLORADO: Annual Report, 1984
Annual.   Mar. 1, 1985.
4+82 p.
LC 81-645891.
SRI/MF/complete

Annual report on Colorado crimes and arrests, 1984, with summary comparisons to 1983.

Covers crimes, and value of property recovered and/or stolen, by Index offense, with detail by circumstances including type of weapon or property involved; total Index offense clearances; adult and juvenile arrests by Index and non-Index offense; and population; all by reporting agency and/or county.

Also includes statewide data on arson offenses, loss value, and total and juvenile clearances, by type of structure; arrest summary by sex; assaults on police by type of weapon and other circumstances, and assaults cleared; and murder victims and offenders, by age, sex, and race (white, black, Indian, Asian, and other).

Index offenses are murder, rape, robbery, assault, burglary, larceny/theft, and motor vehicle theft.

Data are from reports of State and local law enforcement agencies submitted under the Uniform Crime Reporting Program.

Contains contents listing (1 p.); introduction with 3 tables (p. 1-5); and 21 tables, interspersed with narrative summaries (p. 7-82).

Previous report, for 1983, is described in SRI 1984 Annual under S1055-1. Colorado Investigation Bureau has moved from Dept of Local Affairs.

Availability: Colorado Department of Public Safety, Investigation Bureau, Crime Information Center, 2002 S. Colorado Blvd., Denver CO 80222, †; SRI/MF/complete.

S1070   COLORADO
Department of Regulatory Agencies

S1070–2   SEVENTY-FIFTH ANNUAL REPORT OF STATE BANK COMMISSIONER of the State of Colorado, 1984
Annual.   Dec. 31, 1984.
xi+352 p.
SRI/MF/complete

Annual report on financial condition of Colorado State-chartered financial institutions, 1984, presenting assets, liabilities, and equity capital, aggregate and by institution, for commercial and industrial banks, and for trust companies. Aggregate data include comparison to 1983.

Also includes aggregate assets, liabilities, loans, and equity capital of credit unions.

Data are compiled from annual reports submitted to the Division of Banking by all institutions.

Contains lists of State banking personnel and officials, and data on new bank charters (p. II-IV); commercial bank section, with aggregate data on credit unions (p. V-197); trust company section (p. 198-204); and industrial bank section, with regulatory amendments (p. 205-352). Each section generally includes index of institutions listed alphabetically by location, 1-2 summary tables, and 1 table repeated for each institution.

Availability: Colorado Department of Regulatory Agencies, Banking Division, 303 W. Colfax Ave., Suite 700, Denver CO 80204, $15.00; SRI/MF/complete.

S1070–3   FINANCIAL REPORT ON COLORADO STATE CHARTERED SAVINGS AND LOAN ASSOCIATIONS, 1984
Annual.   May 1985.   3+23 p.
SRI/MF/complete

Annual report on financial condition of Colorado State-chartered savings and loan assns, presenting assets, liabilities, and net worth, by institution, 1984; and composite financial and operating data, 1981-84. Composite data include balance sheet totals and ratios, number of investing members, and number and value of mortgage loans.

Data are compiled from reports filed with the Division of Savings and Loan.

Contains table of contents (1 p.); summary, and directory of savings and loan assns and officers (p. 1-12); and 3 tables (p. 13-23).

Availability: Colorado Department of Regulatory Agencies, Savings and Loan Division, 1525 Sherman St., Rm. 110, Denver CO 80203, $2.00; SRI/MF/complete.

S1075   COLORADO
Department of Revenue

S1075–1   ANNUAL REPORT, 1984, Colorado Department of Revenue
Annual.   Nov. 29, 1984.
151 p.
LC 43-52674.
SRI/MF/complete

Annual report on Colorado tax revenues, by type of tax, FY84, with trends from FY50. Includes sales tax by county, municipality, and industry. Also includes data on motor vehicle registrations and accidents, drivers licenses, and State lottery revenues.

Contains contents listing (p. 1-3); 1 table showing Colorado population by county, 1970, 1980, and 1983 (p. 4); narrative report on Revenue Dept organization and State tax legislation (p. 9-32); and 10 statistical sections, with statutory references, tax rates or fees, facsimile tax reporting forms, 1 chart, and 60 tables listed below (p. 35-151).

This is the 43rd annual report.

Availability: Colorado Department of Revenue, Research and Statistics, 1375 Sherman St., Rm. 422, Denver CO 80261, †; SRI/MF/complete.

S1075–1.1: Collections, Refunds, and Administrative Costs
[Data are shown for FY84, unless otherwise noted.]

[1] Total collections and cost of administration, FY50-84. (p. 35)

[2-3] Collections [FY83-84]; and refunds and net collections, FY84; by source. (p. 36-38)

[4] Gross collections and cost of administration, by fund and tax source. (p. 39)

[5] Administrative expenditures, by purpose. (p. 41)

[6] Number of audits, assessments, and refunds [by tax section]. (p. 42)

S1075–1.2: Alcoholic Beverage and Cigarette Taxes

ALCOHOLIC BEVERAGE TAXES
[1] Comparison of [liquor tax] receipts and refunds, FY82-84. (p. 47)

[2] Liquor tax statistical summary [receipts from license fees by type, and from excise tax], FY84. (p. 48)

[3] Taxable gallons of beer, wine, and spirituous liquors, FY72-84. (p. 49)

[4-5] Liquor licenses in force [by type, FY84]; and total number of State liquor licenses issued, by county [1979-83]. (p. 50-51)

[6] Violations of the liquor code and 3.2% Beer Act [hearings, revocations, suspensions, denials, court cases, and local hearings], FY82-84. (p. 52)

CIGARETTE TAX
[7-8] Cigarette tax [gross amount, wholesaler's discount, refunds, and gross and net collections]; and distribution of net collections [city/county and State shares]; FY74-84. (p. 56)

S1075–1.3: Estate and Income Taxes, Checkoff Contributions, and Lottery Revenues

ESTATE TAX
[1] Estate, inheritance, and gift tax activity [returns and documents reviewed/recorded, and statements/certificates/receipts, lien releases, and refunds issued, FY83-84]. (p. 61)

[2] Estate, inheritance, and gift tax net collections, FY71-84. (p. 62)

INCOME TAX
[3-4] Number of taxable and nontaxable returns [also includes partnership returns], FY84; and tax liability, FY73-84; by type of return. (p. 68-69)

[5] Surtax liability [for individual returns, FY74-84]. (p. 69)

[6] Number of individual returns and adjusted gross income, FY71-84. (p. 70)

[7-10] Tax liability, credits, payments, and overpayments, FY84; and tax refunds issued [FY77-84]. (p. 71-72)

[11] Individual and corporation income tax cash flow [FY80-84]. (p. 73)

[12] Number of corporate returns, tax, and tax credits, by industry [division], FY84. (p. 74)

[13] Individual resident returns: number of returns, adjusted gross income, and net normal tax classified, by major planning regions, FY84. (p. 75)

[14] Returns filed for old age property tax/heat credits [and refund/credit amount, FY72-84]. (p. 76)

TAX CHECKOFF CONTRIBUTIONS
[15] Wildlife, domestic abuse, and Olympic Committee checkoffs, number of returns and collections, [various years FY78-84]. (p. 77)

LOTTERY REVENUES
[16] Lottery sales [and days in game, by game], FY83-84. (p. 83)

[17] 1984 lottery distributions by fund. (p. 84)

S1075–1.4: Mileage/Fuel and Motor Vehicle Taxes, and Other Motor Vehicle Data

MILEAGE/FUEL TAXES
[1] Motor fuel: gross gallons, gallons exempted, and net gallons taxes, FY83-84. (p. 89)

[2] Motor and special fuel tax refund, by use [FY83-84]. (p. 90)

[3] Motor fuel: gross gasoline gallonage [by month, FY80-84]. (p. 91)

[4] Special fuel tax gallonage and collections, FY75-84. (p. 92)

[5] Motor fuel, diesel fuel, LPG [liquefied petroleum gas], and other taxable fuel collections [including gasohol], FY83-84. (p. 92)

[6] Gross ton-mile tax [collections and refunds], FY74-84. (p. 93)

[7-8] Port of entry truck activities [includes special fuel permits, agricultural licenses and inspection certificates, and health/brand inspections, FY82-84]; and trucks cleared and weighed, by port, FY84. (p. 94-95)

MOTOR VEHICLE DATA
[9] License fees and ownership tax collected [by county], 1983. (p. 103)

[10] Number of registrations, by type of license, by county, 1983. (p. 104-106)

[11] Motor vehicle emissions program [licensing activity, certificates sold, and collections], FY84. (p. 107)

[12] Standard summary of motor vehicle traffic accidents, [injuries, and fatalities; includes detailed data by accident and vehicle type; location; age and sex of driver and victim, including data for pedestrians and bicyclists; mileage traveled; contributing circumstances; and helmet and eye protection use; 1983, with summary comparisons to 1982]. (p. 108-109)

[13] Driver's license activity [types of licenses and permits issued, endorsements, and examinations, at total State and county offices], 1983. (p. 110)

[14] Driver improvement [license suspensions, revocations, denials, and cancellations, by type; reinstatements; and financial responsibility reports received; 1982-83]. (p. 111)

S1075–1.5: Sales and Use Taxes, and Severance Tax

SALES AND USE TAXES

[Data are shown for FY84, unless otherwise noted. Data by business class are shown by industry division, with additional detail for hotels/lodging and types of retail trade.]

[1-3] Sales tax collections, .5% emergency fund collections, and [consumer and retailer] use tax, [various years] FY74-84. (p. 117-118)

[4-5] Number of returns, gross sales, deductions, and net taxable sales; and retail sales, by county; by business class. (p. 119-121)

[6-7] Retail trade sales and retail sales, by county, 1974-83. (p. 122-123)

[8] Number of returns, sales by type of sales, and sales tax, by county. (p. 124-125)

[9] Number of returns, retail sales, and net tax collected, by business class. (p. 126-128)

[10] Gross sales, retail sales, and net tax collected, for selected cities [and] by county. (p. 129-138)

[11] Summary of local sales tax rates: number of tax jurisdictions, by tax rate. (p. 139)

[12-14] City and county sales tax rates collected by the State [by city or county]; and city sales taxes not collected by the State; as of July 1, 1984. (p. 140-143)

SEVERANCE TAX

[15] Severance tax collections [for oil/gas, coal, and metallic minerals/molybdenum, FY78-84]. (p. 151)

S1085   COLORADO
Department of
Social Services

S1085–1   COLORADO STATE DEPARTMENT OF SOCIAL SERVICES Annual Report, FY83
Annual.   [1985.]   53 p.
LC 81-642327.
SRI/MF/complete

Annual report on Colorado public assistance program cases, recipients, and payments, by program and county, FY83, with trends from FY67. Covers food stamps, AFDC, Medicaid, veteran assistance, aging, pension, child welfare, energy assistance, and other programs. Also includes data on reported child abuse cases.

Contains contents listing (1 p.); and report, with narrative summaries, and 3 charts and 23 tables listed below (p. 1-53).

Availability: Colorado Department of Social Services, 1575 Sherman St., Rm. 619, Denver CO 80203, †; SRI/MF/complete.

CHARTS AND TABLES:
[Data are for Colorado, FY83, unless otherwise noted.]

SUMMARY AND MEDICAL ASSISTANCE

[1] Dept of Social Services expenditures [of State and Federal funds, by function or program]. (p. 3-4)

[2] Estimated Medicaid and OAP [old age pension] health and medical fund [payments] by type of recipient. [chart] (p. 12)

[3] [Social services dept] appropriations/expenditures [by program]. [chart] (p. 13)

[4] Medicaid payments by category of services. [chart] (p. 14)

CHILD WELFARE AND VETERAN SERVICES

[5] [Child abuse cases reported, 1970-83.] (p. 18)

[6] Interstate compact on the placement of children [in- and out-of-State placements by type, and case dispositions, July 1982-June 1983]. (p. 21)

[7] Services summary [recipients by program, including adoptions, daycare, and homemaker and family planning services, by county, FY83]. (p. 22-23)

[8] Veterans affairs program [caseload distribution]. (p. 24)

[9] [Veterans' nursing homes: capacity, occupancy, and cost per day, by facility, FY82-83]. (p. 25)

[10] Veterans affairs [awards and monetary recoveries FY81-83; and awards and payments, by type of benefit, FY83]. (p. 26)

ENERGY ASSISTANCE, AFDC, AND CHILD SUPPORT

[11] Low income energy assistance program [cases and expenditures by program, FY81-83]. (p. 28)

[12-13] AFDC [net expenditures, FY80-83; and average monthly caseloads and recipients, FY67-83]. (p. 29)

[14] Average monthly data, AFDC [cases and expenditures], by county. (p. 30-31)

[15] Child support enforcement program [collections, expenditures, and cases], FY82-83. (p. 33)

REFUGEE SERVICES, PENSIONS, AND MEDICAL ASSISTANCE

[16] Refugee services [cases and expenditures, FY79-83]. (p. 34)

[17-22] OAP, aid to the needy disabled, and aid to blind/blind treatment [expenditures, and cases or recipients, FY79-83, and by county, FY83]. (p. 35-43)

[23] Average monthly Medicaid eligibles [cases by county]. (p. 45)

FOOD ASSISTANCE PROGRAMS

[24] Monthly average number of household participation [in food stamp program, for public assistance recipients and others, FY71-83]. (p. 46)

[25] Food stamp program [value of coupons issued, estimated economic impact, public assistance and other households participating, and recipients, by county and district]. (p. 47-48)

[26] [Donated foods] dollar value and net weight of food issued [by program, including school lunch and breakfast]. (p. 49)

S1090   COLORADO
Department of
State

S1090–1   STATE OF COLORADO ABSTRACT OF VOTES CAST, 1984
Biennial.   [1985.]   2+236 p.
LC 3-11921.
SRI/MF/complete

Biennial report presenting results of the Colorado primary election held Sept. 11, 1984, and the general election held Nov. 6, 1984. Shows voting for President and Vice-President; U.S. and State senators and representatives; judges; State board of education; other State officials; university regents; and 5 State constitutional amendments, including measures limiting State/local funding for abortions and legalizing gambling in Pueblo County.

Also includes voter registration and turnout, and directories of State and county officials.

All data are shown by district or county. Voting is shown by candidate's name and political party.

Previous report, covering 1982 elections, is described in SRI 1983 Annual under this number.

Availability: Colorado Department of State, Elections and Licensing Division, 1560 Broadway, Suite 200, Denver CO 80202, $3.00 if picked up, $3.50 if mailed; SRI/MF/complete.

S1155   CONNECTICUT
Department of Agriculture

S1155-1   CONNECTICUT AGRICULTURAL STATISTICS, 1983
Annual. [1985.] 8+47 p.
ISSN 0573-6269.
LC 82-641380.
SRI/MF/complete

Annual report on Connecticut agricultural production, marketing, and finances, 1983, with some data for 1984 and trends from 1972. Data are generally shown by commodity, with some comparisons to neighboring States or regions and total U.S.

Report covers cash receipts, production, value, prices, and, as applicable, acreage, yield, inventory, or disposition, for field crop, fruit, vegetable, livestock, dairy, and poultry sectors.

Also includes data on weather; number and acreage of farms; aquaculture, including shellfish harvest and licenses; farm assets, debt, and production expenses; farmland preservation program; and U.S. per capita consumption of major food commodities.

Data are primarily from Connecticut Dept of Agriculture and USDA.

Contains contents listing (1 p.); highlights, and statistical section with 8 charts and 58 tables (p. 1-36); and State Dept of Agriculture activities, with 3 text tables (p. 37-47).

Availability: Connecticut Department of Agriculture, Marketing Division, State Office Bldg., Hartford CT 06106, †; SRI/MF/complete.

S1170   CONNECTICUT
Office of the Comptroller

S1170-1   REPORT OF THE STATE COMPTROLLER TO THE GOVERNOR for the Fiscal Year Ended June 30, 1984, Connecticut
Annual. Aug. 31, 1984.
99 p.
Public Document No. 1.
LC 83-645088.
SRI/MF/complete

Annual report on financial condition of Connecticut State government, FY84, presenting assets and liabilities, reserves, fund balances, and surplus; receipts by source; and disbursements by function; for all, general, special revenue, debt service, capital project, internal service, enterprise, and fiduciary funds.

Also includes data on general fund budgeted vs. realized revenues by source, and appropriations vs. expenditures by detailed agency and program; bonded debt; current expenses by type, fixed charges, capital outlays, inventories, and property valuation, by agency.

Data are from the records of the comptroller's office.

Contains contents listing, transmittal letter, and certificate of audit (p. 2-4); and 25 exhibits and schedules (p. 5-99).

Availability: Connecticut Office of the Comptroller, Central Accounting Division, 30 Trinity St., Hartford CT 06106, †; SRI/MF/complete.

S1185   CONNECTICUT
Department of Education

S1185-1   STATEMENT OF ACTIVITIES, 1983/84, Connecticut Department of Education
Annual. 1985. 46 p.
SRI/MF/complete, current & previous year reports

Annual report, for 1983/84, on Connecticut Dept of Education division activities. Covers staff size, and expenditures from State and Federal funds for personal services, equipment, grants/other payments, and other expenses, all by division, bureau, and program.

Contains contents listing (1 p.); overview, with organizational chart and 1 table (p. 1-5); and Commissioner's Office and division reports, with 6 tables (p. 7-46).

Previous report, for 1982/83, has also been reviewed and is also available on SRI microfiche under this number [Annual. 1984. 49 p. ◆].

Report was previously published as volume 1 of a 3-part series on Connecticut public schools. Prior to 1985, SRI covered the entire series under S1185-1. Former volumes 1-3 are now covered as separate reports rather than a series, and are described under S1185-1, S1185-2, and S1185-3, respectively.

Availability: Connecticut Department of Education, Public Information, Rm. 304, PO Box 2219, Hartford CT 06145, ‡; SRI/MF/complete.

S1185-2   CONNECTICUT PUBLIC SCHOOLS: Town and School District Profiles, 1982/83
Annual. 1984. v+374 p.
SRI/MF/complete

Annual report, for 1982/83, profiling Connecticut public school districts and towns. Covers community data, including population, income, and property values; and educational enrollment, programs, finances, personnel, and students. Also includes data for 4 private schools.

Data are compiled from school district reports, State Dept of Education, Census Bureau, and other sources.

Contains contents listing and foreword (p. iii-v); statistical profiles, each generally including tabular listings of educational program offerings and school district officials and grade levels served, and 3-10 tables as indicated below (p. 1-355); and definitions and sources, and index (p. 357-374).

Report was previously published as volume 2 of a 3-part series on Connecticut public schools. Prior to 1985, SRI covered the entire series under S1185-1. Former volumes 1-3 are now covered as separate reports rather than a series, and are described under S1185-1, S1185-2, and S1185-3, respectively.

Availability: Connecticut Department of Education, Public Information, Rm. 304, PO Box 2219, Hartford CT 06145, educational and library communities †, others $8.25; SRI/MF/complete.

TABLES:

STATEWIDE

[1] Community data [including population; per capita income; equalized property value; percent of students enrolled in public schools and population age 25/over completing high school and college; percent of children in single-parent families; median family income; percent of families below poverty level; and median value of housing units; mostly 1979 or 1980]. (p. 2)

[2] District students [including minority, special education, non-English home language, economically disadvantaged, and nonresident students; students in vocational/technical schools and vocational/agriculture centers; and high school graduates by postgraduate activity], 1982/83. (p. 2)

[3] EERA [Education Evaluation and Remedial Assistance] 9th grade proficiency test results [by subject], fall 1982. (p. 2)

[4] Staff data [number of FTE teachers, support staff, and administrators; per pupil ratios; mean age, experience, and salary; percent with Master's/higher degree; and staff cost per pupil], 1982/83. (p. 3)

[5-7] Revenue data and selected State and Federal grants, 1982/83. (p. 3)

[8] Educational equalization data [per capita property value, equalized school tax rate, and student need], 1980/81. (p. 3)

[9] Aid and expenditure data [per pupil equalization aid and minimum expenditure requirement; and percent for special education, transportation, and school construction]; 1983/84. (p. 3)

[10] Expenditure data [total and per pupil, and State median per pupil, by function], 1982/83. (p. 3)

TOWNS THAT OPERATE SCHOOL DISTRICTS

Tables [1-10] are generally repeated for each town operating a school district. Table [8] includes State rankings; table [10] includes expenditure comparisons to State median; and table [3] is omitted for some towns. (p. 6-303).

TOWNS THAT DO NOT OPERATE SCHOOL DISTRICTS

Tables [1] and [8-9] are generally repeated for each town not operating a school district. Table [8] includes State rankings; and table [9] omits detailed distribution. (p. 306-315)

REGIONAL DISTRICTS

Tables [2-7] and [10] are generally repeated for each regional school district. Table [10] includes expenditure comparisons to State median. (p. 318-349)

MISCELLANEOUS SCHOOLS

Tables [2-4] are repeated for 3 endowed/incorporated academies and E. O. Smith School. (p. 352-355)

S1185-3   MEETING THE CHALLENGE: Condition of Education in Connecticut, Elementary and Secondary, 1984
Annual. 1985. 51 p.
LC 85-622221.
SRI/MF/complete

Annual report on Connecticut public schools, presenting data on enrollment, staff, special programs, and finances, primarily 1983/84, with some data for 1984/85 and trends from the 1970s.

Data are compiled from school district reports, State Dept of Education, Census Bureau, and other sources.

Contains contents listing (p. 1); and narrative report interspersed with several summary charts, and 22 more detailed charts and 49 tables described below (p. 4-51).

Report was previously published as volume 3 of a 3-part series on Connecticut public schools. Prior to 1985, SRI covered the entire series under S1185-1. Former volumes 1-3 are now covered as separate reports, under S1185-1, S1185-2, and S1185-3, respectively.

Last previous edition of this report was published during 1982, and is described in SRI 1983 Annual under S1185-1.3.

Availability: Connecticut Department of Education, Public Information, Rm. 304, PO Box 2219, Hartford CT 06145, †; SRI/MF/complete.

CHARTS AND TABLES

[Unless otherwise noted, data are for Connecticut, 1983/84 or 1984/85, with trends from 1970s.]

S1185–3.1: Schools and Enrollment

a. Public schools, by level and for alternative/ prekindergarten/special education; enrollment, for public schools by grade level with projections to 1999, for nonpublic schools, and for vocational/technical schools with detail by sex and for minority and handicapped students; and general population summary. 7 charts and 8 tables (p. 4-8)

b. Instructional time summary, by level; high school graduation requirements by subject, 1980, 1984, and 1988; mean years of study by subject and degree program goals of seniors, by sex; special education students by disability; and public school enrollment of blacks, Hispanics, and other minorities. 6 tables (p. 8-10)

S1185–3.2: Teachers and Staff

a. Full-time teacher/support staff characteristics (including education, State teaching experience, and age) and mean, minimum, and maximum salaries; low, median, and high starting salaries for teachers with bachelor's degree; and threats and/or assaults against administrators, teachers, students, and others. 1 chart and 7 tables. (p. 11-13)

b. Students receiving teacher incentive college loans, by subject; teacher withdrawals/retirements; high school seniors intending to study education; public opinion on quality of education and teachers; State college/university education program graduates, by degree level; teaching certificates issued by specialty; and State expenditures for school staff development. 2 charts and 5 tables. (p. 14-19)

S1185–3.3: Educational Achievement, Programs, and Finances

EDUCATIONAL ACHIEVEMENT

a. Graduates of public, vocational/technical, and nonpublic schools, with public school completion rates; high school equivalency tests administered and passed; postgradu-

ate activities of public high school graduates; and adult education program graduates and selected benefits. 1 chart and 6 tables. (p. 22-24)

b. Average scores for Connecticut Assessment of Educational Progress test by grade and topic, for verbal and mathematics portions of Preliminary Scholastic Aptitude Test/National Merit Scholarship Qualifying Test, and for Standard Written English Test by sex, with some comparisons to U.S.; and advanced placement test participants and scores, for public and private school students. 5 tables. (p. 26-28)

PROGRAMS

c. Prekindergarten and kindergarten public and nonpublic enrollment; and vocational program enrollment by sex, graduates, and postgraduate activities and average hourly wages, by program type and/or sponsor. 5 tables. (p. 31-35)

d. Local education agency adult education enrollment, by program with detail by age and race (including black and Hispanic); Division of Vocational Rehabilitation clients by service; public and nonpublic compensatory education enrollment; students eligible for State-funded bilingual educational programs, by language; and participation in paid, reduced price, and/or free breakfast, lunch, and milk programs. 3 charts and 4 tables. (p. 36-40)

FINANCES

e. Educational funding from State and Federal government, with detail by program or purpose; per pupil expenditures; school district expenditures by major item; and highest, average, and lowest school district spending per pupil, school tax rate, and teacher/professional staff salary. 8 charts and 3 tables. (p. 47-51)

S1200   CONNECTICUT
Department of
Health Services

S1200–1   **STATE OF CONNECTICUT ONE HUNDRED AND THIRTY-SIXTH REGISTRATION REPORT of Births, Marriages, Divorces, and Deaths for the Year Ended Dec. 31, 1983**
Annual.   May 30, 1985.
53 p.
LC 83-643327.
SRI/MF/complete, current & 2 previous years reports

Annual report on Connecticut vital statistics, 1983. Covers population, births, deaths by cause, marriages, and divorces. Includes data by race, sex, age, county, and town.

Data are derived from Connecticut vital event registrations.

Contains contents and table listing, explanatory notes, and summary (p. 3-6); 16 tables, listed below (p. 7-51); and glossary and formulas (p. 52-53).

Reports for 1982 and 1981 have also been reviewed by SRI during 1985, and are also availa-

ble on SRI microfiche under S1200-1 [Annual. May 30, 1985. 52 p. $10.00 (report for 1982); Annual. May 30, 1985. 51 p. $10.00 (report for 1981)]. Report for 1980 is described in SRI 1983 Annual, also under S1200-1.

Availability: Connecticut Department of Health Services, Health Statistics Division, Statistical Analysis Unit, 150 Washington St., Hartford CT 06106, $10.00; SRI/MF/complete.

TABLES:

[Data are for Connecticut, 1983, unless otherwise noted. Data by town include totals for health service areas.]

POPULATION, AND DATA BY TOWN

1. Population, by age and sex. (p. 7)

2. Estimated populations and vital statistics [including occurrence-based and residence-based births, deaths, and marriages, with selected detail by race, all shown by town, with totals for out-of-State]. (p. 8-13)

BIRTHS AND DEATHS

3. Births, [by age of mother and race, crosstabulated by place of delivery (hospital, other, unknown), child's sex, legitimacy, birth weight, gestation period, and plurality]. (p. 14)

4. Live births to residents by race, low birth weights and maternal age [by town]. (p. 15-27)

5. Fetal deaths occurring [detail similar to table 3]. (p. 28)

6. Causes of fetal deaths occurring. (p. 29)

7-8. Causes of death [among all and] nonwhite residents [by sex and age]. (p. 30-37)

9. Deaths under 1 year of age, residents [by town, race, age, and cause]. (p. 38-41)

10. Selected causes of infant deaths, residents [by race, sex, and age]. (p. 42-47)

11. Leading causes of death in certain age groups [by sex]. (p. 48-49)

MARRIAGES AND DIVORCES

12-13. Number of present marriage, and previous marital status, bride and groom. (p. 50)

14. County of dissolution of marriages [also shows State totals by sex of complainant]. (p. 51)

15. Children under 18 affected by marriage dissolution. (p. 51)

16. Duration of marriages dissolved. (p. 51)

S1212   CONNECTICUT
Department of
Housing

**S1212–1   CONNECTICUT HOUSING
PRODUCTION AND PERMIT
AUTHORIZED
CONSTRUCTION: 1984**
Annual. Mar. 1, 1985. 71 p.
ISSN 0069-9020.
LC 76-625065.
SRI/MF/complete, current & 2
previous reports

Annual report on Connecticut construction activity authorized by building permits, by locale, 1984, with trends from 1980. Includes data on volume and value of residential construction by structure type (including mobile homes); residential demolitions and additions/alterations; conversions of structures to and from residential use; and housing losses and gains; by county and/or city/town.

Also includes statewide data on construction of publicly and privately owned residential and nonresidential buildings, by structure type.

Data are based on monthly reports collected by Census Bureau and Connecticut Dept of Housing from local building permit offices.

Contains letter of transmittal, contents listing, and narrative summary (p. 5-11); 2 maps and 15 tables (p. 13-64); and definitions and reporting forms (p. 65-71).

Previous reports, for 1982 and 1983, have also been received, and are also available on SRI microfiche under S1212-1 [Annual. 1982. 48 p. †] and [Annual. 1983. 51 p. †], respectively; previous reports omit detailed nonresidential building construction activity. Report for 1981 is described in SRI 1982 Annual under this number.

Prior to 1982, report was titled *Construction Activity Authorized by Building Permits; and Housing Units in Connecticut.*

Availability: Connecticut Department of Housing, Development, Planning and Research Section, 1179 Main St., Hartford CT 06103-1089, †; SRI/MF/complete.

S1220   CONNECTICUT
Judicial Department

**S1220–1   BIENNIAL REPORT OF THE
CONNECTICUT JUDICIAL
DEPARTMENT, July 1,
1982-June 30, 1984**
Biennial. Jan. 9, 1985.
116 p. var. paging.
ISSN 0098-8138.
LC 75-644536.
SRI/MF/complete

Biennial report, for FY83-84, on Connecticut judicial system, including appellate and trial court caseloads and dispositions. Covers supreme, superior, and probate courts. Includes trial court data by case type and court location.

Case types shown include criminal, motor vehicle, civil, small claims, domestic relations, juvenile, probate, adoption, guardianship, commitment, proceedings for mentally retarded, passport applications, and other case types.

Report also includes data on judicial dept finances, and probation and Bail Commission activities.

Contains preface and contents listing (3 p.); narrative report in 7 sections, with 12 charts and 8 tables (p. 1-57); and 3 appendices, with list of judges and 48 tables (p. A1-C2).

Previous report, for FY81-82, is described in SRI 1983 Annual under this number.

Availability: Connecticut Judicial Department, Chief Court Administrator's Office, Drawer N, Station A, Hartford CT 06106, ‡; SRI/MF/complete.

S1222   CONNECTICUT
Insurance Department

**S1222–1   STATE OF CONNECTICUT
One-Hundred Eighteenth
Annual Report of the
Insurance Commissioner,
1984**
Annual. Aug. 23, 1984.
3+119 p.
SRI/MF/complete

Annual report on Connecticut insurance industry financial condition and underwriting activity, by company and type of insurance, 1983. Covers assets, liabilities, capital/guaranty fund, surplus, and premiums written in Connecticut, for life, fire/casualty, and title companies.

Premium data are generally shown by line of coverage, including accident/health, property, medical malpractice, workmen's compensation, automobile, and surety.

Data are compiled from annual statements submitted by individual insurers.

Contains contents listing (1 p.); 9 tables (p. 1-113); and table addenda (p. 114-119).

Availability: Connecticut Insurance Department, 165 Capitol Ave., Hartford CT 06106, $30.25; SRI/MF/complete.

S1235   CONNECTICUT
Labor Department

**S1235–1   CONNECTICUT LABOR
SITUATION**
Monthly. Approx. 10 p.
SRI/MF/complete, shipped
quarterly

Monthly report on Connecticut nonagricultural employment, earnings, hours, and selected other economic indicators. Data are from State labor records, and are shown by industry group and MSA. Month of coverage is 1 month prior to cover date.

Contains narrative summary with text statistics; 8 monthly tables, listed below; an annual article on labor force demographic composition; and occasional special articles or summary tables, including data from BLS annual area wage surveys.

Monthly tables appear in all issues. Additional features with substantial nonsummary statistical content are described, as they appear, under "Statistical Features." Nonstatistical features are not covered.

Prior to the Feb. 1985 issue, data were shown by labor market area rather than MSA.

The Employment Security Division also issues a biweekly press release on unemployment claims; and monthly or quarterly reviews of conditions in each of the States' 16 labor market areas. These reports are not covered in SRI.

Availability: Connecticut Labor Department, Employment Security Division, Research and Information Office, 200 Folly Brook Blvd., Wethersfield CT 06109, †; SRI/MF/complete, shipped quarterly.

Issues reviewed during 1985: Nov. 1984-Sept. 1985 (P).

MONTHLY TABLES:
[Data are for Connecticut, unless otherwise noted. Tables [1-6] show data for month of coverage, previous month, and same month of previous year.]

[1] Nonagricultural employment (excludes agricultural, private household, self-employed, and unpaid family workers) [by industry division and major group].

[2] Earnings and hours, manufacturing production/related workers [by major industry group] and on-site construction workers.

[3] Unemployment, by [MSA].

[4] U.S. CPI, all urban consumers.

[5] Area nonagricultural wage/salary employment, by place of work [manufacturing and nonmanufacturing, by MSA].

[6] Earnings and hours by [MSA], manufacturing/production/maintenance/related workers.

[7] Economic indicators [employment, average weekly initial unemployment benefit claims, unemployment rate, personal income, auto registration, average workweek hours, and manufacturing output index; monthly for year to date and previous year].

[8] Unemployment insurance benefit financial data [insured unemployed, benefits paid, and employer contributions, monthly for year to date and previous year, with trends from the 1970s; Federal loans and direct repayments, and repayments via employer tax credit reduction, annually from the 1970s; and loans outstanding and State Unemployment Compensation Fund balance, as of 1-2 months prior to cover date].

STATISTICAL FEATURE:

S1235–1.601: May 1985
PROFILE OF THE LABOR FORCE IN CONNECTICUT, 1984, ANNUAL FEATURE

(p. 9-10) Annual article, with 2 tables showing Connecticut population aged 16/over by labor force status; and labor force by employment status, including mean duration of unemployment; all by race and sex, with detail for youth, 1983-84. Data are from BLS.

S1255   CONNECTICUT
Office of
Policy and Management

S1255–4   REVISED AGE AND SEX DISTRIBUTIONS OF POPULATION PROJECTIONS for Connecticut Regions and Municipalities to the Year 2000
Monograph.   Dec. 1984.
225 p. var. paging.
LC 85-621405.
SRI/MF/complete

Report presenting revised Connecticut population projections by sex and age, for the State, and for individual planning regions, health service areas, municipalities, and counties, quinquennially 1985-2000, with actual data for 1980. Also includes number of persons in group quarters and total population, for census tracts with significant proportion of group quarters residents, 1980.

Projections are based on the 1980 census.

Contains contents listing (1 p.); introduction and methodology, with 1 chart and 1 table (p. 1-13); and 1 basic table, repeated for each geographic entity noted above, arranged in 5 separately paginated sections (197 p.).

Data are revisions to a similar report published in 1983; for description, see SRI 1983 Annual under this number.

Availability: Connecticut Office of Policy and Management, Comprehensive Planning Division, Connecticut Census Data Center, 80 Washington St., Hartford CT 06106-4459, $7.00+$2.00 postage and handling; SRI/MF/complete.

S1255–6   DISTRIBUTION OF FAMILY INCOME IN 1979 by Age of Head of Household
Monograph.   May 1984.
1+178 p.
LC 85-621404.
SRI/MF/complete

Report presenting 1980 U.S. Census of Population and Housing data on Connecticut family income, by county and city. Includes number of families by income group, and median and aggregate income, all by age of head of household, 1979.

Data are from Summary Tape File 4B and are based on sample counts.

Contains 1 table repeated for the State (p. 1), each county (p. 2-9), and each municipality (p. 10-178).

Availability: Connecticut Office of Policy and Management, Comprehensive Planning Division, Connecticut Census Data Center, 80 Washington St., Hartford CT 06106-4459, $7.00+$2.00 shipping and handling; SRI/MF/complete.

S1255–7   SELECTED STATISTICS FOR VETERANS IN CONNECTICUT
Monograph.   June 1984.
1+178 p.
SRI/MF/complete

Report presenting 1980 U.S. Census of Population and Housing data on Connecticut veterans, by county and city. Includes civilians by veteran status and sex, and civilian veterans by period of service.

Data are from Summary Tape File 3A and are based on sample counts.

Contains 1 table repeated for the State (p. 1), each county (p. 2-9), and each municipality (p. 10-178).

Availability: Connecticut Office of Policy and Management, Comprehensive Planning Division, Connecticut Census Data Center, 80 Washington St., Hartford CT 06106-4459, $7.00+$2.00 shipping and handling; SRI/MF/complete.

S1256   CONNECTICUT
Department of
Public Safety

S1256–1   CRIME IN CONNECTICUT, 1984
Annual.   [1985.]   iii+246 p.
LC 83-645941.
SRI/MF/complete, current & previous year reports

Annual report on Connecticut crimes and arrests, by offense, 1984, with selected trends from 1980. Includes data by city, county, and reporting agency, and by offender age, sex, and race/ethnicity. Also includes law enforcement employment, and assaults on officers.

Report focuses on 8 Index offenses: murder, rape, robbery, aggravated assault, burglary, larceny/theft, motor vehicle theft, and arson. Arrests are also shown for numerous non-Index offenses.

Data are from State and local agency reports submitted under the Uniform Crime Reporting (UCR) Program.

Contains highlights, crime clock, and contents listing (p. i-iii); UCR Program description (p. 1-3); and 8 statistical sections, with 17 charts and 231 tables described below, in p. 5-246).

This is the 7th annual report. A *Quarterly Crime Index* is also issued, but is not covered by SRI.

Previous report, for 1983, was also reviewed in SRI during 1985, and is also available on SRI microfiche under S1256-1 [Annual. [1984.] iii+244 p. †].

Availability: Connecticut Department of Public Safety, State Police Division, Uniform Crime Reporting Program, 294 Colony St., Meriden CT 06450-2098, †; SRI/MF/complete.

TABLES AND CHARTS
[Data are for 1984, unless otherwise noted. Data by race/ethnicity include white, black, Indian, and Asian.]

S1256–1.1: State Index Offense Summary, and Stolen Property Value
[In addition to the data described below, sections on general and specific Index offenses also include 1 trend chart, and/or 1 table showing total offenses, and crime and clearance rates, 1980-84.]

INDEX OFFENSES, GENERAL
a. Offenses, clearances, and value of property loss, by offense, with selected offense characteristics. 1 chart and 2 tables. (p. 5-6)

SPECIFIC INDEX OFFENSES
b. Murder: victims and offenders, by age, sex, and race/ethnicity (including Hispanic and non-Hispanic); and offenses by victim/offender relationship and type of weapon. 2 charts and 3 tables. (p. 7-9)

c. Rape: forcible rapes and attempted rapes. 2 charts and 1 table. (p. 10)

d. Robbery: offenses and value of property stolen, by place of occurrence; and offenses by weapon type. 2 charts and 2 tables. (p. 11-12)

e. Aggravated assault: offenses by weapon used; and simple and aggravated assaults. 3 charts and 1 table. (p. 13-14)

f. Burglary: offenses and value of property stolen, for day and night residential and nonresidential offenses; and offenses by type of entry. 2 charts and 2 tables. (p. 15-16)

g. Larceny: offenses and value of property stolen, by type and amount of theft. 1 chart and 2 tables. (p. 17-18)

h. Motor vehicle theft: offenses by vehicle type; and locally stolen vehicles recovered, and value of locally stolen and all recovered vehicles. 1 chart and 3 tables. (p. 19-20)

i. Arson: offenses, average value of damage, and percent cleared, by property type. 2 tables. (p. 21)

OFFENSES BY COUNTY, AND STOLEN PROPERTY VALUE
j. Index offense rates by county and offense, for violent and property crimes (excluding Arson). 1 chart and 1 table. (p. 23-24)

k. Value of property stolen and recovered, monthly, and by property type. 1 chart and 2 tables. (p. 26-27)

S1256–1.2: State Arrest Summary, and Data by Jurisdiction
[Detailed data on arrests are shown by age, sex, and race/ethnicity, for 28 Index and non-Index offenses, with summary totals for Hispanic and non-Hispanic arrests. Data by jurisdiction are repeated for 100-101 city, university, and State police depts.]

a. State total Index and non-Index arrests, 1980-84; and detailed arrests by offense. 2 tables. (p. 29-31)

b. Offenses, clearances, and value of property stolen, by Index offense, with selected offense characteristics, arranged by jurisdiction, and usually showing population; and Index crimes by offense (excluding arson), by town. 102 tables. (p. 33-136)

c. Arrest detail by jurisdiction and for total State police. 100 tables. (p. 138-237)

S1256–1.3: Assaults on Police, and Law Enforcement Employment
a. Police officers killed and injured, 1983-84; officers assaulted and clearance rates, by type of activity; and officers assaulted by type of assignment, time of day, and weapon used. 1 chart and 5 tables. (p. 240-241)

b. Full-time sworn and civilian law enforcement employees by sex, and, generally, population served, for city and university agencies grouped by county, and for State police. 1 table. (p. 244-246)

S1265   CONNECTICUT
Office of the
Secretary of the
State

S1265-1   STATEMENT OF VOTE,
General Election, Nov. 6,
1984, Connecticut
Biennial. [1985.] 65 p.
SRI/MF/complete

Biennial report presenting results of the Connecticut general election held Nov. 6, 1984. Shows voting for President/Vice President, U.S. Representatives, and State senators and representatives; and 3 State constitutional amendments, including 1 prohibiting discrimination against disabled persons. Data are shown by district and town, and include party affiliation of candidates.

Also includes voter registration and turnout, by district and town.

Previous report, covering 1982 general election, is described in SRI 1983 Annual under this number.

Availability: Connecticut Office of the Secretary of the State, Publications Division, 30 Trinity St., Hartford CT 06106, †; SRI/MF/complete.

S1275   CONNECTICUT
Department of
Transportation

S1275-1   1983 STATEWIDE
ACCIDENTS: Connecticut
DART Univariate Distribution
Annual. [1984.]
35+5 p.+2 attachments.
SRI/MF/complete

Annual report on Connecticut traffic accidents by accident and vehicle type, location, time, and other detailed circumstances; and driver and pedestrian victim characteristics, including alcohol and drug use, 1983. Also includes data on fatalities and injuries, State of vehicle registration and driver residence, number of vehicles requiring towing, local residence of Connecticut drivers, and safety device usage.

Data are based on reports submitted to the Connecticut Motor Vehicle Dept.

Report contains statistical tabulations (35 p.); 5 indexes (5 p.); and accompanying descriptions of accident reporting criteria (1 p.), and data headings (2 p.).

Availability: Connecticut Department of Transportation, Planning and Research Bureau, Planning Inventory and Data, PO Drawer A, Wethersfield CT 06109-0801, †; SRI/MF/complete.

S1335   DELAWARE
Department of
Agriculture

S1335-1   DELAWARE
AGRICULTURAL
STATISTICS, 1984
Summary
Annual. 1985. 49 p.
SRI/MF/complete

Annual report on Delaware agricultural production, marketing, and income, 1970s-84 with selected trends from 1950. Data are generally shown by commodity, with some detail by county, and with occasional comparisons to total U.S.

Covers production, prices, value, and, as applicable, acres harvested, yield, stocks, inventory, and disposition, for field crop, fruit, vegetable, poultry, livestock, and dairy sectors.

Also includes data on number, acreage, and value of farms; rents for all farms and for cropland; field crop production in Delaware/Maryland portion of Delmarva peninsula; poultry sales; cash receipts from marketings; farm income, production expenses, feed prices, and fertilizer consumption; and farm expenditures by value of sales, by U.S. region.

Data are compiled from reports of USDA and Maryland-Delaware Crop Reporting Service.

Contains listing of contents, tables, and charts (p. 2-3); foreword (p. 4); report in 6 sections, with narrative summaries, 5 charts, and 51 tables (p. 5-48); and highlights (inside back cover).

This is the 3rd edition of the report. SRI coverage begins with this edition, and replaces coverage of *Delaware Farm Income* (see U6600-1 below).

Availability: Maryland-Delaware Crop Reporting Service, 50 Harry S. Truman Pkwy., Rm. 202, Annapolis MD 21401, †; SRI/MF/complete.

S1345   DELAWARE
Department of
Community Affairs

S1345-2   QUARTERLY REVIEW OF
HOUSING PRODUCTION in
Delaware
Quarterly. Approx. 40 p.
SRI/MF/complete

Quarterly report on single- and multi-family residential housing production and construction costs in Delaware counties and major cities. Includes data on new housing, mobile home sales, rehabilitation housing, and demolitions; and on new unit heating fuels used, square footage, and number of bedrooms.

Data are from local building permit records. Report is issued 2-4 months after quarter of coverage.

Contains foreword, contents listing, introduction, and highlights with summary charts and/or text tables; 8 quarterly tables, listed below; and 8 trend charts. Issue for 4th quarter includes an annual summary, with 1 table showing housing production trends from the 1970s.

Availability: Delaware Department of Community Affairs, Housing and Community Development Division, 18 The Green, PO Box 1401, Dover DE 19901, †; SRI/MF/complete.

Issues reviewed during 1985: 3rd Qtr. 1984-2nd Qtr. 1985 (D) (Vol. XII, No. 4; Vol. XIII, Nos. 1-3).

TABLES:
[Data are shown by county and major city, for quarter of coverage, with year-to-date totals, and comparisons to previous quarters and/or year.]

1A-1C. On-site [single- and multi-family housing] permits issued, and mobile home sales.

2A-3C. Total and average cost of on-site [single- and multi-family] construction.

4A-4B. Number of bedrooms in new [single- and multi-family] housing units.

5. Number of [new] units by square foot per unit.

6. Heating fuel [oil, gas, electric, and other] in new housing units.

7. Rehabilitation housing (units and cost).

8. Residential demolitions.

S1345-3   1984 REPORTS OF THE
DELAWARE PUBLIC
LIBRARIES
Annual. [1985.] 40 p.
No. 50-10-85-02-02.
SRI/MF/complete

Annual report on Delaware public library services, holdings, circulation, and finances, for FY84. Data are from reports by individual libraries, and Division of Libraries records.

Contents:

a. Contents listing (1 p.); public library directory, map, trustees and advisory council members, standards for FY85-89, and hours of operation (p. 2-14); local public library statistics, with 6 tables listed below (p. 15-21); and multitype library network members and officers (p. 22-25).

b. State library division statistics, with text data on employment, 4 charts, and 4 tables also listed below. (p. 26-40)

Availability: Delaware Department of Community Affairs, Libraries Division, 33-43 S. DuPont Hwy., PO Box 1401, Dover DE 19903, †; SRI/MF/complete.

TABLES:
[Data are for FY84.]

LOCAL LIBRARIES
[Tables [1-5] show data by library.]

[1] Financial reports [expenditures by category; and income by source, including government levels]. (p. 15-16)

[2-5] Output measures [population served, book circulation and holdings, library visits, programs sponsored and attendance, and registered borrowers]. (p. 17-20)

[6] Public library statistics [population served, expenditures, circulation, and holdings, by county]. (p. 21)

STATE LIBRARY DIVISION

[7] Interlibrary loan statistics [requests filled and unfilled, by network]. (p. 26)

[8] Financial report [including income by source, and expenditures by category and program]. (p. 35)

[9] Library services for the blind/physically handicapped [including user registrations, number of collections by type of facility, and circulation by type of material]. (p. 38)

[10] Institutional library services [expenditures, population served, weekly library hours, available materials, and circulation, by institution]. (p. 39-40)

S1360   DELAWARE
Administrative Office of the Courts

S1360–1   1984 ANNUAL REPORT OF THE DELAWARE JUDICIARY
Annual.   Nov. 30, 1984.
188 p.
ISSN 0098-0927.
LC 75-641321.
SRI/MF/complete

Annual report, for FY84, on Delaware judicial system, including trial and appellate court caseloads and case dispositions. Covers supreme, chancery, public guardian, superior, family, common pleas, municipal, justice of the peace, and alderman's courts. Includes trial court data by case type and city and/or county, with selected trends from FY75 or earlier and projections to FY89.

Case types shown are criminal and civil, for most courts, with some additional detail for juvenile, domestic relations, probate, adoption, traffic, and landlord/tenant cases.

Also includes data on court finances and case processing time.

Data are from court records.

Contains contents listing (p. 3-4); and report, with 21 charts and 65 tables, interspersed with law library and court directories (p. 6-188).

Availability: Delaware Administrative Office of the Courts, Carvel Delaware State Bldg., 11th Floor, 820 N. French St., Wilmington DE 19801, †; SRI/MF/complete.

S1365   DELAWARE
Commissioner of Elections

S1365–1   STATE OF DELAWARE Official Results of General Election, 1984
Biennial.   Jan. 16, 1985.
28 p.
LC 73-615318.
SRI/MF/complete

Biennial report presenting results of the Delaware general election held Nov. 6, 1984. Shows voting for President; U.S. and State senators and representatives; Governor and other State and local officials, including sheriffs; and State referendum on lotteries for charitable causes. Data are shown by county and/or district. Also shows party affiliation of candidates.

Also includes registered voters, by county and district and by age and sex, all by party, with summary trend from 1972; voter turnout by county; and voting for Governor and President since early 1900s.

Previous report, covering the 1982 general election, is described in SRI 1983 Annual under this number.

Availability: Delaware Commissioner of Elections, 101 Court St., PO Box 1401, Dover DE 19903, †; SRI/MF/complete.

S1375   DELAWARE
Executive Office of the Governor

S1375–4   DELAWARE DATA BOOK
Annual.   Mar. 1985.
126 p. var. paging, looseleaf.
Doc. No. 1003-85-02-01.
SRI/MF/complete

Annual looseleaf compilation of economic and social statistics for Delaware, 1985. Data are shown for various periods 1970-86.

Report is designed to present an overview of the State, targeted to businesses considering relocation. Socioeconomic, demographic, and geographic breakdowns are shown, as applicable, for selected topics. These breakdowns include data by city, county, income, industry, occupation, age, and sex. Comparisons to total U.S., neighboring States, and cities in nearby States are also often included.

Data are compiled from State and Federal agencies, and private firms. Data sources appear beneath each table.

Contains transmittal letters and State description, with 1 map (4 p.); and 12 maps, 8 charts, and 54 tables, arranged in 10 sections, described below (122 p.).

This is the 4th edition of the *Data Book*.

Availability: Delaware Development Office, 99 Kings Hwy., PO Box 1401, Dover DE 19903, $25.00; SRI/MF/complete.

SECTIONS:
[Each section generally begins with a 1-page contents listing and narrative highlights.]

a. **Economic Overview:** includes unemployment rates; listing of major employers; and State government expenditures, with cumulative cash balance, budgetary dollar sources and uses, bond and short-term debt issues value, and debt service share of general fund receipts. 6 charts. (p. I.1-I.10)

b. **Taxes:** includes State tax rates for corporations and banks; license fees and taxes; miscellaneous and excise taxes and fees; representative property values and tax rates; unemployment insurance and workers compensation tax rates, and premiums and/or benefits; tax incentives; and income tax rates and liabilities. 15 tables. (p. II.1-II.16)

c. **Financing:** includes business financial assistance programs, including listing of firms recently assisted; and branches and assets of major financial institutions. 3 tables. (p. III.1-III.14)

d. **Labor:** includes labor force; employment; production worker earnings; salary differentials for comparable standard of living in selected areas; starting wages; labor productivity and value added; union membership and union election results; work stoppages, workers involved, and days idle; and average duration of unemployment claims. 1 chart and 10 tables. (p. IV.1-IV.9)

e. **Education/Training:** includes vocational training enrollment, by curriculum; school districts and enrollment; and listing of postsecondary institutions. 2 maps and 1 table. (p. V.1-V.14)

f. **Markets/Transportation:** includes automobile transportation cost index and average insurance premiums; and airports and services. 5 maps and 2 tables. (p. VI.1-VI.12)

g. **Utilities/Resources:** includes residential and industrial electricity costs; and gas utility prices by service class. 2 maps and 4 tables. (p. VII.1-VII.8)

h. **Site Selection:** includes commercial casualty/liability insurance premiums; and cities affected by coastal zoning regulations. 1 map and 1 table. (p. VIII.1-VIII.10)

i. **Construction Costs:** includes comparisons of industrial site acquisition and residential and commercial construction costs; building operating costs; building trades union wage indexes; office space rental rates; and construction costs and specifications for 3 commercial buildings. 9 tables. (p. IX.1-IX.10)

j. **Quality of Life:** includes cost-of-living indexes; housing costs and insurance premiums; residential lot costs; listing of towns/cities and recreation facilities, including State parks and cultural attractions; temperature; crime rates for violent crimes; and health care facilities, medical personnel, and hospital costs. 2 maps, 1 chart, and 9 tables. (p. X.1-X.19)

S1385   DELAWARE
Department of Health and Social Services

S1385–1   PUBLIC ASSISTANCE GRANTS STATISTICAL REPORTS, Delaware
Quarterly.   6 p.
SRI/MF/complete

Quarterly report on Delaware public assistance payments, cases, and recipients, by program. Includes caseload data by county. Covers AFDC, general and emergency assistance, food stamps, and SSI. Report is issued 2-3 months after month of coverage.

Contains 4 tables, listed below.

Availability: Delaware Department of Health and Social Services, Planning, Research, and Evaluation Division, Human Services Planning Bureau, Delaware State Hospital, New Castle DE 19720, †; SRI/MF/complete.

Issues reviewed during 1985: Sept. 1984-June 1985 (D).

TABLES:
[Data are shown by program. Tables [2-4] include detail for AFDC program categories and for SSI State supplementation and Federal payments. Tables [2-3] also include detail for AFDC and general assistance recipients under age 18.]

[1] Financial statement, State funds [amounts available for year and disbursed, for all programs except food stamps, cumulative for fiscal year through month of coverage].

[2-3] Public assistance monthly and cumulative statistics [payments, cases, and/or recipients, for fiscal year through month of coverage, with comparison to same cumulative period of previous fiscal year].

[4] Comparative caseloads by county [cases and/or recipients, for month of coverage].

S1405   DELAWARE
Department of Labor

S1405–1   ANNUAL PLANNING REPORT, FY85, Delaware and Major Subareas
Annual. Dec. 1984.
iv+49 p.
SRI/MF/complete, current & previous year reports

Annual planning report, for FY85, identifying Delaware population groups most in need of employment services. Includes data on population, labor force, and employment by industry and occupation, various years 1970-85.

Data are primarily from State and Federal agencies, including Employment Security Automated Reporting System; and Lawrence Berkeley Laboratory projections.

Contains contents and table listings (p. i-iv); narrative summary (p. 1-12); 31 tables, listed below (p. 14-46); and map, and technical and explanatory notes (p. 47-49).

Previous report, for FY83, was also reviewed in 1985, and is also available on SRI microfiche under this number [Annual. Dec. 1983. iv+48 p. †].

Availability: Delaware Department of Labor, Occupational and Labor Market Information Office, PO Box 9029, Newark DE 19714-9029, †; SRI/MF/complete.

TABLES:
[Unless otherwise noted, tables show data for Delaware. Data for State subareas generally are shown for New Castle County, Wilmington City, and balance of State.]

S1405–1.1: Population, Labor Force, and Employment by Industry
[Tables 1, 3-4 and 7-10D show data for State and each subarea.]

TOTAL AND VETERAN POPULATION

1. Population trends, by race and sex [including data for each county, 1960, 1970, and 1980]. (p. 14)

2-4. 1970 census and projected FY85; and estimated population trends by age, sex, and race. (p. 15-18)

5-6. U.S. veteran population by period of service and age, Mar. 31, 1983. (p. 19)

7. Veteran population for State and counties [by period of service], Mar. 31, 1983. (p. 20)

LABOR FORCE AND EMPLOYMENT

8A-8E. Civilian population, labor force, labor force participation rate, unemployment, and unemployment rate, by age and sex, 1970 and 1985. (p. 21-25)

9A-9E. Labor force participation rates (by sex, age, and race), FY85 (projected) and 1970 census. (p. 26-28)

10A-10D. Labor force, unemployment, and unemployment rate, by age, sex, and race, 1970 and 1985 (projected). (p. 29-32)

11. Labor force, employment, and unemployment annual averages [with comparisons to U.S.], 1976-83. (p. 33)

BY INDUSTRY

12-14. Historical growth perspective, annual average [nonfarm employment], 1982-83; current employment and economic base [distribution of employment, with comparison to U.S.], 1983; and covered employment [Mar. 1983], and business establishments, 1st quarter 1982-83; [all by industry division and major manufacturing group]. (p. 34-36)

S1405–1.2: Employment Service Data by Applicant Characteristics and Occupation, and Income

BY APPLICANT CHARACTERISTICS

15. Employment service applicants registered [by age group, sex, educational attainment, and race-ethnicity (white, black, and Hispanic), and for unemployment insurance claimants, veterans, handicapped, and welfare recipients; all for State and by county], FY84. (p. 37)

BY OCCUPATION

16. Applicant supply per job opening demand [by occupation], FY84. (p. 38)

17. Applicants and job openings for selected occupations [listed] at Division of Employment and Training offices, FY84. (p. 39-44)

18. Occupational employment: State, [4] neighboring States, and U.S., 1983 annual averages. (p. 45)

PERSONAL INCOME

19. Per capita personal income, U.S., State, and subareas [including data for each county, 1977-83]. (p. 46)

S1405–2   DELAWARE AND WILMINGTON SMSA LABOR MARKET TRENDS
Quarterly. Approx. 12 p.
SRI/MF/complete

Quarterly report on Delaware employment, unemployment, earnings, hours, and unemployment insurance (UI), with selected detail for Wilmington SMSA and other State areas. Also includes data on job applicants and Philadelphia CPI. Some data are shown by major industry group. Report is issued approximately 2 months after quarter of coverage.

Contains highlights and narrative summary, interspersed with 7 quarterly tables listed below; and contents and table listing.

Availability: Delaware Department of Labor, Occupational and Labor Market Information Office, PO Box 9029, Newark DE 19714-9029, †; SRI/MF/complete.

Issues reviewed during 1985: 3rd Qtr. 1984-2nd Qtr. 1985 (D) (Vol. 29, Nos. 3-4; Vol. 30, Nos. 1-2).

TABLES:
[Data are shown monthly for quarter of coverage, unless otherwise noted. Most tables include comparisons to same months of previous year.]

1. Civilian labor force, employment, and unemployment, by place of residence [Delaware, Wilmington SMSA, 4 neighboring States, and total U.S.].

[A] Employment and training activities [job applicants available through State Division of Employment and Training, by occupational group, as of end of last month of quarter of coverage].

2-3. Nonagricultural wage/salary employment, by [industry division and selected major manufacturing group, and total persons involved in work stoppages]; and average hourly and weekly earnings and hours worked by production workers in selected [major] manufacturing industry groups; [all for Delaware and Wilmington SMSA].

4. Number and amount of unemployment compensation payments for UI regular and extended benefits programs, by [county and] local office.

5. Delaware UI regular continued claim counts [auto industry and other; includes data for 1 week of each month in quarter of coverage, and same weeks of previous year].

6. CPI [by category] and percent changes for all urban consumers, Philadelphia area [with comparisons to U.S.].

S1430   DELAWARE
Department of Public Instruction

S1430–1   STATE OF DELAWARE REPORT OF EDUCATIONAL STATISTICS, 1983/84
Annual. Oct. 1984.
ix+180 p. Document No. 95-01/84-10-01.
ISSN 0362-8787.
LC 76-641222.
SRI/MF/complete

Annual report, for the 1983/84 school year, on students, staff, finances, and facilities of Delaware elementary and secondary public schools. Also includes data for nonpublic schools and historical trends from 1958/59. Data are compiled from reports of local school districts, by the Delaware Dept of Public Instruction.

Contains foreword, chart and table listings, and definitions (p. i-ix); and 12 charts, and 89 tables listed below, arranged in 8 sections (p. 3-180).

Two less comprehensive reports, *September Enrollments* and *Nonpublic Schools in Delaware,* are also available from the issuing agency, but are not covered in SRI.

Availability: Delaware Department of Public Instruction, Planning, Research, and Evaluation Division, Townsend Bldg., PO Box 1402, Dover DE 19903, †; SRI/MF/complete.

TABLES:
[Tables show public school data for academic year 1983/84, or as of Sept. 30, 1983, unless otherwise noted. Data by racial/ethnic group include American Indian, Asian or Asian/Pacific Islander, and Hispanic.]

S1430–1.1: Statistical Summaries
[Tables show data for 1979/80-1983/84.]

1. Summary of statistics: pupils [enrollment, attendance, and high school graduates]; personnel [administrative, instructional, and other]; and schools. (p. 3)

2. Summary of statistics: public school expenditures [total by function, and per pupil]. (p. 4)

S1430–1.2: Pupils
[Most tables show data by county and/or district.]

ATTENDANCE AND ENROLLMENT

3. Average daily membership (ADM) and average daily attendance (ADA) of pupils [by grade level]. (p. 15)

4-5. Enrollment by grade: FTE; and regular, part-time special, and full-time special students [including data by individual special school]. (p. 16-23)

6. Pupil enrollment by racial/ethnic group. (p. 24)

7. Comparison of Sept. 30 enrollments [by grade level only], 1963-83. (p. 25)

8. Unit allotments based on enrollments reported by local school districts [for regular education by grade level, special education by school and type of handicap, and vocational education]. (p. 26-36)

TEST SCORES, GRADUATES, AND DROPOUTS

9-10. Educational assessment program, average NCE [normal curve equivalent] scores for Delaware students, comprehensive tests of basic skills (regular and special education combined): [by content area only], spring 1984; and total battery [by district], 1983/84; [all for grades 1-11]. (p. 37-38)

11-12. Secondary school graduates, by sex and race, July 1, 1983-June 30, 1984. (p. 40-43)

13-14. Dropouts: by county; and by race and sex, statewide. (p. 44)

S1430–1.3: Staff
[Most tables show data by position.]

PERSONNEL AND SALARIES

15-16. Dept of Public Instruction professional personnel, and educational personnel profile [by sex, race, and educational attainment, and average age and experience]. (p. 47-49)

17-18. Number FTE employees and instructional personnel, by [county and] district. (p. 50-51)

19-20. Salary level [distribution of] full-time educational personnel; and average annual salary for full-time professional personnel, all sources of funding, county and statewide. (p. 52-54)

TEACHER SUPPLY AND DEMAND

21. Demand data: source of full-time educational personnel [new and returning]. (p. 55-56)

22. State awarding bachelor degree: full-time educational personnel. (p. 57-58)

23. Renewals and new certificates issued [by type]. (p. 59-61)

24-25. Demand trend data: professional educational personnel, FTE, by assignment classification; and source of full-time classroom teachers [new and returning; various years 1974/75-1983/84]. (p. 62-63)

26. Supply trend data: occupations of education graduates, University of Delaware/Delaware State College [total and employed in public and nonpublic schools, 1980/81-1982/83 graduates]. (p. 64)

27. Graduates from Delaware State College/University of Delaware, showing the number by subject area trained and teaching in Delaware [1980/81-1983/84]. (p. 65)

28. Trend data: full-time professional personnel [by sex, 1958/59-1983/84]. (p. 66)

S1430–1.4: Finance
[Most tables show data by county and district.]

SUMMARY DATA

29. Income, expense, and balances. (p. 69)

INCOME

30. Income sources. (p. 71)

31-33. Revenue receipts: State appropriations, Federal sources, and local sources. (p. 72-77)

34-35. District revenue receipts per pupil, based on ADA and enrollment. (p. 78-79)

36. Nonrevenue receipts [State and local bonds; other State; and local property sale, insurance adjustments, and other]. (p. 80)

EXPENSES

37-38. Total and current expenses, summary. (p. 81-82)

39-45. Current expenses: administration, instruction, attendance/health services, transportation, maintenance and operation of plant, fixed charges, and food and community services. (p. 84-92)

46. Summary of expenditures per pupil. (p. 93)

47-48. Capital outlay and debt service; and school construction funds. (p. 84-95)

TAXES

49. District assessment, number of capitations, and authorized tax rates for debt service, current expense, tuition, minor capital improvement, and total levies. (p. 96)

50. Combined tax rates on assessed valuation of real estate (rates per $100 of assessed value). (p. 97)

VOCATIONAL PROGRAMS

51. Vocational-technical expenditures [State and Federal funds statewide]. (p. 98)

STATE FUNDING, AND FINANCING REFERENDA

52. Public school State funding: Division II and Division III [1972/73-1983/84]. (p. 99)

53. Referenda by local school districts [votes cast and outcome]. (p. 99)

OTHER PROGRAM COSTS

54. Pupil transportation [buses, pupils, and costs]. (p. 100)

55. Revenue and expenditures: national school lunch/school breakfast/special milk child nutrition programs. (p. 101)

56. National school lunch and school breakfast programs [participants and meals]. (p. 102)

57. Year-round child care food program, nonschool meals, for day care/Headstart/family day care homes/after school hour programs [by county only]. (p. 103)

58. Summer food service program for children, P.L. 94-105 [by sponsor, statewide]. (p. 103)

S1430–1.5: Federal Programs
[Tables generally show grant awards by project, and, where applicable, enrollment and employees, by county and district or specific agency or institution.]

59. Federal grants [by program, statewide]. (p. 107)

60-61. Programs for educationally deprived and delinquent children: P.L. 97-35; and P.L. 89-10, Migrant; ECIA [Education Consolidation and Improvement Act], Chapter I. (p. 108-112)

62-63. Federal programs for the handicapped, funding source: ECIA-Chapter I (H), and P.L. 94-142 EHA(B) [Education of the Handicapped]. (p. 113-120)

64. Federal vocational education programs under amendments of 1976, funded under P.L. 94-482. (p. 121-137)

65. Adult basic education reading, writing, computation, and consumer living skills: P.L. 91-230 as amended. (p. 138-139)

S1430–1.6: Services
[Tables show data by county, district, or institution.]

66. Immunization levels: percent adequately immunized, by vaccine type. (p. 143)

67. Summary of health services provided by school nurses. (p. 143)

68. James H. Groves Adult High School: pregnant students, State grant programs [funding, enrollments, and FTE employees]. (p. 144)

69-70. Adult driver education program; and driver education/traffic safety, public and nonpublic schools; [pupil enrollment and status]. (p. 145-147)

S1430–1.7: Facilities
[Data are shown by county, district, project, or institution, generally for FY84, with some comparisons to FY82 and/or FY83.]

71-73. House Bill No. 387, 132nd General Assembly, 1983 minor capital improvement and school building maintenance programs [allocations and expenditures], and minor capital improvement program contingency allocation. (p. 151-153)

74-76. School construction programs, State Board of Education final approval; status of funded capital improvement projects; and certificates of necessity approved by Board of Education. (p. 153-154)

77-79. House Bill No. 809, 132nd General Assembly, 1983 minor capital improvement program contingency allocation [State and local expenditures], and minor capital improvement and school building maintenance programs [total allocations and expenditures]. (p. 155-157)

80-82. House Bill No. 448, 131st General Assembly, 1982 minor capital improvement program contingency allocation, and minor capital improvement and school building maintenance programs [expenditures]. (158-160)

S1430–1.8: Nonpublic Schools
[Data are for nonpublic schools. School types are Catholic, other religious affiliation, and independent.]

83. Pupils and staff [number of schools, enrollment by racial/ethnic group, June 1983 graduates, and instructional personnel, all by school type]. (p. 163)

84. Enrollment, by grade [by school]. (p. 164-167)

85. Enrollment by district of residence, by grade or program, and by type of school. (p. 168)

86. Trend data: enrollment, 1961-83. (p. 169)

87-89. FTE instructional staff [by position], ADM and ADA of pupils, and pupil transportation cost [by school]. (p. 170-180)

S1435   DELAWARE
Department of Public Safety

S1435–1   ANNUAL STATISTICAL ANALYSIS AND SUMMARIZATION, 1984
Delaware State Police Traffic Control Section
Annual. Apr. 15, 1985.
94 p.
SRI/MF/complete

Annual report on Delaware traffic accidents, injuries, and fatalities, by accident and vehicle type, location, time, and other circumstances; and driver and victim characteristics; 1983, with selected comparisons to 1982, and trends from as early as 1935.

Also includes data on seatbelt and motorcycle helmet use; vehicle registrations, travel mileage, and licensed drivers; first aid treatment at accident scene; vehicle defects; State police law enforcement activity; traffic arrests; and alcohol-related accidents.

Data are from reports by State and local police.

Contains contents listing (2 p.); introduction, highlights, 9 charts, and 113 tables (p. 1-80); and appendix, with National Safety Council summary table repeated for total accidents and 6 accident types (p. 81-94).

Availability: Delaware Department of Public Safety, State Police Traffic Control Section, PO Box 430, Dover DE 19903, †; SRI/MF/complete.

S1445   DELAWARE
Department of State

S1445–1   SIXTY-FIFTH ANNUAL REPORT OF THE STATE BANK COMMISSIONER OF DELAWARE for the Fiscal Year Ended June 30, 1984
Annual. Oct. 22, 1984.
104 p.
Doc. No. 20-15/84/10/02.
LC 21-27231.
SRI/MF/complete

Annual report on financial condition of Delaware financial institutions, FY84, presenting assets, liabilities, and equity or total capital, aggregate and by institution, for State-chartered

commercial banks, nondeposit trust companies, mutual savings banks, national banks, and State and federally chartered savings and loan assns. Aggregate data include comparison to FY83.

Also includes data on Bank Commissioner Office finances; and small loan company aggregate personal and retail loan activity, FY65-84.

Data are compiled from bank call reports and other reports filed with State.

Contains contents listing (p. 4); 10 tables (p. 5-15); statements of individual institutions, arranged by type (p. 17-97); and directories of registered small loan companies and 8 other types of licensed financial companies (p. 100-104).

Prior to FY84, reports are covered by SRI under S1330-1. Bank Commissioner's Office is no longer part of Dept of Administrative Services.

Availability: Delaware Department of State, State Bank Commissioner's Office, 540 S. DuPont Hwy., Third Floor, Thomas Collins Bldg., PO Box 1401, Dover DE 19903, †; SRI/MF/complete.

S1507
DISTRICT OF COLUMBIA
Office of the Controller

S1507–1   DISTRICT OF COLUMBIA COMPREHENSIVE ANNUAL FINANCIAL REPORT, Year Ended Sept. 30, 1984
Annual. Jan. 28, 1985.
2+68 p.
SRI/MF/complete

Annual report on financial condition of District of Columbia government, for FY84, presenting assets, liabilities, revenues by source, expenditures by object and/or function, and fund balances, for general, capital projects, enterprise, and fiduciary funds, with comparisons to FY83.

Also includes data on actual vs. budgeted revenues and expenditures; long-term debt; Federal payments to D.C.; delinquent property taxes; population, median age, and per capita income; property valuations, including market value of top 10 commercial, residential, and tax-exempt properties; construction; bank deposits; and income tax payers and distribution of payments, by income level.

Also includes selected other financial, social, and economic indicators, including land use, public service facilities, government employment by function, and school enrollment; and selected trends from the 1970s.

Data are from records of the controller's office.

Contains listing of contents, fund statements, and tables (p. 1-2); transmittal letter, with summary text data (p. 3-11); financial section, with 21 fund statements (p. 16-58); and statistical section, with 9 charts (2 p.) and 17 tables (p. 59-66).

Availability: District of Columbia Office of the Controller, 415 12th St., NW, Rm. 412, Washington DC 20004, †; SRI/MF/complete.

S1515
DISTRICT OF COLUMBIA
Courts

S1515–1   1984 ANNUAL REPORT, District of Columbia Courts
Annual. [1985.] vii+101 p.
LC 79-642641.
SRI/MF/complete

Annual report, for 1984, on District of Columbia court caseloads and case dispositions, for appeals and superior courts, by case type, with selected trends from 1976.

Case types include criminal and civil, with additional detail for landlord/tenant, small claims, juvenile, domestic relations, mental health and retardation, probate, tax, social service, and traffic cases.

Also includes judicial system revenues and expenditures; bar applications, admissions, disbarments, and other disciplinary actions; juror utilization; marriage bureau activity; and court reporter division personnel and transcript production.

Contains listing of contents, tables, and charts (p. iii-v); and report, with 16 charts and 42 tables (p. 1-99).

Availability: District of Columbia Courts, Executive Office, 500 Indiana Ave., NW, Suite 1500, Washington DC 20001, †; SRI/MF/complete.

S1525
DISTRICT OF COLUMBIA
Board of Elections and Ethics

S1525–1   DISTRICT OF COLUMBIA GENERAL ELECTION, Nov. 6, 1984
Biennial. [1985.] 12 p.
SRI/MF/complete

Biennial report presenting results of the District of Columbia general election held Nov. 6, 1984. Shows voting for President and Vice-President, U.S. House of Representatives delegate, city council member-at-large and other city officials, and 1 initiative. Also includes voter registration and turnout. Data are shown by ward and subarea.

Previous report, covering 1982 general election, is described in SRI 1983 Annual under this number.

Availability: District of Columbia Board of Elections and Ethics, District Bldg., 14th and E Sts., NW, Rm. 7, Washington DC 20004, $1.50; SRI/MF/complete.

S1527
DISTRICT OF COLUMBIA
Department of
Employment Services

S1527-1 ANNUAL PLANNING REPORT, DISTRICT OF COLUMBIA, 1985
Annual. June 1985.
v+87p. var. paging.
SRI/MF/complete.

Annual planning report, for 1984-85, identifying District of Columbia and Washington, D.C. metro area population groups most in need of employment services. Includes data on employment by industry and occupation, and population and labor force characteristics.

Also includes data on unemployment insurance activity, Job Training Partnership Act (JTPA) participant characteristics, and job openings by occupation; selected comparisons to U.S.; and selected trends from 1970 and projections through 2000.

Data are from U.S. Depts of Commerce and Labor; D.C., Maryland, and Virginia State agencies; and private sources.

Contains preface, and listings of contents, tables, and charts (p. i-iv); narrative analysis, with 17 charts, and 25 tables described below (p. 1-53); and appendix, with 11 tables also described below (p. 55-68).

For description of previous report, for FY83, see SRI 1982 Annual under this number.

Availability: District of Columbia Department of Employment Services, Labor Market Information, Research, and Analysis Division, 500 C St., NW, Rm. 201, Washington DC 20001, †; SRI/MF/complete.

TABLES:
[Data are shown for D.C., with selected comparisons to Washington MSA and metro and suburban areas, and some detail by ward, municipality, and jurisdiction.]

a. Metro area economic indicators, including retail sales, CPI, new construction, per capita income, and sales and motor vehicle excise tax collections, 1983-84; gross product, 1960-84; and average pay by industry division, 1981-83. Tables I-V. (p. 2-8)

b. Population, by age, race, and sex, various years 1970-85; and households projected to 2000. Tables VI-XI. (p. 10-16)

c. Labor force by employment status, and labor force participation rates, with selected detail by age, sex, and race, various years 1970-85; and employment by industry division and occupation, various years 1976-90. Tables XII-XXIV. (p. 19-44)

d. JTPA participants, by sex, age, race (including Hispanic, American Indian/Alaskan Native, and Asian/Pacific Islander), education, and public assistance and family status, and for offenders, displaced homemakers, students, unemployed and underemployed, handicapped, and persons with limited English-speaking ability; FY83. Table XXV. (p. 53)

e. Population by race (including Spanish origin); public school enrollment and dropouts by level; per capita and total personal income; and nonagricultural wage/salary employ-

ment by industry division and major group; various years 1969-84. Tables A.I-A.VII. (p. 55-63)

f. Public assistance (AFDC, general, food stamps, and medicaid) cases and recipients, FY70-84; unemployment compensation claims, payments, and exhaustions, 1961-84; OMB poverty guidelines, 1985; and job openings due to growth and separations, for individual occupations with 200/more openings yearly, 1980-90 period. Tables A.-VIII-A.XI. (p. 64-68)

S1527-3 METROPOLITAN WASHINGTON, D.C., AREA LABOR SUMMARY
Monthly. Approx. 15 p.
SRI/MF/complete, shipped quarterly

Monthly report on labor force conditions in District of Columbia and Washington, D.C. MSA. Includes employment, earnings, and hours, by industry. Also includes selected unemployment insurance data. Report is issued approximately 2 months after month of data coverage.

Contains narrative summary interspersed with 7 monthly tables, listed below. Other statistical features include a table showing employment estimates before and after latest benchmark revisions; recurring BLS summaries of D.C. employment, earnings, and hours data; and a recurring table on D.C. CPI.

Most monthly tables appear in all issues. All additional features with substantial D.C. statistics not covered in monthly tables are described, as they appear, under "Statistical Features." Nonstatistical features are not covered.

Availability: District of Columbia Department of Employment Services, Labor Market Information, Research, and Analysis Division, 500 C St., NW, Rm. 201, Washington DC 20001, †; SRI/MF/complete, shipped quarterly.

Issues reviewed during 1985: Sept. 1984-Aug. 1985 (D).

MONTHLY TABLES:
[Tables show data for D.C. and Washington, D.C. MSA, for month of coverage, previous month, and 1-2 comparable months of previous year, unless otherwise noted. Table sequence and titles may vary from issue to issue.]

[1] Employment status for the civilian population: D.C., Washington, D.C. MSA, and the suburban ring.

[2] Wage/salary employment by [major] industry [group] and place of work.

[3] Unemployment in selected cities [shows unemployment rate in D.C. and 23 other central cities, for month prior to month of coverage and same month of previous year].

[4] Selected unemployment insurance benefit statistics [initial claims, weeks claimed, benefits paid, recipients, and average weeks of duration, for State, Federal, and ex-serviceperson's programs; D.C. only].

[5] Earnings [and average hours] of production workers in manufacturing [industry groups], Washington MSA.

[6-7] Insured unemployed: selected characteristics [sex and occupational group; and] length of current spell of [unemployment, with median duration by sex].

STATISTICAL FEATURES:

S1527-3.601: Sept. 1984
PROFILE OF DISTRICT RESIDENTS NOT IN THE LABOR FORCE
(p. 10-11) Article, with 2 tables showing D.C. residents not in the labor force, by sex, race (including Hispanic), age group, and reason, 1983. Data are from Current Population Survey.

AVERAGE PAY IN THE DISTRICT, 1983
(p. 12) Article, with 2 tables showing average annual pay of D.C. workers by industry division, with comparisons to U.S., Maryland, and Virginia, 1983.

DISTRICT OF COLUMBIA CPI (ALL URBAN CONSUMERS), RECURRING FEATURE
(p. 14) Recurring table showing D.C. and U.S. CPI for all items and by sector, Sept. 1984, with percent change from July 1984 and from Sept. 1983. Data are from BLS.

S1527-3.602: Oct. 1984
DISCOURAGED WORKERS IN THE DISTRICT, 1983
(p. 10-11) Article, with 1 table showing D.C. residents not in the labor force, and estimated discouraged workers (persons who would like to work but are not actively seeking employment), by sex and race, 1983. Also includes 1 chart showing D.C. population distribution by labor force status, 1983. Data are based on the Current Population Survey.

INCREASES IN PERSONAL INCOME LAG BEHIND IN THE DISTRICT
(p. 14) Article, with 2 tables showing D.C. personal income, with detail by source and comparison to total U.S., 2nd quarter 1983-84. Data are from Dept of Commerce.

S1527-3.603: Nov. 1984
DISTRICT OF COLUMBIA CPI (ALL URBAN CONSUMERS), RECURRING FEATURE
(p. 11) Recurring table showing D.C. CPI for all items and by sector, Nov. 1984, with percent change from Sept. 1984 and Nov. 1983. Data are from BLS.

S1527-3.604: Dec. 1984
AREA JOBS
(p. 7-11) Article, with 1 table showing D.C. SMSA employment in occupations with employment of 6,000/more, 1980 and 1990. Also includes summary text data and charts. Data are from D.C. Dept of Employment Services.

S1527-3.605: Jan. 1985
DISTRICT'S SERVICES INDUSTRY: A PROFILE
(p. 9-12) Article, with 1 chart and 5 tables showing D.C. service industries employment, average pay, and number of firms, and workers by employment status, sex, and race (including Hispanic), and aged 16-19, with selected comparisons to all and private sector industries, various years 1979-83; and distribution of D.C. workers by occupation (no date). Data are from Census Bureau.

DISTRICT LAGS BEHIND NATION AS PERSONAL INCOME RISES
(p. 16) Article, with 2 tables showing U.S. and D.C. total personal income, with D.C. income

by source, 3rd quarter 1983-84. Data are from Commerce Dept Bureau of Economic Analysis.

DISTRICT OF COLUMBIA CPI (ALL URBAN CONSUMERS), RECURRING FEATURE

(p. 17) Recurring table showing D.C. CPI for all items and by sector, Jan. 1985, with percent change from Jan. and Nov. 1984. Data are from BLS.

S1527–3.606: Mar. 1985

CHARACTERISTICS OF THE DISTRICT'S UNEMPLOYED: 1984, ANNUAL ARTICLE

(p. 7-10) Annual article, with 2 tables showing D.C. unemployment and unemployment rate, by age, sex, race, marital status, and ward, 1983-84. Data are from Current Population Survey, and Employment Services Dept estimates.

For description of previous article, see SRI 1984 Annual under S1527-3.503.

WASHINGTON AREA CPI (ALL URBAN CONSUMERS), RECURRING FEATURE

(p. 18) Recurring table showing CPI for all items and by sector, for Washington, D.C. MSA, Mar. 1985, with percent change from Jan. 1985 and Mar. 1984. Data are from BLS. Includes brief accompanying article.

S1527–3.607: Apr. 1985

WASHINGTON AREA WAGES IN MAR. 1984

(p. 10-14) Article, with 1 table showing Washington MSA weekly and hourly wages, by selected occupation, Mar. 1983-84. Data are from BLS.

S1527–3.608: May 1985

ANALYSIS OF UNEMPLOYMENT IN THE DISTRICT DURING THE 1981-82 RECESSION

(p. 8) Article, with 1 table showing unemployment rates for D.C. (total and for black men and women) and U.S., 1979-84.

WASHINGTON AREA CPI (ALL URBAN CONSUMERS), RECURRING FEATURE

(p. 14-15) Recurring table showing CPI for all items and by sector, for Washington, D.C. MSA, May 1985, with percent change from Mar. 1985 and May 1984. Data are from BLS. Includes brief accompanying article.

S1527–3.609: June 1985

PROFILE OF THE DISTRICT PRIVATE SECTOR INDUSTRIES, EMPLOYERS, EMPLOYEES, AND WAGES, 1984

(p. 7-9) Article, with 1 table showing number of D.C. private employers and employees, and average wages, by major industry group, FY84, with total for FY83. Data are from D.C. Dept of Employment Services.

DISTRICT'S TOP 100 EMPLOYERS

(p. 9-10) Article, with ranked listing of 100 largest employers in D.C., as of Sept. 1984. Listing does not include actual number of employees. Summary data on total employees are included in the article text.

WASHINGTON AREA WAGES IN MAR. 1985

(p. 13, 15) Article, with 1 table showing Washington MSA weekly and hourly wages, by selected occupation, Mar. 1984-85. Data are from BLS.

For description of a similar article, with data for 1983-84, see S1527-3.607 above.

S1527–3.610: July 1985

ANNUAL PAY IN THE DISTRICT: 1984, ANNUAL FEATURE

(p. 6-7) Annual article, with 2 tables showing average annual pay of D.C. workers by industry division, with summary comparisons to U.S., Maryland, and Virginia, 1984.

Previous article, for 1983, is described under S1527-3.601 above.

WASHINGTON AREA CPI (ALL URBAN CONSUMERS), RECURRING FEATURE

(p. 13-14) Recurring table showing CPI for all items and by sector, for Washington, D.C. MSA, July 1985, with percent change from May 1985 and July 1984. Data are from BLS. Includes brief accompanying article.

S1527–3.611: Aug. 1985

EXTENT OF HOLIDAY HIRING

(p. 8) Article, with 1 table showing retail trade employment for D.C. and for Washington, D.C. MSA, Oct. and Dec. 1978-84. Data are from D.C. Dept of Employment Services.

$4.2 BILLION PAID TO DISTRICT WORKERS IN 1ST QUARTER OF THIS YEAR

(p. 13) Article, with 1 table showing D.C. employment and wages (total and annual average), for private employers and for Federal and local governments, 4th quarter 1984 and 1st quarter 1984-85. Data are from D.C. Dept of Employment Services.

S1535
DISTRICT OF COLUMBIA
Executive Office
of the Mayor

S1535–2	**1983 CRIME AND ARREST PROFILE STATISTICAL UPDATE, for the District of Columbia**

Annual. Nov. 1984.
35 p. no paging.
SRI/MF/complete

Annual report on District of Columbia crimes and arrests, by offense, 1983, with trends from 1973. Includes data by police district, and by offender age, sex, and race. Also includes comparisons to selected other cities.

Report focuses on 8 Index offenses: murder/non-negligent manslaughter, forcible rape, robbery, aggravated assault, burglary, larceny/theft, motor vehicle theft, and arson. Arrests are also shown for numerous non-Index offenses.

Data are primarily from agency reports submitted under the Uniform Crime Reporting Program, and unpublished data of the D.C. Metropolitan Police Dept.

Contains narrative summary and table listing (4 p.); and 29 tables, described below (31 p.).

Availability: District of Columbia Executive Office of the Mayor, Statistical Analysis Center, Criminal Justice Plans and Analysis Office, 421 Eighth St., NW, 2nd Floor, Washington DC 20004, †; SRI/MF/complete.

TABLES:

[Unless otherwise noted, data are for D.C., 1983. Index crime data generally are shown by offense and include totals for violent and property crimes.]

a. Index crimes and rates, 1973-83; Index crimes by police district; population, and Index crimes and rates, for D.C. and 20 other cities; robberies, burglaries, and larcenies/thefts, by detailed type of location; and violent Index crimes, and total non-Index crimes, by type of weapon. Tables 1-7. (9 p.)

b. Arrests of adults and juveniles, by Index and non-Index offense, with Index offense detail by age, race, sex, and police district, and selected trends from 1973; and crimes by Index and non-Index offense. Tables 8-21. (14 p.)

c. Drug-related arrests of adults and juveniles, for felonies and misdemeanors, and for drug sales and possession by substance, with detail by sex, race, and police district and division, various years 1979-83. Tables 22-29. (8 p.)

S1535–3	**INDICES: Statistical Index to District of Columbia Services**

Annual. July 1985.
vi+3+194 p.
SRI/MF/complete

Annual compilation, for 1985, presenting detailed social, governmental, and economic statistics for the District of Columbia. Data are shown primarily for 1970s-85, with urban development projections to 2000.

Report is designed to present a comprehensive overview of D.C. Extensive socioeconomic, demographic, and geographic breakdowns are shown, as applicable, for most topics. These breakdowns include data by city ward, income, industry, age, educational attainment, race, and sex. Comparisons to total U.S. and other jurisdictions in the D.C. metro area are also included.

Data are from D.C. and Federal sources. Data sources appear beneath each table.

Contains introductory letter and preamble (p. ii-iii); contents listing (2 p.); 6 data sections, described below, containing 30 charts and maps, and 213 tables (p. 1-188); and index of tables (6 p.).

This is the 2nd annual report.

Availability: District of Columbia Executive Office of the Mayor, Office of Policy and Program Evaluation, District Bldg., Rm. 412, 1350 Pennsylvania Ave., NW, Washington DC 20004, $5.00; SRI/MF/complete.

DATA SECTIONS:

[Each section is preceded by a contents listing.]

S1535–3.1: Washington, the Government and the People

(p. 1-64) Contains 14 charts/maps and 56 tables. Includes elected officials; D.C. council legislative activity; and ward profiles, including land area and taxable acreage, population, public schools and recreation facilities, household size and income, percent of population in poverty, housing units and tenure, and subsidized housing share.

Also includes voter registration and participation in presidential elections; households; personal income by source; income taxes and taxpayers; taxable business receipts; land use; property assessed values and tax rates; D.C.

---

government land acreage, use, and value; and public buildings by agency, and lease and utility costs.

Also includes capital improvement projects and expenditures, and loans outstanding from U.S. Treasury; D.C. government bond issues, total and personnel expenditures, revenues by source (with Federal grant revenues by function), and employment; and tax revenues lost due to Federal exemptions.

S1535–3.2: Economic Development

(p. 65-107) Contains 6 maps/charts and 51 tables. Includes building permits and valuation; commercial construction and costs; downtown D.C. current and planned development; Washington Convention Center bookings and visitors; visits to major museums and historic sites; Commission on the Arts and Humanities expenditures, by fund source; business establishments, employment, and payroll; hotel rooms and occupancy; and banks with assets over $500 million.

Also includes value of exports; foreign-owned property and value; nonprofit and minority firms and contracts with D.C. government; D.C. loans to business, and jobs created/retained; commercial and industrial revitalization projects and finances; licensed service establishments and professionals; top 10 business and nonprofit employers; labor force by employment status; earnings; unemployment insurance recipients and benefits paid; and summer youth employment and job training program enrollees and expenditures.

Also includes housing occupancy and median rent; condominium conversions and new projects; housing sales, average price, and assessment/sales price ratio; housing project financing and assistance provided, by program; urban renewal projects; community development block grants; energy conservation cost savings; energy assistance program caseloads and payments; and CPI.

S1535–3.3: Human Services

(p. 108-139) Contains 6 charts/maps and 45 tables. Includes AFDC, SSI, medicaid, and other welfare program payments and/or recipients; Office on Aging expenditures, services, and beneficiaries; Hispanic resident births and educational enrollment; and food stamp and nutrition program recipients.

Also includes child day care facilities; child abuse and neglect cases; foster care caseload; adoptions; births, and infant deaths; communicable diseases reported; death rates by cause; and medical examiners' investigations and autopsies.

Also includes hospital operations and finances, with selected detail by hospital; health clinic visits; alcohol and drug abuse center services; mental health facilities and services, with detail for St. Elizabeth's Hospital; nursing home beds; homeless shelter operations, by facility; vocational rehabilitation and work incentive program services; and social security eligibilty evaluations.

S1535–3.4: Public Education and Recreation

(p. 140-155) Contains 4 maps/charts and 21 tables. Includes public school and special education program enrollment; educational facilities and utilization, and finances; student performance on basic skills tests and Scholastic Aptitude Test (SAT); promotion rates; and high school graduates.

Also includes University of D.C. enrollment and degrees awarded; public library circulation, holdings, and per capita book expenditures; Recreation Dept facilities, including swimming pools; D.C. and National Park Service park acreage; and water area.

S1535–3.5: Public Works

(p. 156-168) Contains 1 map and 16 tables. Includes miles of streets, sidewalks, and alleys, and number of bridges, street lights, and signal intersections; resurfaced roads; traffic accidents and fatalities (including alcohol-related fatalities and arrests); and parking meters and revenues collected.

Also includes Washington Metropolitan Area Transit Authority rail and bus operations, finances, and ridership; water customers and meters installed/replaced; water/sewer billings and collections; average daily wastewater treatment and sludge generated; and solid waste collection and disposal.

S1535–3.6: Public Safety

(p. 169-188) Contains 4 charts/maps and 24 tables. Includes fire dept operations and fire loss data; ambulance services, by hospital of destination; crimes reported, and adult and juvenile arrests, by major offense; activities of Pretrial Services Agency and Public Defender Service; cases presented to U.S. Attorney; and court case filings and outcomes.

Also includes juvenile detentions and commitments; corrections facility detainees, new commitments, and prisoners; prison academic and vocational training program enrollment; parole population, removals, and revocations; and probation cases and officers.

S1565
DISTRICT OF COLUMBIA
Department of
Human Services

S1565–1 SOCIAL SERVICES MONTHLY STATISTICAL REPORT, District of Columbia
Monthly.   Approx. 15 p. no paging.
SRI/MF/complete, shipped quarterly

Monthly report on District of Columbia public welfare programs, covering AFDC, general assistance (GA), food stamps, emergency shelter, and institutions for children. Includes cases, payments, and/or recipients by program. Also includes quarterly data on emergency assistance, and food stamp race-ethnic group participation. Report is issued 3-8 months after month of coverage.

Contains contents listing, and 9 monthly and 7 quarterly tables, listed below. Monthly tables appear in all issues. Quarterly tables appear in Mar., June, Sept., and Dec. issues.

Availability: District of Columbia Department of Human Services, Policy and Planning Office, Research and Statistics Division, 425 I St., NW, Rm. 3001, Washington DC 20001, †; SRI/MF/complete, shipped quarterly.

Issues reviewed during 1985: Apr. 1984-Mar. 1985 (D).

TABLES:

MONTHLY TABLES
[Tables generally show data for month of coverage, with selected comparisons to prior periods. Table numbers vary when issues include quarterly tables. Tables [1-4] show data from the Income Maintenance or Payments Assistance Administration.]

1. Public assistance cases, [persons], and payments, [by category].

2-3. AFDC and GA applications [and disposition], and cases, by service center [data discontinued as of Jan. 1985, but tables without data continue to appear].

4. Food stamp program cases and persons participating [and value of coupons redeemed and average bonus per family], by type of household [public assistance and other].

5-6. Temporary emergency family shelter, case activity and cumulative admissions and discharges [by shelter]: Office of Emergency Shelter and Support Services.

7-9. Institutions for children: population statistics and cumulative admissions and discharges, and comparison of average population [by specific facility or type of facility]: Youth Services Administration.

QUARTERLY TABLES
[Most data are shown for quarter ending with month of coverage. Tables [A-E] show data from the Income Maintenance Administration.]

[A-B] Reasons for denials of AFDC applications, and AFDC discontinuances by reason for discontinuance.

[C] Average distribution of public assistance [cases, and Medicaid and food stamp families not receiving public assistance], by ward.

[D] Emergency assistance [total families and recipients, total Federal funds, and] amount of payment approved for each type of emergency [including food, rent, and utility assistance, for each month of quarter].

[E] Food stamp program average monthly racial/ethnic group participation [white, black, Oriental, Native American, Spanish American, Vietnamese, Cambodian, and other].

[F] Blair/Pierce temporary shelters for men [total sheltered, 1st time users, and number of nights of shelter]: Family Services Administration [for each month of quarter].

[G] Child protection register, number of child abuse and neglect reports, and ward distribution [all for families and children]: Family Services Administration.

S1565–2 VITAL STATISTICS SUMMARY, 1982, District of Columbia
Recurring (irreg.) [1985.]
100 p.
ISSN 0419-4381.
LC 74-642073.
SRI/MF/complete

Recurring report on District of Columbia vital statistics, 1982, with trends from the 1960s. Covers births, deaths by cause, and population. Includes data by race, age, sex, and ward or census tract.

Data are compiled from D.C. records.

Contains listings of symbols, contents, tables, and charts (p. 2-6); introduction and definitions (p. 7-11); narrative report, interspersed with text tables, 1 map, and 11 tables listed below (p. 12-26); and statistical section, with 28 tables, also listed below (p. 28-100).

For description of previous report, for 1981, see SRI 1984 Annual under this number.

Availability: District of Columbia Department of Human Services, Policy and Planning Office, Research and Statistics Division, 425 I St., NW, Rm. 3107, Washington DC 20001, †; SRI/MF/complete.

TABLES:

[Data are for D.C., 1982, unless otherwise noted.]

S1565–2.1: Narrative Section Tables

POPULATION AND TRENDS

[Tables A-K show data for D.C. residents, 1970-82, unless otherwise noted.]

A. Live births and birth rates, by race and sex. (p. 15)

B-C. Deaths [total], and infant and neonatal deaths, and death rates, by race. (p. 16-17)

D. Three-year moving average of infant mortality rate, by age at death, 1961/63-1980/82. (p. 18)

E-F. Fetal and perinatal deaths and death rates, by race. (p. 19-20)

G. Out-of-wedlock births, by race. (p. 21)

H. Incidence of low birth weight, by race. (p. 22)

I-J. Births to adolescent mothers [under age 20 and under age 18], and maternal mortality, by race. (p. 23-24)

K. Recorded events, and resident events in other States [showing births and deaths in D.C. and resident births and deaths outside D.C.]. (p. 25)

S1565–2.2: Statistical Section Tables

POPULATION AND TRENDS

1. Estimated population by age, race, and sex. (p. 28)

2-4. Number of total, black, and white resident live births and deaths, [and] number and rates of infant, neonatal, and fetal deaths, 1975-82 and averages [for selected periods] 1945-79. (p. 29-31)

BIRTHS

5. Out-of-wedlock ratios [births per 1,000 live births] by age of mother and race, 1976-82. (p. 32)

6. Number and percent distribution of resident live births by live-birth order and race, 1979-82 and averages [for selected periods] 1965-79. (p. 33)

7-12. Live births: by live birth order, age of mother, and plurality, all races; and by live birth order and age of mother, and by ward and age of mother, [by race]. (p. 34-41)

13. Number and percent distribution of resident live births, and births with selected characteristics (out-of-wedlock, premature, immature, and with inadequate prenatal care), by race and ward. (p. 42-44)

DEATHS

14-15. Resident deaths and crude death rates, for 20 leading causes, by race and sex. (p. 45-46)

16. Principal causes of death of residents, by age group and sex, with rates. (p. 47-49)

17. Number of resident deaths and crude and age-adjusted death rates by age, race, and sex. (p. 50)

18. Deaths from 72 selected causes, by age, race, and sex. (p. 51-77)

19. Resident deaths for 20 leading causes, by race and ward. (p. 78-80)

FETAL AND INFANT DEATHS

20. Infant deaths and death rates by age and race, and fetal deaths by race, 1975-82 and averages [for selected periods] 1950-79. (p. 81)

21. Resident infant deaths and death rates by age, 1962-82. (p. 82)

22. Infant death rates by ward and age, 1981-82. (p. 83)

23. Resident infant deaths by cause and age. (p. 84-86)

24. Three-year moving average of infant mortality rate, by age at death, 1962/64-1980/82. (p. 87)

MISCELLANEOUS

25. Live births, out-of-wedlock births, infant deaths, fetal deaths, [and] total deaths, by place of occurrence [D.C. and elsewhere, for events involving D.C. residents], and residence [D.C., Maryland, Virginia, or elsewhere, for events occurring in D.C.]. (p. 88)

26. Recorded number of live births and deaths: number and rates of infant, neonatal, and fetal deaths, by race, 1975-82 and averages [for selected periods] 1940-79. (p. 89-91)

27. Resident live births, out-of-wedlock births, births with no prenatal care, immature births, total deaths, and infant deaths, by census tract. (p. 92-98)

28. Recorded deaths from accidental causes by age and type of accident. (p. 99-100)

S1605
DISTRICT OF COLUMBIA
Public Schools

S1605–1   DISTRICT OF COLUMBIA PUBLIC SCHOOLS DATA RESOURCE BOOK, School Year 1984/85
Annual.   Feb. 1985.
iii+31 p.
SRI/MF/complete

Annual report, for academic year 1984/85, on District of Columbia public and private school enrollment, graduates, standardized test results, finances, and staffing. Data are from D.C. Education Dept reports.

Contains preface and contents listing (p. ii-iii); lists of school board, administration, and regional officials, with 1 map (p. 1-7); and narrative description, interspersed with 15 tables listed below (p. 8-31).

This is the 13th annual data resource book.

Availability: District of Columbia Public Schools, Quality Assurance Division, 415 12th St., NW, Rm. 1013, Washington DC 20004, †; SRI/MF/complete.

TABLES:

[Tables show data for D.C., 1984/85, unless otherwise noted.]

STUDENTS

[Tables A-C generally show enrollment data for elementary, junior high, senior high, career development, and special education schools, including some individual institutions or programs; and tuition grant students and regular and special preschool students; as of Oct. 18, 1984.]

A. Membership [with comparisons to Oct. 1983]. (p. 8-9)

B-C. Student membership: by race [and ethnic group, including American Indian, Asian/Pacific Islander, and Hispanic]; and by region. (p. 10-12)

D. Adult/continuing education [membership by sex and level, as of Feb. 15, 1985]. (p. 13)

E. Graduates [from senior high schools, STAY school, Street Academy, career development centers, and Ellington School of the Arts, 1980/81-1983/84]. (p. 13)

F. Nonpublic [parochial, private, and other, by type] and public school enrollment [all by race]. (p. 14-15)

G. Special education [students served, by local and State program type, 1983/84]. (p. 16)

H. Student assessment [including results of basic skills tests in reading and mathematics, by grade, 1980-84]. (p. 17-18)

I. Food services [number of student meals served 1983/84, and prices 1984/85, by level of education]. (p. 19)

J. School calendar [and day school advisory periods]. (p. 20-21)

ADMINISTRATION

K. Budget [appropriations for capital outlay, and regular and Federal operating expenses and per pupil expenditure, FY83-85]. (p. 23)

L. Federal grants [by source and program, FY85]. (p. 24-25)

M. Staffing [by position, and professional employees by degree level, FY85]. (p. 26)

N-O. Number of schools and instructional programs [by level or program, all by region]; and alphabetical listing and regional designation of the public schools. (p. 27-31)

S1685   FLORIDA
Department of
Agriculture and
Consumer Services

S1685–1   FLORIDA AGRICULTURAL STATISTICS
Annual series.   For individual publication data, see below.
SRI/MF/complete

Series of 6 annual reports on Florida agricultural production, finances, and marketing, for citrus, vegetable, poultry, livestock, field crop, and dairy sectors. Data generally are shown by commodity and/or county, with selected comparisons to other States and total U.S.

Data are from USDA; State and local government agencies; growers assns; and agricultural, transportation, and food industry firms.

Reports reviewed during 1985 are described below.

Related, less comprehensive publications available from the issuing agency, but not covered in SRI, include 2 biennial citrus reports, *Commercial Citrus Inventory* and *Maturity Summary*.

Availability: Florida Crop and Livestock Reporting Service, 1222 Woodward St., Orlando FL 32803, series of 6 reports $12.00, single report $2.50; SRI/MF/complete.

S1685–1.1: Florida Agricultural Statistics, Citrus Summary, 1984

[Annual. Jan. 1985. 46 p. LC 74-644777. SRI/MF/complete.]

Annual report on Florida citrus fruit production, acreage, yield, utilization, prices, value, shipments, and trade, by fruit type. Data are shown for various crop years 1960s-1983/84, with selected trends from 1886.

Includes selected comparisons to Arizona, California, and Texas; production and acreage by county; and U.S. and Florida citrus exports, by country of destination.

Also includes citrus shipments in U.S. and Canada, including cartons received in approximately 25 cities, by transport mode and source (State, Mexico, and other); U.S. per capita citrus consumption; and comparative citrus fruit production of selected foreign countries.

Contains contents listing (1 p.); narrative summary, with 3 tables (p. 1-3); 3 charts and 35 detailed tables (p. 4-44); and data sources (p. 45).

S1685–1.2: Florida Agricultural Statistics, Vegetable Summary, 1984

[Annual. Apr. 1985. iv+69 p. LC A63-7731. SRI/MF/complete.]

Annual report on Florida vegetable, melon, and strawberry production, acreage, yield, prices, shipments, and trade, by commodity, with selected data by county or State area. Most data are shown for 1969/70-1983/84 crop years.

Also includes Florida monthly shipments to other States/Canada and exports, and shipments received in 24 U.S. and Canadian cities by source (Florida and other States), both by transport mode and commodity; and monthly imports of Mexican tomatoes; various periods 1980/81-1983/84.

Contains production calendar and contents listing (p. iii-iv); narrative summary, with 1 table (p. 1-11); and 133 detailed tables (p. 12-69).

S1685–1.3: Florida Agricultural Statistics, Livestock Summary, 1984

[Annual. May 1985. 21 p. LC A64-7767. SRI/MF/complete.]

Annual report on Florida livestock production, value, inventories, shipments, dispositions, marketing, income, slaughter, and prices, by species, mostly 1975-84, with some data for 1985, and some comparisons to other States and total U.S.

Also includes data on apiary sector production, value, inventory, and prices; feeder calf outshipments, by State of destination; U.S. livestock inventories, by State; and U.S. per capita consumption of meat, fish, poultry, and eggs, 1943-84.

Contains contents listing (1 p.); narrative summary and methodology, with 1 table (p. 1); 28 detailed tables (p. 2-20); and directory of cattle/hog auctions (p. 21).

S1685–1.4: Florida Agricultural Statistics, Poultry Summary, 1984

[Annual. July 1985. 32 p. LC A64-7653. SRI/MF/complete.]

Annual report on Florida poultry and egg production, income, and prices, and poultry inventories, mostly 1975-84, with selected trends from 1970, and some comparisons to other States and total U.S.

Contains contents listing (1 p.); narrative summary, with glossary (p. 1); and 2 charts, 3 maps, and 23 tables (p. 2-32).

S1685–1.5: Florida Agricultural Statistics, Dairy Summary, 1984

[Annual. Aug. 1985. 26 p. LC 75-646842. SRI/MF/complete.]

Annual report on Florida dairy production, value, utilization, income, and prices, by county and/or product, mostly 1975-84, with some comparisons to other States and total U.S.

Also includes data on Florida cattle inventories, raw milk inshipments, and cattle inshipments by State of origin; and U.S. per capita dairy product consumption, 1961-84.

Contains contents listing (1 p.); and brief narrative summary, 2 charts, and 24 tables (p. 1-26).

S1685–1.6: Florida Agricultural Statistics, Field Crops Summary, 1984

[Annual. Aug. 1985. 18 p. SRI/MF/complete.]

Annual report on Florida field crop and nut acreage, yield, production, prices, and value, by commodity and/or district and county, 1984, with trends from 1974.

Contains contents listing (1 p.); narrative summary (p. 1-2); and 17 tables (p. 3-18).

S1717   FLORIDA
Office of the Comptroller

S1717–1   ANNUAL REPORT OF THE COMPTROLLER for the Fiscal Year Ended June 30, 1984, State of Florida

Annual. 2 volumes.
For individual publication data, see below.
LC 10-11492.
SRI/MF/complete

Annual report on the financial condition of Florida, FY84, with comparisons from FY75, and historical trends from 1932. Data are from records of the comptroller's office and various State agencies.

Report is published in 2 volumes: main report with detailed cash basis accounting of receipts and disbursements; and audited financial statements, with notes. Individual volumes are further described below. Prior to FY84, report was issued in 1 volume.

Availability: Florida Office of the Comptroller, Banking and Finance Department, Capitol Bldg., Tallahassee FL 32301, †; SRI/MF/complete.

S1717–1.1: Main Report

[Annual. Dec. 15, 1984. 238 p. SRI/MF/complete.]

Presents receipts by source and month; expenditures, by function, object, dept, and institution; and fund balances; for specific general revenue, trust, working capital, and Federal revenue sharing funds, FY84, with selected comparisons from FY75 and earlier.

Also includes data on appropriations compared to disbursements; tax collections and allocations, educational program disbursements, and welfare program assistance, by county; revenue distribution to municipalities; State retirement systems; and pari-mutuel wagering fund receipts and disbursements.

Contains letter of transmittal, foreword, and table listing (p. 3-6); 2 charts and 27 tables (p. 8-235); and agency index (p. 236-238).

S1717–1.2: General Purpose Financial Statements

[Annual. Feb. 6, 1985. v+61 p. SRI/MF/complete.]

Presents assets, liabilities and equity; revenues by source; and expenditures by purpose and/or agency; for government, proprietary, and fiduciary fund types, FY84.

Also includes data on State construction project costs; and long-term debt obligations.

Contains contents listing and letter of transmittal (p. iii-v); auditor's statement (p. 1-2); 7 financial exhibits (p. 3-22); and notes to financial statements (p. 23-61).

S1717–2   ANNUAL REPORT OF THE DIVISION OF BANKING, Florida, 1983

Annual. [1984.] 174 p.
LC 76-643004.
SRI/MF/complete

Annual report on financial condition of Florida financial institutions, presenting assets, liabilities, capital, and operating income and expenses, for commercial banks, industrial savings banks, nondeposit trust companies, savings and loan assns, and credit unions, as of Dec. 31, 1983, with selected comparisons to 1982.

Includes data for State-located national banks and international bank agencies. Commercial bank data are shown by institution and county; in general, only assets are shown individually for other institution types.

Also includes selected summary trends from 1895; bank operating ratios; top 10 State and national banks ranked by assets; and financial data for multi- and 1-bank holding companies, and independent banks, by county.

Contains contents listing (p. 1-2); dept personnel lists (p. 4-9); 5 charts and 40 tables, interspersed with status changes and other lists (p. 10-115); and regulatory information (p. 116-174).

Availability: Florida Department of Banking and Finance, Banking Division, Capitol Bldg., Suite 1301, Tallahassee FL 32301, ‡; SRI/MF/complete.

S1720   FLORIDA
Department of Corrections

S1720–1   ANNUAL REPORT, FY84, Florida Department of Corrections
Annual.   Dec. 31, 1984.
ii+101 p.
LC 80-648829.
SRI/MF/complete

Annual report, for FY84, on corrections in Florida, presenting data on the prison and parole/probation population, including admissions, releases, demographic and socioeconomic characteristics, criminal background, primary offense, and sentence length or supervision period. Includes selected data by institution and county of commitment or supervision, with trends from 1974, and projected prison and parole/probation populations to 1987.

Also includes interstate transfers of parolees and probationers; prison escapes; population under pretrial supervision; inmates' IQ, and alcohol and narcotic use; prison industry trust fund financial statements; corrections dept finances; prison operating costs; and financing for capital projects.

Contains contents listing (p. 1); introduction and narrative summary, with 10 charts and 3 maps (p. 2-42); 2 statistical sections, with 6 charts and 50 tables (p. 43-95); directory of correctional institutions and parole/probation service offices (p. 96-99); and index (p. 100-101).

Availability: Florida Department of Corrections, 1311 Winewood Blvd., Tallahassee FL 32301, †; SRI/MF/complete.

S1725   FLORIDA
Department of Education

S1725–1   FACT BOOK, 1983/84, State University System of Florida
Annual.   Feb. 1, 1985.
xi+207 p.   No. BOR 85-4.
ISSN 0093-9617.
LC 74-642941.
SRI/MF/complete

Annual report, for 1983/84 academic year, on Florida State-supported universities. Covers enrollment, finances, degree programs, contracts and grants, and staff, for 9 universities in the State University System (SUS). Includes enrollment and appropriation trends from 1970s.

Report is based on individual university surveys, State agency studies, and Higher Education General Information Survey (HEGIS) reports.

Contains listing of contents, tables, and charts (p. v-xi); introductory material (p. 1-11); 11 charts and 59 tables (p. 12-189); and functional directory, glossary, and index (p. 193-207).

All tables, and charts presenting substantial data not covered in tables, are described below.

Availability: Florida Department of Education, Board of Regents, State University System of Florida, 107 W. Gaines St., Tallahassee FL 32301, ‡; SRI/MF/complete.

TABLES AND CHARTS:
[Most data are shown for total SUS and by individual institution. Data by race also include Hispanic and, occasionally, Asian/Pacific Islander and American Indian/Alaskan Native.]

a. **Institutional characteristics:** including locale, campus size and housing units, enrollment and financial summaries, number of National Merit Scholars, and endowed faculty chairs, generally 1984; and square footage of facilities (current and under construction), as of June 30, 1984. Tables 1-2. (p. 12-25)

b. **Admissions:** applicants, admissions, and enrollment, by student category; admissions, by entrance examination scores and high school grade point average; 1st-time student enrollment, by county of residence; and community college transfers to SUS; fall 1983. Tables 3-9. (p. 29-45)

c. **Enrollment:** FTE enrollment and average credit hour load, by academic level; headcount enrollment, by county and State of residence, nation of citizenship, full- and part-time status, sex, and race; noncredit programs and participants; continuing education units awarded; FTE enrollment, by on- and off-campus site; and student age; fall 1983 or 1983/84, with enrollment trends from 1974/75. Tables 10-24. (p. 49-82)

d. **Degree programs:** programs offered; headcount enrollment by discipline, cross-tabulated by level, race (also nonresident aliens), and sex; undergraduate and graduate course work distribution, by discipline of student and course; degrees granted, by level, discipline, race, and sex; and participation in exchange programs with other institutions; fall 1983 or 1983/84. Tables 25-37. (p. 85-132)

e. **Student and institution finances:** tuition and required fees, with detail for medical programs, 1984/85; room and board charges, and out-of-State tuition/fee waivers, 1983/84; financial aid, by type and race, 1983/84; appropriations to SUS, by type including libraries, various years 1975/76-1984/85; instructional expenditures, by category, 1983/84; SUS data processing costs, by type, FY84; and summary revenues and expenditures, FY84. Charts 3-4 and tables 38-50. (p. 135-164)

f. **Contracts and grants:** copyrights and patents granted; research/service contract/grant funds by source and expenditures by discipline; contract/grant indirect costs recovered and amounts transferred to trust fund; and Federal contract/grant awards, by sponsoring agency; FY84. Tables 51-56. (p. 167-176)

g. **Personnel:** "manyear" distribution, by budget classification and function; total personnel, by function, race, and sex; and faculty, by tenure status, race, sex, academic rank, and age; 1983/84. Charts 5-11 and tables 57-59. (p. 179-189)

S1725–2   PROFILES OF FLORIDA SCHOOL DISTRICTS, 1983/84
Annual.   [1985.]   ii+213 p.
Profile XIV, Vol. II.
LC 73-640923.
SRI/MF/complete

Annual report, for 1983/84, on Florida public schools, with comparative data for 1982/83 and trends from 1901. Includes statistics on enrollment, finances, graduates, and staff, all by school district. Also includes selected data for nonpublic schools.

Contains contents listing and preface (p. i-ii); introduction, and list of school districts and regions (p. 1-2); historical data, with 4 charts and 3 tables (p. 3-6); State and school district profiles (p. 8-159); appendix, with 3 detailed tables, and notes (p. 162-213); and 1 data map showing population by congressional district, 1980 (inside back cover).

All profiles and tables are described below.

Report is Volume II of the Commissioner of Education's annual report on Florida public schools. Volume I is a narrative description of programs and is not covered by SRI.

Availability: Florida Department of Education, Public Schools Division, Education Information Services/MIS, 275 Knott Bldg., Tallahassee FL 32301, †; SRI/MF/complete.

PROFILES AND TABLES:
[Data by race are generally for white, black, Hispanic, Asian/Pacific Islander, and American Indian/Alaskan Native.]

S1725–2.1: State Historical Data

a. Total population, population aged 5-17, enrollment, high school graduates, teachers, average teacher salary, schools, assessed valuation of property, and total and per pupil expenses, 1901/02-1983/84. 1 table. (p. 3)

b. Percent of class survival, 1st grade through college entrance, for classes beginning 1962-72; and revenue receipts, total and from Federal, State, and local sources, 1959/60-1983/84. 2 tables. (p. 4)

S1725–2.2: School District Profiles

Profiles cover the State (p. 8-9), 3 State schools (p. 10-15), and 5 school regions and 67 school districts (p. 16-159). State school profiles show summary enrollment and financial data for 1983/84. Other profiles show the data described below, generally for 1982/83-1983/84 school years unless otherwise noted.

a. Community: population by race and sex, by age, 1983; and urban and rural population, adults by race and educational attainment, and median family income, 1980.

b. Students: FTE count for elementary/secondary, adult, vocational, and exceptional students; fall membership by race; total graduates and percent entering college and technical school; SSAT (State student assessment test) performance by subject area and grade; number of public schools; and number of nonpublic schools and students.

c. Staff: number of personnel by position and race; personnel distribution and ratios by position, and percent of professional personnel resigning; FTE students per FTE teacher by grade level; and salary range by certification status.

d. Finance: revenues, including receipts by source (Federal, State, and local), categorical/special allocations by program, operating tax millage and yield, assessed property value, and required local effort; and expenditures, including capital outlay, debt service, and expenditures for elementary and secondary education by grade level, and for exceptional, vocational, and adult education by type of program; with per pupil amounts for selected items.

e. Transportation: cost per pupil, and expenditures of State and district funds.

S1725–2.3: Appendix

[Tables show data by school district, fall 1983 or 1983/84.]

I. Student data [nonpublic students and graduates; public graduates and dropouts; SSAT results by subject and grade; public student membership by race; and final unweighted FTE count for vocational (high school and adult) and exceptional student programs, by program or handicap, and for basic education by level, including adult basic/high school and educational alternatives]. (p. 162-172)

II. Staff data [full-time and support staff by position; and full-time professional and support staff by sex and race]. (p. 173-174)

III. Fiscal data [revenues by source (Federal, State, and local), and detail by fund; expenditures by fund and detailed object; and long-term debt]. (p. 175-200)

S1735   FLORIDA
Office of the Governor

S1735–1   ECONOMIC REPORT OF THE GOVERNOR
Annual, discontinued.

Annual report on Florida economic trends and outlook, discontinued with the 1981/82 report (for description, see SRI 1982 Annual under this number).

Issuing agency now publishes a bimonthly report, *Governor's Report on Florida's Economy*, not covered in SRI.

S1745   FLORIDA
Department of Health and Rehabilitative Services

S1745–2   FLORIDA MORBIDITY STATISTICS, 1981
Annual. [1984.] xvi+91 p.
ISSN 0093-8084.
LC 74-642299.
SRI/MF/complete.

Annual report on Florida reported incidence of notifiable communicable diseases, by disease and county, 1981. Includes selected trends from 1957, and selected data by age, race, and sex. Data are compiled by the Health Program Office from State sources.

Contains contents listing, introduction, epidemiologic notes, map of State health districts, and 1 table showing population and health district numbers by county (p. iii-xvi); and 5 sections, with 42 charts and 31 tables described below, interspersed with narrative analysis (p. 1-91).

This is the 37th annual report. Previous report, for 1980, is described in SRI 1983 Annual, under this number.

Availability: Florida Department of Health and Rehabilitative Services, Health Program Office, Preventive Health Services/Epidemiology Program, 1317 Winewood Blvd., Tallahassee FL 32301, †; SRI/MF/complete.

CHARTS AND TABLES:
SUMMARY

a. Cases of selected diseases, by month of onset 1981, and annually (with rates) 1972-81; and cases of diseases of infrequent occurrence, 1967-81. 4 tables. (p. 3-6)

COUNTY DATA

b. By disease: includes cases by month of onset, and rates, by county; and cases by age group; for 13 diseases, 1981, with 1978-80 mean rate by county for most diseases, and detail on meningococcal meningitis testing. 29 charts and 14 tables. (p. 9-47)

c. Animal rabies and zoonoses: animal specimens examined, and confirmed rabies cases by month and county, by species, 1981; confirmed rabies cases by county and species, 1972-81; and cases of 4 types of zoonotic diseases, by county, 1981. 1 chart and 5 tables. (p. 50-64)

d. Venereal diseases: includes cases by county 1981, cases and rates 1957-81, and cases by source of report (private physicians, and public and military clinics) 1981, for syphilis and gonorrhea. 7 charts and 3 tables. (p. 65-79)

e. Tuberculosis: includes cases and rates, with comparison to U.S., 1971-81; cases and rates by age, race, sex, health district, and county, 1981; and cases by disease site, 1981. 5 charts and 5 tables. (p. 81-91)

S1745–3   FLORIDA VITAL STATISTICS, 1984
Annual. Sept. 1985.
v+125 p.
LC 83-643734.
SRI/MF/complete, current & previous year reports

Annual report on Florida vital statistics, including population, births, deaths by cause, and marriages and dissolutions, 1984, with trends from as early as 1959. Includes data by location, race, age, and sex.

Data are derived primarily from records filed with the Office of Vital Statistics; population data are from University of Florida Bureau of Economic and Business Research.

Contents:

a. Map and listing of Florida counties, with Health and Rehabilitative Services (HRS) districts and subdistricts shown for each; and contents and table listings. (p. ii-v)

b. Introduction; and 6 sections with 43 detailed tables listed below, and 38 interspersed summary/trend tables including data on population by age group and sex, fertility, life expectancy, deaths by disposition of remains, underwater diving deaths, and accidental deaths by detailed type and victim characteristics. (p. 1-125)

Previous report, for 1983, was also reviewed in SRI during 1985, and is also available on SRI microfiche under S1745-3 [Annual. Nov. 1984. v+125 p. †].

Availability: Florida Department of Health and Rehabilitative Services, Publications, Public

Health Statistics and Records Registration Section, PO Box 210, Jacksonville FL 32231-0042, 1st copy †, additional copies $5.24; SRI/MF/complete.

TABLES:
[Tables show data for Florida, by race, 1984, unless otherwise noted.]

S1745–3.1: Population and Live Births
[Tables show data by county.]

POPULATION

1. Midyear population estimates, 1980 and 1984. (p. 5)

LIVE BIRTHS

2-3. Recorded and resident live births and birth rates per 1,000 population, 1984 and annual averages 1979-81. (p. 9-10)

4. Live births, by place of occurrence and residence, for 104 incorporated cities of 10,000 or more population. (p. 11)

5. Percent of resident live births attended by physician [in and out of hospital], midwife, and other. (p. 12)

6-7. Resident live births: by sex, by weight at birth; and by age of mother. (p. 13-18)

8-10. Resident live births to unwed mothers [with] rates per 100 total live births, 1984 and annual average 1979-81; and by age of mother and birth order. (p. 19-23)

S1745–3.2: Mortality, Marriages, and Marriage Dissolutions
[Data are shown by county, unless otherwise noted. Causes of death are shown according to the 9th Revision of the International Classification of Diseases. Tables on mortality often include rates.]

MORTALITY

11-16. Resident fetal deaths (stillbirths) of 20 or more weeks gestation; recorded and resident neonatal deaths (age under 28 days); resident perinatal deaths (fetal plus neonatal); and recorded and resident infant deaths (age under 1 year); 1984 and annual average 1979-81. (p. 26-31)

17-18. Resident neonatal and infant deaths from selected causes, by age. (p. 32-37)

19-20. Recorded and resident deaths, 1984 and annual average 1979-81. (p. 50-51)

21. Deaths, by place of occurrence and by place of residence, for 104 incorporated cities of 10,000 or more population. (p. 52)

22. Resident death rates per 100,000 population, 40 important cause groups. (p. 53-62)

23. Resident deaths, by age groups [by sex]. (p. 63-67)

24. Resident deaths for 360 cause groups, by age [not by county]. (p. 68-72)

25. Resident deaths from selected causes, by sex. (p. 73-106)

MARRIAGES AND DISSOLUTIONS
[Data are not shown by race.]

26. [Total] marriages performed, by month. (p. 108)

27. [Total] dissolutions of marriage by month granted, and annulments. (p. 109)

S1745–3.3: HRS Districts

[Tables show data by HRS district and subdistrict. Tables often include rates.]

28-29. Live births, and live births to unwed mothers [resident and recorded]. (p. 111)

30-31. Resident live births to teenage mothers and percent of live births; and resident live births to unwed teenage mothers and percent of live births to unwed mothers; [by age group]. (p. 112)

32-33. Resident first order and low weight live births [total and] to unwed mothers. (p. 113)

34-35. Resident live births in hospital, and nonhospital, by attendant, and percent of live births. (p. 114-115)

36-39. Fetal deaths 20 or more weeks gestation, and neonatal, perinatal, and infant deaths [recorded and resident]. (p. 116-117)

40-41. [Recorded and] resident deaths, and resident deaths for leading causes. (p. 118-121)

42. [Total] accidental deaths by ranked external cause [not by race]. (p. 122-124)

43. Marriages and [total] dissolutions of marriage. (p. 125)

S1745–4   ANNUAL STATISTICAL REPORT, FY83-84, Florida Department of Health and Rehabilitative Services

Annual. Apr. 1985. 3+37 p.
LC 79-644487.
SRI/MF/complete

Annual report, for FY84, on Florida public welfare programs, including cases, recipients, and payments, by program and county. Covers AFDC, SSI, food stamps, low-income home energy assistance, child support enforcement, and medical assistance. Includes demographic characteristics of medical assistance recipients, and types of medical services financed.

Data are compiled by the Office of Revenue Management.

Contains contents listing (1 p.); and 21 tables, listed below (p. 1-37). Some tables are accompanied by charts, generally showing trends from the 1970s.

Report has been published annually since 1967.

Availability: Florida Department of Health and Rehabilitative Services, Revenue Management Office, 1317 Winewood Blvd., Bldg. 3, Rm. 315, Tallahassee FL 32301, †; SRI/MF/complete.

TABLES:

[Data are shown for FY84, unless otherwise noted. Most data by county are also shown by district.]

S1745–4.1: Direct Assistance Programs

SUMMARY

1. Direct assistance payments by county [and program, including SSI, AFDC, and Cuban/Haitian and Indo-Chinese refugee assistance]. (p. 1-6)

AFDC

2. Applications approved [families and persons for financial/medical and medical only], denied/otherwise disposed of, and pending [all by county]. (p. 7-8)

3-4. Recipients [families, children, and persons] and direct assistance [by county and month]. (p. 9-11)

5. Children in foster care [and payments, by month]. (p. 12)

REPATRIATED AMERICANS AND SSI

6. Assistance to repatriated Americans, Federal funds [maintenance/transportation, medical assistance, and repayments, by month]. (p. 13)

7. Optional State supplementation [average monthly cases and direct assistance, by county]. (p. 14)

8. SSI payments [average monthly cases and direct assistance, by county, for Old Age Assistance, Aid to the Blind, and Aid to the Disabled]. (p. 15-16)

S1745–4.2: Food Stamps, Energy Assistance, Child Support Enforcement, and Medical Assistance

FOOD STAMPS

9. Households, persons, and value of food stamps issued, by participating counties [includes households and persons by public assistance status]. (p. 21-22)

ENERGY ASSISTANCE

10. Low-income Home Energy Assistance Program [households, persons, and payments, by county]. (p. 23)

11. Low-income home energy assistance [applications, approvals, and] direct assistance payments [by district; with total State approvals by type of home heating fuel, and for households receiving other types of assistance, and cases involving elderly and handicapped persons]. (p. 24)

CHILD SUPPORT ENFORCEMENT

12. Average intrastate AFDC collections per investigator, [number of investigators, and total collections], by district. (p. 25)

MEDICAL ASSISTANCE

[Data are shown by type of medical facility and service, and are for year ended Sept. 30, 1984, unless otherwise noted.]

13-18. Recipients of medical care, and medical vendor payments: by age in years; by race/ethnicity [including American Indian/Alaskan Native, Asian/Pacific Islander, and Hispanic]; and by sex. (p. 28-31)

19. Comparison of medical assistance program recipients and expenditures, FY83-84. (p. 32)

20. Use and cost: [health care costs and recipients, for aged, blind, disabled, AFDC child and adult categories, and other title XIX]. (p. 33-35)

21. Medical payments by month. (p. 36-37)

S1750   FLORIDA
Department of Highway Safety and Motor Vehicles

S1750–2   FLORIDA TRAFFIC ACCIDENT FACTS, 1984

Annual. [1985.] 33 p.
LC 74-645046.
SRI/MF/complete, current & previous year reports

Annual report on Florida traffic accidents, injuries, and fatalities, by accident and vehicle type, location, time, and other circumstances; and driver and victim characteristics; 1984, with trends from 1964.

Also includes data on accident property damage costs, alcohol involvement, and seat belt use; motor vehicle registrations, licensed drivers, and highway and travel mileage; and summary comparisons to other States.

Data are compiled by Florida Dept of Highway Safety and Motor Vehicles.

Contains contents listing (1 p.); highlights (p. 1); 16 charts and 10 tables (p. 3-25); and standard reporting section, with 5 tables (p. 26-33).

Previous report, for 1983, was also reviewed during 1985 and is also available on SRI microfiche under this number [Annual. [1985.] 25+8 p. †].

Availability: Florida Department of Highway Safety and Motor Vehicles, Administrative Services Division, Traffic Accident Records and Forms Management, Kirkman Bldg., 2900 Apalachee Pkwy., Tallahassee FL 32301-8209, †; SRI/MF/complete.

S1760   FLORIDA
Department of Insurance

S1760–1   REPORT OF THE DEPARTMENT OF INSURANCE, State of Florida, for the Fiscal Year Ending June 30, 1984

Annual. July 1, 1984.
392 p.
SRI/MF/complete

Annual report on Florida insurance industry financial condition and underwriting activity, by company and line of coverage, 1983, with summary comparisons from 1979. Covers assets, liabilities, capital, surplus, premiums written and earned, losses incurred and paid, operating and underwriting gain/loss, dividends paid, and selected operating ratios.

Data are shown, as applicable, for fire, marine/casualty/surety/inter-insurance, title, and life insurance companies; fraternal benefit societies; and accident and health insurance business of life insurance companies.

Data by line of coverage include detail for automobile, worker compensation, and medical malpractice.

Also includes data on fire marshal activities, including liquified petroleum gas regulation, FY84; firefighter and police pension fund tax allocations, by city, 1983; insurance company bail bond business, 1983; and insurance industry employment, investments, payments to State/local government, market shares of top companies by insurance line, and consumer complaints, 1983.

Data are from annual insurer statements filed with the Insurance Dept, and from dept records.

Contains index to contents, transmittal letter, and lists of companies and status changes (p. 3-10); Insurance Dept report, with text tables (p. 11-21); and 41 insurance tables and lists (p. 23-392).

Availability: Florida Department of Insurance, Insurance Commissioner, The Capitol, Tallahassee FL 32301, †; SRI/MF/complete.

S1765   FLORIDA
Department of Labor and Employment Security

S1765-3   FLORIDA EMPLOYMENT STATISTICS
Monthly.   Approx. 6 p.
ISSN 0364-8311.
LC 76-648230.
SRI/MF/complete, shipped quarterly

Monthly report on Florida employment, unemployment, hours, earnings, and unemployment insurance activities. Month of coverage is approximately 2 months prior to cover date.

Contains brief narrative analysis, and 5 monthly tables.

Monthly tables are listed below; most appear in all issues. Issues also occasionally include tables showing trend data for topics covered in monthly tables.

Similar reports for individual MSAs are also available from the issuing agency, but are not covered by SRI.

Availability: Florida Department of Labor and Employment Security, Labor, Employment, and Training Division, Caldwell Bldg., Tallahassee FL 32301, †; SRI/MF/complete, shipped quarterly.

Issues reviewed during 1985: Sept. 1984-Aug. 1985 (P) (Nos. 419-430).

MONTHLY TABLES:
[Unless otherwise noted, data are shown for month of coverage, previous month, and same month of previous year. Table sequence may vary.]

[1] Labor force summary [by employment status].

[2] Nonagricultural employment [by industry division and selected group].

[3] Average hours and earnings in manufacturing [and selected nonmanufacturing] industries.

[4] Seasonally adjusted nonagricultural employment [by industry division].

[5] Unemployment compensation activity [initial claims, weeks claimed, and total payments].

S1770   FLORIDA
Department of Law Enforcement

S1770-1   UNIFORM CRIME REPORTS, State of Florida: 1984 Annual Report
Annual.   Mar. 25, 1985.
x+212 p.
ISSN 0363-9231.
LC 78-643781.
SRI/MF/complete

Annual report on Florida crimes, arrests, and law enforcement employment, 1984 with comparisons from 1982.

Covers crimes by Index offense, and crime rate and clearances; arrests by Index and non-Index offense, arrest rate, and arrests of adults, juveniles, and nonresidents; and law enforcement employment by sex and status (sworn and civilian), and assaults on employees; all by county, municipality, other reporting agency, and judicial circuit.

Also includes statewide data on Index offenses by type of weapon and other circumstances, and type and value of property involved; murder victims, and arrests by Index and non-Index offense, by age, sex and race, with arrest detail for narcotics and gambling violations; law enforcement officers killed, disposition of offenders, and assaults on officers by circumstance; resident and tourist populations, and modified crime rates; and summary crime forecast for 1985.

Index offenses are murder, rape, robbery, assault, burglary, larceny, motor vehicle theft, and arson. Most data by race include white, black, American Indian, Oriental, and other.

Data are from reports of State and local law enforcement agencies, submitted under the Uniform Crime Reporting (UCR) Program.

Contains contents and table/chart listings, and Dept organization (p. vi-x); introduction, with UCR description (p. 2-6); statewide statistical section, with narrative summaries, 23 charts, and 52 tables (p. 7-82); local data section, with 6 extended tables (p. 86-202); and glossary and index (p. 203-212).

This is the 14th annual report.

Availability: Florida Department of Law Enforcement, PO Box 1489, Tallahassee FL 32302, †; SRI/MF/complete.

S1790   FLORIDA
Public Service Commission

S1790-1   FLORIDA PUBLIC SERVICE COMMISSION, 1984-85 Report
Annual.   [1985.]   62 p.
SRI/MF/complete

Annual report presenting Florida public utility regulatory, financial, and operating data, primarily by utility type and company, 1984, with selected trends from 1960. Utility types covered are telephone, gas, and electric, with regulatory data only for railroads and water/sewer systems.

Includes data on Public Service Commission finances and regulatory activities, including consumer complaints; utility plant value, revenue, customers, and return on equity; telephone facilities and call completion rates; average residential electricity consumption, and electricity and gas bills; electric utility fuel costs and conservation practices; nuclear power plant capacity, costs, and employment; and natural gas accidents, injuries, and fatalities.

Also includes data on average U.S. residential electricity use, bill, and revenues, by census division; and electric rates in selected U.S. cities.

Data are from FPSC records and company reports.

Contains contents listing (1 p.); report, with regulatory text tables (p. 1-32); table listing (p. 33); and statistical section, with 33 tables (p. 37-62).

Availability: Florida Public Service Commission, Consumer Affairs Department, 101 E. Gaines St., Tallahassee FL 32301, †; SRI/MF/complete.

S1800   FLORIDA
Department of State

S1800-1   TABULATION OF OFFICIAL VOTES: Florida General Election, Nov. 6, 1984
Biennial.   [1985.]   41 p.
LC 83-621530.
SRI/MF/complete

Biennial report presenting results of the Florida general election held Nov. 6, 1984. Shows voting for President/Vice President, U.S. Representatives, State senators and representatives, State attorneys, public defender, and judges; and 8 State constitutional amendments. Data are shown by county and/or district, and include most candidates' party affiliation.

Also includes registered voters, by race and party, by county.

Previous report, covering 1982 general election, is described in SRI 1983 Annual under this number.

Availability: Florida Department of State, Elections Division, Capitol Bldg., Rm. 1801, Tallahassee FL 32301, †; SRI/MF/complete.

S1800–2   1984 FLORIDA LIBRARY DIRECTORY with Statistics

Annual. Aug. 1984. 176 p.
LC 52-62285.
SRI/MF/complete

Annual report on Florida public, academic, and institution libraries, with data for FY83. Includes finances, holdings, staff, capacity, and population served, by library system, county, and institution. Data are compiled from reports of participating libraries.

Contents:

a. Preface and contents listing (p. 3-5); and directories of library assns, libraries, and school media personnel (p. 7-110).

b. Statistical sections, with 2 maps and 16 tables listed below (p. 112-160); and personnel index (p. 163-176).

Academic library data are generally included in every other edition, but directories appear in every edition. This edition does not include academic library data.

Availability: Florida Department of State, State Library, Library Services Division, R. A. Gray Bldg., Tallahassee FL 32301-8021, $12.50; SRI/MF/complete.

TABLES:

PUBLIC LIBRARIES

[Data are for FY83, and are shown for regional systems, and by county and library.]

1. Volumes of books [and other material, periodical titles, microform and audiovisual titles, and population served]. (p. 114-119)

2. Use of library [registered borrowers; total circulation; interlibrary loans; book turnover rate; and per capita circulation, reference transactions, program attendance, and interlibrary materials use]. (p. 120-124)

3. Service delivery [number of public service outlets, library capacity, and hours per week]. (p. 125-129)

4. Personnel in FTE [by category, and annual salaries for library director and new librarians]. (p. 130-134)

5-7. Financial information: receipts by source [including State and Federal aid and nonresident fees]; financial information ranked by population [operating expenditures and distribution by category, and capital outlay; and libraries and systems] ranked by expenditures. (p. 135-145)

INSTITUTION LIBRARIES

[Data are shown by State agency and institution, FY83.]

1. Number of residents, books and periodicals, and other materials. (p. 150)

2. Library capacity, hours, and staff [with head librarian salary]. (p. 152)

3. Financial information: income by source, and operating expenditures by category. (p. 154-155)

STATE LIBRARY

[A] [Budget expenditures by object and fund, circulation, and holdings by type, 1982/83.] (p. 158)

GENERAL DATA

[B] State library information network [number of borrowing libraries, books supplied by source, subject and title requests received, and percentage supplied], 1982/83. [table and map] (p. 158-159)

[C] Status of library development, 1984 [number of counties, aggregate 1983 population, and percent of State population served and unserved, all by 5 library service categories (regional and countywide systems, and substandard, limited, and no public service); and State and unincorporated population 1980 and 1983]. [table and map] (p. 160)

S1855   GEORGIA
Department of Agriculture

S1855–1   GEORGIA AGRICULTURAL FACTS, 1984

Annual. Nov. 1984.
3+87 p.
SRI/MF/complete

Annual report on Georgia agricultural production, marketing, and finances, mostly 1978-83, with some data for 1984 and selected trends from as early as 1960. Data are generally shown by commodity and/or county or district.

Covers production, prices, sales, value, and, as applicable, acreage, yield, disposition, stocks, and inventory, for field crop, vegetable, fruit and nut, poultry, livestock, and dairy sectors.

Also includes data on number of farms by type, and acreage and value; bee sales; grain storage facilities and capacity; farm income, expenses, assets, and liabilities; prices paid by farmers for selected items; weather; export value of selected commodities; fertilizer consumption; farm labor and wages; value of forest products; and summary comparisons to other States, and U.S. per capita consumption of selected foods.

Data are compiled by the Georgia Crop Reporting Service in cooperation with USDA.

Contains contents listing (1 p.); foreword (p. 1); and report, with 18 maps, 16 charts, and 87 tables (p. 2-85).

Availability: Crop Reporting Board Publications, South Bldg., Rm. 5829, U.S. Department of Agriculture, Washington DC 20250, $5.00; SRI/MF/complete.

S1860   GEORGIA
Department of Audits

S1860–1   REPORT OF THE STATE AUDITOR OF GEORGIA, Year Ended June 30, 1984

Annual. Dec. 31, 1984.
x+355 p.
LC 81-649640.
SRI/MF/complete

Annual report on financial condition of Georgia State government and university system for FY84, covering assets, liabilities and fund equity, fund balances, revenues by source, and expenditures by function and object. Most data are shown by fund type, with selected detail for individual State agencies and higher education institutions, and summary comparisons to FY83.

Governmental and fiduciary funds and account groups covered include general, budget, State revenue collections, debt service, capital projects, public and private trust and agency, and general fixed assets and long-term debt. University system fund types covered include current, loan, endowment, plant, and agency.

Also includes data on bonded debt, and comparisons of budgeted to actual financial activity.

Data are compiled from audit reports submitted by all State agencies and higher education institutions.

Contains transmittal letter and contents listing (p. v-x); and auditor's reports on all funds (p. 3-11), State agencies (p. 13-218), and university system (p. 219-355), with text statistics and 36 tables.

Three supplemental volumes, showing detailed salary, travel, and/or other reimbursed expenses, or professional fees or expenses paid, by recipient, are also available from Georgia Dept of Audits, but are not covered in SRI.

Availability: Georgia Department of Audits, Trinity-Washington Bldg., Rm. 214, 270 Washington St., SW, Atlanta GA 30334, †; SRI/MF/complete.

S1865   GEORGIA
Department of Banking and Finance

S1865–1   DEPARTMENT OF BANKING AND FINANCE, State of Georgia: Sixty-Fifth Annual Report, Year Ending Dec. 31, 1984

Annual. [1985.] xvi+67 p.
ISSN 0095-4039.
LC 74-648638.
SRI/MF/complete

Annual report on financial condition of Georgia financial institutions, presenting assets for individual State and national banks, State-chartered credit unions, and savings and loan assns, all arranged by city, and for international bank agencies; and composite assets, liabilities, capital, income, and expenses, for banks by asset size, and for credit unions and savings and loan assns; as of Dec. 31, 1984, usually with comparative data for 1983.

Also includes dept revenues and disbursements, FY84; unpaid claims and unliquidated assets of State banks and credit unions in liquidation; firms and agents licensed under Georgia Sale of Checks Act; banks absorbed in mergers; and Georgia Credit Union Deposit Insurance Corp. financial statement.

Data are from institution annual reports and dept records.

Contains contents listing (2 p.); dept overview with 1 map and 1 table (p. i-xvi); and 14 financial tables, interspersed with information on regulatory activities and lists of financial institutions (p. 1-67).

Availability: Georgia Department of Banking and Finance, 2990 Brandywine Rd., Suite 200, Atlanta GA 30341, †; SRI/MF/complete.

S1880 GEORGIA
Criminal Justice Coordinating Council

S1880-1 GEORGIA CRIMINAL JUSTICE DATA, 1984
Annual. July 1985.
7+150 p..
SRI/MF/complete

Annual report presenting detailed data on Georgia criminal justice system, primarily 1984 and trends. Includes data on crimes and arrests, law enforcement personnel, assaults on officers, traffic fatalities, court caseloads, correctional institution population, probation, and parole board activity.

Data are from State agency reports.

Contains listings of contents, tables, and charts (6 p.); introduction (p. 1); 4 report sections, with narrative analyses, 56 charts, and 77 tables (p. 1-138); statements from senior officials (p. 140-148); and appendix, with data analysis techniques and 1 table showing 1984 population by county (p. 149-150).

All report section tables, and charts with substantial statistics not covered in tables, are described below.

Availability: Georgia Crime Information Center, PO Box 370748, Decatur GA 30037-0748, †; SRI/MF/complete.

TABLES AND CHARTS:
[Unless otherwise noted, data are for Georgia and are shown for 1984 with selected trends from 1980.]

S1880-1.1: Law Enforcement
[Part I Index crimes are murder/non-negligent manslaughter, forcible rape, robbery, aggravated assault, burglary, larceny, motor vehicle theft, and arson; Part II crimes are 20 other offenses.]

CRIMES

a. Crimes and arrests, aggregated for Part I and Part II offenses; and crimes and crime rate, and offense characteristics, including victim-offender relationship, type of weapon used, place of occurrence, months of highest occurrence, value of property stolen, arrest/crime ratio, and persons arrested by age, sex, and race, all by Part I offense. Tables 1-12. (p. 9-35)

b. Part I crimes and/or rates, by offense; and population; shown by metro area and component county, for total nonmetro areas, and statewide, with comparisons to total and southern U.S. Tables 13-19. (p. 37-44)

c. Part II crimes; and crimes against children, and arrests by sex; all by offense. Tables 20-22B. (p. 46-49)

ARRESTS AND COUNTY PROFILES

d. Arrests, and arrest rates, by Part I and Part II offense, with detail by age, sex, and race; drug arrests by substance; and clearances and clearance rates, by Part I and Part II offense; various years 1972-84. Tables 23-38. (p. 51-65)

e. Part I crimes by offense, and aggregate crime rate; full-time law enforcement sworn and civilian employees, by sex; and law enforcement employees per 100,000 population; all by county, with selected rankings. Tables 39-43. (p. 67-83)

OFFICERS ASSAULTED AND TRAFFIC ENFORCEMENT

f. Officers killed; and officers assaulted, by type of activity and weapon, injury status, type of assignment, and time of day, with total clearances. Table 44. (p. 84)

g. Driving under the influence (DUI) arrests by county, with ranking by arrest rate; and DUI arrests by age. Tables 45-47. (p. 86-91)

h. Traffic fatal accidents and fatalities (total, DUI, and other alcohol-related); monthly traffic fatalities by urban-rural location and type (pedestrian, motorcycle, and other vehicle); and accidents, injuries, and fatalities, by holiday. Tables 48-53. (p. 94-95)

STATE BUREAU OF INVESTIGATION

i. Criminal investigative division caseloads, arrests, and value of property recovered; crime information center activity; and forensic science division caseload by branch office and case type, and other activities. Table 54. (p. 97)

S1880-1.2: Courts and Corrections

COURTS

a. Case filings and/or dispositions, by case type: for superior, State, probate, and juvenile courts, by circuit or county, FY84 with aggregate trends from FY80; and for supreme court, 1983-84. Charts 29-32 and tables 55-59. (p. 103-117)

CORRECTIONS

b. Correctional institution population, by type of facility, individual institution, age, sex, race, length of sentence, number of prior arrests, most serious type of crime, and offense, with various cross-tabulations. Tables 60-69. (p. 122-129)

c. Probation population by race, sex, age, most serious type of crime, offense, and first offender status, with various cross-tabulations, 1985, with selected trends from 1980; and parole board case dispositions and other actions. Tables 70-77. (p. 130-138)

S1885 GEORGIA
Department of Education

S1885-1 FACTS AND TRENDS IN GEORGIA PUBLIC SCHOOLS for 1984-85
Annual. 1984. 39 p.
LC 84-622203.
SRI/MF/complete

Annual report, for 1984/85, presenting data on Georgia public elementary and secondary education, including finances, staff and salaries, and student enrollment, achievement, and transportation. Some data include detail by school system, comparisons to other States, and trends from as early as 1949/50. Data are from Georgia Dept of Education and National Education Assn.

Contains contents listing, 13 charts, and 16 tables. All tables, and charts with detailed data not covered in tables, are listed below.

This is the 4th edition; SRI coverage begins with this report.

Availability: Georgia Department of Education, Public Information and Publications Division, 2052 Twin Towers E., Atlanta GA 30334, †; SRI/MF/complete.

CHARTS AND TABLES:
[Data are for Georgia, unless otherwise noted.]

FINANCES, PERSONNEL, AND SALARIES

[1] Percent of State funds for education, [FY74, FY80, and FY85]. [chart] (p. 7)

[2] State education budget in inflated and July 1973 dollars, [FY74 and FY85]. [chart] (p. 8)

[3-4] Estimated current expenditures for public elementary/secondary schools per pupil in average daily attendance (ADA) [by State (in rank order)], 1982/83-1983/84. (p. 9)

[5] Percent of personal income spent on elementary/secondary education, by State [in rank order], 1981/82. (p. 10)

[6] Local school system supplements [number of systems paying and not paying teachers a local supplement], school year 1982/83. (p. 11)

[7] Beginning teacher salaries [for 11 States] in the Southeast, school year 1984/85. (p. 12)

[8-9] Average annual teacher salaries: percent increase in average salaries of public school teachers, 1973/74-1983/84 [period; and] estimated average salaries of public school teachers, 1983/84; [by State (in rank order)]. (p. 13)

[10] Number of teachers and students and cost per child in ADA, 1949/50-1983/84. (p. 14)

[11] Public school teachers by grade level [and sex, kindergarten and exceptional program teachers, and nonteaching principals/assistant principals, as of June 1, 1984; and teachers/principals by certificate level, 1974 and 1983-84. (p. 15)

STUDENT ACHIEVEMENT AND COMPENSATORY EDUCATION

[12-16] Student achievement, criterion-referenced test [percent of 8th, 4th, and 1st grade students demonstrating mastery of specific skills, and average scores of 8th and 4th grade students, for reading and mathematics, 1983 and/or 1984. [charts] (p. 16-20)

[17] Student achievement 1972-84, scholastic aptitude test, high school verbal and mathematics [scores as percent of national average]. (p. 22)

[18] Compensatory education budget, inflated and July 1971 dollars, [FY72-73 and FY85]. [chart] (p. 23)

ATTENDANCE AND ENROLLMENT

[19-20] Annual ADA of [all and] 1st grade students, [various years] 1964/65-1983/84. [charts] (p. 24-25)

[21] ADA and gross enrollment by grade [including exceptional programs], 1983/84. (p. 26)

[22] Annual ADA, [aggregate] K-12 students by school system, 1983/84. (p. 27-28)

TRANSPORTATION AND OTHER

[23] Multisystem high schools [average daily membership 1983/84, and opening date, by system]. (p. 29)

[24] [State funded] pupil transportation [vehicles and annual mileage operated, by type of ownership; and pupils transported]; 1982/83. (p. 32)

[25] Selected characteristics of boards of education and superintendents [number of boards, board members, and superintendents, by selection method; and superintendents by certificates held]; 1983/84. (p. 33)

[26] Certified tax digest by school system [levy mills and tax digest for maintenance/operation and bonds, 1983]. (p. 34-37)

S1885–2   1984 GEORGIA PUBLIC LIBRARY STATISTICS
Annual.   1985.   83 p.+errata.
LC 83-647279.
SRI/MF/complete

Annual report on Georgia public library holdings, services, construction, and finances, including State agency services and special programs, for FY84.

Contains contents listing and introduction (p. 1-3); 6 tables, listed below (p. 4-21); and library directories (p. 22-83).

Availability: Georgia Department of Education, Public Library Services Division, 156 Trinity Ave., SW, Annex Bldg., Atlanta GA 30303, †; SRI/MF/complete.

TABLES:
[Data are for FY84, unless otherwise noted.]

[1] Statistics for library systems [1983 population, and number of counties and branches, staff, circulation, holdings, funds by source, and expenditures by object, by library system]. (p. 4-9)

[2] Audiovisual materials [by type, by library system]. (p. 10-12)

[3] Analysis of Federal funds received (libraries receiving other than LSCA [Library Services and Construction Act], Title I) [amount and funding source, by library]. (p. 13)

[4] Construction [project status, square feet, and funding by source, by library and location]. (p. 14)

[5] State agency services [large group loans; State film collection holdings, circulation, and audience; technical services, including microforms; and reader services]. (p. 15-20)

[6] LSCA, Title I, special programs directed to national/regional priorities [including disadvantaged, institutionalized, and limited English-speaking; and library for the blind/physically handicapped (holdings and circulation, by medium)]. (p. 21)

S1895   GEORGIA
Department of Human Resources

S1895–1   GEORGIA VITAL STATISTICS REPORT, 1983
Annual.   Nov. 1984.   357 p.
LC 76-646236.
SRI/MF/complete

Annual report, for 1983, on Georgia vital statistics, covering births, abortions, deaths by cause, marriages, divorces, and population, by demographic characteristics and location. Data are primarily from records received by DHR prior to June 30, 1984.

Contains introduction, technical notes, and glossary (p. 1-5); 2 tables, described below, repeated for various geographic breakdowns (p. 9-343); map (p. 345); and appendix, with definitions and methodology (p. 349-357).

This is the 37th annual report.

Availability: Georgia Department of Human Resources, Public Health Division, Vital Records and Health Statistics Unit, 878 Peachtree St., NE, Rm. 200, Atlanta GA 30309, †; SRI/MF/complete.

TABLES:

a. Vital statistics, 1983: live births (total and to unwed mothers), spontaneous abortions/stillbirths, and induced abortions, by age of mother or abortion recipient; births by birth weight; out-of-hospital births; marriages and divorces; and deaths by age and cause; all with number and/or rate by race, repeated for State (p. 9-10), DHR health districts (p. 13-32), health service areas (p. 35-42), SMSAs and total non-SMSA (p. 45-54), counties (p. 57-216), and cities and total outside cities (p. 219-292).

b. Population, by age, race, and sex, 1983, repeated for counties and State (p. 295-334), DHR health districts (p. 335-339), health service areas (p. 339-341), and SMSAs and total non-SMSA (p. 341-343).

S1903   GEORGIA
Judicial Council

S1903–1   ELEVENTH ANNUAL REPORT ON THE WORK OF THE GEORGIA COURTS, July 1, 1983-June 30, 1984
Annual.   Jan. 1985.   40 p.
Rpt. No. J-0185-A-01.
ISSN 0363-9320.
LC 76-644657.
SRI/MF/complete

Annual report, for FY84, on Georgia judicial system, including trial and appellate court caseloads and case dispositions, with trends from FY80. Covers supreme, appeals, superior, State, probate, magistrate, and juvenile courts. Includes trial court data by case type, circuit, and county.

Case types shown are generally civil and criminal, with additional detail for domestic relations, deprived and delinquent children, guardianship, commitment, habeas corpus, and various other cases.

Also includes data on judicial finances, appropriations for FY85, manpower, and seminar attendance and certification; magistrate court search/arrest warrants issued; and sentence review panel caseloads.

Contains contents listing (inside front cover); foreword and report, with 1 map, 4 charts, and 13 tables (p. 1-35); and appendices on judicial personnel and agencies, with 1 table (p. 36-40).

Availability: Georgia Judicial Council, Administrative Office of the Courts, Suite 550, 244 Washington St., SW, Atlanta GA 30334, †; SRI/MF/complete.

S1905   GEORGIA
Department of Labor

S1905–1   GEORGIA LABOR MARKET TRENDS
Monthly.   Approx. 15 p.
LC 77-640866.
SRI/MF/complete, shipped quarterly

Monthly report on Georgia employment and unemployment, by industry and MSA. Also includes data on hours and earnings by manufacturing industry. Data are from Current Employment Statistics program estimates, based on monthly survey responses from approximately 6,200 Georgia businesses; and Local Area Unemployment Statistics program estimates.

Report is issued 1-2 months after month of coverage.

Contains articles and news briefs on economic developments, occasionally with substantial statistics; 2-3 summary charts with trends; and 17 monthly tables, listed below, with interspersed analysis.

Prior to 1985, report included an additional monthly table, showing metro and nonmetro labor force estimates.

Monthly tables appear in all issues. All additional features with substantial statistics are described, as they appear, under "Statistical Features." Nonstatistical features are not covered.

Availability: Georgia Department of Labor, Employment Security Agency, Labor Information Systems, 254 Washington St., SW, Atlanta GA 30334, †; SRI/MF/complete, shipped quarterly.

Issues reviewed during 1985: Sept. 1984-Aug. 1985 (D) (Vol. X, Nos. 9-12; Vol. XI, Nos. 1-8).

MONTHLY TABLES:
[All data are shown for month of coverage, previous month, and same month of previous year.]

PLACE-OF-WORK DATA
[Data on employment are shown by industry division and major group; other data are shown by major manufacturing industry group.]

[1] Nonagricultural employment.

[2] Production workers.

[3] Hours and earnings.

[4-6] [Tables [1-3] are repeated for Atlanta MSA.]

[7-11] [Table [1] is repeated for Albany, Athens, Augusta, Columbus, and Macon-Warner Robins MSAs.]

[12-14] [Tables [1-3] are repeated for Savannah MSA.]

RESIDENCE DATA

[15-17] U.S. and Georgia labor force estimates by place of residence [by employment status, with detail for 7 Georgia MSAs and for Augusta and Columbus MSA residents of Georgia and neighboring States].

STATISTICAL FEATURES:

S1905–1.601: Oct. 1984 (Vol. X, No. 10)

HIGH TECHNOLOGY IN GEORGIA

(p. 1-3) First in a series of articles on high-technology industries in Georgia. Includes 1 table showing employment in high technology by industry group, 1978, 1980, and 1983.

S1905–1.602: Nov. 1984 (Vol. X, No. 11)

HIGH TECHNOLOGY IN GEORGIA

(p. 1-2) Second in a series of articles on high-technology industries in Georgia. Includes 2 tables showing average earnings for 3 industry segments, 1978, 1980, and 1983; and distribution of high-technology employment by occupation, by industry group (no date).

S1905–1.603: Dec. 1984 (Vol. X, No. 12)

HIGH TECHNOLOGY IN GEORGIA

(p. 1-3) Third in a series of articles on high-technology industries in Georgia. Includes 1 table showing States (and 2 territories) ranked by high-technology share of total nonagricultural employment in 3 industry segments, 1982.

S1905–1.604: Jan. 1985 (Vol. XI, No. 1)

HIGH TECHNOLOGY IN GEORGIA

(p. 1-2) Fourth in a series of articles on high technology industries in Georgia, presenting national data based on 691 high-technology companies participating in a study published by Joint Economic Committee of Congress in June 1982.

Includes 2 tables showing study results concerning regional ratings based on selected industrial siting factors; and actual and planned high-technology plant sites by location (U.S. regions, overseas, Canada, and Latin and South America), 1981-86 period.

S1905–1.605: June 1985 (Vol. XI, No. 6)

GEORGIA PER CAPITA PERSONAL INCOME UP

(p. 1-3) Article, with 1 table showing Georgia per capita personal income, by MSA and county, 1983, with comparisons to U.S. Data are from Commerce Dept.

S1905–1.606: July 1985 (Vol. XI, No. 7)

TEXTILES AND APPAREL IN GEORGIA: AN UPDATE

(p. 1-2) Article, with 1 table showing percent of Georgia unemployment insurance claims made by workers from the textile and apparel industries, monthly Jan. 1984-July 1985.

S1915   GEORGIA
Department of Offender Rehabilitation

S1915–1   GEORGIA DEPARTMENT OF OFFENDER REHABILITATION 1984 Annual Report
Annual. [1985.] 39 p.
ISSN 0093-7096.
LC 80-640501.
SRI/MF/complete

Annual report, for FY84, on corrections in Georgia, presenting data on prison admissions and releases; escapes and apprehensions; and inmate population by detailed demographic and other characteristics, including educational level, commitment offense, number of children, and religious affiliation.

Also includes data on probation activities; prison farm production and costs, by commodity; community-based programs and finances; inmate population and costs, by institution; prison health care services and costs; and DOR finances.

Contains contents listing (1 p.); narrative report, interspersed with 2 maps, 5 charts, and 19 tables (p. 1-29); and appendix, with institutional directory, 3 charts, and 8 tables (p. 30-39).

Report returns to annual publication schedule with the FY84 edition; previous edition covered FY82 and FY83.

Availability: Georgia Department of Offender Rehabilitation, Information and Legislative Services Division, Two Martin Luther King Jr. Dr., SE, Floyd Bldg., Twin Towers East, 7th Floor, Atlanta GA 30334, †; SRI/MF/complete.

S1925   GEORGIA
Department of Public Safety

S1925–1   GEORGIA DEPARTMENT OF PUBLIC SAFETY, 1983 Annual Report
Annual. [1984.] 53 p.
SRI/MF/complete

Annual report on Georgia traffic accidents, fatalities, and injuries, by accident and vehicle type, location, and other circumstances; and driver and victim characteristics; 1983, with selected trends from 1973.

Also includes data on miles of travel, traffic law enforcement, and drivers licenses; State police hours and activities; and public safety dept budget.

Contains contents listing (1 p.); highlights and departmental organization, with 3 trend charts (p. 1-14); and statistical summary, with 1 map and 20 tables (p. 17-53).

Availability: Georgia Department of Public Safety, 959 E. Confederate Ave., SE, PO Box 1456, Atlanta GA 30371-2303, †; SRI/MF/complete.

S1950   GEORGIA
Department of Revenue

S1950–1   STATISTICAL REPORT FOR 1984, Georgia Department of Revenue
Annual. Nov. 15, 1984.
vi+42 p.
LC 41-52330.
SRI/MF/complete

Annual report, for FY84, on Georgia Dept of Revenue activities, including tax collections by type and county; State revenue trends from 1900; and tax valuations of general property, public utilities, and intangibles.

Contains foreword and contents listing (p. ii-vi); report in 4 parts, with dept information, narrative highlights, 9 charts, and 23 tables listed below (p. 1-41); and index (p. 42).

Availability: Georgia Department of Revenue, Trinity-Washington Bldg., Rm. 401, 270 Washington St., SW, Atlanta GA 30334, †; SRI/MF/complete.

TABLES:

S1950–1.1: State Revenue Collections and Trends

H1. Net revenue collections, FY39-84. (p. 6)

[H1.A] Monthly revenue collections [FY81-Oct. FY85]. (p. 6)

H2. Net revenue collections by [detailed] kind of tax, FY82-84. (p. 8)

H3. Trend in total State tax revenues by major source, FY74-84. (p. 10)

H4. Comparative trends in personal income and State income tax receipts, FY70-84. (p. 10)

S1950–1.2: Tax Data by Type and/or County

DATA BY TYPE OF TAX

1-2. Sales/use tax revenues, FY84; and adjusted gross sales and use tax receipts, 1983 with index of change [1981-83]; by business group. (p. 15-16)

3. Growth trend of personal income tax [number of returns, adjusted gross and taxable income reported, and tax liability, 1969-82]. (p. 17)

4. Motor fuels and motor carriers: detailed revenue data for FY84. (p. 18)

5. Personal income tax, returns by income class [number of returns, net taxable income, tax, number of dependents, and additional selected statistics], 1982 income. (p. 19)

6. Details of revenue from selective excise taxes and business license fees [for alcoholic beverages, cigars/cigarettes, and motor fuels], FY84. (p. 20)

7-8. Summary of revenues from motor vehicle tags, titles, and related items, FY82-84; and number of motor vehicle tags sold by major category, and number of titles sold, 1981-83. (p. 21)

9. Taxable values and tax rates for general property and public utilities, selected years 1900-83. (p. 22)

10. Summary of net property tax collections, by category, FY84. (p. 22)

11. Taxable values of general property, public utilities, and intangibles, by class of property, 1982-83. (p. 23)

DATA BY COUNTY

[Tables show data by county.]

12. 1981 personal income tax data: 1982 earnings [number of returns, adjusted gross income less deficit, net taxable income, and amount of tax liability; also shows 1980 population]. (p. 24-26)

13. Selected tax statistics and estimates [including sales and use tax receipts, general property and public utility assessed value, and motor vehicle tags sold by vehicle type], 1983. (p. 27-31)

14. Four economic indicators, with ranking and per capita amounts [taxable sales, auto registrations, and net property/utility digest, 1983; and adjusted gross income reported, 1982]. (p. 32-37)

CORPORATE TAX RETURNS

15. [Domestic and foreign] corporation income tax returns [and net taxable income] by taxable income class, 1982 tax year returns. (p. 38)

MILLAGE RATES AND INTANGIBLE ASSESSMENTS

16-17. 1983 millage rates by county, alphabetically and numerically listed. (p. 39-40)

18. Gross intangible tax assessments, by county, 1983. (p. 41)

S2030   HAWAII
Department of
Agriculture

S2030-1   STATISTICS OF HAWAIIAN AGRICULTURE, 1983
Annual.   July 1984.
4+100 p.
SRI/MF/complete

Annual report on Hawaii agricultural production and marketing, mostly 1979-83, with selected trends from 1973 and some data for 1984. Data are generally shown by commodity, with selected detail by island.

Covers production, sales, value and/or price, and, as applicable, number of farms, acreage, yield, disposition, and inventory, for field and specialty crops, including flowers and nursery products, coffee, and sugar, with detail for molasses; and for fruit and nut, vegetable and melon, livestock, dairy, apiary, and poultry sectors.

Also includes data on farm income from government payments; precipitation; market supply of commodities by source (Hawaii and inshipments); outshipments of selected commodities, including detail for anthuriums by country of destination; prices paid by farmers for feed and other production items; fertilizer consumption; and agricultural employment and wage rates.

Data are compiled by Hawaii Agricultural Reporting Service in cooperation with USDA.

Contains contents listing (p. 1); 24 charts and 136 tables, interspersed with brief narrative analyses (p. 2-96); and definitions, methodology, and list of additional reports available from issuing agency (p. 97-100).

Availability: Crop Reporting Board Publications, South Bldg., Rm. 5829, U.S. Department of Agriculture, Washington DC 20250, $5.00; SRI/MF/complete.

S2035   HAWAII
Department of the
Attorney General

S2035-1   CRIME IN HAWAII, 1984: A Review of Uniform Crime Reports
Annual.   May 1985.
ii+89 p.+ errata.
SRI/MF/complete

Annual report on Hawaii crimes and arrests, by offense, 1984, with selected comparisons to 1983 and trends from 1980. Includes data by county and by offender age, sex, and race/ethnicity.

Report focuses on 8 Index offenses: murder, forcible rape, robbery, aggravated assault, burglary, larceny/theft, motor vehicle theft, and arson. Arrests are also shown for numerous non-Index offenses.

Data are from State and local agency reports submitted under the Uniform Crime Reporting Program.

Contains contents and table listings (p. ii); introduction (p. 1-4); and the following:

a. Crime summary, with 40 charts and 16 tables generally showing reported offenses and crime circumstances for each Index crime, including the following: crime rates; monthly distribution of offenses, murder victim characteristics (race/ethnicity, age, and relationship to offender), offenses by location and by type of weapon and property involved, value of stolen property, and crime clocks, with trends from 1980. (p. 5-40)

b. State comparisons, with 1 table showing States ranked by population and total, violent, and property crime rates, 1983. (p. 41-42)

c. Arrest and offense data, with 4 charts, and 31 detailed tables described below; and definitions. (p. 43-89)

This is the 10th annual report.

Availability: Hawaii Department of the Attorney General, Criminal Justice Data Center, Kekuanao'a Bldg., 1st Floor, 465 S. King St., Honolulu HI 96813, †; SRI/MF/complete.

DETAILED TABLES:

S2035-1.1: Arrest and Offense Statistics

[Tables show data for Hawaii, with detail by county, for 1984, with selected monthly trends and comparisons to 1983. Data by race/ethnicity generally include American Indian, Chinese, Japanese, Filipino, Samoan, Korean, and Hawaiian.]

a. Crimes, clearances, and crime rates; and value of property recovered and/or stolen, by property type; all by Index crime (excluding arson), with selected detail by crime location and other circumstances. Tables [A] and 1-9. (p. 43-52)

b. Arrests of adults and juveniles by race/ethnicity, age, and sex, for Index and selected non-Index offenses, with detail for drug

abuse arrests by substance, and including comparisons to total population; and juvenile case dispositions. Tables [B] and 10-29. (p. 54-86)

S2065   HAWAII
Department of
Health

S2065-1   STATISTICAL SUPPLEMENT, DEPARTMENT OF HEALTH, State of Hawaii, 1983
Annual.   Sept. 1984.
iv+236 p.
LC 61-63740.
SRI/MF/complete

Annual report, for 1983, on Hawaii vital statistics; Dept of Health programs and services; incidence and treatment of chronic, communicable, and mental health diseases; types of hospital and nursing care; and environmental and health protection services.

Data are primarily from Hawaii government agencies.

Selected data are shown by demographic characteristics and by county, major city, and/or island.

Contains contents listing (p. iii); and 10 statistical sections, with text statistics, 7 charts, and 237 tables listed below, arranged by health agency and division or branch reporting (p. 2-236).

This report is the statistical supplement to a descriptive report issued separately by the Dept of Health. The descriptive report is not covered in SRI.

Availability: Hawaii Department of Health, Research and Statistics Office, PO Box 3378, Honolulu HI 96801, †; SRI/MF/complete.

TABLES:

[Data are for State of Hawaii, 1983, unless otherwise noted. Data by residence or geographic area generally are shown for counties, cities, and/or islands.

Data by race generally are shown for Caucasian, Hawaiian, part-Hawaiian, Chinese, Filipino, Japanese, Puerto Rican, Korean, Samoan, Negro, Portuguese, Vietnamese, American Indian, other, and unknown.]

S2065-1.1: Vital Statistics

POPULATION

1. Estimated population by residence and military status, 1970, 1980, and 1983. (p. 7)

BIRTHS

2-3. Live births by place of occurrence reallocated to place of residence and race of child and mother. (p. 8-9)

4-7. Live births: by race of mother and type of congenital malformation; by place and month of occurrence; by type of attendant at birth by race of child by place of birth; and by race of father and of mother. (p. 9-11)

8-10. Live births, by race of mother: and month of first prenatal visit, number of children born to mother, and number of children born alive to mother. (p. 11-12)

11-12. Live births by age of mother: and number of children born, and number of children born alive. (p. 13)

13-14. Single live births by weight at birth and race of child and mother. (p. 14)

15-16. Single male and female live births by weight and gestation period. (p. 15)

17-19. Live births: by race, sex, plurality of birth, and low birth weight; by race and age of mother; and by age of father and mother. (p. 16-17)

20-22. Illegitimate live births: by place of occurrence reallocated to place of residence and race of mother; by weight at birth and race of child; and by race and age of mother. (p. 17-18)

23. Resident births occurring outside State by age of mother, and race and sex of child. (p. 19)

DEATHS

24. Total deaths by place of occurrence reallocated to usual residence, by race. (p. 20)

25-27. Resident deaths: by place and month of occurrence; by place of occurrence, age, and sex; and by age and race. (p. 21-22)

28. Total recorded deaths, by age, race, and sex. (p. 22)

29. Total resident deaths recorded by age groups [with median age at death] for selected years 1963-83. (p. 23)

30. Resident deaths by age, sex, and marital status. (p. 23)

31. Leading causes of death for 1983 and comparative data for selected years 1963-83. (p. 24)

32-32E. Resident deaths by [detailed] selected causes of death and by age group by sex [for State and 4 counties]. (p. 25-35)

33. Total recorded deaths from malignant neoplasm by major and [detailed] selected sites, sex, and age [group]. (p. 36-37)

34. Resident deaths occurring outside the State by race, age [group], and sex. (p. 38)

35. Total recorded deaths by island of occurrence, by method of disposition and autopsy performed. (p. 38)

INFANT DEATHS

36. Infant deaths by place of occurrence reallocated to usual residence by race of child. (p. 40)

37-38. Resident infant deaths: by age and race of mother; and by race of mother and month of first prenatal visit. (p. 40-41)

39. Resident infant mortality by race of child: [by] age, [and for] low birth weight infant deaths. (p. 41)

40. Resident infant mortality by selected causes: by birth weight, sex, and age; [and for] neonatal deaths. (p. 42)

FETAL DEATHS

[Standard fetal deaths are deaths due to spontaneous or unknown causes, and exclusive of elective abortion.]

41-42. Standard fetal deaths by place of occurrence reallocated to usual residence of mother and gestation period and by race [of fetus]. (p. 42-43)

43-45. Standard fetal deaths: by cause and gestation period; by age of mother and gestation period; and by race and age of mother. (p. 43-44)

ELECTIVE ABORTIONS

46-49. Elective abortions: by race and age of mother; by age of mother and length of gestation period; and by legitimacy status and race and age of mother. (p. 45-46)

50-51. Elective abortions: by type of procedure and gestation period; and by county of residence and county of occurrence. (p. 46-47)

MARRIAGE

52-54. Marriages: by place and month of occurrence; by age of groom and bride; and by previous marital status of groom and bride by age. (p. 48-49)

55-59. Marriages: by occupation and previous marital status of groom and bride; by number of times groom and bride previously married; and by race and age of groom and bride. (p. 49-51)

60-61. Marriages by residence and race of groom and bride. (p. 51-52)

DIVORCE AND ANNULMENT

62-66. Divorces and annulments: by place and month of occurrence, number of children reported under 18 years, and by race and age of husband and wife. (p. 52-54)

67-70. Divorces and annulments: by legal grounds and duration of marriage; and by education, residence, and age of husband and wife. (p. 54-56)

S2065–1.2: Hawaii Tumor Registry

[Data are shown by sex.]

1-2. Most common cancers reported by site and race [for] residents, 1982. (p. 60)

3-4. Tumor registrations: [by] race and age, 1982. (p. 61)

5-6. Tumor registrations, recent years [of diagnosis, 1979-82]. vital status. (p. 62)

7-8. Tumor status in living patients, recent years [of diagnosis, 1979-82]. (p. 63)

S2065–1.3: Health Surveillance Program, and Health Planning and Development Agency

PREVALENCE OF CHRONIC AND ACUTE DISEASE

[Data are from a 1983 annual survey of 15,250 persons in 6,437 households.]

1-14. Prevalence of selected chronic conditions, and number per 1,000 persons per year, by geographic area and age [by sex], and [by race]. (p. 65-78)

15. Number of [selected] chronic conditions per 1,000 persons per year (1978-83). (p. 79)

16-18. Distribution [and number] of persons by activity limitation status due to chronic conditions according to sex and family income, [by] age. (p. 80-82)

19-28. Incidence of [selected] acute conditions, and number per 100 persons per year, by geographic area, age, [sex] by age, and [race]. (p. 83-92)

29. Number of [selected] acute conditions per 100 persons per year (1978-83). (p. 93)

30-35. [Total and] average number per person per year of restricted and bed days, and of work days lost for persons 17 years of age and older, by geographic area and age. (p. 94-99)

36. Total number and average school days lost per person 6-16 years of age, by geographic area. (p. 100)

HEALTH PLANNING AND DEVELOPMENT AGENCY

1-3. SHPDA [State Health Planning and Development Agency] recognized acute, long-term, and specialty care bed capacity [by specialty or facility type, by individual institution]. (p. 104-105)

4-7. Average length of stay, occupancy rates, average daily [patient] census, and number of admissions, [all] by county [for long-term, total acute, medical/surgical, critical, obstetric, pediatric, and psychiatric care, with selected data for mentally retarded and other care types, 1978-83]. (p. 105-108)

S2065–1.4: Family Health Services Division

MATERNAL AND CHILD HEALTH BRANCH

1. Women receiving family planning services in publicly subsidized clinics, FY83. (p. 113)

2. Number of women and infants receiving services at the maternity and infant care project by type of service [including prenatal care, deliveries, and family planning admissions]. (p. 113)

3. Waimanalo children and youth project activities [by service type]. (p. 114)

4. Infants and children provided public health nursing services in child health conferences [by county, FY83]. (p. 114)

CRIPPLED CHILDREN'S BRANCH

5. Distribution of children receiving services by status [new and old cases] and age, FY83. (p. 114)

6. Staff services provided by branch, by type of service, FY83. (p. 114)

7. Distribution of primary medical conditions among children receiving services by diagnostic group and age of child, FY83. (p. 115)

DEVELOPMENTALLY DISABLED BRANCH

8. Infant and child development services provided by number of children served and geographic area covered [by selected service providers], FY83. (p. 116)

9. Number of mentally retarded in case management services, FY83. (p. 116)

10. Statistical movement of residents from Waimano Training School and Hospital [for the retarded], FY83. (p. 116)

11. Leave population, Waimano, June 30, by measured intelligence, FY82. (p. 116)

SCHOOL HEALTH SERVICES BRANCH

12-13. Activity and respite care programs, numbers served and geographic areas covered, FY82. (p. 117)

14. Total numbers of health room visits, reasons for visit and disposition, by school year 1978/79-1982/83. (p. 117)

15. Requests for administration of medication by [type of] condition [and medication], 1982/83. (p. 118)

16. Health problem summary list [selected health conditions, by district], 1982/83. (p. 119)

17. Number of cases referred to school nurses [by island and school level], 1982/83. (p. 119)

18-19. Vision and hearing statistics [includes screenings, referrals, completed referrals, and deficit findings; by screening source], 1982/83. (p. 120)

20-21. Number of students receiving occupational and physical therapy services, by category and district, FY83. (p. 121)

22-23. Referral source [and school type, by] follow-up recommendations of children evaluated for learning disability, FY83. (p. 122-123)

S2065–1.5: Communicable Disease Division

EPIDEMIOLOGY BRANCH

1. Number of cases and deaths from communicable diseases, 1979-83. (p. 126)

2. Selected communicable disease rates per 100,000 population, 1979-83. (p. 127)

3. Communicable disease report by geographic areas. (p. 127)

4. Venereal disease cases reported to the Dept of Health by diagnosis and source of report. (p. 128)

5-6. Total primary and secondary syphilis and total gonorrhea cases by age, 1978-83. (p. 128)

7. Number and rate per 100,000 population of total reported gonorrhea cases [by age group], 1969-83. (p. 128)

8. Gonorrhea morbidity: case rate per 100,000 population, and by sex and resistance to penicillin (1974-83). (p. 129)

9. Infectious syphilis morbidity trend, by [stage of syphilis] and sex (1974-83). (p. 129)

HANSEN'S DISEASE PROGRAM

1. Total Hansen's disease [leprosy] patients registered by register status, 1976-83. (p. 131)

2-3. Hansen's disease patients [by] Kalaupapa registry status, and total cases of Hansen's disease registered by type and location, 1977-83. (p. 131-132)

4-6. New cases of Hansen's disease by age group, island of residence, and place of birth, 1977-83. (p. 132-133)

7-9. [Cases and rate per 100,000] of Hansen's disease, by island of residence and [age group], and for Hawaii-born vs. foreign-born. (p. 134)

10. New cases of Hansen's disease by place of residence at onset of symptoms. (p. 135)

11. Sex-specific incidence [cases and rate per 100,000] of Hansen's disease. (p. 135)

TUBERCULOSIS (TB) BRANCH

1. X-ray survey activities for TB by county. (p. 137)

2. TB cases reported by geographic area of residence, [1982-83]. (p. 137)

3. TB cases by place of birth and length of residence, and number of persons admitted to Hawaii with permanent visas, [1982-83]. (p. 138)

4-7. TB cases: location of disease, source of report, and reason for examination, by county of residence; and by age, race, and sex. (p. 138-140)

8-9. Reactivations reported: by bacteriology and number of reactivations, by county; and by age, sex, and county. (p. 140-141)

10. Number of TB deaths, and new cases reported by year, [decennially] 1930-80 and 1981-83. (p. 141)

S2065–1.6: Dental Health Division

[Data are for FY83, unless otherwise noted.]

1. Summary of dental health services [prevention and detection, and treatment]. (p. 144)

2. Distribution of dental hygiene services by counties [schools and children served]. (p. 144)

3. Dental treatment status of children in 186 schools [aggregate] by areas, 1982/83 [with totals for 1981/82]. (p. 145)

4. Treatment data: hospital dentistry and community services branch [number of patients and selected procedures]. (p. 145)

S2065–1.7: Environmental Protection and Health Services Division

POLLUTION INVESTIGATION AND ENFORCEMENT BRANCH

1. Summary of air quality data (24-hour sampling) [of suspended particulates and sulfur dioxide at 10 sampling stations]. (p. 147)

2. Water quality on [35] public beaches [includes number of samples and fecal coliform density]. (p. 149)

CONSTRUCTION GRANTS PROGRAM

1. [Federal grants awarded for individual public wastewater treatment construction projects, amount and status of completion.] (p. 151)

2. [Projects completed.] (p. 151)

ENVIRONMENTAL PERMITS BRANCH

1. [National pollutant discharge elimination system] permits issued or renewed. (p. 152)

2. [Air pollution control and solid waste management permits issued.] (p. 152)

FOOD AND DRUG BRANCH

1. Summary of samples examined. (p. 154)

2. Samples and analyses of various dairy products for heptachlor epoxide. (p. 154)

3-4. Samples and analyses of milk, milk products, and frozen desserts. (p. 155)

5. Food and drugs [weight and retail value] condemned/destroyed, by county. (p. 156)

6. Selected activities [including poison permits issued]. (p. 156)

SANITATION BRANCH

[Data are for 3 islands and Maui county, unless otherwise noted.]

1. Average daily production of pasteurized milk. (p. 158)

2. Dairies and milk plants as of Dec. 31, 1983, by type. (p. 158)

3. Distribution of sanitary inspections by type. (p. 159)

4-5. Summary of activities by sanitarians, and daily summary of food service and food establishments [inspection, investigation, enforcement, education, and technical review/consultation provided]. (p. 160-164)

6. Public water systems [by island]. (p. 165)

VECTOR CONTROL BRANCH

1. Principal activities of the vector control branch on [selected] islands [including surveillance, inspections, breeding sources abated, and fish stocked for mosquito control]. (p. 167)

2. Total small mammal retrievals by [selected] island, activity, and species. (p. 168)

3. Summary of zoonosis laboratory activities and findings by [geographic] area. (p. 169)

LITTER CONTROL PROGRAM

1. Community work day program [participants and activities]. (p. 172)

2. State recycling campaign [participants, amount of aluminum and other materials collected, and total earnings], Feb. 1983. (p. 172)

3-4. Litter bags provided for public use; and educational and promotional litter control materials distributed. (p. 173)

S2065–1.8: Medical Health Services Division

CHRONIC DISEASE BRANCH

1-3. Diabetes screening survey by age, sex, race, and [selected] island, FY83. (p. 176-177)

4. Blood pressure screening, FY83. (p. 177)

EMERGENCY MEDICAL SERVICES SYSTEMS BRANCH

1. Emergency ambulance units level of service, by island, FY83. (p. 178)

2. Emergency ambulance calls responded to, by island [1981-83]. (p. 178)

HOSPITALS AND MEDICAL FACILITIES BRANCH

1-2. Number and type of facility, and bed count in facilities, by island. (p. 180-181)

3. Licensed beds by type of facility [1978-83]. (p. 181)

LABORATORIES BRANCH

[Tables 2-8 show data from Central Laboratory on Oahu, FY83.]

1. Number of samples submitted and number of bacteriological, parasitological, serological, and chemical examinations performed upon them by type of specimen and island, FY83. (p. 183)

2-3. Incidence of salmonella by type: [by] age [of individuals affected], and from nonhuman sources. (p. 184-185)

4-6. Incidence of: parasites [by type] from humans, gram negative diplococcus from gonorrhea cultures submitted, and mycobacteria from human sources. (p. 186-187)

7. Viral isolations [type and number of specimens]. (p. 188)

8. Viral serologies [type and number]. (p. 189)

PUBLIC HEALTH NURSING BRANCH

[Data are for FY83.]

1. Cases admitted to public health nursing service and visits made, by county [by type of service]. (p. 191)

2. Clinics conducted by public health nursing service by type of clinic, number of sessions and attendance by county. (p. 192)

3-5. Public health nursing service to schools, day care centers, and care homes, by county [and type of program]. (p. 193)

NUTRITION BRANCH

1. Nutrition branch services [number by type, including nutrition education sessions, consultations and inspections, and special supplemental food program for women, infants, and children]. (p. 195)

S2065–1.9: Mental Health Division

[All data are for State mental health facilities. Mental diagnoses include alcoholism, drug addiction, and mental retardation.]

1-1B. Patients active Dec. 31, 1983, by problems on admission, and age [and sex]. (p. 199-204)

2-3B. Patients [in- and out-care] active Dec. 31, 1983: by catchment area, and problems on admission and age. (p. 205-209)

4-6. Admissions: by age and problems on admission; by [race] and catchment area; and by referral source and community mental health center or service. (p. 210-213)

7-7B. Unduplicated admissions [by sex, race, and] problems at admission, and mean age on admission. (p. 214-225)

8-10. Terminations, by age and problems on admission, and by community mental health center or service and disposition; and unduplicated count of patients served, by problems and age. (p. 226-230)

S2065–1.10: Refugee Screening Project and Waimano Training School and Hospital Division

REFUGEES

1. Demographic breakdown of refugees entering Hawaii (primary arrivals) [by age and sex for 3 Southeast Asian countries and Afghanistan], Oct. 1982-Sept. 1983 [period]. (p. 233)

WAIMANO

1. Waimano Training School and Hospital [for the retarded] statistical movement of patients [FY76-83]. (p. 236)

2. Resident population, Waimano, June 30, distribution by measured intelligence [FY76-83]. (p. 236)

S2077   HAWAII
Office of the Lieutenant Governor

S2077–1   RESULT OF VOTES CAST, GENERAL ELECTION, Tuesday, Nov. 6, 1984, State of Hawaii
Biennial.   Jan. 1985.
226 p. var. paging+errata.
LC 66-63258.
SRI/MF/complete

Biennial report presenting results of the Hawaii general election held Nov. 6, 1984. Shows voting for President/Vice President; U.S. Representatives; State senators and representatives; county offices; Office of Hawaiian Affairs trustees; school board members; State consitutional amendments, including elimination of required refund of excess revenues to taxpayers; and county charter amendments.

Also shows party affiliation of candidates, as applicable; voter registration, by sex; and voter turnout.

Data generally are shown by legislative district and precinct.

Previous report, covering 1982 general election, is described in SRI 1983 Annual under this number.

Availability: Hawaii Office of the Lieutenant Governor, Elections Division, State Capitol, Honolulu HI 96813, $2.40; SRI/MF/complete.

S2090   HAWAII
Department of Planning and Economic Development

S2090–1   STATE OF HAWAII DATA BOOK, 1984: A Statistical Abstract
Annual.   Feb. 1985.   762 p.
ISSN 0073-1080.
LC 68-66724.
SRI/MF/complete

Annual compilation, for 1984, of detailed demographic, social, governmental, and economic statistics for Hawaii. Data are shown primarily for 1970s-83, with trends from as early as 1826 and projections to 2005.

Report is designed to present a comprehensive overview of the State. Extensive socioeconomic, demographic, and geographic breakdowns are shown, as applicable, for most topics. These breakdowns include data by city, county and other State region (including island), urban-rural status, commodity, industry, occupation, age, education, marital status, race, and sex.

Data are primarily from State and Federal sources. Data sources appear beneath each table.

Contents:

a. Contents listing, map of Hawaii counties and districts, introduction, guide to tabular presentation, and weights and measures table. (p. 3-10)

b. 3 population maps and 722 tables arranged in 24 sections, described below. Tables in each section are preceded by a 1-2 page narrative summary, including primary statistical sources. (p. 11-728)

c. Bibliography, with 1 table on printing history of the statistical abstract, and detailed subject index. (p. 729-762)

This is the 18th edition of the *Data Book,* first published in 1962.

Availability: Hawaii Department of Planning and Economic Development, Information Office, PO Box 2359, Honolulu HI 96804, Hawaii residents $5.00, others $15.00; SRI/MF/complete.

TABLE SECTIONS:

S2090–1.1: Section 1: Population

(p. 11-83) Contains 3 maps and 62 tables. Includes population trends from 1831 and projections to 2005; resident, military, and visitor population and characteristics; land area; family and household characteristics; centenarian population, deaths, and social security beneficiaries; farm population; and centers of population.

Also includes resident ancestry; citizenship status, by residence length; population change components and birthplace, by military status; languages comprehended and spoken at home; aliens, immigration, and naturalization, by nationality; Southeast Asian refugee arrivals; and churches, clergy, and members, by religion and denomination.

S2090–1.2: Section 2: Vital Statistics and Health

(p. 84-128) Contains 48 tables. Includes births, deaths, and fertility rates, by military status; illegitimate births; abortions; infant and fetal deaths; most common given names and surnames; catastrophic deaths; deaths by cause, and corpse disposition method; life expectancy; blind persons registered; health conditions resulting in mobility limitations; communicable disease cases and deaths; and survey of use of coffee, cigarettes, alcohol, and legal and illegal drugs.

Also includes hospitals and other care facilities, beds, utilization, and finances; leprosy patients registered; mental health and retardation facility admissions, patients, and beds; physicians, dentists, nurses, and pharmacists; drugstores, sales, and prescriptions filled; health care and insurance costs; dental condition and services received; marriages and dissolutions; body measurements; student nutrition; and daily food intake and nutritive value.

S2090–1.3: Section 3: Education

(p. 129-149) Contains 21 tables. Includes public, private, and parochial schools, teachers, enrollment, and high school graduates; federally connected pupils in public schools; and public school expenditures and capital outlays.

Also includes enrollment and degrees awarded at University of Hawaii and private institutions; Federal aid to higher education; educational attainment; achievement test results; and State and university library operations and/or personnel.

S2090–1.4: Section 4: Law Enforcement, Courts, and Prisons

(p. 150-175) Contains 25 tables. Includes criminal justice system expenditures, employment, and payroll; offenses reported and clearances; arrests; victimization rates; value of stolen and recovered property; white-collar crime losses; marijuana confiscated; disposition of adult and juvenile arrests; and child abuse and neglect cases.

Also includes legal services establishments, employment, and finances; judges and lawyers; court cases, by court and type of action; State correctional facility inmates; average age and sentences of felons; parole activity; and executions since 1826.

S2090–1.5: Section 5: Geography and Environment

(p. 176-217) Contains 38 tables. Includes selected distances from Honolulu, Hilo, and Kure Atoll; channel widths and depths; shorelines, and land and water areas; inhabited and uninhabited islands; topographic features including summits, streams, waterfalls, and lakes; volcanic eruptions, earthquakes, and cyclones; and hurricanes and tsunamis, with resulting deaths and property damage.

Also includes dams; water services and consumption; pollution abatement capital expenditures and costs, and quantities of pollutants removed; public beach water quality; air quality, and pollutant emissions by source; Oahu noise levels; climatic data by station; bird counts by species; trees along streets and in parks; and native flora by endangered status.

S2090–1.6: Section 6: Land Use and Ownership

(p. 218-231) Contains 15 tables. Includes land use and area; Oahu improved acreage uses, structure age, and housing inventory; land parcels; public and private land ownership; leased and unleased private lands; acreage owned by 6 major landowners; and native Hawaiian homestead acreage, lessees, and applicants.

S2090–1.7: Section 7: Recreation and Tourism

(p. 232-282) Contains 52 tables. Includes visitor demographic and travel characteristics, including accommodations and country or world area of residence; visitor arrivals and economic impact projected to 2005; meetings/conventions and attendance; visitor expenditures, and jobs and income generated; Hawaii Visitors Bureau finances; out-of-State travel by Hawaii residents; and passports issued, by destination.

Also includes attendance at museums and other cultural attractions; Oahu performing arts productions, performances, and attendance, by organization; nonprofit cultural organizations, finances, and volunteer hours; Honolulu symphony orchestra personnel, performances, attendance, and expenses; and zoo animals and visitors, by zoo.

Also includes recreational facilities and participation; national, State, and county parks, visits, and/or acres; Honolulu beach visits and water safety/emergency activities; fishing, hunting, and camping permits issued, and participation; public hunting areas and wildlife refuges; sandy shoreline miles; professional baseball, and academic and amateur sports events, results, and attendance; and dog licenses issued.

S2090–1.8: Section 8: Government Finances and Employment

(p. 283-310) Contains 31 tables. Includes tax receipts by level of government and source; tax burden for average Oahu family: State and county revenues by source and expenditures by function; excise and use tax collections; and property tax valuations and tax rates.

Also includes Federal and State individual income tax returns and adjusted gross income; IRS operations; DOD and nondefense Federal outlays; State and county bonded debt; government employment by level; and State civil service employment and salary schedules.

S2090–1.9: Section 9: Social Insurance and Human Services

(p. 311-327) Contains 18 tables. Includes social welfare expenditures; public assistance payments and recipients; food stamp participation; Medicare enrollment and reimbursement; and social security and OASDI beneficiaries and benefits.

Also includes unemployment insurance recipients, benefits, and exhaustion rate; State retirement system pensioners, assets, and benefits; adoptions; nonprofit foundations, assets, and grants; United Way revenues and outlays; social services organizations, employment, payroll, and services provided; and Quality of Life Index rankings.

S2090–1.10: Section 10: National Defense

(p. 328-338) Contains 14 tables. Includes residents on active military duty; military personnel, dependents, and families; Army and Air National Guard strength; DOD military and civilian personnel, by installation; military housing; defense payroll, prime contract awards, and other expenditures; veterans by period of service; and military retirees and pay. Most data are shown by service branch.

S2090–1.11: Section 11: Labor Force, Employment, and Earnings

(p. 339-383) Contains 43 tables. Includes labor force by employment status projected to 2005; characteristics of insured unemployed; job counts; public and private sector employment and wages; covered employers; hours and earnings; hotel and resort condominium executive salaries; minimum wage chronology; manufacturing labor turnover rates; and job-seeker migration to and from mainland.

Also includes work and transportation disability status of population; industrial accidents, deaths, and insurance payments; occupational injuries and illnesses, and lost workdays; labor union and employee assn membership; State and county employees in collective bargaining units; and work stoppages, workers involved, and days lost.

S2090–1.12: Section 12: Income, Expenditures, and Wealth

(p. 384-421) Contains 31 tables. Includes direct income from 4 major export industries; total and per capita GSP, and expenditure account components; personal income by source, and expenditures by object; savings; and construction and nonstructural capital investments.

Also includes State/local and Federal Government revenues and expenditures; imports and exports; visitor personal consumption expenditures; unreported or illegal income; GSP and personal income projections to 2005; and household and family income.

Also includes families and unrelated individuals below poverty level, and income; poverty income guidelines; aggregate characteristics of top wealthholders; and millionaires.

S2090–1.13: Section 13: Prices

(p. 422-438) Contains 12 tables. Includes Honolulu CPI and retail food prices; family and retired couple annual budgets at 3 standard-of-living levels, for Honolulu and Oahu; and Federal employee Hawaii cost-of-living pay adjustment compared to Washington, D.C.

S2090–1.14: Section 14: Elections

(p. 439-462) Contains 25 tables. Includes election districts and precincts, and elected positions by level of government; apportionment of State legislature; voting age population; registered voters; voting residence of military personnel and dependents; and votes cast by type of election, political party, and major candidate and office.

Also includes campaign expenditures by office and party; Oahu neighborhood board election results; votes cast for Office of Hawaiian Affairs Board of Trustees; party affiliation of county councils; and State legislature party affiliation, demographic composition, session length, and bill and resolution dispositions.

S2090–1.15: Section 15: Banking, Insurance, and Business Enterprise

(p. 463-484) Contains 26 tables. Includes firms, branches, assets, and/or deposits of banks, savings and loan assns, industrial loan licensees, trust companies, small loan licensees, and credit unions; bank clearings; consumer credit outstanding at banks; and total resident shareholders, and shareholders in 9 major Hawaii companies.

Also includes insurance premiums and claims/benefits paid, by class; State-based, other U.S., and foreign insurance companies and operating data; health insurance coverage, payments, and premiums, with hospital average stay and costs; and prepaid health plan membership and dues.

Also includes Honolulu fire alarms, deaths, and losses; business establishments, employment, and payroll; corporations and partnerships formed, dissolved/merged, and on record; taxable and nontaxable corporations, partnerships, and proprietorships, and receipts; sales, employees, and revenues of selected Hawaii-based corporations; business failures and liabilities; and women-owned business firms, employment, payroll, and receipts.

S2090–1.16: Section 16: Communications

(p. 485-499) Contains 18 tables. Includes post offices, postal receipts, and mail handled; telegraph messages; telephone service; TV and radio stations; cable TV companies, subscribers, and revenues; TV households and viewers; newspaper circulation; periodicals published; Hawaii University Press books and scholarly journals published, sales, and revenues; and Honolulu postage, telephone, and telegraph rates, and newspaper prices.

S2090–1.17: Section 17: Energy and Science

(p. 500-525) Contains 29 tables. Includes energy consumption, by fuel type and sector; energy expenditures and prices, by sector; electric and natural gas utility customers, capacity and/or sales, average use and rates, and revenues; water and telephone utility rates; liquid fuel consumption, by type; fuel oil and kerosene deliveries, by end use; Oahu gasoline prices since 1903; and gasoline service stations, sales, employment, and payroll.

Also includes Honolulu customs district bunker oil laden on U.S. and foreign vessels; boilers and pressure vessels; sugar plantation energy generation, consumption, and sales; manufacturing energy use and expenditures; and housing units with solar heaters.

Also includes Federal R&D obligations; R&D expenditures at postsecondary institutions; and patents issued to residents.

S2090–1.18: Section 18: Transportation

(p. 526-569) Contains 53 tables. Includes street/highway mileage, bridges, tunnels, traffic signal intersections, and metered parking spaces; motor vehicle sales, registrations, and top makes registered; households by number of vehicles available; vehicle fuel consumption and mileage; highway speed monitoring data; traffic accidents, injuries, and deaths; commuting patterns; auto rental/leasing establishments and receipts; and registered taxicabs and bicycles.

Also includes railroad track mileage and passengers; Oahu bus passengers, service, and revenues; airports and heliports; aircraft traffic and operations by field; Pacific region pilots and flight personnel; inter-island and transpacific air carriers, traffic, fares, and passenger origins and destinations; and local airline operating data.

Also includes commercial harbor specifications, vessel arrivals, and freight and passenger traffic, by harbor; documented and undocumented vessels and characteristics; boating accidents, injuries, fatalities, and property damage; and overseas and inter-island shipping.

S2090–1.19: Section 19: Agriculture

(p. 570-596) Contains 27 tables. Includes farms, acreage, and operating characteristics; farm operators; crop and livestock marketings; livestock inventory; flowers and nursery product production and value; market supply of specified foods; farm productivity rating and soil loss; land use; fertilizer consumption; and freshwater prawn and other aquaculture production, acreage, and value.

S2090–1.20: Section 20: Forests, Fisheries, and Mining

(p. 597-609) Contains 14 tables. Includes forest acreage; commercial timberland ownership, timber volume, and growing stock; forest fires and acres burned; forest products harvested, price, and value; commercial fishermen, vessels, fisheries, and landings; fish inventory at specified sampling sites; mineral industry establishments, employment, and operations; and nonfuel mineral production and value.

S2090 1.21: Section 21: Construction and Housing

(p. 610-655) Contains 47 tables. Includes residential and nonresidential building permits and value; government construction contract awards by level; residential construction and demolition; condominium projects and conversions; Honolulu construction cost indexes; construction industry establishments, employment, and receipts; and contracting excise tax base.

Also includes housing units, occupancy, and structural and financial characteristics; Hawaii Housing Authority units and resident population, assets, revenues, and average rent; Oahu housing in specific neighborhoods; and migration by military status.

Also includes Oahu housing prices and multiple listing service listings and sales; Honolulu office building occupancy rates, available space, and average rent; deeds filed, and value of land conveyed or transferred; real estate licensees; mortgages recorded, foreclosures, and sale agreements; mortgage loans outstanding, by type of financial institution; and FHA-insured housing characteristics and homebuyer profile.

Also includes elevators and escalators; height of tallest structures; and seating capacities of selected Oahu stadiums, theaters, and churches.

S2090–1.22: Section 22: Manufactures

(p. 656-669) Contains 14 tables. Includes manufacturing employment and payroll, production workers and hours and wages, establishments, value added, shipments, production costs, and capital investments, with selected detail for DOD facilities; plant capacity utilization rates; and industrial parks and acreage.

Also includes excise tax base for sugar processing, pineapple canning, and manufacturing; pineapple and sugar companies and plants; processed pineapple, sugar, and molasses production; sugar industry strikes, cane acreage, average price, and government payments; and pineapple and sugar industries employment, earnings, and sales.

S2090–1.23: Section 23: Domestic Trade and Services

(p. 670-709) Contains 41 tables. Includes retail and wholesale trade, and service industries establishments, sales or revenues, excise tax base, and other operations; consumer purchasing habits and shopping center patronage; available retail space; department stores and sales; eating and drinking places, including franchise holders, and sales; restaurant and major shopping center characteristics; and retail stores, employment, and sales for 10 major companies.

Also includes armed forces retail facilities and sales; membership organizations, employment, and expenses; operating data for tourist-oriented businesses, hotels, and motels; condominium properties and units; hotel units under construction/planned; motion picture and TV production data; Oahu liquor licenses and sales; liquor and tobacco tax bases; alcoholic beverage consumption and tax revenues, by beverage type; and funeral service/crematory establishments and receipts.

S2090–1.24: Section 24: Foreign and Interstate Commerce

(p. 710-728) Contains 17 tables. Includes Hawaii-mainland trade; foreign trade through Honolulu customs district, by mode and country; petroleum, integrated circuit, and fireworks imports; foreign trade zone users, user employment, merchandise value, and revenues and expenditures; foreign-owned firms, employment and payroll; foreign direct investment by country; export-related employment; and foreign-owned agricultural land.

S2090–2   QUARTERLY STATISTICAL AND ECONOMIC REPORT, State of Hawaii
Quarterly.   Approx. 50 p.
SRI/MF/complete

Quarterly report on Hawaii business and economic conditions, with data on income, employment, State taxes, tourism, construction activities, and population. Includes selected 10-year trends, U.S. comparisons, and data by county. Data generally are current to 1-2 quarters preceding cover date.

Data are compiled by Dept of Planning and Economic Development (DPED) from Federal and State government and private sources.

Report usually contains listings of contents, tables, and charts; narrative analysis of economic developments, with accompanying charts, and occasionally with tables showing 2-year forecasts for selected U.S. and/or Hawaii economic indicators; and statistical section, with 26 tables described below. Report also occasionally includes special articles with statistics.

Quarterly tables appear in all issues. Articles with substantial statistics are described, as they appear, under "Statistical Features." Nonstatistical features are not covered.

Issuing agency also publishes *The Economy of Hawaii: Annual Economic Report and Outlook,* which includes summary data for many of the topics covered in the quarterly report. The annual report is not covered in SRI.

Availability: Hawaii Department of Planning and Economic Development, Research and Economic Analysis Division, PO Box 2359, Honolulu HI 96804, ‡; SRI/MF/complete.

Issues reviewed during 1985: 4th Qtr. 1984/1st Qtr. 1985-3rd Qtr. 1985 (P) [4th Qtr. 1984/1st Qtr. 1985 is a combined issue].

QUARTERLY TABLES:

[Tables present most recent available data, with comparisons to prior periods. Many tables show data for quarter prior to cover date, with quarterly trends for current and previous year, and annual data for selected earlier years, from 1970.

Labor force, visitor, hotel, construction, and population data include selected detail by county (island).]

a. Total and disposable personal income; and Honolulu CPI for selected items. 3 tables.

b. Jobs by industry (including self-employed and workers involved in labor disputes), and labor force by employment status; value of business transactions subject to State excise/use tax for selected industries; and collections of major State taxes, and distribution to State general fund. 7 tables.

c. Visitors to Hawaii (eastbound and westbound); hotel rooms, occupancy, and rates; value of completed and authorized construction, by type; value of government construction contracts; single- and multi-family housing units authorized; construction employment, hours, and earnings; and Honolulu construction cost indexes. 12 tables.

d. Visitor and defense expenditures; sugar and pineapple production value and/or sales; processed sugar and canned pineapple shipment value subject to excise tax; and economic and demographic summary, including population. 4 tables.

STATISTICAL FEATURES:

S2090–2.601: 2nd Qtr. 1985
UNITED AIRLINES PILOTS STRIKE

(p. 7-12) Article, with 4 tables estimating United Airlines pilot strike's economic impact on Hawaii, including visitors and visitor expenditures, sales of goods/services, employment, household income, and government tax revenues, May 17-Dec. 31, 1985.

S2090–2.602: 3rd Qtr. 1985
GROWTH OF JOBS, INCOME, AND THE "BRAIN DRAIN"

(p. 12-24) Article on employment, income, and out-migration trends in Hawaii. Data are from Federal and State government reports.

Includes 7 tables showing the following for Hawaii: civilian labor force, by employment status, sex, age, occupational group, and industry division; jobs, by industry division and selected major group; civilian population, by age; population change components, by military status; and residency and migration status of newly enrolled college students; various years 1970-85, with labor force and population projections to 1990.

S2090-5 HAWAII POPULATION AND ECONOMIC PROJECTION AND SIMULATION MODEL: Updated State and County Forecasts
Monograph. July 1984.
x+112 p.
LC 85-620638.
SRI/MF/complete

Report forecasting Hawaii population, employment, and income, statewide and by county, quinquennially 1985-2005, with estimates for 1980 and selected trends from 1958. Presents resident and de facto population; jobs by industry division and selected group and for self-employed and military; and total and per capita personal income. Includes alternate forecasts based on various assumptions concerning tourism growth.

Also includes forecast and/or trend data on visitors, visitor expenditures, hotel/condominium units, and hotel employment; export values, with detail for sugarcane and pineapple; Federal defense and nondefense spending; GSP; disposable income; population (including military status) and change components, life expectancy, and labor force participation rates, all by age and sex; fertility rates; and comparisons to other published population projections, with some data through 2030.

Data sources include Census Bureau, Bureau of Economic Analysis, Hawaii Dept of Labor and Industrial Relations, and other agencies. Forecasts were derived with the Population and Economic Projection and Simulation Model, developed by Hawaii Dept of Planning and Economic Development.

Contains listings of contents, tables, and charts (p. vii-x); summary, with 1 chart and 3 tables (p. 1-7); narrative analysis, interspersed with 3 charts and 16 tables (p. 9-52); appendices A-E, with methodology and 22 tables (53-109); and bibliography (p. 110-112).

This report expands *Population and Economic Projections for the State of Hawaii, 1980-2005*, described in SRI 1984 Annual under S2090-4.

Availability: Hawaii Department of Planning and Economic Development, Research and Economic Analysis Division, PO Box 2359, Honolulu HI 96804, †; SRI/MF/complete.

S2120 HAWAII
Department of Taxation

S2120-1 DEPARTMENT OF TAXATION ANNUAL REPORT, 1983-84, Hawaii
Annual. Oct. 1, 1984.
26 p.+App 6 p.
ISSN 0360-2931.
LC 75-647948.
SRI/MF/complete

Annual report of the Hawaii Dept of Taxation, presenting data on tax collections and allocations, FY84, with comparisons to FY83, and selected trends from FY79. Includes data by county.

Contains contents listing (p. 1); narrative report, with 7 summary charts and 12 tables (p. 2-26); and appendix, including contents listing, 4 tables, and outline of Hawaii's tax system (p. A1-A6). All tables are listed below.

Availability: Hawaii Department of Taxation, Tax Research and Planning Office, PO Box 259, Honolulu HI 96809, †; SRI/MF/complete.

TABLES:
[Unless otherwise noted, tables show data for FY83-84, often with average annual percent change, FY79-84 and FY83-84.]

S2120-1.1: Text Tables
[1] Tax litigation [appeals cases, shown for review boards by county, and for supreme and tax appeal courts by case type and court, FY84]. (p. 10)

[2-3] [Income] taxes paid by individuals and corporations [including amount withheld from wages, and refunds]. (p. 12-13)

[4] General excise and use tax base and taxes [by source]. (p. 15)

[5-6] Inheritance and estate taxes, and public service company taxes. (p. 16)

[7] Gallons of fuel consumed [by fuel type and use, including boating and aviation]. (p. 18)

[8] Allocation of fuel taxes [by fund, including detail by fuel type and county]. (p. 18)

[9] Fuel tax rates per gallon [State and county rates, by county, FY84]. (19)

[10] Miscellaneous taxes [collected]. (p. 20)

[11-12] Distribution of collections [by fund; and] tax collections [by county]. (p. 20-21)

S2120-1.2: Appendix Tables
[1-2] Tax collections [by source of revenue] and distribution [to State funds by fund, and total to counties by source]. (p. A1-A2)

[3] State general fund [by source of revenue]. (p. A2)

[4] Dept of Taxation training programs [employees and training hours, FY84]. (p. A3)

S2125 HAWAII
Department of Transportation

S2125-1 MAJOR TRAFFIC ACCIDENTS, State of Hawaii, 1984
Annual. June 1985.
ii+37 p.
LC 78-643965.
SRI/MF/complete, current & previous year reports

Annual report on Hawaii traffic accidents involving injuries, fatalities, and property damage, and number of persons killed and injured, 1984, with trends from 1975. Includes data by accident and vehicle type, location, time, and other circumstances; and driver and victim characteristics, including driver alcohol use.

Also includes data on motor vehicle and driver registrations, vehicle miles traveled, and population.

Data are from State and local agencies.

Contains contents and table listing (p. i-ii); narrative summary (p. 1-3); and 14 charts and 20 tables (p. 4-37).

Report for 1983 has also been reviewed in 1985, and is also available on SRI microfiche under S2125-1 [Annual. June 1984. ii+37 p. †].

SRI coverage begins with the report for 1983.

Availability: Hawaii Department of Transportation, Highways Division, Traffic Branch, 869 Punchbowl St., Honolulu HI 96813, †; SRI/MF/complete.

S2205 IDAHO
Department of Agriculture

S2205-1 IDAHO AGRICULTURAL STATISTICS, 1985
Annual. [1985.] 72 p.
ISSN 0094-1271.
LC 74-642213.
SRI/MF/complete

Annual report on Idaho agricultural production, finances, and marketing, 1970s-84, with selected trends from as early as 1940. Data are generally shown by commodity, with selected data by county, and some comparisons to other States, regions, and total U.S.

Report generally covers production, prices, disposition, value, and, as applicable, acreage, yield, or inventory, for field crop, vegetable, fruit, livestock, dairy, and poultry sectors.

Also includes data on cash receipts by commodity; farm income, production expenses, workers, and wage rates; farms and acreage; range/pasture condition; cattle feedlots and capacity; sheep and lamb losses by cause; mink bred and pelts produced; fertilizer consumption; and potatoes in cold storage, by U.S. region.

Data are compiled by the Idaho Crop and Livestock Reporting Service in cooperation with the USDA Statistical Reporting Service.

Contains contents listing (p. 3); 3 maps and 100 tables, interspersed with brief narrative summaries (p. 5-71); and list of other reports available (p. 72).

This is the 14th edition.

Availability: Idaho Crop and Livestock Reporting Service, PO Box 1699, Boise ID 83701, $5.00; SRI/MF/complete.

S2215   IDAHO
Office of the Auditor

S2215–1   ANNUAL REPORT OF THE STATE AUDITOR, State of Idaho, July 1, 1983-June 30, 1984
Annual. [1985.]
71 var. paging. Foldouts.
SRI/MF/complete

Annual report on financial condition of Idaho State government, for FY84, presenting assets and liabilities, reserves, balances, and fund transfers; receipts by source; and disbursements by functions; by account type, with selected detail by specific agency account.

Also includes data on appropriations vs. expenditures, by function and agency; liquor account distributions to local areas; bond sales, redemptions, and indebtedness; and summary tax levies and collections, 1981-83.

Data are from the records of the auditor's office.

Contains transmittal letter, foreword and contents description, and 4 charts (7 p.); and 15 exhibits and schedules (64 p.).

This is the 11th annual report.

Availability: Idaho Office of the Auditor, 700 W. State St., Boise ID 83720, †; SRI/MF/complete.

S2222   IDAHO
Administrative Office of the Courts

S2222–1   IDAHO COURTS 1984 Annual Report
Annual. 2 volumes.
For individual publication data, see below.
SRI/MF/complete

Annual report, for 1984, on Idaho judicial system, including trial and appellate court caseloads and case dispositions. Covers supreme, appeals, district, and magistrate courts. Includes trial court data by case type, judicial district, and county.

Case types shown are criminal and civil, with additional detail for domestic relations, small claims, drug-related, driving while intoxicated, driver's license suspension, Youth Rehabilitation Act, Child Protective Act, adoption, guardianship, probate, and habeas corpus case types.

Data are from dept records.

Report is presented in 2 parts, individually described below.

Availability: Idaho Administrative Office of the Courts, Supreme Court Bldg., 451 W. State St., Boise ID 83720; SRI/MF/complete.

S2222–1.1: Idaho Courts Annual Report for 1984
[Annual. [1985.] 8 p. Oversized. †. SRI/MF/complete.]

Narrative newspaper-style report, with several articles on Idaho court operations and caseloads, interspersed with 11 charts and 2 tables showing trends for court caseloads, driving under the influence filings, Youth Rehabilitation Act petitions, and drug abuse complaints, from 1975; and appeals and trial court case processing times, 1984.

S2222–1.2: Idaho Courts 1984 Annual Report: Appendix
[Annual. [1985.] i+107 p. ‡. SRI/MF/complete.]

Statistical appendix volume, showing detailed caseload data by Idaho court, judicial district, and county.

Contains contents listing and introduction (2 p.); 4 appellate court tables (p. 1-3); and 2 district and magistrate court tables, repeated for State and each district and county (p. 4-107).

S2225   IDAHO
Department of Education

S2225–1   1984/85 FALL ENROLLMENT REPORT, Idaho
Annual. Oct. 1, 1984.
7 p. Oversized.
SRI/MF/complete

Annual report on Idaho public and nonpublic elementary and secondary school enrollment, by grade, shown by school district and county, as of Oct. 1, 1984, with comparisons to 1983. Contains 1 table.

Availability: Idaho Department of Education, Finance Division, Research and Statistics Unit, Len B. Jordan Bldg., 650 W. State St., Boise ID 83720, †; SRI/MF/complete.

S2225–2   FINANCIAL SUMMARIES, IDAHO SCHOOL DISTRICTS, FY84
Annual. [1985.] iv+154 p.
LC 60-63291.
SRI/MF/complete

Annual report, for FY84, on Idaho public school district revenues by source and expenditures by object, by fund and district. Also includes data on attendance, market valuation, bonded debt, Foundation Program receipts, and transportation.

Data are compiled from annual reports submitted by school districts to the State Dept of Education.

Contains introduction, table listing, and list of school districts (p. i-iv); 3 tables showing State summary statistics, with comparisons to FY82-83 (p. 1-3); and 12 tables, described below, generally showing data by school district (p. 4-153).

Availability: Idaho Department of Education, Finance Division, Research and Statistics Unit, Len B. Jordan Bldg., 650 W. State St., Boise ID 83720, †; SRI/MF/complete.

TABLES:
[Tables show data for FY84.]

a. Attendance and enrollment; market valuation and bonded debt; expenditures per average daily attendance (ADA); maintenance/operation expenditures, including costs for social security, retirement, and administration; Foundation Program State allowance receipts; and transportation data, including number transported, expenditures, and average daily bus miles; all by school district arranged by county. 7 tables. (p. 4-31)

b. District rankings, by ADA, and by general fund expenditures and market value per ADA; and monies requested in successful supplemental maintenance/operation levy elections; all by school district. 4 tables. (p. 32-37)

c. Finances: revenues by source and expenditures by object, all by fund, including general, school plant facility, bond interest/redemption, bond building, adult and driver education, school lunch, insurance adjustment, Federal forest, Elementary and Secondary Education Act by title, Indian education funds, and migrant and other special funds. 1 table, repeated for State and each school district. (p. 38-154)

S2225–3   1984/85 STATISTICAL REPORT: Public School Certified Personnel and Employees in Noncertified Positions, Idaho
Annual. [1985.] iv+22 p.
SRI/MF/complete

Annual report on Idaho public school certified and noncertified personnel characteristics and salaries, by position, 1984/85 school year. Data are from reports submitted by school districts to State Dept of Education in fall 1984.

Contains contents listing (1 p.); introduction (p. i-iv); 1 table showing school districts ranked by enrollment and including number of teachers (p. 1-6); and 14 tables, described below (p. 7-22).

Availability: Idaho Department of Education, Len B. Jordan Bldg., 650 W. State St., Boise ID 83720, †; SRI/MF/complete.

TABLES:
[Most data are shown by position, with selected comparisons by enrollment size, 1984/85.]

a. Certified staff: FTE, actual number, and average base salary and extra pay, by sex; average salary expenditure per child; years of experience in education, age group, highest degree earned, and source of education (Idaho institutions and other); and turnover rates, by sex and reason. 11 tables. (p. 7-17)

b. Noncertified staff: FTE and actual number, and average annual and hourly salary, all by sex. 3 tables. (p. 18-22)

S2230 — IDAHO — Department of Employment

S2230–1   LABOR FORCE IN IDAHO and Basic Economic Data for Idaho
Annual. Sept. 1984. 136 p.
LC 80-641141.
SRI/MF/complete

Annual report on labor force and employment in Idaho, 1982-83. Data are from State Dept of Employment records.

Contains foreword with definitions, and contents listing (2 p.); and 2 tables repeated for the State, each county (including Asotin County, Washington State), and labor market area, showing monthly data for the following:

a. Labor force by employment status (including data for Ada/Boise SMSA), seasonally adjusted and unadjusted, 1982-83. (p. 9-33)

b. Nonagricultural wage/salary employment, by industry division and major manufacturing group, 1982-83. (p. 37-136)

Previous report, presenting data for 1981, is described in SRI 1983 Annual under this number. No separate report for 1982 was published. Issuing agency plans to publish future editions annually, with 1 year's data in each edition.

Availability: Idaho Department of Employment, Research and Analysis Bureau, 317 Main St., Boise ID 83735, †; SRI/MF/complete.

S2230–3   ANNUAL PLANNING INFORMATION REPORT, Idaho, 1986
Annual. Feb. 1985. ii+88 p.
LC 79-640461.
SRI/MF/complete

Annual planning report, for FY86, identifying Idaho population groups most in need of employment services. Includes data on population and labor force, employment, income, public assistance recipients, and characteristics of unemployment insurance claimants and job service applicants. Data are shown by industry, occupation, county, and planning area, various years 1976-FY86.

Data are generally from Census Bureau and State agencies, including Employment Service Automated Reporting System.

Contains contents/table listing (p. i-ii); introduction, highlights, and map (p. 1-4); 51 tables described below, arranged in 7 sections, each preceded by brief narrative (p. 5-85); and appendix, with methodology and data sources (p. 86-88).

Availability: Idaho Department of Employment, Research and Analysis Bureau, 317 Main St., Boise ID 83735, †; SRI/MF/complete.

TABLES:
[Data by race generally include Native American, Asian/Pacific Islander, and Hispanic.]

S2230–3.1: Population, Labor Force, Unemployment Insurance Claimants, and Employment

a. Population: by sex, age, and race, by county; and by sex and age, by planning area; FY86. Tables 1-5. (p. 6-10)

b. Labor force and unemployment, by sex, age, and race, by planning area and/or county, FY86; and monthly unemployment rate trends, 1976-84. Tables 6-20. (p. 12-24)

c. Unemployment insurance claimants by race, educational atttainment, sex, industry division, age, and occupational group, with cross-tabulations by duration of unemployment, all by planning area, 1984; and unemployment, with distribution by reason, 1977-83. Tables 21-28. (p. 27-35)

d. Employment: by industry division and selected group, class of worker, and occupational group, all by county; by occupational group by planning area; and by race and sex, by occupation; 1980 or 1983. Tables 29-33. (p. 37-42)

S2230–3.2: Socioeconomic Characteristics

a. Income for households, families, and unrelated individuals over age 15, by county, 1979; personal income by type and industry division, 1981-83; total and per capita personal income by county, 1980-82; average annual wages by industry division and selected group, by county, 1983; and hourly salaries, by detailed occupation (no date). Tables 34-38. (p. 45-53)

b. High school enrollment and dropouts, by county, 1980-86; economically disadvantaged population by age group, by county and planning area, FY86; poverty guidelines; and persons in poverty by race and county, FY86. Tables 39-43. (p. 54-58)

c. Public assistance recipients by program, FY84 with detail by age and sex for Feb. 1985; and food stamp recipients, FY84; generally by planning area. Tables 44-46. (p. 59-60)

d. Veterans by period of service, and female veterans, by county, 1980; and job service applicants and characteristics, including data for handicapped, veterans, unemployment insurance claimants, migrants, and farm workers, variously shown by age group, sex, education, urban or rural residence, race, family income, and planning area, and for Boise MSA, FY84. Tables 47-51. (p. 61-85)

S2235 — IDAHO — Department of Finance

S2235–1   STATE OF IDAHO DEPARTMENT OF FINANCE Sixty-Sixth Report
Annual. [1985.] 49 p.
LC 6-16846.
SRI/MF/complete

Annual report on financial condition of Idaho State-regulated financial institutions, mostly as of Dec. 31, 1983 or June 30, 1984, presenting assets, liabilities, and generally equity capital or net worth, for State-chartered banks, savings and loan assns, and credit unions. Data are generally shown by institution.

Also includes composite balance sheet data for State-located national banks; composite financial and loan activity of regulated lenders; credit union and regulated lender loan delinquencies; bank consumer loans by purpose; dept staffing and finances; and Securities Bureau registrations and enforcement proceedings, FY81-84.

Contains contents listing and foreword (p. 5-6); and report, with 31 tables, and lists of selected institutions (p. 7-49).

Availability: Idaho Department of Finance, Statehouse, Boise ID 83720, 1st copy †, additional copies $2.00; SRI/MF/complete.

S2245 — IDAHO — Office of the Governor

S2245–2   IDAHO ECONOMIC FORECAST
3 times a year.
Approx. 70-80 p.
SRI/MF/complete

Periodic report, published 3 times a year, on Idaho and U.S. economic trends and forecasts. Includes data on population and change components; housing starts and stock; personal income and components; employment, by industry division and major manufacturing group; Federal transfer payments to State/local governments; and, for U.S. only, GNP and selected price deflators, interest rates, and production indexes.

Historical data are compiled from State and Federal sources. Forecasts are from Data Resources, Inc. Macroeconomic Model and the Idaho Economic Model, and are usually generated in 2nd month of cover date period.

General format:

a. Contents listing and introduction; 2 summary forecast tables; narrative summary; alternative forecasts of selected indicators based on varying assumptions about the national economy, with 1-2 tables; and 1-2 feature articles, occasionally with statistics.

b. Detailed table, showing actual or forecast data for the indicators noted above, annually for 17-18 years beginning 14-15 years prior to cover date, and quarterly for 18 quarters beginning with 3rd quarter of year 2-3 years prior to cover date.

c. Appendix, with descriptions of forecast models.

Summary and detailed tables and alternative forecast appear in all issues. Additional features with substantial statistical content are described, as they appear, under "Statistical Features." Nonstatistical features are not covered.

Availability: Idaho Economic Forecast, Financial Management Division, Statehouse, Rm. 122, Boise ID 83720, Idaho residents $7.50 per yr., others $15.00 per yr.; SRI/MF/complete.

Issues reviewed during 1985: Autumn 1984-Summer 1985 (P) (Vol. VI, No. 3; Vol. VII, Nos. 1-2).

STATISTICAL FEATURE:

S2245–2.601: Autumn 1984 (Vol. VI, No. 3)

IDAHO ECONOMIC REGIONS

(p. 19-24) Article, with 2 tables showing Idaho population, by county and region, 1970, 1980, and 1983, with selected rankings; and employment by major sector, by region, 1967 and 1982, with change for selected intervening periods.

S2250   IDAHO
Department of
Health and Welfare

S2250–1   QUARTERLY WELFARE STATISTICAL BULLETIN, Idaho
Quarterly.   Approx. 20 p.
ISSN 0364-1104.
LC 75-645543.
SRI/MF/complete

Quarterly report on Idaho public welfare program caseloads, recipients, and expenditures, with some data by county and State region. Report is issued 3-6 months after quarter of coverage.

Contains 1 map, chart and table listing, and 7 trend charts; and 2 charts and 9 tables, listed below.

Availability: Idaho Department of Health and Welfare, Welfare Division, Research and Statistics Section, Statehouse, Boise ID 83720, †; SRI/MF/complete.

Issues reviewed during 1985: July/Sept. 1984-Jan./Mar. 1985 (D) (Vol. 29, Nos. 3-4; Vol. 30, No. 1).

QUARTERLY TABLES AND CHARTS:
[Data are for quarter of coverage, or middle month of quarter, unless otherwise noted. Data indicated as monthly are shown for each month of quarter.]

1. Summary of [monthly] obligations incurred, cases, and average payment, by program [including Old Age Assistance (OAA), Aid to the Blind, Aid to the Permanently and Totally Disabled (APTD), aid to dependent children, and medical assistance].

[A] Sources, and uses [by program], of funds. [chart]

2. Medical assistance expenditures [recipients, days/services, and amount paid, by type of service; and expenditures and recipients, by welfare program].

3. Reasons for approving AFDC cases [monthly].

[B] Selected characteristics of AFDC caseload, percent of cases by $50 grant increments and by length of time since most recent case opening [for Feb. or Mar. in 1st-2nd quarter issues, and Aug. or Sept. in 3rd-4th quarter issues]. [chart]

4. Reasons for closing adult program cases [OAA, AB, and APTD]; and cases of AFDC.

5. Percent of population receiving assistance by county and region [with detail for population under 18].

6. Summary of adoption activity [monthly adoptions, by child's age group, and for Indian, Negro, and Mexican children].

7. Foster care statistics [children in and number of foster homes and institutions, and amount paid, by program and region].

8. Food stamp activity [assistance and nonassistance recipients, and value of coupons issued, by county and region].

9. Recovery of child support payments [average amount collected per month, by quarter for current year and annually from 1973].

S2250–2   1983 ANNUAL SUMMARY OF VITAL STATISTICS, Idaho
Annual.   [1984.]   iv+105 p.
ISSN 0362-9279.
LC 76-644913.
SRI/MF/complete

Annual report, for 1983, on Idaho vital statistics, covering population, births, deaths by cause, marriages, and divorces, all by county and health district, with trends from the 1970s and comparison with U.S. Data are compiled from State records and Census Bureau reports.

Contains contents listing and definitions (p. ii-iv); 6 statistical sections, with narrative summaries, 1 map, 13 charts, and 66 tables (p. 1-83); and appendices, with 2 tables (p. 85-105).

All tables, and selected charts showing data not included in tables, are listed below.

Availability: Idaho Department of Health and Welfare, Health Division, Vital Statistics, Standards and Local Health Services Bureau, 450 W. State St., Boise ID 83720, †; SRI/MF/complete.

TABLES AND CHARTS:
[Unless otherwise noted, tables and charts show data for Idaho, 1983. Most data by race also include American Indian, Japanese, other, and Spanish surname or origin.]

S2250–2.1: Population and Trends
POPULATION

[1-5] [Population: U.S., by census division and State; and Idaho, by district and county (including change components and detail by age and sex), by city, and by age and sex; Apr. 1, 1980 census, with selected estimates for July 1, 1981-83.] (p. 2-12)

TRENDS AND SUMMARY

[Tables [6-8] show numbers and rates.]

[6] Vital statistics [live births and deaths by sex, out-of-wedlock and immature live births, and stillbirths, infant and maternal deaths, marriages, and divorces], 1974-83. (p. 15)

[7-8] Summary of vital statistics: births, deaths, marriages, and divorces; and infant, fetal, and perinatal mortality; [by district and county]. (p. 17-18)

S2250–2.2: Natality
ALL BIRTHS

[1-4] Resident live births and rates, 1979-83; and resident live births, by sex of child and race of mother, by age of mother, and by attendant at and place of birth, 1983; [all by district and county of residence]. (p. 21-24)

[5] Idaho live birth [rate, 1983], and fertility rates [1982-83], by district and county of residence. (p. 25)

[6] Resident live births, [by] live birth order by age of mother. (p. 26)

[7] 1983 age-specific fertility rates [compared to 1981 U.S. rate]. (p. 26)

[8-13] Resident live births: trimester of pregnancy when prenatal care began (percent), and educational attainment of mother, [by district and county of residence]; complications and malformations, [total] and by prenatal care; and Apgar scores, 1 minute [by] 5 minutes. (p. 28-31)

IMMATURE BIRTHS

[All tables, except table [17], begin "Immature live births..." Tables [14-15] and [18] show data by district and county of residence.]

[14-15] By race and age of mother. (p. 32-33)

[16] Live birth order by age of mother. (p. 34)

[17] Age-specific immaturity rates. (p. 34)

[18] By weight at birth. (p. 35)

OUT-OF-WEDLOCK BIRTHS

[19-20] [Out-of-wedlock births: U.S. 1981, and Idaho 1983, by race; and] Idaho race-specific ratios [1980-83]. (p. 36)

[21-23] Out-of-wedlock live births: by race and age of mother [by district and county of residence]; and live birth order by age of mother. (p. 37-39)

[24] Age-specific out-of-wedlock live birth ratios. (p. 39)

S2250–2.3: Mortality and Morbidity
DEATH RATES AND CAUSES

[1-3] Resident deaths and rates, 1979-83; and resident deaths, by sex and race, and age at death, 1983; [all by district and county of residence]. (p. 43-45)

[4-6] 10 leading causes of death [by sex]; leading causes by age group [chart]; and malignant neoplasm deaths by primary site [by sex]. (p. 46-51)

[7] Resident deaths from selected causes, by district and county of residence. (p. 52-53)

[8] Accidental deaths occurring in Idaho, by category and age group, 1982-83. (p. 54)

[9-10] Reported morbidity from selected diseases: by district and county of residence, 1983; and reported cases, 1979-83. (p. 56-58)

INFANT MORTALITY

[11-13] Resident infant deaths and rates, 1979-83; and resident infant deaths by sex and race of child, and neonatal and postneonatal, 1983; [all by district and county of residence]. (p. 61-63)

[14-16] Causes of infant deaths: by neonatal and postneonatal periods, and by district of residence, and totals for U.S. and Idaho. (p. 64-65)

[17-18] Resident stillbirths and perinatal deaths and ratios, by district and county of residence, 1979-83. (p. 66-67)

ABORTIONS

[19] [Induced abortions, ratio per live births and per 1,000 females, for U.S., 1981, and Idaho, 1983.] (p. 69)

[20] Induced abortions reported: [total and for residents, by district and county], 1982-83. (p. 70)

[21-26] Induced abortions reported: age of patient by marital status, previous induced abortions and number of living children, termination procedure by length of gestation, reported complications by termination procedure, and age and race of patient by district and county of residence. (p. 71-74)

S2250–2.4: Marriages and Divorces

MARRIAGES

[1-5] Marriages occurring in Idaho: by district and county of occurrence, 1974-83; and by age and race of bride by age and race of groom, and age of bride and groom by previous marital status, 1983. (p. 76-79)

DIVORCES

[6-9] Divorces granted in Idaho: by district and county of occurrence, 1974-83; number of children affected, 1983; and divorces and annulments granted, by legal grounds, 1983; and duration of marriage, 1981-83. (p. 80-83)

S2250–2.5: Appendices

A-B. Vital statistics profile [summary] by district and county; and detailed causes of death by age. (p. 85-105)

S2260   IDAHO
Department of
Insurance

S2260–1   EIGHTY-THIRD ANNUAL REPORT: STATE OF IDAHO, DEPARTMENT OF INSURANCE, for the Year Ended June 30, 1984
Annual.   [1985.]   iii+49 p.
LC 60-45313.
SRI/MF/complete

Annual report on Idaho insurance industry financial condition and underwriting activity, by company and type of insurance, 1983. Covers assets and liabilities, capital, surplus, net income or loss, and premiums written in Idaho.

Data are shown for life, disability, property, marine/transportation, casualty, surety, title, and mortgage guaranty companies; and, in slightly different detail, for fraternal benefit societies, motor clubs, hospital/professional service corporations, hospital liability trusts, and county mutual/fraternal fire companies.

Also includes Insurance Dept FY84 receipts, expenditures, regulatory and licensing activity, and consumer services, with revenue trends from FY79; number of regulated companies with headquarters in Idaho, other States, and foreign countries, by type of company; and 1983 summary of underwriting activity in Idaho, by type of company and line of business (including medical malpractice, workmen's compensation, and automobile insurance).

Contains contents listing (p. i); Insurance Dept report and summary, with 12 tables (p. 1-15); and 7 company financial tables (p. 16-49).

Availability: Idaho Department of Insurance, 700 W. State St., Boise ID 83720, †; SRI/MF/ complete.

S2275   IDAHO
Department of
Law Enforcement

S2275–2   IDAHO UNIFORM CRIME REPORTING PROGRAM: 1984 Annual Report
Annual.   [1985.]   vii+269 p.
LC 80-645204.
SRI/MF/complete

Annual report on Idaho crimes and arrests, by offense, 1984, with selected comparisons to 1983 and trends from 1980. Includes data by county and reporting agency, and by victim and offender age, sex, and race/ethnicity. Also includes law enforcement employment, and assaults on officers.

Report focuses on 8 Index offenses: murder, rape, robbery, aggravated assault, burglary, larceny/theft, motor vehicle theft, and arson. Arrests are also shown for numerous non-Index offenses.

Data are from State and local agency reports submitted under the Uniform Crime Reporting Program.

Contains contents listing (p. v-vii); and 15 statistical sections, with 28 charts and 48 tables, interspersed with narrative summaries (p. 1-269).

All tables, and selected charts containing substantial statistics not included in tables, are described below.

Availability: Idaho Department of Law Enforcement, Police Services Division, Technical Services Unit, PO Box 55, Boise ID 83707, †; SRI/MF/complete.

CHARTS AND TABLES:
[Data are for 1984, unless otherwise noted. Data by race/ethnicity include black, white, American Indian/Alaskan Native, Asian/Pacific Islander, Hispanic, and non-Hispanic.]

S2275–2.1: Offenses, Arrests, and Law Enforcement Personnel

INDEX OFFENSE SUMMARY

a.   Crime clocks; Index offenses and rates, 1980-84; Index offenses by population size group; percent of crimes cleared by arrest; and value of stolen and recovered property, by type of property. 1 chart and 5 tables. (p. 1-11)

INDEX OFFENSES AND VANDALISM
[Data shown for each offense include number and rate, 1983-84; and most frequent month of occurrence and other characteristics. Each offense section also includes narrative summary with text statistics. Additional data are described below.]

b.   Murder victims by age group, sex, and race/ethnicity, and offenses by type of weapon; and forcible rapes and attempted rapes. 2 charts and 5 tables. (p. 14-25)

c.   Robbery offenses and stolen property value by place of occurrence, and offenses by weapon; aggravated assaults by weapon; burglaries and stolen property value, by day and night residence and nonresidence occurrence; and larceny offenses and stolen property value, by type of larceny. 3 charts and 11 tables. (p. 28-51)

d.   Motor vehicle thefts; arson offenses and value of property damage by type of property; and vandalism damage value by month, with offenses, rate, and damage value, by reporting agency and county. 9 tables. (p. 54-71)

ARREST DATA
[Data by offense are shown for Index offenses and 22 non-Index offenses.]

e.   Arrests and rate by offense; police disposition of juveniles; and arrests by offense, by age, sex, and race/ethnicity. 6 tables. (p. 74-83)

f.   Drug arrests by substance: by race/ethnicity; for juveniles and adults by sex, and for sale/manufacturing and possession, by age group. 1 chart and 4 tables. (p. 83-86)

g.   Adult and juvenile arrests by offense, and total rate, by reporting agency and county. 1 table. (p. 87-113)

LAW ENFORCEMENT PERSONNEL AND OFFICERS ASSAULTED

h.   Officers assaulted, by type of activity, assignment, weapon, time of day, and reporting agency and county. 1 chart and 4 tables. (p. 117-122)

i.   Police officer and civilian employees, by sex, and number per 1,000 population, all by agency and county, as of Oct. 31, 1984. 1 table. (p. 126-132)

S2275–2.2: Offenses and Clearances by Agency and County

a.   Index total offense rate by county, with ranked lists, various years 1980-84. 2 tables. (p. 133-134)

b.   Offenses and clearances, with rates, for Index offenses, by reporting agency and county, 1980-84. 1 table. (p. 135-269)

S2290   IDAHO
Public Utilities Commission

S2290–1   1984 ANNUAL REPORT: The Idaho Public Utilities Commission
Annual.   [1985.]   112 p.
LC 14-31884.
SRI/MF/complete, current & previous year reports

Annual report, for 1984, of the Idaho Public Utilities Commission. Presents narrative summaries of developments and regulatory cases for electric, gas, telephone, and water utilities under the Commission's jurisdiction.

Also includes statistics on Commission finances; common/contract intrastate carrier case activity; utility consumer complaints/inquiries received; and average monthly residential bill, and cost per kWh or therm, for individual electric and gas utilities, 1984.

Contains contents listing (1 p.); introduction and narrative report, with 3 tables (p. 1-72); regulated utilities list and directory (p. 73-89); and 10 billing and rate tables (p. 92-112).

Previous report, for 1982-83, was also reviewed in 1985 and is also available on SRI microfiche under this number [Annual. [1984.] 82+App. 20 p. †]. Previous report is substantially similar in format and content, but also includes data on number of motor carriers and permits, and omits data on consumer complaints/inquiries.

Report for 1981-82 is described in SRI 1982 Annual under this number. No report was issued during 1983.

Availability: Idaho Public Utilities Commission, Statehouse, Boise ID 83720, †; SRI/MF/complete.

S2295   IDAHO
Department of
Revenue and Taxation

**S2295–1   FORTIETH ANNUAL
REPORT OF STATE TAX
COMMISSION, State of
Idaho**
Annual.   Dec. 1, 1984.
iv + 79 p.
LC 47-32622.
SRI/MF/complete

Annual report on Idaho tax collections by type, and property valuations, for fiscal or calendar year 1984. Includes selected detail by county, trends from as early as FY63, and tax burden comparisons to other States.

Contains transmittal letter, foreword, and contents listing (p. i-iv); narrative review of legislative developments and Tax Commission activities, with organizational charts and text data (p. 1-22); and 3 charts, and 47 tables described below, some with accompanying narrative (p. 23-79).

Previous editions included data on regulated industry property value by company, and a separately paginated data supplement. The 40th edition omits these features; however, supplemental data are available from the State Tax Commission.

Availability: Idaho Department of Revenue and Taxation, State Tax Commission, Property Tax Section, 700 W. State St., PO Box 36, Boise ID 83722, †; SRI/MF/complete.

TABLES:

a. Cash receipts, by detailed source, FY83-84; tax collections, and collection costs, FY69-84; State Tax Commission expenses, by program, FY84; and audit/collection recoveries on current/delinquent returns, FY71-84. 5 tables. (p. 23-31)

b. Tax collections, by type, FY80-84; individual and corporate income tax returns and tax liability, FY63-84; electric power use for irrigation and industry, and kWh tax collections, FY70-84; taxable sales, sales tax collections, and reimbursements for business inventory exemptions, all by county, various periods FY82-84; allocation of income and sales tax collections, by fund, FY80-84; and tax refund trust fund revenues and expenses, FY84. 11 tables. (p. 31-38)

c. Property market value, by type of property and county, 1983 and/or 1984, with summary comparison to 1970; property tax levied, 1970-83, with selected detail by tax type; number of property taxing districts, by type, 1980-84; tax charges for water pollution control sinking bond fund and private railroad car companies, 1974-84, with 1984 sinking fund detail by county; and urban and rural tax rates, by county, 1983. 12 tables. (p. 41-51)

d. Circuit Breaker Program for property tax relief: selected data including approved applicants and benefits paid, 1974-83, with 1983 detail by applicant category and income bracket. 3 tables. (p. 52-54)

e. Idaho tax burden comparisons to other States, FY82, with trends from FY78; and tax burden data by county, including population, total and per capita income and property taxes, and tax capacity and effort indexes, 1982, with rankings and selected comparisons to 1981. 13 tables. (p. 58-74)

f. Property assessment ratio study results, measuring uniformity of assessed vs. market value by property type, 1982-84. 3 tables. (p 77-79)

S2305   IDAHO
Office of the Secretary of
State

**S2305–1   ABSTRACT OF VOTES CAST
AT THE GENERAL
ELECTION, Nov. 6, 1984,
State of Idaho, and Results
for Legislative Districts**
Biennial.   [1985.]
1 foldout + 88 p. no paging.
SRI/MF/complete

Biennial report presenting results of the Idaho general election held Nov. 6, 1984. Shows voting for President; U.S. and State senators and representatives; and 2 State constitutional amendments and 1 initiative. Also includes voter registration and turnout, and party affiliation of candidates. Data are shown by county, with detail by legislative district and precinct for State offices.

Previous report, covering 1982 general election, is described in SRI 1983 Annual under this number.

Availability: Idaho Office of the Secretary of State, Elections Division, Rm. 203, Statehouse, 700 W. Jefferson St., Boise ID 83720, abstract †, legislative fact sheets $11.00; SRI/MF/complete.

S2315   IDAHO
Department of
Transportation

**S2315–1   STATE OF IDAHO MOTOR
VEHICLE TRAFFIC
ACCIDENTS, Statewide
Summary, from Jan. 1,
1984-Dec. 31, 1984**
Annual.   June 6, 1985.   7 p.
SRI/MF/complete

Annual report on Idaho traffic accidents involving fatalities, injuries, and property damage, and number of persons killed and injured, 1984. Includes data by accident and vehicle type, location, time, and other circumstances; and driver and victim characteristics.

Also includes data on motor vehicle travel mileage; emergency equipment responding to accidents, and ambulance response time; safety device use in accidents; and citations issued by type.

Contains 32 tables (7 p.).

Availability: Idaho Department of Transportation, Traffic Section, 3311 W. State St., PO Box 7129, Boise ID 83707, †; SRI/MF/complete.

S2390   ILLINOIS
Department of
Agriculture

**S2390–1   ILLINOIS AGRICULTURAL
STATISTICS, Annual
Summary, 1984**
Annual.   Oct. 1984.   146 p.
Bull. 84-1.
LC 51-62568.
SRI/MF/complete

Annual report on Illinois agricultural production, marketing, and finances, 1983, with some data for 1984 and trends from as early as 1910. Data generally are shown by commodity and/or district or county.

Report covers production, prices, value, and, as applicable, acreage, yield, disposition, and stocks or inventory, for field crop, fruit, vegetable, livestock, poultry, and dairy sectors.

Also includes data on number and acreage of farms; farm mortgage debt, interest rates, property value and taxes, income by source, production expenses, labor, and wage rates; total and farm population; weather; mink pelt production; grain storage facilities and capacity; fertilizer sales and use; and Illinois export value and share of U.S. agricultural exports.

Data are compiled by the Illinois Cooperative Crop Reporting Service.

Contains contents listing (p. 4-6); and 11 sections, with 15 maps, 21 charts, and 153 tables (p. 7-146).

Related supplemental publications available from the issuing agency, but not covered in SRI, include 2 county estimate reports for corn and soybeans, and wheat.

Availability: Illinois Cooperative Crop Reporting Service, PO Box 429, Springfield IL 62705, Illinois residents †, others $5.00; SRI/MF/complete.

S2395   ILLINOIS
Commissioner of
Banks and Trust Companies

**S2395–1   1983 ANNUAL REPORT,
COMMISSIONER OF BANKS
AND TRUST COMPANIES,
State of Illinois**
Annual.   June 1984.   95 p.
SRI/MF/complete

Annual report on financial condition of Illinois State-chartered banks and trust companies, 1983, presenting assets, liabilities, capital/surplus, and profits/reserves for individual bank and trust companies, arranged by city or ranked by assets.

Also includes Commissioner's Office finances; assets of licensed foreign banks by institution, and aggregate resources and liabilities of institutions with trust powers; bank income and expenses, total and as percents of earnings, by asset size group; number of banks, assets, and liabilities, by county; and number of banks and assets, by State district.

Contains contents listing, and personnel rosters (p. 2-6); 7 financial tables (p. 7-84); and lists of bank status changes, with 1 map and 3 tables (p. 85-95).

Availability: Illinois Commissioner of Banks and Trust Companies, Reisch Bldg., Rm. 400, 119 S. Fifth St., Springfield IL 62701-1296, †; SRI/MF/complete.

S2405   ILLINOIS
Department of Commerce and Community Affairs

S2405–2   ILLINOIS BIMONTHLY ECONOMIC DATA SHEETS
Bimonthly. Approx. 30 p.
SRI/MF/complete

Bimonthly statistical compilation of economic, business, and industrial activity indicators for Illinois. Includes historical trends, and comparisons to total U.S.

Data are compiled from State and Federal agency sources, Dun and Bradstreet, Coldwell Banker, and other private sources. Most forecasts are by Chase Econometrics Associates and Data Resources, Inc. Month of coverage for most data is 1-4 months prior to cover date.

Contains narrative highlights sheet; table listing; and 29 indicator tables, listed below, most accompanied by 2 illustrative charts. Bimonthly tables appear in all issues. Narrative highlights sheet is usually also issued in months when full statistical report is not issued.

Prior to the Jan. 1985 issue, report title was *Illinois Monthly Economic Data Sheets*.

Availability: Illinois Department of Commerce and Community Affairs, Research Office, 620 E. Adams St., Springfield IL 62701, †; SRI/MF/complete

Issues reviewed during 1985: Nov. 1984-Sept. 1985 (P).

INDICATOR TABLES:
[Most tables show trends for previous 2-15 years, and monthly data for current year through month of coverage. Data are for Illinois, unless otherwise noted. Many tables include percent comparisons to U.S.]

[1-2] GSP, and total [and per capita] personal income [annually and by quarter].

[3-5] Cash receipts from farm marketings, bituminous coal production [surface and underground], and contracts for future construction [by type].

[6-11] Labor force, employed and unemployed [and insured unemployed]; total nonagricultural employment; employment by industry [division, for State and 9 MSAs]; manufacturing employment; and hours and earnings of production workers in manufacturing.

[12-14] Unemployment rate [including historical data by race, and data by MSA and county].

[15] Help-wanted advertising indexes [for U.S., East North Central region, Chicago, and St. Louis; monthly for year to date and previous year].

[16-17] New business incorporations [including data by census division]; and [business and nonbusiness] bankruptcy filings [by State district and selected city].

[18-19] Manufacturing production and productivity [including inventories and capacity utilization rate]; and new capital expenditures and gross book value of depreciable assets.

[20] Interest rates [national averages, for approximately 20 types of instrument].

[21] Population [including data for blacks, change components, and projections to 2010, annual data only].

[22] State exports [including agricultural value for 6-8 products, manufacturing value by major industry group, and related employment by industry division; annual data only].

[23] U.S. and Chicago [area] CPI.

[24] Industrial and office vacancy rates [for Chicago and 4-6 other U.S. cities or areas, quarterly for current year through most recent available quarter and previous 3 years].

[25-26] Sales of all retail stores [including data for Chicago, city and MSA]; and retailers sales comparison [by State region and for department, specialty, and other stores, monthly percent change from 1 year ago, current year only].

[27] [Chicago] purchasing managers survey [business activity composite index, and indexes for production, new orders, order backlog, inventories, employment, vendor deliveries, and prices paid, with comparisons to U.S.; monthly for current and/or previous year].

[28-29] State transactions, general funds [revenues and expenditures]; and State employment and payroll [for education and all other agencies; both monthly, for current year only].

S2410   ILLINOIS
Commerce Commission

S2410–1   ILLINOIS UTILITIES STATISTICS
Annual series. For individual publication data, see below.
SRI/MF/complete

Series of 2 annual reports presenting Illinois electric and gas utility financial and operating data, by company and class of service, 1983-84. Data are from annual reports filed with the State Commerce Commission by 12 electric and 16 gas utilities.

Each report contains introduction, contents listing, and 13 tables showing the following data by company, 1983-84: sales revenue, sales volume (kWh or therm), and average number of customers, all by ultimate consumer class of service, and for resale and interdepartmental sales; and other operating revenues.

Ultimate consumer classes of service covered in each report are described below.

Availability: Illinois Commerce Commission, Technical Information Center, 527 E. Capitol Ave., Springfield IL 62706, $2.00 each; SRI/MF/complete.

S2410–1.1: Illinois Gas Utilities: A Comparative Study of Gas Sales Statistics for Calendar Years 1984 and 1983
[Annual. May 1985. ii+34 p. Research Bull. No. 112. SRI/MF/complete.]

Ultimate consumer classes of service covered for gas utilities are: residential and commercial/industrial, with and without space heating; interruptible commercial/industrial; and all other.

S2410–1.2: Illinois Electric Utilities: A Comparative Study of Electric Sales Statistics for Calendar Years 1984 and 1983
[Annual. May 1985. ii+17 p. Research Bull. No. 113. SRI/MF/complete.]

Ultimate consumer classes of service covered for electric utilities are: residential, large industrial, small commercial, public street/highway lighting, other public authorities, and railroads/railways.

S2410–2   OPERATING STATISTICS OF TELEPHONE COMPANIES IN ILLINOIS for Calendar Year 1984
Annual. May 1985.
iii+55 p. Rpt. No. 214r.
LC 81-644032.
SRI/MF/complete

Annual report presenting Illinois Class A and B and cooperative telephone company financial and operating data, by company, 1984. Includes number of facilities, value of plant in service and under construction, capitalization, revenues, expenses, and income.

Contains introduction (1 p.); company index (p. i-iii); and 1 table repeated for 50 companies (p. 1-55).

Availability: Illinois Commerce Commission, Technical Information Center, 527 E. Capitol Ave., Springfield IL 62706, $2.00; SRI/MF/complete.

S2415   ILLINOIS
Office of the Comptroller

S2415–1   1984 ILLINOIS ANNUAL REPORT
Annual. Feb. 1985. 407 p.
ISSN 0360-8719.
LC 80-644544.
SRI/MF/complete

Annual report on financial condition of Illinois State government, for fiscal year ended June 30, 1984, and "lapse period" July 1-Sept. 30, 1984. Presents revenues by source; expenditures of individual agencies, by object and function; and fund balances; for general, highway, university/college income, special State, bond financed, debt service, Federal and State trust, and revolving funds. Includes selected comparisons to FY83.

Also includes Capital Development Board funding for individual projects; and comparison of budgeted vs. actual expenditures.

Data are from records of the comptroller's office.

Contains contents and table listing (p. 3-4); and 9 tables (p. 8-407).

An annual summary report on Illinois financial condition is also available from the Office of the Comptroller, but is not covered by SRI.

Availability: Illinois Office of the Comptroller, Statehouse, Rm. 201, Springfield IL 62706, †; SRI/MF/complete.

S2430   ILLINOIS
Administrative Office of the Courts

S2430–1   ADMINISTRATIVE OFFICE OF THE ILLINOIS COURTS 1983 Annual Report to the Supreme Court of Illinois
Annual. [1985.] 252 p.
ISSN 0536-3713.
LC 74-640509.
SRI/MF/complete

Annual report, for 1983, on Illinois judicial system, including trial and appellate court caseloads and case dispositions. Covers supreme, appellate, and circuit courts. Includes trial court data by case type, judicial district, and county; with extensive detail for Cook County by jurisdiction and type of criminal offense.

Civil and criminal cases are shown for most courts, with trial court detail for chancery, eminent domain, tax, municipal corporations, mental health, divorce, family relations, juvenile, felony, misdemeanor, small claims, probate, ordinance, traffic, and conservation cases.

Also includes data on State judicial budget and salaries, medical experts' court-related activities, legal internship program, judges and workloads, law jury cases and processing time, sentences imposed in felony cases, circuit court revenues and expenditures, probation dept and juvenile detention home personnel and caseloads, and probation dept restitution collections.

Contains contents listing (p. 3-6); narrative report, with 14 summary charts and tables (p. 7-83); statistical section, with 3 charts and 118 tables (p. 84-247); and appendices, with 1 text table (p. 248-252).

Availability: Illinois Administrative Office of the Courts, Supreme Court Bldg., Springfield IL 62706, †; SRI/MF/complete.

S2445   ILLINOIS
Board of Elections

S2445–1   STATE OF ILLINOIS OFFICIAL VOTE Cast at the General Election, Nov. 6, 1984
Biennial. [1985.] 90 p.
ISSN 0160-4325.
LC 78-641783.
SRI/MF/complete

Biennial report presenting results of the Illinois general election held Nov. 6, 1984. Shows voting for President and Vice-President; U.S. and State senators and representatives; judges and other State officials, including university trustees; and a referendum and constitutional amendment. Data are shown by county and/or district, with selected detail by ward and township for Cook County. Also shows party affiliation of candidates.

Also includes voter registration trends, by county.

Previous report, covering 1982 election, is described in SRI 1983 Annual under this number.

Availability: Illinois Board of Elections, 1020 S. Spring St., PO Box 4187, Springfield IL 62708, †; SRI/MF/complete.

S2457   ILLINOIS
Department of Financial Institutions

S2457–1   ILLINOIS CHARTERED CREDIT UNIONS 1984 Annual Report
Annual. Mar. 21, 1985.
2+25 p.
SRI/MF/complete

Annual report on financial condition of Illinois State-chartered credit unions, presenting assets, shares, members, and loans, by institution, as of Dec. 31, 1984.

Also includes data on real estate lending, and mergers and liquidations; consolidated operating ratios, balance sheet, and income and expenses; selected data by credit union type and county; and selected comparisons to 1983, with trends from 1929.

Contains contents listing (p. 1); and report, with text data, 2 charts, and 15 tables (p. 2-25).

Availability: Illinois Department of Financial Institutions, Credit Union Division, 421 E. Capitol Ave., Springfield IL 62706, †; SRI/MF/complete.

S2470   ILLINOIS
Department of Public Health

S2470–1   VITAL STATISTICS, Illinois, 1983
Annual. July 1985.
177 p. var. paging.
LC A60-9072.
SRI/MF/complete, current & previous year reports

Annual report, for 1983, on Illinois vital statistics, covering population, births, deaths by detailed cause, marriages, divorces, and annulments, by demographic characteristics. Includes data by city, county, and health service area (HSA), and selected trends from 1918. Data are from vital statistics certificates filed with the Dept of Health as of Feb. 15, 1984.

Contents:

a. Contents and table listing. (5 p.)

b. Introduction and general summary, with 1 map, 5 text tables, and 23 lettered tables. (p. I.01-I.31)

c. 1 detailed table repeated for State, HSAs, Chicago, and counties, with index (p. II.001-II.115); and 5 tables showing data by city (p. III.01-III.07).

d. Methodology, facsimiles of vital statistics certificates, definitions, and list of causes of death based on International Classification of Diseases, 9th Revision. (p. IV.01-IV.18)

All tables are listed below.

Report for 1982 was also reviewed in SRI during 1985, and is also available on SRI microfiche under S2470-1 [Annual. May 1985. 176 p. var. paging. †]. Previous report is substantially similar in format and content, but also includes data on induced abortions, and does not include data on number of births by educational attainment of mother.

Availability: Illinois Department of Public Health, Health Information and Evaluation Division, 535 W. Jefferson St., Springfield IL 62761, †; SRI/MF/complete.

TABLES:

[Unless otherwise noted, data are for Illinois, 1983. Data on births and deaths are usually for Illinois residents. Data on marriages, divorces, and annulments are for events occurring in Illinois.]

S2470–1.1: Text Tables

1. Live birth rates by age of mother and race of child, 1980, 1982, 1983. (p. I.02)

2. Live births by educational attainment of mother and race of child, 1980-83. (p. I.03)

3. Percent distribution of live births by month of pregnancy prenatal care began, according to race, 1980-83. (p. I.04)

4. Percent of live births with low birth weight by age of mother and race of child, 1980-83. (p. I.04)

5. Deaths and death rates for diabetes mellitus [by age,] 1970, 1980, 1982, and 1983. (p. I.06)

S2470–1.2: Births, Deaths, Marriages, and Divorces

TRENDS

A. Live births, deaths, infant deaths, neonatal deaths, and maternal deaths, with rates for each, and fetal deaths, with ratios, [and total population], 1918-83. (p. I.10)

BIRTHS

B-C. Live births: by birth weight, sex, and race; and by race, classified by sex, place of birth [hospital and nonhospital], attendant [physician, midwife, and other], and by marital status and age of mother; [all for] Illinois, Chicago, and downstate. (p. I.11-I.12)

D. Live births and births to unmarried women, with ratios, 1950-83. (p. I.13)

DEATHS

E. Causes of fetal death among infants born to Illinois mothers, by weight at birth. (p. I.14)

F. Perinatal losses and mortality ratio by race and sex, Illinois, Chicago, and downstate. (p. I.15)

G-H. [10] leading causes: of infant, [neonatal, and post neonatal] deaths, by age; and of deaths among white and nonwhite races. (p. I.16-I.17)

I-K. Components of heart disease deaths; cancer deaths by site; and deaths due to cerebrovascular disease [by lesion type; all by age]. (p. I.17-I.18)

L. Accidental deaths [and rates] by type of accident and age of decedent. (p. I.19)

M. Accidental deaths occurring in Illinois by type of accident and place where accident occurred [metro and nonmetro counties and Chicago], by population [size] class. (p. I.20)

N. Deaths and death rates from the principal diseases affecting the respiratory system, [selected years] 1950-83. (p. I.21)

O-P. 12 leading causes of death, and death rates, by age and race among residents of Illinois, Chicago, and downstate. (p. I.22-I.27)

Q. Leading causes of death by selected age groups. (p. I.28)

MARRIAGES, DIVORCES, AND ANNULMENTS

R. Marriages, divorces, and annulments, 1958-83. (p. I.29)

S. Marriages by age of bride and groom. (p. I.29)

T-U. Number of previous marriages of bride and groom; and marital status of bride and groom at time of marriage. (p. I.30)

V-W. Divorces by age of husband and wife at time of decree; and divorces and annulments classified by the duration of marriage. (p. I.31)

S2470-1.3: Local Area Data

STATE, HSAs, AND COUNTIES

[Table [A] is repeated for total State; 11 HSAs, including city of Chicago; and HSA component counties.]

[A] Selected vital statistics among residents [includes population (total, and age 65/over by sex); live births by sex; total and illegitimate live births and fetal deaths (to all mothers and mothers under age 20); premature live births and fetal deaths; neonatal and infant deaths; perinatal loss, by sex; and nonfetal deaths, total and by 21 causes, with selected data by sex and for age 65/over; all by race, for 1983, with rates for 1979-83 period and 1983]. (p. II.001-II.114)

CITIES

[Data are shown for residents of 66 cities.]

1-2. Live births, infant deaths, neonatal deaths, fetal deaths, and rates, by race. (p. III.01-III.02)

3. Live births with percentage rates for premature births and hospital births, infant deaths by age, with rates, and maternal deaths. (p. III.03)

4-5. Deaths and death rates from important causes. (p. III.04-III.07)

S2475 ILLINOIS
Board of
Higher Education

S2475-1 DATA BOOK ON ILLINOIS HIGHER EDUCATION
Annual. 1985. ix+243 p.
ISSN 0098-5279.
LC 75-643784.
SRI/MF/complete

Annual report on Illinois higher education enrollment, degrees, staff, and finances, 1984 and trends. Presents data for private and public colleges and universities and for community colleges, generally by individual institution. Most data are for fall 1984, 1984/85 academic year, or FY84, with trends from as early as 1951.

Data are from institution surveys conducted or coordinated by Board of Higher Education staff.

Contains preface, and contents and table listings (p. i-ix); introduction (p. 1-4); and 81 tables listed below, grouped into 10 sections, each preceded by descriptions of tables, definitions, and data sources (p. 5-243).

This is the 12th annual report.

Availability: Illinois Board of Higher Education, Four W. Old Capitol Square, 500 Reisch Bldg., Springfield IL 62701, †; SRI/MF/complete.

TABLES:
[Tables show data for Illinois, by individual institution, unless otherwise noted.]

S2475-1.1: Enrollment and Degrees
[Instructional locations are on- and off-campus and home study. Attendance status is full- or part-time. Data are for fall 1984, unless otherwise noted.]

CURRENT ENROLLMENT

I.1. General characteristics of enrollment [summary by institution type]. (p. 13)

I.2-I.4. Characteristics of degree credit enrollment at public universities, public community colleges, and private colleges and universities, by location of instruction, level or type of instruction, and attendance status. (p. 14-20)

I.5. FTE degree credit enrollment at public universities, by level and location of instruction. (p. 21)

I.6-I.11. Degree credit headcount enrollment and FTE degree credit enrollment: at public universities, at public community colleges by instructional program, and at private institutions, [all] by class level. (p. 22-35)

STUDENT CHARACTERISTICS
[Tables II.1-II.13 generally show data for degree credit students.]

II.1. [Headcount, by] sex, by level of instruction. (p. 41-46)

II.2. Course load, by level [of instruction and attendance status]. (p. 47-52)

II.3-II.7. Age distribution: by level of instruction and sex; and of 1st-time freshmen, undergraduate students, and graduate students, by attendance status; by type of institution [only]. (p. 53-57)

II.8. Average age, by sex and level of instruction. (p. 58-64)

II.9-II.10. Race or national origin [white, black, American Indian/Alaskan Native, Asian/Pacific Islander, Hispanic, and nonresident alien]. (p. 65-71)

II.11-II.13. Home State of 1st-time freshmen students; and home county of in-State 1st-time freshmen [by attendance status; aggregate,] by type of institution. (p. 72-79)

ENROLLMENT TRENDS

III.1. Fall degree credit headcount enrollments [U.S. total, and aggregate Illinois by institution type], 1951-84. (p. 83)

III.2-III.3. Fall FTE degree credit enrollment; and fall off-campus/home study headcount enrollment; [aggregate, by level of instruction and type of institution], 1965-84. (p. 84-85)

III.4. Fall degree/certificate credit enrollments [selected years 1965-84]. (p. 86-107)

III.5-III.6. Fall term on-campus degree credit headcount enrollment, by class level; and degree credit enrollments, by location of instruction [and attendance status; aggregate, by type of institution], 1975-84. (p. 108-109)

ACADEMIC PROGRAM ENROLLMENT

IV.1-IV.4. Headcount majors in public universities, by discipline [and instructional level]. (p. 113-116)

ADMISSIONS AND TRANSFERS

V.1-V.2. Applications, acceptances, and enrollments of 1st-time freshmen, transfer students, and entering professional and graduate students. (p. 119-126)

V.3. Institutional origin of undergraduate transfer students. (p. 127-158)

DEGREES

VI.1-VI.2. Number of bachelor, masters, doctorate, and 1st professional degrees conferred; and number of associate degree and certificate awards conferred; 1981/82-1983/84. (p. 161-166)

VI.3-VI.8. Bachelor's, master's, doctoral, and professional degrees conferred, and associate degrees and certificates conferred, by discipline [aggregate for all schools, selected years] 1970/71-1983/84. (p. 167-172)

VI.9-VI.10. Number and percent of degrees conferred, by field of study and level: by type of institution and sex [aggregate data], 1983/84. (p. 173-182)

S2475-1.2: Staffing and Finances

STAFF AND SALARIES
[Tables VII.1-VII.3 and VII.5-VII.9 present data for public universities.]

VII.1-VII.2. State appropriated staff earnings; and budgeted staffing levels in staff years, by staff classification and fund source [appropriated or nonappropriated; both for administrative, faculty, civil service, and student employees], FY85. (p. 189-190)

VII.3-VII.4. Number and sex of full-time faculty in public universities and private colleges and universities, by rank, fall 1984. (p. 191-193)

VII.5-VII.7. Average salary, 1984/85 (9- and 12-month contracts); and percent tenured, fall 1984 (all contracts); of full-time faculty, by rank and sex. (p. 194-196)

VII.8. Staff-year faculty assignment, by instructional activity and level of instruction, 1983/84. (p. 197-199)

VII.9. Statewide student credit hours per staff year faculty (direct instruction) by discipline and level [aggregate], 1983/84. (p. 200)

STUDENT COSTS

VIII.1-VIII.5. Annual tuition and fees of full-time undergraduates, graduates, and [health, law, and theology] professional students; detailed undergraduate fee charges in public universities; public community college charges [by district only]; and annual charges for room and board; 1984/85. (p. 203-211)

STUDENT FINANCIAL AID

[Data are shown by type of institution.]

IX.1. Student financial assistance by source [including Federal, State, and institutional], FY80-84. (p. 214)

IX.2. Number of [undergraduate and graduate] financial aid recipients, FY80-84. (p. 215)

IX.3-IX.5. Undergraduate grants, scholarships, and tuition waivers [number and value, by type of award and source], FY84; and value of undergraduate and graduate level financial assistance, by type, FY80-84. (p. 216-218)

FINANCIAL TRENDS

[Table titles for X.1-X.7 begin "Historical record of..." Only data for public universities are shown by institution.]

X.1. State higher education operating appropriations [summary, including data for public universities], FY80-85. (p. 225)

X.2-X.5. State appropriations: to public community colleges and State scholarship commission for operations and grants; for health education grants to private institutions; and for State universities retirement system; FY80-85. (p. 226-229)

X.6. State appropriations to public universities, by source of funds, FY83-85. (p. 230)

X.7. Total audited revenues [by source] for public community colleges, FY81-84. (p. 231)

CURRENT REVENUES AND EXPENDITURES

X.8-X.9. Current fund revenues by source at nonpublic institutions; and current funds expenditures at public universities by function (all funds); FY84. (p. 232-235)

X.10. Audited expenditures [aggregate] for public community colleges, by functional classification, FY81-84. (p. 236)

X.11-X.12. Current fund expenditures, by function, at public community colleges and nonpublic institutions, FY84. (p. 237-240)

INSTRUCTIONAL COSTS AND CAPITAL APPROPRIATIONS

X.13. Instructional costs per credit hour, by student level, at public universities, FY84. (p. 241)

X.14. Total instructional costs per credit hour, [aggregate for] public universities, by discipline and level, FY84. (p. 242)

X.15. Appropriations [new and reappropriated] for capital projects, FY83-85. (p. 243)

S2485   ILLINOIS
Department of Insurance

S2485-1   49th ANNUAL REPORT AND SUMMARY OF ANNUAL STATEMENTS by the Director of Insurance, Illinois, 1983
Annual. [1984.]
79 p.+errata sheet.
LC 53-23746.
SRI/MF/complete

Annual report on Illinois insurance industry financial condition and underwriting activity, by company and type of insurance, 1983. Covers total assets, liabilities, surplus, risks in force, assessments/fees, operating gain, and premiums written and losses paid; and Illinois premiums written; for Illinois-based, other U.S., and foreign companies.

Data are shown, as applicable, for farm mutual, property/liability, and life/health insurance companies. Life/health data include detail for fraternal benefit societies, HMOs and specialty service plans, and burial societies.

Also includes data on Insurance Dept regulatory activities, securities deposits, personnel, itemized finances, licensing activity, and consumer complaints, various years FY70-83: number of licensed companies; and finances of companies in liquidation/conservation/rehabilitation.

Data are compiled from unaudited annual insurer statements filed with the Insurance Dept, and from dept records.

Contains contents listing (1 p.); Insurance Dept narrative report, with 15 charts and 6 text tables (p. 7-32); and 3 detailed corporate financial tables (p. 33-79).

Previous report, for 1982, is described in SRI 1983 Annual, under this number.

Availability: Illinois Department of Insurance, 320 W. Washington St., Springfield IL 62767, †; SRI/MF/complete.

S2497   ILLINOIS
Department of Law Enforcement

S2497-1   CRIME IN ILLINOIS, 1983
Annual. [1984.] 5+188 p.
LC 81-641713.
SRI/MF/complete

Annual report on Illinois crimes and arrests, 1983, with some monthly data and comparisons to 1982.

Covers crimes and rates by location and reporting agency; clearances; and arrests by offender age, sex, and race/ethnicity; with detail by type of property and weapon involved and other crime circumstances, and data on value of property stolen, recovered, and destroyed, all by Index offense. Index offenses are murder, forcible rape, robbery, assault, burglary, theft, motor vehicle theft, and arson.

Also includes data on murder victims by sex and race; crimes, clearances, and adult and juvenile arrests, for individual non-Index offenses; law enforcement officers killed, and officers assaulted by type of weapon and circumstance; and law enforcement employment by agency.

Data by race/ethnicity are shown for white, black, Mexican, Puerto Rican, other Hispanic, Asian/Pacific Islander, and American Indian/Alaskan.

Data are from law enforcement agency reports submitted under the Uniform Crime Reporting (UCR) Program. Due to reporting problems, data for Chicago are shown separately from the rest of Illinois.

Contains contents listing and preface (2p.); introduction, with UCR Program description (p. 1-4); 5 sections on crimes and arrests, with brief narrative comments, 15 charts, and 56 tables (p. 6-140); Chicago data, with 14 charts and 33 tables (p. 143-171); and law enforcement casualties and employment, with 2 tables (p. 175-188).

This is the 12th annual report.

Availability: Illinois Department of Law Enforcement, Support Services Division, Identification Bureau, 726 S. College, Springfield IL 62704, †; SRI/MF/complete.

S2505   ILLINOIS
Department of Mental Health and Developmental Disabilities

S2505-1   ILLINOIS MENTAL HEALTH STATISTICS, FY84
Annual. Nov. 1984.
4+119 p.
LC 79-644938.
SRI/MF/complete

Annual statistical report on the patient population of mental health facilities in Illinois, FY84. Presents data on admissions, discharges, length of stay, and patient census for Dept of Mental Health and Developmental Disabilities (DMHDD) inpatient facilities, State operated outpatient and grant-in-aid facilities, general hospitals, and private sanitaria. Also includes specific data for Chicago area.

Contains definitions and contents listing (4 p.); and 2 maps, 1 chart, and 64 tables listed below (p. 1-119).

A monthly report with similar but less complete data is also published by DMHDD, but is not covered by SRI.

Availability: Illinois Department of Mental Health and Developmental Disabilities, 401 S. Spring St., Springfield IL 62706, †; SRI/MF/complete.

TABLES:

[Unless otherwise noted, data are for FY84 or as of June 30, 1984. Data by facility include data by region.]

S2505-1.1: Outpatient Data by Age, Treatment, and Facility

[Tables [2-6] show data by individual facility.]

[1] Summary of patient data, by age group, treatment category, and facility type [case openings/admissions, closings/separations, active cases/residents plus home visits, and patients served/client contacts]. (p. 2-3)

[2] Case openings and admissions, by treatment category and facility: State operated outpatient, grant-in-aid facilities, and private/general hospitals. (p. 4-13)

[3] Case movements and number of client contacts/patients served: State operated outpatient, grant-in-aid facilities, and private/general hospitals. (p. 14-24)

[4] Unduplicated count of patients served by treatment category: State operated outpatient and grant-in-aid facilities. (p. 25-33)

[5] Patients served by treatment category: private/general hospitals. (p. 34-35)

[6] Count of client contacts by treatment category: State operated outpatient and grant-in-aid facilities. (p. 36-44)

[7] Unduplicated clients served [and] duplicated client contacts by treatment category and region of facility [State operated outpatient and grant-in-aid facilities]. (p. 45)

[8] Case closings and separations by number of days open, and by treatment category within type of facility [State operated outpatient and grant-in-aid facilities, and private/general hospitals]. (p. 46)

S2505-1.2: DMHDD Inpatient Census, Admissions, and Separations

[All tables show data for DMHDD inpatient facilities.]

CENSUS

[1] Changes in inpatient population: residents plus home visits [by facility, various periods FY82-84]. (p. 47)

[2-3] Residents plus home visits, by age group; and temporary absence data by type of absence; [both] by facility. (p. 48-49)

[4-5] Average daily resident plus home visit population, by treatment category; and average daily populations by sex. (p. 50-51)

[6-7] Residents plus home visits: by age group and diagnosis; and by treatment category [and facility]. (p. 52-53)

[8] Resident plus home visit days for recipients, by treatment category [and facility]. (p. 54)

[9-13] Residents plus home visits: by treatment category; by age group, total and diagnostic category of mentally ill and developmentally disabled; and by facility; all by time in residence. (p. 55-59)

ADMISSIONS AND SEPARATIONS

[14] Net additions and patients served [by facility]. (p. 60)

[15-18] Admissions by mental health code legal status [voluntary and involuntary]; total admissions by age group and sex and by treatment category [by facility]; and admissions by age group, sex, and average age within diagnosis. (p. 61-64)

[19-22] First and readmissions by age group and facility, and by age and diagnosis; and readmissions by type of termination of previous episode, by facility and by days stay in community. (p. 65-68)

[23-25] Live discharges: by age group and facility; by age group and diagnosis; and by treatment category [and facility]. (p. 69-71)

[26-30] Live discharges: by treatment category; by age group, total and diagnostic category of mentally ill and developmentally disabled; and by facility; all by length of stay. (p. 72-76)

[31-33] Total deaths by age group and length of stay, total and diagnostic category of mentally ill and developmentally disabled. (p. 77-79)

[34] Terminations of on-books population, by type of termination [by facility]. (p. 80)

S2505-1.3: Region, Subregion, and County Data, and Employment

[All tables showing data by county and most showing data by region include separate figures for suburban Cook County and Chicago.]

REGIONAL AND COUNTY DATA

[1] Transfers to DMHDD inpatient facilities [by receiving facility] according to region of facility from which transferred. (p. 81)

[2-6] Residents plus home visits: at inpatient facilities, by treatment category and county of residence; at DMHDD inpatient facilities, by region of legal residence [and facility]; by treatment category and recipients region of residence; and at DMHDD inpatient facilities, by age group and by time in residence, by region of residence. (p. 82-88)

[7] Admissions and case openings, by type of service and treatment category within region of residence. (p. 89)

[8] Population movements at DMHDD inpatient facilities, by treatment category and region of residence. (p. 90)

[9-11] Case openings and admissions, by type of facility and county of residence; and admission, discharge, and census data [including rates], by county and region of residence. (p. 91-99)

[12-13] Readmissions: time in residence for previous episodes, and time (in community) since last discharge, by treatment category and region of residence. (p. 100-101)

[14-16] Live discharges from DMHDD inpatient facilities: by treatment category and county to which discharged; by age group and region of residence; and by length of stay and region to which discharged. (p. 102-106)

[17] Absolute discharges to community placement program by region of placement, DMHDD inpatient facilities. (p. 107)

FACILITY EMPLOYMENT DATA

[18] Changes in employment, filled positions (general revenue/federally funded) [by pay facility, various periods June 30, 1982-84]. (p. 108-109)

S2505-1.4: Health Service Area (HSA) and Inpatient Facilities Data

[1] Residents plus home visits and admissions, by patient's HSA, number and rate per 100,000 general population. (p. 111)

[2-3] Residents plus home visits at DMHDD inpatient facilities, and admissions to DMHDD inpatient facilities, by treatment category and HSA. (p. 112-117)

[4] Admissions [and average daily population] of State-operated inpatient facilities, FY70-84. (p. 119)

S2535
Office of the Secretary of State

ILLINOIS

S2535-1   ILLINOIS LIBRARIES: Public Library Statistics, 1983-84
Monthly (selected issue).
Nov. 1984. 118 p.
Vol. 66, No. 9.
ISSN 0019-2104.
LC 29-23175.
SRI/MF/complete

Annual statistical issue of *Illinois Libraries,* presenting public library statistics for FY84. Includes data on library holdings, staff, and finances.

Data are from reports of public libraries, 1980 census, and State agencies. Data were prepared by the Library Research Center, University of Illinois Graduate School of Library and Information Science.

Contents:

a. Contents listing, and definitions. (2 p.)

b. 1 detailed table showing population served, nonresident fee, weekly hours, transactions, FTE staff, volumes added and held, films and recordings held, periodicals received, municipal tax valuation and rate, local government and total receipts, and salary and materials expenditures, all by library, mostly for FY84. (p. 459-484)

c. 1 summary table showing number of district, county, township, city, town, and village libraries. (p. 485)

d. Directories and index of public libraries and librarians. (p. 486-574)

Illinois Libraries is a monthly publication that is primarily narrative; the statistical issue, published each Nov., is the only issue covered in SRI. Issues are paginated cumulatively throughout the year.

Availability: Illinois State Library, Centennial Bldg., Springfield IL 62756, †; SRI/MF/complete.

S2540
Department of Transportation

ILLINOIS

S2540-1   ACCIDENT FACTS, 1984, Illinois
Annual. [1985.] 24 p.
LC 80-620689.
SRI/MF/complete

Annual report on Illinois traffic accidents, fatalities, and injuries, by accident and vehicle type, location, time, and other circumstances; and driver and victim characteristics; 1984, with trends from 1975.

Also includes data on motor vehicle registrations, travel mileage, and licensed drivers; blood alcohol content of driver fatalities by age group; and detailed data on pedestrian, motorcycle, and school bus accidents.

Contains contents listing (inside front cover); and highlights, 2 data maps, 5 charts, and 14 tables (p. 1-24).

A booklet containing additional motorcycle accident data is also available from the issuing agency, but is not covered by SRI.

Availability: Illinois Department of Transportation, Traffic Safety Division, 2300 S. Dirksen Pkwy., Rm. 319, Springfield IL 62764, †; SRI/MF/complete.

S2570   INDIANA
Office of the Auditor

S2570–1   ANNUAL REPORT OF THE AUDITOR OF STATE of the State of Indiana for the Fiscal Year Ending June 30, 1984
Annual.   Dec. 1, 1984.
xii+380 p.
LC 10-13355.
SRI/MF/complete

Annual auditor's report on financial condition of Indiana State government for FY84, covering assets, liabilities and fund equity, revenues by detailed source, appropriations and expenditures by function and object, and fund balances, for general, special revenue, capital projects, enterprise, internal service, and pension and other trust funds, with selected detail by individual account.

Also includes data on State motor vehicle highway fund receipts, administrative expenses, and distributions; property tax levies, assessed values, and collections and distributions, and other tax levies, by county and type; and selected trends from 1974.

Contains introductory material, including 6 summary charts, and contents listing (p. i-xii); general purpose, and combining and individual fund financial statements and schedules, with 30 tables (p. 1-72); and statistical section, with 13 tables (p. 74-380).

Availability: Indiana Office of the Auditor, State House, Rm. 240, Indianapolis IN 46204, †; SRI/MF/complete.

S2620   INDIANA
Employment Security Division

S2620–3   INDIANA LABOR MARKET TRENDS
Quarterly.   Approx. 50 p. no paging.
SRI/MF/complete

Quarterly report on Indiana labor market trends, including employment, earnings, and unemployment insurance data, by industry and local area. Most data are from Indiana Employment Security Division. Report is issued 4-6 months after quarter of coverage.

Issues contain contents and table listing; brief narrative analysis, with 1 quarterly table showing seasonally adjusted employment data; articles on aspects of Indiana economy, often with statistics; 11 other quarterly tables, listed below; and directory of State employment service offices.

Issue for 1st quarter includes additional summary employment data.

Most quarterly tables appear in all issues. All additional features with substantial statistical content are described, as they appear, under "Statistical Features." Nonstatistical features are not covered.

Report is discontinued with the 2nd quarter 1985 issue. Quarterly data on seasonally adjusted employment are now included in the monthly *Labor Market Letter,* not covered in SRI. Other data are available from the issuing agency as individual releases.

Availability: Indiana Employment Security Division, Labor Market Information and Statistical Services, Ten N. Senate Ave., Indianapolis IN 46204, †; SRI/MF/complete.

Issues reviewed during 1985: 2nd Qtr. 1984-2nd Qtr. 1985 (D).

QUARTERLY TABLES:

[Unless otherwise noted, data are for Indiana and are shown annually for 6-11 previous years and monthly for current year through quarter of coverage. Data by industry are shown by industry division and major manufacturing industry group.]

I. CPI [U.S., for all urban wage earners/clerical workers and consumers, by item and for 5 major cities, for final month of quarter of coverage, with change from previous month and year, and 5-year monthly trends].

II. Annual average unemployment rates, U.S. and Indiana [12-13 years through previous year].

III. Indiana labor force summary [by employment status] with U.S. unemployment rates.

IV. Nonagricultural wage/salary employment, by industry.

V. Average weekly earnings for production workers, by industry.

VI. Labor force status summary for major labor market areas.

VII. Nonagricultural wage/salaried employment in establishments in major labor market areas, by industry.

VIII. Summary of unemployment insurance activities [including new and continuing claims; claims exhausted and from other States; payments; and claims and payments for Federal and extended benefit programs; usually for quarter prior to quarter of coverage, previous quarter, same quarter of prior year, and cumulative year to date].

IX-X. Unemployment insurance payments [number and amount] by local office and by industry [usually shown monthly for quarter of coverage and/or previous quarter, with cumulative comparisons to same quarter of previous year].

[XI] Covered employment and payrolls [and average weekly earnings for all and manufacturing workers, by county, for most recent available quarter or quarters, with monthly employment detail].

STATISTICAL FEATURES:

S2620–3.601: 2nd Qtr. 1984

1982 INDIANA PER CAPITA PERSONAL INCOME RISES LESS THAN HALF OF U.S. INCREASE, ANNUAL FEATURE

(3 p.) Annual article, with 2 tables showing Indiana total personal income, by SMSA and county of residence, with comparison to total U.S., 1981-82.

For description of 1980-81 data, see SRI 1983 Annual under S2620-3.404.

SELECTED 1983 DATA FOR INDIANA COUNTIES, ANNUAL FEATURE

(7 p.) Annual feature, with 6 maps showing the following by Indiana county, 1983: manufacturing employment and change from 1982; and average weekly earnings for all and manufacturing employment, with rankings.

Corrected data appear in the 3rd quarter 1984 issue; for description, see S2620-3.602 below.

For description of 1982 data, see SRI 1983 Annual under S2620-3.404.

TOTAL ESTABLISHMENT EMPLOYMENT DATA FOR INDIANA NON-SMSA COUNTIES, 1979-83, ANNUAL TABLE

(10 p.) Annual table showing Indiana employment in nonmanufacturing sector and in durable and nondurable goods manufacturing, for each county not included in an MSA, 1979-83.

1980 CENSUS COMMUTING PATTERNS OF INDIANA COUNTIES

(4 p.) Table and map presenting 1980 census data on commuting patterns in Indiana, covering points of origin and destination for Indiana residents and for nonresidents working in the State. Data are cross-tabulated among Indiana counties and neighboring States.

S2620–3.602: 3rd Qtr. 1984

CORRECTION

(inside front cover) Corrected data for article on Indiana employment and earnings by county, appearing in the 2nd quarter 1984 issue.

For description of orginal article, see S2620-3.601 above.

OCCUPATIONAL WAGE SURVEYS SCHEDULED FOR SERVICE DELIVERY AREAS (SDAS) AS WELL AS FOR INDIVIDUAL COUNTIES

(p. 8 p.) Article, with 3 tables showing Indiana manufacturing employment, median wage, and wage ranges, by occupation, with detail for durable and nondurable sectors and for firms with 1-299 and 300/more employees, 1982/83.

Data are based on the 1982/83 Indiana Occupational Wage Survey of a representative sample of 1,650 manufacturing firms employing 329,277 workers.

S2620–3.603: 4th Qtr. 1984

ECONOMIC RECOVERY AND JOBS IN THE 7TH DISTRICT

(8 p.) By Jerry Szatan and William A. Testa. Article, with 3 tables showing percent change in employment during economic contraction and expansion periods 1969-84, with some detail for manufacturing employment, all for Indiana and 4 neighboring States, 7th Federal Reserve District, and total U.S. Data are from BLS.

INITIAL CLAIMS AND INSURED UNEMPLOYMENT BY WEEKS, ANNUAL FEATURE

(2 p.) Annual table showing Indiana insured unemployment and initial claims by program type, and claims for extended benefits and Federal supplemental compensation, weekly 1984.

S2620–3.604: 2nd Qtr. 1985

GARY-HAMMOND PMSA STEEL MILL EMPLOYMENT LOSSES NOT AS DAMAGING AS ELSEWHERE

(p. 1-5) By Lillian Miles. Article, with 3 tables showing steel industry employment, and overall unemployment rate, for U.S. and for 10 major steel-producing locales, 1984. Data are from BLS.

SELECTED 1984 DATA FOR INDIANA COUNTIES, ANNUAL FEATURE

(8 p.) Annual feature, with 7 maps showing the following by Indiana county, 1984: manufacturing employment and change from 1983; average weekly earnings for all and manufacturing employment, with rankings; and manufacturing employment as percent of total employment, with comparison to 1983.

For description of previous feature, see S2620-3.601 above.

TOTAL ESTABLISHMENT EMPLOYMENT DATA FOR INDIANA NON-MSA COUNTIES, 1980-84, ANNUAL TABLE

(10 p.) Annual table showing Indiana employment in nonmanufacturing sector and in durable and nondurable goods manufacturing, for each county not included in an MSA, 1980-84.

For description of previous table, see S2620-3.601 above.

S2625   INDIANA
Department of Financial Institutions

S2625–1   DEPARTMENT OF FINANCIAL INSTITUTIONS, State of Indiana, July 1, 1983-June 30, 1984
Annual.   [1985.]   71 p.
LC 35-27683.
SRI/MF/complete

Annual report, for FY84, on financial condition of Indiana State-chartered financial institutions. Presents composite assets, liabilities, income, and expenses, for bank/trust companies, industrial loan/investment companies, building and loan assns, pawnbrokers, and credit unions. Also presents assets for individual banks, building and loan assns, and credit unions, with bank detail by asset category.

Also includes composite loan analysis for banks, consumer loan licensees, and pawnbrokers; and dept finances.

Data generally are as of June 30, 1984, or Dec. 31, 1983, with selected comparisons to prior years. Dept finances are for FY82-84.

Contains contents listing (p. 3); dept summary, with 1 table (p. 5-9); and division reports, with 20 tables (p. 12-71).

Availability: Indiana Department of Financial Institutions, 1024 Indiana State Office Bldg., Indianapolis IN 46204, †; SRI/MF/complete.

S2630   INDIANA
Board of Health

S2630–2   HEALTH PROFILE REPORT, 1970-82, by State and County, Indiana
Biennial.   July 1984.
iv+186 p.
LC 85-620748.
SRI/MF/complete

Biennial health profile of Indiana counties, with related data on vital statistics, public assistance, socioeconomic conditions, and public health, 1970 and 1978-82. Data are primarily from Federal and State agencies.

Contains introduction and data references (p. i-iv); and 12 tables, listed below, repeated for the State and each county (p. 1-186).

Previous report, for 1968-80, is described in SRI 1983 Annual, under this number.

Availability: Indiana Board of Health, Public Health Statistics Division, 1330 W. Michigan St., PO Box 1964, Indianapolis IN 46206-1964, †; SRI/MF/complete.

TABLES:
[Tables show data for 1970 and 1978-82, unless otherwise noted.]

1. Geographic data [area and density] and vital statistics [population, live births, deaths, and marriages].

2. Effective buying income [per household and per capita, number of households, household median income, and percent of households in 6 income ranges].

3. Average number of welfare recipients [by program, total for Jan.-June].

4. Employment patterns [average employment by industry division].

5. Selected leading causes of death.

6. Infant and maternal health [total, live, still, premature, and illegitimate births; maternal, infant, neonatal, and perinatal deaths; and abortions].

7. Reported immunizations [of 1st graders, by disease].

8. Selected leading communicable diseases [and reported animal bites and rabid animals].

9. Mental health summary [hospital admissions, patients, and discharges].

10. Tuberculosis summary.

11. Local health [dept] appropriations [total and per capita].

12. Medicare enrollees [by sex and for white race, 1978-82 only].

S2630–3   INDIANA VITAL STATISTICS SUMMARY, 1983
Annual.   [1984.]   3+61 p.
LC 61-64187.
SRI/MF/complete

Annual compilation of vital statistics for Indiana, 1983. Covers births, deaths by cause, estimated population, and marriages, generally by health service area, county, and city. Includes data by age, race, and sex.

Contains narrative summary, with text table showing 10 leading causes of death, 1982-83 (2

p.); table listing (1 p.); 8 tables listed below (p. 1-60); and list of additional tables available from agency on request (p. 61).

Previous report, for 1982, is described in SRI 1983 Annual under this number.

Availability: Indiana Board of Health, Public Health Statistics Division, 1330 W. Michigan St., PO Box 1964, Indianapolis IN 46206-1964, †; SRI/MF/complete.

TABLES:
[Tables 3-6 show data by health service area, county, and city with 1980 census population of 5,000 or more. Data are for 1983, unless otherwise noted.]

1. Residence vital statistics summary [including abortions; fertility rate; births and deaths by month; deaths by age, race, and sex; and deaths and death rates from selected causes]. (p. 1-4)

2. Residence deaths by sex and by age, from each cause (or group of causes), for the 5-year period 1979-83. (p. 5-17)

3. Estimated population, and residence live births, deaths, stillbirths, and rates. (p. 19-23)

4. Residence deaths and death rates for selected causes. (p. 25-41)

5. Residence total births, live births, [and] maternal, infant, neonatal, and perinatal deaths and death rates. (p. 43-47)

6. Residence births by race, sex, attendant [physician and other], and place of delivery [in and not in hospital]. (p. 49-53)

7. Residence deaths from certain leading causes, by age, race, and sex. (p. 55-58)

8. Marriages by health service areas, subareas, and county of marriage and month of occurrence. (p. 59-60)

S2630–5   INDIANA POPULATION CHANGES, 1970-80
Series.   For individual publication data, see below.
SRI/MF/complete

Report, in 3 volumes, covering Indiana population and vital statistics, by Health Service Area (HSA), subarea, and component county, 1970 and 1980 or 1970-80 period. Includes population, deaths, and net migration, by age; and median age; all by race and sex.

Data are from U.S. Census Bureau and State records.

Each volume contains introduction, map, list of HSA subareas and component counties, and contents listing (p. i-vii); 10 tables repeated for total HSA and each subarea (with brief narrative summaries), and 3 tables repeated for each component county (119-189 p.); and appendix with 7 tables comparing State and each HSA (6 p.).

Volumes are listed below.

Availability: Indiana Board of Health, Public Health Statistics Division, 1330 W. Michigan St., PO Box 1964, Indianapolis IN 46206-1964, †; SRI/MF/complete.

VOLUMES:

S2630–5.1: Northern Indiana Population Changes, 1970-80
[Monograph. 1983. vii+127 p. LC 84-623006. SRI/MF/complete.]

S2630–5.2: Central Indiana Population Changes, 1970-80
[Monograph. 1984. vii+157 p. LC 84-622763. SRI/MF/complete.]

S2630–5.3: Southern Indiana Population Changes, 1970-80
[Monograph. 1984. vii+197 p. LC 84-622764. SRI/MF/complete.]

S2635 INDIANA
Commission for Higher Education

S2635–1 INDIANA HIGHER EDUCATION 1984 FACT BOOK
Annual. May 1985.
2 p.+i+72 p.
SRI/MF/complete

Annual report, for 1984, on Indiana higher education, covering enrollment, degrees awarded, and finances, by institution, for public and independent schools. Also includes comparisons to other States, and Scholastic Aptitude Test (SAT) scores for high school seniors.

Contains contents and table listing (2 p.); preface (p. i); and 22 tables listed below (p. 1-72).

Fact Book is accompanied by a primarily narrative summary, *Annual Report of the Commission for Higher Education* [Annual. Mar. 1985. 5+50 p. †]. Narrative summary is also available on SRI microfiche under this number.

Prior to 1984, both narrative and statistical content were included in the *Annual Report.*

Availability: Indiana Commission for Higher Education, 400 Harrison Bldg., 143 W. Market St., Indianapolis IN 46204-2892, †; SRI/MF/complete.

TABLES:
[Unless otherwise noted, data are for 1983/84.]

ENROLLMENTS AND DEGREES
[Data are shown for public and independent institutions, unless otherwise noted. Student characteristics include percent male, State resident, foreign, on-campus, black, other minority, full-time, and over age 25.]

1. Statewide fall enrollments [full- and part-time, fall] 1974-84. (p. 1)

2. Fall headcount enrollment by campus, 1976-84. (p. 2-5)

3. 1982/83-1983/84 annual enrollment statistics by campus [full- and part-time, semester credit hours, and FTE]. (p. 6-9)

4. Selected student characteristics for annual enrollment by campus. (p. 10-13)

5-6B. Annual enrollment headcount by student level and campus; and [annual] enrollments by program area and [degree type]. (p. 14-25)

7A-8. Student characteristics by program; and [annual enrollment] by origin of student [including top 5 States and 5 foreign countries]. (p. 26-34)

9. Student characteristics by [Indiana] county of origin [for all institutions]. (p. 35-38)

10-11B. Degrees awarded by campus and degree type; and by program area and [degree type]. (p. 39-48)

SAT SCORES

12-12. SAT [verbal and mathematics] scores for seniors: [national, midwestern, and Indiana averages, and national averages for students requesting that scores be sent to Indiana higher education institutions (by type of institution), all by sex], in 1983/84 school year; and Indiana and nationwide averages, 1972/73-1983/84. (p. 49-50)

FINANCES
[Tables 16-18 show data for public institutions only, by campus.]

14. Tuition/regularly assessed fees for colleges and universities [by campus, 1976/77-1984/85]. (p. 51-53)

15. Student aid funds in Indiana [by Federal and State grant program], 1977/78-1984/85. (p. 54-55)

16. Funding for higher education institutions, selected general fund data [institutional general operating appropriation, student fees, and fee replacement], 1975/76-1984/85. (p. 56-59)

17. State appropriations and bond authorizations for capital expenditure, by expenditure class, [biennially] 1973/75-1983/85. (p. 60-61)

18. Average annual rates of increase for salaries of continuing employees [by occupational category], 1974/75-1984/85. (p. 62-63)

DEGREE PROGRAMS

19. Degree programs by level and academic area aggregated by type of institution. (p. 64-69)

COMPARISONS TO OTHER STATES

20. Comparison of tuition and fee levels [for in-State and out-of-State students at selected institutions, for Indiana and 6 neighboring States], 1983/84 vs. 1984/85. (p. 70)

21. Comparative State appropriation increases to higher education [for Indiana and 12 other States, 1982/83-1984/85 period]. (p. 71)

22. National rankings of 1984/85 State appropriations [per capita and per $1,000 of personal income, and 2- and 10- year change] for higher education, Indiana and [16] other selected States. (p. 72)

S2675 INDIANA
State Police Department

S2675–1 SUMMARY OF MOTOR VEHICLE TRAFFIC ACCIDENTS in Indiana, 1984
Annual. Feb. 7, 1985. 2 p.
SRI/MF/complete

Annual report on Indiana traffic accidents, injuries, and fatalities, by vehicle and accident type, location, and other circumstances; and by driver and victim characteristics; 1984, with selected comparisons to 1983.

Data are from dept records, based on reports available as of Feb. 7, 1985.

Report contains 21 tables.

Similar reports showing detail for truck, motorcycle, train, interstate, urban, and rural accidents are also available from the issuing agency, but are not covered by SRI.

Availability: Indiana State Police Department, 301 State Office Bldg., 100 N. Senate Ave., Indianapolis IN 46204, †; SRI/MF/complete.

S2685 INDIANA
Department of Public Welfare

S2685–1 GRAPHIC OVERVIEW OF INDIANA'S PUBLIC WELFARE PROGRAMS for FY85
Annual. [1985.]
174 p. var. paging.
LC 82-642200.
SRI/MF/complete

Annual report, for FY85, on Indiana public welfare caseloads, recipients, and expenditures, by program, source of funds, county, and selected recipient demographic characteristics, with trends from FY73. Includes detailed data on child abuse and neglect. Also includes comparisons to U.S., by State and territory.

Contains contents listing, and directories of welfare officials (p. i-ix); 2 summary charts (p. xi-xiii); and 7 sections with 65 charts and 41 tables (p. A1-G12). All tables, and charts with substantial statistics not covered in tables, are listed below.

Availability: Indiana Department of Public Welfare, State Office Bldg., Rm. 701, 100 N. Senate Ave., Indianapolis IN 46204, †; SRI/MF/complete.

TABLES AND CHARTS:
[Unless otherwise noted, data are for Indiana, FY85. Tables showing data by State often include data for various U.S. territories. Data by race generally include Hispanics, and occasionally also include American Indians/Alaskan Natives and Orientals.]

S2685–1.1: Expenditures and Sources of Funds

[1] Expenditures for welfare, FY73-85. [chart] (p. xi)

[2] Expenditures for welfare [by program; assistance repayments; and funding from Federal, State, and county sources]. [chart] (p. xiii)

S2685–1.2: Public Assistance

AFDC SUMMARY

[1] Total expenditures [and average monthly recipients], FY74-85. [chart] (p. A1)

[2] AFDC comparative data [money and non-money grant adult and child recipients, and money payments], for June and 12 months FY84-85. (p. A3)

[3] Average monthly AFDC money payment per family [U.S. and Indiana], Nov. 1984. [chart] (p. A7)

[4-6] Percentage of population receiving AFDC assistance [by county], and comparison of AFDC distribution with population [in 5 largest counties], June 1985; and percentage of population receiving AFDC [for U.S., by State], Nov. 1984. [charts] (p. A11-A15)

AFDC QUALITY CONTROL DATA

[7] Comparison of current activities with initial base period [Apr.-Sept. 1973 and Oct. 1984-Mar. 1985 periods]. [chart] (p. A17)

[8] Payment error rate [Oct. 1982-Sept. 1983 period, and FY83], by State. (p. A19)

AFDC CHARACTERISTICS

[9-10] AFDC [family distribution by] race [Oct. 1984-Mar. 1985 period, and case distribution by] number of children in case [June 1985]. [charts] (p. A21)

[11] Need standards and [maximum legal] payment amounts (family of 4) [by State], as of Oct. 1, 1984. (p. A23)

[12] Average payment per family, excluding medical care, by State, Nov. 1984. [chart] (p. A25)

OTHER ASSISTANCE PROGRAMS

[13] Fair hearings, number of appeals requested, by program [monthly]. (p. A26)

[14] Medical review team: number of cases approved and denied for permanent/total disability [FY77-85]. [chart] (p. A27)

[15-16] Assistance to residents in county homes (ARCH) [monthly recipients and room/board, personal needs, and medical payments], FY85; [and cases and payments for aged and disabled, by county], June 1985. (p. A29-A30)

[17] Room/board assistance program [monthly recipients and payments]. (p. A31)

[18] Eye treatment [monthly caseload and expenditures], FY84-85. (p. A32)

[19] Welfare recipient fraud [suspected cases, and action reported and dollars involved]. (p. A33)

[20-21] Total welfare savings generated by State welfare work incentive program (WIN) [FY76-85, chart]; and WIN summary of total welfare savings and number of persons removed from AFDC [by county], FY85. (p. A35-A37)

S2685–1.3: Child Support

[Data are for the child support program (Title IV-D).]

[1-2] Disbursement of child support collected [by source, and AFDC and non-AFDC recipients, various years] FY78-85. [charts] (p. B1-B3)

[3] Child support collections by intercept program [State revenue dept and employment security division, and IRS], FY83-85. [chart] (p. B5)

[4] Child support amount collected and how distributed [by general fund function, by county and through IRS]. (p. B7-B10)

S2685–1.4: Medicaid

EXPENDITURES

[1] Total Medicaid expenditures, and monthly average number of recipients who received Medicaid, FY75-85. [chart] (p. C1)

PARTICIPATING POPULATION

[2] Number of persons enrolled, as compared to persons who actually received Medicaid (monthly average) [FY75-85]. [chart] (p. C3)

[3] Percentage of population enrolled in Medicaid program [by county], as of June 1985. [chart] (p. C5)

EXPENDITURES BY TYPE OF PROVIDER OR SERVICE

[Data for providers and services include nursing homes, pharmacies, dentists, other facilities/agencies/practitioners/suppliers, physicians, optometrists, clinics, hospitals, and mental hospitals.]

[4] Medicaid program expenditures by counties, selected categories of service. (p. C7-C8)

[5] Total Medicaid payments by type of provider, percentage of total [FY84-85]. [chart] (p. C9)

[6] Medical services payments by category [AFDC, aged, disabled, blind, and intermediate care facilities for the mentally retarded/inpatient psychiatric hospitals, FY84-85]. [chart] (p. C11)

[7] Number of Medicaid claims processed by provider category [and claims denied, suspended, and paid]. [chart] (p. C13)

[8-9] Medicaid program: total expenditures for ancillary services and medical supplies (in descending order by cost), FY84-85; and number of hospitals, nursing homes, and community residential facilities participating [by county], as of June 1985. [chart] (p. C15-C17)

[10] Medical assistance [caseloads by program and total expenditures] for patients in Medicaid certified mental health facilities and intermediate care facilities for the mentally retarded, FY84-85. (p. C19)

[11] Certified mental health facilities and intermediate care facilities for the mentally retarded, location and number of beds. (p. C20)

S2685–1.5: Food Stamps

PARTICIPATION BY COUNTY OR STATE

[1] Total value of ["free" and purchased] food stamps issued [FY77-85]. [chart] (p. D1)

[2-3] Food stamp participation [general public and AFDC households and persons], by month; and total stamps issued by county; FY84-85. (p. D3-D5)

[4] Average monthly value of food stamps received per person [Indiana, July 1984 and June 1985; and U.S., July 1984]. (p. D7)

[5] Number of persons and households certified to receive food stamps (monthly average) [FY78-85]. [chart] (p. D9)

[6-7] Percentage of population certified in food stamp program, June 1985 [chart]; and persons certified for food stamps, June 1984-85; [both by county]. (p. D13-D16)

[8] U.S. percentage of population participating in food stamp program [by State], July 1984. [chart] (p. D17)

[9] Food stamp quality control data: comparison of current activities with initial base period [July-Dec. 1973 and Oct. 1984-Mar. 1985 periods]. [chart] (p. D21)

[10] Food stamp quality control payment error rate, by State, Oct. 1982-/Sept. 1983 [period]. (p. D23)

[11] Food stamp participation by race [by county], July 1985. (p. D25-D26)

S2685–1.6: Child Welfare

SUMMARY DATA

[1] Child welfare expenditures, FY75-85. [chart] (p. E1)

[2] Number of child welfare institutions [foster homes, day care homes and centers, child placing agencies, and child caring institutions] licensed by State welfare, FY77-85. [chart] (p. E3)

CHILD PROTECTION SERVICE PROGRAM

[Titles for tables or charts [3-24] begin "Child Protection Service Program..."]

[3-4] Total number of children reported as victims of abuse and neglect [FY80-85, chart]; and number of children [involved in substantiated, indicated, and unsubstantiated cases, by type by county]. (p. E5-E8)

[5-6] Child abuse and neglect substantiated/indicated cases, action taken [FY84-85]. [charts] (p. E9-E11)

[7-8] [Children involved, by] type of abuse and neglect, by age group, for substantiated/indicated [cases; and total deaths]. (p. E13-E14)

[9-10] Number of children reported as victims of sexual abuse, and fatalities due to abuse/neglect (substantiated/indicated cases) [FY80-85]. [charts] (p. E15)

[11] Source of initial child abuse and neglect reports. [chart] (p. E17)

[12-13] Abuse and neglect, race and sex [distribution] of all children. [charts] (p. E19)

[14-15] Relationship of perpetrator to child abuse and neglect victims (for substantiated/indicated children). [charts] (p. E21)

[16] Number of abuse/neglect children per 1,000 population under the age of 18 [by county]. [chart] (p. E23)

[17] Age group of perpetrators for substantiated/indicated [physical and sexual abuse, and neglect] cases. (p. E25)

[18] Child abuse in sexual abuse reports, only substantiated/indicated cases [demographic characteristics and relationship of child and perpetrator]. (p. E26)

[19] Child abuse and neglect fatalities [by selected sociodemographic characteristics of child and perpetrator, including marital status of parents]. (p. E27)

[20-22] Institutional [physical and sexual] abuse and [total] neglect reports [FY83-85, chart]; and investigations by type of facility; [both for substantiated, indicated, and unsubstantiated]. (p. E28)

[23-24] [Children involved, by] type of institutional abuse and neglect by race, sex, and age [group] (for substantiated/indicated children). (p. E32)

CHILD CARE FACILITIES AND ADOPTION

[Titles for tables on charts [26-32] begin "Substitute Care Program..."]

[25] Child welfare analysis: number of county welfare dept juvenile wards, [total and] per 1,000 population [by county, June 1985]. (p. E33)

[26] Case activity for children in substitute care, for the period July 1984-June 1985 [including children entering and leaving care during period, children leaving care by reason and race, and type of placement for children at end of period by race.] (p. E34)

[27] Characteristics of children in substitute care [by] age, race, and [other] special needs with regard to placement. (p. E35)

[28-29] Type of placement, and reason for entering care, for children in care at end of June 1985. [charts] (p. E37)

[30-31] Children free for adoption by age, sex, and race; and [number of] adoptions finalized by age, sex, and type of adoptive home [foster parent, ralative, and unrelated/not foster parent]. (p. E39)

[32] Children in adoptive placement by length of time free for adoption prior to adoptive placement, by age and race. (p. E40)

[33-34] Number of child caring residential facilities, full-time foster homes, intermediate foster homes, and day care homes and centers licensed by State welfare as of June 30, 1985 [by county]. [charts] (p. E41-E43)

[35] Total number of adoption petitions filed during 1974-84. [chart] (p. E45)

S2685–1.7: Crippled Children

[1] Crippled children program total expenditures, Federal vs. State [and] county disbursement of funds [FY75-85]. [chart] (p. F1)

[2-3] Number of children receiving services for crippled children [FY75-85, chart]; [and by county], FY85. (p. F3-F5)

[4] Diagnostic and treatment centers: location and services available [and number of children assigned, by center]. (p. F6)

S2685–1.8: Miscellaneous

[All tables show data for State Dept of Public Welfare.]

[1] Federal dollars that State [treasury] receives via welfare programs [by program], and percent to total by type of revenue. [chart] (p. G1)

[2] Summarized fund and expenditure report [disbursing agency and source of funds, by program], accumulative FY85.

[3] Caseload information by program [and by type of service and county] for the month of June 1985. (p. G7-G12)

S2702   INDIANA
Office of the Secretary of State

S2702–1   1984 ELECTION REPORT, State of Indiana
Biennial. [1985.]   2+84 p.
LC 78-643490.
SRI/MF/complete

Biennial report presenting results of the Indiana primary and general elections, 1984. Shows voting for President/Vice-President; U.S. Representatives; State senators and representatives; Governor and other officials, including judges and school superintendents; and 2 propositions to amend the State constitution.

Also shows party affiliation of candidates, voter registration and turnout, and number of electoral precincts. Data are shown by district and/or county.

Previous report, covering 1982 elections, is described in SRI 1983 Annual under this number.

Availability: Indiana Office of the Secretary of State, State House, Rm. 201, Indianapolis IN 46204, †; SRI/MF/complete.

S2703   INDIANA
Supreme Court

S2703–1   1984 INDIANA JUDICIAL REPORT
Annual. [1985.]
iii+376 p. Oversized.
SRI/MF/complete

Annual report on Indiana judicial system, covering trial and appellate court caseloads and case dispositions, 1984, with selected trends from 1978. Covers supreme, appeals, circuit and superior, county, Marion County municipal and small claims, and city and town courts. Includes data by case type, and by jurisdiction for trial courts.

Case types shown are criminal and civil for all courts, with some additional detail for juvenile, marital dissolution, probate/adoption, traffic, guardianship, and small claims cases.

Report also includes data on age of pending cases in appeals courts; judicial system finances and personnel, by county and/or city; and trial judges and population, by county.

Data are from reports filed with the Court Administration Division, and from the annual State auditor's report.

Contains contents listing (p. i-iii); introduction and narrative summary, with organizational chart (p. 1-8); and report, with 93 tables, and personnel roster (p. 9-376).

Availability: Indiana Supreme Court, State Court Administration Division, State House, Rm. 323, Indianapolis IN 46204, †; SRI/MF/complete.

S2735   IOWA
Department of Agriculture

S2735–1   IOWA AGRICULTURAL STATISTICS, 1985
Annual. June 1985.
4+177 p.
LC 76-646749.
SRI/MF/complete

Annual report on Iowa agricultural production, marketing, and finances, mostly 1984, with comparisons to 1970s-83, and selected historical trends. Data are generally shown by commodity and/or county or district, with some comparisons to other States and total U.S.

Covers production, prices, marketing, value, and, as applicable, acreage, yield, disposition, and stocks/inventories, for field crop, livestock, dairy, and poultry sectors.

Also includes number of farms, and acreage by land use category (crop, pasture, woodland, and other); corn harvesting and handling methods; wool production and income; farmland rental rates, ownership, value, and debt outstanding; farm income, production expenses, employment, hours, and wages; fertilizer use; weather; Corn Belt cattle and hog prices, feed costs, and margins; and U.S. meat production by State and trade by country, field crop exports, farm-retail price spreads, and food consumption.

Data are compiled by the Iowa Crop and Livestock Reporting Service in cooperation with the USDA.

Contains contents listing (1 p.); and report in 4 sections, with 23 maps, 17 charts, and 170 tables, with interspersed narrative (p. 1-177).

Availability: Iowa Crop and Livestock Reporting Service, Federal Bldg., Rm. 833, 210 Walnut St., Des Moines IA 50309, $4.00; SRI/MF/complete.

S2745   IOWA
Department of Banking

S2745–1   ANNUAL REPORT OF THE SUPERINTENDENT OF BANKING of the State of Iowa, for the Year Ending June 30, 1984
Annual. Aug. 31, 1984.
63 p.
LC 46-37477.
SRI/MF/complete

Annual report on financial condition of Iowa State-chartered bank and trust companies, presenting assets, liabilities, and equity capital, by institution arranged by city, as of June 30, 1984; and composite income, expenses, and financial ratios, 1981-83; with selected summary trends from 1891.

Also includes data on dept receipts and disbursements; consumer loans by type of collateral; small loan licensee composite finances, loan activity, and delinquent account legal action; and loan insurance activity.

Data are compiled from reports filed by the institutions with the Banking Dept.

Contains contents listing (p. 5); lists of State banking officials and banks, 1 trend table, and status changes (p. 6-26); bank financial section, with 5 tables (p. 28-51); small loan licensee statistical section, with 9 tables (p. 54-58); and list of small loan, debt management, and money order companies (p. 59-63).

Availability: Iowa Department of Banking, 530 Liberty Bldg., 418 Sixth Ave., Des Moines IA 50309, †; SRI/MF/complete.

S2755   IOWA
College Aid Commission

S2755–1   DATA DIGEST ON IOWA POSTSECONDARY INSTITUTIONS, 1983/84
Annual. [1985.]   5+177 p.
LC 80-640449.
SRI/MF/complete

Annual report on Iowa higher education, covering enrollment, student expenses and financial aid, degrees conferred, faculty salary and tenure, and finances, by individual institution, 1983/84, with trends from 1975, and student expense data for 1984/85. Most data are from Higher Education General Information Survey.

Contains preface and contents listing (5 p.); directory of colleges, universities, and specialized schools (p. 7-19); and 1 chart and 108 tables described below, arranged in 6 sections, each preceded by a brief narrative (p. 21-177).

This is the 9th annual report.

Availability: Iowa College Aid Commission, 201 Jewett Bldg., Des Moines IA 50309, Iowa State agencies and postsecondary institutions †, others $10.00; SRI/MF/complete.

TABLES AND CHART:

[Data by individual institution are arranged by institution type and generally are accompanied by summary tables. Institution types include regents universities, independent 4- and 2-year institutions, and area, Bible/theological, business, nursing, and professional schools.]

a. Enrollment: undergraduate and graduate students, by institution type, 1975-83; and full- and part-time undergraduate and graduate/professional students, by sex and residency status, by individual institution, fall 1983. 5 tables. (p. 23-30)

b. Student budget expenses and/or tuition/fees: for 2- and 4-year public and private institutions, Iowa and U.S. averages; for regents universities by resident status; and by individual institution; various years 1977/78-1984/85. 6 tables. (p. 33-38)

c. Degrees and other awards conferred: by level and sex, by discipline and individual institution, 1982/83. 20 tables. (p. 41-78)

d. Faculty salaries and tenure: average faculty salaries, by institution type and faculty rank and sex, 1975 and 1983, with comparisons to U.S., 1983/84; and total and tenured employment and mean salary for full-time instructional faculty, by academic rank, sex, length of contract, and individual institution, 1983/84. 13 tables. (p. 81-93)

e. Finances: revenues by source, expenditures by function, net physical plant assets, and endowment, by individual institution, FY83. 57 tables. (p. 99-157)

f. Student financial aid by source (including Federal, State, institutional, and other); aid by institution type, and Independent College Assistance Center aid by individual institution, both by program; nonrepayable student aid, loans, and employment, by program and institution type; and total aid value and students assisted vs. fall enrollment, by individual institution; 1982/83 or 1983/84. 1 chart and 7 tables. (p. 161-177)

S2780   IOWA
Development Commission

S2780-1   IOWA, A PLACE TO GROW: 1985 Statistical Profile of Iowa
Annual. 1985. 6+116 p.
LC 75-650016.
SRI/MF/complete

Annual statistical profile, for 1985, presenting detailed social, economic, and governmental data on Iowa. Data are primarily for various years 1960-83, with population trends from 1840 and projections to 2000.

Report is designed to present a comprehensive overview of the State. Extensive socioeconomic, demographic, and geographic breakdowns are shown, as applicable, for most topics. These breakdowns include data by city, county and other State region, SMSA, urban-rural status, com-

modity, income, industry, occupation, age, educational attainment, race, and sex. Comparisons to other North Central States and U.S. are also often included.

Most data are from State and Federal sources. Data sources appear beneath each table.

Contains contents listing (3 p.); and 41 maps and charts, and 149 tables arranged in 23 sections, described below (p. 1-116).

This is the 14th edition of the *Statistical Profile.*

Availability: Iowa Development Commission, Research and Development Group, 600 E. Court Ave., Suite A, Des Moines IA 50309, †; SRI/MF/complete.

TABLE SECTIONS:

S2780-1.1: Agriculture and Climate

(p. 1-15) Contains 3 maps and charts, and 19 tables. Includes cash receipts from farming; farm real estate value, income, workers, wage rates, and operators; farms by type of organization; Federal farm payments by program; farm machinery inventory and retail sales; and percent of population involved in food production, percent of income spent on food, food trade balance, and minutes of work required to purchase selected food items, compared for U.S. and 10 foreign countries.

Also includes farms, and average size and value; corn and soybean yield and production; livestock and poultry marketings, by species; and monthly climatological data.

S2780-1.2: Communication Industry and Construction

(p. 16-18) Contains 9 tables. Includes telephones in use; newspapers and circulation; radio and TV stations; and cable TV systems and subscriptions.

Also includes construction industry establishments, employment, and payroll; building permits issued and value; new residential construction and value; and housing units, value or rent, and vacancy rate.

S2780-1.3: Crime, Economy, Education, and Libraries

(p. 19-34) Contains 15 maps and 17 tables. Includes crime rates; violent and property crimes reported, by offense; personal income by source; GSP; and nonfarm employment.

Also includes public and nonpublic school enrollment and high school graduation rates; higher education enrollment and degrees; community college enrollment by institution; educational attainment of adult population; teacher salaries; public school expenditures per pupil; and economic development training by program.

Also includes public libraries; and library finances, acquisitions, holdings, and circulation.

S2780-1.4: Energy and Finance

(p. 35-40) Contains 1 map and 15 tables. Includes total and farm energy consumption, by fuel type; industrial electricity kWh prices by State; industrial energy use and cost; average residential electric bills; and gas and electric utilities sales and revenues, by consuming sector.

Also includes bank deposits and loans; mortgages; and bank, savings and loan assn, small loan company, and State-chartered credit union establishments and financial data.

S2780-1.5: Health and Housing

(p. 41-45) Contains 2 maps and 7 tables. Includes physicians; hospitals, beds, admissions, occupancy rates, and average stay length and cost; deaths by cause; reported cases of notifiable diseases; licensed health professionals; and housing units, occupancy, and value or rent.

S2780-1.6: Income, Industry, and Insurance

(p. 46-62) Contains 3 maps and charts, and 22 tables. Includes total and per capita personal income; personal income by source; earnings; effective buying income; and business establishments, employment, and payroll.

Also includes new and expanded industry, capital invested, and jobs created; Fortune 500 firms with Iowa plants; value added per manufacturing worker; industrial, pollution control, and health facility revenue bond financing; and manufacturing firms, employees, payroll, wages, hours, cost of materials, shipments, and capital expenditures, by State.

Also includes insurance companies, and financial and underwriting data, by type of coverage.

S2780-1.7: International, Mining, and Population

(p. 63-79) Contains 4 maps and charts, and 22 tables. Includes farm exports, by country of destination; manufactured product exports and related employment; foreign investments by country; and Iowa export share of U.S. balance of payments.

Also includes mineral production and value; coal production, mine price, and value; population from 1840; land area; housing units; and population projected to 2000.

S2780-1.8: Retail-Wholesale Trade, Service Industries, and Taxes

(p. 80-95) Contains 2 maps and charts, and 11 tables. Includes retail and wholesale trade, and service establishments, employees, and payrolls; and taxable retail sales by type of business.

Also includes per capita public debt, by State; expenditures by function; revenues by source; general fund receipts, and tax revenues and rates, by type; and property valuation and tax levies, by property class.

S2780-1.9: Transportation

(p. 96-102) Contains 6 maps and 12 tables. Includes rail and road mileages; airports and runways; rail, truck, and river freight; transportation industry establishments, employees, and payroll; public transit miles of service and passengers; road construction funding; traffic fatalities; registered aircraft; and motor vehicle registrations.

S2780-1.10: Travel

(p. 103-109) Contains 1 map and 7 tables. Includes fishing and hunting licenses issued; recreation areas and acreage; hunters and game harvested, by major species; State park attendance, by park; travel-generated expenditures, payroll, employment, and State and local tax receipts; and trip and traveler characteristics.

S2780–1.11: Workforce and Employment

(p. 110-116) Contains 4 maps and 8 tables. Includes union membership; work stoppages, workers involved, and days idle; labor force by employment status; labor productivity indicators; nonfarm employment, and manufacturing employment, earnings, and hours; unemployment rates; and manufacturing and construction wages.

S2780–2 IOWA DEVELOPMENT COMMISSION DIGEST

Bimonthly. Approx. 15 p.
ISSN 0193-8460.
LC SC 79-3388.
SRI/MF/complete

Bimonthly report on Iowa business and economic activity, including employment, construction, and agricultural prices. Data are from Iowa Development Commission; Iowa Dept of Job Service; Piper, Jaffray & Hopwood, Inc.; and other sources.

General format:

a. Several news briefs, editorial depts, and feature articles, usually nonstatistical.

b. Bimonthly "Iowa Ag & Business Indicators" feature, with 11 tables, listed below.

c. Bimonthly "Available Buildings" feature, listing square footage, community location, and former use of selected commercial buildings for sale.

d. Quarterly "Iowa Economic Indicators" feature, with 2 tables and accompanying charts showing Iowa GSP, personal income, industrial production index (total and for selected industries), and labor/proprietor/corporate income by industry division and selected major manufacturing group; and selected U.S. indexes; for month or quarter ended 3-8 months prior to cover date, with comparisons to preceding comparable period and 1-2 previous years.

e. Quarterly "Labor Market Information" feature, with 2 tables and 1 chart showing State labor force by employment status, with comparisons to U.S.; and nonagricultural wage/salary employment by industry division; for month 2-4 months prior to cover date, with comparisons to various previous periods.

Most bimonthly tables appear in all issues. All additional features with substantial statistical content are described, as they appear, under "Statistical Features;" page locations and latest dates of coverage for quarterly features are also noted. Nonstatistical features are not covered.

Prior to May/June 1985 issue, report was published monthly; and selected issues included a bimonthly table showing farm marketing value of livestock/products and crops, for U.S. and top 9 States.

Availability: Iowa Development Commission, Communications Group, 600 E. Court Ave., Suite A, Des Moines IA 50309, †; SRI/MF/complete.

Issues reviewed during 1985: Nov. 1984-Mar./Apr. 1985 (monthly); May/June 1985 (bimonthly) (P) (Vol. XIII, Nos. 10-11; Vol. XIV, Nos. 1-4) [Feb. 1985 issue incorrectly reads Vol. XIII, No. 2; Mar./Apr. 1985 is a combined issue; no July/Aug. 1985 issue was published].

TABLES:

[Tables show data for various periods, generally current to 3-6 months prior to cover date, with comparisons to specified prior periods. Data are shown for Iowa, unless otherwise noted.]

[1] Labor demand and supply [State Job Service placements and new applicants/renewals, by service area].

[2-3] U.S. CPI, and composite construction cost index.

[4] Business data [new car registrations, savings and loan assn loans closed and savings, and labor force by employment status].

[5] Value of new dwellings [by major city].

[6] Farm retail price spreads [for 4 commodities].

[7] Personal income.

[8] Stock index [Iowa and Dow Jones Industrial].

[9-11] Average prices received and paid by farmers, and commodity feed price ratios, [by commodity].

STATISTICAL FEATURES:

S2780–2.601: Nov. 1984 (Vol. XIII, No. 10)
QUARTERLY FEATURES

a. Iowa economic indicators, for 1st or 2nd quarter, or Aug. 1984. (p. 9-11)

b. Labor market information, for Aug. 1984. (p. 12)

S2780–2.602: Jan. 1985 (Vol. XIIII, No. 1)
QUARTERLY FEATURES

a. Iowa economic indicators, for 2nd or 3rd quarter, or Oct. 1984. (p. 9-11)

b. Labor market information, for Oct. 1984. (p. 12)

S2780–2.603: May/June 1985 (Vol. XIV, No. 4)
QUARTERLY FEATURES

a. Iowa economic indicators, for 3rd or 4th quarter 1984, or Jan. 1985. (p. 11-13)

b. Labor market information, for Mar. 1985. (p. 14)

S2795 IOWA
Department of Health

S2795–1 VITAL STATISTICS OF IOWA, 1983

Annual. [1985.]
4+89 p.+errata.
LC 79-644698.
SRI/MF/complete

Annual report on Iowa vital statistics, covering population, births, deaths by cause, marriages, and divorces, by demographic characteristics and location. Data are for 1983, with selected trends from 1915, and were compiled from State records and Census Bureau population reports.

Contains chart and table listings (3 p.); narrative analysis with 20 summary charts (p. 2-23); 42 tables listed below (p. 26-86); and definitions (p. 88-89).

Vital Statistics Pocket Guide is also issued by the Iowa Dept of Health, but is not covered in SRI.

Availability: Iowa Department of Health, Statistical Services Unit, Management and Budget Office, Lucas Office Bldg., Des Moines IA 50319, ‡; SRI/MF/complete.

TABLES:

[Tables are for Iowa, 1983, unless otherwise noted. Data by color are for white and nonwhite. Most data show percent or rate and/or number.]

S2795–1.1: Summary Tables

[Unless otherwise noted, tables show resident data. Marriages and dissolutions are shown as occurrences only.]

1-2. Population, live births (total and out-of-wedlock), deaths (total, infant, neonatal, fetal, and maternal), and marriages and dissolutions, 1915-83. (p. 26-27)

3. Summary of vital statistics by event [live births by sex and color, and out-of-wedlock live births; deaths by sex, color, and marital status; and marriages and dissolutions]; by month. (p. 28)

4-6. Summary of selected vital events [including live births with congenital malformations, perinatal deaths, and deaths by 67 selected causes] for the State [occurrence and resident data], and by county and city. (p. 31-56)

S2795–1.2: Natality

[All tables show resident data.]

7. Live births by color and sex of child, live birth order, birth weight, and plural births, all by age of mother. (p. 57)

8-10. Live births by live birth order, and 1st and 2nd live birth orders by age of mother, 1979-83. (p. 58-59)

11. In-wedlock and out-of-wedlock live births, by age and color of mother. (p. 60)

12. Out-of-wedlock live births by year, by age of mother, 1950-83. (p. 61)

13-15. In-wedlock and out-of-wedlock live births, by age of mother; and live births by teenage mothers; 1979-83. (p. 61-62)

16. Live births with prenatal care starting in 1st trimester, by age of mother, 1981-83. (p. 63)

S2795–1.3: Mortality

[All tables except table 28 show resident data.]
CAUSE OF DEATH

17. Selected causes of death, 1973-83. (p. 63)

18. Deaths by color and age, by sex. (p. 64)

19. Leading causes of death, by selected age groups. (p. 65)

20-21. Male and female malignant neoplasms deaths, by 10 leading sites, 1979-83. (p. 66-67)

22. 15 leading causes of death, by number and percent of total deaths, by male and female. (p. 68)

23-25. Heart disease, malignant neoplasms, and cerebrovascular disease deaths, by age, by sex. (p. 69-70)

26-27. Suicide deaths by age, by sex; and by age, by method, by sex. (p. 70-71)

28. Accidental deaths by type of accident [including work-related deaths by industry division], by age, occurrence data. (p. 72)

INFANT MORTALITY

29. Fetal deaths by age of mother, by in-wed-lock and out- of-wedlock. (p. 73)

30-31. Fetal and infant deaths by cause, by color. (p. 74-75)

32-33. Infant deaths by cause, sex, and color; and infant deaths by year, 1960-83; [both] by subdivision of the 1st year of life. (p. 76-77)

S2795–1.4: Marriages and Divorces

[Tables show occurrence data.]

34-36. Marriages: by age of groom and bride, 1979-83; and by age of groom by age of bride. (p. 78-80)

37-38. Dissolutions: by age, by color of husband and wife; and by age by primary marriage and remainder, by husband and wife. (p. 81-82)

39-40. Dissolutions, by age of husband and wife, and by duration of marriage, 1979-83. (p. 83-84)

41-42. Dissolutions by duration of marriage, and involving children under 18 years of age, [both] by color. (p. 85-86)

S2802   IOWA
Department of Human Services

S2802–1   MONTHLY PUBLIC ASSISTANCE STATISTICAL REPORT, Iowa
Monthly.   Approx. 30 p.
Rpt. Series A-1.
SRI/MF/complete, shipped quarterly

Monthly report on Iowa public welfare and social service program caseloads, recipients, and payments, by program and county. Covers aid to dependent children (ADC) and SSI programs. Report is issued 1-2 months after month of coverage.

Contains 2 charts, and 4 tables listed below.

Availability: Iowa Department of Human Services, Management Information Bureau, Management and Budget Division, Research and Statistics Section, Hoover State Office Bldg., 1305 E. Walnut St., Des Moines IA 50319, ‡; SRI/MF/complete, shipped quarterly.

Issues reviewed during 1985: Oct. 1984-Aug. 1985 (D).

MONTHLY TABLES:

ADC

[1] ADC program [regular and unemployed parent ADC cases, total and child recipients, payments, and average costs; and child support recoveries; for month of coverage, previous month, and same month of previous year].

[2] Fiscal year to date information [for ADC total and net costs, child support recoveries, and Federal and State funding; and for same period of previous year.]

[3] Public assistance programs [ADC, ADC-unemployed parent, and subsidized adoption cases, recipients, grant value, and cases opened and closed, by county, for month of coverage].

SSI

[4] SSI program [and Federal and State supplementation cases and payments, for aged, blind, and disabled, by county, for month of coverage].

S2805   IOWA
Insurance Department

S2805–1   1985 REPORT OF THE INSURANCE DEPARTMENT of Iowa
Annual.   May 1985.   188 p.
LC 46-43626.
SRI/MF/complete

Annual report on Iowa insurance industry financial condition and underwriting activity, by company and type of insurance, 1984. Covers assets; liabilities; capital stock; surplus; premiums in force, written, or collected; dividends; taxes; underwriting and investment income and expenses; losses incurred or paid; benefits paid; and other financial data; for companies with headquarters in Iowa and elsewhere.

Data are shown, as applicable, for fire/casualty/multiple line companies, mortgage guaranty insurers, reciprocal exchanges, State and county mutual insurance assns, hospital/medical service corporations, life insurance companies, fraternal beneficiary societies, and HMOs.

Data for fire/casualty/multiple line companies and reciprocal exchanges include additional breakdowns for 21 lines of coverage, including medical malpractice, workers compensation, fidelity/surety, accident/health, and automobile.

Also includes lists of company admissions, withdrawals, mergers, and name changes, 1984; data on value of securities on deposit, by company, Dec. 1984; State Insurance Dept appropriations, receipts, and disbursements, FY84; consumer complaints, 1984; and insurance agent prosecutions and license revocations, 1980-84.

Most data are compiled from annual statements filed by individual insurers.

Contains Insurance Dept summary, with 2 tables and 2 charts (p. 3-16); 47 company financial schedules and tables (p. 17-184); and index (p. 185-188).

This is the 116th annual report.

Availability: Iowa Insurance Department, Lucas State Office Bldg., Des Moines IA 50319, †; SRI/MF/complete.

S2810   IOWA
Department of Job Service

S2810–1   RESOURCE HANDBOOK OF FACTS AND FIGURES: A Guide to Iowa Department of Job Service Statistics and Other Statistics
Annual.   Nov. 1984.
3+iii+201 p.
LC 85-621592.
SRI/MF/complete

Annual report on Iowa employment and earnings, with detail by industry group, MSA, county, and occupation; and population characteristics; 1983, with selected comparisons from 1930s and projections to 2000. Also includes data on unemployment insurance and other unemployment assistance programs. Report is intended as an aid in manpower planning.

Data are derived from Iowa Dept of Job Service records, BLS, and other State and Federal sources.

Contains contents listing (3 p.); introduction and publications list (p. i-iii); glossary (p. 1-20); 6 statistical sections, with 109 tables listed below (p. 21-197); and index (p. 198-201).

For description of previous report, for 1982, see SRI 1983 Annual under this number.

Availability: Iowa Department of Job Service, Audit and Analysis Department, 1000 E. Grand Ave., Des Moines IA 50319, †; SRI/MF/complete.

TABLES:
[Tables show data for Iowa, unless otherwise noted.]

S2810–1.1: Population and Labor Force

POPULATION

[1] Iowa and U.S. population [decennially 1900-70, and annually 1971-83]. (p. 21)

[2] 1980 population of the U.S. and Iowa, by age. (p. 22)

[3-4] Population of [MSAs] and their component counties, and of [all] counties, Apr. 1, 1970 and 1980 [and births, deaths, and net migration, of all counties, 1970-80 period]. (p. 23-26)

[5] Provisional population projections [by county, quinquennially 1980-2000]. (p. 27-29)

[6] Selected population indicators [labor force by employment status, and persons in armed forces and not in labor force, by sex, 1970 and 1980]. (p. 30)

[7-8] Nonwhite population [black, American Indian, Eskimo, Aleut, and Asian/Pacific Islander by national origin], Iowa and selected counties [with summary comparisons to U.S.], 1980. (p. 31-32)

LABOR MARKET INFORMATION

[9-10] U.S. civilian labor force [1960-83]; and Iowa civilian labor force non-CPS [Current Population Survey] adjusted, [1970-83: both including unemployment, and agricultural and nonagricultural employment]. (p. 33-34)

[11] CPI, U.S., for all urban consumers, [monthly 1958-83]. (p. 35)

S2810–1.2: Unemployment Assistance Programs

COVERED WORKERS AND EMPLOYERS: JOB INSURANCE (JI)

CLAIMS ACTIVITY AND BENEFITS PAID

OTHER FEDERAL UNEMPLOYMENT ASSISTANCE PROGRAMS

IOWA JI TRUST FUND

S2810–2   LABOR MARKET INFORMATION FOR IOWA
Job Training Partnership Act
Annual. Feb. 1985.
5+119 p.
SRI/MF/complete

Annual planning report on Iowa labor market conditions, 1984, with selected trends from 1970s and projections to 1995. Presents data on population, labor force, employment by industry and occupation, and characteristics of job service applicants and insured unemployed.

Data are from Iowa Dept of Job Service, Census Bureau, and other State sources.

Contains preface and listings of contents, tables, and charts (5 p.); narrative report, with 1 map, 16 charts, and 15 text tables, (p. 1-48); and appendices with 15 tables, and list of labor market information sources (p. 51-119).

All tables are listed below.

Availability: Iowa Department of Job Service, Audit and Analysis Department, 1000 E. Grand Ave., Des Moines IA 50319, †; SRI/MF/complete.

TABLES:
[Data are for Iowa, unless otherwise noted.]

S2810–2.1: Text Tables

EMPLOYMENT AND POPULATION SUMMARY

WAGES, AND LABOR SUPPLY AND DEMAND

JOB SERVICE CLIENTS

S2810–2.2: Appendix Tables

POPULATION

EMPLOYMENT, HOURS, AND EARNINGS

[10] Report on hours and earnings [by industry division and major manufacturing industry group, monthly] 1984. (p. 73-75)

JOB OPENINGS AND APPLICANTS

[11] Job openings and applicants by [detailed] occupation, 1984. (p. 79-98)

[12] Labor supply and demand for [16] service delivery areas [by occupational group], 1984. (p. 101-106)

UNEMPLOYMENT COMPENSATION

[13-15] Regular/veterans/Federal civilian employees, extended benefits, and Federal supplemental compensation: number of weeks compensated and amount of benefits paid, under State and Federal unemployment insurance programs, by county [and total out of State], 1984. (p. 109-113)

S2815   IOWA
Judicial Department

S2815-1   **1984 ANNUAL STATISTICAL REPORT: Report to the Supreme Court of Iowa by the Court Administrator of the Judicial Department**
Annual.   Apr. 23, 1985.
vii+87 p.
LC 78-640215.
SRI/MF/complete

Annual report on the Iowa judicial system, including trial and appellate court caseloads, case dispositions, and processing time, 1984, with trends from 1956. Covers supreme, appeals, and district courts. Includes trial court data by case type and district.

Case types shown are criminal and civil, for all courts, with some additional detail for lawyer disciplinary, domestic relations, probate, juvenile, hospitalization, and small claims cases.

Also includes data on judicial dept personnel and FY85 appropriations; search warrant applications and seized property hearings; and driving while intoxicated cases; and traffic violations handled by court clerks, by county.

Data are from dept records.

Contains contents listing and highlights (p. ii-vii); report, with text statistics, 1 map, 2 charts, and 30 tables (p. 1-78); and appendices, with 3 maps and 6 tables (p. 79-87).

Availability: Iowa Judicial Department, Capitol Bldg., 10th and Grand, Des Moines IA 50319, †; SRI/MF/complete.

S2825   IOWA
Library Commission

S2825-1   **IOWA PUBLIC LIBRARY STATISTICS, 1983-84**
Annual.   1985.   1+iv+173 p.
LC 81-643203.
SRI/MF/complete

Annual report, for FY84, on Iowa public library finances, holdings, circulation, and staff. Data are shown for individual libraries, grouped by size of population served, operating income, and county. Data are from Library Commission annual survey of city and county libraries, and from Census Bureau.

Contents:

Contents listing (1 p.); introduction and explanatory notes (p. i); and 6 summary tables, including data on acquisitions by type (p. ii-iv).

Section I-III. 3 basic tables, listed below, presenting data for individual libraries. (p. 1-111)

Section IV-VI. Statistical analyses: 3 tables showing average and percentile values for selected operating and financial data and ratios, by population and budget size group; and county summaries, each including city and rural population, municipal income, and municipal library circulation, unit cost, and holdings by city. (p. 112-166)

Survey explanatory notes. (p. 167-173)

Availability: Iowa Library Commission, Library Development Office, Historical Bldg., E. 12th St. and Grand Ave., Des Moines IA 50319, †; SRI/MF/complete.

BASIC TABLES:

[All tables show data for city libraries arranged by population size group, and for county libraries, FY84. Each entry includes location, State region, and population. Types of material include books, periodicals, audiovisual, and microform.]

I. Financial information [income from municipal, county, Federal, and miscellaneous sources; and expenditures for wages/salaries, plant operation, capital outlays, equipment, and materials by type]. (p. 2-45)

II. Materials holdings and circulation [by type]. (p. 48-89)

III. Personnel, hours open, and salary ranges [includes professional staff, by highest degree held; technical/clerical and plant staff; director's salary; and salary ranges for professional, support/technical, and clerical/secretarial staff]. (p. 91-111)

S2850   IOWA
Department of Public Safety

S2850-1   **IOWA UNIFORM CRIME REPORTS, 1983**
Annual.   Fall 1984.
2+v+368 p.
LC 80-645121.
SRI/MF/complete

Annual report on Iowa crimes and arrests, by offense, 1983 with summary trends from 1977. Includes data by county, reporting agency, suburban and nonsuburban cities, and rural areas, and by offender age, race/ethnicity, and sex. Also includes law enforcement employment, and assaults on officers.

Report focuses on 8 Index offenses: murder, rape, robbery, aggravated assault, burglary, larceny, motor vehicle theft, and arson. Arrests are also shown for non-Index offenses.

Data are from State and local law enforcement agency reports submitted under the Uniform Crime Reporting Program.

Contains listings of contents, tables, and charts (p. i-v); introduction and methodology (p. 1-9); State level analysis of reported crimes, with 43 charts described below (p. 12-44); and computer printout data from local reporting jurisdictions, with 69 tables also described below (p. 47-368).

This is the 7th annual report.

Availability: Iowa Department of Public Safety, Research and Development Bureau, Wallace State Office Bldg., Des Moines IA 50319, †; SRI/MF/complete.

CHARTS AND TABLES:

[Unless otherwise noted, data are shown for 1983. Data by race are usually shown for white, black, Indian, and other.]

S2850-1.1: Part I: State Level Analysis of Reported Crimes

[Data on Index offenses and rates are shown for 1977-83.]

a. Index offenses and rates, for total, violent, and property crimes; and stolen property value by type of property, including farm-related theft. Charts 1-9. (p. 13-19)

b. Murder: offenses and rates; victims and offenders by age, sex, and race; and offenses by victim-offender relationship, whether multiple or single victim and offender, weapon, circumstance, and urban-rural location. Charts 10-22. (p. 21-28)

c. Rape, robbery, and aggravated assault offenses and rates; robberies by weapon and type of location; and aggravated assaults by weapon. Charts 23-31. (p. 30-35)

d. Burglary, larceny, and motor vehicle theft offenses and rates; burglaries by day and night residence and nonresidence occurrence, and by type of entry; larcenies by type; and motor vehicle thefts by type of vehicle. Charts 32-41. (p. 37-42)

e. Arson offenses, 1980-83; and arsons by type of structure, 1983. Charts 42-43. (p. 43-44)

S2850–1.2: Part II: Data from Local Reporting Agencies

[Arson is classified as an Index offense. However, in order to maintain comparability with prior years, arson data are presented in tables for non-Index offenses.

Data by reporting agency are shown for individual police depts and sheriffs offices by county, arranged by district. Data by population category include city and/or city population size groups (with totals for suburban and nonsuburban city size groups), aggregate or specific suburban and rural areas, and suburban sheriffs and universities. Some tables also include population totals.]

a. Crimes and rates, and percent of offenses cleared by total and juvenile arrests, by reporting agency and population category; crimes by month; and offenses by circumstance; all by offense. Tables 1–6. (p. 47–93)

b. Value of property stolen by offense and detailed circumstance; and value of stolen and recovered property, by type. Tables 7–8. (p. 94–95)

c. Farm-related thefts and value of farm property stolen and recovered, by property type and population category; arson offenses, clearances by total and juvenile arrests, number of vacant structures involved, and value of property damage, all by type of structure; and arson offenses by time of day. Tables 9–10. (p. 96–99)

d. Arrests and arrest rates by reporting agency and population category; arrests by month; and arrests by age, sex, and race, for total, adult, and juvenile offenders, with detail for aggregate city, suburban, and rural areas; all by Index and non-Index offense, with detail for adult and juvenile drug-related arrests by substance involved and population category. Tables 11–64. (p. 100–348)

e. Law enforcement disposition of juvenile cases; police employment, employees per 1,000 population, and crimes per employee, for officer and civilian employees; total Index and non-Index arrests per officer; and assaults on police by weapon, assignment, activity, time of day, and injury status, with assaults cleared and officers killed; mostly by population category. Tables 65–69. (p. 349–368)

S2860
Department of Revenue

IOWA

S2860–1   IOWA RETAIL SALES AND USE TAX REPORT
Quarterly, with annual summary. Approx. 135 p.
LC 75-648610.
SRI/MF/complete

Quarterly report, with annual fiscal year summary, presenting data on Iowa retail sales and use taxes, by county, town, selected cities, size of computed tax due and gross sales, and kind of business. Types of use tax are motor vehicle/trailer, retailers, hotel/motel, and consumer use.

Data are from business tax returns filed with Iowa Dept of Revenue. Report is issued 7–14 months after period of coverage.

Contains contents listing, foreword, and glossary; and narrative review, with 16 quarterly tables, listed below. Annual summary for FY84 accompanied the 1st quarter 1984 report.

Availability: Iowa Department of Revenue, Research and Management Services Division, Hoover State Office Bldg., 1305 E. Walnut St., Des Moines IA 50319, †; SRI/MF/complete.

Issues reviewed during 1985: 3rd Qtr. 1983–4th Qtr. 1984 (D); and annual summary for FY84.

QUARTERLY TABLES:
[Unless otherwise noted, data are shown for quarter of coverage.]

SUMMARY TABLES
[Tables [1], [4-5], and [8] also show number of businesses.]

[1] Taxable sales tax, by business group [shows computed tax for current quarter and same quarter of preceding year].

[2] Number of returns filed, taxable retail sales, and computed tax, by county.

[3] Computed tax, by population [size] group [of cities and towns, and for rural areas].

[4] Retail sales tax collection, by [size of] computed tax due.

[5] Gross sales and computed tax, by size of gross sales.

[6] Retailers use tax, by business group [number of returns and computed tax].

[7] Comparison of use taxes [number of returns and computed tax value for retailers, motor vehicle registrations, and consumers, for current quarter and same quarter of preceding year].

[8] Retailers use tax collection report, by [size of] computed tax due.

[9] Local option hotel/motel tax [collected and rate, by jurisdiction].

RETAIL SALES AND USE TAXES
[All tables show computed tax. Tables [10-12] and [14] also show number of businesses.]

[10] Retail sales tax [and taxable sales], by county and town.

[11] Retail sales tax by county and selected cities, by business class.

[12] Retail [taxable] sales, by [SIC 3-digit] business classification.

[13] Use tax on motor vehicles/trailers [number of units], by county.

[14] Retailers use tax [and taxable sales], by business classification.

[15-16] Consumer use tax [and number of returns], by [major] business classification and by county.

S2860–2   IOWA CORPORATION INCOME AND FRANCHISE TAX REPORT, Returns Filed in 1984
Annual. [1985.] 50 p.
LC 85-641664.
SRI/MF/complete, current & previous year reports

Annual report on Iowa income taxes paid by corporations, and franchise taxes paid by financial institutions, based on returns filed in 1984. Includes data on returns filed, taxable income, and taxes paid, by industry division, income bracket, residency status, and county.

Contains contents and table listing, and introduction (3 p.); corporate and franchise tax narrative sections, with 9 summary tables (p. 3-24); and statistical appendix, with 16 tables (p. 27-50).

Previous report, for 1983, was also reviewed in SRI during 1985, and is also available on SRI microfiche under S2860-2 [Annual. [1984.] 56 p. †]. Previous report is substantially similar in content and format, but also includes data on corporate tax abatements.

Availability: Iowa Department of Revenue, Research and Management Services Division, Hoover State Office Bldg., 1305 E. Walnut St., Des Moines IA 50319, †; SRI/MF/complete.

S2860–3   1983 IOWA INDIVIDUAL INCOME TAX Annual Statistical Report: Returns Filed in 1984
Annual. [1985.] 51 p.
LC 81-643714.
SRI/MF/complete, current & previous year reports

Annual report on 1983 Iowa individual income tax returns, including data on filings, credits, deductions, adjusted gross and taxable income, withholdings, and taxes paid. Data are shown by income bracket and by county. Also includes data on voluntary political campaign fund checkoffs, and school district tax surcharges.

Data are from individual income tax returns filed in 1984 with the Iowa Dept of Revenue.

Contains contents listing (2 p.); introduction, with text statistics on 1983 tax year income tax law changes and rates (p. 1-3); 4 charts and 8 summary tables, with accompanying narrative (p. 3-17); and statistical appendix, with glossary and 31 detailed tables (p. 18-51). All tables are listed below.

Previous report, covering 1982 tax returns, was also reviewed during 1985 and is also available on SRI microfiche under this number [Annual. [1984.] 46 p. †]. For description of report covering 1981 returns, see SRI 1983 Annual under this number.

Availability: Iowa Department of Revenue, Research and Management Services Division, Hoover State Office Bldg., 1305 E. Walnut St., Des Moines IA 50319, †; SRI/MF/complete.

TABLES:

[Data are for 1983 tax returns filed in 1984, unless otherwise noted.]

S2860–3.1: Summary Tables

[Data by filing status are for single head of household/surviving spouse, and married joint and separate.]

[1] Individual income tax abatements [number of returns, tax, penalty, and interest], 1984. (p. 3)

[2-3] [Individual income tax returns and computed tax, by filing status, 1981-83] (p. 5)

[4] Adjusted gross income (AGI) summary [returns, AGI, and tax paid, by AGI bracket]. (p. 6)

[5] [AGI, tax, and incidence (percent of AGI paid in State income tax), by AGI bracket, 1982 and/or 1983.] (p. 12)

[6] Method of payment. (p. 13)

[7] Iowa fish and game protection fund total returns, [eligibles, participants, and contributions], by filing status. (p. 15)

[8] Income tax [political] checkoff by filing status [number of filers, eligibles, participants, Democrats, Republicans, and split tickets]. (p. 16)

S2860–3.2: Appendix Tables

[Tables 1-28 include number of returns. Tables 1-10 also show AGI, net taxable income, personal and dependent credits, and, as applicable, tax paid.]

1-3. Total, pay, and no-pay returns [by AGI bracket]. (p. 19-21)

4-9. Single, married joint, and married separate: pay and no-pay returns [by AGI bracket]. (p. 22-27)

10. Total pay/no-pay returns, by county. (p. 28-29)

11. Total pay/no-pay returns, by type of payment [total withholding, estimated and additional payments, out-of-State and motor fuel credit, and refunds, by AGI bracket]. (p. 30)

12-23. Total, pay, no-pay, single, married joint, and married separate returns, by itemized and standard deduction [AGI, taxable income, Federal tax and itemized or standard deduction, and tax paid, by AGI bracket]. (p. 31-42)

24-26. Total, pay, and no-pay returns [AGI, taxable income, Federal tax deduction, personal and dependent credits, and tax paid, by taxable income bracket]. (p. 43-45)

27-28. Total pay/no-pay returns, by credit and Federal tax payment [includes child care, out-of-State, and motor fuel credits; political contribution; Federal tax refunds and deductions; AGI; and tax paid; all by AGI bracket]. (p. 46-47)

29-30. Iowa election campaign fund checkoff, all filers [eligibles, participants, Democrats, Republicans, and split tickets], by county and AGI brackets. (p. 48-50)

31. School district surtax collections [by school district]. (p. 51)

S2865   IOWA
Office of the Secretary of State

S2865–1   SUMMARY OF OFFICIAL CANVASS OF VOTES CAST in Iowa General Election, Nov. 6, 1984
Biennial. [1984.]
11 p. no paging.
SRI/MF/complete

Biennial report presenting results of the Iowa general election held Nov. 6, 1984. Shows voting for President and Vice President; U.S. and State senators and representatives; judges; and 2 State constitutional amendments. Also includes results for special election held for State senator, Nov. 8, 1983. Data are shown by county and/or district. Also shows party affiliation of candidates.

Previous report, covering 1982 election, is described in SRI 1983 Annual under this number.

Availability: Iowa Office of the Secretary of State, State Capitol Bldg., 10th and Grand, Des Moines IA 50319, ‡; SRI/MF/complete.

S2880   IOWA
Department of Transportation

S2880–1   1983 IOWA ACCIDENT FACTS
Annual. Jan. 1985.
iv+59 p.+foldouts.
LC 82-647424.
SRI/MF/complete

Annual report on Iowa traffic accidents, fatalities, and injuries, by accident and vehicle type, location, time, and other circumstances; and driver and victim characteristics; 1983, with trends from 1962 and summary comparisons to U.S.

Also includes data on vehicle miles of travel; licensed drivers and vehicle registrations; and accident drug and alcohol involvement, seat belt and motorcycle helmet use, and motor vehicle defects.

Data are from reports filed by law enforcement agencies.

Contains foreword, contents listing, and glossary (p. i-iv); and 4 charts and 207 tables (p. 1-59).

Availability: Iowa Department of Transportation, Motor Vehicle Division, Driver Services Office, Lucas State Office Bldg., Des Moines IA 50319, †; SRI/MF/complete.

S2885   IOWA
Treasurer

S2885–1   REPORT OF THE TREASURER OF STATE, IOWA for the Fiscal Year July 1, 1983-June 30, 1984
Annual. [1985.] 68 p.
LC 80-642423.
SRI/MF/complete

Annual financial report of the Iowa State treasurer, for FY84, presenting receipts/credits, disbursements, and balances, for general and special revenue, capital project, debt service, enterprise, internal service, expendable and nonexpendable trust, pension trust, and agency funds, by detailed fund and account.

Also includes data on revenues by source, FY80-84; appropriations by government function, FY82-85; and bond holdings, and public employees' retirement loan program receipts and expenditures, FY84.

Contains transmittal letter (p. 1); and 14 financial schedules and statements (p. 3-68).

Report is issued as Part II of 2 parts comprising the State Treasurer's biennial report for the biennium ending June 30, 1984. Part I is described in SRI 1984 Annual, under this number.

Availability: Iowa Treasurer, State Capitol Bldg., 10th and Grand, Des Moines IA 50319, †; SRI/MF/complete.

S2900   KANSAS
Department of Administration

S2900–1   STATE OF KANSAS DEPARTMENT OF ADMINISTRATION FINANCIAL REPORT for Period July 1, 1983-June 30, 1984
Annual. 2 volumes.
For individual publication data, see below.
LC 78-642377.
SRI/MF/complete

Annual report on financial condition of Kansas State government, FY84, with comparisons to FY83. Presents financial data for the following funds: general; Federal revenue sharing; special revenue; highway; capital projects; enterprise; intragovernmental service; trust and agency; clearing/rcfund/suspense; and payroll clearing.

Also includes data on bond indebtedness, tax balances by type and county, property valuations, and legislative appropriation limitations.

Data are based on State records.

Report is published in 2 volumes, individually described below. This is the 31st annual report.

Availability: Kansas Department of Administration, Accounts and Reports Division, State Office Bldg., Topeka KS 66612-1574, †; SRI/MF/complete.

S2900–1.1: Volume I
[Annual. Oct. 5, 1984. xxiv+115 p. SRI/MF/complete.]

Presents assets and liabilities, balances, revenues by source, and expenditures by object, for combined funds and by fund type.

Also includes data on revenues by tax type; employment security fund revenues and expenditures; State and Federal assistance to local areas; Federal grants, by purpose; and bonded indebtedness.

Contains contents listing (p. iii); highlights, with 7 charts and 13 tables (p. v-xxiv); 13 sections with 43 exhibits and schedules, and accompanying notes (p. 1-112); and directory to Volume II (p. 115).

S2900–1.2: Volume II

[Annual. Oct. 5, 1984. p. 117-270+4 p. SRI/MF/complete.]

Presents detailed appropriation accounts for 3 funds, fund balances for 8 funds, and revenue statements for 10 funds, by governmental function, agency, and appropriation or fund title.

Also includes tax account balances for 3 capital project building funds; property and motor vehicle tax balances, and property valuations, tax levies, and estimated motor vehicle tax revenues for 2 building funds, all by county; legislative appropriation limitation compared to expenditures, by agency and fund title; and receipts from fees and licenses by type, fines/forfeitures/penalties, interest on idle funds, and sales tax, by county.

Contains contents listing (p. 117); 11 schedules and statements (p. 118-270); and cross-reference index (3 p.).

S2915   KANSAS
Board of
Agriculture

S2915–1   66TH BIENNIAL REPORT AND FARM FACTS, Kansas

Biennial. [1984.] 261 p.
ISSN 0196-0954.
LC sn 85-19280.
SRI/MF/complete

Biennial report on Kansas agricultural production, marketing, and finances, 1982-83, with some data for 1984 and selected trends from 1867. Data generally are shown by commodity and/or county and district, with some comparisons to selected States or U.S.

Generally covers production, prices, disposition, value, and, as applicable, acreage, yield, or inventory, for field crop, fruit, livestock, dairy, and poultry sectors.

Also includes data for Kansas on meat/poultry plant inspection activity; reservoir capacity and water in storage; water appropriation applications; farms and farm acreage; fertilizer use; weather; grain storage capacity and stocks; irrigation; livestock inshipments by State of origin; farm income, production expenses, assets and debts, labor, and wage rates; and cropland and pastureland values and rents.

Also includes data on agricultural export value of various commodities for leading States; and U.S. parity prices.

Data are compiled by the Kansas Crop and Livestock Reporting Service in cooperation with USDA.

Contains introduction, contents listing, highlights, and division reports, with 2 maps and 5 tables (p. 2-93); "Farm Facts" section, with 17 maps, 3 charts, and 130 tables (p. 94-247); and index (p. 248-261).

Previous reports were issued annually. For description of 65th report, issued in 1982, see SRI 1982 Annual, under this number.

Availability: Kansas Crop and Livestock Reporting Service, 109 S.W. Ninth St., Topeka KS 66612-1280, †; SRI/MF/complete.

S2925   KANSAS
Office of the
Attorney General

S2925–1   CRIME IN KANSAS, 1984: Uniform Crime Report

Annual. Apr. 15, 1985.
xix+163 p.
LC 84-641010.
SRI/MF/complete

Annual report on Kansas crimes and arrests, by offense, 1984, with summary trends from 1974. Includes data by city, county, and reporting agency, and by offender age, sex, and race/ethnicity. Also includes law enforcement employment, and assaults on officers.

Report focuses on 8 Index offenses: murder/non-negligent manslaughter, rape, robbery, aggravated assault, burglary, larceny/theft, motor vehicle theft, and arson. Arrests are also shown for non-Index offenses.

Data are from State and local agency reports submitted under the Uniform Crime Reporting Program, and from the State Fire Marshal's Office.

Contains summary, and listings of contents, tables, and charts (p. iii-xix); introduction (p. 3-5); 4 sections, with narrative summaries, and 29 charts and 54 tables described below (p. 9-155); and appendix, with glossary and statutory requirements (p. 159-163).

Availability: Kansas Office of the Attorney General, Investigation Bureau, Statistical Analysis Center, 1620 Tyler, Topeka KS 66612-1837, †; SRI/MF/complete.

TABLES AND CHARTS:

[Data are for 1984, unless otherwise noted. Data by city are shown for cities with over 10,000 population and balance of State. Data by race/ethnicity generally include white, black, American Indian, Asian, Hispanic, and non-Hispanic. Arson is often not included in data shown by Index crime.]

S2925–1.1: Index Offenses, Arson and Fires, and Arrests

INDEX OFFENSES

[A chart showing crime trends and projections, mostly 1975-85, is repeated for total, violent and property crimes, and each individual offense. Crime clocks, showing offense frequency, are also presented for total, violent, and property crimes and most offense categories. Other data are described below.]

a. Crimes and/or crime rates and value of stolen and recovered property, by offense and/or property type, city, and reporting agency; offenses and clearances, by of-

fense, 1974-84; and clearances by city and offense. 5 charts and tables 1-11. (p. 10-55)

b. Murder/non-negligent manslaughter offenses by month, type of weapon, victim-offender relationship, offense circumstances, and victim and offender age, sex, and race/ethnicity. 2 charts and tables 12-17. (p. 59-63)

c. Rapes, by month, time of day, victim and offender age and race/ethnicity, victim-offender relationship, type of weapon, and location; robberies and value of stolen property, by type of location and city; and distribution of robberies and aggravated assaults by type of weapon used. 9 charts and tables 18-26. (p. 66-79)

d. Burglary residence and nonresidence offenses and stolen property value, by day or night occurrence and city; distribution of burglaries by type of entry; larceny offenses and stolen property value, by larceny type and city; motor vehicle theft distribution by type of vehicle (autos, trucks, other); and vehicles recovered locally and elsewhere, by city. 6 charts and tables 27-31. (p. 82-91)

ARSON AND FIRES

e. Arson offenses and value of property loss, by city and/or month, and clearances, all by property type, including uninhabited/abandoned structures. 2 charts and tables 32-34. (p. 94-96)

f. Fires: total and incendiary/suspicious fires by type (structure, vehicle, grass/refuse and/or other), and firefighter and citizen injuries and fatalities, with selected detail by month; incendiary and suspicious fires by property type, day of week, and time of day; and value of property loss from incendiary/suspicious fires, by property type. Tables 35-40. (p. 97-100)

ARRESTS

g. Crime index arrests, 1975-85, with detail by offense, 1974-84; arrests by juvenile or adult status, sex, race/ethnicity, age, and reporting agency, all by Index and non-Index offense; and juvenile dispositions by type. 2 charts and tables 41-48. (p. 104-133)

S2925–1.2: Police Assaults and Employment

ASSAULTS

a. Assaults on officers: by weapon, injury status, circumstance, type of assignment, and time of day, with various cross-tabulations, and summary trends from 1975. 3 charts and tables 49-52. (p. 138-141)

EMPLOYMENT

b. Police and sheriff's office sworn officers and civilian personnel, by sex, race/ethnicity, education, and length of service (total and with agency), and average age; and sworn and civilian personnel by sex, by reporting agency arranged by county. Tables 53-54. (p. 146-155)

S2940   KANSAS
Department of Corrections

S2940–1   STATISTICAL PROFILE: FY84 OFFENDER POPULATION of the Kansas Department of Corrections
Annual.   Oct. 31, 1984.
viii+62 p.
SRI/MF/complete

Annual report on corrections in Kansas, presenting data on prison and parolee population, including inmate admissions, releases, escapes, deaths, and sentence length; and inmate and parolee demographic characteristics, previous convictions and incarcerations, and commitment offense category; FY84, with trends from FY76. Some data are shown by institution and county.

Also includes data on facility capacity outlook to 1985; prisoner employment and work release programs; alcohol and drug use prior to admission; and interstate compact parole and probation transfers, by State.

Contains contents and table listing, and preface with 1 chart and 1 table (p. ii-viii); and narrative report, interspersed with 7 charts, and 21 tables (p. 1-62).

Data in this report also appear as a statistical section of State Dept of Corrections' *Annual Report,* not covered in SRI.

Availability: Kansas Department of Corrections, Planning, Research, Evaluation and Accreditation Unit, Jayhawk Towers, 700 Jackson, Topeka KS 66603, †; SRI/MF/complete.

S2945   KANSAS
Department of Education

S2945–1   ANNUAL STATISTICAL REPORT, 1983/84, Kansas State Department of Education
Annual.   [1985.]   429 p.
LC 80-640571.
SRI/MF/complete

Annual report, for 1983/84, on Kansas public schools, covering finances, students, personnel, facilities, and transportation services. Presents enrollment and financial data by school district and county. Also includes enrollment and operating data for nonpublic schools. Data are compiled from school district annual reports.

Contains the following 2 sections, each beginning with a contents listing:

Part 1. Statistical tables and charts for the State. 4 charts, generally showing trends from 1971/72; and 29 tables listed below. (p. 1-46)

Part 2. Detailed listings. 2 extended tables showing: nonpublic school teachers, enrollment (as of Sept. 15, 1983), and average daily attendance (ADA) by school level, all by school; and public school enrollment, graduates, dropouts by sex, summer school enrollment and staff by school level, expenditures by object and revenues by source for funds covered in Part 1, and pupil transportation service, all by school district arranged by county, 1983/84. (p. 47-429)

Availability: Kansas Department of Education, Kansas State Education Bldg., 120 E. Tenth St., Topeka KS 66612, †; SRI/MF/complete.

STATE TABLES:
[Tables show data for public schools, 1983/84, unless otherwise noted.]

S2945–1.1: Part 1: Statistical Tables and Charts

SCHOOLS AND STUDENTS

1. Number of accredited schools [by level], 1979/80-1983/84. (p. 3)

2. Fall enrollment, ADA, and average daily membership [all by school level]. (p. 3)

3. High school graduates and dropouts [by sex]. (p. 3)

SUMMARY FINANCES
[Expenditure objects are classified as series 100-1400.]

4. Financial statement—general fund [revenue from local, county, State, and Federal sources; total expenditures; and balances]. (p. 4)

5. General fund expenditures by category [series], 1974/75-1983/84. (p. 6)

6. Estimated cost of vandalism. (p. 8)

7-8. Estimated operational costs and cost per pupil in ADA, 100-800 series; and total expenditures 100-1400 series (excluding 1100 and 1300 series); year ending June 30, 1984. (p. 8)

9. General fund expenditures, each series expressed as a percent of year's total, 100-1400 series (excluding 1300 series), 1978/79-1983/84. (p. 10)

10. General fund salaries for administration and instruction, 1980/81-1983/84. (p. 10)

SPECIAL FUNDS

11-21. Special assessment, capital outlay, vocational education, transportation, special education, co-op special education, driver training, food service, adult education, adult supplementary education, and teacher retirement funds [showing for each, opening and closing balances, receipts, and expenditures]. (p. 12-16)

PERSONNEL AND OPERATING DATA

22. Personnel data [certified and noncertified, by position]. (p. 17-18)

23-24. Pupil transportation services and costs. (p. 19-21)

25. School facilities [schools and classrooms in use and abandoned]. (p. 22)

26. Summer school [enrollment, ADA, staff, and expenditures], 1984. (p. 22)

27. Nonpublic schools [teachers and ADA, by school level; graduates and dropouts by sex; and enrollment by grade]. (p. 23-24)

SCHOOL DISTRICTS

[28-29] [State equalization and transportation aid payments; and enrollment (Sept. 1983), income tax rebates, and rebate per pupil; by school district arranged by county.] (p. 25-46)

S2975   KANSAS
Department of Health and Environment

S2975–1   ANNUAL SUMMARY OF VITAL STATISTICS, Kansas, 1983
Annual.   Nov. 1984.
vii+123 p.
ISSN 0364-2372.
LC 76-647679.
SRI/MF/complete

Annual report on Kansas vital statistics, covering births, deaths by cause, population growth and density, abortions, marriages, and divorces and annulments, 1983, with trends from 1953. Includes data by Health Service Area (HSA), county, city, age, race, and sex. Most data are from State vital statistics and health records.

Contents:

a. Listings of contents, tables, and charts; and highlights with 1 chart, introduction, methodology, and definitions. (p. iii-vii, 1-12)

b. Report narrative and appendix, with 36 interspersed numbered tables, listed below; and additional illustrative charts, maps, and text data, including population density by county (p. 24), births by mother's race and child's sex and by birth order (p. 29), abortion trends (p. 37), and fetal deaths by mother's age (p. 39). (p. 14-119)

c. Index of tables and charts. (p. 122-123)

Monthly updated data on births, deaths, diseases, and changes in marital status are provided in *Monthly Summary of Vital Statistics,* not covered by SRI. Copies are available from the Division of Health Resources of the Bureau of Registration and Health Statistics.

Availability: Kansas Department of Health and Environment, Registration and Health Statistics Bureau, Forbes Field, Topeka KS 66620, †; SRI/MF/complete.

TABLES:
[Tables show data for Kansas, 1983, unless otherwise noted.]

S2975–1.1: General Data

SUMMARY

1-2. Vital events and percent change; and by number, rate, and ratio, [various years] 1973-83. (p. 14-16)

3. Population, natural increase, and net migration, 1954-83. (p. 22)

BIRTHS, AND FETAL AND INFANT DEATHS

4. Live births by age group of mother, by selected characteristics [birth weight, prematurity, and illegitimacy]. (p. 32)

5. Perinatal period III mortality [fetal and hebdomadal deaths], selected years 1953-83. (p. 42)

6. Infant deaths by cause of death and age group of infant. (p. 45)

DEATHS

7-8. Deaths by race [including American Indians] and sex; and selected causes of death; by age group and average age at death. (p. 53-54)

9-10. Ten leading causes of death: by sex, by number, rate, and average age at death; and by sex and race [including American Indians]. (p. 56-57)

11. Selected leading causes of death by number and rate, Kansas and U.S. (p. 58)

12. Heart disease deaths by age group and sex. (p. 62)

13. Malignant neoplasm deaths by site of lesion, age group, and sex. (p. 64)

14-16. Cerebrovascular disease, selected chronic disease, and accidental deaths, by [type], age group, and sex. (p. 65-68)

17. Ten leading causes of death: underlying cause by nonunderlying cause. (p. 72)

MARRIAGES, DIVORCES, AND ANNULMENTS

18-19. Marriages by age group and premarital status of bride and groom. (p. 77-78)

20. Divorces and annulments by duration of marriage in years. (p. 83)

21. Divorces and annulments by number and percent by number of minor children. (p. 84)

S2975–1.2: Appendix: Geographical Divisions

HSA DATA

22-23. Vital statistics [summary], and selected causes of death, by HSA. (p. 88-89)

COUNTY DATA

[Unless otherwise noted, data are shown by county of residence.]

24-25. Population, and live births by number and rate, 1979-83. (p. 90-93)

26-27. Live and out-of-wedlock births, by age group of mother. (p. 94-97)

28. Induced abortions by age group of patient. (p. 98-99)

29. Perinatal period III deaths. (p. 100-102)

30. Infant deaths by component [and infant age]. (p. 103-104)

31. Deaths by number and rate, 1979-83. (p. 105-106)

32. Deaths by age group and average age at death. (p. 107-109)

33. 20 leading causes of death. (p. 110-113)

34-35. Marriages by county of marriage and divorces/annulments by county of action, by number and rate, 1979-83. (p. 114-117)

CITY DATA

36. Population, live births, and total deaths by city of residence, 1982-83. (p. 118-119)

S2985   KANSAS
Department of
Human Resources

S2985–1   KANSAS ANNUAL
PLANNING INFORMATION
REPORT, 1985
Annual. July 1985. 3+51 p.
Rpt. Series No. 17.
SRI/MF/complete

Annual planning report, for 1985, identifying Kansas population groups most in need of employment services. Includes data on population and labor force characteristics, personal income, employment by industry division, job openings by occupation, and characteristics of insured unemployed, by county and service delivery area (SDA), various periods 1979-85. Also includes data on top 40 occupations ranked by projected employment growth.

Most data are from Kansas Dept of Human Resources and U.S. Census Bureau.

Contains preface and contents listing (2 p.); 25 tables interspersed with brief narrative (p. 1-44); and appendix with glossary and 1 table (p. 45-51).

All tables are described below.

Availability: Kansas Department of Human Resources, Employment and Training Division, Research and Analysis Section, 401 Topeka Ave., Topeka KS 66603, †; SRI/MF/complete.

TABLES:
[Data are shown for Kansas, by county and/or SDA, unless otherwise noted.]

a. Population, with detail by sex, age, and race/ethnicity (including Hispanic, American Indian, and Hawaiian/Pacific Islander); high school dropouts, handicapped persons, and veterans; total families, families with children (with detail for married couples, female and male householders, and female householders below poverty level), and families below poverty level; per capita personal income; and U.S. urban CPI by major item; various years 1979-84. 10 tables. (p. 1-19)

b. Labor force by employment status, sex, and race/ethnicity (including Hispanic), and participation rate; farm employment, and non-farm wage/salary employment by industry division; characteristics of insured unemployed; workers involved in labor-management disputes; job openings by occupational group; poverty level guidelines; and economically disadvantaged population, with detail by age group; various periods 1980-87. 15 tables. (p. 20-44)

c. Top 40 occupations ranked by share of total projected employment growth, with wage range, minorities and females as percent of total employment, and demand summary; all shown for total State only, 1982-95 period. 1 table. (p. 48-50)

S2990   KANSAS
Department of
Insurance

S2990–1   ONE HUNDRED FIFTEENTH
ANNUAL REPORT OF THE
KANSAS INSURANCE
DEPARTMENT, for Year
Ending Dec. 31, 1984
Annual. [1985.]   3+120 p.
SRI/MF/complete

Annual report on Kansas insurance industry financial condition and underwriting activity, by company and type of insurance, 1984. Covers assets, liabilities, surplus/capital, income, disbursements, net gain, dividends, insurance written and in force, premiums earned or written, claims/benefits or losses paid, losses incurred, loss ratios, and other operating ratios, for companies with headquarters in Kansas and elsewhere.

Data are shown, as applicable, for fraternal and other life insurance companies, with detail for accident/health insurance; hospital and medical service corporations and HMOs; and fire/casualty companies.

Also includes data on Insurance Dept receipts, company admissions, agent/broker certifica-

tions, consumer complaints and assistance, and rate reviews; insurance company security deposits; and underwriting activities of workers compensation assigned risk and State automobile insurance plans.

Data are compiled from Insurance Dept internal records and annual statements filed by individual insurers.

Contains contents listing (1 p.); and report, with narrative and 37 tables (p. 1-120).

Availability: Kansas Department of Insurance, 420 S.W. Ninth St., Topeka KS 66612, Kansas residents †, others $2.75; SRI/MF/complete.

S3000   KANSAS
State
Library

S3000–1   KANSAS PUBLIC LIBRARY
STATISTICS, 1984
Annual. [1985.]
2+iii+138 p.
LC 75-613256.
SRI/MF/complete

Annual report, for 1984, on Kansas public library and library system holdings, population served, staff, and finances, by library and by regional library system. Data are from 312 responses to questionnaires mailed to all 316 public libraries in the State.

Contains contents listing (2 p.); introduction, with summary text data (p. i-iii); directories of public libraries, regional systems of cooperating libraries, State library personnel, and advisory commission members (p. 1-19); and 14 tables, listed below (p. 21-138).

Availability: Kansas State Library, State Capitol, 3rd Floor, Topeka KS 66612, $10.00; SRI/MF/complete.

TABLES:
[All data are for Kansas, 1984. Tables [1-6] show data by library, grouped within 7 regional library systems; tables [7-14] show data by library system only. Tables [1-6] and [9] include data on population served.]

INDIVIDUAL LIBRARIES

[1] Support [from local taxes, Federal revenue sharing, library system grants, State aid, and other]. (p. 21-35)

[2] Expenditures [on books, periodicals, nonbook materials, salaries, and other operations; and total budget for next year]. (p. 36-50)

[3-4] Resources [weekly hours and volumes owned and added; periodical subscriptions; record, reference, art print, and film holdings; number of regular borrowers; and interlibrary loan requests received]. (p. 51-81)

[5] Circulation [adult, juvenile, and other circulation, and interlibrary loans sent]. (p. 82-96)

[6] Personnel [positions at each library, hourly wage, weekly hours, and educational attainment]. (p. 97-126)

LIBRARY SYSTEMS

[7] Support [funds from system tax, State/Federal aid, and other]. (p. 127)

[8] Expenditures [by object]. (p. 128-129)

[9] Types and number of member libraries [public libraries in counties levying system tax; contracting, club, school, and college/university libraries; service outlets; and nonparticipating libraries]. (p. 130)

[10] Resources [total and added volumes; and reference, large-print, periodical, sound recording, art print, film, and slide holdings]. (p. 131)

[11] Circulation [by program; and total circulation and reference questions received]. (p. 132)

[12] Interlibrary loan [transactions]. (p. 133)

[13] Miscellaneous [Mail-a-Book and rotating book services, workshops, and beginning librarian salary]. (p. 134)

[14] Personnel [position titles, salaries, weekly hours, and educational requirements]. (p. 135-138)

S3030   KANSAS
Office of the Secretary of State

S3030-1   ELECTION STATISTICS, STATE OF KANSAS, 1984 Primary and General Elections
Biennial. [1985.] 145 p.
LC 61-63008.
SRI/MF/complete

Biennial report presenting results of Kansas primary and general elections held Aug. 7 and Nov. 6, 1984. Shows voting for President and Vice-President; U.S. and State senators and representatives; district judges and attorneys; State board of education; judicial retention; and questions on methods for selection of judges in 3 judicial districts. Data are shown by district and/or county. Also shows party affiliation of candidates.

Previous report, covering 1982 elections, is described in SRI 1983 Annual, under this number.

Availability: Kansas Office of the Secretary of State, Elections Division, State Capitol, 2nd Floor, Topeka KS 66612, †; SRI/MF/complete.

S3035   KANSAS
Supreme Court

S3035-1   ANNUAL REPORT OF THE COURTS of Kansas, FY84
Annual. Nov. 15, 1984.
5+139 p.
LC 79-644946.
SRI/MF/complete

Annual report, for FY84, on Kansas judicial system, including trial and appellate court caseloads and case dispositions. Covers district, supreme, and appeals courts. Includes trial court data by case type, judicial district, and county.

Trial court case types shown are criminal and civil, with some additional detail for domestic relations, traffic, driving while intoxicated, juvenile, probate, fish/game violations, small claims, adoption, mental illness treatment, and alcoholism treatment cases.

Also includes roster of judges; and data on case processing time.

Contains preface, map, and contents listing (4 p.); and report in 4 sections, with 23 tables (p. 1-139).

This is the 7th annual report.

Availability: Kansas Supreme Court, Judicial Center, Judicial Administration Office, 301 W. Tenth St., Topeka KS 66612, ‡; SRI/MF/complete.

S3040   KANSAS
Department of Transportation

S3040-1   KANSAS MOTOR VEHICLE TRAFFIC ACCIDENTS, 1984
Annual. July 25, 1985.
19 p. no paging+Summary 2 p. Oversized.
SRI/MF/complete, current & previous year reports

Annual report on Kansas traffic accidents, injuries, and fatalities, by vehicle and accident type, location, time, and other circumstances; and driver and victim age; 1984.

Also includes data on vehicle mileage, alcohol involvement in accidents (including blood alcohol levels), citations issued, and vehicle defects.

Report is a computer printout consisting of 12 tables. Issuing agency also publishes an annual summary of traffic accidents, including selected trends from 1981. Summary is also available on SRI microfiche under S3040-1.

Previous report, for 1983, was also reviewed by SRI during 1985, and is also available on SRI microfiche under S3040-1 [Annual. July 9, 1984. 20 p. no paging. †]. Previous report is substantially similar in format and content, but also includes data on use of vehicle safety devices.

An annual *Highway Safety Plan* report, including some accident statistics, is also published by the issuing agency, but is not covered in SRI.

Availability: Kansas Department of Transportation, Rural and Urban Development Bureau, Traffic Safety Section, State Office Bldg., Topeka KS 66612, †; SRI/MF/complete.

S3040-2   SCHOOL BUS LOADING AND UNLOADING SURVEY
Annual. [1985.] 28 p.
SRI/MF/complete

Annual report on children killed during school bus loading/unloading, 1983 and trends. Includes number of States reporting fatalities, and number of fatalities by detailed accident circumstances and by victim age and sex, mostly 1980-83, with selected 1983 data for 24 individual States and summary trends for 1970-83 period.

Data are compiled by Kansas Dept of Transportation from information supplied by State agencies.

Contains introduction and loading/unloading area diagram (p. 1-2); 14 tables (p. 3-16); brief descriptions of individual accidents (p. 17-22); 3 trend charts (p. 23-25); and summary (p. 26-27).

Report has been published since 1970. SRI coverage begins with edition presenting data through 1983.

Availability: Kansas Department of Transportation, Management Services-Safety Bureau, State Office Bldg., 7th Floor, Topeka KS 66612, ‡; SRI/MF/complete.

S3085   KENTUCKY
Department of Agriculture

S3085-1   KENTUCKY AGRICULTURAL STATISTICS, 1984-85
Annual. Sept. 1985. 118 p.
LC 50-63276.
SRI/MF/complete

Annual report on Kentucky agricultural production, marketing, and finances, 1983-84, with selected trends from 1970s or earlier. Data generally are shown by commodity and/or county and district, with some comparisons to other States and total U.S.

Report covers production, value, prices, and, as applicable, acreage, stocks, inventory, and disposition, for field crop, fruit, livestock, poultry, and dairy sectors.

Also includes data on weather; wool production; off-farm grain storage capacity; tobacco production quotas; farm income and production expenses; prices paid by farmers; fertilizer use and sales; farms and acreage; agricultural exports; production rankings and farm value and rents, by selected State; U.S. mink production; and Census of Agriculture summary findings.

Report is prepared by the Kentucky Crop and Livestock Reporting Service.

Contains contents listing, and foreword with 1 chart (p. 2-4); 7 sections, with narrative summaries, 20 maps, 5 charts, and 88 tables (p. 6-115); and directory of agricultural officials and list of reports available from Crop and Livestock Reporting Service (p. 116-118).

Availability: Kentucky Crop and Livestock Reporting Service, PO Box 1120, Louisville KY 40201, †; SRI/MF/complete.

S3095   KENTUCKY
Department of Banking and Securities

S3095-1   ANNUAL REPORT OF THE COMMISSIONER OF BANKING AND SECURITIES, Division of Banking of the Commonwealth of Kentucky
Annual.

SRI now covers this publication under S3121-1.

S3103   KENTUCKY
Council of Economic Advisors

S3103–2   KENTUCKY ECONOMY:
             Review and Perspective
             Quarterly.

SRI now covers this publication under U7138-1.

S3104   KENTUCKY
Department of Economic Development

S3104–1   1985 KENTUCKY
             ECONOMIC STATISTICS
             Annual.   1985.   iv+126 p.
             SRI/MF/complete

Annual compilation of detailed demographic and socioeconomic statistics for Kentucky. Data are shown primarily for 1980-83, with selected population trends from 1930 and projections to 2020.

Report is designed to present a socioeconomic overview of the State by geographic area, including area development district, county, MSA, and city. Various socioeconomic breakdowns are shown, as applicable, for most topics. These breakdowns include income, industry, commodity, race, urban-rural status, age, and sex. Comparisons to total U.S. are also occasionally included.

Most data are from Federal and State agencies. Data sources appear beneath each table.

Contains contents and table listing (p. iii-iv); 4 maps and 49 tables, arranged in 5 sections, described below (p. 1-119); and definitions and index (p. 121-126).

This is the 21st edition.

Availability: Kentucky Department of Economic Development, Research and Planning Division, Capital Plaza Tower, Frankfort KY 40601, $4.00+$1.00 postage and handling; SRI/MF/complete.

TABLE SECTIONS:

S3104–1.1: State Data

(p. 3-13) Contains 15 tables. Includes population from 1930; housing construction; nonresidential construction value; U.S. CPI and poverty thresholds; unemployment rate; households and families; persons and families below poverty level; total and per capita personal income; nonfarm employment; manufacturing hours, earnings, production, value added, and shipment value; farm income; and mineral production and value.

S3104–1.2: Area Development District Data

(p. 17-21) Contains 5 tables. Includes land area; population and change components; population projected to 2020; labor force, farm and nonfarm employment, and unemployment; and total and per capita personal income.

S3104–1.3: County Data

(p. 25-96) Contains 21 tables. Includes land area and county seat; population and change components; percent individuals and families below poverty level; households, and average household size; persons in group quarters; population projected to 2020; labor force, farm and nonfarm employment, and unemployment; and covered wages and manufacturing employment.

Also includes total and per capita personal income; median family income for nonmetro counties; banks and deposits; motor vehicle registrations; and individual income tax and sales tax receipts, and property assessments.

S3104–1.4: MSA and City Data

(p. 100-119) Contains 8 tables. Includes population and change components, by MSA and component county; banks and deposits, median family income, and total and per capita personal income, all by MSA; and population, households, average household size, and persons in group quarters, by city.

S3104–2   COMMUTING IN
             KENTUCKY
             Monograph.   1984.
             vi+213 p.+foldout.
             SRI/MF/complete

Report presenting 1980 census data on commuting patterns in Kentucky, covering points of origin and destination for Kentucky residents and for nonresidents employed in the State. Data are cross-tabulated among counties of Kentucky and neighboring States.

Also includes number of Kentucky workers by means of transportation to work, by county, 1980.

Data are based on unpublished tabulations from Summary Tape File 4 of the 1980 Census of Population and Housing.

Contains preface and contents listing (p. iii-vi); 3 data sections, each with 1 extended table (p. 3-208); and methodology, definitions, and map (p. 211-213, and foldout).

Availability: Kentucky Department of Economic Development, Maps and Publications Office, 133 Holmes St., Frankfort KY 40601, $4.00; SRI/MF/complete.

S3105   KENTUCKY
Administrative Office of the Courts

S3105–1   KENTUCKY COURT OF
             JUSTICE, 1983-84 Annual
             Report
             Annual.   [1985.]   71 p.
             SRI/MF/complete

Annual report, for FY84, on Kentucky judicial system, including trial and appellate court cases and dispositions. Covers supreme, appeals, circuit, and district courts. Includes data on trial court cases by type and court location, with selected comparisons to FY83.

Case types shown include criminal, civil, domestic relations, probate, adoption/termination, mental health, workers compensation, traffic, small claims, juvenile, and other.

Also includes data on Judicial Retirement and Removal Commission cases and dispositions; judicial dept personnel, revenues, and expenditures; State law library reader services and staff attorney activities; pretrial services, including diversion, mediation, and interviewing activities; judicial caseloads; and economical litigation project and baseline dockets.

Contains contents listing (p. 5); and narrative report, interspersed with 9 charts and 20 tables (p. 8-71).

Availability: Kentucky Administrative Office of the Courts, 403 Wapping St., Frankfort KY 40601, †; SRI/MF/complete.

S3110   KENTUCKY
Department of Education

S3110–1   PROFILES OF KENTUCKY
             PUBLIC SCHOOLS, FY84
             Annual.   [1985.]   vii+140 p.
             LC 70-649005.
             SRI/MF/complete

Annual report presenting data for 17 indicators of public education quality in Kentucky, by school district and educational development region, 1983/84, with State trends from 1972/73.

Contents:

a. Foreword and contents listing. (p. v-vii)

b. Introduction and methodology. (p. 1-5)

c. 17 indicators, listed below, repeated as follows: State averages and trends, 1972/73-1983/84, with 17 charts and 1 table (p. 7-26); and by region and district, including deviations from State averages, 1983/84, with 1 map and 18 tables (p. 29-140).

This is the 17th edition of the report. Profiles of individual school districts, as well as annual reports on detailed public school finances, are also available from the issuing agency but are not covered by SRI.

Availability: Kentucky Department of Education, Administrative Services Office, Capital Plaza Tower, Frankfort KY 40601, †; SRI/MF/complete.

INDICATORS:

[1] Annual current expenses per pupil in ADA [average daily attendance].

[2-3] Average annual salaries for classroom teachers; and percent supplement for instructional salaries.

[4] Percent of instructional staff with rank II or higher [standard certificate and master's degree or equivalent].

[5] Percent of 9th graders completing high school.

[6] Percent of attendance.

[7] Local financial index [ratio of local revenue per pupil to assessed value per pupil].

[8-9] Cost per pupil for educational materials and for instruction.

[10] Percent of instructional staff with less than rank III [not fully qualified].

[11] Pupil/teacher ratio.

[12] Percent of high school graduates entering college.

[13] Cost per pupil for administration.

[14-16] Percent of revenue from local, State, and Federal sources.

[17] Percent of economically deprived children.

S3120 KENTUCKY
Finance and Administration Cabinet

S3120–1 COMMONWEALTH OF KENTUCKY ANNUAL FINANCIAL REPORT for the Fiscal Year Ended June 30, 1984
Annual.   Apr. 1, 1985.
xix+94 p.
LC 43-11518.
SRI/MF/complete

Annual report on financial condition of Kentucky State government, for FY84, presenting assets and liabilities, reserves, and fund balances; and revenues by source and expenditures by function and object, with detail for individual agency accounts; all by fund.

Funds covered are general, special, transportation, Federal, trust/agency, debt service, capital projects, enterprise, internal service, and university/college.

Also includes debt service requirements through 1989, finances of debt-issuing authorities, and comparison of budgeted vs. actual revenues and expenditures.

Also includes a general statistical section, covering the following: trends from 1970s, for government revenues and expenditures, property valuations, property tax levies and collections (including delinquent collections), bonded debt, population, per capita income, unemployment rate, construction, bank deposits, and personal income by industry division; and 50 largest manufacturers ranked by number of employees, with number of plants, 1983.

Contains contents listing and introduction, with 4 charts (p. v-xx); financial section, with 44 combined and individual fund statements, and accompanying auditor's notes (p. 3-85); and statistical section, with 10 tables (p. 87-94).

For description of previous report, for FY83, see SRI 1983 Annual under this number.

Availability: Kentucky Finance and Administration Cabinet, Administration Department, Accounts Division, Capitol Annex, Frankfort KY 40601, †; SRI/MF/complete.

S3121 KENTUCKY
Department of Financial Institutions

S3121–1 SEVENTY SECOND ANNUAL REPORT OF THE COMMISSIONER OF BANKING AND SECURITIES, Division of Banking of the Commonwealth of Kentucky
Annual.   June 30, 1984.
73 p.
LC 74-649680.
SRI/MF/complete

Annual compilation of 5 reports on financial condition of Kentucky State-chartered banks and trust companies, credit unions, industrial loan companies, and savings and loan assns, and State-licensed consumer loan companies, as of June 30, 1984, or Dec. 31, 1983. Presents aggregate balance sheets for each type of institution, and assets by institution and city for most types.

Also includes Banking Division expenditures for FY84; summary asset trends from as early as 1912; bank, credit union, and savings and loan status changes; and directories of industrial and consumer loan companies.

Contains 5 reports, with 14 tables (p. 1-73).

This is the 72nd annual bank report, the 50th annual credit union report, the 39th annual industrial loan report, and the 66th annual savings and loan report.

Previous reports are described in SRI under S3095-1. Name of issuing agency has changed from Kentucky Department of Banking and Securities.

Availability: Kentucky Department of Financial Institutions, Banking Division, 911 Leawood Dr., Frankfort KY 40601-3392, †; SRI/MF/complete.

S3140 KENTUCKY
Cabinet for Human Resources

S3140–1 1983 VITAL STATISTICS REPORT, Kentucky
Annual. [1985.] vi+159 p.
LC 51-61842.
SRI/MF/complete

Annual report on Kentucky vital statistics, covering 1982 population; and births, deaths by major cause, and marriages and divorces, with data by age, sex, race, and county, 1983 with trends from as early as 1940. Data are primarily from certificates filed with the State registrar of vital statistics.

Contains introduction, district map, and contents/table listing (p. i-vi); 4 sections, each preceded by narrative summary, with 15 summary charts, and 1 chart and 33 tables listed below (p. 1-153); and appendix, with definitions and rates (p. 155-159).

Data on births to unmarried mothers and data by county of occurrence are no longer included in the report, but are available on request from issuing agency.

Availability: Kentucky Department for Health Services, State Health Planning Division, Health and Vital Statistics Branch, CHR Bldg., 1st Floor, 275 E. Main St., Frankfort KY 40621, $5.00+2.50 postage and handling; SRI/MF/complete.

TABLES:
[Unless otherwise noted, data are for 1983 and are shown by district and county of residence. Most tables show numbers and rates.]

S3140–1.1: Population and Natality

POPULATION

A1-A2. Population by race, sex, and age, 1982. (p. 3-12)

BIRTHS

[Table titles B1-B3, B5, B8-B9, and B11 begin "Resident live births..." or "Live births...." Tables B1-B5 show statewide data only.]

B1. By age of mother, 1975 and 1980-83. (p. 18)

B2-B3. By age of mother: by sex and race, and trimester prenatal care began. (p. 20-22)

B4. Stillbirths by age of mother, by trimester prenatal care began. (p. 24)

B5. By age of mother and birth weight. (p. 26)

B6-B7. Total live births and stillbirths, by race and sex. (p. 29-39)

B8-B9. By age and educational level of mother. (p. 41-53)

B10. Livebirths and stillbirths by trimester prenatal care began. (p. 55-59)

B11. By place of delivery and attendant at birth. (p. 61-64)

B12. Premature live births by age of mother. (p. 65-68)

B13. Selected live birth data: previous births, multiple births, congenital anomalies, and fertility rate. (p. 69-73)

S3140–1.2: Mortality, Marriage, and Divorce

DEATHS

[Tables C1-C8 show statewide data only.]

C1. Live births and deaths; [and] fetal, infant, neonatal, and maternal [deaths]; 1950-83. (p. 78)

C2. Deaths by age group, [selected years] 1950-83. (p. 80)

C3-C6. Deaths from malignant neoplasms, heart disease, accidents, and suicide, 1950-83. (p. 82-85)

C7. Leading causes of deaths by age group. (p. 86)

Chart C7. Leading causes of death, 1940 and 1983. (p. 87)

C8. Leading causes of deaths by sex and race. (p. 88)

C9-C10. Deaths by race, sex, and age group. (p. 91-102)

C11. Birth-related and infant deaths. (p. 103-106)

C12. Leading causes of deaths. (p. 107-124)

C13-C16. Deaths from suicide by age group, accidents by age group and type, and malignant neoplasms by category. (p. 125-144)

MARRIAGE AND DIVORCE

D1. Marriages and divorces [statewide only], 1965-83. (p. 147)

D2. Marriages and divorces by race. (p. 149-153)

S3140–2 PUBLIC ASSISTANCE IN KENTUCKY
Monthly, with semiannual and annual supplements.
Approx. 125 p.
PA-264 Rpt. Series.
LC 73-648644.
SRI/MF/complete.

Monthly report (with semiannual and annual supplements) on Kentucky public assistance program recipients and payments, by program, type of service, and county. Programs covered include AFDC, Medicaid, and State supplementation to aged, blind, and disabled.

Report is issued 2-4 months after month of coverage.

Contains narrative summary and history of programs, contents and table listing, and 24 monthly tables listed below.

A semiannual supplement on Medicaid recipient characteristics by county and selected program, and an annual supplement summarizing data covered in monthly tables, are also issued. The semiannual supplement begins with July 1985 issue.

Availability: Kentucky Cabinet for Human Resources, Social Insurance Department, Management and Development Division, 275 E. Main St., Frankfort KY 40621, †; SRI/MF/complete.

Issues reviewed during 1985: Dec. 1983-July 1985; semiannual supplement for July 1985; and annual supplement for FY84 (D).

MONTHLY TABLES:
[Data are shown for month of coverage. Most tables show data by program or service, by county, and include State guardianship cases.]

PART A: SUMMARY
1. Grand total public assistance payments: money payments and vendor medical payments.

2. Grand total eligible recipients, by eligibility factor: categorically needy and medically needy.

PART B: AFDC
[1] Recipients and payments: money payment cases.

PART C: STATE SUPPLEMENTATION TO AGED, BLIND, AND DISABLED
[1] Recipients and payments, by eligibility factor and type of need: money payment cases: State funds only.

PART D: TITLE XIX, MEDICAID
[All tables except table 2 show data by type of medical service, including hospital, nursing home, physician, drugs, dental, screening, clinic, mental health facilities, lab/X-ray, home health, family planning, ambulance, and alternate care services. Tables 5-12.5 begin "Medicaid payments to..."]

1-1A. State total utilizers (recipients) and utilization rates; and Medicaid payments and average payments per utilizer: categorically needy and medically needy.

2. Utilizers (recipients), by eligibility factor: categorically needy and medically needy.

3-4. Utilizers (recipients), and summary of Title XIX Medicaid payments: categorically needy/medically needy.

5-7. Aged, blind, and disabled, categorically needy cases: receives Title XVI/SSI/State supplementation.

8-8.2. Families with dependent children, categorically needy cases: receives Title IV AFDC (basic/foster care, death/absence/incapacity, and foster care).

9-11. Aged, blind, and disabled: medically needy cases.

12-12.2. Families with children [aggregate]; basic [medical assistance] families with children (death/absence/incapacity of parent); and families with unemployed parents (Federal definition of unemployment): medically needy cases.

12.3-12.5. Children in foster care (non-AFDC), from AFDC families, and in medical institutions: medically needy cases.

S3140–3 KENTUCKY ANNUAL PLANNING INFORMATION, Program Years 1985-86
Annual. July 1985.
v+101 p.
SRI/MF/complete

Annual planning report, for 1985-86, identifying Kentucky population groups most in need of employment services. Includes data on population and labor force characteristics, income, and employment by occupation and industry, by area development district (ADD) and service delivery area (SDA), various years 1968-85, with selected projections to 2020.

Also includes survey data on U.S. high-technology industry siting, by region and world area.

Data are primarily from BLS, Census Bureau, University of Louisville, State Dept for Employment Services, Lawrence Berkley Laboratories, and a high-technology industry survey conducted by Joint Economic Committee of Congress.

Contains contents/table listing (p. ii-v); annual planning information, with 55 tables described below (p. 1-83); special section on high-technology industry, with 4 tables also described below (p. 84-92); and glossary and bibliography (p. 93-101).

Previous report, for FY84, is described in SRI 1983 Annual under this number. Issuing agency also publishes a monthly report, *Kentucky Labor Market Information,* not covered by SRI.

Availability: Kentucky Cabinet for Human Resources, Manpower Services Department, Labor Market Research and Analysis Branch, 275 E. Main St., Frankfort KY 40621, †; SRI/MF/complete.

TABLES:

PLANNING INFORMATION
[Unless otherwise noted, data are shown for Kentucky, mostly with detail by ADD and/or SDA. Comparisons to total U.S. are also often included.]

a. **Population:** total, and by age group, sex, and county; nonwhite and economically disadvantaged population; veterans by period of service (currently in armed forces, Vietnam and post-Vietnam era, other conflicts, and peacetime service); and juvenile and adult offenders released, by age group and county; various years 1980-2020. 7 tables. (p. 6-16)

b. **Employment and earnings:** nonagricultural employment by industry division and major manufacturing group; private and civilian government employment; weekly wages of workers covered by unemployment insurance, by industry division; average hours and earnings in manufacturing (total, and for nondurable and durable goods); and U.S. CPI; various periods 1968-84. 9 tables. (p. 20-38)

c. **Labor force:** civilian labor force by employment status, and labor force participation rates, by sex and race; U.S. labor force by employment status, unemployment by duration and/or reason, and full- and part-time employment, all by sex, race, and for youths age 16-19; and U.S. unemployment rate by State, with State rankings; various periods 1970-84. 9 tables. (p. 41-48)

d. **Education:** employment and labor force status, and percent of population not enrolled in school, for high school graduates and nongraduates by age group; and educational attainment of persons aged 25/over by sex, with comparison to neighboring States and persons age 18-24; 1980. 6 tables. (p. 50-56)

e. **Income:** households with public assistance income and by income group, families below poverty level, and number and median income of households and families, 1979; economically disadvantaged youths and adults (no date); and AFDC/work incentive program registrants (no date). 6 tables. (p. 59-64)

f. **Occupations:** U.S. top 20-26 occupations ranked by projected employment growth or decline, and by job openings, and employment distribution by major occupational group, various periods 1978-95; and Kentucky total and female employment, and job openings due to industry growth and separations, by occupation, mostly 1980. 14 tables. (p. 66-83)

SPECIAL SECTION ON HIGH TECHNOLOGY
g. **High technology:** existing and planned high-technology plants/offices by world area and U.S. region, 1981-86 period; and high-technology company rankings of factors that influence firm location, and U.S. regional preferences, 1982 survey. 4 tables. (p. 88-91)

S3150 KENTUCKY
Department of Justice

S3150–1 1984 UNIFORM CRIME REPORTS, Commonwealth of Kentucky
Annual. [1985.]
5+99 p.+errata.
SRI/MF/complete

Annual report on Kentucky crimes and arrests, by offense, 1984, with selected comparisons to 1983 or earlier. Includes data by county, municipality, district, and reporting agency, and by offender age, sex, and race/ethnicity. Also includes law enforcement employment, and assaults on police.

Report focuses on 8 Index offenses: murder, rape, robbery, aggravated assault, burglary, larceny, auto theft, and arson. Arrests are also shown for numerous non-Index offenses.

Data are from State and local law enforcement agency reports, submitted under the Uniform Crime Reporting (UCR) Program.

Contains contents listing (1 p.); explanation of UCR program (p. 1-2); and report, with narrative summaries, and 8 maps, 39 charts, and 56 tables, described below (p. 4-97, and inside back cover.)

This is the 15th annual report.

Availability: Kentucky Department of Justice, State Police Bureau, Records Section, 1250 Louisville Rd., Frankfort KY 40601, †; SRI/MF/complete.

STATISTICS:

[Unless otherwise noted, data are for 1984, with selected comparisons to 1983. Although arson is classified as an Index crime, data are reported separately, and are not included in tables showing data by Index offense.

Data by district are shown for 15 area development districts. Data by race/ethnicity generally include American Indian/Alaskan Native, Asian/Pacific Islander, Hispanic, and non-Hispanic.]

S3150–1.1: Index Offenses

STATE SUMMARY

a. Index crimes: offenses reported, with percent occurring in aggregate urban, rural, and campus jurisdictions; offenses in counties containing major cities; crime clearance rates; and offenses and cases cleared, with clearances by adult and juvenile arrests, by district; mostly by Index offense. 1 map, 7 charts, and 5 tables. (p. 4-9)

INDIVIDUAL OFFENSES

[Data for each type of offense except arson include a crime clock; and 1 map and 3 tables showing offenses reported (total and by district); clearances; and arrests by offender age, sex, and race/ethnicity, by district. Additional data are noted below.]

b. Murder: offenses by type of weapon involved and other circumstances; and victims by age, sex, race/ethnicity, and relationship to offender. 1 map, 4 charts, and 6 tables. (p. 11-14)

c. Rape: offenses by relationship of offender to victim; victims by marital and injury status; victims and offenders, by age and whether under the influence of alcohol/drugs; and offenses by day of week. 1 map, 7 charts, and 3 tables. (p. 16-19)

d. Robbery: offenses and value of property stolen, by place of occurrence, and type of weapon involved. 1 map, 2 charts, and 5 tables. (p. 21-23)

e. Aggravated assault: offenses by type of weapon involved; and assaults on police, totals 1980-84, and by time of day, circumstances, and type of weapon used (with injury status). 1 map, 4 charts, and 6 tables. (p. 25-28)

f. Burglary: offenses and value of property stolen, by day and night residential and nonresidential occurrence. 1 map, 3 charts, and 5 tables. (p. 30-32)

g. Larceny: value of property stolen and recovered, by property type; and offenses and value of property stolen, by type of theft. 1 map, 3 charts, and 5 tables. (p. 34-37)

h. Auto theft: value of vehicles stolen and recovered; and vehicles stolen by type. 1 map, 4 charts, and 4 tables. (p. 39-41)

i. Arson: crime clock; and offenses, clearances, and value of property damage, by type of structure. 1 chart and 2 tables. (p. 43)

BY LOCATION

j. Index offenses, by city, county, and reporting agency. 1 table. (p. 45-61)

S3150–1.2: Arrests, Law Enforcement Employment, and Identification Activity

a. Arrests by Index and non-Index offense, county, and offender age, sex, and race/ethnicity; and drug-related arrests, by county and substance. 4 charts and 8 tables. (p. 63-87)

b. Municipal police, sheriff dept, and county, university, State, and other police agency officers and civilian employees, by jurisdiction; and police officers and civilian employees, by sex. 5 tables. (p. 89-97)

c. State Police Information Services Branch statistical summary of information and report processing. 1 table. (inside back cover)

S3150–2   KENTUCKY TRAFFIC ACCIDENT FACTS, 1984
Annual. [1985.] 4+34 p.
SRI/MF/complete

Annual report on Kentucky traffic accidents involving fatalities, injuries, and property damage, and number of persons killed and injured, 1984, with trends from 1974. Includes data by accident and vehicle type, location, time, and other circumstances; and driver and victim characteristics.

Also includes data on alcohol involvement (including alcohol test results), and license status of driver, for fatal accidents; and safety restraint use compared to injury results of accidents.

Report is compiled from law enforcement agency accident reports to the State Police.

Contains introduction and contents listing (2 p.); and 18 charts and 44 tables, with interspersed narrative and text data (p. 1-34 and inside back cover).

Availability: Kentucky Department of Justice, State Police Bureau, Records Section, 1250 Louisville Rd., Frankfort KY 40601, †; SRI/MF/complete.

S3165   KENTUCKY
Department for Libraries and Archives

S3165–1   STATISTICAL REPORT OF KENTUCKY PUBLIC LIBRARIES, FY84
Annual. Feb. 1985.
30+18 p.+errata sheets.
SRI/MF/complete

Annual report on Kentucky public library finances and operations, by region and county, FY84, with summary trends from FY81. Includes data on income by source, expenditures by object, tax rates, salaries, employees, volunteers, hours, branches, bookmobiles, interlibrary loans, book holdings, complaints about materials, materials removed as result of complaints, registered borrowers, circulation, and programs and participants.

Data are from public library annual reports.

Contains contents listing (1 p.); definitions and 4 summary tables (p. 1-5); 3 tables showing data by region (p. 6-8), 1980 population by county (p. 9), and data by county (p. 10-29); county index (p. 30); and sample reporting form (18 p.).

Availability: Kentucky Department for Libraries and Archives, Field Services Division, PO Box 537, Frankfort KY 40602-0537, †; SRI/MF/complete.

S3213   KENTUCKY
Office of the Secretary of State

S3213–1   OFFICIAL PRIMARY AND GENERAL ELECTION RETURNS for 1984, Kentucky
Annual. [1985.] 62 p.
SRI/MF/complete, current & previous year reports

Annual report presenting results of Kentucky primary and general elections held in 1984. Shows voting for President and Vice-President; U.S. Senator; U.S. and State representatives; supreme court justice; district judges; commonwealth's attorney; and 1 State constitutional amendment; by district and/or county. Also includes results of a special election for U.S. Representative.

Previous report, covering 1983 elections, was also reviewed by SRI during 1985, and is also available on SRI microfiche under S3213-1 [Annual. [1984.] 123 p. †]. Previous report includes voting for Governor, State senators, judges, and other officials.

Availability: Kentucky Office of the Secretary of State, State Board of Elections, State Capitol, Rm. 71, Frankfort KY 40601, †; SRI/MF/complete.

S3265   LOUISIANA
Department of Commerce

S3265–1   REPORTS OF THE STATE BANKS, SAVINGS AND LOAN ASSOCIATIONS, CREDIT UNIONS, CONSUMER CREDIT, AND SALE OF CHECKS in the State of Louisiana
Annual. [1985.] 459 p.
LC 81-643716.
SRI/MF/complete

Annual report on financial condition of Louisiana State-chartered banks, savings and loan assns, and credit unions, presenting assets, liabilities, and equity or net worth, by institution arranged by city, as of Dec. 31, 1984.

Also includes regulatory activities; number of banks with Federal Reserve System and FDIC membership; branch facilities and capital stock increases for selected institutions; composite bank operating ratios; consumer credit supervised lenders' composite assets, liabilities, income, and expenses; and Sale of Checks Act licensees and branches.

Contains bank section, with status changes and 6 tables (p. 6-255); savings and loan assn and credit union sections, with 2 tables (p. 258-415); and consumer credit division and Sale of Checks Act sections, including supervised lenders directory, and 2 tables (p. 418-459).

Availability: Louisiana Department of Commerce, Financial Institutions Office, PO Box 94095, Capitol Station, Baton Rouge LA 70804-9095, $10.00; SRI/MF/complete.

S3275   LOUISIANA
Department of Culture, Recreation, and Tourism

S3275–1   PUBLIC LIBRARIES IN LOUISIANA, Statistical Report, 1984
Annual.   [1985.]   36 p.
LC 57-36645.
SRI/MF/complete.

Annual report on Louisiana public library personnel, operations, holdings, circulation, and finances, by library, 1984.

Contains contents listing, and list of parishes (p. 2-3); 9 tables, listed below (p. 4-33); and glossary (p. 34-36).

Availability: Louisiana Department of Culture, Recreation, and Tourism, State Library Office, PO Box 131, Baton Rouge LA 70821, ‡; SRI/MF/complete.

TABLES:
[Data are for 1984. Tables 1-7 show data by parish and for 3 municipalities.]

1. Library profile [includes population and land area served, branches, deposit stations, bookmobiles, and holdings by type of material]. (p. 4-11)

2. Additions to resources (gross) [by type of material]. (p. 12-13)

3. Library use: loan transactions [by type of distribution and material, and interlibrary loans]. (p. 14-17)

4. Operating receipts, by source [includes local and Federal funds by type, gifts, and State aid]. (p. 18-21)

5. Operating expenditures, by purpose [salaries and related costs, materials by type, and other]. (p. 22-25)

6. Capital project fund [expenditures, by object]. (p. 26-27)

7. Personnel [work week; head librarian salary; FTE librarians and library associates, and lowest and highest salaries paid; and total FTE staff]. (p. 28-31)

8-9. Library systems: services [including requests received and filled, borrowers' cards issued, and books loaned]; and operating expenditures, by purpose; [all by library system]. (p. 32-33)

S3280   LOUISIANA
Department of Education

S3280–1   LOUISIANA DEPARTMENT OF EDUCATION One Hundred Thirty-Fifth Annual Statistical and Financial Report, Session 1983/84
Annual.   [1985.]   xii+396 p.
Bull. 1472.
LC E11-207.
SRI/MF/complete

Annual report, for 1983/84 school year, on Louisiana public and nonpublic elementary/secondary schools, with enrollment projections through 1987/88, and selected U.S. comparisons and trends from mid-1970s or earlier. Includes enrollment, dropouts, graduates, personnel, facilities, transportation, food services, finances, and special programs, shown for the State and by parish/city school district.

Data are from reports by parish and city school systems and by divisions of the State Dept of Education, and from National Education Assn, NCES publications, and other sources.

Contains listings of contents, tables, and figures (p. iii-xii); narrative report interspersed with 41 figures and 54 detailed tables (p. 1-114); school district profiles, each with 20 tables (p. 115-387); appendix, with 6 summary tables (p. 388-393); and index (p. 394-396).

All tables, and selected figures presenting substantial data not covered in tables, are listed below.

Availability: Louisiana Department of Education, Research and Development Office, Research Bureau, PO Box 94064, Baton Rouge LA 70804-9064, †; SRI/MF/complete.

TABLES AND FIGURES:
[Unless otherwise noted, data are shown for Louisiana public schools, 1974/75-1983/84.]

S3280–1.1: Students, Personnel, and Programs

POPULATION CHARACTERISTICS

1.1. Population of parishes, 1970 and 1980; and 1983 estimates. (p. 13)

1.2. Economic statistics [percent of families in poverty and median family income, by parish and/or MSA, selected years 1979-83]. (p. 14)

1.3-1.4. Birth rates per 1,000 population, and estimated school-age (5-17) population as percent of total population [U.S. and Louisiana, various years 1960-83]. (p. 15)

1.5. Comparison of Louisiana and the U.S.: population characteristics [children of school age, change in resident population, migration rate, and educational attainment measures; various periods 1970-83]. (p. 16)

STUDENT CHARACTERISTICS

1.6. Student registration [by race], with percent increase or decrease over previous year, public and nonpublic. (p. 17)

1.7-1.8. Public/nonpublic student registration in elementary, secondary, kindergarten, and special education; and registration by grade level; [various years] 1974/75-1987/88. (p. 18-19)

1.9. Trends in average daily membership (ADM), average daily attendance (ADA), and percent attendance. (p. 20)

1.10-1.11. Enrollment [secondary and adult] in vocational education programs, 1973/74-1983/84; and adult basic education and R.S. 17:14 adult education programs [including student average age, enrollment by sex and race, achievement, and terminations]. (p. 21-22)

1.12. Comparison of Louisiana and the U.S.: [public and nonpublic school] enrollment [fall 1981-83]; and attendance [1983/84]. (p. 23)

UNIVERSITY ADMISSION REQUIREMENTS

Figure 2.2. Number of Carnegie units [high school courses] required for State university admission, by subject area and State, fall 1982. (p. 28)

RETENTION, DROPOUTS, AND GRADUATES

2.1. Comparison of Louisiana and the U.S.: estimated U.S. and actual Louisiana retention rates, 5th grade through high school graduation, in public/nonpublic schools, selected years [fall 1968-72]. (p. 29)

2.2. Trends in dropouts [by race]. (p. 30)

2.3-2.4. Comparison of white and nonwhite suspension and expulsions, and most frequent reasons for suspension/expulsion, 1983/84. (p. 31-32)

2.5. Number of high school graduates [by race], with percent increase or decrease over previous year, public and nonpublic. (p. 33)

ACHIEVEMENT TESTS

2.6-2.8. Comparison of Louisiana and national ACT [American College Test] and SAT [Scholastic Aptitude Test] scores for freshmen; and students' satisfaction with various aspects of local high schools, [from] 1984 ACT [survey] data. (p. 34-36)

PERSONNEL

3.1-3.2. Professional and nonprofessional personnel; [and] breakdown [by position and sex], 1983/84. (p. 45)

3.3. Sex and race of principals and classroom teachers. (p. 46)

3.4-3.5. Professional training and total experience of principals/teachers. (p. 47-48)

3.6. Average annual salaries of teachers and principals [by race]. (p. 49)

3.7. Student/teacher ratios accompanied by student registration and number of teachers [by grade level and for special education], 1983/84. (p. 50)

3.8-3.9. Comparison of Louisiana and U.S.: pupils enrolled per teacher, fall 1972-83; and staff characteristics [including number of teachers, percent male, and average salary, 1984]. (p. 51-52)

S3280–1.2: Facilities and Finances

FACILITIES

4.1. Number of public and nonpublic schools. (p. 57)

4.2-4.3. Inventory of property [number and/or cost of buildings, sites, and equipment]; and libraries [number of libraries, librarians, and books, value of books/equipment, and total expenses]. (p. 58)

4.4-4.6. Percentage distribution of class size, and mean class size, by classroom type [regular, ungraded, special and compensatory education, vocational education, and other], elementary and secondary grade levels, 1983/84. (p. 59-60)

FINANCES

Figure 5.5-5.6. Where schools get their operating funds [distribution by government level], and average per pupil expenditures [by State], 1982/83. (67-68)

5.1-5.3. Revenue from local, State, and Federal sources for education; and revenue from ESEA [Elementary and Secondary Education Act] Title I funds and ECIA [Education Consolidation and Improvement Act] funds, [various years 1973/74-1982/84]. (p. 69-70)

5.4-5.5. Education expenditure by function, 1979/80-1983/84; and expenditures per pupil. (p. 71-72)

5.6-5.7. State totals for bonded and other debt, 1980/81-1983/84; and cash and security holdings [FY83-84]. (p. 73)

5.8-5.9. Student activity funds [beginning and ending balances and financial activity, 1983-84]; and Minimum Foundation Program [including costs and local support]. (p. 74-75)

5.10-5.11. State and Federal expenditures for special education, and [Federal and State/local] expenditures in vocational education programs. (p. 76-77)

5.12. Revenues [by source] and expenditures [by function and detailed object] for the Dept of Education, FY84. (p. 78-89)

5.13-5.14. Expenditure of State revenues, and of all State revenues (State revenues/Federal grants), by function of State government, 1972/73-1983/84. (p. 90-91)

5.15-5.16. Comparison of Louisiana and U.S.: general financial resources and government revenue [including personal income and tax revenues]; and school revenues [by source] based on 2 independent national reports; [various years 1981/82-1983/84]. (p. 92-93)

5.17-5.19. Comparison of Louisiana and national direct expenditures for all government functions and for education; current expenditure in ADA and ADM; and distribution of school districts, by core current expenditure; [all shown as per capita or per pupil; various periods 1974-1983/84]. (p. 94-95)

5.20. Summary of Louisiana and national expenditure, by purpose, for public elementary/secondary education, as percentage of total expenditure, 1980/81. (p. 96)

S3280–1.3: Regional Trends

[Figures 6.1-6.2, 6.4, and 6.6 show data by region and for 12 southeastern States. Figure 6.9 shows data for all 50 States. Data are for various years, 1965-82.]

Figure 6.1-6.2. Total enrollment, public schools; and private enrollment as percent of total public and private enrollment. (p. 97-98)

Figure 6.4. Classroom teachers as percent of total staff. (p. 100)

Figure 6.6. Students per teacher by school level. (p. 102)

Figure 6.9. Average annual salaries of classroom teachers in real (1967) dollars. (p. 106)

S3280–1.4: Parish/City School District Profiles

INDIVIDUAL DISTRICT PROFILES

[Tables are repeated for total State and each parish/city school district. District profiles also include names of superintendent and school board chairperson, number of school board members, square mile area, and number of school days. Data are for 1983/84, unless otherwise noted.

Data by ethnicity are for American Indian, Asian, black, Hispanic, and white.]

1. Student registration [by] ethnicity and sex [for public and nonpublic schools].

2-3. Public and nonpublic student registration [by grade and for special education, and graduates, actual 1983/84 and (except for special education) projected 1984/85-1987/88].

4. Membership at end of session, ADM, and ADA [public and nonpublic, by level].

5. Number of high school graduates [public and nonpublic, by ethnicity and sex].

6. Dropouts [by ethnicity, by grade and for special education and kindergarten].

7. Number and type of public schools in terms of pupil registration [by grade level].

8. Staff information [by ethnicity, sex, and position].

9. Number and type of nonpublic schools.

10. Experience of teachers [number of elementary and secondary teachers in each category of experience].

11. Pupils in membership being served by exceptional children program [by age group, by type of handicap, and for gifted children].

12. Basic skills and State assessment results [reading, math, and writing; grades 2-4, 7, and 10].

13-16. Sources of revenue, expenditures [by function], and school system bonded status and taxation.

17. School food services [meals served, Federal reimbursements, and State/local support, all for public and nonpublic schools].

18. School transportation [buses, public and nonpublic pupils transported, miles driven, and cost].

19. Rankings [amounts and, for parishes, rank among parishes, for expenditure per pupil; public school pupil/teacher ratios, percent of graduates continuing education, mean salary of teachers, and teacher/administrator ratio; assessed property valuation per student; and 1981-82 per capita income; 1982/83-1983/84].

[20] Additional educational statistics: [including schools with advanced placement programs; computers used for instruction (1982-83); foreign language/second language specialists; schools attaining criteria of excellence; and percent of high school students enrolled in vocational programs].

APPENDIX TABLES

[All tables show data by parish/city school district, 1983/84.]

1-4. Total public and nonpublic registration [by race, level, and] grade.

5. [ADM, ADA, dropouts, graduates, and per pupil expenditure.]

6. [Pupil/teacher ratio, average teacher salary, and number of teachers, principals, and assistant principals.]

S3285
Office of the
Governor

**S3285-2   STATE OF LOUISIANA
ANNUAL FINANCIAL
REPORT, June 30, 1984**
Annual. Mar. 18, 1985.
16+108+2 p.
LC 50-63201.
SRI/MF/complete

Annual report on financial condition of Louisiana State government, presenting assets and liabilities, reserves, and fund balances; revenues by source; and expenditures by function; for general, special revenue, capital projects, debt service, internal service, enterprise, and fiduciary funds; FY84 with trends from FY75.

Also includes data on bonded indebtedness and long-term debt service obligations; and selected detail by State-supported postsecondary institution.

Contains introductory section, including contents listing, transmittal letter, and 4 charts (13 p.); financial section, with auditor's opinion (3 p.), 7 combined financial statements with accompanying notes (p. 2-43), 22 statements arranged by fund category (p. 45-87), and statement of changes in general long-term obligation (p. 89); statistical section, with 9 tables (p. 91-108); and fund index (2 p.).

Availability: Louisiana Office of the Governor, Administration Division, State Accounting Office, State Capitol Bldg., PO Box 44095, Baton Rouge LA 70804, ‡; SRI/MF/complete.

S3295
Department of
Health and Human Resources

**S3295-1   1981 VITAL STATISTICS of
Louisiana**
Annual. [1985.]   xx+123 p.
ISSN 0460-1009.
LC 76-642575.
SRI/MF/complete

Annual report, for 1981, on Louisiana vital statistics, covering population, births, deaths by cause, morbidity, marriages, and divorces. Includes data by age group, race, sex, parish, city, State planning district (SPD), and health service area (HSA). Most data are from State records.

Contains contents and table listings, and 1 map (2 p.); and the following:

a. Introduction, with data sources, definitions, and 3 tables showing U.S. total and infant deaths according to the International Classification of Diseases, 9th Revision, 1976; and 1 table showing Louisiana population by parish, July 1981. (p. i-viii)

b. Summary, with narrative, 3 trend charts, and 7 tables showing selected U.S. vital statistics (total births and deaths, low-weight births, births to unmarried women, leading causes of death, and infant and neonatal deaths), mostly by State and/or census division; and Louisiana births in charity hospitals, leading causes of death (total and infant), and neonatal mortality by selected maternal characteristics; mostly by race, 1981, with charity hospital birth trends from 1974. (p. ix-xx) *c.* 37 tables, listed below, arranged in 5 sections. (p. 1-123)

A semiannual preliminary report on Louisiana births and deaths is also published, Semiannual report will be covered in SRI under S3295-2; coverage will begin in 1986.

Availability: Louisiana Department of Health and Human Resources, Public Health Statistics, PO Box 60630, New Orleans LA 70160, †; SRI/MF/complete.

TABLES:

[Data are for 1981, unless otherwise noted. "A" and "B" versions of tables show data by parish and/or major city, and by SPD and HSA. Data by major city are for cities with over 10,000 population.]

S3295–1.1: Natality

I.A-I.B. Live births by place of occurrence, reallocated to mother's usual residence and shown by age of mother, and by sex and race of child. (p. 1-9)

II. Live births by place of occurrence [parish and major city], reallocated to mother's usual residence and shown by sex of child, race, and attendant [physician, midwife, and other]. (p. 10-12)

III. Live births showing hospital in which birth occurred, by sex and race. (p. 13-17)

IV. Congenital anomalies specified on birth certificates, shown by type of anomaly and age of mother. (p. 18)

V. Immature births [by race, sex, and weight group], showing hospital in which birth occurred. (p. 19-22)

VI. Live births by birth order by weight of child. (p. 23)

VII. Live births by weight of child, shown by sex and race. (p. 23)

VIII. Live births by birth weight, age of mother, and race of child. (p. 24)

IX. Live births by birth order, shown by age of mother and race of child. (p. 25)

X.A.-X.B. Illegitimate births by place of occurrence, reallocated to mother's usual residence and shown by age of mother and race of child. (p. 26-30)

S3295–1.2: Mortality and Morbidity

FETAL MORTALITY

XI.A-XI.B. Stillbirths by place of occurrence, reallocated to mother's usual residence and shown by age of mother and race of child. (p. 31-35)

XII. Stillbirths shown by selected cause, age of mother, and race of child. (p. 36-37)

XIII-XIX. Reported induced terminations of pregnancy occurring in Louisiana: by parish of residence and occurrence; by woman's State of residence; by weeks of gestation, [by] woman's age and race, and type of procedure; and by woman's age and marital status [by] race. (p. 38-41)

OTHER MORTALITY

XX.A-XX.B. Deaths (exclusive of stillbirths) by place of occurrence, reallocated to usual residence of the deceased and shown by sex, race, and age. (p. 43-53)

XXI. Deaths showing hospital in which death occurred, by age. (p. 54-59)

XXII. Principal causes of death, by parish. (p. 60-61)

XXIII. Deaths (exclusive of stillbirths) shown by selected causes, sex, race, and age. (p. 62-91)

XXIV. Accidental deaths by type of accident [motor vehicle, home, occupational, other public, and not stated], shown by geographic location where accident occurred [parish and major city]. (p. 92)

XXV.A-XXV.B. Infant deaths (exclusive of stillbirths) by place of occurrence, reallocated to mother's usual residence and shown by sex, race, and age. (p. 93-101)

XXVI. Infant mortality rates by place of residence, shown by age at death and race, by SPD and HSA. (p. 102)

XXVII. Infant deaths (exclusive of stillbirths) by selected causes, sex, race, and age. (p. 103-109)

XXVIII. Maternal deaths by place of occurrence [parish], reallocated to usual residence of deceased and shown by race and age. (p. 110)

XXIX-XXX. Maternal deaths by cause, race, and age [with trends by cause and race from 1979]. (p. 111-112)

MORBIDITY

XXXI-XXXII. Reportable diseases by parish [and major city], and by race and age. (p. 113-120)

S3295–1.3: Marriage and Divorce

XXXIII. Marriages, final divorces, and annulments granted [by parish]. (p. 121)

XXXIV-XXXVI. Marriages, by month of occurrence; and by race [including American Indian, Chinese, Japanese, and other] and previous marital status of bride and groom. (p. 122)

XXXVII. All marriages by age of bride, by age of groom. (p. 123)

S3310   LOUISIANA
Commissioner of Insurance

S3310–1   STATE OF LOUISIANA REPORT OF COMMISSIONER OF INSURANCE for 1983
Annual. [1984.] 6+200 p. SRI/MF/complete

Annual report on Louisiana insurance industry financial condition and underwriting activity, by company and type of insurance, 1983. Covers assets, net reserves, liabilities, capital stock and surplus; and premiums earned, insurance written and in force, and losses incurred or claims paid; for companies based in Louisiana and elsewhere.

Data are shown, as applicable, for life insurance companies, hospital/medical service companies, domestic service companies, nonprofit funeral assns, fraternal orders, fire/marine/fidelity/surety/casualty companies, title insurers, and surplus line brokers.

Also includes total premiums and losses by line of coverage, including medical malpractice, workers compensation, automobile insurance, and surety bonds; Insurance Dept taxes and fees collected, 1983, and personnel, salaries/benefits, and other operating expenses, FY84.

Data are compiled from annual sworn statements submitted by the individual insurance companies.

Contains transmittal letters with regulatory data, Insurance Dept and industry summary with 4 tables, and contents listing (6 p.); recently enacted insurance laws, and index and directory of companies (p. 1-107); and 13 company financial tables (p. 108-200).

This is the 13th annual report. For description of the 12th report, see SRI 1983 Annual under this number.

Availability: Louisiana Commissioner of Insurance, PO Box 44214, Capitol Station, Baton Rouge LA 70804, †; SRI/MF/complete.

S3320   LOUISIANA
Department of Labor

S3320–1   ANNUAL PLANNING REPORT for Louisiana (Statewide)
Annual. Sept. 1985. 80 p. SRI/MF/complete

Annual planning report, for 1985, identifying Louisiana population groups most in need of employment services. Includes data on labor force, personal income, employment by industry, insured unemployment, and State job service activity. Data generally are current to 1984 or 1st half 1985, with trends from as early as 1965 and employment projections to 1990.

Selected data are shown for individual Job Training Partnership Act (JTPA) service delivery areas, by parish.

Data are compiled by the Louisiana Dept of Labor in conjunction with the U.S. Dept of Labor.

Contains contents listing (1 p.); State description (p. 2-3); population summary and economic profile, with 1 map and 1 table (p. 6-10); and 11 sections, with 3 charts and 30 tables, lists of related publications, and definitions (p. 11-80). All tables are listed below.

Separate planning reports for local areas and MSAs are also available from issuing agency, but are not covered by SRI.

Availability: Louisiana Department of Labor, Employment Security Office, Research and Statistics Unit, PO Box 94094, Baton Rouge LA 70804-9094, †; SRI/MF/complete.

TABLES:

[Data are shown for Louisiana, unless otherwise noted.]

S3320–1.1: Population and Labor Force Characteristics

[1] [Parishes with over 100,000 population and their largest cities, and total State population, 1984.] (p. 8)

[2] Unemployment rates, a comparison [for State and U.S., with State ranking, 1971-84]. (p. 12)

[3] Unemployment rates (not seasonally adjusted), statewide and national [1983 and monthly 1984]. (p. 13)

[4] Total personal and per capita income [1965-83]. (p. 14)

[5] CPI [U.S., for all urban consumers and urban wage/clerical workers, 1967-84 and monthly 1984-July 1985]. (p. 15)

[6-7] 1984 population estimates [by race, sex, minority status, parish, and labor market area (LMA)]. (p. 18-19)

[8] Occupational breakout of civilian labor force by sex and [minority status], 1984. (p. 20)

[9] Labor force summary [showing labor force by employment status, monthly] 1970-84. (p. 22-24)

[10-11] Nonagricultural wage/salary employment [by industry division and selected group, monthly] 1983-84. (p. 26-29)

[12-14] Average weekly earnings and hours of production workers in manufacturing [groups] and mining, and nonsupervisory workers in other selected industries, [monthly] 1984. (p. 30-32)

S3320-1.2: Insured Unemployed, Job Service Applicants and Openings, Local Labor Force, and Employment Projections

1-6. Insured unemployed: by age, industry [division], and occupation [cross-tabulated by] race and sex; and by industry division [cross-tabulated by] duration of unemployment and weekly benefit amount; 2nd quarter 1985. (p. 34-39)

[7] Insured unemployed by industry [division, race], and occupation group for the week including the 19th of May 1985. (p. 40)

[8-9] Characteristics of active file applicants placed [showing total, minority, female, and veteran applicants]; and total agricultural and nonagricultural job openings received, filled, and unfilled; by major occupational groups, July 1984-June 1985 period. (p. 42-43)

[10] [Federal poverty guidelines, Mar. 1985.] (p. 46)

[11-14] SDA [service delivery area] information for JTPA administration [includes labor force by employment status, high school dropouts, AFDC and food stamp recipients, private and government employment, and total and economically disadvantaged population by age group, all by SDA, parish, and/or city, various periods 1980-85. (p. 57-74)

[15-16] Employment projections by major occupational and industrial category [1980 and 1990]. (p. 76-77)

[17] Most rapidly growing occupations, 1980-90 [period]. (p. 78)

S3320-2   LOUISIANA LABOR MARKET INFORMATION
Monthly. 18 p. no paging.
SRI/MF/complete, shipped quarterly

Monthly report on Louisiana employment, hours, and earnings, by industry and labor market area (LMA). Also includes employment data by parish. Report is issued 1 month after month of coverage.

Contains narrative analysis; 4 monthly tables and 1 irregularly recurring table, listed below; and, occasionally, revised data for previous issues.

Monthly tables appear in all issues; irregularly recurring table appears in Dec. 1984 and July 1985 issues.

Availability: Louisiana Department of Labor, Employment Security Office, Research and Statistics Unit, PO Box 94094, Baton Rouge LA 70804-9094, †; SRI/MF/complete, shipped quarterly.

Issues reviewed during 1985: Sept. 1984-Aug. 1985 (D).

TABLES:

MONTHLY TABLES

[Data are shown for month of coverage, previous month, and same month of previous year. Table [2] is repeated for State and each LMA. Table [3] is repeated for State and 3 LMAs, with LMA data shown for manufacturing industries only.]

[1] Civilian labor force summary [by employment status, by LMA].

[2] Nonagricultural wage/salary employment [by industry division and major industry group].

[3] Average hours and earnings in manufacturing [major industry groups] and selected nonmanufacturing [industry divisions].

[4] Employment situation by LMA.

RECURRING TABLE

[5] Insured unemployed by industry [division] and occupational group for the week including the 19th of [month 1-2 months prior to month of coverage, by race and LMA].

S3345   LOUISIANA
Department of Public Safety

S3345-1   STATE OF LOUISIANA SUMMARY OF MOTOR VEHICLE TRAFFIC ACCIDENTS, 1984
Annual. May 9, 1985.
16 p. var. paging.
ISSN 0741-4358.
SRI/MF/complete

Annual report on Louisiana traffic accidents, fatalities, and injuries, by vehicle and accident type, location, time, and other circumstances; and by driver and victim characteristics; 1984, with selected comparisons to 1983.

Also includes data on safety device use and vehicle miles traveled.

Report contains 17 tables.

Availability: Louisiana Department of Public Safety, State Police Office, Traffic Records Section, PO Box 66614, Baton Rouge LA 70896, †; SRI/MF/complete.

S3365   LOUISIANA
Department of Revenue and Taxation

S3365-1   41st REPORT, FY83-84, Louisiana Department of Revenue and Taxation
Annual. [1985.] 49 p.
SRI/MF/complete

Annual report on Louisiana State tax revenue collections, by tax type, FY84 with selected trends from FY70. Includes individual income tax returns and payments by income bracket, sales and severance taxes by parish and commodity group, and collections from audits.

Contains contents listing and introductory matter (p. 1-4); dept profile, with 1 table summarizing operating expenditures (p. 5-6); and 32 tables described below, interspersed with explanatory notes and 21 charts (p. 8-46).

Availability: Louisiana Department of Revenue and Taxation, Public Relations Section, PO Box 201, Baton Rouge LA 70821, †; SRI/MF/complete.

TABLES:

[Data on taxes show value of revenue collections.]

a. Total taxes, FY78-84; and taxes by type, and revenue collections by detailed source, FY83-84. 3 tables. (p. 8-11)

b. Beer and liquor/wine taxes, corporation franchise and income taxes, and individual income taxes, FY79-84; individual income tax returns by filing status, tax year 1983; total returns, and payments and/or income, by income bracket and zip code area, tax year 1983; and contributing taxpayers and value of donations, for 4 charitable organizations with tax refund checkoffs (no date). 9 tables. (p. 14-20)

c. Severance taxes by type of natural resource and parish; petroleum product taxes and inspection fees, with detail for gasoline and special fuels; motor fuel gallonage taxed, by fuel type; sales tax collections, by parish and commodity group; and tobacco product tax; various years FY79-84. 14 tables. (p. 21-36)

d. Audit collections by tax type, and from in-State offices by district and out-of-State offices by city, FY84; tax trends by tax type, FY70-84, with FY84 detail by month; and revenues by source as affected by the State's conversion to a modified accrual basis of accounting, FY84. 6 tables. (p. 40-46)

S3370   LOUISIANA
Office of the Secretary of State

S3370–1   STATE OF LOUISIANA REPORT OF THE SECRETARY OF STATE, from Jan. 1, 1983-Dec. 31, 1984
Biennial. [1985.]
28 p.+10 foldouts.
SRI/MF/complete

Biennial report presenting results of Louisiana primary and general elections, 1983-84. Shows voting for President and Vice-President; U.S. and State senators and representatives; Governor and other State officials, including board of education, superintendent of education, and appellate court judges; and State constitutional amendments, including provision for deposit of State windfall revenues from oil/gas price deregulation in Louisiana Investment Fund for Enhancement. Also includes party affiliation of candidates, voter registration by race and political party, and fees collected by the Secretary of State. Most data are shown by parish.

Previous report, covering 1981-82 elections, is described in SRI 1983 Annual under this number.

Availability: Louisiana Office of the Secretary of State, PO Box 94125, Baton Rouge LA 70804-9125, $3.00; SRI/MF/complete.

S3375   LOUISIANA
Supreme Court

S3375–1   1984 ANNUAL REPORT OF THE JUDICIAL COUNCIL, SUPREME COURT OF LOUISIANA
Annual. Feb. 21, 1985.
26 p.
LC 73-641954.
SRI/MF/complete

Annual report on Louisiana trial and appellate court caseloads and case dispositions, 1984, with selected trends from 1982. Covers supreme, appeals, district, family and juvenile, and city and parish courts. Includes jury trials by case type and jurisdiction.

Case types shown include civil, criminal, traffic, and juvenile.

Data are from court reports to Judicial Administrator's Office.

Contains contents listing, letter of transmittal, and roster of supreme court judges (p. 1-3); narrative report, with rosters of judges and clerks (p. 4-17); and statistical appendix with 2 charts and 6 tables (p. 18-26).

This is the 29th annual report.

Availability: Louisiana Supreme Court, Judicial Administrator's Office, Supreme Court Bldg., Rm. 109, 301 Loyola Ave., New Orleans LA 70112-1887, $15.00; SRI/MF/complete.

S3425   MAINE
Department of Agriculture, Food and Rural Resources

S3425–1   MAINE AGRICULTURAL STATISTICS, 1983-84
Annual. [1985.] 3+92 p.
SRI/MF/complete

Annual report on Maine agricultural production, stocks, marketing, and finances, mostly 1971-83, with selected trends from 1950, and summary estimates for 1984. Data generally are shown by county and/or commodity.

Covers production, prices, value, income and/or sales, and, as applicable, acreage, yield, disposition, and inventory, for potato, field crop, vegetable, fruit, nursery, apiary, maple syrup, dairy, livestock, wool, and poultry sectors.

Also includes data on Maine farms and acreage, weather, and farm balance sheet, income by source, production expenses, feed prices, and fertilizer consumption; farm production expenses for Northeast States and U.S.; and U.S. and Maine food consumption by commodity.

Data are compiled by the New England Crop and Livestock Reporting Service, and Maine Dept of Agriculture, Food and Rural Resources.

Contains contents listing (1 p.); and 13 charts and 101 tables, arranged in 7 sections, generally with narrative highlights (p. 1-92).

For description of previous report, for 1981-82, see SRI 1983 Annual under this number.

Availability: Maine Department of Agriculture, Food and Rural Resources, Statehouse Station 28, Augusta ME 04333, †; SRI/MF/complete.

S3429   MAINE
Department of Business, Occupational and Professional Regulation

S3429–1   ANNUAL STATISTICAL REPORT OF THE BUREAU OF BANKING, Maine
Annual. Apr. 1985.
17 p. no paging.
SRI/MF/complete

Annual report presenting aggregate financial data for Maine financial institutions, by institution type, county, and State economic area, 1977-84, with selected trends from 1950.

Includes assets, deposits or shares, loans, and number of institutions and branches, for commercial bank/trust companies, national banks, savings and industrial banks, and State and Federal savings and loan assns and credit unions.

Also includes loans by type, demand and savings/time deposits, and negotiable orders of withdrawal, all by county; and total and per capita deposits, total loans, per capita installment and real estate debt, and number of offices reporting by institution type, all by State economic area.

Data are compiled by the Banking Bureau from reports filed by individual institutions.

Contains 3 tables, and list of economic areas.

Availability: Maine Department of Business, Occupational and Professional Regulation, Bank

Superintendent's Office, Banking Bureau, State House Station 36, Augusta ME 04333, †; SRI/MF/complete.

S3435   MAINE
Department of Educational and Cultural Services

S3435–1   MAINE EDUCATIONAL FACTS, 1983/84
Annual. [1985.] ii+27 p.
LC 76-626298.
SRI/MF/complete

Annual report on elementary/secondary education in Maine, 1983/84. Covers public and private school enrollment, graduates, postsecondary education, and dropouts. Also includes data on public school units and districts, special education, schooling of Indian children, and growth trends in staffing and expenditures from 1960s. Selected data are shown by county.

Data are from reports submitted by local school administrators.

Contains contents listing (p. ii); brief narrative summary (p. 1); and 24 tables, listed below (p. 2-27).

Availability: Maine Department of Educational and Cultural Services, Management Information Division, Education Bldg., Station 23, Augusta ME 04333, †; SRI/MF/complete.

TABLES:
[Data are for Maine, 1983/84, unless otherwise noted.]

S3435–1.1: Public Schools

[1] Distribution of municipalities [and school systems, by type of school supervision district]. (p. 2)

[2] Units that do not operate schools. [list] (p. 3)

[3] Universe of public school districts [number of local units, nonoperating local units, schools, and average daily membership (ADM)], by county [and for schooling of Indian children and children in unorganized territories]. (p. 4)

[4] One-room schools [enrollment, by school], fall 1984. (p. 5)

[5] Units that do not have kindergarten, 1984/85. [list] (p. 6)

S3435–1.2: Enrollment
[Data by grade include special education and postgraduates. Public school data generally include separate totals for Indian children and children in unorganized territories.]

[1] Net [public school] enrollment, State totals by grade [and high school graduates, total population, and births; 1950-84]. (p. 7-8)

[2-6] Fall enrollment for public and private schools, by grade and county, 1984/85. (p. 9-13)

[7-10] Oct. 1, 1983 and Apr. 1, 1984 resident enrollment, by county and grade. (p. 14-17)

[11] Enrollment comparisons by year [and school level, Oct. 1, 1971-83]. (p. 18)

S3435-1.3: Summary Year-End Data, Dropouts, and Postsecondary Enrollment

[1] Year-end data, as reported in the "Report of the Public School System, 1983/84" [enrollment and dropouts, by grade; average daily attendance and ADM; number of public, private, and discontinued schools; and public and private school pupils conveyed on municipal and private buses]. (p. 19-20)

[2] Dropout [number and] rates, by county. (p. 21)

[3-4] Rate [and number] of 1983 and 1984 graduates [going] on to college, by county. (p. 22-23)

[5-6] 1983 and 1984 [public and private] school students enrolled in postsecondary education or training [postgraduate high school course, junior college, college/university, vocational/commercial/technical, and other continuing education, inside and outside Maine]. (p. 24-25)

S3435-1.4: Finances and Growth Trends

[1] Local school expenditures and source of revenues [local, State, and Federal, including Elementary and Secondary Education Act and school lunch funds, 1967/68-1983/84]. (p. 26)

[2] Growth of public education in Maine [teachers, average salary, expenditures, and resident pupils, 1961/62-1983/84] (p. 27)

S3435-2   LIBRARIES IN MAINE: Directory and Public Library Statistics, 1983

Annual. [1985.]   54 p.
LC 73-646640.
SRI/MF/complete

Annual report, for 1983, on Maine libraries, presenting directory of public, institutional, and special libraries and personnel; and data on holdings, circulation, and finances of individual public libraries, by town. Data are from annual reports submitted by public libraries to the State library.

Contents:

a. Contents listing (1 p.); introduction (p. 1); and directories of library officials and libraries (p. 2-46).

b. Public library statistics: 1 table showing summary data for State, 1982-83 (p. 47); and 1 extended table showing hours, holdings, circulation, expenditures for books and salaries, municipal appropriations, and total operating expenditures, 1983, and population, 1980, for individual public libraries, by town (p. 48-54).

Availability: Maine Department of Educational and Cultural Services, Maine State Library, Library Development Services, State House Station 64, Augusta ME 04333, †; SRI/MF/complete.

S3450   MAINE
Department of Finance and Administration

S3450-1   STATE OF MAINE FINANCIAL REPORT for Period July 1, 1983-June 30, 1984

Annual.   [1984.]   4+138 p.
LC 45-27740.
SRI/MF/complete

Annual report on financial condition of Maine State government for FY84, with comparisons to FY83, presenting assets, liabilities, reserves, and fund balances; revenues by source; and expenditures by object and agency; for general, highway, special revenue, bond proceed, debt and internal service, enterprise, and trust/agency funds.

Also includes data on budgeted vs. actual revenues and expenditures; State bonded debt and fixed assets; and summary trends from FY75.

Contains contents listing (2 p.); and 4 summary charts, and 54 financial exhibits with accompanying notes (p. 1-138).

Availability: Maine Department of Finance and Administration, Accounts and Control Bureau, State Office Bldg., Rm. 300, Station No. 14, Augusta ME 04333, †; SRI/MF/complete.

S3450-2   MAINE STATE GOVERNMENT ANNUAL REPORT, 1983-84

Annual.   1984.   xxvi+758 p.
LC 76-643347.
SRI/MF/complete

Annual compilation of reports, for FY84, of approximately 450 Maine State depts and agencies, with data on selected administrative, regulatory, and financial activities. Data are compiled by the State Bureau of Budget.

Contents:

Foreword, contents listing, and lists of organizational changes. (p. vii-xxvi)

Agency reports, arranged alphabetically by function, with information on agency purpose, activities, organization, employees, and licenses/permits and/or publications issued; tabular summaries of agency expenditures by object and fund, FY84; and additional tables, described below. (p. 1-741)

Index. (p. 743-758)

Availability: Maine Department of Finance and Administration, Purchases Bureau, Reprographics Division, State House Station 91, Augusta ME 04333, $6.24 payable to Maine Treasurer of State; SRI/MF/complete.

ADDITIONAL TABLES:

[Unless otherwise noted, data are shown for FY84.]

a. Baxter State Park Authority: visitor use, revenues, and expenditures, 1979-1983/84. 1 table. (p. 67)

b. Consumer Credit Protection Bureau: licensing activity, by type of lending institution. 1 table. (p. 82)

c. Real Estate Commission: licensing activity, and licenses in effect, by type, as of June 1984. 2 tables. (p. 87-88)

d. Corrections Dept: Parole Board case activity; and supervised probationers and parolees. 2 tables. (p. 162, 166)

e. Civil Emergency Preparedness Bureau: Federal assistance grants, by program. 1 table. (p. 179)

f. Veteran's Services Bureau: claimant and benefit activity by city, FY84 with trends from FY75; Veteran's Memorial Cemetery burials and reservations; and educational dependent benefit applications and enrollment, by type of college. 3 tables. (p. 186-188)

g. Historic Preservation Commission: Federal grant awards, by project category. 1 table. (p. 215)

h. School Management Bureau: school nutrition program meals served, Dec. and summer 1983. 2 tables. (p. 239)

i. Environmental Protection Dept: air, land, and water quality monitoring and enforcement activity; and oil pollution and hazardous material spills/waste control program activities. 6 tables. (p. 268-280)

j. Insurance Advisory Board: premiums and claims paid by major lines of State administered insurance. 1 table. (p. 339-340)

k. Taxation Bureau: elderly householder tax/rent refunds, FY83-84; assessments of individual and corporate nonfilers of State tax returns; sales/income/fuel and property tax revenues. 5 tables. (p. 343-345)

l. Nursing Board: examination results and licensure activity for registered and practical nurses. 4 tables. (p. 417-418)

m. Inland Fisheries and Wildlife Dept: guide licenses passed and denied, by type; fish stocked from State hatcheries/rearing stations; and game warden hours by enforcement activity; 1983. 3 tables. (p. 456-463)

n. Judicial Dept: law bar examination results, various months 1981-84. 1 table. (p. 479)

o. Labor Dept: Bureau of Employment Security detailed finances; consumer protection and industrial safety inspection and regulatory activities; boiler, elevator, and tramway inspections; and apprenticeship program and minimum wage regulatory activities. 7 tables. (p. 494-511)

p. Maritime Academy: revenues and expenditures, by item. 1 table. (p. 573)

q. Public Safety Dept: State police investigative cases; gambling, weapons, and private investigator licensing; motor vehicle inspections; and canine unit and crime laboratory activities; mostly 1983. 6 tables. (p. 635-648)

r. State Retirement System: detailed finances, including assets and trust fund reserves, with selected comparisons to FY83; and payments, contributions, and recipients, FY80-84; for State and local employees, and teachers. 9 tables. (p. 662-669)

s. School Building Authority: construction financed since 1951; and bond activities and debt. 2 tables. (p. 674-675).

t. Transportation Dept: construction div contracts. 1 table. (p. 703)

u. University of Maine: full-time employees, by category and funding source, Oct. 1983; and revenues and expenditures by item. 2 tables. (p. 722-723)

v. Workers' Compensation Commission: premiums written, taxes paid to general fund, and losses, 1964 and 1974-83. 1 table. (p. 740)

S3463   MAINE
Judicial Department

S3463-1   STATE OF MAINE JUDICIAL DEPARTMENT 1984 Annual Report
Annual.   Mar. 15, 1985.
iii+179 p.
SRI/MF/complete

Annual report, for 1984, on Maine judicial system, including trial and appellate court caseloads, case dispositions, and processing time. Covers law court (court of final appeal), and superior, district, and administrative courts. Includes administrative court cases by agency; trial court data by case type, district, county, and city; and trends from 1976.

Case types shown are civil and criminal for all courts, with some detail for workers compensation, damages, personal injury, contract, Uniform Reciprocal Enforcement of Support Act (interstate child support agreement), divorce, habeas corpus, bail review, family abuse, small claims, juvenile, mental health, money judgments, and traffic cases.

Also includes data on court mediation service and case processing time; and judicial dept finances.

Data are from reports submitted to the Administrative Office.

Contains listings of contents and tables/charts (p. i-iii); transcript of a speech by the chief justice (p. 1-7); narrative report with 5 charts and 4 tables (p. 9-41); and 5 statistical appendices, with 8 charts, 47 tables, and 2 maps (p. 43-179).

This is the 9th annual report. Issuing agency also issues an executive summary, not covered in SRI.

Availability: Maine Judicial Department, Administrative Office of the Courts, 66 Pearl St., PO Box 4820 D.T.S., Portland ME 04112, †; SRI/MF/complete.

S3465   MAINE
Department of Labor

S3465-1   MAINE OCCUPATIONAL STAFFING PATTERNS
Series.   For individual publication data, see below.
SRI/MF/complete

Continuing series of reports, published in a 3-year cycle, each covering Maine employment in a group of selected industries, by detailed occupation.

Data are from Occupational Employment Statistics (OES) surveys, conducted over a 3-year period and updated triennially, on the following industries: nonmanufacturing; manufacturing; wholesale and retail trade, and selected regulated industries; Federal, State, and local government; hospitals; and education.

General format of each report:

a. Contents listing; and introduction, sometimes with charts or tables showing trends, summary data, and/or survey sample characteristics.

b. 1 table, repeated for each SIC 2- or 3-digit industry covered, showing estimated employment by detailed occupational group, including percent of surveyed establishments/units reporting each occupation.

c. Methodology.

Reports reviewed in 1985 are described below.

Availability: Maine Department of Labor, Employment Security Bureau, Economic Analysis and Research Division, 20 Union St., Augusta ME 04330, †; SRI/MF/complete.

S3465-1.8: Maine Occupational Staffing Patterns for Wholesale and Retail Trade and Selected Transportation, Communications, Electric, Gas, and Sanitary Services, Second Quarter 1982
[Triennial. Feb. 1985. v+25 p. Pub. Series No. OES-22. SRI/MF/complete.]

Covers occupational employment in the following industries:

a. Transportation and utilities, including local and suburban transit and interurban highway passenger transportation; motor freight transportation and warehousing; water and air transportation; communications; and electric, gas, and sanitary services.

b. Wholesale trade, including durable and nondurable goods.

c. Retail trade, including building materials, hardware, garden supply, and mobile home dealers; general merchandise stores; food stores; automobile dealers and gasoline service stations; apparel and accessory stores; eating and drinking places; and miscellaneous retail stores.

Data are based on mail surveys conducted 2nd quarter 1982.

Previous report, for 2nd quarter 1979, is described in SRI 1981 Annual under S3465-1.2.

S3465-1.9: Maine Occupational Staffing Patterns for Federal Government (Oct. 1982), State Government (May 1982), and Local Government (May 1982)
[Triennial. Mar. 1985. v+19 p. Pub. Series No. OES-23. SRI/MF/complete.]

Covers occupational employment in Federal Government, Oct. 1982, and in State and local governments, May 1982.

Data are based on mail surveys conducted during 1982.

Previous report, for 1979 and 1980, is described in SRI 1982 Annual under S3465-1.4.

S3465-1.10: Maine Occupational Staffing Patterns for Manufacturing Industries, Second Quarter 1983
[Triennial. Mar. 1985. v+38 p. Pub. Series No. OES-24. SRI/MF/complete.]

Covers occupational employment in food/kindred products, textiles, apparel, lumber/wood products, furniture/fixtures, printing/publishing, chemicals/allied products, rubber/plastics, leather/leather products, stone/clay/glass/concrete products, fabricated metal products, nonelectrical machinery, electrical/electronic

machinery/equipment/supplies, transportation equipment, instruments/related products, and miscellaneous manufacturing industries.

Data are based on mail surveys conducted 2nd quarter 1983.

Previous report, for 2nd quarter 1980, is described in SRI 1982 Annual under S3465-1.6.

S3465-1.11: Maine Occupational Staffing Pattern for Hospitals, Apr. 1983
[Triennial. Mar. 1985. v+12 p. Pub. Series No. OES-25. SRI/MF/complete.]

Covers occupational employment in hospitals. Data are based on mail surveys conducted Apr. 1983.

Previous report, for Apr. 1980, is described in SRI 1982 Annual under S3465-1.5.

S3465-2   MAINE LABOR MARKET DIGEST
Monthly.   6 p.
SRI/MF/complete, shipped quarterly

Monthly report on Maine employment trends, earnings, and unemployment insurance claimants. Includes data by industry and MSA. Data are compiled by the Maine Bureau of Employment Security. Report is issued 4-8 weeks after month of coverage.

Contains narrative article, occasionally with statistics; 6 trend charts; and 6 monthly tables and 1 irregularly recurring table, listed below.

Monthly tables appear in all issues. Irregularly recurring table appears in Nov.-Dec. 1984 and Jan.-Apr. and July 1985 issues. All additional features with substantial statistics on topics not covered in recurring tables are described, as they appear, under "Statistical Features." Nonstatistical features are not covered.

Availability: Maine Department of Labor, Employment Security Bureau, Economic Analysis and Research Division, 20 Union St., Augusta ME 04330, †; SRI/MF/complete, shipped quarterly.

Issues reviewed during 1985: Sept. 1984-Aug. 1985 (D).

TABLES:

[Tables generally show data for month of coverage, previous month, and same month of previous year. Data are for Maine, unless otherwise noted. Data for 2 MSAs are for Portland and Lewiston-Auburn.]

MONTHLY TABLES

[1] Nonfarm wage/salary employment by place of work [industry division and major manufacturing group, and total involved in labor-management disputes, for State and for 2 MSAs].

[2] Earnings and workweek of production workers in manufacturing industries [for State by manufacturing group, and totals for 2 MSAs; also shows average hourly earnings for 3 preceding years].

[3] Female labor force [total, unemployed, and resident employed].

[4] U.S. CPI.

[5] Labor force, employment, and unemployment [for Maine labor markets, for 4 MSAs, 5 other New England States, and total U.S.].

[6] Midmonth insured unemployment (less partials) [continued-week claimants and insured unemployment rate, for State and 2 MSAs].

IRREGULARLY RECURRING TABLE

[7] Selected characteristics of unemployment insurance claimants [distribution by occupation and age].

STATISTICAL FEATURES:

S3465–2.601: Sept. 1984

PERSONS OF FRENCH ANCESTRY, MAINE AND MAINE COUNTIES, 1980

(p. 6) Table showing Maine population with French, French/Canadian, and multiple (including French or French/Canadian) ancestry, by county, 1980. Data are from the 1980 Census of Population and Housing.

S3465–2.602: Oct. 1984

ABOVE-AVERAGE NUMBER OF MAINE PERSONS WORKING PART-TIME FOR ECONOMIC REASONS

(p. 1-2, 6) Article, with 1 table showing part-time employment (voluntary and for economic reasons) and full-time employment, for 6 New England States and U.S., 1978 and 1983. Data are from the Current Population Survey.

S3465–2.603: Feb. 1985

SUMMARY OF FEDERAL FUNDS FOR THE U.S. AND NEW ENGLAND STATES, FY84

(p. 6) Table showing Federal expenditures in each of 6 New England States, as follows: per capita, with national ranking; and by purpose (grants to State/local governments, salaries/wages, direct payments for individuals, procurement, and other); FY84. Also includes U.S. totals. Data are from Census Bureau.

S3465–2.604: Apr. 1985

DOWNTOWN RETAIL SALES IN BANGOR'S METROPOLITAN AREA STRONGEST IN MAINE, CENSUS BUREAU REPORTS

(p. 1-2) Article, with 1 table showing Maine retail sales in 3 MSAs, with detail for component central cities and business districts, 1977 and 1982. Data are from Census Bureau.

S3465–2.605: July 1985

RATE OF SELF-EMPLOYMENT ABOVE AVERAGE IN MAINE

(p. 1-2) Article, with 2 tables showing total and nonagricultural employment and self-employed workers, for 6 New England States and total U.S., 1984. Data are from BLS.

S3465–2.606: Aug. 1985

FEMALE PARTICIPATION IN THE LABOR FORCE CONTINUES TO INCREASE

(p. 1-2, 6) Article, with 3 tables showing New England employment by status (full-time, part-time for economic reasons, and voluntary part-time) and by occupational group; and labor force participation rates by age and marital status; all by sex, 1984. Data are from BLS.

S3475   MAINE
Department of Public Safety

S3475–1   CRIME IN MAINE, 1984
Annual. [1985.]
2+v+127 p.
LC 77-643188.
SRI/MF/complete

Annual report on Maine crimes, arrests, and police employment, 1984 with comparisons to 1983.

Covers Index crimes by offense, and crime and clearance rates, by reporting agency arranged by county; value of property stolen and recovered by type of property, sworn and civilian police employment by type of agency, and assaults on police, by county; and arrests by age and sex, by Index and non-Index offense.

Also includes data on murder victims and offenders by age and sex; Index and domestic violence offenses, by type of weapon and other circumstances; and domestic violence offenses by county.

Index offenses are murder, rape, robbery, aggravated assault, burglary, larceny, motor vehicle theft, and arson.

Data are from reports of State and local law enforcement agencies, submitted under the Uniform Crime Reporting (UCR) program.

Contains listings of contents, tables, and charts (p. i-v); highlights and UCR program description (p. 1-6); report, with narrative summaries, and 26 charts and 27 tables (p. 7-96); and UCR reporting procedures (p. 97-127).

This is the 10th annual report.

Availability: Maine Department of Public Safety, Uniform Crime Reporting Division, 36 Hospital St., Augusta ME 04333, †; SRI/MF/complete.

S3475–2   MAINE MOTOR VEHICLE TRAFFIC ACCIDENTS, 1984
Annual. Feb. 25, 1985.
22 p. no paging.
SRI/MF/complete

Annual report on Maine traffic accidents, fatalities, and injuries, by accident circumstances, vehicle type and make, and driver and victim characteristics, 1984.

Also includes accident-related data on use of safety equipment; vehicle defects; alcohol and drug involvement, including results of blood alcohol content tests; and value of damaged property.

Report consists of 13 tables. This is the 3rd edition of the report. SRI coverage begins with this edition.

Availability: Maine Department of Public Safety, 36 Hospital St., Augusta ME 04333, †; SRI/MF/complete

S3490   MAINE
Office of the Secretary of State

S3490–1   STATE OF MAINE GENERAL ELECTION, Nov. 6, 1984
Biennial. 2 volumes.
For individual publication data, see below.
SRI/MF/complete

Biennial report, issued in 2 parts, presenting results of Maine general election held Nov. 6, 1984. Also includes data on registered voters for primary and general election. Individual reports are described below.

For description of previous reports, covering 1982 general election results, see SRI 1983 Annual under this number.

Availability: Maine Office of the Secretary of State, Elections Bureau, Public Administration Division, State House Station 101, Augusta ME 04333, †; SRI/MF/complete.

S3490–1.1: Enrolled and Registered Voters with Comparative Presidential, U.S. Senatorial, and Congressional Votes
[Biennial. 1984. 35 p. SRI/MF/complete.]

Shows primary election enrolled voters and voting for U.S. Senator, by political party; general and primary election registered voters; and general election voting for President, and U.S. Senator and Representatives, by candidate; all by county and municipality, with selected detail by ward and precinct.

S3490–1.2: Official Vote for Statewide, Legislative, and County Officers
[Biennial. [1984.] 33 p. SRI/MF/complete.]

Shows voting for State senators, representatives, and district attorneys, by district; county officers, including probate judges and sheriffs, by county; 4 bond issues; and 4 State constitutional amendments, including 1 concerning equal rights for women.

Also includes summary data on voting for President and U.S. Senator and Representatives.

S3593   MARYLAND
Department of Agriculture

S3593–1   MARYLAND AGRICULTURAL STATISTICS, 1984
Annual. [1985.] 56 p.
Rpt. No. MDA 113-85.
LC 64-64330.
SRI/MF/complete

Annual report on Maryland agricultural production, marketing, and finances, 1984, with some data for 1985 and selected trends from as early as 1970. Data are generally shown by commodity and/or county, with some comparisons to neighboring States and total U.S.

Report covers production, prices, sales, value, and, as applicable, acreage, yield, disposition, and inventory, for field crop, fruit, vegetable, poultry, dairy, and livestock sectors.

Report also includes data on farms; farm acreage, value, rents, income and production expenses; weather; fertilizer sales; and field crop production in Delmarva counties.

Data are compiled by the Maryland Crop Reporting Service in cooperation with USDA.

Contains contents listing and foreword (p. 2-4); and report, with 3 maps, 3 charts, and 60 tables (p. 5-56).

Availability: Maryland Crop Reporting Service, 50 Harry S. Truman Pkwy., Rm. 202, Annapolis MD 21401, †; SRI/MF/complete.

S3600   MARYLAND
Administrative Office of the Courts

S3600–1   ANNUAL REPORT OF THE MARYLAND JUDICIARY, 1983-84
Annual. 2 volumes.
For individual publication data, see below.
SRI/MF/complete

Annual report on Maryland judicial system, for FY84. Covers appeals, special appeals, circuit, and district courts. Report is issued in 2 volumes, a primarily narrative report and a statistical abstract, individually described below.

This is the 8th annual report. Previous report, for FY83, is described in SRI 1983 Annual, under this number.

Availability: Maryland Administrative Office of the Courts, Courts of Appeal Bldg., PO Box 431, Annapolis MD 21404, †; SRI/MF/complete.

S3600–1.1: Annual Report of the Maryland Judiciary, 1983-84: Narrative Report
[Annual. Sept. 25, 1984. vi+34 p. LC 79-643900. SRI/MF/complete.]

Narrative report on Maryland judicial system, for FY84, with selected trends from FY77.

Includes data on revenues, expenditures, and personnel, by court level and/or judicial agency; court caseload summary; judicial system funding sources; jury trial requests before and after passage of trial reduction law, for Baltimore City, selected counties, and State; percent of candidates passing bar exams; State law library use; complaints and disciplinary actions against attorneys; and judicial vacancies, applicants, and nominees, by court level.

Contains contents listing, transmittal letter, introduction, and organizational chart (p. iii-vi); narrative report, in 7 sections, interspersed with 9 charts and 7 tables (p. 1-31); and maps of judicial districts and lists of members of the judiciary (p. 32-34).

S3600–1.2: Annual Report of the Maryland Judiciary, 1983-84: Statistical Abstract
[Annual. [1984.] ix+110 p. LC 79-643892. SRI/MF/complete.]

Statistical abstract on Maryland judicial system, for FY84, including trial and appellate court caseloads and case dispositions and processing times. Includes data by case type and county, with selected trends from 1973.

Case types include equity, law, criminal, and juvenile cases, with some additional detail for tort, contract, traffic, domestic, and landlord-tenant relations cases.

Also includes data on judicial workloads, circuit court appeals from district courts and administrative agencies, and bar examination results.

Data by county are generally arranged by circuit or district and include detail for Baltimore City.

Contains contents and table listings (p. iii-ix); glossary (p. 1-7); report, in 4 sections with 7 charts and 66 tables (p. 11-104); and appendix with lists of legal officials and 1 table (p. 107-110).

S3610   MARYLAND
Department of Education

S3610–1   FACTS ABOUT MARYLAND PUBLIC EDUCATION, 1984/85: A Statistical Handbook
Annual. [1985.]
2+47 p. Pocket size.
LC 73-646032.
SRI/MF/complete

Annual statistical summary, for 1984/85, on Maryland elementary and secondary education, covering public and nonpublic school enrollment and facilities, and public school staff, finances, and programs. Includes selected data by race, and by county and for Baltimore City, with trends from 1979.

Contains contents listing (p. 1), and 7 charts and 25 tables showing the following:

a. Summary: population, July 1984; professional staff, number of public and nonpublic schools, local education budget, cost per pupil, average teacher salary, adult education enrollment, public school enrollment, average daily membership, and high school graduates, 1984/85; teaching certificates issued, 1983/84; and Maryland's rank among the States in selected education-related areas, various periods 1981/82-1983/84. 2 tables. (p. 2-3)

b. Enrollment for public and nonpublic schools by level, and for State institution educational programs, and public schools by county, fall 1979 and 1983-84; and for public schools by level, by county, Sept. 1984. 3 tables. (p. 4-6)

c. Nonpublic schools, and public schools by level, by county, 1984/85. 1 table. (p. 7)

d. Enrollment and professional staff, by race and for American Indian/Alaskan Native, Asian/Pacific Islander, and Hispanic, all by county, 1984/85. 2 tables. (p. 8-9)

e. General Educational Development (GED) test results, by test center, July 1983-June 1984 period; Maryland functional reading test passing rates, for grades 9-12, 1982/83-1983/84; and total 7th-12th grade pupil withdrawals by cause, 1983/84. 1 chart and 2 tables. (p. 10-12)

f. Salaries and employment: minimum and maximum salary for teacher with bachelor's degree; and staff employment, by function; all by county, 1984/85. 2 tables. (p. 13-15)

g. Finances: disbursements by government source and function, and per pupil costs, State aid, and local wealth, by county, 1983/84; and State aid by expenditure category, 1984/85. 4 charts and 1 table. (p. 16-23)

h. Food service programs, including Federal and State revenue, and meals served, by county, 1983/84. 2 tables. (p. 24-27)

i. Federal aid to disadvantaged children, and children eligible and participating, by county; and correctional institution education program enrollment and staff, with number completing 8th grade, high school, and vocational programs, by institution; 1983/84. 2 tables. (p. 28-29)

j. Library media centers, materials, expenditures, and employment, by county, 1982/83; public library income, staff, and book circulation, by county, 1983/84; and distribution of instructional TV broadcast hours, by curriculum area and school level, 1984/85. 1 chart and 2 tables. (p. 30-34)

k. Extended elementary education enrollment, schools, and staff, 1984/85; enrollment in vocational/technical and industrial arts, adult, vocational adult and apprentice, and community education programs, by program, including school volunteers, 1984/85; and students receiving special education and related services, by handicap or type of program, 1983/84; all by county. 5 tables. (p. 35-43)

l. Vocational rehabilitation program caseloads and rehabilitations by county, and rehabilitations by nature of disability, 1984. 1 chart and 1 table. (p. 44-46)

Also includes information on requirements for a high school diploma, 1984/85. (p. 47)

Availability: Maryland Department of Education, 200 W. Baltimore St., Baltimore MD 21201-2595, †; SRI/MF/complete.

S3610–2   MARYLAND PUBLIC SCHOOLS
Series. For individual publication data, see below.
SRI/MF/complete

Series of reports on Maryland elementary and secondary schools, covering enrollment, staff, salaries, finances, and transportation. Data are shown by county and for Baltimore City. Some reports include nonpublic school data.

Most reports are issued on an annual basis. Reports are described in order of receipt. Reports reviewed during 1985 are described below.

Prior to 1985, abstracts for these reports were grouped according to year of issuance. For descriptions of reports covered in 1984, see SRI 1984 Annual under S3610-3.

Issuing agency also publishes a detailed, less current annual report, not covered in SRI, compiling data covered in the series.

Availability: Maryland Department of Education, Management Information Systems Office, 200 W. Baltimore St., Baltimore MD 21201-2595, †; SRI/MF/complete.

S3610–2.1: Public School Enrollment, State of Maryland, Sept. 30, 1984
[Annual. Jan. 1985. 10 p. no paging. Rpt. No. MSDE-OMIS 04100(R)001. SRI/MF/complete.]

Contains 6 tables showing Maryland public school enrollment, by grade (including special education) and sex, by county, Sept. 30, 1984.

S3610–2.2: Number of Maryland Public Schools by Organization and Enrollment, Sept. 30, 1984

[Annual. Jan. 1985. 12 p. no paging. Rpt. No. MSDE-OMIS 04100(R)905. SRI/MF/complete.]

Contains 6 tables showing number of Maryland public schools, by grade organization and pupil membership, by county, Sept. 1984.

Also includes lists of middle schools, vocational/technical schools, and schools with special education programs only.

S3610–2.3: Staff Employed at School and Central Office Levels, Maryland Public Schools, 1984/85

[Annual. Feb. 1985. 10 p. no paging. Rpt. No. MSDE-ADM 04100(R)100. LC 85-621867. SRI/MF/complete.]

Contains table listing, and 8 tables primarily showing Maryland public school staff employment by detailed function and county, 1984/85, with summary per-pupil ratios and comparisons to 1983/84.

S3610–2.4: Statistics on Enrollment and Number of Schools, Public and Nonpublic, Sept. 30, 1984, Maryland

[Annual. Mar. 1985. 20 p. no paging. Rpt. No. MSDE-OMIS 04110(R)003. LC 84-622980. SRI/MF/complete.]

Contains table listing, and 14 tables showing the following for Maryland: public and nonpublic school enrollment trends, by county, 1979 and 1983-84; enrollment and number of schools by grade level, number of FTE teachers, and enrollment by specific grade (including special education), for public, Catholic, and other nonpublic schools, by county, Sept. 30, 1984; and State institution educational program enrollment, by institution and grade level, Sept. 30, 1984.

S3610–2.5: Professional Staff by Race and Sex, Maryland Public School Systems, Sept. 30, 1982

[Biennial. Mar. 1985. 21 p. no paging. Rpt. No. MSDE-ADM 04100(R)104. SRI/MF/complete.]

Contains table listing, introduction, definitions, and 2 charts; and 3 tables showing Maryland public school professional staff employment by function, sex, and race, for total State and by county, Sept. 30, 1982. Racial breakdowns are white, black, Hispanic, Asian, and American Indian (for State data); and white, black, and other (for county data).

For description of previous report, for 1980, see SRI 1982 Annual under S1360-2.13.

S3610–2.6: Professional Staff by Race and Sex, Maryland Public School Systems, Sept. 30, 1984

[Biennial. Mar. 1985. 21 p. no paging. Rpt. No. MSDE-ADM 04100(R)104. LC 85-622869. SRI/MF/complete.]

Contains table listing, introduction, definitions, and 2 charts; and 3 tables showing Maryland public school professional staff employment by function, sex, and race, for to-

tal State, Baltimore City, and by county, Sept. 30, 1984. Racial breakdowns are white, black, Hispanic, Asian, and American Indian (for State data); and white, black, and other (for county and Baltimore data).

For description of previous report, for 1982, see S3610-2.5 above.

S3610–2.7: Selected Financial Data, Maryland Public Schools, 1983/84: Part 2, Expenditures

[Annual. May 1985. 20 p. no paging. Rpt. No. MSDE-OMIS 04110(R)201. LC 79-635530. SRI/MF/complete.]

Contains table listing and 13 tables showing Maryland public school disbursements by detailed function and object, by county, 1983/84.

S3610–2.8: Selected Financial Data, Maryland Public Schools, 1983/84: Part 1, Revenue and Local Unit Wealth

[Annual. May 1985. 6+17 p.+errata sheets. Rpt. No. OMIS 04110(R)200. SRI/MF/complete.]

Contains contents and table listing, introduction, definitions, and 12 tables showing the following for Maryland, by county, for 1983/84:

a. Revenue by source (State, Federal, and local government) and purpose (current expenses, school construction, debt service, and food services); and State and Federal revenues by detailed category.

b. Basic State aid compared to local wealth; assessed property valuation; and local school appropriations compared to total local revenue, assessed valuation, and net taxable income.

S3610–2.9: Selected Financial Data, Maryland Public Schools, 1983/84: Part 3, Analysis of Costs

[Annual. July 1985. 12 p. no paging. Rpt. No. OMIS 04100(R)202. SRI/MF/complete.]

Contains introduction and 11 tables showing the following for Maryland: costs per pupil belonging and attending, by expenditure function, with selected county rankings; local appropriations and per pupil costs for tuition; per pupil costs for textbooks, library books, and materials; school property value per pupil; and average salary per teacher and principal; all by county, 1983/84, with trends from 1973/74.

S3610–2.10: Public School Pupil Transportation in Maryland, 1983/84

[Annual. July 1985. 14 p. no paging. Rpt. No. OMIS 04100(R)300. LC 84-623270. SRI/MF/complete.]

Contains table listing, and 13 tables showing the following for Maryland: public school pupils transported, by grade level; transportation vehicles, by capacity; contract and public vehicle mileage, and driver and aide hours; public and nonpublic school handicapped pupils transported, by means; total disbursements and State aid for transportation; and cost per pupil transported; all by county, 1983/84, with selected trends from 1974.

S3610–2.11: Selected Financial Data, Maryland Public Schools, Part 4: Ten Year Summary, 1974/75-1983/84

[Annual. Aug. 1985. 28 p. no paging. Rpt. No. OMIS 04100(R)203. SRI/MF/complete.]

Contains table listing and 22 tables showing summary time series data by county, 1974/75-1983/84, for selected items covered in Parts 1-3, above.

S3610–2.12: Federal Program Expenditures, Maryland Public Schools, 1983/84

[Annual. Aug. 1985. 21 p. no paging. Rpt. No. OMIS 04100(210). SRI/MF/complete.]

Contains table/chart listing; and 2 charts and 8 tables showing expenditures of Federal funds for Maryland public schools, by program and function, by county, 1983/84.

S3610–2.13: Salary Schedules of Professional Personnel, Maryland Public Schools, 1984/85

[Annual. Nov. 1984. 13 p. var. paging. Rpt. No. MSDE-OMIS 04100(R)250. SRI/MF/complete.]

Contains 5 tables showing Maryland public school salary schedules for teachers and 7 administrative positions, by county, with detail by degree level for most positions, 1984/85. Includes minimum and/or maximum amounts, and amount by salary schedule step (for teachers only). Also includes methods of determining salaries.

S3610–5 MARYLAND PUBLIC LIBRARY STATISTICS, FY83

Annual. [1984.]
6 p. no paging.
SRI/MF/complete

Annual report, for FY83, on Maryland public libraries. Covers finances, staff, holdings, and circulation. Consists of 6 tables showing population, and the following for public libraries, by county, FY83:

a. State operating/capital aid; operating income by source, including Federal and State aid, and local appropriations; and operating expenditures by type, including salaries, materials, and equipment.

b. Professional librarians, library associates, support staff, and CETA employees; minimum salaries for professional librarians; library holdings by type; book and film circulation; and registered borrowers.

Availability: Maryland Department of Education, Library Development and Services Division, 200 W. Baltimore St., Baltimore MD 21201-2595, †; SRI/MF/complete.

S3615   MARYLAND
Administrative Board of Election Laws

S3615–1   NOV. 6, 1984 GENERAL ELECTION RESULTS AND VOTER TURNOUT STATISTICS, Maryland
Biennial. [1985.] 20 p.
LC 85-622904.
SRI/MF/complete

Biennial report presenting results of the Maryland general election held Nov. 6, 1984. Shows voting for President/Vice President, U.S. Representatives, judges, and 1 State constitutional amendment. Also shows voter registration and turnout, by party. Data are shown by county and/or district.

Previous report, covering 1982 general election, is described in SRI 1983 Annual under this number.

Availability: Maryland Administrative Board of Election Laws, PO Box 231, Annapolis MD 21404-0231, $1.50; SRI/MF/complete.

S3616   MARYLAND
Department of Employment and Training

S3616–1   LABOR MARKET DIMENSIONS, Maryland
Monthly. Approx. 18 p.
SRI/MF/complete, shipped quarterly

Monthly report on Maryland employment and unemployment, hourly and weekly earnings, and unemployment insurance (UI) activities. Most employment data are shown by major industry group; separate data are generally shown for Baltimore metro area.

Data are compiled by the Dept of Employment and Training, and are issued approximately 4-5 months after month of coverage.

Contains narrative review of reported data; and 6 monthly tables and 1 quarterly table, listed below.

Dec. 1984 issue includes an additional table showing 1984 annual averages for data in monthly table [1]. Jan. 1985 issue includes an additional table showing civilian labor force by employment status, monthly 1970-84.

Monthly tables appear in all issues. Page locations and latest period of coverage for quarterly table are noted, as the table appears, under "Statistical Features."

Availability: Maryland Department of Employment and Training, Research and Analysis Division, 1100 N. Eutaw St., Baltimore MD 21201, †; SRI/MF/complete, shipped quarterly.

Issues reviewed during 1985: Sept. 1984-June 1985 (D).

RECURRING TABLES:
[Unless otherwise noted, data are shown for current and previous month, and for same month of previous year. Data in tables [2-4] are shown separately for Maryland and Baltimore metro area.]

MONTHLY TABLES

[1] Civilian labor force, employment, and unemployment, by place of residence [by State region and county, for current and previous month].

[2] Nonagricultural payroll employment by industry [group], by place of employment.

[3] Gross average hourly and weekly earnings and hours [worked] by production workers in selected [major] manufacturing industry groups.

[4] UI activities, State regular UI compensation program [claims and payments].

[5] Maryland Federal programs [unemployment compensation initial and continued claims].

[6] Estimated nonagricultural payroll employment by industry [div], by place of employment: Maryland [aggregate] counties in the Washington, D.C. metro area; Baltimore City; western Maryland; and balance of State.

QUARTERLY TABLE

[7] Females and production workers: estimated nonagricultural payroll employment by industry, by place of employment [employed in Maryland; by month for quarter ended 1 month prior to cover date].

STATISTICAL FEATURES:

S3616–1.601: Oct. 1984

QUARTERLY TABLE

[7] Females and production workers nonagricultural employment, July-Sept. 1984. (p. 18)

S3616–1.602: Jan. 1985

QUARTERLY TABLE

[7] Females and production workers nonagricultural employment, Oct.-Dec. 1984. (p. 20)

S3618   MARYLAND
Department of Fiscal Services

S3618–1   LOCAL GOVERNMENT FINANCES IN MARYLAND for the Fiscal Year Ended June 30, 1984
Annual. Mar. 12, 1985.
409 p.
LC 79-615811.
SRI/MF/complete

Annual report presenting data on the financial condition of Maryland counties, incorporated municipalities, and other local taxing jurisdictions, FY84. Also includes status of local pension plans. Data are compiled from State agency and local government reports.

Contents:

Section I. Transmittal letter, and contents and table listing. (p. 1-3)

Section II-III. Report, with 13 detailed financial tables, listed below, showing data for counties and special districts (p. 7-177) and for cities, towns, villages, and special taxing areas (p. 181-384).

Section IV. Appendices, with 12 tables, described below, including data on local tax rates and bond issues. (p. 387-402)

Section V-VI. Notes and index. (p. 403-409)

This is the 36th annual report.

Availability: Maryland Department of Fiscal Services, Fiscal Research Division, Legislative Services Bldg., Rm. 200, 90 State Circle, Annapolis MD 21401-1991, †; SRI/MF/complete.

TABLES:
[Data by county are also shown for Baltimore City.]

S3618–1.1: Detailed Financial Tables
[Data are for FY84, unless otherwise noted.]

BY COUNTY
[Tables show data by county. Data in tables I-II are shown by applicable jurisdictional unit, variously including library, education, community college, social services, and health boards; State highway administration account; sanitary districts; transit authorities; relevant commissions; and others.

Revenues are generally shown by source, including local property and income taxes, licenses/permits, revenue sharing, and Federal and State grants. Expenditures are generally shown by function.]

I. Financial summaries [property valuation, public debt detail, and aggregate revenues and expenditures]. (p. 9-36)

II. Statements of revenue and expenditure [including data for governmental (operating and capital) and enterprise operations]. (p. 39-88)

III. Five-year summary: statements of revenue and expenditure, FY80-84. (p. 91-115)

IV. Statements of revenue and expenditure, percent of total. (p. 119-123)

V. Statements of per capita revenue and expenditure. (p. 127-131)

VI. Analyses of county accounts with boards of education, boards of trustees for community colleges, and library boards. (p. 135-158)

VII. Pension plan disclosures [local pension plan descriptions, groups covered, accounting and funding policies, costs, and funding status (assets compared to nonvested and/or vested benefits), all by individual plan], as of the 2 most recent plan valuation dates. (p. 161-177)

BY MUNICIPAL AREA
[Data are generally arranged by county. Municipal areas are cities, towns, villages, and special taxing areas.]

I-II. [Tables I-II, listed above, are repeated for individual municipal areas; data are not shown by jurisdictional unit, except data in table II are shown for government and enterprise operations funds.] (p. 183-295)

III. [Table III, listed above, is repeated for aggregate municipal areas.] (p. 299-318)

IV-V. [Tables IV-V, listed above, are repeated for individual municipal areas.] (p. 321-354)

VI. [Table VII, listed above, is repeated for individual municipal areas.] (p. 357-384)

S3618–1.2: Appendix Tables
a. Population and land area, by county and municipality or special taxing district, 1984; and municipal and/or county tax rates for property, admissions/amusement,

income, property transfer, recordation, sales/service, and trailer parks, mostly for FY84. App. I-VIII. (p. 387-398)

b. Industrial revenue bond issues, by place of issue and issuing jurisdiction, and issues of State industrial development financing authority, by location, 1984; and county bond ratings, 1983. App. IX-X. (p. 399-402)

S3635   MARYLAND
Department of
Health and
Mental Hygiene

S3635–3   MARYLAND MEDICAL CARE PROGRAMS: The Year in Review, FY84
Annual. Jan. 1985.
iii+87 p.
SRI/MF/complete

Annual report, for FY84, on Maryland health care services for low-income residents. Covers payments and number of enrollees, recipients, and/or services, by eligibility category; by detailed type of health service; by county and Baltimore City; by enrollee and recipient age, race, and sex; and by individual health care facility.

Eligibility categories are 14 federally matched and nonmatched indigent and medically indigent programs. Types of service include hospital inpatient and outpatient, nursing home, physician, pharmacy, dental, home/community health, and special services.

Also includes data on population compared to program enrollment by county and for Baltimore City, fraud investigations and recoveries, program trends from FY79, and summary enrollment from FY67.

Most data are compiled by the State Center for Health Statistics.

Contains contents and table listing (p. i-iii); narrative report, with 4 charts and 8 tables (p. 1-30); 35 detailed tables (p. 32-82); and glossary and technical note, with 1 table (p. 83-86).

Availability: Maryland Department of Health and Mental Hygiene, Medical Care Programs, Policy Analysis and Program Development, 300 W. Preston St., 2nd Floor, Baltimore MD 21201, †; SRI/MF/complete.

S3645   MARYLAND
Department of
Human Resources

S3645–2   INCOME MAINTENANCE ADMINISTRATION Statistical Report, Maryland
Monthly, with annual supplement. Approx. 30 p.
SRI/MF/complete, shipped quarterly

Monthly report, with annual supplement, on Maryland public welfare program applicants, recipients, and expenditures, by program and by county. Also includes data on current welfare fraud investigations. Report is issued approximately 3 months after month of coverage.

Generally contains data revisions or additions for previous reports, 1-6 summary charts, and 20 monthly tables listed below.

Nov. 1984 issue also includes 1 additional table showing number and amount of child support payments refunded to State.

An annual supplement is also issued, summarizing caseload data by program and county for the previous fiscal year.

Availability: Maryland Department of Human Resources, Income Maintenance Administration, Research and Analysis Division, 300 W. Preston St., Rm. 511, Baltimore MD 21201, †; SRI/MF/complete, shipped quarterly.

Issues reviewed during 1985: Aug. 1984-June 1985; and FY84 annual supplement (D).

TABLES:

[Unless otherwise noted, data are for month of coverage, and are shown by county and for Baltimore City.]

SUMMARY TABLES AND AFDC

1-2. Public assistance payments, cases, and recipients [by program, State only; includes selected comparisons of budgeted and actual amounts, year-to-date totals, and previous month data].

3-5. AFDC total and [with and without unemployed parents (AFDC-UP): applications, cases, dispositions, child and adult recipients, and payments].

EMERGENCY, GENERAL PUBLIC, AND MEDICAL ASSISTANCE

6. Emergency assistance (EA) payments: EAFC [emergency assistance to families with dependent children] and EA [paid cases and expenditures].

7-8. General public assistance (GPA) and general public assistance to employables (GPA-E) [applications, cases, dispositions, recipients, and payments].

9-10. Medical assistance [applications received and disposition, for nonpublic assistance (NPA) and SSI].

CHANGES AND RECONSIDERATIONS

11A-11B. Reconsiderations and interim changes completed [by program].

FOOD STAMP PROGRAM

12. Food stamp program, NPA [applications received, and dispositions].

13. Food stamp program [certified households, and participating households and individuals, for public assistance and NPA; and total dollar value of coupons].

CHILD SUPPORT COLLECTIONS

14-15. Child support collections [net, gross, and intra-State incentives]; and case data; [AFDC and non-AFDC].

EMERGENCY ASSISTANCE, AND FRAUD INVESTIGATIONS

16-18. Emergency assistance (EA and EAFC) [applications approved, by program, State only]; emergency requests, number received and number approved; and emergency payment [by program, State only]; [all by type of emergency, for month 1-3 months prior to month of coverage; tables may not appear in every issue].

19. Investigations of recipient fraud [referrals made to investigative units, investigations completed (indicating fraud or nonfraud), and total cases under investigation; for public assistance, medical assistance-NPA, and food stamp-NPA].

S3645–3   STATE OF MARYLAND LABOR MARKET BENCHMARKS AND BAROMETERS
Annual, discontinued.

Annual planning report identifying Maryland population groups most in need of employment services, discontinued with report for FY83 (for description, see SRI 1982 Annual under this number).

Data are now available on request from the Maryland Dept of Employment and Training, 1100 N. Eutaw St., Baltimore MD 21201.

S3655   MARYLAND
Department of
Licensing and Regulation

S3655–1   ONE HUNDRED THIRTEENTH ANNUAL REPORT OF THE INSURANCE COMMISSIONER of the State of Maryland
Annual. Nov. 14, 1984.
ii+72 p.
LC 32-16079.
SRI/MF/complete

Annual report on Maryland insurance industry financial condition and underwriting activity, by company and type of insurance, 1983. Covers assets, liabilities, capital/surplus, premium income, losses or claims incurred and/or paid, insurance in force, and gain from underwriting and investments, for insurers based in Maryland and elsewhere.

Data are shown, as applicable, for property/casualty and title insurance companies, nonprofit hospital service corporations, HMOs, life insurance companies, and fraternal beneficiary assns.

Also includes data on company admission applications processed, regulatory filings, broker and agent licensing, and Insurance Division receipts.

Data are compiled primarily from unaudited annual insurer statements filed with the Insurance Division.

Contains contents listing (p. ii); Insurance Division report, with 5 text tables (p. 1-15); 13

corporate financial tables (p. 17-69); and statement of Insurance Division receipts, with 1 chart and 1 table (p. 71-72).

Availability: Maryland Department of Licensing and Regulation, Insurance Division, 501 St. Paul Pl., Baltimore MD 21202-2272, †; SRI/MF/complete.

S3655–2 **SEVENTY-FOURTH ANNUAL REPORT OF THE BANK COMMISSIONER of the State of Maryland, June 30, 1984**
Annual. [1985.] 5+48 p.
LC 12-33233.
SRI/MF/complete

Annual report on financial condition of Maryland State-chartered banks and other financial institutions for FY84, presenting assets, liabilities, equity capital, income, and expenses, for commercial banks, trust companies, mutual savings institutions, and credit unions, generally as of June 30, 1984 or Dec. 31, 1983. Data on assets and liabilities are generally shown by institution, with composite trends from 1963.

Also includes data on dept fee receipts and disbursements; banks and assets, by county; and credit union financial ratios.

Contains lists of dept personnel, letter of transmittal, and contents listing (5 p.); dept report, with 2 text tables and regulatory activities (p. 1-13); and 11 financial tables, interspersed with lists of financial institutions and licensees (p. 14-48).

Availability: Maryland Department of Licensing and Regulation, State Bank Commissioner, The Brokerage, Suite 800, 34 Market Pl., Baltimore MD 21202, †; SRI/MF/complete.

S3665   MARYLAND
Department of Public Safety and Correctional Services

S3665–1 **1984 STATE OF MARYLAND UNIFORM CRIME REPORTS**
Annual. 2 volumes.
For individual publication data, see below.
SRI/MF/complete

Annual report on Maryland crimes and arrests, by offense, 1984, with trends from 1975. Includes data by region, county, municipality, and law enforcement agency, and by offender age, sex, and race. Also includes law enforcement employment, and assaults on officers.

Report focuses on 8 Index offenses: murder, rape, robbery, aggravated assault, burglary, larceny/theft, motor vehicle theft, and arson. Arrests are also shown for numerous non-Index offenses.

Data are from State and local agency reports submitted under the Uniform Crime Reporting Program.

Report is published in 2 volumes, described below. This is the 10th annual report.

Availability: Maryland Department of Public Safety and Correctional Services, Uniform Crime Reporting Section, Criminal Records-Central Repository, Maryland State Police, Pikesville MD 21208-3899, †; SRI/MF/complete.

S3665–1.1: 1984 Crime in Maryland
[Annual. June 6, 1985. vii+159 p. LC 83-646293. SRI/MF/complete.]

Contains listings of contents, tables, and charts (p. vi-vii); introduction, with 1 summary table (p. 1-9); crime classifications and methodology (p. 11-23); and 13 charts, and 29 tables described below, interspersed with narrative analyses (p. 27-159).

TABLES:
[Data by region are shown for 5 State regions. Data by county are also shown for Baltimore City.]

INDEX OFFENSES

a. Value of property stolen and recovered, by type, 1984, and total 1980-84. 2 tables. (p. 29-33)

b. Murders, by circumstance 1981-84, and by type of weapon used 1980-84. 2 tables. (p. 39-40)

c. Rapes (forcible and attempted), 1980-84. 1 table. (p. 42)

d. Robberies by type of weapon used, 1980-84; and robberies and value of property stolen, by type of location, 1984. 2 tables. (p. 46-50)

e. Aggravated assaults, by type of weapon, 1980-84. 1 table. (p. 52)

f. Breaking/entering offenses (forcible entry, no force, and attempted), 1980-84; and breaking/entering offenses and value of property stolen, by classification (residential and nonresidential day and night), 1984. 2 tables. (p. 56-59)

g. Larcenies, by type, 1980-84. 1 table. (p. 65)

h. Motor vehicles (autos, trucks, and other) stolen, and value of vehicles stolen and recovered; 1980-84. 2 tables. (p. 68-69)

i. Arson offenses, loss value, and clearance rate, by type of property, 1984. 1 table. (p. 75)

LOCAL OFFENSE AND ARREST DATA

j. Index offenses: crime rate and/or offenses by type, all by region, county, law enforcement agency, and municipality, and also including population, clearances, and clearance rates for jurisdictions except municipalities; 1983-84. 2 tables. (p. 80-120)

k. Arrests of juveniles and adults, and for drug abuse violations by substance and gambling violations by type, and arrest rates by Index offense, 1980-84; and arrests by detailed Index and non-Index offense, by sex, race/ethnicity (white, black, American Indian, and Asian), and age, 1984. 6 tables. (p. 124-131)

LAW ENFORCEMENT EMPLOYEES

l. Assaults on police officers, by type of weapon, activity, and injury status, 1980-84; and assaults by type of weapon, injuries, and clearances, by region, county, and law enforcement agency, 1984. 4 tables. (p. 137-148)

m. Employment in law enforcement, and rate per 1,000 population, by region and county; and sworn officers, civilian employees, and total employees by sex, by region, county, and law enforcement agency; 1984. 2 tables. (p. 150-156)

COUNTY TRENDS

n. Population, Index crimes, and law enforcement officers, by county, 1975-84. 1 table. (p. 157-159)

S3665–1.2: Maryland Arrest Data: Supplement to 1984 Crime in Maryland
[Annual. June 1985. 62 p. no paging. SRI/MF/complete.]

(62 p.) Contains 1 extended table showing adult and juvenile arrests, and arrests by detailed Index and non-Index offense, by region, county, and law enforcement agency, and for Baltimore City, 1983-84.

S3665–3 **CRIMINAL JUSTICE AGENCY PROCESSING STATISTICS, Maryland**
Annual Series. For individual publication data, see below.
SRI/MF/complete

Series of 2 annual reports on corrections in Maryland, including Division of Correction (DOC) inmate population, and related data on crimes and parole activities, fiscal and calendar year 1984, with comparisons to 1983 and inmate population summary from 1978. Most data are shown by month.

Covers DOC sentenced inmates and number in local jails, escapes, and prison admissions and releases by reason; inmates and average sentence length, and life and death sentences, by committing jurisdiction; inmates by sex, race (including Indian), age, sentence length, and commitment offense, by facility; and selected detail for Patuxent Institution.

Also includes data on crimes by major offense; adult and juvenile arrests; local jail admissions, departures, and average population by reason for incarceration; Division of Probation and Parole cases added, closed, under active supervision, and being administered, by type of case; and disposition of Parole Commission hearings.

Data are from reports filed with various State agencies.

Series consists of 1 fiscal year and 1 calendar year report. Both reports contain contents listing; and 6 statistical sections, with narrative summaries, and 29 charts and 33 tables.

Reports reviewed in 1985 are listed below.

Availability: Maryland Department of Public Safety and Correctional Services, Research and Statistics Office, One Investment Pl., Suite 500, Towson MD 21204, †; SRI/MF/complete.

REPORT:

S3665–3.1: Criminal Justice Agency Processing Statistics, FY84 vs. FY83
[Annual [1984.] 67 p. Oversized. LC 85-620823. SRI/MF/complete.]

S3665–3.2: Criminal Justice Agency Processing Statistics, CY84 vs. CY83
[Annual. [1985.] 68 p. Oversized. LC 85-621874. SRI/MF/complete.]

S3685   MARYLAND
Comptroller of the Treasury

S3685–1   1983 SUMMARY REPORT, Maryland Income Tax Division
Annual. [1985.]   54 p.
LC 79-643507.
SRI/MF/complete

Annual report on Maryland 1983 individual income tax returns, with data on filings, income, and tax liability, generally shown by State adjusted gross income (AGI) class, county, and city or town.

Data are from a complete tabulation of all resident and nonresident returns filed for 1983 and received by the comptroller of the treasury during FY84.

Contains contents listing (1 p.); introduction with text tables (p. 1-4); and 13 detailed tables, listed below (p. 6-54).

This is the 16th edition of the report.

Availability: Maryland Comptroller of the Treasury, Income Tax Division, State Income Tax Bldg., Annapolis MD 21401, †; SRI/MF/complete.

DETAILED TABLES:
[Unless otherwise noted, data are for 1983. All tables include number of returns filed, usually shown for taxable and nontaxable returns. Tables [1-3] and [6-10] show data by county and for Baltimore City and nonresidents.]

[1-3] Maryland gross income [and Federal AGI and modifications]; net taxable income [and deductions and number and amount of exemptions]; and net State tax [and local tax and tax rate]. (p. 6-8)

[4-5] AGI classes [Maryland AGI, total deductions, exemptions, and net taxable income]; and net State and local tax; by AGI classes. (p. 9-10)

[6] Nontaxable returns, with selected data [Federal AGI, modifications, and Maryland gross income]. (p. 11)

[7] Numbers of returns filed, and net taxable income. (p. 12)

[8] Summary of refunds [number and total amount]. (p. 13)

[9] Selected tax credits [gross State and out-of-State income tax, personal property tax, and net State income tax]. (p. 14)

[10] Resident tax returns filed, 1977-83. (p. 15)

[11] Nonresident return statistics [net taxable income and net and average State tax, by State AGI class]. (p. 16)

[12] [Net taxable income, net State tax, and local tax, for nontaxable returns and by Maryland AGI class; repeated for each county and Baltimore City.] (p. 18-41)

[13] [Total tax, by city and town, and for rural/unincorporated areas, arranged by county.] (p. 44-54)

S3685–2   STATE OF MARYLAND COMPREHENSIVE ANNUAL FINANCIAL REPORT for the Year Ended June 30, 1984
Annual.   Nov. 30, 1984.
79 p.
LC 83-645659.
SRI/MF/complete

Annual report on financial condition of Maryland State government, for FY84, presenting assets and liabilities, revenues by source, and expenditures by function, for general, special revenue, debt service, capital projects, enterprise, trust and agency, and higher education/university hospital funds.

Also includes data on investments by type of instrument; bonded and other long-term debt; retirement fund finances; budgeted vs. actual expenses in FY84, and budgeted revenues and appropriations for FY85; and State aid and property taxes receivable, by county.

Also presents selected trend data, primarily for FY75-84, including fund financial summary; property taxes, assessed value, and tax rates by county; long-term debt; consolidated transportation funding; population, per capita income, school enrollment, and unemployment rate; bank deposits; and property value, by property type.

Data were compiled by the Office of the Comptroller of the Treasury.

Contains contents listing (p. 3-4); introductory section, with text data (p. 7-16); 24 financial statements and schedules, with accompanying notes including text statistics (p. 22-70); and statistical section, with 11 tables (p. 73-79).

Availability: Maryland Comptroller of the Treasury, General Accounting Division, Financial Reporting Section, PO Box 466, Annapolis MD 21404-0466, †; SRI/MF/complete.

S3777   MASSACHUSETTS
Executive Office for Administration and Finance

S3777–1   COMMONWEALTH OF MASSACHUSETTS FINANCIAL REPORT for the Fiscal Year Ended June 30, 1984
Annual.   Dec. 31, 1984.
xiii+105 p.   House No. 500.
LC 82-641564.
SRI/MF/complete

Annual report on financial condition of Massachusetts State government, for FY84, presenting assets, liabilities, and fund balances; revenues by source; and expenditures by agency, object, and agency account; generally by specific fund.

Funds covered are general, special revenue, capital projects, proprietary, and trust and agency.

Also includes data on State bonded debt, budgeted vs. actual revenues and expenditures, and selected trends from FY75.

Contains contents listing, and 2 summary exhibits with accompanying charts and tables (p. iii-xiii); auditor's report, with 6 financial statements (p. 1-23); individual fund sections, with 22 statements (p. 26-67); debt service section, with 6 schedules (p. 70-81); statement of appropriations by fund (p. 84-85); and statistical section, with 9 schedules (p. 88-105).

Availability: Massachusetts Executive Office for Administration and Finance, Comptroller's Division, John W. McCormack Bldg., One Ashburton Pl., Boston MA 02108, †; SRI/MF/complete.

S3805   MASSACHUSETTS
Department of Correction

S3805–1   STATISTICAL DESCRIPTION OF RESIDENTS OF THE MASSACHUSETTS CORRECTIONAL INSTITUTIONS on Jan. 1, 1985
Annual. Aug. 1985. 120 p.
Pub. No.
14209-121-250-10-85-CR.
LC 77-644275.
SRI/MF/complete

Annual report on Massachusetts correctional institutions, with data on the inmate population, including demographic and socioeconomic characteristics, criminal background, drug use history, commitment offense, sentence length, furlough participation and outcomes, and escape record, as of Jan. 1, 1985. Data are shown by institution.

Data are from the Correction and Parole Management Information System.

Contains contents and table listing (p. 1-7); introduction and summary (p. 8-11); 2 statistical sections, with 52 tables repeated for correctional institutions with and without prerelease components (p. 12-117); and glossary (p. 118-120).

Availability: Massachusetts Department of Correction, Leverett Saltonstall State Office Bldg., 100 Cambridge St., Boston MA 02202, †; SRI/MF/complete.

S3807   MASSACHUSETTS
Office of the Chief Administrative Justice of the Trial Court

S3807–1   ANNUAL REPORT OF THE MASSACHUSETTS TRIAL COURT, 1984
Annual. Mar. 1, 1985.
vi+242 p.
LC 80-644980.
SRI/MF/complete

Annual report on Massachusetts trial court caseloads and case dispositions, FY84. Covers Boston municipal court; and district, housing, juvenile, land, probate/family, and superior courts. Includes data by case type and court location, with selected trends from FY80.

Case types shown are criminal and civil, for most courts, with some additional detail for traffic, domestic relations, mental health commitment, violent crime victim claims, spouse abuse, small claims, juvenile, adoption, and other case types. District and Superior court data also include appeals.

Also includes data on age of active trial caseloads; drunk driving cases; land court finances, including assessed value of property involved in land registration cases; child support, alimony, and other court fees collected; and probation dept activities and finances, including probate/family court investigations.

Contains contents listing (p. v); narrative summary of justice administration activities (p. 1-28); court caseload statistics, with narrative summaries, 32 charts, and 47 tables (p. 31-153); and probation office report, with 46 tables (p. 157-242).

Availability: Massachusetts Office of the Chief Administrative Justice of the Trial Court, Trial Court, 300 New Court House, Boston MA 02108, †; SRI/MF/complete.

S3808   MASSACHUSETTS Executive Office of Economic Affairs

S3808–1   MASSACHUSETTS EMPLOYMENT REVIEW
Monthly. Approx. 12 p.
LC sn83-11943.
SRI/MF/complete, shipped quarterly

Monthly report on Massachusetts labor force, employment, and unemployment, including unemployment insurance claims, all by local area, with selected detail by industry. Also includes job service applicants and openings.

Data are from State and Federal sources.

Contains narrative overview of labor market conditions, occasionally with summary text tables or charts; 1 summary table; 9 detailed tables, listed below; and glossary.

Availability: Massachusetts Employment Review, Massachusetts Employment Security Division, Research and Policy Department, Charles F. Hurley Bldg., Government Center, Boston MA 02114, †; SRI/MF/complete, shipped quarterly.

Issues reviewed during 1985: Aug.-Nov. 1984 (D) (Vol. 11, Nos. 8-11).

MONTHLY TABLES:
[Unless otherwise noted, data are for month of coverage, previous month, and same month of previous year. Data for labor areas are shown by SMSA and labor market area (LMA).]

[1] Labor force, employment, and unemployment: Massachusetts and the labor areas.

[2] Job matching service data [available applicants and unfilled openings, for State].

[3-7] Nonagricultural wage/salary employment: Massachusetts, Boston SMSA, Springfield/Chicopee/Holyoke and Worcester LMAs, and by [selected other labor] area [by major manufacturing group and industry division, including Federal, State, and local employees].

[8] Preliminary estimates [labor force by employment status, by city and town, month of coverage only].

[9] Unemployment insurance claims [initial and continued, for State, SMSAs, and labor areas].

S3840   MASSACHUSETTS Department of Food and Agriculture

S3840–1   MASSACHUSETTS AGRICULTURE, 1984
Annual. [1985.] 4+74 p.
ISSN 0092-9794.
LC 74-640739.
SRI/MF/complete

Annual report on Massachusetts agricultural production, marketing, and finances, by commodity, 1970s-84, with selected comparisons to Northeast region and U.S.

Report covers production, prices, income, value, and, as applicable, acreage, yield, inventory, and disposition, for livestock, dairy, poultry, mink, field crop, maple syrup, and fruit and vegetable sectors; and farm income, production expenses, and balance sheet.

Also includes data on farms and acreage, including State agricultural preservation program lands and expenditures; government inspection and licensing/registration activities, including apiary inspections by county; and U.S. food consumption.

Data are compiled by the New England Crop and Livestock Reporting Service.

Contains table of contents (2 p.); and 2 sections, with narrative summaries, 5 charts, and 67 tables (p. 1-74).

Availability: Massachusetts Department of Food and Agriculture, Leverett Saltonstall Bldg., 100 Cambridge St., Government Center, Boston MA 02202, †; SRI/MF/complete.

S3850   MASSACHUSETTS Department of Public Health

S3850–1   ANNUAL REPORT, VITAL STATISTICS OF MASSACHUSETTS, 1983
Annual. June 1985.
xi+176 p. Pub. Doc. No. 1.
LC 79-3383.
SRI/MF/complete, current & previous year reports

Annual report on Massachusetts vital statistics for 1983, with trends from as early as 1900. Covers births, deaths by cause, abortions, marriages, divorces, and population. Includes data by city/town, county, health service area (HSA), age, sex, and race.

Data are from State Registry of Vital Records and Statistics, and Census Bureau.

Contains listing of contents, tables, and charts (p. vii-xi); introduction (p. 1-3); 7 statistical sections, with narrative summaries, 4 text tables, 20 summary and trend charts, and 47 numbered tables listed below (p. 7-159); and appendices, with facsimiles of vital statistics certificates, definitions, and maps (p. 163-176).

This is the 142nd annual report. Previous report, for 1982, was also reviewed during 1985, and is also available on SRI microfiche, under S3850-1 [Annual. Jan. 1985. xi+172 p. †].

Availability: Massachusetts Department of Public Health, Health Statistics and Research

Division, Vital Records and Statistics Registry, 150 Tremont St., 5th Floor, Boston MA 02111, †; SRI/MF/complete.

TABLES:
[Data are for Massachusetts, 1983, unless otherwise noted.]

S3850–1.1: Summary and Natality
SUMMARY
[Tables A1-A2 and A4 include births; deaths (total, fetal, infant, and neonatal); marriages and divorces; and abortions.]

A1-A2. Summary and crude rates of vital events, Massachusetts and U.S., 1982-83. (p. 10-11)

A3-A4. State resident births and deaths and resultant natural increase, [selected years] 1900-83; and vital events, by month. (p. 12-14)

A5a-A5c. Births and deaths, by town, county, and HSA of occurrence and residence [includes resident mature and immature births, total deaths, and infant and neonatal deaths, by sex], with natural increase. (p. 15-32)

NATALITY
B1. Resident births, by sex and race. (p. 39)

B2. Age-specific birth rates among women, [selected years] 1970-83. (p. 42)

B3-B4. Resident births, by age, race, and marital status of mother; and parity by age of mother. (p. 44-45)

B5-B6. Resident births to teenage mothers, 1970-83; and number of cesarean deliveries compared to total births [by race; all by age of mother]. (p. 46-47)

B7. Resident births, by age and marital status of mother and birth weight of infant. (p. 49)

B8. Birthweight, by education of mother. (p. 51)

B9. [Hospital] births, by hospital of occurence [and by HSA], 1980-83. (p. 52-54)

S3850–1.2: Mortality
DEATHS
C1. Resident deaths, by age, sex, and race. (p. 61)

C2-C3. Leading causes of death: Massachusetts and U.S., 1982-83; and by HSA. (p. 62, 65)

C4. Leading causes of death, by age group and sex. (p. 66-69)

C5. Major causes of resident deaths by race and sex. (p. 72)

C6-C7. Selected causes and rates per 100,000 of resident deaths, by age and sex. (p. 74-77)

C8a-C8b. [Total] deaths [and] deaths due to malignant neoplasms, by underlying cause and mentioned conditions. (p. 78-80)

C9. [Deaths due to] artherosclerosis, hypertensive disease, and diabetes [mellitus as] underlying cause and mentioned condition, by age group and sex. (p. 81-82)

C10. Suicides by cause, sex, and age, residents. (p. 83)

C11. Motor vehicle accidents by type [of victim (driver, passenger, motorcyclist, pedestrian, and pedalcyclist), by sex], residents. (p. 84-85)

C12-C13. Medical examiner certified deaths: by cause, sex, race, and age, occurrence; and [total and nonviolent deaths certified, deaths referred but not certified, total deaths, and population], by county. (p. 86-89)

C14a-C14c. Selected causes of death by city/town, county, and HSA of residence. (p. 90-99)

C15. Resident deaths, by [detailed] cause, sex, and race. (p. 100-115)

INFANT AND NEONATAL DEATHS

D1. [Massachusetts] resident infant and neonatal deaths, [and deaths per 1,000 live births in] Massachusetts and U.S.; 1970-83. (p. 122)

D2-D4. Infant and neonatal deaths: by age, sex, and race; and by cause, age, and sex. (p. 124-126)

D4. Neonatal mortality by birth weight [1970-83]. (p. 126)

S3850–1.3: Marriages and Divorces, Abortions, and Population

MARRIAGES AND DIVORCES

E1-E2. Marriages and divorces by county; and marriages and divorces, and rates per 1,000 population, [selected years] 1900-83. (p. 133-135)

E3-E4. Marriages by age and marital status [of bride and groom]; and number of marriages for age of bride by age of groom (p. 136-137)

ABORTIONS

F1. Rate of abortions to births by age of woman. (p. 143)

F2. Number of abortions occurring by type of facility and age of woman. (p. 144)

POPULATION

G1. Population, by race, age, and sex, 1980. (p. 151-152)

G2-G4. Population: by counties [quinquennially 1955-80; and by] cities/towns and HSAs, 1970 and 1980. (p. 153-159)

S3870   MASSACHUSETTS
Board of
Library Commissioners

**S3870–1   DATA FOR
MASSACHUSETTS, FY84:
Comparative Public Library
Report**
Annual. Dec. 1984.
65 p.+addendum.
LC 79-641407.
SRI/MF/complete

Annual report, for FY84, on Massachusetts public library holdings, circulation, finances, and staff, by municipality. Data are based on reports from local libaries.

Contains contents and table listing (1 p.), and the following:

Introduction, with 1 table showing selected library trends for FY82-84; and user guide. (p. 1-11)

Section 1. 9 summary tables showing mean, median, and percentile data for selected library indicators, aggregated for municipalities in 6 population size groups, FY84. (p. 13-17)

Section 2. 7 municipal tables showing library per capita income, municipal appropriations, operating expenditures by object, holdings, and circulation; hours open; FTE employees; and average workweek; all by municipality, arranged in 7 population size groups, FY84, with rankings by 1980 population. (p. 20-43)

Section 3. Facsimile report forms, with definitions. (p. 46-57)

Index to municipal population groups, and addendum. (p. 60-65, 2 p.)

Availability: Massachusetts Board of Library Commissioners, Development of Library Services Office, Planning and Research Unit, 648 Beacon St., Boston MA 02215, ‡; SRI/MF/complete.

S3920   MASSACHUSETTS
Office of
the Secretary of
State

**S3920–1   MASSACHUSETTS
ELECTION STATISTICS,
1984**
Biennial. [1985.] 557 p.
Public Document No. 43.
LC 82-642996.
SRI/MF/complete

Biennial report presenting results of Massachusetts primary elections held Mar. 13 and Sept. 18, 1984, general elections held Nov. 6, 1984, and special elections held in 1983-84. Shows voting for President and Vice President; U.S. and State senators and representatives; sheriffs, and other State and county officials; and State questions, including water fluoridation, alcoholic beverage licensing, "nuclear free zone" in Northampton, and withdrawal of U.S. military aid from Central America.

Also includes voter registration and turnout, by party, with trends from 1948.

Data are shown by city/town, county, district, ward, and precinct.

Previous report, covering 1982 primary and general elections, is described in SRI 1983 Annual under this number.

Availability: Massachusetts State Bookstore, State House, Rm. 116, Boston MA 02133, †; SRI/MF/complete.

S3957   MICHIGAN
Department of
Commerce

**S3957–1   MICHIGAN FINANCIAL
INSTITUTIONS BUREAU
ANNUAL REPORT, 1984**
Annual. [1985.] iii+152 p.
ISSN 0145-4021.
LC 76-649778.
SRI/MF/complete

Annual report, for 1984, on financial condition of Michigan banks, savings and loan assns, safe/collateral deposit companies, credit unions, and loan companies.

For most types of institutions, report presents consolidated assets, liabilities, income, and expenses, 1983-84; assets and various other financial data for individual institutions, 1984; and various trends, including operating ratios and lending activity, from 1970s or 1980. Only individual institution data are presented for safe/collateral deposit companies. Only consolidated and trend data are presented for loan companies.

Also includes data on Financial Institutions Bureau revenues, expenditures, and regulatory activity; bank holding companies and subsidiary deposits; consumer inquiries and complaints; and results of surveys on automated teller machines owned/leased by depository institutions.

Most data are compiled from internal records and reports filed by individual institutions.

Contains contents listing (p. i-iii); summary of Bureau activities and regulatory developments, with 6 tables (p. 1-21); division reports, with text statistics, 4 charts, and 61 statements and tables (p. 23-115); and appendix, with text of selected orders and speeches (p. 117-152).

This is the 96th annual report.

Availability: Michigan Department of Commerce, Financial Institutions Bureau, Reporting and Publications Division, PO Box 30224, Lansing MI 48909, †; SRI/MF/complete.

S3960   MICHIGAN
Department of
Corrections

**S3960–1   MICHIGAN DEPARTMENT
OF CORRECTIONS, 1983,
Statistical Presentation**
Annual. Fall 1984.
6+106 p.
LC 76-646695.
SRI/MF/complete

Annual report, for 1983, on correctional activities in Michigan, presenting data on prison population, including inmate admissions, commitment offenses, criminal background, sentence length, demographic characteristics, and releases. Some data are shown by institution, with selected trends from 1971.

Also includes data on State court cases and dispositions, by district and detailed offense; prison incidents, capacity, and work and education programs; paroles and community programs; dept investigations, finances, and personnel; and inmate litigations.

Data are primarily from the State Bureau of Administrative Services.

Contains contents listing (3 p.); organizational chart (p. 1); and 8 report sections, with narrative and 2 maps, 35 charts, and 30 tables (p. 2-106).

Availability: Michigan Department of Corrections, Public Information Office, Stevens T. Mason Bldg., Lansing MI 48909, †; SRI/MF/complete.

S3962   MICHIGAN
Court Administrative Office

S3962–1   REPORT OF STATE COURT ADMINISTRATOR, Michigan
Annual series. For individual publication data, see below.
SRI/MF/complete

Annual series of 4 reports, for 1984, on Michigan judicial system. Series consists of base report and 3 supplements, described below.

Availability: Michigan Court Administrative Office, 200 Washington Square, PO Box 30048, Lansing MI 48909, ‡; SRI/MF/complete.

S3962–1.1: 1984 Report of State Court Administrator, Michigan

[Annual. [1985.] 3+52 p. SRI/MF/complete, current & previous year reports.]

Annual report, for 1984, on Michigan judicial system, including trial and appellate court caseloads and case dispositions. Covers supreme, appeals, circuit, district, municipal, probate, and claims courts. Includes trial court data by case type, with probate court detail by county, and municipal court detail for 4 cities.

Case types shown are criminal and civil for most courts, with some data for domestic relations, guardianship, adoption, juvenile, child abuse/neglect, traffic, and small claims case types.

Report also includes data on supreme and appeals court caseload trends, assignment of judges, disciplinary actions and/or grievances against judges and lawyers, and public defender caseloads.

Contains contents listing (2 p.); and report, with narrative summaries, 1 chart, 6 maps, and 31 tables (p. 1-52).

Previous report, for FY83, was also reviewed in SRI during 1985, and is also available on SRI microfiche under S3962-1.1 [Annual. [1984.] 3+44 p. ‡].

S3962–1.2: Circuit Court Supplement to the 1984 Annual Report of the State Court Administrator, Michigan

[Annual. [1985.] 3+105 p. SRI/MF/complete, current & previous year reports.]

Annual supplement, for 1984, presenting data on Michigan circuit court caseloads and case dispositions, by case type and county. Case types shown are criminal and civil, including detail for appeals, domestic relations, and child support.

Contains contents listing (3 p.); and 1 table repeated for State, and for each county and circuit, arranged by region. (p. 1-105).

Previous report, for FY83, was also reviewed in SRI during 1985, and is also available on SRI microfiche under S3962-1.2

[Annual. [1984.] 3+102 p. ‡]. Previous report is similar in format and content, but also includes data on product liability and labor relations cases.

S3962–1.3: District Court Supplement to the 1984 Annual Report of the State Court Administrator, Michigan

[Annual. [1985.] 5+190 p. SRI/MF/complete, current & previous year reports.]

Annual supplement, for 1984, presenting data on Michigan district court caseloads and case dispositions, by case type and district. Case types shown are criminal and civil, including detail for traffic and small claims cases.

Contains contents listing (5 p.); and 1 table repeated for State, and for districts and selected municipalities, arranged by region (p. 1-190).

Previous report, for FY83, was also reviewed in SRI during 1985, and is also available on SRI microfiche under S3962-1.3 [Annual. [1984.] 5+195 p. ‡].

S3962–1.4: Probate Court Supplement to the 1984 Annual Report of the State Court Administrator, Michigan

[Annual. [1985.] 2+103 p. SRI/MF/complete, current & previous year reports.]

Annual supplement, for 1984, presenting data on Michigan probate court caseloads and case dispositions, by case type and county. Case types include estates and trusts, guardians, adoption, mental illness, protective orders, and marriages.

Also includes inheritance taxes collected; and detail for juvenile division, including delinquency caseload by type of offense, and child abuse/neglect cases and disposition, by county.

Contains contents listing (2 p.); 1 summary table on fees and taxes collected (p. 1); 1 table, repeated for State and each county (p. 2-85); and juvenile division report, with 8 tables (p. 86-103).

Previous report, for FY83, was also reviewed in SRI during 1985, and is also available on SRI microfiche under S3962-1.4 [Annual. [1984.] 2+91 p. ‡].

S3965   MICHIGAN
Board of Education

S3965–3   1983/84 MICHIGAN K-12 PUBLIC SCHOOL DISTRICTS Ranked by Selected Financial Data
Annual. [1985.] 37 p.
Bull. 1014.
SRI/MF/complete

Annual report on Michigan public school finances, by district, 1983/84. Includes school enrollments, per pupil costs, and average teacher salary. Data are from reports by 528 elementary and secondary school districts.

Contains foreword and glossary (p. 1-5); 1 summary table (p. 7) showing selected data for total school districts grouped by active membership size; and 1 detailed table (p. 8-37) showing the following data for individual school districts arranged by county, 1983/84:

a. Per pupil general fund revenues by source, and expenditures by purpose including salaries.

b. Average salary per teacher; State aid members (pupils), and State equalized valuation per member; and millage rates for operations, building site, and debt retirement.

School district rankings are also shown for most of the items noted above.

Issuing agency also publishes an annual report with similar data, *Analysis of Michigan Public School Revenues and Expenditures,* not covered by SRI.

Availability: Michigan Department of Education, PO Box 30106, Lansing MI 48909, ‡; SRI/MF/complete.

S3980   MICHIGAN
Department of Labor

S3980–2   MICHIGAN LABOR MARKET REVIEW
Monthly.
Approx. 4 p. no paging.
SRI/MF/complete, shipped quarterly

Monthly report on Michigan labor force, including employment, unemployment, hours, earnings, and unemployment insurance claims. Data sources include BLS and Current Employment Statistics program. Selected data are shown by industry and labor market area. Month of coverage is 1 month prior to cover date.

Contains narrative summary, 4 monthly tables listed below, and list of labor surplus areas eligible for Federal procurement preference.

The issuing agency also publishes monthly reports on labor conditions in each of the State's 13 labor market areas. These reports are not covered by SRI.

Due to computer conversion, issuing agency temporarily suspended publication of the monthly report after the combined Sept./Dec. 1984 issue.

Availability: Michigan Employment Security Commission, Research and Statistics Bureau, 7310 Woodward Ave., Detroit MI 48202, †; SRI/MF/complete, shipped quarterly.

Issues reviewed during 1985: July-Sept./Dec. 1984 (P) (Vol. XXXX, Nos. 7-12) [Sept./Dec. 1984 report is a combined issue; no separate data were issued for Oct.-Nov. 1984].

MONTHLY TABLES:

[1-2] Civilian labor force, employment and unemployment estimates [by SMSA and for Upper Peninsula labor market area, for month of coverage; and for total State, including employment by industry division and major manufacturing group, and workers involved in labor disputes, usually for month of coverage, 1-2 previous months, and same month of previous year].

[3] Weekly [initial and continued] claims for unemployment insurance [regular and Federal supplemental programs; weekly for month of coverage].

[4] [Average] hours and earnings [of manufacturing production workers, with detail for se-

lected major industry groups; for month of coverage, previous month, and same month of previous year].

S3985   MICHIGAN
Department of Management and Budget

S3985–2   COMPREHENSIVE ANNUAL FINANCIAL REPORT OF THE STATE OF MICHIGAN, Fiscal Year Ended Sept. 30, 1984
Annual.   Mar. 22, 1985.
ix + 181 p.
ISSN 0095-1463.
LC 74-647935.
SRI/MF/complete

Annual report on financial condition of Michigan State government, for FY84 with comparisons to FY83, presenting assets, liabilities, and fund balances; revenues by source; and expenditures by function and/or object; for general, special revenue, debt service, capital projects, enterprise, internal service, trust, and agency funds.

Also includes bonded debt, and financial and socioeconomic trends from 1974.

Data are compiled by the Dept of Management and Budget.

Contains contents listing, and transmittal letter with State organizational chart and list of principal officials (p. ii-ix); financial section, with auditors reports and 50 statements and schedules, interspersed with explanatory notes and text statistics (p. 4-164); and statistical section with 9 trend tables (p. 168-181).

Availability: Michigan Department of Management and Budget, Accounting Division, PO Box 30026, Lansing MI 48909, †; SRI/MF/complete.

S3997   MICHIGAN
Department of State Police

S3997–1   1983 UNIFORM CRIME REPORT FOR THE STATE OF MICHIGAN
Annual.   [1984.]   103 p.
ISSN 0360-9146.
LC 75-648835.
SRI/MF/complete

Annual report on Michigan crimes and arrests, 1983, with selected summary trends from 1974.

Covers crimes and arrests by Index and non-Index offense, crime rates and clearances, motor vehicle recoveries, juvenile dispositions, value of property stolen and recovered, arsons by type of structure and value of damage, and officers killed and assaulted, all by reporting agency arranged by county, and by population size.

Also includes statewide data on arrests by Index and non-Index offense, and murder victims, by age, sex, and race/ethnicity; police employment, and assaults on police by circumstance; and detail for Index offenses, including total and juvenile clearances, type of weapon and property involved and other circumstances, and value of property stolen and recovered.

Index offenses are murder, rape, robbery, aggravated assault, burglary, larceny, motor vehicle theft, and arson. Data by race/ethnicity are shown for white, black, American Indian/Alaskan Native, Asian/Pacific Islander, and Hispanic.

Data are from reports of State and local law enforcement agencies, submitted under the Uniform Crime Reporting (UCR) Program.

Contains contents listing (1 p.); description of UCR Program, definitions, and summary with 1 table (p. 1-7); statewide section, with 20 charts and 41 tables (p. 9-50); and reporting agency section with 3 detailed tables, and 3 tables on police officers (p. 51-103).

This is the 25th annual report.

Availability: Michigan Department of State Police, 714 S. Harrison Rd., East Lansing MI 48823, ‡; SRI/MF/complete.

S3997–2   MICHIGAN TRAFFIC ACCIDENT FACTS, 1983
Annual.   [1984.]   56 p.
LC 54-63117.
SRI/MF/complete

Annual report on Michigan traffic accidents, fatalities, and injuries, by detailed accident and vehicle type, location, time, and other circumstances; and driver and victim characteristics; 1983, with comparisons from 1970s and trends from as early as 1938.

Also includes data on motor vehicle registrations and revenue, licensed drivers, vehicle miles traveled, vehicle safety restraint use, driver and pedestrian alcohol use, and intoxicated drivers arrested.

Data are compiled by the State Police Dept from State and local police and sheriff reports, and from other State depts.

Contains preface, contents listing, highlights, and trends, with 7 charts and 2 tables (p. 1-8); and report, with 1 map, 1 chart, and 35 tables (p. 9-56).

A related report, *Alcohol Related Fatal Motor Vehicle Traffic Accident Study, Michigan,* is also available from the issuing agency but is not covered in SRI.

Availability: Michigan Department of State Police, Traffic Services Division, Attn: Analysis Section, 7150 Harris Dr., Lansing MI 48913, †; SRI/MF/complete.

S4000   MICHIGAN
Department of Public Health

S4000–3   MICHIGAN HEALTH STATISTICS, 1983
Annual.   [1985.]   379 p.
ISSN 0539-7413.
LC 74-644861.
SRI/MF/complete, current & previous year reports

Annual report, for 1983, on Michigan vital statistics, covering births, deaths by detailed cause, marriages, divorces, and incidence of communicable diseases. Summary data are shown by county. Also includes trends from 1900 and abridged life tables. Data are from State records.

Contents:

a. Listings of contents, tables, and charts; introduction; definitions; and notes on data limitations. (p. 1-27)

b. 3 sections on natality, mortality, and marriages and divorces, with statistical overviews, narrative analyses, 66 summary charts, and 133 detailed tables listed below. (p. 31-320)

c. Appendix section, with 27 tables listed below; 7 summary charts, including vital statistics data for 14 State regions; and facsimiles of health dept certificates and records. (p. 323-379)

Previous report, for 1982, was also reviewed in SRI during 1985, and is also available on SRI microfiche under S4000-3 [Annual. [1984.] 374 p. $11.00].

Report for 1981 is described in SRI 1983 Annual under S4000-3.

Availability: Michigan Department of Public Health, State Registrar's Office and Health Statistics Center, 3500 N. Logan St., PO Box 30035, Lansing MI 48909, $11.00; SRI/MF/complete.

TABLES:

[Unless otherwise noted, tables show data for Michigan residents for 1983. Several tables include comparative data for U.S.]

S4000–3.1: Natality

LIVE BIRTHS

1.1-1.3. Total births, live births and crude birth rates, and fertility rates, selected years 1900-83. (p. 33, 37-38)

1.4. Live births by infant's race or national origin [including American Indian, Chinese, and Filipino], 1970-83. (p. 42)

1.5. Crude birth rates and fertility rates by race, 1970-83. (p. 43)

1.6. Live births and percent distribution by age of mother and race of child. (p. 44)

1.7. Live births and population of women, by age, 1973 and 1983. (p. 45)

1.8. Age-specific live birth rates, by race, 1973 and 1983. (p. 47)

1.9. First births, selected years 1960-83. (p. 51)

1.10-1.11. Live births by live birth order and age of mother, 1973 and 1983. (p. 52)

1.12-1.13. Live births to women reporting prior pregnancy terminations, by time span between last and current termination, 1973 and 1983; and by whether prior termination resulted in a live birth or a fetal death, 1983. (p. 54-55)

1.14. Live births by month prenatal care began and number of prenatal visits. (p. 56)

1.15. Numbers and percents of live births with prenatal care beginning in the 1st trimester, by age of mother and race of child. (p. 59)

1.16. Live births by month of pregnancy prenatal care began and live birth order. (p. 60)

1.17. Live births and percent distribution, by number of the mother's prenatal visits and race of child. (p. 61)

1.18. Live births with no prenatal care, by age of mother and race of child. (p. 63)

1.19. Live births, by birth weight and race. (p. 64)

S4010   MICHIGAN
Department of Social Services

S4010–1   ASSISTANCE PAYMENTS STATISTICS, Michigan
Monthly. Approx. 150 p. no paging. Pub. No. 67. SRI/MF/complete

Monthly report on Michigan public assistance programs, including number of cases, recipients, and payments, by program and county. Programs covered are Aid to Dependent Children (ADC), general assistance, State and federally funded emergency assistance, medical assistance, food stamps, SSI, child welfare, and home help services.

Data are compiled by the Dept of Social Services. Report is issued approximately 9 weeks after month of coverage.

Contains 28 monthly tables, listed below; most tables appear in all issues. Issues also frequently contain additional charts and tables, including revised data for previous monthly tables. Additional tables presenting substantial statistics not covered in monthly tables are described, as they appear, under "Statistical Features."

Prior to Dec. 1984 issue, report also included data on applications for assistance. Report also formerly included a monthly table on LIHEAP, Michigan's home energy assistance program; final table is described below under S4010-1.602.

Availability: Michigan Department of Social Services, 300 S. Capitol Ave., PO Box 30037, Lansing MI 48909, †; SRI/MF/complete.

Issues reviewed during 1985: Sept. 1984-Aug. 1985 (D).

MONTHLY TABLES:
[Data are for month of coverage only, unless otherwise noted. All tables except 18 show data by county; some tables also include data by district.]

SUMMARY

1. Total number of recipients and expenditures under ADC, emergency needs program, general assistance, energy assistance, and food stamps [for month of coverage, and percent change from previous month and same month of previous year].

ADC PROGRAM

2-4. ADC: families and money payments to families: [total, and] regular and unemployed-parent segments [for month of coverage, previous month, and same month of previous year].

5. ADC: number of child and adult recipients, by program segment.

GENERAL ASSISTANCE

6-8. General assistance: number of cases and amount of gross payments [all cases, and] regular and State funded emergency needs cases [for month of coverage, previous month, and same month of previous year].

9. General assistance: number of cases and amount of gross payments by type of case [with and without children], by program segment.

10. General assistance: number of child and adult recipients by type of case and program segment.

EMERGENCY AND MEDICAL ASSISTANCE, FOOD STAMPS, AND SSI

11. State funded emergency needs program, burials: number of cases and amount of gross payments.

12-13. Federal and State funded emergency needs: number of cases and recipients, and amount of gross payments, by basis of eligibility.

14. Food stamps: households, persons, and value of food stamps issued, by type of case [total, ADC, general assistance, and other].

15. Medical assistance: number of cases and persons eligible for medical assistance only (medically needy), by type of case [age 65/over, blind, disabled, families with dependent children, and other children under 21].

16. SSI: number of cases eligible for SSI by basis of eligibility [age 65/over, blind, and disabled].

17. SSI: recipients and money payments to aged/blind/disabled persons [Federal payments and State supplements].

18. Medical assistance: recipients and expenditures, by basis of eligibility, type of case, and type of service.

19-20. Medical assistance (Medicaid): amount of vendor payments and number of recipients, by type of service [inpatient general and mental hospitals, skilled nursing, mentally retarded and other intermediate care facilities, physicians, dental, and 8 other categories].

21-22. General assistance, medical: amount of vendor payments and number of recipients by type of service.

CHILD CARE AND HOME HELP SERVICES
[Tables 23-28 begin in the Jan. 1985 issue.]

23. Day care: number of cases [and children], and amount of day care payments, by eligibility group [ADC, Medicaid, income eligibles, protective services, young parent, and group eligibles (migrants)].

24. ADC, foster care: children, and vendor payments.

25. State child care reimbursement [for month of coverage and fiscal year to date].

26-28. Home help services (Titles XX and XIX): number of cases and amount of vendor payments.

STATISTICAL FEATURES:
[Fiscal year data are for year ending Sept. 30.]

S4010–1.601: Sept. 1984
QUARTERLY AND ANNUAL TABLES

Six quarterly and 6 annual tables showing ADC and general assistance applications approved and denied, and cases closed, by reason and county, with selected detail by district, for quarter ended Sept. 1984 and full year FY84. Includes approvals due to exhaustion of unemployment benefits, layoff/discharge, and strike or strike-related layoff.

S4010–1.602: Oct. 1984
[All tables show data by county.]

LIHEAP

Table showing number of cases and recipients, and amount of gross payments, for the low-income home energy assistance emergency needs program, Sept. 1984.

This table appeared on a monthly basis through the Aug. 1984 issue. Monthly table has been discontinued.

SEMIANNUAL TABLES

Two semiannual tables showing food stamp households, by race-ethnicity (including Hispanic and American Indian), Oct. 1984.

S4010–1.603: Dec. 1984
QUARTERLY TABLES

Six quarterly tables showing ADC and general assistance applications approved and denied, and cases closed, by reason and county, with selected detail by district, for quarter ended Dec. 1984. Includes approvals due to exhaustion of unemployment benefits, layoff/discharge, and strike or strike-related layoff.

S4010–1.604: Jan. 1985
ANNUAL TABLES

Two annual tables showing ADC children by age and county, Jan. 1985.

For description of previous tables, see SRI 1984 Annual under S4010-1.504.

S4010–1.605: Feb. 1985
SEMIANNUAL TABLES

Four semiannual tables showing general assistance and ADC cases by race/ethnicity (including American Indian and Mexican or Hispanic), by county, Dec. 1984.

S4010–1.606: Mar. 1985
QUARTERLY TABLES

Six quarterly tables showing ADC and general assistance applications approved and denied, and cases closed, by reason and county, with selected detail by district, for quarter ended Mar. 1985. Includes approvals due to exhaustion of unemployment benefits, layoff/discharge, and strike or strike-related layoff.

ANNUAL TABLE

Annual table showing average number of applications received per month for public assistance by program (AFDC, general and medical assistance, food stamps and recertifications, emergency needs, county hospitalization, and other), by county, FY84.

Prior to Dec. 1984, data were were included in each monthly issue.

S4010–1.607: Apr. 1985
[All tables show data by county, with selected detail by district.]

RECURRING TABLE

Table showing the following for hospitalization assistance: persons hospitalized, length of stay, central office payments for doctors/surgeons and inpatient care, and total local office payments, FY84.

SPECIAL TABLES

Three tables showing number of applications for children's and other protective services; average number of cases per month for children's protective services by type of case (abuse, neglect, and both); and average number of social service cases per month by program, including adult and child community placement and protection, day care, delinquency service, employment/training program, and family services; FY84.

SEMIANNUAL TABLES

Two semiannual tables showing food stamp households, by race-ethnicity (including American Indian/Alaskan Native, Hispanic, and Asian/Pacific Islander), Apr. 1985.

S4010–1.608: June 1985

[All tables show data by county, with selected detail by district.]

SEMIANNUAL TABLES

Four semiannual tables showing ADC and general assistance cases by race/ethnicity (including American Indian and Hispanic), June 1985.

QUARTERLY TABLES

Six quarterly tables showing ADC and general assistance applications approved and denied, and cases closed, by reason, for quarter ended June 1985. Includes approvals due to exhaustion of unemployment benefits, layoff/discharge, and strike/strike-related layoff.

S4020   MICHIGAN
Secretary of State

S4020–1   STATE OF MICHIGAN GENERAL ELECTION, Nov. 6, 1984: Official Canvass
Biennial. [1985.] 95 p.
SRI/MF/complete

Biennial report presenting results of the Michigan general election held Nov. 6, 1984. Shows voting for President and Vice-President; U.S. and State senators and/or representatives; and State board of education members, university officials, supreme court justices, judges, and proposals. Data are shown by district and/or county.

Previous report, covering 1982 general election, is described in SRI 1983 Annual, under this number.

Availability: Michigan Secretary of State, Elections Division, 208 N. Capitol Ave., 4th Floor, Mutual Bldg., Lansing MI 48918, $3.00; SRI/MF/complete.

S4130   MINNESOTA
Department of Agriculture

S4130–1   MINNESOTA AGRICULTURAL STATISTICS, 1985
Annual. July 1985. 82 p.
SRI/MF/complete

Annual report on Minnesota agricultural production, marketing, and finances, 1984, with trends primarily from 1980 and some data for 1985. Data are generally shown by commodity and/or county and district, with some comparisons to other States and total U.S.

Covers production, prices, value, and, as applicable, acreage, yield, stocks, and inventory, for field crop, vegetable, fruit, livestock, poultry, and dairy sectors.

Also includes data on farms, acreage, and farmland value; farm income, production ex-

penses, and balance sheet; agricultural export values; weather; pesticide use; mink farms, pelts produced, and females bred; prices paid by farmers for selected feed and energy commodities; custom farming rates; and U.S. farm value share of retail price of 12 food items.

Data are compiled by the Minnesota Dept of Agriculture in cooperation with USDA.

Contains contents listing (1 p.); 7 maps, 25 charts, and 63 tables, interspersed with narrative summaries (p. 1-82); and index (inside back cover).

Availability: Minnesota State Documents Center, 117 University Ave., St. Paul MN 55155, $4.75; SRI/MF/complete.

S4140   MINNESOTA
Department of Commerce

S4140–1   MINNESOTA COMMERCE DEPARTMENT ANNUAL REPORT
Annual, discontinued.

Annual report on Minnesota banking, insurance, securities, and real estate industries and regulatory activities, discontinued with the FY82 edition (for description, see SRI 1983 Annual under S4140-2). Report has been discontinued due to reorganization of issuing agency and repeal of State mandate requiring report publication.

Data on banking and insurance are available on request from Minnesota Department of Commerce, 500 Metro Square Bldg., Seventh and Robert Sts., St. Paul MN 55101.

S4160   MINNESOTA
Department of Economic Security

S4160–3   REVIEW OF LABOR AND ECONOMIC CONDITIONS, Minnesota
Quarterly, with monthly supplements.
Approx. 30 p. or 4 p.
LC 77-646692.
SRI/MF/complete

Quarterly report, with monthly supplements, on Minnesota labor and economic conditions, presenting data on employment and unemployment, earnings, hours, characteristics of insured unemployed, and income support and employment services. Includes data by industry and locale, historical trends, and comparisons to total U.S.

Quarterly issues are published 2 months after quarter of coverage, and generally contain contents listing, editorial comment, and the following:

a. "Research Summaries" article; "Job Market" feature, usually including review of employment conditions in a selected Minnesota industry, and supply/demand summary for specific occupations in Minnesota regions; and a feature article; all often including statistics.

b. Narrative review of U.S. and Minnesota economic conditions; and 23 trend charts and 10 quarterly tables.

Monthly supplement, entitled *Current Minnesota Labor Market Conditions,* is published in the 8 months for which no quarterly report is published. Supplement presents selected data also covered in quarterly report. Data are shown for month prior to month of publication, generally with comparisons to previous periods. Monthly supplements are filmed and shipped with the subsequent quarterly issue.

Quarterly tables are listed below; most appear in all quarterly issues. All additional features with substantial statistical content are described, as they appear, under "Statistical Features." Nonstatistical features are not covered.

Availability: Minnesota Department of Jobs and Training, Research and Statistics Office, 390 N. Robert St., St. Paul MN 55101, †; SRI/MF/complete.

Issues reviewed during 1985: Quarterly Review: 3rd Qtr. 1984-2nd Qtr. 1985 (D) (Vol. 11, Nos. 3-4; Vol. 12, Nos. 1-2).

Issues reviewed during 1985: Monthly Supplements: Sept. 1984-July 1985 (P).

QUARTERLY TABLES:

[Unless otherwise noted, data are for Minnesota and U.S. Tables 1, [3], and [5-10] show data for quarter of coverage and/or subsequent month, generally with comparison to prior periods. Most data in tables 1, [3], and [6-8] are also included in monthly supplement. Prior to 1st quarter 1985 issue, economic indicator data were presented in 2 tables, and included data for Minnesota.]

JOB SERVICE APPLICANTS AND OPENINGS

1. Experienced supply [of job service applicants, and] job openings demand, [by occupation, for Minnesota only].

LABOR FORCE

[2] Forecasts of GNP, and Minnesota payroll employment [by industry division, for quarter of coverage and 8 subsequent quarters].

[3] Labor force estimates [by employment status].

[4] Historical labor force series [by employment status, for previous 12-15 years].

[5] Labor force and establishment data [including labor utilization rates; and nonagricultural employment, and average hours and wages, by industry division].

[6] Persons claiming benefits [for unemployment insurance, by age, sex, industry division, occupation, and duration of unemployment; for Minnesota only].

[7] Minnesota nonagricultural wage/salary employment [and production worker] hours and earnings [by industry division and selected industry group].

[8] Labor force [and unemployment] data: State, MSAs, and counties.

ECONOMIC INDICATORS

[9] Spending, output, income, and prices [selected indicators of consumer and government spending, industrial output, personal and family income, money supply and credit, and prices, for U.S. only].

INCOME AND EMPLOYMENT ASSISTANCE

[10] Minnesota income support and employment assistance data [including payments and

recipients of unemployment insurance and general assistance by State region; and participants in job service, vocational rehabilitation, Job Training Partnership Act, trade adjustment assistance, targeted jobs tax credit, food stamp, work incentive, and Minnesota Emergency Employment Development programs; table begins in the 1st quarter 1985 issue].

STATISTICAL FEATURES:

S4160–3.601: 3rd Qtr. 1984 (Vol. 11, No. 3)

JOB MARKET: SALES WORKERS

(p. 5) By B. J. Jones. Includes 1 table showing distribution of Minnesota sales workers by type of occupation, 1980, 1982, and 1990.

PART-TIME WORKERS

(p. 8-16) By Bruce Steuernagel and D. Hilber. Article on part-time employment in Minnesota. Data are from Census Bureau and BLS. Includes 7 tables showing the following:

a. Minnesota: full- and part-time employment, by sex, age, household type, and occupation, 1980; part-time employment, 1980, and production workers' average hours and earnings, 1983, by industry division and selected major group; average earnings of full- and part-time workers, by age and sex, 1979; total and part-time employment, decennially 1950-80; and part-time employment projections for 1990; with selected comparisons to U.S.

b. U.S. voluntary and involuntary part-time employment as percent of total employment, by industry division and for self-employed persons and unpaid family workers, 1970 and 1983.

S4160–3.602: 4th Qtr. 1984 (Vol. 11, No. 4)

RESEARCH SUMMARIES: CONSENSUS ECONOMIC FORECASTS

(p. 2-3) By Bruce Steuernagel. Article, with 1 table showing percent change in real GNP and prices, and unemployment rate, as forecast by 13 econometric services, 4th quarter 1984-85. Data are from *Business Week*.

JOB MARKET: MINNESOTA EMPLOYMENT OUTLOOK TO 1990

(p. 4-5) By B. J. Jones. Includes 2 tables showing Minnesota employment by industry division and occupational group, 1982 and 1990; and job openings caused by growth and separations, by occupational group, 1982-90 period.

1985 ECONOMIC OUTLOOK, ANNUAL FEATURE

(p. 8-16) Annual article, by R. Pinola, analyzing economic outlook for Minnesota and U.S. in 1985. Includes 4 tables showing percent change in GNP and components, 1985; U.S. and Minnesota labor force by employment status, 1984-85; and percent change in selected U.S. economic indicators during economic contraction and expansion periods, 1949-84.

S4160–3.603: 1st Qtr. 1985 (Vol. 12, No. 1)

JOB MARKET: THE AGRICULTURE INDUSTRY

(p. 5-6) By D. Detrick. Includes 1 table showing Minnesota agriculture industry employment distribution by occupational group, 1980, 1982, and 1990.

1979-82, CONTINUOUS RECESSION IN MINNESOTA

(p. 9-16) By B. Boyle. Article on impact of recent periods of economic recession on Minnesota employment. Data are from State Dept of Economic Security.

Includes 6 tables showing employment during business cycle peaks and troughs, by industry group, and 20 industry groups with largest numerical and percentage declines from peak to trough, various months 1978-83; and current employment levels compared to troughs and previous highs, by major industry group, Mar. 1985; with selected comparisons to total U.S.

S4160–3.604: 2nd Qtr. 1985 (Vol. 12, No. 2)

RESEARCH SUMMARIES: YOUNG MINNESOTANS' CAREER GOALS

(p. 3-5) By Bruce Steuernagel. Article on Minnesota high school students' career goals and future plans. Data are from Census Bureau, and a spring 1984 survey of approximately 725 students conducted by University of Minnesota.

Includes 3 tables showing survey response concerning career goals, with comparison to actual employment distribution in 1980, by occupation; and social or economic attributes considered indicators of success and failure; all by sex.

JOB MARKET: THE ELECTRONIC MACHINERY AND EQUIPMENT INDUSTRY

(p. 6-7) By D. Detrick. Includes 1 table showing Minnesota electrical machinery/equipment industry employment distribution by occupational group, 1980, 1982, and 1990.

PROBLEMS WITH COMPARING STATE UNEMPLOYMENT INSURANCE LAWS

(p. 10-16) By J. Berglund. Article describing reasons for difficulty encountered in comparing unemployment insurance data among States. Data are primarily from Dept of Labor.

Includes 2 tables showing Minnesota unemployment rate; unemployment insurance benefit cost rate (benefits as a percent of wages paid); and ratios indicating the effect of unemployment and wage levels on benefit cost rate; with comparison to U.S., various periods 1950-84.

S4165   MINNESOTA Department of Education

S4165–2   MINNESOTA LIBRARIES: Minnesota Public Library Statistics, 1983
Quarterly (selected issue).
Spring 1984. 34 p.
Vol. XXVII, No. 9.
ISSN 0026-5551.
LC 10-33240.
SRI/MF/complete

Annual *Minnesota Libraries* statistical issue, for 1983, on public library holdings, staff, services, circulation, and finances. Data are shown by facility and system for consolidated and federated regional library systems, and for unaffiliated libraries.

Data are from reports of each library.

Contents:

a. Contents listing. (front cover)

b. Introduction, and 2 charts and 1 table showing 1983 summary statistics, including area served for each library system; and library administrative units and branches. (p. 223-227)

c. Individual library statistics, with 1 detailed table showing the following for each system and facility (including bookmobiles), as appropriate: population served, professional and total FTE staff, weekly hours, stations, whether union affiliated and open on Sundays, holdings by type, circulation, loan period, program attendance, local and State/Federal receipts, indirect receipts/expenditures, and personnel and materials expenditures, all for 1983. (p. 228-245)

c. Directory of public libraries. (p. 246-256)

Minnesota Libraries is a quarterly publication that is primarily narrative; the annual statistical issue is the only issue described and filmed by SRI. Issues are paginated cumulatively throughout the year.

Availability: Minnesota Department of Education, Library Development and Services Office, 440 Capitol Square Bldg., 550 Cedar St., St. Paul MN 55101, †; SRI/MF/complete.

S4180   MINNESOTA Department of Finance

S4180–1   STATE OF MINNESOTA COMPREHENSIVE ANNUAL FINANCIAL REPORT, for the Year Ended June 30, 1984
Annual. Dec. 12, 1984.
127 p.
LC 77-646853.
SRI/MF/complete

Annual report on financial condition of Minnesota State government, for FY84, presenting assets and liabilities, revenues by source, expenditures by major function or object, and changes in fund balances; for all, general, special revenue, capital projects, debt service, enterprise, internal service, and fiduciary funds.

Also includes budgeted vs. actual revenues and expenditures; detail on retirement fund finances and investments; debt service obligations to 2004; trends in State government finances, property value, federally insured bank deposits, population, and personal income, generally 1974-83; and sales, assets, and net income for Minnesota-based companies (ranked by sales) included in Fortune 500 list, 1983, with ranking comparison to 1982.

Contains contents listing and financial highlights with State executive branch organizational chart (p. 3-12); report, with 37 financial statements and accompanying notes (p. 15-119); and statistical section with 8 tables (p. 122-127).

This is the 6th annual edition; prior to FY79, report was published biennially.

Availability: Minnesota Department of Finance, 309 State Administration Bldg., St. Paul MN 55155, †; SRI/MF/complete.

S4190   MINNESOTA
Department of
Health

S4190-2   MINNESOTA HEALTH
STATISTICS, 1983
Annual.   June 1985.
6+128 p.
LC 74-645678.
SRI/MF/complete, current &
previous year reports

Annual report, for 1983, on Minnesota vital statistics, by county and city, covering population, births, deaths by cause, marriages, and divorces. Also includes data on occupational injuries and illnesses. Most data were compiled from records submitted to the Dept of Health prior to Aug. 1, 1984. Population data are from U.S. Census Bureau.

Contains foreword, and listings of contents, tables, and charts (6 p.); technical notes (p. 1-6); 7 statistical sections, with narrative analysis, 2 charts, and 31 tables listed below (p. 9-99); and appendices, with definitions, related publications, sample certificates, map of health districts, and lists of diseases according to the 8th and 9th Revisions of the International Classification of Diseases (p. 105-128).

This is the 33rd annual report. Previous report, for 1982, was also reviewed by SRI during 1985, and is also available on SRI microfiche under S4190-2 [Annual. Nov. 1984. 6+124 p. †].

Availability: Minnesota Department of Health, Health Statistics Center, 717 Delaware St., SE, PO Box 9441, Minneapolis MN 55440, †; SRI/MF/complete.

TABLES:
[Unless otherwise noted, data are for Minnesota residents, 1983. Data by race include Indian.]

S4190-2.1: 1983 Vital Statistics
OVERVIEW
1. Percent changes between 1982 and 1983, selected health statistics. (p. 9)

2. Crude rates of vital events, State vs. U.S. [decennially 1950-80 and annually 1981-83]. (p. 10)

3. Births, deaths, infant deaths, fetal deaths, marriages, and divorces/annulments, by month, Minnesota occurrences. (p. 11)

4. Live births, fetal deaths, deaths, infant deaths, and neonatal deaths, by urban area of residence. (p. 12-15)

LIVE BIRTHS
5. Live births by county of occurrence distributed according to residence [in-county, other Minnesota, or out-of-State], and resident live births distributed according to place of birth [in-State or out-of-State, by county of residence]. (p. 20-21)

6. Selected resident natality statistics [including birth and fertility rates; births by selected characteristics (sex, race, legitimacy, birth order, plurality, prematurity, mother's age and education, prenatal care history, presence of congenital anomalies and other significant conditions, and risk status); infant, neonatal, and fetal deaths by race; and maternal deaths], by county and cities over 90,000. (p. 22-33)

7. Live birth weight by live birth order and sex. (p. 34)

8. Live births by age of mother and live birth order. (p. 35)

9. Prenatal care and race by age of mother and by legitimacy status [and fetal deaths by legitimacy, race, and mother's age]. (p. 36)

INFANT MORTALITY AND FETAL DEATHS
10. Infant, neonatal, and postneonatal deaths by cause. (p. 39)

11. Fetal deaths of 20 weeks/over by cause and weight of fetus. (p. 40)

GENERAL MORTALITY
12. Deaths by county of occurrence distributed according to residence, [and] resident deaths distributed according to place of death [same detail as table 5]. (p. 44-45)

13. Deaths from selected causes [arranged by International Classification of Diseases, 9th Revision], by age group and sex. (p. 46-51)

14. Deaths due to selected causes, by race. (p. 52)

15. Fifteen leading causes of death, death rates per 100,000 population, and percent of total deaths. (p. 53)

16. Leading causes of death by selected age groups. (p. 54)

17. Accident fatalities occurring in Minnesota, by accident category and age group, 1982-83. (p. 55)

18. Deaths occurring in Minnesota by cause and autopsy status. (p. 56)

19. Selected resident mortality statistics [including rates by age and numbers by sex, race, and selected causes], by county and cities over 90,000. (p. 57-68)

MARRIAGE AND DIVORCE
20. Marriages reported in Minnesota by State of residence [of bride and groom]. (p. 71)

21. Marriages, divorces, and annulments, by county of occurrence. (p. 72-73)

22-23. Marriages occurring in Minnesota by race and age of bride and groom [also includes data for Chinese, Japanese, and other Asian]. (p. 74-75)

24. Divorces and annulments by age of husband and wife. (p. 76)

S4190-2.2: Occupational Illness/Injury, and Population

OCCUPATIONAL ILLNESS AND INJURY
[Tables 25-30 show data for 1982-83.]

25. Estimated number of injuries and illnesses by major industrial category. (p. 79)

26. Annual average employment, percent of total employment, and rate of occupational injuries/illnesses per 1,000 workers, by industrial category. (p. 80)

27. Number of injuries/illnesses by major occupational category. (p. 81)

28-30. Estimated number of occupational injuries/illnesses, by type of accident, nature of injury, and part of body injured. (p. 82-84)

POPULATION
31. Population estimates by region, county, cities over 90,000, and sex [all cross-tabulated by age]. (p. 89-99)

S4195   MINNESOTA
Higher Education
Coordinating Board

S4195-2   REPORT TO THE
GOVERNOR AND 1985
LEGISLATURE, Minnesota
Higher Education
Coordinating Board
Biennial.   1985.   xii+175 p.
SRI/MF/complete

Biennial report, for 1985, on the Minnesota post-secondary education system. Report focuses on activities of the State Higher Education Coordinating Board (HECB), and includes data on enrollment, student characteristics, educational finances, and student aid programs, mostly by type of public and private school system, various periods 1968-85, with selected projections to 2003.

Data are primarily from HECB, and various Federal and State agencies.

Contains preface, and listings of contents, tables, and charts (p. i-xii); 5 report sections, with narrative, 15 charts, and 82 tables (p. 1-169); and appendices, with narrative summary and comment, listing of additional publications, and 1 enrollment summary table (p. 171-175).

All report section tables, and selected charts showing substantial statistics not covered by tables, are listed below.

Previous report, for 1982/83, was published in 2 parts under the title *Problems, Prospects, Proposals: Report to the Governor and 1983 Legislature, Minnesota Higher Education Coordinating Board.* For description, see SRI 1983 Annual under this number.

Availability: Minnesota Higher Education Coordinating Board, Capitol Square Bldg., Suite 400, 550 Cedar St., St. Paul MN 55101, †; SRI/MF/complete.

TABLES AND CHARTS:
[Data are for Minnesota postsecondary education systems, unless otherwise noted. Data by system are shown by various categories, often including area vocational-technical institute (AVTI), community college, State university, and University of Minnesota systems; and private 2- and 4-year and professional colleges.]

S4195-2.1: Students and Finances
ENROLLMENT, DEGREES, AND STUDENT CHARACTERISTICS
I.1-I.2. On-campus headcount enrollment: public and private systems; and full- and part-time, all systems; 1969-83. (p. 3)

I.3. Full-time, part-time, and total fall headcount enrollment by system, 1969, 1976, and 1983. (p. 4)

I.4. On-campus undergraduate headcount enrollment by sex, all systems, 1973-83. (p. 4)

I.5. Age distribution of on-campus collegiate undergraduate students, all systems, 1974-83. (p. 5)

I.6. Headcount enrollment and percent of total headcount enrollment, by racial/ethnic group [black, American Indian, Asian, Hispanic, and white/other] and system, [selected years] 1974-82. (p. 6-7)

I.7. Resident, nonresident, and foreign headcount enrollment, fall 1976-83. (p. 8)

S4202   MINNESOTA
Department of Human Services

S4202–1   SUMMARY OF MINNESOTA PUBLIC ASSISTANCE TRENDS

Monthly.   Approx. 30 p.
SRI/MF/complete, shipped quarterly

Monthly report on Minnesota public welfare programs, covering general, medical, and supplemental assistance, and AFDC. Includes cases, recipients, and expenditures, by county and program.

Data are compiled by the Assistance Payments Policy and Operations Division of the Dept of Human Services. Report is issued approximately 9 months after month of coverage.

Issues generally include narrative summary, with 1 summary table and scattered text data; 23 detailed monthly tables; and technical notes and glossary.

Detailed monthly tables are listed below; most appear in all issues. Text tables and charts generally show trends for topics covered in monthly tables, often by State subarea; these trends are not described in SRI. All other additional features with substantial statistical content are described, as they appear, under "Statistical Features." Nonstatistical contents are not covered.

Prior to the July 1984 issue, report is covered in SRI under S4240-1. Issuing agency name has changed from Minnesota Department of Public Welfare.

Availability: Minnesota Department of Human Services, Reports and Statistics Section, Assistance Payments Policy and Operations Division, Space Center Bldg., 2nd Floor, 444 Lafayette Rd., St. Paul MN 55101, †; SRI/MF/complete, shipped quarterly.

Issues reviewed during 1985: July 1984-Mar. 1985 (D).

TABLES:

PROGRAM TRENDS

[Tables show data for current month and 12 previous months, unless otherwise noted. Tables [1-9] and [12-14] show number of cases and/or recipients, expenditures or payments, and additional data as indicated below.]

[1] Public assistance programs (excluding food stamps).

[2] Food stamps.

[3] AFDC [including current month data by program category (with detail for child and caretaker recipients) and for special supplements].

[4] Emergency assistance program [including current month data by program category (with detail for adult and child recipients, and maintenance and medical payments) and for defined emergencies].

[5] SSI.

[6] Minnesota supplemental aid [including current month data for aged, blind, and disabled].

[7-8] General assistance, and general assistance medical care [including current month data by case type or category].

[9] General assistance by [Minnesota Emergency Employment Development and/or job service] exemption/referral status of responsible person [for current month and 6-12 previous months].

[10] General assistance subprogram payment trends [including shelter for battered women].

[11] General assistance medical care expenditures by category of service [for current month and fiscal year to date].

[12] Medical assistance program [including eligible persons, recipients, and payments, by basis of eligibility, for current month].

[13] Medical assistance by category of service [for current month, with expenditures also shown for fiscal year to date].

[14] Nursing home care by basis of eligibility [and level of care, current month only].

[15] Public assistance programs: applications and cases [by program, with detail for medical assistance by basis of eligibility; for current month, preceding month, and same month of preceding year].

DATA BY COUNTY

[Tables show cases and/or persons, and payments, and additional data as indicated below. Data are shown by county for current month with some comparisons to previous month.]

I. AFDC [including caretakers and children].

II. SSI and Minnesota supplemental aid.

III. General assistance [including detail for single cases, and families with children and with adults only].

IV-V. General assistance medical care: cases concurrently receiving general assistance, and medical care only cases.

VI-VII. Medical assistance: recipients [including adult and caretaker/child] concurrently receiving SSI, Minnesota supplemental aid, or AFDC, and receiving medical assistance only, [with detail for Indochinese cases.]

PRELIMINARY DATA

[16] Preliminary statistical report on income maintenance [cases, persons, and payments, by program and category, for 3 coming months and selected month of previous year].

STATISTICAL FEATURES:

S4202–1.601: Oct. 1984

MINNESOTA SUPPLEMENTAL AID

(p. 3-4) Includes 1 table showing Minnesota Supplemental Aid recipients by detailed type of living arrangement, including institutionalized persons by type of facility, Sept. 1984.

S4202–1.602: Jan. 1985

AID TO FAMILIES WITH DEPENDENT CHILDREN

(p. 3-4) Includes 2 tables showing Minnesota AFDC eligible children by age and sex, and eligible adults by marital status, as of Jan. 1985. Data are from State Welfare Information File.

S4202–1.603: Feb. 1985

AID TO FAMILIES WITH DEPENDENT CHILDREN

(p. 3) Includes 1 table showing Minnesota AFDC eligible adults, with number employed full- and part-time, by sex and AFDC program segment (regular, and unemployed and incapacitated parent), as of Feb. 28, 1985.

S4230   MINNESOTA
Department of Public Safety

S4230–1   MINNESOTA CRIME INFORMATION, 1983

Annual.   July 1, 1984.
xi+119 p.
LC 74-641518.
SRI/MF/complete

Annual report on Minnesota crimes and arrests, by offense, 1983, with summary trends from 1936. Includes data by county, reporting agency, and municipality, and by offender age, sex, and race/ethnicity. Also includes data on law enforcement employment, assaults on officers, and firearms discharges by officers.

Report focuses on 8 Index offenses: murder, rape, robbery, aggravated assault, burglary, larceny/theft, motor vehicle theft, and arson. Selected data are also shown for numerous non-Index offenses.

Data are from State and local agency reports submitted under the Uniform Crime Reporting Program.

Contains preface, and listings of contents, charts, and tables (p. v-xi); introduction and explanation of offense classifications (p. 1-7); narrative analyses with text data, interspersed with 33 charts and 31 tables described below (p. 8-118); and glossary (p. 119).

Availability: Minnesota Department of Public Safety, Criminal Apprehension Bureau, Criminal Justice Information Systems Section, 1246 University Ave., St. Paul MN 55104, †; SRI/MF/complete.

CHARTS AND TABLES:

[Data are for Minnesota, 1983, unless otherwise noted.]

S4230–1.1: Offenses and Stolen Property

SUMMARY

a. Number of contributing agencies, and population represented, by urban and rural population size group; Index offenses, by quarter, 1980-83 period; and violent and property crimes, by offense, 1978-83. Charts 1-3 and table 1. (p. 8-12)

VIOLENT CRIMES

b. Homicides, by victim/offender relationship, weapon used, situation (multiple or single victims and offenders), and circumstance; and murder victims and offenders, by age, sex, and race (including Indians). Charts 4-5 and tables 2-3. (p. 15-18)

c. Rapes, including percent of reported cases unfounded, percent cleared by arrest, and percent reported as attempts, 1978-83; robberies, and stolen property value, by place of occurrence; and aggravated assaults, by weapon. Charts 6-10. (p. 20-24)

PROPERTY CRIMES

d. Burglaries, by category (attempted, forced entry, and unlawful entry); residence and nonresidence burglaries by time of day, and stolen property value, various years 1977-83; larceny thefts, by stolen property value; and larceny thefts and stolen property value, by property type. Charts 11-17. (p. 26-32)

e. Motor vehicle thefts by vehicle type, stolen and recovered value, and percent of vehicles recovered in same and other jurisdiction, 1979-83. Charts 18-19. (p. 34-35)

f. Arson, including unfounded and actual offenses, total and juvenile clearances, and estimated property damage, all by detailed property type; and arson offenses involving structures not in use, by structure type. Table 4. (p. 37)

MISCELLANEOUS DATA

g. Index crimes by offense, and percent cleared, for sheriff's depts and municipal police depts in 6-7 population size groups; value of property stolen and recovered in same and other jurisdiction, by property type; average loss per property offense, 1982-83; and distribution of dollar loss to serious crimes, by offense. Charts 20-21 and tables 5-8. (p. 38-43)

h. Statewide crimes, unfounded complaints, crime rate, and total and juvenile clearances by arrest, all by Index and non-Index offense; property offenses and value stolen and recovered, by type of property or crime; Index and non-Index crimes reported and percent cleared, by reporting agency area, with population; and Index crimes by offense, 1936-83. Tables 9-12. (p. 45-52)

S4230-1.2: Arrests, Urban-Rural Analysis, and Regional Summary

[Data by offense are shown for Index and non-Index offenses, unless otherwise noted.]

ARRESTS

a. Arrests by age and sex, adult and juvenile arrests by race (including Indian and Asian), and arrests of Hispanics, all by offense; and narcotics arrests, by substance, age, sex, race (including Indian/Alaskan and Asian/Pacific Islander), county, and city; with selected trends from 1974. Charts 22-25 and tables 13-17. (p. 54-68)

URBAN-RURAL AREAS AND REGIONS

b. Urban and rural areas: known/reported and actual crimes, unfounded complaints, crime rate, total and juvenile clearances by arrest, and arrests by sex, all by offense; and property offenses and value recovered and/or stolen, by type of property and Index offense. Tables 18-23. (p. 70-76)

c. Crime and arrest summary by region. Chart 26 and table 24. (p. 78-79)

S4230-1.3: Law Enforcement Employment, Assaults on Police, Firearms Discharges, and Data by Agency

a. Police urban and rural employees (sworn and civilian) as of Oct. 31, 1983, by city, county, and population size group; municipal police and sheriff dept employees, and urban and rural police/population ratios, by population size group; and State patrol employees. Tables 25-28. (p. 82-86)

b. Assaults on law enforcement officers, by type of weapon used, type of activity and assignment, and time of day. Charts 27-30. (p. 88-91)

c. Firearms discharges by law enforcement officers, by type of assignment, weapon used, purpose, result, time of occurrence,

whether felony or misdemeanor involved, and size of community served, with selected detail by type of police activity. Charts 31-33 and tables 29-30. (p. 92-96)

d. Crimes and clearances by Index and non-Index offense, by reporting agency. Table 31. (p. 98-118)

S4230-2   MINNESOTA MOTOR VEHICLE CRASH FACTS, 1984
Annual.   [1985.]
x+95 p.+errata.
LC 79-643000.
SRI/MF/complete

Annual report on Minnesota traffic accidents involving fatalities, injuries, and property damage, and number of persons killed and injured, 1984, with trends from the 1970s. Includes data by accident and vehicle type, location, time, and other circumstances; and driver and victim characteristics.

Also includes data on economic cost of accidents; motor vehicle registrations and mileage; licensed drivers; seatbelt, child restraint, and motorcycle helmet use in accidents; blood alcohol content of driver and pedestrian fatalities; and alcohol-related arrests and license revocations.

Data are compiled by Minnesota Office of Traffic Safety from accident reports submitted by citizens and law enforcement agencies.

Contains listing of contents, charts, and tables (p. i-vi); introduction and summary (p. vii-viii); and 10 parts, with narrative summaries, 1 map, 17 charts, and 93 tables (p. ix-x, 1-95).

Issuing agency also publishes *Minnesota 1984 Motor Vehicle Crash Facts Summary,* not covered by SRI.

Availability: Minnesota Department of Public Safety, Public Information Office, 318 Transportation Bldg., St. Paul MN 55155, †; SRI/MF/complete.

S4235   MINNESOTA Department of Public Service

S4235-1   MINNESOTA DEPARTMENT OF PUBLIC SERVICE Biennial Report, 1983-84
Biennial.   [1984.]   1+37 p.
LC 79-643434.
SRI/MF/complete

Biennial report presenting Minnesota public utility financial and operating data, by utility type, with some detail by company, 1983. Utility types covered are telephone, electric, and natural gas.

Includes data on customers by sector, revenues and expenses including tax payments, value of plant and materials/supplies, average residential bills and consumption or use, and telephone facilities.

Also includes dept financial and regulatory data, including rate increase cases filed and amounts requested and granted, and weights/measures division complaint investigations and other activities, various years 1975-FY84.

Contains contents listing (1 p.); and narrative report, with text data, 3 charts, and 19 tables (p. 1-37).

Previous report, for 1981, is described in SRI 1983 Annual under this number.

Availability: Minnesota Department of Public Service, 790 American Center Bldg., 160 E. Kellogg Blvd., St. Paul MN 55101, †; SRI/MF/complete.

S4240   MINNESOTA Department of Public Welfare

S4240-1   SUMMARY OF MINNESOTA PUBLIC ASSISTANCE TRENDS
Monthly.   Approx. 30 p.
SRI/MF/complete, shipped quarterly

Monthly report on Minnesota public welfare programs, covering general, medical, and supplemental assistance, and AFDC. Includes cases, recipients, and expenditures, by county and program.

Data are compiled by the Operations Review Division of the Dept of Public Welfare. Report is issued approximately 6 months after month of coverage.

Issues generally include narrative summary, with 1 summary table and scattered text data; 23 detailed monthly tables; and technical notes and glossary.

Detailed monthly tables are listed below; most appear in all issues. Text tables and charts generally show trends for topics covered in monthly tables, often by State subarea; these trends are not described in SRI. All other additional features with substantial statistical content are described, as they appear, under "Statistical Features." Nonstatistical contents are not covered.

Beginning with the July 1984 issue, SRI covers this report under S4202-1. Issuing agency name has changed to Minnesota Department of Human Services.

Availability: Minnesota Department of Public Welfare, Operations Review Division, Reports and Statistics Office, Space Center Bldg., 2nd Floor, 444 Lafayette Rd., St. Paul MN 55101, †; SRI/MF/complete, shipped quarterly.

Issues reviewed during 1985: Apr.-June 1984 (D).

TABLES:

PROGRAM TRENDS

[Tables show data for current month and 12 previous months, unless otherwise noted. Tables [1-9] and [12-14] show number of recipients and/or cases, expenditures or payments, and additional data as indicated below.]

[1] Public assistance programs (excluding food stamps).

[2] Food stamps.

[3] AFDC [including current month detail by program category and for special supplements].

[4] Emergency assistance program [including current month detail by program category and for defined emergencies].

[5] SSI.

[6] Minnesota supplemental aid (MSA) [including current month detail for aged, blind, and disabled].

[7-8] General assistance, and general assistance medical care [including current month detail by case type].

[9] General assistance by [Minnesota Emergency Employment Development and/or job service] exemption/referral status of responsible person [for current month and 6-12 previous months].

[10] General assistance subprogram payment trends [including shelter for battered women].

[11] General assistance medical care expenditures by category of service [for current month and fiscal year to date].

[12] Medical assistance program [including eligible persons, recipients, and expenditures, by basis of eligibility, for current month].

[13] Medical assistance by category of service [for current month, with expenditures also shown for fiscal year to date].

[14] Nursing home care by basis of eligibility [and level of care, current month only].

[15] Public assistance programs: applications and cases [by program, with detail for medical assistance by basis of eligibility; for current month, preceding month, and same month of preceding year].

DATA BY COUNTY
[Tables show cases and/or persons, and payments, and additional data as indicated below. Data are shown by county for current month. Several tables also include summary data by type of county (urban, suburban, and/or rural), and change from previous month.]

I. AFDC [including caretakers and children].

II. SSI and MSA.

III. General assistance [including detail for single cases, and families with children and with adults only].

IV-V. General assistance medical care: cases concurrently receiving general assistance, and medical care only cases.

VI-VII. Medical assistance: recipients [including adult and caretaker/child] concurrently receiving SSI, MSA, or AFDC, and receiving medical assistance only, [with detail for Indochinese cases.]

PRELIMINARY DATA
[16] Preliminary statistical report on income maintenance [cases, persons, and payments, by program and category, for 3 coming months and selected month of previous year].

S4250   MINNESOTA
Department of Revenue

S4250–2   MINNESOTA CORPORATION INCOME TAX: Returns Filed During 1983
Annual.   Feb. 1985.
57 p. var. paging.
Bull. No. 61.
LC 79-649271.
SRI/MF/complete, current & previous year reports

Annual summary report on income taxes paid by corporations and banks in Minnesota, based on returns filed in 1983, with selected trends from 1979. Includes data by county, industry, and income size.

Contains contents and table listing (2 p.); summary of filing requirements and definitions, with 1 table showing corporate income tax rates and credits for selected periods 1933-83 (p. 1-3); analysis of returns filed for 1983, with 9 summary tables (p. 4-8); statistical appendix, with 29 tables listed below (p. 11-28); and tax form facsimile (28 p.).

Previous report, for 1982, was also reviewed in 1985, and is also available on SRI microfiche, under this number [Annual. July 1984. 3 + 34 + 5 p. Bull. No. 59. †]. 1982 report is substantially similar in content.

Availability: Minnesota Department of Revenue, Research Office 113, PO Box 64446, St. Paul MN 55164, †; SRI/MF/complete.

TABLES:

CORPORATION AND BANK EXCISE TAX RETURNS
[Data are for 1983. Tables show number of returns, gross sales, cost of goods sold, total and net income, State net and taxable income, and tax liability. Tables titles begin "Minnesota corporation and bank exise tax..." Tables 1-21 show data for all, tax, no-tax, multi-State, 100% Minnesota, unitary, and non-unitary returns.]

1-7. By size of total net income. (p. 11-14)

8-14. By size of State taxable income. (p. 14-17)

15-21. By major industry group. (p. 18-20)

22. By industry classification, all returns. (p. 21-22)

23. By county [where main office is located, and including selected locations in other States, total located in foreign countries, and unclassified], all returns. (p. 23-24)

TRENDS
[Data are for 1979-83. Tables show number of returns, State taxable income, and tax liability. Table titles begin "Minnesota corporation income tax returns..." Data from bank excise tax returns are included in totals for 1983.]

24-26. By size of State taxable income. (p. 25-27)

27-29. By major industry group. (p. 28)

S4255   MINNESOTA
Office of the Secretary of State

S4255–1   MINNESOTA ELECTION RESULTS, 1984: Primary Election and General Election
Biennial.   [1985.]   232 p.
SRI/MF/complete

Biennial report presenting results of the Minnesota primary and general elections held Sept. 11 and Nov. 6, 1984. Shows voting for President and Vice-President, U.S. Senators and Representatives, and State representatives and constitutional amendments. Also includes voter registration and turnout. Data are shown by district and/or county, with detail by precinct. Also shows party affiliation of candidates.

Previous report, covering 1982 elections, is described in SRI 1983 Annual under this number.

Availability: Minnesota Office of the Secretary of State, Election Division, 180 State Office Bldg., St. Paul MN 55155-1299, †; SRI/MF/complete.

S4310   MISSISSIPPI
Department of Agriculture and Commerce

S4310–1   MISSISSIPPI AGRICULTURAL STATISTICS, 1982-83
Annual.   Dec. 1984.
6 + 62 p.   Supplement No. 18.
SRI/MF/complete

Annual report on Mississippi agricultural production, marketing, and finances, 1982-83, with some data for 1984. Data generally are shown by commodity and/or county and district with some comparisons to U.S.

Covers production, value and/or price, and, as applicable, acreage, yield, stocks, inventory, and disposition, for field crop, fruit and nut, livestock, dairy, and poultry sectors.

Also includes data on number and acreage of farms; value of exports; cash receipts by commodity; cotton ginning; off-farm storage facilities; feed prices paid by farmers; and agricultural employment, hours, and wage rates.

Data are compiled by the Mississippi Crop and Livestock Reporting Service in cooperation with the USDA.

Contains contents listing (3 p.); and 12 maps and 66 tables (p. 1-62).

Availability: Mississippi Crop and Livestock Reporting Service, Agricultural Statistician, PO Box 980, Jackson MS 39205, †; SRI/MF/complete.

S4325   MISSISSIPPI
Department of Banking and Consumer Finance

S4325–1   ANNUAL REPORT OF THE DEPARTMENT OF BANKING AND CONSUMER FINANCE, State of Mississippi, Jan. 1, 1984-Dec. 31, 1984
Annual. [1985.]   116 p.
LC 81-643490.
SRI/MF/complete

Annual report on financial condition of Mississippi financial institutions as of Dec. 1984. Covers composite assets, liabilities, equity capital, income, and expenses, for State-chartered commercial banks, small loan lenders, and credit unions; composite assets, liabilities, and equity capital, for nationally chartered banks; and assets of individual banks and credit unions.

Also includes regulatory activity and departmental finances; and lists of banks, branches, and other financial institutions, by location.

Contains contents listing (p. 4-5); and 15 tables, interspersed with rosters, directories, and lists (p. 5-116).

Availability: Mississippi Department of Banking and Consumer Finance, 1206 Woolfolk State Office Bldg., PO Drawer 731, Jackson MS 39205-0731, †; SRI/MF/complete.

S4340   MISSISSIPPI
Department of Education

S4340–1   ANNUAL REPORT OF THE STATE SUPERINTENDENT OF PUBLIC EDUCATION TO THE LEGISLATURE OF MISSISSIPPI, 1985: Statistical Reports 1983/84, Volume II
Annual. [1984.]   135 p.
LC 78-646492.
SRI/MF/complete

Annual report, for 1983/84, on Mississippi public elementary and secondary school enrollment, staff and salaries, and finances, by school district. Also includes data on public and private colleges and selected trends from 1950s.

Contains 7 statistical sections, with 2 charts and 71 tables described below (p. 1-132); and index (p. 133-135).

Volume I of report contains recommendations and summaries of dept activities, and is not covered in SRI.

Availability: Mississippi Department of Education, Administrative and Finance Division, PO Box 771, Jackson MS 39205-0771, †; SRI/MF/complete.

CHARTS AND TABLES:
[Data are for Mississippi, 1983/84, unless otherwise noted. Data by grade usually also include prekindergarten, kindergarten, and special and ungraded elementary and secondary sections. Data by type of position for instructional personnel are generally for principals and assistant principals, supervisors, guidance counselors, librarians, and teachers.]

S4340–1.1: Schools, Enrollment, Staff, and Finances

a. School districts and schools: school districts by type and size; agricultural high schools and junior colleges; school board members by district type; number of schools by education level and size; number of elementary and secondary schools, 1973/74-1983/84; and accredited public and private secondary, elementary, and special schools. 9 tables. (p. 1-6)

b. Students: cumulative and fall enrollment, average daily attendance and membership, promotions and nonpromotions, and dropouts, all by grade level; high school graduates, by sex; grade 1-12 enrollment, for children born in 1966; and retention rate between 5th grade and college; various years 1956/57-1983/84. 9 tables. (p. 7-15)

c. Staff: total staff, by position; characteristics of administrative and instructional personnel, variously including age, salary, training level, and experience, with selected detail by position and district type; teacher salary and training trends, various years 1952/53-1983/84; and instructional personnel, salaries, and expense per pupil, for U.S. and 12 southeastern States. 13 tables. (p. 16-25)

d. Finances: Total expenditures and expenditures per pupil, by function and object, with detail by district type, and comparisons to total U.S. and southeastern States; receipts by source; general fund appropriations and receipts, including detailed appropriations for public education and higher education, FY83-84 or FY84; capital outlays, by function; value of capital facilities and equipment; and school and nonschool food program participation and finances. 2 charts and 10 tables. (p. 26-35)

S4340–1.2: Higher Education, Transportation, and Vocational Education

a. Higher education: public junior college finances, administrative districts and campuses, and transportation and housing services; enrollment in public and nonpublic junior colleges, 4-year Bible colleges and theological schools, and colleges and universities, by program and/or class level, all by institution; and public/nonpublic college enrollment by class level, 1966/67-1983/84. 7 tables. (p. 36-41)

b. Transportation: privately and publicly owned vehicles in use and purchased, mileage traveled, and pupils transported; and school bus accidents, injuries, and property damage. 1 table. (p. 43)

c. Vocational education: vocational enrollment by program and level, including disadvantaged and handicapped students; and vocational/technical education expenditures by source of funds, by program; FY84. 2 tables. (p. 44-45)

S4340–1.3: School Districts
[All tables show data by school district.]

a. Fall enrollment and average daily attendance, by grade level; and instructional personnel and average salaries, by type of position. 3 tables. (p. 46-67)

b. Financial report, including expenditures by function; revenue receipts by detailed local, State, and Federal source, including taxes by type; income from nonrevenue transactions; and tax levies by type and 1983 assessments, for county, consolidated, and municipal separate districts. 12 tables. (p. 68-116)

c. Classroom teachers, pupil/teacher ratios, average salaries, fall enrollment, average daily attendance, expenditures per pupil, revenues, and wealth and ad valorem tax collections per pupil unit; with rankings for each district. 5 tables. (p. 117-132)

S4345   MISSISSIPPI
Employment Security Commission

S4345–1   ANNUAL PLANNING INFORMATION, State of Mississippi, PY85
Annual. Mar. 1985.   123 p.
SRI/MF/complete

Annual planning report, for planning year 1985, identifying Mississippi population groups most in need of employment services, and presenting data on employment by industry and occupation, with selected trends from 1970 and projections through 1995. Includes data on population and labor force, job openings, unemployment insurance, and veterans, with some detail by county.

Planning year 1985 (PY85) is the year ended June 30, 1986. Data are compiled by the Employment Security Commission.

Contains contents and table listing (2 p.); highlights and conclusions, and State geographical description (p. 3-11); 9 narrative sections, interspersed with 5 maps and 35 tables, listed below (p. 15-115); and appendix, with glossary and list of additional reports published by issuing agency (p. 119-123).

Availability: Mississippi Employment Security Commission, Labor Market Information Department, PO Box 1699, Jackson MS 39215-1699, †; SRI/MF/complete.

TABLES:

S4345–1.1: Population, Labor Force, and Unemployment Characteristics
[Tables [1-11] show data by race, sex, and age group, for PY85, unless otherwise noted.]

POPULATION AND LABOR FORCE

[1] [Population, 1970, 1980, and estimated 1986]. (p. 16-17)

[2-3] Labor force; and participation rate [1970, 1980, and 1986]. (p. 18-19)

[4] Veteran status: [male] population 16/over [by period served and race]. (p. 20)

[5] Labor force status [of] Vietnam veterans, by age and race. (p. 21)

UNEMPLOYMENT

[6-8] Number unemployed and unemployment rate, number of different individuals unemployed, and long-termed unemployed (15 weeks or more). (p. 26-28)

[9-10] Experienced unemployed by occupation and service [by race and sex]; and weeks worked. (p. 29-31)

[11] Civilian labor force, total employment, total unemployment, and unemployment rates, [monthly] 1977-84. (p. 36-39)

S4345–1.2: Insured Unemployed and Employment Characteristics

INSURED UNEMPLOYED
[Data are shown quarterly for 1984.]

[1-2] UI [unemployment insurance] claimants, by age, occupation, race, and sex. (p. 44-45)

[3-4] UI claimants by duration of unemployment [by sex and race], and by industry of attachment. (p. 46-47)

EMPLOYMENT BY INDUSTRY AND OCCUPATION

[5] [Residence-based civilian labor force, by employment status; establishment-based employment, by industry division and major manufacturing group; persons involved in labor-management disputes; and insured unemployed]; PY78-85. (p. 52)

[6] Employment [1982 and 1995] and job openings [1982-95 period] by [detailed] occupation. (p. 57-75)

[7-8] 25 occupations/occupational categories projected to grow most rapidly and to have largest job growth [shows employment 1982 and 1995, and job growth 1982-95 period]. (p. 76-77)

S4345–1.3: Employment Services and Characteristics of Economically Disadvantaged

EMPLOYMENT SERVICES
[Data are shown quarterly for 1984, by occupational category.]

[1] Unfilled job openings [total and unfilled 30 days or more]. (p. 83)

[2-3] Job openings received and filled. (p. 84-85)

[4-5] Occupations of job applicants, and experienced applicants available at end of quarter, by sex and minority status. (p. 86-87)

ECONOMICALLY DISADVANTAGED
[Data are by race, for PY85. Tables [7] and [10-14] also show data by sex.]

[6] Economically disadvantaged individuals [total and under age 18] in families with income below poverty level, [and] unrelated individuals [total and over age 65] with income below poverty level. (p. 92)

[7] Civilian family heads: labor force [and/or] poverty status. (p. 93)

[8] Related children under 18 years of age, by type of family [male and female heads], poverty status, and age [group]. (p. 94)

[9] Older individuals [65/over], by poverty status. (p. 95)

[10] Poverty level by age. (p. 96)

[11] Persons 14/above by type of income [wage/salary, nonfarm and farm self-employment, social security/railroad retirement, welfare, and other]. (p. 97)

[12-13] Youth enrolled in school (3-24 years of age), and youth 14-24 not in school, [total and below] poverty level, by age. (p. 98)

[14] Employed part-time for economic reasons [and total employed]. (p. 99)

S4345–1.4: Socioeconomic Characteristics

POPULATION AND HOUSING
[Data are shown by county.]

[1-2] Population: percent change 1980-86 [period]; and percent minority, 1980. [maps] (p. 104-105)

[3-4] Housing units, percent change 1970-80 [period]; and persons per housing unit, 1970 and 1980. [maps] (p. 106-107)

INCOME

[5] Per capita income as percent of national [by county and MSA], 1982. [map] (p. 108)

[6] Total income [distribution by source (interest/dividends/rent, transfer payments, and earnings by industry division) by county], 1982. (p. 109-114)

[7] Average weekly wages, by industry [division and major manufacturing group], 1977-85]. (p. 115)

S4348   MISSISSIPPI
Office of the Governor

S4348–1   UNIFORM CRIME REPORT, State of Mississippi Annual Report, Jan.-Dec. 1983
Annual.   [1985.]   vii+47 p.
SRI/MF/complete

Annual report on Mississippi crimes and arrests by offense, including data by county and/or reporting agency, 1983, with summary crime trends from 1974.

Report focuses on 8 Index offenses: murder, rape, robbery, aggravated assault, burglary, larceny, motor vehicle theft, and arson. Arrests are also shown for numerous non-Index offenses.

Data are compiled from reports of State and local law enforcement agencies, submitted to the FBI under the Uniform Crime Reporting (UCR) Program. (Mississippi's State UCR program has been discontinued, but many agencies continue to participate voluntarily by sending reports directly to the FBI.)

Contains foreword, and listings of contents, tables, and charts (p. iii-vii); introduction (p. 1); State Index crime summaries, with brief narratives, crime clock, 13 charts, and 12 tables (p. 2-27); and local data, with 2 detailed tables (p. 28-47).

This is the 3rd edition of the report. Previous edition also presented data on Index crime characteristics, arrests by age and sex, value of stolen property, and law enforcement personnel.

Availability: Mississippi Office of the Governor, Criminal Justice Planning, Statistical Analysis Center, 301 W. Pearl St., Jackson MS 39203-3088, †; SRI/MF/complete.

S4350   MISSISSIPPI
Department of Health

S4350–1   VITAL STATISTICS, Mississippi, 1984
Annual   [1985.]   iv+138 p.
LC 85-622259.
SRI/MF/complete, current & previous year reports

Annual report, for 1984, on Mississippi vital statistics, covering births, deaths by detailed cause, marriages, and divorces, by county and selected demographic characteristics. Also includes historical trends from 1913 and selected data by city. Data are from records filed with the State Dept of Health.

Contains contents and table listing (p. i-iv); introduction and definitions (p. 1-3); and 64 tables, listed below, arranged in 3 sections (p. 5-138).

Previous report, for 1983, was also reviewed by SRI during 1985, and is also available on SRI microfiche under S4350-1 [Recurring (irreg.) [1984.] v+138 p. †]. Report for 1982 is described in SRI 1983 Annual under S4350-1.

Availability: Mississippi Department of Health, Public Health Statistics Office, PO Box 1700, Jackson MS 39205-1700, †; SRI/MF/complete.

TABLES:
[Most data are shown by race. Data are for 1984, unless otherwise noted.]

S4350–1.1: Summary Tables
LIVE BIRTHS

A1. Live births and average per day, by month. (p. 7)

A2. Percentage of live births in hospitals/clinics [selected years 1940-84]. (p. 7)

A3-A5. Live births and percentage distribution: by type of facility and attendant; by age of mother; and by years of school completed by father and mother. (p. 8-9)

A6. Illegitimate live births and percent of total live births in specified group, by age of mother. (p. 10)

A7. Live births, percentage distribution, and median age of mother, by total-birth order. (p. 11)

A8-A9. Live births and percentage distribution, by whether mother received prenatal care [and] time during pregnancy care began, and by maturity. (p. 12)

A10. Congenital malformations reported on live birth certificates, by malformation. (p. 13)

FETAL DEATHS

B1-B2. Reportable fetal deaths: and percentage distribution, by place of delivery and attendant; and fetal death ratios, by age of mother. (p. 14)

B3. Percentage distribution of live births and reportable fetal deaths, by whether mother received prenatal care. (p. 15)

B4. Reportable fetal deaths and fetal death ratios, by completed weeks of gestation, 1982-84. (p. 16)

DEATHS

C1-C2. Deaths and average per day, by month; and deaths and percentage distribution, by age. (p. 17)

C3. Deaths by age and sex, and male/female ratios by age. (p. 18)

C4-C5. Deaths and percent of total deaths: from 10 leading causes; and from 5 leading causes by age; by cause. (p. 18-19)

C6-C7. Deaths: from malignant neoplasms and percentage distribution, by primary site and sex; and from major chronic respiratory diseases [selected years 1959-84]. (p. 20)

C8. Deaths and percent of total accidental deaths from 5 leading causes of accidental death, by cause. (p. 21)

C9. Deaths from selected types of accidents, by sex, also by age. (p. 22)

C10. Motor vehicle accident deaths occurring in Mississippi and rates, also motor vehicle accident deaths of Mississippi residents and rates [selected years 1950-84]. (p. 23)

C11. Infant deaths, percentage distribution, and mortality rates, by age. (p. 24)

C12. Deaths and mortality rates for 10 leading causes of infant deaths, by cause. (p. 25)

MARRIAGES

D1. Marriages and average per day, by month. (p. 26)

D2. Brides and grooms and percentage distribution, by age. (p. 27)

D3. Median age of bride and groom, for all marriages and 1st marriages. (p. 28)

D4-D5. Brides and grooms and percentage distribution, by marriage order and previous marital status. (p. 29-30)

D6. Marriages and percentage distribution, by residence of bride and groom. (p. 31)

DIVORCES

E1-E3. Divorces and percentage distribution: by cause, number of minor children, and number of years married. (p. 32-33)

S4350–1.2: Major Tables

LIVE BIRTHS

1. Live births by place of occurrence [and] by place of residence (place includes counties, out of State, and towns of 10,000 or more). (p. 37-39)

2. Live births, by county of residence, attendant [and] sex. (p. 40-42)

3A-3C. Live births, by county of residence and age of mother. (p. 43-48)

4. Illegitimate live births and percent of total live births, by county of residence. (p. 49-50)

5A-5C. Illegitimate live births, by county of residence and age of mother. (p. 51-56)

6-7. Immature and premature live births and percent of total live births, by county of residence. (p. 57-60)

FETAL DEATHS

8. Reportable fetal deaths, by county of occurrence; also reportable fetal deaths and fetal death ratios, by county of residence. (p. 61-62)

DEATHS, MARRIAGES, AND DIVORCES

9. Deaths by place of occurrence [and] by place of residence (place includes counties, out of State, towns of 10,000 or more). (p. 63-65)

10. Deaths, by [detailed] cause. (p. 66-80)

11. Deaths from major cause groups and certain selected causes, by sex and age, also rates for major cause groups and certain selected causes. (p. 81-87)

12A-12B. Infant, neonatal, and postneonatal deaths, by county of residence, 1984; and rates, 1980-84 (5-year average). (p. 88-91)

13. Infant deaths from selected causes, by age, also mortality rates for selected causes. (p. 92-93)

14. Accidental deaths, by county of occurrence and type of accident. (p. 94-95)

15. Marriages, by county of licensure, occurrence, and residence of bride. (p. 96-97)

16. Divorces, by county of occurrence. (p. 98-99)

17. Deaths from selected causes used for ranking leading causes [by county of residence]. (p. 101-121)

S4350–1.3: Time Series Tables

18-20. Live births, deaths, maternal deaths, and rates (occurrence data 1913-43, residence data 1944-84). (p. 125-130)

21. Infant deaths and mortality rates (occurrence data 1917-44, residence data 1945-84). (p. 131-132)

22-23. Neonatal and postneonatal deaths and mortality rates (occurrence data 1924-44, residence data 1945-84). (p. 133-136)

24. Marriages and divorces, occurrence data, 1926-84. (p. 137-138)

S4360   MISSISSIPPI
Board of Trustees of State Institutions of Higher Learning

S4360–1   STATISTICAL REPORT OF INFORMATION REGARDING THE ENROLLMENT, STUDENT CREDIT HOURS, DEGREES CONFERRED, AND FINANCES of the State-Supported Universities in Mississippi for the Summer of 1983 and the 1983/84 Regular Session
Annual. Feb. 1985.
5+vi+216 p.
SRI/MF/complete

Annual report on Mississippi public university operations, covering enrollments, degrees conferred, credit hours, and finances, all by institution, summer 1983 and/or academic year 1983/84, with selected trends from 1979/80. Includes detail by student level and field of study.

Contains preface (2 p.); contents and table listing (p. i-vi); and 6 statistical sections, with 1 chart and 61 tables described below (p. 1-216).

Availability: Mississippi Board of Trustees of State Institutions of Higher Learning, 3825 Ridgewood Rd., PO Box 2336, Jackson MS 39225-2336, †; SRI/MF/complete.

TABLES:
[All data are shown by institution, often including on-campus study, off-campus degree granting

and resident centers, and extension classes. Data are generally for 1983 summer session and/or 1983/84 academic year.]

a. Enrollments: FTE and/or headcount enrollments, by term, resident status, class level, and subject area, including medical center, with selected summaries by sex and trends from 1979/80; full- and part-time on-campus enrollments; and summary comparison of total enrollments at all Mississippi institutions of higher learning, including private and junior colleges. 1 chart and 31 tables. (p. 1-38)

b. Degrees conferred and credit hours produced, by level and field of study. 10 tables. (p. 39-188)

c. Finances: restricted and unrestricted revenues by source, including Federal and State appropriations, and expenditures by function, including scholarships/fellowships; and unrestricted on-campus student credit hour cost for instruction/related academic support, by level and field of study. 20 tables. (p. 189-216)

S4365   MISSISSIPPI
Insurance Department

S4365–1   ANNUAL REPORT OF THE INSURANCE DEPARTMENT OF THE STATE OF MISSISSIPPI
Annual, suspended.

Annual report presenting Mississippi insurance industry financial and underwriting data, by company and line of insurance. Report has been suspended indefinitely, due to funding constraints; for description of the last edition, presenting data for 1979, see SRI 1981 Annual under this number.

Summary data on insurance industry underwriting business is available from Mississippi Insurance Department, PO Box 79, Jackson, MS 39205-0079.

S4370   MISSISSIPPI
Library Commission

S4370–1   STATISTICS FOR PUBLIC LIBRARIES: Annual Report of Mississippi Public Libraries, FY84
Annual. [1985.]
21 p. + errata sheet
LC 81-623578.
SRI/MF/complete

Annual report on Mississippi public libraries, FY84. Covers library personnel, operations, holdings, circulation, income, and expenditures.

Contains contents listing (p. 1); 3 tables listed below (p. 2-15); and directories of library administrative units and library commission members (p. 16-21).

Availability: Mississippi Library Commission, PO Box 10700, Jackson MS 39209-0700, †; SRI/MF/complete.

TABLES:

[Tables show data by library, for FY84, unless otherwise noted.]

[1] Administrative units [director, organizational structure, and hours and days open; population served, Sept. 1984; and stationary and mobile service units, personnel, items owned, and circulation, FY83-84]. (p. 2-7)

[2] Income [operating and capital outlay, by funding source]. (p. 8-11)

[3] Expenditures [by object, including salaries/benefits and construction]. (p. 12-15)

S4395   MISSISSIPPI
Department of
Public Accounts

S4395–1   ANNUAL FINANCIAL REPORT OF THE STATE OF MISSISSIPPI for the Fiscal Year Ended June 30, 1984
Annual.   Dec. 31, 1984.
2+iii+295 p.
SRI/MF/complete

Annual report, for FY84, on financial condition of Mississippi State government, presenting revenues by source, expenditures by function and object, and fund balances; for all, general, and special funds, with selected comparisons to FY83 and summary trends from FY75. Most data are also shown by detailed dept and agency.

Also includes data on general fund appropriations vs. expenditures; and apportionments to individual counties, cities, special districts, junior colleges, universities, and hospitals.

Data are from the records of the State auditor of public accounts.

Contains contents listing (1 p.); introduction (p. i-iii); 6 trend tables (p. 3-49); 25 statements (p. 53-291); and roster of State auditors (p. 295).
Availability: Mississippi Department of Public Accounts, State Auditor, PO Box 1060, Jackson MS 39215-1060, †; SRI/MF/complete.

S4400   MISSISSIPPI
Department of
Public Safety

S4400–1   ANNUAL SUMMARY OF TRAFFIC ACCIDENT AND ENFORCEMENT ACTIVITIES of the Mississippi Department of Public Safety, 1983
Annual.   [1985.]   5+106 p.
LC 57-35954.
SRI/MF/complete

Annual report on Mississippi traffic accidents, fatalities, and injuries, by accident and vehicle type, location, time, and other circumstances; and driver and victim characteristics; 1983, with trends from 1938.

Also includes data on travel and highway miles; motor vehicle registrations, licensed drivers, and license testing; value of property damage; highway patrol enforcement personnel and activities including arrests; drunken driving and

related medical tests; license revocations and other administrative procedures; and Driver Services Bureau vehicle use and revenues.

Data are compiled by the Dept of Public Safety.

Contains contents listing (3 p.); highlights, 2 maps, 45 charts, and 45 tables (p. 1-93); and glossary and index (p. 94-106).
Availability: Mississippi Department of Public Safety, Driver Services Bureau, Statistics Division, PO Box 958, Jackson MS 39205, †; SRI/MF/complete.

S4410   MISSISSIPPI
Department of
Public Welfare

S4410–1   MISSISSIPPI STATE DEPARTMENT OF PUBLIC WELFARE ANNUAL REPORT, FY84
Annual.   [1985.]   4+55 p.
ISSN 0098-5120.
LC 75-644224.
SRI/MF/complete

Annual report on Mississippi public welfare cases, recipients, and payments, by program and county, FY84, with trends from 1980. Covers Aid to Dependent Children (ADC), food stamps, adoption, foster care, child support, and general relief. Includes data on suspected fraud cases.

Contains listings of contents, tables, and charts (3 p.); narrative report arranged by division, with 1 map, 1 table, and 1 chart (p. 1-20); statistical section arranged by program type, with 1 chart, 4 maps, and 15 tables (p. 21-42); information on employee attendance at conferences, and related expense (p. 43-54); and organizational chart (p. 55).

All tables, and maps and charts with substantial statistics not covered in tables, are listed below.
Availability: Mississippi Department of Public Welfare, PO Box 352, 515 E. Amite St., Jackson MS 39205, †; SRI/MF/complete.

MAPS, CHARTS, AND TABLES:
[Data are for Mississippi, FY84 or as of June 1984, unless otherwise noted.]

STATE SUMMARY

[1-2] Statement of expenditures by program [by object and funding source; and] total expenditure by program. [table and chart] (p. 1-2 and 20)

FOOD ASSISTANCE

[3] Number of persons and households receiving food stamps [1980-84]. [chart] (p. 21)

[4-5] Food stamp participation [households, persons, and coupon value, by county, and by month], FY84. (p. 23-24)

[6] Percentage of U.S. population participating in food stamp program [national average and by State, no date]. [map] (p. 25)

ADC

[7-9] [ADC:] individuals eligible for assistance, applications handled, and expenditure for assistance payments [by county]. (p. 27-30)

ADOPTION, FOSTER CARE, AND CHILD SUPPORT

[10-11] Total number of certified special needs children receiving adoption assistance payments, and adoption unit placements [by age, and by foster and nonfoster parent race]. (p. 31-32)

[12] Adoption assistance locations [number of adoption assistance recipients by county]. [map] (p. 33)

[13] Foster home care payments by county. (p. 34)

[14] Child support: cases and collections [ADC and non-ADC, by county]. (p. 35-36)

SOCIAL SERVICES, FRAUD, AND GENERAL RELIEF

[15] Social service cases under care: primary and secondary service recipients by county. (p. 37-38)

[16-18] Administrative disqualification hearings and reviews, and fair hearings [by program]. (p. 39-40)

[19] Court survey [suspected food stamp and public assistance fraud cases and dispositions; and fraud/refund investigation referrals and completions, by program]. (p. 41)

[20] General relief [cases and payments]: only counties offering general relief. (p. 42)

S4425   MISSISSIPPI
Office of the
Secretary of
State

S4425–1   MISSISSIPPI OFFICIAL AND STATISTICAL REGISTER, 1984-88
Quadrennial.   Jan. 1985.
518 p.
LC 10-33135.
SRI/MF/complete

Quadrennial report presenting general reference information and electoral statistics for Mississippi, 1985. Data are compiled by the secretary of state.

Contains contents listing and introduction (p. 1-24); and the following sections:

General information: includes State description; land area and population, by county, 1970 and 1980; climatological data by city and State region; lists of famous persons and State parks; and directories of newspapers, TV and radio stations, and public libraries. 4 tables. (p. 25-75)

Education: includes history and organization; number of school districts and schools; revenues, pupils, bus operations, and personnel and salaries; and school trust land acreage, by district; 1983/84. 1 map and 3 tables. (p. 77-87)

Executive, Legislative, and Judicial Branches; Federal Officials; County and Local Governments; and State Agencies, Boards, and Commissions: includes directories and biographies of officials; list of governors since 1798; tabular list of court districts by county; and 12 maps. (p. 89-372)

Elections: includes directory of election commissioners and political party officials; and 62 tables described below. (p. 373-508)

Index. (p. 509-511)

For description of previous edition, see SRI 1981 Annual under this number.

Availability: Mississippi Office of the Secretary of State, Documents and Publications Division, PO Box 136, Jackson MS 39205-0136, †; SRI/MF/complete.

ELECTION RESULTS:

S4425-1.1: Elections

[All tables show data by county.]

a. Voter registration, Oct. 1982, July 1983, and Oct. 1984; and population, 1980. 1 table. (p. 376-377)

b. Election results for special, primary, regular, and general elections held June 23, 1981-Nov. 20, 1984; showing voting for President/Vice President, U.S. and State senators and representatives, Governor, judges, and other officials, and 5 concurrent resolutions; with party affiliation of candidates. 61 tables. (p. 393-508)

S4435   MISSISSIPPI
Tax Commission

S4435-1   SERVICE BULLETIN, FYE June 30, 1984, Mississippi State Tax Commission
Annual. Dec. 31, 1984.
137 p.
SRI/MF/complete

Annual report presenting detailed data on Mississippi tax collections by type of tax, and disbursements by locality and function, FY84. Includes data by industry, county, and city.

Also includes data on property value assessments, reimbursements, motor vehicle fuel consumption and registrations, and Alcoholic Beverage Control (ABC) Division sales and profits.

Data were compiled by the Tax Commission in cooperation with the State auditor.

Contains contents listing (1 p.); and 8 statistical sections, with 7 charts, and 51 tables listed below (p. 7-137).

Availability: Mississippi Tax Commission, PO Box 960, Jackson MS 39205-0960, †; SRI/MF/complete.

TABLES:

[Unless otherwise noted, data are for FY84.]

S4435-1.1: Statistical Sections

SUMMARY

[1-4] General and special fund total receipts [by source] and expenditures [by function]. (p. 11-17)

AD VALOREM TAX, HOMESTEAD EXEMPTION

[5] Assessment [summary of property and utilities by class, and including real property acreage], 1983. (p. 21)

[6] Total assessments of each county [1975-83]. (p. 22)

[7-8] Assessment of personal property and real estate, by classes [and county], 1983. (p. 23-24)

[9] Ad valorem assessments [by type and county], 1983. (p. 25)

[10] Comparative statement of assessments: public utilities [by company], 1977-83. (p. 26)

[11] Assessment of public utilities by classes [and county], 1983. (p. 27)

[12-13] County and separate school district applications classified according to value [by county and district], 1982. (p. 28-29)

[14-15] Counties, municipalities, and municipal separate school districts: reimbursements for elderly/disabled [and regular reimbursements, all by county or district], 1981-82. (p. 30-31)

[16] Adjustments in homestead exemption tax loss claims, counties/municipal separate school districts/municipalities combined [regular and elderly/disabled reimbursements 1981-82, and total adjustments 1981/82, by county]. (p. 32)

[17-18] Exempt assessed valuation [for individual] counties and municipal separate school districts [biennially 1974-82]. (p. 33-34)

ABC FINANCES

[Tables [19-24] begin "ABC Division..."]

[19-20] Collections and distributions of revenue [by major source or recipient], and revolving fund statement of operations, FY83-84. (p. 37-38)

[21] Wet [and] dry counties [list]. (p. 40)

[22] 18-year comparison of revenue collections [by source, 1967-84]. (p. 41)

[23] Schedule of local governing authorities share of permit licenses fees [by county and municipality]. (p. 42-45)

[24] Schedule of sales, and collections [by tax type], by counties. (p. 46)

INCOME AND FRANCHISE TAXES

[25-26] Selected corporate income and franchise tax information [number of taxpayers, income revenue, taxable income, franchise tax, and annual fee, by industry division and county, and for out of State]. (p. 49-51)

[27] Selected personal income tax information [number of taxpayers, gross income tax, and net taxable income, by county and for out of State]. (p. 52-53)

SEVERANCE AND PETROLEUM TAXES

[28] Payments to counties: oil, gas, and timber severance taxes. (p. 57-58)

[29-36] Tax collected on gasoline; interstate fuel tax; fuel tax collected at scales; taxes collected on other motor fuel, and on liquefied compressed gas for highway use; collections on permits and decals; and tax collected on oil and crankcase lubricating oil; [generally showing monthly taxable gallons and amount collected, with some detail by type of fuel or oil]. (p. 61-68)

[37] [Monthly] seawall tax collections [and taxable gallons for 3 counties]. (p. 69)

[38] Petroleum tax distribution to counties [municipal and county share, and surplus]. (p. 70-71)

[39-40] Petroleum tax division receipts [by source] and disbursements [by category]. (p. 72-73)

MOTOR VEHICLE REGISTRATIONS, FEES, AND TAXES

[41] Regular registration/tag fees [and taxes collected, and decals/plates issued, by vehicle type and other classification]. (p. 77)

[42] Motor vehicle license tag plates: number issued by tax collectors [by county], 1982-83. (p. 78-79)

[43-44] Prorate registrations fees and taxes, FY84; and passenger coach [revenue] distribution for 1984 [for 3 cities]. (p. 80)

[45] Privilege tax distribution to counties. (p. 81-82)

[46-47] Privilege tax division and title division [receipts and disbursements]. (p. 83-84)

SALES TAX

[48] Basic classification of sales [number of businesses and gross tax and sales, by kind of business]. (p. 87-90)

[49] Sales tax payments to individual municipalities and amounts diverted for repayment of air/water pollution control grants. (p. 91-97)

[50-51] Sales and tax [and number of taxpayers, by selected] industry group [by county and city, and for total noncity]. (p. 98-137)

S4480   MISSOURI
Department of Agriculture

S4480-1   MISSOURI FARM FACTS, 1985
Annual. May 1985.
iv+60 p.
ISSN 0544-5507.
LC 77-648377.
SRI/MF/complete

Annual report on Missouri agricultural production, marketing, and finances, mostly 1980-84, with some data for 1985, and selected historical trends. Data generally are shown by commodity and/or county, with some comparisons to total U.S.

Covers production, value and/or prices, sales, and, as applicable, acreage, yield, stocks or inventory, and disposition, for field crop, fruit, livestock, dairy, and poultry sectors.

Also includes data on population; weather; fertilizer consumption; grain storage facilities; feeder pig outshipments by State of destination; farm income, production expenses, telephone and electricity use and costs, and balance sheet; value of exports; farm real estate value, rent, taxes, and debt; and Missouri and U.S. farms, farm acreage, and foreign-owned agricultural land.

Data are compiled by the Missouri Crop and Livestock Reporting Service in conjunction with USDA.

Contains contents listing (1 p.); and 4 sections, with narrative summaries, 9 maps, 12 charts, and 99 tables (p. 1-59).

Availability: Missouri Crop and Livestock Reporting Service, PO Box L, Columbia MO 65205, †; SRI/MF/complete.

S4500   MISSOURI
Department of
Consumer Affairs,
Regulation and Licensing

S4500–2   NINETEENTH BIENNIAL
REPORT OF THE DIVISION
OF FINANCE of the
Department of Consumer
Affairs, Regulation and
Licensing, State of Missouri
Biennial.   Nov. 1, 1984.
5+64 p.
SRI/MF/complete, current &
previous year reports

Biennial report, for FY83-84, on financial condition of Missouri State-chartered banks and trust companies, and consumer credit lenders. Includes number of institutions, and aggregate assets, liabilities, equity capital, and operating ratios, quarterly FY82-84, with selected trends from 1934; and assets by institution, as of June 30, 1984; all for banks and trust companies.

Also includes number of consumer credit lenders, and aggregate assets, income, and expenses, 1982-83; and Finance Division appropriations, expenditures, receipts, personnel, and salaries, FY83 and/or FY84.

Contains transmittal letter and contents listing (5 p.); and report, with narrative, selected lists and directories, and 9 tables (p. 1-64).

Previous report, for FY81-82, was also reviewed during 1985, and is also available on SRI microfiche, under this number [Biennial. Nov. 22, 1982. 5+62 p. 1st copy †, additional copies $13.00].

Availability: Missouri Department of Consumer Affairs, Regulation and Licensing, Finance Division, PO Box 716, Jefferson City MO 65102, 1st copy †, additional copies $13.00; SRI/MF/complete.

S4505   MISSOURI
Department of
Elementary and
Secondary Education

S4505–1   135th REPORT OF THE
PUBLIC SCHOOLS OF
MISSOURI for the School
Year Ending June 30, 1984
Annual.   Feb. 1985.   147 p.
ISSN 0145-2975.
LC 80-643870.
SRI/MF/complete

Annual report, for 1983/84 school year, on Missouri public schools, with selected trends from the 1970s. Covers education program activities, finances, enrollment, attendance, graduates, and staff, shown for the State and by school district and county. Also includes State data on vocational, adult, and special education.

Report is prepared by Missouri Board of Education.

Contains contents listing (p. 3), and the following sections:

Part I. Narrative report on dept activities and priorities, with 1 summary table, and 1 additional table (p. 10) showing public high

school graduation requirements, by subject area, before and after fall 1984 revisions. (p. 8-16)

Part II. "Reaching for Excellence: An Action Plan for Educational Reform in Missouri." Reprint of the 1983/84 report developed by the State Board of Education and Dept of Elementary and Secondary Education. (p. 17-25)

Part III. Statewide data, with 2 summary charts, and 44 tables listed below. (p. 27-66)

Part IV. Local data, by county and school district, with 4 extended tables, also listed below. (p. 68-147)

Availability: Missouri Department of Elementary and Secondary Education, PO Box 480, Jefferson City MO 65102, ‡; SRI/MF/complete.

PART III-IV TABLES:
[Tables show data for 1983/84 school year, unless otherwise noted.]

S4505–1.1: Statewide Data
[Several table titles begin "Summary of..." Data by types of district are for districts maintaining elementary schools only and for those also maintaining high schools, often with detail by accreditation classification.]

FINANCES

1a-1b. Receipts by sources available for use for current expenditures; and revenue and nonrevenue receipts [by source] in public schools. (p. 28)

2a-2c. Receipts, expenditures, and levies of public school districts [by fund]; and detailed analysis of receipts [by source and fund] and of expenditures [by function and object]. (p. 29-30)

2d. Expenditures [total and per average daily attendance (ADA), 1970-84]. (p. 30)

3-4. Expenditures [by function and] object, by fund. (p. 31-32)

5-6. Tax levies for districts maintaining high school and 6-director elementary schools; and valuation, levies, value of school property, and indebtedness. (p. 32)

7-8b. Average tax levy per hundred dollars valuation, and bonds outstanding and issued [1976-84]; and short-term borrowing, 1983/84. (p. 33)

9a-9b. Foundation program apportionments and payments [1975/76-1983/84]; and Fair Share [cigarette tax fund] and Proposition C [sales tax fund] payments [1982/83-1983/84]. (p. 33)

10. Expenditure factors [eligible pupils and current expenditures, 1976/77-1983/84]. (p. 33)

TRANSPORTATION

11-12a. Average daily number of pupils transported [1975/76-1983/84]; and transportation of public school pupils [including vehicles, mileage, and costs], 1983/84. (p. 34)

12b. State maximum cost factor, 104%. (p. 34)

ENROLLMENT, ATTENDANCE, AND GRADUATES

13. Live births in Missouri [1974-84]. (p. 34)

14-16. Accumulated enrollment [elementary and high school, 1977/78-1983/84]; and number of districts by fall enrollment range, grades 9-12 [1978-84], and grades K-12, 1983/84. (p. 34)

17. Fall enrollment by grades in public elementary and secondary schools [1978/79-1984/85]. (p. 35)

18-19. Fall enrollment by grades; and accumulated enrollment [by grade level and sex; all by type of district]. (p. 36)

20a-20b. Eligible pupil data [compared to resident ADA and membership, by type of district; and summary trend from 1977/78]. (p. 36)

21-22. ADA [for residents and nonresidents by grade level, including preschool special education and summer schools, by type of district, 1983/84; and for elementary and high school districts, 1976/77-1983/84]. (p. 37-38)

23-24. Graduates [by sex]; and follow-up data on graduates [number entering college, special schools, jobs, and military; various years 1975/76-1984/85]. (p. 38)

25a-25b. Number in graduating classes in high school districts [1979/80-1983/84]; and graduation rate in public high schools [by class level], 1972-84. (p. 38)

TEACHERS, SCHOOL DISTRICTS, AND CURRICULUM
[Tables 26-31 show data for teachers and other professional personnel, by position and type of district, and (except for tables 29-30) by school level.]

26-27. Numbers of teachers and average annual teachers' salaries [by sex]. (p. 39-40)

28. Breakdown of teachers by degree. (p. 41)

29-30. Tenure and experience. (p. 42-43)

31. Teacher turnovers from FY83 to FY84 [total and 1st-year teachers]. (p. 44)

32-33. [Teachers'] certificates issued [by type, 1983/84; and total, 1978/79-1983/84]. (p. 45)

34. Number of school districts [by type, 1976-84]. (p. 45)

35A-35B. Classification data: school district classification; and high schools holding membership in the North Central Assn [including elementary and nonpublic high schools; all by district or school type, including State institutional schools]. (p. 45)

36-37. Courses offered in subject matter fields [number of districts offering courses and enrollment, by course title, 1983/84; and summary trends, 1971/72-1983/84; all by subject]. (p. 46-51)

VOCATIONAL, ADULT, AND SPECIAL EDUCATION

38A-38B. Vocational education: financial and statistical data summary [including Federal and State allotments and expenditures; expenditures by function and program; and number of districts, teachers, and students for secondary, postsecondary, and adult programs, by subject], FY84. (p. 52)

39a-39e. Adult education: employment training section, adult basic education, and veterans education [showing number of schools, teachers or businesses involved, and student enrollment]; high school equivalence [applications and certificates issued]; and community education program [schools, personnel by type, facilities, and funding by source; various years 1977/78-1983/84]. (p. 53)

40A-40C. Special education: financial and statistical data summary, programs data, and school trust funds [selected data on special education programs and State schools for blind, deaf, and severely handicapped, including State and Federal funding, expenditures by object, number of children served, number of teachers, and trust fund balance sheets], FY84. (p. 54-57)

41A-41D. Vocational rehabilitation [selected program data, including number of clients, costs, and client occupations and earnings], year ending Sept. 30, 1984. (p. 58)

TESTS

42A-42J. Testing and assessment program data [including performance on 8th grade basic essential skills test and subtests, and on various statewide tests for selected other grades; and Scholastic Aptitude and American College Test scores as compared to national norms; various years 1971/72-1983/84]. (p. 59-64)

FOOD SERVICE

43a-43g. School food services program [including participation and Federal and State funding]. (p. 65)

EDUCATION CONSOLIDATION AND IMPROVEMENT ACT (ECIA)

44. Distribution of Chapter 1, ECIA services [students served, teachers and aides employed, and number of programs; by] grade levels and subjects [reading, mathematics, and language arts; 1983-84].

S4505-1.2: Local Data

[Tables 1-4 show data by county and school district.]

1. Apportionment and payment of State school and textbook monies. (p. 68-90)

2. Summary of financial data [including resident ADA and membership, eligible pupils, expenditure per pupil, assessed valuation, total levy, and operating tax levy]. (p. 91-112)

3. Classification and organization [including accreditation category, grade span, units of approved credit in high schools, enrollment, and total staff members]. (p. 113-130)

4. Receipts by source [local/county, State, Proposition C, and Federal] available for use for current expenditures. (p. 131-147)

S4520   MISSOURI
Coordinating Board for Higher Education

S4520-1   1984 ANNUAL REPORT, Coordinating Board for Higher Education, Missouri
Annual.   Dec. 1984.
2+21 p.
ISSN 0361-1191.
LC 75-649670.
SRI/MF/complete

Annual report, for 1984, of the Missouri Coordinating Board for Higher Education. Reviews the Board's activities, and presents statistics on the following:

a. Enrollment by type of institution (public and private university and 2- and 4-year college, and technical/professional school), fall 1983-84; and masters degrees (total and in education) conferred by public institutions, 1972 and 1982.

b. Academic program review activity; and results of a survey on high schools' readiness to offer a model college preparatory curriculum.

c. Appropriation and capital improvement recommendations, by public institution, FY85 and/or FY86.

Data are from State records and reports by institutions.

Contains contents and table listings (2 p.); and narrative report, interspersed with 13 tables (p. 1-21).

Availability: Missouri Coordinating Board for Higher Education, Higher Education Department, 101 Adams St., Jefferson City MO 65101, $1.73; SRI/MF/complete.

S4520-2   DIRECTORY OF MISSOURI LIBRARIES: Public, Special, College and University, FY84
Annual.   [1985.]   ix+68 p.
ISSN 0092-4067.
LC 73-645566.
SRI/MF/complete

Annual directory, for FY84, of Missouri public, special, and academic libraries, with data on finances, holdings, circulation, staff, and services.

Contents:

a. Map; lists of higher education board members, State library staff, and library organizations; 3 State summary tables on public library expenditures, income, volumes, and staff, Federal fund expenditures by object, and interlibrary loan activity; and foreword and abbreviation key. (p. ii-ix)

b. Library directory by city, including some or all of the following for each library: address; hours open; assessed valuation; tax rate; income by source, including State and Federal grants, and gifts; population served; staff and total payroll; expenditures by object; volumes; total and juvenile circulation; bookmobile service; branches; and cooperative and Federal program participation. (p. 1-44)

c. Library directory by county, including total county assessed valuation and tax levy rate, and generally operating income, volumes available, and State aid. (p. 45-56)

d. Index. (p. 57-68)

Availability: Missouri Coordinating Board for Higher Education, Missouri State Library, PO Box 387, Jefferson City MO 65102, †; SRI/MF/complete.

S4530   MISSOURI
Department of Labor and Industrial Relations

S4530-2   ANNUAL REPORT, Missouri Department of Labor and Industrial Relations, 1984
Annual.   Dec. 15, 1984.
3+42 p.
LC 57-63397.
SRI/MF/complete

Annual report, for FY84, on Missouri Dept of Labor and Industrial Relations activities and programs, with data on Missouri employment, earnings, unemployment insurance, work injuries and deaths, and mining production.

Contains contents listing, introduction, and organizational chart (2 p.); and 7 departmental reports, interspersed with 2 maps, 2 charts, and 41 tables, listed below (p. 1-42).

This is the 10th annual report.

Availability: Missouri Department of Labor and Industrial Relations, PO Box 59, Jefferson City MO 65104, †; SRI/MF/complete.

TABLES, MAPS, and CHARTS:

S4530-2.1: Labor and Industrial Relations Commission

[1-2] Appeals to the Labor and Industrial Relations Commission: employment security appeals and workers' compensation cases [by type and disposition, 1983-84]. (p. 1)

S4530-2.2: Division of Labor Standards

[1] [Child labor inspections and violations, and serious accident investigations, FY84.] (p. 2)

[2] Mineral production [by commodity, FY83-84]. (p. 2)

[3-8] Clay, coal, iron, lead, zinc, copper, silica sand, and shale [production and fatal accidents, by operator, and, for coal only, by county, FY84; and total production, 1975-84]. (p. 3-4)

[9] Granite [production and fatal accidents, by operator, FY84]. (p. 5)

[10] Fatal accidents in mines [and miners killed, 1983]. (p. 5)

[11] [Prevailing Wage Law enforcement activities, including inspections, violations, and wage/penalties collected, FY83-84]. (p. 6)

[A] Prevailing Wage Section, number of wage determinations [by county (no date)]. [map] (p. 7)

S4530-2.3: Division of Workers' Compensation

WORK REVIEW REPORT

1. Reports of injuries by years reported, 1926-83. (p. 14)

2. Statement of expenses [for personal service, and expense/equipment, monthly] 1983. (p. 16)

STATISTICS ON 1983 CASES

1. Incidence frequency by age. (p. 16)

2-7. Cost by type of disability for all incidences, 1983 and 1978-82 (revised to July 1, 1984) [showing incidences, compensation, and medical payments]. (p. 16-18)

WORK INJURY ANALYSIS

[Tables show data for 1983. Data by severity are for fatalities, disabling cases, medical treatment/1st aid cases, and other. Data by type of accident are for 8 causes of injuries. Data by source of injury are for 9 objects or substances causing injury. Most data by type of disability are for temporary total, permanent partial, fatalities, and others.

Tables 1-5 and 11 show data by industry division.]

1-5. Accidents and diseases by severity, type, source and nature [of injury], and affected [body] part. (p. 18-20)

6A-6D. Cost data by injury category: [accident type, source and type of injury, and affected body part; includes number of cases, compensation, and medical payments]. (p. 20-21)

7-10. Type, source, and nature of injury, and part of body affected, by type [of disability]. (p. 21-22)

11. Cost [compensation and medical payments] by type of disability. (p. 22)

12. Cost by type of disability, by county. (p. 23)

S4530–2.4: Division of Employment Security

[B] Unemployment rates [for counties, SMSAs, and labor market areas], 1983 annual averages. [map] (p. 27)

[1] [Civilian labor force by employment status, and manufacturing and nonmanufacturing employment, FY81-84.] (p. 28)

[2] Labor force summary [by employment status, annual averages 1982-83]. (p. 34)

[3] Employment, [weekly and hourly] earnings, [and weekly hours, all by major manufacturing group and industry division], 1983 annual averages. (p. 35)

[4] Job service activities [job openings, applications, referrals, and placements, by local State employment office], FY84. (p. 36-37)

[5] Unemployment insurance programs [covered workers and employers; wages of covered workers; employer contributions and contribution rates; unemployment insurance fund balance and interest earned on fund; and amount and duration of unemployment insurance payments, selected years FY38-65, and annually FY70-84]. (p. 38)

[6] Unemployment compensation fund [balances at beginning and end of year, and receipts and disbursements by type], FY84. (p. 39)

[C] Employers by contribution rate, 1984. [chart] (p. 39)

[7] Unemployment insurance contributions and benefits, by county of residence: all programs [employer contributions, initial claims, weeks claimed and paid, and amount of State and Federal benefits paid], FY84. (p. 40-41)

[D] Benefit payments, all programs by fund [FY81-84]. [chart] (p. 42)

S4530–3 MISSOURI AREA LABOR TRENDS

Monthly. Approx. 15 p.
ISSN 0148-4214.
SRI/MF/complete, shipped quarterly

Monthly report on Missouri labor market conditions. Covers employment, hours, earnings, insured unemployment, and State Job Service activities. Includes data by industry, MSA, and county. Report usually is issued approximately 2 months after month of coverage.

Contains 1 trend chart, and narrative review of labor conditions statewide and in Kansas City, St. Louis, and Springfield MSAs, interspersed with the following data shown for month of coverage, previous month, and same month of previous year, unless otherwise noted:

a. Labor force by employment status, by MSA, labor market area, and county. 1 table.

b. Total nonagricultural wage/salary employment, and production worker average hours and earnings, by industry division and selected manufacturing industry group; and total employees involved in labor disputes. 1-2 tables, repeated for State (excludes labor dispute data) and for each of the 3 MSAs noted above.

c. Summary labor force data; average weekly insured unemployment; and unemployment insurance average weekly initial claims, exhaustions, and benefits paid. 1 table.

d. Selected Job Service and unemployment data for Kansas City and St. Louis MSAs, including demographic and other characteristics of job applicants and placements; demographic characteristics, industry attachment, and/or occupational distribution, for insured unemployed or for unemployment insurance weeks claimed; and occupational distribution of job openings and placements (St. Louis only); for current month, with selected comparisons to previous months. Text data.

Availability: Missouri Department of Labor and Industrial Relations, Employment Security Division, PO Box 59, Jefferson City MO 65104, †; SRI/MF/complete, shipped quarterly.

Issues reviewed during 1985: Sept. 1984-July 1985 (D) [Nov. 1984 issue incorrectly reads Dec. 1984].

S4560 MISSOURI
Department of Public Safety

S4560–2 1983 MISSOURI CRIME AND ARREST DIGEST

Annual. [1985.]
vii+3+113 p.
SRI/MF/complete, current & 2 previous reports

Annual report on Missouri crimes and arrests, by offense and location, 1983, with selected trends from 1974 and projections through 1987.

Includes crimes and arrests, and crime rates, by Index offense; and total arrests for non-Index offenses; all by reporting agency, arranged by category (municipalities with population 25,000/over and under 25,000, suburban counties, and rural counties).

Also includes statewide data on arrests by sex, age group (adult and juvenile), and race-ethnicity, all by Index offense; arrests by sex and age group, by non-Index offense; Index offense clearance rates; murder victims by sex, age group, and race-ethnicity; value and type of property stolen; value of arson losses by type of property; and circumstances of Index offenses, including types of weapons and locations.

Index offenses are murder, forcible rape, robbery, aggravated assault, burglary, theft, motor vehicle theft, and arson. Most data by race include white, black, and American Indian.

Data are from reports of law enforcement agencies, submitted under the Uniform Crime Reporting Program.

Contains foreword (1 p.); acknowledgments, and listings of contents, tables, and charts (p. i-vii); executive summary (3 p.); introduction (p. 1-2); statewide section, with 17 charts, and 55 tables (p. 3-88); reporting agency section with 8 detailed tables (p. 89-110); and glossary (p. 111-113).

Previous reports, for 1981-82, have also been reviewed and are also available on SRI microfiche under this number [Annual. [1984.] v+2+85 p. †; and Annual. [1984.] v+3+74 p. †]. The 1981 report is the 1st edition.

Availability: Missouri Department of Public Safety, State Highway Patrol, Information Systems Division, PO Box 568, Jefferson City MO 65102, †; SRI/MF/complete.

S4570 MISSOURI
Department of Revenue

S4570–1 ANNUAL COMBINED FINANCIAL REPORT: Missouri Department of Revenue and Office of the State Treasurer, FY84

Annual. [1985.] 74 p.
LC 74-643144.
SRI/MF/complete

Annual financial report on the operations of the Missouri Dept of Revenue and the State Treasurer's Office, FY84. Includes data on Revenue Dept tax collections and distributions, and State fund balance investments held by banks.

Contains contents and table listing (1 p.); Dept of Revenue report, with narrative summary and 20 tables listed below (p. 7-58); and State Treasurer's report, with letter of transmittal, 2 text tables, and 9 detailed tables also listed below (p. 59-74).

Dept of Revenue also publishes a monthly brochure on collections, which is not covered by SRI.

Availability: Missouri Department of Revenue, Management, Planning, and Policy Office, PO Box 311, Jefferson City MO 65105, $11.00; SRI/MF/complete.

TABLES:

[Tables show data for FY84 or June 30, 1984, unless otherwise noted.]

S4570–1.1: Dept of Revenue Report

[Tables show data for the Dept of Revenue, unless otherwise noted.]

GENERAL

1-2. Administrative costs [salaries, equipment, and operations], and 5-year summary [FY80-84]. (p. 10)

3. Review of legislation [bill number and subject of legislation]. (p. 11-13)

COLLECTIONS

4. Major taxes administered [description, tax rate, collections, and disposition, by tax]. (p. 14-16)

5. Individual income tax rates. (p. 17)

6. Five-year tax collection history [by tax, 1980-84]. (p. 17)

7. Summary of activities: Division of Taxation and Collection [individual and corporation income tax returns and senior citizens tax credit claims filed, and number and/or amount of refunds]. (p. 20)

8-8A. State revenue, tax and nontax; and nonrecorded revenue; by funds. (p. 20-26)

9. General revenue fund receipts FY84, and original estimate FY85 [by source]. (p. 27)

DISTRIBUTIONS

10. Distribution summary [of] financial institution taxes [bank, credit institution, farmers cooperative, and total taxes collected, and interest to county treasurer, by county], 1983. (p. 29-30)

11-12. Gasoline tax allocation to counties and to cities [by locality]. (p. 31-40)

13-14. City and St. Louis County sales tax distribution [by city], 1983. (p. 40-45)

15. County sales tax distribution [by county], 1983. (p. 45-46)

16-16A. Major fees and licenses administered [rates, collections, and disposition, by type]; and license plate categories, rates and fees [by type of carrier]. (p. 47-48)

17. Summary of activities, Division of Motor Vehicle and Licensing [drivers licenses, and motor vehicle and marine registrations and titles issued]. (p. 49)

BALANCE SHEETS

18-19. Highway Reciprocity Commission cash report [revenues from motor vehicle and prorate fees, and permits; license plates issued; and] administrative costs. (p. 50)

20. Nonappropriated funds: sources and application [receipts, expenditures, assets, and beginning and ending balances; for State agencies and funds administered by each dept, including universities, mental health centers and hospitals, and correctional institutions]. (p. 51-58)

S4570–1.2: State Treasurer Report

21. Analysis of average daily balances of State funds [by month]. (p. 61)

22-23. Time deposits: general and water pollution bond/interest reports of the transactions of the State treasury, for the month ending June 30, 1984, showing the balances in the [individual] banks. (p. 62-70)

24. List of balances in several funds [current and previous balance, receipts, and disbursements]. (p. 70-72)

25-25A. State indebtedness: water pollution control and 3rd State building bonds [including number, denomination, interest rate, and amount retired and outstanding]. (p. 73)

26-28. Treasury funds invested in U.S. securities; and State seminary and public school fund investments. (p. 73)

29. Report of the transactions of the State treasury for the month ending June 30, 1984, showing [aggregate] balances in the various banks [by type of account or investment]. (p. 74)

S4575   MISSOURI
Department of Social Services

S4575–1   MISSOURI VITAL STATISTICS, 1984
Annual. July 1985.
viii+116 p. Pub. No. 4.30.
ISSN 0098-1974.
LC 75-643234.
SRI/MF/complete, current & previous year reports

Annual report on Missouri vital statistics, covering population, births, abortions, deaths by cause, marriages, and divorces, 1984, with selected trends from 1911. Includes data by county, city, age, sex, and race. Data are compiled from State records and Census Bureau reports.

Contains listing of contents, tables, and charts (p. v-vii); 7 charts and 59 tables, listed below (p. 1-110); and appendix, with methodology and definitions (p. 111-116).

Previous report, for 1983, was also reviewed in SRI during 1985, and is also available on SRI microfiche under S4575-1 [Annual. July 1984. viii+116 p. Pub. No. 4.29. †].

Availability: Missouri Department of Social Services, Health Division, Center for Health Statistics, Broadway State Office Bldg., PO Box 570, Jefferson City MO 65102-0570, †; SRI/MF/complete.

CHARTS AND TABLES:
[Data are for Missouri, 1984, unless otherwise noted. Some tables with historical trends show pre-1970 data quinquennially rather than annually.]

S4575–1.1: Population Trends, and Births
TRENDS

A. Live birth and death rates per 1,000 population, 1911-84. [chart] (p. 1)

1-2. Population, recorded births and deaths with rates per 1,000 population, and natural increase, 1911-44; and resident births and deaths, 1945-84. (p. 2-3)

B. Total fertility rates, 1911-84. [chart and table] (p. 4)

3. Fertility rates per 1,000 females by age of mother, 1911-84. (p. 5)

C. Crude and age-adjusted death rates per 1,000 population, 1911-84. [chart and table] (p. 6)

4. Age-specific death rates per 1,000 population, 1911-84. (p. 7)

BIRTHS

5. Resident live births by selected characteristics [including sex, attendant (physician, midwife, and other), place and month of birth, mother's smoking habits during pregnancy, and complications], by race of child. (p. 8)

6-7. Resident live births and teenage resident live births, by age of mother, by live birth order, by legitimacy, by race of child. (p. 9-10)

8. Percent low birth weight and resident live births, by birth weight, by age of mother, by race of child. (p. 11)

9. Resident live births, by legitimacy, by race, with percentages by county and cities with 25,000 or more population. (p. 12-15)

10A-10C. Resident live births by selected characteristics [including birth weight; type of delivery (including cesarean); whether mother smoked during pregnancy; age, height, and weight of mother; and birth order]; by race, regional planning commission, county, and cities with 25,000 or more population. (p. 16-43)

S4575–1.2: Abortions

11. Resident teenage pregnancies and abortions by selected ages by county of residence. (p. 44-45)

D. Resident abortion ratios per 1,000 live births [and number of abortions], 1971-84. [chart and table] (p. 46)

12. Resident abortions by race, age of woman, type of procedure, and complications, by weeks of gestation. (p. 47)

13. Resident abortions by age, marital status, and education, by race. (p. 48)

14A-14B. Resident abortions and ratios per 1,000 live births by county of residence and regional planning commission. (p. 49-50)

15-16. Resident abortions, by age and marital status of woman, and by number of living children and number of previous abortions. (p. 50)

S4575–1.3: Population Natural Increase, and Deaths
POPULATION NATURAL INCREASE

17. Resident and recorded live births, deaths, and natural increase, with rates, by counties [also shows population] and cities with 25,000 or more population. (p. 51-54)

18. Resident and recorded live births and deaths, by cities with 2,500-24,999 population. (p. 55-57)

DEATHS

19. 12 leading causes of death by race, with percentages, and with rates per 100,000 for all races, resident data. (p. 58)

20. 5 leading causes of death for selected age groups, with percentages, resident data. (p. 59)

21. Resident deaths, age groups by race by sex, with age-specific rates per 1,000 by sex. (p. 60)

22A-22C. Resident deaths [total, male, and female], age groups by selected causes of death. (p. 61-66)

E. Infant death rates per 1,000 live births [and infant deaths], 1911-44 (recorded) and 1945-84 (resident). [chart and table] (p. 67)

23A-23B. Resident perinatal, infant, fetal, neonatal, postneonatal, and maternal deaths: by county and cities with 25,000 or more population; and by regional planning commission, with rates per 1,000 live births. (p. 68-70)

24. Resident infant deaths by age, cause, and race, with rates per 1,000 live births by cause and race. (p. 71)

25-26. Resident infant deaths and rates per 1,000 live births, by age of mother by birth order, and by birth weight by race. (p. 72)

27A–27C. Resident deaths by selected causes of death: for State total by race, with rates per 100,000 for all races; and by regional planning commission, county, and cities with 25,000 or more population. (p. 73-93)

28. Recorded deaths by type of accident, age, and sex. (p. 94)

LIFE EXPECTANCY

29. Abridged life table for total population, and by sex. (p. 95-97)

S4575–1.4: Marriages and Dissolutions
MARRIAGES

F. Marriage rates per 1,000 population [and number of marriages], 1949-84. [chart and table] (p. 98)

30. Reported marriages by age of groom, by age of bride. (p. 99)

31-33. Reported marriages: by age and previous marital status of bride and groom; by previous marital status of bride and groom; and by race of bride by race of groom. (p. 101-102)

34A-34B. Reported marriages by county and regional planning commission of recording, with rates per 1,000 population. (p. 103-104)

DISSOLUTIONS

G. Dissolution rates per 1,000 population [and number of dissolutions], 1949-84. [chart and table] (p. 105)

35. Reported dissolutions of marriage, by type of decree. (p. 106)

36-42. Reported dissolutions/invalidities: by number of previous marriages for husband and wife; by duration of marriage; by number of children affected; by petitioner by disposition of children; by type of maintenance and settlement; and by age and race, wife by husband. (p. 106-108)

43A-43B. Reported dissolutions/invalidities, by county and regional planning commission of recording, with rates per 1,000 population. (p. 109-110)

S4575–2　　ANNUAL REPORT, 1982-83, Missouri Division of Family Services
Annual. 2 volumes.
For individual publication data, see below.
ISSN 0148-5474.
LC 77-640889.
SRI/MF/complete.

Annual report, for FY83, on activities of the Missouri Division of Family Services (DFS), including number of recipients and expenditures for public welfare, medical, and other assistance programs, by program and county, with selected trends from FY38.

Report is issued in 2 volumes: a primarily narrative summary, and a statistical report. Volumes are individually described below. Prior to FY83, report was issued in 1 volume.

Availability: Missouri Department of Social Services, Family Services Division, PO Box 88, Jefferson City MO 65103, †; SRI/MF/complete.

S4575–2.1: Main Report
[Annual. Dec. 1984. 34 p. SRI/MF/complete.]

Contains introduction and contents listing (p. 1-3); and narrative report interspersed with 28

charts and 4 tables primarily showing trends or summary data also included in the statistical report (p. 4-34).

S4575–2.2: Statistical Supplement
[Annual. [1984.] 50+App 17 p. SRI/MF/complete.]

Contains listing of tables and charts (p. 2-7); 5 charts, and 62 tables described below (p. 8-50); and appendix with 6 tables, also described below (p. A1-A17).

TABLES:
[Tables show data for FY83, unless otherwise noted.]

PUBLIC ASSISTANCE TRENDS

a. Public assistance recipients, expenditures, and average monthly payments, by program, FY38-83. Tables 1-3. (p. 8-10)

DFS ACTIVITIES

b. DFS employees, by position; employee turnover, quarterly FY83; and appropriations, by purpose and program, FY84. Tables 4-6. (p. 12-13)

PUBLIC ASSISTANCE PROGRAMS
[Data are often shown by month.]

c. AFDC program: number of recipients and amount of payments; applications received and disposition; cases opened and closed, and applications rejected, by reason; and recipients and payments for dependent children families with foster care status. Tables 7-12. (p. 14-18)

d. General relief, blind pension, supplemental nursing care, and supplemental aid to the blind programs: number of recipients and amount of payments; and caseloads, usually including applications received and disposition, and cases opened and closed, often with detail by reason. Tables 13-28. (p. 18-26)

e. Adult supplementary programs funded by SSI and State supplemental aid (includes Aid to Blind, Aid to Permanently and Totally Disabled, and Old Age Assistance): number of recipients by program and amount of payments. Tables 29-30. (p. 27-28)

f. Appeals/fair hearings caseload analysis; and food stamp and USDA-donated food distribution program participation and distribution amounts. Tables 31-33. (p. 28-29)

MEDICAL, CHILD, AND BLIND SERVICES

g. Medical services: expenditures by service and program, with selected comparisons to FY82; expenditures, recipients, and Medicaid eligibles, by month; number of recipients and cost of payments for physician, inpatient hospital, prescription drug, dental, skilled nursing home, intermediate care facility, outpatient, and clinic services, all by program; medical assistance applications received and disposition, by month; and cases opened and closed, and applications rejected, by reason. Tables 34-48. (p. 30-39)

h. Foster care cases active and opened and average age of child, subsidized adoption cases and payments, protective service cases, and reports of child abuse/neglect, all by month; children receiving interstate compact placement services, by type; and number and capacity of licensed day care facilities, by type, as of June 1983. Tables 49-54. (p. 40-44)

i. Services for the blind: rehabilitation teaching cases and turnover; vocational rehabilitation caseloads, and expenditures by funding source and object; and expenditures for blindness prevention services by type. Tables 55-58. (p. 44-45)

j. Child support enforcement program: cases and/or money collected, by month and district, for AFDC and non-AFDC. Tables 59-60. (p. 46)

EXPENDITURES SUMMARY

k. Expenditures charged against all funds for assistance and administration, by program and fund source (Federal, State, and donated/local); and administrative costs by item. Tables 61-62. (p. 47, 50)

APPENDIX

l. Public assistance recipients and cash payments, by county; and State recipients and cash expenditures, monthly FY82-83; all by program. Tables I-IV. (p. A2-A13)

m. Medical assistance expenditures, by type of service, by month; and food stamp program recipient households and persons, and value of stamps, by county. Tables V-VI. (p. A14-A17)

S4580　　MISSOURI
Office of the Secretary of State

S4580–1　　1985-86 ROSTER OF STATE, DISTRICT, AND COUNTY OFFICIALS, State of Missouri
Biennial. [1985.] 275 p. SRI/MF/complete

Biennial report presenting results of the Missouri general election held Nov. 6, 1984. Covers voting for President and Vice-President; U.S. and State senators and/or representatives; Governor and other State officials, including judges; and propositions and constitutional amendments, including 2 amendments on establishing a State lottery and authorizing wagering on horse racing.

Also includes results for special election held for State representative, Feb. 5, 1985.

Most data are shown by county, circuit, and district, with selected detail by ward and precinct. Also shows party affiliation of candidates.

Contains contents listing (p. 6-8); directories of executive, administrative, legislative, and judicial officials (p. 9-60); voting results (p. 61-230); and directory of county officials (p. 231-275).

Previous report, covering 1982 general election, is described in SRI 1983 Annual under this number.

Availability: Missouri Office of the Secretary of State, 209 State Capitol, PO Box 778, Jefferson City MO 65102, †; SRI/MF/complete.

S4585   MISSOURI
Supreme Court

S4585–1   MISSOURI JUDICIAL REPORT, FY84
Annual.   [1985.]   viii + 104 p.
ISSN 0099-0558.
LC 82-640897.
SRI/MF/complete

Annual report on Missouri judicial system, including trial and appellate court caseloads and case dispositions, FY84, with trends from FY75. Covers supreme, appeals, and circuit courts. Includes data by case type, by district (for appeals courts), and by circuit and county (for circuit courts).

Case types shown are civil and criminal for all courts. Circuit court data include detail for felony, misdemeanor, juvenile, traffic, small claims, probate (including mental health), domestic relations, child abuse/neglect, adoption, tort, contract, eminent domain, and other case types.

Also includes State judicial expenditures; writs of habeas corpus; and number of judges and workload analysis.

Contains listings of contents, charts, and tables (p. iv-viii); narrative analysis, with 22 charts and 21 tables (p. 1-28); statistical section, with 45 tables (p. 29-97); and appendices, with Missouri court profile (p. 99-104).

Availability: Missouri Supreme Court, State Courts Administrator's Office, 1105 Rear Southwest Blvd., Jefferson City MO 65101, $5.68; SRI/MF/complete.

S4653   MONTANA
Department of Administration

S4653–1   MONTANA COMPREHENSIVE ANNUAL FINANCIAL REPORT for the Fiscal Year Ended June 30, 1984
Annual.   Dec. 1, 1984.
160 p.
ISSN 0090-6042.
LC 73-644597.
SRI/MF/complete

Annual report on Montana State government financial condition, for FY84. Presents assets and liabilities, fund balances, revenues by source, and expenditures by function, for general, special revenue, debt service, capital projects, enterprise, internal service, expendable and nonexpendable trust, pension trust, agency, and higher education funds.

Also includes data on budgeted vs. actual revenues and expenditures, long-term bonded indebtedness, participants in State pension systems, and payments under capital and operating leases.

Also includes data on property tax levies and collections; property values and tax rates; population; labor force by employment status; construction activity; bank deposits; personal income; and school enrollment; various years 1974-84.

Report is compiled by Montana Dept of Administration.

Contains contents listing (4 p.); transmittal letter, organizational chart, and auditor's report (p. 1-10); 49 financial statements, with accompanying notes and summary statistics (p. 12-141); and statistical section with 16 tables (p. 144-160).

Availability: Montana Department of Administration, Accounting Division, Mitchell Bldg., Rm. 255, Helena MT 59620, †; SRI/MF/complete.

S4655   MONTANA
Department of Agriculture

S4655–1   MONTANA AGRICULTURAL STATISTICS, 1984
Annual.   Sept. 1984.   81 p.
Vol. XXI.
LC 48-13383.
SRI/MF/complete

Annual report on Montana agricultural production, marketing, prices, and stocks, 1983, with some data for 1984 and selected trends from 1910. Data generally are shown by commodity and/or county and district.

Covers production, prices, value, and, as applicable, acreage, yield, and stock or inventory, for field crop, livestock, dairy, poultry, and apiary sectors, and sweet cherries.

Also includes data on number and acreage of farms; land area by ownership and use; farm income by source; irrigation; fertilizer use; weather; wheat detail, including seeded acreage by variety, and out-of-State shipments by transport mode and region of destination; and value of U.S. and Montana agricultural exports.

Data are compiled by Montana Crop and Livestock Reporting Service.

Contains introduction and contents listing (p. 4-7); 11 maps, 14 charts, and 97 tables (p. 8-80); and list of additional reports available (p. 81).

Availability: Montana Crop and Livestock Reporting Service, PO Box 4369, Helena MT 59604, †; SRI/MF/complete.

S4690   MONTANA
Department of Health and Environmental Sciences

S4690–1   MONTANA VITAL STATISTICS, 1984
Annual.   Sept. 1985.
iii + 86 p.
ISSN 0077-1198.
LC 73-641210.
SRI/MF/complete, current & previous year reports

Annual report on Montana vital statistics, covering population, births, deaths by cause, abortions, reportable diseases, marriages, and divorces, 1984, with selected trends from 1910. Includes data by age, sex, race, and county. Data are compiled from records of the Dept of Health and Environmental Sciences.

Contains contents listing (p. iii); introduction, definitions, and 1 chart (p. 1-6); 8 sections, with narrative summaries, 1 map, 16 charts, and 33 tables listed below (p. 8-85); and note on data availability (p. 86).

Report has been published annually since 1954.

Previous report, for 1983, was also reviewed in SRI during 1985, and is also available on SRI microfiche under S4690-1 [Annual. Sept. 1984. iii + 88 p. †]. Previous report was substantially similar in format and content, but also included data on births attended by midwives.

Availability: Montana Department of Health and Environmental Sciences, Records and Statistics Bureau, Cogswell Bldg., Helena MT 59620, †; SRI/MF/complete.

TABLES:
[Unless otherwise noted, data are for Montana, 1984, and are residence-based for births and deaths and occurrence-based for marriages and divorces.]

S4690–1.1: General Data, Births, and Deaths
[Data prior to 1946 are based on place of occurrence.]

GENERAL

1. [Population], deaths, live births, and fetal, infant, and maternal deaths [quinquennially 1910-25 and annually 1930-84]. (p. 9)

2. Populations [by county], 1980 and 1984. (p. 10)

3. Deaths, live births, [and] fetal, infant, and maternal deaths, [by county of occurrence and residence]. (p. 11)

4. Deaths, live births, and fetal deaths, by race [white, Indian, and other; by county]. (p. 12)

BIRTHS

5. Summary of live births [sex, legitimacy status, multiple births, and number of previous living children], 1983-84. (p. 17)

6. Number and percentage distribution of live births, by attendant [born on arrival/in hospital, and physician and other not in hospital], by [county] of occurrence. (p. 18)

7. Live births, by birth weight group [premature and mature, by county]. (p. 19)

8. Number and percent of live-born infants, by years of education of mother and number of children born alive. (p. 20)

DEATHS

[Causes of death are shown according to the 9th Revision of the International Classification of Diseases.]

[A] [Median age at death for 10 leading causes, by sex.] (p. 22).

9. Deaths, by [detailed] cause, sex, and race. (p. 25-35)

10. Leading causes of death, by age group. (p. 36)

11. Deaths from selected accidents, by age, by place of occurrence. (p. 37)

12. Deaths from selected causes, by county. (p. 38)

13. Infant mortality by race and age group, and 5-year [1980-84 period] infant mortality rates, [all by county]. (p. 39)

14. Infant mortality from selected causes, by age group [and race]. (p. 40)

15-16. Communicable disease historical mortality statistics [10 diseases], and selected cause-specific death rates [quinquennially 1910-25 and annually 1930-84]. (p. 41-44)

S4690–1.2: Abortions, Marriages and Divorces, County Summaries, Pregnancy, and Morbidity

ABORTIONS

17-19. Induced abortions, by woman's total number of previous pregnancies; by 5-year age groups; and by type of procedure and completed week of gestation. (p. 46-47)

[B] Reports of induced abortions by [county of residence and occurrence; and for out-of-State residents in 3 neighboring States, rest of U.S., Canada, and rest of world]. (p. 48)

MARRIAGES AND DIVORCES

20. Marriages, marital dissolutions, and invalid marriages [by county]. (p. 54)

21. Marriages and [divorces/annulments, number and rate], 1944-84. (p. 55)

22-23. Marriages, by month of occurrence, and by age and previous marital status of bride and groom. (p. 55-56)

24-25. First marriages by age of bride by age of groom; and marriages by race [including Indian, Chinese, Japanese, and Hawaiian] of bride and groom. (p. 57)

26-28. Marital terminations: by legal grounds for decree; by age of husband and by age of wife; and by number of children [under 18 years of age] by age of mother. (p. 57-58)

COUNTY SUMMARIES

29. Selected vital statistics [includes population; residence-based live births and deaths by sex, infant and fetal deaths, and 10 leading causes of death; and occurrence-based live births, total and accidental deaths, infant deaths, marriages, and marital terminations; all by county]. (p. 61-68)

PREGNANCY

30. Total reported pregnancies by type of outcome [live births, fetal deaths, and induced abortions], by county of residence and age with percent distribution. (p. 71-82)

MORBIDITY

31. Reported cases of reportable diseases, by [county] of residence. (p. 84-85)

S4690–2 MONTANA HEALTH DATA BOOK and Medical Facilities Inventory, 1984
Annual. [1985.] 95 p.
LC 84-623473.
SRI/MF/complete

Annual report on Montana health care facilities, 1983 with trends from 1978. Covers private hospital and long-term care facility capacity, utilization, and finances, by individual institution and State region. Also includes patient residence data.

Data are primarily from State Dept of Health and Environmental Sciences (DHRS) annual surveys, and from the Montana Hospital Assn.

Contains contents listing and preface (2 p.); and 4 statistical sections with 19 tables described below (p. 3-95).

This is the 5th edition of the report.

Availability: Montana Department of Health and Environmental Sciences, Cogswell Bldg., Helena MT 59620, Montana residents †, others $4.00; SRI/MF/complete.

TABLES:
[Tables show data for individual hospitals or long-term care facilities, grouped by region, with selected detail for total State.]

a. Hospitals: number of licensed beds, bed and patient days, occupancy rate, average daily census and length of stay, and admissions; Medicare and Medicaid admissions, patient days, and average length of stay; and paid expenses, and adjusted expenses per inpatient day and admission; various years 1978-83. 7 tables. (p. 4-37)

b. Patient discharges from hospitals, by region of residence, and for unknown State and out-of-State patients, with distributions based on total discharges from region and each hospital, 1983. 2 tables. (p. 39-50)

c. Long-term care facilities: number of staffed beds; patient days; patients by age group and sex; admissions by patient residence (same county as facility, adjacent county, and other area); and finances, including gross expenditures and revenues, average expenses per patient day, and reimbursement revenues and expenditures from Medicare, Medicaid, private, and other sources; 1983. 10 tables. (p. 52-95)

S4705 MONTANA
Department of Justice

S4705–1 CRIME IN MONTANA, 1984 Annual Report
Annual. July 1985.
vi+49 p.
ISSN 0160-7103.
LC 77-643354.
SRI/MF/complete

Annual report on Montana crimes and clearances, by offense, 1984. Includes data by county and law enforcement agency. Also includes youth court activity, and youth population projections to 1990.

Report focuses on 7 Index offenses: homicide, rape, robbery, aggravated assault, burglary, larceny/theft, and motor vehicle theft. Some data are also shown for non-Index offenses.

Most data are based on law enforcement agency reports, submitted under the Uniform Crime Reporting (UCR) Program.

Contains foreword and contents listing (p. iii-vi); introduction, UCR Program description, and definitions (p. 1-6); and crime clocks, 19 trend or illustrative charts, 7 charts and 11 tables described below, and interspersed narrative, all arranged in 3 sections (p. 7-49).

Availability: Montana Department of Justice, Crime Control Board, Criminal Justice Data Center, 303 N. Roberts St., Helena MT 59620, †; SRI/MF/complete.

CHARTS AND TABLES:

a. State data: offenses (reported/known, unfounded, and actual) and clearances by arrest (total and juveniles), shown by Index and non-Index offense, with detail for motor vehicle thefts by type of vehicle and for narcotics offenses by type of substance, 1984; and Index crime rates, 1984, and Index and non-Index crimes, 1983-84, all by offense. 5 tables. (p. 21-26)

b. By locality: ranking of counties by crime rate; and population, crime rate, and Index crimes by offense, all by county and reporting agency (including Indian tribes and Glacier National Park); 1984. 2 tables. (p. 29-34)

c. Youth population (persons aged 10-17), by sex. 2 charts. (p. 38)

d. Youth court activity, including referrals by type of violation, age, and sex; and referrals detained by reason, sex, and length of stay; 1984, with detention trends (total and for status offenders) from 1977. 5 charts and 4 tables. (p. 40-47)

S4705–2 1984 MONTANA HIGHWAY PATROL ANNUAL REPORT
Annual. Mar. 7, 1985.
78 p. no paging.
SRI/MF/complete

Annual report on Montana traffic accidents, injuries, and fatalities, by accident and vehicle type, location, time, and other circumstances; and driver and victim characteristics, including alcohol consumption; 1984, with fatalities by county from 1935.

Also includes economic loss; accidents by type of traffic control; detailed data on safety device use; and vehicles involved by place of registration (U.S. States and territories, and Canadian Provinces).

Data are from Montana Highway Patrol records.

Contains contents listing, highlights, and analysis, with 1 chart and 3 tables (6 p.); and report in 4 sections, with 2 maps, 12 charts, and 7 tables (72 p.).

Availability: Montana Department of Justice, Highway Patrol, Accident Records Bureau, 303 N. Roberts St., Helena MT 59620, †; SRI/MF/complete.

S4710 MONTANA
Department of Labor and Industry

S4710–1 MONTANA EMPLOYMENT AND LABOR FORCE
Quarterly. Approx. 25 p.
SRI/MF/complete

Quarterly report on Montana employment and unemployment, hours and earnings, and unemployment insurance claims. Also includes new business firms enrolling in unemployment insurance program. Employment data are shown by State area and industry division and group. Data are from BLS and State sources.

Contains contents listing and glossary; narrative analysis, with 1-2 summary tables; 3 charts; and 14 detailed quarterly tables, listed below.

Quarterly tables appear in all issues. First quarter issue also includes 5-11 tables summarizing annual trends for selected data covered in quarterly tables.

Availability: Montana Department of Labor and Industry, Research and Analysis Bureau, PO Box 1728, Helena MT 59624, †; SRI/MF/complete.

Issues reviewed during 1985: 3rd Qtr. 1984-2nd Qtr. 1985 (D) (Vol. 14, Nos. 3-4; Vol. 15, No. 2) [Vol. 14, No. 3 incorrectly reads Vol. 15].

QUARTERLY TABLES:

[Data are for Montana. Data are shown monthly for quarter of coverage, unless otherwise noted, and often include comparisons to previous periods. Labor force data include employment and unemployment. Table sequence may vary from issue to issue.]

I. Civilian labor force, not seasonally adjusted [includes workers involved in labor/management disputes, and unemployment comparisons to U.S.; monthly for current year to date and 2 previous years].

II. Labor force areas, civilian labor force [by area and for Great Falls and Billings MSAs].

III.A.–III.C. Monthly labor force, by county.

IV.A–IV.B Statewide [total] and female employment, by industry [division].

V.A.–V.B. Hours and earnings for private nonagricultural industries [by industry division and selected major group]; and average weekly and real spendable earnings [monthly for year to date and previous 2 years, with taxes withheld during quarter of coverage].

VI. CPI, U.S., all items [by item; also includes data for previous 27 months].

VII. New business firms [enrolling in State unemployment insurance compensation program, by labor force area, county, and MSA, and for multi-county business; includes year-to-date totals for current and previous years].

VIII.A. Selected unemployment insurance activities [claims, payments, and trust fund balance; includes selected year-to-date totals for current and previous year].

VIII.B–VIII.C. Quarterly and cumulative [year-to-date] distribution of regular unemployment insurance [claims and payments, by county and for interstate].

S4710–2 ANNUAL REPORT, FY84, DIVISION OF WORKERS' COMPENSATION, Montana
Annual. [1985.] 38 p.
LC 66-64329.
SRI/MF/complete

Annual report on Montana work injuries, workers' compensation and medical benefit payments, and Division of Workers' Compensation fund balances, revenues, and expenditures, FY84, with selected trends from FY72. Also covers status of crime victim compensation fund.

Contains contents listing and preface (p. 1-2); and 6 sections, with narrative descriptions, and 25 tables described below (p. 3-38).

This is the 70th annual report.

Availability: Montana Department of Labor and Industry, Workers' Compensation Division, Five S. Last Chance Gulch, Helena MT 59601, †; SRI/MF/complete.

TABLES:

a. Financial reports: assets, liabilities, revenues by source, expenditures by program or object, changes in balances, and investments by instrument, shown for various programs and/or funds related to injured worker and crime victim compensation, FY84, with selected comparisons to FY83. 9 tables. (p. 8-22)

b. Insurance coverage plans: employers, annual payroll or premium, number of work injuries and occupational diseases reported, claims filed, compensation and medical/burial bene-

fits paid, and fatality assessments, all for employers using self-insurance, private carriers, and State fund compensation plans, FY82-84. 1 table. (p. 23)

c. State compensation insurance fund: assets and liabilities; reserves, balances, and changes; and income and expenses; FY84. 3 tables. (p. 25-27)

d. Uninsured employers' fund: compensation claims paid, investigations, audits, employers fined, number and amount of collections, revenues by source, and program costs, FY83-84. 2 tables. (p. 29)

e. Crime victims' compensation: claims received, by source, disposition, type of crime, victim characteristics, and crime location; and fund revenue sources and program costs; FY83-84. 2 tables. (p. 31-32)

f. Work injury reports: injuries by degree of disability; fatalities by cause, by industry division and compensation insurance plan type; and injuries and/or accidents, by type, industry division, and victim age and sex; various years FY72-84. 8 tables. (p. 34-38)

S4710–3 ANNUAL PLANNING INFORMATION, CY86, State of Montana
Annual. June 1985. 54 p.
LC 79-642770.
SRI/MF/complete

Annual planning report, for 1986, identifying Montana population groups most in need of employment services. Includes data on labor force; employment and job openings by industry and/or occupation; and data by service delivery area (SDA), and county. Data are shown for various years 1970-86, with selected earlier trends and projections to 1990.

Data are from State and Federal sources, including Census Bureau; and Lawrence Berkeley Laboratory projections.

Contains contents listing (1 p.), and the following:

a. Glossary; State description, with 1 table showing Montana's rank among the States in population, land area, and selected demographic and socioeconomic characteristics, mostly 1980; and narrative analyses of U.S. and State economy, with 3 illustrative charts, and 1 table showing selected U.S. economic indicators for 1983-84. (p. 1-12)

b. Labor force description, with brief narratives, 4 charts, and 37 tables listed below (p. 13-54); and 1 map showing State labor force areas. (inside back cover)

Availability: Montana Department of Labor and Industry, Employment Security Division, Research and Analysis Bureau, PO Box 1728, Helena MT 59624, †; SRI/MF/complete.

TABLES:
[Data are for Montana, unless otherwise noted.]

LABOR FORCE AND POPULATION DATA

[1] Employment status of civilian noninstitutional population 16 years/over [with comparison to U.S., 1970-86]. (p. 14)

[2-10] Population, labor force, labor force participation rate, and unemployment projections [by age, sex, and race, repeated for State and each SDA], July 1986. (p. 15-23)

INDUSTRY AND OCCUPATION DATA

[11] Distribution of employment by major industry groups, [1982 and 1990]. (p. 25)

[12] Industry employment 2-digit SIC [annual average, 1982 and 1990]. (p. 26-27)

[13] Distribution of employment by major occupational group [with annual openings per occupation, and due to growth and separations, 1982 and 1990]. (p. 29)

[14-15] Occupations with most openings (annual average job openings) [total, and due to growth and separations, 1982-90 period]; and [employment in] fastest growing occupations, 1982 and 1990. (p. 30-31)

[16] Annual average nonagricultural employment [by industry division and major group, selected years 1950-84]. (p. 32)

[17-18] Annual labor force report [labor force by employment status, and employment by industry division and major group, monthly] 1983-84. (p. 33-34)

[19-20] Hours and earnings series [by] month: average hours and earnings in private, nonagricultural industries [by industry division and selected major group], 1983-84. (p. 35-36)

[21] Female employment by industry [division, monthly 1983-84]. (p. 37)

[22] New businesses, by industry [division, and for nonclassifiable establishments, monthly] 1984. (p. 38)

COUNTY DATA AND ECONOMICALLY DISADVANTAGED POPULATION

[23] Estimates of the population of counties [and births, deaths, and migration, all by county], 1980-83. (p. 39)

[24] Unemployment rates [by county, and for U.S. by State, 1983-84]. (p. 40)

[25] Annual average covered employment by [selected] major industry groups, [by county], 1984. (p. 41-42)

[26-34] Current population survey data [labor force by employment status, by county], 1976-84. (p. 43-51)

[35] Economically disadvantaged [and total population, by sex, race/ethnicity (including Native American, Asian/Pacific Islander, and Spanish origin), and age group, for State and by SDA], 1980. (p. 52)

[36] Poverty income guidelines [for U.S. contiguous States, Alaska, and Hawaii, by family size], 1985. (p. 52)

[37] Economically disadvantaged [by age/income] categories [and total population, by county], 1980. (p. 53-54)

S4725   MONTANA
Library Commission

S4725-1   MONTANA LIBRARY DIRECTORY, 1984, with Statistics of Montana Public Libraries

Annual. [1985.] 116 p.
ISSN 0094-873X.
LC 74-646588.
SRI/MF/complete

Annual directory, for FY84, of Montana public, institutional, and special libraries and personnel, with public library statistics for FY83-84.

Includes the following data for individual public libraries, arranged by county: total titles and volumes, titles added, and periodicals received; local and bookmobile circulation; hours; staff; nonresident borrower fee; income by source; expenditures by function; and potential tax receipts and spending; FY83-84.

Also includes taxable valuation, mill levies, and 1980 population served, by library and/or county; and summary data for FY82.

Data are from an annual survey of public libraries.

Contains table of contents (1 p.); directories (p. 1-76); and statistical section, with contents listing, 6 summary tables, and 2 detailed tables (p. 77-116).

Previous report, described in SRI 1984 Annual under this number, presented data for FY82. No separate report for FY83 was published.

Availability: Montana Library Commission, 1515 E. Sixth Ave., Helena MT 59620, †; SRI/MF/complete.

S4740   MONTANA
Office of Public Instruction

S4740-1   MONTANA PUBLIC SCHOOL ENROLLMENT DATA, Fall 1984

Annual. [1985.] 41 p.
Rpt. No. FA17784.
SRI/MF/complete

Annual report presenting Montana public school enrollment by sex, by grade (and for special education), shown by school and county, Oct. 1, 1984. Also includes high school graduates (no date).

Contains contents listing (1 p.) and 6 tables.

Availability: Montana Office of Public Instruction, Financial Aid and Transportation Division, State Capitol, Helena MT 59620, †; SRI/MF/complete.

S4750   MONTANA
Department of Revenue

S4750-1   REPORT OF THE STATE DEPARTMENT OF REVENUE for the Period July 1, 1982-June 30, 1984, Montana

Biennial. [1985.] vi+135 p.
LC 75-646983.
SRI/MF/complete

Biennial report, for FY83-84, of the Montana Dept of Revenue, presenting data on tax collections by type, and property values by county. Also includes data on establishments, production, and income, for various taxed industries; selected 1980s trends, and property value trends from 1933; and revenues from non-tax sources. Data are from Dept internal records.

Contains contents listing (2 p.); 9 report sections, interspersed with 55 charts and 136 tables (p. i-vi, 1-134); and appendix report from revenue oversight committee (1 p.).

All tables, and selected charts showing substantial data not covered by tables, are listed below.

Previous report, for FY81-82, is described in SRI 1983 Annual under this number.

Availability: Montana Department of Revenue, Mitchell Bldg., 205 Roberts St., Helena MT 59620, †; SRI/MF/complete.

TABLES AND CHARTS:

S4750-1.1: Revenue Dept Collections Summary, and Specific Taxes Other than Property

[Tables show data for FY80-84, unless otherwise noted.]

SUMMARY

[1] Dept of Revenue collections [by source, including detailed type of tax]. (p. vi)

INCOME TAX

[2] Distribution of income tax collections [allocation to general and sinking funds, and school foundation], FY83. [chart] (p. 1)

[3-4] [Effect of CPI-based indexing of income taxes on tax paid by average family of 4 and individuals, 1981-82.] (p. 1)

[5] Type of deduction claimed on itemized returns [1982]. [chart] (p. 2)

[6-7] Individual income tax returns for 1982-83 [summary of returns received and processed as of Dec. 6, 1983 and Jan. 8, 1985] [includes number of personal exemptions listed, number of returns showing itemized and standard deductions, value of deductions, adjusted gross and taxable income, and taxes paid, all by income bracket]. (p. 4-5)

[8] Income tax credits [number of taxpayers claiming, and average amount claimed, for energy conservation, nonfossil energy, and investment in business-related equipment, by income bracket], 1982. (p. 6)

NONRENEWABLE NATURAL RESOURCE TAXATION

[Tables [21-28] show data by county, for 1982-83 production taxable in 1983-84.]

[9-10] Resource indemnity: tax collections by mineral; and trust [fund] principal and interest; [FY83-84]. (p. 7)

[11] Metaliferous mines license tax [rates, number of producers, gross production value, and taxes paid]. (p. 8)

[12] Micaceous mineral mines license tax [number of mines, production, and taxes paid]. (p. 9)

[13] Oil and gas producers privilege/license tax [collections, FY82-83]. (p. 10)

[14-15] Crude oil and natural gas severance tax [includes oil production volume and value, number of gas producers and sales volume, and taxes collected]. (p. 10-11)

[16-17] Oil and natural gas severance taxes returned to producing counties [by county, FY82-83]. (p. 12)

[18-20] Coal severance tax: collections [including number of producers (total and exempt), volume taxed, production value, and surface mining tax, FY80-84]; and distribution [by State fund], and principal and interest on trust funds, [FY83-84]. (p. 13-14)

[21-24] Coal [production volume and value, contract sales assessed value, and taxable gross proceeds]; and metal mines [production volume and gross and taxable value]. (p. 18-19)

[25-28] Miscellaneous [minerals] and oil and gas [production volume and gross and taxable value, proceeds, and royalty interest]. (p. 20-24)

CORPORATION TAXES

[29-31] Corporate license and income taxes: collections, FY80-84; returns [with detail by industry division], FY84; and top 50 taxpayers [industries, including number of companies and tax liability], FY84. (p. 25-26)

[32-33] Banks/savings and loans [taxes paid and amount refunded to counties]; and [number of corporations claiming credits and amount claimed, by credit type]; FY84. (p. 26)

MOTOR FUEL AND OTHER TAXES

[34-35] Gasoline distributors license tax [collections, and gallons of gasoline consumed and involved in refunds]; and gasoline dealers refund permits [issued and fees collected]. (p. 27-28)

[36-37] Gasohol [gallons sold] and tax incentive [payments]; and special fuel tax [diesel fuel gallons consumed and involved in refunds, and tax rates and collections]. (p. 28-29)

[38] Aviation fuel tax collections. (p. 30)

[39-40] Retail coal dealers and cement/gypsum license taxes [paid, and number of retailers or producers, coal sales volume, and cement/gypsum production]. (p. 31-32)

[41] Electricity/electrical energy license tax [paid, and number of generators and kilowatt hours generated]. (p. 32)

[42-43] Telephone company license and freight line company taxes [paid, number of accounts, and gross income or earnings]. (p. 33-34)

[44] Rural electric/telephone co-op tax [paid and number of cooperatives]. (p. 34)

[45-48] National housing tax, consumer counsel tax, and public contractor's gross receipt tax and license fee collections. (p. 35-37)

[49] Store license tax [paid, and number of wholesale and retail stores]. (p. 37)

[50-51] Camper certificate/decal and tramway gross receipt tax collections. (p. 38-39)

[52-54] Cigarette wholesale/retailer licenses [issued and fees paid]; and cigarette sales tax and tobacco products tax collections. (p. 39, 41-42)

[55] Inheritance taxes paid. (p. 42)

LIQUOR TAXES

[56-59] Liquor license [fees and] tax collections, [liquor profits], and liquor excise and beer tax collections. (p. 43-45)

[60-62] Liquor license, beer, and wine tax allocation [percent to general fund, local areas, and State Dept of Institutions alcoholism programs (no dates)]. [charts] (p. 46)

[63] Wine tax [collections from Dept of Revenue and wine distributors]. (p. 47)

S4750-1.2: Property Tax, Child Support, and Medicaid Fraud

PROPERTY TAX

[Tables show data for 1983-84, unless otherwise noted. Tables [61-76] show data by county.]

[1] Analysis of taxable valuation [of agricultural land and all other real property, livestock, personal property, utilities, and net proceeds, 1933-84]. (p. 54)

[2-58] [County summaries, showing land acreage and personal property items by type; and market and taxable value of land and improved property by type, personal property, and intracounty utilities and cooperatives; repeated for each county and statewide]. (p. 56-112)

[59] Taxable values of cities and towns. (p. 113)

[60] Taxes levied [by function, with State total market and taxable valuations]. (p. 115)

[61-72] Taxes levied for State and county purposes [by type or fund]; and for school purposes]. (p. 116-127)

[73-74] Total average tax, and special [including fire] district taxes. (p. 128-129)

[75-76] Total taxes levied [by purpose]. (p. 130-131)

CHILD SUPPORT AND MEDICAID FRAUD

[77] Child support enforcement collections, [and administration costs, FY83-84]. (p. 132)

[78] Medicaid fraud control bureau [investigation cases opened and closed by provider category, total cases resolved, and overpayment collections, FY83-84]. (p. 133)

S4755   MONTANA
Department of Social and Rehabilitation Services

S4755-1   STATISTICAL REPORT, Montana

Monthly, with annual summary. Approx. 30 p.
ISSN 0091-1143.
LC 73-643173.
SRI/MF/complete, shipped quarterly

Monthly statistical report, with fiscal year summary, on Montana public assistance programs, including number of cases, recipients, and payments, by program and county. Programs covered include AFDC, general and medical assistance, food stamps, and energy assistance.

Data are compiled by the Management Information Office. Report is issued approximately 3 months after month of coverage.

Contains contents listing; 3 summary charts; 11 monthly and 7 quarterly tables, listed below, some with accompanying charts; and occasionally revised data for previous issues.

Most monthly tables appear in all issues; latest period of coverage for quarterly tables is noted under "Statistical Features."

Fiscal year summary, issued with the Aug. report, presents totals for most data covered in the monthly reports. Errata for the FY84 annual summary have been received and are available on SRI microfiche under this number.

Prior to Dec. 1984 issue, report included 2 additional quarterly tables on social service cases (see S4755-1.601 below).

Availability: Montana Department of Social and Rehabilitation Services, Management Information Office, Centralized Services Division, PO Box 4210, Helena MT 59604, †; SRI/MF/complete, shipped quarterly.

Issues reviewed during 1985: Aug. 1984-July 1985 (D); and FY84 annual summary.

TABLES:

[Data are for month of coverage, unless otherwise noted. Tables 2-11 show data by county.]

MONTHLY TABLES

1. Summary of public assistance and medical care [obligations incurred, recipients, and average payments, by program, for month of coverage, previous month, and same month of previous year].

2. Total expenditures for public assistance and medical care [aid to dependent children, medical assistance, and general assistance/county medical].

3. AFDC, by unemployed parent and regular cases [number of cases, adults, and children, and amount; table begins in the July 1985 issue].

4-5. AFDC [cases, recipients, and amount], and medical assistance [cases and amount], compared with the same month last year and 5 years ago.

6. Medical assistance (Medicaid): number of recipients and amount of payments by type of service [hospital inpatient and outpatient, physicians, drugs/supplies, nursing home, other practitioners, lab/X-ray/radiology, dental, and miscellaneous].

7. Medical assistance (Medicaid): number of recipients and amount of payments by basis of eligibility [aged, AFDC adult and child, blind, and disabled].

8. Analysis of general assistance by family and 1-person cases [and payments].

9. Expenditures for general assistance, county medical, burials, and transient relief.

10. Number of households [public assistance and other, and individuals] receiving food stamps, and value of food stamps.

11. Low income energy assistance [including handicapped and senior citizen cases, and payments, cumulatively from Oct. through month of coverage or 1-3 months prior to month of coverage].

QUARTERLY TABLES

[Most data are shown by county for quarter ending in month of coverage, or most recently completed quarter.]

1-2. Activity of WIN [work incentive program] cases, welfare savings resulting from the WIN program; and WIN services provided [by type of service; all by local office].

3-7. Rehabilitation/visual caseload by type of disability and severity of the disability; status of open rehabilitation and visual cases [for month of coverage]; and rehabilitation and visual applications closed and cases closed [including cost per case].

STATISTICAL FEATURES:

S4755-1.601: Aug. 1984

QUARTERLY TABLES

[Tables show data by county, for quarter ended June 1984.]

1. Disposition of social services cases.

2. Social services, number of cases receiving each service [including adoption, day care, foster care, homemaker services, and investigative and protective services].

This is the final appearance of these 2 tables.

S4755-1.602: Sept. 1984

QUARTERLY TABLES

1-7. WIN, rehabilitation, and visual service data, for quarter ended Sept. 1984.

For data description, see S4755-1 above.

S4755-1.603: Dec. 1984

QUARTERLY TABLES

1-7. WIN, rehabilitation, and visual service data, for quarter ended Dec. 1984.

For data description, see S4755-1 above.

S4755-1.604: Mar. 1985

QUARTERLY TABLES

1-7. WIN, rehabilitation, and visual service data, for quarter ended Mar. 1985.

For data description, see S4755-1 above.

S4755-1.605: June 1985

QUARTERLY TABLES

1-7. WIN, rehabilitation, and visual service data, for quarter ended June 1985.

For data description, see S4755-1 above.

S4760   MONTANA
Office of the Secretary of State

S4760–1   REPORT OF THE OFFICIAL CANVASS by County of Votes Cast at the General Election Held in the State of Montana, Nov. 6, 1984
Biennial. [1985.]
2 p. Foldout.
SRI/MF/complete

Biennial report presenting results of Montana general election held Nov. 6, 1984. Shows voting for President and Vice-President; U.S. Senator and Representatives; selected State officials and judges; and 4 constitutional amendments and initiatives on disciplining of judges, congressional district reorganization, milk price decontrol, and licensing and regulation of denture manufacturing (denturitry).

Also shows political affiliation of candidates, and voter registration and turnout. Most data are shown by county and district.

For description of previous report, covering 1982 general election, see SRI 1983 Annual under this number. Primary election results are also available from the issuing agency but are not covered in SRI.

Availability: Montana Office of the Secretary of State, Capitol Bldg., Rm. 202, Helena MT 59620, †; SRI/MF/complete.

S4825   NEBRASKA
Department of Administrative Services

S4825–1   STATE OF NEBRASKA COMPREHENSIVE ANNUAL FINANCIAL REPORT, Year Ending June 30, 1984
Annual. Dec. 20, 1984.
124 p.
SRI/MF/complete

Annual report on financial condition of Nebraska State government, FY84, presenting assets and liabilities, reserves, and fund balances; revenues by source; expenditures by object, function, and agency; and fund balances; all for general, special revenue, debt service, capital projects, internal service, trust and agency, and college and university funds, with selected comparisons from 1975.

Also includes data on long-term debt; State aid to local areas; budgeted vs. actual expenditures, by fund and agency; population, income, and employment comparisons to U.S., various years 1940-83; and educational enrollment by grade and by higher education institution, farm cash receipts, housing units authorized, State highway miles and construction, motor fuel sales volume, and motor vehicle registrations, 1974-83.

Data are compiled from reports of State and Federal agencies.

Contains contents listing (p. 1-2); introductory section with transmittal letters, text data, 3 illustrative charts, and organizational chart (p. 5-14); financial section with 25 fund statements, and accompanying notes with text data (p. 16-77); and statistical section, with 2 charts, 15 tables, and list of budgetary programs and funds arranged by agency and fund type (p. 80-124).

Availability: Nebraska Department of Administrative Services, Accounting Division, State Capitol Bldg., Rm. 1210, Lincoln NE 68509, †; SRI/MF/complete.

S4835   NEBRASKA
Department of Agriculture

S4835–1   NEBRASKA AGRICULTURAL STATISTICS: Annual Report, 1982-83
Annual. Aug. 1984. 174 p.
LC 50-44970.
SRI/MF/complete

Annual report on Nebraska agricultural production, marketing, and finances, mostly 1982-83, with some data for 1984 and selected trends from 1925. Data generally are shown by commodity and/or county and district, with selected comparisons to other States and regions and to total U.S.

Covers production, prices, disposition, value, and, as applicable, acreage, yield, or inventory, for field crop, vegetable, livestock, poultry, and dairy sectors.

Also includes data on irrigation; cattle feedlots; number of farms and acreage; wool production; Omaha market prices; farm labor and wages, income, mortgage debt, land value and rental rates, property tax levies, and production expenses; fertilizer use and sales; retail commercial feed sales; weather; prices paid by farmers; and U.S. food consumption and foreign trade, including export shares for Nebraska.

Also includes selected findings from 1980 Census of Agriculture, including farm operators by age group.

Data are primarily from Nebraska Dept of Agriculture and USDA.

Contains preface, methodology, and contents listing (p. 2-6); and report, in 5 sections, with 8 maps, 1 chart, and 174 tables (p. 7-174).

Previous report, for 1981-82, is described in SRI 1983 Annual, under this number.

Availability: Nebraska Crop and Livestock Reporting Service, PO Box 81069, Lincoln NE 68501, $5.00; SRI/MF/complete.

S4865   NEBRASKA
Department of Education

S4865–1   STATISTICS AND FACTS ABOUT NEBRASKA SCHOOLS, 1984/85
Annual. [1985.] iv + 121 p.
ISSN 0561-9440.
LC 76-646956.
SRI/MF/complete

Annual report on Nebraska public and nonpublic school enrollments by county and district, school districts, high school graduates, and personnel, for school year 1984/85. Includes trends from 1970/71 and projections to 1994.

Contains table and chart listing, and explanation of school district classifications (p. i-iii); and 4 summary charts, and 24 tables listed below (p. 1-121).

Availability: Nebraska Department of Education, Management Information Services, 301 Centennial Mall, S., PO Box 94987, Lincoln NE 68509-4987, $2.50 + postage; SRI/MF/complete.

TABLES:
[Data are for school year 1984/85, unless otherwise noted.]

DISTRICTS, SCHOOLS, AND ENROLLMENTS
[Tables [1-3] and [5] show data for public schools by class of district, and for total State-operated and nonpublic schools.]

1. State total: number of districts, enrollment, and FTE of certified staff. (p. 1)

2. [Number of] operating school districts, and number of schools [by type, including special education]. (p. 2)

3. Enrollment by grade. (p. 3)

4. Enrollment by grade, reported by type of school (public schools only). (p. 4)

5. 3-year comparison of the number of districts and enrollment [1982/83-1984/85]. (p. 5)

ENROLLMENT TRENDS AND PROJECTIONS
6. County enrollments by school system, all schools [individual data for each public, State-operated, and nonpublic school district, arranged by county, all by grade]. (p. 6-50)

7. Percent of change in county enrollment [by county, 1974/75 and 1983/84-1984/85]. (p. 51)

8a-8c. 15-year history of enrollment by grade [and for special education], State total, public/State-operated, and nonpublic schools [1970/71-1984/85]. (p. 52-54)

9. Public/nonpublic schools estimated enrollment [by grade], 1985-94. (p. 57)

10. District ranking by enrollment: [public school district] classes I, II-V, and VI; State-operated; and nonpublic systems; [includes enrollment by grade level, and elementary and secondary FTE teachers and pupil/teacher ratio]. (p. 58-83)

11. Enrollment report by race [Asian/Pacific Islander, Hispanic, American Indian/Alaskan Native, black, and white], and sex [by district and county for public and nonpublic schools]. (p. 84-110)

BIRTHS AND SCHOOL CENSUS

12. Nebraska birth rate, [estimated population, and number of births], 1956-83. (p. 111)

13. School census: number of males and females [age 20 and under] by age and county, as of June 1984. (p. 114-115)

GRADUATES AND STAFF

14. Comparison of high school graduates to [9th and 12th grade] fall enrollment [by graduation year 1972/73-1987/88]. (p. 117)

15a-15d. FTE of certificated personnel by position assignment [and sex], State total, nonpublic, State-operated, and public schools. (p. 118-121)

S4885   NEBRASKA
Department of Health

S4885-1   1984 ANNUAL
STATISTICAL REPORT,
Nebraska Bureau of Vital
Statistics
Annual. [1985.] 5+111 p.
LC 75-640799.
SRI/MF/complete

Annual report on Nebraska vital statistics, covering births, deaths by cause, marriages, divorces, and population, 1984, with selected trends from 1925. Includes data by age, race, sex, and location. Data are compiled primarily from State records.

Contains foreword and contents listing (5 p.); introduction, with 2 tables showing selected vital statistics, 1925-84 and monthly 1984 (p. 1-4); 4 sections, with narrative summaries, text statistics, list of health planning regions, 3 maps, 7 charts, and 62 tables listed below (p. 5-110); and definitions (p. 111).

Availability: Nebraska Department of Health, Health Data and Statistical Research Division, Vital Statistics Bureau, 301 Centennial Mall, S., PO Box 95007, Lincoln NE 68509, †; SRI/MF/ complete.

TABLES:

[Unless otherwise noted, data are for Nebraska, 1984. Data by race are for white, black, Indian, Mexican, and other. Data by place of residence and/or occurrence are usually shown by county and selected city.]

S4885-1.1: Births

[1-2] Births: by place of occurrence and by usual residence of mother, for health planning regions [and for counties and selected cities, 1982-84]. (p. 10-16)

[3] Births: sex, race, and plurality, by place of residence. (p. 17-20)

[4] Birth order by age of mother. (p. 21)

[5-6] Births, prenatal care: gravidity and prenatal visits, by trimester in which prenatal care started (percent). (p. 22)

[7-8] Births: by education of father and mother, and by weight groups. (p. 23-24)

[9-11] Out-of-wedlock births: by place of residence, 1984; by age and race of mother [generally 1980-84]; and by age of mother [and birth order], 1984. (p. 25-28)

[12-14] Births, congenital anomalies: by county of residence, [month of birth, age of mother, birth weight, sex, race, and type of defect]. (p. 29-31)

[15] Births: selected defects by number and rate [per 1,000 live births]. (p. 32)

[16] [Births and deaths for Nebraska residents by State of occurrence, and births and deaths occurring in Nebraska for nonresidents by resident State.] (p. 33)

S4885-1.2: Deaths

[Tables [1-22] begin "Nebraska deaths..."]

DEATHS BY LOCATION AND CAUSE

[1-2] By place of occurrence and by usual residence of deceased, for health planning regions [and for counties and selected cities, 1982-84]. (p. 38-42)

[3] Sex and race, by place of residence. (p. 43-46)

[4-6] Six leading causes by age group and sex; and age-specific rates. (p. 49-50)

[7] Rates for 6 leading causes, by place of residence. (p. 51-54)

[8] Principal and other causes, by place of residence [with totals by sex]. (p. 55-59)

[9] Blacks, by leading cause and sex [and deaths in hospital and not in hospital, and infant deaths and rate]. (p. 60)

[10-11] Principal and other causes and rates per 100,000 population [1980-84]. (p. 61-62)

[12-13] Cancer by site and sex, and rates by site [1980-84]. (p. 63-64)

ACCIDENTAL DEATHS

[14-15] Accidents: by principal and other causes, by place of residence; and for [detailed types of] accidents by occurrence [including at work by industry division, all by age group]. (p. 65-69)

[16] Accidents by cause [and total by sex, and rate per 100,000 estimated population, 1980-84]. (p. 70)

[17-19] Drownings by site; farm fatalities by type; and suicides by type; all by sex and age group. (p. 71-72)

DEATHS OCCURRING IN HOSPITALS AND ELSEWHERE

[20] Hospital and nonhospital, by [place of] occurrence and residence. (p. 73-76)

INFANT AND FETAL DEATHS

[21] Under 1 year of age by cause [and race, by sex; and by birth weight groups]. (p. 78)

[22] Infant, neonatal, perinatal, and fetal, by place of residence. (p. 79-82)

[23-24] Fetal deaths by cause of death, and by month, age group of mother, sex, race, and place of delivery. (p. 83-84)

S4885-1.3: Marriages, Divorces, and Population

MARRIAGES

[Most tables begin "Nebraska marriages..."]

[1] Number and rate, by county [1981-84]. (p. 87-88)

[2] Number of county residents married per 1,000 population [by county]. (p. 89)

[3-7] By education, race, number of marriages, residence status, and previous marital status of bride and groom. (p. 90-92)

[8] Nonresident brides and grooms [by resident State]. (p. 93)

[9-11] Number of marriages, by age of bride and [by age of] groom; [and total] marriages, and 1st marriages, by age of bride and groom. (p. 94-96)

[12] By occupation of bride and groom. (p. 97)

DIVORCES

[Tables begin "Nebraska divorces..."]

[13] Number and rate, by county [1981-84]. (p. 99-100)

[14] By age of husband and wife. (p. 101)

[15] By duration of marriage [1982-84]. (p. 102)

[16-17] By race of husband and wife; and number of children affected. (p. 103)

[18-19] Number of marriage [of] husband and wife; and settlements made [by type]. (p. 104)

[20-21] By education and occupation of husband and wife. (p. 105-106)

POPULATION

[22] Nebraska population by county, U.S. census [decennially 1930-80]. (p. 109-110)

S4890   NEBRASKA
Department of Insurance

S4890-1   SUMMARY OF INSURANCE
BUSINESS IN NEBRASKA
for the Year 1984
Annual. [1985.] 2+424 p.
LC 10-8606.
SRI/MF/complete

Annual report on Nebraska insurance industry financial condition and underwriting activity, by company and type of insurance, 1984. Covers assets, liabilities, capital, surplus, premiums received or written and earned, losses incurred, claims or benefits paid, insurance issued and in force, and membership fees and/or size, for companies with headquarters in Nebraska and elsewhere.

Data are shown, as applicable, for property/ liability and life insurance companies, fraternal benefit societies, assessment companies, county and hospital/physician mutual assns, HMOs, legal and dental service corporations, service contract organizations, and motor clubs.

Property/liability insurance data include additional breakdowns for automobile, accident/ health, medical malpractice, surety, workers' compensation, and other detailed lines of coverage.

Also includes data on Insurance Dept consumer complaints, agent licensing and examination results, and revenues; number of companies by type of insurance; finances of insurers in liquidation; securities on deposit by company; and State guaranty assn financial condition.

Contains contents listing (1 p.); Insurance Dept report, including assorted lists and directories, and 22 tables (p. 1-77); and 13 detailed financial tables (p. 78-424).

Availability: Nebraska Department of Insurance, 301 Centennial Mall, S., PO Box 94699, Lincoln NE 68509-4699, $7.00; SRI/MF/complete.

S4895 NEBRASKA
Department of Labor

S4895–1 NEBRASKA WORK TRENDS
Monthly. Approx. 17 p.
SRI/MF/complete, shipped
quarterly

Monthly report on Nebraska labor force, including employment and unemployment by county and MSA, and employment by industry. Also includes data on unemployment insurance claims.

Reports are issued approximately 3 months after month of coverage, and contain contents listing, 2 illustrative charts, and 11 monthly tables listed below.

Report is discontinued with June 1985 issue. Similar data are included in the quarterly report *Nebraska Labor Market Information Quarterly*. Quarterly report will be covered in SRI under S4895–2; coverage will begin in 1986.

Availability: Nebraska Department of Labor, Employment Division, Research and Statistics Section, PO Box 94600, State House Station, Lincoln NE 68509-4600, †; SRI/MF/complete, shipped quarterly.

Issues reviewed during 1985: Sept. 1984-June 1985 (D).

MONTHLY TABLES:
[Data are for Nebraska, unless otherwise noted.]

[1-2] Estimates: of labor force data [by employment status, for State and Omaha and Lincoln MSAs]; and of nonfarm employment data [by industry group; preliminary for month of coverage, and revised for preceding month and same month of preceding year].

[3] Monthly report on labor force, [employment], and unemployment [by county, MSA, and selected metro area, as of selected date during 1-2 months following month of coverage].

[4-5] Summary of initial and continued claims [for unemployment insurance, monthly for current year to date and previous year].

[6] Estimates of hours and earnings in manufacturing [by selected major group, for State and Omaha and Lincoln MSAs, for month of coverage, previous month, and same month of previous year].

[7-8] [Table [2] is repeated for Omaha and Lincoln MSAs.]

[9] Percent changes in [U.S.] CPI for all urban consumers [by item, for month of coverage and trends].

[10-11] Job training labor force and unemployment report [by State service delivery area and planning district, for month of coverage, previous month, and same month of previous year].

S4900 NEBRASKA
Commission on Law Enforcement and Criminal Justice

S4900–1 UNIFORM CRIME REPORTS, 1984, Nebraska
Annual. [1985.] iv+60 p.
NE Pub. Clearinghouse No.
L2500S001.
ISSN 0090-3221.
LC 75-647156.
SRI/MF/complete

Annual report on Nebraska crimes and arrests, by offense, 1984 with comparison to 1983. Includes data by county and reporting agency, and by offender age, race, and sex. Also includes law enforcement employment and assaults on officers.

Report focuses on 8 Index offenses: murder, rape, robbery, aggravated assault, burglary, larceny/theft, motor vehicle theft, and arson. Arrests are also shown for numerous non-Index offenses.

Data are from State and local agency reports submitted under the Uniform Crime Reporting (UCR) Program.

Contains summary, and listings of contents, tables, and charts (p. ii-iv); description of UCR Program (p. 1-4); and report, with brief narratives, 12 charts, and 39 tables (p. 5-60).

All tables, and selected charts presenting data not included in tables, are described below.

Availability: Nebraska Commission on Law Enforcement and Criminal Justice, Uniform Crime Reporting Section, 301 Centennial Mall South, PO Box 94946, Lincoln NE 68509, ‡; SRI/MF/complete.

CHARTS AND TABLES:
[Data are for Nebraska, 1984, with selected comparisons to 1983.]

S4900–1.1: Offenses and Arrests
[Tables with data by race/ethnicity usually include white, black, Indian, and Asian.]

INDEX OFFENSES

a. Summary: number of offenses, rate, and percent cleared, by Index offense; and value of stolen and recovered property, by type. Tables 1-3. (p. 5-6)

b. Murder victims and offenders, by age, sex, and race/ethnicity; and murder/manslaughter offenses, by circumstance, type of weapon, and victim/offender relationship. Chart 2, tables 4-7. (p. 7-9)

c. Rapes, by type (forcible and attempted), age of victim, place of occurrence, and victim/offender relationship, and value of stolen and recovered property. Chart 4, tables 8-11. (p. 11-12)

d. Robberies, by place of occurrence; robberies and felony assaults, by type of weapon; burglaries, by place and time of occurrence; larceny/theft offenses, by type; and arson offenses, by type of property; also including data on value of property stolen, recovered, and damaged, by type (including motor vehicles). Charts 6 and 7, tables 12-19. (p. 13-25)

ARRESTS

e. Arrest rates per 100,000 population, adult and juvenile arrests, and arrests by age, sex, and race/ethnicity, all by Index and non-Index offense; and drug abuse arrests by substance, by sex and race/ethnicity. Tables 20-30. (p. 27-37)

S4900–1.2: Police Assaulted, Law Enforcement Employees, and Local Data
[Data by agency are shown for county sheriff offices and local police depts.]

a. Officers assaulted: by time of day, and type of activity, weapon, and assignment. Tables 31-34. (p. 38-40)

b. Law enforcement sworn and civilian employees by sex, officers per 1,000 population, and officers assaulted, by agency. Tables 35-37. (p. 41-44)

c. Local data: Index offenses by type, clearances, population, crime rate, adult and juvenile arrests, and arrests by Index and non-Index offense, all by agency arranged by county. 2 tables. (p. 46-60)

S4910 NEBRASKA
Library Commission

S4910–1 NEBRASKA LIBRARIES, 1984
Biennial. [1984.] 49 p.
Rpt. No. L4000DO16-1984.
SRI/MF/complete

Biennial report, for 1984, presenting directories of Nebraska public, academic, and other libraries; and statistics on public library finances and operations, by library, 1979/80 and 1980/81.

Public library data include income by source, including State, local, and revenue sharing funds; expenses by function (personnel and materials); holdings, including books, periodicals, and audiovisual materials; and personnel, total circulation, and population served.

Data are from reports to State Library Commission.

Contains contents listing (1 p.); introduction, library directory, and 1 map (p. 1-25); public library data, with 1 table repeated for 6 networks (p. 26-45); and additional library-related directories (p. 46-49).

This is the 1st edition of the report.

Availability: Nebraska Library Commission, 1420 P St., Lincoln NE 68508, †; SRI/MF/complete.

S4940   NEBRASKA
Public Service Commission

S4940–1   NEBRASKA PUBLIC SERVICE COMMISSION 1982-84 BIENNIAL REPORT

Biennial.   Dec. 1, 1984.
65 p.
ISSN 0098-2083.
LC 75-643112.
SRI/MF/complete

Biennial report presenting Nebraska railroad and telephone company regulatory, financial, and operating data; and regulatory data only for motor transportation, warehousing, and grain sectors; mostly 1982-83 or FY83-84.

Covers licensing and inspection activity, and rate cases, by sector. Also covers railroad and telephone company assets, liabilities, revenues, and expenses; railroad mileage, length of line potentially subject to abandonment, and revenue freight by commodity; and telephone facilities, rate increases, stockholders, and shares and par value; all by company.

Also includes data on railroad track and freight car safety inspections and investigations, including investigations of derailments and cartrain deaths, by railroad; Commission receipts and expenditures, and complaint processing activities; and grain warehouse capacity and licensing trends from 1952.

Contains contents listing (p. 1); departmental overview, with 2 tables (p. 2-18); and statistical section with 24 tables (p. 19-65).

For description of previous report, for 1980-82, see SRI 1983 Annual under this number.

Availability: Nebraska Public Service Commission, 301 Centennial Mall, S., PO Box 94927, Lincoln NE 68509, †; SRI/MF/complete.

S4950   NEBRASKA
Department of Revenue

S4950–1   1983 ANNUAL REPORT, NEBRASKA DEPARTMENT OF REVENUE

Annual.   [1985.]   96 p.
ISSN 0092-9220.
LC 73-647511.
SRI/MF/complete

Annual report on Nebraska State tax revenues, by tax type and county, 1983 with selected trends from 1867. Also includes individual tax returns by income bracket, and sales tax by municipality and detailed industry. Data are from State and Federal sources.

Contains contents and table listing (1 p.), and the following sections:

a. General information, with summary of State Revenue Dept organization and activities, and overview of revenue sources; 2 trend charts; 1 chart showing U.S. per capita tax revenues by State, 1983; and 3 tables showing Nebraska per capita and/or total personal income by county 1981-82, allocation of funds to local governments by type of aid FY83, and chronology of income and sales tax rates as of various dates 1967-84. (p. 1-12)

b. 4 statistical sections, with narrative summaries, 4 charts, and 46 tables (including 2 maps designated as 1 table) listed below. (p. 13-93)

c. Index. (p. 95-96)

Availability: Nebraska Department of Revenue, Research Division, PO Box 94818, Lincoln NE 68509, †; SRI/MF/complete.

TABLES:
[All tables show data for Nebraska.]

S4950–1.1: Income Taxes
[Data are for tax year 1982, unless otherwise noted. Types of tax credits include food sales, motor fuels, elderly, energy, and tax paid to other States.]

1-2. Individual income tax statistics [including exemptions, tax credits by type, Federal adjusted gross income (AGI), and Federal and calculated State taxes]; and liability [total returns, returns with tax liability, and calculated liability, by Federal AGI bracket]; by county. (p. 16-22)

3. Average individual income tax liability per return and per capita [by county]. [maps] (p. 23)

4. Analysis of individual income tax liability [returns with and without liability, and calculated liability, by Federal AGI bracket]. (p. 24)

5-9. Analysis of [tax credits by type, including number of returns claiming credit, and amount claimed, by Federal AGI bracket]. (p. 25-27)

10-12. General fund individual and corporate income tax cash receipts; and withholding tax cash revenues; [by month, 1982-83]. (p. 27-28)

13. Analysis of corporate income tax returns [number of corporations, taxable income, and calculated tax, by State income classification]. (p. 29)

S4950–1.2: Sales Tax
[Data are shown for 1983, unless otherwise noted. Tables 1-4 show net taxable sales and sales tax.]

1. Total net taxable sales and State sales tax [by county and municipality]. (p. 33-37)

2. Sales tax on motor vehicles [by county]. (p. 38)

3-4. Sales tax statistics by [detailed] business classification; and business classification sales by county [by industry division]. (p. 39-53)

5. City sales tax returned to [12] municipalities [1982-83]. (p. 54)

6-7. General fund sales tax cash revenues and receipts [by month, 1982-83]. (p. 55)

S4950–1.3: Miscellaneous Tax

1. General fund miscellaneous tax cash receipts [by source, 1982-83]. (p. 59)

2. Alcoholic beverage gallonage and revenue [beer, alcohol/spirits, and fortified and light wine, by month 1983, with totals annually 1970-83, and tax rates from 1935]. (p. 60)

3. Cigarette tax receipts [and number of packages taxed, 1964-83]. (p. 61)

4. Comparative pari-mutuel report [amounts wagered and taxable, and tax paid, by 5 organizations, 1982-83; and tax rates, 1959-83]. (p. 62)

5-6. Importing dealers and special fuels net taxable gallons and calculated net tax due [monthly 1983]. (p. 63)

7. Interstate motor carriers net taxable gallons and calculated net tax due [used in State, purchased in State, monthly 1983]. (p. 64)

8. Aviation fuels net taxable gallons and calculated net tax due [monthly 1983]. (p. 64)

9-10. Gasohol net taxable gallons and litter fee receipts [monthly 1982-83]. (p. 65)

11. Lodging tax returned to [21] counties, 1982-83; [and] chronology of lodging tax. (p. 66)

S4950–1.4: Property Tax
[Data are shown for 1983, unless otherwise noted. Tables 3 and 5-15 show data by county.]

1. History of assessed valuation and total property tax [and total mill levy, various years 1867-1983]. (p. 71)

2. Tangible property taxes levied [general levies for local governments, and special assessments, 1973-83]. (p. 72)

3. Actual valuation, property taxes levied, rate, and distributions of State aid [to counties and homestead exemption]. (p. 73)

4. Cities and villages valuations and levies. (p. 74-78)

5. Distribution of payments in lieu of taxes by public power districts [by recipient: State, counties, cities/villages, and school and miscellaneous districts]. (p. 79)

6. Selected property taxes levied [by tax type: county, city/village, township, and rural fire district; miscellaneous; education taxes for city/village and rural schools, county/rural high schools, and special education; and payments in lieu of taxes by public power districts]. (p. 80-81)

7. Actual value as set by State Board of Equalization [for tangible property (from assessment abstract), public utilities (from franchise assessment), and railroads]. (p. 82)

8. Valuation of all personal property, [special schedules, and property assessed by State Board]. (p. 83)

9. Valuation of all [urban and rural] real estate, and oil/mineral interest. (p. 84)

10-11. Actual value of personal property [including mobile homes]; and of miscellaneous schedules [utilities and motor vehicles; by property type]. (p. 85-86)

12. Number of [regular and special] property tax schedules returned. (p. 87)

13-15. Actual value of rural, agricultural, and urban real estate [by property type]. (p. 88-93)

S4955
Office of the Secretary of State

NEBRASKA

S4955–1   OFFICIAL REPORT OF THE BOARD OF STATE CANVASSERS of the State of Nebraska: Primary Election, May 15, 1984; General Election, Nov. 6, 1984
Biennial. [1985.] 41 p.
SRI/MF/complete

Biennial report presenting results of the Nebraska primary election held May 15, 1984 and general election held Nov. 6, 1984. Includes voting for President/Vice President, U.S. Senator and Representatives, State legislators, judges, education officials, various other officials, and 4 State constitutional amendments including revision of judicial disciplinary procedures. Data are shown by county and/or district, and include most candidates' party affiliation.

Also includes voter registration by party and county, and voting trends from 1907.

Previous report, covering 1982 elections, is described in SRI 1983 Annual under this number.

Availability: Nebraska Office of the Secretary of State, Administrative and Elections Division, 2300 State Capitol, Lincoln NE 68509, †; SRI/MF/complete.

S4957
Department of Social Services

NEBRASKA

S4957–1   NEBRASKA DEPARTMENT OF SOCIAL SERVICES 1983 Annual Report
Annual. [1984.] 21+15 p.
SRI/MF/complete

Annual report, for FY83, on Nebraska public welfare programs, including cases, recipients, and payments, by program, county, and State region, with trends from FY80. Covers Aid to Dependent Children (ADC), SSI, food stamps, medical assistance, and family services.

Contains narrative report, with 13 charts and 10 tables (p. 1-20); and appendices, with 9 tables (p. 20-21, and 15 p.).

All tables, and charts presenting substantial data not covered in tables, are listed below.

Previous report, for FY82, is described in SRI 1983 Annual under S4945-1. Issuing agency name has changed from Nebraska Dept of Public Welfare.

A quarterly report on public welfare is also available from the issuing agency, but is not covered in SRI.

Availability: Nebraska Department of Social Services, PO Box 95026, Lincoln NE 68509-5026, ‡; SRI/MF/complete.

CHARTS AND TABLES:
[Data are for Nebraska, FY83, unless otherwise noted.]

S4957–1.1: Administration and Income, Medical, and Social Services Programs

ADMINISTRATION

[1] Statement of disbursements [actual program costs, and local and State administration costs]. (p. 3)

INCOME MAINTENANCE
[Table and charts [3-6] show data for FY80-83.]

[2] Average payment per ADC recipient in Nebraska and surrounding States, June 1983. [chart] (p. 4)

[3] ADC total expenditures and average monthly cases. [chart] (p. 5)

[4] SSI and State supplement cases, average monthly number [includes State supplement total, aged, blind, and disabled cases]. (p. 5)

[5-6] Average monthly number of persons and households participating in the food stamp program; and total value of food stamps issued. [charts] (p. 6)

[7] Participation in food distribution program [number of programs, average monthly participants, and amount of allocated food; by program type]. (p. 8)

[8] Income maintenance payments [by program]. [chart] (p. 9)

MEDICAL ASSISTANCE
[Titles for tables and charts [9-14] begin "Medicaid...."]

[9] Vendor expenditures and average monthly recipients, FY80-83. [chart] (p. 10)

[10] Expenditures [and refunds], FY82-83. (p. 10)

[11-12] Expenditures and average monthly recipients, by program area. [charts] (p. 11)

[13-14] Persons and expenditures by maintenance category: by type of service [including hospital, mental health, nursing home, physician, dental, clinic, laboratory/radiology, home health, family planning, sterilization, drugs, and health screening]; and by maintenance payment status. (p. 12-13)

[15] Non-categorical medical programs [emergency assistance, and refugee resettlement and State disability programs: persons and expenditures, by month]. (p. 14)

[16] [Crippled children] clinics and hospitalizations [number of clinic visits, hospitalizations, and days hospitalized, by diagnostic or clinic category]. (p. 15)

SOCIAL SERVICES

[17-18] Contracted expenditures, and unduplicated persons receiving purchased services, Title XX, [for adult, family, and mental retardation services]. [charts] (p. 16)

[19-20] Registered/licensed child care and child placement facilities by [type and] field offices, licensed as of June 30, 1983; and mental retardation services [persons served and units, by type of service], by region. (p. 18)

[21] Title IV-B foster care (maintenance only) total expenditures and average monthly cases, FY80-83. [chart] (p. 19)

S4957–1.2: Appeals, Data by County, and Quality Control

APPEALS

[1] Report on appeals [number, type, principal issue, and disposition, for 8 social service programs]. (p. 21)

DATA BY COUNTY
[Data are shown by multicounty unit and/or county.]

[2] ADC program [family, adult, and child recipients, and maintenance payments, with detail for unemployed parent and foster care program segments]. (2 p.)

[3] State supplementation [cases and payments for aged, blind, and disabled, and cases with and without] Federal SSI. (2 p.)

[4] Food stamp program participants [public assistance and other households and persons, and value of coupons]. (2 p.)

[5-6] Title XIX: persons and [expenditures] by maintenance category, and expenditures by service. (4 p.)

[7] Adult and family contracted service expenditures [by type of service]. (2 p.)

[8] Unduplicated persons receiving purchased social services [by type]. (2 p.)

QUALITY CONTROL

[9] Quality control review error findings, active cases (State findings only), [for ADC, food stamps, and Medicaid, Apr.-Sept. 1982 and Oct. 1982-Mar. 1983 periods]. (1 p.)

S5010
Department of Agriculture

NEVADA

S5010–1   1984 NEVADA AGRICULTURAL STATISTICS
Annual. Sept. 23, 1985.
3+37 p.
SRI/MF/complete

Annual report on Nevada agricultural production, marketing, and finances, 1984, with some data for 1985 and selected trends from 1968. Data generally are shown by county and commodity, with some data for Carson City and comparisons to U.S.

Report generally covers production, value, prices, and, as applicable, acreage, disposition, yield, or inventory, for field crop, livestock, dairy, apiary, and poultry sectors.

Also includes data on number of farms, farm acreage, weather, pesticide use, pasture/rangeland condition, fertilizer consumption, and agricultural production costs and income.

Data are compiled jointly by USDA, University of Nevada, and Nevada Dept of Agriculture.

Contains foreword and contents listing (2 p.); and 43 tables, accompanied by brief narrative summaries (p. 1-36).

Availability: Nevada Department of Agriculture, Statistical Reporting Service, PO Box 8880, Reno NV 89507, †; SRI/MF/complete.

S5025   NEVADA
Office of the Controller

S5025–1   STATE OF NEVADA COMPREHENSIVE ANNUAL FINANCIAL REPORT for the Fiscal Year Ended June 30, 1984

Annual.   Mar. 19, 1985.
3+ix+195 p.
LC 10-33042.
SRI/MF/complete

Annual report on financial condition of Nevada State government, for FY84, presenting balance sheets; and statements of revenue by source, expenditures by function, and fund balances; for all, general, special revenue, debt service, capital projects, enterprise, internal service, trust, and agency funds.

Also includes data on general fixed assets; spending authority compared to actual expenditures, by dept; revenue collections by type and county; cash on deposit with State treasurer; finances of State-assisted postsecondary and correctional institutions; taxable gaming revenues; debt service obligations to 2009; socioeconomic indicators, including per capita income, population by county, employment, persons involved in work stoppages, and deposits in financial institutions; and selected trends from 1960.

Data are from records of the controller's office, and other State and Federal sources.

Contains contents listing (3 p.); letter of transmittal, with text tables and 4 charts (p. i-vii); auditors report and 37 financial exhibits, with accompanying notes (p. 1-181); and statistical section on financial and socioeconomic trends, with 12 tables (p. 184-195).

Availability: Nevada Office of the Controller, State Capitol Bldg., Carson City NV 89710, †; SRI/MF/complete.

S5035   NEVADA
Department of Education

S5035–1   BIENNIAL REPORT OF SELECTED DATA BY THE SUPERINTENDENT OF PUBLIC INSTRUCTION

Biennial, discontinued.

Biennial report on Nevada public education, discontinued with report for 1978/79-1979/80 academic years (for description, see SRI 1982 Annual under this number).

Report has been discontinued because publication is no longer required by law. Issuing agency publishes a report on enrollment, not covered in SRI.

S5040   NEVADA
Employment Security Department

S5040–1   ECONOMIC UPDATE, Nevada

Quarterly.   Approx. 15 p. no paging.
SRI/MF/complete

Quarterly report on Nevada labor market and related economic trends, including employment by industry, average hours and earnings, gaming revenues, and taxable sales, with detail for Las Vegas and Reno. Data are from employer reports and Federal sources. Report is issued approximately 6 weeks after quarter of coverage.

Contains narrative summary of economic changes during quarter of coverage; 1 or more feature articles, occasionally with statistics; and 9 quarterly tables.

Quarterly tables are listed below and appear in all issues. All additional features with substantial statistical content are described, as they appear, under "Statistical Features." Nonstatistical features are not covered.

A monthly summary and additional reports covering various State labor market areas are also published by issuing agency, but are not covered by SRI.

Availability: Nevada Employment Security Department, Employment Security Research Section, 500 E. Third St., Carson City NV 89713-0001, †; SRI/MF/complete.

Issues reviewed during 1985: 3rd Qtr. 1984-2nd Qtr. 1985 (D).

QUARTERLY TABLES:

[Most data are shown for Nevada, Las Vegas, and, except for tables [8-9], Reno. Tables show data for quarter of coverage, generally by month; tables [1-7] also include comparisons to same periods of previous year.]

[1] Economic indicators [unemployment rate, gross gaming revenues, and taxable sales; also includes U.S. unemployment rate and all-urban CPI].

[2-7] Labor force summary [by employment status, and persons involved in work stoppages]; and establishment-based industrial employment [by major industry group].

[8-9] Average hours and earnings in selected industries.

STATISTICAL FEATURES:

S5040–1.601: 3rd Qtr. 1984

1985 TAX RATES FOR UNEMPLOYMENT INSURANCE

(p. 4) By Tom Hills. Article, with 2 charts showing Nevada unemployment insurance taxable wage base, and average tax rate on taxable and total wages, 1976-85.

EMPLOYMENT GAINS FOLLOWING THE 1981-82 RECESSION IN NEVADA

(p. 6-8) By Kim Spielman. Article, with 2 tables showing Nevada employment by industry division and in selected service industry groups, Aug. 1981 and 1984; and average weekly hours worked, by industry division, before, during, and after the 1981-82 recession.

FIRMS AND WAGES IN NEVADA, 1982-83, ANNUAL FEATURE

(p. 10-11) Annual article, by Robert Murdock, with 1 table showing average number of business firms and average wage, by industry division and for hotels/gaming/recreation, for Nevada, Las Vegas SMSA, and Reno SMSA, 1982-83.

ANNUAL PAY LEVELS IN METROPOLITAN AREAS

(p. 12) By George Anastassatos. Article, with 1 table showing average annual pay for all metro areas, and for Las Vegas and Reno SMSAs, 1982-83, with national rankings for the SMSAs. Also includes text data on metro areas with the highest and lowest pay levels and greatest increases and decreases. Data are based on employer reports on workers covered by unemployment insurance.

RISING UNEMPLOYMENT RATES

(p. 17-20) By Jeffrey Milligan and Ken Sceirine. Article, with 2 tables showing Nevada and U.S. unemployment rates during peak and trough quarters of 4 business cycles, 1969-82; and selected trends in U.S. labor force composition, 1970-82 period.

S5040–1.602: 4th Qtr. 1984

EMPLOYMENT GROWTH IN THE LAUGHLIN GAMING INDUSTRY

(p. 8-9) By Kim Spielman. Article, with 2 tables showing gross gaming revenue (GGR) in Laughlin and Clark County, Nev., 1979-84; and GGR in Laughlin and Las Vegas as percents of total GGR in Clark County (no date).

NEVADA OCCUPATIONAL PROJECTIONS

(p. 11-12) By Jeffrey Milligan. Article, with 2 tables showing Nevada nonagricultural employment, by industry division and selected group, and by occupational group, 1983 and projected 1990. Data are from the State Employment Security Dept.

S5040–1.603: 1st Qtr. 1985

MEDIAN WEEKLY EARNINGS OF WORKERS AND THEIR FAMILIES

(p. 5) By George Anastassatos. Article, with 1 table showing U.S. median weekly earnings, for families by type, and for individuals by sex and race/ethnicity (white, black, and Hispanic), 1983-84. Data are from Labor Dept.

DATA REVISION, ANNUAL FEATURE

(p. 6-7) Annual article, by Ken Sceirine, with 2 tables presenting revised estimates of nonagricultural employment by industry division, 1982-84; and labor force by employment status, 1983-84; for Nevada, Las Vegas, and Reno. Data are from Nevada Employment Security Research Dept.

Previous article, for 1981-83, is described in SRI 1984 Annual under S5040-1.503.

GROWTH OF SMALL BUSINESS IN NEVADA

(p. 8-9) By Kim Spielman. Article, with 2 tables showing nonagricultural employment by firm size, for Nevada by industry division, and for Las Vegas, Reno, and balance of State, 1983-84.

NEVADA AFFIRMATIVE ACTION 1985

(p. 10) By Patty Brisbin. Article, with 1 table showing Nevada total and female population by race/ethnicity (white, black, Native American, Asian/Pacific Islander, Hispanic, and other), 1985. Data are from Nevada Employment Security Research Dept.

S5040–1.604: 2nd Qtr. 1985

PER CAPITA PERSONAL INCOME, ANNUAL FEATURE

(p. 4-5) Annual article, by Jeffrey Milligan, with 2 tables showing per capita personal income for total U.S., Far West region, and 4 western States, and by Nevada county, various years 1981-84. Data are from U.S. Commerce Dept.

HIGH TECHNOLOGY PROFILE

(p. 7-9) By George Anastassatos. Article, with 1 chart and 1 table showing Nevada high-technology employment by occupation, 1983 and 1990. Data are from Nevada Employment Security Research.

S5062   NEVADA
Gaming Control Board

S5062–1   NEVADA GAMING
ABSTRACT, 1984
Annual.   2 volumes.
For individual publication data,
see below.
LC 78-641572.
SRI/MF/complete

Annual report on Nevada casino finances and employment, FY84. Includes data on number of establishments; assets and liabilities; long-term debt; revenues, expenses by function, and employment, all by dept; gaming area square footage; financial and operating ratios; and gaming win and drop amounts, and average win per unit, by type of game. Data are shown by casino location and gaming revenue range, with selected detail for hotel/casino complexes and publicly owned casinos.

Also includes hotel/casino available and occupied rooms, by month.

Data are compiled by the Nevada State Gaming Control Board from casino financial reports.

Report is published in 2 parts, further described below.

Monthly Gross Gaming Revenue Report is also available from the issuing agency, but is not covered by SRI.

Availability: Nevada Gaming Control Board, Publications, 1150 E. William St., Carson City NV 89710, $10.00; SRI/MF/complete.

S5062–1.1: Main Report
[Annual. Jan. 1985. 134 p. var. paging. SRI/MF/complete.]

Presents data on finances and employment. Contains introduction, terminology, and contents listing (5 p.); and 3 separately paginated statistical sections, with table listing for each, and 10-11 basic tables repeated by casino location or type, and by gaming revenue range (129 p.).

S5062–1.2: Supplement
[Monograph. [1985.] 1+45 p. SRI/MF/complete.]

Presents data on revenues and average win per unit. Contains introduction (1 p.); contents

listing (p. 1.1); and 2 basic tables repeated by casino location or type, and by gaming revenue range (p. 1.2-1.45).

S5065   NEVADA
Office of the
Governor

S5065–1   NEVADA STATISTICAL
ABSTRACT, 1983-84 Edition
Biennial.   Oct. 1984.
16+282 p.
LC 78-648222.
SRI/MF/complete

Biennial compilation, for 1983/84, of detailed demographic, socioeconomic, and governmental statistics for Nevada. Data are primarily for 1970s-84, with population trends from 1860 and projections to 2000. Data are primarily from State and Federal sources.

Report is designed to present a comprehensive overview of the State. Extensive socioeconomic, demographic, and geographic breakdowns are shown, as applicable, for most topics. These breakdowns include data by city, county and Carson City, SMSA, urban-rural status, commodity, government agency, income, industry, occupation, age, educational attainment, marital status, race, and sex. Comparisons to total U.S., neighboring States, and western region are also occasionally included.

Contains map of Nevada counties and SMSAs, preface, and contents and table listings (16 p.); 213 tables arranged in 16 chapters, described below, each preceded by a brief introduction (p. 1-280); and appendix, with explanatory notes (p. 281).

For description of 1981-82 report, see SRI 1982 Annual under this number.

Availability: Nevada Office of the Governor, Community Services Office, Capitol Complex, Carson City NV 89710, $10.00; SRI/MF/complete.

CHAPTERS:
[Data sources appear beneath each table.]

S5065–1.1: Population

(p. 1-51) Contains 43 tables. Includes population since 1860 and projections to 2000; family and household characteristics; persons in group quarters; births, deaths, and net migration; land area; veterans; and Indian population and tribal affiliation, by reservation.

S5065–1.2: Health and Vital Statistics

(p. 52-67) Contains 13 tables. Includes births and deaths; death rates for 10 leading causes; marriages and divorces; hospital beds and utilization, by facility; and physicians, dentists, nurses, and pharmacists.

S5065–1.3: Housing and Construction

(p. 68-87) Contains 15 tables. Includes housing units, structural characteristics, occupancy, and value or rent; residential and nonresidential construction value; and building permits.

S5065–1.4: Education

(p. 88-101) Contains 12 tables. Includes public, private, and postsecondary schools; public school enrollment; vocational program enrollment and expenditures; teachers, nonteaching personnel, and average salaries; and University of Nevada System enrollment, revenues, expenditures, and faculty, by branch.

S5065–1.5: Employment and Earnings

(p. 102-126) Contains 17 tables. Includes labor force by employment status; average hours and earnings; covered employment and payrolls; unemployment insurance coverage, contributions, and benefit payments; Federal civilian employment; and business establishments.

S5065–1.6: Personal and Per Capita Income

(p. 127-135) Contains 8 tables. Includes total and per capita personal income; and personal income by source.

S5065–1.7: Poverty in Nevada

(p. 136-163) Contains 15 tables. Includes household, residence, employment, and educational characteristics of persons and families in poverty vs. total population.

S5065–1.8: Low Income Benefits

(p. 164-174) Contains 9 tables. Includes recipients and/or expenditures for food stamp, AFDC, medical, housing energy, and weatherization assistance programs.

S5065–1.9: Government and Taxes

(p. 175-194) Contains 17 tables. Includes Federal expenditures, with detail for direct payments to individuals, agency grants, and salaries/wages; State revenues by source, and appropriations and expenditures by function; State tax collections and allocations; gambling revenues and taxes; property assessed valuation; tax revenues; local government budgets; and Bureau of Land Management payments.

S5065–1.10: Tourism and Recreation

(p. 195-209) Contains 12 tables. Includes total and per capita gambling revenues; State park visitors, by park; hunting and fishing licenses issued; game harvest by species, and upland game and waterfowl hunters; licensed trappers, fur harvest by species, and value; boat registrations; museums; and public and academic library holdings, by library or school district.

S5065–1.11: Energy

(p. 210-226) Contains 12 tables. Includes electricity and natural gas consumption, by sector; per capita energy consumption; household fuel expenditures (average and as a percent of family income); average residential electricity and natural gas consumption, revenues, and bills, with detail for electric utilities; electric utility expenditures for R&D; and gasoline consumption.

S5065–1.12: Transportation and Communications

(p. 227-241) Contains 10 tables. Includes State highway expenditures; road/street mileage; motor vehicle registrations; active drivers licenses; traffic fatalities; air passenger and cargo traffic at 2 major airports; aircraft landing facilities and reported abandonments; and general aviation aircraft and airports.

Also includes radio and TV stations; and newspaper and periodical circulation, by publication.

S5065–1.13: Environment and Geography

(p. 242-254) Contains 10 tables. Includes Federal lands and withdrawals in lieu of tax payments; tax exempt public lands; county acreage on tax rolls; average temperatures, precipitation, and growing season; air pollution monitoring by site; and nuclear tests conducted.

S5065–1.14: Agriculture

(p. 255-264) Contains 6 tables. Includes farms, farmland, and property value; crop and irrigated acreage; crop and livestock market value and cash receipts; and gross income and production expenses.

S5065–1.15: Minerals

(p. 265-273) Contains 8 tables. Includes mineral production and value; oil/gas, geothermal, and mineral leases and acreage; oil production by field; oil/gas well completions and depth, by company; and Bureau of Land Management revenues from public lands.

S5065–1.16: Finance, Insurance, and Real Estate

(p. 274-280) Contains 6 tables. Includes banks, assets and liabilities, loans, and deposits; savings and loan assns, assets, savings, and mortgages; life insurance in force, value, and benefit payments; and business failures and liabilities.

S5095   NEVADA
State
Library

S5095–1   **NEVADA LIBRARY DIRECTORY AND STATISTICS, 1985**
Annual. [1985.] 96 p.
LC 77-644335.
SRI/MF/complete

Annual directory of public, academic, and special libraries in Nevada, with statistics on holdings, circulation, finances, and operations, FY84. Data are from reports of individual libraries to the State library.

Contains contents listing (p. 1); directories of libraries and personnel (p. 2-88); and statistical section, with 8 tables listed below (p. 89-96).

Availability: Nevada State Library, Library Development Division, Capitol Complex, Carson City NV 89710, $3.00; SRI/MF/complete.

TABLES:

[Data are for Nevada, FY84, unless otherwise noted.]

[1] Public library resources and support [population served, staff, expenditures, circulation, interlibrary loan activity, hours open, reference questions, and book collection size, all by library]. (p. 90-91)

[2] Tax-supported college and university libraries [same data as described in table [1]]. (p. 90-91)

[3] Public school library resources and support [enrollment, schools, staff, and volumes held, by school district]. (p. 92).

[4] State library statistics [including income, staff, holdings by type, and circulation; reference, archival, and other activities; and blind/handicapped talking book circulation and patrons]. (p. 93)

[5] Libraries statistical summary. (p. 94)

[6] Bookmobile circulation. (p. 94)

[7] Federal Library Services and Construction Act (LSCA) grants to Nevada [FY58-84]. (p. 95)

[8] General fund appropriations to operate the State library [FY61-85], and State aid to library development [FY74-85]. (p. 96)

S5125   NEVADA
Office of the
Secretary of
State

S5125–1   **STATE OF NEVADA 1984 GENERAL ELECTION**
Biennial. [1985.]
15 p. no paging. Oversized.
SRI/MF/complete

Biennial report presenting results of the Nevada 1984 general election. Includes voting for President/Vice President, U.S. Representatives, State senators and assembly members, judges, other State officials, and 12 referenda. Data are shown by county and/or district, and include party affiliation of most candidates.

Also includes voter registration and turnout, by county.

Previous report, covering 1982 general election, is described in SRI 1983 Annual under this number.

Availability: Nevada Office of the Secretary of State, Elections Division, Capitol Complex, Carson City NV 89710, †; SRI/MF/complete.

S5140   NEVADA
Department of
Transportation

S5140–1   **NEVADA TRAFFIC ACCIDENTS, 1983**
Annual. [1984.] 38 p.
LC 78-642127.
SRI/MF/complete

Annual report on Nevada traffic accidents, fatalities, and injuries, by accident and vehicle type, location, and other circumstances, 1983, with selected trends from 1974. Also includes data on vehicle miles traveled, by county; drivers involved in accidents, by age and sex; street location detail for fatal accidents in Reno, Las Vegas, and Clark County; and selected comparisons to U.S.

Report was compiled by Dept of Transportation in cooperation with State Dept of Motor Vehicles and Federal Highway Administration.

Contains contents listing (1 p.); and introduction, 7 maps, 25 charts, and 7 tables (p. 1-38).

Previous report, for 1982, is described in SRI 1983 Annual, under this number.

Availability: Nevada Department of Transportation, Safety Engineering Division, 1263 S. Stewart St., Carson City NV 89712, †; SRI/MF/complete.

S5175   NEW HAMPSHIRE
Department of
Administrative Services

S5175–1   **COMPREHENSIVE ANNUAL FINANCIAL REPORT for the Year Ended June 30, 1984, New Hampshire**
Annual. Dec. 12, 1984.
3+82 p.
SRI/MF/complete

Annual report on financial condition of New Hampshire State government, FY84, presenting assets and liabilities, revenues by source, expenditures by function or object, and fund balances, all by fund, with comparisons to FY83 and earlier.

Funds covered include general, special revenue, highway, fish/game, debt service, capital projects, enterprise, and trust/agency.

Also includes data on bonded indebtedness, and operations of Liquor, Sweepstakes, and Horse and Greyhound Racing Commissions.

Data are from the records of the comptroller's office.

Contains contents listing (3 p.); introduction with 2 charts and 1 summary table (p. 1-7); and report with 63 financial statements and accompanying notes (p. 12-82).

Issuing agency name has changed from New Hampshire Dept of Administration and Control, and title has changed from *Dept of Administration and Control, Annual Report.*

Availability: New Hampshire Department of Administrative Services, Accounting Services Division, State House Annex, Rm. 310, Concord NH 03301, †; SRI/MF/complete.

S5185   NEW HAMPSHIRE
Banking Department

S5185–1   **HUNDRED FORTIETH ANNUAL REPORT OF THE BANK COMMISSIONER of the State of New Hampshire, for the Year Ending Dec. 31, 1984**
Annual. 1984. 223 p.
LC 6-3171.
SRI/MF/complete

Annual report, for 1984, on financial condition of New Hampshire State-chartered financial institutions. Presents assets, liabilities, income, expenses, and other operating data, by institution arranged by city, for trust companies, mutual/guaranty savings banks, cooperative banks, credit unions, and the New Hampshire Business Development Corp., with composite data for 2nd mortgage and small loan licensees.

Also includes data on number of retail sellers and finance companies offering motor vehicle installment loans, and small loan licensee loan activities including legal actions.

Contains contents listing and index of institutions (p. 5-9); foreword, 1 table, and list of status changes (p. 10-15); and 11 sections, with regulatory and legislative information, directories, 6 charts, and 4-7 tables repeated for each type of institution (p. 19-223).

Availability: New Hampshire Banking Department, 97 N. Main St., Concord NH 03301, †; SRI/MF/complete.

S5200 NEW HAMPSHIRE Department of Education

S5200–1 EDUCATIONAL STATISTICS for New Hampshire
Annual series. For individual publication data, see below. SRI/MF/complete

Series of annual reports, each presenting data on an aspect of New Hampshire elementary and secondary education. Topics include public school and academy enrollment, finance, administration and staff, facilities, and programs. Some nonpublic school data are also included.

Data are compiled from individual school and school district reports to the New Hampshire Dept of Education, and other State and local agencies.

Series also includes an annual glossary of related terms.

Reports are described in order of receipt. Reports and annual glossary reviewed during 1985 are described below.

Prior to 1985, abstracts for these reports were grouped according to period of data coverage. For descriptions of reports covered in 1984, see SRI 1984 Annual under this number and under S5200-2 and S5200-3.

Availability: New Hampshire Department of Education, Computer and Statistical Services, 101 Pleasant St., Concord NH 03301-3860, †; SRI/MF/complete.

S5200–1.1: Distribution to School Districts from the Proceeds of the New Hampshire Sweepstakes, 1984/85
[Annual. Aug. 15, 1984. 7 p. SRI/MF/complete.]

Annual table showing State sweepstakes revenue distribution, 1984/85; and school average daily membership in residence, 1982/83; by school and district.

Previous report, issued in 1983, is described in SRI 1983 Annual under S5200-3.1.

S5200–1.2: Fall Enrollments in New Hampshire Public Schools and Approved Public Academies, Oct. 1, 1984
[Annual. Jan. 21, 1985. 4 p. SRI/MF/complete.]

Annual table showing fall 1984 enrollment by school district for elementary, middle/junior high, and high schools, with district and State totals.

S5200–1.3: Enrollments in Grades 9-12 in New Hampshire Approved Public Secondary Schools and Approved Public Academies, Oct. 1, 1984
[Annual. Jan. 9, 1984. 2 p. SRI/MF/complete.]

Annual table showing Oct. 1984 secondary school enrollment by individual school, arranged by size. Includes high school, separate grade 9, and total State enrollments.

S5200–1.4: Fall Enrollments, 1984/85, by School Administrative Unit
[Annual. Jan. 23, 1985. 6 p. SRI/MF/complete.]

Annual table showing fall 1984 enrollments by school administrative unit, for elementary, middle/junior high, and high schools, with State totals.

S5200–1.5: Teacher Salary Schedules 1984/85: New Hampshire School Districts
[Annual. Dec. 10, 1984 4 p. SRI/MF/complete.]

Annual table showing teacher salary rates by school district for the 1984/85 school year. Includes minimum and maximum rates, and number of salary steps between each, for teachers with bachelor's degrees, master's degrees, and additional credit hours.

S5200–1.6: Average Expenditures per Pupil for All Grades, 1983/84, New Hampshire
[Annual. Mar. 7, 1985. 3 p. SRI/MF/complete.]

Annual table showing average expenditures per pupil, by function, for elementary, middle/junior high, and high schools, and general expenses, 1983/84 school year.

S5200–1.7: Preliminary Costs per Pupil for Purposes of Tuition, 1984/85, New Hampshire
[Annual. Mar. 18, 1985. 5 p. SRI/MF/complete.]

Annual preliminary report on cost per pupil for school operations, 1984/85 school year. Costs are estimates based on previous year's spending, and exclude transportation, capital outlay, and debt obligations.

Includes 1 table showing per pupil cost by school district, for elementary, middle/junior high, and high schools.

S5200–1.8: Estimated Expenditures of School Districts, 1984/85, New Hampshire
[Annual. Feb. 28, 1985. 1 p. SRI/MF/complete.]

Annual table estimating school district expenditures, for 1984/85 school year. Includes total and per-pupil expenditures by purpose, and average daily membership, with selected detail for elementary, middle/junior high, and high schools.

S5200–1.9: Preliminary Expenditures of School Districts, 1983/84, New Hampshire
[Annual. Feb. 28, 1985. 1 p. SRI/MF/complete.]

Annual table presenting preliminary data on school district expenditures, for 1983/84

school year. Includes total and per-pupil expenditures by function, and average daily membership, with selected detail for elementary, middle/junior high, and high schools.

S5200–1.10: Total Net Revenue and Expenditures of School Districts, 1983/84, New Hampshire
[Annual. Mar. 7, 1985. 5 p. SRI/MF/complete.]

Two annual tables showing school district revenues by detailed source, including Federal, State, and local governments; and expenditures by function, for elementary, middle/junior high, and high schools, and general expenses; 1983/84 school year.

S5200–1.11: 1983/84 Average Daily Membership Based upon Attendance and Residence, New Hampshire
[Annual. Apr. 25, 1985. 8 p. SRI/MF/complete.]

Annual table showing average daily membership in attendance and residence, by school district, for elementary, middle/junior high, and high school, 1983/84 school year.

S5200–1.12: Valuations, Property Tax Assessments, and School Tax Rates of School Districts, 1983/84, New Hampshire
[Annual. May 1, 1985. 8 p. SRI/MF/complete.]

Annual table showing net assessed and equalized valuations, property tax assessments (total and for schools), and school tax and property tax rates, by school district, 1983/84 school year.

S5200–1.13: 1984 Equalized Valuation per Pupil, 1983/84, of New Hampshire School Districts
[Annual. [1985.] 8 p. SRI/MF/complete.]

Two annual tables showing 1984 equalized valuation by school district, based on 1983/84 enrollment, for districts organized for grades K-12 or 1-12 (table 1), and for districts with grade spans less than 1-12 (table 2).

Includes total and per pupil equalized valuation, and average daily membership. Proportional equalized valuation is shown for table 2.

S5200–1.14: Fact Sheet: Approved Elementary, Middle, Junior High, and High Schools (by District for School Year 1983/84), New Hampshire
[Annual. May 17, 1985. 15 p. SRI/MF/complete.]

Four annual tables showing summary enrollment and financial data, by school district, for elementary, middle, junior high, and high schools, 1983/84 school year. Covers fall enrollment, per pupil cost and assessed property value, property tax levy rates, and district ranks.

S5200–1.15: Glossary of Related Terms
[Annual. May 2, 1985. 2 p. SRI/MF/complete.]

Glossary of terms for *Educational Statistics for New Hampshire* series.

S5205   NEW HAMPSHIRE
Department of
Employment Security

S5205–1   ECONOMIC CONDITIONS in New Hampshire
Monthly.   Approx. 8 p.
LC 72-612932.
SRI/MF/complete, shipped quarterly

Monthly report on employment developments in New Hampshire, including unemployment rates, placements, unemployment insurance activities, and hours and earnings. Data are from local State employment offices, and cooperating employers. Report is issued 3-4 months after cover date.

Contains narrative analysis, 2 summary charts, and 8 monthly tables listed below; and occasional additional tables, usually showing summary, trend, or revised data for topics covered in monthly tables.

Most monthly tables appear in all issues. All other tables with substantial statistics for New Hampshire on topics not covered in monthly tables are described, as they appear, under "Statistical Features." Nonstatistical features are not covered.

Reports for local labor market areas are also available from the issuing agency, but are not covered in SRI.

Availability: New Hampshire Department of Employment Security, Economic Analysis and Reports Section, 32 S. Main St., Concord NH 03301-4857, †; SRI/MF/complete, shipped quarterly.

Issues reviewed during 1985: Aug. 1984-July 1985 (D) (1984 Nos. 8-12; 1985 Nos. 1-7).

MONTHLY TABLES:

[Tables show data for month of coverage, usually with comparison to preceding month and same month of previous year. Data are for New Hampshire, unless otherwise noted. Tables [1] and [6-7] also show data for Manchester and Nashua metro areas.]

[1] Labor force, total employment and unemployment [and persons involved in labor disputes], and nonagricultural wage/salary employment [by industry division and major manufacturing group], as of the middle of the month.

[2] Total unemployment and labor force by [labor market] area and county.

[3] U.S. CPI.

[4] Weekly [unemployment insurance initial and continuing] claims filed during [month of coverage], classified by local office.

[5] Unemployment compensation fund balance [at] end of month [and contributions received, benefits paid, and interest].

[6] Average earnings and hours of production workers in manufacturing industries [by major industry group].

[7] Number of [State employment service total] active applicants and female applicants, by major occupational category.

[8] Employment service activity [applicants, openings received and unfilled, and placements].

STATISTICAL FEATURES:

S5205–1.601: Aug. 1984 (No. 8)

AVERAGE WEEKLY WAGES BY COUNTY FOR THE YEAR 1983

(p. 5) Table showing New Hampshire average weekly manufacturing and nonmanufacturing wage, by county, 1983, with percent change from 1982. Data are based on employer reports filed under the State Unemployment Compensation Law.

S5205–1.602: Sept. 1984 (No. 9)

AVERAGE CONTRIBUTION RATE OF EMPLOYERS COVERED UNDER STATE UNEMPLOYMENT COMPENSATION LAWS, 1983

(p. 5) Chart showing average percent of payroll contributed by employers to unemployment insurance, by State, 1983. Data are from Dept of Labor.

S5205–1.603: Mar. 1985 (No. 3)

FIRMS BY SIZE: UNIT, EMPLOYEES, AND WAGES, AUG. 1984, ANNUAL FEATURE

(p. 5) Annual table showing number of industrial firms and employment, Aug. 1984; and wages, 3rd quarter 1984; all by employment size group. Data are based on State unemployment compensation coverage.

S5205–3   ANNUAL PLANNING INFORMATION, New Hampshire, FY86
Annual.   June 1985.
3+147 p.
LC 78-646549.
SRI/MF/complete

Annual planning report, for FY86, identifying New Hampshire population groups most in need of employment services, and presenting data on employment by industry and occupation through 1991. Also includes data on population and labor force by county, selected years 1980-86. Data are compiled from various State and Federal sources.

Contains 1 map and contents listing (2 p.); narrative analysis, with 11 summary tables (p. 1-14); glossary (p. 15-21); and appendix, with table listing, and 29 detailed tables listed below (p. 22-147).

Separate county reports are also available from issuing agency, but are not covered in SRI.

Availability: New Hampshire Department of Employment Security, Economic Analysis and Reports Section, 32 S. Main St., Concord NH 03301-4857, †; SRI/MF/complete.

APPENDIX TABLES:

[Unless otherwise noted, data are for New Hampshire, 1986 or FY86, and are shown by county. Data by industry are generally shown by major manufacturing industry group, non-manufacturing industry division, and government level.]

S5205–3.1: Population, Labor Force, Employment, Unemployment, and Personal Income

POPULATION

1. Population by sex and minority status [including black, American Indian, Asian, and Hispanic], July 1986. (p. 24)

2. Population estimates for youth [by age group], by sex, with percent distribution. (p. 25)

3-4. Population characteristics by age, sex, and racial status, 1980 and 1986; and population estimated by age, July 1986. (p. 26-38)

LABOR FORCE

5. Population, labor force, and labor force participation rate, by age and sex, 1980 and 1986. (p. 39-50)

UNEMPLOYMENT, EMPLOYMENT, AND WAGES

6. Total unemployment and labor force and percent of labor force unemployed, by sex. (p. 51)

7. Total number of different individuals unemployed during [the fiscal year] and the average number of long-term unemployed, by sex. (p. 52)

8. Nonagricultural wage/salary average annual employment (percentage distribution) by industrial division, New Hampshire and U.S. [only, 1981-84]. (p. 53)

9. Estimated nonagricultural employment in New Hampshire, and Manchester MSA and Nashua Primary MSA [only], 1984 preliminary (excluding the self-employed, domestic service workers, and persons on strike) [by industry, by month]. (p. 54-56)

10. Number of units, average employment, total wages, and percent changes (workers covered by unemployment compensation in private industry) [by industry], 1980-83. (p. 57-68)

11. Average employment, and total and average weekly wages, classified by industry, 3rd quarter 1984. (p. 69-93)

12-13. Employment changes and average weekly wages [and statewide changes in number of establishments], 3rd quarter 1984 and percent change from 1983. (p. 94-95)

DISADVANTAGED, VETERANS, AND JOB SERVICES

14. Nonagricultural employment, and employment part-time for economic reasons, [by sex]. (p. 96)

15. Estimated all poor persons, those 18 years old/over, [those 65 years/older], black, and Hispanic [no date]. (p. 97)

16-17. Cases receiving welfare assistance [AFDC, foster care children, persons age 65/older, and disabled/blind], 1984 and Jan. 1985. (p. 98-99)

18. Estimated civilian labor force status of [total and Vietnam era] veterans. (p. 100)

19. Placements as a percent of applicants available by selected applicant characteristics [female, eligible claimants, handicapped, minority, total and Vietnam era veterans, and age group], July 1, 1984- Apr. 30, 1985. (p. 101)

20. Active applicants [by sex and age group, and for veterans, minority, poor, and handicapped, all by occupational classification], as of Mar. 31, 1985. (p. 102-113)

INSURED UNEMPLOYED

21-22. Exhaustees: by weekly benefit amount [by sex], 1st quarter 1985. (p. 114-126)

23-25. Insured unemployed [by industry division, occupation, weeks of current unemployment, sex, and age, with selected cross-tabulations, shown for State, Hillsborough County, and balance of State only], Apr. 1985. (p. 127-129)

PERSONAL INCOME

26. Total and per capita personal income for the U.S. and [6] States in New England, 1981-83. (p. 130)

27. Percent change of personal income by major industrial division in the U.S. and [6] New England States, 1982-83. (p. 131)

PROJECTED EMPLOYMENT

28. Occupations projected to 1991 [employment 1981, 1986, and 1991; and average annual job openings due to growth and replacement needs, and annual growth rate, 1981-91 period; all by detailed occupation, State only]. (p. 132-146)

29. Occupations with the largest number of employees, 1986, and with the largest percentage employment increase, 1981-86 [State only]. (p. 147)

S5205–4   LABOR MARKET INFORMATION ABOUT YOUTH in New Hampshire
Recurring (irreg.), discontinued.

Recurring report on New Hampshire youth employment and unemployment, discontinued with 1981 report (for description, see SRI 1982 Annual, under this number). Report has been discontinued due to funding constraints.

Data on New Hampshire employment and unemployment, by age, are available in *Annual Planning Information, New Hampshire,* covered in SRI under S5205-3.

S5205–5   COMMUTING PATTERNS, NEW HAMPSHIRE, 1980
U.S. Census
Monograph.   Feb. 1985.
ii+85 p.
SRI/MF/complete

Report presenting 1980 census data on commuting patterns in New Hampshire, covering points of origin and destination for New Hampshire residents and for nonresidents employed in the State. Data are arranged by New Hampshire labor market area (LMA) and MSA and are cross-tabulated among cities of New Hampshire and locations in neighboring States.

Data are based on information gathered from 388,021 workers in the 1980 census.

Contains preface and contents listing (p. i-ii); analysis and highlights, with 1 summary table (p. 1-4); and 3 tables, with accompanying narrative and map, repeated for each LMA and MSA (p. 5-85).

Availability: New Hampshire Department of Employment Security, Economic Analysis and Reports Section, 32 S. Main St., Concord NH 03301-4857, †; SRI/MF/complete

S5227   NEW HAMPSHIRE State Library

S5227–1   NEW HAMPSHIRE LIBRARY STATISTICS, Jan.-Dec. 1983
Annual.   [1984.]
24 p. no paging.
LC 64-63685.
SRI/MF/complete

Annual report, for 1983, on New Hampshire public, college, and State libraries, including finances and holdings, by city and institution.

Contents:

a. Summary statistics, with 3 tables showing holdings, circulation, and expenditures, by type of library, 1982-83. (2 p.)

b. Public library statistics, with 1 detailed table showing the following, by city and library, arranged by population size group: population served; circulation, by type of material; books borrowed from other libraries; weekly hours open; total volumes, and print and nonprint volumes added; city appropriations and total receipts; and expenditures including detail for salaries and books; 1983. (18 p.)

c. College and State library statistics, with 1 table showing the following: total operating expenditures, salaries/wages, and expenditures for books/binding; and volumes added, periodicals received, and total volumes; by college (also shows enrollment), fall 1983, and for State library, FY84. (2 p.)

d. List of towns with no/inactive public library, and population. (1 p.)

Availability: New Hampshire State Library, 20 Park St., Concord NH 03301, $2.00; SRI/MF/complete.

S5255   NEW HAMPSHIRE Department of State

S5255–1   STATE OF NEW HAMPSHIRE MANUAL FOR THE GENERAL COURT, 1985
Biennial.   1985.   604 p.
Rpt. No. 49.
ISSN 0196-4585.
LC SN 79-19165.
SRI/MF/complete

Biennial report presenting results of the New Hampshire presidential primary held Feb. 28, 1984; direct primary held Sept. 11, 1984; and general election held Nov. 6, 1984. Shows voting results for President, including primary recount results; U.S. and State senators and representatives; Governor; various State and county offices; State constitutional convention delegates; and 13 State constitutional amendments.

Also includes voter turnout trends from 1910, by party; and political affiliation of candidates.

Most data are shown by county or district, city, and ward.

Also presents summary data on State forest acreage and other geographic features, and on selected State socioeconomic indicators, including employment of 30 largest employers; employment by major industry; new corporate

formations, by type; and assessed property value and tax rates, median family income, and population, all by town and county; various years 1970-84.

Contains contents listing (1 p.); summary State data section, with 7 tables (p. 1-14); lists of State officials from 1680 (p. 15-42); 1 population table, and list of election districts accompanied by 3 maps (p. 43-52 and 3 p.); tabular presentation of election results (p. 54-483); directory of 1985-86 State government officials (p. 485-598); and index (p. 599-604).

For description of previous report, covering 1982 elections, see SRI 1983 Annual under this number.

Availability: New Hampshire Department of State, Secretary of State, State House, Rm. 204, Concord NH 03301, $4.00; SRI/MF/complete.

S5350   NEW JERSEY Department of Agriculture

S5350–1   NEW JERSEY AGRICULTURE, 1984
Annual.   Oct. 1984.   v+68 p.
Circular 507.
LC 58-63411.
SRI/MF/complete

Annual report on New Jersey agricultural production, finances, and marketing, mostly 1978-83, with some data for 1984 and selected trends from 1967. Data generally are shown by commodity and/or county, with selected comparisons to U.S.

Covers production, value, prices, and, as applicable, acreage, yield, and stocks or inventory, for field crop, vegetable, fruit and berry, livestock, dairy, and poultry sectors.

Also includes data on weather; pasture condition; farm income and production expenses; farms; farm acreage and value; value of exports; fertilizer consumption; U.S. potato production and consumption per capita; and farm expenditures for northeast U.S.

Data are primarily from New Jersey Dept of Agriculture and USDA.

Contains contents listing (p. iv-v); 7 statistical sections, with 11 maps, 13 charts, and 63 tables (p. 1-52); list of issuing agency reports (p. 53); and narrative "Highlights of the Annual Report" (p. 54-68).

Availability: New Jersey Crop Reporting Service, Health and Agriculture Bldg., Rm. 204, CN 330, Trenton NJ 08625-0330, $5.00; SRI/MF/complete.

S5355   NEW JERSEY
Department of Banking

S5355–1   STATE OF NEW JERSEY, COMMISSIONER OF BANKING, Annual Report, 1984
Annual.   July 1, 1985.
xiv + 188 p.
ISSN 0098-8073.
LC 76-644048.
SRI/MF/complete

Annual report on assets and liabilities of New Jersey State-chartered commercial and savings banks, credit unions, insurance premium finance companies, pawnbrokers, secondary mortgage and small loan companies, and savings and loan assns, by institution, as of Dec. 31, 1984.

Also includes data on national bank assets and liabilities; other licensed financial institutions by type; savings and loan assn aggregate membership, deposits, and loan closings by type, by county; asset and deposit rankings for savings and loan assns; consumer complaints by nature and type of institution; State cemetery board trust fund balances, and licensed cemeteries by county; and selected summary trends from 1900.

Contains contents listing and Banking Dept activities, including organizational chart (p. iv-xiv); division reports, with text statistics and 40 tables (p. 1-183); and amendments to State financial statutes (p. 186-188).

Availability: New Jersey Department of Banking, Savings and Loan Associations Division, CN 040, Trenton NJ 08625, $10.00; SRI/MF/complete.

S5360   NEW JERSEY
Casino Control Commission

S5360–1   NEW JERSEY CASINO CONTROL COMMISSION ANNUAL REPORT, Dec. 31, 1984
Annual.   [1985.]   29 p.
LC 80-648401.
SRI/MF/complete, current & previous year reports

Annual report on New Jersey casino industry revenues and operations, and State Casino Control Commission regulatory activities and finances, 1984, with comparisons to 1983.

Includes the following for 10 casino/hotels: revenue, revenue adjusted for uncollectibles, and tax; number of games and devices, by type; square footage of casino and convention space; number of hotel rooms, parking spaces, theater seats, and restaurants; fixed asset investment; and employment.

Also includes data on casino/hotel female and minority employment, by occupation; commission licensing activities; number of registered casino industry labor organizations; revenues by type of game and device; casino revenue fund disbursements; Atlantic City visitors by travel mode, gaming revenues, and convention revenues and attendance; casino control fund balance sheet and detailed revenues and expenditures; and selected comparisons to Las Vegas, Nev.

Contains contents listing and summary of commission activities, with 1 chart and 1 table (p. 1-8); 11 charts and 6 tables (p. 10-17); State auditor's report with 5 financial statements and accompanying notes (p. 20-26); and commission staff (p. 28-29).

Previous report, for 1983, was also reviewed in SRI during 1985, and is also available on SRI microfiche under S5360-1 [Annual. [1984.] 28 p. †]. Previous report is substantially similar in content and format, but shows data for 9 facilities, includes comparisons to total Nevada rather than Las Vegas, and omits data on female and minority employment, and convention revenues and attendance. SRI coverage begins with the 1983 report.

Availability: New Jersey Casino Control Commission, 3131 Princeton Pike, Bldg. No. 5, CN 208, Trenton NJ 08625, †; SRI/MF/complete.

S5362   NEW JERSEY
Department of Commerce and Economic Development

S5362–1   NEW JERSEY PROFILE, 1984
Biennial.   May 24, 1984.
12 + 180 p.
LC 85-622817.
SRI/MF/complete

Biennial compilation, for 1984, of social, governmental, and economic statistics for New Jersey. Data are shown primarily for 1970s-83.

Report is designed to present a comprehensive overview of the State. Socioeconomic, demographic, and geographic breakdowns are shown, as applicable, for many topics. These breakdowns include data by city, county, commodity, industry, educational attainment, race, and sex. Comparisons to total U.S., New England and South Atlantic regions, and neighboring States are also often included.

Most data are from Federal and State agencies. Data sources appear beneath each table.

Contains preface, and listings of contents, tables, and charts (10 p.); introduction (p. 1-2); and 11 sections, with 87 charts and 98 tables, described below (p. 5-180).

This is the 2nd edition of the report; SRI coverage begins with this edition.

Availability: New Jersey Office of Economic Policy, 1 W. State St., Trenton NJ 08625-0823, †; SRI/MF/complete.

S5362–1.1: Population

(p. 13-32) Contains 13 charts and 8 tables. Includes population and density, births, birth and mortality rates, deaths by leading cause, infant deaths, and migration.

S5362–1.2: Employment and Income

(p. 35-65) Contains 18 charts and 12 tables. Includes employment, unemployment rates, total and per capita personal income, median family income, and families and persons below poverty level.

S5362–1.3: Agriculture and Natural Resources

(p. 69-83) Contains 7 charts and 15 tables. Includes farms and farmland; total, cropland, and woodland acreage; cash receipts from crop and livestock marketings; land area and coastline; commercial fishing catch and value; fishing industry plants and employment; forest acreage; commercial timber land and production; State park/recreation area acreage and visitors; and mineral production and value.

S5362–1.4: Construction and Manufacturing

(p. 87-104) Contains 13 charts and 10 tables. Includes construction establishments, employment, receipts, and insured unemployment; housing stock and average construction cost; manufacturing employment, value added, and value of shipments; and manufacturing exports.

S5362–1.5: Transportation, Communication, and Public Utilities

(p. 107-121) Contains 9 charts and 17 tables. Includes employment in transportation, communication, and public utilities; transportation share of State budget; road mileage and vehicle miles traveled; licensed drivers; motor vehicle registrations; gasoline tax rate; highway tolls and total collections; and traffic accident fatalities.

Also includes public transit trips and mileage; freight transportation; railroad mileage; telephone lines and service; natural gas and electric customers; energy consumption by end-use sector; electric power production, capacity, sales, and fuel use; and natural gas sales and prices.

S5362–1.6: Trade and Services; and Finance, Insurance, and Real Estate

(p. 125-145) Contains 12 charts and 14 tables. Includes wholesale/retail trade employment; retail sales; wholesale trade establishments, receipts, and sales; and service industry employment.

Also includes finance/insurance/real estate employment growth; financial institutions and assets, by type of institution; commercial bank deposits; insurance companies, by type of business; life insurance policies and value; and real estate sales, and aggregate selling prices.

S5362–1.7: Education and Culture

(p. 149-166) Contains 9 charts and 13 tables. Includes educational attainment of population age 25/over; illiteracy rate; elementary/secondary enrollment, with private school share; teachers by highest degree held; student/teacher ratios; expenditures for public education, and school revenues; per pupil property valuation; and dropouts as a percent of enrollment.

Also includes freshmen attending college in and out of State; and higher education enrollment, degrees awarded, and revenues from State/local governments.

S5362–1.8: Government

(p. 169-180) Contains 6 charts and 9 tables. Includes State/local government employment, expenditures by function, taxes, and revenues by source; local governments and revenues; and Federal income tax burden.

S5370   NEW JERSEY
Department of Corrections

S5370–1   OFFENDERS IN NEW JERSEY CORRECTIONAL INSTITUTIONS ON JUNE 8, 1983, by Selected Characteristics: Annual Report
Annual.   Jan. 15, 1984.
iii+37 p.
SRI/MF/complete

Annual report on New Jersey correctional institution population, as of June 8, 1983. Presents number of inmates by commitment offense category, length of sentence, ethnic identification (white, black, Hispanic, and other), age group, and county of commitment, all by type of institution and individual facility.

Data were compiled from reports submitted by correctional facilities.

Contains introduction, highlights, and contents listing (p. i-iii); summary table (p. 1); 5 charts and 4 tables repeated for each of the 5 data categories, interspersed with narrative summaries (p. 2-36); and list of county abbreviations (p. 37).

SRI coverage begins with this edition.

Issuing agency also publishes a report on prison parolee population, not covered in SRI.

Availability: New Jersey Department of Corrections, Correctional Information and Classification Services Bureau, Whittlesey Rd., PO Box 7387, Trenton NJ 08628, †; SRI/MF/complete.

S5375   NEW JERSEY
Administrative Office of the Courts

S5375–1   1984 ANNUAL REPORT, NEW JERSEY JUDICIARY, July 1, 1983-June 30, 1984
Annual.   [1985.]   122 p.
LC 81-643674.
SRI/MF/complete

Annual report, for court year ended June 30, 1984, on New Jersey judicial system, including trial and appellate court caseloads and case dispositions. Covers supreme, superior, vicinage (district), tax, and municipal courts. Includes trial court data by case type and county, with selected trends from 1973.

Case types shown are criminal and civil for all courts except tax courts, with some additional detail for traffic, juvenile, small claims, and domestic violence cases.

Also includes data on judges and work hours; criminal trial length, conviction rates, and sentencing; value of tax assessments contested; and probation dept activities.

Contains contents listing (1 p.); and report, with 44 charts and 70 tables (p. 3-122).

Availability: New Jersey Administrative Office of the Courts, State House Annex, CN 037, Trenton NJ 08625, †; SRI/MF/complete.

S5385   NEW JERSEY
Department of Education

S5385–1   VITAL EDUCATIONAL STATISTICS, 1983/84, New Jersey
Annual.   2 volumes.
For individual publication data, see below.
LC 79-644249.
SRI/MF/complete

Annual report on New Jersey elementary and secondary education for the 1983/84 school year, with summary trends from 1979/80. Covers public school students, staff, and facilities, by county. Data are compiled from reports of individual school districts.

Report is published in 2 volumes, described below.

This is the 10th edition of the report. Issuing agency also publishes an additional annual report with detailed breakdowns on enrollments and dropouts by race/ethnicity, sex, county, and district; report is not covered by SRI.

Availability: New Jersey Department of Education, Information Services and Support Office, 225 W. State St., CN 500, Trenton NJ 08625, †; SRI/MF/complete.

VOLUME:
[Most tables show data for public schools by county, as of Sept. 30, 1983. Data by racial/ethnic origin are usually for black, white, Hispanic, American Indian/Alaskan Native, and Asian/Pacific Islander.]

S5385–1.1: Volume I
[Annual. May 1984. vi+36 p.
PTM No. 400.09. SRI/MF/complete.]

Contains contents and table listing (p. v-vi); introduction, with 1 table showing selected trends, 1979/80-1983/84 (p. 1-2); 3 sections with summary analyses and 15 tables listed below (p. 3-25); and glossary, and appendix with sample data collection forms (p. 26-32, and 4 p.).

TABLES:

DISTRICTS AND SCHOOLS

I. Operating and nonoperating school districts. (p. 5)

II. Universe of State, county, and local educational school systems (operational). (p. 6)

III. School districts by enrollment size. (p. 7)

IV. Schools by type of school [elementary, secondary including vocational, and schools for handicapped]. (p. 8)

STUDENTS
[Data by grade include special education, ungraded, and, as appropriate, postgraduates.]

V-VII. Elementary and secondary school enrollments in school districts, by grade. (p. 13-15)

VIII. Students enrolled by racial/ethnic origin. (p. 16)

IX-XI. Summary of known and unknown dropout reasons; and student dropouts, by grade, sex, and racial/ethnic origin; Sept. 1982-Aug. 1983 [period]. (p. 17-19)

XII. Status of 1983 high school graduates during the fall of 1983 [continuing education, employed, and other]. (p. 20)

XIII-XIV. High school graduates by racial/ethnic origin, Sept. 1, 1982-Aug. 31, 1983 [period]; and racial/ethnic distribution of high school graduates (1983) continuing education at a college/university, [and total] by location [in-State, out-of-State]. (p. 21-22)

FACILITIES

XV. Estimated cost [and number] of school district capital improvement projects, Sept. 30, 1983; and [number for which] bids will be received [1983/84-1986/87]. (p. 25)

S5385–1.2: Volume II
[Annual. Dec. 1984. vi+41 p. PTM No. 400.50. SRI/MF/complete.]

Contains contents and table listing (p. v-vi); introduction with 2 tables showing trends in staff characteristics, 1979/80-1983/84 (p. 1-3); 2 sections, with summary analysis and 23 tables listed below (p. 5-35); and glossary and appendix, with sample data collection forms (p. 36-41).

TABLES:

CERTIFICATED STAFF
[Data by major assignment category are for administrators/supervisors, classroom teachers, and educational support services.]

I. Full-time and part-time staff employed by major assignment category. (p. 11)

II-IV. Full-time and part-time certificated staff assigned to elementary school, secondary school, and system-wide positions, by type of position; and to elementary and secondary schools, by major position assignment category. (p. 12-14)

V-VII. Sex, highest degree held, and certificate held by administrators/supervisors, classroom teachers, and educational support services personnel employed. (p. 15-17)

VIII-X. Racial/ethnic distribution of full-time administrators/supervisors, classroom teachers, and educational support services personnel employed in school districts. (p. 18-20)

XI-XVI. Age distribution and total educational experience of administrators/supervisors, classroom teachers, and educational support services personnel in school districts. (p. 21-26)

XVII. Certificated personnel entering and leaving, by [major assignment category] during the period Oct. 1, 1982-Sept. 30, 1983. (p. 27)

XVIII-XX. Number of full-time classroom teachers employed, beginning and reentering, and separations, by position (subject). (p. 28-30)

NONCERTIFICATED STAFF

XXI. FTE assignments of full-time noncertificated personnel employed, by support service program areas. (p. 33)

XXII. Racial/ethnic distribution and sex of full-time noncertificated support services personnel. (p. 34)

XXIII. FTE assignments of all noncertificated personnel employed, by support service program areas. (p. 35)

S5385–2   NEW JERSEY PUBLIC LIBRARY STATISTICS for 1983
Annual. Oct. 1984. 41 p.
LC 73-647717.
SRI/MF/complete

Annual report on New Jersey public library operations, 1983. Covers population served, finances, holdings, staff, and circulation, by county and library. Data are from annual library reports.

Contains contents listing (1 p.); introduction and definitions (p. 1-4); 8 tables, described below (p. 5-39); and staff directories (p. 40 and inside back cover).

Availability: New Jersey Department of Education, State Library Division, 185 W. State St., CN 520, Trenton NJ 08625-0520, †; SRI/MF/complete.

TABLES:
a. Per capita library expenditures, by county, 1983, with county rankings from 1977; and selected State summary data. 6 tables. (p. 5-11)

b. By county and institution: population served; equalized property valuation; income (total, and from local taxes and State aid); expenditures (total, and for salary/wage/benefits and materials); staff; volumes owned and added; circulation; periodical subscriptions; and weekly hours open; 1983. 2 tables. (p. 13-39)

S5405   NEW JERSEY Department of Health

S5405–1   NEW JERSEY HEALTH STATISTICS, 1982
Annual. [1984.]
295 p. looseleaf, var. paging.
LC A65-7393.
SRI/MF/complete

Annual report on New Jersey vital statistics, covering population, births, deaths by cause, marriages and divorces, abortions, and communicable diseases, 1982 with selected trends from 1940. Includes data by location, race, age, and sex. Data are from State records and 1980 Census of Population and Housing.

Contents:

Table of contents and introduction. (p. i-iv)

Section I. Statistical report arranged in 10 chapters, with table listings, narrative summaries, text data, and 92 tables listed below. (p. A1-K14)

Section II. Technical notes, with methodology and definitions. (p. II1-II26)

An additional Section I chapter (on morbidity) and 2 additional sections (related reports and index) are listed in the table of contents but have not yet been published. These portions of the report will be published as supplements, and will be covered in SRI when they are received.

Previous report, for 1981, is described in SRI 1983 Annual under S5405-2.

Availability: New Jersey Department of Health, Health Statistics Center, Rm. 405, CN 360, Trenton NJ 08625, †; SRI/MF/complete.

TABLES:
[Tables show data for New Jersey, 1982, unless otherwise noted. Tables frequently include data on rates. Data by county generally include totals for State institutions and military posts.]

S5405–1.1: Highlights and Historical Trends

HIGHLIGHTS
[Tables 1-10 and 12 show data by county and selected municipality. Data for marriages are shown for place of occurrence. Tables 1-4, 6-11, and 13 begin 'Resident...']

1. Births, marriages, and deaths. (p. A7)

2-4. Births by sex, race, legitimacy, maturity [birth weight], and age of mother. (p. A8-10)

5. Marriages by sex, previous marital status, and average age. (p. A11)

6-7. Deaths by sex and race; and infant fetal, neonatal, and perinatal deaths. (p. A12-A13)

8-9. Deaths by suicide and homicide; and from heart diseases, cancer, all accidents, and diabetes. (p. A14-A15)

10-11. Deaths from cerebrovascular diseases by sex and age; and deaths by age [ranked by principal cause]. (p. A16-A18)

12. Tuberculosis, morbidity, and mortality. (p. A19)

13-14. Cases of syphilis and gonorrhea [with detail for civilian cases by age and sex, and additional detail for syphilis by stage]. (p. A20-A21)

15. Notifiable diseases by county of residence. (p. A22)

HISTORICAL PERSPECTIVES
1-3. Vital statistics of the U.S. [major events summary], 1974-82; and average length of life in years, by race and sex, [selected years] 1950-82. (p. B7-B8)

4-6. Vital statistics summary [major events and fertility rates; detailed] mortality statistics; [and other] vital statistics [including tuberculosis and venereal disease cases; decennially 1940-70 and annually 1971-82]. (p. B9-B11)

7. U.S. and New Jersey selected causes of death. (p. B12)

8. Principal causes of death, [decennially 1940-70 and annually 1971-82]. (p. B13-B14)

S5405–1.2: Natality
[All table titles begin "Resident births..."]

1. By race and legitimacy, 1968-82. (p. C10)

2-6. By sex, legitimacy, month of pregnancy prenatal care began, birth weight groups, and Apgar score [at] 5 minutes; [all by age of mother and race]. (p. C11-C15)

7-10. By birth weight and Apgar score [at] 5 minutes: by [age of mother, race, month of pregnancy prenatal care began], and previous number of pregnancy terminations. (p. C16-C19)

11. By age of mother and previous number of live births. (p. C20)

12-20. By race, sex, legitimacy, age of mother, month of pregnancy prenatal care began, birth weight groups, Apgar score, attendant [including midwife], month, and plurality; [all by county, with various cross-tabulations]. (p. C21-C29)

21. [By] sex, race, and legitimacy, by place of residence [municipality arranged by county]. (p. C30-C49)

S5405–1.3: Mortality
[Table titles 2-12 begin "Resident deaths..." Tables 5-10 show deaths by county.]

1. Mortality by race, sex, and age, 1968-82. (p. D12)

2. By cause group and age; by race and sex. (p. D13-D22)

3-4. Malignant neoplasms: by age group, race, and sex. (p. D23-D24)

5. By cause. (p. D25-D30)

6. By month. (p. D31)

7-9. By age: by sex and race. (p. D32-D38)

10. Maternal, infant, perinatal, neonatal, and fetal totals and by race. (p. D39-D42)

11-12. By place of residence [counties, municipalities, and individual State institutions and military posts]: by age group, sex, and race. (p. D43-D84)

S5405–1.4: Marriages and Divorces

1. Estimated average age at marriage, and previous marital status [by sex], 1968-82. (p. E8)

2. Marriages by sex, previous marital status, and average age; [by county of occurrence]. (p. E9)

3-6. Marriages: by previous marital status, age, and age at 1st marriage; [all shown for husband and wife]. (p. E10-E13)

7. Divorces [including annulments], by county of origin, 1966-82. (p. E14)

S5405–1.5: Municipality Gross Summary

[A-B] Estimated population, marriages, births, deaths, infant deaths, fetal deaths, and neonatal deaths [all by county and municipality of occurence (marriages) or residence (all other data)]. (p. F4-F28)

S5405–1.6: Fertility and Abortions

FERTILITY
[1-2] U.S. and New Jersey births and fertility rate, [various years] 1960-82. (p. G8-G9)

3-5. Births, female population, and age-specific fertility rates; [all by age, for women aged 15-44, selected years] 1950-82. (p. G10)

ABORTIONS
[Tables 2-8 begin "Abortions..."]

1. Characteristics of women receiving abortions [residence, age, race, marital status, previous births and abortions, type of procedure and facility (hospitals or clinics), and weeks gestation]. (p. H8-H9)

2-3. By county of residence, race, and age; and percent distribution by age, race, marital status, gestation, and type of facility. (p. H10-H11)

4-5. By age, race, primary procedure, and length of gestation; and percent distribution by race, marital status, and age. (p. H12-H13)

6. By age, race, marital status, and prior abortions. (p. H14)

7-8. By prior number of abortions and live births; and by prior number of live births, by race and marital status. (H15-H16)

S5405–1.7: Accidental Deaths and Population

ACCIDENTAL DEATHS

1-3. Accidental deaths by type classification in any location or specific setting; [and by detailed setting, with work accidents by industry division; various years] 1970-82. (p. J7-J9)

4-7. Motor vehicle, in the home, public non-motor vehicle, and at-work deaths, 1981-82. (p. J10-J11)

8-9. Accidental deaths by occurrence [type and distribution by age group], 1981-82. (p. J12-J13)

POPULATION

1. Population by age and sex, [for] U.S., New Jersey, New York, and Pennsylvania, Apr. 1, 1980. (p. K10)

2-3. Population by county, sex, race, and age, Apr. 1, 1980. (p. K11-K12)

4. Components of change in resident population, by county [including natural increment and net migration], [selected periods] Apr. 1, 1980 to July 1, 1982. (p. K13)

5. Population estimates for counties and selected [municipalities], July 1, 1982. (p. K14)

S5415   NEW JERSEY
Department of Human Services

S5415–1   **PUBLIC WELFARE STATISTICS, New Jersey**
Monthly, with annual summary. 20 p. var. paging.
SRI/MF/complete, shipped quarterly

Monthly report, with annual summary, on New Jersey public welfare programs, including cases, recipients, payments, and case processing, by program and county or municipality. Covers AFDC, general assistance, State medical assistance for the aged, food stamps, emergency assistance, and child support and paternity programs.

Report is issued 5-12 months after cover date.

Issues generally contain contents listing, 18 monthly tables, and brief narrative with text statistics on State medical assistance for the aged.

Monthly tables are listed below and generally appear in all issues; occasionally selected data are unavailable at time of publication, and affected tables are issued as addenda at a later date. Annual summary is described, as it appears, under "Statistical Feature."

Availability: New Jersey Department of Human Services, Public Welfare Division, Six Quakerbridge Plaza, CN 716, Trenton NJ 08625, †; SRI/MF/complete, shipped quarterly.

Issues reviewed during 1985: Dec. 1984-Apr. 1985 (D).

MONTHLY TABLES:

[Tables [1-3] show data for month of coverage, previous month, and same month of previous year; other tables generally show data for month of coverage only. All tables except tables [1-3] and II.D-II.F show data by county. Table order may vary.]

SUMMARY

[1-3] Public assistance, AFDC, and general assistance programs [including applications processed, cases closed, recipient cases and persons, and expenditures].

AFDC

[Tables show total cases; adults, children, and total persons; and payments.]

I.A-I.D. AFDC program, statistical summary: all segments [also includes applications processed and cases closed]; and C, F, and N segments.

ASSISTANCE AND FOOD STAMP PROGRAMS

II.A-II.F. Statistical summary for general assistance program, [total and] employable and unemployable segments: [by county and] for 21 municipalities; [variously showing applications processed; cases approved, closed, and aided; and persons aided and assistance commitments, with detail for maintenance and hospital assistance].

III.A-III.B. Food stamp program: participating households; and persons participating, coupons issued, and average coupon value per person participating.

IV. Statistical summary for emergency assistance program [federally and nonfederally matchable and total cases, persons, and expenditures].

CHILD SUPPORT COLLECTION ACTIVITY

V-V.A. Child support and paternity account [collections by category (from reporting county, other counties, and other States), and distribution by purpose (incentive payments and refunds to assistance account), shown for total and tax offset (refund withholding) activity; table V.A (on tax offset activity) begins in the Nov. 1984 issue].

STATISTICAL FEATURE:

S5415–1.601: Sept. 1984

ANNUAL REPORT, FY84

(10 p.) Annual report, for FY84, summarizing New Jersey welfare program finances and caseloads, with comparative data for FY82-83. Includes 5 exhibits showing the following:

1. Selected statistics, public assistance programs [gross expenditures; and average monthly cases, recipients, and grants per case and recipient; for assistance to SSI recipients (with detail by program), emergency assistance, 3 AFDC program segments, public and nonpublic assistance food stamps, general assistance, Cuban/Haitian entrant program, refugee resettlement, and home energy assistance], FY82-84.

2. Statistical summary: "Medicaid only" assistance to aged, blind, and disabled; AFDC; "Medicaid only" institutional program; and [State] medical assistance for the aged; [application and caseload activity, and expenditures], FY84.

3. Summary of financial transactions [Federal, State, and county share of net assistance, social services, and administrative expenditures, and of reimbursements, for most programs listed in exhibit 1], FY84.

4. General assistance program statistical and financial summary [caseload activity, average monthly grants, and municipal and State shares of assistance and administrative expenditures], FY84.

5. Child support and paternity program, AFDC: comparison of collections, distribution, and administrative expenditures, FY82-84.

S5420   NEW JERSEY
Department of Insurance

S5420–1   **STATE OF NEW JERSEY, ANNUAL REPORT OF THE COMMISSIONER OF INSURANCE for the Year Ending Dec. 31, 1983**
Annual. Mar. 1, 1984.
197 p.
LC 73-640312.
SRI/MF/complete

Annual report on New Jersey insurance industry financial condition and underwriting activity, by company and type of insurance, 1983, with summary comparisons to 1982.

Covers premiums written, received, or earned; losses incurred; assets and liabilities; capital and/or surplus; gain from underwriting and investments; loss and underwriting expense ratios; insurance in force; income and disbursements; and claims or benefits paid, and claims outstanding; for insurers based in New Jersey and elsewhere.

Data are shown, as applicable, for fire/casualty and life insurance companies; fraternal benefit societies; hospital, medical, and dental service corporations; title insurance and mortgage guaranty companies; and 1 investment assn.

Data on fire/casualty insurance include additional detail by line of coverage, including medical malpractice, workers compensation, automobile, and surety; and policyholders' surplus for surplus lines insurers.

Data are compiled from annual statements submitted by individual insurers.

Contains contents and table listing (p. 3-6); Insurance Dept summary, with lists of company status changes, and 1 summary table (p. 7-21); and 18 financial tables, interspersed with company directories (p. 24-197).

Availability: New Jersey Department of Insurance, Financial Examination Division, 201 E. State St., CN-325, Trenton NJ 08625, †; SRI/MF/complete.

S5425   NEW JERSEY
Department of Labor

S5425–1   **NEW JERSEY ECONOMIC INDICATORS**
Monthly.
ISSN 0098-227X.
LC 80-643168.
SRI/MF/complete, shipped quarterly

Monthly report reviewing selected New Jersey economic indicators, including employment, earnings, business and construction activity, retail sales, and unemployment claims.

Data are from the State Dept of Labor, BLS, and other Federal or private sector sources. Month of coverage is 1-4 months prior to month of publication.

Contents:

a. Article reviewing economic situation in U.S. and in New Jersey for the month of coverage, with 1 table and generally 12 charts.

b. Articles on aspects of New Jersey economy, often with statistics, including annual features on economic conditions and outlook, employment, and population.

c. Statistical section with 13 tables showing 4-year data for 39 indicator series by month, with accompanying charts showing trends from 1960s; and 12 tables showing employment and earnings data by detailed industry sector, and summary indicators.

Monthly statistical section tables are listed below, and appear in all issues. All additional features with substantial statistics pertaining to New Jersey are described, as they appear, under "Statistical Features." Nonstatistical contents, and Federal data not pertaining specifically to New Jersey, are not covered.

Availability: New Jersey Department of Labor, Planning and Research Division, Publications Office, CN 056, Trenton NJ 08625-0056, †; SRI/MF/complete, shipped quarterly.

Issues reviewed during 1985: Dec. 7, 1984-Sept. 30, 1985 (P) (Nos. 244-254)

MONTHLY TABLES:

LONG-TERM INDICATORS, BY MONTH

[Tables I-II show seasonally adjusted official BLS data and "unofficial" data prepared by State analysts from a combination of sources. Most other tables show seasonally adjusted and unadjusted data.

Data are shown monthly, usually for current year through month of coverage, and for preceding 3 years.]

I-II. Resident labor force indicators [labor force and participation rate; employment and ratio to population; and unemployment and rate].

III-IV. Establishment employment indicators [nonfarm, private and public sectors, manufacturing, construction, and service employment].

V. Production workers indicators [manufacturing employment, and weekly hours and manhours].

VI. Earnings and price indicators [weekly earnings of production workers, urban CPI for U.S. and NYC and Philadelphia metro areas, and net spendable earnings of manufacturing workers].

VII. General business indicators [new business incorporations and business failures, and electric power sales volume; electric power data begin with the Mar. 8, 1985 issue].

VIII-IX. Construction contracts and residential building permits indicators, [by type].

X. Trade indicators [retail sales and passenger car registrations].

XI. Labor market indicators [nonfarm job openings and placements, and unemployment insurance average weeks claimed].

XII-XIII. Unemployment insurance claimants indicators [insured unemployment rate, initial claims weekly average, insurance exhaustions; and unemployment in manufacturing, construction, and service industries].

EMPLOYMENT AND EARNINGS, BY INDUSTRY

[Tables [1] and [3-5] show data for month of coverage and 12 preceding months, by SIC 2- and 3-digit industries in New Jersey.]

[1] Nonfarm payroll employment.

[2] Nonfarm payroll workers by major industries [annually for approximately 25 years].

[3-4] Average weekly gross dollar earnings and hours of production workers.

[5] Average hourly gross dollar earnings of production workers.

SUMMARY TABLES

[Tables [6-8] show data for month of coverage, previous month, and same month of previous year.]

[6] Labor force data [by employment status].

[7] Unemployment insurance claims [by program].

[8] Characteristics of insured unemployed [sex, race and ethnic group, industry of previous employment, age, and duration of unemployment].

[9] Residential construction authorized by building permits [units and value; month of coverage, previous month, and current and previous year to date].

[10] Official BLS sample estimates, standard errors, and coefficients of variation [for resident employment, unemployment, and unemployment rate, monthly for current year through month of coverage, and for preceding 1-3 years].

[11] Comparative U.S. and New Jersey civilian labor force trends [by employment status, annually for previous 5-7 years, and monthly for current year through month of coverage and for preceding 1-2 years].

[12] Monthly averages for indicator series 1-39 [monthly tables I-XIII, annually for 11 years to year preceding current year].

STATISTICAL FEATURES:

S5425–1.601: Dec. 7, 1984 (No. 244)

IMPROVEMENT IN PLANNED HOMEBUILDING

(p. 6-10) By Connie O. Hughes. Article, with 1 table showing number of dwelling units authorized, monthly 1982-Aug. 1984. Data are from the New Jersey Dept of Labor.

S5425–1.602: Jan. 4, 1985 (No. 245)

ANNUAL STATEMENT OF THE ECONOMIC POLICY COUNCIL, ANNUAL FEATURE

(p. 6-15) Annual article analyzing economic conditions and outlook for New Jersey and U.S., 1980-85. Includes 1 chart and 1 table showing U.S. and N.J. employment change by industry division, selected periods 1980-84; and distribution of employment by major sector, 1984. Also includes 1 table with selected economic data for U.S., 1984-85.

S5425–1.603: Feb. 1, 1985 (No. 246)

NEW JERSEY'S POPULATION, JULY 1, 1984

(p. 6-7) By Frederick W. Hollmann. Article, with 2 tables showing resident population by U.S. region and for 9 northeastern States; and New Jersey population change due to natural increment and net migration; various periods 1970-84. Data are from the Census Bureau.

S5425–1.604: Mar. 8, 1985 (No. 247)

NONAGRICULTURAL EMPLOYMENT ESTIMATES REVISED TO A 1984 BENCHMARK, ANNUAL FEATURE

(p. 4-7) Annual article, by Waldemar Falk, presenting revised 1984 New Jersey monthly employment and labor force benchmarks. Includes 3 tables showing original and revised monthly nonfarm employment, 1981-84; and estimated and benchmark employment, by State labor area and by industry division and manufacturing group, Mar. 1984.

EFFECT OF A CHANGING LABOR FORCE ON NEW JERSEY'S UNEMPLOYMENT RATE

(p. 8-13) By Robert Vaden. Article, with 4 tables showing New Jersey labor force and population distribution, and labor force participation rates, by age (16-19 and 19/over), sex, and race; and estimated effect of labor force and population changes on unemployment rate; various years 1960-80. Data are from BLS and Census Bureau.

OCCUPATIONAL STAFFING PATTERNS IN MANUFACTURING INDUSTRIES

(p. 14-16) By Patricia McKendrick. Article, with 2 tables showing New Jersey employment in durable and nondurable goods manufacturing, by major industry and occupational group, 1983. Data are from New Jersey Labor Dept.

LABOR SUPPLY ANALYSIS

(p. 17) Article, with 2 tables showing New Jersey unemployment rate, by SMSA, 2nd quarter 1983-2nd quarter 1984; and number of New Jersey and U.S. SMSAs by unemployment level, 2nd quarter 1984. Data are from Labor Dept.

S5425–1.605: Apr. 8, 1985 (No. 248)

EARNINGS OF WOMEN IN NEW JERSEY

(p. 4-7) By Connie O. Hughes. Article, with 5 tables showing the following for New Jersey workers by sex: median income and earnings, with earnings detail by occupation, education, and age, and for persons working year-round and full-time; number in labor force; and number working year-round and less than 50 weeks, by full- or part-time status; with selected comparisons to total U.S., 1969 and/or 1979. Data are from Census Bureau.

RETAIL TRADE IN NEW JERSEY: 1982

(p. 8-12) By Connie O. Hughes. Article, with 3 tables showing New Jersey retail trade establishments, sales, and payroll, by industry group and county, 1977 and/or 1982. Data are from Census Bureau.

NEW JERSEY'S DENSITY SURPASSES 1000

(p. 13) Brief article, with 1 table showing New Jersey population size and density, as of Apr. 1 or July 1, 1980-84. Data are from Census Bureau.

S5425–1.606: Apr. 30, 1985 (No. 249)

PROVISIONAL COUNTY POPULATION ESTIMATES

(p. 4-5) By Alfred Toizer. Article, with 1 table showing New Jersey population by county, Apr. 1, 1980 and July 1, 1984. Data are from Census Bureau.

S5425–1.607: June 5, 1985 (No. 250)

1985 JOB OUTLOOK FOR COLLEGE GRADUATES

(p. 5) By Mary Ann Unger. Article, with 1 text table showing share of bachelor degrees awarded in 4 disciplines (business, liberal arts, education, and computer sciences) by New Jersey institutions, 1977 and 1983-84. Data are from State Dept of Higher Education.

ANNUAL DEMOGRAPHIC PROFILE OF NEW JERSEY: 1984

(p. 6-12) By Charles Crowley. Article on New Jersey demographic characteristics. Data are from the Mar. 1984 Current Population Survey, and previous surveys. Includes 1 summary table, and 7 tables showing the following for New Jersey:

a. Family and nonfamily households, and average number of persons per household; population age 15/over, by sex and marital status; living arrangements of persons under age 18; civilian institutional population, and labor force by employment status, for persons age 16/over by sex and race and for youth age 16-19; 1980-84.

b. Median family and household income in current and 1983 dollars, with detail for families by race, number of workers, householder educational attainment, and type of family, and for households by household size and householder age (over and under 65), tenure status, sex, and race; 1979 and 1982-83.

c. Families in poverty and poverty rate: for all, married couple, and female householder families; and by race, by presence of children under age 18 and age 6, and by number of family members in labor force; 1979 and 1982-83.

S5425–1.608: June 28, 1985 (No. 251)

NONCASINO EMPLOYMENT GROWTH IN THE ATLANTIC CITY MSA

(p. 8-10) By Chester E. Sherman. Article, with 1 table showing Atlantic City labor area nonfarm employment by industry division, with detail for manufacturing durable and nondurable goods and for casinos, 1983-84. Data are from New Jersey Dept of Labor.

S5425–1.609: Aug. 2, 1985 (No. 252)

ESTIMATES OF NEW JERSEY'S POPULATION, BY AGE: JULY 1, 1984, ANNUAL FEATURE

(p. 6) Annual article, by Frederick W. Hollmann, with 1 table showing New Jersey population by age group, Apr. 1, 1980 and July 1, 1983-84, with comparisons to U.S. population. Data are from Census Bureau.

1984 NEW JERSEY PLANNED HOMEBUILDING OUTPACES THE NATION

(p. 7-9) By Connie O. Hughes. Article, with 5 tables showing New Jersey dwelling units authorized by building permits, by month and by size and county, various years 1982-84; with summary comparisons to U.S., 1980-84. Most data are based on reports submitted by building inspectors to State municipalities.

BUSINESS BIRTHS IN NEW JERSEY, 1982-83, ANNUAL ARTICLE

(p. 10-13) Annual article, by Robert Vaden, on New Jersey new business establishments' survival and employment. Data are from employer reports filed with the New Jersey Dept of Labor.

Includes 5 tables showing employment and number of units for new businesses, and survival rates, all by industry division, various periods 1975-84.

For description of previous article, see SRI 1984 Annual under S5425-1.505.

ECONOMIC BRIEF: PROJECTIONS BY BEA FOR NEW JERSEY

(p. 14) Article, with 1 table showing population, personal income, and employment, for New Jersey and U.S., selected years 1973-2000. Data are from U.S. Dept. of Commerce.

S5425–1.610: Aug. 30, 1985 (No. 253)

NEW JERSEY'S BUSINESS COMMUNITY BY SIZE OF ESTABLISHMENT

(p. 6-9) By David Aylesworth. Article, with 4 tables showing New Jersey business establishments and employment, by industry division and employment size class, Mar. 1984, with summary data by county and trends from 1973. Data pertain to private sector businesses covered by unemployment compensation, and are based on reports submitted by employers.

NEW JERSEY MIGRATION SINCE 1970

(p. 10-17) By Charles Crowley. Article, with 3 tables and 2 charts showing New Jersey net migration, selected periods 1970-84; and inmigrants and outmigrants, by race (also including Spanish origin), sex, age, and State of previous or current residence, 1975-80 period; mostly by county. Data are from Census of Population and Housing and New Jersey Dept of Labor.

OCCUPATIONAL OUTLOOK FOR NEW JERSEY: 1995

(p. 18-20) By Thomas S. Charpentier. Article, with 3 tables showing New Jersey employment by occupational category, and top 10 occupations ranked by employment and by average annual job openings, for 1984 and 1995 or 1984-95 period. Data are from New Jersey Dept of Labor.

S5425–1.611: Sept. 30, 1985 (No. 254)

POPULATION ESTIMATES FOR NEW JERSEY COUNTIES AND MUNICIPALITIES, JULY 1, 1984, ANNUAL FEATURE

(p. 6-12) Annual article, by Alfred Toizer, analyzing New Jersey population trends. Includes 5 tables showing population by county and municipality; and population change due to natural increment and migration, and population age 65/over, by county; generally for 1970, 1980, and 1984.

Data are prepared by the New Jersey Labor Dept in cooperation with the U.S. Census Bureau.

COVERED EMPLOYMENT WAGES IN 1984, ANNUAL FEATURE

(p. 13-15) Annual article, by William Saley, with 3 tables showing average wage of New Jersey private-sector employees covered by unemployment insurance, by industry division and by county, with selected comparisons to U.S., 1983-84. Data are from employer reports.

S5425–3   NEW JERSEY RESIDENTIAL BUILDING PERMITS, 1984
Summary
Annual. Aug. 1985. i+44 p.
SRI/MF/complete

Annual report on construction and demolition of residential units authorized by New Jersey building permits, including estimated costs for new construction and additions/alterations, by coun-

ty and municipality, 1984, with selected trends from 1960 and summmary comparisons to total U.S.

Data are based on monthly reports submitted by local agencies.

Contains contents listing (p. i); narrative analysis with 1 chart, and 10 tables listed below (p. 1-39); and technical notes (p. 43-44).

Monthly report on permits and construction costs is also available from issuing agency, but is not covered in SRI.

Availability: New Jersey Department of Labor, Planning and Research Division, Demographic and Economic Analysis Office, CN 388, Trenton NJ 08625-0388, †; SRI/MF/complete.

TABLES:

[Most data are shown for units authorized by building permits, by dwelling unit size. Tables 3-4 and 8 include public housing units and estimated residential construction costs (total, new, and additions/alterations).]

1. Total dwelling units authorized: New Jersey and U.S., 1980-1984. (p. 2)

2. Conversions [dwelling unit gain or loss due to conversion of nonresidential structures to residential use and residential structures to nonresidential use], by municipality, 1984. (p. 7)

3-4. Residential construction [total], 1960-84; and by month, 1984. (p. 11-12)

5-6. Annual average construction costs of dwelling units, 1974-84; and dwelling units authorized for demolition, 1983-84. (p. 13)

7. Change in [total] dwelling units, by county [with rankings for each county], 1983-84. (p. 14)

8. Residential construction [total], by county, 1984. (p. 15)

9-10. Dwelling units [1984; and number of residential demolitions, 1983-84; by county and municipality]. (p. 16-39)

S5425–9   NEW JERSEY POPULATION TRENDS, 1790 TO 1980
Monograph. June 1984.
iv+52 p.
LC 84-622847.
SRI/MF/complete

Report presenting New Jersey population trends, decennially 1930-80, with summary trends from 1790. Includes population and land area by county and municipality, with selected comparisons to U.S. by State and census division and region. Data are from Census Bureau and New Jersey Dept of Community Affairs.

Contains contents and table listing (1 p.); narrative summary (p. i-iv); and 9 tables (p. 1-52).

Availability: New Jersey Department of Labor, Planning and Research Division, Demographic and Economic Analysis Office, CN 388, Trenton NJ 08625-0388, $2.00; SRI/MF/complete.

S5425–10   NEW JERSEY ECONOMIC AND DEMOGRAPHIC FACTBOOK
Biennial. Nov. 1984.
vii+26 p.
LC 85-620914.
SRI/MF/complete

Biennial compilation of general economic and demographic statistics for New Jersey, 1980-83, with trends from 1958 and projections to 2000. Includes data by county, other local area, and industry. Data are from State Dept of Labor and U.S. Census Bureau.

Contains contents and table listing (2 p.); introduction, and explanation of geographic breakdowns, with 2 maps (p. i-vii); and 19 tables, described below (p. 1-25).

This is the 1st edition.

Availability: New Jersey Department of Labor, Planning and Research Division, Demographic and Economic Analysis Office, CN 388, Trenton NJ 08625-0388, $2.00; SRI/MF/complete.

TABLES:

[Data are for 1980-83, unless otherwise noted.]

a. Population by county, MSA, and MSA component, and for municipalities with 50,000/more residents, 1970, 1980, and 1983; net migration by county, 1980-83 period; and projected population by county, quinquennially 1985-2000. Tables 1-6. (p. 1-6)

b. Personal income by county, 1980-82; and authorized housing construction by type and county. Tables 7-10. (p. 7-9)

c. Labor force by employment status, and manufacturing hours and earnings, by labor area; and nonfarm employment by industry division and major manufacturing group, with detail by labor area and trends from 1958. Tables 11-14. (p. 10-20)

d. Employment covered by unemployment insurance, and wages of covered employees, both by county, and covered employment by industry division and for municipalities with 20,000/more employees, selected years 1970-83; and employment by occupation, 1982. Tables 15-19. (p. 21-25)

S5425–11   CENSUS TRENDS, 1970 TO 1980

Series. For individual publication data, see below.
LC 85-620668.
SRI/MF/complete

Series of reports presenting New Jersey population and housing characteristics, 1970 and 1980. Series consists of individual reports for the State and each county. Data are from the 1970 and 1980 Censuses of Population and Housing.

Each report contains preface (p. iii-iv); listing of contents, tables, and charts (p. v-vi); narrative analysis interspersed with a varying number of maps and charts, and approximately 24 tables (30-70 p.); and technical notes (p. A1-A15).

Data topics are described below. Series begins with the reports listed below.

Availability: New Jersey Department of Labor, Planning and Research Division, Demographic and Economic Analysis Office, CN 388, Trenton NJ 08625-0388, $5.00 per volume; SRI/MF/complete.

DATA TOPICS:

[Data are generally shown for 1970 and 1980 or 1970-80 period. Data by local area are shown by county in the State report and by municipality in the county reports. Selected reports include some additional demographic detail, comparisons to U.S., and trends.]

a. **Vital statistics:** total population and population density, by local area; births, deaths, and net migration; and residence relative to 5 years previous, including same or different house and county, same State, different region, and abroad.

b. **Population:** population by sex, age, and race/ethnicity (including white, black, American Indian, Eskimo, and Aleut, and detail by place of ancestry for persons of Asian/Pacific Island, European, and Spanish origin); and black population by local area.

c. **Households and marital status:** total and family households, and persons in group quarters, by local area; population by marital status by sex; and population by type of household (including institutionalized) for all persons and those 18/under and 65/over.

d. **Education:** school enrollment by level; and years of school completed for persons 25/over.

e. **Labor force and commuting:** labor force status for total and black population, by sex; employment by occupational group; and commuting patterns, covering points of origin and destination for residents and nonresident workers.

f. **Income:** families by income level, and median family income, with detail by age of householder; per capita and median family income, and poverty rate, by local area; and population below poverty level for all persons and those 65/over.

g. **Housing units:** housing units and vacancy rate, and owner and renter occupied units and median value or rent, with detail for year round units, by local area; units by tenure and occupancy status, by number of units in structure (and for mobile homes/trailers); households by level of gross rent relative to income; and units by number of persons per room for all occupied units and those with complete plumbing facilities.

REPORTS:

S5425–11.1: State of New Jersey
[Monograph. July 1984. vi+47+15 p. SRI/MF/complete.]

S5425–11.2: Bergen County
[Monograph. Oct. 1984. vi+57+15 p. SRI/MF/complete.]

S5425–11.3: Cape May County
[Monograph. Oct. 1984. vi+32+15 p. SRI/MF/complete.]

S5425–11.4: Cumberland County
[Monograph. Oct. 1984. vi+36+15 p. SRI/MF/complete.]

S5425–11.5: Gloucester County
[Monograph. Oct. 1984. vi+35+15 p. SRI/MF/complete.]

S5425–11.6: Mercer County
[Monograph. Oct. 1984. vi+32+15 p. SRI/MF/complete.]

S5425–11.7: Monmouth County
[Monograph. Oct. 1984. vi+67+15 p. SRI/MF/complete.]

S5425–11.8: Passaic County
[Monograph. Oct. 1984. vi+34+15 p. SRI/MF/complete.]

S5430   NEW JERSEY
Department of
Law and Public Safety

S5430–1   UNIFORM CRIME REPORTS, State of New Jersey, 1984

Annual. [1985.] viii+194 p.
ISSN 0548-5851.
LC 82-643666.
SRI/MF/complete

Annual report on New Jersey crimes and arrests, by offense, 1984, with trends from 1975. Includes data by county and municipality, and by offender age, race, and sex. Also includes law enforcement employment, and assaults on officers.

Report focuses on 7 Index offenses: murder, rape, robbery, aggravated assault, burglary, larceny/theft, and motor vehicle theft. Report also includes detail for arson, but State does not classify arson as an Index offense. Arrests are also shown for numerous non-Index offenses.

Data are from State and local agency reports submitted under the Uniform Crime Reporting (UCR) Program.

Contains listings of contents and tables/charts (p. v-viii); explanation of UCR Program (p. 1-8); report in 9 sections, interspersed with narrative summaries and text statistics, and 20 charts and 55 tables described below (p. 9-191); and glossary and calculations (p. 192-194).

Availability: New Jersey Division of State Police, Uniform Crime Reporting Unit, PO Box 7068, West Trenton NJ 08625, †; SRI/MF/complete.

CHARTS AND TABLES:

[Data are for 1984, with selected comparisons to 1983, unless otherwise noted. Data by race are for white, black, American Indian/Alaskan Native, and Asian/Pacific Islander.]

S5430–1.1: Index Offenses

SUMMARY

a. Index offense frequency; number of offenses, rate, and clearances, by weapon, method, and other crime characteristics; and adult and juvenile clearances; all by offense. 3 charts and 2 tables. (p. 10-14)

b. Value of property stolen and recovered, by property type. 1 table. (p. 15)

c. Trend in number of Index offenses, by crime characteristics, 1980-84; and percent change in offenses for New Jersey, U.S., and northeastern States; all by offense. 2 tables. (p. 16-20)

INDEX OFFENSES

d. Murder: offenses by day of week; by victim age, sex, and race; and by type of weapon, victim/offender relationship, and circumstance. 4 charts and 1 table. (p. 22-25)

e. Robbery, assault, and burglary: robberies and value of stolen property, by place of occurrence; weapons used in robberies and assaults; and residential and nonresidential burglaries and value of stolen property, by day or night entry. 2 charts and 2 tables. (p. 28-32)

f. Larceny/theft, motor vehicle theft, and arson: larceny/theft offenses and value of property stolen, by theft type and size; motor vehicle thefts by vehicle type, and number and value of vehicles stolen and recovered; and arson offenses, value of damage, and total and juvenile clearances, by type of property. 2 charts and 4 tables. (p. 34-38)

S5430–1.2: State and County Arrests, and County Offenses

ARRESTS

a. Arrests by Index and non-Index offenses: total arrests, by age; total and juvenile arrests, by sex; and total, adult, and juvenile arrests, by race and ethnic origin (Hispanic and not Hispanic). 8 tables. (p. 40-49)

b. Arrests by county: total, adult, and juvenile arrests by Index and non-Index offenses, and rates; adult and juvenile arrests by sex and race; and police disposition of juveniles taken into custody. 8 tables. (p. 50-61)

c. Drug abuse arrests, by type of substance. 3 charts. (p. 66-67)

OFFENSES BY COUNTY

[All data are shown by county.]

d. Index offenses by type, total violent and nonviolent crimes, and rates; robberies by place of occurrence; residential and non-residential burglaries, by day or night entry; and larceny offenses, by type. 3 tables. (p. 72-79)

e. Value of property stolen and recovered, by type. 1 table. (p. 80-81)

S5430–1.3: Urban, Rural, University, and Municipal Data

a. Index offenses by university and college institution and campus (including arson), and by 7 municipal population size groupings. 2 tables. (p. 92-93)

b. Index offenses and total violent and nonviolent crimes 1980 and 1984, and rates 1983-84, for urban, suburban, and rural areas. 4 tables. (p. 94-97)

c. Index offenses for State and 2 urban population size categories, 1975 and 1984 and total period; and 6 street crimes, aggregate for 15 urban municipalities, 1975-84. 3 tables. (p. 100-104)

d. Municipal profiles: Index offenses (including arson) and crime rates; population and land area; whether urban, suburban, or rural; and number of police officers by sex, and civilian police employees; all by municipality and county. 1 table. (p. 106-161)

S5430–1.4: Police Employee and Domestic Violence Data

a. Law enforcement employment: number of officers by sex, and civilian employees, for municipal, county, and State, and other police; and by State agency, university and college campus, county, and dept. 1 chart and 5 tables. (p. 164-169)

b. Police assaults: police officers killed 1975-84; police assaulted, by type of weapon, activity, and time of day; and municipal police employed and assaulted, by county. 2 charts and 3 tables. (p. 174-178)

c. Domestic violence: offenses, by victim/offender relationship, type of weapon, extent of injury, day of week, time of day, month, and county; and arrests; with selected detail by type of offense. 3 charts and 5 tables. (p. 183-191)

S5430–2   FATAL MOTOR VEHICLE ACCIDENT COMPARATIVE DATA REPORT, 1983, New Jersey State Police

Annual. [1984.]   2+44 p.
LC 75-642363.
SRI/MF/complete

Annual report on New Jersey fatal traffic accidents and fatalities, by accident and vehicle type, location, and other circumstances; and driver and victim characteristics, including alcohol and drug use; 1983, with trends from 1970s. Includes detailed chronology of fatal accidents by county.

Also includes summary trends for total and injury accidents, and data on interstate highway mileage.

Data are compiled by the Fatal Accident Unit of the New Jersey State Police.

Contains contents listing (1 p.); and report with 1 chart, 30 tables, and 1 map (p. 1-44).

Availability: New Jersey Department of Law and Public Safety, State Police Division, PO Box 7068, West Trenton NJ 08625, †; SRI/MF/complete.

S5440   NEW JERSEY
Department of State

S5440–1   STATE OF NEW JERSEY RESULTS OF THE GENERAL ELECTION Held Nov. 6, 1984

Biennial. [1985.]   25 p.
LC 35-27506.
SRI/MF/complete

Biennial report presenting results of the New Jersey general election held Nov. 6, 1984. Shows voting for President/Vice President, U.S. Senator and Representatives, various county offices including sheriff, and 6 public questions including a State constitutional amendment to prohibit taxation of social security/railroad retirement benefits. Data are shown by county or district, and include candidates' party affiliation.

Also includes voter registration, and total ballots cast and rejected, by county; election trends from 1952; and results of 3 special elections held during 1984.

Previous report, covering 1982 elections, is described in SRI 1983 Annual under this number.

Availability: New Jersey Department of State, Elections Division, State House, PO Box 1330, Trenton NJ 08625, †; SRI/MF/complete.

S5455   NEW JERSEY
Department of the Treasury

S5455–1   STATE OF NEW JERSEY ANNUAL FINANCIAL REPORT for the Year Ended June 30, 1984

Annual. Nov. 30, 1984.
187 p.
LC 82-621084.
SRI/MF/complete

Annual report on financial condition of New Jersey State government, presenting assets, liabilities, and fund balances; revenues by source; and expenditures by function; for all, general, special revenue, debt service, capital projects, and trust and agency funds, FY84, with comparisons to FY83 and summary trends from FY75.

Also includes data on long-term debt, projected to 2008; property tax relief, gubernatorial election, and casino control and revenue funds; and appropriations compared to expenditures.

Also presents socioeconomic indicators, including property valuation, population, personal income, labor force by employment status, employment and earnings by industry, employment of top 50 employers, retail sales, new housing value, farm cash receipts, and school enrollments with detail for higher education by selected institution, various years 1973-84.

Data are compiled by the Dept of the Treasury from State, Federal, and private sources.

Contains contents listing (2 p.); introduction with 2 text tables, 2 illustrative charts, and organizational chart (p. 1-5); financial section, with 22 financial statements, and accompanying notes with 14 text tables (p. 8-120); and statistical and economic data section with narrative and 24 tables (p. 121-187).

Issuing agency also publishes an interim financial report with data for the 1st half of the fiscal year. SRI does not cover the interim report.

Availability: New Jersey Department of the Treasury, Budget and Accounting Division, CN 221, State House, Trenton NJ 08625, †; SRI/MF/complete.

S5455–2   STATE OF NEW JERSEY ANNUAL REPORT OF THE DIVISION OF TAXATION in the Department of the Treasury, for FY84

Annual. [1985.]   xii+438 p.
LC 51-30726.
SRI/MF/complete

Annual report, for FY84, on sources of New Jersey State revenue, with detailed data on tax rates, assessments, collections, and apportionment to local governments, by type and county. Includes summaries of new tax legislation and history of each current tax, tax court decisions, comparative data on other States' taxes, and revenue trends from as early as 1960.

Contents:

Transmittal letter, with 1 chart; listings of contents, tables, and charts; and organizational chart. (p. iv-xii)

Chapters I-II. Taxation Division history and activities: including audit report, with text data showing financial results of the audits; processing and administration activities, with text tables; local property assessment and taxes; and report of special procedures and investigations branch, with text data summarizing branch collections, by type of activity. Includes 2 charts and 7 numbered tables. (p. 1-36)

Chapters III-IV. Sources of revenue administered by the Division, with description, history, and disposition for each current tax, including text data on collection trends, rates, and/or licensing activity; and recent tax legislation and court decisions. Includes 1 chart and 12 numbered tables. (p. 37-172)

App. I-IV. Miscellaneous statistics; tax calendars; directories of tax court justices, county boards of taxation, and county tax assessors and collectors; and description of State distributions to local governments. Includes 9 numbered tables. (p. 173-431)

Index. (p. 433-438)

All numbered tables, and selected other tables with substantial statistical content not described above or covered in the numbered tables, are listed below.

Availability: New Jersey Department of the Treasury, Taxation Division, 50 Barrack St., Trenton NJ 08646, †; SRI/MF/complete.

TABLES:
[Data are for FY84, unless otherwise noted.]

S5455–2.1: Chapter Tables
SUMMARY TRENDS

1. Major State tax collections (net) [by source], FY82-84. (p. 4-5)

LOCAL PROPERTY AND PUBLIC UTILITY TAXES

2. Public utilities gross receipts and franchise taxes collected by the State for distribution to municipalities [for electric, gas, water, sewer, telephone/telegraph, and municipal electric companies, 1984]. (p. 11)

3. Local property tax growth by years, net [1975-84]. (p. 21)

4. 1983 summary of farm assessment: regular farm (3a) and qualified farm (3b) [by county]. (p. 24)

5-6. Summary of exempt property values reported in county abstract of ratables; and summary of local property taxes [by tax type; 1983-84]. (p. 29)

7. Summary of local property net valuations taxable [by county, 1983-84]. (p. 30)

SOURCES OF REVENUE
[Most tables showing tax rates include comparisons to 5-7 other States, and selected additional citics.]

8-9. Alcoholic beverage tax collections and gallonage, FY82-84; and tax rates; [for beer, liquor, and wines]. (p. 39-40)

10. Cigarette tax rates. (p. 45)

[A] [Cigarette] license fees [licenses issued, and amount, by type of licensee]. (p. 45)

11. New Jersey comparative sales, packs of cigarettes [FY75-84]. (p. 46)

12. Corporation business tax: [rate and basis of tax]. (p. 53)

13. Motor fuels tax [rates per gallon of gasoline and diesel]. (p. 69)

14. Motor fuels distributors, jobbers, and dealers license fees [and licenses issued]. (p. 70)

15. Realty transfer fee tax rates. (p. 82)

16. Sales and use tax exemptions [on 9 items], comparisons with [6] other States. (p. 88)

17. Sales and use tax rates. (p. 88)

18. State taxes on banks and financial institutions [rate and basis of tax]. (p. 91)

19. Transfer inheritance/estate tax [rates]. (p. 99)

S5455–2.2: Appendix Tables
COMPARATIVE DATA AND COLLECTIONS

20. Major State tax rates [by State, for sales, motor fuels, cigarette, and corporate and personal income taxes]. (p. 174-175)

21-22. Sales and use tax cash collections, 1982-83; and sales tax base and sales and use tax cash collections, 1983; by type of business [including number of vendors]. (p. 176)

23. State tax collections and property taxes, adjusted for changes in population and in the purchasing power of the dollar [1960-83]. (p. 177)

24. State and local taxes [total], as a percent of personal income, and per capita, by State [with selected rankings], FY82. (p. 178-179)

25. State and local taxes [total and property taxes, by State], FY82. (p. 180)

CORPORATE TAX RETURNS

26-28. Corporation tax returns, [payments, credit, and penalties/interest]: by total, net income, and net worth tax liability, 1982. (p. 181-183)

MUNICIPALITY TAX RATES AND ASSESSMENT APPEALS

[B] Effective property tax rates by municipality [arranged by county], 1982-84. (p. 208-213)

[C] Summary of county tax board appeals [number of appeals by property class and filing fee category; dispositions; and value of original assessments, and assessment reductions and increases]; 1983. (p. 218-219)

STATE REVENUE SHARING

[D] Taxes collected by the State for distribution to municipalities [by tax type and municipality, with totals by county], 1984. (p. 244-270)

[E] State revenue sharing distribution [municipalities' share, property tax and veteran deductions, and homestead rebate, including number of claims; by county and municipality], 1984. (p. 272-295)

LOCAL PROPERTY TAX RATES AND EXEMPTIONS

[F] Abstract of ratables and exemptions in the State [by county and municipality, generally including for each: taxable value of land and improvements thereon, partial exemptions, taxable value of machinery/equipment of telephone/telegraph/messenger system companies, general rate, true value of Class II railroad property, equalization, apportionment of taxes by general function, miscellaneous revenues for local municipal budget, and deductions allowed for senior citizens and veterans], 1984. (p. 298-401)

[G] State equalization table [assessed value of personal and real property, percent by which assessed value of real property should be increased, and true value of real property, by county], 1984. (p. 402)

[H] Compilation of equalized valuation in the State as of Oct. 1, 1984 [aggregate real property assessed valuation and true value, assessed valuation of Class II railroad and all personal property, and equalized valuation; by county and municipality]. (p. 404-431)

S5530   NEW MEXICO
Department of
Agriculture

**S5530–1   NEW MEXICO
AGRICULTURAL
STATISTICS, 1984**
Annual. July 1985. 72 p.
Bull. No. 24.
LC 63-54681.
SRI/MF/complete

Annual report on New Mexico agricultural production, finances, and marketing, 1984, with selected trends from 1940 and some data for 1985. Data are generally shown by county and/or commodity.

Report covers production, prices, value, and, as applicable, acreage, yield, disposition, stocks, and inventory, for field crop, vegetable, fruit and nut, livestock, dairy, and poultry sectors.

Report also includes data on weather; irrigated acreage; fertilizer inshipments; commercial feed sales; number of farms; farm acreage; range/pasture condition; cattle feedlots; farm assets and debts, and income including government payments; and in- and out-shipments by State of origin and destination, and for Mexico and/or Canada.

Data are compiled by the New Mexico Crop and Livestock Reporting Service in conjunction with USDA.

Contains contents listing and transmittal letters (p. 1-3); and 8 maps, 5 charts, and 88 tables, interspersed with narrative (p. 4-72).

This is the 24th annual report.

Availability: New Mexico Crop and Livestock Reporting Service, PO Box 1809, Las Cruces NM 88004, †; SRI/MF/complete.

S5545   NEW MEXICO
Commerce and Industry
Department

S5545–2   NEW MEXICO FACT BOOK
Recurring (irreg.)
June 1984-Aug. 1985.
140 p. looseleaf, no paging.
LC 83-620901.
SRI/MF/complete

Recurring report (with periodic update supplements) presenting economic and social statistics for New Mexico. Current abstract covers a compilation of supplements issued June 1984-Aug. 1985; these supplements show data primarily for 1970s-84, with selected projections to 2005.

Report presents an overview of the State, and is primarily intended to promote economic development. Geographic, socioeconomic, and demographic breakdowns are shown, as applicable, for most topics. These breakdowns include data by city, school district, county, MSA, urban-rural status, commodity, income, industry, occupation, age, education, race, and sex. Comparisons to total U.S. and neighboring States are also often included.

Most data are from State and Federal agencies. Data sources are noted beneath each table.

Compilation of supplements for June 1984-Aug. 1985 contains contents listing and index (4 p.); and 26 maps, 15 charts, and 93 tables, arranged in 14 sections, described below (136 p.).

The base edition of the *Fact Book* and supplement issued June 1983 are described in SRI 1983 Annual under S5545-2.

Availability: New Mexico Commerce and Industry Department, Economic Development Division, Bataan Memorial Bldg., Santa Fe NM 87503, $40.00 (includes updates for 1 yr.); SRI/MF/complete.

SECTIONS:

S5545–2.1: Section I: Introduction

(8 p.) Contains 2 maps, 2 charts, and 10 tables. Includes population, per capita income growth, and employment projected to 1990; temperature extremes and precipitation; State/local expenditures for parks/natural resources; State income from permanent funds; State appropriations by function and revenues by source.

Also includes housing units, occupancy by tenure status, median value or rent, and average purchase price; physicians, dentists, and hospital beds per 100,000 population; police per 10,000 population; and TV and radio stations and newspapers.

S5545–2.2: Section II: Population

(8 p.) Contains 2 maps, 5 charts, and 6 tables. Includes population projected to 2005; and births, deaths, and net migration.

S5545–2.3: Section III: Income/Employment

(16 p.) Contains 2 maps, 5 charts, and 17 tables. Includes average earnings and hours; entry-level wages; labor force by employment status; personal income; nonagricultural employment, income growth, and job openings, projected to 1990 or 2000; agricultural employment; and households and effective buying income.

S5545–2.4: Section IV: Education

(18 p.) Contains 1 map and 9 tables. Includes higher education enrollment, degree programs by field, and degrees conferred by level, by institution; elementary/secondary teachers, average salary, and experience; pupil/teacher ratio; and college entrance test scores.

S5545–2.5: Section V: Energy/Natural Resources

(6 p.) Contains 6 maps, 1 chart, and 4 tables. Includes mineral and energy production rankings; mineral, energy, and other natural resource reserves, production, and/or State revenues; and underground water basins area.

S5545–2.6: Section VI: Major Industries

(10 p.) Contains 2 maps, 2 charts, and 23 tables. Includes employment and establishments; 15 largest nonmanufacturing employers and 10 largest manufacturers; retail and wholesale employment; retail sales; visitors to State and national tourist attractions; fishing and hunting licenses; ski area attendance; and lodging and eating/drinking place employment.

Also includes racing days, attendance, and pari-mutuel wagering, by racetrack; convention attendance and expenditures; agricultural cash receipts; construction employment and contract value; new housing units; financial institutions and balance sheet data; and government employment and wages.

S5545–2.7: Section VII: High Technology

(12 p.) Includes tabular descriptions of laboratories, research facilities, military and missile bases, and universities.

S5545–2.8: Section VIII: Taxes and Incentives

(14 p.) Contains text statistics and 11 tables. Includes tax rates; property value and tax; workers compensation rates and premiums; unemployment benefits-contributions ratio; unemployment trust fund net worth per covered worker; industrial revenue bonds, by company; and investment and energy tax credit information.

S5545–2.9: Section IX: Permits and Fees

(4 p.) Contains 1 table. Includes regulatory information; and residential and nonresidential building valuations.

S5545–2.10: Section X: Business Services

(6 p.) Includes directories of business development organizations and chambers of commerce.

S5545–2.11: Section XI: Utilities

(10 p.) Contains 6 maps and 9 tables. Includes residential electricity costs by U.S. region; coal mines; electricity generation by fuel type; electricity, gas, and telephone rates; water and sewer capacity, average demand, and reserve; and water withdrawals by use category.

S5545–2.12: Section XII: Transportation

(4 p.) Contains 3 maps and 3 tables. Includes interstate highway mileage, by completion status; road mileage; truck size and weight restrictions; truck and rail delivery times; and airline and railroad service.

S5545–2.13: Section XIII: Industrial Parks

(10 p.) Includes directory of industrial parks and site characteristics.

S5545–2.14: Section XIV: International Trade

(10 p.) Contains 2 maps. Includes lists of U.S. Customs offices, international development programs, major products exported, and foreign consulates.

S5550   NEW MEXICO
Corporation Commission

S5550–1   STATE OF NEW MEXICO DEPARTMENT OF INSURANCE 1983 Life, Accident and Health, and Property and Casualty Insurance Business
Annual.   Dec. 31, 1983.
221 p.
LC 63-63121.
SRI/MF/complete

Annual report, for 1983, on New Mexico insurance industry financial condition and underwriting activity, by company and line of coverage. Covers total assets, liabilities, capital, and surplus; and New Mexico premiums written and/or earned, dividends paid, and losses, for companies with headquarters in New Mexico and elsewhere.

Data are shown, as applicable, for health care, fire/casualty, and life insurance companies; fraternal benefit societies; and title companies; with detail for life insurance companies' accident/health business, and for fire/casualty companies' specific lines of coverage (including medical malpractice, workers compensation, auto, and surety).

Also includes data on insurance company taxes/fees, and State Insurance Dept finances, FY75-84.

Data are compiled from annual statements and reports filed by individual insurers.

Contains contents listing (1 p.); and 16 tables (p. 1-221).

This is the 59th annual report. Previous report, for 1981, is described in SRI 1983 Annual under this number. No report with data for 1982 was published.

Availability: New Mexico Corporation Commission, Insurance Department, PERA Bldg., PO Box 1269, Santa Fe NM 87504-1269, †; SRI/MF/complete.

S5575   NEW MEXICO
Department of Education

S5575–2   NEW MEXICO SCHOOL DISTRICT PROFILE, 1983/84 School Year
Annual.   [1985.]
200 p. var. paging.
LC 80-642386.
SRI/MF/complete

Annual report presenting selected statistics on New Mexico's public elementary/secondary schools, by school district, 1981/82-1983/84 school years. Includes data on students and graduates, staff, educational test scores, and vocational education. Data are from State Dept of Education.

Contains contents listing (1 p.); introduction (p. 1); State overview, with 11 charts and 1 summary table (p. 2-20); and 1 detailed table repeated for each district (176 p.).

Detailed table is described below. Charts primarily illustrate data in tables, but also include dropout and proficiency test score trends from

1977 or 1979; distribution of staff by function, 1983/84; and amount earned by cooperative education students, 1979-84.

This is the 14th edition of the report.

Availability: New Mexico Department of Education, Evaluation, Testing, and Data Management Unit, Education Bldg., Santa Fe NM 87501-2786, †; SRI/MF/complete.

DETAILED TABLE:

[Table shows the following data for each school district, for 1981/82-1983/84:]

a. Enrollment by grade level; percent of students in special and bilingual education programs, and served by Federal Title I program for the disadvantaged; student dropout and mobility rates; Anglo, Hispanic, and Native American students and teachers; student/teacher ratios, and teacher load per day; certified FTE staff; and teaching staff average years of experience, and percent with masters'/higher degree.

b. High school graduates; percent of students and graduates passing high school proficiency exams; vocational education classes as percent of all classes, and available class hours per student; test scores on comprehensive basic skills tests, by grade level; and scores on American College Test, and number of students taking test.

S5578   NEW MEXICO
Employment Security
Department

S5578–1   NEW MEXICO ANNUAL MANPOWER PLANNING REPORT

Annual.   May 1985.   3+87 p.
LC 78-642503.
SRI/MF/complete

Annual planning report identifying New Mexico population groups most in need of employment services, 1970s-84. Includes data on employment by industry division; population; job openings by occupation; income; and poverty; with detail by location and demographic characteristics, and selected projections through 2000.

Data are from 1980 census, New Mexico Employment Security Dept, University of New Mexico, and other State sources.

Contains statement of purpose, and contents listing (3 p.); descriptions of Employment Security Dept programs and publications (p. 1-3); 9 report sections, with narrative, 3 maps, 18 charts, and 51 tables (p. 4-80); and technical notes and definitions (p. 81-87).

All tables, and 1 chart presenting data not shown in tables, are described below.

Previous edition was titled *Job Training Partnership Act: Labor Market Information.*

Availability: New Mexico Employment Security Department, Economic Research and Analysis, PO Box 1928, Albuquerque NM 87103, †; SRI/MF/complete.

TABLES AND CHART:

[Data are for New Mexico, unless otherwise noted. Some data include U.S. comparisons. Data by MSA are for Albuquerque and Las Cruces. Data by race are usually shown for white, black, Indian, Asian/Pacific Islander, and Spanish origin.]

POPULATION AND LABOR FORCE

a. Population: by county and race; by planning district and MSA; by age and sex, with age detail for Bernalillo County; and by city; various years 1970-84, with projections by county and planning district through 2000. 7 tables. (p. 10-17)

b. Labor force and unemployment, 1970-84; labor force by employment status, by month, by county and MSA, and by race and sex, 1984, with selected comparisons to 1980; and persons registered with State employment service, by age, sex, education, race, and veteran and welfare status, and for handicapped, seasonal and migrant farmworkers, and economically disadvantaged registrants, for State and Bernalillo County, Dec. 1984. 9 tables. (p. 18-28)

c. Agricultural employment by county; and nonagricultural employment by industry division and major group, with detail by MSA; various years 1974-84. 6 tables. (p. 35-42)

d. Projected employment by industry division and major group, 1990; job openings in high-demand occupations (with detail for Albuquerque), and openings by occupational group, annual average 1981-90 period; job openings in occupations with 140/more employment service applicants, and job orders in occupations with 50/more orders, July 1984; and employment and/or new hires, by industry division and selected major group, FY83, with detail by quarter. 1 chart and 7 tables. (p. 47-60)

INCOME AND POVERTY

e. Per capita personal income, compared to western regions and other western States, and by county and city, various years 1979-83; and U.S. CPI, monthly 1978-Mar. 1985. 4 tables. (p. 61-65)

f. Percent of population below poverty level, by race, with detail by MSA, 1979; population below poverty level (individuals by race, total families, and female-headed families), by county and planning district, 1979; and distribution of households by income size and of persons below poverty level by race, and percent of households receiving income from wage/salary, self-employment, social security, and public assistance, with detail by MSA, 1980. 5 tables. (p. 66-69)

JOB TRAINING PARTNERSHIP ACT TARGET GROUP DATA

g. Labor force by employment status; youth unemployment rate and population, by county; labor force by employment status, for all youths and for high school dropouts, with detail for Bernalillo County; and unemployment and labor force participation rates for high school graduates and dropouts; with selected detail by age group, various years 1980-84. 5 tables. (p. 71-75)

h. Economically disadvantaged age 16-21 and 22/over, by county (no date); unemployment and rate, by county, 1984; veterans by age, period of service, race, and labor force status, with period of service detail by county, 1980; and recipients of AFDC and medical and food assistance, by planning district and county, Feb. or Mar. 1985. 5 tables. (p. 76-80)

S5578–2   NEW MEXICO LABOR MARKET REVIEW

Monthly.   Approx. 10 p.
LC 60-29817.
SRI/MF/complete, shipped quarterly

Monthly report on New Mexico employment, unemployment, hours, and earnings, by industry and local area. Data are compiled by the Employment Security Dept in cooperation with the U.S. Labor Dept. Reports are issued approximately 1 month after month of coverage.

Contains narrative summary interspersed with 8 monthly tables, and occasional special statistical features. Jan. issue also includes 4-6 annual tables showing revised estimates for New Mexico labor force and employment, for current and/or previous year.

Monthly tables are listed below, and appear in all issues. All additional features with substantial statistical content are described, as they appear, under "Statistical Features." Nonstatistical features are not covered.

Availability: New Mexico Employment Security Department, Economic Research and Analysis, PO Box 1928, Albuquerque NM 87103, †; SRI/MF/complete, shipped quarterly.

Issues reviewed during 1985: Sept. 1984-Aug. 1985 (D) (Vol. 13, Nos. 9-12; Vol. 14, Nos. 1-8) [Vol. 13, No. 9 incorrectly reads No. 10].

MONTHLY TABLES:

[Data are shown for New Mexico, for month of coverage, previous month, and same month of previous year, unless otherwise noted.]

[1] Summary [civilian labor force by employment status].

[2] Estimated nonagricultural wage/salary employment [by industry division and major group].

[3] [Table [1] is repeated for Albuquerque MSA.]

[4-5] [Table [2] is repeated for Albuquerque and Las Cruces MSAs.]

[6] Average hours and earnings estimates [of production/construction/nonsupervisory employees, for State by selected industry division, and for Albuquerque manufacturing employees].

[7] U.S. CPI [month of coverage only].

[8] Labor force estimates [by employment status, for State and by MSA and county].

STATISTICAL FEATURES:

S5578–2.601: Oct. 1984 (Vol. 13, No. 10)
CHARACTERISTICS OF INSURED UNEMPLOYED IN NEW MEXICO

(p. 6) Brief article, with 1 table showing New Mexico insured unemployed, by industry division, occupational category, age group, number of weeks unemployed, and sex, quarterly 1983-3rd quarter 1984.

S5578–2.602: Feb. 1985 (Vol. 14, No. 2)
NONAGRICULTURAL EMPLOYMENT IN NEW MEXICO AND ITS BORDER STATES

(p. 8) Article, with 1 table showing percent change in employment, by industry division, for New Mexico and 5 neighboring States, 1984 vs. 1983 and 1980.

S5578–2.603: Apr. 1985 (Vol. 14, No. 4)

NEW MEXICO MINING EMPLOYMENT

(p. 6) Article, with 2 tables showing New Mexico mining employment, by type of mineral or operation; and distribution of mining employment by county; June 1981 and Sept. 1984.

S5585   NEW MEXICO
Department of
Finance and Administration

S5585–1   ANNUAL FINANCIAL
           REPORT, 72nd Fiscal Year,
           State of New Mexico
           Annual. [1985.] 286 p.
           LC 76-615237.
           SRI/MF/complete

Annual report on financial condition of New Mexico State government, for FY84, presenting revenues by source, disbursements by function, and fund balances, for combined, general, special revenue, bond, working capital, and trust and agency funds.

Also includes assets and liabilities for combined funds and selected fund categories; State bonded indebtedness; detailed cash transactions, and appropriations and actual expenditures, by agency and function; and selected comparisons for FY83 and estimates for FY85.

Data are from Financial Control Division records.

Contains contents listing, and general comments (p. 3-8); 8 sections with contents listings, 3 charts, and 28 statements and exhibits (p. 9-286).

This is the 22nd annual report.

Availability: New Mexico Department of Finance and Administration, Financial Control Division, 166 Bataan Memorial Bldg., Santa Fe NM 87503, †; SRI/MF/complete.

S5585–2   STATISTICS: OFFICE OF
           EDUCATION, State of New
           Mexico
           Annual. Dec. 1984.
           273 p. var. paging.
           LC 59-63589.
           SRI/MF/complete

Annual report of the New Mexico Dept of Finance and Administration, on public school finances, 1983/84 and projected 1984/85, with selected trends from 1970s. Also includes data on pupil membership, personnel, salaries, and vocational schools. Most data are shown for individual school districts grouped by county.

Contains foreward and contents listing (2 p.); lists of school districts and superintendents (p. A1-A2); and 3 charts, and 43 tables listed below (p. B1-G9).

This is the 21st edition of the report. Additional data on New Mexico public school pupils, teachers, and finances are available in *New Mexico School District Profile,* covered in SRI under S5575-2.

Availability: New Mexico Department of Finance and Administration, Public School Finance Division, 515 Don Gaspar Ave., Santa Fe NM 87501-4498, $20.00; SRI/MF/complete.

TABLES:

[Tables show data by school district for 1983/84, unless otherwise noted.]

S5585–2.1: School Districts and Membership

[1] Number of school districts in State, Sept. 1 [decennially 1950-80, by county]. (p. A3)

[2] Average daily membership [ADM, aggregate for] grades 1-12, special education C & D [more and less severely handicapped students], nonprofit (private special education), and early childhood education FTE (State funded only). (p. B1-B4)

[3-4] Statewide membership: by grade by funding period [and for various] reporting periods, 1974/75-1983/84. (p. B5-B6)

S5585–2.2: Income, Expenditures, and Cash Balances

INCOME

[Tables [3-5], [10], and [12] show State totals only.]

[1-2] Actual income by fund; and actual revenue [by detailed source], operational fund. (p. C1-C17)

[3] Total appropriations and distributions [by fund]. (p. C18)

[4] State appropriations to public schools [by function], 10-year comparison, 1974/75-1984/85. (p. C19)

[5] Analysis of receipts [by source]. (p. C22)

[6] Special education ADM served in private nonprofit training centers, and program cost generated by ADM. (p. C23)

EXPENDITURES AND CASH BALANCES

[7] Expenditures by line item. (p. C24-C98)

[8-9] Supporting information, actual expenditures: 11. series special projects (operational); and 17. series Federal projects (non-operational). (p. C99-C103)

[10] Expenditure comparison by budget category, 1980/81-1983/84 inclusive. (p. C104)

[11] Operational expenditures per pupil, by school size. (p. C105-C107)

[12] Net operational expenditures per pupil, 10-year study, 1974/75-1983/84. (p. C108)

[13] Cash balances as of June 30, 1984, operational fund, and other funds [by fund]. (p. C109-C116)

S5585–2.3: Income Projections and Budgets

[Tables show projected data for 1984/85.]

[1-2] Appropriations [State total], and projected income; by fund. (p. D1-D6)

[3] Estimated revenue [by detailed source], operational fund. (p. D7-D19)

[4] Final approved budget [by function and object]. (p. D20-D94)

[5-6] Supporting information, final approved budgets: 11. series special projects (operational); and 17. series Federal projects (non-operational). (p. D95-D99)

[7] Reconciliation of estimated revenue and budget [by fund, State total]. (p. D100)

S5585–2.4: Assessed Valuations and Bonded Indebtedness

[1] Comparison of actual assessed valuations: local, corporate, and oil/gas, actual 1982-83. (p. E1-E4)

[2] District tax rates and statewide average tax rates, 1984/85. (p. E5-E9)

[3] Bonded debt of school districts, as of June 30, 1984. (p. E10-E13)

S5585–2.5: Personnel and Salaries

[1] Average teacher salary, 10-year study [State total, 1974/75-1984/85]. (p. F1)

[2] School district ranking by average salaries of full-time classroom teachers, and related information [including number of teachers, pupil/teacher ratio, beginning and highest salary on schedule, average years of experience, and percent of teachers with master's/higher degree]. (p. F2-F4)

[3-4] Certified and noncertified personnel average annual salaries, by [position and] school size (paid from operational budgets). (p. F5-F22)

[5] One-time, non-recurring salary increases [by position]. (p. F23).

[6] Total number of Federal employees, by Federal project employed [and position; State total]. (p. F24)

S5585–2.6: Vocational Schools

[Data are shown for 3 technical and/or vocational institutions: Albuquerque Technical-Vocational Institute, Luna Area Vocational-Technical School, and Tucumcari Area Vocational School.]

[1-2] FTE and operational fund distributions summary; and capital outlay appropriations summary; [various periods 1979/80-1983/84]. (p. G1-G2)

[3-4] Degree and nondegree personnel average annual salaries (paid from operational budget) [by position]. (p. G3)

[5-10] Budget report or ending cash balance, 1983/84; and finalized budget, 1984/85. (p. G4-G9)

S5605   NEW MEXICO
Health and Environment
Department

S5605–1   SELECTED HEALTH
           STATISTICS, New Mexico,
           1982-83
           Biennial. Oct. 1985.
           3+119 p.
           ISSN 0161-5416.
           LC 80-640288.
           SRI/MF/complete

Biennial report on New Mexico vital statistics, including population, births, deaths, and disease, by location and demographic characteristics, 1983 with selected trends from 1940. Also includes special analysis of New Mexico prenatal care and mortality, and selected comparisons to U.S.

Data are primarily from dept records, other State agencies, and Federal sources.

Contents:

a. Map of State health districts, and contents listing (2 p.); highlights and definitions (p.

1-3); and 4 statistical sections, with narrative analyses interspersed with 69 charts/maps and 95 tables (p. 4-70).

b. "New Mexico Levels of Prenatal Care." Special feature, with 6 tables and 3 charts showing live births, and infant, neonatal, and post-neonatal mortality rates, by county and level of prenatal care (high, middle, low); and live births with little/no prenatal care, by age of mother and race/ethnicity of child; various periods 1980-83. (p. 71-74)

c. "New Mexico Matched Infant Death File Statistical Summary." Special feature, with 1 table and 12 charts showing infant mortality rates, by birth weight, mother's marital status and age group, race/ethnicity, and other characteristics, with comparison to neonatal and post-neonatal mortality; and distribution of births by level of prenatal care, birth weight, and age of mother; 1980-82 period or 1983. (p. 75-80)

d. "New Mexico Standardized Mortality Ratios." Special feature, with 3 tables showing number of deaths recorded and expected under standardized national rates, by race/ethnicity, age group, and county, all by cause, 1979-82 period. (p. 81-86)

e. "New Mexico Years of Potential Life Lost." Special feature, with 1 table and 4 charts showing years of potential life lost (a measurement of premature mortality based on age-specific death rates), by county and cause of death; with ranking of major causes responsible for greatest loss (including detail by race/ethnicity and comparison to U.S.), 1979-82 period. (p. 87-94)

f. Appendix, with table listing, and 19 tables. (p. 95-119)

All statistical section and appendix tables, and selected statistical section charts presenting State statistics on topics not covered in tables, are listed below.

Previous report, for 1981, is described in SRI 1983 Annual under this number. Periodicity of previous reports was erroneously designated in SRI as annual.

Availability: New Mexico Health and Environment Department, Health Services Division, PO Box 968, Santa Fe NM 87504-0968, †; SRI/MF/ complete.

TABLES AND CHARTS:

[All tables show data for New Mexico, often with comparisons to total U.S. Data by race/ethnicity are generally shown for Hispanic and non-Hispanic white, and for black and Indian. Data shown by county are generally grouped for 7 health districts.]

S5605–1.1: Selected Vital Statistics

POPULATION

1.1. 12 fastest growing States [cumulative percent increase], 1980-83 and 1970-80. (p. 4)

1.2. Components of population change [increase or decrease in number, and share caused by natural increase and net migration, 1950-60 period, and annually 1961-1983]. (p. 5)

1.3-1.5. Population percentage distribution: by age group [various years 1950-2000]; and by age group, by county, 1980. (p. 5-6)

1.6-1.8. Population by county [various years 1970-2000]. (p. 7-9)

1.9-1.12. Ethnic/racial composition, 1970 census and 1980 estimate; population growth characteristics by [race/ethnicity], 1970-80 [period]; and racial distribution, by county, and by age group, 1980. (p. 11)

Figure 1.12. Population distribution by age, [race/ethnicity, and sex], 1980 census. (p. 12)

INCOME

1.13. Per capita personal income, 1975-83. (p. 12)

Figure 1.14. Per capita personal income, ranking by county, 1982. (p. 13)

1.14. Percentage of persons at/below poverty level, by race/ethnicity, 1980 census. (p. 13)

Figure 1.15. [Percentage of] families below poverty, ranking by county, 1980 census. (p. 14)

Figure 1.16. Financial/food stamp recipients percent of county population, ranking by county, July 1982. (p. 14)

MARRIAGES AND DIVORCES

1.15-1.16. Marriages and dissolutions of marriages: rates per 1,000 population, selected years 1940-83; [and number and rate, by county], 1980-81. (p. 15)

ABORTIONS

[Tables show data for 1980-83, unless otherwise noted. All tables, except tables 1.22 and 1.24, begin "New Mexico residents; reported legal induced abortions...," and show data by race/ethnicity.]

1.17. Abortions, and ratio per 1,000 live births. (p. 16)

1.18-1.21. Percentage distribution by age group, level of education, marital status, and [number of] previous induced abortions. (p. 16-17)

1.22. Resident abortions, percentage distribution by age group and gestation period. (p. 17)

1.23. Percentage distribution by weeks gestation. (p. 18)

1.24. Residents reported legal induced abortions, percentage [distribution] by facility [physician's office, clinic, and hospital], 1978-83. (p. 18)

Figure 1.18. Abortion ratios (per 1,000 live births), [by county], 1980-83 [period]. (p. 18)

S5605–1.2: Births

LIVE BIRTHS

[Tables 2.2-2.3, 2.5-2.7, and 2.9-2.10 begin "New Mexico resident(s)..."]

2.1. Birth rate by county of residence, 1975-83. (p. 20)

Figure 2.3. Birth rate by race/ethnicity, 1978-83. (p. 20)

2.2. Fertility rates, and birth rates by age of mother, [selected years 1960-83]. (p. 21)

2.3-2.6. Live births, [and/or] percentage distribution, by age of mother and race/ethnicity, [various years 1960-83]. (p. 21-22)

Figure 2.4. Percentage of births to teen-aged mothers, [by race/ethnicity], 1978-83. (p. 22)

2.7. Fertility rates, and birth rates by age of mother [all by race/ethnicity], 1979-83. (p. 23)

2.8. Percent [distribution] of live births, by age of mother and age of father, 1983. (p. 23)

2.9-2.10. Live births, [and] percentage distribution by live birth order, by age of mother [and race/ethnicity, various years 1960-83]. (p. 24-25)

2.11. Births to single mothers, percentage of total births by county of residence, [selected periods 1973-83]. (p. 26)

Figure 2.8. Births to single mothers, percentage by race/ethnicity [including 3 specific Indian tribes], 1978-83. (p. 27)

2.12-2.14. Births to single mothers, percentage of total births: by age of mother, by race/ethnicity and county, 1983; and by age of mother, 1976-83. (p. 27-28)

INCIDENCE OF LOW BIRTH WEIGHT

Figure 2.12. Low birth weight [births as percent of total births] by race/ethnicity [including 3 specific Indian tribes], 1978-83. (p. 29)

2.15-2.17. Percent low birth weight: by county, by age of mother, 1982/83 average; by race/ethnicity and sex, 1982-83; and by county of residence, selected periods 1973-83. (p. 29-30)

2.18-2.19. Percent of live births by birth weight distribution and weeks of gestation, 1982 and/or 1983. (p. 30-31)

CONGENITAL ANOMALIES

[Tables and figures begin "Live births with congenital anomalies..."]

2.20. Rate per 100,000 live births, by selected types of anomalies, 1980-83 [period] average. (p. 32)

Figures 2.16-2.17. Percent reported by race/ethnic group and age of mother, 1980-83 [period] average. (p. 32)

2.21. Number and percent reported, by county of residence, 1980-83. (p. 33)

MISCELLANEOUS CHARACTERISTICS

Figure 2.19. Percent of live births by education of mother and father, 1983. (p. 33)

2.22. Percentage of live births in hospital by county of occurrence, [selected years] 1956-83. (p. 34)

2.23. Resident births [occurring in and out of county, and out of State, by county of residence], 1983. (p. 34)

2.24. Live births, percentage occurring in [and out of] hospitals, and [distribution] by attendant [1965 and 1971-83]. (p. 34)

2.25-2.26. Natality characteristics by county [number and rate; sex ratio; percent of births of low weight, single mothers, and mothers age 19 and under; and births by race/ethnicity of child], 1982-83. (p. 35)

S5605–1.3: Deaths and Communicable Diseases

[Death cause categories are from the 9th revision of the *International Classification of Diseases.*]

DEATHS AND DEATH RATES

3.1. Crude and adjusted death rates [by sex and race/ethnicity, selected periods 1979-83]. (p. 36)

3.2. Age specific death rates, [by sex], 1981-83 [period] average. (p. 36)

3.3. Average years of life remaining based on 3-year average mortality rates (1979-81) [by age and sex, by race/ethnicity]. (p. 37)

DEATHS BY CAUSE

3.4-3.6. Death rates from [13] leading causes, 1980-83. (p. 38-39)

3.7. Resident deaths, percentage distribution by cause, by race/ethnicity, 1980-83 [period] average. (p. 40)

3.8. Crude and age-adjusted death rates [by sex, race/ethnicity, and cause, 1981-83 period average]. (p. 41)

DEATHS BY AGE

[Tables 3.9-3.20 show average data for 1981-83 period.]

3.9. [Number of deaths,] and percentage [distribution] by age groups, [by] sex and race/ethnic groups. (p. 42)

3.10-3.17. Age specific death rates, [for 8 age groups], leading causes: by race/ethnicity [and sex]. (p. 42-46)

3.18. Age adjusted mortality rates by [12] selected causes, by [sex and] county. (p. 47)

3.19-3.20. Age specific death rates [of] males and females for [13] selected causes [by race/ethnicity]. (p. 48-49)

INFANT AND MATERNAL DEATHS

3.21-3.24. Infant mortality rate: by race/ethnicity, 1972-83; by cause, 1980-83; and by race/ethnicity and sex, 1982-83. (p. 50-53)

3.25. Infant mortality, number and rate by county, 1979-83 aggregate. (p. 53)

3.26-3.27. Infant mortality rates by cause and age, 1982-83. (p. 54-55)

3.28-3.29. Maternal mortality by race/ethnicity and age of mother [number and rate], various periods 1979-83. (p. 56)

Figure 3.14. Fetal death ratio by age of mother, 1981-83 [period] average. (p. 57)

3.30-3.32. Fetal deaths: number and ratio by county, 1977-83; and by cause and race/ethnicity, 1982-83. (p. 58-59)

3.33-3.34. Mortality by county [total by sex, total rate, maternal deaths, and number and rate for neonatal, postneonatal, infant, and fetal deaths], 1982-83. (p. 60)

COMMUNICABLE DISEASES

4.1. Gonorrhea, age specific case rates, 1976-83. (p. 62)

4.2-4.3. Occurrence by county, gonorrhea and syphilis cases reported, 1982-83. (p. 62)

4.4. Primary/secondary syphilis, age specific case rates, 1976-83. (p. 62)

Figures 4.5-4.6. Plague, total cases reported by county, 1982-83. (p. 63)

4.5. Plague occurrence [for month acquired and by age group and sex], 1976-83. (p. 64)

Figures 4.8-4.9. Rabies, number of cases reported [by county], 1982-83. (p. 65)

4.6. Tuberculosis morbidity and mortality [rates, selected years] 1930-83. (p. 65)

4.7. Tuberculosis death rates by race/ethnicity, 1978-83. (p. 66)

4.8. Tuberculosis case rate per 100,000 population, specific age groups, 1981-83. (p. 67)

Figure 4.17. Rubella, number of cases reported per 100,000 population [by county], 1982. (p. 68)

4.9-4.10. Notifiable diseases, reported cases and case rates, 1982-83. (p. 69)

4.11. Selected communicable diseases, number of reported cases, 1967-83. (p. 70)

S5605–1.4: Appendix Tables

A1. City populations [1970 and] 1980 census. (p. 96)

A2. Resident live births, [and] percentage by age of mother, [by county], 1970, 1980, and 1982-83. (p. 97)

A3. Fertility rates, [and] birth rates by age of mother, by county, 1970, 1980, and 1982-83. (p. 98-99)

A4-A5. Live births by age of mother, [and] percentage distribution by live birth order, [by county], 1982-83. (p. 100-103)

A6-A7. Births by county of occurrence, by facility and attendant at birth, 1982-83. (p. 104-105)

A8-A9. Births and deaths, by place of residence [county and urban-rural status], 1982-83. (p. 106-109)

A10. Age specific death rates by county and sex, 1981-83 [period] average. (p. 110-111)

A11. Resident deaths, number and crude death rate by cause, 1982-83. (p. 112)

A12-A17. Selected causes of death by county [for total, males, and females], 1982-83. (p. 113-118)

A18. Summary of trends in health statistics [mid-year population estimate; number and rate of births, deaths, and maternal, infant, and fetal deaths; and neonatal and post-neonatal death rates; 1950-83]. (p. 119)

S5623   NEW MEXICO
Judicial Department

S5623–1   ANNUAL REPORT, JULY 1, 1983-JUNE 30, 1984, Judicial Department, State of New Mexico
Annual.   Nov. 1, 1984.
3+32 p.
LC 73-645091.
SRI/MF/complete

Annual report on New Mexico judicial system, including trial and appellate court caseloads and case dispositions, FY84, with summary trends from 1966. Covers supreme, appeals, district, magistrate, and Bernalillo County metro courts. Includes trial court data by case type, district, and county, with detail for magistrate courts by city.

Case types include civil, criminal, domestic, juvenile, and traffic cases including driving while intoxicated.

Also includes data on judicial system finances and personnel; case processing time for appeals; bond forfeitures, and crime laboratory and other fees; and metro court probation dept activities.

Data are from reports filed with the administrative office of the courts.

Contains contents listing (1 p.); and report, with 1 map and 18 tables (p. 1-32).

This is the 72nd fiscal year report. Previous report, for FY83, is unavailable for review. For description of FY82 report, see SRI 1983 Annual under this number.

Availability: New Mexico Judicial Department, Administrative Office of the Courts, Supreme Court Bldg., Rm. 130, Santa Fe NM 87503, †; SRI/MF/complete.

S5627   NEW MEXICO
State Library

S5627–1   LIBRARY STATISTICS, FY84, New Mexico State Library
Annual.   Jan. 1985.   23 p.
LC 81-649870.
SRI/MF/complete

Annual report, for FY84, on New Mexico public library holdings, circulation, finances, services, and staff. Data are from reports of libraries, and the 1980 census.

Contains introduction and library directories (p. 1-7); and 7 tables, listed below (p. 8-23).

Availability: New Mexico State Library, 325 Don Gaspar Ave., Santa Fe NM 87503, †; SRI/MF/complete.

TABLES:

[Data are shown for FY84, generally by location and/or library. Tables show data for some or all of the following: hours open; FTE staff; circulation; holdings (including volumes, titles, periodical subscriptions, technical reports, microforms, and audiovisual); interlibrary loans; municipal, county, State, and/or other income; population, communities, and/or borrowers served; and salary, materials, and other operating expenditures. Additional data are noted below.]

[1-3] Public, community, and academic libraries. (p. 8-17)

[4] Special libraries [also includes library subject specialty]. (p. 18-19)

[5] State institutions [residents' libraries in correctional, health/environment, and vocational rehabilitation/educational institutions, including State schools for the deaf and visually handicapped; income sources are institution, Library Services and Construction Act funds, and other Federal funds]. (p. 20-21)

[6] State library program statistics [shows selected data for books-by-mail, library for the blind/physically handicapped, large-print book circuit, and information and other services; and expenditures by object]. (p. 22)

[7] State library bookmobile service [by region; also includes data on stops, mileage, and deposit collections]. (p. 23)

[8] Book stations. (p. 23)

S5645   NEW MEXICO
Public Service Commission

**S5645–1   FORTIETH ANNUAL
REPORT, 72nd Fiscal Year,
July 1, 1983-June 30, 1984:
New Mexico Public Service
Commission**
Annual.   Oct. 31, 1984.
82 p.
LC 43-52821.
SRI/MF/complete

Annual report presenting New Mexico public utility financial and operating data, primarily for 1982-83, and regulatory data, for FY84; for electric, gas, and water utilities.

Covers operating summary, including plant investment, operating revenue and expenses, stockholders' equity, and bonded and long-term debt; selected financial and operating ratios; and customers, sales volume, gross revenues, average customer use and bill, and monthly rates by community and company, all by customer class; for all utility types.

Also includes security issuances, by company; and Commission receipts, disbursements, and regulatory caseloads, including rate cases and consumer complaints.

Data are compiled from Commission records and utility company reports.

Contains contents and table listing, introduction, and Commission authority and financial summary (p. 4-10); list of regulated companies (p. 11-13); utility data, with 13 tables (p. 14-39); and regulatory caseload dispositions (p. 40-82).

Availability: New Mexico Public Service Commission, Bataan Memorial Bldg., Santa Fe NM 87503, †; SRI/MF/complete.

S5652   NEW MEXICO
Regulation and
Licensing Department

**S5652–1   70th ANNUAL REPORT,
New Mexico Financial
Institutions Division, 1984**
Annual.   [1985.]   106 p.
LC 79-644636.
SRI/MF/complete

Annual report on the financial condition of New Mexico State- and/or federally-chartered financial institutions for 1984, presenting assets and liabilities for banks, savings and loan assns, and credit unions, all by institution. Includes equity capital, net worth, or reserves, and number of branches, as appropriate; and consolidated statements of income and expenses for each type of State-chartered institution.

Also includes Financial Institutions Division activities; State bank loans outstanding by type; Consumer Credit Bureau composite financial, loan, and legal data for small loan licensees; State Securities Bureau applications and fees received; and selected trends from as early as 1920.

Contains transmittal letter and contents listing (3 p.); and report, with 23 tables, directories, and summary of regulations (p. 4-106).

Availability: New Mexico Regulation and Licensing Department, Financial Institutions Division, Lew Wallace Bldg., Santa Fe NM 87503, ‡; SRI/MF/complete.

S5655   NEW MEXICO
Office of the
Secretary of
State

**S5655–1   STATE OF NEW MEXICO
OFFICIAL RETURNS: 1984
General, Primary, and
Special Primary Returns**
Biennial.   Jan. 14, 1985.
360 p. var. paging. Oversized.
LC 81-645986.
SRI/MF/complete

Biennial report, for 1984, presenting results of New Mexico primary and general elections held June 5, Sept. 18, and Nov. 6, 1984. Includes voting for President/Vice President; U.S. Senator and Representatives; State senators, representatives, judges, board of education, and other State and county offices including sheriffs; 1 constitutional amendment; and several referenda, including Sunday sales of liquor "by the drink." Data are shown by precinct, county, and district, and include party affiliation of candidates.

Also includes voter registration and turnout, by party and location.

For description of previous report, covering 1982 elections, see SRI 1983 Annual, under this number.

Availability: New Mexico Office of the Secretary of State, Executive Legislative Bldg., Santa Fe NM 87503, †; SRI/MF/complete.

S5700   NEW YORK STATE
Department of
Agriculture and Markets

**S5700–1   NEW YORK AGRICULTURAL
STATISTICS, 1984**
Annual.   June 1985.   83 p.
LC 79-648711.
SRI/MF/complete

Annual report on New York State agricultural production, marketing, and finances, mostly 1975-84, with some data for 1985. Data generally are shown by commodity, with some detail by county and area, and selected comparisons to other States and total U.S.

Covers production, cash receipts, value, prices, and, as applicable, acreage, yield, inventory, and disposition, for field crop, vegetable, fruit, livestock, dairy, poultry, and floriculture sectors.

Also includes data on farms and acreage; farm finances, utility use, pasture condition, labor and wages, acreage, and value; apple processing plants and holdings in cold storage; dairy product manufacturing plants; maple syrup and mink industries; weather; farm labor, wage rates, and hours worked; fertilizer consumption; and U.S. farm real estate value by State, and food consumption by commodity.

Data are compiled by the New York State Crop Reporting Service and USDA in cooperation with the State Dept of Agriculture and Markets.

Contains contents listing (p. 5); 2 maps, 7 charts, and 108 tables, with interspersed narrative summaries (p. 6-82); and list of State agriculture reports available (p. 83).

Availability: New York State Crop Reporting Service, One Winners Circle, Albany NY 12235-0001, †; SRI/MF/complete.

S5710   NEW YORK STATE
Department of
Audit and Control

**S5710–1   STATE OF NEW YORK 1984
ANNUAL REPORT OF THE
COMPTROLLER**
Annual.   July 20, 1984.
63 p.
ISSN 0098-6372.
LC 75-644665.
SRI/MF/complete

Annual report on financial condition of New York State, FY84, presenting assets, liabilities, equity, revenues by source, expenses by function, and balances, for individual general fund accounts; special revenue, debt service, capital project, and trust/agency funds; and public benefit corporations.

Also includes data on finances of State-administered retirement systems, bonded debt, and budgeted vs. actual receipts and disbursements.

Data are compiled by the comptroller's office.

Contains transmittal letter, overview, and contents listing (p. 1-3); and 15 financial statements, explanatory notes with text data, and 8 summary charts (p. 4-63).

An annual financial report on municipal affairs is also available from the comptroller's office, but is not covered by SRI.

Availability: New York State Department of Audit and Control, Comptroller's Press Office, Alfred E. Smith State Office Bldg., Albany NY 12236, †; SRI/MF/complete.

S5720   NEW YORK STATE
Department of
Commerce

**S5720–2   BUSINESS STATISTICS,
New York State**
Quarterly, with annual
summary.   Approx. 20 p.
SRI/MF/complete

Quarterly report, with annual summary, on New York State business activity indicators, with detail by location and comparisons to U.S. Includes data on industrial production, domestic and foreign trade, employment and unemployment, construction activity, income and finance, air traffic, motor vehicle registrations, social services, and newspaper advertising linage.

Data are from specified State, Federal, and private sources. Report is issued 12-20 months after quarter of data coverage.

Contains contents listing, and 9 tables listed below. Annual summary presents 9-year trends for data covered in quarterly tables.

Report has been published since 1939. SRI coverage begins with the Oct./Dec. 1983 issue.

A less detailed monthly report is also available from the issuing agency, but is not covered by SRI.

Availability: New York State Department of Commerce, Economic Research and Statistics Division, Business Research Bureau, One Commerce Plaza, Albany, NY 12245, †; SRI/MF/ complete.

Issues reviewed during 1985: Oct./Dec. 1983; and annual summary for 1975-83 (D).

TABLES:

[Data are for New York State, unless otherwise noted, and often include comparisons to total U.S. Most data are shown monthly for quarter of coverage and 2 preceding months, with comparisons to same quarter of previous year.]

[1] Indexes of business activity [summary by industry sector and metro area].

[2] Production [factory output and electricity production indexes, and utilities' natural gas sales volume; and (U.S. only) value of manufacturers' shipments, inventories, and new orders].

[3] Domestic trade [retail and wholesale activity indexes; and retail sales in nondurable goods, general merchandise/apparel/furniture/appliance, and department stores, with detail for NYC area].

[4] Foreign trade [value, through New York State customs districts (Canadian border and other), and for waterborne trade through Port of New York].

[5] Employment, hours, and earnings [nonagricultural employment by industry division and major group, manufacturing hours and earnings, unemployment, unemployment benefit claims, and unemployment insurance fund balance and covered employment, with selected detail by metro area and county].

[6] Construction and real estate [construction activity index; construction contract value for residential and nonresidential buildings and for nonbuilding structures; and, occasionally, new housing units authorized and building permit value; all by metro area].

[7] Income, savings, and finance [finance/insurance/real estate activity index; personal income; savings bank savings; savings and loan assn shares outstanding; sales of U.S. savings bonds; volume and/or value of NYSE stocks listed and sold, and aggregate average price for 30 industrial stocks; value of bank time and demand deposits and commercial/agricultural/industrial loans, for NYC, aggregate leading cities, and/or New York Federal Reserve District; and debits of NYC and other banks].

[8] Price levels [includes index of milk prices received by farmers, CPI for 2 metro areas, and U.S. PPI].

[9] Miscellaneous measures [activity indexes for transportation/communication/public utility and service sectors; overseas and domestic passenger and freight traffic and plane movements, for aggregate NYC area airports; motor vehicle registrations; NYC and other cases for home relief and Aid to Dependent Children (unemployed father) programs; new incorporations; newspaper advertising linage by metro area; and, occasionally, business failures and liabilities].

S5720-3   NEW YORK STATE BUSINESS FACT BOOK, 1984 Supplement
Annual.   1984.   25 p.
LC 77-640471.
SRI/MF/complete

Annual report presenting New York State business and economic indicators, by locale, various periods 1981-83. Includes residential and nonresidential construction value; nonagricultural employment, and employment covered by unemployment insurance; labor force and unemployment rate; business establishments; personal income; high school graduates; bank deposits; motor vehicle registrations; and population.

Also includes index of overall business activity, with trends from 1975; and list of major manufacturing plant additions and expansions under construction/completed during 1983.

Most data are shown by labor area, SMSA, and county, with some comparisons to other industrial States and total U.S. Employment and establishment data include detail by major manufacturing group and/or industry division.

Data are from specified Federal, State, and private sources.

Contains contents listing (1 p.); narrative summary, with 1 chart and 1 table (p. 1-5); list of plant additions and expansions (p. 6-8); 10 tables, and list of SMSAs (p. 9-23); and State Commerce Dept directory, and map (p. 24-25).

Report has been published since 1929. SRI coverage begins with the 1984 edition.

Availability: New York State Department of Commerce, Economic Research and Statistics Division, One Commerce Plaza, Albany, NY 12245, †; SRI/MF/complete.

S5720-4   OFFICIAL POPULATION PROJECTIONS FOR NEW YORK STATE COUNTIES: 1980-2010
Monograph.   Apr. 1985.
203 p.
SRI/MF/complete

Report presenting projections of New York State population by age and sex, by county, SMSA, and region, quinquennially 1985-2010, with actual data for 1980. Also includes fertility and migration rates, by county, 5-year periods 1980-2010.

Data are based on 1980 census findings.

Contains introduction, highlights, methodology, and data sources (p. 3-6); 2 maps and 3 tables (p. 7-15); and 1 basic table and 1 chart, repeated for the State and each county, SMSA, and region (p. 20-203).

Availability: New York State Department of Commerce, State Data Center, One Commerce Plaza, Rm. 905, Albany NY 12245, †; SRI/MF/ complete.

S5725   NEW YORK STATE Department of Correctional Services

S5725-1   CHARACTERISTICS OF INMATES, New York State
Series.   For individual publication data, see below.
SRI/MF/complete

Series of 2 annual reports on corrections in New York State, presenting data on characteristics of inmates committed to and released on parole from State correctional facilities. Data are based on Correctional Services Dept records.

Individual reports are described below. SRI coverage begins with the 1983 reports.

Availability: New York Department of Correctional Services, Program Planning, Research, and Evaluation Division, State Office Bldg. Campus, Bldg. No. 2, Albany NY 12226, †; SRI/ MF/complete.

S5725-1.1: Characteristics of New Commitments to the Facilities of the Department of Correctional Services, 1983
[Annual. [1984.] ix+84 p. Vol. XVIII, No. 1. SRI/MF/complete.]

Annual report on characteristics of offenders committed to New York State correctional facilities, 1983, with selected trends from 1978. Includes data by inmate commitment offense, sentence length, and prior criminal record; region of commitment (NYC, upstate, and suburban); selected demographic and socioeconomic characteristics; and drug use history.

Contains listings of contents, charts, and tables (p. i-vi); introduction and highlights (p. vii-ix); and 13 charts and 82 tables, with accompanying narrative (p. 1-84).

S5725-1.2: Characteristics of First Parole and Conditional Releases from the Department of Correctional Services, 1983
[Annual. [1985.] ix+86 p. Vol. XVIII, No. 2. SRI/MF/complete.]

Annual report on characteristics of offenders released on parole for the 1st time from New York State correctional facilities, 1983, with selected trends from 1978. Includes data on parolee sentence length, time served, prior criminal record, commitment offense, region of commitment (NYC, upstate, and suburban NYC), and other demographic and socioeconomic characteristics, with various cross-tabulations.

Also includes data on total offenders discharged by type of release, including escapes and deaths, 1983.

Contains listings of contents, charts, and tables (p. i-vii); highlights and introduction (p. viii-ix); and 13 charts and 51 tables, with accompanying narrative (p. 1-86).

S5730   NEW YORK STATE
Office of
Court Administration

S5730–1   STATE OF NEW YORK REPORT OF THE CHIEF ADMINISTRATOR OF THE COURTS for the Calendar Year Jan. 1, 1982-Dec. 31, 1982
Annual.   Mar. 15, 1983.
xiii+173 p.
Legislative Doc. No. 90.
LC 81-640443.
SRI/MF/complete

Annual report, for 1982, on New York State judicial system, including trial and appellate court caseloads and case dispositions. Covers court of appeals; supreme, claims, family, surrogate, county, district, and town/village courts; and NYC civil and criminal courts. Includes data by case type and court location, and selected trends from 1979.

Case types shown are generally civil and criminal, with additional detail for tort, tax, housing, traffic, medical malpractice, probate, family relations, child abuse, and juvenile delinquency cases.

Also includes data on number of judges, by court level; case processing time; children in child abuse cases, by age and sex; attorney registrations, disciplinary actions, and retainer statements; and monetary settlements and judgments, by type of court and amount of recovered funds.

Contains listings of contents, charts, and tables (p. vii-xiii); narrative report in 4 chapters, with 8 charts and 18 tables (p. 1-108); and appendices with narrative and 45 tables (p. 109-173).

This is the 5th annual report.

Previous report, for 1981, is described in SRI 1983 Annual under this number.

Availability: New York State Office of Court Administration, 270 Broadway, New York NY 10007, †; SRI/MF/complete.

S5745   NEW YORK STATE
Education Department

S5745–1   ANNUAL EDUCATIONAL SUMMARY, 1982/83: Statistical and Financial Summary of Education in New York State for the Year Ending June 30, 1983
Annual.   [1984.]   x+198 p.
ISSN 0085-4077.
LC 74-644306.
SRI/MF/complete

Annual report on education in New York State, 1982/83 academic year, with selected trends from 1960/61. Presents detailed data on public elementary and secondary schools, including enrollment and finances by county and school district. Also includes selected data on nonpublic schools, colleges and universities, Boards of Cooperative Educational Services (BOCES) programs, and public libraries.

Most data are from the State Education Dept's Information Center on Education.

Contains foreword and listings of contents, tables, and charts (p. iii-x); 7 chapters, interspersed with 2 charts and 53 tables (p. 1-58); and appendix, with 14 tables (p. 59-198). All tables are listed below.

Availability: New York State Education Department, Information Center on Education, Publications Distribution Desk, State Education Bldg., Albany NY 12234, †; SRI/MF/complete.

TABLES:
[Types of school districts are: NYC, other cities, independent superintendencies, and supervisory districts. Data by location are generally for 5 major cities and rest of State.]

S5745–1.1: Statistical Highlights of 1982/83; and Public Elementary and Secondary Schools, Classrooms, and Staff

1. Education summary [for elementary/secondary schools, colleges/universities, and libraries], 1980/81-1982/83. (p. 2)

2-4. Number of public school districts by [enrollment] size and type of organization; and number of public schools by level; [various years] 1960/61-1982/83. (p. 5-7)

5. Professional positions in public day schools [and BOCES positions, various years] 1960/61-1982/83. (p. 8)

6-7. Pupil/staff ratios in public school districts, by type of district; and major pupil personnel services [medical, psychologists, guidance counselors, attendance, and social work] in public schools; 1980/81-1982/83. (p. 9-10)

S5745–1.2: Public Elementary and Secondary School Students

ENROLLMENT
[Tables 9-12 show data for 1960/61-1982/83.]

8. Fall enrollment in public schools by grade [including ungraded handicapped and BOCES], 1980/81-1982/83. (p. 12)

9-10. Fall enrollment in public schools by [grade] level and by type of district [and BOCES]. (p. 13-14)

11. Percentage of pupils enrolled in public school districts, by type of school district and [urban and nonurban] location. (p. 15)

12. Fall enrollment and average daily attendance (ADA) in public schools [in NYC and rest of State]. (p. 16)

SPECIAL PROGRAMS

13. Resident handicapped children [by type of handicap], by agency where services are received [in home district and by type of service], fall 1982. (p. 17)

14. Enrollment in occupational education programs by type of agency, [level of program], and major program area, 1982/83. (p. 18)

HIGH SCHOOL GRADUATES ENTERING COLLEGE

15-16. Percent of public high school graduates entering institutions of higher education [by type], within and outside New York State [various periods 1970/71-fall 1983]. (p. 19)

MINORITY STUDENTS

17-18. Percent distribution of public school students by racial/ethnic origin [black, Hispanic, and other]; and distribution of black and Hispanic students; [by location, various years] 1978/79-1982/83. (p. 20-21)

SUMMER SCHOOL

19. Public summer high schools [number and enrollment], 1981-83. (p. 21)

S5745–1.3: Finances of Public Elementary and Secondary Schools

20-22. Public school general, debt service, and Federal aid fund: revenues by major source and expenditures [by type, with selected detail by district type, various years] 1960/61-1982/83. (p. 23-25)

23-24. Public school general and debt service fund expenditures: per pupil in weighted average daily attendance (WADA) [by type of expense]; and percent distribution by major object of expense; [by district type, various years] 1980/81-1982/83. (p. 26-27)

25. Trends in public school expenditures [by type of fund], 1960/61-1982/83. (p. 28)

26. Public school capital funds [receipts and disbursements], 1980/81-1982/83. (p. 29)

S5745–1.4: Nonpublic Schools, Enrollment, and Staff

27. Fall enrollment in nonpublic schools by grade [including ungraded handicapped], 1980/81-1982/83. (p. 31)

28-29. Number of nonpublic schools and enrollment by religious [and other group] affiliation [and grade level]; and distribution of enrollment by location and racial/ethnic origin [including American Indian/Alaskan Native, Asian/Pacific Islander, and Hispanic]; 1982/83. (p. 32-34)

30-31. Number of nonpublic high school graduates, 1963/64-1982/83; and percent entering institutions of higher education [by type], fall 1965-83. (p. 35-36)

32. Professional positions in nonpublic schools [by position], 1980/81-1982/83. (p. 37)

33. Nonpublic summer high schools [number and enrollment], 1981-83. (p. 37)

S5745–1.5: Colleges and Universities
[All tables show data for institutions of higher education. Data by type of institution are generally for 2- and 4-year or more public, independent, and proprietary institutions. Data by institutional classification are basically for same categories, with additional detail by type of SUNY (State University of New York), CUNY (City University of New York), and independent institution.]

INSTITUTIONS AND APPLICATIONS

34. Number of degree-granting institutions [by type], 1978/79-1982/83. (p. 39)

35-36. Undergraduate applications received, accepted, and full-time students actually enrolled in class, fall 1982; and graduate and 1st-professional applications received and accepted for full- and part-time study, July 1, 1981-June 30, 1982; by institutional classification. (p. 40-41)

ENROLLMENT AND DEGREES CONFERRED

37. Degree-credit enrollment [by type of institution], fall 1978-82. (p. 42)

38. Degree-credit [full- and part-time] and noncredit enrollment by level of program and institutional classification, fall 1982. (p. 43)

39. Degree trends by type of institution, level of degree, and year, 1978/79-1982/83. (p. 44)

40. Degrees conferred by level of degree [by sex] and institutional classification, 1982/83. (p. 45)

FACULTY AND STAFF

41-42. Number, tenure status, and mean salary of full-time instructional faculty by length of contract; and number of full- and part-time employees by occupational activity; [both by] institutional classification, 1982/83. (p. 46-47)

S5745–1.6: Special Services of the State Education Dept

CONTINUING EDUCATION, LIBRARIES, AND REGENTS EXAMINATIONS

43. Continuing education in public school districts by field of study [number of districts, classes, and registrations], 1982/83. (p. 49)

44. Public/free assn libraries [number and population served, holdings, circulation, staff, and expenditures], 1980-82. (p. 50)

45. Number of State Regents examination papers written in secondary schools, by subject area, 1960/61-1982/83. (p. 51)

STUDENT AID

46-47. Number and cost of State scholarships, fellowships, and tuition assistance program awards, by year and type, 1981/82-1982/83. (p. 52)

48. Student loan program administered by the New York State Higher Education Services Corp. [recipients and amount], 1980/81-1982/83. (p. 53)

49. State-funded programs of postsecondary opportunity [student characteristics, number of graduates, funds per student, and freshmen scholastic and income background; for SUNY, CUNY, and independent institution programs], 1982/83. (p. 54)

PROFESSIONAL CERTIFICATES

50. Teaching and administrative certificates issued [permanent and provisional, by type of position], 1979-81. (p. 55)

51. Professional certificates and licenses, other than educational, issued FY81-83. (p. 56)

52. Professional registration [by occupation], FY83. (p. 57)

HIGH SCHOOL EQUIVALENCY GRADUATES

53. High school equivalency diplomas issued, 1960/61-1982/83. (p. 58)

S5745–1.7: Appendix Tables: District, County, and Region Data

[All data are shown by region, county, and school district. Tables 56-67 show data for 1982/83.]

54-55. Public school enrollment by grade [and ungraded handicapped; includes data for BOCES], fall 1982. (p. 60-83)

56-57. Unadjusted ADA [by grade level] and WADA. (p. 84-96)

58-61. General fund, debt service fund, and Federal aid fund revenues [by source] and expenditures [by type]. (p. 98-151)

62-63. Expenditures per pupil in WADA [by fund and expenditure type]. (p. 152-177)

64-67. Real property valuation and tax levy [total, and] per pupil in resident WADA. (p. 178-198)

S5745–2 **PUBLIC AND ASSOCIATION LIBRARIES STATISTICS, 1983, New York State**
Annual. Aug. 10, 1984.
vi+184 p.
ISSN 0077-9326.
LC 76-646730.
SRI/MF/complete

Annual report on New York State public and assn libraries, 1983. Presents data on population and area served, holdings, circulation, staff, and finances, by library. Data are based on reports from individual libraries.

Contains contents listing, introduction, and reference notes (p. iv-vi); 10 tables, listed below (p. 1-89); and 6 appendices, with report forms and instructions, abbreviations, and indexes (p. 91-184).

This agency also issues *Institution Libraries Statistics* and *Directory of College and University Libraries in New York State,* not covered by SRI.

Availability: New York State Education Department, Library Development, Cultural Education Center, Rm. 10B41, Empire State Plaza, Albany NY 12230, †; SRI/MF/complete.

TABLES:

[Tables II-V show data for 1983.]

I. Comparative study [population and counties served by system/nonsystem libraries, number of systems and libraries, holdings and circulation, staff, and finances, 1957 and 1981-83]. (p. 1)

II-IIA. System summary [population, land area, and number of counties served; book stock; circulation; operating fund disbursements for salaries/benefits and library materials; total operating/capital fund disbursements; and operating fund receipts, by source]; and public outlets [including bookmobiles; all by library system]. (p. 2-3)

IIIA. System statistics—general [book and nonbook holdings, professional and nonprofessional staff, book and audiovisual additions, circulation, and interlibrary loan use, by library, arranged by system and county]. (p. 4-23)

IIIB-IIIC. System statistics—financial disbursements [by object] and receipts [by source; by library, arranged by system and county]. (p. 24-65)

IVA-IVC. [Tables IIIA-IIIC are repeated for nonsystem libraries.] (p. 66-71)

V. System and nonsystem statistics, by [library, ranked by size of] population served [books added, book holdings, circulation, hours open per week, staff, and finances]. (p. 72-89)

S5750 **NEW YORK STATE Board of Elections**

S5750–1 **BALLOT BILLBOARD: Biennial Election Results**
Quarterly (selected issue).
[Jan. 1985.] 36 p. no paging.
SRI/MF/complete

Biennial feature presenting results of the New York State general election held Nov. 6, 1984. Shows voting for President/Vice-President, 2 proposed State constitutional amendments, U.S. Representatives, State senators, and State Assembly members, all by county or district.

Also includes voter registration and presidential election turnout, by county.

Ballot Billboard is a quarterly newsletter on New York State election and campaign activities, and is generally narrative. The biennial election results feature appears as an insert in the issue for the winter quarter following a general election. The winter issue is the only one covered by SRI.

For description of previous feature, see SRI 1983 Annual under this number.

Availability: New York State Board of Elections, PO Box 4, One Commerce Plaza, Albany NY 12260, †; SRI/MF/complete.

S5760 **NEW YORK STATE Executive Department**

S5760–3 **NEW YORK STATE CRIME AND JUSTICE Annual Report, 1983**
Annual. [1984.] x+286 p.
ISSN 0095-4047.
LC 74-648505.
SRI/MF/complete

Annual report presenting detailed data on New York State crimes and arrests, and summary data on law enforcement personnel, court operations, and corrections, 1983 with trends from as early as FY67.

Covers crimes and clearances; and arrests by offender age, sex, and race/ethnicity; all by Index and non-Index offense, with detail by county and/or reporting agency. Index offenses are murder, rape, robbery, assault, burglary, larceny, motor vehicle theft, and arson. Index offense data also include value of property stolen and recovered, types of weapons and property involved, and other crime circumstances (including detailed analyses for murder, arson, and domestic violence).

Also presents data on felony indictments, case prcessing time, and dispositions, including convictions, jury trials, probation placements, incarceration, and sentence lengths, with detail by offense; law enforcement expenditure summary; officers killed and assaulted by circumstance; and law enforcement employment by sex, and vehicles owned, by local agency.

Also includes caseloads and dispositions by type of court; correctional institution inmates, admissions, and releases, with data for juveniles, and detail by commitment offense (and whether 1st or 2nd commitment), sentence length, race/ethnicity, age, education, sex, and individual facility; incidents occurring in correctional facilities, by type; and activities of Parole Board and Crime Victims Board, including crime victim claims and payments.

Data are often shown for NYC, suburban NYC, upstate region, and individual counties. Data by race/ethnicity variously include white, black, Indian, Asian, and Hispanic.

Data are from reports of State and local agencies, including filings submitted under the Uniform Crime Reporting (UCR) Program.

Contains contents, table, and chart listing (4 p.); introduction, with description of UCR Program and county map (p. ix-x, 1-4); and report in 2 sections, with 44 charts and 128 tables, interspersed with narrative summaries (p. 1-294).

This is the 9th annual report.

Availability: New York State Executive Department, Criminal Justice Services Division, Policy Analysis Office, Research and Statistical Services, Executive Park Tower, 10th Floor, Stuyvesant Plaza, Albany NY 12203-3764, $5.00; SRI/MF/complete.

S5765   NEW YORK STATE Department of Health

S5765-1   VITAL STATISTICS of New York State, 1983
Annual. [1985.] 162 p.
ISSN 0097-9449.
LC 75-642675.
SRI/MF/complete

Annual report, for 1983, on New York State vital statistics, including births, deaths by cause, marriages, and marriage dissolutions, for the State, NYC, all counties, and cities over 10,000 population, 1981-83, with birth and death trends from 1900.

Data are primarily from certificates filed with the Bureau of Health Statistics, and from related Federal and State information systems.

Contains listings of contents, maps, charts, and tables (3 p.); narrative report, with 6 charts, 14 maps, and 4 summary tables (p. 1-43); 36 tables, listed below (101 p.); technical notes (7 p.); and list of articles appearing in other New York State vital statistic publications (6 p.).

Other Bureau of Health Statistics publications include a quarterly report, *Vital Statistics Monitor,* that contains provisional summary data and special studies. Quarterly report is not covered by SRI.

This is the 104th annual report.

Availability: New York State Department of Health, Health Statistics Bureau, Rm. 321, ESP Tower Bldg., Albany NY 12237, †; SRI/MF/ complete.

TABLES:
[Upstate New York is the State exclusive of NYC.]

S5765-1.1: Trends, 1963-83
[Tables 1-6 show data for State, NYC, and upstate New York. Tables 2-6 show data for 1963-83.]

1. Estimated population by sex and age, July 1, 1983. (1 p.)

2. Live births, live birth rates, and general fertility rates. (1 p.)

3. Spontaneous fetal deaths 20+ weeks gestation and fetal mortality rates. (1 p.)

4. Deaths, crude death rates, and age-sex-adjusted death rates. (1 p.)

5. Infant deaths (deaths under 1 year of age) and infant mortality rates. (1 p.)

6. Neonatal deaths (deaths under 28 days of age) and neonatal mortality rates. (1 p.)

S5765-1.2: State Data
[All tables show data for 1983. Tables show data for State and upstate New York, unless otherwise noted. Data by color are shown for white and nonwhite.]

LIVE BIRTHS

7-8. Live births by birth weight and color, month in which prenatal care began and color, by age of mother. (2 p.)

9-10. Live births by sex and color, live birth order and color, by age of mother. (2 p.)

DEATHS

11. Deaths and death rates by age and sex. (1 p.)

12-14. Deaths and death rates from selected causes [includes data for NYC]. (3 p.)

15-16. Deaths from 5 leading causes, by age and color. (2 p.)

17-20. Infant deaths (under 1 year of age) from selected causes, [total and] among non-whites, by age and sex. (4 p.)

S5765-1.3: County Data
[Tables show data by resident county and mother's age, 1983.]

21. Live births. (1 p.)

22. Induced abortions. (1 p.)

23. Fetal deaths (gestation 20 weeks and over) excluding induced abortions. (1 p.)

24. Total pregnancies (including spontaneous fetal deaths gestation 20 weeks and over). (1 p.)

25. Out-of-wedlock live births. (1 p.)

26. Live births with live birth order 4 or higher. (1 p.)

S5765-1.4: Marriages and Dissolutions of Marriage

27. Marriages occurring in upstate New York by ages of bride and groom, 1983. (1 p.)

28. Dissolutions of marriage by duration of marriage and type of dissolution: certificates of dissolution of marriage filed in New York State, 1983. (1 p.)

S5765-1.5: Detail by Community, and Reportable Diseases

29.01-29.60. Basic New York State vital statistics by county and by cities and villages with 10,000 or more population: 1981-83 [including estimated population, live births, fetal deaths, deaths by age and 5 causes, nonwhite deaths, marriages, and dissolutions of marriage by type of decree]. (60 p.)

30. Reportable diseases, cases, and deaths: New York State, NYC, and upstate New York, 1982-83. (1 p.)

S5765-1.6: Trends, 1900-83
[Tables show data for State, NYC, and upstate New York, 1900-83.]

31-33. Live births, deaths, fetal deaths, infant deaths, neonatal deaths, and rates. (6 p.)

34-36. Deaths and death rates from [5] selected causes. (6 p.)

S5770   NEW YORK STATE Insurance Department

S5770-2   ANNUAL REPORT OF THE SUPERINTENDENT OF INSURANCE TO THE LEGISLATURE: Statistical Tables from Annual Statements, New York State
Annual. [1985.]
462 p. + errata sheet.
LC 60-29817.
SRI/MF/complete

Annual report on New York State insurance industry financial condition and underwriting activity, by company and line of coverage, 1980. Covers assets, including bond classifications; liabilities; income; disbursements; dividends and benefits paid; premiums written, earned, and/or received; policies in force, issued, and terminated; annuities; surplus; reserves; and losses incurred and paid; for companies based in New York State and elsewhere, including foreign countries.

Data are shown, as applicable, for life and accident/health insurance companies; health/hospital service/medical/dental expense indemnity corporations; HMOs; retirement systems/pension funds; fraternal benefit and charitable annuity societies; fire/casualty insurance companies; assessment cooperative fire companies; title insurance and mortgage guaranty companies; and New York State insurance exchanges.

Data on fire/casualty insurance include additional breakdowns by detailed line of coverage, including automobile, medical malpractice, workmen's compensation, and surety. Automobile data include loss trends from 1974.

Data are from annual statements filed by individual insurers.

Contains contents listing (p. 3-4); 73 tables (p. 6-388); and lists of status changes (p. 389-462). Previous report, for 1979, is described in SRI 1982 Annual under this number.

Availability: New York State Insurance Department, Empire State Plaza, Agency Bldg. One, 5th Floor, Publications Office, Albany NY 12257, $6.50; SRI/MF/complete.

S5775   NEW YORK STATE
Department of
Labor

S5775–1   EMPLOYMENT REVIEW,
New York State
Monthly.
ISSN 0013-6883.
LC 75-645033.
SRI/MF/complete

Monthly report on employment, earnings, and hours, for workers in New York State, NYC, and selected areas of upstate New York. Also covers women's employment. Data are shown by SIC 1- to 3-digit industries.

Data are from Federal and State government records. Report is issued approximately 4 months after month of coverage.

Contents:

a. Contents listing and narrative review of labor situation.

b. 4 monthly summary tables showing employment, unemployment, and unemployment rate, by county and major labor area, for month of coverage, previous month, and same month of previous year; and labor force status of State and NYC population, for current month, 12 previous months, and annually from 1970s.

c. 27 detailed monthly tables on employment, earnings, hours, and women's employment, by industry.

d. 20 quarterly tables on insured employment and payrolls.

e. Special features, usually with tables.

f. Occasional data revisions for previous months, data explanations, and publications list.

Detailed monthly and quarterly tables are listed below. Monthly tables appear in all issues. All additional features with substantial statistical content are described, as they appear, under "Statistical Features;" page locations and latest periods of coverage for quarterly tables are also noted. Nonstatistical features are not covered.

Availability: New York State Department of Labor, Research and Statistics Division, Publications Office, State Campus, Bldg. No. 12, Albany NY 12240, †; SRI/MF/complete.

Issues reviewed during 1985: Aug. 1984-Apr. 1985 (D) (Vol. 37, Nos. 8-12; Vol. 38, Nos. 1-4).

DETAILED MONTHLY TABLES:

[Monthly tables A3-D3 generally show data for month of coverage, with comparisons to previous month and/or same month of previous year.]

NEW YORK STATE EMPLOYMENT, EARNINGS, AND HOURS

A1. Employees in nonagricultural establishments, by industry division [annually from 1939 and monthly for 13 or more consecutive months through month of coverage].

A2. Earnings and hours of production workers in manufacturing establishments [annually from 1947 and monthly for 13 or more consecutive months through month of coverage].

A3. Employees, earnings, and hours in nonagricultural establishments, by [SIC 2- and 3-digit] industry.

A4. Average weekly hours and average overtime hours of production workers in selected [SIC 2-digit] manufacturing industries.

NEW YORK COMBINED AREA AND UPSTATE AREA EMPLOYMENT, EARNINGS, AND HOURS

B1-B7. [Data in table A3 are repeated for New York combined area, New York and Nassau/Suffolk Primary MSAs, NYC, and Westchester, Rockland, and Putnam labor market areas.]

C1-C13. [Data in table A3 are repeated for 13 upstate counties or areas.]

WOMEN'S EMPLOYMENT

D1-D3. Women as percent of all employees in manufacturing industries [for New York State and combined area, and upstate areas].

QUARTERLY TABLES:

[All quarterly tables begin "Reporting units, employment, and payrolls covered by unemployment insurance..." Tables show employment for each month of the quarter ending 5-8 months prior to month of coverage, and payroll for the total quarter.]

1-10. In New York State, NYC, and 8 State areas, by industry [division and major group].

11. [By county and industry division.]

12-20. [In 9 counties with employment of 100,000 or more, by industry division and major group; prior to Mar. 1985 issue, tables were numbered C1-C9.].

STATISTICAL FEATURES:

S5775–1.601: Aug. 1984 (Vol. 37, No. 8)
QUARTERLY TABLES

1-11 and C1-C9. Reporting units, employment, and payrolls covered by unemployment insurance, by industry, labor market area, and county, 4th quarter 1983, with average employment and total payroll 1983. (p. 35-67, 78-87)

AVERAGE WEEKLY EARNINGS IN INSURED EMPLOYMENT, 1979-83, ANNUAL FEATURE

(p. 68-77) Annual feature presenting 5 tables showing the following:

a. Average weekly earnings of employees covered by New York State unemployment insurance law: by industry division and major group, for New York State and NYC; by industry division for 8 major labor market areas; and by county; 1979-83.

b. Reporting units, average monthly employment, and average weekly earnings of Federal and State/local government employees covered by unemployment insurance, New York State, 1983.

S5775–1.602: Oct. 1984 (Vol. 37, No. 10)
QUARTERLY TABLES

1-11 and C1-C9. Reporting units, employment, and payrolls covered by unemployment insurance, by industry, labor market area, and county, 1st quarter 1984. (p. 35-77)

S5775–1.603: Nov. 1984 (Vol. 37, No. 11)
UNEMPLOYMENT INSURANCE TAX RATES, 1984, ANNUAL FEATURE

(p. 6-25) Annual article, by Elias D. Loizides, on New York State unemployment insurance taxes, with 10 tables showing tax data, including number of employer accounts and average tax rates for 1984, tax contributions and benefit charges for 1983, and total and taxable payrolls for year ending Sept. 30, 1983, all by SIC 1- and 2-digit industry and size of firm.

S5775–1.604: Dec. 1984 (Vol. 37, No. 12)
QUARTERLY TABLES

1-11 and C1-C9. Reporting units, employment, and payrolls covered by unemployment insurance, by industry, labor market area, and county, 2nd quarter 1984. (p. 38-77)

S5775–1.605: Jan. 1985 (Vol. 38, No. 1)
ANNUAL REVISIONS OF NONFARM EMPLOYMENT ESTIMATES, NEW YORK STATE, NYC, AND SELECTED AREAS BY INDUSTRY, 1983-84, ANNUAL TABLE

(p. 7-107) Annual table, repeated for New York State, New York combined area including NYC and neighboring counties, and 13 upstate counties or areas, presenting revisions of monthly employment estimates by industry, based on the 1984 benchmark. Revisions supersede estimates previously published for 1983-84 in the Jan.-Dec. 1984 issues of *Employment Review.*

EARNINGS AND HOURS IN NONAGRICULTURAL ESTABLISHMENTS, ANNUAL AVERAGES, 1984, ANNUAL FEATURE

(p. 108-118) Annual table, repeated for New York State, New York combined area (including NYC and neighboring counties), and 13 upstate counties or areas, showing manufacturing hours and earnings, generally by industry group, 1984.

REVISIONS OF DEC. 1984 DATA FOR NEW YORK STATE, NYC, AND UPSTATE AREAS

(p. 122-123) Table, repeated for New York State, NYC and neighboring counties, and 5 upstate areas, presenting revised data for manufacturing hours and earnings, generally by industry group, Dec. 1984.

S5775–1.606: Feb. 1985 (Vol. 38, No. 2)
1984 IN REVIEW, ANNUAL FEATURE

(p. 6-10) Annual article, by Vincent F. DeSantis et al., with 4 tables showing New York State population and labor force by employment status, by sex and race and for Hispanics, with selected detail for youth aged 16-19; wage/salary employment by industry division, and change from 1978; and employment and unemployment, by State labor area; 1983-84.

Data are from Current Population Survey of Households.

REVISIONS OF JAN. 1985 DATA FOR NEW YORK STATE, NYC, AND UPSTATE AREAS

(p. 11) Table, repeated for New York State, NYC and neighboring counties, and 5 upstate areas, presenting revised data for manufacturing hours and earnings, generally by industry group, Jan. 1985.

S5775–1.607: Mar. 1985 (Vol. 38, No. 3)
QUARTERLY TABLES

1-20. Reporting units, employment, and payrolls covered by unemployment insurance, by industry, labor market area, and county, 3rd quarter 1984. (p. 53-101)

S5775–2   **ANNUAL LABOR AREA REPORT, New York State, FY85**
Annual. Sept. 1984.
v + 109 p.
BLMI Rpt. No. 22.
LC 77-646372.
SRI/MF/complete

Annual planning report, for FY85, identifying New York State population groups most in need of employment services, and presenting data on labor force and population characteristics, employment by industry and occupation, hours and earnings, and job supply and demand, for various years 1970-83. Includes data by SMSA, county, and Job Training Partnership Act service area.

Data are from State Labor Dept, Census Bureau, and other State and Federal agencies.

Contains contents and table listings, and introduction (p. i-v); highlights, and narrative analysis interspersed with 3 charts and 39 tables (p. 1-78); appendix, with 10 tables (p. 81-101); and glossary (p. 105-109). All tables are listed below.

Report was previously titled *Annual Planning Information, New York State;* report for FY84 is described in SRI 1983 Annual under this number.

Availability: New York State Department of Labor, Research and Statistics Division, State Analysis Unit, State Campus, Bldg. 12, Rm. 405, Albany NY 12240, †; SRI/MF/complete.

TABLES:
[Unless otherwise noted, data are for New York State. Data for "selected population groups" are shown for whites, blacks, and various ethnic groups.]

S5775–2.1: Population and Labor Force

1. Total population and percent change, State and selected areas [SMSAs, NYC, and metro and nonmetro], 1970 and 1980. (p. 3)

2. Components of change [births, deaths, and migration] of the population, State and selected areas [SMSAs, and metro and nonmetro], 1970-80 [period]. (p. 5)

3-4. Population and percent change, by age and selected population group [includes American Indian, and Asian/Pacific Islander by country of ancestry], 1970 and 1980. (p. 7)

5. Hispanic population, State and selected areas [SMSAs and NYC], 1980. (p. 8)

6. Median age and percent distribution of the population by selected population group [includes Hispanics] and age, 1980. (p. 8)

7. Percent distribution of educational attainment, persons 25 years of age/over, 1970 and 1980. (p. 9)

8. Median years of school completed and percent distribution of educational attainment for persons 25 years of age/over, by selected population group [includes Hispanic, American Indian/Eskimo/Aleut, and Asian/Pacific Islander], 1980. (p. 10)

9-10. Persons aged 3 years/older enrolled in school: by age group, 1970 and 1980; and by type of school [nursery, kindergarten, elementary, high school, college], 1980. (p. 11)

11. Trends and projections of public and non-public school enrollment, 1980/81-1989/90. (p. 12)

12. Veteran population and percent distribution, by sex and period of service, 1980. (p. 13)

13-14. Civilian labor force summary [by employment status]; and participation rates by sex and race; [with selected U.S. comparisons], 1970-83. (p. 15-17)

S5775–2.2: Unemployment, Employment, and Occupations

UNEMPLOYMENT

15-17. Number unemployed and unemployment rates, 1973-83; and percent distribution of the unemployed, by reason and duration of unemployment; State and U.S., 1983. (p. 22-24)

18-21. Annual average unemployment rates, and percent distribution of unemployed persons, by sex, age group, and selected population group [includes Hispanics]; State and U.S., 1982 and/or 1983. (p. 25-28)

22. Selected characteristics of individuals receiving unemployment insurance [age group, race, ethnic group (including American Indian and Hispanic), education, occupational group, and industry division], 1983. (p. 30-31)

EMPLOYMENT AND EARNINGS

23-24. Nonagricultural wage/salary employment: [by industry division], 1973-83; and by selected areas [including NYC and selected counties and metro areas], 1973 and 1983. (p. 35-37)

25. Projected job growth by major industry division, U.S., [selected periods] 1982-95. (p. 47)

26. Nonagricultural wage/salary employment by industry [group], 1982-83. (p. 48-51)

27-28. Nonagricultural industries registering the largest employment increases and decreases, 1973-83 and 1978-83 [periods]. (p. 53-55)

29. Hours and earnings in selected industries, 1982-83. (p. 58)

OCCUPATIONS

30-32. Ratios [of job] applicants to openings, applicants placed to applicants registered, and openings filled to openings received; and job service applicants and openings; by occupational category; FY83. (p. 60-62)

33-36. Occupations with lowest and highest ratios of job applicants to job openings, and with substantial number of openings and applicants, FY83. (p. 64-71)

37-39. Occupations with the largest projected job growth; anticipated fastest growing occupations; and projected rapidly declining occupations; U.S., 1982-95 [period]. (p. 74-77)

S5775–2.3: Appendix Tables
[Data by race include Hispanics.]

A1. Population and percent change [by county], 1960, 1970, 1980. (p. 81-82)

A2-A3. Job service applicants: selected characteristics [including minorities, economically disadvantaged, veterans, women, handicapped, welfare recipients, and youth], by age and/or occupational group, FY83. (p. 83-85)

A4. Full- and part-time status of the civilian labor force 16 years/over, 1970-83 [with 1980-83 detail by sex and race]. (p. 86-88)

A5-A6. Distribution of unemployed persons 16 years/over by reason for and duration of unemployment [by race and for Hispanics, by sex, and for persons age 16-19, various years] 1970-83. (p. 89-93)

A7. Selected characteristics of residents in service delivery areas under the Job Training Partnership Act [including unemployment (with detail for persons unemployed 15 weeks/longer) and economically disadvantaged (with detail for youths), 1980 or 1983]. (p. 94-95)

A8. Total and per capita personal income [by county], 1981-82. (p. 97-98)

A9. Monthly average number of persons or cases, public assistance programs, by program, 1975-82. (p. 100)

A10. Public high school dropouts and rates, State and NYC, 1970/71-1982/83. (p. 101)

S5775–4   **1980 COMMUTATION PATTERNS, New York State Counties and Metropolitan Statistical Areas**
Monograph. 1984. vi + 87 p.
BLMI Rpt. No. 11, FY1984.
SRI/MF/complete

Report presenting 1980 census data on commuting patterns in New York State, covering points of origin and destination for New York residents and for nonresidents employed in the State. Data are cross-tabulated among counties and MSAs of New York and similar areas of neighboring States.

Data are primarily from Summary Tape File 4 of the 1980 Census of Population and Housing.

Contains contents listing (p. iii-iv); introduction (p. v-vi); and 1 table repeated for each county and MSA (p. 1-87).

A report on commuting patterns in the NYC area is also available from the issuing agency, but is not covered by SRI.

Availability: New York State Department of Labor, Research and Statistics Division, Labor Market Information Bureau, State Office Bldg. Campus, Albany NY 12240, †; SRI/MF/complete.

S5775–5   **COUNTY PROFILES: SOCIO-ECONOMIC CHARACTERISTICS, New York State**
Series. For individual publication data, see below.
LC 84-623501.
SRI/MF/complete

Series of profiles presenting detailed demographic and socioeconomic statistics for counties of New York State, 1970s-83. Series consists of profiles for individual counties, or occasionally for 2-3 counties. Data were compiled by the New York State Dept of Labor, generally from State and Federal sources.

Each profile contains contents and table listing; introduction; narrative report, in 6-7 sections, interspersed with maps, charts, and 21-28 tables; and appendices, with 1-14 tables, and glossary.

Data topics covered in most profiles are described below. Individual profiles received to date are listed below; additional data topics in individual profiles are also noted.

SRI coverage of this series begins with profiles produced since the 1980 census; similar profiles were also produced during the 1970s.

Availability: New York State Department of Labor, Labor Market Information Bureau, Bldg. No. 12, Rm. 445, State Campus, Albany NY 12240, †; SRI/MF/complete.

DATA TOPICS:

[Data are for various periods 1970s–83, unless otherwise noted, and include some comparisons to total State and U.S.

Data by race/ethnicity are generally for white, black, Hispanic, American Indian/Eskimo/Aleut, Asian/Pacific Islander, and other. Data by industry division usually include detail for manufacturing durable and nondurable goods.]

a. **Geographic and population characteristics:** land area and use, 1968; total population, decennially 1900–80; and population by county subdivision, sex, age, and race/ethnicity, various decennial years 1950–80.

b. **Employment:** commuting patterns for persons living and working in county; labor force by employment status, with participation rates by sex; employment, with distribution by industry division, and impact of national and local employment factors on area employment changes; manufacturing average monthly turnover rate (new hires, recalls, quits, layoffs); and employment changes resulting from company openings, expansions, closings, and contractions, by firm.

c. **Income:** personal income by source; labor/proprietor income, and average weekly wages for persons covered by unemployment insurance, both by industry division; and poverty and lower living standard levels by family size, with number of persons below these levels.

d. **Social programs:** public assistance recipients by type of program, including aid to dependent children.

e. **Education:** enrollment for public and non-public elementary and secondary schools, with distribution of public school students by race/ethnicity (total and for each school district); and number of public and nonpublic high school graduates, by type of post-high school activity (continuing education by type of institution, enlistment in armed forces, employment, and other).

f. **Employment and job training services:** CETA enrollment by type of service provided; population 14 years/older and persons meeting eligibility requirements for receiving services, by sex, age, and race/ethnicity; and New York State Job Service activities, including total or registered and active applicants, openings received or applicants placed, and percent of openings filled, all by detailed occupation.

g. **Population and housing data from 1980 census:** population, by urban/rural and marital status and by sex; families and households; housing units by type (urban, rural, year-round occupied and vacant, and seasonal/migratory); occupied housing units, by tenure and number of persons per unit; owner-occupied units by value; and householders by tenure and race/ethnicity.

h. **Income and poverty data from 1980 census:** families by income level, and mean income, both by race/ethnicity; poverty status of individuals, by age and race/ethnicity, and income as percent of poverty level; households and mean income, by income type (including earnings, interest/dividends/net profit, social security, and public assistance); and families and mean income, by number of workers in family.

Data on population by age and sex, activities of high school graduates, and 1980 census data on population and housing, all begin with profiles published in spring 1982. Data on impact of national and local employment factors on area employment appear only in profiles published prior to spring 1982. CETA data appear only in profiles published prior to fall 1982. Income and poverty data from the 1980 census begin with profiles published in winter 1983.

PROFILES:

S5775–5.1: Warren and Washington Counties

[Recurring (irreg.) Summer 1981. iv+43 p. BLMI Rpt. No. FY1981-93. SRI/MF/complete.]

Profile also includes employment by major industry. Job service and selected employment data are aggregated for Warren/Washington labor area.

S5775–5.2: Clinton County

[Recurring (irreg.) Fall 1981. v+41 p. BLMI Rpt. No. FY1982-6. SRI/MF/complete.]

S5775–5.3: Columbia County

[Recurring (irreg.) Fall 1981. v+39 p. BLMI Rpt. No. FY1982-7. SRI/MF/complete.]

S5775–5.4: Cortland County

[Recurring (irreg.) Fall 1981. v+37 p. BLMI Rpt. No. FY1982-8. SRI/MF/complete.]

S5775–5.5: Fulton County

[Recurring (irreg.) Fall 1981. v+39 p. BLMI Rpt. No. FY1982-9. SRI/MF/complete.]

S5775–5.6: Genesee County

[Recurring (irreg.) Fall 1981. v+38 p. BLMI Rpt. No. FY1982-10. SRI/MF/complete.]

S5775–5.7: Herkimer County

[Recurring (irreg.) Fall 1981. v+40 p. BLMI Rpt. No. FY1982-11. SRI/MF/complete.]

S5775–5.8: Putnam County

[Recurring (irreg.) Fall 1981. v+35 p. BLMI Rpt. No. FY1982-12. SRI/MF/complete.]

S5775–5.9: Sullivan County

[Recurring (irreg.) Fall 1981. v+36 p. BLMI Rpt. No. FY1982-13. SRI/MF/complete.]

S5775–5.10: Tompkins County

[Recurring (irreg.) Fall 1981. v+40 p. BLMI Rpt. No. FY1982-14. SRI/MF/complete.]

S5775–5.11: Cayuga County

[Recurring (irreg.) Spring 1982. v+51 p. BLMI Rpt. No. FY1982-54. SRI/MF/complete.]

S5775–5.12: Essex County

[Recurring (irreg.) Spring 1982. vii+48 p. BLMI Rpt. No. FY1982-55. SRI/MF/complete.]

S5775–5.13: Franklin County

[Recurring (irreg.) Spring 1982. vi+51 p. BLMI Rpt. No. FY1982-56. SRI/MF/complete.]

S5775–5.14: Greene County

[Recurring (irreg.) Spring 1982. v+50 p. BLMI Rpt. No. FY1982-57. SRI/MF/complete.]

S5775–5.15: Livingston County

[Recurring (irreg.) Spring 1982. vii+51 p. BLMI Rpt. No. FY1982-58. SRI/MF/complete.]

S5775–5.16: Madison County

[Recurring (irreg.) Spring 1982. vi+52 p. BLMI Rpt. No. FY1982-59. SRI/MF/complete.]

S5775–5.17: Montgomery County

[Recurring (irreg.) Spring 1982. vi+52 p. BLMI Rpt. No. FY1982-60. SRI/MF/complete.]

S5775–5.18: Ontario County

[Recurring (irreg.) Spring 1982. v+52 p. BLMI Rpt. No. FY1982-61. SRI/MF/complete.]

S5775–5.19: St. Lawrence County

[Recurring (irreg.) Spring 1982. vi+61 p. BLMI Rpt. No. FY1982-62. SRI/MF/complete.]

S5775–5.20: Wayne County

[Recurring (irreg.) Spring 1982. v+52 p. BLMI Rpt. No. FY1982-63. SRI/MF/complete.]

S5775–5.21: Allegany, Cattaraugus, and Chautauqua Counties

[Recurring (irreg.) Spring 1982. vii+126 p. BLMI Rpt. No. FY1982-71. SRI/MF/complete.]

Profile also includes the following by county: labor/proprietors' income, for persons living and working in each county, 1978; average monthly public assistance payments, 1980; and projections of public school enrollment and high school graduates, through 1990/91.

Poverty and CETA enrollment data are aggregated for entire region.

S5775–5.22: Steuben County

[Recurring (irreg.) Summer 1982. vi+62 p. BLMI Rpt. No. FY1982-72. SRI/MF/complete.]

S5775–5.23: Chenango County

[Recurring (irreg.) Fall 1982. vi+54 p. BLMI Rpt. No. FY1983-2. SRI/MF/complete.]

S5775–5.24: Delaware County

[Recurring (irreg.) Winter 1983. vi+56 p. BLMI Rpt. No. FY1983-26. SRI/MF/complete.]

S5775–5.25: Otsego County

[Recurring (irreg.) Winter 1983. ix+60 p. BLMI Rpt. No. FY1983-27. SRI/MF/complete.]

S5775–5.26: Jefferson County

[Recurring (irreg.) Sept. 1983. vi+64 p. BLMI Rpt. No. FY1984-1. SRI/MF/complete.]

S5775–5.27: Lewis County

[Recurring (irreg.)   Sept. 1983.   vi+58 p.
BLMI Rpt. No. FY1984-2.   SRI/MF/complete.]

S5775–5.28: Suffolk County

[Recurring (irreg.)   Oct. 1984.   vii+60 p.
BLMI Rpt. No. FY1985-14.   SRI/MF/complete.]

Profile also includes workers age 16 years/over by employment class (private wage/salary, government, self-employed, unpaid family), 1970 and 1980; companies employing 1,000/more workers, ranked by employment size, with headquarters and type of business, 1984; persons below poverty level by age group, with detail for blacks and Hispanics, 1980; and public assistance expenditures, monthly 1983.

Also includes educational attainment, 1980; year-round and seasonal hotels/motels and rooms, and overnight camping facilities (no dates); and year-round and seasonal households, 1970-83; all for various municipalities and other locations.

S5775–5.29: Schuyler County

[Recurring (irreg.)   Dec. 1984.   ix+50 p.
BLMI Rpt. No. FY1985-12.   SRI/MF/complete.]

Profile also includes median income for families and individuals holding full-time jobs, and number of families and persons below poverty level, with selected detail by sex and age group and for blacks and Hispanics; families below poverty level, by whether householder worked during year and by presence of children for female householders; and households and families receiving public assistance, with mean value of assistance; generally with comparisons to urban and rural New York State, 1979 or 1980.

S5775–5.30: Chemung County

[Recurring (irreg.)   Apr. 1985.   ix+60 p.
BLMI Rpt. No. FY1985-6.   SRI/MF/complete.]

Profile also includes data on labor-management disputes, including workers affected and company and union involved, 1983-June 1984 period; and data on income, poverty, and public assistance recipients, as described for Schuyler County under S5775-5.29 above.

S5782   NEW YORK STATE Legislative Commission on Rural Resources

S5782–1   SOCIOECONOMIC TRENDS IN RURAL NEW YORK STATE: Toward the 21st Century
Monograph.   Sept. 1984.
xv+422 p.
SRI/MF/complete

By Paul R. Eberts. Report comparing socioeconomic trends for urban and rural counties in New York State, 1950-80, with population projections to 2010. Includes the following indicators for each county and for 6 urban-rural county classifications, decennially 1950-80:

a. Demography: population, percent age 21-65 and 65/over, and percent nonwhite; population density; and occupied housing.

b. Industry: employment, with detail by industry division and for persons age 21-65, females, and managerial/professional employees; manufacturing units with 20/more and 100/more employees; and number of farms, percent of land in agriculture, acres harvested, and value of agricultural marketings.

c. Socioeconomic: median family income; percent of population with some college education; percent of population unemployed; and percent of families in poverty and affluence.

d. Personal well-being: percent of housing with plumbing; and rates of infant mortality, suicide, homicide, and marital disruption (divorce/separation/spouse death).

Also includes the following for each county: population by age and sex, selected years 1970-2010; and 1980 data on which urban-rural classification is based (total and rural population, population of largest city, and percent of population commuting).

Data are derived from 1950-80 censuses, and U.S. and New York State health dept records. Report is intended to facilitate rural affairs policy development.

Contains contents listing, foreword, listing of tables and charts, and map (p. iii-xv); narrative analysis in 7 sections, interspersed with 36 charts and 9 tables (p. 1-120); Appendix A, with 36 tables presenting data by county classification (p. 121-139); Appendix B presenting county profiles, each with narrative summary, 1 chart, and 2 tables (p. 141-413); Appendix C, with 1 chart and 1 table (p. 415-417); and Appendix D, with data sources and notes (p. 419-422).

Availability: New York State Legislative Commission on Rural Resources, PO Box 7019, Alfred E. Smith State Office Bldg., Albany NY 12225, †; SRI/MF/complete.

S5795   NEW YORK STATE Department of Public Service

S5795–1   FINANCIAL STATISTICS OF THE MAJOR PRIVATELY OWNED UTiLITIES WITHIN NEW YORK STATE, 1983
Annual.   Aug. 1984.
473 p. var. paging.
LC 76-645041.
SRI/MF/complete

Annual report presenting financial and operating data for major privately-owned utilities in New York State, by utility type and company, 1979-83. Utility types covered are combination gas and electric, gas only, telephone, and water.

Includes detailed data on assets, liabilities, revenues, and expenses, by item. Also includes sales, customers, and average bill, by customer type, for combination, gas, and water utilities; telephones in service, by type; and electricity output by type of generation (1982-83 only).

Data are from company reports filed with the Public Service Commission.

Contains summary table (2 p.); contents listing (2 p.); preface, and highlights with text data (p. 1-34); 4 sections with 22 tables grouped by utility type (27 p.); 4 sections with 5 tables repeated for each company, grouped by utility type (391 p.); 3 sections with 7 tables on company rates of return (12 p.); and index to companies (2 p.).

This is the 14th annual report. SRI coverage begins with this edition.

Availability: New York State Department of Public Service, Accounting and Finance Office, Three Empire State Plaza, Albany NY 12223, $6.00; SRI/MF/complete.

S5800   NEW YORK STATE Department of Social Services

S5800–2   STATISTICAL SUPPLEMENT, 1983 ANNUAL REPORT, New York State Department of Social Services
Annual.   [1985.]   5+65 p.
SRI/MF/complete

Annual report on New York State public assistance and social service caseloads and expenditures, by program, 1983, with selected trends from 1973. Includes data by source of funds and by social service district (New York City and counties).

Contains table and chart listings (4 p.); 1 summary table (p. 1); and 19 charts and 47 tables, arranged in 5 sections (p. 2-65). All tables are listed below.

Report is the statistical supplement to *Department of Social Services Annual Report,* which is largely narrative. Narrative report is published 6-8 months prior to supplement and is not covered in SRI.

A monthly report with similar but less detailed data on New York State welfare is also issued, but is not covered in SRI.

Availability: New York State Department of Social Services, Ten Eyck Bldg., 40 N. Pearl St., Albany NY 12243, †; SRI/MF/complete.

TABLES:

[Tables show data for New York State, NYC, and rest of State, 1983, unless otherwise noted. Sources of funds are local and/or Federal and State aid.]

S5800–2.1: Program Summary and Income Maintenance

SUMMARY

1. Expenditures in the State-aided public assistance and services programs [by source of funds and program (including refugee resettlement)]. (p. 1)

INCOME MAINTENANCE

[Tables 3, 6-7, and 18 show data by social service district.]

2. Annual expenditures by source of funds, and monthly average cases, persons, and payments [by program]. (p. 2)

3. Expenditures for major programs. (p. 3)

4-5. Cases and persons, and expenditures, by program and month. (p. 4-5)

6-7. Monthly average number of cases and persons, and payment per case and per person, by program. (p. 6-7)

8-9. Monthly average number of cases and persons, and expenditures by source of funds, 1973-83. (p. 8-9)

10-17. AFDC and home relief: monthly average number of cases and persons receiving assistance, annual expenditures, and monthly average payment per person; and reasons for opening and closing cases [New York State only]; 1973-83. (p. 13-25)

18. Child support: cases making payments, cases with payments due, and amount of collections. (p. 26)

S5800–2.2: Medical Assistance

[Tables 19-23 show data by social service district.]

19. Monthly average number of medical assistance eligible persons by category of eligibility. (p. 27)

20-22. Medical assistance expenditures by source of funds and major types of care; and percentage distribution of medical assistance by major types of care (parts I and II). (p. 29-33)

23. Estimated monthly average number of medical assistance beneficiaries. (p. 35)

24-26. Monthly average number of beneficiaries receiving care, expenditures by source of funds, and average annual payment, 1973-83. (p. 36-39)

S5800–2.3: Child and Adult Services, Food Stamps, and Other Programs

[Tables 27-28, 33, 36-38, 41, 43, and 45-46 show data by social service district.]

SERVICES SUMMARY

27-28. Cases and expenditures for services by type [including day and foster care, children preventive and protective, adoption, adult care, administrative, and other]; and services expenditures, by local district claiming schedule. (p. 40-41)

CHILD SERVICES

[Data by type of foster care are shown for some or all of the following: institutions; group, foster family, and boarding homes; and other.]

29. Children in foster care, by type of care, and county of residence, Dec. 31, 1983. (p. 42)

30. Children in foster care, by type of care, end of year 1973-83. (p. 44)

31. Foster care and adoption subsidies, annual expenditures, 1973-83. (p. 46)

32. Adoptions: number completed [by sex, age, race including Hispanic, and subsidy status]. (p. 47)

33. Day care: monthly average number of children [including cash grant, and family/in-home and group care Title XX and WIN recipients]. (p. 48)

34. Child protection: trends in abuse and neglect reports registered, 1973-83. (p. 49)

ADULT SERVICES

[Facility types are family and adult homes, licensed shelters, and others. Client categories are SSI, home relief, and private pay.]

35. Expenditures by service type. (p. 50)

36. Protective services to adults: monthly average number of recipients and hours of service. (p. 51)

37-38. Capacity and vacancy rate by type of facility; and reported occupancy and distribution by client category in adult care facilities. (p. 52-53)

39. Adult care facilities, reported occupancy and distribution by client category and type of facility. (p. 54)

FOOD STAMPS

[Tables show data for public assistance recipients and others.]

40. Food stamp program participants and total coupon values, by month. (p. 55)

41. Monthly average number of households and persons participating in the food stamp program, and total coupon values. (p. 56)

42. Annual coupon values, monthly average number of households and persons participating in the food stamp program, 1975-83. (p. 57)

SSI

43. Recipients and expenditures [Federal and State supplement]. (p. 60)

44a-44b. Monthly average number of SSI recipients by living arrangement and location and category of assistance [aged, blind, and disabled]. (p. 61)

HOME ENERGY ASSISTANCE PROGRAM (HEAP)

45-46. Number of households receiving HEAP by eligibility status [public assistance, non-public assistance, SSI, and emergency]; and local expenditures by eligibility status and administration, Federal fiscal year Oct. 1982-Sept. 1983. (p. 62-63)

LOCAL ADMINISTRATION

47. Expenditures for local administration of social services programs, by source of funds [and program]. (p. 65)

S5800–3   HOMELESSNESS IN NEW YORK STATE, A Report to the Governor and the Legislature

Monograph. Oct. 1984.
159 p. var. paging.
SRI/MF/complete

Report on New York State homeless population, emergency shelter services provided, and service needs and proposals, 1984. Includes data on shelter facilities, bed-capacity, operations, and client characteristics, shown for NYC, NYC suburbs, and 7 upstate regions.

Data on shelter operations include type of program (direct or purchased/arranged services); seasons and hours open; average number of persons sheltered each night, and average length of stay; limitations on types of persons sheltered, length of stay, and number of stays; sources of referrals and funding; and whether meals, information/referral, and support services are provided.

Data on shelter client characteristics include age; sex; race-ethnicity (black, white, Hispanic, or other); living arrangement prior to homelessness; geographic origin (same county as shelter, other county, or out of State); cause of homelessness; degree of self-sufficiency; and whether mentally or physically disabled, substance abuser, or victim of domestic violence; with selected detail for single persons and family members.

Also includes data on unmet needs as perceived by shelter operators; community residential facilities and capacity, by type of facility and county; poverty and unemployment rates, by county; and waiting lists for 4 assisted housing programs.

Most data are based on 250 responses to a May 1984 survey of New York State social service agencies.

Contents:

Introduction and acknowledgments. (3 p.)

Volume I. Condition and Needs of the Homeless. Includes contents listing, narrative analysis with text data, and bibliography. (51 p.)

Volume II. Opportunities for Action. Includes contents listing and proposals. (45 p.)

App. A-G. Includes State agency service summary, facsimile of survey questionnaire, and 28 tables. (58 p.)

Availability: New York State Department of Social Services, Ten Eyck Bldg., 40 N. Pearl St., Albany, NY 12243, †; SRI/MF/complete.

S5880   NORTH CAROLINA Department of Administration

S5880–2   INDICATORS OF CHILDREN'S NEEDS IN NORTH CAROLINA
Monograph.   Jan. 1985.
iv+193 p.
SRI/MF/complete

Report presenting North Carolina socioeconomic data relevant to the well-being and needs of children and youth, 1984 and trends. Includes data on child and family characteristics, child care, health, juvenile justice, and education. Data are primarily from 1980 Census of Population and Housing, and State Dept of Human Resources.

Contains contents listing (p. iv); foreword and historical trends, with text data, and 1 chart and 5 tables described below (p. 3-22); list of detailed tables (p. 25-32); 148 detailed tables, also described below (p. 33-180); and glossary and list of data sources (p. 182-193).

Availability: North Carolina Department of Administration, Policy and Planning Office, 116 W. Jones St., Raleigh NC 27611, †; SRI/MF/ complete.

TABLES AND CHART:

S5880–2.1: Historical Trends
a. Population by age group, selected years 1950-2000. 1 table. (p. 8)
b. Exceptional children in public schools, including disabled students by type of disability, gifted/talented students, and pregnant students; child/youth population and admissions to State mental retardation centers, psychiatric hospitals, and correctional training schools; and population distribution by years of school completed; various years 1940-1983/84. 1 chart and 4 tables. (p 15-21)

S5880–2.2: Indicator Tables
[All tables show data by county; most also include county rankings.]

a. Population: total population; child population, by age group and race-ethnicity (including American Indian, Spanish origin, and Asian/Pacific Islander); and urban children; 1980, with child population change from 1970. Tables A1-A15. (p. 33-47)
b. Families: families, and children in 1- and 2-parent families, by race; and average family size; 1980. Tables B1-B5. (p. 48-52)
c. Income status: families below poverty level and number of children affected, and mean income, by race, 1979; and children receiving AFDC, Medicaid, food stamps, Women and Infant Care (WIC) services, and subsidized school lunch/breakfast, 1984. Tables C1-C23. (p. 53-75)
d. Child care needs: mothers age 16/over in labor force, by age of children and presence of husband, 1980; licensed day care centers and family day care plans, 1984; and children receiving subsidized day care services, FY83-84. Tables D1-D12. (p. 76-87)

e. Children living outside the family: social service agency child placement caseload; total, black, and Indian children in foster care, and average age and stay; children for whom long-term care is permanent plan; children returned to biological parents/kin; foster children adopted; and children in child-caring institutions, group homes, mental health facilities, community-based programs, correctional training schools, and schools for visually and hearing impaired; mostly 1984. Tables E1-E16. (p. 88-103)
f. Health: total and illegitimate births, with detail for teenage mothers; premature births, and fetal, neonatal, and infant deaths, with rates by race; teenagers with inadequate prenatal care; teenage abortions; sexually transmitted disease rate among youths; child deaths, with detail for motor vehicle and other accidents, suicide, and homicide; child abuse/neglect cases; and assaultive children classified as mentally/neurologically/emotionally handicapped); mostly 1982 Tables F1-F29. (p. 104-132)
g. Juvenile justice: total and juvenile arrests; juvenile arrests for violent and property crimes; juvenile court caseload and number of first offenders; runaways arrested; juveniles detained in secure detention facilities; complaints regarding delinquent and undisciplined youth; juveniles in community-based alternative programs; and juveniles arrested for driving under the influence, and sentenced to alcohol/drug education schools; mostly 1983. Tables G1-G16. (p. 133-148)
h. Education: enrollment by level; enrollment in extended school day program; children not promoted from kindergarten and 1st grade, and nonpromotion rates for all grades; reading and math competency test failures, and achievement test scores by grade; high school dropouts; adults with less than 8th grade education; high school graduates; student absenteeism; and disabled/handicapped children in public schools, by disability; mostly for various periods 1983-84. Tables H1-H32. (p. 149-180)

S5885   NORTH CAROLINA Department of Agriculture

S5885–1   NORTH CAROLINA AGRICULTURAL STATISTICS, 1984
Annual.   Oct. 1984.   76 p.
No. 153.
SRI/MF/complete

Annual report on North Carolina agricultural production, marketing, and finances, mostly 1982-83, with some data for 1984 and selected trends from the 1970s. Data generally are shown by commodity and/or county and district, and include selected comparisons to other States.

Covers production, prices, sales, value, and, as applicable, acreage, yield, and stocks or inventory, for field crop, fruit and nut, livestock, poultry, and dairy sectors.

Also includes North Carolina data on number, acreage, and value of farms; farm rent, income, expenses, and labor; agricultural exports; fertilizer shipments; and weather.

Also includes number of North Carolina farm operators by ownership status, and other preliminary findings from the 1982 Census of Agriculture; cash receipts from marketings and Government payments, by State; and farm workers, hours, and wage rates, in 7 southeastern States compared to U.S.

Data are compiled by the North Carolina Crop and Livestock Reporting Service in cooperation with the USDA.

Contains contents listing (p. 2); list of additional reports available from State Crop and Livestock Reporting Service (p. 4); report, with 18 maps, 2 charts, and 114 tables, grouped in 4 sections (p. 5-76); and map of counties by crop reporting districts (inside back cover).

Availability: North Carolina Crop and Livestock Reporting Service, Agricultural Statistician, PO Box 27767, One W. Edenton St., Raleigh NC 27611, †; SRI/MF/complete.

S5900   NORTH CAROLINA Department of Correction

S5900–1   NORTH CAROLINA DEPARTMENT OF CORRECTION STATISTICAL ABSTRACT
Quarterly, suspended.

Quarterly report on North Carolina correctional institution population, admissions, and separations, suspended with the Apr./June 1984 issue (for description, see SRI 1984 Annual under this number). Report has been suspended pending conversion to new computer.

Issuing agency plans to resume publication with the issue presenting data for 3rd quarter 1985.

S5910   NORTH CAROLINA Department of Cultural Resources

S5910–1   STATISTICS AND DIRECTORY OF NORTH CAROLINA PUBLIC LIBRARIES, July 1, 1983-June 30, 1984
Annual.   Jan. 1985.   34 p.
ISSN 0164-0844.
LC 78-647664.
SRI/MF/complete

Annual report, for FY84, on North Carolina public library finances, holdings, circulation, and personnel, by library system. Also includes directory.

Contains contents listing (p. 4); statistical summary table (p. 5); 6 tables, listed below (p. 6-23); and directory (p. 25-34).

State library also publishes *Statistics of North Carolina Special Libraries* and *Statistics of North Carolina University and College Libraries,* not covered by SRI.

Availability: North Carolina Department of Cultural Resources, State Library Division, 109 E. Jones St., Raleigh NC 27611, ‡; SRI/MF/ complete.

TABLES:

[All tables show data by regional, county, municipal, and Indian reservation library system, FY84. Tables I and III-IV also show estimated 1982 population.]

I. Finance [operating receipts, by source; and operating expenditures for personnel, books, periodicals, audiovisuals, microforms, binding, and processing; and capital outlay]. (p. 6-9)

II. Sources of local receipts [county, municipality, other, and balance brought forward]. (p. 10-11)

III. Public library collections [total, adult, and juvenile books; volumes and titles added, and volumes withdrawn; and periodicals, recordings, slides, microform titles, films, and film-strips]. (p. 12-15)

IV. Use of books [circulation by type of book; circulation for main library, branches, mobile units, mail, and in-house; reference questions answered; and interlibrary loans]. (p. 16-19)

V. Use of nonbook materials [and audience for library-sponsored and nonlibrary-sponsored progams]. (p. 20-21)

VI. Miscellaneous [professional and non-professional FTE personnel; and vehicles operated, by type]. (p. 22-23)

S5915 NORTH CAROLINA Department of Public Education

S5915–1 STATISTICAL PROFILE, 1985, North Carolina Public Schools
Annual. 1985.
400 p. var. paging.
ISSN 0148-2742.
LC 75-622263.
SRI/MF/complete

Annual report on North Carolina elementary and secondary public school pupils, personnel, and finances, 1983/84 academic year, with selected data for 1984/85, trends from 1972/73, and enrollment projections through 1994. Includes data by local education agency (LEA) and regional education center.

Data are compiled by the Public Education Dept.

Contents:

Introduction, and contents and table listings. (p. iii-x)

Part I. State Summary. Includes 1 map; and 1 chart and 34 tables, listed below, with interspersed narrative. (p. I.1-I.87)

Part II. Local Education Agencies. Includes definitions; and 4 tables, also listed below, repeated for each LEA and 8 regional education centers. (p. II.1-II.303)

This is the 11th annual report.

Availability: North Carolina Department of Public Education, Information and Publications, Education Bldg., Rm. 352, Raleigh NC 27611, $12.00+$1.20 postage and handling; SRI/MF/ complete.

CHART AND TABLES:

S5915–1.1: State Summary

GRADE ENROLLMENT, ATTENDANCE, AND PROMOTIONS

[Tables 1-7 show data for kindergarten and grades 1-12, and usually for elementary and high school exceptional children classes. Tables 1-6 show data for 1974/75-1983/84 school years; tables 1-3 also show data for 1st month, 1984/85 school year.]

1. Final enrollment. (p. I.3)

2-3. Final average daily membership and attendance. (p. I.4-I.5)

4. Membership last day. (p. I.6)

5-6. Promotions and nonpromotions. (p. I.7-I.8)

7. Nonpromotion rate, 1976/77-1983/84. (p. I.9)

8. Extended day program enrollment [grades 9-12, by LEA], 1984/85. (p. I.10-I.12)

ENROLLMENT PROJECTIONS AND CHARACTERISTICS

[Tables 10-12 show data by LEA.]

9. Projected final average daily membership [by grade], 1984/85-1988/89. (p. I.14)

10. Projected final average daily membership, 1985/86-1989/90. (p. I.15-I.17)

11. Pupils in membership being served by exceptional children programs [by type of handicap, and for gifted students and pregnant students, as of Dec. 1, 1984]. (p. I.18-I.20)

12. Pupils in membership by race [and ethnic origin, including American Indian, Asian, and Hispanic], and sex, 1984/85. (p. I.21-I.23)

13. Pupil membership by race/ethnic origin [including American Indian/Alaskan Native, Asian/Pacific Islander, and Hispanic, 1972/73-1984/85]. (p. I.24)

HIGH SCHOOL GRADUATES AND DROPOUTS

[Intentions include postsecondary enrollment, by institution type and whether in- or out-of-State; military enlistment; and seeking employment.]

14. 1984 high school graduates intentions including 1983 summer school [by sex, by race and for American Indian and other ethnic groups]. (p. I.26)

15. Intentions of high school graduates: a 5-year history [1980-84]. (p. I.27)

16. Projection of public high school graduates [by LEA], 1985-94. (p. I.29-I.31)

17. Estimated annual high school dropout rate [for regular and extended day program, 1983/84; and estimated retention rate (1983/84 graduates as percent of 1980/81 9th grade enrollment); all by LEA]. (p. I.33-I.35)

PUBLIC SCHOOL PERSONNEL

[Tables 19-22 show data for 1984/85.]

18. Public school full-time personnel [by position, by source of funds (government level and vocational funding), and by sex and race], as of October 1, 1984. (p. I.37)

19. [Employment] experience status of instructional personnel [by LEA]. (p. I.38-I.40)

20. Highest degree held by professional personnel [by LEA]. (p. I.41-I.43)

21. Teacher profile by subject area (grades 7-12) [and sex]. (p. I.44)

22. Selected characteristics of public school staff [percent of teachers with graduate certificate and with no prior experience, and percent of professional staff paid entirely from local funds, with rankings, by LEA]. (p. I.46-I.48)

FINANCES AND PERSONAL INCOME

[Unless otherwise noted, data are for 1983/84. Sources of funds are Federal, State, and local.]

23. Current expense expenditures by source of funds [and object, total and per pupil]. (p. I.50)

24. Distribution of the dollar for public education. [chart] (p. I.51)

25. Comparison of per pupil expenditures, current expense expenditures only [by source of funds, 1974/75-1983/84]. (p. I.52)

26. Per pupil expenditure ranking [and amount by source of funds, by LEA]. (p. I.53-I.55)

27. Per pupil expenditure ranking (excludes school food service expenditures) [and amount by source of funds, by LEA]. (p. I.56-I.58)

28. Revenue [current expense and capital outlay, by detailed item]. (p. I.59)

29. Current expense expenditures by [detailed program including special, adult, and vocational education, and support services; by object and source of funds]. (p. I.60-I.67)

30. Capital outlay expenditures by source of funds [for 3 project categories and other]. (p. I.68)

31. County revenue and expenditures for public education [total and per pupil, by county, with selected rankings], 1982/83. (p. I.70-I.71)

32. 1982 per capita personal income by counties [with ranking]. (p. I.72)

TRANSPORTATION AND COURSE MEMBERSHIP

33. Student transportation on public school buses (excludes contract transportation) [number of buses and miles, and cost, by LEA], 1983/84. (p. I.74-I.76)

34. Course membership summary [number of classes and students, by course, aggregate for grades 7-12], 1983/84. (p. I.77-I.86)

S5915–1.2: Local Education Agencies

[The 4 tables listed below are repeated for each LEA and regional education center. Data for LEAs also include number of elementary and secondary schools.]

[1] Pupil accounting [enrollment, average daily membership, and average daily attendance, 1983/84 and 1st month 1984/85; and membership last day, promotions, and nonpromotions, 1983/84; all by grade and for exceptional children classes].

[2] 1983/84 high school graduate intentions [same breakdowns as in State summary table 14].

[3] 1984/85 public school personnel summary (full-time personnel only) [same breakdowns as in State summary table 18].

[4] 1983/84 current expense expenditures by source of funds [same breakdowns as in State summary table 23].

S5920   NORTH CAROLINA
Board of Elections

S5920-1   STATE OF NORTH CAROLINA CERTIFICATION OF VOTES CAST in the General Election Conducted on Nov. 6, 1984
Biennial. [1985.]
8 p. Oversized.
SRI/MF/complete

Biennial report presenting results of the North Carolina general election held Nov. 6, 1984. Shows voting for President, U.S. Senator and Representatives, and Governor, by county and/or district. Includes candidates' party affiliation.

Previous report, covering 1982 general election, is described in SRI 1983 Annual under this number.

Availability: North Carolina Board of Elections, PO Box 1166, Raleigh NC 27602-1166, †; SRI/MF/complete.

S5925   NORTH CAROLINA
Employment Security Commission

S5925-5   STATE LABOR SUMMARY, North Carolina
Monthly. 10 p.
SRI/MF/complete, shipped quarterly

Monthly report on North Carolina nonagricultural employment, hours, and earnings, by industry division and group. Also includes demographic characteristics of registered job applicants, and number of job openings by occupation.

Report, compiled by the Employment Security Commission, is issued approximately 2 months after month of coverage.

Contains narrative summary and 7 monthly tables, listed below.

Additional monthly and bimonthly reports showing labor force data by SMSA are also available from issuing agency, but are not covered in SRI.

Availability: North Carolina Employment Security Commission, Labor Market Information Division, PO Box 25903, Raleigh NC 27611, ‡; SRI/MF/complete, shipped quarterly.
Issues reviewed during 1985: Sept. 1984-Aug. 1985 (D).

MONTHLY TABLES:
[Unless otherwise noted, tables show data for North Carolina for month of coverage, preceding month, and usually same month of previous year. Order of tables may vary from issue to issue.]

[1] Civilian labor force [unadjusted and seasonally adjusted, by employment status].

[2] Statewide active applicant file [including by age group, sex, race, and ethnic group (Hispanic, American Indian/Alaskan Native, and other); and whether eligible claimant, veteran, handicapped, seasonal farmworker, or welfare recipient; for last day of month of coverage only].

[3] Statewide job openings data [number received and filled, for month of coverage and fiscal year to date; and number unfilled as of last day of month of coverage, total and for 30 days or more; all by occupational group].

[4-5] Estimated wage/salary employment in nonagricultural industries [unadjusted and seasonally adjusted, by industry division and group].

[6] Estimated number of production workers in selected manufacturing industries.

[7] Estimated average weekly earnings, average weekly hours, and average hourly earnings of production workers in selected manufacturing industries and nonsupervisory employees in selected nonmanufacturing industries.

S5925-6   OCCUPATIONAL EMPLOYMENT REPORTS, North Carolina
Series. For individual publication data, see below.
SRI/MF/complete

Continuing series of reports covering employment in selected groups of North Carolina industries, by detailed occupation.

Data are from Occupational Employment Statistics (OES) surveys of employers in the various industry groups, conducted over a 3-year cycle and covering the following sectors: manufacturing, hospitals, trade, transportation and communication, public utilities, nonmanufacturing, government, and education.

General format of each report:

a. Contents listing; introduction, with 3-5 summary and trend charts; and methodology.

b. 1 table, repeated for each SIC 2- or 3-digit industry covered, showing estimated employment by detailed occupation, at survey date.

Report reviewed during 1985 is described below.

Availability: North Carolina Employment Security Commission, Labor Market Information Division, PO Box 25903, Raleigh NC 27611, †; SRI/MF/complete.

S5925-6.7: Occupational Employment in Manufacturing and Hospitals, North Carolina, 1983
[Triennial. Aug. 1984. iv+65 p. SRI/MF/complete.]

Covers occupational employment in 18 SIC 2-digit manufacturing industry groups, and in hospitals. Based on responses of approximately 3,300 establishments to a survey conducted June 1983-Mar. 1984.

This is the 4th report on manufacturing industries and the 2nd on hospitals.

Previous report, for 1980, is described in SRI 1982 Annual, under S5925-6.4.

S5930   NORTH CAROLINA
Office of the Governor

S5930-6   NORTH CAROLINA COMMUTING PATTERNS: 1980 Census of Population and Housing
Monograph. Feb. 1985.
1+166 p.
Technical Rpt. No. 5.
LC 85-621916.
SRI/MF/complete

Report presenting 1980 census data on commuting patterns in North Carolina, covering points of origin and destination for North Carolina residents and for nonresidents employed in the State. Data are cross-tabulated among North Carolina counties and counties and cities of other States, and for persons working abroad and at sea.

Also includes summary trends from 1960 and 1970.

Data are primarily from Summary Tape File 4 of the 1980 Census of Population and Housing.

Contains contents listing (1 p.); data sources and definitions (p. 1-3); summary and conclusions, with 3 maps and 4 tables (p. 4-11); and 1 table repeated for each county (p. 13-166).

Availability: Librarian, State Budget and Management Office, Research and Planning Services, 116 W. Jones St., Raleigh NC 27611, $5.00; SRI/MF/complete.

S5940   NORTH CAROLINA
Department of Human Resources

S5940-1   NORTH CAROLINA VITAL STATISTICS, 1983
Annual. 2 volumes.
For individual publication data, see below.
LC 79-644285.
SRI/MF/complete

Annual report presenting North Carolina vital statistics, by county, region, and selected city, 1983, with trends from 1979. Covers population, births, deaths by cause, marriages, and divorces/annulments. Includes data by race.

Report is issued in 2 volumes, described below.
This is the 68th annual vital statistics report. Every 3 years Vol. 2 is expanded to include sociodemographic detail and analyses. Vol. 2 for 1981 is the most recent expanded edition.

Other reports available from the issuing agency, but not covered in SRI, include *Detailed Mortality Statistics,* showing deaths by cause, by age, race, and sex; and *North Carolina Vital Statistics: Annual Provisional Report,* presenting provisional data on births, deaths, marriages, and divorces/annulments, by county and major city.

Availability: North Carolina Department of Human Resources, Health Services Division, State Center for Health Statistics, PO Box 2091, Raleigh NC 27602-2091, †; SRI/MF/complete.

S5940–1.1: Volume 1: Births, Deaths, Population, Marriages, Divorces

[Annual. Dec. 1984. iv+210 p. var. paging. SRI/MF/complete.]

Contains contents listing (1 p.); introduction, trend analysis, methodology, technical notes, definitions and formulas, and references, with illustrative charts and tables (p. 1.1-1.46); and 1 detailed table, described below, repeated for the State (p. 2.1), and by Dept of Human Resources (DHR) region (p. 3.1-3.4), health service area (p. 4.1-4.6), perinatal care region (p. 5.1-5.6), county (p. 6.1-6.100), and city (p. 7.1-7.43).

Counties and cities are arranged in alphabetical order.

TABLE:

[Births and deaths are shown in detail for residents, with totals for all occurrences regardless of residency. Marriages and divorces/annulments are shown by place of occurrence only.

Table shows numbers for 1983, and rates for 1983 and the period 1979-83. Data are shown for whites and nonwhites, unless otherwise noted.]

a. Population, by sex, and natural increase; live births, by sex, and by type of attendant; premature and out-of-wedlock births; and total live birth occurrences.

b. Perinatal deaths, fetal deaths by type of attendant, and out-of-wedlock fetal deaths; neonatal, postneonatal, and infant deaths; and deaths (excluding fetal deaths), by sex, age group, and location (hospital, other institution, home/noninstitution), and total occurrences.

c. Marriages, and divorces/annulments [data are not shown by race].

Tables for cities omit data on population, marriages, and divorces/annulments.

S5940–1.2: Volume 2: Leading Causes of Mortality

[Annual. Dec. 1984. vii+175 p. var. paging. SRI/MF/complete.]

Contains contents listing, 2 maps showing DHR and health service areas, and preface (p. iii-vii); and the following sections:

Sections I-IV. Technical Notes, and Mortality Highlights. Includes 2 tables showing North Carolina death rates 1983 and 1979-83 period, and deaths by cause, 1983, with age/race/sex adjusted rates for selected counties. (p. 1.1-4.3)

Section V. Mortality Statistics. Includes 47 maps, and basic table showing deaths and death rates for State, and by DHR region, health service area, and county, 1983 and 1979-83 period. Table is repeated for each of 25 death causes and for infant deaths. (p. 5.3-5.149)

Section VI. Multiple Conditions Present at Death. Includes 6 maps, and 2 tables showing underlying causes of death related to primary cause, 1983. (p. 6.3-6.17)

S5950   NORTH CAROLINA Judicial Department

S5950–1   NORTH CAROLINA COURTS, 1983-84: Annual Report of the Administrative Office of the Courts

Annual. Feb. 1985.
iii+172 p.
LC 70-626501.
SRI/MF/complete, current & previous year reports

Annual report on the North Carolina judicial system, including trial and appellate court caseloads and case dispositions, FY84. Covers supreme, appeals, superior, and district courts. Includes trial court data by case type, judicial district, and county, with selected comparisons from as early as 1978.

Case types shown are criminal and civil, for all courts, with some additional detail for estates and special proceedings, domestic relations, juvenile, and traffic case types.

Report also includes data on judicial dept finances, personnel, and salaries; legal services for indigents and mental hospital patients; fine and fee collection and distribution by county; and court case processing time.

Data are from Dept records.

Contains listings of contents, tables, and charts (p. i-iii); and report, in 4 parts, with personnel listings, 34 charts, and 41 tables (p. 1-172).

This is the 18th annual report. Previous report, for FY83, was also reviewed during 1985, and is also available on SRI microfiche, under this number [Annual. Feb. 1984. iii+170 p. ◆].

Availability: North Carolina Judicial Department, ◆; SRI/MF/complete.

S5955   NORTH CAROLINA Department of Justice

S5955–1   STATE OF NORTH CAROLINA UNIFORM CRIME REPORT, 1984

Annual. [1985.] x+212 p.
ISSN 0096-3208.
LC 75-641275.
SRI/MF/complete

Annual report on North Carolina crimes and arrests, 1983-84, with selected trends from 1980 and forecasts for 1985. Includes data by county and reporting agency, and by offender age, sex, and race/ethnicity. Also includes law enforcement employment, and assaults on officers.

Report focuses on 8 Index offenses: murder, rape, robbery, aggravated assault, burglary, larceny, motor vehicle theft, and arson. Arrests are also shown for numerous non-Index offenses.

Data are from State and local agency reports submitted under the Uniform Crime Reporting Program.

Contains contents listing (p. ix-x); reporting methodology and definitions, with 1 map, 2 charts, and 1 summary table (p. 1-19); 5 statistical sections with 3 maps and 50 charts, and 75 tables described below, interspersed with narrative (p. 21-201); history of contributing agency participation, with 3 tables (p. 204-207); and glossary (p. 210-212).

Maps and charts with substantial data not included in tables are also described below.

Availability: North Carolina Department of Justice, Police Information Network, PO Box 629, Raleigh NC 27602, $15.00; SRI/MF/complete.

MAPS, CHARTS, AND TABLES:

[Data are shown for North Carolina, 1984 or 1983-84, unless otherwise noted. Arson is classified as an Index offense, but data are reported separately and usually are not included in the Crime Index tables.

Data by race are generally shown for white, black, Indian, and Asian; data by ethnicity are for non-Hispanic and Hispanic.]

S5955–1.1: Crime Index

BY INDEX OFFENSE

[With the exception of arson, data for each individual Index offense, and for total, violent, and property Index offenses, include 2 tables showing offenses by month 1983-84; and total offenses, rate per 100,000 population, and percent cleared, annually 1980-84. All additional data are described below.]

a. Index total and violent crime distribution by offense; and crime clocks. 2 charts and 4 tables. (p. 22-31)

b. Murders: by day of week; by age, sex, race, and ethnicity of victim and offender, and victim/offender relationship; by weapon type, circumstance, and county; and by occurrence in conjunction with other felonies by type. 1 map, 2 charts, and 7 tables. (p. 34-39)

c. Forcible rapes: by whether actual or attempted and intraracial or interracial; by place, time, and day of week; alcohol/drug influence on victim and offender; by victim race, age group, injury status, and relationship to offender; by offender race and age; number of offenders involved per offense; and by weapon used. 2 charts and 14 tables. (p. 42-47)

d. Robberies by type of weapon, and offenses and value stolen by type of location; bank robberies by institution type and time of day, and value of property stolen and recovered; and aggravated assaults by weapon type. 1 chart and 7 tables. (p. 50-55)

e. Property crime distribution by offense; burglaries by type of entry, and offenses and value stolen by residence and nonresidence day and night occurrence; larceny offenses by type and value stolen; and motor vehicle thefts by vehicle type, with total value stolen and recovered. 3 charts and 11 tables. (p. 58-71)

f. Arson: offenses, rate per 100,000 population, and percent cleared, 1980-84; and offenses by property type, with total value of property damage. 1 table. (p. 74)

PROJECTIONS

g. Projected and actual Index crimes by offense, 1980-85. 10 charts and 1 table. (p. 76-81)

BY COUNTY AND REPORTING AGENCY

h. Rates for total, violent, and nonviolent crimes, by county; and Index crimes by offense, community type and population, employed sworn officers by sex, and civilian employees, all by county and reporting agency, with totals for urban and rural communities. 4 tables. (p. 88-143)

STOLEN PROPERTY VALUES

i. Value of property stolen and recovered by month, property type, and county; and value stolen by selected Index offense, with detail by type or circumstance. 10 tables. (p. 146-156)

S5955-1.2: Arrests, Officers Assaulted, and Summary Data

ARRESTS

a. Arrests for Index and non-Index offenses, by offender age, sex, race, and ethnicity, and by county. 5 tables. (p. 158-188)

b. Drug arrests of adults and juveniles for sale and possession by substance, by sex. 1 table. (p. 190)

OFFICERS ASSAULTED

c. Officers killed, by circumstance, 1975-84 period, and offenders by prior arrest record, annually 1975-84; assaults by month, type of circumstance and assignment, time of day, weapon, and injury status; and assault clearances. 3 charts and 5 tables. (p. 192-195)

SUMMARY

d. Index offenses, clearances and arrests with rates, and value of stolen property, all by offense; value of recovered property; offenses by crime circumstance and/or type, 1980-84; and U.S. Index crimes and rates by State, with population, 1983. 1 chart and 5 tables. (p. 198-201)

S5990   NORTH CAROLINA
Department of Transportation

S5990-1   NORTH CAROLINA TRAFFIC ACCIDENT FACTS, 1984
Annual. [1985.] 2+55 p.
LC 80-648618.
SRI/MF/complete

Annual report on North Carolina traffic accidents, fatalities, and injuries, by circumstances, location, vehicle type, and driver and victim characteristics, 1984, with trends from as early as 1930.

Also includes data on motor vehicle registrations and mileage; alcohol involvement in accidents, and arrests for driving while intoxicated; licensed drivers; and seat belt and child restraint use during accidents.

Contains contents listing (1 p.); accident summary (p. 1-2); 8 charts and 12 tables (p. 3-20); 2 basic tables with accompanying index, repeated for all accidents (p. 21-31), rural accidents (p. 33-43), and urban accidents (p. 45-54); and definitions (p. 55).

Availability: North Carolina Department of Transportation, Motor Vehicles Division, 1100 New Bern Ave., Raleigh NC 27697, †; SRI/MF/complete.

S6020   NORTH CAROLINA
Utilities Commission

S6020-1   NORTH CAROLINA UTILITIES COMMISSION: 1985 Report
Annual. July 1, 1985.
vii+158 p. Vol. XVI.
LC 37-27878.
SRI/MF/complete

Annual report presenting North Carolina public utility financial, operating, and regulatory data, by utility type and/or company, 1982-83 with selected trends from as early as 1960. Utility types are electric, gas, telephone, water/sewer, motor freight and passenger carriers, and railroads.

Includes revenues, expenses, assets, liabilities, rates, customers, employment, salaries/wages, and security issuances, for most utility types; electricity capacity by type of generation; telephones and exchanges; water/sewer systems and customers by county; motor passenger carrier fleet and mileage; and railroad track mileage, freight tons by commodity, highway grade crossings, and grade crossing accident injuries and fatalities.

Also includes number of utilities regulated; Commission finances, regulatory caseload, and motor carrier inspections; economic impact of utilities on employment, compensation, and selected taxes and fees; Western Union offices in North Carolina and U.S.; and comparative residential electric bills in 10 States and U.S.

Data are from reports filed with the Commission, and Federal and State agency and industry assn published reports.

Contains listings of contents, tables, and charts (p. iii-vii); and 12 chapters, with 31 maps/charts and 58 tables (p. 3-158).

This is the 16th annual report.

Availability: North Carolina Utilities Commission, Office of the Chief Clerk, PO Box 29510, Raleigh NC 27626-0510, $6.00; SRI/MF/complete.

S6060   NORTH DAKOTA
Office of the
Attorney General

S6060-2   NORTH DAKOTA CORRECTIONAL FACILITIES REPORT, 1984
Annual. 1985. vi+40 p.
SRI/MF/complete, current & previous year reports

Annual report on North Dakota local correctional facility incarcerations, 1984, with trends from 1977. Covers number, demographic characteristics, and physical condition of persons incarcerated; incarceration reasons and duration; and means of release. Most data include detail for individual city and county jails, and juvenile detention facilities.

Data are from the North Dakota Jail Information System.

Contains listings of contents, tables, and charts (p. ii-v); and narrative report, with 3 charts and 28 tables (p. 1-40).

This is the 3rd edition of the report. No report was issued for 1983. Report for 1982 was also reviewed in SRI during 1985 and is also available on SRI microfiche under S6060-2 [Annual. Oct. 1983. vi+39 p. †]. Report for 1981 was titled *North Dakota Jail Population.*

Data on State prison inmates are included in *North Dakota Director of Institutions Biennial Report to the Governor,* covered in SRI under S6130-1.

Availability: North Dakota Office of the Attorney General, Criminal Justice Training and Statistics Division, State Capitol, Bismarck ND 58505, †; SRI/MF/complete.

S6080   NORTH DAKOTA
Economic Development
Commission

S6080-1   NORTH DAKOTA GROWTH INDICATORS
Recurring (irreg.) Nov. 1984.
iv+82 p.
SRI/MF/complete, Apr. & Nov. 1984 reports

Recurring compilation of economic and demographic indicators for North Dakota, primarily 1970s-83, with selected trends from 1900 and population projections to 2030.

Report is designed to present a socioeconomic overview of the State. Economic, demographic, and geographic breakdowns are shown, as applicable, for most topics. These breakdowns include data by city, county, urban-rural status, income, industry, occupation, age, education, marital status, and sex. Comparisons to total U.S., other States, and major cities are also included.

Data are from reports of Census Bureau, USDA, State agencies, university research organizations, and commercial publications. Data sources appear beneath each table.

Contains introduction and contents listing (p. II-IV); and 13 charts and 81 tables arranged in 3 sections, described below (p. 1-82).

Previous report for Apr. 1984 has also been received, and is also available on SRI microfiche under S6080-1 [Recurring (irreg.). Apr. 1984. iv+89 p. †]. For description of Nov. 1982 report, see SRI 1983 Annual under this number.

Availability: North Dakota Economic Development Commission, 1050 E. Interstate Ave., Bismarck ND 58505-0291, †; SRI/MF/complete.

SECTIONS:

S6080-1.1: State Data

a. Economic development: GSP; personal income by source; business establishments, employment, and payroll; population, employment, and income projected to 2030; and occupational supply and demand. 1 chart and 12 tables. (p. 1-10)

b. Agriculture: summary findings from 1978 Census of Agriculture on farm size, value, production, income, operators, and forms of organization; and cash receipts from farm marketings, and agricultural production costs. 5 charts and 6 tables. (p. 11-15)

c. Mineral production and value; natural gas and crude oil production; and construction awards and establishments, employment, and receipts. 3 charts and 3 tables. (p. 16-20)

d. Manufacturing statistics (establishments, employment, payroll, value added, cost of materials, capital expenditures, shipments, and production workers, hours, and earnings); and union membership rates, productivity indexes, and work stoppages, workers involved, and days lost, by State. 7 tables. (p. 21-24)

e. Wholesale and retail trade, and service industries establishments, sales or receipts, payroll, and employment, and inventories (wholesale only); and export-related shipments and employment. 5 tables. (p. 25-29)

f. Population, education, labor force, employment, housing and income findings from Census of Population and Housing; and population projected to 2000. 4 charts and 5 tables. (p. 30-40a)

g. Miscellaneous: elementary and secondary schools, enrollment, and teachers; crime rates; population density; State government revenues by source and expenditures by function; truck freight delivery time from Bismarck to 21 cities; and general flying conditions and average snow/sleet. 9 tables. (p. 41-46)

S6080–1.2: County Data
[All tables show data by county.]

a. Business establishments, employment, and payroll; labor force and employment; farms, acreage, and real estate value; and mineral industry and manufacturing statistics (similar to data described above, under "State Data"). 5 tables. (p. 48-52)

b. Wholesale trade and service establishments, sales or receipts, inventories (wholesale trade only), payroll, and employees; retail sales by kind of business; consumer buying power index; taxable sales; property tax mill levies; and motor vehicle registrations. 8 tables. (p. 53-61)

c. Demographic data: population and components of change, and social and economic characteristics, including education, labor force participation, income, and poverty; elementary and secondary schools, enrollment, personnel, and districts; personal income; and housing structural and occupancy characteristics, including monthly owner costs and gross rent. 9 tables. (p. 62-70)

S6080–1.3: City Data
[All tables show data by city.]

a. Economic data: nonagricultural employment; manufacturing, and retail and wholesale trade statistics (similar to data described above, under "State Data"); consumer buying power index; services sales; and property tax mill levies. 8 tables. (p. 72-78)

b. Demographic data: population, and social and economic characteristics, including education, labor force participation, income, and poverty; and housing structural and occupancy characteristics, including owner costs and gross rent. 5 tables. (p. 79-82)

S6110   NORTH DAKOTA
Board of
Higher Education

S6110–1   FALL 1984 ENROLLMENTS, NORTH DAKOTA INSTITUTIONS OF HIGHER EDUCATION
Annual.   Nov. 1984.
vi+36 p.
ISSN 0147-5037.
LC 74-622476.
SRI/MF/complete

Annual report on enrollment in 13 North Dakota higher education institutions, fall 1984. Presents data on headcount enrollment by institution, county, and selected student characteristics.

Contains definitions, abbreviations, and contents and table listings (p. iii-vi); and 14 maps and 12 tables, listed below (p. 1-36).

Availability: North Dakota Board of Higher Education, Postsecondary Education Commission, State Capitol, 10th Floor, Bismarck ND 58505-0154, †; SRI/MF/complete.

TABLES:
[Unless otherwise noted, data are shown by institution, fall 1984. Tables 1-6 and 12 show number of students in 4 undergraduate levels, special and unclassified status, and graduate and professional degree programs.]

1-2. Headcount and full-time enrollments. (p. 1-2)

3-4. Total student credit hours and FTE enrollments of part-time students. (p. 3-4)

5. Total of full-time and FTE of part-time enrollment. (p. 5)

[6] FTE enrollments based on total student credit hours. (p. 6)

7-8. Nonresident headcount undergraduate and graduate/professional enrollments, by State [and from Canada and other foreign countries]. (p. 7-11)

9. Headcount enrollments by county of residence for North Dakota students. (p. 12-14)

[9A-9B] Total in-State enrollment [and enrollment for each institution], by county of origin [1979-84]. 14 maps. (p. 15-28)

10-11. Headcount enrollments at North Dakota colleges by race [American Indian, Afro-American, Oriental American, Spanish surname American, American white, and other]; and by citizenship, veteran status, sex, marital status, and transfer status. (p. 29-30)

12. Total student credit hours produced by course level. (p. 31-36)

S6115   NORTH DAKOTA
Highway Department

S6115–1   NORTH DAKOTA HIGHWAY STATISTICS
Annual, discontinued coverage.
Annual report on North Dakota highway and street use and finances. SRI selection criteria now exclude State reports on highway finances.

Coverage of this report is discontinued with the 1983 edition; for description, see SRI 1984 Annual under this number.

S6115–2   1984 NORTH DAKOTA VEHICULAR ACCIDENT FACTS
Annual.   July 1985.   27 p.
ISSN 0362-9171.
LC 76-644562.
SRI/MF/complete

Annual report on North Dakota traffic accidents involving fatalities, injuries, and property damage, and number of persons killed and injured, 1984, with trends from 1975. Includes data by accident and vehicle type, location, time, and other circumstances; and driver and victim characteristics.

Also includes data on vehicle miles traveled, blood alcohol content of traffic fatalities, licensed drivers, traffic violations/convictions, and use of safety devices in accidents.

Data are compiled primarily from State law enforcement reports.

Contains contents listing (1 p.); introduction and highlights (p. 1-2); and 1 map, 3 charts, and 28 tables (p. 3-27).

Availability: North Dakota Highway Department, Planning Division, 600 E. Boulevard Ave., Bismarck ND 58505-0178, †; SRI/MF/complete.

S6140   NORTH DAKOTA
Job Service

S6140–2   ANNUAL PLANNING REPORT, FY86, North Dakota
Annual.   Sept. 1985.
4+101 p.
LC 82-644178.
SRI/MF/complete

Annual planning report, for FY86, identifying North Dakota population groups most in need of employment services. Includes data on population and labor force characteristics, employment and earnings by industry, poverty, job service clients, and agriculture.

Most data are current to 1983 or 1984, with trends from the 1970s. Selected data are also shown by county.

Data are primarily from Census Bureau and other Federal agencies.

Contents:

a. Contents and table listing, and map. (4 p.)

b. Narrative report, with interspersed summary and text statistics, including 1 chart showing personal income by source, 1983; 2 tables showing covered employment and earnings for 1983-84, and employment for various periods 1970-86, all by industry division; and 1 footnote table showing unemployment insurance claimants residing out of State, quarterly 1981-2nd quarter 1985. (p. 1-43)

c. Appendices, with 31 tables listed below (p. 45-98); bibliography (p. 99-101); and directory of local job service offices (inside back cover).

Availability: North Dakota Job Service, Research and Statistics Section, 1000 E. Divide Ave., PO Box 1537, Bismarck ND 58502, †; SRI/MF/complete.

TABLES:
[Data are for North Dakota, unless otherwise noted. Data by county are arranged by State planning regions, and data by industry generally are shown by industry division. Data by race/ethnicity are shown for total, American Indians, and other minorities.]

S6140-2.1: Appendices

POPULATION

1. Population projections to 1985 and 1987 [and population in 1980], by age. (p. 47)

2. Persons enrolled in grades 1-12 for urban and rural portions [including detail for aggregate rural counties strongly affected by synthetic natural gas plant construction], by school year [1980/81-1984/85]. (p. 48)

3-4. Enrollment in grades 7-12 for the 1984/85 school year [by county, by grade]; and persons enrolled in grades 1-12 by county and school year [1980/81-1984/85]. (p. 49-50)

5. Population by age, sex, and county, 1980. (p. 51-53)

LABOR FORCE AND OCCUPATIONS

6. Civilian population, and labor force [by employment status], estimates by sex and age, 1984. (p. 57)

7. Profile of employment by industry [including self employed/unpaid family worker] and occupation, 1982. (p. 58)

8-9. Labor force [by employment status], by county [and MSA, 1983-84]. (p. 59-60)

EMPLOYMENT

10-12. Nonagricultural job insurance covered wage/salary employment by industry and county, 1980-82 annual averages. (p. 63-65)

13. Quarterly and annual average nonagricultural wage/salary employment for goods-producing and services-producing industries, [quarterly, 1981-1st quarter 1985]. (p. 66)

14-15. Industry [group] of employed persons by class of worker [private wage/salary, government by level, self-employed, and unpaid family] and by sex, 16 years/older, [1970 and 1980]. (p. 67-72)

POVERTY

16. Persons receiving food stamps, by county, 1st quarter average, 1982-85. (p. 75)

17. Characteristics of persons below the poverty level, by age, sex, and race/ethnicity, 1980. (p. 76)

18. Family [median] income [and number of families (total and by income group)] by family type [including sex of householder], 1979. (p. 77)

19. Poverty status in 1979 of persons with public assistance income [by selected characteristics including age group, for total and rural areas]. (p. 78)

20. Poverty status in 1979 of families and persons [by selected characteristics, by place of residence (inside and outside SMSAs, rural, and farm)]. (p. 79)

EARNINGS AND INCOME

21. Average monthly earnings per covered job, by industry, 1980-84. (p. 83)

22. Job insurance covered employment, average monthly earnings per job, and total earnings, by quarter, 1978-84. (p. 84)

CHARACTERISTICS OF JOB SERVICE CLIENTS

23-27. Characteristics of job service clients [including race/ethnicity, age, sex, and education; economically disadvantaged, handicapped, and veteran clients; and unemployment insurance claimants and exhaustees by age; mostly shown by State region and/or occupational group, 1984]. (p. 87-91)

AGRICULTURE

28. Farm income [by source, including government payments] and expenditures [by type, 1978-83]. (p. 95)

29. Summary data from the 1982 Census of Agriculture [number of farms, by size; farm operators by age, by principal occupation (farming and nonfarming) by residence (on and off farm), and by days of off-farm work; and selected production expenditures; 1978 and 1982]. (p. 96)

30-31. Number of farms, and change in number of farms, by county and size class, 1982 or 1978-82 period. (p. 97-98)

S6140-4   NORTH DAKOTA LABOR MARKET ADVISOR
Monthly.   Approx. 10 p. no paging.
SRI/MF/complete, shipped quarterly

Monthly report on North Dakota employment, hours, and earnings, by industry division and/or location. Report is published approximately 2 months after month of coverage.

Contains brief narrative, with a related chart (front cover) and occasionally with additional statistics; 8 monthly tables; and definitions. Feb. issue also includes 5 annual tables showing previous year totals for most data covered in monthly tables.

Monthly tables are listed below and appear in all issues. Additional features presenting substantial statistics not covered in monthly tables are described, as they appear, under "Statistical Features." Nonstatistical features are not covered.

Availability: North Dakota Job Service, Research and Statistics Section, 1000 E. Divide Ave., PO Box 1537, Bismarck ND 58502, †; SRI/MF/complete, shipped quarterly.

Issues reviewed during 1985: Oct. 1984-Jan. 1985 (D) (Vol. 3, Nos. 10-12; Vol. 4, No. 1); Feb.-Aug. 1985 (Vol. 1, Nos. 1-7).

MONTHLY TABLES:
[Data are for North Dakota, unless otherwise noted, and generally are shown for month of coverage, preceding month, and same month of previous year.]

[1-2] Nonagricultural wage/salary employment [by industry division and selected major group, for State and 3 MSAs].

[3-4] U.S. CPI, all urban consumers; and PPI, U.S. average.

[5] Manufacturing hours and earnings [for U.S., North Dakota, and Fargo-Moorhead MSA].

[6] Labor force, by county, by region [by employment status].

[7] Labor force [by employment status, for U.S., North Dakota, and 3 MSAs].

[8] Bordering State labor force comparisons [by employment status for North Dakota and 3 bordering States, for month prior to month of coverage; table begins with Feb. 1985 issue].

STATISTICAL FEATURES:

S6140-4.601: July 1985 (Vol. 1, No. 6)

HOW 'BIG' OR 'SMALL' ARE NORTH DAKOTA EMPLOYERS?

(1 p.) Article, with 1 table showing North Dakota business establishments, employment, and payroll, by employment size group, 1st quarter or Mar. 1985. Cover of report also includes a related chart showing distribution of establishments with fewer than 10 employees, by industry division, Mar. 1985.

S6140-4.602: Aug. 1985 (Vol. 1, No. 7)

LABOR MARKET INFORMATION FOR CAREER PLANNERS

(front cover and 1 p.) Article, with 1 chart showing distribution of North Dakota job openings by educational requirement (high school, up to 3 years postsecondary training, and bachelor degree/higher), 1982-90 period.

S6205   NORTH DAKOTA Office of the Secretary of State

S6205-1   OFFICIAL ABSTRACT OF VOTES CAST AT THE GENERAL ELECTION Held Nov. 6, 1984, North Dakota
Biennial.   [1985.]
2 p. Oversized.
SRI/MF/complete

Biennial report presenting results of North Dakota general election held Nov. 6, 1984. Includes voting for President, U.S. Representative, Governor/Lieutenant Governor, various other State officials, and judges; and 4 referenda, including 1 concerning right to bear arms. Data are shown by county, and include party affiliation of most candidates.

For description of previous report, covering the 1982 general election, see SRI 1983 Annual under this number.

Availability: North Dakota Office of the Secretary of State, State Capitol, Bismarck ND 58505, †; SRI/MF/complete.

S6210   NORTH DAKOTA
Supreme Court

S6210–1   ANNUAL REPORT OF THE NORTH DAKOTA JUDICIAL SYSTEM, 1984
Annual. [1985.]   38 p.
LC 78-646491.
SRI/MF/complete

Annual report on North Dakota judicial system, including trial and appellate court caseloads and case dispositions, 1983-84, with selected trends from 1977. Covers supreme, district, county, and municipal courts. Includes trial court data by case type and court location.

Case types shown are civil and criminal, for all courts, with detail for juvenile cases; and some data for traffic, small claims, probate, mental health commitment, and guardianship cases.

Also includes data on supreme court case processing time; State judicial budget; lawyer and judge disciplinary complaints and dispositions; and State bar applications and certifications.

Contains contents listing (p. 3); report, with text statistics, 11 charts, and 22 tables (p. 4-36); and judicial council directory (p. 37-38).

Availability: North Dakota Supreme Court, Court Administrator's Office, State Capitol, Bismarck ND 58505, †; SRI/MF/complete.

S6250   OHIO
Office of the
Auditor

S6250–1   STATE OF OHIO ANNUAL REPORT
Annual, discontinued.

Annual report on financial condition of Ohio State government, discontinued with 1982 report (for description, see SRI 1983 Annual under this number).

Report is discontinued due to budgetary restraints. Data are available on request from the issuing agency at Ohio Office of the Auditor, PO Box 1140, Columbus OH 43216-1140.

S6260   OHIO
Department of
Development

S6260–1   OHIO ECONOMIC INDICATORS QUARTERLY
Quarterly.   Approx. 10 p.
SRI/MF/complete

Quarterly report presenting economic activity indicators for Ohio and the U.S. Data are from Federal agencies and Ohio Dept of Employment Services. Quarter of coverage is quarter ending 4 months prior to cover date.

Contains highlights; 8 quarterly tables, listed below, with accompanying narrative analysis and 2 illustrative charts; and business activity indexes for 8 metro areas, with text data and 8 charts.

Please note that issue with Jan. 1985 cover date (presenting data through 4th quarter 1984) was published in Sept. 1985.

Availability: Ohio Department of Development, Data Users Center, PO Box 1001, Columbus OH 43216-1001, $7.50 per yr.; SRI/MF/complete.

Issues reviewed during 1985: Oct. 1984-Jan. 1985 (P) (Vol. 4, No. 4; Vol. 5, No. 1).

QUARTERLY TABLES:
[Unless otherwise noted, tables show data for Ohio and U.S., for quarter of coverage, previous quarter (Ohio only), and same quarters of preceding year.]

1. Personal income [by type, including farm, nonfarm by industry division, unemployment insurance benefits, and transfer payments].

2. Labor force [by employment status, and employment by industry division].

3. CPI [all items and 7 major components for U.S. and Cleveland and Cincinnati MSAs, for quarter of coverage, previous quarter, and same quarters of preceding year].

4. Retail sales [durable and nondurable goods].

5. Commercial banking indicators [loans by type, and demand and time/savings deposits].

6. Permit authorized private construction [units and value, by detailed type of structure].

7. Electric energy sales, by type of consumer.

8. Collection of selected State taxes [general sales/gross receipts, motor fuel, tobacco product and alcoholic beverage sales, individual and corporate income, and other].

S6260–2   OHIO COUNTY PROFILES
Annual, discontinued.

Annual compilation of basic economic and social statistics for Ohio's counties, discontinued with Mar. 1984 report.

For description of report, see SRI 1984 Annual under this number.

Data are available from the issuing agency on computer disk only.

S6260–5   1984 OHIO ENERGY STATUS REPORT
Annual.   May 1, 1985.
5+52 p.
SRI/MF/complete

Annual report, for 1984, on Ohio energy supply-demand situation. Includes data on consumption by end-use sector, and production, all by energy type, mostly 1970s-83, with consumption projections to 1994.

Also includes distribution of natural gas supply, by pipeline company; energy consumption compared to GSP; electric utility generating capacity and production, and environmental and R&D expenditures, by utility; electric and natural gas utility customers, sales, and revenues, by utility; electricity and natural gas consumption, by industry; consumption of refined petroleum products; retail gasoline sales, by company; and average gasoline prices in Cincinnati and Cleveland.

Data are from State, Federal, and private sources.

Contains listings of contents, tables, and charts (5 p.); introduction (p. 1-3); 5 narrative sections, interspersed with 18 charts and 3 tables (p. 1-24); statistical section, with 4 charts and 23 tables (p. 25-50); and definitions and sources (p. 51-52).

Availability: Ohio Department of Development, Energy Division, 65 E. State St., Suite 206, Columbus OH 43215, †; SRI/MF/complete.

S6260–6   ASSESSMENT OF THE SUPPLIES OF NATURAL GAS AND FUELS FOR GENERATING ELECTRICITY IN OHIO, Nov. 1984-Oct. 1985
Semiannual.   Dec. 15, 1984.
vii+99 p.
SRI/MF/complete, current and 2 previous reports

Semiannual report forecasting Ohio electricity and natural gas supply and demand, by utility system, monthly Nov. 1984-Oct. 1985, with selected trends from 1982 or earlier. Includes data on fuel supplies by type and source, and energy demand by consuming sector. Also includes degree-day and natural gas price trends.

Data are primarily from individual utility reports, and Federal and private agency reports.

Contains summary, and listings of contents, tables, and charts (p. i-vii); introduction, with 1 chart and 1 table (p. 1-6); electricity report, with 8 charts and 8 tables (p. 7-32); natural gas report, with 8 charts and 13 tables (p. 33-62); and 2 appendices, with 13 charts and 21 tables (p. 64-99).

Report is issued in Dec. of each year for the Nov.-Oct. forecast, and in Aug. for the July-June forecast.

The following previous forecasts were also reviewed during 1984 and are also available on SRI microfiche under this number: Nov. 1983-Oct. 1984 [Semiannual. Dec. 15, 1983. 110 p. †]; and July 1984-June 1985 [Semiannual. Aug. 15, 1984. 106 p. var. paging. †].

Availability: Ohio Department of Development, Energy Division, 65 E. State St., Suite 206, Columbus OH 43215, †; SRI/MF/complete.

S6265   OHIO
Department of
Education

S6265–1   ANNUAL FINANCIAL AND STATISTICAL REPORT, School Year 1983/84, Division of Special Education, Ohio
Annual.   Mar. 1985.
2+59 p.
LC 60-64038.
SRI/MF/complete

Annual report on Ohio special education expenditures, services, and enrollments, by type of handicap and by school district and county, 1983/84, with summary trends from 1979/80. Data are from Division of Special Education.

Contains contents listing (2 p.); and 15 tables, listed below (p. 1-59).

Availability: Ohio Department of Education, Special Education Division, 933 High St., Worthington OH 43085-4087, †; SRI/MF/complete.

TABLES:
[Data by county and school district are shown for 1983/84; other data are shown for 1979/80-1983/84.]

SUMMARY

[1] Comparison of the number of pupils and approved costs paid for all special education services [including transportation, teacher training, and total costs certified for payment]. (p. 1-3)

INDIVIDUAL INSTRUCTIONAL SERVICES

[Tables show number of pupils, hours instructed, and amount paid, for total State, and by county and school district.]

[2-4] Individual instructional services: home instruction [total and for] orthopedically/other health impaired and severe behavioral handicaps. (p. 4-28)

[5-6] Individual instructional services: [for specific learning disabled, and hearing and visually handicapped]. (p. 29-48)

INDIVIDUAL SUPPLEMENTAL SERVICES

[Tables show number of pupils and amount paid, for total State and by county and school district, unless otherwise noted.]

[7] Individual supplemental services [aggregate, State only]. (p. 49)

[8-12] Interpreter services; and reader and guide services, for visually handicapped children. (p. 50-54)

[13-14] Attendant services for crippled children. (p. 55-58)

ADMINISTRATION

[15] Administration monies [from general revenue and Federal Education of the Handicapped Act, FY81-84]. (p. 59)

S6265-2   STATE BOARD OF EDUCATION OF OHIO ANNUAL REPORT, 1984: Communicating Excellence in Education
Annual. Dec. 1984. 33 p.
LC 59-62559.
SRI/MF/complete

Annual report on public education in Ohio, covering enrollment, test scores, staff, finances, special and vocational education, and Federal assistance, 1983/84, with trends from 1978/79.

Contains contents listing (1 p.); narrative report, with 1 table showing educational expenditures for FY83-84, and appropriations for FY85, by program (p. 1-24); and statistical section, with 6 charts and 25 tables (p. 25-33).

All statistical section tables, and charts containing data not covered in tables, are listed below.

Additional detailed reports on costs per pupil and salaries of educational personnel are also available from the issuing agency but are not covered by SRI.

Availability: Ohio Department of Education, Educational Media Center, Rm. 808, 65 S. Front St., Columbus OH 43215, †; SRI/MF/complete.

TABLES AND CHARTS:

[Data are for Ohio, 1979/80-1983/84 or 1980-84, unless otherwise noted.]

S6265-2.1: Enrollment, Staff, Test Scores, School Districts, and Finances

[1-2] Total public school enrollment and public high school graduates. (p. 25)

[3] Enrollment by grades, 1983/84. (p. 25)

[4] Pupil/teacher ratio [with number of full-time teachers, and total enrollment]. (p. 25)

[5] Degree status [of teachers] in Ohio [distribution for nondegree, bachelor, 5-year, master, and doctorate], 1984. [chart] (p. 25)

[6-7] American College Test Composite and Scholastic Aptitude Test math and verbal [test scores, Ohio and total U.S., FY79-84]. [charts] (p. 26)

[8] Number of public school districts [city, exempted village, local, and total, 1979-84]. (p. 26)

[9] Disadvantaged pupil program funds (DPPF) [expenditures and number of programs]. (p. 26)

[10-11] Revenue by source , all funds [local, State, and Federal, FY83-84]; and average expenditure per pupil [city, exempted village, local, and State, 1978/79-1982/83]. (p. 27)

[12] Ohio school districts total property valuation, valuation per pupil, State average millage, and local revenue generated. (p. 27)

[13] SF-12 [School Foundation] calculation. (p. 27)

S6265-2.2: Special Educational Services, Federal Assistance, and Transportation

[1] Handicapped children receiving full services [by type of handicap, program placement, and age group], as of Dec. 1, 1983. (p. 28)

[2] Special education foundation units [and districts, by program type], 1983/84. (p. 29)

[3-6] Vocational education: secondary and adult enrollment [in agriculture, business/office, distributive, home economics, and trade/industrial], and total enrollment [secondary, adult, and career education]; and State expenditures for secondary vocational education. (p. 29-30)

[7] Students served in DPPF programs [by type of program, 1983/84]. [chart] (p. 31)

[8-9] Chapter 1 programs for disadvantaged pupils: percent of participants by grades, and district participation and funds available [1979-84]. (p. 32)

[10-12] Chapter 1 programs for migrant children and for neglected/delinquent children in State-operated schools [participants and funds]; and grants through Public Laws 81-874 [maintenance/operation]; [1979-84]. (p. 32)

[13] Funds administered by the Division of Federal Assistance [by program], 1983/84. (p. 33)

[14-15] Pupil transportation statistics [pupils transported, annual miles, and average cost per pupil and per mile]; and driver education [pupils served and subsidy]. (p. 33)

[16] Adult basic education programs [funded, enrollment, and Federal, State, and local funding]. (p. 33)

S6270   OHIO
Bureau of Employment Services

S6270-1   OHIO LABOR MARKET REVIEW
Monthly. Approx. 45 p.
SRI/MF/complete, shipped quarterly

Monthly report on Ohio employment, hours, and earnings, by industry, and job service and unemployment insurance activities, all by MSA. Data are compiled by the State in cooperation with the U.S. Dept of Labor. Report is issued approximately 1 month after month of coverage.

Contains sections for the State and each MSA, with narrative summaries, charts, and 9 monthly tables listed below; occasional additional features with statistics; and definitions.

Prior to the Jan. 1985 issue, report format varied, and report was titled *Employment, Hours, and Earnings in Ohio.*

Most monthly tables appear in all issues. All additional features with substantial statistical content are described, as they appear, under "Statistical Features." Nonstatistical features are not covered.

Bureau of Employment Services also issues an annual edition of the monthly report. Annual report is not covered in SRI.

Availability: Ohio Bureau of Employment Services, Labor Market Information Division, 145 S. Front St., PO Box 1618, Columbus OH 43216, †; SRI/MF/complete, shipped quarterly.

Issues reviewed during 1985: Oct. 1984-Aug. 1985 (D).

MONTHLY TABLES:

[Unless otherwise noted, data are for the entire State, and are shown for month of coverage or previous month, with comparison to preceding 12 months and 11 years.]

[1] Civilian labor force estimates [by employment status, with U.S. unemployment rate].

[2-3] Nonagricultural wage/salary employment [manufacturing and nonmanufacturing], and nonmanufacturing wage/salary employment [by industry division].

[4] Employment, hours, and earnings in [durable and nondurable] manufacturing.

[5] Employment and average weekly earnings in selected major manufacturing industries.

[6-7] Nonagricultural wage/salary employment, and hours and gross earnings of production/nonsupervisory workers [by SIC 2- and 3-digit industry, for month of coverage, previous month, and same month of previous year; repeated for State and each MSA].

[8] Labor force and employment data [including civilian labor force by employment status, nonagricultural wage/salary and manufacturing employment, and manufacturing production workers and average hours and earnings (hourly and/or weekly); repeated for each MSA only].

[9] Selected administrative program activities [including employment service applicants, active job seekers, and job openings and placements; and unemployment insurance claims and payments; for month of coverage, previous month, and same month of previous year; repeated for State and each MSA; table begins in Jan. 1985 issue].

STATISTICAL FEATURES:

S6270–1.601: Feb. 1985

SPECIAL TABLE

(p. 13) Table showing civilian labor force by employment status, by county, 1984. Also includes accompanying map showing unemployment rates by county, 1984 (p. 12).

S6270–1.602: Apr. 1984

PERSONAL INCOME

(p. 13) Brief article, with 2 tables showing per capita personal income comparisons for U.S., Ohio, and Ohio MSAs, 1979-83. Data are from Commerce Dept.

S6285   OHIO
Department of Health

S6285–1   REPORT OF VITAL STATISTICS for Ohio, 1983
Annual. Dec. 1984.
6+172 p.
LC 77-646834.
SRI/MF/complete

Annual report on Ohio vital statistics, covering births, deaths by cause, marriages, and divorces, by county and selected demographic characteristics, 1983. Also includes trends from 1940 and data on abortions and population. Most data are from Division of Vital Statistics records as of Mar. 23, 1984.

Contains summary charts, and contents and table listings (6 p.); methodology and definitions (p. 1-4); and 66 tables, listed below (p. 5-172).

Availability: Ohio Department of Health, Statistical Analysis Unit, Data Services Division, 246 N. High St., Columbus OH 43215, †; SRI/MF/complete.

TABLES:
[Tables show data for Ohio, 1983, unless otherwise noted.]

S6285–1.1: Summary Data and Births
VITAL STATISTICS SUMMARY

[A] Vital statistics summary [births by sex, type of delivery (single, twin, and triplets/more), and whether born in hospital, premature, and with congenital anomaly; median age of mother; fertility ratio; illegitimate births; and deaths (maternal, infant, neonatal, fetal, and perinatal); all by race]; 1982-83. (p. 5-6)

BIRTHS

[Tables 9-18 show data by county.]

1. Total live, premature, and illegitimate births, classified by color: number and rate, by county, city, and balance of county. (p. 7-18)

2. Live births, by month: number and percentage distribution, by sex and color. (p. 19)

3. Number of live births and premature births, by age of mother and color, and by birth weight. (p. 20)

4. Live births, classified by maturity status, color, and length of pregnancy in weeks: number and percent. (p. 21)

5. Number of live births, by live birth order and color, and by age of mother. (p. 22)

6. Live births, classified by color, and age and selected completed levels of education of mother. (p. 23)

7-8. Live births, classified by color and time of 1st prenatal visit, [cross-tabulated by] age of mother and number of prenatal visits. (p. 24-25)

9. Number of live births by age of mother. (p. 26-28)

10. Resident live births to mothers under 20 years of age, classified by single years of age. (p. 29-31)

11. Number of live births by live birth order. (p. 32-34)

12. Number of births, classified by month of birth. (p. 35-37)

13. Resident live births, classified by place of birth [hospital, clinic, home, and other]. (p. 38-39)

14. Live births with malformations/anomalies indicated on birth certificate, number and rate per 1,000 live births. (p. 40)

15. Resident and recorded live births. (p. 41)

16. Live births by trimester prenatal care began [or no prenatal care]. (p. 42-43)

17. Live births with birth weights 2,500 grams/under (premature), by weight group. (p. 44-45)

18. Number of resident illegitimate births by age of mother. (p. 46-48)

S6285–1.2: Deaths
[Most tables include rates.]

19. Classification of leading causes of death according to 9th Revision of the International Classification of Diseases [list of code numbers for 37 causes]. (p. 49)

20-23. Resident deaths: total all causes, fetal, neonatal, infant, and maternal; and from [15] leading causes; by county, city, and balance of county. (p. 50-97)

24. Resident and recorded deaths, classified by county. (p. 98)

25-26. 10 leading causes of death, classified by sex and by color, with percent of all deaths. (p. 99-100)

27. 5 leading causes of death, classified by sex and age group. (p. 101-105)

28. Deaths: all causes and [detailed] selected causes, classified by sex and color and by age group. (p. 106-114)

29. Total deaths: by age group, color, and sex. (p. 115)

30. Number of resident deaths, classified by month of death and county. (p. 116-118)

31. Resident and recorded fetal deaths, classified by county. (p. 119)

32-33. Fetal deaths, classified by maturity status, color, and length of pregnancy in weeks; and by color, time of 1st prenatal visit, and age of mother. (p. 120-121)

34. Resident fetal deaths, by selected cause of death and color. (p. 122)

35. Resident and recorded infant deaths, classified by county. (p. 123)

36. 10 leading causes of infant deaths, classified by color, with percent of all infant deaths. (p. 124)

37. Number of reported sudden unexpected deaths in infants, classified by county and [whether autopsy was performed]. (p. 125-126)

38. 10 leading causes of neonatal deaths, classified by color, with percent of all neonatal deaths. (p. 127)

39. Perinatal deaths, classified by county. (p. 128)

40. Number of maternal deaths, classified by selected cause, color, and age. (p. 129-130)

S6285–1.3: Marriages and Divorces

41-43. Marriages: by age and number of present marriage of bride and groom; and by month of occurrence, [by] marriage order of bride and groom. (p. 131-133)

44-46. Number of marriages with rates per 1,000 population, classified by month and by age of bride and groom, [all] by county where license was issued. (p. 134-142)

47. Number of divorces/annulments/dissolutions, with rates per 1,000 population, classified by county where decree was issued and by month of final decree. (p. 143-145)

48. Divorces and annulments, by legal grounds for decree. (p. 146)

49-50. Divorces, annulments, and dissolutions, by number of children reported under 18 years of age, and by duration of marriage. (p. 147-148)

S6285–1.4: Trends, Population, and Abortions

TRENDS

51. Live births by color: number and rate per 1,000 population, and percent occurring in hospitals, 1940-83. (p. 149)

52. Resident live births, classified by color and age of mother, 1957-83. (p. 150-152)

53. Number of illegitimate births, classified by color, with rate per 1,000 live births, 1949-83. (p. 153)

54. Fertility rates, classified by color and age of mother, 1973-83. (p. 154)

55. Deaths, by color: number and rate per 1,000 population, 1940-83. (p. 155)

56-59. Infant, fetal, maternal, and neonatal deaths: number and rate per 1,000 or 10,000 live births, classified by color, 1940-83. (p. 156-159)

60. Deaths, classified by age group, 1949-83. (p. 160)

61. Leading causes of death, with rates per 100,000 population, 1973-83. (p. 161)

62. Marriages and divorces/annulments: number and rate per 1,000 population, 1950-83. (p. 162)

POPULATION

63-64. Enumerated population, by county, city, and balance of county; and by age, sex, and color; [revised data as of Apr. 1, 1980]. (p. 163-169)

ABORTIONS

65. Number of induced abortions, by ethnic group [white, black, all others, and not reported], age group, and marital status. (p. 171-172)

S6290   OHIO
Department of Highway Safety

S6290–1   1983 OHIO TRAFFIC ACCIDENT FACTS
Annual.   Dec. 1984.
4+67 p.
SRI/MF/complete

Annual report on Ohio traffic accidents, fatalities, and injuries, by vehicle and accident type, location, time, and other circumstances; and by driver and victim characteristics; 1983, with selected trends from as early as 1936.

Also includes data on death rates and traffic fatalities, for Ohio and 8 other industrial States; accident economic costs, for Ohio and U.S.; and Ohio highway mileage, licensed drivers, registered vehicles, accidents involving alcohol and uninsured drivers, traffic violation convictions, and safety device use in accidents (including child restraint law effects).

Data are from dept records and the National Safety Council.

Contains contents listing (2 p.); 6 sections, with highlights, 52 charts, and 74 tables (p. 1-66); and definitions (p. 67).

Previous report, for 1982, is described in SRI 1983 Annual under this number.

Availability: Ohio Department of Highway Safety, 240 Parsons Ave., PO Box 7167, Columbus OH 43205, †; SRI/MF/complete.

S6310   OHIO
Department of Insurance

S6310–1   117th ANNUAL REPORT OF THE DIRECTOR OF INSURANCE, Ohio
Annual.   Dec. 1984.
v+307 p.
ISSN 0360-4799.
LC 41-21841.
SRI/MF/complete

Annual report on Ohio insurance industry financial condition and underwriting activity, by company and line of coverage, 1983. Covers assets, liabilities, capital, surplus, net premium and total income, losses and/or claims paid, disbursements, underwriting gain/loss, and types of policies and risks written and in force; and Ohio direct premiums written and losses and/or dividends paid; for companies headquartered in Ohio and elsewhere.

Data are shown, as applicable, for fire/casualty/multiple line companies, title and title guaranty/trust companies, mutual protective assns, life insurance companies, fraternal benefit societies, nonprofit hospital service and health/dental care assns, and HMOs.

Ohio underwriting data for fire/casualty companies include breakdowns for specific lines of coverage, including automobile, accident/health, medical malpractice, surety, and workers' compensation. Data for life insurance companies include detail for accident/health depts.

Also includes number of companies by type of insurance; and underwriting tax, fee, and expenditure trends from 1974.

Most data are compiled from annual statements filed by individual insurers.

Contains contents listing (p. iii-v); introduction, with regulatory summary and 4 tables (p. 1-13); and 2 statistical sections, with 68 tables (p. 15-307).

Availability: Ohio Department of Insurance, Examination Division, 2100 Stella Ct., Columbus OH 43266-0566, ◆; SRI/MF/complete.

S6380   OHIO
Office of the Secretary of State

S6380–1   OHIO ELECTION STATISTICS, 1983-84
Biennial.   [1985.]   407 p.
SRI/MF/complete, current & previous report

Biennial report presenting results of Ohio general elections held Nov. 8, 1983 and Nov. 6, 1984, and primary elections held May 8, 1984. Shows voting for President and Vice President; U.S. and State representatives; State senators, supreme court justices, judges, sheriffs, board of education members, coroners, and other State and county officials; and 3 State constitutional amendments, including raising the minimum drinking age for beer.

Results are generally shown by county, district, and/or municipality, and often include party affiliation of candidates.

Also includes voter turnout and registration, and number of precincts, by political subdivision and/or county, various years 1974-84; and selected trends from as early as 1802, including election results, presidential electors and national political convention delegates, and voting for proposed laws and State constitutional amendments.

Previous report, covering 1981-82 elections, was also reviewed in SRI during 1985, and is also available on SRI microfiche under S6380-1 [Biennial. [1983.] 385 p. †]. Previous report was substantially similar in format and content, with the following exceptions: current election results covered Governor and U.S. Senators as well as the offices noted above (except President and Vice President), 5 constitutional amendments (including authorization of high-speed intercity rail transportation system), and voting in special elections for U.S. Representatives.

Availability: Ohio Office of the Secretary of State, Elections Section, 30 E. Broad St., Columbus OH 43216, †; SRI/MF/complete.

S6385   OHIO
Supreme Court

S6385–1   TWENTY-FOURTH SUMMARY EDITION, 1983: Ohio Courts
Annual.   [1985.]   3+154 p.
LC 72-613073.
SRI/MF/complete

Annual report on Ohio judicial system, including trial and appellate court caseloads and case dispositions, 1983, with trends from 1979. Covers supreme, appeals, common pleas, claims, municipal, and county courts. Includes trial court data by case type, county and district.

Case types shown are criminal and civil, for all courts, with some additional detail for workers' compensation, traffic, small claims, crime victim claims, domestic relations, probate, estate, guardianship, adoption, mental illness/retardation, juvenile, driving while intoxicated, and contract case types.

Report also includes ratios of judges to filings and population by court.

Data are from court records.

Contains contents listing (p. 1); and report in 6 sections, with contents listings, 1 map, 26 charts, and 45 tables, interspersed with brief narrative summaries (p. 2-154).

Previous report, for 1982, is described in SRI 1983 Annual under this number.

Availability: Ohio Supreme Court, Administrative Director's Office, State Office Tower, 30 E. Broad St., Columbus OH 43215, †; SRI/MF/complete.

S6390   OHIO
Department of Taxation

S6390–1   ANNUAL REPORT OF THE OHIO DEPARTMENT OF TAXATION for the Fiscal Year Ending June 30, 1984
Annual.   July 31, 1985.
viii+135 p.
LC 44-25537.
SRI/MF/complete, current & previous year reports

Annual report, for FY84, on Ohio tax collections by tax type. Also includes characteristics of individual tax returns, corporate tax liability by industry, revenue distribution and assessed property values by county, and energy credit applications. Data generally are shown for 1983 or FY84, with trends from as early as 1979.

Contents:

a. Listing of contents, charts, and tables; and dept organizational chart, and map. (p. iii-viii)

b. Dept summary, with text data, and 2 charts and 8 tables listed below. (p. 1-9)

c. 73 tables, also listed below, and 1 chart, arranged in 17 sections generally by tax type, with accompanying narrative summaries, statutory references, and synopses of court decisions. (p. 10-135)

Previous report, for FY83, was also reviewed in SRI during 1985, and is also available on SRI microfiche under S6390-1 [Annual. Sept. 12, 1984. viii+143 p. †].

Report for FY82 is described in SRI 1983 Annual under this number.

Availability: Ohio Department of Taxation, Research and Statistics Section, PO Box 530, Columbus OH 43216, †; SRI/MF/complete.

TABLES AND CHARTS:

S6390–1.1: Summary

[Unless otherwise noted, data are for FY84.]

1. Dept of Taxation staff structure and number of employees. (p. 2)

2. Expenditures of the Dept of Taxation. (p. 2)

3. Number of pollution control, conversion facility, and thermal efficiency improvement facility final certificates issued and value of exemptions granted [by type of facility]. (p. 4)

4. Total audit production for sales, income, property, and estate tax divisions, FY80-84. (p. 4)

5. Personal property tax assessments, 1982-83. (p. 5)

6. Sales and excise tax assessments levied and unpaid assessments certified for payment, FY83-84. (p. 5)

7. Personal income tax and corporate franchise tax assessments levied, FY81-84. (p. 5)

8. Collections for taxes administered by tax commissioner [State-collected taxes, FY83-84; and locally collected taxes assessed, 1982-83]. (p. 7)

Figure 1-2. All revenue receipts [by source]; and general revenue fund sources. (p. 8-9)

S6390–1.2: Alcoholic Beverage, Cigarette, and Corporate Franchise Taxes

ALCOHOLIC BEVERAGE AND CIGARETTE TAXES

9-10. Alcoholic beverage tax payments and credits, FY84; and tax liability, as reported on returns, FY82-84; [by beverage type]. (p. 13)

11. Cigarette excise tax receipts [by payment type], FY84. (p. 16)

CORPORATE FRANCHISE TAX

12. Corporate franchise tax collections [and refunds], FY80-84. (p. 23)

13-16. Number of corporations and reported tax liability by tax base [and tax credits by type, all] by industry [division] and tax liability class, tax year 1983. (p. 24-26)

17-20. [Repeats tables 13-16 for manufacturing corporations, with detail by major industry group.] (p. 27-29)

21. Number of financial institutions and reported tax liability by type of institution, tax year 1983. (p. 30)

S6390–1.3: Energy Credit Program; and Estate, Highway Use, Horse Racing, and Income Taxes

ENERGY TAX CREDITS

22. Energy credit program: number of applications by county and type of aid [cash payment or credit], 1983/84 heating season. (p. 32)

ESTATE TAXES

[Data are for resident estate taxes only.]

23-25. Distribution of taxable estates, gross and net values, and estate taxes assessed and paid; and number of estates, aggregate gross and net taxable estate valuations, and aggre-gate taxes assessed; by selected gross value brackets and net taxable value (tax rate) brackets, FY84. (p. 39-40)

26. Distribution of estates generating estate tax and of tax paid among estates over and under $100,000 gross value, FY81-84. (p. 41)

27. Estates generating tax and estate taxes assessed, according to amounts of tax generated, FY83-84. (p. 41)

28. Number of estates, aggregate gross and net taxable values, amounts of tax assessed and paid, and average amounts of tax paid per estate, by county of probate, FY84. (p. 42-43)

HIGHWAY USE TAX

29-30. Highway use tax liability: [total] FY80-84; and by tax rate classification, FY84; by type of permit holder [Ohio, foreign, and uni-dentified]. (p. 46)

31. Average number of highway use tax permits and total mileage subject to tax, by tax rate classification [and type of permit holder], FY84. (p. 46)

HORSE RACING TAX

32. Amount wagered on horse racing and total tax and special fund receipts, by type of event, FY80-84. (p. 53)

33. Amount wagered on horse racing, [number of racing days, and] tax receipts and allocation to funds, by [type of] meet, FY84. (p. 54)

PERSONAL INCOME TAX

[Tables 34 and 37-44 show data for 1982. Tables 34-42 show data by income bracket, and generally include number of returns, Federal adjusted gross income, and Ohio taxable income and/or tax liability. Most table titles begin "Personal income tax..."]

34. Returns by income class. (p. 61)

35-36. Comparison of 1981-82 personal income tax returns. (p. 62)

37-42. Returns: for all filing status categories; claiming married joint, single, and married separate filing status; according to Ohio taxable income class; and claiming the joint filer credit. (p. 63-65)

43-44. Returns, [Federal adjusted gross income, and Ohio tax], by county; and rank of counties by average income, as reported on 1982 Ohio personal income tax returns. (p. 66-67)

45. Personal income taxes required to be returned to counties of origin, school foundation payments, and property tax relief reimbursement payments, 1983, by county. (p. 68)

46. Returns filed [and taxes paid] by employers and individuals, FY83-84. (p. 69)

47. Collections [employer withholding, individual and other collections, and refunds], by month, FY84. (p. 69)

S6390–1.4: Revenue Distribution; and Intangible Property, Motor Vehicle Fuel, and Public Utility Taxes

INTANGIBLE PROPERTY TAX

48. Taxes levied, by level of collection [county and State], and distribution of funds, 1983. (p. 78)

49-51. Taxes levied: by level of collection and form of property, 1979-83; by form of property, 1982-83; and for local government purposes by [level of collection and] county, 1983. (p. 79-81)

REVENUE DISTRIBUTION

[Tables 53-55 show data by county.]

52. Total State-collected revenues distributed for general local governmental purposes, 1979-83. (p. 84)

53. State local government fund: amounts distributed to counties and municipalities by source, 1983. (p. 85-86)

54. County undivided local government funds: amounts distributed to counties for redistribution to subdivisions by county budget commissions, by source, 1983. (p. 87)

55. Distribution of county undivided local government funds [to counties, townships, and municipalities], 1983. (p. 88)

MOTOR VEHICLE FUEL TAX

56-57. Gross amount of motor vehicle fuel tax certified for collection, refunds, and net tax after refunds; and taxable gallons of motor vehicle fuel [gasoline and special]; FY80-84. (p. 92)

58. Motor vehicle fuel taxes distributed to local governments, by county, 1983. (p. 93)

PUBLIC UTILITY TAXES

59. Public utility excise taxes levied, by class of utility, 1979-83 [and 1983 tax rate]. (p. 97)

60-61. Assessed value of public utility real and personal property: by class of utility, 1979-83; and taxes charged, by county, 1983. (p. 101-102)

S6390–1.5: Real Property, Sales, Severance, and Tangible Personal Property Taxes

REAL PROPERTY TAXES

[Tables 64-65 and 67-69 show data by county.]

62. Assessed value of taxable real estate/public utility property, taxes charged, average tax rates, and tax relief [reduction and homestead exemption], 1979-83. (p. 108)

63. Assessed value of taxable real estate and public utility property inside and outside municipalities, 1979-83. (p. 109)

64. Total real property taxes, values, and effective tax rates (including public utility real property), 1983. (p. 110)

65. Taxes charged on real/public utility property and property tax relief, 1982 (including public utility real/tangible property). (p. 111-112)

66. Assessed valuation of exempt real property, by selected [public and private] ownership classifications, 1979-83. (p. 113)

67. Assessed value of exempt real property compared to potential tax base, 1983. (p. 114)

68. Delinquent real and personal property taxes due/payable, 1983. (p. 115)

69. Number of homestead exemptions granted, average reduction in taxable value, and total amount of reduction in taxes, tax year 1983. (p. 116)

SALES AND USE TAXES

70. Sales and use tax collections, by type of payment, FY80-84. (p. 123)

71. Number of accounts by type and payment schedule, as of June 30, 1984. (p. 123)

72. County and transit authority permissive tax collections [by county and authority], FY80-84. (p. 124-125)

SEVERANCE TAX

73. Severance tax collections [by natural resource], FY82-84 [and tax rate as of July 1, 1983]. (p. 127)

TANGIBLE PERSONAL PROPERTY TAX

74. Assessed value and taxes levied, 1979-83. (p. 132)

75-76. Taxes levied [total and in cities, by type of jurisdictional] subdivision, 1979-83. (p. 132)

77. Assessed value of property of intercounty corporations by industry class and class of property, 1983. (p. 133)

78. Assessed value of property [of intercounty corporations and all businesses], by class of property, 1982-83. (p. 133)

79. Percentages applied to true value of property [by class of property] to determine taxable value, tax years 1976-85. (p. 133)

80. Assessed value of property, taxes levied, and average county rates, 1983, by county. (p. 134)

81. Taxes levied currently by school districts and all local governments, 1983, by county. (p. 135)

S6405   OKLAHOMA
Department of Agriculture

S6405–1   OKLAHOMA AGRICULTURAL STATISTICS, 1984
Annual. [1985.] v+103 p.
LC 80-643362.
SRI/MF/complete

Annual report on Oklahoma agricultural production, finances, and marketing, 1984, with trends from 1960 and some data for 1985. Data generally are shown by commodity and/or county and district, and include some comparisons to neighboring States and U.S.

Covers production, prices, disposition, value, and, as applicable, stocks, inventories, and total and irrigated acreage and yield, for crop, fruit and nut, livestock, dairy, and poultry sectors.

Also includes data on farms, acreage, value, tax rates, and rent; weather; pasture condition; farm income and production expenses; and agricultural exports.

Also includes selected findings from the 1982 Census of Agriculture, including data on farm operators by ownership status and age.

Data are compiled by the State Crop and Livestock Reporting Service, and are based primarily on sample surveys of farmers and ranchers.

Contains contents listing and methodology (p. iii-v); overview, with 10 tables (p. 1-5); 7 sections, with narrative reviews, 15 maps, 15 charts, and 66 tables (p. 6-101); and list of other reports available (p. 101-102).

Availability: Oklahoma Crop and Livestock Reporting Service, PO Box 1095, Oklahoma City OK 73101, $5.00; SRI/MF/complete.

S6422   OKLAHOMA
Department of Economic and Community Affairs

S6422–2   PLACE OF WORK FROM THE 1980 CENSUS: A Summary Report on Commuting Patterns in Oklahoma Counties
Monograph.   2 volumes.
For individual publication data, see below.
SRI/MF/complete

Report presenting 1980 census data on commuting patterns in Oklahoma, covering points of origin and destination for Oklahoma residents and for nonresidents employed in the State. Includes data cross-tabulated among counties of Oklahoma and neighboring States.

Report is issued in 2 parts, described below.

Availability: Oklahoma Department of Economic and Community Affairs, State Data Center, Lincoln Plaza Bldg., Suite 285, 4545 N. Lincoln Blvd., Oklahoma City OK 73105-3481, †; SRI/MF/complete

S6422–2.1: Part I
[Monograph. Mar. 1984. 6 p. no paging. Oversized. SRI/MF/complete.]

Presents commuting summary for each Oklahoma county, including major work areas (cities or counties) for residents working outside the county.

Contains introduction, definitions, and highlights (1 p.); and 1 table (5 p.).

S6422–2.2: Part II
[Monograph. Apr. 1985. 98 p. SRI/MF/ complete.]

Presents detailed commuting patterns for each Oklahoma county, including in- and out-commuters by county of origin or destination. Also presents summary comparisons to 1970; and summary of interstate commuting, and persons working at sea and outside the U.S.

Contains listing of contents and tables (1 p.); introduction, definitions, highlights, and 4 maps (p. 1-8); 2 summary tables (p. 9-15); and 1 table repeated for each county (p. 19-98).

S6423   OKLAHOMA
Department of Education

S6423–1   1983/84 ANNUAL REPORT, OKLAHOMA STATE DEPARTMENT OF EDUCATION
Annual.   3 volumes.
For individual publication data, see below.
LC 76-646002.
SRI/MF/complete

Annual report on Oklahoma public schools, covering finances, programs, personnel, and students, 1983/84, with trends from 1924/25. Presents valuations and Federal, State, and local funding data by school district and county. Also includes data on teacher education and salaries, special education, Indian education, and pupil transportation.

Report is issued in 3 volumes, individually described below, and also includes a detached foldout table showing summary educational revenues, by source and county, FY84.

Prior to 1983/84, report was issued in 1 volume.

Availability: Oklahoma Department of Education, Communications Section, Administration Division, Oliver Hodges Memorial Education Bldg., 2500 N. Lincoln Blvd., Oklahoma City OK 73105-4599, ‡ ($1.00 postage); SRI/MF/ complete.

VOLUMES:
[Tables show data by county for 1983/84 school year or FY84, unless otherwise noted.]

S6423–1.1: Volume 1
[Annual. [1985.] 118 p.+foldout. SRI/MF/ complete.]

Contains contents listing (1 p.); and 52 tables, listed below (p. 1-118).

TABLES:

STATE PROGRAMS

[1] Career education (H.B. 1179) [funding amount received, by school district]. (p. 1)

[2] Driver and safety education section, reimbursements to public schools [by object, and number of pupils]. (p. 2-4)

[3] Library media improvement [funding amount received, by school district]. (p. 5-7)

[4-5] School lunch [State and Federal] funds distributed to districts; and disbursements [by program]. (p. 8-12)

[6] County superintendents' salaries, showing amount paid by the State, number of dependent districts, and number of teachers employed. (p. 13)

[7] State aid paid [by purpose]. (p. 14-22)

[8] Report of State education agency expenditures [by function and object, for total State, with total Federal spending]. (p. 23)

[9-10] Textbooks section: allocations [and enrollment]; and State textbook committee [member listing]. (p. 24-25)

FEDERAL AID PROGRAMS

[11-13] Federal programs [amount received for adult basic education, compensatory education, and education consolidation and improvement; by school district or agency]. (p. 26-49)

[14] Federal funds paid to school districts and certain other agencies under [9] major Federal education assistance acts. (p. 50-53)

[15] Federal programs [amount received for Indian education, by school district or agency]. (p. 54-59)

[16] Indian education section, Johnson-O'Malley funds distributed to districts [for special programs and educational support]. (p. 60-63)

[17-18] School plant services section, P.L. 874: actual [total] receipts; and section 7 actual receipts for disaster payments; [by school district]. (p. 64-70)

[19-22] Federal programs [amount received for special education and pre-school incentive programs, and transition program for refugee children; by school district or institution]. (p. 71-78)

STATISTICAL INFORMATION

[23] Annexations and consolidations of State school districts [mandatory and elective, and number of school districts, Jan. 1, 1946-July 31, 1984 period]. (p. 79-80)

[24-43] Approved teacher education programs in State [tabular listing of program subjects, grade levels, and degrees, repeated for 20 institutions]. (p. 81-110)

[44] Attendance, membership, and transportation [State totals from superintendents' and auditing section reports]. (p. 111)

[45] Enrollment [for all grades and for 11th and 12th grades, and high school graduates, State totals, 1960/61-1983/84]. (p. 112)

[46] Number of high school districts, high schools, mid-high schools, junior high schools, and elementary schools [and middle, dependent elementary, vocational/technical, and north central schools], 1982/83-1983/84. (p. 113-114)

[47-48] Public school statistics: 20-year comparison [of] original entries and total average daily attendance, [State totals by school level, 1964/65-1983/84]. (p. 115)

[49-50] Scholastic population, and high school graduates [by sex]. (p. 116)

[51-52] Statistical information on teachers [State total teachers by years of experience, and average salaries, by degree level; and number of FTE personnel and total and average salaries for 35 positions]. (p. 117-118)

S6423–1.2: Volume 2

[Annual. [1985.] 99 p. SRI/MF/complete.]

Contains contents listing (1 p.); worksheet for calculating State foundation and salary incentive aid (p. 1); and 166 tables listed below (p. 2-99).

TABLES:

[1] Comparable data concerning State public schools, [State totals for average daily attendance (ADA), number of teachers, average salary, State aid, total and per capita expenditures, and net valuation], 1924/25-1983/84. (p. 2-3)

[2-4] School district net valuations as certified to State board of equalization; total revenue received by school districts [by source]; and classification of general fund expenditures of public schools; [State totals]. (p. 4)

[5-159] School district net valuations [including value of real and personal property and public services, total and per capita valuation, levies by fund, and July 1984 general fund surplus], 1984/85; and total revenue received by school district [total, per capita, and by local/county, State, and Federal source, 1983/84; all by school district, repeated for each county]. (p. 5-81)

[160] Per capita revenues by source, and per-centage of total revenue. (p. 82-83)

[161] Classification of general fund expenditures [by function]. (p. 84-91)

[162] County valuations per ADA. (p. 92)

[163] Pupil transportation [number of buses, miles traveled, average daily pupils transported, and State aid and total expenditures]. (p. 93-94)

[164] Original entries, kindergarten through 12th grade [by specific grade and for ungraded special education]. (p. 95-96)

[165] State totals for sources of revenue and the amount collected from each source by the common schools. (p. 97)

[166] Finance Division, comparative data [State totals for number of districts and teachers, average salary, and revenues by source, 1963/64-1983/84]. (p. 98-99)

S6423–1.3: Volume 3

[Annual. [1985.] 51 p. SRI/MF/complete.]

Narrative report on State Dept of Education activities in 1983/84, with text data on various programs and services, including teacher certification, creative arts programs, gifted/talented students, and preschool programs.

Contains 1 summary table, organizational chart, and contents listing (p. 2-5); and narrative report (p. 7-51).

S6425   OKLAHOMA
Election Board

S6425–1   STATE OF OKLAHOMA ELECTION RESULTS AND STATISTICS, 1984

Biennial. [1985.] 98 p.
LC 81-644395.
SRI/MF/complete

Biennial report presenting results of Oklahoma primary, primary run-off, and general elections held during 1984. Shows voting for presidential electors; U.S. and State senators and representatives; Governor; other State officials, including judges; and 14 State questions.

Also shows party affiliation of candidates, number of precincts, and general election voter registration by party and turnout. Data are generally shown by county or district.

Previous report, covering 1982 elections, is described in SRI 1983 Annual under this number.

Availability: Oklahoma Election Board, PO Box 53156, Oklahoma City OK 73152, †; SRI/MF/complete.

S6430   OKLAHOMA
Employment Security
Commission

S6430–2   OKLAHOMA LABOR MARKET

Monthly.   Approx. 10 p.
ISSN 0030-1744.
LC 52-44621.
SRI/MF/complete, shipped quarterly

Monthly report on Oklahoma labor force, covering employment and unemployment, hours and earnings, and characteristics of the insured unemployed. Includes data by industry, MSA, and county.

Data are from Federal and State agencies. Month of coverage is 1-2 months prior to cover date.

Contains narrative summary; usually 3 summary charts; and 5 monthly and 3 quarterly tables, listed below.

Monthly tables appear in all issues; quarterly tables appear in Oct. 1984 and Jan. and Apr. 1985 issues.

Availability: Oklahoma Employment Security Commission, Research and Planning Division, 310 Will Rogers Memorial Office Bldg., Oklahoma City OK 73105, †; SRI/MF/complete, shipped quarterly.

Issues reviewed during 1985: Aug. 1984-Aug. 1985 (P).

TABLES:

[Data are for Oklahoma, unless otherwise noted. Tables [1-2] show data for month of coverage, previous month, and same month of previous year. Table sequence may vary.]

MONTHLY TABLES

[1] Labor force summary [by employment status, agricultural and domestic service/self-employed/unpaid family workers, and workers idled by labor disputes; and nonfarm wage/salary employment, by industry group].

[2] Hours and earnings in selected industries [by major industry group].

[3] Labor force data [employment, unemployment, and unemployment rate, by county and selected MSA, and for 12 service delivery areas, for month of coverage, with unemployment rate also for previous month and same month of previous year].

[4] U.S. CPI, all urban consumers [monthly for current year to date and previous year, and annually from 1970s].

[5] Comparisons of unemployment rates, U.S. and Oklahoma [unadjusted and seasonally adjusted, monthly current year to date and 2-3 previous years].

QUARTERLY TABLES

[I-III] Characteristics of the insured unemployed: industry [division and group], major occupational group, age, sex, duration [of unemployment], and race [variously cross-tabulated, for a selected week of month of coverage].

S6445   OKLAHOMA
Department of
Health

S6445–1   OKLAHOMA HEALTH
STATISTICS, 1984
Annual.   [1985.]   7+228 p.
ISSN 0098-5651.
LC 75-643676.
SRI/MF/complete

Annual report, for 1984, on Oklahoma vital statistics, covering population, births, deaths by cause, marriages, and divorces. Includes data by location, race, and age, and selected trends from 1920.

Data were compiled from birth and death certificates filed with the State Dept of Health prior to Apr. 15, 1985; and from reports by county court clerks on marriages and divorces.

Contains prefatory material, and contents and table listing (7 p.); methodology, notes on vital records, and guide to symbols used in tables (p. 1-4); 20 tables, listed below (p. 5-221); and technical appendix, with definitions and sample birth and death certificates (p. 222-228).

A less detailed monthly vital statistics report is also published by the issuing agency, but is not covered in SRI.

Availability: Oklahoma Department of Health, Public Health Statistics Section, Data Management Division, 1000 N.E. Tenth St., PO Box 53551, Oklahoma City OK 73152, †; SRI/MF/complete.

TABLES:
[Tables present data for Oklahoma, 1984, unless otherwise noted. Data by race are shown for white, black, and Indian.

Tables I-II, V-VII, and X-XI show live and stillbirths by attendant (physician in and out of hospital, and midwife/other/unknown). Tables I-II and V-VII also show population.]

BIRTH AND MORTALITY TRENDS
I-II. Resident births, fetal deaths (stillbirths), [total, infant, and neonatal] deaths, and deaths by 34 selected causes: number and rate, 1930-84; and by race, 1984. (p. 5-25)

III. Births and deaths, number and rate, 1920-84. (p. 26)

BIRTH WEIGHTS
IV. Resident live births by age of mother, race, and number and percent of low-weight births. (p. 27)

BIRTHS AND DEATHS BY LOCALITY
V-VII. Resident births, fetal deaths (stillbirths), [total, infant, and neonatal] deaths, and deaths by 34 selected causes: number and rate, by race, by county, MSA, and cities of 2,500 or more. (p. 28-134)

VIII-IX. Resident births and deaths by county, race, and sex. (p. 135-136)

DEATHS BY CAUSE AND AGE
X-XI. Resident births, fetal deaths (stillbirths), [total, infant, and neonatal deaths], and deaths by 34 selected causes: by month, and by age, race, and sex. (p. 137-186)

XII-XIII. [10] leading causes of deaths, number and rank: by race and sex, and by age. (p. 187-188)

XIV. Resident deaths by 3-digit ICDA [International Classification of Diseases Adapted] codes, number and rate, and race. (p. 189-212)

XV. Fetal deaths by ICDA, by race. (p. 213)

BIRTHS AND DEATHS BY PLACE OF OCCURRENCE AND RESIDENCE
XVI. Births and deaths of Oklahoma residents by State of occurrence; and births and deaths of out-of-State residents occurring in Oklahoma, by State of residence. (p. 214)

XVII. Births, fetal deaths (stillbirths), [total] deaths, and infant and neonatal deaths, by county of residence and occurrence. (p. 215)

MARRIAGES AND DIVORCES
XVIII. Marriages, divorces, [and annulments], number and rate, [by county]. (p. 216)

LIFE EXPECTANCY
XIX. Life expectancy [by age group, with calculation]. (p. 219)

XX. Estimated average life expectancy, by county and age. (p. 220-221)

S6450   OKLAHOMA
Regents for
Higher Education

S6450–1   TWENTY-SECOND
BIENNIAL REPORT, PART II,
Oklahoma State Regents for
Higher Education, Fiscal
Year Ending June 30, 1984
Biennial.   Dec. 19, 1984.
4+192 p.
LC 43-52673.
SRI/MF/complete

Biennial report on Oklahoma higher education programs and activities for 2- and 4-year accredited colleges and universities, with data on State supported institution enrollment, finances, and operations, for FY84.

Report is published in 2 parts, presenting separate data for each fiscal year of the biennium. Part I is published in even-numbered years; Part II is published in odd-numbered years. Current Part II presents data for FY84, with selected trends from as early as FY09.

Data are from Oklahoma State System of Higher Education and other sources.

Contents:

Table of contents. (2 p.)

Chapter I: Progress and Plans. Narrative analysis of statewide programs; and reports of individual State supported and independent institutions, with various text statistics summarizing 1983/84 academic year. (p. 1-75)

Chapter II: Historical and Statistical Information. Includes descriptions of financial aid, entrance examination, and selected programs and procedures; summaries of State Regents' FY83 budgeting resolutions and guidelines; and 18 tables, listed below. (p. 79-135)

Chapter III: Historical Record of Boards, Institutions, and Presidents. Narrative, lists of officials, and expiration dates of office terms. (p. 139-191)

Index. (p. 192)

Part I of the 22nd biennial report is described in SRI 1984 Annual under this number.

Availability: Oklahoma Regents for Higher Education, 500 Education Bldg., State Capitol Complex, Oklahoma City OK 73105, †; SRI/MF/complete.

TABLES:
[Unless otherwise indicated, all data are for Oklahoma State System of Higher Education.]

S6450–1.1: Enrollment and Degrees
[Tables [3-6] show data by institution.]

ENROLLMENT
[1] Oklahoma high school graduates, by county [and sex], 1984. (p. 79)

[2] Geographic origin of students enrolled in public institutions in 1983/84, by county, State, and country. (p. 80-81)

[3] Summary of fall off-campus enrollments, 1982/83-1983/84. (p. 82)

[4] Comparison of main and branch campus fall semester enrollments, 1973-83. (p. 83)

[5] Enrollment by county, 1st semester 1983/84. (p. 84-87)

DEGREES
[6] Summary of degrees granted [by level and subject area], 1982/83. (p. 88-91)

S6450–1.2: Finances
STUDENT AID
[1] State scholarships granted [students helped, and funds used and authorized, by institution], 1983/84. (p. 94)

[2-3] Guaranteed student loan program "in-school" loans, as of June 30, 1984; and tuition aid grant/SSIG [State student incentive grants] program [recipients and value, by institution, for State and other institutions, FY84]. (p. 96-99)

EXPENDITURES AND BUDGETS
[Tables [6-7] and [10-12] show data by institution.]

[4] Regents' office expenditures [by object and summary of budgeted] State and Federal funds, 1983/84. (p. 111)

[5] Summary of appropriation acts [and amounts], 39th Oklahoma Legislature, FY84. (p. 112)

[6-7] Educational and general operating budget: Part I summary [State and other funds available], FY84, and Part II, allocations for sponsored research/other sponsored programs [FY83-84]. (p. 113-115)

[8] State Regents' No. 220 loan fund [status, as of June 30, 1984]. (p. 122)

[9] Expenditures for State purposes since statehood: budget office totals [FY09-84]. (p. 123)

[10] Current operating income [by source] and expenditures [by function], 1983/84. (p. 124-127)

[11] Bonded indebtedness, as of June 30, 1984. (p. 128-131)

[12] Section 13 and new college funds [available and expended], 1983/84. (p. 134)

S6450–2   COLLEGE AND UNIVERSITY SALARIES IN TEN MID-WESTERN STATES, 1983/84 Academic Year
Annual.   Apr. 1984.
12 p. Oversized.
SRI/MF/complete

Annual report, for academic year 1983/84, on public college and university faculty salaries in Oklahoma and 9 surrounding States, by institution and faculty academic rank. Also includes data on student/faculty ratios, staff benefits, and selected administrative salaries.

Data are based on a questionnaire survey of 178 institutions in Arizona, Arkansas, Colorado, Iowa, Kansas, Missouri, Nebraska, New Mexico, Oklahoma, and Texas.

Contains table listing (1 p.); list of participating institutions, and highlights (p. 1-2); and 10 tables (p. 3-12).

Availability: Oklahoma Regents for Higher Education, 500 Education Bldg., State Capitol Complex, Oklahoma City OK 73105, †; SRI/MF/complete.

S6455   OKLAHOMA
Department of Human Services

S6455–1   OKLAHOMA DEPARTMENT OF HUMAN SERVICES Annual Report, FY84
Annual.   2 volumes.
For individual publication data, see below.
SRI/MF/complete

Annual report on Oklahoma public welfare programs, cases, clients, services, and finances, by county, FY84, with selected historical trends from FY37. Data are from Dept of Human Services (DHS) records and other State sources.

Report is issued in 2 volumes: a narrative report and a statistical report. Volumes are individually described below.

Availability: Oklahoma Department of Human Services, Research and Statistics Division, Editorial Office, PO Box 25352, Oklahoma City OK 73125, †; SRI/MF/complete.

S6455–1.1: Main Report
[Annual. [1984.] 20 p. DHS Pub. No. 84-92. SRI/MF/complete.]

Contains contents listing (front cover); and narrative report, interspersed with 27 charts and 4 tables showing summary data generally included in the statistical report (p. 4-19).

S6455–1.2: Statistical Report
[Annual. [1984.] 48 p. DHS Pub. No. 84-101. SRI/MF/complete.]

Contains 3 charts and 4 tables (p. 2); table listing (p. 3); 36 charts and 33 tables (p. 4-46); and listing of committee members (p. 47).

All tables, and selected charts with substantial statistics for Oklahoma not included in tables, are listed below.

TABLES AND CHARTS:
[Data are for FY84, unless otherwise noted. Data by category generally cover State supplemental payments for aged, blind, and disabled;

AFDC; and, sometimes, payments for medically needy, food stamps, general assistance, and AFDC emergency. Data by race are for white, black, Indian, and other].

SUMMARY EXPENDITURES, EMPLOYEES, AND COLLECTIONS
[A-D] Services delivered to clients, and employees providing the services [by program]; how it is spent [expenditures by program or function]; and sources of DHS revenue; [various periods FY83-84]. (p. 2)

1. Expenditures [by program/activity area], FY83-84. (p. 4)

2. DHS program expenditures: by [State and Federal] source of funds, FY37-84. (p. 5)

3. State tax dollar: collections, expenditures, and amounts returned [by State region and county, with total out-of-State collections]. (p. 6-7)

PUBLIC ASSISTANCE
4-7. Public assistance payments, monthly average payment, and monthly average cases and persons, [all] by category, FY37-84; and payments by category and county, FY84. (p. 8-12)

[E] Percent of population receiving supplemental payments/AFDC [by county]. [chart] (p. 12)

8-11. Application and case movement; public assistance cases opened and closed, by reason; and appeals and dispositions; [all by category]. (p. 13-14)

FOOD STAMP ASSISTANCE AND DONATED FOOD
12. Food stamp program: cases, persons, and value, by category [AFDC and non-AFDC] and county. (p. 15-16)

[F] Percent of population receiving food stamps, by county. [chart] (p. 15)

[G] Percent of population below poverty level by county. [chart] (p. 17)

13. Donated food commodities: average retail value, by issue [schools, institutions, elderly nutrition, child care, summer camps, and needy Indian and other families], by county. (p. 17-18)

STATE SUPPLEMENTAL AND AFDC RECIPIENTS
14-15. Total recipients of State supplemental payments [to the aged, blind, and disabled]; and AFDC recipients [families and children]; by race, sex, and county. (p. 19-25)

16. Total children in AFDC by age and sex. (p. 25)

17-19. Recipients of State supplemental payments to the aged, blind, and disabled, by age, race, and sex. (p. 26)

SOCIAL SERVICES
[H-I] [Number of] social services for adults and children; and children in DHS-paid day care and number of licensed day care slots; [by county, as of June 1984]. [charts] (p. 27)

MEDICAL ASSISTANCE
[Data by type of service generally include hospitals, physicians, and prescribed drugs and/or other services.]

20. Medical payments by category [combined adult, AFDC, medically needy by age group, vocational rehabilitation, and crippled children], and type of service. (p. 28)

21-22. Medicaid payments and recipients, by type of service and county. (p. 29-32)

[J] Percent of population receiving Medicaid benefits [by county]. [chart] (p. 31)

23. Hospitalization: persons, days, and payments, by hospital [and related facility, FY83-84]. (p. 33-36)

24. Vocational rehabilitation medical services, cases and payments, by type of service and county. (p. 37-38)

[K-L] Rehabilitation clients by type of disability; rehabilitation expenditures by type of service; and persons served and rehabilitated through rehabilitative/visual services, by county. [charts] (p. 38)

SERVICES FOR ELDERLY AND CHILDREN
25. Nutrition programs for the elderly: meals served by type [congregate and at-home] and by county. (p. 39)

26-27. Adoptive homes: placements [by age group; and applications, completed studies, and trial adoptions]. (p. 40)

28. Foster homes [applications and approvals]. (p. 40)

29. Child abuse and neglect [cases alleged and confirmed], by county. (p. 41)

30. Children receiving services from court related and community services, by [State] region and county. (p. 42-43)

[M-N] Services to developmentally disabled/mentally retarded, by type of service; and level of retardation [among residents] at State schools; June 1984. [charts] (p. 44)

[O] Developmental disability services [children in State schools for mentally retarded and in community services], by county. [chart] (p. 44)

31. Homes and schools: population movement by facility. (p. 44)

32. Child support enforcement: collections and absent parent cases, by category [AFDC and non-AFDC] and activity, FY83-84. (p. 45)

TEACHING HOSPITALS
33. Oklahoma teaching hospitals [beds, admissions, discharges, average occupancy, and outpatient clinic visits, by hospital, FY82-84]. (p. 46)

[P] OTH [Oklahoma teaching hospital] inpatient admissions [by county]. [chart] (p. 46)

S6465   OKLAHOMA
Bureau of Investigation

S6465–1   STATE OF OKLAHOMA UNIFORM CRIME REPORT, Jan.-Dec. 1984
Annual.   [1985.] ix + 125 p.
LC 78-648358.
SRI/MF/complete

Annual report on Oklahoma crimes and arrests, by offense, 1984, with comparisons to 1982-83. Includes data by county and reporting agency, and by offender age, race/ethnicity, and sex. Also includes law enforcement employment by sex, and assaults on officers.

Report focuses on 8 Index offenses: murder, rape, robbery, aggravated asault, burglary, larceny/theft, motor vehicle theft, and arson. Arrests are also shown for numerous non-Index offenses.

Data are from State and local agency reports submitted under the Uniform Crime Reporting (UCR) Program.

Contains listings of contents, tables, and charts, and introduction (p. vi-ix); crime summary, with 1 table, and UCR Program description (p. 2-11); 6 statistical sections, with 27 charts and 52 tables described below (p. 14-117); statement of policy for release of UCR information (p. 120); and appendix, with 1 table showing law enforcement employment by sex, 1984, and glossary (p. 122-125).

This is the 11th annual report. A quarterly report with summary data is also available from the issuing agency, but is not covered by SRI.

Availability: Oklahoma Bureau of Investigation, Uniform Crime Reporting Division, Cimarron Station, PO Box 11497, Oklahoma City OK 73136, †; SRI/MF/complete.

CHARTS AND TABLES:

[Data are shown for 1982-84, unless otherwise noted. Arson is generally not included in data shown by Index offense.]

S6465–1.1: Index Offenses, Stolen Property, and Arrests

[Data by race/ethnic group generally are shown for white, black, Indian, Hispanic, non-Hispanic, and other, including Asian.]

INDEX OFFENSES

[For most individual Index offenses, tables and charts include number of offenses by month for 1982-84 and by season for 1984, in addition to the data described below.]

a. Total, violent, and nonviolent offenses, by month; and frequency of occurrence, by offense. 7 charts and 3 tables. (p. 14-19)

b. Murder: offenses by day of week, and victims by age, sex, and race/ethnic group, 1982-84; and offenses by circumstance, victim-offender relationship, and weapon, 1984. 2 charts and 6 tables. (p. 21-23)

c. Rape: forcible and attempted rapes. 2 charts and 3 tables. (p. 25)

d. Robbery and aggravated assault: robberies and value of property stolen, by place of occurrence; and robberies and aggravated assaults, by weapon. 4 charts and 7 tables. (p. 26-29)

e. Burglary, larceny, and motor vehicle theft: burglary offenses, by type of entry; residence and nonresidence burglary offenses and value of property stolen, by day or night occurrence; larceny offenses by value of property stolen, and offenses and value by type of theft; and motor vehicle thefts, by type of vehicle. 8 charts and 15 tables. (p. 31-38)

f. Arson: offenses and value of property damage, by type of property. 1 table. (p. 40)

STOLEN PROPERTY

g. Value of property stolen and recovered, by month, 1982-84, with 1984 detail by offense and/or type of property. 1 chart and 5 tables. (p. 43-46)

ARRESTS AND CLEARANCES

h. Clearances: total, number involving adults and juveniles, and rates, by Index offense, 1984, with rate trends from 1982. 2 charts and 1 table. (p. 49-50)

i. Arrests of juveniles and adults, by sex, age, race/ethnic group, and offense, including drug-related by substance, 1984; and juvenile dispositions (releases and referrals), 1982-84. 3 tables. (p. 51-56)

S6465–1.2: Police Assaulted, Offenses by Locale, and UCR Participation

a. Assaults on officers, by type of assignment, circumstance, weapon, injury status, and time of day. 5 tables. (p. 58-61)

b. Population, Index crime rate, and Index offenses by type, by county and law enforcement agency. 1 table. (p. 65-106)

c. UCR participation, by agency, 1984, with totals for police depts and sheriffs offices, 1982-84, all by month. 2 tables. (p. 110-117)

S6470   OKLAHOMA
Department of Libraries

S6470–1   ANNUAL REPORT OF OKLAHOMA LIBRARIES, 1984
Annual.   [1985.]   78 p.
LC 84-642174.
SRI/MF/complete

Annual report, for FY84, on Oklahoma library holdings, finances, circulation, and staff, for public, academic, institutional, school, and special libraries, by facility.

Includes some or all of the following for each library and for public library systems: population served; income by source, including governmental level; expenditures by function, including salaries, materials, and operations; circulation, total and added volumes, periodical subscriptions, and audiovisual materials; FTE staff (total and with master of library science degrees); hours of operation; and available seating, services, and programs.

Also includes data on public library registered borrowers.

Data are from State library annual reports and the Census Bureau.

Contains contents listing (1 p.); and summary analysis, and 16 tables (p. 1-78).

Report previously included a directory, published separately beginning in 1984. The directory is not covered in SRI.

Availability: Oklahoma Department of Libraries, 200 N.E. 18th St., Oklahoma City OK 73105, ‡; SRI/MF/complete.

S6482   OKLAHOMA
Department of Public Safety

S6482–1   1984 OKLAHOMA TRAFFIC ACCIDENT DATA
Annual.   June 1985.
35 p. + back cover.
LC 80-646638.
SRI/MF/complete, current & previous year reports

Annual report on Oklahoma traffic accidents, fatalities, and injuries, by accident type, location, time, and other circumstances; and driver and victim characteristics; 1984, with selected trends from as early as 1937.

Also includes data on highway mileage, vehicle miles traveled, number of licensed drivers and registered vehicles, value of property damaged in accidents, and motorcycle helmet use; and details for school bus accidents.

Contains contents listing (1 p.); statistical highlights (p. 1-2); and 19 charts and 17 tables (p. 3-35 and back cover).

Previous report, for 1983, was also reviewed during 1985 and is also available on SRI microfiche, under this number [Annual. [1984.] 35 p. †]. Previous report is substantially similar in format and content, but also includes data on breathalyzer and blood alcohol test results.

Availability: Oklahoma Department of Public Safety, Services and Records Division, PO Box 11415, 3600 N. King Ave., Oklahoma City OK 73136-0415, †; SRI/MF/complete.

S6493   OKLAHOMA
Supreme Court

S6493–1   ANNUAL REPORT ON THE OKLAHOMA JUDICIARY, 1983-84
Annual.   Jan. 2, 1985.
225 p. var. paging.
LC 79-641067.
SRI/MF/complete

Annual report on Oklahoma judicial system, including trial and appellate court caseloads and case dispositions, for FY84, with selected trends from 1979. Covers supreme, appeals, and district courts. Includes trial court data by case type and county.

Trial court case types shown are civil, domestic relations, probate, small claims, and criminal misdemeanor and felony (including traffic, with detail for driving under influence cases).

Also includes data on special jurisdiction courts and councils, including tax review and judicial complaints activity; State judicial appropriations; local court fund collections and disbursements by fund, by county; and district court bond forfeitures, by case type and county.

Contains contents listing (p. i-iv); introduction and legislative review (p. 1-6); 2 sections on judicial system and funding, with narrative, 2 charts, and 7 tables (p. 8-36); district court caseload statistics, with 33 tables (p. 39-192); and 4 appendices, with 6 tables and accompanying charts, lists of judges and clerks, and 4 maps (p. A1-A28).

Availability: Oklahoma Supreme Court, Administrative Services, 5005 N. Lincoln, Suite 225, Oklahoma City OK 73105, †; SRI/MF/complete.

S6495   OKLAHOMA
Tax Commission

S6495–1   ANNUAL REPORT OF THE OKLAHOMA TAX COMMISSION, Fiscal Year Ended June 30, 1984
Annual.   Mar. 15, 1985.
ii + 22 p.
LC 32-27747.
SRI/MF/complete

Annual report presenting detailed data on Oklahoma tax revenues by source, and apportionment to local governments and State agencies and funds, FY84, with trends from FY46.

Data are compiled by the Oklahoma Tax Commission.

Contains narrative summary (p. i-ii); and 1 chart, and 5 detailed tables listed below (p. 1-22).

Availability: Oklahoma Tax Commission, McConnors Bldg., 2501 Lincoln Blvd., Oklahoma City OK 73194-0001, †; SRI/MF/complete.

TABLES:
[Major tax sources are alcoholic beverage, beverage, cigarette, corporation franchise, gasoline/fuels excise, gross production, income, estate, motor vehicle excise, sales, tobacco, and vehicle taxes and/or license fees.

Breakdowns for revenue apportionment are for counties by function, cities/towns, and individual State agencies and funds.]

[1] Review of 1983/84 taxes and collections [tax rate, definitions, and amounts, by type of tax]. (p. 1-5)

[2] Comparative statement of all tax collections [by type, FY83-84]. (p. 6-9)

[3] Apportionment of statutory revenues [FY83-84]. (p. 10-11)

[4] State revenue [by source] and apportionment. (p. 12-17)

[5] Revenue growth from major tax sources [by type], FY46-84. (p. 18-21)

S6575   OREGON
Department of Agriculture

S6575–1   OREGON AGRICULTURAL STATISTICS BULLETIN, 1983-84
Annual.   Nov. 1984.
5 + 56 p.
LC 84-645404.
SRI/MF/complete

Annual report on Oregon agricultural production, marketing, and finances, 1983, with trends from as early as 1870. Data are shown by commodity and/or county or district.

Report covers production, value, prices, and, as applicable, acreage, yield, stocks or inventory, and disposition, for field crop, fruit, nut, berry, vegetable, livestock, dairy, and poultry sectors.

Also includes number of farms and acreage; farm income and expenses; precipitation; fertilizer consumption; cold storage holdings of selected fruits and vegetables; manufactured dairy products production; mink breeding and pelt production; and U.S. potato consumption, and production and stocks by State.

Data are compiled by the Oregon Crop and Livestock Reporting Service in cooperation with USDA.

Contains foreword and contents listing (2 p.); and 7 charts and 76 tables, interspersed with brief narrative summaries (p. 1-56).

This is the 3rd annual report.

Availability: Oregon Department of Agriculture, 635 Capitol St., NE, Salem OR 97310-0110, †; SRI/MF/complete.

S6580   OREGON
Department of Commerce

S6580–1   SEVENTY-SEVENTH ANNUAL REPORT OF THE SUPERINTENDENT OF BANKS, 1984, Oregon
Annual.   [1985.]   77 p.
SRI/MF/complete

Annual report on financial condition of Oregon financial institutions, presenting assets, liabilities, revenues, and expenses, for banks/trust companies, credit unions, and consumer finance licensees, all as of Dec. 31, 1984, with selected trends for 1980s. Most data on assets and liabilities are shown by institution.

Also includes data on State Banking Fund receipts and disbursements; capital stock changes; aggregate trust balance sheet; number and resources of banks since 1909; bank deposits and loans, by institution and location; and pawnbroker and consumer finance loan analyses.

Contains contents listing (p. 5); 20 tables interspersed with lists of status changes and directories (p. 6-76); and index (p. 77).

Availability: Oregon Department of Commerce, Banking Division, 280 Court St., NE, Salem OR 97310, †; SRI/MF/complete.

S6585   OREGON
Economic Development Department

S6585–1   OREGON: A Statistical Profile
Biennial.   Apr. 1985.   104 p.
LC 79-623551.
SRI/MF/complete

Biennial compilation of Oregon economic data, 1983 and trends. Covers population, employment, GSP, income, agriculture, trade, tourism, and timber harvest. Most data are from State and Federal sources.

Contains contents listing, summary, and map (p. 5-11); 7 report chapters, with 31 charts and 28 tables (p. 13-71); chart and table listings (p. 74-79); and 6 appendix tables (p. 80-103). All tables are listed below.

For description of 1982 report, see SRI 1983 Annual under this number.

Availability: Oregon Economic Development Department, Research and Information Services, 595 Cottage St., NE, Salem OR 97310, $10.00; SRI/MF/complete.

TABLES:
[All tables show data for Oregon, unless otherwise noted.]

S6585–1.1: Report Tables
[Most data are shown for 1983, occasionally with trends from 1970, 1960, or late 1950s. Data by sector generally are shown for agriculture, manufacturing and nonmanufacturing industries, and government.]

POPULATION AND LABOR FORCE

[1-3] Population and components of change [natural increase and net migration]; population estimates by county; and population distribution [by age and sex]. (p. 16-18)

[4] Population, labor force, employment, and unemployment. (p. 21)

[5-6] Employment by major sector; and percent distribution of employed labor force [and average employment, by industry sector, including self-employed]. (p. 22)

[7-8] Percent distribution of [and average] manufacturing and nonmanufacturing employment by industry [group]. (p. 33-35)

OUTPUT AND INCOME

[9-12] GSP: percent of total by sector; annual average percent change by industry [division and major manufacturing group]; and in current and constant 1972 dollars, by sector. (p. 38-46)

[13-14] GNP [in current and constant 1972 dollars (U.S. only)]; and GSP and GNP annual percent change. (p. 47-48)

[15] Personal and per capita income. (p. 50)

[16] Composition of personal income [net earnings, divident/interest/rent, and transfer payments]. (p. 52)

[17] Labor/proprietors' income [by sector]. (p. 53)

[18-19] Income by county, selected types [total personal, per capita, and average wage/salary]; and median family income by county or MSA. (p. 54-55)

FARMING, FOREIGN TRADE, AND TOURISM

[20] Agricultural commodities [production value and] percent distribution. (p. 59)

[21-22] Gross farm sales [from crops and livestock] by district and county. (p. 60-61)

[23] Agricultural statistics [number of farms, and total and average acreage; livestock and poultry sales by species; and crops harvested by commodity]. (p. 62)

[24-27] Value of exports and imports through the Oregon customs district; top 10 exports and imports; 20 leading trading partners [by country]; and commerce of major ports. (p. 66-68)

[28] Out-of-State visitors (pleasure travelers) [estimated number and expenditures]. (p. 70)

S6585-1.2: Appendix Tables

[1] GSP by industry [division and manufacturing industry group, in current and constant dollars], 1958-83. (p. 80-85)

[2] Resident labor force, unemployment, and employment by place of work [industry group, with total farm employment and total workers in labor-management disputes, various years 1960-83]. (p. 86-90)

[3-4] Leading agricultural commodities, by commodity group [gross farm sales]; and by value of sales, [1981-83]. (p. 91-96)

[5] Gross farm sales [by district, county, and commodity], preliminary 1983, and revised estimates, 1979-82. (p. 97-101)

[6] Timber harvest report [volume removed, by county and owner category], 1982-83. (p. 102-103)

S6585-2 COUNTY ECONOMIC INDICATORS 1984, Oregon

Annual. Nov. 1984.
ii+22 p.
LC 83-645972.
SRI/MF/complete

Annual report on Oregon economic and business activity indicators, by county, 1983, with trends from 1975. Data are compiled by Business Information Division, State Economic Development Dept, primarily from Federal and State sources.

Contains table listing and preface (p. i-ii); 19 tables, described below (p. 1-21); and county map (p. 22).

Report has been issued since early 1970s. Previous report, for 1983, is described in 1983 SRI Annual under this number.

Availability: Oregon Economic Development Department, Research and Information Services, 595 Cottage St., NE, Salem OR 97310, $2.50; SRI/MF/complete.

TABLES:

[Data are shown by county, for 1976-83 unless otherwise noted.]

a. Resident population; and civilian labor force by employment status (also shown for 4 MSAs and 1 multicounty labor market area). 6 tables. (p. 1-6)

b. Income: total, per capita, and farm income, based on place of residence, and labor/proprietor, manufacturing, nonmanufacturing, and government income, and average earnings per job, based on place of work, 1975-82; and estimated median family income (also shown for 2 MSAs), 1978-83. 9 tables. (p. 7-15)

c. Commercial bank deposits; retail sales; assessed taxable property valuation; and residential single- and multi-family building permits issued, and cost, 1978-83. 4 tables. (p. 16-21)

S6590   OREGON
Department of Education

S6590-1   OREGON EDUCATIONAL STATISTICS

Annual series. For individual publication data, see below.
SRI/MF/complete

Series of annual reports, each presenting data on an aspect of Oregon elementary and secondary education. Topics include public school enrollment, finance, and staff. A report on nonpublic schools is also included.

Reports are described in order of receipt. Reports reviewed during 1985 are described below.

Prior to 1985, abstracts for these reports were grouped according to period of data coverage. For descriptions of reports covered in 1984, see SRI 1984 Annual, under this number and under S6590-2 and S6590-3.

Two nonstatistical reports in the series, listing 1-teacher schools and middle schools, are not covered in SRI.

Availability: Oregon Department of Education, School District Services Office, School Finance and Data Information Services, 700 Pringle Pkwy., SE, Salem OR 97310, †; SRI/MF/complete.

S6590-1.1: Summary of 1983/84 School District and ESD Budget Resources and Tax Extensions, Oregon

[Annual. May 1984. 2+50 p. Oversized. SRI/MF/complete, current & previous year reports.]

Annual table showing estimated school district budget requirements, and budget resources by source; uncollected taxes; offsets and extended levy; property assessed valuation and tax rate; certified levy within, outside, and not subject to 6% tax base limitations; and amount of levy to be used for operating and other purposes; all by school district and educational service district/county, 1983/84.

Previous report, for 1982/83, has also been received, and is also available on microfiche under this number [Annual. [1983.] 2+50 p. Oversized.]; for description of report for 1981/82, see SRI 1983 Annual under S6590-2.8.

S6590-1.2: 1983 Summary of School District Financial Elections, Oregon

[Annual. May 1984. 16 p. SRI/MF/complete.]

Annual table showing date and type of financial election, yes and no votes cast, election number, amount submitted to voters in election, and existing tax base, all by school district, grouped by county, 1983.

Previous report, for 1982, is described in SRI 1983 Annual under S6590-2.18.

S6590-1.3: Audited Current Expenditures for Resident Students, 1982/83, Oregon

[Annual. May 1984. 10 p. SRI/MF/complete.]

Two annual tables showing public school expenditures per average resident daily membership, and expenditures by function, all by educational service district/county and school district, 1982/83.

S6590-1.4: School District Audit Summary, 1982/83, Oregon

[Annual. [1984.] 12 p. Oversized. SRI/MF/complete.]

Two annual tables showing public school revenues by source by fund; and expenditures by fund, function, and object; for the total State, 1982/83.

S6590-1.5: Summary of 1982/83 Audited Resources of Oregon School Districts and ESDs

[Annual. [1984.] 15 p. Oversized. SRI/MF/complete.]

Annual table showing public school resources by source, by school district and educational service district/county, 1982/83.

S6590-1.6: School District Budget Summary, 1983/84, Oregon

[Annual. [1984.] 10 p. SRI/MF/complete.]

Two annual tables showing public school revenues by source and fund, and expenditures by fund, function, and object, budgeted for the total State, 1983/84.

Previous report, for 1982/83, is described in SRI 1983 Annual under S6590-3.6.

S6590-1.7: Apportionment of the Basic School Support Fund for the Fiscal Year Ending June 30, 1984, Oregon

[Annual. [1984.] 25 p. SRI/MF/complete.]

Three annual tables, with accompanying narrative, showing basic school support fund apportionment by account, by county and school district; equalization summary, by county; and apportionment financial statement; FY84.

Previous report, for FY83, is described in SRI 1983 Annual under S6590-3.7.

S6590-1.8: Oregon School District Census (Between Ages 4 and 20 Years) by ESD Lines

[Annual. May 1984. 4 p. SRI/MF/complete.]

Annual table showing population age 4-20, by school district and county, Oct. 1983.

S6590-1.9: Summary of 1983/84 Oregon Private and Parochial Schools

[Annual. June 15, 1984. 33 p. SRI/MF/complete.]

Two annual tables showing the following for private/parochial schools:

a. School address, district, denomination, grades taught, enrollment, average daily membership (ADM), and high school graduates by sex, for individual schools, arranged by county, 1983/84.

b. Enrollment by grade for grades P-12 and unclassified elementary and secondary; and ADM for grade ranges P-8, 9-12, and P-12; all by county, Dec. 31, 1983.

S6590–1.10: 1984 Oregon Public High School Graduates

[Annual. Sept. 13, 1984. 8 p. SRI/MF/complete.]

Annual table showing public high school graduates, by sex, by school, arranged by county and school district, 1984.

S6590–1.11: Oregon Public and Private High School Graduates, Actual and Projected

[Annual. Oct. 1984. 1 p. SRI/MF/complete.]

Annual table showing number of public and private high school graduates, 1964/65-1987/88.

S6590–1.12: Approved Secondary Schools in Oregon, Fall of 1984

[Annual. Nov. 1984. 14 p. SRI/MF/complete.]

Annual table showing estimated enrollment in public junior high schools and high schools, grouped by county and school district, fall 1984.

S6590–1.13: Number of Public Schools, 1984/85, Oregon

[Annual. Dec. 1984. 1 p. SRI/MF/complete.]

Annual table showing number of elementary, secondary, and special public schools, by educational service district/county and type of school, as of Oct. 1, 1984.

S6590–1.14: Estimated Full-Time Equivalency of Public School District Personnel, as of Oct. 1, 1984, Oregon

[Annual. Jan. 1985. 1 p. SRI/MF/complete.]

Annual table showing number of FTE official/administrative, professional/educational, and nonprofessional public school personnel, by position, sex, and race/ethnicity (including Hispanic, Asian/Pacific Islander, and American Indian/Alaskan Native), as of Oct. 1, 1984.

S6590–1.15: Estimated 1984/85 per Student Current Expenditures, Oregon

[Annual. Jan. 1985. 19 p. SRI/MF/complete.]

Two annual tables estimating public school expenditures per resident average daily membership (ADM), assessed value per ADM, and total school tax rate, by school district and county, and by school district arranged by type and size, 1984/85.

S6590–1.16: 1984 Summary of School District Financial Elections, Oregon

[Annual. Jan. 1985. 14 p. SRI/MF/complete.]

Annual table showing date and type of financial election, yes and no votes cast, election number, amount submitted to voters in election, and existing tax base, all by school district, grouped by county, 1984.

Previous report, for 1983, is described in S6590-1.2 above.

S6590–1.17: 1984/85 Summary of Valuations and Taxes Levied, Oregon

[Annual. Feb. 1985. 25 p. SRI/MF/complete.]

Three annual tables showing assessed value, local extended levy, county school fund levy, and ESD (educational service district) levy amounts, by ESD, county, and school district; and tax rates, by school district; 1984/85.

S6590–1.18: Oregon School District Census (Between Ages 4 and 20 Years) by ESD Lines

[Annual. Mar. 1985. 4 p. SRI/MF/complete.]

Annual table showing population age 4-20, by school district and county, Oct. 1984.

Previous report, for 1983, is described in S6590-1.8 above.

S6590–1.19: Summary of 1984/85 Oregon Private and Parochial Schools

[Annual. May 15, 1985. 32 p. SRI/MF/complete.]

Two annual tables showing the following for private/parochial schools:

a. School address, district, denomination, grades taught, enrollment, average daily membership (ADM), and high school graduates by sex, for individual schools, arranged by county, 1984/85.

b. Enrollment by grade for grades P-12 and unclassified elementary and secondary; and ADM for grade ranges P-8, 9-12, and P-12; all by county, Dec. 31, 1984.

Previous report, for 1983/84 and 1983, is described in S6590-1.9 above.

S6590–1.20: Audited Current Expenditures for Resident Students, 1983/84, Oregon

[Annual. [1985.] 10 p. SRI/MF/complete.]

Two annual tables showing public school expenditures per average resident daily membership, and expenditures by function, all by educational service district/county and school district, 1983/84.

Previous report, for 1982/83, is described in S6590-1.3 above.

S6590–1.21: School District Audit Summary, 1983/84, Oregon

[Annual. [1985.] 12 p. SRI/MF/complete.]

Two annual tables showing public school revenues by source by fund; and expenditures by fund, function, and object; for the total State, 1983/84.

Previous report, for 1982/83, is described in S6590-1.4 above.

S6590–1.22: School District Budget Summary, 1984/85, Oregon

[Annual. [1985.] 11 p. SRI/MF/complete.]

Two annual tables showing public school revenues by source and fund, and expenditures by fund, function, and object, budgeted for the total State, 1984/85.

Previous report, for 1983/84, is described in S6590-1.6 above.

S6603 OREGON
Executive Department

S6603–2 ANNUAL FINANCIAL REPORT for the Year Ended June 30, 1984, State of Oregon

Annual. Oct. 31, 1984.
102 p.
LC 80-647882.
SRI/MF/complete

Annual report on financial condition of Oregon State government, FY84. Presents assets and liabilities, reserves, and fund balances; revenues by source; and expenditures by object and program area; for all, general, special revenue, debt service, capital project, enterprise, internal service, and trust and agency funds, with selected comparisons from FY80.

Also includes data on budgeted vs. actual revenues and expenditures; fixed assets; long-term debt; analyses of cash holdings, investments by type of instrument, and bonded debt; economic indicator trends, and employment projections; and energy consumption by type.

Data are compiled from reports of State and Federal agencies.

Contains contents listing (1 p.); and 14 report sections, with introduction (p. 1-6), and 3 charts and 71 tables, interspersed with narrative analyses (p. 7-102).

Availability: Oregon Executive Department, Accounting Division, 155 Cottage St., NE, Salem OR 97310, †; SRI/MF/complete.

S6603–3 REPORT OF CRIMINAL OFFENSES AND ARRESTS, 1984, Oregon

Annual. June 1985.
iii+159 p.
ISSN 0145-6903.
LC 77-644178.
SRI/MF/complete, current & previous year reports

Annual report on Oregon crimes and arrests, by offense, 1984, with trends from 1975. Includes data by reporting agency and county, and by offender age, sex, and race/ethnicity. Also includes law enforcement employment, and assaults on officers.

Report covers 8 Index offenses (murder, rape, robbery, aggravated assault, burglary, larceny, motor vehicle theft, and arson), and numerous non-Index offenses.

Data are from State and local agency reports submitted under the Uniform Crime Reporting (UCR) Program.

Contents:

a. Contents, table, and chart listing. (p. i-iii)

b. Crime summary, with 11 charts and 8 tables showing summary data, and offense and arrest trends from 1981. (p. 1-20)

c. 5 sections, with 5 charts and 26 tables, described below. (p. 21-151)

d. 2 appendices, with offense definitions and methodology. (p. 155-159)

This is the 11th annual report.

Report for 1983 has also been reviewed in 1985, and is also available on SRI microfiche under S6603-3 [Annual. May 1984. iii+133 p.†].

Report for 1982 was issued by the Oregon Dept of Justice and is described in SRI 1984 Annual under S6620-1.

Availability: Oregon Executive Department, Law Enforcement Data System, Data Systems Division, 155 Cottage St., NE, Salem OR 97310, †; SRI/MF/complete.

CHARTS AND TABLES:

[Unless otherwise noted, data by offense are shown for Index and non-Index crimes.]

S6603-3.1: Statewide Data

a. Offenses, crime rates, and adult and juvenile arrests, by offense, 1983-84; and Index offense and arrest distribution by metro and nonmetro region, 1984. 4 charts and 2 tables. (p. 22-27)

b. Index and non-Index offenses by detailed type of circumstance, including victim/offender relationship (murder offenses), entry method (burglary offenses), property type or value, blood alcohol content (BAC) test data (driving under the influence offenses), and type of weapon used, 1983-84. 2 tables. (p. 28-35)

c. Non-Index sex crimes by type, 1977-84, with detail for adult and juvenile victims by sex, 1983-84; drug arrests by detailed activity and type of substance, 1983-84; number of crimes involving loss, and value of property lost and recovered, by property type, 1984; and Index and non-Index offenses by type of location and month, 1984. 6 tables. (p. 36-41)

S6603-3.2: Local Data, and Law Enforcement Personnel

a. Population, Index crimes by offense, and total non-Index crimes, all by county, 1975 and 1980-84, with crime rates and county rankings for 1984; adult and juvenile arrests by age, sex, and race/ethnicity (white, negro/black, Indian, Hispanic, and other Asian), with age detail by county, all by offense, 1984. 8 tables. (p. 44-93)

b. Law enforcement officers and support staff by sex, and ratio to population; officers and total law enforcement staff by county; officers assaulted by type of weapon and by whether alone or with another officer, and assault clearances, all by type of activity; assaults by time of day; and assaults with and without injury by type of weapon, agency type (sheriff and police depts, and State police), and county; 1984 with selected trends from 1981. 1 chart and 7 tables. (p. 96-102)

c. Agency summary: law enforcement officers and total staff; officers assaulted; population; and crimes, arrests, and clearances, by offense; all by agency arranged by county, 1984 with comparisons to 1983. 2 tables. (p. 104-151)

S6615   OREGON
Department of Human Resources

S6615-2   OREGON LABOR TRENDS
Monthly. 8 p.
LC sn82-21132.
SRI/MF/complete, shipped quarterly

Monthly report on Oregon labor force, employment, and average hours and earnings. Data are compiled from employers' reports and readership surveys, and generally are current to 1-2 months prior to publication date.

Contains features on economic and employment conditions, occasionally statistical, including recurring labor force data by county and MSA; 1-3 charts; and 4 monthly tables listed below. Some issues include additional tables presenting recent trends for data covered in monthly tables.

Monthly tables appear in all issues. All additional features presenting Oregon data not covered in monthly tables are described, as they appear, under "Statistical Features." Nonstatistical features are not covered.

Dept of Human Resources also issues a monthly table entitled *Resident Oregon Labor Force and Unemployment by Area;* and 16 monthly reports on employment in local areas. These publications are not covered in SRI. The latter may be requested from the issuing agency, either as a group or for individual counties or regions.

Availability: Oregon Department of Human Resources, Employment Division, Attention: R&S-LMI, 875 Union St., NE, Salem OR 97311, †; SRI/MF/complete, shipped quarterly.

Issues reviewed during 1985: Oct. 1984-Sept. 1985 (P).

MONTHLY TABLES:

[Tables [2-4] show data for most recent month available, preceding month, and same month of previous year.]

[1] [Month] indicators [including CPI for Portland MSA, and selected summary comparisons to U.S. and to various previous months].

[2] Resident Oregon labor force [by employment status, and seasonally adjusted unemployment rate].

[3] Nonagricultural wage/salary employment [by industry division and major group; and workers involved in labor-management disputes, and Oregon diffusion index].

[4] Average hours and earnings of industrial production workers [by industry division and manufacturing group].

STATISTICAL FEATURES:

S6615-2.601: Nov. 1984

OCCUPATIONAL IMPACTS OF THE RECESSION

(p. 5-6) Article, with 2 tables showing Oregon employment 1979 and 1982, for 21-22 occupations with significant increases and decreases during the 1979-82 period; and percent of dentists, physicians, and lawyers who are self-employed, 1970 and 1980.

S6615-2.602: Jan. 1985

RESIDENT OREGON LABOR FORCE AND UNEMPLOYMENT BY AREA, RECURRING FEATURE

(p. 6) Recurring table showing Oregon labor force by employment status, by MSA and county, Dec. 1984.

S6615-2.603: Feb. 1985

MONTHLY ECONOMIC ANALYSIS

(p. 1, 4-5) Article, with 2 tables showing recent Oregon plant shutdowns/curtailments and openings/expansions, with jobs created or lost, effective date, and location, by company.

OREGON GAINS POPULATION

(p. 5-6) Article, with 1 table showing population gain or loss, natural increase, and net migration, each for top 5 Oregon counties, for year ended July 1984.

S6615-2.604: Apr. 1985

LOCAL AREA UNEMPLOYMENT STATISTICS, ANNUAL FEATURE

(p. 5-6) Annual article, by Fred Klatz, with 1 table ranking Oregon counties and MSAs by unemployment rate, 1984, with comparisons to 1983.

For description of previous article, see SRI 1984 Annual under S6615-2.504

S6615-2.605: May 1985

OCCUPATIONAL EMPLOYMENT STATISTICS PROGRAM

(p. 5-6) By Bill Kimball. Article, with 1 table showing Oregon employment in 5 occupations with greatest projected increase in demand, 1982 and 1990. Data are from Oregon Employment Division.

S6615-2.606: June 1985

RESIDENT OREGON LABOR FORCE AND UNEMPLOYMENT BY AREA, RECURRING FEATURE

(p. 8) Recurring table showing Oregon labor force by employment status, by MSA and county, May 1985.

S6615-2.607: July 1985

STATE OF OREGON UNEMPLOYMENT RATES BY AREA, RECURRING FEATURE

(p. 8) Recurring table showing Oregon labor force by employment status, by MSA and county, June 1985.

S6615-3   ADULT AND FAMILY SERVICES in Oregon
Monthly 11 p.
SRI/MF/complete, shipped quarterly

Monthly report on Oregon public welfare caseloads, recipients, and expenditures, by program or type of medical service received, city, and State region. Report is issued approximately 3 months after month of coverage.

Contains contents listing, 4 maps, list of counties and cities in each State region, and 3 monthly tables listed below.

Report is discontinued with July 1985 issue. Similar data are included in the monthly report, *Adult and Family Services Public Assistance Programs, Regional and Branch Data.* Report will be described in SRI under S6615-8; coverage will begin in 1986.

Availability: Oregon Department of Human Resources, Adult and Family Services Division, 400 Public Service Bldg., Salem OR 97310-0380, $15.00 per yr.; SRI/MF/complete, shipped quarterly.

Issues reviewed during 1985: Aug. 1984-July 1985 (D) (Vol. 49, Nos. 8-12; Vol. 50, Nos. 1-7).

MONTHLY TABLES:

[All tables show data for month of coverage, by city branch office and State region. July 1985 issue omits data on old age, blind, and disabled assistance.]

A. [Persons and/or] cases receiving nonmedical payments [and total and average payments, for general assistance, Old Age Assistance, Aid to Blind, aid to disabled, aid to dependent children, and 2- and 1-parent emergency assistance].

B. Persons and payments for medical services [for physicians, hospitals, drugs, and dental, visual, and miscellaneous services].

C. Food stamp activity [value of coupons issued, and number of public assistance and nonassistance persons and households participating].

S6615–5   OREGON PUBLIC HEALTH STATISTICS REPORT for Calendar Year 1983

Annual.   Aug. 1985.
148 p.+errata.
LC 73-640513.
SRI/MF/complete

Annual report on Oregon vital statistics, 1983. Covers population, births, deaths by cause, reportable diseases, and marriages and dissolutions. Includes data by county, age, sex, and race; and trends from as early as 1908.

Data are primarily from reports filed with the Oregon State Health Division.

Contents:

a. Listings of contents, charts, and tables. (4 p.)

b. 6 statistical sections, with narrative analyses, 1 summary table, 9 charts, and 67 tables listed below. (p. 3-127)

c. Technical notes, with methodology, and definitions and abbreviations. (p. 131-148)

Availability: Oregon Department of Human Resources, Health Division, Center for Health Statistics, State Office Bldg., PO Box 116, Portland OR 97207, †; SRI/MF/complete.

TABLES:

[Data by race are generally shown for white (total and Hispanic), black, Indian, Chinese, Japanese, other Asian/Pacific Islander, Filipino, and other nonwhite. Data are for Oregon, 1983, unless otherwise noted.]

S6615–5.1: Summary

1-6. Population; live births; births to unwed mothers; marriages; dissolution of marriages; deaths; and maternal, infant, neonatal, and fetal deaths; [for] U.S. 1945-83, and Oregon 1908-83 [with 1983 detail by county of residence or occurence]. (p. 4-11)

7. Population, births, and deaths, by city of residence. (p. 12)

S6615–5.2: Natality

NATALITY

[Tables 9-13 and 15-16 begin "Resident births..."]

8. Age specific birth rates, fertility rates, and total fertility rates, [decennially] 1940-70 [and annually] 1975-83. (p. 20)

9. By age group of mother, 1955-83. (p. 21)

10. By race of child, 1955-83. (p. 22)

11-12. [Total and] to unwed mothers, by age of mother and birth weight. (p. 23)

13. By age of mother and live birth order. (p. 24)

14. Total pregnancies by type of outcome [including induced abortions] and age groups. (p. 25)

15-16. [To all and] to unwed mothers, by [county of residence and] age [groups] of mother. (p. 26-27)

17. Births by county of residence, by sex and race of child. (p. 28)

18. Resident low birth weight infants [by county of residence]. (p. 29)

19. Congenital malformations by site reported on birth certificate by county of residence. (p. 30-31)

20. Births by county of occurrence by type of institution [in or not in hospital] and by delivery attendant [including midwives]. (p. 32-33)

21. Maternal risk factors [inadequate care; 4/ higher birth order; plural birth; and selected maternal characteristics (age 17/younger or 35/older, nonwhite, unwed, and less than 12 years education)], by county of residence. (p. 34)

S6615–5.3: Mortality

LEADING CAUSES OF DEATH

[A] Selected death statistics [crude and age-adjusted death rates, comparative mortality figure, years of life lost index, and selected rankings], by county of residence, 1977-83 [period]. (p. 44)

22. Age specific death rates by sex. (p. 47)

23. Selected leading causes of deaths with rates, 1965-83. (p. 48)

24. Five principal causes of death, by age groups [and sex]. (p. 49-50)

25. Leading causes of death, by rank order for resident males and females. (p. 51)

26. Age specific death rates, by sex, for the leading causes of death. (p. 52-53)

27. Deaths by marital status, sex, and age groups. (p. 54)

28. Resident deaths for selected causes, by age and sex. (p. 55-64)

HOMICIDE, SUICIDE, AND ACCIDENTAL DEATHS

29. Resident deaths due to or mentioning external factors [by cause]. (p. 65)

30. Resident deaths from suicide, homicide, [and] external causes undetermined whether accidentally or purposely inflicted, by age, sex, and method. (p. 66)

31. Resident accidental deaths, by type or source of injury, age groups, and sex. (p. 67)

32. Deaths occurring in Oregon, by type of accident and age groups. (p. 68)

INFANT DEATHS

33. Infant, neonatal, and post-neonatal deaths, 1979-83 [period], by maternal risk factors and infant characteristics, for residents at birth. (p. 69)

34-35. Resident infant deaths by cause and county of residence [by] age at time of death. (p. 70-71)

DEATHS BY LOCATION

[Data are shown by county of residence, unless otherwise noted.]

36. Deaths, by age groups and sex. (p. 72-73)

37. Leading causes of death. (p. 74-75)

38. Deaths, by sex and race. (p. 76)

39. Accidental deaths, by principal classes and county of accident. (p. 77)

40. All deaths and medical examiner's cases, by county of occurrence and autopsy. (p. 78)

41. Deaths occurring in Oregon by disposal of remains. (p. 79)

42-43. Deaths, by selected causes with rates, for Oregon, [3] selected cities, and by county. (p. 80-89)

S6615–5.4: Marriage and Divorce

[Tables 44, 51-52, and 55-56 begin "Dissolution of marriages and annulments..."]

[B] Median duration of marriage before divorce [by order of marriage for wife and husband], 1978 and 1983. (p. 96)

44. By number of minor children affected. (p. 97)

45. Marriages and dissolution of marriages (including annulments), by month of occurrence. (p. 97)

46-47. Marriages, by age groups and previous marital status of groom and bride. (p. 98)

48. All marriages and 1st marriages for both bride and groom, by age groups. (p. 99)

49-50. Marriages, by county of occurrence, by age groups of bride and groom. (p. 100-101)

51-52. By age of husband and wife, [by] duration and order of marriage. (p. 102-103)

53-54. Dissolution of marriages by county of occurrence, by age groups of wife and husband. (p. 104-105)

55. By duration and order of marriage for husband and wife. (p. 106)

56. By State or region where marriage occurred [census division, Mountain and Pacific division State, Virgin Islands, and foreign country], by duration of marriage. (p. 107)

S6615–5.5: Morbidity and Population

MORBIDITY

57. Reported cases [and occurrence rates] of gonorrhea, by sex and age groups, 1979-83. (p. 112)

58. Reported cases [and occurrence rates] of syphilis, by age groups and year, 1978-83. (p. 113)

59. Reported cases with rates of syphilis and gonorrhea, by year, 1945-83. (p. 114)

60. Reported cases [and occurrence rates] of syphilis and gonorrhea, by county of residence and type of infection. (p. 115)

61. Reported tuberculosis cases and deaths with rates, 1950-83. (p. 116)

62-63. Cases of reportable diseases [by type], by month of report, and by county of residence. (p. 117-119)

POPULATION

64. Population distribution by age and sex, 1950, 1960, 1970, and 1975-83. (p. 123)

65. Estimated 5 year age groups by sex, [by county]. (p. 124-127)

S6655   OREGON
Public Utility Commissioner

S6655–2   1984 OREGON UTILITY STATISTICS
Annual. [1985.] 100 p.
ISSN 0091-0546.
LC 73-642994.
SRI/MF/complete

Annual report presenting Oregon public utility financial and operating data, by type of utility and company, 1984 with selected trends from 1975. Utility types covered are electric, gas, steam heat, telephone, and water. Data are grouped by type of ownership or revenue class within each utility type.

Includes assets, liabilities, revenues, and expenses, by detailed item; and sales and/or customers, by sector; for most utility types. Also includes income and balance sheet data for joint utilities; electric and gas utility residential conservation activities; electricity output and capacity, by type of generation; gas production; and telephone access lines.

Data are from unaudited company reports filed with the Commissioner.

Contains contents listing (2 p.); and 12 charts and 23 tables grouped in 6 sections, each preceded by foreword and company index (p. 1-100).

Availability: Oregon Public Utility Commissioner, Research Division, Labor and Industries Bldg., Salem OR 97310, $7.50 (prepaid); SRI/MF/complete.

S6665   OREGON
Office of the
Secretary of
State

S6665–1   OFFICIAL ABSTRACT OF VOTES, GENERAL ELECTION, Nov. 6, 1984, State of Oregon
Biennial. Dec. 1984.
x+43 p.
SRI/MF/complete

Biennial report presenting results of the Oregon general election held Nov. 6, 1984. Includes voting for President, U.S. and State senators and representatives, secretary of state, attorney general, treasurer, judges, and district attorneys; and 9 referenda, including State constitutional amendments or other measures concerning State lottery, death penalty, and radioactive waste disposal. Data are shown by county and/or district, and include party affiliation of most candidates.

Also includes voter registration and turnout, by party, county, and district, with summary comparisons to primary elections and trends from 1954.

Previous report, covering 1982 general election, is described in SRI 1983 Annual under this number.

Availability: Oregon Office of the Secretary of State, Elections Division, State Capitol, Salem OR 97310-0722, †; SRI/MF/complete.

S6670   OREGON
Supreme Court

S6670–1   THIRTIETH ANNUAL REPORT RELATING TO JUDICIAL ADMINISTRATION in the Courts of Oregon, 1983
Annual. [1984.] 56 p.
LC 78-643534.
SRI/MF/complete

Annual report on Oregon judicial system, including trial and appellate court caseloads and case dispositions, 1983, with trends from 1974. Covers supreme, appeals, tax, circuit, district, justice, and municipal courts. Includes selected court data by case type and county, municipality, and/or district.

Case types shown are criminal and civil for most courts, with some additional detail for small claims, traffic, marital dissolution, mental competency, estate and guardianship, adoption, juvenile, workers' compensation, parole board review, and other case types.

Report also includes data on judges, workloads, and case processing time; and lawyer disciplinary cases filed. Data are from court reports.

Contains contents and table listing (1 p.); and 7 sections with 29 tables (p. 1-56).

Previous report, for 1982, is described in SRI 1983 Annual, under this number.

Availability: Oregon Supreme Court, State Court Administrator's Office, Supreme Court Bldg., Salem OR 97310, †; SRI/MF/complete.

S6680   OREGON
Department of
Transportation

S6680–1   OREGON TRAFFIC ACCIDENTS, 1984: Summary
Annual. June 1985.
141 p. no paging.
ISSN 0093-1934.
LC 82-641440.
SRI/MF/complete

Annual report on Oregon traffic accidents involving fatalities, injuries, and property damage, and number of persons killed and injured, 1984, with summary trends from 1980. Includes data by accident and vehicle type, location, and other circumstances; and driver and victim characteristics.

Data are compiled by the Motor Vehicles Division.

Contains 14 tables, repeated for State, rural and urban areas, and each city and county; interspersed with 5 summary tables.

Traffic accident reports for trucks, pedestrians, motorcycles, and bicycles are also available from

the issuing agency, along with reports on accidents involving alcohol, and on licensed drivers, accident involvement, and violation convictions. These reports are not covered in SRI.

Availability: Oregon Department of Transportation, Motor Vehicles Division, 1905 Lana Ave., NE, Salem OR 97314, †; SRI/MF/complete.

S6760   PENNSYLVANIA
Department of
Agriculture

S6760–1   1984 CROP AND LIVESTOCK Annual Summary, Pennsylvania
Annual. [1985.] ii+75 p.
Order No. 995.
ISSN 0079-046X.
LC A55-9126.
SRI/MF/complete

Annual report on Pennsylvania agricultural production, marketing, and finances, 1984, with some data for 1985 and trends from 1940. Data generally are shown by commodity and county, with selected comparisons to other States.

Covers production, value, prices, and, as applicable, acreage, yield, inventory, and disposition, for livestock, poultry, dairy, mink, field crop, vegetable, fruit, and nursery sectors.

Also includes data on weather; farm income and expenses; custom work rates; fertilizer consumption; number, acreage, and value of farms; U.S. food consumption; value of agricultural sales for 100 leading U.S. counties; and mink industry data, cropland rental fees, and farm property value, by State.

Data are compiled by the Pennsylvania Crop Reporting Service in cooperation with USDA.

Contains contents listing (p. ii); 3 maps, 2 charts, and 98 tables, interspersed with narrative summaries (p. 1-73); facsimile of data reporting form and list of State agricultural reports available (p. 74-75).

Availability: Crop Reporting Board Publications, South Bldg., Rm. 5829, U.S. Department of Agriculture, Washington DC 20250, Pennsylvania farmers †, others $5.00; SRI/MF/complete.

S6775   PENNSYLVANIA
Department of Commerce

S6775–1   1985 PENNSYLVANIA STATISTICAL ABSTRACT
Annual. 1985. viii+261 p.
ISSN 0476-1103.
ISBN 0-8182-0069-3.
LC A59-9073.
SRI/MF/complete

Annual compilation, for 1985, of detailed social, demographic, governmental, and economic statistics for Pennsylvania. Data are primarily for 1970s-84, with population trends from 1790 and projections to 2030.

Report presents a comprehensive overview of the State. Extensive geographic, socioeconomic, and demographic breakdowns are shown, as applicable, for most topics. These breakdowns include data by city, county and other State region, SMSA, urban-rural status, commodity, income, industry, occupation, age, educational attainment, marital status, race, and sex. Comparisons to total U.S. are also occasionally included.

Data are primarily from reports of State and Federal agencies. Data sources appear beneath each table.

Contains listings of contents, tables, charts/maps, and Pennsylvania SMSAs (p. iv-viii); 21 charts/maps and 239 tables arranged in 9 sections, described below (p. 1-253); and subject index (p. 254-261). Tables in each section are preceded by a listing of data sources and definitions.

This is the 27th edition.

Availability: State Book Store, Management Services Bureau, PO Box 1365, Harrisburg PA 17125, $11.05; SRI/MF/complete.

TABLE SECTIONS:

S6775–1.1: Section 1: Population, Births, Deaths, Marriages, and Divorces

a. **Population:** projections to 2030 and trends from 1790; household, family, and fertility characteristics; land area; educational attainment, labor force, and income characteristics; characteristics of persons age 60/over; and veterans by period of service. Tables 1-15. (p. 4-19)

b. **Vital statistics:** births; total and accidental deaths by cause; suicides and homicides; and marriages and divorces. Tables 16-23. (p. 20-25)

S6775–1.2: Section 2: Commerce, Manufacturing, and Banking

a. **Economic development:** State industrial development projects, costs, loans, and planned employment and payroll; revenue bond and mortgage program projects, cost, and jobs created and preserved; Federal coastal energy impact and small community planning allocations; and State grants for housing, development, and small communities. Tables 24-29. (p. 27-30)

b. **Finance:** financial institutions (including pawnbrokers), and balance sheet data, by institution type; and savings and loan assn and credit union membership and assets. Tables 30-35. (p. 31-37)

c. **Business, trade, and construction:** State liquor stores and sales; insurance companies and underwriting data by type of company; and nonresidential construction value and housing units constructed. Tables 36-40. (p. 38-41)

d. **Housing units:** housing tenure and occupancy; median number of rooms and rent or value; vacancy rate; housing units by fuel type; and monthly housing costs. Tables 41-42. (p. 42-43)

e. **Foreign trade:** manufacturing exporters and exports; and ports of Philadelphia cargo traffic, customs receipts, and imports and exports by country of origin and destination. Tables 43-47. (p. 44-48)

f. **Industry:** establishments, employment, and payroll, with additional operating data for retail and wholesale trade (including sales), construction (including receipts, value added, and capital expenditures), and services (including receipts); and travel-generated expenditures, payroll, employment, and State and local tax receipts. Tables 48-54. (p. 49-59)

g. **Commerce:** State funding and project summaries for partnership, community facilities, site development, and Appalachian region programs; State capital loan fund activity; and minority business development projects, loans, and jobs created or preserved. Tables 55-60. (p. 60-61)

S6775–1.3: Section 3: Employment and Income

a. **Employment:** labor force by employment status; covered employment and wages/salaries; unemployment compensation and job service activities; and hours and earnings. Tables 61-73. (p. 64-84)

b. **Income:** household, family, and unrelated individual income; median family income; families and persons below poverty level; total and per capita personal income; and GSP. Tables 74-80. (p. 85-92)

c. **Industrial injuries:** fatal and nonfatal injuries. Table 81. (p. 93)

S6775–1.4: Section 4: Education

a. **Elementary and secondary education:** public and private school enrollment; and public school buildings and classrooms, and buildings deactivated. Tables 82-86. (p. 94-97)

b. **Vocational education:** enrollment, completers, and posteducation status, by level and program. Tables 87-89. (p. 97-98)

c. **Educational personnel and finance:** personnel, education, salary, and years of service; State and Federal expenditures by function or program; total and per pupil expenditures; revenues by level of government; school districts; and tax districts and collections. Tables 90-98. (p. 99-108)

d. **Higher education:** enrollment; expenditures and average tuition/fees; faculty and average salaries; State financial assistance applicants and grants; State funding, by institution; Federal funding for scientific education and R&D; and degrees conferred, by field and level. Tables 99-112. (p. 109-123)

e. **Libraries:** public libraries, holdings, staff, population served, operations, finances, and Federal and State aid, with detail by selected library. Tables 113-114. (p. 124-126)

S6775–1.5: Section 5: Social Services

a. **Health care:** occupational disease compensation cases and payments; hospitals, admissions, and beds; State supported residents in private mental retardation facilities; State mental retardation center residents by facility, and applicants awaiting admission; vocational rehabilitation caseload and expenditures; and VA expenditures. Tables 115-120. (p. 127-131)

b. **Public welfare:** public assistance and medical assistance recipients and/or expenditures; children receiving in-home, foster home, adoptive, and institutional services; and blind caseload. Tables 121-130. (p. 132-140)

S6775–1.6: Section 6: State and Local Government and Taxes

a. **Elections:** population of congressional and State legislative districts; voter registration by political party; election trends from 1900; and votes cast for President, Governor, and other Federal and State offices. Tables 131-142. (p. 141-168)

b. **Local government:** county seats and municipalities; municipal employment, payroll, revenues by source, expenditures by function, indebtedness, and borrowing capacity; property valuations and tax rates; municipal authorities; and bond issues, projects, and debt. Tables 143-154. (p. 169-180)

c. **State government:** expenditures by object, and revenues by source and fund; bonded indebtedness; lottery income and expenses; State employment by dept or agency and employment status; and State Human Relations Commission complaints and disposition. Tables 155-163. (p. 181-188)

d. **Taxes:** individual income tax returns and taxable income; municipal tax levies; and sales/use tax receipts. Tables 164-168. (p. 189-192)

S6775–1.7: Section 7: Law Enforcement, Crime, and Correction

a. **Corrections and sentencing:** correctional admissions, releases, and inmates by institution; and State Board of Probation and Parole operations, caseload, and parolees and parole agents. Tables 169-180. (p. 193-201)

b. **Courts:** common pleas court cases, dispositions, and inventory. Table 181. (p. 202)

c. **Crime and law enforcement:** State police traffic arrests by violation; Part I and Part II offenses and clearances, by type of offense; and Crime Index offenses. Tables 182-185. (p. 203-206)

S6775–1.8: Section 8: Agriculture, Natural Resources, and Conservation

a. **Agriculture:** farms, income by source, and production cost components; crop acreage, production, and value; livestock, dairy, and poultry farms, production, and value; milk prices; and cash receipts. Tables 186-194. (p. 207-216) *b.* **Climate:** temperature and precipitation extremes and/or averages. Tables 195-196. (p. 217-218)

c. **Resources:** coal production, employment, productivity, fatalities, and exports; production value of extracted minerals and cement; crude oil shipments and connected wells; and watershed projects and costs. Tables 197-201. (p. 219-223)

d. **Conservation and environment:** conservation program acreage and landowner participation; forest fires, area burned, and cost of extinction; pollution abatement and capital expenditures; State Bureau of Air Quality Control expenditures and caseload; and river basins showing water quality change. Tables 202-210. (p. 224-229)

e. **Recreation:** attendance at State and national parks, historical sites, and museums, by site; hunting and fishing licenses issued; game released and sport fish stocked, by species; and motorboat registrations. Tables 211-217. (p. 229-236)

S6775-1.9: Section 9: Communications, Utilities, Energy, and Transportation

a. **Communications and utilities:** finances and operations of electric, natural gas, telephone, and water utilities, and sewer authorities; regulated transportation and other utilities, and revenues; energy production; and energy consumption by fuel type and sector. Tables 218-229. (p. 237-244)

b. **Accidents:** traffic accidents, fatalities, and injuries; and vehicle traffic, average speeds, and percent exceeding speed limit. Tables 230-233. (p. 245-247)

c. **Transportation:** State Motor License Fund financial statement; transportation program expenditures; urban mass transit total and senior citizen patronage and fleet characteristics, by agency; Pennsylvania Turnpike vehicle flow; highway mileage; and motor vehicle registrations. Tables 234-239. (p. 247-253)

S6775-2   PENNSYLVANIA PUBLIC UTILITY SERIES
Series. For individual publication data, see below.
SRI/MF/complete

Series of 5 annual reports presenting financial and operating data for Pennsylvania electric, telephone, sewer, gas, and water utilities. Data are from the Census of Public Utilities in Pennsylvania.

Each report covers one utility category, and presents all or most of the following data: investment in plant, capital expenditures, revenues and expenses, net income, taxes, employment, wages/salaries, customers (usually by customer class), and selected financial ratios.

Data generally are shown as aggregates, with selected data also shown for individual utilities.

Each report contains highlights (inside front cover), contents listing, introduction, definitions and explanations, and tables.

Individual reports presenting data for 1982 are further described below. SRI coverage begins with the 1982 reports.

Availability: Pennsylvania Department of Commerce, Statistics, Research, and Planning Bureau, Rm. 474, Forum Bldg., Harrisburg PA 17120, †; SRI/MF/complete.

S6775-2.1: Statistics for Electric Utilities in Pennsylvania, 1982
[Annual. Dec. 1983. 9 p. LC 74-644929. SRI/MF/complete.]

Annual report on Pennsylvania electric utilities, presenting financial and operating data as described above, for 1982, with comparisons to 1972 and 1981. Also includes data on electricity prices; and generating capacity and output, by fuel source. Includes 10 tables.

S6775-2.2: Statistics for Telephone Companies in Pennsylvania, 1982
[Annual. Jan. 1984. 5 p. LC 74-644852. SRI/MF/complete.]

Annual report on Pennsylvania telephone utilities, presenting financial and operating data as described above, for 1982, with comparisons to 1972 and 1981. Also includes data on number of telephones and telephone exchanges in use. Includes 4 tables.

S6775-2.3: Statistics for Sewer Authorities in Pennsylvania, 1982
[Annual. Apr. 1984. 13 p. LC 74-643221. SRI/MF/complete.]

Annual report on Pennsylvania sewer authorities, presenting financial and operating data as described above, for 1982, with trends from 1977. Also presents data by county. Includes 5 tables.

S6775-2.4: Statistics for Gas Utilities in Pennsylvania, 1982
[Annual. Oct. 1984. 7 p. LC 73-647214. SRI/MF/complete.]

Annual report on Pennsylvania gas utilities, presenting financial and operating data as described above, for 1982, with comparisons to 1972. Also includes data on gas cost to consumers; natural and manufactured gas production and purchases; oil and gas wells, drilling activity, and well sales and abandonments; and underground gas storage. Includes 7 tables.

S6775-2.5: Statistics for Water Utilities Including Water Authorities in Pennsylvania, 1982
[Annual. Nov. 1984. 19 p. LC 74-644956. SRI/MF/complete.]

Annual report on Pennsylvania water utilities, presenting financial and operating data as described above, for 1982, with comparisons to 1980-81. Also presents data by county. Includes 12 tables.

S6782   PENNSYLVANIA Department of Corrections

S6782-1   PENNSYLVANIA DEPARTMENT OF CORRECTIONS 1984 Annual Statistical Report
Annual. May 1985.
iii+62 p.
LC 80-645286.
SRI/MF/complete

Annual report, for 1984, on corrections in Pennsylvania, presenting data on prison population, including inmate admissions, demographic characteristics, commitment offense, sentence length, releases, and average time served. Includes data by institution and committing county; with trends from 1974.

Also includes data on incarceration costs and staff positions, by institution; Probation and Parole Board activities; inmate assaults and escapes; and inmates serving life sentences, and under sentence of death.

Contains contents listing (1 p.); introduction, definitions, and summary (p. 1-5); and 6 charts and 51 tables (p. 6-62).

Availability: Pennsylvania Department of Corrections, Finance, Planning, and Research Division, PO Box 598, Camp Hill PA 17011, †; SRI/MF/complete.

S6790   PENNSYLVANIA Department of Education

S6790-2   1983-84 PENNSYLVANIA PUBLIC LIBRARY STATISTICS
Annual. [1985.] 2+i+102 p.
LC A60-9149.
SRI/MF/complete

Annual report on Pennsylvania public libraries, covering personnel, holdings, circulation, and finances, FY84, with some comparisons to FY83. Report is compiled from public library annual reports.

Contains contents listing, and map of district library centers (2 p.); introduction (p. i); and 9 report sections, with 5 charts, and 15 tables described below (p. 1-102).

Availability: Pennsylvania Department of Education, State Library, PO Box 1601, Harrisburg PA 17108, †; SRI/MF/complete.

TABLES:

a. Services and finances, including population served; hours; new and total registrations; volunteer and salaried staff; book and periodical holdings; circulation; interlibrary loans; income by source, including State and Federal aid; capital expenditures; and operating expenditures by object and source of funds; shown for public libraries arranged by county, and district library centers, FY84. 8 tables. (p. 1-60)

b. Rankings of libraries by total operating expenditures, population served, holdings, and circulation, FY84. 5 tables. (p. 63-99)

c. State library operating hours, professional and clerical staff, holdings, interlibrary loans, and services; and summary of public library operations; FY83-84. 2 tables. (p. 101-102)

S6790-5   STATISTICAL REPORTS

Series. For individual publication data, see below. SRI/MF/complete

Series of annual statistical reports, each presenting data on a selected aspect of Pennsylvania elementary and secondary education, higher education, and vocational education.

Reports reviewed during 1985 are described below.

Data on public schools and higher education are also included in the annual *Status Report on Education in Pennsylvania,* not covered in SRI.

Availability: Pennsylvania Department of Education, Data Services Division, 333 Market St., Harrisburg PA 17126-0333, †; SRI/MF/complete.

S6790-5.1: Basic Student Charges at Institutions of Higher Education, 1984/85, Pennsylvania

[Annual. [1984.] 21 p. SRI/MF/complete.]

Annual report on Pennsylvania higher education tuition/fees and room/board charges at public and private institutions, 1984/85 with trends from 1975/76. Presents resident and nonresident tuition/fees by program level, and room and board charges, all by institution and institutional category. Also includes detail for professional school tuition/fees, by field of study.

Contains listings of contents, tables, and charts (1 p.); introduction, 3 charts, and 7 tables (p. 1-20); and appendix, with name of nonresponding institution (p. 21).

For description of report for 1983/84, see SRI 1983 Annual under S6790-5.10.

S6790-5.2: Degrees and Other Formal Awards Conferred, 1983/84, Pennsylvania

[Annual. Mar. 1985. 3+24 p. SRI/MF/complete.]

Annual report on Pennsylvania higher education degrees conferred, by degree level, sex, detailed field of study, and institution arranged by type, 1983/84, with trends from 1974/75.

Contains highlights and listing of contents, tables, and charts (1 p.); introduction, 4 charts, and 6 tables (p. 1-22); and 2 appendices, including glossary (p. 23-24).

Note that publication date in document incorrectly reads Mar. 1984.

S6790-5.3: Public and Nonpublic School Enrollments, 1984/85, Pennsylvania

[Annual. Apr. 1985. 3+23 p. LC 84-623502. SRI/MF/complete.]

Annual report on Pennsylvania elementary and secondary public and nonpublic schools and enrollment, 1984/85, with trends from 1975/76.

Includes enrollment detail by grade and county; public school enrollment by race/ethnicity (including American Indian/Alaskan Native, Asian/Pacific Islander, and Hispanic), and type of secondary school (including middle schools, and technical/vocational and special education institutions); and private school enrollment by religious affiliation of institution.

Also includes data on number of public and nonpublic elementary and secondary schools in operation.

Contains highlights, and listing of contents, tables, and charts (3 p.); introduction, 5 charts, and 15 tables (p. 1-21); and glossary (p. 23).

S6790-5.4: Higher Education Summer and Fall Enrollments, 1984, Pennsylvania

[Annual. May 1985. 3+40 p. SRI/MF/complete.]

Annual report on Pennsylvania higher education enrollment, by sex, full- or part-time status, degree level, and race/ethnicity (including American Indian/Alaskan Native, Asian/Pacific Islander, and Hispanic), and for non-resident aliens, all by institution, summer and/or fall 1984, with trends from 1975.

Covers State and private colleges and universities, State-related commonwealth universities, private State-aided institutions, community colleges, theological seminaries, private junior colleges, specialized degree-granting institutions, and State school of technology.

Contains highlights and contents listing (2 p.); introduction, 4 charts, and 12 tables (p. 1-37); and 2 appendices, including glossary (p. 39-40).

S6790-5.5: Public School Professional Personnel, 1984/85, Pennsylvania

[Annual. [1985.] 2+46 p. LC 84-641002. SRI/MF/complete.]

Annual report on Pennsylvania public school professional employees, 1984/85. Presents number of employees by sex, educational attainment, years of service, salary range, and age; and average educational attainment, years of service, and salary, by sex; for 46 positions in 3 occupational categories (administrative/supervisory, classroom teachers, and coordinate services), and/or by certified assignment category.

Also includes withdrawals by reason, by certified assignment category; number of personnel by sex, total and average salary, and average years of service and educational attainment, with selected rankings, all by administrative unit; and summary trends from 1975/76.

Contains highlights, and listing of contents, tables, and charts (2 p.); and introduction, 4 charts, and 10 tables (p. 1-46).

S6790-5.6: Public and Nonpublic High School Graduates, 1984, Pennsylvania

[Annual. Aug. 1985. 3+33 p. SRI/MF/complete.]

Annual report on Pennsylvania public and nonpublic high school graduates, by sex, race/ethnicity (including American Indian/Alaskan Native, Asian/Pacific Islander, and Hispanic), and type of post-high school activity (including continuing education by type of institution, enlistment in armed forces, employment in selected occupations, and unemployment); mostly by county, 1984, with selected trends from 1975.

Also includes public school enrollment and institutions, by level, 1984/85; and high school graduates by sex, and graduates enrolled in college and other postsecondary schools, 1984; all by administrative unit.

Contains highlights, and listing of contents, tables, and charts (3 p.); introduction, and 5 charts and 10 tables (p. 1-32); and glossary (p. 33).

S6790-5.7: Higher Education Financial Statistics, 1983/84, Pennsylvania

[Annual. Aug. 1985. 3+20 p. LC 84-644822. SRI/MF/complete.]

Annual report on Pennsylvania higher education finances, FY84, with summary trends from FY75. Presents data on revenues by source; expenditures by function; physical plant assets and indebtedness; and endowment and other fund balances; all by type of institution.

Contains highlights, and listing of contents, tables, and charts (3 p.); introduction, and 4 charts and 12 tables (p. 1-18); and appendices (p. 19-20).

S6790-5.8: Higher Education Faculty and Staff, 1984/85, Pennsylvania

[Annual. Sept. 1985. 2+14 p. LC 84-622484. SRI/MF/complete.]

Annual report on Pennsylvania higher education faculty employment and compensation at public and private institutions, 1984/85, with trends from 1975/76. Presents the following data for instructional faculty with 9- and 12-month contracts: number, mean salary, and percent with tenure, by rank, sex, and type of institution; and number of faculty covered by and expenditures for fringe benefits, by type of benefit.

Contains highlights, and listing of contents, tables, and charts (2 p.); introduction, and 2 charts and 9 tables (p. 1-12); and appendices (p. 13-14).

S6790-5.9: Preparation and Occupational Pursuits of Teachers, 1983/84, Pennsylvania

[Annual. Sept. 1985. 2+15 p. LC 84-623256. SRI/MF/complete.]

Annual report on newly certified teachers prepared by Pennsylvania higher education institutions, by type of certification, field of preparation, occupational status, and institution type, 1974/75-1983/84, with selected detail by institution for 1983/84.

Certification types are elementary, secondary, combined, and special education. Occupational status categories are teaching in and out of State, otherwise employed, continuing study, seeking teaching and nonteaching position, and other.

Contains highlights, and listing of contents, tables, and charts (2 p.); introduction, 3 charts, and 7 tables (p. 1-13); and glossary (p. 15).

S6820   PENNSYLVANIA
Department of Health

S6820–1   PENNSYLVANIA VITAL STATISTICS Annual Report, 1983
Annual. Feb. 15, 1985.
xiii + 187 p.
LC 81-645516.
SRI/MF/complete

Annual report on Pennsylvania vital statistics, covering population, births, deaths by cause, marriages, and divorces, by location and demographic characteristics, 1983, with selected trends from 1906. Data are from State records.

Contains listings of contents, tables, and charts (p. iii-xiii); preface (p. 1); and report, in 5 sections, with narrative summaries, 5 maps, 22 charts, and 78 tables listed below (p. 5-174); and technical notes and methodology (p. 177-187).

Availability: Pennsylvania Department of Health, State Health Data Center, PO Box 90, Harrisburg PA 17108, †; SRI/MF/complete.

TABLES:
[Unless otherwise noted, tables show data for Pennsylvania, 1983. Tables often include rate per 1,000 population, and occasionally comparisons to U.S.]

S6820–1.1: Population and Natality
POPULATION
A1-A4. Population, 1950-83; and by State health service area (HSA), county, and selected municipality, 1980 and 1983. (p. 7-9)

NATALITY
[Most table titles begin "Resident live births..."]
B1-B2. [Trends], 1915-83; and general and total fertility rates, 1950-83. (p. 17-18)

B3-B4. By age of mother [quinquennially 1965-80 and 1983]; and by age of mother, [by] sex and race of child, 1983. (p. 20-21)

B5-B6. By age of mother and trimester of 1st prenatal visit; and by birth weight, [by] sex and race of child. (p. 21-22).

B7-B13. By age of mother: by birth weight, number of previous pregnancies and live births, marital status and education of mother, place of delivery and attendant at birth, type of medical condition, and method of delivery. (p. 22-26)

B14a-B14b. By Apgar score at 1 and 5 minutes, by race and sex of child. (p. 27)

B15-B21. By sex and race, age of mother, number of previous pregnancies and live births, birth weight, and education and marital status of mother; all by HSA. (p. 28-31)

B22-B32. By sex and race, age of mother, birth weight, number of previous pregnancies and live births, education and marital status of mother, month [of birth], trimester of 1st prenatal visit, place of delivery and attendant at birth, and type of medical condition; all by county. (p. 32-55)

B33-B37. By sex and race, age of mother, birth weight, marital status of mother, and trimester of 1st prenatal visit; all by selected municipality. (p. 56-61)

S6820–1.2: Mortality
C1-C2. Resident deaths, live births, and fetal, infant, neonatal, and maternal deaths, 1950-83. (p. 73-74)

C3. Leading causes of death [decennially 1930-80 and 1983]. (p. 78)

C4. Resident deaths by age group [decennially 1940-80 and 1983]. (p. 81)

C5a-C5e. Leading causes of death by age group [by sex and race]. (p. 82-86)

C6-C8. Resident deaths, resident infant deaths by age at death, and fetal deaths, all by cause. (p. 87-100)

C9a-C11b. Heart disease, malignant neoplasm, and accidental deaths, 1950-83; and resident deaths by type [of heart disease and accident, and neoplasm site], by age, 1983. (p. 101-107)

C12-C14. Pneumonia/influenza, suicide, and homicide deaths, 1950-83. (p. 110-112)

C15-C23. Resident deaths, live births, and fetal, infant, and neonatal deaths; resident deaths by age group; and leading causes of death; all by HSA, county, and selected municipality. (p. 113-151)

D1. Resident deaths by underlying cause and selected conditions mentioned on death certificate. (p. 157-161)

S6820–1.3: Marriage and Divorce
E1-E3. Marriages, 1906-83; and marriages by age of bride and groom, [selected years 1970-83]. (p. 167-168)

E4-E5. Previous marital status by race and age of bride and groom. (p. 169)

E6-E7. Prior marriages by age of bride and groom. (p. 170)

E8-E10. All marriages by age and residence of bride and groom, and by month [of occurrence]. (p. 171-172)

E11-E12. Divorces/annulments, 1945-83; and by duration of marriage, 1983. (p. 173)

E13. Marriages and divorces, by county. (p. 174)

S6820–3   PENNSYLVANIA DEPARTMENT OF HEALTH ANNUAL MARRIAGE AND DIVORCE STATISTICS, 1982
Monograph. [1984.] 3 p.
SRI/MF/complete

Two tables showing Pennsylvania divorces, annulments, and marriages, by county, 1982.

Tables are issued as a supplement to the 1982 Pennsylvania vital statistics report; for description see SRI 1984 Annual, under S6820-1.

Availability: Pennsylvania Department of Health, State Health Data Center, PO Box 90, Harrisburg PA 17108, †; SRI/MF/complete.

S6835   PENNSYLVANIA
Insurance Department

S6835–1   REPORT OF THE INSURANCE COMMISSIONER OF THE COMMONWEALTH OF PENNSYLVANIA for the Period July 1, 1983-June 30, 1984
Annual. Dec. 21, 1984.
3 + 168 p.
LC 10-33069.
SRI/MF/complete

Annual report on Pennsylvania insurance industry financial condition and underwriting activity, by company and type of insurance, 1983. Covers assets; surplus or surplus/assets ratio; operating income/premium earnings, and loss ratios; premiums written and/or earned; dividends or benefits paid; insurance and certificates in force; and losses incurred; for companies with headquarters in Pennsylvania and elsewhere.

Data are shown, as applicable, for fire/casualty insurance companies; fraternal benefit societies; title and life insurance companies; nonprofit hospital and medical service corporations; and HMOs.

Data are also shown for companies ranked by Pennsylvania market share in each line of coverage, including property, workmen's compensation, automobile, surety, medical malpractice, and accident/health insurance.

Also includes data on Insurance Dept licensing activities and finances, including premium tax revenues by type of insurance, FY84.

Most data are compiled from annual statements filed by individual companies with the Insurance Dept.

Contains contents listing (1 p.); Insurance Dept regulatory activities, with 5 tables (p. 1-8); and 36 company financial tables (p. 9-168).

Availability: Pennsylvania Insurance Department, Companies Division, Strawberry Sq., Rm. 1311, Harrisburg PA 17120, $15.00; SRI/MF/complete.

S6845   PENNSYLVANIA
Department of Labor and Industry

S6845–1   PENNSYLVANIA EMPLOYMENT AND EARNINGS
Quarterly, with interim monthly supplements.
Approx. 10 p. or 5 p.
SRI/MF/complete, shipped quarterly

Quarterly report, with interim monthly supplements, on Pennsylvania labor force, employment, unemployment, hours, and earnings, by industry, with summary data by labor market area (LMA). Report is issued 1-2 months after month of coverage.

Each issue contains narrative summary, and 1 or more summary trend charts; quarterly issues include occasional articles, and 7 tables listed below; and monthly supplements include 2 tables, also listed below.

Reports for individual LMAs are also available from the issuing agency, but are not covered in SRI.

Availability: Pennsylvania Department of Labor and Industry, Employment Security Office, Research and Statistics Division, Labor and Industry Bldg., Rm. 1200, Seventh and Forster Sts., Harrisburg PA 17121, †; SRI/MF/complete, shipped quarterly.

Issues reviewed during 1985: Aug. 1984-July 1985 (D) (Vol. XXIX, Nos. 8-12; Vol. XXX, Nos. 1-7) [July 1985 issue incorrectly reads Vol. XXIX].

TABLES:

QUARTERLY ISSUES
[Data are shown for month of coverage, previous 3 months, and same month of previous year, unless otherwise noted.]

[A] Quarterly average adjusted unemployment by LMAs: number and rate [for quarter ending in month of coverage, previous quarter, and same quarter of previous year].

1. Resident employment, unemployment, and unemployed rate [Pennsylvania and U.S., for month of coverage, several previous months and quarters, and 14-18 previous years].

2. Nonagricultural wage/salary employment [by industry group and division; and total workers involved in labor disputes].

3. Selected employment indices [for selected industry groups and divisions; includes annual averages for 3 previous years].

4. Actual and real gross earnings of manufacturing production workers [for previous 11-13 years].

5. Employment, payrolls, and manhours of manufacturing production workers.

6. Hours and earnings for manufacturing and selected nonmanufacturing industry [groups].

MONTHLY SUPPLEMENTS
[Data are for month of coverage, previous month, and same month of previous year.]

[A] Total civilian labor force, employment, and unemployment.

[B] Manufacturing and selected nonmanufacturing industry detail [employment, and production worker average hours and earnings, by industry division and major group; and total workers involved in labor disputes].

S6860   PENNSYLVANIA
State
Police

S6860–1   UNIFORM CRIME REPORT: Commonwealth of Pennsylvania, Annual Report, 1984
Annual. [1985.]
226 p. var. paging.
ISSN 0095-5752.
LC 75-640313.
SRI/MF/complete

Annual report on Pennsylvania crimes and arrests, by type of offense, 1984, with trends from 1980. Includes data by county, jurisdiction, MSA, and State region, and by offender age, sex, and race. Also includes law enforcement employment, and assaults on officers.

Report focuses on 8 Index offenses: murder, rape, aggravated assault, robbery, burglary, larceny/theft, motor vehicle theft, and arson. Substantial data are also shown for numerous non-Index offenses.

Data are from State and local agency reports submitted under the Uniform Crime Reporting Program.

Contents:

a. Listings of contents, tables, and charts. (3 p.)

b. Introduction, with 3 summary tables on 1984 reported offenses, clearances, and arrests. (p. 1-13)

c. Crime Index offenses: narrative summary interspersed with 34 charts and 54 summary tables, including data on trends for each offense, 1980-84; and crime frequency, stolen property value, murders by victim/offender relationship and circumstances, burglaries by type of entry and time occurred, motor vehicle theft by vehicle type, arson by property classification, and weapons used in offenses, mostly for 1984. (p. 14-68)

d. Non-Index offenses: narrative with 15 charts and 22 summary tables showing offenses, arrests, and clearances, including detail for selected categories, 1984, with trends from 1980. (p. 69-95)

e. Law enforcement employees, with 2 charts and 6 tables on employment trends, 1980-84; and police depts by size, 15 largest local police agencies ranked by employment, and assaults on law enforcement officers by type of weapon used and by month, 1984. (p. 96-104)

f. Appendix A, with 25 detailed tables, listed below. (p. A1-A20)

g. Appendix B-C, with computer tabulations of Part I and Part II offenses and clearances, by offense, county, and jurisdiction, with jurisdiction populations, 1984. (p. B1-B42, C1-C57)

Availability: Pennsylvania State Police, Research and Development Bureau, 1800 Elmerton Ave., Harrisburg PA 17120, †; SRI/MF/complete.

APPENDIX A TABLES:
[Tables show data for Pennsylvania, 1984.]

S6860–1.1: Appendix A
[Data by county are also shown by State region.]

OFFENSES AND CLEARANCES

1. Offenses reported [and cleared, by Part I and Part II offense]. (p. A1)

2-3. Part I offenses and clearances reported [by offense], by county. (p. A2-A3)

4. Offenses by MSA [totals for Part I and Part II offenses]. (p. A4)

5-6. Murder victims and offenders, by age, sex, and race. (p. A5)

7-8. Part II offenses and clearances reported [by offense], by county. (p. A6-A7)

9-10. Part I and Part II arrests reported [by offense], by county. (p. A8-A9)

11. Persons arrested by age, sex, and race [includes Indian and Asian; and by offense charged]. (p. A10-A11)

12-14. Arrests by major age grouping, sex, and race [by detailed offense, including drug possession and sales by substance]. (p. A12-A14)

15. Persons charged and disposition of persons charged by police [by offense]. (p. A15)

LAW ENFORCEMENT EMPLOYEES AND OFFICERS ASSAULTED
[Tables 17-25 begin "Assaults on Pennsylvania law enforcement officers..." Data "by population group" are shown for Philadelphia, Pittsburgh, 5 municipality size groups, State police, and sheriffs/other county police.]

16. Law enforcement employees [officers and civilians by sex], by county. (p. A16)

17-19. Injury rates and clearances, percent distribution of weapons used, and number of assaults and percent with injury; [all] by population group. (p. A17)

20. Type of weapon and type of police activity. (p. A18)

21. Percent cleared by type of police activity and population group. (p. A18)

22-24. Police activity by type of weapon; and type of assignment by police activity. (p. A19-A20)

25. Time of assaults by population group. (p. A20)

S6900   PENNSYLVANIA
Supreme Court

S6900–1   1983 ANNUAL REPORT, Administrative Office of Pennsylvania Courts
Annual. [1985.] 93 p.
ISSN 0148-9925.
LC 77-647649.
SRI/MF/complete

Annual report, for 1983, on Pennsylvania judicial system, including trial and appellate court caseloads and case dispositions. Covers supreme, superior, commonwealth, common pleas, district justice, Philadelphia traffic and municipal, and Pittsburgh magistrate courts. Includes trial court data by case type and county, and trends from 1979.

Data are shown for criminal and civil cases for most courts, with trial court detail for traffic, small claims, landlord/tenant, probate (orphans' court), divorce, domestic relations, adoption, custody, and juvenile cases, and for cases involving fugitives.

Report also includes data on disciplinary actions against judges and lawyers; civil cases handled through arbitration; crime victim compensation costs; authorized judges by county; and judicial dept finances.

Data are from dept records.

Contains listings of contents, tables, and charts (p. 3); report, with 6 charts and 23 tables (p. 6-74); and judicial directory (p. 75-93).

Availability: Pennsylvania Supreme Court, Administrative Office of the Courts, Three Penn Center Plaza, Rm. 1414, Philadelphia PA 19102, †; SRI/MF/complete.

S6905   PENNSYLVANIA
Department of
Transportation

S6905–2   REPORT OF
REGISTRATIONS FOR
CALENDAR YEAR 1984,
PENNSYLVANIA
Annual. [1985.]   2+37 p.
LC 75-647301.
SRI/MF/complete

Annual report on Pennsylvania registered motor vehicles, by detailed vehicle type and county, as of Dec. 31, 1984.

Contains introduction and 5 tables.

Availability: Pennsylvania Department of Transportation, Motor Vehicles and Licensing Bureau, Transportation and Safety Bldg., G 132, Harrisburg PA 17122, †; SRI/MF/complete.

S6905–3   PENNSYLVANIA TRAFFIC
ACCIDENTS
Annual. [1985.]
21 p. no paging.
SRI/MF/complete

Annual report on Pennsylvania traffic accidents, fatalities, and injuries, by accident and vehicle type, location, time, and other circumstances; and by driver and pedestrian victim characteristics; 1984.

Report consists of 16 tables.

Report has been published since mid-1960s. SRI coverage begins with this edition.

A report on alcohol-related accidents is also available from the issuing agency, but is not covered by SRI.

Availability: Pennsylvania Department of Transportation, Accident Analysis Bureau, 1210 Transportation and Safety Bldg., Harrisburg PA 17120, †; SRI/MF/complete.

S6930   RHODE ISLAND
Department of
Administration

S6930–1   ANNUAL FINANCIAL
REPORT OF THE STATE OF
RHODE ISLAND AND
PROVIDENCE
PLANTATIONS for the
Fiscal Year Ended June 30,
1984
Annual.   Jan. 15, 1985.
6+292 p.
LC 42-13379.
SRI/MF/complete

Annual report on financial condition of Rhode Island State government, FY84, presenting assets and liabilities, fund equity and balances, revenues by source, and expenditures by function or agency, for all, general, special revenue, capital projects, university/college, enterprise, internal service, trust/agency, and public authorities/corporations funds, with selected comparisons to FY83 and earlier.

Also includes data on budgeted vs. actual revenues and expenditures; expenditures vs. appropriations by agency and program; State retirement system finances and employee benefit costs; bonded indebtedness; State aid to individual cities and towns; investments by fund; and employment insurance program finances.

Data are from the records of the controller's office.

Contains contents listing (6 p.); introduction, with 3 charts and 5 summary tables (p. 1-9); and 3 sections, 6 charts, and 110 exhibits and schedules (p. 12-292).

A condensed version of the annual report is available from the Office of the State Controller, but is not covered by SRI.

Availability: Rhode Island Department of Administration, State Controller's Office, Accounts and Control Division, 544 Elmwood Ave., Providence RI 02907, †; SRI/MF/complete.

S6930–3   1980 CENSUS OF
POPULATION BY AGE, SEX,
AND TRACT, Rhode Island
Monograph. Sept. 1984.
iii+261 p.
Technical Paper No. 111.
SRI/MF/complete

Report presenting Rhode Island population by age group, sex, and race, by municipality and census tract, 1980.

Data are from Summary Tape File 2 of the 1980 Census of Population and Housing.

Contains preface, and contents and table listings (p. i-iii); introduction and census tract designations (p. 1-3); 1 basic table repeated for each location (p. 5-259); and glossary (2 p.).

Availability: Rhode Island Department of Administration, Statewide Planning Program, 265 Melrose St., Providence RI 02907, †; SRI/MF/complete.

S6930–4   1980 CENSUS OF
POPULATION AND
HOUSING: SELECTED DATA,
Rhode Island
Monograph. Dec. 1984.
30 p. var. paging+foldout.
Technical Paper No. 115.
SRI/MF/complete

Report presenting Rhode Island population size and number of housing units, by census tract and municipality, 1970 and 1980. Includes total and white population; and total, owner- and renter-occupied, and vacant year-round and/or seasonal housing units.

Data are from Summary Tape Files (STF) 1A and 3A of the 1980 Census of Population and Housing, and First Count Tape of the 1970 census.

Contains preface, and contents and table listings (p. i-iii); introduction, and STF and census questionnaire descriptions (p. 1-6); 3 extended tables (p. 7-24 and foldout); and appendix, with glossary and census tract designations (p. A1-A3).

Availability: Rhode Island Department of Administration, Statewide Planning Program, 265 Melrose St., Providence RI 02907, †; SRI/MF/complete.

S6930–5   1980 CENSUS OF
POPULATION INCOME AND
POVERTY DATA BY TRACT
Monograph. Jan. 1985.
iv+259+App 6 p.
Technical Paper No. 117.
SRI/MF/complete

Report presenting income and poverty status data for Rhode Island municipalities and census tracts, 1980. Includes the following data for families and individuals in each locale: total number, number below poverty level, and distribution by income, with selected detail for families with female household heads and minor children, for persons age 65/over, and by race/ethnicity (including American Indian/Eskimo/Aleut, Asian/Pacific Islander, and Spanish origin).

Also includes 1980 median family income and 1979 median and per capita income for each locale; and U.S. poverty trends from 1979.

Data are from Summary Tape File 3A of the Census of Population and Housing.

Contains preface, and contents and table listings (p. i-iv); introduction, with 1 table (p. 1-3); 1 basic table repeated for State and each locale (p. 5-259); and appendices, with 3 tables, technical notes, census tract designations, and glossary (6 p.).

Availability: Rhode Island Department of Administration, Statewide Planning Program, 265 Melrose St., Providence RI 02907, †; SRI/MF/complete.

S6930–6   SELECTED POPULATION,
HOUSING, AND AREA
DATA, BY CENSUS TRACT,
FOR 1970-80, Rhode Island
Monograph.   Apr. 1985.
33 p. var. paging.
Technical Paper No. 118.
SRI/MF/complete

Report presenting Rhode Island population and housing units for 1970 and 1980, and land and inland water acreage, all by municipality and census tract.

Most data are from Census Bureau.

Contains contents and table listings (p. ii-iii); introduction and 4 tables (p. 1-15); census tract maps (p. 16-29); and appendices, with census tract designations (2 p.).

Availability: Rhode Island Department of Administration, Statewide Planning Program, 265 Melrose St., Providence RI 02907, †; SRI/MF complete.

S6945   RHODE ISLAND
Department of
Business Regulation

S6945–1   SEVENTY-SEVENTH ANNUAL REPORT OF THE BANKING DIVISION to the General Assembly, 1984, Rhode Island
Annual. [1984.]   x+56 p.
LC 9-6541.
SRI/MF/complete

Annual report on assets and liabilities of Rhode Island State-chartered savings banks, commercial banks and trust companies, loan and investment companies, building-loan assns, and credit unions, by institution, as of Dec. 31, 1983, with selected summary comparisons to 1982 and trends from 1974.

Also includes banking taxes assessed/paid and fees collected; composite balance sheet for finance companies; and assets of individual State-located national banks and Federal savings and loan assns.

Contains contents and index listings, and Banking Division report with 3 text tables (p. iii-x); and 43 financial statements and tables (p. 2-56).

Availability: Rhode Island Department of Business Regulation, Banking Division, 100 N. Main St., Providence RI 02903, $8.00; SRI/MF/complete.

S6945–2   ONE HUNDRED TWENTY-FIRST ANNUAL REPORT OF THE INSURANCE DIVISION Made to the General Assembly, 1983, Rhode Island
Annual.   July 1, 1983.
232 p.
LC 45-27257.
SRI/MF/complete

Annual report on Rhode Island insurance industry financial condition and underwriting activity, by company and type of insurance, 1982. Covers assets, liabilities, capital, surplus, direct premiums, losses or claims/benefits paid, and annuities; and insurance in force, issued, and terminated; for companies based in Rhode Island and elsewhere.

Data are shown, as applicable, for stock and mutual fire/casualty and life insurance companies, fraternal organizations, hospital/physician/ dental service corporations, and reciprocals.

Data on fire/casualty insurance include additional breakdowns by detailed line of coverage, including medical malpractice, accident/health, worker compensation, automobile, and surety.

Also includes data on licenses issued and fees collected, FY83.

Data are compiled from annual statements filed by individual insurers.

Contains contents listing (p. 1); Insurance Division regulatory summary with 3 tables, and directory of companies (p. 4-31); 34 company financial statements (p. 32-66); and 2 statistical sections, with 15 tables (p. 68-232).

Availability: Rhode Island Department of Business Regulation, Insurance Division, 100 N. Main St., Providence RI 02903, $15.00; SRI/ MF/complete.

S6960   RHODE ISLAND
Department of
Corrections

S6960–1   CHARACTERISTICS OF INMATE POPULATION, Rhode Island Adult Correctional Institution, Apr. 1, 1982
Recurring (irreg.)   [1984.]
5+150 p.
SRI/MF/complete

Recurring report on characteristics of the Rhode Island Adult Correctional Institution inmate population, 1982, with selected trends from 1974. Covers inmate sociodemographic characteristics, criminal background, commitment offense, sentence length, and substance abuse; and time served by inmates released during 1982. Includes separate data for male and female inmates, sentenced inmates by level of security (high, maximum, medium, minimum, work release), and inmates awaiting trial.

Contains contents and table listings (5 p.); introduction, definitions, and narrative analysis with 33 summary tables (p. 1-46); and 36 detailed tables (p. 47-150).

Report is issued every 2-3 years. Previous report, presenting data primarily for 1980, is described in SRI 1982 Annual under this number.

Availability: Rhode Island Department of Corrections, 75 Howard Ave., Cranston RI 02920, †; SRI/MF/complete.

S6970   RHODE ISLAND
Department of
Education

S6970–1   1983/84 STATISTICAL TABLES, Rhode Island Department of Education
Annual.   [1985.]   xii+43 p.
LC 50-63458.
SRI/MF/complete

Annual report on Rhode Island educational enrollment, graduates, personnel, and finances, by school district, community, and institution, for academic year 1983/84. Data are from records of State Depts of Education and Community Affairs.

Contains foreword, statistical overview, and contents and table listings (p. i-xii); 29 tables, listed below (p. 2-42); and glossary (p. 43).

Availability: Rhode Island Department of Education, Research and Evaluation Bureau, Educational Statistics, Roger Williams Bldg., 22 Hayes St., Providence RI 02908, †; SRI/MF/complete.

TABLES:
[Tables show data for Rhode Island, 1983/84, unless otherwise noted.]

S6970–1.1: Students
[Tables S1, S4-S5, and S9-S10 show data for fall 1983-84.]

DISTRICT SCHOOLS
[Tables show data by Local Education Agency (LEA) school district. Data for "others" are shown for prekindergarten, ungraded/unclassified, and postgraduate students.]

S1. Pupil summary [membership, attendance, and enrollment]. (p. 2)

S2-S3. Summary of daily membership by grade grouping, and "others" in daily membership. (p. 3-4)

S4-S4A. Enrollment by grades, and "others" in fall enrollment. (p. 5-10)

S5. Enrollment by grade grouping. (p. 11)

S6. Enrollment by race/ethnic origin [including American Indian/Alaskan Native, Asian/ Pacific Islander, and Hispanic], and sex, fall 1984. (p. 12)

OTHER SCHOOLS
S7-S8. Enrollment by grade and place of residence, for Catholic diocesan and independent schools, fall 1984. (p. 13-16)

S9-S10. Enrollment by grade grouping [by] place of residence and schools, for State-operated schools. (p. 17-18)

S6970–1.2: Graduates and Personnel
GRADUATES
D1-D3. Graduates of LEA and nonpublic high schools and State-operated schools, by sex [by school or State institution]. (p. 20-22)

D4. Summary of Rhode Island high school graduates [for regular and GED (general education development) diploma, by sex, by type of school]. (p. 23)

PERSONNEL
[Tables show data for personnel paid with funds from all sources, by LEA and sex.]

P1. Classroom teachers: number of FTE positions, by level [including special education]. (p. 25)

P2. Professional instructional personnel, by position. (p. 26-27)

S6970–1.3: Finances
[Tables FO1-FO6 and FC1 show data by LEA.]

OPERATIONS
FO1. Total operating expenditures [by function, including adult basic and continuing education, and transportation]. (p. 29)

FO2. Net resident expenditures, by source of funds [including tuition]. (p. 30)

FO3. Federal aid paid [by program]. (p. 31)

FO4. Per pupil costs based on average daily membership and total current operating expenditures for day schools and debt service expenditures. (p. 32)

FO5. State support for school operations [including programs for disadvantaged children, and vocational and bilingual education]. (p. 33)

FO6. State entitlements for school operations, 1983/84-1984/85. (p. 34)

FO7. State funds expended for education: Rhode Island Board of Regents for elementary and secondary education [by area of expenditure, including special populations], 1983/84-1984/85. (p. 35)

CAPITAL EXPENDITURES

FC1. Expenditures for debt service commitments for school construction. (p. 37)

S6970–1.4: Taxation

[All tables show data by community.]

T1. Assessed, full, and equalized weighted assessed property valuations, 1981. (p. 39)

T2. Rank of communities by effective tax rates on full property values for operation and construction of schools. (p. 40)

T3. Municipal tax rates per $1,000 assessed property value, 1983-84. (p. 41)

T4. Full property value per pupil in RADM [resident average daily membership]. (p. 42)

S6980   RHODE ISLAND
Department of
Employment Security

**S6980–1   RHODE ISLAND
EMPLOYMENT BULLETIN**
Monthly.   4 p.
SRI/MF/complete, shipped
quarterly

Monthly report on Rhode Island employment and unemployment, hours and earnings, and job service and unemployment insurance activities. Includes data by industry and locale. Data are current to 1-2 months preceding publication date.

Contains narrative highlights, and 6 monthly tables and 1 quarterly table, listed below.

Monthly tables appear in all issues; quarterly table appears in Sept., Dec., Mar., and June issues.

Availability: Rhode Island Department of Employment Security, Research and Statistics Unit, 24 Mason St., Providence RI 02903-1082, †; SRI/MF/complete, shipped quarterly.

Issues reviewed during 1985: Oct. 1984-Sept. 1985 (P) (Vol. 30, Nos. 10-12; Vol. 31, Nos. 1-9).

TABLES:

[Most data are shown for month of coverage, same month of previous year, and previous month.]

MONTHLY TABLES

[1] Employment service activities [placements, applications, and openings received].

[2] Employment security activities [claims, payments, and exhaustions].

[3] Federal supplemental compensation [claims and payments].

[4] Labor force and unemployment estimates, for State and Providence, Pawtucket/Woonsocket/Attleboro, and Newport metro areas.

[5-6] Total establishment employment [by industry division]; and employment, earnings, and hours in manufacturing industries [by major industry group].

QUARTERLY TABLE

[7] Characteristics of the insured unemployed [number and percent by sex, age (under and over 45), industry division, and occupation; for selected week of month of coverage].

**S6980–3   ANNUAL PLANNING
INFORMATION for State of
Rhode Island**
Annual.   May 1985.
iv + 52 p. + addenda.
SRI/MF/complete

Annual planning report, for FY86, identifying Rhode Island population most in need of employment services, and projecting job openings by occupation through 1990. Also includes data on population, labor force, and employment by industry.

Data are from Federal and State agencies.

Contains listings of contents, maps, and tables, and preface (p. ii-iv); narrative report in 5 sections, with 1 map, and 11 tables listed below (p. 1-45); and appendix, with data sources and explanatory notes (p. 47-52).

Additional tables, presenting labor force data for Providence and Pawtucket-Woonsocket-Attleboro MSAs, are also available from the issuing agency. MSA tables, which are comparable to state tables [2-3] and [8-9] described below, once were included in the annual planning report but now must be requested separately. MSA tables are also available on SRI microfiche under this number.

Availability: Rhode Island Department of Employment Security, Labor Market Information Section, 24 Mason St., Providence RI 02903-1082, †; SRI/MF/complete.

TABLES:

[Data are for Rhode Island, unless otherwise noted.]

[1] Population change, 1970 and 1980, in the U.S. and Rhode Island. (p. 3)

[2-3] Establishment employment [by industry division and major manufacturing group, and persons in labor disputes, monthly] 1983-84. (p. 6-7)

[4] Occupations with job openings unfilled for 30 days or more during 1984: range and monthly average number of openings unfilled. (p. 12-13)

[5] Occupations with 10 or more job openings unfilled for 30 days or more at the end of Mar. 1985. (p. 16)

[6] Average annual number of job openings, by [detailed] occupation, during 1980-90 period. (p. 19-37)

[7] Occupations with 100 or more active applicants at the end of Feb. 1985. (p. 39)

[8-9] Labor force and unemployment, [monthly] 1983-84. (p. 41-42)

[10-11] Characteristics of the insured unemployed [by sex, age, industry division, and occupation], 1983-84. (p. 44-45)

S6995   RHODE ISLAND
Department of
Health

**S6995–1   VITAL STATISTICS
ANNUAL REPORT, 1983,
Rhode Island**
Annual.   Feb. 1985.
v + 145 p.
LC 80-645335.
SRI/MF/complete

Annual report on Rhode Island vital statistics, covering population, births, deaths by cause, marriages, and divorces, 1983, with selected trends from 1954. Includes data by age, sex, race, and locality. Data are from State records.

Contains chart and table listing (p. i-v); introduction, with narrative summary, 1 map, 17 charts, and 7 tables presenting selected summary data and trends (p. 1-36); and 48 detailed tables, listed below (p. 37-145).

Availability: Rhode Island Department of Health, Vital Statistics Division, Cannon Bldg., Rm. 101, 75 Davis St., Providence RI 02908, †; SRI/MF/complete.

TABLES:

[Tables show data for Rhode Island, 1983, unless otherwise noted. Tables showing births and deaths are generally for State residents. Marriages and divorces are shown for occurrences in State.]

S6995–1.1: Population and Summary

1. U.S. census population by race and sex, and age by sex, 1970 and 1980. (p. 39)

2. Population of cities and towns, by county, census of 1970 and 1980, and 1983 estimate. (p. 40)

3. Number of live births, deaths, and marriages, with rates, by city and town. (p. 41)

4. Population, live births, deaths, marriages, and divorces, with rates per 1,000 population, 1954-83. (p. 42)

S6995–1.2: Births and Deaths

DEATHS

5. Number of infant, neonatal, perinatal, and maternal deaths, with rates, 1954-83. (p. 43)

6. Deaths, by city or town of residence, by age, race, and sex. (p. 44-49)

7. Deaths and death rates for [20] leading causes in 1983, with comparability ratios and for comparable causes in 1974-82. (p. 50)

LOCAL DATA

8. Selected health characteristics [total and infant deaths, and total live, out-of-wedlock, and low-weight births], by neighborhood and city or town, 5-year totals with average rates, 1979-83; [and 1980 population for each locale]. (p. 51-53)

BIRTHS

9. Number of births out of wedlock, with ratio per 1,000 live births, 1960-83. (p. 54)

10. Births out of wedlock, with ratio per 1,000 total births in specified age group, 1974-83. (p. 54)

11-12. Live births and births out of wedlock, by sex and race of child, age of mother, and live birth order. (p. 55-62)

13-15. Live births: [total], plural, and out of wedlock, by age of mother, race, and birth weight. (p. 63-71)

16. Births, by city or town, by selected characteristics [total, in-hospital, out-of-wedlock, and low birth weight, by race]. (p. 72)

17. Live births, by city or town, by month. (p. 73)

18. Selected natality data [total, out-of-wedlock, and low birth weight; births with malformation; and births by month prenatal care began]; by city or town, by census tract. (p. 74-81)

18A. Births and births out of wedlock, all ages and under age 20, by city or town of residence. (p. 82)

FETAL DEATHS
[Tables show data for occurrences in Rhode Island. Modes of delivery are spontaneous and induced.]

19A-19B. Fetal deaths, by race of fetus and weeks of uterogestation, and mode of delivery; and by month of delivery, by weeks of uterogestation. (p. 83)

20. Resident fetal deaths occurring in Rhode Island, by mode of delivery, by city or town and census tract of mother's residence, by marital status of mother. (p. 84-91)

21. Induced fetal deaths, by age and marital status of mother, and by number and nature of previous deliveries to mother. (p. 92-95)

22A-22B. Spontaneous fetal deaths of 20 weeks or more uterogestation and [total] spontaneous fetal deaths, by number of child in total birth order, number of previous fetal deaths, and age of mother. (p. 96-97)

23. Spontaneous fetal deaths of 20 weeks or more uterogestation, by weight of fetus and age of mother. (p. 98)

24. Fetal deaths, by selected cause of death and weeks of uterogestation. (p. 99)

DEATHS BY CAUSE AND LOCALITY

25. Deaths from 72 selected causes, by race, age, and sex. (p. 100-112)

26. Deaths, by city or town, by month. (p. 113)

27. Infant deaths from 61 selected causes, by age. (p. 114)

28. Accidental deaths, with non-motor vehicle accidents shown by New England Standard Locations [type or place of accident], by sex and age. (p. 115-116)

29A-29B. Selected mortality data [deaths by cause], by city or town, by census tract. (p. 117-132)

30. Accident deaths, by type and age. (p. 133)

31-32. 10 leading causes of death, by sex; and 5 leading causes of death in specified age groups; 1983 [with 1982-83 rates]. (p. 135-136)

S6995–1.3: Marriages and Divorces

MARRIAGES

33. Number of marriages and persons married, by city and town of residence of bride and groom. (p. 137)

34-35. Marriages, by age of bride by age of groom; and by age at marriage and previous marital status of bride and groom. (p. 138-139)

36. Number of times married for brides, by number of times married for grooms. (p. 140)

37-38. Marriages, by previous marital status of bride and groom; and according to last grade of school completed by bride and groom. (p. 140-141)

DIVORCES

39-40. Divorces, by age of wife by age of husband; and by number of times married before this divorce, by sex. (p. 142)

41. Divorces, by marital status and age of husband and wife. (p. 143)

42. Number of divorces of remarried persons, by previous marital history. (p. 143)

43. Number of divorces by county, with number of children under 18 known to be affected. (p. 144)

44. Divorces according to last grade of school completed, by sex. (p. 145)

S7015   RHODE ISLAND
Department of
Social and
Rehabilitative Services

S7015–1   **STATISTICS ON ASSISTANCE CASELOADS AND PAYMENTS, by City and Town, State of Rhode Island**
Quarterly, with fiscal year summary. 8 p.
LC 80-643749.
SRI/MF/complete

Quarterly report, with fiscal year summary, on Rhode Island public assistance programs, including caseloads, recipients, and payments, by program and city. Covers AFDC, general public assistance (GPA), Medicaid, food stamps, and SSI.

Report is issued 2-6 months after month of coverage. Issuing agency compiles data on a monthly basis, but publishes data only for the last month of each quarter.

Contains contents listing, narrative comments, and 6 quarterly tables, listed below.

Availability: Rhode Island Department of Social and Rehabilitative Services, Research and Statistics Office, 600 New London Ave., Cranston RI 02920, †; SRI/MF/complete.

Issues reviewed during 1985: Sept. 1984-June 1985 (D) [No Dec. 1984 and Mar. 1985 issues were published].

QUARTERLY TABLES:
[Tables show data by city for month of coverage.]

AFDC
[Data are shown for regular and unemployed segments.]

I. AFDC cases, current, last month, and last year.

II. AFDC children, parents, and total persons.

GPA

I. All GPA maintenance/medical caseloads and payments [family cases and persons, and individuals].

MISCELLANEOUS

I. Medicaid: [family] cases and persons eligible for medical assistance only [includes aged, blind, and disabled; and totals for recipients in State institutions].

II. Food stamps: [AFDC, GPA, and SSI/other] cases and persons authorized as of 1st of month.

III. SSI: persons receiving [adult and child blind and disabled, and aged].

S7025   RHODE ISLAND
Department of
Transportation

S7025–1   **RHODE ISLAND TRAFFIC ACCIDENTS**
Annual. [1985.]
24 p. no paging.
SRI/MF/complete

Annual report on Rhode Island traffic accidents involving fatalities, injuries, and property damage, and number of persons killed and injured, 1983. Includes data by accident and vehicle type, location, time, and other circumstances; and driver and victim characteristics.

Also includes data on use of seatbelts and motorcycle helmets in accidents, property damage costs, vehicle defects contributing to accidents, and severity of personal injuries.

Contains 24 tables (24 p.).

Report has been published since 1974. SRI coverage begins with this edition.

Availability: Rhode Island Department of Transportation, Planning Division, State Office Bldg., Smith St., Providence RI 02903, †; SRI/MF/complete.

S7125   SOUTH CAROLINA
Budget and Control Board

S7125–1   **SOUTH CAROLINA STATISTICAL ABSTRACT, 1984**
Annual. [1985.] 371 p.
LC 72-611159.
SRI/MF/complete

Annual compilation, for 1984, of detailed social, economic, and governmental statistics for South Carolina. Data are shown primarily for 1970s-84 with decennial population trends from 1790 and projections to 2000.

Report is designed to present a comprehensive overview of the State. Extensive socioeconomic, demographic, and geographic breakdowns are shown, as applicable, for most topics. These breakdowns include data by city, county, MSA, urban-rural status, commodity, income, industry, occupation, age, educational attainment, marital status, race, and sex. Comparisons to other southeastern States and total U.S. are occasionally included.

Most data are from State and Federal agencies. Data sources appear beneath each table.

Contents:

a. Preface and contents listing. (p. 3-7)

b. State rankings section, with contents listing and 6 tables showing comparative State rankings in selected socioeconomic and demographic areas. (p. 9-16)

c. 32 maps, 38 charts, and 259 tables arranged in 17 sections, described below, each preceded by a contents listing and usually a glossary. (p. 17-352)

d. Appendix, with guide to data sources, and index. (p. 353-371)

Availability: South Carolina Budget and Control Board, Research and Statistical Services Division, Rembert C. Dennis Bldg., Rm. 337, 1000 Assembly St., Columbia SC 29201, $15.00; SRI/MF/complete.

TABLE SECTIONS:

S7125-1.1: Sections 2-3: Agriculture and Seafood Production; and Area, Geography, and Natural Resources

a. Agricultural acreage, yield, production, and value; cash receipts and government payments; farms and acreage, and average size and value; farm operator characteristics; and commercial fish and shellfish landings and value. 2 charts and 10 tables. (p. 19-28)

b. Land and water area; population; temperature and precipitation; land use; forest fires and acreage burned by cause, and acreage protected; mineral production value; and tree seedlings planted, by landowner class and company. 8 maps and 10 tables. (p. 31-46)

S7125-1.2: Section 4: Banking, Finance, and Capital Investment

a. State bank and savings and loan assn balance sheets; consumer finance licensees, assets, and loans; credit unions, members, and finances; banks and deposits; State debt and trust fund holdings; and insurance premiums and claims, and life insurance in force, since 1910. 9 tables. (p. 49-54)

b. Manufacturing and nonmanufacturing firms and employment; new and expanded plants, employment, and capital investments; and foreign manufacturing employment, and investments by country. 1 map, 2 charts, and 10 tables. (p. 55-60)

S7125-1.3: Section 5: Education

a. Public and private schools and enrollment; vocational and adult education enrollment; handicapped children receiving public school services; and high school graduates and postsecondary plans. 2 charts and 6 tables. (p. 64-69)

b. Educational receipts and expenditures; professional staff; average teacher salaries; educational attainment; postsecondary enrollment and tuition/fees, by institution; technical college enrollment; and degrees conferred. 2 maps, 5 charts, and 22 tables. (p. 70-92)

S7125-1.4: Sections 6-8: Employment, Energy Resources, and Government and Politics

a. Labor force by employment status; nonfarm, manufacturing, and textile employment; average covered employment; State

and local government employment by function; union membership and bargaining contracts, by union; and establishments, employment, and payroll. 3 charts and 23 tables. (p. 95-132)

b. Electric utilities financial and operating data, by privately-owned company; electric and natural gas utility customers, sales, and consumption, by sector; electricity generation by fuel source; and gasohol, gasoline, and diesel fuel consumption. 3 charts and 12 tables. (p. 135-140)

c. Local government jurisdictions, including school and special districts; population and social characteristics of congressional and other State districts; and voting age population, registered voters, and voter turnout for 1980 presidential election. 4 maps and 6 tables. (p. 144-154)

S7125-1.5: Sections 9-10: Health and Housing

a. Nursing school graduates, and licensed and active nurses; dentists and physicians, by specialty; and nonfederal health professionals. 5 tables. (p. 157-163)

b. Mental retardation patients; vocational rehabilitants, by disability; health care facilities, beds, admissions/discharges, and patient days; State mental hospital admissions, population, and patient movement; and alcohol/drug abuse clients treated. 4 maps and 7 tables. (p. 164-170)

c. Housing units, occupancy, and financial and structural characteristics; persons, families, and households; median household income and percent below poverty level; and value of residential and nonresidential construction permits, and new housing authorized. 1 map and 13 tables. (p. 173-198)

S7125-1.6: Section 11: Income and Selected Economic Indicators

a. Total and per capita personal income; personal income by source; median family and household income; persons below poverty level; adjusted gross income, tax collections, and number of returns; manufacturing, nonmanufacturing, textile, and total industry payroll; and manufacturing hours and earnings. 6 charts and 19 tables. (p. 201-226)

b. Economic indicators, including net taxable and gross sales; auto registrations; construction permits; retail sales; and farm income, expenses, and inventory changes. 2 maps, 3 charts, and 6 tables. (p. 227-234)

S7125-1.7: Section 12: Law Enforcement, Courts, Crime, and Corrections

a. Crime Index rates, offenses, arrests, and clearances, by offense; homicide circumstances and victim characteristics; police assaults by weapon and activity; and stolen and recovered property value. 2 charts and 8 tables. (p. 237-242)

b. Court caseload and disposition; correctional institution inmate admissions, by offense and sentence length; and parole and probation cases, by offense; and probationer and parolee characteristics. 10 tables. (p. 243-250)

S7125-1.8: Sections 13-14: Population and Public Welfare

a. Population trends from 1790 and projections to 2000; population change components; land area; churches and membership, by denomination; elderly population characteristics, including employment, income, household size, and home ownership; and population by birthplace and selected European country of ancestry. 5 maps, 3 charts, and 30 tables. (p. 253-292)

b. Medicare enrollment and payments; AFDC and SSI cases and payments; food stamp participants and benefits; and unemployment insurance initial claims and benefits. 2 charts and 9 tables. (p. 295-302)

S7125-1.9: Sections 15-16: Recreation and Tourism; and Revenues and Expenditures

a. State park attendance, by use and park; travel expenditures, and travel-generated payroll, employment, and tax revenues; boat registrations; hunting and fishing licenses and sales; and land contributed to game management area programs, by landowner. 2 maps and 10 tables. (p. 305-312)

b. State tax allocations, collections, and tax rate changes, by tax type; State revenues by source and expenditures by function; and population and county government finances, for counties with populations over 100,000. 1 chart and 10 tables. (p. 315-324)

S7125-1.10: Sections 17-18: Transportation and Vital Statistics

a. Waterborne foreign trade and customs receipts; railroad and bus operations, by company; motor vehicle registrations; railroad track mileage operated, by railroad; bus passengers, by company; highway and vehicle mileage; traffic accidents, fatalities, injuries, and property loss; airports and air traffic; gasoline demand; and labor force, by mode of transport to work and place of work. 2 maps, 1 chart, and 13 tables. (p. 327-338)

b. Vital statistics, including population, net migration, births, total and infant deaths, deaths by leading cause, marriages, divorces/annulments, marital status of population, and life expectancy. 1 map, 3 charts, and 11 tables. (p. 341-352)

S7125-4   POPULATION PROJECTIONS FOR SOUTH CAROLINA by County, 1985, 1990, 1995, 2000
Monograph.   July 1, 1984.
129 p.
SRI/MF/complete

Report presenting South Carolina population projections by age, sex, and race, quinquennially 1985-2000. Shows data for the State, and by county, planning district, and health service area.

Also includes population by county, as of July 1, 1970, and quinquennially 1980-2000.

Projections are based on 1980 U.S. census.

Contains brief narrative, and 1 summary table (p. 2-3); and 1 extended table (p. 3-129).

Report updates the Dec. 1982 projections described in SRI 1983 Annual under this number.

Availability: South Carolina Budget and Control Board, Research and Statistical Services Division, Rembert C. Dennis Bldg., Rm. 337, 1000 Assembly St., Columbia SC 29201, $7.00; SRI/MF/complete.

S7125-6   PROFILE OF INCORPORATED PLACES of Over 5,000 Population in South Carolina
Monograph.   July 1, 1985.
64 p.
SRI/MF/complete

Report presenting selected demographic and socioeconomic data for South Carolina municipalities with population over 5,000. Includes the following data for each municipality:

a. Population by race, sex, marital status, age, and educational attainment; persons aged 16/over by labor force status and occupation; households and average size; occupied, vacant, and renter-occupied housing units; median value of owner-occupied units; and median rent; 1980.

b. Households and families, by income level; per capita and average household and family income; and poverty status of families (total and with female household head by presence and age of children); 1979.

Also includes aggregate population trends from 1900, and selected summary data for various years 1970-82.

Data are from Census Bureau.

Contains contents listing (p. 3); introduction, with 1 map and 6 summary trend tables (p. 5-11); 1 basic table repeated for each municipality (p. 12-63); and 1 summary chart (p. 64).

Availability: South Carolina Budget and Control Board, Research and Statistical Services Division, Rembert C. Dennis Bldg., Rm. 337, 1000 Assembly St., Columbia SC 29201, $4.00; SRI/MF/complete.

S7127   SOUTH CAROLINA Office of the Comptroller General

S7127-1   STATE OF SOUTH CAROLINA, 1984 ANNUAL REPORT OF THE COMPTROLLER GENERAL
Annual.   [1985.]   4+54 p.
LC 8-13085.
SRI/MF/complete

Annual report on financial condition of South Carolina State government, for FY84, presenting assets, liabilities, and fund equity; revenues by source; and expenditures by function or object; for general, special revenue, capital projects, debt service, enterprise, internal service, trust/agency, and higher education/university hospital funds.

Includes detail on budgeted vs. actual financial activity; bonded debt; appropriations; State public education finances; State shared revenues, by type and county; homestead exemptions and value by county; and selected trends from 1979.

Also includes population; labor force and employment status; State and local government employment by government level; public and private college enrollment; and total, per capita, and disposable personal income, for State, U.S., and southeast region; mostly 1970s-83, with population trends from 1790 and labor force trends from 1940.

Contains transmittal message (1 p.); contents listing (2 p.); introductory section, with 6 trend charts (p. 1-7); financial section, with 10 financial exhibits (p. 9-37); and statistical section, with 20 tables (p. 38-54).

For description of previous report, for FY83, see SRI 1984 Annual under S7127-2.1. An annual report on county government finances is also published: for description of report for FY82, see SRI 1984 Annual under S7127-1.1.

Availability: South Carolina Office of the Comptroller General, Wade Hampton State Office Bldg., PO Box 11228, Columbia SC 29211, †; SRI/MF/complete.

S7135   SOUTH CAROLINA Department of Corrections

S7135-1   ANNUAL REPORT OF THE BOARD OF CORRECTIONS and the Commissioner of the South Carolina Department of Corrections, for the Period July 1, 1983-June 30, 1984
Annual.   [1985.]   129 p.
LC 77-648588.
SRI/MF/complete

Annual report, for FY84, on corrections in South Carolina, presenting data on prison population, including inmate admissions, releases, selected demographic characteristics, commitment offense, and sentence length, time served, and time remaining . Some data are shown by committing county and State district, with selected trends from 1960.

Also includes data on prison capacity, and personnel, by institution; corrections expenditures; work credit, parole, and community programs; and juvenile corrections population.

Data are compiled by Division of Resource and Information Management.

Contains listings of contents, tables, and charts (p. 2-7); directories and description of Corrections Dept organization (p. 9-17); report, with 3 maps, 24 charts, and 32 tables (p. 8-117); and narrative appendices (p. 118-129).

Availability: South Carolina Department of Corrections, PO Box 21787, Columbia SC 29221-1787, †; SRI/MF/complete.

S7145   SOUTH CAROLINA Department of Education

S7145-1   RANKINGS OF THE COUNTIES AND SCHOOL DISTRICTS of South Carolina, 1983/84
Annual.   Apr. 1985.
xiv+335 p.
ISSN 0093-5115.
LC 74-642137.
SRI/MF/complete

Annual report ranking South Carolina counties and school districts by educational and socioeconomic characteristics, 1983/84, with selected comparisons to 1973/74. Covers pupils, staff, and finances. Data are from State Dept of Education, county and district superintendents of education, other State agencies, and Census Bureau.

Contents:

a. Foreword, contents and table listings, and explanatory notes (iii-xiv); and 107 tables, listed below (p. 1-319).

b. Footnotes with data sources for each table, and appendices A-D, including lists of area vocational centers for which revenues or expenditures were prorated among 2 or more school districts; multidistrict counties, with distribution of monies and average daily membership (ADM); revenue and expenditure accounts used in compiling data for financial tables; and code identification for staff positions. (p. 320-335)

This is the 15th annual report.

Educational Trends in South Carolina, an annual report presenting comparative summaries of data for 4-5 years, is also available from the Dept of Education, but is not covered in SRI.

Availability: South Carolina Department of Education, Management Information Section, Research Office, Rutledge Bldg., Rm. 605, 1429 Senate St., Columbia SC 29201, $6.00; SRI/MF/complete.

TABLES:
[Unless otherwise noted, tables 1-34 show data for 1983 by county, and tables 35-107 show data for 1983/84 by school district. Counties and school districts are arranged both alphabetically and by rank.

Tables that show percent generally also show data from which percentages were derived.]

S7145-1.1: Population

1-2. Total population as of Apr. 1, 1980; and percent change from Apr. 1, 1970. (p. 1-4)

3-4. Percent of population classified as nonwhite and as under 18 years of age, 1980. (p. 5-8)

5. Median age of population, by school district, as of Apr. 1, 1980. (p. 9-10)

6. Percent of 5-17 year old population classified as nonwhite, by school district, 1980. (p. 11-14)

7. Percent of population 18 years old or over not completing high school, by school district, 1980. (p. 15-16)

8. Median school years completed by population 25 years old or over, 1980. (p. 17)

9. Percent of population classified as rural, by school district, 1980. (p. 18-21)

10. Percent of households headed by a single parent, by school district, 1980. (p. 22-25)

11-12. Estimated population and percent classified as nonwhite, as of July 1, 1983. (p. 26-29)

13-14. Percent change in white and nonwhite population, Apr. 1, 1980-July 1, 1983. (p. 30-33)

15. Percent of population in public/nonpublic school membership (K-12), 1983/84. (p. 34-35)

16. Percent of 1980 families below poverty level in 1979, by school district. (p. 36-39)

S7145–1.2: Economic Data

17. Median household income, by school district, 1979. (p. 40-41)

18-19. Per capita personal income, 1982; and percent increase, 1980-82. (p. 42-45)

20-23. Percent of income tax returns with adjusted gross income of [4 income groups]. (p. 46-49)

24. Percent of total civilian labor force unemployed. (p. 50-51)

25. Average weekly salary of workers covered in employment. (p. 52)

26-32. Percent of nonagricultural wage/salary employment in manufacturing, contract construction, transportation/public utilities, wholesale/retail trade, finance/insurance/real estate, services/mining, and government. (p. 53-66)

33-34. Per capita value of farm products and net taxable sales. (p. 67-70)

S7145–1.3: Pupil Data

35-36. ADM (K-12), by school district and by county. (p. 71-73)

37. Percent of total school membership in private/special/denominational schools, by county [only]. (p. 74-75)

38. 35-day enrollment (K-12). (p. 76-77)

39. Percent change in enrollment (grades 1-12) [1973/74 and 1983/84]. (p. 78-81)

40. Percent of enrollment classified as nonwhite. (p. 82-85)

41-42. Percent change in white and nonwhite enrollment [1973/74 and 1983/84]. (p. 86-93)

43-44. Percent change in enrollment from 1st grade 1972/73 and from 9th grade 1980/81 to 12th grade 1983/84. (p. 94-101)

45. Percent of ADM in average daily attendance. (p. 102-105)

46-48. Percent of 1983 graduates entering junior/senior colleges, other postsecondary schools, and employment/other activities. (p. 106-117)

49. Enrollment in basic and high school adult education programs, by county [only]. (p. 118-119)

50. Percent of pupils eligible for free/reduced-price lunches, Oct. 1983. (p. 120-123)

51-57. Membership weighted according to the Education Finance Act [for] kindergarten, primary, elementary, high school, handicapped/homebound, vocational, and all classifications. (p. 124-149)

58. Dropouts as percent of enrollment for grades 9-12. (p. 150-153)

S7145–1.4: Professional Staff

59-61. Percent of professional staff with bachelor's degrees, master's degrees, and 6-year certificates/doctorates. (p. 154-165)

62-66. Average number of years of total education experience of the administrative, supervisory, kindergarten/elementary/secondary teaching, special education teaching, and library/guidance staffs. (p. 166-175)

67-70. Ratio of school membership to the administrative, supervisory, kindergarten/elementary/secondary teaching, and library/guidance staffs. (p. 176-191)

71. Percent of teachers who are men. (p. 192-195)

72. Percent of teachers teaching out of certification at least 50% of the time. (p. 196-199)

73. Teacher turnover rate, 1982/83-1983/84. (p. 200-201)

S7145–1.5: Financial Data, and Miscellaneous

TEACHERS' SALARIES

74-77. Salary schedules for teachers: with bachelor's and master's degrees and zero years experience; with bachelor's degree plus 18 hours and 10 years experience; and with master's degree and 17 years experience. (p. 202-209)

78. Average total annual salary for classroom teachers. (p. 210-211)

TAX ASSESSMENTS AND REVENUES

79-80. Total tax per capita assessed against real/personal property excluding motor vehicles for county and school purposes, 1983, by county [only]. (p. 212-215)

81. Per capita total expenditures for public schools, by county [only]. (p. 216-217)

82-85. Amount of revenue for operating funds received per pupil in ADM from local, State, and Federal sources, and from [all] sources [combined]. (p. 218-233)

86-88. Percent change in revenue for operating funds received from local taxes, State sources, and local/State/Federal sources, 1982/83-1983/84. (p. 234-245)

89. Increase in revenue received per pupil for operating purposes, 1973/74 and 1983/84. (p. 246-249)

90. Revenue received per pupil in ADM for capital outlay and debt retirement purposes. (p. 250-253)

91-92. Assessed valuation per pupil in ADM, 1983/84; and change from 1973/74. (p. 254-261)

93. Wealth (fiscal capacity) per pupil [in ADM]. (p. 262-265)

94-95. Total tax levy in mills, 1983/84; and change from 1973/74. (p. 266-273)

96. Local tax effort [including ability index, equalized and actual tax revenues, and tax effort]. (p. 274-277)

EXPENDITURES

97. Current operating expenditures per pupil in ADM. (p. 278-281)

98. Increase in expenditures per pupil, 1973/74 and 1983/84. (p. 282-285)

99-102. Current operating expenditures per pupil in ADM for general administration, instructional services, plant operations/maintenance, and auxiliary services. (p. 286-301)

103-104. Expenditures per pupil in ADM for capital outlay and debt retirement. (p. 302-309)

MISCELLANEOUS

105. Average number of pupils in membership per school plant. (p. 310-313)

106. Percent of school plants on sites of 11 or more acres. (p. 314-317)

107. Area in square miles. (p. 318-319)

S7155   SOUTH CAROLINA Employment Security Commission

S7155–2   **SOUTH CAROLINA EMPLOYMENT TRENDS**
Monthly. Approx. 25 p. SRI/MF/complete, shipped quarterly

Monthly report on South Carolina employment, earnings, hours, and production workers, by industry group. Includes employment data for women, and by county and MSA. Data are compiled by the Employment Security Commission, and are issued approximately 2 months after month of coverage.

Report generally contains brief articles on economic and employment conditions; summary features on employment service activities and plant openings/expansions; and 15 monthly tables.

Monthly tables are listed below; most appear in all issues. All additional features with substantial statistical content on topics not covered in monthly tables are described, as they appear, under "Statistical Features." Nonstatistical features are not covered.

Availability: South Carolina Employment Security Commission, Labor Market Information Division, PO Box 995, Columbia SC 29202, †; SRI/MF/complete, shipped quarterly.

Issues reviewed during 1985: Sept. 1984-Aug. 1985 (D).

MONTHLY TABLES:
[Data are shown for current month, preceding month, and same month of preceding year.]

1. Civilian labor force summary [by employment status, for State and 3 MSAs].

2. Summary of monthly earnings of manufacturing workers [for State and 3 MSAs].

3. Summary of monthly overtime hours of [durable and nondurable goods] manufacturing workers.

4. Productivity index [for production workers, durable and nondurable goods, textiles, and apparel].

5. Nonfarm wage/salary employment by major industry division and selected industry group.

6. Wage/salary manufacturing employment [by selected industry group].

7. Seasonally adjusted nonfarm wage/salary employment by industry [division and selected group].

8-10. [Data in table 5 are repeated for 6 MSAs and for female employment.]

11-12. Estimated number of production workers and average earnings and hours in manufacturing [by industry group, for State and 3 MSAs].

13. Nonfarm wage/salary [manufacturing and nonmanufacturing] employment for [individual] counties.

14. Labor force and unemployment by county.

15. Labor force, employment, and unemployment for selected cities.

STATISTICAL FEATURES:

S7155–2.601: Sept. 1984

1983 ANNUAL PAY FOR SOUTH CAROLINA'S METROPOLITAN AREAS

(p. 10) Article, with 1 table showing South Carolina average annual wages, by MSA, 1982-83, with comparison to U.S. and rankings among all MSAs.

EMPHASIS ON VETERAN SERVICES DURING NOV.

(p. 11) Article, with 2 tables showing South Carolina veterans by period of service, Mar. 31, 1984; and veterans receiving various job services, July 1-Sept. 1984 period. Data are from the Veterans Administration and the South Carolina Employment Security Commission.

S7155–2.602: Nov. 1984

NONAGRICULTURAL EMPLOYMENT PROJECTED TO 1990, ANNUAL FEATURE

(p. 8, 23) Annual article, with 1 table showing South Carolina nonagricultural employment, by industry group, 1982-83 and projected 1990. Data are from the South Carolina Employment Security Commission.

S7155–3   SOUTH CAROLINA LABOR MARKET REVIEW, 1985
Annual.   July 1985.
198 p. var. paging.
SRI/MF/complete

Annual planning report, for 1985, identifying South Carolina population groups most in need of employment services. Includes data on employment by industry and occupation, and population and labor force characteristics. Also includes data on State economic outlook, labor turnover, job service activities and applicants, the insured unemployed, and other topics; selected data by county and MSA; and selected trends from as early as 1930 and projections through 2000.

Data are primarily from State agencies, Census Bureau, and BLS.

Contents:

a. Contents listing and introduction (p. iii-vi); geography and area statistics summary, including 1 summary population table, and 2 tables showing climatic characteristics by State division and selected MSA (p. I.1-I.5).

b. Economic developments and outlook, with 6 tables showing trends in industry wages and employment, various periods 1973-83; number of plants, new employment, and investment, for new and expanded plants, 1960-84; and textile mill employment losses, by county, 1973-84 period. (p. II.1-II.11)

c. Labor and population data, in 8 sections, with narrative summaries, 6 maps, 51 charts, and 102 tables; tables, and selected charts with substantial data not covered in tables, are described below. (p. III.1-X.23)

d. Appendix, with glossary and directories. (p. A1-A13)

Availability: South Carolina Employment Security Commission, Labor Market Information Division, PO Box 995, Columbia SC 29202, †; SRI/MF/complete.

TABLES AND CHARTS:
[Data are for South Carolina, unless otherwise noted.]

S7155–3.1: Employment, Tourism, and Population

EMPLOYMENT AND TOURISM

a. Nonfarm wage/salary employment by industry division and major manufacturing group, for U.S., South Carolina, and 3 MSAs, 1984. 4 tables. (p. III.2-III.5)

b. Travel expenditures by type; travel industry payroll and employment by industry category; and travel-generated tax revenues by level of government; with detail by county; 1983. 5 tables. (p. III.7-III.10)

POPULATION

c. Population, by age, sex, race (also including Indian/Eskimo/Aleut and Asian/Pacific Islander), MSA, and county, various periods 1950-2000; births and deaths, 1980-82 period, and migration, various periods 1965-82, all by county; and population aged 65/over employment, median income, poverty status, living alone, and home ownership, by county, 1980. 15 tables. (p. IV.2-IV.18)

S7155–3.2: Labor Force, Insured Unemployment, and Job Service Activities

LABOR FORCE

a. Labor force by employment status; unemployment by duration and reason; employment and/or unemployment, by occupation, full- and part-time status, and county; and monthly unemployment rates; generally by race and sex, with selected data by age group and comparisons to total U.S., including unemployment rates by State; various years 1960-86. 23 tables. (p. V.1-V.28)

EMPLOYMENT

b. Nonfarm total and female employment, and manufacturing average earnings and hours, generally by major industry group, 1983-84, with some projections for 1990, and female employment trends from 1930; employment covered by employment security law, by industry division, 3rd quarter 1983-84; manufacturing overtime hours, by month, 1983-84; South Carolina employment as percent of U.S. total, by selected industry group, June 1984; and U.S. employment and average wages, by State, year ended June 1984. 1 chart and 12 tables. (p. VI.2-VI.19)

c. Job openings due to growth and separations, and occupations with fastest employment growth, and greatest employment decrease, all by detailed occupation, 1980-

90 period; manufacturing and non-manufacturing labor turnover (new hires, separations, and rehires), FY80-84; and new hire, separation, and rehire rates, by industry division and county, FY84. 8 tables. (p. VI.21-VI.31)

INSURED UNEMPLOYMENT

d. Insured unemployment average volume and rate, by MSA and county of residence, 1983-84; insured unemployment, by industry division, occupation, duration of unemployment, sex, and age; and long-term unemployment distribution, and percent of unemployment insurance claimants experiencing long-term unemployment, by county, 1984. 7 tables (p. VII.2-VII.7)

JOB SERVICE

e. Job service applicants by service provided and occupational category, and work incentive program registrants, all by applicant characteristics, variously including age, sex, race, educational attainment, and veteran, handicapped, and migrant status; job applicants, openings received and filled, and average wage, by occupational group and detailed job title; and Targeted Jobs Tax Credit program eligibility determinations and certifications; various periods, FY84. 7 tables. (p. VIII.2-VIII.14)

f. Labor force groups especially in need of job services: as percent of total population and total job service applicants; and distribution by age, race, sex, occupation, and other characteristics; for veterans, minorities, youth, handicapped, and women, FY84 or CY84. 29 charts. (p. IX.3-IX.13)

S7155–3.3: Income and Education

a. Income: total and/or per capita personal income, by county, MSA, and source (including earnings by industry division, transfer payments, and dividends/interest/rent), with selected comparisons to other States and U.S.; median household and family income, by county; and persons below poverty level, by age, race, and county; various years 1969-84. 12 tables. (p. X.2-X.13)

b. Education: public and private/special/denominational schools and enrollment, public school vocational and adult education enrollment, public high school graduates and percent entering higher education and employment, and population age 25/over by educational attainment, all by county; and public and private higher education enrollment, by institutional category; various years 1960/61-1982/83. 8 tables. (p. X.15-X.22)

c. Education summary trends, including instructional staff by type and educational attainment; public and private/special/denominational schools by level and/or type; and handicapped children receiving services in public schools; 1970 and 1982-83. 1 table. (p. X.23)

S7165   SOUTH CAROLINA
Board of
Financial Institutions

S7165–1   SEVENTY-EIGHTH ANNUAL REPORT OF THE STATE BOARD OF FINANCIAL INSTITUTIONS of the State of South Carolina, 1984
Annual. Sept. 5, 1984. 70 p.
LC 81-642985.
SRI/MF/complete

Annual report on financial condition of South Carolina State-chartered financial institutions, FY84, presenting assets and liabilities, by institution, for banks, trust companies, and savings and loan assns; and restricted and supervised consumer finance company finances and loan activity, 1983.

Also includes data on Board of Financial Institutions revenues, expenditures, and licensing activity; aggregate bank income and expense analysis by deposit size; credit unions and funeral homes, by city; and consumer finance company delinquent account legal actions.

Contains contents listing (p. 2); and reports of Commissioner of Banking and Director of Consumer Finance Division, with lists of financial institution branches, offices, and status changes, and 24 tables (p. 4-70).

Availability: South Carolina Board of Financial Institutions, Commissioner of Banking, 1026 Sumter St., Rm. 217, Columbia SC 29201, †; SRI/MF/complete.

S7175   SOUTH CAROLINA
Department of
Health and
Environmental Control

S7175–1   SOUTH CAROLINA VITAL AND MORBIDITY STATISTICS, 1983, Volume I
Annual. Jan. 1985.
9+vii+153 p.
ISSN 0094-6338.
LC 78-645478.
SRI/MF/complete

Annual report on South Carolina vital statistics, covering population, births, deaths by cause, marriages and divorces, and communicable diseases, 1983, with selected trends from 1950. Includes data by sex, race, age, county, and city. Data are from State records.

Contains preface, and listings of contents, tables, and charts (9 p.); and the following:

a. Introduction, methodology, and definitions, with 2 tables showing births and deaths allocated by residence and occurrence, by race, 1983; and resident live births, by race (including Indian, Chinese, Japanese, and other) of mother and father, 1983. (p. i-vii)

b. 9 summary and trend charts, and 1 chart and 87 tables listed below, arranged in 6 sections. (p. 1-145)

c. Appendix, with facsimiles of vital statistics certificates, and list of codes and comparabili-

ty ratios for 72 causes of death, and 10 causes of infant death, according to the International Classification of Diseases, 8th and 9th Revisions. (p. 146-153)

Companion Vol. II, *Detailed Mortality Statistics,* is covered in SRI under S7175-2.

Availability: South Carolina Department of Health and Environmental Control, Biostatistics Division, Vital Records and Public Health Statistics Office, 2600 Bull St., Columbia SC 29201, ‡; SRI/MF/complete.

TABLES:
[All tables show data for South Carolina.]

S7175–1.1: Vital Statistics and Population Summary
[Unless otherwise noted, data are for 1964-83. Most tables show residence data and include rates.]

1. Population, live births, deaths, marriages, and divorces, by race. (p. 1)

2. Out-of-wedlock, low weight births, fetal deaths, death under 1 year and under 28 days, and maternal deaths, by race. (p. 2)

3. Mortality from selected causes of death, by race, 1974-83. (p. 3-4)

[A] [Population by age group, 1970 and 1980.] (p. 5)

4. Population, live births, deaths, and natural increase. (p. 6)

5. Estimates of population, by race by county, July 1983. (p. 8)

S7175–1.2: Births
[Unless otherwise noted, data are for 1983. Most tables show residence data. Data by attendant are shown for physician, midwife (generally with breakdowns for in and out of hospital), other, and self-attended.]

STATE TOTALS
[Tables 6, 8, and 11-15 show data by race.]
6. Total live births and birth rate, 1950-83. (p. 10)

7. Live births by attendant by place of delivery [hospital/clinic, doctor's office, en route, and residence]. (p. 11)

8. Percentages of births occurring in hospitals, 1974-83. (p. 11)

9-10. Percentage distribution of out-of-wedlock and [total] live births, by age of mother, 1979-83. (p. 12)

11. Live births by birth weight, with percentages of births in weight group. (p. 13)

12. Percent of births less than 2,500 grams, by age of mother. (p. 13)

13-14. Fertility rates and population of females age 15-44 [selected years 1960-83]. (p. 15)

15. Sex ratio of males per 100 females, 1979-83. (p. 16)

BIRTHS BY COUNTY
[Tables 16-30 generally show data by race and/or county.]

16-17. Live births and birth rates: each county and places of 2,500 or more population (residence and occurrence data). (p. 17-24)

18-19. Live births by sex (residence and occurrence data). (p. 25-26)

20-20A. Live births by number of prenatal care visits. (p. 27-29)

21-23A. Live births by month prenatal care began and by attendant (residence and occurrence data). (p. 30-38)

24. Live births and percent of live births, by marital status, by age of mother. (p. 39)

25-27. Live births: by age of mother; to mothers less than 20 years old; and by birth weight and age of mother. (p. 40-44)

28-29A. Low weight live births, and percent of low weight live births; and low weight live births by age of mother. (p. 45-48)

30. Live births by birth weight. (p. 49-54)

31. Out-of-wedlock live births and percent of live births out-of-wedlock. (p. 55)

32. Out-of-wedlock live births by age of mother. (p. 56)

CONGENITAL ANOMALIES

33-34. Live births with reported congenital malformations [and rates; and] by type [State total only]; 1981-83. (p. 57-58)

S7175–1.3: Deaths
[Tables show residence data, 1983, unless otherwise noted. Many tables show data by race.]

STATE TOTALS
35. Total deaths and death rate, 1950-83. (p. 60)

36. Percentage distribution of deaths, by age, 1964 and 1983. (p. 61)

37. Leading causes of infant death, by age at death. (p. 62)

38. Maternal deaths by cause and age. (p. 63)

39. Violent deaths with rates, by type, 1979-83. (p. 64)

40. Types of accidental deaths, by sex. (p. 64)

41-42. Methods of suicidal and homicidal deaths, by sex. (p. 65)

43. Distribution of malignant neoplasms, by site. (p. 66)

44. Deaths from major cardiovascular diseases. (p. 67)

45. Mortality from 10 leading causes of death. (p. 68)

[B] Percentage distribution of the 10 leading causes of death and deaths from all causes, by sex. [chart] (p. 68)

46. Mortality from 5 leading causes of death in specified age groups. (p. 69)

DEATHS BY COUNTY
[Tables 47-64 show data by race and county, unless otherwise noted.]

47-48. Deaths and death rates: each county and places of 2,500 or more population (residence and occurrence data). (p. 70-77)

49-50. Deaths by sex (residence and occurrence data). (p. 78-79)

TL 51-51A. Deaths and death rates from selected causes, by sex [rates shown for State only]. (p. 80-103)

52. Deaths from selected causes, by age and sex [State total only]. (p. 104-113)

53-54A. Deaths by certifier and burial disposition (occurrence data). (p. 114-116)

55-56. Major causes of accidental death (residence and occurrence data) [not by race]. (p. 117-118)

57-58. Deaths from suicides by method and from homicides by type (occurrence data) [not by race]. (p. 119-120)

59-62. Infant, neonatal, and postneonatal deaths and mortality rates. (p. 120-127)

63-65. Fetal and perinatal deaths and mortality rates, and fetal deaths by age of mother. (p. 128-130)

66-67. Maternal deaths and maternal mortality rate (residence and occurrence data). (p. 131)

S7175–1.4: Marriages, Divorces, and Annulments

[All data are for 1983. Data by residential status are for resident and nonresident.]

68. Marriages by race [white, black, Indian, Chinese, Japanese, and other] of bride and groom. (p. 133)

69. Marriages by county in which license was issued, by residential status [of bride and groom]. (p. 134)

70. Marriages by residential status [of bride and groom], by county of marriage. (p. 135)

71-72. Marriages by race, by residential status, by age groups of brides and grooms. (p. 136-137)

73. Marriages by age of bride, by age of groom. (p. 138)

74. Divorces/annulments [and] number of children involved, by race: each county. (p. 139)

75. Divorces by plaintiff [and] legal grounds for decree; [and annulments]: each county. (p. 140)

76. Divorces by age groups, by race [of husband and of wife]. (p. 141)

77. Divorces by duration of marriage, by plaintiff, by legal grounds for decree; [and annulments]. (p. 142)

S7175–1.5: Morbidity

[Data are shown by county of occurrence, 1983, with 1982 totals.]

78. Reported cases of selected communicable diseases. (p. 143-144)

79. Reported cases of venereal disease [by type]. (p. 145)

S7175–2   DETAILED MORTALITY STATISTICS, South Carolina, 1983, Volume II
Annual. Oct. 1984.
4+141 p.
SRI/MF/complete

Annual report on South Carolina deaths, by cause, age, sex, and race, 1983, compiled by the Office of Vital Records and Public Health Statistics.

Contains data interpretation, and contents and code guides (4 p.); and 1 extended table showing resident deaths, by detailed cause, cross-tabulated by age, sex, and race (p. 1-141). Data are arranged according to the *International Classification of Diseases, 9th Revision.*

Companion Vol. I, *Vital and Morbidity Statistics,* is covered in SRI under S7175-1.

Availability: South Carolina Department of Health and Environmental Control, Biostatistics Division, Vital Records and Public Health Statistics Office, 2600 Bull St., Columbia SC 29201, ‡; SRI/MF/complete.

S7185   SOUTH CAROLINA Commission on Higher Education

S7185–2   STATE OF SOUTH CAROLINA HIGHER EDUCATION STATISTICAL ABSTRACT, Seventh Edition
Annual. Apr. 1985.
iii+69 p.
LC 72-624835.
SRI/MF/complete

Annual report on South Carolina higher education enrollment, faculty, degrees awarded, and finances, 1984, with trends from fall 1975. Most data are shown by public and/or private institution.

Contains table index (p. iii); and 1 chart, and 20 tables described below.

Availability: South Carolina Commission on Higher Education, 1429 Senate St., Rm. 1104, Columbia SC 29201, †; SRI/MF/complete.

TABLES:
[Unless otherwise noted, data by institution are shown for public senior colleges and universities.]

a. Enrollment trends: head count and FTE, by degree level and institution, fall 1975-84. 4 tables. (p. 1-4)

b. Fall 1984 enrollment, FTE and/or head count: by degree level and for entering freshmen, with summary percent change from 1982-83; by race for undergraduates and graduate students; and by sex for all students and nonresident aliens; all by public and private institution, including technical and junior colleges. 6 tables. (p. 5-16)

c. Faculty/student data: selected student characteristics, including percent from South Carolina; FTE faculty, by academic rank; faculty credit hour production and teaching hours; student/faculty ratio; and average students per class; all by institution, fall 1983-84. 2 tables. (p. 17-35)

d. Degrees awarded: aggregate by sex, race, and academic discipline; and by public and private institution; all by degree level, for the period July 1, 1983-June 30, 1984. 3 tables. (p. 36-42)

e. Finances: revenues by source and expenditures by function, by institution, 1983/84; State appropriations by institution, and aggregate for technical education, tuition aid grants to private colleges, and education dept appropriations, with comparisons to total State revenues, 1975/76-1984/85. 4 tables. (p. 43-65)

f. FTE employees, by function and institution, fall 1984. 1 table. (p. 67-68)

S7190   SOUTH CAROLINA Department of Highways and Public Transportation

S7190–1   ANNUAL REPORT OF THE SOUTH CAROLINA DEPARTMENT OF HIGHWAYS AND PUBLIC TRANSPORTATION to the General Assembly, for Period July 1, 1983-June 30, 1984
Annual. [1985.]
132 p.+foldout.
LC 78-646535.
SRI/MF/complete, current & previous year reports

Annual report of the South Carolina Dept of Highways and Public Transportation, FY84, with trends from FY30. Covers revenues and expenditures, highway construction and maintenance, motor vehicle registrations, driver's licenses, and support services. Also includes summary traffic arrest and accident data, and dept employment and payroll.

Contains contents listing, personnel lists, and introduction with 1 summary financial chart and table (p. 3-15); and narrative report, with 53 tables, as follows:

a. Highway construction costs by type of material, compared to Federal Highway Administration construction cost index and Atlanta CPI, 1967-83; fuel consumption, selected years 1940-83; average speed and percent of motorists exceeding limits, by highway type, FY82-83; and highway mileage by road width and traffic volume, road surveys, bridge and railroad crossing projects and finances, and expenditures for right-of-way, FY84 with trends from 1970s. 10 tables. (p. 17-34)

b. Highway maintenance program costs, with detail by highway type, FY83-84; and highway patrol arrests for traffic and truck size/weight violations, FY84. 4 tables. (p. 36-40)

c. Motor vehicle registrations and receipts, primarily 1982-84, with trends from 1945; driver exam and licensing activities, various years FY82-84; vehicle titles issued, 1958-FY84; Interagency Council on Public Transportation activities, FY84-85; number of traffic accidents and fatalities, 1982-83; and economic loss from accidents by county, 1981-83. 14 tables. (p. 41-59)

d. Damage claims/suits and State damage recoveries, various years FY75-84; and worker's compensation payments by type, equipment costs, and radio and other electronic equipment in use, FY84. 6 tables. (p. 61-69)

e. Statistical section, with 19 detailed tables listed below, and dept organizational chart. (p. 76-132, and foldout)

Previous report, for FY83, was also reviewed in 1985, and is also available on SRI microfiche, under this number [Annual. [1984.] 120 p.+foldout. ‡]. Previous report is substantially similar in format and content, but omits detailed data on traffic law violations.

Availability: South Carolina Department of Highways and Public Transportation, PO Box 191, Columbia SC 29202, ‡; SRI/MF/complete.

DETAILED TABLES:

S7190-1.1: Highway Dept Finances and Employment, Vehicle Registrations and Driver's Licenses, and Traffic Law Violations

FINANCIAL STATEMENTS AND NET EXPENDITURES

[Data are for FY83-84.]

1-2. Comparative balance sheet; and comparative statement of general fund revenues [and] other receipts [by source], and expenditures [by agency and object]. (p. 77-85)

3A-5B. Statement of changes in invested capital, reserves, and fund balances; and of receipts and disbursements [for] trust funds, and special deposits fund [by category of deposit]. (p. 86-96)

6. Net expenditures by objective classification. (p. 97-101)

CONSTRUCTION FUNDS, FUNDED DEBT, DEPT PAYROLL, AND HIGHWAY MILES

[Data are as of June 30, 1984.]

7. Status of allocated highway construction funds [Federal and State]. (p. 102-105)

8. Funded debt, digest of obligations [by year due], and comparison with debt limitation. (p. 106)

9. Payroll statistics report [employment by category, and total employment and payroll compared to June 1983, all by organizational unit]. (p. 107-113)

10. Mileage summary record by counties [and road type]. (p. 114-115)

VEHICLE REGISTRATION, DRIVER'S LICENSES, AND TRAFFIC LAW VIOLATIONS

11-13. Net motor vehicle registrations and receipts, by classification and counties, 1982 and/or 1983. (p. 116-124)

14-15. Passenger vehicle and truck registrations by counties, 1977-83. [Table 15 is erroneously numbered 14 in the document.] (p. 125-126)

16. Net permanent and 5-year vehicle registration by classification.(p. 127-128)

17. Driver's licenses issued and withdrawn [FY30-84]. (p. 129-130)

18. Summary by counties of driving privileges withdrawn [by cause and age group], FY84. (p. 131)

19. Traffic law violations [warnings issued, caseloads, case dispositions, and bonds posted with county/city courts, by type of violation], FY84. (p. 132)

S7190-2   1984 SOUTH CAROLINA TRAFFIC ACCIDENTS
Annual. [1985.] 64 p.
LC 41-52472.
SRI/MF/complete

Annual report on South Carolina traffic accidents, injuries, and fatalities, by accident and vehicle type, location, time, and other circumstances; and by driver, victim, and vehicle characteristics; 1984, with trends from 1955.

Also includes data on economic loss from accidents, by county; licensed drivers, motor vehicle registrations, and miles of travel; driver and pedestrian alcohol use, including driver blood alcohol content levels; safety belt use; and detail for motorcycle, school bus, urban and rural, and military vehicle accidents.

Report contains highlights and contents listing (p. 2-9); and 25 charts and 27 tables (p. 10-63).

Availability: South Carolina Department of Highways and Public Transportation, PO Box 191, Columbia SC 29202, †; SRI/MF/complete.

S7195   SOUTH CAROLINA Department of Insurance

S7195-1   SEVENTY-SEVENTH ANNUAL REPORT OF THE DEPARTMENT OF INSURANCE of South Carolina
Annual. [1984.]   iii+249 p.
LC 9-7968.
SRI/MF/complete

Annual report on South Carolina insurance industry financial condition and underwriting activity, by company, 1983. Covers total assets, liabilities, capital, surplus, and South Carolina premiums written, for property/casualty/allied line and life/accident/health insurance companies; with detailed balance sheet and income/expense data for South Carolina State-chartered companies.

Also includes underwriting trends from 1950; and Insurance Dept revenues by source, expenditures by object, allocation to counties of additional premium tax and fire dept fund tax, and regulatory and consumer assistance caseloads, 1983 or FY84.

Company data are from annual statements filed by individual insurers.

Contains contents listing and legislative recommendations (p. iii, 1-9); Insurance Dept report, with 14 tables (p. 12-37); financial tables, arranged alphabetically by company (p. 41-167); and directory and detailed data for South Carolina State-chartered companies (p. 170-249).

Availability: South Carolina Department of Insurance, PO Box 4067, Columbia SC 29240, ‡; SRI/MF/complete.

S7197   SOUTH CAROLINA Judicial Department

S7197-1   ANNUAL REPORT, 1983, Judicial Department of South Carolina
Annual. [1985.] 133 p.
SRI/MF/complete

Annual report on South Carolina judicial system, including caseloads and case dispositions for supreme, appellate, general sessions, common pleas, family, magistrate, and municipal courts, 1983, with trends from 1973.

Trial court data are shown by court location (and by presiding official for magistrate courts); data include criminal and civil proceedings, with detail as applicable for driving under the influence and other traffic cases, jury and nonjury trials, bail proceedings, and arrest and search warrant issuances.

Also includes data on judicial dept appropriations; expenditures for defense of indigents, by county; grievances and disciplinary actions concerning attorneys and judges; bar examinations and results; age of pending cases; and court employees, costs, and revenues, by county.

Contains contents listing (p. 4-5); and report in 5 sections, with narrative description interspersed with 7 charts and 47 tables (p. 6-133).

This is the 5th annual report.

Availability: South Carolina Judicial Department, Court Administrator's Office, PO Box 50447, Columbia SC 29250, †; SRI/MF/complete.

S7205   SOUTH CAROLINA Law Enforcement Division

S7205-1   CRIME IN SOUTH CAROLINA, 1984
Annual.   Apr. 15, 1985.
2+61 p.
LC 78-620956.
SRI/MF/complete

Annual report on South Carolina crimes and arrests, 1984, with selected trends from 1982 and aggregate summary of police fatalities from 1969.

Covers crimes by Index offense, by reporting agency arranged by county; and arrests by Index and non-Index offense, by county, and by age, race, and sex; with selected rates.

Also includes statewide data on crime clearances, and crimes by type of weapon and property involved and other circumstances, by Index offense; value of property stolen and recovered; murder victims by sex, and rape victims, by age and race; and police officers killed and assaulted, by type of weapon and other circumstances.

Index offenses are murder, rape, robbery, aggravated assault, breaking/entering, larceny, motor vehicle theft, and arson.

Data are from reports of State and local law enforcement agencies, submitted under the Uniform Crime Reporting (UCR) Program.

Contains contents listing (1 p.); UCR Program description (p. 1-3); and 12 charts and 42 tables, interspersed with brief narrative summaries (p. 4-61).

Availability: South Carolina Law Enforcement Division, Uniform Crime Report Section, PO Box 21398, Columbia SC 29221-1398, †; SRI/MF/complete.

S7210   SOUTH CAROLINA State Library

S7210-1   FIFTEENTH ANNUAL REPORT: THE SOUTH CAROLINA STATE LIBRARY, July 1, 1983-June 30, 1984
Annual. [1984.]
63 p.+foldouts.
LC 78-648699.
SRI/MF/complete

Annual report on South Carolina public and institutional library finances, services, holdings, and staff, FY84.

Contains contents listing (p. 2); narrative report, with text statistics, on South Carolina library history, services, and activities (p. 3-48); and 9 tables, listed below, interspersed with directories (p. 49-63 and 3 foldouts).

Availability: South Carolina State Library, PO Box 11469, Columbia SC 29211, ‡; SRI/MF/complete.

TABLES:
[Tables show data for FY84, unless otherwise noted.]

[1] State library collections [summary of holdings by detailed type, as of June 30, 1983-84, with additions and withdrawals during year]. (p. 49-50)

[2] State library loan statistics [including requests received, books loaned, and photocopies sent, by requesting library; and total loans, by type of library and material]. (p. 51)

[3] State library, State expenditures [includes salaries/wages and 28 other expense items]. (p. 52)

[4] State library, Federal expenditures [by title and project, FY82-84 funds]. (p. 53-54)

[5] Public library [per capita] bookstock, circulation, and [total and local] support, by county. (p. 62)

[6] Public library statistics [libraries and librarians; bookstock, circulation, and population; and library income; FY44, FY56, FY74, and FY84]. (p. 63)

[7] Public libraries, annual library statistics [1980 population of area taxed for support; and operating income by source, expenditures by object, capital outlay, holdings, total and juvenile users and book circulation, interlibrary loans and borrowings, average weekly reference transactions, and number of branches/stations and bookmobiles; all by library]. (1 foldout)

[8] State supported institutions library statistics [residents, operating expenses by object, and funding; and summary data on holdings and professional and nonprofessional personnel; all by institution, FY85]. (1 foldout)

[9] Colleges and universities annual library statistics [operating expenses by object, holdings, and professional and nonprofessional FTE personnel; hours of student assistance; and total enrollment; all by institution]. (1 foldout)

S7252   SOUTH CAROLINA
Department of
Social Services

S7252–1   STATISTICAL REPORT, South Carolina Department of Social Services
Monthly.   Approx. 25 p.
SRI/MF/complete, shipped quarterly

Monthly report on South Carolina public welfare programs, including cases, recipients, and payments, by program and county. Covers AFDC, general disability assistance (GDA), medical assistance, food stamps, and work incentive (WIN) activities. Report is issued approximately 4 months after month of coverage.

Contains table and chart listings; 5-9 charts primarily illustrating recent trends, but also showing percent of population participating in food stamp program and receiving AFDC; and 22 monthly tables, listed below.

A slightly less detailed annual report on this subject is also available from the Office of Public Information of the issuing agency, but is not covered in SRI.

Availability: South Carolina Department of Social Services, Research and Statistics, PO Box 1520, Columbia SC 29202-1520, †; SRI/MF/complete, shipped quarterly.

Issues reviewed during 1985: Sept. 1984-July 1985 (D) (Vol. 48, Nos. 3-12; Vol. 49, No. 1).

MONTHLY TABLES:
[Data are for month of coverage, unless otherwise noted. Tables 4-13 and 15-22 show data by county. Table order may vary.]

APPLICATIONS

1-3. Cases approved, applications denied/otherwise terminated, and cases closed, for public assistance money payments, by category [AFDC and GDA], by reason.

4. AFDC money payment applications [pending, received, approved, and not approved].

ASSISTANCE PAYMENTS AND SERVICES

5-6. AFDC money payments [and cases, recipients, and children, for month of coverage and fiscal year] to date.

7. GDA and SSI optional supplement gross money payments [and cases, and GDA persons].

8. CWS [child welfare service] foster care recipients and gross payments [total, State and local funds, and adoption supplement].

9. AFDC foster care and IV-E adoption supplement recipients and payments.

FOOD STAMPS

10-11. Food stamp participation [coupon issuance and SSI/cash out, for households, persons, and benefits, for month of coverage and fiscal year] to date.

12-13. Food stamp monthly activity report [applications and disposition]; and Project Fair food stamp recipient claim collections, by type [intentional program violation/fraud and non-fraud client and agency error].

MEDICALLY NEEDY
[Titles of tables 14-16 begin "Medically needy program..." Tables show data for total, pregnant women, and children under 18. Tables 14 and 16 begin with Dec. 1984 issue. Table 15 begins with Jan. 1985 issue.]

14. Approvals, denials, and closures, by reason.

15. Applications [received, dispositions, and pending applications].

16. Cases receiving assistance.

WIN ACTIVITIES

17. WIN activities [initial certifications, and amounts of AFDC grant reductions].

SERVICES, VOLUNTEERS, AND LOCAL FUNDS

18. Title XX services authorization summary [including adoption, homemaker, and adult and child protective services].

19. Volunteer services report [hours worked, volunteers, and cash and in-kind contributions, month of coverage and fiscal year to date].

20. Disbursement of local funds [cases, persons, and payments, for medical and other payments].

MEDICAL ASSISTANCE
[Tables begin with the July 1985 issue.]

21-22. Medical assistance only: applications [pending, received, approved, and not approved, total excluding nursing homes, and for nursing homes only]; and recipients by category [including eligibility limitations, nursing homes, foster care, general hospital, and 1977 pass-along].

S7255   SOUTH CAROLINA
Tax Commission

S7255–1   SEVENTIETH ANNUAL REPORT OF THE SOUTH CAROLINA TAX COMMISSION, 1984
Annual.   Sept. 1, 1984.
105 p.
LC 16-27141.
SRI/MF/complete

Annual report, for FY84, on South Carolina tax revenues and collections by type, allocations to localities, and property assessments by county and company, with selected comparisons to FY80. Also includes data on corporate income tax returns by business classification, and personal income tax returns by tax liability bracket.

Data are compiled by the State Tax Commission.

Contains contents and table listing (p. 6-7); summary Tax Commission information, including 4 summary charts, and 4 tables listed below (p. 8-17); 4 division reports, with 48 tables, also listed below (p. 18-92); narrative report of attorney general on tax litigation (p. 93-103); and subject index (p. 104-105).

Availability: South Carolina Tax Commission, Box 125, Columbia SC 29202, †; SRI/MF/complete.

TABLES:
[Data are shown for South Carolina, FY84, unless otherwise noted.]

S7255–1.1: Summary Data, and Income and Estate Division

SUMMARY DATA

1-3. Tax Commission comparative revenue statement (net), and percent change for major tax collections, FY83-84; and total General Fund revenue collections, [FY80-84; all by tax type]. (p. 15-16)

4. Expenses of the Tax Commission [with appropriations and unexpended balance, by object], FY84. (p. 17)

INCOME TAXES

5. Statement showing amount of cash collected by the Income and Estate Division: [from bank, savings and loan assn, corporation license, estate, gift, income, and insurance taxes, and unclaimed property]. (p. 18)

6. Distribution of 7½% income tax to counties. (p. 19)

7-8. Analysis of 1982-83 corporation returns by [SIC 4-digit] business classification [number of returns and amount of tax]. (p. 21-22)

9-12. Analysis of 1982-83 corporation and individual income tax returns [number of returns and amount of tax, by tax liability bracket]. (p. 23-25)

13-14. Number of returns, adjusted gross income, taxable income, income tax liability, total exemptions and deductions, and total tax, by adjusted gross income classes, 1983. (p. 26-27)

ESTATE AND BANK TAXES

15. Recapitulation of probate judges' commissions paid [by county] on account of inheritance/estate taxes. (p. 29)

16. Bank tax distributions [to cities arranged by county]. (p. 30-35)

S7255–1.2: Sales and License Division

SUMMARY

17. Statement showing the amount of cash collected by the Sales and License Division [for 21 tax types]. (p. 36)

LICENSES

18-20. Business license, coin operated devices, and documentary stamp tax total net collections. (p. 38-39)

GASOLINE

21-22. Gasoline tax collected [by month]; and distributions to counties. (p. 40-41)

23. Gasoline tax refunded on gasoline purchased and used solely for agricultural purposes [number of claims and amount by county]. (p. 42-43)

24. Distribution of watercraft gasoline tax to counties [boats registered and amount distributed]. (p. 44-45)

25. Refund on tax paid on motor fuels purchased by carriers in excess of that used on South Carolina highways [by month]. (p. 46)

BEVERAGES

26. Soft/bottled drinks tax total net collections [by type]. (p. 47)

27-28. Alcoholic liquors tax collections [from retail, wholesale, additional case, and excise taxes; surtax; and penalties; all by month]. (p. 48-49)

29-30. Alcoholic liquors tax distributions [total to counties and selected cities arranged by county; and by county for] mini bottles. (p. 50-57)

31-32. Beer and wine tax net collections; and beer/wine tax distributions [to counties and selected cities arranged by county]. (p. 57-64)

SALES AND USE TAXES

33. Collections from the retail license tax [number of returns and amount paid, by license fee amount]. (p. 66)

34. Collections of sales/use tax by [SIC 4-digit] business classification [FY82-84]. (p. 67-68)

35. Analysis of sales/use tax returns [number of returns and amount of tax, by tax liability size]. (p. 69)

36. Sales and use tax total active accounts. (p. 69)

S7255–1.3: Property Tax and Field Services Divisions

PROPERTY TAXES

[Tables 38-50 show assessments for 1984.]

37. Statement showing the amount of cash collected by the Property Tax Division [from aircraft and private car line taxes]. (p. 70)

38. Business personal property assessments [number of returns, inventory value, consigned merchandise, equipment depreciation value, and total and assessed values, by county]. (p. 71)

39. Assessed value of all classes of property [by type, by county]. (p. 72-73)

40. Manufacturing property: property tax assessments [and number of accounts, by county]. (p. 74-75)

41. Pipeline companies: property tax assessments [for 11 companies, by county]. (p. 76)

42. Water companies: property tax assessments [by company and location]. (p. 77-78)

43-44. Assessed value of all railroad property [and miles of track] used in daily operation of [all] railroads and of the Seaboard Coastline Railroad System [by county]. (p. 79-80)

45-46. Assessed value of all property [and miles of track] used in the daily operation of the Southern Railway System and of the local railroads [by railroad]. (p. 81)

47-49. Light, heat, and power companies; electric cooperatives; and local telephone companies: property tax assessments [by company and county]. (p. 82-89)

50. Major communications companies [AT&T, Southern Bell, and Western Union]: property tax assessments [by county]. (p. 90)

FIELD SERVICES

51-52. Total additional tax collections [from audits, delinquent accounts, and other, by tax type], Field Services Division, FY84; and comparison of field collections, FY82-84. (p. 91-92)

S7300   SOUTH DAKOTA
Department of
Commerce and Regulation

S7300–1   PUBLIC UTILITIES COMMISSION ANNUAL REPORT, FY83-84, South Dakota
Annual. Jan. 24, 1985.
2+48 p.
LC 9-14652.
SRI/MF/complete, current & previous year reports

Annual report presenting South Dakota public utility regulatory and operating data, by company and/or utility type, primarily FY83-84, with selected trends from FY79. Utility types are electric, gas, and telephone.

Covers regulatory cases and dispositions, including detailed reports on consumer complaint and rate actions; telephone rates by type of customer, and aggregate revenues and expenses; and miles of electric transmission lines and natural gas pipelines, and capacity of energy conversion facilities.

Also includes Public Utilities Commission finances; and summary data on licensing of motor carriers and public warehouses, including warehouses used for grain storage and value of stored grain.

Previous report, for FY80-82, has also been reviewed and is also available on SRI microfiche under this number [Annual. [1983.] 2+58 p. †].

Report for FY80-82 is substantially similar in format and content, but also includes data on gas and electric utility revenues, expenditures, consumption, and average bills.

Report was temporarily suspended following publication of the FY79 edition (for description, see SRI 1980 Annual under this number). Combined editions for FY80-82 and FY83-84 are designed to allow continuity of data. Future issues will be published annually.

Availability: Public Utilities Commission, 500 E. Capitol Ave., Pierre SD 57501, †; SRI/MF/complete.

S7300–2   COMPARATIVE STATEMENT OF INSURANCE BUSINESS in South Dakota During the Years 1983-84
Annual. May 1, 1985. 48 p.
LC 75-19531.
SRI/MF/complete, current & previous year reports

Annual report on South Dakota insurance industry underwriting activity, by company and type of insurance, 1983-84. Covers premiums written or collected, assets or policyholder surplus, and losses paid, for insurers based in South Dakota and elsewhere.

Data are shown, as applicable, for fire/casualty insurers, hospital/medical/dental services companies, farm mutual assns, and fraternal benefit societies; and life insurers, including amount of policies issued and detail for accident/health insurance companies.

Includes company directories, and 11 tables.

Previous report, for 1982-83, was also reviewed during 1985, and is also available on SRI microfiche, under S7300-2 [Annual. May 1, 1984. 48 p. †].

Availability: South Dakota Department of Commerce and Regulation, Insurance Division, Insurance Bldg., 320 N. Nicollet St., Pierre SD 57501-2297, †; SRI/MF/complete.

S7300–3   1984 SOUTH DAKOTA MOTOR VEHICLE TRAFFIC ACCIDENT SUMMARY
Annual. [1985.] 3+55 p.
ISSN 0147-0760.
LC 84-623404.
SRI/MF/complete

Annual report on South Dakota traffic accidents involving fatalities, injuries, and property damage, and number of persons killed and injured, 1984, with trends from 1960. Includes data by accident and vehicle type, location, time, and other circumstances; and age of driver and victim.

Also includes data on alcohol involvement in accidents, travel mileage, motor vehicle registrations, licensed drivers and motorcyclists, safety device use, arrests for driving while intoxicated, and fatality rate comparison with 6 neighboring States.

Data are from accident reports submitted to State Dept of Commerce and Regulation.

Contains listings of contents, tables, and charts (3 p.); introduction, highlights, 15 charts, and 33 tables, with narrative analyses (p. 1-47); glossary (p. 49); and appendix, with 6 tables (p. 51-55).

This is the 12th annual report.

Availability: South Dakota Department of Commerce and Regulation, Accident Records Section, 118 W. Capitol Ave., Pierre SD 57501-2080, †; SRI/MF/complete.

S7302   SOUTH DAKOTA Department of State Development

S7302-1   SOUTH DAKOTA AGRICULTURE, 1979-85
Annual.   May 1985.   100 p.
LC 85-622298.
SRI/MF/complete

Annual report on South Dakota agricultural production, marketing, and finances, mostly 1979-84. Data are generally shown by commodity, with crop data by county and district. Includes selected comparisons to other States and total U.S.

Covers production, disposition, prices, sales, value, and, as applicable, acreage, yield, and inventory, for field crop, livestock, poultry, and dairy sectors.

Also includes data on number and acreage of farms, with trends from 1955; fertilizer consumption; and farm income, production expenses, real estate value and taxes, title transfers, and cash rents.

Data are compiled by the South Dakota Crop and Livestock Reporting Service in cooperation with USDA.

Contains preface and contents listing (p. 1-2); and 12 maps, 42 charts, and 114 tables, interspersed with narrative summaries (p. 3-100).

Availability: South Dakota Crop and Livestock Reporting Service, 3528 S. Western Ave., PO Drawer V, Sioux Falls SD 57117, †; SRI/MF/complete.

S7315   SOUTH DAKOTA Department of Education and Cultural Affairs

S7315-1   1983/84 SOUTH DAKOTA EDUCATIONAL STATISTICS DIGEST
Annual.   [1985.]
60+App 98 p.+addendum.
Research Bull. 3.4-13.
ISSN 0360-4772.
LC 75-646389.
SRI/MF/complete

Annual report on South Dakota elementary and secondary schools and school districts, covering students, staff, finances, and transportation, 1983/84, with selected trends from 1968/69. Also includes data on tax valuations and levies, and on nonpublic schools.

Data are compiled by the Office of Support Services.

Contents:

a. Contents listing (1 p.); and 1 table and accompanying map showing number of schools by educational level, 1- and 2-teacher schools, and school districts by county (p. 1).

b. 19 State summary and 6 detailed district tables, listed below. (p. 2-59)

c. Appendix with school district profiles, arranged alphabetically by district, including data on 1983 mill levies by fund, taxable valuation of property, school calendar, staff, average daily attendance (ADA), average daily membership (ADM), revenues by government level of source, State aid entitlements, expenditures by function and fund, and number of bus routes and pupils transported. (App. p. 1-98)

Less comprehensive annual reports not covered in SRI but also available from the issuing agency are: *Public School Districts Fall Enrollment, Nonpublic Schools Fall Enrollment,* and *South Dakota Elementary and Secondary Educational Comparisons.*

Availability: South Dakota Department of Education and Cultural Affairs, Elementary and Secondary Education Division, Support Services Office, Kneip Bldg., 700 N. Illinois St., Pierre SD 57501-2281, †; SRI/MF/complete.

TABLES:
[Data are for 1983/84, unless otherwise noted.]

S7315-1.1: State Summary

OVERVIEW

[1] A look at enrollments and costs [1968/69-1985/86]. (p. 2)

[2-3] General information [cumulative enrollment, and ADM and ADA by grade level, with distribution by educational level 1979/80-1983/84; public and nonpublic 1984 high school graduates, by sex and postgraduation status (attending college or other educational institution, employed, and military service); and number of school districts, by enrollment size, fall 1983]. (p. 3-4)

FINANCES
[Funds shown include general, capital outlay, special education, pension, bond redemption, and sometimes trust/agency funds.]

[4] Statement of changes in fund balances [by fund, July 1983-June 1984]. (p. 5)

[5] General fixed assets [by type]. (p. 5)

[6] Receipts by funds [and by government source]. (p. 6)

[7-8] [General and special education funds] educational expenditures by functions and by objects. (p. 7-8)

[9] Capital outlay fund expenditures. (p. 9)

[10] Bond redemption fund disbursements. (p. 9)

[11] Costs of special programs [kindergarten and summer programs]. (p. 9)

[12] Per pupil costs [for general/special education and capital outlay funds]. (p. 9)

ENROLLMENT, STAFF, AND MISCELLANEOUS DATA

[13] 1984 fall data [public and nonpublic school enrollment and FTE teachers]. (p. 10)

[14] 1984 fall enrollment: public and nonpublic [by grade and sex]. (p. 10)

[15] Miscellaneous data [including number of districts, and taxable valuation of agricultural and nonagricultural property, by nonagricultural mill levy range; and districts with levies above and below certain levels]. (p. 11)

[16] Staff information [certified and noncertified personnel by position, by sex]. (p. 12)

[17] Summary information [including State aid entitlements for 1984/85, and average classroom units (CRU) per district, cost per CRU, tax raised per resident child, ADM, and cost per pupil ADM]. (p. 12)

[18] Transportation data [number of districts reporting bus service, number of buses, pupils transported, mileage, and costs, for public and private ownership]. (p. 13)

NONPUBLIC SCHOOLS

[19] Summary of South Dakota nonpublic schools [schools and enrollment; teaching positions by sex, enrollment, ADM, and ADA, all by educational level; and special enrollment, by program]. (p. 14)

S7315-1.2: School District Summaries
[Tables show data for individual school districts.]

[1] Selected school data [ADM, expenditures, CRUs, tax raised per resident child, agricultural and nonagricultural property value and levies, special education levy, and transportation State aid entitlement]. (p. 15-23)

[2] General information: enrollment [by grade]; and instructional staff [and ADM, by educational level, and ADM in 1- and 2-teacher schools]. (p. 24-31)

[3] Information for financial receipts [by government level; and from general, capital outlay, special education, and bond redemption funds]. (p. 32-40)

[4] Sale of securities [general fund and capital outlay, for selected districts]. (p. 40)

[5] Information for financial expenditures [for instruction, support services, community services, nonprogrammed, debt service, co-curricular, special education, capital outlay, and bond redemption]. (p. 41-49)

[6] School bus transportation [cost, ADM, and mileage]. (p. 50-58)

S7345   SOUTH DAKOTA Department of Health

S7345-1   SOUTH DAKOTA VITAL STATISTICS ANNUAL REPORT, 1984
Annual.   Aug. 1985.
vi+93+6 p.
ISSN 0095-4802.
LC 74-648589.
SRI/MF/complete, current & previous year reports

Annual report on South Dakota vital statistics, covering population, births, deaths by cause, marriages, divorces, abortions, and communicable disease, 1984, with trends from as early as 1906. Includes data by age, sex, race, and county. Most data are from State Dept of Health records as of Apr. 15, 1984.

Contains preface and listings of contents, tables, and charts (p. ii-vi); 7 statistical sections with narrative summaries, 13 mostly illustrative charts, 4 other charts showing infant death and induced abortion trends from 1974, and 42 tables listed below (p. 3-88); notes and definitions (p. 91-93); and facsimiles of reporting forms (6 p.)

Previous report, for 1983, was also reviewed in SRI during 1985, and is also available on SRI microfiche under S7345-1 [Annual. Aug. 1984. iv + 85 p. + errata. $3.00]. Previous report is substantially similar in format and content, but also includes migration and population demographic characteristics by county, and detailed data on fetal and injury deaths; and omits data on characteristics of women receiving prenatal care, babies with low birth weight, and number of pregnancies.

Availability: South Dakota Department of Health, Health Statistics Center, 523 E. Capitol Ave., Pierre SD 57501-9975, $5.00; SRI/MF/complete.

TABLES:

[Unless otherwise noted, data are for South Dakota, 1984; and data by race are for whites, American Indians, and other.]

S7345–1.1: Overview, Population, and Live Births

OVERVIEW

1. Selected health statistics [summary], 1983-84. (p. 3)

2. Vital statistics [population, and number and rate of births, deaths, marriages, divorces, and fetal and infant deaths, various years 1906-84]. (p. 4)

3. Population [actual for Apr. 1980, and revised] estimates [for July 1, 1981-83], by county. (p. 5)

4. Vital statistics by county ([number and rate for] births, deaths, abortions and fetal deaths by county of residence, and marriages and divorces by county of occurrence). (p. 6)

LIVE BIRTHS

5. Births and birth rate, by county of residence, race, and sex. (p. 11)

6. Births by county of residence of mother by mother's age. (p. 12)

7. Resident births by age, race, and marital status of mother. (p. 13)

8. Out-of-wedlock births [and rates] by resident county and race [of mother]. (p. 14)

9. Live births by age of mother, race, and month prenatal care began. (p. 17)

10-11. Trimester prenatal care began, and prenatal care visits, by county of residence. (p. 19-20)

12. Prenatal care by mother's race, marital status, and education. (p. 21)

13. Births by county of residence and birthweight. (p. 24)

14. Low birth weight babies by county of residence and race of mother. (p. 25)

15. Resident births with reported congenital anomalies, by [mother's] race and [child's] sex. (p. 26)

16. Births by county of occurrence, by attendant at birth [physician, midwife, other medical, and nonmedical]. (p. 27)

17. [Resident] births by State of occurrence and [births in South Dakota by] State of mother's residence. (p. 28)

18. Resident pregnancies by county of residence and mother's age. (p. 29)

S7345–1.2: Infant and Fetal Deaths, General Mortality, and Accidental/Violent Deaths

INFANT AND FETAL DEATHS

19. Infant and neonatal deaths by county of mother's residence and race. (p. 38)

20. Resident infant deaths by age, [race], and cause. (p. 39)

21. Fetal deaths by mother's county of residence, race, and age. (p. 40)

GENERAL MORTALITY

A. Leading causes of death [number and percent of total deaths], by age [group]. (p. 44)

B. Suicides [and rates, and percent committed by males and whites], 1960-84. (p. 45)

22. Deaths by county of residence and occurrence, by race. (p. 47)

23. [Resident] deaths by State of ocurrence and [deaths in South Dakota by] State of residence. (p. 48) 3

24. Deaths by county of occurrence and place of death [hospital, other institution, and other]. (p. 49)

25. Resident leading causes of death [by race]. (p. 50)

26. Resident deaths from selected causes by age and race. (p. 53-55)

27. Deaths from malignant neoplasms by [body site and] county of residence. (p. 56)

ACCIDENTAL/VIOLENT DEATHS

28. Deaths from selected external causes by race and sex. (p. 58)

29. External cause of death by county of injury. (p. 60)

S7345–1.3: Induced Abortions, Marriages and Divorces, and Communicable Diseases

INDUCED ABORTIONS

[Data are shown by age of patient.]

30. Resident induced abortions by county of residence. (p. 65)

31-34. Induced abortions occurring in South Dakota: by State of patient's residence, race of patient [including black], number of previous abortions, and number of living children. (p. 66-69)

MARRIAGES AND DIVORCES

35. County of marriage and number of licenses issued. (p. 74)

36. Marriages by county of occurrence, by residence status of bride and groom. (p. 75)

37-38. Marital terminations by county of residence of party to whom granted, and by number of children affected and age of mother. (p. 76-77)

COMMUNICABLE DISEASES

39. Reported cases of specified notifiable diseases, 1975-84. (p. 87)

40. Reported cases of selected notifiable diseases by month of report. (p. 88)

S7355   SOUTH DAKOTA Department of Labor

S7355-1   SOUTH DAKOTA LABOR BULLETIN
Monthly.   Approx. 10 p.
LC 72-17677.
SRI/MF/complete, shipped quarterly

Monthly report on South Dakota labor force, covering employment, unemployment, hours and earnings, characteristics of the insured unemployed, and unemployment insurance claims and payments. Includes State and local data, shown by industry.

Data are based on State records, and are published approximately 1 month after month of coverage.

Issues contain narrative summary and feature articles, occasionally with statistics; 8 monthly tables, listed below; and occasional summary or trend tables on topics covered in monthly tables.

Monthly tables appear in all issues. All additional features with substantial statistics on topics not covered in monthly tables are described, as they appear, under "Statistical Features." Nonstatistical features are not covered.

Availability: South Dakota Department of Labor, Labor Market Information Center, Box 4730, Aberdeen SD 57401, †; SRI/MF/complete, shipped quarterly.

Issues reviewed during 1985: Sept. 1984-Aug. 1985 (D).

MONTHLY TABLES:

[Tables generally show data for month of coverage, previous month, and same month of previous year. Table sequence may vary from issue to issue. Prior to Apr. 1985 issue, table numbering varies from this listing.]

1. Labor force, employment, and unemployment [for U.S., State, Sioux Falls MSA, and by county].

2-3. South Dakota and Sioux Falls MSA (Minnehaha County) nonagricultural wage/salary employment [by industry division, with detail by major group for the State].

4. Hours and earnings of [manufacturing] production workers [for the State and Sioux Falls MSA].

5. CPI: all urban consumers [by major item, for total U.S.].

6. Characteristics of the insured unemployed, statewide [including sex, race, age group, industry and occupational attachment, and duration of unemployment].

7. Selected Labor Dept activities, statewide [unemployment insurance initial claims, weeks claimed, benefit payments, and fund balance; and job service applicants, placements, and job openings].

8. Joint job service and social service activity [number of AFDC recipients finding employment, and resultant savings for the State due to discontinued and reduced benefits].

STATISTICAL FEATURES:

S7355–1.601: Sept. 1984

NONAGRICULTURAL WAGE AND SALARIED INDUSTRY EMPLOYMENT PROJECTIONS

(p. 1-2) Article, with 1 table showing South Dakota employment by industry division, 1982, 1985, and 1990. Data are from State Dept of Labor.

S7355–1.602: Oct. 1984

RETAIL TRADE EMPLOYMENT: CHRISTMAS HOLIDAY TRENDS

(p. 1) Article, with 1 table showing South Dakota retail employment, by kind of business, monthly Oct. 1983-Jan. 1984. Data are from State Dept of Labor.

DID YOU KNOW IN SOUTH DAKOTA

(p. 10) Brief article, with 1 table showing value of agricultural products sold in South Dakota, by commodity, 1982. Data are from the Census of Agriculture.

S7355–1.603: Nov. 1984

TOP GROWTH OCCUPATIONS TO 1990

(p. 1-2) Article, with 2 tables showing top 10 South Dakota occupations ranked by growth rate and by number of new jobs, 1980-90 period. Data are from the State Labor Market Information Center.

S7355–1.604: Jan. 1985

COST OF LIVING SURVEY

(p. 1-2) Article, with 1 table showing cost-of-living indexes for selected items in 4 South Dakota cities, with comparison to 14 other major cities, 3rd quarter 1984. Data are from American Chamber of Commerce Researchers Assn.

DID YOU KNOW IN SOUTH DAKOTA

(p. 10) Brief article, with 1 table showing population, for South Dakota and 6 neighboring States, as of Apr. 1, 1980 and July 1, 1983-84. Data are from Census Bureau.

S7355–1.605: Feb. 1985

YOUTH EMPLOYMENT

(p. 1-2) Article, with 1 table showing South Dakota population, labor force, and unemployment, for all persons, and for persons age 16-19 and 20-24 by sex, 1984.

S7355–1.606: May 1985

DID YOU KNOW IN SOUTH DAKOTA

(p. 10) Brief article, with 1 table showing grants to South Dakota State/local governments, by Federal agency, FY84. Data are from Census Bureau.

S7355–1.607: June 1985

NONAGRICULTURAL WAGE AND SALARIED INDUSTRY EMPLOYMENT PROJECTIONS

(p. 1-2) Article, with 1 table showing South Dakota nonagricultural wage/salary employment by industry division, 1983 and 1995. Data are from State Dept of Labor.

S7355–1.608: July 1985

SUMMERTIME EMPLOYMENT CHANGES

(p. 1) Article, with 1 table showing South Dakota employment in tourism-related and construction industries, selected months 1984.

S7355–1.609: Aug. 1985

SIZE OF BUSINESS IN SOUTH DAKOTA: LARGE AND SMALL

(p. 1-2) Article, with 1 chart and 1 table showing South Dakota business establishments, employment, and wages paid, for firms covered by unemployment insurance, by employment size group, 1984. Data are from State Dept of Labor.

S7355–2   SOUTH DAKOTA ANNUAL PLANNING REPORT
Annual, discontinued.

Annual planning report identifying South Dakota population groups most in need of employment services, discontinued with June 1983 report (for description, see SRI 1983 Annual under this number).

South Dakota employment data are available in the monthly *South Dakota Labor Bulletin,* covered in SRI under S7355-1.

S7380   SOUTH DAKOTA
Department of Revenue

S7380–1   SOUTH DAKOTA DEPARTMENT OF REVENUE ANNUAL STATISTICAL REPORT, FY84
Annual. 2 volumes.
For individual publication data, see below.
LC 76-649355.
SRI/MF/complete

Annual report, for FY84, on South Dakota Revenue Dept activities, including data on State tax revenues by source, and distribution to local governments, Indian tribes, and State funds or agencies. Also includes data on 1983-84 property valuations and taxes payable in 1984. Most data are shown by type of tax and local area.

Report is published in 2 volumes: a statistical report, and a supplementary report on county property taxes. Volumes are further described below.

Prior to FY84, report was published in 1 volume.

Availability: South Dakota Department of Revenue, Kneip Bldg., 700 N. Illinois St., Pierre SD 57501-2276, ‡; SRI/MF/complete.

S7380–1.1: Annual Statistical Report, FY84

[Annual. Nov. 30, 1984. ii+70 p. SRI/MF/complete.]

Contains listings of contents, tables, and charts (p. i-ii); and 7 report sections, with descriptions of dept and division functions, and 3 charts and 18 tables (p. 1-70).

All tables, and a chart showing substantial statistics not included in tables, are listed below.

TABLES AND CHART:

REVENUES AND DISBURSEMENTS

I.1-I.2. Taxes [rate-base and description], and disposition of revenues generated by taxes administered by the Dept of Revenue. [tabular lists] (p. 3-10)

I.3. Dept of Revenue statement of receipts, FY81-84. (p. 11)

IV.1. Sales/use tax collections remitted to municipalities and Indian tribes [by city or tribe, FY83-84]. (p. 14-15)

V.1. Motor fuel tax fund distribution by county highway/bridge funds, FY84. (p. 19)

VI.1. Sales/property tax refunds [and claims] for the elderly and disabled: [singles and households (chart); and] by county; FY84. (p. 21-22)

PROPERTY VALUATIONS AND TAXES

VII.1-VII.2. Summarization of valuations and amount of taxes payable for principal classifications of property, and local government ad valorem tax dollar distribution, [both for] taxes payable in 1984. (p. 25)

[A] State summary [shows full/true value of real estate and utilities, by classification, 1983-84; taxable values and/or taxes, for total local areas and special county purposes, 1984; and number, valuation, and taxes paid, for mobile homes, 1984]. (p. 26-27)

[B] Property taxes collected from all sources [for counties, schools, townships, cities/towns, conservancy subdistricts, railroad authority, and rural fire protection districts, by county], 1982 taxes collected in 1983. (p. 28-29)

VII.4. 1983 amount of taxable valuation levies and taxes [by type], for municipalities payable in 1984 [and population, all by city]. (p. 30-46)

VII.5. 1984 valuations [full/true value for real estate, and taxable value for railroad, utility, telephone, and telegraph assessments, by county]. (p. 48-49)

GOVERNMENT FINANCES AND LAND OWNERSHIP

VII.7. Unaudited financial report [shows current, fixed, and other assets; current and long-term liabilities; equity; revenue; and expenditures; by county with detail for selected cities and schools], 1983. (p. 50-60)

VII.8. County warrants and encumbrances [by function and county], 1983. (p. 62-67)

IX.1-IX.4. Federally owned land by agency, FY82; and State owned land by agency, privately owned Indian and non-Indian land, and nonfederal and Federal acres [with detail by purpose for nonfederal land, no dates]. (p. 68-69)

[IX.5] Property tax replacement distribution [by county, lst and 2nd half FY84]. (p. 70)

S7380–1.2: Supplement to Annual Statistical Report, FY84

[Annual. [1984.] 137 p. SRI/MF/complete.]

Contains brief narrative (p. 1-2); 2 summary tables (p. 3); and 1 detailed table, repeated for the State (p. 4-5) and each county (p. 6-137).

Detailed table shows the following: full/true value of real estate and utilities, by classification, 1983-84; taxable value, mill levy, and taxes, for townships, schools, cities/towns, special districts, and county purposes, 1984; and mobile homes, valuation, and taxes paid.

S7385   SOUTH DAKOTA
Department of Social Services

S7385–1   SOUTH DAKOTA DEPARTMENT OF SOCIAL SERVICES Annual Statistical Report, FY84

Annual. [1984.]   iv+57 p.
ISSN 0147-6467.
LC 77-641772.
SRI/MF/complete

Annual report on South Dakota public welfare recipients and payments, by county, for FY84. Covers Aid to Dependent Children (ADC); SSI for the aged, blind, and disabled; and medical assistance. Also includes data on mental health services, food stamps, low income energy assistance, assistance to Asian refugees, and Work Incentive Program (WIN) grant reductions.

Contains listing of contents, tables, and charts (p. i-iv); 29 tables, interspersed with 1 map and 3 trend charts, showing statewide data (p. 1-33); and 14 tables showing district and county data (p. 35-57). All tables are listed below.

Statistical Analysis Report, a monthly publication presenting similar but less detailed data, is also issued, but is not covered by SRI.

Availability: South Dakota Department of Social Services, Statistical Analysis and Reports, Management Information Office, Kneip Bldg., 700 N. Illinois St., Pierre SD 57501-2291, †; SRI/MF/complete.

TABLES:
[Unless otherwise noted, data are for FY84.]

S7385–1.1: Statewide Data
[Tables usually include average monthly recipients and/or cost.]

ADULT SERVICES AND AGING
[Tables 1-2 include data for economically and socially needy and by race/ethnic group, including Indians, Asians, and Hispanics.]

1. Elderly nutrition projects [including total meals and/or average monthly persons served congregate and home delivered meals]. (p. 2)

2. Social services for the elderly [number of persons served by type of service]. (p. 3-4)

DEVELOPMENTAL DISABILITIES SERVICES

3. Office of development disabilities [recipients and payments, by type of service]. (p. 5)

4. Number of clients served in adjustment training centers, community residential facilities, community habilitation facilities, and follow-along, by funding source, as of June 30, 1984; and admissions and terminations, FY84. (p. 6)

ASSISTANCE PAYMENTS AND FOOD STAMP PROGRAM

5-7. Total ADC and Asian refugee payments [to families, adults, and children]; and recipients and payments of optional supplements. (p. 8)

8-9. Reasons for closing cases on money payment status; and denials and other dispositions of applications, by reason; ADC program, FY83-84. (p. 9-10)

10-11. Grant reductions [and closures] for WIN, [monthly] FY84; and WIN ADC reductions [including cases closed, grants reduced, and dollars saved], FY80-84. (p. 11-12)

12. Recipients and payments of SSI and the mandatory supplement [for aged, blind, and disabled.] (p. 14)

13. Food stamps program participation [public and nonpublic assistance households and persons participating, and value of coupons]. (p. 16)

MEDICAL SERVICES

14-16. Total recipients eligible for medical utilization, by basis of eligibility; and ADC [adult and children] recipients and Asian refugees eligible for medical utilization; [all by whether receiving money or nonmoney payment, monthly]. (p. 17- 19)

17-18. Average number of recipients per month receiving medical care, and [amount of] medical care payments, by type of service [including Indian health service] and basis of eligibility. (p. 20-21)

19-20. Supplemental medical insurance premiums, by basis of eligibility, FY84; and medical assistance payments from Title XIX funds for Office of Children, Youth, and Family Services foster care, FY83-84. (p. 22-23)

21-23. Medical assistance payments for families with dependent children recipients, FY83-84; and for Asian refugees and renal disease services, FY84. (p. 23-24)

24. Total number of recipients and payments of skilled nursing homes, intermediate care facilities, and crippled children's hospital [by type of care and physical and/or mental health status]. (p. 25)

25-26. Medical assistance payments for aged, blind, and disabled recipients; and total number of recipients and payments of supplemental long-term care (SB-201); [both by type of care and physical and/or mental health status]. (p. 26-29)

27. Supplemental payments for long-term care of aged, blind, and disabled (SB-201) [aggregate persons, by type of care and mental health status]. (p. 30)

28. Medical assistance payments from Title XIX funds for Indian health services [for aged, blind, disabled, ADC, and foster care cases]. (p. 31)

CHILD SUPPORT ENFORCEMENT

29. Child support enforcement collections [and average number of paying cases, by region]. (p. 33)

S7385–1.2: County and District Data
[Data are shown by county and/or office location, usually grouped by State district, with district totals.]

CHILDREN, YOUTH, FAMILIES, AND ADULT AND AGING SERVICES

30. Purchased services [including adoption] provided by Office of Children, Youth, and Family Services [number of recipients and amount of payments]. (p. 35)

31-32. Children/youth/family services, and adult services and aging: number of persons receiving direct services [by type]. (p. 36-37)

MENTAL HEALTH SERVICES, ADC, SSI, AND FOOD STAMPS

33. Developmentally disabled services provided to persons under Title XX [number of recipients and amount of payments, by type of service]. (p. 38-39)

34. Percent of population receiving ADC. (p. 40)

35-37. ADC maintenance; mandatory [supplement for SSI recipients] and SSI [for aged, blind, and disabled]; and optional supplement; [number of recipients and amount of payments]. (p. 42-46)

38. Percent of population participating in food stamp program. (p. 47)

39. Food stamp program participation [number of households and persons participating by public assistance status, and value of coupons]. (p. 48-49)

MEDICAL AND ENERGY ASSISTANCE

40. Average number of [aged, blind, disabled, and ADC] recipients per month eligible for medical utilization. (p. 50-51)

41. Supplemental long-term care [number of aged, blind, and disabled recipients, and amount of payments, by type of care]. (p. 52-53)

42. Medical [assistance] by type of service [average recipients per month, and amount of payments]. (p. 54-55)

43. Low income energy assistance [eligible clients and amount of payments]. (p. 56-57)

S7390   SOUTH DAKOTA
Office of the Secretary of State

S7390–1   OFFICIAL ELECTION RETURNS AND REGISTRATION FIGURES FOR SOUTH DAKOTA, General Election, Nov. 6, 1984

Biennial. [1985.]   24 p.
LC 82-620849.
SRI/MF/complete

Biennial report presenting results of the South Dakota general election held Nov. 6, 1984. Includes voting for President/Vice President, U.S. and State senators and representatives, judges, and other officials; 1 State constitutional amendment; and 3 referenda, including measures concerning nuclear waste disposal and nuclear arms freeze. Data are shown by county and/or district, and include party affiliation of most candidates.

Also includes voter registration, by county and party.

Previous report, covering 1982 general election, is described in SRI 1983 Annual under this number.

Availability: South Dakota Office of the Secretary of State, Capitol Bldg., 500 E. Capitol, Pierre SD 57501-5077, †; SRI/MF/complete.

S7395   SOUTH DAKOTA
Supreme Court

S7395–1   **BENCHMARK 1984: Annual Report of the South Dakota Unified Judicial System**
Annual.   Jan. 1985.   4+50 p.
LC 79-642739.
SRI/MF/complete

Annual report on South Dakota judicial system, including supreme and circuit court caseloads and case dispositions, for FY84, with trends from FY80. Circuit court data are shown by case type, county, and circuit.

Case types shown are criminal and civil, with detail for divorce, small claims, probate, adoption, mental illness, guardianship, juvenile, and driving under the influence case types.

Also includes data on population trends; and judicial system personnel, receipts (including fines and child support) and disbursements, and expenditures for court-appointed attorneys/public defenders.

Data are from reports of clerks of court and court services officers.

Contains listing of contents, tables, and charts (2 p.); and report, including narrative, 21 charts, and 19 tables (p. 1-50).

Availability: South Dakota Supreme Court, State Court Administrator's Office, 500 E. Capitol Ave., Pierre SD 57501, †; SRI/MF/complete.

S7460   TENNESSEE
Department of Agriculture

S7460–1   **TENNESSEE AGRICULTURAL STATISTICS, 1984 Annual Bulletin**
Annual.   Oct. 1984.
4+112 p.   Bull. T-21.
LC 64-64265.
SRI/MF/complete

Annual report on Tennessee agricultural production and marketing, by commodity and/or county and district, 1970s-83, with some data for 1984 and trends from as early as 1945. Covers production, value, prices, and, as applicable, acreage, yield, stocks, inventory, and disposition, for field crop, fruit, vegetable, livestock, poultry, and dairy sectors.

Also includes data on farm income by source; production expenses and prices paid by item, with comparison to Appalachian region; number, acreage, and value of farms; farm real estate taxes and debt; fertilizer consumption; and value of U.S. and Tennessee agricultural exports.

Data are compiled by the Tennessee Crop Reporting Service.

Contains contents listing (2 p.); 10 sections, with narrative summaries, 15 maps, 12 charts, and 114 tables (p. 1-109); and list of reports available from State Crop Reporting Service (p. 111-112).

Availability: Crop Reporting Board Publications, South Bldg., Rm 5829, U.S. Department of Agriculture, Washington DC 20250, †; SRI/MF/complete.

S7466   TENNESSEE
Department of Commerce and Insurance

S7466–1   **ANNUAL REPORT OF THE COMMISSIONER OF DEPARTMENT OF COMMERCE AND INSURANCE, Business of 1983, Tennessee**
Annual.   Sept. 1, 1984.
2+121 p.
ISSN 0364-2534.
LC 76-646352.
SRI/MF/complete

Annual report on Tennessee insurance industry financial condition and underwriting activity, by company and type of insurance, 1983. Covers assets, liabilities, surplus, earned premiums, incurred losses, underwriting and investment gains/losses, dividends, and loss/premium ratios; for companies based in Tennessee and elsewhere.

Data are shown, as applicable, for life, captive, fire/casualty, county mutual fire, and title insurance companies; fraternal assns; nonprofit hospital/medical assns; and surplus line companies.

Also includes data on Insurance Dept receipts by source, with trends from 1930; consumer complaints; trust funds on deposit in U.S. from surplus lines companies based in other countries; and regulatory, inspection, and investigative activity involving insurance, fires, securities, and licensed professionals. Most of these data are for 1983, or fiscal year ended June 30, 1983.

Data are from dept internal records and annual statements filed by individual insurers.

Contains contents listing (p. 1); Insurance Division summary, with 8 tables (p. 2-11); directory of insurance companies and listings of corporate status changes (p. 12-60); 13 company financial tables, with interspersed directories (p. 61-94); listings of self-insured companies and auto clubs (p. 95-97); and activity summaries for Divisions of Fire Prevention, Consumer Affairs, Securities, and Regulatory Boards, with 40 text tables (p. 98-121).

This is the 111th annual report. Previous reports are described in SRI under S7540-1. Issuing agency name has changed from Tennessee Dept of Insurance.

Report for 1982 is described in SRI 1983 Annual under S7540-1.

Availability: Tennessee Department of Commerce and Insurance, Examination Section, 114 State Office Bldg., Nashville TN 37219, †; SRI/MF/complete.

S7490   TENNESSEE
Department of Education

S7490–2   **ANNUAL STATISTICAL REPORT of the Department of Education for the Scholastic Year Ending June 30, 1984, State of Tennessee**
Annual.   June 1985.   171 p.
LC 58-27757.
SRI/MF/complete

Annual report, for 1983/84, on Tennessee public schools, presenting data on students, staff, finances, operations, and special programs, shown for the State and by county, city, and special school district.

Contents:

a. Contents and table listing, and lists of public school and municipal officials. (p. 7-20)

b. State special schools: 3-4 tables showing enrollment by county or by sex and level, graduates by sex, staff, allotment, and expenditures by object, for State agricultural institute, preparatory school, and schools for blind and deaf. (p. 21-27)

c. Vocational-technical education: 2 tables showing enrollment by delivery system and instructional area. (p. 28-29)

d. State data: 20 summary tables presenting data for grades K-12 and special schools. (p. 32-38)

e. County and school district data: 39 detailed tables, listed below. (p. 40-171)

Availability: Tennessee Department of Education, Research and Development Division, 100 Cordell Hull Bldg., Nashville TN 37219, †; SRI/MF/complete.

COUNTY AND SCHOOL DISTRICT TABLES:

[Tables show data by county, city, and special school district, for 1983/84 school year, unless otherwise noted.]

S7490–2.1: Schools and Staff

I. Number of schools [by grade span, and for vocational and special education]. (p. 40-42)

II. Training of teachers [highest level of education attained, and number of years at college, by sex]. (p. 43-45)

III-IV. Assignment of teachers, administrators, and members of boards of education; and other employees of boards of education; [by position, mostly by elementary and secondary level]. (p. 46-54)

V. Average annual salary of instructional personnel. (p. 55-57)

S7490–2.2: Graduates, Attendance, and Enrollment

VI. Number of 12th grade graduates [regular and equivalency diplomas, by sex]. (p. 58-60)

VII. Average daily membership [and] average daily attendance [in kindergarten, grades 1-12, and special education], and length of school term in days. (p. 61-63)

VIII. Net enrollment [by grade, and for special education, by sex]. (p. 64-75)

IX. Record of pupil progress [number enrolled, dropped from rolls, re-entered, promoted, and failing]. (p. 76-78)

S7490-2.3: Special Programs, Transportation, and Buildings

X. Programs of education other than K-12 run by local boards of education [Head Start, summer school, adult education, and other pupils]. (p. 79-81)

XI. Number of handicapped children receiving special education services [by type of handicap, and for intellectually gifted students]. (p. 82-84)

XII. Pupil transportation [including mileage, vehicles, pupils transported, drivers by sex and salaries, and accidents by resulting injury, fatality, and damage]. (p. 85-87)

XIII-XIV. Complete new buildings and additions to existing buildings contracted for between July 1, 1983 and June 30, 1984 [including type of building and addition, and costs]. (p. 88-90)

XV-XVI. Maintenance of buildings/grounds [including number of schools receiving repairs and funding, acreage and costs of new and existing sites, classrooms available, and school property value]. (p. 91-96)

S7490-2.4: Finances

XVII. Distribution of school funds [including State, Federal, and vocational funds, by object and program]. (p. 97-105)

XVIII-XXIV. Receipts [State revenue, Federal funds received through the State and received directly, county and city or special district revenue receipts, other revenue receipts, and nonrevenue receipts, all by detailed source]. (p. 106-126)

XXV. Summary of receipts. (p. 127-129)

XXVI-XXXVII. Expenditures [for administration, instruction, education for handicapped, vocational education, pupil transportation, operation and maintenance of plant, food service, fixed charges, other services, capital outlay, and debt service, all by detailed object]. (p. 130-165)

XXXVIII. Current expenditures [by object, and total per pupil in average daily attendance]. (p. 166-168)

XXXIX. Financial statement summary as of June 30, 1984 [assets, liabilities, reserves, and fund balance for general purpose, Federal projects, and capital projects]. (p. 169-71)

S7495   TENNESSEE
Department of
Employment Security

S7495-1   TENNESSEE COVERED EMPLOYMENT AND WAGES BY INDUSTRY, Statewide and by County, 1983

Annual. Nov. 1984.
3+204 p.
ISSN 0094-4734.
LC 74-645399.
SRI/MF/complete

Annual report, for 1983, on Tennessee employment and wages, by county and industry, for employers covered by unemployment insurance. Also includes number of units reporting, unemployment insurance contributions, and average premium rates.

Data are compiled from contribution and wage reports submitted by employers to the Tennessee Dept of Employment Security.

Contains contents listing and introduction (2 p.); and 5 tables, listed below (p. 1-204).

Availability: Tennessee Department of Employment Security, Research and Statistics Division, 519 Cordell Hull Bldg., Nashville TN 37219, †; SRI/MF/complete.

TABLES:
[All data are for Tennessee, 1983.]

[1-3] Covered employment and wages, by industry [group, showing reporting units and employment, total and taxable wages, unemployment insurance premiums due, and premium rates], statewide, by county, [and for firms not reporting in any particular county]. (p. 1-202)

[4-5] County ranking by average weekly wage; and by annual average employment. (p. 203-204)

S7495-2   TENNESSEE LABOR MARKET REPORT

Monthly. 8 p.
SRI/MF/complete, shipped quarterly

Monthly report on Tennessee labor force, employment, hours, and earnings, and employment service activities, by industry group and/or MSA. Reports are issued 2-4 months after month of coverage.

Contains narrative summary, 8 trend charts, and 5 monthly tables listed below.

Availability: Tennessee Department of Employment Security, Research and Statistics Division, 519 Cordell Hull Bldg., Nashville TN 37219, †; SRI/MF/complete, shipped quarterly.

Issues reviewed during 1985: Sept. 1984-Aug. 1985 (D).

MONTHLY TABLES:
[Data are shown mostly for current month, preceding month, and same month of preceding year. Tables [1-4] are shown for State and 5 MSAs.]

[1] Civilian labor force summary [by employment status].

[2] Estimated nonagricultural employment [by major industry group].

[3] Job service activities [new applications, testing, enrolled in training, nonagricultural placements, and counseling; totals, and for nonwhite, veteran, and female; for current and previous month; table may not appear in every issue].

[4] Hours and earnings of production workers [by major industry group].

[5] CPI for all urban consumers.

S7495-4   1986 ANNUAL PLANNING INFORMATION, Tennessee

Annual. May 1985.
1+399 p.
LC sc84-1577.
SRI/MF/complete

Annual planning report, for FY86, identifying Tennessee population groups most in need of employment services. Includes data on population and labor force, employment by occupation and industry, unemployment insurance recipients, veterans, and high school graduates; by service delivery area (SDA). Also includes employment and wage data by county. Most data are for various years 1983-85, with selected projections for 1990.

Data are from U.S. Census Bureau and Dept of Labor, Lawrence Berkeley Laboratory, and Tennessee Dept of Employment Security.

Contains contents listing (1 p.); introduction and table listing (p. 1-2); 1 map, narrative summary, and 15 tables listed below, repeated for each of 14 SDAs (p. 3-393); and appendix, with references and directory of field analysts (p. 395-399).

Availability: Tennessee Department of Employment Security, Research and Statistics Division, 519 Cordell Hull Bldg., Nashville TN 37219, †; SRI/MF/complete.

TABLES:
[Data by race often also include Hispanics.]

1-3. 1985 population summary and male and female population [by race and age].

4-7. 1985 total and civilian labor force [by age, race, employment status, and sex].

8. Nonagricultural wage/salary employment by industry [division and major manufacturing group, 1983-84].

9. Projected employment by broad occupational category, [1984 and 1990].

10-11. UI [unemployment insurance] claimant characteristics and occupations [number of claimants, with distribution by sex, educational attainment, age, and race, and for veterans, welfare recipients, and handicapped; summary and by detailed occupation, July 1-Dec. 31, 1984].

12. Persons below poverty level [by race and age, 1983].

13. Veteran population [by county and period of service], Mar. 31, 1984.

14. 1984 high school graduates [continuing education and entering labor force; and 12th-grade dropouts and total school dropouts; all for city, county, and private schools].

15. Average annual covered wage [and employment, and total wages, by county, for total and service industries, 1983].

S7505   TENNESSEE
Department of Finance and Administration

S7505-1   TENNESSEE COMPREHENSIVE ANNUAL FINANCIAL REPORT for the Year Ended June 30, 1984
Annual.   Dec. 26, 1984.
viii+87 p.
SRI/MF/complete

Annual report on financial condition of Tennessee State government, for FY84, with comparisons to FY83. Covers assets and liabilities, revenues by source, expenditures by function and/or object, and fund balances; for all, general, special revenues, debt service, capital projects, enterprise, internal service, trust/agency, and college/university funds.

Also includes data on general fund expenditures by dept; budgeted vs. actual revenues and expenditures; selected debt ratios; bond repayment schedules; and financial and economic indicator trends from 1974.

Economic indicators include GSP, earnings, manufacturing gross product, and employment, all by industry; personal and farm income; industrial expansions and capital investments; employees and plants of top 50 industrial employers; population; bank deposits; IRS collections; retail sales; building permit and property values; and educational enrollments, by level and postsecondary institution.

Data are compiled by the Finance and Administration Dept primarily from internal records and reports of other State agencies.

Contains contents listing (3 p.); introduction, with text data and 7 charts (p. i-viii); 51 financial statements (p. 1-72); and statistical and economic data sections, with 26 tables (p. 73-87).

The annual *Report of the Treasurer of the State of Tennessee,* presenting less comprehensive data on State treasury finances and retirement funds, is also available from the Treasury Department, State Capitol, Nashville TN 37219. Report is not covered by SRI.

Availability: Tennessee Department of Finance and Administration, Rm. 314, Andrew Jackson State Office Bldg., Nashville TN 37219, †; SRI/MF/complete.

S7507   TENNESSEE
Department of Financial Institutions

S7507-1   1984 ELEVENTH ANNUAL REPORT, State of Tennessee Department of Financial Institutions
Annual.   Apr. 15, 1985.
iv+103 p.
LC 78-642408.
SRI/MF/complete

Annual report, for 1984, on financial condition of Tennessee State-chartered financial institutions. Includes assets, deposits, and/or loans, for individual banks, credit unions, and savings and loan assns, as of Dec. 31, 1984, with selected comparisons to 1983 and/or earlier years.

Also includes aggregate balance sheet and income statement data for banks and credit unions; bank operating ratios; bank holding company assets; bank deposit and population data by county and SMSA; credit union shares, special accounts, and membership trends; and aggregate loan activity and financial data for industrial loan/thrift companies, 1983.

Most data are from required year-end call reports submitted by individual institutions.

Contains contents listing (p. iii); introductory matter and legislative summary (p. 1-7); status change lists and 24 tables, arranged in 3 sections (9-98); and 4 illustrative charts (p. 99-103).

Availability: Tennessee Department of Financial Institutions, James K. Polk State Office Bldg., 505 Deaderick St., 2nd Floor, Nashville TN 37219-5384, †; SRI/MF/complete.

S7520   TENNESSEE
Department of Health and Environment

S7520-1   TENNESSEE MORBIDITY STATISTICS, 1983, Including Summary Tables for 1974-83
Annual.   Sept. 1984.
v+24 p.
ISSN 0361-5324.
LC 74-647396.
SRI/MF/complete

Annual report on the occurrence in Tennessee of 32 diseases requiring notification of State health authorities, 1983, with trends from 1974. Includes number and/or rate of cases, by disease, age, race, and county. Data are based on reports to the Tennessee Health and Environment Dept.

Contains listings of contents, tables, charts, and diseases (p. iii-v); introduction and narrative, with 2 maps, 4 charts, and 4 summary tables (p. 1-14); and 4 detailed tables (p. 15-24).

This is the 54th annual report.

Availability: Tennessee Department of Health and Environment, Information and Referral Unit, State Center for Health Statistics, C1-136 Cordell Hull Bldg., Nashville TN 37219-2505, †; SRI/MF/complete.

S7520-2   ANNUAL BULLETIN OF VITAL STATISTICS for the Year 1981, Tennessee
Annual.   [1985.]   80 p.
LC 34-6645.
SRI/MF/complete, current & previous year reports

Annual report on Tennessee vital statistics, covering population, births, deaths by cause, marriages, divorces, and abortions, 1981. Includes data by race, sex, age, city, county, and health dept region, and selected trends from 1952. Data are primarily from reports filed with the Office of Vital Records as of Mar. 31, 1982.

Contains listings of contents, tables, and charts (p. 3-5); narrative analysis, including definitions and description of reporting criteria, 1 map, 9 charts, and 36 text tables (p. 7-27); and 12 detailed tables (p. 28-80). All tables are listed below.

This is the 55th report. Previous report, for 1980, was also reviewed in 1985 and is also available on SRI microfiche under this number [Annual. [1984.] 79 p. †]. Issuing agency name has changed from Tennessee Dept of Public Health.

Issuing agency also publishes *Induced Abortions Reported in Tennessee,* not covered by SRI.

Availability: Tennessee Department of Health and Environment, State Center for Health Statistics, Cordell Hull Bldg., Nashville TN 37219-2505, †; SRI/MF/complete.

TABLES:
[Tables show resident data for Tennessee, 1981, unless otherwise noted. Rates are expressed as per 100,000 population, unless otherwise noted.

Causes of death are shown according to the *9th Revision, International Classification of Diseases.*]

S7520-2.1: Text Tables
INTRODUCTORY DATA
1. Cities of 10,000 or more population for counties, 1980. [list] (p. 10)

2. Birth and death rates and rate of natural increase per 1,000 population, by race. (p. 12)

BIRTHS
3-4. Number of births by month, with average per day; and number and percentage of births according to attendant [physician, nurse/midwife, midwife, and other], by race. (p. 13)

5. Percentage of births occurring in hospitals, by race, 1962-81. (p. 13)

6-7. Number and percentage of births: according to weight group, by race; and according to age of mother, by race of child. (p. 13-14)

8. Live births by number of prenatal visits, by month of pregnancy prenatal care began and race of child. (p. 14)

9. Percentage of live births reported to be illegitimate, by race, 1952-81. (p. 14)

DEATHS
[Data by urban character of county are shown for SMSA and non-SMSA counties, with detail for 6 SMSAs.]

10-11. Number and percentage of fetal deaths, according to weight group and cause, by race. (p. 15)

12-13. Number of reported induced abortions: according to race of woman, with ratios per 1,000 recorded live births, 1974-81; and number and percent distribution according to age and race of woman, 1981. (p. 16)

14. Age-adjusted death rates per 1,000 population, by race, 1970-81. (p. 16)

15-16. Death rates per 1,000 population: by race, sex, and age; and by urban character of county, by race. (p. 17)

17. Number of deaths by month, with average per day. (p. 18)

18. Infant mortality rates per 1,000 live births, by urban character of county, by race. (p. 18)

19-20. Number of infant deaths, by cause and by age at death, with rates per 1,000 live births, [all] by race. (p. 19)

21-23. Principal causes of death with rates: [total], by sex, and for 5 age groups. (p. 20-21)

24. Number of deaths from malignant neoplasms according to primary site, with rates, by race. (p. 22)

25-27. Average annual death rates for malignant neoplasms, for diseases of heart, and for accidents/adverse effects; by race, sex and age, 1979-81 [period]. (p. 23-24)

28-29. Number of deaths from accidents and adverse effects: according to type of accident, with rates; and by class of accident, with percentages. (p. 24-25)

30. Average annual death rates for accidents/ adverse effects according to class of accident, by age, 1979-81 [period]. (p. 25)

31-32. Number of deaths: from home accidents according to type of accident, with rates, by race; and from motor vehicle accidents by type of accident, with percentages. (p. 25-26)

MARRIAGES AND DIVORCES

33-35. Number of marriages recorded: and persons married, with rates per 1,000 population, 1972-81; and by month with average per day, and according to previous marital status of bride and groom, 1981. (p. 26-27)

36. Number of divorces recorded and persons divorced, with rates per 1,000 population, 1972-81. (p. 27)

S7520–2.2: Detailed Tables

[Tables I, III-VIII, and XI show data by race. Data by city are for cities of 10,000 or more population.]

I. Population; births and deaths with rates per 1,000 population; and fetal, infant, and neonatal deaths, with rates per 1,000 live births; recorded and resident data, 1962-81. (p. 28)

II-III. Deaths from selected infectious and parasitic diseases, and from selected causes by sex, [both] with rates, 1962-81. (p. 29-33)

IV. Deaths according to cause, by sex and age. (p. 34-36)

V. Deaths according to 211 selected causes, with rates. (p. 37-38)

VI-VIII. Births, infant deaths, fetal deaths, induced abortions, and deaths by cause, with rates; for the State and for the counties, cities, and health dept regions. (p. 39-75)

IX. Births and deaths in hospitals, with percentages, for cities, and for counties inclusive of cities, resident and recorded data. (p. 76)

X. Selected recorded data regarding [live] births [and] fetal deaths [in hospital, and out of hospital attended by physician, midwife, or other], and [total, neonatal, and infant] deaths, for cities, and for counties inclusive of cities. (p. 77-78)

XI. Number of induced abortions, by county, resident and recorded data. (p. 79)

XII. Selected data on marriages and divorces by recorded county. (p. 80)

S7525   TENNESSEE
Higher Education
Commission

S7525–1   STATISTICAL ABSTRACT OF TENNESSEE HIGHER EDUCATION, 1984/85
Annual. [1985.] ii+123 p.
Rpt. No. CB50-SATHE0985.
ISSN 0149-8339.
LC 77-645180.
SRI/MF/complete, current & previous year reports

Annual report on Tennessee postsecondary education for the 1984/85 school year. Covers enrollment, finances, graduates, degree programs, and faculty, for public universities, community colleges, and technical institutes. Also covers private institution enrollment and student finances. Most data are shown by institution.

Data are from institution surveys, higher education governing boards, NCES, and other sources.

Contains introduction (p. ii); listings of contents, tables, and charts (p. 1-6); report notes, organizational chart, 4 maps, and 2 charts (p. 7-15); 8 statistical sections, with 4 summary charts, and 56 tables listed below (p. 16-119); and glossary and abbreviations (p. 120-123).

This is the 10th annual report. Previous report, for 1983/84, was also reviewed in SRI during 1985 and is also available on SRI microfiche under S7525-1 [Annual. [1985.] ii+115 p. †].

Report for 1982/83 is described in SRI 1983 Annual under this number.

Availability: Tennessee Higher Education Commission, 501 Union Bldg., Suite 300, Nashville TN 37219, †; SRI/MF/complete.

TABLES:

[Data are for Tennessee public institutions of higher education, and are shown by institution, unless otherwise noted. Figure 7 is numbered in sequence with maps and charts in the report, but presents tabular data.]

S7525–1.1: Enrollment and Transfers

[Tables show data for 1984 unless otherwise noted; all data are shown for fall.]

CURRENT ENROLLMENT

1. General characteristics of headcount enrollment [residence status, sex, full- or part-time, class level, and race; aggregates for public institutions by type, and total private institutions]. (p. 16)

2-5. Student headcount enrollment: by class level; and in-State, out-of-State, foreign enrollment, and percentage ratio; for public and private institutions. (p. 17-20)

6. Resident and nonresident enrollment [including number of nonresidents from 14 southeastern States, other States, and foreign countries]. (p. 21-24)

7-8. Part- and full-time enrollment and percentage ratio, public and private institutions. (p. 25-26)

9-10. Enrollment by major [academic program] division, by student level, [and by individual institution]. (p. 27-31)

11. Enrollment and percent of total by race, sex, and age, [for total] public institutions. (p. 32)

12-13. Undergraduate and graduate/professional enrollment by age. (p. 33-34)

14-15. Enrollment: by race and student level, public institutions; and by race [including foreign students], private institutions. (p. 35-39)

16-17. Enrollment by sex and by class, public institutions; and enrollment by sex and percentage ratio, private institutions. (p. 40-41)

18. Degree credit enrollment for off-campus center locations. (p. 42)

ENROLLMENT TRENDS

Figure 7. Percent/headcount enrollment by type of institution and type of student [freshmen, women, part-time, black, 25/older, and/ or graduate/professional, biennially 1978-84]. (p. 43-44)

19. Student enrollment [for U.S., and for total Tennessee public institutions by type and private institutions], 1974-84. (p. 45)

20-21. Student enrollment [at] public universities, community colleges, and technical institutes, 1974-84. (p. 46-47)

22-24. Student enrollment: public institutions FTE, and private institutions headcount and FTE, 1974-84. (p. 48-50)

25-28. First-time freshman enrollment [at] public institutions, full-time freshman enrollment [at] private institutions, undergraduate and graduate/professional enrollment [at] public institutions; and percentage change, 1980-84. (p. 51-54)

29. Enrollment by major [academic program] division and by student level [not by institution]. (p. 55)

30. Total resident enrollment, 1976-84, and percent change, 1983/84, by county of origin, [not by institution]. (p. 56-58)

UNDERGRADUATE TRANSFERS

31-32. Undergraduate transfers to public institutions and percentage ratio, by type of transfer institution [and student level]. (p. 60-64)

33. Undergraduate transfers from public institutions to other public institutions. (p. 65-68)

S7525–1.2: Finances, Degrees, and Faculty

STUDENT FINANCES

34. Student fees per academic year [resident and nonresident rates for undergraduates and graduates], 1983/84-1984/85. (p. 69)

35-36. 1984/85 mandatory fees/tuition and State grant awards; and resident tuition per academic year 1980/81-1984/85 and percent change [by public and private institution]. (p. 70-73)

DEGREES CONFERRED

[Data are shown by degree level.]

37. Degrees awarded, 1983/84. (p. 75)

38. Community college/technical institute transfer report, graduates of 1983/84 matched with fall 1984 enrollment. (p. 76-77)

39-40. 1983/84 graduates: by race [Caucasian, Black, Oriental, American Indian, and Hispanic]; and by permanent address [4 State subregions, out-of-State, and foreign]. (p. 78-87)

41-43. Five years of graduates, 1979/80-1983/84; and 1983/84 graduates, by term of award and sex. (p. 88-103)

44. 1983/84 graduates by major taxonomy [not by institution]. (p. 104)

FACULTY AND SALARIES

45. Number of full-time teaching faculty and average annual salary by [academic] rank and group [faculty with doctorate degrees, faculty with master's degrees, and 2-year institutions], 1984/85. (p. 105)

INSTITUTIONAL FINANCES
[Tables 46-50 show data for FY83-85.]

46-48. State appropriations; and unrestricted educational and general expenditures and transfers, formula and nonformula units [by institution and function]. (p. 107-109)

49-50. Revenues and expenditures for auxiliary enterprises and restricted items, and percentage increases. (p. 110-111)

51. Capital outlay appropriations, total dollars and percentage ratio, FY81-85. (p. 112)

THEC ACTIONS
[Data are for Tennessee Higher Education Commission (THEC).]

52-53. Programs approved [by degree level], 1968-1984 period; and action on academic programs [by institution type], 1982-84; [not by institution]. (p. 113-114)

54-55. Program reorganizations and new programs approved, 1982-84. (p. 115-119)

S7535   TENNESSEE
Department of
Human Services

S7535–1   TENNESSEE DEPARTMENT OF HUMAN SERVICES STATISTICS
Monthly. Approx. 30 p.
ISSN 0361-896X.
LC 76-641878.
SRI/MF/complete, shipped quarterly

Monthly report on Tennessee public welfare program caseloads, recipients, services, and payments, covering AFDC, food stamps, medical assistance, and social services. Most data are shown by county.

Report is compiled by Research and Statistics Division of State Dept of Human Services, and is issued 5-6 months after month of coverage.

Contains listings of contents, tables, and charts; narrative review; 14 monthly tables, listed below; and 3 trend charts.

A less detailed annual report, containing additional data on public assistance funding and expenditures, is also available from the issuing agency, but is not covered in SRI.

Monthly tables appear in all issues.

Availability: Tennessee Department of Human Services, Research and Statistics Section, 1720 West End Ave., Rm. 501, Nashville TN 37203, †; SRI/MF/complete, shipped quarterly.

Issues reviewed during 1985: July 1984-Apr. 1985 (D).

MONTHLY TABLES:
[Data are shown for month of coverage, generally by county.]

1. AFDC: applications on hand [number received, and disposition].

2-3. AFDC: reason for need (approvals) and reason for rejection [State only].

4. AFDC: applications pending, by length of time.

5-8. AFDC: approvals and closings; cases reviewed [total and per worker]; cases receiving money payments [families, total individuals, and children]; and amount of money payments.

9. AFDC: reason for closing [State only].

10. Food stamps [household and individual] certifications and participants, and value of coupons.

11-12. Medical assistance applications [received, disposed of, and pending]; and medical assistance approvals and caseload; [for medically needy women/children and for categorically needy aged, blind, disabled, and women/children].

13. Social service work load report [recipients by type of service, for general and protective services, foster care, adoption, other services, and information/referral, by county and State region].

14. Nursing home care (SSI) activity [income certification requests completed and cases terminated, and total cases active during month].

S7565   TENNESSEE
Public
Service Commission

S7565–1   ANNUAL REPORT, TENNESSEE PUBLIC SERVICE COMMISSION, for the Year 1984
Annual. Dec. 31, 1984.
95 p.
LC 9-14680.
SRI/MF/complete

Annual report, for 1984, on regulatory activities of the Tennessee Public Service Commission, with property valuation, financial, and operating data for industries within the commission's jurisdiction. Industries covered include electric and telephone companies and cooperatives; and gas, pipeline, water/sewerage, bus, truck, railroad, railroad car, airline, barge, mobile phone, and other types of companies.

Includes assessed property values, by industry, individual company, county, and city, 1984, with summary trends from 1877; and plant value, revenues, expenses, and customers, shown for gas, water, telephone, and radio common carrier (mobile phone) industries, 1979-83.

Also includes commission disbursements and revenues; number of companies regulated; and rate reviews, consumer complaints, and other types of regulatory activities.

Data are from commission records.

Contains contents listing (1 p.); commission information and report, interspersed with text data and 6 tables (p. 2-45); and 4 tables on property valuation (p. 46-95).

Availability: Tennessee Public Service Commission, Cordell Hull Bldg., Nashville TN 37219, †; SRI/MF/complete.

S7570   TENNESSEE
Department of
Revenue

S7570–1   BIENNIAL REPORT, Tennessee Department of Revenue, FY83-84
Biennial. Dec. 31, 1984.
viii+62 p.
LC 76-645919.
SRI/MF/complete

Biennial report, for FY83-84, on Tennessee tax revenues by source, and apportionments by county, municipality, and fund, all by type of tax. Also includes trends from 1975.

Contains listings of contents, tables, and charts (p. v-vi); narrative description of Revenue Dept organization, State taxes and fees, and tax legislation and court decisions (p. 4-32); and statistical section, with 2 summary charts, and 9 tables listed below (p. 35-62).

This is the 31st biennial report. Previous report, for FY81-82, is described in SRI 1983 Annual under this number.

Availability: Tennessee Department of Revenue, Research Section, 927 Andrew Jackson State Office Bldg., 500 Deaderick St., Nashville TN 37242, †; SRI/MF/complete.

TABLES:
[Tables show data by type of tax.]

1-2. Department collections, and percentage of total tax collections, 1975-84. (p. 37-38)

3. Sales/use tax collections by county, FY78-84. (p. 39-40)

4-5. Apportionment and percentage apportionment of collections, by fund [general, general earmarked revenue, highway, and sinking funds; and to counties, municipalities, and miscellaneous]; FY80-84 (p. 41-44)

6-9. 1983-84 county and municipality fund distributions. (p. 45-62)

S7580   TENNESSEE
Office of the
Secretary of
State

S7580–1   CERTIFICATION OF ELECTION RETURNS for the General Election Held Nov. 6, 1984, Tennessee
Biennial. [1985.]
32 p. Oversized.
SRI/MF/complete

Biennial report presenting results of Tennessee general election held Nov. 6, 1984. Shows voting for President, Vice-President, U.S. and State senators and representatives, State public service commissioners, and judges. Data are shown by district and/or county. Also shows party affiliation of candidates.

Previous report, covering 1982 general election results, is described in SRI 1983 Annual under this number. Additional reports, covering the Democratic and Republican primary elections, are also available from issuing agency, but are not covered in SRI.

Availability: Tennessee Office of the Secretary of State, James K. Polk Bldg., Suite 500, Nashville TN 37219-5040, †; SRI/MF/complete.

S7580–2   TENNESSEE PUBLIC LIBRARY STATISTICS, July 1, 1983-June 30, 1984
Annual. [1985.] ii+43 p.
LC 58-62849.
SRI/MF/complete

Annual report, for FY84, on Tennessee public library collections, finances, services, and staff, for metro and local libraries, regional centers, and Tennessee Regional Library for the Blind and Physically Handicapped. Data are compiled from individual library reports.

Contains contents listing (i-ii); 4 summary tables (p. 1-2); and 6 sections with 28 detailed tables, described below (p. 3-43).

Availability: Tennessee State Library and Archives, Development and Extension Services Section, 403 Seventh Ave., N., Nashville TN 37219, †; SRI/MF/complete.

TABLES:
[Data for libraries serving the general public cover population and area served, number of libraries/branches, book and nonbook holdings and circulation, bookmobiles, professional and nonprofessional staff, income by source, expenditures by object, and other topics as noted below.]
a. Metro and city libraries, by library; also including area resource center expenditures and services. 10 tables. (p. 3-12)
b. Regional centers and local libraries, by region and county; also including bookmobile operating data; books withdrawn, lost, and paid; and reference and loan services. 15 tables. (p. 13-38)
c. Tennessee Regional Library for the Blind and Physically Handicapped, including patrons served by service type, region, and county; and materials circulation. 3 tables. (p. 40-43)

S7585   TENNESSEE
Supreme Court

S7585–1   1984 ANNUAL REPORT: Office of the Executive Secretary, Tennessee State Supreme Court
Annual. [1985.] 154 p.
LC 73-640219.
SRI/MF/complete

Annual report, for 1984, on Tennessee judicial system, including trial and appellate court caseloads and case dispositions. Covers supreme, appeals, circuit, criminal, chancery, and general sessions courts. Includes trial court data by case type and county, and selected trends from 1964.

Case types shown are criminal and civil, for most courts, with additional detail for domestic relations (including adoption), damages/torts, workers compensation, probate, administrative

hearing appeal, contempt proceeding, mental health, tax, trust, and other case types (including specific criminal offenses).

Contains contents listing (1 p.); 4 report sections, with narrative summaries, 1 chart, and 2-4 tables repeated for each court type and jurisdiction (p. 1-141); and appendix, with glossary, 2 tables, and listings of court officials and courts (p. 142-154).

Availability: Tennessee Supreme Court, Executive Secretary's Office, Judicial Information System, Rm. 416, Supreme Court Bldg., Nashville TN 37219, †; SRI/MF/complete.

S7620   TEXAS
Advisory Commission on Intergovernmental Relations

S7620–1   NET MIGRATION IN TEXAS: 1970-80 by Age and Sex for Whites and Nonwhites
Monograph. Mar. 1985.
272 p. No. 1, Series 1985.
SRI/MF/complete

Report on Texas migration patterns, for the State and each county, 1970-80 period. Shows net migration and migration rates, by age, by sex and race. Data were compiled from Census Bureau population figures.

Contains contents listing (1 p.); introduction, methodology, and bibliography (p. 1-14); and statistical section, with 1 table repeated for State and each county (p. 15-272).

Availability: Texas State Data Center, Data Management Program, PO Box 13206, Austin TX 78711, $15.24; SRI/MF/complete.

S7630   TEXAS
Department of Agriculture

S7630–1   1983 TEXAS COUNTY STATISTICS
Annual. Sept. 1984.
3+273 p. Bull. No. 223.
LC 72-622638.
SRI/MF/complete

Annual report on Texas agricultural production and marketing, by commodity and crop reporting district and county, 1982-83.

Covers production and, as applicable, acreage, yield, marketing, and inventory, for field crop, vegetable, fruit and nut, livestock, dairy, and poultry sectors.

Also includes data on farm income, irrigation, and farm/ranch and pasture/rangeland acreage, by district and county.

Data are compiled by Texas Crop and Livestock Reporting Service.

Contains map, foreword, and contents listing (3 p.); State agricultural rankings (p. 2-3); and 5 basic tables, repeated for the State and each district and county (p. 4-273).

Availability: Commissioner, Texas Department of Agriculture, PO Box 12847, Austin TX 78711; or Agricultural Statistician, Texas Crop and Livestock Reporting Service, PO Box 70, Austin TX 78767, †; SRI/MF/complete.

S7655   TEXAS
Comptroller of Public Accounts

S7655–2   STATE OF TEXAS 1984 ANNUAL FINANCIAL REPORT, Fiscal Year Ended Aug. 31, 1984
Annual. 2 volumes.
For individual publication data, see below.
LC 76-648987.
SRI/MF/complete

Annual report on financial condition of Texas State government, for FY84. Report is issued in 2 volumes, individually described below.

A much less detailed report, *Summary of the Annual Financial Report,* is also available from the comptroller, but is not covered in SRI.

Availability: Texas Comptroller of Public Accounts, Planning and Research Office, 111 E. 17th St., Rm. 806, Austin TX 78774, †; SRI/MF/complete.

S7655–2.1: Financial Summary Report
[Annual. Nov. 5, 1984. vii+55 p. SRI/MF/complete.]

Annual report presenting an overview of Texas State government finances, FY84 and trends.

Includes data on economic impact of tax law changes; cash condition summary, by fund category; fund investments, by fund and type of instrument; bonded debt; securities deposited in trust with State treasurer; transactions of departmental suspense and petty/travel/imprest cash advance funds; motor fuel tax fund and dedicated revenue receipts and allocations; foundation school budget and expenditures; and funding for local governments; primarily for FY84.

Also includes trends in State revenues by detailed source and expenditures by function and object, for FY80-84.

Contains listings of contents, tables and charts, and introduction (p. iii-vii); brief economic overview, with 10 charts (p. 1-8); and report, with narrative summaries, 9 charts, and 29 financial tables (p. 9-55).

S7655–2.2: Detailed Report
[Annual. [1984.] vii+567 p. SRI/MF/complete.]

Annual report presenting revenues by source, expenditures by object, and cash balances, for over 300 Texas State government funds, FY84, with summary comparison to FY83.

Contains contents listing and introduction (p. i-vii); and 7 extended tables (p. 1-567).

S7657   TEXAS
Coordinating Board, Texas College and University System

S7657-1   STATISTICAL SUPPLEMENT TO THE ANNUAL REPORT, FY84, Coordinating Board, Texas College and University System
Annual.   Jan. 1985.
iv + 141 p.
LC 74-648444.
SRI/MF/complete

Annual statistical supplement on Texas higher education, presenting data on individual public and private universities, colleges, and junior colleges, 1983/84 and trends. Includes statistics on enrollment, faculty, curricula, funding for education, and student aid.

Contains contents listing (p. iii-iv); lists of institutions by type (p. 1-3); and 54 tables listed below (p. 7-141).

Separate reports with data on research expenditures, funding formulas, degrees awarded, and degree program requests are also available from the issuing agency but are not covered by SRI.

Availability: Texas Coordinating Board, Texas College and University System, Publications Office, PO Box 12788, Austin TX 78711, †; SRI/MF/complete.

TABLES:

S7657-1.1: Student Enrollments and Faculty Data
[Tables [1-17] show data for fall semester. Tables [2-12] and [15-21] show data by institution. Data by ethnic origin are shown by race and for Hispanics, Asians, Indians, and aliens.]

STUDENTS
[Tables [1-14] show data for independent and/or public senior colleges/universities and junior colleges. Tables [1-10] include data for other professional, health-related, and/or medical and dental schools.]

[1] Summary of headcount enrollment [by type of institution, including public technical institutes], 1979-83. (p. 7)

[2-4] Headcount enrollment, 1979-83. (p. 8-14)

[5-10] Headcount enrollment by [academic] classification, ethnic origin, and sex, 1983. (p. 15-46)

[11-12] Resident and nonresident [and foreign] students [at public institutions], 1983. (p. 47-49)

[13-14] Texas resident students by county of origin; and out-of-State enrollments [by State or territory of origin; aggregate for public institutions], 1983. (p. 50-53)

FACULTY
[Tables [18-20] show data for public senior colleges/universities.]

[15-17] Faculty headcount: [total] and tenured, by [academic] rank, public senior colleges/universities; [and totals for] public community junior colleges; [all] by ethnic origin and sex, 1983. (p. 57-72)

[18] Faculty salaries [averages], all [academic] ranks, 1979/80-1983/84. (p. 73)

[19] Faculty salaries [and ranges], by [academic] rank, (9 months) 1983/84. (p. 74-76)

[20] Student-faculty ratios, 1979/80-1983/84. (p. 77)

[21] Faculty salaries [and ranges], public community junior colleges, 1983/84. (p. 78)

S7657-1.2: Credit Hours and Physical Plant
[Tables [1-9] and [11-17] show data by institution.]

CREDIT HOURS

[1-5] Semester credit hours by [degree] level; and undergraduate, master's, doctoral, and special/professional semester credit hours, by program; [all for] public senior colleges/universities, FY84. (p. 81-92)

[6-8] Semester credit hours, fall 1983 and spring and summer 1984 [by degree level, for] public senior colleges/universities. (p. 93-95)

[9] Semester credit hour enrollments by curriculum area, public community junior colleges, fall 1983. (p. 96-101)

PHYSICAL FACILITIES
[Tables [10-12] show data for public senior colleges/universities and junior colleges. Tables [10-13] also show data for Texas A&M University System agricultural and engineering services, health-related units, and other agencies.]

[10] Investment in physical plant [by type of institution], FY83. (p. 105)

[11-13] Investment in physical plant [and value of land, buildings, other improvements, construction in progress, and equipment], FY83. (p. 106-108)

[14-17] Net assignable facilities space by function, in square feet, as of Oct. 31, 1984. (p. 109-113)

S7657-1.3: Financial Data

LEGISLATIVE APPROPRIATIONS

[1-2] Legislative appropriations, all funds and general revenue, agencies of higher education [by agency, FY84-85]. (p. 117-123)

[3] Legislative appropriations for educational and general purposes [by function, for] public senior colleges/universities [FY84-85]. (p. 124)

[4-5] Biennial legislative appropriations per FTE student, all funds and general revenue, public senior colleges/universities [1953/55-1983/85]. (p. 125-126)

STUDENT AID
[Tables [6-16] show data for FY84 or cumulative through FY84.]

[6-7] Hinson-Hazlewood College Student Loan Act: summary of loan transactions [by type of public and independent institution], and statement of collections [by status of account]. (p. 129-131)

[8-13] Hinson-Hazlewood College Student Loan Act: institutional status of accounts with payments seriously past due [by type of institution, and by individual institution, for public and independent senior colleges/universities and junior colleges, and other agencies of higher education]. (p. 133-138)

[14-16] Tuition equalization grants, State student incentive grants, and Texas public educational/State student incentive grants programs: [summaries of grants administered by type of institution]. (p. 139-141)

S7660   TEXAS
Department of Corrections

S7660-1   TEXAS DEPARTMENT OF CORRECTIONS 1984 Fiscal Year Statistical Report
Annual.   [1985.]   xii + 165 p.
LC 83-642724.
SRI/MF/complete

Annual report, for FY84, on corrections in Texas, presenting data on the prison population, including inmate admissions, releases, demographic characteristics, criminal background, commitment offense, and sentence length. Includes summary data by institution (including halfway houses) and by SMSA of conviction and residence.

Also includes data on corrections dept finances; inmate enrollment in educational and vocational programs, and degrees awarded; inmate intelligence quotient (IQ) and achievement test results; detail for inmates paroled and for inmates discharged under mandatory supervision, including average time served and violators; and selected trends from 1967.

Contains preface, and contents and table listing (p. ii-xii); introduction (p. 1-4); and 10 statistical sections, with 3 charts and 113 tables (p. 6-165).

This is the 8th annual report.

Availability: Texas Department of Corrections, Management Services, Box 99, Huntsville TX 77340, †; SRI/MF/complete.

S7670   TEXAS
Education Agency

S7670-1   TEXAS EDUCATION STATISTICS
Annual series.   For individual publication data, see below.
SRI/MF/complete

Annual series of reports, each presenting data on a selected aspect of Texas elementary and secondary education. Topics include personnel and salaries; enrollment, attendance, and graduates; and possibly others.

Data are compiled by the Texas Education Agency.

Each report consists of 1 extended table showing data by county and school district.

Reports are described in order of receipt. Reports reviewed during 1985 are described below.

Prior to 1985, abstracts for these reports were grouped according to period of data coverage. For descriptions of reports covered in 1984, see SRI 1984 Annual, under this number and under S7670-2.

Series previously was entitled *Statistical Brief, Texas,* and each report included narrative analysis and several detailed tables. Beginning in summer 1984, issuing agency publishes only frequently requested data in this series; other data may be requested from the agency.

Availability: Texas Education Agency, Publications Distribution Office, 201 E. 11th St., Austin TX 78701; SRI/MF/complete.

S7670–1.1: 1983/84 Personnel and Salaries by District with Pupil/Personnel Ratios (Excluding Special Ed Personnel)
[Annual. Aug. 29, 1984. 157 p. $3.00. SRI/MF/complete.]

Annual table showing Texas elementary/secondary school FTE aides, teachers, and support/administrative personnel, by funding source; salaries; pupil/personnel ratios; and average daily attendance; by county and school district (including special districts and State-administered schools), 1983/84.

For description of report showing similar data for 1981/82, see SRI 1983 Annual under S7670–2.7. No report with data for 1982/83 was issued.

S7670–1.2: 1983/84 Pupil Count Data
[Annual. Oct. 5, 1984. 48 p. $2.00. SRI/MF/complete.]

Annual table showing Texas elementary/secondary school original entries, average daily membership, average daily attendance (ADA), and graduates (with percent planning to enter college), by county, school district (including special districts and State-administered schools), and district subcategories (including ADA size, urban-rural classification, average market property value, and tax effort classification), 1983/84.

For description of report showing similar data for 1981/82, see SRI 1984 Annual under S7670–2.8.

S7670–1.3: Texas 1983/84 PPR Full-Time Equivalent Personnel (FTE)
[Annual. [1984]. 144 p. $3.00. SRI/MF/complete.]

Annual table showing Texas elementary/secondary school FTE teachers, administrative/support personnel, and aides/secretaries, by sex and race/ethnic group (white, black, Hispanic, Asian, Indian, and other), by county and school district, 1983/84.

For description of report showing similar data for 1981/82, see SRI 1983 Annual under S7670–2.6. No report with data for 1982/83 was issued.

S7675   TEXAS
Employment Commission

S7675–1   TEXAS OCCUPATIONAL EMPLOYMENT STATISTICS
Series. For individual publication data, see below. SRI/MF/complete

Continuing series of 6 reports, published in a 3-year cycle, each presenting data on employment in a selected Texas industry sector, by detailed occupation. Sectors covered are manufacturing, nonmanufacturing, State and local government, trade and regulated industries, educational services, and hospitals.

Data are from Occupational Employment Statistics Program surveys of employers in the various sectors, conducted over the 3-year cycle and updated triennially.

General format of each report:

a. Contents listing, introduction, and methodology.

b. 1 table, repeated for each SIC 2- or 3-digit industry covered, usually showing estimated employment and relative standard error, by occupation.

c. Glossary and/or bibliography.

Reports reviewed during 1985 are described below.

Availability: Texas Employment Commission, Economic Research and Analysis Department, TEC Bldg., 15th and Congress Ave., Austin TX 78778, †; SRI/MF/complete.

S7675–1.11: Industry Staffing Patterns for Hospitals, 2nd Quarter 1983
[Recurring (irreg.) Oct. 1984. v + 10 p. SRI/MF/complete.]

Covers occupational employment in private/State government/local government hospitals. Excludes Federal and prison hospitals. Presents estimated employment only.

Based on a mail survey of 565 hospitals, conducted in Apr. 1983.

Previous report, for 1980, is described in SRI 1982 Annual under S7675–1.7.

S7675–1.12: Industry Staffing Patterns for Selected Manufacturing Industries, 2nd Quarter 1983
[Recurring (irreg.) Dec. 1984. xi + 331 p. LC 82-622401. SRI/MF/complete.]

Covers Texas occupational employment in food, textiles, apparel, lumber, furniture and fixtures, paper, printing and publishing, chemicals, petroleum, rubber and plastics, leather, cement and concrete, primary and fabricated metal, machinery, transportation equipment, instruments, and other manufacturing industries.

Based on mail surveys conducted 2nd quarter 1983.

For description of previous report on manufacturing employment, see SRI 1982 Annual under S7675–1.6.

S7675–3   TEXAS LABOR MARKET REVIEW
Monthly. 8 p.
LC sc84-7310.
SRI/MF/complete, shipped quarterly

Monthly report on Texas labor force, covering employment, hours, and earnings, by MSA and industry group; and unemployment insurance claims and benefits. Data are from the Texas Employment Commission. Month of data coverage is 1 month prior to publication date.

Contains narrative summary, and 7 monthly tables and 1 quarterly table described below.

Monthly tables appear in all issues. Quarterly table appears in Nov. 1984 and Jan., Apr., and July 1985 issues.

Availability: Texas Employment Commission, Economic Research and Analysis Department, TEC Bldg., 15th and Congress Ave., Austin TX 78778, †; SRI/MF/complete, shipped quarterly.

Issues reviewed during 1985: Oct. 1984-Aug. 1985 (P).

TABLES:
[Unless otherwise noted, tables show data for Texas, for month of coverage, preceding month, and same month of preceding year.]

MONTHLY TABLES

a. U.S. and Texas labor force, actual and seasonally adjusted, by employment status. 1 table.

b. Nonagricultural wage/salary employment, by MSA and industry division, and statewide by industry group. 2 tables.

c. Labor force, by employment status and MSA. 1 table.

d. Hours and earnings: statewide by industry division and selected group; and for durable and nondurable goods manufacturing in selected MSA. 2 tables.

e. Texas Employment Commission activities, including placements, and unemployment insurance claims and benefits, for month of coverage and same month of preceding year. 1 table.

QUARTERLY TABLE

f. Unemployment insurance benefits paid, by MSA, for quarter ending 1 month prior to issue date. 1 table.

S7685   TEXAS
Department of Health

S7685–1   TEXAS VITAL STATISTICS, 1984
Annual. [1985.] vi + 99 p.
ISSN 0495-257X.
LC 76-641131.
SRI/MF/complete

Annual report on Texas vital statistics, covering births, deaths by cause, marriages, and divorces, by location and selected demographic characteristics, 1984, with trends from 1950. Data are compiled from State records and Census Bureau reports.

Contains listings of contents, tables, and charts (p. iii-vi); and 1 map, 7 charts, and 29 tables listed below, arranged in 4 sections (p. 1-99).

Availability: Texas Department of Health, Vital Statistics Bureau, Statistical Services Division, 1100 W. 49th St., Austin TX 78756-3199, †; SRI/MF/complete.

TABLES:
[Data are for 1984, unless otherwise noted.]

TRENDS
[Tables I-VI show data for 1950-84.]

I. Births and deaths, and rates per 1,000 population. (p. 2)

II-III. Births, by attendant [physician and midwife/other], and place of delivery [hospital and home/other], and by race and sex. (p. 3-4)

IV. Deaths by race and sex. (p. 5)

V. Infant, maternal, and fetal deaths, and rates [or] ratios per 1,000 births. (p. 6)

VI. Infant deaths by age, and rates per 1,000 births. (p. 8)

VII. [Ten] leading causes of death in selected years and rates per 100,000 population based on census as of Apr. 1 each year [decennially 1950-80]. (p. 9)

VIII. Mortality from selected causes and rates per 100,000 estimated population, 1980-84. (p. 10)

BIRTHS AND DEATHS

IX-X. Births, by age of mother and birth weight, by race and sex. (p. 11)

XI. Births, deaths, and fetal deaths [number and rate or ratio] by month. (p. 12)

XII. [Ten] leading causes of death and rate per 100,000 estimated population. (p. 13)

XIII. Five leading causes of death by sex and age. (p. 14)

XIV. Deaths from selected causes, by race, sex, and age. (p. 15-26)

XV. Deaths from selected types of accidents, by race, sex, and age. (p. 28-29)

XVI-XVII. Deaths under 1 year and under 28 days from selected causes, by race and sex [with] rates per 1,000 births. (p. 30-33)

XVIII-XIX. Deaths under 1 year, and under 28 days, by age, race, and sex [with] rates per 1,000 births. (p. 34)

XX. Births and deaths [by sex and race] by public health region, county [including rural areas], and city of residence [for] cities over 2,500 population. (p. 36-47)

XXI.A.-XXI.B. Deaths from selected causes, by public health region and county of residence; and by city of residence [for] cities over 10,000 population. (p. 48-69)

XXII. Births; [and] infant, neonatal, maternal, and fetal deaths [with] rates [or] ratios per 1,000 births; by public health region, county [including rural areas], and city of residence. (p. 70-76)

MARRIAGES AND DIVORCES

XXIII. Marriages by age of bride and age of groom. (p. 77)

XXIV. Marriages by county, sex, and age. (p. 78-87)

XXV-XXVI. Divorces by age of wife and age of husband; and by number of children [with total children affected]. (p. 88)

XXVII-XXVIII. Divorces by age of wife and age of husband [by] duration of marriage. (p. 89)

XXIX. Divorces by county, sex, and age. (p. 90-99)

S7695   TEXAS
Department of Human Resources

S7695–1   **1984 ANNUAL REPORT, Texas Department of Human Resources**
Annual. Dec. 1984.
2+73 p.
SRI/MF/complete

Annual report, for FY84, on Texas Dept of Human Resources (DHR) social, medical, and financial services, expenditures, and administration, mostly by county.

Contains contents listing (1 p.); introduction (p. 3-5); 4 narrative sections, with 10 charts (p. 9-40); and statistical summary, with 1 chart and 5 tables described below (p. 43-73).

Availability: Texas Department of Human Resources, PO Box 2960, Austin TX 78769, †; SRI/MF/complete.

CHART AND TABLES:

[Data are for FY84, and are shown by county unless otherwise noted.]

a. Statewide estimated expenditures for services to families/children and aged/disabled adults, agency administration, and health care services, with percent from Federal, State, and other sources, all by function; and expenditures on AFDC, food stamps, families/children, and aged/disabled adults, by DHR region. 1 table and 1 chart. (p. 44-45)

b. Food stamp and AFDC monthly average participants and total value or payments, and aggregate fraud case dispositions. 1 table. (p. 46-52)

c. Families and children benefits: payments for prescribed medicines and hospital/other services, and average monthly active Medicaid eligibles, number of clients served by protective services for children, children in day care purchased by DHR, and licensed day care and 24-hour child care facilities. 1 table. (p. 53-59)

d. Aged/disabled benefits: nursing home/mentally retarded/intermediate care facility clients and payments, payments for prescribed medicines and hospital/other services, average monthly active Medicaid eligibles, and clients served by community care services. 1 table. (p. 60-66)

e. DHR employees, medical assistance payments, food stamp value, and AFDC payments. 1 table. (p. 67-73)

S7710   TEXAS
State Library

S7710–1   **TEXAS PUBLIC LIBRARY STATISTICS for 1983**
Annual. 1984.
iii+233 p. var. paging+addendum.
ISSN 0082-3120.
LC 75-646379.
SRI/MF/complete

Annual report, for FY83, on Texas public libraries, presenting data on collections, services, finances, and personnel, for individual libraries. Also includes library directories.

Data are from reports submitted by 429 public libraries.

Contains foreword and contents listing (p. i-iii); and 4 sections, each individually paginated, as follows:

Section I. General information, including directories of library officials, interlibrary loan centers, and historical resource and State document depositories. (p. 1-11)

Section II. Directory of public libraries and branches. (p. 1-69)

Section III. Statistical information with narrative introduction (2 p.); and 3 tables, listed below. (p. A1-C11)

Section IV. Index to directory section. (p. 1-42)

Issuing agency also publishes *Texas Academic Library Statistics,* not covered by SRI.

Availability: Texas State Library, Library Development Division, PO Box 12927, Capitol Station, Austin TX 78711, †; SRI/MF/complete.

TABLES:

[Data on library personnel are for Jan. 1984; total population data in table C are from 1980 census counts. All other data are for local FY83.]

[A] Statistics by library [arranged alphabetically by library system, and including location; 1983 population served; holdings by type; collection turnover rate; in-library usage; interlibrary loan items received; program attendance; library visits; reference transactions; expenditures by object including salaries and utilities, and by funding source; per capita tax support; budgeted FTE staff; and librarians with master's degrees in library science]. (p. A1-A86)

[B] Summary statistics [repeats most data in Table [A], by regional library system and for State; also includes State total bookmobiles]. (p. B1-B12)

[C] Statistics by county [total population, 1983 population served, maximum property tax allocation to libraries, and total library expenditures]. (p. C1-C11)

S7735   TEXAS
Department of Public Safety

S7735–2   **TEXAS CRIME REPORT, 1984**
Annual. [1985.] iv+75 p.
SRI/MF/complete

Annual report on Texas crimes and arrests, by offense, 1984, with selected trends from 1974. Includes data by county and reporting agency, and by offender age, sex, and race. Also includes law enforcement employment, assaults on officers, and data on child sexual abuse and domestic violence.

Report focuses on 8 Index offenses: murder, rape, robbery, aggravated assault, burglary, theft, motor vehicle theft, and arson. Arrests are also shown for numerous non-Index offenses.

Data are from State and local agency reports submitted under the Uniform Crime Reporting (UCR) Program. Child sexual abuse data are based on a sample survey of 21 agencies. Domestic violence data are based on a sample survey of 24 agencies.

Contains contents listing (p. iii-iv); UCR Program description and offense classification (p. 3-7); 16 charts and 43 tables, with interspersed narrative and text data (p. 9-72); and glossary (p. 75). All tables, and selected text data and charts presenting data not covered in tables, are described below.

Availability: Texas Department of Public Safety, Uniform Crime Reporting Bureau, PO Box 4143, Austin TX 78765, †; SRI/MF/complete.

DATA:

[Unless otherwise noted, data are for 1984. Arson data are not included in the Crime Index tables.]

S7735–2.1: Offenses

INDEX OFFENSES

[In addition to the tables described below, 1 table showing arrests by age, sex, and race is repeated for each Index offense except arson.]

a. Summary: stolen property value and percent recovered, by property type and/or offense; clearance rates, by offense; and percent property and violent crime. 4 charts and 1 table. (p. 11-13)

b. Murder: offense distribution by weapon, victim-offender relationship, circumstances, and victim age, sex, and race. 1 chart and 4 tables. (p. 14-15)

c. Rape: offense distribution by classification (forcible and attempted forcible). 1 chart and 1 table. (p. 16)

d. Robbery: offenses and stolen property value, by setting; and offense distribution by weapon. 2 charts and 2 tables. (p. 17)

e. Aggravated assault: offense distribution by weapon. 1 chart and 1 table. (p. 18)

f. Burglary: offenses and stolen property value by circumstances (residence or nonresidence, night or day); and offense distribution by type of entry (forcible, no force, and attempted forcible). 2 charts and 2 tables. (p. 19)

g. Theft: offenses and stolen property value, by type and size of theft. 1 chart and 2 tables. (p. 20)

h. Motor vehicle theft: offense distribution by vehicle type; and vehicles recovered in and outside jurisdiction where stolen. 1 chart and 2 tables. (p. 21)

i. Arson offenses, clearances, clearances involving juveniles, offenses involving uninhabited structures, and property damage value, by property classification. 1 table. (p. 22)

j. Crime frequency, 1984; population, offenses, and crime rate, 1974-84; and offenses, by urban-rural location, by area population size, and on college/university campuses, 1984; all by offense. 1 chart and 15 tables. (p. 23-27)

CHILD SEXUAL ABUSE AND DOMESTIC VIOLENCE

k. Child sexual abuse analysis, including distribution by victim age and offense type. Text data and 1 chart. (p. 28)

l. Domestic violence analysis including police response to calls, nature of violence, and victim and offender characteristics. Text data. (p. 29-30)

LOCAL OFFENSE DATA

m. Index offenses by type, by contributing agency (sheriffs' offices, police depts, and colleges/universities), grouped by county. 1 table. (p. 33-58)

S7735-2.2: Arrests and Law Enforcement Employee Data

ARRESTS

a. Juvenile and adult arrests, by sex and age, for 39 Index and non-Index offense classifications, including detailed breakdown for drug offenses. 4 tables. (p. 61-66)

LAW ENFORCEMENT EMPLOYEES

b. Law enforcement officers killed, 1975-84; and officers assaulted, by type of assignment, activity, weapon, whether injury resulted, and time of day, 1984. 1 chart and 5 tables. (p. 71-72)

c. Sworn and civilian law enforcement employees, by sex; and survey forms returned; by dept type. 2 tables. (p. 72)

S7735-3   MOTOR VEHICLE TRAFFIC ACCIDENTS, 1984, Texas
Annual. [1985.] 48 p.
LC 54-28420.
SRI/MF/complete

Annual report on Texas traffic accidents involving fatalities, injuries, and property damage, and number of persons killed and injured, 1984, with selected trends from 1937. Includes data by vehicle and accident type, location, time, and other circumstances; and driver and victim characteristics.

Also includes data on accident economic loss, vehicle registrations and mileage, licensed drivers, use of safety devices, breath alcohol test results, incidence of driving while intoxicated, and vehicle defects.

Contains contents listing and highlights (p. 1-3); and 5 charts and 34 tables (p. 4-48).

Availability: Texas Department of Public Safety, Statistical Services, PO Box 4087, Austin TX 78773, †; SRI/MF/complete.

S7795   UTAH
Department of Administrative Services

S7795-1   STATE OF UTAH COMPREHENSIVE ANNUAL FINANCIAL REPORT for the Year Ended June 30, 1984
Annual. Dec. 21, 1984.
vii+123 p.
LC 84-641831.
SRI/MF/complete, current & previous year reports

Annual report on financial condition of Utah State government for FY84, presenting assets, liabilities, and fund equity; revenues by source; and expenditures by object, function, and agency or institution; for general, special revenue, capital projects, debt service, enterprise, internal service, trust and agency, and college and university funds, with selected trends from 1977.

Also includes data on long-term bonded debt; financial and debt ratios; and selected socioeconomic trends, including population; retail sales, personal income, and labor force, by industry division and/or kind of business; unemployment rate; bank deposits; and employment of 25 largest employers; various years 1940-84.

Most data are from internal records of the State Administrative Services Dept Finance Division.

Contains transmittal letter and contents listing (p. iii-vii); highlights, with 4 charts and 4 tables (p. 1-5); financial section with 38 fund statements, and accompanying notes with text data (p. 10-104); and statistical trend section, with 3 charts and 20 tables (p. 107-123).

Previous report, for FY83, has also been reviewed and is also available on SRI microfiche under this number [Annual. Oct. 5, 1983. vii+111 p. †]. Report for FY82 is described in SRI 1983 Annual, under this number.

Availability: Utah Department of Administrative Services, Finance Division, 2110 State Office Bldg., Salt Lake City UT 84114, †; SRI/MF/complete.

S7800   UTAH
Department of Agriculture

S7800-1   UTAH AGRICULTURAL STATISTICS, 1985
Annual. [1985.] 100 p.
LC 72-623245.
SRI/MF/complete

Annual report on Utah agricultural production, finances, and marketing, 1984, with selected data for 1985 and trends from as early as 1850. Data are generally shown by commodity and/or county, with some comparisons to total U.S.

Report generally covers production, prices, disposition, value, and, as applicable, acreage, yield, stocks, and inventory, for field crop, fruit, vegetable, livestock, dairy, and poultry sectors.

Also includes data on urban and rural population by county, and farm population; number, acreage, and value of farms; irrigation; farm income, production expenses, balance sheet, labor, and wages; mink operations; and weather.

Data are primarily from Utah Dept of Agriculture and USDA.

Contains introduction and contents listing (p. 4-5); 1 map, 11 charts, and 95 tables, interspersed with narrative summaries (p. 6-93); article on model enterprise budgets, with 6 tables (p. 94-99); and a list of other publications available (p. 100).

Availability: Crop and Livestock Reporting Service, Crop and Livestock Reporting Service, PO Box 25007, Salt Lake City UT 84125, †; SRI/MF/complete.

S7815   UTAH
Office of Education

S7815-1   ANNUAL STATISTICAL REPORT OF SCHOOL DISTRICTS, 1983/84, Utah
Annual. Dec. 1984.
ii+266 p.
SRI/MF/complete

Annual report, for school year 1983/84, on Utah public school enrollment, attendance, and personnel, by school district and type of program. Also includes data on school dropouts, special and adult education, and pupil transportation.

Data are from reports of 40 school districts, compiled by the Office of Education.

Contains table listing (p. i-ii); and 44 tables, listed below (p. 1-266).

This is the most comprehensive report published by the Utah Dept of Education, which also issues 3 other annual reports not covered in SRI: *Salary Schedule Information on Utah School Districts, Status of Teacher Personnel in Utah,* and *Annual Report of the State Superintendent.*

Availability: Utah Office of Education, Administrative Services Division, 250 East Fifth South, Salt Lake City UT 84111, †; SRI/MF/complete.

TABLES:
[Tables show data by school district, 1983/84, unless otherwise noted. Data by racial break-

down include American Indian/Alaskan Native, Hispanic, black, Caucasian, and Asian/Pacific Islander.]

S7815-1.1: Enrollment, Dropouts, and Attendance

[Tables [3], [5], and [7-9] show data for elementary, middle, and secondary schools, by grade and type of handicap or learning disability, and number in or not in training centers.]

[1] Number of public day schools in school district, by type of organized unit. (p. 1)

[2] Total year-end enrollment, ranked from highest to lowest [school district]. (p. 2)

[3] Year-end enrollment. (p. 3-11)

[4] Dropouts, by racial breakdown, grade [7th-12th, and self-contained classes], and sex. (p. 12-29)

[5] Aggregate days attendance. (p. 30-38)

[6] Comparison of pupils in average daily attendance [ADA], 1982/83-1983/84. (p. 39)

[7] ADA. (p. 40-48)

[8-10] Aggregate and average days membership; and percentage aggregate daily attendance is of aggregate daily membership. (p. 49-67)

S7815-1.2: School Personnel

[Tables show data by sex.]

[1] FTE classified personnel [by function and type of position, with detail by school level]. (p. 68-118)

[2] Number of classified personnel, by racial breakdown (FTE). (p. 119-120)

[3] FTE classified personnel, nonregular day school [by type of position]. (p. 121-125)

[4] Number of classified personnel, by racial breakdown [nonregular day school]. (p. 126-127)

[5] FTE certificated nonteaching personnel [by function and type of position]. (p. 128-160)

[6] FTE certificated teaching personnel [kindergarten and regular teachers grades 1-12; and] resource programs [by specialty], self-contained handicapped [by type of handicap], teacher interns, and subtotal regular/handicapped teachers [all by school level]. (p. 161-209)

[7] Grand total FTE, all certificated professional personnel [by school level]. (p. 210-212)

[8] Certificated professional personnel by racial breakdown. (p. 213-214)

[9-10] FTE extended year. summer school [elementary, secondary, and vocational home economics/agricultural] teachers who teach. (p. 215-216)

[11] FTE certificated personnel [by function and position], nonregular day school. (p. 217-223)

[12] Certificated professional personnel, by racial breakdown (FTE), nonregular day school. (p. 224-225)

S7815-1.3: Special Programs and Pupil Data

SPECIAL PROGRAMS

[1-2] Handicapped resource program, and handicapped in self-contained classes: total elementary/secondary by student count and average daily membership (ADM) [by type of handicap]. (p. 226-234)

[3-4] Special needs students [total and number homebound/hospitalized]; and extended year program for severely multiple handicapped [number of students and aggregate membership and attendance]. (p. 235-236)

[5] Driver education program for private school pupils, classroom instruction only [ADA and ADM by grade]. (p. 237)

[6] Behind-the-wheel driver education, number of students [full-time and private school students, and adults] completing program. (p. 238)

[7-8] Extended year/summer/day program (summer 1984) direct instruction enrollments, and teacher training participant hours. (p. 239-240)

HIGH SCHOOL GRADUATES

[9] High school graduates by racial breakdown [and sex]. (p. 241-242)

ADULT EDUCATION

[10-11] Adult basic education/adult high school enrollees, by age and sex; and by sex, race, and selected ethnic groups. (p. 243-245)

[12-13] Adult basic education/adult high school: programs [graduates and transfers from regular day school, by sex]; and personnel (head count only, not FTE) [by type of position]. (p. 246-247)

[14] Adult basic education/adult high school impact data [including level of education achieved; public assistance discontinued; and job, citizenship, voter registration, and drivers license obtained]. (p. 248-249)

[15] Adult high school impact data: number of units of adult high school completion credit awarded from all sources, by [source]. (p. 250-251)

[16] Adult basic education/adult high school reasons for separation. (p. 252-253)

TRANSPORTATION

[17] Transportation: total annual bus mileage [by type]. (p. 254-255)

[18] Transportation: number of regular bus drivers by male/female (not FTE); [and number of pupils transported by district buses, contracted services, and parents, and number receiving subsistence in lieu of transportation, all by eligibility category]. (p. 256-259)

[19] Number of school buses purchased during FY84. (p. 260)

[20-21] Number of [regular, spare], and contracted school buses in use in pupil transportation program, by seating capacity. (p. 261-264)

[22] School bus accidents data [mileage, accidents, and accident rates, 1982-84]. (p. 265-266)

S7820-1   UTAH EMPLOYMENT, WAGES, AND REPORTING UNITS by Firm Size, 1984

Annual. Jan. 1985. 49 p.
SRI/MF/complete

Annual report, for 1984, presenting data on Utah nonagricultural employment, wages, and reporting business units, by firm employment size. Data are shown by SIC 2-digit industry and by county and planning district, for 1st quarter 1984, with summary trends from 1970.

Data are compiled from employer reports to the Dept of Employment Security.

Contains contents listing (1 p.); introduction (p. 1); and report in 3 sections, with brief narrative summary and 3 tables (p. 3-49).

Availability: Utah Department of Employment Security, Labor Market Information Services Section, 174 Social Hall Ave., PO Box 11249, Salt Lake City UT 84147, †; SRI/MF/complete.

S7820-3   UTAH LABOR MARKET REPORT

Monthly. Approx. 10 p.
SRI/MF/complete, shipped quarterly

Monthly report on Utah nonagricultural employment, hours, and earnings, by industry, with selected data by locale. Also includes employment security activities.

Data are from reports of State and Federal agencies, and the American Chamber of Commerce Research Assn (ACCRA). Report is issued 1 month after month of coverage.

Contains brief narrative analysis, with 1-2 summary employment trend charts; recurring summary data on trends in Utah composite index of leading economic indicators and U.S. CPI; and 10 monthly tables.

Issues also occasionally contain additional statistical features, including quarterly cost-of-living data for selected western cities.

Monthly tables are listed below; most tables appear in all issues. All additional features with substantial statistical content are described, as they appear, under "Statistical Features." Non-statistical features are not covered.

Quarterly reports for each planning district are also available from the issuing agency, but are not covered by SRI.

Availability: Utah Department of Employment Security, Research and Analysis Section, 174 Social Hall Ave., PO Box 11249, Salt Lake City UT 84147, †; SRI/MF/complete, shipped quarterly.

Issues reviewed during 1985: Oct. 1984-Sept. 1985 (D).

MONTHLY TABLES:

[Tables generally show data for month of coverage, with comparisons to varying prior periods. Some data are current only to 1-3 months prior to month of coverage. Data are for Utah, unless otherwise noted.]

1. Civilian labor force [by employment status, and total involved in labor disputes].

2. Employees on nonagricultural payrolls, by industry [division and major group, and total involved in labor disputes].

3. Employment status of Utah's population, and nonagricultural jobs by industry [division] (seasonally adjusted).

4. Distribution of nonagricultural employment by sex, and production workers, by industry [division].

5. Labor force [by employment status] and employment [by industry division] in MSAs [Salt Lake/Ogden and Provo/Orem].

6. Civilian labor force and components unemployment rate and nonagricultural wage/salary jobs], by planning district and county.

7-8. Hours and earnings of production workers in Salt Lake-Ogden labor area and in Utah [by industry division and selected major group].

9. Employment security activities [including job openings, applicants, placements, and unemployment insurance claims and benefits].

10. Current price indexes, U.S. [including CPI for all urban consumers by item, and PPI by commodity category].

STATISTICAL FEATURES:

S7820–3.601: Oct. 1984

LOWER UNEMPLOYMENT INSURANCE TAX RATES FOR MANY UTAH EMPLOYERS IN 1985

(p. i-vi) Article, with 1 chart and 2 tables showing number of Utah employers, as follows:

a. By unemployment insurance tax rate, 1984 and estimated 1985 under revised rate schedule.

b. With and without former workers applying for/receiving unemployment benefits, FY84; and with lower unemployment tax rates in 1985 than in 1984; all by industry division.

Data are from Utah Dept of Employment Security.

COMPARATIVE GROWTH IN NONAGRICULTURAL EMPLOYMENT: UTAH AND U.S.

(p. 7) Table showing nonagricultural employment for Utah and U.S., 1970-84. Data are from Utah Dept of Employment Security and BLS.

S7820–3.602: Nov. 1984

UTAH LABOR MARKET REVIEW FOR 1984 AND OUTLOOK FOR 1985, ANNUAL FEATURE

(p. A-F) Annual articles presenting Utah employment review and outlook. Data are from Utah Dept of Employment Security. Includes 1 table showing civilian labor force by employment status, and employment by industry division, 1981-83 and forecast 1984-85.

S7820–3.603: Jan. 1985

ACCRA COMPOSITE COST-OF-LIVING COMPARISONS FOR SELECTED METRO AREAS, QUARTERLY FEATURE

(1 p.) Quarterly table showing cost-of-living index for U.S., selected western cities, and cities with highest and lowest index, by item, 3rd quarter 1984.

Data are from American Chamber of Commerce Researchers Assn.

S7820–3.604: Apr. 1985

YOUTH SURVEY HIGHLIGHTS EMPLOYMENT AND CAREERS

(p. D) Brief article, with 1 chart showing distribution of high school seniors by hours worked per week, by sex, 1982. Data are from a survey conducted by the Institute for Social Research at the University of Michigan.

ACCRA COMPOSITE COST-OF-LIVING COMPARISONS FOR SELECTED METRO AREAS, QUARTERLY FEATURE

(p. F) Quarterly table showing cost-of-living index for U.S., selected western and other cities, and cities with highest and lowest index, by item, 4th quarter 1984.

Data are from American Chamber of Commerce Researchers Assn.

S7820–3.605: May 1985

LABOR MARKET IMPACTS OF KMC CLOSURE

(8 p.) Article on effects of Kennecott Minerals Corp. (KMC) closure of Utah operations on State's labor market. Data are from Utah Dept of Employment Security. Includes 4 tables showing KMC role in Utah employment and unemployment trends, various periods 1950-85.

SUMMARY OF KEY LABOR MARKET INFORMATION FOR UTAH, ANNUAL FEATURE

(12 p.) Eleven annual tables showing Utah population, labor force by employment status, nonagricultural payroll employment and wages, establishments reporting in 1st quarter, and total and per capita personal income, all by planning district and county, various years 1970-84.

S7820–3.606: June 1985

ACCRA COMPOSITE COST-OF-LIVING COMPARISONS FOR SELECTED METRO AREAS, QUARTERLY FEATURE

(1 p.) Quarterly table showing cost-of-living index for U.S., selected western and other cities, and cities with highest and lowest index, by item, 1st quarter 1985.

Data are from American Chamber of Commerce Researchers Assn.

S7820–3.607: July 1985

ITEM OF ECONOMIC INTEREST

(p. 7) Table showing nonagricultural employment and civilian unemployment rates, for Utah, 7 other Rocky Mountain States, and total U.S., 1977-84. Data are from BLS.

S7820–3.608: Aug. 1985

UNEMPLOYMENT INSURANCE BENEFIT PAYMENTS SOFTENS UNEMPLOYMENT IMPACTS IN UTAH

(4 p.) Article, with 1 table and 2 charts showing the following for Utah: unemployment insurance benefits paid, weeks compensated, and average nonagricultural wage, 1938-84; and economic impact of unemployment insurance (in terms of payment value or employment equivalent) compared to impact (employment or payroll) of 6 major types of employers, 1984. Data are from Utah Dept of Employment Security.

CHARACTERISTICS OF UTAH'S UNEMPLOYED, 1984 ANNUAL AVERAGES

(p. 7) Table showing Utah unemployed by age, marital status, and unemployment circumstances and duration, all by sex, 1984. Data are from BLS and Census Bureau.

S7820–3.609: Sept. 1985

ACCRA COMPOSITE COST-OF-LIVING COMPARISONS FOR SELECTED METRO AREAS, QUARTERLY FEATURE

(1 p.) Quarterly table showing cost-of-living index for U.S., selected western and other cities, and cities with highest and lowest index, by item, 2nd quarter 1985.

Data are from American Chamber of Commerce Researchers Assn.

CURRENT LABOR MARKET INFORMATION FOR SMALL AREAS IN UTAH

(4 p.) By Richard W. Newman. Article, with 2 tables showing the following for Salt Lake County, Utah, by community; and for selected nonmetro Utah cities: nonagricultural employment, total and average monthly wages, and number of firms, various years 1971-1984. Data are from Utah Dept of Employment Security.

S7830   UTAH
Department of
Financial Institutions

S7830–1   **FOURTH ANNUAL AND THIRTY-EIGHTH REPORT OF THE COMMISSIONER OF FINANCIAL INSTITUTIONS,** State of Utah, for the Period July 1, 1983-June 30, 1984
Annual. [1984.] 109 p.
SRI/MF/complete

Annual report on financial condition of Utah State-chartered banks and other financial institutions, FY84, presenting assets, liabilities, and generally income and expenses, for commercial banks and trust companies, savings/building and loan assns, industrial loan corporations, credit unions, and supervised lenders. Asset and liability data are generally shown by institution.

Also includes data on dept appropriations, fee receipts, and expenditures; selected balance sheet data for State-located national banks and federally chartered savings/building and loan assns; and selected trends from 1978.

Contains contents listing (p. 2); dept report, with 4 tables (p. 4-10); and 36 financial tables, interspersed with directories and status change listings (p. 12-109).

Availability: Utah Department of Financial Institutions, 160 East 300 South, PO Box 89, Salt Lake City UT 84110, †; SRI/MF/complete.

S7835
Department of Health

UTAH

S7835–1   UTAH'S VITAL STATISTICS: Annual Report, 1982
Annual.   Oct. 1984.
xiii+91 p.
ISSN 0500-7720.
LC 74-642626.
SRI/MF/complete

Annual report on Utah vital statistics, by district and county, 1982 with selected trends from 1935. Presents detailed data on births and on deaths by cause, including selected demographic breakdowns. Also includes data on population, abortion, marriages, and divorces, and some U.S. comparisons.

Data are from local filings with the State Bureau of Health Statistics, and from U.S. Census Bureau.

Contains preface (p. iii); listings of contents, tables, charts, and additional tables available from issuing agency (p. iv-xi); definitions (p. xii-xiii); narrative report, interspersed with 6 charts, and 22 text tables described below (p. 1-30); 47 detailed reference tables, listed below (p. 31-83); and technical appendix (p. 84-91).

Previous report, for 1981, is described in SRI 1983 Annual, under this number.

Availability: Utah Department of Health, Health Statistics Bureau, PO Box 45500, Salt Lake City UT 84145-0500, $10.00 (prepaid); SRI/MF/complete.

TABLES:
[Unless otherwise noted, data are shown for Utah, 1982. Data by race generally are for white, black, American Indian, and other nonwhite. Data by residence are for district and county of residence.]

S7835–1.1: Text Tables
a. Overview: population, live births, deaths, marriages, and divorces/annulments, 1935-82, and rates with U.S. comparison, 1950-82; population by district and county, 1980-82; and number and rate of births, deaths, and abortions, by district and county, with birth and death totals for urban, rural, and SMSA classifications, 1982. Tables 1-6. (p. 3-11)

b. Birth summary: births, fertility rates, sex ratios of births, and low-weight birth rates by race, with selected U.S. comparisons, various years 1950-82; births to resident mothers in Utah and out of State, and to nonresident mothers in Utah, by district and county of residence or occurrence, 1982; and out-of-wedlock births and rates, by age of mother, 1970-82. Tables 7-12. (p. 14-18)

c. Death summary: mortality rates by leading cause, with U.S. comparisons, 1982; deaths and rates 1970-82, and expected total and working years of life lost by sex 1982, by selected cause; infant mortality rates, by age, 1960-82; and deaths and rates, for Spanish-origin and others, by selected cause and age, 1982. Tables 13-19. (p. 21-26)

d. Violent deaths: number and rate by type, 1981-82, with U.S. comparison; and suicides, by sex and age, 1960-82. Tables 20-22. (p. 28-30)

S7835–1.2: Births
[All tables, except A1, show data for Utah residents. Table titles A1-A15 and A18-A29 begin "Live births..."]

A1-A2. By county of occurrence, sex, attendant [physician, and midwife], and hospital delivery; and by sex, number born, birth order, and residence of mother. (p. 31-32)

A3-A4. By month of occurrence and residence of mother; and by age and residence of mother. (p. 33-34)

A5-A8. By residence of mother: by race and birth weight of infant, month prenatal care began, and number of prenatal visits. (p. 35-38)

A9-A11. By age of mother and race of infant: by birth order of infant, month prenatal care began, and prenatal visits. (p. 39-41)

A12-A13. By birth weight: by sex and race of infant, and weeks gestation. (p. 42-43)

A14-A15. By age and education of mother by number of previous live births; and by age and education of parents. (p. 44-45)

A16-A17. Out-of-wedlock live births by age and education of parents; and by age and residence of mother. (p. 46-47)

A18. By age and marital status of mother, and race of infant. (p. 48)

A19. By age of mother and birth weight of infant. (p. 49)

A20-A23. By birth weight of infant, month prenatal care began, age of mother, and residence, [all for births] with 1/more complications [or congenital anomalies] reported. (p. 50-53)

A24. By 5-minute Apgar score and birth weight of infant. (p. 54)

A25-A29. By residence, age of mother, race of infant, number of prenatal visits, month prenatal care began, and marital status of mother; and by age of mother, 1/more complications [or congenital anomalies] reported; [all for] mother of Spanish origin. (p. 55-59)

S7835–1.3: Deaths
BIRTHS AND DEATHS
A30. Live births and deaths by community [county and city] of occurrence and residence. (p. 60-63)

FETAL AND INFANT DEATHS
A31. Live births, premature live births, fetal deaths, and selected causes of infant mortality, by institutions and county of occurrence. (p. 64-65)

A32-A33. Fetal deaths: by age and residence of woman, and by sex and selected cause. (p. 66-67)

A34. Infant mortality for selected causes, by age, race, and sex, [for] residents. (p. 68)

A35. Infant, neonatal, and perinatal mortality by [age of infant and] residence of mother. (p. 69)

TOTAL DEATHS
A36. Deaths by month of occurrence and residence. (p. 70)

A37-A39. Deaths by race, sex, residence, and age [various cross-tabulations]. (p. 71-74)

A40-A41. Deaths by selected causes, by county of residence and age. (p. 75-77)

A42. Deaths by place where death occurred [including hospitals and nursing homes] by county of occurrence. (p. 78)

VIOLENT AND ACCIDENTAL DEATHS
A43-A45. Violent deaths by age, sex, residence, and race, [all] by cause. (p. 79-81)

A46-A47. Accidental death occurrences: by month and type of accident; and by age, sex, and type of accident. (p. 82-83)

S7835–2   UTAH MARRIAGE AND DIVORCE, 1980-82
Annual.   Jan. 1985.
xiv+128 p.
ISSN 0093-9641.
LC 80-645335.
SRI/MF/complete

Annual report on Utah marriages and divorces, 1982, with summary trends from 1940. Includes data by educational level, age, race, type of ceremony, and previous marital status. Data are from county reports and certificates filed with the Health Statistics Bureau.

Contents:

a. Listings of contents, tables, and charts. (p. iii-xiv)

b. Introduction and narrative summary, interspersed with 7 charts and 16 tables primarily showing summary data, but also including population and marriage and divorce trends from 1940, and comparisons to selected western States and total U.S. (p. 1-29)

c. Statistical section, with 87 reference tables listed below. (p. 30-122)

d. Appendix, with technical notes and facsimiles of report forms and certificates. (p. 123-128)

Previous report, for 1979, is described in SRI 1981 Annual under this number.

Issuing agency also publishes *Utah Vital Statistics: Annual Report,* which includes summary data on marriages and divorces. Report is described in SRI under S7835-1.

Availability: Utah Department of Health, Health Statistics Bureau, PO Box 45500, Salt Lake City UT 84145-0500, $10.00 (prepaid); SRI/MF/complete.

TABLES:
[Data by race are shown for white, black, Indian, and other. Tables show data for 1980-82.]

S7835–2.1: Reference Tables
MARRIAGES
[Data by type of officiant are shown for Catholic, Jewish, Latter Day Saints (L.D.S.), Protestant, all other religions, and unspecified religious ceremonies; and county clerk, judge, justice of the peace, and unspecified civil ceremonies. Tables show data for total marriages, unless otherwise noted.]

R1-R3. By county of residence of groom and bride. (p. 30-32)

R4-R9. By county of residence of groom and bride, and county of occurrence of marriage. (p. 33-38)

R10-R15. [Total and] 1st marriages, by age of bride and groom. (p. 39-50)

R16-R18. By State of residence of bride and groom. (p. 51-53)

R19-R21. By age and number of present marriage of bride and groom. (p. 54-56)

R22-R24. By age and previous marital status of bride and groom. (p. 57-59)

R25-R30. [Total and] first marriages by age and race of bride and groom. (p. 60-65)

R31-R33. Remarriages by age and race of bride and groom. (p. 66-68)

R34-R36. By race of bride and groom. (p. 69-71)

R37-R42. By education, previous marital status, and race of bride and groom. (p. 72-77)

R43-R45. By order of this marriage and education of husband and wife. (p. 78-80)

R46-R51. By order of marriage, education of groom and bride, and type of officiant. (p. 81-86)

R52-R54. By previous marital status of bride and groom, and type of officiant. (p. 87-89)

R55-R57. Remarriages [of] bride and groom by year previous marriage terminated and age at remarriage. (p. 90-92)

R58-R60. By month and county of occurrence. (p. 93-95)

R61-R63. Marriages and remarriages of bride and groom by month of occurrence. (p. 96-98)

R64-R69. By resident status of couples marrying and type of officiant, [total and for] teenage brides. (p. 99-104)

DIVORCES AND ANNULMENTS

[All tables begin "Divorces and annulments..."]

R70-R72. By month and county of occurrence. (p. 105-107)

R73-R75. Occurring in Utah, according to State where marriage was performed. (p. 108-110)

R76-R78. By duration of marriage in years. (p. 111-113)

R79-R84. By age of husband and wife, and number of times married. (p. 114-119)

R85-R87. By number of dependent children under 18 years of age. (p. 120-122)

S7850   UTAH
Judicial Council

S7850-1   UTAH COURTS, 1983-84
Annual. [1984.] 66 p.
ISSN 0098-9045.
LC 75-644191.
SRI/MF/complete

Annual report, for FY84, on Utah judicial system, including trial and appellate court caseloads and case dispositions. Covers supreme, district, circuit, and justice of the peace courts. Includes trial court data by case type and county or other jurisdiction, with selected comparisons to FY83 and forecasts for FY85.

Case types shown are criminal and civil, by detailed case type, including specific criminal offenses; and domestic relations, child abuse, probate, adoption, guardianship, mental competency hearings, contract, property rights, small claims, driving while intoxicated, and traffic cases.

Also includes data on crime victim compensation; case processing time; and judicial dept finances, including trial court revenues by source and expenditures by object.

Data are from court clerk's reports filed under the State Judicial Information System.

Contains contents listing (1 p.); introduction (p. 1-4); and report, in 8 sections, with text statistics, 9 charts, and 23 tables (p. 5-66).

This is the 11th annual report.

Availability: Utah Judicial Council, State Court Administrator's Office, 255 South Third East, Salt Lake City UT 84111, †; SRI/MF/complete.

S7875   UTAH
Office of the Lieutenant Governor/Secretary of State

S7875-1   GENERAL ELECTION REPORT Nov. 6, 1984, State of Utah
Biennial. [1985.]
17 p. no paging.
SRI/MF/complete

Biennial report presenting results of the Utah general election held Nov. 6, 1984. Includes voting for President/Vice President, U.S. Representatives, Governor/Lieutenant Governor, attorney general, State senators and representatives, judges, and other State officials; referendum on Cable TV Decency Act; and 5 constitutional amendments, including 1 concerning the right to bear arms. Data are shown by county and/or district, and include party affiliation of candidates.

Also includes voter registration and turnout, by county.

For description of previous report, covering 1982 general election, see SRI 1983 Annual under this number. Reports on primary elections are also available from the issuing agency, but are not covered in SRI.

Availability: Utah Office of the Lieutenant Governor/Secretary of State, 203 State Capitol Bldg., Salt Lake City UT 84114, †; SRI/MF/complete.

S7890   UTAH
Department of Public Safety

S7890-2   UTAH TRAFFIC ACCIDENT SUMMARY, 1984
Annual. July 1, 1985.
1+40 p.
LC 85-620874.
SRI/MF/complete

Annual report on Utah traffic accidents involving fatalities, injuries, and property damage, and number of persons killed and injured, 1984, with selected trends from 1948. Includes data by accident and vehicle type, location, time, and other circumstances; and driver and victim characteristics.

Also includes data on miles traveled; detail for accidents involving pedestrians, motorcycles, alcohol (including blood alcohol content of drivers), and vehicle defects; and use of safety devices in accidents.

Data are primarily from Utah Highway Safety Office records.

Contains contents listing (1 p.); introduction (p. 1-2); and 27 charts and 38 tables (p. 3-40).

Availability: Utah Department of Public Safety, Highway Safety Division, 4501 South 2700 West, Salt Lake City UT 84119, †; SRI/MF/complete.

S7890-3   CRIME IN UTAH, 1984
Annual. [1985.]
2+35 p.+errata.
LC 81-649761.
SRI/MF/complete

Annual report on Utah crimes and arrests, by offense, 1984, with summary trends from 1979. Includes data by county, reporting agency (including State protective service), and victim and offender age group. Also includes law enforcement employment, and assaults on officers.

Report focuses on 8 Index offenses: murder, rape, robbery, assault, burglary, larceny/theft, motor vehicle theft, and arson. Arrests are also shown for numerous non-Index offenses.

Data are from State and local agency reports submitted under the Uniform Crime Reporting Program.

Contains contents listing (1 p.); introduction, reporting procedures, and definitions, with crime clocks, and 1 table showing crime trends and State population, 1979-84 (p. 2-8); and 12 charts and 26 tables (p. 11-35).

All tables, and selected charts with substantial statistics not covered by tables, are described below.

This is the 7th annual report. A less detailed semiannual report on crimes and arrests is also available from the issuing agency, but is not covered by SRI.

Availability: Utah Department of Public Safety, Uniform Crime Reporting Section, Criminal Identification Bureau, 4501 South 2700 West, Salt Lake City UT 84119, †; SRI/MF/complete.

CHARTS AND TABLES:

[Unless otherwise noted, data are for 1984, with selected comparisons to 1983.]

INDEX CRIME SUMMARY

[In addition to tables and charts described below, data for each offense include 1 table showing offenses, offense rate, and clearances.]

a. Murder victims and offenders, by age group, sex, and race/ethnicity (including Indian and Asian/Pacific Islander); murders, by type of weapon, day of week, and victim/offender relationship; rape offenses and attempts; robberies and value of property stolen, by crime location; and aggravated assaults, by type of weapon. 5 charts and 9 tables. (p. 11-15)

b. Burglaries and value of property stolen, by day or night residential and nonresidential occurrence; larceny/theft offenses and value of property stolen, by theft type; value of motor vehicles stolen and recovered; and arson offenses involving structures, mobile property, and other types of property, and value of property damaged. 4 charts and 6 tables. (p. 16-18)

c. Value of property stolen and/or recovered, by offense and property type. 2 charts. (p. 19)

LAW ENFORCEMENT OFFICERS AND COUNTY DATA

d. Assaults on law enforcement officers, by time of day, circumstance, weapon, and injury status; and full-time sheriffs and municipal officers, by county. 1 chart and 4 tables. (p. 21-23)

e. Index crimes by offense, full-time law enforcement officers, and population, all by county and reporting agency. 2 tables. (p. 25-30)

ARRESTS

f. Adult and juvenile arrests: by Index and non-Index offense, 1982-84; and by county and reporting agency. 5 tables. (p. 32-35)

S7895   UTAH
Board of Regents/Office of the Commissioner of Higher Education

S7895–1   FIFTEENTH ANNUAL REPORT TO THE GOVERNOR AND THE LEGISLATURE, Utah State Board of Regents, 1983/84
Annual.   Jan. 1985.
xvi+100 p.
ISSN 0360-8123.
LC 75-649010.
SRI/MF/complete

Annual report on Utah postsecondary education for the 1983/84 school year, with trends from 1979/80. Includes data on State-supported institution finances and degrees awarded; and private institution degrees awarded.

Data sources include Higher Education General Information Survey .

Contents:

Foreword, contents listing, and lists of higher education officials. (p. iv-xvi)

Chapter I-II: Commissioner's Report and Events of the Year. (p. 1-33)

Chapter III: Academic Affairs. Includes summary of regent activities and program approvals and changes, and 6 tables showing: degrees awarded, variously cross-tabulated by institution type (public and private), individual institution, degree type and level, and field of study, various years 1979/80-1983/84. (p. 34-51)

Chapter IV: Budgets and Finance. Includes table listing (p. 53), narrative summary, and 4 tables showing: general fund appropriations, expenditures, operating and total revenues, and tuition and fees, by public institution, with selected detail for board of regents administration, and statewide and related programs; various years 1980/81-1984/85. (p. 53-60)

Chapter V-VII. Planning, Capital Facilities, and Profiles of Member Institutions. Includes narrative summaries, and text statistics showing capital facility funding requests 1985/86, and student fees and requirements, by public institution. (p. 62-98)

Index. (p. 100)

Availability: Utah Board of Regents/Office of the Commissioner of Higher Education, 355 West North Temple, 3 Triad Center, Suite 550, Salt Lake City UT 84180-1205, †; SRI/MF/complete.

S7905   UTAH
Tax Commission

S7905–1   TWENTY-SEVENTH BIENNIAL REPORT OF THE UTAH STATE TAX COMMISSION, Volume II
Biennial.   Jan. 10, 1985.
v+161 p.
LC 33-27803.
SRI/MF/complete

Biennial report volume, for FY84, on Utah State tax collections by source, and distribution of tax revenues to local areas and State government funds. Also includes data on taxable retail purchases by industry, property valuations, Federal tax returns of Utah residents, and tax commission activities.

Report is published in 2 volumes, presenting separate data for each fiscal year of the biennium. Volume I is published in even-numbered years; Volume II is published in odd-numbered years. Current Volume II presents data for FY84; for description of Volume I for FY83, see SRI 1984 Annual under this number.

Contains contents listing (p. iii-v); 3 sections on commission activities, tax trends, and taxation in Utah and neighboring States, with 11 charts and 12 tables (p. 5-39); and 20 sections on specific tax types, with facsimile tax reporting forms, descriptions of taxes, statutory references, tax rates or fees, 15 charts, and 26 tables (p. 41-161).

All tables, and selected charts showing substantial statistics not included in tables, are described below.

Availability: Utah Tax Commission, Heber M. Wells Office Bldg., 160 East Third South, Salt Lake City UT 84134, †; SRI/MF/complete.

TABLES AND CHARTS:
[Unless otherwise noted, tables show data for Utah.]

UTAH TAX OVERVIEW

a. Tax commission net State/local collections, commission expenditures by division and item, commission employees compared to State population, and tax audit refunds/deficiency assessments by tax type, various years FY73-84. 5 tables. (p. 11-14)

b. Net tax collections by type, FY75-84; gross collections and refunds/adjustments by source and fund, FY83-84; and State population by county, 1970, 1980, and 1982-83. 3 tables. (p. 18-23)

TAXATION IN UTAH AND NEIGHBORING STATES

c. Income taxes paid by 8 types of corporations in Utah and 7 neighboring States; Utah taxpayer tax liability under current and 3 alternative tax systems, by income group; and business share of State taxes, distribution of State revenues by major tax type, and index of tax burdens on households, all for Utah and 9 neighboring States; various years 1980-83. 1 chart and 4 tables. (p. 29-39)

SPECIFIC UTAH TAXES

d. Sales/use tax collections FY65-84; and gross taxable retail sales/use tax purchases, by industry division and major group, FY82-84, with detail for FY84 by quarter. 4 tables. (p. 43-52)

e. State individual income tax collections FY65-84; and Federal tax returns filed, adjusted gross income, tax rate and taxes paid, and number of net exemptions, by county and/or income group, with county rankings by average adjusted gross income, mostly for 1982. 5 tables. (p. 55-65)

f. Property tax collections by property class, and distributions to public schools and other local entities, 1983; property assessed value and taxes, by property class, 1982-83; tax collections for motor fuel tax and for local option sales/use tax, FY65-84; and sales/use tax distribution to participating counties and cities, FY83-84. 2 charts and 4 tables. (p. 71-93)

g. Collections for corporate income/franchise, insurance premium, mine occupation (oil/gas and metalliferous ore), local transit authority, special fuel, cigarette/tobacco, inheritance, transient room, beer, and oil gas/conservation taxes; and local transit authority and transient room tax distributions to participating counties and cities; various years FY64-84. 13 tables. (p. 97-145)

S7978   VERMONT
Department of Agriculture

S7978–1   AGRICULTURE OF VERMONT, 1983-84
Biennial.   [1984.]   39+26 p.
SRI/MF/complete

Biennial report, for 1983-84, of the Vermont Dept of Agriculture. Includes data on agricultural production, value, cash receipts, prices, and, as applicable, inventory, acreage, and yield, for the dairy, livestock, poultry, crop, and maple syrup sectors, primarily 1973-83, with some data for 1984.

Also includes data on State Agriculture Dept finances and operations, including inspection activity; pesticide sales and use; damage to beehives by bears; meat-handling establishments and operations; dairy industry plants and operations, by county; fertilizer consumption; feed prices; number and acreage of farms, and farm income, production expenditures, and balance sheet, with selected comparisons to northeast region or New England and to U.S.; and U.S. per capita consumption of major food commodities.

Contains contents listing (1 p.); reports from State agricultural divisions, with narrative and 38 tables (p. 5-39); and separately paginated section on agricultural statistics, with contents listing (1 p.), and 8 charts and 46 tables (p. 1-26).

This is the 42nd biennial report. Previous report, for 1981-82, is described in SRI 1983 Annual under this number.

Availability: Vermont Department of Agriculture, State Office Bldg., 116 State St., Montpelier VT 05602, †; SRI/MF/complete.

S7995   VERMONT
Department of Banking and Insurance

S7995-2   ANNUAL REPORT OF THE BANK COMMISSIONER of the State of Vermont, for the Year Ended Dec. 31, 1984
Annual.   June 1, 1985.   67 p.
LC 76-626902.
SRI/MF/complete

Annual report on financial condition of Vermont State-chartered financial institutions, presenting assets and liabilities by institution, and composite income and expense data, for savings and commercial banks/trust companies, savings and loan assns, credit unions, and licensed lenders, 1984, with selected trends from 1855. Includes data for national banks and Federal credit unions.

Also includes data on banking division receipts and disbursements; populations for bank locations; rankings of banks by assets; trends in number of banks and value of deposits, from 1855; bank trust dept balance sheet; family financial counseling service clients and trust account value; and number of credit unions and members.

Other data include development credit corporation balance sheets; and Vermont Home Mortgage Guarantee Board loan guarantees, and trust fund finances, FY84.

Contains contents listing (p. 3-4); preface, lists of financial institutions and status changes, and banking division finances, with 2 tables (p. 7-22); and 23 financial tables, interspersed with directories (p. 23-67).

Availability: Vermont Department of Banking and Insurance, Banking Division, State Office Bldg., 120 State St., Montpelier VT 05602-9974, †; SRI/MF/complete.

S8020   VERMONT
Department of Education

S8020-1   VERMONT EDUCATION STATISTICS
Annual series.   For individual publication data, see below.
SRI/MF/complete

Series of 4 annual reports, each presenting data on an aspect of Vermont elementary and secondary education. Topics covered are enrollment, facilities, administration and staff, and finances. Some reports include nonpublic school data.

Data are compiled by the Dept of Education from reports by individual school districts.

Reports are described in order of receipt. Reports reviewed during 1985 are described below.

Prior to 1985, abstracts for these reports were grouped according to period of data coverage. For descriptions of reports covered in 1984, see SRI 1984 Annual under S8020-2 and S8020-3.

Availability: Vermont Department of Education, Statistics and Information Office, State Office Bldg., 120 State St., Montpelier VT 05602, †; SRI/MF/complete.

S8020-1.1: 1983/84 Vermont School Enrollment
[Annual. [1984.] 10+30 p. SRI/MF/complete.]

Contains introduction and 1 summary table (2 p.); lists of school districts, including county and superintendence, and school type codes (7 p.); and 1 table repeated for public, State administered, parochial, and private schools, showing enrollment, by sex and grade (including ungraded and postgraduate), by school, 1983/84 school year, for elementary schools (p. 1-18) and secondary schools (p. 19-30).

For description of report for 1982/83, see SRI 1983 Annual under S8020-3.2.

S8020-1.2: 1983/84 Vermont School Data
[Annual. [1984.] 9+25 p. SRI/MF/complete.]

Contains introduction, and lists of school districts, including county and superintendency, and school type codes (8 p.); and 1 table repeated for public schools (p. 1-19), State administered schools (p. 20), parochial schools (p. 21), and private schools (p. 22-25), showing number of instructional rooms, building area, teacher and total staff, and total enrollment, by school, 1983/84 school year.

For description of report for 1982/83, see SRI 1983 Annual under S8020-3.1.

S8020-1.3: 1984/85 Vermont Education Profiles Study
[Annual. May 1985. 9 p. no paging. SRI/MF/complete, current & 2 previous reports.]

Contains 1 table repeated for 15 professional and nonprofessional Vermont public school positions, showing mean, median, high, and low age, years in State and public school systems, and salary, 1984/85 school year.

Previous reports, for 1982/83 and 1983/84, have also been reviewed and are also available on SRI microfiche under S8020-1 [Annual. Sept. 1983. 9 p. no paging. †] and [Annual. May 1984. 9 p. no paging. †].

Report for 1981/82 is described in SRI 1982 Annual under S8020-2.3.

S8020-1.4: 1984/85 Vermont School Enrollment
[Annual. [1985.] 10+30 p. SRI/MF/complete.]

Contains introduction and 1 summary table (2 p.); lists of Vermont school districts, including county and superintendency, and school type codes (8 p.); and 1 table repeated for public, State administered, parochial, and private schools, showing enrollment, by sex and grade (including ungraded and postgraduate), by school, 1984/85 school year, for elementary schools (p. 1-18) and secondary schools (p. 19-30).

Previous report, for 1983/84, is described under S8020-1.1, above.

S8020-1.5: 1984/85 Vermont School Data
[Annual. [1985.] 10+25 p. SRI/MF/complete.]

Contains introduction, and lists of Vermont school districts, including county and superintendency, and school type codes (9 p.); and 1 table repeated for public schools (p. 1-18), State administered schools (p. 20), parochial schools (p. 21), and private schools (p. 22-25), showing number of instructional rooms, building area, teacher and total staff, and total enrollment, by school, 1984/85 school year.

Previous report, for 1983/84, is described under S8020-1.2, above.

S8020-1.6: 1983/84 Financial Statistics, Vermont School Systems
[Annual. [1985.] 182 p. Rpt. No. 052. SRI/MF/complete.]

Contains contents listing (1 p.); and 6 extended tables showing the following data, by county, town, supervisory union, and/or school district:

a. State aid distributed, including total aid, and wealth indexes, FY85; resident pupil long-term average daily attendance, FY84; and current expenses, FY83. (p. 2-15)

b. Transportation costs (total and as percent of operating expenditures), number of students transported, and average cost per student, 1983/84. (p. 17-48)

c. Revenues, by source; operating and other expenditures, by function; and cost per pupil; 1983/84. (p. 49-182)

Two additional tables are listed in the table of contents, but have not yet been published. These tables will be issued as supplements and will be covered in SRI when they are received.

Previous report, for 1982/83, is described in SRI 1984 Annual, under S8020-3.3.

S8025   VERMONT
Department of Employment and Training

S8025-1   WOMEN: LABOR FORCE, EMPLOYMENT, UNEMPLOYMENT, WAGES, 1983, Vermont
Annual.   [1984.]   37 p.
SRI/MF/complete

Annual report on Vermont women's labor force participation and earnings, 1983, with comparisons to men and selected trends from the 1950s. Includes data by employment status, age, educational attainment, occupation, industry division and selected major group, county, and unemployment reason and duration.

Also includes data on U.S. median earnings by sex and occupation; and Vermont female employers and sole business owners, and their employees, by SIC 4-digit industry.

Data are from Census Bureau, BLS, and quarterly reports of employees subject to Vermont's Unemployment Compensation Law.

Contains listing of contents, tables, and charts (1 p.); report, with summary, 5 charts, and 18 tables (p. 1-24); special section on female employers, with brief narrative and 1 table (p. 25-35); and glossary (p. 36-37).

Availability: Vermont Department of Employment and Training, Research and Statistics Section, PO Box 488, Montpelier VT 05602-0488, $5.00; SRI/MF/complete.

S8025–2   VERMONT ANNUAL PLANNING INFORMATION, 1985

Annual.   Sept. 1985.   54 p.
SRI/MF/complete

Annual report, for 1985, identifying Vermont population groups most in need of employment services. Includes data on population and labor force by county and labor market area; employment by industry; income comparisons to U.S.; socioeconomic characteristics of the unemployed; and job service activity; various years 1970-84, with selected earlier trends, and employment projections for 1990.

Data are compiled from reports by various Federal and State agencies.

Contents:

a. Listings of contents, tables, and charts. (2 p.)

b. Foreword and highlights; and narrative report, interspersed with 2 maps showing Vermont counties and labor market areas, 2 charts, and 22 tables listed below. (p. 1-32)

c. Economic profiles of the State, Burlington MSA, and each county; summary of U.S. poverty income guidelines with 1 table; and additional sources of information, glossary, and description of labor market areas. (p. 33-54)

Availability: Vermont Department of Employment and Training, Research and Statistics Section, PO Box 488, Montpelier VT 05602-0488, †; SRI/MF/complete.

TABLES:

[Data are for the State of Vermont, unless otherwise noted.]

S8025–2.1: Employment, Population, and Income

[Population data are shown for 1970, 1980, and estimated 1983.]

1. Population of major cities and towns. (p. 6)

2. Major employment centers, by county. [list] (p. 7)

3. Top 10 industries, estimated nonagricultural wage and salary employment, 1984. (p. 7)

4. Population by age group and sex. (p. 8)

5-6. Population of counties and labor market areas. (p. 9-10)

7-7A. Per capita income, annual average wages in covered employment, average hourly earnings, and the CPI, 1970-84; and per capita disposable personal income, 1948-83; [for Vermont and/or U.S.]. (p. 11-12)

8. Annual average wages and per capita income, by county, 1983. (p. 13)

S8025–2.2: Labor Force, Characteristics of the Unemployed, and Job Services

[Labor force data are shown by employment status. Tables 11-16 and 20-21 show current population survey estimates.]

9. Average estimated nonagricultural wage/salary employment [by industry division, major manufacturing group, and government level], 1980 and 1983-84. (p. 15)

10. Employment by industry [division with detail for manufacturing durable and nondurable goods, and government employment by level], 1980 and 1990. (p. 17)

11. Labor force estimates, annual averages, 1976-84. (p. 20)

12. Labor force by age group, [total and by race,] 1984. (p. 22)

13. Labor force by sex and race, 1980 and 1984. (p. 23)

14. Comparison of unemployment rates: annual averages, U.S., New England, and Vermont, 1976-84. (p. 24)

15-16. Labor force estimates: counties and labor market areas, annual averages, 1984. (p. 25-26)

17. Characteristics of the insured unemployed [receiving] regular benefits [sex, age, industry of previous employment, occupation, and duration of unemployment], 1984 annual averages. (p. 27)

18. Characteristics of fully registered active applicants [sex, occupation, age, educational attainment, total and Vietnam-era veterans, and handicapped], Vermont job service, FY83-84. (p. 29)

19. Job openings received [by occupational category and duration of job], Vermont job service, FY83-84. (p. 30)

20-21. Full- or part-time status of the civilian labor force; and unemployed persons by reason for unemployment [job losers, leavers, entrants, and reentrants]; by sex and age [group (16-19 and 20/older)], 1984 annual averages, population controlled. (p. 31-32)

S8035   VERMONT
Department of Finance and Information Support

S8035–1   ANNUAL REPORT OF THE COMMISSIONER OF FINANCE AND INFORMATION SUPPORT, State of Vermont, for the Fiscal Year Ended June 30, 1984

Annual.   Dec. 31, 1984.
160 p.
ISSN 0093-2965.
LC 74-641290.
SRI/MF/complete

Annual report on financial condition of Vermont State government for FY84, presenting assets, liabilities, and fund balance; revenues by source; and expenditures by function, object, and/or agency; for all, general, transportation, fish/wildlife, special, Federal revenue, general and transportation bond, enterprise, internal service, and agency funds.

Also includes data on appropriations compared to actual expenditures; long-term bonded debt; and finances of State lottery.

Contains contents and table listing (p. 2-3); general comments, with summary data (p. 4-7); auditors' letters (p. 9-11); report, with 46 financial exhibits and schedules, and notes (p. 14-152); and supplemental section, with 5 exhibits and schedules (p. 153-160).

An annual summary report on financial condition, *Vermont, a Fiscal Summary of 1984,* is also published by the Finance and Information Support Dept but is not covered by SRI.

Availability: Vermont Department of Finance and Information Support, Agency of Administration, 133 State St., Montpelier VT 05602, †; SRI/MF/complete.

S8054   VERMONT
Department of Health

S8054–1   1983 ANNUAL REPORT OF VITAL STATISTICS in Vermont

Annual.   Jan. 1985.
ix + 144 p.
LC 77-641747.
SRI/MF/complete

Annual report, presenting Vermont vital statistics, including population estimates, births, deaths by detailed cause, marriages, and divorces, 1983, with trends from 1857. Data are shown by county of residence and/or occurrence and selected demographic characteristics. Data are from State health dept records.

Contains listings of contents, tables, and charts (p. iii-ix); introduction, with 2 charts and definitions (p. 1-7); report in 5 sections, with summaries including 2 tables, 11 trend charts, and 78 detailed tables (p. 10-136); and 4 appendices, with listings of State hospitals, death and injury classifications, and Public Health Statistics Division staff directory (p. 138-144).

All tables are listed below. Report is the 99th in a series begun in 1857.

Availability: Vermont Department of Health, Public Health Statistics Division, 60 Main St., PO Box 70, Burlington VT 05402, †; SRI/MF/complete.

TABLES:

[Tables show data for Vermont, 1983, unless otherwise noted. Data by State include Canada and aggregate other countries. Some data by county of residence include totals for out-of-State residents.]

S8054–1.1: Vital Events Summary

[A] Summary of vital events. (p. 10)

1. Vital statistics [historical] summary [includes midyear population; live births; pregnancies; infant, neonatal, fetal, and total deaths; marriages; and divorces; selected years] 1857-1983. (p. 13)

2. Estimated population by sex, age, and county. (p. 14)

3. Selected statistics [population, births, deaths, marriages, and divorces], by town of event [and/or] residence [includes births at home and with low birth weight; and infant deaths]. (p. 16-22)

S8054–1.2: Resident Births

[Table titles 5-21 begin "Vermont resident births..."]

[B] Births [by 10 boys' and girls'] names most frequently given. (p. 24)

4. Geographic distribution of births [occurring in Vermont, by State of residence; and Vermont resident births, by State of occurrence]. (p. 27)

5-7. Sex, by month of birth; and selected characteristics [sex, legitimacy, plurality, and birth order] by age of mother and by county of residence. (p. 27-28)

8-9. Race of child [including American Indian], by age of mother and county of residence. (p. 29)

10-11. Age of mother by county of residence: [births], age specific fertility rates, and crude birth rates [total for all ages]. (p. 30-31)

12-15. Month of birth, education of mother, number of prenatal visits, and month prenatal care began, [all] by county of residence. (p. 32-35)

16-18. Birth weight in grams: by county of residence, weeks gestation, and age of mother and sex of child. (p. 36-40)

19-21. Month prenatal care began, by education of mother, number of prenatal visits, and age of mother. (p. 41-43)

22. [Vermont births by] county of residence, by place of birth. (p. 44)

23. [Births occurring in Vermont, by] attendant [doctor, midwife, nurse, family member, and other], by place of birth [including at home, individual hospitals, and physician's office]. (p. 45)

S8054–1.3: Resident Deaths

[Table titles 27-40 begin "Vermont resident deaths..."]

24. 10 leading causes of death, by sex, Vermont residents, 1983, with trends [for selected periods 1952-81, and] rates per 100,000 population. (p. 50-51)

25. Leading causes of death by age groups and sex, rates per 100,000 population. (p. 52)

26. Geographic distribution of deaths [occurring in Vermont, by State of residence; and Vermont resident deaths, by State of occurrence]. (p. 55)

27-28. Age at death, and age specific and crude death rates per 100,000 population, by county of residence. (p. 56)

29. Age at death by marital status and sex. (p. 57)

30-31. Month of death by county of residence and disposition of body [including burial, cremation, and medical study]. (p. 58)

32. Race by county of residence. (p. 59)

33. Autopsy by certifier to death [doctor, medical examiner, and pathologist]. (p. 59)

34-39. Sex, county of residence, age at death, and month of death; and assignment of selected causes as the underlying cause of death or as a multiple cause of death, and the ratio of multiple to underlying causes; [all] by 72 selected causes. (p. 60-71)

40. Number of deaths with mention of an external cause of death, by nature of injury; number of events and row percents. (p. 72)

41-42. Resident accidental deaths, [by] weekday of death by place of accident, number of events and row percents; and age at death by place of accident and sex. (p. 73-74)

43. Deaths [by] county of residence by place of death. (p. 75)

44. Residents: [detailed] cause of death, by age at death and sex. (p. 76-106)

S8054–1.4: Infant and Fetal Deaths, and Abortions

45-51. Resident fetal, perinatal, neonatal, and infant deaths and rates, by age of mother, county of residence, weeks of gestation, and birth weight. (p. 110-114)

52. Resident fetal deaths: birth weight in grams by cause of death. (p. 115)

53. Resident infant deaths: [detailed] cause of death by age at death, and sex. (p. 116-118)

54-61. Abortions: age and race of patient, by State of residence; month of procedure by type of facility; age and education of patient, by county of residence; county of residence by county of abortion; patient's marital status by number of living children; and weeks of gestation by abortion procedure. (p. 120-124)

S8054–1.5: Marriages and Divorces

62-68. Marriages: State of residence of groom and bride; county of residence, education, age, marriage number, and race of bride [crosstabulated by the same factors for groom]; and month of marriage by county of marriage. (p. 128-131)

69-73. Divorces: plaintiff and legal grounds for decree, month of divorce, length of separation, number of years married, and number of children under 18, [all] by county of decree. (p. 132-134)

74-78. Divorces: education, age, and marriage number of wife, by education, age, and marriage number of husband; and length of marriage by husband's and wife's age at marriage. (p. 134-136)

S8080 — VERMONT Department of Libraries

S8080–1   VERMONT DEPARTMENT OF LIBRARIES 8th Biennial Report, Statistics of Local Libraries, July 1, 1982-June 30, 1984; Vermont Library Directory, 1985
Biennial. [1985.]   114 p.
LC 73-618230.
SRI/MF/complete

Biennial report on Vermont public and other libraries, for FY83-84. Includes data on finances, resources, circulation, and population served, by municipality and library.

Contents:

a. Contents listing; and narrative report, with staff listings and 3 tables showing total system resources, circulation, reference services, and appropriations and expenditures by function and object, FY83-84. (p. 1-12)

b. Glossary, and public library statistics, with 1 table showing the following by municipality and library: population, 1980; town property tax valuation, 1984; and tax appropriation and revenue sharing income, total income, per capita tax support, total and library materials expenditures, volumes added, total volumes, registered borrowers, circulation, and hours open, for various fiscal years (identified for each library) ending Dec. 1983-Jan. 1985. (p. 13-31)

c. Other library statistics, with 1 undated table showing book stock, other holdings, and circulation, by municipality, institution, and library. (p. 32-40)

d. 1985 library directory arranged by municipality; list of library-related assns; lists of libraries by type, region, name, and subject strength; and list of catalog symbols. (p. 41-114)

Previous report, for FY81-82, is described in SRI 1983 Annual under this number.

Availability: Vermont Department of Libraries, c/o State Office Bldg. Post Office, Montpelier VT 05602, †; SRI/MF/complete.

S8100 — VERMONT Public Service Department

S8100–1   BIENNIAL REPORT OF THE DEPARTMENT OF PUBLIC SERVICE, State of Vermont, July 1, 1982-June 30, 1984
Biennial. [1985.] vi+46 p.
LC 74-641290.
SRI/MF/complete

Biennial report presenting Vermont public utility financial and operating data, by utility type and company, primarily for 1982-83. Utility types include electric, gas, telecommunications, and water.

Covers revenues, expenses, taxes paid, and plant investment, for electric, gas, and telephone utilities; electric and gas utility sales and/or customers, by sector; electric utility assets and liabilities; residential electric rates; typical gas bills; telephones in use; and cable TV and private water system customers and rates.

Also includes revenues and disbursements for Vermont Public Service Dept and New York State Power Authority, FY83-84; and trends in electric power allocations to Vermont by New York (including detail for Niagara and St. Lawrence projects), and in Vermont telephones in use, from 1960s.

Contains contents listing and introduction (p. ii-vi); and 5 chapters, with 11 charts, 23 tables, and interspersed narrative (p. 1-46).

Previous report, with data for 1980-81, is described in SRI 1983 Annual under this number.

Availability: Vermont Public Service Department, State Office Bldg., 120 State St., Montpelier VT 05602, †; SRI/MF/complete.

S8120 — VERMONT Supreme Court

S8120–1   JUDICIAL STATISTICS, State of Vermont, for the Year Ending June 30, 1985
Annual. [1985.]
54 p. no paging.
SRI/MF/complete, current & previous year reports

Annual report, for FY85, on Vermont trial court caseloads, case dispositions, and processing time. Covers supreme, superior, district, and probate courts. Includes data by case type and county or district, and selected trends from FY80.

Case types shown are civil and criminal for most courts, with detail for habeas corpus, mental health, juvenile, small claims, domestic relations, fish/game, traffic, child support, testamentary trust, guardianship, adoption, and other case types. Also includes data on district court petitions for protective services.

Contains brief narrative highlights, 1 chart, and 55 tables.

Previous report for FY84, was also reviewed by SRI during 1985, and is also available on SRI microfiche, under S8120-1 [Annual. [1985.] 62 p. no paging. †].

Quarterly report on lower court caseloads is also available from issuing agency, but is not covered in SRI.

Availability: Vermont Supreme Court, Court Administrator's Office, 111 State St., Montpelier VT 05602, †; SRI/MF/complete.

S8125   VERMONT
Department of
Taxes

S8125–1   1983 VERMONT TAX STATISTICS
Annual.   Nov. 1984.   90 p.
ISSN 0149-1385.
LC 77-623630.
SRI/MF/complete

Annual report on 1983 Vermont individual income tax returns. Includes data on income, filings, refunds, exemptions, tax credits, and Federal and State taxes, all by income class, county, and town. Also includes property and sales tax refunds, by income class and county.

Data are from 1983 individual income tax returns filed in 1984 with the Dept of Taxes.

Contains table listing (1 p.); and 18 tables, listed below (p. 1-90).

A biennial report with detail on other major State taxes is also issued by Vermont Dept of Taxes, but is not covered in SRI.

Availability: Vermont Department of Taxes, Pavillion Office Bldg., 109 State St., Montpelier VT 05602, †; SRI/MF/complete.

TABLES:

S8125–1.1: Personal Income Tax Returns
[Most table titles begin "1983 Vermont personal income tax returns..."]

STATE SUMMARY BY INCOME CLASS
[Tables [1-7] show data by adjusted gross income class. Tables [1-3] and [5-6] include returns for out-of-State and unclassified residence.]

[1] Number of returns filed, by marital status and type of tax credits [also shows number of exemptions, returns with refunds and no tax owed, taxes withheld and estimated, and adjusted tax]. (p. 1)

[2-3] Amount of [adjusted and taxable] income, [Federal and State] tax, and tax-offsets (credits). (p. 2-3)

[4] [Number of returns, by Vermont State taxable income]. (p. 4)

[5] Distribution of 1983 income tax refunds by refund range. (p. 5)

[6] Filed by aged 65/over individuals [including number by marital status, number of exemptions, number and amount of $7,000 credits, number with refunds, and amounts of Vermont income and Federal and State tax]. (p. 6)

[7] 1983 Vermont energy schedule statistics [including number of claims by energy system type, and total amount of claims], June 30/earlier and July 1/later. (p. 7-8)

COUNTY AND TOWN DATA
[Tables [10], [12], and [15] include number of exemptions and/or returns with no tax owed, and amounts of income and State tax.]

[8-9] [Data similar to tables [1-2], repeated by county.] (p. 9-10)

[10] County distribution by income class. (p. 11-13)

[11] [Data similar to table [6], repeated by county.] (p. 14)

[12] Age 65, county distribution by income class. (p. 15-17)

[13-14] Distribution of numbers [data similar to table [1]; and of dollars [adjusted gross income, Federal and State tax, and credits by type]; by town. (p. 18-37)

[15] Town distribution by income class. (p. 38-74)

S8125–1.2: Property and Sales Tax Refunds
[Data are shown by county.]

[1-2] 1983 Vermont homeowner or renter [under and over age 65] rebates distribution [by household] income class. (p. 75-89)

[3] 1983 individual income tax system: sales tax refund statistics [number of claims and exemptions, and amount of refund, by income category], as of Nov. 6, 1984. (p. 90)

S8160   VIRGINIA
Department of
Agriculture and
Consumer Services

S8160–1   VIRGINIA AGRICULTURAL STATISTICS
Annual.   Sept. 1984.   112 p.
Bull. No. 52.
ISSN 0360-3830.
LC 75-647372.
SRI/MF/complete

Annual report on Virginia agricultural production, marketing, and finances, 1970s-83, with some data for 1984 and selected trends from as early as 1937. Data generally are shown by commodity and/or county, with some comparisons to total U.S.

Report covers production, prices, sales, value, and, as applicable, acreage, yield, or inventory, for field crop (particularly tobacco), livestock, dairy, poultry, vegetable, and fruit sectors; farm income, production methods and expenses, labor, and wages; and number of farms, acreage, and value.

Also includes data on precipitation and temperature, soil condition, tobacco exports and price supports, fertilizer and liming material sales by city or county, fruit orchards and trees, population, personal income, U.S. food consumption, and CPI.

Data are compiled by the Virginia Crop Reporting Service in cooperation with the USDA.

Contains contents listing and foreword (2 p.); 9 sections, with 8 maps, 26 charts, 86 tables, and interspersed narrative highlights (p. 2-108); and methodology, calendar of report releases, and 2 maps (p. 109-112).

Previous report, issued Sept. 1983, is described in SRI 1983 Annual, under this number.

Availability: Crop Reporting Board Publications, Rm. 5829, South Bldg., U.S. Department of Agriculture, Washington DC 20250, †; SRI/MF/complete.

S8170   VIRGINIA
Office of the
Comptroller

S8170–1   ANNUAL REPORT OF THE COMPTROLLER TO THE GOVERNOR OF VIRGINIA for the Fiscal Year Ended June 30, 1984
Annual.   Dec. 14, 1984.
4+102 p.
LC 77-647681.
SRI/MF/complete

Annual report on financial condition of Virginia State government, FY84, presenting assets and liabilities, revenues by source, expenditures by object and major function, and fund balances, for general, special revenue, debt service, capital projects, enterprise, internal service, public benefit corporations, trust and agency, and higher education funds, with comparisons to FY83 and selected trends from FY75.

Also includes general fund budgeted vs. actual revenues and expenditures; bonded debt obligations through 2022; State aid to localities by program; and nonagricultural wage/salary employment by industry division, 1979-83.

Contains contents and chart listings (3 p.); transmittal letter and summary sections, with 21 summary charts and tables, and organizational chart (p. 2-11); 2 financial sections, with 38 fund statements, accompanying footnotes, 23 text tables, and 9 charts (p. 14-94); and statistical section, with 7 tables (p. 96-102).

Availability: Virginia Office of the Comptroller, PO Box 6-N, Richmond VA 23215, †; SRI/MF/complete.

S8180   VIRGINIA
Corporation Commission

S8180–2   1984 ANNUAL REPORT OF THE BUREAU OF FINANCIAL INSTITUTIONS, State Corporation Commission, Commonwealth of Virginia
Annual.   Dec. 31, 1984.
135 p.
LC 80-642269.
SRI/MF/complete

Annual report presenting assets and liabilities for Virginia State-chartered banks, mutual and stock savings and loan assns, industrial loan assns, and credit unions, as of Dec. 31, 1984. Includes data for individual banks and savings and loan assns, arranged by city.

Also includes bank and credit union consolidated income and expenses; aggregate financial and operating ratios for banks by asset size; Virginia Credit Union Share Insurance Corp. assets and liabilities/equity; and summary comparisons to 1983.

Data are from reports filed with the State Bureau of Financial Institutions.

Contains contents listing (p. 2); and report, with institution status changes and directories, 1 chart, and 9 tables (p. 8-135).

Availability: Virginia Corporation Commission, Financial Institutions Bureau, PO Box 2AE, Richmond VA 23205, †; SRI/MF/complete.

S8190   VIRGINIA
Department of Education

S8190-1   VIRGINIA SCHOOL CENSUS, 1983
Triennial.   July 1984.   20 p.
ISSN 0360-5124.
LC 72-191934.
SRI/MF/complete

Triennial report presenting Virginia population under age 20, by age, sex, county, city, and race/ethnicity (American Indian/Alaskan Native, Asian/Pacific Islander, black, Hispanic, and white), as of Jan. 1, 1984 with aggregate trends from 1968. Also presents detail for handicapped persons under age 22, including data by type of handicap.

Report is based on filings of individual school districts, and is intended for use in determining distribution of State sales tax funds to school divisions.

Contains contents and table listing (inside front cover); brief introduction, with 1 trends table (p. 1); and 4 detailed tables (p. 2-20).

Previous report, with data as of Jan. 1981, is described in SRI 1981 Annual under this number.

Availability: Virginia Department of Education, Management Information Services Division, PO Box 6Q, Richmond VA 23216-2060, †; SRI/MF/complete.

S8190-2   FACING UP—19: Statistical Data on Virginia's Public Schools, 1983/84 School Year
Annual.   June 1985.   62 p.
LC A68-7576.
SRI/MF/complete

Annual report on public education in Virginia, for school year 1983/84, covering enrollment, staff, salaries, finances, graduates, and test scores, by county and municipality. Includes selected trends from 1981/82.

Contains contents and table listing, and introduction with 1 summary table (p. 1-2); and 12 tables, listed below (p. 3-62).

Availability: Virginia Department of Education, Management Information Services Division, PO Box 6Q, Richmond VA 23216-2060, †; SRI/MF/complete.

TABLES:
[Tables show data for Virginia, by county and municipality, 1983/84, unless otherwise noted.]

ENROLLMENT, CLASS SIZE, TEACHERS, AND SALARIES

1. Student membership, Sept. 30 [and] end-of-year membership [1981/82-1983/84]. (p. 3-7)

2-3. Ratio of [elementary and secondary] pupils to classroom teaching positions, regular day school; ratio of pupils to instructional personnel K-6; average salaries of classroom teaching positions; instructional personnel positions per 1,000 students in ADM [average daily membership; and] average salaries based on instructional positions; 1983/84 [and 1982/83 salaries]. (p. 8-17)

STUDENT PROMOTIONS AND TEST SCORES

4. Students promoted, 3-year period [1981/82-1983/84]. (p. 18-22)

5. National percentile equivalents of selected average scores, Virginia State Assessment Program [reading, language arts, and math; grades 4, 8, and 11]. (p. 23-27)

GRADUATES, POSTGRADUATE ACTIVITIES, AND DROPOUTS

6. Graduates [number and] as percent of 9th grade membership 4 years earlier [1981/82-1983/84]. (p. 28-32)

7. Graduates continuing education [including number attending 2- and 4-year colleges]; graduates [not continuing education, and percent] with marketable skills; and dropouts, grades 8-12. (p. 33-38)

FINANCES

8. 1982-84 composite index of local ability-to-pay costs of *Standards of Quality* [includes property value, personal income, taxable retail sales, and population (no dates), and ADM as of Mar. 31, 1980]. (p. 39-43)

9. Total local expenditures for operations, and sources of financial support for expenditures. (p. 44-48)

10. State basic aid and categorical aid to localities for operations [by purpose, including special and vocational education, and pupil transportation; with per pupil totals]. (p. 49-52)

11. Per pupil expenditure for operations from local, State, and Federal funds. (p. 53-57)

12. Expenditures for capital outlay [buildings/sites, buses/other vehicles, furniture/equipment, and other] and debt service. (p. 58-62)

S8195   VIRGINIA
Board of Elections

S8195-1   COMMONWEALTH OF VIRGINIA OFFICIAL ELECTION RESULTS, 1984
Annual.   [1985.]   26 p.
SRI/MF/complete

Annual report presenting results of the Virginia primary election held June 12, 1984 and general election held Nov. 6, 1984. Includes voting for President; U.S. Senator and Representatives; and 2 State constitutional amendments, including 1 requiring balanced State budget. Data are shown by county, city, and/or district, and include candidates' party affiliation.

Also includes total voter registration, and voter turnout by district, for the general election.

Availability: Virginia Board of Elections, 101 Ninth St. Office Bldg., Richmond VA 23219-3497, †; SRI/MF/complete.

S8205   VIRGINIA
Employment Commission

S8205-4   VIRGINIA ECONOMIC INDICATORS
Quarterly.   Approx. 20 p.
ISSN 0042-6490.
LC 81-1095.
SRI/MF/complete

Quarterly report on performance of selected Virginia economic indicators, including employment, manufacturing production worker hours and earnings, new business incorporations, value of building permits, motor vehicle registrations, electric power sales, and taxable retail sales. Data are from State agencies.

Contains contents listing; summary analysis; 6 quarterly tables, with accompanying charts; occasional special articles with statistics; and approximately 15 charts illustrating trends from the 1970s.

Prior to 4th quarter 1984 issue, report also included an additional quarterly table showing seasonally adjusted employment by major industry group.

Quarterly tables are listed below and appear in all issues. Issues for 4th quarter 1984 and 1st quarter 1985 also include an additional table showing employment by major industry group, 1983-84. All additional features with substantial statistical content not covered in quarterly tables are described, as they appear, under "Statistical Features." Nonstatistical features are not covered.

Report had been discontinued in Dec. 1981 (for description, see SRI 1982 Annual under this number). Report resumes with the 2nd quarter 1984 issue.

Availability: Virginia Employment Commission, Research and Analysis Division, 703 E. Main St., PO Box 1358, Richmond VA 23211-1358, †; SRI/MF/complete.

Issues reviewed during 1985: 2nd Qtr. 1984-2nd Qtr. 1985 (D) (Vol. XVI, Nos. 1-3; Vol. XVII, Nos. 1-2).

QUARTERLY TABLES:
[Tables [1-3] show seasonally adjusted and unadjusted data, by month, for current year through quarter of coverage and preceding year.]

[1] Employment and unemployment indicators [nonagricultural wage/salary and manufacturing employment, total unemployment rate, average weekly insured unemployment rate, and unemployment insurance final payments and average weekly initial claims].

[2] Manufacturing production worker indicators [average hours and earnings, and aggregate man-hours].

[3] Business indicators [new business incorporations and motor vehicle registrations, building permit value, electric power sales, and (beginning with 3rd quarter 1984 issue) taxable retail sales].

[4-6] Data summary [showing seasonally adjusted indicators from tables [1-3] for each month of quarter, with comparison to preceding month, and same month of previous year].

STATISTICAL FEATURES:

S8205–4.601: 3rd Qtr. 1984 (Vol. XVI, No. 2)

COAL MINING IN VIRGINIA: FACTS AND FIGURES

(p. 13) Two charts, with brief accompanying narrative, showing Virginia coal mining production and employment, 1980-84. Data are from DOE.

S8205–4.602: 4th Qtr. 1984 (Vol. XVI, No. 3)

TUR-IUR GAP

(p. 12-13) Article, with 1 table showing Virginia total unemployment rate (TUR) and unemployment rate for persons eligible for unemployment insurance benefits (IUR), 1970-84.

S8205–4.603: 1st Qtr. 1985 (Vol. XVII, No. 1)

PERSONAL INCOME

(p. 11-12) Article, with 1 table showing Virginia personal income, 1972-84. Data are from Bureau of Economic Analysis.

S8205–5   EMPLOYMENT, HOURS, AND EARNINGS in Virginia and Its Metropolitan Areas
Monthly.   Approx. 20 p.
SRI/MF/complete, shipped quarterly

Monthly report on Virginia labor force, employment, hours, and earnings, shown by industry group, MSA, and selected labor market areas. Includes data on female employment.

Most data are collected by the State Employment Commission in cooperation with BLS, and are based on payroll records of a sample of approximately 7,500 establishments. Month of coverage is 1 month preceding cover date.

Contains contents and table listing; narrative summary; 21 monthly tables, listed below; and explanatory notes.

Prior to Feb. 1985 issue, report differed slightly from this description.

Another monthly report, *Labor Force and Unemployment Insurance Status Report,* showing data by Virginia congressional district and city, is also available from issuing agency, but is not covered by SRI.

Availability: Virginia Employment Commission, Research and Analysis Division, 703 E. Main St., PO Box 1358, Richmond VA 23211-1358, †; SRI/MF/complete, shipped quarterly.

Issues reviewed during 1985: Oct. 1984-Sept. 1985 (P) (Vol. 34, Nos. 10-12; Vol. 35, Nos. 1-9) [Vol. 35, No. 5 incorrectly reads No. 4].

MONTHLY TABLES:
[Most data are shown for month of coverage, preceding month, and same month of preceding year.]

A1. Estimated employment in nonagricultural industries [by industry group].

A2. Employees in nonagricultural establishments, by industry divisions, annual averages [for 10 previous years, and monthly for current year to date and 4 preceding years].

A3. Estimated female employment in nonagricultural industries [by industry group].

A4. Estimated number of production workers in manufacturing industries [by industry group].

A5-A12. Estimated employment in nonagricultural industries [by industry division and major manufacturing group, by MSA and labor market area].

C1-C8. Hours and gross earnings of production workers in manufacturing industries [by industry group, by MSA and labor market area].

E1. CPI for all urban consumers, U.S. city average [monthly for current year to date and 13-15 preceding years].

S8225   VIRGINIA
Department of Health

S8225–1   1983 VITAL STATISTICS ANNUAL REPORT, Virginia
Annual. [1984.] v+171 p.
LC 56-32221.
SRI/MF/complete

Annual report, for 1983, on Virginia vital statistics, covering population, births, deaths by cause, marriages, and divorces, by demographic characteristics and location. Also includes trends from 1964, and data on communicable diseases. Data are from State records.

Contents:

a. Listing of contents, charts, and tables. (p. i-v)

b. Introduction, definitions, and narrative analysis, with 10 charts and 60 text tables including the following data: births, deaths, and marriages involving residents of Virginia and bordering States; suicides and homicides, by method; marriages and divorces, by educational attainment of husband and wife; and cremations, by place of occurrence and month. (p. 1-47)

c. 55 detailed tables, listed below. (p. 50-158)

d. Communicable disease analysis, with 5 tables, also listed below. (p. 160-171)

This is the 71st annual report.

Availability: Virginia Department of Health, Health Statistics Center, PO Box 1000, Richmond VA 23208-1000, $5.00; SRI/MF/complete.

TABLES:
[Data by location, place of residence, or place of occurrence are shown for individual counties, independent cities, and 22 health planning districts. Data by location generally refer to place of residence. Data are for 1983, unless otherwise noted.]

S8225–1.1: Summary, Population, Births, and Deaths

SUMMARY AND POPULATION

1. Vital events with rates [by location]. (p. 50-51)

2. Projected population for July 1, 1983, by race [by location]. (p. 52)

TRENDS
[Tables 3-5 show data by race, 1964-83, with rates.]

3. Estimated population, births, deaths, marriages, and divorces. (p. 53)

4. Resident illegitimate births and immature births with percent of total births, and deaths under 1 year and under 28 days. (p. 54)

5. Resident total pregnancy terminations, live births, all fetal deaths, induced abortions, and natural fetal deaths. (p. 55)

BIRTHS AND FETAL DEATHS

6. Live births by place of occurrence and place of residence, with resident rate per 1,000 population, by race. (p. 56-57)

7-9. Live births by place of delivery [hospital, and nonhospital physician and midwife/other]; illegitimate live births, immature births, and congenital anomalies, with percent of total births; and resident live births by age of mother; [by location, by race]. (p. 58-68)

10-11. Resident live births, by birth order by birth weight, and by birth weight by race and age of mother. (p. 68-69)

12-13. Resident live births and percent distribution, by live birth order, by age and race of mother. (p. 70)

14-15. Resident live births by education of mother, by birth order and trimester care began. (p. 71)

16-17. Resident live births by birth order and age of mother, by trimester care began. (p. 71)

18-19. Resident births with Apgar score, by age of mother, race, and sex. (p. 72)

20-21. Complications of pregnancy and congenital anomalies reported for resident live births, by trimester care began. (p. 73)

22. Resident live births and natural fetal deaths, by race and sex, by month of delivery and number of individuals delivered per confinement. (p. 74)

23. Resident live births by sex, and sex ratio, by race, 1974-83. (p. 74)

24. Resident pregnancy terminations (live births/induced abortions/natural fetal deaths) by race and legitimacy status, with percent illegitimate, by age of mother. (p. 74)

25-27. Resident live births, natural fetal deaths, and induced abortions, by race and legitimacy status, with percent illegitimate, by age of mother. (p. 75)

28. Teenage total pregnancy terminations, live births, induced abortions, and natural fetal deaths [by age group, by location]. (p. 76-77)

29-32. Natural fetal deaths by length of gestation, by race; resident natural fetal deaths by age of mother; induced abortions by race and legitimacy status, with percent illegitimate; and resident induced abortions by age of mother; [all by location]. (p. 78-85)

33. Resident natural fetal deaths and length of gestation, by race, by cause of death. (p. 86)

INFANT DEATHS
[Tables 34-36 show data by race, by location.]

34. Neonatal deaths with rates per 1,000 live births. (p. 87)

35. Infant deaths by place of occurrence and place of residence; with resident rate per 1,000 live births. (p. 88-89)

36. Perinatal mortality rate with infant deaths under 1 week and fetal deaths 28 weeks/over gestation. (p. 90-91)

37-38. Resident infant deaths: by race and sex, by cause of death, with rates per 100,000 live births; and by age and cause of death. (p. 92-95)

ALL DEATHS

39. Deaths by place of occurrence and place of residence, with resident rate per 1,000 population, by race. (p. 96-97)

40. Resident deaths from important causes, with rates per 100,000 population, by race, 1974-83. (p. 98-99)

41. Resident deaths by age, by cause, race, and sex. (p. 100-106)

42. Five leading causes of death in specified age groups, by race. (p. 107)

43-44. Resident accidental and resident home accidental deaths, by age, by type of accident. (p. 108-109)

45. Deaths by place of occurrence and place of residence, by race, by cause. (p. 110)

46. Deaths by race, by cause [and location]. (p. 111-149)

S8225–1.2: Marriages, Divorces, and Communicable Diseases

MARRIAGES

47. Marriages by place of [occurrence], residence of bride, and residence of groom, by race. (p. 150-151)

48-49. Marriages: by type of ceremony, by month; and by previous marital status of bride [and] groom, according to race of groom. (p. 152)

50. Marriages by age of bride by age of groom. (p. 153)

DIVORCES

[Table titles 51-55 begin "Divorces (including annulments)..."]

51. By race of husband and cause of divorce, by [location] where granted. (p. 154-155)

52. By race, by month of decree [also includes separate data for annulments]. (p. 156)

53. By race of husband, by place of marriage [Virginia and elsewhere], and number of minor children in family. (p. 156)

54-55. By duration of marriage and person granted divorce, by plaintiff and cause of divorce; and by age of wife by age of husband. (p. 157-158)

COMMUNICABLE DISEASES

[A-B] New, active tuberculosis cases: [by] age by race; and [physiological] location of disease by bacteriologic status. (p. 163)

56. Reported cases and deaths from certain communicable diseases, with case rates per 100,000 estimated population, 1974-83. (p. 165)

57. Reported cases of certain communicable diseases [by location]. (p. 166-169)

58. Reported cases of venereal disease [by type and location]. (p. 170-171)

S8230 VIRGINIA
Council of
Higher Education

S8230–1   VIRGINIA PLAN FOR HIGHER EDUCATION, 1983

Biennial. [1984.] 114 p.
ISSN 0098-0609.
LC 68-7596.
SRI/MF/complete

Biennial report, for 1983, on Virginia public and private higher education enrollments and operations , including data on students and faculty and selected comparisons to other States. Data are from Virginia State supported and independent colleges and universities, National Research Council, and U.S. Dept of Education.

Contents:

a. Contents, listing of Higher Education Council membership, preface, and introduction. (p. 2-8)

b. Statistical profile of Virginia system of higher education, with narrative analysis and 19 tables, listed below, including historical data from 1960. (p. 9-25)

c. Narrative review of educational issues, with 1 table showing number of private and public institution PhD programs receiving National Research Council above-average ratings for scholarly/research quality of faculty; and 7 other tables, listed below. (p. 27-43)

d. Narrative profiles of history, objectives, and development plans of 51 State-supported and independent higher education institutions. (p. 45-114)

Previous reports were issued in 2 volumes. Report described below is similar to Vol. I. Vol. II contained statistical profiles of individual institutions. For description of previous Vol. I report, for 1981, see SRI 1982 Annual under S8230-1.1; Vol. II for 1981 is described in SRI 1983 Annual under S8230-1.2.

Availability: Virginia Council of Higher Education, 700 Fidelity Bldg., Ninth and Main Sts., Richmond VA 23219, †; SRI/MF/complete.

TABLES:

[Unless otherwise noted, data are for Virginia higher education institutions.]

S8230–1.1: Statistical Profile

[All tables except 4-6, 11, 14-16, and 18 show data for Virginia's State-supported 2- and 4-year institutions.]

ENROLLMENT

1. Fall headcount and regular session FTE enrollment [selected years] 1965-82 (on-campus students only) [by institution]. (p. 11)

2-3. Enrollment at State-supported institutions [by full- or part-time status, residency status, and sex], fall term 1982; and fall 1983 headcount enrollment; (on-/off-campus students) [by institution]. (p. 12-13)

4. Independent college and university enrollment, [selected years] 1960-83. (p. 14)

5-6. [Data in Tables 2-3 are repeated for independent institutions.] (p. 14-15)

7-8. Actual 1982 fall headcount and 1982/83 regular session FTE enrollment, [and] projected fall headcount enrollment and regular ses-

sion FTE, [selected years] 1983/84-1994/95 (on-campus students only) [all by institution]; and full- and part-time fall session headcount, fall 1970 and fall 1982. (p. 16-17)

9-10. Ages of students, fall 1981; and estimated [white and] minority headcount enrollments [1973 and 1982]. (p. 17, 19)

FINANCES AND FACILITIES

11. Biennial appropriations for operating expenses [total, general, and special funds for all State-supported institutions, 1972/74-1982/84]. (p. 19)

12. Net additional educational and general space needs by 1994 [for classroom, laboratory, faculty office, library, physical education, and instructional support; includes data for doctoral institutions]. (p. 20)

DEGREES AND FACULTY

[Tables 17-19 show data by institution.]

13. Number of degrees conferred [1971/72 and 1981/82]. (p. 21)

14-15. Total degrees conferred in selected [and] high technology disciplines (senior State-supported institutions), 1981/82. (p. 21)

16. Total degress conferred in selected disciplines (independent institutions), 1981/82. (p. 21)

17-18. Faculty tenure at State-supported institutions, (1975/76 and 1982/83); and at independent institutions, (1982/83). (p. 22-23)

19. Distribution of faculty by rank [includes data for doctoral institutions](1975/76 and 1982/83). (p. 24)

S8230–1.2: Educational Issues

NATIONAL DATA

[Tables 1-3 show data by State, with rankings for each data category.]

1. 1981 population and [higher education] enrollment statistics. (p. 39)

2. [Percent of general tax revenues allocated to public higher education, and general fund appropriation and estimated tuition per student, 1982/83.] (p. 40)

3. Average salaries of full-time faculty [1978/79-1981/82]. (p. 41)

VIRGINIA FACULTY DATA

4. Distribution of faculty and percent of faculty with tenure status, [both] by rank [for U.S. and Virginia, 1981/82]. (p. 42)

5-6. National ranking of Virginia's full-time faculty salaries [and actual average salary] by [faculty] rank and [institution] classification [3 doctoral levels, comprehensive master, baccalaureate, specialized, and 2-year], for public institutions [1978/79-1981/82]. (p. 42)

7. Salary averages [actual and as percent of national average at State-supported institutions, by institution grouped by classification], 1978/79 and 1981/82. (p. 43)

S8270   VIRGINIA
Department of Labor and Industry

S8270–1   1984 ANNUAL REPORT, Department of Labor and Industry, Virginia

Annual.   June 30, 1985.
77 p.
LC 9-219.   SRI/MF/complete

Annual report, for 1984, of the Virginia Dept of Labor and Industry. Includes data on labor law enforcement, apprenticeship programs, occupational health and safety, employment, food prices, and mineral production and related data.

Contains introductory matter and contents listing (p. 1-7); departmental functions (p. 8-9); and 7 division reports, with brief narrative summaries and the following charts and tables:

a. Boiler/pressure vessel safety division activities, including registrations, inspections, inspectors, and inspector examination results; and number of reported violations, injuries, and fatalities; 1983-84. 1 table. (p. 11)

b. Labor law court cases, dispositions, and complaint investigations, and value of child labor civil money penalties, with children involved and violations by type, 1983-84; employment certificates issued to minors, 1975-84; and wages collected under State minimum wage/garnishment statutes, 1980-84. 2 charts and 4 tables. (p. 13-18)

c. Apprenticeship programs and participants, by type of system, bargaining agency (labor union), State region, occupation, and company employment size; and field staff activities, by State region; 1984, with some trends from 1940. 1 chart and 8 tables. (p. 20-29)

d. Inspections and other activities of the occupational safety division and voluntary safety compliance and training division, 1983 and/or 1984. 2 tables. (p. 31-33)

e. Workers' compensation case distribution by type of accident, industry division, and occupation, 1983; and occupational injury/illness incidence rates and lost workdays, by SIC 2- and 3-digit industry, 1975-83, with summary data for 1982-83 and comparisons to 1983 employment. 3 tables. (p. 35-40)

f. Retail food price comparison for 3 metro areas, by detailed commodity, Jan. and Dec. 1984. 1 table. (p. 42)

g. Manufacturers annual survey, showing employment and salaries/wages (total and for production workers), value added by manufacturers, and actual and anticipated capital expenditures, by industry group, for State and 9 metro areas, 1983; and capital expenditures (State only), 1978-83. 1 chart and 10 tables. (p. 43-53)

h. Mine inspections by type, and violations and closure orders; miner education and training activities; and certificates and cards/permits issued; 1984. 4 tables. (p. 56-57)

i. Natural gas and/or crude oil wells, production, acreage under lease, and drilling activity; and natural gas reserves and deliveries to pipelines; by county and/or company, 1984 with quarterly detail. 11 tables. (p. 58-67)

j. Coal mines, production, employment, wages, days worked, injuries, and fatalities, by coun-

ty; characteristics of fatal coal mining accidents and victims; and selected data for other minerals, including production, employment, salaries/wages, hours worked, capital expenditures, injuries, and fatalities; 1984. 8 tables. (p. 68-75)

Availability: Virginia Department of Labor and Industry, PO Box 12064, Richmond VA 23241, †; SRI/MF/complete.

S8275   VIRGINIA
State Library

S8275–1   STATISTICS OF VIRGINIA PUBLIC LIBRARIES AND INSTITUTIONAL LIBRARIES, 1982-83

Annual.   1984.
41 p.+addendum.
LC 74-648420.
SRI/MF/complete

Annual report, for FY83, on Virginia public and institutional library services, holdings, finances, personnel, and related data, by library.

Contains summary table (inside front cover); contents listing (p. 1); 15 other tables (p. 2-33); and directory of public libraries (p. 34-39). All tables are listed below.

Availability: Virginia State Library, Library Development Branch, 11th at Capitol Square, Richmond VA 23219, †; SRI/MF/complete.

TABLES:
[Tables I-IV are repeated for Virginia regional and city libraries, and county and town libraries. Funding sources are generally local, State, and Federal aid, and other. Data are for FY83, unless otherwise noted.]

[A] Public library statistical summary [circulation, total volumes, and operating expenditures by source of income, for regional, county, city, and town public libraries; Federal and State-funded operating expenditures for library development programs, by program; number of public libraries by type; and population with and without library service]. (inside front cover)

I. Analysis of income and expenditures [population and square miles served, distribution of income by source and operating expenditures by object, local and total operating expenditures per capita, and unexpended income by source]. (p. 2-3, 10-11)

II. Analysis of circulation [books by type; nonbook materials; outlets by type, including branches and bookmobiles; and headquarters hours per week]. (p. 4-5, 12-13)

III. Analysis of collections [books by type; volumes and titles added and volumes withdrawn; and nonbook materials, including filmstrips, recordings, microforms, and number of periodical and newspaper titles]. (p. 6-7, 14-15)

IV. Additional statistics [full- and part-time personnel; outlets, including branches and bookmobiles; bookmobile hours open; interlibrary loan transactions; computer services; and registered borrowers]. (p. 8-9, 16-17)

[B] Local income sources [county, city/town, revenue sharing, common governmental fund, and other, by library; with summary]. (p. 18-22)

[C] Comparative summary of public library statistics [population, counties, and cities served; book stock; circulation and operating expenditures by type; and number of libraries, bookmobiles, branches, and librarians]; FY79-83. (p. 23)

[D] Virginia State library service data [volumes added and withdrawn, newspaper and periodical titles, government documents received and distributed, interlibrary and film loans, and reference inquiries]. (p. 23)

[E] Institutional libraries [under Rehabilitative School Authority, Dept of Mental Health/Mental Retardation, and Dept of Rehabilitative Services: residents, hours, operating expenditures, and collections, by library]. (p. 24-25)

[F] College and university libraries [list, with name, librarian, total collection, students, computer services and lending restrictions]. (p. 26-28)

[G] Special libraries [list, with name, librarian, subject specialty, computer services, and lending restrictions]. (p. 28-33)

S8293   VIRGINIA
Department of Social Services

S8293–2   PUBLIC WELFARE STATISTICS, Virginia

Quarterly.   Approx. 60 p.
LC 39-28484.
SRI/MF/complete

Quarterly report on Virginia public welfare programs, including caseloads, recipients, and expenditures, by program, county, and city. Covers aid to dependent children (ADC), emergency assistance to needy families, and general relief including aid to refugees, foster care, adoptions, food stamps, day care, and child support collections.

Issuing agency collects data on a monthly basis, but presents most data only for last month of each quarter. Report is issued approximately 6 months after month of coverage.

Report contains table listing, and 21 quarterly tables, listed below.

Report has been published since 1939. A biennial report with similar data is also published, and is covered in SRI under S8293-1.

Availability: Virginia Department of Social Services, Research and Reporting Bureau, 8007 Discovery Dr., Richmond VA 23288, †; SRI/MF/complete.

Issues reviewed during 1985: June 1984-June 1985 (D) (Vol. XLV, No. 4; Vol. XLVI, Nos. 1-4).

QUARTERLY TABLES:
[Data are shown for month of coverage, unless otherwise noted.]

STATE SUMMARY
I-II. Cases receiving assistance and amount of assistance; and cases under care; [with comparisons to same month of previous year].

III. Application and case information [approvals, other dispositions, and payment discontinuations, for general relief, ADC, and Medicaid, for quarter ending month of coverage].

BY LOCALITY

[Tables generally show cases and/or recipients, and expenditures, by county and city, unless otherwise noted.]

IV. Auxiliary grant payments for the aged and disabled.

V-VI. ADC [regular]; and ADC foster care [entrusted and nonentrusted].

VII. Emergency assistance to needy families with children [by ADC status].

VIII. General relief [medical, short-term emergency, and maintenance].

IX. General relief for refugees and Cuban/Haitians.

X-XI. Foster care and adoptions.

XII-XIV. Food stamp program: monthly participation record [households and persons, by public assistance status, and total stamps issued]; State participation [summary, compared with previous month and same month of previous year]; and percent of population participating, by local agency.

XV. Report of collections on food stamp overissuance claims [by type of error, for quarter ending month of coverage].

XVI. Fraud activity report [including number and disposition of cases, and restitution received, for ADC and food stamps].

XVII. Service cases under care [by recipient category, including SSI/auxiliary grants for aged/blind/disabled, and Medicaid cases; expenditure data are omitted].

XVIII-IX. Employment services program (ESP) day care/other purchased services; and day care other than ESP.

XX. Aid to refugees and Cuban/Haitians: ADC eligible/other.

XXI. Support enforcement collection summary for ADC and non-ADC cases, by region [amount collected during quarter of coverage, with comparison to same period of previous year].

S8295   VIRGINIA
Department of State Police

S8295–1   VIRGINIA TRAFFIC CRASH FACTS, 1984
Annual. Mar. 1985. 114 p.
LC A44-5266.
SRI/MF/complete

Annual report on Virginia traffic accidents involving fatalities, injuries, and property damage, and number of persons killed and injured, 1984, with trends from 1954. Includes data by accident and vehicle type, location, time, and other circumstances; and driver and victim characteristics.

Also includes data on driver and pedestrian alcohol use, vehicle mileage and registrations, insurance coverage of vehicles in accidents, motor fuel consumption, vehicle defects, and safety device use by accident victims.

Contains 2 charts, foreword, contents listing, and highlights (inside front cover and p. 1-5); report, with 13 charts and 23 tables (p. 6-41); and computer printouts of total State and rural accident detailed data, with 29 tables (p. 44-114).

Availability: Virginia Department of State Police, Safety Division, PO Box 27472, Richmond VA 23261-7472, †; SRI/MF/complete.

S8295–2   CRIME IN VIRGINIA, 1984
Annual. [1985.] vii+169 p.
ISSN 0146-5759.
LC 77-648613.
SRI/MF/complete

Annual report on Virginia crimes and arrests, by offense, 1984, with selected comparisons to 1983. Includes data by county, municipality, planning district, and reporting agency, and by offender age, sex, and race/ethnicity. Also includes law enforcement employment, and assaults on officers.

Report focuses on 8 Index offenses: murder, rape, robbery, aggravated assault, burglary, larceny, motor vehicle theft, and arson. Arrests are also shown for numerous non-Index offenses.

Data are from State and local agency reports submitted under the Uniform Crime Reporting (UCR) Program.

Contents:

Foreword, highlights, and contents listing. (p. iii-vii)

Section I. UCR Program description, with 1 summary table on Index offenses, rates, and clearances, 1983-84. (p. 1-4)

Section II-VI. Index offenses by offense and local jurisdiction, reporting agencies and employment, Index offense summary, and value of property stolen and recovered; with 30 charts and 44 tables, described below. (p. 5-81)

Section VII-IX. Arrests, law enforcement officers killed and assaulted, and planning district data; with 3 charts and 21 tables, described below. (p. 83-169)

Availability: Virginia Department of State Police, Uniform Crime Reporting Section, PO Box 27472, Richmond VA 23261-7472, †; SRI/MF/complete.

TABLES AND CHARTS:

[All tables and charts present data for 1984; many include comparative data for 1983. Data by race/ethnicity generally include American Indian/Alaskan Native, Asian/Pacific Islander, Hispanic, and non-Hispanic. Arson is classified as an Index offense, but it is sometimes not included in data shown by Index crime.]

S8295–2.1: Sections II-VI

HIGHLIGHTS

a. Monthly summary for Index offenses, including negligent manslaughter and simple assaults; and crime clocks, showing frequency of Index offenses. 1 chart and 3 tables. (p. 6-8)

BY OFFENSE

[Sections on individual offenses are prefaced with 1 summary table; all sections except arson also include 1 monthly trend chart. Additional data are described below.]

b. Murder/non-negligent manslaughter: victims and offenders, by age, sex, and race/

ethnicity; and offenses, by victim-offender relationship, circumstances of murder, and type of weapon and situation (single or multiple victims/offenders). 3 charts and 5 tables. (p. 9-14)

c. Rape: forcible and attempted rapes; and arrests, by age. 3 charts and 2 tables. (p. 15-17)

d. Robbery: offenses and value of property stolen, by place of occurrence; and offenses, by type of weapon. 3 charts and 4 tables. (p. 18-21)

e. Aggravated assault: offenses by type of weapon; and simple and aggravated assaults. 3 charts and 2 tables. (p. 22-24)

f. Burglary: offenses, and value of stolen property, for day and night, residence and nonresidence occurrences; offenses, by type of entry; and arrests, by age. 3 charts and 5 tables. (p. 25-28)

g. Larceny: offenses and value of property stolen, by type and amount of theft. 1 chart and 4 tables. (p. 29-32)

h. Motor vehicle theft: offenses by vehicle type; vehicles recovered, by location of theft and recovery (locally or elsewhere); and arrests, by age. 3 charts and 4 tables. (p. 33-35)

i. Arson: offenses and value of property damage, by property type. 2 tables. (p. 36-37)

CRIME AND POLICE, BY LOCAL AGENCY

j. Population, crime and clearance rates, and Index offenses by type, by reporting agency in each county and independent city; and clearance rates and offenses, by college and university and other agency. 1 table. (p. 40-56)

k. Law enforcement employment, including sworn officers by sex, and civilians, all by reporting agency in each county, city, and other jurisdiction. 1 table. (p. 58-61)

SUMMARY, AND STOLEN PROPERTY

l. Total Index, violent, and property crime and clearance summary, by offense, with offenses by quarter, and juvenile and adult clearance rates. 8 charts and 5 tables. (p. 64-72)

m. Value of stolen property, by property type and offense; and value of recovered property, by type; with detail by month. 2 charts and 6 tables. (p. 74-81)

S8295–2.2: Sections VII-IX
[Arrest data by offense are shown for Index and non-Index offenses.]

ARRESTS AND POLICE ASSAULTS

a. Monthly arrests; arrests by age, race/ethnicity, and sex, by offense; arrests for drug sale/manufacture and possession by substance, by age; arrest rates, by offense; and juvenile arrest dispositions. 1 chart and 13 tables. (p. 84-96)

b. Officers killed by felonious act and accidentally; officers assaulted, by type of activity, weapon, injury status, assignment, and time of day; and percent of officer assaults cleared, by type of activity. 2 charts and 4 tables. (p. 98-100)

DATA BY PLANNING DISTRICT

[The following tables are repeated for each of 22 planning districts.]

c. Index offenses and clearance rates; value of property stolen, by type of offense; and total value of property stolen and recovered, by type of property. 2 tables. (p. 103-124)

d. Arrest totals for adults and juveniles, by age and offense. 2 tables. (p. 126-169)

S8300 VIRGINIA
Supreme Court

S8300–1   **1984 STATE OF THE JUDICIARY REPORT, Virginia**
Annual. [1985.] 428 p.
LC 79-644178.
SRI/MF/complete

Annual report on Virginia judicial system, including trial and appellate court caseloads and case dispositions, 1984, with selected trends from the 1960s. Covers supreme, circuit, and district courts. Includes trial court data by case type and locality.

Case types shown are civil and criminal, for all courts, with some additional detail for habeas corpus, traffic, juvenile, and domestic relations case types.

Report also includes data on case processing time, medical malpractice claims, indigent defense and involuntary commitment costs by district, judicial personnel and salaries, magistrates' activities, detailed court finances, and judges and workloads.

Data are from dept records.

Contains contents listing (p. 3-6); report, with 27 charts, 265 tables, and lists of judges (p. 9-427); and list of related publications (p. 428).

This is the 10th annual report.

Availability: Virginia Supreme Court, Executive Secretary's Office, Supreme Court Bldg., 100 N. Ninth St., 3rd Floor, Richmond VA 23219, †; SRI/MF/complete.

S8305 VIRGINIA
Department of Taxation

S8305–1   **DEPARTMENT OF TAXATION ANNUAL REPORT, 1983-84, Commonwealth of Virginia**
Annual. [1985.] vii+36 p.
LC 30-27254.
SRI/MF/complete

Annual report, for FY84, on Virginia tax revenues, by tax type, county, and independent city. Includes individual and corporate tax returns by income bracket, and taxable retail sales by major industry group. Also includes trends from 1973.

Contains contents listing and tax dept organizational summary (p. iii-vii); and the following:

a. Introduction and narrative sections, with 2 charts and 2 tables showing general and special fund revenue collections by source, FY83-84; and tax dept expenditures by budget program, FY84. (p. 1-8)

b. Appendix, with table listing, and 34 tables listed below. (p. 9-36)

State Taxation Dept also issues several related publications, including a quarterly taxable retail sales report, an annual real estate assessment/sales ratio study, and a summary of tax facts. These reports are not covered by SRI.

Availability: Virginia Department of Taxation, 2220 W. Broad St., PO Box 6-L, Richmond VA 23282, †; SRI/MF/complete.

APPENDIX TABLES:
[Data by locality are shown by county and independent city.]

S8305–1.1: Income Taxes

INDIVIDUAL INCOME TAX

[Data are shown for 1982 taxable year, unless otherwise noted.]

1.1. Adjusted gross income (AGI), total exemptions, total deductions, total taxable income, and total tax, by AGI classes. (p. 10)

1.2-1.4. Number and type of returns and exemptions, total AGI, total tax, and effective tax rate, by AGI classes. (p. 10-11)

1.5-1.7. Total AGI and total exemptions, total deductions, number of returns, total net taxable income, total amount taxed and income tax paid at each tax rate, and total income tax paid, all by locality. (p. 12-17)

1.8. Statewide individual income taxes, 1973-82. (p. 18)

CORPORATE INCOME TAX

2.1-2.2. Number of corporate returns, taxable income, and tax assessed [by tax bracket], FY75-84. (p. 18-19)

S8305–1.2: Sales and Other Taxes

RETAIL SALES AND USE TAX

3.1. Retail sales/use tax business classification code. [list] (p. 20-21)

3.2. Annual sales by business classification made during FY84, as reflected by deposits of sales tax revenues made during the period Aug. 1, 1983-July 31, 1984. (p. 22)

3.3-3.4. State and local retail sales/use tax, FY75-84. (p. 23)

3.5. Aircraft sales/use tax, FY75-84. (p. 23)

3.6. Sales tax distribution [by locality], FY84. (p. 24)

OTHER STATE TAXES

4.1-4.3. Inheritance and gift taxes, FY75-84; and estate taxes [replacing inheritance/gift taxes], FY81-84. (p. 25)

4.4. State recordation taxes, FY75-84. (p. 26)

4.5. Taxes on capital not otherwise taxed, tax years 1974-83. (p. 26)

4.6. Assessed value of capital not otherwise taxed for the tax year 1983, and the State tax thereon at 30 cents per $100 valuation [by locality]. (p. 27)

4.7. Statement showing [county and city] assessment for the tax year beginning Jan. 1, 1984, of the net taxable capital of banks/trust companies. (p. 28)

4.8. [State and local] franchise tax on net capital of bank/trust companies, FY75-84. (p. 28)

4.9-4.11. Malt beverage, tobacco products, and miscellaneous excise taxes, FY75-84. (p. 29)

S8305–1.3: Local Property Taxes

[Tables 5.4-5.7 show data by locality, tax year 1983.]

5.1-5.3. Assessed values, levies assessed, and average nominal tax rates [by property type], tax years 1974-83. (p. 31)

5.4. Real estate: [land] area, fair market values, taxable values, and local levies on land books. (p. 32-33)

5.5-5.6. Tangible personal property, machinery/tools, and merchants' capital: local values and levies assessed on property books. (p. 34-35)

5.7. Public service corporations: assessed values and local levies. (p. 36)

S8310 VIRGINIA
Department of the Treasury

S8310–1   **ANNUAL REPORT OF THE TREASURER to the Governor of Virginia for the Fiscal Year Ended June 30, 1984**
Annual. [1985.] 55 p.
LC 10-17712.
SRI/MF/complete

Annual financial report of the Virginia Dept of the Treasury, presenting data for FY84, with comparisons to FY83, and trends from FY75. Includes financial statements, variously showing receipts, disbursements, fund balances, assets, liabilities, and long-term debt detail, for the following funds: public debt, construction, Richmond-Petersburg Turnpike, literary, special capital improvement, and public school authority.

Also includes data on State investment portfolio performance; revenues from unclaimed property; Treasury checks issued; constitutional debt limit; and bond activity of Virginia Public School Authority by locality and of individual higher education institutions.

Contains contents listing (p. 2-3); letter of transmittal, highlights, summary, and organizational chart (p. 4-7); description of dept operations with 1 table and 11 charts (p. 8-17); and 18 financial statements (p. 21-55).

Annual Report of the Comptroller to the Governor of Virginia, presenting data on the State's general financial condition, is covered in SRI under S8170-1.

Availability: Virginia Department of the Treasury, PO Box 6-H, Richmond VA 23215, †; SRI/MF/complete.

S8325
WASHINGTON STATE
Department
of General
Administration

S8325-1 **STATE OF WASHINGTON, SEVENTY-SEVENTH ANNUAL REPORT of the Supervisor of Banking, for the Year 1983**
Annual. [1984.] 64 p.
LC 74-647170.
SRI/MF/complete

Annual report on financial condition of Washington State financial institutions, 1983, with summary trends from 1908. Covers State-chartered commercial and savings banks/trust companies and industrial loan and consumer finance companies, and State branches of alien (foreign) banks.

Includes number of institutions and aggregate assets, liabilities, income, and expenses for most institution types; and assets of individual State-chartered banks and industrial loan companies.

Also includes data on State Banking Division examination activities and finances; bank financial ratios; and finance company aggregate loan activities.

Contains historical table and highlight contents listing (p. 3-5); and 6 charts and 26 tables, interspersed with institution directories (p. 6-64).

Previous report, for 1982, is described in SRI 1983 Annual, under this number.

Availability: Washington State Department of General Administration, Banking Division, General Administration Bldg., Rm. 219, Olympia WA 98504, †; SRI/MF/complete.

S8328
WASHINGTON STATE
Department of
Agriculture

S8328-1 **WASHINGTON AGRICULTURAL STATISTICS, 1983-84**
Annual. Dec. 1984. 86 p.
ISSN 0095-4330.
LC 74-648858.
SRI/MF/complete, current & previous year reports

Annual report on Washington State agricultural production, marketing, and finances, 1980-83, with some data for 1984 and trends from 1959. Data are generally shown by commodity and/or district or county, with selected comparisons to U.S.

Report covers production, prices, value, and, as applicable, acreage, disposition, yield, and stock or inventory, for field crop, fruit and nut, vegetable, berry, livestock, dairy, poultry, and nursery/greenhouse sectors.

Also includes data on farm income and expenses; prices paid by farmers for selected items; number and acreage of farms; weather; mink production; U.S. cold storage holdings of apples and berries, with detail for Washington State, and Pacific region; and U.S. potato consumption and production.

Data are prepared by the Washington State Crop and Livestock Reporting Service.

Contains contents listing (p. 3); and 6 sections, with narrative summaries, 22 charts, 13 maps, and 91 tables (p. 4-85).

Previous report, for 1982-83, has also been reviewed and is also available on SRI microfiche under this number [Annual. Dec. 1983. 84 p. †]. Previous report is substantially similar in format and content, but also includes data on apiary and seed crop sectors, and does not include mink production data.

Availability: Washington State Crop and Livestock Reporting Service, 417 W. Fourth Ave., Olympia WA 98501, †; SRI/MF/complete.

S8340
WASHINGTON STATE
Employment Security
Department

S8340-3 **WASHINGTON LABOR MARKET**
Monthly. Approx. 12 p.
LC sc84-111.
SRI/MF/complete, shipped quarterly

Monthly report on Washington State labor force, employment, unemployment, earnings, and hours. Includes data by industry group and labor market area. Month of coverage is 1-2 months prior to cover date.

Issues generally contain narrative summary, with 1 text table; 1-5 summary charts; and 5 monthly tables, listed below. Feb. issue also includes 2 annual tables showing monthly labor force and employment data revisions for previous year, with trends from the 1970s.

Similar reports for selected MSAs are available from the issuing agency on a quarterly basis, but are not covered in SRI.

Availability: Washington State Employment Security Department, Labor Market and Economic Analysis Branch, KG-11, Olympia WA 98504-5311, †; SRI/MF/complete, shipped quarterly.

Issues reviewed during 1985: Oct. 1984-Sept. 1985 (P) (Vol. 8, Nos. 10-12; Vol. 9, Nos. 1-9) [Oct. 1984, Vol. 8, No. 10 incorrectly reads Aug. 1984, Vol. 9, No. 10; June 1985 report was issued in 2 parts].

MONTHLY TABLES:
[Data are for Washington State, unless otherwise noted. Data are shown for month of coverage and selected previous periods. Table sequence may vary.]

[1] CPI [urban consumers, for U.S. city average and Seattle-Everett MSA; table may not appear in every issue].

[2] Nonagricultural wage/salary workers, place of work [by industry division and major manufacturing industry group; and total workers involved in labor-management disputes].

[3-4] Resident labor force and employment; and labor force and employment estimates for Federal program purposes; in Washington State and labor market areas [including 6 MSAs and 3 PMSAs].

[5] Estimated average hours and earnings of production workers in manufacturing and of nonsupervisory workers in nonmanufacturing activities [by major manufacturing industry group and for selected nonmanufacturing industries; table may not appear in every issue].

S8345
WASHINGTON STATE
Office of
Financial Management

S8345-3 **STATE OF WASHINGTON ANNUAL FINANCIAL REPORT for the Fiscal Year Ended June 30, 1984**
Annual. Dec. 21, 1984.
iv+74 p.
LC 84-641027.
SRI/MF/complete

Annual report on financial condition of Washington State government, FY84. Presents assets, liabilities, and fund equity and balances; revenues by source; and expenditures by object and major function; for general, special revenue, debt service, capital projects, trust, enterprise, and internal service funds.

Also includes data on budgeted vs. actual revenues and expenditures; bonded debt by agency, institution, and purpose; and trends in fiscal and economic indicators, with selected comparisons to U.S.

Indicators covered include selected State financial and debt ratios; State government staff funding; educational enrollments; population size and change components; labor force; employment, wages, and business income, by industry; personal income; bank deposits; agricultural production value by commodity; international trade; and property valuations and tax rates; various years 1974-FY84.

Contains contents and table listing (p. iii); transmittal letter with 1 text table, listing of elected officials, and 4 charts and 3 summary tables (p. 1-12); auditor's report; and 5 combined financial statements with accompanying notes and text data (p. 14-46); and statistical section with 6 schedules and 21 indicator tables (p. 48-74).

Availability: Washington State Office of Financial Management, Accounting and Fiscal Services Division, Insurance Bldg., M.S. AQ-44, Olympia WA 98504, †; SRI/MF/complete.

S8345-4 **1985 POPULATION TRENDS for Washington State**
Annual. Aug. 1985.
vi+59 p.+errata.
LC 74-648666.
SRI/MF/complete

Annual report on Washington State population trends, including data by county and city, various years 1910-1985. Also includes some data on households and housing units. Data are from Census Bureau and various State sources.

Contains contents listing, preface, and listings of tables and charts (p i-vi); 2 trend charts, and 1 other chart and 14 tables described below (p. 3-33); and 4 special report sections with population survey methodology, text data, and 5 tables also described below (p. 37-59).

Availability: Washington State Office of Financial Management, Policy Analysis and Forecasting Division, M.S. AQ-44, Olympia WA 98504-0201, †; SRI/MF/complete.

TABLES AND CHART:
[Data by city are shown for cities and towns, and usually also include totals for unincorporated places. Data by race/ethnicity variously include Hispanic, Indian, and/or Asian.]

a. Population and housing units, 1980-85, with 1985 housing units by structure type, by city and county; population age 65/over, institutional population, and military personnel, by county, 1970-85; and population by age and race/ethnicity, with race/ethnicity detail by county, various years 1970-85. 1 chart and 8 tables. (p. 3-18)

b. Population change components (births, deaths, and migration), selected years 1910-85, and by county for 1980-85 period; fertility rates, marriages, and divorces/dissolutions, various years 1930-85; city and town annexations (parcels, land area, dwelling units, and population), by county and/or city, various periods 1960-85; and population by city and town, Apr. 1985. 9 tables. (p. 21-39)

c. Group quarter population and number of mobile homes/trailers, by selected city, 1980 city and Federal census counts; and average household size by type of structure, by city, 1985 and most recent previous census (specified for each city). 2 tables (p. 52, 58)

S8365
WASHINGTON STATE
Office of the
Insurance Commissioner

S8365-1 **STATE OF WASHINGTON INSURANCE COMMISSIONER'S NINETIETH ANNUAL REPORT, 1983 Data**
Annual. [1985.] iv+158 p.
LC 62-57499.
SRI/MF/complete, current & 2 previous year reports

Annual report on Washington State insurance industry financial condition and underwriting activity, by company and type of insurance, 1983. Covers assets, liabilities, capital, and surplus; premiums written and/or earned; and losses and claims incurred or paid; for insurers based in Washington State and elsewhere.

Data are shown, as applicable, for life/annuity, accident/health, property/casualty, and title insurance companies; HMOs; surplus line brokers (premiums only); and nonauthorized insurers.

Data for property/casualty insurance include breakdowns for homeowners, automobile, medical malpractice, fidelity and surety, and workers compensation.

Also includes data on State insurance commissioner receipts by source; fireworks licenses issued; and fire marshal investigations by county, month, and structure type, and inspections of licensed facilities by type.

Data are compiled from reports submitted by individual insurers and from insurance dept internal records.

Contains contents listing (p. 1); reviews of State insurance commissioner/fire marshal activities, with list of insurance company status changes, and 7 tables (p. 3-24); and 7 financial tables with composite and company data (p. 25-158).

Reports for 1982 and 1981 were also reviewed in 1985 and are also available on SRI microfiche under this number [Annual. 1985. iv+233 p. † (report for 1982); Annual. 1984. iv+161 p. † (report for 1981)]. Report for 1980 is described in SRI 1983 Annual, also under this number.

Availability: Washington State Office of the Insurance Commissioner, Insurance Bldg., Olympia WA 98504, $13.00; SRI/MF/complete.

S8375
WASHINGTON STATE
Library

S8375-1 **ANNUAL STATISTICAL BULLETIN: Public Library Statistics, 1984, Washington State Library**
Annual. Dec. 1984. 47 p.
SRI/MF/complete

Annual report on Washington State public library finances, holdings, circulation, staff, and population served, shown by library or library system, primarily for 1983.

Contents:

a. Contents listing. (1 p.)

b. Library directory, 1 map, and 1 summary table, including population without library service and number of municipalities and counties unserved. (p. 1-5)

c. List of libraries by county; and 1 table showing population served, professional and non-professional staff, hours of operation, circulation, and holdings by type, by library. (p. 7-19)

d. Assessed valuation, tax revenue and other income, expenditures by item, population served, circulation by outlet, holdings by type, hours of operation, professional and nonprofessional staff, and outlets and facilities served by type, 1983; and salaries by position, 1984; by system, arranged by size group of population served. 10 tables. (p. 20-47)

Availability: Washington State Library, Documents Distribution Center, Olympia WA 98504-0111, †; SRI/MF/complete.

S8405
WASHINGTON STATE
Office of the
Superintendent of
Public Instruction

S8405-1 **MINORITY ENROLLMENTS IN PUBLIC AND PRIVATE SCHOOLS, State of Washington, Oct. 1984**
Annual. Mar. 1985.
1+114 p. var. paging
SRI/MF/complete

Annual report on minority enrollment in Washington State public and private schools for 1984/85 school year. Contains 2 detailed tables showing enrollment for black, Asian/Pacific Islander, American Indian/Alaskan Native, Hispanic, and white pupils, by county, district, and school, for public schools (p. 1-73) and private schools (p. 1-41).

Availability: Washington State Office of the Superintendent of Public Instruction, Information Services, Old Capitol Bldg., FG-11, Olympia WA 98504, †; SRI/MF/complete.

S8415
WASHINGTON STATE
Department of Revenue

S8415-1 **STATE OF WASHINGTON, 1984 TAX STATISTICS**
Annual. [1984.] 85 p.
ISSN 0094-6885.
LC 64-6271.
SRI/MF/complete

Annual report on Washington State tax collections, with actual and assessed real and personal property values, FY84, with trends from FY27. Also includes valuation of operating property of intercounty public service companies, including transportation, communication, and energy utilities.

Data are from State Revenue Dept and Office of Financial Management records.

Contains contents listing (p. 1); and 4 statistical sections, each preceded by table listing, with 42 tables listed below (p. 3-85).

Availability: Washington State Department of Revenue, Research and Information Division, General Administration Bldg., MS-AX-02, Olympia WA 98504, ‡; SRI/MF/complete.

TABLES:
[Tables show data for Washington State, FY84, unless otherwise noted.]

S8415-1.1: Excise Taxes

1-2. Summary of taxes, FY83-84; and net tax collections [by source, including general and selective sales taxes, gross receipts, property and in-lieu excises, other State taxes, and licenses], selected years FY27-84. (p. 4-11)

3. General fund revenues [by source, including Federal revenue]. (p. 12)

4. Dept of Revenue collections [including State taxes by type, and administrative and local tax collections], FY83-84. (p. 13)

5. County/city sales/use tax distributions [by jurisdiction], FY80-84. (p. 14)

6. Public transportation systems: local sales/ use tax distributions [by transit district], FY82-84. (p. 15)

7. Timber excise tax distributions by county, 1984. (p. 16)

8. Local leasehold excise tax distributions [by county], FY82-84 [with amounts for cities, FY84]. (p. 17)

9. Public utility district (PUD) excise tax, distributions [by county] in FY80-84. (p. 18)

10. Retail sales/use tax distributions for local stadium/convention center facilities [total for cities and counties], FY77-84. (p. 19)

11. Real estate excise tax statistics [number and taxable value of sales, and tax revenue], FY75-84. (p. 19)

12. Number of State excise taxpayers, registered accounts by county [and for out of State] and reporting frequency, beginning of FY84-85. (p. 20)

S8415-1.2: Property Tax Levies and Collections

[Types of taxing districts include State, counties, cities/towns, school, fire, water, cemetery, hospital, and various others. Tables 13-16 show data for year due.]

13-14. Property tax levies, by [type of] major taxing district, 1981-84; and by county, 1983-84. (p. 22-24)

15. Property tax levies by county, countywide average rates per $1,000 assessed value, 1980-84. (p. 25)

16. Property tax [county, and State assessed] valuations, [total tax] levies, and average tax rates, [quinquennially 1910-50 and annually 1951-85]. (p. 26)

17. Number of taxing districts by type, 1979-84. (p. 27)

18-19. Property tax collections and year-end delinquency: amounts by county, 1983; and statewide totals [quinquennially 1935-70 and annually 1971-83]. (p. 28-31)

S8415-1.3: Property Valuations and Assessment Ratios

[Tables show data for 1984, unless otherwise noted. All tables show data by county.]

20-21. Indicated property tax ratios: by assessment years 1979-84; and real, personal, and combined indicated ratios, assessment years 1983-84. (p. 34-35)

22. Assessed valuation of lands/improvements: locally assessed property [platted and unplatted lands in unincorporated areas, cities/towns, and total taxable value]. (p. 36)

23. Valuation of current use land: agricultural/timber/open space lands approved for current use assessment. (p. 37)

24. Valuation of forest land: privately owned classified and designated forest land [acres and value]. (p. 38)

25. Other property valuation statistics: valuation of reforestation lands, and senior citizens exempt property. (p. 36)

26-27. Assessed valuation of personal property [including farm and logging/mining machinery/equipment, supplies/materials, and mobile homes; household head exemption];

and valuation of State assessed vessels (commercial boats subject to property tax). (p. 40-42)

28. Assessed and actual value of taxable real and personal property, and computation of State property tax levy. (p. 43-45)

S8415-1.4: State-Assessed Utility Valuations

[Data are for 1984, unless otherwise noted. Tables 30-42 show actual and equalized assessed value of real and personal property, by county and/or company.]

29. Summary of public service company values: [number of firms, and actual and equalized] values, by type of utility [transportation, communication, and energy], 1983-84. (p. 48)

30-41. Air transportation, electric light/power, gas, [motor carrier] freight and passenger transportation [for nonvehicle property], pipeline, private car, railroad, telegraph, telephone, water transportation, and domestic water companies. (p. 49-73)

42. Recapitulation [of public utility companies]. (p. 74-85)

S8420
WASHINGTON STATE
Department of Social and Health Services

S8420-1   VITAL STATISTICS SUMMARY, Washington State, 1982
Annual.   [1984.]   xii+93 p.
LC 72-625420.
SRI/MF/complete

Annual report on Washington State vital statistics, covering births, deaths by cause, marriages and dissolutions, and population, 1982, with selected trends from 1920. Data are shown by selected demographic characteristics and by county and city. Data are from State and local records.

Contents:

a. Contents and table listing, map, highlights, and 3 charts (p. v-xii); and narrative report, with 16 charts primarily showing trends (p. 3-30).

b. Statistical section, with 42 tables listed below. (p. 32-85)

c. Appendices A-E, including methodology, definitions, conversion table, and 2 tables showing population by age group, sex, city, and county, as of Apr. 1, 1982. (p. 88-93)

Previous report, for 1981, is described in SRI 1983 Annual, under this number.

Availability: Washington State Department of Social and Health Services, Health Statistics Center, Health Data Section, ET 14, PO Box 9709, Olympia WA 98504, †; SRI/MF/complete.

TABLES:

[Tables show data for 1982, unless otherwise noted. Data by race generally are shown for white, black, Mexican/Chicano, Indian, Japanese, Chinese, Filipino, other Asian, and other.]

SUMMARY

1. Summary of [population, and] the number of live births, deaths, deaths of infants under 1 year of age, maternal deaths, and fetal deaths, with rates, 1920-82. (p. 32-33)

NATALITY

[Tables 4-9 and 12-13 show data by county and city.]

2A-2H. Live births by selected topics [residence live births, by race and mother's age by sex, and by birth order and type of attendant; multiple live births; occurrence live births by type of place of birth; and residence and occurrence live births by sex and birth weight, and live births and fetal deaths by month]. (p. 36-37)

[3] Live birth inter-county travel patterns [live births cross-tabulated by county of residence and occurrence, and total out-of-State]. (p. 38-39)

4-5. Live births with rates by place of residence and occurrence, by sex; and live births by race by place of residence. (p. 40-41)

6-7. Live births by mother's age group and by month [both] by place of residence. (p. 42-43)

8. Live births by institutions [general hospital, Federal facility, home, birth center, born on arrival, and other], by place of occurrence. (p. 44)

9. Live births by birth weight in grams by place of residence. (p. 45)

10-11. Live births by race and mother's age [both] by birth weight. (p. 46-47)

12. Multiple live births and immature live births, by place of residence. (p. 48)

13. Live births [resulting in] infant deaths by mother's age group, by place of residence. (p. 49)

S8420-1.2: Mortality

[Causes of death are coded according to the *9th Revision of the International Classification of Diseases, Adapted.*]

SUMMARY

1A-1G. Deaths by selected topics [residence deaths by race, marital status, and age group, all by sex; residence infant deaths by race; residence deaths by 10 leading causes; residence and occurrence deaths by month; and occurrence deaths by type of place of death]. (p. 52-53)

BY PLACE AND CAUSE

[Tables 2-12 and 15-16 show data by county and city.]

2. Deaths with rates by place of residence and occurrence. (p. 54)

3-4. Deaths by sex, race, and age group, [all] by place of residence. (p. 55-56)

5-7. Deaths with rates by selected causes, place of residence. (p. 57-59)

8. Deaths by certain infective and parasitic diseases, by place of residence. (p. 60)

9-12. Deaths with rates by external causes by place of residence and place of occurrence. (p. 61-64)

13. Residence deaths with rates by selected causes, by sex. (p. 65-67)

14. Residence deaths with rates and percent by age group and sex, by 5 leading causes. (p. 68-69)

15-16. Deaths, by month of occurrence by place of residence; and by type of place [general and psychiatric hospitals, State and Federal facilities, nursing home, home, dead on arrival, and other], by place of occurrence. (p. 70-71)

17. Deaths, occurrence, by month by selected causes. (p. 72)

18. Deaths, resident, by nontransport causes, by place of accident [home, farm, industrial, recreation, street/highway, public building, resident institution, and other]. (p. 73)

INFANT MORTALITY
[Tables 19-20, 23, and 25 show data by county and city.]

19-20. Fetal, perinatal, neonatal, and infant mortality by place of residence and occurrence. (p. 74-75)

21. Residence fetal mortality by sex and weight. (p. 76)

22. Fetal mortality by cause. (p. 77)

23. Infant mortality by race, by place of residence. (p. 78)

24. Infant mortality by age and sex, by cause. (p. 79)

25. Infant mortality by leading causes, by place of residence. (p. 80)

S8420–1.3: Marriages and Dissolutions

1. Marriages by county of marriage, by bride and groom age group. (p. 82)

2. Dissolutions, annulments, and separate maintenance, by county of decree. (p. 83)

3-4. Dissolutions, by total living children by place of residence, and by county of divorce by husband and wife age group. (p. 84-85)

S8425
WASHINGTON STATE
Office of the Secretary of State

S8425–1   **OFFICIAL ABSTRACT OF THE RESULTS OF THE NOV. 6, 1984 WASHINGTON STATE GENERAL ELECTION**
Biennial.   2 volumes.
For individual publication data, see below.
SRI/MF/complete

Biennial report presenting results of the Washington State 1984 general elections. Report is published in 2 sections, described below. Data on the primary elections are also available from this issuing agency, but are not covered in SRI.

Previous report, covering the 1982 general election, was titled *County-by-County Abstract of the 1982 State General Election, Washington State* (for description, see SRI 1983 Annual, under this number).

Availability: Washington State Office of the Secretary of State, Elections Division, Legislative Bldg., Olympia WA 98504, †; SRI/MF/ complete.

S8425–1.1: 1984 General Election Returns for Legislative Races
[Biennial. [1984.] 30 p. SRI/MF/complete.]
Shows voting for State senators and representatives, by county and district.

S8425–1.2: 1984 General Election
[Biennial. [1984.] 25 p. SRI/MF/complete.]
Shows registration and votes cast; and voting for President/Vice President, U.S. Representatives, Governor, Lieutenant Governor, secretary of state and 6 other State offices, State supreme court justices, court of appeals and superior court judges, and 3 initiative measures. All data are shown by county.

S8428
WASHINGTON STATE
Traffic Safety Commission

S8428–1   **STATE OF WASHINGTON DATA SUMMARY AND ANALYSIS OF 1984 TRAFFIC COLLISIONS**
Annual.   [1985.]   60 p.
SRI/MF/complete, current & previous year reports

Annual report on Washington State traffic accidents, fatalities, and injuries, by vehicle and accident type, location, time, and other circumstances; and driver and victim characteristics; 1984, with selected trends from 1980.

Also includes data on vehicle registrations and miles traveled; miles of highways; licensed drivers; alcohol involvement in accidents and chemical test results; vehicle defects contributing to accidents; and use of safety devices by vehicle occupants involved in accidents.

Contains contents listing (1 p.); and 2 maps, 57 charts, and 50 tables, interspersed with narrative analyses (p. II.1-II.60).

Previous report, for 1983, was also reviewed during 1985, and is also available on SRI microfiche under S8428-1 [Annual. [1984.] 60 p.+errata sheet. †].

Availability: Washington State Traffic Safety Commission, 1000 S. Cherry St., Olympia WA 98504, †; SRI/MF/complete.

S8440
WASHINGTON STATE
Uniform Crime Reporting

S8440–1   **CRIME IN WASHINGTON STATE, 1984**
Annual.   [1985.]   vii+152 p.
SRI/MF/complete

Annual report on Washington State crimes and arrests, by offense, 1984, with selected comparisons to 1983. Includes data by county and law enforcement agency, and by offender age, sex, and race/ethnicity. Also includes law enforcement employment, and assaults on officers.

Report focuses on 8 Index offenses: murder, rape, robbery, aggravated assault, burglary, larceny/theft, motor vehicle theft, and arson. Arrests are also shown for numerous non-Index offenses.

Data are compiled from State and local agency reports, submitted under the Uniform Crime Reporting (UCR) Program.

Contains summary, and listings of contents, tables, and charts (p. i-vii); introduction and explanation of UCR program, with 1 summary chart (p. 1-12); 15 charts and 24 tables, described below (p. 14-146); and glossary (p. 148-152). This is the 5th annual crime report issued by the Washington Assn of Sheriffs and Police Chiefs.

Availability: Washington Association of Sheriffs and Police Chiefs, PO Box 826, Olympia WA 98507, ‡; SRI/MF/complete.

TABLES AND CHARTS:
[Data are shown for 1984, with selected comparisons to 1983. Data by race/ethnicity generally include American Indian, Asian, Hispanic, and non-Hispanic. Unless otherwise noted, data by offense are shown for Index crimes.]

a. Violent crime analysis: murders by type of weapon, city and county population size, month, victim/offender relationship, and circumstance; murder victims and offenders, by age, sex, and race/ethnicity; attempted and forcible rapes; value of property stolen, by type of robbery location; and robberies and assaults, by type of weapon. 7 charts and tables 1-5. (p. 14-25)

b. Property crime and arson analysis: burglaries by type of entry; value of property stolen, for residence and nonresidence, day and night burglaries; larceny offenses and value of property stolen, by offense type; motor vehicle thefts, by vehicle type; and arson offenses (total and abandoned structures), property damage value, and clearances, by type of structure. 6 charts and table 6. (p. 26-33)

c. Arrest analysis and stolen property value: adult and juvenile arrests, by age, sex, and race/ethnicity, for Index and non-Index offenses (with detail for Seattle); reported and actual offenses, and clearances, by offense (excluding arson); and value of property stolen and recovered, by offense (excluding arson) and/or property type. Tables 7-10. (p. 34-46)

d. Local data: Index crimes and rates, and total and juvenile clearances, by agency and county; and offenses, by city and county population size group; with lists of reporting agencies. Tables 11-15. (p. 47-101)

e. Assaults on officers, by weapon, injury status, time, and type of assignment and circumstance; and clearances by circumstance. 2 charts and tables 16-19. (p. 108-114)

f. Law enforcement personnel: commissioned and civilian law enforcement employees by sex, by agency, county, and agency type; and total and commissioned employees, by population size group, city, and county; with population for each agency and location. Tables 20-24. (p. 115-146)

S8450
WASHINGTON STATE
Utilities and
Transportation Commission

S8450–1   STATISTICS OF UTILITY COMPANIES, Washington State
Annual series.   For individual publication data, see below.
SRI/MF/complete

Series of 3 annual reports on the financial and operating conditions of utilities regulated by the Washington State Utilities and Transportation Commission. Covers electric, gas, and telephone companies. Data are compiled from annual reports filed by the companies with the commission.

Reports generally include individual company balance sheets and other financial data, and selected operating statistics.

Reports reviewed during 1985, presenting data for 1983, are described below.

Prior to editions presenting data for 1981, series also included an annual report on water companies.

Availability: Washington State Utilities and Transportation Commission, Accounting Division, Highways-Licenses Bldg., Olympia WA 98504-8002, †; SRI/MF/complete.

S8450–1.1: Statistics of Gas Companies, 1983
[Annual. [1984.] 17 p. Oversized. ISSN 0090-9068. LC 45-51236. SRI/MF/complete.]

Annual report presenting Washington State Class A gas utility financial and operating data, by company, 1983, with selected aggregate trends from 1979.

Includes balance sheet, income statement, operating ratios, plant in service, production, and sales and customers by customer class.

Contains contents listing (1 p.); brief narrative, with 2 charts and 1 summary text table (p. 1-3); and 9 tables generally showing company data (p. 4-17).

Previous report, for 1982, is described in SRI 1983 Annual, under this number.

S8450–1.2: Statistics of Electric Companies, 1983, Washington State
[Annual. [1985.] 21 p. Oversized. LC 45-51104. SRI/MF/complete.]

Annual report presenting Washington State Class A electric utility financial and operating data, by company 1983, and aggregate 1982-83, with selected trends from 1979.

Includes balance sheet, operating ratios, income statement, fuel sources, sales and customers by customer class, generating capacity by fuel type, plant value, and equipment in use.

Also includes typical residential bill.

Contains contents listing and company index (p. 1-2); brief narrative with text tables (p. 3-4); 3 charts and 8 tables generally showing aggregate data (p. 5-15); and 6 tables showing company data (p. 16-21).

S8450–1.3: Statistics of Telephone Companies, 1983, Washington State

[Annual. [1985.] i+31 p. Oversized. SRI/MF/complete.]

Annual report presenting Washington State Class A-B telephone company financial and operating data, by company 1983, and aggregate 1982-83. Includes balance sheet, income statement, plant value, equipment in use, and operating ratios.

Contains contents listing (1 p.); company index (p. i); brief narrative, and 2 charts and 3 tables showing aggregate data (p. 1-7); and 7 tables showing company data (p. 8-31).

S8450–3   QUARTERLY STATISTICS OF CLASS I AND CLASS II MOTOR CARRIERS OF PROPERTY
Quarterly (selected issue).
Apr. 1985.   33 p. Oversized.
SRI/MF/complete

Annual compilation of statistics on the financial condition of Washington State Class I and II motor carriers of property, 1984, with comparisons to 1983 and detail for 4th quarter. Includes revenues, expenditures, and operating ratios, by company, with itemized detail by carrier type group.

Carrier groups are local/statewide and large interstate scheduled line-haul general freight and household goods carriers; and nonscheduled general freight, Greater Puget Sound area, bulk commodity, agricultural/allied products, heavy machinery/building materials/forest products, refrigerated products, and miscellaneous commodity carriers.

Data are compiled from company reports filed with the Washington State Utilities and Transportation Commission.

Contains table of contents (1 p.); brief narrative (p. 1-2); and 2 basic tables, repeated for each carrier group (p. 3-33).

Annual data are published each year in the 4th quarter issue of *Quarterly Statistics of Class I and Class II Motor Carriers of Property;* 4th quarter issue is the only issue covered by SRI.

The Commission also issues a series of annual reports on Washington State utility financial and operating statistics. Series is covered in SRI under S8450-1.

Availability: Washington State Utilities and Transportation Commission, Accounting Section, Highways-Licenses Bldg., Olympia WA 98504-0087, †; SRI/MF/complete.

S8510   WEST VIRGINIA
Department of
Agriculture

S8510–1   WEST VIRGINIA AGRICULTURAL STATISTICS, 1984
Annual. Jan. 1985.   3+90 p.
C. R. Bull. No. 15.
LC 44-41812.
SRI/MF/complete

Annual report on West Virginia agricultural production, marketing, and finances, 1983, with some estimates for 1984, and trends from 1970s. Data are generally shown by commodity and/or county.

Covers production, prices, sales, value, and, as applicable, acreage, yield, disposition, and inventory, for field crop, fruit, livestock, dairy, poultry, and apiary sectors.

Also includes data on West Virginia precipitation, pasture condition, feed and fertilizer sales, prices paid by farmers for selected production items, and farm income; Appalachian region farm production expenditures; Northeastern region agricultural employment, hours, and wages; and number of farms and acreage, by State.

Data are compiled by the West Virginia Crop Reporting Service in cooperation with USDA.

Contains listing of contents (1 p.); and 7 charts, 11 maps, and 82 tables, interspersed with narrative summaries (p. 1-90).

Availability: West Virginia Department of Agriculture, Crop Reporting Service, Charleston WV 25305, contributors to publication †, others $5.00; SRI/MF/complete.

S8530   WEST VIRGINIA
Department of
Banking

S8530–1   STATE OF WEST VIRGINIA, Eighty-Second Report of Financial Institutions
Annual. [1985.]   113 p.
LC 10-11565.
SRI/MF/complete

Annual report on the financial condition of West Virginia State-chartered banks, trust companies, building and loan assns, industrial loan companies, and credit unions, showing composite liabilities, assets, income, and expenses, and liabilities and/or assets by institution, as of Dec. 31, 1982-83, with selected comparisons from as early as June 30, 1891.

Also includes data on Banking Dept receipts and expenditures; State-located national bank total assets and liabilities, and deposits by institution; bank failures by city and institution; licensed small loan companies composite assets; and floating mortgage rate ceilings.

Contains contents listing and Banking Dept summary with 1 table (p. 2-8); and 16 financial tables, interspersed with tabular lists (p. 9-113).

Previous report, presenting data as of Dec. 1980-81, is described in SRI 1983 Annual under this number.

Availability: West Virginia Department of Banking, State Office Bldg. No. 6, Rm. B406, Charleston WV 25305, †; SRI/MF/complete.

S8540   WEST VIRGINIA Department of Education

S8540-1   SEVENTIETH REPORT (TWENTY-NINTH ANNUAL REPORT) OF THE STATE SUPERINTENDENT OF SCHOOLS, West Virginia
Annual.   3 volumes.
For individual publication data, see below.
LC 72-621530.
SRI/MF/complete

Annual report, for 1982/83, on West Virginia public elementary and secondary education, with selected data for private schools. Report is published in 3 volumes as follows:

Vol. 1. Narrative report, describing Dept of Education activities, with selected facility and funding statistics.

Vol. 2. Statistical summary, presenting data on educational personnel, pupils, transportation, and facilities for public schools, and selected data for nonpublic schools.

Vol. 3. Financial report.

Volume 3 is described below.

For description of Volumes 1 and 2 for 1982/83, see SRI 1984 Annual under this number.

Availability: West Virginia Department of Education, Public Information Office, Capitol Complex, Bldg. 6, Rm. B-215, Charleston WV 25305, †; SRI/MF/complete.

S8540-1.3: Volume 3 (Financial Report)
[Annual. [1984.] 158 p. SRI/MF/complete.]
Contains contents listing (1 p.); and 24 tables, listed below (p. 3-158).

TABLES:
[All data are for the 1982/83 school year. All tables except table [22] show data by county.]
[1] Current expense fund receipts [by detailed source]. (p. 3-30)
[2] Current expense fund: summary of receipts, expenditures, and balances. (p. 31-33)
[3] Current expenditures: summary by major classification. (p. 34-39)
[4-18] Current expenditures [by detailed classification]. (p. 40-122)
[19-21] Debt service, bond construction, and permanent improvement funds [including opening and closing balances, revenues, expenditures, and interfund transfers]. (p. 123-155)
[22] Financial summary statement for all funds. (p. 156)
[23] Total expenditures for all funds. (p. 157)
[24] Per pupil expenditure and average annual salary for instructional personnel. (p. 158)

S8540-2   ANNUAL REPORT, EDUCATION 1983/84, West Virginia
Annual.   3 volumes.
For individual publication data, see below.
LC 72-621530.
SRI/MF/complete

Annual report, for 1983/84, on West Virginia public elementary and secondary education, with selected data for private schools. Report is published in 3 volumes as follows:

Vol. I. Narrative report, describing Dept of Education activities, with selected facility and funding statistics.

Vol. II. Statistical summary, presenting data on educational personnel, pupils, transportation, and facilities for public schools, and selected data for nonpublic schools.

Vol. III. Financial report.

Volumes covering 1983/84 are described below.

Volumes for 1982/83 are covered in SRI 1984 and 1985 Annuals under S8540-1.

Availability: West Virginia Department of Education, Public Information Office, Capitol Complex, Bldg. 6, Rm. B-215, Charleston WV 25305, †; SRI/MF/complete.

S8540-2.1: Volume I: Seventy-First Report (Thirtieth Annual Report) of the Superintendent of Schools
[Annual. Nov. 1, 1984. vi+27 p. SRI/MF/complete.]

Contains contents listing (p. v); introduction and organizational chart (p. 1-2); and narrative report interspersed with 5 tables, listed below (p. 3-27).

TABLES:

BETTER SCHOOL BUILDING PROGRAM
[Tables I-IV show data by county.]
I-III. Comprehensive educational facilities [budget] plans and school construction projects approved by the State board of education; and school facilities projects completed/inspected to date; [all including project costs by funding source (State, Federal/State, and local bond issue and levies/other), as of June 29, 1984]. (p. 20-21, 23)
IV. Bond elections attempted since inception of Better School Building Program [including value of bond issues proposed, and value and percent of voter approval of approved and defeated issues, selected years 1971-83]. (p. 22)

EDUCATIONAL FUNDS
[A] Board of education funds processed [by expenditure category, and function or program], 1983/84. (p. 26-27)

S8540-2.2: Volume II: 1983/84 Educational Statistical Summary
[Annual. [1984.] 99 p. SRI/MF/complete.]
Contains contents listing (1 p.); and 40 tables, listed below (p. 3-99).

TABLES:
[All tables show data for 1983/84 school year. All tables except tables [8-12] and [14-15] show data by county. Pupil data by grade generally include ungraded and/or special education.]

PERSONNEL
[1] Personnel, FTE [by detailed position]. (p. 3-18)
[2-7] Instructional personnel, by grade of certificate and years of experience: elementary, secondary, and unclassified. (p. 19-27)
[8] Certificate type and number issued. (p. 28)

[9] Professional administrative certificates endorsements. (p. 29)
[10] Original professional certificates issued [for graduates: by State institution, and by State for out-of-State institutions]. (p. 30)
[11] Endorsements on provisional certificates, by West Virginia colleges where degree was granted [and teaching field]. (p. 31-34)
[12] Endorsements on original professional certificates. (p. 35-36)
[13] Teaching permits issued [by type]. (p. 37)
[14] Endorsements on teaching permits [by field and permit type]. (p. 38-39)
[15] Instructional personnel, number and average salary [by position]. (p. 40)

PUPILS
[16-18] Public school net enrollment: elementary, junior high, and high school [by sex and grade]. (p. 43-49)
[19] Public school net [elementary, secondary, and postgraduate] enrollment [by sex]. (p. 50-51)
[20] Promotions, retentions, and withdrawals, by grades, public elementary schools. (p. 52-55)
[21-22] Total days present and average daily attendance [prekindergarten/kindergarten, elementary, junior high, and high school]. (p. 56-57)
[23] Public high school graduates [by sex]. (p. 58)
[24] Pupils previously enrolled in other States/other West Virginia nonpublic schools [elementary, junior high, and high school]. (p. 59)

TRANSPORTATION
[25] Number of school buses and school bus operators. (p. 63)
[26] Number of pupils and passengers transported on regular and contract buses. (p. 64)
[27] Miles traveled by regular and contract buses [and extracurricular and curricular miles traveled]. (p. 65)

SCHOOL PLANT AND FACILITIES
[28] School buildings [elementary and secondary: number of schools and buildings, and number of square feet in buildings in use at beginning of school year, new buildings, and additions; number of buildings and additions completed; seating capacity; and rooms vacant and needed because of population shifts]. (p. 69-74)
[29] Value of buildings, grounds, and equipment [including furniture, apparatus, libraries, teaching aids/materials, school buses, and transportation equipment]. (p. 75-76)

NONPUBLIC SCHOOLS
[30] Nonpublic schools [number of schools and net enrollment for church related and other private schools]. (p. 79)
[31-32] Church related schools: number of [elementary and secondary] schools, term, and [instructional and noninstructional] staff; and high school graduates [by sex]. (p. 80-81)
[33-35] Church related schools: net enrollment, elementary and secondary [by grade and sex]. (p. 82-89)
[36-40] Other private schools [same data breakdowns as tables 31-35]. (p. 90-99)

S8540–2.3: Volume III (Financial Report)

[Annual. [1985.] 165 p. SRI/MF/complete.]

Contains contents listing (1 p.); and 24 tables, listed below (p. 3-165).

TABLES:

[All data are for the 1983/84 school year. All tables except table [23] show data by county.]

[1-2] Current expense fund receipts [by detailed source; and summary of receipts, expenditures, and balances]. (p. 3-31)

[3] Current expenditures [summary by major classification]. (p. 32-37)

[4-18] Current expenditures [by detailed classification]. (p. 38-129)

[19-21] Debt service, bond construction, and permanent improvement funds [including opening and closing balances, revenues, expenditures, and interfund transfers]. (p. 130-162)

[22] Total expenditures for all funds. (p. 163)

[23] Financial summary statement for all funds. (p. 164)

[24] Per pupil expenditure and average annual salary for instructional personnel. (p. 165)

S8545   WEST VIRGINIA Department of Employment Security

S8545–2   ANNUAL PLANNING INFORMATION, State of West Virginia, and West Virginia Less Kanawha County Service Delivery Area, FY86

Annual. [1985.] iii+49 p.
Rpt. No. LER-LMI 121.
SRI/MF/complete, current & previous year reports

Annual planning report, for FY86, identifying West Virginia population groups most in need of employment services, and presenting data on employment by industry, population, labor force, personal income, and production workers' hours and earnings, various years 1970-FY86. Also includes occupational employment projections through 1996.

Data are from Federal, State, and private sources.

Contains contents and table listings (p. i-iii); 4 narrative chapters (p. 1-5); 22 tables, listed below (p. 6-40); and notes, glossary, and data sources (p. 41-49).

Previous report, for FY85, was also reviewed during 1985 and is also available on SRI microfiche under this number [Annual. [1984.] iii+42 p. †]. Previous report is substantially similar in format and content, but omits occupational employment projections and data on dislocated workers. For description of report for FY84, see SRI 1983 Annual under this number.

Reports for individual MSAs are also available from issuing agency but are not covered in SRI.

Availability: West Virginia Department of Employment Security, Labor and Economic Research Section, 112 California Ave., Charleston WV 25305, †; SRI/MF/complete.

TABLES:

[Data are for West Virginia, unless otherwise noted. Several tables are in 2 parts, generally presenting data for the State and for the State minus the Kanawha County service delivery area.]

POPULATION AND INCOME

1-2. Population characteristics, 1980 census and FY86; and composition of the labor force, 1970 and FY86; [all] by age, sex, and race. (p. 6-9)

3. Population by race, by county, census: 1970 and 1980. (p. 10)

4. Per capita personal income, by county [and metro-nonmetro status], 1982-83. (p. 11)

EMPLOYMENT, HOURS, AND EARNINGS

5-6. Nonagricultural wage/salary employment, by industry [division or major group], annual averages 1982-84, projected FY86, and [monthly] 1984. (p. 12-14)

7-9. Labor force statistics [civilian labor force, employment, and unemployment: monthly 1970-84]; by county, annual averages 1984; and FY77-85. (p. 15-21)

10. Labor force, employment, and unemployment characteristics by race, sex, and age, FY86. (p. 22-23)

11. Insured unemployment by industry [division], weeks of duration, sex, and age, annual averages 1983-84. (p. 24)

12. Industrial employment historical growth perspective [by industry division and major group], annual averages 1970, 1980, and 1984. (p. 25)

13. Nonagricultural wage/salary employment by industrial classification [and labor force by employment status, for] U.S., State, and [by] MSA, annual averages 1984. (p. 26-27)

14. Federal poverty income guidelines, FY85. (p. 28)

15-16. Production workers: hours and earnings (current dollars); and real earnings (adjusted to constant 1967 dollars by CPI; [by industry division or major group], annual averages 1983-84. (p. 29-30)

DISADVANTAGED PERSONS AND DISLOCATED WORKERS

17. Economically disadvantaged [by county and age group], Aug. 1984. (p. 31)

18. Dislocated workers, by county and industry [division], Apr. 1983. (p. 32)

JOB SERVICE ACTIVITIES AND OCCUPATIONAL PROJECTIONS

19-20. Applicants and job openings listed with [and openings filled by] the job service offices [by occupation]; and labor demand (occupations for which 50/more openings were received in job service offices); Jan.-Sept. 1984. (p. 33-34)

21-22. Fast and slow growth occupations [based on projected annual average openings, 1983-96 period]; and U.S. 40 occupations with largest job growth, and 20 fastest growing and most rapidly declining occupations [based on employment change, 1982-95 period]. (p. 36-40)

S8560   WEST VIRGINIA Department of Health

S8560–1   THIRTY-SEVENTH ANNUAL REPORT: Vital Health Statistics of West Virginia, 1983

Annual. Dec. 1984.
iii+6+117 p.
LC 80-648783.
SRI/MF/complete

Annual report on West Virginia vital statistics, covering population, births, deaths by cause, marriages, and divorces, for 1983, with selected trends from 1920s.

Data usually are shown by county; selected data are shown by city and region. Most data were compiled from records submitted to the Dept of Health prior to June 1, 1984. Population data are from U.S. Census Bureau.

Contains foreword (p. iii); listing of contents, charts, and tables (6 p.); summary, methodology, and definitions (p. 1-11); 2 summary tables (p. 12-13); 4 statistical sections with 20 exhibits (each generally 1 chart with accompanying table) and 47 tables, listed below (p. 17-107); and appendices, with facsimile record forms and listing of ICDA (International Classification of Diseases, Adapted) codes (p. 111-117).

Availability: West Virginia Department of Health, Health Statistics Center, Health Planning and Evaluation Office, 1800 Washington St., E., Charleston WV 25305, †; SRI/MF/complete.

STATISTICAL SECTION EXHIBITS AND TABLES:

[Unless otherwise noted, tables show data for 1983. Data by city are shown for cities with population over 10,000. Exhibits are indicated by an "E" before the table number.]

S8560–1.1: Population

E1. Population [quinquennially 1925-80, and 1981-83]. (p. 17)

1A-1B. Population, 1970 and 1980; and 1981-82, [by] region and county. (p. 18-19)

E2-E4. Population characteristics: age group, sex, and race distribution, 1980 [includes data for American Indians/Eskimos/Aleuts, Asian/Pacific Islanders, and persons of Spanish origin, and selected comparisons to 1970]. (p. 20-22)

E5. Population age group distribution [decennially 1950-80]. (p. 23)

2. Population, 1980: age group distribution by county. (p. 24-25)

3. Population [and] birth and death rates, 1940-83. (p. 26)

S8560–1.2: Births

[Most tables and exhibits begin "West Virginia resident births..."]

E6. Number and rate [quinquennially 1920-75 and 1978-83]. (p. 29)

4. Summary totals [by sex, race, attendant at birth, hospital and nonhospital, and marital status by race]. (p. 30)

E7. Rates per 1,000 population [by] region and county. (p. 31)

5. Births, number by [county of] residence and occurrence, [and] rate [by county] of residence. (p. 32)

6. Number by county of residence, 1979-83. (p. 33)

E8-E9. [By] birth weight in grams and [by] age of mother. (p. 34-35)

7-8. [By] birth weight by age of mother, and [by] age of mother by region and county of residence. (p. 36-37)

E10. [By] marital status by age of mother. (p. 38)

9. [By] place of delivery [hospital or nonhospital], race and sex of child, and marital status of mother, by county of residence. (p. 39)

10-11. [By] trimester prenatal care began, by county of residence, race, and marital status and education of mother. (p. 40-41)

12. [By] prenatal care visits by county of residence. (p. 42)

13. Number and rate [and 1980 population], by city. (p. 43)

14. Out-of-State occurrences [by State, 1980-83]. (p. 44)

S8560–1.3: Deaths
[Most tables and exhibits begin "West Virginia resident deaths..."]

E11. Number and rate [quinquennially 1920-75 and 1978-83]. (p. 47)

15-16. [By] county of residence by race and sex, and by county of occurrence. (p. 48-49)

17. Out-of-State occurrences [by State]. (p. 50)

18-20. Number, 1979-83; and by age at death and [type of] place death occurred, 1983; [all] by county of residence. (p. 51-53)

E12-E14. Leading causes of death [number and rate: for West Virginia total and by sex, and U.S.]. (p. 54-56)

21. Leading causes by age group and sex. (p. 57-60)

22-23. [By type of] diseases of the heart and malignant neoplasms (cancer): number and rate by sex. (p. 61)

E15. [By] types of accidental deaths. (p. 62)

E16. Nontransport accidental deaths [by type of] place of occurrence. (p. 63)

24-25. [By type of] nontransport and home accidental deaths. (p. 64)

E17. Fetal, neonatal and infant deaths: number and ratio [quinquennially 1920-75 and 1978-83]. (p. 65)

26. Infant deaths [by] causes of death by age. (p. 66)

27-28. Fetal deaths: number by county of residence and occurrence, and ratio by county of residence, 1983; and number and ratio by county of residence, 1979-83. (p. 67-68)

29. [By] selected causes by race and sex. (p. 69)

30. [By detailed] causes of death: number and rate. (p. 70-78)

31-33. [By] selected causes: number and rate by region, county, and city. (p. 79-90)

34-35. [By] selected causes: by age groups and by month of occurrence. (p. 91-92)

36. Autopsies by region and county. (p. 93)

S8560–1.4: Marriages and Divorces
[Tables E19-41 begin "West Virginia resident marriages..."]

E18. Resident marriages and divorces, 1968-83. (p. 97)

E19. [By] month of occurrence. (p. 98)

37-38. [By] month of occurrence by region and county, 1983; and number by county, 1979-83. (p. 99-100)

E20. [By] age of bride and groom. (p. 101)

39. [By] age of bride by age of groom. (p. 102)

40-41. [By] previous marital status and number of previous marriages, [cross-tabulated] for bride and groom. (p. 103)

42-44. Divorces and annulments, [by] region and county of occurrence, 1983; and divorces/annulments, number by county, 1979-83, and by age of husband and wife, 1983. (p. 104-106)

45-47. Divorces and annulments, [by] plaintiff by duration of marriage, [and by] number of [minor] children; and divorces/annulments [by] plaintiff by age group. (p. 106-107)

S8565   WEST VIRGINIA
Department of
Highways

S8565–1   WEST VIRGINIA ACCIDENT DATA, 1984
Annual. [1985.] iv + 32 p.
SRI/MF/complete

Annual report, for 1984, on West Virginia traffic accidents involving fatalities, injuries, and property damage, and number of persons killed and injured. Includes data by accident and vehicle type, location, time, and other circumstances.

Also includes traffic accident economic loss by county, and incidence of alcohol use in fatal accidents.

Data are compiled by State Highway Dept from accident reports filed with State Motor Vehicle Dept.

Contains contents listing (p. iv); and report, with 1 map, 5 charts, and 15 tables (p. 1-32).

Availability: West Virginia Department of Highways, Public Information Office, 1900 Washington St., E., Charleston WV 25305, †; SRI/MF/complete.

S8573   WEST VIRGINIA
Department of
Human Services

S8573–1   HUMAN SERVICES STATISTICS, West Virginia
Monthly.   51 p.
LC 75-6823.
SRI/MF/complete, shipped quarterly

Monthly report on West Virginia public welfare and social service program caseloads, recipients, and expenditures, by program and type of service rendered, and by area and county. Report is issued approximately 2-3 months after month of coverage.

Contains contents listing; 34 monthly tables, listed below; and glossary.

Most monthly tables appear in all issues.

Availability: West Virginia Department of Human Services, Statistical Unit, Bldg. No. 6, 8th Floor, Charleston WV 25305, †; SRI/MF/complete, shipped quarterly.

Issues reviewed during 1985: Aug. 1984-Aug. 1985 (D).

MONTHLY TABLES:
[Tables generally show data for month of coverage. Data by program category usually include AFDC regular and unemployed parent (AFDC-U) segments, medically needy, and often food stamps and general assistance (GA).]

SUMMARY

1. Monthly statistical bulletin: caseloads, expenditures, and paid medical invoices [by program category, current and previous month].

2. Comparison facts [caseload and payment changes for AFDC, AFDC-U, and GA; current month, previous month, and same month of previous year; text statistics].

3. Trends in public assistance [AFDC, AFDC-U, and GA cases and grants, monthly for 13 consecutive months ending month of coverage].

ASSISTANCE PROGRAMS
[Tables show data by area and county.]

4. Net cases receiving assistance [AFDC and AFDC-U master payroll; and new, closed, and total cases].

5-6. Classified assistance: cases assisted, total grants, and average grant per case [includes children and adults eligible for AFDC by reason of death/absence/incapacity, and for AFDC-U].

7. GA, [adult boarding care], and burials [cases and expenditures].

8. Emergency assistance to needy families with children [cases, recipients, and expenditures, for AFDC and other].

9. Food stamp authorizations [total, public assistance, and nonpublic assistance cases and value of stamps].

10. Transportation renumeration incentive program (TRIP) tickets issued [cards redeemed, number of eligibles, cash, ticket value, and bonus].

WORK PROGRAM

11. Work and training program: human services savings [by area].

MEDICAL SERVICES

[Tables 12-13 show data by program category, including Old Age Assistance, Aid to Blind, Aid to Disabled, State custody, and handicapped children's services.

Vendor types include physicians, hospitals, dental, nursing homes, pharmacy, and screening.]

12. Medical service program [current month and cumulative year-to-date expenditures, Federal and State].

13. Medical service expenditures, by category and vendor type.

14-15. Medical invoices processed, in error, and denied, including percentage factors [by group number and by vendor type; shown through Feb. 1985 only].

HEARINGS AND SUPPORT ENFORCEMENT

16. Report on human services and work and training hearings, statewide during [current and previous month; includes hearings by program category, processing time, and type].

17. Child support enforcement program, public assistance collections [cases on file, open for collections, and with payment credits; absent parents involved with payments; and current collections received; by area and county].

SOCIAL SERVICES

[Tables 18-33 begin "Division of Social Services..." and generally show data by area. Tables 27-32 and 34 show number of children or clients, and expenditure amounts.

Data by type of service include day care, home management, homemaker, foster care, nursing home, family planning, adoptive home, emergency shelter, protective services, and volunteer services.

Living arrangements include independent living, with relatives by relationship, adoptive homes, foster family home, correctional institutions, and halfway houses.]

18-19. Living arrangements of children receiving social services; and social services provided to children [by type of service].

20-22. Children entering, leaving, and in foster care [includes children by age, custodial program, and living arrangement; and case closures by reason].

23. Social services provided to adults [by type].

24-25. Living arrangements of aged/blind/disabled social service recipients; and social services provided [by type] to aged/blind/disabled adults.

26. Providers of social services [includes chore services, day care, emergency shelter, foster care for children, personal care, adult family care, and adoptive homes].

27-28. Day care expenditures: numbers and source of funds [Title XX AFDC and income eligible, and work incentive program], and type of care [in home, day care center, and family care home].

29-31. Foster care expenditures: numbers and type of care [foster family, institutions, and relatives], and source of funds [State funds, AFDC foster care (AFDC-FC), and Title XX emergency shelter]; and children in foster care, expenditures and average amounts [State funds, and AFDC-FC, for foster homes/relatives, and institutions/group homes].

32. Services to adults expenditures [by type of service].

33. Child protective services report [suspected child abuse and neglect referrals, clearances, and worker/caseload information].

34. Division of Special Projects: Medicaid waiver [by type of service and area].

S8575   WEST VIRGINIA Department of Insurance

S8575–1   SEVENTY-FIFTH ANNUAL REPORT OF THE INSURANCE COMMISSIONER of the State of West Virginia, Year Ending Dec. 31, 1983
Annual. Oct. 23, 1984.
1+iii+368 p.
LC 74-18892.
SRI/MF/complete

Annual report on West Virginia insurance industry financial condition and underwriting activity, by company and type of insurance, 1983. Covers assets, liabilities, and capital/surplus or net worth; premiums collected, or written and earned; losses incurred and paid; expenses or claims/benefits paid; and dividends; for insurers based in West Virginia and elsewhere.

Data are shown, as applicable, for title insurance companies; fraternal benefit societies; fire/casualty, life, and accident/health insurance companies; and health service organizations and HMOs (also includes enrollment).

Includes detail for life, accident/health, and fire/casualty companies by line of coverage, including workmen's compensation, automobile, surety, and medical malpractice.

Also includes data on Insurance Dept expenditures; finances of State post-assessment insurance guaranty assn; rate changes; excess line brokers, policy premiums, number of policies, and taxes paid; consumer complaints; agent licensing examination activity; taxes paid by top 20 life and fire/casualty insurers; number of companies by type; and lists of company status changes; various calendar or fiscal years 1980-84.

Data are compiled from statements filed by insurers with the Insurance Commissioner.

Contains contents listing (p. ii-iii); narrative report on dept activities, with text data and 18 tables (p. 1-112); and 35 tables and statistical directories (p. 113-368).

Availability: West Virginia Department of Insurance, Insurance Commissioner's Office, 2100 Washington St., E., Charleston WV 25305, $10.00; SRI/MF/complete.

S8590   WEST VIRGINIA Library Commission

S8590–1   1984 WEST VIRGINIA LIBRARY COMMISSION Statistical Report
Annual. [1985.] 26 p.
ISSN 0094-6486.
LC 74-645697.
SRI/MF/complete

Annual report, for 1984, on West Virginia public, academic, and special libraries. Includes holdings, finances, staff, and services provided.

Contains contents listing (1 p.), and the following:

a. Statistical summary with 6 tables showing statewide data on number of libraries, services, finances, and population served; and directory of public libraries. (p. 1-10)

b. By library: population served, volumes added and total volumes, periodicals, recordings, book and nonprint circulation, staff, hours open weekly, income by source, and expenditures by object, shown for each public library arranged by library service area, and for direct service area libraries arranged by county. 4 tables. (p. 11-16)

c. By county: local library population served; total and per capita volumes, circulation, and receipts; and number of libraries, branches, and bookmobiles. 1 table. (p. 17)

d. Film service activity, including number of films shown and viewers by library, and for State institutions, government depts, and Southern Community College. 4 tables. (p. 18-19)

e. College and university enrollment, library volumes held, interlibrary loans, microforms, audiovisual materials, periodicals, hours open weekly, staff, and total expenditures; and special library book and periodical holdings, by municipality; all by institution. 2 tables. (p. 20-25)

A narrative annual report on State library construction and services, with summary statistics, is also available from the issuing agency, but is not covered by SRI.

Availability: West Virginia Library Commission, Cultural Center, Charleston WV 25305, †; SRI/MF/complete.

S8610   WEST VIRGINIA
Department of Public Safety

S8610–1   CRIME IN WEST VIRGINIA, 1984
Annual.   May 1, 1985.
iii+2+227 p.
ISSN 0095-1641.
LC 74-648125.
SRI/MF/complete

Annual report on West Virginia crimes and arrests, by type of offense, 1984, with comparisons to 1983 and selected trends from 1980. Includes data by reporting agency, county, and municipality, and by offender age, sex, and race. Also includes law enforcement employment, and assaults on officers.

Report focuses on 8 Index offenses: murder, rape, robbery, felonious assault, breaking and entering, larceny-theft, motor vehicle theft, and arson. Arrests and crime rates are also shown for numerous non-Index offenses. Report also includes an analysis of domestic violence complaints and reported child abuse.

Data are from State and local agency reports submitted under the Uniform Crime Reporting Program.

Contains listings of contents, tables, and charts (2 p.); introduction, offense classifications, methodology, and statistical synopsis (p. 1-17); 8 statistical sections, interspersed with narrative summaries, and 11 charts and 59 tables described below (p. 19-217); and summary of UCR contributor participation, and glossary (p. 218-227).

This is the 13th annual report.

Availability: West Virginia Department of Public Safety, Uniform Crime Reporting Section, 725 Jefferson Rd., South Charleston WV 25309, †; SRI/MF/complete.

CHARTS and TABLES:
[Data are shown for 1984 unless otherwise noted, and usually include comparisons to 1983. Data by race/ethnicity are generally shown for white, black, American Indian/Alaskan Native, Asian/Pacific Islander, Hispanic, and non-Hispanic. Data by agency type are generally shown for county sheriff's offices, and rural, State, and municipal police.

Part I offenses are Index offenses. Arson is classified as an Index offense, but arson data are not included in the Crime Index tables. Part II offenses are all other crimes.]

S8610–1.1: Index Offenses and Arrests, Law Enforcement Employment, and Assaults on Police

STATE INDEX OFFENSES
[One table, with illustrative chart, showing offenses by month, annual offense rate, and adult and juvenile clearances, is repeated for total, violent, and property crime, and for each individual Index offense. Additional data are described below.]

a. Index offense summary; stolen property value, by Index offense; and Index crimes and rates, by offense, 1980-84. 3 charts and 5 tables. (p. 20-25)

b. Murders by type of weapon and circumstance; murder victims, by age, sex, and race/ethnicity; and forcible rapes. 2 charts and 4 tables. (p. 26-30)

c. Robbery offenses by weapon, and offenses and value stolen by place of occurrence; felonious assaults by weapon; breaking/entering offenses by type of entry, and offenses and value stolen for day and night residential and nonresidential occurrences; larceny/theft offenses and value stolen, by type of theft; and motor vehicle thefts by vehicle type. 5 charts and 12 tables. (p. 31-43)

STATE ARRESTS
d. Arrests by month, crime rate, and adult and juvenile arrests, for aggregate Part I and Part II offenses, with disposition of juveniles arrested; crime rate, and arrests by race/ethnicity, sex, and age, for individual Part I and Part II offenses; and narcotic arrests by substance and age. 1 chart and 9 tables. (p. 47-53)

LAW ENFORCEMENT EMPLOYEE DATA
e. Sworn and civilian law enforcement employees, by sex and agency type (including Natural Resources Dept); officers assaulted, by type of weapon, time of day, and injury status, and clearances and population, all by agency type; officers killed; and assaults by type of assignment and circumstance. 3 tables. (p. 56-58)

S8610–1.2: Data by Agency and County, Natural Resources Dept Arrests, Arson, and Domestic Violence

DATA BY AGENCY AND COUNTY
a. Population, Index offenses by type, and total Index clearances; and Part I and Part II arrests by offense type, and total adult and juvenile arrests; all by county, agency type, and municipal agency. 3 tables. (p. 62-191)

NATURAL RESOURCES DEPT ARRESTS
b. Dept of Natural Resources: juvenile and adult arrests, by age, race/ethnicity, and Part I and Part II offense, including narcotics violations by substance, for 6 districts. 12 tables. (p. 194-205)

ARSON AND DOMESTIC VIOLENCE
c. Arson offenses, including number reported and number determined to be unfounded; total and juvenile clearances; offenses involving uninhabited structures; and property damage value; all by property classification. 1 table. (p. 208)

d. Domestic violence: victims, offenders, and complainants, by sex; repeat complainants; complaints by weapon used, extent of abuse, police action taken, victim-offender relationship, day of week, and month; and child abuse/neglect caseloads, by month; with selected data by agency. 10 tables. (p. 210-215)

S8620   WEST VIRGINIA
Board of Regents

S8620–4   STATISTICAL PROFILE OF HIGHER EDUCATION in West Virginia, 1984
Annual.   Mar. 1985.
ix+127 p.
SRI/MF/complete

Annual report on West Virginia higher education, 1984. Covers enrollment, degrees conferred, and programs offered, for public and private institutions; and faculty characteristics and finances, for public institutions. Most data are shown by institution. Also includes selected trends from as early as 1972.

Contains contents and table listings, 1 map, and introduction (p. iii-ix); and 4 chapters, with narrative summaries, and 73 tables listed below (p. 1-127).

This is the 3rd annual report.

Availability: West Virginia Board of Regents, PO Box 3368, Charleston WV 25333, †; SRI/MF/complete.

TABLES:
[Data are shown by institution, as of fall 1984 or academic year 1983/84, unless otherwise noted.]

S8620–4.1: Enrollment and Degrees
[Data are shown for public and private institutions, unless otherwise noted.]

ENROLLMENT
[Data by attendance status show full- and part-time, and data by residence show in- and out-of-State.]

[A-D] [Trends in] credit headcount enrollment; and FTE enrollments, medical and dental student headcounts included [for public institutions only; various years 1971-84]. (p. 4-7)

1.1. Credit headcount enrollment [aggregated for public and private institutions] by level of institution, [by] sex, attendance status, residence, [and level] of student, together with total noncredit headcount enrollment. (p. 8-9)

1.2-1.8. Credit headcount enrollment by residence, sex, attendance status, and level of student [with various cross-tabulations]. (p. 10-29)

1.9. In-State credit headcount enrollment, by county of residence. (p. 30-33)

1.10. Out-of-State credit headcount enrollment, by State of residence [with total for U.S. territories/foreign]. (p. 34-37)

1.11-1.12. FTE enrollment in public institutions, by course level and student enrollment categories, and by course level. (p. 38-39)

[E] Age distribution of students enrolled in public institutions. (p. 40)

DEGREES CONFERRED
[F] Total degrees conferred by public institutions [1973/74-1983/84]. (p. 42)

[G-H] Degrees conferred by institutions, by level; and degrees awarded by level, sex, 1973/74-1983/84, public institutions. (p. 43-44)

2.1-2.3. Total degrees conferred [aggregated for public and private institutions], by sex of student, level of degree, level of institution, and academic area of study [with various cross-tabulations]. (p. 45-49)

2.4-2.7. Total degrees conferred, by level of degree and sex of student; and number of different degree programs offered and total degrees conferred, by academic area of study and by level of degree. (p. 50-57)

S8620-4.2: Faculty and Finances
[Data are for public institutions only.]

FACULTY CHARACTERISTICS
[Tables 3.1-3.8 and 3.10-3.13 include aggregate trends for 1980-84.]

3.1-3.5. Academic rank of full-time faculty; highest earned academic degree held by full- and part-time faculty; and full-time faculty members' years of experience at institution of present employment and years of total experience in higher education. (p. 60-64)

3.6-3.8. Age and sex of full- and part-time faculty. (p. 65-67)

3.9. Tenure analysis of full-time faculty. (p. 68)

3.10-3.13. Average 9-month salary of full-time faculty engaged exclusively in teaching, and engaged in teaching and some other function, by academic rank and highest degree held (medical colleges excluded). (p. 69-72)

3.14. Number of FTE resident teaching faculty, total resident teaching salary cost, and average 9-10 months instructional salary cost per FTE resident faculty. (p. 73)

3.15-3.30. Number of faculty, average 9-month salary, average years of experience at institution of present employment, average total years of higher education experience, and average age of full-time faculty members engaged exclusively in resident instruction, by academic rank, highest degree held, and by sex. (p. 74-105)

FINANCIAL DATA
[Data are for FY84, unless otherwise noted. Fund types are educational/general, auxiliary enterprises, medical schools/medical center, and student aid.]

4.1-4.2. Total operating revenue and expenditures [by fund type]. (p. 109-110)

4.3-4.4. Total operating revenue and expenditures [aggregate data, by fund type], FY80-84. (p. 111)

4.5-4.7. Educational/general revenue [from 6 sources, with] percentage distribution, and [amount] per FTE student. (p. 114-116)

4.8-4.9. Comparison of educational/general revenue and State general fund revenue [total and per FTE student], FY80-84. (p. 117-118)

4.10-4.12. Educational/general expenditures [for 7 functions, with] percentage distribution, and [amount] per FTE student. (p. 120-122)

4.13. Comparison of educational/general expenditures [total and per FTE student], FY80-84. (p. 123)

4.14-4.15. Auxiliary enterprise revenue [by source] and expenditures [by function]. (p. 125-126)

4.16. Total operating revenue [by source] and expenditures [by function], medical schools and medical center. (p. 127)

S8630   WEST VIRGINIA
Office of the Secretary of State

S8630-1   STATE OF WEST VIRGINIA OFFICE OF SECRETARY OF STATE, OFFICIAL RETURNS OF THE PRIMARY ELECTION, JUNE 5, 1984, AND GENERAL ELECTION, NOV. 6, 1984
Biennial. [1985.] 1+71 p.
SRI/MF/complete

Biennial report presenting results of the West Virginia primary election held June 5, 1984, and general election held Nov. 6, 1984. Shows voting for President and Vice President; U.S. and State senators and representatives; Governor; judges and other State and local officials, and delegates to national political conventions; and 5 State constitutional amendments, including questions concerning a State lottery, school prayer, bonds for veterans housing, and equitable taxation/exemption. Data are shown by district and/or county.

Also includes voter registration, by party and county; population by county, 1970 and 1980; number of precincts and voting methods for each county; and voter turnout.

Previous report, covering 1982 general election, is described in SRI 1983 Annual under this number.

Availability: West Virginia Office of the Secretary of State, Elections Division, State Capitol, Charleston WV 25305, †; SRI/MF/complete.

S8675   WISCONSIN
Department of Administration

S8675-2   WISCONSIN ANNUAL FISCAL REPORT for the Year Ending June 30, 1985
Annual. 2 volumes.
For individual publication data, see below.
LC 75-642705.
SRI/MF/complete, current and previous year reports

Annual report on financial condition of Wisconsin State government, for FY85, presenting financial data for general, conservation, transportation, higher education, unemployment reserve, retirement, building trust, and capital improvement funds.

Report is issued in 2 volumes, individually described below.

Availability: Wisconsin Department of Administration, Financial Operations Bureau, PO Box 7864, Madison WI 53707, †; SRI/MF/complete.

S8675-2.1: Main Report
[Annual. Oct. 11, 1985. 62 p. SRI/MF/complete, current & previous year reports.]

Presents assets, liabilities, receipts by source, disbursements by function and object, and fund balances, by fund, FY85, with comparisons from FY83.

Also includes comparison of appropriations and actual expenditures; population, and State payments to localities for property tax relief and shared revenues, by county; State and Federal local assistance payments and aid to individuals and organizations, by agency and program; State bonded indebtedness; and property valuation.

Contains contents listing and transmittal letter (p. 1-3); economic highlights, with 3 charts (p. 5-9); general purpose financial statements, with 4 exhibits (p. 11-22); financial section, with 4 charts and 10 exhibits (p. 24-43); and statistical section, with 2 charts and 8 exhibits (p. 45-62).

Previous report, for FY84, was also reviewed in SRI during 1985, and is also available on SRI microfiche under S8675-2.1 [Annual. Oct. 5, 1984. 64 p. †].

S8675-2.2: Appendix
[Annual. [1985.] 49 p. SRI/MF/complete, current & previous year reports.]

Presents detailed statements of appropriations by source (general purpose or program); expenditures for State operations, aid, and local assistance; and balances; shown by function, agency, program, and fund, FY84-85.

Contains 1 summary exhibit and 8 detailed schedules.

Previous report, for FY83-84, was also reviewed in SRI during 1985, and is also available on SRI microfiche under S8675-2.2 [Annual. [1984]. 49 p. †].

S8680   WISCONSIN
Department of Agriculture, Trade and Consumer Protection

S8680-1   1985 WISCONSIN AGRICULTURAL STATISTICS
Annual. June 1985.
ii+95 p.
ISSN 0512-1329.
LC 66-63464.
SRI/MF/complete

Annual report on Wisconsin agricultural production, marketing, and finances, 1970s-84, with some data for 1985 and selected trends from 1950. Data are generally shown by commodity and/or county and district, with selected comparisons to other States and total U.S.

Covers production, value and prices, marketing, and, as applicable, acreage, yield, stocks or inventory, and disposition, for field crop, vegetable, fruit, livestock, poultry, apiary, and dairy sectors.

Also includes data on Wisconsin farm income, production expenses, balance sheet, real estate value and taxes, and land sales and prices; number of farms and acreage, with detail by type of ownership; farm operators by sex, age group, and farm tenure status; mink operations; cattle and hog outshipments by destination; and weather.

Also includes U.S. value of agricultural exports and imports, consumer expenditures for food, per capita meat consumption, labor force by employment status, and total and farm population.

Data are compiled by the Wisconsin Agriculture Reporting Service.

Contains contents listing (p. ii); foreword, and 6 sections with narrative summaries, 29 maps, 32 charts, and 156 tables (p. 1-94); and planting dates and glossary (inside back cover).

This is the 21st annual report.

Availability: Wisconsin Agriculture Reporting Service, PO Box 9160, Madison WI 53715, $3.00; SRI/MF/complete.

S8700   WISCONSIN
Council on
Criminal Justice

S8700–1   WISCONSIN CRIME AND ARRESTS, 1984
Annual. [1985.] iii + 158 p. SRI/MF/complete

Annual report on Wisconsin crimes and arrests, by offense, 1984, with summary trends from 1973. Includes data by county and reporting agency, and by offender age, sex, and race/ethnicity. Also includes law enforcement employment, and assaults on officers.

Report focuses on 8 Index offenses: murder, rape, robbery, aggravated assault, burglary, larceny/theft, motor vehicle theft, and arson. Arrests are also shown for numerous non-Index offenses.

Data are from State and local agency reports submitted under the Uniform Crime Reporting Program (UCR).

Contains contents listing (p. iii); introduction and overview, crime clock, and 2 maps and 3 summary tables (p. 1-10); 40 charts and 91 tables, with accompanying narrative summaries (p. 11-155); and glossary (p. 157-158).

All tables, and selected chart showing substantial data not included in tables, are described below.

Availability: Wisconsin Council on Criminal Justice, Statistical Analysis Center, 30 W. Mifflin St., Suite 1000, Madison WI 53702, $1.50 + postage; SRI/MF/complete.

TABLES AND CHART:
[Data are for 1984 with selected comparisons to 1983, unless otherwise noted. Data by race/ethnicity include Asian and/or American Indian.]

INDEX OFFENSES
[Summary and individual offenses (except sexual assault/forcible rape) each include 5 tables showing offenses and rates by population size group and for total suburban and rural sheriffs' offices; adult and juvenile arrests by sex and race/ethnicity; and clearance rates. Additional data are noted below.]

a. Summary: for total, violent, and property Index offenses. 15 tables. (p. 12-27)

b. Murder: victims and offenders, by age group, sex, and race/ethnicity; and offenses, by type of weapon and victim/offender relationship. 1 chart and 8 tables. (p. 30-35)

c. Sexual assault/forcible rape: offenses, victims and offenders by age group and sex, victim injury status by type of weapon (dangerous and personal), victim/offender relationship, and arrests, all for rapes and/or total sexual assaults, with selected detail by degree of offense. 9 tables. (p. 38-40)

d. Robbery and aggravated assault: offenses by type of weapon, 1980-84; and value of property stolen in robberies by location. 13 tables. (p. 42-51)

e. Burglary: offenses by type of entry; and offenses and value of property stolen, for residential and non-residential day and night occurrences. 7 tables. (p. 54-57)

f. Thefts and value of property stolen, by type and amount of theft; motor vehicle theft by vehicle type, 1980-84; value of vehicles stolen and recovered; and arson. 19 tables. (p. 60-74)

TRENDS, AND ASSAULTS ON OFFICERS

g. Offenses and rates, clearance rates, and ratio of arrests/offenses, for total, violent, property, and individual Index crimes, 1974-84. 4 tables. (p. 78-81)

h. Officers assaulted, by time of day, injury status, type of weapon and assignment, and activity. 4 tables. (p. 83-85)

LOCAL DATA, ARRESTS, AND STOLEN PROPERTY

i. Offenses and rates, clearance rates, and juvenile clearances as percent of all clearances, for total, violent, property, and individual Index crimes; and adult and juvenile arrests, by Index and non-Index offense; all by county and local law enforcement agency. 8 tables. (p. 90-144)

j. Arrests of adults and juveniles by sex, age, and race/ethnicity (including Hispanic and non-Hispanic), for Index and non-Index offenses; and value of stolen property, by selected Index offense, with detail by offense characteristics. 3 tables. (p. 146-148)

LAW ENFORCEMENT EMPLOYMENT

k. Law enforcement full-time officers and civilians, by agency. 1 table. (p. 149-155)

S8715   WISCONSIN
Department of
Health and
Social Services

S8715–2   DIVISION OF CORRECTIONS STATISTICAL BULLETINS, Wisconsin
Annual series. For individual publication data, see below. SRI/MF/complete

Series of annual and semiannual reports on corrections in Wisconsin, covering prisons, juvenile correctional facilities, community residential centers, and probation and parole programs. Includes data on admissions, releases, and offender characteristics.

Most data are shown by sex. Some data are shown by individual institution. Data by race/ethnic group generally include white, black, American Indian or Native American, and Asian, with selected data for Hispanics and non-Hispanics.

Reports are described in order of receipt. Reports reviewed during 1985, presenting data for 1983-84, are described below.

Prior to 1985, abstracts for these reports were grouped according to period of data coverage.

Issuing agency also publishes a monthly report on prison population movements, not covered in SRI.

Availability: Wisconsin Department of Health and Social Services, Corrections Division, Information Management and Operations Office, PO Box 7925, Madison WI 53707, †; SRI/MF/complete.

S8715–2.1: Fiscal Year Summary Report of Population Movement, 1984
[Annual. Sept. 1984. 15 p. Statistical Bull. C-60A. LC 79-640446. SRI/MF/complete.]

Annual report covering Wisconsin inmate population, admissions, transfers, releases, deaths, and absences, for adult and juvenile correctional facilities, by institution; juvenile institutional and billable absence days, by facility type; and probation and parole adult and juvenile population, admissions, terminations, and absconders; FY84, with summary trends from FY80.

Contains summary with 1 trend table (p. 1-3); 5 detailed tables (p. 4-13); and footnotes (p. 14-15).

S8715–2.2: Offenders Admitted to Adult Correctional Institutions, 1983
[Annual. Nov. 1984. 29 p. Statistical Bull. C-53. SRI/MF/complete.]

Annual report covering Wisconsin prison admissions by admission status category; and 1st admissions and readmissions by offense, length of sentence, county of commitment, age at admission, race/ethnic group, marital status, previous felony convictions and penal experience, juvenile institutional experience, highest grade completed, tested grade level, estimated intelligence, current disabilities, whether served in the military, and primary work skill, 1983.

Contains narrative analysis, with 2 maps (p. 1-5); and 18 tables (p. 6-29).

Previous report, for 1982, is described in SRI 1983 Annual under S8715-2.5.

S8715–2.3: Offenders Released from Adult Correctional Institutions, 1983
[Annual. Nov. 1984 33 p. Statistical Bull. C-54. SRI/MF/complete.]

Annual report covering Wisconsin adult prison 1st releases and rereleases, 1983, with selected trends from 1979. Includes data by institution and type of release; offense; length of sentence and stay; county of commitment; race/ethnic group; participation in educational, alcohol and drug, work and study release, and vocational programs; college credits earned; and intended residence (Wisconsin counties, other U.S., or foreign country).

Contains narrative highlights, with 2 maps (p. 1-5); 22 detailed tables (p. 6-30); and 3 summary trend tables (p. 31-33).

Previous report, for 1982, is described in SRI 1983 Annual under S8715-2.6.

S8715–2.4: 1983 Calendar Year Summary of Population Movement
[Annual. Aug. 1984. 15 p. Statistical Bull. C-60B. LC 79-642600. SRI/MF/complete.]

Annual report covering Wisconsin inmate population, admissions, transfers, releases, deaths, and absences, for adult and juvenile correctional facilities, by institution; juvenile institutional and billable absence days, by facility type; and probation and parole adult and juvenile population, admissions, terminations, and absconders; 1983 with summary trends from 1979.

Contains highlights, with 1 summary trend table (p. 1-3); 4 detailed tables (p. 4-13); and footnotes (p. 14-15).

Previous report, for 1982, is described in SRI 1983 Annual under S8715-2.3.

S8715–2.5: Residents in Wisconsin Adult Correctional Facilities on June 30, 1984, with Five-Year Trends for 1980-84

[Semiannual. Mar. 1985. 39 p. Statistical Bull. C-57. SRI/MF/complete.]

Semiannual report covering adult correctional institution inmates in Wisconsin, by admission status, race/ethnic group, offense, length of sentence, county of commitment, age, county or State of birth, disability status, military service, education, tested grade level and intelligence, length of stay, and conviction for new offense after admission, all by institution, as of June 30, 1984, with selected trends from 1980.

Contains narrative highlights, with 3 charts and 2 summary trend tables (p. 1-7); and 15 detailed tables (p. 8-39).

S8715–2.6: 1984 Calendar Year Summary of Population Movement, Wisconsin

[Annual. May 1985. 16 p. Statistical Bull. C-60B. LC 79-642600. SRI/MF/complete.]

Annual report covering Wisconsin inmate population, admissions, transfers, releases, deaths, and absences, for adult and juvenile correctional facilities, by institution; juvenile institutional and billable absence days, by facility type; and probation and parole adult and juvenile population, admissions, terminations, and absconders; 1984 with summary trends from 1980.

Contains highlights, with 1 summary trend table (p. 1-3); 4 detailed tables (p. 4-13); and footnotes (p. 14-16).

Previous report, for 1983, is described under S8715-2.4 above.

S8715–4   PUBLIC HEALTH STATISTICS, Wisconsin

Annual. For individual publication data, see below.
ISSN 0190-5708.
LC 79-640448.
SRI/MF/complete

Annual report, for 1982, on Wisconsin vital statistics, covering population estimates, births, deaths by cause, marriages and divorces, and cases of reportable disease, with trends from the 1930s and selected data by county, age, sex, and race. Data are from records filed in the Section of Vital Statistics prior to Apr. 1, 1983.

Report is published in 2 parts, described below. Part I presents vital statistics; Part II presents both population data and vital statistics.

Part II of this edition also includes a separately paginated Part II for the 1981 edition. For description of Part I of 1981 edition, see SRI 1983 Annual under this number.

Availability: Wisconsin Department of Health and Social Services, Health Division, Health Statistics Bureau, PO Box 309, Madison WI 53701, †; SRI/MF/complete.

PARTS I AND II:

[Table numbers are shown as they appear in the report. Omitted numbers are for additional tables available by request from the issuing agency; these tables are listed, along with the tables appearing in the report, in the contents listing of Part II for 1982.

Tables show data for Wisconsin residents, unless otherwise noted. Data by race generally are shown for white and nonwhite, with selected detail for American Indians.]

S8715–4.1: Public Health Statistics, 1982, Wisconsin, Part I

[Annual. [1984.] xii+43 p. SRI/MF/complete.]

Contains contents listing, introduction, definitions, sample certificates, and methodological notes (p. iii-xii); and 14 tables, listed below (p. 1-43).

TABLES:

[All tables show data for 1982.]

NATALITY AND OTHER INFANT DATA

14. Live births by county, and live births by wedlock status, by race and sex of child. (p. 1)

17. Live births by age of mother, by birth order and race of mother. (p. 2)

20. Live births by education of mother, by gravidity, by age of mother. (p. 3)

21. Live births of children born with reported congenital anomalies, by age of mother [and by sex of child]. (p. 4)

23. Live births, fetal deaths, deaths, and infant deaths; by county, selected MCDs [minor civil divisions], and balance of county (residence and occurrence data). (p. 5-10)

MORTALITY

25. Fetal and infant deaths by birth weight group and age of mother, white and nonwhite (occurrence data). (p. 11)

28, 30. Deaths by major causes: by county; and by sex and race. (p. 12-18)

31. Deaths by individual cause, ICD-9 [International Classification of Diseases, 9th Revision]. (p. 19-27)

32. Deaths by cause, age, and sex. (p. 28-32)

34. Accidental deaths by cause, age, and sex (occurrence data). (p. 33-40)

40. Mortality by age, sex, and occupation. (p. 41)

MARRIAGE AND DIVORCE

44, 44A. Marriages, and divorces/annulments granted, by month and county (occurrence data). (p. 42-43)

S8715–4.2: Public Health Statistics, 1981-82, Wisconsin, Part II

[Annual. [1984.] 79 p. var. paging. SRI/MF/complete.]

Contents:

a. Part II for 1981: table listing (1 p.); and 9 tables (p. 1-20).

b. Part II for 1982: listing of contents and all available tables, index, introduction, definitions, and methodological notes (p. iii-xii); and report on population (p. 1-12) and vital statistics (p. 14-35), with narrative summaries, 6 charts, 3 text tables, and 11 other tables.

All tables appearing in Part II for 1981 and 1982, and 2 charts presenting data not covered in tables, are listed below.

TABLES:

PART II FOR 1981

1. Population by counties enumerated in 1980 [by race] and estimated July 1, 1981, with amount and rate of change. (p. 1-2)

3. Population characteristics [sex and age] by county, July 1, 1981 estimate. (p. 3-4)

4. Population by age and sex, 1980 census [by race] and 1981 estimate. (p. 5)

5-6. Abridged life tables for males and females, 1979-81 (1980 average) [includes probability of death, life expectancy, and average age at death, by age intervals]. (p. 6)

8. Leading causes of death, by sex and age groups, 1981. (p. 7-11)

9. Live births and deaths by county, 1972-81. (p. 12-15)

41, 43. Cases from reportable disease, by county and by month, [by disease], 1981. (p. 16-20)

PART II FOR 1982

Charts 3-4. Total population growth, and percent change in population due to migration, by counties, 1970-80 [period]. (p. 5)

1. [Table 1 listed above under Part II for 1981 is repeated, with 1980 and 1982 data.] (p. 6-7)

2. Population growth due to natural increase and migration [shows total population, births, deaths, natural increase, and percent gain or loss through migration, 1945-82, with decennial trends from 1930]. (p. 8)

3-6. [Tables 3-6 listed above are repeated, with 1982 data substituted for 1981; tables 5-6 show data for 1980-82 with 1981 average.] (p. 9-12)

7. Vital events and rates [estimated population; live births; infant, fetal, maternal, and total (excluding fetal) deaths; marriages; and divorces/annulments/separations]; 1930-82. (p. 15)

8-9. [Tables 8-9 listed above are repeated, with data for 1982 and 1973-82 respectively.] (p. 16-24)

Text tables 1-2. Fertility rates for women 20-24; and age-specific fertility rates; [various years] 1940-82. (p. 25-26)

Text table 3. Total death and death rates by sex and age groups, 1982. (p. 27)

41, 43. [Tables 41 and 43 listed above are repeated, with 1982 data.] (p. 31-35)

S8715–5   PUBLIC HEALTH STATISTICS, Wisconsin

Annual. For individual publication data, see below.
ISSN 0190-5708.
LC 79-640448.
SRI/MF/complete

Annual report, for 1983, on Wisconsin vital statistics, covering population estimates, births, deaths by cause, marriages and divorces, and cases of reportable disease, with selected data by county, age, sex, and race. Data are from records filed in the Section of Vital Statistics prior to Apr. 1, 1984.

Report is published in 2 parts. Part I presents vital statistics; Part II presents both population data and vital statistics. Part I is described below; Part II has not yet been published.

For description of 1982 Parts I and II, see S8715-4 above.

Availability: Wisconsin Department of Health and Social Services, Health Division, Health Statistics Center, PO Box 309, Madison WI 53701, †; SRI/MF/complete.

PART I:

[Tables show data for Wisconsin residents, unless otherwise noted. Data by race generally are shown for white and nonwhite, with selected detail for American Indians.]

S8715–5.1: Public Health Statistics, 1983, Wisconsin, Part I

[Annual. [1985.] xii+46 p. SRI/MF/complete.]

Contains contents and table listing, introduction, definitions, sample certificates, and methodological notes (p. iii-xii); 14 tables, listed below (p. 1-43); and list of supplemental and rate tables available from issuing agency (p. 44-46).

TABLES:

[All tables show data for 1983.]

NATALITY AND OTHER INFANT DATA

1.1. Live births by county, and live births by wedlock status, by race and sex of child. (p. 1)

1.2. Live births by age of mother, by birth order and race of mother. (p. 2)

1.3. Live births by education of mother, by gravidity, by age of mother. (p. 3)

1.4. Live births of children born with reported congenital anomalies, by age of mother [and by sex of child]. (p. 4)

1.5. Live births, fetal deaths, deaths, and infant deaths; by county, selected MCDs [minor civil divisions], and balance of county (residence and occurrence data). (p. 5-10)

MORTALITY

2.1. Fetal and infant deaths by birth weight group and age of mother, white and nonwhite (occurrence data). (p. 11)

2.2-2.3. Deaths by major causes: by county; and by sex and race. (p. 12-18)

2.4. Deaths by individual cause, ICD-9 [International Classification of Diseases, 9th Revision]. (p. 19-27)

2.5. Deaths by cause, age, and sex. (p. 28-32)

2.6. Accidental deaths by cause, age, and sex (occurrence data). (p. 33-40)

2.7. Mortality by age, sex, and occupation. (p. 41)

MARRIAGE AND DIVORCE

3.1-3.2. Marriages, and divorces/annulments granted, by month and county (occurrence data). (p. 42-43)

S8750   WISCONSIN
Department of Industry, Labor and Human Relations

S8750–1   WISCONSIN ECONOMIC INDICATORS

Monthly. Approx. 15 p.
ISSN 0147-6106.
LC 77-646943.
SRI/MF/complete, shipped quarterly

Monthly report on Wisconsin employment and economic conditions, including data on 27 economic indicators; and employment, hours, and earnings, by industry group and locality. Data sources include State and Federal agencies. Month of data coverage is 1-2 months prior to cover date.

Contains list of data sources; narrative analysis of employment and economic developments during the month of coverage; 5 monthly tables; 1 feature article, often with statistics, including a quarterly economic outlook feature; and usually several economic trend charts.

Monthly tables are listed below and appear in all issues. Report sometimes includes additional tables showing summary or trend data for topics covered in monthly tables; these tables are not described. All other additional features with substantial statistical content, are described, as they appear, under "Statistical Features." Nonstatistical features are not covered.

Another monthly report, *Wisconsin Employment Picture,* presenting detailed employment data, is also available from the issuing agency, but is not covered in SRI.

Prior to the Dec. 1984 issue, report was titled *Wisconsin Employment and Economic Indicators.*

Availability: Wisconsin Department of Industry, Labor and Human Relations, Job Service Division, Labor Market Information Section, 201 E. Washington Ave., PO Box 7944, Madison WI 53707, †; SRI/MF/complete, shipped quarterly.

Issues reviewed during 1985: Oct. 1984-Sept. 1985 (P).

MONTHLY TABLES:

[Data are for Wisconsin, unless otherwise noted. All tables show data for month of coverage or latest available month, preceding month, and same month of previous year. Tables [1-2] show both seasonally adjusted and unadjusted data. Tables [3-5] show unadjusted data.]

[1] Economic indicators [27 leading, coincident, and other indicators, including average manufacturing workweek and overtime hours; average unemployment compensation claims; job openings; new incorporations; net gain in business and residential phone access lines; building plans examined; Milwaukee help-wanted index and CPI; natural gas and electric power sales; auto registrations; securities registrations; cash receipts from farm marketing; birth, death, and marriage registrations, and population gain; prices received by farmers; workers involved in labor disputes; and unemployment compensation exhaustees; prior to Apr. 1985 issue, table also included personal income].

[2] Labor force estimates [civilian employment and unemployment for Wisconsin and U.S., and Wisconsin nonfarm wage/salary employment by industry division].

[3-4] Manufacturing employment, and earnings and hours data [both by industry group].

[5] Summary of recent data [production workers' average hours and earnings, and manufacturing employment; for U.S., Wisconsin, 3 SMSAs, and 12 counties and cities].

STATISTICAL FEATURES:

S8750–1.601: Nov. 1984

WISCONSIN'S ECONOMIC OUTLOOK, QUARTERLY FEATURE

(p. 9-12, 14) Quarterly article, by David H. Peterson and Gene Schubert, analyzing the economic outlook for Wisconsin through 1987. Includes 2 tables showing Wisconsin employment by industry division, with quarterly detail by manufacturing industry group, various periods 1983-87.

S8750–1.602: Feb. 1985

WISCONSIN'S ECONOMIC OUTLOOK, QUARTERLY FEATURE

(p. 9-11, 14) Quarterly article, by David H. Peterson and Gene Schubert, analyzing the economic outlook for Wisconsin through 1987. Includes 1 table showing Wisconsin employment by industry division, 1983-87.

S8750–1.603: Mar. 1985

WAGE SURVEY AIDS ECONOMIC RESEARCH

(p. 9-11) By Joseph Tumpach Jr. and Bill Beutel. Article on occupational concentration for men and women in Wisconsin, with 2 undated tables showing the following for 14-19 occupations held predominantly by 1 sex: average wage, and predominant sex's share of total employment. Data are from Census Bureau and Wisconsin Dept of Industry, Labor and Human Relations.

S8750–1.604: May 1985

WISCONSIN'S ECONOMIC OUTLOOK, QUARTERLY FEATURE

(p. 9-12, 14) Quarterly article, by David H. Peterson and Gene Schubert, analyzing the economic outlook for Wisconsin through 1987. Includes 1 table showing Wisconsin employment by industry division, 1983-87.

S8750–1.605: June 1985

EXTENDED UNEMPLOYMENT: THE QUIET CRISIS

(p. 9-11) By Stephen B. Blumenfeld. Article, with 2 tables showing Wisconsin total and insured unemployment rates; and distribution of unemployed persons by duration of unemployment; 1975-84. Data are from Current Population Survey and other sources.

S8750–1.606: Aug. 1985

WISCONSIN'S ECONOMIC OUTLOOK, QUARTERLY FEATURE

(p. 9-12, 14) Quarterly article, by David H. Peterson and Gene Schubert, analyzing the economic outlook for Wisconsin through 1987. Includes 1 table showing Wisconsin employment by industry division and selected manufacturing group, 1983-87.

S8755   WISCONSIN
Office of the
Commissioner of
Insurance

S8755–1   WISCONSIN INSURANCE
REPORT, Business of 1984
Annual. [1985.]
3+iii+188 p.
LC 80-644240.
SRI/MF/complete

Annual report on Wisconsin insurance industry financial condition and underwriting activity, by company and type of insurance, 1984. Covers assets, capital/surplus, premiums/annuity considerations, losses and benefits incurred, gain from operations, benefits paid, net income, premiums written and/or earned, and loss and expense ratios; for companies based in Wisconsin and elsewhere.

Data are shown, as applicable, for property/liability and life/health insurers, including accident/health assns; fraternal societies; HMOs; and mutual, stock, and reciprocal insurance companies.

Selected data are also shown for companies ranked by Wisconsin market share within specific lines of coverage, including medical malpractice, workers compensation, automobile, and surety.

Also includes data on finances of Insurance Commissioner's Office and 4 State-administered insurance funds, mostly for FY84; regulatory activities; finances of companies in liquidation; and consumer complaint caseloads.

Contains contents listing (1 p.); narrative report, with 16 tables (p. i-ii, 1-61); statistical section, with 7 tables (p. 64-112); and directory of licensed insurers (p. 114-188).

This is the 116th annual report.

Availability: Wisconsin Office of the Commissioner of Insurance, PO Box 7873, Madison WI 53707-7873, $2.00; SRI/MF/complete.

S8795   WISCONSIN
Department of
Public Instruction

S8795–1   WISCONSIN LIBRARY
SERVICE RECORD, 1983
Annual. July 1984. i+83 p.
Bull. No. 5025.
LC 76-640787.
SRI/MF/complete

Annual report, for 1983, on Wisconsin libraries, presenting directories of academic, special, and public libraries; and statistics for individual public libraries, including holdings by type, income by source, expenditures (wages/salaries, materials, and other), capital outlays, staff, circulation, interlibrary loan activity, and hours open. Also includes summary public library trends from 1981, and data on special library holdings.

Contains contents listing (p. i); directories of academic and special libraries (p. 1-27); and public library section, with 1 State trend table, narrative summary with 7 text tables, 1 detailed table, and directory (p. 28-83).

Availability: Wisconsin Department of Public Instruction, Library Services Division, 125 S. Webster St., PO Box 7841, Madison WI 53707, †; SRI/MF/complete.

S8795–2   BASIC FACTS About
Wisconsin's Elementary and
Secondary Schools,
1984/85
Annual. [1985.]
110 p. var. paging.
Bull. No. 5320.
SRI/MF/complete

Annual report, for 1984/85, on Wisconsin elementary and secondary school enrollment, staff, costs, and State aid distribution, by school district. Also includes data on pupils and staff by race/ethnicity, and trends from 1981/82. Data are from State Depts of Public Instruction and Revenue, and reports of local school districts and private schools.

Contains listings of contents, school districts, and union high schools (UHS) (2 p.); 5 statistical sections, with brief narratives, 2 maps, and 13 tables listed below (101 p.); and glossary (7 p.).

Availability: Wisconsin Department of Public Instruction, Publications Section, 125 S. Webster St., PO Box 7841, Madison WI 53707, $3.50; SRI/MF/complete.

TABLES:
[Most data by ethnic category generally include American Indian/Alaska Native, Asian/Pacific Islander, black, white, and Hispanic. Data by scope are for grades prekindergarten-8, prekindergarten-12, and 9-12 or UHS.]

STATEWIDE
[Tables 1-6 show data for 1983/84-1984/85.]

1. School summary information [number and enrollment of public and private schools, and professional staff of public schools]. (p. A1)

2. School district analysis summary [districts by scope and type; and total and high school districts by enrollment size]. (p. A2)

3. Student enrollments [for public and private schools, by grade, including prekindergarten and ungraded]. (p. A3)

4-5. Ethnic category enrollments and [professional and nonprofessional] staff. (p. A4)

6. Pupil/teacher [by scope] and pupil/total staff ratios. (p. A5)

7. Complete annual school cost per member [and cost less transportation, and Federal, State, and local shares, by scope and for total State, 1981/82-1983/84]. (p. A6)

8. Distribution of State aid dollars [including amounts paid to districts and counties, by program] for 1983/84. (p. A7)

9. General school aid eligibility [costs, aid, and valuation, total and per member, and levy rate, by scope and for total State] for 1984/85. (p. A8)

BY DISTRICT
[Tables [10-13] show data by district.]

[10] Student and staff data [public and private enrollments, for grades prekindergarten-8 and 9-12; public minority enrollments, by ethnic category; public high school graduates; public school FTE teachers and total professional staff; and school census; as of fall 1984]. (p. B2-B12)

[11] Complete annual school cost per member [and cost less transportation, and Federal, State, and local shares, 1981/82-1983/84]. (p. C1-C12)

[12] Distribution of State aid dollars [by program, including equalization, integration, transportation, tuition, common school fund, driver and handicapped children education, bilingual/bicultural, alcohol/drug abuse, school lunch, and food service for elderly], 1983/84. (p. D6-D16)

[13] Estimated general school aid eligibility for 1984/85 [costs, State aid, and property valuation, total and per member, and levy rate]. (p. E3-E51)

S8815   WISCONSIN
Department of
Transportation

S8815–1   WISCONSIN ACCIDENT
FACTS, 1984
Annual. 1985. 32 p.
LC 44-31829.
SRI/MF/complete

Annual report on Wisconsin traffic accidents involving fatalities, injuries, and property damage, and number of persons killed and injured, 1984, with selected trends from 1973. Includes data by accident and vehicle type, location, time, and other circumstances; and driver and victim characteristics.

Also includes data on vehicle registrations and travel miles; licensed drivers by age; driver fatality blood alcohol level, by age and sex; alcohol involvement in accidents, by county and age; and helmet use in motorcycle accidents.

Data are compiled from law enforcement accident reports.

Contains contents listing (inside front cover); and highlights, 5 charts, and 34 tables (p. 1-32).

Availability: Wisconsin Department of Transportation, Traffic Accident Data Section, Motor Vehicles Division, Rm. 694, PO Box 7917, Madison WI 53707, †; SRI/MF/complete.

S8855   WYOMING
Department of
Administration
and Fiscal Control

S8855–1   WYOMING SALES TAX
REVENUE REPORT, 10th
Edition, 1985
Annual. 1985. 2+71+iv p.
LC 78-643743.
SRI/MF/complete

Annual report on Wyoming sales tax collections, by industry division and retail sector, shown by county, FY74-85. Also includes monthly total collections statewide, FY70-85; and general fund revenues by source, FY83-85.

Data are compiled by Division of Research and Statistics from Dept of Revenue and Taxation reports.

Contains preface, and listings of contents, tables, and charts (2 p.); introduction, with 1 table, list of tax rate adoption dates by county, and list of taxable events and exemptions (p. 1-6); 3 report sections, with brief narratives, 3 charts, and 5 tables (p. 8-71); and glossary (p. i-iv).

This is the 10th edition. Previous edition was titled *Wyoming Tax Revenue Report*.

Availability: Wyoming Department of Administration and Fiscal Control, Research and Statistics Division, Emerson Bldg., Rm. 302, Cheyenne WY 82002-0060, †; SRI/MF/complete.

S8860   WYOMING
Department of Agriculture

S8860–1   WYOMING AGRICULTURAL STATISTICS, 1984
Annual. [1985.] 91 p.
ISSN 0363-9339.
LC 76-646923.
SRI/MF/complete

Annual report on Wyoming agricultural production, marketing, and finances, mostly 1970s-83, with some data for 1984. Data generally are shown by commodity and/or county, with selected comparisons to total U.S.

Covers production, sales, prices, cash receipts, and, as applicable, acreage, yield, inventory, stocks, value, and disposition, for livestock, poultry, dairy, apiary, and field crop sectors.

Also includes data on number of farms; farm acreage, value, taxes, income, and production expenses; climatological conditions; sheep and lamb losses to weather and predatory animals; irrigation; prices paid by farmers; telephone and electricity use and costs; and agricultural employment, hours and wages for western States.

Data are compiled by the Wyoming Crop and Livestock Reporting Service.

Contains contents listing (p. 2); introduction, and list of reports published by issuing agency (p. 3-4); 3 maps, 15 charts, and 94 tables, interspersed with analyses (p. 7-88); and directory of USDA field offices (p. 91).

Availability: Wyoming Crop and Livestock Reporting Service, Agricultural Statistician, Box 1148, Cheyenne WY 82003, †; SRI/MF/complete.

S8875   WYOMING
Office of the Auditor

S8875–1   STATE OF WYOMING, 1984 Annual Report of the State Auditor
Annual. Oct. 1, 1984.
iii+149 p.
LC 78-643833.
SRI/MF/complete

Annual report, for FY84, on financial condition of Wyoming State government, presenting revenues by source and expenditures by function for agency accounts; and assets, liabilities, reserves, and fund balances; all by individual fund.

Funds covered are general, earmarked revenue, Federal revenue, trust and agency, debt service, intragovernmental, highway, game and fish, University of Wyoming, permanent land, permanent land income, permanent Wyoming mineral trust, and enterprise.

Also includes data on appropriations vs. expenditures for selected funds; State bonded debt; activities of the State Auditor's Office, including value of warrants issued, and audits and mineral site inspections conducted; and summary trends from FY73.

Contains listings of contents and financial schedules (p. i-iii); introduction and summary report, interspersed with text tables and 5 charts (p. 1-24); 1 chart and 66 financial schedules (p. 25-148); and notes to financial statements (p. 149).

Availability: Wyoming Office of the Auditor, State Capitol Bldg., Rm. 114, Cheyenne WY 82002, †; SRI/MF/complete.

S8885   WYOMING
Department of Economic Planning and Development

S8885–1   1984 WYOMING MINERAL YEARBOOK
Annual. Nov. 1984. 134 p.
ISSN 0096-9842.
LC 75-641349.
SRI/MF/complete

Annual report, by John T. Goodier and Dale S. Hoffman, on Wyoming taxable mineral production, assessed valuation, and tax income, various years 1969-84, with selected trends from 1865.

Data are compiled from reports of the Wyoming Dept of Revenue and Taxation, State Geological Survey, and Oil and Gas Conservation Commission, and from mineral company estimates of production.

Contents:

a. Contents listing (1 p.); and introduction with text tables and 4 summary charts (p. 1-4).

b. 10 mineral industry tax tables, listed below. (p. 5-15)

c. Review of mineral production, with 11 summary charts, and 7 tables showing production of bentonite, coal, iron ore, natural gas, petroleum, trona, and uranium, various years 1865-1983. (p. 17-70)

d. Narrative county profiles of mineral production and valuation, with text statistics for 23 counties; and 2 charts repeated for 17 counties, showing property valuation with distribution by mineral and for all other property, 1979 and 1984. (p. 71-111)

e. 20 tables showing production 1979-83, assessed valuation (total and per standard unit of measurement) 1980-84, and production projections 1984-88, for 8 major minerals (types noted above, plus gypsum), by county; and list of references. (p. 113-134)

Availability: Wyoming Department of Economic Planning and Development, Mineral Division, Herschler Bldg., 3rd Floor, Cheyenne WY 82002, †; SRI/MF/complete.

MINERAL TAX TABLES:
[Tables I-VI show data for oil, gas, coal, uranium, trona, and usually other, for 1969-84 unless otherwise noted.]

I-II. Assessed valuation and ad valorem tax paid on production. (p. 6-7)

III. Assessed valuation per unit of production. (p. 8)

IV-V. Severance tax collections and tax rates. (p. 9-10)

VI. Severance tax distribution [by recipient], 1984. (p. 11)

VII. Sales and use tax [for oil/natural gas, coal, metal mining, and other mining, FY71-84]. (p. 12)

VIII. Government royalty (mineral royalty returns to State) [1970-84; and distribution of returns, by recipient]. (p. 13)

IX. Summary table [assessed valuation per unit, severance tax, average tax levy (mills), tax as percent of valuation, and average tax paid per unit, all by mineral, 1969 and 1984]. (p. 14)

X. Mineral income to the State of Wyoming [by type of tax, rent, and royalty], 1971-84. (p. 15)

S8885–2   1984 COMMUNITY PROFILES, WYOMING
Recurring (irreg.) [1985.]
23 rpts., 4 p. each.
SRI/MF/complete

Set of profiles for 23 Wyoming cities, compiling governmental, economic, and social statistics, primarily for 1983-84.

Contains a 4-page profile for each city. Profiles include the following information, as available:

a. Proximity to selected cities; city and county population, various years 1970-84; climate; type of local govt; size of police force and fire dept; and whether city has planning commission, industrial plan approval, zoning regulations, and industrial revenue bond financing.

b. Elementary and secondary schools, enrollment, and teachers; colleges; private/parochial and vocational/technical schools; libraries and holdings; day care centers; and churches, by major denomination.

c. Shopping centers and department stores; lodging, recreational vehicle parks, and convention facilities; financial institutions by type; and health facilities, physicians, and dentists.

d. Newspapers, radio stations, cable TV availability, telephone and telegram service, and post offices; and recreational facilities, including parks and acreage.

e. Housing data for county, including occupied and vacant units, by type; city and county assessed valuation, tax levies, and property taxes; school and special district tax levies; and selected tax and fee rates.

f. Utilities, including electricity, natural gas, and water suppliers, capacity, demand, and rates; and sewage treatment capacity and load.

g. Transportation facilities; county labor force and unemployment rate; business firms, employment, and weekly earnings, by industry division; list of major employers, with employment size; and available industrial properties.

Profiles are published as information and funding become available. The last set was published in 1983 (for description, see SRI 1983 Annual under this number). Communities covered vary from set to set.

Availability: Wyoming Department of Economic Planning and Development, Herschler Bldg., 3rd Floor, Cheyenne WY 82002, †; SRI/MF/complete.

S8890   WYOMING
Department of Education

S8890-1   STATISTICAL REPORT SERIES, Wyoming
Annual Series.   For individual publication data, see below.
ISSN 0093-5530.
LC 74-642288.
SRI/MF/complete

Series of 3 annual reports on Wyoming public schools, enrollments, and staff as of fall 1984, and finances for FY84 or 1984 tax year. Includes data on property valuations, tax levies, bonded debt, and revenues and expenditures.

Data are from school district reports submitted to the State Dept of Education. Most data are shown by county and district.

Reports are described below.

Availability: Wyoming Department of Education, Administration Division, Data Collection, Hathaway Bldg., Cheyenne WY 82002, †; SRI/MF/complete.

S8890-1.1: 1984 School District Property Valuations, Mill Levies, and Bonded Debt, Wyoming
[Annual.   Mar. 1985.   2+11 p. Oversized. Rpt. No. 1.   ISSN 0146-7948.   SRI/MF/complete.]

Annual report, for tax year 1984, on Wyoming public school district property valuations, tax levies, and bonded debt, by county and district. Includes preface, contents listing, and 4 tables showing the following:

a. Property valuation 1983-84, and average daily membership 1983/84, by district arranged by county; and valuation by county for detailed types of real property, mineral production, utilities, and personal property, 1984. (p. 1-5)

b. Tax levies, by type (State school foundation, mandatory county, operating, bond/interest, and other school), 1984; and

bonded debt as of June 1983 and 1984, election amount approved, bonds issued, refunds, principal and interest paid, and percent of bonding capacity obligated; all by district arranged by county. (p. 6-11).

S8890-1.2: 1984 School Districts Fall Report of Staff, Teachers/Pupils/Schools, Enrollments, Special Education Student Count, Wyoming
[Annual.   Mar. 1985.   2+121 p. Oversized. Rpt. No. 2.   ISSN 0146-7972.   LC 77-648346. SRI/MF/complete.]

Annual report, for fall 1984, on Wyoming public schools, staff, and enrollments. Includes preface, contents listing, and 4 tables showing the following, generally as of fall 1984:

a. FTE and other staff, by position and sex; and teachers, enrollment, and schools by level, with 1983/84 average daily membership; all by district arranged by county. 2 tables. (p. 1-53)

b. Enrollment by grade, including ungraded; and special education students by disability; all by county, district, and school. 2 tables. (p. 54-121)

S8890-1.3: Wyoming Public Schools Fund Accounting and Reporting, 1983/84
[Annual.   Mar. 1985.   3+64 p. Oversized. Rpt. No. 3.   ISSN 0146-793X.   SRI/MF/complete.]

Annual report, for FY84, on Wyoming public school revenues and expenditures, by school district. Includes preface, contents listing, and the following data for FY84:

a. General fund revenues, by specific local, county, State, and Federal source; and expenditures, by program and object. 3 charts and 2 tables. (p. 1-3)

b. Average daily membership (ADM) by grade, including exceptional students; classroom units by type; general fund revenues per ADM, by source; general fund expenditures, by program and object; and general fund expenditures per pupil and classroom unit; all by district, generally arranged by county. 6 tables. (p. 4-14)

c. Profiles for individual districts and the State, including revenues by source and expenditures by program, all by fund; costs per ADM and per classroom unit; and schools, fall enrollment, graduates by sex, dropout rate, average daily attendance, ADM, classroom units and value, staff, assessed valuation, bonded debt, students transported daily, annual bus miles, and district-owned buses. 3 tables repeated for each profile. (p. 15-64)

S8895   WYOMING
Employment Security Commission

S8895-1   WYOMING LABOR FORCE TRENDS
Monthly.   7 p.
ISSN 0512-4409.
LC SC 79-4113.
SRI/MF/complete, shipped quarterly

Monthly report on Wyoming employment and unemployment, unemployment insurance claims and payments, and job openings and placements. Also includes data on mining industry hours and earnings. Report is based on employer reports to the Employment Security Commission, and is issued approximately 2 months after month of coverage.

Contains narrative analyses with 1 summary trend chart; 5 monthly tables, listed below; and occasional articles and additional tables, some with substantial statistics, but most presenting summaries or recent trends for data covered in monthly tables.

Monthly tables appear in all issues. Feb. 1985 issue also includes 4 annual tables showing monthly labor force and employment data, by county, 1984. Additional features presenting substantial Wyoming data not covered in monthly tables are described, as they appear, under "Statistical Features." Nonstatistical features and U.S. data reprinted from Federal sources are not covered.

Availability: Wyoming Employment Security Commission, Research and Analysis Section, PO Box 2760, Casper WY 82602, †; SRI/MF/complete.

Issues reviewed during 1985: Sept. 1984-July 1985 (D) (Vol. 21, Nos. 8-11; Vol. 22, Nos. 1-4) [No issues for Mar.-May 1985 were published].

MONTHLY TABLES:
[Tables 1-3 show data for month of coverage, previous month, and same month of previous year.]

[A] Trend setters [shows summary data, for month of coverage and previous month].

[B] [U.S.] CPI [by item, for month of coverage; occasionally includes trends from 1960s and data for Denver].

1. Economic indicators [including labor force and employment; agricultural employment; total and insured unemployment rates; average hours and earnings for mining production workers; unemployment insurance claims filed, weeks compensated, and payments; and employment service applications, openings, and placements; with selected U.S. comparisons].

2. Civilian labor force and unemployment [by county].

3. Nonfarm wage/salary employment [by industry division and selected major group, for Wyoming, Casper, and Cheyenne].

STATISTICAL FEATURES:

S8895-1.601: Nov. 1984 (Vol. 21, No. 10)

RECORD NUMBER OF BANKRUPTCIES IN WYOMING

(p. 3, 5) Article, with 1 table and 1 chart ranking Wyoming counties by number of bankruptcies, and also showing bankruptcy rate per 10,000 population, Oct. 1983-Sept. 1984 period. Data are from U.S. Bankruptcy Court, Cheyenne, Wyo.

S8895–1.602: Dec. 1984 (Vol. 21, No. 11)

PRE AND POST RECESSION EMPLOYMENT COMPARISONS

(p. 3) Article, with 1 table showing employment for Wyoming, Casper, and Cheyenne, as reported under 3 estimating procedures used by Wyoming Employment Security Commission, June 1979 and June 1984.

S8895–1.603: July 1985 (Vol. 22, No. 4)

WYOMING PER CAPITA INCOME TUMBLES

(p. 2) Brief article, with 1 table showing Wyoming per capita income, with ranking among States and comparison to U.S. average, 1976-84. Data are from Commerce Dept.

S8895–2   WYOMING ANNUAL PLANNING REPORT, FY85
Annual.   Nov. 1984.
vii+103 p.
LC 78-645546.
SRI/MF/complete

Annual planning report, for FY85, identifying Wyoming population groups most in need of employment services and projecting employment by industry and occupation through 1990 or 1994. Includes data on population and labor force by county, earnings, and job openings and applicants. Most data are for 1983, with selected trends from 1970s and earlier, and comparisons to total U.S.

Data are from Wyoming Employment Security Commission, BLS, Commerce Dept, and other sources.

Contents:

a. Listings of contents, charts, and tables (p. iii-vii); introduction (p. 1-2); and narrative report in 9 sections, interspersed with text statistics, 9 charts, and 28 tables (p. 1-57).

b. Appendix, with 2 maps, 11 charts, and 17 tables. (p. 60-97)

c. Glossary. (p. 98-103)

All tables, and selected charts providing Wyoming data not shown in tables, are listed below.

Availability: Wyoming Employment Security Commission, Research and Analysis Section, PO Box 2760, Casper WY 82602, †; SRI/MF/complete.

CHARTS AND TABLES:
[Unless otherwise noted, charts and tables show data for Wyoming, often with comparisons to total U.S.]

S8895–2.1: Report Tables

NATIONAL DATA

[A] U.S. GNP growth [1981-2nd quarter 1984]. (p. 4)

1. Average prime rate charged by banks [monthly 1982-July 1984]. (p. 5)

2. U.S. CPI, all urban, all items [monthly 1967-Aug. 1984]. (p. 6)

POPULATION, LABOR FORCE, INFLATION, AND INCOME

3-5. Total population [decennially 1870-1970 and annually 1971-83]; population, by county [including per square mile] for selected years [1970-83]; and 1983 population, by age. (p. 10-13)

6. 1983 labor force [by employment status, by month]. (p. 13)

7. Total unadjusted unemployment rates [compared to U.S., monthly] 1976-Oct. 1984. (p. 15)

8. Summary table of economic assumptions [shows labor force and insured unemployment data, 1976-85]. (p. 18)

9. Comparative cost-of-living index prices [for 23 cities and Lakewood County] as of July 11/12/13, 1984. (p. 19)

10. Annual inflation rates by [State] region and by [expenditure] category, weighted by population (2nd quarter 1983-84). (p. 20)

EARNINGS AND EMPLOYMENT

11. Average annual pay for covered workers, by industry [division], 1982-83. (p. 21)

12. Per capita income [including national ranking, 1975-83]. (p. 22)

13. Average covered employment by industry [division], 2nd quarter 1978-83. (p. 24)

14. Annual average nonagricultural employment [by industry division and selected major group, 1976-83]. (p. 25)

15. Major sources of personal income [wage/salary disbursements by industry division], 1st quarter 1981-84. (p. 26)

[B] Severance tax rate changes [by mineral type, 1972 and 1982]. (p. 29)

[C] Total State assessed valuation [with distribution by mineral type and for all other property], 1973, 1978, and 1983. [chart] (p. 30)

16-17. Mining and manufacturing hours and earnings [July 1983-84]. (p. 35)

JOB OPENINGS

18. Job openings [by occupation] with ESARS [Employment Service Automated Reporting System] record showing no action taken for 30 days or more, period ending June 30, 1984. (p. 39)

19. Quarterly summary report of job openings [by occupational group] at job service centers, quarter ending June 30, 1984. (p. 40)

MINORITIES AND ECONOMICALLY DISADVANTAGED

20-22. Population, and annual average labor force and unemployed [all] by sex and race/ethnic group [white, black, Native American, Asian, Hispanic, and other, by county], for 1983. (p. 44-46)

23. Estimated total population of economically disadvantaged [total, female, and age 16/over, by race and for Hispanics], for 1980 and 1983. (p. 48)

JOB APPLICANTS AND EMPLOYMENT OUTLOOK

24. Number of active file applicants [total, female, veteran, minority, age 22-30, and age 45/over] by occupation [group], for Oct. 1, 1983-June 30, 1984. (p. 50)

25-26. Employment by industrial sector and by major occupational group, for 1983, and projected for 1990. (p. 51-52)

S8895–2.2: Appendix Tables

MINERAL RESOURCES

[A] Assessed mineral valuation [distribution by county], 1983. [chart] (p. 71)

LABOR FORCE TRENDS AND PROJECTIONS
[Tables 2-13 and 15-16 show data by county.]

1. Total unemployment rate (not seasonally adjusted) [monthly 1960-Sept. 1984]. (p. 73)

2-9. Labor force, employment, unemployment, and unemployment rate [monthly 1983, and annual average 1970-83]. (p. 74-81)

10. Employment for SIC [industry divisions], 1983-86. (p. 82-85)

11. Age distribution [of the population, by sex], 1983-86. (p. 86-89)

12-13. Final population and employment matrices [1980-94]. (p. 90-91)

14. Historical coal production, employment, and productivity, [various years] 1865-1983. (p. 92-94)

15-16. 1983 annual average covered employment and weekly wages of covered employment [by industry division]. (p. 95-96)

17. Total wages, and annual averages [for] UI [unemployment insurance] covered employment by industry [division], 1955-83. (p. 97)

S8920   WYOMING
Department of Health and Social Services

S8920–1   MANAGEMENT INFORMATION AND STATISTICAL REPORT, FY84, Wyoming
Annual.   [1984.]   41 p.
SRI/MF/complete, current & previous year reports

Annual report, for FY84, on Wyoming public welfare programs, including recipients, expenditures, and caseload, by program, county, and month. Also includes data on child support collections, adoption and foster care, child abuse and neglect, Work Incentive Program (WIN), and other social services.

Contains table listing (1 p.); and 41 tables, listed below (p. 1-41).

Report for FY83 has also been received, and is also available on SRI microfiche under this number [Annual. [1983.] 40 p. †]. Report for FY83 also contains data for 1st 2 quarters of FY84. For description of report for FY82, see SRI 1983 Annual, under this number.

Availability: Wyoming Department of Health and Social Services, Public Assistance and Social Services Division, Hathaway Bldg., Cheyenne WY 82002, †; SRI/MF/complete.

TABLES:
[Unless otherwise noted, tables show data by county and month, for FY84.]

CHILD SUPPORT ENFORCEMENT AND FOOD STAMPS

[1] Child support enforcement: total amount child support collected, PA [public assistance]. (p. 1)

[2-5] Food stamp issuance: dollar value of coupons issued, and total number of households, recipients, and AFDC households. (p. 2-5)

PUBLIC ASSISTANCE

[6-8] AFDC: number of grants paid and recipients, and cost in dollars. (p. 6-8)

[9-10] Supplemental Security Income (SSI): number of clients, and cost of $20 payments. (p. 9-10)

[11-14] Sheltered care: number of persons under Title XIX, number [receiving] State payment only and SSI only, and total cost. (p. 11-14)

[15-18] General welfare: emergency and general assistance, and prescription drugs dollar value; and total MMP [Minimum Medical Program] expenditures. (p. 15-18)

SOCIAL SERVICES AND ENERGY ASSISTANCE

[19-20] Adoption: number of approved homes waiting placement, and number of children adopted. (p. 19-20)

[21-24] Child abuse and neglect victim statistics [including type of maltreatment, child's age, relationship to perpetrator, and sex, and source of report, quarterly FY84]. (p. 21-24)

[25-26] Foster care: number of children in care, and number of foster home providers. (p. 25-26)

[27-29] WIN: number of new registrants; number of persons in employment; and dollar reduction achieved from AFDC grants. (p. 27-29)

[30-32] Purchase of service: homemaker, day care, and total expenditures. (p. 30-32)

[33] Low income energy assistance payments, [persons involved, and number of households approved and denied], year to date, Aug. 2, 1984. (p. 33)

CASELOAD SUMMARIES

[Tables [34-41] show data by program, for last month of each quarter, FY84.]

[34-37] Caseload management report. (p. 34-37)

[38-41] Caseload income maintenance by relative value. (p. 38-41)

S8920–2   SUMMARY OF WYOMING VITAL STATISTICS, 1983
Annual.   Apr. 1985.   ii+55 p.
LC 59-62576.
SRI/MF/complete

Annual report on Wyoming vital statistics, 1983, with selected trends from as early as 1922, and comparisons to U.S. Covers population, births, deaths by cause, marriages, and divorces, by demographic characteristics and/or county. Most data are from documents filed with the State as of Apr. 15, 1984.

Contains contents and table listings (p. i-ii), introduction, definitions, and summary report, interspersed with 4 charts and 8 text tables, generally showing trends and summary data (p. 1-20); and statistical section, with 34 tables listed below (p. 23-55).

Availability: Wyoming Department of Health and Social Services, Health and Medical Services Division, Vital Records Services, Hathaway Bldg., Cheyenne WY 82002, †; SRI/MF/complete.

STATISTICAL SECTION TABLES:

[Data are for 1983, unless otherwise noted. Data by race also include Indians. Data by county generally include Yellowstone National Park.]

S8920–2.1: Population, Births, and Deaths
POPULATION AND HISTORICAL DATA

1. Population by county, 1980-83. (p. 23)

2. Births, deaths, infant deaths, stillbirths, maternal deaths, [and population], 1922-83. (p. 24)

BIRTHS

[Tables 3-9 and 12 show data by county of residence.]

3. Births and rates, 1979-83. (p. 25)

4-5. Births by sex, race, and age of mother. (p. 26-27)

6. Births to unmarried mothers, by age of mother and race. (p. 28)

7. Low weight births, 1979-83. (p. 29)

8-9. Births by weight at birth and by live birth order. (p. 30-31)

10-11. Births by age of mother, by live birth order and trimester prenatal care began. (p. 32)

12. Births by trimester prenatal care began. (p. 33)

13. Births by county of occurrence, attendant, and place of delivery. (p. 34)

14. Birth travel patterns: county of residence by county of occurrence. (p. 35)

DEATHS

[Tables 15-17, 23-24, and 26 show data by county of residence.]

15. Deaths and rates, 1979-83. (p. 36)

16-17. Deaths by sex, race, age, and selected cause. (p. 37-38)

18. Leading cause of death by age group. (p. 39)

19-21. [Total], male, and female resident deaths by selected cause and age. (p. 40-42)

22. Accidental deaths occurring in State by age and sex [by type of accident]. (p. 43)

23. Infant deaths by age. (p. 44)

24. Infant and neonatal deaths [and rates], 1979-83. (p. 45)

25. Resident infant deaths by selected cause and age at death. (p. 46)

26. Stillbirths, 1979-83. (p. 47)

BIRTHS AND DEATHS

27. Births and deaths, by county of occurrence, 1979-83. (p. 48)

S8920–2.2: Marriages and Divorces
[Most tables show data by county of occurrence.]

28. Marriages and rates, 1979-83. (p. 49)

29. Marriages by month. (p. 50)

30-31. Marriages by age and previous marital status of bride and groom. (p. 51-52)

32. Divorces/annulments with rates, 1979-83. (p. 53)

33-34. Divorces/annulments by duration of marriage, and by number of children affected. (p. 54-55)

S8925   WYOMING
Highway Department

S8925–1   WYOMING'S COMPREHENSIVE REPORT ON TRAFFIC ACCIDENTS, 1983
Annual.   [1984.]   ix+244 p.
LC 63-62626.
SRI/MF/complete

Annual report on Wyoming traffic accidents, injuries, and fatalities, by vehicle type and make; accident type, location, time, and other circumstances; and driver and victim characteristics; 1983, with trends from 1974.

Also includes data on vehicle registrations and travel miles; accident costs; alcohol involvement in accidents, and blood alcohol content test results; safety device use; and accidents involving youthful drivers.

Data are compiled from dept reports and National Safety Council records.

Contains contents listing, introduction, and definitions (p. i-ix); and 10 statistical sections, with 1 map, 48 charts, and 243 tables (p. 1-244).

Availability: Wyoming Highway Department, Highway Safety Branch, Safety Analysis Section, PO Box 1708, Cheyenne WY 82002-9019, 1st copy †, additional copies $5.00; SRI/MF/complete.

S8990   WYOMING
Department of Revenue and Taxation

S8990–1   ANNUAL REPORT OF THE STATE BOARD OF EQUALIZATION, 1984, State of Wyoming
Annual.   [1984.]   15+224 p.
LC 74-642856.
SRI/MF/complete

Annual report on Wyoming assessed property valuations and tax levies, including data by property type, tax purpose, county, city, and company, 1984 with summary trends from 1944.

Contains narrative summary with 1 text table, and index (12 p.); 16 tables, described below (p. 1-223); and listing of county assessors and treasurers (p. 224).

Availability: Wyoming Department of Revenue and Taxation, Ad Valorem Tax Division, 122 W. 25th St., Cheyenne WY 82002-0110, †; SRI/MF/complete.

TABLES:

[Unless otherwise noted, data are for 1984.]

a. Detailed valuations, by property type and county, including land acreage where applicable. Table I. (p. 1-22)

b. Mineral, energy resource, and utility taxable production (1983) and/or valuation, by company: for coal, natural gas and crude oil (including detail by field), sand/gravel, trona, uranium, and other minerals, with ad valorem and collectible severance taxes by mineral type; and for pipeline companies, municipally and privately owned utilities, rural electricity cooperatives, railroads, and telephone and telegraph companies. Table II. (p. 23-200)

c. Taxes levied, by purpose, type (including school taxes), and county; municipal property valuation and taxes levied, by city or town; private railroad car valuation and taxes levied, by county; county tax summary; and special taxes on animals, by county. Tables III-VII. (p. 201-214)

d. Miscellaneous tax information, including average tax levies; distribution of valuation and taxes by property type and/or county; and veterans exemption valuations and tax benefits, by county. Tables VIII-XII. (p. 215-219)

e. State mill levies and taxable valuation, 1944-84; ad valorem taxes levied, by type, 1950-84; property tax expenditure distribution; and county valuation summary. 4 tables. (p. 220-223)

S9000   WYOMING
Office of the Secretary of State

S9000-1   1985 WYOMING OFFICIAL DIRECTORY
Annual. [1985.] vii+280 p.
ISSN 0363-8421.
LC 79-4177.
SRI/MF/complete

Annual directory, for 1985, of Wyoming Federal, State, and county government officials, with results of the State's general and primary elections held during 1984, and population and electoral trends from 1870.

Contents:

a. Contents listing (p. vii); and directories of State officials and agencies, and Federal and local officials (p. 1-152).

b. Election results: voting for President/Vice-President, U.S. and State senators and representatives, judges, other State officials, and 3 constitutional amendments, by county, district, and precinct, for general election held Nov. 6, 1984; and selected results by county, for primary election held Sept. 11, 1984; with party affiliation of candidates. Includes 6 tables. (p. 153-228)

c. Historical rosters and trends: State urban and rural population, and population by county; list of cities and towns; rosters of U.S. Senators and Representatives, Governors, and other State officials including women legislators; presidential and gubernatorial summary election results; and political party composition of State legislature; all for various years 1870-1985. Includes 5 tables. (p. 229-255)

d. Subject and surname indexes. (p. 257-280)

Directory is issued annually, but is covered in SRI only when major election results are included. Directory presenting 1982 election results is described in SRI 1983 Annual under this number.

Availability: Wyoming Office of the Secretary of State, Capitol Bldg., Cheyenne WY 82002-0020, Wyoming residents †, others $3.50 (prepaid); SRI/MF/complete.

S9010   WYOMING
Office of the Treasurer

S9010-1   ANNUAL REPORT OF THE TREASURER OF THE STATE OF WYOMING for the Period July 1, 1983-June 30, 1984
Annual. Sept. 28, 1984.
5+32 p.
LC 10-17749.
SRI/MF/complete

Annual report on the financial transactions of the Wyoming State Treasurer's Office, FY84, with selected trends from FY75. Includes the status of State investments and major funds, and distributions of various appropriated and Federal funds to counties and municipalities. Distributions to localities include government mineral royalties and severance tax, and gasoline tax refunds to airports and agricultural users.

Contains foreword, description of Treasurer's office duties, organizational chart, and contents listing (4 p.); 20 financial tables, listed below (p. 1-30); explanation of public employee deferred compensation plan, with text data on participants and fund status, FY84 and trends (p. 31); and list of legislative mandates (p. 32).

Previous report, for FY83, is described in SRI 1983 Annual, under this number.

Availability: Wyoming Office of the Treasurer, State Capitol Bldg., Cheyenne WY 82002, †; SRI/MF/complete.

TABLES:

[Unless otherwise noted, data are for FY84, or as of June 30, 1984.]

S9010-1.1: Fund Financial Status

[1-2] State treasurer's distribution of cash, and statement of investments [by account and fund]. (p. 1-2)

[3] Summary of receipts and disbursements. (p. 3)

[4] Account balances [by fund]. (p. 4)

[5] Report of State Board of Deposits [deposits by individual bank and savings/loan institution]. (p. 5-7)

[6] [Aggregate State deposits in Wyoming banks and savings/loan institutions, and interest rates, 1976-84.] (p. 8)

[7] State treasurer's bid program [including number and value of bids, and deposits by individual bank and savings/loan institution]. (p. 9)

[8] Investments by major type at cost. (p. 10)

[9] Income vs. disbursements [monthly FY84 and annual totals FY75-83]. (p. 11)

[10] Total interest to income funds and interest on other funds. (p. 12)

S9010-1.2: Distribution of Funds

[1] Government [mineral] royalty distribution [by type or function, FY83-84]. (p. 13)

[2] Permanent land funds [balances, and revenues by type of land lease royalty, for 12 funds]. (p. 14-17)

[3-4] State treasurer's mortgage purchase program: mortgage pass-through certificates ser-

ies [including commitment and closing amounts, closing dates, number of lenders, and number and amount of loans; and deliveries, by individual banking, savings/loan, and mortgage banker institution; various periods 1981-84]. (p. 18-20)

[5] Permanent Wyoming mineral trust fund [tax collections, balance, and interest received/transferred to general fund, FY75-84; and loans outstanding to political subdivisions]. (p. 21)

[6] Distributions to counties [of funds from homestead exemption, Taylor grazing, forest reserve, car company tax, veterans' exemption, and gasoline and severance taxes, all by county]. (p. 22)

[7] Distributions to cities and towns [of funds from police officers' retirement, gasoline tax, government royalty, and severance tax, by city or town]. (p. 23-26)

S9010-1.3: Gasoline Tax Refunds, and Gifts/Forfeitures

[1] Agricultural gasoline tax refunds, by counties [including number of applicants, FY83-84]. (p. 27)

[2] Gasoline tax refunds [to municipalities and airports, FY83-84]. (p. 28-29)

[3] Gifts/escheats/forfeitures [including beginning and ending balances], FY80-84. (p. 30)

U0280
Arizona State University:
Bureau of Business
and Economic Research

U0280–1   ARIZONA BUSINESS
Monthly. Approx. 12 p.
ISSN 0093-0717.
LC 74-640105.
SRI/MF/complete, shipped
quarterly

Monthly report on Arizona business and economic trends and conditions. Includes a monthly survey of Arizona purchasing managers, and recurring data on CPI, construction activity, and other indicators. Data are from Arizona State University survey studies, and various State, Federal, and commercial sources.

Contains feature articles, most with statistics; and 3 monthly and 8 quarterly tables, listed below, generally accompanied by narrative analyses, with occasional supplementary charts or tables.

Monthly tables appear in all issues. All additional features with substantial statistical content are described, as they appear, under "Statistical Features;" page locations and latest periods of coverage for quarterly tables are also noted. Nonstatistical features are not covered.

Prior to the Mar. 1985 issue, report was published quarterly.

Availability: Arizona State University: Bureau of Business and Economic Research, College of Business, Tempe AZ 85287, †; SRI/MF/complete, shipped quarterly.

Issues reviewed during 1985: 3rd-4th Qtrs. 1984 (quarterly); and Mar.-Oct. 1985 (monthly) (P) (Vol. 31, Nos. 3-4; Vol. 32, Nos. 1-8).

MONTHLY TABLES:
[Data in table [1] generally are current to 2 months prior to cover date. Data in tables [2-3] are current to 2-7 months prior to cover date.]

[1] Purchasing survey [percent of surveyed members of Arizona Purchasing Management Assn indicating higher, lower, or same levels for commodity prices, vendor delivery time, inventory levels, new orders, production, employment, and purchases; generally for current month and 2 previous months].

[2] Arizona economic indicators [generally includes GSP, Phoenix CPI, leading indicator index, building permit value and housing units authorized in 2 metro counties and balance of State, Maricopa County home sales and median price, and electrical power sales; shown for latest month or quarter and year to date, with percent change from previous periods. Table begins with Mar. 1985 issue].

[3] Net contribution of individual components to the Arizona Index of Leading Economic Indicators [shows overall value of index, and net index contribution of each component, including selected indicators from ta-

bles [1-2], unemployment insurance claims, manufacturing workweek, and money supply, generally for current month and 2-3 previous months. Table begins with Apr. 1985 issue; an article introducing the feature is described under U0280-1.604 below].

QUARTERLY TABLES:
[Data are shown for most recent available quarter (generally current to 3-6 months prior to cover date), with selected comparisons to prior periods. Tables [1-5] include accompanying narrative summaries. Tables [6-7] show data by Arizona county and local area. Table titles and sequence may vary.]

[1-3] [CPI by item, for Phoenix, U.S., and 2 cities outside Arizona.]

[4] Economic growth [Arizona GSP compared to U.S. GNP; occasionally includes GSP breakdowns by industry division].

[5] Key sector construction activity [number and value of building permits issued for single-family units, apartments, office buildings, retail stores, and industrial, for Maricopa County, Pima County, and rest of State].

[6] Building permits [number and value of residential, commercial, industrial, and other permits].

[7] New housing starts [residential building permits by unit size (1-family, duplex, 3-4 family, and 5 or more) and mobile home permits].

[8] Metro Phoenix home sales [volume and median price for new and resale single-family and townhouse/condominium units].

STATISTICAL FEATURES:

U0280–1.601: 3rd Qtr. 1984 (Vol. 31, No. 3)

QUARTERLY TABLES
[1-3] CPI, for 2nd quarter 1984. (p. 42-44)

[4] Economic growth, for 1st quarter 1984 [includes additional data by industry division; table title varies]. (p. 36-37)

[5] Key sector construction activity, for 2nd quarter 1984. (p. 22)

[6] Building permits, for 2nd quarter 1984. (p. 27-28)

[7] New housing starts, for 2nd quarter 1984. (p. 26)

[8] Metro Phoenix home sales, for 2nd quarter 1984. (p. 29)

1983-84 ECONOMIC IMPACT OF ARIZONA STATE UNIVERSITY
(p. 3-9) By Timothy D. Hogan and Lee R. McPheters. Article on impact of Arizona State University (ASU) on the State economy, 1983/84. Data are based on a survey of 300 faculty/staff and 4,000 students, and on ASU records.

Includes 5 charts and 8 tables primarily showing institutional, staff, and student expenditures, by category; faculty/staff payroll, and computation of disposable income; staff and

student purchases of homes and autos; employment directly and indirectly attributable to ASU; and out-of-State funding brought into Arizona by ASU; mostly for FY84.

HOUSING APPRECIATION IN THE PHOENIX METROPOLITAN AREA
(p. 10-14) By Jay Q. Butler and Tom R. Rex. Article, with 3 tables showing Phoenix housing value appreciation rate, by quarter, 2nd quarter 1981-2nd quarter 1984, with detail by geographic district and comparison to Phoenix CPI and housing sales volume and price. Data are from Arizona State University. Appreciation rate is based primarily on analysis of 4,507 single-family homes sold at least twice during 1982-83.

ARIZONA BUSINESS SCENE: DEMOGRAPHICS OF THE URBAN SOUTHWEST
(p. 38-40) By Tom R. Rex. Article, with 2 tables showing the following for 7 southwestern cities and total U.S., 1980: population, growth since 1970, and percent Hispanic, born in State of residence, having attended college, and employed by government; median family income; and employment distribution by industry division. Data are from Census Bureau.

U0280–1.602: 4th Qtr. 1984 (Vol. 31, No. 4)

QUARTERLY TABLES
[1-3] CPI, for 3rd quarter 1984. (p. 37-39)

[4] Economic growth, for 2nd quarter 1984 [table title varies]. (p. 34)

[5] Key sector construction activity, for 3rd quarter 1984. (p. 21)

[6] Building permits, for 3rd quarter 1984. (p. 25-26)

[7] New housing starts, for 3rd quarter 1984. (p. 27)

[8] Metro Phoenix home sales, for 3rd quarter 1984. (p. 24)

SURVEY OF ARIZONA BUSINESS CONDITIONS AS A LEADING ECONOMIC INDICATOR
(p. 3-9) By Harold Fearon and Tom R. Rex. Article comparing U.S. and Arizona economic cycles with indicators of State economic activity as reported in monthly surveys of Arizona-based purchasing managers, 1960s-84. Includes 2 tables.

Recent purchasing survey results are a regular feature of *Arizona Business;* for description, see U0280-1 above.

FORECASTING ARIZONA ECONOMIC ACTIVITY
(p. 10-14) By Luke Koons and Tom R. Rex. Article, with 2 tables showing Arizona and U.S. personal income, unemployment rate, wage/salary employment, and population; and Arizona GSP, Phoenix CPI, and U.S. GNP and CPI; actual and forecast for various periods 1982-85. Forecast data include results from an econometric model developed by Arizona State University Bureau of Business and Economic Research.

ARIZONA BUSINESS SCENE: 1982 CENSUS OF RETAIL TRADE

(p. 31-33) By Tom R. Rex. Article, with 2 tables showing retail establishments, sales, employment, and payroll, for Arizona by kind of business, and for Phoenix and Tucson MSAs, 1982. Data are from U.S. Census Bureau.

U0280–1.603: Mar. 1985 (Vol. 32, No. 1)

QUARTERLY TABLES

[1-3] CPI, for 4th quarter 1984. (p. 4)

[4] Economic growth, for 3rd quarter 1984. (p. 5)

[8] Metro Phoenix home sales, for 4th quarter 1984. (p. 11)

INFLATION RATE ACCELERATES IN 1984, ANNUAL FEATURE

(p. 1-3) Annual article, with 2 tables showing annual data for quarterly tables [2-3] on Phoenix CPI by item, 1983-84.

ANTICIPATED EXPENDITURES FOR NEW PLANT AND EQUIPMENT, ANNUAL FEATURE

(p. 7) Annual table accompanying monthly purchasing survey, showing anticipated expenditure levels for new plant/equipment, compared with previous year, 1976-85. Data are from Purchasing Management Assns of Arizona and Southern Arizona.

PHOENIX AREA HOMES APPRECIATE 3% IN '84

(p. 8-10) Article, with 2 tables showing Phoenix housing value appreciation rate, with detail by geographic district and comparison to Phoenix CPI and housing sales price, various periods 1981-84. Data are from Arizona State University.

Article updates an article appearing in the 3rd quarter 1984 issue; for description, see U0280-1.601 above.

U0280–1.604: Apr. 1985 (Vol. 32, No. 2)

NEW INDEX TO SIGNAL STATE'S ECONOMIC TURNING POINTS

(p. 1-4) Article, with 1 table showing overall value of Arizona leading economic indicators index, and value and net index contribution of each component, Oct. 1984-Jan. 1985. Data are from Bureau of Business and Economic Research.

INCONSISTENT ECONOMIC GROWTH LIKELY THROUGH '85, QUARTERLY FEATURE

(p. 1, 4-6) Quarterly article examining Arizona and Maricopa County economic outlook for 1985. Includes 1 table showing GSP, personal income, retail sales, CPI, unemployment rate, wage/salary employment, population, and residential building permits, 1984-85.

ARIZONA CONSTRUCTION REPORT, ANNUAL FEATURE

(p. 8-15) Annual compilation of features on Arizona construction activity and housing financing in 1984. Data are from Arizona Real Estate Institute and Arizona State University. Includes 4 tables showing the following:

a. Construction activity: annual data for quarterly tables [5-7], 1984, with selected comparisons to 1983.

b. Expectations of Maricopa County homebuilders, financial services, real estate brokers, and other groups, for conventional and FHA mortgage, prime and commercial interest, inflation, Treasury bill, Phoenix unemployment, and apartment vacancy rates, 1985.

U0280–1.605: May 1985 (Vol. 32, No. 3)

QUARTERLY TABLES

[1-3] CPI, for 1st quarter 1985. (p. 9)

ARIZONA'S "FOUR Cs" DECLINE

(p. 1, 4-5) Article, with 1 chart showing distribution of Arizona personal income, by industry division, 1929 and 1983. Data are from Bureau of Business and Economic Research.

MORE LARGE HOMES SOLD DURING '84

(p. 8) Article, with 1 chart showing metro Phoenix median housing sales price per square foot by presence of selected features, including garage, carport, air conditioning, patio, and swimming pool, 1984. Data are from Bureau of Business and Economic Research.

U0280–1.606: June 1985 (Vol. 32, No. 4)

QUARTERLY TABLES

[4] Economic growth, for 4th quarter 1984. (p. 3)

[8] Metro Phoenix home sales, for 1st quarter 1985. (p. 6)

ASTRONOMY ADDS $84 MILLION TO ARIZONA ECONOMY

(p. 1-3) Article on economic impact of astronomical facilities in Arizona. Data are from Arizona State University. Includes 1 table showing number of astronomical agencies, employment, observatory and visiting scientist expenditures, value of physical plant and planned projects, and tourists, FY83.

Also includes tabular list of major Arizona observatories and their locations.

GSP GROWTH SETS RECORD IN '84

(p. 1, 3-5) Article, with 1 table showing annual data for quarterly table [4] on Arizona GSP, 1980-84; and also including 1 chart showing GSP distribution by industry division, 1984.

U0280–1.607: July 1985 (Vol. 32, No. 5)

QUARTERLY TABLES

[5] Key sector construction activity, for 1st quarter 1985. (p. 10)

[6] Building permits, for 1st quarter 1985. (p. 12)

[7] New housing starts, for 1st quarter 1985. (p. 13)

MIGRATION PATTERNS NET ARIZONA MORE RESIDENTS

(p. 1-5) Article, with 1 chart and 3 tables on population migration patterns in Arizona and 11 other western States, including Arizona detail by county and age group, 1975-80 period. Data are from 1980 Census and Arizona State University.

ECONOMY TO CONTINUE ON ROLLER COASTER, QUARTERLY FEATURE

(p. 1, 5-8) Quarterly article examining Arizona and Maricopa County economic outlook through 1986. Includes 1 table showing GSP, personal income, retail sales, CPI, unemployment rate, wage/salary employment, population, and residential building permits, 1984-86.

COUNCIL OF 100 ECONOMIC OUTLOOK

(p. 9) Article, with 2 tables showing Arizona business executives' expectations for selected national economic indicators, and for business conditions nationally and in their own organizations, various periods 1985-86. Data are from a semiannual survey of the Arizona State University College of Business Dean's Council of 100.

U0280–1.608: Aug. 1985 (Vol. 32, No. 6)

QUARTERLY TABLES

[1-3] CPI, for 2nd quarter 1985. (p. 5-6)

ECONOMIC FORECASTS: VALUABLE DESPITE LARGE ERRORS

(p. 1-5) Article, with 3 tables primarily showing accuracy of GNP forecasts based on Index of Leading Economic Indicators, with comparison to *Blue Chip Economic Indicators* forecasts, 1970s-85. Most data are from Bureau of Business and Economic Research, Arizona State University.

INDUSTRY CHARACTERISTICS, ECONOMIC IMPACT REVEALED

(p. 6-8) Article, with 1 chart showing distribution of Arizona manufacturing employment by major industry group, 1982. Data are from 1982 Census of Manufactures.

ARIZONA LEADING INDEX REVISED; STILL SIGNALS INCONSISTENT GROWTH

(p. 8-11) Article, with 1 chart and 1 table showing trends in Arizona Index of Leading Economic Indicators, including average contributions by each index component during Jan. 1984-May 1985 period, and overall performance during 1977-79 and 1983-85 periods.

Corrected data appear in the Sept. 1985 issue. For description, see U0280-1.609 below.

U0280–1.609: Sept. 1985 (Vol. 32, No. 7)

QUARTERLY TABLES

[4] Economic growth, for 1st quarter 1985. (p. 4)

[8] Metro Phoenix home sales, for 2nd quarter 1985. (p. 5)

NEW INDEXES REVEAL HIGHER HOME AFFORDABILITY IN '85

(p. 1-4) Article, with 2 tables showing affordability index for new and resale homes in Phoenix metro area, annually 1981-84 and quarterly 1984-2nd quarter 1985. Tables also include index components (median sales price, interest rate, loan amount, monthly payment, and gross income).

Data are from Arizona State University, FHLBB, and *Sales and Marketing Management.*

CORRECTION

(p. 7) Data correction for article on Arizona index of leading economic indicators, appearing in Aug. 1985 issue; for description, see U0280-1.608 above.

U0280–1.610: Oct. 1985 (Vol. 32, No. 8)

QUARTERLY TABLES

[5] Key sector construction activity, for 2nd quarter 1985. (p. 10)

[6] Building permits, for 2nd quarter 1985. (p. 12)

[7] New housing starts, for 2nd quarter 1985 [table title varies]. (p. 11)

Quarterly tables are accompanied by special table (p. 13) showing selected cities and counties ranked by total value of building permits, 2nd quarter 1985.

ARIZONA VOTERS TO DECIDE REVENUE/IMPROVEMENT LEVEL

(p. 1-6) Article, with 1 undated table showing estimated development costs for 8 Arizona highways with highest development priority. Data are from State Transportation Dept.

1985-86 ARIZONA FORECAST, QUARTERLY FEATURE

(p. 6-9) Quarterly article examining Arizona and Maricopa County economic outlook through 1986. Includes 2 tables showing GSP, personal income, retail sales, CPI, unemployment rate, wage/salary employment, population, and residential building permits, 1984-86.

U1075
Clemson University: South Carolina Agricultural Experiment Station

U1075-1   SOUTH CAROLINA LIVESTOCK AND POULTRY STATISTICS, Inventory Numbers, 1980-85; and Production and Value of Livestock and Poultry Products, 1979-84
Annual.   July 1985.   3+27 p.
Rpt. No. AE437.
LC 81-640886.
SRI/MF/complete

Annual report on South Carolina livestock and poultry inventories, value, and disposition; and production, value, and sometimes prices, for dairy and poultry products; mostly 1979-84, with some data for 1985 and selected trends from 1867. Data are generally shown by species or commodity, and by district and/or county, with some comparisons to total U.S.

Also includes data on farms and acreage, 1978-84, with 1984 detail by county.

Data are compiled by the South Carolina Crop and Livestock Reporting Service in cooperation with Clemson University and USDA.

Contains contents listing (1 p.); and report, with narrative review, and 34 tables (p. 1-26, and inside back cover).

Availability: South Carolina Crop and Livestock Reporting Service, PO Box 1911, Columbia SC 29202, †; SRI/MF/complete.

U1075-2   SOUTH CAROLINA CROP STATISTICS, 1980-84
Annual.   June 1985.   3+70 p.
Rpt. No. AE436.
LC 81-640880.
SRI/MF/complete

Annual report on South Carolina agricultural acreage, yield, production, value, and selected prices, for field crops, vegetables, and fruit, by commodity and county, 1980-84.

Also includes number and acreage of farms, 1978-84; grain stocks on and off farms, 1979-84; and fertilizer consumption, by county, FY84.

Data are compiled by South Carolina Crop and Livestock Reporting Service.

Contains table of contents (1 p.); narrative summary (p. 1-5); and 10 maps and 73 tables (p. 6-70).

Availability: South Carolina Crop and Livestock Reporting Service, PO Box 1911, Columbia SC 29202, †; SRI/MF/complete.

U1120
College of William and Mary: Bureau of Business Research

U1120-1   VIRGINIA BUSINESS REPORT
Monthly.   4 p.
LC sc77-177.
SRI/MF/complete, shipped quarterly

Monthly report (11 issues per year) on Virginia business and economic conditions. Report is issued 1 month after month of coverage.

Presents all or most of the following indexes (base period=1977) for the State and each of 17 cities or MSAs: bank debits, building permits, electricity and water consumption, newspaper advertising linage, new auto registrations, nonagricultural employment, retail sales, and postal receipts. Also includes a composite index for each city and MSA.

Most indexes are shown for month of coverage, with percent change from same month and same year-to-date period of previous year. Occasionally comparisons to other previous periods are also included.

Issues generally contain narrative summary; feature article, occasionally with statistics; summary charts; and 2-5 tables.

Monthly index data appear in all issues. All additional features with substantial statistical content are described, as they appear, under "Statistical Features." Nonstatistical features are not covered.

Availability: College of William and Mary: Bureau of Business Research, School of Business Administration, Williamsburg VA 23185, †; SRI/MF/complete, shipped quarterly.

Issues reviewed during 1985: Oct. 1984-Aug. 1985 (D) (Nos. 294-303) [No Nov. 1984 issue was published].

STATISTICAL FEATURES:

U1120-1.601: Jan. 1985 (No. 296)
EMPLOYMENT GROWTH IN VIRGINIA SMSAs, ANNUAL FEATURE

(2 p.) Annual article, with 2 tables showing Virginia nonagricultural employment by industry division, statewide and for 10 SMSAs, 1984 with percent change from 1983. Data are from State Employment Commission and Bureau of Business Research.

U1120-1.602: Feb. 1985 (No. 297)
VIRGINIA IN 1985 AND 1986

(2 p.) Article, with 2 tables showing Virginia manufacturing and nonmanufacturing employment, and total personal income, 1983-86. Data are from State Employment Commission and from Mar. 1985 estimates of the Bureau of Business Research.

U1120-1.603: June 1985 (No. 301)
STATE AND URBAN AREA PERSONAL INCOME, 1980-83

(2 p.) Article, with 1 table showing Virginia per capita personal income, by MSA and labor market area, 1980 and 1983, with comparison to U.S. Data are from U.S. Dept of Commerce.

U1120-1.604: Aug. 1985 (No. 303)
FUTURE FEDERAL DEFICITS—HOW LARGE?

(2 p.) Article, with 1 table showing GNP and Federal budget deficit under optimistic and pessimistic economic assumptions, 1985-90 or 1986-90. Data are from Congressional Budget Office.

U1245
Columbia University: Center for International Business Cycle Research

U1245-1   INTERNATIONAL ECONOMIC INDICATORS
Monthly.   Approx. 70 p.
SRI/MF/complete, delayed

Monthly report presenting detailed economic time series data for U.S., Canada, UK, West Germany, France, Italy, Japan, Australia, and Taiwan. Presents 11-18 individual leading and coincident indicators for each country, and multicountry composite leading and coincident indicators aggregated for all countries, North America, 4 European and 3 Pacific countries, and all countries excluding U.S. Data for Taiwan and aggregate data for North America and 3 Pacific countries begin with the Jan. 1985 issue.

Data are shown by month, generally for current year to date and 3 previous years, with summary trends from the 1970s. Most data are current to 2-3 months prior to cover date.

June and Dec. issues also include appendices showing economic growth cycle trends for 8-14 countries, including dates of peaks and troughs since 1948, and median lead or lag of selected economic indicators at peaks and troughs.

Data are prepared by Columbia University Center for International Business Cycle Research.

Contains contents listing; notes on changes for current issue; and 3 statistical sections, with 2 summary tables, 35-38 charts, and detailed tabulations of country and composite indicators. June and Dec. appendices include growth cycle analysis with 4 tables, and user instructions.

Historical data for the indicators covered in this report are available from the issuing agency.

Availability: Center for International Business Cycle Research, Graduate School of Business, 323 Uris Hall, Columbia University, New York NY 10027, university or public libraries $250.00 per yr., corporations $450.00 per yr.; SRI/MF/complete, delayed shipment 4 months from cover date.

Issues reviewed during 1985: Nov. 1984-Oct. 1985 (P) (Vol. 7, Nos. 11-12; Vol. 8, Nos. 1-10).

U1245-2   RECESSION-RECOVERY WATCH
Bimonthly, with annual supplement.   Approx. 25 p.
SRI/MF/complete

Bimonthly report analyzing U.S. business cycles as measured by changes in approximately 60 economic indicators. Data are primarily from Columbia University Center for International Business Cycle Research, and are generally current to 1-3 months preceding cover date.

Contains narrative analysis, with 1 or more summary tables and/or charts; list of indicator charts and user instructions; and 3 detailed tables, with accompanying illustrative indicator charts, showing indicator levels and change from preceding business cycle peak or trough, for current cycle as of most recent month or quarter available, and for 7-8 comparable recessionary or expansionary periods, 1940s-82. Indicators are as follows:

a. Composite leading, coincident, and lagging indexes, including employment index and 6-8 country leading index.

b. Output, income, and sales, including real GNP, personal income, consumer expenditures, and retail sales; and industrial production index.

c. Employment and unemployment, including employment diffusion index, nonfarm employee hours, part-time employment ratio, manufacturing average workweek and overtime hours, layoff rate, and unemployment insurance initial claims.

d. Investment and inventory, including housing starts and permits, contracts/orders for plant/equipment, inventory/sales ratio, and capital appropriations.

e. Productivity and profitability, including output per hour, hourly compensation, unit labor costs, selling price index, price/labor cost ratio, corporate profit margin, business failures, industrial materials price index, CPI, and leading index of inflation.

f. Financial, including money supply; total, business/consumer, and Federal debt; and Treasury bill rate, corporate bond yield, and stock price index.

An annual supplement, presenting detailed trend data for the indicators covered in this report, has also been received, and is also available on SRI microfiche under U1245-2. [Annual. [1985.] 3+93 p. $100.00]. Supplement is not included in the bimonthly report subscription, and must be ordered separately.

Availability: Center for International Business Cycle Research, Graduate School of Business, 323 Uris Hall, Columbia University, New York NY 10027, $75.00 per yr., annual supplement $100.00 additional; SRI/MF/complete.

Issues reviewed during 1985: Dec. 1984-Oct. 1985 (P) (Vol. 6, No. 6; Vol. 7, Nos. 1-5) [Vol. 7, No. 2 incorrectly reads No. 1]; and annual supplement for 1985.

U1380
Cornell University: New York State College of Agriculture and Life Sciences

U1380–1 **OPERATING RESULTS OF SELF-SERVICE DISCOUNT DEPARTMENT STORES and the Mass Retailers' Merchandising Report, 1983-84**
Annual. Sept. 1984.
xii+162 p.
ISSN 0474-2656.
LC 77-640100.
SRI/MF/complete

Annual report, by Gene A. German and Gerard F. Hawkes, providing detailed data on sales, expenses, earnings, and operating ratios of self-service discount department stores, by sales size category. Also includes "Mass Retailers' Merchandising Report" showing operating data by sales department. Data are shown for FY84, with selected trends from FY79.

Data are based on survey responses of 30 firms operating 2,892 stores with aggregate sales of $17.0 billion, and are shown separately for all firms and for 23 "identical" firms with 2 or more years of consecutive responses to the annual survey.

Report is sponsored by the National Mass Retailing Institute, and is intended to permit individual stores to compare their performance with industry averages.

Contents:

Foreword and contents listing. (p. ii-viii)

Section 1, Highlights. (p. ix-xii)

Section 1, Part I. Six-year trends for all firms and identical firms. Includes 30 charts and 30 tables showing trends in 30 financial and operating indicators, including average sales per store and square foot, average sales and occupancy cost per selling area, and cumulative markup and stockturns for owned depts, mostly FY79-84. (p. 1-30)

Section 1, Part II-III. Identical and all firm analysis. Includes 1 highlights table, and 4 detailed tables listed below, repeated for identical firms (p. 32-77) and all firms (p. 79-130).

Section 2, Part I-II. Mass Retailers' Merchandising Report. Includes 7 tables showing FY83-84 averages and FY84 middle range for net sales by payment type, and for the following by dept: sales as percent of store total, stockturns, markup as percent of original retail, stock shortage and markdown as percent of owned dept sales, and gross margin as percent of owned dept sales; repeated for identical firms (p. 135-141) and all firms (p. 145-151).

Appendix. Includes survey methodology and questionnaire facsimiles. (p. 154-162)

This is the 20th annual report. Subsequent editions will be covered in SRI under A8060-6; for description of 21st edition, see A8060-6 above.

Availability: National Mass Retailing Institute, 570 Seventh Ave., New York NY 10018, members $60.00, nonmembers $75.00, educational institutions $32.00; SRI/MF/complete.

DETAILED TABLES:
[Data include FY83-84 averages and FY84 middle range. All data are shown by sales size; data in tables [1] and [3-4] are also shown by gross margin, expense, and payroll levels.]

[1] Gross margin, expense[s], and earnings [as] percent of sales [including expenses for payroll, advertising, taxes/licenses, utilities, and 13 other items].

[2] Responsibility centers [expenses as percent of sales for 12 expense categories, including advertising/promotion, accounting, data processing, employee benefits, warehousing, and transportation].

[3] Assets [as] percent of total assets [for components of current and other assets and of property/equipment, and for total intangible assets].

[4] Liabilities and net worth [as] percent of total [for components of current liabilities, long-term debt, and net worth].

U1380–3 **OPERATING RESULTS OF FOOD CHAINS, 1983-84**
Annual. Oct. 1984.
iv+103 p.
SRI/MF/complete

Annual report, by Gene A. German et al., on operating performance of food store chains, FY84. Presents data on gross margins, and on expenses, earnings, assets, liabilities, net worth, and other indicators as percent of gross annual sales, for firms by item, sales class, and region, with trends from FY79.

Data are presented for all firms and for firms with 5 or more consecutive years of participation in the report (identical firms), and allow companies to compare their operations with averages of other companies of similar size and region. Data are compiled by Cornell University, from reports of 46 companies operating 5,232 stores in the U.S. and Canada.

Contains foreword and contents listing (p. ii-iv); introduction with 3 summary tables (p. 3-4); 3 sections, with 20 charts and 31 tables (p. 6-93); and appendix, with methodology, definitions, and questionnaire facsimile (p. 94-103).

Availability: Cornell University: New York State College of Agriculture and Life Sciences, Department of Agricultural Economics, 205 Warren Hall, Ithaca NY 14853, $35.00; SRI/MF/complete.

U1380–4 **AGRICULTURAL FINANCE REVIEW, 1983**
Annual. 1983. 60 p.
Vol. 43.
ISSN 0002-1466.
SRI/MF/complete

Annual compilation, for 1983, of research articles on agricultural finance. Articles analyze results of surveys and/or model simulations pertaining to agricultural credit and investment, farm financial condition and taxation, and related topics.

Contains 6 articles. Articles presenting original survey findings or other substantial nontechnical statistics are described below. Articles presenting only technical, theoretical, or localized statistics are not described.

This is the 43rd volume of the report. SRI coverage begins with this volume. Previous volumes were published by USDA, and were covered by *American Statistics Index,* a companion Congressional Information Service index to Federal statistical publications.

For description of Volume 42, see ASI 1982 Annual under 1544-1. For description of Volume 44, see U1380-5 below.

Availability: Cornell University: New York State College of Agriculture and Life Sciences, Department of Agricultural Economics, 157 Warren Hall, Ithaca NY 14853, †; SRI/MF/ complete.

U1380-4.1: Statistical Articles

IMPACTS OF RECENT CHANGES IN PERSONAL INCOME AND BUSINESS PROFIT TAXES ON INVESTMENTS IN THE FARMING SECTOR

(p. 1-8) By Dean W. Hughes and Ann Laing Adair. Article examining effect of 1981-82 tax law changes on agricultural investments. Includes 1 table showing econometric analysis results on percent change in general economic and agricultural financial indicators with and without tax law changes, 1982-84.

EVALUATION OF STATE LEGISLATIVE PROGRAMS TO ASSIST BEGINNING FARMERS

(p. 9-20) By James Lowenberg-DeBoer and Michael Boehlje. Article, with 2 tables showing State and Federal costs for programs to assist beginning farmers, by program type (direct loan, guarantee/payment adjustment, farmland lease/purchase, savings subsidy, and tax incentives for sale and lease), based on 1981 conditions in Iowa.

LOAN PRICING AND PROFITABILITY ANALYSIS BY AGRICULTURAL BANKS

(p. 21-29) By Peter J. Barry and Jeffrey D. Calvert. Article reporting survey results on farm loan policies of agricultural banks. Data are from responses of 451 banks to a 1981 survey conducted by the authors.

Includes 4 undated tables showing survey response on methods for determining farm loan base interest rates, for pricing loans, and for evaluating loan profitability; farm loan interest rates compared to rates for other types of loans; and competition from other lenders; with selected detail by bank size, structure, and ratio of farm loans to total loans.

COOPERATIVE EQUITY REDEMPTION PLANS AND FINANCIAL STRENGTH: NEW EMPIRICAL EVIDENCE

(p. 41-49) By Mark D. Newman. Article examining equity redemption policies of farm cooperatives, and associated financial performance. Data are from a 1981 survey of 241 grain marketing and supply cooperatives in Kansas, conducted by the author.

Includes 1 table showing Kansas cooperatives' assets, sales, members, annual cash patronage dividends, and selected financial ratios, by type of equity retirement policy, 1980/81.

INFLUENCE OF THE FARM CREDIT SYSTEM STOCK REQUIREMENT ON ACTUAL INTEREST RATES

(p. 50-60) By Eddy L. LaDue. Article on stock purchase plans used by Farm Credit System in making farm loans, and effects of stock requirement on interest rates paid by farmers. Data are based in part on information from 7 Federal intermediate credit banks, covering 198 Farm Credit System product credit assns (PCAs).

Includes 7 undated tables showing distribution of PCAs by stock requirement percentage for farm loans; and annual equivalent interest rates for selected stock requirement percentages, under 2 types of PCA stock cancellation plans, and for production loans when stock is not retired.

U1380-5 AGRICULTURAL FINANCE REVIEW, 1984

Annual. 1984. 72 p.
Vol. 44.
ISSN 0002-1466.
SRI/MF/complete

Annual compilation, for 1984, of research articles on agricultural finance. Articles analyze results of surveys and/or model simulations pertaining to agricultural credit and investment, farm financial condition and taxation, and related topics.

Contains 9 articles. Articles presenting original survey findings or other substantial nontechnical statistics are described below. Articles presenting only technical, theoretical, or localized statistics are not described.

This is the 44th volume of the report. For description of the 43rd volume, see U1380-4 above.

Availability: Cornell University: New York State College of Agriculture and Life Sciences, Department of Agricultural Economics, 157 Warren Hall, Ithaca NY 14853, †; SRI/MF/ complete.

U1380-5.1: Statistical Articles

CURRENT FINANCIAL STRESS AMONG FARMERS IN SOUTH GEORGIA

(p. 1-7) By Wesley N. Musser et al. Article examining financial condition of farmers in south Georgia. Most data are from responses of 192 Georgia peanut producers to a spring/ summer 1982 survey, conducted by the authors.

Includes 3 tables showing debt-asset ratios for farmers in various land tenure and peanut allotment tenure categories; growth rates for selected commodity prices and production expenses, 1974-82 period; and statistical simulation results analyzing impact of farm expansion on financial condition.

IMPACT OF RECENT TAX LEGISLATION AND INFLATION ON THE TAXATION OF FARM CAPITAL

(p. 36-42) By Ron L. Durst and Ronald A. Jeremias. Article examining effect of 1981-82 tax law changes on incentives for investment in farm capital. Includes 3 tables showing taxable income, marginal tax rates, and estimated effective income tax rates for farm capital by asset type, 1980-84; and effective tax rates under alternative capital cost recovery systems, 1980; all for low- and high-income investors.

BANKS AND FARM CREDIT AS AGRICULTURAL LENDERS IN INDIANA

(p. 43-48) By David A. Sherman and Lee F. Schrader. Article comparing farm loan activity and financial performance of Farm Credit System vs. commercial banks in Indiana. Data are from responses of 80 commercial banks, 10 production credit assns, and 23 Federal land bank assns to a 1981 survey, conducted by the authors.

Includes 4 tables showing number of farm borrowers, average loan size, interest rates, and other loan characteristics; trend in use of various loan terms; selected financial ratios; and percent of borrowers who paid debt easily, paid with difficulty, and did not pay (by whether still farming); all by type of lender, primarily for spring 1980-summer 1981 period.

EQUITY LEVELS NECESSARY FOR SUCCESSFUL ENTRY INTO DAIRY PRODUCTION

(p. 49-57) By William Grisley and Matthew C. Grady. Article, with 1 table presenting statistical simulation results on initial equity financing required for new dairy farmers to achieve financial solvency within 5 years. Table includes beginning and ending equity for various combinations of farm structure, financing source, milk production levels, and cow rental rates.

U1880
Georgia State University:
Economic Forecasting Center

U1880-1 GEORGIA STATE UNIVERSITY FORECAST: The Nation

Quarterly. Approx. 15 p. var. paging.
SRI/MF/complete

Quarterly report presenting 8-quarter forecasts of U.S. expenditures, income components of the GNP, derivation of personal income, Federal Government activity, export/import balance, and approximately 30 other indicators of the U.S. economy.

Data are from Economic Forecasting Project econometric model, and are current to quarter preceding publication date.

Contains narrative analysis, forecast assumptions, and brief summary; and 9 quarterly tables, listed below.

Availability: Georgia State University: Economic Forecasting Project, University Plaza, Atlanta GA 30303-3083, $100.00 per yr.; SRI/MF/complete.

Issues reviewed during 1985: Nov. 15, 1984-Aug. 1985 (P).

TABLES:

[Data are shown quarterly for 10 quarters beginning 2 quarters prior to cover date, and annually for 3-4 years, unless otherwise noted.]

1-2. Expenditures and real expenditures [by component].

3. Income related GNP components [including employee compensation by industry sector, proprietors' and rental income, and national income].

4. Derivation of personal income [including government transfer payments by type, disposable personal income, and personal savings rate].

5. Federal Government activity [including receipts and expenditures by line item, and Federal debt held by individuals].

6. Selected economic variables of the economy [approximately 30 indicators, including percent change in wages and productivity; and CPI, PPI, corporate profits, checkable deposits, money supply, prime rate, Treasury bill

and Aaa corporate bond interest rates, FHA mortgage rates, housing starts, auto sales, and industrial production index].

7. Foreign trade accounts [exports and imports of merchandise by type, and balance of payments; annually only].

8. Implicit price deflators for personal consumption expenditures [by component].

9. Implicit price deflators with annual percentage changes [in approximately 15 indicators, including personal consumption, private domestic investment, foreign trade, and Federal and State/local government purchases and value added].

U1880-2   GEORGIA STATE UNIVERSITY FORECAST: Georgia and Atlanta
Quarterly. Approx. 15 p. var. paging.
SRI/MF/complete

Quarterly report presenting 2-year forecasts of employment and personal income levels in Georgia and the Atlanta MSA. Data are from Economic Forecasting Project econometric model, and are current to quarter preceding publication date.

Contains narrative analysis and summary; and statistical section, with 6 quarterly tables, listed below.

Feb. and Aug. issues include 2 additional tables showing 5-year employment and income forecasts for Georgia (Feb.) and Atlanta (Aug.).

Availability: Georgia State University: Economic Forecasting Project, University Plaza, Atlanta GA 30303-3083, $50.00 per yr.; SRI/MF/complete.

Issues reviewed during 1985: Nov. 15, 1984-Aug., 1985 (P).

QUARTERLY TABLES:
[Tables 1-4 and 6 present data for current, 1-2 previous, and 1-2 future years, revised each quarter. Income data are shown by industry division and source; employment data are shown by industry division and major manufacturing industry group.]

1-2. Georgia wage/salary employment, and personal income.

3-4. [Tables 1-2 are repeated for Atlanta MSA.]

5. Seasonally adjusted nonagricultural employment [for Georgia and Atlanta MSA, quarterly for 4-5 quarters ending quarter preceding publication, and for final month of most recent quarter].

6. Metro Atlanta [single- and multi-unit] housing permits [by county].

U1880-3   GSU ECONOMIC FORECASTING PROJECT NEWSLETTER: Monthly Projections
Monthly. Approx. 15 p. var. paging.
SRI/MF/complete, shipped quarterly

Monthly report presenting forecasts of economic indicators in the consumer, industrial, construction, and financial sectors, for approximately 18 months. Data are from Economic Forecasting Project econometric model, and are revised each month. Report is issued approximately 2 months after each forecast revision.

Contains narrative analysis, usually with 1 table showing quarterly deflators for real, price, and nominal GNP; and 9 monthly indicator tables, described below.

Availability: Georgia State University: Economic Forecasting Project, University Plaza, Atlanta GA 30303-3083, $75.00 per yr.; SRI/MF/complete, shipped quarterly.

Issues reviewed during 1985: Oct. 1984-Sept. 1985 (D).

INDICATOR TABLES:
[Data usually are shown for approximately 18 consecutive months beginning 5-7 months prior to month of current forecast revision, and include comparison to previous month's forecast. Table order may vary slightly from issue to issue.]

a. Employment, and personal income: including payroll and household employment, unemployment rate, indexes of hours worked and hourly earnings; and wage/salary income, disposable income, and personal savings and expenditures. 2 tables.

b. Consumption, and retail sales: including consumption and/or sales of durables, non-auto durables, autos, nondurables, and services; total real and personal consumption; and total retail sales. 2 tables.

c. Construction, and business activity: including housing starts and permits, construction expenditures, and private nonresidential, residential, and public construction; and business inventories, durable and nondefense capital goods orders, defense and nondefense shipments, and industrial production and capacity utilization indexes. 2 tables.

d. Prices, and miscellaneous: including CPI, PPI, merchandise trade balance, index of leading indicators, corporate inventory valuation adjustment (IVA) rate, and estimated GNP. 2 tables.

e. Financial markets: including money supply; and interest rates for Federal funds, 6-month Treasury bills, Aaa corporate and municipal bonds, commercial paper, 90-day certificates of deposit, and prime rate. 1 table.

U2030
Harvard University: Russian Research Center

U2030-1   RRC NEWSLETTER
Monthly. Approx. 5 p.
SRI/MF/complete, shipped quarterly

Monthly report on Soviet Union economy, including industrial production, currency exchange rates, and balance of trade. Data are from published Soviet sources and U.S. Commerce Dept.

Issues typically contain narrative briefs on recent events affecting U.S.-Soviet economic relations, and on upcoming conferences; and 3 monthly tables. Report also includes 2 irregularly recurring tables, 2 quarterly tables, and occasional special tables.

Recurring tables are listed below. Monthly tables appear in all issues. Special tables are described, as they appear, under "Statistical

Features;" page locations and latest periods of coverage for irregularly recurring and quarterly tables are also noted. Nonstatistical features are not covered.

Availability: Harvard University: Russian Research Center, Gary Eynatian, 1737 Cambridge St., Cambridge MA 02138, subscriptions †, single copy ‡; SRI/MF/complete, shipped quarterly.

Issues reviewed during 1985: Nov. 8, 1984-Oct. 8, 1985 (P) (Vol. IX, Nos. 3-12, Vol. X, Nos. 1-2) [Sept. 1985 issue omits date and volume and issue numbers].

RECURRING TABLES:

MONTHLY TABLES

[1] Industrial production figures [for approximately 20 varying products, including electricity, petroleum, natural gas, coal, steel, fertilizer, metal cutting tools, industrial robots, computer technology, tractors, paper, cement, meat, margarine, watches, radios, TV sets, and automobiles; for month 2 months prior to cover date and/or year to date, with comparisons to previous year].

[2] Currency figures [rates of exchange for rubles and 8-9 foreign currencies, including U.S. dollar; for month prior to cover date, previous 1-2 months, and same month of previous year].

[A] Livestock herds [inventories for cattle, cows, hogs, sheep/goats, and chickens, for month prior to cover date, with comparisons to previous year; table begins with the June 5, 1985 issue].

IRREGULARLY RECURRING TABLES

[Data are current to approximately 4 months prior to cover date, and are shown for year to date, same period of previous year, and 3-5 previous full years.]

[3] [Value of U.S. exports to and imports from Soviet Union, by principal commodity group and detailed commodity.]

[4] [Value of U.S. exports to and imports from Eastern Europe, by principal commodity group, occasionally with detail by country.]

QUARTERLY TABLES

[5] Balance of trade [value of exports from and imports to Soviet Union, for U.S. and approximately 20 other non-Communist countries, for year to date through quarter ending 3-6 months prior to cover date, and same period of several previous years].

[6] Soviet balance of trade with Eastern Europe [value of exports from and imports to Soviet Union, for 6 countries, usually for year to date through quarter ending 3-6 months prior to cover date, and same period of previous 1-4 years].

STATISTICAL FEATURES:

U2030-1.601: Nov. 8, 1984 (Vol. IX, No. 3)

QUARTERLY TABLE

[5] Balance of trade [Soviet Union with U.S. and 19 other non-Communist countries], 1st half 1984. (p. 4)

U2030-1.602: Dec. 6, 1984 (Vol. IX, No. 4)

QUARTERLY TABLE

[6] Soviet balance of trade with Eastern Europe, 1st half 1984. (p. 5)

U2030-1.603: Jan. 9, 1985 (Vol. IX, No. 5)

IRREGULARLY RECURRING TABLES

[3-4] [Value of U.S. exports to and imports from USSR and Eastern Europe, by commodity, through Sept. 1984.] (4 p.)

U2030-1.604: Feb. 8, 1985 (Vol. IX, No. 6)

QUARTERLY TABLE

[5] Balance of trade [Soviet Union with U.S. and 19 other non-Communist countries], 1st 9 months 1984. (p. 4)

U2030-1.605: Mar. 4, 1985 (Vol. IX, No. 7)

IRREGULARLY RECURRING TABLES

[3-4] [Value of U.S. exports to and imports from USSR and Eastern Europe, by commodity, through 1984.] (p. 5-8)

QUARTERLY TABLE

[6] Soviet balance of trade with Eastern Europe, 1st 9 months 1984. (p. 4)

U2030-1.606: May 5, 1985 (Vol. IX, No. 9)

QUARTERLY TABLE

[5] Balance of trade [Soviet Union with U.S. and 19 other non-Communist countries], 1984. (p. 3)

U2030-1.607: June 5, 1985 (Vol. IX, No. 10)

IRREGULARLY RECURRING TABLE

[3] [Value of U.S. exports to and imports from USSR, by commodity, through Mar. 1985.] (p. 3-5)

U2030-1.608: July 3, 1985 (Vol. IX, No. 11)

IRREGULARLY RECURRING TABLE

[4] [Value of U.S. exports to and imports from Eastern Europe, by commodity, through Jan.-Mar. 1985.] (p. 6-7)

QUARTERLY TABLE

[6] Soviet balance of trade with Eastern Europe, full year 1984. (p. 3)

U2030-1.609: Aug. 9, 1985 (Vol. IX, No. 11)

QUARTERLY TABLE

[5] Balance of trade [Soviet Union with U.S. and 19 other non-Communist countries], 1st quarter 1985. (p. 4)

U2030-1.610: Sept. 1985 (Vol. X, No. 1)

[Issue omits date and volume and issue numbers.]

IRREGULARLY RECURRING TABLE

[4] [Value of U.S. exports to and imports from Eastern Europe, by commodity, through Jan.-June 1985.] (p. 5-8)

QUARTERLY TABLE

[6] Soviet balance of trade with Eastern Europe, 1st quarter 1985. (p. 4)

U2030-1.611: Oct. 8, 1985 (Vol. X, No. 2)

IRREGULARLY RECURRING TABLE

[3] [Value of U.S. exports to and imports from USSR, by commodity, through June 1985.] (p. 5-7)

QUARTERLY TABLE

[5] Balance of trade [Soviet Union with U.S. and 19 other non-Communist countries], 1st half 1985. (p. 4)

U2160
Indiana University:
Graduate School of Business

U2160-1   INDIANA BUSINESS REVIEW

Bimonthly.   Approx. 20 p.
ISSN 0019-6541.
LC sf83-1130.
SRI/MF/complete

Bimonthly report on Indiana business activities and economic trends. Data are generally from Federal and State agencies.

Issues generally contain feature articles, occasionally statistical, on a specific aspect of the Indiana economy; and 3 recurring tables. Report also includes a semiannual business conditions review and outlook analysis.

Recurring tables are listed below, and appear on a space available basis. All additional features with substantial statistical content are described, as they appear, under "Statistical Features;" page locations and latest periods of coverage for recurring tables are also noted. Nonstatistical features are not covered.

Availability: Indiana University: Graduate School of Business, Division of Research, 10th and Fee Lane, Bloomington IN 47405, Indiana residents †, others ‡; SRI/MF/complete.

Issues reviewed during 1985: July/Aug. 1984-May/June 1985 (P) (Vol. 59-60).

RECURRING TABLES:

[Data are shown for latest available month and selected prior periods. Most data are seasonally adjusted. Table content may vary.]

[1] Indiana industrial electricity sales [by city].

[2] U.S. and Indiana business indicators [including indexes of employment and construction activity; weekly hours and earnings in manufacturing; unemployment rate; production indexes for bituminous coal, industrial electricity, manufacturing, and raw steel; personal income; and auto sales and registrations].

[3] U.S. and Indiana man-hours in industrial production [by manufacturing group].

STATISTICAL FEATURES:

U2160-1.601: July/Aug. 1984 (Vol. 59)

INDIANA EMPLOYMENT GROWTH, 1960-81: AN EXAMINATION OF THE INDUSTRIAL MIX HYPOTHESIS

(p. 2-9) By William M. Ritteman. Article, with 5 tables showing Indiana and U.S. employment, and Indiana indexes and adjusted data relative to U.S. employment experience, for each recessionary and expansion period, Apr. 1960-July 1981.

INPUT-OUTPUT ANALYSIS FOR THE INDIANA ECONOMY

(p. 10-16) By Thomas W. Hertel and Lance McKinzie. Article examining theoretical effect on Indiana economy of additional in-State in-

---

dustrial processing of goods produced in Indiana, based on input-output analysis of data from the authors' research.

Includes 6 tables showing Indiana production value and amount shipped out of State, wages, number of jobs, and sales multipliers, with production comparisons to U.S., 1977; industrial input requirements for production in selected metals sectors, 1977; and employment multipliers, and estimated effect of additional processing on wages and jobs (no date); for various industries.

U2160-1.602: Sept./Oct. 1984 (Vol. 59)

TENTATIVE HOUSEHOLD PROJECTIONS FOR INDIANA COUNTIES

(p. 2-5) By Morton J. Marcus and John C. S. Lim. Article, with 3 tables showing Indiana population change, selected periods 1880-2000; occupied households, total population, and population age 20/older, decennially 1960-2000; and households by county, decennially 1980-2000.

U2160-1.603: Nov./Dec. 1984 (Vol. 59)

RECURRING TABLES

(p. 18-20) Most data are current to Sept. 1984. Data on business indicators and industrial man-hours are shown for U.S. only.

For data descriptions, see U2160-1 above.

FORECAST OF THE ECONOMY, SEMIANNUAL FEATURE

Semiannual economic review and forecast issue, presenting analyses for U.S., Indiana, and 11 Indiana urban areas. Data are generally from State agency and university research center reports. Includes the following analyses with statistics:

ANOTHER GOOD YEAR: A LOOK AHEAD FOR INDIANA

(p. 3-4) By Richard L. Pfister. Includes 3 tables showing personal income and establishment employment, 1976-85; and change in personal income, real wages/salaries, and employment by major sector, for economic recovery periods 1975-76 and 1983-84.

SOUTH BEND AND ELKHART

(p. 7-8) By John E. Peck. Includes 2 tables showing unemployment rate; residential real estate active listings, and average days listed and prices for closed sales; and indexes of employment by major sector, help-wanted advertising, industrial electricity and commercial and industrial gas sales, new car and truck sales, and housing permit volume and value; for Elkhart and/or South Bend, Aug. 1983 and July-Aug. 1984.

GARY-HAMMOND-EAST CHICAGO (CALUMET AREA)

(p. 10-11) By Leslie P. Singer. Includes 2 tables showing Calumet area unemployment rate; employment by major sector; personal income; payroll for export, steel, and private sectors; and business activity index; various periods 1973-85.

LAFAYETTE

(p. 11-12) By William C. Dunkelberg et al. Includes 6 undated tables presenting data on Lafayette area business trends and outlook, including expected changes in employment, real sales, and capital outlays; recent changes in sales and profits; and business problems perceived as most important. Data are from 59 responses to a Chamber of Commerce membership survey conducted by the authors.

Also includes 1 table showing Lafayette area employment by industry division, and total payroll, various periods 1979-Sept. 1984.

EVANSVILLE

(p. 13-14) By Maurice Tsai. Includes 1 table showing Evansville area business index for industrial production, 4 industry divisions, and employment, monthly Jan.-Sept. 1984, and annually 1981-85.

JEFFERSONVILLE-NEW ALBANY (LOUISVILLE AREA)

(p. 14-16) By Fay Ross Greckel. Includes 2 tables showing unemployment rate, and manufacturing and nonmanufacturing employment, for Louisville, Kentucky metro area (total and Indiana portion); and residential building permits issued, for Jefferson County, Ky. and Clark and Floyd Counties, Ind.; various periods 1979-84.

U2160–1.604: Jan./Feb. 1985 (Vol. 60)

INDIANA CHAMBER OF COMMERCE'S POSITION ON ECONOMIC DISPATCH

(p. 8-9) By Lisa Kobe. Article examining costs and benefits of implementing an economic dispatch system in Indiana, in which electric utilities would form a cooperative energy pool and distribute the lowest-cost energy first. Data are from R. W. Beck and Associates, and Stone and Webster Management Consultants, Inc. Includes 1 table presenting 2 cost/benefit analyses, 1985-94 period.

HOME HEATING FUELS IN INDIANA

(p. 11-12) By John Spellman. Article, with 2 tables showing number of Indiana housing units by type of fuel used for heating, and percent of units using electric and utility gas heat, by county, 1970 and/or 1980. Data are from Census Bureau, and Indiana Information Retrieval System.

U2160–1.605: Mar./Apr. 1985 (Vol. 60)

EXPENDITURES ON HIGHER EDUCATION AND ECONOMIC GROWTH IN MANUFACTURING

(p. 2-7) By Leslie P. Singer and Edith Allen-Schult. Article analyzing theoretical effect of increased higher education expenditures and increased capital investment on selected indicators of economic growth in the manufacturing sector, by U.S. region, 1975-78. Includes 4 tables presenting regression analysis results.

RECESSION AND RECOVERY REVISITED

(p. 14-16) By Morton J. Marcus. Article, with 4 tables showing personal income trends for Indiana, neighboring States, and U.S. regions, with comparisons to total U.S., and Indiana data by income source and industry, various periods 1978-84. Data are from Commerce Dept.

U2160–1.606: May/June 1985 (Vol. 60)

MIDYEAR REVIEW OF THE INDIANA ECONOMY, SEMIANNUAL FEATURE

Semiannual economic review and forecast issue, presenting analyses for U.S., Indiana, and 10 Indiana urban areas. Data are generally from State agency and university research center reports. Includes the following analyses with statistics:

MIDYEAR REVIEW OF THE INDIANA ECONOMY IN 1985

(p. 3-4) By Richard L. Pfister. Includes 1 table showing State personal income, wages/salaries, manufacturing and nonmanufacturing employment, and unemployment rate (seasonally adjusted), Nov. 1984 and June 1985.

INDIANAPOLIS

(p. 4-6) By Robert J. Kirk. Includes 4 tables showing percent employment growth for Indianapolis and 3 metro areas, by selected industry sector, with summary comparisons to U.S., Indiana, and 4 midwestern States; percent population change for Indianapolis, U.S., and 6 metro areas; and absolute and percent employment change for Indianapolis, by service industry sector; various periods 1980-84.

SOUTH BEND AND ELKHART

(p. 6-7) By John E. Peck. Includes 1 table showing unemployment rate; residential real estate active listings, and average days listed and prices for closed sales; and indexes of employment by major sector, help-wanted advertising, industrial electricity and commercial and industrial gas sales, new car and truck sales, and housing permit volume and value; for South Bend and Elkhart, Feb. 1984 and Jan.-Feb. 1985.

ANDERSON-MUNCIE

(p. 11-12) By Robert R. Jost. Includes 2 tables showing Muncie business index and establishment employment annual averages, by selected industry division, 1979-84.

GARY-HAMMOND-EAST CHICAGO (CALUMET AREA)

(p. 13-15) By Leslie P. Singer. Includes 2 tables showing Northwest Indiana employment by major sector, total payroll, and payroll for steel and manufacturing production workers and nonsupervisory employees in nonmanufacturing industries, 1st quarter 1984-2nd quarter 1986.

EVANSVILLE

(p. 16-17) By Maurice Tsai. Includes 1 table showing Evansville area business index, composite and for industrial production, 4 industry divisions, and employment, July 1984-Feb. 1985, and annually, 1981-85.

LAFAYETTE

(p. 17-18) By William C. Dunkelberg. Includes 1 table showing Lafayette employment by selected industry division, May 1984-85.

JEFFERSONVILLE-NEW ALBANY (LOUISVILLE AREA)

(p. 18-20) By Fay Ross Greckel. Includes 2 tables showing unemployment rate and persons unemployed, and manufacturing and nonmanufacturing employment, for Louisville, Ky. metro area (total and Indiana portion); and residential building permits issued for Clark and Floyd Counties, Ind., and Jefferson County, Ky.; various periods 1981-85.

U2420
Iowa State University: North Central Regional Educational Materials Project

U2420–1   U.S. FARMERS' VIEWS ON AGRICULTURAL AND FOOD POLICY: A Seventeen-State Composite Report

Monograph. Dec. 1984.
2+44 p.
North Central Regional Extension Pub. 227.
North Central Regional Research Pub. 300.
LC 85-620885.
SRI/MF/complete

By Harold D. Guither et al. Survey report on farmers' opinions concerning agricultural and food policies of the Federal Government, by selected State, 1984. Also includes selected characteristics of farmers and farm operations.

Data are based on responses of 8,085 farmers to sample surveys conducted in 17 States during Mar.-June 1984. The surveyed States represented approximately 50% of all farms and farm cash receipts in 1982.

The survey project was a joint effort of the North Central Public Policy Education Committee and the North Central Regional Policy Research Project, and was sponsored by Cooperative Extension Services in 12 States, USDA Extension Service, and Agricultural Experiment Stations in 17 States.

Contains contents and table listings (2 p.); introduction and narrative analysis (p. 1-14); 1 table on survey sample (p. 15); 46 tables, described below, presenting survey findings (p. 15-39); and questionnaire facsimile (p. 41-44).

Availability: University of Illinois: Agricultural Experiment Station, Mumford Hall, 1301 W. Gregory Dr., Urbana IL 61801, ‡; SRI/MF/complete.

TABLES:

[Data are shown for individual survey States, grouped by region.]

OPINIONS ON FARM POLICY

a. General farm policy direction after 1985; continuation of target prices/deficiency payments, acreage diversion payments, and farmer-owned grain reserves; future target prices and payment limitations; market price as basis for loan rates; reestablishment of Payment-in-Kind Program; and benefit preference for small farms. 9 tables. (p. 15-19)

b. Soil conservation as requirement for benefits; distribution of soil conservation funds; continuation of milk production cutback incentives (and expected trend in number of milk cows); natural disaster payment policy; Federal crop insurance value, coverage adequacy, and complexity; FmHA credit policy; and locus of farm commodity policy decisions. 12 tables. (p. 20-25)

OPINIONS ON FOOD ASSISTANCE, AGRICULTURAL TRADE, AND FISCAL POLICY

c. Food stamp expenditure level; and whether U.S. should match competitors' export subsidies, encourage lower trade barriers by importers, lower support prices in order to increase exports, establish a marketing board, promote bilateral trade agreements, join an export cartel, increase foreign food aid, strengthen tariff/trade agreement, expand farmer-financed foreign market development program, and set up 2-price plan for domestic vs. export commodities. 11 tables. (p. 26-31)

d. Federal budget issues, including importance of balanced budget and methods of reducing deficit. 5 tables. (p. 31-33)

FARMER AND FARM OPERATION CHARACTERISTICS

e. Participation in specific farm programs during 1983; acreage farmed, and percent of farmed acreage owned; annual gross sales, most important commodity income source in 1983, and share of income from off-farm employment/investments; membership in specific farm and commodity organizations; and age and education. 9 tables. (p. 34-39)

U2480
Iowa State University: World Food Institute

U2480–1 WORLD FOOD TRADE AND U.S. AGRICULTURE, 1960-83
Annual.   Aug. 1984.
vi+81 p.
ISSN 0733-2378.
LC 82-643729.
SRI/MF/complete

Annual report on U.S. and world agricultural production and trade, with selected data by country and commodity, various years 1960/61-1984/85. Includes data on value of U.S. agricultural imports and exports, including Government food assistance programs, by commodity. Most data are from USDA and UN Food and Agriculture Organization.

Contains listings of contents, tables, and charts (p. ii-v); narrative analysis, interspersed with 50 charts and 26 tables (p. 1-65); bibliography and notes (p. 66-69); and 4 appendices, with country economic classifications, 11 trend charts, 2 maps, and 3 tables (p. 70-81).

All tables, and selected charts showing data not included in tables, are described below.

This is the 4th annual report.

Availability: Iowa State University: World Food Institute, 102 E. O. Bldg., Ames IA 50011, †; SRI/MF/complete.

TABLES AND CHARTS:

a. World grain production, utilization, trade, and ending stocks, for wheat, coarse grains, and milled rice; oilseed product production; soybean, wheat, and coarse grain yield and harvested area; cassava, pulses (legumes), pork, poultry, and beef/veal production; and poultry exports; with selected detail by major producing or exporting country and world area, various years 1960/61-1984/85. Tables 1-15. (p. 4-30)

b. USSR: imports of wheat, coarse grain, soybeans, and soybean meal, with percent from U.S.; wheat, and coarse and total grain yield and harvested area; and soybean, cottonseed, and sunflower seed production; various years 1965/66-1984/85. Tables 16-18. (p. 33-34)

c. PRC: wheat, coarse grain, and rice production; grain imports by country or world area of origin; and purchases of U.S. soybeans, and share of total U.S. soybean and soybean oil exports; various periods 1970/71-1984/85. Tables 19-21. (p. 35-36)

d. Outstanding external debt of 13 countries, 1983; and prices for Chicago cash corn and soybeans in dollars and selected foreign currencies, quarterly 1977-2nd quarter 1984. Tables 22-23. (p. 37-38)

e. Concessional (Government-financed) exports as percent of total exports, by commodity, FY77-83; and Commodity Credit Corporation (CCC) program value, by destination and commodity, FY83. Chart 31 and table 24. (p. 41-42)

f. Agricultural trade, including export and import value by commodity, with selected export detail by destination and leading exporting State; corn, wheat, and soybean exports by port area of departure; concessional exports, by commodity and aid category, and CCC programs value; various periods 1972/73-1983/84. Charts 36-39, tables 25-26, and 3 appendix tables. (p. 44-81)

U2505
Johns Hopkins University: Center for Social Organization of Schools

U2505–1 QUALITY OF AMERICAN HIGH SCHOOL GRADUATES: What Personnel Officers Say and Do about It
Monograph.   May 1984.
4+40 p.   Rpt. No. 354.
SRI/MF/complete

By Robert L. Crain. Survey report assessing employers' concerns with the quality of high school education, based on analysis of their hiring practices. Compares factors influencing hiring decisions, and status of positions assigned, for job applicants with high school and college degrees, with detail by race and sex and for graduates of suburban and inner-city high schools. Also includes applicant qualities valued most by employers.

Data are from 1,912 responses to a survey of employers conducted in the summer of 1983.

Contains narrative analysis (p. 1-30); bibliography (p. 31); and 1 chart and 8 tables (p. 32-40).

This is the 1st in a series of reports analyzing findings from the Johns Hopkins University Survey of American Employers.

Availability: Johns Hopkins University: Center for Social Organization of Schools, 3505 N. Charles St., Baltimore MD 21218, $3.00; SRI/MF/complete.

U2520
Johns Hopkins University: Population Information Program

U2520–1 POPULATION REPORTS
Series.   For individual publication data, see below. Cumulative pagination throughout individual series.
ISSN 0275-8792.
LC 82-5055.
SRI/MF/complete

Continuing series of reports on world family planning and fertility trends, covering aspects of health and reproduction, population growth and government policy, fertility research, and contraceptive practices in developing countries.

Most data are from research studies, UN agencies, foreign government reports, World Fertility Surveys, and U.S. Agency for International Development (USAID).

Each report focuses on a selected topic. Reports are presented in 13 subject series; each series is paginated consecutively.

General format:

a. Summary, and discussion of research findings, with illustrative charts, and tables presenting results of selected studies and/or more broad-based statistics.

b. Tabular description of studies, and research bibliography.

Only reports with substantial, broad-based statistics are described in SRI. Reports presenting only clinical data or narrowly focused research results are not covered.

Reports reviewed during 1985 are described below.

Availability: Johns Hopkins University: Population Information Program, Hampton House, 624 N. Broadway, Baltimore MD 21205, health personnel in developing countries †, individual copies for others $0.50 each; SRI/MF/complete.

U2520–1.29: Laws and Policies Affecting Fertility: A Decade of Change
[Monograph. Nov. 1984. p. E105-E151. Vol. XII, No. 6 (Series E, Law and Policy, No. 7). SRI/MF/complete.]

Report on worldwide status of laws, policies, and programs regarding fertility, family planning, and womens rights. Includes 10 tables presenting status summaries for individual developing and developed countries, 1970s-84. Also includes 1 table showing number of countries with and without restrictions on family planning, and with government support of family planning, by selected world region or country grouping, 1983.

U2520–1.30: Impact of Family Planning Programs on Fertility
[Monograph. Jan./Feb. 1985. p. J733-J771. Vol. XIII, No. 1 (Series J, Family Planning Programs, No. 29). SRI/MF/complete.]

Report on the impact of national family planning programs on fertility and birth rates, with focus on developing countries. Data are from World Bank and various specified studies. Includes 10 tables showing the following, primarily for various periods 1951-82:

a. Population, and birth, death, and fertility rates, for 24 developed and developing countries.

b. Birth rate changes and contributing factors, including female population of reproductive age, and marital fertility; birth rates before and during national family planning programs; and number of births averted by planning programs and contraceptive methods provided; for various developing countries, with some detail based on socioeconomic level and strength of family planning effort.

c. India population, birth and infant mortality rates, prevalence of contraceptive use, and female literacy rate, by State; Indonesia fertility rates and percent of married women of reproductive age using any and modern contraception, for 6 Provinces in Java and Bali; and knowledge and use of modern contraception among Thailand married women age 15-44, by urban or rural residence.

U2520–1.31: Minilaparotomy and Laparoscopy: Safe, Effective, and Widely Used

[Monograph. May 1985. C125-C167 Vol. XIII, No. 2 (Series C, Female Sterilization, No. 9). SRI/MF/complete.]

Report on worldwide female sterilization methods, use, reliability, benefits, and risks. Data are from a variety of specified studies conducted 1970s-85, and are shown for various developed and developing countries or world areas.

Includes 7 tables showing incidence of female sterilizations for contraceptive purposes; prevalence of contraceptive use among married women, and reliance on male and female sterilization; pregnancy rates following female sterilization, and pregnancy outcomes following reversals by method; incidence of deaths and selected health complications related to sterilization, by method; and contraceptive preferences among women not currently using any method; various years 1973-85.

U2520–1.32: Contraceptive Social Marketing: Lessons from Experience

[Monograph. July-Aug. 1985. J773-J812. Vol. XIII, No. 3 (Series J, Family Planning Programs, No. 30). SRI/MF/complete.]

Report on the development, management, and finances of contraceptive social marketing (CSM) programs that advertise and sell subsidized contraceptives in developing countries. Most data are from reports of individual CSM programs.

Includes 3 tables showing wholesale and retail prices for 2 contraceptives in Nepal and India; sales, and operating costs by item, for CSM programs in 3 countries; and CSM programs in 8-10 countries ranked by volume of products dispensed, population reached, and operating costs; 1984 or 1985.

Also includes listing of CSM programs by country, including starting dates, products sold and prices, funding sources, distribution methods, and advertising media used.

U2730
Louisiana State University: Center for Energy Studies

U2730–1   LOUISIANA ENERGY INDICATORS
Quarterly.
Approx. 6 p. no paging.
Foldout.
SRI/MF/complete

Quarterly report on Louisiana energy industry trends and developments, including production, consumption, employment, prices, and related State revenues.

Data are compiled from reports of State and Federal agencies, and energy publications. Quarter of data coverage is 2 quarters prior to quarter of publication.

Issues generally contain brief feature article, occasionally with statistics; quarterly historical presentation, with 1 or more tables and/or charts; and 3 quarterly tables accompanied by illustrative charts.

Quarterly tables are listed below and appear in all issues. All other features with substantial statistics are described, as they appear, under "Statistical Features."

Availability: Louisiana State University: Center for Energy Studies, E. Fraternity Circle, Baton Rouge LA 70803-0301, †; SRI/MF/complete.

Issues reviewed during 1985: Winter 1984-Summer 1985 (P).

QUARTERLY TABLES:

[Tables show data monthly for quarter of coverage, quarterly for 3 preceding quarters, annually for 5 previous years, and cumulative year to date for current and previous year. Table format and content may vary from issue to issue. Data covered in "Historical Presentation" feature are often omitted from quarterly tables in that issue.]

[1] Drilling [oil and gas wells completed, dry holes drilled, total and wildcat active rigs, running rigs, and crude oil allowable production, for north and south regions of State, and offshore; and exploratory and developmental drilling permits].

[2] Production, consumption, and employment [oil and gas production for north and south regions of State, and offshore; refinery runs; crude oil stock; electricity production by type of fuel; gasoline consumption in State and total U.S.; electricity consumption by sector; and employment by energy-related SIC 2-digit industry].

[3] Prices and revenues [electricity prices by utility and user sector; interstate and intrastate natural gas prices; wellhead oil prices; retail gasoline prices in New Orleans and total U.S.; energy-related State revenues by source, compared to total State revenues; and GNP, PPI, and CPI].

STATISTICAL FEATURES:

U2730–1.601: Winter 1984
HISTORICAL PRESENTATION: CRUDE OIL, ANNUAL FEATURE

(1 p.) Annual table showing Louisiana oil stocks, and northern, southern, and offshore wells completed and production; and U.S. wellhead oil price; 4th quarter 1978-3rd quarter 1984.

U2730–1.602: Spring 1985
HISTORICAL PRESENTATION: REVENUES, ANNUAL FEATURE

(1 p.) Annual table showing Louisiana State revenues from energy-related sources, including taxes, bonuses, rentals, and royalties, with comparison to total State revenues, quarterly 1979-84.

For description of previous annual table, see SRI 1984 Annual under U2730-1.505.

U2730–1.603: Summer 1985
DRILLING COST CHANGES IN LOUISIANA

(2 p.) By Fred M. Wrighton. Article, with 1 table showing number of wells drilled per active rig in north and south regions of Louisiana, 1979-84.

HISTORICAL PRESENTATION: DRILLING

(1 p.) Table showing Louisiana exploratory and developmental drilling permits issued; and exploratory wells drilled and well completions, for north and south regions of the State and offshore; 2nd quarter 1979-1st quarter 1985.

U2735
Louisiana State University: College of Business Administration

U2735–1   LOUISIANA BUSINESS REVIEW
Quarterly.   Approx. 25 p.
ISSN 0024-6751.
LC 40-35372.
SRI/MF/complete

Quarterly review of Louisiana business and economic developments, presenting articles on recent commercial activity, finance, foreign investments in the State, labor-management relations, projected socioeconomic conditions, and other topics.

Issues generally contain narrative editorial depts and feature articles, some with statistics.

Report has been suspended with the Fall 1984 issue, due to funding restrictions. Statistical feature appearing in the Fall 1984 issue is described below.

Availability: Louisiana State University: College of Business Administration, Division of Research, Baton Rouge LA 70803, †; SRI/MF/complete.

Issues reviewed during 1985: Fall 1984 (P) (Vol. 48, No. 3).

STATISTICAL FEATURE:

U2735–1.601: Fall 1984 (Vol. 48, No. 3)
LOUISIANA'S ECONOMIC PREDICTIONS, ANNUAL FEATURE

(p. 7-24) Annual article, by Loren C. Scott et al., presenting economic outlook for Louisiana through 1986, based on Louisiana Econometric Model. Data sources include Louisiana Dept of Labor and U.S. Bureau of Economic Analysis.

Includes 26 tables, primarily showing Louisiana employment and earnings by industry division and MSA, personal income by type, population, bank and savings and loan assn financial activity, and energy supply-demand and prices, 1982-86, with selected comparisons to U.S. economic indicators.

U2735-2 LOUISIANA ECONOMIC INDICATORS
Monthly. Approx. 25 p.
ISSN 0279-6392.
LC sc82-1131.
SRI/MF/complete, shipped quarterly

Monthly report (except July and Nov.-Dec.) on Louisiana State and local business and economic activity. Data are from State agencies, the Federal Government, and private or commercial sources. Data are current to month of publication or 1-3 months prior.

Issues generally contain brief narrative with summary charts and text tables, and 19 monthly economic indicator tables.

Monthly indicator tables are listed below and appear in most issues. All additional features with substantial statistical content are described, as they appear, under "Statistical Features." Nonstatistical features are not covered.

Oct. 1984 issue also includes 2 tables showing oil and natural gas severance tax collections by parish, various periods 1982-July 1984; and May 1985 issue includes 1 table showing motor vehicle sales tax collections by local governments, arranged by parish, monthly Nov. 1984-May 1985.

Additional data may be found in the semiannual *Louisiana Business Survey,* available from the University of New Orleans, Division of Business and Economic Research, New Orleans LA 70148. *Business Survey* is not covered by SRI.
Availability: Louisiana State University: College of Business Administration, Division of Research, Louisiana Economic Indicators, Baton Rouge LA 70803, †; SRI/MF/complete, shipped quarterly.
Issues reviewed during 1985: Oct. 1984-June 1985 (P) (Vol. 4, No. 7; Vol. 5, Nos. 1-6).

MONTHLY TABLES:
[Unless otherwise noted, tables show data for month of coverage and 4-11 preceding months, with selected comparisons to previous periods. Data for parishes and other local areas generally include population. Table sequence and content of economic indicator tables may vary from issue to issue.

Prior to Feb. 1985 issue, indicator tables also included data on births and deaths, and data on new car and truck sales were shown in separate tables. Prior to Mar. 1985 issue, indicator tables included data on welfare recipients and payments.]

[1] Unemployment rate and leading indicators [index, for State and U.S., monthly for current year through month of coverage and 1-2 preceding years].

[2] Economic indicators: Louisiana [including employment by industry division; unemployment; unemployment insurance claims, payments, and exhaustions; manufacturing hours and earnings; retail sales; tax revenues; construction contracts and value; residential and commercial/industrial building permits and

value; FHLBB construction and other loans; corporate filings; telephone lines; coal trade; motor fuel consumption; petroleum production by company; volume of oil handled by Louisiana Offshore Oil Port (by country or area of origin); drilling rigs; natural gas activity; State employee retirement benefit disbursements; new car and truck sales by make; and beer sales].

[3-10] Economic indicators [for 8 metro areas; repeats selected data in table [2]; also includes number of department stores, classified advertising linage, port activity, airline traffic, sales and severance tax collections, and convention attendance and hotel/motel occupancy (New Orleans only); prior to Jan. 1985 issue, table showing data for Houma metro area also included Thibodaux].

[11-12] State sales tax collections by parish and commodity.

[13-15] Local sales tax collections, by parish school boards, cities and towns, and police juries.

[16] Severance tax collections by parish.

[17] Economic indicators: U.S. [including PPI, CPI, industrial production indexes, bond yields, money supply, bank debits, financial institution deposits, employment and unemployment, life insurance data, and energy production, consumption, and trade].

[18-19] Louisiana tourist traffic data: visitors to selected tourist attractions and information stations.

U2735-2.601: Apr. 1985 (Vol. 5, No. 4)
SPECIAL TABLES
[A] Standard cases of beer sold [and population], by parish [July 1984-Jan. 1985, with percent change from Jan. 1984]. (p. 34)

[B-C] New car and truck sales, by parish [and by domestic and import make, 1984]. (p. 35-37)

U3040
Memphis State University: Bureau of Business and Economic Research

U3040-1 MID-SOUTH BUSINESS JOURNAL
Quarterly. Approx. 20 p.
Pub. 885720.
LC 79-617891.
SRI/MF/complete

Quarterly report on economic, financial, and labor conditions in the U.S. and 5 Midsouth States (Alabama, Arkansas, Louisiana, Mississippi, and Tennessee). Data are from Federal, State, and private assn publications. Report is issued 1-2 months after quarter of coverage.

Each issue contains feature articles, occasionally with statistics; and a statistical supplement insert, with 3 charts on economic indicator trends, and 4 tables listed below. An annual analysis of changes in the Midsouth economy appears in the 1st quarter issue.

Quarterly supplement statistics appear in all issues. All additional features with substantial statistical content are described, as they appear, under "Statistical Features." Nonstatistical features are not covered.

Availability: Memphis State University: Bureau of Business and Economic Research, Fogelman College of Business and Economics, Memphis TN 38152, †; SRI/MF/complete.
Issues reviewed during 1985: 3rd Qtr. 1984-2nd Qtr. 1985 (D) (Vol. IV, No. 4; Vol. V, Nos. 1-3).

QUARTERLY SUPPLEMENT TABLES:
[Most data are shown for 1 month of current or previous quarter, with percent change from same month of previous year and/or during year to date. Data shown as percent change only are noted below. Data are shown by Midsouth State, with selected comparisons to U.S. and total Midsouth.]

[1] Labor [labor force, unemployment, manufacturing and nonmanufacturing employment, and average hours and earnings of manufacturing production workers].

[2] Construction [percent change in residential and nonresidential construction value, and dwelling unit permits issued].

[3] Finance [percent change in demand, time, and savings deposits].

[4] Savings and loan activity [mortgage loans made; and net savings flow].

STATISTICAL FEATURE:

U3040-1.601: 1st Qtr. 1985 (Vol. V, No. 2)
ANALYSIS OF ANNUAL CHANGES IN THE MID-SOUTH ECONOMY, ANNUAL FEATURE
(4 p.) Annual summary review of Midsouth economic indicator performance in 1984. Includes 6 tables cumulating data appearing in quarterly tables and also showing personal income for 1st 9 months and sales tax collections for full year 1984, with comparisons to 1983. Data generally are shown for 5 Midsouth States and U.S.

U3130
Michigan State University: Placement Services

U3130-1 RECRUITING TRENDS, 1984-85: A Study of 658 Businesses, Industries, Governmental Agencies, and Educational Institutions Employing New College Graduates
Annual. Nov. 30, 1984.
xii + 67 p.
LC 78-641579.
SRI/MF/complete

Annual report, by John D. Shingleton and L. Patrick Scheetz, on employer practices and plans with regard to hiring new college graduates, 1984/85 with selected comparisons to 1983/84.

Includes data on anticipated changes in new hires and starting salaries, by degree level, academic field, and employer type, and for women and minorities; employment offers vs. acceptances; use of on-campus interviews, and percent of interviews resulting in hires; factors affecting selection of applicants for interviews and plant visits; and sources of new hires.

Also includes data on total salaried employment; average starting salary, by degree field and level; employment outlook for new graduates, by region; work environment changes affecting future hiring needs; courses to increase liberal arts graduates' employability; criteria for measuring effectiveness of recruiting programs; measures to increase college staff familiarity with student career opportunities; policy on hiring handicapped persons; and factors influencing starting salary size.

Data are based on survey responses of 658 organizations employing new college graduates.

Contains summary (p. iii-xii); 43 tables, interspersed with brief narrative analyses (p. 1-59); and list of respondents (p. 60-67).

This is the 14th annual survey.

Availability: Michigan State University: Placement Services, Student Services Bldg., East Lansing MI 48824-1113, $10.00; SRI/MF/complete.

U3255
Mississippi State University: College of Business and Industry

U3255–2   MISSISSIPPI BUSINESS REVIEW
Monthly.
ISSN 0026-6167.
LC 54-40725.
SRI/MF/complete, shipped quarterly

Monthly report on Mississippi business activity, employment, industrial expansion, and other economic indicators. Also includes southeastern regional economic indicators, for 6 States and selected cities. Data are from Federal, State, and private sources. Month of data coverage is 2-3 months prior to cover date.

Each issue usually contains feature articles, occasionally with statistics; and 11 monthly tables, listed below.

Most monthly tables appear in all issues. Additional tables are sometimes included showing U.S. data reprinted from Federal sources; these tables are not described. All other additional features with substantial statistical content are described, as they appear, under "Statistical Features." Nonstatistical features are not covered.

Full report was discontinued with the June 1985 issue, and was replaced by *Mississippi Business Review Statistical Report,* which continues selected data series from the full report. The statistical report is available only to current subscribers, and consists of monthly tables most requested by subscribers (tables [3-6] and [9] in most issues), and occasional special tables. Special tables are also described under "Statistical Features."

Availability: Mississippi Business Review, PO Box 5288, Mississippi State MS 39762-5288, available to paid subscribers; others ◆; SRI/MF/complete, shipped quarterly.

Issues reviewed during 1985: Mississippi Business Review: Oct. 1984-June 1985 (P) (Vol. XLVI, Nos. 4-12) [Vol. XLVI Nos. 6-12 incorrectly read Vol. XLVL].

Issues reviewed during 1985: Mississippi Business Review Statistical Report: July-Oct. 1985 (P).

MONTHLY TABLES:
[Data are for Mississippi, unless otherwise noted. Most data are shown for month of coverage, preceding month, and same month of previous year. Table order may vary.]

[1] [Employment in] new and expanded industry [by location, firm, and product; no date; presents data available at time of publication].

[2] Indexes of selected economic indicators [retail and electric sales, and gasoline consumption].

[3] State economic indicators [employment by industry division, unemployment rate, average manufacturing earnings and hours, crude oil production, gasoline delivered to dealers, electricity sales, and retail sales; prior to June 1985 issue, table also included data on agricultural receipts].

[4] Business activity by city [sales tax collections and building permits].

[5] SMSAs [employment data, and city sales tax collections, for Jackson and Biloxi-Gulfport].

[6] Sales indicated by sales tax collections, by county.

[7] Food stamp participation [payments and recipient households and persons], by county.

[8] Agriculture report [prices received and paid by farmers, by commodity].

[9] General fund transfers [by source].

[10] Financial transactions, banks and S&L's, regional and U.S. [commercial bank, credit union, and savings and loan assn deposits, by type; and savings and loan assn mortgage commitments and mortgages outstanding; for U.S., Southeast region, and 6 southeastern States; table appeared in Oct. 1984, and Jan. and May 1985 issues only].

[11] Southeast regional economic indicators [including nonfarm employment, unemployment rate, plane passenger arrivals, value of nonresidential building permits, and number of residential single- and multi-family building permits, total and by selected city, for 6 southeastern States; table appeared in Nov. 1984 and June 1985 issues only].

STATISTICAL FEATURES:

U3255–2.601: Oct. 1984 (Vol. XLVI, No. 4)
RETAIL SALES BY STORE GROUP

(back cover) Table showing Mississippi retail sales by type of business, by county, 1983.

U3255–2.602: Nov. 1984 (Vol. XLVI, No. 5)
FINANCIAL SERVICES: IMPLICATIONS FOR MARKET SEGMENTATION

(p. 3-7) By Ronald D. Taylor and Blaise J. Bergiel. Article presenting survey findings on financial institution patronage. Data are from 931 responses to a survey conducted in 6 midwestern towns. Includes 5 undated tables showing respondents using 1 or more than 1 financial institution, by type or combination of types; and results of statistical analyses comparing single- and multi-institution users, including types of bank and savings and loan services used, factors influencing institution choice, and selected sociodemographic characteristics.

MORTGAGES OWNED BY U.S. LIFE INSURANCE COMPANIES

(p. 18) Table showing value of farm and nonfarm mortgages owned by U.S. life insurance companies, by State, and for Puerto Rico, other U.S. territories/possessions, Canada, and all other foreign countries, 1982. Data are from the American Council of Life Insurance.

U3255–2.603: Dec. 1984 (Vol. XLVI, No. 6)
[Issue incorrectly reads Vol. XLVL.]
CASH RECEIPTS FROM FARM MARKETINGS, MISSISSIPPI, 1981-83

(p. 8) Table showing cash receipts from farm marketings by commodity, government payments to farmers, and value of products consumed on farms, for Mississippi, 1981-83. Data are from Mississippi Crop and Livestock Reporting Service.

For description of a similar table covering 1980-82, see SRI 1984 Annual under U3255-2.503.

U3255–2.604: Mar. 1985 (Vol. XLVI, No. 9)
[Issue incorrectly reads Vol. XLVL.]
1984 ANNUAL CROP SUMMARY: ESTIMATED ACREAGE, YIELD AND PRODUCTION OF CROPS WITH 1983 COMPARISONS

(p. 9) Annual table showing acres planted and harvested, yield, and production, by crop, for Mississippi and U.S., 1983-84. Data are from Federal and State agencies.

COVERED EMPLOYMENT, ANNUAL FEATURE

(p. 16) Annual table showing average monthly employment covered by Mississippi Employment Security Law, by county, 1982-83.

U3255–2.605: Apr. 1985 (Vol. XLVI, No. 10)
[Issue incorrectly reads Vol. XLVL.]
RETAIL SITE SELECTION: A STUDY OF METHODS USED BY RETAILING EXECUTIVES

(p. 3-10) By Carol H. Anderson et al. Article on siting methods used by retail chain executives for selection of new outlet locations, with regression analyses relating siting methods to chain size, type of store, and executive's education and tenure with company. Data are from 115 responses to a survey of chain store executives conducted by the authors. Includes 7 tables.

U3255–2.606: Aug. 1985
SPECIAL TABLE

(1 p.) Table showing Mississippi employment, average workweek and salaries, and number of business firms, by occupation (no date). Data are from Mississippi Employment Security Commission.

U3255–2.607: Sept. 1985
SPECIAL TABLE

(1 p.) Table showing Mississippi total and median household effective buying income (EBI), households by EBI group, and buying power index, all by metro area and county, 1984. Data are from *Sales and Marketing Management.*

U3255–2.608: Oct. 1985

SPECIAL TABLE

(1 p.) Table showing Mississippi retail sales, by kind of business, by county and selected metro area and city, 1984. Data are from *Sales and Marketing Management*.

U3255–4   MISSISSIPPI STATISTICAL ABSTRACT, 1984
Annual.   Dec. 1984.
viii + 827 p.
LC 75-629881.
SRI/MF/complete

Annual compilation, for 1984, of detailed demographic, social, governmental, and economic statistics for Mississippi. Data are mostly for 1981-83, with selected historical trends. Data are from Federal and State governments, private industry, and research and trade assns.

Report is designed to present a comprehensive overview of the State. Extensive socioeconomic, demographic, and geographic breakdowns are shown, as applicable, for most topics. These breakdowns include data by city, county and other State district, SMSA, urban-rural status, commodity, industry, age, marital status, race, and sex. Comparisons to U.S. and selected neighboring States are also often included.

Contains introduction, and contents and chart listings (p. iii-viii); 50 maps/charts and 331 tables arranged in 16 sections, described below, each preceded by a summary of data sources and listings of tables and charts (p. 1-817); and a subject index (p. 818-827).

This is the 16th annual edition of the *Abstract*.

Availability: Mississippi State University: College of Business and Industry, Research Division, PO Box 5288, Mississippi State MS 39762-5288, $23.00+$1.50 postage and handling; SRI/MF/complete.

TABLE SECTIONS:
[Data sources appear beneath each table.]

U3255–4.1: Section 1: Recreation, Geography, and Climate

(p. 1-68) Contains 3 maps/charts and 10 tables. Includes land area; temperature and precipitation averages and extremes, by station; Federal lands; recreation areas, acreage, and attendance; parks, reservoirs, and national forests, and facilities; lake acreage and fishermen, by lake; and certified boats.

U3255–4.2: Section 2: Population

(p. 69-97) Contains 4 maps/charts and 12 tables. Includes population since 1900; housing units; land area; and births, deaths, and net migration.

U3255–4.3: Section 3: Health and Vital Statistics

(p. 98-176) Contains 3 maps/charts and 42 tables. Includes births; deaths by leading cause; infant and maternal deaths; marriages; and divorces by cause, years of marriage, and number of minor children.

Also includes licensed nursing homes, capacity, admissions, patients by source of fees, discharges, and deaths; hospitals, capacity, utilization, and staff; physicians by specialty; and dentists.

U3255–4.4: Section 4: Education

(p. 177-256) Contains 4 maps/charts and 29 tables. Includes State finances; public and private schools; public school enrollment, attendance, finances, and teachers and administrative staff and average salaries; high school graduates; and school dropouts, retention, and attrition.

Also includes postsecondary enrollment, by public and private institution; public junior college finances and facilities; education appropriations, by legislative bill and postsecondary institution; wealth and property tax collections per pupil; and vocational/technical enrollment and finances.

U3255–4.5: Section 5: Labor Force, Employment, and Earnings

(p. 257-339) Contains 1 map/chart and 19 tables. Includes nonfarm employment; hours and earnings; covered business establishments, employment, wages, and payroll; unemployment benefits, insurance tax rates, employer contributions, and trust fund balances; and labor force by employment status.

U3255–4.6: Section 6: Manufacturing and Trade

(p. 340-457) Contains 3 charts and 12 tables. Includes business establishments, employment, and wages; wholesale/retail sales, gross sales and taxes, and taxpayers; new and expanded industries, employment, and capital investment, by firm; and business births and deaths, active establishments, and ownership changes.

U3255–4.7: Section 7: Transportation

(p. 458-504) Contains 3 maps/charts and 26 tables. Includes motor vehicle registrations; government vehicles; highway and motor use tax revenues; licensed passenger and property motor carriers and revenues; railroad employment, and mileage operated by railroad; and ICC rail abandonment applications and status.

Also includes foreign and/or domestic freight traffic at 3 harbors; Mississippi River freight and passenger traffic at 8 ports; Yazoo River freight traffic; aircraft departures, passengers, and cargo, including U.S. and foreign mail, by airport and/or type of aircraft; pilots and flight instructors; active and abandoned airports; and airport specifications.

U3255–4.8: Section 8: Communications and Public Utilities

(p. 505-530) Contains 2 maps/charts and 17 tables. Includes newspapers; energy consumption by sector and fuel source; radio and TV stations; post offices; electricity generation and capacity by type of fuel; and electric and natural gas utility customers, revenues, and sales and/or prices, by service class; public utility commission membership and employment; and telephones in use and percent of households with telephone service.

U3255–4.9: Section 9: Banking, Finance, and Insurance

(p. 531-572) Contains 1 chart and 27 tables. Includes assets, liabilities, income, and expenses, for credit unions, small loan companies, and banks; failed banks, and FDIC disbursements, losses, and recoveries; banks,

branches, deposits, and equity capital; bank assets by bank; and savings and loan assns, assets, and mortgage loan holdings.

Also includes life insurance underwriting data and guaranty funds; health insurance benefit payments and hospitalization data; mortgages owned by life insurance companies; and loans by Veterans Farm and Home Board.

U3255–4.10: Section 10: Law Enforcement, Courts, and Crime

(p. 573-616) Contains 7 maps/charts and 23 tables. Includes State police employment and enforcement activities, including duty hours; traffic accidents, injuries, fatalities, and property damage; juvenile court cases and dispositions; prisoners; and crimes and crime rates.

U3255–4.11: Section 11: Forest and Mineral Products

(p. 617-655) Contains 3 maps/charts and 27 tables. Includes forest land area, by ownership; forest fires and acreage burned; national forest acreage, timber sales and harvest, grazing use, visitors, reforestation and improvement needs, cooperative management activities, and road and bridge construction; State forestry commission finances; timber severance tax collections; and commercial timberland ownership, sawtimber, and growing stock.

Also includes mineral production and value; sand, gravel, and clay sales/use; principal producers of quarry products; natural gas marketed production; producing wells and oil, water, and gas production; petroleum refinery capacity, by refinery, and working storage capacity; liquefied petroleum gas and ethane sales; and energy consumption by sector and energy source.

U3255–4.12: Section 12: Public Finance and Tax Revenue

(p. 656-686) Contains 6 charts and 9 tables. Includes State revenues by source and expenditures by function; sales tax payments to cities, including amount to air/water pollution board; corporation taxpayers, revenue, taxable income, franchise tax collections, and annual fees; personal income taxpayers, taxable income, and gross tax; and oil, gas, and timber severance tax payments.

U3255–4.13: Section 13: Social Insurance and Welfare Services

(p. 687-709) Contains 4 maps/charts and 11 tables. Includes welfare appeals hearings; welfare program caseloads, finances, and payments; child support cases and collections; foster home and adoption placements; individuals eligible for assistance under Aid to Dependent Children; food stamp program participation and coupon value; and social service cases.

U3255–4.14: Section 14: Government and Politics

(p. 710-762) Contains 3 maps/charts and 31 tables. Includes votes cast for presidential electors, President, and U.S. Representatives, by party; voting age population; composition of U.S. Congress by party; and defense contract awards and payroll.

Also includes State/local government employment and payroll; Federal civilian employment; State/local government indebtedness and expenditures by function; veterans and veterans' benefits; rosters of State elected and appointed officials; and court districts.

U3255–4.15: Section 15: Construction and Housing

(p. 763-772) Contains 1 chart and 6 tables. Includes housing units authorized and value; HUD disbursements; construction contract value; savings assn and FHA mortgage activity; and savings and loan assn loans closed and savings activity.

U3255–4.16: Section 16: Agriculture

(p. 773-817) Contains 2 maps/charts and 30 tables. Includes farm cash receipts and State rankings; farm income and production expenses; Federal payments, by program; production, use, sales, and/or value, for selected field crops, sweet potatoes, pecans, and peaches; cattle inventory and calf crop; and egg and broiler production.

U3270
Mississippi State University: Mississippi Agricultural and Forestry Experiment Station

U3270–1 MISSISSIPPI COUNTIES: SOCIAL AND ECONOMIC ASPECTS, A Compendium of Statistical Data

Recurring (irreg.) Apr. 1984.
vii+140 p.
Rpt. No. MAFES 5826.
LC 85-621198.
SRI/MF/complete

Recurring report presenting general social and economic profile of Mississippi, by county. Data are shown primarily for 1980, with selected trends from 1930.

Report is designed to present an overview of the State. All data are shown by county and include State totals. Socioeconomic and demographic breakdowns are shown, as applicable, for selected topics. These breakdowns include urban-rural status, occupation, education, age group, marital status, race (including Hispanic), and sex.

Most data are from 1980 U.S. Census.

Contains contents and table listings (p. iii-vii); introduction and definitions (p. 1-3); 58 tables described below (p. 5-138); and subject index (p. 139-140).

This is the 5th edition of the report. SRI coverage begins with this edition.

Availability: Mississippi State University: Mississippi Agricultural and Forestry Experiment Station, Department of Sociology and Anthropology, PO Box C, Mississippi State MS 39762, $10.00; SRI/MF/complete.

TABLES:

a. **Population and vital statistics:** includes population size and migration; population by place of residence 5 years earlier; population density; births; deaths; families and households; and population by living arrangements. Tables 1-37. (p. 5-117)

b. **Education:** includes population age 25/over by educational attainment; and private and public school enrollment. Tables 38-41. (p. 118-121)

c. **Employment and income:** includes employed workers by type of employer and occupational group; total and female labor force, by employment status; individual, household, and family median incomes; and percent of population in poverty. Tables 42-48. (p. 122-128)

d. **Housing:** includes housing units by occupancy status, water source, type of sewage disposal, and presence of bathrooms, kitchens, telephones, and air conditioning; and median persons, rooms, and value per unit. Tables 49-58. (p. 129-138)

U3340
New Mexico State University: Agricultural Experiment Station

U3340–1 PEOPLE OF NEW MEXICO, 1980

Monograph. June 1984.
4+66 p. Bulletin 710.
SRI/MF/complete

Report on New Mexico population and housing characteristics, primarily 1980, with decennial population trends from 1850. Includes the following data, generally by city and county:

a. Population: by urban-rural and farm status, race (including Native American and Hispanic), poverty status, age, sex, marital status, educational attainment, language spoken at home (English, Spanish, or other), and English-speaking ability, with selected comparison to U.S. and 7 other mountain States.

b. Housing and income: housing units, families, and households (total and by type); housing units with plumbing, gas, water, sewer services, and central heating, and with 1/more persons per room; median housing value, rent, and monthly owner costs with and without mortgage; families by income level; sources of household income; and median household and family income.

c. Mobility: natives by place of birth (New Mexico, different State, abroad/at sea, and foreign), and population by place of residence 5 years earlier; commuters by travel time, transportation mode, and number of riders in car pool; and housing units by number of available vehicles.

Data are primarily from Census Bureau.

Contains highlights and contents listing (3 p.); and narrative report interspersed with 24 charts and 23 tables (p. 1-66).

Availability: New Mexico State University: Agricultural Experiment Station, Bulletin Office, Department of Agricultural Information, Drawer 3AI, Las Cruces, NM 88003, †; SRI/MF/complete.

U3515
New York University: Salomon Bros Center for the Study of Financial Institutions

U3515–2 MONOGRAPH SERIES IN FINANCE AND ECONOMICS

Series. For individual publication data, see below.
SRI/MF/complete

Continuing series of reports on selected financial and economic topics of interest to the higher education community, corporations, banks, and government agencies. Reports are generally issued 4-5 times a year and include data from government agencies, university and private research organizations, individual authors, and other sources.

Only those reports with substantial statistical content are covered by SRI.

Reports reviewed during 1985 are described below.

Availability: New York University—Salomon Bros Center for the Study of Financial Institutions, 90 Trinity Pl., New York NY 10006, $15.00 per yr., full-time teachers $7.50 per yr., single copy $5.00; SRI/MF/complete.

U3515–2.6: U.S. Payments System: Costs, Pricing, Competition and Risk

[Monograph. 1984. 11+137 p. Monograph 1984-1/2. $7.50. SRI/MF/complete.]

By David Burras Humphrey. Report presenting economic analysis of the payments system, 1983 and trends. Focuses on impact of 1980 Depository Institutions Deregulation and Monetary Control Act on costs and pricing of payment methods, on competition among providers of wholesale payments services, and on payments system risks.

Includes data on transaction volume, value, costs, and prices, by payment method (cash, check, automated clearinghouse, and wire); Federal Reserve float levels; scale economy analysis for Federal Reserve processing of checks (including detail by city) and automated clearinghouse transactions, and for commercial banking services; and overdraft analysis for wire transfers; 1983, with selected trends from 1973.

Also includes Treasury Dept revenue changes associated with Monetary Control Act, 1981-88.

Data are from Federal Reserve System.

Contains listings of contents, tables, and charts (7 p.); 10 chapters, with narrative analysis, 5 charts, and 13 tables (1-129); and appendix and bibliography (p. 130-135).

U3515–2.7: Role of Gold in Consumer Investment Portfolios

[Monograph. 1984. 5+69 p. Monograph 1984-3. SRI/MF/complete.]

By Lawrence S. Ritter and Thomas J. Urich. Report examining suitability of gold as an investment vehicle. Includes data on gold prices and investment return rates, with comparisons to other types of investments (silver, stocks, housing, Treasury bills, and bonds), 1968-83.

Data are from Handy and Harman, Federal agencies, and other sources.

Contains listings of contents, tables, and charts (2 p.); introduction (p. 1-2); and 5 chapters, with narrative analysis, 5 charts, and 30 tables (p. 3-67).

U3600
North Dakota State University: Agricultural Experiment Station

U3600–1   NORTH DAKOTA AGRICULTURAL STATISTICS, 1985
Annual. June 1985. 132 p.
Ag. Statistics No. 54.
ISSN 0737-1624.
LC 83-641803.
SRI/MF/complete

Annual report on North Dakota agricultural production and marketing, mostly 1980-84, with trends from the 1970s and some data for 1985. Data generally are shown by commodity, county, and/or district.

Report covers production, prices, sales, value, and, as applicable, acreage, yield, disposition, inventory, and stocks, for crop, livestock, dairy, poultry, and apiary sectors.

Also includes data on number and acreage of farms; farm income, production expenses, real estate value, rent, taxes, and debt; irrigated acreage; grain shipments and storage facilities; fertilizer consumption; pesticide use; wages and custom work rates; and share of U.S. exports.

Data are compiled by North Dakota Crop and Livestock Reporting Service.

Contains contents listing (2 p.); 5 sections, with brief narrative summaries, 47 charts and maps, and 210 tables (p. 6-131.

This is the 28th annual report.

Availability: North Dakota Crop and Livestock Reporting Service, 345 U.S. Post Office, Federal Bldg., PO Box 3166, Fargo ND 58108, $5.00; SRI/MF/complete.

U3600–3   REPORT SERIES
Series. For individual publication data, see below.
SRI/MF/complete

Series of reports analyzing selected population data for North Dakota, based on findings from the 1980 Census of Population and Housing.

The series begins with the reports described below. Issuing agency also publishes a less detailed population bulletin series, not covered in SRI.

Availability: North Dakota State University: Agricultural Experiment Station, Department of Agricultural Economics, Morrill Hall, Rm. 207, PO Box 5636, Fargo ND 58105, †; SRI/MF/complete.

U3600–3.1: Single Parents in North Dakota: A Statistical Portrait
[Monograph. Apr. 1985. 2+ii+29 p. Rpt. No. 1. SRI/MF/complete.]

By Polly Fassinger and Richard Rathge. Report analyzing demographic characteristics and economic circumstances of single parents in North Dakota, 1979 or 1980, with selected comparisons to 1970. Includes the following data:

a. Families with children; and children (total and preschool age), by family size; all by householder type (married couple, and male and female single parent).

b. Single parents, by marital status, sex, race/ethnicity (including Native American, Asian, and Spanish origin), and age group.

c. Impoverished householders with children, by householder type and race/ethnicity; impoverished single parents (white and Native American), by sex and employment status; female single parents, by marital and labor force status; and distribution of all and impoverished families, by householder type.

Data are based on Public Use Microdata Samples drawn from Census of Population and Housing.

Contains preface (2 p.); listings of contents, charts, and tables (p. i-ii); narrative analysis (p. 1-8); and appendices, with 12 tables, 4 charts, data sources, and references (p. 9-29).

U3730
Northwestern University: Placement Center

U3730–1   NORTHWESTERN ENDICOTT REPORT: Trends in the Employment of College and University Graduates in Business and Industry, 1985
Annual. 1984. 19 p.
ISSN 0097-6297.
LC 75-642040.
SRI/MF/complete

Annual survey report, by Victor R. Lindquist, on corporate plans for hiring 1985 college/university graduates. Includes number of bachelor's and master's degree recipients to be hired at various salary levels, by field, with comparison to 1984.

Also includes corporate outlook and performance assessment; recruiting trends and outlook; factors in selection of colleges for campus interviews, and results of interviews; recruiting success ratios in difficult-to-recruit academic disciplines; and opinions on career counseling.

Data are based on responses of 250 companies in 29 States and D.C. to a Nov. 1984 survey. Most respondents are national large or medium-sized companies that have recruited college graduates for many years.

Contains introduction (p. 3); survey findings, with text statistics and 3 tables (p. 5-17); and summary (1 p.).

This is the 39th annual survey.

Availability: Northwestern University: Placement Center, Scott Hall, Evanston IL 60201, $10.00; SRI/MF/complete.

U3780
Ohio State University: Center for Human Resource Research

U3780–1   CENTER FOR HUMAN RESOURCE RESEARCH REPORTS
Series. For individual publication data, see below.
SRI/MF/complete

Continuing series of reports by the Center for Human Resource Research on contemporary issues, with emphasis on labor market research and manpower planning.

Most reports are based upon statistical analysis of data from the National Longitudinal Surveys (NLS) of Labor Market Experience, covering 20,000 older men, middle-aged women, and young men and women. The surveys have been conducted annually or biennially by the Census Bureau since 1966.

Beginning in 1979, the NLS project also includes an additional youth panel survey of approximately 13,000 young men and women, including military personnel. The youth panel is interviewed annually by National Opinion Research Center.

Only reports containing statistics are covered in SRI. Reports reviewed during 1985 are described below.

Availability: Ohio State University: Center for Human Resource Research, College of Administrative Science, 650 Ackerman Rd., Suite A, Columbus OH 43202-1501, $1.00 for postage and handling; SRI/MF/complete.

U3780–1.19: From Work to Retirement: The Experience of a National Sample of Men
[Monograph. Feb. 1983. xix+127 p. SRI/MF/complete.]

By Herbert S. Parnes and Lawrence Less. Report on the retirement experience of men, various periods 1966-80. Includes data on reasons for retiring and different measures of retirement; age at retirement; levels and detailed sources of income; labor force participation, including comparison to preretirement employment; leisure activities; and perceptions about adequacy of income and quality of life.

Data are shown generally by race and age group, and occasionally by other characteristics including health condition, previous occupation type, and marital status, with various cross-tabulations.

Data are based on responses of over 3,000 men age 45-59 in 1966, participating in the National Longitudinal Surveys of the Labor Market Experience of Men. The sample was surveyed annually or biennially during 1967-80.

Contains contents listing, introductory matter, and summary (p ii-xix); 3 chapters, with narrative analysis and 39 interspersed tables showing sample characteristics, response distributions, and results of statistical analyses (p. 1-123); and references (p. 124-127).

U3780-4   PATHWAYS TO THE FUTURE: A Report on the National Longitudinal Surveys of Youth
Series. For individual publication data, see below.
SRI/MF/complete

Series of reports examining youth employment and educational experiences, including participation in employment training programs.

Reports present detailed analyses based on sociodemographic characteristics, including sex, age, region, school enrollment status (high school student or dropout, college student, and nonenrolled high school graduate), educational attainment, marital and employment status, income, race (including Hispanic), occupation, and industry division.

Data are primarily from the National Longitudinal Survey of Youth Labor Market Experience, consisting of a base survey covering approximately 12,500 persons age 14-21 in 1979, and annual follow-up surveys through 1984.

Each report includes contents listing, introductory section, and 4-6 survey-related articles interspersed with a varying number of tables.

Results from the 1980-81 surveys are presented in preliminary and final reports; the final reports focus on narrative analyses and are not covered in SRI. Results from the 1982 and later surveys are presented in single reports.

Preliminary reports covering the 1980-81 surveys, and reports covering the 1982-83 surveys, are described below.

Report based on the original 1979 survey was published by the Dept of Labor and is described in *American Statistics Index* (ASI), a companion CIS publication; for description, see ASI 1981 Annual under 6406-8.4.

Availability: Ohio State University—Center for Human Resource Research, College of Administrative Science, 650 Ackerman Rd., Suite A, Columbus OH 43202-1501, $1.00 postage and handling; SRI/MF/complete.

U3780-4.1: Preliminary Report on the 1980 Survey
[Monograph. Dec. 1981. 172 p. SRI/MF/complete.]

Includes 64 tables presenting 1980 survey results on the following, with some comparisons to the 1979 survey:

a. Labor force participation; employment/population ratio; employment and school enrollment status, and other major activity (including keeping house and serving in military); hours and weeks worked, wages, and number of jobs held during past year; and government employment training program participation, employment and related services used, and perceived effectiveness of and satisfaction with training program experiences.

b. School characteristics, including student/teacher and student/counselor ratios, vocational programs offered by type, and presence of minority students and faculty members; student participation in remedial English and math courses, and Hispanic student participation in bilingual education and English as a 2nd language programs; students dropping out and returning to school; and high school graduates immediately entering college.

c. Criminal activities, including reported involvement and convictions by type of offense, and results of other encounters with law enforcement/judicial agencies; portion of income earned from illegal activities; and involvement in school disciplinary actions.

U3780-4.2: Preliminary Report on the 1981 Survey
[Monograph. Nov. 1982. 111 p. SRI/MF/complete.]

Includes 36 tables presenting 1981 survey results on the following, with some comparisons to the 1979-80 surveys:

a. Labor force participation rates, unemployment, and employment/population ratios, with detail for persons reporting general health restrictions and problems with obesity; and 1st and current job characteristics, including wage, length of employment, and hours worked, with comparison to median weekly earnings of all workers by occupational group and sex.

b. Government employment training program participation, employment and related services used, and perceived effectiveness of and satisfaction with training program experiences, with summary of CETA program participation among total population.

c. Time spent in various activities related to work, school, work training programs, leisure, employment search (by method), household chores, and child care; and mean time and distance to school or work, by mode of transportation.

U3780-4.3: Labor Market Experience in 1982
[Monograph. Apr. 1984. ix+276 p. Vol. IV. SRI/MF/complete.]

Includes 80 tables presenting 1982 survey results on the following, with some comparisons to previous surveys:

a. Employment: school year employment, hours and weeks worked, average wage, and number of employers, by grade level; multivariate regression analyses of the effect of student employment on lifestyle, education, and post-school employment, and the effect of sociodemographic characteristics on employment probability, wages, job search duration, and job satisfaction; and ratings of effectiveness of various job search techniques.

b. Education: educational attainment and expectations; and school dropouts, probability of dropping out by grade level, and reasons for dropping out; with various regression analyses, including probability of meeting education goals, and the impact of education, experience, and household situation on earnings and employment.

c. Government training programs: regression analyses of effect of participation in selected programs on earnings, job satisfaction, school enrollment and graduation, and reliance on public assistance.

U3780-4.4: Report on the National Longitudinal Surveys of Youth Labor Market Experience in 1983

[Monograph. Jan. 1985. vi+196 p. Vol. V. SRI/MF/complete.]

Includes 59 tables presenting 1983 survey results on the following, with some comparisons to previous surveys:

a. Government employment and training program participation, including detail for summer programs and specific services; with analyses relating program participation to employment and earnings.

b. Employment: weeks of employment and unemployment in year following end of schooling; weeks elapsed between end of schooling and 1st job; weeks elapsed and number of jobs held between end of schooling and 1st permanent full-time job; characteristics of 1st post-school job, including occupation, industry, hours, wage, and tenure; tenure in 1st permanent full-time job; and regression analyses relating family background, education, and socioeconomic characteristics to unemployment and wages.

c. College enrollment and retention rates, with detail by college type (2- and 4-year, in- and out-of-State), and by student full- and part-time status; major field of study, and retention of major field; use of student aid by type, and mean value of grants and earnings; and youth income by source; with various regression analyses, including impact of selected characteristics on college attendance and use of student aid.

d. Public assistance use by young mothers compared to other young women, with mothers' use before and during 1st pregnancy and after 1st birth; expected and achieved educational attainment of mothers, by public assistance status; and number of children in household upon 1st use of assistance, months between 1st birth and 1st use, and duration of use; all shown for welfare and AFDC, with selected regression analyses.

U3830
Ohio State University: Ohio Agricultural Research and Development Center

U3830-1   OHIO AGRICULTURAL STATISTICS, 1984
Annual. July 1985. 58 p.
LC 58-40536.
SRI/MF/complete

Annual report on Ohio agricultural production, marketing, and finances, mostly 1983-84, with some data for 1985 and trends from 1962. Data generally are shown by commodity and county and/or district, with selected comparisons to other States and total U.S.

Generally covers production, prices, value, and, as applicable, acreage, yield, inventory, and disposition, for field crop, vegetable, fruit, livestock, poultry, and dairy sectors.

Also includes data on number and acreage of farms; commercial grain storage capacity; weather; exports; fertilizers; mink operations; prices paid by farmers for selected items; and farm value, rent, income, production costs, credit, and debt outstanding.

Data are compiled by the Ohio Crop Reporting Service.

Contains contents listing (p. 1); and 11 maps, 11 charts, and 83 tables, with interspersed narrative summaries (p. 2-58).

Availability: Ohio Crop Reporting Service, Rm. 608, Federal Bldg., 200 N. High St., Columbus OH 43215, ‡; SRI/MF/complete.

U4110
Pennsylvania State University:
College of Business Administration

U4110-1   PENNSYLVANIA BUSINESS SURVEY
Monthly.   Approx. 5 p.
ISSN 0031-4382.
LC A53-9621.
SRI/MF/complete, shipped quarterly

Monthly report on economic conditions in Pennsylvania. Includes data on industrial production, employment, and construction activity.

Contents:

a. Narrative analysis with approximately 5 trend charts, and occasional summary tables, including 1 table showing State leading and coincident indexes for month of publication and several previous months; and occasional special features with substantial statistical content.

b. Monthly table on Pennsylvania economic indicators, showing number and seasonally adjusted indexes for manufacturing and nonmanufacturing jobs, manufacturing hours and payroll, steel and coal mining production, industrial electric power sales, construction contracts awarded, labor force by employment status, initial unemployment benefit claims, and CPI in 3 metro areas, for month 2 months prior to cover date, previous month, and same month of previous year.

c. Quarterly personal income table, showing Pennsylvania and U.S. seasonally adjusted income, by type and industry division, for quarter ended approximately 6 months prior to cover date, with percent change from previous quarter and same quarter of previous year.

d. Quarterly employment table, showing Pennsylvania and U.S. employment percent change, employment, and unemployment and labor force participation rates, by sex and race and for youths, for quarter ended approximately 5 months prior to cover date and selected previous periods.

e. Quarterly "Around the State" feature, with trend charts and 1 table, repeated for each Pennsylvania MSA and metro area, showing most of the economic indicators covered in the monthly State table, for quarter prior to cover date, previous quarter, and same quarter of previous year; feature presenting 4th quarter data also includes full year summary.

Quarterly features are accompanied by narrative summaries.

Monthly table appears in all issues. Special features with substantial statistical content are described, as they appear, under "Statistical Features;" latest periods of coverage for quarterly data are also noted. Nonstatistical features are not covered.

Availability: Pennsylvania State University: College of Business Administration, Division of Research, 103 Business Administration Bldg. II, University Park PA 16802, $7.00 per yr.; SRI/MF/complete, shipped quarterly.

Issues reviewed during 1985: Nov. 1984-Oct. 1985 (P) (Vol. 25, Nos. 11-12; Vol. 26, Nos. 1-10).

STATISTICAL FEATURES:

U4110-1.601: Nov. 1984 (Vol. 25, No. 11)
QUARTERLY DATA
(p. 4-12) "Around the State" local economic indicators, for 3rd quarter 1984.

U4110-1.602: Dec. 1984 (Vol. 25, No. 12)
QUARTERLY DATA
(p. 4) Personal income, for 2nd quarter 1984.

U4110-1.603: Jan. 1985 (Vol. 26, No. 1)
QUARTERLY DATA
(p. 4) Employment, for 3rd quarter 1984.

U4110-1.604: Feb. 1985 (Vol. 26, No. 2)
QUARTERLY DATA
(p. 7-16) "Around the State" local economic indicators, for 4th quarter 1984.
ANNUAL REVIEW OF MAJOR ECONOMIC INDICATORS, PENNSYLVANIA AND THE U.S.
(p. 4-5) Annual table, with accompanying charts, presenting Pennsylvania and U.S. data for most items covered in monthly table on Pennsylvania economic indicators, and also including wage/salary jobs by industry division, 1983-84.

U4110-1.605: Mar. 1985 (Vol. 26, No. 3)
QUARTERLY DATA
(p. 3) Personal income, for 3rd quarter 1984.

U4110-1.606: Apr. 1985 (Vol. 26, No. 4)
PENNSYLVANIA'S FEMALE-MALE UNEMPLOYMENT MARGIN
(p. 3) Article, with 2 tables showing Pennsylvania unemployment and labor force participation rates, by sex, 1981-84; and average employment by industry division, 1984, with percent change from 1972, and projections for 1984-90.

U4110-1.607: May 1985 (Vol. 26, No. 5)
QUARTERLY DATA
(p. 4-12) "Around the State" local economic indicators, for 1st quarter 1985.

U4110-1.608: June 1985 (Vol. 26, No. 6)
QUARTERLY DATA
(p. 3) Personal income, for 4th quarter 1984.

U4110-1.609: July 1985 (Vol. 26, No. 7)
QUARTERLY DATA
(p.7) Employment, for 1st quarter 1985.

No table with data for 4th quarter 1984 was published.

U4110-1.610: Aug. 1985 (Vol. 26, No. 8)
QUARTERLY DATA
(p. 4-12) "Around the State" local economic indicators, for 2nd quarter 1985.

U4110-1.611: Sept. 1985 (Vol. 26, No. 9)
QUARTERLY DATA
(p. 4) Personal income, for 1st quarter 1985.

U4110-1.612: Oct. 1985 (Vol. 26, No. 10)
AVERAGE PAY RISES SLIGHTLY IN 1984
(p. 3) Article, with 1 table showing average pay by industry division, for Pennsylvania and U.S., 2nd quarter 1984 with percent change from 1980 and 1983. Data are from BLS.

U4360
Purdue University:
Agricultural Experiment Station

U4360-1   INDIANA ANNUAL CROP AND LIVESTOCK SUMMARY, 1984
Annual.   June 1985.
ii+144 p.   Rpt. No. A 85-1.
SRI/MF/complete

Annual report on Indiana agricultural production, marketing, and finances, mostly 1979-84, with some data for 1985 and selected historical trends from as early as 1866. Data generally are shown by commodity, with some detail by county and district, and selected comparisons to other States and total U.S.

Generally covers production, prices, income, value, and, as applicable, acreage, yield, inventory, and disposition, for field crop, fruit and vegetable, livestock, dairy, poultry, apiary, and mink sectors.

Also includes data on weather; number, acreage, and value of farms; grain storage and livestock slaughter facilities; pasture condition and forage acreage; fertilizer; farm cash receipts, income, expenses, prices paid, labor and wages, and utility rates; agricultural exports; and U.S. food consumption.

Data are compiled by the Indiana Crop and Livestock Reporting Service in cooperation with the USDA.

Contains map of crop reporting districts (inside front cover); foreword and contents listing (p. 1-3); 4 sections, interspersed with brief narrative summaries, 17 maps, 9 charts, and 116 tables (p. 4-143); metric conversion table (p. 144); and lists of USDA agriculture reports available (inside back cover).

Availability: Indiana Crop and Livestock Reporting Service, Agricultural Administration Bldg., Purdue University, West Lafayette IN 47907, $2.00 (4th class mail), $4.00 (1st class mail); SRI/MF/complete.

U4370
Purdue University: Credit Research Center

U4370–1   CREDIT RESEARCH CENTER WORKING PAPERS
Series.   For individual publication data, see below.
SRI/MF/complete

Continuing series of preliminary drafts of research study reports examining consumer and mortgage credit trends and practices, and their impact on the credit industry, consumers, and government.

Reports generally contain narrative analyses with interspersed tables and charts presenting data from government and private published sources, or from original surveys and/or survey analyses.

SRI covers only reports with substantial, broad-based statistics.

Report reviewed during 1985 is described below.

Availability: Purdue University—Credit Research Center, Krannert Graduate School of Management, West Lafayette IN 47907, $6.00 each; SRI/MF/complete.

U4370–1.22: Consumers' Choice of Consumer Loan Contract Terms
[Monograph. 1985. 31+6 p. Working Paper No. 51. SRI/MF/complete.]

By A. Charlene Sullivan. Report examining factors affecting consumer selection of adjustable- vs. fixed-rate auto loans. Compares the following for consumers choosing fixed-rate loans, and those choosing adjustable-rate loans with fixed- and adjustable-payment schedules: expectations for inflation and auto loan interest rates, and income growth vs. inflation; willingness to take financial risks; and variability in level of monthly income, and income relative to fixed obligations.

Data are from 247 responses to a July 1984 survey of consumers obtaining auto loans during Apr.-May 1984.

Contains summary (p. 1); report, with 12 interspersed tables on survey results and sample characteristics (p. 2-31); and questionnaire facsimile (6 p.).

U4900
South Dakota State University: Department of Rural Sociology

U4900–2   POPULATION CHANGE OF COUNTIES AND INCORPORATED PLACES IN SOUTH DAKOTA: 1950-1980
Monograph.   Mar. 1984.
39 p.
Update Series C229, No. 13.
LC 84-622167.
SRI/MF/complete

By Marvin P. Riley et al. Report presenting South Dakota population, by county and incor-

porated place, decennially 1950-80. Also includes population rankings for each location covered.

Data are from U.S. census reports.

Contains contents and table listing, introduction, and definitions (p. 2-4); and 7 tables and 1 map (p. 5-39).

Availability: South Dakota State University: Department of Rural Sociology, 226 Scobey Hall, Brookings SD 57007, †; SRI/MF/complete

U4900–3   POPULATION AND HOUSING INFORMATION, South Dakota School Districts: 1980
Monograph.   Dec. 1984.
37 p.
Update Series C229, No. 19.
LC 85-621499.
SRI/MF/complete

Report presenting selected education-related population and housing data for South Dakota school districts. Includes the following data for each district, 1980:

a. Population (total and rural), families and households, households with children aged 18/under by type of family structure, and children aged 18/under by type of living arrangement, including institutionalized children.

b. Persons aged 21/under by age, with median age of total population by sex; occupied, vacant, and renter-occupied houses; and houses by value, with median value.

Data are from the 1980 U.S. Census of Population and Housing.

Contains introduction, definitions, and contents and table listing (p. 1); and 3 tables (p. 2-37).

Availability: South Dakota State University: Department of Rural Sociology, 226 Scobey Hall, Brookings SD 57007, †; SRI/MF/complete.

U5025
Stanford University: Institute for Research on Educational Finance and Governance

U5025–1   EDUCATIONAL CONSEQUENCES OF HIGH TECHNOLOGY
Series.   For individual publication data, see below.
SRI/MF/complete

Series of reports discussing the potential impact of high-technology developments on employment, occupational demand, job skill requirements, and the educational system. Data are from Census Bureau, BLS, and other private and government sources.

Reports are part of special study project sponsored by the National Institute of Education; project began Dec. 1, 1982 and is scheduled for completion Nov. 30, 1985.

Most reports contain summary abstract, narrative analysis, bibliography, and a varying number of charts and tables. Only those reports with substantial statistics will be covered in SRI. Series begins with the reports described below.

Availability: Stanford University: Institute for Research on Educational Finance and Governance, CERAS Bldg., Stanford CA 94305, $2.00 per volume; SRI/MF/complete.

U5025–1.1: Educational Implications of High Technology
[Monograph. Feb. 1983. iii+16+3 p. Project Rpt. No. 83-A4. SRI/MF/complete.]

By Henry M. Levin and Russell W. Rumberger. Report on potential impact of advances in high technology on employment, job skill requirements, and education.

Includes 2 tables showing employment 1978 and 1990, and job growth during 1978-90 period, with detail for occupations with greatest anticipated growth; and employment growth distribution, by occupational group, selected periods 1960-90.

U5025–1.2: Forecasting the Impact of New Technologies on the Future Job Market
[Monograph. Feb. 1984. 3+27+5 p. Project Rpt. No. 84-A4. SRI/MF/complete.]

By Russell W. Rumberger and Henry M. Levin. Report on occupational employment projections, and methods used by BLS and other major organizations to account for the future impact of high technology. Includes 5 tables showing the following:

a. Employment distribution by industry division and occupational group, selected years 1900-95; and employment in 1982, and growth during 1982-95 period, aggregated for all and high-technology industries and occupations, and individually for fastest growing occupations (with data on educational requirements and earnings relative to all workers).

b. Growth rates for employment in selected occupations as projected by BLS, NSF, and Institute for Economic Analysis, under various scenarios of high-technology growth, various periods 1978-2000.

U5025–1.3: State Planning for Higher Education and Jobs in an Age of High Technology
[Monograph. Feb. 1984. 3+16 p. Policy Paper No. 84-C1. SRI/MF/complete.]

By Henry M. Levin. Report relating high-technology developments to State government planning for employment and education. Includes 2 tables showing occupations with greatest projected employment growth, 1982-95 period.

U5025–1.4: High Technology and Job Loss
[Monograph. May 1984. iii+28+7 p. Project Rpt. No. 84-A12. SRI/MF/complete.]

By Russell W. Rumberger. Report on technological advances and their impact on employment, with focus on potential worker displacement. Includes 6 tables showing the following:

a. Employment: for declining occupations; for fastest declining and growing occupations, including earnings as percent of all occupations and average years of education required; by industry division, including mean earnings; and for occupations potentially most affected by technological advances; various periods 1960-95.

b. Manufacturing and total economy output, capital stock, and employment, decennially 1960-80.

U5025–1.5: Bandwagon Once More: Vocational Preparation for High-Tech Occupations

[Monograph. May 1984. 3+36 p. Program Rpt. No. 84-B6. SRI/MF/complete.]

By W. Norton Grubb. Report discussing the role of high technology in development of vocational education programs, with detail for Texas. Includes 5 tables showing the following:

a. Texas: high-technology and standard manufacturing employment distribution by education and occupational group, 1980; and regression analysis of impact of education and other variables on income in selected high-technology and other industries, 1979.

b. U.S.: technician and computer specialist share of employment in all and selected high-technology industries, 1978 and 1990; employment in selected high-technology occupations, 1982 and 1995; and associate/other pre-bachelor degrees awarded by field, selected years 1970/71-1981/82.

U5025–1.6: Technology and the Redesign of Work in the Insurance Industry

[Monograph. Nov. 1984. 3+23+4 p. Project Rpt. No. 84-A22. SRI/MF/complete.]

By Eileen Appelbaum. Report on insurance industry automation and the effects on employment and job requirements.

Includes 3 tables showing insurance industry employment by occupation, selected years 1960-90; and total and female employment, for property/casualty and life/health insurers, and insurance agencies/brokers, various years 1960-82.

U5025–1.7: Potential Impact of Technology on the Skill Requirements of Future Jobs

[Monograph. Nov. 1984. 3+30 p. Project Rpt. No. 84-A24. SRI/MF/complete.]

By Russell W. Rumberger. Report on high technology and future job skill requirements.

Includes 3 tables showing economic output and employment by industry division, 1947 and 1981; and employment growth by major occupational group, various periods 1900-95.

U5025–1.8: Integrated Circuits/Segregated Labor: Women in Three Computer-Related Occupations

[Monograph. Nov. 1984. 3+46 p. Project Rpt. No. 84-A27. SRI/MF/complete.]

By Myra H. Strober and Carolyn L. Arnold. Report on women's employment in computer-related occupations and high-technology industries. Includes 9 tables showing the following:

a. Computer-related employment, with distribution by sex and race (including Spanish origin); earnings for men, with female/male earnings ratio; regression analysis of impact of education, age, and sex on earnings; and employment and men's earnings by industry division, with comparison to women; all for 3-15 computer-related occupations, 1970 and/or 1980.

b. High-technology and non-high-technology industry employment by sex and occupation, 1970 and 1980; and occupations with highest median weekly earnings for women, 1981.

U5025–1.9: Labor Market in Silicon Valley and Its Implications for Education

[Monograph. May 1985. 3+32 p. Project Rpt. No. 85-A8. SRI/MF/complete.]

By Martin Carnoy. Report analyzing the employment and wage structure of Santa Clara County, Calif. (Silicon Valley), and the impact of labor market and industry trends on current and future education policies.

Includes 9 tables showing Santa Clara County employment by industry division and selected major group; earnings by educational attainment and selected age group, with comparisons to total U.S.; and selected labor force characteristics; all shown for white and Hispanic workers by sex, with selected detail for electronics industry white employees (including employment by occupation and education); 1979 or 1980.

U5100
State University of New York: Nelson A. Rockefeller Institute of Government

U5100–1   1984-85 NEW YORK STATE STATISTICAL YEARBOOK
Annual. May 1985. 484 p.
ISSN 0077-9334.
ISBN 0-914341-02-2.
LC 68-65956.
SRI/MF/complete

Annual compilation, for 1984-85, of social, governmental, and economic statistics for New York State. Data are primarily for 1970s-84, with historical data from as early as 1899 and population projections to 2010.

Report is designed to present a comprehensive overview of the State. Extensive socioeconomic, demographic, and geographic breakdowns are shown, as applicable, for most topics. These breakdowns include data by city, county, SMSA, commodity, income, industry, occupation, age, educational attainment, race, and sex. Many tables include breakdowns for NYC, often by borough. Comparisons to U.S. by State are occasionally included.

Most data are from State and Federal government sources. Data sources appear beneath each table.

Contains contents listing, transmittal letter, introduction, SMSA overview, and map of counties (p. 3-8); 13 maps, 13 charts, and 405 tables arranged in 14 sections, described below (p. 9-438); appendices with State government organizational chart and agency directory (p. 439-474); and subject and data source indexes (p. 475-484).

This is the 11th edition.

Availability: State University of New York: Nelson A. Rockefeller Institute of Government, 411 State St., Albany NY 12203, $17.00+$2.00 postage and handling; SRI/MF/complete.

TABLE SECTIONS:
[Tables in each section are preceded by user notes, a table listing, and reproductions of segments from the 1860 *Historical and Statistical Gazetteer of New York State;* statistics from 1860 report are not described below. Some sections also include glossaries.]

U5100–1.1: Section A: Population and Vital Statistics

(p. 9-41) Contains 3 maps and 31 tables. Includes population trends from 1930, and projections to 2010; older population by household type; median age; land area; migration; households; families; persons in group quarters; life expectancy; births; deaths by cause; infant deaths; induced abortions; communicable diseases; and marriages and dissolutions.

U5100–1.2: Section B: Housing

(p. 43-60) Contains 2 maps and 12 tables. Includes housing units and characteristics, including occupancy, tenure, median value, number of units, age, type of heating equipment, and type of fuel; and housing construction and costs.

U5100–1.3: Section C: Health and Human Services

(p. 61-100) Contains 4 charts and 37 tables. Includes hospital discharges, services, reimbursement sources, and patient days and average stay; most common diagnostic and surgical procedures; psychiatric center admissions, residents, and patients served; local mental health and drug abuse programs and patients; alcoholism treatment programs, admissions, discharges, patients served, and State appropriations; and developmental disability facilities, residents, admissions, and patients served.

Also includes public assistance recipients and expenditures, by program; medical assistance beneficiaries and expenditures; food stamp recipients and coupon value; food distribution program staples distributed; child support cases and collections; children in foster care; adoptions; and child abuse and maltreatment cases reported.

U5100–1.4: Section D: Education

(p. 101-136) Contains 43 tables. Includes school districts; public and nonpublic school enrollment; nonpublic schools by type; teachers and other professional staff; high school graduates, dropout rates, and percent of graduates entering higher education; and educational attainment of population age 25/over.

Also includes higher education enrollment and degrees conferred; scholarship and award grants and recipients; tuition assistance; guaranteed student loans and defaults purchased; and State university system enrollment, degrees, and employment, by campus.

Also includes public school revenues by source, and expenditures by object; public and academic libraries, holdings, staff, and budget; State archives accessions, holdings, and research inquiries; science service collection; art, history, and science museums, employment, and budgets; and public broadcasting stations, broadcast hours, audience, and contract value.

U5100–1.5: Section E: Employment and Personal Income

(p. 137-167) Contains 2 maps and charts, and 29 tables. Includes labor force by employment status; labor/proprietors' and personal income, and earnings; 20 largest private employers; licensed professionals; government employment by level; manufacturing employment, payroll, and production worker hours and earnings; unemployment insurance beneficiaries and payments; work stoppages, workers involved, and days idle; worker compensation accidents and disabilities; and CPI.

U5100–1.6: Section F: Commerce and Industry

(p. 169-203) Contains 2 charts and 25 tables. Includes selected economic and business activity indicators; business establishments, employment, and payroll; manufacturing establishments, employment, capital expenditures, shipments, and value added; and service, wholesale, and retail establishments, sales or receipts, payroll, and employment.

Also includes value of exports and imports; mining establishments, employment, payroll, production, and value of shipments/receipts; construction sand/gravel sold/used; and construction contract values.

U5100–1.7: Section G: Banking and Insurance

(p. 205-219) Contains 20 tables. Includes bank deposits and savings, market value and sales of NYSE-listed stocks, and business loans outstanding; and financial institutions, branches, offices, and resources, by type of institution.

Also includes insurance industry firms, assets, liabilities, premiums, losses, and income, by type of coverage; savings bank and other life insurance in force; public and private retirement/pension assets and payments; property insurance underwriting assn policies issued; auto assigned risk insurance policies written, coverage, and discount/surcharge categories; auto and fire/contents insurance coverage; and hospital and medical/dental insurance coverage by health service corporations.

U5100–1.8: Section H: Energy and Utilities

(p. 221-244) Contains 6 charts and 24 tables. Includes energy production; oil and gas wells, reserves, gas stored underground, and State income from leasing/royalties; energy consumption, customer bills, and prices, by fuel type and sector; and State Power Authority energy sources and disposition.

Also includes electric utility kWh generated; private electric and gas utility revenues, sales, and average bills and consumption per customer; natural gas supply outlook to 1999; energy requirement projections to 2000, by provider; and energy conversion factors.

U5100–1.9: Section I: Transportation

(p. 245-268) Contains 2 charts and 27 tables. Includes motor vehicle registrations; driver's licenses issued and in force; traffic accidents and contributing factors, with injuries and fatalities; vehicle miles traveled; traffic violation convictions; highway mileage and condition; new car fuel efficiency; and New York State Thruway traffic, tolls, revenues, and accidents.

Also includes Amtrak ridership; public transit service passengers, vehicle miles, and related data, by individual authority; rail and canal freight traffic; waterborne freight and vessel traffic by port; airfields; airport passenger and freight traffic, and aircraft departures; and commuter airline passengers.

U5100–1.10: Section J: Agriculture

(p. 269-285) Contains 2 maps, 1 chart, and 16 tables. Includes farms, acreage, and average farm value; leading counties for selected agricultural products; harvested acreage and production of principal crops; livestock, dairy, and poultry inventory and/or production; livestock and crop marketings; and apple and grape prices and utilization.

U5100–1.11: Section K: Natural Resources, Conservation, and Tourism

(p. 287-305) Contains 2 maps and 20 tables. Includes land acreage under jurisdiction of State Environmental Conservation Dept; acreage and/or attendance for State recreational, camping, park, and historic sites; tourists at Empire State Plaza; motorboat and snowmobile registrations; and fish distributed by State hatcheries.

Also includes forest fires and acres burned; seedlings distributed; State forest product sales; hunting, fishing, and trapping licenses; deer take; significant earthquakes since 1737; air pollution severity and point sources; municipal sewage treatment plants; and solid waste disposal sites.

U5100–1.12: Section L: Public Safety, Law Enforcement, and the Courts

(p. 307-338) Contains 38 tables. Includes State and local criminal justice expenditures; State criminal justice staff by agency; municipal police, sheriff's dept, and local probation agency employees; State police information network entries and inquiries; and pistol licenses.

Also includes crimes and arrests, by offense; criminal case processing time, dispositions, and sentences; inmate population and characteristics; county jail/penitentiary admissions and releases; recidivism; parolees and parole; juvenile residential facility admissions; appellate court case activity, including bar admissions and attorney disciplinary proceedings; and community dispute resolution centers intake and dispositions.

U5100–1.13: Section M: Government Finance and Operations

(p. 339-410) Contains 72 tables. Includes State receipts and disbursements by fund, appropriations by agency, and tax collections by type (with related data); motor vehicle registration and driver's license fees; horse racing revenues; sales/use tax rates; and income tax collections, refunds, taxpayers, income, deductions and exemptions claimed, tax liability, and returns.

Also includes revenues from public land and surplus property disposition, and from use of State facilities; licenses issued and revenues; State lottery sales and prizes; public debt; local government entities, revenues, expenditures, State aid, and bonds issued and redeemed; taxable property value, equalization rates, and/or acreage; and value of exempt real property.

Also includes commodity contracts awarded to resident bidders, and small and minority businesses; State highway contract awards; professional service and construction contracts awarded to minority/female-owned firms; public employee and teacher retirement system contributions, benefits, and assets; on- and off-track betting; government space leased and rent paid; and capital projects and financing.

U5100–1.14: Section N: Elections

(p. 411-438) Contains 9 maps and 11 tables. Includes voter registration; political party enrollment; votes cast for President, U.S. Senator and Representatives, Governor, and State comptroller, attorney general, senators, and assembly members; and population of political districts.

U5680
University of Alabama:
Center for Business
and Economic Research

U5680–1   ALABAMA BUSINESS
Monthly. Approx. 8 p.
ISSN 0002-4163.
LC 52-25749.
SRI/MF/complete, shipped quarterly

Monthly report on Alabama business activity indicators, with data on industrial production and consumption, construction, finance, prices, employment, and trade. Data are current to 3-4 months preceding cover date.

Data are compiled by the Center for Business and Economic Research from reports of Federal and State agencies, and various private sources.

Each issue includes articles or brief commentaries, occasionally containing statistics; and 1 detailed table on general business indicators, including the following:

a. Industrial and construction activities, including production of selected energy commodities and pulp/paper/paperboard; consumption of cotton, industrial electricity, and cement; and value of building contracts awarded, by type.

b. Finance and prices, including savings and loan assn savings; tax collections by tax type; and index of prices received by Alabama farmers.

c. Labor force: unemployment; employment by industry division, and manufacturing and selected other industry groups; State employment service job applicants and placements; unemployment compensation initial claims and payments; and labor force and unemployment rate, by county.

d. Trade: imports, exports, and total shipments through Port of Mobile; non-industrial electric energy consumption; gasoline sales volume; new car registrations; and taxable retail sales, by kind of business, MSA, and county.

e. Building activity: value of total, residential, and nonresidential building permits, for State and selected cities.

Table presents most data for month of coverage and the preceding 12 months, and annually for the preceding 2 years.

Please note that retail sales data for current months, suspended in the Feb.-Aug. 1984 issues, have been resumed. The Sept. 1984 issue presents monthly retail sales data for 1983. Beginning in the Oct. 1984 issue, the data cover taxable sales only, and are presented for Jan. 1984 through month of coverage. The Oct. 1984 issue includes an explanation of changes in the retail data series.

Monthly table appears in all issues. All additional features with substantial statistical content are described, as they appear, under "Statistical Features." Nonstatistical features are not covered.

Availability: University of Alabama: Center for Business and Economic Research, PO Box AK, University AL 35486, †; SRI/MF/complete, shipped quarterly.

Issues reviewed during 1985: Sept. 1984-Aug. 1985 (P) (Vol. 53, Nos. 9-12; Vol. 54, Nos. 1-8).

STATISTICAL FEATURES:

U5680-1.601: Nov. 1984 (Vol. 53, No. 11)

FORECAST CALLS FOR IMPROVED STATE ECONOMY

(p. 1-2) Article, with 1 table forecasting Alabama population and selected economic indicators, including total and per capita GSP and personal and disposable income; employment and unemployment rate; manufacturing wages; retail trade; tax revenues; energy consumption indexes; and per capita gasoline consumption; with selected comparisons to U.S.; 1984-93.

Most monetary values are shown in current and constant 1972 dollars. Data are from the Alabama Econometric Model developed by University of Alabama.

U5680-1.602: June 1985 (Vol. 54, No. 6)

TRAVEL IN ALABAMA: THE ECONOMIC IMPACT

(p. 2, 8) By James W. Adams. Article, with 1 table and text statistics showing top 10 States ranked by percent of travel parties traveling to Alabama, 1984, with comparisons to 1983; and distribution of Alabama travel expenditures by State region, and travel-related employment vs. 3 other industries, 1984. Most data are from Alabama Bureau of Tourism and Travel.

U5750
University of Alaska: Agricultural Experiment Station

U5750-1   ALASKA AGRICULTURAL STATISTICS, 1984
Annual.   June 1984.   27 p.
LC 79-640359.
SRI/MF/complete

Annual report on Alaska agricultural production and income, mostly 1981-83, with some data for 1984 and summary trends from 1960. Data generally are shown by commodity and/or district.

Report covers production, value, cash receipts, and, as applicable, acreage, yield, and/or inventory, for field crop, vegetable, livestock, poultry, and dairy sectors.

Also includes data on fertilizer consumption, reindeer, and weather.

Data are compiled by Alaska Crop and Livestock Reporting Service in cooperation with USDA, Alaska Dept of Natural Resources, and University of Alaska.

Contains contents listing and foreword (p. 1-2); and 30 tables arranged in 4 sections, each preceded by a narrative summary (p. 3-27).

Previous report, for 1980-82, is described in SRI 1983 Annual, under this number.

Availability: Alaska Crop and Livestock Reporting Service, PO Box 799, Palmer AK 99645, $5.00; SRI/MF/complete.

U5780
University of Alaska: Institute of Social and Economic Research

U5780-1   ALASKA REVIEW OF SOCIAL AND ECONOMIC CONDITIONS
Series.   For individual publication data, see below.
ISSN 0162-5403.
LC 78-645273.
SRI/MF/complete

Continuing series of reports on Alaska socioeconomic developments, including industrial activity, employment, prices, income, energy resources and consumption, and State revenue, expenditures, programs, and services.

Each report covers a single topic and contains narrative analysis, often with tables and charts presenting data from Federal and State agencies, University of Alaska, and private sources and surveys. Only reports with statistical content are described in SRI.

Reports reviewed during 1985 are described below.

Availability: University of Alaska: Institute of Social and Economic Research, 707 "A" St., Suite 206, Anchorage AK 99501, †; SRI/MF/complete.

U5780-1.10: Prices and Incomes, Alaska and the U.S., 1980-84

[Monograph. Sept. 1984. 28 p. Vol. XXI, No. 2. SRI/MF/complete.]

By Linda Leask. Report on prices, cost of living, and personal income in Alaska, 1960s-84. Data are from BLS, Census Bureau, and other governmental and private sources.

Includes 4 trend charts, and 27 tables showing the following data, for Alaska and/or Anchorage unless otherwise noted, with selected comparisons to the U.S., various periods 1967-84:

a. CPI for all urban consumers, by component; and average annual budget and costs for a family of 4, by expense category, and Federal taxes as a percent of family budget, all at 3 standard-of-living levels. Tables 1-4. (p. 4-9)

b. Transportation costs for water shipment of selected commodities from Seattle to 3 Alaskan cities; rates for air freight and parcel post, from Anchorage to 8 other Alaskan cities; and round-trip air fares from 13 Alaskan cities to Seattle. Tables 5-7. (p. 11-12)

c. Housing characteristics, including percent lacking complete plumbing; median value of owner-occupied houses, and median price of houses sold; and median monthly rents, and rent increase. Tables 8-12. (p. 13-15)

d. Construction cost indexes for public works projects, by city and State region, and for labor and materials of large construction projects in Anchorage, Fairbanks, and 6 other U.S. cities; and weekly food costs for a family of 4 under State low-cost food budget plan, for 9 cities. Tables 13-15. (p. 15-16)

e. Residential electric rates, average bills and State assistance, and average monthly electricity use, with detail by city or State region; and daily revenues per patient in community hospitals, for 4 States with highest and lowest hospital costs. Tables 16-19. (p. 17-19)

f. Earnings indexes for entry-level State and State university employees; median household income, with detail for home owners and renters and for households headed by women with children; percent of families below poverty level; per capita personal income; and distribution of employment, and median annual earnings, by occupational group and sex; with selected detail by city or State region. Tables 20-27. (p. 20-26)

U5780-1.11: Changes in the Well-being of Alaska Natives Since ANCSA

[Monograph. Nov. 1984. 12 p. Vol. XXI, No. 3. SRI/MF/complete.]

By John A. Kruse. Report on Alaska Native population characteristics since the passage of the Alaska Native Claims Settlement Act, with comparison to non-Native population, 1970 and 1980. Most data are from Census Bureau.

Includes 10 charts and 1 table showing the following data, generally as percents for Alaska Natives and non-Natives, mostly for 1970 and 1980:

a. Population by age, community size, and State region; death rates by general cause, and infant mortality rates; and educational attainment.

b. Labor force by employment status and sex; self-employment, and employment in government by level and private sector; portion of food supplied by personal subsistence activities; and median family income, families receiving public assistance, and population below poverty level.

U5830
University of Arizona: Arizona Crop and Livestock Reporting Service

U5830-1 **1984 ARIZONA AGRICULTURAL STATISTICS**
Annual.   July 1985.
iv+102+9 p.   Bull. S-20.
SRI/MF/complete

Annual report on Arizona agricultural production, marketing, and finances, mostly 1980-84, with some data for 1985. Data generally are shown by commodity and/or county, with selected comparisons to U.S.

Report covers production, prices, value, and, as applicable, acreage, yield, inventory, and disposition, for field crop, vegetable, fruit, livestock, dairy, wool, and poultry sectors.

Also includes data on Arizona farm income, production expenses, debt, and balance sheet; grain storage facilities; weather; reservoir storage; farm employment, hours, and wages; agricultural export value; irrigation; energy costs; electricity and telephone use and costs; motor fuel prices; cotton ginning; fertilizer use; pesticide sales; land ownership by county and type of owner; and public land grazing fees.

Also includes number and acreage of farms/ranches in U.S. and 14 western States.

Data are compiled by Arizona Crop and Livestock Reporting Service in conjunction with University of Arizona.

Contains contents listing (p. ii-iii); introduction (p. 1); 1 map, 3 charts, and 284 tables accompanied by brief narrative summaries (p. 2-101); directory of agricultural statistical offices, by State (p. 102); lists of related Arizona and USDA reports (7 p.); and 1 summary table (2 p.).

This is the 20th edition of the report.

Availability: University of Arizona: Arizona Crop and Livestock Reporting Service, Agricultural Statistician, 201 E. Indianola, Suite 250, Phoenix AZ 85012, †; SRI/MF/complete.

U5920
University of Arkansas: Agricultural Experiment Station

U5920-1 **1983 ARKANSAS AGRICULTURAL STATISTICS**
Annual.   Sept. 1984.   56 p.
Rpt. Series 288.
LC 59-63340.
SRI/MF/complete

Annual report on Arkansas agricultural production, marketing, and finances, 1983, with trends from as early as 1867. Data generally are shown by commodity, county, and district, with selected comparisons to U.S. and other States.

Covers production, prices, value, and, as applicable, acreage, yield, inventory, and disposition, for field crop, vegetable, fruit and nut, livestock, dairy, and poultry sectors.

Also includes farm income and expenses; land area, number and acreage of farms, and irrigated acreage; fertilizer consumption; farm workers and wages; aquaculture production; and farm real estate value for 7 southeastern States.

Data are compiled by Arkansas Crop and Livestock Reporting Service and University of Arkansas.

Contains contents listing and narrative summary (p. 1-4); 8 maps and 61 tables (p. 5-55); and list of additional reports issued (p. 56).

Previous report, for 1982, is described in SRI 1983 Annual, under this number.

Availability: Arkansas Crop and Livestock Reporting Service, PO Box 1417, Little Rock AR 72203, †; SRI/MF/complete.

U5925
University of Arkansas: Arkansas Rehabilitation Research and Training Center

U5925-1 **U.S. CENSUS AND DISABLED ADULTS: The 50 States and the District of Columbia**
Monograph.   Apr. 1984.
vi+63+App 13 p.
Rpt. No. 1250.
LC 85-620534.
SRI/MF/complete

By Frank Bowe. Report on labor force participation of disabled population, by State, 1980. Includes data on percent of population disabled; labor force status of disabled population age 16-64, by sex and race, and for Hispanics; and prevalence of transportation disabilities in noninstitutional disabled population aged 16-64 and 65/over; all shown by State, with selected State rankings and comparisons to total U.S.

Data are from 1980 U.S. census.

Contains contents listing (p. iii-iv); introduction, and narrative report interspersed with 2 summary charts repeated for each Bureau of Vocational Rehabilitation region (p. 4-60); references and list of tables (p. 61-63); and 13 tables (13 p.).

Availability: Arkansas Rehabilitation Research and Training Center, Dissemination Clerk, PO Box 1358, HSRC, Hot Springs AR 71902, $6.00; SRI/MF/complete.

U5930
University of Arkansas: Bureau of Business and Economic Research

U5930-1 **ARKANSAS BUSINESS AND ECONOMIC REVIEW**
Quarterly.   Approx. 50 p.
ISSN 0004-1742.   LC 78-510.
SRI/MF/complete

Quarterly report on business activity and management in Arkansas, Southeastern States, and the U.S. Data are mainly from Commerce Dept, BLS, and State agency reports.

Issues contain feature articles, usually statistical; and economic indicators section, with narrative review of quarter covered and 10 quarterly economic indicator tables. The 4th quarter issue includes an annual index of articles.

Quarterly economic indicator tables are listed below and appear in all issues. All additional features with substantial statistical content are described, as they appear, under "Statistical Features;" page locations and quarter of coverage for quarterly tables are also noted. Nonstatistical features are not covered.

Availability: University of Arkansas: Bureau of Business and Economic Research, College of Business Administration, Fayetteville AR 72701, †; SRI/MF/complete.

Issues reviewed during 1985: Vol. 17, Nos. 3-4, 1984; Vol. 18, No. 1, 1985 (P).

QUARTERLY TABLES:
[Tables show data for Arkansas quarterly for current year through quarter of coverage, and annually or quarterly for 7 or more previous years, unless otherwise noted. Tables [1-8] are generally accompanied by text data showing percent change for 4 preceding quarters and from 1967 base year, some with comparisons to U.S.]

[1] Labor force and employment [manufacturing wage/salary, agricultural, and total; and unemployment rate; shown monthly for 12-18 months generally through quarter following quarter of coverage, and annually for 4 preceding years; prior to Vol. 18, No. 1, table included data by major industry group].

[2] Personal income.

[3] Value added by manufacture.

[4] Cash receipts from farm marketings.

[5] Economic activity of savings and loan assns [value of new loans and net new savings].

[6] Freight traffic, Arkansas River commerce [inbound, outbound, and internal tonnages].

[7-8] Residential and nonresidential construction contracts [value].

[9] Labor force estimates [total labor force, unemployment rate, and employment, for U.S., Arkansas, 4 MSAs, and each county; generally as of month following quarter of coverage].

[10] Consumer prices [U.S. CPI, by item, monthly for 13 months generally through quarter following quarter of coverage, and annually for 8 preceding years].

STATISTICAL FEATURES:

U5930-1.601: Vol. 17, No. 3, 1984

QUARTERLY TABLES

(p. 30-40) Quarter of coverage is 2nd quarter 1984. For data descriptions, see U5930-1 above.

FOREIGN DIRECT INVESTMENT PATTERNS IN ARKANSAS: WHAT ARE THE ISSUES?

(p. 12-17) By Donald L. Bumpass. Article, with 3 tables showing foreign investment in U.S. affiliates, by major industry group; gross book value, employment share, and employment of U.S. affiliates, by region and for 6 Southeastern States; and number of foreign-owned manufacturing firms by country of owner, for 7 Southeastern States and total U.S.; various years 1977-82.

Data are from Commerce Dept and *Directory of Foreign-Owned Manufacturers in the U.S.*

ECONOMIC FORECAST FOR ARKANSAS THROUGH 1985, ANNUAL FEATURE

(p. 20-26) Annual article, by Harry French and Betty Weeks, presenting survey results on Arkansas economic outlook, and selected U.S. issues, 1984-85. Data are based on 75 responses to a July 1984 survey of Arkansas academicians, businessmen, and government officials, conducted by the issuing agency.

Includes 1 extended table showing respondents' expectations (increase, decrease, same level) for selected State economic indicators; and views on selected U.S. economic issues; 1984-85.

U5930-1.602: Vol. 17, No. 4, 1984

QUARTERLY TABLES

(p. 39-51, passim) Quarter of coverage is 3rd quarter 1984.

For data descriptions, see U5930-1 above.

PLANT LOCATION: A CONFLICT BETWEEN MANUFACTURERS AND COMMUNITY INTEREST GROUPS

(p. 1-8) By G. Michael Epping and Herman S. Napier. Article comparing perceptions of manufacturing executives and local community officials regarding factors of greatest importance in industrial siting decisions. Data are from an author survey receiving responses from 118 manufacturing executives locating a plant in Arkansas, 73 executives choosing not to locate in the State, and 209 local community leaders. Includes 2 undated tables.

INVESTING IN ELECTRIC UTILITY STOCK

(p. 9-12) By Wallace N. Davidson, III. Article, with 1 undated table presenting a measure of overall regulatory environment for utilities in each State, based on a composite index utilizing data from 5 unspecified investor services.

UNION ORGANIZING ACTIVITY AMONG SOUTHERN DEPOSITORY INTERMEDIARIES

(p. 13-19) By Duane B. Graddy and Gary A. Hall. Article, with 3 tables showing number and results of labor unionization elections involving financial institutions in the South, by institution type, individual union, and employment size, various periods 1962-80. Data are from National Labor Relations Board.

AHRP PANEL INDICATORS SUGGEST MILD DOWNTURN IN ARKANSAS ECONOMY, RECURRING FEATURE

(p. 23-34) Recurring article, by William R. Darden et al., on Arkansas economic conditions and prospects as perceived by State residents, 1978-84. Data are from quarterly surveys of the Arkansas Household Research Panel (AHRP).

Includes 10 tables showing survey response regarding current assessment and expectations for family financial status and general economic conditions; whether conditions are favorable for durable goods purchases; and intentions to purchase life insurance, securities, and investment real estate during the coming year; most accompanied by constant 1978 and seasonally adjusted indexes, quarterly Mar. 1978-Sept. 1984.

For description of previous survey, see SRI 1983 Annual under U5930-1.403.

MINERAL INDUSTRY OF ARKANSAS IN 1984, ANNUAL FEATURE

(p. 50) Annual article, with 1 table showing Arkansas nonfuel mineral production value and quantity, by commodity, 1983-84. Data are from U.S. Dept of Interior.

U5930-1.603: Vol. 18, No. 1, 1985

QUARTERLY TABLES

(p. 35-44) Quarter of coverage is 1st quarter 1985, with the following exceptions: table [4] shows data for 4th quarter 1984; tables [2] and [6-8] show data for 2nd quarter 1985; and table [1] shows data through May 1985.

For data descriptions, see U5930-1 above.

PERCEPTIONS OF ARKANSAS AS A MANUFACTURING LOCATION

(p. 1-7) By Philip Taylor and Mary Hirsch. Article on Arkansas manufacturing establishments' economic conditions and outlook for expansion. Data are based on 95 responses to a mid-1984 survey of Arkansas Power and Light Company industrial customers.

Includes 1 table showing survey response on 1983 capacity utilization, economic outlook over next 5 years, and likelihood of expansion in Arkansas, all by SIC 2-digit industry.

MULTI-STATE COMPARISON OF NONMETRO MIGRATION GROWTH

(p. 8-16) By Ronald J. Gunderson. Article, with 3 tables showing number of nonmetro counties and change in net migration rates, for 4 midwestern States; and regression analysis relating growth of nonmetro counties to selected demographic and socioeconomic variables; 1970-80 period. Data are from Census Bureau.

MEASURING THE SEASONALITY OF ARKANSAS' INSURED LABOR FORCE DATA

(p. 25-28) By Philip Taylor and Mary Hirsch. Article, with 2 tables showing Arkansas seasonally adjusted indexes of labor force by employment status, quarterly 1984; and actual and seasonally adjusted unemployment rate, quarterly 1970-83.

U5935
University of Arkansas: Center for Information Services

U5935-1   ARKANSAS STATE AND COUNTY ECONOMIC DATA
Annual.   Oct. 1984.
iii + 18 p.
SRI/MF/complete

Annual compilation, by Frank H. Troutman and Neva Wayman, of Arkansas social and economic data, by MSA and/or county, 1984.

Data are primarily from State and Federal agencies. Report is compiled by the University of Arkansas Center for Information Services, for the Arkansas Industrial Development Commission.

Contains contents listing (p. iii); and 17 tables showing data for various periods 1959-83, by MSA and/or county, as follows:

a. Population and components of change; labor force, employment, and unemployment rate; total and manufacturing employment, payrolls, and average weekly earnings, covered by State employment security law; and total and per capita personal income. 9 tables. (p. 2-10)

b. Sales for retail, wholesale, and service establishments; bank deposits; manufacturing value added; market value of agricultural products sold; property assessments; and public school enrollment. 8 tables. (p. 11-18)

This is the 3rd annual edition. Previous reports are covered by SRI under U5945-1; issuing agency has changed from University of Arkansas: Industrial Research and Extension Center.

Availability: University of Arkansas: Center for Information Services, Socio-Economic Data Services Division, 33rd and University Ave., Little Rock AR 72204, $1.00 for postage and handling; SRI/MF/complete.

U5945
University of Arkansas: Industrial Research and Extension Center

U5945-1   ARKANSAS STATE AND COUNTY ECONOMIC DATA
Annual.

SRI now covers this publication under U5935-1.

U5960
University of Arkansas: Office of Institutional Research

U5960–1   EIGHTEENTH ANNUAL RANK-ORDER DISTRIBUTION OF ADMINISTRATIVE SALARIES PAID, 1984/85
Annual. Dec. 31, 1984.
iii + 121 p.
LC 82-640747.
SRI/MF/complete

Annual report, for 1984/85, on administrative salaries paid in doctoral-granting public universities. Data are based on a survey of 151 State-supported single campus universities in 47 States, and 33 multicampus university systems in 27 States.

Contains introduction, and contents and table listing (p. i-iii); and tables I-III showing ranked and average salaries for the following: approximately 75 administrative positions in single campus universities (p. 4-41), selected positions in 9 equal employment opportunity regions (p. 43-114), and approximately 30 positions in multicampus university systems (p. 116-121).

Salaries are not specified by university; however a list of universities surveyed is presented at the beginning of each table.

Availability: University of Arkansas: Office of Institutional Research, 318 Administration Bldg., Fayetteville AR 72701, $7.00; SRI/MF/ complete.

U6215
University of California at Los Angeles: Graduate School of Education

U6215–1   AMERICAN FRESHMAN: National Norms for Fall 1984
Annual. Dec. 1984.
ii + 178 p.
ISSN 0278-6990.
LC sc80-1315.
SRI/MF/complete

Annual survey report, by Alexander W. Astin et al., on characteristics of full-time students entering college for the 1st time in fall 1984. Presents data on freshman biographic and demographic characteristics, career plans, educational aspirations, and financial arrangements.

Study is part of the Cooperative Institutional Research Program ongoing longitudinal study of U.S. higher education system, sponsored by the American Council on Education and currently administered by the University of California at Los Angeles Graduate School of Education.

Data for the 1984 survey are from responses of 182,370 freshmen entering 345 2- or 4-year colleges and universities, and are weighted to provide representative data (national norms) for all entering full-time students.

Contains contents listing (2 p.); introduction, and summary with 6 charts (p. 1-7); and 1 extended table presenting weighted national norms for 43 items, listed below and repeated for the following:

a. Freshman men (p. 11-26); freshman women (p. 27-42); and all freshmen (p. 43-58); all shown by type of institution (2-year public and private; 4-year public, private-nonsectarian, Protestant, and Catholic; public and private universities; and public and private predominantly black colleges).

b. Universities (public and private, of low, medium, and high selectivity), by sex (p. 59-74); and 4-year colleges (public, private-nonsectarian, other sectarian, and Catholic colleges, of low, medium, and high selectivity) (p. 75-90).

c. Geographic regions (East, Midwest, South, and West), by sex. (p. 91-106).

Also contains appendices A-F (p. 107-178), including research methodology, facsimile of student questionnaire form, list of participating institutions, and facsimile of report furnished to participating institutions.

This is the 19th annual report.

Availability: University of California at Los Angeles: Graduate School of Education, Cooperative Institutional Research Program, Los Angeles CA 90024, $8.25; SRI/MF/complete.

TABLE ITEMS:

U6215–1.1: Weighted Norms

Weighted national norms are presented for the following items:

BIOGRAPHIC DATA

[1] Year graduated from high school [1981-84 or earlier; high school equivalency, or never completed high school].

[2] Age by Dec. 31, 1984.

[3] Racial background [white/Caucasian, black/Negro/Afro- American, American Indian, Asian-American/Oriental, Mexican-American/Chicano, Puerto Rican-American, and other].

[4] Political orientation [far left, liberal, middle-of- the-road, conservative, and far right].

[5-6] [Average] grade and academic rank in high school.

[7] Estimated parental income.

[8-9] Persons currently dependent on parents for support; and number of other dependents currently attending college.

[10] Miles from home to college.

[11] Marital status.

[12] U.S. citizen.

[13] Permission to use student I.D.

[14-15] Have met or exceeded recommended years of study in [English, math, foreign language, physical and biological sciences, history/government, other social studies, computer science, and art/music]; and type of high school attended [public or private].

[16-17] Have had or will need remedial work in [English, reading, math, social studies, science, and foreign language].

[18] Disabilities [by type].

[19] Twin status.

CHOICE OF COLLEGE

[20] This college is student's [1st, 2nd, 3rd, or less than 3rd choice].

[21-22] Reasons noted as very important in deciding to go to college; and as very important in selecting this college.

[23-24] Number of other colleges applied to for admission this year; and number of other college acceptances this year.

RELIGION

[25-27] Current religious preference; and father's and mother's religious preference.

ACADEMIC AND OTHER PLANS

[28] [Probable major field of study:] arts and humanities, biological science, business, education, engineering, physical science, professional, social science, technical, and other fields; [each field includes 6-11 subfields].

[29-33] Probable career occupation [by 44 categories]; and father's and mother's education and occupation.

[34] Activities engaged in by students during the past year [including participation in speech/debate, arts, sports, and student organizations; computer use; religious service attendance; class absences; smoking; vitamin and tranquilizer use; volunteer work; recital/ concert attendance; jogging or other exercise; beer drinking; and work in political campaign].

[35-36] Highest degree planned [at this institution and] anywhere.

[37] Students estimate chances are very good [for 26 alternative possibilities, including changing major field, career choice, and college; obtaining a job to pay college expenses; joining fraternity/sorority; making at least a "B" average; participating in student protests; getting a bachelor's degree; marrying; and finding a job in preferred field].

[38] Objectives considered to be essential or very important [including being an authority in chosen field; raising a family; being very well off financially; and keeping up with political affairs].

METHODS OF FINANCING EDUCATION

[39] Sources for educational expenses [parental aid; spouse; savings from summer work; other savings; grants, scholarships, and loans (including Pell Grants, Federal Guaranteed Student Loans, and college work/study grants); part- or full-time employment; own and parent's G.I. benefits; and other sources of support].

[40] Concern about financing college [no, some, or major concern].

RESIDENCY PLANS AND POLITICAL/SOCIAL ATTITUDES

[41-42] Residence planned and preferred during fall term [with parents/relatives, other private home/apartment, college dormitory, fraternity/sorority house, and other campus housing].

[43] Agree strongly or somewhat [on approximately 30 public policy, social, and academic issues, including consumer and environmental protection; disarmament; energy use; defense spending; capital punishment; national health policy; abortion; school busing and grading; women's employment; sexual behavior; taxation; marijuana; college officials' right to regulate student behavior and ban speakers; student evaluation of faculty; preferential treatment for disadvantaged persons and competency standards for college graduation].

U6250
University of California at Los Angeles: Latin American Center

U6250–1   STATISTICAL ABSTRACT OF LATIN AMERICA

Annual. 1984. lii+886 p.
Vol. 23.
ISBN 0- 87903-244-8 (cloth).
LC 56-63569.
SRI/MF/not filmed

Annual report, for 1984, presenting detailed social, governmental, and economic statistics for Latin America. Data are primarily for 1970s-81, with historical trends from as early as 1774, and population projections to 2025.

Most data are from Latin American governmental sources, and international agencies such as UN, OAS, AID, and IMF. Data sources appear beneath each table. Report is edited by James W. Wilkie and Adam Perkal.

Contents:

a. Contents listing and preface, with 3 maps and 6 tables described below; list of tables; methodology, with 1 map showing major cities and summary population; explanation of terms; list of major sources; and measurement conversion table. (p. v-lii)

b. 34 maps and charts, and 802 tables grouped in 34 chapters, described below. (p. 1-731)

c. 6 narrative chapters with 53 charts and 89 tables, also described below. (p. 733-874)

d. Index. (p. 875-886)

This is the 23rd edition of the report. For description of 22nd edition, see SRI 1983 Annual under this number.

Availability: University of California at Los Angeles: Latin American Center, 405 Hilgard Ave., Los Angeles CA 90024, $100.00; SRI/MF/not filmed.

CHAPTERS:

[Most tables show data for the following countries: Argentina, Bolivia, Brazil, Chile, Colombia, Costa Rica, Cuba, Dominican Republic, Ecuador, El Salvador, Guatemala, Haiti, Honduras, Mexico, Nicaragua, Panama, Paraguay, Peru, Uruguay, and Venezuela. Some tables also show comparisons with U.S. and other countries.]

U6250–1.1: Preface: On Defining the Concepts of Latin America, the Caribbean, and Economically Questionable Nations (EQNs)

(p. vii-xxv) By James W. Wilkie. Report identifying countries and territories traditionally and nontraditionally associated with Latin America, and describing the political and economic status of countries gaining independence since the 1960s.

Includes 3 maps and 6 tables showing summary population, land area, and GDP trends; year of independence and/or country of current prior affiliation; membership in international organizations; and Central American Common Market (CACM) trade; all by Latin American country and/or area, with selected comparisons to other world areas; various years 1960-83. Also includes population of major Latin American metro areas with population of 1 million or over, 1972.

Part I: Main Indicators

U6250–1.2: Chapter 1: Main Social Indicators

(p. 2-11) Contains 13 tables. Includes gap between U.S. and Latin America for selected health, education, and communication (HEC) developmental indicators; and demographic trends including population by age, urban population, population density, birth and death rates, life expectancy, quality of life, and world population, rankings, and growth rates, by country.

Also includes indexes of central government expenditures and tax revenues, infant mortality, literacy, food consumption and production, and intake of protein, fat, and calories.

U6250–1.3: Chapter 2: Main Economic Indicators

(p. 14-37) Contains 22 charts and 23 tables. Includes total and per capita GDP; consumption; domestic investment; and economic profiles, including GDP by sector, central government finances, money and price trends, balance of payments, and external debt.

Part II: Geographic and Land Tenure Data

U6250–1.4: Chapter 3: Geography

(p. 40-83) Contains 2 maps and 31 tables. Includes population and density; land area of major civil divisions; altitudes of principal mountains; last eruption date and altitude of volcanoes; principal rivers, lakes, and deserts; distances between cities; monthly temperature and precipitation, by weather station; and average temperature and days without rain in capital cities.

U6250–1.5: Chapters 4-5: Land Use and Population in Agriculture, and Land Tenure

(p. 86-101) Contains 12 tables. Includes agricultural and nonagricultural land uses; cultivated, irrigated, and arable land; tractors in use; crop and pasture land development and investment; and agricultural population and employment.

Also includes number and size of agricultural landholdings; single and mixed land tenure systems; and land reform program beneficiaries and hectares distributed.

Part III: Social Data

U6250–1.6: Chapter 6: Demography

(p. 104-152) Contains 65 tables. Includes population estimates and growth rate, 1774-2025; population and density by major civil division; population of capital and principal cities; urban and rural population, by sex and age; indigenous (Indian) population and percent of total; and U.S. Hispanic population and elected officials in top 15 States and top 20 cities with largest Hispanic populations.

U6250–1.7: Chapter 7: Vital Statistics and Disease

(p. 154-168) Contains 13 tables. Includes life expectancy projected to 2025, by sex; births by age of mother; fertility and birth rates; deaths and top 5 causes by sex; death rates, including fetal, infant, and maternal deaths; and marriages, divorces, and divorce rates.

U6250–1.8: Chapter 8: Health Care, Welfare, and Family Planning

(p. 170-177) Contains 14 tables. Includes hospitals by type and ownership; hospital beds and utilization; urban and rural outpatient health facilities; and mental health clinics, rehabilitation centers, and dental clinics.

Also includes physicians, nurses by function, dentists, and other professional and auxiliary health personnel; population per physician; child health services and children attended; and infant immunizations.

U6250–1.9: Chapter 9: Construction, Housing, and Utilities

(p. 180-184) Contains 5 tables. Includes population with water supply and sewage systems, by urban-rural status; housing access to water supply by source, and sanitary facilities by type; and Mexico construction index based on cement consumption, by State.

U6250–1.10: Chapter 10: Education and Science

(p. 186-205) Contains 22 tables. Includes urban and rural illiteracy by sex; proportions of school-age population enrolled, by age; elementary and secondary educational enrollment and attainment by urban-rural status, by age and sex; teachers by level and sex; pre-primary and primary schools, teachers, and pupils; postsecondary enrollment by sex and field of study; postsecondary teachers by sex and type of institution; and graduates by sex, degree level, and field of study.

Also includes public expenditures on education by object and level; libraries by type; and scientific and technical personnel by field, and R&D expenditures.

U6250–1.11: Chapter 11: The Military and Religion

(p. 208-247) Contains 37 tables. Includes armed forces expenditures, personnel, vessels, and aircraft; military expenditure per capita, and as a percent of total government expenditures and GDP; U.S. military aid and sales agreements, deliveries, and transfer costs; and U.S. expenditures and students trained under international military education and training program.

Also includes Catholic Church clerical hierarchy, charitable institutions, and schools; population per Catholic priest; Jehovah's Witnesses publishers and members; religious affiliation and participation since 1900, by religion and selected denomination; and Bibles distributed since 1900.

Part IV: Socioeconomic Data

U6250–1.12: Chapter 12: Communication

(p. 250-257) Contains 12 tables. Includes daily newspapers and circulation; newsprint consumption and imports; books published, by subject; mail and telegram traffic; telephones in use; cinemas and attendance; and radio and TV stations and receivers.

U6250–1.13: Chapter 13: Employment, Underemployment, Unemployment, and Class Structure

(p. 260-278) Contains 4 charts and 20 tables. Includes "economically active" population, by sex, industry, occupation, and urban and agricultural activity; manufacturing employment and hours of work; labor force participation, by sex; underemployment and unemployment survey topics; unemployment by age, and sex; and urban open unemployment.

Also includes distribution of middle and upper social classes; Mexico social modernization index; household income distribution; and urban and rural households in poverty.

U6250-1.14: Chapter 14: Wages, Income Distribution, and Cooperatives

(p. 280-297) Contains 26 tables. Includes minimum and real wages in selected industries; real wage indexes; CPI; urban legal minimum wages; and labor disputes, workers involved, and workdays lost.

Part V: Economic Data

U6250-1.15: Chapters 15-18: Agricultural, Fisheries, Ranching, and Forestry Production

(p. 300-332) Contains 1 map and 51 tables. Includes area, production, and yield for selected grain crops, cotton, coffee, cocoa beans, selected vegetable crops, bananas, oranges/tangerines, sugar cane, tobacco, and copra; agricultural production indexes; fertilizer consumption, production, and foreign trade; fish catch from marine areas and inland waters; and seaweed production.

Also includes livestock inventory by species; horses; milk production and yield; wool output; lumber and wood panel production; wood pulp output; and newsprint, paper, and paperboard production.

U6250-1.16: Chapter 19: Industrial Production

(p. 334-344) Contains 17 tables. Includes industrial production index; production of autos, butter, cheese, cement, cigarettes, copper, cotton fabric and yarn, fertilizer, iron, meat, sheet metal, steel, sugar, and wheat flour; Argentina shipbuilding; and Cuba vs. world sugar production since 1850.

U6250-1.17: Chapters 20-21: Mining Production and Energy Resources

(p. 346-377) Contains 46 tables. Includes mine output of antimony, bauxite, chromite, copper, fluorspar, gold, gypsum, iron, lead, manganese, mercury, molybdenum, nickel, phosphate rock, salt, silver, sulphur, tin, tungsten, and zinc.

Also includes total energy production, total and per capita consumption, and indexes; oil and gas production and reserves; refined oil products and offshore oil production; oil refinery distillation capacity; fuelwood and bagasse (sugarcane residue) production; coal production and resources; electrical energy production, installed capacity, and consumption; and geothermal energy installed capacity.

U6250-1.18: Chapter 22: Transportation

(p. 380-389) Contains 13 tables. Includes civil aviation passenger, freight, and mail traffic; airline passenger load factors; railroad freight and passenger traffic, track length, vehicles, and equipment; total and paved road length; commercial and passenger motor vehicle registrations; and international shipping, including vessels entered and cleared, and cargo loaded and unloaded.

U6250-1.19: Chapter 23: National Accounts

(p. 392-428) Contains 53 tables. Includes real GDP, by sector and by component, with trends from 1896.

U6250-1.20: Chapters 24-25: Government Plans, Finance, and Money Supply; and Exchange Rates

(p. 430-467) Contains 1 chart and 58 tables. Includes growth in employment, agriculture, and exports, and investments under current national development plans; central government expenditures by function, revenues by source, and deficits and financing methods; money supply; Mexico inflation indexes; and U.S. dollar exchange rate index.

Also includes free/black market, Special Drawing Rights, and real exchange rates; and exchange agreements.

U6250-1.21: Chapter 26: Price Changes, Commodity Prices, and Interest Rates

(p. 470-507) Contains 38 tables. Includes changes in consumer prices, GDP deflators, and Cuba food prices; cost-of-living index in capital cities; UN and IMF indexes of wholesale prices and export and import unit values; wholesale prices by commodity; and OPEC crude oil prices.

Also includes average financing terms of U.S. and international agency loans to Latin America; and 90-day, prime, and U.S. Federal funds interest rates.

Part VI: International Statistics

U6250-1.22: Chapters 27-28: Balance of Payments and International Liquidity; and Foreign Trade

(p. 510-610) Contains 2 charts and 97 tables. Includes detailed balances of current and capital accounts; international reserves and foreign exchange; gold physical holdings; exports, imports, and trade distribution by commodity and industry; trade and purchasing power indexes; and trade with selected regions and countries, including data for Latin American Integration Assn, Economic Commission for Latin America, and Central American Common Market.

U6250-1.23: Chapters 29-30: Nonagricultural and Agricultural Commodities in Foreign Trade

(p. 612-657) Contains 2 charts and 55 tables. Includes exports and imports of crude and refined oil; OPEC oil production and U.S. imports; wood panel, sawnwood, and paper/paperboard trade; silver supply and consumption; machinery, manufacturing, and fuel trade shares; and forest product and fishery export shares of consumption.

Also includes value of agricultural trade, by commodity group; and trade volume of bana-nas, selected grains, butter, cacao, coffee, cotton, meat, milk, soybean oil, sugar, and wool.

U6250-1.24: Chapter 31: Loans, Grants, and Assistance

(p. 660-694) Contains 40 tables. Includes IMF fund accounts; AID and general U.S. assistance; Eximbank loans; Peace Corps volunteers; cumulative foreign loans to Mexico; external public debt outstanding and interest, amortization, and debt service payments; cumulative loan exposure of 13 U.S. banks, UK, and all international banks; Japanese lead management of loans; and Inter-American Development Bank loans.

U6250-1.25: Chapter 32: Investments

(p. 696-708) Contains 12 tables. Includes direct and portfolio investment flows; direct U.S. foreign investment and capital flows, and capital expenditures and gross product of U.S. majority-owned foreign affiliates, by industry; UK direct investment; and direct investment by OECD Development Assistance Committee countries.

U6250-1.26: Chapter 33: Immigration and Tourism

(p. 710-722) Contains 17 tables. Includes immigrants to the U.S., by occupation, country of birth, and immigration status; U.S. naturalizations; legal Mexican immigration since 1900; deportable aliens, with detail for Mexicans and Haitians; aliens deported by country and cause; temporary workers admitted to U.S.; tourists by travel mode, and receipts; lodging capacity; and Cuba immigration and emigration.

Part VII: Political Data

U6250-1.27: Chapter 34: Political Statistics

(p. 724-731) Contains 12 tables. Includes country rankings for political and civil rights (Freedom House survey and Fitzgibbon-Johnson Index); and presidential and legislative election results.

Part VIII: Development of Data

U6250-1.28: Chapter 35: New Research on Food Production in Latin America Since 1952

(p. 733-781) By James W. Wilkie and Manuel Moreno-Ibanez. Report examining Latin American food production since 1952, and interrelating food supply with population growth, land reform, and revolution.

Includes 45 charts and 15 tables showing Latin American food production indexes, per capita daily caloric supply, food trade balances by commodity group and for principal commodities, fish consumption, agricultural population, and agricultural shares of total population and GDP, generally by country, various years 1950-81.

Also includes 2 tables on methodology.

U6250-1.29: Chapter 36: Problems in Comparative Crime Statistics for Latin America and the English-Speaking Caribbean, 1973-78

(p. 785-793) By Luis P. Salas and Raymond B. Surette. Report on reliability of Latin American crime statistics and data comparability among countries.

Includes 1 chart and 5 tables showing availability of statistics on crimes by offense, arrests, sentences, and prisoners, by country, 1973-78; and Chile homicide rates, by victim sex and age, 1976.

U6250-1.30: Chapter 37: Survey Research in Authoritarian Regimes: Brazil and the Southern Cone of Latin America Since 1970

(p. 795-814) By Brian H. Smith and Frederick C. Turner. Report on reliability of opinion surveys in South American countries under military rule.

Includes 6 tables presenting data on voting intentions in national elections in Uruguay, Chile, and Argentina, with selected comparisons to election results; and popularity of Argentine political leaders; various periods 1980-83.

U6250-1.31: Chapter 38: Losses and Lessons of the 1982 War for the Falklands

(p. 815-835) By Adam Perkal. Report on the 1982 conflict between UK and Argentina over the Falkland Islands. Includes 3 charts and 13 tables showing the following:

a. Chronology of events; Argentine and UK military personnel engaged in combat, injured, killed, and taken prisoner, and aircraft and ships engaged and lost; and UK task force composition; Mar.-Nov. 1982 period.

b. Central bank claims and reserves, defense expenditures, and military manpower, for Argentina and UK, various periods 1950-83.

c. Falkland Islands government revenues by source, expenditures by function, and cash flows; UK development expenditures; and Falkland Islands population, personal and national income, GNP, and GDP; various years 1973/74-1981/82.

U6250-1.32: Chapter 39: Sources of Investment Capital in Twentieth-Century Mexico

(p. 837-856) By Dale Story. Report evaluating the extent of private domestic, public, and foreign investment in Mexico's industrial sector since 1895.

Includes 3 charts and 8 tables showing Mexican government expenditures, with selected detail by function; total foreign and U.S. investment in Mexico; industrial ownership and capital investment shares, by source; and industrial value added; various years 1895-1979.

U6250-1.33: Chapter 40: Revisando la Deuda Publica Mexicana, 1970-82

(p. 857-874) By Samuel Schmidt. Report analyzing Mexico's public debt, 1970-82. Includes 40 tables showing Mexico's internal and external debt compared with the following financial indicators, various years 1970-82:

a. GDP by industry; government revenues, expenditures, investments, and budgetary deficit; CPI; U.S. export price index; dollar exchange rate and currency flow to U.S.; debt service and amortization; tax revenues; monetary reserves; exports; and trade balance.

b. Petroleum industry exports and taxes paid; and external debt of 5 government corporations.

Report is in Spanish and updates a similar report published in the 22nd edition of the *Abstract;* for description, see SRI 1983 Annual under U6250-1.30.

U6250-2   STATISTICAL ABSTRACT OF THE UNITED STATES-MEXICO BORDERLANDS
Recurring (irreg.)   1984.
xiv + 121 p.
Statistical Abstract of Latin America Supplement Series, Supplement 9.
ISBN 0-87903-243-X.
LC 83-24922.
SRI/MF/not filmed

Recurring report, for 1984, presenting detailed social, economic, and governmental statistics for the U.S.-Mexico borderland region. Data are shown primarily for 1970s-81, with historical trends from 1900, and population projections to 2000.

Most data are from U.S. and Mexican universities and Government agencies. Data sources appear beneath each table.

Contents:

Contents and table listings; explanation of terms; and preface, with 1 map. (p. v-xiv)

Part One. Statistical Time Series. 50 tables grouped in 10 chapters, described below. (p. 1-84)

Part Two. Development of Data. 4 narrative chapters with 18 tables, also described below. (p. 85-120)

Report is edited by Peter L. Reich. This is the 1st edition. Report is designed as a supplement to the annual *Statistical Abstract of Latin America,* covered in SRI under U6250-1.

Availability: University of California at Los Angeles: Latin American Center, 405 Hilgard Ave., Los Angeles CA 90024, $45.00; SRI/MF/not filmed.

CHAPTERS:
[Most chapters show data for Arizona, California, New Mexico, and Texas; and the Mexican States of Baja California Norte, Chihuahua, Coahuila, Nuevo Leon, Sonora, and Tamaulipas. Comparisons to border and national totals are also included.]

Part One: Statistical Time Series

U6250-2.1: Chapters 1-3: Demography, Vital Statistics, and Religion

(p. 4-32) Contains 17 tables. Includes population since 1900 and projected to 2000; population density; border city populations, with detail by Mexican State of origin; births, deaths, marriages, and divorces; U.S. population and births of Mexican origin/descent, and as percent of total Hispanics; and population by religious affiliation.

U6250-2.2: Chapter 4: Immigration

(p. 34-39) Contains 6 tables. Includes U.S.-Mexico immigration; Mexican workers departing to and returning from U.S.; undocumented Mexicans in U.S., number working in agriculture and other industries, and number apprehended and considered "deportable"; and U.S. Immigration and Naturalization Service man-hours for border patrol and criminal investigation activities.

U6250-2.3: Chapters 5-6: Employment, Wages, and Prices; and Maquiladoras

(p. 42-58) Contains 12 tables. Includes Mexican border city labor force by employment status, employment by industry, urban and rural minimum wages, and CPI; Mexico City minimum wages and CPI; U.S. border employment by industry; and U.S. Hispanic labor force by employment status, and total unemployent rate.

Also includes maquiladora establishments, total employment, average work hours, production workers by sex, technicians, and supervisors, by border city and industry. (Maquiladoras are foreign-owned assembly plants in Mexico producing goods for export and using imported materials and domestic labor. Export market is generally the U.S.)

U6250-2.4: Chapters 7-8: Transportation and Communication; and Agricultural and Fisheries Production

(p. 60-71) Contains 8 tables. Includes road mileage; motor vehicle registrations; airports; telephones in use; and motion pictures shown in Mexico, by national origin.

Also includes corn, cotton, and wheat production and acreage; and fishery production.

U6250-2.5: Chapters 9-10: Mexican-U.S. Economic Relations; and Tourism

(p. 74-84) Contains 7 tables. Includes peso-dollar exchange rates; bilateral trade since 1900; and U.S. Government grants/credits to Mexico and share of total Western Hemisphere and total foreign grants.

Also includes Mexican border tourists by city; Mexican tourism-related revenue and expenditures; and U.S. tourists in Mexico.

Part Two: Development of Data

U6250-2.6: Chapter 11: Economy of Baja California

(p. 88-99) By Mike Farrell. Report on the economic development of the Mexican State of Baja California, 1950s-70. Includes 10 tables showing the following:

a. Baja California: rural and urban population since 1930; GDP share by industry division, and compared to aggregate GDP of approximately 60 countries grouped by GDP level; imports and exports by commodity group, with detail for trade under the Border Industrialization Program; and percent of housing with selected structural characteristics, utility connections, and TV, with comparison to total Mexico.

b. Labor force participation rates by age and sex; and distribution of workers by monthly income; for total Mexico, and for Baja California and 2 border cities.

c. Deportable Mexican nationals in California, U.S., 1970-76.

U6250–2.7: Chapter 12: Gap Between Theoretical Modeling and the Application of These Models to the U.S.-Mexican Border Economy

(p. 102-104) By Jerry R. Ladman. Narrative methodological report.

U6250–2.8: Chapter 13: Industrial Technology Transfer for Borderlands Development: The Need for a U.S.-Mexican Data Base

(p. 106-113) By Martin E. Rosenfeldt. Report examining the relationship between the adjoining cities of McAllen, Tex., and Reynosa, Mexico. Includes 1 table showing pedestrian and vehicular border crossings between the cities; and McAllen and Reynosa population, and manufacturing employment, payroll, value added, GDP, and establishments, with co-variate analyses; 1970 and 1975.

U6250–2.9: Chapter 14: U.S.-Mexico Border Economic Interdependence: Input-Output Model Perspectives of the Effects of the 1982 Peso Devaluations on the San Diego Economy

(p. 116-120) By Kenneth L. Shellhammer. Report, with 4 tables showing econometric analyses of San Diego, Calif., bilateral trade with Mexico, 1982; and effects of 1982 peso devaluation on San Diego industrial production, income, and employment; all by industry division and manufacturing group.

U6250–3   LATIN AMERICAN POPULATION AND URBANIZATION ANALYSIS: Maps and Statistics, 1950-82

Monograph.   1984.
xxii+433 p.
Statistical Abstract of Latin America Supplement Series, Supplement 8.
ISBN 0-87903-242-1.
LC 83-620019.
SRI/MF/not filmed

By Richard W. Wilkie. Report presenting detailed analysis of population and urbanization changes in Latin American countries, primarily 1950s-82, with selected historical trends including population census data from as early as 1774.

Most data are from Government censuses, UN, and *Statistical Abstract of Latin America.* Data sources appear beneath each table.

Contents:

Contents, illustration, and table listings. (p. vii-xxi)

Part One. Overview. Introduction, 41 maps, 7 charts, and 17 tables, arranged in 4 chapters. (p. 3-91)

Part Two. Country Data. Detailed data on 20 Latin American countries, including brief narrative, 169 maps, 10 charts, and 131 tables, arranged in 20 chapters. (p. 95-431)

Data topics covered by tables in Part One and Part Two are described below.

Report is designed as a supplement to the annual *Statistical Abstract of Latin America,* covered in SRI under U6250-1.

Availability: University of California at Los Angeles: Latin American Center, 405 Hilgard Ave., Los Angeles CA 90024, $65.00; SRI/MF/ not filmed.

DATA TOPICS:

[Most data are shown for the following countries: Argentina, Bolivia, Brazil, Chile, Colombia, Costa Rica, Cuba, Dominican Republic, Ecuador, El Salvador, Guatemala, Haiti, Honduras, Mexico, Nicaragua, Panama, Paraguay, Peru, Uruguay, and Venezuela.

Urban-rural classifications generally are as follows: dispersed settlement (population of 1-99); village (100-2,500); simple urban (2,501-20,000); complex urban (20,001-500,000); and metropolitan (over 500,000).]

U6250–3.1: Part One: Overview

Tables cover the following data topics: population by urban rural classification, population density, and rankings, by country; population and rankings of major metro areas; and agricultural population as percent of total, agricultural landholdings by type of tenure system, land reform program beneficiaries and land distributed, land area, and internal migration as percent of total urban growth, all by country.

U6250–3.2: Part Two: Country Data

Tables cover the following data topics for each country: population and density, land area, and civil subdivisions, by Province or other political division; population by urban center and by urban-rural classification; historical trends in population census; population change indicators, including birth and death rates, life expectancy at birth, percent of population under age 15, and years required for population to double; and per capita GNP.

Data for Argentina also include number of urban centers, by population size; and in- and out-migration by Province and urban center.

U6395
University of Chicago: National Opinion Research Center

U6395–1   GENERAL SOCIAL SURVEYS, 1972-85: Cumulative Codebook

Annual.   July 1985.
v+554 p.
Social Science Series No. 6.
ISSN 0161-3340.
ISBN 0-932132-32-4.
SRI/MF/complete

Annual report cumulating responses to General Social Survey interviews on selected values and socioeconomic attitudes of adult Americans. Results are shown for all respondents, 1972-82 period and 1983-85, and for an over-sample of black Americans, 1982. Covers questions pertaining to politics, government, religion, women's issues, racial issues, employment and economic situation, and other social and ethical matters. Also includes detailed data on respondents' background and family characteristics.

Data are from 12 national survey samples of approximately 1,500 persons each, conducted Feb.-Apr. 1972-78, 1980, and 1982-85, by the National Opinion Research Center, University of Chicago. General Social Surveys include 3 types of questions: permanent, occurring in each survey; rotating, occurring in 2 out of every 3 surveys; and 1-time questions.

Report is intended to be used in conjunction with a separately published machine-readable data file, not covered by SRI.

Contains contents listing and preface (p. iii-v); introduction, with index to data by mnemonic code and question number (p. 1-19); 329 survey questions, described below (p. 21-325); appendices A-Q, on survey methodology (p. 327-547); and subject index (p. 548-554).

Availability: Roper Center, University of Connecticut, Box U-164R, Storrs CT 06268; or University of Chicago: National Opinion Research Center, 6030 S. Ellis Ave., Chicago IL 60637 (single copies only), $12.00; SRI/MF/complete.

QUESTION AREAS:

U6395–1.1: Respondent Characteristics and Political Attitudes

a. Background of respondent, including employment, occupation, and industry; marital status; employment, occupation, and industry of spouse and father; number of siblings and children; age and education; parents' and spouse's education; and sex and race. Questions 1-21. (p. 21-41)

b. Home characteristics at 16 years of age; mother's work history; whether birthplace in or outside of U.S.; country of ancestry; household size, composition, and income; military service; work hours for self and spouse; residence location; housing type and tenure; and occupational relationship with data, people, and things, for self, spouse, and father. Questions 22-60. (p. 42-79)

c. Party affiliation, voting history, and political ideology; adequacy of government spending for space exploration, environment, health, urban problems, crime reduction, drug problems, education, blacks, defense, foreign aid, welfare, transportation, Social Security, and parks/recreation; agreement with specified opinions on government, business, and society; support for government reduction of income differences between rich and poor; and opinions on amount of Federal income tax paid. Questions 61-78. (p. 80-105)

d. Attitudes regarding censorship and civil liberties of persons with ideas considered bad or dangerous by others; attitudes regarding death penalty, gun control, courts, crime and law enforcement, wiretapping, legalization of marijuana, prospects of war, U.S. role in world affairs, continuation of U.S. in UN, and communism; and popularity rating of 8 countries. Questions 79-103. (p. 106-122)

U6395–1.2: Religious Preference, Quality of Life, and Selected Attitudes

a. Religious preferences, background, and beliefs, including view of life after death and image of God; spouse's religious preference and background; attitudes regarding prayer in public schools, the Bible, and human nature; and attitudes regarding race-related matters, including interracial marriage, personal race relations, community and school integration, busing, and equal employment opportunities for blacks, with some detail for black respondents only. Questions 104-151. (p. 122-161)

b. General attitudes toward life and society, including satisfaction with marriage and health; confidence in other people and in selected institutions; qualities desirable in children; social activities, and membership in 15 types of organizations; use of alcohol and tobacco; and attitudes regarding money, quality of life, and public officials. Questions 152-177. (p. 162-199)

c. Job security and satisfaction; importance ratings for selected job characteristics; social class; satisfaction with financial situation; family income category, and minimum income needed; job supervision; unemployment history and receipt of government aid; and labor union membership. Questions 178-194. (p. 199-211)

d. Opinions about selected social issues, including women's rights and participation in politics and business, abortion, ideal family size, birth control, sex education, divorce, extramarital sex, homosexuality, pornography, euthanasia, and suicide. Questions 195-228. (p. 211-228)

e. Participation in labor strike, and in civil rights, anti- or pro-war, and school-related demonstrations; assault and other crime victimization experiences; attitudes regarding justifiability of violence; perception of neighborhood safety; gun ownership; police record; and hunting participation. Questions 229-240. (p. 229-237)

f. Media use; and interview characteristics of respondent. Questions 241-248. (p. 237-239)

U6395–1.3: Social Issues, Military Service, and Miscellaneous

a. Opinions about women and race, including abortion, working mothers, Equal Rights Amendment, married women in business/industry, programs encouraging integration of suburbs, and racial differences. Questions 249-266. (p. 240-249)

b. Frequency with which interview topics are thought about; and family 5-year history of traumatic events including divorce, unemployment, hospitalization/disability, and death. Questions 267-278. (p. 250-259)

c. Opinions about level of defense spending, Federal Government efforts for minority groups, and Government services. Questions 279-281. (p. 259-262)

d. Value attached to various aspects of life, including family, work, leisure, friends, relatives, religion, and politics; concern about threats to privacy; interest in public affairs; personal time management; and perceptions of survey validity. Questions 282-287. (p. 262-266)

e. Attitudes on compulsory national service; armed service personnel and pay/benefits; proportion of women, Hispanics, and blacks in armed forces, and women's suitability for selected combat vs. noncombat jobs; draft vs. volunteer army; draft exemptions and penalties for refusal to register;

and education and career training responsibilities of military. Questions 288-302. (p. 267-278)

f. Expectations for nuclear, conventional, and guerilla war; U.S.-USSR relations and arms reductions; experiences regarding civilian employment with military/DOD or defense contractors; and perceived economic dependency of local area on defense business. Questions 303-307. (p. 279-282)

g. Opinions on civic responsibilities, including voting, community volunteer work, jury duty, reporting crimes witnessed, ability to speak and understand English, keeping informed about public affairs, and military service; Federal Government responsibility for poverty relief, medical assistance, and improvement of living standards for blacks; social contacts and relationships; vocabulary knowledge; and sample frames/methods and weights. Questions 308-329. (p. 283-325)

U6430
University of Colorado:
Business Research Division

U6430–1 COLORADO BUSINESS REVIEW
Monthly. Approx. 8 p.
ISSN 0010-1524.
LC 59-33322.
SRI/MF/complete, shipped quarterly

Monthly report on selected Colorado State and city business indicators, including employment, energy production, construction, and farm prices. Data are from Colorado Dept of Labor and Employment, and Federal, other State, local, and private agencies. Month of data coverage is 4 months prior to cover date.

Contains 2 monthly tables on economic indicators; and occasional special articles.

Monthly tables are listed below and appear in all issues. All additional features with substantial statistical content are described, as they appear, under "Statistical Features." Nonstatistical features are not covered.

Report is discontinued with the Dec. 1984 issue.

Availability: University of Colorado: Business Research Division, Graduate School of Business Administration, Campus Box 420, Boulder CO 80309, Colorado residents †, others $5.00 per yr.; SRI/MF/complete, shipped quarterly.

Issues reviewed during 1985: Oct.-Dec. 1984 (P) (Vol. LVII, Nos. 10-12).

MONTHLY TABLES:
[Tables show data for month of coverage, previous month, and same month of preceding year.]

[1] Colorado business indicators [including unemployment, agricultural employment, nonagricultural employment by industry division and selected major group; weekly hours and earnings in construction and manufacturing; bankruptcies; unemployment claims; State revenues and expenditures; energy production and consumption; construction permits; highway contractor payments; savings and loan assn new savings; national park visits; motor

vehicle title applications; Denver airport activity; and prices received by farmers for 6 agricultural commodities].

[2] Local business conditions [electric power use; banks and deposits; and residential and nonresidential construction value; for approximately 40 Colorado cities].

STATISTICAL FEATURE:

U6430–1.601: Oct. 1984 (Vol. LVII, No. 10)

EVOLUTION OF THE COLORADO ECONOMY, 1940-80
(p. 2-4) By Michael C. Bird. Article, with 1 table showing Colorado employment, by industry division and selected major industry group, and for armed forces, decennially 1940-80, with "shift-share" analysis of Colorado employment trends relative to national trends. Data are from Census Bureau.

U6430–2 TRAVEL TRENDS IN THE U.S. AND CANADA, 1984 Edition
Triennial. 1984. ix+262 p.
ISBN 0-89478-078-6.
LC 82-620698.
SRI/MF/complete

Triennial report, by Charles R. Goeldner and Karen P. Duea, presenting detailed data on U.S. and Canadian travel and tourism, various years 1960-87. Includes data on visits to parks, travel economic impact, transportation use, government tourism dept expenditures and budgets, trip and traveler characteristics, and international travel.

Data are from national and local governments, traveler surveys, and selected private sources.

Contains preface, and listings of contents and tables (p. ii-ix); U.S. data, with narrative and 59 tables (p. 2-139); Canadian data, with narrative and 49 tables (p. 141-225); and information source listings (p. 227-262).

All tables are described below.

This is the 7th edition of the report. For description of the 6th edition, see SRI 1982 Annual, under this number.

Availability: University of Colorado: Business Research Division, Graduate School of Business Administration, Campus Box 420, Boulder CO 80309, $45.00; SRI/MF/complete.

TABLES:

U6430–2.1: U.S. Travel Data by State
[Data are by State, unless otherwise noted.]

PARKLAND AND OUT-OF-STATE VISITS

a. National park total, recreation, and overnight visits, and camper days; State park total and overnight visits; national forest total and campground recreational visits; Federal outdoor recreation area visits, by agency (not by State); and total out-of-State visitors, and average length of stay and persons per party; various years 1960-82. Tables 1-11. (p. 15-43)

ECONOMIC IMPACT

b. Expenditures by visitors/tourists: total; and average for each person and party per day and per visit, and for each person per day by object; various years 1970-82. Tables 12-14. (p. 46-50)

c. Hotel/other lodging average annual employment, wages/salaries paid, and taxable sales; number and receipts of hotels and motels/motor hotels/tourist courts; and percent of visitors using 6 types of accommodation; various years 1963-82. Tables 15-19. (p. 54-66)

d. Eating/drinking place average annual employment and wages/salaries paid, 1970-82; number and receipts of travel agencies/tour operators/related services, 1967, 1972, and 1977; annual revenue from travel taxes, 1976-82; and travel-generated employment (total and as percent of all employment), 1978 and 1981. Tables 20-24. (p. 67-78)

TRANSPORTATION AND GOVERNMENT TOURISM SPENDING

e. Transportation use distribution, and aggregate U.S. intercity passenger miles and fuel efficiency, all by transportation mode, various years 1965-82; and gasoline service stations and sales, 1977-83. Tables 25-29. (p. 81-87)

f. Tourism advertising expenditures, with detail for total U.S. by media, and for selected tourist areas spending $100,000/more, various years 1965-82; and travel dept total, advertising, and printing budgets, FY75-84. Tables 30-37. (p. 91-101)

U6430–2.2: U.S. Trip Characteristics and International Travel

TRIP AND TRAVELER CHARACTERISTICS

a. Trips by distance, duration, purpose, means of transportation, type of lodging, travel party size and composition, region of origin and destination, and traveler family income and age; and traveler distribution by selected personal and household characteristics, including sex, marital status, age, income, and region of residence, with comparison to U.S. population; 1981 and/or 1982. Tables 38-40. (p. 104-107)

b. Recreational sport participants, and frequency of participation, by sport; interest in sports, by sex, age, education, and income; reasons for participating in sports; and household participation in selected leisure activities; various years 1973-83. Tables 41-45. (p. 110-115)

c. Travel price index and CPI, monthly 1972-82. Table 46. (p. 117-118)

INTERNATIONAL TRAVEL

d. Passport recipients by sex, age, occupation, and trip purpose, various years 1975-82; and passports issued, monthly 1970-82. Tables 47-50. (p. 120-124)

e. Passenger fare and other travel expenditures, and number of travelers, for U.S. residents traveling abroad and for foreign visitors to U.S., with detail by country or world area of origin or destination, various years 1970-82. Tables 51-59. (p. 127-139)

U6430–2.3: Canadian Travel Data by Province

[Data are by Province, unless otherwise noted.]

PARKLAND AND OUT-OF-PROVINCE VISITS

a. National and provincial park total and overnight visits; visits to national historic parks/major sites; out-of-Province visitors; and average length of stay, and persons per party; various years 1970-83. Tables 60-66. (p. 143-149)

ECONOMIC IMPACT

b. Expenditures by visitors/tourists: total; and average for each person and party per day and per visit, and for each person per day by object, various years 1970-82. Tables 67-69. (p. 151-153)

c. Lodging/food service employment; lodging establishments by type, and receipts by establishment type and source; and percent of visitors using 6 types of accommodation; various years 1970-82. Tables 70-73. (p. 156-161)

TRANSPORTATION AND GOVERNMENT TOURISM SPENDING

d. Transportation use distribution, by mode; nonresident motorists and passenger cars entering Canada; and aggregate Canadian intercity revenue passengers carried, by transportation mode; various years 1970-82. Tables 74-77. (p. 163-166)

e. Tourism advertising expenditures by Canadian governments in U.S. media, 1972-82; and travel dept total, advertising, and printing budgets, FY74-84. Tables 78-81. (p. 168-172)

U6430–2.4: Canadian Trip Characteristics and International Travel

TRIP AND TRAVELER CHARACTERISTICS

a. Trips, person nights, and expenditures, for trips of 80/more kilometers, by Province of origin and destination, transportation mode, type of accommodation, and trip purpose, distance, and duration; trips by traveler age, education, and occupation; travel expenditures by object; and intra- and inter-provincial trips, by Province of origin; 1980 and 1982, with selected detail by quarter. Tables 82-87. (p. 175-182)

b. Recreational activities participated in during trips, by quarter and Province, 1982; and participation in various athletic activities, 1976 and 1981. Tables 88-91. (p. 184-187)

c. Travel and consumer price indexes, 1972-82. Table 92. (p. 189)

INTERNATIONAL TRAVEL

d. Trips, person nights, and expenditures, for Canadians traveling abroad, by country or world area of destination (with detail for U.S. regions and States), trip purpose and duration, quarter of return to Canada, and (for travelers to U.S.) transportation mode, various years 1973-82. Tables 93-98. (p. 192-203)

e. Foreign visitors to Canada, by country of residence; and trips, person nights, and expenditures, for visitors from U.S. and other countries, shown variously by place of residence (U.S. region or country or world area), trip purpose and duration, quarter of entry to Canada, transportation mode, traveler sex and age group (under and over age 12), and whether 1st trip to Canada; various years 1972-82. Tables 99-104. (p. 205-219)

f. Canadian travel receipts from and payments to U.S. and all others, 1970-82; and international travel total receipts and payments, and number of U.S. and other visitors to Canada and of Canadian visitors to U.S. and all other countries, 1972-87. Tables 105-108. (p. 221-225)

U6430–3 **ECONOMIC ANALYSIS OF NORTH AMERICAN SKI AREAS, 1983-84 Season**

Annual. 1984. xviii+139 p.
ISSN 0147-4243.
ISBN 0-89478-081-6.
LC 76-622253.
SRI/MF/complete

Annual report, by Charles R. Goeldner et al., on the U.S. and Canadian ski industry, presenting detailed data on facility characteristics and finances for the 1983/84 ski season, with selected trends from 1979/80. Includes data by geographic region, average area profitability and vertical transport capability, area type (day, weekend, or vacation), ski season length, and for areas with snowmaking and night operations.

Facility characteristics include acreage; skier capacity; proximity to SMSA and competitive areas; lodging capacity; site ownership; business characteristics, including involvement in land development by type; age; days/nights of operation; skier visits; day vs. night use; ski lift and other ticket prices; other activities available; computer use; concession operations; and employment by dept.

Financial data include profits; revenues and expenses; balance sheets and ratios; economic ratios; and departmental margins.

Regions covered are New England/Quebec, Eastern States/Ontario, Midwest, Central and Northern Rockies, California/Nevada, and Pacific Northwest/Alberta/British Columbia.

Report is based on responses of 113 National Ski Areas Assn members to a July 1984 survey, and is intended to permit ski area managers to compare their operations with averages of other areas with similar characteristics.

Contains executive summary, comments, preface, and acknowledgments, with 3 tables and 1 chart (p. ii-xii); contents and table listings (p. xiii-xviii); 10 chapters, with narrative summaries and 91 tables (p. 1-123); and 4 appendices, including directory of survey respondents, questionnaire facsimile, and glossary (p. 124-139).

This is the 16th annual report.

Availability: University of Colorado: Business Research Division, Graduate School of Business Administration, Campus Box 420, Boulder CO 80309, $50.00; SRI/MF/complete.

U6600
University of Delaware: Agricultural Experiment Station

U6600–1   DELAWARE FARM INCOME: Crop and Livestock Production, 1983; Acreage of Crops and Livestock Numbers
Annual. Feb. 1985. 15 p.
A. E. Pamphlet No. 85.
SRI/MF/complete

Annual report, by Raymond C. Smith, on Delaware agricultural production, marketing, and income, 1982-83, with some data for 1984 and selected trends from 1960. Data are shown by county and/or commodity.

Covers farm income, production, sales, prices, and, as applicable, acres harvested, yield, and inventory, for field crop, fruit, vegetable, livestock, poultry, and dairy sectors.

Also includes data on government subsidies; production expenses; and summary findings from the Census of Agriculture, including number and value of farms, total and irrigated acreage, and farm operators by age group and ownership status, selected years 1964-82.

Data are compiled from reports of USDA and Maryland-Delaware Crop Reporting Service.

Contains table listing (p. 1); and report, with narrative summary and 14 tables (p. 2-15).

SRI coverage of *Delaware Farm Income* ends with this edition. Coverage is being discontinued in favor of a more comprehensive report, *Delaware Agricultural Statistics;* for description, see S1335-1.

Availability: University of Delaware: Agricultural Experiment Station, Agricultural Economics Department, Newark DE 19717-1303, †; SRI/MF/complete.

U6600–2   EMPLOYMENT GROWTH IN THE NORTHEAST: 1970-79
Monograph. Aug. 1984.
iv+69 p. Bull. No. 455.
LC 84-623590.
SRI/MF/complete

By Steven E. Hastings and Jeffrey D. White. Report analyzing Northeast area employment growth during the 1970s, by industry division, region, and State, and for aggregate metro and nonmetro counties by size, with various cross-tabulations. Presents actual employment for 1970 and 1979, and/or analysis of 1970s employment growth relative to the U.S. and/or total Northeast area.

"Northeast area" comprises States in the New England and Middle Atlantic census divisions, and Maryland, Delaware, Virginia, West Virginia, and Washington, D.C.

Data are from Dept of Commerce.

Contains listings of contents and tables (p. i-iv); narrative analysis, interspersed with 22 tables (p. 1-51); bibliography (p. 52-55); and 2 statistical appendices, with 24 tables (p. 56-69).

Availability: University of Delaware: Agricultural Experiment Station, Agricultural Economics Department, Newark DE 19717-1303, †; SRI/MF/complete.

U6660
University of Florida: Bureau of Economic and Business Research

---

U6660–1   1984 FLORIDA STATISTICAL ABSTRACT
Annual. Aug. 1984.
6+707 p.
ISBN 0- 8130-0798-4 (cloth).
ISBN 0- 8130-0799-2 (pbk.).
LC A67-7393.
SRI/MF/complete

Annual compilation of social, governmental, and economic statistics for Florida. Data are primarily for 1970s-84, with selected historical data from as early as 1830, and population projections to 2020. Most data are from Federal censuses, and other Federal and State sources.

Report is designed to present a comprehensive overview of the State. Extensive socioeconomic, demographic, and geographic breakdowns are shown, as applicable, for most topics. These breakdowns include data by city, county and other State district, MSA, urban-rural status, commodity, income, industry, occupation, age, educational attainment, marital status, race, and sex. Comparisons to Sun Belt States, other populous States, and U.S. are also often included.

Contains introduction, contents listing, and 3 maps (6 p.); 460 tables and 3 maps arranged in 25 sections, described below (p. 1-662); guide to statistical sources and index of census tables in previous *Abstract* editions (p. 663-679); and subject index (p. 681-707).

Report has been published annually since 1966. Tables are not generally repeated from previous *Abstract* if updated data are not available at time of printing. This applies to most census data.

Availability: University Presses of Florida, 15 NW 15th St., Gainesville FL 32603, $27.95 (cloth), $19.95 (pbk.), +$1.50 handling charge for 1st copy, $0.50 for each additional copy; SRI/MF/complete.

TABLE SECTIONS:
[Data source is given beneath each table.]

HUMAN RESOURCES

U6660–1.1: Section 1: Population

(p. 1-59) Contains 1 map and 28 tables. Includes population since 1830 and projected to 2020; nonpermanent residents; migration; land area; institutional inmates/patients; veterans; Federal expenditures for veterans; and resident and naturalized aliens.

U6660–1.2: Section 2: Housing

(p. 60-75) Contains 8 tables. Includes housing units by occupancy status and tenure; households and household size; persons in group quarters; residential and nursing homes for aged; public lodgings by type; and mobile home and recreational vehicle license sales.

U6660–1.3: Section 3: Vital Statistics and Health

(p. 76-90) Contains 15 tables. Includes births, deaths, and rates; births by age of mother;

pregnancies and abortions; infant deaths; deaths by cause, with detail for accidents and suicide; reportable diseases; marriages and annulments/dissolutions; and State mental hospital admissions and discharges by institution, and resident patients by type of disorder.

U6660–1.4: Section 4: Education

(p. 91-111) Contains 15 tables. Includes public and nonpublic schools and enrollment; graduates; dropouts; disciplinary measures; students referred to alternative programs and court/juvenile authorities; teachers and average salaries; assessed property value; education expenditures; achievement test performance; school lunch program participation and cost; transportation costs; educational attainment of population; and postsecondary enrollment by institution.

U6660–1.5: Section 5: Income and Wealth

(p. 112-171) Contains 30 tables. Includes income tax returns and tax liability; personal income by source; assets of top wealthholders; median family income; families and persons below poverty level; and proprietorship tax returns, receipts, depreciation, and net income.

U6660–1.6: Section 6: Labor Force, Employment, and Earnings

(p. 172-199) Contains 11 tables. Includes labor force by employment status; farm and nonfarm proprietors; earnings; covered employment and payroll; top 50 employers and location of corporate headquarters; and average annual pay.

U6660–1.7: Section 7: Social Insurance and Welfare

(p. 200-218) Contains 1 map and 14 tables. Includes Medicare and social security beneficiaries and payments; public assistance payments and caseload, by program; medical assistance recipients; food stamp value and participants; unemployment insurance contributions, disbursements, and claimants exhausting benefits; and worker compensation payments.

PHYSICAL RESOURCES AND INDUSTRIES

U6660–1.8: Section 8: Geography and Climate

(p. 219-229) Contains 7 tables. Includes land and water area, coastline, and elevations; Federal and Indian lands; temperature and precipitation at National Weather Station offices; climate characteristics for Jacksonville, Miami, and 4 other U.S. cities; and air quality by specific sampling location.

U6660–1.9: Section 9: Agriculture

(p. 230-286) Contains 1 map and 51 tables. Includes farm population; veterinarians; farm proprietors and employees; migrant and foreign seasonal workers; fertilizer consumption; agricultural production and service establishments, employment, and payrolls; income from Federal payments and farm marketings; value of home consumption; and production expenses.

Also includes farms and farmland, including foreign-owned acreage; Agricultural Stabilization and Conservation Service payments; farm loans outstanding; farm property values; total and female farm operators; and farm taxes.

Also includes citrus fruit production, value, acreage, and average price; orange juice sales; crop production data; livestock and poultry inventory and/or marketing; and apiary and commercial dairy production.

U6660–1.10: Section 10: Forestry, Fisheries, and Minerals

(p. 287-303) Contains 19 tables. Includes hardwood and softwood net annual growth and harvest; forest product income and value added; national forest land acreage, by forest; commercial forest acreage, by ownership class; and tree farms and acreage, by State.

Also includes fisheries; fish and shellfish landings and value; and forestry, fishing/hunting, and mining establishments, employment, and payroll.

Also includes nonfuel mineral production and value; and phosphate rock production, value, use, trade, apparent consumption, stocks, and reserves.

U6660–1.11: Section 11: Construction

(p. 304-325) Contains 10 tables. Includes residential and nonresidential construction value; new housing units authorized; mobile home shipments; U.S. construction cost indexes and PPI for construction materials; and construction establishments, employment, and payroll.

U6660–1.12: Section 12: Manufacturing

(p. 326-354) Contains 21 tables. Includes manufacturing establishments, employment, payroll, value added, new capital expenditures, and value of shipments; export related employment; and employment and location of individual firms with 500 or more employees.

U6660–1.13: Section 13: Transportation

(p. 355-384) Contains 26 tables. Includes workers by means of transportation to work; road and vehicle mileage; highway receipts and expenditures, by government level; highway bridges; average driving speeds; vehicle registrations, license tags sold and revenue, and drivers licenses issued.

Also includes transportation industry establishments, employment, and payroll; out-of-State vehicle registrations, by State of previous registration; traffic accidents, injuries, and fatalities; and accident circumstances.

Also includes waterborne and air foreign trade volume, by port; railroad mileage, taxes, employment, and earnings; assessed value of railroad property, by company; and civil and military aviation operations, and civil air passenger and cargo traffic, by airport.

U6660–1.14: Section 14: Communications

(p. 385-399) Contains 9 tables. Includes circulation of daily, weekly, university, black, and Spanish-language newspapers; post office zip codes and receipts; communications industry establishments, employment, and payroll; and telephone company finances, customers, exchanges, and access lines, by company.

U6660–1.15: Section 15: Power and Energy

(p. 400-421) Contains 23 tables. Includes energy consumption by fuel type and sector; oil and gas production by field; electricity sales and customers, by utility and rural cooperative; establishments, employment, and payrolls for electric/gas/sanitary services; and electrical generating capacity, generation by prime mover and type of fuel and ownership, and production costs and retail prices.

Also includes finances, customers, and residential bills, by electric and gas company; energy expenditures; nuclear power plant capacities; natural gas production, movement, value, and consumption; motor fuel consumption; and gasoline prices.

SERVICES

U6660–1.16: Section 16: Wholesale and Retail Trade

(p. 422-433) Contains 10 tables. Includes wholesale and retail establishments, sales, employment, and payroll; and gross and taxable sales, by type of business.

U6660–1.17: Section 17: Finance, Insurance, and Real Estate

(p. 434-457) Contains 25 tables. Includes commercial banks and trust companies, and financial and operating data, with detail for holding company affiliates; failed banks; credit unions and finances; and foreign bank offices and assets, by country.

Also includes mortgage loan characteristics; savings assns, assets, and offices; finance, insurance, and real estate establishments, employment, and payroll; licensed real estate brokers and salespersons; and insurance premiums, losses, and underwriting activity.

U6660–1.18: Section 18: Personal and Business Services

(p. 458-467) Contains 11 tables. Includes selected service industry establishments, receipts, employment, and payroll; and licensed accountants, architects, and engineers.

U6660–1.19: Section 19: Tourism and Recreation

(p. 468-484) Contains 15 tables. Includes visitors, expenditures, and average stay, by mode of travel; origin and destination of visitors; highway traffic; registered boats; attendance at individual State and national parks and memorials; and gross and taxable sales and tax collections, by type of business.

Also includes hotels, motels, and capacity; eating places and seating capacity; and establishments, employment, and payroll, for travel- and recreation-related businesses.

U6660–1.20: Section 20: Health, Education, and Cultural Services

(p. 485-525) Contains 30 tables. Includes establishments, employment, and payroll, for health services and facilities, educational, social, and cultural services, and membership organizations; hospitals and beds; VA hospital utilization; nursing homes and capacity; hospital costs; and health practitioners.

Also includes public library expenditures and volumes, by library; public school teachers and staff, and salaries; student-teacher ratios; public school finances, tax structure, and property assessed valuations; community college finances, by institution; State appropriations for arts agencies; and number and finances of foundations.

PUBLIC RESOURCES AND ADMINISTRATION

U6660–1.21: Section 21: Government and Elections

(p. 526-540) Contains 14 tables. Includes State and local government units, and school and special districts; voting-age population; registered voters by party; votes cast for President, U.S. Senator, and Governor; women and blacks holding public office; U.S. and State legislators, by party; and apportionment in U.S. House of Representatives since 1840.

U6660–1.22: Section 22: Courts and Law Enforcement

(p. 541-558) Contains 14 tables. Includes Crime Index offenses, arrests, rates, and clearances; drug seizures and arrests; prisoners under death sentence; prisoners; parolees/probationers; legal service, justice, public order, and safety units, employment, and payroll; and lawyers by type of practice.

U6660–1.23: Section 23: Government Finance and Employment

(p. 559-631) Contains 40 tables. Includes Federal outlays in Florida, by program; defense contract awards and payroll; State revenues by source, expenditures by function and object, and fund balances; indebtedness; sales tax collections by trade classification; and tax collections and fund distributions.

Also includes gasoline and gasohol sales; alcoholic beverage licenses issued; horse and dog racing and jai alai performances, days, attendance, and pari-mutuel wagering revenues and taxes; and State retirement system membership, finances, and benefits.

Also includes Federal, State, and local government units, employment, and payroll; local government revenues, expenditures, and indebtedness; special district revenues and expenditures; real, personal, and railroad property valuations; and property tax rates and collections.

ECONOMIC AND SOCIAL TRENDS

U6660–1.24: Section 24: Economic Indicators and Prices

(p. 632-647) Contains 13 tables. Includes State economic indicators, including unemployment rate, employment, and sales tax collections; residential building permits; gross and taxable sales, and sales taxes paid; CPI and PPI; consumer characteristics and average weekly expenditures; Miami energy prices; electricity prices; price level index, by major item; and business failures.

U6660-1.25: Section 25: Quality of Life

(p. 648-662) Contains 1 extended table. Includes quality-of-life data, covering population and housing characteristics; health care, educational, and economic conditions; climate; and other indicators.

U6660-2   BUSINESS AND ECONOMIC DIMENSIONS

Quarterly, discontinued.

Quarterly review of selected topics related to business and economic conditions in Florida, discontinued with 4th Quarter 1983 issue (for description, see SRI 1984 Annual under this number).

Discontinued publication has been replaced by a monographic series available from University of Florida: Bureau of Economic and Business Research, College of Business Administration, 221 Matherly Hall, Gainesville FL 32611. Series is not covered in SRI.

U6660-3   POPULATION STUDIES BULLETIN

Series.   For individual publication data, see below.
ISSN 0071-6030.
LC 77-648516.
SRI/MF/complete

Continuing series of reports on Florida population and household composition. Reports generally contain a narrative analysis, with 1-3 accompanying tables showing data for the State and, often, by county and demographic characteristics.

Reports reviewed during 1985 are described below.

Availability: University of Florida: Bureau of Economic and Business Research, College of Business Administration, 221 Matherly Hall, Gainesville FL 32611, $20.00 per yr., single copy $6.00; SRI/MF/complete.

U6660-3.17: Number of Households and Average Household Size in Florida: Apr. 1, 1984

[Annual. Feb. 1985. 4 p. Bull. No. 71. SRI/MF/complete.]

Annual report, by Stanley K. Smith, with 1 table showing Florida households and average household size, by county, as of Apr. 1, 1970 and 1980 (census), and 1984 (estimated). Data are from Census Bureau and estimates by the issuing agency.

U6660-3.18: County Population Estimates by Age, Race, and Sex: Apr. 1, 1984

[Recurring (irreg.) Mar. 1985. 8 p. Bull. No. 72. SRI/MF/complete.]

Recurring report, by Faith Sincich, with 1 table showing Florida population estimates by race and sex, by county and age group, as of Apr. 1, 1984. Data are based primarily on 1970 and 1980 census counts.

Previous report, for 1982, is described in SRI 1984 Annual under U6660-3.12.

U6660-3.19: Projections of Florida Population by Age and Sex, 1985-2020

[Annual. May 1985. 4 p. Bull. No. 73. SRI/MF/complete.]

Annual report, by Stanley K. Smith and Faith Sincich, presenting high, low, and medium projections of Florida population by age group and sex, quinquennially 1985-2020, with actual data for 1980. Data are based primarily on Apr. 1, 1980 census counts. Includes 1 table.

No report was issued in 1984; for description of previous report, see SRI 1983 Annual under U6660-3.10. During 1984, series included 2 reports presenting population projections by age and sex, for individual counties and for blacks (see SRI 1984 Annual, under U6660-3.15 and U6660-3.16 respectively).

U6660-3.20: Projections of Florida Population by County, 1987-2020

[Annual. June 1985. 8 p. Bull. No. 74. SRI/MF/complete.]

Annual report, by Stanley K. Smith and Faith Sincich, estimating Florida population as of Apr. 1, 1984, and presenting high, low, and medium projections, selected years 1987-2020, all by county. Data are primarily based on Apr. 1, 1980 census counts. Includes 1 table.

U6660-4   FLORIDA ESTIMATES OF POPULATION, Apr. 1, 1984, State, Counties, and Municipalities

Annual. Feb. 1985.   48 p.
LC 73-623497.
SRI/MF/complete

Annual report estimating Florida population by county, city, and MSA, as of Apr. 1, 1984. Estimates are used for State revenue-sharing distribution for FY86. Includes comparisons with decennial censuses from 1960.

Also includes data on births and deaths, by race; population by age; and county land area.

Data are estimated from number of occupied housing units, based on residential building permits, electric utility customer records, and U.S. censuses.

Contains contents and table listing, analysis of population trends, and estimation methodology, with 1 text table (p. 3-7); and 2 maps, and 10 tables listed below (p. 8-48).

Availability: University of Florida: Bureau of Economic and Business Research, College of Business Administration, 221 Matherly Hall, Gainesville FL 32611, $14.00; SRI/MF/complete.

TABLES:

[All data are as of Apr. 1. Data are shown for 1970, 1980, and 1984, unless otherwise noted.]

1. Estimates of population [1980 and 1984; and inmates/patients in Federal/State-operated institutions, 1984]; by county and municipality [and unincorporated area]. (p. 8-27)

2-3. Components of population change [natural increase and net migration]; and resident live births and deaths, by race; by county, 1980-84 [period]. (p. 28-31)

4-6. Population change, by county, MSA, and planning district [decennially 1960-80 and 1984]. (p. 32-37)

7. Rank in population and percentage change, for [35] specified cities. (p. 38)

8-9. Rank of counties by population size, and population distribution; and population per square mile and rank according to density [with 1980 land area]; by county. (p. 40-43)

10. Age distribution (percentages) of the population of Florida and its counties. (p. 44-47)

U6660-5   BUILDING PERMIT ACTIVITY in Florida

Monthly, with annual summary. 8 p.
ISSN 0007-3555.
LC sn80-12467.
SRI/MF/complete, shipped quarterly

Monthly report, with annual summary, on the value of construction authorized by building permits in Florida, by county, city, and type of dwelling. Report is issued 1-2 months after month of coverage.

Contains 1 table showing value of private housekeeping and nonhousekeeping residential units, nonresidential units, and additions/alterations; number of housekeeping units in private 1-family houses and multi-family buildings; and value of public building permits; by county and city, with totals for county unincorporated areas, all for month of coverage.

Also includes a similar table showing late reports of building permit activity for previous months.

An annual summary issue (No. 13) is also published.

Availability: University of Florida: Bureau of Economic and Business Research, College of Business Administration, 221 Matherly Hall, Gainesville FL 32611, $15.00 per yr., annual summary $4.00, single copy $2.00; SRI/MF/complete, shipped quarterly.

Issues reviewed during 1985: Sept. 1984-Aug. 1985; and annual summary for 1984 (D) (Vol. XXX, Nos. 9-13; Vol. XXXI, Nos. 1-8) [Apr.-May 1985 issues incorrectly read Vol. XXXII].

U6660-7   1980 CENSUS HANDBOOK, FLORIDA COUNTIES

Monograph. May 1984.
x + 404 p.
ISBN 0-8130-0807-7.
SRI/MF/complete

Report presenting detailed demographic and socioeconomic statistics for Florida, by county. Data are primarily for 1970 and 1980, with income data for 1979 and population trends from 1930.

Data are from primarily from Census Bureau. Data sources appear beneath each table.

Contents:

a. Introduction and listing of contents, maps, and charts (p. iii-v); and 2 tables showing general population and housing characteristics for U.S., by State, 1980 (p. vii-x).

b. 18 maps/charts and 72 tables arranged in 6 sections, described below (p. 1-275).

c. 2 maps/charts and 22 tables arranged in 2 sections, presenting summary population and housing characteristics for elderly population and for State's 19 congressional districts, and including data on persons living in nursing homes, on population by national ancestry, and on voting-age, farm, and veteran populations (p. 278-369).

d. Appendices, with explanation of sources and terms (p. 371-396); and subject index (p. 397-402).

Report is issued as a supplement to the *Florida Statistical Abstract*, covered in SRI under U6660–1.

Availability: University Presses of Florida, 15 N.W. 15th St., Gainesville FL 32603, $15.00+$1.50 postage and handling charge for 1st copy, $0.25 for each additional copy; SRI/MF/complete.

TABLE SECTIONS:

[Data are shown by county, generally for 1970 and/or 1980, unless otherwise noted. Data by ethnic group generally include American Indian/Eskimo/Aleut, Asian/Pacific Islander, and Spanish origin. Tables are not sequentially numbered.]

U6660–7.1: Population

(p. 3-73) Contains 10 maps/charts and 15 tables. Includes population by sex, age, urban-rural and marital status, and race-ethnicity, with selected trends from 1930; land area and population density; and household and family characteristics, including composition, size, and presence of own children, with detail for rural households.

Also includes residents of group quarters by type (mental hospital, home for aged, military quarters, college dormitory, and other); place of birth, including foreign-born and natives born in State, different region, and elsewhere; and residence in 1975 relative to residence in 1980, including same or different house, county, and State (with detail by region for persons residing in another State), and abroad.

Also includes nonpermanent households and persons by age and/or region of usual residence (including outside U.S. and not reported).

U6660–7.2: Housing

(p. 76-139) Contains 2 maps/charts and 21 tables. Includes housing occupancy status (including vacant held for occasional use) and current householder's tenure by race-ethnicity and year moved in, with detail for rural and farm housing units; and persons in occupied housing units, by tenure and race-ethnicity.

Also includes year-round housing units by tenure; presence of complete plumbing facilities, air conditioning, and telephone; year built; number of units (including mobile homes) in structure; and median number of rooms and persons, and percent with 1/more persons per room, by race-ethnicity.

Also includes housing units by tenure, housing value and contract rent, race-ethnicity of householder, monthly owner costs with and without a mortgage, and heating, water heating, and cooking fuel; and year-round condominium units and/or value (owner- and renter-occupied), by race-ethnicity of householder.

U6660–7.3: Transportation and Education

(p. 142-174) Contains 2 maps/charts and 11 tables. Includes travel time and means of transportation to work, including number of occupants in private vehicles; availability of vehicle at housing unit; and persons with public transportation and work disability status.

Also includes school enrollment by level, with detail for private schools; persons age 3/over enrolled in school, with distribution by age group; educational attainment of persons

18-24 and 25/over, by race-ethnicity and/or sex; and English speaking ability, and language spoken at home.

U6660–7.4: Income

(p. 176-220) Contains 1 map/chart and 13 tables. Includes family income by age of householder, presence and age of children, number of workers, and race-ethnicity, with detail for married-couple families and women with no husband present; personal income by sex and employment status; and household income by type (including earnings, interest/dividend/rent, social security, and public assistance) and by race-ethnicity.

Also includes poverty thresholds by family size; and poverty status of families and unrelated individuals, with detail for families by race-ethnicity and presence of children, and for female householders with no husband present.

Data reflect 1969 and/or 1979 income and poverty levels for households, families, and individuals surveyed in 1970 and 1980.

U6660–7.5: Employment

(p. 222-275) Contains 3 maps/charts and 12 tables. Includes labor force by employment status, with detail for all women, for women by presence of spouse and presence and age of children, for married couples, and by race-ethnicity.

Also includes employment by occupational group, industry division, and class of worker (including self-employed, government, and unpaid family worker); proximity of workplace to residence, including same or different county; and work disability status.

U6730
University of Georgia: College of Business Administration

U6730–1   GEORGIA STATISTICAL ABSTRACT, 1984-85
Biennial. Aug. 1984.
3+452 p.
ISSN 0085-1043.
LC 52-62944.
SRI/MF/complete

Biennial compilation of social, governmental, and economic statistics for Georgia. Data are primarily for 1970s-83, with selected trends from as early as 1940. Most data are from Federal and State government sources; data sources are identified for each table.

Report is designed to present a comprehensive overview of the State. Extensive socioeconomic, demographic, and geographic breakdowns are shown, as applicable, for most topics. These breakdowns include data by city, county, SMSA, urban-rural status, commodity, industry, occupation, age, marital status, race, and sex. Comparisons to total U.S. and other southeastern States are also often included.

Contains contents and map listings (2 p.); 16 maps and 282 tables, described below, arranged in 24 sections, with a table listing preceding each section (p. 1-444); and index (p. 447-452).

An annual companion report, *Georgia Economic Outlook,* is also available from the issuing

agency, and may be ordered with the Statistical Abstract for $20.00, or separately for $7.00. The *Economic Outlook* is not covered by SRI.

For description of *Statistical Abstract* for 1982, see SRI 1983 Annual under this number.

Availability: University of Georgia: College of Business Administration, Division of Research, Athens GA 30602, $18.00; SRI/MF/complete.

TABLE SECTIONS:

U6730–1.1: Sections 1-2: Population; and Vital Statistics and Health

(p. 1-75) Contains 48 tables. Includes population and net migration; land and inland water areas; population density; and households and persons in households.

Also includes births and deaths; illegitimate and immature births; abortions; infant, maternal, and fetal deaths; leading causes of death; marriages and divorces/annulments; physicians and dentists; hospital, nursing home, and mental health facilities and patients; hospitalization costs; and Federal food stamp and school lunch program participants and costs.

U6730–1.2: Section 3: Education

(p. 77-97) Contains 1 map and 14 tables. Includes educational enrollment and attendance; teachers certified, and other public school personnel; State/local educational employment and payroll; school systems; school buses, children carried, and cost; public school system receipts and expenditures; educational cost per pupil; school dropouts; and degrees conferred, enrollment, and income, by State-supported institution.

U6730–1.3: Sections 4-6: Labor, Employment, and Earnings; Income, GSP, and Wealth; and Prices

(p. 99-168) Contains 51 tables. Includes labor force by employment status, and unemployment rate; payroll; production workers, hours, and earnings; and labor union membership.

Also includes total and per capita GSP, and per capita output; personal income per capita and by source; families, and median income; persons and families below poverty level; CPI, and urban intermediate budgets for 4-person families and retired couples, in selected U.S. cities; and U.S. PPI.

U6730–1.4: Sections 7-8: Area, Geography, and Climate; and Agriculture

(p. 169-220) Contains 8 maps and 27 tables. Includes land and water areas; and climatological data, including average temperature and precipitation.

Also includes number of farms, average size, and value of land/buildings and products sold; tenant farm operators and land in tenancy; harvested acreage, production, value, and yield; livestock and poultry farms and stocks; poultry and egg production, prices, and income; farm income; mortgage loans; and cooperatives, membership, and net business.

U6730–1.5: Sections 9-11: Forestry, Fisheries, and Minerals

(p. 221-244) Contains 1 map and 13 tables. Includes national forest land area; forest fires and acreage burned; seedling shipments; pulpwood production; and forest product manufacturing establishments, payroll, and employment.

Also includes fish and shellfish catch and values; manufactured fishery product value; sport fish distributed; and mineral production and value.

U6730–1.6: Sections 12-13: Business Enterprise, and Manufactures

(p. 245-274) Contains 17 tables. Includes proprietorships and partnerships, and receipts; business establishments; business failures, and liabilities; Georgia-based firms among Fortune 500, and net income; and new business incorporations.

Also includes manufacturing employment, payroll, production worker hours and wages, value added, capital expenditures, and establishments.

U6730–1.7: Section 14: Distribution and Services

(p. 275-295) Contains 1 map and 17 tables. Includes total sales; retail and wholesale trade establishments and sales; wholesale trade operating expenses, payroll, and employment; service industry and amusement/recreation establishments and receipts; and service industry proprietorships, partnerships, and payroll.

U6730–1.8: Sections 15-16: Transportation, and Highways and Highway Vehicles

(p. 297-309) Contains 10 tables. Includes ocean port domestic and foreign commerce; coastwise traffic shipments and receipts; and airport facilities.

Also includes highway/street mileage; State aid for public roads; highway construction and maintenance expenditures; motor vehicle registrations; motor fuel consumption; and traffic accident fatalities.

U6730–1.9: Sections 17-18: Communication and Power

(p. 311-332) Contains 18 tables. Includes business and residential telephones; telephone carrier miles of wire, central offices, calls per year, and State taxes; newspapers and periodicals published; and newspaper circulation.

Also includes electric power production, plants, and capacity; electric utility fuel consumption; energy consumption by type and end-use sector; kWh sales; developed and undeveloped water power capacity by U.S. census division; and gas utility customers, sales, revenues, and prices.

U6730–1.10: Section 19: Banking and Finance

(p. 333-356) Contains 21 tables. Includes commercial banks and branches, and deposits by type, assets, liabilities, and equity capital; Banks for Cooperatives, Production Credit Assns, and Federal land bank loans; and credit unions, savings, members, and loans.

Also includes life insurance companies and benefits paid; and insurance in force, premiums received or paid, and losses paid, shown as applicable for life, domestic fire/casualty, and mutual fire insurance companies, fraternal insurance societies, and nonprofit hospitalilzation assns.

U6730–1.11: Section 20: Construction and Housing

(p. 357-372) Contains 6 tables. Includes construction contract values; residential building permits; construction contractor employment; housing structural, occupancy, and financial characteristics; and owner occupied mobile homes.

U6730–1.12: Sections 21-22: Government and Politics, and Public Finance

(p. 373-402) Contains 3 maps and 25 tables. Includes number of local governments, by type of district; county elective offices; votes cast for selected State and Federal offices; voting age population; and voters registered and voting.

Also includes State and city government revenues by source, expenditures by function, and outstanding debt; Federal aid received; payments by local governments to the State; and State aid to local governments.

U6730–1.13: Section 23: Law Enforcement and Courts

(p. 403-432) Contains 2 maps and 7 tables. Includes Index crime offenses and rates; offenses known to police; law enforcement employment; State/Federal prisoners; inmate admissions and departures; correctional institution expenditures; and superior court circuits and judges.

U6730–1.14: Section 24: Public Welfare

(p. 433-444) Contains 8 tables. Includes unemployment insurance coverage, claims, payments, and average weekly benefits; State unemployment insurance fund employer contributions, interest, benefits, and balance; employment service placements; Old-Age and Survivors Insurance benefits; and public assistance program recipients and payments.

U6730–2   GEORGIA BUSINESS AND ECONOMIC CONDITIONS

Bimonthly.   Approx. 20 p.
ISSN 0279-3857.
LC 33-21288.
SRI/MF/complete

Bimonthly report on Georgia economic conditions and business indicators. Most data are from Federal and State sources, and are current to 2 months prior to cover date.

General format:

a. Feature articles, some with statistics; and occasional special tables.

b. Bimonthly table showing Georgia leading and coincident economic indicator indexes, employment, manufacturing employment and earnings, retail sales, building permits, construction value, agricultural price index, and personal income; Atlanta help-wanted advertising index; and CPI for southern U.S. and Atlanta; generally for month of coverage, previous 2 months, and same month of previous year.

Bimonthly table appears in most issues. All additional features with substantial statistical content are described, as they appear, under "Statistical Features." Nonstatistical features are not covered.

Availability: University of Georgia: College of Business Administration, Division of Research, Athens GA 30602, $12.00 per yr.; SRI/MF/complete.

Issues reviewed during 1985: Nov./Dec. 1984-Sept./Oct. 1985 (P) (Vol. 44, No. 6; Vol. 45, Nos. 1-5).

STATISTICAL FEATURES:

U6730–2.601: Nov./Dec. 1984 (Vol. 44, No. 6)

TRENDS AND CONSTRAINTS IN GEORGIA'S GROWTH

(p. 1-5) By James E. Kundell and Howard A. Schretter. Article, with 2 tables showing Georgia land distribution by use (no date); and population, 1980 and projected 2000; by State region. Data are from USDA, Census Bureau, and Georgia Office of Planning and Budget.

PERSONAL INCOME IN GEORGIA: THE EARLY 1980s

(p. 6-17) By Suzanne A. Lindsay. Part 2 of a series of articles discussing trends in Georgia personal income. Data are from U.S. Dept of Commerce.

Includes 3 maps, 5 summary tables, and 3 detailed tables showing the following for per capita personal income, by Georgia MSA and/or county: nominal and real income, and income as percent of U.S. average, 1970, 1980, and 1982, with selected rankings and growth rates.

For description of Part 1, see SRI 1984 Annual, under U6730-2.507.

U6730–2.602: Jan./Feb. 1985 (Vol. 45, No. 1)

GEORGIA'S ECONOMIC SUCCESS AND FUTURE PROSPECTS

(p. 1-5) By Albert W. Niemi, Jr. Article, with 9 tables showing Georgia real GSP and growth rate in labor productivity by industry division, and real output per capita, with comparisons to 13 other southern States and total U.S., various periods 1950-83.

CHANGING REGIONAL STRUCTURE OF THE U.S. ECONOMY

(p. 6-15) By Phillip A. Cartwright. Part 1 of a 2-part article analyzing demographic and economic variations among U.S. regions, primarily 1970s-83. Data are from Commerce and Labor Depts.

Includes 8 tables showing population and components of change, and personal income in current and constant 1972 dollars, by selected region and State, various periods 1950-83; and indexes of principal household expenses by item, for selected metro areas and aggregate nonmetro areas in 3 regions, 1981; with some comparisons to total U.S.

U6730–2.603: Mar./Apr. 1985 (Vol. 45, No. 2)

THE 'TWO GEORGIAS' PROBLEM

(p. 3-13) By Charles F. Floyd. Article presenting economic indicators primarily for Georgia. Most data are from University of Georgia, Georgia Labor Dept, and U.S. Commerce Dept. Includes 7 tables showing the following:

a. GSP and employment, by industry division, decennially 1950-80; manufacturing employment by industry group, 1982; and population and net migration, 1970 and 1980, and personal income (with comparison to U.S. average), 1981, all by MSA.

b. Selected income, population, and housing data, by selected State area and county (no date); and communities with 10,000/over population, by interstate and multi-lane highway access, for 9 Southeastern States, 1984.

CHANGING REGIONAL STRUCTURE OF THE U.S. ECONOMY

(p. 14-21) By Phillip A. Cartwright. Part 2 of a 2-part article analyzing demographic and economic variations among U.S. regions, 1970s-85. Data are from BLS and other sources.

Includes 4 tables showing the following for selected regions and/or States: employment, 1972, 1980, and 1983; employment distribution by industry division, 1982; production worker average earnings as percent of U.S. average, 1972 and 1982; Federal tax burden, 1983-85; and Federal grants to State/local governments, FY83.

SPECIAL TABLE

(p. 22) Table showing taxable sales in Georgia by kind of business and county, 1983-84. Data are from University of Georgia.

Data for 1981-83 appeared in Mar./Apr. 1984 issue as part of an annual compilation of tables (for description, see SRI 1984 Annual under U6730-2.504).

U6730-2.604: May/June 1985 (Vol. 45, No. 3)

TRENDS IN GEORGIA'S TEXTILE AND APPAREL INDUSTRIES

(p. 1-5) By Joe D. Tanner. Article, with 2 tables showing employment in textile and apparel industries for 8 southeastern States and total U.S., 1984; and unemployment rates in Georgia counties with high concentrations of employment in these industries, 1984 and Jan.-Feb. 1985. Data are from the Georgia Dept of Labor.

ECONOMIC GROWTH IN THE SOUTHEASTERN PIEDMONT

(p. 13-19) By Suzanne A. Lindsay. Article, with 3 tables showing the following for Alabama, Georgia, North Carolina, and South Carolina:

a. Number of counties (total, MSA, and Piedmont MSA), 1980.

b. Population, population density, total employment, and nonfarm proprietor and wage/salary employment, with employment change detail by industry division and for manufacturing durable and nondurable goods; for State and aggregate metro areas, and by MSA for Piedmont region, 1982 with comparisons to 1970.

Data are from the U.S. Dept of Commerce.

U6730-2.605: July/Aug. 1985 (Vol. 45, No. 4)

RECENT CHANGES IN GEORGIA EMPLOYMENT

(p. 5-8) By Elizabeth S. Kasner. Article, with 1 table showing Georgia nonagricultural employment, by industry division and selected group, 1981 and 1984, with shift-share analysis comparing State and national employment changes. Data are from BLS.

ECONOMIC RECOVERY AND EMPLOYMENT IN GEORGIA

(p. 9-18) By Suzanne A. Lindsay. Article, with 5 tables showing nonagricultural employment, and durable and nondurable manufacturing employment and production workers, for Georgia and U.S., 1972-84, and average annual growth, selected periods 1973-84. Data are from BLS and Georgia Dept. of Labor.

U6730-2.606: Sept./Oct. 1985 (Vol. 45, No. 5)

IS THERE GROWTH OUTSIDE ATLANTA?

(p. 3-12) By Suzanne A. Lindsay. Article on Georgia employment trends, 1982-84. Data are from Georgia Dept of Labor.

Includes 8 tables showing Georgia labor force by employment status, for the State, for aggregate metro and nonmetro areas, and by MSA; unemployment rate, and change in labor force, employment, and unemployment, by county; and aggregate analyses of county unemployment rate trends; various periods 1982-84.

U6750
University of Georgia:
Rural Development Center

U6750-1   GEORGIA COUNTY GUIDE, Fourth Edition
Annual.   Spring 1984.
4 + 161 p.
SRI/MF/complete

Annual compilation of economic, social, and governmental statistics for individual Georgia counties. Data are shown primarily for 1970s-84, with population projections to 2000. Most data are from Federal and State agencies.

Contains contents listing (3 p.); statistical section, with 18 maps, and 64 tables listed below (p. 1-155); and notes and data sources (p. 156-161).

SRI coverage begins with the 4th edition.

Availability: University of Georgia: Rural Development Center, PO Box 1209, Tifton GA 31793, $7.00; SRI/MF/complete.

TABLES

[Tables show data by county, unless otherwise noted.]

U6750-1.1: Agriculture, Courts, Crime, and Economics

AGRICULTURE

[1] County extension directors, 1984. [list] (p. 2-4)

[2-4] Crop production: corn, soybeans, peanuts, cotton, tobacco, wheat, oats, rye, and sorghum, 1981-82. (p. 5-10)

[5] Irrigated farm land [acreage], 1974 and 1978-82. (p. 12-13)

[6] Livestock and poultry production [cattle/calves and commercial layers, Jan. 1982-83; hogs/pigs, Dec. 1981-82; and commercial broilers, 1981-82]. (p. 14-15)

[7] Number of farms, [and] harvested cropland [acreage], 1974, 1978, 1982. (p. 16-17)

COURTS AND CRIME

[8-9] Juvenile courts' commitments, FY75 and FY79-83; and superior courts' caseloads [dockets filed and dispositions, for all, criminal, and civil cases], 1983. (p. 20-23)

[10] Number of crimes reported [by Part I offense], 1982. (p. 24-25)

[11] State prison inmates' home county [women, and men by age, 1983; and totals], 1982-83. (p. 26-27)

ECONOMICS

[12] Business patterns [number of establishments and employees], 1978-81. (p. 28-29)

[13] Deposits in commercial banks [total, 1981-82; and demand, time, and savings deposits], 1982. (p. 31-32)

[14] Establishments insured by employment security law [by industry], 1st quarter 1983. (p. 33-34)

[15] Personal income tax [returns, adjusted gross and net taxable income, and tax liability], 1981. (p. 35-36)

[16] Manufacturing plants, major products, [and employees by sex], 1983. (p. 37-40)

[17] Master economic rank, taxable sales, [adjusted gross] income, [and] property [tax] digest [and] millage rates, 1981-82. (p. 41-42)

[18] Poverty characteristics [including percent of population below poverty level, with detail by race, for persons age 65/over, and for female-headed households], 1979. (p. 43-44)

[19] Total personal, per capita, median household, and median family income, 1979 and 1981. (p. 47-48)

U6750-1.2:   Education, Government, Health, Housing, Labor, Libraries, and Media

EDUCATION

[1-4] County and independent city systems: number of schools, enrollment, graduates, dropouts, black and white enrollment, number of teachers [total and with advanced degrees], beginning [teacher] salary, cost per pupil, and [percent of students buying lunch vs. receiving free lunch, 1982 or 1983]. (p. 49-54)

[5] Educational levels [population age 25/over by level of education], 1980. (p. 55-56)

[6] Universities, colleges, and vocational-technical schools [and enrollment by sex], 1983. [list] (p. 57-59)

GOVERNMENT

[7] Registered voters, [selected years] 1968-82. (p. 63-64)

HEALTH

[8] Hospitals and nursing homes [facilities, bed capacity, and admissions], 1982. (p. 68-69)

[9] Leading [7] causes of death, 1981. (p. 70-73)

[10] Licensed health professionals [chiropractors, dentists, osteopaths, physicians, public health nurses, and veterinarians], 1983. (p. 74-75)

[11] Life expectancy at birth [by race and sex, for persons born 1969-71]. (p. 76-77)

HOUSING

[12] Housing characteristics [owner or renter occupied, mobile homes, housing units built before 1939, and units lacking complete plumbing], 1980. (p. 78-79)

[13] New privately owned housing units authorized in permit issuing places, 1976-82. (p. 80-81)

LABOR

[14] Commuters, travel time, and mode of transportation, 1980. (p. 82-83)

[15] Total civilian labor force annual averages [by employment status, 1983, with 1982 unemployment rate]. (p. 84-85)

LIBRARIES AND MEDIA

[16] Public library facilities [and total books/ media and funds], 1983. (p. 87-88)

[17] Commercial [AM and FM] radio and TV stations, 1983. (p. 89-90)

[18] Newspapers [number of dailies and weeklies, location, and total circulation], 1983. (p. 91-92)

U6750–1.3: Natural Resources, Occupations, and Population

NATURAL RESOURCES

[1-2] Area of commercial forest land by stand-size class [including sawtimber, poletimber, and sapling/seedling] and by ownership class [Federal, State, county/municipal, forest industry, farmer, corporate and private], 1982. (p. 94-97)

[3] Land and water area, rank of size, population per square mile, and population rank per square mile, 1980. (p. 98-99)

[4] Mineral production [and value, principal minerals produced, and numbers of active surface mines and acres permitted], 1980-83. (p. 100-101)

OCCUPATIONS

[5-7] [Employment in selected occupational categories, 1980.] (p. 102-107)

POPULATION

[8] Black population, [decennially] 1960-80. (p. 108-109)

[9] County seat population, 1970 and 1980. (p. 110-111)

[10] Farm, rural, urban [and rural farm and nonfarm populations], 1980. (p. 112-113)

[11] Households, families, female-headed households, and divorced persons, 1980. (p. 114-115)

[12] MSAs [shows population (total, under age 18, and age 65/over), and population and households (by race and for Hispanics), all by MSA], 1983. (p. 117)

[13] Population by age, 1980. (p. 118-119)

[14] Population change [1980 vs. 1st year of each decade from 1930]. (p. 120-121)

[15] Population projections [1990 and 2000]. (p. 122-123)

[16] Total population, [decennially] 1930-80. (p. 124-125)

U6750–1.4: Public Assistance, Recreation, Transportation, and Vital Statistics

PUBLIC ASSISTANCE

[1-2] Medicaid recipients, and households participating in food stamp program; and social welfare, AFDC to families and to persons under 18 years of age, 1981. (p. 126-129)

RECREATION

[3] State parks and historic sites, 1984. [list] (p. 131)

TRANSPORTATION

[4] Accidents, injuries, deaths [with detail for speeding accidents, and drinking accidents and deaths], 1982. (p. 133-134)

[5] Airports open to the public [and characteristics], 1984. (p. 135-136)

[6] Highway mileage [total and paved, and on State routes, county roads, and city streets], 1983. (p. 137-138)

[7] Motor vehicle registrations [passenger cars, trucks, trailers, motorcycles, and buses], 1982. (p. 140-141)

VITAL STATISTICS

[Tables [8] and [10-13] show number and/or rate, by race, 1981.]

[8] Births. (p. 142-143)

[9] Child abuse and child protective services [cases and children involved], 1982. (p. 144-145)

[10] Divorces. (146-147)

[11-12] Infant deaths, 1 year and under; and live births to unwed teenage mothers, and induced abortions. (p. 148-151)

[13] Marriages. (p. 152-153)

[14] Sexually transmitted diseases and suicides [and rates], 1981. (p. 154-155)

U6875
University of Idaho: Center for Business Development and Research

U6875–1   IDAHO STATISTICAL ABSTRACT
Recurring (irreg.), discontinued.

Recurring compilation of detailed social, governmental, and economic statistics for Idaho, discontinued with 1980 edition (for description, see SRI 1981 Annual under this number).

Report has been discontinued due to lack of funding.

U6910
University of Illinois: Bureau of Economic and Business Research

U6910–1   ILLINOIS BUSINESS REVIEW
Bimonthly. Approx. 12 p.
ISSN 0019-1922.
LC A44-1688.
SRI/MF/complete

Bimonthly review of Illinois economic conditions and business indicators, and selected U.S. and world economic developments. Data are compiled by the Bureau of Economic and Business Research from Federal and State government and private agency reports. Most data are current to approximately 3 months prior to cover date.

Issues generally include articles, often with statistics; and a bimonthly Illinois business index table showing the following:

a. Manufacturing employment and weekly hours and earnings, Chicago and St. Louis help-wanted advertising, retail sales, coal and petroleum production, vendor performance, building permits and value, and CPI; generally for month of coverage, 3 previous months, and selected months of preceding year.

b. Personal income, for 5-6 consecutive quarters through quarter ending 5-10 months prior to month of publication.

Bimonthly table appears in all issues. All additional features with substantial statistical content are described, as they appear, under "Statistical Features." Nonstatistical features are not covered.

Availability: University of Illinois: Bureau of Economic and Business Research, College of Commerce and Business Administration, 428 Commerce W., 1206 S. Sixth St., Champaign IL 61820, †; SRI/MF/complete.

Issues reviewed during 1985: Oct. 1984-Aug. 1985 (P) (Vol. 41, Nos. 5-6; Vol. 42, Nos. 1-4).

STATISTICAL FEATURES:

U6910–1.601: Oct. 1984 (Vol. 41, No. 5)
SMALL ILLINOIS BANKS AND THE FEDERAL FUNDS MARKET

(p. 1-5, 10) By J. W. Abraham. Article on federal funds market activity (borrowing and lending of funds among commercial banks) of Illinois banks with assets of less than $50 million. Includes 1 table showing number of banks lending funds, by loans' percent of bank assets, semiannually 1972-82.

REAL ESTATE DEVELOPMENTS: RESTRUCTURING CITY TAXES—THE EFFECTS ON BUSINESS AND HOUSEHOLD TAX BURDENS

(p. 6-11) By Kalman Goldberg and Robert C. Scott. Article analyzing effect of city tax restructuring in Peoria, Ill., 1981. Includes 5 analytical tables.

Also includes 1 table ranking the 50 States and D.C. by the following: State/local total and property taxes, and individual income tax, per capita; and percent of income remaining after taxes; FY82. Data are from Commerce Dept.

U6910–1.602: Dec. 1984 (Vol. 41, No. 6)
ECONOMIC OVERVIEW OF RECENT ADMINISTRATIONS

(p. 1-3, 11) By David Lee and Deborah Mustell. Article, with 6 charts showing distribution of Federal expenditures by general purpose, and value of GNP and components, during Nixon/Ford, Carter, and Reagan (through 1983) Administrations. Data are from Citibank and Commerce Dept.

REAL ESTATE DEVELOPMENTS: ADJUSTABLE RATE MORTGAGE AND ILLINOIS CONSUMERS, A SUMMARY OF A 1984 SURVEY

(p. 4-8) By Mona J. Gardner and Dixie L. Mills. Article on Illinois consumers' familiarity with alternate mortgage instruments (A-MIs). Data are from 352 responses to an Apr.-May 1984 survey.

Includes 7 tables showing responses concerning familiarity with types of AMIs and various mortgage features, perceived reasons AMIs are offered, whether fixed-rate mortgages (FRMs) are generally preferred, acceptability of particular adjustable rate mortgage (ARM) features, and highest acceptable FRM payment/rate relative to capped ARM with a 12% initial rate.

MOVIE BOX OFFICE SUCCESSES: COMPARING THE OLDIES WITH NEW HITS

(p. 10-11) By Deborah Mustell. Article, with 3 tables showing all-time top 10 movies ranked by gross, inflation-adjusted, and per capita rental income in U.S./Canada, as of 1983. Data are from *Variety*.

U6910–1.603: Feb. 1985 (Vol. 42, No. 1)

FEDERAL GOVERNMENT EXPENDITURES IN ILLINOIS

(p. 10-11) By Carolyn Woj. Article, with 1 table showing Federal Government per capita expenditures or obligations by type, for top 5 Illinois counties, balance of State, and total U.S., 1983.

U6910–1.604: Apr. 1985 (Vol. 42, No. 2)

WHO'S ON FIRST

(p. 1-4) By Larry E. White. Article, with 1 table showing salaries of prominent baseball players, selected years 1907-85, with 1984 dollar equivalent amount. Data are from Federal and other publications.

U6910–1.605: June 1985 (Vol. 42, No. 3)

ECONOMIC LOOK AT LOTTO

(p. 1-3) By David Lee. Article, with 1 table and 1 chart showing Illinois State Lottery odds of winning selected prizes, and allocation of receipts among top 3 lottery prizes and State government (no dates).

U6910–1.606: Aug. 1985 (Vol. 42, No. 4)

HEALTH CARE COST CONTAINMENT

(p. 8-10) By Carolyn Woj. Article, with 1 table showing U.S. health care costs (amount and/or as percent of GNP), 1965 and 1970-83.

LIGHTS, CAMERA, ILLINOIS

(p. 11) By Carolyn Woj. Article, with 1 table showing number of motion picture/TV productions filmed in Illinois, expenditures, and local residents hired; and number of productions sought by State film office; 1976-83.

U7085
University of Kansas: Center for Public Affairs

U7085–1   KANSAS STATISTICAL ABSTRACT, 1983-84
Annual. [1984.] vii+260 p.
LC 80-647969.
SRI/MF/complete

Annual compilation, by Wendy A. Murray, of demographic, social, governmental, and economic statistics for Kansas, 1983/84. Data are primarily for 1970s-84, with population and oil and gas production trends from 1800s. Data are from reports of State and Federal agencies, League of Kansas Municipalities, University of Kansas, and industry assns.

Report is designed to present a comprehensive overview of the State. Extensive socioeconomic, demographic, and geographical breakdowns are shown, as applicable, for most topics. These breakdowns include data by State region, city, county, SMSA, urban-rural status, commodity, industry, age, educational attainment, race, and sex. Comparisons to total U.S. are also often included.

Contains foreword, preface, and contents listing (p. ii-vii); 16 statistical sections, with 19 maps, 10 charts, and 120 tables, described below (p. 1-254); and subject index (p. 257-260).

This is the 19th annual edition.

Availability: Institute for Public Policy and Business Research, University of Kansas, 607 Blake Hall, Lawrence KS 66045, $13.00; SRI/MF/complete.

TABLE SECTIONS:
[Data sources appear beneath each table.]

U7085–1.1: Population, Vital Statistics, and Health

(p. 3-50) Contains 7 maps, 2 charts, and 23 tables. Includes population trends from 1860; land area and density; median age; and families and households.

Also includes births, deaths, marriages, and divorces/annulments; infant and fetal deaths; induced abortions; hospitals, beds, admissions, and personnel; medical and osteopathic physicians; and adult care homes and beds.

U7085–1.2: Housing and Construction

(p. 53-61) Contains 5 tables. Includes housing units and structural characteristics, including presence of public water and sewer services, central heating, and air conditioning; new housing construction authorized; and value of building permits issued.

U7085–1.3: Education

(p. 65-79) Contains 1 map and 8 tables. Includes accredited schools; public school enrollment, and high school graduates and dropouts; 2- and 4-year college enrollment, by institution; and school district costs per pupil, assessed valuation, and tax levy.

U7085–1.4: Climate

(p. 83-91) Contains 4 maps and 4 tables. Includes precipitation and temperature; and tornadoes, injuries, and deaths.

U7085–1.5: Employment and Earnings, and Personal Income

(p. 95-121) Contains 2 maps, 3 charts, and 10 tables. Includes labor force, employment, unemployment, payroll, and business establishments.

Also includes personal income by source; household and family income; and poverty incidence.

U7085–1.6: Banking and Finance

(p. 125-129) Contains 4 tables. Includes banks, deposits, assets, and loans; savings and loan assns, assets, and 1st mortgages; and life insurance policies and value in force.

U7085–1.7: State and Local Government Finances and Employment

(p. 133-155) Contains 1 chart and 16 tables. Includes State and local revenues by source, expenditures by function, and indebtedness; State and local employees and payroll; property tax levies, rates, and assessed valuation; sales tax collections, by kind of business; and municipal population and property tax base.

U7085–1.8: Courts, Crime, and Public Safety

(p. 159-186) Contains 1 map, 1 chart, and 18 tables. Includes criminal and civil court caseload activities; Index crime offenses and ar-

rests; correctional institution admissions and releases, and population by institution; and inmate characteristics.

Also includes State and local criminal justice expenditures and employment; law enforcement personnel; and fire depts and responses, and fire-related damages, injuries, and deaths.

U7085–1.9: Parks and Recreation

(p. 189-192) Contains 1 map and 3 tables. Includes State park acreage and visitors; Federal reservoir drainage and surface areas, and storage; and hunting and fishing license sales and value.

U7085–1.10: Communications and Transportation

(p. 195-207) Contains 6 tables. Includes circulation of daily newspapers; and radio and TV stations.

Also includes motor vehicle registration trends from 1900, and special license plates issued; motor fuel consumption and gallons taxed; and expenditure of funds from Federal Highway Administration.

U7085–1.11: Agriculture

(p. 211-235) Contains 1 map, 3 charts, and 13 tables. Includes farms, total and harvested acreage, and production value; average farm size and property value; prices received and paid by farmers; livestock and poultry production value; farm marketing cash receipts and government payments; and income per farm.

Also includes agricultural production, plants, and value, for meat, flour and mill feed, dairy, hatchery, and soybean products; fertilizer sales; commercial feed manufacturers, sales, and production; and summary crop and livestock production, and grain storage capacity, with State rankings.

Also includes livestock inshipments by State of origin; cattle feedlots; commercial livestock slaughter; and farm wages.

U7085–1.12: Mining and Mineral Products, and Manufacturing

(p. 239-254) Contains 2 maps and 10 tables. Includes mineral production and value; and oil and gas production and value since 1880s, and producing wells.

Also includes new and expanded industries, jobs created, capital expenditure, and payroll; and GSP.

U7095
University of Kansas: Institute for Public Policy and Business Research

U7095-1   KANSAS BUSINESS REVIEW

Quarterly.   Approx. 30 p.
ISSN 0164-8632.
LC 79-642737.
SRI/MF/complete

Quarterly report on Kansas business, employment, retail sales, farm prices, and financial activity.

Data are from State agencies, USDA, and private sources. Most data are current to 1-3 months prior to cover date.

General format:

a. Feature articles; and "Economic Conditions," quarterly feature containing 2 articles on U.S. and Kansas economies.

b. "Economic Indicators," with 5 charts and 9 quarterly tables presenting national and State economic data.

Quarterly economic indicator tables are listed below and appear in all issues. All additional features with substantial statistical content are described, as they appear, under "Statistical Features." Nonstatistical features are not covered.

Availability: University of Kansas: Institute for Public Policy and Business Research, 607 Blake Hall, Lawrence KS 66045-2965, †; SRI/MF/complete.

Issues reviewed during 1985: Fall 1984-Spring/Summer 1985 (P) (Vol. 8, Nos. 1-3/4) [Spring/Summer 1985 is a combined issue].

QUARTERLY TABLES:

[Tables generally show data for latest date/period available, with percent change from previous period and/or year. Data are for Kansas, unless otherwise noted.]

1. Economic indicators [personal income, employment, unemployment rate, retail sales, and Kansas City CPI, all with comparisons to U.S.; and construction activity, new incorporations, oil production, and State tax revenues and expenditures].

2. National indicators [selected U.S. income, labor force, unemployment, general business, price, and banking and finance measures].

3. Employment [labor force, employment on farms and by industry division and major manufacturing group, unemployment insurance initial claims, and manufacturing average weekly hours].

4. Income [farm and nonfarm income, and earnings by industry division].

5. Retail sales subject to sales tax [by kind of business].

6. Employment [labor force and total employment; and retail] sales; for [3] SMSAs, [Kansas portion of Kansas City SMSA], and [7] counties; [prior to Winter 1984/85 issue, table also showed farm employment].

7. Agricultural indicators [crop and livestock prices received by commodity; prior to Winter 1984/85 issue, table also showed index of prices paid].

8-9. Banking activity [loans and/or deposits by type, for Federal Reserve member banks]; and savings and loan assn activities [loans and net savings gain; all for State, Kansas City, Topeka, and Wichita; prior to Spring/Summer 1985 issue, data on loans and deposits were also shown for all commercial banks].

STATISTICAL FEATURES:

U7095-1.601: Fall 1984 (Vol. 8, No. 1)

KANSAS ECONOMIC DEVELOPMENT IN THE DECADE AHEAD: A METHOD AND APPLICATION

(p. 1-7) By Robert A. McLean. Article on outlook for Kansas economic growth. Data are from Commerce Dept. Includes lists of potential high growth industries; and 1 table showing establishments and employment, by SIC 2-digit industry, 1980.

WAGE STRUCTURE OF THE KANSAS ECONOMY

(p. 19-23) Article, with 4 tables showing Kansas average annual wages by industry division, by State region and major county, with comparisons to 4 neighboring States and U.S., various years 1980-83.

KANSAS ECONOMY

(p. 25-27) Article, with 1 table showing Kansas actual employment, and estimated employment based on national growth/recession, by industry division and major manufacturing group, various periods 1971-84.

U7095-1.602: Winter 1984/85 (Vol. 8, No. 2)

LONG-TERM STRUCTURAL CHANGES IN THE KANSAS ECONOMY

(p. 1-9) By Anthony Redwood et al. Article analyzing long-term demographic and economic trends in Kansas. Most data are from Federal agencies.

Includes 3 charts, 5 maps, and 6 tables showing Kansas employment, personal income, and GSP, by industry division; distribution of farms and agricultural sales, by sales size; migration, median age, and percent of population aged 65/over, by county; population growth vs. 3 neighboring States; and CETA eligibility rates by sex and educational attainment; with some U.S. comparisons, various years 1950-84, with employment projections to 1990.

ECONOMIC CONDITIONS: THE NATIONAL REVIEW

(p. 22-23) Article, with 1 table showing peak unemployment rate and month of occurrence, for 7 recessionary periods during 1954-1982.

U7095-1.603: Spring/Summer 1985 (Vol. 8, No. 3-4)

RECENT BUSINESS FORMATION IN KANSAS

(p. 1-7) By Charles E. Krider and Daniel L. Petree. Article on development of new business in Kansas, 1978-82. Data are from Census Bureau.

Includes 16 tables showing business establishments, by industry division, manufacturing and oil/extraction industry group, State region, SMSA, and establishment size; and employment, by establishment size; for Kansas, with selected comparisons to U.S. and 4 neighboring States, mainly 1982 with trends from 1978. Data are actual numbers and/or percent change. Establishment size categories are based on number of employees.

INCOME TAX REFORM

(p. 12-15) By David J. Faurot. Article, with 1 table showing Federal income taxes paid by individuals in the top 2 income brackets, with share of total taxes, 1981-83. Data are from IRS.

INDUSTRIAL REVENUE BOND USER REVISITED: LARGE CORPORATIONS OR SMALL BUSINESS?

(p. 16-21) By Loran B. Smith. Article, with 3 tables showing the following for industrial revenue bonds in Kansas: number issued, by purpose and city: number and value issued to Fortune 500 corporations, by corporation, with city of issuance; and Fortune 500 corporations' aggregate share of total bonds (number and value), by purpose; 1962-83 period. Data are from survey responses of 17 cities.

U7095-2   KANSAS STATISTICAL ABSTRACT, 1984-85

Annual.   [1985.]   ix+258 p.
LC 80-647969.
SRI/MF/complete

Annual compilation, by Wendy A. Murray, of demographic, social, governmental, and economic statistics for Kansas, 1984/85. Data are primarily for 1970s-85, with population projections to 1990, and population and oil and gas production trends from 1800s.

Report is designed to present a comprehensive overview of the State. Extensive geographic, socioeconomic, and demographic breakdowns are shown, as applicable, for most topics. These breakdowns include data by State region, city, county, MSA, urban-rural status, commodity, industry, age, educational attainment, race, and sex. Comparisons to total U.S. are also often included.

Data are from reports of State and Federal agencies, League of Kansas Municipalities, University of Kansas, and industry assns. Data sources appear beneath each table.

Contains foreword, preface, contents listing, and map of counties (p. ii-ix); 16 statistical sections, with 17 maps, 8 charts, and 115 tables, described below (p. 1-252); and subject index (p. 255-258).

This is the 20th annual edition. Prior to 1984/85 edition, report is covered in SRI under U7085-1; issuing dept name has changed from Institute for Economic and Business Research. Previous report, for 1983/84, is described under U7085-1, above.

Availability: University of Kansas: Institute for Public Policy and Business Research, 607 Blake Hall, Lawrence KS 66045-2965, $14.00; SRI/MF/complete.

TABLE SECTIONS:

U7095-2.1: Population, Vital Statistics, and Health

(p. 3-55) Contains 6 maps and 24 tables. Includes population, with trends from 1860 and projections to 1990; land area and density; median age; and families and households.

Also includes births, deaths, marriages, and divorces/annulments; infant and fetal deaths; induced abortions; hospitals, beds, admissions, and personnel; medical and osteopathic physicians; dentists; and adult care homes and beds.

U7095-2.2: Housing and Construction

(p. 59-67) Contains 5 tables. Includes housing units and structural characteristics, including presence of public water and sewer services, central heating, and air conditioning; new housing construction authorized; and value of building permits issued.

U7095-2.3: Education

(p. 71-85) Contains 1 map and 8 tables. Includes accredited schools; public school enrollment, and high school graduates and dropouts; higher education enrollment, by 2- and 4-year institution; and school district costs per pupil, assessed valuation, and tax levy.

U7095-2.4: Climate

(p. 89-97) Contains 4 maps and 4 tables. Includes precipitation and temperature; and tornadoes, injuries, and deaths.

U7095-2.5: Employment and Earnings, and Personal Income

(p. 101-126) Contains 1 map, 3 charts, and 13 tables. Includes labor force by employment status; payroll; business establishments; average annual pay; and wholesale and retail sales.

Also includes personal income by source.

U7095-2.6: Banking and Finance

(p. 129-133) Contains 4 tables. Includes banks, banking offices, deposits, assets, and loans; savings and loan assns, assets, and mortgage loans; and life insurance policies and value in force.

U7095-2.7: State and Local Government Finances and Employment

(p. 137-158) Contains 1 chart and 13 tables. Includes State and local revenues by source, expenditures by function, and indebtedness; property tax levies, rates, and assessed valuation; sales tax collections; and local population and property tax base.

U7095-2.8: Courts, Crime, and Public Safety

(p. 161-182) Contains 1 map, 1 chart, and 12 tables. Includes judicial system structure and number of judges; criminal and civil court caseload activities; Index crime offenses and arrests; correctional institution admissions and releases, and population by institution; and inmate characteristics.

Also includes law enforcement personnel; and fire depts and responses, fires, and fire-related losses, injuries, and deaths.

U7095-2.9: Parks and Recreation

(p. 185-188) Contains 1 map and 3 tables. Includes State park acreage and visitors; Federal reservoir drainage and surface areas, storage capacity, shoreline, and number of public access areas; and hunting and fishing license sales and value.

U7095-2.10: Communications and Transportation

(p. 191-203) Contains 6 tables. Includes circulation of daily newspapers; and radio and TV stations.

Also includes motor vehicle registrations, with trends from 1900, and special license

plates issued; motor fuel consumption and gallons taxed; and expenditure of funds from Federal Highway Administration.

U7095-2.11: Agriculture

(p. 207-231) Contains 1 map, 3 charts, and 13 tables. Includes farms, total and harvested acreage, and production value; average farm size and property value; prices received and paid by farmers; farm marketing cash receipts and government payments; livestock and poultry production value; and income per farm.

Also includes agricultural production, value, and/or plants, for meat, flour and mill feed, dairy, hatchery, and soybean products; fertilizer sales; commercial feed manufacturers, sales, and production; and summary crop and livestock production, and grain storage capacity, with Kansas ranking among States.

Also includes livestock inshipments by State of origin; cattle feedlots; commercial livestock slaughter; and farm wages.

U7095-2.12: Mining and Mineral Products, and Manufacturing

(p. 235-252) Contains 2 maps and 10 tables. Includes mineral production and value; and oil and gas production and value since 1880s, and number of producing wells.

Also includes new and expanded industries, jobs created, capital expenditure, and payroll; and GSP.

U7138
University of Kentucky:
Center for Business
and Economic Research

U7138-1 KENTUCKY ECONOMY: Review and Perspective
Quarterly. Approx. 15 p.
ISSN 0270-1421.
LC sn80-12933.
SRI/MF/complete

Quarterly report on Kentucky business activity and economic performance indicators and trends, with selected U.S. comparisons. Data are current to quarter preceding cover date, and are compiled from reports of various Federal, State, and private agencies.

General format:

a. Newsbriefs; and feature articles, often with statistics.

b. "Selected Indicators of Economic Activity" section, with 2 quarterly tables described below.

Quarterly tables appear in all issues. All additional features with substantial statistical content are described, as they appear, under "Statistical Features." Nonstatistical features are not covered.

Prior to the Fall 1984 issue, report was described in SRI under S3103-2. Issuing agency has changed from Kentucky Council of Economic Advisors.

Availability: University of Kentucky: Center for Business and Economic Research, College of Business and Economics, 301 Mathews Bldg., Lexington KY 40506-0047, †; SRI/MF/complete.

Issues reviewed during 1985: Fall 1984-Summer 1985 (P) (Vol. 8, No. 3; Vol. 9, Nos. 1-2) [No Winter 1984 issue was published].

QUARTERLY INDICATOR TABLES:

[Data are shown for quarter prior to cover date, total and by month, with percent change from previous quarter and same quarter of previous year.]

[1] U.S. data [including CPI and PPI, by major item, with detail for energy sector; labor force and employment; GNP; personal income; index of industrial production; residential building permits; and outstanding installment credit].

[2] Kentucky data [including labor force; employment by industry division; manufacturing hours and earnings; coal mining output, hours, earnings, and severance tax receipts; residential construction permits and value; loans by savings and loan assns; car registrations; and State government sales, income, and other tax receipts].

STATISTICAL FEATURES:

U7138-1.601: Fall 1984 (Vol. 8, No. 3)

KENTUCKY ECONOMIC REVIEW

(p. 1, 14) By Merl M. Hackbart. Article, with 1 table showing Kentucky seasonally adjusted employment by industry division, and unemployment rate, Sept. 1983-Aug. 1984. Data are from the Kentucky Economic Information System.

FORECASTING THE REAL ESTATE MARKET IN KENTUCKY

(p. 3-5) By G. S. Laumas. Article, with 3 tables showing Kentucky mortgage rates and housing unit sales projected under 3 economic scenarios, 1984-90. Data are derived from Kentucky Economic Information System.

KENTUCKY REVENUES IN 1983-84 AND THE OUTLOOK FOR 1984-85, ANNUAL FEATURE

(p. 6-7, 10) Annual article, by Lawrence K. Lynch, presenting actual and forecast tax receipts for Kentucky general and transportation funds by tax source, various periods FY80-85. Actual data are from the Kentucky Revenue Dept; forecasts are the author's. Includes 4 tables.

CURRENT REVENUE SITUATION IN KENTUCKY

(p. 11-13) By Gary W. Gillis and James A. Street. Article, with 3 tables showing sales, income, and property taxes as percent of personal income; business taxes as percent of all taxes; and per capita personal income; for Kentucky, 7 neighboring States, and U.S., various years 1957-83. Data are from the U.S. Dept of Commerce and Advisory Commission on Intergovernmental Relations.

KENTUCKY PERSONAL INCOME: SUMMARY, BY QUARTERS, RECURRING FEATURE

(p. 15) Recurring table showing Kentucky personal income by source and earnings by industry division, and contributions to social insurance, 2nd quarter 1983-2nd quarter 1984. Data are from U.S. Bureau of Economic Analysis.

U7138-1.602: Spring 1985 (Vol. 9, No. 1)

KENTUCKY ECONOMIC REVIEW

(p. 1, 6-7) By Merl M. Hackbart. Article, with 2 tables showing growth in total personal income, for U.S., southeastern States, and Kentucky, quarterly 1983-84 and annually 1982-84; and average annual employment growth rates for U.S. and Kentucky, by industry division, 1979-84 and 1982-84 periods. Data are from the Kentucky Economic Information System.

SUPPLY AND DEMAND FOR U.S., APPALACHIAN, AND KENTUCKY COAL

(p. 10-13) By Curtis E. Harvey. Article, with 4 tables showing coal production by region (Appalachian, interior, and western), with detail by State; shipments of Appalachian coal by end user (including exports to Canada); and shipments of Kentucky coal to electric utilities (total and as a percent of all Kentucky coal shipments and of all coal received by utilities), by State; various years 1970-83.

Data are from U.S. Depts of Energy and Interior.

U7138-1.603: Summer 1985 (Vol. 9, No. 2)

KENTUCKY PERSONAL INCOME: SUMMARY, BY QUARTERS, RECURRING FEATURE

(p. 9) Recurring table showing Kentucky personal income by source and earnings by industry division, and contributions to social insurance, 1st quarter 1984-1st quarter 1985. Data are from U.S. Bureau of Economic Analysis.

KENTUCKY COUNTY-LEVEL PER CAPITA PERSONAL INCOME, 1982-83, ANNUAL FEATURE

(p. 11) Annual table showing Kentucky per capita personal income, by county, 1982-83. Data are from U.S. Commerce Dept.

Previous table is described in SRI 1984 Annual under S3103-2.504.

U7138-2 **ANNUAL ECONOMIC REPORT, 1984,**
Commonwealth of Kentucky
Annual. [1985.] xiii+89 p.
ISSN 0270-238X.
LC 80-647821.
SRI/MF/complete

Annual report on Kentucky economic conditions compared to U.S., generally 1970-83. Includes data on population, labor force, income and earnings, State/local government revenues, and coal and construction industries.

Data are primarily from U.S. Commerce Dept, and Kentucky Economic Information System.

Contains listings of contents, tables, and charts (p. v-ix); foreword and preface (p. xi-xiii); report, with 26 charts, and 37 tables described below (p. 1-85); and glossary (p. 87-89).

This is the 13th annual report. Prior to 1984 edition, report was issued by Kentucky Council of Economic Advisors under the title *Council of Economic Advisors Annual Report,* and was covered in SRI under S3103-4.

Availability: University of Kentucky: Center for Business and Economic Research, College of Business and Economics, 301 Mathews Bldg., Lexington KY 40506-0047, public and nonprofit institutions †, others $10.00; SRI/MF/complete.

TABLES:

[Unless otherwise noted, most data are shown for Kentucky and U.S., various years 1970-83, with trends from as early as 1920.]

a. Population size and density; net migration; labor force participation and unemployment rates; and average earnings by industry division. 5 tables. (p. 3-11)

b. Personal income per capita as percent of U.S. average, for Kentucky and Southeast U.S.; and distribution of income by source, and indexes of growth rates, for wages/salaries by industry division, and durable and nondurable manufacturing by industry group. 12 tables. (p. 13-38)

c. Area Development District population, unemployment, income, and earnings as percent of State, and income distribution by source, by district; Fayette County commuting patterns with surrounding counties; and income, earnings, and labor force participation rates for selected high- and low-income counties, with economic comparison of Carlisle and Martin Counties. 7 tables. (p. 43-55)

d. State/local government revenue distribution and indexes by source and tax type, FY78-83; actual vs. potential State/local revenues by tax type, FY83; and State/local tax revenues per capita and as percent of income, FY70-83. 7 tables. (p. 58-71)

e. Coal production indexes for 2 State and 3 U.S. regions; coal production distribution by selected State; and coal mine production, employment, and wage/salary indexes. 3 tables. (p. 73-76)

f. Farm income and expenditure indexes; farm labor/proprietors' income as percent of total income; and indexes of construction contracts awarded and wages/salaries. 3 tables. (p. 80-84)

U7175
University of Louisville: Urban Studies Center

U7175-3 **HOW MANY KENTUCKIANS: Population Forecasts, 1980-2020**
Recurring (irreg.) Fall 1984.
ii+149 p. var. paging.
SRI/MF/complete

Recurring report presenting Kentucky population projections by age and sex, by area development district and county, selected years 1985-2020, with actual or estimated data for 1980 and 1982. Also includes projected survival rates, by age, race, and sex; and fertility rates, by age and race.

Projections are based on Census Bureau data.

Contains contents listing (p. ii); introduction and methodology summary, with 4 tables (p. A1-A10); and 1 basic table, repeated for State and each area development district and county (p. B1-B138).

For description of previous edition, for 1983, see SRI 1983 Annual under this number.

More detailed projections are available on request from the issuing agency.

Availability: University of Louisville: Urban Studies Center, College of Urban and Public Af-

fairs, Attention: Publications, Gardencourt Campus, 1020 Alta Vista Rd., Louisville KY 40292, $10.00; SRI/MF/complete.

U7360
University of Massachusetts: Management Research Center

U7360-1 **MASSACHUSETTS BUSINESS AND ECONOMIC REPORT**
Quarterly.
Approx. 6 p. no paging.
SRI/MF/complete

Quarterly report presenting forecasts of selected Massachusetts business and economic indicators, and articles on topics affecting the Massachusetts economy. Forecasts are from a model developed by Data Resources, Inc.

Issues usually contain articles, occasionally with substantial statistics; and 1 quarterly table, "Control Forecast," including data on employment, wages, average weekly hours in manufacturing, rate of inflation, personal and disposable income, and business cost index.

Table usually presents data annually for current, prior, and coming years, and quarterly for 5 quarters beginning 1-2 quarters prior to date of issue.

Quarterly table has been discontinued, beginning with the Winter 1985 issue. Issues reviewed by SRI during 1985 contained no statistical articles.

Because the quarterly table has been discontinued, SRI coverage of this publication ends with the Spring/Summer 1985 issue.

Availability: University of Massachusetts: Management Research Center, Business Publications Services, School of Management, Amherst MA 01003, †; SRI/MF/complete.

Issues reviewed during 1985: Fall 1984-Spring/Summer 1985 (P) (Vol. 11, No. 4; Vol. 13, No. 2) [Vol. 11, No. 4 incorrectly reads Vol. 12; subsequent issues begin with Vol. 13, No. 1].

U7475
University of Michigan: Institute for Social Research

U7475-1 **SURVEYS OF CONSUMER ATTITUDES, Quarterly Report**
Quarterly.
Summary approx. 15 p., tables approx. 70 p. no paging.
SRI/MF/complete

Quarterly report on survey examining changes in consumer attitudes and expectations concerning personal finances and general business and market conditions. Covers attitudes affecting consumer decisions on discretionary purchases and savings, including perceptions of inflation and buying conditions for household goods, automobiles, and houses.

Survey is conducted by the University of Michigan Survey Research Center as part of a program monitoring economic change. Data are based on approximately 2,000 interviews conducted over several weeks and concluded in the final month of each quarter. Report is published 2-3 weeks after the end of quarter surveyed.

Survey report is presented in 2 parts:

a. Narrative summary of survey highlights, including changes during the quarter in consumer attitudes and outlook, usually with 1 or more charts and tables.

b. 34 tables (under separate cover), listed below, presenting survey results, most with 1-2 accompanying charts showing recent and historical trends; and contents listing, explanatory charts, and definitions.

A less comprehensive monthly report is also published (see U7475-2, below).

Availability: University of Michigan—Institute for Social Research, Monitoring Economic Change Program, Survey Research Center, PO Box 1248, Ann Arbor MI 48106-1248, members $2000.00 per yr., sponsors $2500.00 per yr., nonprofit groups $1200.00 per yr. (includes working papers series of same title); SRI/MF/complete.

Issues reviewed during 1985: Dec. 1984-Sept. 1985 (D).

TABLES:

[Tables 1-3 show quarterly data for current and preceding 6-7 years. Tables 4-34 show quarterly data for current and preceding 2-3 years, for all families, and families with incomes over $20,000.]

1. Index of consumer sentiment [for all families, and families with incomes over $20,000 and over $25,000].

2. Index of consumer sentiment within region and age subgroups [for all families].

3. Components of the index of consumer sentiment [for all families].

4-5. Current financial situation compared to a year ago, and selected reasons for opinions about personal financial situation.

6-7. Expected change in financial situation, and trend in personal financial situation.

8. Expected family income change during the next 12 months.

9-10. Past and expected changes in real family income.

11. Trend in family income and prices comparisons.

12-13. News heard and selected items of news heard of recent changes in business conditions.

14-16. Current business conditions compared to a year ago, expected change in a year, and reasons for opinions about [expected] changes.

17-19. Trend in past and expected changes in business conditions, and business conditions expected during the next 12 months and the next 5 years.

20-21. Expected change in unemployment and in interest rates.

22-23. Change in prices during the last 12 months and expected during the next 12 months.

24. Unemployment or inflation more serious economic hardship.

25. Opinions about the government's economic policy.

26-27. Buying conditions for large household goods, and selected reasons for opinions about buying conditions.

28-29. Buying conditions for houses, and selected reasons for opinions about buying conditions.

30-31. Buying conditions for cars, and selected reasons for opinions about buying conditions.

32-34. Plans to purchase an automobile during the next 12 months, and current and future vehicle purchase intentions.

U7475–2   SURVEYS OF CONSUMER ATTITUDES, Monthly Report

Monthly.
Summary approx. 10 p., tables approx. 60 p. no paging.
SRI/MF/complete

Monthly report on survey measuring changes in consumer attitudes and expectations concerning their personal financial situation and general business and market conditions. Questions cover attitudes affecting consumer decisions on discretionary purchases and savings, including perceptions of inflation and buying conditions for household goods, automobiles, and houses.

Data are based on approximately 700 interviews conducted over several weeks and concluded in the 3rd week of each month. Report is published 2-3 weeks after end of month of coverage.

Survey is presented in 2 parts:

a. Narrative summary of changes in consumer attitudes from preceding month, usually with 1 or more charts and text tables.

b. 34 tables (under separate cover), listed below, most with 1-2 accompanying charts showing recent and longer-term trends; and contents listing, explanatory charts, and definitions.

Survey report is a companion to the more comprehensive quarterly survey, described in SRI under U7475-1. Quarterly survey includes additional detail by income group.

Availability: University of Michigan—Institute for Social Research, Monitoring Economic Change Program, Survey Research Center, PO Box 1248, Ann Arbor MI 48106-1248, members $3350.00 per yr., sponsors $3900.00 per yr., nonprofit groups $2100.00 per yr. (subscription includes quarterly report and working papers series of same title); SRI/MF/complete.

Issues reviewed during 1985: Oct. 1984-Sept. 1985 (D).

TABLES:

[Tables 1-3 show data for month of coverage and preceding 36 months. All other tables show data for month of coverage and preceding 12 months.]

1. Index of consumer sentiment [all families, and families with incomes over $20,000, and over $25,000].

2. Index of consumer sentiment within region and age subgroups.

3. Components of the index of consumer sentiment.

4-5. Current financial situation compared to a year ago, and selected reasons for opinions about personal financial situation.

6-7. Expected change in financial situation, and trend in personal financial situation.

8. Expected family income change during the next 12 months.

9-10. Past and expected changes in real family income.

11. Trend in family income and prices comparisons.

12-13. News heard and selected items of news heard of recent changes in business conditions.

14-16. Current business conditions compared to a year ago, expected change in a year, and reasons for opinions about [expected] changes.

17-19. Trend in past and expected changes in business conditions, and business conditions expected during the next 12 months and the next 5 years.

20-21. Expected change in unemployment and in interest rates.

22-23. Change in prices during the last 12 months, and expected during the next 12 months.

24. Unemployment or inflation more serious economic hardship.

25. Opinions about the government's economic policy.

26-27. Buying conditions for large household goods, and selected reasons for opinions about buying conditions.

28-29. Buying conditions for houses, and selected reasons for opinions about buying conditions.

30-31. Buying conditions for cars, and selected reasons for opinions about buying conditions.

32-34. Plans to purchase an automobile during the next 12 months, and current and future vehicle purchase intentions.

U7475–3   ECONOMIC OUTLOOK USA

Quarterly. Approx. 20 p. cumulative pagination throughout year.
ISSN 0095-3830.
LC 74-648918.
SRI/MF/complete

Quarterly journal analyzing current economic conditions, and presenting selected measures of consumer economic expectations and buying attitudes.

Data are from the Commerce Dept, National Bureau of Economic Research, National Assn of Business Economists (NABE), and University of Michigan econometric forecast model and consumer surveys. Quarter of data coverage is 1 quarter prior to cover date.

Issues generally contain 2-6 "Economic Prospects" trend charts for selected economic indicators; quarterly consumer survey feature, with 1 consumer sentiment index trend chart, and occasionally 1 or more tables; other articles, many with statistics; 2 quarterly economic indicator tables; and 12 quarterly trend charts on consumer attitudes and economic indicators.

Statistical articles include a recurring feature presenting national economic forecasts.

An annual author index appears in autumn issue.

Quarterly economic indicator tables are described below. Most quarterly charts and tables appear in all issues. All additional features with substantial statistical content, including consumer survey tables, are described as they appear, under "Statistical Features." Nonstatistical features are not covered.

Availability: University of Michigan—Institute for Social Research, Survey Research Center, 426 Thompson St., PO Box 1248, Ann Arbor MI 48106-1248, $27.00 per yr., academic subscribers $13.00 per yr.; SRI/MF/complete.

Issues reviewed during 1985: Autumn 1984; and 1st-3rd Qtrs. 1985 (P) (Vol. 11, No. 4; Vol. 12, Nos. 1-3).

QUARTERLY TABLES:

a. Actual and projected data for 17 indicators, including industrial production index, corporate profits and bond yield, housing starts, Treasury bill rate, government purchases, and change in business inventories, shown quarterly for quarter of coverage and previous 6 and following 4-5 quarters, and annually for previous, current, and coming years; projections are from American Statistical Assn-National Bureau of Economic Research panel.

b. Current-dollar GNP accounts: 7 indicators including personal consumption expenditures, private domestic investment, government purchases, net exports, disposable personal income, and personal saving rate; quarterly for quarter of coverage and preceding 11 quarters, and annually for current and/ or 2-3 preceding years.

STATISTICAL FEATURES:

U7475-3.601: Autumn 1984 (Vol. 11, No. 4)

BUSINESS ECONOMISTS FAVOR REAGANOMICS BUT STILL EXPECT RECESSION WITHIN 18 MONTHS

(p. 81-84) By Richard E. Barfield. Article on business economists' opinions on current economic issues and outlook. Data are from a survey of National Assn of Business Economists (NABE) members, conducted by University of Michigan Survey Research Center, Sept. 1984.

Includes 5 tables showing survey findings on recent economic trends in respondents' own company/industry; forecasts for selected economic indicators, various periods through 1988; satisfaction with fiscal and monetary policy, with trends from Nov. 1983; and expected year for current business cycle peak.

Article previously appeared on a quarterly basis.

U7475-3.602: 1st Qtr. 1985 (Vol. 12, No. 1)

U.S. ECONOMIC OUTLOOK FOR 1985-86, RECURRING FEATURE

(p. 3-10) Recurring article, by Joan P. Crary et al., presenting national economic forecasts through 1986. Data are from Federal agencies, and from forecasts developed by University of Michigan Research Seminar in Quantitative Economics.

Includes 1 summary chart covering 6 major indicators, 1984-86; and 4 tables showing the following:

a. Change in 23 economic indicators, various periods 1958-83; and Federal Government expenditures by type, and total receipts, FY84-86.

b. Forecasts for 27 economic indicators, including GNP and components, unemployment rate, corporate profits, 3-month Treasury bill rate, real disposable income, and personal saving rate, quarterly 4th

quarter 1984-4th quarter 1986, and annually 1985-86, with actual data for 3rd quarter 1984.

c. Potential economic impact of taxation changes incorporating broadened tax base, modified indexation, and value added tax (no date).

SURPRISES OF 1983-84 AND SCENARIOS FOR 1985-86, ANNUAL FEATURE

(p. 11-14) Annual article, by Victor Zarnowitz, assessing the accuracy of economic forecasts through 1986. Data sources include forecasts derived from American Statistical Assn-National Bureau of Economic Research (ASA-NBER) surveys, and actual data from Commerce Dept.

Includes 3 tables showing actual and/or forecast changes in selected economic indicators, including GNP, implicit price deflator, industrial production index, unemployment rate, corporate profits, housing starts, consumption expenditures, nonresidential fixed investment, business inventories, 3-month Treasury bill rate, and net exports, various periods 1982-86.

For description of previous article, see SRI 1983 Annual under U7475-3.402.

RECESSION NARROWLY AVERTED?

(p. 15-16) By Paul W. McCracken. Article, with 3 tables showing percent of firms reporting increases in production, new orders, and inventory, monthly 1984; annual rates of increase in GNP, final demand, and domestic demand for output, quarterly 1984; and export and Federal surplus values, exchange rate index, and Moody's Aaa bond yields, 1977-84.

Data are from National Assn of Purchasing Management and Commerce Dept.

U7475-3.603: 2nd Qtr. 1985 (Vol. 12, No. 2)

CONSUMER OPTIMISM MAINTAINED, QUARTERLY FEATURE

(p. 31-33) Quarterly consumer survey article, by Richard T. Curtin, with 2 tables on expectations concerning income tax simplification proposal, Jan.-Feb. 1985. Tables cover the proposal's likelihood of passage, and impact on personal finances.

THE CHANGING AMERICAN FAMILY: LIVING ARRANGEMENTS AND RELATIONSHIPS WITH KIN

(p. 34-38) By Arland Thornton and Deborah Freedman. Article on trends in household structure. Data are from the Census Bureau.

Includes 3 tables showing distribution of households by size, and average household size, 1790-1980; and living arrangements of married and unmarried persons age 65/over, 1900-75, and of never-married men and women age 25-34 maintaining their own households, 1950-82. Data are shown for selected years within the periods noted.

SOME CONSEQUENCES OF RECENT CHANGES IN HOUSEHOLD COMPOSITION

(p. 39-43) By Duane F. Alwin. Article on trends in living arrangements. Data are based on 3,692 responses to a 1978 survey conducted by the University of Michigan Survey Research Center.

Includes 3 tables showing respondents' living arrangements, by sex and marital status; and statistical analyses correlating living arrangements with social activity (visiting friends) and distress.

U7475-3.604: 3rd Quarter 1985 (Vol. 12, No. 3)

MID-YEAR REVIEW AND FORECAST: THE U.S. ECONOMIC OUTLOOK FOR 1985-86, RECURRING FEATURE

(p. 54-59) Recurring article, by Saul H. Hymans and Joan P. Crary, presenting national economic forecasts through 1st half 1987. Data sources include forecasts developed by University of Michigan Research Seminar in Quantitative Economics. Includes 4 tables showing the following:

a. Demand for domestically produced and total goods/services, and for U.S. production worldwide, and real GNP, semiannually 2nd half 1982-1st half 1985; Federal Government expenditures by type, and total receipts, FY84-87; and percent change in GNP and money supply, and 3-month Treasury bill rates, semiannually 4th quarter 1982-2nd quarter 1985.

b. Forecasts for 21 economic indicators, including GNP and components, wages, productivity, prices, personal consumption, exchange rate, unemployment, exports, auto sales, housing starts, Treasury bill and corporate bond rates, corporate profits, and Federal deficit; shown as level or percent change, semiannually 2nd quarter 1985-2nd quarter 1987, with actual data for 4th quarter 1984-2nd quarter 1985 period.

ECONOMIC SELF-SUFFICIENCY AMONG RECENTLY-ARRIVED REFUGEES FROM SOUTHEAST ASIA

(p. 60-63) By Nathan Caplan et al. Article, with 2 charts and 1 table showing Southeast Asian refugee unemployment rates and poverty status, by number of months in U.S. and/or household composition, late summer 1982. Data are from a survey of 1,384 households of refugees who had arrived in the U.S. since Oct. 1978. Survey was conducted by Institute for Social Research.

U7475-4   SURVEYS OF CONSUMER ATTITUDES: Working Paper Series

Series. For individual publication data, see below.
SRI/MF/complete

Series of special reports covering consumer and household financial transactions, credit and consumption patterns, durable goods ownership, and related topics. Includes data on consumer attitudes, and breakdowns by sociodemographic characteristics.

Data are primarily from monthly Surveys of Consumer Attitudes and other Institute for Social Research studies.

Reports usually contain analysis of survey findings, with text statistics, and 3 or more detailed tables showing response breakdowns.

Report reviewed during 1985 is described below.

Availability: University of Michigan—Institute for Social Research, Monitoring Economic Change Program, Survey Research Center, PO Box 1248, Ann Arbor MI 48106-1248, included in subscription to *Surveys of Consumer Attitudes,* available individually at $50.00 each; SRI/MF/ complete.

U7475–4.17: Consumer Outlook: Early Vigor to Mature Recovery

[Monograph. Nov. 1984. 12+20 p. No. WP20. SRI/MF/complete.]

By Richard T. Curtin. Report on recent trends in consumer attitudes and expectations. Includes consumer opinions concerning the 1984 presidential election and effect on personal income tax rates; Federal budget deficit changes and impact on business; and influence of interest rates on decision to purchase durable goods, houses, and vehicles.

Also includes indexes of consumer sentiment based on responses to the topics described above, and expected changes in personal financial situation and business and market conditions.

Data are from Surveys of Consumer Attitudes conducted Mar. and Sept. 1984, with selected trends from as early as 1961.

Contains narrative report (p. 1-12); and 29 trend charts and 9 tables (20 p.).

U7475–5   MONITORING THE FUTURE: Questionnaire Responses from the Nation's High School Seniors, 1983

Annual. 1985. x+273 p.
ISR Code No. 4653.
ISSN 0190-9185.
ISBN 0-87944-300-6.
LC 79-640937.
SRI/MF/complete

Annual survey, for 1983, by Lloyd D. Johnston et al., of the values, behavior, and lifestyle of U.S. high school seniors. Principal focus is on drug use and related attitudes, but study also includes responses on life satisfaction, leisure activities, personal relationships, changing roles of women, attitudes toward social institutions, conservation and ecology issues, and social and ethical attitudes.

Data are based on a national survey sample of 16,947 students in 112 public and 22 private high schools, conducted by the Survey Research Center of the University of Michigan in 1983.

The survey, 9th in a series begun in 1975, is designed to study trends in attitudes and behavior, and repeats a majority of the 1,300 questions asked each year. Questions are divided into 5 questionnaire forms answered by approximately 3,400 seniors for each form; approximately 100 questions appear on all 5 forms and are answered by the total sample.

Contents:

a. Contents listing; preface; and introduction, presenting study background and methodology, with 2 tables showing sample size and response rates, 1975-83, and list of 19 subject areas covered. (p. v-x, 1-11)

b. Descriptive results, with explanation of table format (p. 13-15); and responses to questions appearing on all survey forms (p. 16-33), and to questions on each form (p. 34-201).

c. Cross-time index of questionnaire items, 1975-83. (p. 203-243)

d. Appendices A-C, presenting sampling error estimates and methodology, with 2 charts and 5 tables; sample of questionnaire; and list of references. (p. 245-273)

Question topics are described below.

Availability: University of Michigan—Institute for Social Research, Publications Sales, PO Box 1248, Ann Arbor MI 48106-1248, $40.00, $215.00 for 8 volume set; SRI/MF/complete.

QUESTION TOPICS:

[All responses are shown by sex, race, census region, 4-year college plans (yes or no), and life-time illicit drug use (none, marijuana only, few pills, more pills, and any heroin).]

U7475–5.1: Questionnaire Forms 1-5

[Data show responses to approximately 100 questions appearing on all 5 questionnaire forms.]

a. Background data including ethnicity; marital status; household composition; parents' schooling; political beliefs; religious preferences; self-rating on ability and intelligence; and school grades and attendance record; questions C01-C20. (p. 16-20)

b. Activities including future plans; employment and recreation; weekly income; vehicle use; traffic violations and accidents while drinking or using drugs; and expectations of military service; questions C21-C34. (p. 20-24)

c. Frequency and quantity of cigarette smoking; drinking of alcoholic beverages; and use of drugs, by type including marijuana, LSD, cocaine, heroin, and other narcotics and inhaled substances; questions B01-B17C. (p. 25-33)

U7475–5.2: Questionnaire Form 1

a. Views on personal happiness and relations with others, life satisfaction and goals, and the political system; questions A001-A011J. (p. 34-41)

b. Detailed questions on circumstances, frequency, and attitudes with respect to cigarette, alcohol, and drug use; questions B001-B104L. (p. 41-82)

c. Experiences in and attitudes toward school; experiences with school counselors; and health; questions D001-D018. (p. 83-89)

U7475–5.3: Questionnaire Form 2

a. Frequency of participation in leisure time activities including watching TV and reading; attitudes toward the economic system, social protest, marriage, and working couples sharing responsibilities; political attitudes and participation; U.S. foreign policies; frequency of delinquent behavior; and experiences of victimization; questions A01-A20G. (p. 90-104)

b. Drug availability; life satisfaction and self-ratings, and ratings for 12 types of organizations or institutions; assessment of the frequency with which friends engage in drug use by specific drug, and drink alcoholic beverages; and personal drug use, school grade in which first tried different drugs, and parents' knowledge of alcohol and drug use; questions A21-E06. (p. 104-113)

c. Reactions to anger; views on military service and draft; assessment of the influence of people in authority on the school system; experiences with school drug education; views on tests of basic academic skills; and eating, exercise, and sleep habits; questions E07-E20F. (p. 113-118)

U7475–5.4: Questionnaire Form 3

a. Attitudes toward equal employment of women; willingness to change behavior to conserve resources; importance of leisure and work; relations with other racial groups; plans for marriage and having children; and ratings for 12 types of organizations or institutions; questions A01-A26. (p. 119-128)

b. Personal use of nonprescription drugs; attitudes toward and association with different types of drug users; frequency of selected physical symptoms; and attempts to stop using drugs and reasons; questions A27-D04. (p. 128-135)

c. Views on value of conservation and anti-pollution efforts and need for population and birth control; experiences with school sex education; ratings of behaviors that give high status in high school; experiences of victimization; desire for material possessions; and school grade in which first tried different drugs; questions E01-E10M. (p. 136-145)

U7475–5.5: Questionnaire Form 4

a. Attitudes concerning the future, including resolution of environmental problems; views on characteristics of a good job, and expected job at age 30; attitudes toward premarital relationships and marriage; amount of TV watched daily, and reading habits; and influence various institutions should exert on society; questions A01-A19J. (p. 146-158)

b. Views on legalization of drugs; life and job satisfaction, and job experiences; world problems; frequency of use of alcoholic beverages; views on military life; similarity of student's, parents', and friends' attitudes on selected issues including drug use and drinking alcohol; and student and parental involvement in groups concerned with drug or alcohol abuse; questions A20-E15. (p. 158-172)

U7475–5.6: Questionnaire Form 5

a. Concern with social problems; preparation for marriage and parenting; rating of work setting; experiences with other racial groups; driving; consumer behavior; concern for others; and types of organizations likely to receive student's charitable contributions in the future; questions A01-A21. (p. 173-183)

b. Views on discrimination against women; risk of harmful effects from cigarettes, selected drugs, and alcohol; attitudes about self and others; financial and job security; and saving and spending habits; questions A22-D05E. (p. 183-193)

c. Personal attitudes and opinion on others' attitudes toward users of marijuana and other illegal drugs, and cigarette smoking; and consumption of caffeinated beverages; questions E01-E15. (p. 193-201)

U7475–10 IMPACT OF WORK SCHEDULES ON THE FAMILY
Monograph. 1983.
xix + 166 p. + errata sheet.
ISR Code No. 4550.
ISBN 0-87944-284-0.
LC 83-8451.
SRI/MF/complete

Survey report analyzing the impact of work schedules on family life. Presents survey findings and regression analyses relating family life quality measures to selected work schedule and socioeconomic characteristics.

Family life quality measures include time spent on child care and housework, perceived conflict between work and family, and satisfaction with family life. Work schedule characteristics include number and variability of hours and days worked, weekend work, and shiftwork. Socioeconomic characteristics include worker's sex and education, presence and employment status of spouse, and family's life-cycle stage.

Also presents detailed analysis of dual-earner couples' work schedules, including data by blue/white-collar status and use of child day care.

Data are based on responses of 1,090 workers to the 1977 Quality of Employment Survey conducted by the Institute for Social Research.

Contains introductory material, and contents and table listings (p. v-xix); 7 chapters, with narrative analysis and 40 interspersed tables (p. 1-130); appendices, with questionnaire facsimile and 4 tables (p. 131-159); and references (p. 161-166).

Availability: University of Michigan—Institute for Social Research, Publications Sales, PO Box 1248, Ann Arbor MI 48106-1248, $22.00; SRI/MF/complete.

U7475–11 YEARS OF POVERTY, YEARS OF PLENTY: The Changing Economic Fortunes of American Workers and Families
Monograph. 1984.
xvi + 184 p.
ISR Code No. 4591.
ISBN 0-87944-285-9 (cloth), ISBN 0-87944-289-0 (pbk.).
LC 81-12923.
SRI/MF/complete

By Greg J. Duncan et al. Survey report analyzing changes in economic status of individuals and families over the 10-year period 1969-78. Includes survey findings and regression analyses pertaining to income changes, persistence of poverty and welfare dependence, and economic status of women and black males relative to that of white males.

Data are based on annual interviews with over 5,000 families conducted since 1968 for the continuing Panel Study of Income Dynamics.

Contents:

Introductory matter and contents listing (p. v-xvi); and introduction (p. 1-7).

Chapter 1. Overview of Family Economic Mobility. Includes 5 tables showing trends in income levels and income/needs ratio, including impact of changes in family composition; and frequency of undesirable life events among married men. (p. 9-31)

Chapter 2-3. Dynamics of Poverty and Welfare Use. Includes 2 charts and 10 tables showing incidence and persistence of poverty and welfare dependence, and correlation with demographic characteristics. (p. 33-94)

Chapter 4. Dynamics of Work Hours, Unemployment, and Earnings. Includes 6 tables showing changes in work hours, by race and sex; demographic characteristics of chronically unemployed male household heads; and earnings changes for white men, including contributing factors. (p. 95-128)

Chapter 5. Recent Trends in the Relative Earnings of Black Men. Includes 3 tables primarily comparing changes in earnings levels of black men relative to white men. (p. 129-152)

Chapter 6. Do Women "Deserve" To Earn Less Than Men? Includes 1 table showing work skill/attachment measures (education, work experience and continuity, self-imposed job restrictions, absenteeism) for white men and white and black women, and extent to which each measure explains the male-female wage gap. (p. 153-172)

References and glossary. (p. 173-184)

Annual reports based on the Panel Study of Income Dynamics are covered in SRI under U7475-7.

Availability: University of Michigan—Institute for Social Research, Publications Sales, PO Box 1248, Ann Arbor MI 48106-1248, $14.00 (pbk.), $24.00 (cloth); SRI/MF/complete.

U7730
University of Missouri: College of Business and Public Administration

U7730–1 STATISTICAL ABSTRACT FOR MISSOURI, 1985
Biennial. [1985.] xiii + 258 p.
LC 81-644761.
SRI/MF/complete

Biennial compilation, for 1985, of detailed social, governmental, and economic statistics for Missouri. Data are primarily for 1970s-85, with selected trends from 1940.

Report is designed to present a comprehensive overview of the State. Extensive socioeconomic, demographic, and geographic breakdowns are shown, as applicable, for most topics. These breakdowns include data by city, county, SMSA, commodity, industry, age, educational attainment, race, and sex. Comparisons to total U.S. and other States are also often included.

Most data are fom Federal and State agencies. Data sources appear beneath each table.

Contains preface, map, and listings of tables and charts (p. iii-xiii); and 16 charts and 104 tables arranged in 7 sections, described below (p. 3-258).

This is the 3rd edition. Previous report, for 1983, is described in SRI 1983 Annual under this number.

Availability: University of Missouri: College of Business and Public Administration, Research Center, Ten Professional Bldg., Columbia MO 65211, $17.50; SRI/MF/complete.

TABLE SECTIONS:

U7730–1.1: Section A: Population and Vital Statistics

(p. 3-28) Contains 4 charts and 13 tables. Includes population; births, deaths, and migration; public and private elementary, secondary, and higher education enrollment; and marriages and divorces.

U7730–1.2: Section B: Income, Employment, and Prices

(p. 30-146) Contains 5 charts and 33 tables. Includes personal income by source; transfer payments by program, with detail for income maintenance and unemployment insurance; labor force by employment status; government employment by level; manufacturing employment, hours, and earnings; CPI for State, St. Louis, and Kansas City; and U.S. PPI.

U7730–1.3: Section C: Transportation

(p. 148-160) Contains 1 chart and 6 tables. Includes waterborne freight at St. Louis and Kansas City ports; U.S. motor vehicle production; motor vehicle registrations; State share of passenger car assemblies; airport specifications; and civil and military aircraft operations at selected airports.

U7730–1.4: Section D: Business, Finance, and Construction

(p. 162-175) Contains 1 chart and 8 tables. Includes investment and jobs created by new and expanding manufacturers; liquid assets; interest rates on U.S. Government securities, and municipal and corporate bonds; financial institution assets and liabilities; and number and value of new housing units authorized.

U7730–1.5: Section E: Agriculture and Natural Resources

(p. 177-197) Contains 1 chart and 10 tables. Includes number and acreage of farms; farm income vs. total personal income; farm production expenditures and prices received; lead and total mineral production volume and/or value; and nonfuel mineral production value, by State.

U7730–1.6: Section F: Energy

(p. 199-214) Contains 12 tables. Includes energy consumption by fuel type and end-use sector, including input at electric utilities.

U7730–1.7: Section G: Public Sector

(p. 216-258) Contains 4 charts and 22 tables. Includes revenues by government level and source, with detail for tax collections; State and Federal income tax returns and tax liability; State/local revenues and expenditures per $1,000 personal income; assessed property values; education finances, including average teacher salaries; and registered voters.

U7860
University of Nebraska: Bureau of Business Research

U7860–1   BUSINESS IN NEBRASKA
Monthly.   Approx. 6 p.
ISSN 0149-4163.
LC sn82-8107.
SRI/MF/complete, shipped
quarterly

Monthly review of business and economic activity in Nebraska. Data are from Federal and State agencies and private sources. Month of data coverage is 4 months prior to month of publication.

Each issue contains 1-2 feature articles, often with statistics; and 3 charts and 5 monthly tables, accompanied by narrative analysis.

Monthly tables are listed below and appear in all issues. All additional features with substantial statistical content are described, as they appear, under "Statistical Features." Nonstatistical features are not covered.

Availability: University of Nebraska: Bureau of Business Research, College of Business Administration, Rm. 200, Lincoln NE 68588-0406, †; SRI/MF/complete, shipped quarterly.

Issues reviewed during 1985: Oct. 1984-Oct. 1985 (P) (Vol. 40, Nos. 481-491; Vol. 41, Nos. 492-493).

MONTHLY TABLES:
[Tables show data for month of coverage and/or current year to date, both as percent of same periods of previous year.]

1-2. Economic indicators: Nebraska and U.S. [indexes of physical output and dollar volume for agricultural, nonagricultural, construction, manufacturing, distributive, and government sectors; also shows change from 1967].

3. Net taxable retail sales of Nebraska regions and cities.

4. City business indicators [employment, building activity, and electric power/natural gas consumption, by city trading center].

5. Price indexes [consumer and wholesale for U.S., and agricultural for Nebraska and U.S.].

STATISTICAL FEATURES:

U7860–1.601: Oct. 1984 (Vol. 40, No. 481)

EXCESS FARM SUPPLY: PERMANENT OR TRANSITORY?

(p. 1-3) Article, with 2 tables showing U.S. percent change in farm output supply and demand, various periods 1949-82; and economic analysis of farm unit costs, efficiency, and parity price requirements, by farm sales size, 1981. Data are from Council of Economic Advisers and USDA.

U7860–1.602: Nov. 1984 (Vol. 40, No. 482)

NEBRASKA PER CAPITA PERSONAL INCOME

(p. 1-3, 6) Article, with 3 tables showing Nebraska farm and nonfarm total personal income, 1972-76; and per capita personal income, by State region, county, and total metro and nonmetro areas, with rankings, 1972 and 1982. Data are from U.S. Bureau of Economic Analysis.

U7860–1.603: Dec. 1984 (Vol. 40, No. 483)

EMPLOYMENT CHANGES IN NEBRASKA AND NEARBY STATES, 1982-84

(p. 1-3) Article, with 1 chart and 3 tables showing total employment and employment in 3 industry divisions, for 9 Plains States and U.S., May/June 1982 and 1984. Data are from BLS.

U7860–1.604: Feb. 1985 (Vol. 40, No. 485)

PERSPECTIVE ON AGRICULTURAL DEBT IN NEBRASKA

(p. 1-3, 6) Article, with 7 tables showing Nebraska agricultural debt (real estate and other) by lender type, with average interest rate, total interest payments, and comparisons to farm production expenses and income; various years 1960-84. Data are from USDA.

U7860–1.605: Mar. 1985 (Vol. 40, No. 486)

WAGE AND SALARY EARNINGS: NEBRASKA AND THE U.S.

(p. 1-3, 6) Article, with 3 tables showing Nebraska and U.S. employment distribution and average earnings, by industry division and/or detailed industry, 1983, with summary earnings trends from 1978. Data are from Bureau of Economic Analysis.

U7860–1.606: Apr. 1985 (Vol. 40, No. 487)

REVIEW AND OUTLOOK

(p. 4) Brief article, with 2 tables showing Nebraska total and nonfarm personal income, 4th quarter 1981-3rd quarter 1984; and Nebraska and U.S. employment in manufacturing, construction, and service industry sectors, with detail for Omaha and Lincoln metro areas, Jan. 1984-85.

U7860–1.607: May 1985 (Vol. 40, No. 488)

GROSS FARM PRODUCT: NEBRASKA AND THE PLAINS STATES

(p. 1-3, 6) Article, with 2 charts and 4 tables showing gross farm product for 7 Plains States, with detail by component and aggregate comparison to U.S.; and Nebraska nominal and real gross farm and nonfarm product, and GSP distribution by industry division; various periods 1960-83.

Data are from USDA, and University of Nebraska Bureau of Business Research calculations.

U7860–1.608: Aug. 1985 (Vol. 40, No. 491)

NEBRASKA RETAIL SALES, 1983-84, ANNUAL FEATURE

(p. 1-3) Annual article, with 2 tables showing Nebraska net taxable retail sales, by planning/development region, county, and selected trading center, 1983-84, with price-adjusted and unadjusted percent change.

HOUSING UNITS AUTHORIZED

(p. 6) Article, with 1 table showing Nebraska new housing authorized, by permit-issuing city or county, 1977 and 1982-84. Data are from Census Bureau.

U7860–1.609: Sept. 1985 (Vol. 41, No. 492)

PERSONAL INCOME IN THE PLAINS STATES

(p. 1-3) Article, with 2 tables showing total personal income for 7 Plains States, and for the U.S. by region; and Nebraska and U.S. nonfarm and wage/salary income; selected quarters 1978-1985. Data are from U.S. Bureau of Economic Analysis.

U7860–1.610: Oct. 1985 (Vol. 40, No. 493)

AGRICULTURAL ALTERNATIVE? FRUIT AND VEGETABLE PRODUCTION IN NEBRASKA

(p. 1-3, 6) Article, with 1 chart showing Nebraska vegetable acreage planted, by crop, 1984. Data are from University of Nebraska Cooperative Extension Service.

U7870
University of Nebraska: Bureau of Sociological Research

U7870–1   NEBRASKA ANNUAL SOCIAL INDICATORS SURVEY
Series.   For individual publication data, see below.
SRI/MF/complete

Continuing series of reports on Nebraska residents' attitudes toward selected economic and social issues relating to quality of life.

Series is based on Nebraska Annual Social Indicators Survey (NASIS) of 900-1800 persons, conducted by telephone by the Bureau of Sociological Research at the University of Nebraska-Lincoln. Series began in 1977, and a panel selected from 1977 respondents, supplemented by some new respondents, is reinterviewed each odd-numbered year. A new cross-sectional sample is interviewed each even-numbered year.

Each year, series includes 1 report documenting survey methodology; and a varying number of topical reports, each presenting narrative analysis and summary of survey findings pertaining to a selected issue, with tables showing sample characteristics and detailed breakdowns of responses.

Reports reviewed during 1985 are described below; reports are based on data from the 7th and 8th annual NASIS surveys, conducted in 1983 and 1984, respectively.

Availability: University of Nebraska: Bureau of Sociological Research, 732 Oldfather Hall, Lincoln NE 68588-0325; SRI/MF/complete.

1983 SERIES

U7870–1.47: Angling in Nebraska
[Monograph. Dec. 1984. 14 p. NASIS-83, No. 4. $1.50. SRI/MF/complete.]
By Gene Zuerlein and Helen A. Moore. Report on recreational fishing activities of Nebraskan adults and children.

Includes 7 tables showing survey responses concerning fishing months; number of fishing trips to rivers/streams and lakes/reservoirs; fish harvested, by species; support for State law requiring mandatory water levels in streams/rivers; fisherman characteristics; miles driven on fishing trips; and preference for official State fish; mostly for 1981 and/or 1982.

1984 SERIES

U7870-1.48: Designs, Procedures, Instruments, and Forms for the 1984 NASIS

[Annual. [1985.] 131 p. var. paging. NASIS-84, No. 1. $7.50. SRI/MF/complete.]

Annual report, by David R. Johnson, on methodology and respondent characteristics of NASIS, 1984.

Contents:

a. Narrative summary, with 5 tables showing sample data, population distribution by State region, and survey costs. (p. 1-25)

b. Appendices, including study prospectus, questionnaire facsimile, interviewer manual, codes, and variables. (106 p.)

U7870-1.49: Nebraskans View Their University

[Monograph. [1985.] 7 p. NASIS-84, No. 2. $0.75. SRI/MF/complete.]

By Alan Booth. Report on Nebraskans' attitudes concerning the University of Nebraska's goals and performance, with detail by type of contact with the university. Includes 2 tables.

U7870-1.50: Participation of Nebraskans in Voluntary Groups

[Monograph. [1985.] 10+6 p. NASIS-84, No. 3. $1.00. SRI/MF/complete.]

By David R. Johnson and Laurie K. Scheuble. Report on Nebraskans' participation in church- and job-related, recreational, fraternal/service, civic/political, and other types of organizations. Includes 4 tables showing average number of organizations joined; and membership and office-holding, by organization type; all by member characteristics.

U7920
University of Nevada:
Bureau of Business
and Economic Research

U7920-1   NEVADA REVIEW OF BUSINESS AND ECONOMICS
Quarterly. Approx. 30 p.
ISSN 0148-5881.
LC 77-643077.
SRI/MF/complete

Quarterly report on Nevada business and economic activity indicators, including employment data by industry division, SMSA, and county. Quarter of data coverage is 2 quarters prior to cover date.

Data are from Federal, State, and local government reports, and from F. W. Dodge Co. and other private sources.

Contains feature articles, some with statistics; and "Nevada Economic Indicators" section, with 5 quarterly tables.

Quarterly tables are listed below and appear in most issues. All additional features with substantial statistical content are described, as they appear, under "Statistical Features." Nonstatistical features are not covered.

Availability: University of Nevada: Bureau of Business and Economic Research, College of Business Administration, Nevada Review of Business and Economics, Reno NV 89557-0016, †; SRI/MF/complete.

Issues reviewed during 1985: Fall 1984-Spring 1985 (P) (Vol. VIII, Nos. 3-4; Vol. IX, No. 1).

QUARTERLY TABLES:

[All tables show total and monthly data for quarter of coverage, with percent change from previous quarter and same quarter of preceding year.]

[1] Statewide statistical data [including all or most of the following: labor force by employment status; employment by industry division and selected group; average earnings and hours in 5 industry divisions; construction value by type, and number of new dwellings; liquor, cigarette, and fuel tax collections; taxable sales; gaming revenues; and highway traffic flow].

[2-3] Las Vegas and Reno SMSAs [including labor force by employment status, employment by industry division and selected major group, construction value by type, number of new dwellings or permits, taxable sales, gaming revenues, air passenger and cargo traffic, highway traffic flow, and room tax collections, with selected detail for SMSA component areas; and electricity sales and customers (Las Vegas only)].

[4] Nevada statistical data by county [including all or most of the following: labor force by employment status; construction value by type, and number of new dwellings; taxable sales; and gaming revenues].

[5] Selected U.S. economic indicators [CPI and PPI by major item or commodity grouping, and labor force by employment status].

STATISTICAL FEATURES:

U7920-1.601: Fall 1984 (Vol. VIII, No. 3)

ACADEMIC EXCELLENCE: AN ACHIEVABLE GOAL FOR THE UNIVERSITY OF NEVADA, RENO?

(p. 11-18) By Michelle I. Austin. Article analyzing factors affecting the quality of education at the University of Nevada, Reno. Data are from *Nevada Public Affairs Review* and other published and unpublished sources.

Includes 6 tables showing enrollment and faculty compensation trends for the university, with compensation comparisons to Mountain/Pacific region and U.S., various years 1974/75-1983/84; single-family home resale prices in Reno and 15 other cities, July 1983 and Jan. 1984; and rankings of States by tax capacity, tax effort (revenues as percent of capacity), and share of tax revenues allocated to public higher education, 1982 or 1983/84.

PRICING AS A CONSERVATIVE PRACTICE OF NEVADA WATER COMPANIES: A SURVEY

(p. 19-23) By Donald E. Agthe and Kambiz Raffiee. Article, with 3 tables on Nevada water systems, showing number of systems and customers, by rate structure; and customers, rate structure, fixed monthly charge, and typical

bill, by major system; all for commercial and residential service; 1981 or 1984. Data are from Resource Concepts, Inc.

U7920-1.602: Spring 1985 (Vol. IX, No. 1)

PATTERNS OF PUBLIC RESPONSE TO LOTTERY, HORSERACE, AND CASINO GAMBLING ISSUES

(p. 12-22) By William N. Thompson. Article discussing public opinion on legalized gambling. Data are primarily from Public Gaming Research Institute, Inc. Includes 5 tables comparing public opinion poll-based predictions with actual outcomes, for campaigns to legalize lotteries, horserace betting, and casino gambling, by State, 1980s, with selected legalization campaign outcome trends from 1956.

U7980
University of New Mexico:
Bureau of Business
and Economic Research

U7980-1   NEW MEXICO BUSINESS, Current Economic Report
Monthly. Approx. 8 p.
LC 65-79758.
SRI/MF/complete, shipped quarterly

Monthly report (Jan./Feb. combined) reviewing economic, demographic, and other developments affecting business activity in New Mexico, the Southwest, and the U.S. Data are from Federal and State agencies, and private or commercial sources. Month of coverage for most data is 2 months prior to cover date.

Issues generally contain a narrative summary of recent State economic developments; 7 monthly economic indicator tables; and occasional special articles and tables. Jan./Feb. issue also includes an annual State economic profile.

Monthly tables are listed below and appear in all issues. All other features with substantial statistical content on topics not covered in monthly tables are described, as they appear, under "Statistical Features." Nonstatistical features are not covered.

Availability: University of New Mexico: Bureau of Business and Economic Research, Institute for Applied Research Services, Albuquerque NM 87131, $15.00 per yr., single copy $1.85; SRI/MF/complete, shipped quarterly.

Issues reviewed during 1985: Oct. 1984-Aug. 1985 (P) (Vol. 5, Nos. 9-11; Vol. 6, Nos. 1-7).

MONTHLY TABLES:

[Table [1] shows quarterly averages for most recent available quarter and 3 preceding quarters, and monthly averages for month of coverage and 2 preceding months, with percent change from same periods of previous year. Unless otherwise noted, all other tables show data for month of coverage, preceding month, and same month of previous year.]

[1] Economic indicators [including unemployment insurance claims, new business incorporations, business failure liabilities, agricultural receipts, mineral production, construction permits and contracts, manufacturing hours worked, bank loans and deposits, savings and loan assn deposits and savings, national park visits, and others].

[2] CPI and indexes of selected categories, U.S. city average.

[3] Hours and earnings of production/construction/nonsupervisory employees [for 6 industry divisions, and durable and nondurable goods manufacturing].

[4] Estimated civilian labor force and employment [by industry division, for State, and Albuquerque and Las Cruces MSAs].

[5] Albuquerque banking data [net bank loans, and total assets and deposits; and savings/loan deposits and new savings; for most recent available quarter and previous quarter].

[6-7] Number and value of [residential and nonresidential] building permits [for 18 selected cities and remainder of State; for month of coverage, current year to date, and same periods of previous year].

STATISTICAL FEATURES:

U7980–1.601: Jan./Feb. 1985 (Vol. 6, No. 1)

NEW MEXICO ECONOMY 1984, ANNUAL FEATURE

(p. 1-22) Annual article reviewing performance of the New Mexico economy in 1984, with analysis of employment and economic trends in 8 industry sectors, selected years 1974-84. Data are from Federal agencies, New Mexico Employment Security Dept, and other sources.

Includes 20 trend charts; and the following tables, showing data for New Mexico unless otherwise noted, generally for 1974 and 1978-84:

a. Per capita income in selected western States and MSAs; and U.S. PPI, CPI, and construction cost index. 3 tables. (p. 1-3)

b. Civilian employment: labor force by employment status; and employment and current and constant dollar hourly earnings, by industry division. 3 tables. (p. 4-6)

c. Agriculture and mining: livestock prices and cash marketings of farm products; and mining production volume and value by mineral, employment by sector, and hours and earnings. 4 tables. (p. 7-10)

d. Construction and manufacturing: construction employment, value of contracts awarded, and number and value of building permits; and manufacturing employment by sector, and hours and earnings. 2 tables. (p. 12, 15)

e. Transportation, communications, utilities, and wholesale and retail trade: employment by sector, and wholesale/retail trade hours and earnings. 2 tables. (p. 16-17)

f. Finance, insurance, and real estate: employment by sector; bank assets, deposits, and loans; savings and loan assn deposits and new savings; life insurance sales; and new business incorporations. 2 tables. (p. 18-19)

g. Services, recreation, and tourism: employment in lodging establishments, eating/drinking places, and various other service businesses; and visits to State and national parks/monuments. 2 tables. (p. 20-21)

h. Government: civilian employment in Federal, State, and local government. 1 table. (p. 22)

1983 COUNTY POPULATION ESTIMATES FOR NEW MEXICO, ANNUAL FEATURE

(p. 23) Annual article, with 1 table showing New Mexico population estimates, by county, as of Apr. 1, 1980 and July 1, 1981-83. Data are from Census Bureau.

U7980–1.602: May 1985 (Vol. 6, No. 4)

NEW STATE AND COUNTY PERSONAL INCOME DATA NOW AVAILABLE

(p. 8) Brief article, with 1 table showing top 10 New Mexico counties ranked by per capita personal income, 1983. Data are from Commerce Dept.

U7980–1.603: July 1985 (Vol. 6, No. 6)

NEW COUNTY POPULATION PROJECTIONS NOW AVAILABLE

(p. 8) Brief article, with 1 table showing New Mexico population, for total State and 10 most populous counties, quinquennially 1980-2005. Data are from University of New Mexico Bureau of Business and Economic Research.

U7980–1.604: Aug. 1985 (Vol. 6, No. 7)

NEW CITY POPULATION AND INCOME ESTIMATES NOW AVAILABLE

(p. 8) Brief article, with 1 table showing population of New Mexico's 20 largest cities, 1984, with comparison to 1980 and 1982. Data are from Census Bureau.

U7980–3   THIRD ANNUAL MOUNTAIN REGION ECONOMIC OUTLOOK CONFERENCE
Annual. Mar. 12, 1985.
101 p. var. paging.
SRI/MF/complete, current & previous year reports

Annual report, for 1985, on Mountain States' and U.S. economic trends and outlook. Includes data on various socioeconomic indicators for Arizona, Colorado, and New Mexico, with selected data by SMSA and comparisons to neighboring States, primarily 1970s-85, with some trends from 1960 and projections to 2005.

State indicators include labor force, employment by industry, income and earnings, retail sales, population, CPI, government finances and taxes, nonfuel mineral and energy production, construction activity, unemployment compensation claims, and agricultural sales. Not all indicators are shown for each State.

Additional indicators for Arizona include high-technology employment by sector and major company, value of high-technology shipments and DOD procurement, and copper production by mine.

Also includes analysis of U.S. economy, including data on GNP, prices, wages, inflation, industrial production, construction activity, employment, money supply, interest rates, income, consumer spending, and corporate finances, various periods 1983-87; and savings and investment projections to 1994.

Data are from State and Federal agencies and Data Resources, Inc., and are presented in papers prepared for delivery at the annual Mountain States Region Economic Outlook Conference.

Contains U.S. economic analysis, with 35 charts and 11 tables (p. 1-15); and 3 separately paginated State research papers, with 33 charts and 25 tables (85 p.).

This is the 3rd annual report. SRI coverage begins with the previous report, which was also reviewed during 1985, and is also available on SRI microfiche under U7980-3 [Annual. Mar. 13, 1984. 227 p. $50.00+$3.00 handling fee]. Previous report was similar in content, but omitted data on U.S. economy and additional data for Arizona, and included State reports for Utah, Nevada, Wyoming, Idaho, and Montana. State indicators covered in previous report also vary slightly.

Availability: University of New Mexico: Bureau of Business and Economic Research, Institute for Applied Research Services, Albuquerque NM 87131, $25.00+$3.00 handling fee, summary and outlook for New Mexico available separately for $5.00+$3.00 handling fee; SRI/MF/complete.

U8013
University of North Carolina

U8013–1   STATISTICAL ABSTRACT OF HIGHER EDUCATION in North Carolina, 1984/85
Annual. Apr. 1985.
xii+179 p.
Research Rpt. 1-85.
LC 79-647373.
SRI/MF/complete

Annual report, for academic year 1984/85, on North Carolina higher education. Covers enrollment, degrees, faculty, and library resources; and student costs, financial aid, and housing; for public and private colleges and universities. Includes selected trends from as early as 1900. Most data are shown by individual institution.

Data are compiled from information supplied by individual institutions.

Contains listings of contents, tables, and charts (p. ii-x); introduction and map (p. xi-xii); 11 statistical sections, with 14 charts and 83 tables listed below (p. 1-169); and appendices, with data sources and definitions (p. 173-179).

This is the 18th annual report.

Availability: University of North Carolina, General Administration, Planning Division, PO Box 2688, 910 Raleigh Rd., Chapel Hill NC 27514, †; SRI/MF/complete.

TABLES:

[Unless otherwise noted, tables show data for North Carolina colleges and universities, by individual institution, usually including Bible colleges and theological seminaries.]

U8013–1.1: Enrollment
[Unless otherwise noted, enrollment data are shown for headcount enrollment.]

CURRENT ENROLLMENT
[Tables 1-25 and 27-29 show data for fall 1984.]

1. General characteristics of enrollment [aggregates for public and private institutions]. (p. 8)

2-4. Enrollment by residence status, full-time and part-time [status], and sex; by class and level of instruction; and by level of instruction and residence status. (p. 9-17)

5. FTE enrollment by level of instruction and residence status. (p. 18-20)

6. Enrollment in community colleges and technical institutes/colleges [by type of curriculum]. (p. 21)

7-10. Percentage of enrollment by age distribution [by sex, full- and part-time status, and level of instruction; for] University of North Carolina [and total] private colleges/universities; for transfer enrollment at [total] community colleges; and for vocational/technical enrollment at [total] community colleges/technical institutes/technical colleges. (p. 22-23)

11-16. Average age of enrollment [by sex, full- and part-time status, and level of instruction, for individual institutions grouped by type, and including data for community college transfer students]. (p. 24-26)

17-20. Home county of in-State undergraduate enrollment and home State of out-of-State undergraduate enrollment, [aggregated] by type of institution, and for University of North Carolina [by campus]. (p. 27-32)

21-22. Home county and home State of total enrollment in [aggregate] community colleges/technical institutes/technical colleges [by type of curriculum]. (p. 33-35)

23. Geographic origin of undergraduate enrollment [same county as institution, adjacent counties, other in-State counties, and out-of-State]. (p. 36-38)

24. Graduate and 1st professional enrollment [by residence status and sex]. (p. 39)

25. Upper-division undergraduate and post-baccalaureate enrollment in the University of North Carolina by field of study. (p. 40)

26. Summer school unduplicated enrollment and credit hours registered [by level of instruction and residence status], 1984. (p. 41-42)

27. Foreign students enrolled by level of instruction [and sex]. (p. 43-44)

28. Racial composition of enrollment. (p. 45-47)

29. Extension credit enrollment in the University of North Carolina [by residence status and level of instruction]. (p. 48)

ENROLLMENT TRENDS
[Tables show data for fall 1974-84, unless otherwise noted.]

30. Enrollment trends [aggregate] in public and private colleges/universities, [selected years] fall 1900-84. (p. 51)

31. Enrollment. (p. 52-54)

32. Enrollment by residence status [aggregates for public and private institutions]. (p. 55)

33. Percentages of out-of-State enrollment in public colleges and universities [by University of North Carolina campus, and aggregates for military centers and community colleges; all for entering freshmen, undergraduate, and total enrollment]; fall 1979-84. (p. 56)

34. Enrollment trends by level of instruction [aggregates for public and private institutions]. (p. 57)

35-36. Trend in county origin of in-State undergraduate enrollment and State origin of out-of-State undergraduate enrollment [aggregate for all institutions]. (p. 58-62)

UNDERGRADUATE TRANSFERS

37. Undergraduate transfers to colleges and universities [aggregates by type of institution transferred to and from], fall 1974-84. (p. 65)

38-42. Undergraduate transfer students: [aggregate] by type of institution and sex; and by institutions [transferred to and from]; fall 1984. (p. 66-72)

43. Undergraduate transfer students from out-of-State colleges/universities to North Carolina colleges/universities [aggregates by State by type of institution transferred to], fall 1984. (p. 73)

44. Transfers into noncollege parallel programs at community colleges and technical institutes/colleges from other colleges and universities [by type of institution transferred from and specific institution transferred to], fall 1984. (p. 74)

U8013-1.2: Degrees, Faculty, and Library Resources
[Data are for 1983/84, unless otherwise noted.]

DEGREES CONFERRED

45. Number of degrees conferred [by level], 1980/81-1983/84. (p. 80)

46. Number and percent of degrees conferred by field of study, type of institution [public and private], and level of degree. (p. 81-83)

47. Degrees conferred by field of study, level of degree, race [black, American Indian/Alaskan Native, Asian/Pacific Islander, Hispanic, and white, and for nonresident aliens], and sex, [aggregated for all institutions]. (p. 84-85)

48-51. Number of bachelor's, 1st professional, master's, and doctorate degrees conferred, by sex and field of study. (p. 86-93)

52. Degrees and awards based on less than 4 years work beyond high school [by type and field of study]. (p. 94-95)

FACULTY

53. Academic rank and sex of full-time faculty, fall 1984. (p. 99-101)

54. Highest earned degree held by full-time faculty by academic rank, fall 1984. (p. 102-110)

LIBRARY RESOURCES

55. Library resources [by type]. (p. 112-114)

56. Library operating expenditures [by type, including salaries and for microforms]. (p. 115-117)

U8013-1.3: Student Costs, Admissions, Financial Aid, and Housing

TUITION AND FEES
[Tables 58-61 show data for 1984/85.]

57. Undergraduate tuition/required fees combined [by residence status], 1979/80-1984/85. (p. 120-122)

58. Costs [tuition by residence status, fees, dormitory rooms, and board] to undergraduate students. (p. 123-124)

59. Detailed listing of required fees charged to regular undergraduate students. (p. 125-126)

60-61. Costs [tuition/academic fee by residence status, and fees] to students in 1st professional degree programs by type of program, and to graduate students. (p. 127)

ADMISSIONS
[Tables 63-72 show data for fall 1984.]

62. Average SAT [Scholastic Aptitude Test] scores of entering freshmen in the University of North Carolina [by campus], fall 1974-84. (p. 132)

63-64. Distribution of SAT scores of entering freshmen in the University of North Carolina [by campus]; and average SAT scores of entering freshmen in private colleges/universities [by residence status]. (p. 133-134)

65-66. High school class rank of entering freshmen. (p. 135-136)

67-70. Number of freshman and undergraduate transfer applications, acceptances, and enrollees [by residence status and sex]. (p. 137-144)

71-72. Number of graduate and 1st professional applications, acceptances, and enrollees in the University of North Carolina [by campus, by residence status and sex]. (p. 145)

FINANCIAL AID
[Data show number of students and amounts received, 1983/84.]

73. Employment [college work/study and other] of undergraduate students. (p. 148-149)

74. Scholarships, grants, and awards [by type] for undergraduate students. (p. 150-152)

75. Pell Grants. (p. 153-155)

76. Loans [by type] provided to undergraduate students. (p. 156-158)

77-78. Financial aid [by type] for 1st professional and graduate students. (p. 159-160)

STUDENT HOUSING

79. Capacity and utilization of dormitories in the University of North Carolina, fall 1974-84. (p. 163)

80-81. Enrollment by type of housing, fall 1984. (p. 164-165)

STATE AID TO STUDENTS IN PRIVATE INSTITUTIONS

82. Fall 1984 undergraduate FTE enrollment and total allocations made to private colleges and universities in 1984/85. (p. 168)

83. North Carolina legislative tuition grants [students and amounts], 1984/85. (p. 169)

U8080
University of North Dakota: Bureau of Governmental Affairs

U8080-1   **1984 ELECTION IN NORTH DAKOTA**
Biennial. July 1985.
ii+49 p. Special Rpt. No. 76.
SRI/MF/complete

Biennial report, by Phil Harmeson, presenting results of North Dakota general election, 1984. Shows voting for President; Governor; U.S. Representative; State senators and representatives; other State officials; and 4 State referenda, including measure affirming the right to bear arms.

Also includes voter turnout, with comparisons to 1976 and 1980; and party affiliation of candidates.

Data are shown by county or district, with some detail by city.

Previous report, covering 1982 primary and general elections, is described in SRI 1983 Annual under this number.

Report presenting official results of 1984 North Dakota general election, including voting for judges, is covered in SRI under S6205-1.

Availability: University of North Dakota: Bureau of Governmental Affairs, Grand Forks ND 58202, †; SRI/MF/complete.

U8080–2   VOTE OF THE PEOPLE: Initiated and Referred Measures in North Dakota from Statehood Through 1984
Recurring (irreg.)   May 1985.
42 p.   Special Rpt. No. 75.
LC 85-622756.
SRI/MF/complete

Recurring report on North Dakota State constitutional amendments and referenda, 1889-1984.

Includes narrative analysis, with summary statistics (p. 1-6); and voting for 384 constitutional amendments, initiatives, or referenda, by election, 1889-1984 (p. 7-42).

Previous report, for 1889-1980, is described in SRI 1982 Annual under this number.

Availability: University of North Dakota: Bureau of Governmental Affairs, Grand Forks ND 58202, †; SRI/MF/complete.

U8130
University of Oklahoma: Center for Economic and Management Research

U8130–1   OKLAHOMA BUSINESS BULLETIN
Monthly.   Approx. 4 p.
ISSN 0030-1671.
LC 40-25254.
SRI/MF/complete, shipped quarterly

Monthly report on Oklahoma economic indicators, including employment, retail trade, construction, and banking, shown variously by metro area or city. Data are based on Federal, State, and commercial sources, and are current to 3 months prior to cover date.

Issues usually contain 6 monthly tables, listed below. Mar., June, Sept., and Dec. issues also include "Business Highlights" narrative feature, and additional quarterly data as noted below. "Business Highlights" occasionally includes additional tables. These tables are described, as they appear, under "Statistical Features."

Availability: University of Oklahoma: Center for Economic and Management Research, 307 W. Brooks St., Rm. 4, Norman OK 73069, $4.00 per yr., single copy $0.50; SRI/MF/complete, shipped quarterly.

Issues reviewed during 1985: Oct. 1984-Sept. 1985 (P) (Vol. 52, Nos. 10-12; Vol. 53, Nos. 1-9).

MONTHLY TABLES:
[Data are generally for month of coverage, and year to date for current and previous year, with percent changes from previous month and previous year. Not all data appear in all issues.]

[1] Summary of indicators [includes personal income (monthly average), crude oil production, industrial power sales, bank demand and savings deposits, savings and loan assn assets and new mortgages, and usually general business index and/or labor force, employment, and unemployment rate].

[2-3] Retail trade in selected cities; and in metro areas and State [by kind of business].

[4-5] [Employment and permit-authorized construction, for 4 MSAs and Muskogee area, with additional data for Oklahoma City and Tulsa MSAs on mortgage loans and bank deposits; in the 3rd issue of each quarter, data are usually presented in 4 tables and also include industrial power sales and, for Oklahoma City and Tulsa only, average weekly earnings and water and/or air transportation.]

[6] Construction, State [permit-authorized construction units and value by type; in the 3rd issue of each quarter, table is titled "Selected Economic Indicators" and includes employment trends by industry division, and average weekly hours and earnings].

U8130–2   STATISTICAL ABSTRACT OF OKLAHOMA, 1984
Biennial.   Sept. 1984.   520 p.
ISSN 0078-4354.
LC 79-642515.
SRI/MF/complete

Biennial compilation, for 1984, of detailed demographic, social, governmental, and economic statistics for Oklahoma. Data are primarily for 1970s-83. Most data are from State and Federal Government sources.

Report is designed to present a comprehensive overview of the State. Extensive socioeconomic, demographic, and geographic breakdowns are shown, as applicable, for most topics. These breakdowns include data by city, county and other State region, SMSA, urban-rural status, commodity, industry, occupation, educational attainment, race, and sex. Comparisons to total U.S. and neighboring States are also occasionally included.

Contents:

a. Contents listing, and section 1, summarizing Oklahoma tax system and rates (p. 1-11); and sections 2-22, with 198 tables, described below (p. 13-500).

b. Section 23, with 5 tables showing selected U.S. economic indexes (p. 502-505); section 24, guide to statistical sources (p. 506-515); and subject index (p. 517-520).

Sections 2-23 are preceded by table listings. Data sources appear beneath each table.

For description of previous report, for 1982, see SRI 1983 Annual under this number.

Availability: University of Oklahoma: Center for Economic and Management Research, 307 W. Brooks St., Rm. 4, Norman OK 73069, $18.00; SRI/MF/complete.

TABLE SECTIONS:

U8130–2.1:   Section 2-4:   Population, Agriculture, and Geography

a. **Population:** population, births, deaths, and net migration. 6 tables. (p. 14-24)

b. **Agriculture:** farms and acreage; farm population; cash receipts; crop production and value, with detail for wheat and peanuts; and livestock inventory and value. 12 tables. (p. 26-38)

c. **Geography:** average temperature and precipitation; land and water area; tornadoes; and tornado deaths and injuries. 9 tables. (p. 40-47)

U8130–2.2: Section 5-6: Finance and Communication

a. **Finance:** financial institutions and balance sheet data; credit union members; life insurance companies, underwriting data, and mortgages owned; commercial bank operating income and expenses; and savings and loan assn and insurance company summary finances, by institution. 13 tables. (p. 50-93)

b. **Communication:** newspaper circulation by paper, telephones and telephone companies, and radio and TV stations. 6 tables. (p. 96-111)

U8130–2.3: Section 7-8: Construction and Trade

a. **Construction:** residential and nonresidential building permits issued and value. 4 tables. (p. 114-133)

b. **Trade:** retail sales; service industry establishments, receipts, payroll, and employment; and wholesale trade establishments, sales, and payroll. 7 tables. (p. 136-145)

U8130–2.4: Section 9-10: Education and Resources

a. **Education:** public school enrollment, attendance, and revenues; higher education and vocational enrollment by institution, and degrees granted or completions by field of study; years of school completed; and classroom teacher and higher education faculty average salaries. 18 tables. (p. 148-174)

b. **Resources:** production and value of nonfuel minerals, oil, natural gas, and casinghead gas; coal production; oil wells drilled and operating rotary rigs; production, reserves, and wells at giant oil fields; water use; lake area, capacity, use, and dam location and height; and national forest land area. 17 tables. (p. 177-206)

U8130–2.5: Section 11-12: Government and Taxation

a. **Government:** number of precincts; voter registration by party; votes cast in general election, Nov. 1982; composition and members of State legislature, by party; and legislative activity and bills vetoed. 6 tables. (p. 208-217)

b. **Taxation:** per capita State/local taxes, by State; State revenues by source and expenditures by function; revenue apportionment by receiver, with detail for city/town governments, schools, and roads; tax collections; ad valorem tax rates; county funds by source; property assessed valuation; bonded debt; sinking fund; tax collections; and retail sales tax collections, and collections returned to cities. 16 tables. (p. 220-306)

U8130–2.6: Section 13-14: Highways and Income

a. **Highways:** construction and maintenance expenditures; road/street and vehicle mileage; fuel use; motor vehicle registrations and fees; licensed drivers; traffic accidents, injuries, and fatalities; and miscellaneous highway fee collections. 9 tables. (p. 308-318)

b. **Income:** total and per capita personal income; and personal income by source. 5 tables. (p. 320-370)

U8130–2.7: Section 15-16: Labor and Legal System

a. **Labor:** manufacturing hours and earnings; average weekly hours; unemployment rate; median earnings; labor force and employment; and county and State/local government employment and payroll. 12 tables. (p. 372-402)

b. **Legal system:** Index crimes by offense; Federal and State prison population; and criminal justice system employment, payrolls, and expenditures. 6 tables. (p. 404-413)

U8130–2.8: Section 17-18: Manufactures and Energy

a. **Manufactures:** employment, payroll, and establishments; major employers grouped by employee size, by company; and business failures and liabilities. 5 tables. (p. 416-424)

b. **Energy:** electric and gas utility sales, by sector; electricity generated by fuel type; natural gas production, revenues, and customers; gasoline consumption; energy consumption and expenditures, by sector; and petroleum drilling permits and well completions. 10 tables. (p. 426-436)

U8130–2.9: Section 19-20: Recreation and Welfare Services

a. **Recreation:** hunting seasons, hunters, and harvest, by species; hunting and fishing license fees and sales; fish hatchery operations; acreage and attendance for State parks and recreation areas and sites; public library volumes, circulation, population served, income, and expenditures, by library; and high school library volumes, circulation, and students, by school. 11 tables. (p. 438-463)

b. **Welfare services:** average hospital stay cost; total and per capita Federal aid to State/local governments, by function; unemployment and benefits paid; Medicare enrollment and payments; social security beneficiaries and payments, by State; income for State sales tax supported programs; and public assistance payments by program. 9 tables. (p. 466-474)

U8130–2.10: Section 21-22: Transportation and Vital Statistics

a. **Transportation:** railroads, bus lines, and airlines, and cities served; railroad track mileage; passenger and freight traffic at 2 major airports; and Tulsa Port of Catoosa barge traffic and freight carried. 6 tables. (p. 476-483)

b. **Vital statistics:** births; deaths by leading cause; infant deaths; marriages and divorces; net migration; physicians; hospitals, nursing homes, and beds; and beds in State mental hospitals, State veterans centers, and Federal hospitals. 11 tables. (p. 486-500)

U8250
University of Pennsylvania: Annenberg School of Communications

U8250–2   GRATUITOUS VIOLENCE AND EXPLOITIVE SEX: WHAT ARE THE LESSONS?
Recurring (irreg.)
Sept. 21, 1984.
17 p. +24 p. no paging.
SRI/MF/complete

Recurring report, by George Gerbner, on TV violence trends, and the impact of TV on viewer attitudes concerning crime and sexism.

Includes TV violence index, by program time and network, and for children's programming (total and cartoons), 1967/68-1983. Index shows prevalence, rate, and duration of violence in programs; and frequency with which major characters commit and are subjected to fatal and nonfatal violence; with number of programs, program hours, and major characters analyzed.

Also includes TV violence victim/perpetrator ratios for selected demographic groups; and correlation of TV viewing habits with attitudes toward sexism and toward crime and violence in everyday life, controlled for selected viewer demographic characteristics.

Report is a continuation of the Cultural Indicators research project begun in 1967. Most data are from the project's monitoring of TV programs; and from Opinion Research Corporation and National Opinion Research Center surveys, various years 1975-83.

Contains introduction (p. 1-2); narrative report, with 1 text table (p. 2-15); bibliography (p. 16-17); and statistical appendix, with 17 tables and 7 charts (24 p.).

Report was discontinued with the Apr. 1980 edition. Publication resumes on an irregularly recurring basis with Sept. 1984 edition. For description of Apr. 1980 edition, see SRI 1980 Annual under this number.

Availability: University of Pennsylvania—Annenberg School of Communications, Attention: Dr. Nancy Signorielli, 3620 Walnut St., Philadelphia PA 19104, Price on request.; SRI/MF/complete

U8595
University of South Dakota: Business Research Bureau

U8595–1   SOUTH DAKOTA BUSINESS REVIEW
Quarterly.   Approx. 12 p.
ISSN 0038-3260.
LC 58-24864.
SRI/MF/complete

Quarterly report on business trends and economic conditions in South Dakota. Includes new car and truck sales, employment, retail and service sales by city, and crop production and prices.

Data are from Dept of Commerce, BLS, State agencies, and private business, and are usually current to 1-3 months prior to cover date for data shown by month, or to quarter ending 2-6 months prior to cover date for data shown by quarter.

Issues generally contain:

a. Special articles, occasionally statistical, including a recurring labor market forecast feature, and annual features on personal income and crop plantings.

b. Business trends analysis, generally including 1 quarterly table showing State unemployment rate; and indexes for personal and farm proprietor incomes, nonagricultural and construction employment, and new car and truck sales; for quarter of coverage and preceding 5-6 quarters.

c. 7 quarterly economic indicator tables.

d. Semiannual table on retail sales by county and/or city.

Quarterly tables are listed below; most appear in all issues. Semiannual table and all additional features with substantial statistical content are described, as they appear, under "Statistical Features." Nonstatistical features are not covered.

A bimonthly report showing taxable sales and other tax collection data, issued as a supplement to this report, is covered in SRI under U8595-2.

Availability: University of South Dakota: Business Research Bureau, School of Business, 414 E. Clark St., Vermillion SD 57069, †; SRI/MF/complete.

Issues reviewed during 1985: Sept. 1984-June 1985 (P) (Vol. XLIII, Nos. 1-4).

QUARTERLY TABLES:
[Unless otherwise noted, tables show data for South Dakota, for current and 1-2 preceding years. Table order may vary from issue to issue.]

[1] General indicators [South Dakota and U.S. personal and farm proprietor incomes, nonagricultural employment, unemployment rate, and total employment, for quarter of coverage].

[2] Total personal income, U.S., Plains Region, and [7] States [for quarter of coverage and preceding 4-6 quarters].

[3] Nonagricultural wage/salary employment [by industry division and selected industry group, and average manufacturing hours and earnings, for month of coverage].

[4] Crop production summary [by crop, cumulative through month of coverage].

[5] Prices received by farmers for commodities sold [for month of coverage, and compared to 1910-14 base price].

[6] Local conditions indicators [percent change in taxable sales (total, retail, and services), telephone access lines, housing starts, postal sales, and employment; by selected city, for month or quarter of coverage vs. same period of previous year].

[7] CPI, U.S. [by major item, monthly through month of coverage, current year only].

STATISTICAL FEATURES:

U8595–1.601: Sept. 1984 (Vol. XLIII, No. 1)

FINANCING PUBLIC EDUCATION IN SOUTH DAKOTA
(p. 1, 4-7) By Raymond J. Ring. Part 1 of a 2-part article on South Dakota public education financing. Data are from Federal and State sources.

Includes 8 tables showing enrollment, and expenditures per capita, per $1,000 of personal income, and per student, all for local (elementary/secondary) and higher education; percent of local school revenues received from Federal, State, and local governments; and tuition/fees compared to State/local government as source of higher education funds; for South Dakota, with selected comparisons to total U.S. and 6 neighboring States, various years 1962/63-1982/83.

UPDATE: THE POSSIBILITY OF DUAL ECONOMIES IN SOUTH DAKOTA

(p. 1, 8) By Randall Stuefen. Article, with 2 tables showing top 10 South Dakota cities ranked by 1980 population, with comparison to 1970; and percent change in retail sales, for total State, counties containing the 10 largest cities, and all other counties, bimonthly July/Aug. 1983-May/June 1984 vs. same periods of previous year.

For description of a related article, see SRI 1984 Annual, under U8595-1.502.

GROSS SALES AND USE TAXABLE ITEMS, SEMIANNUAL FEATURE

(p. 9) Semiannual table showing South Dakota retail sales, by region, county, and selected city, 1st half 1983-84.

U8595-1.602: Dec. 1984 (Vol. XLIII, No. 2)

PERSONAL INCOME 1983, ANNUAL FEATURE

(p. 1, 4-7) Annual article, by Boyden Kneen, analyzing trends in South Dakota total and per capita personal income, by type, industry source, and county, with comparisons to U.S. and other Plains Region States, and growth in current and constant 1967 dollars, various years 1974-83. Data are from U.S. Dept of Commerce. Includes 12 tables.

FINANCING PUBLIC EDUCATION IN SOUTH DAKOTA

(p. 1, 7-9) By Raymond J. Ring. Part 2 of a 2-part article on South Dakota public education financing. Data are from Federal and State sources.

Includes 5 tables showing South Dakota average salaries and tax-adjusted salaries for elementary/secondary and higher education teachers, and per capita taxes, with comparisons to U.S. and 6 neighboring States, various years 1969/70-1983/84; and South Dakota workers' median earnings by sex and occupational category, 1979.

U8595-1.603: Mar. 1985 (Vol. XLIII, No. 3)

MORE ON SOUTH DAKOTA'S DUAL ECONOMY

(p. 1-12, passim) By Randall Stuefen. Article comparing economic and business conditions in South Dakota rural and urban areas. Data are from various sources, including 125 responses to a Sept. 1984 *South Dakota Business Review* reader survey.

Includes 4 tables showing South Dakota's 10 largest cities ranked by population in 1980, with comparison to 1970; retail sales growth rate, with aggregate data for counties containing 10 largest cities and all other counties, bimonthly 1984; and survey responses concerning reasons young people are not taking over businesses in smaller communities.

For description of a related article, see U8595-1.601 above.

U8595-1.604: June 1985 (Vol. XLIII, No. 4)

SOUTH DAKOTA'S TAX BURDEN: AN UPDATE

(p. 1, 4-5) By Raymond J. Ring. Article, with 2 tables showing South Dakota government revenues by source; and taxes per capita and per $1,000 personal income, with comparison to U.S. and 6 neighboring States; various years FY63-83. Data are from Census Bureau and other sources.

Article updates a previous feature appearing in the May 1983 issue; for description, see SRI 1983 Annual under U8595-1.403.

SOUTH DAKOTA RANKS

(p. 5-6) By DeVee Goss. Tabular listing showing South Dakota totals or averages, and ranking among the States, for selected socioeconomic indicators, including income, employment, farm values, farmland, agricultural energy and interest expenses, population, State revenues, welfare recipients, teacher salaries, physicians and hospital beds per 100,000 population, crime rate, prisoners per 100,000 population, and housing starts, various years 1980-84. Data are from State Data Center.

SOUTH DAKOTA LABOR MARKET MODEL FORECAST HIGHLIGHTS, RECURRING FEATURE

(p. 8) Recurring article, with 1 table showing South Dakota total personal, nonfarm personal, wage/salary, and farm income, in current and constant 1972 dollars; total, nonagricultural, and manufacturing employment; and unemployment rate; quarterly 4th quarter 1984-3rd quarter 1986 and annually 1984-86. Also includes selected U.S. economic indicators.

Previous feature is described in SRI 1984 Annual under U8595-1.503.

TAXABLE SALES COMPARISONS BY POPULATION SIZE, SEMIANNUAL FEATURE

(p. 9) Semiannual table showing South Dakota taxable sales by city, 1st and 2nd half 1983-84, with comparisons to 1980 population.

PROSPECTIVE PLANTINGS, ANNUAL FEATURE

(p. 11) Annual table showing South Dakota acreage planted for 10 field crops, actual 1983-84 and intended 1985.

U8595-2   SOUTH DAKOTA DATA SUPPLEMENT
Bimonthly.
Approx. 8 p. no paging
SRI/MF/complete

Bimonthly report on South Dakota gross sales/use tax purchases and taxable retail sales, by region, county, and selected city; and total sales/use tax collections (beginning with Jan. 1985 issue). Also includes rankings for cities and counties, and summary U.S. comparisons.

Data are from State and Federal sources. Most data are shown for 2-month period ending approximately 3 months prior to cover date, with comparison to same period of previous year; sales/use tax collection data are shown quarterly or bimonthly from 1981 through period of coverage.

Contains brief narrative; 4-12 trend charts; 7-8 tables showing data described above; and 1-6 additional tables.

Additional tables usually show various tax-related data, such as year-to-date comparisons,

excise tax collections, and semiannual taxable sales for cities ranked by population. Additional tables occasionally present substantial non-tax-related data; these tables are described, as they appear, under "Statistical Features."

Bimonthly report supplements the quarterly *South Dakota Business Review,* covered in SRI under U8595-1.

Availability: University of South Dakota: Business Research Bureau, School of Business, 414 E. Clark St., Vermillion SD 57069, $6.00 per yr.; SRI/MF/complete.

Issues reviewed during 1985: Nov. 1984-Sept. 1985 (P) (Vol. I, Nos. 5-6; Vol. II, Nos. 1-4).

STATISTICAL FEATURE:

U8595-2.601: July 1985 (Vol. II, No. 3)

1982 CENSUS OF RETAIL TRADE SELECTED STATISTICS

(p. 3) Table showing South Dakota retail trade establishments and sales (total and for establishments with payroll), and retail employment, all by county, 1982. Data are from Census Bureau.

U8710
University of Tennessee: Center for Business and Economic Research

U8710-1   SURVEY OF BUSINESS
Quarterly.   Approx. 30 p.
ISSN 0099-0973.
LC 75-646621.
SRI/MF/complete

Quarterly journal on business trends and economic conditions in Tennessee and occasionally the U.S. Most data are from the Federal Government, the Business Center Tennessee Econometric Model, and private research firms.

Issues usually contain analytical articles focusing on a single topic, often with statistics. Winter issue features an annual economic outlook forecast.

Features with substantial statistical content are described, as they appear, under "Statistical Features."

Availability: University of Tennessee: Center for Business and Economic Research, College of Business Administration, Glocker Bldg., Suite 100, Knoxville TN 37996-4170, †, back issues $1.25; SRI/MF/complete.

Issues reviewed during 1985: Fall 1984-Spring 1985 (P) (Vol. 20, Nos. 2-4) [Vol. 20, No. 4 incorrectly reads No. 3 on contents page].

STATISTICAL FEATURES:

U8710-1.601: Fall 1984 (Vol. 20, No. 2)

TAX REFORM IN TENNESSEE: NEEDS AND OPTIONS

(p. 4-11) By William F. Fox and Kenneth E. Quindry. Article on current Tennessee fiscal condition and tax reform efforts. Data sources include the Tennessee State Budget. Includes 5 charts showing the following:

a. General expenditure per capita, 1982; and income and sales tax collections as a percent of all collections, 1983; all for Tennessee and 10 other southeastern States.

b. Distribution of typical Tennessee tax dollar by major expenditure category, 1963/64 and 1984/85; and distribution of U.S. and Tennessee tax collections by type of tax, 1983.

TAX ISSUES AND ALTERNATIVES

(p. 16-19) By Stanley M. Chervin. Article, with 1 chart showing State sales tax revenues as a percent of all tax revenues, for U.S. and 8 southeastern States, 1982/83.

U8710-1.602: Winter 1985 (Vol. 20, No. 3)

ECONOMIC OUTLOOK 1985, ANNUAL FEATURE

Annual analysis of Tennessee economic outlook. Includes 2 statistical articles, described below. This is the 16th annual analysis.

1985 SURVEY OF BUSINESS ATTITUDES, ANNUAL FEATURE

(p. 5-17) Annual survey article, by David A. Hake et al., on the economic expectations of 134 Tennessee executives for 1985. Includes 7 charts showing survey response for the following, often by State region or industry sector: expected level of change in overall economy (Tennessee and U.S.) and for 8 key economic indicators; appropriate response to Federal deficit; and preferred source for additional Federal revenue.

Also includes 1 table showing Federal budget receipts and expenditures, by major category, FY83 and estimated FY85.

OUTLOOK FOR TENNESSEE, ANNUAL FEATURE

(p. 26-33) Annual article, by William F. Fox and Richard A. Hofler, on Tennessee economic outlook through 1985. Data are from the Tennessee econometric model. Includes 3 charts and 1 table showing the following, generally for U.S. and Tennessee:

a. Nonagricultural jobs: distribution by industry division, 1983, with estimated growth rate for 1985.

b. GNP, personal income, nonagricultural and manufacturing jobs, unemployment rates, and manufacturing average weekly hours, 1st quarter 1984-3rd quarter 1986 and annually 1983-85; and average annual growth rates for output, jobs, and wages/salaries, by industry division with overall State average, 1984-93 period.

U8710-1.603: Spring 1985 (Vol. 20, No. 4)

BANK FAILURES: ORIGINS AND IMPLICATIONS

(p. 4-9) By Ronnie J. Clayton and David S. Kidwell. Article, with 4 tables showing number of bank failures, with comparison to total active banks, various periods 1890-1972; bank failures and FDIC problem banks, annually 1967-84; list of 10 all-time largest bank failures, including bank name and location, assets, and failure date; and Federal deposit insurance limits, selected years 1934-80. Data are from FDIC.

CONSOLIDATING FINANCIAL RESOURCES: INTERSTATE BANKING

(p. 10-18) By Ronnie J. Clayton and David S. Kidwell. Article, with 7 tables on banking structure in U.S., foreign countries, and Tennessee. Tables show the following:

a. Commercial banks, banking offices, population per office, and 5 largest banks' aggregate share of total deposits, for U.S. and 7 foreign countries, 1982; out-of-State offices (nonbanking subsidiary and banking), and number of States with offices, for 10 largest U.S. bank holding companies, 1980; and U.S. interstate nonbanking subsidiaries, by type of activity (no date).

b. Tennessee: deposits, share of State total deposits, affiliates, and number of counties with offices, for 10 bank holding companies, 1983; and market shares of independent banks vs. holding companies in 8 counties, selected years 1974-83.

Data are from Federal, State, and industry sources.

FINANCIAL SERVICES INDUSTRY AND THE CONSUMER: COMPETITION, INNOVATION AND TECHNOLOGY

(p. 19-23) By Robert J. Rogowski. Article, with 4 tables on financial services industry trends, showing the following:

a. Financial institution aggregate assets, by type of institution, selected years 1900-82; commercial bank return on assets and capital, 1972-81; and value of mortgage and installment/revolving loans, for top 15 consumer lenders ranked by total loans, as of Dec. 1981.

b. Types of financial services offered by banks, savings and loan assns, insurance companies, retailers, and security dealers, 1960 and 1984.

Data are from Federal Reserve Bank of Chicago and a variety of published sources.

THRIFTS: PROBLEMS AND PROSPECTS

(p. 24-31) By Ronnie J. Clayton and James A. Verbrugge. Article, with 2 tables showing assets and liabilities, by type, for U.S. federally insured savings and loan assns, selected years 1960-83; and average net assets and selected financial ratios, for Tennessee and U.S. savings and loan assns, Dec. 1983 and Sept. 1984. Data are from FHLBB.

U8710-2   TENNESSEE STATISTICAL ABSTRACT, 1985/86

Annual. Aug. 1985.
xvi+759 p.
LC 68-66499.
SRI/MF/complete, current & previous year reports

Annual compilation, for 1985/86, of detailed demographic, social, governmental, and economic statistics for Tennessee. Data are primarily for 1970s-84, with historical trends from the 1950s and earlier.

Report is designed to present a comprehensive overview of the State. Extensive geographic, socioeconomic, and demographic breakdowns are shown, as applicable, for most topics. These breakdowns include data by city, county and other State region, MSA, urban-rural status, commodity, industry, occupation, age, educational attainment, race, and sex. Comparisons to other southeastern States and total U.S. are also often included.

Most data are from Federal and State government reports. Data sources appear beneath each table.

Contents:

a. Preface and listings of contents and charts; and introduction, with directory of State data centers and map of Tennessee MSAs and counties. (p. v-xvi)

b. 23 maps, 15 charts, and 395 tables arranged in 19 chapters, described below, each preceded by table listing and brief narrative. (p. 1-719)

c. Tennessee rankings section, with 10 tables showing comparative State rankings in selected socioeconomic areas; and subject index. (p. 721-759)

This is the 8th edition. Previous report, for 1984/85, was also reviewed in SRI during 1985, and is also available on SRI microfiche under U8710-2 [Annual. Aug. 1984. xiv+761 p. $20.95+$1.75 postage]. Previous report is substantially similar in format and content; but some tables differ in content, as indicated below, for chapters 1, 3-7, 9, 11, and 17.

Availability: University of Tennessee: Center for Business and Economic Research, College of Business Administration, Glocker Bldg., Suite 100, Knoxville TN 37996-4170, $22.95+$2.05 postage and handling; SRI/MF/complete.

CHAPTERS:

U8710-2.1: Chapter 1: Population

(p. 1-35) Contains 1 map, 1 chart, and 18 tables. Includes population from 1790; persons naturalized by country of birth; land area; persons living in group quarters; and net migration, with detail by U.S. region of origin and destination.

Previous report also included data on resident aliens by country of birth.

U8710-2.2: Chapter 2: Income and Prices

(p. 37-90) Contains 1 map, 2 charts, and 23 tables. Includes GSP; per capita personal income, and total personal income by source; transfer payments; poverty incidence; U.S. CPI; and purchasing power of dollar.

U8710-2.3: Chapter 3: Employment and Earnings

(p. 91-142) Contains 2 maps, 2 charts, and 24 tables. Includes covered employment, employers, wages, tax rate, and unemployment insurance premiums due; employment and unemployment rate; unemployment insurance claimants; State and local government employment and payroll, by function; and DOD, USPS, VA, and other employment.

Also includes work stoppages, workers involved, and days idle; labor force by employment status; scientists and engineers, and median salaries; and labor union membership.

Previous report also included data on CETA enrollment, and Federal funding for work and training programs.

U8710-2.4: Chapter 4: Manufacturing

(p. 143-183) Contains 1 chart and 23 tables. Includes manufacturing establishments, employment, value added, payroll, shipment value, and capital expenditures; manufacturing production workers, hours, and earnings; export employment and shipment value; pollution abatement capital expenditures, operating costs, and pollutants removed; and capacity utilization rates.

Previous report also included data on employment for 50 largest manufacturing companies, and top 5 in each county.

U8710–2.5: Chapter 5: Mining

(p. 185-203) Contains 1 map and 16 tables. Includes nonfuel mineral production and value; coal mines, production, prices, capacity, utilization, reserves, stocks, miners, days worked, and productivity; mineral establishments by major activity; and oil and gas wells and production.

Previous report also included data on natural gas pipeline mileage.

U8710–2.6: Chapter 6: Construction and Housing

(p. 205-237) Contains 1 map, 1 chart, and 17 tables. Includes construction contract valuations; residential building permits issued for public and private housing; apartment rents and vacancy rates; housing units, tenure, occupancy, and financial characteristics; mobile homes; additions to private housing stock; housing demand through 1990; construction employment; housing prices and price index; and savings assn mortgage activity.

Previous report also included data on construction wages and benefits by trade.

U8710–2.7: Chapter 7: Trade and Services

(p. 239-277) Contains 1 chart and 17 tables. Includes retail, wholesale, and service establishments, sales or receipts, payroll, and employment; department stores and sales; wholesale inventories; and business failures and liabilities.

Previous report also included data on retail and service establishment ownership.

U8710–2.8: Chapter 8: Communications

(p. 279-301) Contains 1 map and 14 tables. Includes newspapers and circulation; telephones, and telephone equipment, calls originated, taxes, and central offices; postal facilities, rural routes, and revenues; radio and TV stations; and cable TV communities, subscribers, and subscription rates.

U8710–2.9: Chapter 9: Transportation

(p. 303-337) Contains 2 maps and 25 tables. Includes highway construction and maintenance expenditures; commuting data, including persons with public transportation disabilities; motor vehicle registrations; motor freight terminals; truck size and weight limits, and major uses; airports; Airport Development Aid Program status; and passenger and freight air traffic.

Also includes private investment in Tennessee River industries/terminals; public river terminals and facilities, by river; river freight tonnage; road mileage; motor fuel consumption and taxes; trucks and mileage; truck transport of hazardous materials; active civilian pilots; general aviation aircraft; and Southern District Class I railroad finances and operations.

Previous report also included data on Federal transportation grants.

U8710–2.10: Chapter 10: Energy

(p. 339-383) Contains 2 maps, 1 chart, and 27 tables. Includes energy consumption by fuel type and sector; fuel oil and kerosene deliveries; electric power generation by fuel type, and fuel consumption and costs; and TVA generating plants and capacity.

Also includes electric utility customers, sales, revenues, consumption, and bills and rates, by sector for distributors using TVA power; and gas utility sales, customers, consumption, and prices, by sector.

U8710–2.11: Chapter 11: Agriculture and Forestry

(p. 385-438) Contains 1 map, 1 chart, and 34 tables. Includes farms by tenure, land use, and property value and taxes; farm income sources and production expenses; crop production; livestock inventory and value; dairy and poultry production; and farm price indexes and prices received.

Also includes rural farm population; characteristics of farm operators; rural cooperatives, membership, and revenues; commercial forest land, growing stock and sawtimber, growth and removals, and acreage additions and diversions.

Previous report also included data on lumber industry establishments, employment, payroll, production workers and wages, value added, shipments, and capital expenditures.

U8710–2.12: Chapter 12: Climate, Land Use, and Recreation

(p. 439-464) Contains 2 maps and 15 tables. Includes monthly climatological data; minimum temperatures and heating degree days, by weather station; travel-generated employment, expenditures, payroll, and State and local taxes; and land and inland water area.

Also includes land ownership by Federal agency; national forest acreage; national and State parks and recreation areas, acreage, and visitors; visitors to Great Smoky Mountains National Park and Cherokee National Forest, by outdoor activity; and State expenditures for parks/recreation areas.

U8710–2.13: Chapter 13: Banking and Insurance

(p. 465-510) Contains 1 chart and 27 tables. Includes banks, assets and liabilities, income and expenses, employment, and deposits, with detail by institution; and savings and loan assns, assets, mortgage loans, savings capital, and cash flow.

Also includes insurance companies, assets and liabilities, and underwriting and loss data; life insurance in force, and benefit payments; nonprofit hospitalization assn premiums and claims; credit union membership and loans outstanding; and savings banks and assets.

U8710–2.14: Chapter 14: Government Organization and Elections

(p. 511-538) Contains 4 maps and 13 tables. Includes county and municipal governments; judicial districts, judges, and assistant district attorneys; composition of State legislature by party; votes cast for selected State and Federal offices, by party; voting age population; and registered voters and electoral participation.

U8710–2.15: Chapter 15: Government Finances

(p. 539-599) Contains 1 map, 1 chart, and 26 tables. Includes State revenues by source and expenditures by function; local and Federal payments to State funds, by function; Federal tax collections; and county revenues, and expenditures by function.

Also includes sales/use tax collections; property taxes and rates, and actual and assessed value; Federal grants by program, and funds received; municipal revenues and expenditures; State tax collections; and Federal tax burden.

U8710–2.16: Chapter 16: Education

(p. 601-636) Contains 3 maps and 25 tables. Includes public schools, total and minority enrollment, attendance, finances, teachers and average salaries, pupil transportation services, and high school graduates; private school enrollment; and public library staff, holdings, circulation, and expenditures, by library.

Also includes public and private higher education institutions, enrollment, degrees conferred, and finances, with detail by institution; vocational/technical education enrollment; Federal educational funding; educational attainment of population; and State and local educational employment and payrolls.

U8710–2.17: Chapter 17: Health and Vital Statistics

(p. 637-676) Contains 1 map, 2 charts, and 24 tables. Includes births and deaths, and rates; deaths by major cause; infant and neonatal deaths; teenage and illegitimate births; abortion recipient characteristics; and reported cases of communicable diseases.

Also includes hospital facilities, patients, length of stay and expenses, and personnel and trainees; nursing homes, beds, and occupancy; physicians, dentists, and osteopaths; and marriages and divorces.

Previous report also included data on patients in mental health facilities.

U8710–2.18: Chapter 18: Public Assistance and Social Insurance

(p. 677-698) Contains 1 map and 12 tables. Includes expenditures and sources of funds for human services programs; unemployment insurance program contributions, benefit payments, assets, and covered workers and wages; AFDC cases and payments; and food stamp participation and coupon value.

Also includes medical assistance applications, approvals, and caseload; Medicare and Medicaid benefits paid and enrollment or recipients; sources of public health program expenditures, and persons served; food/nutrition program funds; social security benefits and payments; and SSI for aged, blind, and disabled recipients, and average payments.

U8710–2.19: Chapter 19: Law Enforcement

(p. 699-719) Contains 1 chart and 15 tables. Includes crimes and rates, by type of offense; adult and juvenile correctional institutions and rehabilitative service center population, capacity, and per capita expenditures, by institution; and State prison population and criminals received from court.

Also includes traffic accidents, deaths, and injuries; law enforcement personnel; adult and juvenile commitments to State correctional institutions; State police employment, and vehicles registered and highway miles patrolled; and criminal justice expenditures.

U8960
University of Utah: Bureau of Economic and Business Research

U8960-2 UTAH ECONOMIC AND BUSINESS REVIEW
Monthly. Approx. 12 p.
ISSN 0042-1405.
LC 55-38145.
SRI/MF/complete, shipped quarterly

Monthly report (with 2 or more combined issues each year) on Utah business and economic activity. Data are from Federal and State agencies and private sources. Month of data coverage is 2 months prior to cover date.

Each issue contains 1 feature article, usually with statistics; a list of data sources; and 3 monthly tables, listed below.

Annual statistical features include population estimates; economic trends by county; and personal income by source and county.

Monthly tables appear in all issues; combined issues include separate tables for each month covered. All additional features with substantial statistical content are described, as they appear, under "Statistical Features." Nonstatistical features are not covered.

Availability: University of Utah: Bureau of Economic and Business Research, Graduate School of Business, Kendall D. Garff Bldg., Rm. 401, Salt Lake City UT 84112, †; SRI/MF/complete, shipped quarterly.

Issues reviewed during 1985: Sept. 1984-June 1985 (P) (Vol. 44, Nos. 9-11/12; Vol. 45, Nos. 1-6) [Nov./Dec. 1984 and Apr./May 1985 are combined issues].

MONTHLY TABLES:
[Most data are shown for month of coverage, with comparisons to previous year.]

[1] Utah data [personal income, new corporations, motor vehicle sales, and detailed breakdowns under each of 7 categories: agriculture; construction; employment; finance; production (including electricity, oil, gas, coal, and, in some issues, copper); tourism/travel; and utilities (customers and telephone lines)].

[2] [County data: nonagricultural employment, unemployment rate, value of authorized construction, new dwelling units, postal receipts, natural gas and electric customers, and telephone lines in service, all for 4 counties.]

[3] National data [selected economic indicators for U.S.].

STATISTICAL FEATURES:

U8960-2.601: Sept. 1984 (Vol. 44, No. 9)

UTAH'S EXPANDING SERVICE SECTOR

(p. 1-5) By Constance C. Steffen and James A. Wood. Article, with 3 tables showing Utah service industry receipts, payroll, and employees, by type of business, with receipt detail for Salt Lake City/Ogden and Provo/Orem SMSAs, 1982 with trends from 1977. Data are from U.S. Commerce Dept.

U8960-2.602: Oct. 1984 (Vol. 44, No. 10)

UPDATE ON RETAIL TRADE IN UTAH

(p. 1-5) By Constance C. Steffen. Article, with 4 tables showing Utah retail trade establishments, sales, payroll, and employment, with sales comparisons to total U.S., all by type of business, various years 1974-84; and total and per capita retail sales by county, 1982.

U8960-2.603: Nov.-Dec. 1984 (Vol. 44, Nos. 11-12)

UTAH'S NEXT QUARTER CENTURY: REVISED UTAH PROJECTIONS, 1985-2010

(p. 1-7) By Rodger Weaver et al. Article presenting Utah population and employment projections to 2010. Data are derived from Utah Office of Planning and Budget.

Includes 6 tables showing population, households, and employment, by State planning district; births, deaths, and migration; population aged 5-11 and 12-17; and number of jobs by industry division; various years 1970-2010.

U8960-2.604: Jan. 1985 (Vol. 45, No. 1)

1984 POPULATION ESTIMATES FOR UTAH, ANNUAL FEATURE

(p. 1-8) Annual article, by Brad T. Barber et al., presenting population estimates for Utah as of July 1, 1984. Data are from Utah Population Estimates Committee.

Includes 5 tables showing Utah land area, population density, enrollment in grades 1-8 and 2-9, net migration (students and total), and population based on 5 estimating methods, all by county, 1984, with selected comparisons to 1983; population, by State planning district, July 1, 1975-84; and births and deaths, 1960-83.

U8960-2.605: Feb. 1985 (Vol. 45, No. 2)

FISCAL IMPACTS OF THE INTERMOUNTAIN POWER PROJECT

(p. 1-9) By Constance Steffen and Boyd Fjeldsted. Article on economic impact of construction of a power plant (Intermountain Power Project) in Millard County, Utah. Data are from the University of Utah. Includes 3 tables showing project-related employment, wages, and State/local tax collections, various years 1981-90.

U8960-2.606: Mar. 1985 (Vol. 45, No. 3)

CHANGING CONDITIONS OF THE SALT LAKE COUNTY APARTMENT MARKET

(p. 1-5) By James A. Wood. Article, with 1 table showing distribution of Salt Lake County housing construction by type (duplex, 3/4 units, 5 units/larger, and single family), 1977-84. Data are from *Utah Construction Report.*

U8960-2.607: Apr./May 1985 (Vol. 45, Nos. 4/5)

SELECTED BUSINESS STATISTICS, UTAH COUNTIES, ANNUAL FEATURE

(p. 1-15) Annual feature, by Ronda Brinkerhoff, analyzing economic trends in Utah counties for 1984.

Includes 2 summary charts, 1 summary table, and 1 table, repeated for each county and total State, showing: population; labor force and employment; monthly wage, annual payroll, and total and per capita personal income;

property valuation and taxes, gross taxable sales, and sales tax collections; construction activity; car/truck registrations; and Federal payments in lieu of property tax under P.L. 94-565; 1981-84.

U8960-2.608: June 1985 (Vol. 45, No. 6)

PERSONAL INCOME IN UTAH COUNTIES, 1983, ANNUAL FEATURE

(p. 1-13) Annual article, by Boyd L. Fjeldsted, reviewing Utah personal income, by type, industry source, and county, 1983. Data are from the Regional Economics Information System of the U.S. Dept of Commerce.

Includes 2 tables showing Utah per capita personal income, percent of U.S. average, and State rank, 1962-84; and personal income by type, earnings by industry division (including government by level), and per capita income, by county, 1983, with percent change from 1978.

U9080
University of Virginia: Tayloe Murphy Institute

U9080-1 DISTRIBUTION OF VIRGINIA ADJUSTED GROSS INCOME by Income Class and Locality, 1983
Annual. Apr. 1985. 33 p.
ISSN 0148-6772.
LC 77-641301.
SRI/MF/complete

Annual report, by John L. Knapp and Beverly H. Capone, on income distribution among Virginia MSAs, cities, counties, and planning districts, as shown by adjusted gross income (AGI) on individual and married couple income tax returns, 1983. Data are based on State tax records.

Contains narrative analysis, with 3 charts and 1 table (p. 1-10); 6 detailed tables, listed below (p. 11-31); and lists of MSAs and planning districts (p. 32-33).

This is the 12th annual report.

Availability: University of Virginia—Tayloe Murphy Institute, Dynamics Bldg., 4th Floor, 2015 Ivy Rd., Charlottesville VA 22903-1780, †; SRI/MF/complete.

DETAILED TABLES:
[All tables show data for 1983, by county, city, MSA, and planning district, unless otherwise noted. Tables A1 and A3-A4 show number of returns, total AGI, median AGI per return, and distribution of returns by AGI size class.]

A1. AGI on all returns. (p. 11-15)

A2. Ranking by percentage change in median AGI for married couple returns [by county and city], 1978 and 1983. (p. 16-17)

A3-A4. AGI on married couple and individual returns. (p. 18-27)

A5. AGI per exemption [amount and index relative to State average]. (p. 28-29)

A6. Index of income concentration. (p. 30-31)

U9080–6 VIRGINIA ANNUAL GROSS STATE PRODUCT, 1958-83
Annual. Dec. 1984. 8 p.
SRI/MF/complete

Annual report, by Beverly H. Capone, estimating Virginia GSP in current and constant (1972) dollars, 1958-83, by industry division and per capita, with comparisons to U.S. GNP. Most estimates of data prior to 1983 are revisions which supersede figures published in previous Institute reports. Data are based on Commerce Dept and USDA publications.

Contains narrative summary, with 3 charts and 1 text table (p. 1-4); and 4 tables (p. 5-8).

Availability: University of Virginia—Tayloe Murphy Institute, Dynamics Bldg., 4th Floor, 2015 Ivy Rd., Charlottesville VA 22903-1780, †; SRI/MF/complete.

U9080–9 ESTIMATES OF THE POPULATION OF VIRGINIA COUNTIES AND CITIES: July 1983 (Final) and July 1984 (Provisional)
Annual. Aug. 1985. 30 p.
LC 81-645110.
SRI/MF/complete, current & previous year reports

Annual report, by Julia H. Martin and David W. Sheatsley, presenting Virginia actual and estimated population and net migration, by county, independent city, planning district, and MSA, and for metro and nonmetro areas, various periods 1980-84. Also includes county and city rankings, and summary comparisons to 7 South Atlantic States and D.C.

Estimates are prepared by Tayloe Murphy Institute in cooperation with Census Bureau.

Contains narrative analysis (p. 1-5); 1 map and 4 tables, with brief narrative (p. 6-25); and appendices with MSA list and methodology (p. 26-30).

Previous report, issued Feb. 1985, was also reviewed in SRI during 1985, and is also available on SRI microfiche under U9080-9 [Annual. Feb. 1985. 29 p. †].

Availability: University of Virginia—Tayloe Murphy Institute, Dynamics Bldg., 4th Floor, 2015 Ivy Rd., Charlottesville VA 22903-1780, †; SRI/MF/complete.

U9080–10 HOUSING UNITS AUTHORIZED IN VIRGINIA'S PLANNING DISTRICTS, COUNTIES, AND CITIES
3 per year. Approx. 25 p.
SRI/MF/complete

Recurring report (issued 3 times per year), by Michael A. Spar and Julia H. Martin, on Virginia local housing unit building permits issued and estimated construction costs, by construction type and location. Also includes some data for nonresidential buildings. Report is published in combined 1st/2nd and 3rd/4th quarter issues and an annual issue.

Data are from reports of local building officials to the Census Bureau.

Reports are issued 4-12 months after period of coverage.

Issues generally include narrative introduction and summary of trends, with 3 illustrative charts; and 3 recurring tables listed below.

Issues also occasionally include a directory of county and city planning district membership. Annual issue includes full-year data for quarterly table 1 on housing units and value authorized, and 1 additional table with similar full-year data for 9 types of nonresidential buildings.

Prior to the 3rd/4th quarter issue, report periodicity was designated as quarterly, with combined 1st/2nd quarter issue.

Availability: University of Virginia—Tayloe Murphy Institute, Dynamics Bldg., 4th Floor, 2015 Ivy Rd., Charlottesville VA 22903-1780, †; SRI/MF/complete.

Issues reviewed during 1985: 4th Qtr./Entire Year 1983-Annual 1984 (D).

RECURRING TABLES

A. Aggregate residential construction costs [in constant (1972 and 1977) and current dollars; and Census Bureau construction cost index; 1970 to most recent full year].

B. Aggregate nonresidential construction costs [in constant (1977) and current dollars; and American Appraisal Co. "Boeckh Index" for commercial buildings; for current and previous 3-4 years].

1. Housing units authorized in localities [and value, for mobile, private, single-family, duplex, and 3-4 and 5/more units; and number of private and public units demolished; by county, city, and planning district, for quarter or quarters of coverage].

U9080–17 TAKING STOCK: Virginia's Housing Inventory, 1980
Monograph. Dec. 1984.
iii+105 p.
1980 Census Analysis Series, Vol. 3.
LC 85-621291.
SRI/MF/complete

By David W. Sheatsley. Report on Virginia housing inventory, occupancy, and structural and financial characteristics, by city and county, 1970 and 1980, with selected trends from 1930s. Data are from U.S. census reports.

Contains contents listing (p. iii); introduction (p. 1); narrative report, with 10 maps, 4 charts, and 24 tables described below (p. 3-104); and references (p. 105).

Availability: University of Virginia—Tayloe Murphy Institute, Dynamics Bldg., 4th Floor, 2015 Ivy Rd., Charlottesville VA 22903-1780, $10.40; SRI/MF/complete.

TABLES:

[Data by locality are shown by county and independent city. Most data are for 1970 and 1980, with some trends from as early as 1930.]

a. Structural characteristics: number of housing units by period built, single- and multi-family units, mobile homes, median rooms per unit and persons per household, and median age of housing, all by locality; housing units by type of structure, by tenure; housing units by number of rooms; and housing units removed, by period built. Tables 1-9. (p. 5-48)

b. Occupancy characteristics: occupied housing units by tenure; owner-occupied housing units by locality; owner- and renter-occupied housing units by period occupant established residence, with aggregate detail by locality; and housing units by persons per room. Tables 10-14. (p. 59-74)

c. Housing condition: housing units with and without plumbing, kitchen facilities, air conditioning, and telephones; and housing units by number of bathrooms, source of water, method of sewage disposal, type of heating equipment, number of autos present, and type of house and water heating fuel and cooking fuel. Tables 15-17. (p. 75-79)

d. Financial characteristics: upper and lower limits of housing value and rent for census reporting purposes; housing units by tenure, by housing value or contract rent; median value and rent by locality; and home owning and renting costs as a percent of household income. Tables 18-24. (p. 89-104)

U9120 University of Washington: Graduate School of Business Administration

U9120–1 PACIFIC NORTHWEST EXECUTIVE
Quarterly. Approx. 25 p.
SRI/MF/complete

Quarterly report on economic and industrial trends and outlook for Pacific Northwest region (Washington State, Oregon, and Idaho). Most data are from Census Bureau and State agencies.

Issues contain feature articles, often with statistics. July issue features an annual supplement with detailed data on economic indicators for the Pacific Northwest.

Features with substantial statistical content are described, as they appear, under "Statistical Features."

Report for July 1985 is the 1st issue.

Availability: University of Washington: Graduate School of Business Administration, 336 Lewis Hall, DJ-10, Seattle WA 98195, †; SRI/MF/complete.

Issues reviewed during 1985: July 1985 (P) (Vol. 1, No. 1).

STATISTICAL FEATURES:

U9120–1.601: July 1985 (Vol. 1, No. 1)
FOSTERING ECONOMIC DEVELOPMENT IN WASHINGTON

(p. 2-5) By Booth Gardner. Article, with 1 table showing Washington State labor force and unemployment, quinquennially 1985-2000. Data are from Washington State Employment Security Dept.

WAGE RATES IN WASHINGTON STATE

(p. 8) Article, with 2 charts showing Washington State average manufacturing earnings, and percent by which they exceed U.S. average, by selected industry group, 1984; and lumber/wood products industry average production worker earnings, for Washington State and 10 other States, 1983.

ECONOMIC FORECASTING IN THE PACIFIC NORTHWEST STATES

(p. 9-11) Article, with 1 table showing percent change in personal income, employment, average earnings, housing starts, and CPI, for Washington State, Oregon, and Idaho, 1985-86. Data are based on State agency forecasts.

PACIFIC NORTHWEST ANNUAL ECONOMIC INDICATORS, ANNUAL FEATURE

(p. 12-13) Annual compilation of tables presenting selected economic indicators for Pacific Northwest region. Data are from Federal, State, and private sources. Includes 26 tables showing data on the following, selected years 1960-84:

a. Population; personal and farm income; unemployment rate; employment (total and wage/salary, and by selected industry); average manufacturing earnings; construction contracts and building index; lumber production (with detail for plywood and wood pulp) and average prices; log exports; and aluminum and electricity production; all shown variously for Washington State, Oregon, and Idaho, with selected aggregate data.

b. U.S. implicit price deflator; CPI, for Portland, Oreg., and Seattle-Everett, Wash.; imports and exports, for Portland/Seattle customs districts; and Bonneville Power Administration energy sales and average prices.

This is the 1st annual compilation.

U9190
University of Wisconsin: Applied Population Laboratory

U9190-1   POPULATION SERIES
Series. For individual publication data, see below. SRI/MF/complete

Series of reports analyzing selected population data for Wisconsin, the U.S., and various U.S. regions. Most reports are based on findings from the 1980 Census of Population and Housing. Data are compiled by the University of Wisconsin, Applied Population Laboratory.

Series begins with the reports described below. A similar series (not covered in SRI) was published following the 1970 Census.

Availability: University of Wisconsin: Applied Population Laboratory, Department of Rural Sociology, 1450 Linden Dr., Rm. 316, Madison WI 53706; SRI/MF/complete.

U9190-1.1: Demographic Characteristics of Wisconsin's Welfare Recipients
[Monograph. Jan. 1984. iii+65 p. Population Series 80-2. $5.00. LC 83-83391. SRI/MF/complete.]

By Mark R. Rank and Paul R. Voss. Report analyzing demographic characteristics of Wisconsin residents receiving AFDC, food stamp, and Medicaid assistance, 1981.

Covers direct recipients and/or persons residing in recipient households, by sex, race, age, metro vs. nonmetro location, household composition and size, living arrangement (home, nursing home, and other), marital and school enrollment status, education, disability and employment status, and income and assistance grant level.

Also includes average household size and number of children, mean age and education, and mean income and grant award.

Data are shown for each program and include various cross-tabulations and comparisons to total population.

Data are based on a survey of 3,587 Wisconsin households receiving assistance payments as of July 31, 1981. Survey households represent 10,393 residents.

Contains contents and table listings (p. i-iii); summary and narrative report (p. 1-40); and 24 tables (p. 41-64).

U9190-1.2: Poverty in Wisconsin
[Monograph. Feb. 1985. ii+205 p. Population Series 80-3. $5.00. LC 84-620017. SRI/MF/complete.]

Compilation of papers examining aspects of poverty in Wisconsin. The papers, which were presented at a Nov. 1983 conference held at University of Wisconsin-Madison, focus on the effects of poverty on selected groups, including women, minorities, the elderly, and rural residents.

Contains table of contents (1 p.); preface (p. i-ii); 8 papers, described below, with narrative analyses, 36 maps and charts, and 45 tables (p. 1-204); and conference agenda (p. 205).

PAPERS:
[Data generally are from Census Bureau, unless otherwise noted.]

RECENT INCREASES IN POVERTY: A COMPARISON OF WISCONSIN AND THE U.S.

(p. 1-9) By Sheldon H. Danziger. Includes 3 tables showing poverty rates, by State, 1978 and 1982, with 1982 detail for rates including and excluding cash social insurance and public assistance benefits; and U.S. poverty line compared to median family income and CPI, selected years 1965-82.

ALTERNATIVE MEASURES OF THE RECENT RISE IN POVERTY

(p. 10-27) By Sheldon H. Danziger. Includes 5 tables showing U.S. poverty rates under alternative measures, various years 1965-82; and composition of households below poverty line, 1982; with data by head-of-household category, and detail for poverty definitions including and excluding cash social insurance and public assistance benefits.

Head-of-household categories variously include white, black, Hispanic, female, elderly, student, disabled, and persons working full-time and less than full-time.

POVERTY AMONG MINORITIES IN WISCONSIN

(p. 28-53) By Stephen J. Tordella. Includes 5 tables showing selected socioeconomic indicators for Wisconsin minority groups (black, Indian, Asian/Pacific Islander, and Spanish origin), 1979 or 1980, including the following:

a. Poverty rates, by county; families (total and female-headed), children, and individuals below poverty level; households, by income level; and median household income.

b. Labor force participation and unemployment rates; employment by occupation; educational status of adult population (percent high school graduates, and median years of school completed); and high school dropouts.

FEMALE-HEADED FAMILIES IN POVERTY IN WISCONSIN

(p. 54-71) By Ann Nichols-Casebolt. Includes 4 charts and 4 tables showing the following data for female-headed households or families in Wisconsin, 1980:

a. Number, distribution, and poverty rates, by selected characteristics (presence and age of children, age and race of household head, and marital, employment, and welfare status of household head).

b. Number, percent of all families, and poverty rate, by county; and percent receiving cash social security and public welfare benefits, average amount received, and poverty levels including and excluding benefit income, with detail by presence of children and for elderly household heads.

POVERTY AMONG WISCONSIN'S ELDERLY

(p. 72-108) By Patricia A. Guhleman and Doris P. Slesinger. Includes 14 charts and 3 tables showing the following data primarily for persons age 65/over in Wisconsin:

a. Population share, decennially 1910-2010; and selected socioeconomic indicators, including living arrangements, poverty status, income levels and sources, and median income, mostly 1979; with selected detail by sex, race, and urban-rural status.

b. Population and poverty rate, by county, 1969 and 1979; and population, poverty rate, and percent receiving income from social security, wages/dividends/interest, public assistance, and private pension/other sources, all shown by sex and living arrangement, with poverty rate detail by marital status, and income source detail for persons below poverty level, 1979.

RURAL POVERTY IN WISCONSIN

(p. 109-129) By William E. Saupe and John W. Belknap. Includes 4 charts and 5 tables, primarily showing poverty levels, by county, employment status of household head, and public welfare status of family, for farm and nonfarm rural residents of Wisconsin, with selected comparisons to urban residents, 1979.

EVALUATION OF IMPACTS OF THE REAGAN BUDGET CUTS ON WISCONSIN FOOD STAMP COSTS AND CASELOAD

(p. 130-175) By Maurice MacDonald. Analysis of changes in Wisconsin food stamp and AFDC program participation and benefits after enactment of the Omnibus Reconciliation Act of 1981, which tightened eligibility rules, reduced some food stamp entitlements, and changed AFDC work incentives. Includes 6 charts and 9 tables, primarily presenting supporting data from 1981-82 Wisconsin Basic Needs Surveys covering approximately 2,000 households.

WISCONSIN'S WELFARE POPULATION: A LONGITUDINAL STUDY

(p. 176-204) By Mark R. Rank and Paul R. Voss. Includes 11 tables showing distribution of Wisconsin welfare recipients, Sept. 1980, as follows: type of benefit received (AFDC, food stamp, and Medicaid); welfare history prior to 1980; region (Milwaukee, other metro, and nonmetro); sex, race, age, education, and employment status; whether incapacitated; number of children; and monthly income.

Tables show data for all recipients and for selected household-head categories (female with children, married, single, and elderly). Tables also include comparisons by welfare status in 1982, and former recipients' reasons for leaving welfare programs.

Data are from a longitudinal study involving a random sample of 2,796 recipient households.

U9190–1.3: Demographic Change in Wisconsin: Trends and Outlook

[Monograph. Jan. 1984. iii+121 p. Population Series 80-1. $5.00. LC 83-83392. SRI/MF/complete.]

Compilation of papers analyzing Wisconsin population characteristics and change from the 1950s. The papers were originally presented at a May 26, 1982 conference held in Madison.

Data are primarily from Census Bureau.

Contains contents listing (1 p.); preface (p. i-iii); 5 papers, with narrative analyses, 19 maps and charts, and 15 tables (p. 1-119); and conference agenda (p. 121).

Papers with substantial statistics are described below; charts and maps are generally illustrative and are not described.

PAPERS:

[Unless otherwise noted, data are shown for Wisconsin.]

LIVING ARRANGEMENTS: 1980 CENSUS REVEALS CHANGES IN THE WAY WE LIVE

(p. 1-19) By Cynthia Bautista and Doris P. Slesinger. Includes 4 tables showing households by composition (families and non-families by type, with detail for family householders by sex); change in household composition for Milwaukee and aggregate other metro and nonmetro counties; and labor force and employment status of family household head, by age and sex; 1970 and 1980 or 1970-80 period.

HOUSING WISCONSIN'S POPULATION: THREE DECADES OF CHANGE

(p. 21-46) By Patricia A. Guhleman and Paul R. Voss. Includes 4 tables showing population, households, housing units, and average household size, for Wisconsin, North Central region, and U.S., with selected Wisconsin detail by county; and percent of Wisconsin housing units that are year-round occupied and seasonal, by county; various periods 1950-80.

NET MIGRATION FOR WISCONSIN COUNTIES, 1960 TO 1980

(p. 47-86) By Stephen J. Tordella. Includes 4 tables showing net migration and rate, by sex and age group, for each county and for county type groupings (metro, nonmetro, recreational, agricultural, manufacturing, and University of Wisconsin system), various periods 1960-80.

Also includes listing of counties included in each type grouping.

URBAN AND RURAL POPULATION CHANGE IN WISCONSIN

(p. 87-110) By Balkrishna D. Kale and Robert K. Naylor. Includes 3 tables showing population, natural increase, and net migration, for metro and nonmetro areas by population size group and municipality type (urban, partly urban/partly rural, and entirely rural); and number of cities/villages with population over 2,500 by rate of population increase and net migration; 1970 and 1980 or 1970-80 period.

U9200
University of Wisconsin: Center for Demography and Ecology

U9200–1   CENTER FOR DEMOGRAPHY AND ECOLOGY WORKING PAPER SERIES

Series. For individual publication data, see below.
SRI/MF/complete

Continuing series of reports on aspects of world and U.S. demography, including mobility, socialization, employment, and socioeconomic development.

Each report focuses on a single topic and contains narrative analysis, often interspersed with charts and tables. Approximately 40 reports are published each year; SRI covers only those reports with substantial data on topics of general interest.

Series has been published since 1971. SRI coverage begins with the reports described below.

Availability: University of Wisconsin: Center for Demography and Ecology, 4412 Social Science Bldg., 1180 Observatory Dr., Madison WI 53706, †; SRI/MF/complete.

U9200–1.1: Breaking Tradition: Schooling, Marriage, Work, and Childrearing in the Lives of Young Women, 1960-80

[Monograph. [1984.] 24+18 p. CDE Working Paper No. 84-13. SRI/MF/complete.]

By James A. Sweet and Ruy Teixeira. Report on changes in life patterns among young adult (age 18-29) white non-Hispanic women, 1960, 1970, and 1980. Presents data on proportion of young adult years spent single, married, with and without children, employed and unemployed, and enrolled and not enrolled in school, with cross-tabulations and additional breakdowns by educational attainment.

Data are based on Census Bureau findings.

Contains narrative analysis (p. 1-24); and 13 tables and 4 charts (18 p.).

U9200–1.2: "Hispanicity" and the 1980 Census

[Monograph. July 1984. 24+5 p. CDE Working Paper No. 84-23. SRI/MF/complete.]

By Marta Tienda and Vilma Ortiz. Report examining Hispanic ethnic identification based on 1980 census findings. Analyzes consistency between respondents' self-identification as Hispanic and their responses to various census questions indicative of Hispanic background (including birthplace, ancestry, language, and surname). Compares sociodemographic characteristics of respondents classified according to certainty of Hispanic ethnicity.

Contains narrative analysis (p. 1-24); and 1 chart and 4 tables (5 p.).

U9350
University of Wyoming: Institute for Policy Research

U9350–2   WYOMING QUARTERLY UPDATE

Quarterly. Approx. 50 p.
LC sn83-11924.
SRI/MF/complete

Quarterly report on Wyoming business conditions and economic activity, including employment, finance, and energy production. Data are from State and Federal agencies, and private data bases. Most data are current to 1-2 quarters preceding cover date.

Contents:

a. Economic outlook commentaries and industry profiles for agriculture, mineral, and selected other sectors, and sometimes 1 or more additional articles, occasionally with statistics.

b. 10 quarterly economic indicator tables, listed below, with accompanying notes and charts.

c. 2 additional quarterly tables showing the following for Wyoming: cost-of-living index rankings, by city and component, for a 3-day period in quarter prior to cover date; and average rent for apartments and trailer lots in 23 cities, for quarter ending 2 quarters prior to cover date.

d. Table code keys and data sources.

Quarterly tables appear in all issues. All additional features with substantial statistical content are described, as they appear, under "Statistical Features." Nonstatistical features are not described.

A more detailed cost-of-living index, not covered by SRI, is available from the Dept of Administration and Fiscal Control, 302 Emerson Bldg., Cheyenne WY 82002.

Availability: University of Wyoming: Institute for Policy Research, University Station, PO Box 3925, Laramie WY 82071, †; SRI/MF/complete.

Issues reviewed during 1985: Winter-Summer 1985 (P) (Vol. 4, Nos. 2-4).

QUARTERLY ECONOMIC INDICATOR TABLES:

[Tables show data for 12 consecutive quarters, ending 1-2 quarters prior to cover date. Data are for Wyoming, with selected U.S. comparisons. Table numbering and sequence may vary.]

[1] Energy and mineral production [including coal, oil, and natural gas].

[2] Agriculture [including national forest timber harvesting, and farm price indexes].

[3] Tourism [including national park visits by site, daily traffic count, hotel/motel/camp sales tax, and gasoline sales].

[4] Employment and labor [including labor force by employment status, unemployment insurance claims, nonfarm job openings and placements, and mining earnings and hours].

[5] Business conditions [including new domestic and foreign incorporations, number and value of business failures, and personal bankruptcies].

[6] Construction [including building values and permits].

[7] Utilities [including electricity and natural gas consumption and connections, by consuming sector].

[8] Consumers [including new motor vehicle registrations, liquor sales, and personal income].

[9] Government [including sales/use tax revenues, stolen property value and recovery rate, violent and nonviolent crimes, and percent of crimes cleared].

[10] Banking and finance [including bank loans, total and noninterest bearing deposits, and savings and loan mortgage loans and deposits].

STATISTICAL FEATURES:

U9350-2.601: Winter 1985 (Vol. 4, No. 2)

INDUSTRY PROFILE: A WYOMING OIL REVIEW

(p. 16-26) Article, with 3 tables showing Wyoming oil production, 1894-1983; top 20 crude oil fields ranked by 1983 production, with county location, year discovered, and cumulative production; and taxable oil production and value, by county, 1980-83. Data are from U.S. Bureau of Mines, and Wyoming Oil and Gas Conservation Commission, and Dept of Revenue and Taxation.

U9350-2.602: Spring 1985 (Vol. 4, No. 3)

SPRING MINERALS OUTLOOK: OIL AND GAS

(p. 4-6) Article, with 2 tables showing Wyoming new field wildcat and total well completions, by type (oil, gas, and dry), 1982-84; and natural gas and oil production, 1980-91. Data are from Petroleum Information Corp. and Wyoming Geological Survey.

SPRING MINERALS OUTLOOK: COAL, RECURRING FEATURE

(p. 6-9) Recurring article on Wyoming coal activity. Data are from Wyoming State Inspector of Mines and Geological Survey. Includes 2 tables showing coal production, mines, and employment, by county arranged by basin, 1984; and coal production by county, with aggregate contracted production, 1981-90.

SPRING MINERALS OUTLOOK: URANIUM AND INDUSTRIAL MINERALS

(p. 10) Article, with 1 table showing Wyoming trona production, 1981-89. Data are from Wyoming Geological Survey.

INDUSTRY PROFILE: WYOMING CATTLE REVIEW

(p. 16-24) Article, with 1 table and 1 chart showing Wyoming cattle/calf inventory, by county, 1979-84; and distribution of farm cash receipts, by commodity group, 1983. Data are from Wyoming Crop and Livestock Reporting Service.

U9350-2.603: Summer 1985 (Vol. 4, No. 4)

WYOMING CONSTRUCTION REVIEW

(p. 16-24) Article, with 3 tables showing Wyoming State highway construction and maintenance expenditures, 1944-83; and construction industry earnings, by county, and for U.S. and Rocky Mountain region, 1979-83. Data are from DOT and Bureau of Economic Analysis.

U9350-4   POVERTY IN WYOMING, 1980 CENSUS
Monograph.   Dec. 1984.
21 p.   Rpt. No. 84-2.
SRI/MF/complete

By Judy Denison and G. Fred Doll. Report analyzing demographic characteristics of persons in poverty in Wyoming, 1979 or 1980. Includes number and percent of persons in poverty, shown as follows: for racial/ethnic groups, Indians in Fremont County, farm residents, and urban and rural areas, all by age and/or sex; and for farm and nonfarm residents, by county. Racial/ethnic groups include black, white, Indian, Asian, and Spanish.

Data are from 1980 Census Summary Tape Files 3 and 4.

Contains narrative analysis interspersed with 4 charts (p. 1-10); 3 appendices, with definitions and sampling information (p. 11-14); and 5 tables (p. 15-21).

Availability: University of Wyoming: Institute for Policy Research, Census Retrieval Information Service, University Station, PO Box 3925, Laramie WY 82071, †; SRI/MF/complete.

U9640
Washington University:
Center for the
Study of American Business

U9640-1   REGULATORY CUTBACKS RESUME: Reagan's 1986 Plans for the Regulatory Agencies
Annual.   Apr. 1985.   22 p.
Rpt. No. OP41.
SRI/MF/complete

Annual report, by Paul N. Tramontozzi, on Federal regulation, with data on expenditures and staff of 54 major agencies, selected years FY70-84 and estimated FY85-86. Regulatory areas covered are consumer and job safety, environment/energy, finance/banking, industry-specific, and general business.

Data are from *Budget of the U.S. Government.*

Contains analysis of regulatory budget and staffing trends, interspersed with 3 tables (p. 1-10); and appendix, with 2 detailed tables and notes (p. 11-22).

Please note that publication date on cover incorrectly reads April 1984; correct date is April 1985.

Report updates *Hazards of "Purse Strings" Regulatory Reform: Regulatory Spending and Staffing Under the Reagan Administration,* described in SRI 1984 Annual under this number.

Availability: Washington University: Center for the Study of American Business, Campus Box 1208, St. Louis MO 63130, ‡; SRI/MF/complete.

U9640-2   FORMAL PUBLICATION SERIES
Series.   For individual publication data, see below.
SRI/MF/complete

Continuing series of reports examining effects of Federal regulatory policies on business, and related economic trends, developments, and issues.

Each report covers one topic and generally includes contents and table listings, introduction, and narrative analysis, often with tables and charts. Only reports with statistical content are described in SRI.

Reports in this series have been published since Apr. 1975. SRI coverage begins with the reports described below.

Availability: Washington University: Center for the Study of American Business, Campus Box 1208, St. Louis MO 63130, †; SRI/MF/complete.

U9640-2.1: American Steel: Responding to Foreign Competition
[Monograph. Feb. 1985. 2+25 p. Formal Pub. No. 66. SRI/MF/complete.]

By Arthur T. Denzau. Report examining impact of steel imports and Federal trade regulation on U.S. steel industry. Data are from various Federal, private, and industry sources. Includes 1 chart, and 9 tables showing the following for U.S., with selected comparisons to other steel-producing countries and world regions (including Japan and EC):

a. Iron/steel and manufacturing production worker hourly wages; steel worker productivity, by steel and mill type; new steel mill production costs; and imports of steel mill products, by area of origin; various years 1958-83.

b. Steel consumption and capacity, 1980, 1985, and 1990; U.S. steel industry productivity and employees, and domestic steel usage, imports, and shipments, with detail by mill type, 1984, 1990, and 2000; and dollar exchange rate index, and effects of 15% steel import quota on consumer costs and on employment in selected steel-using SIC 2-digit industries, various years 1970-89.

U9640-2.2: Reforming Regulation of Hazardous Waste
[Monograph. Mar. 1985. 2+i+33 p. Formal Pub. No. 67. SRI/MF/complete.]

By Ronald J. Penoyer. Report examining Federal regulation of the handling and disposal of hazardous and toxic substances. Data are from EPA and Westat, Inc.

Includes 3 tables showing distribution of industrial hazardous waste generated by SIC 2-digit industry, and cost of hazardous waste disposal by method (no dates); and hazardous waste facility operating permits requested and issued by EPA through 1984, by facility type.

U9640-2.3: Reforming Water Pollution Regulation
[Monograph. Aug. 1985. 2+32 p. Formal Pub. No. 69. SRI/MF/complete.]

By Paul N. Tramontozzi. Report examining Federal policy on water pollution control. Data are from EPA, *Water Resources Bulletin,* and Resources for the Future. Includes 3 tables showing the following:

a. Distribution by source, for each of 5 pollutants discharged into waterways (no date).

b. Costs of complying with Clean Water Act, for government and for private industry by sector, 1972-84 period; and estimated clean water compliance cost under existing standards and proposed effluent fee system, for 6 corporate and 2 municipal polluters along Black Warrior River, Alabama (no date).

U9660
Wayne State University: School of Business Administration

U9660–1   MICHIGAN STATISTICAL ABSTRACT, Eighteenth Edition, 1984
Annual.   Aug. 1984.
4+689 p.
ISBN 0-942650-02-6.
LC 74-644904.
SRI/MF/complete

Annual compilation, for 1984, of detailed demographic, governmental, and economic statistics for Michigan. Data are shown primarily for 1970s-83, with trends from as early as 1820. Data are primarily from State and Federal sources.

Report is designed to present a comprehensive overview of the State. Extensive socioeconomic, demographic, and geographic breakdowns are shown, as applicable, for most topics. These breakdowns include data by city, county, SMSA, urban-rural status, commodity, government agency, industry, occupation, age, race, and sex. Data by county often include rankings. Data for Detroit and comparisons to total U.S. and other neighboring States are also often included.

Contains State map, preface, and contents listing (4 p.); 404 tables, arranged in 25 chapters described below (p. 1-674); appendix, with list of Michigan SMSAs and component counties (p. 675-676); and index (p. 677-689).

Availability: Wayne State University: School of Business Administration, Bureau of Business Research, 209 Prentis Bldg., Detroit MI 48202, $20.00; SRI/MF/complete.

TABLE CHAPTERS:
[Tables in each chapter are preceded by a brief narrative and a table listing. Data sources are given beneath each table.]

U9660–1.1: Chapter I-II: Population and Housing

(p. 1-68) Contains 30 tables. Includes population trends from 1820, and change components; households, families, and population in group quarters; and migration by census division and State.

Also includes housing units, by occupancy status, tenure, structural characteristics, and type of fuel used; median value and contract rent; FHA-insured home financial characteristics; and percent multi-family units and mobile homes.

U9660–1.2: Chapter III: Health and Vital Statistics

(p. 69-91) Contains 22 tables. Includes births; fertility rates; infant, perinatal, fetal, and maternal deaths; deaths by cause; life expectancy at birth; communicable diseases reported; marriages; divorces; residents and employees in State mental health centers, with patients by institution; and community hospitals, admissions, and beds.

U9660–1.3: Chapter IV: Education

(p. 92-126) Contains 15 tables. Includes educational attainment of population; public and nonpublic school enrollment; public school districts, staff, teachers and average salaries, and revenues and expenditures; school lunch program participation and cost; higher education degrees conferred; and higher education enrollment, student expenses, and revenues and expenditures, by institution.

U9660–1.4: Chapter V: Labor Market

(p. 127-180) Contains 23 tables. Includes labor force by employment status; unemployment reasons and duration; wage/salary employment; unemployment compensation fund transactions; covered employment, payroll, and average earnings; worker compensation payments; and miner black lung benefit recipients and payments.

U9660–1.5: Chapter VI: Income and Cost of Living

(p. 181-223) Contains 23 tables. Includes personal income by source; labor/proprietor earnings; dividend, interest, and rental income; residence adjustment for earnings; income distribution and median income of households, families, and unrelated individuals; persons in poverty; and Detroit CPI.

U9660–1.6: Chapter VII: Social Welfare

(p. 224-266) Contains 28 tables. Includes transfer payments; public assistance and social security recipients and benefits, by program; VA expenditures; railroad retirement and unemployment insurance benefits; food stamp recipients and value; medical assistance recipients, expenditures, and vendor payments; AFDC mispayment and error rates; and social security and public assistance income households.

U9660–1.7: Chapter VIII-IX: Law Enforcement and the Courts, and Elections and Government Organization

(p. 267-292) Contains 13 tables. Includes Index and non-Index crimes by offense.

Also includes local government units; votes cast for U.S. and State offices, by candidate; State representatives; and bills introduced, passed, and vetoed.

U9660–1.8: Chapter X: Governmental Finance and Employment

(p. 293-344) Contains 29 tables. Includes government employment, tax collections, and expenditures, by level; State and local revenues by source, expenditures by function, and employee payroll and earnings; and Federal personal income tax returns.

Also includes DOD military prime contract awards in State and top 5 contractors; expenditures and military and civilian personnel, by installation; property valuations and tax levies; and local government debt.

U9660–1.9: Chapter XI: Outdoor Environment

(p. 345-360) Contains 10 tables. Includes average temperatures and precipitation, by weather station; State park and forest use; State park acreage, campsites, and use, by park; national forest, park, and lakeshore use, by site; hunting and fishing licenses issued; forest fires and acres burned; and land and inland water area.

U9660–1.10: Chapter XII: Agriculture and Forestry

(p. 361-393) Contains 27 tables. Includes farms and acreage since 1900; farm income, production expenses, and prices; crop acreage, production, yield, and value; fruit trees; livestock and poultry inventory and production; farm workers; agricultural earnings measures; and pulpwood production.

U9660–1.11: Chapter XIII: Mining

(p. 394-418) Contains 17 tables. Includes mining employment, hours, earnings, establishments, payroll, and value added; mineral production and value; iron ore mines active, shipments by range, and employment; cement plants and shipments; and consumption of crushed stone and industrial sand/gravel.

Also includes oil and gas drilling permits issued, and well completions and footage, with detail for 4 major companies; State revenues from oil/gas production; principal mineral producing companies; and natural gas input, pipeline sales, and liquefied petroleum gas recovered, by field/plant.

U9660–1.12: Chapter XIV: Construction

(p. 419-444) Contains 14 tables. Includes construction industry employment, hours, earnings, establishments, receipts, payroll, value added, and summary operating data; residential and nonresidential construction authorized and value; and construction contract awards.

U9660–1.13: Chapter XV: Manufacturing

(p. 445-468) Contains 21 tables. Includes manufacturing employment, hours, earnings, utilization rates, and expenditures for pollution abatement; steel production and shipments; oil refinery capacity, by company; inorganic chemical production; wine and beer shipments, by manufacturer; and commercial wheat milling and flour production.

U9660–1.14: Chapter XVI: Automotive Economy

(p. 469-496) Contains 12 tables. Includes world motor vehicle production by country; motor vehicle production from 1925, with detail by plant from 1977; and U.S. and Canada vehicle and/or parts factory sales and bilateral trade.

Also includes motor vehicle industry employment and earnings; related manufacturing employment; General Motors Corp. employment and earnings; and new auto and truck registrations, by domestic make.

U9660–1.15: Chapter XVII: Transportation

(p. 497-536) Contains 21 tables. Includes State transportation fund revenues; vehicle and road mileage; motor vehicle registrations; traffic accidents, injuries, and deaths; aircraft landing facility characteristics; active pilots and civil aircraft; passenger and freight traffic, and operations, by airport; and flights, seats, and cities served, by carrier.

Also includes mass transit ridership and vehicle hours; domestic and foreign freight traffic on Michigan Great Lakes system, and on principal waterways by port or waterway; revenue vehicles reported by toll authorities; and commuting patterns.

U9660–1.16: Chapter XVIII: Communications

(p. 537-550) Contains 7 tables. Includes newspaper circulation, by paper; radio and TV stations; telephones; telephone equipment, offices, and calls; and telephone main stations by company.

U9660–1.17: Chapter XIX: Energy Production and Consumption

(p. 551-595) Contains 39 tables. Includes energy consumption and prices, by sector and fuel type, with detail for coal, electricity, and natural gas; reserves of natural gas, natural gas liquids, and crude oil; crude oil runs to stills; gasoline production; refinery receipts and capacity; oil wells, production, and value; and natural gas production, disposition, value, interstate and Canadian movements, and storage capacity.

Also includes electricity generating capacity and production; electric utility customers, sales, and peak demand, by company; natural gas utility revenues, and customers and sales by company; and housing units by type of fuel used.

U9660–1.18: Chapter XX-XXI: Wholesale and Retail Trade

(p. 596-620) Contains 14 tables. Includes wholesale trade employment, hours, earnings, establishments, sales, and payroll.

Also includes retail trade employment, hours, earnings, establishments, sales, and payroll; department stores and sales; food service licensing and establishments; machine locations; food service establishments; and branded gasoline retail outlets, by company.

U9660–1.19: Chapter XXII: Finance, Insurance, and Real Estate

(p. 621-655) Contains 24 tables. Includes employment in finance/insurance/real estate; establishments and financial activity of commercial banks, savings and loan assns, credit unions, and small loan companies; savings and loan assn assets, by assn; and credit union membership.

Also includes life insurance in force, beneficiaries, and payments; insurance companies, assets, capital/surplus, premiums, losses, and mortgages owned; stock brokerage firms; and corporation shareholders.

U9660–1.20: Chapter XXIII: Selected Services

(p. 656-661) Contains 4 tables. Includes employment, establishments, receipts, and payroll, for service industries.

U9660–1.21: Chapter XXIV-XXV: International Trade, and Other Enterprise Statistics

(p. 662-674) Contains 11 tables. Includes manufacturing export value; export-related employment; and waterborne and airborne trade through Detroit customs district.

Also includes proprietorship and partnership receipts, payrolls, depreciation, and net profits; franchise establishments; industrial R&D expenditures by funding source; new business incorporations; patents issued to Michigan residents; and small businesses.

U9660–2   MICHIGAN ECONOMY
Bimonthly.   Approx. 8 p.
ISSN 0730-272X.
SRI/MF/complete

Bimonthly report on Michigan business activity and economic indicators, including manufacturing hours and earnings, consumer and farm price indexes, construction, and personal income, with selected comparisons to total U.S. Month of coverage for most data is 2nd month of cover date.

Data are from Census Bureau, BLS, State Crop Reporting Service, and other government and private sources.

Issues contain feature articles, usually statistical; 2 bimonthly tables; and 1 recurring table.

Bimonthly and recurring tables are listed below. All additional features with substantial statistical content are described, as they appear, under "Statistical Features;" page locations and latest periods of coverage for recurring table are also noted. Nonstatistical features are not covered.

Availability: Wayne State University: School of Business Administration, Bureau of Business Research, 209 Prentis Bldg., Detroit MI 48202, †; SRI/MF/complete.

Issues reviewed during 1985: July/Aug. 1984-May/June 1985 (P) (Vol. 3, Nos. 4-6; Vol. 4, Nos. 1-3).

TABLES:

BIMONTHLY TABLES

[1] Michigan economic indicators [State and U.S. average hours and earnings in manufacturing, electricity consumption, and raw steel production; CPI for Detroit area and U.S.; U.S. motor vehicle production and PPI; and State farm price index; for month of coverage, previous month, and same month of preceding year].

[2] Permit authorized construction [residential, industrial, office, and mercantile] in [20-21] selected counties [and the State, current and previous year through month of coverage].

RECURRING TABLE

[1] Quarterly personal income in Michigan [includes labor/proprietors income, by type and industry division; and other types of income, including transfer payments and unemployment insurance benefits; for 7-8 quarters, through quarter ending 3-5 months prior to cover date].

STATISTICAL FEATURES:

U9660–2.601: July/Aug. 1984 (Vol. 3, No. 4)

FOCUS ON DETROIT

(p. 1-3, 5-7) By David I. Verway. Article, with 6 tables showing population by residence 5 years prior (same house, different house in Detroit and surrounding area, rest of U.S., and abroad); population age 16/over, and labor force by employment status, by sex; and families by income group, and mean and median income; all by race, for Detroit, and Detroit SMSA or surrounding area, various years 1970-83.

Also includes text data on population distribution by age group, and distribution of owner-occupied housing, both by race, 1970 and 1980; and manufacturing employment, 1963, 1972, and 1977; for Detroit and/or surrounding suburbs.

Data are from Census Bureau and BLS.

U9660–2.602: Sept./Oct. 1984 (Vol. 3, No. 5)

RECURRING TABLE

[1] Quarterly personal income in Michigan, for 2nd quarter 1984. (p. 8)

U9660–2.603: Nov./Dec. 1984 (Vol. 3, No. 6)

HOME VALUES AND EXPECTATIONS IN MICHIGAN COUNTIES

(p. 1, 3-8) By Robert E. Fish. Article on outlook for Michigan housing markets. Data are from Census Bureau. Includes 2 tables showing median home values, 1960, 1970, and 1980; median family income, 1959, 1969, and 1979; and "expectation factor" measuring expected market trend based on home values and family incomes, 1980; all by county.

U9660–2.604: Jan./Feb. 1985 (Vol. 4, No. 1)

UPDATE ON HISPANIC MICHIGAN

(p. 1, 3-7) By David I. Verway. Article, with 5 tables showing Michigan Hispanic population distribution by age; employment distribution, and median earnings and worker age, by sex and occupation; and median household income and poverty rates; shown for all Spanish origin and/or for Mexican, Puerto Rican, Cuban, and other Spanish origin population, with comparison to total State population, 1980.

Data are from Census Bureau.

U9660–2.605: Mar./Apr. 1985 (Vol. 4, No. 2)

SPECIAL TABLE

(p. 2) Table showing value of residential and nonresidential building contract awards in Michigan, 11 Michigan MSAs, Toledo MSA, and U.S., 1983-84.

UPDATE ON MICHIGAN'S WORKING WOMEN

(p. 1-6) By David I. Verway. Article, with 3 tables showing the following data by sex, for Michigan: employment by occupational group, 1970 and 1980; employment, median earnings, and percent of workers employed full-time, for top 6-12 occupations in terms of men's and women's employment and earnings, 1979; and median earnings, by race and for Spanish origin, Native American, and Asian, with U.S. comparison, 1979. Data are from Census Bureau.

BRIEF

(p. 7-8) Article, with 2 tables showing labor force by employment status, by race and sex, for Michigan, Detroit (city and MSA), and U.S., 1980-84. Data are from BLS.

U9660–2.606: May/June 1985 (Vol. 4, No. 3)

PATH TO PROSPERITY

(p. 1, 3-8) Article, with 1 table showing increase or decrease in Michigan manufacturing earnings, with comparisons to total U.S. and shift-share analysis of industry-mix and competitive factors, all by industry group, 1969-79 period. Data are from Commerce Dept.